Oxford Student's Dictionary of Current English

A S Hornby
with the assistance of
Christina Ruse

1478
1978

Oxford University Press
1978

Oxford University Press, Walton Street, Oxford OX2 6DP

OXFORD LONDON GLASGOW
NEW YORK TORONTO MELBOURNE WELLINGTON
IBADAN NAIROBI DAR ES SALAAM LUSAKA CAPE TOWN
KUALA LUMPUR SINGAPORE JAKARTA HONG KONG TOKYO
DELHI BOMBAY CALCUTTA MADRAS KARACHI

© Oxford University Press 1978
First Published 1978

Computer typeset in
Times and Univers by
Oxford University Press and
Unwin Brothers Ltd

Printed in Great Britain
at the University Press, Oxford
by Vivian Ridler
Printer to the University

Contents

Preface

This dictionary is a new adaptation of the *Oxford Advanced Learner's Dictionary of Current English*. It has been specially prepared for those learning English up to the Intermediate level.

Learning a language has to be distinguished from studying a language. We become able to understand and use the mother tongue without using books. If we ever *study* the mother tongue, it is likely to be at a time when we have fully learnt to use it.

Language is made up of words (the vocabulary) and of the accepted ways of putting these words together (the syntax). We learn words and expressions in the mother tongue by hearing them used, again and again, in infancy, and always in particular situations. We are strongly motivated because we have to communicate. Words may have numerous meanings for many different situations. It is only when we have heard or seen a word repeatedly that we begin to know it. The first step is the identification of the word. The second and more important step is the close association of the word (the symbol) with what it stands for (the object, concept, etc). When this second stage has been achieved we have learnt the word. We know it. This process of coming to know words is universal for the mother tongue.

For a foreign language (eg English for a German child) or for a second language (eg English for a Nigerian child in a home where English is spoken by the family), there are other ways of identifying words. The equivalent in the mother tongue may be given by the teacher, or found by the learner in a bilingual dictionary. By this means identification is immediate and can be (but is not always) accurate. This is a first step only, however. The reaching of complete association between symbol and what is symbolized remains the final aim. Until the learner can use the words confidently and accurately, until he has instant recognition and recall of the word, he does not know it.

A good teacher will use well-tried methods to give the meaning of new words without the use of the mother tongue. He may use drawings and diagrams. A very competent teacher may explain a new word by using other words already known. This is what a monolingual dictionary (such as this one) attempts to do. This is not an easy task and cannot be effective until the learner is past the beginning stage.

What, then, are the advantages of a monolingual dictionary such as this, in which English words are dealt with in English? Modern textbooks encourage learners to think, write and speak in English only. This may be difficult at first but the rewards are well worth it. It is the more natural way of acquiring competence in a language. As soon as a learner has the confidence to read simple English sentences, he can use a monolingual dictionary if it provides simple definitions and notes to help him to use the vocabulary in context.

A bilingual dictionary has some claims to usefulness. There are some words for which there is usually a clear and unambiguous equivalent (*tulip, panther, chisel, valve*). But there are thousands of words with no exact equivalent, which, even when defined clearly, need examples before they are fully known. A word in isolation is a dead word. It comes to life when it occurs in a sentence. There are hundreds of verbs for which patterns must be learnt. *Set* is a short and easy-looking verb but if you look up *set* in this dictionary you will find that it has several meanings, that it is used in several sentence patterns, that it combines with adverbs and prepositions in meanings far removed from the simple usage of 'The sun sets in the west'. These phrasal verbs, *set about/back/down/out*, etc all need illustrative phrases or sentences to show the meaning. In this dictionary the illustrative phrases and sentences help the learner to become familiar with words in their normal contexts. He may know that the verb *sever* means 'cut'. He must learn, from seeing examples the contexts in which *sever* is correct. We do not 'sever meat at meals' but our government may 'sever diplomatic relations with a neighbouring country'.

Remember, there are very few real synonyms in English. Small bilingual dictionaries which give equivalents can encourage errors. A good monolingual dictionary such as this one will not.

English nouns, if they stand for objects that can be counted, have plural forms (*one box, many boxes*). There are some nouns which are not used in the plural. We distinguish between *machine* and *machinery*, *poem* and *poetry*, (simple enough), but nouns such as *hair*, *furniture* and *news* are not so simple. *Hair* is not usually used as a plural so we say 'She has beautiful hair'. But an elderly person may have 'a few white hairs'. In some languages the equivalents of these words may have plural forms when they do not in English. *News* appears to be plural, but is singular – 'Is there any news of him?'. This dictionary provides detailed guidance.

The learner may think that because a bilingual dictionary provides a quick and apparently complete answer to problems of word meanings he need not use a good monolingual dictionary. If he can be encouraged to use this dictionary systematically, he will soon see its advantages.

London 1978   A S Hornby

Acknowledgements

This dictionary is adapted from the *Oxford Advanced Learner's Dictionary* and changes made during the rewriting do not necessarily reflect the opinion of the contributors to the parent volume. We are particularly grateful to A P Cowie for his advice during the preparation of the manuscript and to the many teachers throughout the world who have offered advice and suggestions.

Finally, we are grateful to the staff of the computer department of Oxford University Press for their untiring work on the material.

London 1978   A S Hornby
                                                                                                Christina A Ruse

Sample entries

phonetic transcription for each headword

word-division

ac·cu·racy /ˈækjərəsı/ *n* [U] exactness; correctness.

part of speech

baby /ˈbeɪbɪ/ *n* [C] (*pl* -ies) **1** very young child: *She has a* '~*-boy*/~*girl.* *Which of you is the* ~ (= the youngest member) *of the family?* **2** (*sl*) girl; sweetheart.

style marker

`baby-face(d)`, (of an adult) (having a) youthful face.

`baby 'grand`, small grand piano.

`baby-hood`, state, period, of being a baby.

`baby-ish`, of, like a baby: ~*ish behaviour.*

`baby-minder`, woman paid to look after a baby for long periods, (e g while the mother is out working).

simple definitions

`baby-sitter`, person paid to look after a baby for a short time, (e g while the parents are at the cinema). Hence, **baby-sit** *vi* (-tt-).

examples of usage (with stress-marks where necessary)

doubled consonants

burst² /bɜːst/ *vi, vt* (*pt, pp* ~) (For uses with *adverbial particles* and *prepositions.* ⇨ **5** below.)...

special arrangement of phrasal verbs. Parentheses ( ) show where words may be omitted. Obliques / show where alternative words may be used.

5 (uses with *adverbial particles* and *prepositions*):

burst in (*on/upon*), (a) interrupt: *He* ~ *in on our conversation.* (b) appear or arrive suddenly.

burst into, (a) send out suddenly; break out into: *The coat fell in the fire and* ~ *into flames.* (b) ~ *into tears/laughter/song, etc,* suddenly begin to cry/laugh, etc. ~ *into blossom,* begin to bloom.

burst out laughing/crying, suddenly begin to laugh/cry.

com·ment /ˈkɒment/ *n* [C,U] opinion given briefly in speech or writing about an event, or in explanation or criticism: *Have you any* ~*s to make on my story?* □ *vi* give opinions: ~ *on an essay*

countable/uncountable uses of nouns

example sentences showing current usage

know¹ /nəʊ/ *vt, vi* (*pt* knew /njuː *US:* nuː/, *pp* ~n /nəʊn/) **1** have in the mind as the result of experience ...

irregular tenses with phonetic transcription

American English pronunciations

pretty /ˈprɪtı/ *adj* (-ier, -iest) **1** pleasing and attractive without being beautiful or magnificent; *a* ~ *girl/garden/picture/piece of music.* **2** fine; good: *A* ~ *mess you've made of it!* **3** (*informal*) large in amount or extent: *a* ~ *big fine for such a minor offence.* **a** `pretty kettle of fish,` ⇨ fish¹ (1). **a pretty penny,** ⇨ penny(1). □ *adv*...

cross reference to other words

comparative and superlative forms of adjectives

idiomatic expressions in bold type

The arrangement of the entries

Headwords

Headwords are printed in **bold type**:

fact   fac·tion   fac·tor

The bold dot (·) in the headword shows where the word may be divided in written English. It is usual to divide a word when it needs more space than is left at the end of a line.

fac·sim·ile   false·hood

Where two headwords have the same spelling they are numbered:

fan¹ /fæn/ *n*

fan² /fæn/ *vt,vi*

Compounds

Compounds (whether written as one word, with a hyphen or as two separate words are printed in **bold type** after the entry for the first word of the compound as a sub-group:

fam·ily /ˈfæmlɪ/ *n*
  family name = surname
  family planning, (use of birth control, contraceptives, for) planning the number of children, intervals between births, etc in a family.
  family tree, genealogical chart.

Derivatives

Derivatives follow the headword entry in the same way:

fa·natic /fəˈnætɪk/ *n*
  fa·nati·cally /fəˈnætɪklɪ/ *adv*
  fa·nati·cism /fəˈnætɪsɪzm/ *n* [U] excessive enthusiasm; [C] instance of this.

Idiomatic expressions

Idiomatic expressions are included at the end of the appropriate definition and are printed in ***bold italic type:***

gain² /geɪn/ *vt,vi **gain time,*** improve one's chances by delaying something, making excuses, etc. ***gain the upper hand,*** be victorious.

Phrasal verbs

Phrasal verbs are printed in ***bold italic type*** before the appropriate definition:

gain² /geɪn/ *vt,vi* ... 4 ***gain on/upon,*** (a) get closer to (a person or thing pursued): ∼ *on the other runners in a race.* (b) go faster than, get further in advance of: ∼ *on one's pursuers.*

Some verbs, such as *be, bring, come, get, go, make, take,* are used with a variety of prepositions and adverbial particles to form special expressions. These combinations are given as a separate section at the end of the entry for the verb and are listed in alphabetical order:

close³ /kləʊz/ *vt,vi* . . .
  5 (uses with *adverbial particles* and *prepositions*):
  close down, (a) (of a factory, business, etc) stop production, shut completely. (b) (of a broadcasting station) stop transmitting: *The*

time is just after midnight and we are now
closing down. Hence, **close-down** n.
close in, the days are closing in, getting
shorter.
close in on/upon, (a) envelop: Darkness
∼d in on us. (b) come near(er) and attack:
The enemy ∼d in on us.

Note the use of parentheses ( ) and obliques / in idiomatic
expressions and phrasal verbs.

The parentheses surround words which can be omitted when using the
expression in a sentence.

fall² /fɔl/ vi,vt **fall flat (on one's face),** . . .

look² /lʊk/ vi
    look away (from sth),
    look back (on sth),

The oblique is used to give optional words in an expression·

fate /feɪt/ vt . . . **be fated to/that,**

fashion /ˈfæʃən/ n . . . **come into/go out of fashion,**

Nouns

Noun entries are marked [C], [U], or [C,U].

[C] means that the noun has a singular and a plural form. It can be used
with a, an, another and with numbers. Nouns used in these ways are
countable.

[U] means that the noun does not have a plural form. It is used with
some, a lot of, enough, etc. Nouns used in these ways are uncountable.

[C,U] means that the noun can be used as either countable or
uncountable.

Adjectives

Adjectives sometimes have comparative or superlative forms by the
addition of -r, -st; -er, -est; or -ier, -iest. The dictionary will tell you
when this is possible by printing these endings in parentheses at the
beginning of the entry.

blue¹ /blu/ adj (-r, -st)

deep¹ /dip/ adj (-er, -est)

funny /ˈfʌnɪ/ adj (-ier, -iest)

A few adjectives have special comparative and superlative forms

good² /gʊd/ adj (better, best)

bad /bæd/ adj (worse, worst)

**Irregular
forms**

Whenever the forms of a verb (past participle, present participle, past
tense) are irregular, these forms are given at the beginning of an entry
in parentheses:

fall² /fɔl/ vi,vt (pl fell /fel/, pp ∼en /ˈfɔlən/)

lose /luz/ vt,vi (pt,pp lost /lɔst US: lɔst/)

fry /fraɪ/ vt,vi (3rd person sing pres tense fries, pt,pp fried)

**Doubled
consonants**

Many verbs that end in a single consonant have this letter repeated to
make the past participle or the present participle. Some adjectives
repeat the last consonant in the same way. The Dictionary shows this
by printing the ending in parentheses:

flap² /flæp/ vt,vi (-pp-)

sad /sæd/ adj (-der, -dest)

Speaking and writing good English is not only a problem of grammatical correctness. The word or expression must be right for the particular context. Entries are marked *formal, informal, slang, dated*, etc to help you.

Often, the Dictionary will tell you which word is more usual:

gal /gæl/ *n (dated informal)* = girl

va·liant /ˈvælɪənt/ *adj* brave (the usual word).

American variants for spelling, pronunciation and meaning are shown by *US* before the information.

Each headword and derivative has a phonetic spelling of the word immediately after the ordinary spelling. Phonetic spelling is a way of writing so that one symbol always represents only one sound. By learning the symbols you will be able to pronounce the words in the Dictionary. A list of the phonetic symbols used in this Dictionary is printed on the inside cover for easy reference.

When a word has more than one syllable, one of them is pronounced with more force than the rest. This is called *stress* and the syllable which is stressed is shown with a stress-mark /ˈ/ before it in the Dictionary. In longer words, other syllables may also be pronounced with more force than the rest but this stress is not as strong as those marked /ˈ/. The stress-mark /ˌ/ is used to show this. So, /ˈ/ is used to mark the *primary stress* and /ˌ/ is used to mark the *secondary stress*:

fal·si·fi·ca·tion /ˌfɔlsɪfɪˈkeɪʃən/

fam·ili·ar·ity /fəˌmɪlɪˈærətɪ/

Stress-marks are also given for compounds and expressions whenever this information is useful:

ˈfancy ˈfree

ˈgad aˈbout

in ˈany case

ˈtake sb ˈdown a peg or two

The pronunciations recommended are those which research has shown are the most common and the most useful for those learning English. If English people around you repeatedly use a pronunciation not given here, either discuss the choice with them or join them in their usage. A particular difference is the omission of /ə/ sounds in words, particularly from the endings. Spoken English has speeded up during the last thirty years with the effect of reducing such endings as /-bəl/, /-əl/, /-ʃən/, /-əns/ (as in *able, coastal, musical, civil, station, appearance*).

You should aim to use these shorter pronunciations as your familarity and confidence with spoken English increases. The *Oxford Advanced Learner's Dictionary of Current English* gives these shorter forms

Symbols and abbreviations used

abbr	abbreviation	*n*	noun
adj	adjective	*(naut)*	nautical
adv	adverb	(P)	Proprietary name
(anat)	anatomy	*pl*	plural
(astron)	astronomy	*pp*	past participle
[C]	countable noun	*prep*	preposition
(chem)	chemistry	*pron*	pronoun
(C of E)	Church of England	*pt*	past tense
(comm)	commerce	*(RC)*	Roman Catholicism
conj	conjunction	**sb**	somebody
e g	For example	*sing*	singular
esp	especially	**sth**	something
(fig)	figurative	[U]	uncountable noun
(Fr)	French	*(US)*	American
(GB)	British	*vi*	verb intransitive
(geom)	geometry	*vt*	verb transitive
i e	in other words	⇨	look at (cross-reference)
(It)	Italian		
(maths)	mathematics	⚠	taboo
(med)	medicine	▫	shows a change in the part of speech in an entry
(mil)	military		
(myth)	mythology		

Aa

A[1], **a** /eɪ/ (*pl* A's, a's /eɪz/) the first letter of the English alphabet.
A1 /'eɪ 'wʌn/ (**a**) (of ships) first class. (**b**) (*informal*) excellent: *feeling A1*, in excellent health.
a[2] /ə strong form: eɪ/, **an** /ən strong form: æn/ *indefinite article* (*an* is used before a vowel) **1** one (but no particular one): *I have a pen* (*pl = some pens*). *Have you a pen* (*pl = any pens*)? *I said 'a train was coming, not 'the train.* **2** (used when speaking or writing about number, quantity, groups, etc): *a lot of money; a little more; a few books; half a dozen; half an hour; a friend of mine*, one of my friends. (*Note:* When several objects, etc are parts of a known group, the *indefinite article* is not repeated: *a knife and fork.*) **3** each: *60 miles an hour; twice a week; 20p a metre.* **4** that which is called; every: *A horse is an animal* (*pl = Horses are animals*). **5** another; one like: *He thinks he is a Napoleon.*
aback /ə'bæk/ *adv* **be 'taken a'back,** be suddenly surprised or upset.
aba·cus /'æbəkəs/ *n* [C] (*pl* ~es or -ci /'æbəsaɪ/) frame with beads or balls sliding on rods, for teaching numbers to children, or (still in East Asia) for calculating.
abaft /ə'bɑːft US: ə'bæft/ *adv, prep* (*naut*) at, in, toward, behind, the stern half of a ship .
aban·don[1] /ə'bændən/ *n* [U] careless freedom without thinking of the consequences or of convention.
aban·don[2] /ə'bændən/ *vt* **1** go away from, not intending to return to: *The order was given to ~ ship*, for all on board to leave the (sinking) ship. *He ~ed his wife and child.* **2** give up; stop: *They ~ed the game because of rain.* **3** **abandon oneself to,** allow oneself to feel, act, etc because of necessity, extreme emotion, etc: *He ~ed himself to despair.*
aban·doned *adj* (**a**) immoral; having no shame: *an ~ed girl.* (**b**) left or deserted (with no intention to return or reclaim): *an ~ed car/wife.*
aban·don·ment *n* [U]
abase /ə'beɪs/ *vt* **abase oneself,** (*formal*) lower oneself in dignity or respect.
abase·ment *n* [U]
abashed /ə'bæʃt/ *adj* (*formal*) very embarrassed or ashamed.
abate /ə'beɪt/ *vt, vi* **1** (of winds, storms, floods, pain, etc) make or become less: *The ship sailed when the storm ~d.* **2** (*legal*) bring to an end: *We must ~ the smoke nui-*

sance in our big cities
abate·ment *n* [U] abating; decrease.
ab·at·toir /'æbətwɑː(r) US: 'æbə'twɑr/ *n* [C] slaughter-house (for cattle, sheep, etc).
ab·bess /'æbes US: 'æbɪs/ *n* [C] woman (*Mother Superior*) at the head of a convent or nunnery.
ab·bey /'æbɪ/ *n* [C] (*pl* ~s) **1** building(s) in which monks or nuns live as a community in the service of God. **2** the community.
ab·bot /'æbət/ *n* [C] man (*Father Superior*) at the head of an abbey or monastery.
ab·brevi·ate /ə'briːvɪeɪt/ *vt* shorten (a word, title, etc): *~ January to Jan.*
ab·brevi·ation /ə'briːvɪ'eɪʃən/ *n* **1** [U] abbreviating or being abbreviated. **2** [C] shortened form (esp of a word).
ABC /'eɪ biː 'siː/ *n* the alphabet. *as easy as ABC,* very easy.
ab·di·cate /'æbdɪkeɪt/ *vt, vi* **1** surrender or renounce a high office, control or responsibility. **2** give up the throne: *King Edward VIII ~d in 1936.*
ab·di·ca·tion /'æbdɪ'keɪʃən/ *n* **1** [U] abdicating. **2** [C] instance of this.
ab·do·men /'æbdəmən/ *n* [C] **1** part of the body that includes the stomach and bowels. **2** last of the three divisions of an insect, spider, etc.
ab·domi·nal /æb'dɒmɪnəl/ *adj* in, of, for, the abdomen: *~ pains.*
ab·duct /æb'dʌkt/ *vt* take or lead (esp a woman or child) away unlawfully, by force or fraud. ⇨ **kidnap.**
ab·duc·tion /æb'dʌkʃən/ *n* [C,U]
abeam /ə'biːm/ *adv* (*naut*) on a line at a right angle to the length of a ship or aircraft.
ab·er·ra·tion /'æbə'reɪʃən/ *n* **1** [U] (usually *fig*) turning away from what is expected, normal or right: *stealing something in a moment of ~.* **2** [C] instance of this; defect: *an ~ in the computer.*
abet /ə'bet/ *vt* (-tt-) *abet (in),* (*legal*) help or encourage (in vice, crime). *aid and abet sb,* (*legal*) help him to do wrong.
abey·ance /ə'beɪəns/ *n* [U] condition of not being in force or in use for a time. *be in abeyance,* suspended, e g until more information is obtained. *fall/go into abeyance,* (*legal*) (of a law, rule, custom, etc) be suspended; be no longer observed.
ab·hor /əb'hɔː(r)/ *vt* (-rr-) (*formal*) think of with hatred and disgust: *~ cruelty to both children and animals.*
ab·hor·rence /əb'hɒrəns US: -'hɔr-/ *n* [U] (*formal*) hatred and disgust: *hold something in ~rence.*
ab·hor·rent /əb'hɒrənt US: -'hɔr-/ *adj* (*formal*) hateful; causing horror.
abide /ə'baɪd/ *vt, vi* **1** *abide by,* (*formal*) be faithful to; keep: *~ by a promise/decision.* **2** *cannot/can't/couldn't abide,* cannot/ could not tolerate; hate(d): *She can't ~ that man.*
abid·ing /ə'baɪdɪŋ/ *adj* (*liter*) lasting.

abil·ity /ə`bɪlətɪ/ n (pl -ies) **1** [U] (possible) capacity or power (to do something physical or mental). **to the best of my ability,** as well as I can. **2** [U] cleverness; intelligence: a man of great ~. **3** [C] mental power; talent: a man of many abilities.

ab·ject /`æbdʒəkt/ adj (formal) **1** (of conditions) poor; miserable: living in ~ poverty. **2** (of a person, his behaviour) disliked or thought to be worthless because cowardly or undignified: an ~ apology.
ab·ject·ly adv

ablaze /ə`bleɪz/ adj, adv (formal) **1** on fire: The whole building was soon ~. **2** (fig) shining; bright; excited: The streets were ~ with lights.

able /`eɪbəl/ adj **1 be able to do sth,** have the power, means or opportunity: Will you be ~ to come? ⇨ can², could. **2** (-r, -st) clever; capable; having or showing knowledge or skill: an ~ lawyer/speech; the ~st/most ~ man I know.
'able-'bodied adj physically strong.

-able (also **-ible**) /-əbəl/ suffix **1** (noun + ~ = adj) showing qualities of: fashionable; responsible. **2** (verb + ~ = adj) that can be, fit to be: eatable; reducible.
-ably, -ibly adv

ab·lu·tions /ə`bluʃənz/ n pl ceremonial washing of the hands or the body, esp as an act of religion.

ably /`eɪblɪ/ adv in an able manner.

ab·nor·mal /`æb`nɔməl/ adj different from what is normal, ordinary or expected.
ab·nor·mally /-məlɪ/ adv

ab·nor·mality /`æbnɔ`mælətɪ/ n [U] quality of being abnormal; [C] (pl -ies) thing that is abnormal.

aboard /ə`bɔd/ adv, prep on, in, onto or into a ship, aircraft, or (US) a train or motor-coach: It's time to go ~. All ~! Welcome ~!

abode /ə`bəʊd/ n of/with no fixed ~, (legal) having no permanent home.

abol·ish /ə`bolɪʃ/ vt put an end to, do away with, e g war, slavery, an old custom.

abol·ition /`æbə`lɪʃən/ n [U] abolishing or being abolished (esp used, in the 18th and 19th centuries, of Negro slavery).
abol·ition·ist /-ɪst/ n [C] (esp) person who wished to abolish Negro slavery.

A-bomb /`eɪ bom/ n ⇨ atomic.

abom·in·able /ə`bomɪnəbəl/ adj **1** causing hatred and disgust. **2** (informal) unpleasant; bad: ~ weather/food.
abom·in·ably /-əblɪ/ adv

abom·in·ate /ə`bomɪneɪt/ vt **1** (formal) feel hatred or disgust for. **2** (informal) dislike.

abom·in·ation /ə`bomɪ`neɪʃən/ n (formal) **1** [U] horror and disgust: hold something in abomination. **2** [C] something that arouses horror and disgust.

abo·rig·inal /`æbə`rɪdʒənəl/ adj (of people, living creatures, etc) belonging to, existing in, a region from earliest times, or from the

time when the region was first known. □ n [C] earliest inhabitant, plant, etc of a region.

Abo·rig·ine /`æbə`rɪdʒənɪ/ n [C] Australian aboriginal person.
the abo·rig·ines /`æbə`rɪdʒɪnɪz/ the aboriginal inhabitants.

abort /ə`bɔt/ vt, vi **1** come to nothing; cancel: ~ a space mission, e g because of mechanical trouble. **2** give birth to an undeveloped foetus.

abor·tion /ə`bɔʃən/ n **1** [U] (legal) expulsion of the foetus from the womb during the first 28 weeks of pregnancy; helping or causing this. **2** [C] instance of this: have an illegal ~.
abor·tion·ist /-ɪst/, person who brings about an abortion; person who favours and supports legal abortion.

abor·tive /ə`bɔtɪv/ adj unsuccessful: an ~ rebellion.
abor·tively adv

abound /ə`baʊnd/ vi have, exist, in great numbers or quantities: The river ~s with fish. Fish ~ in the river.

about¹ /ə`baʊt/ adv of degree a little more or less than; a little before or after: ~ as high as that tree; for ~ three miles; ~ six o'clock; on or ~ the fifth of May. ⇨ exactly, just²(5). **be about time...,** (informal) time to do something immediately: It's ~ time you stopped being so rude. **be about it/the size of it,** (informal) be how I assess it, how I see it.

about² /ə`baʊt/ adverbial particle **1** (used with verbs of movement) here and there, in no particular direction: The children were rushing ~. The boys were climbing ~ on the rocks. **2** (used with other verbs, showing position, etc): There were books lying ~ on the floor. **3** (used with be): There was no one ~, no one to be seen. **be (out and) about again,** able to get out, work, etc after an illness. **be up and about,** out of bed and active. **4 bring sth about,** ⇨ bring(5). **come about,** ⇨ come(13). **5** facing round; in the opposite direction: It's the wrong way ~. A~ turn! (GB), A~ face! (US), (mil commands) turn round to face the other way. **(do sth) turn and turn about,** ⇨ turn¹(4). **a'bout-'face** vi turn and face the other way. □ n [C] complete reversal of opinions, etc: He did a complete ~-face!

about³ /ə`baʊt/ prep **1** (used with verbs of movement) here and there, in no particular direction: walking ~ the town; travelling ~ the world. **2** (used with other verbs showing position, state, etc): idle men standing ~ street corners; books and papers lying ~ the room. **3** near to: I dropped the key somewhere ~ here. **4** concerning; regarding; in connection with: He is careless ~ his personal appearance. What do you know ~ him? Tell me all ~ it. **How/What about...,** (used to ask for information, to make a suggestion or to get a person's opinion): How ~ going to France for our holidays? **5** concerned or occupied with: *And while you're ~ it...*, while you're doing that... **go/set about sth,** deal with it: *Do you know how to go ~ it?* **6** round (the usual word): *the fields ~ Oxford. She hung ~ his shoulders.* **7 be about to** + *inf,* be just going to (do something): *As I was (just) ~ to say, when you interrupted me... He was ~ to start.*

above¹ /ə'bʌv/ *adv* **1** at a higher point; overhead; on high: *My bedroom is just ~. A voice from ~ shouted a welcome.* **2** earlier (in a book, article, etc): *As I mentioned/ stated ~ ...*

a'bove-'board *adv* without deceiving; honourably. □ *adj* frank; open(8). ⇨ underhand.

a'bove-'mentioned/-'named *adj* mentioned/named earlier in this book article, list, etc.

above² /ə'bʌv/ *prep* **1** higher than: *The sun rose ~ the horizon. The water came ~ our knees. We were flying ~ the clouds.* (*Note:* Compare: *We flew over/across the Sahara.*) **2** greater in number, price, weight, etc: *The temperature has been ~ the average recently. It weighs ~ ten tons. Applicants must be ~ the age of 21.* **3** more than. **above all,** more than anything else. **over and above,** in addition to. **4** too great, good, difficult, etc for: *If you want to learn, you must not be ~ asking* (= not be too proud to ask) *questions. He is ~ deceit,* does not practise deceit. **5** out of reach of (because too great, good, etc): *His conduct has always been ~ reproach/suspicion.* **6** (various uses): *the waterfall ~* (= up stream from) *the bridge.*

ab·ra·ca·dabra /ˌæbrəkə'dæbrə/ *n* [U] word used to encourage magic.

ab·ra·sion /ə'breɪʒən/ *n* **1** [U] rubbing, scraping, or wearing off. **2** [C] area where something has been worn or scraped away: *an ~ of the skin.*

ab·ras·ive /ə'breɪsɪv/ *n* [C,U] substance (e g emery) used for rubbing or grinding down surfaces. □ *adj* **1** causing abrasion. **2** (*fig*) harsh, rough: *an ~ voice/character.*

abreast /ə'brest/ *adv* (of persons, ships, etc) on a level, side by side, and facing the same way: *walking three ~; warships in line ~.* **be/keep abreast (of/with),** up to date: *keep ~ of the news.*

abridge /ə'brɪdʒ/ *vt* make shorter, esp by using fewer words: *an ~d edition of 'David Copperfield'.*

abridge·ment, abridg·ment *n* [U] abridging; [C] thing, e g a book, that is abridged.

abroad /ə'brɔːd/ *adv* **1** in or to a foreign country or countries; away from one's own country: *be/go/live/travel ~; visitors who have come from ~.* **2** (*dated*) far and wide; everywhere: *There's a rumour ~ that...,* People are saying that...

abrupt /ə'brʌpt/ *adj* **1** unexpectedly sud-

den: *The road is full of ~ turns.* **2** (of speech, writing, behaviour) rough; bad-tempered; unfriendly: *sound ~ on the telephone.* **3** (of a slope) steep.

abrupt·ly *adv*

abrupt·ness *n* [U]

ab·scess /'æbses/ *n* [C] collection of thick yellowish-white liquid (called *pus*) formed in a cavity in the body: *~es on the gums.*

ab·scond /əb'skɒnd/ *vi* go away, suddenly, secretly, and aware of having done wrong, esp to avoid arrest.

ab·sence /'æbsəns/ *n* **1** [U] being away: *He met her during his ~ in America, while he was there. In the ~ of the Manager* (= While he is away) *Mr X is in charge of the business.* **leave of absence,** ⇨ leave²(1). **2** [C] occasion or period of being away: *after an ~ of three months.* **3** [U] non-existence: *in the ~ of definite information.*

ab·sent¹ /'æbsənt/ *adj* **1 absent from,** not present at: *~ from school/work.* **2** lost in thought; having one's attention elsewhere: *When I spoke to him he looked at me in an ~ way but did not answer.*

'absent-'minded /'mɑːndɪd/ *adj* so deep or far away in thought that one is unaware of what one is doing, what is happening, etc.

absent-minded·ly *adv*

absent-minded·ness *n* [U]

ab·sent² /əb'sent/ *vt* (*formal*) stay away (from): *Why did you ~ yourself from school yesterday?*

ab·sen·tee /ˌæbsən'tiː/ *n* [C] person who is absent, e g a landlord who lives away from his property: (attrib) *~ landladies.*

ab·sen·tee·ism /-ɪzm/ *n* [U] frequent failure to be present, e g the practice of often being away from work without a satisfactory reason.

ab·so·lute /'æbsəluːt/ *adj* **1** complete; perfect: *When giving evidence in a law court, we must tell the ~ truth.* **2** unlimited; having complete power: *An ~ ruler need not ask anyone for permission to do anything.* **3** real; undoubted: *It is an ~ fact. Do you have ~ proof of his guilt?*

'absolute 'zero, lowest temperature theoretically possible, = −273·15°C.

ab·sol·ute·ly /'æbsəluːtlɪ/ *adv* **1** completely: *~ impossible; ~ right.* **2** unconditionally: *He refused ~.* **3** /'æbsə'luːtlɪ/ (*informal*) (in answer to a question, or as a comment) I agree; certainly.

ab·so·lut·ism /'æbsə'luːtɪzm/ *n* [U] (*politics*) despotism.

ab·sol·ution /'æbsə'luːʃən/ *n* [U] (R C Church) freeing from consequences of sin: *grant ~ from sin.*

ab·solve /əb'zɒlv/ *vt* **absolve (from),** declare free (from sin, guilt, a promise, duty, etc): *I ~ you from all blame/from your vows.*

ab·sorb /əb'sɔːb/ *vt* **1** take or suck in, e g a liquid, heat, light. **2** (*fig*) gain knowledge, etc: *The clever boy ∼ed all the knowledge his teachers could give him.* **3** use up a great deal of the attention, interest or time of: *He is completely ∼ed in his work.*

ab·sorb·ent /əb`zɔːbənt/ *adj* able to absorb: ∼ *cotton-wool.* □ *n* [C] absorbent material.

ab·sorp·tion /əb`sɔːpʃən/ *n* [U] absorbing or being absorbed: *Complete ∼ in sport interferred with his studies.*

ab·stain /əb`steɪn/ *vi* hold oneself back: *His doctor told him to ∼ from beer and wine. At the last election he ∼ed (from voting).*

ab·stainer, person who abstains.

'total `abstainer, person who never takes alcoholic drinks.

ab·stemi·ous /əb`stiːmɪəs/ *adj* sparing or moderate, esp in taking food and drink.

ab·stemi·ously *adv*

ab·stemi·ous·ness *n* [U]

ab·sten·tion /əb`stenʃən/ *n* [U] abstaining, esp not using one's vote at an election, etc; [C] instance of this: *six votes for, three against and two ∼s.*

ab·sti·nence /`æbstɪnəns/ *n* [U] abstaining, e g from food, enjoyment and esp alcoholic drink.

'total `abstinence, not taking any alcoholic drink.

ab·stract¹ /`æbstrækt/ *adj* thought of separately from facts, objects or particular examples: *A flower is beautiful, but beauty itself is ∼. In the abstract,* regarded in an ideal or theoretical way.

'abstract `art, art which does not represent objects, scenes, etc in an obvious way.

'abstract `noun, (*gram*) one that is the name of a quality or state, e g *length, goodness, virtue.*

ab·stract² /əb`strækt/ *vt* take out; separate: ∼ *metal from ore.*

ab·stract³ /`æbstrækt/ *n* [C] short account, e g of the chief points of a piece of writing, a book, speech, etc.

ab·stracted /əb`stræktəd/ *adj* not paying attention.

ab·stract·ed·ly *adv*

ab·strac·tion /əb`strækʃən/ *n* **1** [U] abstracting or being abstracted. **2** [U] absent-mindedness: *in a moment of ∼.* **3** [C] idea of a quality apart from its material accompaniments: *Don't lose yourself in ∼s,* Keep a firm hold on reality. **4** [U] formation of such an idea or ideas.

ab·struse /əb`struːs/ *adj* (*formal*) whose meaning or answer is hidden or difficult to understand.

ab·struse·ly *adv*

ab·struse·ness *n* [U]

ab·surd /əb`sɜːd -`zɜːd/ *adj* unreasonable; foolish; ridiculous: *What an ∼ suggestion!*

ab·surd·ity *n* [C] (*pl* -ies) **1** [U] state of being absurd. **2** [C] absurd act or statement.

ab·surd·ly *adv*

abun·dance /ə`bʌndəns/ *n* [U] **1** great amount: *food and drink in ∼.* **2** an abun-

dance of, more than enough: *an ∼ of good things.*

abun·dant /ə`bʌndənt/ *adj* more than enough; plentiful: *We have ∼ proof of his guilt.*

abuse¹ /ə`bjuːs/ *n* **1** [U] wrong use; [C] instance of this: *an ∼ of trust.* **2** [C] unjust custom or practice that has become established. **3** [U] angry or violent attack in words; bad language; cursing: *shower ∼ on somebody.*

abuse² /ə`bjuːz/ *vt* **1** make a bad or wrong use of: *Don't ∼ the confidence they have placed in you.* **2** say severe, cruel or unjust things to or about a person.

abus·ive /ə`bjuːsɪv/ *adj* using, containing, curses: ∼ *language.*

abus·ive·ly *adv*

abys·mal /ə`bɪzməl/ *adj* (esp *fig* and *informal*) extreme: ∼ *ignorance.*

abys·mal·ly *adv*

abyss /ə`bɪs/ *n* [C] (*pl* ∼es) **1** hole so deep as to appear bottomless; hell. **2** deepest degree: (*fig*) *the ∼ of despair.*

aca·demic /ˌækə`demɪk/ *adj* **1** of teaching, studying; of schools, colleges, etc; scholarly, literary or classical (contrasted with technical or scientific): ∼ *subjects; the ∼ year.* **2** too concerned with theory and not sufficiently practical: *The question is ∼,* is of no practical importance. □ *n* [C] professional scholar.

academic freedom, liberty to teach and to discuss problems without outside e g Government, interference.

aca·demi·cally /-klɪ/ *adv*

aca·dem·ician /əˌkædə`mɪʃən US: ˌækədə`mɪʃən/ *n* [C] member of an academy, e g of the Royal Academy of Arts.

acad·emy /ə`kædəmɪ/ *n* [C] (*pl* -ies) **1** school for higher learning, usually for a special purpose: *a `naval/`military ∼; an ∼ of music.*

ac·cede /ək`siːd/ *vi* (*formal*) **1** agree, e g to a request. **2** take or succeed to (a position of authority).

ac·cel·er·ate /ək`seləreɪt/ *vt,vi* **1** increase the speed of; cause to move faster or happen earlier. **2** (of a motion or process) become faster.

ac·cel·er·ator /ək`seləreɪtə(r)/ *n* [C] **1** device, e g the pedal in a car, for controlling speed. **2** (*physics*) device for accelerating particles or nuclei.

ac·cent¹ /`æksənt US: `æksent/ *n* [C] **1** force when speaking (by means of stress or intonation) given to a syllable: *In the word 'today' the ∼ is on the second syllable.* **2** mark or symbol used in writing and printing to show a vowel sound or syllabic stress. ⇨ acute, circumflex and grave³. **3** [C, sometimes U] individual, local or national way of pronouncing: *speaking English with a foreign ∼.* **4** (*informal*) emphasis given to one aspect of a display, performance, etc· *At* *this year's Motor Show the* ~ *is on sports cars.*

ac·cent² /æk`sent/ *vt* **1** pronounce with an accent(3). **2** put emphasis on (a syllable or word).

ac·cen·tu·ate /ək`sentʃveɪt/ *vt* give more force or importance to.

ac·cept /ək`sept/ *vt,vi* **1** (agree to) receive (something offered): ~ *a gift/an invitation.* **2** agree; recognize; approve: *I* ~ *that the change may take some time. It is an* ~*ed truth/fact,* It is something that everyone believes. **3** take responsibility for: ~ *delivery of goods.*

ac·cept·able /-əbəl/ *adj* worth accepting; welcome: *if this proposal is* ~*able to you.*

ac·cept·ance /ək`septəns/ *n* [U] **1** accepting or being accepted. **2** approval (the usual word).

ac·cess /`ækses/ *n* [U] **1** way (in) to a place: *The only* ~ *to the farmhouse is across the fields.* **2** **access to,** right, opportunity or means of reaching, using or approaching: *Students must have* ~ *to good books.*

ac·cess·ible /ək`sesəbəl/ *adj* able to be reached, used, visited, influenced, etc: *a collection of paintings not* ~*ible to the general public.*

ac·cessi·bil·ity /ək`sesɪ`bɪlətɪ/ *n* [U]

ac·cess·ary /ək`sesərɪ/ *n* [C] (*pl* -ies), *adj* (US = **accessory**(1)) (*legal*) person who helps in any act, esp a crime. **accessary before/after the fact,** ⇨ fact(1).

ac·ces·sion /æk`seʃən/ *n* **1** [U] reaching a rank, position or state: *the Queen's* ~ *to the throne.* **2** [C,U] (*formal*) (an) addition; (an) increase: *recent* ~*s to the school library.*

ac·cess·ory /ək`sesərɪ/ *n* [C] (*pl* -ies) **1** = accessary. **2** thing that is extra, helpful, useful, but not an essential part of: *the accessories of a bicycle,* e g the lamp, a pump.

ac·ci·dent /`æksɪdənt/ *n* **1** [C] something that happens without a cause that can be seen at once, usually something unfortunate and undesirable: *He was killed in a* `*car* ~. *Accidents will happen,* (*proverb*) Some unfortunate events must be accepted as inevitable. ⇨ prone. **2** [U] instance; fate. **by accident,** by chance: *We met by* ~. `*accident prone,* frequently involved in accidents.

ac·ci·den·tal /`æksɪ`dentəl/ *adj* happening unexpectedly and by chance: *an* ~ *meeting with a friend.*

ac·ci·den·tally /-təlɪ/ *adv*

ao·claim /ə`kleɪm/ *vt* **1** welcome with shouts of approval; applaud loudly: ~ *the winner of a race;* ~ *him as a great actor.* **2** make a person a ruler: *They* ~*ed him King.* □ *n* [U] applause; approval: *The film received great critical* ~.

ac·cla·ma·tion /`æklə`meɪʃən/ *n* [U] (*formal*) loud and enthusiastic approval of a proposal, etc: *elected/carried by* ~

ac·cli·ma·tize /ə`klaɪmətaɪz/ *vt,vi* **1** get (oneself, animals, etc) used to a new climate. **2** (*fig*) get used to a new environment, new conditions, etc: *You will soon become* ~*d.*

ac·cli·mat·iz·ation /ə`klaɪmətaɪ`zeɪʃən US: -tɪ`z-/ *n* [U]

ac·col·ade /`ækəleɪd US: `ækə`leɪd/ *n* [C] **1** granting of a knighthood by a tap on the shoulder with the flat of a sword. **2** (*fig*) praise; approval.

ac·com·mo·date /ə`komədeɪt/ *vt* **1** have, provide, lodging for: *This hotel can* ~ *600 guests.* **2** (*formal*) change a plan so that it fits with something else: *I will* ~ *my plans to yours.*

ac·com·mo·dat·ing /ə`komədeɪtɪŋ/ *adj* willing to do things to please others; easy to deal with.

ac·com·mo·da·tion /ə`komə`deɪʃən/ *n* [U] (*GB*) furnished or unfurnished room(s), e g in a flat, hotel, etc: *Hotel* ~ *was scarce during the Olympic Games.*

ac·com·pani·ment /ə`kʌmpnɪmənt/ *n* [C] **1** thing that naturally or often goes with another thing: *Disease is often an* ~ *of famine.* **2** (*music*) (usually) instrumental part to go with a voice, choir or solo instrument: *a song with a piano* ~.

ac·com·pan·ist /ə`kʌmpənɪst/ *n* [C] person who accompanies a musician.

ac·com·pany /ə`kʌmpnɪ/ *vt* (*pt,pp* -ied) **1** go with: *He was accompanied by his secretary.* **2** occur or do at the same time as: *fever accompanying a headache.* **3** (*music*) play an accompaniment(2) to.

ac·com·plice /ə`kʌmplɪs US: ə`kom-/ *n* [C] helper or companion (in doing something illegal).

ac·com·plish /ə`kʌmplɪʃ US: ə`kom-/ *vt* succeed in doing; finish successfully: ~ *a task.*

ac·com·plished *adj* well trained; skilled: *an* ~*ed dancer.*

ac·com·plish·ment /ə`kʌmplɪʃmənt US: ə`kom-/ *n* (*formal*) **1** [U] completion; finishing: *the* ~*ment of their aims.* **2** [C] thing well done or successfully completed; skill.

ac·cord¹ /ə`kɔd/ *n* [U] *of one's own accord,* without being asked or forced; willingly. *in/out of accord (with),* agreeing/not agreeing with. *with one accord,* everybody agreeing.

ac·cord² /ə`kɔd/ *vi,vt* **1** be in agreement or harmony: *His behaviour does not* ~ *with his principles.* **2** (*formal*) give; grant: *He was* ~*ed a warm welcome.*

ac·cord·ance /ə`kɔdəns/ *n* *in accordance with,* in agreement with; as is expected of: *in* ~ *with your wishes/the regulations.*

ac·cord·ing /ə`kɔdɪŋ/ *according to,* *prep* **1** on the authority of: *A* ~ *to the Bible, God created the world in six days.* **2** in proportion to: *He will be punished* ~ *to the seriousness of his crime.* **3** in a manner consistent with: *The books are arranged on the shelves ~ to subjects.*

ac·cord·ing·ly *adv* for that reason.

ac·cord·ion /əˈkɔːdɪən/ *n* [C] portable musical instrument with a box of air, metal reeds and a keyboard.

ac·cost /əˈkɒst US: əˈkɔːst/ *vt* go up to and speak to first, esp a stranger in a public place: *I was ~ed by a beggar.*

ac·count[1] /əˈkaʊnt/ *n* **1** [C] (*commerce*) statement of money (to be) paid or received (for goods, services, etc): *I have an ~ with the Midland Bank,* keep my money with this Bank. **open an account; open a bank/post office, etc account,** start to keep one's money at a bank, etc. **settle one's account (with),** (a) pay what one owes. (b) (*fig*) do something to get revenge for an injury, etc. **square/balance accounts (with sb),** (a) receive or pay the difference between debit and credit. (b) (*fig*) end a quarrel, etc. by giving or taking punishment. ⇨ current(3), deposit[1](1), joint[2], private(1) and save[1](2). **2** [C] counting; calculation: *He is quick at ~s,* can do arithmetic quickly. **3** [U] benefit; profit. **turn/put sth to (good) account,** use money, abilities, talent, etc profitably. **4 give a good account of oneself,** do well; act in a way that brings credit. **5** [C] report; description: *Don't always believe newspaper ~s of events.* **by one's own account,** according to what one says oneself. **by/from all accounts,** according to what everybody, all the papers, etc. say. **6** [U] **take sth into account; take account of sth,** note or consider it; pay attention to it. **take no account of sth,** pay no attention to it. **7** [U] **on account of,** because of. **on this/that account,** for this/that reason: *Don't stay away on ~ of John/ on John's ~.* **on no account,** not for any reason: *Don't on any ~ leave the baby alone in the house.*

ac·count[2] /əˈkaʊnt/ *vt,vi* **1 account for,** (a) be an explanation of: *His illness ~s for his absence. Ah, that ~s for it!* (b) give an explanation of money spent. **2** consider to be: *In English law a man is ~ed innocent until he is proved guilty.*

account·able /-əbəl/ *adj* responsible; expected to give an explanation: *A mental patient is not ~able for his actions.*

ac·count·an·cy /əˈkaʊntənsɪ/ *n* [U] profession of an accountant.

ac·count·ant /əˈkaʊntənt/ *n* [C] (*GB*) person whose profession is to keep and examine business accounts.

ac·credit /əˈkredɪt/ *vt* appoint or send a person as an ambassador.

ac·crue /əˈkruː/ *vi* come as a natural growth or development: *If you keep your money in the Savings Bank,* interest ~s.

ac·cu·mu·late /əˈkjuːmjʊleɪt/ *vt,vi* make or become greater in number or quantity: *Dust soon ~s if the rooms are not swept.*

ac·cu·mu·la·tion /əˈkjuːmjʊˈleɪʃən/ *n* [C,U] collection: *an ~ of books/rubbish.*

ac·cu·mu·lat·ive /əˈkjuːmjʊlətɪv US: -leɪtɪv/ *adj* growing by being added to.

ac·cu·racy /ˈækjərəsɪ/ *n* [U] exactness; correctness.

ac·cu·rate·ly *adv*

ac·cu·rate /ˈækjərət/ *adj* **1** careful and exact: *be ~ in one's work/in what one says.* **2** free from error: *Clocks in railway stations should be ~.*

ac·cursed, ac·curst /əˈkɜːst/ *adj* under a curse; hateful.

ac·cu·sa·tion /ˌækjuːˈzeɪʃən/ *n* **1** [U] accusing or being accused. **2** [C] charge of doing wrong, of having broken the law: *bring an ~ (of theft) against a person.*

ac·cuse /əˈkjuːz/ *vt* say that he has done wrong, broken the law, is to be blamed: *~ him of theft/ be ~d of stealing.*

the accused, the person(s) charged in a criminal case.

ac·cuser, person who accuses.

ac·cus·ing·ly /əˈkjuːzɪŋlɪ/ *adv* in an accusing manner: *He pointed ~ at me.*

ac·cus·tom /əˈkʌstəm/ *vt* make oneself used to: *This is not the kind of treatment I'm ~ed to,* not the kind I usually receive.

ac·customed *adj* usual: *in his ~ed seat.*

ace /eɪs/ *n* [C] **1** the one on dice, playing-cards, etc; card so marked: *the ~ of spades.* **2** (*informal*) person who is first rate or an expert. **3 within an ace of,** (of bad or unlucky incidents) only just escaping: *within an ace of death/of being killed.*

acetic /əˈsiːtɪk/ *adj* of vinegar.

acety·lene /əˈsetəliːn/ *n* [U] (*chem*) colourless gas (C_2H_2) which burns with a bright light, used for welding and cutting metal: *an ~ torch.*

ache /eɪk/ *n* [C] dull continuous pain: *have ~s and pains all over; have a `head~; suffer from head~s.* (*Ache* is only combined with *back, ear, face, head, heart, stomach, tummy* and *tooth.*) □ *vi* **1** have a steady or continuous dull pain: *My head ~s/is aching.* **2** want very much: *He was aching for freedom.*

achieve /əˈtʃiːv/ *vt* **1** complete; get (something) done: *He will never ~ anything,* will not do anything successfully. **2** gain or reach by effort: *~ success/distinction in public life.*

achiev·able /-əbəl/ *adj* that can be achieved.

achieve·ment /əˈtʃiːvmənt/ *n* **1** [U] achieving: *the ~ of one's aims.* **2** [C] thing done successfully, with effort and skill: *The inventor was rewarded by the Government for his scientific ~.*

acid /ˈæsɪd/ *adj* **1** sour; sharp to the taste: *A lemon is an ~ fruit. Vinegar has an ~ taste.* **2** (*fig*) sarcastic: *an ~ wit; ~ remarks.* □ *n* [C,U] (*chem*) substance that contains hydrogen, which can react with metals to form a

salt: *Some ~s burn holes in wood and cloth.*
`acid test, (*fig*) test that proves of the value
of something.

acid·ify /əˈsɪdɪfaɪ/ *vt,vi* (*pt,pp* -ied) make
or become acid.

acid·ity /əˈsɪdətɪ/ *n* [U] state or quality of
being acid.

ac·knowl·edge /əkˈnɒlɪdʒ/ *vt* 1 admit the
truth, existence or reality of: *He refused to
~ defeat/that he was defeated.* 2 report that
one has received (something): *~ (receipt
of) a letter.* 3 express thanks for: *We must
~ his services to his country.* 4 show that
one recognizes (somebody) by giving a
greeting, a smile, a nod of the head, etc: *I
met her in town but she didn't even ~ my
wave.*

**ac·know·ledge·ment, ac·knowl·edg·
ment** /əkˈnɒlɪdʒmənt/ *n* 1 [U] act of acknowledging: *We are sending you a gift in ~
of your kindness.* 2 [C] something given or
done to acknowledge: *We have had no ~ of
our letter,* no reply.

acne /ˈæknɪ/ *n* [U] disease (common among
adolescents) in which there are pimples and
blackheads on the face and neck.

acorn /ˈeɪkɔːn/ *n* [C] seed or fruit of the oak
tree.

acous·tic /əˈkuːstɪk/ *adj* of sound, the
science of sound and the sense of hearing. □
n [C] studio, hall, etc from the consideration
of how well music, speech, etc can be heard.
acous·tics *n* 1 (used with a *sing verb*) the
scientific study of sound. 2 (used with a *pl
verb*) the physical qualities of sound; the
design of a hall etc, that makes it good,
poor, etc for hearing music or speeches: *The
~s of the new concert hall are excellent.*

ac·quaint /əˈkweɪnt/ *vt* 1 **ac·quaint sb/
oneself with,** make known: *~ oneself/
become ~ed/make oneself ~ed with one's
new duties.* 2 **be acquainted (with sb),**
have met (him) personally: *We are not ~ed.*

ac·quaint·ance /əˈkweɪntəns/ *n* 1 [U]
knowledge or information gained through
experience. **make sb's acquaintance,** get
to know him, e g by being introduced. 2 [C]
person whom one knows (less intimate than
a friend): *He has a wide circle of ~s.*

ac·quiesce /ˌækwɪˈes/ *vi* accept silently or
without protest.
ac·qui·escence /-ˈesəns/ *n* [C] (act of)
acquiescing.

ac·quire /əˈkwaɪə(r)/ *vt* gain by skill or
ability, by one's own efforts or behaviour:
*~ a good knowledge of English/a reputation
for dishonesty.* **an acquired taste,** one that
comes when one has experimented with food
or drink and, in the end, likes it.

ac·qui·si·tion /ˌækwɪˈzɪʃn/ *n* 1 [U] (*formal*) gaining; collecting: *He devotes his time
to the ~ of knowledge.* 2 [C] person or thing
acquired: *Mr Brown will be a valuable ~ to
(= a valuable new member of) the teaching
staff of our school.*

ac·quis·itive /əˈkwɪzətɪv/ *adj* fond of, in
the habit of, collecting, buying, more and
more things.

ac·quit /əˈkwɪt/ *vt* (-tt-) 1 **acquit sb (of/on
sth),** give a legal decision that (he) is not
guilty, e g of an offence. 2 (*formal*) conduct
(oneself): *He ~ted himself well/like a hero.*

ac·quit·tal /əˈkwɪtəl/ *n* [C,U] judgement
that a person is not guilty: *three convictions
and two ~s.*

acre /ˈeɪkə(r)/ *n* [C] measure of land, about
4 000 sq metres.

acre·age /ˈeɪkərɪdʒ/ *n* [U] area of land
measured in acres.

ac·rid /ˈækrɪd/ *adj* (of smell or taste) sharp;
bitter.

ac·ri·moni·ous /ˌækrɪˈməʊnɪəs/ *adj* (*formal*) (of arguments, etc) showing hate, disappointment.

ac·ri·mony /ˈækrɪmənɪ US: -məʊnɪ/ *n* [U]
(*formal*) temper, manner, language, showing hate, disappointment.

ac·ro·bat /ˈækrəbæt/ *n* [C] person who can
do clever or unusual physical acts, e g on a
tightrope or trapeze.

ac·ro·batic /ˌækrəˈbætɪk/ *adj* of or like an
acrobat.
ac·ro·bat·ics *n pl* (used with a *sing verb*)
acrobatic tricks or feats.

ac·ro·nym /ˈækrənɪm/ *n* [C] word formed
from the initial letters of a name, e g *NASA*
/ˈnæsə/, National Aeronautics and Space
Administration.

across[1] /əˈkrɒs US: əˈkrɔːs/ *adv* from one
side to the other: *Can you swim ~? The
river is a mile ~,* wide.

across[2] /əˈkrɒs US: əˈkrɔːs/ *prep* (for combinations with *verbs,* ⇨ the verb entries, e g
come, get, put, run.) 1 from side to side of:
*walk ~ the street; draw a line ~ a sheet of
paper.* 2 on the other side of: *My house is
just ~ the street.* 3 so as to form a cross; so
as to cross or intersect: *He sat with his arms
~ his chest.*

a·cross-the-`board, including all groups,
members, etc. in a business or industry: *an
~-the-board wage increase.*

act[1] /ækt/ *n* [C] 1 thing done: *To kick a dog
is a cruel ~.* 2 process of, instant of, doing;
action. **(catch sb) in the (very) ~ (of
doing sth),** while doing it: *The thief was
caught in the act of breaking into the house.*
3 law made by a government: *an ~ of Parliament.* 4 main division of a play: *a play in
five ~.* 5 one of a series of short performances in a programme: *a circus/variety ~.*
put on an act, pretend (in order to get one's
own way, etc).

Act of God, something which is the result of
uncontrollable natural forces, e g storms,
floods, earthquakes.

act[2] /ækt/ *vi,vt* 1 do something: *The time for
talking is past; we must ~ at once.* **act on**
(*a suggestion/sb's advice/an order*), do
what is suggested, advised, etc. 2 do what is

required or normal: *The brakes wouldn't ~ properly.* **3** do one's professional or official duty: *The police refused to ~,* would not interfere. **act for/on behalf of,** represent (a person) as a solicitor, barrister in a legal case: *A solicitor ~s for his clients.* **4** take the part of, eg a character in a play or cinema film, or in real life: *Who is ~ing (the part of) Hamlet? She's not really crying; she's only ~ing* (= pretending) *in order to gain your sympathy.* **act up,** *(informal)* behave badly so as to attract attention.

act·ing /ˈæktɪŋ/ *adj* doing the duties of another person for a time: *The ~ Manager/ Headmaster.* □ *n* [U] (art of) performing in a play for the theatre, cinema, TV, etc: *She did a lot of ~ while she was at college.*

ac·tion /ˈækʃən/ *n* **1** [U] process of doing things; (way of) using energy, influence, etc: *The time has come for ~, We must act now.* **bring/call (sth) into action,** cause (it) to act. **put (sth) out of action,** stop (it) working; make (it) unfit for use. **take action,** begin to act. **2** [C] thing done; act: *We shall judge you by your ~s, not by your promises.* **3** [C] **bring an action against sb,** (legal) seek judgement against him in a law court. **4** [C,U] fight(ing) between bodies of troops, between warships, etc: *go into ~,* start fighting.

`**action painting,** form of abstract painting in which paint is splashed, dribbled, etc on to the canvas.

`**action stations,** (mil) positions to which soldiers, etc go when fighting is expected to begin.

ac·ti·vate /ˈæktɪveɪt/ *vt* make active.

ac·tive /ˈæktɪv/ *adj* doing things; able to do things; in the habit of doing things: *He's over 90 and not very ~. Mount Vesuvius is an ~ volcano,* is one that erupts. **under active consideration,** being considered.

active voice, (gram) (a) form of a *verbal phrase* not containing *be* + a *past participle,* as in: *He was driving.* Compare: *He was being driven.* (b) sentence containing a *transitive verb* in which the *noun* or *pronoun* in front of the *verb* refers to the doer of the action: *The children finished off the cake.* Compare: *The cake was finished off by the children.*

ac·tive·ly *adv*

ac·tiv·ist /ˈæktɪvɪst/ *n* [C] person taking an active part, eg in a political movement.

ac·tiv·ity /ækˈtɪvətɪ/ *n* (*pl* -ies) **1** [U] being active or lively: *When a man is over 70, his time of full ~ is usually past.* **2** [C] thing (to be) done; occupation: *My numerous activities leave me little leisure.*

ac·tor /ˈæktə(r)/ *n* [C] man who acts on the stage, TV or in films.

ac·tress /ˈæktrəs/ *n* [C] woman who acts on the stage, TV or in films.

ac·tual /ˈæktʃʊəl/ *adj* existing in fact; real: *Can you give me the ~ figures,* not an esti-

mate or a guess?

ac·tu·al·ly /ˈæktʃəlɪ/ *adv* **1** really: *the political party ~ly in power. He looks honest, but ~ly he's a thief.* **2** strange or surprising as it may seem: *He not only ran in the race; he ~ly won it!*

ac·tu·al·ity /ˌæktʃʊˈælətɪ/ *n* (*pl* -ies) **1** [U] actual existence; reality. **2** (usually *pl*) actual conditions or facts.

acu·men /əˈkjuːmən/ *n* [U] ability to understand quickly and clearly: *business ~.*

acu·punc·ture /ˈækjʊpʌŋktʃə(r)/ *n* [U] (*med*) pricking of the flesh of the human body with fine needles to relieve pain and as a local anaesthetic.

acute /əˈkjuːt/ *adj* **1** (of the senses, sensations, intellect) keen, quick to react: *A bad tooth can cause ~ pain.* **2** (of diseases) coming quickly to a crisis: *the ~ stage of the disease,* the brief period during which the disease is severe and at a turning point. ⇨ chronic. **3** (of sounds) high; shrill.

acute angle, angle of less than 90°.

acute accent, mark over a vowel (ˊ), as over *e* in *café.*

acute·ly *adv*

acute·ness *n* [U]

ad /æd/ *n* [C] (*informal*) (abbr for) advertisement.

ad·age /ˈædɪdʒ/ *n* [C] old and wise saying.

Adam /ˈædəm/ *n* **not know sb from Adam,** have no knowledge of what he looks like.

`**Adam's apple,** part that projects in the front of the throat, esp in men, and moves up and down when one speaks.

ada·mant /ˈædəmənt/ *adj* refusing to give in: *On this point I am ~,* Nothing can change my decision.

adapt /əˈdæpt/ *vt* make suitable for a new use, need, situation, etc: *When you go to a new country, you must ~ (yourself) to new manners and customs. Novels are often ~ed for the stage, television and radio.*

adap·ter, adap·tor /-tə(r)/, (a) person who adapts. (b) thing that makes it possible for something to be used in a different way from that for which it was designed, eg a fitting for an electric socket so that more than one plug(3) may be used.

adapt·able /əˈdæptəbəl/ *adj* able to adapt or be adapted: *an ~ man can change according to circumstances, etc.*

ad·ap·ta·tion /ˌædæpˈteɪʃən/ *n* **1** [U] state of being adapted; adapting. **2** [C] thing made by adapting: *An ~ (of a novel) for the stage/for television.*

add /æd/ *vt,vi* **1** join, unite, put (one thing to another): *If you ~ 5 and/to 5 you get 10.* **add to,** increase: *This ~s to our difficulties.* **add together,** combine two or more things. **add sth up,** find the sum of: *~ up a column of figures; ~ them up.* **add up (to),** (a) give as a result, when joined: *The figures add up to 365.* (b) (*informal*) indicate; amount to:

All that this ~*s up to is that you don't want
to help, so why not say so?* (c) (*informal*)
make sense; be believable: *It just doesn't* ~
up. 2 say something more; go on to say:
'*And I hope you'll come early,' he* ~*ed.*
`adding-machine,` machine for calculating
mechanically.

ad·den·dum /ə`dendəm/ *n* [C] (*pl* -da
/-də/) thing (omitted) that is to be added.

ad·der /`ædə(r)/ *n* [C] 1 any of several small
poisonous snakes, e g the viper, common in
Europe. 2 any of several non-poisonous
snakes of N America.

ad·dict /ə`dɪkt/ *vt* **be addicted to,** drink,
smoke, etc without being able to stop wanting to: *He is* ~*ed to alcohol/smoking/
lying/drugs.* □ *n* /`ædɪkt/ person who is
addicted to something harmful: *A* `*drug* ~.
ad·dic·tion /ə`dɪkʃən/ *n* [C,U] (instance of)
being addicted.
ad·dic·tive /ə`dɪktɪv/ *adj* causing addiction:
~*ive drugs.*

ad·di·tion /ə`dɪʃən/ *n* **1** [U] action of
adding: *The sign* + *stands for* ~. **2** [C] person or thing added or joined: *He will be a
useful* ~ *to the staff of the school,* a useful
new teacher. *In addition (to),* as well (as).

ad·di·tional /ə`dɪʃənəl/ *adj* extra; added: ~
charges.
ad·di·tion·ally /-ʃənəlɪ/ *adv*

ad·di·tive /`ædɪtɪv/ *n* [C] substance added in
small amounts for a special purpose: *food
~s,* e g to add colour.

ad·dress[1] /ə`dres *US:* `ædres/ *n* **1** [C] particulars of where a person lives, works, etc
and where letters, etc may be delivered:
What's your home/business ~? **2** [C] speech
or talk (to an audience).

ad·dress[2] /ə`dres/ *vt* **1** make a speech to;
speak to, using a title: *Mr Green will now* ~
the meeting. Don't ~ *me as 'Colonel'; I'm
only a major.* **2** write the name and
address(1) on a letter, etc. **3** *address sth to,*
send (a remark, complaint, etc) to: *Please* ~
complaints to the manager, not to me.

ad·dres·see /`ædre`si/ *n* [C] person to
whom a speech is made.

ad·duce /ə`djus *US:* ə`dus/ *vt* (*formal*) put
forward (as proof, as an example)

ad·en·oidal /`ædɪ`nɔɪdəl/ *adj* of, concerning, the adenoids.

ad·en·oids /`ædɪnɔɪdz *US:* -dən-/ *n pl* soft,
sponge-like growth between the back of the
nose and the throat, in some cases making
breathing and speech difficult.

adept /`ædept/ *adj* expert, skilled: ~ *in*
photography.

ad·equacy /`ædɪkwəsɪ/ *n* [U] (*formal*) state
of being adequate: *He often doubts his* ~ *as
a husband and father.*

ad·equate /`ædɪkwət/ *adj* satisfactory; suf-
ficient: *Are you getting* ~ *payment for the
work you're doing?*
ad·equate·ly *adv*

ad·here /əd`hɪə(r)/ *vi* (*formal*) **1** stick (to):

Glue is used to make one surface ~ *to
another.* **2** remain faithful (to); support
firmly: ~ *to an opinion/a political party.*
ad·her·ence /-əns/ *n* [U]

ad·her·ent /əd`hɪərənt/ *n* [C] supporter (of a
cause, party, etc but not necessarily a member): *The proposal is gaining more and more*
~*s.*

ad·hesion /əd`hiʒən/ *n* [U] being or becom-
ing attached or united.

ad·hesive /əd`hisɪv/ *adj* able to stick or
join: ~ *tape/plaster.* □ *n* [C,U] substance
that sticks or joins, e g *gum.*

adieu /ə`dju *US:* ə`du/ *int, n* [C] (*pl* ~*s* or
~*x* /ə`djuz *US:* ə`duz/) (*formal*) goodbye:
bid her ~.

ad in·fi·ni·tum /`æd ˌɪnfɪ`naɪtəm/ (*Latin*)
without end; for ever.

ad inter·im /`æd ˌɪntərɪm/ (*Latin*) in the
meantime.

ad·jac·ent /ə`dʒeɪsənt/ *adj* next, lying near
(to) but not necessarily touching: ~ *to the
cinema;* ~ *angles.*

ad·jec·tival /`ædʒɪk`taɪvəl/ *adj* (*gram*) of
or like an adjective: *an* ~ *phrase/clause.*

ad·jec·tive /`ædʒɪktɪv/ *n* (*gram*) word that
names a quality, or that defines or limits a
noun; e g *green, pretty, bad.*

ad·join /ə`dʒɔɪn/ *vt,vi* be next or nearest
(to): *The two houses* ~.

ad·journ /ə`dʒɜn/ *vt,vi* **1** stop, e g discus-
sion at a meeting, etc. for a time: *The meeting was* ~*ed for a week.* **2** (of a meeting,
etc) stop or be stopped for a time.
ad·journ·ment *n* [C,U]

ad·judge /ə`dʒʌdʒ/ *vt* decide officially, by
law.

ad·ju·di·cate /ə`dʒudɪkeɪt/ *vt,vi* **1** (*legal*)
(of a judge or court) give a judgement or
decision: ~ *a claim for damages.* **2** (*formal*) sit in judgement in order to decide: ~
on/upon a disagreement.
ad·ju·di·ca·tion /ə`dʒudɪ`keɪʃən/ *n* [C,U]
ad·ju·di·ca·tor /-tə(r)/, judge; member of a
group of judges, e g in a competition.

ad·junct /`ædʒʌŋkt/ *n* [C] **1** something
which is part of a more important thing. **2**
(*gram*) word(s) or phrase added to explain,
describe or define another word in a sentence.

ad·just /ə`dʒʌst/ *vt* set right; put in order;
regulate; make suitable or convenient for
use: *The body* ~*s itself to changes in temperature.*
`well-`adjusted, (*psych*) getting on well
with other persons.
adjust·able /-əbəl/ *adj* that can be adjusted.
ad·just·ment *n* [U] adjusting; settling of, e g
insurance, claims; [C] act or means of
adjusting.

ad·ju·tant /`ædʒutənt/ *n* [C] army officer
responsible for general administration and
discipline in a battalion.

ad lib /`æd `lɪb/ *adv* (*abbr of ad libitum*)
(*informal*) freely. □ **ad-lib** *vi* (-bb-) (*infor-*

9

mal) improvise, e g by making additions to one's part in a play. □ *adj* made by ad-libbing: ~ *comments.*

ad·min·is·ter /əd`mɪnɪstə(r)/ *vt,vi* **1** control, manage, look after business affairs, a household, etc: ~ *a country*, govern it. **2** apply; put into operation; hand out; give: ~ *the law;* ~ *relief/help to people who are suffering from floods.* **3** cause to take: ~ *the last sacraments*, i e to a dying man.

ad·min·is·tra·tion /əd`mɪnɪ`streɪʃən/ *n* [U] **1** management of affairs, etc, esp public affairs, government policy, etc. **2** the administering of justice, an oath, a sacrament, relief, a remedy, a punishment.

ad·min·is·tra·tive /əd`mɪnɪstrətɪv *US:* -streɪtɪv/ *adj* of the management of affairs: *lacking in* ~ *ability.*

ad·min·is·tra·tor /əd`mɪnɪstreɪtə(r)/ *n* [C] **1** person who administers; person with ability to organize. **2** (*legal*) person officially appointed to manage the property of others, to take charge of an estate, etc.

ad·mir·able /`ædmrəbəl/ *adj* excellent; to be admired.

ad·mir·ably /-əblɪ/ *adv*

ad·mir·al /`ædmərəl/ *n* [C] officer in command of a country's warships, or of a fleet or squadron.

Ad·mir·al·ty /`ædmərəltɪ/ *n* **1** office of admiral. **2** that branch of Government which controls the Navy.

ad·mir·ation /`ædmə`reɪʃən/ *n* [U] feeling of pleasure, satisfaction, respect: *She speaks English so well that her friends are filled with* ~.

ad·mire /əd`maɪə(r)/ *vt* **1** look at with pleasure or satisfaction; have a high opinion of: *admiring Britain's legal system.* **2** express admiration of: *Don't forget to* ~ *the baby.*

ad·mirer, person who admires; man who finds a woman attractive: *Mary and her many* ~*s.*

ad·mir·ing *adj* showing or feeling admiration.

ad·mir·ing·ly *adv*

ad·miss·ible /əd`mɪsəbəl/ *adj* (*legal*) that can be allowed as proof in a law court: ~ *evidence.*

ad·mis·sion /əd`mɪʃən/ *n* **1** [U] admitting, being admitted, to a club, a school, a theatre, a museum, etc; fee, charge or condition for this: *A*~ *to the school is by examination only. A*~ *free.* **2** [C] statement admitting or confessing something: *make an* ~ *of guilt. by/on his own admission*, as he himself admitted.

ad·mit /əd`mɪt/ *vt,vi* (-tt-) **1** allow to enter; let in: *The secretary opened the door and* ~*ted me* (*into the office*). **2** have room enough for: *The cinema is small and* ~*s only 300 people.* **3** acknowledge; confess; accept as true or valid: *The accused man* ~*ted his guilt. I* ~ *my mistake/that I was*

mistaken. **admit to,** confess: *I must* ~ *to feeling ashamed of my conduct.*

ad·mit·tance /əd`mɪtəns/ *n* [U] act of admitting, being admitted (esp to a place that is not public); right of entry: *No* ~ *except on business.*

ad·mit·ted·ly /əd`mɪtɪdlɪ/ *adv* without denial; by general agreement: *A*~, *he has not misbehaved before, but ...*

ad·mon·ish /əd`mɒnɪʃ/ *vt* (*formal*) give a mild warning or show disapproval: *The teacher* ~*ed the boys for being lazy.*

ad·mo·ni·tion /`ædmə`nɪʃən/ *n* [C,U]

ad nauseam /`æd `nɔːsɪəm/ *adv* (*Latin*) **1** to the point of being disgusted. **2** (*informal*) so as to cause (great) annoyance, e g because of continuing for too long or repetition.

ado /ə`duː/ *n* [U] fuss: *Without more/much/further* ~, *he signed the agreement.*

adobe /ə`dəʊbɪ/ *n* [U] sun-dried brick (not fired in a kiln), of clay and straw: (as an *adjective*) *an* ~ *house.*

ado·les·cence /`ædə`lesəns/ *n* [U] period of life between childhood and maturity; growth during this period.

ado·les·cent /`ædə`lesənt/ *adj, n* [C] (person) growing up (age 12 or 13 to 18).

adopt /ə`dɒpt/ *vt* **1** take (a child) into one's family as a relation, esp as a son or daughter, with legal guardianship: *As they had no children of their own, they* ~*ed an orphan.* ⇨ foster. **2** take, e g an idea or custom, and use: *European dress has been* ~*ed by people in many parts of the world.* **3** accept, e g a report or recommendation: *Congress* ~*ed the new measures.*

·adop·tion /ə`dɒpʃən/ *n* [U] adopting or being adopted: *The country of his* ~.

adop·tive /ə`dɒptɪv/ *adj* taken by adoption: *His* ~ *parents.*

ador·able /ə`dɔrəbəl/ *adj* lovable; delightful.

ador·ably /-əblɪ/ *adv*

ador·ation /`ædə`reɪʃən/ *n* [U] worship; love: *his* ~ *for Jane.*

adore /ə`dɔ(r)/ *vt* **1** worship (God); love deeply and respect highly. **2** (*informal*) like very much: *The baby* ~*s being tickled.*

adorer, person who adores (another person)

ador·ing *adj* showing love: *adoring looks.*

ador·ing·ly *adv*

adorn /ə`dɔn/ *vt* add beauty or ornament(s) to; decorate (the usual word) (oneself with jewels, etc.)

adorn·ment *n* [U] adorning; [C] (*formal*) ornament; decoration.

ad·renal /ə`drɪnəl/ *adj* (*anat*) of or near the kidneys: ~ *glands.*

adrift /ə`drɪft/ *adv, adj* (of ships and boats) afloat, not under control; loose: *cut a boat* ~ *from its moorings.*

adroit /ə`drɔɪt/ *adj* (*formal*) clever; skilful

adroit·ly *adv*

adroit·ness *n* [U]

adu·la·tion /`ædjʊ`leɪʃən *US:* -dʒʊˈl-/ *n* [U]

(the giving of) too much praise or respect, esp to win favour.

adult /ˈædʌlt/ *adj* grown to full size or strength; (of persons) intellectually and emotionally mature. □ *n* [C] **1** person or animal grown to full size and strength. **2** (*legal*) person old enough to vote, marry, etc.

adult·hood /ˈædʌlthʊd/ *n* [U] the period or state of being adult.

adul·ter·ate /əˈdʌltəreɪt/ *vt* (*formal*) make impure, make poorer in quality.

adul·ter·ation /əˈdʌltəˈreɪʃən/ *n* [U]

adul·terer /əˈdʌltərə(r)/ *n* [C] man who commits adultery.

adul·ter·ess /əˈdʌltərəs/ *n* [C] woman who commits adultery.

adul·ter·ous /əˈdʌltərəs/ *adj* of adultery.

adul·tery /əˈdʌltəri/ *n* (*pl* -ies) **1** [U] voluntary sexual intercourse of a married person with a person to whom he or she is not married. **2** [C] instance of this.

ad·vance¹ /ədˈvɑns US: -ˈvæns/ *n* [C,U] **1** forward movement; progress: *Science was made great ~s during the last fifty years.* **in advance (of),** before(hand): *Send your luggage in ~, before you yourself leave. Galileo's ideas were (well) in ~ of the age in which he lived.* **2** (as an *adjective*) before; early: *have ~ notice, e g of somebody's arrival.*

ad·vance² /ədˈvɑns US: -ˈvæns/ *vi,vt* **1** come or move forward: *Our troops have ~d two miles.* **2** make progress: *Has civilization ~d during this century?* **3** (of costs, values, prices) rise: *Property values continue to ~.* **4** bring forward: *The date of the meeting was ~d from the 10th to the 3rd June. Such actions are unlikely to ~ your promotion.* **5** pay (money) before the due date: *He asked his employer to ~ him a month's salary.*

ad·vance·ment *n* [U]

ad·vanced /ədˈvɑnst US: -ˈvæn-/ *adj* far on in life or progress, etc: *~d in years, very old; ~d courses of study.* ⇨ elementary.

ad·van·tage /ədˈvɑntɪdʒ US: -ˈvæn-/ *n* **1** [C] something useful, helpful or likely to bring success, esp in competition: *the ~s of a good education.* **have/gain/win an advantage (over),** (have, give, etc) a better position or opportunity: *Tom's university education gave him an ~ over boys who had not been to a university.* **have the advantage of sb,** know a person or thing that he does not know. **2** [U] benefit; profit: *He gained little ~ from his visit to London.* **take advantage of sb,** deceive him, play a trick on him. **take (full) advantage of sth,** use it profitably, for one's own benefit: *He always takes full ~ of every opportunity.* **to advantage,** in a way that enables a thing to be seen, used, etc in the best way: *The painting is seen to better ~ from a distance.* **be/prove to sb's advantage,** be profitable or helpful to him.

ad·van·tage·ous /ˌædvənˈteɪdʒəs/ *adj* profitable; useful.

ad·van·tage·ous·ly *adv*

advent /ˈædvənt/ *n* **1** (usually **the ~**) coming or arrival of an important development, season, etc): *Since the ~ of atomic power, there have been great changes in industry.* **2** **A~,** (*eccles*) the coming of Christ; the season (with four Sundays) before Christmas Day. **3** the second coming of Christ at the Last Judgement.

ad·ven·ti·tious /ˌædvenˈtɪʃəs/ *adj* (*formal*) obtained or happening by chance: *~ aid.*

ad·ven·ture /ədˈventʃə(r)/ *n* **1** [C] strange or unusual event, esp an exciting or dangerous journey or activity: *The explorer told the boys about his ~s in the Arctic.* **2** [U] risk; danger, e g in travel and exploration: *He's fond of ~.*

ad·ven·turer, (a) daring or adventurous person. (b) person who is ready to make a profit by risky or dishonest methods.

ad·ven·tur·ess, woman adventurer.

ad·ven·tur·ous /ədˈventʃərəs/ *adj* **1** fond of, eager for, adventure. **2** full of danger and excitement: *an ~ voyage.*

ad·verb /ˈædvɜb/ *n* [C] (*gram*) word that answers questions with *how, when, where* and explains or limits a verb, adjective or another adverb, e g *quickly, now, here.*

ad·verb·ial /ædˈvɜbɪəl/ *adj* of the nature of an adverb: *In the sentence — I put my hand out of the window, 'out of the window' is an ~ phrase.* □ *n* [C] adverb or adverbial phrase.

ad·verbi·ally *adv*

ad·ver·sary /ˈædvəsəri US: -seri/ *n* [C] (*pl* -ies) enemy; opponent (in a contest).

ad·verse /ˈædvɜs/ *adj* unhelpful or unuseful: *~ weather conditions.*

ad·verse·ly *adv*

ad·ver·sity /ədˈvɜsəti/ *n* [C,U] (*pl* -ies) trouble: *Try to be patient/cheerful in ~.*

ad·vert² /ˈædvɜt/ *n* [C] (*GB informal*) (abbr of) advertisement(2).

ad·ver·tise /ˈædvətaɪz/ *vt,vi* make known to people (by printing notices in newspapers, announcements on TV, etc: *~ for a typist.*

ad·ver·tiser, person who advertises.

ad·ver·tise·ment /ədˈvɜtɪsmənt US: ˈædvərˈtaɪzmənt/ *n* **1** [U] advertising: *A~ helps to sell goods.* **2** [C] public announcement (in the press, TV, etc.): *put an ~ in the newspaper.*

ad·vice /ədˈvaɪs/ *n* [U] informed opinion about what to do, how to behave: *You won't get well unless you follow your doctor's ~.* **act on sb's advice,** do what he suggests. **(give sb) a piece/a bit/a word/a few words of advice,** (give) an opinion about what to do, etc.

ad·vis·able /ədˈvaɪzəbəl/ *adj* sensible; to be recommended: *Do you think it ~ to wait?*

ad·vise /ədˈvaɪz/ *vt,vi* **1** give advice to; recommend: *The doctor ~d a complete rest.*

What do you ~ me to do? **2** (*comm*) inform; notify: *Please ~ us when the goods are ready.* **ill-/well-advised,** ⇨**ill, well.**

ad·vis·er, person who gives advice, esp one who is regularly consulted: *an ~r to the Government.*

ad·vis·ory /əd'vaɪzərɪ/ *adj* of advice; having the power to advise: *an ~ committee.*

ad·vo·cate /'ædvəkət/ *n* [C] **1** person who speaks in favour of a person or thing (esp a cause): *an ~ of equal opportunity for men and women.* **2** (*legal*) person who does this professionally in a court of law in Scotland. □ *vt* /'ædvəkeɪt/ support (the usual word): *Do you ~ euthanasia?*

ad·vo·cacy /'ædvəkəsɪ/ *n* [U] pleading in support.

adze, adz /ædz/ *n* [C] carpenter's tool (with a blade at right angles to the handle) for cutting or shaping wood.

aer·ate /'eəreɪt/ *vt* let or put air into: *~ the soil by digging.*

aer·ation /'eə'reɪʃən/ *n* [U]

aer·ial¹ /'eərɪəl/ *adj* **1** existing in, moving through, from the air: *an ~ photograph.* **2** of or like air.

aer·ial² /'eərɪəl/ *n* [C] that part of a radio or TV system which receives or sends out signals.

aer(o)- /eər(ə)-/ *prefix* of aircraft: *aerodynamics.*

aero·bat·ics /'eərə'bætɪks/ *n* [U] (used with a *sing verb*) performance of acrobatic feats by pilots, e g flying upside down.

aero·drome /'eərədrəʊm/ *n* [C] airport (the usual word).

aero·dy·nam·ics /'eərəʊdaɪ'næmɪks/ *n* [U] (used with a *sing verb*) science dealing with the flow of air and the motion of aircraft, bullets, etc through air.

aero·naut·ics /'eərə'nɔːtɪks/ *n* [U] (used with a *sing verb*) aviation (the more usual word).

aero·plane /'eərəpleɪn/ *n* [C] aircraft with one or more engines.

aero·sol /'eərəsɒl US: -sɔl/ *n* [C] container with compressed gas for spraying a mist of scent, paint, etc.

aero·space /'eərəʊspeɪs/ *n* [U] the earth's atmosphere and the space beyond: (as an *adjective*) *an ~ vehicle.*

aes·thete /'iːsθiːt US: 'esθiːt/ *n* [C] person who claims to have great love of and understanding of what is beautiful, esp in the arts.

aes·thetic, es·thetic /iːs'θetɪk US: 'es-/ *adj* of the appreciation of beauty in music, painting, nature etc; (of persons) having such appreciation: *~ standards.* □ *n* particular set of such principles: *the ~ in which he believed.*

aes·thet·ics *n* [U] (used with a *sing verb*) branch of philosophy which tries to make clear the laws and principles of beauty.

afar /ə'fɑː(r)/ *adv* far off or away. *from afar,* from a distance

af·fable /'æfəbəl/ *adj* polite and friendly: *~ to everybody.*

af·fably /-əblɪ/ *adv*

affa·bil·ity /'æfə'bɪlətɪ/ *n* [U] quality of being affable.

af·fair /ə'feə(r)/ *n* [C] **1** something (to be) done or thought about: *That's my ~, not yours.* **2** (*pl*) business of any kind: *A prime minister is kept busy with ~s of state,* the task of government. **mind one's own affairs,** not ask personal questions. **state of affairs,** conditions. **3 have an affair (with sb),** have an emotional (and sexual) relationship. **4** (*informal*) event: *The plane crash was a terrible ~.*

af·fect¹ /ə'fekt/ *vt* **1** influence; have an effect on: *The cold climate ~ed his health,* injured it. **2** produce sad, grateful, etc feelings: *He was much ~ed by the sad news.* **3** (of diseases) cause a particular condition in: *The left lung is ~ed,* e g by cancer.

af·fect² /ə'fekt/ *vt* pretend to have or feel or to do: *He ~ed ignorance.*

af·fec·ted *adj* not natural or genuine: *~ed manners/speech.*

af·fec·ta·tion /'æfek'teɪʃən/ *n* [C,U] (kind of) behaviour that is not natural or genuine, esp for effect: *The ~s in the way she speaks* (e g her vocabulary, accent) *annoy me.*

af·fec·tion /ə'fekʃən/ *n* [U] kindly feeling; love: *Every mother has ~ for/feels ~ toward her children.* **gain/win sb's affection(s),** win the love of.

af·fec·tion·ate /ə'fekʃənət/ *adj* loving: *an ~ wife.*

af·fec·tion·ately *adv* **Yours affectionately,** used to end a letter, e g from a man to his sister.

af·fi·da·vit /'æfɪ'deɪvɪt/ *n* [C] (*legal*) written statement, made on oath, (to be) used as legal proof or evidence: *swear/make/take an ~.*

af·fili·ate /ə'fɪlɪeɪt/ *vt,vi* (of a society or an institution, of a member) enter into association: *The College is ~d to the University.*

af·fili·ation /ə'fɪlɪ'eɪʃən/ *n* [C,U]

af·fin·ity /ə'fɪnətɪ/ *n* (*pl* -ies) **1** [C] close connection, relation; structural similarity (between animals and plants, languages, etc or of one thing with another). **2** [C] strong liking or attraction: *She feels a strong ~ to/ for him.*

af·firm /ə'fɜːm/ *vt,vi* declare positively: *~ the truth of a statement/~ that it is true.*

af·firm·ation /'æfə'meɪʃən/ *n* [C,U]

af·firm·ative /ə'fɜːmətɪv/ *adj, n* (answering) 'yes': *The answer is the ~,* is 'Yes'.

af·fix¹ /ə'fɪks/ *vt* fix or attach (the usual words): *~ a seal/stamp to a document.*

af·fix² /'æfɪks/ *n* [C] suffix or prefix, e g *-ly, -able, un-, co-.*

af·flict /ə'flɪkt/ *vt* cause bodily or mental harm: *~ed with rheumatism.*

af·flic·tion /ə'flɪkʃən/ *n* **1** [U] suffering; distress: *help people in ~.* **2** [C] cause or occasion of suffering: *the ~s of old age*, e g deafness, blindness.

af·fluence /ˈæflʊəns/ *n* [U] wealth.

af·fluent /ˈæflʊənt/ *adj* wealthy: *the ~ society*, members of society who are wealthy and are concerned with prosperity.

af·ford /əˈfɔd/ *vt* **1** (usually with *can/could, be able to*) spare or find enough time or money for: *We can't ~ a holiday/can't ~ to go away this summer.* **2** (with *can/could*) run the risk of: *I can't ~ to neglect my work.* **3** (*formal*) provide: *The trees ~ a pleasant shade.*

af·fray /əˈfreɪ/ *n* [C] fight in a public place, causing or likely to cause a disturbance of the peace: *The men were all charged with causing an ~.*

af·front /əˈfrʌnt/ *vt* insult on purpose, esp in public: *feel ~ed at having one's word doubted.* □ *n* [C] public insult; deliberate show of disrespect: *an ~ to his pride.*

afield /əˈfild/ *adv* *far afield*, far away from home; to or at a distance.

aflame /əˈfleɪm/ *adj* (*poetic*) in flames; red as if burning: *~ with passion.*

afloat /əˈfləʊt/ *adj* **1** floating; carried along on air or water: *The ship crashed on the rocks and we couldn't get it ~ again.* **2** at sea; on board ship: *life ~*, the life of a sailor. **3** (of a business) started; making enough profit.

afoot /əˈfʊt/ *adj* in progress or operation; being prepared: *There's a scheme ~ to improve the roads.*

afore·said /əˈfɔ sed/ *adj* (*legal*) said or written before.

afore·thought /əˈfɔ θɔt/ ⇨ malice.

afraid /əˈfreɪd/ *adj* **1** frightened: *There's nothing to be ~ of.* **2** doubtful or anxious about what may happen: *I was ~ of hurting his feelings/that I might hurt his feelings.* **3** *be afraid*, (with *that* usually omitted) (a polite way of saying or writing something that may be unwelcome): *I'm ~ we shall be late.*

afresh /əˈfreʃ/ *adv* again; in a new way: *Let's start ~.*

Afro- /ˈæfrəʊ/ *prefix* of Africa or Africans: *an ~ hairstyle.*

'Afro-ˈAsian *adj* of Africa and Asia.

'Afro-Aˈmerican *adj*, *n* [C] (of an) American of African descent.

aft /ɑft *US:* æft/ *adv* (*naut*) at or near the stern of a ship.

after¹ /ˈɑftə(r) *US:* ˈæf-/ *adj* **1** later; following: *in ~ years.* **2** (*naut*) toward the stern of a ship: *the ~ cabin.*

after² /ˈɑftə(r) *US:* ˈæf-/ *adv* later in time; behind in place: *He fell ill on Monday and died three days ~* (*later* is more usual). *Soon ~* (*afterwards* is more usual), *he went to live in Wales.*

after³ /ˈɑftə(r) *US:* ˈæf-/ *conj* at or during a time later than: *I arrived ~ he* (*had*) *left.*

after⁴ /ˈɑftə(r) *US:* æf-/ *prep* **1** following in time; later than: *~ dinner/dark/two o'clock.*

after that, then; next. **2** next in order to; following: *'Against' comes ~ 'again' in a dictionary.* **3** behind: *Shut the door ~ you.* **4** as a result of: *I shall never speak to him again ~ what he has said about me.* **5** in spite of: *A~ all my care, it was broken. He failed ~ all*, in spite of all that had been done, etc. **6** *noun after noun*, repeatedly; very often: *day ~ day.* **7** in the style of; in imitation of: *a painting ~ Rembrandt.* **8** (used with *verbs*, showing pursuit, search, inquiry): *Did they ask ~ me*, ask for news of me? *The police are ~* (= trying to find and arrest) *my brother.* ⇨ also **look**, **name** and **take**.

after- /ɑftə(r) *US:* æf-/ *prefix* second or later.

'after-care, further treatment given to a person, e g who has been ill.

'after-effect, effect that occurs afterwards, e g a delayed effect of a drug used medically.

(the) 'after-life, (a) the life believed to follow death. (b) the later part of a person's lifetime (esp after a particular event).

'after-math /-mæθ/, (*fig*) outcome; consequence: *Misery is usually the ~math of war.*

'after-thought, thinking afterwards; thought that comes afterwards.

after·noon /ˈɑftəˈnun *US:* ˈæf-/ *n* [C] time between morning and evening: *in/during the ~; this/yesterday/tomorrow ~; on Sunday ~;* (as an *adjective*) *an ~ sleep.*

after·wards /ˈɑftəwədz *US:* ˈæf-/ *adv* after; later.

again /əˈgen/ *adv* **1** once more: *If you fail the first time, try ~. now and again*, occasionally. *again and again; time and (time) again*, repeatedly; very often. **2** *not ever/never again*, not any more: *Don't ever do that ~.* **3** to or in the original condition, position, etc: *You'll soon be well ~. He was glad to be home ~.* **4** *as many/much again*, (a) the same number/quantity. (b) twice as many/much; the same in addition. **5** *then again*, furthermore, besides: *Then ~, I doubt whether...*

against /əˈgenst/ *prep* **1** (showing opposition): *Public opinion was ~ the proposal.* Compare *for, in favour of.* **2** (used with *verbs* showing protest): *vote/cry out/write ~ a proposal.* **3** (used with *verbs* showing collision or impact): *The rain was beating ~ the windows.* **4** in contrast to: *The trees were black ~ the morning sky.* **5** in preparation for; to prevent: *have an injection ~ smallpox.* **6** (showing support or closeness) by the side of (and touching): *Place the ladder ~ the tree. Put the piano ~ the wall. He was leaning ~ a post.*

ag·ate /ˈægɪt/ *n* [C,U] (sorts of) very hard stone with bands or patches of colour.

age¹ /eɪdʒ/ *n* **1** [C] length of time a person has lived or a thing has existed: *What's his ~*, How old is he? *Their ~s are 4, 7 and 9. be/come of age*, be/become old enough to be responsible in law. *be of an age,* reach a stage in life when one ought to do something: *He's of an ~ when he ought to try settling down,* e g get a good job, marry. *over age,* having passed a certain age or age limit: *He won't be allowed a child's fare; he's over age. under age,* too young. **2** [U] later part of life (contrasted with *youth*): *His back was bent with ~.* **3** [C] great or long period of time, with special characteristics or events: *the atomic ~.* ⇨ also *middle*(3), *stone*(1). **4** (*pl*) (*informal*) very long time: *We've been waiting for ~s.*

`age-bracket, period of life between two specified ages, e g between 20 and 30.

`age-group, number of persons of the same age.

age² /eɪdʒ/ *vt,vi* (*present participle ~*ing or *ageing, pp ~*d /eɪdʒd/) (cause to) grow old: *He's ag(e)ing fast.*

`age-less *adj* eternal; always young.

`age limit, minimum or maximum age at which a person can take part in an activity, become a member of an organisation.

`age-long *adj* lasting for a very long time.

'age of con`sent, age at which the law recognizes a girl's responsibility for agreeing to sexual intercourse, a person's right to marry, etc.

'age-`old *adj* that has been known, practised, etc for a long time: *~-old customs/ceremonies*

-age /-ɪdʒ, -ɑdʒ/ *suffix* (used to form a *noun*): *postage; sabotage.*

aged¹ /eɪdʒd/ *adj* of the age of: *a boy ~ ten.*

aged² /eɪdʒɪd/ *adj* very old: *the poor and the ~.*

age-ing, ag-ing /eɪdʒɪŋ/ *n* [U] process of growing old; changes that occur as the result of the passing of time.

agency /eɪdʒənsɪ/ *n* (*pl* -ies) **1** [C] business, place of business, of an agent(1): *He found a job through an em`ployment ~.* **2** [U] *the agency of,* the action, help or cause of: *Rocks are worn smooth through the ~ of water.*

agenda /ə`dʒendə/ *n* [C] (*pl ~*s) (list of) things to be done, business to be discussed, e g by a committee: *the next item on the ~.*

agent /eɪdʒənt/ *n* [C] **1** person who acts for, or who manages or arranges the affairs of another or others: *a `house-~,* one who buys, sells, lets and rents houses. **2** person used to achieve something or to get a result. **3** (*science*) substance producing an effect: *Rain and frost are natural ~s that wear away rocks.*

ag-glom-er-ation /ə`glɒmə`reɪʃən/ *n* [U] action of collecting into a mass; [C] (esp untidy or unplanned) heap or collection.

ag-grand-ize-ment /ə`grændɪzmənt/ *n* [C] increase in power, rank, wealth, importance: *a man bent on personal ~.*

ag-gra-vate /`ægrəveɪt/ *vt* **1** make worse or

more serious: *~ an illness/offence.* **2** (*informal*) irritate: *How aggravating!*

ag-gra-va-tion /`ægrə`veɪʃən/ *n* [C,U]

ag-gre-gate /`ægrɪgət/ *n* [C] total obtained by adding together.

ag-gres-sion /ə`greʃən/ *n* **1** [U] attack that has no (obvious) cause, often beginning a quarrel or war: *It was difficult to decide which country was guilty of ~.* **2** [C] instance of this.

ag-gress-ive /ə`gresɪv/ *adj* **1** capable of attacking or quarrelling without a reason: *an ~ man.* **2** of or for attacking: *~ weapons.* **3** not afraid of opposition, energetic and able to argue powerfully: *A man who goes from door to door selling things has to be ~ if he wants to succeed.*

ag-gress-ive-ly *adv*

ag-gress-ive-ness *n* [U]

ag-gres-sor /ə`gresə(r)/ *n* [C] country, person, making an aggressive attack.

ag-grieve /ə`griv/ *vt* (*formal*) (usually passive) feel great sorrow (esp because of unjust treatment): *be ~d.*

ag-gro /`ægrəʊ/ *n* [U] (*GB sl*) aggression as shown by gangs of teenagers towards other gangs, racial minorities, etc.

aghast /ə`ɡɑst US: ə`ɡæst/ *adj* filled with fear or surprise: *He stood ~ at the terrible sight.*

agile /`ædʒaɪl US: `ædʒəl/ *adj* (of living things) moving, acting, quickly and effortlessly: *an ~ mind.*

agile-ly *adv*

agil-ity /ə`dʒɪlətɪ/ *n* [U]

ag-ing /eɪdʒɪŋ/ *n* ⇨ ageing.

agi-tate /`ædʒɪteɪt/ *vt,vi* **1** move or shake (a liquid). **2** cause anxiety to (a person), often making one's mind or feelings): *He was ~d about his wife's health.* **3** *agitate for,* argue publicly in favour of, take part in a campaign for: *agitating for higher wages.*

agi-tated *adj* anxious.

agi-ta-tion /`ædʒɪ`teɪʃən/ *n* **1** [U] moving or shaking (of a liquid). **2** [U] anxiety: *She was in a state of ~.* **3** [C,U] discussion or debate (for the purpose of bringing about a change); [U] social or political unrest or trouble caused by such discussion: *Small businesses carried on a long ~ against the government.*

agi-ta-tor /`ædʒɪteɪtə(r)/ *n* [C] person who agitates for, esp political, change.

aglow /ə`ɡləʊ/ *adj* **1** bright with colour: *The sky was ~ with the setting sun* **2** (of persons) showing warmth from exercise or excitement: *~ with pleasure.*

ag-nos-tic /æɡ`nɒstɪk/ *n* [C] person who believes that nothing can be known about God or of anything except things we can see, touch, etc. □ *adj* of this belief.

ag-nos-ti-cism /æɡ`nɒstɪsɪzm/ *n* [U] this belief.

ago /ə`ɡəʊ/ *adv* (used to show time measured back to a point in the past; always placed after the word or words it describes and used with the *past tense*): *The train left a few minutes* ∼/*not long* ∼/*a long while* ∼. *It was seven years* ∼ *that my brother died*. (*Note:* compare, It is seven years *since* my brother died.)

agog /ə'gɒg/ *adj* full of interest; excited: ∼ *for news/to hear the news*.

ag·o·ny /'ægənɪ/ *n* (*sing,* or *pl* -ies) great pain or suffering (of mind or body): *She looked on in* ∼ *at her child's sufferings*.

ag·on·ized /'ægənɑɪzd/ *adj* expressing agony: ∼ *shrieks*.

ag·on·iz·ing /'ægənɑɪzɪŋ/ *adj* causing agony.

agora·phobia /'ægərə'fəʊbɪə/ *n* [U] extreme fear of (crossing) open spaces.

agrar·ian /ə'greərɪən/ *adj* of land (esp farmland) or land ownership: ∼ *policies*.

agree /ə'griː/ *vi,vt* **1** say 'Yes'; consent: *I asked him to help me and he* ∼*d*. **2** be of the same opinion(s): *We* ∼*d to start early/on making an early start/that we should start early. Have you* ∼*d about/on the price yet?* **3** (of two or more persons) be happy together; get on well with one another (without arguing, etc): *We shall never* ∼. **4** be the same: *This bill does not* ∼ *with your original estimate*. **5** suit, e g the health of: *The climate doesn't* ∼ *with me*. **6** (*gram*) correspond in number, person, etc with: *The verb* ∼*s with its subject in number and person*. **7** (of figures, accounts, proposals, etc) accept or approve (as being correct): *The Manager has* ∼*d your expenses*.

agree·able /ə'grɪəbəl/ *adj* **1** pleasant (the usual word): *She has an* ∼ *voice*. **2** ready to agree: *Are you* ∼ *to the proposal?*

agree·ably /-əblɪ/ *adv* pleasantly: *I was agreeably surprised*.

agree·ment /ə'griːmənt/ *n* **1** *be in agreement,* have the same opinion(s): *We are in* ∼ *on that point. I'm quite in* ∼ *with what you say*. **2** [C] arrangement or understanding (spoken or written) made by two or more persons, governments, etc: *sign an* ∼. *come to/arrive at/make/reach an agreement (with sb),* agree.

ag·ri·cul·tural /'ægrɪ'kʌltʃərəl/ *adj* of farming.

ag·ri·cul·ture /'ægrɪkʌltʃə(r)/ *n* [U] science or practice of farming.

aground /ə'grɑʊnd/ *adv, adj* (of ships) touching the bottom in shallow water: *The ship went* ∼.

ah /ɑ/ *int* cry of surprise, pity, etc.

aha /ɑ'hɑ/ *int* cry of surprise, triumph, satisfaction, etc.

ahead /ə'hed/ *adv* in front; in advance: *Standard time in Turkey is two hours* ∼ *of Greenwich Mean Time. Full speed ahead!* Go forward at full speed! *go ahead,* (a) make progress: *Things are going* ∼. (b) (*informal*) continue (with what you're about to say or do). *look ahead,* think of and prepare for future needs

ahem /ə'hem/ *int* (usual spelling form of the) noise made when clearing the throat or to get a person's attention.

ahoy /ə'hɔɪ/ *int* greeting or warning cry used by seamen.

aid /eɪd/ *vt* help (the usual word): *aid a poor family with money*. □ *n* **1** [U] help: *He came to my* ∼, helped me. *What is the collection in* ∼ *of,* What is the money to be used for? ⇨ also first¹(2), legal. **2** [C] something that helps. ⇨ visual aid.
`deaf-aid,` appliance that helps a deaf person to hear.

aide-de-camp /'eɪd də 'kæmp/ *n* [C] (*pl* aides-de-camp) naval or military officer who helps a superior.

ail /eɪl/ *vt,vi* **1** (*old use*) trouble: *What* ∼*s him?* What's wrong with him? **2** be ill: *The children are always* ∼*ing,* always in poor health.

ail·ment /'eɪlmənt/ *n* [C] illness (the usual word).

aim¹ /eɪm/ *n* **1** [U] act of aiming, e g with a gun: *Take careful* ∼ *at the target*. **2** [C] purpose; objective: *He has only one* ∼ *and object in life—to make a fortune before he is fifty*.

aim·less *adj* having no aim(2).

aim·less·ly *adv* in no particular direction, purpose, etc: *changing* ∼*lessly from one job to another*.

aim² /eɪm/ *vt,vi* **1** point (a gun, etc) towards: *He* ∼*ed* (*his gun*) *at the lion, fired and missed*. **2** send, direct, e g a blow: *Tom got angry with his brother and* ∼*ed a heavy book at his head*. **3** (*fig*) (of criticism, praise, etc) be meant for: *My remarks were not* ∼*ed at you*. **4** have as a plan or intention: *Harry* ∼*s at becoming a doctor*.

ain't /eɪnt/ (incorrect) short form of *are/is/ am not,* and *have/has not: I* ∼ *going. We* ∼ *got any*.

air¹ /eə(r)/ *n* **1** [U] the mixture of gases that surrounds the earth and which we breathe: *Let's go out and enjoy the fresh* ∼. *in the air,* (a) uncertain: *My plans are still in the air.* (b) (of opinions, etc) passing from one person to another: *There are rumours in the air that... clear the air,* (a) make the air (in a room, etc) fresh again. (b) (*fig*) lessen suspicion, doubt, etc by giving facts, etc. ⇨ also hot¹(8). **2** *by air,* in aircraft: *travel/ send goods, etc by air*. **3** [U] *on the air,* broadcast(ing): *The Prime Minister will be on the* ∼ *at 9.15 p m. go off the air,* stop broadcasting. **4** [C] (*music, dated*) tune, melody. **5** [C] appearance; manner: *He has an* ∼ *of importance,* seems to be, looks, important. *give oneself/put on airs,* behave in an unnatural way in the hope of impressing people. *airs and graces,* foolish, exaggerated ways of behaving.
`air-bed,` mattress inflated with air.
`air-borne` *adj* (a) transported by air (b) (of an aircraft) in flight: *We were soon* ∼*borne*

'air-con`ditioned adj (of a room, building, etc) supplied with air that is purified and kept at a certain temperature and degree of humidity.

`air-conditioner, machine for air-conditioning.

'air-con`ditioning, process of producing an air-conditioned building, etc.

'air-`cooled adj cooled by a current of air: an ~-cooled engine.

`air-craft, (used with a sing or pl verb) aeroplane(s); airship(s).

`air-craft car-rier, ship with a long, wide deck for aircraft to take off and land

`air-crew, crew of an aircraft.

`air duct, device, e g in an aircraft or a ship's cabin, for directing a flow of air for the comfort of passengers.

`air-field, area of open, level ground, with buildings, offices, etc for operations of (esp military) aircraft.

`air hostess, stewardess in an airliner.

`air letter, sheet of light paper (to be) folded and sent, without an envelope, by airmail.

`air lift, large-scale transport of persons or supplies by air, esp in an emergency.

`air-line, regular service of aircraft for public use.

`air-liner, passenger-carrying aircraft.

`air-mail, mail (to be) carried by air.

`air-plane, (US) = aeroplane.

`air-port, public flying ground for use by airliners.

`air raid, attack by aircraft that drop bombs.

`air-screw, propeller of an aircraft.

`air-ship, lighter-than-air flying-machine with engine(s).

`air space, part of the earth's atmosphere above a country: violation of our ~ space by military aircraft.

`air speed, speed of an aircraft relative to the air through which it is moving.

`air-strip, strip of ground for the use of aircraft, esp one made for use in war or in an emergency.

`air terminal, building(s) (in a town or city centre) to or from which passengers, etc travel to or from an airport.

`air-tight adj not allowing air to enter or escape. (b) (fig) leaving no possibility of misunderstanding or not succeeding, etc.

'air-to-`air adj (of missiles) fired from one aircraft to hit another.

'air-to-`ground adj fired from an aircraft to hit a target on the ground.

`air-way, route regularly followed by airliners; company operating a service of airliners: British Airways.

air² /eə(r)/ vt 1 put (clothing, etc) into the open air or into a warm place to make it quite dry: The blankets need to be ~ed. 2 let fresh air into (a room, etc). 3 cause others to know (one's opinions, troubles etc): He likes to ~ his views.

air-ing /`eərɪŋ/ n give sth an airing, (a)

expose it to the fresh air. (b) discuss it.

`airing-cupboard, warm cupboard in which to store bed-clothes, towels, etc.

air-less /`eələs/ adj not having enough fresh air: an ~ room.

airy /`eəri/ adj (-ier, -iest) 1 having plenty of fresh air moving through it: a nice ~ room. 2 of or like air. 3 not sincere; superficial: ~ promises.

aisle /aɪl/ n [C] 1 passage in a church, esp one that is divided by a row of columns from the nave; (in a small church) passage between rows of pews (= seats). 2 passage between any rows of seats, e g in a theatre or cinema.

aitch /eɪtʃ/ n [C] the letter H. **drop one's aitches,** not sound /h/ at the beginning of a word, e g by saying at for hat.

ajar /ə`dʒɑ(r)/ adj (of doors) slightly open.

akin /ə`km/ adj (liter) of similar character: Pity is often ~ to love.

-al /-əl/ suffix (noun + ~ = adj): magical.

ala-bas-ter /`æləbɑstə(r) US: -bæs-/ n [U] soft, white stone like marble in appearance used for ornaments.

alarm /ə`lɑm/ n 1 [C] (sound or signal giving a) warning of danger: give/raise the ~. 2 apparatus used to give such a warning: a `fire-~. 3 [U] fear and excitement caused by the expectation of danger: He jumped up in ~. □ vt give a warning or feeling of danger to; cause anxiety to: Everybody was ~ed at the news that war might break out.

alarm-ing adj causing fear or anxiety.

alarm-ist /-ɪst/, person who is easily alarmed.

alas /ə`læs/ int cry of sorrow or regret.

alb /ælb/ n [C] white vestment reaching to the feet, worn by some Christian priests at ceremonies.

al-ba-tross /`ælbətros/ n [C] large, white, web-footed seabird, common in the Pacific and Southern Oceans.

al-beit /`ɔl`biːt/ conj (formal) although.

al-bino /`æl`biːnəʊ US: -`baɪ-/ n [C] (pl ~s) animal or human being born without natural colouring matter in the skin and hair (which are white) and the eyes (which are pink).

al-bum /`ælbəm/ n [C] 1 blank book in which a collection of photographs, autographs, postage stamps, etc can be kept. 2 holder for a set of discs. 3 long-playing record with several pieces (often) by the same musician(s), singer(s).

al-bu-men /`ælbjʊmən/ n [U] white of egg.

al-chem-ist /`ælkəmɪst/ n [C] person who studied or practised alchemy.

al-chemy /`ælkəmɪ/ n [U] chemistry of the Middle Ages, attempting to discover how to change ordinary metals into gold.

al-co-hol /`ælkəhɒl US: -hɔl/ n [U] (pure, colourless liquid as present in) such drinks as beer, wine, brandy, whisky.

al-co-holic /`ælkə`hɒlɪk US: -`hɔl-/ adj of or containing alcohol. □ n [C] person whose desire for drink is so great that his health is affected.

al·co·hol·ism /-ızm/ n [C] (effect of the) action of alcohol on the human system.

al·cove /ˈælkəʊv/ n [C] part of a wall set back from the rest, often having a bed or seats.

al·der·man /ˈɔːldəmən/ n [C] (pl -men /-mən/) senior member of a city or borough council in England and Ireland.

ale /eɪl/ n [C,U] light-coloured beer.

alert /əˈlɜːt/ adj fully awake and ready to act, speak, etc: ~ in answering questions. □ n 1 **on the alert**, ready to act, attack, etc. 2 [C] (mil) period of being on the alert. □ vt quickly tell a person to be on the alert

al·fresco /ˈælˈfreskəʊ/ adj, adv (of meals) in the open air: lunching ~.

alga /ˈælgə/ n [C] (pl ~e /ˈældʒiː/) water plant of very simple structure.

al·gebra /ˈældʒıbrə/ n [U] branch of mathematics in which signs and letters are used to represent quantities.

al·ge·braic /ˈældʒıˈbreɪk/, **al·ge·braical** /-kəl/ adj

alias /ˈeɪliəs/ n [C] (pl ~es) name which a person, esp a criminal, uses to hide his own. □ adv also called.

alibi /ˈælıbaɪ/ n [C] (pl ~s) 1 (legal) plea that one was in another place at the time of an act, esp a crime: The accused man was able to establish an ~. 2 (informal) excuse (for failure, etc).

alien /ˈeɪliən/ n [C] person who is not a subject of the country in which he is living: An Englishman is an ~ in the United States. □ adj 1 foreign: an ~ environment. 2 (formal) different in nature or character: These principles are ~ from our religion.

alien·ation /ˈeɪliəˈneɪʃən/ n [U] (esp) mental illness of feeling no relationship with other people.

alien·ate /ˈeɪliəneɪt/ vt cause (a person) to become unfriendly or indifferent (by unpopular or unpleasant actions): The Prime Minister's policy ~d many of his followers.

alight¹ /əˈlaɪt/ adj on fire; lit: The sticks were damp and wouldn't catch ~.

alight² /əˈlaɪt/ vi 1 get down from a horse, etc. 2 (of a bird) come down from the air and settle (on a branch, etc).

align /əˈlaɪn/ vt,vi 1 arrange in a line; e g of soldiers, form a line. 2 agree with (and join): They ~ed themselves with us.

align·ment /əˈlaɪnmənt/ n [C,U] (an) arrangement in a straight line: The desks are in/out of ~

alike /əˈlaɪk/ adj like one another: The two sisters are very much ~. □ adv in the same way: treat everybody ~; the same: summer and winter ~

ali·men·tary /ˈælıˈmentrı/ adj of food and digestion
the ˈalimentary canal, parts of the body through which food passes (from the mouth

to the anus).

ali·mony /ˈælımənı US: -məʊnı/ n [U] money allowance (to be) paid by a man to his wife, or former wife, by a judge's order. e g after a legal separation or divorce.

alive /əˈlaɪv/ adj 1 living: Who's the greatest man ~? 2 in existence: An awareness of the dangers of air-pollution should be kept ~ by the press and TV. **alive to**, aware of: He is fully ~ to the dangers of the situation. **alive with**, full of (living or moving things): The lake was ~ with fish.

al·kali /ˈælkəlaɪ/ n [C] (pl ~s) (chem) one of a number of substances (such as soda, potash, ammonia) that combine with acids to form salts.

al·ka·line /ˈælkəlaɪn/ adj

all¹ /ɔːl/ adj 1 (used with pl nouns) the whole number of: A~ horses are animals. (Note: compare Every horse is an animal.) 2 (used with uncountable nouns and in all the...) the whole extent or amount: A~ hope is lost. They walked ~ the way home. **all (of)**, the whole (of): He spent ~ (of) that year in London. 3 any: It's beyond ~ doubt. There is no reason for doubt.

all² /ɔːl/ adv 1 entirely: They were dressed ~ in black. (Note: compare They were all dressed (=All of them were dressed) in black. 2 (used with comparatives) much; so much: You'll be all the better for a holiday. 3 (uses with prepositions and particles): **all alone**, (a) not in the company of others. (b) without the help and company of other persons. **all along**, (a) for the whole length of: There are trees ~ along the road. (b) (informal) all the time: But I knew that ~ along! **all for**, (informal) strongly in favour of: I'm ~ for accepting the offer. **all the same**, = nevertheless. **all the same to**, a matter of indifference to: It's ~ the same to me whether you go or stay. **all in**, (a) (informal) exhausted; He was ~ in at the end of the race. (b) inclusive of everything: an ~-in price. **all out**, (informal) using all possible strength, energy, etc: He was going ~ out/was making an ~-out effort. **all over**, (a) in every part of: He has travelled all over the world. (b) at an end. **all right**, (alright is a common incorrect spelling) (a) satisfactory, satisfactorily; safe and sound; in good order: I hope they've arrived all right. (b) (as a response to a suggestion, etc) Yes, I consent. **all there**, (informal) mentally alert. **not all there**, (informal) not sane. **all told**, altogether; as the total: There were six people ~ told (= in all).

all³ /ɔːl/ n [U] (used in such phrases as my/ his/their, etc all) everything: He gave his ~, tried as hard as he could.

all⁴ /ɔːl/ pron 1 everything or everybody: They were ~ broken. Take it ~. We ~ want to go. **all of**, every one, the whole: Take ~ of them/it. 2 (uses with prepositions): **above all**, ⇨ above. **after all**, ⇨ after.

(not) at all /ə ˈtɔːl/, (not) in any way: *She's not at ~ suitable. Are you at ~ worried?* **not at all,** polite reply when receiving thanks. *once (and) for all,* now and for the last or only time. **in all,** ⇨ in. **all in all,** considering all the facts: *A~ in ~ he's a nice man.* **not as/so + adj/adv as ~ that,** not to that extent: *It's not as easy as ~ that,* not as easy as it seems. **not all that,** not to that extent: *It's not ~ that easy.*

all- /ɔːl/ *prefix* completely: '*~-ˈpowerful.*
'**all-ˈround** *adj* having various abilities: *an ~-round athlete.* Hence, '**all-ˈrounder** *n.*
'**all-star** *adj* with many famous actors: *an ˈ-star ˈcast.*

Allah /ˈælə/ *n* name of God among Muslims.

al·le·ga·tion /ˌælɪˈɡeɪʃən/ *n* [U] alleging; [C] statement, esp one made without proof: *You have made serious ~s, but can you prove them?*

al·lege /əˈledʒ/ *vt* put forward, esp as a reason or excuse, in support of a claim or in denial of a charge: *In your statement you ~ that the accused man was seen at the scene of the crime.*
al·leg·ed·ly /-ɪdlɪ/ *adv*

al·le·giance /əˈliːdʒəns/ *n* [U] duty, support, loyalty, due (to a ruler or government): *Members of Parliament took the oath of ~ to the Queen.*

al·le·goric /ˌælɪˈɡɒrɪk US: -ˈɡɔːr-/, **al·le·gori·cal** /-kəl/ *adj* of allegory.

al·le·gory /ˈælɪɡərɪ US: -ɡɔːrɪ/ *n* [C] (*pl* -ies) story or description in which ideas such as patience, purity and truth are symbolized by persons who are characters in the story.

al·ler·gic /əˈlɜːdʒɪk/ *adj* of allergy. *allergic to,* (a) having an allergy to. (b) (*informal*) having a dislike of; unable to get on well with.

al·lergy /ˈælədʒɪ/ *n* [C] (*pl* -ies) (*med*) (condition of) being affected by particular foods, fur, insect stings, etc.

al·levi·ate /əˈliːvɪeɪt/ *vt* make (pain, suffering) less or easier to bear.
al·levi·ation /əˌliːvɪˈeɪʃən/ *n* [U]

al·ley /ˈælɪ/ *n* [C] (*pl* ~s) **1** narrow passage or street. **2** narrow enclosure for such games as bowls and skittles.
'**blind ˈalley, (a)** narrow street closed at one end. (b) (*fig*) profession, career with no opportunity for progress.

al·li·ance /əˈlaɪəns/ *n* **1** [U] association or connection. **2** [C] union, e g of states (by treaty): *enter into an ~.*

al·lied /əˈlaɪd/ ⇨ ally.

al·li·ga·tor /ˈælɪɡeɪtə(r)/ *n* [C] reptile (like a crocodile but with a shorter head) living in southeastern US.

al·lit·er·ation /əˌlɪtəˈreɪʃən/ *n* [U] repetition of the first sound or letter of a succession of words, e g *safe and sound.*

al·lit·er·ative /əˈlɪtrətɪv US: -təreɪtɪv/ *adj*

al·lit·er·ative·ly *adv*

al·lo·cate /ˈæləkeɪt/ *vt* give, put on one side, as a share or for a purpose: *~ a sum of money to education.*

al·lo·ca·tion /ˌæləˈkeɪʃən/ *n* **1** [U] allocating or distributing. **2** [C] person or thing allocated.

al·lot /əˈlɒt/ *vt* (-tt-) make a distribution of; decide a person's share of: *Can we do the work within the time ~ted (to) us?*

al·lot·ment *n* [C] part or share, esp (in GB) a small area of public land rented as a vegetable garden.

al·low /əˈlaʊ/ *vt,vi* **1** give permission: *Smoking is not ~ed here.* **2** give, let (a person or thing) have; agree to give: *How much money are you ~ed to have? allow for,* take into consideration: *It will take an hour to get to the station, ~ing for traffic delays.*

al·low·able /-əbəl/ *adj* that is or can be allowed (by law, the rules, etc).

al·low·ance /əˈlaʊəns/ *n* **1** [C] sum of money, amount, allowed. **2** *make allowance(s) for,* allow for: *We must make ~(s) for his youth,* remember that he is young, etc.

al·loy /ˈælɔɪ/ *n* [C,U] mixture of metals, esp a metal of low value mixed with a metal of higher value: *~ steel.*

all·spice /ˈɔːlspaɪs/ *n* [U] spice made from the dried berries of a W Indian tree called the pimento.

al·lude /əˈluːd/ *vi* mention (now the more usual word): *In your remarks you ~d to certain dangerous developments.*

allur·ing /əˈlʊərɪŋ/ *adj* attractive (the usual word).

al·lu·sion /əˈluːʒən/ *n* [C] (*formal*) indirect reference to: *His books are full of classical ~s which few people understand.*

al·lus·ive /əˈluːsɪv/ *adj* containing allusions.

al·luv·ial /əˈluːvɪəl/ *adj* made of sand, earth, etc left by rivers or floods: *~ soil.*

ally¹ /ˈælaɪ/ *n* [C] (*pl* -ies) **1** person, state, etc allied to another. **2** person who gives help or support.

ally² /əˈlaɪ/ *vt* (*pt,pp* -ied) **1** *ally (oneself) with/to,* unite by treaty, marriage, etc: *Great Britain was allied with the United States in both World Wars;* Hence: *the Allied* /ˈælaɪd/ *Powers.* **2** *be allied to,* (of things) related to: *The English language is allied to the German language.*

al·ma·nac /ˈɔːlmənæk/ *n* [C] annual book or calendar of months and days, with information about the sun, moon, tides, anniversaries, etc.

Al·mighty /ɔːlˈmaɪtɪ/ *n* **the A~,** God.

almond /ˈɑːmənd/ *n* [C] (long, flat nut inside the) hard seed of a tree similar to the peach and plum.
'**almond-ˈeyed** *adj* having eyes shaped like an almond.

almoner /ˈɑːmənə(r) US: ˈælm-/ *n* [C] **1** (formerly) official who gave money and help to the poor. **2** (*GB*) hospital official in charge of social service work for patients.

al·most /ˈɔːlməʊst/ *adv* very nearly: *He slipped and* ~ *fell.* **almost no/none/no one/nothing/never,** (= hardly any/any one/anything/ever, scarcely any/anything): *She says* ~ *nothing of importance.*

alms /ɑːmz/ *n* [U] (used with a *sing* or *pl verb*) money, clothes, food, etc given to the poor.

aloft /əˈlɒft *US*: əˈlɔːft/ *adv* high up, esp at the masthead of a ship, or up in the rigging.

alone /əˈləʊn/ *adj, adv* ⇨ **lonely.** **1** (= *by oneself/itself*) without the company or help of others or other things: *He likes living* ~. *You can't lift the piano* ~, *without help.* **2** (*noun/pronoun* + *alone*) and no other: *Smith* ~ *knows what happened.* **be (not) alone in,** not the only persons who are: *We are not* ~ *in thinking that.* **4 let alone,** without considering: *He cannot afford his fares let* ~ *cigarettes.* **let/leave sb/sth alone,** not touch, move, interfere with: *You had better leave that dog* ~; *it will bite you if you kick it.*

along /əˈlɒŋ *US*: əˈlɔːŋ/ *adv* **1** (used to show onward movement, often with the same sense as on): *Come* ~*! The dog was running* ~ *behind its owner.* **2** (used like *over, across, up, down,* in informal requests): *Come* ~ *to my office.* **all along,** ⇨ all²(3). **get along,** ⇨ get(17). □ *prep* from one end of to the other end of; through any part of the length of: *We walked* ~ *the road.*

along·side /əˈlɒŋˈsaɪd/ *adv, prep* close to, parallel with, the side of (a ship, pier, wharf).

aloof /əˈluːf/ *adv* apart. □ *adj* (of a person's character) keeping away, taking no part in: *I find him rather* ~.
aloof·ness *n* [U]

aloud /əˈlaʊd/ *adv* **1** in a voice loud enough to be heard, not in a whisper: *Please read the story* ~. **2** loudly, so as to be heard at a distance: *He called* ~ *for help.*

alp /ælp/ *n* [C] high mountain, esp one of those (**the Alps**) between France and Italy.

al·pha /ˈælfə/ *n* the first letter (A, α) in the Greek alphabet.

al·pha·bet /ˈælfəbet/ *n* [C] the letters used in writing a language, arranged in order: *the Greek* ~.

al·pha·beti·cal /ˈælfəˈbetɪkəl/ *adj* in the order of the alphabet: *The words in a dictionary are in* ~ *order.*
al·pha·beti·cally /-klɪ/ *adv*

al·pine /ˈælpaɪn/ *adj* of the Alps; of alps: ~ *plants.*

al·ready /ɔːlˈredɪ/ *adv* (usually used to show emphasis) **1** by this/that time: *The postman has* ~ *been/has been* ~. **2** (used to show surprise): *You're not leaving us* ~, *are you?* **3** previously; before now: *I've* ~ *been there/been there* ~.

Al·sa·tian /ælˈseɪʃən/ *n* [C] large breed of dog, like a wolf, often trained for police work. (*US = German shepherd*).

also /ˈɔːlsəʊ/ *adv* too; besides; as well: *Tom has been to Canada. Harry has* ~ *been to Canada.* **not only... but also,** both... and: *He not only read the book but* ~ *remembered what he had read.*

al·tar /ˈɔːltə(r)/ *n* [C] **1** raised place (flat-topped table or platform) on which offerings are made to a god. **2** (in Christian churches) the Communion table.

al·ter /ˈɔːltə(r)/ *vt, vi* make or become different; change in character, appearance, etc: *These clothes are too large; they must be* ~ed. *He has* ~ed *a great deal since I saw him a year ago.*
al·ter·able /-əbəl/ *adj* that alters or that can be altered.

alter·ation /ˈɔːltəˈreɪʃən/ *n* [U] altering; [C] act of changing; change that is the result of altering: *A* ~s *to clothes can cost a lot of money.*

al·ter·nate¹ /ɔːlˈtɜːnət/ *adj* (of things of two kinds) by turns, first the one and then the other: *Tom and Harry do the work on* ~ *days,* e g Tom on Monday, Harry on Tuesday, Harry on Wednesday, etc.
al·ter·nate·ly *adv*

al·ter·nate² /ˈɔːltəneɪt/ *vt, vi* arrange or do by turns; cause to take place, appear, one after the other: *She* ~s *boiled eggs with fried eggs for breakfast.* **alternate between,** pass from one state, etc to a second, then back to the first, etc: *He* ~s *so easily between happiness and sadness.*
'alternating 'current, electric current that regularly changes to the opposite direction and back, the number of complete changes per second being known as the *frequency.* ⇨ direct current.

al·ter·na·tive /ɔːlˈtɜːnətɪv/ *adj* (of two things) that may be had, used, etc in place of something else: *There are* ~ *answers to your question.* □ *n* [C] **1** choice between two things: *You have the* ~ *of working hard and succeeding or of not working and being unsuccessful.* **2** one of more than two possibilities.
al·ter·na·tive·ly *adv* as a choice: *a fine of £5 or* ~*ly six weeks imprisonment.*

al·though /ɔːlˈðəʊ/ *conj* ⇨ though.

al·ti·tude /ˈæltɪtjuːd *US*: -tuːd/ *n* **1** [C] (not of living things) height, esp above sea-level. **2** (*pl*) place high above sea-level: *It is difficult to breathe at these* ~s.

alto /ˈæltəʊ/ *n* [C] (*pl* ~s) **1** (musical part for or a person having a) male singing voice between tenor and treble; female voice of similar range (*contralto*). **2** instrument with the same range: *an* ~*-saxophone.*

al·to·gether /ˈɔːltəˈgeðə(r)/ *adv* **1** entirely; wholly: *I don't* ~ *agree with him.* **2** considering everything: *The weather was bad and the trains were crowded;* ~, *it was a bad journey.*

al·tru·ism /ˈæltruɪzm/ *n* [U] principle of considering the well-being and happiness of others first; [C] instance of this.

al·tru·ist /ˈæltruɪst/ *n* [C] person who is altruistic.

al·tru·is·tic /ˌæltruˈɪstɪk/ *adj*

al·tru·is·ti·cally /-klɪ/ *adv*

alu·min·ium /ˌæljʊˈmɪnɪəm/ (*US* = **alu·mi·num** /əˈlumɪnəm/) *n* [U] light white metal, used for saucepans, electrical apparatus, etc.

al·ways /ˈɔːlweɪz/ *adv* 1 at all times; without exception: *The sun ~ rises in the east.* (*Note: Always* may be used with *almost, nearly* or *not: He's nearly ~ at home in the evening.*) 2 again and again; repeatedly: *He ~ asks for money.*

am /*after* 'I': m *usually:* əm, *strong form:* æm/ ⇨ **be¹**.

amal·ga·mate /əˈmælɡəmeɪt/ *vt,vi* (of classes, societies, races of people, business companies) mix; combine; unite.

amal·ga·ma·tion /əˌmælɡəˈmeɪʃən/ *n* [U] mixing; combining. [C] instance of this.

amass /əˈmæs/ *vt* pile or heap up, collect: *~ a fortune/riches.*

ama·teur /ˈæmətə(r)/ *n* [C] 1 person who paints pictures, performs music, plays, etc, for the love of it, not professionally. 2 person playing a game, taking part in sports, without receiving payment: (as an *adjective*) *an ~ painter/photographer.* ⇨ **professional.**

ama·teur·ish /ˈæmətərɪʃ/ *adj* inexpert; imperfect.

ama·teur·ism /-ɪzm/ *n* [U]

amaze /əˈmeɪz/ *vt* fill with great surprise or wonder: *I was ~d at the news/~d to hear that...*

amaz·ing *adj*

amaz·ing·ly *adv: He's doing amazingly well.*

amaze·ment /əˈmeɪzmənt/ *n* [U] surprise: *I heard with ~ that...*

Ama·zon /ˈæməzən *US:* -zɑn/ *n* [C] 1 (in old Greek stories) female warrior. 2 (with a small *a*) tall, strong, active woman.

am·bas·sa·dor /æmˈbæsədə(r)/ *n* [C] 1 minister representing the Government of his country in a foreign country: *the British A~ to Greece.* 2 authorized representative.

am·bas·sa·dress /ˈæmˈbæsədrəs/ *n* [C] female ambassador.

am·bas·sa·dor·ial /æmˈbæsəˈdɔrɪəl/ *adj* of an ambassador or his duties.

am·ber /ˈæmbə(r)/ *n* [U] hard, clear yellowish-brown gum used for making ornaments, etc; its colour.

ambi- /æmbɪ-/ *prefix* both, double, two: *ambiguous; ambidextrous.*

am·bi·dex·trous /ˌæmbɪˈdekstrəs/, (also **-ter·ous**) /-tərəs/ *adj* able to use the left hand or the right hand equally well.

am·bi·ence /ˈæmbɪəns/ *n* [C] environment; atmosphere: *a friendly ~.*

am·bi·ent /ˈæmbɪənt/ *adj* (*formal*) (of air, etc) on all sides; surrounding.

am·bi·guity /ˌæmbɪˈɡjuətɪ/ *n* (*pl* -ies) 1 [U] state of being ambiguous. 2 [C] expression, etc that can have more than one meaning.

am·bigu·ous /æmˈbɪɡjʊəs/ *adj* uncertain: *'400 cadets passed out last year' is ~.*

am·bigu·ous·ly *adv*

am·bi·tion /æmˈbɪʃən/ *n* 1 [U] strong desire, esp to be successful: *A man who is filled with ~ usually works hard.* 2 [C] particular desire of this kind: *He has great ~s.* 3 [C] object of such a desire: *achieve one's ~(s).*

am·bi·tious /æmˈbɪʃəs/ *adj* 1 full of ambition: *an ~ woman; ~ to succeed in life.* 2 showing or needing ambition; *~ plans; an ~ attempt.*

am·bi·tious·ly *adv*

am·biva·lence /æmˈbɪvələns/ *n* [U] 1 existence of two or more opposite or conflicting feelings. 2 (esp) inability to make up one's mind.

am·biva·lent /æmˈbɪvələnt/ *adj* having either or both or two contrary or similar values, meanings, etc.

amble /ˈæmbəl/ *vi* (of a horse) move along without hurrying; (of a person) ride or walk without hurrying. □ *n* [C] slow, gentle, pace.

am·brosia /æmˈbrəʊzɪə *US:* -əʊʒə/ *n* 1 (*Greek myth*) the food of the gods. 2 (*fig*) anything that has a delightful taste or smell.

am·bu·lance /ˈæmbjʊləns/ *n* [C] vehicle for carrying people who are ill, wounded or hurt in accidents.

am·bush /ˈæmbʊʃ/ *n* [C,U] (the placing of) troops, etc, waiting to make a surprise attack: *be attacked from an ~.* □ *vt* attack from such a position.

ameli·or·ate /əˈmiːlɪəreɪt/ *vt,vi* (*formal*) (cause to) become better.

amen /ˈeɪˈmen *in church services:* æˈmen/ *int* (*eccles*) word used at the end of a prayer or hymn and meaning 'May it be so'.

amen·able /əˈminəbəl/ *adj* 1 (of persons) willing to be guided or controlled: *be ~ to kindness/advice/reason.* 2 (*legal*) in a position where one must do certain things or be punished for not doing them: *We are all ~ to the law.*

amend /əˈmend/ *vt,vi* 1 improve; correct: *He'll have to ~ his ways,* improve his behaviour. 2 make changes in the wording of a rule, a proposed law, etc.

amend·able /-əbəl/ *adj*

amend·ment /əˈmendmənt/ *n* [U] correcting; [C] change proposed or made to a rule, etc.

amends /əˈmendz/ *n pl* **make amends (to sb) (for sth),** make a suitable payment; apologise: *make ~ to a friend for being unkind.*

amen·ity /əˈminətɪ/ *n* (*pl* -ies) 1 (*pl*) things, circumstances, surroundings, that make life easy or pleasant: *a town with many amenities,* e g a park, a public library, playing fields. **2** [U] pleasantness: *the* ~ *of the Mediterranean climate.*

Ameri·can·ism /ə`merɪkənɪzm/ *n* **1** [C] word or phrase typical of American English. **2** [U] loyalty to the U S or to things typically American.

am·ethyst /`æmɪθɪst/ *n* [C] precious stone which is purple or violet.

ami·able /`eɪmɪəbəl/ *adj* (*formal*) friendly: *I found him a most* ~ *person.*
ami·a·bil·ity /`eɪmɪə`bɪlətɪ/ *n* [U] friendliness (the usual word).
ami·ably /-əblɪ/ *adv*

amic·able /`æmɪkəbəl/ *adj* done in a friendly way: *They settled their dispute in an* ~ *way.*
amic·ably /-əblɪ/ *adv*

amid /ə`mɪd/, **amidst** /ə`mɪdst/ *prep* among, in, the middle of.

amid·ships /ə`mɪdʃɪps/ *adv* (*naut*) half-way between the bows and stern of a ship.

amir, ameer, emir /ə`mɪə(r)/ *n* title used by some Muslim rulers.

amiss /ə`mɪs/ *adj, adv* wrong(ly); out of order: *There's not much* ~ *with it.* **take sth amiss,** be hurt in one's feelings (esp too strongly): *Don't take it* ~ *if I point out your errors.*

am·me·ter /`æmɪtə(r)/ *n* [C] meter that measures electric current in amperes.

am·mo·nia /ə`məʊnɪə/ *n* [U] strong, col-ourless gas (NH_3) with a sharp smell, used in refrigeration and for the manufacture of explosives and fertilizers; solution of this gas in water.

am·mu·ni·tion /`æmjʊ`nɪʃən/ *n* [U] mili-tary stores, esp of explosives (shells, bombs, etc).

am·nesia /æm`nɪzɪə *US:* -ɪʒə/ *n* [U] (*med*) partial or total loss of memory.

am·nesty /`æmnəstɪ/ *n* [C] (*pl* -ies) general pardon, esp for political offences: *The rebels returned home under an* ~.

amoeba /ə`miːbə/ *n* [C] (*pl* ~s or ~e /-bi/) microscopic form of living matter, found in water, soil, etc.

amoebic /ə`miːbɪk/ *adj* of, caused by, amoebae: ~ *dysentery.*

amok, amuck /ə`mɒk/ *adv* **run amuck,** run about wildly (as with a desire to kill people).

among /ə`mʌŋ/, **amongst** /ə`mʌŋst/ *prep* **1** (showing position) surrounded by; in the middle of: *a village* ~ *the hills; hiding* ~ *the bushes.* (*Note:* the noun or pronoun must be *pl.* Compare: Sweden is situated *between* Norway and Finland.) **2** (showing associa-tion, connection): *You are only one* ~ *many who need help.* 3 (used with a *superlative*) one of: *Leeds is* ~ *the largest industrial towns in England.* **4** (showing division, dis-tribution, possession, activity, to, for or by more than two persons): *You must settle the matter* ~ *yourselves.* (*Note:* between is used of two.) **5** (used after a *prep*): *Choose one*

from ~ *these.*

amoral /`eɪ`mɒrəl *US:* -`mɔːrəl/ *adj* not con-cerned with or having morals.

am·or·ous /`æmərəs/ *adj* easily moved to love; showing love; of (esp sexual) love: ~ *looks;* ~ *poetry.*
am·or·ous·ly *adv*

amount /ə`maʊnt/ *vi* **amount to,** add up to; be equal to: *His debts* ~ *to £5 000. Rid-ing on a bus without paying the fare* ~ *s to* (= is the same thing as) *stealing.* □ *n* [C] **1** total; whole: *He owed me £100 but could pay only half that* ~, could only pay £50. **2** [C] quantity: *A large* ~ *of money is spent on tobacco every year.*

amp /æmp/ *n* [C] (abbr for) ampere.

am·pere /`æmpeə(r) *US:* `æmpɪər/ *n* [C] unit for measuring electric current.

am·phib·ian /æm`fɪbɪən/ *n* [C] **1** animal able to live both on land and in water, e g a frog. **2** aircraft designed to take off from and land on either land or water. **3** vehicle able to move in water and on land.

am·phibi·ous /æm`fɪbɪəs/ *adj* adapted for both land and water.

amphi·theatre (*US* = **-ter**) /`æmfɪ-θɪətə(r)/ *n* [C] round or oval unroofed build-ing with rows of seats rising behind and above each other round an open space, used for public games and amusements.

ample /`æmpəl/ *adj* (-r, -st) **1** with plenty of space: *There's* ~ *room for the children.* **2** plentiful: *He has* ~ *resources,* is wealthy. **3** sufficient: *£5 will be* ~ *for my needs.*
am·ply /`æmplɪ/ *adv*

am·plify /`æmplɪfaɪ/ *vt* (*pt,pp* -ied) **1** make larger or fuller; esp give fuller information, more details, etc, about. **2** increase the strength of, esp sound.
am·pli·fi·ca·tion /`æmplɪfɪ`keɪʃən/ *n* [U]
am·pli·fier /`æmplɪfaɪə(r)/, appliance for amplifying, esp sound.

am·pu·tate /`æmpjʊteɪt/ *vt* cut off, e g an arm, a leg, by surgery.
am·pu·ta·tion /`æmpjʊ`teɪʃən/ *n* [C,U]

amuck /ə`mʌk/ *adv* ⇨ amok.

amu·let /`æmjʊlət/ *n* [C] thing worn in the belief or hope that it will protect (against evil, etc).

amuse /ə`mjuːz/ *vt* **1** make time pass pleasantly for: *Keep the baby* ~*d with these toys.* **2** make (a person) laugh or smile: *His funny stories* ~*d all of us.*

amuse·ment /ə`mjuːzmənt/ *n* **1** [U] state of being amused: *To the great* ~*ment of every-body, the actor's beard fell off.* **2** [C] some-thing that makes time pass pleasantly: *There are plenty of* ~*ments here—cinemas theatres, concerts, football matches, etc.*

amus·ing /ə`mjuːzɪŋ/ *adj* causing laughtei or smiles: *an* ~ *story/storyteller.*

an /ən *strong form:* æn/ ⇨ a[2].

an- /æn-, ən-/ *prefix* not, without: *anony-mous, anaesthetic.*

-an /-ən/ *suffix* (*proper noun* + ~ = *noun*

or *adj*): *Mexican; Italian.*

anach·ron·ism /ə'nækrənızm/ *n* [C] **1** something out of date either now or in a description of past events: *In the sentence 'Julius Caesar looked at his wrist-watch and lifted the telephone receiver' there are two ∼s.* **2** person, attitude, etc regarded (unfavourably) as out of date: *Is the House of Lords an ∼?*

anach·ron·is·tic /ə'nækrə'nıstık/ *adj*

ana·conda /'ænə'kɒndə/ *n* [C] (*pl* ∼s) large snake, esp the boa-constrictor.

anae·mia (*US* = **anemia**) /ə'nimıə/ *n* [U] lack of enough blood; poor condition of the blood, causing paleness.

anae·mic (*US* = **anemic**) /ə'nimık/ *adj* suffering from anaemia.

an·aes·thesia (*US* = **an·es-**) /'ænıs'θizıə *US*: -'θiʒə/ *n* [U] state of being unable to feel (pain, heat, cold, etc).

an·aes·thetic (*US* = **an·es-**) /'ænıs'θetık/ *n* [C] substance, e g ether, chloroform, or technique, that produces anaesthesia: *be given an ∼.* ⇨ general, local anaesthetic.

an·aes·the·tize (*US* = **an·es-**) /ə'nisθət- aız/ *vt* make insensible to pain, etc.

an·aes·the·tist (*US* = **an·es-**) /ə'nisθətıst/, person trained to administer anaesthetics.

ana·gram /'ænəgræm/ *n* [C] word made by changing the order of the letters in another word (e g plum—lump).

anal /'eınəl/ *adj* (*anat*) of the anus.

an·al·gesia /'ænıl'dʒiziə *US*: -iʒə/ *n* [U] (*med*) absence of, condition of not feeling, pain.

an·al·gesic /'ænıl'dʒizık/ *n* [C] substance, e g an ointment, which relieves pain.

ana·logue, -log /'ænəlɒg *US*: -lɔg/ *n* [C] something that is similar to another thing: *meat ∼,* artificial prepared substitute for meat (usually of soya beans).

anal·og·ous /ə'næləgəs/ *adj* similar or parallel: *The two processes are not ∼ (with each other).*

anal·og·ous·ly *adv*

anal·ogy /ə'nælədʒı/ *n* (*pl* -ies) **1** [C] partial likeness or agreement: *The teacher drew an ∼ between the human heart and a pump.* **2** [U] process of reasoning between parallel cases: *argue by/from ∼; on the ∼ of.*

ana·lyse (*US* = **-lyze**) /'ænəlaız/ *vt* **1** examine (a thing) in order to learn what it is made up of: *If we ∼ water, we find that it is made up of two parts of hydrogen and one part of oxygen.* **2** (*gram*) split up (a sentence) into its grammatical parts. **3** study or examine in order to learn about: *The leader tried to ∼ the causes of our failure.* **4** = psychoanalyse.

analy·sis /ə'næləsıs/ *n* (*pl* -ses /-siz/) **1** [U] (e g of a book, a character, a situation) separation into parts possibly with comment and judgement: *a critical ∼ of literary texts;* [C] instance of this; statement of the result of doing this. **2** = psychoanalysis.

ana·lyst /'ænəlıst/ *n* [C] **1** person skilled in making (esp chemical) analyses: *a food analyst.* **2** = psychoanalyst.

ana·lytic /'ænə'lıtık/, **-i·cal** /-kəl/ *adj* of or using analysis.

ana·lyti·cally /-klı/ *adv*

ana·lyze ⇨ analyse.

an·archic /ə'nɑkık/ *adj* (person, state) believing in or having no government.

an·arch·ism /'ænəkızm/ *n* [U] political theory that government and laws are undesirable.

an·arch·ist /'ænəkıst/ *n* [C] person who favours anarchism.

an·archy /'ænəkı/ *n* [U] absence of government or control; disorder.

anath·ema /ə'næθəmə/ *n* [C] (*pl* ∼s) **1** (*eccles*) formal declaration excommunicating a person or condemning something as evil. **2** thing that is detested.

anat·omy /ə'nætəmı/ *n* [U] science of the structure of animal bodies; study of their structures by separation into parts.

ana·tomi·cal /'ænə'tɒmıkəl/ *adj*

anat·om·ist /-ıst/, person who dissects corpses; person who studies anatomy.

-ance (also **-ence**) /-əns/ *suffix* (*verb* + ∼ = *noun*): *assistance; confidence.*

an·ces·tor /'ænsestə(r)/ *n* [C] any one of those persons from whom one is descended, esp one more remote than a grandparent.

an·ces·tral /æn'sestrəl/ *adj* belonging to, having come from, one's ancestors: *his ∼ home.*

an·ces·try /'ænsestrı/ *n* [C] (*pl* -ies) line of ancestors.

an·chor /'æŋkə(r)/ *n* [C] heavy piece of iron used for keeping a ship fast to the sea bottom or a balloon to the ground; thing or person that gives stability or security. □ *vt, vi* make (a ship) secure with an anchor.

an·chor·age /'æŋkərıdʒ/ *n* [C] place where ships may anchor safely.

an·chovy /'æntʃəʊvı/ *n* [C] (*pl* -ies) small fish of the herring family.

ancient /'eınʃənt/ *adj* **1** belonging to times long past: *∼ Rome and Greece.* **2** (often *humorous*) very old: *an ∼-looking hat.*

'ancient 'history, up to A D 476 when the Western Roman Empire was destroyed.

an·cil·lary /æn'sılərı *US*: 'ænsəlerı/ *adj* **1** helping, providing a service to those carrying on the main business. **2** secondary: *∼ roads/undertakings/industries.*

and /ənd/ *strong form:* ænd/ *conj* **1** (connecting words, clauses, sentences): *a table ∼ four chairs; learning to read ∼ write.* (*Note:* when two *nouns* stand for things or persons closely connected, *a* or *the* is not repeated before the second *noun: a knife and fork.*) **2** (replacing an *if*-clause): *Work hard ∼ you will pass* (= If you work hard, you will pass) *the examination.* **3** (showing repetition or continuation): *for hours ∼ hours; better ∼ better.* **4** (*informal*) to: *Try ∼*

come early.

an·ec·dote /ˈænɪkdəʊt/ n [C] short, usually amusing, story about a real person or event.

anemia, anemic ⇨ anaemia, anaemic.

anem·one /əˈneməni/ n [C] 1 small star-shaped woodland flower; cultivated varieties of this flower. 2 = sea anemone.

an·es·the·sia ⇨ anaesthesia.

anew /əˈnjuː US: əˈnuː/ adv again; in a new or different way.

angel /ˈeɪndʒəl/ n 1 (esp in Christian belief) messenger from God (usually shown in pictures as a human being in white with wings). 2 lovely or innocent person. 3 (as a compliment to a kind, thoughtful, etc person): *Thanks, you're an ~!*

an·gel·ic /ænˈdʒelɪk/ adj of or like an angel. **an·gel·i·cal·ly** /-klɪ/ adv

an·gelus /ˈændʒɪləs/ n (also A~) (bell rung in R C churches at morning, noon and sunset to call people to recite a) prayer to the Virgin Mary.

anger /ˈæŋɡə(r)/ n [U] the strong feeling that comes when one has been wronged or insulted, or when one sees cruelty or injustice; the feeling that makes people want to quarrel or fight: *filled with ~; done in a moment of ~.* □ vt make (a person) angry: *He is easily ~ed.*

angle¹ /ˈæŋɡəl/ n 1 space between two lines or surfaces that meet: *an acute/obtuse ~.* 2 (fig) point of view: *What ~ are you using in the story?* □ vt make an angle of; bend.

angle² /ˈæŋɡəl/ vi 1 fish with a hook and bait. 2 (fig) use tricks, hints, etc in order to get something: *~ for an invitation to a party.*

angler /ˈæŋɡlə(r)/ n [C] person who fishes with a rod and line.

Ang·li·can /ˈæŋɡlɪkən/ n [C], adj (member) of the Church of England.

ang·li·cize /ˈæŋɡlɪsaɪz/ vt make English or like English: *~ a French word.*

Anglo- /ˈæŋɡləʊ/ prefix English: *~-French relations*, between GB and France.

'Anglo-'Saxon n [C], adj (person) of English descent; race of people who settled in England before the Norman Conquest; their language (also called *Old English*).

Anglo·mania /ˌæŋɡləʊˈmeɪnɪə/ n [U] excessive love of and admiration for English customs, etc.

Anglo·phile /ˈæŋɡləʊfaɪl/ adj, n [C] (person) loving England or English things to excess.

Anglo·phobe /ˈæŋɡləʊfəʊb/ adj, n [C] (person) hating England or English things to excess.

Anglo·pho·bia /ˌæɡələʊˈfəʊbɪə/ n [U] excessive hatred of England and of English things.

angry /ˈæŋɡrɪ/ adv (-ier, -iest) 1 filled with, showing anger: *He was ~ at being kept waiting.* 2 (of a cut, sore, wound) red; inflamed. 3 (of the sea, sky, clouds) stormy;

threatening.

angri·ly adv

an·guish /ˈæŋɡwɪʃ/ n [U] severe mental suffering: *She was in ~ until she knew that her husband's life had been saved.*

an·guished adj expressing suffering: *~ed looks.*

angu·lar /ˈæŋɡjʊlə(r)/ adj 1 having angles or sharp corners. 2 (of persons) thin and bony; (of a person's nature, etc) rather stiff and awkward.

ani·mal /ˈænɪməl/ n [C] 1 living thing that can feel and move about: *Men, horses, birds, flies, fish, snakes are all ~s.* 2 four-footed animal such as a dog or horse. 3 any animal other than man. 4 (as an *adjective*) physical, not spiritual; of animals(1).

the 'animal kingdom, as contrasted with the *vegetable* or *mineral* ones.

ani·mate¹ /ˈænɪmət/ adj living; lively.

ani·mate² /ˈænɪmeɪt/ vt give life to; make lively: *There was an ~d (= lively) discussion.*

'animated car'toon, cinema film made by photographing a series of drawings.

ani·ma·tion /ˌænɪˈmeɪʃən/ n [U] 1 liveliness; spirit. 2 process of making animated cartoons.

ani·mos·ity /ˌænɪˈmɒsətɪ/ n (pl -ies) (formal) 1 [U] strong hatred, active hostility. 2 [C] instance of this.

an·ise /ˈænɪs/ n [C] plant with sweet-smelling seeds.

ani·seed /ˈænɪsiːd/ n [U] seed of anise, used for flavouring.

ankle /ˈæŋkəl/ n [C] joint connecting the foot with the leg; thin part of the leg between this joint and the calf.

an·nals /ˈænəlz/ n pl story of events year by year; record of new knowledge or discoveries written year by year; yearly record of the work of a learned society.

an·nex¹, an·nexe /ˈænəks/ n [C] smaller building added to, or situated near, a larger one: *a hotel ~.*

an·nex² /əˈneks/ vt 1 take possession of (territory, etc). 2 add or join (something) (as a secondary part).

an·ni·hi·late /əˈnaɪəleɪt/ vt destroy completely; end the existence of (e g an army, a fleet): *The invasion force was ~d.*

an·ni·hi·la·tion /əˌnaɪəˈleɪʃən/ n [U] complete destruction (of military or naval forces, etc).

an·ni·ver·sary /ˌænɪˈvɜːsərɪ/ n [C] (pl -ies) yearly return of the date of an event; celebration of this: *my 'wedding ~; the ~ of Shakespeare's birth.*

an·no Dom·ini /ˌænəʊ ˈdɒmɪnaɪ/ (Latin, shortened to A D /ˌeɪ ˈdiː/) in the year of our Lord: *in A D 250,* 250 years after the birth of Jesus. ⇨ B C. (*Note:* A D is never used except when contrasting the year with the time before the birth of Jesus and for the years up to 1 000.)

an·no·tate /ˈænəteɪt/ vt add notes (to a book, etc) explaining difficulties, giving opinions, etc: an ∼d text/version.

an·no·ta·tion /ˌænəˈteɪʃən/ n [U] annotating; [C] note or comment.

an·nounce /əˈnaʊns/ vt 1 make known to the public: Mr Green ∼d (to his friends) his engagement to Miss White. 2 make known the arrival of: The secretary ∼d Mr and Mrs Brown, spoke their names as they entered. 3 say that somebody is about to speak, sing, etc.

an·nounce·ment, something said, written or printed to make known what has happened or (more often) what will happen: An ∼ment will be made next week.

an·nouncer, (esp) person who announces speakers, singers, etc on the radio or TV.

an·noy /əˈnɔɪ/ vt irritate; make angry: Do stop ∼ing me!

an·noy·ing adj irritating: The ∼ing thing is that..

an·noy·ance /əˈnɔɪəns/ n 1 [U] anger; being annoyed: with a look of ∼; much to our ∼. 2 [C] something that annoys.

an·nual /ˈænjʊəl/ adj 1 coming or happening every year. 2 lasting for only one year or season. 3 of one year: his ∼ income. □ n[C] 1 book, etc that appears under the same title but with new contents every year. 2 plant that lives for one year or less.

an·nual·ly adv

an·nu·ity /əˈnjuːətɪ/ US: -ˈnu-/ n [C] (pl -ies) fixed sum of money paid yearly as income during a person's lifetime; form of insurance to provide such a regular, annual income.

an·nul /əˈnʌl/ vt (-ll-) 1 put an end to, e g an agreement, a law, etc. 2 declare (that something, e g a marriage, is) invalid.

an·nul·ment n [C,U]

an·ode /ˈænəʊd/ n [C] (electricity) 1 positively charged electrode (from which current enters). ⇨ **cathode.** 2 negative terminal of a battery.

anoint /əˈnɔɪnt/ vt apply oil or ointment to (as a religious ceremony): ∼ him with oil.

an·noint·ment n [C,U]

anom·al·ous /əˈnɒmələs/ adj different in some way from what is normal.

anomalous verb, verb that forms a question and negative without the verb do, e g must, ought.

anom·al·ous·ly adv

anom·aly /əˈnɒmälɪ/ n [C] (pl -ies) abnormal thing: A bird that cannot fly is an ∼.

anon¹ /əˈnɒn/ adv (old use) soon.

anon² /əˈnɒn/ (in footnotes, etc) short for by an anonymous author.

anon·ym·ity /ˌænəˈnɪmətɪ/ n [U] state of being anonymous.

anony·mous /əˈnɒnɪməs/ adj without a name, or with a name that is not made known: an ∼ gift.

anony·mous·ly adv

anoph·eles /əˈnɒfɪliːz/ n [C] (kinds of) mosquito, esp the kinds that spread malaria.

an·or·ak /ˈænəræk/ n [C] jacket with a hood attached, worn as protection against rain, wind and cold.

an·other /əˈnʌðə(r)/ pron, adj 1 an additional (one): Would you like ∼ cup of coffee/∼ (one)? 2 a similar (one): He thinks he's another Napoleon, a man like Napoleon. 3 a different (one): We can do that ∼ time. That's quite ∼ matter.

answer¹ /ˈɑːnsə(r) US: ˈæn-/ n 1 something done in return; reply: Have you had an ∼ to your letter? in **answer to,** as a reply to: in ∼ to your letter. 2 solution; result of working with numbers, etc: The ∼ to 3 × 17 is 51.

answer² /ˈɑːnsə(r) US: ˈæn-/ vt,vi 1 say, write or do in return or reply: Have you ∼ed his letter?. No one ∼ed. **answer the door,** open the door when somebody has knocked or rung the bell. **answer the (tele)phone,** pick up the receiver when it has rung. 2 be suitable or satisfactory for: Will this ∼ your purpose? 3 (uses with prepositions and particles):

answer back, be impolite, esp when told one has done wrong.

answer for, (a) be responsible for: I can't ∼ for his honesty. **(b)** be punished for: If the police catch you, you'll have a lot to ∼ for.

answer·able /ˈɑːnsrəbəl US: ˈæn-/ adj 1 that can be answered. 2 responsible.

ant /ænt/ n [C] small insect, known to be very active, that lives in highly organized societies. ⇨ white ant.

ant-eater, name of various animals that live on ants.

ant-hill, pile of earth, etc, over an underground nest of ants; cone-shaped nest of white ants.

-ant (also **-ent**) /-ənt/ suffix 1 (verb + ∼ = adjective): significant; different. 2 (verb + ∼ = noun): assistant; confident.

an·tag·on·ism /ænˈtægənɪzm/ n [C,U] (instance of) fighting against or opposing: the ∼ between the two men; feel a strong ∼ for/toward a person.

an·tag·on·ist /ænˈtægənɪst/ n [C] opponent (the usual word).

an·tag·on·is·tic /ænˈtægəˈnɪstɪk/ adj 1 opposed. 2 (of forces) acting against each other.

an·tag·on·is·ti·cally /-klɪ/ adv

an·tag·on·ize /ˈænˈtægənaɪz/ vt make an enemy of; irritate a person until he attacks: I advise you not to ∼ him.

ant·arc·tic /ænˈtɑːktɪk/ adj of the south polar regions.

the 'Antarctic 'Circle, the line of latitude 66½°S

ante- /æntɪ/ prefix before, previous to: antenatal.

ante·ced·ence /ˈæntɪˈsiːdəns/ n [U] (formal) priority.

ante·ced·ent /ˌæntɪˈsiːdənt/ adj previous (to). □ n 1 [C] preceding event or circumstance. 2 (pl) ancestors; past history of a person or persons. 3 [C] (gram) noun, clause or sentence, to which a following pronoun or adverb refers.

ante·date /ˌæntɪˈdeɪt/ vt 1 put a date on, e g a letter, document, etc, earlier than the true one; give an earlier date than the true one to (an event). 2 come before in time: This event ~s the arrival of Columbus by several centuries.

ante·di·luvian /ˌæntɪdɪˈluːvɪən/ adj 1 of, suitable for, the time before the Flood. 2 (fig) very old-fashioned; out of date.

ante·lope /ˈæntɪləʊp/ n [C] deer-like, fast-running animal with thin legs.

ante meridiem /ˌæntɪ məˈrɪdɪəm/ (Latin) (shortened to a m /ˈeɪ ˈem/) time between midnight and noon: 7.30 a m.

ante·natal /ˌæntɪˈneɪtəl/ adj existing or occurring before birth: ~ clinics, for pregnant women.

an·tenna /ænˈtenə/ n [C] (pl ~e /-niː/) jointed organ found in pairs on the head of insects, shell-fish, etc, used for feeling, etc.

an·ter·ior /ænˈtɪərɪə(r)/ adj coming before (in time or position).

an·them /ˈænθəm/ n [C] musical composition to be sung in churches. ⇨ national anthem.

an·ther /ˈænθə(r)/ n [C] part of a flower containing pollen.

an·thol·ogy /ænˈθɒlədʒɪ/ n [C] (pl -ies) collection of poems or pieces of prose, or of both, by different writers, or a selection from the work of one writer.

an·thro·poid /ˈænθrəpɔɪd/ adj like man. □ n [C] animal like man, e g a gorilla.

an·thro·po·logi·cal /ˌænθrəpəˈlɒdʒɪkəl/ adj of anthropology.

an·thro·pol·ogist /ˌænθrəˈpɒlədʒɪst/ n expert in, student of, anthropology.

an·thro·pol·ogy /ˌænθrəˈpɒlədʒɪ/ n [U] science of man, esp of the beginnings, development, customs and beliefs of mankind.

anti- /ˈæntɪ US: ˈæntaɪ/ prefix 1 opposed to, against: antisocial; antiseptic. 2 instead of: anti-hero.

anti-air·craft /ˌæntɪ ˈeəkrɑːft US: -kræft/ adj used against enemy aircraft: ~ guns.

anti·biotic /ˌæntɪbaɪˈɒtɪk/ n [C], adj (substance produced by moulds and bacteria, e g pencillin) capable of destroying or preventing the growth of bacteria

anti·body /ˈæntɪbɒdɪ/ n [C] (pl -ies) (kinds of) substance formed in the blood tending to inhibit or destroy harmful bacteria, etc.

an·tics /ˈæntɪks/ n pl unusual or clever movement, step, attitude, intended to amuse, e g by a clown at a circus; odd behaviour.

an·tici·pate /ænˈtɪsɪpeɪt/ vt 1 do, make use of, before the right or natural time. 2 do before somebody else does it: It is said that Columbus discovered America, but he was probably ~d by sailors from Norway who reached Labrador 500 years earlier. 3 see what needs doing, what is likely to happen, etc and do what is necessary: He tries to ~ all my needs, satisfy them before I mention them. 4 expect: We don't ~ much trouble.

an·tici·pa·tion /ænˌtɪsɪˈpeɪʃən/ n [U] action of anticipating; something anticipated: Thanking you in ~, in advance and expecting you to do what I have asked.

anti–cli·max /ˌæntɪ ˈklaɪmæks/ n [C] sudden change or fall from something (expected to be) important, sensible, enjoyable etc; descent that contrasts with a previous rise.

anti·cyc·lone /ˌæntɪˈsaɪkləʊn/ n [C] area in which atmospheric pressure is high compared with that of surrounding areas, giving quiet, settled weather. ⇨ depression(4).

anti·dote /ˈæntɪdəʊt/ n [C] medicine used against a poison or to prevent a disease from having an effect: an ~ against/for/to snake-bite.

anti·freeze /ˈæntɪfriːz/ n [U] substance added to another liquid to lower its freezing point, e g as used in the radiator of a motor-vehicle.

anti·hero /ˈæntɪ hɪərəʊ/ n [C] (pl ~es) (in fiction and drama) leading character lacking the traditional characteristics of a hero, such as courage and dignity.

an·tipa·thy /ænˈtɪpəθɪ/ n (pl -ies) 1 [U] strong dislike; 2 [C] instance or object of this: feel/show a strong ~ to a place/against a person.

an·tipo·des /ænˈtɪpədiːz/ n pl the ~, (two) place(s) on the opposite sides of the earth, esp the region opposite our own, e g Australia and New Zealand.

anti·quated /ˈæntɪkweɪtɪd/ adj obsolete; out of date; (of persons) having old-fashioned ideas and ways.

an·tique /ænˈtiːk/ adj belonging to the distant past; existing since old times; in the style of past times. □ n [C] material, (e g a piece of furniture, a work of art) of a past period (in GB at least 50 years old, in US 100 years).

an·tiquity /ænˈtɪkwətɪ/ n (pl -ies) 1 [U] old times, esp before the Middle Ages: a city of great ~, e g Athens. 2 (pl) buildings, ruins, works of art, remaining from ancient times: Greek and Roman antiquities.

anti·sep·tic /ˌæntɪˈseptɪk/ n [C], adj (chemical substance) preventing disease, esp by destroying germs.

anti·so·cial /ˌæntɪˈsəʊʃəl/ adj 1 opposed to social laws or to organized societies. 2 (modern informal) likely, tending to interfere with or spoil public amenities: It is ~ to leave litter in public places.

an·tith·esis /ænˈtɪθəsɪs/ n (pl -ses /-siːz/) 1 [U] direct opposite. 2 [U] opposition: the ~ of good to evil; [C] instance of this; contrast of ideas vividly expressed, as in 'Give me liberty, or give me death'.

ant·ler /ˈæntlə(r)/ n [C] branch of a horn (of a stag or other deer).

an·to·nym /ˈæntənɪm/ n [C] word that is contrary in meaning to another: *Hot is the ~ of cold.* ⇨ synonym.

anus /ˈeɪnəs/ n [C] (pl ~es) (anat) opening at the end of the alimentary canal, through which solid waste matter passes out.

an·vil /ˈænvɪl/ n [C] **1** large, heavy block of iron on which a smith hammers heated metal into shape. **2** (anat) bone in the ear.

anxiety /æŋˈzaɪətɪ/ n (pl -ies) **1** [U] emotional condition in which there is fear and uncertainty about the future: *We waited with ~ for news of her safe arrival.* **2** [C] instance of such a feeling: *All these anxieties made him look pale and tired.* **3** [U] keen desire: *~ to please his employers.*

anxious /ˈæŋʃəs/ adj **1** feeling anxiety; troubled: *I am very ~ about my son's health.* **2** causing anxiety: *We have had an ~ time.* **3** **anxious to/for/about/that,** strongly wishing: *He was ~ to meet you/~ for his brother to meet you. We were ~ that help should be sent /~ for help to be sent.*
anxious·ly adv

any[1] /ˈenɪ/ adj **1** (showing amount or quantity or a number, usually more than two): *Have you ~ milk? They haven't ~ children. Are there ~ flowers left?* (Note: *any* is used in questions and negatives; *some* is used in statements, etc: *There are some flowers. There is some milk. Any* and *some* are pl forms of *a* and *an.* ⇨ a[2](1).) **2** (used with verbs such as *prevent* and after *without, hardly,* etc): *We did it without ~ help. I've hardly ~ left.* ⇨ also **almost.** **3** no matter which: *Come ~ day you like.* **4** (informal) a, one: *This is useless — it hasn't ~ handle.* **5** *in* `any case,` whatever happens; even considering the facts: *It's too late now, in ~ case.* *at* `any rate,` at least; in any case.

any[2] /ˈenɪ/ adv at all; to even a little extent: *Is he feeling ~ better? We can't go ~ further.* (Note: *any* is used in questions, negative sentences and with *comparatives.* Compare: *We can go no further.)*

any[3] /ˈenɪ/ pron = some[2].

any·body /ˈenɪbɒdɪ/ n, pron **1** a person, but not a particular one: *Is ~ there? We couldn't see ~.* (Note: *anybody* is used in questions and negative sentences. Compare: *Somebody's there. We could see someone in the garden.)* **2** (used in statements, etc) no matter who: *A~ will tell you where the bus stop is.* **3** person of importance: *You must work harder if you wish to be ~.* **anybody else,** ⇨ else.

any·how /ˈenɪhaʊ/ adv **1** in any possible way; by any possible means: *The house was empty and ~ I couldn't get in.* **2** = in any case: *It's too late now. ~.*

any·one /ˈenɪwʌn/ n, pron = anybody.

any·thing /ˈenɪθɪŋ/ n, pron **1** an event,

happening, but not a particular one: *Has ~ unusual happened?* (Note: *anything* is used in questions, negative sentences, etc. Compare: *Something's* happened.) **2** no matter what: *I want something to eat; ~ will do. He is ~ but mad,* far from being mad. **3** (used to intensify a meaning): *The thief ran like ~ when he saw the policeman.* **(as) easy as anything,** (informal) very easy.

any·way /ˈenɪweɪ/ adj = anyhow.

any·where /ˈenɪweə(r)/ US: -hweər/ adv **1** to any place: *I'm not going ~ without you. Are we going ~ (in) particular?* (Note: *anywhere* is used in questions, negative sentences, etc. Compare: *Let's go somewhere different tomorrow.)* **2** a place, but not a particular one: *That leaves me without ~ to keep all my books.* **3** no matter where: *Put the box down ~. We'll go ~ you like.*

aorta /eɪˈɔːtə/ n [C] (pl ~s) chief bloodvessel through which blood is carried from the left side of the heart.

apart /əˈpɑːt/ adv **1** distant: *The two houses are 500 metres ~. They are still miles ~,* show no signs of agreeing. **2** to or on one side (the usual words): *He took me ~ in order to speak to me alone.* **joking apart,** speaking seriously. **3** separate(ly): *He was standing with his feet wide apart.* **apart from,** independently of; leaving on one side: *~ from these reasons.* **tell/know two things or persons apart,** distinguish one from the other. ⇨ also **come**(13), **pull**[1](7), **take**[1](16).

apart·heid /əˈpɑːtheɪt/ n [U] (S Africa) (policy of) racial segregation; separate development of Europeans and non-Europeans.

apart·ment /əˈpɑːtmənt/ n **1** [C] single room in a house. **2** (pl) set of rooms as a residence, furnished or unfurnished.

apa·thetic /ˈæpəˈθetɪk/ adj showing or having apathy.
apa·theti·cally /-klɪ/ adv

apa·thy /ˈæpəθɪ/ n [U] absence of sympathy or interest.

ape /eɪp/ n [C] **1** tailless monkey (gorilla, chimpanzee, orang-outan, gibbon). **2** person who copies the behaviour of others. **3** (informal) clumsy, ill-bred person. □ vt copy (a person's behaviour, etc).

aperi·tif /əˈperətɪf US: əˈperəˈtiːf/ n [C] alcoholic drink, (e g sherry) taken before a meal.

ap·er·ture /ˈæpətʃʊə(r)/ n [C] opening, esp one that admits light, e g to a camera lens.

apex /ˈeɪpeks/ n [C] (pl ~es or apices /ˈeɪpɪsɪz/) top or highest point: *the ~ of a triangle/his career/fortunes.*

aph·ro·dis·iac /ˈæfrəˈdɪzɪæk/ n, adj [C,U] (substance, drug) exciting sexual desire and activity.

apiece /əˈpiːs/ adv to, for or by, each one of a group: *They cost a penny ~,* each.

apish /ˈeɪpɪʃ/ adj of or like an ape; copying a person's behaviour, etc.

aplomb /əˈplɒm/ n [U] self-confidence (in

speech or behaviour): *He answered with perfect* ∼.

apoc·ry·phal /əˈpɒkrɪfəl/ *adj* of doubtful authority or authorship.

apolo·getic /əˌpɒləˈdʒetɪk/ *adj* making an apology; excusing a fault or failure: *He was* ∼ *for arriving late.*
apolo·geti·cally /-klɪ/ *adv*

apolo·gize /əˈpɒlədʒaɪz/ *vi* make an apology; say one is sorry: *You must* ∼ *to your sister for being so rude.*

apol·ogy /əˈpɒlədʒɪ/ *n* [C] (*pl* -ies) statement of being sorry (for doing wrong, hurting a person's feelings): *make one's apologies* (*to a friend*), e g for being late, for not being able to come. *an apology for*, a poor example of.

apo·plec·tic /ˌæpəˈplektɪk/ *adj* **1** causing, having, apoplexy. **2** (*informal*) red in the face; easily made angry.

apostle /əˈpɒsl/ *n* [C] **1** one of the twelve men chosen by Jesus to spread His teaching, also St Barnabas and St Paul. **2** leader or teacher of a new faith or movement.

apos·tolic /ˌæpəˈstɒlɪk/ *adj* **1** of the twelve apostles(1) or the times when they lived. **2** of the Pope.

apos·trophe /əˈpɒstrəfɪ/ *n* [C] the sign ' used to show omission of letter(s) or number(s), (as in *can't*, *I'm*, *'05*, for *cannot*, *I am*, *1905*), for the possessive (as in *boy's*, *boys'*), and for the plurals of letters (as in *There are two l's in 'Bell'*).

apoth·ecary /əˈpɒθɪkərɪ/ *US*: -keri/ *n* [C] (*pl* -ies) (*old use*) person who prepares and sells medicines and medical goods.

ap·pal (*US* also **ap·pall**) /əˈpɔl/ *vt* (-ll-) fill with fear or dismay; shock deeply: *They were* ∼*led at the news.*
ap·pal·ling *adj*

ap·par·atus /ˌæpəˈreɪtəs/ *US*: -ˈrætəs/ *n* [C] (*pl* ∼es) set of tools, instruments or machinery put together for a purpose.

ap·parel /əˈpærəl/ *n* [U] (*old use* or *literary*) dress; clothing.

ap·par·ent /əˈpærənt/ *adj* **1** clearly seen or understood: *It was* ∼ *to all of us...,* We all saw clearly... **2** appearing but not necessarily true or genuine: *the* ∼ *cause but not the real one.*
ap·par·ent·ly *adv*

ap·par·ition /ˌæpəˈrɪʃən/ *n* [C] the coming into view, esp of a ghost or the spirit of a dead person.

ap·peal /əˈpil/ *vi* **1** make an earnest request: *The prisoner* ∼*ed to the judge for mercy.* **2** (*legal*) take a question (to a higher court, etc) for rehearing and a new decision. **3** (*sport*) go (to a person) for a new decision: ∼ *against the referee's decision.* **4** attract; move the feelings of: *Do these paintings* ∼ *to you?* □ *n* **1** [C] earnest call for: *make an* ∼ *for help.* **2** [C] act of appealing(2,3): *an* ∼ *to a higher court/to the referee.* **3** (power of) attraction: *That sort of music hasn't much* ∼

for *me/has lost its* ∼. **4** [U] asking for help or sympathy: *with a look of* ∼ *on her face.*

ap·peal·ing /əˈpilɪŋ/ *adj* **1** moving; touching the feelings or sympathy. **2** attractive.
ap·peal·ing·ly *adv*

ap·pear /əˈpɪə(r)/ *vi* **1** come into view, become visible: *When we reached the top of the hill, the town* ∼*ed below us.* **2** arrive: *He promised to come at 4 but didn't* ∼ *until 6.* **3** (**a**) (of an actor, singer, lecturer, etc) come before the public: *He has* ∼*ed in every large concert hall in Europe.* (**b**) (of a book) be published: *When will your new novel* ∼*?* (**c**) (*legal*) present oneself: *The defendant failed to* ∼ *before the court.* **4** give the impression of being (but not necessarily a true or genuine one): *Why does she* ∼ *so sad?*

ap·pear·ance /əˈpɪərəns/ *n* [C] **1** act of appearing: *make one's first* ∼, (of an actor, singer, etc) appear in public for the first time. *put in an appearance*, show oneself, attend (a party, meeting, etc). **2** that which shows or can be seen; what a thing or person appears to be: *The child had the* ∼ *of being* (= looked as if it were) *half starved.* **3** style of dressing: *have an untidy* ∼.

ap·pease /əˈpiz/ *vt* make quiet, less angry or calm.
ap·pease·ment *n* [U]

ap·pend /əˈpend/ *vt* (*formal*) add in writing or in print; add something at the end: ∼ *a signature to a document.*

ap·pend·age /əˈpendɪdʒ/ *n* [C] something added to, fastened to or forming a natural part of, a larger thing.

ap·pen·di·ci·tis /əˌpendɪˈsaɪtɪs/ *n* [U] diseased condition of the appendix[2].

ap·pen·dix[1] /əˈpendɪks/ *n* [C] (*pl* -dixes /-dɪsɪz/) something added, esp at the end of a book.

ap·pen·dix[2] /əˈpendɪks/ *n* [C] (*pl* ∼es or -dices /-dɪsiz/) small out-growth on a bodily organ, esp the large intestine.

ap·per·tain /ˌæpəˈteɪn/ *vi* (*formal*) belong to as a right: *the duties* ∼*ing to his office.*

ap·pe·tite /ˈæpɪtaɪt/ *n* **1** [C,U] physical desire esp for food: *The long walk gave him a good* ∼. **2** (*fig*) desire: *He had no* ∼ *for the fight.*

ap·pe·tizer /ˈæpɪtaɪzə(r)/ *n* [C] something done (e g a walk) or served (e g a short alcoholic drink) in order to encourage the appetite(1).

ap·pe·tiz·ing *adj* exciting the appetite: *an appetizing smell from the kitchen.*

ap·plaud /əˈplɔd/ *vi, vt* **1** show approval (of) by clapping the hands: *The audience* ∼*ed* (*the singer*) *for five minutes. He was loudly* ∼*ed.* **2** express approval of; agree with: *I* ∼ *your decision.*

ap·plause /əˈplɔz/ *n* [U] loud approval; hand-clapping.

apple /ˈæpl/ *n* [C] (tree with a) round fruit with firm juicy flesh and a thin skin. *the apple of one's eye*, thing or person dearly loved. ⇨ Adam's apple.

ap·pli·ance /ə'plaɪəns/ n [C] instrument or apparatus: an ~ (= tool) for opening tin cans; household ~s, eg a washing-machine.

ap·pli·cable /'æplɪkəbəl/ adj that can be applied; that is suitable and proper: Is the rule ~ to this case?

ap·pli·cant /'æplɪkənt/ n [C] person who applies (esp for a job).

ap·p·li·ca·tion /ˌæplɪ'keɪʃən/ n 1 [U] making of a request: A sample will be sent on ~. [C] request (esp in writing): We made an ~ to the manager for an interview. 2 [U] putting one thing on to another: He suggests an ~ of this cream to small cuts only. [C,U] substance used: This ~ is for burns and cuts. 3 [U] putting to a special or practical use: the ~ of a new technical process to industry. 4 [U] effort: If you show ~ in your studies (= If you work hard) you will succeed.

'ap·pli·'ca·tion form, one to be filled in when asking for a job, membership, etc.

ap·plied /ə'plaɪd/ adj put to practical use: ~ mathematics.

applied science, engineering, etc as a subject for study.

ap·ply /ə'plaɪ/ vt,vi (pt,pp -ied) 1 ask for: ~ to the Consul for a visa. 2 a) lay one thing on or in another: ~ a plaster to a cut. b) put into operation: We intend to ~ economic sanctions. 3 (cause to) have a bearing (on); concern: What I have said does not ~ to you. 4 **apply oneself/one's mind/one's energies (to sth/to doing sth),** give all one's thought, energy or attention to: ~ your mind to your work. 5 make practical use of (research, a discovery).

ap·point /ə'pɔɪnt/ vt 1 fix or decide: The time ~ed for the meeting was 8.30 p m. 2 choose for a post; set up by choosing members: They ~ed White (to be) manager. We must ~ a committee.

ap·poin·tee /əˌpɔɪn'tiː/ n [C] person appointed to an office or position.

ap·point·ment /ə'pɔɪntmənt/ n 1 [U] act of appointing: meet by ~, after fixing a time and place. 2 [C] arrangement to meet: make/ fix an ~; keep/break an ~. 3 [C] position or office: He got the ~ as manager.

ap·por·tion /ə'pɔːʃən/ vt divide; distribute (the usual words): This sum of money is to be ~ed among the six boys.

ap·po·site /'æpəzɪt/ adj very apt for a purpose or occasion: an ~ remark.

ap·prais·al /ə'preɪzəl/ n [C,U] opinion, judgement of how good, valuable, etc somebody or something is.

ap·praise /ə'preɪz/ vt fix a price for: ~ property (at a certain sum) for taxation.

ap·preci·able /ə'priːʃəbəl/ adj that can be seen or felt: an ~ change in the temperature.

ap·preci·ably /-əblɪ/ adv

ap·preci·ate /ə'priːʃɪeɪt/ vt,vi 1 judge rightly the value of; understand and enjoy: We all ~ a holiday after a year of hard work. 2 put a high value on: We greatly ~ all your help. 3 (of land, goods, etc) increase in value: The land has ~d greatly since the new motorway was built.

ap·preci·ation /əˌpriːʃɪ'eɪʃən/ n 1 [C,U] (statement giving) judgement, valuation: She showed little or no ~ of good music. 2 [U] understanding and recognition: in sincere ~ of your valuable help. 3 [U] rise in value, e g of land, business shares.

ap·preci·ative /ə'priːʃətɪv/ adj feeling or showing appreciation(2): an ~ audience.

ap·pre·hend /ˌæprɪ'hend/ vt (legal) arrest: ~ a thief.

ap·pre·hen·sion /ˌæprɪ'henʃən/ n 1 [U] understanding: quick/slow of ~. 2 [U] (also pl) fear; unhappy feeling about the future: feel ~ for her safety. 3 (legal) arresting: the ~ of a thief.

ap·pre·hen·sive /ˌæprɪ'hensɪv/ adj uneasy; worried: ~ for his safety.

ap·pren·tice /ə'prentɪs/ n [C] learner of a trade who has agreed to work for a number of years in return for being taught. □ vt put in the care of an apprentice: The boy was ~d to a carpenter.

ap·pren·tice·ship /-ʃɪp/, (time of) being an apprentice.

ap·proach /ə'prəʊtʃ/ vt,vi 1 come near(er) (to): As winter ~ed the weather became colder. 2 (fig) be (nearly) as good as: Few writers can even ~ Shakespeare in greatness. 3 go to (a person) with a request or offer: When is the best time to ~ him about an increase in salary? □ n 1 [U] act of approaching: The enemy ran away at our ~. 2 [C] way, path, road: All the ~es to the Palace were guarded by soldiers.

ap·proach·able /-əbəl/ adj (of a person or place) that can be approached; accessible.

ap·pro·pri·ate¹ /ə'prəʊprɪət/ adj 1 suited to: That dress is not ~ for a formal wedding. 2 in keeping with: Write in a style ~ to your subject.

ap·pro·pri·ate·ly adv

ap·pro·pri·ate² /ə'prəʊprɪeɪt/ vt 1 put on one side for a special purpose: £20 000 has been ~d for the new building. 2 take and use as one's own: He often ~s my ideas.

ap·pro·pri·ation /əˌprəʊprɪ'eɪʃən/ n 1 [U] appropriating or being appropriated; [C] instance of this. 2 [C] thing, esp a sum of money, that is appropriated: make an ~ for payment of debts.

ap·prov·al /ə'pruːvəl/ n [U] feeling, showing or saying, that one is satisfied, that something is right, that one agrees: Your plans have my ~. Does what I have done meet with your ~?

ap·prove /ə'pruːv/ vt,vi 1 give one's approval of: Her father will never ~ of her marriage to you. 2 agree to: The minutes (of the meeting) were read and ~d. 3 confirm: our *expenses have been* ∼*d.*

ap·prov·ing·ly *adv*

ap·proxi·mate¹ /ə`prɒksɪmət/ *adj* very near (to); about right: *The* ∼ *speed was 30 miles an hour.*

ap·proxi·mate·ly *adv*

ap·proxi·mate² /ə`prɒksɪmeɪt/ *vi,vt* come near to (esp in quality or number): *His description of the event* ∼*d to the truth but there were a few errors.*

ap·proxi·ma·tion /ə͵prɒksɪ`meɪʃən/ *n* [C] almost correct amount or estimate; [U] being or getting near (in number or quality).

après-ski /͵æpreɪ `skiː/ *adj* of the evening period after skiing: ∼ *clothes.*

apri·cot /`eɪprɪkɒt/ *n* 1 [C] (tree with) round, orange-yellow or orange-red fruit with soft flesh and a hard stone-like seed. 2 [U] colour of this fruit when ripe.

April /`eɪprəl/ *n* fourth month of the year.

'**April** '**fool**, person who has a practical joke played on him on 'All `Fools' Day (1 April).

apron /`eɪprən/ *n* [C] loose garment worn over the front part of the body to keep clothes clean; any similar covering.

'**apron stage**, (in some theatres) part of the front of a stage extending into the audience.

apse /æps/ *n* [C] semi-circular or many-sided recess, with an arched or domed roof, esp at the east end of a church.

apt /æpt/ *adj* (-er, -est) 1 intelligent: ∼ *at learning a new subject.* 2 well suited: *an* ∼ *remark.* 3 having a tendency, likely (to do something): *He's a clever boy but* ∼ *to get into mischief.*

apt·ly *adv* suitably: ∼*ly named.*

apt·ness *n* [U]

ap·ti·tude /`æptɪtjud *US:* -tud/ *n* [C,U] natural or acquired talent: *He shows an* ∼ *for languages.*

aqua-lung /`ækwəlʌŋ/ *n* [C] (*P*) breathing unit (mask cylinder(s)) used for underwater swimming or diving.

aqua·mar·ine /͵ækwəmə`rin/ *n* [C,U] bluish-green (jewel).

aquar·ium /ə`kweərɪəm/ *n* [C] (*pl* ∼s, -ria /-rɪə/) (building with an) artificial pond or tank for keeping and showing living fish and water plants.

Aquar·ius /ə`kweərɪəs/ *n* the Water Carrier, the eleventh sign of the zodiac.

aquatic /ə`kwætɪk/ *adj* 1 (of plants, animals, etc) growing or living in or near water. 2 (of sports) taking place on or in water, e g rowing, swimming.

aque·duct /`ækwɪdʌkt/ *n* [C] artificial channel for supplying water, esp. one built of stone or brick and higher than the surrounding land.

Ara·bic /`ærəbɪk/ *adj* of the Arabs. □ *n* [U] language of the Arabs.

Arabic numeral, the sign 0, 1, 2, 3, etc.

ar·able /`ærəbəl/ *adj* (of land) suitable for ploughing; usually ploughed.

ar·bit·rary /`ɑbɪtrərɪ *US:* -trerɪ/ *adj* 1 based on opinion, accident or sudden decision only, not on reason. 2 using unlimited power.

ar·bi·trate /`ɑbɪtreɪt/ *vt,vi* decide by arbitration: *Mr Smith has been asked to* ∼ *between the employers and their workers.*

ar·bi·tra·tion /͵ɑbɪ`treɪʃən/ *n* [U] settlement of a dispute by the decision of a person or persons chosen and accepted as judges or umpires: *The Union agreed to (go to)* ∼, i e for a settlement of their claims.

ar·bi·tra·tor /`ɑbɪtreɪtə(r)/ *n* [C] person appointed by two parties to settle a dispute.

ar·bour (*US* = **ar·bor**) /`ɑbə(r)/ *n* [C] shady place among trees.

arc /ɑk/ *n* [C] part of the circumference of a circle or other curved line.

ar·cade /ɑ`keɪd/ *n* [C] covered passage, usually with an arched roof, e g a passage with shops or market stalls along one or both sides; covered market.

arch /ɑtʃ/ *n* [C] 1 curved structure supporting the weight of what is above it, as in bridges, gateways, etc. 2 (also '**arch·way**) passageway under an arch, built as an ornament or gateway: *a triumphal* ∼. 3 any curve in the shape of an arch, e g the curved part under the foot. □ *vt,vi* 1 form into an arch: *The cat* ∼*ed its back when it saw the dog.* 2 be like an arch: *The trees* ∼ *over the river.*

arch- /ɑtʃ/ *prefix* 1 chief, first; head: *archbishop.* 2 notable; extreme: *my* ∼*-enemy.*

ar·chae·ologi·cal (also **ar·che·ol-**) /͵ɑkɪə`lɒdʒɪkəl/ *adj* of archæology.

ar·chae·ol·ogist (also and *US* **ar·che·ol-**) /͵ɑkɪ`ɒlədʒɪst/ *n* [C] expert in, student of, archæology.

ar·chae·ol·ogy (also and *US* **ar·che·ol-**) /͵ɑkɪ`ɒlədʒɪ/ *n* [U] study of ancient things, esp remains of prehistoric times.

ar·chaic /ɑ`keɪɪk/ *adj* 1 (of languages, words) not now used. 2 of ancient times.

ar·chaism /ɑ`keɪɪzm/ *n* [C] archaic word or expression; [U] use or imitation of what is archaic.

arch·angel /`ɑk͵eɪndʒəl/ *n* [C] angel of the highest rank.

arch·bishop /`ɑtʃ`bɪʃəp/ *n* [C] chief bishop.

arch·bishop·ric, position, rank or district of an archbishop.

arch·deacon /`ɑtʃ`dikən/ *n* [C] (in the C of E) priest next below a bishop, in charge of rural deans.

arch·deaconry, position, rank, residence, of an archdeacon.

archer /`ɑtʃə(r)/ *n* [C] person who shoots with a bow and arrows.

arch·ery /`ɑtʃərɪ/ *n* [U] (art of) shooting with a bow and arrows.

archi·pel·ago /͵ɑkɪ`peləgəʊ/ *n* [C] (*pl* ∼s, ∼es) (sea with a) group of many islands.

archi·tect /`ɑkɪtekt/ *n* [C] person who designs (and supervises the construction of) buildings, etc.

archi·tec·tural /ˈɑːkɪˈtekʃərəl/ *adj* of architecture: *the ∼ beauties of a city.*

archi·tec·ture /ˈɑːkɪtektʃə(r)/ *n* [U] art and science of building; style of building(s).

ar·chives /ˈɑːkaɪvz/ *n pl* (place for keeping) public or government records; other historical records.

archi·vist /ˈɑːkɪvɪst/ *n* [C] person in charge of archives.

arch·way /ˈɑːtʃweɪ/ *n* ⇨ arch(2).

arc·tic /ˈɑːktɪk/ *adj* of the north polar regions: *the A∼ Ocean; ∼ weather,* very cold weather.

ar·dent /ˈɑːdənt/ *adj* very enthusiastic: *∼ supporters of the new movement.*
ar·dent·ly *adv*

ar·dour (*US* = **ar·dor**) /ˈɑːdə(r)/ *n* [C,U] enthusiasm (the more usual word).

ar·du·ous /ˈɑːdjʊəs *US:* -dʒʊ-/ *adj* needing and using up much energy.
ar·du·ous·ly *adv*

are /ə(r) *strong form:* ɑ(r)/ ⇨ be¹.

area /ˈeərɪə/ *n* [C] **1** surface measure: *If a room measures 3 × 5 metres, its ∼ is 15 square metres/it is 15 square metres in ∼.* **2** region of the earth's surface: *desert ∼s of North Africa.* **3** (*fig*) scope or range of activity: *The ∼s of disagreement were clearly indicated at the Board Meeting.*

arena /əˈriːnə/ *n* [C] (*pl ∼s*) **1** central part, for games and fights, of a Roman amphitheatre. **2** (*fig*) any scene of competition or struggle: *the political ∼.*

aren't /ɑːnt/ = *are not.*

ar·gu·able /ˈɑːgjʊəbl/ *adj* that can be supported by facts; that can be disagreed with.
ar·gu·ably /-əblɪ/ *adv*

ar·gue /ˈɑːgjuː/ *vi,vt* **1** express disagreement; quarrel: *arguing over/about the decision. Don't ∼ with me; my decision is final.* **2 argue (for/against/that...),** give reasons (in support of, for, against, esp with the aim of persuading a person): *You can ∼ either way, for or against. He was arguing that poverty may be a blessing.* **3** debate: *The lawyers ∼d the case for hours.*

ar·gu·ment /ˈɑːgjʊmənt/ *n* **1** [C] (serious) disagreement; quarrel: *endless ∼s about money; an ∼ with the referee.* **2** [C,U] discussion giving reasons for agreeing or disagreeing: *It is beyond ∼ that...*

ar·gu·men·ta·tive /ˈɑːgjʊˈmentətɪv/ *adj* fond of arguing(1).

aria /ˈɑːrɪə/ *n* [C] (*pl ∼s*) melody for a single voice in an opera, etc.

-arian /-eərɪən/ *suffix* practiser of: *vegetarian.*

arid /ˈærɪd/ *adj* **1**(of soil, land) dry, barren. **2** (of climate, regions) having not enough rainfall to support plants, etc.

Aries /ˈeərɪz/ *n* the Ram, the first sign of the zodiac.

arise /əˈraɪz/ *vi* (*pt* arose /əˈrəʊz/, *pp* arisen /əˈrɪzən/) **1** come into existence; be noticed: *A new difficulty has ∼n.* **2** result

from: *Serious effects may ∼ from your mistakes.* **3** (*old use*) get up; stand up.

ar·is·toc·racy /ˈærɪˈstɒkrəsɪ/ *n* (*pl -ies*) **1** [U] government by persons of the highest social rank; [C] country or state with such a government. **2** [C] ruling body of nobles; the social class from which these nobles come.

ar·is·to·crat /ˈærɪstəkræt *US:* əˈrɪst-/ *n* [C] member of the class of nobles; person of noble birth.

ar·is·to·cratic /ˈærɪstəˈkrætɪk *US:* əˈrɪstə-/ *adj* of the aristocracy; like an aristocrat: *with an ∼ walk.*
ar·is·to·crati·cally /-klɪ/ *adv*

arith·me·tic /əˈrɪθmətɪk/ *n* [U] science of numbers; working with numbers.
ar·ith·meti·cal /ˈærɪθˈmetɪkəl/ *adj* of arithmetic.

ark /ɑːk/ *n* (in the Bible) covered ship in which Noah and his family were saved from the Flood.

Ark of the Covenant, wooden chest in which writings of Jewish law were kept.

arm¹ /ɑːm/ *n* [C] **1** either of the two upper limbs of the human body, from the shoulder to the hand: *She was carrying a child in her ∼s.* **keep sb at arm's length,** (*fig*) avoid becoming familiar with him. (*welcome sb/ sth*) **with open arms,** warmly, with enthusiasm. **walk 'arm-in-'arm,** (of two persons) walk side by side, with the arm of one round the arm of the other. **2** sleeve: *The ∼s of this coat are too long.* **3** anything shaped like or suggesting an arm: *the ∼s of a chair.* **4** *the* (**long**) *arm of the law,* the authority or power of the law. **5** branch or division of a country's armed forces: *the infantry/air ∼.* **6** weapon: *a 'fire-∼.*
'arm-chair, chair with supports for the arms.
'arm-ful, as much as one arm or both arms can hold: *an ∼ful of books.*
'arm-hole, hole (in a shirt, jacket, etc) through which the arm is put.
'arm-pit, hollow under the arm near the shoulder.

arm² /ɑːm/ *vt,vi* supply, fit, weapons and armour; prepare for war: *a warship ∼ed with nuclear weapons.*
the armed forces/services, the military forces.

ar·mada /ɑːˈmɑːdə/ *n* [C] (*pl ∼s*) great fleet of warships, esp the Spanish fleet sent against England in 1588.

ar·ma·dillo /ˈɑːməˈdɪləʊ/ *n* [C] (*pl ∼s*) small burrowing animal of S America, with a body covered with a shell of bony plates, and the habit of rolling itself up into a ball when attacked.

ar·ma·ment /ˈɑːməmənt/ *n* **1** (usually *pl*) military forces and their equipment; navy, army, air force. **2** (usually *pl*) weapons, esp the large guns on a warship, military tank, etc: *the ∼s industry.* **3** [U] process of getting military forces equipped; preparation for war.

ar·mis·tice /ˈɑːmɪstɪs/ n [C] agreement during a war or battle to stop fighting for a time.

ar·mour (US = **ar·mor**) /ˈɑːmə(r)/ n [U] 1 defensive covering, usually metal, for the body, worn in fighting: a suit of ∼. 2 metal covering for warships, tanks, motorvehicles, etc. 3 (collective) tanks, motorvehicles, etc protected with amour.

ar·moured adj (a) covered with armour: an ∼ed car. (b) equipped with tanks, vehicles, guns, etc that are protected with armour: an ∼ed column.

ar·mourer, manufacturer or repairer of arms and armour.

ar·moury /ˈɑːmərɪ/, place where arms are kept.

arms /ɑːmz/ n pl 1 weapons: The soldiers had plenty of ∼ and ammunition. **lay down (one's) arms,** stop fighting. **take up arms; rise up in arms (against),** (literally or fig) get ready to fight. **(be) up in arms (about/over),** (fig) be protesting strongly. 2 (heraldry) pictorial design used by a noble family, town, university, etc. ⇨ also coat of arms, fire-arms, small arms.

`**arms-race,** competition among nations for military strength.

army /ˈɑːmɪ/ n [C] (pl -ies) 1 the ∼, the military forces of a country, organized for fighting on land: be in the ∼, be a soldier. 2 large number: an ∼ of workmen/officials/ants.

aroma /əˈrəʊmə/ n [C] sweet smell: the ∼ of a cigar.

aro·matic /ˈærəˈmætɪk/ adj fragrant; spicy: the ∼ bark of the cinnamon tree.

arose /əˈrəʊz/ pt of arise.

around /əˈraʊnd/ adv, prep 1 on every side, in every direction. 2 about; round; here and there: I'll be ∼ (= not far away) if you should want me.

arouse /əˈraʊz/ vt 1 awaken: behaviour that might ∼ suspicion. 2 cause (somebody) to become active: fully ∼d.

ar·raign /əˈreɪn/ vt (legal) bring a criminal charge against (a person); bring (a person) before a court for trial: ∼ed on a charge of theft.

ar·range /əˈreɪndʒ/ vt,vi 1 put in order: She's good at arranging flowers. 2 make plans in advance; see to the details of: I have ∼d to meet her at ten o'clock. The meeting ∼d for tomorrow has been postponed. 3 come to an agreement: I've ∼d a loan with Harry for the car. 4 adapt (a piece of music): ∼ a piece of music for the violin.

ar·range·ment /əˈreɪndʒmənt/ n 1 [U] putting in order; arranging or being arranged: The ∼ of the furniture in our new house took a long time. 2 (pl) plans; preparations: Have you made ∼s for your journey to Scotland? 3 [U] agreement; settlement: We can come to some sort of ∼ over expenses. 4 [C] result or manner of arranging: an ∼ (e g of orchestral music) for the piano. I have an ∼ by

which I can cash my cheques at banks anywhere in Europe.

ar·ray /əˈreɪ/ vt (literary) 1 position (esp armed forces, troops) in order for battle. 2 dress: ∼ed in ceremonial robes. □ n [C] (literary) 1 order: troops in battle ∼. 2 clothes: in military ∼. 3 display (of): an impressive ∼ of statistics.

ar·rears /əˈrɪəz/ n pl 1 money that is owing and that ought to have been paid: ∼ of rent/wages. **be in/fall into arrears (with),** be late in paying. 2 work still waiting to be done.

ar·rest /əˈrest/ vt 1 seize (somebody) by the authority of the law: The police ∼ed the thief and put him in prison. 2 put a stop to (a process or movement): Poor food ∼s the natural growth of children. 3 catch (a person's) attention): The bright colours of the flowers ∼ed the child's attention. □ n [C] act of arresting (a wrongdoer, etc): The police made several ∼s. **(be/place/put) under arrest,** (be/be made) a prisoner.

ar·rest·ing adj likely to hold the attention.

ar·ri·val /əˈraɪvəl/ n 1 [U] act of arriving: waiting for the ∼ of news; to await ∼, (on a letter, parcel, etc) to be kept until the addressee arrives. 2 [C] person or thing that arrives: The new ∼ (= The newborn child) is a boy.

ar·rive /əˈraɪv/ vi 1 reach a place, esp the end of a journey: ∼ home. 2 come: At last the day ∼d. Her baby ∼d (= was born) yesterday. 3 **arrive at,** reach (a decision, a price, the age of 40, manhood, etc). 4 (modern use) establish one's position or reputation: The publicity he received at the airport proved he'd ∼d.

ar·ro·gance /ˈærəgəns/ n [U] arrogant behaviour, manner.

ar·ro·gant /ˈærəgənt/ adj behaving in a proud, superior manner; (of behaviour, etc) showing too much pride in oneself and too little consideration for others: speaking in an ∼ tone.

ar·ro·gant·ly adv

ar·row /ˈærəʊ/ n [C] 1 thin, pointed stick (to be) shot from a bow. 2 mark or sign (→) used to show direction or position, e g on a map or as a road sign.

`**arrow-head,** pointed end of an arrow.

ar·senal /ˈɑːsənəl/ n [C] government building(s) where weapons and ammunition are made or stored.

ar·senic /ˈɑːsnɪk/ n [U] (chem) chemical element (symbol As), used in glass-making, dyes, etc; strong poison.

ar·son /ˈɑːsən/ n [U] act of starting a fire intentionally and unlawfully.

art¹ /ɑːt/ n 1 [U] the creation or expression of what is beautiful, esp in visual form; fine skill or aptitude in such expression: the ∼ of the Renaissance; children's ∼; an ∼ historian. 2 [C] something in which imagination and personal taste are more important than exact measurement and calculation: *History and literature are among the ~ (subjects)* (contrasted with science). **3** [C,U] trickery; trick: *In spite of all her ~s, the young man was not attracted to her.* ⇨ also black art, fine art.

`art gallery,` one for the display of paintings, sculpture, etc.

`art school,` one where painting, sculpture, etc are taught.

'Bachelor/'Master of Arts, (abbr = B A/ M A) person who has passed an examination, etc. for the award of a university degree in an arts(2) subject.

black art, magic (used for evil purposes).

fine art, drawing, painting, sculpture, design, music, dancing, etc.

'work of `art,` good painting, sculpture, etc.

art² /ɑt/ v (pres t form of be) used with thou: thou art.

ar·te·fact ⇨ artifact.

ar·ter·ial /ɑˈtɪərɪəl/ adj 1 of or like an artery: ~ blood. 2 (fig) ~ roads, important main roads.

ar·tery /ˈɑtərɪ/ n [C] (pl -ies) 1 one of the tubes carrying blood from the heart to all parts of the body. 2 main road or river; chief channel in a system of communications, etc.

art·ful /ˈɑtfəl/ adj cunning; deceitful; clever in getting what one wants.
art·ful·ly /-fəlɪ/ adv
art·ful·ness n [U]

ar·thri·tic /ɑˈθrɪtɪk/ adj of arthritis.

ar·thri·tis /ɑˈθraɪtɪs/ n [U] inflammation of a joint or joints.

ar·ti·choke /ˈɑtɪtʃəʊk/ n [C] 1 globe ~, plant like a large thistle, with a head of thick, leaf-like scales used as a vegetable. 2 Jerusalem ~, plant with white roots used as a vegetable.

ar·ticle /ˈɑtɪkəl/ n [C] 1 particular or separate thing: ~s of clothing, e g shirts, coats; toilet ~s, e g soap, toothpaste. 2 piece of writing, complete in itself, in a newspaper or other periodical. 3 (legal) separate clause or item in an agreement: ~s of apprenticeship. 4 (gram): definite ~, 'the'; indefinite ~, 'a', 'an'. □ vt bind, e g an apprentice by articles.

ar·ticu·late¹ /ɑˈtɪkjʊlət/ adj 1 (of speech) in which the separate sounds and words are clear. 2 (of a person) able to put thoughts and feelings into clear speech.
ar·ticu·late·ly adv

ar·ticu·late² /ɑˈtɪkjʊleɪt/ vt, vi 1 speak (distinctly). 2 connect by joints: bones that ~/ are ~d with others.

articulated vehicle, having parts joined in a flexible manner, e g a lorry with a trailer.

ar·ticu·la·tion /ɑˌtɪkjʊˈleɪʃən/ n [U] 1 production of speech sounds: The speaker's ideas were good but his ~ was poor. 2 (connection by a) joint.

ar·ti·fact, ar·te·fact /ˈɑtɪfækt/ n [C] something made by human being(s), e g a simple

tool or weapon of archaeological interest.

ar·ti·fice /ˈɑtɪfɪs/ n (formal) 1 [C] skilful way of doing something. 2 [U] cunning; ingenuity; trickery; [C] trick.

ar·ti·fi·cial /ˌɑtɪˈfɪʃl/ adj not natural or real; made by man: ~ flowers/teeth/light.

artificial respiration, method of forcing air into the lungs, e g to a man nearly drowned.
ar·ti·fi·cial·ly /-ʃəlɪ/ adv

ar·til·lery /ɑˈtɪlərɪ/ n [U] big guns (mounted on wheels, etc); branch of an army that uses these.

ar·ti·san /ˈɑtɪzæn US: ˈɑtɪzən/ n [C] skilled workman in industry or trade; mechanic.

art·ist /ˈɑtɪst/ n [C] 1 person who practises one of the fine arts, esp painting. 2 person who acts with skill and good taste: an ~ in words.

art·iste /ɑˈtist/ n [C] professional singer, actor, dancer, etc.

ar·tis·tic /ɑˈtɪstɪk/ adj 1 done with skill and good taste, esp in the arts; able to appreciate what is beautiful. 2 having or showing good taste. 3 of art or artists.
ar·tis·ti·cally /-klɪ/ adv

art·istry /ˈɑtɪstrɪ/ n [U] artistic skill or work; qualities of taste and skill possessed by an artist.

arty /ˈɑtɪ/ adj (informal) pretending or falsely claiming to be artistic.

-ary /-ərɪ, -rɪ/ suffix 1 (used to form an adj): planetary. 2 (pl -ies) (used to form a noun): dictionary.

as¹ /əz strong form: æz/ adv as .. as, in the same degree: I'm ~ tall ~ you. (Note: In a negative sentence as is often replaced by so: It's not so difficult as I expected.)

as² /əz strong form: æz/ conj 1 when; while: I saw him ~ he was getting off the bus. A~ he grew older he became less active. 2 (expressing reason) since; seeing that: A~ he wasn't ready in time, we went without him. 3 (used in comparisons of equality): I want a box twice ~ large ~ this. It's ~ easy ~ ABC. 4 (usually replaceable by a construction with although): Much ~ I like you (= Although I like you), I will not marry you. 5 in the way in which: Do ~ I do. Leave it ~ it is. 6 like: Why is he dressed ~ a woman? 7 (used to avoid repetition): Harry is unusually tall, ~ are his brothers, and his brothers are also unusually tall. 8 in the capacity or character of: He was respected both ~ a judge and ~ a man. 9 (used after regard, view, represent, treat, acknowledge, etc): Most people regarded him (= looked on him) ~ a fool. (Note: compare. Most people considered him (to be) a fool.) 10 such as, for instance, for example, like: Countries in the north of Europe, such ~ Finland, Norway, Sweden. 11 as if; as though, (introducing a clause of manner) a) (with a pt in the clause): He talks ~ though he knew all about it. b) (followed by a to-infinitive): He opened his lips ~ if to say something. **12 as for,** /'æz fə(r)/ with reference to (sometimes suggesting indifference or contempt): *A~ for you, I never want to see you here again.* **13** (used as a conjunction, usually after *same* and *such*): *You must do the same things ~ he does?* **14** *Cyprus,* ~ (= which fact) *you all know, is in the Mediterranean.* **15 so as to,** /'səʊ əz/ **(a)** *He stood up so ~ to* (= in order to) *see better.* **(b)** *It is foolish to behave so ~ to annoy* (= in ways that annoy) *your neighbours.* **16 as good as,** the same thing as: *He's ~ good ~ dead,* almost dead, sure to die soon. **17 as/so long as, (a)** on condition that: *You can go where you like so long ~ you get back before dark.* **(b)** while: *You shall never enter this house ~ long ~ I live in it.* **18 as much,** so; what really amounts to that: *I thought ~ much.* ⇨ also far¹(2), soon(3,5), well²(8).

as·bes·tos /æs'bestəs/ *n* [U] soft, grey, mineral substance that can be made into fire-proof fabrics or heat-proof solid sheeting.

as·cend /ə'send/ *vt,vi* **1** (*formal*) go or come up (a mountain, river, etc): *We watched the mists ~ing from the valley. The path ~s here.* **2 ascend the throne,** become king or queen.

as·cend·ancy, (also **-ency**) /ə'sendənsɪ/ *n* [U] (position of) having power.

as·cen·sion /ə'senʃən/ *n* [C] act of ascending.

the Ascension, the departure of Jesus from the earth, on the fortieth day after the Resurrection.

as·cent /ə'sent/ *n* [C] act of ascending; way up; upward movement: *The ~ of the mountain was not difficult.*

as·cer·tain /ˌæsə'teɪn/ *vt* find out (in order to be certain about); get to know: *~ the facts; ~ what really happened.*

as·cer·tain·able /-əbəl/ *adj* that can be found.

as·cetic /ə'setɪk/ *adj* self-denying; leading a life of severe self-discipline. □ *n* [C] person who (often for religious reasons) leads a severely simple life without ordinary pleasures.

ascor·bic /ə'sɔːbɪk/ *adj* **ascorbic acid,** (also known as *vitamin C*) vitamin found in citrus fruits and vegetable products, used against skin diseases.

as·cribe /ə'skraɪb/ *vt* consider to be the cause, origin, reason or author, of: *He ~d his failure to bad luck. He has ~d a wrong meaning to a word.*

asep·tic /ə'septɪk/ *adj* (of wounds, dressings, etc) free from bacteria; surgically clean.

asex·ual /ˌeɪ'sekʃʊəl/ *adj* **1** without sex or sex organs: *~ reproduction.* **2** (of a person) showing no interest in sexual relations

asex·ual·ity /ˌeɪseksʃʊ'ælətɪ/ *n* [U]

ash¹ /æʃ/ *n* [C] forest-tree with silver-grey bark and hard, tough wood; [U] wood of this

tree.
`ash-key,` winged seed of the ash.

ash² /æʃ/ *n* [U or *pl*, but not with numerals] **1** powder that is left after something has burnt: *Don't drop cigar`ette ~ on the carpet. The house was burnt to ~es.* **2** (*pl*) the burnt (= cremated) remains of a human body.

`ash-tray,` small (metal, glass, etc) receptacle for tobacco ash.

Ash Wednesday, first day of Lent.

ashamed /ə'ʃeɪmd/ *adj* feeling shame: *You should be ~ of yourself/of what you have done.*

ashen /'æʃən/ *adj* of ashes; pale; ash-coloured: *His face turned ~ at the news.*

ashore /ə'ʃɔː(r)/ *adv* on, on to, the shore. **go ashore,** leave a ship to go on land.

ashy /'æʃɪ/ *adj* of or like ashes; covered with ashes; ash-coloured, pale.

Asian /'eɪʃən US: 'eɪʒən/ *n* [C] *adj* (native) of Asia.

Asi·atic /ˌeɪʃɪ'ætɪk/ *n* [C], *adj* (native) of Asia (*Asian* is the preferred word).

aside /ə'saɪd/ *adv* on or to one side: *He laid the book ~,* put it down and stopped reading it. *Please put this ~ for me,* reserve it. *Joking ~,* Speaking seriously,... □ *n* [C] word(s) spoken, esp (on the stage) words that other persons (on the stage) are supposed not to hear.

as·in·ine /'æsɪnaɪn/ *adj* **1** of asses. **2** (*informal*) stupid.

ask /ɑːsk US: æsk/ *vt,vi* (*pt,pp ~ed*) **1** call for an answer to; request information or service: *Did you ~ the price? We must ~ him about it. I will ~ (him) how to get there. Please ~ (her) when she will be back.* **2** invite: *Mr Brown is at the door; shall I ~ him in?* **ask for trouble,** behave in such a way that trouble is likely. **3** request to be allowed: *I must ~ you to excuse me/~ to be excused.* **4** demand as a price: *What are they ~ing for the house?*

ask·ing *n* **the ~:** *You may have it/It's yours for the ~ing,* You have only to ask for it and it will be given to you.

askew /ə'skjuː/ *adv, adj* out of the straight or usual (level) position: *have a hat on ~.*

aslant /ə'slɑːnt US: ə'slænt/ *adv, prep* in a slanting direction: *The wrecked coach lay ~ the railway track.*

asleep /ə'sliːp/ *adj* **1** sleeping: *He fell/dropped ~ during the lecture.* **fast asleep,** in a deep sleep. **2** (of the arms or legs) without feeling (as when under pressure).

asp¹ /æsp/ *n* [C] = aspen.

asp² /æsp/ *n* [C] small poisonous snake of Egypt and Libya.

as·para·gus /ə'pærəgəs/ *n* [U] plant whose young shoots are cooked and eaten as a vegetable; the shoots.

as·pect /'æspekt/ *n* [C] **1** look or appearance (of a person or thing): *a man of fierce ~; a* man with *a serious* ~. **2** front that faces a particular direction: *a house with a southern* ~. **3** (*fig*): *study every* ~ *of a subject*, study it thoroughly.

as·per·ity /ə`sperətɪ/ *n* [U] (*formal*) roughness; harshness (of manner); extreme cold (of weather): *speak with* ~.

as·per·sion /ə`spɜ:ʃən *US:* -ɜ:ʒən/ *n* **cast aspersions on/upon sb/sb's honour, etc,** say false things about him.

as·phalt /`æsfælt *US:* -fɔːlt/ *n* [U] black, sticky substance like coal-tar used for making roofs, etc waterproof, and making road surfaces. □ *vt* surface (a road) with asphalt.

as·phyxia /əs`fɪksɪə/ *n* [U] condition caused by lack of air in the lungs; suffocation.

as·phyxi·ate /əs`fɪksɪeɪt/ *vt* make ill, cause the death of, through lack of sufficient air in the lungs: *The men in the coalmine were* ~*ted by bad gas*.

as·phyxi·ation /əs`fɪksɪ`eɪʃən/ *n* [U]

as·pic /`æspɪk/ *n* [U] clear meat jelly: *chicken in* ~.

as·pir·ant /ə`spaɪərənt/ *n* [C] (*formal*) person who is ambitious for fame, etc: *an* ~ *to high office.*

as·pir·ate¹ /`æspərət/ *n* [C] the sound of 'h'; sound with an 'h' in it.

as·pir·ate² /`æspəreɪt/ *vt* say with an 'h' sound: *The 'h' in 'honour' is not* ~*d.*

as·pir·ation /`æspə`reɪʃən/ *n* [C,U] ambition: *the* ~*s of the developing countries.*

as·pire /ə`spaɪə(r)/ *vi* be filled with ambition: ~ *to become an author.*

as·pirin /`æsprɪn *US:* -pər-/ *n* (*P*) [U] medicine used to relieve pain and reduce fever; [C] tablet or measure of this: *Take two* ~*s for a headache.*

ass /æs/ *n* [C] **1** animal of the horse family with long ears; donkey. **2** (*fig*) stupid person.

as·sail /ə`seɪl/ *vt* attack (the usual word): ~ *a speaker with questions/insults; be* ~*ed with doubts.*

as·sail·able /-əbəl/ *adj* that can be attacked.
as·sail·ant /-ənt/ *n* [C] attacker (the usual word).

as·sas·sin /ə`sæsɪn/ *n* [C] person, often one hired by others, who assassinates.

as·sas·sin·ate /ə`sæsɪneɪt *US:* ə`sæsən-/ *vt* kill a person (esp an important politician, ruler), for political reasons.

as·sas·sin·ation /ə`sæsɪ`neɪʃən/ *n* [U] murder of this kind; [C] instance of this.

as·sault /ə`sɔːlt/ *n* [C] violent and sudden attack: *They made an* ~ *on the enemy's positions.* **assault and battery,** (*legal*) beating or hitting a person. □ *vt* attack (e g a fortress) by a sudden rush.

as·semble /ə`sembəl/ *vt,vi* **1** gather together; collect: *The pupils* ~*d/were* ~*d in the school hall.* **2** fit or put together (the parts of): ~ *a car.*

as·sem·bly /ə`semblɪ/ *n* [C] (*pl* -ies) **1** number of persons who have come together: *the Legislative A*~; *the school* ~, the daily

meeting of staff and pupils. **2** military call, by drum or bugle, for soldiers to assemble.

as·`sembly hall, one where a school meets for prayers, etc.

as·`sembly line, stage of mass production in which parts of a machine, vehicle, etc move along for fixing together.

as·sent /ə`sent/ *n* [C] official agreement, e g to a proposal; (royal) agreement (to a bill passed by Parliament): *by common* ~, everybody agreeing. □ *vi* (*formal*) give agreement (to, e g a proposal).

as·sert /ə`sɜːt/ *vt* **1** make a claim to: ~ *one's rights.* **2** declare: ~ *one's innocence/that one is innocent.*

as·ser·tion /ə`sɜːʃən/ *n* **1** [U] insisting on one's rights. **2** [C] strong statement; claim: *make an* ~.

as·sert·ive /ə`sɜːtɪv/ *adj* having or showing confidence: *speaking in an* ~ *tone.*
as·sert·ive·ly *adv*

as·sess /ə`ses/ *vt* **1** decide or fix the amount of (e g a tax or a fine): *Damages were* ~*ed at £100.* **2** fix or decide the value of (e g property), the amount of (e g income), for purposes of taxation. **3** (*fig*) test the value of: ~ *a speech at its true worth.*

as·sess·ment *n* [C,U].

as·ses·sor /ə`sesə(r)/ *n* [C] **1** person who assesses property, income, taxes, etc. **2** person who advises a judge, a committee, etc on technical matters.

as·set /`æset/ *n* [C] **1** (usually *pl*) anything owned by a person, company, etc that has money value and that may be sold to pay debts. ⇨ **liability.** **2** valuable or useful quality or skill: *Good health is a great* ~.

as·sign /ə`saɪn/ *vt* **1** give for use or enjoyment, or as a share or part in, e g of work, duty: *Those rooms have been* ~*ed to us. Your teacher* ~*s you work to be done at home.* **2** name, put forward as a time, place, reason, etc: *Has a day been* ~*ed for the trial? Can one* ~ *a cause to these events?* **3** appoint: *A*~ *your best man to the job.* **4** (*legal*) transfer property, rights, etc to.

as·sign·able /-əbəl/ *adj* that can be assigned: ~*able to several causes.*

as·sign·ment *n* [C,U]

as·simi·late /ə`sɪmələt/ *vt,vi* **1** absorb (food) into the body (after digestion); be thus absorbed: *We* ~ *some kinds of food more easily than others.* **2** (allow people to) become part of another social group or state: *The USA has* ~*d people from many European countries,* has absorbed them, so that they are Americans.

as·simi·la·tion /ə`sɪmə`leɪʃən/ *n* [U]

as·sist /ə`sɪst/ *vt,vi* (*formal*) help: ~ *an applicant to fill in the forms. Two men are* ~*ing the police in their enquiries,* answering questions which may lead to the arrest of the criminal(s), or perhaps their own arrest as the criminals.

as·sist·ance /ə`sɪstəns/ *n* [U] help: *give/*

lend ∼ (to a person).

as·sist·ant /ə'sɪstənt/ n [C] helper: *an ∼ to the Manager; a `shop-∼,* one who serves customers.

as·so·ci·ate¹ /ə'səʊʃɪət/ adj (of colleagues, etc) joined in function or level: *an ∼ judge.* □ n /ə'səʊsɪət/ [C] person joined with others in work, business or crime; person given certain limited rights in an association; companion.

as·so·ci·ate² /ə'səʊʃɪeɪt/ vt,vi 1 join or connect: *∼ one thing with another. We ∼ Egypt with the Nile.* 2 be often in the company of: *Don't ∼ with dishonest boys.*

as·so·ci·ation /ə,səʊʃɪ'eɪʃən/ n 1 [U] associating; being associated; companionship (with): *I benefited much from my ∼ with him/from our ∼. In association (with),* together. 2 [C] group of persons joined together for some common purpose: *the `Automobile A∼.*

As'sociation 'football, (common abbr = *soccer*) game in which two teams of eleven players kick a round ball that must not be touched with the hands except by the goalkeeper or when throwing in.

as·sorted /ə'sɔtɪd/ adj of various sorts; mixed: *a pound of ∼ chocolates.*

as·sort·ment /ə'sɔtmənt/ n [C] assorted collection of different examples or types: *This shop has an ∼ of goods to choose from.*

as·sume /ə'sjum US: ə'sum/ vt 1 believe before there is proof: *You ∼ his innocence/ him to be innocent/that he is innocent before hearing the evidence against him.* 2 undertake: *∼ office,* begin to govern. 3 take for oneself something not genuine or sincere: *∼ a new name.*

as·sump·tion /ə'sʌmpʃən/ n 1 [C] something regarded as true or likely to happen; something thought to be true but not proved: *Their ∼ that the war would end quickly was proved wrong. I am going on the ∼ that ... I am supposing that...* 2 [C] *assumption of,* a) the act of assuming(2): *his ∼ of office/ power/the presidency.* b) the adopting of a manner, etc which is not genuine: *with an ∼ of indifference,* pretending not to be interested. 4 the A∼, reception into Heaven in bodily form of the Virgin Mary; Church feast commemorating this.

as·sur·ance /ə'ʃʊərəns/ n 1 [U] (often *self-∼*) belief and trust in one's own powers: *He answered all the questions with ∼.* 2 [C] promise; statement made to give confidence: *He gave me a definite ∼ that the repairs would be finished by Friday.* 3 [U] (chiefly GB) insurance: *life ∼,* because death is certain.

as·sure /ə'ʃʊə(r)/ vt 1 say positively, with confidence: *I ∼ you (that) there's no danger.* 2 cause (a person) to be sure, to feel certain: *We tried to ∼ the nervous old lady that flying was safe.* 3 insure, esp against death.

as·sured adj sure; confident.

as·sur·ed·ly /ə'ʃʊərɪdlɪ/ adv surely; confidently

as·ter /'æstə(r)/ n [C] garden plant with flowers that have white, pink or purple petals round a yellow centre.

as·ter·isk /'æstərɪsk/ n [C] the mark *, used to call attention to something or to show that letters are omitted, as in *Mr J***s,* for *Mr Jones.*

astern /ə'stɜn/ adv in or at the stern of a ship.

as·ter·oid /'æstərɔɪd/ n [C] any of many small planets between the orbits of Mars and Jupiter.

asthma /'æsmə US: 'æzmə/ n [U] chronic chest disease marked by difficult breathing.

asth·matic /'æs'mætɪk US: 'æz-/ adj suffering from asthma; of asthma.

astir /ə'stɜ(r)/ adv, adj (formal) in a state of excitement: *The whole village was ∼ when news came that the Queen was coming.*

as·ton·ish /ə'stɒnɪʃ/ vt surprise greatly: *The news ∼ed everybody.*

as·ton·ish·ing adj very surprising.

as·ton·ish·ment n [U] great surprise: *I heard to my ∼ment that... He looked at me in ∼ment.*

astound /ə'staʊnd/ vt shock (the usual word).

as·tral /'æstrəl/ adj of or from the stars.

astray /ə'streɪ/ adv, adj out of, off, the right path, esp (fig) into doing wrong: *The boy was led ∼ by bad friends.*

astride /ə'straɪd/ adv, adj, prep with one leg on each side (of): *sitting ∼ his father's knee.*

as·trin·gent /ə'strɪndʒənt/ n [C] (kind of) substance that shrinks soft skin tissues and contracts blood-vessels. □ adj of or like an astringent.

astr(o)- /'æstr(ə)-/ prefix of the stars, of outer space: *astronomy.*

as·trol·oger /ə'strɒlədʒə(r)/ n [C] expert in, student of, astrology.

as·tro·logi·cal /'æstrə'lɒdʒɪkəl/ adj of astrology.

as·trol·ogy /ə'strɒlədʒɪ/ n [U] art of observing the positions of the stars in the belief that they influence human affairs.

as·tro·naut /'æstrənɔt/ n [C] person who travels in a spacecraft.

as·tron·omer /ə'strɒnəmə(r)/ n [C] expert in, student of, astronomy.

as·tro·nomi·cal /'æstrə'nɒmɪkəl/ adj 1 of the study of astronomy. 2 (informal) enormous: *an ∼ sum.*

as·tron·omy /ə'strɒnəmɪ/ n [U] science of the sun, moon, stars and planets.

as·tute /ə'stjut US: ə'stut/ adj 1 quick at seeing how to gain an advantage. 2 clever; sensible: *an ∼ lawyer/businessman.*

as·tute·ly adv

as·tute·ness n [U]

asy·lum /ə'saɪləm/ n 1 [C,U] (place of

refuge or safety **2** (formerly) institution where mentally ill people were cared for, now called a *mental home* or *mental hospital*. **3** protection from cruel treatment, etc: *ask for political ∼*.

at /ət *strong form:* æt/ *prep* **1 (a)** in or near: *∼ my uncle's; ∼ the station*. (*Note: In* is used for countries and large towns, and places important to the speaker.) **(b)** (towards; in the direction of): *look ∼ him; laugh ∼ the joke; throw it ∼ her*. **(c)** (showing an attempt to get or reach something): *He had to guess ∼ the meaning*. **(d)** (showing distance): *It looks better ∼ a distance*. **2 (a)** (showing a point of time): *∼ 2 o'clock; ∼ any moment*. ⇨ in²(4). ⇨ on²(2). **(b)** (of age): *He left school ∼ (the age of) 15*. **(c)** (showing order): *∼ the third attempt; ∼ first; ∼ last*. **(d)** (showing the rate of occurrence): *∼ (all) times; ∼ regular intervals*. **3 (a)** (showing occupation): *∼ work; ∼ play*. **hard `at it**, working hard. **(b)** (used after *adjectives*): *good ∼ translation*. **(c)** (state, condition): *∼ war*. **4 (a)** (rate): *∼ full speed; ∼ a snail's pace*. **(b)** (value, cost, etc): *buy articles ∼ 20p and sell them ∼ 25p*. **(c)** (used with *superlatives*): *∼ least; ∼ the worst*. **5** (cause): *The pupils were shocked ∼ the news*.

ate /et *US:* eɪt/ *pt* of **eat**.

-ate *suffix* **1** /-ət/ (used to form a *noun*): *electorate*. **2** /-eɪt/ (used to form a *verb*): *stimulate*.

athe·ism /ˈeɪθɪɪzm/ *n* [U] belief that there is no God.

athe·ist /ˈeɪθɪɪst/ *n* [C] person who believes that there is no God.

athe·is·tic /ˈeɪθɪˈɪstɪk/ *adj* of atheism or atheists.

ath·lete /ˈæθliːt/ *n* [C] person trained for competing in physical exercises and outdoor games, e g a person good at running, jumping, swimming, boxing.

ath·letic /æθˈletɪk/ *adj* **1** of athletes. **2** physically strong, with a well-balanced body: *an ∼-looking young man*.

ath·let·ics *n pl* (usually with a *sing verb*) practice of physical exercises and sports, esp competitions in running, jumping, etc.

-ation *suffix* -tion.

atishoo /əˈtɪʃuː/ *int* spelling form used to indicate a sneeze.

-ative /-ətɪv/ *suffix* (used to form an *adjective* from an *-ate* verb): *illustrative*.

-atively, (used to form an *adverb*).

at·las /ˈætləs/ *n* [C] book of maps.

at·mos·phere /ˈætməsfɪə(r)/ *n* **1 the ∼,** mixture of gases surrounding the earth. **2** [C] air in any place. **3** [C] feeling, e g of good, evil, from a place, conditions, etc: *There is an ∼ of peace and calm in the country quite different from the ∼ of a big city*.

at·mos·pheric /ˈætməsˈferɪk/ *adj* of, connected with, the atmosphere: *∼ conditions*.

atoll /ˈætɒl/ *n* [C] ring of coral reef(s) round a lagoon.

atom /ˈætəm/ *n* [C] **1** smallest unit of an element that can take part in a chemical change: *A molecule of water* (H_2O) *is made up of two ∼s of hydrogen and one ∼ of oxygen*. ⇨ electron, neutron, nucleus, proton. **2** (*fig*) very small bit: *There's not an ∼ of truth* (= no truth at all) *in what he said*.

atomic /əˈtɒmɪk/ *adj* of an atom, or atoms.

ˈatomic `bomb, bomb of which the destructive power comes from atomic energy.

ˈatomic `energy, energy obtained as the result of splitting an atom.

atone /əˈtəʊn/ *vi* make repayment: *How can I ∼ for hurting your feelings?*

atone·ment *n* [U] atoning: *make ∼ment for a fault*. **(b) the A∼ment,** the sufferings and death of Jesus.

-ator /eɪtə(r)/ *suffix* object or person performing an *-ate* verb: *illustrator*.

atro·cious /əˈtrəʊʃəs/ *adj* **1** very wicked or cruel: *an ∼ crime*. **2** (*informal*) very bad: *an ∼ dinner; ∼ weather*.

atro·cious·ly *adv*

atroc·ity /əˈtrɒsətɪ/ *n* (*pl* -ies) [U] wickedness; [C] wicked or cruel act: *Shooting prisoners of war is an ∼*.

at·tach /əˈtætʃ/ *vt,vi* **1** fasten or join (one thing to another): *∼ labels to the luggage; a house with a garage ∼ed. A∼ed you will find/A∼ed please find…*, (business style) You will find, attached to this letter… **2 be attached to**, be fond of: *She is deeply ∼ed to her young brother*. **3** consider to have; connect with: *Do you ∼ much importance to what he says?* **4** go with, be joined (to): *No suspicion/blame ∼es to him*, He cannot be suspected/blamed. **5** join as a member: *I am ∼ed to the Sixth battalion/to the European group*.

at·tach·ment /əˈtætʃmənt/ *n* **1** [U] act of joining; being attached. **2** [C] something attached. **3** [C] affection; friendship: *have an ∼ for her*.

at·taché /əˈtæʃeɪ *US:* ˈætəˈʃeɪ/ *n* [C] person who is attached to the staff of an ambassador: *the naval/ military/press ∼*.

attaché case /əˈtæʃɪ keɪs/, small, flat, rectangular case for documents.

at·tack /əˈtæk/ *n* **1** [C] violent attempt to hurt, overcome, defeat: *make an ∼ on the enemy*; [U] *The enemy came under ∼*. **2** [C] hostile criticism in speech or writing: *a strong ∼ against/on the Government's policy*. **3** [C] start, e g of disease: *an ∼ of fever; a `heart ∼*, pain in the region of the heart, with irregular beating. □ *vt* make an attack on: *∼ the enemy; a disease that ∼s children. Rust ∼s metals*.

at·tacker, person who attacks.

at·tain /əˈteɪn/ *vt,vi* (*formal*) achieve (the usual word): *∼ one's hopes*.

at·tain·able /-əbəl/ *adj* that can be attained.

at·tain·ment, **(a)** [U] act of attaining: *for*

the ~ment of (= in order to achieve) *his purpose.* **(b)** [C] (usually *pl*) skill in some branch of knowledge, etc: *legal ~ments.*

at·tempt /ə'tempt/ *vt* make a start at doing something; try: *The prisoners ~ed to escape but failed. Don't ~ impossibilities,* Don't try to do impossible things. □ *n* [C] **1** *attempt to do sth/at doing sth,* trying; effort to do something: *They made no ~ to escape/at escaping.* **2** *attempt at,* thing not very well done: *Her ~ at a Christmas cake had to be thrown away.* **3** *attempt on/ upon,* try: *make an ~ on the world speed record.*

at·tend /ə'tend/ *vi,vt* **1** give care and thought to: *~ to one's work. You're not ~ing,* not listening, not paying attention. **2** wait (*on/upon*); serve; look after: *Which doctor is ~ing you?* **3** go to; be present at: *~ school/church/a meeting.*

at·tend·ance /ə'tendəns/ *n* **1** [C,U] being present, at school etc: *The boy was given a prize for regular ~,* for attending school regularly. **2** [C] (with *adjectives*) number of persons present: *There was a large ~ at church this morning.* **3** [U], act of attending(2): *Now that the patient is out of danger, the doctor is no longer in ~.*

at·tend·ant /ə'tendənt/ *n* [C] servant or companion. □ *adj* accompanying (the usual word): *famine and its ~ diseases.*

at·ten·tion /ə'tenʃən/ *n* **1** [U] act of directing one's thoughts: *Pay ~ to what you're doing. He shouted to attract ~,* to make people notice him. **2** (often *pl*) kind or polite act: *A pretty girl usually receives more ~(s) than a plain girl,* finds men more willing to do things for her. **3** [U] drill position in which a man stands straight and still: *come to/stand at ~;* (as a military command): *A~!* (shortened to *'shun* /ʃʌn/).

at·tent·ive /ə'tentɪv/ *adj* giving or paying attention: *A speaker likes to have an ~ audience.*

at·tent·ive·ly *adv.* *They listened ~ly to the teacher.*

at·test /ə'test/ *vt,vi* **1** be or give clear proof of: *These papers ~ the fact that...* **2** declare on oath; put (a person) on oath; cause (a person) to declare solemnly: *I have said nothing that I am not ready to ~,* to say on oath. **3** *attest to,* bear witness to: *feats which ~ to his strength of will.*

at·tic /'ætɪk/ *n* [C] space within the roof of a house: *two small rooms in the ~.*

at·tire /ə'taɪə(r)/ *n* [U] (*literary* or *poetic*) dress: *in holiday ~.* □ *vt* (*old use*) dress: *~d in white/satin.*

at·ti·tude /'ætɪtjud *US:* -tud/ *n* [C] **1** way of feeling, thinking or behaving: *What is your ~ towards this question?* What do you think about it, how do you propose to act? **2** manner of placing or holding the body: *He stood there in a threatening ~.*

at·tor·ney /ə'tɜːnɪ/ *n* [C] (*pl ~s*) person

with legal authority to act for another in business or law: *power of ~,* authority so given.

at·tract /ə'trækt/ *vt* **1** pull towards (by unseen force): *A magnet ~s steel.* **2** get the attention of: *Bright lights ~ moths. He shouted to ~ attention.* **3** find attractive; find pleasure in: *Do you feel ~ed to her?* Do you like her?

at·trac·tion /ə'trækʃən/ *n* **1** [U] power of pulling towards: *He cannot resist the ~ of the sea on a hot day/of a pretty girl.* **2** [C] that which attracts: *the ~s of a big city,* e g concerts, cinemas, large shops.

at·trac·tive /ə'træktɪv/ *adj* having the power to attract; pleasing: *a most ~ girl; ~ prices.*

at·trac·tive·ly *adv*

at·tribu·table /ə'trɪbjutəbəl/ *adj* that can be attributed.

at·tribute¹ /ə'trɪbjut/ *vt* consider as a quality of, as being the result of, as coming from: *He ~s his success to hard work.*

at·tribute² /'ætrɪbjut/ *n* [C] **1** quality considered to be naturally or necessarily belonging to a person or thing: *Mercy is an ~ of God.* **2** object recognized as a symbol of a person or his position: *The crown is an ~ of kingship.*

at·tune /ə'tjun *US:* ə'tun/ *vt* make used to: *ears ~d to the sound of gunfire.*

auber·gine /'əʊbeəʒɪn/ *n* [C] fruit of the eggplant, used as a vegetable.

auburn /'ɔːbən/ *adj* (usually of hair) reddish-brown.

auc·tion /'ɔːkʃən/ *n* [C,U] public sale at which goods are sold to the persons making the highest bids or offers: *sale by ~.* □ *vt* sell by auction.

auc·tion·eer /'ɔːkʃə'nɪə(r)/ *n* [C] person in charge of an auction.

aud·acious /ɔː'deɪʃəs/ *adj* daring; bold.

aud·acious·ly *adv*

aud·ac·ity /ɔː'dæsətɪ/ *n* [U] daring; cheek.

aud·ible /'ɔːdəbəl/ *adj* loud enough to be heard: *The speaker was scarcely ~.*

aud·ibly /-əblɪ/ *adv*

audi·ence /'ɔːdɪəns/ *n* [C] **1** gathering of persons for the purpose of hearing a speaker, singer, etc: *There was a large ~ at the pop concert.* **2** persons listening, watching, reading: *The Radio programme has an ~ of several million. His book has reached a wide ~.* **4** formal interview given by a ruler, the Pope, etc: *The Pope granted him an ~.*

audio- /'ɔːdɪəʊ/ *prefix* of hearing, of sound: *~-visual.*

'audio-visual 'aids, teaching aids such as record players and film projectors.

audit /'ɔːdɪt/ *n* [C] official examination of accounts to see that they are in order. □ *vt* examine accounts officially.

aud·ition /ɔː'dɪʃən/ *n* [C] trial hearing to test the voice of a singer or of an actor wishing to take part in a play. □ *vt* give an audition to.

audi·tor /ˈɔːdɪtə(r)/ n [C] person who audits.

audi·tor·ium /ˌɔːdɪˈtɔːrɪəm/ n [C] (pl ~s) building, or part of a building, in which an audience sits.

audi·tory /ˈɔːdɪtrɪ US: -tɔːrɪ/ adj of the sense of hearing: the ~ nerve.

aught /ɔːt/ n (literary) anything: for ~ I know/care, (used to show that the speaker does not know/care at all).

aug·ment /ɔːɡˈment/ vt, vi (formal) make or become greater; increase: ~ one's income by writing short stories.

augur /ˈɔːɡə(r)/ n [C] (in ancient Rome) religious official who claimed to foretell future events. □ vi, vt foretell, be a sign of.

augury /ˈɔːɡjʊrɪ/ n [C] (pl -ies) omen; sign.

august /ɔːˈɡʌst/ adj majestic; causing feelings of respect or awe.

August /ˈɔːɡəst/ n the eighth month.

auk /ɔːk/ n [C] northern seabird.

aunt /ɑːnt US: ænt/ n [C] sister of one's father or mother; wife of one's uncle.

aun·tie, aun·ty /ˈɑːntɪ US: ˈæntɪ/ n (informal) aunt.

au pair /ˌəʊ ˈpeə(r)/ adj (Fr) (in GB) girl from overseas who, in return for light household duties, receives board and lodging, and facilities for study.

aura /ˈɔːrə/ n [C] (pl ~s) atmosphere surrounding a person or object and thought to come from him or it: There seemed to be an ~ of holiness about the Indian saint.

aural /ˈɔːrəl/ adj of the organs of hearing: an ~ surgeon.

au re·voir /ˌəʊ rəˈvwɑː(r)/ int (Fr) till we meet again; good-bye.

aur·icle /ˈɔːrɪkəl/ n [C] (anat) 1 the external part of the ear. 2 either of the two upper cavities of the heart.

aur·ora aus·tra·lis /ɔːˌrɔːrəɔːˈstreɪlɪs/ n bands of coloured light, usually red and green, seen in the sky in the regions of the South Pole.

aur·ora bor·ea·lis /ɔːˌrɔːrəˈbɔːrɪˈeɪlɪs/ n bands of coloured light, usually in red and green, seen in the sky in the regions of the North Pole.

aus·pices /ˈɔːspɪsɪz/ n pl under the auspices of, helped and favoured by.

aus·pi·cious /ɔːˈspɪʃəs/ adj showing signs, giving promise, of future success; favourable; prosperous.

aus·pi·cious·ly adv

aus·tere /ɔːˈstɪə(r)/ adj 1 of a person, his behaviour, severely moral and strict. 2 of a way of living, of places, styles, simple and plain; without ornament or comfort.

aus·tere·ly adv

aus·ter·ity /ɔːˈsterətɪ/ n (pl -ies) 1 [U] quality of being austere. 2 (pl) austere practices, e g fasting, living in a cell, for religious reasons.

aut·archy /ˈɔːtɑːkɪ/ n [U] country under absolute sovereignty.

aut·arky /ˈɔːtɑːkɪ/ n [U] self-sufficiency, esp

of a State in its economy.

auth·en·tic /ɔːˈθentɪk/ adj genuine; known to be true: ~ news; an ~ signature.

auth·en·ti·cally /-klɪ/ adv

auth·en·ti·cate /ɔːˈθentɪkeɪt/ vt prove beyond doubt the origin, authorship, etc of.

auth·en·ti·ca·tion /ɔːˌθentɪˈkeɪʃən/ n [U]

auth·en·tic·ity /ˌɔːθenˈtɪsətɪ/ n [U] quality of being genuine: feel confident of the ~ of a signature.

author /ˈɔːθə(r)/ n [C] 1 writer of a book, play, etc: Dickens is his favourite ~. 2 person who creates or begins something.

author·ess /ˈɔːθərəs/ n [C] woman author.

author·ship /ˈɔːθəʃɪp/ n [U] 1 occupation of an author: It's risky to take to ~ (= begin to write books) for a living. 2 origin of a book, etc: Nothing is known of the ~ of the book.

auth·ori·tar·ian /ɔːˌθɒrɪˈteərɪən/ adj supporting or requiring obedience to authority, esp that of the State. □ n [C] supporter of this principle.

auth·ori·tat·ive /ɔːˈθɒrɪtətɪv/ adj 1 having, given with, authority: ~ orders. 2 having an air of authority; commanding: in an ~ manner. 3 that can be trusted because from a reliable source: an ~ report.

auth·ori·tat·ive·ly adv

auth·or·ity /ɔːˈθɒrətɪ/ n (pl -ies) 1 [U] power or right to control, give orders and make others obey: Who is in ~ here? Only the treasurer has ~ to make payments. 2 [C] person or (pl) group of persons having authority: the health authorities. 4 [C,U] person with special knowledge; book, etc that supplies reliable information or evidence: The 'Oxford English Dictionary' is the best ~ on English words.

auth·or·ize /ˈɔːθəraɪz/ vt 1 give authority to: I have ~d him to act for me while I am abroad. 2 give authority for: The Finance Committee ~d the spending of £10 000 on a new sports ground.

'Authorized Version, (common abbr **A V**) the English translation of the Bible, first published 1611.

auth·or·iz·ation /ˌɔːθəraɪˈzeɪʃən US: -rɪˈz-/ n [U] authorizing; giving legal right; the right given.

auto /ˈɔːtəʊ/ n [C] (US informal) (abbr of) automobile.

auto- /ˈɔːtəʊ/ prefix 1 of oneself: autobiography. 2 without help, independently: automatic.

auto·bio·graphic /ˈɔːtəˈbaɪəˈɡræfɪk/, **auto·bio·graphi·cal** /-kəl/ adj of, engaged in, autobiography.

auto·bi·ogra·phy /ˌɔːtəʊbaɪˈɒɡrəfɪ/ n (pl -ies) 1 [C] story of a person's life written by himself. 2 [U] the art and practice of this sort of writing.

autoc·racy /ɔːˈtɒkrəsɪ/ n (pl -ies) 1 [U] government by a ruler who has unlimited power. 2 [C] (country with a) government of this kind.

auto-crat /ˈɔːtəkræt/ n [C] ruler with unlimited power; person who gives orders without considering the wishes of others.

auto-cratic /ˌɔːtəˈkrætɪk/ adj of or like an autocrat: *Don't be so ~ic!*

auto-crati-cal-ly /-klɪ/ adv

auto-graph /ˈɔːtəgrɑːf US: -græf/ n [C] person's own handwriting, esp his signature. □ vt write one's name on or in: *a book ~ed by the author.*

auto-mate /ˈɔːtəmeɪt/ vt convert to, control by, automation.

auto-matic /ˌɔːtəˈmætɪk/ adj 1 (of a machine) able to work or be worked without attention: *~ weapons,* weapons that continue firing until pressure on the trigger is released. 2 (of actions) done without thought; unconscious: *Breathing is ~.* □ n [C] small automatic gun.

auto-mati-cal-ly /-klɪ/ adv

auto-ma-tion /ˌɔːtəˈmeɪʃən/ n [U] (use of) methods and machines to save labour.

auto-mo-bile /ˈɔːtəməbiːl US: ˈɔːtəməˈbiːl/ n [C] (esp US) motorcar.

auton-omous /ɔːˈtɒnəməs/ adj (of states) self-governing.

auton-omy /ɔːˈtɒnəmɪ/ n [C,U] (pl -ies) (right of) self-government.

au-topsy /ˈɔːtɒpsɪ/ n [C] (pl -ies) (med) examination of a body (by cutting it open) to learn the cause of death.

autumn /ˈɔːtəm/ n [C] (US = fall) third season of the year, between summer and winter (Sept, Oct and Nov in the northern hemisphere).

autum-nal /ɔːˈtʌmnəl/ adj of autumn.

aux-ili-ary /ɔːgˈzɪlɪərɪ/ adj helping; supporting: *~ troops.*

avail /əˈveɪl/ vt,vi **avail oneself of,** (formal) make use of, profit by, take advantage of: *You should ~ yourself of every opportunity to practise speaking English.* □ n of *no/little avail,* not helpful; not effective: *His intervention was of little ~. without avail; to no avail,* without regret; unsuccessfully: *We pulled him out of the river and tried to revive him, but to no ~.*

avail-able /əˈveɪləbəl/ adj that may be used or obtained: *There were no tickets ~ for Friday's performance.*

avail-abil-ity /əˈveɪləˈbɪlətɪ/ n [U]

ava-lanche /ˈævəlɑːnʃ US: -læntʃ/ n [C] 1 great mass of snow and ice at a high altitude, caused by its own weight to slide down a mountain side, often carrying with it thousands of tons of rock. 2 (fig) great many: *an ~ of words/letters/questions.*

avant-garde /ˈævɒn ˈɡɑːd/ n (Fr) (fig) radical leader(s) of any movement (in art, drama, literature, etc).

av-ar-ice /ˈævərɪs/ n [U] greed (the usual word); great eagerness to get or keep.

av-ar-icious /ˈævəˈrɪʃəs/ adj greedy

av-ar-icious-ly adv

avenge /əˈvendʒ/ vt get or take revenge for:

~ an insult.

av-enue /ˈævənjuː US: -nuː/ n [C] 1 road with trees on each side, esp the private road going up to a large country house. 2 wide street with buildings on one or both sides. 3 (fig) way (to an object or aim): *~s to success/promotion.*

av-er-age /ˈævərɪdʒ/ n [C] 1 result of adding several quantities together and dividing the total by the number of quantities: *The ~ of 4, 5 and 9 is 6.* 2 standard or level regarded as ordinary or usual: *Tom's work at school is above/below the ~.* □ adj 1 found by making an average: *The ~ age of the boys in this class is fifteen.* 2 of the ordinary or usual standard: *boys of ~ ability.* □ vt,vi 1 find the average of: *If you ~ 7, 14 and 6, you get 9.* 2 amount to, do, as an average: *~ 200 miles a day during a journey.*

averse /əˈvɜːs/ adj opposed, unwilling: *He is ~ to hard work/from taking action.*

aver-sion /əˈvɜːʃən US: əˈvɜːʒən/ n 1 [C,U] strong dislike: *He has a strong ~ to getting up early.* 2 [C] thing or person disliked: *my pet ~,* thing I specially dislike.

avert /əˈvɜːt/ vt (formal) 1 turn away (one's eyes, thoughts, etc): *~ one's eyes/gaze from a terrible spectacle.* 2 prevent, avoid: *~ an accident.*

avi-ary /ˈeɪvɪərɪ US: -vɪerɪ/ n [C] (pl -ies) place for keeping birds, e.g. in a zoo.

avi-ation /ˌeɪvɪˈeɪʃən/ n [U] (art and science of) flying in aircraft.

avi-ator /ˈeɪvɪeɪtə(r)/ n [C] airman (now usually pilot or captain) who controls an aircraft, etc.

avid /ˈævɪd/ adj (formal) eager, greedy: *~ for fame/applause.*

avid-ly adv

avo-cado /ˌævəˈkɑːdəʊ/ n [C] (pl ~s) pear-shaped tropical fruit.

avoid /əˈvɔɪd/ vt keep or get away from; escape: *Try to ~ danger.*

avoid-able /-əbəl/ adj that can be avoided.

avoid-ance /-əns/ n [U] act of avoiding.

avoir-du-pois /ˌævədəˈpɔɪz/ n [U] system of weights used, before metrication, in most English-speaking countries (1 pound = 16 ounces), used for all goods except precious metals and stones, and medicines.

avow /əˈvaʊ/ vt (formal) admit; declare openly: *~ a fault. He ~ed himself (to be) a Christian.*

avowal /-əl/ n [U] free and open confession; [C] instance of this.

await /əˈweɪt/ vt 1 (of persons) wait for: *I ~ your instructions.* 2 be in store for; be waiting for: *Death ~s all men.*

awake[1] /əˈweɪk/ vi (pt,pp awoke /əˈwəʊk/) 1 = wake (the usual word). 2 become conscious of, realize: *He awoke to his opportunities.*

awake[2] /əˈweɪk/ adj roused from sleep: *Is he ~ or asleep? awake to,* aware of: *be ~ to danger.*

awaken /ə`weikən/ vt = wake.

awaken·ing /ə`weikniŋ/ n [C] act of becoming aware, of realizing, esp something unpleasant: *It was a rude ~ing when to be told that he was to be dismissed.*

award /ə`wɔd/ vt give or grant (by official decision): *He was ~ed the first prize.* □ n [C] **1** decision made by a judge or arbitrator. **2** thing given as the result of such a decision, e g a prize in a competition.

aware /ə`weə(r)/ adj **aware of/that,** having knowledge: *We are fully ~ of the facts.*
aware·ness n [U]

awash /ə`wɒʃ/ adj washed over by, level with, the waves: *rocks ~ at high tide. The ship's deck was ~.*

away /ə`wei/ adverbial particle **1** to or at a distance (from the place, person, etc in question): *The sea is two miles ~. Take these things ~,* Remove them. **2 away with,** (used in exclamations without a verb): *A~ with them!* Take them ~! **3** continuously; constantly: *He was working ~.* **4** (used to show loss, lessening, weakening, exhaustion): *The water has all boiled ~,* There is no water left. **5 far and away,** very much: *This is far and ~ the best.* **right/ straight away,** at once, without delay.

awe /ɔ/ n [U] fear and respect: *He had a feeling of ~ as he was taken before the judge.*
`awe-inspiring adj filling with awe: *an ~-inspiring sight.*
`awe-stricken, `awe-struck adj filled with awe.
`awe-some /-səm/ adj causing awe.

aw·ful /`ɔfəl/ adj **1** terrible; dreadful: *He died an ~ death.* **2** (*informal*) very bad; very great; extreme of its kind: *What an ~ nuisance! What ~ handwriting/weather!*

aw·fully /`ɔflɪ/ adv very (much): *It has been ~ly hot this week. I'm ~ly sorry.*

awhile /ə`wail US: ə`hwail/ adv for a short time: *Please stay ~.*

awk·ward /`ɔkwəd/ adj **1** (of objects, places) not well designed for use; (of circumstances, etc) likely to cause inconvenience or difficulty: *This is an ~ corner; there have been several road accidents here.* **an awkward customer,** ⇨ customer. **2** (of living things) clumsy; having little skill: *Some animals are ~ on land but able to move easily in the water.* **3** embarrassed: *an ~ silence/pause.*
awk·ward·ly adv
awk·ward·ness n [U]

awl /ɔl/ n [C] small pointed tool for making holes, esp in leather.

awn·ing /`ɔnɪŋ/ n [C,U] canvas covering (against rain or sun), e g over a ship's deck, over or before doors or windows.

awoke ⇨ awake.

awry /ə`rai/ adv, adj crooked(ly); wrong(ly): *Our plans have gone ~,* have gone wrong.

axe /æks/ n [C] (*pl ~s* /`æksiz/) tool for felling trees or splitting wood. **`have an `axe to grind,** (*fig*) have reasons to quarrel. □ vt reduce, e g costs, public services; dismiss: *He's just been ~d.*

ax·iom /`æksiəm/ n [C] statement accepted as true without argument.
axio·matic /`æksiə`mætik/ adj obviously true: *It is ~atic that a whole is greater than any of its parts.*

axis /`æksis/ n [C] (*pl ~s* /`æksiz/) **1** line round which a turning object spins. **2** line that divides a figure into two symmetrical parts, e g the diameter of a circle. **3** political connection (not always an alliance) between two or more states: *the Berlin—Rome—Tokyo A~* (before 1939).
the earth's axis, the imaginary line joining the North and South Poles through the centre of the earth, on which the earth rotates once in twenty-four hours.

axle /`æksəl/ n [C] **1** rod on or with which a wheel turns. **2** bar or rod that passes through the centres of a pair of wheels: *the back ~ of a bus.*

ay, aye /ai/ int, adv (*Scot, regional*) yes; (*naval*) usual reply to an order: *~, ~, sir!* □ n pl vote or person supporting a proposal: *The ~s have it,* Those in favour are in the majority.

az·ure /`æʒə(r)/ adj, n [U] (*poetic*) bright blue colour: *an ~ sky.*

Bb

B, b /bi/ (*pl B's, b's* /biz/) the second letter of the English alphabet.

baa /bɑ/ n [C] cry of a sheep or lamb. □ vi make this cry; bleat.

babble /`bæbəl/ vi, vt **1** talk quickly so that it is difficult to understand; make sounds like a baby, streams, etc. **2** tell (a secret): *~ (out) nonsense/secrets.* □ n [U] **1** childish or foolish talk; talk not easily understood (as when many people are talking together). **2** sound of water flowing over stones, etc.

babe /beib/ n [C] **1** (*literary*) baby. **2** inexperienced and easily deceived person. **3** (*US sl*) girl or young woman.

babel /`beibəl/ n [C] **1** *the Tower of B~,* (*Biblical*) tower built to try to reach heaven during which language became mixed and confused. **2** [U] scene of noisy and confused talking.

ba·boon /bə`bun US: bæ-/ n [C] large monkey (of Africa and southern Asia) with a dog-like face.

baby /`beibi/ n [C] (*pl -ies*) **1** very young child: *She has a '~-`boy/`girl. Which of you is the ~* (= the youngest member) *of* *the family?* **2** (*sl*) girl; sweetheart.

'baby-face(d), (of an adult) (having a) youthful face.

'baby 'grand, small grand piano.

'baby-hood, state, period, of being a baby.

'baby-ish, of, like a baby: ∼*ish behaviour*.

'baby-minder, woman paid to look after a baby for long periods, (e g while the mother is out working).

'baby-sitter, person paid to look after a baby for a short time, (e g while the parents are at the cinema). Hence, **baby-sit** *vi* (-tt-).

bach-elor /ˈbætʃələ(r)/ *n* [C] **1** unmarried man. ⇨ spinster. **2** of, suitable for, an unmarried person: ∼ *flats*. **3** (man or woman who has taken the) first university degree: *B*∼ *of Arts/Science.*

ba-cil-lus /bəˈsɪləs/ *n* [C] (*pl* -cilli /-laɪ -li/) name given to types of long bacterium, one of which causes disease.

back¹ /bæk/ *adverbial particle* **1** to or at the rear; away from the front: *Stand* ∼, *please! Sit* ∼ *in your chair and be comfortable.* **go back on one's word,** fail to keep a promise. **2** in (to) an earlier position or condition: *Throw the ball* ∼ *to me. We shall be* ∼ (= *home again*) *before dark. How far is it there and* ∼? **3** in return: *If I hit you, would you hit me* ∼? **have/get one's 'own back (on sb),** (*informal*) have one's revenge. **4** (of time) ago; into the past: *a few years* ∼.

back² /bæk/ *n* [C] **1** (of the human body) surface of the body from the neck to the buttocks: *If you lie on your* ∼, *you can look up at the sky.* **break the back of sth,** (e g of a piece of work) finish the hardest or larger part of it. **do/say sth behind sb's back,** without his knowledge (always in connection with something unpleasant, such as slander). **get off sb's back,** stop being a burden or nuisance. **be glad to see the back of sb,** feel pleased to see him go away. **have/with one's back to the wall,** in a difficult position, forced to defend oneself. **put one's back into sth,** work very hard at it. **put/get sb's back up,** make him angry. **turn one's back on sb,** rudely turn away from him. **2** upper surface of an animal's body: *Fasten the saddle on the horse's* ∼. **3** that part of a chair or seat on which a person's back rests. **4** that surface of an object that is less used, less visible or important: *the* ∼ *of one's hand.* **5** that part of a thing that is farthest from the front: *a room at the* ∼ *of the house.* **6** (*sport*) player whose position is behind the forwards, near the goal.

'back-ache, pain in the back.

'back-bencher, member of Parliament in a seat at the back of the House of Commons because he does not have a Government appointment. Hence, 'back-benches *n pl*

'back-bite *vt,vi* say things to damage a person's reputation.

'back-bone, (a) column of bones down the middle of the back; spine. (b) (*fig*) (of a person's character) strength.

'back-breaking *adj* (of work) exhausting.

'back-chat, (*informal*) (exchange of) rude replies.

'back-'date *vt* date back to a time in the past: ∼*date a wage increase.*

'back 'door, door at the back of a building.

'back-fire *n* [U] sound caused by the pistons in an engine when gas explodes. □ *vi* (a) produce this sound. (b) (*fig*) fail; have an unpleasant result.

'back-ground, (a) that part of a view, scene, etc at the back. (b) existing or relevant conditions: *the political* ∼*ground*. (c) person's past experiences, education, etc. (d) **in the background,** away from publicity; not being clearly seen or heard.

'back-hand, stroke (in tennis, etc) with the back of the hand forward.

'back-'handed, *adj* (*fig*) not genuine, sarcastic: *a* ∼*handed compliment.*

'back-ing, (a) help; support; body of supporters: *The new leader has a large* ∼*ing.* (b) material used to form a support or lining to something. (c) musical background for a pop singer.

'back-lash, (*fig*) (in social or race relations) unpleasant or violent reaction.

'back-less *adj* (of a dress) not covering the back.

'back-log, business affairs (e g correspondence) still to be attended to.

'back-num-ber (a) issue of a newspaper, etc now out-of-date. (b) (*fig*) old-fashioned person, method, thing, etc.

'back-'pedal *vi* (a) (on a bicycle, etc) pedal backwards. (b) (*fig*) go back on a promise, offer, etc.

'back 'seat, (of a car, etc) seat at the back. **take a back seat,** (*fig*) stay in the background.

'back-'side, (*informal*) buttocks.

'back-'stage, (in a theatre, etc) behind the stage.

'back-stroke, style of swimming on one's back.

'back-water, (a) part of a river not reached by its current. (b) (*fig*) place, etc not affected by progress, important events, etc: *They live in a* ∼ *water.*

'back-yard, small area or garden at the back of a terraced house.

back³ /bæk/ *vt,vi* **1** go or cause to go back: *He* ∼*ed the car into/out of the garage.* **2** support: ∼ *a friend in an augument or quarrel.* **back sb up,** support him in every way. **3** bet money on (a horse, etc). **4** *back down (from),* give up a claim, etc: *I see he has* ∼*ed down from the position he took last week. back out (of),* withdraw (from a promise or undertaking): *He's trying to* ∼ *out (of his bargain),* escape from the agreement. **5** put or be a lining to; put on as a surface at the back: ∼*ed with sheet iron.* **6** be situated at the back of: *Their house* ~*s on to our garden.*

backer, (a) person who bets on a horse. (b) person who gives support or help (e g to a political movement). (c) person who gives financial support to an undertaking.

back·gam·mon /ˈbækˌgæmən/ *n* [U] game for two players, played on a board with draughts and dice.

back·sheesh ⇨ baksheesh.

back·ward /ˈbækwəd/ *adj* **1** towards the back or the starting-point: *a* ~ *glance/ movement.* **2** having made, making, less than the usual or normal progress: *This part of the country is still* ~*; there are no railways or roads and no electricity.* ⇨ backwater. **3** shy; reluctant; hesitating: *He is* ~ *in giving his views.*

back·ward(s) *adv* (a) away from one's front; towards the back: *He looked* ~*s over his shoulder.* (b) with the back or the end first: *Can you say the alphabet* ~*(s)*, ie ZYXWV, etc? *know sth backwards,* know it perfectly. *backwards and forwards,* first in one direction and then in the other: *travelling* ~*s and forwards between London and Brighton.*

bacon /ˈbeɪkən/ *n* [U] salted or smoked meat from the back or sides of a pig.

bac·terial /bækˈtɪərɪəl/ *adj* of bacteria: ~ *diseases.*

bac·terium /bækˈtɪərɪəm/ *n* [C] (*pl* -ria /-rɪə/) (kinds of) simplest and smallest form of plant life, existing in air, water and soil, and in living and dead creatures and plants, essential to animal life and sometimes a cause of disease.

bad¹ /bæd/ *adj* (worse, worst) **1** wicked, evil, immoral: *It is* ~ *to steal.* **2** unpleasant; disagreeable; unwelcome: *We've had* ~ *news. What* ~ *weather we're having!* **3** of things that are unpleasant) serious; noticeable: *That was a* ~ *mistake. He's had a* ~ *accident.* **4** inferior; worthless; incorrect; of poor quality: *His pronunciation of English is* ~*. What a* ~ *drawing! be in a bad way,* be very ill or unfortunate; be in trouble or difficulty. *go from bad to worse,* get worse every day. *with bad grace,* showing unwillingness. *not (so) bad,* (*informal*) quite good. *not half bad,* very good. **5** not able to be eaten; rotten: ~ *eggs/meat. go bad,* become unfit to eat. **6** *bad for,* hurtful or injurious for; unsuitable for: *Smoking is* ~ *for the health.* **7** in ill health, diseased: *a* ~ (= sore) *finger. She was taken* ~ (= fell ill) *during the night.* **8** (*informal*) unfortunate: *It's too* ~ *she's so ill.* **9** (*informal*) sorry: *I feel so* ~ *about not being able to help you.*

bad debt, one that is unlikely to be paid.

bad language, swear-words; improper use of words connected with holy or things.

bad word, swear-word; obscenity.

bad·ly *adv* (worse, worst) (Compare *well, better, best.*) (a) in a bad manner; roughly;

untidily, etc: ~*ly made/dressed/wounded.* (b) by much: ~*ly beaten at football.* (c) *want/need badly,* very much: *She wants it* ~*ly.* (d) *badly off,* poor.

bad·ness *n* [U] quality of being bad: *the* ~*ness of the weather/climate.*

bad² /bæd/ *n* [U] that which is bad: *take the* ~ *with the good,* take bad fortune with good fortune.

bade /bæd/ ⇨ bid¹(3).

badge /bædʒ/ *n* [C] something (usually a design on cloth or metal brooch) worn to show a person's occupation, rank, etc or membership of a society.

badger¹ /ˈbædʒə(r)/ *n* [C] small, grey animal living in holes in the earth and going about at night.

badger² /ˈbædʒə(r)/ *vt* worry or annoy (with questions, requests, etc for): *Tom has been* ~*ing his uncle to buy him a camera.*

bad·min·ton /ˈbædmɪntən/ *n* [U] game played with rackets and shuttlecocks across a high, narrow net.

baffle¹ /ˈbæfəl/ *vt* be too difficult to do, understand, etc prevent (a person) from doing something: *One of the examination questions* ~*d me completely.*

baffle² /ˈbæfəl/ *n* [C] plate, board, screen, etc used to prevent or control the flow of a gas, a liquid or sound.

bag¹ /bæg/ *n* [C] **1** container made of flexible material (paper, cloth, leather) with an opening at the top, used for carrying things from place to place: *a* `*travelling*-~; *a* `*hand*-~. *a bag of bones,* lean person or animal. *let the cat out of the bag,* tell a secret (without intending to do so). **2** *bags of,* (*sl*) plenty of: *There's* ~*s of room. He has* ~*s of money.*

bag² /bæg/ *vt,vi* (-gg-) **1** put into a bag or bags: *to* ~ (*up*) *wheat.* **2** (of sportsmen) kill or catch: *They* ~*ged nothing except a couple of rabbits.* **3** (*informal*) take (somebody else's property, etc without permission, but not intending to steal): *Who has* ~*ged my matches?* **4** hang loosely: *trousers that* ~ *at the knees.*

bag·gage /ˈbæɡɪdʒ/ *n* [U] **1** luggage (the usual word). **2** tents, bedding, equipment, etc of an army: *a* `~ *train.*

baggy /ˈbæɡɪ/ *adj* (-ier, -iest) hanging in loose folds: ~ *trousers.*

bag·pipes /ˈbæɡpaɪps/ *n pl* musical instrument with air stored in a bag of wind held under one arm and pressed out through pipes in which there are reeds.

bags /bæɡz/ *n pl* (*informal, dated*) trousers: *Oxford* ~, style with wide legs.

bah /bɑː/ *int* used as a sign of contempt.

bail¹ /beɪl/ *n* [U] sum of money demanded by a law court, paid by or for a person accused of wrongdoing, as security that he will appear for his trial, until which time he is allowed to go free. □ *vt bail sb out,* obtain his freedom until trial by payment of bail.

ball² /beɪl/ n [C] (*cricket*) either of the two cross pieces over the three stumps.

bail³ /beɪl/ vt,vi throw water out of a boat with buckets, etc: ∼ing water (out).

bailey /ˈbeɪlɪ/ n [C] outer wall of a castle; courtyard of a castle enclosed by strong walls.

Old Bailey, London Central Criminal Court.

bail-iff /ˈbeɪlɪf/ n [C] **1** law officer who helps a sheriff. **2** landowner's agent or manager.

bait¹ /beɪt/ n [U] **1** food, or an imitation, put on a hook to catch fish, or in nets, traps, etc to attract prey. **2** (*fig*) anything that entices or tempts.

bait² /beɪt/ vt,vi **1** put food, real or imitation, (on a hook, etc) to catch fish, etc: ∼ a hook with a worm. **2** torment by making cruel or insulting remarks

baize /beɪz/ n [U] thick woollen cloth, usually green, used for covering (tables, etc): green ∼ for the card-table.

bake /beɪk/ vt,vi **1** cook, be cooked, by dry heat in an oven: ∼ bread/cakes. **2** make or become hard by heating: The sun ∼d the ground hard. **3** be warmed or tanned: We are baking in the sun.

ˈbaking-ˈhot adj very hot: a baking-hot day.

ˈbaking-powder, mixture of powders used to make bubbles of gas in cakes, etc and so cause them to be light.

baker, person who bakes bread, etc.

baker's dozen, thirteen.

bak-ery, place where bread and cakes are baked (and sold).

bala-laika /ˈbæləˈlaɪkə/ n [C] stringed musical instrument (triangular, with three strings), popular in Russia and other countries in eastern Europe.

bal-ance¹ /ˈbæləns/ n **1** [C] apparatus for weighing, with two scales or pans. *be/hang in the balance,* (*fig*) (of a result) be still uncertain. **2** [U] condition of being steady; condition that exists when two opposing forces are equal. *in the balance,* undecided. *keep one's balance,* keep steady, remain upright: A small child has to learn to keep its ∼ before it can walk far. *lose one's balance,* become unsteady; fall. *balance of power,* condition in which no one country or group of countries is much stronger than another. **3** [U] (in art) harmony of design and proportion: a picture lacking in ∼ **4** (*accounts*) difference between two columns of an account (money received and money paid out, etc). *on balance,* taking everything into consideration. **5** amount still owed after a part payment: ∼ to be paid within one week **6** the ∼, (*informal*) the remainder of anything; what is left.

ˈbalance-sheet, (*accounts*) written statement showing credit and debit

ˈbalance wheel, small wheel which regulates the speed of a clock or watch

bal-ance² /ˈbæləns/ vt,vi **1** keep or put (something, oneself) in a state of balance: Can you ∼ a stick on the end of your nose? **2** (of accounts) compare debits and credits and record the sum needed to make them equal; (of the two sides of a balance-sheet) be equal: My accounts ∼. **3** compare (two objects, plans, arguments, etc) (in order to judge the relative weight, value, truth, etc).

a balanced diet, one with the quantity and variety of food needed for good health.

bal-cony /ˈbælkənɪ/ n [C] (*pl* -ies) **1** platform (with a wall or rail) built on an outside wall of a building, reached from an upstairs room. **2** (in a theatre or concert hall) series of rows of seats above floor-level and (usually) rising one above the other

bald /bɔːld/ adj (-er, -est) **1** (of men) having no or not much hair on the scalp; (of animals) hairless; (of birds) featherless; (of trees) leafless; (of land, hills, etc) without trees or bushes. **2** (*fig*) dull; without ornament: a ∼ statement of the facts, one that gives the facts in an uninteresting way

bald-ly adv (*fig*): speaking ∼ly; to put it ∼ly, frankly, without trying to soften what one says.

bald-ness n [U]

bale¹ /beɪl/ n [C] heap of material pressed together and tied with rope or wire: ∼s of cloth. □ vt make into, pack in, bales.

bale² /beɪl/ vt *bale out (of),* (of an airman) jump with a parachute from an aircraft.

balk, baulk /bɔːk/ vt,vi **1** purposely get in the way of: ∼ a person's plans, prevent him from carrying them out. **2** (eg of a horse) refuse to go forward· The horse ∼ed at the high hedge. **3** hesitate: Her husband ∼ed at the expense of the plans she had made.

ball¹ /bɔːl/ n [C] **1** any solid or hollow sphere as used in games (ˈfootˈ, ˈtennis-∼, ˈcricket-∼, etc). *be on the ball,* be alert, competent (in what one is doing) *keep the ball rolling,* keep the conversation, etc going *play ball,* (*informal*) co-operate: The management refused to play ∼. **2** material gathered, rolled or wound, into a round mass: a ∼ of wool/string; a ˈsnow-∼; a ˈmeat-∼, of minced meat **3** metal missile to be fired from a gun. **4** round part: the ∼ of the thumb, near the palm, the ∼ of the foot, near the base of the big toe □ int ⚠ (*pl, vulgar*) Nonsense! □ vi form into a ball; wind or squeeze into a ball

ball² /bɔːl/ n [C] social gathering for dancing, with an organized programme, and (often) special entertainment.

ˈball-dress, woman's gown to be worn at balls

ˈball-room, large room for balls.

bal-lad /ˈbæləd/ n [C] song or poem, esp one that tells a story

bal-lade /bæˈlɑːd/ n [C] **1** poem of stanzas with 7, 8 or 10 lines, each ending with the same refrain line. **2** musical composition of a romantic nature.

43

bal·last /ˈbæləst/ n [U] 1 heavy material (e g rock, iron, sand) loaded into a ship to keep it steady. 2 sand or other material carried in a balloon, to be thrown out to make the balloon go higher. 3 gravel, crushed rock, etc used to make a foundation for a road, esp a railway. □ vt supply with ballast.

bal·ler·ina /ˌbæləˈriːnə/ n [C] woman ballet dancer, esp one who takes one of the chief classical roles.

bal·let /ˈbæleɪ/ n [C,U] 1 dramatic performance, without dialogue or singing, illustrating a story by a group of dancers. 2 the dancers: a member of the ∼.
the ballet, this kind of stage performance as an art.
`**ballet-dancer,** person who dances in ballets.

bal·lis·tic /bəˈlɪstɪk/ adj of rockets, bullets, etc: intercontinental ∼ missiles, long-range rockets for use in war.
bal·lis·tics n pl (used with a sing verb) study, science, of projectiles.

bal·loon /bəˈluːn/ n [C] 1 bag or envelope filled with air, or with gas lighter than air. 2 (in a strip cartoon, etc) outline for dialogue, exclamations, etc. □ vi swell like a balloon.
hot-air balloon, apparatus for travel in the air with a basket (for the passengers, etc) suspended beneath a large balloon of hot gas.
bal·loon·ist, person who flies in balloons.

bal·lot /ˈbælət/ n 1 [C] piece of paper (usually `∼-paper`), ticket or ball, used in secret voting; [U] secret voting; [C] instance of this. 2 votes so recorded. □ vi give a vote: draw lots
`**ballot-box,** box into which ballot-papers are put by voters.

balm /bɑːm/ n [U] 1 sweet-smelling oil or ointment obtained from certain kinds of trees, used for soothing pain or healing. 2 (fig) that which gives peace of mind; consolation.
balmy adj (-ier, -iest) (a) (of air) soft and warm. (b) healing; fragrant.

balsa /ˈbɔːlsə/ n [C,U] (light-weight wood of a) tropical American tree.

bal·sam /ˈbɔːlsəm/ n 1 = balm(1). 2 flowering plant grown in gardens.

bal·us·ter /ˈbæləstə(r)/ n [C] one of the upright posts supporting a handrail; (pl) banisters.

bal·us·trade /ˌbæləˈstreɪd/ n [C] row of banisters with the stonework or woodwork that joins them on top, round a balcony, terrace, flat roof, etc.

bam·boo /ˌbæmˈbuː/ n (pl ∼s) 1 [U] tall plant with hard, hollow, jointed stems, of the grass family. 2 [C] stem, used as a stick or support.

bam·boozle /bæmˈbuːzl/ vt (informal) 1 bewilder: You can't ∼ me. 2 cheat, trick: ∼ him into/out of doing it.

ban /bæn/ vt (-nn-) order with authority that a thing must not be done, said, etc: The play was ∼ned by the censor. □ n [C] order that bans something.

ba·nal /bəˈnɑːl US: ˈbeɪnəl/ adj dull, ordinary and uninteresting: ∼ remarks.

ba·nana /bəˈnɑːnə US: bəˈnænə/ n [C] long, finger-shaped, thick-skinned (yellow when ripe) fruit growing in bunches on the banana-tree in tropical and semi-tropical countries.

band /bænd/ n [C] 1 flat, thin strip of material, esp for fastening things together or for placing round an object to strengthen it: papers kept together with a rubber ∼. 2 flat, thin strip of material forming part of an article of clothing: a long skirt with a wide `waist∼. 3 strip or line, different from the rest in colour or design, on something: a white plate with a blue ∼ round the edge. 4 group of persons under a leader and with a common purpose: a ∼ of robbers. 5 group of persons who play popular or light music together: a `dance ∼; a `jazz ∼; a `steel ∼. 6 = wave-band. □ vt,vi 1 put a band, strip or line on. 2 unite in a group: They ∼ed together to protest.
`**band-stand,** raised, open-air platform for a band(5).
`**band-wagon,** vehicle carrying the band(5) at the front of a procession. **jump on the bandwagon,** join in but only because success is guaranteed.

ban·dage /ˈbændɪdʒ/ n [C] strip of material as used for binding round a wound or injury. □ vt tie up with, wrap in, a bandage.

ban·dit /ˈbændɪt/ n [C] robber, one of an armed band (e g attacking travellers in forests or mountains or, today, banks and offices).

bandy¹ /ˈbændɪ/ adj (of the legs) curving outwards at the knees.
bandy² /ˈbændɪ/ vt exchange (words, blows). **have one's name bandied about,** be talked about in an unfavourable way, be a subject for gossip.

bang¹ /bæŋ/ n [C] violent blow; sudden, loud noise: boom. He fell and got a nasty ∼ on the head. He always shuts the door with a ∼. □ vt,vi 1 hit violently; shut with a noise: He ∼ed at the door. He ∼ed his fist on the table. Don't ∼ the lid down. The door ∼ed shut. 2 make a loud noise: The guns ∼ed away. □ adv, int go bang, burst with a loud noise. **bang in the middle,** exactly in the middle.

banger /ˈbæŋə(r)/ n (sl) 1 sausage. 2 noisy firework. 3 old worn car.

bangle /ˈbæŋɡəl/ n [C] ornamental rigid band worn as jewelry.

ban·ish /ˈbænɪʃ/ vt 1 send away, esp out of the country, as a punishment: He was ∼ed from the realm. 2 put away from, out of (the mind): ∼ care.
banish·ment n [U]

ban·is·ter /ˈbænɪstə(r)/ n [C] post supporting the handrail of a staircase; (*pl*) posts and handrail together.

banjo /bæn`dʒəʊ/ *n* [C] (*pl* ~s, ~es) musical instrument played by plucking the strings with the fingers.

bank[1] /bæŋk/ *n* [C] **1** land along each side of a river or canal; ground near a river: *A river flows between its* ~s. **2** sloping land or earth, often forming a border or division: *There were flowers growing on the* ~s *on each side of the country lanes.* **3** (also `sandbank) part of the seabed higher than its surroundings, but covered with enough water for ships except at low tide. **4** flat-topped mass of cloud, snow, etc esp one formed by the wind: *The sun went down behind a* ~ *of clouds.* **5** artificial slope made to enable a car to go round a curve with less risk.

bank[2] /bæŋk/ *vt,vi* **1 bank up,** (a) make or form into banks, ⇨ **4** above: *The snow has* ~ed up. (b) heap up (the fire in a fireplace or furnace) with coal, etc so that the fire burns slowly for a long time. **2** (of a motor-car or aircraft) travel with one side higher than the other (e g when turning).

bank[3] /bæŋk/ *n* [C] **1** establishment for keeping money and valuables safely, the money being paid out on the customer's order (by means of cheques): *have money in the* ~, *have savings.* **2** (place for storing) supplies: *a* `blood-~.

`bank-account, arrangement for keeping money in a bank.

'bank `holiday, day (except Sundays) when banks are closed by law.

`bank-note, piece of paper money.

`bank-robber, person who steals from a bank.

`bank-roll, (person's) ready cash.

bank[4] /bæŋk/ *vt,vi* **1** place (money) in a bank[3](1): *He* ~s *half his salary every month.* **2** keep money in a bank. **3 bank on/upon,** base one's hopes on: *I'm* ~ing on *your help.*

banker, person who owns or is a partner in a joint-stock bank, or is a governor or director.

bank-ing, business of keeping a bank: ~ing *hours, 10 a m to 3 p m.*

bank-rupcy /bæŋkrəpsɪ/ *n* (*pl* -ies) **1** [U] bankrupt condition. **2** [C] instance of this.

bank-rupt /bæŋkrʌpt/ *n* [C] (*legal*) person judged by a law court to be unable to pay his debts in full, his property being distributed for the benefit of his creditors. □ *adj* **1** unable to pay one's debts. **2** completely without: ~ *in ideas.* □ *vt* make bankrupt.

ban-ner /bænə(r)/ *n* [C] **1** flag (now chiefly *fig*): *the* ~ *of freedom.* **2** flag or announcement, usually on two poles, carried in (e g political) processions, making known principles, slogans, etc.

banner headline, (in newspapers) prominent headline in large type.

ban-nis-ter /bænɪstə(r)/ *n* [C] = banister.

banns /bænz/ *n pl* public announcement in church that two persons are to be married: *put up/publish the* ~; *have one's* ~ *called.*

ban-quet /bæŋkwɪt/ *n* [C] elaborate meal, usually for a special event, at which speeches are made: *a* `wedding ~. □ *vt,vi* give or take part in a banquet.

ban-tam /bæntəm/ *n* [C] **1** kind of small domestic fowl, esp the cock, which fights. **2** boxer between 112 and 118 pounds.

ban-ter /bæntə(r)/ *vt,vi* tease in a playful way. □ *n* [U] good-humoured teasing.

bao-bab /beɪəbæb *US:* `baʊbæb/ *n* [C] tree of tropical Africa with a trunk that grows to an enormous size.

bap-tism /bæptɪzm/ *n* **1** [U] ceremony of sprinkling a person with, or immersing a person in, water, accepting him as a member of the Christian Church and (usually) giving him a name or names (in addition to the family name); [C] instance of this: *There were six* ~s *at this church last week.* **2** (*fig*) first experience of a new kind of life: *a soldier's* ~ *of fire,* his first experience of warfare.

bap-tis-mal /bæptɪzməl/ *adj* of baptism: ~al *water.*

Bap-tist /bæptɪst/ *n* [C] one of those Christians who object to infant baptism and believe that baptism should be by immersion and at an age when a person is old enough to understand the meaning of the ceremony.

bap-tize /bæptaɪz/ *vt* give baptism to: *He had been* ~d *a Roman Catholic.*

bar[1] /bɑ(r)/ *n* [C] **1** long-shaped piece of hard, stiff material (e g metal, wood, soap, chocolate). **2** rod or rail, rigid length of wood or metal, across a door, window or gate, etc: *He was placed behind prison* ~s, put into a prison cell. **3** (in a hotel, public house, etc) room, counter, where drinks (such as beer and spirits) are served. **4** counter at which meals, etc are served and also eaten: *a* `coffee ~. **5** barrier (across a road) that could not be passed (in former times) until a sum of money (called a *toll*) was paid: *a* `toll ~. **6** bank or ridge of sand, etc across the mouth of a river or the entrance to a bay: *The ship crossed the* ~ *safely.* **7** (*fig*) barrier or obstacle; thing that hinders or stops progress: *Poor health may be a* ~ *to success in life.* **8** narrow band (of colour, light, etc): *As the sun went down, there was a* ~ *of red across the western sky.* **9** (*music*) vertical line across the stave marking divisions of equal value in time; one of these divisions and the notes in it: *the opening* ~s *of the National Anthem.* **10** railing or barrier in a law court, separating the part where the business is carried on from the part for spectators. *the prisoner at the bar,* the accused person.

the Bar, profession of barrister; barristers. *be called to the Bar,* be received as a member of the Bar.

`bar·maid,` woman who serves drinks at a bar(3).

`bar·man,` man who does this.

`bar·ten·der,` barmaid or barman.

bar² /bɑ(r)/ *vt* (-rr-) **1** fasten (a door, gate, etc) with a bar or bars¹(2). **2** keep in or out: *He ~red himself in,* fastened doors, windows, etc so that no one could enter the building. **3** obstruct: *Soldiers were ~ring the way and we couldn't go any farther.* **4** ban: *~ a person from a competition,* order that he shall not take part.

bar³ /bɑ(r)/, **bar·ring** /ˈbɑrɪŋ/ *prep* (*informal*) except: *We shall arrive at noon barring accidents,* unless there are accidents. *bar none,* without exception. *bar one,* except one.

barb /bɑb/ *n* [C] curving point of an arrow, spear, fish-hook, etc.

`barbed` *adj* having a barb or barbs: *~ed wire,* wire with short, sharp points, used for fences, etc.

bar·bar·ian /bɑˈbeərɪən/ *adj* uncivilized or uncultured. □ *n* [C] barbarian person.

bar·baric /bɑˈbærɪk/ *adj* of or like barbarians; rough and rude (esp in art and taste).

bar·bar·ism /ˈbɑbərɪzm/ *n* **1** [U] state of being uncivilized, ignorant, or rude: *living in ~.* **2** [C] instance of this.

bar·bar·ity /bɑˈbærətɪ/ *n* (*pl* -ies) **1** [U] savage cruelty. **2** [C] instance of this: *the barbarities of modern warfare,* eg the bombing of cities.

bar·bar·ize /ˈbɑbəraɪz/ *vt* make barbarous.

bar·bar·ous /ˈbɑbərəs/ *adj* uncivilized; cruel; savage; unrefined in taste, conduct, or habits.

`bar·bar·ous·ly` *adv*

bar·be·cue /ˈbɑbɪkju/ *n* [C] **1** grill, iron framework, for cooking an animal whole. **2** (outdoor) social occasion at which food cooked over a charcoal fire is eaten. □ *vt* roast (meat, etc) in this way.

bar·ber /ˈbɑbə(r)/ *n* [C] person whose trade is shaving and men's hair-cutting.

bar·bitu·rate /bɑˈbɪtʃʊrət/ *n* [C,U] (*chem*) (kinds of) substance causing sleep; pill for settling the nerves or inducing sleep.

bard /bɑd/ *n* [C] (*literary*) poet: *the ~ of Avon,* Shakespeare.

`bar·dic` *adj* of bards or their songs.

bare¹ /beə(r)/ *adj* (-r, -st) **1** without clothing, covering, protection, or decoration: *fight with ~ hands,* without boxing gloves; *in his ~ skin,* naked; *~ floors,* without carpets, rugs, etc; *a ~ hillside,* without shrubs or trees. *lay bare,* uncover, expose, make known (something secret or hidden). **2** not more than: *the ~ necessities of life,* things needed just to keep alive; *earn a ~ living,* only just enough money to live on: *approved by a ~ majority,* a very small one.

`bare·back` *adv* (of a horse) ridden without a saddle: *ride ~back.*

`bare-faced` *adj* insolent; shameless; undisguised: *It's ~faced robbery to ask £15 for such an old bicycle!*

`bare-foot` *adv* without shoes and socks: *be/go/walk ~foot.*

`bare-ˈfooted` *adj* with bare feet.

`bare-ˈheaded` *adj* not wearing a hat.

`bare-ˈlegged` *adj* with the legs bare; not wearing stockings.

`bare·ly` *adv* only just; scarcely: *We ~ly had time to catch the train. I ~ly know her.*

`bare·ness` *n* [U]

bare² /beə(r)/ *vt* uncover; reveal: *~ one's head,* take one's hat off. *bare one's heart,* make known one's deepest feelings. *bare it's teeth,* (of an animal) show them in anger.

bar·gain /ˈbɑgɪn/ *n* [C] **1** agreement to buy, sell or exchange something, made after discussion. *a good/bad bargain,* one that favours/does not favour oneself. *into the bargain,* as well; in addition; moreover. *drive a hard bargain,* try to force an agreement favourable to oneself. *make/strike a bargain,* reach agreement. **2** (in industry) agreement between management and labour over wages, hours, etc; something obtained as the result of such an agreement. **3** thing offered, sold or bought cheap: *~-basement,* lowest floor of a shop, where goods are offered at reduced prices; *~ price,* low price. □ *vi,vt* **1** talk for the purpose of reaching an agreement (about buying or selling, doing a piece of work, etc): *We ~ed with the farmer for a supply of milk and butter.* **2** *bargain away,* give up in return for something; sacrifice: *~ away one's freedom,* give it up in return for some advantages or other. *bargain for,* be ready or willing to accept or agree to: *He got more than he ~ed for,* (*informal*) was unpleasantly surprised. *I didn't ~ for John arriving so soon,* didn't expect it.

barge¹ /bɑdʒ/ *n* [C] **1** large flat-bottomed boat for carrying goods and people on rivers and canals, towed by a tug or horse; similar boat with its own engine. **2** warship's boat, for the use of the officers.

barge² /bɑdʒ/ *vi* (*informal*) **1** *barge into/ against,* rush or bump heavily into/ against. **2** *barge about,* move clumsily, without proper control of one's movements or without care. **3** *barge in/into,* intrude; rudely interrupt: *Stop barging into our private conversation.*

bari·tone /ˈbærɪtəʊn/ *n* [C] male voice between tenor and bass.

bark¹ /bɑk/ *n* [U] outer coverings or skin on the trunks, boughs and branches of trees. □ *vt* **1** take the bark off (a tree). **2** scrape the skin off (one's knuckles, knee, etc) (by falling, etc).

bark² /bɑk/ *n* [C,U] **1** the cry made by dogs and foxes. **2** (*fig*) sound of a deep cough or an angry voice. *His bark is worse than his bite,* He is not as dangerous as he pretends

46

to be. □ *vi, vt* **1** (of dogs, etc) give a bark or barks: *The dog ∿s at strangers.* **bark up the wrong tree,** (*fig*) direct one's complaint, accusation, etc wrongly. **2** say (something) in a fierce, commanding voice: *The officer ∿ed (out) his orders.*

bar·ley /ˈbɑlɪ/ *n* [U] grass-like plant and its seed (called *grain*), used for food and for making beer and whisky.

`**barley-sugar,** solid sweet substance, made from pure sugar.

barmy /ˈbɑmɪ/ *adj* (ier, -iest) (*informal*) mad; foolish.

barn /bɑn/ *n* [C] covered building for storing hay, grain, etc on a farm.

`**barn dance,** kind of country dance.

`**barn-yard,** = farmyard.

bar·nacle /ˈbɑnəkəl/ *n* [C] small sea-animal that fastens itself to rocks, the bottoms of ships, etc.

ba·rom·eter /bəˈrɒmɪtə(r)/ *n* [C] **1** instrument for measuring the pressure of the atmosphere, used for forecasting the weather and measuring height above sea-level. **2** (*fig*) something which forecasts changes (e g in public opinion, market prices).

baro·met·ric /ˈbærəˈmetrɪk/ *adj*

bar·on /ˈbærən/ *n* [C] **1** (in GB) member of the lowest rank of Peer. **2** (*US*) great industrial leader: `*oil ∿s.*

bar·on·ess /ˈbærənes/ *n* [C] baron's wife; woman holding the rank of a baron in her own right.

bar·onet /ˈbærənɪt/ *n* [C] member of the lowest hereditary titled order, lower in rank than a baron but above a knight; shortened to *Bart,* added to the name, as *Sir John Williams, Bart.*

baro·nial /bəˈrəʊnɪəl/ *adj* of, suitable for, noblemen.

ba·roque /bəˈrəʊk/ *n, adj* (of the) ornamental or extravagant style in the arts (esp architecture) in Europe in the 17th and 18th centuries.

bar·rack /ˈbærək/ *vt, vi* shout and laugh rudely at; make cries of protest against.

bar·racks /ˈbærəks/ *n pl* large building(s) for soldiers to live in.

bar·rage /ˈbærɑʒ US: bəˈrɑʒ/ *n* [C] **1** artificial obstacle built across a river for storing water to be diverted into canals for irrigation (as on the Nile). ⇨ **dam. 2** (*mil*) barrier made by heavy, continuous gunfire directed onto a given area.

bar·red /bɑd/ *pt, pp* of **bar³.**

bar·rel /ˈbærəl/ *n* [C] **1** round container, made of curved strips of wood with bands or hoops, or of plastic; the amount that a barrel holds. **2** metal tube of a rifle, revolver or pistol. □ *vt* (-ll-) put in a barrel or barrels.

`**barrel-organ,** instrument from which music is produced by turning a cylinder to make it act mechanically on keys.

bar·rel·led *adj* stored in a barrel: *∿led beer.*

bar·ren /ˈbærən/ *adj* **1** (of land) not able to

produce crops. **2** (of plants, trees) not producing fruit or seeds. **3** (of women, animals) unable to have young ones. **4** (*fig*) without value, interest, or result: *a ∿ discussion.*

bar·ri·cade /ˈbærɪkeɪd/ *n* [C] barrier of objects (e g sacks of defence. □ *vt* block (a street, doorway, etc): *They ∿d themselves in.*

bar·rier /ˈbærɪə(r)/ *n* [C] **1** something (e g a rail, gate, turnstile) that prevents, hinders or controls progress or movement: *The Sahara Desert is a natural ∿ that separates North and Central Africa. Show your ticket at the ∿,* e g in a railway station. **2** limit or boundary: *the `sound-∿.* **3** (*fig*) hindrance: *Poor health and lack of money may both be ∿s to educational progress.*

bar·ring /ˈbɑrɪŋ/ ⇨ **bar³.**

bar·ris·ter /ˈbærɪstə(r)/ *n* [C] (not US) lawyer who has the right to speak and argue in higher law courts. ⇨ **counsel.**

bar·row /ˈbærəʊ/ *n* **1** = wheelbarrow. **2** small cart with two wheels, pulled or pushed by hand. **3** metal frame with two wheels used by porters for luggage (at railway-stations, in hotels, etc).

bar·ter /ˈbɑtə(r)/ *vt, vi* exchange (goods, property, etc) (for other goods, etc): *∿ wheat for machinery;* (*fig*) *∿ away one's rights/honour/freedom.* □ *n* [U] exchange made in this way.

bar·terer, person who barters.

base¹ /beɪs/ *n* [C] **1** lowest part of anything, esp the part on which a thing rests or is supported: *the ∿ of a pillar.* **2** place at which armed forces, expeditions, etc have their stores, hospitals, etc: *a `naval ∿; a ∿ camp,* e g for an Everest expedition. **3** (*geometry*) line or surface on which a figure stands or can stand: *B C is the ∿ of the triangle A B C.* **4** (*maths*) the number (usually 10) which is the starting point for a numerical system. **5** (*chem*) substance capable of combining with an acid to form a salt and water only; substance into which other things are mixed. **6** (*baseball*) one of four stations or positions.

base·less *adj* without cause or reason: *∿less fears.*

base² /beɪs/ *vt* **base on/upon,** use as a basis for: *Direct taxation is usually ∿d on income.*

base³ /beɪs/ *adj* (of persons, their behaviour, thoughts, etc) dishonourable: *acting from ∿ motives.*

base metal, non-precious metal.

base·ball /ˈbeɪsbɔl/ *n* [U] popular game of the US, played with a bat and ball, by two teams of nine players each, on a field with four bases.

base·ment /ˈbeɪsmənt/ *n* [C] lowest part of a building, partly or wholly below ground level; inhabited room(s) in this part.

bases /ˈbeɪsɪz/ **1** *pl* of basis. **2** *pl* of base¹.

bash /bæʃ/ *vt* (*informal*) strike heavily so as

to break or injure: ~ *in the lid of a box;* ~ *him on the head with a stick;* ~ *one's head in the dark.* □ *n* [C] violent blow or knock: *I gave him a* ~ *on the nose.* **have a bash at sth,** (*sl*) attempt it.

bash·ful /'bæʃfəl/ *adv* shy (the usual word). **bash·fully** /-fəlɪ/ *adv*

basic /'beɪsɪk/ *adj* of or at the base or start; fundamental: *the* ~ *vocabulary of a language,* the words that must be known. **ba·si·cally** /-klɪ/ *adv* fundamentally.

basil /'bæzəl/ *n* [U] sweet-smelling herb like mint, used in cooking.

ba·sil·ica /bə'zɪlɪkə/ *n* [C] (*pl* ~s) 1 oblong hall divided by rows of columns (used in ancient Rome as a law court). 2 building of this type used as a church: *the* ~ *of St Peter's in Rome.*

basin /'beɪsən/ *n* [C] 1 round, open dish for holding liquids; its contents. ⇨ **wash-basin.** 2 bowl for preparing or serving food in. 3 hollow place where water collects (e g a stone structure at the base of a fountain, a deep pool at the base of a waterfall, deep part of a harbour). 4 area of country drained by a river and its tributaries: *the Thames* ~.

basis /'beɪsɪs/ *n* [C] (*pl* bases /-siz/) 1 substance into which others are mixed; most important part of a mixture. 2 (usually *fig*) foundation: *arguments that have a firm* ~, that are easily supported by facts; *On the* ~ *of our sales forecasts* (i e From what these show) *we may make a profit next year.*

bask /bɑsk *US:* bæsk/ *vi* 1 enjoy warmth and light: *sitting in the garden,* ~*ing in the sunshine.* 2 (*fig*) enjoy(approval, success, etc): ~*ing in her approval.*

bas·ket /'bɑskɪt *US:* 'bæskɪt/ *n* [C] 1 container, usually made of materials that bend and twist easily (canes, rushes): *a* '*shopping* ~; *a* '*waste-*'*paper* ~. 2 as much as a basket holds: *They ate a* ~ *of plums.*

bas·ket·ball /'bɑskɪtbɔl *US:* 'bæs-/ *n* [U] indoor game played by two teams of five players (men) who try to throw a large ball into baskets fixed 10 ft above the ground at each end of the court.

bas-relief /'bæsrɪ'lif/ *n* [U] (= *low relief*) sculpture in which a flat surface of metal or stone is cut away so that a design or picture stands out; [C] example of this.

bass¹ /bæs/ *n* [C] (*pl* unchanged) kinds of fish (perch) used as food, caught in rivers, lakes and in the sea.

bass² /beɪs/ *adj* deep-sounding; low in tone. □ *n* [C] lowest part in music (voice and instruments); singer or instrument with lowest notes.

bas·soon /bə'sun/ *n* [C] musical wind-instrument with double reeds made of wood, giving very low notes.

bas·tard /'bɑstəd *US:* 'bæs-/ *n* [C] 1 illegitimate child: *a* ~ *child/daughter/son.* 2 ⚠ (*vulgar*) (also as *int*) ruthless insensitive person (used as a term of abuse): *He's a real*

~, *leaving his wife in that way.* (used without abuse): *Harry, you old* ~! *Fancy meeting you here!* 3 ⚠ unfortunate man: *Poor* ~! *He's been sacked and he won't find another job very easily.* 4 (of an incident, etc) annoying, very bad, etc: *This is a* ~ *of a headache/essay.* 5 (of things) not geniune or authentic.

baste¹ /beɪst/ *vt* sew cloth with long temporary stitches (*tacks*(2)).

baste² /beɪst/ *vt* pour fat, juices, etc over meat which come from it during cooking.

bas·tion /'bæstɪən/ *n* [C] 1 (often five-sided) part of a fortification that stands out from the rest. 2 (*fig*) military stronghold near hostile territory.

bat¹ /bæt/ *n* [C] small animal like a mouse with large wings that flies at night and feeds on fruit and insects. **as blind as a bat,** unable to see, not seeing, clearly.

bat² /bæt/ *n* [C] 1 shaped wooden implement for striking the ball in games, esp cricket and baseball. **do sth off one's own bat,** (*fig*) do it without help. 2 = batsman: *He's a useful* ~. □ *vi,vt* (-tt-) use a bat: *Green* ~*ted for two hours,* was at the wicket for two hours.

'bats·man, (a) (*cricket*) player who bats: *He's a good* ~*sman but no good as a bowler.* (b) man who uses a pair of bats (like those used in table-tennis) to guide an aircraft as it lands.

bat³ /bæt/ *vt* (-tt-) **not bat an eyelid,** (a) not sleep at all. (b) not show any surprise.

batch /bætʃ/ *n* [C] 1 number of persons or things receiving attention as a group: *a* ~ *of letters to be answered.* 2 number of loaves, cakes, etc baked together: *baked in* ~*es of twenty.*

bath /bɑθ *US:* bæθ/ *n* (*pl* ~s /bɑðz *US:* bæðz/) 1 [C] washing of the body, by sitting or lying in water: *I shall have a hot* ~ *and go to bed.* 2 [U] water for a bath: *Your* ~ *is ready.* 3 [C] (container for) liquid in which something is washed or dipped. 4 (*pl*) building, rooms, where baths may be taken, often with a large indoor swimming pool: *public swimming* ~*s; the Turkish* ~*s.* 5 = bathtub. □ *vt,vi* 1 give a bath to: ~ *the baby.* 2 have a bath.

'Bath-'chair, three-wheeled chair for an invalid, pushed or pulled by hand.

'bath·room, room in which there is a bath.

'bath·tub, oblong vessel in which baths are taken.

bathe /beɪð/ *vt,vi* 1 apply water to; soak in water; put in water: *The doctor told him to* ~ *his eyes twice a day.* 2 go into the sea, a river, lake, etc for sport, swimming, to get cool, etc. 3 **be bathed in,** be made wet or bright all over: *Her face was* ~*d in tears.* ⇨ also sun(4). □ *n* swimming, playing, etc in the sea, a river, lake, etc: *Let's go for a* ~. **bather** /'beɪðə(r)/, person who bathes.

bath·ing /'beɪðɪŋ/ *n* [U] act or practice of

going into the sea to swim, etc: *The* ~ *here is safe*, It is safe to swim here.

`bathing-costume,` one-piece garment worn by women and girls for swimming.

ba·tik /ˈbætɪk/ *n* **1** [U] method (originally in Java) of printing coloured designs on textiles by waxing the parts not to be dyed. **2** [C] piece of cloth dyed in this way.

bat·man /ˈbætmən/ *n* [C] (*pl* -men) (*GB mil*) army officer's personal servant.

baton /ˈbætɒn *US:* bəˈtɒn/ *n* [C] **1** policeman's short, thick stick, used as a weapon. **2** short, thin stick as used by the conductor of a band or an orchestra.

bats /bæts/ *adj* (*sl*) mad; eccentric.

bat·tal·ion /bəˈtælɪən/ *n* [C] army unit made up of several companies and forming part of a regiment or brigade.

bat·ten /ˈbætən/ *n* [C] **1** long board, e g one used to keep other boards in place, or to which other boards are nailed; (on a ship) strip of wood or metal used to fasten down covers or tarpaulins over a hatch. □ *vt bat·ten down,* make secure with battens.

bat·ter[1] /ˈbætə(r)/ *vt,vi* strike hard and often; beat out of shape: *Let's* ~ *the door down. He was driving a badly* ~*ed old car.*
`bat·ter·ing ram,` (*mil*) big, heavy log with an iron head (formerly) used for knocking down walls.

bat·ter[2] /ˈbætə(r)/ *n* [U] beaten mixture of flour, eggs, milk, etc for cooking.

bat·tery /ˈbætərɪ/ *n* [C] (*pl* -ies) **1** group of connected electric cells from which current will flow: *This transistor radio has four small batteries.* **2** army unit of big guns, with men and vehicles. **3** group of big guns on a warship, or for coastal defence. **4** set of similar utensils or instruments used together: *a* ~ *of lenses/ovens.* **5** *assault and battery,* (*legal*) attack on or threatening touch. **6** series of boxes, etc in which hens are kept for laying eggs or for fattening: ~ *hens.* ⇨ free-range.

battle /ˈbætəl/ *n* **1** [C] fight, esp between organized and armed forces. *die in battle,* die fighting. **2** [C] (*fig*) any struggle: *the* ~ *of life.* **3** [U] victory; success: *Youth is half the* ~, Youthful strength brings likelihood of success. □ *vi* struggle: *battling against poverty. They* ~*d with the winds and waves.*
`battle-axe,` (a) axe with a long handle, formerly used as a weapon. (b) (*informal*) aggressive, strict, older woman.
`battle-cruiser,` large, fast cruiser with heavy guns and lighter armour than a battleship.
`battle-dress,` soldier's uniform.
`battle-field,` place where a battle is or was fought.
`battle-ship,` large kind of warship, with big guns and heavy armour.

battle·ments /ˈbætəlmənts/ *n pl* flat roof of a tower or castle with openings through which to shoot.

batty /ˈbætɪ/ *adj* (*sl*) crazy; slightly mad.

bauble /ˈbɔbəl/ *n* [C] pretty, bright and pleasing ornament of little value.

baulk /bɔk/ ⇨ balk.

baux·ite /ˈbɔksaɪt/ *n* [U] clay-like substance from which aluminium is obtained.

bawd /bɔd/ *n* [C] (*old use*) woman who keeps a brothel.
`bawd·ily` *adv*
`bawdy` *adj* (-ier, -iest) (of talk, persons) vulgar; using rude subjects to laugh at, etc: ~*y talk/stories.*

bawl /bɔl/ *vt,vi* shout or cry loudly: *The frightened child* ~*ed for help.*

bay[1] /beɪ/ *n* [C] (also `~-tree,` `~ laurel`) kind of tree or shrub with leaves that are used in cooking and are spicy when crushed.

bay[2] /beɪ/ *n* [C] part of the sea or of a large lake, enclosed by a wide curve of the shore: *Hudson B*~.

bay[3] /beɪ/ *n* [C] **1** space between pillars that divide a wall, building etc. **2** extension of a room beyond the line of one or two of its walls; recess. **3** compartment in an aircraft: *the* `bomb` ~. **4** part of a college campus, etc for those who are ill or injured: *the* `sick`-~. **5** compartment in a warehouse, barn etc for storing things: *Clear No 3* ~ *to make room for new stock.*

bay[4] /beɪ/ *n* [C] long, deep bark, esp of hounds while hunting. *keep/hold sb at bay,* keep an enemy, etc at a distance; prevent him from coming too near. □ *vi* (esp of large dogs, hounds) bark with a deep note, esp continuously, when hunting.

bay[5] /beɪ/ *adj, n* [C] reddish-brown (horse): *He was riding a dark* ~.

bay·onet /ˈbeɪənɪt/ *n* [C] dagger-like blade that can be fixed to the muzzle of a rifle. □ *vt* stab with a bayonet.

ba·zaar /bəˈzɑ(r)/ *n* [C] **1** shop for the sale of cheap goods of great variety. **2** (place where there is a) sale of goods for charitable purposes: *a church* ~. **3** (in Iran, India and other Eastern countries) street of workshops and shops; that part of a town where the markets and shopping streets are.

ba·zoo·ka /bəˈzukə/ *n* [C] (*pl* ~s) portable weapon for firing armour-piercing rockets.

be[1] /bi/ *vi* (*present tense* **am** /after 'I': m *otherwise:* əm, *strong form:* æm/, **is** /z *but* s *after* p, t, k, f, θ, *strong form:* ɪz/, **are** /ə(r) *strong form:* ɑ(r)/; *pt* **was** /wəz *strong form:* wɒz/, **were** /wə(r) *strong form:* wɜ(r)/; *contracted forms,* **I'm** /aɪm/, **he's** /hiz/, **she's** /ʃiz/, **it's** /ɪts/, **we're** /wɪə(r)/, **you're** /juə(r)/, **they're** /ðeə(r)/; *negatives* **isn't** /ˈɪzənt/, **aren't** /ɑnt/, **wasn't** /ˈwɒzənt/, **weren't** /wənt/; *present participle* **being** /ˈbiɪŋ/, *pp* **been** /bin *US:* bɪn/) **1** (with a *noun* or *pronoun*, identifying or asking about the subject): *Today is Monday. Is Peter a teacher/a Catholic?* **2** (with an *adjective* or a *preposition*, in descriptions): *The world is round. He is ten years old.* **3**

(with a *preposition* or *adverbial particle* of place): *The lamp is on the table. Mary's upstairs.* **4** (with a *noun* or a *preposition*, showing possession): *The money's not yours, it's John's.*

be² /biː/ *vi* (For pronunciations, etc ⇨ be¹) (showing a change from one quality, place, etc to another): *He wants to be* (= become) *a fireman when he grows up. You can be* (= get) *there in five minutes.*

be³ /biː/ *vi* (For pronunciations, etc ⇨ be¹) **1** (with *there*): *There's a bus-stop down the road. There were six of us.* **2** (with *there*, meaning 'exist'): *There is a God.* **3** go; come (esp the *pp* been): *I've been to see my uncle. He has been to Paris. Has the postman been* (= called) *yet?* **for the time being,** until some other arrangement, etc is made ⇨ also being.

the...to-ˈbe, the future...: *the ˈbride-to-ˈbe.* **ˈwould-be,** who wishes to be or imagines himself to be: *a would-be poet.*

be⁴ /biː/ *auxiliary verb* (used with other verbs) (For pronunciations, etc ⇨ be¹) **1** (used with *present participles* to form the progressive or continuous tenses): *They are/were reading. I shall be seeing him soon. What have you been doing this week?* **2** (used with a *pp* to form the passive voice): *He was killed in the war.* **3** (used with a *to*-infinitive) **(a)** (= must or ought, showing duty, necessity, etc): *You are to be congratulated.* **(b)** intention: *They are to be married in May.* **(c)** mutual arrangement: *Every member of the party was to pay his own expenses.* **(d)** the expressed wish of another person: *At what time am I* (= do you want me) *to be there?*

be- /bɪ-/ *prefix* **1** (~ + *verb* = *verb*): all over; all around; in all directions: *bedeck.* **2** (~ + *noun* or *adj* = *verb*) wake, become: *befriend.* **3** (+ *vi* = *vt*): *bemoan.*

beach /biːtʃ/ *n* [C] coastline covered with sand or pebbles. □ *vt* push or pull (a boat, a ship) up on to the shore or beach.

ˈbeach ball, large light-weight one used for games on the beach.

ˈbeach-comber /-kəʊmə(r)/, **(a)** long wave rolling in from the sea. **(b)** man who makes a poor living on the waterfront in ports in the Pacific.

ˈbeach-head, fortified position established on a beach by an invading army. ⇨ bridgehead.

ˈbeach-wear, clothes for sunbathing, swimming, etc.

bea-con /ˈbiːkən/ *n* [C] **1** (*old use*) (also **ˈ~-fire**) fire lit on a hill-top as a signal. **2** light on a hill or mountain, or on the coast, on rocks, etc to give warning of a danger or for the guidance of ships, etc. **3** (also **ˈ~-light**) fixed lantern to warn or guide ships; flashing light to warn aircraft of high mountains, etc.

bead /biːd/ *n* [C] **1** small ball of wood, glass,

etc with a hole through it for threading with others on a string or wire. **2** (*pl*) necklace of beads. **3** drop of liquid: *His face was covered with ~s of sweat.*

beady /ˈbiːdɪ/ *adj* (of eyes) small, round and bright.

beagle /ˈbiːgəl/ *n* [C] small, short-legged dog used for hunting when those who take part are on foot, not on horse-back.

beak /biːk/ *n* [C] hard, horny part of bird's mouth, esp when curved.

beaker /ˈbiːkə(r)/ *n* [C] **1** open glass vessel with a lip (as used for chemical experiments, etc). **2** similar plastic vessel used as a drinking glass.

beam /biːm/ *n* [C] **1** long horizontal piece of squared timber, or of steel, etc used to carry the weight of a building, etc. **2** **(a)** ray or stream of light (e g from a lamp or lighthouse, the sun or moon). **(b)** (*fig*) bright look or smile, showing happiness, etc: *with a ~ of delight.* **(c)** radio signal used to direct an aircraft on its course. **3** crosspiece of a balance, from which the scales hang. □ *vt,vi* **1** (of the sun, etc) send out light and warmth. **2** (*fig*) smile happily and cheerfully: *~ing on his friends; ~ing with satisfaction.* **3** send (a radio programme, etc) in a particular direction: *~ed from Britain to S America.*

bean /biːn/ *n* [C] **1** (any of several plants with) seed in long pods (all used as vegetables): *ˈbroad ~s; ˈkidney ~s; ˈsoya ~s.* **2** seed similar in shape of other plants (e g *ˈcoffee-~s*). **full of beans,** lively; in high spirits. **spill the beans,** make a secret known.

ˈbean-stalk, stalk of tall-growing varieties of bean.

bear¹ /beə(r)/ *n* [C] **1** large, heavy animal with thick fur. **2** rough, clumsy ill-mannered person ⇨ Great Bear, Little Bear.

bear² /beə(r)/ *vt,vi* (*pt* bore /bɔː(r)/, *pp* borne /bɔːn/) **1** carry: *~ a heavy load.* **2** have; show: *~ the marks/signs of blows/wounds/punishment; a document that ~s your signature.* **3** have; be known by: *a family that bore an ancient and honoured name.* **4** feel: *the love/hatred she bore him,* felt towards him. **5** support; sustain: *The ice is too thin to ~ your weight. Who will ~ the responsibility/expense?* **6** (used with *can/could*) tolerate; put up with: *I can't ~ (the sight of) that old man. The pain was almost more than he could ~. How can you ~ to look at her?* **7** be fit for: *His language doesn't ~ repeating.* **8** give birth to: *~ a child. She has borne him six sons.* (*Note: born:* The eldest son was born in 1932.) **9** turn: *When you reach the top of the hill, ~ (to the) right.*

10 (uses with *adverbial particles* and *prepositions*):

bear on/upon, be connected; have influence on: *These are matters that ~ on the welfare of the community.* **bring to bear**

on/upon, make (a thing) relate to, have influence on: *bring pressure on ~ on a person.* ⇨ bearing(2).

bear *(sth or sb)* out, confirm (something); support (somebody): *John will ~ me out/will ~ out what I've said.*

bear up *(against/under sth),* be strong in the face of (sorrow, etc): *Tell her to ~ up,* to have courage, not give way.

bear with *(sb),* treat patiently: *Please ~ with me* (i e listen patiently to me) *a little longer.*

bear·able /ˈbeərəbəl/ *adj* (from bear²(6)) that can be endured.

beard /bɪəd/ *n* [C] **1** hair of the lower part of the face (excluding the moustache): *a man with a ~.* **2** similar growth of hair on an animal: *a goat's ~.* □ *vt* defy openly, oppose.
bearded *adj* having a beard.

bearer /ˈbeərə(r)/ *n* [C] **1** person who brings a letter or message: *the ~ of good news.* **2** person who helps to carry a coffin to a grave, who carries a stretcher, flag, etc. **3** person who presents a cheque at a bank.

bear·ing /ˈbeərɪŋ/ *n* **1** [U] way of behaving; way of standing, walking, etc: *a man of military ~.* **2** [C,U] relation, aspect: *What he said has no/not much ~ on* (= is not connected with) *the subject.* **3** [U] possibility of being tolerated; endurance: *His conduct was beyond (all) ~.* ⇨ bear²(6). **4** [C] direction in which a place, etc lies: *take a compass ~ on a lighthouse.* **5** (*pl*) relative position; direction. **find one's bearings,** (*fig*) finds one's position, become confident, etc. **lose one's bearings,** (*fig*) be lost, puzzled, etc.

beast /biːst/ *n* [C] **1** four-footed animal (*animal* is the usual word). **2** cow or bullock; animal for riding or driving. **3** (*informal*) cruel or disgusting person.
beast·ly *adj* **(a)** like a beast; unfit for human use. **(b)** (*informal*) nasty: *What ~ly weather!*

beat¹ /biːt/ *n* [C] **1** regular repeated stroke, or sound of this: *We heard the ~ of a drum. His heart ~s were getting weaker.* **2** recurring emphasis marking rhythm in music or poetry. **3** route over which a person (e g a policeman) goes regularly.

beat² /biːt/ *vt,vi* (*pt ~, pp ~en* /ˈbiːtən/) **1** hit repeatedly (e g with a stick): *He was ~ing a drum. The boy was ~en until he was black and blue,* covered with bruises. *Somebody was ~ing at/on the door.* **beat a retreat, (a)** give the signal (by drum) to retreat. **(b)** (*fig*) go back, retire. **2** (of the sun, rain, wind, etc) strike: *The rain was ~ing against the windows.* **3** mix thoroughly and let air into by using a fork or similar utensil: *~ eggs.* **4** hammer, change the shape of by blows: *~ something flat.* **5** defeat; do better than: *Our army was ~en. He ~ me at chess.* **beat the record,** make a new and better record. **6** be too difficult for: *That problem*

has *~en me.* **7** move up and down regularly: *His heart was still ~ing.* **beat time,** measure time (in music) by making regular movements (with the hands, etc). **8** *beat about the bush,* talk about something without coming to the point. **dead beat,** tired out. **beat it,** (*sl*) go away.

9 (uses with *adverbial particles* and *prepositions*):

beat down (on), The sun was ~ing down on our heads, shining with great heat. **beat sb/sth down:** *He wanted £800 for the car but I ~ him down* (= made him lower his price) *to £600.*

beat sb/sth off, repel: *The attacker/attack was ~en off.*

beat sth out, (a) (of a fire) put out **(b)** (of rhythm, etc) be played: *He ~ out* (= drummed) *a tune on a tin can.*

beat sb up, fight and hurt badly.

beaten /ˈbiːtən/ *adj* (esp) **1** shaped by beating: *~ silver.* **2** (of a path) worn hard by use: *a well-~ path.* **go off/keep to the beaten track,** do something/not do anything unusual.

beater /ˈbiːtə(r)/ *n* [C] utensil used for beating: *an `egg-~.*

bea·tif·ic /ˌbiːəˈtɪfɪk/ *adj* (*formal*) showing great happiness; making blessed.

be·ati·fi·ca·tion /bɪˌætɪfɪˈkeɪʃən/ *n* [C,U] beatifying or being beatified; first step before canonization.

be·atify /bɪˈætɪfaɪ/ *vt* (*pt,pp* -ied) (in the R C church) announce that a dead person is among the Blessed (i e those who will live for ever with God in supreme happiness).

beat·ing /ˈbiːtɪŋ/ *n* [C] (esp punishment by hitting or striking repeatedly) defeat: *give him a good ~.*

be·ati·tude /bɪˈætɪtjuːd *US:* -tuːd/ *n* [U] great happiness; blessedness.

beau /bəʊ/ *n* [C] (*pl ~x* /bəʊz/) **1** (*old use*) rather old man who is greatly interested in the fashion of his clothes. **2** (*dated*) girl's admirer or lover.

beau·te·ous /ˈbjuːtɪəs/ *adj* (*poetic*) beautiful.

beau·ti·cian /bjuːˈtɪʃən/ *n* [C] person who runs a beauty-parlour.

beau·ti·ful /ˈbjuːtəfəl/ *adj* giving pleasure or delight to the mind or senses: *a ~ face/flower/voice;* ~ *weather/music.*
beau·ti·fully /-fəlɪ/ *adv* in a beautiful manner: *She plays the piano ~ly.*

beau·tify /ˈbjuːtəfaɪ/ *vt* (*pt,pp* -ied) make beautiful.

beauty /ˈbjuːtɪ/ *n* (*pl* -ies) **1** [U] combination of qualities that give pleasure to the senses (esp the eye and ear) or to the moral sense or the intellect: *the ~ of a sunlit rose-garden.* **2** [C] person, thing, specimen, feature, characteristic, that is beautiful or particularly good: *Isn't she a ~! Look at this horse. Isn't it a ~!*
`beauty-parlour, = beauty-salon.

`beauty queen`, girl voted the most beautiful in a contest.

`beauty-salon`, place where women have treatment (of the figure, skin, hair, etc) to be more beautiful.

`beauty-sleep`, sleep before midnight.

`beauty-spot`, (a) place with beautiful scenery. (b) birthmark or artificial patch on the face, said to increase beauty.

bea·ver /ˈbiːvə(r)/ n **1** [C] fur-coated animal that lives both on land and in water, with strong teeth with which it cuts down trees and makes dams across rivers. **2** [U] its fur.

be·calmed /bɪˈkɑːmd/ adj (of a sailing-ship) stopped because there is no wind.

be·came pt of become.

be·cause /bɪˈkɔz, -kəz/ conj **1** for the reason that: I did it ∼ they asked me to do it. (Note: when the reason is obvious, or is thought to be known, it is preferable to use as or so: As it's raining, you'd better take a taxi. It's raining, so you'd... After the noun reason, that is preferred to because: The reason why we were late is that...) **2** `because of`, prep by reason of; on account of: B∼ of his bad leg, he couldn't walk as fast as the others.

beckon /ˈbekən/ vt,vi call a person's attention by a movement of the hand or arm, usually to show that he is to come nearer to or to follow.

be·come /bɪˈkʌm/ vi,vt (pt became /bɪˈkeɪm/, pp become) **1** come or grow to be; begin to be: He became a doctor. It's becoming much more expensive to travel abroad. **2** `become of`, happen to: What will ∼ of the children if their father dies? **3** be right or fitting: He used language (e g vulgar language) that does not ∼ a man of his age and education.

be·com·ing adj attractive; suitable: with a modesty becoming to his low rank.

be·com·ing·ly adv

bed¹ /bed/ n [C] **1** piece of furniture, or other arrangement, on which to sleep (Note: the example sentences show when the articles are used): go to ∼; get into/out of ∼; put the children to ∼; sit on the ∼; find a ∼ for her. `bed and board`, food and lodging. `get out of bed on the wrong side`, be bad-tempered after waking up. `make the bed`, put the bedclothes (sheets, blankets, etc) in order, ready for use. **2** flat base on which something rests: The dam is built on a ∼ of concrete. **3** bottom of the sea, a river, lake, etc: the `sea-∼`. **4** layer of rock, stone, etc as a foundation for a road or railway; layer of clay, rock, etc below the surface soil: If you dig here, you will find a ∼ of clay. **5** garden plot, piece of ground (for flowers, vegetables, etc): `flower-∼s`.

`bed-clothes` n pl sheets, blankets, etc for a bed.

`bed-pan`, vessel for urine, etc used by an invalid in bed.

`bed·rid·den` adj confined to bed by weakness or old age.

`bed-room`, room for sleeping in.

`bed-side`, side of (esp a sick person's) bed: Dr Green has a good ∼side manner, is tactful, knows how to fill his patients with confidence in himself; a ∼side table.

`bed·sitting-room`, (informal = `bed·sitter`) room used (e g by students, single persons away from home) for both living in and sleeping in.

`bed-sore`, sore caused by lying in bed for a long time.

`bed-spread`, covering spread over a bed during the day.

`bed-stead`, framework of wood and metal to support the mattress.

`bed-time`, time for going to bed: His usual ∼time is eleven o'clock.

bed² /bed/ vt (-dd-) **1** plant (seedlings, etc): He was ∼ing out some young cabbage plants. **2** place or fix in a foundation: The bullet ∼ded itself in (= went deep into) the wall. **3** `bed down`, give bedding to: ∼ down a soldier.

bed·ding /ˈbedɪŋ/ n [U] **1** = bedclothes. **2** straw, etc for animals to sleep on.

be·decked /bɪˈdekt/ adj adorned, decorated (with flowers, jewels, etc).

be·dev·il /bɪˈdevəl/ vt (-ll-, US -l-) confuse; complicate: The issue is ∼led by Smith's refusal to co-operate with us.

be·dev·il·ment n [U]

bed·lam /ˈbedləm/ n [C] **1** (old use) asylum for mad people. **2** scene of noisy confusion: When the teacher was called away the classroom was a regular ∼.

be·drag·gled /bɪˈdrægəld/ adj made wet or dirty, e g by being dragged in mud.

bee /biː/ n [C] small, four-winged, stinging insect that produces wax and honey. `have a bee in one's bonnet`, be obsessed by an idea. `make a bee-line for`, go towards by the shortest way, go quickly towards.

`bee-hive`, ⇨ hive.

beech /biːtʃ/ n [C] forest tree with smooth bark and shiny dark-green leaves and small triangular nuts; [U] its wood.

beef /biːf/ n [U] flesh of an ox, bull or cow, used as meat. □ vi (sl) complain: Stop ∼ing so much!

`beef-steak`, ⇨ steak.

beefy /ˈbiːfɪ/ adj (of a person) well covered with flesh; strong.

been ⇨ be¹.

beep /biːp/ n [C] repeated signal or note (as during a phone conversation, indicating that it is being timed).

beer /bɪə(r)/ n [U] alcoholic drink made from malt and flavoured with hops; other drinks made from roots, etc: `ginger-∼`.

beery adj like beer in taste or smell; (e g of a person) smelling of beer.

bees·wax /ˈbiːzwæks/ n [U] wax made by bees for honeycomb, used for polishing wood. □ *vt* polish with beeswax.

beet /biːt/ *n* [C] sorts of plant with a sweet root.

`**beet·root** /ˈbiːtruːt/ red beet used as a vegetable, esp in salads.

`**sugar beet,** white beet used for making sugar.

beetle /ˈbiːtl/ *n* [C] insect with hard, shiny wing-covers.

be·fall /bɪˈfɔːl/ *vt,vi* (*pt* befell /bɪˈfel/ *pp* ~ /bɪˈfɔːlən/) (*literary*) (used only in the *3rd person*) happen (to): *What has* ~*en him?*

be·fit /bɪˈfɪt/ *vt* (-tt-) (used only in the *3rd person*) be right and suitable for: *It does not* ~ *a man in your position to...*

be·fit·ting *adj* right and proper.

be·fore¹ /bɪˈfɔː(r)/ *adv* at an earlier time; in the past; already: *I've seen that film* ~. *You should have told me so* ~, earlier.

be·fore² /bɪˈfɔː(r)/ *conj* previous to the time when: *I must finish my work* ~ *I go home. Do it now* ~ *you forget.*

be·fore³ /bɪˈfɔː(r)/ *prep* **1** earlier than: *the day* ~ *yesterday; the year* ~ *last; two days* ~ *Christmas. before long, soon.* **2** in front of (esp with reference to order or arrangement): *B comes* ~ *C.* (*Note:* Except in a few phrases, *in front of* is preferred to *before* when referring to position, e g There are some trees *in front of* the house.) **3** in the presence of; face to face with: *He was brought* ~ *the judge.* **4** in preference to: *Death* ~ *dishonour.*

be·fore·hand /bɪˈfɔːhænd/ *adv* earlier; before³(1): *I knew what he would need, so I made preparations* ~, in advance, in readiness. □ *adj* early; in advance: *She's always* ~ *with the rent,* pays it, or is ready to pay it, before it is due.

be·friend /bɪˈfrend/ *vt* make a friend of; be kind and helpful to (esp a younger person who needs help).

beg /beg/ *vt,vi* (-gg-) **1** ask for (food, money, clothes, etc); make a living by asking for money (in the streets, etc): *He made a living by* ~*ging from door to door.* **2** ask earnestly, or with deep feeling: *They* ~*ged us not to punish them. I* ~ (*of*) *you not to take any risks. go begging,* (of things) be unwanted: *If these things are going* ~*ging* (= if nobody wants them), *I'll take them.* **3** take the liberty of (saying or doing something): *I* ~ *to differ.*

be·gan ⇨ begin.

be·get /bɪˈget/ *vt* (-tt-) (*pt* begot /bɪˈgot/, *old use* begat) **1** father: *Abraham begat Isaac.* **2** (*literary*) be the cause of: *War* ~*s misery and ruin.*

beg·gar /ˈbegə(r)/ *n* [C] **1** person who lives by begging, e g for money, food; poor person. *Beggars can't be choosers,* People asking for help must take whatever is offered them. **2** (*informal*) (playful or friendly use) person: *You lucky* ~! □ *vt* make poor, ruin.

beg·gar·ly *adj* very poor; deserving con-

tempt.

be·gin /bɪˈgɪn/ *vt,vi* (*pt* began /bɪˈgæn/, *pp* begun /bɪˈgʌn/) (-nn-) (For notes on the use of *begin* and *start,* ⇨ start.) **1** start: *It's time to* ~ *work. The meeting will* ~ *at seven o'clock.* **2** (used of activities and states that come into existence): *She began to feel ill/afraid. I'm* ~*ning to understand. The water is* ~*ning to boil. She began crying/to cry.* **3** *begin at,* start from: *Today we* ~ *at page 30, line 12. to begin with,* in the first place: *We can't appoint Smith; to* ~ *with, he's too young; secondly, I want my son to have the job.*

be·gin·ner, (esp) person still learning and without much experience.

be·gin·ning, starting point: *I've read the book from* ~*ning to end.*

be·grudge /bɪˈgrʌdʒ/ *vt* (intensive form of *grudge*) feel or show dissatisfaction or envy at: *We don't* ~ *your going to Italy.*

be·guile /bɪˈgaɪl/ *vt* (*formal*) cheat, deceive: *They were* ~*d into forming an unwise alliance.*

be·gun ⇨ begin.

be·half /bɪˈhɑːf *US:* -ˈhæf/ *n on behalf of,* for, in the interest of, on account of, as the representative of. *on my/his/our/John's, etc behalf,* for me/him/us/John, etc: *On* ~ *of my colleagues and myself,* speaking for them and me.

be·have /bɪˈheɪv/ *vi* **1** act; conduct oneself: *Can't you make your little boy* ~ (*himself*), show good manners, be polite? **2** (of machines, etc) work; function: *How's your new car behaving?*

`**well-/ˈbadly-be·haved,** behaving well/badly.

be·hav·iour (*US* = **-ior**) /bɪˈheɪvjə(r)/ *n* [U] way of behaving, manners (good or bad); treatment shown towards others: *His* ~ *towards me shows that he does not like me. Tom won a prize for good* ~ *at school. be on one's best behaviour,* take great care to behave well.

be·head /bɪˈhed/ *vt* cut off the head of (as a punishment).

be·held ⇨ behold.

be·hest /bɪˈhest/ *n* (*old use*) (only in) *at sb's behest,* on a person's orders: *at the King's* ~.

be·hind¹ /bɪˈhaɪnd/ *adv* **1** in the rear: *The dog was running* ~. *The others are a long way* ~. *stay/remain behind,* stay after others have left. **2** *be behind in/with,* be in arrears with: *He was* ~ *in his payments,* had not made payments (e g of rent) when they were due.

be·hind² /bɪˈhaɪnd/ *n* (*informal*) buttocks: *He fell on his* ~.

be·hind³ /bɪˈhaɪnd/ *prep* **1** to the rear of: *The boy was hiding* ~ *a tree. The sun was* ~ (= hidden by) *the clouds.* **2** not having made so much progress as: ~ *other boys of his age; a country far* ~ *its neighbours.* **3**

remaining after, when one has left a place: *The storm left a trail of destruction ~ it.* **4** (of time): *Your schooldays will soon be far ~ you.*

be·hind·hand /bɪ'haɪndhænd/ *adj* **1** in arrears: *be ~ with the rent.* **2** late; after all the others: *He did not want to be ~ in generosity.*

be·hold /bɪ'həʊld/ *vt* (*pt,pp* beheld /bɪ'held/) (*old* or *literary use*) notice.

beige /beɪʒ/ *n* [U] **1** soft fabric of undyed and unbleached wool. **2** colour of sand. □ *adj* sand-coloured.

be·ing /'biːɪŋ/ *n* **1** [U] existence. *come into being,* begin to exist: *We do not know when this world came into ~.* **2** [C] human creature: *Men, women and children are 'human `~s.*

be·jew·elled (*US* = -eled) /bɪ'dʒuːld/ *adj* decorated, adorned, with jewels.

be·lated /bɪ'leɪtɪd/ *adj* coming very late or too late: *a ~ apology.*

belch /beltʃ/ *vt,vi* **1** send out, e g smoke, flames: *A volcano ~es out smoke and ashes.* **2** send out gas from the stomach noisily through the mouth. □ *n* [C] **1** act or sound of belching. **2** thing belched out (e g smoke from a chimney).

be·leaguer /bɪ'liːgə(r)/ *vt* surround with an army.

bel·fry /'belfrɪ/ *n* [C] (*pl* -ies) (church) tower in which bells hang.

be·lief /bɪ'liːf/ *n* **1** [U] the feeling that something is real and true; trust; confidence: *I haven't much ~ in his honesty,* cannot feel sure that he is honest. *He has lost his ~ in God,* no longer accepts the existence of God as true. *to the best of my belief,* in my genuine opinion. **2** [C] something accepted as true or real. **3** [C] (something taught as part of a religion): *the ~s of the Christian Church.*

be·lieve /bɪ'liːv/ *vt,vi* **1** feel sure of the truth of something, that somebody is telling the truth: *I ~ that man. I ~ what that man says. They ~d that he was insane. Will they be ready tomorrow? Yes, I ~ so. No, I ~ not.* **2** *believe in,* (a) have trust in: *I ~ in that man.* (b) feel sure of the existence of: *~ in God.* (c) feel sure of the value or worth of: *He ~s in getting plenty of exercise.* **3** *make believe,* pretend: *The boys made ~ that they were explorers in the African forests.* Hence, `make-believe *n*: *Don't be frightened, it's all make-~,* is all pretence.

be·liever, person who believes, esp in a religious faith.

be·liev·ing, *n seeing is believing,* you will believe something only if you see it.

be·little /bɪ'lɪtl/ *vt* cause to seem unimportant or of small value: *Don't ~ yourself,* be too modest about your abilities, etc.

bell /bel/ *n* [C] **1** metal, usually shaped like a cup, that makes a ringing sound when struck. *as sound as a bell,* (*fig*) in first-rate

condition. *ring a bell,* (*informal*) recall to memory something half forgotten. **2** (*naut*) *one to eight bells,* bells sounded every half hour.

`bell-`bottomed, (of trousers) made very wide at the bottom of the leg.

`bell-`bottoms, trousers made this way.

`bell-push, button pressed to ring an electric bell.

`bell-ringer, person who rings church bells.

`bell-tent, bell-shaped tent.

belle /bel/ *n* [C] beautiful girl or woman. *the belle of the ball,* the most beautiful woman present.

bel·li·cose /'belɪkəʊs/ *adj* (*formal*) willing to fighting; anxious to fight.

-bel·lied /-belɪd/ *suffix*: 'big-~having a big abdomen.

bel·liger·ency /bɪ'lɪdʒərənsɪ/ *n* [U] (*formal*) being warlike; state of being at war.

bel·liger·ent /bɪ'lɪdʒərənt/ *adj, n* [C] (state, party, nation) eager to be at war.

bel·low /'beləʊ/ *vi,vt* **1** make a loud, deep noise (like a bull); roar; shout: *He ~ed even before the dentist had started.* **2** sing, shout loudly or angrily: *They ~ed out a drinking song.*

bel·lows /'beləʊz/ *n pl* (also *a pair of* ~) apparatus for blowing or forcing air into something, e g a fire, an accordian, the pipes of an organ, e g in a church.

belly[1] /'belɪ/ *n* [C] (*pl* -ies) **1** (*informal*) = abdomen. **2** the stomach: *have a `~-ache.* **3** bulging part (concave or convex) of anything, e g the surface of a violin across which the strings pass.

`belly-ache *vi* (*informal*) grumble or complain, esp without a good reason.

`belly-button, (*informal*) = navel.

`belly-landing, landing of an aircraft without its undercarriage in position.

`belly-laugh *n* [C] loud, coarse laugh. □ *vi* laugh in this way.

belly-ful, as much as one wants of anything: *He's had his ~ful of fighting,* refuses to go on fighting.

belly[2] /'belɪ/ *vi,vt* (*pt,pp* -ied) (cause to) swell out: *The wind bellied (out) the sails.*

be·long /bɪ'lɒŋ/ *vi* **1** *belong to,* (a) be the property of: *These books ~ to me,* are mine. (b) be a member of, be connected with: *Which union do you ~ to?* **2** have as a right or proper place: *Does it ~ here?*

be·long·ings /bɪ'lɒŋɪŋz/ *n pl* clothes, personal articles, luggage; furniture, possessions (not land, buildings, a business, etc): *I hope you've left none of your ~ in the hotel.*

be·loved /bɪ'lʌvd/ *adj* dearly loved: *~ by all.* □ *n* /bɪ'lʌvɪd/ [C] dearly loved person.

be·low[1] /bɪ'ləʊ/ *adv* **1** at or to a lower level: *From the hilltop we saw the blue ocean ~. We heard voices from ~.* **2** at the foot of a page, etc; later (in a book, article, etc): *see paragraph six ~.* **3** *down below,* in the lower part of a building, in a ship's hold, etc (according to context). **here below,** on earth.

be·low[2] /bɪˈləʊ/ prep (*Note: Below can sometimes be replaced by under; when under is possible, it is given in the examples.*) **1** lower than: *Skirts this year reach just ~ the knees. Your work is ~ (the) average. Shall I write my name on, above or ~ the line? The Dead Sea is ~ sea level. There is nothing ~/under 50p, costing less than this. He can't be much ~/under sixty (years of age).* **2** down stream from: *a few yards ~ the bridge.*

belt /belt/ n [C] **1** band or strip of cloth, leather, etc worn round the waist to support or keep clothes in place: *He ate so much that he had to loosen his ~ two holes.* **hit below the belt,** fight unfairly. **2** similar strip of leather, etc worn over the shoulder to support weapons, etc. **3** endless strap, used to connect wheels and so drive machinery: *a ˈfan-~,* in the engine of a car. **4** any wide strip or band, surrounding area, etc. ⇨ green belt. □ vt **1** fasten with a belt: *The officer ~ed his sword on.* **2** hit with a belt; (*informal*) strike with the fist(s): *if you don't shut up, I'll ~ you.*

comˈmuter belt, residential area outside a large town, e g London, from which people travel to and from work.

belt·ing n: *give the boy a good ~ing,* hit him hard (with a belt).

be·moan /bɪˈməʊn/ vt moan for; show great sorrow for: *~ one's sad fate.*

bench /bentʃ/ n [C] **1** long seat of wood or stone, e g in a public park. **2** (in the House of Commons) seat occupied by members. ⇨ back-benches; cross-benches; front-benches. **3** worktable at which a shoemaker, carpenter, etc works. **4** the ~, judges; magistrates; judge's seat or office; law court.

ˈbench seat, (in a car) seat (for 2 or 3 persons) extending the width of the car.

bend[1] /bend/ n [C] **1** curve or turn: *a sharp ~ in the road.* **round the bend,** (*sl*) mad. **2** sailor's knot (in a rope). **3** the ~s, (*informal*) pains in the joints, caused by coming to the surface too fast after skin-diving.

bend[2] /bend/ vt,vi (pt,pp bent /bent/) **1** cause (something rigid) to be out of a straight line or surface; force into a curve or angle: *B~ the end of the wire up/down/back. Her head was bent over her book.* **bend a rule,** (*informal*) interpret it loosely (to suit the circumstances). **2** become curved or angular; bow down: *The branches were ~ing (down) with the weight of the fruit. Can you ~ down and touch your toes without ~ing your knees? The road ~s to the left here.* **3** direct: *All eyes were bent on me, Every one was looking at me.* **4** submit: *~ to a person's will;* make (a person) submit: *~ a person to one's will.* **5** **be bent on,** determined: *He is bent on mastering English.*

be·neath /bɪˈniːθ/ prep, adv **1** (*old use* or *literary*) below, under(neath). **2** not worthy of: *His accusations are ~ contempt/notice,* should be ignored.

ben·edic·tion /ˌbenɪˈdɪkʃən/ n [C] blessing (esp one given by a priest at the end of a church service): *pronounce the ~.*

ben·efac·tion /ˌbenɪˈfækʃən/ n **1** [U] doing good. **2** [C] good deed (esp the giving of money for charity); charitable gift.

ben·efac·tor /ˈbenɪfæktə(r)/ n [C] person who has given help, esp financial help, to a school, hospital or charitable institution.

ben·efac·tress /ˈbenɪfæktrəs/ n [C] woman benefactor.

ben·efice /ˈbenɪfɪs/ n [C] income-producing property (called a *church living*) held by a priest or clergyman (esp a vicar or rector).

be·nefi·cence /bɪˈnefɪsəns/ n [U] (*formal*) doing good; active kindness.

be·nefi·cent /bɪˈnefɪsənt/ adj (*formal*) doing good; kind.

ben·efi·cial /ˌbenɪˈfɪʃəl/ adj having good effect, helpful: *Fresh air and good food are ~ to the health.*

ben·efi·ci·ary /ˌbenɪˈfɪʃəri US: -ˈfɪəri/ n [C] (pl -ies) person who receives a benefit, esp one who receives money, property, etc under a will.

beni·fit /ˈbenɪfɪt/ n **1** [U] advantage; profit; help: *Did you get much ~ from your holiday? Did you feel better afterwards? The money is to be used for the ~ of the poor,* to help poor people. **give sb the benefit of the doubt,** assume that he is innocent because there is insufficient evidence that he is guilty. **2** [C] act of kindness; favour; advantage: *the ~s of a good education.* **3** [C] allowance of money to which a person is entitled as a citizen or as a member of an insurance society, etc: *unemployment/sickness ~.* □ vt,vi do good to: *The sea air will ~ you. You will ~ by a holiday.*

ben·ev·ol·ence /bɪˈnevələns/ n [U] wish to do good; activity in doing good: *His ~ made it possible for many poor boys to attend college.*

ben·ev·ol·ent /bɪˈnevələnt/ adj kind and helpful (towards, to).
ben·ev·ol·ent·ly adv

be·nign /bɪˈnaɪn/ adj **1** (of persons) kind and gentle. **2** (of soil, climate) mild, favourable. **3** (of a disease, tumour) not dangerous ⇨ malignant(2).

bent[1] /bent/ n [C] inclination or aptitude; natural skill in and liking: *She has a ~ for sewing/music.* **follow one's bent,** do what one is interested in and what one enjoys doing.

bent[2] /bent/ adj (*sl*) dishonest; corrupt; mad.

bent[3] pt,pp bend[2].

be·numbed /bɪˈnʌmd/ adj made numb: *~ with cold.*

be·queath /bɪˈkwið/ **1** arrange (by making a will) to give (property, etc) at death: *He has ~ed me his gold watch.* **2** hand down to those who come after: *discoveries ~ed to us by the scientists of the last century.*

be·quest /bɪˈkwest/ *n* **1** [U] bequeathing. **2** [C] thing bequeathed: *He left ~s of money to all his staff.*

be·reave /bɪˈriːv/ *vt* (*pt,pp* bereft /bɪˈreft/ or bereaved; usually bereft in (1) and bereaved in (2)) **1** rob or take away from: *bereft of hope,* without hope; *bereft of reason,* mad. **2** (of death) cause sadness: *the ~d husband,* the man whose wife had died.

be·reave·ment *n* [C,U]

be·reft ⇨ bereave.

be·ret /ˈbereɪ *US:* bɪˈreɪ/ *n* [C] flat, round cap of felt or cloth, as worn and by soldiers.

berg /bɜːg/ *n* [C] = iceberg.

beri-beri /ˈberɪ ˈberɪ/ *n* [U] disease, common in oriental and tropical countries, caused by lack of vitamins, etc.

berry /ˈberɪ/ *n* [C] (*pl* -ies) **1** kinds of small fruit with seeds: `straw~`; `black~`; `rasp~`. **2** coffee bean.

ber·serk /bəˈsɜːk/ *adj* be/go/send sb berserk, be, go, etc uncontrollably wild: *He went completely ~.*

berth /bɜːθ/ *n* [C] **1** sleeping-place in a train, ship, etc. **2** place at a wharf, etc where a ship can be tied up. □ *vt,vi* **1** (*naut*) find, have, a sleeping-place (for). **2** moor (a ship) in harbour, tie up (a ship) at a wharf, etc.

be·seech /bɪˈsiːtʃ/ *vt* (*pt,pp* besought /bɪˈsɔːt/) (*old use* or *literary*) ask earnestly or urgently: *Spare him, I ~ you.*

be·seech·ing *adj* (of a person's look, tone of voice, etc) appealing.

be·set /bɪˈset/ *vt* (*pt,pp* ~) (-tt-) close in, have, on all sides: *a problem ~ with difficulties;* *~ by doubts,* troubled by doubts.

be·side /bɪˈsaɪd/ *prep* **1** at the side of; close to: *Come and sit ~ me.* **2** beside the point/ mark/question, having nothing to do with (what is being discussed, etc). **3** beside oneself, at the end of one's self-control: *He was ~ himself with joy/rage.*

be·sides /bɪˈsaɪdz/ *adv* moreover; also: *I don't like that new dictionary; ~, it's too expensive.* □ *prep* in addition to; as well as: *I have three other brothers ~ John.*

be·siege /bɪˈsiːdʒ/ *vt* **1** surround (a place) with armed forces and keep them there; attack from all sides: *Troy was ~d by the Greeks for ten years.* **2** besiege with, crowd round (with requests, etc): *The teacher was ~d with questions. He was ~d by his fans.*

be·sieger, person who besieges.

be·smirch /bɪˈsmɜːtʃ/ *vt* make dirty: (*fig*) *His reputation was ~ed.*

be·sot·ted /bɪˈsɒtɪd/ *adj* stupefied (by alcoholic drink, drugs, love, etc).

be·sought ⇨ beseech.

be·spat·tered /bɪˈspætəd/ *adj* covered with: *~ with mud.*

best[1] /best/ *adj* of the most excellent kind: *the ~ poetry/poets; the ~* (= quickest, most convenient, etc) *way from London to Paris.* make the best use of one's time, etc, use one's time, etc in the most useful way. put one's best foot forward, ⇨ foot(1). with the best will in the world, even making every effort to be fair, etc. ⇨ good, better.

'best `man,** bridegroom's friend, supporting him at his wedding.

best[2] /best/ *adv* in the most excellent way: *He works ~ in the morning. Do as you think ~. She was the ~-dressed woman in the village.* ⇨ well, better.

'best-'seller,** book that is sold in very large numbers.

best[3] /best/ *pron* the outstanding person, thing, etc among several; the most excellent part, aspect: *We're the ~ of friends,* very close friends. be (all) for the best, be good in the end (although not at first seeming to be good). All the best! (used when parting) With warmest wishes! at best, taking the most hopeful view: *We can't arrive before Friday at ~.* at its/their/his, etc best, in the best condition: *The garden is at its ~ this month.* (even) at the best of times, (even) when circumstances are most favourable. with the best of intentions, intending only to help. do one's best/the best one can, make the greatest possible effort. (do sth) to the best of one's ability/ power, use all one's ability/ power when doing it. make the best of a bad job/ business, do what one can, in spite of misfortune, failure, etc. make the best of it/ things, be contented (although things are not satisfactory). to the best of my knowledge, etc, so far as I know (though my knowledge, etc may be imperfect).

best[4] /best/ *vt* (*informal*) get the better of; defeat.

bes·tial /ˈbestɪəl/ *adj* of or like a beast; brutish; savage.

be·stow /bɪˈstəʊ/ *vt* give as an offering: *~ an honour/a title on him.*

be·stowal, action, instance of, bestowing.

be·stride /bɪˈstraɪd/ *vt* (*pt* bestrode /bɪˈstrəʊd/, *pp* bestridden /bɪˈstrɪdən/) sit, stand, with one leg on each side of: *~ a horse.* ⇨ astride.

bet /bet/ *vt,vi* (*pt,pp* ~ or occasionally ~ted) (-tt-) **1** risk money on a race or an event of which the result is doubtful: *He ~ me a pound that he would win.* **2** (*informal*) be certain: *I ~ I win.* □ *n* [C] agreement to risk money, etc on an event of which the result is doubtful; the money, etc offered: *make a ~; win/lose a ~.*

be·tray /bɪˈtreɪ/ *vt* **1** be disloyal to; act deceitfully towards: *He ~ed his principles.* **2** allow (a secret) to become known, either by accident or on purpose. **3** be or give a sign of, show: *His accent at once ∼ed the fact that he was a foreigner.*

be·tray·al /bɪˈtreɪəl/ *n* (**a**) [U] betraying or being betrayed. (**b**) [C] instance of this.

be·tray·er, person who betrays.

be·trothed /bɪˈtrəʊðd/ *adj* (*literary*) engaged. □ *n* [C] person engaged to be married.

be·trothal /-ðəl/, engagement to marry.

bet·ter¹ /ˈbetə(r)/ *adj* **1** having more qualities or abilities: *This is good but that is ∼. He's a ∼ man than his brother.* **no better than**, practically the same as: *He's no ∼ than a fool.* **see better days,** be not so poor or unfortunate as at present. **his better half,** (*informal*) his wife. **2** (of health) improving: *He feels ∼ today but is still not well enough to get up.* **quite better,** recovered: I'm quite ∼ now. ⇨ good, best.

bet·ter² /ˈbetə(r)/ *adv* **1** (of qualities, etc such as kindness, health, beauty, etc) more: *You would write ∼ if you had a good pen. You play tennis ∼ than I do. You'll like it ∼* (= more) *when you understand it more.* **be better off**, richer; more comfortable. **be better off without**, happier: *We'd be ∼ off without all that noise.* **know better**, (**a**) be wise or experienced enough not to do something: *You ought to know ∼ than to go out with wet hair.* (**b**) refuse to accept a statement (because one knows it is not true): *He says he didn't cheat, but I know ∼,* feel sure that he did. **2 had better,** would find it more suitable, more to your advantage, etc: *You had ∼ mind your own business. You'd ∼ not say that,* I advise you not to say that. *Hadn't you ∼ take an umbrella?* ⇨ best, well.

bet·ter³ /ˈbetə(r)/ *n* **get the better of sb/ sth**, overcome; defeat; win (an argument, etc): *She always gets the ∼ of the quarrels/ him.* **for better (f)or worse**, whether one has good or bad fortune.

bet·ter⁴ /ˈbetə(r)/ *vt* improve; do better than: *Your work last year was good; I hope you will ∼ it, this year. She hopes to ∼ herself* (= earn more, etc) *in the Civil Service.*

bet·ter⁵, **bet·tor** /ˈbetə(r)/ *n* [C] person who bets.

be·tween¹ /bɪˈtwiːn/ *adv* in or into a place or time that is between: *We visited the Museum in the morning and the Art Gallery later, with a quick lunch ∼.* **few and far between,** few and widely scattered or separate: *In this part of Canada houses are few and far ∼.* **in between,** spaced out among.

be·tween² /bɪˈtwiːn/ *prep* **1** (of place): *The letter B comes ∼ A and C.* (*Note:* Between usually involves only two limits, but when boundaries are concerned, there may be more than two limits: *Switzerland lies ∼ France, Italy, Austria and Germany.* ⇨ among.) **2** (of order, rank, etc): *An army major ranks ∼ a captain and a colonel.* **3** (of time): ∼ *the two world wars;* ∼ *1 o'clock and 2 o'clock.* **4** (of distance,

amount, etc): ∼ *five and six miles; somewhere ∼ thirty and forty years old.* **5** to and from: *This liner sails ∼ Southampton and New York.* **6** (showing connection): *after all there has been ∼ us,* in view of our past friendship, the experiences we have shared, etc. **7** (to show sharing; used of two only): *Divide/Share the money ∼ you.* **between ourselves/you, me and the gatepost/you and me,** in confidence. **8** (to show combination, used of two, or more than two to show several independent relationships): *We* (two or more) *saved up for a year and bought a second-hand car ∼ us.* **9** (showing relationship): *the distinction ∼ right and wrong; wars ∼ nations.*

bevel /ˈbevəl/ *n* [C] sloping edge; surface with such a slope, e g at the side of a picture frame. □ *vt* (-ll-, *US* = -l-) give a sloping edge to.

bev·er·age /ˈbevərɪdʒ/ *n* [C] any sort of drink except water, e g milk, tea, wine, beer.

be·ware /bɪˈweə(r)/ *vi, vt* (usually *imperative* or *infinitive*) be on guard, take care: *B∼ of the dog! B∼ of pickpockets!*

be·wil·der /bɪˈwɪldə(r)/ *vt* puzzle; confuse: *The old woman from the country was ∼ed by the crowds and traffic in the big city.*

be·wilder·ing *adj*

be·wilder·ment *n* [U]

be·witch /bɪˈwɪtʃ/ *vt* **1** work magic on; put a magic spell on. **2** charm; delight very much: *She danced so well that she ∼ed all the young men.*

be·witch·ing *adj: a ∼ing smile.*

be·witch·ing·ly *adv*

be·yond¹ /bɪˈjɒnd/ *adv* at or to a distance; farther on: *India and the lands ∼.*

be·yond² /bɪˈjɒnd/ *prep* **1** at, on or to, the farther side of: *The house is ∼ the bridge.* **2** (of time) later than: *Don't stay out ∼ 6 o'clock* (*after* is more usual) **3** surpassing, exceeding; out of reach of: *That's going ∼ a joke,* passes the limits of what is reasonable as a joke. *He lives ∼ his income,* spends more than he earns. *It's quite ∼ me,* is more than I can understand.

bi- /ˈbaɪ/ *prefix* **1** happening twice (in one period): *bi-monthly; bi-annual.* **2** lasting for two, happening every two: *bicentennial.* **3** having two: *bilingual; biped.*

bias /ˈbaɪəs/ *n* [C] (*pl* ∼es) **1** particular inclination or tendency: *He has a strong ∼ towards/against the plan,* is in favour of it/ opposed to it without having full knowledge of it. **2 cut on the bias,** (dress-making, etc) cut across, slantingly. □ *vt* (*pt, pp* ∼ed) give a bias to; influence (usually unfairly): *The government used newspapers and the radio to ∼ the opinions of the people.*

bib /bɪb/ *n* [C] **1** piece of cloth tied under a child's chin. **2** upper part of an apron.

bib·li·ogra·pher /ˈbɪblɪˈɒɡrəfə(r)/ *n* [C] person who writes or studies bibliographies.

bib·lio·graph·ical /ˈbɪblɪəˈɡræfɪkəl/ *adj* of,

concerning a, bibliography.

bib·li·og·ra·phy /ˈbɪblɪˈɒgrəfɪ/ *n* [C] (*pl* -ies)
1 [C] list of books and writings of one author
or about one subject. **2** [U] study of the
authorship, editions, etc of books.

bib·lio·phile /ˈbɪblɪəfaɪl/ *n* [C] person who
loves and collects books.

bi·cen·ten·ary /ˈbaɪˈsen'tinərɪ *US:*
-ˈsentərɪ/ *n* [C] (*pl* -ies) (celebration of
the) 200th anniversary of an event.

bi·cen·ten·nial /ˈbæɪˈsentenɪəl/ *adj* **1** happening once in 200 years. **2** lasting for 200
years. **3** of a 200th anniversary: *The ∼ celebrations in the USA in 1976.* □ *n* [C] 200th
anniversary.

bi·ceps /ˈbaɪseps/ *n* [C] (*pl unchanged*)
large muscle in the front part of the upper
arm

bi·cycle /ˈbaɪsɪkəl/ [C] *n* two-wheeled
machine propelled by using pedals, for riding on. □ *vi* (usually shortened to *cycle*) ride
a bicycle; go (*to*) on a bicycle.

bid¹ /bɪd/ *n* [C] **1** (at an auction sale) offer of
a price: *Are there no ∼s for this very fine
painting?* **2** *make a bid for*, try to obtain (by
offering something): *make a ∼ for popular
support.* **4** (in card-games, esp bridge) statement of the number of tricks a player proposes to win: *a ∼ of 2 hearts.*

bid² /bɪd/ *vt,vi* (*pt,pp ∼*) (-dd-) **1** (at an
auction sale) make an offer of money; offer
(a certain price): *Will anyone bid £5 for this
painting?* **2** (playing certain card-games)
make a bid: *∼ 2 hearts.* ⇨ outbid.

bid³ /bɪd/ *vt,vi* (*pt bade* /bæd/, *pp ∼*den
/ˈbɪdən/, *∼*) (*old use*) **1** command; tell: *He
bade me* ⟨*to*⟩ *come in.* **2** say (as a greeting,
etc): *∼ him good morning.*

bid·der /ˈbɪdə(r)/ *n* [C] person who bids at
cards.

bid·ding /ˈbɪdɪŋ/ *n* [C] **1** *do sb's bidding*,
do what he commands. **2** [U] act of offering
a price at an auction sale: *∼ was brisk,
There were many bids, quickly made.* **3** (at
cards) the making of bids(4).

bi·en·nial /ˈbaɪˈenɪəl/ *adj* lasting for two
years; happening every alternate year.

bier /bɪə(r)/ *n* [C] movable wooden stand for
a coffin or a dead body.

biff /bɪf/ *n* [C] (*sl*) sharp blow. □ *vt* (*dated
sl*) strike: *He ∼ed me on the nose.*

bi·focal /ˈbaɪˈfəʊkəl/ *adj* (esp of lenses in
spectacles) designed for both distant and
near vision.
bi·focals *n pl* spectacles with bifocal lenses.

big /bɪg/ *adj* (-ger, -gest) (opposite = *little*;
⇨ *large*, *small*) of large size, capacity,
extent, importance, etc: *∼ feet/ideas/
gardens/cups; a ∼ day*, an important one;
'*big-'hearted*, (*informal*) generous, kind; *to
think ∼*, have big ideas.

'**big 'business, (a)** powerful financial or
business resources. **(b)** (*informal*) very
important concern.

'**big·head**, (*informal*) conceited person.

'**big·wig**, (*sl*) important person.

big·am·ist /ˈbɪgəmɪst/ *n* [C] person guilty of
bigamy.

big·am·ous /ˈbɪgəməs/ *adj* guilty of, involving, bigamy.

big·amy /ˈbɪgəmɪ/ *n* [U] having two wives
or husbands living, a crime in Christian
countries.

bight /baɪt/ *n* [C] curve in a coast, larger
than, or with not so much curve as, a bay.

bigot /ˈbɪgət/ *n* [C] person with an opinion
or belief and who not change it in spite of
reason or argument.
big·oted *adj* intolerant and narrow-minded.

bike /baɪk/ *n* (*informal* and common abbr
for) bicycle. □ *vi* = cycle.

bi·kini /bɪˈkɪnɪ/ *n* [C] (*pl ∼s*) two-piece
garment (bra and briefs) worn by girls and
women for swimming and sun-bathing.

bi·lat·eral /ˈbaɪˈlætərəl/ *adj* **1** of, on, with
two sides. **2** (*legal*) (of an agreement, etc)
made between two (persons, governments).
bi·lat·er·ally *adv*

bile /baɪl/ *n* [U] brownish-yellow bitter
liquid produced by the liver to help in
digesting food.

bilge /bɪldʒ/ *n* [U] **1** ship's bottom, inside or
outside; (also '*∼-water*) the dirty water that
collects here. **2** (*sl*) foolish or worthless talk
or writing.

bil·har·zia /bɪlˈhɑːzɪə/ *n* [U] tropical disease
caused by parasites in the blood and bladder.

bi·lin·gual /ˈbaɪˈlɪŋgwəl/ *adj* **1** speaking,
using, two languages. **2** written, printed, in
two languages.

bil·ious /ˈbɪlɪəs/ *adj* feeling sick, because of
too much bile: *a ∼ attack; ∼ patients.*

bill¹ /bɪl/ *n* [C] horny part of the mouth of
some birds. □ *vi* *bill and coo,* (of doves)
exchange caresses.

bill² /bɪl/ *n* [C] **1** written statement of
charges for goods delivered or services
given: *There are some ∼s to pay/to be paid.
foot the bill,* ⇨ foot². **2** written or printed
notice, poster, etc. *fill the bill,* be, do, all
that is required or expected. **3** (*legal*) proposed law, to be discussed by a parliament
(and called an *Act* when passed). **4** (*US*)
banknote: *a ten-dollar ∼.* **5** certificate: *∼ of
entry*, one from Customs to show final clear-
ance of goods; *a clean ∼ of health*, one certifying that a person is healthy. □ *vt* **1** make
known by means of bills(2); announce,
advertise in, a programme: *Olivier was ∼ed
to appear as Lear.* **2** *bill sb for sth,* give or
send a bill(1) to.

bil·let /ˈbɪlɪt/ *n* [C] place (usually a private
house) where soldiers are boarded and
lodged. □ *vt* place (troops) in billets.

bil·liards /ˈbɪlɪədz/ *n* (used with a *sing verb*)
game played with balls and long tapering
sticks (called *cues*) on an oblong, cloth-
covered table.

bil·lion /ˈbɪlɪən/ *n* [C] **1** (*GB*) million millions or 10^{12}. **2** (*Fr, US*) thousand millions

or 10⁹.

bil·low /'bɪləʊ/ **1** *n* [C] (*literary*) great
wave. **2** (*pl*) (*poetic*) the sea. **3** (*fig*) anything that sweeps along like a great wave. □
vi rise or roll like waves: *The flames ~ed
over the roof.*

bil·lowy *adj* rising or moving like billows.

billy-goat /'bɪlɪ gəʊt/ *n* [C] male goat.

bin /bɪn/ *n* [C] large rigid container usually
with a lid, for storing bread, coal, etc: *a
`dust~, bin for rubbish, etc; a `litter~.*

bi·nary /'baɪnərɪ/ *adj* of or involving a pair
or pairs: *a ~ system,* two stars revolving
round a common system or one round the
other; *the ~ scale,* (*maths*) with only two
digits, 0 and 1, i e 1 = 1, 2 = 10, 3 = 11, 4
= 100, etc.

bind /baɪnd/ *vt,vi* (*pt,pp* bound /baʊnd/) **1**
tie or fasten, with rope, etc: *They bound his
legs (together) so that he couldn't escape.* **2**
(*fig*) closely linked: *We are bound to him by
gratitude/by a close friendship.* **3** secure the
edge of something with tape, etc. *~ the cuffs
of a jacket with leather.* **4** tie or wind
something round: *~ up a wound.* **5** fasten
(sheets of paper) into a cover: *a book bound
in leather.* **6** hold (a person) (by legal agreement, a promise, or under penalty) to a certain course of action: *~ him to secrecy,*
make him promise to keep a secret. *bind sb
over (to keep the peace, etc),* order that he
must appear before the judge again (if he
fails to keep the peace, etc). ⇨ **bound⁴** for
special uses of the *pp.*

binder, person or thing that binds, especially in the sense of 5 above.

`bind·ery, place where books are bound.

bind·ing, (a) book-cover. (b) strip, tape, etc
for protecting an edge or a seam (of a garment, etc).

bingo /'bɪŋgəʊ/ *n* [U] popular gambling
game, played with cards on which numbered
squares are covered as the numbers are
called.

bin·nacle /'bɪnəkəl/ *n* [C] (*naut*) non-
magnetic stand for a ship's compass.

bin·ocu·lars /bɪ'nɒkjʊləz/ *n pl* (also *a pair
of ~*) instrument with lenses for both eyes,
making distant objects seem nearer.

bio- /baɪə- baɪ'ɒ-, baɪəʊ-/ *prefix* of life, of
living organisms: *biographic; biology; bio-
chemistry.*

bio·chem·is·try /'baɪəʊ'kemɪstrɪ/ *n* [U]
chemistry of living organisms.

bi·ogra·pher /baɪ'ɒgrəfə(r)/ *n* [C] person
who writes a biography.

bio·graphic, -i·cal /'baɪəʊ'græfɪk, -ɪkəl/
adj of biography.

bi·ogra·phy /baɪ'ɒgrəfɪ/ *n* **1** [C] person's
life-history written by another. **2** [U] branch
of literature dealing with the life-history of
persons.

bio·logi·cal /'baɪə'lɒdʒɪkəl/ *adj* of biology:
~ warfare, the deliberate use of germs, etc
for spreading disease.

bi·ol·ogist /baɪ'ɒlədʒɪst/ *n* [C] student of,
expert in, biology.

bi·ol·ogy /baɪ'ɒlədʒɪ/ *n* [U] science of the
physical life of animals and plants.

bi·par·ti·san /'baɪpɑːtɪ'zæn *US:* baɪ-
'pɑːtɪzən/ *adj* of, supported by, consisting
of, two otherwise opposed (esp political)
parties: *a ~ foreign policy.*

bi·ped /'baɪped/ *n* [C] two-footed animal,
e g a man or a bird.

bi·plane /'baɪpleɪn/ *n* [C] aircraft with two
pairs of wings, one above the other.

birch /bɜːtʃ/ *n* **1** [C] (kinds of) forest tree
growing in northern countries with a smooth
bark and slender branches. **2** [U] its wood.

bird /bɜːd/ *n* [C] **1** feathered creature with
two legs and two wings, usually able to fly.
*A bird in the hand is worth two in the
bush,* (*proverb*) Something which one has,
though small, is better than anything one has
not or cannot have. *kill two birds with one
stone,* achieve two aims at the same time. **2**
(*sl*) young girl, esp a girlfriend.

`bird-cage, cage for birds.

'bird's-'eye 'view, (a) wide view seen from
high up. **(b)** (*fig*) general survey without
details.

`bird-watcher, one who studies the habits
of birds.

biro /'baɪərəʊ/ *n* [C] (*pl ~s*) (*P*) (kind of)
ball-pen.

birth /bɜːθ/ *n* **1** [C,U] (process of) being
born, coming into the world: *The baby
weighed seven pounds at ~,* when it was
born. *give birth to,* produce (a child). **2** [U]
origin, descent: *She is Russian by ~ and
British by marriage.*

`birth-control, (method of) preventing
unwanted conception(2).

`birth·day, (anniversary of the) day of one's
birth.

`birth-mark, mark on the body at or from
birth.

`birth-place, house or district in which one
was born.

`birth-rate, number of births in one year for
every 1 000 persons.

bis·cuit /'bɪskɪt/ *n* [C] **1** flat, thin, crisp cake
of many kinds, sweetened or unsweetened.

bi·sect /'baɪ'sekt/ *vt* cut or divide into two
(usually equal parts).

bi·sec·tion /'baɪ'sekʃən/ *n* [U] division into
two (equal) parts.

bishop /'bɪʃəp/ *n* [C] **1** Christian clergyman
of high rank who organizes the work of the
Church in a city or district. **2** chess piece.

bishop·ric /-rɪk/, office, district, etc of a
bishop.

bi·son /'baɪsən/ *n* [C] (*pl* unchanged)
European wild ox; American buffalo.

bis·tro /'bistrəʊ/ *n* [C] (*pl ~s*) small bar or
nightclub.

bit¹ /bɪt/ *n* [C] **1** mouth-piece (metal bar)
forming part of a horse's bridle. **2** part of a
tool that cuts or grips when twisted; tool for

boring or drilling holes.

bit[2] /bɪt/ *n* [C] small piece of anything: *He ate every ~ of* (= all) *his dinner.* **a bit,** a little: *She's feeling a ~ tired.* **a bit of a,** to a small degree: *He's a ~ of a coward.* **not a bit,** not at all; not in the least: *He doesn't care a ~.* **wait a bit,** a short time. **bit by bit,** slowly, gradually. **every bit as good, etc as,** equally (good, etc). **go/come to bits,** into small pieces. **pull/cut/tear sth to bits,** into small pieces.

bit[3] /bɪt/ ⇨ bite[2].

bitch /bɪtʃ/ *n* [C] **1** female dog, wolf or fox. **2** (*informal*) spiteful woman or girl. □ *vi* (*informal*) complain bitterly; speak spitefully to or about a person.

bite[1] /baɪt/ *n* **1** [C] act of biting. **2** [C] injury resulting from a bite or sting: *His face was covered with `insect ~s.* **3** [C] piece cut off by biting: *I haven't had a ~ since morning, have eaten nothing.* **4** [C] catching of a fish on a hook: *He had been fishing all morning but hadn't had a ~.* **5** [U] sharpness; sting: *There's a ~ in the air this morning.* **6** [U] grip; hold: *a file/screw with plenty of ~.*

bite[2] /baɪt/ *vt,vi* (*pt* bit /bɪt/, *pp* bitten /ˈbɪtn/), **1** cut in with the teeth: *The dog bit me in the leg.* **bite off more than one can chew,** attempt too much. **bite the dust,** (*fig*) fall to the ground; be killed. **bite one's lip,** try to conceal one's anger or annoyance. **2 (a)** (of fleas, mosquitoes, etc) sting. **(b)** (of fish) accept the bait: *The fish wouldn't ~.* **3** cause a smarting pain to; injure: *His fingers were bitten by the frost/ were `frost-bitten.* **4** take strong hold of; grip: *The roads were covered with sand and the wheels did not ~.*

bit·ing /ˈbaɪtɪŋ/ *adj* sharp; cutting: *a biting wind; biting words.*
bit·ing·ly *adv*

bit·ten /ˈbɪtən/ ⇨ bite[2].

bit·ter /ˈbɪtə(r)/ *adj* **1** (opposite = *sweet*) tasting sharp and unpleasant. **2** unwelcome to the mind; unpleasant; causing sorrow: *~ disappointments/memories.* **3** filled with, showing, caused by, envy, hate, or disappointment: *~ quarrels/enemies.* **4** extremely sharp and cold: *a ~ wind.* **5 to the bitter end,** until all that is possible has been done, even until death. □ *n* **1** [U] bitter beer: *a pint of ~.* **2** (*pl*) liquor made from herbs, etc taken to help digestion or used to flavour gin, etc.
bit·ter·ly *adv*
bit·ter·ness *n* [U]

bit·tern /ˈbɪtən/ *n* [C] any of several kinds of wading birds that live on marshes.

bitu·men /ˈbɪtjʊmən/ *n* [U] black, sticky substance (from petroleum) used for making roads, etc.

bi·valve /ˈbaɪvælv/ *n* [U] water animal with a hinged double shell, e g an oyster, a mussel, a clam.

bi·week·ly /ˌbaɪˈwiːklɪ/ *adj* lasting for two weeks; happening every alternate week.

bi·zarre /bɪˈzɑː(r)/ *adj* very odd to look at, to have occurred, etc.

blab /blæb/ *vt,vi* (-bb-) talk foolishly or indiscreetly; tell (a secret).

black /blæk/ *adj* (-er, -est) **1** without light or almost without light; the colour of this printing-ink; opposite to white. **be black and blue,** covered with bruises. **in black and white,** written down. **black in the face,** dark red or purple (as with anger). **be in sb's black book(s),** ⇨ book[1](6). **be not so black as one is painted,** be not so bad as one is said to be. **2** (various uses, mostly to intensify the meaning of the *noun*): *~ despair/moods.* **3** (of work in a factory, shipyard, etc during a strike; of the materials, etc) not to be done, handled, etc: *The strikers declared the work/cargo ~.* **4** Negroid. □ *n* **1** [U] black colour. **2** [C,U] Negro (formerly discrediting, but now widely used): *B~ is beautiful* □ *vt* **1** make black; clean (boots, etc) with shoe-polish. **2** declare black(3): *The strikers ~ed the ship/ the cargo.*

black art/magic, used for evil purposes.

`black·ball *vt* prevent (a person) from being elected a member of a club by voting against him at a secret ballot.

`black·berry, small berry, black when ripe, growing on bushes (called *brambles*).

`black·bird, common European songbird.

`black·board, board used in schools for writing and drawing on with chalk.

`black·cur·rant, kind of currant with black fruit.

`black·guard /ˈblægɑːd/ *n* [C] person who is quite without honour; scoundrel. □ *vt* call (a person) a blackguard; use very bad language about or to (a person).

`black·head, (kind of) pimple on the skin, the top being black.

'black `ice, ice, esp on a road surface, which is invisible and dangerous to drive on.

'black-`lead, soft, grey-black substance as used for lead pencils.

`black-leg *n* [C] person who offers to work when the regular workers are on strike. □ *vi,vt* (-gg-) betray (fellow workers) by doing this.

`black-list, list of persons who are considered dangerous or who are to be punished. □ *vt* enter a person's name on such a list.

'black `magic, ⇨ black art.

`black·mail** *vt, n* [U] (force a person to make a) payment of money for not making known something to harm his character. Hence, **`black·mailer, person who does this.

'black `market, unlawful buying and selling of goods, currencies, etc that are officially controlled; place where such trading is carried on.

`black·out *n* [C] **(a)** (during wartime) the keeping of all buildings, streets, etc dark in order to prevent any light being seen, esp from the air. (b) temporary complete failure of the memory or consciousness. (c) putting out of all lights on the stage of a theatre, e g for a change of scenery. □ *vt,vi* cause a blackout ((a) and (c) above); lose one's memory, etc temporarily.

'Black `Power, militant Negro movement in the USA for their advancement.

'black `pudding, dark sausage made of blood, suet, etc.

'black `sheep, worthless person.

`black-smith, man who makes and repairs things of iron, esp who shoes horses.

blacken /ˈblækən/ *vt,vi* 1 make or become black. 2 say harmful things about (a person).

black-ing /ˈblækɪŋ/ *n* [U] black paste or liquid for polishing shoes (now called *shoe-polish*).

blad-der /ˈblædə(r)/ *n* [C] 1 bag of skin in which urine collects in human and animal bodies. ⇨ also gall-bladder. 2 bag of rubber, etc that can be filled with air, e g in a football.

blade /bleɪd/ *n* [C] 1 sharp cutting part of a knife, sword, chisel, etc. 2 (`razor-~) thin, flat piece of steel with a sharp edge for shaving: *a packet of five razor -~s.* 3 flat wide part of an oar (the part that goes into the water), bat, propeller, etc. 4 flat, long, narrow leaf, esp of grass and cereals (wheat, barley, etc).

blame /bleɪm/ *vt* accuse a person of being responsibile for something: *He ~d the teacher for his failure. I am not to ~,* am not responsible. □ *n* [U] responsibility for failure, etc: *Where does the ~ lie?* Who or what is responsible?

blame-less *adj* free from responsibility or faults; innocent.

blame-less-ly *adv*

blame-worthy *adj* deserving blame.

blanch /blɑntʃ US: blæntʃ/ *vt,vi* 1 make or become pale or white, e g by taking the skin off almonds. 2 make or become pale with fear, cold, etc.

bland /blænd/ *adj* 1 gentle or polite in manner or talk (usually not genuine). 2 (of air, food, drink) mild; comforting.

bland-ly *adv*

bland-ness *n* [U]

blank /blæŋk/ *adj* 1 (of paper) with nothing written, printed or drawn on it: *a ~ sheet of paper.* 2 (of a document) with spaces in which details, signature, etc are to be filled in: *a ~ cheque.* 3 empty; without interest or expression: *There was a ~ look on his face, He seemed not to be interested, not to understand, etc. My mind went ~,* I could not recall things, esp things I needed to remember. □ *n* [C] 1 space left empty or to be filled (in an application form, etc). 2 empty surface; emptiness: *His mind/memory was a complete ~,* he could remember nothing. 3 cartridge without a bullet

blank cartridge, ⇨ blank *n* (4).

blank cheque, signed but with no amount stated.

blank verse, (a) without rhyme. **(b)** (usually 10 lines) with a rhythm common in English epic and dramatic poems.

blank-ly *adv*

blan-ket /ˈblæŋkɪt/ *n* [C] 1 thick, woollen covering as used on beds. 2 (*fig*) similar covering or layer: *a ~ of snow.* ⇨ wet blanket. □ *vt* be thickly covered with: *The valley was ~ed with fog.*

blare /bleə(r)/ *n* [U] sound or noise (as of trumpets or horns). □ *vi,vt* make or produce such sounds: *The trumpets ~d (forth). He ~d out a warning,* shouted.

blasé /ˈblɑzeɪ US: blɑˈzeɪ/ *adj* tired of pleasure; bored.

blas-pheme /blæsˈfim/ *vi,vt* speak in an irreverent way about God and sacred things; use violent language: *~ the name of God.*

blas-phemer, person who blasphemes.

blas-phem-ous /ˈblæsfəməs/ *adj* (of persons) using blasphemy; (of language) containing blasphemy.

blas-phem-ous-ly *adv*

blas-phemy /ˈblæsfəmɪ/ *n* [U] contemptuous or irreverent talk about God and sacred things; [C] instance of this.

blast /blɑst US: blæst/ *n* [C] 1 strong, sudden rush of wind: *A ~ of hot air came from the oven.* 2 strong rush of air or gas spreading outwards from an explosion: *Thousands of windows were broken by the `bomb-~.* at full blast, (*informal*) with the maximum activity. 3 sound made by a wind-instrument: *The hunter blew a ~ on his horn.* 4 quantity of explosive (e g dynamite) used at one time (e g in a quarry). □ *vt* 1 blow up (rocks, etc) with explosives. 2 cause to come to nothing; injure: *The tree had been ~ed by lightning. His hopes were ~ed.* 3 *blast off,* (of spacecraft, etc) be forced upwards by expanding gases.

`blast-furnace, for melting iron-ore by forcing heated air into it.

`blast-off, (time of) launching of a spacecraft. ⇨ 3 above.

blast /blɑst US: blæst/ *int* (used in curses or in anger): *B~ you/it!*

blasted *adj* (used to show how strongly one feels): *What a ~ed nuisance!*

bla-tant /ˈbleɪtənt/ *adj* noisy and rough; attracting attention in a vulgar and shameless way; too obvious.

bla-tant-ly *adv*

blaze¹ /bleɪz/ *n* [C] 1 bright flame or fire: *We could see the ~ of a fire through the window.* 2 fire; burning building: *It took the firemen two hours to put the ~ out.* 3 (*pl*) hell: *Go to ~s! He was working like ~s,* working very hard. 4 glow of colour; bright light: *The red tulips made a ~ of colour in the garden.* 5 violent outburst: *in a ~ of anger.*

blaze² /bleɪz/ *vi, vt* **1** burn with flame: *When the firemen arrived the whole building was blazing.* **2** be bright with colour; shine brightly or with warmth: *The sun ~d down on us* **3** burst out with strong feeling: *He was blazing with anger/indignation.*
blaz·ing *adj*

blaze³ /bleɪz/ *n* [C] white mark on a horse's or an ox's face; mark made on a tree by cutting the bark. □ *vt* mark (a tree) by cutting off part of the bark. *blaze a trail*, (*fig*) do something and show others how to do it.

blaze⁴ /bleɪz/ *vt* make known far and wide: *~ the news* (*abroad*).

blazer /ˈbleɪzə(r)/ *n* [C] loose-fitting jacket (sometimes in the colours of a school, club, team, etc).

bla·zon /ˈbleɪzən/ *n* [C] coat of arms, esp on a shield.

bleach /bliːtʃ/ *n* [U] chemical used for bleaching or sterilizing. □ *vt, vi* make or become white (by chemical action or sunlight): *~ linen; bones of animals ~ing on the desert sand.*

bleak /bliːk/ *adj* (-er, -est) **1** (of the weather) cold and miserable; (of a place) bare, swept by cold winds: *a ~ hillside.* **2** (*fig*) depressing: *~ prospects.*
bleak·ly *adv*

bleary /ˈblɪəri/ *adj* dim; blurred.
'bleary-'eyed /ˈblɪər aɪd/ *adj* having blurred vision.

bleat /bliːt/ *n* [C,U] cry of a sheep, goat or calf. □ *vi, vt* make a cry of this kind.

bleed /bliːd/ *vi, vt* (*pt, pp* bled /bled/) **1** lose, send out, blood; suffer wounds (for a cause, etc): *If you cut your finger it will ~.* **2** feel great distress: *Our hearts ~ for homeless people during this cold winter.* **3** (*informal*) force (a person) to pay money unjustly: *The blackmailers bled him for £500.*

bleep /bliːp/ *n* [C] (word used for a) high-pitched sound or signal as sent out by radio (and used, e g by a doctor in a hospital, to summon a person when needed). □ *vi* make such sounds.

blem·ish /ˈblemɪʃ/ *n* [C,U] mark, etc that spoils the beauty or perfection; moral defect: *without ~, faultless.* □ *vt* spoil the perfection of.

blench /blentʃ/ *vi* make a quick movement of fear.

blend /blend/ *vt, vi* **1** mix together, esp sorts of coffee, tobacco, spirits, etc to get a certain quality. **2** mix, form a mixture: *Oil does not ~ with water.* **3** go well together; have no sharp or unpleasant contrast *how well their voices ~!* **4** (esp of colours) pass by degrees into each other: *These two colours ~ well.* □ *n* [C] mixture made of various sorts (of tea, tobacco, etc): *This coffee is a ~ of Java and Brazil.*

bless /bles/ *vt* (*pt, pp* ~ed /blest/ and blest, as in 5 below) **1** ask God's favour for: *They brought the children to Jesus and he ~ed*

them. **2** wish happiness or favour to: *B~ you, my boy!* **3** consecrate; make sacred or holy: *bread ~ed at the altar.* **4** *be blessed with*, be fortunate in having: *May you always be ~ed with good health.* **5** (*informal*) (in exclamations): *B~ my soul! I'm blest if I know!* i e I don't know at all. *B~ you!* (said to a person who has sneezed.)

bles·sed /ˈblesɪd/ *adj* **1** holy, sacred: *the B~ Virgin*, the mother of Jesus; *the B~ Sacrament*, Holy Communion. **2** fortunate: *B~ are the poor in spirit.* **3** *the B~*, those who are with God in paradise. **4** (*sl*) = blasted: *I've broken the whole ~ lot.*

bless·ing /ˈblesɪŋ/ *n* [C] **1** the favour of God; prayer for God's favour; thanks to God before or after a meal: *ask a ~.* **2** something that one is glad of, that brings comfort or happiness: *What a ~ it is you didn't get caught in the storm yesterday! a blessing in disguise*, something that seemed unfortunate, but that is seen later to be fortunate.

blew /bluː/ ⇨ **blow²**.

blight /blaɪt/ *n* **1** [U] (sorts of) plant disease; mildew. **2** [C] evil influence of obscure origin: *a ~ on his hopes.* □ *vt* be a bad influence on: *His hopes were ~ed.*

blind¹ /blaɪnd/ *adj* **1** without the power to see: *Tom helped the ~ man across the road.* *turn a blind eye (to sth)*, pretend not to see it. **2** unable to see effects, to judge or understand well: *Mothers are sometimes ~ to the faults of their children.* **3** reckless; thoughtless: *In his ~ haste he almost ran into the river.* **4** not having a purpose: *Some people think that the world is governed by ~ forces.*
'blind 'alley, ⇨ alley.
'blind 'date, ⇨ date¹.
'blind 'drunk, very drunk.
'blind-man's 'buff, game in which a person is blindfolded and tries to catch and identify others.
'blind spot, (a) point on the retina insensible to light. (b) (*fig*) something one does not seem able to understand or know in spite of having information.
blind turning, one in a road that cannot easily be seen by drivers.

blind² /blaɪnd/ *vt* **1** make blind: *a ~ing light.* **2** (*fig*) take away the power of judgement: *His feelings for her ~ed him to her faults.*
blind·ly *adv*
blind·ness *n* [U]

blind³ /blaɪnd/ *n* [C] **1** roll of cloth fixed on a roller and pulled down to cover a window: *pull down/lower, draw up/raise the ~s.* **2** (*fig*) deception: *It was only a ~.*

blind·fold /ˈblaɪndfəʊld/ *vt* cover the eyes of (a person) with a bandage, scarf, etc so that he cannot see. □ *n* [C] such a cover. □ *adj* with the eyes bandaged, etc.

blink /blɪŋk/ *vi, vt* **1** shut and open the eyes quickly: *~ the eyes; ~ away a tear.* **2** (of lights, esp when in the distance) come and go; shine in an unsteady way: *We saw the lighthouse* ∼*ing on the horizon.* □ *n* [C] act of blinking.

blink·ers /ˈblɪŋkəz/ *n pl* leather squares to prevent a horse from seeing sideways.

blip /blɪp/ *n* [C] spot of light on a radar screen.

bliss /blɪs/ *n* [U] perfect happiness; great joy.
ˈbliss·ful /-fʊl/ *adj*
ˈbliss·fully /-fəlɪ/ *adv*

blis·ter /ˈblɪstə(r)/ *n* [C] **1** small swelling under the skin, filled with liquid (caused by rubbing, burning, etc): *If your shoes are too tight, you may get* ∼*s on your feet.* **2** similar swelling on the surface of metal, painted or varnished wood, etc. □ *vt,vi* cause, get, a blister or blisters on.

blitz /blɪts/ *n* [C] rapid, violent attack (esp from the air). □ *vt* damage or destroy in this way.

bliz·zard /ˈblɪzəd/ *n* [C] violent and heavy snowstorm.

bloated /ˈbləʊtɪd/ *adj* **1** swollen; fat and large in an unhealthy way: *a* ∼ *face.* **2** (*fig*): ∼ *with pride*, very proud.

blob /blɒb/ *n* [C] drop of liquid, e g paint; small round mass, e g of wax; spot of colour. □ *vt* (-bb-) drop (paint, etc) in blobs.

bloc /blɒk/ *n* [C] combination of parties, groups, states, etc with a special interest: *the sterling* ∼, of countries with currencies related to sterling.

block¹ /blɒk/ *n* [C] **1** large, solid piece of wood, stone, etc: *A butcher cuts up his meat on a large* ∼ *of wood.* **2** mass of buildings (shops, offices, apartments, etc) joined together; (esp *US*) area of buildings bounded by four streets; the length of one side of such an area: *To reach the post office, walk two* ∼*s and then turn left.* **3** division of seats in a theatre, concert hall, etc. **4** large quantity of shares in a business. **5** obstruction: *There was a* ∼ *in the pipe and the water couldn't flow away.* ⇨ road block. **6** the ∼, (in olden times) large piece of wood on which a person put his neck to have his head cut off as a punishment. **7** shaped piece of wood on which hats are moulded. **8** (often ∼ *and tackle*) pulley, or system of pulleys, in a wooden case. **9** piece of wood or metal with designs, etc cut (engraved) on it for printing. **10** (*sl*) (person's) head: *I'll knock your* ∼ *off!*
ˈblock ˈletters/ˈwriting, with each letter separate and in capitals: *Write your name in* ∼ *letters.*

block² /blɒk/ *vt* **1** make movement difficult or impossible; obstruct: *All roads were* ∼*ed by the heavy snowfall.* **2** make (action) difficult or impossible: *The general succeeded in* ∼*ing the enemy's plans.* **3** (chiefly in the *pp*) restrict the use or expenditure of (currency, etc): ∼*ed sterling.* **4** shape (e g hats) on a block¹(7). **5** **block in/out,** make a rough

sketch or plan of the general arrangement (of objects in a drawing, etc).

block·ade /blɒˈkeɪd/ *n* [C] the enclosing or surrounding of a place, e g by armies or warships, to keep goods or people from entering or leaving. **run the blockade,** get through it. □ *vt* make a blockade of, e g a fort, etc.

block·age /ˈblɒkɪdʒ/ *n* [C] **1** state of being blocked. **2** thing that blocks: *There's a* ∼ *in the drain-pipe.*

block·head /ˈblɒkhed/ *n* [C] slow and stupid person.

bloke /bləʊk/ *n* [C] (*sl*) man.

blond /blɒnd/ *n* [C], *adj* (man of European race) having fair complexion and hair.

blonde /blɒnd/ *n* [C], *adj* (woman who is) blond.

blood /blʌd/ *n* [U] **1** red liquid flowing throughout the body: **2** passion; temper: *He makes my* ∼ *boil*, makes me very angry. **make one's blood boil,** make one very angry. **(kill sb) in cold blood,** when one is not feeling angry or excited; deliberately. **make one's ˈblood run cold,** fill one with fear or horror. **3** relationships; family: *They are of the same* ∼, have ancestors in common. **one's own flesh and blood,** one's relations. **Blood is thicker than water,** (*proverb*) The ties of one's family are more important.
ˈblood bank, ⇨ bank¹(3).
ˈblood·bath, large-scale slaughter, e g during a revolution.
ˈblood count, (counting of the) number of red and white corpuscles in a certain volume of blood.
ˈblood-curdling *adj* producing feelings of horror.
ˈblood-donor, person who gives blood for transfusions.
ˈblood feud, serious quarrel between families.
ˈblood-group/-type, any of several distinct classes of human blood.
ˈblood-ˈheat, the normal temperature of human blood (about 98.5°F, 37°C).
ˈblood·hound, large dog able to trace a person by scent.
ˈblood-poisoning, condition that results when poisonous germs enter the blood, esp through a cut or wound.
ˈblood pressure, the force exerted by blood within the arteries.
ˈblood ˈred *adj* having the colour of blood.
ˈblood relation, related by blood, not by marriages.
ˈblood·shed, killing or wounding of people; putting to death.
ˈblood·shot *adj* (of the white of the eyes) red.
ˈblood-sports *n pl* outdoor sports in which animals or birds are killed.
ˈblood·stream, flow of blood, system of blood vessels, in the body.
ˈblood·thirsty *adj* (-ier, -iest) cruel and

taking pleasure in killing.

ˋblood-transfusion, transfer of blood (originally taken) from the veins of one person to those of another.

ˋblood-vessel, tube (vein or artery) through which blood flows in the body.

blood·less adj (a) without bloodshed: a ⁓less victory. (b) pale; unfeeling and cold-hearted.

blood·less·ly adv

bloody /ˈblʌdɪ/ adj 1 bleeding; covered with blood: a ⁓ nose. 2 with much bloodshed: a ⁓ battle. 3 (vulgar) (used to show emphasis, either bad or good, but often with no meaning): What a ⁓ shame! You're a ⁓ fool! You're a ⁓ genius! □ adv (vulgar sl): Not ⁓ likely! Certainly not!

ˋbloody-ˋminded, (sl) unwilling to cooperate.

bloom /blum/ n 1 [C] flower, esp of plants admired chiefly for their flowers (e g roses, tulips, chrysanthemums): The tulips are in full ⁓ now. 2 (sing only) (time of) greatest beauty or perfection: She was in the ⁓ of youth. □ vi 1 be in flower; bear flowers: The roses have been ⁓ing all summer. 2 (fig) be in full beauty and perfection.

bloom·ing /ˈblumɪŋ/ adj 1 (used in the senses of the verb). 2 (dated) (often /ˈblʊmɪŋ/) = bloody(3).

bloomer /ˈbluːmə(r)/ n [C] (sl) mistake: He made a tremendous ⁓.

bloom·ers /ˈbluːməz/ n pl (also a pair of ⁓) loose garment covering each leg to the knee and hanging from the waist, formerly worn by girls and women for games, cycling, etc, with or without a skirt.

blos·som /ˈblosəm/ n 1 [C] flower, esp of a fruit-tree. 2 [U] mass of flowers on a bush or tree: The apple-trees are in ⁓. □ vi 1 open into flowers: The cherry-trees will ⁓ next month. 2 develop: He ⁓ed out as a first-rate athlete.

blot /blot/ n [C] 1 mark caused by ink spilt on paper. 2 fault; disgrace; something that takes away the beauty or goodness: a ⁓ on his character; a ⁓ on the landscape, e g an ugly building or advertisement. □ vt (-tt-) 1 make a blot or blots on (paper with ink). 2 dry up (wet ink) with blotting-paper. 3 blot out, (a) make a blot over (words that have been written): Several words in his letter had been ⁓ted out. (b) hide from view: The mist came down and ⁓ted out the view. (c) destroy, exterminate (enemies, etc).

blot·ter, piece or pad of blotting-paper.

ˋblot·ting-paper, absorbent paper used to dry up wet ink.

blotch /blotʃ/ n [C] large, discoloured mark (e g on the skin).

blouse /blaʊz US: blaʊs/ n [C] outer garment from neck to waist, worn by women and girls, etc.

blow¹ /bləʊ/ n [C] 1 hard stroke (given with the hand, a stick, etc): He struck his enemy a heavy ⁓ on the head. come to blows, fight. strike a blow for, (perform a single act of) support for; struggle for: strike a ⁓ for freedom. 2 shock; disaster: His wife's death was a great ⁓ to him.

blow² /bləʊ/ vi,vt (pt blew /bluː/, pp ⁓n /bləʊn/, or, 9 below, ⁓ed) 1 (with air, wind, or it as the subject) move along, flow as a current of air: The wind was ⁓ing round the street-corners. 2 (of the wind) cause to move: The wind blew my hat off. I was almost ⁓n over by the wind. 3 (of objects, etc) be moved or carried by the wind or other air current: The door blew open. 4 send or force a strong current of air on, into or through: ⁓ (on) one's food (to cool it); ⁓ one's nose, in order to clear it. 5 make by blowing: ⁓ bubbles. 6 produce sound from (a trumpet, etc) by sending air into it; (of a wind-instrument, etc) produce sound: The referee blew his whistle. We heard the bugles ⁓ing. 7 breathe hard and quickly: The old man was puffing and ⁓ing when he got to the top of the hill. 8 (of a fuse) melt because the electric current is too strong; cause to do this: The fuse has ⁓n. 9 (sl uses) spend (money) recklessly or extravagantly: ⁓ £10 on a dinner with a girlfriend. Well, I'm ⁓ed! I'm amazed! blow one's top, (sl) lose one's temper.

11 (uses with adverbial particles and prepositions):

blow back, (of gas in a tube, etc) explode.

blow off steam, release tension by arguing, being noisy, etc: Parents must let children ⁓ off steam sometimes.

blow (sth) out, (be) put out by blowing: The candle was ⁓n out by the wind. blow one's brains out, kill oneself by shooting in the head.

blow over, pass by; be forgotten: The storm/scandal will soon ⁓ over.

blow up, (a) explode: The barrel of gunpowder blew up. (b) lose one's temper: I'm sorry I blew up at you. blow sb up, (informal) scold severely: The teacher blew John up for not doing his homework. blow sth up, (a) break or destroy by explosion: The soldiers blew up the bridge. (b) inflate with air or gas: ⁓ up a tyre. (c) enlarge greatly: ⁓ up a photograph. (d) exaggerate: David's abilities have been greatly ⁓n up by the newspapers.

ˋblow-fly, common meat fly.

ˋblow-ing-ˋup, scolding.

ˋblow-lamp/-torch, for directing an intensely hot flame on to a surface.

ˋblow-out, (a) sudden (often violent) escape of air, steam, etc; (esp) bursting of a tyre. (b) blowing out of an electric fuse. (c) (sl) big meal; feast.

ˋblow-pipe, (esp) tube for increasing the heat of a flame by forcing air into it.

ˋblow-up, greatly enlarged photograph.

blow³ /bləʊ/ n [C] blowing: Give your nose

a good ~, clear it thoroughly.
blow[4] /bləʊ/ *vi* (*pp* ~n /bləʊn/) (chiefly in *pp* as) *full-*~ *roses,* wide open, with petals about to fall.
blower /ˈbləʊə(r)/ *n* [C] **1** apparatus for forcing air, etc into or through something. **2** person who makes things by blowing (eg *a* `*glass-*~). **3** (*GB sl*) telephone: *Get Jones on the* ~ *for me.*
blown /bləʊn/ *pp* of blow[2]. ⇨ also blow[4].
blowzy /ˈblaʊzɪ/ *adj* (of a woman) red-faced, untidy and cheaply dressed.
blub·ber /ˈblʌbə(r)/ *n* [U] fat of whales and other sea-animals from which oil is obtained.
bludgeon /ˈblʌdʒən/ *n* [C] short, thick stick with a heavy end, used as a weapon. □ *vt* **1** strike with a stick: *He had been* ~*ed to death.* **2** (*fig*) force or bully somebody into doing something.
blue[1] /blu/ *adj* (-r, -st) coloured like the sky on a clear day or the deep sea when the sun is shining: *His face was* ~ *with cold.* **once in a blue moon,** very rarely.
blue[2] /blu/ *n* **1** colour: *dark/light* ~. **2** (the) sky. **out of the blue,** unexpectedly. **a bolt from the blue,** unexpected. **3** (*poetic*) (the) sea. **4 a true blue,** a loyal member (of a pol-itical party, esp Conservative). **5 the** ~**s,** (a) (dances, dance tunes, for) haunting jazz melodies originally of Negroes in the south-ern US. (b) (*informal*) condition of being sad, melancholy.
ˈblue-ˈblooded *adj* of aristocratic birth.
ˈblue-bottle, meat fly or blowfly.
blue cheese, kinds which have been pierced with copper rods to produce a blue mould.
ˈblue-ˈcollar *adj* used of workers in fac-tories, etc (contrasted with *white-collar* workers in offices, etc).
ˈblue-eyed *adj* (a) having blue eyes. (b) favourite: *He's mummy's* ~*-eyed boy!*
ˈblue ˈfilm, obscene film.
ˈblue ˈjoke, obscene joke.
ˈblue-print, (a) photographic print, white on blue paper, usually for building plans. (b) (*fig*) plan, scheme.
ˈblue-stock-ing, woman who is regarded as having superior literary tastes and intellec-tual interests.
blu·ish /ˈbluːʃ/ *adj* tending towards blue: *bluish green.*
blue[3] /blu/ *vt* **1** make blue. **2** (*sl*) spend (money) recklessly.
bluff[1] /blʌf/ *n* [C] headland with a broad and very steep face. □ *adj* **1** (of headlands, cliffs, a ship's bows) with a broad, perpendicular front. **2** (of a person, his manner, etc) abrupt; rough but honest and kind, simple and good-natured.
bluff-ness *n* [U]
bluff[2] /blʌf/ *vt,vi* deceive by pretending. **bluff it out,** survive a difficult situation by pretence. □ *n* [U] deception of this kind; (the use of) threats that are intended to get results

without being carried out. **call sb's bluff,** invite him to carry out his threats.
blu·ish /ˈbluːʃ/ ⇨ blue[2].
blun·der /ˈblʌndə(r)/ *vi,vt* **1** move about uncertainly, as if blind: ~ *into a wall.* **2** make foolish mistakes: *Our leaders have* ~*ed again.* □ *n* [C] careless mistake.
blunt /blʌnt/ *adj* (-er, -est) **1** without a point or sharp edge: *a* ~ *knife.* **2** (of a per-son, what he says) plain; not troubling to be polite: *He's a* ~ *man.* □ *vt* make blunt: *If you try to cut stone with a knife, you will* ~ *the edge.*
blunt·ly *adv: to speak* ~*ly,* frankly.
blunt·ness *n* [U]
blur /blɜ(r)/ *n* [C] **1** dirty spot or mark; smear of ink. **2** confused or indistinct effect: *If, when you read, you see only a* ~, *you need glasses.* □ *vt,vi* (-rr-) make a dirty mark or smear on; make or become unclear in appearance: *Tears* ~*red her eyes. The writing was* ~*red.*
blurb /blɜb/ *n* [C] description of the contents of a book, printed on the jacket, etc.
blurt /blɜt/ *vt* **blurt sth out,** tell, eg a sec-ret, suddenly, often thoughtlessly.
blush /blʌʃ/ *vi* **1** become red (in the face) from shame or confusion. **2** be ashamed. □ *n* [C] **1** reddening of the face, eg from shame, etc: *She turned away to hide her* ~*es.*
blus·ter /ˈblʌstə(r)/ *vi,vt* **1** (of the wind, waves, etc) storm; be rough or violent. **2** (of persons) act and speak in a forceful but rather unsteady, often rather boastful way. **3** utter in this way: ~ *out threats.* □ *n* [U] **1** noise of violent wind or waves. **2** forceful, noisy talk, behaviour, threats.
blus·tery *adj* (of the weather) rough and windy.
boa /ˈbəʊə/ *n* [C] (also `**boa-constrictor**) large non-poisonous snake that kills by crushing its prey.
boar /bɔ(r)/ *n* [C] **1** wild male pig. **2** uncas-trated male domestic pig.
board[1] /bɔd/ *n* [C] **1** long, thin, flat piece of wood with squared edges, used in building walls, floors, boats, ship's decks, etc. **2** flat piece of wood or other material for a special purpose: *a* `*notice-*~; *a* `*diving* ~, (at a swimming pool). **3** flat surface with pat-terns, etc on which games, eg chess, are played. **4** (from the boards that form the deck of a ship) *be/go on board,* be/go on a ship or airliner. **go by the board,** (*fig*) (of plans, hopes, etc) be given up or abandoned; fail completely. **5** council-table; council-lors; committee; group of persons control-ling a business, or a government department: *the* ˈB~ *of* `*Trade; a Se*`*lection B*~, one that selects (future staff, etc) from applicants or candidates. **across the board,** ⇨ across[2](1). **6** [U] food served at table, esp meals supplied by the week or month (eg at a lodging-house) or as part payment for ser-vice: *B*~ *and lodging £15 weekly.* **7** =

65

cardboard.

`board-room, room in which meetings (of a Board of Directors, etc) are held.

board² /bɔːd/ vt 1 make or cover with boards(1): ~ up a window. 2 get, supply with, meals for a fixed weekly/monthly, etc payment: In a university town, many people make a living by ~ing students (⇨ board¹(6)). 3 get on or into (a ship, train, bus, etc).

boarder, (a) person who boards with somebody. ⇨ 2 above. (b) schoolboy or girl at a boarding-school (⇨ below).

board-ing, (a) structure of boards(1). (b) the providing or receiving of board(6).

`boarding-card, embarkation card, esp for an airliner or ship.

`boarding-house, private house that provides board and lodging.

`boarding school, one at which pupils live.

boast /bəʊst/ n [C] words used in praise of oneself, one's acts, belongings, etc; cause for satisfaction or pride: It was his ~ that he had never failed in an examination. □ vt,vi 1 make a boast or boasts: He ~s of being/~s that he is the best tennis-player in the town. 2 possess with pride: Our school ~s a fine swimming-pool.

`boast-ful /-fəl/ adj (of persons) fond of boasting.

`boast-fully /-fəlɪ/ adv

boat /bəʊt/ n [C] small open vessel for travelling in on water, esp the kind moved with oars (`rowing ~), sails (`sailing ~), engines (`motor-~); also used of fishing-vessels and small steamers: We crossed the river by ~/in a ~. be (all) in the same boat, have the same dangers to face. □ vi travel in a boat, esp for pleasure: We ~ed down the river.

`boat-house, shed in which boats are stored.

`boat-man, man who rows or sails a small boat for pay; man from whom boats may be hired.

`boat-race, race between boats.

`boat-train, train that takes people to or from a steamer, e g between London and Dover. ⇨ also ferry, house¹(7), life(14).

boat-swain /ˈbəʊsən/ n [C] senior seaman who controls the work of other seamen and is in charge of a ship's rigging, boats, sails, anchors, etc.

bob¹ /bɒb/ vi (-bb-) move up and down: The cork on his fishing-line was ~bing on the water. □ n [C] quick up and down movement; curtsy.

bob² /bɒb/ vt (-bb-) cut (a woman's or girl's hair) so that it is short and hangs loosely: She wears her hair ~bed.

bob-bin /ˈbɒbɪn/ n [C] small roller or spool for holding thread, yarn, wire, etc in a machine.

bobby /ˈbɒbɪ/ n [C] (GB dated informal) policeman.

bob-sleigh, bob-sled /ˈbɒbsleɪ, -sled/ n [C] racing sleigh for two or more persons. □ vi ride in a bobsleigh.

bode /bəʊd/ vt,vi bode well/ill for, be a good/bad sign of: His idle habits ~ ill for his future, suggest that his future career will be a failure. ⇨ forbode.

bod-ice /ˈbɒdɪs/ n [C] close-fitting part of a woman's dress from the shoulders to the waist.

bod-ily /ˈbɒdəlɪ/ adj of or in the human body or physical nature: ~ (= physical) assault. □ adv 1 as a whole or mass; completely: The shed was transported ~ (= as a whole, without being pulled down) to the end of the garden. 2 in person; in the body.

bod-kin /ˈbɒdkɪn/ n [C] blunt, thick needle.

body /ˈbɒdɪ/ n [C] (pl -ies) 1 the whole physical structure of a man or animal: We wear clothes to keep our bodies warm. 2 dead body; corpse: His ~ was brought back to England for burial. 3 main portion of a man or animal without the head, arms and legs: He received one wound in the left leg and another in the ~. 4 main part of a structure: the ~ of a car. 5 group of persons who do something together or who are united in some way: Large bodies of unemployed men marched through the streets demanding work. in a body, all together; as a whole: The staff resigned in a ~. 6 mass, quantity, collection: A lake is a ~ of water. 7 the heavenly bodies, the sun, moon and stars. ⇨ also anybody, everybody, nobody, somebody.

`body-guard, man or men guarding an important person.

`body-snatcher, person who steals corpses from graves.

`body-work, main part, material, of (esp) a motor-vehicle.

bog /bɒg/ n [C] (area of) soft, wet, spongy ground (chiefly decayed or decaying vegetable matter). □ vt,vi (-gg-) bog down, (cause to) be stuck fast, unable to make progress: The tanks were ~ged down in the mud.

boggy adj (-ier, -iest) (of land) soft and wet.

bo-gey /ˈbəʊgɪ/ = bogy.

boggle /ˈbɒgəl/ vi be unwilling, hesitate, to do something: The mind/imagination ~s (at the idea), is alarmed at the idea.

bo-gus /ˈbəʊgəs/ adj not genuine.

bogy, bo-gey /ˈbəʊgɪ/ n [C] (pl -ies, ~s) evil spirit; cause of fear.

boil¹ /bɔɪl/ n [C] hard (usually red, often painful) poisoned swelling under the skin, which bursts when ripe.

boil² /bɔɪl/ n [U] boiling point. be on the boil, be boiling. bring sth to the boil, heat it until it boils. come to the boil, (a) begin to boil. (b) (fig) reach a crisis.

boil² /bɔɪl/ vi,vt 1 (of water or other liquid, also of the vessel that contains it) reach the temperature at which change to gas occurs; bubble up: *When water ∼s it changes into steam. The kettle is ∼ing.* **2** (of the sea, of a person's feelings, etc) be very disturbed: *He was ∼ing (over) with rage.* **3** cause water or other liquid to boil; cook in boiling water: *Please ∼ my egg for three minutes.* **4** (uses with *adverbial particles* and *prepositions*):

boil away, (a) continue to boil: *The kettle was ∼ing away merrily on the fire.* (b) boil until nothing remains: *The water had all ∼ed away and the kettle was empty.*

boil down, be reduced in quantity: *It all ∼s down to this...,* (*informal*) the essence (of the statement, proposal, etc) is...

boil over, flow over the side: *The milk had ∼ed over.*

ˈboiling ˈhot *adj* (*informal*) very hot: *a ∼ing hot day.*

ˈboiling-point, (a) temperature at which a liquid boils. (b) (*fig*) height of excitement, anger, etc.

boiler /ˈbɔɪlə(r)/ *n* [C] metal container in which water, etc is heated, e g for producing steam in an engine, for supplying hot water.

ˈboiler-suit, overalls, for rough or dirty work.

bois·ter·ous /ˈbɔɪstərəs/ *adj* (of a person, his behaviour) noisy and cheerful.

bold /bəʊld/ *adj* (-er, -est) **1** without fear; showing absence of fear. **2** without feelings of shame. **as bold as brass,** daring. **3** well marked; clear: *the ∼ outline of a mountain.*

bold·ly *adv*

bold·ness *n* [U]

boll /bəʊl/ *n* [C] pod for seeds (of cotton and flax).

ˈboll ˈweevil, small destructive insect in cotton-plants.

bol·lard /ˈbɒləd/ *n* [C] **1** post on a quay or a ship's deck for making ropes secure. **2** similar post on a traffic island, or a roadway, for organizing parking, directing traffic.

bol·ster[1] /ˈbəʊlstə(r)/ *n* [C] long pillow for the head of a bed.

bol·ster[2] /ˈbəʊlstə(r)/ *vt* give (greatly needed encouragement or) support to, e g a person, theory, etc: *She'll need ∼ing up if you want her to win the race.*

bolt[1] /bəʊlt/ *n* [C] **1** metal fastening for a door or window, consisting of a sliding pin or rod and a staple into which it fits. **2** metal pin with a head at one end and a thread (as on a screw) at the other, used with a nut for holding things together. **3** discharge of lightning. ⇨ **thunder-bolt.** □ *vt,vi* fasten with a bolt or bolts(1): *∼ the doors.*

bolt[2] /bəʊlt/ *vi,vt* **1** (esp of a horse) run off out of control. **2** run away quickly: *As soon as I came downstairs the burglar ∼ed through the back door.* **3** swallow (food) quickly: *We ∼ed a few mouthfuls of food and hurried on.* □ *n* [C] act of running away. **make a bolt for it,** run away quickly.

bolt[3] /bəʊlt/ *adv* (only in) **bolt upright,**

suddenly and completely upright.

bomb /bɒm/ *n* [C] hollow metal ball or shell filled either with explosive or with smoke, gas, etc. **go like a bomb,** (*sl*) be very efficient, successful, etc: *My new car/The new play goes like a ∼.* □ *vt,vi* attack with bombs.

bomber, (a) aircraft used for bombing. **(b)** soldier trained in bombing.

ˈbomb-shell, (*fig*) thing that causes great surprise or shock.

bom·bard /bɒmˈbɑːd/ *vt* **1** attack with shells from big guns. **2** (*fig*) worry with many questions, requests, complaints, etc.

bom·bard·ment *n* [C,U]

bond /bɒnd/ *n* [C] **1** agreement or engagement that a person is bound to observe, esp one that has force in law; document, signed and sealed, containing such an agreement. **2** (usually *fig*) something that joins or unites: *the ∼(s) of affection.* **3** printed paper issued by a government or a corporation acknowledging that money has been lent to it and will be paid back with interest.

bond·age /ˈbɒndɪdʒ/ *n* [U] slavery, servitude: *in hopeless ∼ to his master.*

bone /bəʊn/ *n* [C] one of the parts that make up the framework of an animal's body: *This fish has a lot of ∼s in it.* **feel in one's bones that,** feel certain that. **have a bone to pick with sb,** have something to argue or complain about. **make no bones about doing sth,** not hesitate to do it. □ *vt* take bones out of (a chicken, etc).

ˈbone ˈdry *adj* completely dry.

ˈbone-ˈidle/-ˈlazy *adj* very idle.

bon·fire /ˈbɒnfaɪə(r)/ *n* [C] large fire made out of doors either to celebrate some event or to burn up rubbish, etc

bon·kers /ˈbɒŋkəz/ *adj* (*sl*) insane.

bon·net /ˈbɒnɪt/ *n* [C] **1** close-fitting head-dress with a soft brim, usually tied under the chin, as worn by babies. **2** protective cover of various sorts, e g over the engine of a motor-vehicle.

bonny /ˈbɒnɪ/ *adj* healthy looking; with a glow of health: *a ∼ baby.*

bo·nus /ˈbəʊnəs/ *n* [C] (*pl* ∼es) payment in addition to what is usual, necessary or expected, e g an extra dividend to stock-holders of a business company or an extra payment to workers.

no ˈclaims bonus, percentage reduction in an insurance premium (for a motor-vehicle) if claims are not made.

bony /ˈbəʊnɪ/ *adj* (-ier, -iest) **1** full of bones: *a ∼ fish,* e g a herring. **2** having big or prominent bones: *∼ fingers.*

boo /buː/ *int* **1** sound made to show disapproval or contempt. **2** exclamation used to surprise or startle. □ *vt,vi* make such sounds: *The speaker was ∼ed off the platform.*

boob[1] /buːb/ *n* [C] (*informal*) silly mistake. □ *vi* make a silly mistake.

boob[2] /buːb/ *n* [C] (*sl*) woman's breast.

booby /ˈbubɪ/ n [C] silly or stupid person.
ˈbooby prize, prize given as a joke, e g to the person who is last in a race, etc.
ˈbooby-trap, apparently harmless object that will kill or injure when picked up or interfered with.

book¹ /bʊk/ n [C] **1** number of sheets of paper, either printed or blank, fastened together in a cover; literary composition that would fill such a set of sheets: write a ∼. **2** main division of the Bible: the B∼ of Genesis. **3** packet of similar items fastened together, e g postage stamps, matches. **4** (pl) business accounts, records, etc: The firm has full ˈorder ∼s, orders for goods. **be in sb's good/bad/black books,** have/have not his favour or approval.
ˈbook-case, piece of furniture with shelves for books.
ˈbook-club, organization that sells books at a discount to members who agree to buy a minimum number.
ˈbook-ends, pair of props used to keep a row of books upright.
ˈbook-keeper, person who keeps accounts, e g of a business, public office.
ˈbook-keep-ing, (profession of) keeping (business) accounts.
ˈbook-maker, person whose business is taking bets on horse-races, etc.
ˈbook-mark(er), something put in a book to mark the place.
ˈbook-seller, person who sells books.
ˈbook-stall, kiosk, etc at which books, newspapers, etc are sold, in a railway station, a hotel lobby, etc.
ˈbook token, receipt (on an attractive card) exchangeable for a book at the value stated.
ˈbook-worm, (a) small maggot that eats holes in books. (b) person who is very fond of reading.

book² /bʊk/ vt **1** write down (orders, etc) in a notebook. **2** (of the police) record a charge against (a person): be ∼ed for speeding. **3** give or receive an order for, e g tickets for a journey. **4** engage (a person) as a speaker, entertainer, etc.
ˈbook-able /-əbəl/ adj (of seats, etc) that can be reserved: all seats ∼able in advance.
ˈbook-ing clerk, person who sells tickets, e g at a railway station.
ˈbook-ing office, office where tickets are sold (for travel, the theatre).

bookie /ˈbʊkɪ/ n [C] (informal) = bookmaker.

book-let /ˈbʊklət/ n [C] pamphlet, thin book.

boom¹ /bum/ n [C] **1** long pole used to keep the bottom of a sail stretched out. **2** long, movable arm for a microphone. **3** long pole fastened to a crane¹, used for (un)loading cargo. **4** heavy chain, mass of floating logs, etc held in position across a river or harbour entrance.

boom² /bum/ vt,vi **1** (of big guns, etc)

make deep, hollow sounds. **2** boom out, say in a loud deep voice: ∼ing out Shakespearian verses. □ n [C] deep, hollow sound: the ∼ of supersonic aircraft.

boom³ /bum/ n [C] sudden increase in trade activity, esp a time when money is being made quickly. □ vi **1** have a boom: Business is ∼ing. **2** become well known and successful: Jones is ∼ing as a novelist.

boom-er-ang /ˈbuməræŋ/ n [C] **1** curved stick of hard wood (used by Australian aborigines), which can be thrown so that, if it fails to hit anything, it returns to the thrower. **2** (fig) argument or scheme that comes back and harms its author. □ vi (of a scheme) cause harm in this way.

boon /bun/ n [C] advantage; blessing, comfort: Parks are a great ∼ to people in big cities.

boor /bʊə(r)/ n [C] ill-mannered person.
boor-ish adj of or like a boor.

boost /bust/ vt **1** increase (e g the value, reputation, of): Seeing him ∼ed my morale. **2** increase the performance of the engine of a car. □ n [C] act of boosting.

boo-ster /ˈbustə(r)/ n [C] **1** thing that boosts: His work got a welcome ∼. **2** (also ∼ injection) supplementary dose of vaccine to strengthen the effect of an earlier dose.
booster rocket, rocket used to give initial speed to a missile, after which it drops and leaves the missile to continue under its own power.

boot¹ /but/ n [C] **1** outer covering for the foot and ankle, made of leather or rubber. **get the boot,** (sl) be dismissed. **give sb the boot,** (sl) dismiss him from his job. **put the boot in,** (sl) kick a person in a fight. **2** (GB) place for luggage at the back of a motor-car or coach. □ vt kick, dismiss, (a person): He was ∼ed out of the house.
ˈboot-lace, string or leather strip for tying a boot.

boot² /but/ n (only in) **to boot,** as well; in addition.

bootee /ˈbuti/ n [C] baby's knitted wool boot.

booth /buð/ n [C] **1** shelter of boards, canvas or other light materials, esp one where goods are sold at a market or a fair. **2** enclosure for a public telephone. ⇨ kiosk. **3** = polling booth.

booty /ˈbutɪ/ n [U] things taken by robbers or captured from the enemy in war.

booze /buz/ n [U] (informal) **1** alcoholic drink. **2** period of drinking alcoholic drink. □ vi drink (too much) alcoholic drink.
ˈbooze-up, period of boozing.

boozer /ˈbuzə(r)/ n [C] (GB sl) **1** person who often has (too much) alcoholic drink. **2** pub.

boozy /ˈbuzɪ/ adj (-ier, -iest) (sl) drunk; fond of boozing.

bor-der /ˈbɔdə(r)/ n [C] **1** edge; part near the edge: We camped on the ∼ of a lake. There *is a ~ of flowers round the lawn.* **2** (land near the) line dividing two states or countries: *The criminal escaped over the ~.* □ *vt,vi* **1** put or be an edge to: *Our garden is ~ed by a stream.* **2 border on/upon, (a)** be next to: *My land ~s on yours.* **(b)** be almost the same as: *The proposal ~s on the absurd.*

'border·land, (a) district on either side of a boundary. **(b) the ~,** the condition between: *the ~land between sleeping and waking.*

'border·line, line that marks a boundary *a* **'borderline `case,** one that is doubtful, e g a person who may or may not pass an examination.

bore¹ /bɔ(r)/ *vt,vi* make a narrow, round deep hole with a revolving tool; make (a hole, one's way) by doing this or by digging out soil, etc: *boring a hole in wood/a tunnel through a mountain.* □ *n* [C] **1** (also `~-hole`) hole made by boring. **2** hollow inside of a gun barrel; its diameter.

bore² /bɔ(r)/ *vt* make (a person) feel tired by being dull or tedious: *Am I boring you?* □ *n* [C] person who, that which, bores.

bor·ing *adj: a boring evening.*

bore·dom /-dəm/ *n* [U] state of being bored.

bore³ /bɔ(r)/ *pt* of **bear²**.

born /bɔn/ (one of the *pp's* of **bear²**) **1 be born,** come into the world by birth. **2** destined to be: *He was ~ a poet.*

borne /bɔn/ *pp* of **bear²** except of birth; ⇨ **bear²**(10).

bor·ough /ˈbʌrə US: ˈbɜːrəʊ/ *n* [C] (in England) town, or part of a town, that sends one or more members to Parliament; town with a municipal corporation and rights of self-government conferred by royal charter.

bor·row /ˈbɒrəʊ/ *vt,vi* **1** get something, or its use, on the understanding that it is to be returned: *May I ~ your pen?* ⇨ **lend**. **2** take and use as one's own: *~ a person's ideas/methods.*

bor·rower, person who borrows.

bor·stal /ˈbɔstəl/ *n* [C] place where young offenders live and receive training designed to reform them.

bo'sn /ˈbəʊsən/ = **boatswain.**

bosom /ˈbʊzəm/ *n* [C] **1** (*old use*) person's breast; part of dress covering this. **2** centre or inmost part, where one feels joy or sorrow: *a ~ friend,* one who is dear and close.

boss¹ /bɒs/ *n* [C] (*sl*) master; person who controls or gives orders: *Who's the ~ in this house?* □ *vt* give orders to: *He wants to ~ the show,* to make all the arrangements. *boss sb about/around,* give him orders.

bossy *adj* (-ier, -iest) fond of being in authority.

boss-eyed /ˈbɒs aɪd/ *adj* (*sl*) blind in one eyed; cross-eyed.

bo'sun /ˈbəʊsən/ = **boatswain.**

botan·ical /bəˈtænɪkəl/ *adj* of botany: *~ gardens.*

bot·an·ist /ˈbɒtənɪst/ *n* [C] student of, expert in, botany.

bot·any /ˈbɒtənɪ/ *n* [U] science of the structure of plants.

botch /bɒtʃ/ *vt* repair badly; spoil by poor, clumsy work: *a ~ed piece of work.* □ *n* [C] piece of clumsy, badly done work: *make a ~ of it.*

both¹ /bəʊθ/ *adj* (opposite = *neither*) (of two things, persons, etc) the two; the one and also the other: *I want ~ books. I saw him on ~ occasions.* (*Note:* Compare *both* and *each: There are shops on ~ sides of the street. There is a butcher's shop on each side of the street.*)

both² /bəʊθ/ *pron* (opposite = *neither*) (of two persons, things, etc) the two; not only the one: *B~ are good. B~ of them are good. We ~ want to go.* ⇨ **all, each.**

bother /ˈbɒðə(r)/ *vt,vi* **1** be or cause trouble to; worry: *Don't ~ me with foolish questions.* **2** take trouble: *Don't ~ about getting/~ to get dinner for me today; I'll eat out.* **3** (used as an exclamation of impatience or annoyance): *Oh, ~ (it)!* □ *n* **1** [U] worry, trouble: *Don't put yourself to any ~,* inconvenience yourself. **2** person or thing that gives trouble: *His lazy son is quite a ~ to him. This drawer won't shut; isn't it a ~!*

'bother·some /-səm/ *adj* troublesome or annoying.

bottle /ˈbɒtəl/ *n* [C] container with a narrow neck, for liquids; its contents: *Mary drinks two ~s of milk a day.* □ *vt* **1** put into, store in, bottles: *~ fruit.* **2 bottle up,** (*fig*) be unable or unwilling to express, hold in, keep under control, e g anger.

'bottle-fed, (of a child) given milk from a bottle, not fed from its mother's breast.

'bottle-'green *adj* dark green.

'bottle-neck, (a) narrower strip of road, between two wide parts, where traffic is slowed down or held up. **(b)** that part of a manufacturing process, etc where production is slowed down (e g by shortage of materials).

bot·tom /ˈbɒtəm/ *n* [C] **1** lowest part of anything, inside or outside: *We were glad to reach the ~ (= foot) of the mountain.* **2** part farthest from the front or more important part: *at the ~ of the garden.* **3** bed of the sea, a lake, river, etc: *The ship went to the ~,* sank. **4** seat (of a chair, etc.). **5** (*informal*) part of the body on which a person sits: *She smacked the child's ~.* **6** lowest, last, (level); foundation: *Put it on the ~ shelf. Who came ~ in the exam? get to the bottom of sth,* find out how it began. *from the bottom of my heart,* genuinely, deeply.

bot·tom·less *adj* very deep: *a ~less pit.*

bough /baʊ/ *n* [C] large branch coming from the trunk of a tree.

bought /bɔt/ *pt,pp* of **buy.**

boul·der /ˈbəʊldə(r)/ *n* [C] large piece of rock or stone, esp one that has been rounded

69

by water or weather.

bounce /ˈbaʊns/ *vi,vt* **1** (of a ball, etc) (cause to) move away or back when sent against something hard: *The ball ~ed over the wall. She was bouncing a ball.* **2** (cause to) move up and down violently or noisily; rush noisily or angrily: *The boy was bouncing* (*up and down*) *on the bed. He ~d into/ out of the room.* **3** (*informal*) (of a cheque) be returned by a bank because there is no money in the account. □ *n* [C] (of a ball) art of bouncing: *catch the ball on the ~.*

bounc·ing /ˈbaʊnsɪŋ/ *adj* big strong, healthy: *a ~ boy.*

bound¹ /baʊnd/ *vt* jump, spring, bounce; move or run in jumping movements: *His dog came ~ing to meet him.* □ *n* [C] jumping movement upward or forward: *at one ~.* **by leaps and bounds,** very quickly.

bound² /baʊnd/ *adj* (*literary*) ready to start, having started: *Where are you ~* (*for*)? *Where are you going to?*

bound³ /baʊnd/ *vt* set limits to; be the boundary of: *England is ~ed on the north by Scotland.*

bound⁴ /baʊnd/ *pp* of **bind**. (special uses) certain, destined, obliged: *~ to win; ~ to come.* **bound up in,** much interested in, very busy with: *He is ~ up in his work.*

bound·ary /ˈbaʊndrɪ/ *n* [C] (*pl* -ies) **1** line that marks a limit; dividing line: *This stream forms a ~ between my land and his.* **2** hit to or over the boundary of a cricket field.

bound·less /ˈbaʊndləs/ *adj* without limits: *his ~ generosity.*

bound·less·ly *adv*

bounds /baʊndz/ *n pl* limit: *It is beyond the ~ of human knowledge,* Man can know nothing about it. **out of bounds,** outside the limits of areas that one is allowed to enter.

boun·te·ous /ˈbaʊntɪəs/ *adj* generous; giving or given freely; abundant: *a ~ harvest.*

boun·ti·ful /ˈbaʊntɪfəl/ *adj* = bounteous.

bounty /ˈbaʊntɪ/ *n* (*pl* -ies) **1** [U] freedom in giving; generosity. **2** [C] something given out of kindness (esp to the poor). **3** [C] reward or payment offered (usually by a government) to encourage something (e g to kill dangerous animals).

bou·quet /buˈkeɪ/ *n* [C] **1** bunch of flowers (to be) carried in the hand. **2** perfume of wine.

bour·bon /ˈbɜːbən/ *n* [U] kinds of whisky distilled from maize and rye.

bour·geois /ˈbʊəʒwɑ US: ˈbʊəˈʒwɑ/ *n* [C], *adj* **1** (person) of the class that owns property or engages in trade. **2** (person) concerned chiefly with material prosperity and social status.

bour·geosie /ˌbʊəʒwɑˈzi/ *n* [U] **the ~,** bourgeois(1) persons.

bourse /bʊəs/ *n* [C] foreign money-market (esp that of Paris).

bout /baʊt/ *n* [C] **1** period of exercise, work or other activity: *a ˈwrestling ~; a ~ of*

drinking. **2** fit (of illness): *a ~ of influenza.*

bou·tique /buˈtik/ *n* [C] small shop selling articles (clothes, cosmetics, hats, etc) of the latest fashion.

bov·ine /ˈbəʊvaɪn/ *adj* of, like, an ox.

bow¹ /bəʊ/ *n* [C] **1** piece of wood curved by a tight string, used for shooting arrows. **have two strings to one's bow,** have more than one plan, more resources than one. **2** rod of wood with horse-hair stretched from end to end, used for playing the violin, cello, etc. **3** curve; rainbow. **4** knot made with a loop or loops; ribbon, etc tied in this way: *She had a ~ of pink ribbon in her hair.* □ *vt* use a bow on (a violin, etc).

'bow ˈlegged *adj* with the legs curved outwards at the knees.

'bow ˈtie, one made into a bow.

bow² /baʊ/ *vi,vt* **1** bend the head or body (as a greeting, or in submission or respect, or to show agreement); bend (the head or body): *They ~ed their heads in prayer.* **bow to sb's opinion, etc,** submit to it. **2** bend: *The branches were ~ed down with the weight of the snow.* □ *n* [C] bending of the head or body (in greeting, etc): *He answered with a low ~.*

bow³ /baʊ/ *n* [C] **1** (often *pl*) front or forward end of a boat or ship from where it begins to curve. **2** (in a rowing-boat) oarsman nearest the bow. ⇨ **stroke**¹(3).

bowd·ler·ize /ˈbaʊdləraɪz/ *vt* take out of (a book, etc) words, scenes, etc that might be considered improper, unsuitable for young readers, etc.

bowel /ˈbaʊəl/ *n* **1** [C] (usually *pl*) division of the food canal below the stomach; intestine. **2** (always *pl*) innermost part: *in the ~s of the earth,* deep underground.

bowl¹ /bəʊl/ *n* [C] **1** deep, round, hollow dish: *a ˈsalad-/ˈsugar-~.* **2** contents of such a dish: *She ate three ~s of rice.* **3** thing shaped like a bowl: *the ~ of a spoon/pipe.*

bowl² /bəʊl/ *n* **1** [C] heavy, wooden or composition ball made so that it rolls with a bias. **2** (*pl*) game played with these balls: *have a game of ~s; play* (*at*) *~s.*

bowl³ /bəʊl/ *vi,vt* **1** send a ball to the batsman in cricket: *The first two batsmen were ~ed* (*out*), dismissed. **2 bowl along,** go quickly and smoothly on wheels: *Our car ~ed along over the smooth roads.* **3 bowl** (*sb*) *over,* (a) knock down. (b) make helpless, overcome: *He was ~ed over by the news.* **4** play bowls. ⇨ **bowl**²(2).

bowler¹ /ˈbəʊlə(r)/ *n* [C] **1** person who bowls in cricket. **2** person who plays bowls²(2).

bowler² /ˈbəʊlə(r)/ *n* [C] (also **¹~ ˈhat**) hard, rounded, usually black hat.

bowls *n* ⇨ **bowl**²(2).

bow win·dow /ˈbəʊ ˈwɪndəʊ/ *n* [C] curved bay window.

bow-wow /ˈbaʊ ˈwaʊ/ *int* imitation of a dog's bark. □ *n* /ˈbaʊ waʊ/ [C] (young child's word for a) dog.

box¹ /boks/ n [C] **1** container, usually with a lid, made of wood, cardboard, plastic, metal, etc used for holding solids: *a ~ of matches; a `tool-~.* **2** separate compartment, with seats for several persons, in a theatre, concert hall, etc. **3** compartment in a law court for a special purpose: *a `jury-~; a `witness-~.* **4** small hut or shelter, e g for a sentry or railway signalman. **5** separate compartment in a stable or railway truck for a horse. ⇨ also Christmas-box, letter-box, money-box, pillar-box. □ *vt* put into a box. *box up,* (a) shut up in a small space. (b) (*fig*) keep (a fear, problem, etc) to oneself (and suffer because of doing so).
`box-number, (a)` number used in a newspaper advertisement as an address to which answers may be sent (and forwarded from the newspaper office). (b) (*PO Box No.*) postal number used as an address.
`box-office,` office for booking seats in a cinema, etc.
`box-ful` /-fʊl/, full box¹(1) (*of* something).
box² /boks/ *vt, vi* fight with the fists, usually with thick gloves, for sport. *box sb's ears,* give him a blow with the open hand on the ears. □ *n* [C] slap or blow with the open hand (on the ear(s).
`boxing-glove,` padded glove for use in boxing.
`boxing-match,` fight between two boxers.
boxer /`boksə(r)/ n [C] **1** person who boxes. **2** breed of bulldog.
Box·ing Day /`boksɪŋ deɪ/ n first weekday after Christmas Day.
boy /bɔɪ/ n [C] **1** male child up to the age of 17 or 18. **2** son of any age: *He has two ~s and one girl.*
`boy-friend,` favoured male companion of a girl or young woman.
`boy-hood,` time when one is/was a boy.
'**Boy** `Scout,` member of an organization of boys intended to develop character and teach self-reliance, disipline and social awareness.
`boy-ish` *adj* of, for like, a boy.
boy·cott /`bɔɪkɒt/ *vt* (join with others and) refuse to have anything to do with, to trade with (a person, business firm, country, etc); refuse to handle (goods, etc). □ *n* [C] treatment, example, of this kind.
bra /bra/ n [C] (*informal*) (common abbr of) brassière.
brace¹ /breɪs/ n [C] **1** thing used to clasp, tighten or support, e g the roof or walls of a building. **2** revolving tool for holding another tool, e g a *bit* for boring holes, etc. **3** (*GB*) (*pl*) straps passing over the shoulders, used to keep trousers up. **4** (often *pl*) appliance of bands and wires fastened to the teeth to correct their alignment.
brace² /breɪs/ *vt, vi* **1** support; give firmness to: *The struts are firmly ~d.* **2** steady oneself; stand firm: *He ~d himself to meet the blow.*

brace·let /`breɪslət/ n [C] ornamental band or chain of metal etc, for the wrist or arm.
brac·ing /`breɪsɪŋ/ *adj* stimulating: *a ~ climate, ~ air.*
bracken /`brækən/ n [U] large fern that grows on hillsides/waste land, etc; mass of such fern.
bracket /`brækɪt/ n [C] **1** wood or metal support for a shelf, etc. **2** either of the two symbols {} used in writing and printing. **3** grouping; classification: an *`income ~,* e g of incomes of £1 000 to £1 500. □ *vt* put inside, join with, brackets; put together to imply connection or equality: *Jones and Smith were ~ed together at the top of the list.*
brack·ish /`brækɪʃ/ *adj* (of water) slightly salty.
bract /brækt/ n [C] leaf-like part of a plant, highly coloured, situated below a flower or cluster of flowers.
brad·awl /`brædɔl/ n [C] small tool for piercing holes for screws.
brag /bræg/ *vi* (-gg-) boast: *~ of what one has done.*
brag·gart /`brægət/ n [C] person who brags.
Brah·min /`brɑmɪn/ n member of the highest Hindu priestly caste.
braid /breɪd/ n **1** [C] number of strands of hair woven together: *She wears her hair in ~s.* **2** [U] silk, linen, etc woven into a band, used for edging or decorating cloth or garments: *gold/silver ~.* □ *vt* **1** make into braids. **2** trim with braid.
braille /breɪl/ n [U] system of writing and reading (using raised dots) for blind people, to enable them to read by touch.
brain /breɪn/ n [C] **1** (*sing*) (in man and animals) the mass of soft grey matter in the head, centre of the nervous system: *The human ~ is a complex organ.* **2** (as in 1 above, *informal* and usually *pl*): *I'll knock your ~s out if you do it again!* **3** (*pl*) animal's brain, eaten as food: *calf's/sheep's ~s.* **4** (*informal*) mind; intellect: *have a good ~; use your ~s.* **have sth** (e g money) **on the brain,** think constantly about it. **pick sb's brain(s),** learn and use his ideas. **5** [C] clever, brilliant person: *He's the ~ of the college.* □ *vt* kill by a heavy blow on the head.
`brain-child,` original idea, etc attributed to a person or group.
`brain drain,` movement of trained technical and scientific personnel from one country to another (because of better opportunities, etc).
`brain-storm, (a)` mental upset with uncontrolled emotion, e g weeping, and violence. (b) = brain-wave.
`brain-teaser,` difficult problem; puzzle.
`brain-washing,` process of forcing a person to reject old beliefs and accept new beliefs by use of extreme mental pressure.
`brain-wave,` (*informal*) sudden inspiration

or bright idea.

brain-less adj stupid.

brainy adj (-ier, -iest) intelligent.

braise /breɪz/ vt cook (meat) slowly, first in fat and then in a little water: ~d beef/ chicken.

brake /breɪk/ n [C] **1** device for reducing speed or stopping motion, e g of a bicycle, motor-vehicle, train, etc. **2** act as a brake on (progress, initiative, etc), try to prevent it; control it. □ vt,vi use the brake(1): The driver ~d suddenly.

bramble /ˈbræmbəl/ n [C,U] rough shrub with long prickly shoots; blackberry bush.

bran /bræn/ n [U] outer covering (husks) of grain (wheat, rye, etc) separated from flour by sifting.

branch /brɑːntʃ US: bræntʃ/ n [C] **1** part of a tree growing out from the trunk like an arm; smaller division growing from a bough: He climbed up the tree and hid among the ~es. **2** division or subdivision of a river, road, railway, mountain range, etc. **3** division or subdivision of a family, subject of knowledge, organization, etc: The bank has ~es in all parts of the country. □ vi send out, divide into, branches: The road ~es here. **branch off**, (of a car, road, train, etc) leave a main route and take a minor one. **branch out**, (of a person, business firm, etc) expand in a new direction, open new departments or lines of activity.

brand /brænd/ n [C] **1** trademark or trade-name; particular kind of goods with such a mark: an excellent ~ of coffee. **2** piece of burning wood (in a fire). **3** (also `~ing-iron`), iron used red-hot, for burning a design into a surface; mark made in this way. **4** (fig) mark of guilt or disgrace. □ vt **1** mark (cattle, goods, etc) with a branding-iron. **2** give (a person) a bad name: She has been ~ed as a thief.

'brand-'new adj completely new.

bran-dish /ˈbrændɪʃ/ vt wave about (to display, threaten, etc): ~ing a sword.

brandy /ˈbrændɪ/ n [C,U] (pl -ies) (portion of) strong alcoholic drink distilled from wine of grapes: Two brandies, please.

bran-new /ˈbræn ˈnjuː/ adj = brand-new.

brash /bræʃ/ adj (informal) **1** saucy; cheeky. **2** hasty; rash.

brass /brɑːs US: bræs/ n **1** [U] bright yellow metal made by mixing copper and zinc. **get down to brass tacks,** consider the essential facts only. **2** [U] or (pl) thing(s) made of brass, e g ornaments. **3** the ~, musical instruments made of brass. **4** [U] (GB sl) money. **5** [U] (sl) impudence. ⇨ brazen. **6** ⇨ top brass.

'top 'brass, (informal) senior officials, e g high-ranking officers in the armed forces.

'brass 'band, group of musicians with brass instruments.

brassy adj (a) like brass in colour or sound. (b) (sl) impudent.

brass-iere, brass-ière /ˈbræzɪə(r) US: brəˈzɪr/ n [C] (always shortened to **bra**) woman's close-fitting support for the breasts.

brat /bræt/ n [C] (badly behaved) child.

bra-vado /brəˈvɑːdəʊ/ n (pl ~es, ~s) **1** [U] display of boldness or daring: do something out of ~, in order to show one's courage. **2** [C] instance of this.

brave /breɪv/ adj (-r, -st) **1** ready to face danger, pain or suffering; having no fear: as ~ as a lion. **2** needing courage: a ~ act. □ n [C] Red-Indian warrior. □ vt face, go into, meet, without showing fear: He had ~d death a hundred times.

brave-ly adv

brav-ery /ˈbreɪvərɪ/ n [U] courage.

bravo /ˈbrɑːˈvəʊ/ int, n [C] (pl ~es, ~s) (cry of approval) Well done! Excellent!

brawl /brɔːl/ n [C] noisy quarrel or fight. □ vi quarrel noisily; take part in a brawl.

brawler, person who takes part in a brawl.

brawn /brɔːn/ n [U] **1** muscle; strength. **2** meat (esp pork) cut up, spiced and pickled, and compressed.

brawny adj muscular.

bray /breɪ/ n [C] **1** cry of an ass. **2** sound of, or like the sound of, a trumpet. □ vt make a cry or sound of this kind.

brazen /ˈbreɪzən/ adj **1** made of brass; like brass: a ~ (= hard-sounding) voice; the ~ notes of a trumpet. **2** (often `~-faced`) shameless.

braz-ier /ˈbreɪzɪə(r)/ n [C] portable open metal framework for holding a charcoal or coal fire.

breach /briːtʃ/ n [C] **1** breaking or neglect (of a rule, duty, agreement, etc): a ~ of the peace, unlawful fighting in a public place, e g the streets; a ~ of promise, (esp of a promise to marry). **2** opening, e g one made in a defensive wall, gap: The waves made a ~ in the sea wall. **step into/ fill the breach,** come forward to help. □ vt make a gap in, break through (a defensive wall, etc).

bread /bred/ n [U] **1** food made by mixing flour with water and yeast, kneading, and baking in an oven: a loaf/slice/piece of ~. **2** (sl) money.

bread and butter, (a) slice(s) of bread spread with butter. (b) (sl) means of living: earn one's ~ and butter by writing.

'bread-crumb, tiny bit of a loaf, esp for use in cooking.

'bread-board, wooden board on which bread is sliced.

'bread-fruit, tree with starchy fruit, grown in the South Sea Islands and W Africa.

'bread-knife, one of slicing bread.

'bread-line, line of people waiting for food given as charity or relief. **on the bread line,** very poor.

'bread-win-ner, person who works to support a family.

breadth /ˈbretθ/ n ⇨ broad¹(2) **1** distance or measure from side to side: *ten feet in* ∼. **2** largeness (of mind or view); boldness of effect (in music or art).
ˈbreadth-ways/-wise *adv* so that the broad side is in front.

break¹ /breɪk/ n **1** [C] breaking; broken place: *a* ∼ *in the water pipes*. **2** [U] ∼ *of day* (= *day*∼), dawn. **3** interval (in space of time): *a* ∼ *in the conversation; an hour's* ∼ *for lunch*. **without a break**, continuously: *He has been writing since 2 o'clock without a* ∼. **4** change, disturbance: *a* ∼ *in the weather*. **5** **give sb a break**, (*informal*) an opportunity (to make a new start or remedy an error). **a lucky break**, a piece of good fortune. **6** (= ∼*out*) (attempt to) escape (esp from prison). **make a break for it,** (try to) escape.

break² /breɪk/ vt,vi (*pl* broke /brəʊk/ pp broken /ˈbrəʊkən/) (For uses with *adverbial particles* and prepositions, ⇨ 11 below.) **1** (of a whole thing) (cause to) go or come into two or more separate parts as the result of force, a blow or strain (but not by cutting): *The boy fell from the tree and broke his leg. If you pull too hard you will* ∼ *the rope.* **2** (of a part or parts) (cause to) be separate or discontinuous because of force or strain: *He broke a branch from the tree.* **3** make (something) useless by injuring an essential part (of a machine, apparatus, etc): ∼ *a clock/toy.* **4** (uses with *adjectives*) **break even,** make neither a profit nor a loss. **break sth open**, get it open by using force. ∼ *open a safe/door/the lid of a box.* **5** (uses with various subjects): *The abscess/blister/ bubble broke,* burst. *Day was beginning to* ∼, daylight was beginning. ⇨ daybreak. *The storm broke,* began. *The fine weather/ The heat-wave/The frost broke,* The period of fine weather, etc ended. *The enemy broke* (= developed gaps in their lines, fell into confusion) *and fled.* **6** (uses with various objects): ∼ *the bank,* exhaust its funds, win all the money that the person managing a public gaming-table has; ∼ *fresh/new ground,* (*fig*) start work at something new; ∼ *a person's heart,* reduce him to despair; ∼ *a man,* ruin him; ∼ *the news,* make it known; ∼ *a* (*Commonwealth/Olympic/ World, etc*) *record,* do better than it; ∼ *a set of books/china, etc,* cause it to be incomplete by giving away or selling a part or parts of it; ∼ *step,* (of soldiers) stop marching rhythmically in step; ∼ *a strike,* end it by compelling the workers to return to work. **7** train or discipline: ∼ *a horse* (*in*), bring it to a disciplined state. **8** subdue, keep under, end by force: ∼ *a person's spirit/will.* **9** act in opposition to; infringe: ∼ *the law/the rules/a regulation;* ∼ *a contract/an agreement;* ∼ *one's word/a promise,* fail to keep a promise; ∼ *an appointment,* fail to keep it. **10** interrupt or destroy the continuity of; end the action or duration of: ∼ (*the*) *silence;* ∼ *one's journey; a broken night's sleep,* one that is disturbed or interrupted.

11 (uses with *adverbial particles* and prepositions):
break away (from), (a) go away suddenly or abruptly. (b) give up (habits, belief): *About twenty members of the Party have broken away.*
break down, (a) collapse: *Negotiations have broken down.* (b) become disabled or useless: *The car/engine/machinery broke down.* (c) suffer a physical or mental weakening: *His health broke down.* ⇨ breakdown. (d) be overcome by emotion, e g by bursting into tears: *She broke down when she heard the news.* **break sth down,** (a) get (a door, wall, etc) down by hitting it. (b) overthrow by force; suppress: ∼ *down all resistance/opposition.* (c) divide, analyse, classify (statistical material): ∼ *down expenditure,* give details of how money is spent.
break in, enter a building by force: *Burglars had broken in while we were away on holiday.* Hence, ˈbreak-in: *The police are investigating a* ∼*-in at the local bank.*
break in on/upon, disturb; interrupt: *Please don't* ∼ *in on our conversation.*
break into, (a) force one's way into (a building, etc): *His house was broken into* (i e by burglars or thieves) *last week.* (b) burst suddenly into: ∼ *into a song.* (c) change one's method of movement suddenly: ∼ *into a run.* (d) occupy, take up, undesirably: *Social duties* ∼ *into my time/leisure.* (e) (of coins and notes): ∼ *into a pound note,* use one to pay for something costing less than this sum.
break off, (a) stop speaking: *He broke off in the middle of a sentence.* (b) pause; stop temporarily: *Let's* ∼ *off for half an hour and have some tea.* **break (sth) off,** (a) (cause to) separate (a part of something): *The mast broke off/was broken off.* (b) end abruptly: ∼ *off diplomatic relations.*
break out, (of fire, disease, war, rioting, violence) appear, start, suddenly: *A fire broke out during the night.* ⇨ outbreak. **break out (of),** escape: *Several prisoners broke out of the gaol.* **break out in,** (a) suddenly become covered with: *His face broke out in spots.* (b) show sudden violence in speech or behaviour: *He broke out in a rage/in curses.*
break through, make a way through (an enclosure, obstacles, etc): *The enemy's defences were strong but our soldiers broke through. The sun broke through* (*the clouds*). ⇨ breakthrough.
break up, (a) come to pieces: *The ship was* ∼*ing up on the rocks. The gathering broke up in disorder.* (b) (*fig*) (of persons) mentally collapse; become weak: *He broke up under the strain.* (c) (of a school, etc) sepa-

rate at the end of term for holidays. (**d**) (of a couple, a relationship) come to an end: *Their marriage is* ∼*ing up.* (**e**) divide: *Sentences* ∼ *up into clauses.* **break sth up,** (**a**) smash; demolish: ∼ *up a box for firewood.* (**b**) (cause to) split, or divide: ∼ *up a piece of work* (*among several persons*). (**c**) (cause to) disperse: *The police broke up the crowd/meeting.* (**d**) bring to an end: *They broke up the alliance.* Hence, `**break-up** n (end of a marriage, coalition, etc).

break with, (**a**) end a friendship with: ∼ *with an old friend.* (**b**) give up; make an end of: ∼ *with old habits.*

break·able /ˈbreɪkəbəl/ *adj* easily broken.

break·age /ˈbreɪkɪdʒ/ *n* [C] **1** act of breaking. **2** place in, part of, something that has been broken. **3** (usually *pl*) broken articles; loss by breaking: *The hotel allows £150 a year for* ∼*s.*

break·down /ˈbreɪkdaʊn/ *n* [C] **1** failure in machinery: *A* ∼ *on the motorway caused a huge traffic-jam.* **2** collapse of physical or mental health: *He had a 'nervous '*∼*.* **3** analysis of statistics: *a* ∼ *of expenses.*

breaker /ˈbreɪkə(r)/ *n* [C] **1** large wave breaking into foam as it advances towards the shore; wave breaking against a rock, etc. **2** person or thing that breaks.

`**ice-breaker,** strongly built ship used to break up ice in harbours, etc.

break·fast /ˈbrekfəst/ *n* [C] first meal of the day. □ *vi* have breakfast.

break·neck /ˈbreknek/ *adj* **at (a) break-neck speed,** at a dangerously fast speed.

break·through /ˈbreɪkθruː/ *n* [C] **1** movement through or beyond the enemy's defenses. **2** major discovery or achievement in science, medicine, technology, etc.

break·water /ˈbreɪkwɔːtə(r)/ *n* [C] structure built out into the sea to shelter (part of) a harbour.

bream /briːm/ *n* [C] (*pl* unchanged) **1** freshwater fish of the carp family. **2** (also `**sea-**∼) salt-water variety of this.

breast /brest/ *n* [C] **1** either of the milk-producing parts of a woman's chest. **2** chest; upper front part of the human body, or of a garment covering this: *a troubled* ∼, a sad, anxious, etc feeling. **make a clean breast of sth,** confess. **3** part of an animal corresponding to the human breast. **4** (of a chimney) projection into the room for the fireplace, etc.

`**breast pocket,** small pocket in the breast of a jacket, etc.

`**breast-stroke,** stroke (in swimming) in which both the arms are brought at the same time from in front of the head to the sides of the body.

breath /breθ/ *n* **1** [U] air taken into and sent out of the lungs. **2** [C] single act of taking in and sending air out: *take a deep* ∼, fill the lungs with air. **catch/hold one's breath,** stop breathing for a moment (from fear,

excitement, etc). **in the same breath,** at the same moment: *They are not to be mentioned in the same* ∼, cannot be compared. **out of breath,** unable to breathe quickly enough. **take sb's breath away,** startle or surprise him. Hence, `**breath-taking** *adj* exciting; amazing. **waste one's breath,** talk in vain. **3** [C] air in movement; light breeze: *There wasn't a* ∼ *of air/wind,* the air was quite still. **4** [C] (*fig*) suggestion: *not a* ∼ *of suspicion/scandal.*

breath·less *adj* (**a**) out of breath; likely to cause a shortness of breath. (**b**) unstirred by wind: *a* ∼*less* (= calm) *evening.*

breath·less·ly *adv*

breath·alys·er /ˈbreθəlaɪzə(r)/ *n* [C] device (into which a person breathes) to test the alcoholic content of a person's breath.

breathe /briːð/ *vi,vt* **1** take air into the lungs and send it out again: ∼ *in/out. He's still breathing,* is still alive. **2** say quietly; send out, e g a scent, feeling: *Don't* ∼ *a word of this,* keep it secret.

breather, short pause for rest or excercise: *take/go for a* ∼*r.*

breath·ing /ˈbriːðɪŋ/ *n* [U] **1** act of one who breathes; single breath. **2** use of an *h*-sound.

`**breath·ing space,** time to pause, rest.

bred /bred/ *pt,pp* of breed.

breech /briːtʃ/ *n* [C] back part of a rifle or gun barrel, where the cartridge or shell is placed.

breeches /ˈbrɪtʃɪz/ *n pl* (also *a pair of* ∼) garment fitting round the waist and below the knees. ⇨ *riding-breeches.*

breed /briːd/ *vt,vi* (*pt,pp* bred /bred/) **1** keep (animals, etc) for the purpose of producing young, esp by selection of parents: ∼ *horses/cattle.* **2** give birth to young; reproduce: *Rabbits* ∼ *quickly.* **3** train, educate, bring up: *a well-bred boy,* one who has been trained to behave well. **4** be the cause of: *Dirt* ∼*s disease.* □ *n* [C] kind or variety (of animals, etc) with hereditary qualities: *a good* ∼ *of cattle.*

breeder, person who breeds animals.

breed·ing *n* [U] (**a**) (in verbal senses): *the* ∼*ing of horses; the* ∼*ing season for birds.* (**b**) knowledge of how to behave resulting from upbringing: *a man of good* ∼*ing.*

breeze /briːz/ *n* [C,U] wind, esp a gentle wind. □ *vi* **breeze in/out,** (*informal*) come in/go out happily, or unexpectedly.

breez·ily *adv*

breezi·ness *n* [U]

breezy *adj* (**a**) pleasantly windy: *breezy weather.* (**b**) (of persons) lively: good-humoured.

breth·ren /ˈbreðrɪn/ *n pl* (*old use*) brothers.

breve /briːv/ *n* musical [C] note equal to two semibreves.

brev·ity /ˈbrevətɪ/ *n* [U] shortness (of statements, human life and other non-material things).

brew /bruː/ *vt,vi* **1** prepare (beer, tea, etc). **2**

(*fig*) bring about; gather, be forming: *A storm is* ∼*ing*, gathering force. *There's trouble* ∼*ing between them*, They are likely to quarrel. □ *n* [C] result of brewing: *a good, strong* ∼ (*of tea*).

brew·ery, place where beer is brewed.

briar /ˈbraɪə(r)/ *n* **1** [U] hard wood (root of a bush) used esp for making tobacco pipes. **2** [C] pipe made of this wood. **3** [C] thorny bush, esp the wild rose.

bribe /braɪb/ *n* [C] something given, offered or promised in order to influence or persuade a person (often to do something wrong): *offer/take* ∼*s*. □ *vt* offer, give, a bribe to: ∼ *a judge/witness*.

bri·bery, giving or taking of bribes.

bric-a-brac /ˈbrɪk ə bræk/ *n* [U] bits of old furniture, china, ornaments, etc esp of no great value.

brick /brɪk/ *n* **1** [C,U] (usually rectangular block of) clay moulded and baked by fire or sun, used for building purposes. *drop a brick*, (*informal*) do or say something indiscreet. **2** child's rectangular block used for building toy houses, etc. **3** rectangular block, e g of ice-cream. □ *vt* **brick up/in**, block (an opening) with bricks.

brick·layer, workman who builds with bricks.

brick·work, (part of a) structure made of bricks.

bri·dal /ˈbraɪdəl/ *adj* of a bride or wedding.

bride /braɪd/ *n* [C] woman on her wedding-day; newly married woman.

bride·groom /ˈbraɪdgrum/ *n* [C] man on his wedding-day; newly married man.

brides·maid /ˈbraɪdzmeɪd/ *n* [C] girl or young unmarried woman attending a bride at her wedding. ⇨ best man.

bridge¹ /brɪdʒ/ *n* [C] **1** structure of wood, stone, brickwork, steel, concrete, etc providing a way across a river, canal, railway, etc. **2** platform over and across the deck of a ship for the use of the captain and officers. **3** upper, bony part of the nose. **4** movable part over which the strings of a violin, etc are stretched. □ *vt* join by means of a bridge.

bridging loan, loan (esp from a bank) to cover a period of time, e g between the purchase of one house and the sale of another.

bridge² /brɪdʒ/ *n* [U] card-game in which two players (partners) play to win a certain number of tricks against another two players acting as defenders.

bridle /ˈbraɪdəl/ *n* [C] that part of a horse's harness that goes on its head, including the metal bit for the mouth, the straps and the reins. □ *vt,vi* **1** put a bridle on (a horse). **2** (*fig*) control, check: *Try to* ∼ *your passions*. **3** showing pride, contempt, vanity, etc: ∼ *at her remarks*.

brief¹ /brif/ *adj* (-er, -est) (of time, events, writing, speaking) lasting only for a short time. *in brief*, in a few words.

brief·ly *adv*

brief² /brif/ *n* **1** [C] summary of the facts of a case, drawn up for a barrister. *hold a/no brief for (sb)*, argue in support/not be prepared to support. **2** information, instructions, advice, etc given in advance, e g to an aircraft crew before a combat mission. **3** instructions: *My* ∼ *did not include the buying of new materials*. □ *vt* **1** instruct or employ (a barrister). **2** give a brief(2) to. ⇨ debrief. **3** summarize the facts, e g of a business programme.

brief·case, flat leather or plastic case, for documents, etc.

briefs /brifs/ *n pl* (also *a pair of* ∼) woman's pants without legs, held in position by an elastic waistband.

brier /ˈbraɪə(r)/ *n* [C] = briar(3).

brig·ade /brɪˈɡeɪd/ *n* [C] **1** army unit, usually of three battalions, forming part of an army division; corresponding armoured unit. **2** organized body of persons in uniform with special duties: *the* ˈfire-∼.

briga·dier /ˌbrɪɡəˈdɪə(r)/ *n* [C] officer commanding a brigade(1).

brig·and /ˈbrɪɡənd/ *n* [C] member of a band of robbers, esp one that attacks travellers in forests or mountains.

bright /braɪt/ *adj* (-er, -est) **1** giving out or reflecting much light; shining: *Sunshine is* ∼. *The leaves on the trees are* ∼ *green in spring*. **2** cheerful and happy; lit up with joy or hope: ∼ *faces*; *a* ∼ *smile*. **3** clever: *A* ∼ *boy learns quickly*. □ *adv* (usually with *shine*) = brightly.

brighten /-tən/ *vt,vi* make or become brighter, lighter or more cheerful, etc: *These flowers* ∼*en up the classroom*.

bright·ly *adv*

bright·ness *n* [C]

bril·liance /ˈbrɪliəns/ *n* [U] **1** radiance, splendour. **2** intelligence.

bril·liant /ˈbrɪliənt/ *adj* **1** sparkling; very bright(1): *a week of* ∼ *sunshine*. **2** very clever: *a* ∼ *scientist*.

bril·liant·ly *adv*

brim /brɪm/ *n* [C] **1** edge of a cup, bowl, glass, etc: *full to the* ∼. **2** out-turned part (rim) of a hat. □ *vi* (-mm-) **brim over**, (a) be so full that some spills over the top. (b) (*fig*) = overflow(2).

brine /braɪn/ *n* [U] salt water, esp for pickling food.

bring /brɪŋ/ *vt* (*pt,pp* brought /brɔt/) (For uses with *adverbial particles* and *prepositions*, ⇨ 5 below.) **1** cause to come towards the speaker, writer, etc carrying something or accompanying somebody: *Take this empty box away and* ∼ *me a full one*. **2** cause to come; produce: *Spring* ∼*s warm weather and flowers*. *The sad news brought tears to her eyes*. **3** **bring sb/oneself to do sth**, persuade, induce, lead: *She couldn't* ∼ *herself to speak about the matter*. **4** (*legal*) start, put forward: ∼ *an action against her*. **5** (uses with *adverbial particles* and *preposi-*

tions):

bring about, (a) cause to happen: ~ about a war/reforms. **(b)** (naut) cause (a sailing-ship) to change direction: The helmsman brought us about.

bring back, (a) return: Please ~ back the book tomorrow. **(b)** call to mind; cause to remember: Seeing you brought back many memories. **(c)** restore; reintroduce: ~ back hanging.

bring down, (esp) (a) cause to fall; cause to be down: ~ down a hostile aircraft, shoot it down; ~ down prices, lower them; ~ down a government, force an election. **(b)** kill or wound: He aimed, fired and brought down the antelope.

bring forward, (a) cause to be seen, discussed, etc: Please ~ the matter forward at the next meeting. **(b)** advance: The meeting has been brought forward from May 10 to May 3, is to be a week earlier. ⇨ post-pone. **(c)** (abbr = b/f) (book-keeping) carry the total of a column of figures at the foot of one page to the top of the next page.

bring in, (a) produce as profit: He does odd jobs that ~ him in ten to twelve pounds a month. **(b)** introduce: ~ in a new fashion. **(c)** introduce (legislation): ~ in a Bill on road safety. **(d)** admit (as a partner, adviser, etc): They've brought in experts to advise on the scheme. **(e)** (of the police) arrest or bring to a police station for questioning, etc: Two suspicious characters were brought in. **(f)** (of a jury) pronounce (a verdict): ~ in a ver-dict of guilty.

bring off, (esp) manage to do something successfully: It was a difficult task but we brought it off.

bring on, lead to, (help to) produce: He was out all day in the rain and this brought on a bad cold.

bring out, (a) cause to appear, show clearly: ~ out the meaning of a passage of prose. **(b)** publish (a book, etc): When are the publishers ~ing out his new book? **(c)** call forth (a quality): Danger ~s out the best in him. **(d)** cause to strike: The shop-stewards brought out the miners.

bring round, (a) cause (sb) to regain con-sciousness after fainting. **(b)** convert to one's views, etc: He wasn't keen on the plan, but we managed to ~ him round.

bring to, = bring round(a).

bring under, (a) subdue; discipline: The rebels were quickly brought under. **(b)** include (within a category): The various points to be dealt with can be brought under three main headings.

bring up, (a) educate; rear: She has brought up five children. **(b)** vomit: ~ up one's din-ner. **(c)** call attention to: These are matters that you can ~ up in committee.

brink /brɪŋk/ n [C] 1 upper edge of a steep place, a sharp slope, etc; border (of water, esp when deep): He stood shivering on the ~, hesitating to plunge into the water. 2 (fig) edge of something unknown, danger-ous or exciting: on the ~ of war/an exciting discovery.

brisk /brɪsk/ adj (-er, -est) (of persons and movement) active; lively; quick-moving: a ~ walk. Trade is ~.
brisk·ly adv

bristle /ˈbrɪsəl/ n [C] one of the short stiff hairs on an animal; one of the short stiff hairs in a brush: a toothbrush with stiff ~s. □ vi 1 (of hair) stand up, rise on end: The dog was angry and ~d up/its hair ~d. 2 (fig) show anger, indignation, etc: ~ with anger.

Brit·ish /ˈbrɪtɪʃ/ adj 1 of the ancient Britons. 2 of Great Britain, the British Common-wealth or its inhabitants: the ~, British people; ~ citizenship; a Jamaican with a ~ passport.

brittle /ˈbrɪtəl/ adj 1 hard but easily broken (eg coal, ice, glass). 2 (fig): He has a ~ temper, quickly loses his temper.

broach /brəʊtʃ/ vt (fig) begin a discussion of (a topic).

broad¹ /brɔːd/ adj (-er, -est) 1 wide: The river grows ~er as it nears the sea. 2 (after a phrase showing width) from side to side: a river fifty feet ~. 3 full and complete. in broad daylight, when it is unmistakably light: a bank raid in ~ daylight. 4 general, not small or detailed: a ~ distinction. in broad outline, a general impression, with-out details. it's as broad as it is long, it's all the same, however you look at the prob-lem. 5 (of the mind and ideas) liberal; not kept within narrow limits: a man of ~ views, a tolerant man. 6 (of speech) with a strong accent, showing that the speaker is from a definite part of the country.
ˈbroad bean, a common variety growing in large pods.
ˈbroad-ˈminded adj willing to listen sym-pathetically to the views of others even though one cannot agree with them; having a liberal and tolerant mind.
broad·ly adv. ~ly speaking, speaking in a general way, without going into detail.

broad² /brɔːd/ n [C] the wide part: the ~ of the back.

broad·cast /ˈbrɔːdkɑːst/ US: -kæst/ vt,vi (pt,pp ~) send out (speech, music, etc) in all directions, esp by radio or TV: ~ the news/a speech/a concert. □ n [C] something broadcast: a ~ of a football match.

broad·side /ˈbrɔːdsaɪd/ n [C] 1 the whole of a ship's side above the water; (the firing on the same target of) all the guns on one side of a ship. 2 (fig) strong attack of any kind made at one time against one person or group.

broad·ways, broad·wise /ˈbrɔːdweɪz, -waɪz/ adv in the direction of the breadth.

bro·cade /brəˈkeɪd/ n [C,U] woven material richly ornamented with designs (eg in raised gold or silver thread). □ vt decorate (cloth) with raised patterns.

broc·coli /ˈbrokəlɪ/ n [C,U] (pl unchanged) hardy kind of cauliflower with numerous white or purple sprouts (flower-heads), each like a small cauliflower.

bro·chure /ˈbrəʊʃʊə(r) US: brəʊˈʃʊər/ n [C] short, usually illustrated, pamphlet, esp as an advertisement: travel/holiday ∼s.

brogue¹ /brəʊg/ n [C] strong, thick-soled shoe for country wear.

brogue² /brəʊg/ n [C] provincial way of speaking, esp the Irish way of speaking English.

broil¹ /brɔɪl/ vt,vi 1 cook, be cooked, by direct contact with fire; grill. 2 (fig) be very hot: sit ∼ing in the sun.

broke /brəʊk/ pt of break. **(stony/flat) broke,** (sl) penniless.

bro·ken /ˈbrəʊkən/ pp of break: a ∼ marriage, one that has failed; a ∼ home, one in which the parents have separated or are divorced; ∼ (= imperfect) English; ∼ (= disturbed) sleep.

'broken-'hearted, filled with grief.

bro·ker /ˈbrəʊkə(r)/ n [C] (usually `stock-∼`) person who buys and sells (business shares, etc) for others.

brolly /ˈbrolɪ/ n [C] (pl -ies) (informal) umbrella.

bron·chi /ˈbroŋkaɪ/ n pl (sing bronchus) two main branches into which the windpipe divides before entering the lungs, also called bronchial tubes.

bron·chial /ˈbroŋkɪəl/ adj of or affecting the bronchi: bronchial asthma.

bron·chi·tis /broŋˈkaɪtɪs/ n [C] inflammation of the bronchi.

bronze /bronz/ n 1 [U] alloy of copper and tin: a ∼ statue. 2 [U] reddish brown colour. 3 [C] work of art made of bronze: Benin ∼. □ vt,vi make or become bronze in colour: faces ∼d by the sun and wind.

the `Bronze Age,` period when men used tools and weapons made of bronze (between the Stone Age and the Iron Age).

brooch /brəʊtʃ/ n [C] ornamental pin for fastening or wearing on part of a woman's dress.

brood /bruːd/ n [C] 1 all the young birds hatched at one time in a nest. 2 (humorous) family of children. □ vi 1 (of a bird) sit on eggs to hatch them. 2 (fig) think about (troubles, etc) for a long time: ∼ing over/on his misfortunes.

broody /ˈbruːdɪ/ adj 1 (of hens) wanting to brood(1). 2 (informal) (of women) feeling the desire to have children.

brook¹ /brʊk/ n [C] small stream.

brook² /brʊk/ vt put up with; tolerate: He cannot ∼ interference. (Note: Usually used in the negative or in questions.)

broom /bruːm/ n [C] 1 long-handled implement for sweeping floors, etc. 2 shrub with yellow or white flowers growing on sandy banks, etc.

broth /broθ/ n [U] water in which meat has been boiled (flavoured and thickened with vegetables, etc, served as soup).

brothel /ˈbroθəl/ n [C] house at which prostitutes may be visited.

brother /ˈbrʌðə(r)/ n [C] 1 son of the same parents as another person. 2 person united to others by membership of the same society, profession, etc: ∼ officers, in the same regiment. 3 fellow member of a socialist organization, trade union, etc. 4 (pl = brethren /ˈbreðrən/) fellow member of a religious society.

`brother·hood,` (a) [U] feeling (as) of brother for brother. (b) [C] (members of an) association of men with common interests and aims, esp a religious society or socialist organization.

`brother-in-law` /ˈbrʌðər ɪn lɔː/ n [C] (pl ∼s-in-law) brother of one's husband or wife; husband of one's sister.

`brother·ly` adj: ∼ly affection.

brought /brɔːt/ pt,pp of bring.

brow /braʊ/ n 1 (usually pl; also `eye-brow`) arch of hair above the eye. 2 forehead. ⇨ highbrow, lowbrow 3 top of a slope; steep slope: the ∼ of a hill

brow·beat /ˈbraʊbiːt/ vt (pt ∼, pp ∼en /-bitən/) bully: a ∼en little woman.

brown /braʊn/ n adj (-er, -est) (having the) colour of toasted bread, or coffee mixed with milk. □ vt,vi make or become brown. **`browned `off,`** (sl) bored; fed up.

browse /braʊz/ vi 1 feed, as animals do (on grass, etc): cattle browsing in the fields. 2 read (parts of a book, newspaper) without any definite plan, for interest or enjoyment: browsing among books in the public library. □ n (act, period, of) browsing: have a good ∼.

bruise /bruːz/ n [C] injury by a blow or knock to the body, or to a fruit, so that the skin is discoloured but not broken: He was covered with ∼s after falling off his bicycle. □ vt,vi 1 cause a bruise to: Pack the peaches carefully so that they won't get ∼d. 2 show the effects of a blow or knock: A child's flesh ∼s easily.

brunch /brʌntʃ/ n [C] late morning meal instead of breakfast and lunch.

bru·nette /bruːˈnet/ n [C] woman (of one of the white races) with dark skin and dark-brown or black hair.

brunt /brʌnt/ n [C] chief stress or strain: bear the ∼ of an attack.

brush¹ /brʌʃ/ n [C] 1 implement of bristles, hair, wire, etc fastened in wood, plastic, or other material, used for scrubbing, sweeping, cleaning (e g `tooth-∼`, `nail-∼`), or tidying the hair (`hair∼`); tuft of hair, etc set in a handle, used by painters and artists: a `paint-∼`. 2 (act of) using a brush: He gave his clothes a good ∼. 3 [U] rough low-growing bushes; undergrowth: a ∼ fire. ⇨ bush(2). 4 short, sharp fight or encounter: a

~ *with the enemy.*

brush² /brʌʃ/ *vt,vi* **1** use a brush on; clean, polish, make tidy or smooth: ~ *your hat/ clothes/shoes/hair/teeth.* **2 brush off,** come off as the result of being brushed: *The mud will* ~ *off when it dries.* **brush sth away/ off,** remove with a brush, one's hand, etc: *He* ~*ed away a fly from his nose.* **brush sth aside/away,** (*fig*) pay no or little attention to (difficulties, objections, etc). **brush up (on),** study or practise in order to get back skill that has been lost: *If you're going to France you'd better* ~ *up* (*on*) *your French.* **3** touch when passing: *He* ~*ed past/by/ against me in a rude way.*

brusque /brusk/ *adj* (of speech or behaviour) rough and abrupt.
brusque·ly *adv*
brusque·ness *n* [U]

Brus·sels sprout /ˈbrʌsəlz ˈspraʊt/ *n* [C] green vegetable with buds growing thickly on the stem; one of the buds.

bru·tal /ˈbruːtəl/ *adj* savage; cruel.
bru·tally *adv*
bru·tal·ity /bruˈtæləti/, (**a**) [U] cruelty; savagery. (**b**) [C] cruel or savage act.

brute /bruːt/ *n* [C] **1** animal (except man). **2** stupid, savage or cruel person. □ *adj* **1** cruel, savage. **2** unthinking and physical: ~ *strength.*
brut·ish /ˈbruːtɪʃ/ *adj* of or like a brute: ~ *appetites.*
brut·ish·ly *adv*

bubble /ˈbʌbl/ *n* [C] **1** (in air) floating ball formed of liquid and containing air or gas: `*soap* ~*s.* **2** (in liquid) ball of air or gas that rises to the surface, e g in boiling water, in sparkling wine. **3** air-filled cavity in a solidified liquid, e g glass. □ *vi* send up, rise in, make the sound of, bubbles: *She was bubbling over with joy/laughter.*
`**bubble–gum,** chewing-gum which can be blown into bubbles.
bub·bly /ˈbʌblɪ/ *adj* full of bubbles. □ *n* [U] (*informal*) champagne.

buc·ca·neer /ˌbʌkəˈnɪə(r)/ *n* [C] pirate.

buck¹ /bʌk/ *n* [C] male of a deer, hare or rabbit. ⇨ **doe.**

buck² /bʌk/ *vi,vt* **1** (of a horse) jump up with the four feet together and the back arched; throw (the rider) to the ground by doing this. **2** (*informal*) make haste; make or become more energetic or cheerful: *The good news* ~*ed us all up.*

buck³ /bʌk/ *n* [C] (*sl*) US dollar.

buck⁴ /bʌk/ *n pass the buck (to sb),* (*sl*) shift the responsibility (to).

bucket /ˈbʌkɪt/ *n* [C] **1** vessel of wood, plastic, etc for holding or carrying water, etc. **2** (also `**bucket·ful**) the amount a bucket holds.

buckle /ˈbʌkəl/ *n* [C] metal, plastic, etc fastener, with one or more spikes made to go through a hole in a belt, etc □ *vt,vi* **1** fasten, be fastened with a buckle: ~ *a belt;* ~ *on a*

sword. **2 buckle to/down to** (*work, etc*), begin (work) in earnest: *The sooner he* ~*s down to it, the better.* **3** (of metal work, etc) bend, become twisted, etc from strain or heat.

bud /bʌd/ *n* [C] leaf, flower or branch, at the beginning of its growth. *in bud,* having buds or sending out buds: *The trees are in* ~. *nip sth in the bud,* put an end to, e g a plot, while it is in the beginning stage. □ *vi* (**-dd-**) put out buds.
bud·ding *adj* beginning to develop: *a* ~ *lawyer/poet.*

Bud·dhism /ˈbʊdɪzm/ *n* the religion founded by Gautama /ˈɡaʊtəmə/ or Siddartha /sɪˈdɑːtə/ Buddha /ˈbʊdə/ (teacher) in N India, in about the 6th century.
Bud·dhist /ˈbʊdɪst/ *n* [C] follower of Buddha. □ *adj* of Buddhism.

buddy /ˈbʌdɪ/ *n* [C] (*pl* -ies) (*sl*) pal; mate.

budge /bʌdʒ/ *vt,vi* (usually in the *negative* and with *can, could* or with *won't, wouldn't*) **1** (cause to) move very little, make the slightest movement. **2** (*fig*) (cause to) change a position or attitude: *It won't* ~ *an inch.*

bud·geri·gar /ˈbʌdʒərɪɡɑː(r)/ *n* [C] Australian kind of small parakeet.

budget /ˈbʌdʒɪt/ *n* [C] **1** estimate of probable future income and expenditure, esp that made by the Chancellor of the Exchequer in the House of Commons. **2** similar estimate made by a business company, society, private person, etc. □ *vi* **budget for,** allow or arrange for: ~ *for the coming year.*

buff /bʌf/ *n* [U] **1** thick, strong, soft leather. **2** dull yellow colour. *stripped to the* ~, naked. □ *vt* polish (metal) with a buff.

buf·falo /ˈbʌfələʊ/ *n* [C] (*pl* ~s) **1** kinds of ox in India, Asia, Europe and Africa. **2** (used incorrectly for) N American bison.

buf·fer /ˈbʌfə(r)/ *n* [C] apparatus for lessening the effect of a blow or collision, e g on a railway engine or van.

buf·fet¹ /ˈbʊfeɪ *US*: bəˈfeɪ/ *n* [C] **1** counter where food and drink may be bought and consumed, e g in a railway station or on a train. **2** sideboard or table from which (usually cold) food is served, e g in a hotel.

buf·fet² /ˈbʌfɪt/ *n* [C] blow, generally one given with the hand. □ *vt,vi* give a blow to: *flowers* ~*ed by rain and wind.*

buf·foon /bəˈfuːn *US*: bʌˈfuːn/ *n* [C] clown; fool.

bug /bʌɡ/ *n* [C] **1** small, flat, ill-smelling, blood-sucking insect that infests dirty houses and beds. **2** (esp US) any small insect. **3** (*informal*) germ; virus infection: *You've got the Asian 'flu* ~. **4** (*sl*) defect, snag, e g in a computer **5** small hidden microphone (for listening to conversations, etc). **6** (*modern informal*) addiction: *She's always in the library; she really has got the* ~*!* □ *vt* (**-gg-**) **1** (*informal*) use electronic devices (in a room, etc) in order to listen secretly to conversations. **2** (*sl*) annoy: *That* *man really ∼s me.*

bug·bear /'bʌgbeə(r)/ *n* [C] thing feared or disliked, with or without good reason: *the ∼ of rising prices.*

bugle /'bju:gəl/ *n* [C] musical wind-instrument of copper or brass (like a small trumpet but without keys or valves), used for military signals.

bugler, person who plays a bugle.

build¹ /bɪld/ *vt,vi* (*pt,pp* built /bɪlt/) **1** make by putting parts, materials, etc together: *∼ a house/railway.* **2** put parts together to form a whole: *He has built these scraps of metal into a very strange-looking sculpture.* **3** base (hopes, etc) on; rely on: *Don't ∼ too many hopes on his helping us.* **4** *build up,* (**a**) accumulate; form a block: *Traffic is ∼ing up* (= The number of vehicles is increasing steadily) *along the roads to the coast.* (**b**) come or build together (so as to increase or intensify): *Their pressure on the enemy is ∼ing up.* *build sb/sth up,* (**a**) try to increase a person's, an institution's reputation (through publicity, praise): *Don't ∼ me up too much; I may disappoint you.* (**b**) make, acquire, steadily and gradually: *He has built up a good business.* (**c**) become covered with buildings: *The district has been built up since I was last there.*

`**build-up,** (**a**) increase: *a ∼-up of forces/pressure.* (**b**) accumulation: *a ∼-up of traffic.* (**c**) flattering publicity, etc: *The press gave him a tremendous ∼-up.*

builder, person who builds, esp houses. (**b**) (*fig*) person who builds up(b): *a great* `*empire ∼er,* person who controls many businesses, etc.

build² /bɪld/ *n* [U] general shape or structure; (of the human body) general characteristics of shape and proportion: *a man of powerful ∼.*

build·ing /'bɪldɪŋ/ *n* **1** [C] house or other structure: *Houses, schools, churches, factories and sheds are all ∼s.* **2** [U] (art of) constructing houses, etc: *∼ materials.*

`**building-society,** organization for making loans with interest to members who wish to build or buy a house, using funds supplied by its members.

bulb /bʌlb/ *n* [C] **1** almost round, thick, underground part of a plant sending roots downwards and leaves upwards. **2** thing like a bulb in shape, e g the swollen end of a glass tube, e g in a thermometer. **3** glass case for an electric light.

bul·bous /'bʌlbəs/ *adj* of, having, like, growing from, a bulb.

bulge /bʌldʒ/ *n* [C] **1** irregular swelling; place where a swelling or curve shows. **2** temporary increase in volume or numbers. □ *vi,vt* (cause to) swell beyond the usual size; curve outwards: *His pockets were bulging with apples.*

bulk /bʌlk/ *n* [U] quantity, volume, esp when large. *in bulk.* (**a**) in large amounts: *buy in ∼.* (**b**) loose, not packed in boxes, tins, etc. *the bulk of,* the greater part or number of: *He left the ∼ of his property to his brother.* □ *vi* appear large or important.

bulky *adj* (-ier, -iest) taking up much space; clumsy to move or carry.

bulk·head /'bʌlkhed/ *n* [C] water-tight or air-tight division or partition in a ship or tunnel, spacecraft, etc.

bull¹ /bʊl/ *n* [C] **1** uncastrated male of any animal of the ox family (⇨ cow): *a man with a neck like a ∼,* with a thick neck. *a bull in a china shop,* person who is rough and clumsy where skill and care are needed. *take the bull by the horns,* meet a difficulty boldly instead of trying to escape from it. **2** male of the whale, elephant and other large animals.

`**bull-dog,** large, powerful breed of dog, with a short, thick neck, noted for its strong grip and its courage.

`**bull-doze** *vt* (**a**) remove earth, flatten obstacles, with a bull-dozer. (**b**) force a person into doing something by using physical strength or by intimidating him.

bull-dozer, powerful tractor with a broad steel blade in front, used for shifting large quantities of earth, etc.

`**bull-finch,** small songbird with a rounded beak and coloured feathers

`**bull-frog,** large American species of frog.

'**bull-'headed** *adj* clumsy, impetuous, obstinate.

`**bull's-eye,** centre of target (for archers, gunners, etc).

'**bull-'terrier,** cross between a bulldog and a terrier.

bull² /bʊl/ *n* [C] official order from the Pope.

bul·let /'bʊlɪt/ *n* [C] shaped piece of lead, usually coated with another metal, (to be) fired from a rifle or revolver. (*Note: shells* are fired from guns.)

`**bullet-proof** *adj* able to stop bullets: *a ∼-proof jacket.*

bul·letin /'bʊlətɪn/ *n* [C] **1** official statement of news: *The doctors issued ∼s twice a day.* **2** printed sheet of paper with official news or announcements.

bul·lion /'bʊlɪən/ *n* [U] gold or silver in bulk or bars.

bul·lock /'bʊlək/ *n* [C] castrated bull.

bully¹ /'bʊlɪ/ *n* [C] (*pl* -ies) person who uses his strength or power to frighten or hurt those who are weaker. □ *vt* (*pt,pp* -ied) use strength, etc in this way.

bul·rush /'bʊlrʌʃ/ *n* [C] (kinds of) tall rush or reed with a thick head.

bul·wark /'bʊlwək/ *n* [C] **1** wall, esp one built of earth, against attack. **2** (*fig*) thing that defends or protects: *Law is the ∼ of society,* gives us security. **3** (usually *pl*) wall round (esp a sailing) ship's deck.

bum¹ /bʌm/ *n* [C] (*informal*) part of the

body on which one sits; buttocks.

bum² /bʌm/ n [C] (sl) habitual beggar or lazy person. □ vi (-mm-) **bum around,** wander about doing nothing.

bumble·bee /ˈbʌmbəl biː/ n [C] large kind of hairy bee.

bump /bʌmp/ vt,vi 1 come into contract with a blow or knock: *The room was dark and I ∼ed (my head) against the door. The blind man ∼ed into me.* 2 move with a jerky, jolting motion (like a cart on a bad road): *The heavy bus ∼ed along the rough mountain road.* 3 **bump sb off,** (sl) murder him. □ adv suddenly; violently: *Our bus ran ∼ into the wall.* □ n [C] 1 blow or knock; dull sound made by a blow (as when two things come together with force). 2 swelling on the body as caused by such a blow. 3 irregularity on a road surface. 4 (jolt felt in an aircraft, caused by a) sudden change in air-pressure.

bumpy adj (-ier, -iest) with many bumps: *a ∼y road/ride.*

bum·per¹ /ˈbʌmpə(r)/ n [C] steel bar on a bus, motor-vehicle (front and rear) to lessen the effect of a collision; fender (on the side of a boat or ship).

bum·per² /ˈbʌmpə(r)/ adj unusually large or abundant: *a ∼ harvest.*

bump·kin /ˈbʌmpkɪn/ n [C] awkward person with unpolished manners, esp from the country.

bump·tious /ˈbʌmpʃəs/ adj conceited: *∼ officials.*

bun /bʌn/ n [C] 1 small round, sweet cake. 2 twisted knot of hair above the back of the neck.

bunch /bʌntʃ/ n [C] 1 numbers of small, similar things naturally growing together: *a ∼ of grapes/bananas.* 2 collection of things of the same sort placed or fastened together: *a ∼ of flowers/keys.* □ vt,vi **bunch up,** form into a bunch.

bundle /ˈbʌndəl/ n [C] number of things fastened, tied or wrapped together: *The books were tied up in ∼s of twenty.* □ vt,vi 1 **bundle up,** make into a bundle. 2 put together or away in a confused heap; *We ∼d everything into a drawer.* 3 send or go in a hurry: *They ∼d him into a taxi.*

bung /bʌŋ/ n [C] large (usually rubber, cork or plastic) stopper for closing a hole in a cask or barrel. □ vt put a bung into. **bunged up,** (a) (of the nose) stopped up with mucus. (b) (of drains) clogged with dirt.

bun·ga·low /ˈbʌŋɡələʊ/ n [C] small house with only one storey.

bungle /ˈbʌŋɡəl/ vt,vi do (a piece of work) badly and clumsily; spoil (a task, etc) by lack of skill.

bun·ion /ˈbʌnɪən/ n [C] inflamed swelling, esp on the large joint of the big toe.

bunk¹ /bʌŋk/ n [C] 1 narrow bed fixed on the wall, e g in a ship. 2 one of two narrow beds built one above the other, usually for children.

bunk² /bʌŋk/ n **do a bunk,** (sl) run away.

bunker /ˈbʌŋkə(r)/ n [C] 1 that part of a ship where coal or fuel oil is stored. 2 sandy hollow, made as an obstacle, on a golf-course. 3 (mil) underground shelter, fortified point, of steel and concrete. □ vt,vi fill a ship's bunkers with fuel.

bunny /ˈbʌnɪ/ n [C] (pl -ies) (child's word for a) rabbit.

buoy /bɔɪ/ n [C] 1 floating object, anchored to the bottom, to show a navigable channel or to indicate reefs, submerged wrecks, etc. 2 = life-buoy. □ vi 1 mark the position of with a buoy: *∼ a wreck/channel.* 2 **buoy up,** (a) keep afloat. (b) (fig) keep up hopes, dreams, etc.

buoy·ancy /ˈbɔɪənsɪ/ n [U] 1 power to float or keep things floating. 2 (fig) lightness of spirits; cheerfulness. 3 (fig) (of the stock market) tendency of prices to rise.

buoy·ant /ˈbɔɪənt/ adj 1 able to float or to keep things floating. 2 (fig) cheerful: *a ∼ disposition.* 3 (fig) (of the stock market, etc) maintaining high prices.
buoy·ant·ly adv

bur, burr /bɜː(r)/ n [C] (plant with a) seedcase or flower-head that clings to the hair or fur of animals.

burble /ˈbɜːbəl/ vi make a gentle murmuring or bubbling sound: *burbling with happiness.*

bur·den /ˈbɜːdəl/ n [C] 1 load (esp one that is heavy): *beast of ∼,* animal that carries packs on it's back. 2 (literary or fig) something difficult to bear: *the ∼ of taxation on industry.* 3 [U] ship's carrying capacity, tonnage; *a ship of 3 000 tons ∼.* 4 obligation to prove: *The ∼ of proof rests with him.* □ vt load; put a burden on: *∼ oneself with a heavy overcoat/with useless facts.*
bur·den·some /-səm/ adj hard to bear; making tired.

bureau /ˈbjʊərəʊ/ n [C] (pl ∼x /-rəʊz/) 1 writing desk with drawers. 2 government or municipal department or office: *the 'Information B∼*

bureauc·racy /bjʊəˈrɒkrəsɪ/ n [U] government by paid officials not elected by the people, officials who keep their positions whatever political party is in power; [C] this system of government; the officials as a body.

bureau·crat /ˈbjʊərəkræt/ n [C] official who works in a bureau or government department, esp one who obeys the rules of his department without exercising much judgement.
bureau·cratic /ˈbjʊərəˈkrætɪk/ adj of or like a bureaucrat; too much attached to rules
bureau·crati·cally /-klɪ/ adv

bur·glar /ˈbɜːɡlə(r)/ n [C] person who breaks into a house at night in order to steal.
'burglar-alarm, device to give warning of burglars.
'burglar-proof adj made so that burglars

cannot break in or into.

bur·glary /ˈbɜːglərɪ/ n (pl -ies) [U] crime of breaking into a house by night to steal; [C] instance of this.

burgle /ˈbɜːgəl/ vt,vi break into (a building) to commit burglary; commit burglary.

bur·ial /ˈberɪəl/ n [U] burying; [C] instance of this.

`**burial-ground,** cemetery.

bur·lesque /bɜːˈlesk/ n 1 [C] imitation, e g of a book, speech, person's behaviour, for the purpose of making fun of it or of amusing people. 2 [U] amusing imitation.

burly /ˈbɜːlɪ/ adj (-ier, -iest) (of a person) big and strong.

burn[1] /bɜːn/ n [C] injury, mark, made by fire, heat or acid: He died of the ~s he received in the fire.

burner, (a) person who burns or makes something by burning: a `charcoal-~er. (b) (that part of an) apparatus from which the light or flame comes: an `oil-~er.

burn·ing adj intense; exciting: a ~ing thirst/desire/question.

burn[2] /bɜːn/ vt,vi (pt,pp ~t /bɜːnt/, occasionally ~ed /bɜːnd/) (For uses with adverbial particles and prepositions, ⇨ 6 below.) 1 use for the purpose of lighting or heating: Most large steamships now ~ oil instead of coal. 2 damage, hurt, destroy by fire, heat or the action of acid: Be careful not to ~ the meat. Wood ~s easily. 3 make by heat; ~ a hole in a carpet, e g by dropping a cigarette end. 4 be hurt or spoilt by fire or heat; be or feel warm or hot: She has a skin that ~s easily, is quickly hurt by the sun. 5 (fig) be filled with strong feeling: He was ~ing with anger.

6 (uses with adverbial particles and prepositions):

burn away, (a) continue to burn: The fire was ~ing away cheerfully. **(b)** make, become less, by burning: Half the candle had ~t away.

burn down, be destroyed, destroy to the foundations, by fire: The house (was) ~t down.

burn out, (a) become extinguished: The fire ~t (itself) out. **(b)** (of a rocket) use up its fuel. **(c)** be destroyed by fire: ~t-out factories/tanks.

burn up, (a) burst into flames, flare up: Put some wood on the fire and make it ~ up. **(b)** get rid of, by burning: We ~t up all the garden rubbish. **(c)** (of a rocket, etc re-entering the atmosphere from space) catch fire and be destroyed.

bur·nish /ˈbɜːnɪʃ/ vt,vi polish by, or as if by, rubbing.

burp /bɜːp/ n [C] (sl) belch. □ vi make a burp.

burr[1] n ⇨ bur.

burr[2] /bɜː(r)/ n [C] whirring sound made by parts of machines that turn quickly.

bur·row /ˈbʌrəʊ US: ˈbɜːrəʊ/ n [C] hole

made in the ground (by foxes, rabbits, etc). □ vi,vt make a burrow.

bur·sar /ˈbɜːsə(r)/ n [C] 1 treasurer (esp of a college). 2 (student holding a) scholarship or grant: British Council ~s in Great Britain.

bur·sary, (a) scholarship, grant. (b)office of a bursar.

burst[1] /bɜːst/ n [C] 1 bursting explosion: the ~ of a shell/bomb; a ~ in the water main. 2 brief, violent effort: a ~ of energy/speed. 3 outbreak: a ~ of applause; a ~ of gunfire. 4 ⇨ bust[2].

burst[2] /bɜːst/ vi,vt (pt,pp ~) (For uses with adverbial particles and prepositions, ⇨ 5 below.) 1 (of a bomb, shell, etc) (cause to) fly or break apart from internal pressure; explode. 2 (of river banks, a dam, an abscess, a boil) (cause to) break outwards; (of a bubble) break; (of leaf and flower buds) open out. **be bursting to,** be eager to: He was ~ing to tell us the news. 3 be full to over-flowing; be able to contain with difficulty: They were ~ing with happiness/impatience/health. 4 make a way or entry suddenly or by force: He ~ into the room. The sun ~ through the clouds.

5 (uses with adverbial particles and prepositions):

burst in (on/upon), (a) interrupt: He ~ in on our conversation. **(b)** appear or arrive suddenly.

burst into, (a) send out suddenly; break out into: The coat fell in the fire and ~ into flames. **(b)** ~ into tears/laughter/song, etc, suddenly begin to cry/laugh, etc. ~ into blossom, begin to bloom.

burst out laughing/crying, suddenly begin to laugh/cry.

bury /ˈberɪ/ vt (pt,pp -ied) 1 place (a dead body) in the ground, in a grave or in the sea; (of a clergyman) perform the Burial Service over: He's dead and buried. 2 put underground; cover with earth, leaves, etc; cover up and forget; hide from view: buried treasure. She buried (= hid) her face in her hands.

bus /bʌs/ n (pl ~es) (= omnibus which is not now used) public motor-vehicle that travels along a fixed route and takes up and sets down passengers at fixed points: Shall we walk or go by ~? **miss the bus,** (sl) be too late to use an opportunity. □ vi,vt (-ss-) 1 go, take, by bus. 2 (esp US) transport children to their schools: the ~sing of children to achieve racial integration.

`**bus stop,** signed stopping place for buses.

bush /bʊʃ/ n 1 [C] low-growing plant with several or many woody stems coming up from the root: a `rose-~. 2 [U] (often the ~) wild, uncultivated land, with or without trees or bushes, esp in Africa and Australia.

`**bush·man,** member of certain tribes in the S African bush.

`**bushy** adj (-ier, -iest) **(a)** covered with bushes. **(b)** growing thickly; thick and rough: ~y *eyebrows.*

bushel /ˈbʊʃəl/ n [C] (before metrication) measure for grain and fruit (= 8 gallons).

busier, busiest, busily ⇨ busy.

busi·ly /ˈbɪzəlɪ/ adv in a busy way: ~ *engaged in working.*

busi·ness /ˈbɪznəs/ n 1 [U] buying and selling; commerce; trade: *We do not do much* ~ *with them.* **on business,** for the purpose of doing business: *Are you here on* ~ *or for pleasure?* 2 [C] shop; commercial enterprise, etc: *He is the manager of three different* ~*es.* 3 [U] task, duty, concern; what has to be done: *It is a teacher's* ~ *to help his pupils.* **get down to business,** start the work that must be done. **mind one's own business,** attend to one's own duties and not interfere with those of others.

`**business-like** adj using, showing, system, promptness, care, etc.

business-man, man who is engaged in buying and selling, etc (not a lawyer, doctor, etc).

busk /bʌsk/ vi entertain people for tips, e g sing to queues outside cinemas.

busker, person who busks.

bust¹ /bʌst/ n [C] 1 head and shoulders of a person cut in stone, or cast in bronze, etc. 2 woman's breast; measurement round the chest and back.

bust² /bʌst/ vt,vi (sl for burst) **bust sth,** smash in: *The business went* ~, failed.

bustle¹ /ˈbʌsəl/ vi,vt (cause to) move quickly and excitedly: *Everyone was bustling about/in and out.* □ n [U] excited activity: *the* ~ *of city streets.*

bustle² /ˈbʌsəl/ n [C] frame formerly used to puff out a woman's skirt at the back.

busy /ˈbɪzɪ/ adj (-ier, -iest) 1 working; occupied; having much to do: *The doctor is a* ~ *man.* 2 full of activity: *a* ~ *day;* (of places) filled with active people, traffic, etc: *The shops are* ~ *before Christmas.* 3 (of a telephone line) in use. □ vt keep busy, occupy oneself with: *He busied himself with all sorts of little tasks.*

but¹ /bʌt/ adv only (now the usual word): *We can* ~ *try. He's* ~ *a boy.*

but² /bət strong form: bʌt/ conj 1 (coordinating): *Tom was not there* ~ *his brother was. Never a month passes* ~ *she writes* (= in which she does not write) *to her old parents.* 2 (formal) (with cannot or could not): *I could not choose* ~ *go* (= had no alternative).

but³ /bət strong form: bʌt/ prep (The uses of but as a prep and as a conj are not always easily distinguished.) (used with negatives, e g no one, none, nothing, and interrogatives, e g who, and such words as all, every one) except, excluding: *Nothing* ~ *disaster would come from such a plan. No one* ~ *he/him showed much interest in the proposal.* `**but for,** except for, without: *B*~ *for your help we should not have finished in*

time. **but then,** on the other hand: *London is a noisy place,* ~ *then it's also the place where you get the best entertainment.*

butcher /ˈbʊtʃə(r)/ n 1 person who kills, cuts up and sells animals for food. 2 person who has caused unnecessary death, e g a general who wastes the lives of soldiers. 3 person who kills savagely and needlessly. □ vt 1 prepared meat for selling as food. 2 kill violently, esp with a knife.

butch·ery, (esp) needless and cruel killing of people.

but·ler /ˈbʌtlə(r)/ n [C] head of a household staff (in charge of the wine-cellar, pantry, etc).

butt¹ /bʌt/ n [C] 1 large cask for wine or ale. 2 large barrel for storing rainwater, e g from roofs.

butt² /bʌt/ n [C] 1 thicker, larger end (esp of a fishing-rod or rifle). 2 unburned end, e g of a smoked cigar or cigarette.

butt³ /bʌt/ n 1 **the** ~**s,** shooting-range; the targets and the mound of earth behind them (used for practice in firing rifles). 2 [C] person who is a target for ridicule, jokes, etc: *He is the* ~ *of the whole school.*

butt⁴ /bʌt/ vt,vi 1 push with the head (as a goat does): ~ *a man in the stomach.* 2 **butt** `**in,** (informal) force oneself into the conversation or company of others.

but·ter /ˈbʌtə(r)/ n [U] 1 fatty food substance made from cream, used on bread, in cooking, etc: *She looks as if* ~ *would not melt in her mouth,* has an innocent appearance. 2 substance similar to butter, made from other materials: *peanut* ~. □ vt 1 spread, cook with, butter. 2 **butter sb up,** flatter.

`**but·ter·cup,** wild plant with small yellow flowers.

`**but·ter·fin·gers,** person unable to hold or catch things well.

`**but·ter·milk,** liquid that remains after butter has been separated from milk.

`**but·ter·scotch,** [U] sweet substance made by boiling sugar and butter together.

but·ter·fly /ˈbʌtəflaɪ/ n [C] (pl -ies) insect with four wings, often brightly coloured.

but·tock /ˈbʌtək/ n [C] either side of that part of the body on which a person sits· *a smack on the* ~*s.*

but·ton /ˈbʌtən/ n [C] 1 small, usually round, bit of plastic, metal, etc for fastening articles of clothing, or sewn on as an ornament. 2 small, round object, esp one that, when pushed, makes an electrical contact, e g for a bell: *press/push/touch the* ~. 3 small, unopened mushroom. □ vt,vi fasten with a buttons: ~ (*up*) *one's coat.*

`**button-hole** n [C] (**a**) hole through which a button is passed. (**b**) flower worn in a hole (e g in the lapel of a jacket or coat). □ vt hold a person (to get his attention).

but·tress /ˈbʌtrəs/ n [C] 1 support against a wall. 2 (fig) prop; thing that supports: *the ~es of society/the constitution.* □ *vt* strengthen, support *~ up an argument.*

buxom /'bʌksəm/ *adj* (of women) large and healthy-looking.

buy /baɪ/ *vt,vi* (*pt,pp* bought /bɔt/) **1** get in return for money, get by paying a price: *Can money ~ happiness?* **2** obtain at a sacrifice: *Victory was dearly bought.* □ *n* (*informal*) purchase: *a good ~, a bargain.*

buyer, (a) person who buys articles on sale. **(b)** person who chooses articles to be sold in a shop.

buzz /bʌz/ *vi,vt* **1** make a humming sound (as of bees or machinery in quick motion). **2** move quickly or excitedly: *~ about/around; ~ing along the road.* **buzz off,** (*sl*) go away. **3** (of the ears) be filled with a buzzing noise: *My ears ~.* **4** (of an aircraft) fly near to or low over (another plane) in a threatening manner: *Two fighters ~ed the airliner.* □ *n* [C] **1** sound of people talking, of whirling machinery, etc. **2** humming (of bees or other insects).

buz·zer, electrical bell that produces a buzzing note when the current flows.

buz·zard /'bʌzəd/ *n* [C] kinds of falcon.

by¹ /baɪ/ *adverbial particle* **1** near: *He hid the money when nobody was ~.* **2** past: *He hurried ~ without a word.* **by and by,** later on. **by and large,** on the whole; taking everything into consideration.

by² /baɪ/ *prep* **1** near; at or to the side of: *Come and sit ~ me/~ my side.* **by oneself,** alone: *He was (all) ~ himself.* ⇨ 13 below. **stand by sb,** support him. **2** (showing direction of movement) through, along, across, over: *We came ~ the fields, not by the roads.* **3** past: *He walked ~ me without speaking.* **5** (of time, esp to show conditions and circumstances) during: *The enemy attacked ~ night.* **6** (of time) as soon as; not later than; when (the time indicated) comes: *Can you finish the work ~ tomorrow?* **7** (in phrases of a unit of time, length, weights, measurements, etc): *rent a house ~ the year; sell cloth ~ the metre/eggs ~ the dozen, etc.* **8** through the agency, means, of: *He makes a living ~ teaching. He was killed ~ lightning.* **9** (of means of travel, transport, conveyance): *travel ~ land/sea/air; ~ bus/car/boat, etc.* **10** (of a part of the body that is touched, etc): *grab him ~ the arm.* **11** according to: *B~ my watch it is 2 o'clock.* **12** to the extent of: *The bullet missed me ~ two inches.* **13** know/learn sth by heart, so that one can repeat it from memory. **by accident/mistake/chance,** not on purpose or intentionally. **by oneself,** without help. ⇨ 1 above.

bye-bye /'baɪ 'baɪ/ *int* (*informal*) goodbye.

by-elec·tion /'baɪ ɪlekʃən/ *n* [C] election made necessary by the death or resignation of a member during the life of Parliament. ⇨ general election.

by·gone /'baɪgɒn/ *adj* past: *in ~ days,* in the time now past. □ *n* (*pl*) **Let bygones be bygones,** Forgive and forget the past.

by-law, bye-law /'baɪ lɔ/ *n* [C] law or regulation made by a local authority (e g a town or railway company).

by-pass /'baɪ pas *US:* pæs/ *n* [C] wide road passing round a heavily populated urban area or village, to take through traffic. □ *vt* **1** provide with, make a bypass. **2** (*fig*) ignore.

by-prod·uct /'baɪ prɒdʌkt/ *n* [C] substance obtained during the manufacture of some other substance.

by·stander /'baɪ stændə(r)/ *n* [C] person standing near but not taking part in an event or activity.

by·word /'baɪwɜd/ *n* [C] person, place, etc regarded and spoken of as a notable example of a (bad) quality.

Cc

C, c /si/ (*pl* C's, c's /siz/) the third letter of the English alphabet.

cab /kæb/ *n* [C] **1** motor-vehicle (`taxi-~`) that may be hired for short journeys, usually in towns: *Shall we go by bus or take a ~?* **2** part of a railway engine, bus, lorry etc for the driver. **3** (*formerly*) horse-drawn carriage.

cab·aret /'kæbəreɪ/ *n* [C] **1** entertainment (songs, dancing, etc) provided in a restaurant, etc while guests are dining or drinking.

cab·bage /'kæbɪdʒ/ *n* [C] (kinds of) plant with a round head of thick green leaves; [U] these leaves as a vegetable.

ca·ber /'keɪbə(r)/ *n* [C] trunk of a young fir-tree thrown in Highland games (Scotland) as a trial of strength and skill: *toss the ~.*

cabin /'kæbɪn/ *n* [C] **1** room in a ship or aircraft, esp (in a ship) one for sleeping in. **2** small house, usually made of logs; railway signal-box.

`cabin cruiser,` large motor-boat with a cabin.

cabi·net /'kæbɪnət/ *n* [C] **1** piece of furniture with drawers or shelves for storing or displaying things: *a `medicine ~; a `filing ~,* for storing letters, documents. **2** plastic, wooden or metal container for radio or record-playing equipment. **3** group of men (chief ministers of state) chosen by the head of the government (the prime minister in GB) to be responsible for government administration and policy: *C~ Minister,* one of these men.

cable /'keɪbəl/ *n* **1** [C,U] (length of) thick, strong rope (of fibre or wire), used on ships, bridges, etc. **2** protected bundle of insulated wires for carrying electrical power or messages by electric telegraph; message so carried. □ *vt,vi* send (a message) by cable.

`cable-car/railway,` one up a steep slope, worked by a cable(1).

`cable-gram,` telegram sent via a cable(2).

ca·cao /kə`kaʊ/ *n* [C] **1** (also `~-bean`) seed of a tropical tree from which cocoa and chocolate are made. **2** (also `~-tree`) the tree.

cackle /`kækəl/ *n* **1** [U] noise made by a hen after laying an egg. **2** [C] loud laugh; [U] foolish talk. □ *vi* **1** (of a hen) make this noise. **2** (of a person) talk or laugh noisily.

cac·tus /`kæktəs/ *n* [C] (*pl* ~es, cacti /`kæktaɪ/) (sorts of) plant from hot, dry climates with a thick, fleshy stem, often with no leaves and covered with clusters of spines or prickles.

ca·dence /`keɪdəs/ *n* [C] rhythm in sound; the rise and fall of the voice in speaking.

ca·det /kə`det/ *n* [C] **1** student at a naval, military or air force college. **2** young person under training for a profession: *po`lice ~s.*

cadge /kædʒ/ *vt,vi* (*informal*) beg; (try to) get by begging: *be always cadging.*

cad·ger, person who cadges.

Caesar·ian /sɪ`zeərɪən/ *adj, n* [C] (of a) delivery of a child by cutting the walls of the abdomen and uterus: *~ section.*

café /`kæfeɪ *US:* kæ`feɪ/ *n* [C] **1** (in Europe) place where the public may buy and drink coffee, beer, wine, spirits, etc. **2** (in GB) small, usually self-service, restaurant at which meals, drinks (but not alcoholic drinks) may be bought.

cafe·teria /ˌkæfɪ`tɪərɪə/ *n* [C] = café(2).

caf·tan /`kæftən/ *n* [C] **1** long tunic with a cord at the waist, worn by men in the Near East. **2** woman's loosely hanging dress.

cage /keɪdʒ/ *n* [C] **1** framework, fixed or portable, with wires or bars, in which birds or animals may be kept. **2** framework in which cars are lowered or raised in the shaft of a mine. □ *vt* put, keep, in a cage.

ca·jole /kə`dʒəʊl/ *vt* use flattery or deceit to persuade or to get information, etc.

cake /keɪk/ *n* **1** [C,U] sweet mixture of flour, eggs, butter, etc baked in an oven: *a slice of ~.* *a piece of cake,* (*sl*) something very easy and pleasant. **2** [C] shaped mixture of other kinds of food: *`fish-~s.* **3** [C] shaped piece of other materials or substances: *a ~ of soap.* □ *vt,vi* coat thickly, become coated (with mud, etc).

cala·bash /`kæləbæʃ/ *n* [C] (tree with a) fruit or gourd of which the hard outer skin (or shell) is used as a container or ornament.

ca·lam·ity /kə`læmətɪ/ *n* [C] (*pl* -ies) great and serious misfortune or disaster (e g a big earthquake or flood).

cal·cium /`kælsɪəm/ *n* [U] soft white metal (symbol Ca), the chemical basis of many compounds essential to life, occurring in bones and teeth and forming part of limestone, marble and chalk.

cal·cu·lable /`kælkjʊləbəl/ *adj* that may be measured, reckoned or relied on.

cal·cu·late /`kælkjʊleɪt/ *vt,vi* **1** find out by working with numbers: *~ the cost of a journey.* **2** planned or designed to: *This advertisement is ~d to attract the attention of housewives.* **3** consider, etc and be confident (that something will happen, etc).

cal·cu·lat·ing *adj* scheming; crafty.

cal·cu·la·tion /ˌkælkjʊ`leɪʃən/ *n* [U] act of calculating; careful thought; [C] result of this: *I'm out in my ~s,* have made a mistake in them.

cal·cu·la·tor /`kælkjʊleɪtə(r)/ *n* [C] **1** person who calculates. **2** machine that calculates automatically.

cal·cu·lus /`kælkjʊləs/ *n* [C] (*pl* -li /-laɪ/ or ~es) **1** branch of mathematics that deals with variable quantities, used to solve many mathematical problems. **2** (*med*) stone in some part of the human body.

cal·en·dar /`kælɪndə(r)/ *n* [C] **1** list of the days, weeks, months, of a particular year; list with dates that are important to certain people. **2** system by which time is divided into fixed periods, and marking the beginning and end of a year: *the Muslim ~.*

`calender `month,` month as marked on the calendar (contrasted with a *lunar month* of 28 days).

calf[1] /kɑf *US:* kæf/ *n* **1** [C] (*pl* calves /kɑvz *US:* kævz/) young of the domestic cow; young of the seal, whale and some other animals for the first year. **2** [U] (also `~ skin`) leather from the skin of a calf.

calf[2] /kɑf *US:* kæf/ *n* [C] (*pl* calves /kɑvz *US:* kævz/) fleshy part of the back of the human leg, between the knee and the ankle.

cali·brate /`kælɪbreɪt/ *vt* determine or correct the scale of a thermometer, gauge or other graduated instrument.

`cali·bra·tion /ˌkælɪ`breɪʃən/ *n* [C] degree marks, etc on a measuring instrument.

cal·ibre (*US* = **cal·iber**) /`kælɪbə(r)/ *n* **1** [C] inside diameter of a tube/gun/barrel, etc. **2** [U] quality of mind or character: *a man of considerable ~,* importance.

cali·pers /`kælɪpəz/ *n pl* (*US*) = callipers.

ca·liph, ca·lif /`keɪlɪf/ *n* [C] title once used by rulers who were descendants and successors of Muhammad; chief civil and religious ruler: *the C~ of Baghdad.*

`cal·iph·ate /`keɪlɪfeɪt/, caliph's position and residence.

call[1] /kɔl/ *n* [C] **1** shout; cry: *a ~ for help.* **2** characteristic cry of a bird. **3** military signal (on a bugle, etc). **4** short visit (to a house, etc); short stop (at a place): *Pay a ~ on a friend. I have several ~s to make.* **5** message; summons; invitation: *`telephone ~s.* **on call,** (of doctors, nurses, etc) prepared to go on duty if asked. **6** [U] (chiefly *negative* or *interrogative*) need; occasion: *There's no ~ for you to worry.* **7** (in card games) player's right or turn to make a bid; bid thus made.

`call-box,` small public kiosk with a telephone.

call² /kɔl/ vt,vi (For special uses with *adverbial particles* and *prepositions*, ⇨ 9 below.) **1** say in a loud voice; cry; speak or shout to attract attention: *She ∼ed to her father for help.* **call out,** cry or shout when needing help, or from surprise, pain, etc. ⇨ 9 below. **2** pay a short visit: *I ∼ed on Mr Green. This train ∼s at every station.* **call for,** visit (a house, etc) to get something, or to go somewhere with somebody: *I'll ∼ for you at 6 o'clock and we'll go to the cinema together.* **3** name; describe as: *His name is Richard but we all ∼ him Dick.* **call sb names,** abuse or insult him. **call it a day,** ⇨ day(3). **4** consider; regard as: *I ∼ that a shame.* **5** summon; wake; send a message to: *Please ∼ a doctor. Please ∼ me* (= wake me up) *at 6 tomorrow morning. Please ∼ me a taxi/∼ a taxi for me.* **6** (special uses with nouns) **call attention to,** require (a person) to give his attention to. **call a meeting,** announce that one will be held and summon people to attend. **call a strike,** order workers to come out on strike. **7** make a bid in card games. ⇨ call¹(7). **be called to the bar,** ⇨ bar¹(12).
9 (uses with *adverbial particles* and *prepositions*):
call by, (*informal*) visit for a short time.
call for, demand, require: *You must take such steps as seem* (to be) *∼ed for.*
call sth in, order or request the return of: *The librarian has ∼ed in all books.*
call (sth) off, (a) tell it to go/come away: *Please ∼ your dog off.* **(b)** decide, give orders, to stop: *The strike/attack was ∼ed off,* was either not started or was stopped.
call on, make a short visit.
call on/upon, appeal to; invite; require: *I now ∼ on* (= invite) *Mr Grey to address the meeting.*
call out, (a) summon, esp to an emergency: *The fire brigade was ∼ed out twice yesterday.* **(b)** instruct (workers) to come out on strike.
call sb/sth up, (a) telephone to: *I'll ∼ you up this evening.* **(b)** bring back to the mind: *∼ up scenes of childhood.* **(c)** summon for (military, etc) service: *If war breaks out, we shall be ∼ed up at once.* Hence, `**call-up** n
cal·ler /ˈkɔlə(r)/ n [C] person who makes a visit.
cal·ligra·phy /kəˈlɪgrəfɪ/ n [U] handwriting; (art of) beautiful handwriting.
cal·ling /ˈkɔlɪŋ/ n [C] (esp) occupation, profession or trade.
cal·li·pers /ˈkælɪpəz/ n pl **1** instrument for measuring the diameter of round objects or the inside measurement of tubes, etc. **2** metal supports attached to the legs of a disabled person to enable him to walk.
cal·lous /ˈkæləs/ adj **1** (of the skin) made hard (by rough work, etc). **2** (*fig*) hard-hearted. unsympathetic.

cal·low /ˈkæləʊ/ adj young; inexperienced: *a ∼ youth.*
cal·lus /ˈkæləs/ n [C] (pl ∼es) area of thick, hardened skin.
calm /kɑm/ adj (-er, -est) **1** (of the weather) quiet; not windy; (of the sea) still; without large waves. **2** not excited; untroubled; quiet: *keep ∼.* □ n a ∼, a time when everything is quiet and peaceful. □ vt,vi make or become calm: *He asked the workers to ∼ down.*
calm·ly adv
calm·ness n [U]
cal·orie /ˈkælərɪ/ n [C] unit of heat; unit of energy supplied by food: *An ounce of sugar supplies about 100 ∼s.*
cal·or·ific /ˈkæləˈrɪfɪk/ adj producing heat: *calorific value,* (of food or fuel) quantity of heat produced by a given quantity.
cal·umny /ˈkæləmnɪ/ n [C] (pl -ies) false statement about a person, made to damage his character; [U] slander.
ca·lyp·so /kəˈlɪpsəʊ/ n [C] (pl ∼s) improvised popular song, as composed by West Indians, on a subject of current interest.
ca·lyx /ˈkeɪlɪks/ n [C] (pl ∼es or calyces /ˈkeɪlɪsɪz/) ring of leaves (called *sepals*) forming the outer support of the petals of an unopened flower-bud.
cam·ber /ˈkæmbə(r)/ n [C] slight rise in the middle of a surface (e g a road, to let rain run off).
came /keɪm/ pt of come.
camel /ˈkæməl/ n [C] long-necked animal, with either one or two humps on its back, used in desert countries for riding and for carrying goods.
cameo /ˈkæmɪəʊ/ n [C] (pl ∼s) piece of hard stone with a raised design, often of a different colour, used as a jewel or ornament.
cam·era /ˈkæmrə/ n [C] **1** apparatus for taking single photographs or (`film/`movie ∼) moving pictures, or, (`T V ∼) for broadcasting programmes, etc. **2** in camera, privately.
cam·ou·flage /ˈkæməflɑʒ/ n [U] **1** that which makes it difficult to recognize the presence or real nature of something or somebody: *The white fur of the polar bear is a natural ∼, because the bear is not easily seen in the snow.* **2** (in war) the use of paint, netting, branches, etc to deceive the enemy. □ vt try to conceal by means of camouflage.
camp /kæmp/ n [C] **1** place where people (e g people on holiday, soldiers, explorers) live in tents or huts. **2** number of people with the same ideas (esp on politics or religion): *We're in the same ∼,* are in agreement, are working together. **3** (also `holiday-∼) organized centre, usually near the sea, for family holidays. □ vi make, live in, a camp: *Where shall we ∼ tonight?* **go camping,** spend a holiday in tents, etc: *The boys have decided to go ∼ing next summer.*

camper, person who camps, esp on holiday.

cam·paign /kæmˈpeɪn/ n [C] **1** group of military operations with a set purpose, usually in one area. **2** series of planned activities to gain a special object: an `advertising ~. □ vi take part in, go on, a campaign.

cam·paigner, person who campaigns.

cam·pus /ˈkæmpəs/ n [C] (pl ~es) grounds of a school, college or university.

can¹ /kæn/ n [C] **1** metal container for liquids, etc: an `oil-~. **2** (formerly US but now also GB) tin-plated airtight container (for food, etc); contents of such a container: a ~ of beer. ⇨ tin. **3** (US sl) prison. □ vt (-nn-) preserve (food, etc) by putting in a can(2).

can·nery, place where food is tinned or canned.

can² /kən strong form: kæn/ auxiliary verb (negative cannot /ˈkænɒt/, can't /kɑnt US: kænt/, pt could /kəd strong form: kʊd/, negative couldn't /ˈkʊdənt/) **1** be able to; know how to: C~ you lift this box? She ~ speak French. **2** (used with verbs of perception): I ~ hear people talking in the next room. We could hear someone singing in the bathroom. **3** (informal) (used to show permission; may is more formal): You ~ go home now. The children asked whether they could go for a swim. You can't travel first-class with a second-class ticket.**4** (used to show possibility): That couldn't be true. **5** (used in questions to show surprise, doubt, etc): What '~ he `mean? **6** (used to what is considered characteristic, what somebody or something is considered capable of being or doing): It ~ be very cold here, even in May.

ca·nal /kəˈnæl/ n [C] **1** channel cut through land for use of boats or ships (eg the Suez C~) or to carry water to fields for irrigation. **2** tube or pipe (or system of these) in a plant or animal body for food, air, etc: the alimentary ~.

ca·nary /kəˈneərɪ/ n (pl -ies) **1** [C] small, yellow-feathered songbird. **2** [U] its colour, light yellow.

can·cel /ˈkænsəl/ vt,vi (-ll-, US -l-) **1** cross out, draw a line through (words or figures); make a mark on (eg postage stamps to prevent re-use). **2** say that something already arranged or decided will not be done, will not take place, etc: The sports meeting was ~led.

can·cel·la·tion /ˈkænsəˈleɪʃən/ n [C,U]

can·cer /ˈkænsə(r)/ n [C,U] diseased growth in the body, often causing death: lung ~.

can·cer·ous /ˈkænsərəs/ adj of, like, having, cancer.

Can·cer /ˈkænsə(r)/ n **1** Tropic of ~, the parallel of latitude 32½°N. **2** the Crab, fourth sign of the zodiac.

can·did /ˈkændɪd/ adj straightforward, frank: I will be quite ~ with you: I think you acted foolishly.

can·did·ly adv

can·di·date /ˈkændɪdət, -deɪt/ n [C] **1** person who wishes, or who is put forward by others, to take an office or position (eg for election to Parliament): The Labour ~ was elected. **2** person taking an examination.

candle /ˈkændəl/ n [C] round stick of wax, etc with a string (wick) through it, for giving light.

`candle·stick, holder for a candle.

can·dour (US = **can·dor**) /ˈkændə(r)/ n [U] quality of saying freely what one thinks.

candy /ˈkændɪ/ n [U] (also 'sugar-~) sugar made hard by boiling; [C] (pl -ies) piece of this. □ vt,vi (pt,pp -ied) preserve (eg fruit) by boiling or cooking in sugar: candied lemon peel.

cane /keɪn/ n [C] **1** long, hollow, jointed stem of tall reeds and grass-like plants (eg bamboo); [U] this material: a chair with a ~ seat. **2** [C] length of cane used as an instrument for punishing children. □ vt punish with a cane(2).

ca·nine /ˈkæmaɪn US: `keɪnaɪn/ adj of, as of, a dog or dogs.

can·is·ter /ˈkænɪstə(r)/ n [C] **1** small box (usually metal) with a lid, used for holding tea, etc. **2** cylinder which, when thrown or fired from a gun, bursts and scatters its contents: a `tear-gas ~.

can·ker /ˈkæŋkə(r)/ n [U] **1** disease that destroys the wood of trees. **2** disease that causes the formation of ulcers. **3** (fig) evil influence or tendency that causes decay. □ vt destroy by canker.

can·ker·ous /ˈkæŋkərəs/ adj of, like, causing, canker.

can·na·bis /ˈkænəbɪs/ n [U] drug smoked or chewed as an intoxicant. ⇨ hemp.

can·nery ⇨ can¹.

can·ni·bal /ˈkænəbəl/ n [C] person who eats human flesh; animal that eats its own kind.

can·ni·bal·ism /-ɪzm/, practice of eating the flesh of one's own kind.

can·ni·bal·is·tic /ˈkænəbəlˈɪstɪk/ adj of or like cannibals.

can·non /ˈkænən/ n **1** [C] (pl often unchanged) large, heavy gun, fixed to the ground or to a guncarriage, esp the old kind that fired a solid ball of metal (called a `~-ball). (Note: gun and shell are the words used for modern weapons). **2** [C] heavy, automatic gun, firing explosive shells, used in modern aircraft.

can·non·ade /ˈkænəˈneɪd/ n [C] continued firing of big guns.

can·not /ˈkænət/ ⇨ can².

ca·noe /kəˈnu/ n [C] light boat moved by one or more paddles. □ vi travel by canoe.

ca·noe·ist, person who paddles a canoe.

canon /ˈkænən/ n [C] **1** church law. **2** general standard or principle by which something is judged: the ~s of conduct/ good taste. **3** body of writings accepted as genuine (esp those of the Bible). **4** official list (esp of RC saints). **5** priest (the Rev

Canon) who is one of a group with duties in a cathedral.

ca·noni·cal /kə'nɒnɪkəl/ *adj* according to church law; of the canon(3): ~ *books*.

canon·ize /'kænənaɪz/ *vt* place (a person) in the list of saints.

ca·non ⇨ canyon.

can·opy /'kænəpɪ/ *n* [C] (*pl* -ies) (usually cloth) covering over a bed, throne, etc or held (on poles) over a person; cover for the cockpit of an aircraft.

cant /kænt/ *n* [U] 1 insincere talk; hypocrisy. 2 special talk, words, used by a particular class of people.

can't /kɑnt *US:* kænt/ = cannot. ⇨ can².

can·ta·loup, -loupe /'kæntəlup/ *n* [C] kind of melon.

can·tank·er·ous /kæn'tæŋkərəs/ *adj* bad-tempered; quarrelsome.

can·tata /kæn'tɑtə/ *n* [C] (*pl* ~s) short musical work to be sung by soloists and a choir, usually a dramatic story, but not acted.

can·teen /kæn'tin/ *n* [C] 1 place (esp in factories, offices, barracks) where food, drink and other articles are sold and meals bought and eaten. 2 box or chest of table silver and cutlery (knives, forks, spoons). 3 soldier's, camper's, eating and drinking utensils.

can·ter /'kæntə(r)/ *n* [C] (of a horse) slow gallop. □ *vt, vi* (cause to) gallop slowly.

can·ticle /'kæntɪkəl/ *n* [C] short hymn.

can·ti·lever /'kæntɪlivə(r)/ *n* [C] long, large bracket extending from a wall or base (e g to support a balcony).

canto /'kæntəʊ/ *n* [C] (*pl* ~s) chief division of a long poem.

can·vas /'kænvəs/ *n* (*pl* ~ses) 1 [U] strong, coarse cloth used for tents, sails, bags, etc and by artists for oil-paintings. 2 [C] (piece of this for an) oil-painting.

can·vass /'kænvəs/ *vt, vi* go from person to person and ask for votes, orders for goods, subscriptions, etc or to learn about people's views on a question. □ *n* [C,U]

can·yon, cañon /'kænjən/ *n* [C] deep gorge (usually with a river flowing through it).

cap /kæp/ *n* [C] 1 soft head-covering, worn by boys and men, without a brim, but with a peak. 2 special cap showing membership of a team, occupation, etc. 3 waterproof head-covering for swimming, etc. 4 indoor headdress worn by nurses and formerly by old women. 5 cover (e g on a milk bottle, tube of toothpaste). *and to cap it all...*, and the final, best, etc reason, description, etc is ... □ *vt* (-pp-) 1 put a cap on; cover the top of. 2 do or say something better than somebody else. *cap a joke/story*, tell a better one. 3 award (a player) a cap(2) (as a member of a football team, etc): *He's been* ~*ped 36 times for England*.

ca·pa·bil·ity /'keɪpə'bɪlətɪ/ *n* (*pl* -ies) 1 [U] power, fitness or capacity: *nuclear* ~,

power to wage nuclear war. 2 (*pl*) talent that can be developed: *The boy has great capabilities.*

ca·pable /'keɪpəbəl/ *adj* 1 talented; able: *a very* ~ *teacher*. 2 *capable of*, (a) (of persons) having the power, ability or inclination: *He's* ~ *of any crime*. (b) (of things, situations, etc) ready for; open to: *The situation is* ~ *of improvement*.
ca·pably *adv*

ca·pac·ity /kə'pæsətɪ/ *n* (*pl* -ies) 1 [U] ability to hold, contain, get hold of, learn: *The hall has a seating* ~ *of 500*, has seats for 500 people. 2 [C] position; character: *I am your friend, but in my* ~ *as your Manager I must ask you to resign.*

cape¹ /keɪp/ *n* [C] loose sleeveless garment, hanging from the shoulders.

cape² /keɪp/ *n* [C] high point of land going out into the sea: *the C~ of Good Hope.*

cap·il·lary /kə'pɪlərɪ *US:* 'kæpəlerɪ/ *n* [C] (*pl* -ies) small, narrow tube, esp a very small blood-vessel.

capi·tal /'kæpɪtəl/ *n* [C] (often used as an *adjective*) 1 town or city where the government of a country, state or county is carried on: *Melbourne is the* ~ *of Victoria. London, Paris and Rome are* ~ *cities.* 2 (of letters of the alphabet) not small: *Write your name in* ~ *letters/in* ~*s.* 3 [U] wealth, money or property that may be used for the production of more wealth; money with which a business, etc is started: *The company has a* ~ *of £500 000.* 4 head, top part, of a column(1). □ *adj* 1 punishable by death: ~ *offences.* 2 (*informal*) excellent, first-rate: *What a* ~ *idea!*

capi·tal·ism /'kæpɪtəlɪzm/ *n* [U] economic system in which a country's trade and industry are organized and controlled by the owners of capital(3), the chief elements being competition, profit, supply and demand. ⇨ socialism.

capi·tal·ist, (a) supporter of capitalism. (b) person who controls much capital(3).

capi·tal·is·tic /'kæpɪt'lɪstɪk/ *adj*

capi·tal·ize /'kæpɪtəlaɪz/ *vt, vi* 1 write or print with a capital letter. 2 convert into, use as, capital(3). 3 (*fig*) take advantage of; use to one's advantage or profit.

ca·pitu·late /kə'pɪtʃʊleɪt/ *vt* surrender (on stated conditions).
ca·pitu·la·tion /kə'pɪtʃʊ'leɪʃən/ *n* [U]

ca·pon /'keɪpɒn *US:* -pɒn/ *n* [C] cock (male domestic fowl) castrated and fattened for eating.

ca·price /kə'pris/ *n* [C] (tendency towards a) sudden change of mind or behaviour that has no obvious cause.

ca·pri·cious /kə'prɪʃəs/ *adj* often changing; irregular; unreliable.
ca·pri·cious·ly *adv*

Cap·ri·corn /'kæprɪkɒn/ *n* 1 Tropic of ~, the parallel of latitude 23½°S. 2 the Goat tenth sign of the zodiac.

cap·si·cum /ˈkæpsɪkəm/ n [C] (pl ~s) kinds of plant (green pepper) with seed-pods containing hot-tasting seeds; such pods prepared for use in cooking, etc.

cap·size /kæpˈsaɪz/ vt,vi (esp of a boat in the water) (cause to) overturn, upset.

cap·stan /ˈkæpstən/ n [C] upright device, like a bollard, turned to raise anchors, sails, etc and for pulling a ship to a wharf, etc.

cap·sule /ˈkæpsjul US: ˈkæpsəl/ n [C] 1 seed-case that opens when the seeds are ripe. 2 tiny soluble container for a dose of medicine. 3 metal cap for a bottle. 4 (recoverable or non-recoverable) compartment which can be ejected from a spacecraft.

cap·tain /ˈkæptɪn/ n [C] 1 leader or chief commander: the ~ of a ship/football team. 2 (in the army) officer (below a major and above a lieutenant) who commands a company. 3 (in the navy) officer below an admiral and above a commander. □ vt act as captain.

cap·tion /ˈkæpʃən/ n [C] 1 short title or heading of an article in a periodical, etc. 2 words printed with a photograph or illustration.

cap·ti·vate /ˈkæptɪveɪt/ vt fascinate: He was ~d by Helen.

cap·tive /ˈkæptɪv/ n [C], adj (person, animal) taken prisoner, kept as a prisoner.
'captive 'audience, one that cannot get away easily and so avoid being persuaded.

cap·tiv·ity /kæpˈtɪvətɪ/ n [U] state of being held captive: Some birds will not sing in ~.

cap·tor /ˈkæptə(r)/ n [C] person who takes a person captive.

cap·ture /ˈkæptʃə(r)/ vt make a prisoner of; take or obtain as a prize by force, trickery, skill, etc: Our army ~d 500 of the enemy. □ n 1 [U] act of capturing: the ~ of a thief. 2 [C] thing that is caught.

car /kɑ(r)/ n [C] 1 = motor-car. 2 = tram-car (street-car). 3 coach of a train: the 'dining-~. 4 that part of a lift, etc used by passengers.
'car-ferry, ferry (sea or air) for taking cars (e g across the English Channel).
'car-park, place, building, for parking motor-vehicles.
'car-port, open-sided shelter for a motor-vehicle.

cara·mel /ˈkærəməl/ n 1 [U] burnt sugar used for colouring and flavouring. 2 [C] small, shaped piece of boiled sugar.

cara·pace /ˈkærəpeɪs/ n [C] shell on the back of a tortoise, etc.

carat /ˈkærət/ n [C] 1 unit of weight (about three and one-fifth grains) for precious stones. 2 measure of the purity of gold, pure gold being 24 carat.

cara·van /ˈkærəvæn/ n [C] 1 company of persons (e g pilgrims, merchants) making a journey together for safety, usually across desert country. 2 covered cart or wagon used for living in, e g by gipsies. 3 modern kind

on two wheels, used by people on holiday and pulled behind a motor-vehicle. ⇨ also trailer.

carbo·hy·drate /ˈkɑːbəʊˈhaɪdreɪt/ n 1 [C,U] (kinds of) organic compound including sugars and starches. 2 (pl) starchy foods, considered to be fattening.

car·bolic acid /ˈkɑːˈbɒlɪk ˈæsɪd/ n [U] strong-smelling, powerful liquid used as an antiseptic and disinfectant.

car·bon /ˈkɑːbən/ n 1 [U] non-metallic element (symbol C) that occurs in all living matter, in its pure form as diamonds and graphite and in an impure form in coal and charcoal. 2 [C,U] (also ~-paper) (sheet of) thin paper coated with coloured matter, used between sheets of writing paper for taking copies. 3 [C] copy made by the use of a carbon(2).

car·buncle /ˈkɑːbʌŋkəl/ n [C] (esp) red (usually painful) inflamed swelling under the skin.

car·bu·ret·tor, (also -retor, -retter) /ˈkɑːbjʊˈretə(r) US: ˈkɑːbəreɪtər/ n [C] that part of an internal-combustion engine, e g in a car, in which petrol and air are mixed to make an explosive mixture.

car·cass, car·case /ˈkɑːkəs/ n [C] dead body of an animal (esp one prepared for cutting up as meat).

card /kɑːd/ n [C] 1 (usually small, oblong-shaped) piece of stiff paper or thin cardboard, as used for various purposes: a 'Christmas/New 'Year/'Birthday ~, sent with greetings at Christmas, etc. ⇨ also postcard, etc. 2 programme for a race meeting or game, with details, and space for marking results: a 'score ~. 3 (often 'playing-~) one of the 52 cards used for various games (whist, bridge, poker, etc) and for telling fortunes. on the cards, likely or possible. put one's cards on the table, make one's plans, intentions, etc, known.
'card game, game using playing-cards.
'card 'index, index, catalogue, on cards.

car·da·mom /ˈkɑːdəməm/ n [U] aromatic spice from various East Indian plants.

card·board /ˈkɑːdbɔːd/ n [U] thick, stiff kind of paper or pasteboard, used for making boxes, etc.

car·diac /ˈkɑːdɪæk/ adj of the heart: ~ muscle/surgery.

car·di·gan /ˈkɑːdɪgən/ n [C] knitted woollen jacket that buttons up the front, made with sleeves.

car·di·nal¹ /ˈkɑːdənəl/ adj chief; most important; on which something depends: the ~ virtues.
cardinal number, any number e g 2, 5, 17, (contrasted with second, fifth, etc).
cardinal points, chief points of the compass (N, S, E and W).

car·di·nal² /ˈkɑːdənəl/ n 1 [C] member of the Sacred College of the R C Church, which elects Popes. 2 [U] bright red

care¹ /keə(r)/ n 1 [U] serious attention or thought: *You should take more ~ over your work.* **take care of,** (*informal*) deal with, be responsible for. 2 [U] protection; charge; responsibility: *The child was left in its sister's ~.* **care of,** (often written c/o) used in addresses before the name of the person(s) to whose house, office, etc a letter is sent. 3 [U] sorrow; anxiety; troubled state of mind caused by doubt or fear: *C~ has made him look ten years older.* 4 [C] (usually pl) cause of sorrow and anxiety: *He was poor and troubled by the ~s of a large family.*
`care-free` adj free from care(3).
`care-taker,` person in charge of a building: *the school ~taker.*
`care-worn` adj troubled by anxiety.

care² /keə(r)/ vi 1 feel interest, anxiety or sorrow: *He failed in the examination but I don't think he ~s very much/he doesn't seem to ~.* **be past caring,** without interest, energy, feeling. 2 (only in the *negative* or in *questions*) like; be willing: *Would you ~ to go for a walk?* 3 **care for,** (a) like (to have): *Would you ~ for a drink?* (b) have a taste for; like: *Do you ~ for modern music?* (c), look after, provide food, attendance, etc: *Who will ~ for the children if their mother dies?*

ca-reer /kə'rɪə(r)/ n 1 [C] progress through life; development and progress of a political party, principle etc: *We can learn much by reading about the ~s of great men.* 2 [C] way of making a living; profession: *All ~s should be open to women.* 3 [U] quick or violent forward movement. □ *vi* rush wildly: *~ about/past.*

care-ful /'keəfəl/ adj 1 (of a person) cautious; thinking of, paying attention to, what one does, says, etc: *Be ~ not to break the eggs. Be more ~ with your work.* 2 done with, showing, care: *a ~ piece of work.*
`care-fully` /-flɪ/ adv
`care-ful-ness` n [U]

care-less /'keələs/ adj 1 (of a person) not taking care; thoughtless: *A ~ driver is a danger to the public.* 2 done or made without care: *a ~ mistake.* 3 unconcerned about: *He is ~ of his reputation.*
`care-less-ly` adv
`care-less-ness` n [U]

ca-ress /kə'res/ n [C] loving or affectionate touch; kiss. □ *vt* give a caress to.

cargo /'kɑːgəʊ/ n [C,U] (pl ~es) goods carried in a ship, aircraft or other vehicle.

cari-ca-ture /'kærɪkətʃʊə(r)/ US: 'kærɪkətʃʊər/ n 1 [C] picture, imitation of a person's voice, behaviour, etc stressing certain features in order to cause amusement or ridicule. 2 [U] art of doing this. □ *vt* make, give, a caricature of.

car-ies /'keərɪz/ n [U] decay (of bones or teeth): *dental ~.*

car-nage /'kɑːnɪdʒ/ n [U] killing of many people.

car-nal /'kɑːnəl/ adj of the body or flesh; sensual: *~ desires.*

car-na-tion /kɑː'neɪʃən/ n [C] garden plant with sweet-smelling white, pink or red flowers; the flower.

car-ni-val /'kɑːnɪvəl/ n [U] public entertainment and feasting, usually with processions of persons in fancy dress; [C] festival of this kind.

car-ni-vore /'kɑːnɪvɔː(r)/ n [C] flesh-eating animal.
car-ni-vor-ous /kɑː'nɪvərəs/ adj flesh-eating.

carol /'kærəl/ n [C] song of joy or praise, esp a Christmas hymn. □ *vi* sing joyfully.

ca-rouse /kə'raʊz/ vt drink heavily and be merry (at a noisy feast, etc).

carp¹ /kɑːp/ n [C] (pl unchanged) freshwater fish that lives in lakes and ponds.

carp² /kɑːp/ vt make unnecessary complaints about small matters: *She's always ~ing at her husband.*

car-pal /'kɑːpəl/ adj (anat) of the wrist. □ *n* [C] (anat) bone in the wrist.

car-pen-ter /'kɑːpɪntə(r)/ n [C] workman who makes and repairs (esp) the wooden parts of buildings and other structures of wood.
`car-pen-try,` work of a carpenter.

car-pet /'kɑːpɪt/ n [C] 1 thick covering for floors or stairs, often with a pattern. 2 something suggesting a carpet: *a ~ of moss.* □ *vt* cover (as) with a carpet: *to ~ the stairs.*

car-riage /'kærɪdʒ/ n 1 [C] vehicle, esp one with four wheels, pulled by a horse or horses, for carrying people. 2 [C] car or coach for passengers on a railway train. 3 [U] (cost of) carrying of goods from place to place. 4 [C] wheeled support on which a heavy object may move or be moved (e g a `gun-~`). 5 [C] moving part of a machine, changing the position of other parts (e g the roller of a typewriter). 6 [U] manner of holding the head or the body (when walking, etc): *She has a graceful ~.*
`car-riage-way,` (part of a) road used by vehicles. ⇨ dual carriageway.

car-rier /'kærɪə(r)/ n [C] 1 person or company that carries goods or people for payment. 2 support for luggage, etc fixed to a bicycle, etc. 3 person, animal, etc that carries or transmits a disease without himself or itself suffering from it. 4 vehicle, ship, etc used for the transport of troops, aircraft, tanks, etc: *an `aircraft-~.*
`carrier `bag,` strong paper or plastic bag for carrying away purchases from shops.
`carrier-pigeon,` pigeon used to carry messages because it can find its way home from a distant place.

car-rion /'kærɪən/ n [U] dead and decaying flesh.

car-rot /'kærət/ n [C] (plant with a) yellow or orange root used as a vegetable.

carry /'kærɪ/ vt,vi (pt,pp -ied) (For uses with *adverbial particles* and *prepositions*, ⇨

11 below.) **1** support the weight of and move from place to place; take a person, a message, etc from one place to another: *He was* ~*ing a box on his shoulder. Some kinds of seeds are carried by the wind for great distances. The police seized the spy and carried him off to prison.* **2** have with one; wear; possess: *Do you always* ~ *an umbrella? Can you* ~ *all these figures in your head,* remember them without writing them down? **3** support: *These pillars* ~ *the weight of the roof.* **4** involve; have as a result: *The loan carries 3% interest.* **5** (of pipes, wires, etc) conduct; take: *Wires* ~ *sound. Copper carries electricity.* **6** make longer; extend; take (to a specified point, in a specified direction, etc): ~ *pipes under a street. carry a joke too far,* be no longer amusing. **7** win; capture; persuade; overcome: *The bill/motion/ resolution was carried,* There were more votes for it than against it. *carry the day,* be victorious. **8** hold oneself, head, etc in a particular way: *He carries himself like a soldier,* stands and walks like one. **9** (of missiles, sounds, voices, etc) (have the power to) go to: *The sound of their voices carried many miles.* **10** (of a newspaper, etc) print in its pages: *a newspaper that carries several pages of advertisements.*

11 (uses with *adverbial particles* and *prepositions*):

be carried away, lose self-control: *He was carried away by his enthusiasm,* was so enthusiastic that he was unable to judge calmly, etc.

carry back, take back in the memory: *an incident that carried me back to my schooldays,* made me remember them.

carry forward, transfer (a total of figures on a page) to the head of a new column or page.

carry off, win: *Tom carried off all the school prizes. carry it off (well),* succeed in a difficult situation; cover a mistake, etc.

carry on, (a) conduct; manage: *Rising costs made it hard to* ~ *on the business.* (b) talk loudly and complainingly; behave strangely or suspiciously: *Did you notice how they were* ~*ing on?* *carry on (with),* (a) continue: *C*~ *on (with your work).* (b) (often suggesting disapproval) have a love affair with.

carry out, complete something: ~ *out a plan.*

carry through, (a) help (through difficulties, etc): *Their courage will* ~ *them through.* (b) complete something: *Having made a promise, you must* ~ *it through.*

carry-cot /ˈkærɪ kɒt/ n [C] portable cot for a baby.

cart /kɑt/ n [C] two-wheeled vehicle pulled by a horse. *put the cart before the horse,* do or put things in the wrong order. □ *vt* **1** carry in a cart: ~*ing away the rubbish.* **2** (*informal*) carry in the hands, etc: *Have you really got to* ~ *these parcels around for the*

rest of the day?

`cart-horse, strong horse for heavy work.

`cart-load, as much as a cart holds.

carte blanche /ˈkɑt ˈblɑnʃ/ n (*Fr*) full authority or freedom (to use one's own judgement about how to proceed, etc): *be given* ~ *to do it.*

car·ti·lage /ˈkɑtlɪdʒ/ n [C,U] (structure, part, of) tough, white tissue attached to the joints in animal bodies.

car·tog·ra·pher /kɑˈtɒgrəfə(r)/ n [C] person who makes maps and charts.

car·to·graphic /ˈkɑtəˈgræfɪk/ adj of cartography.

car·tog·ra·phy /kɑˈtɒgrəfɪ/ n [U] the drawing of maps and charts.

car·ton /ˈkɑtən/ n [C] cardboard box for holding goods: *a* ~ *of cigarettes.*

car·toon /kɑˈtun/ n [C] **1** drawing dealing with contemporary (esp political) events in an amusing way. **2** full-size preliminary drawing on paper, used as a model for a painting, etc. **3** (also *animated* ~) cinema film made by photographing a series of drawings: *a Walt Disney* ~. □ *vt* represent (a person, etc) in a cartoon.

car·toon·ist, person who draws cartoons(1).

car·tridge /ˈkɑtrɪdʒ/ n [C] **1** case containing explosive (for blasting), or explosive with a bullet or shot (for firing from a rifle or shotgun). **2** detachable head of the device which picks up sound (on a record-player), holding the stylus. **3** (large) cassette.

carve /kɑv/ vt,vi **1** form by cutting away material from a piece of wood or stone: ~ *a statue out of wood; a boy* ~*d from marble;* (*fig*) ~ *out a career for oneself,* achieve one by great effort. **2** inscribe by cutting on a surface: ~ *one's initials.* **3** cut up (cooked meat) into pieces or slices at or for the table: ~ *a leg of lamb.*

carver, (a) carving-knife. (b) person who carves.

`carv·ing, something carved (in wood, etc): *a* `wood-~.

cas·cade /kæˈskeɪd/ n [C] **1** waterfall. **2** similar fall of lace, cloth, etc. □ *vi* fall like a cascade.

case¹ /keɪs/ n [C] **1** instance or example of the occurrence of something; actual state of affairs; circumstances or special conditions relating to a person or thing: *If that's the* ~ (= If the situation is as stated or suggested), *you'll have to work much harder. No, that's not the* ~, is not true. *I can't make an exception in your* ~, for you and not for others. *It's a clear* ~ *of cheating,* is clear that cheating has taken place. *(just) in case,* if it should happen that; because of a possibility: *It may rain; you'd better take an umbrella (just) in* ~. *In* ~ *I forget, please remind me of my promise. in* `any case, whatever happens or may have happened. *in this/that case,* if this/that happens, has happened, should happen. **2** person suffering from a disease; instance of this: *There were five ~s of influenza.* **3** (*legal*) question to be decided in a law court; the facts, arguments, etc used on one side in a law case: *When will the ~ come before the Court?* **make out a case (for/against)**, give arguments in favour of/against. **4** (*gram*) (change in the) form of a noun or pronoun that shows its relation to another word: *The first person pronoun has three ~s, 'I', 'me' and 'my'*.

`case-book`, record kept, e g by a doctor, of cases(2) dealt with.

`case-'history`, record of the past history of a person's health, social state, etc.

`case-law`, law based on decisions made by judges.

`case-load`, list of cases(2) to be dealt with in a particular period: *Dr Jones has a heavy (= large) ~-load tomorrow.*

`case-work`, work involving study of individuals or families with social problems.

case² /keɪs/ *n* [C] **1** box, bag, covering, container: *a `pillow-~*, of cloth for covering a pillow. ⇨ also suitcase, bookcase and other compounds. **2** (in printing): *upper ~*, capital letters; *lower ~*, small letters. □ *vt* enclose in a case or casing.

case·ment /ˈkeɪsmənt/ *n* [C] window that opens outwards or inwards like a door, not up or down or from side to side.

cash /kæʃ/ *n* [U] **1** money in coin or notes: *I have no ~ with me; may I pay by cheque?* **cash on delivery**, payment on delivery of the goods. ⇨ credit¹(1). **2** money in any form: *be short of ~*, without money. □ *vt,vi* **1** give or get cash for: *Can you ~ this cheque for me/~ me a cheque?* **2** take advantage of; benefit from: *shopkeepers who ~ in on shortages by putting up prices.*

`cash crop`, food-crop (e g coffee, groundnuts) to be sold for cash (not for use by the growers).

`cash desk`, desk or counter (in a shop, etc) where payment (by cash or cheque) are made.

`cash price`, price if payment is immediate.

`cash register`, cash box with a device for recording and storing cash received.

ca·shew /ˈkæʃuː/ *n* [C] (tropical American tree with a) small kidney-shaped nut (` ~-nut).

cash·ier /kæˈʃɪə(r)/ *n* [C] person who receives and pays out money in a bank, store, hotel, restaurant, etc.

cash·mere /ˈkæʃmɪə(r)/ *n* [U] fine soft wool of Kashmir /kæʃˈmɪə(r)/ goats of India.

cas·ing /ˈkeɪsɪŋ/ *n* [C,U] covering; protective wrapping: *copper wire with a rubber ~*.

ca·sino /kəˈsiːnəʊ/ *n* [C] (*pl* ~s) public room or building for music, dancing, etc and (usually) for gambling.

cask /kɑːsk *US*: kæsk/ *n* [C] **1** barrel for liquids. **2** amount that a cask holds.

cas·ket /ˈkɑːskɪt *US*: ˈkæskɪt/ *n* [C] **1** small box to hold letters, jewels, cremated ashes, etc. **2** (*US*) coffin.

cas·sava /kəˈsɑːvə/ *n* [C,U] (tropical plant with) starchy roots eaten as food.

cas·ser·ole /ˈkæsərəʊl/ *n* [C] heat-proof dish with a lid in which food is cooked; food so cooked: *a ~ of lamb.*

cas·sette /kəˈset/ *n* [C] (*US* = *cartridge*) sealed container for magnetic tape or for photographic film.

cas·sock /ˈkæsək/ *n* [C] long, close-fitting outer garment, worn by some priests.

cast¹ /kɑːst *US*: kæst/ *n* [C] **1** act of throwing (e g a net or fishing line). **2** thing made by casting(3) or by pressing soft material into a mould: *His leg was in a plaster ~.* **3** mould for a casting. **4** set of actors in a play; the distribution of the parts among these actors: *a play with an all-star ~.* **5** type or quality: *~ of/mind.* **6** (of the eyes) slight squint.

cast² /kɑːst *US*: kæst/ *vt,vi* (*pt,pp* ~) **1** throw; allow to fall or drop: *The fisherman ~ his net into the water.* **be cast down**, be depressed, unhappy. ⇨ downcast. **cast a vote**, give a vote. **2** turn or send in a particular direction. **cast one's eye over sth**, look at, examine, it. **3** pour (liquid metal) into a mould; make in this way: *a figure ~ in bronze.* **4** give (an actor) a part in a play: *He was ~ for the part of Hamlet.* **5** **cast sb or sth aside**, abandon; throw away as useless or unwanted. **cast off, (a)** unloose (a boat) and let go. **(b)** (*fig*) abandon; throw away as unwanted. **(c)** remove the last row of stitches from a knitting needle. **cast on**, make the first row of stitches when knitting.

`cast iron` *n* [U] iron in a hard, brittle form, made in moulds after melting the ore in a blast furnace. Hence, **'cast-'iron** *adj* **(a)** made of cast iron. **(b)** (*fig*) hard; strong; unyielding: *a man with a ~-iron will/constitution.*

`'cast·ing 'vote`, one given (e g by the chairman) to decide a question when votes on each side are equal.

cas·ta·nets /ˌkæstəˈnets/ *n pl* instruments of hardwood, etc used in pairs on the fingers to make rattling sounds as a rhythm for dancing.

cast·away /ˈkɑːstəweɪ *US*: ˈkæst-/ *n* [C] shipwrecked person, esp one reaching a strange country or lonely island.

caste /kɑːst *US*: kæst/ *n* **1** [C] one of the Hindu hereditary social classes; any exclusive social class. **2** [U] this system.

cas·tel·lated /ˈkæstəleɪtɪd/ *adj* having turrets or battlements (like a castle).

cas·ti·gate /ˈkæstɪgeɪt/ *vt* punish severely with blows or by criticizing.

cas·ti·ga·tion /ˌkæstɪˈgeɪʃən/ *n* [C,U]

cast·ing /ˈkɑːstɪŋ/ *n* [C] thing made by being poured into a mould. ⇨ cast²(3).

castle /ˈkɑːsl *US*: ˈkæsl/ *n* [C] **1** large building or group of buildings fortified against attack, esp as in olden times; house that was once such a fortified building. **2** piece (also called *rook*) used in the game of chess. □ *vi* (in chess) move the king sideways two squares and place the castle on the square the king moved across.

cas·tor, cas·ter /ˈkɑstə(r) *US:* ˈkæs-/ *n* [C] **1** wheel fixed to the legs of a chair, etc (so that it may be turned easily). **2** bottle or metal pot, with holes in the top, for sugar, salt, etc.

`castor sugar,` white, finely powdered sugar.

cas·tor oil /ˈkɑstər ˈɔɪl *US:* ˈkæstər ɔɪl/ *n* [U] thick oil, used as a medicine.

cas·trate /kæˈstreɪt *US:* ˈkæstreɪt/ *vt* make (a male animal) useless for breeding purposes.

cas·tra·tion /kæˈstreɪʃən/ *n* [C,U]

cas·ual /ˈkæʒʊəl/ *adj* **1** happening by chance: *a ~ meeting.* **2** careless; informal: *a ~ glance; ~ clothes,* for informal occasions, holidays, etc. **3** irregular; not continued: *~ labourers,* not permanently engaged by one employer.

cas·ual·ly *adv*

casu·alty /ˈkæʒʊəltɪ/ *n* [C] (*pl* -ies) **1** accident, esp one involving loss of life or serious injury. **2** person killed or seriously injured in war or an accident: *The enemy suffered heavy casualties.*

`Casualty Ward/Department,` part of a hospital to which injured persons are taken.

cat /kæt/ *n* [C] **1** small, fur-covered animal often kept as a pet, to catch mice, etc. *not room to swing a cat (in),* very small, narrow space. **2** any animal of the group that includes cats, tigers, lions, panthers and leopards.

`cat burglar,` one who enters a building by climbing up walls, drainpipes, etc.

`cat-call` *vi, n* [C] (make a) loud, shrill whistle expressing disapproval (e g at a political meeting).

`cat-nap,` short sleep or doze (in a chair, etc not in bed).

`cat-o'-nine-tails,` knotted whip formerly used to punish offenders.

`cat suit,` woman's or child's close-fitting one-piece garment for the whole body.

`cat-walk,` narrow footway along a bridge, or through machinery, engines, etc.

`cat's whisker,` (esp) excellent example, proposal, person.

cata·clysm /ˈkætəklɪzm/ *n* [C] sudden and violent change (e g an earthquake, a political or social revolution).

cata·clys·mic /ˈkætəˈklɪzmɪk/ *adj*

cata·combs /ˈkætəkumz/ *n pl* series of underground galleries with openings along the sides for the burial of the dead (as in ancient Rome).

cata·falque /ˈkætəfælk/ *n* [C] decorated stand or stage for a coffin at a funeral.

cata·logue (*US* also **catalog**) /ˈkætəlɒg *US:* -lɔg/ *n* [C] list of names, places, goods, etc in a special order: *a library ~.* □ *vt* make, put in, a catalogue.

cata·maran /ˈkætəməˈræn/ *n* [C] boat with twin hulls.

cat·a·pult /ˈkætəpʌlt/ *n* [C] **1** Y-shaped stick with a piece of elastic, for shooting stones, etc from. **2** (in ancient times) machine for throwing heavy stones in war. **3** apparatus for launching aircraft without a runway (e g from the deck of a carrier). □ *vt* **1** shoot (as) from a catapult. **2** launch (aircraft) with a catapult.

cata·ract /ˈkætərækt/ *n* [C] **1** large, steep waterfall. **2** growth over the eyeball, that progressively obscures sight.

ca·tarrh /kəˈtɑ(r)/ *n* [U] inflamation in the nose and throat, causing flow of liquid, as when one has a cold.

ca·tas·trophe /kəˈtæstrəfɪ/ *n* [C] sudden event causing great suffering and destruction (e g a flood).

cata·strophic /ˈkætəˈstrofɪk/ *adj*

catch[1] /kætʃ/ *n* [C] **1** act of catching (esp a ball): *That was a difficult ~.* **2** that which is caught or worth catching: *a fine ~ of fish.* **3** something intended to trick or deceive: *There's a ~ in it somewhere.* **4** device for fastening or securing a lock, door, etc.

catch[2] /kætʃ/ *vt,vi* (*pt,pp* caught /kɔt/) **1** stop (something in motion) (e g by getting hold of it with the hands, by holding out something into which it may come): *I threw the ball to him and he caught it.* **2** capture; seize; intercept: *~ a thief. How many fish did you ~?* **3** surprise a person doing something (wrong): *I caught the boys stealing apples from my garden. catch sb out,* detect an offender. **4** be in time for: *~ a train/the bus, etc.* **5** *catch sb up/up with sb,* (a) come up to a person who is going in the same direction; overtake. (b) do all the work that has not yet been done: *Tom has got to work hard to ~ up with the rest of the class.* **6** (cause to) become fixed or prevented from moving; (cause to) be trapped: *I caught my fingers in the door.* **7** get (the meaning of); hear (the sound); receive (punishment, etc): *I don't quite ~ your meaning. I didn't ~ the end of the sentence. You'll ~ it!* You'll be scolded, punished, etc! *catch sb's eye,* look at him to attract his attention when he looks in your direction. *catch sight/a glimpse of,* see for a short time. **8** become infected with: *~ a disease/a cold.* **9** (try to) grasp: *A drowning man will ~ at a straw. He caught hold of my arm.* **10** hit: *She caught him one* (= gave him a blow) *on the cheek.* **11** *catch one's breath,* fail to breathe regularly for a moment (from surprise, etc). *catch fire,* begin to burn.

`catch-word,` (a) word placed so as to draw attention to an article, the subject of a paragraph, etc. (b) phrase or slogan in frequent current use.

catch·ing /ˈkætʃɪŋ/ adj (esp of diseases) infectious.

catchy /ˈkætʃɪ/ adj (-ier, -iest) 1 (of a tune, etc) easily remembered. 2 tricky, deceptive.

cat·echism /ˈkætɪkɪzm/ n 1 [U] instruction (esp about religion) by question and answer. 2 [C] number, succession, of questions and answers designed for this purpose.

cat·echize /ˈkætɪkaɪz/ vt teach or examine by asking many questions.

cat·egor·i·cal /ˈkætɪˈgorɪkəl US: -ˈgɔr-/ adj (of a statement) unconditional; absolute: the ~ truth.

cat·egor·i·cally adv

cat·egor·ize /ˈkætɪgəraɪz/ vt place in a category.

cat·egory /ˈkætɪgərɪ US: -gɔrɪ/ n [C] (pl -ies) division or class in a complete system or grouping.

ca·ter /ˈkeɪtə(r)/ vi 1 cater for, provide food: Weddings and parties ~ed for. 2 cater for/to, supply amusement, etc: TV programmes usually ~ for all tastes.

ca·terer, person who provides meals, etc to clubs, etc.

cat·er·pil·lar /ˈkætəpɪlə(r)/ n [C] 1 larva of a butterfly or moth. 2 endless belt passing over toothed wheels on tanks, etc.

cat·gut /ˈkætgʌt/ n [U] material used for the strings of violins, tennis rackets, etc.

ca·thar·sis /kəˈθɑːsɪs/ n (pl -ses /-siːz/) 1 [U] emptying of the bowels. 2 [C] outlet for strong emotion (e g as given by an account of deep feelings given to another person).

ca·thar·tic /kəˈθɑːtɪk/ adj.

ca·the·dral /kəˈθiːdrəl/ n [C] chief church in a diocese.

cath·ode /ˈkæθəʊd/ n [C] negative electrode in a battery, etc; electrode which releases negative electrons in a [1] ~ ray tube.

cath·olic /ˈkæθəlɪk/ adj 1 liberal; general; including many or most things: a man with ~ tastes and interests. 2 C~, = Roman Catholic. □ n C~, = Roman Catholic.

Ca·tholi·cism /kəˈθɒləsɪzm/ n [U] teaching, beliefs, etc of the Church of Rome.

cat·kin /ˈkætkɪn/ n [C] spike of soft, downy flowers hanging down from twigs of such trees as willows and birches.

catty /ˈkætɪ/ adj (-ier, -iest) (esp) sly and spiteful.

cattle /ˈkætəl/ n pl bulls, bullocks, cows: twenty head of ~.

cau·cus /ˈkɔːkəs/ n [C] (pl ~es) (meeting of the) organization committee of a political party (making plans, decisions, etc).

caught /kɔːt/ pt,pp of catch [2].

caul·dron /ˈkɔːldrən/ n [C] large, deep, open pot in which things are boiled.

cauli·flower /ˈkɒlɪflaʊə(r) US: ˈkɔlɪ-/ n [C,U] (vegetable with a) large, white flowerhead.

caulk /kɔːk/ vt make (joins between planks, etc) tight with fibre or a sticky substance.

cau·sal /ˈkɔːzəl/ adj of cause and effect; of, expressing, cause.

cau·sal·ity /kɔːˈzælətɪ/ n [C] (pl -ies) relation of cause and effect; the principle that nothing can happen without a cause.

cau·sa·tive /ˈkɔːzətɪv/ adj acting as, expressing, cause.

cause /kɔːz/ n 1 [C,U] that which produces an effect, that makes something happen: The ~ of the fire was carelessness. 2 [U] reason: You have no ~ for complaint/no ~ to complain. 3 [C] purpose for which efforts are being made: fight in the ~ of justice. □ vt be the cause of: What ~d his death?

cause·less adj without any natural or known reason.

cause·way /ˈkɔːzweɪ/ n [C] raised road or footpath, esp across wet land or a swamp.

caus·tic /ˈkɔːstɪk/ adj 1 able to burn or destroy by chemical action: ~ soda. 2 (fig) sarcastic: ~ remarks.

caus·ti·cally /-klɪ/ adv

cau·ter·ize /ˈkɔːtəraɪz/ vt burn (e g a snakebite) with a caustic substance or with a hot iron (to destroy infection).

cau·tion /ˈkɔːʃən/ n 1 [U] taking care; paying attention (to avoid danger or making mistakes): When crossing a busy street we must use ~. 2 [C] warning words: The judge gave the prisoner a ~ and set him free. □ vt give a caution to: I ~ed him against being late. The judge ~ed the prisoner.

cau·tion·ary /ˈkɔːʃənərɪ US: ˈkɔːʃənerɪ/ adj giving advice or warning: ~ tales.

cau·tious /ˈkɔːʃəs/ adj having or showing caution.

cau·tious·ly adv

cav·al·cade /ˈkævəlˈkeɪd/ n [C] procession of persons on horseback or in carriages. ⇨ motorcade.

cava·lier /ˈkævəˈlɪə(r)/ n 1 [C] (old use) horseman or knight. 2 (in the Civil War, England, 17th century) supporter of Charles I. □ adj discourteous.

cav·alry /ˈkævəlrɪ/ n (sing or pl, -ies) soldiers who fight on horseback.

cave /keɪv/ n [C] hollow place in the side of a cliff or hill; large natural hollow under the ground. □ vi,vt cave ˈin, (cause to) fall in, give way to pressure: The roof of the tunnel ~d in.

ˈcave-man, cave dweller.

cav·ern /ˈkævən/ n [C] (literary) cave.

caviar, cavi·are /ˈkævɪɑː(r)/ n [U] pickled roe (eggs) of the sturgeon or certain other large fish.

cav·ity /ˈkævətɪ/ n [C] (pl -ies) empty space; small hole, within a solid body: a ~ in a tooth.

ca·vort /kəˈvɔːt/ vi (informal) prance or jump about like an excited horse.

caw /kɔː/ n [C] cry of a raven, rook or crow □ vi,vt make this cry.

cay·enne /keɪˈen/ n [U] (also ~ pepper) very hot kind of red pepper.

cease /siːs/ vt,vi stop (the usual word): C~

fire!

cease·less *adj* never ending.

cease·less·ly *adv*

cedar /ˈsidə(r)/ *n* **1** [C] evergreen tree with hard, red, sweet-smelling wood. **2** [U] the wood.

cede /sid/ *vt* **cede to,** give up (rights, land, etc to another state, etc).

ce·dilla /sɪˈdɪlə/ *n* [C] mark put under the c (ç) in the spelling of some French, Spanish and Portuguese words (as in *façade*) to show that the sound is /s/.

ceil·ing /ˈsilɪŋ/ *n* [C] **1** upper or overhead surface of a room. **2** highest (practicable) level (to be) reached by an aircraft: *an aircraft with a ~ of 20 000 ft.* **3** maximum height, limit or level: *price ~s; wage ~s.*

cel·ebrate /ˈseləbreɪt/ *vt* **1** do something to show that a day or an event is important, or an occasion for rejoicing: *~ Christmas/one's birthday; ~ Mass,* consecrate the Eucharist. **2** praise and honour: *The names of many heroes are ~d by the poets.*

cel·ebrated *adj* famous: *a ~d painter.*

cel·ebra·tion /ˌseləˈbreɪʃən/ *n* [C,U]

ce·leb·rity /sɪˈlebrətɪ/ *n* (*pl* -ies) **1** [U] being celebrated; fame and honour. **2** [C] famous person.

cel·ery /ˈselərɪ/ *n* [U] garden plant of which the white stems are eaten raw as salad or cooked as a vegetable: *~ soup.*

ce·les·tial /sɪˈlestɪəl *US:* -tʃəl/ *adj* **1** of the sky; of heaven: *~ bodies,* e g the sun and the stars. **2** divinely good or beautiful.

celi·bacy /ˈselɪbəsɪ/ *n* [U] state of living unmarried, esp as a religious obligation.

celi·bate /ˈselɪbət/ *adj, n* [C] (of an) unmarried person (esp for religious reasons).

cell /sel/ *n* [C] **1** small room for one person (esp in a prison or a monastery). **2** compartment in a larger structure, esp in a honeycomb. **3** unit of an apparatus for producing electric current by chemical action. **4** microscopic unit of living matter. **5** (of persons) centre of (usually revolutionary) propaganda: *communist ~s in an industrial town.*

cel·lar /ˈselə(r)/ *n* [C] underground room for storing coal, wine, etc; (person's) store of wine.

cel·list /ˈtʃelɪst/ *n* [C] cello player.

cello, 'cello /ˈtʃeləʊ/ *n* [C] (*pl ~s*) (common abbr for) violoncello.

cel·lu·lar /ˈseljʊlə(r)/ *adj* consisting of cells(4): *~ tissue.*

Cel·sius /ˈselsɪəs/ *n* (of thermometers) = centigrade.

ce·ment /sɪˈment/ *n* [U] **1** grey powder (made by burning lime and clay) which, after being wetted, becomes hard like stone and is used for building, etc. ⇨ **concrete. 2** any similar soft substance that sets firm, used for filling holes (e g in the teeth), or for joining things. □ *vt* **1** put on or in, join with cement. **2** (*fig*) strengthen; unite firmly: *~ a friendship.*

ce·ment-mixer, (vehicle with a) revolving drum in which concrete is mixed.

cem·etery /ˈsemətrɪ *US:* ˈseməterɪ/ *n* [C] (*pl* -ies) area of land, not a churchyard, used for burials.

ceno·taph /ˈsenətɑf *US:* -tæf/ *n* [C] monument put up in memory of a person or persons buried elsewhere.

cen·sor /ˈsensə(r)/ *n* [C] (esp) official with authority to examine letters, books, periodicals, plays, films, etc and to cut out anything regarded as immoral or in other ways undesirable, or, in time of war, helpful to the enemy. □ *vt* examine, cut out, parts of (a book, etc).

ˈcen·sor·ship, office, duties, etc of a censor.

cen·sure /ˈsenʃə(r)/ *vt* criticize unfavourably: *censuring her for being lazy.* □ *n* [U] rebuke; disapproval: *pass a vote of ~;* [C] expression of disapproval: *unfair ~s of a new book.*

cen·sus /ˈsensəs/ *n* [C] (*pl ~es*) official counting of the population, traffic, etc.

cent /sent/ *n* [C] the 100th part of a dollar and some other metric units of currency; metal coin of this value. *per cent,* (%) in, by or for, every 100. (*agree, etc*) *one hundred per cent,* completely.

cen·taur /ˈsentɔ(r)/ *n* [C] (in old Greek stories) creature, half man and half horse.

cen·ten·ar·ian /ˌsentɪˈneərɪən/ *n* [C] *adj* (person who is) (more than) 100 years old.

cen·ten·ary /senˈtinərɪ *US:* ˈsentənerɪ/ *adj, n* [C] (*pl* -ies) **1** (having to do with a) period of 100 years. **2** 100th anniversary.

cen·ten·nial /senˈtenɪəl/ *adj, n* = centenary.

cen·ten·nial·ly *adv*

cen·ter /ˈsentə(r)/ *n* (*US*) = centre.

cent(i)- /sent(ɪ)-/ *prefix* a hundred; a hundredth part.

cen·ti·grade /ˈsentɪgreɪd/ *adj* in or of the temperature scale that has 100 degrees between the freezing-point and the boiling-point of water: *100° ~ (100°C).*

cen·ti·gram(me) /ˈsentɪgræm/ *n* [C] the 100th part of a gram(me).

cen·ti·metre (*US* = **-meter**) /ˈsentɪmitə(r)/ *n* [C] the 100th part of a metre.

cen·ti·pede /ˈsentɪpid/ *n* [C] small, long, crawling creature with numerous joints and feet.

cen·tral /ˈsentrəl/ *adj* **1** of, at, from or near, the centre: *My house is very ~,* is in or near the middle of the town. **2** chief; most important: *the ~ idea of an argument.*

ˈcentral ˈheating, system of heating a building from a central source through radiators, etc.

cen·tral·ly *adv*

cen·tral·ize /ˈsentrəlaɪz/ *vt,vi* **1** bring to the centre. **2** come, put, bring, under central (esp government) control.

cen·tral·iz·ation /ˌsentrəlaɪˈzeɪʃən *US:* -lɪˈz-/ *n* [U]

centre (US = **cen·ter**) /ˈsentə(r)/ n [C] **1** middle part or point: *the ~ of London.* **'centre of `gravity,** that point in an object about which the weight is evenly balanced in any position. **2** place of great activity, of special interest, etc: *a `health-~; the `shopping ~ of a town.* **3** person or thing that attracts interest, attention etc: *She loves to be the ~ of attraction.* **4** that which occupies a middle position, e g in politics, persons with moderate views. □ *vt,vi* **1** place in, pass to, come to, be at, the centre: *The defender ~d the ball.* **2** *centre on/upon:* *Our thoughts ~ on one idea.*

cen·tri·fu·gal /senˈtrɪfjʊɡl/ *adj* moving, tending to move, away from the centre or axis: *~ force,* the force which causes a body spinning round a centre to tend to move outwards.

cen·tury /ˈsentʃərɪ/ n [C] (*pl* -ies) **1** 100 years. **2** one of the periods of 100 years before or since the birth of Jesus Christ: *in the 20th ~,* AD 1901-2000. **3** 100 runs made in cricket by a batsman in one innings.

ce·ramic /sɪˈræmɪk/ *adj* of the art of pottery.

ce·ram·ics, (a) art of making and decorating pottery. (b) (used with a *pl verb*) articles made of porcelain, clay, etc.

cer·eal /ˈsɪərɪəl/ n [C] (usually *pl*) **1** any kind of grain used for food. **2** food prepared from cereals: *breakfast ~s.*

cer·ebral /ˈserəbrəl/ *adj* of the brain: *a ~ haemorrhage.*

cer·emo·nial /ˌserəˈməʊnɪəl/ *adj* formal; as used for ceremonies: *~ dress.* □ *n* [C,U] special order of ceremony, formality, for a special event, etc.

cer·emo·nial·ly *adv*

cer·emo·ni·ous /ˌserəˈməʊnɪəs/ *adj* fond of, marked by, formality.

cer·emo·ni·ous·ly *adv*

cer·emony /ˈserəmənɪ US: -məʊnɪ/ n [C] (*pl* -ies) **1** [C] special act(s), religious service, etc on an occasion such as a wedding, funeral, the opening of a new public building, etc. **2** [U] behaviour required by social customs, esp among officials, people of high class, etc: *There's too much ~ on official occasions.* **stand on ceremony,** pay great attention to rules of behaviour.

cert¹ /sɜːt/ n [C] (*sl*) something looked on as certain to happen or that certainly has happened: *a dead ~,* an absolute certainty.

cert² /sɜːt/ n [C] (*informal*) (abbr for) certificate.

cer·tain /ˈsɜːtən/ *adj* **1** settled; of which there is no doubt: *It is ~ that two and two make four.* **2** convinced; having no doubt; confident: *I'm ~ (that) he saw me.* **for certain,** without doubt: *I cannot say for ~ (=* with complete confidence) *when he will arrive.* **make certain,** (a) inquire in order to be sure: *I think there's a train at 8.20 but you ought to make ~.* (b) do something in

order to be assured: *I'll go and make ~ of our seats.* **3** reliable; sure to come or happen: *There is no ~ cure for this disease.* **4** not named, stated or described, although it is possible to do so: *on ~ conditions; a ~ person I met yesterday.* **5** some, but not much: *There was a ~ coldness in her attitude towards me.*

cer·tain·ly *adv* (a) without doubt: *He will ~ly die if you don't get a doctor.* (b) (in answer to questions) yes: *'Will you pass me the towel, please?' 'C~ly!'*

cer·tain·ty, (a) thing that is certain: *Prices have gone up—that's a ~ty.* (b) state of being sure; freedom from doubt: *We can have no ~ty of success.*

cer·ti·fi·able /ˈsɜːtɪfaɪəbl/ *adj* that can be certified.

cer·tifi·cate /səˈtɪfɪkət/ n [C] written or printed statement, that may be used as proof or evidence: *a `birth/`marriage ~.*

cer·tify /ˈsɜːtɪfaɪ/ *vt,vi* (*pt,pp* -ied) declare (usually by giving a certificate) that one is certain, that something is true, correct, in order: *I ~ (that) this is a true copy of...*

cer·ti·tude /ˈsɜːtɪtjuːd US: -tuːd/ n [U] certainty (the more usual word).

cer·vi·cal /ˈsɜːvaɪkəl US: `sɜːvɪkəl/ *adj* of the neck: *a ~ smear,* smear taken from the cervix, to test for cancer.

cer·vix /ˈsɜːvɪks/ n [C] (*anat*) narrow part of the womb.

ces·sa·tion /seˈseɪʃən/ n [U] (*formal*) ceasing: *the ~ of hostilities.*

ces·sion /ˈseʃən/ n [U] (*legal*) act of ceding or giving up lands/rights etc by agreement; [C] thing ceded.

cess·pit /ˈsespɪt/, **cess·pool** /ˈsespuːl/ n [C] (usually covered) hole, pit or underground tank into which drains (esp for sewage) empty.

chafe /tʃeɪf/ *vi,vt* **1** rub (the skin, one's hands) to get warmth. **2** make or become rough or sore by rubbing: *Her skin ~s easily.* **3** feel irritation or impatience: *~ at the delay/inefficiency; ~ under restraints.* □ *n* [C] sore place on the skin.

chaff¹ /tʃɑːf US: tʃæf/ n [U] **1** outer covering (husks) of grain, removed before the grain is used as human food. **2** hay or straw cut up as food for cattle. □ *vt* cut up (hay, straw).

chaff² /tʃɑːf US: tʃæf/ n [U] good-humoured teasing or joking. □ *vt* tease.

chaf·finch /ˈtʃæfɪntʃ/ n [C] small European songbird.

cha·grin /ˈʃæɡrɪn US: ʃəˈɡrɪn/ n [U] feeling of disappointment or annoyance (at having failed, made a mistake, etc): *Much to his ~, he did not win the race.* □ *vt* affect through disappointment, etc.

chain /tʃeɪn/ n [C] **1** flexible line of connected rings or links for connecting, continuing, restraining, ornament, etc. **2** (*pl*) kind used for prisoners. **3** number of connected things, events, etc: *a ~ of events/*

ideas/mountains. **4** measure of length (66 ft). □ *vt* make fast with a chain.

`chain-armour/-mail,` armour made of metal rings linked together.

`chain-gang,` gang of prisons in chains while at work outside their prison.

`chain reaction,` chemical change forming products that themselves cause more changes so that the process is repeated again and again.

`chain-smoker,` person who smokes cigarettes one after the other.

`chain-stitch,` kind of sewing in which each stitch makes a loop through which the next stitch is taken.

`chain-store,` one of many shops owned and controlled by the same company.

chair /tʃeə(r)/ *n* [C] **1** separate movable seat for one person, usually with a back and in some cases with arms (`arm~`): *Won't you take a ~,* sit down? **2** seat, office, of a person who presides at a meeting. *be in/take the chair,* act as chairman. **3** position of a professor: *the C~ of Philosophy.* □ *vt* **1** place in a chair; raise up and carry (a person who has won a contest): *The newly elected MP was ~ed by his supporters.* **2** ~ *a meeting,* act as chairman.

`chair-man,` person controlling a meeting.

chalet /ʃælei/ *n* [C] **1** Swiss mountain hut or cottage built of wood and with a sharply sloping and overhanging roof. **2** summer cottage built in the same style. **3** small hut in a holiday camp, etc.

chal-ice /tʃælis/ *n* [C] wine-cup, esp that used for the Eucharist.

chalk /tʃɔk/ *n* **1** [U] soft, white substance (a kind of limestone) used for making lime. **2** [C,U] this material, or a material similar in texture, white or coloured, made into sticks for writing and drawing. □ *vt* write, draw, mark, whiten, with chalk.

chalky *adj* of, containing, like, chalk.

chal-lenge /tʃæləndʒ/ *n* [C] **1** invitation or call to play a game, run a race, have a fight, etc to see who is better, stronger, etc. **2** order given by a sentry to stop and explain who one is: *'Who goes there?' is the ~.* □ *vt* give, send, be, a challenge to; ask for facts (to support a statement, etc): *~ a person's right to do something.*

chal-lenger, person who challenges.

cham-ber /tʃeimbə(r)/ *n* **1** *(old use)* room, esp a bedroom. **2** *(pl)* judge's room for hearing cases that need not be taken into court; rooms in a large building to live in or to use as offices. **3** (hall used by a) group of legislators, often distinguished as the `Upper C~` and the `Lower C~.` **4** offices of barristers, etc esp in the Inns of Court. **5** group of persons organized for purposes of trade: *a C~ of Commerce.* **6** enclosed or walled space in the body of an animal or plant, in a gun, in some kinds of machinery.

`chamber concert,` concert of chamber music.

`chamber-maid,` housemaid who keeps bedrooms in order (now chiefly in hotels).

`chamber music,` music for a small number of players (e g a string quartet).

`chamber-pot,` vessel for urine, used in a bedroom.

cha-meleon /kə`miliən/ *n* [C] **1** small lizard with a long tongue whose colour changes according to its background. **2** *(fig)* person who changes his voice, manner, etc to suit his audience.

chammy-leather /ʃæmi leðə(r)/ *n* = chamois-leather.

cham-ois /ʃæmwa US: ʃæmi/ *n* [C] small animal like a goat that lives in the high mountains of Europe and S W Asia.

`chamois-leather,` soft leather from the skin of goats and sheep.

champ[1] /tʃæmp/ *vt,vi* **1** (of horses) bite (food, the bit) noisily. **2** *(fig)* show impatience: *~ with rage.*

champ[2] /tʃæmp/ *n* [C] *(informal)* (abbr for) champion(2).

cham-pagne /ʃæm`pein/ *n* [C,U] (kinds of) white sparkling French wine.

cham-pion /tʃæmpiən/ *n* [C] **1** person who fights, argues or speaks in support of another or of a cause: *a ~ of free speech/of woman's rights.* **2** person, team, animal, etc taking the first place in a competition: *a `boxing/ `tennis ~.`* □ *vt* support; defend.

cham-pion-ship, [U] act of championing; [C] position of a champion.

chance[1] /tʃɑns US: tʃæns/ *n* **1** [U] the happening of events without any warning or cause that can be seen or understood; the way things happen; fortune or luck: *Let's leave it to ~.* *by chance,* unexpectedly, not by design or on purpose. *take one's chance(s),* trust to luck, take whatever happens to come. **2** [C,U] possibility: *He has no/not much ~/a poor ~ of winning. The ~s are that you'll lose.* *on the off chance of doing sth,* in the hope of doing it. **3** [C] opportunity; occasion when success seems very probable: *It's the ~ of a lifetime,* a favourable opportunity that is unlikely ever to come again. *stand a (good, fair) chance (of...),* have a (good) hope (of). □ *adj* coming or happening by chance(1): *a ~ meeting.*

chance[2] /tʃɑns US: tʃæns/ *vi,vt* **1** find, happen or meet by chance: *I ~d to be there.* **2** take a risk, esp *chance it/one's arm,* *(informal)* take a risk.

chan-cel /tʃɑnsəl US: tʃænsəl/ *n* [C] eastern part of a church, round the altar, used by the priest(s) and choir.

chan-cel-lor /tʃɑnsələ(r) US: tʃæns-/ *n* [C] **1** State or law official of various kinds: *the C~ of the Exchequer.* **2** (of some universities) honorary head or president (the duties being performed by the Vice-C~). **3** chief secretary of an embassy. **4** (in some coun-

tries, e g Germany) chief minister of state.
chancy /'tʃɑnsɪ US: 'tʃænsɪ/ adj (-ier, -iest)
(informal) risky; uncertain.
chan·de·lier /ˌʃændə'lɪə(r)/ n [C] branched
support, hanging from a ceiling, for a number of lights.
chan·dler /'tʃɑndlə(r) US: 'tʃænd-/ n [C] 1
person who makes or sells candles, paint,
etc. 2 ship's ∼, dealer in canvas, ropes and
other supplies for ships.
change¹ /tʃeɪndʒ/ n 1 [C] changed or different condition(s); thing used in place of
another or others; move from one place to
another: a welcome ∼ from town to country
life. Take a ∼ of clothes with you, extra
clothes to ∼ into. **a change of air/climate,**
e g a holiday away from home. 2 [U] money
in small(er) units; money that is the difference between the price or cost and the sum
offered in payment: Can you give me ∼ for a
one-pound note? Don't leave your ∼ on the
shop counter! 3 [C,U] alteration; changing:
Let's hope there will be a ∼ in the weather.
for a change, for the sake of variety; to be
different from one's routine: Why not pay
for me for a ∼?
change¹ /tʃeɪndʒ/ vt,vi 1 leave one place
and go to, enter, another: I've ∼d my
address, moved to a different house. 2 take
off something and put something else on: It
won't take me five minutes to ∼, to put on
different clothes. 3 give and receive in
return: He ∼d his Italian money before leaving Rome. I ∼d places with her. 4 make or
become different: That has ∼d my ideas.
The wind has ∼d from north to east.
change one's mind, decide on a new plan,
have a new opinion, etc. **change up/down,**
change to a higher/lower gear when driving
a motor-vehicle.
change·able /-əbəl/ adj likely to alter; able
to be changed: ∼able weather.
chan·nel /'tʃænəl/ n [C] 1 stretch of water
joining two seas; the English C∼, between
France and England. 2 natural or artificial
bed of a stream of water; passage along
which a liquid may flow. 3 (fig) any way by
which news, ideas, etc may travel: He has
secret ∼s of information. **through the
usual channels,** by the usual means of
communication. 4 band of radio or TV fre-
quencies within which signals from a transmitter must be kept. □ vt (-ll-, US also -l-) 1
form a channel in; cut out (a way): The river
had ∼led its way through the soft rock. 2
cause to go through channels.
chant /tʃɑnt US: tʃænt/ n [C] often-repeated
tune for psalms and canticles; several syllables or words to one note. ⇨ hymn. □ vi,vt
sing; sing a chant.
chaos /'keɪɒs/ n [U] complete absence of
order or shape; confusion: The room was in
complete ∼ when the burglars had left.
cha·otic /keɪ'ɒtɪk/ adj in a state of chaos;
confused

cha·oti·cally /-klɪ/ adv
chap¹ /tʃæp/ n [C] (informal) man; boy.
chap² /tʃæp/ vt,vi (-pp-) 1 (of the skin)
become sore, rough, cracked: My skin soon
∼s in cold weather. 2 cause to become
cracked or rough: hands and face ∼ped by
the cold. □ n [C] crack, esp in the skin.
chapel /'tʃæpəl/ n [C] 1 place (not a parish
church) used for Christian worship, e g in a
school, prison, etc. 2 small place within a
Christian church, used for private prayer,
with an altar. 3 service held in a chapel. 4
trade union group in a factory, etc.
chap·er·on /'ʃæpərəʊn/ n [C] married or
elderly person (usually a woman) in charge
of a girl or young unmarried woman on
social occasions. □ vt act as a chaperon to.
chap·lain /'tʃæplɪn/ n [C] priest or clergyman, esp in the armed forces, or of a
chapel(1).
chap·ter /'tʃæptə(r)/ n [C] 1 (usually numbered) division of a book. **'chapter and
'verse,** the exact reference. 2 period: the
most brilliant ∼ in our history. 3 (general
meeting of the) whole number of canons of a
cathedral church, or the members of a
monastic order.
'chapter-house, building used for meetings
of chapters(3).
char¹ /tʃɑ(r)/ vt,vi (-rr-) (of a surface) make
or become black by burning: ∼red wood.
char² /tʃɑ(r)/ vi (-rr-) do the cleaning of
offices, houses, etc with payment by the
hour or the day: go out ∼ring. □ n [C] =
charwoman.
'char·woman, woman who earns money by
charring.
char³ /tʃɑ(r)/ n [U] (GB sl) tea: a cup of ∼.
char·ac·ter /'kærɪktə(r)/ n 1 [U] (of a person, community, race, etc) mental or moral
nature; mental or moral qualities that make
one person, race, etc different from others: a
woman of fine/strong/noble, etc ∼; the ∼ of
of the French. **in/out of character,** appro-
priate/inappropriate to a person's known
character. 2 [U] moral strength; reputation: a
man of ∼. 3 [U] all those qualities that make
a thing, place, etc what it is and different
from others: the ∼ of the desert areas of N
Africa. 4 [C] person who is well known;
person in a novel, play, etc: the ∼s in the
novels of Charles Dickens. 5 [C] letter, sign,
mark, etc used in a system of writing or
printing: Greek/Chinese ∼s.
char·ac·ter·less adj undistinguished; ordinary.
char·ac·ter·is·tic /ˌkærɪktə'rɪstɪk/ adj
forming part of, showing, the known character of: It's so ∼ of him. □ n [C] special
mark or quality.
char·ac·ter·is·ti·cally /-klɪ/ adv
char·ac·ter·ize /'kærɪktəraɪz/ vt show or
mark in a special way: Your work is ∼d by
lack of attention to detail.
cha·rade /ʃə'rɑd US: -'reɪd/ n [C] 1 game in

which a word is guessed by the onlookers after each syllable of it has been suggested by acting a little play. **2** pointless action.

char·coal /ˈtʃɑːkəʊl/ n [U] black substance, used as fuel, for drawing, etc made by burning wood slowly in an oven with little air.

charge¹ /tʃɑːdʒ/ n [C] **1** accusation; statement that a person has done wrong, esp that he has broken a law. **bring a charge against sb,** accuse him of (a crime). **2** sudden and violent attack at high speed (by soldiers, animals, a football player, etc). **3** price asked for goods or services: *hotel* ~s. **4** amount of powder, etc (to be) used in a gun or for causing an explosion; quantity of energy (to be) contained in an electrical battery, etc: *a positive/negative* ~. **5** [C,U] work, responsibility, given to a person as a duty: *Mary was in* ~ *of the baby*. **take charge of,** be responsible for. **6** instructions: *the judge's* ~ *to the jury*, instructions concerning their duty (in reaching a verdict).

charge² /tʃɑːdʒ/ vt,vi **1** accuse; bring a charge(1) against: *He was* ~d *with murder*. **2** rush forward (and attack): *The wounded lion suddenly* ~d *at me*. **3** ask in payment: *He* ~d *me fifty pence for it*. **4** load (a gun); fill, put a charge(4) into: ~ *a battery*. **5** **charge with,** give as a task or duty: *He was* ~d *with an important mission*. **6** (esp of a judge, a bishop or person in authority) command; instruct: *I* ~ *you not to forget what I have said*.

charge·able /ˈtʃɑːdʒəbəl/ adj **1** that can be, is liable to be, charged: *If you steal, you are* ~ *with theft*. **2** that may be added (to an account); that may be made an expense: *Costs of repairs are* ~ *to the owner*.

chargé d'affaires /ˌʃɑːʒeɪ dæˈfeə(r)/ n [C] (*pl* chargés d'affaires, pronunciation unchanged) official who takes the place of an ambassador or minister when the ambassador, etc is away.

char·iot /ˈtʃærɪət/ n [C] horse-drawn vehicle with two wheels, used in ancient times in fighting and racing.
char·io·teer /ˌtʃærɪəˈtɪə(r)/ n [C] driver of a chariot.

cha·risma /kəˈrɪzmə/ n [C] (*pl* ~s) **1** spiritual grace. **2** creative ability of an unusually high degree. **3** ability to inspire devotion and enthusiasm.
char·is·matic /ˌkærɪzˈmætɪk/ adj

chari·table /ˈtʃærɪtəbəl/ adj showing, having, for, charity: ~ *trusts*.
chari·tably /-əblɪ/ adv

char·ity /ˈtʃærətɪ/ n (*pl* -ies) **1** [U] (kindness in giving) help to the poor; money, food, etc so given. **2** [C] society or organization for helping the poor. **3** [U] willingness to judge other persons with kindness or love.

char·la·tan /ˈʃɑːlətən/ n [C] person who claims to have more skill, knowledge or ability than he really has.

charm /tʃɑːm/ n **1** [U] attractiveness; power

to give pleasure. **2** [C] pleasing quality or feature: *Her* ~ *of manner made her very popular*. **3** [C] thing believed to have magic power, good or bad: *a good-luck* ~. □ vt,vi **1** attract; give pleasure to: *We were* ~ed *with the scenery*. **2** use magic on; influence or protect as if by magic: *She* ~ed *away his sorrow*.

charm·ing adj delightful: *a* ~ing *young lady*.

chart /tʃɑːt/ n [C] **1** map used by sailors, showing the coasts, depth of the sea, position of rocks, lighthouses, etc. **2** sheet of paper with information, in the form of curves, diagrams, etc: *a* ˈweather ~. □ vt make a chart of; show on a chart.

char·ter /ˈtʃɑːtə(r)/ n [C] **1** (written or printed statement of) rights, permission, esp from a ruler or government (e g to a town, city or university). **2** hiring or engagement (of an aircraft, a ship, etc): *a* ˈ~ *flight*. □ vt **1** give a charter to. **2** hire or engage a ship, an aircraft, etc for an agreed time, purpose and payment.
ˈchartered acˈcountant, (in GB) member of the Institute of Accountants.
char·woman /ˈtʃɑːwʊmən/ n ⇨ char².

chary /ˈtʃeərɪ/ adj cautious; careful: ~ *of catching cold*.
char·ily /ˈtʃeərəlɪ/ adv

chase¹ /tʃeɪs/ vt,vi **1** run after in order to capture, kill, overtake or drive away: *Dogs like to* ~ *rabbits*. **2** (*informal*) hurry; rush: *The children all* ~d *off after the procession*. □ n [C] **1** act of chasing: *After a long* ~, *we caught the thief*. **2** hunted animal, person or thing being pursued.

chase² /tʃeɪs/ vt cut patterns or designs on; engrave: ~d *silver*.

chasm /ˈkæzm/ n [C] **1** deep opening, crack in the ground. **2** (*fig*) wide difference (of feeling or interests, between persons, groups, nations, etc).

chas·sis /ˈʃæsɪ/ n [C] (*pl* unchanged) **1** framework of a motor-vehicle on which the body is fastened or built. **2** landing gear of an aircraft.

chaste /tʃeɪst/ adj **1** virtuous in word, thought and deed. **2** (esp) abstaining from unlawful or immoral sexual intercourse. **3** (of style, taste) simple.
chaste·ly adv

chas·ten /ˈtʃeɪsən/ vt **1** punish in order to correct. **2** make chaste(2).

chas·tise /tʃæˈstaɪz/ vt punish severely.
chas·tise·ment n [U] punishment.

chas·tity /ˈtʃæstətɪ/ n [U] state of being chaste.

chat /tʃæt/ n [C] friendly, informal talk: *I had a long* ~ *with him*. □ vi,vt (-tt-) **1** have a chat: *They were* ~ting (*away*) *in the corner*. **2** **chat sb up,** (*informal*) talk to in order to win friendship: ~ *up a pretty barmaid*.
chatty adj (-ier, -iest) fond of chatting.

châ·teau /ˈʃætəʊ/ n [C] (*pl* ~x /-təʊz/)

castle or large country house in France.

chat·tel /ˈtʃætəl/ n [C] (*legal*) article of personal movable property (e g a chair, a car).

chat·ter /ˈtʃætə(r)/ vi **1** (of a person) talk quickly or foolishly; talk too much. **2** (of the cries of monkeys and some birds, of a person's upper and lower teeth striking together from cold or fear) make quick, indistinct sounds. □ n [C] sounds of the kind noted above: *the ~ of children.*

`chat·ter·box, person who chatters(1).

chauf·feur /ˈʃəʊfə(r) US: ˈʃəʊˈfɜr/ n [C] man paid to drive a private car.

chau·vin·ism /ˈʃəʊvɪnɪzm/ n [U] unreasoning enthusiasm for national military glory, sexual superiority, etc.

`chau·vin·ist, person with such enthusiasm: *a male ~.*

chau·vin·is·tic /ˌʃəʊvɪnˈɪstɪk/ adj

cheap /tʃip/ adj (-er, -est) **1** costing little money: *travel by the ~est route.* **2** worth more than the cost. **3** of poor quality: *~ and nasty.* **4** shallow; insincere: *~ emotion.*

cheap·ly adv

cheap·ness n [U]

cheapen /ˈtʃipən/ vt,vi make or become cheap; lower the price or quality of: *Don't ~ yourself.*

cheat /tʃit/ vi,vt act in a dishonest way to win an advantage or profit: *~ a person out of his money; ~ in an examination.* □ n [C] person who cheats; dishonest trick.

check¹ /tʃek/ n [U] **1** control; person or thing that checks or restrains: *Wind acts as a ~ on speed.* **2** examination to make certain of accuracy; mark or tick (usually written✓) to show that something has been proved to be correct. **3** receipt given temporarily in return for something handed over.

`check-up, (esp a medical) examination.

check² /tʃek/ vt,vi **1** examine in order to learn whether something is correct: *Will you please ~ these figures?* **check up on sb/ sth,** examine to see whether he/it is, has done, etc. **2** hold back; cause to go slow or stop: *He couldn't ~ his anger.* **3** threaten an opponent's king in chess. **4** **check in,** arrive and register at a hotel, etc. **check out,** pay one's bill and leave.

`check-out, (esp) place (e g in a supermarket) where one pays the bill, wraps one's goods and leaves.

checker, person who checks orders, etc.

check³ /tʃek/ n [U] pattern of crossed lines forming squares (often of different shades or colours); cloth with such a pattern.

check·mate /ˈtʃekmeɪt/ vt **1** make a move in chess that prevents the opponent's king from being moved away from a direct attack (and so win the game). **2** (*fig*) obstruct and defeat (a person, his plans). □ n [C] complete defeat.

cheek /tʃik/ n [C] **1** either side of the face below the eye. **2** [U] impudence: *He had the ~ to ask me to do his work for him!* □ vt be

impudent to: *Stop ~ing your mother!*

`cheek-bone, bone below the eye.

cheeky adj (-ier, -iest) impudent.

cheek·ily /-əlɪ/ adv

cheep /tʃip/ vi, n [C] (make a) weak, shrill note (as young birds do).

cheer¹ /tʃɪə(r)/ n **1** [U] state of hope, gladness: *words of ~,* of encouragement. **2** [C] shout of joy or encouragement.

cheer² /tʃɪə(r)/ vt,vi **1** fill with gladness, hope, high spirits; comfort: *Your visit has really ~ed me (up).* **2** take comfort, become happy: *He ~ed up when I promised to go.* **3** give shouts of joy, approval or encouragement: *The speaker was loudly ~ed.*

cheer·ing n [U] *The ~ing could be heard half a mile away.* □ adj: *That's ~ing news.*

cheer·ful /ˈtʃɪəfəl/ adj **1** bringing or suggesting happiness: *a ~ day/room/smile.* **2** happy and contented; willing: *~ workers.*

cheer·fully /-flɪ/ adv

cheer·ful·ness n [U]

cheerio /ˈtʃɪərɪˈəʊ/ int (*informal*) (used when parting) goodbye.

cheer·less /ˈtʃɪələs/ adj without comfort; gloomy; miserable: *a wet and ~ day.*

cheery /ˈtʃɪərɪ/ adj (-ier,-iest) lively; merry: *a ~ smile/greeting.*

cheer·ily /ˈtʃɪərɪlɪ/ adv

cheese /tʃiz/ n **1** [U] kinds of solid food made from milk curds. **2** [C] shaped and wrapped portion of this.

`cheese-cloth, (a) thin cotton cloth (gauze) put round some kinds of cheese. (b) similar (thicker) cloth used to make shirts, etc.

`cheese-paring, excessive carefulness in the spending of money.

chee·tah /ˈtʃitə/ n [C] kind of leopard.

chef /ʃef/ n [C] (*pl ~s*) head male cook in a hotel, restaurant etc.

chef-d'oeuvre /ˈʃeɪ ˈdəvr/ n [C] (*pl chefs-d'oeuvre, pronunciation unchanged*) (*Fr*) (person's) masterpiece.

chemi·cal /ˈkemɪkəl/ adj of, made by, chemistry: *~ warfare,* using poison gas, smoke, etc. □ n [C] (often *pl*) substance used in, or obtained by, chemistry.

chem·ically /-klɪ/ adv

chem·ist /ˈkemɪst/ n [C] **1** person who is expert in chemistry. **2** person who prepares and sells medical goods, toilet articles, etc.

chem·is·try /ˈkemɪstrɪ/ n [U] branch of science that deals with how substances are made up, how they (their elements) combine, how they act under different conditions.

cheque /tʃek/ n [C] (*US = check*) written order to a bank to pay money: *a ~ for £10; pay by ~.*

`cheque-book, number of blank cheques fastened together.

cher·ish /ˈtʃerɪʃ/ vt **1** care for tenderly. **2** keep alive (hope, ambition, feelings, etc) in one's heart: *For years she ~ed the hope that her husband might still be alive.*

cherry /ˈtʃerɪ/ n [C] (pl -ies) (tree with) soft, small, round fruit, red, yellow or black when ripe and with a stone-like seed in the middle. □ adj bright red: ~ lips.

cherub /ˈtʃerəb/ n [C] 1 (pl ~s) small beautiful child; (in art) such a child with wings. 2 (pl ~im /-bɪm/) one of the second highest order of angels.

chess /tʃes/ n [U] board game for two players with sixteen pieces each (called `~ men /-men/), on a board with sixty-four squares (called a `~ board).

chest /tʃest/ n [C] 1 large, strong (usually wooden) box with a lid for storing things. 2 upper front part of the body, enclosed by the ribs, containing the heart and lungs. **get sth off one's chest,** (sl) say something that one is anxious to say.
'**chest of 'drawers,** large chest(1) with drawers for clothes.

chest-nut /ˈtʃesnʌt/ n 1 [C,U] (sorts of, wood of) tree with smooth, bright reddish-brown nut (some being edible). 2 colour of the nut. 3 horse of this colour. □ adj reddish-brown.

chew /tʃu/ vt,vi 1 move (food, etc) about between the teeth in order to crush it: C~ your food well before you swallow it. 2 **chew sth over/on sth,** (informal) think over, consider. □ n [C] act of chewing; thing to chew.
'**chew·ing-gum,** sticky substance sweetened and flavoured for chewing.

chic /ʃik/ n [U] (of clothes, their wearer) style that gives an air of superior excellence. □ adj stylish.

chick /tʃik/ n [C] 1 young bird, esp a young chicken. 2 small child. 3 (sl) girl.

chicken /ˈtʃikin/ n [C] 1 young bird, esp a young hen. **(Don't) count your chickens before they are hatched,** (Don't) be too hopeful of your chances of success, etc. 2 [U] its flesh as food.
'**chicken-'hearted** adj lacking in courage.
'**chicken-pox,** disease producing red spots on the skin.
'**chicken-run,** fenced-in area for chickens.

chic-ory /ˈtʃikərɪ/ n [U] 1 plant used as a vegetable and for salad. 2 the root roasted and made into a powder (used with or instead of coffee).

chide /tʃaid/ vt,vi (pt ~d or chid /tʃid/, pp ~d,) scold; complain.

chief /tʃif/ n [C] 1 leader or ruler: the ~ of the tribe. 2 head of a department; highest official. □ adj 1 principal; most important: the ~ thing to remember. 2 first in rank: the C~ Justice.
-**in-'chief,** supreme: the Commander-in-~.
chief·ly adv (a) above all; first of all. (b) mostly; mainly.

chief-tain /ˈtʃiftən/ n [C] chief of a highland clan or of a tribe.

chi-gnon /ˈʃinjɒn US: -njɑn/ n [C] (Fr) knot or roll of hair worn at the back of the

head by women.

child /tʃaild/ n [C] (pl children /ˈtʃildrən/) 1 young human being. 2 son or daughter (of any age).
'**child-birth,** the process of giving birth to a child.
'**child-hood,** state, time, of being a child.
'**child-ish** adj of, behaving like, suitable for, a child: ~ish games/arguments.
child-less adj having no child(ren).
'**child-like** adj simple, innocent.
'**child's play,** something very easily done.

chill /tʃil/ n 1 (sing only) unpleasant feeling of coldness: There's quite a ~ in the air this morning. 2 (sing only) (fig) something that causes a depressed feeling: The bad news cast a ~ over the gathering. 3 [C] illness caused by cold and damp, with shivering of the body. □ adj unpleasantly cold: a ~ breeze; a ~ welcome. □ vt,vi make or become cold or cool: He was ~ed to the bone, very cold.
chilly adj (-ier, -iest) (a) rather cold: feel ~y. (b) (fig) unfriendly: a ~y interview.

chilli /ˈtʃilɪ/ n [C,U] dried pod of red pepper, often made into powder and used to give a hot flavour.

chime /tʃaim/ n [C] (series of notes sounded by a) tuned set of bells: a ~ of bells; □ vi,vt 1 (of bells, a clock) make (bells) ring; ring bells: The bells are chiming. 2 break in on the talk of others: 'Of course,' he ~d in.

chim-ney /ˈtʃimni/ n [C] (pl ~s) 1 structure through which smoke from a fire is carried away through the wall or roof of a building. 2 narrow opening by which a cliff face may be climbed.
'**chimney-pot,** pipe fitted to the top of a chimney(1).
'**chimney-stack,** group of chimneys.
'**chimney-sweep(er),** man who sweeps soot from chimneys.

chimp /tʃimp/ n [C] (informal) (abbr for) chimpanzee.

chim-pan-zee /ˌtʃimpænˈziː/ n [C] African ape, smaller than a gorilla.

chin /tʃin/ n [C] part of the face below the mouth; front of the lower jaw.

china /ˈtʃainə/ n [U] 1 baked and glazed fine white clay. 2 articles (eg cups, saucers, plates) made from this.

chink¹ /tʃiŋk/ n [C] narrow opening or crack.

chink² /tʃiŋk/ vt,vi, n [C] (make or cause the) sound of coins, glasses, etc striking together.

chip /tʃip/ n [C] 1 small piece cut or broken off (from wood, stone, china, glass, etc). **have a chip on one's shoulder,** resent or exaggerate prejudice against oneself. 2 strip cut from a potato, etc: fish and ~s, fried fish and potato ~s. 3 place (eg in a cup) from which a chip has come. 4 flat plastic counter used as money (esp in gambling). □ vt,vi (-pp-) 1 cut or break (a piece off or from):

All the plates have ~*ped edges.* **2** make into chips(2). **3** (of things) be broken at the edge: *These cups* ~ *easily.* **4 chip in,** (*informal*) (**a**) interrupt. (**b**) contribute money (to a fund).

chi·rop·odist /kɪˈrɒpədɪst/ *n* [C] person who is expert in the treatment of troubles of the feet and toe-nails.

chi·rop·ody /kɪˈrɒpədɪ/ *n* [U] work of a chiropodist.

chirp /tʃɜːp/ *vi,vt, n* [C] (make) short, sharp note(s) or sound(s) (as of small birds or insects).

chirpy /ˈtʃɜːpɪ/ *adj* (-ier,-iest) lively, happy, cheerful.

chir·rup /ˈtʃɪrəp/ *vt, n* [C] (make a) series of chirps.

chisel /ˈtʃɪzəl/ *n* [C] steel tool used for shaping wood, stone or metal. □ *vt* (-ll-) **1** cut or shape with a chisel. **2** (*informal*) cheat.

chit[1] /tʃɪt/ *n* [C] **1** young child. **2** young, small, slender woman.

chit[2] /tʃɪt/ *n* [C] note of a sum of money owed.

chit-chat /ˈtʃɪt tʃæt/ *n* [U] light, informal conversation.

chiv·alry /ˈʃɪvəlrɪ/ *n* [U] **1** laws and customs (religious, moral and social) of the knights in the Middle Ages. **2** qualities such as courage, honour, courtesy, loyalty, devotion to the weak and helpless, to the service of women).

chiv·al·rous /ˈʃɪvəlrəs/ *adj*

chloro·form /ˈklɒrəfɔːm US: ˈklɔr-/ *n* [U] thin, colourless liquid given to make a person unconscious during a surgical operation. □ *vt* use chloroform.

chloro·phyl(l) /ˈklɒrəfɪl US: ˈklɔr-/ *n* [U] green colouring matter in the leaves of plants.

choc·olate /ˈtʃɒklət/ *n* **1** [U] substance (powder or bar) made from the crushed seeds of the cacao tree. **2** drink made by mixing this with hot water or milk. **3** [C,U] sweet(1) made from this: *a bar of* ~; *a box of* ~s. **4** [U] the colour of this substance, dark brown. □ *adj* dark brown.

choice /tʃɔɪs/ *n* **1** [C] act of choosing: *take your* ~. **2** [U] right or possibility of choosing: *I have no* ~ *in the matter*, must act in this way. **3** [C] variety from which to choose: *This shop has a large* ~ *of bags.* **4** [C] person or thing chosen: *This is my* ~. □ *adj* unusually good: ~ *fruit.*

choir /ˈkwaɪə(r)/ *n* [C] **1** company of persons trained to sing together, esp to lead the singing in church. **2** part of a church building for the choir.

choke[1] /tʃəʊk/ *vi,vt* **1** be unable to breathe because of something in the windpipe, or because of emotion: ~ *over one's food;* ~ *with anger.* **2** stop the breathing of, by pressing the windpipe from outside or blocking it up inside, or (of smoke, etc) by being unfit to breathe: *She was* ~*d with sobs.* **3**

fill, partly or completely, a passage, space, etc that is usually clear: *a drain* ~*d* (*up*) *with dirt.* **4 choke it back/down,** hold or keep it back/down: ~ *back one's tears.*

choke[2] /tʃəʊk/ *n* [C] valve in a petrol engine to control the intake of air.

chol·era /ˈkɒlərə/ *n* [U] infectious and often fatal disease, common in hot countries.

choose /tʃuːz/ *vt,vi* (*pt* chose /tʃəʊz/, *pp* chosen /ˈtʃəʊzn/) **1** pick out from a greater number; show what or which one wants by taking: *She took a long time to* ~ *a new dress. There's nothing/not much/little to* ~ *between them,* They are about equal, are equally good/bad, etc. **2** decide; be pleased or determined: *He chose to stay at home.*

choosy /ˈtʃuːzɪ/ *adj* (-ier, -iest) (*informal*) (of persons) careful and cautious in choosing; difficult to please.

chop[1] /tʃɒp/ *n* [C] **1** chopping blow. **2** thick slice of meat with the bone in it, (to be) cooked for one person. **3** (*informal*) = sack[2].

chop[2] /tʃɒp/ *vt,vi* (-pp-) cut into pieces by blow(s) with an axe, etc: *Meat is often* ~*ped up before being cooked. I'm going to* ~ *that tree down.*

chop[3] /tʃɒp/ *vi* (-pp-) **chop and change,** be inconsistent: *He's always* ~*ping and changing,* always changing his mind.

chop·per /ˈtʃɒpə(r)/ *n* [C] heavy tool with a sharp edge for chopping meat, wood, etc.

choppy /ˈtʃɒpɪ/ *adj* (-ier, -iest) **1** (of the sea) moving in short, irregular waves. **2** (of the wind) continually changing.

chop·sticks /ˈtʃɒpstɪks/ *n pl* pair of sticks (of wood, ivory, etc) used by Chinese and Japanese for lifting food to the mouth.

choral /ˈkɔːrəl/ *adj* of, for, sung by or together with, a choir: *a* ~ *society.*

chord /kɔːd/ *n* [C] **1** straight line that joins two points on the circumference of a circle or the ends of an arc. **2** combination of three or more musical notes sounded together in harmony. **3** = cord(2).

chore /tʃɔː(r)/ *n* [C] **1** small duty or piece of work, esp an ordinary everyday task (e g in the home). **2** small unpleasant task.

chor·eogra·phy /ˌkɒrɪˈɒɡrəfɪ US: ˌkɔr-/ *n* [U] art of designing ballet and other dance patterns.

chor·eogra·pher, person who designs ballet and other group dancing.

chorus /ˈkɔːrəs/ *n* [C] (*pl* ~es) **1** (music for a) group of singers. **2** (part of a) song for all to sing (after solo verses): *Mr White sang the verses and everybody joined in the* ~. **3** something said or cried by many people together: *The proposal was greeted with a* ~ *of approval.* □ *vt* sing, speak, in chorus.

chose, chosen ⇨ choose.

Christ /kraɪst/ *n* title given to Jesus, now used as part of or for His name.

christen /ˈkrɪsən/ *vt* **1** receive (an infant) into the Christian church by baptism; give a name to at the baptism. **2** give a name to (a new ship when it is launched).

`**christen·ing** /-snɪŋ/ n [C] ceremony of baptizing or naming.

Christen·dom /ˈkrɪsəndəm/ n all Christian people and Christian countries.

Chris·tian /ˈkrɪstʃən/ adj **1** of Jesus and his teaching. **2** of the religion, beliefs, church, etc based on this teaching. □ n [C] person believing in the religion of Christ.

`**Christian name,** name given at baptism; forename.

Chris·ti·an·ity /ˈkrɪstɪˈænətɪ/ n [U] the Christian faith, religion, or character.

Christ·mas /ˈkrɪsməs/ n [C] (pl -es) (also '~ `Day) yearly celebration of the birth of Jesus Christ, 25 Dec; the week beginning on 24 Dec: the ~ holidays.

`**Christmas-box,** money given at Christmas to the postman, etc.

`**Christmas card,** sent as a greeting to friends at Christmas.

`**Christmas cracker,** roll of brightly coloured paper, which explodes harmlessly when the ends are pulled.

`**Christmas-tree,** small decorated evergreen tree set up at Christmas.

chrome /krəʊm/ n [U] yellow colouring matter used in paints, etc.

chro·mium /ˈkrəʊmɪəm/ n [U] element (symbol Cr) used for covering taps, motor-car fittings, etc and in stainless steel.

chro·mo·some /ˈkrəʊməsəʊm/ n [C] one of the tiny threads in every nucleus in animal and plant cells, carrying genes.

chronic /ˈkrɒnɪk/ adj (of a disease or condition) continual, lasting for a long time: ~ rheumatism; a ~ illness.

chroni·cally /-klɪ/ adv

chron·icle /ˈkrɒnɪkəl/ n [C] record of events in the order of their happening. □ vt make, a chronicle.

chrono·logi·cal /ˈkrɒnəˈlɒdʒɪkəl/ adj in order of time: Shakespeare's plays in ~ order, the order in which they were written.

chrono·logi·cally /-klɪ/ adv

chron·ol·ogy /krəˈnɒlədʒɪ/ n (pl -ies) **1** [U] science of fixing dates. **2** [C] arrangement or list of events with dates.

chron·ometer /krəˈnɒmɪtə(r)/ n [C] kind of watch that keeps very accurate time.

chrysa·lis /ˈkrɪsəlɪs/ n [C] (pl ~es) **1** form taken by an insect between the time when it creeps or crawls as a larva and the time when it flies as a moth, butterfly, etc. **2** the sheath that covers it during this time.

chry·san·the·mum /krɪˈsænθɪməm/ n [C] (pl ~s) (flower of a) garden plant blooming in autumn and early winter.

chubby /ˈtʃʌbɪ/ adj (-ier, -iest) fat, round: ~ cheeks.

chuck[1] /tʃʌk/ vt (informal) **1** throw: ~ away rubbish; ~ a drunken man out of a pub. **2** abandon, give up (in disgust): ~ up one's job.

chuck[2] /tʃʌk/ n [C] **1** part of a lathe which grips the work to be operated on. **2** part which grips the bit on a drill.

chuckle /ˈtʃækəl/ n [C] low, quiet laugh with closed mouth (showing satisfaction or amusement). □ vt laugh in this way: He was chuckling to himself.

chug /tʃʌg/ vi (-gg-) make the short explosive sound (of an oil-engine or small petrol-engine running slowly): The boat ~ged along. □ n [C] this sound.

chum /tʃʌm/ n [C] close friend (esp among boys). □ vi (-mm-) chum up (with sb), form a friendship (with).

chummy adj (-ier, -iest) friendly.

chump /tʃʌmp/ n [C] **1** short, thick block of wood. **2** thick piece of meat: a ~ chop. **3** (sl) fool.

chunk /tʃʌŋk/ n [C] thick, solid piece or lump cut off a loaf, a piece of meat, etc.

chunky adj (-ier, -iest) short and thick.

church /tʃɜːtʃ/ n [C] **1** building for public Christian worship. **2** [U] service in such a building: What time does ~ begin? **enter the Church,** become a minister of religion.

`**church-goer,** person who goes to church regularly.

`**church-yard,** burial ground round a church. ⇨ cemetery.

churn /tʃɜːn/ n [C] **1** tub in which cream is shaken or beaten to make butter. **2** very large can in which milk is carried from the farm. □ vt,vi **1** make (butter) in a churn. **2** stir or move about violently: The ship's propellers ~ed up the waves.

chute /ʃuːt/ n [C] **1** long, narrow, steep slope down which things may slide: an e`scape ~, canvas tunnel by which passengers leave an aircraft in an emergency. **2** smooth, rapid fall of water over a slope.

chut·ney /ˈtʃʌtnɪ/ n [U] hot-tasting mixture of fruit, peppers, etc eaten with curry, cold meat, etc.

cic·ada /sɪˈkɑːdə/ n [C] (pl ~s) winged insect with transparent wings. The male chirps shrilly in hot, dry weather.

cider /ˈsaɪdə(r)/ n [U] fermented apple juice.

cigar /sɪˈgɑː(r)/ n [C] tight roll of tobacco leaves with pointed end(s) for smoking.

ciga·rette /ˈsɪgəˈret/ n [C] roll of shredded tobacco enclosed in thin paper for smoking.

`**ciga·rette-case,** small one for carrying cigarettes.

`**ciga·rette-holder,** tube in which a cigarette may be put for smoking.

cinch /sɪntʃ/ n [C] (sl) something that is certain, easy or sure.

cin·der /ˈsɪndə(r)/ n [C] small piece of coal, wood, etc partly burned, no longer flaming, and not yet ash.

cine- /sɪnɪ/ prefix form used for cinema in compounds.

`**cine-cam·era,** one used for taking moving pictures.

`**cine-pro·jec·tor,** machine for showing

films on a screen.

cin·ema /ˈsɪnəmə/ n 1 [C] place where films are shown. 2 [U] moving pictures as an artform or industry.

cin·na·mon /ˈsɪnəmən/ n [U] 1 spice from the inner bark of an E Indian tree, used in cooking. 2 its colour, yellowish brown.

cipher, cypher /ˈsaɪfə(r)/ n [C] 1 the symbol 0, representing nought or zero. 2 any Arabic numeral, 1 to 9. 3 (fig) person or thing of no importance. 4 (method of, key to) secret writing: a message in ~. □ vt,vi put into secret writing. ⇨ **decipher**.

circa /ˈsɜːkə/ prep (Latin) (abbr = c, ca) about (with dates): born ~ 150 B C.

circle /ˈsɜːkl/ n [C] 1 space enclosed by a curved line, every point on which is the same distance from the centre; the line enclosing this space. 2 ring: a ~ of trees; standing in a ~. 3 block of seats in curved rows, between the highest part (the gallery) and the floor of a theatre or hall. 4 number of persons bound together by having the same or similar interests: He has a large ~ of friends. □ vt,vi move in a circle; go round: The aircraft ~d (over) the landing-field.

cir·cuit /ˈsɜːkɪt/ n [C] 1 journey round, from place to place: The ~ of the racing track is three miles. 2 closed path for an electrical current; apparatus for using an electric current: ~ diagram, one that shows the connections in such an apparatus. ⇨ **short**[1]. 3 chain of cinemas, theatres, etc under a single management.

cir·cu·itous /sɜːˈkjuːɪtəs/ adj going a long way round: a ~ route.

cir·cu·lar /ˈsɜːkjʊlə(r)/ adj round or curved in shape; moving round: a ~ tour/trip, ending at the starting-point without visiting a place more than once. □ n [C] printed letter, advertisement, announcement, etc of which many copies are made and distributed.

cir·cu·lar·ize vt send circulars to.

cir·cu·late /ˈsɜːkjʊleɪt/ vi,vt 1 go round continuously; move from place to place freely: Blood ~s through the body. Don't stand in the corner — ~ among the other guests. 2 cause to circulate: I'll ~ this book among you.

cir·cu·la·tion /ˌsɜːkjʊˈleɪʃən/ n 1 [U] circulating or being circulated, esp the movement of the blood from and to the heart: He has a good/bad ~. 2 [U] state of being circulated: When were the British decimal coins put into ~? 3 [C] number of copies of a newspaper or other periodical sold to the public.

cir·cum·cise /ˈsɜːkəmsaɪz/ vt remove the skin at the end of the male sex organ.

cir·cum·ci·sion /ˌsɜːkəmˈsɪʒən/ n [C,U]

cir·cum·fer·ence /sɜːˈkʌmfrəns/ n [C] 1 line that marks out a circle or other curved figure. 2 distance round: The ~ of the earth is almost 25 000 miles.

cir·cum·flex /ˈsɜːkəmfleks/ n [C] mark placed over a vowel to show how it is to be sounded (as in French rôle).

cir·cum·navi·gate /ˌsɜːkəmˈnævɪgeɪt/ vt sail round (esp the world).

cir·cum·navi·ga·tion /ˌsɜːkəmˈnævɪˈgeɪʃən/ n [C,U]

cir·cum·stance /ˈsɜːkəmstəns US: -stæns/ n [C] 1 (usually pl) conditions, facts, etc connected with an event or person: Don't judge the crime until you know the ~s. in/ under the circumstances, such being the state of affairs. in/under no circumstances, never. 2 fact or detail: He has plenty of money, which is a fortunate ~. 3 (pl) financial condition.

cir·cum·stan·tial /ˌsɜːkəmˈstænʃəl/ adj 1 (of a description) giving full details. 2 (of evidence) based on, with details that suggest strongly but do not provide direct proof.

cir·cum·vent /ˌsɜːkəmˈvent/ vt 1 gain advantage over; defeat (a person's plans). 2 prevent (a plan) from being carried out; find a way to get round (a law, rule, etc).

cir·cum·ven·tion /ˌsɜːkəmˈvenʃən/ n [U]

cir·cus /ˈsɜːkəs/ n [C] (pl ~es) 1 (round or oval) place with seats on all sides for (in modern times) a show of performing animals, acrobats, etc; persons and animals giving such a show. 2 (esp in proper names) open space where a number of streets converge: Piccadilly C~, in London.

cir·rus /ˈsɪrəs/ n [C,U] type of cloud, high in the sky, delicate and feathery in appearance.

cis·tern /ˈsɪstən/ n [C] water tank, eg as above the bowl of a lavatory, or for storing water in a building.

cite /saɪt/ vt 1 give or mention as an example (esp by quoting from a book, to support an argument, etc). 2 (legal) summons at law: be ~d in divorce proceedings.

ci·ta·tion /saɪˈteɪʃən/ n [U] citing; [C] (esp) a statement, that is cited.

citi·zen /ˈsɪtɪzən/ n [C] 1 person who lives in a town, not in the country: the ~s of Paris. 2 person who has full rights in a State, either by birth or by gaining such rights: immigrants who have become ~s of the United States.

`citizen·ship`, being, rights and duties of, a citizen.

cit·ric /ˈsɪtrɪk/ adj ~ acid, acid from such fruits as lemons and limes.

cit·ron /ˈsɪtrən/ n [C] (tree with) pale yellow fruit like a lemon but larger, less acid, and thicker skinned.

cit·rous /ˈsɪtrəs/ adj of the citrus fruits.

cit·rus /ˈsɪtrəs/ n [C] (pl ~es) kinds of tree including the lemon, lime, citron, orange and grapefruit. □ adj of these trees: `~ fruit.

city /ˈsɪtɪ/ n [C] (pl -ies) 1 large and important town; town given special rights in self-government. 2 the C~, the oldest part of London, now the commercial and financial centre. 3 people living in a city.

civic /ˈsɪvɪk/ adj of the official life and affairs of a town or a citizen: ~ pride; a ~

centre, where the official buildings, e g the town hall, library, etc, are grouped together.

civ·ics /ˈsɪvɪks/ *n pl* (used with a *sing verb*) study of city government, the rights and duties of citizens, etc.

civil /ˈsɪvəl/ *adj* **1** of human society; of people living together: *We all have ∼ rights and ∼ duties.* **2** not of the armed forces. **3** politely helpful: *Can't you be more ∼?* **'civil 'engi'neering,** the design and building of roads, railways, canals, docks, etc. **'civil 'law,** law dealing with private rights of citizens, not with crime. **'civil 'marriage,** without religious ceremony but recognized by law. **'civil 'rights,** rights of a citizen to political, racial, legal, social freedom or equality. **'civil 'servant,** official in the Civil Service. **the 'Civil 'Service,** all government departments except the Navy, Army and Air Force.
civil·ly *adv* politely.

ci·vil·ity /sɪˈvɪlətɪ/ *n* **1** [U] politeness. **2** (*pl*) polite acts.

ci·vil·ian /sɪˈvɪlɪən/ *n* [C], *adj* (person) not serving with the armed forces: *In modern wars ∼s as well as soldiers are killed.*

civi·li·za·tion /ˌsɪvəlaɪˈzeɪʃən US: -lɪˈz-/ *n* **1** [U] civilizing or being civilized; state of being civilized: *The ∼ of mankind has taken thousands of years.* **2** [C] system, stage of, social development: *the ∼s of ancient Egypt, Babylon and Persia.* **3** [U] civilized States collectively: *acts that horrified ∼.*

civi·lize /ˈsɪvəlaɪz/ *vt* **1** bring out of a savage or ignorant state (by education, moral teaching, etc). **2** improve and educate.

clack /klæk/ *vi, n* [C] (make the) short, sharp sound of objects struck together.

claim¹ /kleɪm/ *n* **1** [C] act of claiming(1): *His ∼ to own the house is invalid.* **2** [C] sum of money demanded, e g under an insurance agreement: *make/put in a ∼ (for a refund).* **3** [U] right to ask for: *You have no ∼ on my sympathies.* **4** [C] something claimed; piece of land (esp in a gold-bearing region) given to a miner.

claim² /kleɪm/ *vt,vi* **1** demand recognition of the fact that one is, or owns, or has a right to (something): *He ∼ed to be the owner of/ ∼ed that he owned the land.* **claim damages,** ⇨ damage. ⇨ also bonus. **2** **lay claim to,** demand as a right: *lay ∼ to your father's land.* say that something is a fact: *He ∼ed to be the best tennis player in the school.* **3** (of things) need; deserve: *There are several matters that ∼ my attention.*

claim·ant /ˈkleɪmənt/ *n* [C] person who makes a claim, esp in law.

clair·voy·ance /kleəˈvɔɪəns/ *n* [U] abnormal power of seeing in the mind what is happening or what exists beyond the normal range of the senses.
clair·voy·ant /-ənt/, person with such power.

clam /klæm/ *n* [C] large shellfish, with a shell in two halves, used for food.

clam·ber /ˈklæmbə(r)/ *vi* climb with difficulty, using the hands and feet: *∼ up/over a wall.* □ *n* [C] awkward or difficult climb.

clammy /ˈklæmɪ/ *adj* (-ier, -iest) damp and sticky to the touch: *∼ hands.*

clam·our (*US* = **clam·or**) /ˈklæmə(r)/ *n* [C,U] loud confused noise or shout, esp of people complaining angrily or making a demand. □ *vi, vt* make a clamour: *The foolish people were ∼ing for war.*

clamp /klæmp/ *n* [C] **1** appliance for holding things together tightly by means of a screw. **2** band of iron, etc for strengthening or tightening. □ *vt, vi* **1** put a clamp on; put in a clamp. **2** **clamp down (on),** (*informal*) put pressure on or against (in order to stop something): *They ∼ed down on drug pushers.* Hence, **'clamp-down** *n* [C]

clan /klæn/ *n* [C] large family group, as found in tribal communities, esp Scottish Highlanders.

clan·des·tine /klænˈdestɪn/ *adj* secret; done secretly; kept secret: *a ∼ marriage.*

clang /klæŋ/ *vt,vi, n* [C] (make a) loud ringing sound: *The ∼ of the firebell alarmed the village.*

clank /klæŋk/ *vt,vi, n* [C] (make a) ringing sound (not so loud as a clang): *Prisoners ∼ing their chains.*

clan·nish /ˈklænɪʃ/ *adj* showing family feeling; in the habit of supporting one another against outsiders.

clap¹ /klæp/ *vt,vi* (-pp-) **1** show approval, by striking the palms of the hands together; do this as a signal (e g to summon a waiter, etc): *When the violinist finished the audience ∼ped for five minutes.* **2** strike or slap lightly with the open hand, usually in a friendly way: *∼ somebody on the back.* **3** put quickly or energetically: *∼ed in prison.* **clap eyes on sb,** (*informal*) catch sight of: *I haven't ∼ped eyes on him since 1960.* □ *n* **1** loud explosive noise (of thunder). **2** sound of the palms of the hands brought together. (*Note:* Clapping is the usual word for applause, not *claps.*)

claret /ˈklærət/ *n* [U] **1** (kind of) red table wine from Bordeaux. **2** its colour. □ *adj* dark red.

clar·ify /ˈklærɪfaɪ/ *vt,vi* (*pt,pp* -ied) **1** make or become clear or intelligible. **2** make (a liquid, etc) free from impurities.
clari·fi·ca·tion /ˌklærɪfɪˈkeɪʃən/ *n* [U] being clarified.

clari·net /ˌklærɪˈnet/ *n* [C] musical woodwind instrument, with finger holes and keys.
clari·net·tist, person who plays the clarinet.

clar·ion /ˈklærɪən/ *n* [C] loud, shrill call made to rouse and excite.

clar·ity /ˈklærətɪ/ *n* [U] clearness: *∼ of thought.*

clash /klæʃ/ *vi, vt* **1** make a loud, broken, confused noise (as when metal objects strike together): *The cymbals ~ed.* **2** come suddenly together; meet in conflict: *The two armies ~ed outside the town.* **3** (of events) interfere with each other because they are (to be) at the same time on the same date: *It's a pity the two concerts ~, I want to go to both.* **4** be in disagreement or at variance: *I ~ed with him/We ~ed at the last meeting of the Council. The (colours of the) curtains ~ with (the colours of) the carpet.* □ *n* [C] **1** clashing noise. **2** disagreement; conflict: *a ~ of views/colours.*

clasp /klɑsp US: klæsp/ *n* [C] **1** device with two parts that fasten, used to keep together two things or two parts of one thing (e g the ends of a necklace or belt). **2** firm hold (with the fingers or arms). □ *vt,vi* **1** hold tightly or closely: *~ed in each other's arms; with his hands ~ed behind him.* **2** fasten with a clasp(1).

class /klɑs US: klæs/ *n* [C] **1** group having qualities of the same kind; kind, sort or division: *As an actor A is not in the same ~ as/with B,* is not so good as B. **2** [U] system of ranks in society; caste system: *It will be difficult to abolish ~; the ~ struggle.* **3** [C] all persons in one of these ranks: *Should society be divided into upper, middle and lower ~es?* **4** group of persons taught together; their course of teaching. **5** (*US*) group of pupils or students who enter school or college in the same year and leave together: *the ~ of 1973.* **6** grade or merit after examination: *take a first-/second-~ degree.* **7** (*informal*) distinction; excellence; style: *He's a top ~ tennis player. There's not much ~ about her.* □ *vt* place in a class(1): *a ship ~ed A1.*

class-room, room where a class(4) is taught.

class-less *adj* without distinctions of class(2): *Is a ~less society possible?*

clas-sic /ˈklæsɪk/ *adj* **1** of the highest quality; having a recognized value or position recognized. **2** of the standard of ancient Greek and Latin literature, art and culture. **3** famous because of a long history: *The Derby* (horse-race) *is a ~ event.* **4** (of fashion) traditional: *a ~ suit.* □ *n* [C] **1** writer, artist, book, etc of the highest class: *Milton is a ~. 'Robinson Crusoe' is a ~.* **2** ancient Greek or Latin writer. **3** (*pl*) **the ~s,** (literature of the) ancient languages of Greece and Rome. **4** university course in the classics(3): *He read ~s at Oxford.* **5** classic(3) event.

clas-si-cal /ˈklæsɪkəl/ *adj* **1** in, of, the best (esp ancient Greek and Roman) art and literature: *a ~ education.* **2** of proved value because of having passed the test of time: *~ music,* usually taking traditional form as a symphony, etc, e g of Mozart. ⇨ **light²**(6).

clas-si-cally /-klɪ/ *adv*

clas-si-cist /ˈklæsɪsɪst/ *n* [C] **1** follower of classic style. **2** classical scholar: *Milton was a ~.*

clas-si-fi-ca-tion /ˌklæsɪfɪˈkeɪʃən/ *n* **1** [U] classifying or being classified. **2** [C] group into which something is put.

clas-sify /ˈklæsɪfaɪ/ *vt* (*pt,pp* -ied) **1** arrange in classes or groups. **2** put into a class(1): *In a library books are usually classified by subjects.*

clas-si-fied *adj* (a) arranged in classes(1): *classified advertisements.* (b) officially secret: *classified information.*

clat-ter /ˈklætə(r)/ *n* [U] **1** long, continuous, resounding noise (as of hard things falling or knocking together): *the ~ of cutlery.* **2** noisy talk: *The boys stopped their ~ when the teacher came into the classroom.* □ *vi,vt* make a clatter(1): *Pots and pans were ~ing in the kitchen.*

clause /klɔz/ *n* [C] **1** (*gram*) part of a sentence, with its own subject and predicate, esp one doing the work of a noun, adjective or adverb. **2** (*legal*) complete paragraph in an agreement, legal document, etc.

claus-tro-pho-bia /ˌklɔstrəˈfəʊbɪə/ *n* [U] abnormal fear of confined places (e g a lift).

clavi-chord /ˈklævɪkɔd/ *n* [C] early stringed instrument with a keyboard, like the piano.

clav-icle /ˈklævɪkəl/ *n* [C] collar-bone.

claw /klɔ/ *n* [C] **1** one of the pointed nails on the feet of some animals and birds; foot with such nails. **2** pincers of a shellfish (e g a lobster). **3** instrument or device like a claw (e g a steel hook on a machine for lifting things). □ *vt* get hold of, pull, scratch, with claws or hands.

clay /kleɪ/ *n* [U] **1** stiff, sticky earth that becomes hard when baked. **2** material from which bricks, pots, earthenware, etc are made.

clean¹ /klin/ *adj* (-er, -est) **1** free from dirt: *~ hands. Wash it ~.* **2** not yet used; fresh: *Give me a ~ sheet of paper.* **3** pure; innocent; free from offense or indecency: *a ~ joke; He has a ~ record,* is not known to have done wrong. **4** even; regular; with a smooth edge or surface: *A sharp knife makes a ~ cut.* **5** having clean habits: *a ~ waitress.* **6** fit for food: *~/un~ animals,* those that are/are not considered fit for food (by religious custom). **7** thorough, complete. ⇨ **sweep²**(1). □ *adv* completely; entirely: *I ~ forgot about it.* **come clean,** make a full confession. □ *n* [U] (with *a*) cleaning: *give it a good ~.*

'clean-'cut *adj* sharply outlined.

'clean-'shaven *adj* with the hair of the face shaved off.

clean² /klin/ *vt,vi* **1** make clean (of dirt, etc): *I must have this suit ~ed,* sent to the dry-cleaner's. ⇨ **dry¹**(13). **2** (uses with *adverbial particles and prepositions*):

clean down, clean by brushing or wiping: *~ down the walls.*

clean sb out, win or take all the money of.

clean sth out, clean the inside of: *It's time you ~ed out your bedroom.*

clean up, make clean or tidy; put in order: *You should always clean up after a picnic,* collect litter, empty bottles, etc. **clean sth up, (a)** get rid of criminal and immoral elements, etc: *The mayor has decided to ~ up the city,* end corruption, etc. **(b)** (*informal*) win or take all the money.

cleaner /ˈkliːnə(r)/ *n* [C] **1** person or thing that ~s. **2** tool, machine, substance, etc for cleaning: *send/take a suit to the* (ˈdry-) `~ers; a `vacuum-~er.

clean·ly[1] /ˈklenlɪ/ *adj* (-ier, -iest) having clean habits; usually clean: *Are cats ~ animals?*

clean·li·ness *n* [U]

clean·ly[2] /ˈkliːnlɪ/ *adv* exactly, sharply; neatly: *He caught the ball ~,* without fumbling.

cleanse /klenz/ *vt* make thoroughly clean or pure: *~ the heart of/from sin.*

clear[1] /klɪə(r)/ *adj* (-er, -est) **1** easy to see (through): *the ~ water of a mountain lake; a ~ sky/light.* **2** free from guilt or blame: *a ~ conscience.* **3** (of sounds, etc) easily heard; distinct; pure: *the ~ note of a bell.* **4** (of and to the mind) free from doubt or difficulty: *It was ~ (to everyone) that the war would not end quickly.* **make oneself/one's meaning clear,** make oneself understood. **5** free from obstacles, dangers, etc: *Is the road ~?* **6** confident; certain: *I am not ~ as to what you expect me to do.* **7** free: *I wish I were ~ of debt.* **8** complete: *for three ~ days; a ~ profit of £5.* □ *n* [U] **in the clear,** free from suspicion, danger, etc.

'clear-ˈheaded, having good understanding.

'clear-ˈsighted, able to see, think, understand well.

`clear·way, (in GB) section of a main road on which vehicles must not stop or park.

clear[2] /klɪə(r)/ *adv* **1** distinctly: *speak loud and ~.* **2** quite; completely: *The prisoner got ~ away.* **3** apart; without touching; at or to a distance: *He jumped three inches ~ of the bar.*

clear·ness *n* [U] state of being clear: *the ~ness of vision.*

clear[3] /klɪə(r)/ *vt,vi* **1** remove, get rid of, what is unwanted or unwelcome: *~ the streets of snow; ~ oneself (of a charge),* prove one's innocence. **clear the air,** ⇨ air[1](1). **clear one's throat,** e g by coughing. **2** get past or over without touching: *Our car only just ~ed the gatepost.* **3** make as a net gain or profit: *~ £50.* **4** get (a ship or its cargo) free by doing what is necessary (signing papers, paying dues, etc) on entering or leaving a port: *~ goods through customs.*

5 (uses with *adverbial particles* and *prepositions*):

clear away, (a) take away, get rid of: *~ away the plates.* **(b)** pass away: *The clouds have ~ed away.*

clear off, (a) get rid of, make an end of: *~ off a debt.* **(b)** (of unwanted persons) go away: *This is my garden, so ~ off!*

clear out, (a) empty; make clear by taking out the contents of: *~ out a drain/a cupboard.* **(b)** (*informal*) go away; leave: *The police are after you, you'd better ~ out!*

clear up, become clear: *The weather/The sky is ~ing up.* **clear sth up, (a)** put in order; make tidy: *Who's going to ~ up the mess?* **(b)** make clear; solve (a mystery, etc): *~ up a misunderstanding.*

clear·ance /ˈklɪərəns/ *n* [C] **1** clearing up, removing, making tidy. **2** [C,U] free space; space between, for moving past: *There is not much/not enough ~ for large lorries passing under this bridge.*

clear·ing /ˈklɪərɪŋ/ *n* [C] open space from which trees have been cleared in a forest.

`clearing-house, office at which banks exchange cheques, etc and settle accounts, the balance being paid in cash.

clear·ly /ˈklɪəlɪ/ *adv* **1** distinctly: *speak/see ~.* **2** (in answers) undoubtedly: *'Was he mistaken?' 'C~'.*

cleav·age /ˈkliːvɪdʒ/ *n* [C] **1** (direction of a) split or division. **2** (*informal*) the cleft between a woman's breasts.

cleave /kliːv/ *vt,vi* (*pt* clove /kləʊv/, cleft /kleft/ or cleaved /kliːvd/, *pp* cleft or cloven /ˈkləʊvən/) **1** cut into two (with a blow from a heavy axe, etc); come apart: *~ a block of wood in two.* **2** make by cutting: *~ one's way through the crowd/the jungle.* **in a cleft stick,** (*fig*) in a dilemma.

'cleft `palate, division in the roof of the mouth from birth.

clef /klef/ *n* [C] musical symbol placed at the beginning of a stave to show the pitch of the notes.

cleft /kleft/ ⇨ cleave.

clema·tis /ˈklemətɪs/ *n* [U] (kinds of) climbing plant with clusters of white, yellow or purple flowers.

clem·ency /ˈklemənsɪ/ *n* [U] **1** mercy. **2** mildness (of temper or weather).

clem·ent /ˈklemənt/ *adj* **1** showing mercy. **2** (of the weather, a person's temper) mild.

clench /klentʃ/ *vt* **1** press or clasp firmly together, close tightly: *~ one's teeth; a ~ed-fist salute.*

clergy /ˈklɜːdʒɪ/ *n pl* persons ordained as priests or ministers of the Christian Church.

`clergy·man, (not used of a bishop) ordained minister, esp of the Church of England.

cleric /ˈklerɪk/ *n* [C] = clergyman.

cleri·cal /ˈklerɪkəl/ *adj* **1** of the clergy: *~ dress; a ~ collar.* **2** of, for, made by, a clerk or clerks(1): *a ~ error,* one made in copying or writing.

clerk /klɑːk *US*: klɜːk/ *n* [C] **1** person employed in a bank, office, shop, etc to keep records and accounts, copy letters, etc: *a `bank ~.* **2** officer in charge of records, etc: *the C~ to the Council.* **3** lay officer of the church with various duties: *the parish ~*

clever /ˈklevə(r)/ adj (-er, -est) **1** quick in learning and understanding things; skilful: *He's ~ at arithmetic/at making excuses.* **2** (of things done) showing ability and skill: *a ~ speech/book.*
clever·ly adv
clever·ness n [U]

cliché /ˈkliːʃeɪ US: kliˈʃeɪ/ n [C] idea or expression that has been used too much (and is now out-dated).

click¹ /klɪk/ vi, n [C] (make a) short, light sound (like that of a key turning in a lock): *The door ~ed shut.*

click² /klɪk/ vi (sl) (of two persons) become friends easily.

cli·ent /ˈklaɪənt/ n [C] **1** person who gets help or advice from a lawyer or any professional man: *a successful lawyer with hundreds of ~s.* **2** customer (at a shop).

cli·en·tele /ˈkliːɒnˈtel/ n (collective) customers.

cliff /klɪf/ n [C] steep face of rock, esp at the edge of the sea.
`cliff-hanger, episode in a story or contest with an uncertain end, leaving the reader or spectator in suspense.

cli·mac·tic /ˈklaɪˈmæktɪk/ adj forming a climax.

cli·mate /ˈklaɪmɪt/ n [C] **1** weather conditions of a place or area; conditions of temperature, rainfall, wind, etc. **2** [C] area or region with certain weather conditions: *A drier ~ would be good for her health.* **3** current condition: *the political ~,* general political attitudes.
cli·matic /ˈklaɪˈmætɪk/ adj of climate.
cli·mati·cally /-klɪ/ adv

cli·max /ˈklaɪmæks/ n [C] (pl ~es) event, point, of greatest interest or intensity (e g in a story or drama): *bring matters to a ~.* □ vt, vi bring or come to a climax.

climb /klaɪm/ vt, vi **1** go or get up (a tree, wall, rope, mountain, etc) or down. **2** (of aircraft) go higher. **3** (of plants) grow upwards. **4** rise by effort in social rank, position, etc. **climb down,** (fig) admit that one has been mistaken, unreasonable, etc. □ n [C] instance of climbing.
climber, (a) person who climbs. (b) climbing plant.

clinch /klɪntʃ/ vt, vi **1** settle (a bargain, an argument) conclusively: *That ~es the argument.* **2** make (a nail or rivet) fast by hammering sideways the end that protrudes. **3** put one or both arms round a person's body: *The boxers/lovers ~ed.* □ n [C] instance of clinching.

cling /klɪŋ/ vi (pt, pp clung /klʌŋ/) hold tight; resist separation: *~ to a hope of being rescued. They clung together when the time came to part. She's the ~ing sort,* depends on others.

clinic /ˈklɪnɪk/ n [C] **1** (part of a) hospital or institution where medical advice and treatment are given and where students are taught

through observation of cases; teaching so given; class of students taught in this way. **2** medical establishment for a specified purpose: *an ˈante-ˈnatal ~.*
clini·cal /ˈklɪnɪkəl/ adj

clink¹ /klɪŋk/ vi, vt, n [C] (make the) sound of small bits of metal, glass, etc knocking together: *the ~ of keys/glasses.*

clink² /klɪŋk/ n [C] (sl) prison: *be in ~.*

clip¹ /klɪp/ n [C] (esp) wire or metal device for holding things (e g papers) together. □ vt (-pp-) put or keep together with a clip: *~ papers together.*

clip² /klɪp/ vt (-pp-) **1** cut with scissors or shears; make short or neat: *~ a hedge.* **2** omit or abbreviate (esp the end of) sounds of (words) (e g by saying *shootin'* /ˈʃuːtɪn/ instead of *shooting* /ˈʃuːtɪŋ/). **3** (sl) hit or punch sharply: *~ him on the jaw.* □ n [C] **1** instance of clipping. **2** smart blow: *a ~ on the jaw.*
`clip·ping, (esp) something cut from a newspaper, etc.

clip·pers /ˈklɪpəz/ n pl (also *a pair of ~s*) instrument for clipping: `hair-~s

clique /kliːk/ n [C] group of persons united by common interests.

cloak /kləʊk/ n [C] **1** loose outer garment, without sleeves. **2** (fig) something used to hide or keep secret: *under the ~ of darkness.* □ vt hide (thoughts, purposes, etc).
`cloak-room, place where coats, etc may be left for a short time (e g in a theatre).

clock /klok/ n [C] instrument (not carried or worn like a watch) for measuring and showing the time. **round the clock,** all day and night. □ vt, vi **1** do something (e g run a race) in a measured period of time: *He ~ed 9·6 seconds for the 100 metres.* **2** clock in/out; clock on/off, record the time of (e g the arrival and departure of workers).
`clock-face, surface of a clock showing figures marking the hours, etc.
`clock-tower, tall structure (forming part of a building, e g a church) with a clock high up on an outside wall.
`clock·wise/ˈanti-ˈclock·wise adv moving in a curve in the same direction/in the opposite direction to that taken by the hands of a clock.

clod /klod/ n [C] lump (of earth, etc).

clog¹ /klog/ n [C] shoe with a wooden sole; shoe carved out of a block of wood.

clog² /klog/ vt, vi (-gg-) **1** (cause to) be or become blocked with dirt, grease, etc so that movement, flow of liquid, etc is difficult or prevented. **2** (fig) *Don't ~ your memory with useless facts.*

clois·ter /ˈklɔɪstə(r)/ n [C] **1** covered walk, usually on the sides of an open courtyard, with a wall on the outer side and columns or arches on the inner side. **2** (life in a) convent or monastery. □ vt put in, live in, a cloister(2).

close¹ /kləʊs/ adj (-r, -st) **1** near (in space

or time): *fire a gun at ~ range.* **close at hand; close to/by,** near. **2** with little or no space in between: *The soldiers advanced in ~ order,* with little space between them. **3** strict; severe: *be (kept) under ~ arrest.* **keep a close watch on,** watch carefully. **4** thorough: *on ~r examination.* **5** intimate: *a ~ friend/friendship.* **6** (of competitions, games, their results) in which the competitors are almost equal: *a ~ contest/election.* **7** (of vowels) pronounced with the roof of the mouth and the tongue near each other (e g the *e* of 'they' but not the *e* of 'there', which is an 'open' vowel). **8** (of the weather or air) uncomfortably heavy; (of a room, etc) having little fresh air. **9** hidden; secret; not in the habit of talking about one's affairs: *keep/lie ~ for a while,* keep one's whereabouts secret, not show oneself. □ *adv* in a close manner; near together; tightly: *stand/ sit ~ against the wall; come ~r together.* ⇨ closely below.

'close-'fitting *adj* fitting close (to the body, etc).

'close-'grained *adj* having a grain in which the lines in the pattern made by growth are close together.

'close-'question *vt* interrogate thoroughly.

'close-'set *adj* set, placed, close together: *~-set eyes.*

'close-up, (a) photograph, taken near to an object, etc and showing it in large scale. (b) close view.

close·ly *adv* in a close manner: *listen ~ly. She ~ly resembles her mother.*

close·ness *n* [U]

close² /kləʊs/ *n* [C] **1** grounds of a cathedral, abbey or school, usually with its buildings round it. **2** = cul-de-sac.

close³ /kləʊz/ *vt,vi* **1** = shut: *If you ~ your eyes, you can't see. This box/The lid of this box doesn't ~ properly.* **close one's eyes/ ears to,** ⇨ shut. **2** (not usually replaceable by *shut*) be, declare, be declared, not open: *This road is ~d to heavy traffic.* **3** bring or come to an end: *close a discussion; the closing* (= last, final) *day for applications.* **4** bring or come together by making less space or fewer spaces between.

5 (uses with *adverbial particles* and *prepositions*):

close down, (a) (of a factory, business, etc) stop production, shut completely. **(b)** (of a broadcasting station) stop transmitting: *The time is just after midnight and we are now closing down.* Hence, **'close-down** *n*

close in, The days are closing in, getting shorter. **close in on/upon, (a)** envelop: *Darkness ~d in on us.* **(b)** come near(er) and attack: *The enemy ~d in on us.*

'closed 'shop, factory, profession or trade in which employment is open only to members of an approved trade union.

close⁴ /kləʊz/ *n* [U] **1** end (of a period of time): *towards the ~ of the century.* **2** con-

clusion (of an activity, etc): *(at) ~ of play,* (cricket) (at the) end of play for the day.

closet /'klɒzɪt/ *n* [C] **1** (now chiefly *US*) small room for storing things. ⇨ cupboard, storeroom. **2** (*old use*) lavatory.

clo·sure /'kləʊʒə(r)/ *n* [C] **1** act of closing (down): *pit ~s.* **2** (in Parliament) device to end debate by taking a vote on a question: *apply the ~ to a debate.*

clot /klɒt/ *n* [C] **1** semi-solid lump formed from liquid, esp blood. **2** (*sl*) idiot, fool. □ *vt,vi* (-tt-) form into clots: *~ted cream.*

cloth /klɒθ *US:* klɔːθ/ *n* (*pl ~s* /klɒθs *US:* klɔːðz/) **1** [U] material made by weaving (cotton, wool, etc): *three metres of ~.* **2** [C] piece of this material for special purpose: *a `dish~.*

clothe /kləʊð/ *vt* wear clothes; put clothes on, supply clothes for: *He has to work hard in order to ~ his family.*

clothes /kləʊðz *US:* kləʊz/ *n pl* coverings for a person's body; dress: *`baby-~; a `~-brush.*

'bed-clothes, sheets, blankets, etc for or on a bed.

'clothes-peg, one used for fastening clothes to a washing-line.

cloth·ing /'kləʊðɪŋ/ *n* [U] (collective) clothes: *articles of ~.*

cloud /klaʊd/ *n* **1** [C,U] (mass of) visible water vapour floating in the sky: *The top of the mountain was hidden under ~.* **2** [C] similar mass of smoke, etc in the air: *a ~ of insects.* **3** [C] vague patch on or in a liquid or a transparent object. **4** [C] something that causes unhappiness or fear: *the ~s of war.* **under a cloud,** under suspicion, in disgrace. □ *vi,vt* become, make, indistinct (as) through cloud: *The sky ~ed over,* became cloudy. *Her eyes were ~ed with tears.*

cloudy *adj* (-ier, -iest) **(a)** covered with clouds: *a ~y sky.* **(b)** (esp of liquids) not clear.

clove¹ ⇨ cleave¹.

clove² /kləʊv/ *n* [C] dried, unopened flower-bud of a tropical tree, used as a spice.

clove³ /kləʊv/ *n* [C] one of the small, separate sections of some bulbs: *a ~ of garlic.*

clo·ver /'kləʊvə(r)/ *n* [U] low-growing plant with (usually) three leaves on each stalk.

'clover-leaf, highway intersection with flyovers, etc forming the pattern of a leaf of clover.

clown /klaʊn/ *n* [C] **1** person (esp in a circus or pantomime) who makes a living by dressing up and performing foolish tricks and antics for fun. **2** person acting like a clown. **3** rude, clumsy man. □ *vt* behave like a clown: *Stop all this ~ing!*

cloy /klɔɪ/ *vt,vi* make or become distasteful or weary by too much of something, sweetness, richness (of food, pleasure, etc): *~ed with pleasure.*

club¹ /klʌb/ *n* [C] **1** heavy stick with one

thick end, used as a weapon. **2** stick with a curved head for playing golf and hockey. □ *vt* (-bb-) hit with a club: *He had been ~bed to death.*

'club-'foot, foot that is (from birth) thick and badly formed. Hence, **'club-'footed** *adj*

club² /klʌb/ *n* **1** [C] one of the thirteen playing-cards with black leaf-like designs printed on it. **2** (*pl*) suit of these cards.

club³ /klʌb/ *n* [C] **1** society of persons who pay money to provide themselves with sport, social entertainment, etc. **2** the rooms or building(s) used by such a society. □ *vi* (-bb-) **club together,** join or act (together, with others) for a common purpose: *The staff ~bed together to buy a present for the Manager.*

cluck /klʌk/ *vi*, *n* [C] (make the) noise made by a hen, e g when calling her chickens.

clue /klu/ *n* [C] fact, idea, etc that suggests a possible answer to a problem: *He hasn't a ~*, (*informal*) is completely ignorant of, unable to understand or explain (what is in question).

clump¹ /klʌmp/ *n* [C] group or cluster (of trees, shrubs or plants): *growing in ~s.* □ *vt* plant in groups.

clump² /klʌmp/ *vi* tread heavily: *~ about,* e g walk in heavy boots.

clumsy /ˈklʌmzɪ/ *adj* (-ier, -iest) **1** ungraceful in movement or construction; not well designed for its purpose: *The ~ workman put his elbow through the window and broke it.* **2** tactless; unskilful: *a ~ apology/ remark.*

'clum-sily /-səlɪ/ *adv*
'clum-si-ness *n* [U]

clung /klʌŋ/ *pt,pp* of cling.

clunk /klʌŋk/ *vi*, *n* [C] (make the) sound of heavy metals striking together.

clus-ter /ˈklʌstə(r)/ *n* [C] **1** number of things of the same kind growing closely together: *a ~ of flowers/curls.* **2** number of persons, animals, objects, etc in a small, close group: *a ~ of spectators/islands; consonant ~s,* (in phonetics, e g *str* in **strong**). □ *vi* be in, form, a close group round.

clutch¹ /klʌtʃ/ *vt,vi* seize; (try to) take hold of tightly with the hand(s): *He ~ed (at) the rope we threw to him.* □ *n* [C] **1** act of clutching. **2** (esp in *pl*) control; power: *He's in his mother-in-law's ~es.* **3** device, e g a pedal, in a machine or engine for connecting and disconnecting working parts: *let the ~ in/out.*

clutch² /klʌtʃ/ *n* [C] **1** set of eggs placed under a hen to hatch at one time. **2** number of chicks hatched from these.

clut-ter /ˈklʌtə(r)/ *vt* make untidy or confused: *a desk ~ed up with papers.* □ *n: in a ~,* in disorder or confusion.

co- /ˈkəʊ/ *prefix* together, jointly, equally: *co-author; co-education.*

coach¹ /kəʊtʃ/ *n* [C] **1** (also `*motor-~*) long-distance, single-decked bus: *travel by ~; a `~-tour of Europe.* **2** (*US* = *car*) railway carriage, often divided into compartments. **3** four-wheeled carriage pulled by four or more horses, used to carry passengers and mail before railways were built. ⇨ state coach.

coach² /kəʊtʃ/ *n* [C] **1** teacher, esp one who gives private lessons to prepare students for a public examination. **2** person who trains athletes for contests: *a `football ~.* □ *vt,vi* teach or train.

co-agu-late /ˈkəʊˈægjʊleɪt/ *vt,vi* (of liquids) change to a thick and solid state, as blood does in air.

co-agu-la-tion /ˈkəʊˈægjʊˈleɪʃən/ *n* [U]

coal /kəʊl/ *n* **1** [U] black mineral that burns and supplies heat. **2** [C] piece of this material.

`coal-face, part of a coal-seam from which coal is being cut.

`coal-gas, the mixture of gases made from coal, used for lighting and heating.

`coal-mine, mine from which coal is dug.

`coal-scuttle, container for coal near a fireside.

`coal-seam, underground layer of coal.

`coal-tar, thick, black, sticky substance produced when coal-gas is made.

co-alesce /ˈkəʊəˈles/ *vi* come together and unite into one substance, group, etc.

co-ales-cence /ˈkəʊəˈlesəns/ *n* [U]

co-ali-tion /ˈkəʊəˈlɪʃən/ *n* **1** [U] uniting. **2** [C] union of political parties for a special purpose: *a ~ government; form a ~.*

coarse /kɔːs/ *adj* (-r, -st) **1** (of substances) not fine and small; rough, lumpy: *~ sand/ sugar; ~ cloth; a ~ skin/complexion.* **2** (of behaviour, language, etc) vulgar; not delicate or refined. **3** (of food) common; inferior: *~ fish.*

coarse-ly *adv*
coarse-ness *n* [U]

coarsen /ˈkɔːsən/ *vt,vi* make or become coarse.

coast¹ /kəʊst/ *n* [C] seashore and land near it: *There are numerous islands off the ~.*

`coast-guard, officer on police duty on the coast (to prevent or detect smuggling, report passing ships, etc).

`coast-line, shoreline, esp when referring to its shape: *a rugged ~line.*

coast² /kəʊst/ *vi,vi* **1** go in, sail, a ship along the coast. **2** ride or slide down a hill or slope without using power (e g without pedalling a bicycle).

coastal /ˈkəʊstəl/ *adj* of the coast: *~ waters/fishing.*

coat /kəʊt/ *n* [C] **1** outer garment with sleeves, buttoned in the front. **2** woman's tailored jacket. **3** any covering that is compared to a garment, e g an animal's hair or wool. **4** layer of paint or other substance put on a surface: *The woodwork has had its final ~ of paint.* □ *vt* cover with a layer: *furniture ~ed with dust.*

'coat of 'arms, design used by a noble family, town, university, etc, e g on a shield.

'coat-hanger, device on which clothes are hung in wardrobes, etc.

coat·ing /ˈkəʊtɪŋ/ n 1 [C] thin layer or covering: *two ~s of paint.* 2 [U] cloth for coats(1,2).

coax /kəʊks/ vt,vi 1 persuade a person or thing to act by kindness or patience: *~ a child to take its medicine; ~ a fire to burn.* 2 get by coaxing: *~ a smile from the baby.*

cob /kob/ n [C] 1 male swan. 2 strong short-legged horse for riding. 3 (also `~-nut*) large kind of hazel-nut. 4 (also `corn-~*) inner part of an ear of maize on which the grain grows: *corn on the ~.*

cobble¹ /ˈkobəl/ n [C] (also `~-stone*) stone worn round and smooth by the water and used for paving. □ vt pave with these stones: *~d streets.*

cobble² /ˈkobəl/ vt (dated) mend (esp shoes), or put together roughly.

cob·bler /ˈkoblə(r)/ n [C] (dated) = shoe-repairer.

co·bra /ˈkəʊbrə/ n [C] poisonous snake of Asia and Africa.

cob·web /ˈkobweb/ n [C] fine network or single thread made by a spider.

coca-cola /ˌkəʊkə ˈkəʊlə/ n [C,U] (P) popular brown non-alcoholic fizzy drink (also called *coke*).

co·caine /kəʊˈkeɪn/ n [U] product (from a shrub) used as a local anaesthetic, and also used by drug addicts.

cochi·neal /ˈkotʃɪnil/ n [U] bright red colouring-matter used in cooking.

coch·lea /ˈkoklɪə/ n [C] (anat) spiral-shaped part of the inner ear.

cock¹ /kok/ n [C] 1 adult male chicken. 2 (in compounds) male of other kinds of bird: *a `pea~; a '~-~robin.*

'cock-crow, (a) cock's cry. **(b)** early dawn.

'cock-fight, fight (form of gambling) between specially bred and trained cocks.

cock² /kok/ n [C] 1 tap and spout for controlling the flow of a liquid or a gas, e g from a pipe. 2 lever in a gun; position of this lever when it is raised and ready to be released by the trigger. **go off at half cock,** (fig) (of an event, etc) be organized, happen, without success because not fully prepared.

cock³ /kok/ vt 1 turn upwards, cause to be erect (showing attention, inquiry, defiance, etc): *The horse ~ed its ears. The horse stopped with its ears ~ed up.* 2 raise the cock of (a gun) ready for firing. ⇨ cock²(2). 3 (sl) make a mess of; upset: *They completely ~ed up the arrangements for our holiday.* Hence, **'cock-up** n

cock-a-doodle-doo /ˌkok ə ˈdudəl ˈdu/ n [C] (informal) imitation of a cock's crow.

cocka·too /ˌkokəˈtu/ n [C] crested parrot.

cocker /ˈkokə(r)/ n [C] (usually '~-`spaniel*) breed of spaniel.

cock·erel /ˈkokrəl/ n [C] young cock¹(1).

cock-eyed /ˈkokaɪd/ adj (sl) 1 squinting; crooked; turned or twisted to one side. 2 badly organised, ill-judged: *a ~ scheme.*

cockle /ˈkokəl/ n [C] edible shellfish; (also `~-shell*) its shell.

cock·ney /ˈkoknɪ/ adj, n [C] (characteristic of a) native, esp working-class, of London: *a ~ accent; ~ humour.*

cock·pit /ˈkokpɪt/ n [C] 1 enclosed space for cock-fighting. 2 (fig) area where battles have often been fought: *Belgium, the ~ of Europe.* 3 compartment in a small aircraft for the pilot.

cock·roach /ˈkokrəʊtʃ/ n [C] large, dark-brown insect that comes out at night in kitchens and places where food is kept.

cocks·comb /ˈkokskəʊm/ n [C] (esp) red crest of a cock¹(1).

cock·sure /ˈkokˈʃʊə(r)/ adj offensively sure or confident.

cock·tail /ˈkokteɪl/ n [C] 1 mixed alcoholic drink, esp one taken before a meal, e g gin and vermouth. 2 mixture of fruit, fruit juices, small quantities of shellfish, etc served as an appetizer.

cocky /ˈkokɪ/ adj (-ier, -iest) (informal) = cocksure.

co·coa /ˈkəʊkəʊ/ n [U] powder of crushed cacao seeds; hot drink made from this with water or milk.

coco·nut /ˈkəʊkənʌt/ n [C,U] large seed (of the `~-palm*) filled with milky juice and with a solid white lining and a hard shell.

co·coon /kəˈkun/ n [C] silky covering made by a caterpillar to protect itself while it is a chrysalis, esp that of the silkworm. □ vt protect (an aircraft, engine, car, etc) by covering completely with a plastic material.

cod /kod/ n 1 [C] (pl unchanged) (also `~ fish*) large sea-fish. 2 [U] its flesh as food. **'cod-liver 'oil,** used as a medicine.

coddle /ˈkodəl/ vt 1 treat with great care and tenderness: *~ a child because it is in poor health.* 2 cook, e g eggs, in water just below boiling-point.

code /kəʊd/ n [C] 1 collection of laws arranged in a system. 2 system of rules and principles that has been accepted by society or a class or group of people: *a high moral ~; a ~ of honour.* 3 system of signs, secret writing, etc used to ensure secrecy, e g in war or economy, in sending cables or to a computer: *the Morse ~.* **break a code,** discover how to interpret a code(3). □ vt (also **en·code** /enˈkəʊd/) put in a code(3).

co·deine /ˈkəʊdin/ n [U] drug from opium used as a medicine.

codi·fy /ˈkəʊdɪfaɪ US: ˈkodəfaɪ/ vt (pt,pp -ied) put into the form of a code(1): *~ the laws.*

co-ed /ˌkəʊ ˈed/ n [C] (informal) (student at a) co-educational school.

co-edu·ca·tion /ˌkəʊ ˈedʒʊˈkeɪʃən/ n [U] education of boys and girls together.
co-edu·ca·tional /-nəl/ adj

co·erce /kəʊˈɜːs/ vt use force to make (a person) obedient, do something, etc.

co·ercion /kəʊˈɜːʃən US: -ɜːrʒən/ n [U] coercing or being co-erced; government by force.

co·ercive /kəʊˈɜːsɪv/ adj of, using, co-ercion: *coercive methods/measures.*

co·exist /ˌkəʊɪgˈzɪst/ vi exist at the same time.

co·exist·ence /-təns/ n [U] (esp) peaceful existence of states with opposed political systems.

cof·fee /ˈkɒfɪ US: ˈkɔːfɪ/ n [U] bush or shrub with berries containing seeds (called *beans*) used for making a drink; the seeds; the powder; [C,U] the drink.

`**coffee bar**, small café serving drinks and light refreshments.

`**coffee-pot**, vessel for making or serving coffee.

cof·fer /ˈkɒfə(r)/ n [C] (esp) large, strong box, esp for holding money or valuables.

cof·fin /ˈkɒfɪn/ n [C] box or case for a dead person to be buried in.

cog /kɒg/ n [C] one of a series of teeth on the rim of a wheel which transfers motion by locking into the teeth of a similar wheel.

co·gency /ˈkəʊdʒənsɪ/ n [U] force or strength (of arguments).

co·gent /ˈkəʊdʒənt/ adj (of arguments) strong and convincing.

cogi·tate /ˈkɒdʒɪteɪt/ vi,vt meditate (the usual word).

cognac /ˈkɒnjæk/ n [U] fine French brandy.

cog·nate /ˈkɒgneɪt/ adj 1 having the same source of origin: *Dutch is ∼ with German.* 2 related: *Physics and astronomy are ∼ sciences.* □ n [C] word, etc that is cognate with another.

co·habit /kəʊˈhæbɪt/ vi (of an unmarried couple) live together and behave as, like, husband and wife.

co·habi·ta·tion /ˌkəʊˈhæbɪˌteɪʃən/ n [U]

co·here /kəʊˈhɪə(r)/ vi 1 stick together; be or remain united. 2 (of arguments, etc) be consistent.

co·her·ence /-rəns/, **co·her·en·cy** /-rənsɪ/ n [U]

co·her·ent /-rənt/ adj

co·her·ent·ly adv

coif·feur /kwɑːˈfɜː(r)/ n (Fr) = hairdresser.

coif·fure /kwɑːˈfjʊə(r)/ n [C] style of hair-dressing.

coil /kɔɪl/ vt,vi wind or twist into a continuous circular or spiral shape; curl round and round: *The snake ∼ed (itself) round the branch.* □ n [C] 1 something coiled; a single turn of something coiled: *the thick ∼s of a python.* 2 length of wire wound in a spiral to conduct electric current. 3 (*informal*) intrauterine contraceptive device in the shape of a coil.

coin /kɔɪn/ n [C,U] (piece of) metal money: *a small heap of ∼(s).* □ vt 1 make (metal) into coins. **be `coining money,** be earning

money quickly or easily. 2 invent (esp a new word).

coin·age /ˈkɔɪnɪdʒ/ n 1 [U] making coins; the coins made. 2 [C] system of coins in use: *a decimal ∼.* 3 [U] inventing (of a new word); [C] newly invented word.

co·incide /ˌkəʊɪnˈsaɪd/ vi 1 (of two or more objects) correspond in area and outline. 2 (of events) happen at the same time; occupy the same period of time: *His free time never ∼d with hers.* 3 (of ideas, etc) be in harmony or agreement: *His tastes and habits ∼ with those of his wife.*

co·inci·dence /kəʊˈɪnsɪdəns/ n [U] the condition of coinciding; [C] instance of this, happening by chance: *by a curious ∼.*

co·inci·dent /-dənt/ adj coincident.

co·inci·den·tal /ˌkəʊˌɪnsɪˈdentəl/ adj of the nature of a, suggesting, coincidence.

coke¹ /kəʊk/ n [U] substance that remains when gas has been taken out of coal, used as a fuel. □ vt turn (coal) into coke.

coke² /kəʊk/ n [C,U] (*informal*) = coca-cola.

col /kɒl/ n [C] depression or pass in a mountain range.

col·an·der, cul·len·der /ˈkʌləndə(r)/ n [C] vessel with many small holes, used to drain off water from vegetables, etc in cooking.

cold¹ /kəʊld/ adj (-er, -est) 1 of low temperature, esp when compared with the human body: *∼ weather; a ∼ wind; feel ∼.* **have cold feet,** feel afraid or reluctant. **throw cold water on sth,** discourage it. **(kill sb) in cold blood; make one's blood run cold,** ⇨ blood¹. 2 (*fig*) unkind; unfriendly: *a ∼ greeting/welcome.* 3 (of colours) suggesting cold, e g grey and blue.

`**cold-`blooded** adj (a) having blood that varies with the temperature (e g fish, reptiles). (b) (*fig*) of persons, their actions) without emotion.

cold comfort, poor consolation.

`**cold cream,** ointment for cleansing and softening the skin.

`**cold `front,** ⇨ front.

`**cold-`hearted** adj without sympathy; indifferent.

`**cold `meat,** meat that has been cooked and cooled.

cold snap, short period of cold weather.

`**cold-`shoulder, n give sb the cold-shoulder,** ignore him. □ vt snub, ignore.

`**cold `war,** struggle for superiority using propaganda, economic measures, etc without actual fighting.

cold·ness n [U]

cold² /kəʊld/ n 1 [U] relative absence of heat; low temperature (esp in the atmosphere): *He was shivering with ∼. He disliked both the heat of summer and the ∼ of winter. Don't stay outside in the ∼, come indoors by the fire.* **(be left) out in the cold,** (*fig*) (be) ignored or neglected. (*Note:* often used with *the.*) 2 [C,U] illness (catarrh) of the nose or throat: *have a* ∼; *catch (a)* ∼.

col·lab·or·ate /kə`læbəreɪt/ *vi* **1** work in partnership: ∼ *on writing biography.* **2** *collaborate with,* act treasonably, esp with enemy forces occupying one's country.

col·lab·or·ation /kə`læbə`reɪʃən/ *n* [U] collaborating: *working in collaboration with others.*

col·lab·or·ator /kə`læbəreɪtə(r)/, person who collaborates(1,2).

col·lage /`kola3 US: kə`la3/ *n* [C] picture made by an unusual combination of bits of paper, cloth, photographs, etc.

col·lapse /kə`læps/ *vi,vt* **1** fall down or in; come or break to pieces suddenly: *The roof* ∼*d under the weight of the snow.* **2** lose physical strength, courage, mental powers, etc: *If you work too hard you may* ∼. *Our plans will* ∼ *unless we get more help.* **3** (of apparatus, e g a chair) close or fold up. □ *n* [C] **1** collapsing: *the* ∼ *of a table/tent/ tower, etc.* **2** (*fig*): *the* ∼ *of their plans/ hopes; suffer a nervous* ∼.

col·laps·ible, -able /-əbəl/ *adj* that can be collapsed(3) (for packing, etc): *a collapsible chair.*

col·lar /`kolə(r)/ *n* [C] **1** part of a garment that fits round the neck; turned-over neck-band of a shirt, dress, etc. ⇨ white-collar. **2** separate article of clothing (linen, lace, etc) worn round the neck and fastened to a shirt or blouse. **3** band of leather, etc put round the neck of a dog, horse or other animal. **4** metal band joining two pipes, rods or shafts, e g in a machine. □ *vt* seize (roughly) by the collar: *The policeman* ∼*ed the thief.*

`**col·lar·bone**, bone joining the shoulder and the breast bone.

`**collar stud**, small button-like device for fastening a collar to a shirt.

col·late /kə`leɪt/ *vt* make a careful comparison between (manuscripts, books, etc) to note the differences: ∼ *a new edition with an earlier edition.*

col·lat·eral /kə`lætərəl/ *adj* **1** secondary or subordinate but from the same source: ∼ *evidence.* **2** descended from a common ancestor but in a different line, i e through different sons or daughters.

col·league /`kolig/ *n* [C] person working with another or others: *When he left the company, his* ∼*s bought him a present.*

col·lect¹ /`kolekt/ *n* [C] short prayer of the Church of Rome or the Church of England, to be read on certain days.

col·lect² /kə`lekt/ *vt,vi* **1** bring or gather together; get from a number of persons or places: *Please* ∼ *all the empty bottles and put them over here.* **2** obtain specimens of (books, stamps, etc), e g as a hobby or in order to learn things: ∼ *foreign stamps.* **3** come together: *A crowd soon* ∼*s when there's an accident.* **4** fetch: ∼ *a child from school.* **5** gather together, recover control of

(one's thoughts, energies, oneself): *Before you begin to make a speech, you should* ∼ *your thoughts and ideas.*

col·lected *adj* (esp of a person) calm; not distracted.

col·lec·tion /kə`lekʃən/ *n* **1** [U] collecting, [C] instance of this: *How many* ∼*s of letters are there every day?* **2** [C] group of objects that have been collected and that belong together: *a fine* ∼ *of paintings.* **3** heap of materials or objects that have come together: *a* ∼ *of dust/rubbish.* **4** [C] money collected (at a meeting, a Church service, etc).

col·lec·tive /kə`lektɪv/ *adj* of a group or society (of persons, nations, etc) as a whole: ∼ *leadership,* (emphasis on) government by a group rather than an individual.

collective noun, (*gram*) one that is singular in form but stands for many individuals, as *cattle, crowd, audience: In 'to catch fish', fish is a* ∼ *noun.*

col·lec·tor /kə`lektə(r)/ *n* [C] person who collects: *a* `*tax*-∼; *a* `*ticket*-∼, e g at a railway station.

col·lege /`kolɪdʒ/ *n* [C] **1** school for higher or professional education; body of teachers and students forming part of a university; their building(s): *go to* ∼; *be at* ∼; `*training* ∼*s.* **2** union of persons with common purposes and privileges: *the C*∼ *of Surgeons; the C*∼ *of Cardinals,* who elect and advise the Pope.

col·le·giate /kə`lidʒɪət/ *adj* of or like a college (student): *collegiate life.*

col·lide /kə`laɪd/ *vi* **1** come together violently; meet and strike: *As the bus came round the corner, it* ∼*d with a van. The ships* ∼*d in the fog.* **2** be opposed; be in conflict: *If the aims of two countries* ∼, *there may be war.*

col·lier /`kolɪə(r)/ *n* [C] **1** coalminer. **2** ship that carries coal as cargo.

col·liery /`koljərɪ/ *n* [C] (*pl* -ies) coalmine (and the buildings, etc connected with it).

col·li·sion /kə`lɪʒən/ *n* [U] colliding; [C] instance of this: *a railway* ∼.

col·lo·cate /`koləkeɪt/ *vi* (of words) combine in a way characteristic of language: *'Weak'* ∼*s with 'tea'* (i e *weak tea* is acceptable) *but 'feeble' does not* (i e *feeble tea* is not good English).

col·lo·cation /`kolə`keɪʃən/ *n* [C,U] coming together; collocating of words: *'Strong tea' and 'heavy drinker' are English collocations.*

col·lo·quial /kə`ləʊkwɪəl/ *adj* (of words, phrases, style) belonging to, suitable for, ordinary conversation; not formal or literary.

col·lo·qui·ally /-əlɪ/ *adv*

col·lo·qui·al·ism /-ɪzm/, colloquial word or phrase.

col·lu·sion /kə`luʒən/ *n* [U] secret agreement or understanding for a deceitful or fraudulent purpose: *act in* ∼ *with a thief.*

co·lon¹ /`kəʊlən/ *n* [C] lower and greater

part of the large intestine.

co·lon² /ˈkəʊlən/ n [C] punctuation mark (:) used in writing and printing.

co·lonel /ˈkɜːnəl/ n [C] army officer above a major (and in US) commanding a regiment.

co·lo·nial /kəˈləʊnɪəl/ adj **1** of a colony or colonies(1). **2** (esp US) in the style of architecture in the British colonies in N America before and during the Revolution. □ n [C] inhabitant of a colony(1), esp one who helps or helped to found and develop it.

co·lo·nial·ism /-ɪzm/, policy of having colonies(1) and keeping them dependent.

co·lo·nial·ist, supporter of colonialism.

col·on·ist /ˈkɒlənɪst/ n [C] pioneer settler in a colony(1).

col·on·ize /ˈkɒlənaɪz/ vt establish a colony; establish in a colony: *The ancient Greeks* ∼*d many parts of the Mediterranean.*

col·on·iz·ation /ˌkɒlənaɪˈzeɪʃən US: -nɪˈz-/ n [U]

col·on·nade /ˌkɒləˈneɪd/ n [C] row of columns(1).

col·ony /ˈkɒlənɪ/ n [C] (pl -ies) **1** country or territory extensively settled by migrants from a mother country, and, for a time, controlled by it, e g (formerly) Australia. **2** country, territory, controlled, administered, and (often) developed by another, e g Hong Kong. **3** group of people from another country, or of people with the same trade, profession or occupation, living together: *a* ∼ *of artists.* **4** number of animals or plants, living or growing together: *a* ∼ *of ants.*

color (US) = colour.

co·los·sal /kəˈlɒsl/ adj immense.

co·los·sus /kəˈlɒsəs/ n [C] (pl -si /-saɪ/, ∼es) **1** immense statue (esp of a man). **2** immense person or personification.

col·our¹ (US = **color**) /ˈkʌlə(r)/ n **1** [U] sensation produced in the eye by rays of decomposed light; [C] effect produced by a ray of light of a particular wavelength, or by a mixture of these: *Red, blue and yellow are* ∼*s. There isn't enough* ∼ *in the picture.* **2** [U] redness of the face: *She has very little* ∼*, has a pale face.* **be/feel/look off colour,** (*informal*) be/look unwell. **3** (pl) materials used by artists; paint: `*water*∼*s;* bright/ dark ∼*s.* **4** [U] (of events, descriptions) appearance of reality or truth. **local colour,** use of details to make a description of a place, scene or time realistic. **5** (pl) ribbon, dress, cap, etc worn as a symbol of a party, a club, a school, etc: *The jockey wears the owners* ∼*s.* **6** (pl) flag (of a ship); ensign or standard of a regiment: *salute the* ∼*s.* **come off with flying colours,** make a great success of something. **show one's true colours,** show what one really is. **7** race or race-mixture other than European.

`**colour-bar,** social distinction between white and coloured races.

`**colour-blind** adj unable to distinguish between or to see certain colours.

`**colour scheme,** scheme for combination of colours in a design (e g decorating a room).

col·our·ful adj full of colour; bright; gay; exciting: *a* ∼*ful scene; lead a* ∼*ful life.*

col·our·less adj pale; dull: *a* ∼*less style; a* ∼*less existence.*

col·our² (US = **color**) /ˈkʌlə(r)/ vt,vi **1** give colour to; put colour on: ∼ *a wall green.* **2** take on colour: *The leaves have begun to* ∼, to turn yellow, brown, etc. **3** blush: *The girl is so shy that she* ∼*s whenever a man speaks to her.* **4** change or misrepresent in some way: *News is often* ∼*ed.*

col·oured adj **(a)** having the colour specified: `*cream*∼*ed;* `*flesh*∼*ed.* **(b)** (of persons) not wholly of white or European descent: *Cape C*∼*eds,* South African people of mixed race.

col·our·ing, (esp) style in which something is described; style in which an artist uses colour.

colt¹ /kəʊlt/ n [C] young male horse up to the age of 4 or 5. ⇨ **filly.**

`**colt·ish** adj like a colt; frisky

colt² /kəʊlt/ n (US) (P) early type of revolver or pistol.

col·umn /ˈkɒləm/ n [C] **1** tall, upright pillar, usually of stone, either supporting or decorating part of a building, or standing alone as a monument. **2** something shaped like or suggesting a column: *a* ∼ *of smoke; the spinal* ∼, the backbone. **3** vertical division of a printed page, (e g of this page or of a newspaper). **4** series of numbers arranged under one another: *add up a long* ∼ *of figures.* **5** line of soldiers, etc one behind the other. **6** line of ships following one another.

coma /ˈkəʊmə/ n [C] **in a coma,** in an unnatural deep sleep usually from injury or illness.

comb /kəʊm/ n [C] **1** piece of metal, rubber, plastic, etc with teeth for making the hair tidy, keeping it in place, etc or as an ornament. **2** part of a machine with a look or purpose like a comb, esp for tidying and straightening wool, cotton, etc for manufacture. ⇨ also **honeycomb, cockscomb.** □ vt,vi **1** use a comb on (the hair). **2** prepare (wool, flax, etc) for manufacture using combs. **3** search thoroughly: *The police* ∼*ed the whole city in their efforts to find the murderer.* **4 comb out,** (*fig*) take out (unwanted things, persons) from a group: ∼ *out a government department,* get rid of officials who are not really needed.

com·bat /ˈkɒmbæt/ n [C] fight; struggle. □ vt,vi fight; struggle: ∼ *the enemy; a ship* ∼*ing with the wind and waves.*

com·bat·ant /ˈkɒmbətənt/ adj fighting. □ n [C] person who fights: *In modern wars both* ∼*s and non-*∼*s are killed in air attacks.*

com·bi·na·tion /ˌkɒmbɪˈneɪʃən/ n **1** [U] joining or putting together; state of being joined: *in* ∼ *with.* **2** [C] number of persons or things that are joined: *The college is supported by a* ~ *of income from the government and fees from students.* **3** (also ~**-lock**) formula, complicated arrangement, for the lock of a safe, etc: *How did the thieves learn the* ~?

com·bine[1] /kəmˈbaɪn/ *vt,vi* (cause to) join together; possess at the same time: *We can't always* ~ *work with pleasure. Hydrogen and oxygen* ~/*Hydrogen* ~*s with oxygen to form water.*

com·bine[2] /ˈkɒmbaɪn/ *n* [C] group of persons, trading companies, etc joined for a purpose (such as controlling prices). **ˈcombine-ˈharvester**, machine that both reaps and threshes (grain).

com·bust·ible /kəmˈbʌstəbəl/ *adj* catching fire and burning easily.

com·bus·tion /kəmˈbʌstʃən/ *n* [U] process of burning; destruction by fire.

come /kʌm/ *vi* (*pt* **came** /keɪm/, *pp* ~) (For uses with *adverbial particles and prepositions*, ⇨ **13** below). **1** move towards or nearer to, the speaker; arrive where the speaker is, was or will be: *Are you coming to my party this evening? They came to a river. She'll* ~ *to the party with John. He's* ~ *to get/* ~ *for his book. The children came running to meet us.* **2** move into, etc the place where the speaker is: *C*~ *in out of the rain. Can you* ~ *out with me for a walk? The sunshine came streaming through the windows.* **3** reach; rise or fall to (a particular level, figure, point): *Your bill* ~*s to £20. When it* ~*s to helping his wife with the housework, John never grumbles.* **come to an agreement,** agree. **come into flower,** begin to have flowers. **come to a decision,** decide. **come to light,** be revealed or discovered. **come to one's notice/attention,** be noticed. **come into view,** appear. (*Note:* In phrases of this kind *come* indicates that the state or condition of the *noun* has been reached. For similar phrases, ⇨ the *noun* entries.) **4 come to sb (from sb),** be left or willed: *The farm came to him on his father's death.* **5 come to sb,** occur to, happen to: *The idea came* (= occurred) *to him in his bath.* **6** reach a point where one sees, understands, etc: *He came to realize that he was mistaken.* **7** (used when asking for an explanation or reason): *How did you* ~ *to find out where she's living? Now that I* ~ (= happen) *to think of it...* **8** occur; be found; have as its place: *May* ~*s between April and June.* **9** be; become; prove to be: *The handle has* ~ *loose.* **come true,** (of wishes, dreams) be realized. **10** (with *adjectives* prefixed with un-, showing undesirable conditions, etc) be; become: *My shoelaces have* ~ *undone.* **11** play the part of; behave, talk etc as if one were (often with the suggestion of overdoing something): *Don't* ~ *the bully over me, Don't* (try to) *bully me.* **12** (used of the future): *in years to* ~; *the life to* ~, life

in the next world; *for some time to* ~, for a period of time in the future.

13 (uses with *adverbial particles and prepositions*):

come about, happen: *It came about in this way...*

come across (sb/sth), (a) find or meet by chance: *I came across this old brooch in a curio shop.* (b) occur to: *The thought came across my mind that...,* occurred to me...

come along, (a) (*imperative*) try harder; make more effort: *C*~ *along, now! Someone must know the answer.* (b) (*imperative*) hurry up; make haste: *C*~ *along, we'll be late!* (c) progress: *The garden is coming along quite nicely.* (d) appear; arrive: *When the right opportunity* ~*s along, he'll take it.*

come apart, fall to pieces: *It just came apart in my hands.*

come away (from), become detached: *The light switch came away from the wall.*

come back, return; (of fashions) become popular again: *Will pointed shoes* ~ *back?* **come back at,** retaliate: *He came back at me with some useful advice.* **come back (to one),** return to the memory: *Their names are all coming back to me now.* Hence, **ˈcome-back** *n* (a) (e g of actors, politicians, athletes, etc) successful return to a former position: *Can he stage a* ~*-back?* (b) recompense (for a loss, etc): *If you're not insured and you're burgled, you'll have no* ~*-back.*

come before sb/sth, (a) be dealt with by: *The complaint will come before the United Nations Assembly next week.* (b) have precedence over: *Baronets* ~ *before knights.*

come between, (a) interfere with a relationship: *It is not advisable to* ~ *between a man and his wife.* (b) prevent a person from having, doing something: *He never lets anything* ~ *between him and his evening paper.*

come by sth, obtain by effort; become possessed of: *Jobs were hard to* ~ *by.*

come down, (a) collapse: *The ceiling came down on our heads.* (b) (of rain, snow, hail) fall: *The rain came down heavily.* (c) (of prices, temperature, etc) fall. **come down in the world,** lose social position; become poor. Hence, **ˈcome-down,** fall in social position: *He has had to sell his house and furniture. What a* ~*-down for him!* **come down in favour of/on the side of sb/sth,** decide to support: *He came down on the side of the government.* **come down to,** (a) reach to: *Her hair* ~*s down to her waist.* (b) can be reduced to: *Your choices in the matter* ~ *down to these.* (c) (of traditions, etc) be handed down: *legends that have* ~ *down to us,* i e from our ancestors. **come down to earth,** return to reality: *Now that his money has all been spent, he's had to* ~ *down to earth.*

come forward, offer or present oneself:

Will no one ~ forward as a candidate?
come from, have as a birthplace, place of origin, etc: *He ~s from Kent.*
come in, (a) (of the tide) rise: *The tide is coming in.* (b) become fashionable: *When did mini skirts first ~ in?* (c) be received as income, etc: *There's not much money coming in at present.* **come in handy/useful**, happen to be useful, serve a purpose: *Don't throw it away; it may ~ in handy one day.* **come in on**, join; take part in: *If you want to ~ in on the scheme, you must decide now.*
come of, (a) be descended from: *She ~s of a good family.* (b) be the result of: *He promised his help, but I don't think anything will ~ of it.* **come of age,** ⇨ age¹(1).
come off (sth), (a) become detached or separated (from): *A button has ~ off my coat.* (b) fall (from): *~ off a horse/bicycle.* (c) get down (from): *C~ off that wall before you fall off it.* **come off it,** (informal) (imperative) stop pretending, or talking nonsense. **come off,** (a) take place: *Did your holiday in Italy ever ~ off?* (b) (of plans, attempts) succeed: *The experiment did not ~ off.*
come on, (a) follow: *You go first, I'll ~ on later.* (b) (as a challenge): *C~ on! Let's race to the bottom of the hill.* (c) make progress; develop: *How's your garden coming on?* (d) (of rain, the seasons, night, illness, etc) start; arrive: *He said he felt a cold coming on,* beginning. (e) (of an actor) appear on the stage; (of a play) be performed: *'Macbeth' is coming on again next month.*
come out, (a) appear; become visible: *The sun/stars came out.* (b) become known: *If the truth ever ~s out...* (c) be published: *When will his new book ~ out?* (d) (of workmen) strike: *The car workers have all ~ out again.* (e) (of details, etc in a photograph; of qualities) appear: *You have ~ out well in that photograph, It is a good likeness.* (f) (of stains, etc) be removed: *These ink stains won't ~ out.* (g) (of dyes, etc) fade; disappear: *Will the colour ~ out if the material is washed?* **come out at,** (of totals, averages, etc) amount to: *The total ~s out at 756,* is 756. **come out in,** be (partly) covered in (pimples, a rash, etc): *She's ~ out in spots!* **come out with,** say: *He came out with a most extraordinary story.*
come over, (a) come from a distance: *Won't you ~ over to England for a holiday?* (b) change sides or opinions: *He will never ~ over to our side.*
come over sb, (of feelings, influences) take possession of: *What has ~ over you?*
come round, (a) come by an indirect route: *The road was blocked so we had to ~ round by the fields.* (b) pay an informal visit to: *Won't you ~ round and see me some time?* (c) occur again: *Christmas will soon ~ round,* be here again. (d) change views, etc: *He has ~ round,* has accepted/agreed. (e)

regain consciousness: *Pour a jug of water on his face. He'll soon ~ round.*
come through, (a) recover from a serious illness or injury: *With such a weak heart, he was lucky to ~ through.* ⇨ pull²(7). (b) arrive (by telephone, radio, etc): *Listen; a message is just coming through.* (c) pass through official channels: *Your posting has just ~ through: it's Hong Kong!*
come 'to, = come round(e).
come under sth, (a) be in (a certain category, etc): *What heading does this ~ under?* (b) be subjected to: *~ under her notice/influence.*
come up, (a) (of seed, etc) show above the ground: *The seeds/snowdrops haven't ~ up yet.* (b) arise; be put forward: *The question hasn't ~ up yet.* (c) occur; arise: *We shall write to you if a vacancy ~s up.* **come up against,** meet (difficulties, opposition). **come up (to),** (a) reach: *The water came up to my waist.* (b) equal: *Your work has not ~ up to my expectations.* **come up with,** (a) draw level with: *We came up with a party of hikers.* (b) produce; find: *~ up with a solution.*
come upon, (a) attack by surprise; strike: *the disaster that came upon them. Fear came upon us.* (b) arrive at suddenly or by surprise: *come upon a thief in the garden.*
com·e·dian /kə'mɪdɪən/ n [C] **1** actor who plays comic parts in plays, etc. **2** person who behaves in a comic way and who cannot be taken seriously.
com·e·di·enne /kə'mɪdɪ'ɛn US: kə'mɪdɪen/ n [C] female comedian.
com·edy /'kɒmədɪ/ n (pl -ies) **1** [U] branch of drama that deals with everyday life and humorous events: *He prefers ~ to tragedy.* **2** [C] play for the theatre, of a light, amusing kind. **3** [C,U] amusing activity or incident in real life: *There's not much ~ in modern war.*
come·ly /'kʌmlɪ/ adj (-ier, -iest) (of a person) pleasant to look at.
comet /'kɒmɪt/ n [C] heavenly body (looking like a star with a bright centre and a less bright tail) that moves round the sun.
com·fort /'kʌmfət/ n **1** [U] state of being free from suffering, anxiety, pain, etc: *living in great ~.* **2** [U] help or kindness to a person who is suffering: *a few words of ~.* **3** [C] person or thing that brings relief or help: *Your letters/You have been a great ~ to me.* □ vt give comfort to: *~ those who are in trouble.*
com·fort·able /'kʌmftəbəl US: -fərt-/ adj **1** giving comfort to the body: *a ~ chair/bed.* **2** having or providing comfort: *a ~ life/income.* **3** at ease; free from (too much) pain, anxiety, etc: *to be/feel comfortable.*
com·fort·ably /-əblɪ/ adv in a comfortable manner: *a car that holds six people comfortably.*
comic /'kɒmɪk/ adj **1** causing people to

laugh: *a ~ song;* intended to amuse: *~ strip,* series of drawings telling an amusing story, as printed in newspapers, etc. **2** of comedy: *~ opera.* □ *n* [C] **1** periodical with comic strips. **2** comedian.

comi·cal /ˈkɒmɪkəl/ *adj* amusing; odd: *a ~ old hat.*

com·ing /ˈkʌmɪŋ/ *n* [C] arrival. □ *adj* which is to come or which will come: *in the ~ years.*

'**comings and 'goings,** arrivals and departures.

comma /ˈkɒmə/ *n* [C] punctuation mark (,) used to indicate a slight pause or break between parts of a sentence. ⇨ inverted commas.

com·mand[1] /kəˈmɑnd *US:* -ˈmænd/ *n* **1** [C] order: *His ~s were quickly obeyed.* **2** [U] authority; power (to control): *General X is in ~ of the army.* **have/take command (of),** have/take authority: *When the major was killed, the senior captain took ~ (of the company).* **3** [C] part of an army, air force, etc under separate command: *Bomber C~.* **4** [U] possession and skill: *He has a good ~ of the English language,* is able to use it well.

com·mand[2] /kəˈmɑnd *US:* -ˈmænd/ *vt, vi* **1** order (usually with the right to be obeyed): *Do as I ~ (you). The officer ~ed his men to fire.* **2** have authority over; be in control of: *The captain of a ship ~s all the officers and men.* **3** be in a position to use; have at one's service: *He ~s great sums of money,* is able to use them if he so wishes. **4** deserve and get: *Great men ~ our respect.* **5** (of a place) be in a position that overlooks (and may control): *The fort ~s the road to the valley.*

com·mand·ing *adj*: *the ~ing officer; in a ~ing tone/position.*

com·man·dant /ˈkɒmənˈdænt/ *n* [C] officer in command of a fortress or other military establishment.

com·man·deer /ˈkɒmənˈdɪə(r)/ *vt* seize (provisions etc) for military purposes under martial law.

com·man·der /kəˈmɑndə(r) *US:* -ˈmæn-/ *n* [C] person in command: *the ~ of the expedition; ~-in-ˈchief,* commander of all the military forces of a State.

com·mand·ment /kəˈmɑndmənt *US:* -ˈmænd-/ *n* [C] divine command, esp one of the ten laws given by God to Moses.

com·mando /kəˈmɑndəʊ *US:* -ˈmæn-/ *n* [C] (*pl* ~s or ~es) (member of a) body of men specially trained for carrying out raids and making assaults.

com·mem·or·ate /kəˈmeməreɪt/ *vt* keep or honour the memory of (a person or event); (of things) be in memory of: *A monument was built to ~ the victory.*

com·mem·or·ation /kəˈmeməˈreɪʃən/ *n* **1** [U] act of commemorating: *in ~ of the victory.* **2** [C] (part of a) service in memory of a person or event.

com·mem·or·ative /kəˈmemrətɪv *US:* -ˈmemərert-/ *adj* serving to commemorate: *~ stamps/medals.*

com·mence /kəˈmens/ *vt, vi* (*formal*) begin; start (the more usual words).

com·mence·ment, beginning.

com·mend /kəˈmend/ *vt* (*formal*) **1** praise; speak favourably of: *His work was highly ~ed.* **2** **commend sth to,** give for safekeeping to.

com·mend·able /-əbəl/ *adj* worthy of praise.

com·men·sur·ate /kəˈmenʃʊrət/ *adj* in the right proportion: *Was the pay you received ~ with the work you did?*

com·ment /ˈkɒment/ *n* [C,U] opinion given briefly in speech or writing about an event, or in explanation or criticism: *Have you any ~s to make on my story?* □ *vi* give opinions: *~ on an essay.*

com·men·tary /ˈkɒməntrɪ *US:* -terɪ/ *n* [C] (*pl* -ies) **1** collection of comments, e g on a book: *a Bible ~.* **2** series of continuous comments (on an event): *a radio ~ on a football match.*

com·men·tate /ˈkɒmənteɪt/ *vi* give a commentary (on).

com·men·ta·tor /ˈkɒmənteɪtə(r)/, person who gives a radio or TV commentary or writes on an event, e g a horse-race.

com·merce /ˈkɒmɜs/ *n* [U] **1** trade (esp between countries). **2** the exchange and distribution of goods: *a Chamber of C~.*

com·mer·cial /kəˈmɜʃəl/ *adj* of commerce: *~ banks.* □ *n* [C] advertisement inserted in a TV or radio programme.

com'mercial 'radio/'television, financed by charges made for commercial advertising in programmes.

'**commercial 'traveller,** travelling salesman.

commercial vehicle, van, lorry, etc for the transport of goods.

com·mer·ci·ally /-əlɪ/ *adv*

com·miser·ate /kəˈmɪzəreɪt/ *vt, vi* feel, say that one feels, pity for: *~ (with) a friend on his misfortunes.*

com·miser·ation /kəˈmɪzəˈreɪʃən/ *n* [C,U] (expression of) pity or sympathy.

com·mis·sion /kəˈmɪʃən/ *n* **1** [U] the giving of authority to a person to act for another. **2** [C] instance of this; action or piece of business that is done: *He has got two ~s to design buildings for a local authority.* **3** [U] payment for selling goods, etc rising in proportion to the amount sold: *He receives a ~ of 10 per cent on sales, as well as a salary.* **4** [C] official paper signed by the Sovereign appointing an officer in the armed services: *get/resign one's ~.* **5** [C] body of persons given the duty of making an inquiry and writing a report: *a Royal C~ to report on betting and gambling.* **out of commission,** (*fig*) not working, not available. □ *vt* give a commission to: *~ an artist* *to paint a portrait.*

com·mis·sion·aire /kəˈmɪʃənˈeə(r)/ *n* [C] uniformed porter at the entrance to a cinema, hotel, large shop, etc.

com·mis·sioner /kəˈmɪʃənə(r)/ *n* [C] **1** member of a commission(5), esp one with particular duties: *the Civil Service C~s*, who conduct the Civil Service examinations. **2** person who has been given a commission: *a C~ for Oaths*, solicitor (given commission by the Lord Chancellor) before whom documents are sworn on oath. **3** government representative of high rank: *the British High C~ in Accra.*

com·mit /kəˈmɪt/ *vt* (-tt-) **1** perform (a crime, etc): *~ murder/suicide/an offence.* **2** give up, hand over to, for guarding or treatment: *~ a man to prison; ~ a patient to a mental hospital.* **commit to memory**, learn by heart. **3** *commit oneself (to...)*, make oneself responsible; undertake: *He has ~ted himself to support his brother's children.* **4** pledge; bind (oneself): *I won't ~ myself to anyone who is dishonest.* ⇨ **uncommitted.**

com·mit·ment *n* [C] (esp) something to which one is committed(3,4): *If you have to pay your son's expenses and give your daughter £100 a year for clothes, you have quite a lot of ~ments.*

com·mit·tee /kəˈmɪtɪ/ *n* [C] group of persons appointed (usually by a larger group) to attend to special business: *to attend a ~ meeting; to be/sit on the ~.*

com·mod·ity /kəˈmɒdətɪ/ *n* [C] (*pl* -ies) useful thing, esp an article of trade: *household commodities, e g pots and pans.*

com·mo·dore /ˈkɒmədɔː(r)/ *n* [C] naval officer having rank above a captain and below a rear-admiral; senior captain of a shipping line.

com·mon¹ /ˈkɒmən/ *adj* (-er, -est) **1** belonging to, used by, coming from, done by, affecting, all or nearly all members of a group or society: *His wife is German but they have English as a ~ language.* **2** usual and ordinary; happening or found often and in many places: *a ~ experience. Is this word in ~ use?* **3** ordinary or average, not of noble birth. **4** (of persons, their behaviour and possessions) of inferior quality or taste: *speak with a ~ accent.* **5** (in maths) belonging to two or more quantities: *~ factor/ multiple.*

'**common ˈground,** (*fig*) agreed basis for argument in a dispute, etc.

'**common ˈknowledge,** what is generally known: *It is ~ knowledge that you are dating Mary.*

'**common ˈlaw,** (in England) unwritten law from customs and earlier legal decisions.

the ˈCommon ˈMarket, (officially the *European Economic Community*) economic, social and political union of 9 European countries with associate membership (for economic preferences) by other countries.

'**common-room,** sitting-room for teachers or for students in a college, school, etc.

'**common ˈsense,** practical good sense from general experience of life, not by special study.

com·mon·ly *adv* (**a**) usually: *That very ~ly happens. Thomas, ~ly called Tom.* (**b**) in a common(3) way: *~ly dressed.*

com·mon² /ˈkɒmən/ *n* **1** [C] area of unfenced grassland for all to use: *Saturday afternoon cricket on the village ~.* **2** **in common**, for or by all (of a group). **have in common (with)**, share (with): *They have nothing in ~ with one another*, have no similar interests, etc.

com·moner /ˈkɒmənə(r)/ *n* [C] one of the common people, not one of the nobility.

com·mon·place /ˈkɒmənpleɪs/ *adj* ordinary or usual.

Com·mons /ˈkɒmənz/ *n pl* **the ~,** (usually *the ' House of ˈ~*) assembly of the British Parliament elected by the people.

com·mon·wealth /ˈkɒmənwelθ/ *n* [C] **1** body of people of a nation or state. **2** group of States (e g *the C~ of Australia*) associating politically for their common good. **3 the C~,** free association of independent states (formerly colonies and dominions of GB).

com·mo·tion /kəˈməʊʃən/ *n* **1** [U] noisy confusion; excitement. **2** [C] instance of this; uprising or disturbance: *You're making a great ~ about nothing.*

com·mu·nal /ˈkɒmjʊnəl/ *adj* **1** of or for a community: *~ facilities.* **2** for common use: *~ land/kitchens.*

com·mune¹ /ˈkɒmjuːn/ *n* [C] **1** (in France, Belgium, Italy, Spain) smallest territorial district for purposes of administration, with a mayor and council. **2** organized group of people promoting local interests. **3** group of people living together and sharing property and responsibilities.

com·mune² /kəˈmjuːn/ *vi* feel at one with; feel, be, in close touch with; talk with in an intimate way: *communing with nature/God in prayer.*

com·muni·cable /kəˈmjuːnɪkəbəl/ *adj* (of ideas, illness, etc) that can be communicated or passed on.

com·muni·cant /kəˈmjuːnɪkənt/ *n* [C] **1** person who (regularly) receives Holy Communion. **2** (*formal*) informer.

com·muni·cate /kəˈmjuːnɪkeɪt/ *vt, vi* **1** pass on (news, information, feelings, an illness, etc). **2** share or exchange (news, etc): *We can ~ with people in most parts of the world by telephone.* **3** (of rooms, gardens, roads, etc) be connected (which is more usual): *My garden ~s with the garden next door by a gate.*

com·muni·ca·tion /kəˈmjuːnɪˈkeɪʃən/ *n* **1** [U] the act of communicating: *Among the deaf and dumb ~ is by means of the finger alphabet.* **2** [C] that which is communicated (e g news): *This ~ is confidential.* **3** [C,U]

117

means of communicating; roads, railways, telephone or telegraph lines connecting places, radio and TV: *All* ∼ *with the north has been stopped by snowstorms.*

com·mu·ni·cat·ive /kə`mjunɪkətɪv US: -keɪtɪv/ *adj* ready and willing to talk and give information.

com·mu·nion /kə`mjunɪən/ *n* 1 [U] sharing in common; participation (with). 2 [U] exchange of thought and feelings. 3 [C] group of persons with the same religious beliefs: *We belong to the same* ∼. **'Holy Com`munion,** (in the Christian Church) celebration of the Lord's Supper.

com·muniqué /kə`mjunɪkeɪ/ *n* [C] official announcement, e g as issued to the press.

com·mu·nism /`komjʊnɪzm/ *n* [U] 1 (belief in a) social system in which property is owned by the community and used for the good of all its members. 2 (usually **C**∼) political and social system in which all power is held by the highest members of the Communist Party, which controls the land and its resources, the means of production, transport, etc, and directs the activities of the people.

com·mu·nist /-ɪst/ *n* [C] believer in, supporter of, communism. □ *adj* of communism.

com·mun·ity /kə`mjunətɪ/ *n* [C] (*pl* -ies) 1 [C] **the** ∼, the people living in one place, district or country, considered as a whole: *work for the good of the* ∼. 2 [C] group of persons having the same religion, race, occupation, etc or with common interests: *a* ∼ *of monks; the Jewish* ∼ *in London.* 3 [U] condition of sharing, having things in common, being alike in some way: ∼ *of religion/interests.*

com·mu·ta·tion /`komjʊ`teɪʃən/ *n* 1 [U] making one kind of payment instead of another, e g money instead of service. 2 [C] payment made in this way. 3 [C] reduced punishment: *a* ∼ *of the death sentence to life imprisonment.*

com·mute /kə`mjut/ *vt,vi* 1 exchange one thing (esp one kind of payment) for another: ∼ *one's weekly pension for a single payment.* 2 reduce the severity of a punishment: ∼ *a death sentence* (*to one of life imprisonment*). 3 travel regularly, e g by train or car, between one's work in a town and one's home in the country or suburbs. **com·muter,** person who commutes(3).

com·pact¹ /`kompækt/ *n* [C] agreement between parties; contract; covenant.

com·pact² /kəm`pækt/ *adj* closely packed together; neatly fitted. □ *vt* join firmly together.
com·pact·ly *adv*
com·pact·ness *n* [U]

com·pact³ /`kompækt/ *n* [C] small, flat container for face-powder.

com·pan·ion /kəm`pænɪən/ *n* [C] 1 person who goes with, or is often or always with,

another: *my* ∼*s on the journey.* 2 person who shares in or has a similar interest in the work, pleasures, misfortunes, etc of another: ∼*s in arms,* fellow soldiers. *He's an excellent* ∼. 3 one of two things that go together; thing that matches another or is one of a pair: *the* ∼ *volume.* 4 woman paid to keep another person company. 5 handbook or reference book: *the Gardener's C*∼.
com·pan·ion·ship, state of being companions: *a* ∼*ship of many years.*
com·pan·ion·way /kəm`pænɪənweɪ/ *n* [C] staircase from the deck of a ship to the saloon or cabins.

com·pany /`kʌmpənɪ/ *n* (*pl* -ies) 1 [U] being together with another or others: *I shall be glad of your* ∼ (= to have you with me) *on the journey. He came in* ∼ *with* (= together with) *a group of boys.* **part company (with),** separate; leave: *It's sad that we have to part* ∼. 2 [U] group of persons; number of guests: *We're expecting* ∼ (= guests, visitors) *next week.* 3 [U] persons with whom one spends one's time: *You may know a man by the* ∼ *he keeps,* judge his character by his friends. 4 [C] number of persons united for business or commerce: *a steamship* ∼. 5 [C] number of persons working together: *a theatrical* ∼. 6 [C] subdivision of an infantry battalion, commanded by a captain or major.

com·par·able /`komprəbəl/ *adj* that can be compared: *His achievements are* ∼ *with the best/to yours.*

com·para·tive /kəm`pærətɪv/ *adj* 1 having to do with comparison or comparing: ∼ *religion.* 2 measured or judged by comparing: *living in* ∼ *comfort,* e g comfortably compared with others, or with one's own life at an earlier period. 3 (*gram*) form of adjectives and adverbs expressing 'more', as in *worse, more likely, more prettily.* □ *n* [C] comparative form: *'Better' is the* ∼ *of 'good'.*
com·para·tive·ly *adv*

com·pare /kəm`peə(r)/ *vt,vi* 1 examine, judge to what extent persons or things are similar or not similar: ∼ *two translations.* 2 point out the likeness or relation between: *Poets have* ∼*d sleep to death.* 3 **compare with,** be able to be compared: *He cannot* ∼ *with Shakespeare.* 4 (*gram*) make the comparative and superlative form (of adjectives and adverbs).

com·pari·son /kəm`pærɪsən/ *n* 1 [U] **by/in comparison (with),** when compared (with): *The tallest buildings in London are small in* ∼ *with those of New York.* 2 [C] act of comparing; instance of this: *It is often useful to make a* ∼ *between two things.* 3 be able to be compared favourably with: *That's a good dictionary, but it won't/can't stand* ∼ *with this.* 4 (*gram*) comparative and superlative position (of adjectives and adverbs), e g *good, better, best.*

com·part·ment /kəmˈpɑːtmənt/ n [C] one of several separate divisions of a structure, esp of a railway carriage or coach: *The first-class ~s are in front.*

com·pass /ˈkʌmpəs/ n [C] (pl ~es) **1** device with a needle that points to the magnetic north: *the points of the ~* (N, NE, E, SE, S, etc). **2** similar device, e g *a radio ~,* for determining direction. **3** (pl) (also *a pair of ~es*) V-shaped instrument with two arms joined by a hinge, used for drawing circles, measuring distances on a map or chart, etc. **4** extent; range: *outside the ~* (= range) *of her voice.*

com·pas·sion /kəmˈpæʃən/ n [U] pity; feeling for the sufferings of others, prompting one to give help: *be filled with ~ for the refugees.*

com·pas·sion·ate /kəmˈpæʃənət/ adj showing or feeling compassion: *The soldier was granted ~ leave,* allowed to go home, e g because of personal affairs.

com·pat·ible /kəmˈpætəbəl/ adj (of ideas, arguments, principles, etc) suited to, in accord with, able to exist together with: *driving a car at a speed ~ with safety.*

com·pat·ibly /-əblɪ/ adv

com·pa·triot /kəmˈpætrɪət US: -ˈpeɪt-/ n [C] person born in or citizen of the same country as another.

com·pel /komˈpel/ vt (-ll-) force (a person or thing to do something); get, bring about, by force: *His conscience ~led him to confess.*

com·pen·sate /ˈkompənseɪt/ vt,vi make a suitable payment, give something, to make up (for loss, injury, etc): *Nothing can ~ for the loss of one's health.*

com·pen·sa·tion /ˌkompənˈseɪʃən/ n [U,C] compensating; something given to compensate: *He received £5 000 in ~/by way of ~ for the loss of his right hand.*

com·pen·sa·tory /kəmˈpensətərɪ US: -tɔːrɪ/ adj compensating.

com·père /ˈkompeə(r)/ n [C] (Fr) organizer of a cabaret or broadcast entertainment who introduces the performers, speakers, etc. □ vt act as compère for.

com·pete /kəmˈpiːt/ vi take part in a race, contest, examination, etc: *to ~ against/with other countries in trade.*

com·pet·ence /ˈkompɪtəns/ n **1** [U] being competent; ability: *his ~ in handling money/to handle money.* **2** (of a court, etc) legal capacity: *business that is within/beyond the ~ of the court.*

com·pet·ent /ˈkompɪtənt/ adj **1** (of persons) having ability, power, authority, skill, knowledge, etc (to do what is needed): *Is Miss X ~ in her work/~ as a teacher/~ to teach French?* **2** (of qualities) sufficient, adequate: *Has she a ~ knowledge of French?*

com·pet·ent·ly adv

com·pe·ti·tion /ˌkompəˈtɪʃən/ n **1** [U] com-

peting; activity in which persons compete: *At the Olympic Games our representatives were in ~* (= were competing) *with the best swimmers from all parts of the world.* **2** [C] instance of competing; contest; meeting(s) at which skill, strength, knowledge, etc is tested: *chess ~s.*

com·peti·tive /kəmˈpetətɪv/ adj in or for which there is competition: *We offer ~ prices,* prices that compete with those of other firms.

com·peti·tor /kəmˈpetɪtə(r)/ n [C] person, firm, etc that competes.

com·pi·la·tion /ˌkompɪˈleɪʃən/ n [U] compiling; [C] thing that is compiled.

com·pile /kəmˈpaɪl/ vt collect (information) and arrange (in a book, list, report, etc): *~ a dictionary.*

com·piler, person who compiles (a list, dictionary, etc).

com·pla·cence /kəmˈpleɪsəns/ n [U] self-satisfaction; feeling of personal contentment.

com·placent /kəmˈpleɪsənt/ adj pleased with oneself, one's ability (usually in an annoying way): *with a ~ smile/air.*

com·pla·cency /-sənsɪ/ n [U]

com·pla·cent·ly adv

com·plain /kəmˈpleɪn/ vi say that one is not satisfied, that something is wrong, that one is suffering: *We have nothing to ~ of/about.*

com·plain·ant /kəmˈpleɪnənt/ n [C] (legal) person who makes a complaint in a law court.

com·plaint /kəmˈpleɪnt/ n **1** [U] complaining. **2** [C] statement of, grounds for, dissatisfaction: *Some children are full of ~s about their food.* **3** [C] illness; disease: *a heart/liver ~.*

com·plais·ance /kəmˈpleɪzəns/ n [U] easy-going habit of mind; readiness and willingness to do what pleases others.

com·plais·ant /-zənt/ adj obliging; ready to please: *a complaisant wife.*

com·ple·ment /ˈkomplɪmənt/ n **1** that which makes something complete; the full number or quality needed. **2** (gram) word(s) esp *adjectives* and *nouns,* used after *verbs* such as *be* and *become* and qualifying the subject. □ vt complete; be the complement to.

com·ple·ment·ary /ˌkomplɪˈmentrɪ/ adj serving to complete: *~ volumes.*

com·plete¹ /kəmˈpliːt/ adj **1** having all its parts; whole: *a ~ edition of Shakespeare's plays.* **2** finished; ended: *When will the work be ~?* **3** thorough; in every way: *It was a ~ surprise to me,* I wasn't expecting it and hadn't even thought of it.

com·plete·ly adv wholly; in every way: *~ly successful.*

com·plete·ness n [U]

com·plete² /kəmˈpliːt/ vt finish; bring to an end; make perfect: *I need one more volume to ~ my set of Dickens.*

E

com·ple·tion /kəmˈpliːʃən/ n [U] act of completing; state of being complete: *You may occupy the house on ~ of contract*, when the contract of sale has been completed.

com·plex[1] /ˈkɒmpleks *US:* komˈpleks/ adj made up of closely connected parts; difficult to understand or explain: *a ~ argument/ proposal/situation.*
com·plex·ity /kəmˈpleksətɪ/ n [C,U]

com·plex[2] /ˈkɒmpleks/ n [C] **1** number of different parts intricately related. **2** mental state of obsessive concern or fear. ⇨ **inferiority, superiority.**

com·plex·ion /kəmˈplekʃən/ n [C] **1** natural colour, appearance, etc of the skin, esp of the face: *a good/dark/fair ~.* **2** general character or aspect (of conduct, affairs, etc): *This victory changed the ~ of the war.*

com·pli·ance /kəmˈplaɪəns/ n [U] action of complying: *in ~ with your wishes*, as you wish(ed) us (to do).

com·pli·ant /kəmˈplaɪənt/ adj ready to comply.

com·pli·cate /ˈkɒmplɪkeɪt/ vt make complex; make difficult to do or understand: *This ~s matters.*
com·pli·cated adj made up of many parts: *a ~d machine/business deal.*

com·pli·ca·tion /ˌkɒmplɪˈkeɪʃən/ n [C] state of being complex, confused, difficult; something that makes new difficulties (e g of a person who is ill): *Here are further ~s to worry us. She'll live; if no further ~s set in.*

com·plic·ity /kəmˈplɪsətɪ/ n [U] taking part with another person (in doing wrong).

com·pli·ment /ˈkɒmplɪmənt/ n [C] **1** expression of admiration, approval, etc, either in words or by action, e g by asking a person for his advice or opinions, or by imitating him. **2** (pl) greetings: *My ~s to your wife*, Please give her a greeting from me. □ vi /ˈkɒmplɪment/ express admiration, etc: *I ~ed him on his skill.*

com·pli·men·tary /ˌkɒmplɪˈmentrɪ *US:* -terɪ/ adj **1** expressing admiration, praise, etc. **2** given free, out of courtesy or kindness: *a ~ ticket.*

com·ply /kəmˈplaɪ/ vt (pt,pp -ied) act in accordance with a request, command, a wish, etc): *He refused to ~.*

com·po·nent /kəmˈpəʊnənt/ adj helping to form (a complete thing): *~ parts.* □ n [C] part of a larger or more complex object: *the ~s of a camera.*

com·port /kəmˈpɔːt/ vt,vi (formal) **1** behave; conduct: *~ oneself with dignity.* **2** suit, be in harmony with: *His conduct did not ~ with his high position.*

com·pose /kəmˈpəʊz/ vt,vi **1** (of elements) make up: *Our party was ~d of teachers, pupils and their parents.* **2** put together (words, musical notes, etc) in literary, musical, etc form: *~ a poem/a song/a speech.* **3** (printing) set up (type) to form pages, etc. **4**

get under control; calm: *~ one's thoughts/ passions.*

com·posed adj calm; with feelings under control.
com·posed·ly adv

com·po·ser /kəmˈpəʊzə(r)/ n [C] (esp) person who composes music.

com·pos·ite /ˈkɒmpəzɪt/ adj made up of different parts or materials: *a ~ illustration*, made by putting together two or more drawings, etc.

com·po·si·tion /ˌkɒmpəˈzɪʃən/ n **1** [U] act or art of composing, e g a piece of writing or music. **2** [C] that which is composed, e g a piece of music, an arrangement of objects to be painted or photographed. **3** [C] (esp) exercise in writing by one who is learning a language. **4** [U] the parts of which something is made up: *Scientists study the ~ of the soil.* **5** [C] substance composed of more than one material, esp an artificial substance: *~ floors.*

com·pos·i·tor /kəmˈpɒzɪtə(r)/ n [C] skilled person who composes type for printing.

com·pos men·tis /ˌkɒmpəs ˈmentɪs/ adj (Latin) sane: *He's not quite ~.*

com·post /ˈkɒmpɒst/ n [U] prepared mixture, esp of rotted food, leaves, manure, etc for use as a fertiliser. □ vt make into, treat with compost.

com·po·sure /kəmˈpəʊʒə(r)/ n [U] condition of feeling calm: *behave with great ~.*

com·pound[1] /ˈkɒmpaʊnd/ n, adj **1** [C] (thing) made up of two or more combined parts: *Common salt is a ~ of sodium and chlorine.* **2** (gram) word made up of two or more parts, themselves usually words, e g *safety-pin.*
'compound 'fracture, breaking of a bone with an open wound in the skin.
'compound 'interest, interest on capital and on accumulated interest.

com·pound[2] /kəmˈpaʊnd/ vt,vi (formal) **1** mix together: *~ a medicine.* **2** settle (a quarrel, a debt) by mutual agreement. **3** agree terms: *He ~ed with his creditors for a remission of what he owed.* **4** add to, increase the seriousness of (an offence or injury): *That simply ~s the offence.*

com·pound[3] /ˈkɒmpaʊnd/ n [C] enclosed area with buildings, etc, e g a number of houses.

com·pre·hend /ˌkɒmprɪˈhend/ vt (formal) **1** understand fully. **2** include; consist of.

com·pre·hen·sible /ˌkɒmprɪˈhensəbəl/ adj that can be understood fully: *a book that is ~ only to specialists.*
com·pre·hen·si·bil·ity /ˌkɒmprɪˈhensəˈbɪlətɪ/ n [U]

com·pre·hen·sion /ˌkɒmprɪˈhenʃən/ n **1** [U] the mind's act or power of understanding: *The problem is above/beyond my ~.* **2** [C,U] exercise aimed at improving or testing one's understanding. **3** (formal) power of including: *a term of wide ~*, that has many meanings, uses, etc.

com·pre·hen·sive /ˈkɒmprɪˈhensɪv/ adj that comprehends(2): a ~ description. □ n [C] comprehensive school.

comprehensive school, that provides all types of secondary education.

comprehensive·ly adv

com·pre·hen·sive·ness n [U]

com·press[1] /kəmˈpres/ vt 1 press, get into a small(er) space: ~ed air. 2 put (ideas, etc) into fewer words.

com·press[2] /ˈkɒmpres/ n [C] pad or cloth pressed on to part of the body (to stop bleeding, reduce fever, etc): a cold/hot ~.

com·pres·sion /kəmˈpreʃən/ n [U] compressing; being compressed.

com·prise /kəmˈpraɪz/ vt be composed of; have as parts or members: The committee ~s men of widely different views.

com·pro·mise /ˈkɒmprəmaɪz/ n [U] settlement of a dispute by which each side gives up something it has asked for; [C] instance of this; settlement reached in this way: A ~ was at last arrived at. □ vt, vi 1 settle a dispute, etc, by making a compromise: if they agree to ~. 2 bring under suspicion by unwise action, etc: You will ~ yourself/ your reputation if you stay in that hotel. 3 risk the safety of: The battalion's safety was ~d by the general's poor judgement.

com·pul·sion /kəmˈpʌlʃən/ n [U] compelling or being compelled.

com·pul·sive /kəmˈpʌlsɪv/ adj having a tendency or the power to compel; caused by an obsession: a ~ eater/liar.

com·pul·sive·ly adv

com·pul·sory /kəmˈpʌlsərɪ/ adj that must be done; required: Is English a ~ subject?

com·pul·sor·ily /kəmˈpʌlsərəlɪ/ adv

com·punc·tion /kəmˈpʌŋkʃən/ n [U] uneasiness of conscience; feeling of regret for one's action: She kept me waiting without the slightest ~.

com·pu·ter /kəmˈpjuːtə(r)/ n [C] electronic device which stores information on discs or magnetic tape, analyses it and produces information as required from the data on the tapes, etc.

com·pu·ter·ize vt store (information) with or in a computer; supply with a computer (system).

com·rade /ˈkɒmreɪd US: -ræd/ n [C] 1 trusted companion; loyal friend: ~s in arms, fellow soldiers. 2 fellow member of a trade union, a (left-wing) political party, etc.

com·rade·ship /ˈkɒmrɪdʃɪp/ n

con- /kɒn-, kən-/ prefix with, together: congregate.

con·cave /ˈkɒŋkeɪv/ adj (of an outline or surface) curved inwards like the inner surface of a sphere or ball.

con·cav·ity /ˈkɒnˈkævətɪ/ n [U] concave condition; [C] (pl -ies) concave surface.

con·ceal /kənˈsiːl/ vt hide; keep secret: He tried to ~ the truth from me.

con·ceal·ment n [U] (state) of being concealed.

con·cede /kənˈsiːd/ vt admit; grant; allow: ~ a point in an argument. We cannot ~ any of our territory, allow another country to have it.

con·ceit /kənˈsiːt/ n [U] too high opinion of, too much pride in, oneself or one's abilities, etc: He's full of ~.

con·ceited adj

con·ceit·ed·ly adv

con·ceiv·able /kənˈsiːvəbəl/ adj that can be thought of or believed: It is hardly ~ (to me) that...

con·ceiv·ably /-əblɪ/ adv

con·ceive /kənˈsiːv/ vt, vi 1 form (an idea, plan, etc) in the mind: Who first ~d the idea of the wheel? 2 (of a woman) become pregnant: ~ a child.

con·cen·trate /ˈkɒnsəntreɪt/ vt, vi 1 bring or come together at one point: to ~ soldiers in a town. 2 keep one's attention on: You'll solve the problem if you ~ on it. 3 increase the strength of (a solution) by reducing its volume (e g by boiling it). □ n [C] product made by concentrating(3).

con·cen·trated adj (a) intense: ~d hate. (b) increased in strength or value by evaporation of liquid: ~d orange-juice.

con·cen·tra·tion /ˈkɒnsənˈtreɪʃən/ n 1 [C] that which is concentrated: ~s of enemy troops. 2 [U] concentrating or being concentrated: a book that requires great ~, great attention.

'concen'tration camp, place where civilian political prisoners are brought together.

con·cen·tric /kənˈsentrɪk/ adj (of circles) having a common centre.

con·cept /ˈkɒnsept/ n [C] idea underlying a class of things; general notion.

con·cep·tion /kənˈsepʃən/ n 1 [U] conceiving of an idea or plan; [C] idea or plan that takes shape in the mind: A good novelist needs great powers of ~. 2 conceiving(2).

con·cern[1] /kənˈsɜːn/ vt 1 have relation to; affect; be of importance to: Does this ~ me? So/As far as I'm ~ed..., So far as the matter is important to me or affects me... 2 be busy with, interest oneself in: I'm ~d about/with child-psychology. 3 make unhappy or troubled: We are all ~ed for/about her safety.

con·cern·ing prep = about[3](4).

con·cern[2] /kənˈsɜːn/ n 1 [C] relation or connection; something in which one is interested or which is important: It's no ~ of mine, I have nothing to do with it. 2 [C] business or undertaking: The shop has now become a paying ~, is making profits. 3 [C] share: He has a ~ in the business, is a part-owner. 4 [U] anxiety: There is some cause for ~.

con·cerned adj anxious: with a ~ed look.

con·cert /ˈkɒnsət/ n 1 [C] musical entertainment, esp one given to an audience by players or singers. **2** [U] combination of voices or sounds: *voices raised in* ∼. **3** [U] agreement; harmony: *working in* ∼ *with his colleagues.*

con·cert·ed /kənˈsɜːtɪd/ *adj* planned, performed, designed (by two or more together): *to make a* ∼ *effort.*

con·cer·tina /ˌkɒnsəˈtiːnə/ *n* [C] (*pl* ∼s) musical wind instrument held in the hands and played by pressing keys at each end.

con·certo /kənˈtʃɜːtəʊ/ *n* [C] (*pl* ∼s) musical composition for one or more solo instruments supported by an orchestra: *a pi`ano* ∼.

con·ces·sion /kənˈseʃən/ *n* **1** [U] conceding; [C] that which is conceded, esp after discussion, an argument, etc: *As a* ∼ *to public opinion, the Government reduced the tax on petrol.* **2** [C] (esp) right given by owner(s) of land, or by a Government, to do something (eg take minerals from land): *American oil* ∼*s in the Middle East.*

con·cili·ate /kənˈsɪlɪeɪt/ *vt* win the support, goodwill or friendly feelings of; calm the anger of; soothe.

con·cili·atory /kənˈsɪlɪətrɪ US: -tɔːrɪ/ *adj* tending or likely to conciliate: *a conciliatory act/spirit.*

con·cili·ation /kənˌsɪlɪˈeɪʃən/ *n* [U] conciliating or being conciliated: *The dispute is being dealt with by a* ∼ *board,* a group of persons who arbitrate, etc.

con·cise /kənˈsaɪs/ *adj* (of a person, his speech or style, of writings, etc) giving much information in few words.
con·cise·ly *adv*
con·cise·ness *n* [U]

con·clave /ˈkɒŋkleɪv/ *n* [C] private or secret meeting (eg of cardinals to elect a Pope).

con·clude /kənˈkluːd/ *vt,vi* **1** come or bring to an end: *He* ∼*d by saying that...* **2** arrange; bring about: *to* ∼ *a treaty with...* **3** arrive at a belief or opinion: *The jury* ∼*d, from the evidence, that the accused man was not guilty.*

con·clu·sion /kənˈkluːʒən/ *n* [C] **1** end: *at the* ∼ *of his speech. in conclusion,* lastly. **2** arrangement; decision; settlement: *the* ∼ *of a peace treaty.* **3** belief or opinion which is the result of reasoning: *to come to/reach the* ∼ *that...*

con·clus·ive /kənˈkluːsɪv/ *adj* (of facts, evidence, etc) convincing; ending doubt: ∼ *evidence/proof of his guilt.*
con·clus·ive·ly *adv*

con·coct /kənˈkɒkt/ *vt* **1** prepare by mixing together: *to* ∼ *a new kind of soup.* **2** invent (a story, an excuse, a plot for a novel, etc).
con·coc·tion /kənˈkɒkʃən/ *n* [U] mixing; [C] mixture.

con·cord /ˈkɒŋkɔːd/ *n* [U] agreement or harmony (between persons or things): *live in* ∼ (*with...*). **2** [C] instance of this.

con·cord·ance /kənˈkɔːdəns/ *n* **1** [U] agreement. **2** [C] arrangement in ABC order of the

important words used by an author or in a book: *a* `*Shakespeare* ∼.

con·course /ˈkɒŋkɔːs/ *n* [C] **1** coming or moving together of things, persons, etc: *an unforeseen* ∼ *of circumstances.* **2** place where crowds come together.

con·crete /ˈkɒŋkriːt/ *adj* **1** of material things; existing in material form; that can be touched, felt, etc: *A lamp is* ∼ *but light is abstract.* **2** definite; positive: ∼ *proposals/ evidence/proof.* □ *n* [U] building material made by mixing cement with sand, gravel, etc: *a* `∼ *mixer* machine that makes concrete. □ *vt* cover with concrete: ∼ *a road.*

con·cu·bine /ˈkɒŋkjʊbaɪn/ *n* [C] (in some countries, where polygamy is legal) lesser wife.

con·cur /kənˈkɜː(r)/ *vi* (-rr-) **1** agree in opinion: *I* ∼ *with the speaker in condemning what has been done.* **2** (of circumstances, etc) happen together: *Everything* ∼*red to produce a successful result.*

con·cur·rence /kənˈkʌrəns US: -ˈkɜːrəns/ *n* [U] agreement; coming together.

con·cur·rent /kənˈkʌrənt US: -ˈkɜːrənt/ *adj* concurring; happening together; co-operating.
con·cur·rent·ly *adv*

con·cuss /kənˈkʌs/ *vt* injure (the brain) by concussion.

con·cus·sion /kənˈkʌʃən/ *n* [C,U] (an) injury or (a) violent shaking or shock (to the brain) (as caused by a blow, knock or fall).

con·demn /kənˈdem/ *vt* **1** say that a person is, or has done, wrong or that something is wrong or unfit for use: *We all* ∼ *cruelty to children.* **2** (*legal*) give judgement against: ∼ *a murderer to life imprisonment.* **3** force, send, appoint (to do something unwelcome or painful): *an unhappy housewife,* ∼*ed to spend hours at the kitchen sink.* **4** declare (smuggled goods, property, etc) to be forfeited: *Merchant ships captured in war were often* ∼*ed.*

con·dem·na·tion /ˌkɒndəmˈneɪʃən/ *n* [U]

con·den·sa·tion /ˌkɒndenˈseɪʃən/ *n* **1** [U] condensing or being condensed: *the* ∼ *of steam to water.* **2** [C,U] (mass of) drops of liquid formed when vapour condenses: *A cloud is a* ∼ *of vapour.*

con·dense /kənˈdens/ *vt,vi* **1** (of a liquid) (cause to) increase in density or strength; to become thicker: ∼*ed milk;* (of a gas or vapour) (cause to) change to a liquid; (of light) focus; concentrate (by passing through a lens). **2** put into fewer words: *a* ∼*d account of an event.*

con·den·ser /kənˈdensə(r)/ *n* [C] **1** apparatus for cooling vapour and condensing it to liquid. **2** apparatus for receiving and accumulating static electricity.

con·de·scend /ˌkɒndɪˈsend/ *vi* **1** (agree to) do something, accept a position, etc that one's rank, merits, abilities, etc do not require one to do. *The Duke has graciously*

~ed to open the new playing field. **2** lower oneself: *He occasionally ~ed to trickery/to take bribes.* **3** behave graciously, but in a way that shows one's feeling of superiority: *Mrs Hope doesn't like being ~ed to.*
con·de·scend·ing *adj*

con·di·ment /ˈkɒndɪmənt/ *n* [C,U] (*formal*) = seasoning.

con·di·tion[1] /kənˈdɪʃn/ *n* **1** [C] something on which another thing depends: *Ability is one of the ~s of success in life.* **on condition that,** only if; provided that: *You can go on ~ that you come home early.* **2** [U] the present state of things; quality, character of: *The ~ of my health prevents me from working. He's in no ~ to travel,* is not well or strong enough. **3** (*pl*) circumstances: *under existing/favourable ~s.*

con·di·tion[2] /kənˈdɪʃn/ *vt* **1** determine; govern; regulate: *My expenditure is ~ed by my income.* **2** bring into a desired state or condition: *We'll never ~ the workers to a willing acceptance of a wage freeze.*

con·di·tioned *adj* (a) subject to certain provisions or conditions; having a specified condition: `air-~ed cinemas.` (b) in a desired mental state through persuasion, force, etc: *~ed to feeling inferior.*

con·di·tional /kənˈdɪʃənl/ *adj* depending on, containing, a condition.
conditional clause, (*gram*) one beginning with 'if' or 'unless'.
con·di·tion·al·ly /-əlɪ/ *adv*

con·dol·ence /kənˈdəʊləns/ *n* [C] (usually *pl*) expression of sympathy: *Please accept my ~s.*

con·done /kənˈdəʊn/ *vt* **1** (of a person) overlook or forgive (an offence): *~ a child's behaviour.* **2** (of an act) make up for: *good qualities that ~ his many shortcomings.*

con·duc·ive /kənˈdjuːsɪv US: -ˈduːs-/ *adj* helping to produce: *Good health is ~ to happiness.*

con·duct[1] /ˈkɒndʌkt/ *n* [U] **1** moral behaviour: *good/bad ~.* **2** manner of directing or managing affairs: *People were not at all satisfied with the ~ of the war,* the way in which the leaders were directing it.

con·duct[2] /kənˈdʌkt/ *vt,vi* **1** lead or guide: *Mr Y ~ed the visitors round the museum.* **2** control; direct; manage: *to ~ a meeting/ negotiations.* **3** direct (an orchestra). **4** behave: *He ~s himself well.* **5** (of substances) allow (heat, electric current) to pass along or through: *Copper ~s electricity.*

con·duc·tion /kənˈdʌkʃn/ *n* [U] transmission, e g of electric current along wires, of liquids through pipes, of heat by contact.

con·duc·tive /kənˈdʌktɪv/ *adj* able to transmit (heat, electric current, etc).

con·duc·tor /kənˈdʌktə(r)/ *n* [C] **1** person who conducts esp a group of singers, a band, an orchestra. **2** person who collects fares on a bus or tram. **3** substance that conducts heat or electric current.

con·duc·tress /kənˈdʌktrəs/ *n* [C] woman conductor(2).

cone /kəʊn/ *n* [C] **1** solid body which narrows to a point from a round, flat base. **2** something of this shape whether solid or hollow. **3** fruit of certain evergreen trees (fir, pine, cedar).

con·fec·tion /kənˈfekʃn/ *n* (*formal*) **1** [C] mixture of sweet things; sweet cake. **2** [U] mixing; compounding.
con·fec·tioner, person who makes and sells pastry, pies, cakes, etc.
con·fec·tion·ery /kənˈfekʃənrɪ US: -nerɪ/ *n* (a) [U] sweets, chocolates, cakes, pies, pastry, etc. (b) [C] (*pl* -ies) place, business, of a confectioner.

con·fed·er·acy /kənˈfedrəsɪ/ *n* [C] (*pl* -ies) union of states, parties or persons: *the Southern C~,* the eleven States that separated from the Union (US, 1860—61) and brought about the Civil War.

con·fed·er·ate[1] /kənˈfedərət/ *adj* joined together by an agreement or treaty: *the C~ States of America.* ⇨ above. □ *n* [C] **1** person or State joined with another or others. **2** accomplice (in a plot, etc).

con·fed·er·ate[2] /kənˈfedəreɪt/ *vt,vi* bring into or come into alliance.
con·fed·er·ation /kənˌfedəˈreɪʃn/ *n* (a) [U] confederating or being confederated. (b) [C] alliance; league.

con·fer /kənˈfɜː(r)/ *vt,vi* (-rr-) **1** *confer sth on/upon,* give or grant (a degree, title, favour): *The Queen ~red knighthoods on several distinguished men.* **2** consult or discuss: *~ with one's lawyer.*
con·fer·ment *n* [C,U]

con·fer·ence /ˈkɒnfrəns/ *n* [C,U] (meeting for) discussion; exchange of views: *The Director is in ~/holding a ~.*

con·fess /kənˈfes/ *vt,vi* **1** say or admit (that one has done wrong): *He ~ed that he had stolen the money. I ~ to having a fear of spiders.* **2** (esp in the R C Church) make known one's sins to a priest; (of a priest) listen to a person doing this: *~ one's sins.*
con·fess·ed·ly *adv* as, by one's own confession.

con·fes·sion /kənˈfeʃn/ *n* **1** [U] confessing; [C] instance of this: *The accused man made a full ~. She is a good Catholic and goes to ~ regularly.* **2** [C] declaration (of religious beliefs, or of principles of conduct, etc): *a ~ of faith.*

con·fes·sional /kənˈfeʃənl/ *n* [C] private place in a church where a priest sits to hear confessions.

con·fes·sor /kənˈfesə(r)/ *n* [C] priest who has authority to hear confessions

con·fetti /kənˈfetɪ/ *n pl* (used with a *sing verb*) small bits of coloured paper showered on people at weddings, etc.

con·fi·dant /ˈkɒnfɪdænt/ *n* [C] person who is trusted with private affairs or secrets (esp about love affairs).

con·fide /kən`faɪd/ *vt, vi* **1** tell a secret; give to be looked after; give (a task or duty to a person): *He ∼d his troubles to a friend.* **2** *confide in,* have trust or faith in: *Can I ∼ in his honesty?*

con·fid·ing *adj* truthful; trusting: *She's of a confiding nature.*

con·fi·dence /`kɒnfɪdəns/ *n* **1** [U] (act of) confiding in or to. *in strict confidence,* expecting something to be kept secret. **2** [C] secret, confidential information, which is confided to a person: *The two girls sat in a corner exchanging ∼s about the young men they knew.* **3** [U] belief in oneself or others or in what is said, reported, etc; belief that one is right or that one is able to perform: *to have/lose ∼ in oneself/her. He answered the questions with ∼.*

`confidence trick,` persuasion of a person to entrust valuables to one as a sign of confidence.

`confidence trickster/man,` person who cheats people in this way.

con·fi·dent /`kɒnfɪdənt/ *adj* feeling or showing confidence; certain: *He feels fairly ∼ of passing/that he will pass the examination.*

con·fi·dent·ly *adv*

con·fi·den·tial /ˌkɒnfɪ`denʃəl/ *adj* **1** (to be kept) secret: *∼ information.* **2** having the confidence of another or others.

con·fi·den·ti·ally /-ʃəlɪ/ *adv*

con·fine /kən`faɪn/ *vt* **1** keep or hold, restrict, within limits: *Please ∼ your remarks to the subject we are debating.* **2** keep shut up: *Is it cruel to ∼ a bird in a cage?*

con·fined *adj* (of space) limited; narrow; restricted.

con·fine·ment *n* (a) [U] being confined; imprisonment: *He was placed in ∼ment.* (b) [U] giving birth to a child; [C] instance of this.

con·fines /`kɒnfaɪnz/ *n pl* limits; borders; boundaries: *beyond the ∼ of human knowledge/this valley.*

con·firm /kən`fɜm/ *vt* **1** make (power, ownership, opinions, rights, feelings, etc) firmer or stronger; provide proof: *The report of an earthquake in Greece has now been ∼ed, We now know that the report was true.* **2** agree definitely to (a treaty, an appointment, etc). **3** admit to full membership of the Christian Church: *She was baptized when she was a month old and ∼ed when she was thirteen.*

con·firmed *adj* (esp) unlikely to change or be changed: *a ∼ed invalid.*

con·fir·ma·tion /ˌkɒnfə`meɪʃən/ *n* [C,U] confirming or being confirmed (all senses): *We are waiting for ∼ of the news.*

con·fis·cate /`kɒnfɪskeɪt/ *vt* (as punishment or in enforcing authority) take possession of (private property) without compensation or payment: *If you try to smuggle goods into the country, they may be ∼d by the Customs authorities.*

con·fis·ca·tion /ˌkɒnfɪ`skeɪʃən/ *n* [C,U]

con·flict[1] /`kɒnflɪkt/ *n* [C] **1** fight; struggle; quarrel: *a bitter ∼ between employers and workers.* **2** (of opinions, desires, etc) opposition; difference: *the ∼ between duty and desire.*

con·flict[2] /kən`flɪkt/ *vi* be in opposition or disagreement: *His account of the war ∼s with mine. They ∼.*

con·flict·ing *adj*: *∼ing evidence/passions.*

con·form /kən`fɔm/ *vi, vt* **1** be in agreement with, comply with (generally accepted rules, standards, etc): *You should ∼ to the rules/to the wishes of others.* **2** make similar to; adapt oneself to: *∼ one's life to certain principles.*

con·form·ist /kən`fɔmɪst/ *n* [C] person who conforms, e g to the customs of the Established Church.

con·form·ity /kən`fɔmɪtɪ/ *n* [U] **1** action, behaviour, in agreement with what is usual, accepted or required by custom, etc: *C∼ to fashion* (= Having things of the latest fashions) *is not essential to the happiness of all women.* **2** agreement: *Was his action in ∼ with the law?*

con·found /kən`faʊnd/ *vt* **1** fill with, throw into, confusion: *His behaviour amazed and ∼ed her.* **2** mix up, confuse (ideas, etc): *Don't ∼ excuses with reasons.*

con·front /kən`frʌnt/ *vt* **1** bring, come, be face to face: *When ∼ed with the evidence of his guilt, he confessed at once. A soldier has to ∼ danger.*

con·fron·ta·tion /ˌkɒnfrən`teɪʃən/ *n* [C,U] (instance of) defiant opposition, of being face to face: *the ∼ between the police and the demonstrators.*

con·fuse /kən`fjuz/ *vt* **1** put into disorder; mix up in the mind: *They asked so many questions that they ∼d me/I got ∼d.* **2** mistake one thing for another: *Don't ∼ Austria with/and Australia.*

con·fus·ed·ly *adv* in a confused manner.

con·fu·sion /kən`fjuʒən/ *n* [U] being confused; disorder: *His unexpected arrival threw everything into ∼. There has been some ∼; it was Mr Smythe who came, not Mr Smith.*

con·fute /kən`fjut/ *vt* (*formal*) **1** prove (a person) to be wrong. **2** show (an argument) to be false.

con·geal /kən`dʒil/ *vt, vi* make or become stiff or solid (esp as the effect of cold, or of the air on blood).

con·gen·ial /kən`dʒinɪəl/ *adj* **1** (of persons) having the same or a similar nature, common interests, etc: *In this small village he found few persons ∼ to him.* **2** (of things, occupations, etc) in agreement with one's tastes, nature: *a ∼ climate; ∼ work.*

con·gen·ially /-ɪəlɪ/ *adv*

con·geni·tal /kən`dʒenɪtəl/ *adj* (of diseases, etc) present, belonging to a person, from or before birth.

con·ger eel /ˈkɒŋgə(r) iːl/ *n* [C] ocean eel of large size.

con·gested /kənˈdʒestɪd/ *adj* **1** too full; overcrowded: *streets ~ with traffic.* **2** (of parts of the body, e g the brain, the lungs) having an abnormal accumulation of blood.

con·ges·tion /kənˈdʒestʃən/ *n* [U] being congested: *~ of the lungs/ of traffic in town.*

con·glom·er·ate¹ /kənˈglɒmərət/ *adj, n* [C] (made up of a) number of things or parts stuck together in a mass or ball (e g rock made up of small stones held together).

con·glom·er·ate² /kənˈglɒməreɪt/ *vt, vi* collect into a mass.

con·glom·er·ation /kənˈglɒməˈreɪʃən/ *n* **1** [U] conglomerating or being conglomerated. **2** [C] mass of conglomerated things.

con·gratu·late /kənˈgrætʃʊleɪt/ *vt* **1** tell somebody that one is pleased about something happy or fortunate that has come to (him): *~ him on his marriage.* **2** consider (oneself) fortunate: *I ~d myself on my escape/on having escaped unhurt.*

con·gratu·la·tory /kənˈgrætʃʊˈleɪtərɪ US: -tɔːrɪ/ *adj* that congratulates: *a congratulatory telegram.*

con·gratu·la·tion /kənˈgrætʃʊˈleɪʃən/ *n* [C] (often *pl*) words that congratulate: *C~s on passing the exam! Please give my heartiest ~s to her.*

con·gre·gate /ˈkɒŋgrɪgeɪt/ *vi, vt* come or bring together: *People quickly ~d round the speaker.*

con·gre·ga·tion /ˈkɒŋgrɪˈgeɪʃən/ *n* **1** [U] congregating; [C] gathering of people. **2** (esp) body of people taking part in religious worship.

con·gre·ga·tional /-nəl/ *adj* of a congregation(2).

con·gress /ˈkɒŋgres US: -grɪs/ *n* **1** [C] meeting, series of meetings, of representatives (of societies, etc) for discussion: *a medical ~; the Church C~.* **2** C~, law-making body of US and some other republics in America; political party in India.

ˈcon·gress·man/woman, member of Congress.

con·gres·sional /kənˈgreʃnəl/ *adj*

con·gru·ent /ˈkɒŋgrʊənt/ *adj* **1** suitable; agreeing (with). **2** having the same size and shape: *~ triangles.*

con·gru·ous /ˈkɒŋgrʊəs/ *adj* fitting; proper; harmonious (with).

conic /ˈkɒnɪk/ *adj* of a cone: *~ sections.*

coni·cal /ˈkɒnɪkəl/ *adj* cone-shaped.

coni·fer /ˈkɒnɪfə(r)/ *n* [C,U] tree of the kind (e g pine, fir) that bears cones.

co·nifer·ous /kəˈnɪfərəs/ *adj*

con·jec·ture /kənˈdʒektʃə(r)/ *vi, vt* (formal) guess; put forward an opinion formed without facts as proof: *It was just as I ~d.* □ *n* [C,U] (formal) guess; guessing: *I was right in my ~s.*

con·jec·tural /kənˈdʒektʃərəl/ *adj* invol-

ving, inclined to, conjecture.

con·ju·gal /ˈkɒndʒʊgəl/ *adj* (formal) of marriage and wedded life; of husband and wife: *~ happiness/infidelity.*

conjugal rights, right of a sexual relationship with a husband or wife.

con·ju·gally /-glɪ/ *adv*

con·ju·gate /ˈkɒndʒʊgeɪt/ *vt* (gram) **1** give the forms of a verb (for number, tense, etc) **2** (of a verb) have these forms.

con·ju·ga·tion /ˈkɒndʒʊˈgeɪʃən/ *n* (a) [C,U] scheme or system of verb forms: *Appendix 1 of this dictionary list the ~s of irregular verbs.* (b) [C] class of verbs conjugated alike.

con·junc·tion /kənˈdʒʌŋkʃən/ *n* **1** [C] (gram) word that joins other words, clauses, etc, e g *and, but, or.* **2** [U] joining; state of being joined: *the ~ of skill and imagination in planning a garden.* **in conjunction with**, together with. **3** [C] combination (of events, etc): *an unusual ~ of circumstances.*

con·junc·tive /kənˈdʒʌŋktɪv/ *adj* serving to join; connective. □ *n* [C] = conjunction(1).

con·junc·ture /kənˈdʒʌŋktʃə(r)/ *n* [C] (formal) combination of events or circumstances.

con·jure /ˈkʌndʒə(r)/ *vt, vi* **1** do clever tricks which appear magical: *~ a rabbit out of a hat.* **2** *conjure up*, (a) cause to appear as if from nothing, or as an image in the mind: *~ up visions of the past.* (b) compel (a spirit) to appear by invocation: *~ up the spirits of the dead.* (c) (informal) prepare (a meal): *~ up a stew.*

con·jurer, con·juror /ˈkʌndʒərə(r)/, person who performs conjuring(1) tricks.

con·nect /kəˈnekt/ *vt, vi* **1** join, be joined (by things, by personal relationships, etc): *The two towns are ~ed by a railway. Mr Smith has been ~ed with this firm since 1950. If you ring the operator, he will ~ you* (i e by telephone) *with the airport.* **2** think of (different things or persons) as being related to each other: *to ~ Malaya with rubber and tin.*

con·nec·tion /kəˈnekʃən/ *n* **1** [C,U] connecting or being connected; point where two things are connected; thing which connects: *How long will the ~ of the new telephone take,* How long will it take to connect the house by telephone? *What is the ~ between the two ideas?* **2** [C] train, boat, etc arranged to leave a station, port, etc soon after the arrival of another, so that passengers can change from one to the other: *The train was late and I missed my ~.* **3** [C] number of customers, clients, etc: *He started a business and soon had a good ~/good ~s.* **4** *in connection with*, concerning: *The principal would like to see you in ~ with your examination fees.*

con·nect·ive /kəˈnektɪv/ *adj* serving to connect. □ *n* [C] (esp) word that connects (e g a conjunction).

con·nexion /kəˈnekʃən/ occasional GB

spelling for *connection*.

con·nive /kəˋnaɪv/ *vi* **connive at,** take no notice of (what is wrong, what ought to be opposed) (suggesting consent or approval): ~ *at an escape from prison.*

con·niv·ance /-əns/ *n* [U] conniving (at or in a crime): *done with the connivance of/in connivance with...*

con·nois·seur /ˏkɒnəˋsə(r)/ *n* [C] person with good judgement on matters in which (artistic) taste is needed: *a ~ of/in painting/ wine.*

con·note /kəˋnəʊt/ *vt* (of words) suggest something in addition to the basic meaning: *The word 'Tropics' is a geographical area; it also ~s heat.*

con·no·ta·tion /ˏkɒnəˋteɪʃən/ *n* [C] that which is suggested: *Be careful not to use slang words which may have obscene ~s.*

con·quer /ˋkɒŋkə(r)/ *vt* **1** defeat or overcome enemies, bad habits, etc. **2** take possession of by force: ~ *a country.*

con·queror /-rə(r)/, person who conquers.

con·quest /ˋkɒŋkwəst/ *n* **1** [U] conquering (e g a country and its people). **2** [C] something got by conquering: *make a ~ (of),* win the affections (of).

con·science /ˋkɒnʃəns/ *n* [C,U] the consciousness within oneself of the choice one ought to make between right and wrong: *have a clear/guilty ~.* **have no conscience (about),** be as ready to do wrong as right. **(have sth/sb) on one's conscience,** (feel) troubled about something one has done, or failed to do.

`con·science money,` money paid because one has a guilty conscience.

con·scien·tious /ˏkɒnʃɪˋenʃəs/ *adj* **1** (of persons) guided by one's sense of duty. **2** (of actions) done carefully and honestly: ~ *work.*

conscientious objector, person who objects to doing something (e g serving in the armed forces) because he thinks it is morally wrong.

con·scien·tious·ly *adv*

con·scien·tious·ness *n* [C]

con·scious /ˋkɒnʃəs/ *adj* **1** awake; aware; knowing things because one is using the bodily senses and mental powers: *They were ~ of being/that they were being watched.* **2** (of actions, feelings, etc) realized by oneself: *He spoke/acted with ~ superiority.*

con·scious·ly *adv*

con·scious·ness /ˋkɒnʃəsnəs/ *n* [U] **1** being conscious: *We have no ~ during sleep. He didn't recover/regain ~ until two hours after the accident.* **2** all the ideas, thoughts, feelings, wishes, intentions, recollections, of a person or persons: *the moral ~ of a political party.*

con·script /kənˋskrɪpt/ *vt* compel by law, summon, to serve in the armed forces: ~*ed into the army.* ⇨ draft¹(3). □ *n* /ˋkɒnskrɪpt/ [C] person who is conscripted.

con·scrip·tion /kənˋskrɪpʃən/ *n* [U] conscripting; system, practice, taxation, confiscation, property (as a penalty or for war needs).

con·se·crate /ˋkɒnsɪkreɪt/ *vt* set apart as sacred or for a special purpose; make sacred: *to ~ one's life to the service of God/to the relief of suffering. He was ~d Archbishop last year.*

con·se·cra·tion /ˏkɒnsɪˋkreɪʃən/ *n* [C,U] (instance of) being consecrated.

con·secu·tive /kənˋsekjʊtɪv/ *adj* coming one after the other in regular order: *on five ~ days.*

con·secu·tive·ly *adv*

con·sen·sus /kənˋsensəs/ *n* [C] (*pl* ~es) general agreement: *a ~ of opinion.*

con·sent /kənˋsent/ *vi* give agreement or permission: *Anne's father would not ~ to her marrying him.* □ *n* [U] agreement; permission: *He was chosen leader by general ~,* everyone agreed. ⇨ age of consent.

con·se·quence /ˋkɒnsɪkwəns *US:* -kwens/ *n* **1** [C] that which follows or is brought about as the result or effect: *If you behave so foolishly you must be ready to take the ~s,* accept what happens as a result. **2** [U] importance: *It's of no ~.*

con·se·quent /ˋkɒnsɪkwənt/ *adj* (*formal*) following as a consequence: *the rise in prices ~ on the failure of the crops.*

con·se·quent·ly *adv* therefore: *I crashed the car and ~ly I must pay for the repairs.*

con·se·quen·tial /ˏkɒnsɪˋkwenʃəl/ *adj* (*formal*) **1** = consequent. **2** (of a person) self-important

con·se·quen·tial·ly *adv*

con·ser·va·tion /ˏkɒnsəˋveɪʃən/ *n* [U] perservation; prevention of loss, waste, damage, etc: *the ~ of forests/fuel. Energy ~ is a problem throughout the world.*

con·serva·tism /kənˋsɜːvətɪzm/ *n* [U] tendency to maintain a state of affairs (esp in politics) without great or sudden change.

con·serva·tive /kənˋsɜːvətɪv/ *adj* **1** opposed to great or sudden change: *Old people are usually more ~ than young people.* **2** **the C~ Party,** one of the main political parties in Great Britain. **3** cautious; moderate: *a ~ estimate of one's future income.* □ *n* [C] **1** conservative (1) person. **2** C~, member, supporter, of the Conservative Party.

con·serva·tive·ly *adv*

con·serva·toire /kənˋsɜːvətwɑː(r)/ *n* [C] (*Fr*) (in Europe) school of music or other arts.

con·serva·tory /kənˋsɜːvətrɪ *US:* -tɔːrɪ/ *n* [C] (*pl* -ies) **1** building, or part of a building, with glass walls and roof in which plants are protected from cold. **2** school of music or dramatic art.

con·serve /kənˋsɜːv/ *vt* keep from change, loss or destruction: ~ *one's strength/ energies/health.* □ *n* (usually *pl*) jam (the usual word).

con·sider /kənˋsɪdə(r)/ *vt* **1** think about:

Please ∼ *my suggestion. We are* ∼*ing going to Canada.* **2** take into account; make allowances for: *We must* ∼ *the feelings of other people.* **all things considered,** taking everything into account: *We hoped to win the competition, but all things* ∼*ed we did well to reach the final.* **3** be of the opinion; regard as: *They* ∼*ed themselves very important. Do you* ∼ *it wise to interfere?*

con·sid·er·able /kən'sɪdrəbəl/ *adj* great; much; important: *bought at a* ∼ *expense.*

con·sid·er·ably /-əblɪ/ *adv* much; a great deal: *It's considerably colder this morning.*

con·sid·er·ate /kən'sɪdərət/ *adj* thoughtful (of the needs, etc of others): *It was* ∼ *of you to bring me flowers.*

con·sid·er·ate·ly *adv*

con·sid·er·ation /kən'sɪdə'reɪʃən/ *n* **1** [U] act of considering, thinking about: *Please give the matter your careful* ∼. **take sth into consideration,** (esp) make allowances for: *When marking the examination, I took Tom's long illness into* ∼. **under consideration,** being thought about: *Your request for permission to be absent on Friday is under* ∼. **2** [U] quality of being considerate; thoughtful attention to the wishes, feelings, etc, of others: *in* ∼ *of/out of* ∼ *for his youth.* **3** [C] something which must be thought about; fact, thing, etc thought of as a reason: *Time is an important* ∼ *in this case.*

con·sid·er·ing /kən'sɪdərɪŋ/ *prep* in view of; having regard to: *She's very active,* ∼ *her age.*

con·sign /kən'saɪn/ *vt* **1** send (goods, etc) for delivery: *The goods have been* ∼*ed by rail.* **2** hand over, give up: ∼ *a child to its uncle's care.*

con·sign·ment *n* [U] consigning; [C] goods consigned.

con·sist /kən'sɪst/ *vi* **1 consist of,** be made up of: *The committee* ∼*s of ten members.* **2 consist in,** have as the chief or only element: *The happiness of a country* ∼*s in the freedom of its citizens.*

con·sist·ence /kən'sɪstəns/ *n* = consistency.

con·sist·ency /kən'sɪstənsɪ/ *n* (*pl* -ies) **1** [U] the state of always being the same in thought, behaviour, etc; keeping to the same principles: *His actions lack* ∼. **2** [C,U] degree of thickness, firmness or solidity (esp of a thick liquid, or of something made by mixing with a liquid): *mix flour and milk to the right* ∼.

con·sist·ent /kən'sɪstənt/ *adj* (of a person, his behaviour, principles, etc) having a regular pattern or style; in agreement (with): *The ideas in his various speeches are not* ∼. *What you say now is not* ∼ *with what you said last week.*

con·sist·ent·ly *adv*

con·so·la·tion /'kɒnsə'leɪʃən/ *n* **1** [U] consoling or being consoled; something that consoles: *a few words of/a letter of* ∼. **2** [C] circumstances or person that consoles: *Your friendship has been a great* ∼ *to me.*

con'so'lation prize, one given to a competitor who has just missed the main prize.

con·sola·tory /kən'sɒlətrɪ US: -tɔrɪ/ *adj* intended to give comfort: *-a* ∼ *letter.*

con·sole¹ /kən'səʊl/ *vt* give comfort or sympathy to: ∼ *him in his disappointment;* ∼ *oneself with the thought that it might have been worse.*

con·sol·able /-əbəl/ *adj* that can be comforted.

con·sole² /'kɒnsəʊl/ *n* [C] **1** bracket to support a shelf. **2** frame containing the keyboards, stops, etc of an organ. **3** panel for the controls of electronic or mechanical equipment.

con·soli·date /kən'sɒlɪdeɪt/ *vt,vi* **1** make or become (more) solid or strong: ∼ *one's position/influence.* **2** unite or combine into one: ∼ *debts/business companies. The different States have been* ∼*d into one federation.*

con·soli·da·tion /kən'sɒlɪ'deɪʃən/ *n* **1** [U] consolidating or being consolidated. **2** [C] instance of this.

con·sommé /kən'sɒmeɪ/ *n* [U] (*Fr*) clear, meat soup.

con·son·ant /'kɒnsənənt/ *n* [C] speech sound produced by a complete or partial stoppage of the breath; letter of the alphabet or symbol (e g phonetic) for such a sound: *b, c, d, f,* etc.

con·sort¹ /'kɒnsɔt/ *n* [C] **1** husband or wife, esp of a ruler: *the prince* ∼, *the reigning queen's husband.* **2** ship sailing with another (esp for safety during a war).

con·sort² /kən'sɔt/ *vi* **consort with, 1** pass time in the company of: ∼ *with criminals.* **2** (*formal*) be in harmony, go well: *His behaviour does not* ∼ *with his beliefs.*

con·sort·ium /kən'sɔtɪəm/ *n* [C] (*pl* -tia /-tɪə/) association of businesses, States, etc.

con·spicu·ous /kən'spɪkjʊəs/ *adj* easily seen; attracting attention: ∼ *for his bravery. Traffic signs should be* ∼. **make oneself conspicuous,** attract attention by unusual behaviour, wearing unusual clothes, etc: *He made himself* ∼ *at the party by wearing silver boots.*

con·spicu·ous·ly *adv*

con·spir·acy /kən'spɪrəsɪ/ *n* (*pl* -ies) **1** [U] act of conspiring. **2** [C] plan made by conspiring: *There were rumours of a* ∼ *to overthrow the Government.*

con·spira·tor /kən'spɪrətə(r)/ *n* [C] person who conspires.

con·spira·tor·ial /kən'spɪrə'tɔrɪəl/ *adj* of conspirators or a conspiracy: *a* ∼*ial manner.*

con·spire /kən'spaɪə(r)/ *vi* **1** make se.. plans (with others, esp to do wrong): ∼ *a friend against the teacher.* **2** (of eve.. together; combine: *events that* ∼*d*..

about his ruin.

con·stable /ˈkʌnstəbəl *US:* ˈkon-/ *n* [C] (*dated*) policeman (the usual word).

chief constable, senior police officer.

con·stabu·lary /kənˈstæbjʊlərɪ *US:* -lerɪ/ *n* [C] (*pl* -ies) (*dated*) police force (the usual term).

con·stancy /ˈkonstənsɪ/ *n* [U] quality of being firm, faithful, unchanging: ~ *of purpose.*

con·stant /ˈkonstənt/ *adj* **1** going on all the time; frequently recurring: ~ *complaints.* **2** (*formal*) firm; faithful; unchanging: *a* ~ *friend.*

con·stant·ly *adv* continuously; frequently: *She complains* ~*ly about the cold weather.*

con·stel·la·tion /ˌkonstəˈleɪʃən/ *n* [C] named group of fixed stars (e g *the Great Bear*).

con·ster·na·tion /ˌkonstəˈneɪʃən/ *n* [U] surprise and fear; dismay: *News of the highjacking filled him with* ~.

con·sti·pate /ˈkonstɪpeɪt/ *vt* cause constipation.

con·sti·pated /ˈkonstɪpeɪtɪd/ *adj* having bowels that are emptied infrequently or only with difficulty.

con·sti·pa·tion /ˌkonstɪˈpeɪʃən/ *n* [U] difficult or infrequent emptying of the bowels.

con·stitu·ency /kənˈstɪtʃʊənsɪ/ *n* [C] (*pl* -ies) (body of voters living in a) town or district that sends a representative to Parliament.

con·stitu·ent /kənˈstɪtʃʊənt/ *adj* **1** having the power or right to make or alter a political constitution: *a* ~ *assembly.* **2** forming or helping to make a whole: *a* ~ *part.* □ *n* [C] **1** member of a constituency. **2** part (of something else): *the* ~*s of happiness.*

con·sti·tute /ˈkonstɪtjut *US:* -tut/ *vt* **1** establish; give legal authority to (a committee, etc). **2** make up (a whole); amount to; be the components of: *Twelve months* ~ *a year.* **3** (*formal*) give authority to hold (a position, etc): *They* ~*d him chief adviser to the planning committee.*

con·sti·tu·tion /ˌkonstɪˈtjuʃən *US:* -ˈtuʃən/ *n* [C] **1** system of government; laws and principles according to which a state is governed: *Great Britain has an unwritten* ~. **2** general physical structure and condition of a person's body: *Only men with strong* ~*s should climb in the Himalayas.* **3** general structure of a thing; act or manner of constituting: *the* ~ *of the solar spectrum.*

con·sti·tu·tional /ˌkonstɪˈtjuʃənəl *US:* -ˈtu-/ *adj* **1** of a constitution(1): ~ *government/reform.* **2** of a person's constitution(2): *a* ~ *weakness.*

con·strain /kənˈstreɪn/ *vt* use force or strong persuasion; (of conscience, inner forces) compel: *I feel* ~*ed to write and ask for your forgiveness.*

con·straint /kənˈstreɪnt/ *n* [U] constraining or being constrained: *to act under* ~,

because one is forced to do so.

con·strict /kənˈstrɪkt/ *vt* make tight or smaller; inhibit; cause (a vein or muscle) to become tight or narrow.

con·stric·tion /kənˈstrɪkʃən/ *n* (**a**) [U] tightening. (**b**) [C] thing that constricts; feeling of being constricted: *a* ~*ion in the chest because of heavy smoking.*

con·stric·tive *adj*

con·stric·tor /kənˈstrɪktə(r)/ *n* [C] **1** muscle that tightens or narrows. **2** ⇨ boa.

con·struct /kənˈstrʌkt/ *vt* build: *to* ~ *a factory/a sentence/a theory.*

con·struc·tor /-tə(r)/, person who builds things: *building* ~*ors.*

con·struc·tion /kənˈstrʌkʃən/ *n* **1** [U] act or manner of constructing; being constructed: *The new railway is still under* ~, being built. **2** [C] structure; building. **3** [C] meaning; sense in which words, statements, acts, etc are taken: *Please do not put a wrong* ~ *on his action,* misunderstand its purpose. **4** [C] arrangement and relationships of words in a sentence: *This dictionary gives the meanings of words and also gives examples to illustrate their* ~*s.*

con·struc·tional *adj* of, involving, construction: ~*al toys.*

con·struc·tive /kənˈstrʌktɪv/ *adj* helping to construct; giving helpful suggestions: ~ *criticism/proposals.*

con·struc·tive·ly *adv*

con·strue /kənˈstru/ *vt,vi* (*formal*) **1** translate or explain the meaning of words, sentences, acts: *His remarks were wrongly* ~*d,* were misunderstood. **2** analyse (a sentence); combine (words with words) grammatically.

con·sul /ˈkonsəl/ *n* [C] **1** State's agent living in a foreign town to help and protect his countrymen there. **2** (in ancient Rome) either of the two Heads of the State before Rome became an Empire.

con·su·lar /ˈkonsjʊlə(r) *US:* -səl-/ *adj* of a consul or his work.

consu·late /ˈkonsjʊlət *US:* -səl-/ *n* [C] consul's position or office.

con·sult /kənˈsʌlt/ *vt,vi* **1** go to a person, a book, etc for information, advice, opinion, etc: *to* ~ *one's lawyer/a map/the dictionary.* **2 consult with,** take advice, opinion from.

con·sulting room, one in which a doctor examines patients.

con·sul·tant /kənˈsʌltənt/ *n* [C] person who gives expert advice (e g in medicine, business): *a* ~ *surgeon; a firm of* ~*s.*

con·sul·ta·tion /ˌkonsəlˈteɪʃən/ *n* **1** [U] consulting or being consulted: *in* ~ *with the director.* **2** [C] meeting for consulting: *The doctors held a* ~ *to decide whether an operation was necessary.*

con·sul·ta·tive /kənˈsʌltətɪv/ *adj* of, for the purpose of, consulting: *a* ~ *committee.*

con·sume /kənˈsjum *US:* -ˈsum/ *vt,vi* (*formal*) **1** eat or drink. **2** use up; get to the end of; destroy by fire or wastefulness: ~ *all one's energies. This is* `time-consuming work.`

con·sum·er /kən`sjumə(r) *US:* -`su-/ *n* [C] person who uses (manufactured) goods: ~ *research.* ⇨ producer(1).

con·sum·ing *adj* possessing or dominating: *a consuming ambition.*

con·sum·mate² /`kɒnsəmeɪt/ *vt* 1 (*formal*) accomplish; make perfect: *Her happiness was ~d when her father took her to Paris.* 2 make complete (esp marriage by sexual intercourse).

con·sum·ma·tion /`kɒnsə`meɪʃən/ *n* [C,U] action, point of completing; perfecting, or fulfilling: *the ~ of one's ambitions/a marriage.*

con·sump·tion /kən`sʌmpʃən/ *n* [U] 1 using up, consuming (of food, energy, materials, etc); the quantity consumed: *The ~ of beer did not go down when the tax was raised.* 2 (popular name for) tuberculosis of the lung.

con·sump·tive /kən`sʌmptɪv/ *n* [C], *adj* (person) suffering from, having a tendency to, consumption(2).

con·tact /`kɒntækt/ *n* 1 [U] (state of) touching or communication; (process of) coming together. **be in/out of, come/bring into, contact (with):** *Our troops are in ~ with the enemy. A steel cable came into ~ with an electric power line.* **make contact (with),** (esp after searching, etc): *I finally made ~ with him in Paris.* 2 [C] (meeting with a) person: *He made many business ~s while he was in Canada.* 3 [C] connection (for electric current); device for effecting this. 4 [C] person recently exposed to a contagious disease. □ *vt* get into touch with: *Where can I ~ Mr Green?*

`contact lens,` one of thin plastic made to fit over the eyeball to improve vision.

con·ta·gion /kən`teɪdʒən/ *n* 1 [U] the spreading of disease by contact or close association. 2 [C] disease that can be spread by contact. 3 (*fig*) the spreading of ideas, false rumours, feelings, etc; influence, etc that spreads: *A ~ of fear swept through the crowd.*

con·ta·gi·ous /kən`teɪdʒəs/ *adj* 1 (of disease) spreading by contact: *Scarlet fever is ~.* 2 (of a person) in such a condition that he may spread disease. 3 (*fig*) spreading easily by example: *~ laughter/enthusiasm.*

con·ta·gi·ous·ly *adv*

con·tain /kən`teɪn/ *vt* 1 have or hold within itself: *The atlas ~s forty maps.* 2 be equal to: *A metre ~s 100 centimetres.* 3 be capable of holding: *How much does this bottle ~?* 4 keep feelings, enemy forces, etc under control: *Can't you ~ your enthusiasm?*

con·tain·er /kən`teɪnə(r)/ *n* [C] 1 box, bottle, etc designed to contain something. 2 large metal box, etc for transport of goods by road, rail, sea or air.

con·tami·nate /kən`tæmɪneɪt/ *vt* make dirty, impure or diseased (by touching, or adding something impure): *Flies ~ food.*

con·tami·na·tion /kən`tæmɪ`neɪʃən/ *n* 1 [U] contaminating or being contaminated: *the contamination of the water supply.* 2 [C] that which contaminates.

con·tem·plate /`kɒntəmpleɪt/ *vt* 1 look at; think about: *She stood contemplating herself in the mirror.* 2 have in view as a purpose, intention or possibility: *She was contemplating a visit to London.*

con·tem·pla·tion /`kɒntəm`pleɪʃən/ *n* [U] contemplating; deep thought; intention; expectation.

con·tem·pla·tive /kən`templətɪv *US:* `kɒntəmpleɪtɪv/ *adj* (*formal*) thoughtful.

con·tem·por·aneous /kən`tempə`reɪnɪəs/ *adj* (*formal*) originating, existing, happening, during the same period of time: ~ *events.*

con·tem·por·ary /kən`tempərɪ *US:* -pərerɪ/ *adj* 1 of the time or period to which reference is being made; belonging to the same time: *Dickens was ~ with Thackeray.* 2 of the present time. 3 (*informal*) in the most modern style: ~ *music.* □ *n* [C] (*pl* -ies) person of the same age, belonging to the same period, etc as another: *Jack and I were contemporaries at college.*

con·tempt /kən`tempt/ *n* [U] 1 condition of being looked down on or despised: *A man who is cruel to his children should be held in ~.* 2 mental attitude of despising: *We feel ~ for liars.* 3 disregard or disrespect: *in ~ of all rules and regulations.*

con·`tempt of `court, disobedience to an order made by a court; disrespect shown to a judge.

con·tempt·ible /kən`temptəbəl/ *adj* deserving, provoking, contempt.

con·temptu·ous /kən`temptʃʊəs/ *adj* showing contempt: ~ *of public opinion.*

con·tend /kən`tend/ *vi,vt* 1 struggle, be in rivalry or competition: ~*ing with difficulties/for a prize.* 2 argue, assert (that...).

con·tender, competitor, rival, eg one who challenges the holder of a boxing title.

con·tent¹ /kən`tent/ *adj* 1 not wanting more; satisfied with what one has: *Are you ~ with your present salary?* 2 willing or ready (to do something): *I am ~ to remain where I am now.* □ *n* [U] the condition of being satisfied: *to one's heart's ~,* to the extent that brings as much satisfaction or happiness as one wants. □ *vt* satisfy: *As there's no milk we must ~ ourselves (= be satisfied) with black coffee.*

con·tented *adj* satisfied; showing or feeling satisfaction, happiness: *with a ~ed look/smile.*

con·tent·ed·ly *adv*

con·tent·ment *n* [U] state of being content.

con·tent² /`kɒntent/ *n* 1 (*pl*) that which is contained: *the ~s of a room/a book/a* pocket. **2** (*pl*) the amount which a vessel will hold: *the ~s of this bottle.* **3** [C] substance (of a book, speech, etc as opposed to its form): *Do you approve of the ~ of the article/speech?*

con·ten·tion /kənˈtenʃən/ *n* **1** [U] quarrelling or disputing: *This is not a time for ~.* **2** [C] argument used in contending: *My ~ is that...*

con·ten·tious /kənˈtenʃəs/ *adj* quarrelsome; likely to cause argument: *a ~ clause in a treaty.*

con·test¹ /ˈkɒntest/ *n* [C] struggle; fight; competition: *a keen ~ for the prize; a ~ of skill; heavyweight ~.*

con·test·ant /kənˈtestənt/, person who contests.

con·test² /kənˈtest/ *vt,vi* **1** argue; debate; dispute: *~ a statement/point,* try to show that it is wrong. **2** = contend(1). **3** try to win: *~ a seat in Parliament.*

con·text /ˈkɒntekst/ *n* [C,U] **1** what comes before and after a word, phrase, etc helping to fix or illustrate the meaning: *Can't you guess the meaning of the word from the ~?* **2** circumstances in which an event occurs.

con·tex·tual /kənˈtekstʃʊəl/ *adj* according to the context.

con·ti·nent /ˈkɒntɪnənt *US:* -tənənt/ *n* [C] **1** one of the main land masses (Europe, Asia, Africa, etc). **2** the C~, the mainland of Europe.

con·ti·nen·tal /ˌkɒntɪˈnentəl *US:* -tənˈentəl/ *adj* **1** belonging to, typical of, a continent: *a ~ climate.* **2** of the mainland of Europe: *~ breakfast; ~ quilt,* duvet. □ *n* [C] inhabitant of the mainland of Europe.

con·tin·gency /kənˈtɪndʒənsɪ/ *n* (*pl* -ies) **1** [U] uncertainty of occurrence. **2** [C] uncertain event; event that happens by chance: *be prepared for all contingencies; ~ plans.*

con·tin·gent /kənˈtɪndʒənt/ *adj* (*formal*) **1** uncertain; accidental. **2** **contingent on/upon,** dependent on (something that may or may not happen). □ *n* [C] **1** body of troops, number of ships, lent or supplied to form part of a larger force. **2** group of persons forming part of a larger group.

con·tin·ual /kənˈtɪnjʊəl/ *adj* going on all the time without stopping, or with only short breaks: *Aren't you tired of this ~ rain?*

con·tin·ually /-əlɪ/ *adv* again and again; without stopping.

con·tin·uance /kənˈtɪnjʊəns/ *n* [U] **1** duration (the more usual word): *during the ~ of the war.* **2** remaining; staying: *a ~ of prosperity.*

con·tinu·ation /kənˌtɪnjʊˈeɪʃən/ *n* **1** [U] continuing; starting again after a stop. **2** [C] part, etc by which something is continued: *The next issue will contain an exciting ~ of the story.*

con·tinue /kənˈtɪnju/ *vi,vt* **1** go farther; go on (being); go on (doing); stay at/in; remain at/in: *The desert ~d as far as the eye could*

reach. *I hope this wet weather will not ~. How long will you ~ working?* **2** start again after stopping: *The story will be ~d in next month's issue.* **3** retain (in office, etc): *The Colonial Secretary was ~d in office.*

con·ti·nu·ity /ˌkɒntɪˈnjuːɪtɪ *US:* -ˈnuː-/ *n* [U] **1** the state of being continuous: *There is no ~ of subject in a dictionary.* **2** (in films, TV) arrangement of the parts of a story: *Films are often made out of ~,* e g a scene near the end may be filmed before a scene near the beginning. **3** comments, announcements, etc made between broadcast programmes.

con·tinu·ous /kənˈtɪnjʊəs/ *adj* going on without a break: *a ~ performance, 1.00 p m to 11.30 p m,* e g at a cinema.

con·tinu·ous·ly *adv*

con·tort /kənˈtɔːt/ *vt* force or twist out of the usual shape or appearance: *a face ~ed with pain.*

con·tor·tion /kənˈtɔːʃən/ *n* **1** [U] contorting or being contorted (esp of the face or body). **2** [C] instance of this; contorted condition: *the ~s of an acrobat.*

con·tour /ˈkɒntʊə(r)/ *n* **1** [C] outline (of a coast, a human figure, etc). **2** = contour line. □ *vt* **1** mark with contour lines. **2** make (a road) along the contour of a hill, etc.

ˈcontour line, line (on a map) joining points at the same height above sea-level.

contra- /ˈkɒntrə/ *prefix* against; opposite to: *contraception; contradict.*

contra·band /ˈkɒntrəbænd/ *n* [U] **1** bringing into, taking out of, a country goods contrary to the law. **2** (trade in) goods so brought in or taken out.

contra·cep·tion /ˌkɒntrəˈsepʃən/ *n* [U] practice, method, of preventing or planning conception(2).

contra·cep·tive /ˌkɒntrəˈseptɪv/ *n* [C] device or drug intended to prevent conception(2). □ *adj* preventing conception: *~ pills/devices.*

con·tract¹ /ˈkɒntrækt/ *n* [C,U] binding agreement (between persons, groups, states); agreement to supply goods, do work, etc at a fixed price: *enter into/make a ~ (with a person)* (*for the purchase of a house*); *work to be done by private ~; a breach of ~.* (*Note:* The article is not used in phrases like the last two examples.)

con·tract² /kənˈtrækt/ *vt,vi* **1** be bound, bind, by agreement: *~ a marriage; ~ an alliance with another country.* **ˈcontract ˈout (of sth),** reject, abandon, the terms of an agreement. **2** become liable (for debts). **3** catch (an illness): *~ measles.* **4** form; acquire (e g bad habits).

con·trac·tor /-tə(r)/, person, business firm, that enters into contracts: *building ~ors.*

con·trac·tual /kənˈtræktʃʊəl/ *adj* of (the nature of) a contract.

con·tract³ /kənˈtrækt/ *vt,vi* **1** make or become smaller or shorter: *'I will' can be*

~ed to 'I'll'. 2 make or become tighter or narrower: to ~ a muscle.

con·tract·ible /-əbəl/ adj that can be contracted.

con·trac·tion /kən'trækʃən/ n 1 [U] contracting or being contracted: the ~ of a muscle. 2 [C] something contracted; shortened form, such as can't for cannot.

con·tra·dict /ˌkɒntrə'dɪkt/ vt 1 deny the truth of (something said or written); deny (the words of a person): to ~ a statement. Don't ~ me. 2 (of facts, statements, etc) be contrary to: The reports ~ each other.

con·tra·dic·tion /ˌkɒntrə'dɪkʃən/ n 1 [U] contradicting; [C] instance of this. 2 [U] absence of agreement; [C] instance of this: Your statements today are in ~ with what you said yesterday.

con·tra·dic·tory /ˌkɒntrə'dɪktərɪ/ adj contradicting: ~ statements/reports.

con·tralto /kən'træltəʊ/ n [C] (pl ~s) lowest female voice; woman with, musical part to be sung by, such a voice.

con·trap·tion /kən'træpʃən/ n [C] (informal) strange-looking apparatus or device.

con·trary¹ /'kɒntrərɪ US: -trerɪ/ adj 1 contrary to, opposite (in nature or tendency): What you have done is ~ to the doctor's orders. 2 (of the wind and weather) unfavourable (for sailing). 3 (informal) (usually /kən'treərɪ/) obstinate; self-willed. 4 contrary to, in opposition to; against: to act ~ to the rules; events that went ~ to my interests.

con·trar·ily /kən'treərɪlɪ US: -rerəlɪ/ adv in an obstinate manner.

con·trari·ness /'kɒntrərɪnəs US: -rer-/ n [C] being obstinate; refusing advice.

con·trary² /'kɒntrərɪ US: -trerɪ/ n (pl -ies) opposite: The ~ of 'wet' is 'dry'. on the contrary, (denying or contradicting what has been said, written): 'You've nothing to do now, I think.'—'On the ~, I have a lot of work to do.' to the contrary, to the opposite effect: I will come on Monday unless you write me to the ~, telling me not to come.

con·trast¹ /kən'trɑːst US: -ræst/ vt,vi 1 compare so that differences are made clear: C~ these imported goods (with/and the domestic product). 2 show a difference when compared: His actions ~ unfavourably with his promises.

con·trast² /'kɒntrɑːst US: -ræst/ n 1 [U] the act of contrasting: C~ may make something appear more beautiful than it is when seen alone. 2 [C] difference which is clearly seen when unlike things are put together; something showing such a difference: The ~ between the two brothers is remarkable. By ~ with Harry's marks, Tom's were good.

con·tra·vene /ˌkɒntrə'viːn/ vt 1 act in opposition to; go against (a law, a custom). 2 dispute, attack (a statement, a principle). 3 (of things) conflict with.

con·tra·ven·tion /ˌkɒntrə'venʃən/ n [C,U] (act of) contravening (a law, etc): in ~ of the rules.

con·trib·ute /kən'trɪbjuːt/ vt,vi 1 join with others in giving help, money, etc; give ideas, suggestions, etc: ~ money to a charity/new information on a scientific problem. 2 have a share in; help to bring about: Drink ~d to his ruin. 3 write (articles, etc) and send in (to): Mr Green has ~d (poems) to the magazine for several years.

con·tribu·tor /-tə(r)/, person who contributes.

con·tri·bu·tion /ˌkɒntrɪ'bjuːʃən/ n [U] act of contributing; [C] something contributed: ~s to the relief fund.

con·tribu·tory /kən'trɪbjʊtərɪ US: -tɔːrɪ/ adj 1 helping to bring about: ~ negligence, e g that helped to cause an accident. 2 for which contributions are to be made: a ~ pension scheme.

con·trite /'kɒntraɪt/ adj filled with, showing, deep sorrow for doing wrong.

con·tri·tion /kən'trɪʃən/ n [U] deep sorrow (for sins, etc).

con·triv·ance /kən'traɪvəns/ n 1 [U] act or manner of contriving. 2 [U] capacity to invent: Some things are beyond human ~. 3 [C] something contrived; invention.

con·trive /kən'traɪv/ vt,vi invent; design; find a way of doing or causing (something): to ~ a means of escape from prison.

con·trol /kən'trəʊl/ n 1 [U] power or authority to direct, order, or restrain: Some children lack parental ~, are not kept in order by parents. be in control (of), be in command, in charge. be/get out of control, in a state where authority, etc is lost: The children are/have got out of ~. have/get/keep control (over/of), have, get, keep authority, power, etc: That teacher has no ~ over his class. lose control (of), be unable to manage or contain: lose ~ of one's temper. take control (of), take authority: We must find someone to take ~ of the situation. 2 [U] management; guidance: ~ of traffic/ traffic ~. 3 [C] means of regulating, restraining, keeping in order: Government ~s on trade and industry. ⇨ birth control. 4 [C] standard of comparison for results of an experiment: The tests were given to three groups, one being used as a ~. 5 (usually pl) means by which a machine, etc is operated or regulated: the ~s of an aircraft, for direction, altitude, etc. □ vt (-ll-) 1 have control of; check: to ~ expenditure/one's temper. 2 regulate (prices, etc).

con·trol·lable /-əbəl/ adj that can be controlled.

con·trol·ler /kən'trəʊlə(r)/ n [C] person who controls expenditure and accounts or directs a department of a large organization: the C~ of the B B C.

con·tro·ver·sial /ˌkɒntrə'vɜːʃəl/ adj 1 likely to cause controversy: a ~ speech. 2 (of persons) fond of controversy.

con·tro·ver·sial·ly /-ʃəlɪ/ *adv*

con·tro·ver·sy /ˈkɒntrəvɜːsɪ, kənˈtrɒvəsɪ/ *n* [C,U,] (*pl* **-ies**) prolonged argument, esp over social, moral or political matters: *engage in (a)* ~ *with/against him; a question that has given rise to much* ~.

con·va·lesce /ˈkɒnvəˈles/ *vi* regain health and strength after an illness: *She is convalescing by the sea.*

con·va·les·cence /ˈkɒnvəˈlesəns/ *n* [U] gradual recovery of health and strength.

con·va·les·cent /ˈkɒnvəˈlesənt/ *n* [C], *adj* (person who is) recovering from illness.

con·vec·tion /kənˈvekʃən/ *n* [U] the conveying of heat from one part of a liquid or gas to another by the movement of heated substances.

con·vene /kənˈviːn/ *vt,vi* **1** call (persons) to come together (for a meeting, etc). **2** come together (for a meeting, council, etc).

con·vener, person who convenes meetings.

con·veni·ence /kənˈviːnɪəns/ *n* **1** [U] the quality of being convenient or suitable; freedom from difficulty or worry: *I keep my reference books near my desk for* ~. *Please come at your earliest* ~, at the earliest time suitable to you. **2** [C] appliance, device, arrangement, etc that is useful, helpful or convenient: *The house has all modern* ~s, e g central heating, hot water supply, points for electric current.

con·veni·ent /kənˈviːnɪənt/ *adj* suitable; handy; serving to avoid trouble or difficulty; easy to get to or at: *Will it be* ~ *for you to start work tomorrow?*

con·veni·ent·ly *adv*

con·vent /ˈkɒnvənt US: -vent/ *n* [C] **1** society of women (*nuns*) living apart from others in the service of God. ⇨ monastery. **2** building(s) in which they live and work: *enter a* ~, become a nun.

con·ven·tion /kənˈvenʃən/ *n* **1** [C] conference of members of a society, political party, etc or of persons in business, commerce, etc: *the Democratic Party C*~. **2** [C] agreement between States, rulers, etc (less formal than a treaty): *the Geneva C*~s, about the treatment of prisoners of war, etc. **3** [C] practice or custom based on general consent: *It is silly to be a slave to* ~.

con·ven·tional /kənˈvenʃənəl/ *adj* **1** based on convention(3): ~ *greetings.* **2** following what has been customary; traditional: *a* ~ *design for a carpet.*

con·ven·tion·al·ly /-ʃəlɪ/ *adv*

con·verge /kənˈvɜːdʒ/ *vi,vt* (of lines, moving objects, opinions) come, cause to come, towards each other and meet at a point; tend to do this: *armies converging on the capital.*

con·ver·gence /-dʒəns/ *n* [U]

con·ver·gent /-dʒənt/ *adj*

con·ver·sant /kənˈvɜːsənt/ *adj* (*formal*) having a knowledge of: ~ *with all the rules.*

con·ver·sa·tion /ˈkɒnvəˈseɪʃən/ *n* [U] talk-

ing; [C] talk: *I saw him in* ~ *with a friend. I've had several* ~s *with him.*

con·ver·sa·tional /-nəl/ *adj* (of words, etc) used in, characteristic of, talk.

con·verse[1] /kənˈvɜːs/ *vi* (*formal*) talk.

con·verse[2] /ˈkɒnvɜːs/ *n* [U with the] *adj* (idea, statement which is) opposite (to another).

con·verse·ly *adv*

con·ver·sion /kənˈvɜːʃən US: -ˈvɜːrʒən/ *n* **1** [U] converting or being converted: *the* ~ *of cream into butter/of pagans to Christianity.* **2** [C] instance of this: *building firms which specialize in house* ~s, e g of large houses into flats.

con·vert[1] /ˈkɒnvɜːt/ *n* [C] person converted, esp to a different religion (or from no religion), or to different principles: *a* ~ *to socialism.*

con·vert[2] /kənˈvɜːt/ *vt* **1** change (from one form, use, etc into another): *to* ~ *pounds into francs.* **2** cause (a person) to change his beliefs, etc: *to* ~ *a man to Christianity.* **3** (Rugby football) complete (a try) by kicking a goal.

con·verted *adj* that has been converted: *a* ~*ed house.*

con·vert·ible /kənˈvɜːtəbəl/ *adj* that can be converted: *Banknotes are not usually* ~ *into gold nowadays.*

con·vex /ˈkɒnveks/ *adj* with the surface curved like the outside of a ball: *a* ~ *lens.* ⇨ concave.

con·vey /kənˈveɪ/ *vt* **1** take, carry: *Pipes* ~ *hot water from this boiler to every part of the building.* **2** make known ideas, views, feelings, etc to another person: *This picture will* ~ *to you some idea of the beauty of the scenery.* **3 convey to,** (*legal*) give full legal rights (in land or property): *The land was* ~*ed to his brother.*

con·veyer, -or /-ˈveɪə(r)/, person who, that which, conveys.

ˈconveyer-belt, (e g in a factory) band or chain moving over wheels for carrying packages, etc.

con·vey·ance /kənˈveɪəns/ *n* **1** [U] conveying. **2** [C] something which conveys.

con·vict[1] /ˈkɒnvɪkt/ *n* [C] person convicted of crime and being punished.

con·vict[2] /kənˈvɪkt/ *vt* **1** (of a jury or a judge) declare in a law court that (a person) is guilty: *He was* ~*ed of murder.* **2** cause (a person) to be certain that he has done wrong, made a mistake: ~ *somebody of his errors.*

con·vic·tion /kənˈvɪkʃən/ *n* **1** [U] the convicting of a person for a crime; [C] instance of this: *He has had six previous* ~s. **2** [U] the act of convincing, of bringing certainty to the mind. (*not*) *carry much conviction,* (not) be convincing. **3** [C,U] firm or assured belief: *He spoke with such* ~.

con·vince /kənˈvɪns/ *vt* make (a person) feel certain; cause (a person) to realize: *I am* ~*d of his honesty. We couldn't* ~ *him of his* *mistake.*

con·vinc·ing *adj* that convinces: *a convincing speaker/argument.*

con·vinc·ing·ly *adv*

con·vo·ca·tion /ˈkɒnvəˈkeɪʃən/ *n* **1** [U] calling together. **2** [C] legislative assembly of the Church or of graduates of some universities (e g Leeds, Durham, Oxford).

con·voke /kənˈvəʊk/ *vt* call together, summon (a meeting): *to ~ Parliament.*

con·vol·uted /ˈkɒnvəlutɪd/ *adj* coiled; twisted (e g like a ram's horn).

con·vol·ution /ˈkɒnvəˈluʃən/ *n* [C] coil; twist: *the ~s of a snake.*

con·voy¹ /ˈkɒnvɔɪ/ *n* **1** [U] convoying or being convoyed; protection: *The supply ships sailed under ~.* **2** [C] protecting force (of warships, troops, etc). **3** [C] ship(s), supplies under escort: *The ~ was attacked by submarines.*

con·voy² /ˈkɒnvɔɪ/ *vt* (esp of a warship) go with, escort (other ships) to protect (them): *The troopships were ~ed across the Atlantic.*

con·vulse /kənˈvʌls/ *vt* cause violent movements or disturbances: *~d with laughter; a country ~d by civil war.*

con·vul·sion /kənˈvʌlʃən/ *n* [C] **1** violent disturbance: *a ~ of nature, e g an earthquake.* **2** (usually *pl*) violent irregular movement of a limb or limbs, or of the body, caused by contraction of muscles: *The child's ~s filled us with fear.* **3** (*pl*) violent fit (of laughter): *The story was so funny that we were all in ~s.*

con·vuls·ive /kənˈvʌlsɪv/ *adj* having or producing convulsions: *~ movements.*

coo /ku/ *vi,vt, n* [C] (make a) soft, murmuring sound (as of doves).

cook /kʊk/ *vt,vi* **1** prepare (food) by heating (e g boiling, baking, roasting, frying). **2** be cooked: *These apples ~ well.* **3 cook up**, invent a story, excuse, etc. **4** falsify: *~ the books/the accounts.* □ *n* [C] person who cooks food.

cook·ing *n* [U]

cooker /ˈkʊkə(r)/ *n* **1** apparatus, stove, for cooking food: *a ˈgas-~.* **2** kind of fruit, etc (esp apples, pears, plums) grown for cooking.

cook·ery /ˈkʊkərɪ/ *n* [U] art and practice of cooking.

ˈcookery-book, one with recipes.

cool¹ /kul/ *adj* (-er, -est) **1** between warm and cold: *~ autumn weather. The coffee's not ~ enough to drink.* **2** calm; unexcited: *Keep ~! He was always ~ in the face of danger. He has a ~ head, is not easily excited, etc.* Hence, **ˈcool-ˈheaded** *adj.* **play it cool,** deal calmly with a situation. **3** impudent in a calm way; without shame: *How ~ to take my lawn-mower without asking my permission!* **4** (of behaviour) not showing interest or enthusiasm: *They gave the prime minister a ~ reception.* □ *n* [U

with *the*] cool air or place; coolness: *in the ~ of the evening.*

cool·ly *adv*

cool·ness *n* [U]

cool² /kul/ *vt,vi* make or become cool: *The rain has ~ed the air. Has his anger ~ed yet?* **cool down/off,** (fig) become calm, less excited or enthusiastic: *I told him to ~ down.*

ˈcooling-tower, tall structure like a wide chimney for cooling hot water before reuse.

coop /kup/ *n* [C] cage, esp for hens with small chickens. □ *vt* **coop up,** put in a coop; confine (a person): *How long are we going to stay ~ed up in here?*

co-op /ˈkəʊ ɒp/ *n* **the ~,** (*informal*) the co-operative society (shop, store).

cooper /ˈkupə(r)/ *n* [C] maker of tubs, barrels, casks, etc.

co-op·er·ate /kəʊˈɒpəreɪt/ *vi* work or act together in order to bring about a result: *~ with friends in starting a social club.*

co-op·er·ator, person who co-operates.

co-op·er·ation /kəʊˈɒpəˈreɪʃən/ *n* [U] working or acting together for a common purpose: *The workers, in ~ with the management, have increased output by 10 per cent.*

co-op·er·ative /kəʊˈɒprətɪv/ *adj* of co-operation; willing to co-operate: *a ~ society,* group of persons who co-operate, e g to buy machines and services for all to share, or to produce, buy and sell goods among themselves for mutual benefit, or to save and lend money. □ *n* [C] (shop of a) co-operative society or group: *agricultural ~s in India and China.*

co-opt /kəʊ ˈɒpt/ *vt* (of a committee) add (a person) as a member by the votes of those who are already members: *~ a new member on to the committee.*

co-or·di·nate¹ /ˈkəʊˈɔːdənət/ *adj* equal in importance. □ *n* [C] co-ordinate thing or person.

co-or·di·nate² /ˈkəʊˈɔːdəneɪt/ *vt* make co-ordinate; bring or put into proper relation: *to ~ the movements of the arms and legs.*

co-or·di·na·tion /ˈkəʊˈɔːdənˈeɪʃən/ *n* [C] act of co-ordinating; state of being co-ordinate.

coot /kut/ *n* [C] name of several kinds of swimming and diving birds. **as bald as a coot,** very bald.

cop¹ /kɒp/ *n* [C] (*sl*) = policeman.

cop² /kɒp/ *vt* (-pp-) (*sl*) catch: *You'll ~ it,* be punished. □ *n* [C] (*sl*) capture.

co-part·ner /ˈkəʊ ˈpɑːtnə(r)/ *n* [C] partner, e g an employee, who has a share in the profits of a business, etc in addition to his salary or wages.

co-part·ner·ship /-ʃɪp/ *n* [C] such a system, practice, in business or industry.

cope /kəʊp/ *vi* manage successfully; be equal to: *coping with difficulties.*

cop·ing /ˈkəʊpɪŋ/ *n* [C] line of (sometimes overhanging) stonework or brickwork on top of a wall.

`coping-stone, (*fig*) final act, finishing, of a piece of work.

copi·ous /ˈkəʊpɪəs/ *adj* plentiful: *a ~ supply/meal*.

copi·ous·ly *adv*

cop·per[1] /ˈkɒpə(r)/ *n* 1 [U] common reddish-brown metal (symbol Cu): *~ wire/cable/alloy*. 2 [C] coin made of copper (alloy). 3 [C] large vessel made of metal, esp one in which clothes are boiled. ⇨ boiler(1). 4 [U] reddish-brown colour. □ *adj* reddish-brown.

`copper beech, kind of beech with copper-coloured leaves.

'copper-'bottomed *adj* (a) (of a ship) having the bottom plated with copper (and therefore seaworthy). (b) (*fig*) safe in every way: *~-bottomed guarantees*.

`copper-plate *n* [U] polished copper plate on which designs, etc, are engraved. □ *adj* ornate, round and clear.

`copper-smith, person who works in copper.

cop·per[2] /ˈkɒpə(r)/ *n* [C] (*sl*) policeman.

copra /ˈkɒprə/ *n* [U] dried kernels of coconuts, from which oil is extracted for making soap, etc.

copse /kɒps/ *n* [C] small area of shrubs and small trees.

copu·late /ˈkɒpjʊleɪt/ *vi* (esp of animals) unite in sexual intercourse.

copu·la·tion /ˌkɒpjʊˈleɪʃən/ *n* [C,U] act or process of copulating.

copy[1] /ˈkɒpɪ/ *n* [C] (*pl* -ies) 1 thing made to be like another; reproduction of a letter, picture, etc: *Make three carbon copies of the letter*. 2 one example of a book, newspaper, etc of which many have been made: *If you can't buy a ~ of the book, perhaps you can borrow one from the library*. 3 [U] material to be sent to a printer: *The printers are waiting for more ~*.

`copy-cat, (*informal*) person who copies another person's actions, ideas, etc.

copy[2] /ˈkɒpɪ/ *vt,vi* (*pt,pp* -ied) 1 make a copy of: *~ notes (out of a book, etc)*; *~ an address down (from a notice-board)*. 2 do, try to do, the same as; imitate: *You should ~ his good example*. 3 cheat (by looking at a neighbour's paper, etc): *He was punished for ~ing during the examination*.

copy·right /ˈkɒpɪraɪt/ *n* [U] sole legal right, held for a certain number of years, by the author or composer of a work, or by someone delegated by him, to print, publish, sell, broadcast, film or record his work or any part of it. □ *vt* protect in this way.

coral /ˈkɒrəl US: ˈkɔːrəl/ *n* [U] 1 hard, red, pink or white substance built on the seabed by small creatures. 2 red or pink colour. □ *adj* red or pink: *~ lips*.

'coral 'island, one formed by the growth of coral.

`coral-reef, one of coral.

cord /kɔːd/ *n* 1 [C,U] (length of) twisted strands, thicker than string, thinner than rope. 2 [C] part of the body like a cord: *the spinal ~; the vocal ~s*. □ *vt* put a cord round.

cor·dial /ˈkɔːdɪəl/ *adj* 1 warm and sincere (in feeling, behaviour): *a ~ smile*. 2 strongly felt: *~ dislike*. 3 (of food and drink, or medicine) making the heart beat faster.

cord·ially /-ɪəlɪ/ *adv*

cor·don /ˈkɔːdən/ *n* [C] 1 line, ring, persons, military posts, etc acting as guards: *a po`lice ~*. 2 ornamental ribbon of an Order[1](10) (usually worn across the shoulder). □ *vt cordon off*, separate, keep at a distance, by means of a cordon(1).

cor·du·roy /ˈkɔːdərɔɪ/ *n* [U] thick, cotton cloth with raised lines on it.

core /kɔː(r)/ *n* [C] 1 (usually hard) centre, with seeds, of such fruits as the apple and pear. 2 central or most important part of anything: *the ~ of an electro-magnet*. *to the core*, thoroughly: *He is English to the ~*, completely English in manner, speech, dress, etc. *rotten to the core*, (*fig*) thoroughly bad. □ *vt* take out the core of: *to ~ an apple*.

cork /kɔːk/ *n* 1 [U] light, brown, tough substance, the thick outer bark of the tree called the `cork-oak. 2 [C] round piece of this material used as a stopper for a bottle. □ *vt* stop with, or as with, a cork.

`cork-screw, tool for pulling corks from bottles.

corn[1] /kɔːn/ *n* 1 [U] (seed of) any of various grain plants, chiefly wheat, oats, rye and (esp US) maize; such plants while growing: *a field of ~; a `~-field*. 2 [C] single grain (of wheat, pepper, etc).

`corn-cob, part of an ear of maize, on which the grains grow.

`corn-flour (US `corn-starch), flour made from maize, rice or other grains.

corn[2] /kɔːn/ *n* [C] small area of hardened skin on the foot, esp on a toe, often with a painful centre and root. *tread on sb's corns*, (*fig*) hurt his feelings.

cor·nea /ˈkɔːnɪə/ *n* [C] (*pl ~s*) tough transparent covering for the iris of the eyeball.

cor·ner /ˈkɔːnə(r)/ *n* [C] 1 (position of the) angle where two lines, sides, edges or surfaces meet: *a shop on/at the ~; sitting in the ~ of the room*. *cut corners*, (a) (of the driver of a motor-vehicle) go across, not round them when travelling fast. (b) (*fig*) simplify proceedings, ignore regulations, etc to get work done quickly: *We've had to cut a few ~s to get your visa ready in time*. *turn the corner*, (*fig*) pass a critical point in an illness, a period of difficulty, etc. *just round the corner*, very near (in position, time, etc.). *be in a tight corner*, in an awkward or difficult situation. 2 hidden, secret, place: *money hidden in odd ~s*. 3 region;

quarter: *to the four ~s of the earth.* **5** (in Association football) kick from the corner of the field, allowed when the ball has been kicked by an opponent over his own goal-line. □ *vt,vi* **1** force into a corner; put into a difficult position: *The escaped prisoner was ~ed at last.* **2** (of a vehicle, its driver) turn a corner (on a road, etc): *My new car ~s/ takes ~s well.*

`corner-stone, (a)` stone forming a corner of a foundation for a building. **(b)** (*fig*) foundation: *Charm was the ~stone of his success.*

cor·net /`kɔnɪt/ *n* [C] **1** small musical instrument of brass, like a trumpet. **2** piece of paper, biscuit, etc twisted into the shape of a cone, to hold ice-cream, etc.

cor·nice /`kɔnɪs/ *n* [C] **1** projecting part above the frieze in a column(1); ornamental moulding (e g in plaster) round the walls of a room, just below the ceiling; horizontal strip of carved wood or stone along an outside wall. **2** overhanging mass of snow above a precipice.

corny /`kɔnɪ/ *adj* (-ier, -iest) (*sl*) dull because often heard or repeated: *~ jokes/ music.*

co·rol·lary /kə`rɒlərɪ US:* `kɔrəlerɪ/ *n* [C] (*pl -ies*) natural sequence or obvious outcome.

co·rona /kə`rəʊnə/ *n* [C] (*pl ~s, ~e* /-niː/) ring of light seen round the sun or moon, e g during an eclipse.

cor·on·ary /`kɔrənrɪ US:* `kɔrənerɪ/ *adj* of arteries supplying blood to the heart: *~ thrombosis,* formation of a clot in a coronary artery. □ *n* [C] (*pl-ies*) (*informal*) coronary thrombosis.

cor·on·ation /`kɔrə`neɪʃən US:* `kɔr-/ *n* [C] ceremony of crowning a king, queen or other sovereign ruler.

cor·oner /`kɔrənə(r) US:* `kɔr-/ *n* [C] official who inquires the cause of any death thought to be from violent or unnatural causes: *~'s inquest,* such an inquiry (held with a jury).

cor·onet /`kɔrənet US:* `kɔr-/ *n* [C] small crown worn by a peer or peeress; band of precious materials worn as (part of) a woman's head-dress; garland of flowers.

cor·poral¹ /`kɔprəl/ *adj* of the human body: *~ punishment,* e g whipping, beating.

cor·poral² /`kɔprəl/ *n* [C] lowest non-commissioned officer (below a sergeant) in the army.

cor·por·ate /`kɔpərət/ *adj* **1** of or belonging to a corporation(2): *~ property.* **2** of, shared by, members of a group of persons: *~ responsibility/action.* **3** united in one group: *a ~ body.*

cor·por·ation /`kɔpə`reɪʃən/ *n* [C] **1** group of persons elected to govern a town: *the municipal ~.* **2** group of persons authorized to act as an individual, e g for business purposes: *In Great Britain the Electricity Authority and the National Coal Board are*

public ~s.

cor·por·eal /kɔ`pɔrɪəl/ *adj* (*formal*) **1** of or for the body. **2** physical (contrasted with *spiritual*).

corps /kɔ(r)/ *n* [C] (*pl ~ /kɔz/*) **1** one of the technical branches of an army: *the 'Royal 'Army `Medical C~.* **2** military force made up of two or more divisions.

`corps de 'ballet, (*Fr*) company of dancers in a ballet.

the 'Corps 'Diploma'tique, (*Fr*) all the ambassadors, ministers and attachés of foreign states at a capital or Court.

corpse /kɔps/ *n* [C] dead body (esp of a human being).

cor·pu·lent /`kɔpjulənt/ *adj* (*formal*) (of a person or his body) fat and heavy.

cor·pus /`kɔpəs/ *n* [C] (*pl* corpora /`kɔpərə/*) body, collection, esp of writings on a specified subject or of material for study (e g for linguists, a collection of examples of spoken and written usages).

cor·puscle /`kɔpʌsəl/ *n* [C] one of the red or white cells in the blood.

cor·ral /kə`rɑl US:* -`ræl/ *n* [C] enclosure for horses and cattle or the capture of wild animals. □ *vt* (-ll-) drive (cattle, etc) into, shut up in, a corral.

cor·rect¹ /kə`rekt/ *adj* **1** true; right: *the ~ time.* **2** (of conduct, manners, dress, etc) proper; in accord with good taste or convention: *the ~ dress for a ceremony.*

cor·rect·ly *adv*

cor·rect·ness *n* [U]

cor·rect² /kə`rekt/ *vt* **1** make right; take out mistakes from: *Please ~ my pronunciation.* **2** point out the faults of; punish: *~ a child for disobedience.*

cor·rec·tion /kə`rekʃən/ *n* **1** [U] correcting: *the ~ of schoolchildren's work.* **2** [C] something put in place of what is wrong: *a written exercise with ~s in red ink.*

cor·rect·ive /kə`rektɪv/ *n, adj* (something) serving to correct: *~ training,* e g for young offenders.

cor·re·late /`kɔrəleɪt US:* `kɔr-/ *vt,vi* have a mutual relation, bring (one thing) into such a relation (with another): *Research workers find it hard to ~ the two sets of figures/to ~ one set with the other.*

cor·re·la·tion /`kɔrɪ`leɪʃən US:* `kɔr-/ *n* [C] mutual relationship: *the ~ between climate and vegetation.*

cor·re·spond /`kɔrɪ`spɒnd US:* `kɔr-/ *vi* be in harmony: *His actions do not ~ with his words.* **2** correspond to, be equal (to); be similar (in position, etc) (to): *The American Congress ~s to the British Parliament.* **3** exchange letters: *We've been ~ing with each other for years.*

cor·re·spond·ing *adj* that correspond(s)(1): *Imports for 1—10 July this year are larger by 10 per cent than for the ~ing period last year.*

cor·re·spond·ing·ly *adv*

cor·re·spon·dence /ˈkɒrɪˈspɒndəns US: ˈkɔr-/ n 1 [C,U] agreement; similarity: *There is not much ∼ between their ideals and ours.* 2 [U] letter-writing; letters: *I have been in ∼ with him about the problem.*

cor·re·spon·dent /ˈkɒrɪˈspɒndənt US: ˈkɔr-/ n [C] 1 person with whom one exchanges letters: *He's a good/bad ∼, writes regularly/seldom.* 2 person regularly contributing local news or special articles to a newspaper: *a ∼war–∼.*

cor·ri·dor /ˈkɒrɪdɔː(r) US: ˈkɔr-/ n [C] long narrow passages from which doors open into rooms or compartments.

cor·rob·or·ate /kəˈrɒbəreɪt/ vt give support or certainty to (a statement, belief, theory, etc).

cor·rob·or·at·ive /kəˈrɒbəreɪtɪv/ adj tending to corroborate: *∼ evidence.*

cor·rode /kəˈrəʊd/ vt,vi wear away, destroy slowly by chemical action or disease; be worn away thus: *Rust ∼s iron.*

cor·ro·sion /kəˈrəʊʒən/ n [U] corroding or being corroded.

cor·ros·ive /kəˈrəʊsɪv/ n [C], adj (substance) that corrodes: *Rust and acids are ∼.*

cor·ru·gate /ˈkɒrəgeɪt US: ˈkɔr-/ vt,vi make into folds, wrinkles or furrows: *∼d cardboard,* used for packing fragile goods.

cor·ru·ga·tion /ˈkɒrəˈgeɪʃən US: ˈkɔr-/ n [C,U] fold(s); wrinkle(s).

cor·rupt¹ /kəˈrʌpt/ adj 1 (of persons, their actions) immoral; dishonest (esp through taking bribes): *∼ practices,* (esp) the offering and accepting of bribes. 2 impure: *∼ air/blood.* 3 (of languages, texts, etc) debased by errors or alterations: *a ∼ form of English.*

cor·rupt·ly adv

cor·rupt·ness n [U]

cor·rupt² /kəˈrʌpt/ vt,vi make or become corrupt: *young persons whose morals have been ∼ed.*

cor·rupt·ible /-əbəl/ adj that can be corrupted: *∼ible government officials.*

cor·rup·tion /kəˈrʌpʃən/ [U] corrupting or or being corrupt; decay: *the ∼ of the body after death; the ∼ of a language.*

cor·set /ˈkɔːsɪt/ n [C] close-fitting reinforced undergarment confining the waist and hips, to shape the body to the current style.

cor·tege, cor·tège /kɔːˈteɪʒ/ n [C] (Fr) procession, e g at the funeral of a king or president.

cor·tex /ˈkɔːteks/ n [C] (pl cortices /ˈkɔːtɪsiːz/) 1 outer layer of grey matter of the brain. 2 outer shell or covering (e g the bark of a tree).

cor·ti·cal /ˈkɔːtɪkəl/ adj of the cortex.

cos¹ /kɒs/ n [C] (kind of) long-leaved lettuce.

cosh /kɒʃ/ vt, n [C] (GB sl) (strike with a) length of lead pipe, flexible rubber tubing filled with metal, etc.

co-sig·na·tory /ˈkəʊ ˈsɪgnətrɪ US: -tɔːrɪ/

adj, n [C] (pl -ies) (person) signing jointly with others.

cos·metic /kɒzˈmetɪk/ adj, n [C] preparation, substance, esp one that adds colour, designed to make the skin or hair beautiful, e g face-cream, lipstick.

cos·mic /ˈkɒzmɪk/ adj of the whole universe or cosmos: *∼ rays,* radiations that reach the earth from outer space.

cos·mo·naut /ˈkɒzmənɔːt/ n [C] = astronaut (the usual word).

cos·mo·poli·tan /ˈkɒzməˈpɒlɪtən/ adj 1 of or from all, or many different parts of, the world: *the ∼ gatherings at the United Nations Assembly.* 2 free from national prejudices because of wide experience of the world: *a statesman with a ∼ outlook.* □ n [C] cosmopolitan(2) person.

cos·mos /ˈkɒzmɒs/ n the ∼, the universe, all space, seen as a well-ordered system.

cost¹ /kɒst US: kɔːst/ n 1 [C,U] price (to be) paid for a thing: *the ∼ of living. He built his house without regard to ∼,* without considering how much money would be needed. 2 that which is used, needed or given to obtain something: *The battle was won at a great ∼ in human lives.* **at all costs,** whatever the cost(2) may be. **count the cost,** consider the risks, possible losses, etc. **to one's cost,** to one's loss or disadvantage: *Wasps' stings are serious, as I know to my ∼,* as I know because of personal suffering from them. 3 (pl) (legal) expense of having an action settled in a law court: *He had to pay a £10 fine and £3 ∼s.*

cost² /kɒst US: kɔːst/ vi (pt,pp ∼) 1 be obtainable at the price of; require the payment of: *The house ∼ him £8 000.* 2 result in the loss of: *Careless driving may ∼ you your life.* 3 bring injury or disadvantage: *The boy's bad behaviour ∼ his mother many sleepless nights.* □ vt (pt,pp ∼ed) estimate the price to be charged for an article based on the expense of producing it.

co-star /ˈkəʊ ˈstɑː(r)/ vi,vt (-rr-) present one film star as having equal status with another or others: *The film ∼red John Wayne.*

cos·ter·monger /ˈkɒstəmʌŋgə(r)/ n [C] person who sells fruit, vegetables, etc from a barrow in the street.

cost·ly /ˈkɒstlɪ US: ˈkɔːst-/ adj (-ier, -iest) of great value; costing much: *a ∼ mistake,* one involving great loss or sacrifice.

cos·tume /ˈkɒstjuːm US: -tuːm/ n 1 [U] style of dress: *actors wearing historical ∼,* clothes in the style of a period in the past. 2 [C] woman's suit (short coat and skirt of the same material). ⇨ swimming costume.

cosy¹ /ˈkəʊzɪ/ adj (-ier, -iest) warm and comfortable: *a ∼ little room.*

cosily /-əlɪ/ adv

cosi·ness n [U]

cosy² /ˈkəʊzɪ/ n [C] covering for a teapot, or an egg in an egg cup.

cot¹ /kɒt/ n [C] 1 bed for a young child (usually with sides to prevent the child from falling out). **2** (*US*) camp-bed; bunk bed on board ship.

cot² /kɒt/ *n* [C] small building for sheltering animals: *a* ~ *sheep-*~.

cote /kəʊt/ *n* [C] shed or shelter for domestic animals or birds: *a* `dove-`~.

cot·tage /ˈkɒtɪdʒ/ *n* [C] small house, esp in the country: *farm labourers'* ~*s*; ~ *industries*, those that can be carried on in ~s, e g pottery, some kinds of weaving.

cot·ton /ˈkɒtən/ *n* [U] **1** soft, white fibrous substance round the seeds of the `cotton-plant`, used for making thread, cloth, etc: ~ *yarn/cloth*. **2** thread spun from cotton: *a* `needle and ` ~.

`cotton-`wool, cleaned raw cotton; absorbent cotton as used for padding, bandaging, etc.

couch¹ /kaʊtʃ/ *n* [C] **1** long bed-like seat for sitting on or lying on during the day: *a studio-*~. **2** (*literary*) bed.

couch² /kaʊtʃ/ *vt,vi* **1** (*formal*) put (a thought, etc, in words): *The reply was* ~*ed in insolent terms.* **2** (of animals) lie flat (either in hiding, or ready for a jump forward).

cou·gar /ˈkuːɡə(r)/ *n* [C] large wild cat, also called a *puma*.

cough¹ /kɒf *US*: kɔːf/ *n* [C] **1** act or sound of coughing: *He gave me a warning* ~. **2** condition, illness, that causes a person to cough often: *to have a bad* ~.

cough² /kɒf *US*: kɔːf/ *vi,vt* **1** send out air from the lungs violently and noisily. **2** **cough up**, get out of the throat by coughing. **3** (*sl*) confess a crime, esp to the police: *Jones refused to* ~.

could /kʊd *weak form* kəd/ (*negative* ~*n't* /ˈkʊdənt/) *auxiliary verb*; *pt* of *can*, used in indirect speech in place of *can* if the main verb is *pt*; used to express conditions, and to express occasional occurrence and inclination. ⇨ **can**.

coun·cil /ˈkaʊnsəl/ *n* [C] group of persons appointed, elected or chosen to give advice, make rules, and carry out plans, manage affairs, etc, esp of government: *a city/county* ~; *the municipal* ~.

`council-chamber`, in which a council meets.

`council estate`, housing estate built by a city, county, etc council. ⇨ **housing**.

`council-house`, house on a council estate.

coun·cil·lor (*US* also **coun·cil·or**) /ˈkaʊnsələ(r)/ *n* [C] member of a council.

coun·sel¹ /ˈkaʊnsəl/ *n* **1** [U] advice; consultation; opinions; suggestions. **2** *a* ~/~*s of perfection*, excellent advice that cannot be followed. **3** [C] (*pl* unchanged) barrister, or group of barristers, giving advice in a law case: *when the jury had heard* ~ *on both sides*, the barristers for the prosecution and the defence.

coun·sel² /ˈkaʊnsəl/ *vt* (*-ll-*, *US* also *-l-*)

(*formal*) advise: *to* ~ *patience.*

coun·sel·lor (*US* also **coun·sel·or**) /ˈkaʊnsələ(r)/ *n* [C] adviser.

count¹ /kaʊnt/ *n* **1** [C] act of counting; number got by counting: *Four* ~*s were necessary before we were certain of the total.* **2** [U] (*legal*) one of a number of things of which a person has been accused: *He was found guilty on all* ~*s.*

count² /kaʊnt/ *vt,vi* **1** say or name (the numerals) in order: *to* ~ *from 1 to 10. He can't* ~ *yet.* **2** find the total of: *Don't forget to* ~ *your change.* **3** include, be included, in the calculation: *fifty people, not* ~*ing the children.* **4** consider to be: *I* ~ *myself fortunate in being here.* **5** **count (sth) against sb**, be considered, consider, to the disadvantage of: *He is young and inexperienced, but please do not* ~ *that against him.*

6 (uses with *adverbial particles* and *prepositions*):

count down, count seconds backwards (e g 10, 9, 8, 7...) as when launching a rocket, etc into space. Hence, `count-down` *n* [C]

count in, include: *If you're all going to the pub for a drink, you can* ~ *me in.*

count on/upon, expect with confidence; rely on: *We are* ~*ing on you to help.*

count out, **(a)** count things (slowly), one by one: *The old lady* ~*ed out fifteen pence and passed it to the salesgirl.* **(b)** count up to ten over a boxer who has been knocked out: *The referee* ~*ed him out in the first round.* **(c)** not include: *If it's going to be a drunken party*, ~ *me out.*

count up, find the total of: *Just you* ~ *up the number of times he has failed to keep a promise!*

count³ /kaʊnt/ *n* [C] title of nobility in France, Italy, etc (but not in GB).

count·able /ˈkaʊntəbəl/ *adj* that can be counted.

countable noun, one that may be used with *a*, *an* or *many* and with numerals and the plural form.

coun·ten·ance¹ /ˈkaʊntɪnəns/ *n* (*formal*) **1** [C] face, including its appearance and expression: *a woman with a fierce* ~. **2** [U] support; approval: *to give* ~ *to a person/a plan.*

coun·ten·ance² /ˈkaʊntɪnəns/ *vt* (*formal*) give support or approval to: *to* ~ *a fraud.*

coun·ter¹ /ˈkaʊntə(r)/ *n* [C] table or flat surface on which goods are shown, customers served, in a shop or bank. **under the counter**, (of goods in shops or business dealings) bought, sold or arranged dishonestly.

coun·ter² /ˈkaʊntə(r)/ *n* [C] **1** small (round) flat piece of plastic, etc used for keeping count in games, etc. **2** (in compounds) device for keeping count (in machinery, etc): *a* `speed-`~.

coun·ter³ /ˈkaʊntə(r)/ *adv* **counter to**, in the opposite direction (to); in opposition (to): *to act ~ to a person's wishes.*

coun·ter⁴ /ˈkaʊntə(r)/ *vt, vi* oppose; meet an attack (with a return attack): *They ~ed our proposal with one of their own.*

coun·ter- /ˈkaʊntə(r)-/ *prefix* **1** opposite in direction: ¹*counter-pro`ductive.* **2** made in answer to: `*counter-attack.* **3** corresponding: `*counterpart.*

coun·ter·act /ˌkaʊntəˈrækt/ *vt* act against and make (action, force) of less or no effect: *~ (the effects of) a poison.*

coun·ter-at·tack /ˈkaʊntər ətæk/ *n* [C] attack made in reply to an attack by the enemy. □ *vt, vi* make such an attack.

coun·ter·bal·ance /ˈkaʊntəbæləns/ *n* [C] weight, force, equal to another and balancing it. □ *vt* /ˈkaʊntəˈbæləns/ act as a counterbalance to.

coun·ter·clock·wise /ˈkaʊntə ˈklɒkwaɪz/ *adv* (*dated*) = anti-clockwise.

coun·ter·espion·age /ˈkaʊntər ˈespiənaʒ/ *n* [U] spying directed against the enemy's spying.

coun·ter·feit /ˈkaʊntəfɪt/ *n* [C], *adj* (something) made or done in imitation of another thing in order to deceive: *~ money.* □ *vt* copy (coins, handwriting, etc) in order to deceive.

coun·ter·foil /ˈkaʊntəfɔɪl/ *n* [C] section of a cheque, receipt, etc kept by the sender as a record.

coun·ter-in·tel·li·gence /ˈkaʊntər ɪnˈtelɪdʒəns/ *n* [U] = counter-espionage.

coun·ter·mand /ˈkaʊntəˈmɑːnd *US:* -ˈmænd/ *vt* take back, cancel, a command already given.

coun·ter·offer /ˈkaʊntərɒfə(r)/ *n* [C] offer made in reply to an offer.

coun·ter·pane /ˈkaʊntəpeɪn/ *n* [C] (*dated*) bedspread.

coun·ter·part /ˈkaʊntəpɑːt/ *n* [C] person or thing exactly like, or closely corresponding to, another.

coun·ter·plot /ˈkaʊntəplɒt/ *n* [C] plot made to defeat another plot. □ *vt, vi* (-tt-) make such a plot.

coun·ter·rev·ol·ution /ˈkaʊntə ˈrevəˈluʃən/ *n* [C] political movement directed against a revolution.

'**coun·ter-'rev·o'l·ution·ary** *adj* characteristic of a counter-revolution. □ *n* [C] (*pl* -ies) supporter of counter-revolution(s).

coun·ter·sign /ˈkaʊntəsaɪn/ *n* [C] password; secret word(s) to be given, on demand, to a sentry: '*Advance and give the ~*'. □ *vt* add another signature to (a document) to give it authority.

count·ess /ˈkaʊntɪs/ *n* [C] **1** wife or widow of a count or earl. **2** woman to whom an earldom has descended.

count·less /ˈkaʊntləs/ *adj* that cannot be counted (because too numerous).

coun·tri·fied /ˈkʌntrɪfaɪd/ *adj* rural; having the unsophisticated ways, habits, outlook, etc of those who live in the country(4), not

of towns.

coun·try /ˈkʌntrɪ/ *n* (*pl* -ies) **1** [C] land occupied by a nation: *European countries.* **2** [C] land of a person's birth or citizenship: *to return to one's own ~.* **3 the ~,** the people of a country(1); the nation as a whole: *Does the ~ want war?* **4 the ~,** land used for farming, land consisting of open spaces, etc; the contrary of town and suburb: *to live in the ~.* **5** area of land (esp considered with reference to its physical or geographical features): *We passed through miles of densely wooded ~.* (*Note:* used without *a* or *the.*) **6** (as an *adjective*) of or in the country(4): *~ life; ~ roads.*

coun·try·man /ˈkʌntrɪmən/, **coun·try·woman** /ˈkʌntrɪwʊmən/ *n* [C] (*pl* -men, -women) **1** person living in the country(4). **2** person of one's own (or a specified) country(1).

coun·try·side /ˈkʌntrɪsaɪd/ *n* [U] rural area(s) (contrasted with urban areas): *The English ~ looks its best in May and June.*

county /ˈkaʊntɪ/ *n* (*pl* -ies) **1** [C] division of GB, the largest unit of local government: *the ~ of Kent; the home counties,* those round London. **2** (in US and other countries) subdivision of a State.

county council, body of persons elected to administer a county.

coup /kuː/ *n* [C] (*pl* ~s /kuːz/) (*Fr*) **1** sudden action taken to get power, obtain a desired result, etc: *He made/pulled off a great ~,* succeeded in what he attempted. **2** = coup d'état.

coup d'état /ˈkuː deɪˈtɑː/, *n* [C] violent or unconstitutional change in government.

coupé /ˈkuːpeɪ *US:* kuːˈpeɪ/ *n* [C] (*pl* ~s) roofed two-door motor-car with a sloping back.

couple¹ /ˈkʌpəl/ *n* [C] **1** two persons or things, seen together or associated: *He came back with a ~ of rabbits and a hare.* **2** man and his wife: *married ~s;* partners in a dance, relationship, etc: *They make a handsome ~.*

couple² /ˈkʌpəl/ *vt, vi* **1** fasten, join (two things) together: *We ~ the name of Oxford with the idea of learning.* **2** marry; (of animals) unite sexually; (of things) come together; unite.

coup·let /ˈkʌplət/ *n* [C] two successive lines of verse, equal in length and with rhyme.

coup·ling /ˈkʌplɪŋ/ *n* **1** [U] act of joining. **2** [C] link, etc that joins two parts, esp two railway coaches or other vehicles.

cou·pon /ˈkuːpɒn/ *n* [C] **1** ticket, part of a document, paper, bond, etc, which gives the holder the right to receive or do something, e g a voucher given with a purchase to be exchanged for goods. **2** entry form for a competition; form(7) in a newspaper, etc for buying by post, obtaining brochures, etc: *Fill in the ~ below and send it to...*

cour·age /ˈkʌrɪdʒ *US:* ˈkɜr-/ *n* [U] quality

that enables a person to control fear in the face of danger, pain, misfortune, etc: *take* ~, *be brave*.

cou·ra·geous /kəˈreɪdʒəs/ *adj* brave; fearless: *It was ~ of him to chase the gunman.*
cou·ra·geous·ly *adv*

cour·gette /kʊəˈʒet/ *n* (*US* = *zucchini*) small green marrow(3) eaten as a vegetable.

cour·ier /ˈkʊrɪə(r)/ *n* [C] **1** person who is paid to attend to details of travel (e g buying tickets, arranging for hotels, etc) and (sometimes) accompanying travellers. **2** messenger carrying news or important government papers.

course¹ /kɔːs/ *n* **1** [U] forward movement in space or time: *a river in its ~ to the sea; the ~ of events. In due course*, in the natural order; at the normal time: *Sow the seed now and in due ~ you will have the flowers. In the course of*, during: *in the ~ of conversation.* **2** [C] direction taken by something; line along which something moves; line of action: *a map that shows the ~s of the chief rivers; The ship is on/off (her) right ~*, is going/not going in the right direction. *The ~ of the argument suddenly changed*, went in a different direction. *The disease must run its ~*. *(as) a matter of course*, that which one would expect to be or happen, for which no effort is needed: *You needn't ask him to come; he'll come as a matter of ~.* *of course*, naturally; certainly: *'Do you study hard?' 'Of ~ I do'.* **3** [C] ground for games, sport: *a `golf-~; a `race-~.* **4** [C] series of talks, treatments, etc: *a ~ of lectures; a ~ of X-ray treatment.* **5** [C] continuous layer of brick, stone, etc in a wall: *a `damp-~.* **6** [C] one of the several parts of a meal, e g soup, fish, dessert: *a five-~ dinner; the main ~.*

course² /kɔːs/ *vt,vi* chase (esp hares) with greyhounds. **2** move quickly; (of liquids) run: *The blood ~d through his veins.*

cours·ing /ˈkɔːsɪŋ/ *n* [U] sport of chasing hares with greyhounds (by sight, not scent).

court¹ /kɔːt/ *n* **1** [C] place where legal cases are held; the judges, magistrates, and other officers who administer justice: *a `~ of `law/a `law ~; a `~-room. The prisoner was brought to ~ for trial.* **2** (residence of a) great ruler, king, queen, emperor, his family and officials, councillors, etc; state gathering or reception given by a ruler: *The C~ went into mourning when the Queen's uncle died.* **3** [C] space marked out for certain games: *a `tennis-~.*
`court-card, playing card with a king, queen or Jack.
`court-yard, unroofed space with walls or buildings round it.

court² /kɔːt/ *vt,vi* **1** try to win the affections of, with a view to marriage: *He had been ~ing Jane for six months. There were several ~ing couples in the park.* **2** try to win or obtain: *to ~ a person's approval/*

support. **3** act in such a way that one may meet or receive (something disagreeable): *That would be ~ing disaster.*

cour·teous /ˈkɜːtjəs/ *adj* having, showing, good manners; polite and kind (to).
cour·teous·ly *adv*

cour·tesy /ˈkɜːtəsɪ/ *n* (*pl* -ies) **1** [U] courteous behaviour. **2** [C] courteous act. **3** *by courtesy of*, by favour or permission, usually free of charge: *a radio programme presented by ~ of...*

court·ier /ˈkɔːtɪə(r)/ *n* [C] person in attendance at the court of a sovereign: *the King and his ~s.*

court·ly /ˈkɔːtlɪ/ *adj* (-ier, -iest) (*formal*) polite and dignified.

court-mar·tial /ˈkɔːt ˈmɑːʃəl/ *n* [C] (*pl* courts-martial) court for trying offences against military law; such a trial. □ *vt* (-ll-) try (a person) in a court of this kind.

court·ship /ˈkɔːtʃɪp/ *n* [U] courting(1); [C] period during which this lasts: *after a brief ~.*

cousin /ˈkʌzən/ *n* [C] (*first* ~), child of one's uncle or aunt; *second* ~, child of one's parent's first cousin.

cove /kəʊv/ *n* [C] small bay².

cov·en·ant /ˈkʌvənənt/ *n* [C] **1** (*legal*) formal agreement that is legally binding. **2** undertaking to make regular payments to a charity, trust, etc. □ *vt,vi* make a covenant.

Cov·en·try /ˈkɒvəntrɪ/ *n* *send a person to Coventry*, refuse to associate with him.

cover² /ˈkʌvə(r)/ *n* **1** [C] thing that covers: *Some chairs are fitted with loose ~s.* **2** [C] binding of a book, magazine, etc; back or front half of this: *The book needs a new ~. from cover to cover*, from beginning to end: *The child read the book from ~ to ~.* **3** [C] wrapper or envelope. *under separate cover*, in a separate parcel or envelope. **4** [U] place or area giving shelter or protection: *There was nowhere where we could take ~*, e g from rain. *take cover*, place oneself where one is concealed or protected from enemy fire. **5** [U] woods or undergrowth protecting animals, etc. **6** [U] *under cover of*, with a pretence of: *under ~ of friendship/darkness.* **7** [U] force of aircraft protecting a land or sea operation. **8** insurance against loss, damage, etc: *Does your policy provide adequate ~ against fire?*

cover² /ˈkʌvə(r)/ *vt* **1** place (one substance or thing) over or in front of (another); hide or protect (something) in this way; lie or extend over; occupy the surface of: *C~ the table with a cloth. Snow ~ed the ground. He laughed to ~ (= hide) his nervousness. cover up*, wrap up: *C~ yourself up well.* Put on warm clothes, etc. *How can we ~ up our tracks/our mistakes?* **2** *be covered with*, (a) have a great number or amount of: *trees ~ed with blossom/fruit.* (b) have as a natural coat: *Cats are ~ed with fur.* (c) be overcome by: *~ed with shame/confusion.* **3**

sprinkle or strew with: *The table is ~ed with/in dust.* **4** bring on oneself: *~ oneself with glory/honour/disgrace.* **5** protect: *He ~ed his wife from the man's blows with his own body. Are you ~ed*(= insured) *against fire and theft?* **6** travel (a certain distance): *By sunset we had ~ed thirty miles.* **7** keep a gun aimed at a person (so that he cannot shoot or escape): *Keep them ~ed!* **8** (of guns, fortresses, etc) command(6); dominate: *Our heavy artillery ~ed every possible approach to the town.* **9** (of money) be enough for: *We have only just ~ed our expenses,* made enough for our expenses, but no profit. **10** include; extend over; be adequate for: *His researches ~ed a wide field. This book does not fully ~ the subject,* does not deal with all aspects of it. **11** (in games such as cricket and baseball) stand behind (a player) to stop balls that he may miss. **12** (of a journalist) report (what is said and done at meetings, on public occasions, etc): *~ the Labour Party's conference.*

cover·age /ˈkʌvərɪdʒ/ *n* [U] covering of events, etc: *TV ~ of the election campaign,* e g by televising political meetings, interviews with candidates and voters. ⇨ cover²(12).

cover·ing /ˈkʌvərɪŋ/ *n* [C] thing that covers: *a leafy ~,* the trees. □ *adj: a ~ing letter,* one sent with a document or with goods, etc.

cover·let /ˈkʌvələt/ *n* [C] bedspread.

cov·ert¹ /ˈkʌvət *US* also ˈkəʊvət/ *adj* (of glances, threats, etc) half-hidden; disguised. **cov·ert·ly** *adv*

cov·ert² /ˈkʌvət/ *n* [C] area of thick undergrowth in which animals hide.

covet /ˈkʌvɪt/ *vt* desire eagerly (esp something belonging to somebody else).

covet·ous /ˈkʌvətəs/ *adj* (*formal*) *covetous of,* eagerly desirous (esp of things belonging to somebody else). **covet·ous·ly** *adv*

cow¹ /kaʊ/ *n* [C] **1** fully grown female of any animal of the ox family, esp the domestic kind kept by farmers for producing milk. **2** also female elephant, rhinoceros, whale, etc.
'**cow·boy,** man (usually on horseback) who looks after cattle in the western parts of the US.
'**cow·hand,** '**cow·herd,** person who looks after grazing cattle.
'**cow·hide,** leather (or a strip of leather as a whip) made from a cow's hide.
'**cow·shed,** building in which cows are kept, or to which they are taken to be milked.
'**cow·man,** man responsible for milking cows.

cow² /kaʊ/ *vt* frighten (a person) into submission: *The child had a ~ed look,* looked frightened because of threats of violence, etc.

cow·ard /ˈkaʊəd/ *n* [C] **1** person unable to control his fear. **2** person who runs away from responsibility, dangerous situations, etc.

cow·ard·ly *adj* (**a**) not brave. (**b**) of or like a coward: *~ly behaviour.*

cow·ard·ice /ˈkaʊədɪs/ *n* [U] feeling, way of behaviour, of a coward.

cower /ˈkaʊə(r)/ *vi* lower the body; shrink back from cold, misery, fear, shame: *The dog ~ed under the table when its master raised the whip.*

cowl /kaʊl/ *n* [C] **1** long, loose gown (as worn by monks) with a hood that can be pulled over the head; the hood itself. **2** metal cap for a chimney, ventilating pipe, etc often made so as to revolve with the wind and improve the draught(1).

cow·pox /ˈkaʊpɒks/ *n* [C] contagious disease of cattle, caused by a virus which is the source of vaccine for smallpox.

cox /kɒks/ *n* [C] (*informal*) (abbr of) cox-swain. □ *vt,vi* act as coxswain.

cox·swain /ˈkɒksən/ *n* [C] **1** person who steers a rowing-boat, esp in races. **2** person in charge of a ship's boat and crew.

coy /kɔɪ/ *adj* (-er, -est) (esp of a girl) (pretending to be) shy, modest).
coy·ly *adv*

coy·ote /ˈkɔɪəʊt *US:* ˈkɔɪəʊt/ *n* [C] prairie wolf of western N America.

crab /kræb/ *n* [C] ten-legged shellfish; [U] its meat as food.

crab-apple /ˈkræb æpəl/ *n* [C] wild apple-tree; its hard, sour fruit: *~ jelly.*

crab·bed /ˈkræbɪd/ *adj* **1** bad-tempered; easily irritated. **2** (of handwriting) difficult to read; (of writings, authors) difficult to understand.

crack¹ /kræk/ *n* [C] **1** line of division where something is broken, but not into separate parts: *a cup with bad ~s in it.* **2** sudden, sharp noise (as of a rifle or whip): *the ~ of thunder.* **3** sharp blow which can be heard: *give/get a ~ on the head.* **4** *have a crack at sth,* make an attempt at something which is difficult. **6** first-rate; very clever or expert: *He's a ~ shot,* expert at using a rifle.

crack² /kræk/ *vt,vi* **1** get or make a crack or cracks(1) in: *I can ~ it, but I can't break it.* **2** make, cause to make, a crack or cracks(2): *to ~ a whip/the joints of the fingers.* **3** (of the voice) become harsh; (of a boy's voice when he is reaching puberty) undergo a change and become deeper (*Note: break* is more usual.) **4** *crack down on (sb/sth),* take disciplinary action against: *~ down on gambling. crack up,* lose strength (in old age); suffer a mental collapse. *crack a joke,* make one. *get cracking,* get busy (with work waiting to be done).

cracker /ˈkrækə(r)/ *n* [C] **1** thin, flaky, dry biscuit (as eaten with cheese). **2** firework that makes cracking noises when set off: *The Chinese use ~s to frighten away evil spirits.* ⇨ also Christmas cracker, nut-crackers.

crackers /ˈkrækəz/ *adj* (*sl*) mad; crazy.

crackle /ˈkrækəl/ vi make a series of small cracking sounds, as when one treads on dry twigs, or when dry sticks burn: *A cheerful wood fire was crackling on the hearth.* □ n [U] small cracking sounds, as described above: *the distant ~ of machine-gun fire.*

crack·ling /ˈkræklɪŋ/ n [U] **1** crackle. **2** crisp skin of roast pork.

crack·pot /ˈkrækpɒt/ n [C] eccentric person with strange ideas: *~ ideas.*

-cracy /-krəsɪ/ suffix (used to form a *noun*) government, rule, class, characterized by: *democracy; aristocracy.*

cradle /ˈkreɪdəl/ n **1** small, low bed sometimes mounted on rockers, for a newborn baby. *from the cradle to the grave,* from birth to death. **2** (*fig*) place where something is born or begins: *Greece, the ~ of Western culture.* **3** framework resembling a cradle or which is used like a cradle, e g a structure on which a ship is supported while being built or repaired; part of a telephone apparatus on which the receiver rests. □ vt place, hold, in or as in a cradle: *~ a baby in one's arms.*

craft /krɑft US: kræft/ n **1** [C] occupation, esp one in which skill in the use of the hands is needed; such a skill or technique: *the potter's ~; `needle~, `wood~, `handi~.* **2** [C] those engaged in such an occupation, organized in a guild or union: *the ~ of masons.* **3** [C] (*pl* unchanged) boat(s), ship(s): *The harbour was full of all kinds of ~.* ⇨ also aircraft, spacecraft. **4** [U] cunning; trickery; skill in deceiving: *Be careful when you do business with him; he's full of ~.*

craft·ily /-əlɪ/ adv

crafti·ness n [U]

crafts·man /ˈkrɑftsmən US: ˈkræfts-/ n [C] (*pl* -men) skilled workman who practises a craft.

crafty /ˈkrɑftɪ US: ˈkræftɪ/ adj (-ier, -iest) cunning; showing skill in trickery or deceit.

crag /kræg/ n [C] high, steep, sharp or rugged mass of rock.

craggy adj (-ier, -iest) having many crags.

cram /kræm/ vt,vi (-mm-) **1** *cram into/ with,* make too full; put, push, very much or too much into: *to ~ food into one's mouth/ ~ one's mouth with food.* **2** fill the head with facts (for an examination): *to ~ pupils.*

'cram-`full adj,adv as full as cramming can make it.

cramp¹ /kræmp/ n [U] sudden and painful tightening of the muscles, usually caused by cold or overwork, making movement difficult: *The swimmer was seized with ~ and had to be helped out of the water.*

cramp² /kræmp/ vt **1** keep in a narrow space; hinder or prevent the movement or growth of: *All these difficulties ~ed his progress. We are/feel ~ed for space here.* **2** cause to have, affect with, cramp¹. **3** fasten with a cramp³.

cramp³ /kræmp/ n [C] **1** (also `~-iron) metal bar with the ends bent, used for hold-

ing together masonry or timbers. **2** tool with a moveable part which can be screwed up to hold things.

cram·pon /ˈkræmpɒn/ n [C] (usually *pl*) iron plate with spikes, worn on shoes for walking or climbing on ice.

cran·berry /ˈkrænbrɪ US: -berɪ/ n [C] (*pl* -ies) small, red berry of a shrub, used for making jelly and sauce.

crane¹ /kreɪn/ n [C] **1** large wading bird with long legs and neck. **2** machine with a long arm that can be swung round, used for lifting and moving heavy weights.

crane² /kreɪn/ vt,vi stretch (the neck): *to ~ forward; to ~ one's neck in order to see.*

crane-fly /ˈkreɪn flaɪ/ n [C] (*pl* -ies) kind of fly with very long legs.

cran·ial /ˈkreɪnɪəl/ adj (*anat*) of the skull.

cran·ium /ˈkreɪnɪəm/ n [C] (*anat*) bony part of the head enclosing the brain.

crank¹ /kræŋk/ n [C] L-shaped arm and handle for transmitting rotary motion. □ vt move, cause to move, by turning a crank: *to ~ up an engine.*

`crank-shaft, shaft that turns or is turned by a crank.

crank² /kræŋk/ n [C] person with fixed (and often strange) ideas, esp on one matter: *Don't go to that doctor—he's a ~!*

cranky adj (-ier, -iest) **(a)** (of people, ideas) odd; eccentric. **(b)** (of buildings, machines, etc) unsteady; shaky.

cranny /ˈkrænɪ/ n [C] (*pl* -ies) small crack or opening, e g in a wall.

crap /kræp/ n [U] (*sl*) nonsense.

crash¹ /kræʃ/ n [C] **1** (noise made by a) violent fall, blow or breaking: *The tree fell with a great ~. He was killed in a `plane ~.* **2** ruin; collapse (e g in trade, finance): *The great ~ on Wall Street in 1929 ruined international trade.* □ adv with a crash.

`crash-barrier, fence, railing, etc used to keep people, vehicles, etc apart (e g along the centre of a motorway).

`crash-course/-programme, one designed to achieve quick results.

`crash-helmet, hard helmet worn, e g by a motor-cyclist, to protect the head in a crash.

`crash-land** vi,vt (of aircraft) land, be landed, wholly or partly out of control. Hence, **`crash-landing n [C,U]

crash² /kræʃ/ vt,vi **1** fall or strike suddenly, violently, and noisily (esp of things that break): *The bus ~ed into a tree. The aircraft ~ed.* **2** cause to crash: *to ~ an aircraft.* **3** force or break through violently: *elephants ~ing through the jungle.* **4** (of a business company, government, etc) come to ruin; meet disaster: *His great financial scheme ~ed.*

crass /kræs/ adj (of such qualities as ignorance, stupidity, etc) complete; very great.

-crat /-kræt/ suffix (used to form a *noun*) member, support, of a government, class, etc: *democrat; aristocrat.*

-cratic /-ˈkrætɪk/ (used to form an *adjective*): democratic.

crate /kreɪt/ *n* [C] large framework of light boards or basketwork for goods in transport. □ *vt* put in a crate.

cra·ter /ˈkreɪtə(r)/ *n* [C] mouth of a volcano; hole in the ground made by the explosion of a bomb, shell, etc.

cra·vat /krəˈvæt/ *n* [C] piece of cloth loosely folded and worn as a tie.

crave /kreɪv/ *vt, vi* ask earnestly for, have a strong desire for: *to ~ (for) forgiveness; to ~ for a drink.*

crav·ing /ˈkreɪvɪŋ/ *n* [C] strong desire: *a ~ for whisky.*

crawl /krɔl/ *vi* 1 move slowly, pulling the body along the ground or other surface (as worms and snakes do); (of human beings) move in this way, or on the hands and knees: *The wounded soldier ~ed into a shell-hole.* 2 go very slowly: *Our train ~ed over the damaged bridge.* 3 be full of, covered with, things that crawl: *The ground was ~ing with ants.* 4 (of the flesh) feel as if covered with crawling things: *She says that the sight of snakes makes her flesh ~.* □ *n* 1 [U] crawling movement: *Traffic in Oxford Street was reduced to a ~ during the rush hours.* 2 the ~, high-speed swimming stroke in which the head is kept low in the water.

crawler, (a) person or thing that crawls. (b) (*pl*) overall garment made for a baby to crawl about in.

cray·fish /ˈkreɪfɪʃ/ *n* [C] freshwater shellfish like a lobster.

crayon /ˈkreɪən/ *n* [C] stick or pencil of soft coloured chalk, wax or charcoal. □ *vt* draw with crayons.

craze /kreɪz/ *vt* make wildly excited or mad: *a ~d look/expression; a half-~d prophet.* (*Note:* usually used as a *pp.*) □ *n* [C] enthusiastic interest that may last for a comparatively short time; the object of such interest: *the modern ~ for rock music.* ⇨ rage(3).

crazy /ˈkreɪzɪ/ *adj* (-ier, -iest) 1 wildly excited or enthusiastic: *I'm ~ about/for you, darling.* 2 suffering from mental disorder; foolish: *You were ~ to lend that man your money.* 3 (of pavements, etc) made up of irregularly shaped pieces fitted together: *'~ 'paving.*
craz·ily /-əlɪ/ *adv*
crazi·ness *n* [U]

creak /krik/ *n, vi* (make a) sound like that of an unoiled hinge.
creaky *adj* (-ier, -iest) making creaking sounds: *~y stairs.*

cream /krim/ *n* [U] 1 fatty or oily part of milk which rises to the surface and can be made into butter. 2 kind of food containing or resembling cream: *~ cheese; ice-~.* 3 substance like cream in appearance or consistency, used for polishing, as a cosmetic, etc: *'furniture ~; 'face-~.* 4 part of a liquid that gathers at the top: *~ of tartar/lime.* 5 best part of anything: *the ~ of society,* those of highest rank. 6 yellowish-white colour. □ *adj* yellowish-white. □ *vt* take cream from (milk); add cream to: *~ed potatoes.*

creamy *adj* (-ier, -iest) smooth and rich like cream; containing cream: *~y butter.*

cream·ery /ˈkriməri/ *n* [C] (*pl* -ies) 1 place where milk, cream, butter, cheese, etc are sold. 2 butter and cheese factory.

crease /kris/ *n* [C] 1 line made (on cloth, paper, etc) by crushing, folding or pressing: *~-resisting cloth.* 2 white line on a cricket pitch to mark the positions of certain players. □ *vt, vi* make, get a crease in: *This material ~s easily.*

cre·ate /krɪˈeɪt/ *vt* 1 cause something to exist; make (something new or original): *God ~d the world. Dickens ~d many wonderful characters in his novels.* 2 give rise to; produce: *His behaviour ~d a bad impression.* 3 invest (a person) with a rank: *He was ~d Baron of Bunthorp.*

cre·ation /krɪˈeɪʃn/ *n* 1 [U] the act of creating (eg the world): *the ~ of great works of art/of an Empire.* 2 [U] all created things. **the C~,** the world or universe as created by God. 3 [U] production of the human intelligence, esp one in which imagination has a part: *the ~s of poets, artists, composers and dramatists. The women were wearing the newest ~s of the Paris dressmakers.*

cre·ative /krɪˈeɪtɪv/ *adj* having power to create; of creation: *useful and ~ work,* i e requiring intelligence and imagination.
cre·ative·ly *adv*

cre·ator /krɪˈeɪtə(r)/ *n* [C] person who creates. **the C~,** God.

crea·ture /ˈkritʃə(r)/ *n* [C] 1 living animal. 2 living person: *a lovely ~,* a beautiful woman.
'creature comforts, material needs such as food and drink.

crèche /kreɪʃ/ *n* [C] 1 (*GB*) public nursery where babies are looked after while their mothers are at work. 2 (*US*) = crib¹(3).

cre·dence /ˈkridəns/ *n* [U] **give/attach credence to,** (*formal*) believe (gossip, what is said, etc).

cre·den·tials /krɪˈdenʃəlz/ *n pl* letters or papers showing that a person is what he claims to be: *His ~ were so satisfactory that he was given the post of manager.*

cred·ible /ˈkredəbəl/ *adj* that can be believed: *~ witnesses.*
cred·ibly /-əblɪ/ *adv* in a credible manner.
credi·bil·ity /ˈkredəˈbɪlətɪ/ *n* [U]

credit¹ /ˈkredɪt/ *n* 1 [U] belief of others that a person, business company, etc can pay debts, or will keep a promise to pay: *No ~ is given at this shop,* payment must be in cash. 2 [U] money shown as owned by a person, company, etc in a bank account: *You have a ~ balance of £250.* 3 [C] sum of money advanced or loaned (by a bank, etc): *The bank refused further ~s to the company.* 4

(*book-keeping*) record of payments received: *Does this item go among the ~s or the debits?* **5** [C] (*US*) entry on a record to show that a course of study has been completed: *~s in history and geography.* **6** [U] honour, approval, good name or reputation: *a man of the highest ~.* **get/take credit for sth),** receive recognition, etc; take it: *He's cleverer than I gave him ~ for,* than I thought. **7** add to a person's reputation: *The work does you ~.* **be a credit to sb/sth,** add to the good name of: *The pupils are a ~ to their teacher.* **8** [U] belief; trust; confidence; credence: *The rumour is gaining ~.* **9** [C] (usually *pl*) names on a film of persons responsible for acting, directing, etc.

`credit account,` account with a shop, etc with an agreement for payments at a later date, e g monthly or quarterly.

`credit card,` **(a)** one issued by a business firm allowing the holder to obtain goods on credit(1). **(b)** one issued by a bank allowing the holder to have money from its branches or use cheques to buy goods up to a written amount.

`credit side,` **(a)** right-hand side of an account(1) showing payments received. **(b)** (*fig*) favourable comments about a person: *He is easily annoyed, but on the ~ side he is generous.*

`credit-squeeze,` government policy of making it difficult to borrow money (as part of an anti-inflation policy).

credit-titles, n pl = credit(9).

`credit-worthy,` *adj* (accepted as being) safe to offer credit to.

credit² /'kredɪt/ vt **1** believe that a person or thing has something: *Until now I've always ~ed you with more sense. The relics are ~ed with miraculous powers. Miraculous powers are ~ed to the relics.* **2** enter on the credit side of an account: *~ a customer with £10; ~ £10 to a customer/to his account.*

credi·table /'kredɪtəbl/ *adj* that brings credit(1,2,3): *a ~ attempt.*
credi·tably /-əblɪ/ *adv*

credi·tor /'kredɪtə(r)/ *n* [C] person to whom one owes money: *run away from one's ~s.*

cre·du·lity /krə'dʒuːlətɪ *US:* -'duː/ *n* [U] too great a readiness to believe things.

credu·lous /'kredjʊləs *US:* -dʒʊ-/ *adj* (too) ready to believe things: *~ people who accept all the promises of the politicians.*
credu·lous·ly *adv*

creed /kriːd/ *n* [C] (system of) beliefs or opinions, esp on religious doctrine. **the C~,** (*formal*) summary of Christian doctrine.

creek /kriːk/ *n* [C] **1** (*GB*) narrow inlet of water on the coast or in a river-bank. **2** (*N America*) small river.

creep /kriːp/ *vi* (*pt,pp* crept /krept/) **1** move along with the body close to the ground or floor: *The cat crept silently towards the bird.* **2** move slowly, quietly or secretly: *The thief crept along the corridor.* **3** (of time,

age, etc) come on gradually: *Old age ~s on one unawares.* **3** (of plants, etc) grow along the ground, over the surface of a wall, etc: *Ivy had crept over the ruined castle walls.* **4** (of the flesh) have the feeling that things are creeping over it (as the result of fear, repugnance, etc): *The sight of the cold, damp prison cell, with rats running about, made her flesh ~.* ⇨ crawl(4).

creeper /'kriːpə(r)/ *n* [C] **1** insect, bird, etc that creeps. **2** plant that grows along the ground, over rocks, walls, etc.

creepy /'kriːpɪ/ *adj* (-ier, -iest) having or causing fear: *The ghost story made us all ~.*

cre·mate /krɪ'meɪt/ *vt* burn (a corpse) to ashes: *He says he wants to be ~d, not buried.*

cre·ma·tion /krɪ'meɪʃən/ *n* [U] cremating; [C] instance of this.

cre·ma·tor·ium /'kremə'tɔːrɪəm/ *n* [C] (*pl* ~s) furnace, building, place, for the cremating of corpses.

cre·ma·tory /'kremətərɪ *US:* -tɔːrɪ/ *n* [C] (*pl* -ies) = crematorium.

crêpe, crepe /kreɪp/ *n* [U] name for kinds of wrinkled cloth other than the black cloth formerly used for mourning.

`crepe `paper,` thin paper with a wavy or wrinkled surface.

crepe rubber, raw rubber with a wrinkled surface, used for the soles of shoes, etc.

crept /krept/ ⇨ creep.

cres·cendo /krɪ'ʃendəʊ/ *n* [C] (*pl* ~s), *adj* **1** (passage of music to be played, something heard) with, of, increasing loudness. **2** (*fig*) progress towards a climax.

cres·cent /'kresənt/ *n* [C] **1** (something shaped like) the curve of the moon in the first quarter. **2** row of houses in the form of a crescent.

cress /kres/ *n* [U] name of various plants, esp the kind with hot-tasting leaves (used in salads and sandwiches).

crest /krest/ *n* [C] **1** tuft of feathers on a bird's head. **2** decoration like a crest formerly worn on the top of a helmet. **3** design over the shield of a coat of arms, or used separately (e g on a seal, or on notepaper): *the family ~,* one used by a family. **4** top of a slope or hill; white top of a large wave. **on the crest of a wave,** (*fig*) at the most favourable moment of one's fortunes. □ *vt* reach the crest of a hill, a wave.

`crest-fallen,` (*fig*) very disappointed.

cre·tin /'kretɪn *US:* 'kriːtən/ *n* [C] deformed and mentally undeveloped person (diseased because of weakness of the thyroid gland).

cre·vasse /krɪ'væs/ *n* [C] deep, open crack, esp in ice on a glacier.

crev·ice /'krevɪs/ *n* [C] narrow opening or crack (in a rock, wall, etc).

crew¹ /kruː/ *n* [C] **1** all the persons working a ship or aircraft; all these except the officers: *officers and crew.* **2** person or persons on a yacht or plane working under the direction of the helmsman or pilot. **3** group of persons working together; gang. □ *vi* act as crew(2): *Will you ~ for me in tomorrow's race?*

crib[1] /krɪb/ *n* [C] **1** wooden framework (manger) from which animals can pull out fodder. **2** representation (e g in a church at Christmas) of the nativity. **3** bed for a new-born baby.

crib[2] /krɪb/ *n* [C] **1** something copied dis-honestly from the work of another. **2** word-for-word translation of a foreign text used by students of the language. □ *vt, vi* (-bb-) **1** use a crib(2). **2** copy (another pupil's written work) dishonestly.

cricket[1] /ˈkrɪkɪt/ *n* [C] small, brown jump-ing insect which makes a shrill noise by rub-bing its front wings together.

cricket[2] /ˈkrɪkɪt/ *n* [U] ball game ('~-match) played on a field by two teams of eleven players each, with bats and wickets.
cricketer, cricket player.

cried /kraɪd/ ⇨ cry[2].

crier /ˈkraɪə(r)/ *n* [C] **1** officer who makes public announcements in a court of law. **2** person (esp a young child) who cries(2) a lot.

cries /kraɪz/ *pres tense* of cry[2]; *pl* of cry[1].

crime /kraɪm/ *n* **1** [C] offence for which there is severe punishment by law; [U] such offences collectively; serious law-breaking: *to commit a serious ~. It is the business of the police to prevent and detect ~ and of the law courts to punish ~.* **2** foolish or wrong act, not necessarily an offence against the law: *It would be a ~ to send the boy out on such a cold, wet night.*
'**crime-wave**, period when many crimes are committed.

crimi-nal /ˈkrɪmənəl/ *adj* of crime: *a ~ act.* □ *n* [C] person who commits a crime or crimes.
crimi-nally /-nəlɪ/ *adv*

crimi-nol-ogy /ˌkrɪmɪˈnɒlədʒɪ/ *n* [U] the study of crime.

crim-son /ˈkrɪmzən/ *adj, n* [U] deep red (colour). □ *vt, vi* make or become crimson; blush.

cringe /krɪndʒ/ *vi* **1** move (the body) back or down in fear: *The dog ~d at the sight of the whip.* **2** behave (towards a superior) in a way that shows lack of self-respect; be too hum-ble: *cringing to/before a policeman.*

crinkle /ˈkrɪŋkəl/ *n* [C] small, narrow wrinkle (in material such as foil or paper). □ *vt, vi* make or get crinkles in: *~d paper*, e g crêpe paper.

cripple /ˈkrɪpəl/ *n* [C] person unable to walk or move properly, through injury or weak-ness in the spine or legs. □ *vt* make a cripple of; damage or weaken seriously: *~d sol-diers; activities ~d by lack of money.*

cri-sis /ˈkraɪsɪs/ *n* [C] (*pl* crises /-siz/) **1** turning-point in illness, life, history. **2** time of difficulty, danger or anxiety about the

future: *a cabinet/financial ~.*

crisp /krɪsp/ *adj* (-er, -est) **1** (esp of food) hard, dry and easily broken: *~ toast/ biscuits.* **2** (of the air, the weather) frosty, cold: *the ~ air of an autumn morning.* **3** (of hair) tightly curled. **4** (of style, manners) quick, precise and decided; showing no doubts or hesitation: *a man with a ~ manner of speaking.* □ *n* [C] (*US* = chips) thin slices of potatoes, fried and dried (usually sold in packets). □ *vt, vi* make or become crisp.
crisp-ly *adv*
crisp-ness *n* [C]

criss-cross /ˈkrɪskrɒs *US:* -krɔs/ *adj* with crossed lines: *a ~ pattern/design.* □ *adv* crosswise. □ *vt, vi* move crosswise; mark with lines that cross.

cri-terion /kraɪˈtɪərɪən/ *n* [C] (*pl* -ria /-rɪə/ *or* ~s) standard of judgement; principle by which something is measured for value: *Success in money-making is not always a good ~ of real success in life.*

critic /ˈkrɪtɪk/ *n* [C] **1** person who forms and gives judgements, esp about literature, art, music, etc: *musical/dramatic/literary ~s.* **2** person who finds fault, points out mistakes, etc: *I am my own worst critic ~.*

criti-cal /ˈkrɪtɪkəl/ *adj* **1** of or at a crisis: *We are at a ~ time in our history. The patient's condition is ~, He is dangerously ill.* **2** of the work of a critic: *~ opinions on art and literature.* **3** fault-finding: *~ remarks.*
criti-cally /-klɪ/ *adv* in a critical(1) manner: *He's ~ly ill.*

criti-cism /ˈkrɪtɪsɪzm/ *n* **1** [U] the work of a critic; the art of making judgements (con-cerning art, literature, etc). **2** [C] judgement or opinion on literature, art, etc. **3** [U] fault-finding; [C] remark, etc that finds fault.

criti-cize /ˈkrɪtɪsaɪz/ *vt, vi* form and give a judgement of; find fault with: *~ somebody for doing something.*

cri-tique /krɪˈtiːk/ *n* [C] critical essay or review.

croak /krəʊk/ *n* [C] deep, hoarse sound (as made by frogs). □ *vt, vi* **1** make this kind of sound. **2** say in a croaking voice; express dismal views about the future. **3** (*sl*) = die[2].

cro-chet /ˈkrəʊʃeɪ *US:* krəʊˈʃeɪ/ *vt, vi* make with a thread looped over others with the help of a small hooked needle (called a '~-hook). □ *n* [U] material (e g lace) made or being made in this way.

crock /krɒk/ *n* [C] pot or jar made of baked earth, e g for containing water; broken piece of such a pot.

crock-ery /ˈkrɒkərɪ/ *n* [U] pots, plates, cups, dishes and other utensils (made of baked clay).

croco-dile /ˈkrɒkədaɪl/ *n* [C] **1** large river reptile with a long body and tail, covered with a hard skin. **2** (*informal*) (school chil-dren) walking in procession, two by two.

`crocodile tears,` insincere sorrow.

cro·cus /ˈkrəʊkəs/ n [C] (pl ~es) (kind of) small plant growing from a corm, with coloured flowers early in spring.

croft /kroft US: krɔft/ n [C] small, enclosed field; small farm.

crofter, person who rents or owns a small farm, esp a joint tenant of a farm in Scotland.

crook /krʊk/ n [C] **1** stick or staff with a rounded hook at one end, esp such a stick used by a shepherd. **2** bend or curve, eg in a river or path. **3** (informal) person who makes a living by dishonest or criminal means. □ vt,vi bend into the shape of a crook: to ~ one's finger/arm.

crooked /ˈkrʊkɪd/ adj **1** not straight or level; twisted; bent: a ~ little man. You've got your hat on ~. **2** (of a person or his actions) dishonest; not straightforward.

crook·ed·ly adv

croon /kruːn/ vt,vi hum or sing gently in a narrow range of notes: ~ a lullaby.

crop¹ /krop/ n [C] **1** yearly (or season's) produce of grain, grass, fruit, etc: the `potato ~`. **2** (pl) agricultural plants in the fields: to get the ~s in. **3** group of persons or things, amount of anything, appearing or produced together: The Prime Minister's statement produced a ~ of questions.

crop² /krop/ n [C] **1** bag-like part of a bird's throat where food is broken up for digestion before passing into the stomach. **2** very short hair-cut.

crop³ /krop/ vt,vi (-pp-) **1** (of animals) bite off the tops of (grass, plants, etc); graze: The sheep had ~ped the grass short. **2** cut short (a person's hair, a horse's tail or ears). **3** sow or plant: to ~ ten acres with wheat. **4** bear a crop: The beans ~ped well this year. **5** crop up/out, (of rock, minerals) show up above the earth's surface. **6** crop up, appear or arise (esp unexpectedly): All sorts of difficulties ~ped up.

cro·quet /ˈkrəʊkeɪ US: krəʊˈkeɪ/ n [U] game played on short grass with wooden balls which are knocked with wooden mallets through hoops.

cro·sier, cro·zier /ˈkrəʊzɪə(r) US: -ʃər/ n [C] bishop's staff, usually shaped like a shepherd's crook.

cross¹ /kros US: krɔs/ adj **1** (informal) bad-tempered; easily or quickly showing anger: Don't be ~ with the child for being late. **2** (of winds) contrary; opposed: Strong ~ winds made it difficult for the yachts to leave harbour.

cross·ly adv

cross·ness n [U]

cross² /kros US: krɔs/ n [C] **1** mark made by drawing one line across another, eg ×, + : The place is marked on the map with a ~. **2** line or stroke forming part of a letter (eg the horizontal stroke on a 't'). **3** stake or post with another piece of wood across it like

T, † or X, as used in ancient times for crucifixion, esp the C~, that on which Christ died; model of this as a religious emblem; sign of a cross made with the right hand as a religious act. **4** (fig) suffering; affliction; burden of sorrow: to bear one's ~. **5** emblem, in the form of a cross or a star, (to be) worn by an order of knighthood; decoration for personal valour: the Victoria C~. **6** (place of) crossing. (cut) on the cross, diagonally: This skirt material was cut on the ~. **7** offspring of animals or plants of different sorts or breeds: A mule is a ~ between a horse and an ass.

cross³ /kros US: krɔs/ vt,vi **1** go across; pass from one side to the other side of: to ~ a road/river/bridge/the sea/the Sahara. cross one's mind, (of ideas, etc) occur to one: The idea has just ~ed my mind that... **2** draw a line or lines across or through: Two of the words had been ~ed out. I ~ed his name off the list. cross a cheque, draw two parallel lines across it so that it can only be paid into a bank account. **3** put or place across or over: to ~ one's legs. keep one's fingers crossed, (fig) hope for the best, that nothing will happen to upset one's plans, etc. **4** cross oneself, make the sign of the cross on or over oneself as a religious act, to invoke God's protection, or as a sign of awe. **5** (of persons travelling, letters in the post) meet and pass: We ~ed each other on the way. Our letters ~ed in the post. **6** oppose or obstruct (somebody, his plans, wishes, etc): He was angry at having his plans ~ed. **7** produce a cross(7) by mixing breeds.

cross·bar /ˈkrosbɑː(r) US: ˈkrɔs-/ n [C] bar going across, eg the bar joining the two upright posts of the goal (in football, etc) or the front and rear ends of a bicycle frame.

cross·beam /ˈkrosbiːm US: ˈkrɔs-/ n [C] beam placed across, esp one that supports parts of a structure.

cross·benches /ˈkrosbentʃɪz US: ˈkrɔs-/ n pl those benches in the House of Commons used by members who do not vote regularly with either the Government or the Opposition. Hence, **cross·bencher** n [C].

cross·bow /ˈkrosbəʊ US: ˈkrɔs-/ n [C] old kind of bow placed across a grooved wooden support, used for shooting arrows, bolts, stones, etc.

cross·bred /ˈkrosbred US: ˈkrɔs-/ adj produced by crossing breeds: ~ sheep.

cross·breed /ˈkrosbriːd US: ˈkrɔs-/ n [C] (in farming, etc) animal, plant, etc produced by crossing breeds.

cross·country /ˈkros ˈkʌntrɪ US: ˈkrɔs-/ adj, adv across the country or fields, not along roads: a ~ race.

cross·check /ˈkros ˈtʃek US: krɔs/ vt,vi verify, eg a method, calculation, by using a different method, etc: We ~ed the results twice. □ n [C] verification of this sort: We'd *better do a ~ on these figures.*

cross-cur·rent /ˈkrɒs kʌrənt US: ˈkrɔs kərənt/ *n* [C] (*fig*) body of opinion contrary to that of the majority.

cross-division /ˈkrɒs dɪˈvɪʒən US: ˈkrɔs/ *n* [C] division of a group according to more than one factor at the same time so that subdivisions interrelate; instance of this.

cross-exam·ine /ˈkrɒs ɪɡˈzæmɪn US: ˈkrɔs/ *vt* question closely, esp to test answers already given to someone else, as in law court, by counsel, etc.

cross-exam·iner, person who crossexamines.

cross-exam·in·ation /ˈkrɒs ɪɡˌzæmɪˈneɪʃn US: ˈkrɔs/ *n* [C]

cross-eyed /ˈkrɒsaɪd US: ˈkrɔs-/ *adj* with one or both eyeballs turned towards the nose.

cross-fer·ti·lize /ˈkrɒs ˈfɜːtəlaɪz US: ˈkrɔs/ *vt* carry pollen from the stamens of one plant to the pistil of another plant.

cross-fer·ti·li·za·tion /ˈkrɒs ˌfɜːtəlaɪˈzeɪʃən US: ˈkrɔs -lɪˈz-/ *n* [U]

cross-fire /ˈkrɒsfaɪə(r) US: ˈkrɔs-/ *n* [U] 1 firing of guns from two or more points so that the lines of fire cross. 2 (*fig*) situation in which questions are put from persons in different places.

cross-grained /ˈkrɒs ˈɡreɪnd US: ˈkrɔs/ *adj* 1 (of wood) with the grain in crossing directions. 2 (*fig*) difficult to please or get on with.

cross·ing /ˈkrɒsɪŋ US: ˈkrɔs-/ *n* [C] 1 the act of going across, esp by sea: *We had a rough ~ from Dover to Calais.* 2 place where two roads, two railways, or a road and a railway cross. 3 *street ~,* place on a street where pedestrians are requested to cross. ⇨ level-crossing.

cross-legged /ˈkrɒs ˈleɡd US: ˈkrɔs ˈleɡɪd/ *adv* (of a person sitting) with one leg placed across the other.

cross-pur·poses /ˈkrɒs ˈpɜːpəsɪz US: ˈkrɔs/ *n pl* **be at cross-purposes,** (of two persons or groups) misunderstand one another; have different and conflicting purposes.

cross-question /ˈkrɒs ˈkwestʃən US: ˈkrɔs/ *vt* = cross-examine.

cross-ref·er·ence /ˈkrɒs ˈrefrəns US: ˈkrɔs/ *n* [C] reference from one part of a book, index, file, etc to another, for further information.

cross·road /ˈkrɒsrəʊd US: ˈkrɔs-/ *n* [C] 1 road that crosses another. 2 (*pl*, used with a *sing verb*) place where two or more roads meet: *We came to a ~s.*

cross-sec·tion /ˈkrɒs ˈsekʃən US: ˈkrɔs/ *n* [C] 1 (drawing of a) piece or slice made by cutting across, e g a tree trunk. 2 (*fig*) typical or representative sample of the whole: *a ~ of the electors.*

cross-stitch /ˈkrɒs stɪtʃ US: ˈkrɔs/ *n* [C] (needlework using a) stitch formed of two stitches that cross.

cross-wise /ˈkrɒs waɪz US: ˈkrɔs/ *adv* across; diagonally; in the form of a cross.

cross·word /ˈkrɒswɜːd US: ˈkrɔs-/ *n* [C] (also *~ puzzle*) puzzle in which words have to be written (from numbered clues) vertically and horizontally (up and down) in spaces on a chequered square or oblong.

crotch /krɒtʃ/ *n* [C] 1 place where a branch forks from a tree: *The child was sitting in a ~ of a tree.* 2 place where a pair of trousers or a person's legs fork from the trunk.

crotchet /ˈkrɒtʃɪt/ *n* [C] 1 (*music*) (*US = quarter note*) black-headed note with stem (♩), half of a minim. 2 strange, unreasonable idea.

crotchety *adj* unreasonably bad tempered.

crouch /kraʊtʃ/ *vi* lower the body with the limbs together (in fear or to hide, or, of animals, ready to spring). □ *n* [C] crouching position.

croup[1] /kruːp/ *n* [U] children's disease in which there is inflammation of the windpipe, with coughing and difficulty in breathing.

croup[2] /kruːp/ *n* [C] rump or buttocks of certain animals.

crou·pier /ˈkruːpɪeɪ/ *n* [C] person who rakes in the money at a gaming table and pays out winnings.

crow[1] /krəʊ/ *n* [C] (kinds of) large, black bird with a harsh cry. **as the `crow flies,** in a straight line.

`crow's feet *n pl* network of little lines on the skin near the outer corners of a person's eyes.

`crow's-nest, protected look-out platform fixed at the mast-head of a ship for the lookout man.

crow[2] /krəʊ/ *vi* 1 (of a cock) make a loud, shrill cry. 2 (of a baby) make sounds showing happiness. 3 (of persons) express gleeful triumph: *to ~ over an unsuccessful rival.* □ *n* [C] crowing sound.

crow·bar /ˈkrəʊbɑː(r)/ *n* [C] straight, iron bar, often with a forked end, used as a lever for moving heavy objects.

crowd /kraʊd/ *n* [C] 1 large number of people together, but without order or organization: *He pushed his way through the ~.* 2 (*informal*) company of persons associated in some way; set of persons: *I can't afford to go about with that ~; they're too extravagant.* 3 large number (of things, usually without order): *a desk covered with a ~ of books and papers.* □ *vi,vt* 1 come together in a crowd: *Now, don't all ~ together!* **crowd round,** form a circle (round): *People quickly ~ round when there is a car accident.* 2 (cause to) move through, etc in a crowd; fill with: *They ~ed through the gates into the stadium. They ~ed the buses with passengers/~ed people into the buses.* 3 (*informal*) put pressure on: *Don't ~ me; give me time to think!*

crowded *adj* having large numbers of

people: ~ed cities/trains.

crown¹ /kraʊn/ n [C] **1** ornamental head-dress of gold, jewels, etc worn by a sovereign ruler; royal power: *succeed to the ~,* become the sovereign ruler. **2** circle or wreath of flowers or leaves worn on the head, esp as a sign of victory, or as a reward: *a martyr's ~.* **3** (until 1971) a 'half-~, British coin worth 2s 6d; *half a ~,* the sum of 2s 6d (= 12½ new pence). **4** top of the head or of a hat; part of a tooth that shows. **5** (fig) perfection, completion: *the ~ of one's labours.*

crown prince, next in succession to the throne.

crown witness, = witness for the Prosecution in a criminal case.

crown² /kraʊn/ vt **1** put a crown on (a king or queen): *the ~ed heads* (= kings and queens) *of Europe.* **2** reward with a crown; give honour to; reward: *efforts that were ~ed with success.* **3** be or have at the top of: *The hill is ~ed with a wood.* **4** put a happy finishing touch to: *to open a bottle of wine to ~ a feast.* **to crown (it) all,** to complete good or bad fortune: *It rained, we had no umbrellas, and, to ~ all, we missed the last bus and had to walk home.* **5** put an artificial cover on a broken tooth.

crown·ing adj completing; making perfect: *Her ~ing glory is her hair.*

cro·zier /ˈkrəʊzɪə(r) US: -ʒər/ n [C] = crosier.

cru·cial /ˈkruːʃəl/ adj decisive; critical: *the ~ test/question; at the ~ moment.*
cru·cially /-ʃəlɪ/ adv

cru·cible /ˈkruːsəbəl/ n [C] pot in which metals are melted (e g in a chemistry laboratory).

cru·ci·fix /ˈkruːsɪfɪks/ n [C] model of the Cross with the figure of Jesus on it.

cru·ci·fixion /ˌkruːsɪˈfɪkʃən/ n [U] putting to death, being put to death, on a cross(3); [C] instance of this. **the C~,** that of Jesus.

cru·cify /ˈkruːsɪfaɪ/ vt (pt,pp -ied) put to death by nailing or binding to a cross.

crude /kruːd/ adj (-r, -st) **1** (of materials) in a natural state; not refined or manufactured: *~ oil,* petroleum. **2** not having grace, taste or refinement: *~ manners.* **3** not finished properly; badly worked out: *~ schemes/methods/ideas.*
crude·ly adv

crud·ity /ˈkruːdətɪ/ n [U] the state or quality of being crude; [C] (pl -ies) instance of this; crude act, remark, etc.

cruel /ˈkruːəl/ adj (-er, -est) **1** (of persons) taking pleasure in the suffering of others; prepared to give pain to others: *a man who is ~ to animals.* **2** causing pain or suffering; showing indifference to the sufferings of others: *a ~ blow/punishment/disease/war.*
cruel·ly /ˈkruːəlɪ/ adv

cruel·ty /ˈkruːəltɪ/ n (pl -ies) **1** [U] readiness to give pain or cause suffering to others: *C~*

to children is severely punished in England. **2** [C] cruel act.

cruise /kruːz/ vi **1** sail about, either for pleasure, or, in war, looking for enemy ships. **2** (of cars, aircraft) travel at the speed (and of aircraft at the altitude) most economical of fuel, less than the top speed: *The car has a cruising speed of 50 miles an hour.* □ n [C] cruising voyage: *to go on/for a ~.*

cruiser /ˈkruːzə(r)/ n [C] **1** fast warship. **2** (also *cabin-~r*) motor-boat (with sleeping accommodation, etc) designed for pleasure cruises.

crumb /krʌm/ n [C] **1** very small piece of dry food, esp a bit of bread or cake rubbed off or dropped from a large piece: *sweep up the ~s* **2** (fig) small amount: *a few ~s of information/comfort.*

crumble /ˈkrʌmbəl/ vt,vi **1** break, rub or fall into very small pieces: *crumbling walls,* that are falling into ruin. **2** (fig) be destroyed, decay: *hopes that ~d to dust,* came to nothing.

crum·bly /ˈkrʌmblɪ/ adj (-ier, -iest) easily crumbled.

crum·pet /ˈkrʌmpɪt/ n [C] flat, round, soft, unsweetened cake, usually toasted and eaten hot with butter spread on it.

crumple /ˈkrʌmpəl/ vt,vi **1** press or crush into folds or creases: *to ~ one's clothes,* e g by packing them carelessly. **2** become full of folds or creases: *Some kinds of material ~ more easily than others.* **3** crumple up, crush; collapse: *to ~ up a sheet of paper into a ball.*

crunch /krʌntʃ/ vt,vi **1** crush noisily with the teeth when eating: *People who ~ nuts in the cinema can be very annoying.* **2** crush, be crushed, noisily under one's feet, under wheels, etc: *The frozen snow ~ed under the wheels of our car.* □ n [C] the act of, noise made by, crunching.

cru·sade /kruːˈseɪd/ n [C] **1** any one of the military expeditions made by the Christian rulers and people of Europe during the Middle Ages to recover the Holy Land from the Muslims. **2** any struggle or movement in support of something believed to be good or against something believed to be bad: *a ~ against racial hatred.* □ vi take part in a crusade.
cru·sader, person taking part in a crusade.

crush /krʌʃ/ n **1** [U] crowd of people pressed together: *There was a frightful ~ at the gate into the stadium.* **2** [C] *have a crush on sb,* (sl) be, imagine oneself to be, in love with.

crush² /krʌʃ/ vt,vi **1** press, be pressed, so that there is breaking or injury: *Wine is made by ~ing grapes.* **2** (cause to) become full of creases or irregular folds; lose shape: *Her dresses were badly ~ed when she took them out of the suitcase.* **3** be completely victorious: *He was not satisfied until he had ~ed his enemies.* **4** press or push in, etc: *They all tried to ~ into the front seats.*

crush·ing /ˈkrʌʃɪŋ/ adj **1** overwhelming: *a*

~ing defeat. 2 in a manner intended to have a strong effect, esp to disconcert: *a ~ing reply.*

crush·ing·ly *adv*

crust /krʌst/ *n* 1 [C,U] (piece of the) hard-baked surface of a loaf; outer covering (pastry) of a pie or tart. 2 [C,U] hard surface: *a thin ~ of ice/frozen snow; the earth's ~,* the surface. □ *vt,vi* **crust over,** cover, become covered, with a crust; form into a crust: *The snow ~ed over* (= froze hard on top) *during the night.*

crus·ta·cean /krʌˈsteɪʃən/ *n* [C] shellfish.

crusty /ˈkrʌstɪ/ *adj* (-ier, -iest) 1 having a crust; hard like a crust: *~ bread.* 2 (of persons, their behaviour) quick to show irritation, etc.

crutch /krʌtʃ/ *n* [C] 1 stick used as a support under the arm to help a lame person to walk: *a pair of ~es.* 2 support that is like a crutch in shape or use. 3 (*fig*) any moral support. 4 = crotch(2).

crux /krʌks/ *n* [C] (*pl ~es*) part (of a problem) that is the most difficult to solve: *The ~ of the matter is this...*

cry[1] /kraɪ/ *vi,vt* (*pt,pp* cried) 1 (of persons, animals, birds) make sounds that express feelings (e g pain, fear): *A baby can ~ as soon as it is born. He cried with pain when the dentist pulled the tooth out.* 2 (of persons) weep; shed tears (with or without sounds): *The boy was ~ing because he had lost his money.* **cry one's `heart out,** weep very bitterly. **cry oneself to sleep,** cry until one falls asleep. 3 exclaim; call out loudly in words: *'Help! Help!' he cried.* 4 announce for sale; make known by calling out: *to ~ the news all over the town.*

cry[2] /kraɪ/ *n* [C] (*pl* cries) 1 loud sound of fear, pain, grief, etc; loud, excited statement: *a ~ for help; the ~ of an animal in pain; angry cries from the mob.* **a `far/`long cry,** a long way from; very different from: *Being a junior clerk is a far ~ from being one of the Directors.* 2 words spoken loudly to give information: *the ~ of the night watchman.* 3 watchword or phrase, used for a principle or cause: *a `war-~. 'Asia for the Asians' was their ~.* 4 fit of weeping: *have a good ~.*

`cry-baby, young person who cries often or easily without good or apparent cause.

cry·ing /ˈkraɪɪŋ/ *adj* (esp of evils) demanding attention: *a ~ shame/evil/need.*

crypt /krɪpt/ *n* [C] underground room, esp of a church.

cryp·tic /ˈkrɪptɪk/ *adj* secret; with a hidden meaning, or a meaning not easily seen: *a ~ remark.*

cryp·ti·cal·ly /-klɪ/ *adv*

crys·tal /ˈkrɪstəl/ *n* 1 [U] transparent, natural substance like quartz; [C] piece of this as an ornament: *a necklace of ~s.* 2 [U] glassware of best quality, made into bowls, vases, etc: *The dining-table shone with silver and ~.* 3

[C] definite and regular shape taken naturally by the molecules of certain substances: *sugar and salt ~s; snow and ice ~s.*

crys·tal·line /ˈkrɪstəlaɪn/ *adj* made of crystal(s); like crystal; very clear.

crys·tal·lize /ˈkrɪstəlaɪz/ *vt,vi* 1 form, cause to form, into crystals(3). 2 cover (fruit, etc) with sugar-crystals: *~d ginger.* 3 (*fig*) (of ideas, plans) become, cause to be, clear and definite: *His vague ideas ~d into a definite plan.*

crys·tal·li·za·tion /ˌkrɪstəlaɪˈzeɪʃən/ *US:* -lɪˈz-/ *n* [U]

cub /kʌb/ *n* [C] young lion, bear, fox, tiger.

cubby-hole /ˈkʌbɪ həʊl/ *n* [C] small, enclosed space.

cube /kjub/ *n* [C] 1 solid body having six equal square sides; block of something so shaped or similarly shaped. 2 (*maths*) product of a number multiplied by itself twice: *The ~ of 5 (5³) is 5 × 5 × 5 (125).* □ *vt* multiply a number by itself twice: *10 ~d is 1 000.*

cu·bic /ˈkjubɪk/ *adj* having the shape of a cube; of a cube: *one ~ metre,* volume of a cube whose edge is one metre.

cu·bi·cal /ˈkjubɪkəl/ *adj* = cubic (the usual word).

cu·bi·cle /ˈkjubɪkəl/ *n* [C] small division of a larger room, walled or curtained to make a separate compartment, e g for sleeping in, or for (un)dressing, e g at a swimming-pool.

cub·ism /ˈkjubɪzm/ *n* [U] style in art in which objects are represented so that they appear to be largely of geometrical shapes.

cub·ist /ˈkjubɪst/, artist who practises cubism.

cuckoo /ˈkʊku/ *n* [C] bird whose call is like its name, a migratory bird which lays its eggs in the nests of other birds.

`cuckoo-clock, one that strikes the hours with notes like the call of a cuckoo.

cu·cum·ber /ˈkjukʌmbə(r)/ *n* [C,U] (creeping plant with a) long, green-skinned fleshy fruit, sliced and eaten in salads, or made into pickle. **as cool as a cucumber,** unexcited.

cud /kʌd/ *n* [U] food which oxen, etc bring back from the first stomach and chew again. **chew the cud,** (*fig*) reflect; ponder.

cuddle /ˈkʌdəl/ *vt,vi* 1 hold close and lovingly in one's arms: *She likes to ~ her doll.* 2 lie close and comfortably: *The children ~d up* (*together*) *under the blankets.* □ *n* [C] act of cuddling; hug.

cud·dly /ˈkʌdlɪ/ *adj* suitable for, inviting, cuddling: *a nice cuddly doll.*

cud·gel /ˈkʌdʒəl/ *vt,* *n* (-ll-; *US* also -l-) (hit with a) short, thick stick or club.

cue[1] /kju/ *n* [C] 1 something (e g the last words of an actor's speech) which shows when somebody else is to do or say something. 2 hint about how to behave, what to do, etc. **take one's cue from sb,** observe what he does as a guide to one's own action.

cue[2] /kju/ *n* [C] billiard-player's long, tapering, leather-tipped rod, for striking the ball.

cuff¹ /kʌf/ n [C] end of a shirt or coat sleeve at the wrist.

`cuff-link, used for fastening a cuff.

cuff² /kʌf/ vt, n [C] (give a) light blow with the open hand.

cui·sine /kwɪˈziːn/ n [U] (*Fr*) style of cooking; cooking: *a hotel where the ~ is excellent.*

cul-de-sac /ˈkʌl də ˈsæk/ n [C] street with an opening at one end only.

cu·li·nary /ˈkʌlɪnərɪ US: -nerɪ/ adj of cooking or a kitchen: *~ plants,* good for cooking.

cull /kʌl/ vt select: *extracts ~ed from the best authors.*

cul·len·der /ˈkʌləndə(r)/ n [C] = colander.

cul·mi·nate /ˈkʌlmɪneɪt/ vt *culminate in,* (of efforts, hopes, careers, etc) reach the highest point: *misfortunes that ~d in bankruptcy.*

cul·mi·na·tion /ˌkʌlmɪˈneɪʃən/ n [C] highest point: *the culmination of his career.*

culp·able /ˈkʌlpəbəl/ adj (*legal*) blameworthy; deserving punishment: *hold a person ~.*

culp·ably /-əblɪ/ adv

cul·prit /ˈkʌlprɪt/ n [C] person who has done wrong.

cult /kʌlt/ n [C] **1** system of religious worship. **2** devotion to a person or practice and ritual (esp of a single deity): *the ~ of archery; the ~ of Browning.* **3** (group of persons devoted to a) popular fashion or craze.

cul·ti·vate /ˈkʌltɪveɪt/ vt **1** prepare (land) for crops by ploughing, etc; help (crops) to grow (e g by breaking up the soil around them, destroying weeds, etc). **2** give care, thought, time, etc in order to develop something: *to ~ the mind/a person's friendship.*

cul·ti·vated /ˈkʌltɪveɪtɪd/ adj (of a person) having good manners and education.

cul·ti·va·tion /ˌkʌltɪˈveɪʃən/ n [U] cultivating or being cultivated: *the ~ of the soil; land that is under ~.*

cul·ti·va·tor /ˈkʌltɪveɪtə(r)/ n [C] **1** person who cultivates. **2** machine for breaking up ground, destroying weeds, etc.

cul·tural /ˈkʌltʃərəl/ adj having to do with culture: *~ studies,* e g art, literature.

cul·ture /ˈkʌltʃə(r)/ n **1** [U] advanced development of the human powers; development of the body, mind and spirit by training and experience: *Physical ~ is important, but we must not neglect the ~ of the mind.* **2** [U] evidence of intellectual development (of arts, science, etc) in human society: *Universities should be centres of ~.* **3** [U] state of intellectual development among a people; [C] particular form of intellectual development: *We owe much to Greek ~.* **4** [U] all the arts, beliefs, social institutions, etc characteristic of a community, race, etc: *the*

Arabic ~. **5** [U] cultivating; the rearing of bees, silkworms, etc: *He has five acres devoted to bulb ~,* to the growing of such flowers as daffodils and tulips. **6** [C] growth of bacteria (for medical or scientific study): *a ~ of cholera germs.*

cul·tured adj (of persons) cultivated; (of tastes, interests, etc) refined.

cul·vert /ˈkʌlvət/ n [C] sewer or drain that crosses under a road, railway or embankment; channel for electrical cables under the ground.

cum·ber·some /ˈkʌmbəsəm/ adj heavy and awkward to carry: *a ~ parcel.*

cumu·lat·ive /ˈkjuːmjʊlətɪv US: -leɪtɪv/ adj increasing in amount by one addition after another.

cumu·lus /ˈkjuːmjʊləs/ n [C] (*pl* -li /-lɪ/) cloud made up of rounded masses on a flat base.

cunei·form /ˈkjuːnɪɪfɔːm/ adj wedge-shaped: *~ characters,* as used in old Persian and Assyrian writing.

cun·ning¹ /ˈkʌnɪŋ/ adj clever at deceiving; showing this kind of cleverness: *a ~ old fox; a ~ trick.*

cun·ning·ly adv

cun·ning² /ˈkʌnɪŋ/ n [U] quality of being cunning: *The boy showed a great deal of ~ in getting what he wanted.*

cup¹ /kʌp/ n [C] **1** small porcelain bowl, with a handle, used with a saucer, for tea, coffee etc; contents of a cup: *a `tea~; a `~ of `coffee. not my cup of tea,* (*informal*) not what I like, not what suits me. **2** = chalice. **3** vessel (usually of gold or silver) given as a prize in competitions: *I hope Arsenal will win the ~!* **4** thing shaped like a cup: *the ~ of a flower; an `egg-~; the ~s of a bra.*

`cup final, football match to decide the winner of a competition between many teams.

`cup-tie, football match to eliminate teams competing for a cup(3).

cup-ful /ˈkʌpfʊl/ n [C] (*pl ~s*) as much as a cup will hold.

cup² /kʌp/ vt (-pp-) **1** put into the shape of a cup: *to ~ one's hands,* e g to catch a ball. **2** put round or over like a cup: *with her chin ~ped in her hand.*

cup·board /ˈkʌbəd/ n [C] set of shelves with doors, either built into a room as a fixture, or a separate piece of furniture, used for dishes, provisions, clothes, etc.

Cu·pid /ˈkjuːpɪd/ n **1** Roman god of love; (picture or statue of a) beautiful boy (with wings and a bow and arrows). **2** symbol of love.

cu·pola /ˈkjuːpələ/ n [C] (*pl ~s*) small dome forming (part of) a roof; ceiling of a dome.

cur /kɜː(r)/ n [C] **1** bad-tempered or worthless dog (esp low-bred). **2** cowardly or badly behaved man.

cur·able /ˈkjʊərəbəl/ adj that can be cured.

cura·bil·ity /ˌkjʊərəˈbɪlətɪ/ n [U]

cur·acy /ˈkjʊərəsɪ/ n [C] (pl -ies) office and work of a curate.

curate /ˈkjʊərət/ n [C] clergyman who helps a parish priest (rector or vicar).

cura·tive /ˈkjʊərətɪv/ adj helping to, able to, cure (disease or ill health): the ~ value of sunshine and sea air.

cu·ra·tor /kjʊˈreɪtə(r)/ n [C] official in charge of (esp) of a museum or art gallery.

curb /kɜːb/ n [C] 1 chain or leather strap passing under a horse's jaw, used to control it. 2 (fig) something that holds one back or restrains: put/keep a ~ on one's anger/ passions. 3 = kerb. □ vt 1 control (a horse) by means of a curb. 2 keep (feelings, etc) under control: to ~ one's impatience.

curd /kɜːd/ n 1 [C] (often pl) thick, soft substance, almost solid, formed when milk turns sour, used to make cheese. 2 [U] (in compounds) substance resembling curd: 'lemon-~, made from eggs, butter and sugar, flavoured with lemon.

curdle /ˈkɜːdəl/ vi,vt 1 form, cause to form, into curds: The milk has ~d. 2 (fig): What a blood-curdling (= horrifying) yell!

cure¹ /kjʊə(r)/ n [C] 1 curing or being cured(1): The doctor cannot guarantee a ~. 2 substance or treatment which cures(1): Is there a ~ for cancer yet?

cure² /kjʊə(r)/ vt,vi 1 bring (a person) back to health; provide and use successfully a remedy for a disease, ill health, suffering; get rid of (an evil): to ~ a man of a disease; to ~ a child of bad habits. 2 treat meat, fish, skin, tobacco, etc in order to keep it in good condition by salting, smoking, drying, etc: 'well-~d bacon.

cur·few /ˈkɜːfjuː/ n [C] (modern use) time or signal (under martial law) for people to remain indoors: to impose a ~ on a town; to lift/end the ~.

curi·os·ity /ˌkjʊərɪˈɒsətɪ/ n (pl -ies) 1 [U] being curious(1,2): to be dying of/burning with ~ to know what was happening. 2 [C] curious(3) thing; strange or rare object.

curi·ous /ˈkjʊərɪəs/ adj 1 eager (to learn, know): I'm ~ to know what he said. 2 having or showing too much interest in the affairs of others: ~ neighbours. 3 strange; unusual; hard to understand: What a ~ mistake! Isn't he a ~-looking little man!
curi·ous·ly adv

curl¹ /kɜːl/ n 1 [C] something naturally like or twisted into a shape like the thread of a screw, esp a lock of hair of this shape: ~s (of hair) falling over a girl's shoulders; a ~ of smoke rising from a cigarette. 2 [U] the state of being curly: How do you keep your hair in ~?

curl² /kɜːl/ vt,vi make into curls; twist; grow or be in curls: Does her hair ~ naturally? The dog ~ed (itself) up on the rug.

cur·lew /ˈkɜːljuː/ n [C] wading bird with a long, slender, down-curved bill.

curly /ˈkɜːlɪ/ adj (-ier, -iest) having curls;

arranged in curls: ~ hair; a ~-headed girl.

cur·rant /ˈkʌrənt US: ˈkɜːr-/ n [C] 1 small, sweet, dried seedless grape (grown in Greece and neighbouring countries) used in buns, cakes, puddings, etc. 2 (cultivated bush with) small black, red or white juicy fruit growing in clusters.

cur·rency /ˈkʌrənsɪ US: ˈkɜːr-/ n (pl -ies) 1 [U] the state of being in common or general use: The rumour soon gained ~, was repeated until many people were aware of it. 2 [C,U] money that is in use in a country: foreign currencies; a decimal ~.

cur·rent¹ /ˈkʌrənt US: ˈkɜːr-/ adj 1 in common or general use; generally accepted: ~ opinions/beliefs; words that are no longer ~. 2 now passing; of the present time: the ~ year, this year; a newsreel showing ~ events.

'current account, (with a bank) one from which money may be drawn without previous notice.

cur·rent·ly adv at the present time: It is ~ly reported that…

cur·rent² /ˈkʌrənt US: ˈkɜːr-/ n [C] 1 stream of water, air, gas, esp one flowing through slower moving or still water, etc: A cold ~ of air came in when the door was opened. Although he was a strong swimmer he was swept away by the ~ and was drowned. 2 flow of electricity through something or along a wire or cable. 3 course or movement (of events, opinions, thoughts, etc): The government used the radio to influence the ~ of thought.

cur·ric·u·lum /kəˈrɪkjʊləm/ n [C] (pl ~s or -la /-lə/) course of study in a school, college, etc.

'curriculum vitae /ˈviːtaɪ/ (Latin) brief written account of one's past history (e g education, employment), used when applying for a job, etc.

curry¹ /ˈkʌrɪ US: ˈkɜːrɪ/ n (pt, pp -ies) [C,U] (dish of) meat, fish, eggs, etc cooked with hot-tasting spices: Madras curries. □ vt (pt, pp, -ied) prepare curry.

curry² /ˈkʌrɪ US: ˈkɜːrɪ/ vt (pt -ied) 1 rub down and clean (a horse). 2 prepare (tanned leather) by soaking, scraping, etc. 3 **curry favour (with sb),** try to win favour or approval (by using flattery, etc).

curse¹ /kɜːs/ n [C] 1 word, phrase or sentence calling for the punishment, injury or destruction. 2 cause of misfortune or ruin: Gambling is often a ~. The rabbits are a ~ (i e do a lot of damage to crops, etc) in this part of the country. 3 word or words used in violent language expressing anger. 4 the ~, (informal) = menses.

curse² /kɜːs/ vt,vi 1 use a curse against; use violent language against. 2 utter curses: to ~ and swear; cursing at a stupid mistake. 3 **be cursed with,** suffer misfortune, trouble, etc because of: to be ~d with a violent temper.

cursed /kɜst, ˈkɜːsɪd/ *adj* **1** damnable; hateful. **2** (*informal*) very bad: *This work is a ~ nuisance.*

cur·sive /ˈkɜːsɪv/ *adj* (of handwriting) with elaborate letters rounded and joined together.

cur·sory /ˈkɜːsərɪ/ *adj* (of work, reading, etc) quick; hurried; done without attention to details: *a ~ glance/inspection.*
cur·sor·ily /ˈkɜːsərɪlɪ/ *adv*

curst /kɜst/ *adj* = cursed.

curt /kɜt/ *adj* (of a speaker, his manner, what he says) abrupt: *I gave him a ~ answer.*
curt·ly *adv*
curt·ness *n* [U]

cur·tail /kɜˈteɪl/ *vt* make shorter than was first planned; cut off a part of: *to ~ a speech/one's holidays.*
cur·tail·ment *n* [C,U] act or result of curtailing.

cur·tain /ˈkɜːtən/ *n* [C] **1** piece of cloth, etc as hung up at a window: *Please draw the ~s,* pull them across the window(s). **2** sheet of heavy material to draw or lower across the front of the stage in a theatre before and after each scene of a play. **3** (various senses indicating cover or protection): *A ~ of mist hid the view.* □ *vt* **1** furnish or cover with curtains: *enough material to ~ all the windows.* **2** *curtain off,* separate or divide with curtains: *to ~ off part of a room.*

curt·sey, curtsy /ˈkɜːtsɪ/ *n* [C] (*pl* ~s, -ies) gesture of respect (bending the knees) made by women and girls (e g to a queen) □ *vi* (*pt,pp* ~ed, -ied) make this gesture.

cur·va·ture /ˈkɜːvətʃə(r)/ *US:* -tʃʊər/ *n* [C] curving; the state of being curved: *to suffer from ~ of the spine; the ~ of the earth's surface.*

curve /kɜv/ *n* [C] line of which no part is straight and which changes direction without angles: *a ~ in the road.* □ *vt,vi* have, cause to have, the form of a curve: *The river ~s round the hill.*

cushion /ˈkʊʃən/ *n* [C] **1** small bag filled with feathers or other soft material (e g foam rubber), to make a seat more comfortable, or to kneel on, etc. **2** something soft and like a cushion in shape or function: *a ~ of moss; a `pin-~; a ~ of air,* as for a hovercraft. □ *vt* **1** supply with cushions; **2** protect from shock with cushions: *~ed seats.* **3** (*fig*) protect from harmful changes: *farmers who are ~ed against falls in prices,* e g by subsidies.

cushy /ˈkʊʃɪ/ *adj* (-ier, -iest) (*sl*) (of a job, etc) not requiring much effort: *get a ~ job in the Civil Service.*

cusp /kʌsp/ *n* [C] pointed end (esp of a leaf).

cuss /kʌs/ *n* [C] (*sl*) **1** curse. **not worth a tinker's cuss,** worthless. **2** person: *a queer old ~.*

cus·tard /ˈkʌstəd/ *n* [C,U] **1** (`egg-~) (dish of) mixture of eggs and milk, sweetened and flavoured, baked or boiled; **2**

similar mixture prepared by adding sugar and milk to flavoured cornflour (`~-powder), eaten with fruit, pastry, etc

cus·to·dian /kʌˈstəʊdɪən/ *n* [C] **1** person who has custody of something or somebody **2** caretaker of a public building.

cus·tody /ˈkʌstədɪ/ *n* [U] **1** (duty of) caring for, guarding: *A father has the ~ of his children while they are young. You should leave your jewellery in safe ~,* e g with your bank. **2** imprisonment. **(be) in custody,** in prison (e g awaiting trial).

cus·tom /ˈkʌstəm/ *n* **1** [U] usual and generally accepted behaviour among members of a social group (either small or large, e g a nation): *Don't be a slave to ~,* Do not do things merely because most people do them and have always done them. **2** [C] particular way of behaving which, because it has been long established, is observed by individuals and social groups: *Social ~s vary in different countries.* (*Note:* Compare *habit,* a word that means something that a person does regularly and that he cannot easily give up.) **3** [U] regular support given to a tradesman by those who buy his goods: *We should very much like to have your ~.* **4** (*pl*) taxes due to the government on goods imported into a country; import duties; department of government (*the C~s*) that collects such duties: *How long will it take us to pass* (= get through) *the C~s?* **5** (esp *US*) made to order.

cus·tom·ary /ˈkʌstəmərɪ *US:* -merɪ/ *adj* in agreement with, according to, custom(1,2): *the ~ vote of thanks to the chairman.*
cus·tom·ar·ily /ˈkʌstəmərəlɪ *US:* ˈkʌstəˈmerɪlɪ/ *adv*

cus·tomer /ˈkʌstəmə(r)/ *n* [C] **1** person who buys things, esp one who gives his custom(3) to a shop: *Mr Jones has lost some of his best ~s.* **2** (*informal*) person or fellow, (esp): *a queer/awkward ~,* person who is difficult to deal with.

cut¹ /kʌt/ *n* [C] **1** act of cutting; stroke with a sword, whip, etc; result of such as a stroke; opening made by a knife or other sharp-edged tool, etc: *a deep ~ in the leg.* **2** reduction in size, amount, length, etc: *a ~ in prices/salaries/expenditure.* **3** a cutting out; part that is cut out: *There were several ~s in the film,* Parts of it had been deleted **4** something obtained by cutting: *a nice ~ of beef.* **5** style in which clothes, hair, etc are made by cutting. **6** remark, etc that wounds a person's feelings: *That remark was a ~ at me.* **7** refusal to recognise a person. **8** a way across (from one place to another) that shortens the distance: *Let's take a `short ~.* **9** *a cut a`bove,* (*informal*) rather superior to: *She's a cut above the other girls in the office.*

cut² /kʌt/ *vt,vi* (*pt,pp* ~) (-tt-) (For uses with *adverbial particles* and *prepositions,* ⇨ **9** below; for uses with *adjectives* ⇨ **7** below·

for uses with *nouns* or *pronouns* ⇨ 6 below.) **1** make an opening, incision, mark, wound, etc (with a sharp-edged instrument, e g a knife, a pair of scissors, or other edged tool): *He ∼ his face/himself while shaving. I'm having my hair ∼*(= shortened) *tomorrow. Has the wheat been ∼*(= harvested, reaped) *yet? Please ∼ a slice of cake for me/∼ me a slice of cake. Two scenes/episodes were ∼*(= deleted) *by the censor. Was your salary ∼*(= reduced)*? He cut a tunnel through a hill.* **2 (a)** (of a sharp tool, instrument, etc) be suitable to use: *This knife does not ∼ well.* **(b)** (of a material) be capable of being cut: *Sandstone ∼s easily.* **3** stay away from, be absent from: *to ∼ a class/a lecture.* **4** (of lines) cross: *Let the point where AB ∼s CD be called E.* **5** (sport, esp cricket, tennis, billiards) strike (a ball) so that it spins or is deflected; hit the edge of (a ball). **6** (used with *nouns* or *pronouns*) **cut the cards/pack,** lift part of a pack of playing-cards lying face downwards and turn it up to decide something (e g who is to deal). **cut (off) a corner,** go across, not round it. **cut corners,** (*fig*) take a short-cut. **cut a disc/record,** record music, etc on to a gramophone record. **cut the ground from under sb/from under sb's feet,** leave him in a weak or illogical position; destroy the foundation of his plan, argument, etc. **cut no/not much ice (with sb),** have little or no effect or influence (on). **cut one's losses,** abandon a scheme that has caused financial losses before one loses too much. **cut both ways,** (of an action or argument) have an effect both for and against. **7** (used with *adjectives*) **cut sb dead,** pretend not to have seen somebody; treat as a complete stranger: *She ∼ me dead in the street,* ignored me completely. **cut sth/sb loose (from),** make loose or separate by cutting: *∼ oneself loose from one's family,* live an independent life. **cut sth open,** make an opening or split in: *He fell and ∼ his head open.* **cut sth short,** make shorter: *to ∼ a long story short; a career ∼ short by illness.* **8** (as a *pp*) **cut and dried,** (of opinions, etc) already formed and unlikely to be changed. **9** (uses with *adverbial particles* and *prepositions*):

cut across sth, (a) take a shorter route across (a field, etc). **(b)** be contrary to: *Opinion on the Common Market ∼ clean across normal political loyalties.*

cut sth away, remove by cutting: *We ∼ way all the dead wood from the tree.*

cut sth back, (a) (of shrubs, bushes, etc) prune close to the stem. **(b)** reduce: *∼ back production.* Hence, **'cut-back** n [C].

cut sth/sb down, (a) cause to fall by cutting: *to ∼ down a tree.* **(b)** kill or injure with a weapon. **(c)** deprive of life or health (by disease, etc): *He was ∼ down in his prime.* **(d)** reduce in quantity, amount, etc: *I won't*

have a cigarette, thanks—I'm trying to ∼ down, reduce the number of cigarettes 1 smoke. **(e)** persuade (a person) to reduce a price, charge, etc: *We managed to ∼ him down by £30.* **(f)** reduce the length of: *∼ down a pair of trousers.* **cut down on,** reduce one's consumption of: *He's trying to ∼ down on cigarettes and beer.*

cut in, (a) (of the driver of a motor-vehicle, etc who has overtaken another vehicle) return too soon to his own side of the road (with possibility of collision, etc): *Accidents are often caused by drivers who ∼ in.* **(b)** interrupt (a conversation, etc): *cut in half/two/three, etc, divide.*

cut sb/sth off (from), (a) remove by cutting: *He ∼ off a metre of cloth from the roll.* **(b)** stop; interrupt; isolate: *be ∼ off while talking by telephone; ∼ off the gas/electricity supply; be ∼ off from all possibility of help.*

cut out, stop functioning: *One of the aircraft's engines ∼ out.* **cut sth out, (a)** remove by cutting (e g from a periodical): *That's an interesting article—I'll ∼ it out.* **(b)** make by cutting: *∼ out a path through the jungle.* **(c)** shape (a garment) by cutting the outlines of the parts on cloth: *∼ out a dress.* **(d)** (*informal*) leave out; omit: *Let's ∼ out unimportant details.* **(e)** (*informal*) stop doing or using: *My doctor told me 1 must ∼ out tobacco,* stop smoking. **cut sb out,** defeat, eliminate (a rival, esp in a competition. *(not) be cut out for,* (not) have the qualities and abilities needed for: *He's not ∼ out for that sort of work.*

cut sth/sb up, (a) cut into pieces: *∼ up one's meat.* **(b)** destroy: *∼ up the enemy's forces.* **(c)** (*informal*) cause mental suffering to: *He was badly ∼ up by the news of his son's death.* **cut up rough,** (*sl*) be violent and aggressive: *He'll ∼ up rough if you don't give him what he asked for.*

'cut 'glass, glassware with designs cut or engraved in it.

'cut-out n **(a)** article, etc cut out of a newspaper, etc. **(b)** device that disconnects an electric circuit.

'cut 'price, (esp) reduced below those of rivals or the manufacture's recommend price.

'cut-'rate *adj* at a reduced price.

cute /kjut/ *adj* (-r, -st) **1** sharp-witted; quick-thinking. **2** (*informal*) attractive; pretty and charming.
cute-ly *adv*
cute-ness n [U]

cu-ticle /'kjutɪkəl/ n [C] outer layer of hardened skin at the base of a finger-nail or toe-nail.

cut-lass /'kʌtləs/ n [C] **1** (sailor's) short, one-edged sword with a slightly curved blade. **2** cutting tool as used by cacao-growers and copra-growers.

cut-ler /'kʌtlə(r)/ n [C] man who makes and

repairs knives and other cutting tools and instruments.

cut·lery /ˈkʌtlərɪ/ n [U] **1** implements used at table (knives, forks). **2** trade of, things made or sold by, cutlers.

cut·let /ˈkʌtlət/ n [C] slice of meat or fish for one person: *a veal* ∼.

cut·ter /ˈkʌtə(r)/ n [C] **1** person or thing that cuts: *a tailor's* ∼, who cuts out cloth; `*wire-*∼s. **2** sailing-vessel with one mast; ship's boat, for use between ship and shore.

cut-throat /ˈkʌtθrəʊt/ n [C] murderer. □ adj murderous: ∼ *competition*, likely to ruin the weaker competitors.

cut·ting¹ /ˈkʌtɪŋ/ adj **1** sharp; piercing: *a* ∼ *wind*. **2** sarcastic: *a* ∼ *remark*.

cut·ting² /ˈkʌtɪŋ/ n [C] **1** unroofed passage dug through the ground for a road, railway, canal, etc. **2** something cut from a newspaper, etc and kept for reference: `*press* ∼s. **3** short piece of the stem of a plant, to be used for growing a new plant: *chrysanthemum* ∼s; **4** [U] process of editing cinema films, tape recordings, etc, by cutting out unwanted parts.

cuttle·fish /ˈkʌtlfɪʃ/ n [C] sea-animal with long arms (tentacles) which sends out a black liquid when attacked.

cy·an·ide /ˈsaɪənaɪd/ n [U] poisonous compound substance: *potassium* ∼; *sodium* ∼.

cycle /ˈsaɪkəl/ n [C] **1** series of events taking place in a regularly repeated order: *the* ∼ *of the seasons*. **2** complete set or series: *a song* ∼, e g by Schubert. **3** (common abbr for) bicycle or motor-cycle. □ vi ride a bicycle.

cyc·list /ˈsaɪklɪst/, person who cycles.

cyc·lone /ˈsaɪkləʊn/ n [C] violent wind rotating round a calm central area; violent windstorm.

cyc·lonic /saɪˈklɒnɪk/ adj of or like a cyclone.

cyg·net /ˈsɪɡnɪt/ n [C] young swan.

cyl·in·der /ˈsɪlɪndə(r)/ n [C] **1** solid or hollow body shaped like a pole or log. **2** cylinder-shaped chamber (in an engine) in which gas or steam works a piston: *a six-*∼ *engine/motor-car*.

cy·lin·dri·cal /sɪˈlɪndrɪkəl/ adj cylinder-shaped.

cym·bal /ˈsɪmbəl/ n [C] one of a pair of round brass plates struck together to make clanging sounds.

cynic /ˈsɪnɪk/ n [C] person who sees little or no good in anything and who has no belief in human progress; person who shows this by sneering and being sarcastic.

cyni·cism /ˈsɪnɪsɪzm/ n [U] cynic's opinions or attitude of mind; [C] expression of this attitude.

cyni·cal /ˈsɪnɪkəl/ adj of or like a cynic; sneering or contemptuous: *a* ∼ *smile/ remark*.

cyni·cally /-klɪ/ adv

cy·pher /ˈsaɪfə(r)/ n [C] = cipher.

cy·press /ˈsaɪprəs/ n [C] (kinds of) evergreen tree with dark leaves and hard wood.

cyst /sɪst/ n [C] enclosed hollow organ in the body containing liquid matter.

czar /zɑ(r)/ n (also **tsar**) emperor (of Russia before 1917).

czar·ina /zɑˈriːnə/ n Russian empress.

Dd

D, d /diː/ (pl D's, d's /diːz/) **1** the fourth letter of the English alphabet. **2** Roman numeral for 500.

'd, used for *had* or *would* (esp after *I, we, you, he, she, they, who*).

dab¹ /dæb/ vt,vi (-bb-) touch, put on, lightly and gently: ∼ *one's eyes with a handkerchief*. □ n [C] **1** small quantity (of paint, etc) dabbed on. **2** slight tap; brief application of something to a surface (without rubbing).

dabble /ˈdæbəl/ vt,vi **1** splash (the hands, feet, etc) about in water; put in and out of water. **2** (in art, politics, etc) engage in, study, as a hobby, not professionally: ∼ *in philosophy*.

dachs·hund /ˈdækshʊnd/ n [C] small short-legged breed of dog.

dad /dæd/ n [C] (*informal*) = father.

daddy /ˈdædɪ/ n [C] (pl -ies) child's word for 'father'.

'daddy-'long-legs, crane-fly (a long-legged flying insect).

daf·fo·dil /ˈdæfədɪl/ n [C] plant with a yellow flower and long narrow leaves, growing from a bulb.

daft /dɑːft US: dæft/ adj (-er, -est) (*informal*) silly; foolish; reckless.

daft·ly adv

dag·ger /ˈdæɡə(r)/ n [C] short, pointed, two-edged knife used as a weapon.

dah·lia /ˈdeɪlɪə US: ˈdælɪə/ n [C] (pl ∼s) garden plant with brightly coloured flowers, growing from tuberous roots.

daily /ˈdeɪlɪ/ adj, adv happening, done, appearing, every day (or every weekday): *Most newspapers appear* ∼. *Thousands of people cross this bridge* ∼. □ n [C] (pl -ies) **1** newspaper published every day or every weekday. **2** (*informal*) woman who is paid to come and do housework every day.

dainty /ˈdeɪntɪ/ adj (-ier, -iest) **1** (of persons) pretty, neat and delicate(1,3) in appearance and tastes: *a* ∼ *little girl*. **2** (of persons and animals) rather difficult to please because of delicate tastes: *She's* ∼ *about her food*. **3** (of things) pretty; delicate(3), easily injured or broken: ∼ *cups and saucers*. **4** (of food) delicate(8) and delicious: ∼ *cakes*.

dain·tily /-təlɪ/ adv

dainti·ness n [U]

dairy /ˈdeərɪ/ n [C] (pl -ies) **1** shop where milk, butter, eggs, etc, are sold. **2** (part of a) building where milk and milk products are prepared.

`dairy cattle, cows raised to produce milk, not meat.

`dairy·maid, woman who works in a dairy.

`dairy·man, dealer in milk, etc.

dais /ˈdeɪs/ n [C] (pl ~es /-zɪz/) platform (esp at the end of a hall) for a throne or for a desk (for a lecturer, etc).

daisy /ˈdeɪzɪ/ n [C] (pl -ies) small white flower with a yellow centre; other similar plants of various sorts. **push up the daisies,** ⇨ push¹(8).

dale /deɪl/ n [C] (esp in N England and in poetry) valley.

dally /ˈdælɪ/ vi (pt,pp -ied) **1** trifle; think idly about: ~ with an idea or proposal. **2** waste time: Don't ~ over your work.

dam¹ /dæm/ n [C] barrier built to keep back water and raise its level (e g to form a reservoir, or for hydro-electric power). □ vt (-mm-) **1** make a dam across (a narrow valley, etc); hold back by means of a dam: ~ up a river. **2** (fig) hold back: to ~ up one's feelings.

dam² /dæm/ n [C] mother (of four-footed animals). ⇨ sire.

dam·age /ˈdæmɪdʒ/ n **1** [U] harm or injury that causes loss of value: The insurance company will pay for the ~ to my car. **2** (pl) (legal) money claimed from or paid by a person causing loss or injury: He claimed £5 000 ~s from his employers for the loss of his right arm. □ vt cause damage(1) to: furniture ~d by fire.

dame /deɪm/ n [C] **1** (title of a) woman who has been awarded the highest grade of the Order of the British Empire: D~ Agatha Christie. ⇨ lady(6). **2** (US sl) woman.

damn /dæm/ vt **1** (of God) condemn to everlasting punishment. **2** condemn; say that something or somebody is worthless, bad, etc: The book was ~ed by the critics. **3** (used to express anger, annoyance, impatience, etc): I'll be ~ed if I'll go, I refuse to go. Oh ~! D~ you/your impudence! □ in **not (be) worth a damn,** (be) worthless.

dam·nable /ˈdæmnəbəl/ adj **1** hateful; deserving to be damned. **2** (informal) very bad: ~ weather.

dam·nably /ˈdæmnəblɪ/ adv

dam·na·tion /dæmˈneɪʃən/ n [U] being damned; ruin: to suffer eternal ~. □ int Curse it, you, etc.

damned /dæmd/ adj **1** the ~, souls in hell. **2** (informal) deserving to be damned: You ~ fool! □ adv (informal) extremely: ~ hot/funny.

damp¹ /dæmp/ adj (-er, -est) not thoroughly dry; having some moisture (in or on): ~ clothes. □ n [U] state of being damp; damp atmosphere; moisture on the surface of, or existing throughout, something: The ~ rising from the ground caused the walls to stain badly.

damp·ish adj rather damp.

damp·ness n [U]

damp² /dæmp/ vt,vi **1** make damp(1): to ~ clothes before ironing them. **2** (also `damp·en) make sad or dull: Nothing could ~ his spirits. **3** **damp down,** make (a fire) burn more slowly (e g by heaping ashes on it, or by controlling the draught of air entering a stove, etc).

dampen /ˈdæmpən/ vt,vi = damp²(2.

damper /ˈdæmpə(r)/ n [C] **1** movable metal plate that regulates the flow of air into a fire in a stove or furnace. **2** person or thing that checks or discourages: His complaints were a ~ on the evening.

dam·sel /ˈdæmzəl/ n [C] (old use) girl; young unmarried woman.

dam·son /ˈdæmzən/ n **1** [C] (tree producing) small dark-purple plum. **2** [U] dark-purple colour.

dance¹ /dɑns US: dæns/ n [C] **1** (series of) movements and steps in time with music; special form (e g a waltz), tune, piece of music, for such movements and steps: May I have the next ~? **2** social gathering for dancing.

dance² /dɑns US: dæns/ vi,vt **1** move in rhythmical steps, usually with music, either alone, or with a partner, or in a group: They went on dancing until after midnight. **2** perform (a named kind of) such movements or the named (style of) music for it): to ~ a waltz/Swanlake. **3** move in a lively way, quickly, up and down, etc: The leaves were dancing in the wind. **4** cause to dance(3): to ~ a baby on one's knee.

dancer, person who dances.

danc·ing adj (of or that dances). □ n [U] (in compounds) `dancing-teacher, professional teacher of dancing; `dancing-partner, person with whom one (usually) dances; `ballet-dancing; `tap-dancing.

dan·de·lion /ˈdændɪlaɪən/ n [C] small wild plant with bright-yellow flowers.

dan·druff /ˈdændrʌf/ n [U] dead skin in small scales among the hair of the scalp.

dandy /ˈdændɪ/ n [C] (pl -ies) man who pays too much care to his clothes and personal appearance.

dan·ger /ˈdeɪndʒə(r)/ n **1** [U] chance of suffering, liability to suffer, injury or loss of life: Is there any ~ of fire? **in danger (of):** His life was in ~. He was in ~ of losing his life. **out of danger:** He has been very ill, but the doctors say that he is now out of ~, not likely to die. **2** [C] something or somebody that may cause danger: That man is a ~ to society.

dan·ger·ous /ˈdeɪndʒərəs/ adj likely to cause danger: a ~ bridge/journey/illness. The river is ~ to bathe in.

dan·ger·ous·ly adv

dangle /ˈdæŋgəl/ vi,vt **1** hang or swing loosely; carry (something) so that it hangs or swings loosely: a bunch of keys dangling at the end of a chain. **2** dangle round/about, remain near (as an admirer) hoping to obtain something: She keeps her men dangling (about her).

dank /dæŋk/ adj (-er, -est) damp in an unpleasant or unhealthy way: a ~ and chilly cave.

dapple /ˈdæpəl/ vt mark, become marked, with rounded patches of different colour or shades of colour, esp of an animal, or of sunlight and shadow: a ~d horse; ~d shade, as when sunlight comes through the leaves of trees. (Note: usually used as a pp.)
'dapple-'grey adj, n [C] (horse) of grey with darker patches.

dare¹ /deə(r)/ auxiliary verb (3rd person sing is dare, not dares) have the courage, impudence, to: He wanted to fight me but he ~n't. How ~ he say rude things about me!

dare² /deə(r)/ vt,vi **1** be brave enough to: They wouldn't ~ (to be so rude)! **2** take the risk of; face: He will ~ any danger. **3** suggest that somebody has not the courage or ability to do sth: I ~ you (to say that again)! □ n (only in) **do sth for a dare**, do it because one is dared(3) to do it.
'dare-devil, person who is foolishly bold or reckless.

dar·ing /ˈdeərɪŋ/ n [U] adventurous courage: the ~ of the paratroops. □ adj bold and adventurous: a ~ robbery. What a ~ thing to do!
dar·ing·ly adv

dark¹ /dɑːk/ adj (-er, -est) **1** with no or very little light: a ~, moonless night. It's getting too ~ to take photographs. **2** (of colour) not reflecting much light; nearer black than white: ~ blue/green/brown; `~-brown eyes. **3** (of the skin) not fair: a ~ complexion. **4** (fig) hidden, mysterious: a ~ secret, one that is closely guarded. **keep it dark**, keep a secret. **a dark horse**, (fig) person whose capabilities may be greater than they are known to be. **5** hopeless; sad; cheerless: Don't look on the ~ side of things. **6** unenlightened (morally or intellectually).
the 'Dark Ages, (in European history), from the 6th to the 12th centuries.
dark·ly adv
dark·ness n [U] the state of being dark: The room was in complete ~ness.

dark² /dɑːk/ n [U] **1** absence of light: All the lights went out and we were left in the ~. **before/after dark**, before/after the sun goes down. **2** (fig) ignorance: We were completely in the ~ about his movements.

dar·ling /ˈdɑːlɪŋ/ n [C] person or object very much loved.

darn¹ /dɑːn/ vt,vi mend (esp something knitted, eg a sock) by passing thread in and out and in two directions: My socks have been ~ed again and again. □ n [C] place mended by darning.
'darning-needle, large sewing needle used for darning.

darn² /dɑːn/ vt(sl) = damn(3).

dart¹ /dɑːt/ n [C] **1** quick, sudden, forward movement: The child made a sudden ~ across the road. **2** small, sharp-pointed missile (feathered and pointed), to be thrown at a target (marked with numbers for scoring) in the game called darts.

dart² /dɑːt/ vi,vt (cause to) move forward suddenly and quickly; send suddenly and quickly: The deer ~ed away when it saw us. She ~ed into the shop.

dash¹ /dæʃ/ n **1** [C] sudden rush; violent movement: to make a ~ for shelter/ freedom. **2** [C] (sound of) liquid striking something or being thrown or struck: the ~ of the waves on the rocks. **3** [C] small amount of something added or mixed: water with a ~ of whisky in it; red with a ~ of blue. **4** [C] stroke of the pen or a mark (—) used in printing. **5** short race: the 100-metres ~. **6** [U] (capacity for) vigorous action; energy: an officer famous for his skill and ~.
'dash-board, panel beneath the windscreen of a motor-vehicle, with the speedometer, various controls, etc.

dash² /dæʃ/ vt,vi **1** send or throw violently; move or be moved violently: The huge waves ~ed over the rocks. **2** dash sb's hopes, destroy, discourage, them. **3** (dated informal) (used as a mild substitute for) Damn!: D~ it!
dash·ing adj impetuous; lively; full of, showing, energy: a ~ing cavalry charge.

data /ˈdeɪtə/ n pl **1** facts; things certainly known (and from which conclusions may be drawn): unless sufficient ~ are available. **2** information prepared for and operated on a computer programme: The ~ is ready for processing. (Note: usually used with a sing verb.)
'data bank, centre with a comprehensive (computer) file of data.
'data 'processing, the performing of operations on data to obtain more information, solutions to problems, etc.

date¹ /deɪt/ n [C] **1** statement of the time, day, month, year, one or all three of these, when something happened or is to happen: D~ of birth, 20 April 1974; the ~ of the discovery of America by Columbus (1492). What's today's ~? **2** period of time, e g one to which antiquities belong: Many ruins of Roman ~ (= of the time of ancient Rome) are to be seen in the south of France. (be/ go) out of date, no longer used; old-fashioned: out-of-~ ideas. to date, so far; until now. (be/bring) up to date, (a) in line with, according to, what is now known, used, etc: up-to-~ ideas/methods. (b) up to the present time: to bring a catalogue up to ~. **3** (informal) social meeting arranged at a certain time and place; appointment: *I have a ~ with her next month.* **4** (*informal*) companion of the other sex with whom dates (3) are arranged.

blind date, with a person one has not met before.

date·less *adj* endless; immemorial.

date² /deɪt/ *vt,vi* **1** have or put a date(1) on: *Don't forget to ~ your letters.* **2** give a date(2) to: *to ~ old coins. That suit ~s you,* shows your age (because it is old-fashioned). ⇨ **4** below. **3 date from/back to,** have existed since: *The castle ~s back to the 14th century,* was built then. **4** show signs of becoming out of date: *Isn't this text-book beginning to ~?* **5** make a date(3) with.

dated *adj* out of fashion; (of words and phrases) used in the past but not now current.

date³ /deɪt/ *n* [C] small, brown, sweet, edible fruit of the `date-palm, common in N Africa and S W Asia.

dat·ive /ˈdeɪtɪv/ *n* (in Latin and other inflected languages) form of a word showing that it is an indirect object of the verb.

datum /ˈdeɪtəm/ *n* (*sing* of) data.

daub /dɔb/ *vt,vi* **1** put (paint, clay, plaster, etc) roughly on a surface: *to ~ a wall with paint.* **2** paint (pictures) without skill or artistry. **3** make dirty: *trousers ~ed with paint.* □ *n* [C,U] (covering of) soft, sticky material, e g clay.

daugh·ter /ˈdɔtə(r)/ *n* [C] one's female child.

daughter-in-law /ˈdɔtr ɪn lɔ/ (*pl* ~s-in-law) wife of one's son.

daunt /dɔnt/ *vt* discourage: *nothing ~ed,* not at all discouraged.

daunt·less /ˈdɔntləs/ *adj* not discouraged.

dau·phin /ˈdɔfɪn/ *n* [C] title of the King of France's eldest son (from 1349 to 1830).

davit /ˈdævɪt/ *n* [C] one of a pair of small cranes(2), curved at the top, for supporting, lowering and raising a ship's boat.

dawdle /ˈdɔdəl/ *vi,vt* be slow; waste time: *Stop dawdling and do something useful!*

dawn¹ /dɔn/ *n* [C] **1** first light of day; daybreak: *We must start at ~.* **2** (*fig*) beginning; birth: *the ~ of civilization.*

dawn² /dɔn/ *vi* **1** begin to grow light: *The day was just ~ing.* **2** begin to appear; grow clear (to the mind): *The truth began to ~ on him.*

day /deɪ/ *n* **1** [U] time between sunrise and sunset: *He has been working all (the) ~. We travelled ~ and night/night and ~ without stopping.* **by day,** during daylight: *We travelled by ~ and stayed at hotels every night.* **pass the time of day (with sb),** exchange greetings, chat. **2** [C] period of twenty-four hours (from midnight): *There are seven ~s in a week.* **day after day; every day,** for many days together. **day in, day out,** continuously. **one day,** on a day (past or future). **the other day,** a few days

ago. **some day,** some time in the future. **one of these (fine) days,** (used in making a promise or a prophecy) before long. **3** [C] the hours of the day given to work: *I've done a good ~'s work.* **call it a day,** stop working. **4** [C] (often *pl*) time; period. **better days,** times when one was, or will be, richer, more prosperous, etc: *Let's hope we'll soon see better ~s.* **make sb's day,** make him very happy. **the present day,** the time we are now living in: *present-~* (= modern) *writers; in these ~s* (= nowadays); *in those ~s* (= then); *in the ~s of Queen Victoria; in ~s to come,* in future times. **5** *his/her, etc day,* lifetime; period of success, prosperity, power, etc: *Colonialism has had its ~.* **6 the ~,** contest: *We've won/carried/lost the ~.*

`day·break, dawn.

`day-dream *vi, n* [C] (have) idle and pleasant thoughts.

`day-long *adj, adv* (lasting) for the whole day.

`day nursery, place where small children may be left (while their mothers are at work).

`day shift, (workers working a) period during the day, esp in a mine.

`day-time, day(1), esp: *in the ~-time.*

day·light /ˈdeɪlaɪt/ *n* [U] **1** light of day: *Can we reach our destination in ~,* before it gets dark? **2** dawn: *We must leave before ~.*

daze /deɪz/ *vt* make (a person) feel stupid or unable to think clearly: *He looked ~d with drugs/was in a ~d state.* □ *n* **in a daze,** in a bewildered condition.

dazzle /ˈdæzəl/ *vt* make (a person) unable to see clearly or act normally because of too much light, brilliance, splendour, etc: *~d by bright lights; dazzling opportunities.*

de- /di-, dɪ-/ *prefix* (used with a *verb*) negative, reverse, opposite of: *depopulate.*

dea·con /ˈdikən/ *n* [C] minister or officer who has various duties in certain Christian churches (e g in the Church of England, below a bishop or priest; in nonconformist churches, a layman attending to secular affairs).

dea·con·ess /ˈdikənɪs/ *n* [C] woman deacon.

dea·con·ry *n* [C] (*pl* -ies) (office of) deacons.

dead /ded/ *adj, n* [U] **1** (plants, animals, persons) no longer living: *the ~,* dead persons; *~ flowers/leaves. The hunter fired and the tiger fell ~.* **2** never having had life: *~ matter,* e g rock. **3** without movement or activity: *in the ~ of (the) night,* when everything is quiet. **4** (of languages, customs, etc) no longer used or observed: *a ~ language.* **5** (of the hands, etc) numbed, e g by cold; unable to feel anything: *~ fingers.* **dead to,** unconscious of, hardened against. **dead to the world,** (*fig*) fast asleep. **6** complete; abrupt; exact: *to come to a ~*

stop. **7** that can no longer be used: *a ~ match*, one that has been struck. *The telephone went ~*, did not transmit sounds. **8** (of sound) dull, heavy. **9** (of colours) lacking brilliance. **10** (in cricket, tennis, etc) (of the surface of the ground) such that balls move slowly: *a ~ pitch*; (of the ball, in various games) out of play. □ *adv* completely; absolutely; thoroughly: *~ `beat/`tired/ ex`hausted*; *~ `certain/`sure*; *~ `drunk*; *~ ahead*, directly ahead. *You're ~ right!*
dead centre, exact centre.
'dead `end, cul-de-sac.
'dead `heat, race in which two contestants reach the winning-post together.
dead language, ⇨ dead(4).
`dead-line, fixed date for finishing (doing) something.
dead loss, complete loss, failure.
dead march, slow, solemn music for a funeral.
`dead-pan *adj* (of a face) showing no emotion.
dead silence, complete silence.
deaden /ˈdedən/ *vt* take away, deprive of, strength, feeling, brightness: *drugs to ~ the pain; thick walls that ~ the noise*.
dead·lock /ˈdedlɒk/ *n* [C,U] total failure to reach agreement, to settle a quarrel or grievance.
dead·ly /ˈdedlɪ/ *adj* (-ier, -iest) **1** causing, likely to cause, death: *~ weapons/poison*. **2** filled with hate: *~ enemies*. **3** that may result in damnation: *the seven ~ sins*. **4** like that of death: *a ~ paleness*. □ *adv* like that of death: *~ pale*.
deaf /def/ *adj* (-er, -est) **1** unable to hear at all; unable to hear well: *to become ~; the ~ and dumb alphabet*, one in which signs made with the hands are used for letters or words. **2** unwilling to listen: *~ to all advice/entreaty*. **turned a deaf ear to**, refused to listen to.
`deaf-aid, small device, usually electronic, that helps a deaf person to hear.
'deaf `mute, person who is deaf and dumb.
deaf·ness *n* [U]
deafen /ˈdefən/ *vt* make so much noise that hearing is difficult or impossible: *We were almost ~ed by the uproar. There were ~ing cheers when the speaker finished*.
deal[1] /diːl/ *n* [C,U] (board of) fir or pine wood.
deal[2] /diːl/ *n* [U] large or considerable quantity; quite a lot: *He has had to spend a good ~ of money on medicines. I have spent a great ~ of trouble over the work*. □ *adv* very much, often: *They see each other a great ~/a great ~ of each other*.
deal[3] /diːl/ *n* [C] **1** (in games) distribution of playing cards: *It's your ~*. **a raw deal**, ⇨ raw(7). **2** business transaction or agreement. **3** (*informal*) bargain: *I'll do a ~ with you*, make a bargain.
deal[4] /diːl/ *vt,vi* (*pt,pp ~t* /delt/) **1** give out

to a number of persons: *The money must be ~t out fairly. Who ~t the cards?* **2** **deal in sth**, stock, sell: *a shop that ~s in goods of all sorts*. **3** do business: *Do you ~ with Smith, the butcher?* **4** **deal with**, (a) have relations with: *That man is easy/difficult/ impossible to ~ with*. (b) behave towards: *How would you ~ with an armed burglar?* (c) (of affairs) manage; attend to: *How shall we ~ with this problem?* (d) be about; be concerned with: *a book ~ing with West Africa*.
dealer /ˈdiːlə(r)/ *n* [C] **1** person who deals out playing-cards. **2** trader: *a `car ~*.
deal·ing /ˈdiːlɪŋ/ *n* **1** [U] dealing out or distributing; behaviour towards others: *He is well known for fair ~*. **2** (*pl*) business relations: *I've always found him honest in his ~s with me*.
dealt /delt/ *pt,pp* of deal[4].
dean /diːn/ *n* [C] **1** clergyman at the head of a cathedral chapter; clergyman who, under an archdeacon, is responsible for a number of parishes: *a rural ~*. **2** (in some universities) person with authority to maintain discipline; head of a department of studies.
dean·ery /ˈdiːnərɪ/ *n* [C] (*pl* -ies) office, house, of a dean; group of parishes under a rural dean.
dear /dɪə(r)/ *adj* (-er, -est) **1** loved; lovable: *What a ~ little child!* **2** (used as a form of address in speech, or at the beginning of letters): *D~ Madam/Sir; D~ Mr Green*. **3** high in price: (of a shop) asking high prices: *Everything is getting ~er*. **4** precious (to); greatly valued: *He lost everything that was ~ to him*. □ *adv* at a high cost: *If you want to make money, you must buy cheap and sell ~*. □ *n* [C] **1** lovable person: *Isn't she a ~!* **2** (used to address a person): *'Yes, ~'*; (used with a, esp when encouraging somebody): *'Drink your milk up, Anne, there's a ~ '*. □ *int* (used to express surprise, impatience, wonder, dismay, etc): *Oh ~! D~ me!*
dear·ly *adv* (a) very much: *He would ~ly love to see his mother again. He loves his mother ~ly*. (b) at great cost: *Victory was ~ly bought*, e g when hundreds of soldiers were killed.
dear·ness *n* [U]
dearth /dɜːθ/ *n* [U] shortage (the usual word): *a ~ of food*.
deary, dearie /ˈdɪərɪ/ *n* [C] (*pl* -ies) (*informal*) dear one; darling (used, esp by an elderly woman to a younger person, or a mother to her child).
death /deθ/ *n* [C,U] **1** dying; ending of life: *There have been several ~s from drowning here this summer. Two children were burnt to ~ in the fire*. **sick to death of**, extremely tired, bored, etc. **bore sb to death**, bore him extremely. **2** killing or being killed: *The murderer was sentenced to ~*, to be executed. **put to death**, kill. **3** state of being dead: *lie still in ~; united in ~*, e g of hus-

band and wife in the same grave. **(a fate) worse than death,** to be greatly dreaded. **4 be the death of sb,** be the cause of: *That old motor-bike will be the ~ of you.* **catch one's death of cold,** (*informal*) catch a cold that will be fatal. **5** (*fig*) destruction; end: *the ~ of one's hopes/plans.*
`death-bed,` on which one dies: *She's on her ~-bed,* is dying.
`death-certificate,` official document giving cause of death.
`death-duties,` taxes (to be) paid on a person's property after death.
`death-mask,` cast of a dead person's face.
`death rattle,` unusual rattling sound in the throat of a dying person.
`death-roll,` list of persons killed (in a war, etc).
`death-trap,` place, circumstances, etc likely to cause death.
`death-warrant,` official document giving authority for an execution.
death-ly /ˈdeθlɪ/ *adj* like death: *a ~ stillness.* □ *adv* like death: *~ pale.*
deb /deb/ *n* [C] (abbr of) débutante.
de-bar /dɪˈbɑː(r)/ *vt* (-rr-) shut out; prevent a person by a regulation (from doing or having): *~ persons who have been convicted of crime from voting at elections.*
de-base /dɪˈbeɪs/ *vt* make lower in value, poorer in quality, character, etc: *to ~ the coinage,* e g by reducing the percentage of silver.
de-base-ment *n* [U]
de-bat-able /dɪˈbeɪtəbəl/ *adj* that can be debated or disputed; open to question.
de-bate /dɪˈbeɪt/ *n* [C,U] formal discussion, e g at a public meeting, in Parliament; contest between two speakers, or two groups of speakers, to show skill and ability in arguing: *After a long ~ the bill was passed by the House of Commons and sent to the House of Lords.* □ *vt, vi* have a debate about; think over in order to decide: *We were debating whether to go to the mountains or to the seaside.*
de-bater, person who debates.
de-bauch /dɪˈbɔːtʃ/ *vt* cause a person to lose virtue, to act immorally; □ *n* [C] occasion of excessive drinking, immoral behaviour: *a drunken ~.*
de-bauch-ery /dɪˈbɔːtʃərɪ/ *n* [U] taking part in a debauch(2): *a life of ~ery;* [C] (*pl* -ies) instance of this.
de-bili-tate /dɪˈbɪlɪteɪt/ *vt* make (a person, his constitution) weak: *a debilitating climate.*
de-bil-ity /dɪˈbɪlətɪ/ *n* [U] weakness (of health, purpose): *After her long illness she is suffering from general ~.*
debit /ˈdebɪt/ *n* [C] **1** (book-keeping) entry (in an account) of a sum owing. **2** (also `~-side`) left-hand side of an account, on which such entries are made. □ *vt* put on the debit side of an account: *~ a person's account (with £5).*

de-brief /ˈdiːˈbriːf/ *vt* question, examine someone who has returned from a mission to obtain information. Hence, **'de-brief-ing,** *n* [C].
de-bris, dé-bris /ˈdeɪbriː *US:* dəˈbriː/ *n* [U] scattered broken pieces; wreckage: *searching among the ~ after the explosion.*
debt /det/ *n* [C,U] payment which must be, but has not yet been, paid to somebody; obligation: *If I pay all my ~s I shall have no money left. I owe him a ~ of gratitude for all he has done for me.*
debtor /-tə(r)/, person who is in debt to another.
debut, début /ˈdeɪbjuː *US:* deɪˈbjuː/ *n* [C] (of an actor, musician, etc) first appearance on a public stage: *to make one's ~.*
débu-tante /ˈdebjʊtɑːnt *US:* 'debjʊˈtɑːnt/ *n* [C] upper-class girl making her first appearance in high society.
dec-ade /ˈdekeɪd/ *n* [C] period of ten years: *the first ~ of the 20th century,* i e 1900—1909.
deca-dence /ˈdekədəns/ *n* [U] falling to a lower level (in morals, art, literature, etc esp after a period at a high level).
deca-dent /ˈdekədənt/ *adj* in a state of decadence. □ *n* [C] person in this state.
de-cant /dɪˈkænt/ *vt* pour (wine, etc) from a bottle into another vessel slowly so as not to disturb the sediment.
de-canter, vessel, usually of glass with a stopper, into which wine is decanted.
de-capi-tate /dɪˈkæpɪteɪt/ *vt* behead.
de-cay /dɪˈkeɪ/ *vi* go bad; lose power, health: *~ing teeth/vegetables.* □ *n* [U] decaying: *The house is in ~.*
de-cease /dɪˈsiːs/ *vi* die. □ *n* (esp *legal*) (a person's) death. **the ~d,** person who has, persons who have, recently died.
de-ceit /dɪˈsiːt/ *n* **1** [U] causing a person to accept as true or genuine something that is false: *She is incapable of ~,* would never tell lies, etc. **2** [C] lie; dishonest trick.
de-ceit-ful /dɪˈsiːtfəl/ *adj* **1** in the habit of deceiving: **2** intended to deceive; misleading in appearance, etc: *~ words/acting.*
de-ceit-fully /-fəlɪ/ *adv*
de-ceit-ful-ness *n* [U]
de-ceive /dɪˈsiːv/ *vt* cause a person to believe something that is false; play a trick on; mislead (on purpose): *You can't pass the examination without working hard, so don't ~ yourself.*
de-ceiver, person who deceives.
De-cem-ber /dɪˈsembə(r)/ *n* twelfth month of the year.
de-cency /ˈdiːsnsɪ/ *n* [U] (the quality of) being decent; (regard for the) general opinion as to what is decent: *an offence against ~,* e g appearing naked in public.
de-cent /ˈdiːsnt/ *adj* **1** right and suitable; respectful: *Put on some ~ clothes before you call on the Smiths.* **2** modest; not likely to

shock or embarrass others: ∼ *langauge and behaviour*. (*Note*: this is the only sense for which *indecent* is the opposite.) **3** (*informal*) likeable; satisfactory: *He's a very ∼ person*.

de·cent·ly *adv* in a decent(1,2) manner: ∼*ly dressed; behave* ∼*ly*.

de·cen·tra·lize /ˌdiːˈsentrəlaɪz/ *vt* give greater powers (for self-government, etc) to (places, branches, etc away from the centre). **de·cen·tra·liz·ation** /ˌdiːsentrəlaɪˈzeɪʃən *US*: -lɪˈz-/ *n* [U]

de·cep·tion /dɪˈsepʃən/ *n* **1** [U] deceiving; being deceived: *to practise* ∼ *on the public*. **2** [C] trick intended to deceive: *a gross* ∼.

de·cep·tive /dɪˈseptɪv/ *adj* deceiving: *Appearances are often* ∼.
de·cep·tive·ly *adv*

deci·bel /ˈdesɪbel/ *n* [C] unit for measuring the relative loudness of sounds.

de·cide /dɪˈsaɪd/ *vt,vi* **1** settle (a question or a doubt); give a judgement: *The judge* ∼*d the case. It's difficult to* ∼ *between the two. The judge* ∼*d for/in favour of/against the plaintiff.* **2** think about and come to a conclusion; make up one's mind: *The boy* ∼*d not to/∼d that he would not become a sailor. In the end she* ∼*d on it/∼d to buy it. We* ∼*d against going/∼d not to go for a holiday in Wales.* **3** cause to decide(2): *What* ∼*d you to give up your job?*
de·cided *adj* (**a**) clear; definite: *There is a* ∼*d difference between them.* (**b**) (of persons) determined: *He's quite* ∼*d about it.*
de·cid·ed·ly *adv* definitely; undoubtedly: ∼*dly better*.

de·cidu·ous /dɪˈsɪdjʊəs/ *adj* (of trees) losing their leaves annually (esp in autumn).

deci·mal /ˈdesɪməl/ *adj* of tens or one-tenths: *the* `∼ *system*, for money, weights, etc; *a* ∼ *fraction*, e g 0·091.
decimal point, the point in 15·61.
deci·mal·ize /-aɪz/ *vt* change to a decimal system: ∼*ize the currency*.
deci·mal·iz·ation /ˌdesɪməlaɪˈzeɪʃən *US*: -lɪˈz-/ *n*[U]

deci·mate /ˈdesɪmeɪt/ *vt* kill or destroy one-tenth or a large part of: *a population* ∼*d by disease*.

de·cipher /dɪˈsaɪfə(r)/ *vt* find the meaning of (something written in code, bad handwriting, etc).
de·cipher·able /-əbəl/ *adj* that can be deciphered.

de·ci·sion /dɪˈsɪʒən/ *n* **1** [U] deciding; judging; [C] result of this; settlement of a question: *give a* ∼ *on a case. Have they reached/come to/arrived at/taken/made a* ∼ *yet?* **2** [U] ability to decide and act accordingly; the quality of being decided(2): *A man who lacks* ∼ (= who hesitates, cannot decide questions) *cannot hold a position of responsibility*.

de·cis·ive /dɪˈsaɪsɪv/ *adj* **1** having a decided or definite outcome or result; *a* ∼ *battle*,

deciding which side wins the war. **2** showing decision(2); definite: *He gave a* ∼ *answer*.
de·cis·ive·ly *adv*

deck[1] /dek/ *n* [C] **1** any of the floors of a ship, in or above the hull: *My cabin is on E* ∼. *Shall we go up on* ∼? **2** any similar surface, e g the floor of a bus: *on the top* ∼ *of a bus.* **3** pack of playing cards.
`**deck-chair**, collapsible chair of canvas, on a wooden or metal frame, used out of doors.
`**deck hand**, member of a ship's crew who works on deck.
-decker *suffix*: *a three-*∼*er*, ship with three decks; *single-/double-*`∼*er bus. She ate a double-*∼ *sandwich*, one with three slices of bread.

deck[2] /dek/ *vt* decorate: *streets* ∼*ed with flags*.

de·claim /dɪˈkleɪm/ *vi,vt* **1** *declaim against*, speak with strong feeling; attack in words. **2** speak in the manner of addressing an audience or reciting poetry.

dec·la·ma·tion /ˌdekləˈmeɪʃən/ *n* [U] declaiming; [C] speech full of strong feeling; formal speech.
de·clama·tor /dɪˈklæmətərɪ *US*: -tɔrɪ/ *adj*

dec·lar·ation /ˌdekləˈreɪʃən/ *n* [U] declaring; [C] that which is declared: *a* ∼ *of war; the D*∼ *of Independence*, that made by the N American colonies of Great Britain, on 4 July 1776, that they were politically independent; *a* ∼ *of income*, one (to be) made to the Inspector of Taxes.

de·clare /dɪˈkleə(r)/ *vt,vi* **1** make known clearly or formally; announce: *to* ∼ *the results of an election. I* ∼ *this meeting closed.* **declare war** (*on/against*), announce that a state of war exists. **2** say solemnly; say in order to show that one has no doubt: *The accused man* ∼*d that he was not guilty/∼d himself innocent.* **3** *declare for/against*, say that one is/is not in favour of. **4** make a statement (to customs officials) of dutiable goods brought into a country, or (to a Tax Inspector) of one's income: *Have you anything to* ∼?
de·clar·able /dɪˈkleərəbəl/ *adj* that must be declared(4).

de·class·ify /ˌdiːˈklæsɪfaɪ/ *vt* (*pt,pp* -ied) remove from a special class: ∼ *information concerning nuclear arms.*
de·class·ifi·ca·tion /ˌdiːˈklæsɪfɪˈkeɪʃən/ *n*[U]

de·clen·sion /dɪˈklenʃən/ *n* (*gram*) [U] varying the endings of *nouns, pronouns,* and *adjectives* according to their use in a sentence; [C] class of words whose endings for different cases are alike.

de·cline[1] /dɪˈklaɪn/ *n* [C] declining; gradual and continued loss of strength: *the* ∼ *of the Roman Empire; a* ∼ *in prices/prosperity*.

de·cline[2] /dɪˈklaɪn/ *vt,vi* **1** say 'No' (to); refuse (something offered): *to* ∼ *an invitation to (go to) a party.* **2** continue to become smaller, weaker, lower: *declining birthrate; declining sales.* **3** (of the sun) go down. **4**

give the cases of (a word).

de·clutch /ˌdiˈklʌtʃ/ vi disconnect the clutch (of a motor-vehicle) in order to change gear.

de·code /ˌdiˈkəʊd/ vt decipher (a code).

de·com·pose /ˌdikəmˈpəʊz/ vt, vi 1 separate (a substance, light, etc) into its parts: *A prism ∼s light.* 2 (cause to) become bad or rotten; decay.

de·com·po·si·tion /ˌdiˈkɒmpəˈzɪʃən/ n [U]

dé·cor /ˈdeɪkɔː(r) US: deɪˈkɔːr/ n [C] (usually *sing*) all that makes up the general appearance, e g of a room or the stage of a theatre.

dec·or·ate /ˈdekəreɪt/ vt 1 put ornaments on; make (more) beautiful by placing adornments on or in: *to ∼ a street with flags/the house at Christmas.* 2 paint, plaster, etc the outside of (a building); put paint, wallpaper, etc on the inside rooms of (a building). 3 give (a person) a mark of distinction (e g a medal, an order): *Several soldiers were ∼d for bravery.*

dec·or·ator /ˈdekəreɪtə(r)/ n [C] workman who decorates(2): *interior ∼s.*

dec·or·a·tion /ˌdekəˈreɪʃən/ n 1 [U] decorating or being decorated. 2 [C] thing used for decorating: *Christmas ∼s.* 3 [C] medal, ribbon, etc given and worn as an honour or award.

dec·or·ative /ˈdekrətɪv US: ˈdekərətɪv/ adj suitable for decorating(1): *Holly, with its bright red berries, is very ∼.*

de·coy /ˈdiːkɔɪ/ n [C] 1 (real or imitation) bird (e g a duck) or animal used to attract others so that they may be shot or caught; place designed for this purpose. 2 (fig) person or thing used to tempt somebody into a position of danger. □ vt /dɪˈkɔɪ/ trick into a place of danger by means of a decoy: *He had been ∼ed across the frontier and arrested as a spy.*

de·crease /dɪˈkriːs/ vt, vi (cause to) become shorter, smaller, less: *The population of the village has ∼d from 1000 to 500.* □ n /ˈdiːkriːs/ [U] decreasing; [C] amount by which something decreases: *There has been a ∼ in our imports this year.*

de·cree /dɪˈkriː/ n [C] 1 order given by a ruler or authority and having the force of a law: *issue a ∼; rule by ∼.* 2 judgement or decision of some law courts: *a ∼ of divorce.* □ vt, vi issue a, order by, decree: *It had been ∼d that...*

decree nisi /dɪˈkriː ˈnaɪsaɪ/, order for a divorce unless cause to the contrary is shown within a fixed period.

de·crepit /dɪˈkrepɪt/ adj made weak by old age or hard use: *a ∼ horse.*

de·cry /dɪˈkraɪ/ vt (pt, pp -ied) try, by speaking against something, to make it seem less valuable, useful, etc.

dedi·cate /ˈdedɪkeɪt/ vt 1 give up, devote (one's time, energy, etc to a noble cause or purpose): *He ∼d his life to the service of his country.* 2 devote with solemn ceremonies (to God, to a sacred use). 3 (of an author)

write (or print) a person's name at the beginning of a book (to show gratitude or friendship to).

dedi·ca·tion /ˌdedɪˈkeɪʃən/ n (a) [U] dedicating: *the dedication of a church.* (b) [C] words used in dedicating a book.

de·duce /dɪˈdjuːs US: dɪˈduːs/ vt arrive at (knowledge, a theory, etc) by reasoning; reach a conclusion: *If you saw a doctor leaving a house, you might ∼ the fact that someone in the house was ill.*

de·duct /dɪˈdʌkt/ vt take away (an amount or part).

de·duc·tion /dɪˈdʌkʃən/ n 1 [U] deducting; [C] amount deducted: *∼s from pay for insurance and pension.* 2 [U] deducing; [C] conclusion reached by reasoning from general laws to a particular case.

deed /diːd/ n [C] 1 something done; act: *D∼s are better than promises.* 2 (legal) written or printed signed agreement, esp about ownership or rights.

deep¹ /diːp/ adj (-er, -est) 1 going a long way down from the top: *a ∼ well/river.* 2 going a long way from the surface or edge: *a ∼ wound.* 3 (fig) serious; not superficial: *a ∼ thinker.* 4 placed or extending down, back or in (with words to show extent): *a hole two feet ∼; to be ∼ in debt.* 5 (of sounds) low: *in a ∼ voice.* 6 *in a ∼ sleep,* from which one is not easily awakened. 7 (of colours) strong; intense: *a ∼ red.* 8 brought from far down: *a ∼ sigh;* strongly felt: *∼ sorrow/feelings/sympathy.* 9 **deep in,** absorbed in; having all one's attention centred on: *∼ in thought/study/a book.* 10 (fig) difficult to understand or learn about: *a ∼ mystery.*

deep·ly adv intensely: *He is ∼ly interested in the subject.*

deep·ness n [U]

deep² /diːp/ adv far down or in: *We had to dig ∼ to find water.*

'deep-'freeze vt freeze (food) quickly in order to preserve it for long periods: *∼-frozen fish.* □ n [C] special type of refrigerator (or a special part of an ordinary refrigerator) used for this purpose: *put fruit and vegetables in the ∼-freeze.*

'deep-'rooted, not easily removed: *his ∼-rooted dislike of hard work.*

'deep-'seated, firmly established: *The causes of the trouble are ∼-seated.*

deep³ /diːp/ n **the ∼,** (poetry) the sea.

deepen /ˈdiːpən/ vt, vi make or become deep.

deer /dɪə(r)/ n [C] (pl unchanged) (kinds of) graceful, quick-running animal, the male of which has horns.

'deer-skin, (leather made of) deer's skin.

de·esca·late /ˌdiˈeskəleɪt/ vt decrease the area or intensity of, e g a war.

de·face /dɪˈfeɪs/ vt spoil the appearance of (by marking or damaging the surface of).

de·face·ment n [C,U]

de·fame /dɪˈfeɪm/ *vt* attack the good reputation of; say evil things about.

defa·ma·tion /ˈdefəˈmeɪʃən/ *n* [U] defaming or being defamed; harm done to a person's reputation.

de·fama·tory /dɪˈfæmətrɪ *US:* -tɔrɪ/ *adj*

de·fault¹ /dɪˈfɔlt/ *n* [U] act of defaulting: *to win a case/a game by* ~, because the other party (team, player, etc) does not appear. *in default of,* in the absence of.

de·fault² /dɪˈfɔlt/ *vi* fail to perform a duty, or to appear (eg in a law court) when required to do so, or to pay a debt.

de·faulter, person who defaults.

de·feat /dɪˈfit/ *vt* 1 overcome; win a victory over: *to* ~ *another school at football.* 2 make useless; cause to fail: *Our hopes were* ~*ed.* □ *n* [U] defeating or being defeated: *Our team that has not yet suffered* ~; [C] instance of this: *six victories and two* ~*s.*

de·fect¹ /ˈdifekt/ *n* [C] fault; imperfection; something lacking in completeness or perfection: ~*s in a system of education.*

de·fect² /dɪˈfekt/ *vi* desert one's country, one's allegiance, etc: *the ballerina who* ~*ed to the West,* eg by asking for political asylum.

de·fec·tor /-tə(r)/, person who defects: ~*ors from the Republican Party.*

de·fec·tion /dɪˈfekʃən/ *n* [U] falling away from loyalty to a political party (or its leader), religion or duty; [C] instance of this: ~*s from the Socialist Party.*

de·fec·tive /dɪˈfektɪv/ *adj* imperfect: ~ *in workmanship/moral sense.*

de·fec·tive·ly *adv*

de·fec·tive·ness *n* [U]

de·fence (*US =* **de·fense**) /dɪˈfens/ 1 [U] defending from attack; fighting against attack: *money needed for national* ~. 2 [C] thing used for defending or protecting; means of defending: *People used to build strong walls round their towns as a* ~ *against enemies.* 3 [C,U] (*legal*) argument(s) used to contest an accusation; the lawyer(s) acting for an accused person: *The accused man made no* ~. *Counsel for the* ~ *put in a plea for mercy.*

de·fence·less *adj* unable to defend oneself.

de·fence·less·ly *adv*

de·fence·less·ness *n* [U]

de·fend /dɪˈfend/ *vt* guard; protect; make safe: *to* ~ *one's country against enemies.* 2 speak or write in support of: ~ (= uphold) *a claim;* ~ (= contest) *a lawsuit.*

de·fend·ant /dɪˈfendənt/ *n* [C] person against whom a legal action is brought. ⇨ plaintiff.

de·fender /dɪˈfendə(r)/ *n* [C] 1 person who defends. 2 (in sport, eg football) player who guards his goal area against attacks from the other side.

de·fense ⇨ defence.

de·fens·ible /dɪˈfensəbəl/ *adj* able to be defended.

de·fens·ive /dɪˈfensɪv/ *adj* used for, intended for, defending: ~ *warfare/ measures.* □ *n* **be on the defensive,** state or position of defence.

de·fens·ive·ly *adv*

de·fer¹ /dɪˈfɜ(r)/ *vt* (-rr-) put off to a later time: *to* ~ *one's departure for a week.*

de·fer² /dɪˈfɜ(r)/ *vi* (-rr-) give way; yield (often to show respect): ~ *to one's elders/to his opinions.*

de·fer·ence /ˈdefərəns/ *n* [U] giving way to the wishes, accepting the opinions or judgements, of another or others; respect: *to show* ~ *to a judge.* *in deference to,* out of respect for.

de·fer·en·tial /ˈdefəˈrenʃəl/ *adj* showing respect.

de·fer·en·tially /-ʃəlɪ/ *adv*

de·fiance /dɪˈfaɪəns/ *n* [U] open disobedience or resistance; refusal to recognize authority; defying. *in defiance of,* showing contempt or indifference of: *to act in* ~ *of orders.*

de·fiant /dɪˈfaɪənt/ *adj* showing defiance; openly disobedient.

de·fiant·ly *adv*

de·fi·ciency /dɪˈfɪʃənsɪ/ *n* (*pl* -ies) 1 [U] the state of being short of, less than, what is correct or needed; [C] instance of this: *suffering from a* ~ *of food.* 2 [C] amount by which something is short of what is correct or needed: *a* ~ *of £5.* 3 [C] something imperfect: *Cosmetics do not always cover up the deficiencies of nature.*

de·ficient /dɪˈfɪʃənt/ *adj* not having enough of: ~ *in courage; a mentally* ~ *person,* one who is mentally subnormal.

defi·cit /ˈdefəsɪt/ *n* [C] amount by which something, esp a sum of money, is too small; amount by which payments exceed receipts. ⇨ surplus.

de·file /dɪˈfaɪl/ *vt* make dirty or impure: *rivers* ~*d by waste from factories; to* ~ *one's mind.*

de·fine /dɪˈfaɪn/ *vt* 1 state precisely the meaning of (eg words). 2 state or show clearly: *The powers of a judge are* ~*d by law.*

de·fin·able /-əbəl/ *adj* that can be defined.

defi·nite /ˈdefənɪt/ *adj* clear; not doubtful or uncertain: *I want a* ~ *answer: 'Yes' or 'No'.*

'definite 'article, the word 'the'

defi·nite·ly *adv* (a) in a definite manner. (b) (*informal*) (used in answer to a question) yes, certainly.

defi·ni·tion /ˈdefəˈnɪʃən/ *n* 1 [U] defining; [C] statement that defines: *To give a* ~ *of a word is more difficult than you think.* 2 [U] clearness of outline; making or being distinct in outline; power of a lens (in a camera or telescope) to show clear outlines.

de·fin·itive /dɪˈfɪnətɪv/ *adj* to be considered decisive and without the need for, or possibility of, change or addition· *a* ~ *offer/*

answer.

de·flate /dɪˈfleɪt/ *vt* **1** make (a tyre, balloon, etc) smaller by letting out air or gas. **2** (*fig*) lessen the conceit of: ～ *a pompous politician.* **3** /diˈfleɪt/ take action to reduce the amount of money in circulation in order to lower or keep steady the prices of salable goods.

de·fla·tion /dɪˈfleɪʃən/ *n* [U]

de·fla·tion·ary /-nrɪ *US:* -nerɪ/ *adj* produced, designed or tending to produce deflation: *deflationary measures by the Chancellor.*

de·flect /dɪˈflekt/ *vt,vi* (cause to) turn aside (from): *The bullet struck a wall and was ～ed from its course.*

de·flec·tion /dɪˈflekʃən/ *n* [C,U]

de·form /dɪˈfɔm/ *vt* spoil the form or appearance of; put out of shape.

de·formed *adj* (of the body, or a part of it) badly shaped; unnaturally shaped: *The boy has a ～ed foot and cannot play games.*

de·form·ity /dɪˈfɔmətɪ/ *n* [U] being deformed; [C] (*pl* -ies) deformed part (esp of the body).

de·fraud /dɪˈfrɔd/ *vt* trick (a person) out of what is rightly his.

de·fray /dɪˈfreɪ/ *vt* supply the money needed, pay (the expenses) for something.

de·frayal /-əl/ *n* [U]

de·fray·ment *n* [U]

de·frost /ˈdiˈfrɒst *US:* -ˈfrɔst/ *vt* remove, get rid of, ice or frost (e g in a refrigerator, on the windscreen of a motor-vehicle).

deft /deft/ *adj* quick and clever (esp with the fingers).

deft·ly *adv*

deft·ness *n* [U]

de·funct /dɪˈfʌŋkt/ *adj* (of things, e g laws) extinct.

de·fuse /ˈdiˈfjuz/ *vt* remove or make useless the fuse of, e g an unexploded bomb or shell.

defy /dɪˈfaɪ/ *vt* (*pt,pp* -ied) **1** resist openly. **2** refuse to obey or show respect to: *to ～ one's superiors.* **3** offer difficulties that cannot be overcome: *The problem defied solution,* could not be solved. **4** dare(3) (the usual word).

de·gen·er·ate[1] /dɪˈdʒenərət/ *adj* having lost qualities (physical, moral or mental) that are considered normal and desirable: *He didn't let riches and luxury make him ～.* □ *n* [C] degenerate person or animal.

de·gen·er·ate[2] /dɪˈdʒenəreɪt/ *vi* pass from a state of goodness to a lower state by losing qualities which are considered normal and desirable: *Young men of today are not degenerating,* e g not becoming less hard-working, less honest, than those of earlier times.

de·grade /dɪˈgreɪd/ *vt* **1** reduce in rank or status. **2** cause to be less moral or less deserving of respect: *degrading oneself by cheating.*

degra·da·tion /ˈdegrəˈdeɪʃən/ *n* [U] degrading or being degraded.

de·gree /dɪˈgri/ *n* [C] **1** unit of measurement (of a circle) for angles: *an angle of ninety ～s,* (90°) a right angle; *a ～ of latitude,* about 69 miles. **2** unit of measurement for temperature: *Water freezes at 32 ～s Fahrenheit* (32°F) *or zero ～s Centigrade* (0°C). **3** step or stage in a scale or process: *The boys show various ～s of skill in their use of carpentry tools. He was not in the slightest ～ interested,* was completely uninterested. **by degrees,** gradually: *Their friendship grew by ～s into love.* **to a high/the highest degree,** intensively; exceedingly. **4** position in society: *persons of high ～.* **5** academic title; rank or grade given by a university to one who has passed an examination: *studying for/take a ～; the ～ of Master of Arts* (M A). **6** (*music*) interval from one note to another on a stave. **7** (*gram*) one of the three forms of comparison of an *adjective* or *adverb.*

first degree, most extreme stage of seriousness: *first ～ burns, first ～ murder.*

third degree, severe and long examination (e g by the police) of an accused man to get information or a confession: *Are third-～ methods used in your country?*

de·hy·drate /ˈdihaɪˈdreɪt/ *vt* deprive (a substance) of water or moisture: *～d vegetables.*

de·ice /ˈdiˈaɪs/ *vt* free, e g the surfaces of an aircraft, from ice.

de·ify /ˈdiːɪfaɪ/ *vt* (*pt,pp* -ied) worship as a god.

deign /deɪn/ *vi* be kind or gracious enough to: *He passed by without ～ing to look at me.*

de·ity /ˈdeɪɪtɪ *US:* ˈdiːətɪ/ *n* (*pl* -ies) **1** [U] divine quality or nature; state of being a god or goddess. **2** [C] god or goddess: *Roman deities,* e g Neptune, Minerva.

de·ject /dɪˈdʒekt/ *vt* make sad or gloomy: *Why is she looking so ～ed,* in such low spirits? (*Note:* usually used as a *pp.*)

de·ject·ed·ly *adv*

de·jec·tion /dɪˈdʒekʃən/ *n* [U] dejected state: *He left in ～.*

de·lay /dɪˈleɪ/ *vt,vi* **1** make or be slow or late: *The train was ～ed two hours.* **2** put off until later: *Why have they ～ed opening the new school?* □ *n* **1** [U] delaying or being delayed: *We must leave without ～.* **2** [C] instance, time, of this: *after a ～ of three hours.*

de·lec·table /dɪˈlektəbəl/ *adj* delightful, pleasant.

del·egacy /ˈdelɪgəsɪ/ *n* [C] (*pl* -ies) system of delegating; body of delegates.

del·egate[1] /ˈdelɪgət/ *n* [C] person to whom something is delegated (e g an elected representative sent to a conference or convention).

del·egate[2] /ˈdelɪgeɪt/ *vt* appoint and send as a representative to a meeting; entrust (duties, rights, etc): *to ～ her to perform a task; to ～ rights to a deputy.*

del·e·ga·tion /ˌdelɪˈɡeɪʃən/ n (a) [U] delegating or being delegated. (b) [C] group of delegates.

de·lete /dɪˈliːt/ vt strike or take out (something written or printed): *Several words had been ~d by the censor.*

de·le·tion /dɪˈliːʃən/ n [U] deleting; [C] instance of this.

de·lib·er·ate¹ /dɪˈlɪbərət/ adj 1 done on purpose; intentional: *a ~ lie/insult.* 2 slow and cautious (in action, speech, etc): *He entered the room with ~ steps.*

de·lib·er·ate·ly adv

de·lib·er·ate² /dɪˈlɪbəreɪt/ vt, vi (formal) consider, talk about, carefully: *We were deliberating whether to buy a new car.*

de·lib·er·ation /dɪˌlɪbəˈreɪʃən/ n (formal) 1 [C,U] careful consideration and discussion; debate: *After long ~, they decided to go to Paris.* 2 [U] being deliberate(2); slowness of movement: *to speak/take aim with great ~.*

deli·ca·cy /ˈdelɪkəsɪ/ n (pl -ies) 1 [U] quality of being delicate (all senses): *The political situation is one of great ~, requires very careful handling.* 2 [C] delicate(8) kind of food: *all the delicacies of the season.*

deli·cate /ˈdelɪkət/ adj 1 soft; tender; of fine or thin material: *the ~ skin of a young girl.* 2 fine; exquisite: *jewellery of ~ workmanship.* 3 easily injured; becoming ill easily; needing great care: *~ china/plants; a `~-looking child.* 4 requiring careful treatment or skilful handling: *a ~ surgical operation.* 5 (of colours) soft; not strong: *a ~ shade of pink.* 6 (of the senses, of instruments) able to appreciate or show very small changes or differences: *the ~ instruments needed by scientists,* eg for weighing or measuring. 7 taking great care not to be immodest, not to hurt the feelings of others. 8 (of food, its flavour) pleasing to the taste and not strongly flavoured: *Some kinds of fish have a more ~ flavour than others.*

deli·cate·ly adv

deli·ca·tes·sen /ˌdelɪkəˈtesən/ n [C,U] (shop selling) prepared foods ready for serving (esp cooked meat, smoked fish, pickles).

de·li·cious /dɪˈlɪʃəs/ adj giving delight (esp to the senses of taste and smell, and to the sense of humour): *a ~ cake.*

de·li·cious·ly adv

de·light¹ /dɪˈlaɪt/ n 1 [U] great pleasure; joy: *To his great ~ he passed the examination.* **take delight in,** find pleasure in: *The naughty boy takes great ~ in pulling the cat's tail.* 2 [C] cause or source of great pleasure: *Dancing is her chief ~.*

de·light·ful /-fəl/ adj giving pleasure: *a ~ful holiday.*

de·light·ful·ly /-fəlɪ/ adv

de·light² /dɪˈlaɪt/ vt, vi 1 give great pleasure to; please greatly: *Her singing ~ed everyone.* 2 **be delighted,** be greatly pleased: *I was ~ed to hear the news of your success/ ~ed at the news/~ed that you were suc-*

cessful. 3 take or find great pleasure: *He ~s in teasing his young sister.*

de·lin·quency /dɪˈlɪŋkwənsɪ/ n (pl -ies) 1 [U] wrong-doing; neglect of duty: *the problem of juvenile ~,* doing wrong by young persons. 2 [C] instance of this.

de·lin·quent /dɪˈlɪŋkwənt/ n [C], adj (person) doing wrong, failing to perform a duty.

de·liri·ous /dɪˈlɪrɪəs/ adj 1 suffering from, showing, delirium: 2 wildly excited: *We were ~ with joy.*

de·liri·ous·ly adv

de·lir·ium /dɪˈlɪrɪəm/ n [U] 1 violent mental disturbance, often accompanied by wild talk, esp during feverish illness. 2 (fig) wild excitement.

de·liver /dɪˈlɪvə(r)/ vt 1 take (letters, parcels, goods, etc) to houses, to the person(s) to whom they are addressed, to the buyer(s): *Did you ~ my message?* 2 **deliver from,** (formal) rescue, save, set free: *May God ~ us from all evil.* 3 give forth in words: *to ~ a sermon/a course of lectures.* 4 (of a medical attendant, eg a midwife) help (a woman) in childbirth. 5 surrender; give up; hand over: *to ~ up stolen goods; to ~ over one's property to one's son.* 6 send against: *to ~ a blow in the cause of freedom.*

de·liverer, person who delivers; rescuer.

de·liver·ance /dɪˈlɪvərəns/ n [U] delivering(2); rescue; being set free.

de·liv·ery /dɪˈlɪvərɪ/ n (pl -ies) 1 [U] delivering (of letters, goods, etc): *We guarantee prompt ~.* 2 [C] periodical performance of this: *How many deliveries are there in your town* (= How often does the postman deliver letters) *every day?* 2 [U] manner of speaking (in lectures, etc): *His sermon was good, but his ~ was poor.*

dell /del/ n [C] small valley, usually with trees.

delta /ˈdeltə/ n [C] (pl ~s) 1 Greek letter d. 2 land in this shape (Δ) at the mouth of a river between two or more branches: *the Nile D~.*

de·lude /dɪˈluːd/ vt deceive; mislead (on purpose): *to ~ oneself with false hopes; to ~ him/oneself into believing that...*

del·uge /ˈdeljuːdʒ/ n [C] 1 great flood; heavy rush of water; violent rainfall. 2 anything coming in a heavy rush: *a ~ of words/ questions/protests.* □ vt flood: *He was ~d with questions.*

de·lu·sion /dɪˈluːʒən/ n [U] deluding or being deluded; [C] false opinion or belief, esp one that may be a symptom of madness: *to be under a ~/under the ~ that...; to suffer from ~s.*

de·lu·sive /dɪˈluːsɪv/ adj not real; deceptive.

de·lu·sive·ly adv

de luxe /dɪ ˈlʌks/ adj (Fr) of very high quality, high standards of comfort, etc: *a ~ edition of a book.*

delve /delv/ vt, vi **delve into,** investigate, look into: *to ~ into his past.*

dema·gogue /ˈdeməgɒg US: -gɔg/ n [C] political leader who tries, by speeches appealing to the feelings instead of to reason, to stir up the people.

de·mand¹ /dɪˈmɑnd US: -ˈmænd/ n 1 act of demanding(1); something that is demanded(1): *The workers' ~s* (e g for higher pay) *were refused by the employers. on demand*, when demanded: *a cheque payable on ~.* 2 [U] (or with *a* and an *adjective*) desire, by people ready to buy, employ, etc: *There is a great ~ for typists but a poor ~/not much ~ for clerks. Our goods are in great ~.*

de·mand² /dɪˈmɑnd US: -ˈmænd/ vt 1 ask for as if ordering, or as if one has a right to: *~ an apology from her.* 2 need; require: *This sort of work ~s great patience.*

de·mar·cate /ˈdiːmɑːkeɪt/ vt mark or fix the limits of, e g a frontier.

de·mar·ca·tion /ˌdiːmɑːˈkeɪʃən/ n [U] marking of a boundary or limit; separation: *a line of ~.*

de·mean /dɪˈmiːn/ vt (formal) lower oneself in dignity, social esteem.

de·mean·our (US = **-or**) /dɪˈmiːnə(r)/ n [U] way of behaving: *I dislike his pompous ~our.*

de·mented /dɪˈmentɪd/ adj 1 mad. 2 (informal) extremely worried.

de·mented·ly adv

deme·rara /ˌdeməˈreərə/ n [U] (also *`demerara sugar`*) light brown raw cane sugar (from Guyana).

de·mili·tar·ized /ˌdiːˈmɪlɪtəraɪzd/ adj (of a country, or part of it) required, by treaty or agreement, to have no military forces or installation in it.

de·mise /dɪˈmaɪz/ n [C] (legal) death.

de·mist /ˈdiːmɪst/ vt remove the mist from, e g the windscreen of a motor-vehicle.

demo /ˈdeməʊ/ n [C] (informal) (abbr for) demonstration(2).

de·mo·bil·ize /dɪˈməʊbəlaɪz/ vt release from military service.

de·mo·bil·iz·ation /dɪˌməʊbəlaɪˈzeɪʃən US: -lɪˈz-/ n [U]

democ·racy /dɪˈmɒkrəsɪ/ n (pl -ies) 1 [C,U] (country with principles of) government in which all adult citizens share through their elected representatives. 2 [C,U] (country with a) government which encourages and allows rights of citizenship such as freedom of speech, religion, opinion and association, the assertion of the rule of law, majority rule, accompanied by respect for the rights of minorities. 3 [C,U] (society in which there is) treatment of each other by citizens as equals and absence of class feeling: *Is there more ~ in Australia than in Great Britain?*

demo·crat /ˈdeməkræt/ n [C] 1 person who favours or supports democracy. 2 D~, (US) member of the Democratic Party.

demo·cratic /ˌdeməˈkrætɪk/ adj 1 of, like, supporting, democracy(1,2). 2 (esp) of, supporting, democracy(3); paying no or little attention to class divisions based on birth or wealth.

the Democratic Party, (US) one of the two main political parties. ⇨ Republican.

demo·crati·cally /-klɪ/ adv

de·moc·ra·tize /dɪˈmɒkrətaɪz/ vt make democratic.

de·mol·ish /dɪˈmɒlɪʃ/ vt 1 pull or tear down, e g old buildings. 2 destroy, e g an argument; make an end of.

demo·li·tion /ˌdeməˈlɪʃən/ n [C,U]

de·mon, dae·mon /ˈdiːmən/ n [C] 1 evil, wicked or cruel supernatural being or spirit. 2 (informal) fierce or energetic person: *He's a ~ for work.*

de·mon·strable /dɪˈmɒnstrəbəl/ adj that can be logically proved.

de·mon·strably /-blɪ/ adv

dem·on·strate /ˈdemənstreɪt/ vt,vi 1 show clearly by giving proof(s) or example(s): *How would you ~ that the world is round?* 2 take part in a demonstration(2): *The workers marched through the streets with banners to ~ against the rising cost of living.*

dem·on·stra·tion /ˌdemənˈstreɪʃən/ n [C,U] 1 demonstrating(1): *a ~ of affection*, e g when a child puts its arms round its mother's neck. 2 public display of feeling by a group, e g of workers, students: *a student ~ that ended in violence.*

de·mon·stra·tive /dɪˈmɒnstrətɪv/ adj 1 (of persons) showing the feelings: *Some children are more ~ than others.* 2 marked by open expression of feelings: *~ behaviour.* 3 serving to point out. 4 (gram): *~ pronoun*, (this, these, that, those).

de·mon·stra·tive·ly adv

dem·on·stra·tor /ˈdemənstreɪtə(r)/ n [C] 1 person who demonstrates(2): *The ~s were dispersed by the police.* 2 person who teaches or explains by demonstrating(1).

de·moral·ize /dɪˈmɒrəlaɪz US: -ˈmɔːr-/ vt 1 hurt or weaken the morals of: *drugs that have a demoralizing effect.* 2 weaken the courage, confidence, self-discipline, etc of, e g an army.

de·mote /ˈdiːˈməʊt/ vt reduce to a lower rank or grade.

de·mo·tion /ˈdiːˈməʊʃən/ n [U]

de·motic /dɪˈmɒtɪk/ adj of, used by, the common people: *~ Greek*, the everyday form of modern Greek.

de·mur /dɪˈmɜː(r)/ vi (-rr-) (formal) raise an objection: *to ~ to a demand; to ~ at working on Sundays.* □ n [C] hesitation or objection: (chiefly in) *without ~.*

de·mure /dɪˈmjʊə(r)/ adj 1 quiet and serious: *a ~ young lady.* 2 pretending to be, suggesting that one is, demure: *She gave him a ~ smile.*

de·mure·ly adv

den /den/ n [C] 1 animal's hidden lying-place, e g a cave. 2 secret resort: *an `opium*

~; *a* ~ *of thieves*. **3** (*informal*) room in which a person works and studies without being disturbed.

de·na·tion·al·ize /'diˈnæʃnəlaɪz/ *vt* transfer (a nationalized industry, etc) to private ownership again.

de·na·tion·al·iz·a·tion /'diˈnæʃnəlaɪˈzeɪʃən US: -lɪˈz-/ *n* [U]

de·ni·able /dɪˈnaɪəbəl/ *adj* that can be denied.

de·ni·al /dɪˈnaɪəl/ *n* **1** [U] denying; refusing a request; [C] instance of this: *the* ~ *of justice/a request for help*. **2** [C] statement that something is not true: *the prisoner's repeated* ~*s of being involved in the robbery*.

de·nim /ˈdenɪm/ *n* **1** [U] (usually pale blue) cotton cloth (used for jeans, overalls, etc). **2** (*pl*) (*informal*) jeans made from denim.

de·nom·i·na·tion /dɪˈnomɪˈneɪʃən/ *n* [C] **1** name, esp one given to a class or religious group or sect: *The Protestant* ~*s include the Methodists, Presbyterians and Baptists*. **2** class or unit (in weight, length, numbers, money, etc): *The US coin of the lowest* ~ *is the cent*.

de·nom·i·na·tional /-nəl/ *adj* of religious groups.

de·nom·i·na·tor /dɪˈnommeɪtə(r)/ *n* [C] number or quantity below the line in a fraction, e g 4 in ¾.

de·note /dɪˈnəʊt/ *vt* (*formal*) **1** be the sign or symbol of; be the name of: *In algebra the sign x usually* ~*s an unknown quantity*. **2** indicate: *The mark* (ₐ) ~*s that something has been omitted*.

de·nounce /dɪˈnaʊns/ *vt* **1** speak publicly against; give information against: *to* ~ *her as a spy*. **2** give notice that one intends to end (a treaty or agreement).

dense /dens/ *adj* (-*r*, -*st*) **1** (of liquids, vapour) not easily seen through: *a* ~ *fog;* ~ *smoke*. **2** (of people and things) crowded together in great numbers: *a* ~ *crowd/forest*. **3** stupid; having a mind that ideas can penetrate only with difficulty.

dense·ly *adv*: *a* ~*ly populated country*.

dense·ness *n* [U]

den·sity /ˈdensətɪ/ *n* (*pl* -ies) **1** [U] the quality of being dense: *the* ~ *of a forest/the population*. **2** [C,U] (in physics) relation of weight to volume.

dent /dent/ *n* [C] **1** hollow, depression, in a hard surface made by a blow or by pressure. **2** (*fig*) (*informal*) damage, effect badly: *a* ~ *in one's pride*. □ *vt, vi* make or get a dent in: *a car badly* ~*ed in a collision*.

den·tal /ˈdentəl/ *adj* of or for the teeth: *a* ~ *surgeon*.

den·tist /ˈdentɪst/ *n* [C] person whose work is filling, cleaning, taking out teeth and fitting artificial teeth.

den·tistry, work of a dentist.

den·ture /ˈdentʃə(r)/ *n* [C] device (fitted to the gums) with artificial teeth.

de·nun·ci·ation /dɪˈnʌnsɪˈeɪʃən/ *n* [C,U] denouncing: *the* ~ *of a traitor*.

deny /dɪˈnaɪ/ *vt* (*pt,pp* -ied) **1** say that (something) is not true: *The accused man denied the charge. It cannot be denied that* .../*There is no* ~*ing the fact that*..., Everyone must admit that... **2** say that one knows nothing about; refuse to acknowledge: *He denied the signature*, said that it was not his. **3** say 'no' to a request; refuse to give (something asked for or needed): *He denies himself/his wife nothing*.

de·odor·ant /'diˈəʊdərənt/ *n* [C] substance that disguises or absorbs (esp body) odours.

de·odor·ize /'diˈəʊdəraɪz/ *vt* remove unwanted smells from.

de·part /dɪˈpɑt/ *vi* **1** go away; leave: *the train* ~*s* (*from Euston*) *at 3.30 pm*. **2** behave in a way that differs from: ~ *from routine/the truth*.

de·parted *n* the ~*ed*, (*sing*) person who has recently died; (*pl*) those who have died: *pray for the souls of the* ~*ed*.

de·part·ment /dɪˈpɑtmənt/ *n* [C] one of several divisions of a government, business, shop, university, etc: *the Education D*~/ *D*~ *of Education*.

de·part·ment store, large shop where many kinds of goods are sold in different departments.

de·part·mental /ˈdipɑtˈmentəl/ *adj* of a department (contrasted with the whole): ~*al duties/administration*.

de·par·ture /dɪˈpɑtʃə(r)/ *n* **1** [U] departing; going away; [C] instance of this: *There are notices showing arrivals and* ~*s of trains over there*. **2** [C,U] turning away or aside, changing: *a* ~ *from old custom; a new* ~ *in physics*, e g the discovery of nuclear fission.

de·pend /dɪˈpend/ *vi* **1** need, rely on (the support, etc of) in order to exist or to be true or to succeed: *Children* ~ *on their parents for food and clothing. That/It all depends*, the result depends on something else. **2** trust; be certain about: *You can always* ~ *on John to be there when he is needed*.

de·pend·able /-əbəl/ *adj* that may be relied on.

de·pend·ant (also **-ent**) /dɪˈpendənt/ *n* [C] person who depends on another or others for a home, food, etc. ⇨ **dependent** *adj*.

de·pend·ence /dɪˈpendəns/ *n* [U] **1** the state of depending; being supported by others: *Why don't you find a job and end this* ~ *on your parents?* **2** confident trust; reliance: *He's not a man you can put much* ~ *on*, You can't rely on him. **3** the state of being determined or conditioned by: *the* ~ *on drugs*.

de·pend·ency /dɪˈpendənsɪ/ *n* [C] (*pl* -ies) country governed or controlled by another: *The Hawaiian Islands are no longer a* ~ *of the USA*.

de·pend·ent /dɪˈpendənt/ *n* [C] = dependant. □ *adj* depending: *Promotion is* ~ *on your record of success*.

de·pict /dɪˈpɪkt/ vt show in the form of a picture; describe in words: *Mediterranean scenes ~ed in these photographs.*
de·pic·tion /dɪˈpɪkʃən/ n [U]

de·plete /dɪˈplit/ vt use up, empty until little or none remains: *to ~ a lake of fish; ~d supplies.*
de·ple·tion /dɪˈpliʃən/ n [U]

de·plore /dɪˈplɔː(r)/ vt show, say, that one is filled with sorrow or regret for.
de·plor·able /dɪˈplɔːrəbəl/ adj that is, or should be, deplored: *deplorable conduct.*
de·plor·ably /-əblɪ/ adv: *deplorably ignorant children.*

de·ploy /dɪˈplɔɪ/ vt,vi (of troops and warships) (cause to) spread out, e g into line of battle.

de·popu·late /ˌdiˈpɒpjʊleɪt/ vt lessen the number of people living in a place: *a country ~d by war/famine.*
de·popu·la·tion /ˌdiˈpɒpjʊˈleɪʃən/ n [U].

de·port[1] /dɪˈpɔːt/ vt expel (an unwanted person) from a country: *The spy was imprisoned for two years and then ~ed.*
de·port·ation /ˌdipɔːˈteɪʃən/ n [U].

de·port[2] /dɪˈpɔːt/ vt (formal) behave: *to ~ oneself with dignity.*
de·port·ment n [U] (esp); way of holding oneself in standing and walking: *Many young ladies used to have lessons in ~ment.*

de·pose /dɪˈpəʊz/ vt,vi remove, esp a ruler such as a king, from a position of authority.

de·posit[1] /dɪˈpɒzɪt/ n [C] 1 money that is deposited(2,3): *The shopkeeper promised to keep the goods for me if I left/paid/made a ~.* 2 layer of matter deposited(4): *A thick ~ of mud covered the fields after the floods went down.* 3 layer of solid matter (often buried in the earth): *Valuable new ~s of tin have been found in Bolivia.*
de·posit account, money deposited in a bank, not to be withdrawn without notice, on which interest is payable.

de·posit[2] /dɪˈpɒzɪt/ vt 1 lay or put down: *Some insects ~ their eggs in the ground.* 2 put or store for safe-keeping: *to ~ money in a bank/papers with one's lawyer.* 3 make part payment of money that is or will be owed: *We should like you to ~ a tenth of the price of the house.* 4 (esp of a river) leave (a layer of material on): *When the Nile rises it ~s a layer of mud on the land.*

de·posi·tor /dɪˈpɒzɪtə(r)/ n [C] person who deposits, e g money in a bank.

de·pot /ˈdepəʊ US: ˈdipəʊ/ n [C] 1 storehouse, esp for military supplies; warehouse. 2 (US) railway or bus station.

de·prave /dɪˈpreɪv/ vt make morally bad; corrupt: *~d children; ~d (= vicious or perverted) tastes.* (Note: usually used as a pp.)
de·prav·ity /dɪˈprævətɪ/ n [U] depraved state. [C] vicious act.

de·pre·ci·ate /dɪˈpriːʃɪeɪt/ vt,vi make or become less in value: *Shares in this com-*

pany have ~d.
de·preci·ation /dɪˈpriːʃɪˈeɪʃən/ n [U] lessening of value or estimation.

de·press /dɪˈpres/ vt 1 press, push or pull down: *to ~ a lever/the keys of a piano.* 2 make sad, low in spirits: *The newspapers are full of ~ing news nowadays,* e g of war, crime, natural disasters, rising prices. 3 make less active; cause (prices) to be lower: *When business is ~ed there is usually an increase in unemployment.*
de·pressed ˈarea, part of a country where industry is depressed (producing poverty and unemployment).
de·pres·sion /dɪˈpreʃən/ n 1 [U] being depressed(2): *He commited suicide during a fit of ~.* 2 [C] hollow, sunk place, in the surface of something, esp the ground: *It rained heavily and every ~ in the bad road was soon filled with water(3).* 3 [C] time when business is depressed(3). 4 [C] lowering of, area of, atmospheric pressure; the system of winds round it: *a ~ over Iceland.*

de·pri·va·tion /ˌdeprɪˈveɪʃən/ n [U] depriving or being deprived; [C] something which one is deprived: *~ of one's rights as a citizen.*

de·prive /dɪˈpraɪv/ vt take away from; prevent from having, using or enjoying: *trees that ~ a house of light.*
de·prived adj = underprivileged.

depth /depθ/ n 1 [C,U] being deep; distance from the top down, from the front to the back, from the surface inwards: *Water was found at a ~ of 10 metres. The snow is three feet in ~.* **be/go out of one's depth,** (a) be/go in water too deep to stand in: *If you can't swim, don't go out of your ~.* (b) (fig) attempt something too difficult: *When people start talking about nuclear physics I'm out of my ~.* 2 [C] deep learning, thought, feeling, etc: *She showed a ~ of feeling that surprised us.* 3 the ~(s), deepest or most central part(s): *in the ~ of winter; in the ~s of despair.*

depu·ta·tion /ˌdepjʊˈteɪʃən/ n [C] group of representatives; number of persons given the right to act or speak for others.

de·pute /dɪˈpjuːt/ vt give (one's work, authority, etc) to a substitute; give (another person) authority to act as one's representative.

depu·tize /ˈdepjʊtaɪz/ vi act as deputy: *Can you ~ for me?*

deputy /ˈdepjʊtɪ/ n [C] (pl -ies) 1 person to whom work, authority, etc is given: *I must find someone to act as (a) ~ for me during my absence.* 2 (in some countries, e g France) member of a legislative assembly.

de·rail /dɪˈreɪl/ vt cause (a train, etc) to run off the rails: *The engine was ~ed.*
de·rail·ment n [C,U].

de·range /dɪˈreɪndʒ/ vt put out of working order; put into confusion; disturb: *He is mentally ~d,* insane.

der·el·ict /ˈderəlɪkt/ adj abandoned; deserted and left to fall into ruin: a ~ house.
der·el·ic·tion /ˈderəˈlɪkʃən/ n (a) making derelict: the dereliction caused by the invading armies. (b) (deliberate) neglect of duty.
de·re·strict /ˈdiːrɪˈstrɪkt/ vt cancel a restriction on: ~ a road, remove a speed limit from it.
de·ride /dɪˈraɪd/ vt laugh scornfully at: They ~d his efforts as childish.
de·ri·sion /dɪˈrɪʒn/ n [U] deriding or being derided; [C] something that is derided: be/ become an object of ~.
de·ris·ive /dɪˈraɪsɪv/ adj showing or deserving derision: a ~ offer, eg £50 for a car that is worth £250.
de·ris·ory /dɪˈraɪsərɪ/ adj = derisive.
deri·va·tion /ˈderɪˈveɪʃən/ n 1 [U] deriving or being derived; origin; descent: the ~ of words from Latin; a word of Latin ~. 2 [C] first form and meaning of a word; statement of how a word was formed and how it changed: to study the ~s of words.
de·riva·tive /dɪˈrɪvətɪv/ adj, n [C] (thing, word, substance) derived from another: 'Assertion' is a ~ of 'assert'.
de·rive /dɪˈraɪv/ vt, vi 1 get: to ~ great pleasure from one's studies. 2 have as a source or origin: Thousands of English words are ~d from/~ from Latin.
der·ma·tol·ogist /ˈdɜːməˈtɒlədʒɪst/ n [C] expert in skin diseases.
der·ma·tol·ogy /ˈdɜːməˈtɒlədʒɪ/ n [U] medical study of the skin, its diseases, etc.
dero·gate /ˈderəgeɪt/ vi (formal) take away (a merit, good quality, right).
dero·ga·tion /ˈderəˈgeɪʃən/ n [U] lessening (of authority, dignity, reputation, etc).
de·roga·tory /dɪˈrɒgətrɪ US: -tɔːrɪ/ adj tending to damage or take away from (one's credit, etc): Is the slang word 'cop' as ~ as 'pig' for 'policeman'?
der·rick /ˈderɪk/ n [C] 1 (also ~-crane) large crane for moving or lifting heavy weights, esp on a ship. 2 framework over an oil-well or bore-hole, to hold the drilling machinery, etc.
derv /dɜːv/ n [U] fuel oil for diesel engines (from Diesel Engined Road Vehicle).
des·cant /ˈdeskænt/ n [C] (music) additional independent accompaniment (often improvised) to a melody.
de·scend /dɪˈsend/ vi, vt 1 (formal) come or go down: On turning the corner, we saw that the path ~ed steeply. 2 **be descended from**, have as ancestors: According to the Bible, we are all ~ed from Adam. 3 (of property, qualities, rights) pass (from father to son) by inheritance; come from earlier times. 4 attack suddenly: The bandits ~ed on the defenceless village. 5 lower oneself: You would never ~ to fraud/cheating.
de·scend·ant /dɪˈsendənt/ n [C] person who is descended from (the person or persons named): the ~s of Queen Victoria.

de·scent /dɪˈsent/ n 1 [C,U] coming or going down: The ~ of the mountain took two hours. 2 [U] ancestry: of French ~, having French ancestors. 3 [C] sudden attack: The Danes made numerous ~s on the English coast during the 10th century. 4 [U] handing down, eg of property, titles, qualities, etc by inheritance.
de·scribe /dɪˈskraɪb/ vt 1 say what (a person or thing) is like: Words cannot ~ the beauty of the scene. 2 say that (a person or thing) has certain qualities: He ~s himself as a doctor. 3 mark out, draw (esp a geometrical figure): It is easy to ~ a circle if you have a pair of compasses.
de·scrip·tion /dɪˈskrɪpʃən/ n 1 [C,U] describing; picture in words: Her beauty is beyond ~, too beautiful to be expressed in words. Can you give me a ~ of the thief? 2 [C] (informal) sort: The harbour was crowded with vessels of every ~.
de·scrip·tive /dɪˈskrɪptɪv/ adj serving to describe; fond of describing.
des·ecrate /ˈdesɪkreɪt/ vt use (a sacred thing or place) in an unworthy or wicked way.
des·ecra·tion /ˈdesəˈkreɪʃən/ n [U] desecrating or being desecrated.
de·seg·re·gate /ˈdiːˈsegrɪgeɪt/ vt abolish (esp racial) segregation in: ~ schools in Alabama.
de·seg·re·ga·tion /ˈdiːˈsegrɪˈgeɪʃən/ n [U]
de·sert[1] /dɪˈzɜːt/ vt, vi 1 go away from: The streets were ~ed, No people were to be seen. 2 leave without help or support, esp in a wrong or cruel way: He ~ed his wife and children and went abroad. 3 run away from; leave (esp service in a ship, the armed forces) without authority or permission: A soldier who ~s his post in time of war is punished severely. 4 fail: His courage ~ed him.
de·serter, person who deserts, esp in the sense of 3 above.
de·ser·tion /dɪˈzɜːʃən/ n [C,U]
des·ert[2] /ˈdezət/ n [C,U] (large area of) barren land, waterless and treeless, often sand-covered: the Sahara D~. □ adj 1 barren; uncultivated: the ~ areas of N Africa. 2 uninhabited: wrecked on a ~ island.
de·serts /dɪˈzɜːts/ n pl what a person deserves: to be rewarded/punished according to one's ~.
de·serve /dɪˈzɜːv/ vt, vi be entitled to (because of actions, conduct, qualities): He ~s to be sent to prison.
de·serv·ed·ly /dɪˈzɜːvɪdlɪ/ adv according to what is deserved; rightly: to be ~dly punished.
de·serv·ing /dɪˈzɜːvɪŋ/ adj having merit; worthy (of): to give money to a ~ cause; to be ~ of sympathy.
des·ic·cate /ˈdesɪkeɪt/ vt dry out all the moisture from, esp solid food, to preserve it: ~d fruit/coconut.

de·sign /dɪˈzaɪn/ n 1 [C] drawing or outline from which something may be made: ~s for a dress/garden. 2 [U] art of making such drawings, etc: a school of ~. 3 [U] general arrangement or planning (of a picture, book, building, machine, etc): The building seats 2000 people, but is poor in ~. 3 [C] pattern; arrangement of lines, shapes, details, as ornament: a vase with a ~ of flowers on it. 4 [C,U] purpose; intention; mental plan: Was it by accident or ~ that he arrived too late to help? **have designs on,** (a) intend (selfishly or evilly) to get possession of: That man has ~s on your money/your life. (b) (informal) He has ~s on that young girl, wants to be intimate with her. □ vt,vi 1 prepare a plan, sketch, etc (of something to be made): ~ a dress/garden. He ~s for a large firm of carpet manufacturers. 2 set apart, intend, plan: This room was ~ed for the children.

de·sign·er /dɪˈzaɪnə(r)/ n [C] person who designs, e g machinery, clothes.

de·sign·ing /dɪˈzaɪnɪŋ/ adj (esp) artful and cunning; fond of intrigue. □ n [U] art of making designs (for machinery, etc).

des·ig·nate[1] /ˈdezɪɡneɪt/ adj appointed to office (but not yet installed): the bishop ~.

des·ig·nate[2] /ˈdezɪɡneɪt/ vt 1 mark or point out clearly; give a name or title to: to ~ boundaries. 2 appoint to a position or office: He ~d Smith as his successor.

des·ig·na·tion /ˌdezɪɡˈneɪʃən/ n [U] appointing to an office; [C] name, title or description.

de·sir·able /dɪˈzaɪərəbəl/ adj to be desired; worth having: This ~ property to be sold, as in an estate agent's advertisement.

de·sir·abil·ity /dɪˌzaɪərəˈbɪlətɪ/ n [U]

de·sire[1] /dɪˈzaɪə(r)/ n 1 [U] strong longing; [C] instance of this: He has no/not much ~ for wealth. 2 [C] thing that is wished for: I hope you will get all your heart ~s, all you wish for. 3 (formal) request: at the ~ of Her Majesty.

de·sire[2] /dɪˈzaɪə(r)/ vt (formal) long for; wish; have a desire(1) for: We all ~ happiness and health. 2 (official style) request: It is ~d that this rule shall be brought to the attention of the staff.

de·sir·ous /dɪˈzaɪərəs/ adj (formal) feeling desire: ~ of peace.

de·sist /dɪˈzɪst/ vi (formal) stop: ~ from gossiping.

desk /desk/ n [C] 1 piece of furniture (not a table) with a flat or sloping top and drawers at which to read, write or do business, e g one for office use. 2 = reception desk.

deso·late /ˈdesələt/ adj 1 (of a place) in a ruined, neglected state; (of land or a country) unlived in; unfit to live in: a ~, windswept moorland area. 2 friendless; wretched; lonely and sad: a `~-looking child. □ vt /ˈdesəleɪt/ make desolate.

deso·late·ly adv

deso·la·tion /ˌdesəˈleɪʃən/ n [U] making or

being desolate: the desolation caused by war.

des·pair[1] /dɪˈspeə(r)/ n [U] 1 the state of having lost all hope: You will drive me to ~. He gave up in ~. He was filled with ~ when he read the examination questions. 2 the despair of, that causes loss of hope: This boy is the ~ of all his teachers, They no longer hope to teach him anything.

des·pair[2] /dɪˈspeə(r)/ vi be in despair: to ~ of success/of ever succeeding.

des·pair·ing·ly adv

des·patch /dɪˈspætʃ/ n, v = dispatch.

des·per·ate /ˈdespərət/ adj 1 (of a person) filled with despair and ready to do anything, regardless of danger (often because of violent behaviour): The prisoners became ~ in their attempts to escape. They are all ~ criminals. 2 extremely serious or dangerous: The economic state of the country is ~. 4 giving little hope of success; tried when all else has failed: ~ remedies.

des·per·ate·ly adv

des·per·ation /ˌdespəˈreɪʃən/ n [U] the state of being desperate(1): The people rose in ~ against their rulers.

des·pic·able /dɪˈspɪkəbəl/ adj deserving to be despised; contemptible.

des·pic·ably /-əblɪ/ adv

des·pise /dɪˈspaɪz/ vt feel contempt for; consider worthless: Strike-breakers are ~d by their workmates.

des·pite /dɪˈspaɪt/ prep in spite of: D~ what she says...

de·spon·dency /dɪˈspondənsɪ/ n [U] loss of hope: to fall into ~.

de·spon·dent /dɪˈspondənt/ adj having or showing loss of hope: Don't become too despondent.

de·spon·dent·ly adv

des·pot /ˈdespot/ n [C] ruler with unlimited powers, esp one who uses these powers wrongly or cruelly.

des·potic /dɪˈspotɪk/ adj of or like a despot or tyrant.

des·sert /dɪˈzɜt/ n [C] course of fruit, etc at the end of a meal.

des·`sert-spoon, medium-sized spoon.

des·`sert-spoon·ful /-fʊl/. as much as a desertspoon will hold.

des·ti·na·tion /ˌdestɪˈneɪʃən/ n [C] place to which a person or thing is going or is being sent.

des·tine /ˈdestɪn/ vt set apart, decide in advance: They were ~d never to meet again, Fate had determined that they should never meet again.

des·tiny /ˈdestɪnɪ/ n (pl -ies) 1 [U] power believed to control events: tricks played on human beings by ~. 2 [C] that which happens to a person, thought of as determined in advance by fate, etc: It was his ~ to die in a foreign country, far from his family.

des·ti·tute /ˈdestɪtjut US: -tut/ adj without food, clothes and other things necessary for life: *When Mr Hill died, his wife and children were left ~.*

des·ti·tu·tion /ˌdestɪˈtjuːʃən US: -ˈtuː-/ n [U] being destitute: *a war that brought desolation and destitution.*

de·stroy /dɪˈstrɔɪ/ vt break to pieces; make useless; put an end to: *Don't ~ that box—it may be useful. All his hopes were ~ed.*

de·stroyer /dɪˈstrɔɪə(r)/ n [C] 1 person or thing that destroys. 2 small, fast warship for protecting larger ships.

de·struc·tible /dɪˈstrʌktəbəl/ adj that can be destroyed.

de·struc·ti·bil·ity /dɪˈstrʌktəˈbɪlətɪ/ n [U]

de·struc·tion /dɪˈstrʌkʃən/ n [U] 1 destroying or being destroyed: *the ~ of a town by an earthquake.* 2 that which ruins or destroys: *Gambling was his ~.*

de·struc·tive /dɪˈstrʌktɪv/ adj causing destruction; fond of, in the habit of, destroying: *Are all small children ~?*

de·tach /dɪˈtætʃ/ vt 1 unfasten and take apart; separate: *to ~ a coach from a train.* 2 send (a party of soldiers, ships, etc) away from the main body: *A number of men were ~ed to guard the right flank.*

de·tached adj (a) (of the mind, opinions, etc) not influenced by others: *to take a ~ed view of an event.* (b) (of a house) not joined to another on either side.

de·tach·able /-əbəl/ adj that can be separated: *a ~able lining in a coat.*

de·tach·ment /dɪˈtætʃmənt/ n 1 [U] detaching or being detached: *the ~ of a letter from a file.* 2 [U] the state of being detached(1,2); being uninfluenced by surroundings, opinions, etc; being indifferent and uninterested. 3 [C] group of men, ships, etc detached(2) from a larger number (for a special duty, etc).

de·tail[1] /ˈdiːteɪl US: dɪˈteɪl/ n 1 [C] small, particular fact or item: *Please give me all the ~s.* 2 [C] collection of such small facts or items. 3 [U] (in art) the smaller or less important parts considered as a whole: *The composition of the picture is good but there is too much ~.* 4 [C] = detachment(3).

de·tail[2] /ˈdiːteɪl US: dɪˈteɪl/ vt 1 describe fully: *a ~ed description.* 2 appoint for special duty: *Three soldiers were ~ed to guard the bridge.* ⇨ detail[1](4).

de·tain /dɪˈteɪn/ vt keep waiting; keep back; prevent from leaving or going forward: *He told his wife that he had been ~ed in the office.*

de·tainee /ˈdiːteɪˈniː/ n [C] person who is detained (esp by the authorities, who is suspected of doing wrong, etc).

de·tect /dɪˈtekt/ vt discover (the existence or presence of, etc): *The dentist could ~ no sign of decay in her teeth.*

de·tect·able /-əbəl/ adj that can be detected.

de·tec·tor /-tə(r)/, device for detecting, e g changes of pressure, temperature or a radio signal.

de·tec·tion /dɪˈtekʃən/ n [U] detecting; being discovered: *He tried to escape ~ by disguising himself as an old man.*

de·tec·tive /dɪˈtektɪv/ n [C] person whose business it is to detect criminals.

de·tective story/novel, one in which the main interest is crime and the process of solving it.

de·ten·tion /dɪˈtenʃən/ n [U] detaining or being detained, e g detaining a pupil in school after ordinary hours, as a punishment.

de·ter /dɪˈtɜː(r)/ vt (-rr-) discourage: *Failure did not ~ him from trying again.*

de·ter·gent /dɪˈtɜːdʒənt/ n [C,U], adj (substance) that removes dirt, esp from the surface of things.

de·terio·rate /dɪˈtɪərɪəreɪt/ vt,vi make or become of less value, or worse (in quality): *Health quickly ~s in a cold, damp house.*

de·terio·ra·tion /dɪˈtɪərɪəˈreɪʃən/ n [U]

de·ter·mi·nate /dɪˈtɜːmɪnət/ adj (formal) definite; fixed.

de·ter·mi·na·tion /dɪˈtɜːmɪˈneɪʃən/ n [U] 1 determining or being determined; deciding: *The ~ of the meaning of a word is often difficult without a context.* 2 calculation or finding out: *the ~ of the amount of metal in ore.* 3 firmness of purpose; resolution: *his ~ to learn English.*

de·ter·mine /dɪˈtɜːmɪn/ vt,vi 1 decide; fix (the usual word): *to ~ a date for a meeting.* 2 calculate; find out precisely: *to ~ the speed of light.* 3 decide firmly, resolve, make up one's mind: *His future has not yet been ~d, but he may study medicine.* 4 cause to decide: *What ~d you to accept the offer?* 5 be the fact that decides: *The size of your feet ~s the size of your shoes.*

de·ter·min·able /-əbəl/ adj that can be determined.

de·ter·rent /dɪˈterənt US: -ˈtɜːr-/ n [C], adj (thing) tending to, intended to, deter: *Do you believe that the hydrogen bomb is a ~, that it will discourage countries from making war?*

de·test /dɪˈtest/ vt hate strongly: *to ~ dogs.*

de·test·able /-əbəl/ adj hateful: deserving to be hated.

de·throne /dɪˈθrəʊn/ vt 1 remove (a ruler) from the throne. 2 (fig) remove from a position of authority or influence.

de·throne·ment n [U]

det·on·ate /ˈdetəneɪt/ vt,vi (cause to) explode with a loud noise.

det·on·ation /ˈdetəˈneɪʃən/ n [C,U] explosion; noise of an explosion.

det·on·ator /ˈdetəneɪtə(r)/, part of a bomb or shell that explodes first, causing the substance in the bomb, etc to explode.

de·tour /ˈdiːtʊə(r) US: dɪˈtʊər/ n [C] roundabout way, e g a way used when the main road is blocked; diversion: *to make a ~.* □ vt make a detour.

169

de·tract /dɪˈtrækt/ vi take away (from the credit, value, etc, of): to ~ from his merit, make it less.

de·trac·tor /-tə(r)/, person who tries to make a person's reputation, etc smaller.

det·ri·ment /ˈdetrɪmənt/ n [U] damage; harm: I know nothing to his ~, nothing against him.

det·ri·men·tal /ˈdetrɪˈmentəl/ adj harmful: activities that would be ~al to our interests.

det·ri·men·tal·ly /-təlɪ/ adv

deuce[1] /djus US: dus/ n [C] **1** the two on playing-cards or dice. **2** (in tennis) the score of 40 all after which either side must gain two successive points to win the set.

de·value /ˈdiˈvælju/ vt make (the value of a currency) less (esp in terms of gold): to ~ the dollar/pound.

de·valu·ation /ˈdiˈvæljuˈeɪʃən/ n [C] (of currency) change to a new, lower fixed value.

dev·as·tate /ˈdevəsteɪt/ vt ruin; make desolate: towns ~d by fire/floods/war.

dev·as·ta·tion /ˈdevəˈsteɪʃən/ n [U]

de·velop /dɪˈveləp/ vt, vi **1** (cause to) grow larger, fuller or more mature, organized: Plants ~ from seeds. We must ~ the natural resources of our country. Amsterdam ~ed into one of the greatest ports in the world. **2** (of something not at first active or visible) come or bring into a state in which it is active or visible: He ~ed a cough. **3** treat (an exposed film or plate) with chemicals so that the photographed image can be seen. **4** use (an area of land) for the building of houses (or shops, factories, etc) and so increase its value.

de·vel·oper, **(a)** person who, authority which, develops land, etc. **(b)** substance used to develop films and plates.

de·vel·op·ment /dɪˈveləpmənt/ n **1** [U] developing or being developed (all senses): He is engaged in the ~ of his business. The ~ of photographic films requires a dark-room. **2** [C] new stage which is the result of developing: The latest ~s in medical research.

de·vi·ate /ˈdiːvɪeɪt/ vi turn away (what is usual, customary, right, etc): to ~ from the truth/a rule/one's custom.

de·vi·ation /ˈdiːvɪˈeɪʃən/ n [U] turning aside or away: ~ from the rules; [C] instance or amount or degree of this: slight ~s of the magnetic needle, in a compass.

de·vi·ation·ist, person who deviates, esp from the principles of a social or political system, e g Marxism.

de·vice /dɪˈvaɪs/ n [C] **1** plan; scheme; trick: a ~ to put the police off the scent. **2** something thought out, invented or adapted, for a special purpose: a nuclear ~, e g an atomic or hydrogen bomb. **3** sign, symbol or figure used in a decoration, e g a crest on a shield.

devil /ˈdevəl/ n [C] **1** the spirit of evil; wicked spirit; cruel or mischievous person.

the D~, the supreme spirit of evil, Satan. **2** wretched or unfortunate person: Oh, you poor ~! **3** (informal) (used in exclamations): What/Who/Where/Why the ~...?

'devil–may–'care adj without thinking of the consequences.

devil·ment /ˈdevəlmənt/ (also **dev·ilry** /ˈdevəlrɪ/) n **1** [C] mischief: She's up to some ~ or other. **2** [U] high spirits: full of ~.

de·vi·ous /ˈdiːvɪəs/ adj **1** winding; round-about: to take a ~ route to avoid busy streets. **2** cunning, deceitful: to get rich by ~ means.

de·vi·ous·ly adv

de·vi·ous·ness n [U]

de·vise /dɪˈvaɪz/ vt think out; plan: to ~ a scheme for making money.

de·void /dɪˈvɔɪd/ adj devoid of, without; empty of: ~ of shame/sense.

de·vol·ution /ˈdiːvəˈluːʃən US: ˈdev-/ n [U] deputing, delegating or decentralizing (of power or authority).

de·volve /dɪˈvɒlv/ vi, vt (formal) **1** (of work, duties) be transferred or passed to: When the President is ill, his duties ~ on the Vice-President. **2** pass, transfer (work, duties).

de·vote /dɪˈvəʊt/ vt give up (oneself, one's time, energy, etc) to: to ~ one's life to sport. He ~d himself to mission work in Africa.

de·voted adj very loving or loyal: a ~d friend.

de·vot·ed·ly adv

devo·tee /ˈdevəˈtiː/ n [C] person who is devoted to something: a ~ of sport/music.

de·vo·tion /dɪˈvəʊʃən/ n **1** [U] deep, strong love: the ~ of a mother for her children. **2** [U] devoting or being devoted: ~ to duty. **3** (pl) prayers: The priest was at his ~s.

de·vo·tional /-nəl/ adj of, used in devotions(3): ~al literature, for use in worship.

de·vour /dɪˈvaʊə(r)/ vt **1** eat hungrily or greedily: The hungry boy ~ed his dinner. **2** (fig) absorb, use up, destroy, occupy, etc completely: The fire ~ed twenty acres of forest.

de·vout /dɪˈvaʊt/ adj **1** paying serious attention to religious duties: a ~ old lady. **2** (of prayers, wishes, etc) serious; sincere: a ~ supporter; ~ wishes for your success.

de·vout·ly adv eagerly; sincerely.

de·vout·ness n [U]

dew /dju US: du/ n [U] tiny drops of moisture condensed on cool surfaces between evening and morning from water vapour in the air: The grass was wet with dew.

'dew drop, small drop of dew.

dewy adj (-ier, -iest) wet with dew.

dex·ter·ity /ˈdekˈsterətɪ/ n [U] skill, esp in handling things.

dex·ter·ous, **dex·trous** /ˈdekstrəs/ adj clever, skilful with the hands.

dex·ter·ous·ly adv

dhow /daʊ/ n [C] single-masted ship, esp as used by Arab sailors for coastal voyages.

di- /daɪ-, dɪ-/ prefix twice, double: dilemma.

dia- /daɪə-, daɪæ-/ prefix through, across: diagonal.

dia·betes /ˌdaɪəˈbiːtiːz/ n [U] disease of the pancreas in which sugar and starchy foods cannot be properly absorbed.

dia·betic /ˌdaɪəˈbetɪk/ adj of diabetes. □ n [C] person suffering from diabetes.

dia·bolic /ˌdaɪəˈbɒlɪk/ (also **dia·boli·cal** /-kəl/) adj 1 of or like a devil. 2 very cruel or wicked.

dia·boli·cally /-klɪ/ adv

di·aer·esis, di·er·esis /daɪˈerəsɪs/ n [C] (pl -eses /-əsiz/) mark (as in naïve) placed over a vowel to show that it is sounded separately from a preceding vowel.

di·ag·nose /ˈdaɪəɡˈnəʊz US: -əʊs/ vt determine the nature of (esp a disease) from observation of symptoms: The doctor ~d the illness as diptheria.

di·ag·nosis /ˌdaɪəɡˈnəʊsɪs/ n (pl -noses /-ˈnəʊsiz/) 1 [U] diagnosing. 2 [C] (statement of the) result of this.

di·ag·nos·tic /ˌdaɪəɡˈnɒstɪk/ adj of diagnosis: symptoms that were of no ~ value.

di·ag·onal /daɪˈæɡənəl/ n [C], adj (straight line) going across a straight-sided figure, e g an oblong, from corner to corner; slanting; crossed by slanting lines.

di·ag·on·ally /-əlɪ/ adv

dia·gram /ˈdaɪəɡræm/ n [C] drawing, design or plan to explain or illustrate something.

dia·gram·matic /ˌdaɪəɡrəˈmætɪk/ adj

dia·gram·mati·cally /-klɪ/ adv

dial /ˈdaɪəl/ n [C] 1 marked face or flat plate with a pointer for measuring (weight, volume, pressure, consumption of gas, etc). 2 plate, disc, etc on a radio set with names or numbers, for tuning into broadcasting stations. 3 part of a telephone, with numbers and/or letters, used to make a connection. 4 face (of a clock or watch). □ vt (-ll-) telephone: to ~ 01—230 1212.

dia·lect /ˈdaɪəlekt/ n [C,U] form of a language (grammar, vocabulary and pronunciation) used in a part of a country or by a class of people: the Yorkshire ~.

dia·lec·tal /ˌdaɪəˈlektəl/ adj of dialects: ~al differences between two counties.

dia·logue (US also **dia·log**) /ˈdaɪəlɒɡ US: -lɔːɡ/ n 1 [U] (writing in the form of a) conversation or talk: Plays are written in ~. 2 [C] exchange of views; talk: a ~ between the two Prime Ministers.

di·am·eter /daɪˈæmɪtə(r)/ n [C] measurement across any geometrical figure or body; (length of a) straight line drawn from side to side through the centre, esp of a circular, spherical or cylindrical form: the ~ of a tree-trunk.

dia·metri·cally /ˌdaɪəˈmetrɪklɪ/ adv com-

pletely; entirely: ~ opposed views.

dia·mond /ˈdaɪəmənd/ n [C] 1 brilliant precious stone, the hardest substance known: a ring with a ~ in it; a ~ ring/necklace. 2 piece of this substance (often artificially made) as used in industry, or as a stylus for playing gramophone records. 3 figure with four equal sides whose angles are not right angles; this shape (as printed in red on playing-cards): the ten of ~s.

diamond wedding, sixtieth anniversary of a wedding.

dia·phragm /ˈdaɪəfræm/ n [C] 1 wall of muscle between the chest and the abdomen. 2 arrangement of thin plates that control the inlet of light, e g through a camera lens. 3 vibrating disc or cone in some instruments, e g a telephone receiver, producing soundwaves.

di·ar·rhoea (also **-rrhea**) /ˌdaɪəˈrɪə/ n [U] too frequent and too watery emptying of the bowels.

diary /ˈdaɪərɪ/ n [C] (pl -ies) (book for a) daily record of events, thoughts, etc: keep a ~.

dia·rist /ˈdaɪərɪst/, person who keeps a diary.

dice /daɪs/ n pl (sing die which is rarely used) small cubes of wood, bone, etc marked with spots, used in games. □ vi,vt 1 play dice. **dice with death**, (informal) act dangerously and at the risk of death. 2 cut (food, e g carrots) into small cubes.

dicey /ˈdaɪsɪ/ adj (informal) risky; uncertain.

di·chot·omy /daɪˈkɒtəmɪ/ n [C] (pl -ies) division into two (usually contradictory classes or mutually exclusive pairs): the ~ of truth and falsehood.

dic·tate /dɪkˈteɪt US: ˈdɪkteɪt/ vt,vi 1 say or read aloud (words to be written down by another or others): to ~ a letter to a secretary. 2 state with the force of authority: to ~ terms to a defeated enemy. 3 give orders: I won't be ~d to, I refuse to accept orders from you. □ n [C] (usually pl) direction or order: the ~s of common sense.

dic·ta·tion /dɪkˈteɪʃən/ n 1 [U] dictating, being dictated to: The pupils wrote at their teacher's ~. 2 [C] passage, etc that is dictated.

dic·ta·tor /ˈdɪkˈteɪtə(r) US: ˈdɪkteɪtər/ n [C] ruler who has absolute authority, esp one who has obtained such power by force.

dic·ta·tor·ship, [C,U] (country with) government by a dictator.

dic·ta·tor·ial /ˌdɪktəˈtɔːrɪəl/ adj (a) of or like a dictator: ~ial government. (b) fond of giving orders: his ~ial manner.

dic·ta·tori·ally /-əlɪ/ adv

dic·tion /ˈdɪkʃən/ n [U] choice and use of words; style or manner of speaking and writing.

dic·tion·ary /ˈdɪkʃənrɪ US: -nerɪ/ n [C] (pl -ies) book dealing with the words of a language, or with words or topics of a special subject, and arranged in A B C order.

did /dɪd/ ⇨ do.

di·dac·tic /dɪˈdæktɪk/ adj **1** intended to teach: ∼ poetry. **2** having the manner of a teacher.

diddle /ˈdɪdəl/ vt (informal) cheat: I was ∼d (out of my fee).

die¹ /daɪ/ n [C] **1** (pl dice) ⇨ dice. **2** (pl ∼s) block of hard metal with a design, etc cut in it, used for shaping coins, type¹(3), medals, etc or stamping paper, leather, etc.

`die-cast adj made by casting metal in a mould.

die² /daɪ/ vi (pt,pp ∼d, present participle dying) **1** come to the end of life: Flowers soon ∼ if they are left without water. She ∼d of a fever. **die hard**, only after a struggle. **2** have a strong wish: We're all dying for a drink. **3** pass from human knowledge; be lost: His fame will never ∼.

4 (uses with adverbial particles and prepositions):

die away, lose strength, become faint or weak: The breeze/noise ∼d away.

die down, (a) (of a fire) burn with less heat. (b) (of excitement, etc) become less strong. (c) (of noise, etc) become less loud.

die off, die one by one: The leaves of this plant are dying off.

die out, become extinct; come to a complete end: Many old customs are gradually dying out.

die·sel engine /ˈdiːzəl endʒɪn/ n [C] oil-burning engine (as used for buses, locomotives) which burns `diesel oil (heavy fuel oil, not petrol).

diet¹ /ˈdaɪət/ n [C] **1** sort of food usually eaten (by a person, community, etc): Too rich a ∼ (= Too much rich food) is not good for you. **2** sort of food to which a person is limited, eg in order to lose weight: The doctor put her on a ∼. □ vt,vi restrict, be restricted, to a diet(2): Is he still ∼ing?
die·tary /ˈdaɪətrɪ US: -terɪ/ adj of diet: ∼ary rules.

diet² /ˈdaɪət/ n [C] series of meetings for discussion of national, international or church affairs: the Japanese D∼, legislative assembly.

dif·fer /ˈdɪfə(r)/ vi **1** be unlike: They look like each other but ∼ widely in their tastes. How does French ∼ from English? **2** disagree; have another opinion: I'm sorry to ∼ from you about/on/upon that question. **agree to differ,** give up the attempt to convince each other.

dif·fer·ence /ˈdɪfrəns/ n [C,U] **1** the state of being unlike: the ∼ between summer and winter. **2** amount, degree, manner, in which things are unlike: The ∼ between 7 and 18 is 11. I can't see much ∼ between/in them. **3** **make a/some/no/any/not much, etc difference,** be of some/no, etc importance: It won't make much ∼ whether you go today

or tomorrow. **4** disagreement: Why can't you settle your ∼s and be friends again?

dif·fer·ent /ˈdɪfrənt/ adj **1** not the same: She wears a ∼ dress every time I see her. Life today is ∼ from life long ago. **2** separate; distinct: I called three ∼ times, but he was out.
dif·fer·ent·ly adv

dif·fer·en·tial /ˌdɪfəˈrenʃəl/ adj of, showing, depending on, a difference: ∼ taxes, that differ according to circumstances. □ n [C] (also **wage** ∼) difference (expressed in a percentage) in wages between skilled and unskilled workers in the same industry: The increase for all workers would upset the wage ∼.

dif·fer·en·ti·ate /ˌdɪfəˈrenʃɪeɪt/ vt **1** see as different; show to be different: to ∼ varieties of plants; to ∼ one variety from another. **2** treat as different: It is wrong to ∼ between pupils according to their family background.

dif·fi·cult /ˈdɪfɪkəlt/ adj **1** not easy; requiring effort, strength, skill or ability: a ∼ problem/language. The sound is ∼ to pronounce. It is a ∼ sound to pronounce. **2** (of persons) not easily pleased or satisfied; easily offended: He's a ∼ man to get on with.

dif·fi·culty /ˈdɪfɪkəltɪ/ n (pl -ies) **1** [U] the state or quality of being difficult: Do you have any ∼ in understanding spoken English? **2** [C] something hard to do or understand: to be in financial difficulties, short of money, in debt, etc.

dif·fi·dence /ˈdɪfɪdəns/ n [U] lack of confidence; shyness.

dif·fi·dent /ˈdɪfɪdənt/ adj not having, not showing, much belief in one's own abilities: to be ∼ about doing something.
dif·fi·dent·ly adv

dif·fuse¹ /dɪˈfjuːz/ vt,vi **1** send out, spread, in every direction: to ∼ knowledge/light/heat. **2** (of gases and liquids) (cause to) mix slowly.

dif·fu·sion /dɪˈfjuːʒən/ n [U] diffusing or being diffused.

dif·fuse² /dɪˈfjuːs/ adj **1** using too many words: a ∼ writer/style. **2** spread out; scattered: ∼ light.
dif·fuse·ly adv
dif·fuse·ness n [U]

dig¹ /dɪg/ n [C] (informal) **1** push or thrust: Give her a ∼ in the ribs. That was a ∼ at me, a remark directed against me. **2** site being excavated by archaeologists. **3** (pl) (GB informal) lodgings: Are you living at home or in ∼?

dig² /dɪg/ vt,vi (pt,pp dug /dʌg/) (-gg-) **1** use a tool (eg a spade), a machine, claws, etc to break up and move earth, etc; make a way (through, into, etc) by doing this; make (a hole, etc) by doing this; get (something) by doing this: It is difficult to ∼ the ground when it is frozen hard. They are ∼ging a tunnel through the hill. **2** (sl) enjoy; appre-

ciate; understand; follow: *I don't ~ modern jazz.* **3** (uses with *adverbial particles* and *prepositions*):

dig sth in/into sth, push, thrust. poke: *to ~ a fork into a potato. The rider dug his spurs in.*

dig sb/sth out (of sth), (a) get out by digging: *He was buried by the avalanche and had to be dug out.* (b) get by searching: *to ~ information out of books and reports.*

dig sth up, (a) break up (land) by digging: *to ~ up land for a new garden.* (b) remove from the ground by digging: *We dug the tree up by the roots.* (c) bring to light (what has been buried or hidden) by digging: *An old Greek statue was dug up here last month.* (d) (*fig*): *The newspapers love to ~ up scandals.*

di-gest[1] /ˈdaɪdʒest/ *n* [C] short, condensed account; summary: *a ~ of the week's news.*

di-gest[2] /daɪˈdʒest/ *vt, vi* **1** (of food) change, be changed, in the stomach and bowels, so that it can be used in the body. *Some foods ~/are ~ed more easily than others.* **2** take into the mind; make part of one's knowledge; reduce (a mass of facts, etc) to order: *Have you ~ed everything that is important in the book?*

di-gest-ible /-əbəl/ *adj* that can be digested.

di-ges-tion /daɪˈdʒestʃən/ *n* [U] digesting; person's ability to digest food.

di-ges-tive /daɪˈdʒestɪv/ *adj* of digestion (of food).

the di`gestive system, the alimentary canal.

dig-ger /ˈdɪgə(r)/ *n* [C] **1** person who digs: *a `gold-~,* one who digs for gold. **2** mechanical excavator.

dig-ging /ˈdɪgɪŋ/ *n* [U] action of digging.

digit /ˈdɪdʒɪt/ *n* [C] **1** any one of the ten Arabic numerals 0 to 9: *The number 57306 contains five ~s.* **2** finger or toe.

digi-tal /ˈdɪdʒɪtəl/ *adj* of, using, digits.

dig-nify /ˈdɪgnɪfaɪ/ *vt* (*pt, pp* -ied) cause to appear worthy or honourable; give dignity to.

dig-ni-fied *adj* having or showing dignity: *a dignified old lady.*

dig-ni-tary /ˈdɪgnɪtrɪ US: -terɪ/ *n* [C] (*pl* -ies) person holding a high office, esp in the church, e g a bishop.

dig-nity /ˈdɪgnɪtɪ/ *n* (*pl* -ies) **1** [U] true worth; the quality that earns or deserves respect: *A man's ~ depends on his character, not his wealth.* **2** [U] calm and serious manner or style: *He's afraid of losing ~* (e g of being made to look foolish) *and won't speak a foreign language.* **3** [C] high or honourable rank or title: *The Queen conferred the ~ of a peerage on him.*

di-gress /daɪˈgres/ *vi* (esp in speaking or writing) turn or move away (from the main subject)

di-gres-sion /daɪˈgreʃən/ *n* [U] digressing; [C] instance of this

digs /dɪgz/ *n pl* (*GB informal*) lodgings

dike, dyke /daɪk/ *n* [C] **1** ditch (for carrying away water from land) **2** long wall of earth, etc (to keep back water and prevent flooding). □ *vi* make dikes: *diking in the Fens.*

dil-api-dated /dɪˈlæpɪdeɪtɪd/ *adj* falling to pieces; in a state of disrepair: *a ~ old house.*

dil-api-da-tion /dɪˈlæpɪˈdeɪʃən/ *n* [U]

di-late /daɪˈleɪt/ *vi, vt* (cause to) become wider, larger, further open: *The pupils of your eyes ~ when you enter a dark room.* **2** (*formal*) speak or write comprehensively about: *If there were time I could ~ on this subject.*

di-la-tion /ˈdaɪˈleɪʃən/ *n* [U]

dila-tory /ˈdɪlɪtrɪ US: -tɔrɪ/ *adj* slow in doing things; causing delay.

di-lemma /dɪˈlemə/ *n* [C] (*pl* ~s) situation in which one has to choose between two things, two courses of action, etc.

dili-gence /ˈdɪlɪdʒəns/ *n* [U] steady effort showing care and effort

dili-gent /ˈdɪlɪdʒənt/ *adj* hard-working, showing care and effort

dili-gent-ly *adv*

dill /dɪl/ *n* [U] herb with spicy seeds e g as used for flavouring pickles.

di-lute /daɪˈljuːt US: -ˈluːt/ *vt* make (a liquid or colour) weaker or thinner (by adding water or other liquid): *to ~ orange squash with water.* □ *adj* (of acids etc) weakened by diluting.

di-lu-tion /daɪˈljuːʃən US: -ˈluː-/ *n* [C,U]

dim /dɪm/ *adj* (-mer, -mest) **1** not bright; not (to be) seen clearly: *the ~ outline of buildings on a dark night; ~ memories/ recollections of my childhood.* **2** (of the eyes, eyesight) not able to see clearly: *His eyesight is getting ~mer.* **take a dim view of,** (*informal*) regard with disapproval or as hopeless. **3** (*informal*) unintelligent. □ *vt, vi* (-mm-) make or become dim: *eyes ~med by tears.*

dim-ly *adv* in a dim manner. *a ~ly lit room.*

dim-ness *n* [U]

dime /daɪm/ *n* [C] coin of US and Canada worth ten cents.

di-men-sion /dɪˈmenʃən/ *n* **1** [C] measurement of any sort (breadth, length, thickness, height, etc): *What are the ~s of the room?* **2** (*pl*) size; extent: *the ~s of the problem.*

-di-men-sional /-nəl/ *suffix*: *'two-/ 'three-di`mentional,* having two, three, dimensions.

dim-in-ish /dɪˈmɪnɪʃ/ *vt, vi* make or become less: *~ing food supplies.*

dim-inu-tive /dɪˈmɪnjutɪv US: -nu-/ *adj* **1** unusually or remarkably small. **2** (*gram*) (of a *suffix*) indicating smallness. □ *n* [C] word formed by the use of a *suffix* of this kind, e g *streamlet,* a small stream.

dimple /ˈdɪmpəl/ *n* [C] **1** small natural hollow in the chin or cheek (either permanent, or which appears, for example, when a person smiles). **2** slight hollow on water (made, for example, by a breeze). □ *vt,vi* make, form, a dimple.

din /dɪn/ *n* [U] loud, confused noise that continues: *The children were making so much ~/such a ~ that I couldn't study.* □ *vi,vt* (-nn-) make a din: *The cries of his tormentors were still ~ning in his ears.*

dine /daɪn/ *vi,vt* **1** have dinner: *to ~ off roast beef.* **dine out,** eat outside one's home (e g at the house of friends or at a restaurant). **2** give a dinner for.
`dining-car,` railway coach in which meals are served.
`dining-room,` room (in a house) in which meals are eaten.
`dining-table,` table used for dining.

diner /ˈdaɪnə(r)/ *n* [C] **1** person who dines. **2** dining-car on a train. **3** (*US*) restaurant shaped like a diner(2).

ding-dong /ˈdɪŋ ˈdɒŋ/ *n* [C], *adv* (with the) sound of bells striking repeatedly.

din·ghy, din·gey /ˈdɪŋɡɪ/ *n* [C] (*pl* -ies, ~s) **1** (kinds of) small open boat. **2** inflatable rubber boat (e g for use in an emergency).

dingy /ˈdɪndʒɪ/ *adj* (-ier, -iest) dirty-looking; not fresh or cheerful: *a ~ room.*
ding·ily /-əlɪ/ *adv*
dingi·ness *n* [U]

din·ing /ˈdaɪnɪŋ/ ⇨ dine.

din·ner /ˈdɪnə(r)/ *n* [C] main meal of the day, whether eaten at midday or in the evening: *It's time for ~/~-time. He ate too much ~. Shall we give a ~/~-party for her? Shall we ask him to ~?* (*Note: a* and *the* are rarely used.)
`dinner-jacket,` black jacket worn by men in the evening for formal occasions.
`dinner-service/-set,` set of plates, dishes, etc for dinner.

dino·saur /ˈdaɪnəsɔː(r)/ *n* [C] large extinct reptile.

di·ocesan /daɪˈɒsɪsən/ *adj* of a diocese.

dio·cese /ˈdaɪəsɪs/ *n* [C] (*pl* ~s /-sɪzɪz/) bishop's district.

dip¹ /dɪp/ *n* [C] **1** act of dipping. **2** (*informal*) quick bathe or swim: *to have/take/go for a ~.* **3** downward slope: *a ~ in the road.*

dip² /dɪp/ *vt,vi* (-pp-) **1** put, lower, into a liquid: *to ~ one's pen into the ink.* **2** **dip into,** (*fig*): *to ~ into one's purse,* spend money; *to ~ into a book/an author, etc,* take a hurried look. **3** go below a surface or level: *The sun ~ped below the horizon.* **4** (cause to) go down and then up again: *to ~ the headlights of a car,* lower their beams (in order not to dazzle the driver of another car). *The land ~s gently to the south.*

diph·theria /dɪfˈθɪərɪə/ *n* [U] serious disease of the throat causing difficulty in breathing.

diph·thong /ˈdɪfθɒŋ *US:* -θɔŋ/ *n* [C] union of two vowel sounds or vowel letters, e g the sounds /aɪ/ in *pipe* /paɪp/.

di·ploma /dɪˈpləʊmə/ *n* [C] (*pl* ~s) educa-

tional certificate of proficiency: *a ~ in architecture.*

di·plo·macy /dɪˈpləʊməsɪ/ *n* [U] **1** management of a country's affairs by ambassadors and ministers living overseas and their direction by ministries of Foreign Affairs at home; skill in this. **2** art of, skill in, dealing with people so that business is done smoothly.

diplo·mat /ˈdɪpləmæt/ *n* [C] person engaged in diplomacy for his country (e g an ambassador).

diplo·matic /ˈdɪpləˈmætɪk/ *adj* **1** of diplomacy: *the ~ service.* **2** tactful; having diplomacy(2): *a ~ answer; to be ~ in dealing with people.*
diplo·mati·cally /-klɪ/ *adv*

di·ploma·tist /dɪˈpləʊmətɪst/ *n* [C] **1** = diplomat. **2** person clever at dealing with people.

dire /ˈdaɪə(r)/ *adj* **1** dreadful; terrible: *~ news.* **2** extreme: *to be in ~ need of help.*

di·rect¹ /dɪˈrekt/ *adj* **1** (going) straight; not curved or crooked; not turned aside: *in a ~ line.* **2** with nothing or no one in between; in an unbroken line: *as a ~ result of this decision. He's a ~ descendant of the Duke of Kent.* **3** straightforward; going straight to the point: *He has a ~ way of speaking/doing things.* **4** exact: *the ~ opposite.* □ *adv* without interrupting a journey; without going by a roundabout way: *The train goes there ~.* (*Note: direct* is usually pronounced /ˈdaɪrekt/ in these compounds.)
`direct action,` use of strikes by workmen to get their demands.
`direct current,` electric current flowing in one direction.
`direct object,` (*gram*) the *noun* or clause in a sentence to which the action of the *verb* is related.
`direct speech,` (*gram*) speaker's actual words.
di·rect·ness *n* [U]

di·rect² /dɪˈrekt/ *vt,vi* **1** tell or show how to do something, how to get somewhere: *Can you ~ me to the post office?* **2** address (the more usual word): *Shall I ~ the letter to his office or to his home?* **3** speak or write to: *My remarks were not ~ed to all of you.* **4** manage; control: *Who is ~ing the play?* **5** turn: *Our energies must be ~ed towards higher productivity.* **6** order: *The officer ~ed his men to advance slowly.*

di·rec·tion /dɪˈrekʃən/ *n* **1** [C] course taken by a moving person or thing; point towards which a person or thing looks or faces: *Tom went off in one ~ and Harry in another (~).* **2** [U] **have a good/poor sense of direction,** be able/unable to determine well one's position when there are no known or visible landmarks. **3** [C] (often *pl*) information or instructions about what to do, where to go, how to do something, etc: *D~s about putting the parts together are printed on the* *card.* **4** [U] management; control; guidance: *He did the work under my ~.*

di·rec·tion·al /-nəl/ *adj* of direction in space (esp of radio signals transmitted over a narrow angle): *a ~al aerial.*

di·rec·tive /dɪˈrektɪv/ *n* [C] general or detailed instructions as given to staff to guide them in their work.

di·rect·ly /dɪˈrektlɪ/ *adv* **1** in a direct manner: *He was looking ~ at us.* **2** at once; without delay: *Come in ~.* **3** in a short time: *I'll be there ~.* □ *conj* (*informal*) as soon as; *D~ I'd done it, I knew I'd made a mistake.*

di·rec·tor /dɪˈrektə(r)/ *n* [C] **1** person who directs, esp one of a group (called *the Board of D~s*) who manage the affairs of a business company. **2** person who supervises and instructs actors and actresses, the lighting, camera crew, etc in plays and films.

di·ˈrec·tor·ship, position of a company director; time during which he holds his position.

di·rec·tor·ate /dɪˈrektərət/ *n* [C] **1** office or position of a director. **2** board of directors.

di·rec·tory /dɪˈrektərɪ/ *n* [C] (*pl* -ies) **1** (book with a) list of persons, business firms, etc in a district. **2** list of telephone subscribers and their addresses in A B C order.

dirge /dɜːdʒ/ *n* [C] song sung at a burial or for a dead person.

dirt /dɜːt/ *n* [U] **1** unclean matter (e g dust, soil, mud) esp when it is where it is not wanted (e g on the skin, clothes, in buildings): *His clothes were covered with ~.* **2** loose earth or soil: *a ~ road. treat sb like dirt,* treat him as if he were worthless. **3** obscene, rude talk.

'dirt-ˈcheap, very cheap, almost valueless.

'dirt-track, one made of cinders, etc (for, e g motor-cycle races).

dirty¹ /ˈdɜːtɪ/ *adj* (-ier, -iest) **1** not clean; covered with dirt: *~ hands/clothes.* **2** causing one to be dirty: *~ work.* **3** (of the weather) rough; stormy: *I'm glad I haven't to go out on such a ~ night.* **4** obscene: *scribble ~ words on lavatory walls.* **5** (*informal*) mean, dishonourable: *play a ~ trick on her; get/give him a ~ look,* one of severe disapproval or disgust.

dirt·ily /-əlɪ/ *adv*

dirty² /ˈdɜːtɪ/ *vt,vi* (*pt,pp* -ied) make or become dirty: *Don't ~ your new dress.*

dis- /dɪs-/ *prefix* (used with a *verb* or *noun*) negative, reverse, opposite of: *disorder; disagree.*

dis·abil·ity /ˌdɪsəˈbɪlətɪ/ *n* (*pl* -ies) **1** [U] state of being disabled. **2** [C] something that disables or disqualifies a person.

dis·able /dɪsˈeɪbəl/ *vt* make unable to do something, esp take away the power of using the limbs: *He was ~d in the war.*

dis·able·ment *n* [U]

dis·ad·van·tage /ˌdɪsədˈvɑːntɪdʒ *US:* -ˈvæn-/ *n* **1** [C] unfavourable condition; something that stands in the way of progress,

success, etc: *It is a ~ to be small when you're standing in a crowd at a football match.* **2** [U] loss; injury: *rumours to his ~,* that hurt his reputation, etc.

dis·ad·van·tage·ous /ˌdɪsædvənˈteɪdʒəs/ *adj* causing a disadvantage (to): *in a ~ position.*

dis·ad·van·tage·ous·ly *adv*

dis·af·fected /ˌdɪsəˈfektɪd/ *adj* (*formal*) unfriendly; (inclined to be) disloyal.

dis·af·fec·tion /ˌdɪsəˈfekʃən/ *n* [U] political discontent; disloyalty.

dis·agree /ˌdɪsəˈgriː/ *vi* **1** take a different view; have different opinions; not agree: *I'm sorry to ~ with you/with your statement/ with what you say.* **2** (of food, climate) have bad effects on; prove unsuitable: *The climate/That fish ~s with me.*

dis·agree·able /-əbəl/ *adj* unpleasant: *~able weather; a ~able old man.*

dis·agree·ably /-əblɪ/ *adv*

dis·agree·ment /ˌdɪsəˈgriːmənt/ *n* **1** [U] act of disagreement; absence of agreement: *to be in ~ with him/the plan.* **2** [C] instance of this; difference of opinion; slight quarrel: *~s between husbands and wives.*

dis·al·low /ˌdɪsəˈlaʊ/ *vt* refuse to allow or accept as correct: *The judge ~ed the claim.*

dis·ap·pear /ˌdɪsəˈpɪə(r)/ *vi* go out of sight; be seen no more: *Let's hope our difficulties will soon ~.*

dis·ap·pear·ance /-rəns/ *n* [C,U].

dis·ap·point /ˌdɪsəˈpɔɪnt/ *vt* fail to do or be equal to what is hoped for or expected: *The book ~ed me.*

dis·ap·pointed *adj* sad at not getting what was hoped for, etc: *We were ~ed when we heard that you could not come. What are you looking so ~ed about?*

dis·ap·point·ed·ly *adv*

dis·ap·point·ing *adj* causing a person to be disappointed: *Our holiday was so ~ing.*

dis·ap·point·ment /ˌdɪsəˈpɔɪntmənt/ *n* **1** [U] being disappointed: *To her great ~, it rained on the day of the picnic.* **2** [C] person or thing that disappoints: *He had suffered many ~s in love.*

dis·ap·pro·ba·tion /ˌdɪsæprəˈbeɪʃən/ *n* [U] (*formal*) disapproval.

dis·ap·proval /ˌdɪsəˈpruːvəl/ *n* [U] disapproving: *He shook his head in ~,* to show that he disapproved.

dis·ap·prove /ˌdɪsəˈpruːv/ *vi,vt* have, express, an unfavourable opinion: *She wants to become an actress but her parents ~ (of her intentions).*

dis·ap·prov·ing·ly *adv* in a way that shows disapproval: *When Mary lit a cigarette, her father looked at her disapprovingly.*

dis·arm /dɪsˈɑːm/ *vi,vt* **1** take away weapons and other means of attack from: *Five hundred rebels were captured and ~ed.* **2** (of nations) reduce the size of, give up the use of, armed forces: *It is difficult to persuade the Great Powers to ~.* **3** make it difficult for a person to feel anger, suspicion, doubt: *I felt angry, but her smiles ~ed me.*

dis·arma·ment /dɪsˈɑːməmənt/ *n* [U] disarming or being disarmed(2): *~ament conferences.*

dis·array /ˈdɪsəˈreɪ/ *n, vt* (put into) disorder: *The troops were in ~.*

dis·as·sociate /ˈdɪsəˈsəʊʃɪeɪt/ *vt* = dissociate.

dis·as·ter /dɪˈzɑːstə(r) *US:* -ˈzæs-/ *n* 1 [C] great or sudden misfortune; terrible accident (e g a great flood or fire, an earthquake, a serious defeat in war, the loss of a large sum of money). 2 [U] great misfortune or suffering: *a record of ~.*

dis·as·trous /dɪˈzɑːstrəs *US:* -ˈzæs-/ *adj* causing disaster: *~ floods; a defeat that was ~ to the country.*
dis·as·trous·ly *adv*

dis·band /dɪsˈbænd/ *vt,vi* (of organized groups) break up: *The army (was) ~ed when the war ended.*

dis·be·lief /ˈdɪsbɪˈliːf/ *n* [U] lack of belief; refusal to believe.

dis·be·lieve /ˈdɪsbɪˈliːv/ *vt,vi* refuse to believe; be unable or unwilling to believe in.

dis·burse /dɪsˈbɜːs/ *vt,vi* pay out (money).
dis·burse·ment *n* [U] paying out (of money); [C] sum of money paid out.

disc, (also **disk**) /dɪsk/ *n* [C] 1 thin, flat, round place, e g a coin, a gramophone record; round surface that appears to be flat: *the sun's ~.* 2 layer of gristle between vertebrae: *a slipped ~,* one that is slightly dislocated.
`**disc jockey,** radio or T V broadcaster who introduces performers and comments on records and tapes (esp) of light and popular music.

dis·card /dɪˈskɑːd/ *vt* 1 (*formal*) throw out or away; put aside, give up (something useless or unwanted): *to ~ old beliefs.* 2 remove and put back, take away, a playing-card from those in one's hand. □ *n* [C] card or cards discarded(2).

dis·cern /dɪˈsɜːn/ *vt* (*formal*) 1 see clearly (with the eyes or with the mind). 2 (esp) see with an effort: *It is often difficult to ~ the truth of what we are told.*
dis·cern·ing *adj* able to see and understand well.
dis·cern·ible /-əbəl/ *adj* that can be discerned.
dis·cern·ment *n* [U] (good) ability to judge, form opinions.

dis·charge[1] /dɪsˈtʃɑːdʒ/ *n* [C] discharging or being discharged (all senses).

dis·charge[2] /dɪsˈtʃɑːdʒ/ *vt,vi* 1 unload (cargo from) a ship. 2 give or send out (liquid, gas, electric current, etc): *Where do the sewers ~ their contents? Lightning is caused by clouds discharging electricity.* 3 fire (a gun, etc). 4 send (a person) away; allow (a person) to leave: *to ~ a patient from hospital. The accused man was found*

not guilty and was ~d. The typist was ~d (= dismissed) *for being dishonest.* 5 pay (a debt); perform (a duty).

dis·ciple /dɪˈsaɪpəl/ *n* [C] 1 follower of any leader of religious thought, art, learning, etc. 2 one of the twelve personal followers of Jesus Christ.

dis·ci·pli·nar·ian /ˈdɪsəplɪˈneərɪən/ *n* [C] person able to maintain discipline(5): *a good/strict/poor ~.*

dis·ci·plin·ary /ˈdɪsɪˈplɪnərɪ *US:* -nerɪ/ *adj* of or for discipline: *to take ~ action; ~ punishment.*

dis·ci·pline[1] /ˈdɪsəplɪn/ *n* 1 [U] training, esp of the mind and character, to produce self-control, habits of obedience, etc: *school ~; military ~.* 2 [U] the result of such training; order kept (e g among soldiers): *The soldiers showed perfect ~ under the fire of the enemy.* 3 [C] set rules for conduct; method by which training may be given: *Pronunciation drill and question and answer work are good ~s for learning a foreign language.* 4 [U] punishment. 5 [C] branch of knowledge; subject of instruction.

dis·ci·pline[2] /ˈdɪsəplɪn/ *vt* apply discipline(1) to; train and control the mind and character of; punish: *to ~ badly behaved children.*

dis·claim /dɪsˈkleɪm/ *vt* say that one does not own, that one has no connection with: *to ~ responsibility for something; to ~ all knowledge of an incident.*

dis·close /dɪsˈkləʊz/ *vt* 1 uncover; allow to be seen. 2 make known: *to ~ a secret.*
dis·clos·ure /dɪsˈkləʊʒə(r)/ *n* [U] disclosing or being disclosed; [C] that which is disclosed (esp what has been kept secret).

dis·colour (*US* = **-color**) /dɪsˈkʌlə(r)/ *vt,vi* 1 change, spoil, the colour of: *walls ~ed by damp.* 2 become changed in colour: *paper that ~ in strong sunlight.*
dis·colour·ation (*US* = **-color-**) /dɪskʌləˈreɪʃən/ *n* [C,U]

dis·com·fort /dɪsˈkʌmfət/ *n* 1 [U] absence of comfort; uneasiness of mind or body. 2 [C] something that causes uneasiness; hardship: *the ~s endured by explorers in the Antarctic.*

dis·con·cert /ˈdɪskənˈsɜːt/ *vt* 1 upset the calmness or self-possession of: *The Manager was ~ed to discover that he had gone to the office without his diary.* 2 spoil or upset (plans).

dis·con·nect /ˈdɪskəˈnekt/ *vt* detach from; take (two things) apart: *You should ~ the T V set* (e g by pulling out the plug) *before you make adjustments inside it.*
dis·con·nected *adj* (of speech or writing) having the ideas, etc badly ordered.

dis·con·so·late /dɪsˈkɒnsələt/ *adj* unhappy at the loss of something; without hope or comfort.
dis·con·so·late·ly *adv*

dis·con·tent /ˈdɪskənˈtent/ *n* [U] dissatis

faction; absence of contentment; [C] cause of this. □ vt make dissatisfied: to be ∼ed with one's job. (Note: usually used as a pp.)
dis-con-tent-ed-ly adv

dis-con-tinue /ˈdɪskənˈtɪnjuː/ vt, vi (formal) stop; give up; put an end to; come to an end: I'm so busy that I shall have to ∼ (paying) these weekly visits.

dis-con-tinu-ous /ˈdɪskənˈtɪnjuəs/ adj not continuous.

dis-cord /ˈdɪskɔːd/ n 1 [U] disagreement; quarrelling: What has brought ∼ into the family, caused its members to quarrel? 2 [C] difference of opinion; dispute. 3 [U] lack of harmony between sounds, notes, etc sounded together; [C] instance of this.

dis-cor-dance /dɪˈskɔːdəns/ n [U] lack of harmony; disagreement.

dis-cor-dant /dɪˈskɔːdənt/ adj (a) not in agreement: ∼ant opinions. (b) (of sounds) not harmonious: the ∼ant noises of motor-car horns.

dis-cor-dant-ly adv

dis-co-theque /ˈdɪskətek/ n [C] club where people dance to amplified pop music.

dis-count[1] /ˈdɪskaʊnt/ n [C] amount of money which may be taken off the full price, e g of (a) goods bought by shopkeepers for resale, (b) an account if paid promptly.

dis-count[2] /dɪˈskaʊnt US: ˈdɪskaʊnt/ vt (esp) refuse complete belief to a piece of news, a story, etc: Some reporters like sensational news, so you should ∼ a great deal of what appears in the popular press.

dis-coun-ten-ance /dɪˈskaʊntɪnəns/ vt (formal) refuse to approve of.

dis-cour-age /dɪˈskʌrɪdʒ US: -ˈskɜːr-/ vt 1 lessen, take away, the courage or confidence of: Don't let one failure ∼ you; try again. 2 put difficulties in his way; try to persuade him not to do it: The wet weather is discouraging people from going to the meeting.

dis-cour-age-ment n [C,U]

dis-course /ˈdɪskɔːs/ n 1 [C] speech; lecture; sermon; treatise. 2 [U] (old use) conversation: in ∼ with. □ vi /dɪˈskɔːs/ (formal) talk, preach or lecture.

dis-cour-teous /dɪˈskɜːtɪəs/ adj impolite (the usual word): It was ∼ of you to arrive late.

dis-cour-teous-ly adv

dis-cour-tesy /dɪˈskɜːtəsɪ/ n [C,U]

dis-cover /dɪˈskʌvə(r)/ vt find out; get knowledge of, (something existing but not yet known): Columbus ∼ed America, but did not explore the new continent.

dis-cover-er, person who has made a discovery.

dis-covery /dɪˈskʌvərɪ/ n (pl -ies) 1 [U] discovering or being discovered: a voyage of ∼; the ∼ of new chemical elements. 2 [C] something that is discovered: He made wonderful scientific discoveries.

dis-credit[1] /dɪˈskredɪt/ vt refuse to believe or have confidence in; cause the truth, value

or credit to seem doubtful: The judge advised the jury to ∼ the evidence of one of the witnesses.

dis-credit[2] /dɪˈskredɪt/ n 1 [U] loss of credit or reputation: If you continue to behave in this way, you will bring ∼ on yourself. 2 a discredit to, person, thing, causing such loss: a ∼ to the school. 3 [U] doubt; disbelief.

dis-credit-able /-əbəl/ adj bringing discredit: ∼able conduct.

dis-credit-ably /-əblɪ/ adv

dis-creet /dɪˈskriːt/ adj careful, tactful, in what one says and does: to maintain a ∼ silence.

dis-creet-ly adv

dis-crep-ancy /dɪˈskrepənsɪ/ n [C,U] (pl -ies) (of statements and accounts) difference; absence of agreement: There was considerable ∼/There were numerous discrepancies between the two accounts of the fighting.

dis-cre-tion /dɪˈskreʃən/ n [U] 1 being discreet: You must show more ∼ in choosing your friends. 2 freedom to act according to one's own judgement, to do what seems right or best: Use your ∼.

dis-cre-tion-ary /-nrɪ US: -nerɪ/ adj having discretion(2): ∼ary powers.

dis-crimi-nate /dɪˈskrɪmɪneɪt/ vt, vi 1 be, make, see, a difference between: Can you ∼ good books from bad/∼ between good and bad books? 2 treat differently; make distinctions: laws which do not ∼ against anyone, that treat all people in the same way.

dis-crimi-nat-ing adj (a) able to see or make small differences: a discriminating taste in literature. (b) giving special or different treatment to certain people, countries, etc: discriminating duties.

dis-crimi-na-tion /dɪˈskrɪmɪˈneɪʃən/ n [U] discriminating; ability to discriminate: Some people do not show much ∼ in their choice of books. Is there racial ∼ in your country?

dis-crim-i-na-tory /dɪˈskrɪmɪˈneɪtərɪ US: -tɔːrɪ/ adj discriminating(2): discriminatory legislation.

dis-cur-sive /dɪˈskɜːsɪv/ adj (of a person, what he says or does, his style) wandering from one point or subject to another.

dis-cur-sive-ly adv

dis-cus /ˈdɪskəs/ n [C] (pl ∼es) heavy, round plate of stone, metal or wood, thrown in ancient Roman and Greek athletic contests and in modern contests (e g the Olympic Games).

dis-cuss /dɪˈskʌs/ vt examine and argue about (a subject): to ∼ (with one's friends) what to do/how to do it/how something should be done.

dis-cus-sion /dɪˈskʌʃən/ n [U] discussing or being discussed; [C] talk for the purpose of discussing: after much ∼; after several long ∼s. under discussion, being discussed: The question is still under ∼.

dis·dain /dɪsˈdeɪn/ vt (formal) look on with contempt; think (it) dishonourable, be too proud, (to do something): A good man should ~ flattery. He ~ed my offer of help. □ n [U] contempt; scorn: No one likes to be treated with ~.
dis·dain·ful /-fəl/ adj showing contempt: ~ful looks.
dis·dain·fully /-fəlɪ/ adv

dis·ease /dɪˈziz/ n [U] illness; disorder of body or mind or of plants; [C] particular kind of illness or disorder.
dis·eased /dɪˈzizd/ adj suffering from, injured by, disease.

dis·em·bark /ˈdɪsɪmˈbɑk/ vt, vi put, go, on shore: ~ from the liner.
dis·em·bar·ka·tion /ˌdɪsˈembɑːˈkeɪʃən/ n [C,U]

dis·en·chant /ˈdɪsɪnˈtʃɑnt US: -ˈtʃænt/ vt free from enchantment or illusion: He is quite ~ed with the Government.
dis·en·chant·ment n [C,U]

dis·en·gage /ˈdɪsɪnˈgeɪdʒ/ vt, vi separate, detach (oneself or something): to ~ the gears of a car.

dis·en·tangle /ˈdɪsɪnˈtæŋgəl/ vt, vi 1 free, from complications, tangles or confusion: to ~ truth from falsehood. 2 become clear of tangles: I can't ~ this wool.

dis·favour (US = -favor) /ˈdɪsˈfeɪvə(r)/ n [U] (formal) state of being out of favour; disapproval: to be in ~; to fall into ~. □ vt disapprove of.

dis·fig·ure /dɪsˈfɪgə(r) US: -gjə(r)/ vt spoil the appearance or shape of: beautiful scenery ~d by ugly advertising signs; a face ~d by a broken nose/an ugly scar.
dis·fig·ure·ment n [C,U]

dis·fran·chise /dɪsˈfræntʃaɪz/ vt deprive of rights of citizenship; (esp) deprive (a place) of the right to send a representative to parliament or (a citizen) of the right to vote for a parliamentary representative.

dis·gorge /dɪsˈgɔdʒ/ vt 1 throw up or out from, or as from, the throat. 2 (fig) give up (esp something taken wrongfully).

dis·grace¹ /dɪsˈgreɪs/ n 1 [U] loss of respect, favour, reputation: A man who commits a crime and is sent to prison brings ~ on himself and his family. 2 [U] state of having lost respect, etc: He told a lie and is in ~. 3 a ~, thing, state of affairs, person, that is a cause of shame or discredit: These slums are a ~ to the city authorities.
dis·grace·ful /-fəl/ adj bringing or causing disgrace: ~ful behaviour.
dis·grace·fully /-fəlɪ/ adv: to behave ~fully.

dis·grace² /dɪsˈgreɪs/ vt 1 bring disgrace on; be a disgrace to: Don't ~ the family name. 2 put (a person) out of favour.

dis·gruntled /dɪsˈgrʌntəld/ adj discontented; in a bad mood.

dis·guise¹ /dɪsˈgaɪz/ vt 1 change the appearance, etc of, in order to deceive or to hide the identity of: He ~d his looks but he could not ~ his voice. 2 conceal: He ~d his sorrow beneath a cheerful appearance/by appearing cheerful.

dis·guise² /dɪsˈgaɪz/ n 1 [U] disguising; disguised condition: He went among the enemy in ~. 2 [C,U] dress, actions, manner, etc used for disguising: He had tried all sorts of ~s.

dis·gust¹ /dɪsˈgʌst/ n [U] strong feeling of dislike or distaste (e g caused by a bad smell or taste, a horrible sight, evil conduct): He turned away in ~.

dis·gust² /dɪsˈgʌst/ vt cause disgust in: We were ~ed at/by/with what we saw.
dis·gust·ing adj: behaviour that is ~ing to everybody.
dis·gust·ing·ly adv

dish¹ /dɪʃ/ n [C] 1 shallow, flat-bottomed vessel, of earthenware, glass, metal, etc from which food is served at table: a ~meat-~. 2 the ~es, all the plates, bowls, cups and saucers, etc used for a meal: to wash up the ~es. 3 meal: His favourite ~ is steak and kidney pie. 4 large concave reflector for receiving radio-waves from outer space, or in radio-telescopes, etc. 5 (sl) attractive girl: She's quite a ~!
`dish-cloth, cloth for washing dishes, etc.
`dish-washer, power-operated machine for washing dishes, cutlery, etc.
`dish-water, water in which crockery has been washed.
dishy adj (-ier, -iest) (sl) (of a man or girl) attractive.
`dish·ful /-fʊl/ n [C] as much as a dish will contain.

dish² /dɪʃ/ vt 1 put on or into a dish: to ~ (up) the dinner, get it ready for serving. 2 (fig) prepare, serve up facts, arguments, etc: to ~ up the usual arguments in a new form.
dish sth out, distribute: to ~ out programmes.

dis·hearten /dɪsˈhɑtən/ vt cause to lose courage or confidence: Don't be ~ed by what he says.

di·shev·elled (US = -eled) /dɪˈʃevəld/ adj (of the hair and clothes) untidy.

dis·hon·est /dɪsˈɒnɪst/ adj not honest; intended to cheat, deceive or mislead.
dis·hon·est·ly adv
dis·hon·esty /dɪsˈɒnɪstɪ/ n [U] being dishonest; [C] dishonest act, etc.

dis·hon·our (US = -honor) /dɪsˈɒnə(r)/ n [C] 1 disgrace or shame; loss, absence, of honour and self-respect: to bring ~ on one's family. 2 person or thing that brings honour: He was a ~ to his regiment. □ vt 1 bring shame, discredit. 2 (of a bank): ~ a cheque, etc, refuse to pay money on it (because the bank's customer has not enough credit).
dis·hon·our·able /-nrəbəl/ adj without honour; shameful.
dis·hon·our·ably /-nrəblɪ/ adv

dis·il·lu·sion /ˈdɪsɪˈluʒən/ vt set free from

mistaken beliefs: *They had thought that the holiday would be restful, but they were soon ~ed.* □ *n* [U] the state of being disillusioned.

dis·il·lu·sion·ment *n* [C] freedom from illusions: *in a state of complete ~ment.*

dis·in·cli·na·tion /ˈdɪsɪnklɪˈneɪʃən/ *n* [C,U] (formal) unwillingness: *Some schoolboys have a strong ~ for work.*

dis·in·clined /ˈdɪsɪnˈklaɪnd/ *adj* (formal) reluctant or unwilling: *He was ~d to help me.*

dis·in·fect /ˈdɪsɪnˈfekt/ *vt* make free from infection by bacteria: *The house was ~ed after Tom had had scarlet fever.*

dis·in·fec·tant /ˈdɪsɪnˈfektənt/ *adj, n* [C,U] disinfecting (chemical).

dis·in·gen·u·ous /ˈdɪsɪnˈdʒenjʊəs/ *adj* (formal) insincere (the usual word).

dis·in·gen·u·ous·ly *adv*

dis·in·herit /ˈdɪsɪnˈherɪt/ *vt* take away the right to inherit.

dis·in·heri·tance /ˈdɪsɪnˈherɪtəns/ *n* [C,U] (act of) disinheriting.

dis·in·te·grate /dɪsˈɪntɪgreɪt/ *vt, vi* (cause to) break up into small parts or pieces: *rocks ~d by frost and rain.*

dis·in·te·gra·tion /dɪsˈɪntɪˈgreɪʃən/ *n* [U]

dis·in·ter /ˈdɪsɪnˈtɜː(r)/ *vt* (-rr-) dig up (a body) from the earth (e g from a grave).

dis·in·ter·ment *n* [C,U]

dis·in·ter·ested /dɪsˈɪntrəstɪd/ *adj* not influenced by personal feelings or interests: *His action was not altogether ~.* ⇨ uninterested.

dis·in·ter·est·ly *adv*

dis·jointed /dɪsˈdʒɔɪntɪd/ *adj* (e g of speech and writing) not connected; incoherent.

dis·jointed·ly *adv*

dis·jointed·ness *n* [U]

dis·junc·tive /dɪsˈdʒʌŋktɪv/ *adj* (gram): *~ conjunction,* one expressing opposition of or contrast between ideas (e g *either... or*).

disk /dɪsk/ *n* ⇨ disc.

dis·like /dɪsˈlaɪk/ *vt* not like: *to ~ getting up early/being disturbed.* □ *n* [C] feeling of not liking; feeling against: *to have a ~ of/for cats; to take a ~ to him,* begin to dislike him.

dis·lo·cate /ˈdɪsləkeɪt US: -ləʊk-/ *vt* 1 put (esp a bone in the body) out of position: *He fell from his horse and ~d his shoulder.* 2 put traffic, machinery, business, etc out of order: *Traffic was badly ~d by the heavy fall of snow.*

dis·lo·ca·tion /ˈdɪsləˈkeɪʃən US: -ləʊˈk-/ *n* [C,U]

dis·lodge /dɪsˈlɒdʒ/ *vt* move, force, from the place occupied: *to ~ a stone from a building/the enemy from their positions.*

dis·lodge·ment *n* [C,U]

dis·loyal /dɪsˈlɔɪəl/ *adj* not loyal (to).

dis·loyal·ly *adv*

dis·loyal·ty *n* [C,U]

dis·mal /ˈdɪzməl/ *adj* sad, gloomy; miserable; comfortless: *~ weather; in a ~ voice.*

dis·mal·ly /-əlɪ/ *adv*

dis·mantle /dɪsˈmæntəl/ *vt* 1 take away fittings, furnishings, etc from: *The old warship was ~d.* 2 take to pieces: *to ~ an engine.*

dis·may /dɪsˈmeɪ/ *n* [U] feeling of fear and discouragement: *The news that the enemy were near filled/struck them with ~.* □ *vt* fill with dismay: *We were ~ed at the news.*

dis·mem·ber /dɪsˈmembə(r)/ *vt* 1 tear or cut the limbs from: *He was ~ed by the lion.* 2 (fig) divide up (a country, etc).

dis·miss /dɪsˈmɪs/ *vt* 1 send away (from one's employment, from service): *She was ~ed for being lazy and dishonest.* 2 allow to go: *The teacher ~ed his class when the bell rang.* 3 put away from the mind; stop thinking or talking about: *to ~ all thoughts of revenge.* 4 (in cricket, of the team that is fielding) put a batsman or a team out: *The fast bowler ~ed Smith for ten runs.*

dis·mis·sal /-səl/ *n* [C,U]

dis·mount /ˈdɪsˈmaʊnt/ *vi, vt* 1 get down (from a horse, bike etc). 2 remove (something) from its mount: *to ~ a gun* (from the gun-carriage).

dis·obedi·ence /ˈdɪsəˈbiːdɪəns/ *n* [U] failure or refusal to obey: *acts of ~; ~ to orders.*

dis·obedi·ent /ˈdɪsəˈbiːdɪənt/ *adj* not obedient (to).

dis·obedi·ent·ly *adv*

dis·obey /ˈdɪsəˈbeɪ/ *vt* pay no attention to orders; not obey a person, a law, etc.

dis·order /dɪsˈɔːdə(r)/ *n* 1 [U] absence of order; confusion: *The burglars left the room in great ~.* 2 [U] absence of order caused by political troubles; [C] angry outburst of rioting caused by political troubles, etc: *Troops were called out to deal with the ~s in the capital.* 3 [C,U] disturbance of the normal working of the body or mind: *suffering from mental ~.* □ *vt* put into disorder: *a ~ed mind.*

dis·order·ly /dɪsˈɔːdəlɪ/ *adj* 1 in disorder: *a ~ room/desk.* 2 causing disturbance; unruly; lawless: *~ crowds/behaviour.*

dis·or·gan·ize /ˈdɪsˈɔːɡənaɪz/ *vt* throw into confusion; upset the working or system of: *The train service was ~d by fog.*

dis·or·gan·iz·ation /ˈdɪsˈɔːɡənaɪˈzeɪʃən US: -nɪˈz-/ *n* [U]

dis·orien·tate /dɪsˈɔːrɪənteɪt/ (also **dis·orient** /dɪsˈɔːrɪənt/) *vt* confuse (a person) so that he does not know where he is, the time, date, etc.

dis·own /dɪsˈəʊn/ *vt* say that one does not know, that one has not, or no longer wishes to have, any connection with (a person or thing): *The boy was so cruel that his father ~ed him.*

dis·par·age /dɪˈspærɪdʒ/ *vt* say things to suggest that (a person or thing) is of little value or importance.

dis·par·age·ment *n* [U]

dis·par·ag·ing·ly *adv* in a disparaging way.

dis·par·ate /ˈdɪspərət/ *adj* that cannot be

compared in quality, amount, kind, etc.

dis·par·ity /dɪˈspærɪtɪ/ n [U] inequality; difference; [C] (pl -ies) instance or degree of this.

dis·pas·sion·ate /dɪˈspæʃənət/ adj free from passion; not taking sides, not showing favour (in a quarrel, etc between others).
dis·pas·sion·ate·ly adv

dis·patch¹, des·patch /dɪˈspætʃ/ n 1 [U] dispatching or being dispatched (all senses): Please hurry up the ~ of these telegrams. 2 [C] thing dispatched(1), esp, a government, military or newspaper report: London newspapers receive ~es from all parts of the world. 3 [U] (formal) speed: to act with ~.

dis·patch², des·patch /dɪˈspætʃ/ vt 1 send off, to a destination, on a journey, for a special purpose: to ~ letters/telegrams. 2 finish, get through, business, etc. 3 kill: The executioner quickly ~ed the condemned man.

dis·pel /dɪˈspel/ vt (-ll-) drive away: The wind soon ~led the fog. How can we ~ their doubts and fears?

dis·pens·able /dɪˈspensəbəl/ adj that can be done without; not necessary.

dis·pens·ary /dɪˈspensərɪ/ n [C] (pl -ies) place where medicines are given out (eg in a hospital).

dis·pen·sa·tion /ˌdɪspenˈseɪʃən/ n 1 [U] the act of dispensing(1) or distributing: the ~ of justice/medicine/food. 2 [C,U] permission to do something that is usually forbidden, or not to do something that is usually required, esp by ecclesiastical law: to be granted ~ from fasting during a journey.

dis·pense /dɪˈspens/ vt,vi 1 deal out; distribute; administer: to ~ charity/justice. 2 mix; prepare, give out (medicines): to ~ a prescription; dispensing chemist, one qualified to do this. 3 **dispense with, (a)** do without: He is not yet well enough to ~ with the doctor's services. **(b)** make unnecessary: The new design ~s with gears.
dis·penser, (a) person who dispenses, esp medicines. **(b)** container from which something can be obtained without removing a cover, lid, etc: a ~r for liquid soap/paper cups.

dis·perse /dɪˈspɜːs/ vt,vi (cause to) go in different directions: The police ~d the crowd. The crowd ~d when the police arrived.
dis·per·sal /dɪˈspɜːsəl/ n [U].
dis·per·sion /dɪˈspɜːʃən US: -ʒən/ n = dispersal, esp of light.

dis·pir·ited /dɪˈspɪrɪtɪd/ adj discouraged; disheartened.

dis·place /dɪˈspleɪs/ vt 1 put out of the right or usual position. 2 take the place of; put in the place of: Tom has ~d Harry in Mary's affections.

dis·place·ment /dɪˈspleɪsmənt/ n [U] 1 displacing or being displaced: the ~ of human labour by machines. 2 amount of water displaced by a solid body in it, or floating in it: a ship of 10 000 tons ~.

dis·play¹ /dɪˈspleɪ/ n [C,U] displaying; show or exhibition: a `fashion ~, a showing of new styles in clothes, etc; a ~ of bad temper.

dis·play² /dɪˈspleɪ/ vt 1 show; place or spread out so that there is no difficulty in seeing: Department stores ~ their goods in the windows. 2 allow to be seen; show signs of having: to ~ one's ignorance. She ~ed no sign of emotion.

dis·please /dɪˈspliːz/ vt not please; offend; annoy; make indignant or angry: to be ~d with her (for doing that); to be ~d at her conduct.
dis·pleas·ing adj not pleasing (to a person).
dis·pleas·ing·ly adv

dis·pleas·ure /dɪˈspleʒə(r)/ n [U] displeased feeling; dissatisfaction: He incurred his father's ~.

dis·pos·able /dɪˈspəʊzəbəl/ adj made so that it may be (easily) disposed of after use: ~ nappies, of soft paper which disintegrates quickly in water.

dis·posal /dɪˈspəʊzəl/ n [U] 1 the act of disposing(1,2): the ~ of rubbish, getting rid of it; a `bomb ~ squad, group of men who, when unexploded bombs are found, try to make them harmless and remove them. 2 control; management. **at one's disposal**, to be used as one wishes: My desk is at your ~.

dis·pose /dɪˈspəʊz/ vi,vt 1 finish with; get rid of; deal with: to ~ of rubbish. He doesn't want to ~ of (eg sell) the land. 2 place (persons, objects) in good order or in suitable positions: The cruisers were ~d in a single line. 3 (formal) make willing or ready: I'm not ~d/don't feel ~d to help my lazy sister.

dis·po·si·tion /ˌdɪspəˈzɪʃən/ n [C] 1 arrangement(the more usual word): the ~ of furniture in a room. 2 person's natural qualities of mind and character: a man with a cheerful ~. 3 inclination: There was a general ~ to leave early, Most people seemed to wish to leave early. 4 power of ordering and disposing: Who has the ~ of this property, the power or authority to dispose of it?

dis·pos·sess /ˌdɪspəˈzes/ vt take away (property, esp land) from; compel (a person) to give up (the house he occupies): The nobles were ~ed of their property after the Revolution.

dis·pro·por·tion·ate /ˌdɪsprəˈpɔːʃənət/ adj out of porportion; relatively too large or small, etc: to give a ~ate amount of one's time to games.
dis·pro·por·tion·ate·ly adv

dis·prove /dɪˈspruːv/ vt prove to be wrong or false.

dis·put·able /dɪˈspjuːtəbəl/ adj that may be disputed; questionable.

dis·pu·tant /dɪˈspjuːtənt/ n [C] person who

disputes.

dis·pute[1] /'dɪspjut/ n 1 [U] debate, argument: *The matter in* ∼ (= *being disputed*) *is the ownership of a house.* 2 [C] quarrel; controversy: *There were many religious* ∼s *in England during the 17th century.*

dis·pute[2] /dɪ'spjut/ vi,vt 1 argue, debate, quarrel. 2 discuss, question the truth or validity of: *to* ∼ *a statement/a claim/a decision.* 3 oppose; resist: *to* ∼ *an advance by the enemy.*

dis·qual·ify /dɪs'kwolɪfaɪ/ vt (pt,pp -ied) make unfit or unable: *As he was a professional, he was disqualified from taking part in the Olympic Games.*

dis·quali·fi·ca·tion /dɪs'kwolɪfɪ'keɪʃən/ n [C,U]

dis·quiet /dɪs'kwaɪət/ vt (formal) make troubled, anxious, uneasy: ∼ed *by apprehensions of illness.* □ n [U] anxiety: *The President's speech caused considerable* ∼ *in some European capitals.*

dis·quiet·ing adj causing anxiety: ∼ing *news.*

dis·re·gard /'dɪsrɪ'gɑd/ vt pay no attention to; show no respect for: *to* ∼ *a warning.* □ n [U] inattention; indifference; neglect: ∼ *of a rule;* ∼ *for one's teachers.*

dis·re·pair /'dɪsrɪ'peə(r)/ n [U] the state of needing repair: *The building was in bad* ∼.

dis·repu·table /dɪs'repjutəbəl/ adj having a bad reputation; not respectable: *a* ∼ *appearance.*

dis·repu·tably /-əblɪ/ adv

dis·re·pute /'dɪsrɪ'pjut/ n [U] condition of being disreputable; discredit. *fall into disrepute,* no longer have a good reputation.

dis·re·spect /'dɪsrɪ'spekt/ n [U] rudeness; want of respect: *He meant no* ∼ *by that remark,* did not intend to be impolite.

dis·re·spect·ful /-fəl/ adj showing disrespect.

dis·re·spect·fully /-fəlɪ/ adv: *to speak* ∼fully of/about him.

dis·rupt /dɪs'rʌpt/ vt break up, split, separate by force a State, an empire, communications, etc: *Their quarrels seem likely to* ∼ *the meeting.*

dis·rup·tion /dɪs'rʌpʃən/ n [U] disrupting or being disrupted: *the* ∼ion *of the Roman Empire.*

dis·rup·tive /dɪs'rʌptɪv/ adj causing disruption: ∼ive *forces.*

dis·sat·is·fac·tion /'dɪ'sætɪs'fækʃən/ n [U] the state of being dissatisfied.

dis·sat·isfy /dɪ'sætɪsfaɪ/ vt (pt,pp -ied) fail to satisfy; make discontented: *to be dissatisfied with one's salary.*

dis·sect /dɪ'sekt/ vt 1 cut up (parts of an animal body, plant, etc) in order to study its structure.

dis·sec·tion /dɪ'sekʃən/ n [C,U]

dis·semi·nate /dɪ'semɪneɪt/ vt distribute or spread widely ideas, doctrines, etc.

dis·semi·na·tion /dɪ'semɪ'neɪʃən/ n [U]

dis·sen·sion /dɪ'senʃən/ n [U] angry quarrelling; [C] instance of this: ∼(s) *between rival groups in politics.*

dis·sent[1] /dɪ'sent/ n [U] dissenting; (expression of) disagreement: *to express strong* ∼.

dis·sent[2] /dɪ'sent/ vi 1 have a different opinion (from); refuse to agree to: *I strongly* ∼ *from what the last speaker has said.* 2 (esp) refuse to accept the religious doctrine of the Church of England.

dis·sen·ter, person who dissents(2).

dis·ser·ta·tion /'dɪsə'teɪʃən/ n [C] long written or spoken account (e g as submitted for a higher university degree): *a* ∼ *on/upon/concerning...*

dis·ser·vice /dɪ'sɜvɪs/ n [U] harmful or unhelpful action: *You are doing her a great* ∼ *spreading such rumours.*

dis·si·dent /'dɪsɪdənt/ adj disagreeing. □ n [C] person who disagrees; dissenter.

dis·simi·lar /dɪ'sɪmələ(r)/ adj not the same; not similar: *people with* ∼ *tastes.*

dis·simi·lar·ity /'dɪ'sɪmə'lærətɪ/ n [U] lack of similarity; [C] (pl -ies) point, area, of difference.

dis·si·pate /'dɪsɪpeɪt/ vt,vi 1 (cause to) disperse, go away: *to* ∼ *fear/doubt/ignorance.* 2 waste time, leisure, money foolishly: *Don't* ∼ *your efforts.*

dis·sipated adj behaving in a foolish and often harmful way: *to lead a* ∼ *life.*

dis·si·pa·tion /'dɪsɪ'peɪʃən/ n [U] dissipating or being dissipated: *a life of* ∼.

dis·so·ciate /dɪ'səʊʃɪeɪt/ vt separate (in thought, feeling); not associate with: *A politician's public and private life should be* ∼d. *I wish to* ∼ *myself from what has just been said.*

dis·socia·tion /dɪ'səʊʃɪ'eɪʃən/ n [U]

dis·sol·uble /dɪ'soljubəl/ adj that can be dissolved, disintegrated or annulled.

dis·solu·bil·ity /'dɪ'soljʊ'bɪlətɪ/ n [U]

dis·so·lute /'dɪsəljut US: -lut/ adj (of persons, their behaviour) immoral, evil: *to lead a* ∼ *life.*

dis·so·lute·ly adv

dis·sol·ution /'dɪsə'luʃən/ n [C,U] 1 breaking up; undoing or ending (of a marriage, partnership, etc). 2 (esp) ending of Parliament before a general election.

dis·solve /dɪ'zolv/ vt,vi 1 (of a liquid) soak into a solid so that the solid itself becomes liquid: *Water* ∼s *salt.* 2 (of a solid) become liquid as the result of being taken into a liquid: *Salt* ∼s *in water.* 3 cause (a solid) to dissolve: *He* ∼d *the salt in water.* 4 disappear; fade away: *The view* ∼d *in mist.* 5 bring to, come to, an end: *to* ∼ *a business partnership/a marriage/Parliament.*

dis·son·ance /'dɪsənəns/ n 1 [U] discord. 2 [C] combination of notes that is discordant.

dis·son·ant /'dɪsənənt/ adj harsh in tone.

dis·suade /dɪ'sweɪd/ vt advise against: *I tried to* ∼ *her from marrying him.*

dis·sua·sion /dɪˈsweɪʒən/ n [U]

dis·taff /ˈdɪstɑːf US: -tæf/ n [C] stick round which wool, flax, etc is wound for spinning by hand.

dis·tance /ˈdɪstəns/ n [C,U] 1 measure of space, between two points, places, etc: *In the USA ~ is measured in miles, not in kilometres. The town is a great ~ off,* a long way off. *in the distance,* far away: *A ship could be seen in the ~.* 2 space of time: *to look back over a ~ of fifty years.* ⇨ also long distance, middle distance.

dis·tant /ˈdɪstənt/ adj 1 far away in space or time: *We had a ~ view of Mount Everest.* 2 far off in family relationship: *She's a ~ cousin of mine.* 3 (of degree of similarity) not easily seen: *There is a ~ resemblance between the cousins.* 4 reserved; not showing familiarity: *She's always very ~ with strangers.*
dis·tant·ly adv in a distant manner: *He is ~ly related to me.*

dis·taste /dɪsˈteɪst/ n [U] dislike: *a ~ for hard work.*
dis·taste·ful /-fəl/ adj disagreeable; unpleasant: *It is ~ful to me to have to say this, but...*
dis·taste·fully /-fəlɪ/ adv

dis·tend /dɪˈstend/ vt,vi (cause to) swell out (by pressure from within): *a ~ed stomach/vein.*

dis·til (*US = -till*) /dɪˈstɪl/ vt,vi (-ll-) 1 change (a liquid) to vapour by heating, cool the vapour and collect the drops of liquid that condense from the vapour; purify (a liquid) this way: *Salt water can be ~led and made into drinking water.* 2 make (whisky, etc) by distilling.
dis·til·la·tion /ˈdɪstɪˈleɪʃən/ n [C,U]
dis·til·ler /dɪˈstɪlə(r)/ n [C] person who distils (esp whisky).
dis·til·lery, place where liquids (e g gin, whisky) are distilled.

dis·tinct /dɪˈstɪŋkt/ adj 1 easily heard, seen, understood; clearly marked: *a ~ pronunciation. There is a ~ improvement in her typing.* 2 different in kind; separate: *Keep the two ideas ~, the one from the other.*
dis·tinct·ly adv in a clear manner: *I remember ~ly.../He ~ly remembers* (= clearly, leaving no room for misunderstanding) *telling you not to do it.*

dis·tinc·tion /dɪˈstɪŋkʃən/ n 1 [U] being, keeping things, different or distinct(2); distinguishing, being distinguished, as different; [C] instance of this: *The President shook hands with everyone, without ~ of rank. It is difficult to make exact ~s between all the meanings of a word.* 2 [C] point of difference; that which makes one thing different from another: *The ~ between poetry and prose is obvious.* 3 [U] quality of being superior, excellent, distinguished: *a writer/novel of ~.* 4 [C] mark of honour; title; decoration; reward: *academic ~s,* e g a doc-

tor's degree.

dis·tinc·tive /dɪˈstɪŋktɪv/ adj serving to mark a difference or make distinct: *Soldiers often have ~ badges on their caps.*
dis·tinc·tive·ly adv

dis·tin·guish /dɪˈstɪŋgwɪʃ/ vt,vi 1 see, hear, recognize, understand well, the difference: *The twins were so alike that it was impossible to ~ one from the other.* 2 make out by looking, listening, etc: *A person with good eyesight can ~ distant objects.* 3 be a mark of character, difference: *Speech ~es man from the animals.* 4 behave so as to bring credit to oneself: *to ~ oneself in an examination.*
dis·tin·guish·able /-əbəl/ adj that can be distinguished between: *Tom is hardly ~able from his twin brother.*
dis·tin·guished /dɪˈstɪŋgwɪʃt/ adj famous; well known; remarkable; showing distinction(3): *He is ~ for his good knowledge of economics/~ as an economist.*

dis·tort /dɪˈstɔːt/ vt 1 pull, twist, out of the usual shape: *a face ~ed by pain.* 2 give a false account of: *Newspaper accounts of international affairs are sometimes ~ed.*
distorted adj with the mind confused or bewildered: *to be ~ed with/by anxiety/grief.*
dis·tor·tion /dɪˈstɔːʃən/ n [C,U]

dis·tract /dɪˈstrækt/ vt take away a person's attention, concentration, etc: *The noise in the street ~ed me from my reading.*
dis·trac·tion /dɪˈstrækʃən/ n 1 [U] distracting or being distracted. 2 [C] something (annoying and unwelcome) that distracts: *Noise is a ~ when you are trying to study.* 3 [C] something that holds the attention and gives pleasure: *He complained that there were not enough ~s in the village.* 4 [U] wildness or confusion of mind: *He loves her to ~. You'll drive me to ~ with your silly questions.*

dis·traught /dɪˈstrɔːt/ adj distracted; extremely upset: *~ with grief.*

dis·tress¹ /dɪˈstres/ n [U] 1 (cause of) great pain, discomfort or sorrow: *He was a great ~ to his mother.* 2 (suffering caused by) want of money or other necessary things. 2 serious danger or difficulty: *a ship in ~; a ~ signal.*

dis·tress² /dɪˈstres/ vt cause distress(2) to: *What are you looking so ~ed about?*
dis·tress·ing adj causing or experiencing distress.

dis·trib·ute /dɪˈstrɪbjuːt/ vt 1 give or send out: *The teacher ~d the books to the class.* 2 spread out (over a larger area): *to ~ manure over a field.* 3 put into groups or classes.

dis·tri·bu·tion /ˈdɪstrɪˈbjuːʃən/ n [U] distributing or being distributed; manner of being distributed; [C] instance or occasion of distributing: *They could not agree about the ~ of the profits. Is the ~ of wealth uneven in your country?*

dis·tribu·tive /dɪˈstrɪbjʊtɪv/ adj 1 of distribution: *the ~ trades*, e g shop-keeping. 2 (*gram*) of each individual, each member of a class: *'Each', 'every', 'either'* and *'neither'* are ~ pronouns.
dis·tribu·tive·ly adv
dis·tri·bu·tor /dɪˈstrɪbjʊtə(r)/ n [C] 1 person who distributes. 2 part of the engine (in a motor-vehicle) that sends electricity to the sparking plugs.
dis·trict /ˈdɪstrɪkt/ n [C] 1 part of a country: *a mountainous ~; the `Lake D~*, in England. 2 part of a town or country marked out for a special purpose: *the London postal ~s*, e g NW 5, EC 4.
'district 'nurse, nurse who visits people at home, not in hospitals.
dis·trust /dɪsˈtrʌst/ n [U] doubt or suspicion; want of trust or confidence: *The child looked at the stranger with ~.* □ vt have no trust in; be doubtful about: *He ~ed his own father.*
dis·trust·ful /-fəl/ adj suspicious (the usual word).
dis·trust·fully /-fəlɪ/ adv
dis·turb /dɪsˈtɜːb/ vt break the quiet, calm, peace or order of; put out of the right or usual position: *She opened the door quietly so as not to ~ the sleeping child. He was ~ed to hear of your illness/was ~ed by the news of your illness.*
dis·turb·ance /dɪsˈtɜːbəns/ n [U] disturbing or being disturbed; [C] instance of this; something that disturbs; disorder (esp social or political): *Were there any political ~s in the country last year?*
dis·unity /dɪsˈjuːnətɪ/ n [U] lack of unity.
dis·use /dɪsˈjuːs/ n [U] state of no longer being used: *rusty from ~; a machine that has fallen into ~.*
dis·used /dɪsˈjuːzd/ adj no longer used: *a ~d railway-line.*
ditch /dɪtʃ/ n [C] narrow channel dug in or between fields, or at the sides of a road, etc to hold or carry off water. **as dull as `ditch water**, very dull(3). □ vt, vi 1 send or throw into a ditch. 2 (*fig*) abandon: *The pilot had to ~ his plane*, make a forced landing on the sea. *He's ~ed his girlfriend,* (*informal*) suddenly stopped seeing her.
dither /ˈdɪðə(r)/ vi (*informal*) hesitate about what to do; be unable to decide.
ditto /ˈdɪtəʊ/ n [C] (*pl ~s*) the same (used in lists to avoid writing words again): *One hat at £2.25; ~ at £4.50.*
ditty /ˈdɪtɪ/ n [C] (*pl -ies*) short, simple song.
di·van /dɪˈvæn US: `daɪvæn/ n [C] long, low, soft, backless seat or bed.
dive¹ /daɪv/ n [C] 1 act of diving into water: *a graceful ~.* 2 disreputable place for the sale of drink, or for gambling.
dive² /daɪv/ vi 1 go head first into water: *He ~d from the bridge and rescued the drowning child.* 2 (of a submarine, divers) go

under water. 3 go quickly to a lower level: *The aircraft ~d steeply.* 4 move (e g the hand) quickly and suddenly downwards (into something): *He ~d into his pocket and pulled out a handful of coins.*
`diving-board, from which to dive (e g into a swimming pool).
`diving-suit, suit with heavy boots and a helmet worn when diving.
diver, person who dives, esp a person who works under water in a diving-suit.
di·verge /daɪˈvɜːdʒ/ vi (of lines, opinions, roads, etc) get farther apart from a point or from each other as they progress; turn or branch away from: *to ~ from the beaten track.*
di·ver·gence /daɪˈvɜːdʒəns/, **-gency** /-nsɪ/ n [U] diverging; [C] (*pl ~s, -ies*) instance of this.
di·ver·gent /-dʒənt/ adj
di·vers /ˈdaɪvəz/ adj (*old use*) several; more than one.
di·verse /daɪˈvɜːs/ adj of different kinds: *The wild life in Africa is extremely ~.*
di·verse·ly adv
di·ver·sify /daɪˈvɜːsɪfaɪ/ vt (*pt,pp -ied*) make diverse; give variety to.
di·ver·si·fi·ca·tion /daɪˌvɜːsɪfɪˈkeɪʃən/ n [U]
di·ver·sion /daɪˈvɜːʃən US: -ʒən/ n 1 [U] diverting; the act of turning something aside or giving it a different direction: *the ~ of a stream;* [C] instance of this: *traffic ~s*, e g when traffic is directed along different routes because of road repairs. 2 [C] something amusing or which gives rest or amusement: *Chess and tennis are his favourite ~s.* 3 [C] method used to turn the attention from something that one does not wish to be noticed, as when, in war, the enemy's attention is drawn from one place by an unexpected attack at another place: *to create/make a ~.*
di·ver·sion·ary /daɪˈvɜːʃənrɪ US: -ˈvɜːʒənerɪ/ adj
di·ver·sity /daɪˈvɜːsətɪ/ n [U] the state of being diverse; variety.
di·vert /daɪˈvɜːt/ vt 1 turn in another direction: *to ~ a river from its course.* 2 amuse; entertain: *Some people are easily ~ed.*
di·vest /daɪˈvest/ vt (*formal*) 1 take off (clothes): *to ~ a king of his robes.* 2 take away from: *to ~ an official of power and authority.*
di·vide¹ /dɪˈvaɪd/ vt,vi 1 separate, be separated (into); split or break up: *We ~d the money equally. They ~d the cash between/among themselves. The road ~s at this point.* 2 find out how often one number is contained in another: *If you ~ 6 into 30/~ 30 by 6, the answer is 5.* 3 arrange in groups: *The teacher ~d the boys from the girls.* 4 cause disagreement; cause to disagree: *Opinions are ~d on the question.* 5 (in Parliament, at debates, etc) (cause to) part in order to vote: *After a long debate, the House ~d, voted on the question.*

di·vide[2] /dɪˈvaɪd/ *n* [C] something that divides, e g a line of high land that separates two different river systems.

divi·dend /ˈdɪvɪdənd/ *n* [C] (usually periodical) payment of a share of profit, to shareholders in a business company, to a policy holder in a mutual insurance company, etc: *to pay a ~ of 10 per cent.*

di·vid·ers /dɪˈvaɪdəz/ *n pl* (also *a pair of ~*) measuring-compasses used for dividing lines or angles, measuring or marking distances, etc.

di·vine[1] /dɪˈvaɪn/ *adj* **1** of, from, or like God or a god: *D~ Service,* the public worship of God. **2** (*informal*) excellent; very beautiful: *~ weather. She looks ~ in that new dress.*

di·vine·ly *adv*

di·vine[2] /dɪˈvaɪn/ *vt,vi* discover or learn (something) about future events, hidden things, etc by means not based on reason: *to ~ what the future has in store.*

di·viner /dɪˈvaɪnə(r)/ *n* [C] person who divines, esp one who claims to have the power of finding water, metal, etc by using a Y-shaped stick or rod (called a *dīˈvining-rod*).

div·ing ⇨ dive.

di·vin·ity /dɪˈvɪnətɪ/ *n* **1** [U] the quality of being divine, ⇨ divine[1]: *the ~ of Christ;* [C] (*pl* -ies) divine being. **2** [U] the study of theology: *a doctor of ~* (abbr = **DD**).

di·vis·ible /dɪˈvɪzəbəl/ *adj* that can be divided without remainder: *8 is ~ by 2.*

div·ision /dɪˈvɪʒən/ *n* **1** [U] dividing or being divided: *the ~ of time into months, weeks and days; a simple problem in ~* (e g 50 ÷ 5). **2** [C] the effect of dividing; one of the parts into which something is divided: *Is that a fair ~ of the money? He plays in the Second D~ of the Football League.* **3** [C] unit of two or more brigades. **4** [C] line that divides: *A hedge forms the ~ between his land and mine.* **5** [C] disagreement; separation in thought, feeling, etc: *Agitators who stir up ~s in society are dangerous.* **6** [C] (in Parliament, etc) separation into two groups for the counting of votes: *The Bill was read for the second time without a ~.*

di·vorce[1] /dɪˈvɔːs/ *n* **1** [U] legal ending of a marriage so that husband and wife are free to marry again; [C] instance of this: *to sue for a ~; to take/start ~ proceedings; to obtain a ~ (from...).* **2** [C] ending of a connection or relationship: *the ~ between religion and science,* as when science claims or seems to show that religious beliefs are not true.

di·vorce[2] /dɪˈvɔːs/ *vt* **1** put an end to a marriage by law: *Did Mr Hill ~ his wife or did she ~ him?* **2** (*fig*) separate (things usually together): *What happens to the soul when it is ~d from the body?*

di·vor·cee /dɪˈvɔːsiː/, divorced person.

di·vulge /daɪˈvʌldʒ/ *vt* make known (a secret).

dizzy /ˈdɪzɪ/ *adj* (-ier, -iest) **1** (of a person) feeling as if everything were turning round, as if unable to balance; mentally confused. **2** (of places, conditions) causing such a feeling: *a ~ height.* □ *vt* (*pt,pp* -ied) make dizzy.

diz·zily /-əlɪ/ *adv*

diz·zi·ness *n* [U]

do[1] /də strong form: duː/ auxiliary verb (*1st person sing, present tense* negative **don't** /dəʊnt/, *3rd person sing, present tense* **does** /dʌz/, negative **doesn't** /ˈdʌzənt/, *pt* **did** /dɪd/, negative **didn't** /ˈdɪdənt/, *pp* **done** /dʌn/) **1** (used with the main verb) (**a**) for negative sentences with *not*: *He didn't go. Don't go yet.* (**b**) for *questions: Does/Did he want it?* (**c**) (for emphasis): *That's exactly what he `did say.* **2** (**a**) (used in comparisons): *She plays the piano better now than she did* (i e played) *last year.* (**b**) (used in question phrases): *He lives in London, doesn't he?* (**c**) (used in answers, comments, etc): *'Who broke the window?'—'I did!'*

do[2] /duː/ *vt,vi* (For pronunciations, etc ⇨ do[1]) (For uses with *adverbial particles* and *prepositions* ⇨ 14 below.) **1** perform, carry out (an action): *What are you ~ing now? What does he ~ for a living,* What is his job? *I have nothing to ~. It's easier said than done,* easier to talk about than to do. *do it yourself,* (abbr **DIY**) (esp) do house decorating, etc oneself (instead of paying professional workers). **2** (used with *nouns* in many senses) (**a**) produce; make: *I have done* (i e made) *six copies.* (**b**) work at; be busy with: *She's ~ing her knitting.* (**c**) perform: *D~ your duty.* (**d**) study; learn: *Are you ~ing science at school?* (**e**) find the answer to: *I can't ~ this sum.* (**f**) put in order; arrange: *Go and ~ your hair.* (**g**) clean, sweep, etc: *Have you done* (i e brushed) *your teeth?* (**h**) deal with, attend to: *I have a lot of correspondence to ~.* (**i**) use, exert: *~ one's best/all one can to help.* **3** (as a *pp*) bring to an end; finish: *It's done. I've done it. A woman's work is never done.* **4** *do (for),* be satisfactory or convenient, good, enough: *These shoes won't do* (i e are not strong enough) *for mountain-climbing.* **5** be fitting, suitable, tolerable: *This will never ~, cannot be accepted or allowed! It doesn't ~ to be rude to your father.* **6** (*informal*) happen: *He came to ask what was ~ing,* = being done, happening. **7** (**a**) get on well, badly, etc: *Everything in the garden is ~ing* (= growing) *well. He's ~ing well at school.* (**b**) (esp of health) make progress: *The patient is ~ing quite well. How do you do?* (formula used when people are formally introduced). **8** complete (a journey); travel (a distance); go (at a certain speed): *How many miles a day did you ~? We did the journey in six hours.* **9** play the part of: *He does Hamlet well.* **10** cheat, swindle, get the better of: *He once tried to ~ me out of my*

job. **11** (*informal*) see the sights of: *Some Americans think they can ~ England in a fortnight*. **12** cook in the right degree: *How would you like your steak done?* **13** (*with have*) **have to do with,** be connected with: *I know he behaves badly—It all has to ~ with the way he was brought up*. **have to do with/ nothing/not much/a great deal with,** be/not be connected or concerned with: *Hard work had a great deal to ~ with* (= contributed greatly to) *his success.*
14 (uses with *adverbial particles* and *prepositions*):
do away with, abolish, get rid of: *That department was done away with two years ago.*
(be) hard done by, (be) treated unfairly: *He complains that he has been hard done by.*
do for, (*informal*) **(a)** perform, esp domestic services for: *Old Mrs Green has been ~ing for me since my wife died.* **(b)** manage: *What/How will you ~ for water* (= manage to have supplies of water) *while you're crossing the desert?* **(c)** ruin; destroy; kill: *The country's done for,* ruined.
do sb in, (*sl*) kill him. *be done in,* exhausted: *The horse was done in after the race.*
do sb out of sth, ⇨ **10** above.
do sth out, sweep or clean out; put in order: *This room needs ~ing out.*
do sth up, **(a)** restore, repair: *The house needs to be done up/needs ~ing up,* to be decorated. **(b)** change the shape of, put new trimmings, etc on: *She has been ~ing up her last summer's clothes.* **(c)** tie or wrap up; make into a bundle or parcel: *Please ~ up these books and post them to Mr Smith.* **(d)** fasten (a dress or other garment) with buttons, hooks and eyes, etc: *Please ~ your coat up at the back.* **(e)** (of a dress, etc) fasten with buttons, etc: *This dress does up at the back.*
do with, **(a)** (meanings as in the examples): *What did you ~ with my umbrella,* Where did you put it, leave it, etc? *What are we to ~ with* (= How shall we deal with) *this naughty boy? She didn't know what to ~ with herself,* how to occupy her time. **(b)** get on with; live or work with: *I can't ~ with him and his temper.* **(c)** (with *can, could*) expressing a need or wish: *You look as if you could ~ with* (= as if you need) *a good night's sleep.*
do without, manage without: *We shall have to ~ without a holiday this summer.*
do³ /duː/ *n* [C] (*pl* dos or do's /duːz/) **1** (*informal*) entertainment; party: *We're going to a big ~ at the Green's this evening.* **2** customs, rules: *Some teachers have too many ~'s and don'ts.* **3 fair do's,** (*GB sl*) (as an exclamation) Let's be fair (e g in sharing something).

do⁴, doh /dəʊ/ *n* (*music*) first of the syllables used in the scale *do, re, mi, fa, sol, la, ti, do.*

doc·ile /ˈdəʊsaɪl US: ˈdɒsəl/ *adj* easily trained or controlled: *a ~ child/horse.*
do·cil·ity /dəʊˈsɪlətɪ/ *n* [U] the quality of being docile.
dock¹ /dɒk/ *n* **1** [C] place in a harbour, river, etc with gates through which water may be let in and out, where ships are (un)loaded or repaired: *to be in ~.* **2** (*pl*) number or row of docks with the wharves, sheds, offices, etc round them.
docker, dockyard labourer.
ˈ**dock·yard,** enclosure with docks and facilities for building and repairing ships.
dock² /dɒk/ *vi, vt* **1** (of a ship) come or go into a dock. **2** bring, take, (a ship) into a dock. **3** join together (two or more spacecraft) in space.
dock³ /dɒk/ *n* [C] enclosure in a criminal court for the prisoner: *to be in the ~.*
dock⁴ /dɒk/ *vt* (esp) make allowances, wages, supplies, less: *to ~ a workman's wages; to have one's salary ~ed.*
docket /ˈdɒkɪt/ *n* [C] **1** summary of the contents of a letter, document, etc. **2** list of goods delivered, jobs done, etc; label on a package listing the contents, or giving information about use, method of assembly, etc. □ *vt* enter in or write on a docket.
doc·tor /ˈdɒktə(r)/ *n* [C] **1** person who has received the highest university degree: *D~ of Laws/Divinity, etc.* **2** person who has been trained in medical science. ⇨ physician, surgeon. □ *vt* **1** (*informal*) give medical treatment to: *~ a cold/a child.* **2** (*informal*) neuter(5). **3** make (esp food, drink) inferior by adding something; add drugs to. **3** (*fig*) falsify accounts, evidence.
doc·tor·ate /ˈdɒktərət/ *n* [C] doctor's(1) degree.
doc·tri·naire /ˌdɒktrɪˈneə(r)/ *adj* theoretical; dogmatic: *~ teachers/socialism.*
doc·tri·nal /ˈdɒkˈtraɪməl US: ˈdɒktrɪnəl/ *adj* of doctrine(s).
doc·trine /ˈdɒktrɪn/ *n* [C,U] body of teaching; beliefs and teachings of a church, political party, school of scientists, etc: *the ~ that the Pope is infallible.*
docu·ment /ˈdɒkjʊmənt/ *n* [C] something written or printed, to be used as a record or in evidence (e g birth, marriage and death certificate). □ *vt* prove by, supply with, documents: *to be well ~ed.*
doc·u·men·ta·tion /ˌdɒkjʊmenˈteɪʃən/ *n* [U]
doc·u·men·tary /ˌdɒkjʊˈmentrɪ/ *adj* consisting of documents: *~ proof/evidence.* □ *n* [C] (*pl* -ies) (also *~ film*) (non-fiction) film describing ideas, social topics, studies of the natural world, science, etc.
dod·der /ˈdɒdə(r)/ *vi* (*informal*) walk, move, in a shaky way, as from weakness or old age: *to ~ along.*
dod·derer, person who dodders.
dod·der·ing (also **dod·dery**) *adj* weak and uncertain in movement.
doddle /ˈdɒdəl/ *n* [C] (*informal*) something

done very easily.

dodge[1] /dɒdʒ/ *n* [C] **1** quick movement to avoid something. **2** (*informal*) trick: *He's up to all the ~s,* knows them all. **3** (*informal*) clever way of doing something.

dodge[2] /dɒdʒ/ *vt,vi* **1** move quickly to one side, change position or direction, in order to escape or avoid something: *I ~d behind a tree so that he should not see me.* **2** get round (difficulties), avoid (duties, etc) by cunning or trickery: *to ~ military service.* **dodger,** artful or cunning person.

dodgy /dɒdʒɪ/ *adj* (-ier, -iest) (*informal*) **1** artful. **2** involving risk or loss.

dodo /dəʊdəʊ/ *n* [C] (*pl ~es, ~s*) extinct, large, flightless bird of Mauritius.

doe /dəʊ/ *n* [C] female fallow-deer, rabbit or hare.

`doe skin,` (esp) soft leather made from this skin.

doer /dʊə(r)/ *n* [C] person who does things (contrasted with persons who merely talk, etc): *He's a ~, not a talker.* (*Note:* also used in compounds, *evil-~*).

does /dʌz/, **doesn't** /dʌzənt/ ⇨ do[1].

dog[1] /dɒg *US:* dɔg/ *n* [C] **1** common domestic animal of which there are many breeds; male of this animal and of the wolf and the fox. ⇨ **bitch. go to the dogs,** be ruined. **lead a dog's life,** be troubled all the time. **lead sb a dog's life,** give him no peace; worry him all the time. **let sleeping dogs lie,** leave something alone; not look for trouble. **not stand (even) a dog's chance,** have no chance at all of beating a stronger enemy, surviving a disaster, etc. **be top dog,** be in a position where one rules. **be (the) underdog,** be in a position where one must always submit. **2** (*informal*) **the ~s,** greyhound race-meetings. **3** (*informal*) person: *He's a dirty/sly/lucky ~.*

`dog-collar,` (*informal*) clerical collar.

`dog-eared,` (of a book) having the corners of the pages turned down with use.

`dog-fight,` (*sl*) fight in which two or more aircraft are involved.

`dog-fish,` small kind of shark.

`dog-house,` (*sl*) disgrace or disfavour: *be in the ~house.*

`dog-like` *adj* like or as of a dog, esp *~-like devotion,* the kind of devotion given by a dog to its master.

`dog paddle,` simple swimming stroke in which the arms and legs are moved in short, quick splashing movements.

`dogs-body,` overworked person.

doggy /dɒgɪ *US:* dɔgɪ/, (child's word for a) dog.

dog[2] /dɒg *US:* dɔg/ *vt* (-gg-) **1** keep close behind, in the footsteps of: *~ a suspected thief.* **2** (*fig*) follow: *~ged by misfortune.*

dog-ged /dɒgɪd *US:* dɔg-/ *adj* stubborn.
dog-ged-ly *adv*
dog-ged-ness *n* [U]

dogma /dɒgmə *US:* dɔg-/ *n* (*pl ~s*) **1** [C]

belief, system of beliefs, put forward by some authority (esp the Church) to be accepted as true without question. **2** [U] such beliefs collectively.

dog-matic /dɒgˈmætɪk *US:* dɔg-/ *adj* **1** put forward as dogmas: *~ theology.* **2** (of a person) giving opinions as if they were dogmas, esp in an arrogant way; (of statements) put in this way.

dog-mati-cally /-klɪ/ *adv*

dog-ma-tism /dɒgmətɪzm *US:* dɔg-/ *n* [U] (the quality of) being dogmatic: *His ~ was unbearable.*

do-ings /duːɪŋz/ *n pl* (*informal*) things done or being done: *Tell me about all your ~ in London.*

dol-drums /dɒldrəmz/ *n pl* **in the doldrums,** (*fig*) miserable, depressed.

dole /dəʊl/ *vt* distribute food, money, etc in small amounts (e g to poor people). □ *n* [C] **1** something distributed. **2** (*informal*) weekly payment from the State to an unemployed worker. **be/go on the dole,** receive/begin to receive, such payments.

dole-ful /dəʊlfəl/ *adj* miserable, depressed.
dole-fully /-fəlɪ/ *adv*

doll[1] /dɒl/ *n* [C] **1** model of a baby or person, usually for a child to play with. **2** (*dated sl*) pretty but empty-headed girl or woman.

doll[2] /dɒl/ *vt,vi* (*informal*) dress (oneself) up smartly: *She was all ~ed up for the party.*

dol-lar /dɒlə(r)/ *n* [C] unit of money (symbol $) in the US, Canada, Australia and other countries.

dol-lop /dɒləp/ *n* [C] (*informal*) shapeless quantity of food, etc: *a ~ of ice-cream.*

dolly /dɒlɪ/ *n* [C] (*pl* -ies) **1** child's word for a doll. **2** small wheeled frame or platform for moving heavy objects; mobile platform for a heavy camera.

dol-phin /dɒlfɪn/ *n* [C] sea-animal like a porpoise.

dolt /dəʊlt/ *n* [C] stupid person.

-dom /-dəm/ *suffix* (used to form a *noun*) **1** condition, state: *boredom; freedom.* **2** domain: *kingdom.*

do-main /dəʊˈmeɪn/ *n* [C] (*formal*) **1** lands under the rule of a government, ruler, etc. **2** (*fig*) area or topic of thought, knowledge, activity: *in the ~ of science.*

dome /dəʊm/ *n* [C] rounded roof with a circular base; something shaped like a dome: *the rounded ~* (= summit) *of a hill.*

domed *adj* rounded: *a man with a ~d forehead.*

do-mes-tic /dəˈmestɪk/ *adj* **1** of the home, family, household: *He has had a good many ~ troubles.* **2** not foreign; native; of one's own country: *This newspaper provides more foreign news than ~ news.* **3** (of animals, etc) kept by, living with, man: *Horses, cows and sheep are ~ animals.* ⇨ wild. □ *n* [C] person who is employed in household work.

do·mes·ti·cate /dəˈmestɪkeɪt/ *vt* **1** make able to do, interested in, household work and duties: *She's not at all ~d*, is not good at cooking, housekeeping, etc. **2** tame (animals).
do·mes·ti·ca·tion /dəˈmestɪˈkeɪʃən/ *n* [U]
do·mes·tic·ity /ˌdəʊmeˈstɪsətɪ/ *n* [U] home or family life.
domi·cile /ˈdɒmɪsaɪl/ *n* [C] (*formal*) home; (*legal*) place where a person lives permanently.
domi·nance /ˈdɒmɪnəns/ *n* [U] being dominant.
domi·nant /ˈdɒmɪnənt/ *adj* **1** having control or authority; dominating; most important or influential: *the ~ partner in a business*. **2** (of heights) overlooking others: *a ~ cliff*.
domi·nant·ly *adv*
domi·nate /ˈdɒmɪneɪt/ *vt,vi* **1** have control, authority or influence: *The strong usually ~ (over) the weak. Mary ~d the conversation.* **2** (of a place, esp a height) overlook: *The whole valley is ~d by this mountain.*
domi·na·tion /ˈdɒmɪˈneɪʃən/ *n* [U]
domi·neer /ˈdɒmɪˈnɪə(r)/ *vi* act, speak, in a dominating manner; be overbearing: *Big boys sometimes ~ over their small sisters.*
domi·neer·ing *adj*: *He's a very ~ing man.*
Dom·ini·can /dəˈmɪnɪkən/ *adj* of St Dominic /ˈdɒmɪnɪk/ (1170—1221, a Spanish priest) or the order of friars he founded in 1212, under vows of poverty and chastity. □ *n* [C] one of these friars.
do·min·ion /dəˈmɪnɪən/ *n* **1** [U] authority to rule; control (over). **2** [C] territory of a sovereign government. **3** [C] one of the self-governing territories of the British Commonwealth of Nations: *the D~ of Canada.*
dom·ino /ˈdɒmɪnəʊ/ *n* [C] (*pl* ~es or ~s) **1** small, flat, oblong piece of wood or bone, marked with spots. **2** (*pl*) (used with a *sing verb*) game played with 28 of these.
don /dɒn/ *n* [C] **1** (at Oxford and Cambridge) senior resident member of university staff. **2** Spanish gentleman: *D~ Juan.*
don·nish /ˈdɒnɪʃ/ *adj* of or like a don(1).
do·nate /dəʊˈneɪt/ *US*: /ˈdəʊneɪt/ *vt* give (e g money, to a charity, etc); contribute.
do·na·tion /dəʊˈneɪʃən/ *n* [U] giving; something given: *donations to the refugee fund.*
done /dʌn/ ⇨ **do**[1].
don·key /ˈdɒŋkɪ/ *n* [C] (*pl* ~s) (the usual word for an) ass.
'donkey-work, work needing great (physical) effort.
do·nor /ˈdəʊnə(r)/ *n* [C] person who gives something: *a 'blood ~*, person who gives his own blood for transfusion.
don't /dəʊnt/ **1** = *do not*. ⇨ **do**[1]. **2** ⇨ **do**[3](3).
doodle /ˈduːdəl/ *vi, n* [C] (*informal*) (make a) meaningless scrawl or scribble.
doom[1] /duːm/ *n* [U] ruin; death; something

evil that is to come: *to send a man to his ~.*
doom[2] /duːm/ *vt* condemn (esp in *pp*): *~ed to failure.*
Dooms·day /ˈduːmzdeɪ/ *n* the day of Judgement; end of the world. *from now until Doomsday,* for ever.
door /dɔː(r)/ *n* [C] **1** that which closes the entrance to a building, room, cupboard, etc: *The ~ opened/was opened and a man came out.* **lay sth at sb's door,** say that he is responsible for it. **next door,** (in, to) the next house: *I'm just going next ~ to see Mrs Jones.* **out of doors,** in the open air: *It's cold out of ~s; put an overcoat on.* **at death's door,** near death. **2** (*fig*) means of obtaining or approaching something: *a ~ to success.*
'door-bell, bell inside a building, operated by a button, etc outside by somebody seeking admittance.
'door-keeper, person on duty or on guard at a door or other entrance.
'door·man, uniformed attendant at the entrance to a hotel, cinema, etc.
'door·mat, rough mat by a door on which shoes may be wiped.
'door·step, step in front of a door.
'door-stop·per, heavy object placed in a doorway to prevent the door from closing.
'door·way, opening into which a door fits: *standing in the ~way.*
dope /dəʊp/ *n* [U] **1** (*informal*) harmful drug (e g opium). **2** (*sl*) information (e g on the probable winners at a race meeting). □ *vt* give dope(2) to.
dopey, dopy /ˈdəʊpɪ/ *adj* (*sl*) (**a**) half asleep. (**b**) (as if) drugged. (**c**) stupid.
dor·mant /ˈdɔːmənt/ *adj* in a state of inactivity but awaiting development or activity: *a ~ volcano.*
dor·mi·tory /ˈdɔːmɪtrɪ/ *US*: -tɔrɪ/ *n* [C] (*pl* -ies) sleeping-room with several or many beds, esp in a school or institution.
dor·mouse /ˈdɔːmaʊs/ *n* [C] (*pl* dormice /ˈdɔːmaɪs/) small animal (like a mouse) that sleeps during cold weather in winter.
dor·sal /ˈdɔːsəl/ *adj* of, on, near, the back(1,2): *the ~ fin*, e g of a shark.
dos·age /ˈdəʊsɪdʒ/ *n* [U] giving of medicines in doses; [C] quantity of a single dose.
dose /dəʊs/ *n* [C] **1** amount (of medicine) to be taken at one time: *The bottle contains six ~s.* **2** (*informal, fig*) something given or taken: *give her a ~ of her own medicine,* behave as she does, etc. □ *vt* give dose(s) to: *to ~ oneself with aspirin.*
doss /dɒs/ *vi* (*GB sl*) **doss down,** make a (cheap) temporary bed and go to sleep.
'doss-house, cheap lodging-house.
dos·sier /ˈdɒsɪeɪ/ *US*: /ˈdɒs-/ *n* [C] set of papers giving information about a person or event, esp a personal record.
dot /dɒt/ *n* [C] **1** small round mark (as over the letters i and j); decimal points. **on the dot,** (*informal*) at the precise moment. **2**

thing like a dot in appearance: *We watched the ship until it was a mere ~ on the horizon.* □ *vt* (-tt-) **1** mark with a dot. **2** make with, cover with, dots: *a ~ted line,* e g on a document, for a signature. **dotted about,** scattered here and there.

do·tage /ˈdəʊtɪdʒ/ *n* [U] weakness of mind caused by old age: *He's in his ~,* is becoming unable to remember things, fails to notice things, etc.

do·tard /ˈdəʊtəd/ *n* [C] person in his dotage.

dote /dəʊt/ *vi* show much, or too much, fondness: *She ~s on her grandson. He's a doting* (= very loving) *husband.*

doth /dʌθ/ old form used for **does.**

dotty /ˈdɒtɪ/ *adj* (-ier, -iest) (*informal*) mad; idiotic; eccentric.

double[1] /ˈdʌbəl/ *adj* **1** twice as much, large, good, etc: *His income is ~ what it was two years ago.* **2** having two like things or parts: *a railway with a ~ track; a man with a ~ chin,* with a fold of loose flesh below the chin. **3** made for two persons or things: *a ~ bed.* **4** combining two things, qualities, etc: *a piece of furniture that serves a ~ purpose,* e g one that is a settee and can be opened out to make a bed.

'**double-'barrelled** *adj* **(a)** (of a gun) having two barrels. **(b)** (*fig*) (of a compliment, etc ambiguous. **(c)** (of a surname) hyphenated.

'**double-'bass,** largest and lowest-pitched instrument in the violin family.

'**double-'breasted** *adj* (of a coat or waistcoat) made so as to overlap across the front of the body.

'**double-'check** *vt* check[1](1) twice in order to be certain.

'**double-'cross** *vt* (*informal*) cheat or betray (each of two parties, usually by pretended support for both). □ *n* act of this kind.

'**double-'dealer,** person who says one thing and means another.

'**double-'dealing** *n, adj* deceit(ful) (esp in business).

'**double-'decker,** (esp) bus with two decks. ⇨ **deck**[1](2).

'**double-'Dutch,** (*informal*) (of speech) unable to be understood.

'**double 'figures,** any number from 10 to 99 inclusive.

'**double-'first,** a first-class honours degree in two principal subjects gained at the same time.

'**double-'jointed** *adj* having joints that allow the fingers (or arms, legs) to move or bend in unusual ways.

'**double-'quick** *adj, adv* very quick(ly): *in ~-quick time.*

'**double-'talk,** kind of talk that really means the opposite of, or something quite different from, what it seems to mean.

double[2] /ˈdʌbəl/ *adv* **1** twice (as much): *Many things now cost ~ what they did a year ago.* **2** in twos, in pairs or couples. **see double,** see two things when there is only one.

double[3] /ˈdʌbəl/ *n* [C] **1** twice the quantity: *Ten is the ~ of five.* **2** person or thing that looks exactly, or almost exactly, like another: *She's the ~ of her sister.* **3** slow run (about twice as fast as ordinary walking): *The troops advanced at the ~.* **4** game of tennis played with two on each side: *mixed ~s,* a man and woman against another man and woman.

double[4] /ˈdʌbəl/ *vt,vi* **1** make or become twice as great: *to ~ one's income.* **2** bend or fold in two: *If you are cold, ~ the blanket (over).* **3** turn sharply back in flight (when running to escape pursuit): *The fox ~d (back) on its tracks.* **4** **double back,** turn or fold back. **double up, (a)** fold (something) up: *He ~d up his legs and kicked out,* e g when swimming. **(b)** be capable of folding up or rolling up: *This carpet is too thick to ~ up.* **(c)** (of persons) (cause to) bend the body with pain or in helpless laughter: *The stone struck him in the stomach and ~d him up. He ~d up with laughter.* **5** (of an actor) act two parts in the same play: *He's doubling the parts of a servant and a farm worker.*

doub·let /ˈdʌblət/ *n* [C] close-fitting garment for the upper part of the body, worn by men (about 1400—1600).

doubly /ˈdʌblɪ/ *adv* to twice the extent or amount: *to be ~ careful/sure.* (*Note:* used before an *adjective.*)

doubt[1] /daʊt/ *n* [U] uncertainty of thought; [C] feeling of uncertainty; uncertain state of things: *I have no ~ that you will succeed/no ~ of your ability. There is no ~ about it,* It is certain. *When in ~* (= uncertain) *about the meaning of a word, consult a dictionary.* **throw/cast doubt on,** suggest that it is not true or reliable. **no doubt, (a)** certainly. **(b)** (*informal*) very probably: *He meant to help, no ~, but in fact he forgot to come.*

doubt[2] /daʊt/ *vt,vi* feel doubt about; question the truth of: *You cannot ~ your own existence. Do you ~ my word,* think I am not telling the truth? *I ~ whether he will come.*

doubt·ful /ˈdaʊtfəl/ *adj* feeling doubt; causing doubt: *I am/feel ~ (about) what I ought to do. The future/weather looks very ~.*

doubt·fully /-fəlɪ/ *adv*

doubt·less /ˈdaʊtləs/ *adv* **1** without doubt. **2** (*informal*) very probably.

dough /dəʊ/ *n* [U] **1** mixture of flour, water, etc in a paste (for making bread, pastry, etc) **2** (*sl*) money.

'**dough-nut,** sweetened dough cooked in deep fat.

doughy *adj* of or like dough; soft.

dour /dʊə(r)/ *adj* gloomy; severe; stern: *~ looks/silence.*

dour·ly *adv*

douse, dowse /daʊs/ *vt* **1** put into water; throw water over. **2** (*informal*) put out (a light).

dove[1] /dʌv/ n [C] **1** kind of pigeon; symbol of peace. **2** (*informal*) member of a group promoting peace. ⇨ **hawk**[1](2).
`dove-cote, small shelter or house with nesting-boxes for doves.

dove[2] /dəʊv/ (*US*) alternative *pt* form of dive[2].

dove-tail /ˈdʌvteɪl/ n [C] joint for two pieces of wood. □ *vt,vi* **1** join together with these joints. **2** (*fig*) fit (together): *My plans ∼ed with his.*

dowa-ger /ˈdaʊɪdʒə(r)/ n [C] woman with property or a title from her dead husband: *the ∼ duchess.*

dowdy /ˈdaʊdɪ/ *adj* (-ier, -iest) (of clothes, etc) shabby or unfashionable; (of a person) dressed in such clothes.
dow-dily /-əlɪ/ *adv*
dow-di-ness n [U]

dowel /ˈdaʊəl/ n [C] headless pin or peg for keeping two pieces of wood, metal, stone, etc together.

down[1] /daʊn/ n [U] **1** first, soft feathers of young birds; soft feathers of birds (as used for pillows and cushions). **2** similar fine soft hair, e g on a boy's face, on some fruit.

down[2] /daʊn/ *adverbial particle* **1** (used with *verbs* of motion) (a) from a high(er) level to a low(er) level: *The sun went ∼. If you can't jump ∼, climb ∼. Some kinds of food go ∼* (= can be swallowed) *more easily than others.* (b) from an upright position to a horizontal position: *He was knocked ∼ by a bus. If you're tired, go and lie ∼.* **2** (used with *verbs* of change of position but not because of movement in space) to or in a lower position or direction: *Sit ∼, please. The tall man bent ∼ to speak to me.* **3** (used with *verbs* of position or station): *Mary isn't ∼ yet,* is not yet dressed and downstairs. *We can't use the telephone—the lines are all ∼,* on the ground, e g after a storm. **4** from a more important place to a less important place; from an inland place to the coast; from the university: *We went ∼ to Brighton* (e g from London) *for the weekend. The Bill was sent ∼* (from the House of Lords) *to the House of Commons. He has been sent ∼,* expelled from the University for misbehaving, etc. **5** (used with *verbs* to show reduction to a smaller volume, a lower degree, a state of less activity, etc): *The heels of my shoes have worn ∼. The wind died ∼. One of the back tyres is ∼,* is flat or getting flat. *The temperature has gone ∼. The price of fruit is ∼. The factory was closed ∼* (= Work stopped) *because of the steel shortage.* **6** (used with reference to writing): *to write something ∼; Put me ∼/Put my name ∼ for 50p,* e g as willing to give this sum to a charity or an appeal for a fund. **7** from an earlier time (to a later time): *the history of Europe ∼ to 1914.* **8** including the lower limit in a series: *everyone, from the Director ∼.*

Down with, Let us be rid of: *D∼ with grammar!* **down under,** (*informal*) in the other side of the world. **be down and out,** (*informal*) (a) (in boxing) be knocked out, unable to resume the fight. (b) (*fig*) be unemployed and without money. **get down to sth,** start work, etc in real earnest. **be down in the dumps/mouth,** (*informal*), sad; depressed. **be down on one's luck,** (*informal*) having suffered misfortune. **come down in the world,** fall to a lower social position.
'down-to-'earth, concerned with realities; practical (contrasted with *impractical, vague, idealistic*): *He's a ∼-to-earth sort of man.*

down[3] /daʊn/ *prep* **1** from a high(er) to a low(er) level: *to run ∼ a hill. The tears ran ∼ her face.* **2** at a lower part of: *Oxford is farther ∼ the river.* **3** along (not necessarily with reference to a lower level): *I was walking ∼ the street.* **4** (of time) from a farther to a nearer period: *∼ the ages.*

down[4] /daʊn/ *vt* (*informal*) bring, put, knock, down: *to ∼ a glass of beer,* drink it. **down tools,** (of workers) go on strike.

down[5] /daʊn/ n **ups and downs,** changes in fortune, prosperity, etc: *have one's ups and ∼s.* **have a down on sb,** feel ill-will towards him.

down-beat /ˈdaʊnbiːt/ n [C] first beat of a bar in music (when the conductor's hand moves down).

down-cast /ˈdaʊnkɑːst US: -kæst/ *adj* **1** (of a person) depressed; discouraged; sad. **2** (of eyes) looking downwards.

down-fall /ˈdaʊnfɔːl/ n [C] **1** heavy fall (of rain, etc). **2** (*fig*) ruin; fall from fortune or power: *His ∼ was caused by gambling and drink.*

down-grade /ˈdaʊnˈɡreɪd/ *vt* reduce to a lower grade or rank.

down-hearted /ˈdaʊnˈhɑːtɪd/ *adj* sad; depressed.

down-hill /ˈdaʊnˈhɪl/ *adv* in a downward direction. **go downhill,** (*fig*) go from bad to worse (in health, fortune, etc).

down-pour /ˈdaʊnpɔː(r)/ n [C] heavy fall of rain.

down-right /ˈdaʊnraɪt/ *adj* **1** honest; frank: *He is a ∼ sort of person.* **2** thorough; nothing less than: *It's a ∼ lie.* □ *adv* thoroughly: *He was ∼ rude.*

downs /daʊnz/ n *pl* expanse of low hills, esp the chalk hills of S England: *Walking on the North/South D∼s.*

down-stairs /ˈdaʊnˈsteəz/ *adv* **1** to, at, on, of, a lower floor; down the stairs: *Our neighbours ∼* (= on the lower floor) *are very noisy. Your brother is waiting ∼.* **2** (often without the final *s*) used as an *adjective*: *the ∼(s) rooms.*

down-town /ˈdaʊntaʊn/ *adj, adv* towards or in the centre of a town or city: *∼ New York; go ∼.*

down·trod·den /ˈdaʊnˌtrɒdən/ adj kept down and treated badly.

down·ward /ˈdaʊnwəd/ adj moving, leading, going, pointing, to what is lower: *a ~ slope; prices with a ~ tendency.*

down·wards /ˈdaʊnwədz/ adv towards what is lower: *He laid the picture face ~s on the table.*

dowry /ˈdaʊərɪ/ n [C] (pl -ies) property, money, brought by a bride to her husband.

dowse /daʊs/ vt ⇨ douse.

doze /dəʊz/ vi sleep lightly; be half asleep: *He ~d off during the sermon.* □ n [C] short, light sleep.

dozen /ˈdʌzən/ n (pl unchanged) twelve: *Eggs are 50p a ~. I want three ~ of these.* **dozens of,** a large number of: *I've been there ~s of times.*

drab /dræb/ adj (fig) dull; uninteresting; monotonous: *a ~ existence.*
drab·ly adv
drab·ness n [U]

draft¹ /drɑːft US: dræft/ n [C] 1 outline (usually in the form of rough notes) of something to be done: *a ~ for a speech/letter.* 2 written order for payment of money by a bank; drawing of money by means of such an order: *a ~ for £500 on London,* e g one written by a Paris bank on its London branch. Hence, `**bank-draft** n.` 3 (US) = draught. 4 group of men selected to do something esp to serve in the armed forces.

draft² /drɑːft US: dræft/ vt make a draft(1) of: *to ~ a speech.* 2 select (a man) for the armed forces.
draft·ing, the act, method, of drafting.

drafts·man /ˈdrɑːftsmən US: ˈdræfts-/ n [C] 1 person who prepares drafts(1), esp in engineering and architecture. 2 person responsible for the careful and exact wording of a legal document, or a (clause in a) parliamentary bill.

drafty /ˈdrɑːftɪ US: ˈdræftɪ/ adj (US) = draughty.

drag¹ /dræg/ n 1 [C] something that is dragged, e g a net pulled over the bottom of a river to catch fish. 2 [C] (informal) person or thing that slows down progress because dull, etc: *Do we have to take your sister with us? She's such a ~.* ⇨ drag²(3). 3 [U] (sl) woman's clothes worn by a man: *'As you Like It' performed in ~,* with the women's parts acted by men dressed as women. [C] (sl) puff at a cigarette or cigar.

drag² /dræg/ vt,vi (-gg-) 1 pull along (esp with effort and difficulty): *to ~ a heavy box out of a cupboard.* 2 (allow to) move slowly and with effort; (allow to) trail: *He could scarcely ~ himself along.* **drag one's feet,** (usually fig) make slow progress: *We suspect the Government of ~ging their feet.* 3 (of time, work, an entertainment) go on slowly in a dull manner: *Time seemed to ~.* 4 use nets, tools, etc to search the bottom of a river, lake, etc: *They ~ged the river for*

the missing child.

dragon /ˈdrægən/ n [C] 1 fictional creature like a crocodile or snake, but with wings and claws, able to breathe out fire. 2 elderly, strict woman.

drag·on·fly /ˈdrægənflaɪ/ n [C] (pl -flies) insect with a body like a stick and two pairs of large wings.

drain¹ /dreɪn/ n [C] 1 pipe, channel, etc for carrying away water, sewage and other unwanted liquids; (pl) system of such pipes, etc: *There's a bad smell; something wrong with the ~s, I suppose.* 2 (fig) something that continually uses up force, time, wealth, etc; cause of weakening or loss: *Defence costs have been a great ~ on the country's resources.* ⇨ brain drain.
`**drain-pipe,** pipe used in a system of drains.

drain² /dreɪn/ vt,vi 1 *drain away/off,* (of liquid) (cause to) run or flow away: *The water will soon ~ away/off.* 2 (of land, crockery etc) make, become dry as water flows away: *Land must be well ~ed for some crops. Leave the dishes to ~.* 3 (fig) (cause to) lose (strength, wealth, etc) by degrees: *The country was ~ed of its manpower and wealth by war.*
`**drain·ing-board,** board at the side of a sink, on which dishes, etc are placed to drain.

drain·age /ˈdreɪnɪdʒ/ n [U] 1 draining or being drained. 2 system of drains(1). 3 that which is drained away or off.

drake /dreɪk/ n [C] male duck.

dram /dræm/ n 1 unit of weight. 2 (Scot) small drink of alcoholic spirits: *He's fond of a ~,* e g of whisky.

drama /ˈdrɑːmə/ n 1 [C] play for the theatre, radio or TV; [U] composition, presentation and performance of such plays: *a student of (the) ~; to be interested in (the) ~.* 2 [C,U] series of exciting or disturbing events.

dra·matic /drəˈmætɪk/ adj 1 of drama(1): *~ performances/criticism.* 2 sudden or exciting: *~ changes in the international situation.* 3 (of a person, his speech, behaviour) showing feelings or character in a lively way.
dra·mati·cally /-klɪ/ adv
dra·mat·ics, (a) dramatic works or performances: *Are you interested in amateur ~s?* (b) (informal) hysterical, excited behaviour.

dram·a·tist /ˈdræmətɪst/ n [C] writer of plays.

dram·a·tize /ˈdræmətaɪz/ vt 1 put a story, novel, etc into the form of a drama. 2 (informal) exaggerate, esp to cause excitement.
dram·a·tiz·ation /ˌdræmətaɪˈzeɪʃən US: -tɪˈz-/ n [C,U]

drank /dræŋk/ pt of drink².

drape /dreɪp/ vt 1 hang curtains, cloth, a cloak or other garment in folds round or over something: *to ~ curtains over a window; to ~ a flag over the coffin.* 2 **drape with,** cover or decorate: *walls ~d with flags.* 3

allow to rest loosely: *He ~d his legs over the arms of his chair.* □ *n* [C] (*US*) curtain.

dra·per /ˈdreɪpə(r)/ *n* (*GB*) shopkeeper who sells cloth, linen, clothing, etc.

dra·pery, (a) goods sold by a draper: *a ~y business/store.* **(b)** materials used for garments, curtains, etc.

dras·tic /ˈdræstɪk/ *adj* (of actions, methods, medicines) having a strong or violent effect: *~ measures to cure inflation/an illness.*

dras·ti·cally /-klɪ/ *adv*

draught (*US* = **draft**) /drɑːft *US*: dræft/ *n* **1** [C,U] current of air in a room, chimney or other enclosed place: *You'll catch cold if you sit in a ~.* **2** [C] the pulling in of a net of fish(es). **3** [U] depth of water needed to float a ship: *a ship with a ~ of ten feet.* **4** [U] drawing of liquid from a container (e g a barrel): *~ beer.* **5** (amount drunk during) one continuous process of swallowing: *a ~ of water.* **6** (of animals) used for pulling: *a `~-horse,* one that pulls heavy loads, **7** (*pl*) (*US* = **checkers**) board game for two players using twenty-four round pieces (called `*~s(men)*). □ *vt* = **draft²**.

draughts·man /ˈdrɑːftsmən *US*: `dræ-/, (a)** = draftsman. (b) ⇨ **7** above.

draughty (*US* = **drafty**) /ˈdrɑːftɪ *US*: `dræftɪ/ *adj* (-ier, -iest) with draughts(1) blowing through: *a ~ room.*

draw¹ /drɔː/ *n* [C] **1** the act of drawing (in various senses): *the ~ for the fourth round of the tennis tournament. The game ended in a ~,* neither side won. **2** person or thing that attracts attention: *Mr A is always a great ~ at political meetings,* is a popular speaker. ⇨ **draw²**(6). **3 be quick/slow on the draw,** quick/slow at pulling out a gun, etc.

draw² /drɔː/ *vt,vi* (*pt* **drew** /druː/, *pp* ~n /drɔːn/) (For uses with *adverbial particles* and *prepositions* ⇨ **17** below.) **1** move by pulling: *to ~ a boat* (*up*) *out of the water/on to the beach; to ~ one's chair up to the table; to ~ a person aside,* e g to speak to him quietly; *to ~ a curtain across a window. The fisherman drew in his net. When you shoot an arrow, you ~ the bow,* bend it by pulling the string. ⇨ **bow¹**(1). **2** (esp) move by pulling after or behind: *The wagon was being ~n by two horses.* ⇨ **draught**(6). **3** take or get out by pulling; extract: *to ~ a cork,* out of a bottle; *to ~ nails from a plank/a sword from its sheath; to ~ a chicken* (etc), remove the entrails before cooking it; *to ~ cards from a pack; to ~ for partners,* e g when about to play a card game, allow this to decide the question; *to ~ the winner,* get a ticket, etc at a lottery, on which there is a payment, prize, etc; *to ~ a gun* (*on* a person), take it from its holster, ready for use. **draw a blank,** find nothing. **draw lots,** ⇨ **lot²**(1). **4** (of gloves) pull *on/off.* **5** obtain from a source: *to ~ water from a well; to ~ beer from a barrel; to ~ one's salary; to ~ money from the bank/from*

one's account; *to ~ inspiration from nature What moral are we to ~ from this story?* **6** attract: *Street accidents always ~ crowds He drew* (= called) *my attention to a point I had overlooked.* **7** take in: *to ~ a deep breath.* **8** (of a chimney, etc) allow a current of air to flow through: *This chimney/cigar does not ~ well.* **9** cause, persuade, (a person) to talk, show his feelings, etc: *He was not to be ~n,* He refused to say anything about the matter. **10** (cause to) move; come (in the direction shown by the *adverb,* etc): *Christmas is ~ing near. The day drew to its close. The two ships drew level.* **11** make with a pen, pencil, chalk, etc; (*fig*) describe in words: *to ~ a picture/a straight line/a circle. The characters in Jane Austen's novels are well ~n.* **draw the line (at),** set limits; refuse to go as far as or beyond: *This noisy behaviour cannot be allowed; we must ~ the line somewhere.* **12** write out: *to ~ a bill/cheque/order* (*on* a banker, etc, *for* a sum of money). **13** (of a ship) require (a certain depth of water) in order to float, ⇨ **draught**(3): *The ship ~s 20 feet of water.* **14** end (a game, etc) without either winning or losing: *to ~ a football match. The teams drew.* **15** extract the essence of: *to let the tea ~ for three minutes.* **16** (usually in *pp*) (of the features) pull out of shape: *a face ~n with pain/anxiety.*

17 (uses with *adverbial particles* and *prepositions*):

draw away, go ahead of: *The horse quickly drew away from the others.*

draw back, (a) move away from: *He drew back in horror from the accident.* **(b)** (*fig*) show unwillingness: *~ back from a proposal.* ⇨ **drawback.**

draw in, (a) (of a particular day) reach its end. **(b)** (of daylight) become shorter: *the days begin to ~ in after midsummer.*

draw on, take or use as a source: *journalists sometimes ~ on their imaginations for stories. We mustn't ~ on our savings.*

draw out, (a) (of days) become longer: *After Christmas the days began to ~ out.* **(b)** persuade (a person) to talk, show feelings: *He has many interesting stories if you can ~ him out.* **(c)** (cause to) become longer: *a long-~-out discussion.*

draw up, (a) write out: *~ up a contract.* **(b)** (cause to) come near to: *The taxi drew up at the station.* **(c) draw oneself up,** stand up straight: *He drew himself up to his full height.*

draw·back /ˈdrɔːbæk/ *n* [C] something which lessens one's satisfaction, or makes progress less easy.

draw·bridge /ˈdrɔːbrɪdʒ/ *n* [C] bridge that can be pulled up at the end(s) by chains (e g across the moat of a castle, or across a river or canal to allow ships to pass).

drawer /drɔː(r)/ *n* [C] **1** box-like container (with a handle or handles) which slides in and out of a piece of furniture, etc. ⇨ **chest of drawers. 2** (*pl*) old-fashioned two-legged undergarment for the lower part of the body; knickers. **3** (usually /ˈdrɔːə(r)/) person who draws pictures, a cheque, etc.

draw·ing /ˈdrɔːɪŋ/ *n* [U] the art of representing objects, scenes, etc by lines, with a pencil, chalk, etc; [C] sketch, picture, plan, etc. `**drawing-board**, flat board on which to fasten paper for drawing: *still on the* ∼*board*, (*fig*) in the planning stage. `**drawing-pin**, flat-headed pin for fastening paper to a notice-board, etc.

draw·ing-room /ˈdrɔːɪŋ rʊm *US:* rʊm/ [C] room in which guests are received.

drawl /drɔːl/ *vi, vt* speak so that the sounds of the vowels are longer than usual: *The speaker* ∼*ed on.* □ *n* [U] slow way of speaking.

drawn /drɔːn/ *pp* of **draw²**. ⇨ esp **2, 9, 10** and **16**.

dread /dred/ *n* [U] (or with *a*) great fear and anxiety: *to live in constant* ∼ *of poverty. Cats have a* ∼ *of water.* □ *vt, vi* fear greatly: *to* ∼ *a visit to/*∼ *having to visit the dentist.*
dreaded *adj* greatly feared.
dread·ful /-fəl/ *adj* (**a**) causing anxiety: *a* ∼*ful disaster.* (**b**) (*informal*) very unpleasant: *What* ∼*ful weather!*
dread·fully /-fəlɪ/ *adv* (esp) (*informal*) extremely: *I'm* ∼*fully sorry!*

dream¹ /driːm/ *n* [C] **1** something which one seems to see or experience during sleep: *to have a* ∼ (*about …*); *to awake from a* ∼. **2** state of mind in which things going on around one seem unreal: *to live/go about in a* ∼. **3** mental picture(s) of the future: *to have* ∼*s of wealth and happiness.* **4** beautiful or pleasing person, thing, experience, etc: *His new car went like a* ∼. *She looked a perfect* ∼.
`**dream·land/·world**, region outside the laws of nature, as experienced in sleep or in the imagination.
dream·less *adj*
`**dream·like** *adj*

dream² /driːm/ *vi, vt* (*pt, pp* ∼**ed** or ∼**t** /dremt/) **1** have dreams; see, experience, in a dream; imagine; suppose: *The soldier often* ∼*t of/about home. I wouldn't* ∼ *of doing such a thing, The idea would never occur to me.* **2** ∼ *away one's time/the hours, etc,* pass one's time idly. **3** **dream sth up,** (*informal*) imagine, think up (a plan, etc).
dreamer, (a) person who dreams. (**b**) person with impractical ideas, plans, etc.

dreamy /ˈdriːmɪ/ *adj* (-ier, -iest) **1** (of a person) with thoughts far away from his surroundings or work. **2** (of things, experiences) vague; unreal: *a* ∼ *recollection of what happened.*
dream·ily /-əlɪ/ *adv*

dreary /ˈdrɪərɪ/ *adj* (-ier, -iest) dull; gloomy; causing depression: ∼ *work/*

weather.
drear·ily /-əlɪ/ *adv*

dredge¹ /dredʒ/ *n* [C] apparatus for bringing up mud, specimens, etc from the bed of the sea, rivers, etc. □ *vt, vi* bring up, clean, clear: *to* ∼ (*up*) *mud; to* ∼ *a channel/harbour.*
dredger, boat carrying a dredge.

dredge² /dredʒ/ *vt* sprinkle or scatter: *to* ∼ *sugar over a cake.*
dredger, box with holes in the lid for dredging sugar, etc on food.

dregs /dregz/ *n pl* **1** bits of worthless matter which sink to the bottom of a glass, bottle, barrel, etc of liquid. **2** (*fig*) worst or useless part: *the* ∼ *of society/humanity.*

drench /drentʃ/ *vt* make wet all over or all through: *to be* ∼*ed with rain/*∼*ed to the skin.*
drench·ing, thorough wetting: *We got a* ∼*ing.*

dress¹ /dres/ *n* **1** [C] one-piece outer garment with a top part and skirt worn by a woman or girl. **2** [U] clothing in general (for both men and women): *He doesn't care much about* ∼, is not much interested in clothes. ⇨ **evening dress.**
`**dress circle**, lowest gallery in a theatre.
`**dress coat**, black coat with long tails worn by men for evening dress.
`**dress-maker**, woman who makes dresses.
`**dress rehearsal**, final rehearsal of a play, at which actors wear the costumes to be worn at actual performances.

dress² /dres/ *vt, vi* **1** put on (clothes): *Mary was* ∼*ing her doll. Jim isn't old enough to* ∼ *himself. Have you finished* ∼*ing?* **dress up,** put on special clothes, as for a play, for fun, etc: *The children* ∼*ed* (*themselves*) *up as pirates.* **2** put on evening dress: *We don't* ∼ *for dinner nowadays.* **3** (of what is habitual) wear clothes: *He has to* ∼ *well in his position.* **be dressed in,** be wearing: *She was* ∼*ed in white.* **4** provide clothes for: *How much does it cost him to* ∼ *his wife and daughters?* **5** make ready to use; prepare: *to* ∼ *leather,* make it soft and smooth; *to* ∼ *a salad,* ⇨ **dressing(3). 6** brush and comb, arrange (one's) hair. **dress sb down,** (*fig*) scold him severely. Hence, '**dressing-`down** *n* **7** clean and bandage a wound, etc. **8** make cheerful and attractive: *to* ∼ *a shop-window/Christmas tree.*

dress·age /ˈdresɑːʒ/ *n* [U] (*Fr*) training of horses for show-jumping, etc.

dresser¹ /ˈdresə(r)/ *n* [C] **1** person who helps a surgeon to dress wounds in a hospital. **2** person who helps actors and actresses to dress ready for the stage.

dresser² /ˈdresə(r)/ *n* [C] **1** piece of kitchen furniture with shelves for dishes, and cupboards below, often with drawers for cutlery, etc. **2** (*US*) dressing-table.

dress·ing /ˈdresɪŋ/ *n* **1** [U] process of dressing (putting on clothes, cleaning and ban-

daging a wound, etc). **2** [C,U] something used for dressing wounds, e g an ointment, bandage, etc. **3** [C,U] mixture of oil, vinegar, etc used as a sauce for salads and other dishes.
`dressing-gown,` loose gown worn over pyjamas, etc.
`dressing-table,` one with a mirror, used in a bedroom.

drew /druː/ pt of draw².

dribble /ˈdrɪbəl/ vt,vi **1** (of liquids) flow, allow to flow, drop by drop or slowly (esp from the side of the mouth): Babies often ∼ on their bibs. **2** (in football) take (the ball) forward by means of quick, short kicks.
`drib-bler,` person who dribbles.

dried /draɪd/ pt,pp of dry².

drier /ˈdraɪə(r)/ adj ⟹ dry¹. □ n ⟹ dryer.

drift¹ /drɪft/ n **1** [U] drifting movement; being carried along by currents: the ∼ of the tide. **2** [C] something caused by drifting: Big ∼s of snow/ˈsnow ∼s made progress slow and difficult. **3** [U] general tendency or meaning: Did you get/catch the ∼ of the argument? **4** [U] the way in which events, etc tend to move: The general ∼ of affairs was towards war. **5** [U] the state of being inactive and waiting for things to happen: Is the government's policy one of ∼?
`drift-age` /-ɪdʒ/, (of a ship) general movement off course due to currents, winds, tides, etc.
`drift-ice,` broken ice carried along on the surface of the sea, etc by currents of water or air.
`drift-net,` large net into which fish drift with the tide.
`drift-wood,` wood carried along by currents and washed up on beaches.

drift² /drɪft/ vi,vt **1** be carried along by, or as by, a current of air or water: The boat ∼ed out to sea. **2** (fig) (of persons, etc) be without aim, purpose or self-control: Is the government/the country ∼ing towards bankruptcy? She ∼s from one job to another. **3** cause to drift: The logs were ∼ed down the stream to the saw-mills.
`drifter,` (a) boat used in drift-net fishing and, during war, for mine-sweeping. (b) person who drifts(2) or moves from place to place.

drill¹ /drɪl/ n [C] instrument that turns quickly for making holes in hard substances: a dentist's ∼. □ vt,vi make a hole with a drill.

drill² /drɪl/ n [C,U] **1** army training in the handling of weapons; formal movements, e g marching, turning, etc: The soldiers were at ∼ in the barrack square. **2** thorough training by practical experiences, usually with much repetition: ∼s in the English vowel sounds. **3** routine procedure to be followed, e g in an emergency: ˈfire-∼; ˈlife-boat ∼. □ vt,vi train, be trained, by means of drills: to ∼ troops.

drill³ /drɪl/ n [C] long channel where seeds are to be sown; machine for making these, sowing seeds in them, and covering the seeds; row of seeds sown in this way. □ vt sow (seeds) in drills.

drily /ˈdraɪli/ ⟹ dry¹.

drink¹ /drɪŋk/ n [C,U] **1** liquid for drinking: We have plenty of bottled ∼s, lemonade, beer, etc in bottles. **2** alcoholic liquor: He's too fond of ∼. **3** the ∼, (sl) the sea.

drink² /drɪŋk/ vt,vi (pt drank /dræŋk/, pp drunk /drʌŋk/) **1** take (liquid) into the mouth and swallow: to ∼ a pint of milk. D∼ (up) your coffee. **2** (of plants, the soil, etc) take in, absorb (liquid): The thirsty plants drank (up) the water I gave them. **3** take alcoholic liquors, beer, wine, etc, esp too much: He'll ∼ himself to death. **5** wish good (to a person) while raising one's glass: to ∼ a person's health; to ∼ to her success/ health.
`drink-able` /-əbəl/ adj suitable, fit, for drinking.
`drinker,` (esp) person who drinks(3) too often or too much: He's a heavy ∼er.
`drink-ing,` process or habit of taking liquid(s), esp alcoholic liquor: He's too fond of ∼ing.

drip /drɪp/ vi,vt (-pp-) (of a liquid) fall, allow to fall, in drops: The tap was ∼ping. His hand was ∼ping blood. `ˈdripping ˈwet,` very wet. □ n [C] **1** the drop-by-drop falling of a liquid: the ∼s of the rain. **2** (sl) dull, foolish person.
`ˈdrip-ˈdry` n [U] drying of shirts, sheets, etc (of special texture) by allowing them to drip until they are dry (so that they do not need to be ironed): (as an adjective) ∼-dry shirts. □ vt (pt,pp -ied) dry in this way.

drip-ping /ˈdrɪpɪŋ/ n **1** [U] (esp) fat from roasted meat. **2** (pl) liquid that drips or has dripped: the ∼s from the roof.

drive¹ /draɪv/ n **1** [C] journey (in a car, etc not in a public bus, etc): to go for a ∼. The station is an hour's ∼ away. **2** [C] (also `∼ way`) private road through a garden or park to a house; approach from a public road to a garage. **3** (in games played with a ball, e g golf) [U] force given to a ball when it is struck; [C] stroke or hit: a ∼ to the boundary. **4** [U] energy; capacity to get things done: The new headmaster is lacking in ∼. **5** motivation: the ˈsex-∼. **6** [C] organized effort or campaign: the ˈexport ∼, to increase exports. **7** [C] tournament: the ˈwhist-∼. **8** (mechanics) apparatus for driving: a four-wheel ∼, with four wheels connected to the source of power.

drive² /draɪv/ vt,vi (pt drove /drəʊv/, pp ∼n /ˈdrɪvən/) **1** cause animals, people to move in some direction by using cries, blows, threats or other means: to ∼ cattle to market. `drive sb into a corner,` (fig) force him (e g during an argument) into a position from which escape will be difficult. **2** operate, direct the course of a motor-car or other vehicle; control, direct the course of an animal or animals drawing a cart, plough, etc: *to ~ a taxi; to take driving lessons.* **3** travel or go in a car, carriage, etc: *Shall we ~ home or walk?* (*Note:* ride is used of buses, trains, etc.) **4** carry, convey, (a person) in a car, etc (not a public vehicle): *He drove me to the station.* **5** (of steam, electricity or other kind of power) set or keep going; be the power to operate: *The machinery is ~n by steam.* **6** (of wind, water) send, throw, (lifeless things) in some direction: *The gale drove the ship on to the rocks. The wind was driving the rain against the window-panes.* **7** go or move along fast or violently: *The ship drove on the rocks.* **8** force a nail, screw, etc into something: *With one blow he drove the nail into the plank.* **9** hit or strike with force: *to ~ a ball to the boundary.* **drive sth home,** (*fig*) use great force or effort to be believed or understood. **10** cause or force (a person) to be (in a certain state): *Failure drove him to despair/to drink. You'll ~ me mad.* **11** (cause to) work very hard: *He ~s himself very hard.* **12** bore (a tunnel); make (a horizontal excavation): *to ~ a tunnel through a hill.* **13** carry on: *to ~ a roaring trade,* sell a lot of things very fast. **drive a hard bargain,** not give way easily to another person in a business deal. **14** mean, intend: *What's he driving at,* What's he trying to do, explain, etc?.

drivel /ˈdrɪvəl/ *vt* (-ll-, *US* -l-) talk nonsense; talk childishly: *What's he ~ling (on) about?* □ *n* [U] silly nonsense; foolish talk.

drivel·ler, (*US*) **driveler,** person who drivels.

driven /ˈdrɪvən/ *pp* of drive².

driver /ˈdraɪvə(r)/ *n* [C] **1** person who drives (vehicles): *a ˈtaxi-~; a ˈbus-~.* ⇨ chauffeur. **2** person who drives animals. ⇨ drover.

drizzle /ˈdrɪzəl/ *vt* rain (in many small fine drops): *It ~d all day.* □ *n* [U] fine rain.

driz·zly /ˈdrɪzlɪ/ *adj* drizzling: *drizzly weather.*

drom·edary /ˈdrɑmədərɪ *US:* ˈdrɒmədərɪ/ *n* [C] (*pl*-ies) fast, one-humped camel.

drone /drəʊn/ *n* **1** [C] male bee. **2** [C] person who does no work and lives on others. **3** [U] low humming sound (as) made by bees: *the ~ of distant motorway traffic.* **4** [C] monotonous speech, sermon, speaker: *He's a boring old ~.* □ *vt, vi* **1** make a drone(3). **2** talk or sing in a low, boring way: *droning on about his misfortunes.*

drool /druːl/ *vi* be very excited, enthusiastic.

droop /druːp/ *vi, vt* **1** bend or hang downwards (through tiredness or weakness): *The flowers were ~ing for want of water. His spirits ~ed,* He became sad. **2** let (the head, face, eyes) move forward or down. □ *n* [C] bending position.

drop¹ /drɒp/ *n* **1** [C] very small quantity of liquid: *ˈrain~s.* **2** (*pl*) liquid medicine taken in drops: *ˈear/ˈeye/ˈnose ~s.* **3** very small quantity: *There isn't a ~ of milk left.* **a drop in the ocean,** a negligible or unimportant quantity. **4** (glass of) intoxicating liquor: *He has had a ~ too much,* is drunk. **5** something like a drop in shape or appearance. **6** movement from a higher to a lower level, esp distance of a fall: *a sudden ~ in the temperature,* e g from 30°C to 20°C; *a ~ in the price of meat.* **at the ˈdrop of a ˈhat, (a)** as soon as a signal is given. **(b)** at once; readily or willingly. **7** thing that drops or is dropped(1).

ˈdrop-kick, (in Rugby football) one in which the ball is dropped and kicked as it rises.

drop² /drɒp/ *vt, vi* (-pp-) (For uses with *adverbial particles* and *prepositions,* ⇨ **12** below.) **1** (of liquids), fall, cause to fall, in drops. ⇨ drip. **2** (allow to) fall (by the force of gravity, by not being held, etc): *The apple blossom is beginning to ~. She ~ped the teapot.* **drop anchor,** lower the anchor. **drop a stitch,** (in knitting) let it slip off the needle. **3** (allow to) become weaker or lower: *The wind/temperature has ~ped. His voice ~ped/He ~ped his voice to a whisper.* **4** (cause to) fall or sink to the ground, etc: *They were ready to ~ with fatigue. He ~ped (on) to his knees,* knelt down. **6** omit; *Supplies were ~ped by parachute.* **5** express; send casually: *to ~ him a hint,* give him one; *to ~ a word in her ear; to ~ her a postcard/a few lines/a short note.* **6** omit; fail to pronounce, write or insert: *He ~s his h's,* e g by saying 'at for hat. **7** stop (a car, etc) to allow a person to get out: *Please ~ me at the post office.* **8** stop associating with: *He seems to have ~ped most of his friends,* no longer meets them. **9** give up: *to ~ a bad habit.* **10** (cause to) come to an end; no longer deal with or discuss: *Let's ~ the subject.* **11** (in Rugby football) *~ a goal,* score one by a drop-kick.

12 (uses with *adverbial particles* and *prepositions*):

drop away, = drop off (a).

drop back/behind, come to a position behind: *They ~ped behind the rest of the party.*

drop in (on sb); drop by, pay a casual visit to: *Some friends ~ped in to tea/~ped by to see me.*

drop off, (a) (also *~ away*) become fewer or less: *The doctor's practice has ~ped off,* He now has fewer patients. **(b)** fall asleep: *He ~ped off during the sermon.*

drop out, (a) (of persons, horses, etc taking part in a contest, etc) cease to compete: *Three of the runners ~ped out.* **(b)** (of persons doing, or about to do, something) not take part; give up the idea: *Smith has ~ped out of the team.* **(c)** withdraw from conventional social activities, attitudes. Hence, `drop-out, (a)` person who drops out, e g one who withdraws from a course of instruction: *the ~-out rate in a language course.* (b) person who deliberately lives in an unconventional style.

drop-pings /dropiŋz/ *n pl* dung of animals.

drought /draʊt/ *n* [C,U] continuous (period of) dry weather causing distress.

drove[1] /drəʊv/ *pt* of drive[2].

drove[2] /drəʊv/ *n* [C] 1 large number of animals (sheep, cattle) being driven together 2 crowd of people moving together: *~s of sightseers; visitors in ~s.*

drover, man who drives cattle, sheep, etc to market.

drown /draʊn/ *vt,vi* 1 (cause a person to) die in water because unable to breathe: *a ~ing man. He ~ed the kittens.* 2 *(fig)* drenched: *~ed in tears.* 3 (of sound) be strong enough to prevent another sound from being heard: *The noises in the street ~ed the teacher's voice. be drowned out, (a)* be flooded out. (b) *(fig)* be stopped from being heard.

drowse /draʊz/ *vi,vt* be half asleep: *drowsing away a hot afternoon.* □ *n* sleepy condition: *in a ~.*

drowsy /ˈdraʊzɪ/ *adj* (-ier, -iest) feeling sleepy; making one feel sleepy.

drows-ily /-əlɪ/ *adv*

drow-si-ness *n* [U]

drudge /drʌdʒ/ *n* [C] person who must work hard and long at unpleasant tasks. □ *vi* work as a drudge does.

drudg-ery, hard, unpleasant, uninteresting work.

drug /drʌg/ *n* [C] 1 substance used for medical purposes, either alone or in a mixture. 2 substance that changes the state or function of cells, organs or organisms. 3 substance (often habit-forming) inducing sleep or producing stupor or insensibility, e g opium: *a ~ addict; ~ addiction.* □ *vt* (-gg-) 1 add harmful drugs to (food and drink): *His wine had been ~ged.* 2 give drugs to, esp in order to make unconscious: *They ~ged the caretaker and then robbed the bank.*

`drug-store, (US)` place where a wide variety of articles is sold, where prescriptions can be made up, and where food and drink may be bought and eaten.

drug-gist /ˈdrʌgɪst/ *n* [C] 1 *(GB)* tradesman who sells drugs. 2 *(US)* person who sells medicines, toilet articles and other goods, and usually food and drinks. ⇨ drug-store.

drum[1] /drʌm/ *n* [C] 1 musical instrument made of a hollow cylinder or hemisphere with parchment stretched over the open side(s); sound (as) of a drum or drums. 2 thing shaped like a drum, e g a container for oil. ⇨ also eardrum.

`drum-stick, (a)` stick for beating a drum. (b) lower part of the leg of a cooked chicken, turkey, etc.

drum[2] /drʌm/ *vt,vi* (-mm-) 1 play a drum.

2 beat or tap continuously on something: *to ~ on the table with one's fingers.* 3 *(fig)* encourage support for a cause. 4 cause a person to remember something by using repetition: *~ the spelling into his head.*

drum-mer, person who plays a drum.

drunk /drʌŋk/ *adj* (*pp* of drink[2]) *be drunk,* be overcome by drinking alcoholic liquor: *He was ˈdead/ˈblind/ˈhalf ˈ~. get drunk,* (a) become intoxicated: *It's easy to get ~ on brandy.* (b) *(fig)* become greatly excited: *He was ~ with joy/success.* □ *n* [C] person who is drunk.

drunken /ˈdrʌŋkən/ *adj* 1 in the habit of drinking; often drunk: *a ~ and destitute man.* 2 caused by drinking; showing the effects of drinking: *a ~ fight.*

drunken-ly *adv*

drunken-ness *n*

dry[1] /draɪ/ *adj* (-ier, -iest) 1 not wet; free from moisture: *Is this wood ~ enough to burn?* `dry as a ˈbone;` `ˈbone-ˈdry,` quite dry. 2 not rainy: *~ weather;* having a small rainfall: *a ~ climate.* 3 not supplying water: *a ~ well;* not supplying milk: *The cows are ~.* 4 solid, not liquid: *~ goods* (contrasted with *meat, groceries,* etc). 5 without butter, etc: *~ bread/toast.* 6 (of drink) not sweet, not fruity in flavour: *~ wines.* 7 *(informal)* thirsty; causing thirst: *to feel ~.* 8 uninteresting; dull: *a ~ lecture.* 9 plain; undisguised: *~ facts.* 10 not connected with liquid: *a ~ cough.* 11 (of a State, country, its legislation) prohibiting or restricting the sale of alcoholic liquor: *Will the country go ~,* Will it pass and accept legislation of this kind?

`dry-ˈclean` *vt* clean (clothes, etc) by using spirits (e g petrol) instead of water. Hence `dry-ˈcleaners,` `dry-ˈcleaning.`

`dry ˈdock,` one from which water can be pumped out.

`dry ˈrot,` decay of wood (causing it to crumble to powder), occurring when there is no movement of air over its surface.

drily /ˈdraɪlɪ/ *adv*

dry-ness *n* [U]

dry[2] /draɪ/ *vt,vi* (*pt,pp* dried) 1 make or become dry: *~ your hands on this towel. The stream dries up during the hot summer.* 2 (usually the *pp*) preserve by extracting moisture: *dried eggs/milk.* 3 *(fig)* Come to an end: *My thoughts have dried up. I've dried up,* have no more ideas.

dryer, drier /ˈdraɪə(r)/ *n* 1 [C] thing that dries: *a ˈhair-~; a ˈspin-~.* 2 thing on or in which clothes, etc are placed to dry: *a ˈclothes-~.*

dual /ˈdjuːəl *US:* ˈduːəl/ *adj* of two; double; divided in two: *~ ownership;* `ˈ~-ˈpurpose,` adapted so as to, intended to, serve two purposes.

`dual ˈcarriageway,` road divided down the centre (by a barrier, strip of grass) with two lanes in each direction.

dub /dʌb/ vt (-bb-) **1** make (a person) a knight by touching him on the shoulder with a sword. **2** give (a person) a petname: *They ~bed him 'Shorty' because he was so tall.* **3** replace or add to the sound-track of a film or magnetic tape, esp in a different language.

du·bi·ous /ˈdjuːbɪəs US: ˈduː-/ adj **1** (of persons) feeling doubt: *I feel ~ of/about his honesty.* **2** (of persons) causing doubt (because probably not very good or reliable): *He's a ~ character.* **3** (of things, actions, etc) causing doubt; of which the value, truth, etc is doubtful: *a ~ compliment.*
du·bi·ous·ly adv
du·bi·ous·ness n [U]

duch·ess /ˈdʌtʃɪs/ n [C] wife or widow of a duke; woman whose rank is equal to that of a duke.

duchy /ˈdʌtʃɪ/ n [C] (pl -ies) (also *dukedom*) land ruled by a duke or duchess.

duck¹ /dʌk/ n (pl ~s, but often unchanged when collective) **1** [C] common water-bird, both wild and domestic; female of this, ⇨ drake; [U] its flesh as food. *(take to sth) like a duck to water,* naturally, without fear, hesitation or difficulty. *like water off a duck's back,* without producing any effect. **2** batsman's score of nought, 0, in cricket: *to be out for a ~.*
ˈlame ˈduck, ⇨ lame.

duck² /dʌk/ vt,vi **1** move quickly down (to avoid being seen or hit): *to ~ one's head.* **2** go, push (a person), quickly under water for a short time: *The big boy ~ed all the small boys in the swimming-pool.* □ n [C] quick downward or sideways movement of the head or body; quick dip below water (when bathing in the sea, etc).
duck·ing, thorough wetting.

duck-billed platypus /ˈdʌkbɪld ˈplætɪpəs/ n [C] small Australian egg-laying water mammal with webbed feet and a beak like a duck.

duck·ling /ˈdʌklɪŋ/ n [C] **1** young duck. **2** *ugly ~ling,* plain or stupid child who grows up to be attractive or brilliant.

duct /dʌkt/ n [C] **1** tube or canal through which liquid in the body flows. **2** metal tube and outlet for air (e g in an aircraft): *The air ~s above your seat may be adjusted to your convenience.*

dud /dʌd/ n [C], adj (sl) (thing or person) of no use, e g a shell or bomb that fails to explode or a banknote or cheque of no value.

due¹ /djuː US: duː/ adj **1** owing; to be paid: *When is the rent ~? The wages ~ to him will be paid tomorrow.* **2** suitable; right; proper: *after ~ consideration.* **in due course,** at the right and proper time. **3** (to be) expected; appointed or agreed (for a certain time or date): *The train is ~ (in) at 1.30.* **4** *due to,* that may be attributed to: *The accident was ~ to careless driving.* (*Note:* compare 'owing to': *Owing to* (= Because of) *his careless driving, we had a*

bad accident.) □ adv (of points of the compass) exactly: *~ east/north.*

due² /djuː US: duː/ n **1** (*sing* only) that which must be given to a person because it is right or owing: *give the man his ~.* **2** (*pl*) sums of money to be paid, e g for membership of a club; legal charges paid by ship-owners for the use of a harbour, etc.

duel /ˈdjuːəl US: ˈduːəl/ n [C] **1** (illegal) fight (usually with swords or pistols) agreed between two persons, esp to decide a point of honour, at a meeting arranged and conducted according to rules, in the presence of two other persons called *seconds*. **2** any two-sided contest: *a ~ of wits.* □ vi (-ll-, US also -l-) fight a duel.
duel·list, (*US*) **duel·ist,** person who fights a duel.

duet /djuːˈet US: duː-/ n [C] piece of music for two voices or for two players.

duffle (also **duf·fel**) /ˈdʌfəl/ n [U] coarse thick woollen cloth: *a ~ coat,* one of this material, with toggles instead of buttons.

dug¹ /dʌg/ pt,pp of dig.

dug² /dʌg/ n [C] udder or teat of a female mammal.

dug-out /ˈdʌg aʊt/ n [C] **1** rough covered shelter made by digging, esp by soldiers for protection in war. **2** canoe made by hollowing a tree trunk.

duke /djuːk US: duːk/ n [C] **1** nobleman of high rank (next below a prince). **2** (in some parts of Europe) independent sovereign ruler of a small State.
ˈduke·dom, (a) position, duties, rank of a duke. (b) (= *duchy*) land ruled by a duke(2).

dul·cet /ˈdʌlsɪt/ adj (of sounds) sweet; pleasing.

dull /dʌl/ adj (-er, -est) **1** not clear or bright: *a ~ colour/sound/mirror/day/sky; ~ weather.* **2** slow in understanding: *~ pupils; a ~ mind.* **3** monotonous; not exciting or appealing: *a ~ book/speech/ sermon/play.* **4** not sharp: *a ~ knife.* **5** (of pain) not felt distinctly: *a ~ ache.* **6** (of trade) not active; (of goods) not in demand. □ vt,vi make or become dull: *to ~ the edge of a razor; drugs that ~ pain.*
dull·ness n [U]

duly /ˈdjuːlɪ US: ˈduː-/ adv in a right or suitable manner; at the right time.

dumb /dʌm/ adj (-er, -est) **1** unable to speak: *~ from birth; ~ animals,* animals other than human beings. **2** temporarily silent: *The class remained ~ when the teacher asked a difficult question.* **strike dumb,** make unable to talk because of surprise, fear, etc: *He was struck ~ with horror.* **3** (*informal*) stupid; dull.
dumb·ly adv
dumb·ness n [U]

dumb·bell /ˈdʌmbel/ n [C] short bar of wood or iron with a metal ball at each end for exercising the muscles of the arms and shoulders.

dumb·found (*US* also **dum·found**) /dʌm'faʊnd/ *vt* astonish; strike dumb with surprise.

dummy /'dʌmɪ/ *n* [C] (*pl* -ies) **1** object made to look like and serve the purpose of the real person or thing: *a tailor's* ~, for fitting clothes; *a baby's* ~, sucked like the nipple of a mother's breast. **2** (in card games, esp bridge) player whose cards are placed upwards on the table and played by his partner; the cards so placed. **3** person who is present at an event, etc but who takes no real part, because he is acting for another person.

'dummy 'run, trial or practice attack, shoot, performance, etc.

dump /dʌmp/ *n* [C] **1** place where rubbish, etc may be unloaded and left; heap of rubbish, etc. **2** (place where there is a) temporary store of military supplies: *an* 'ammu'nition ~. **3** (*sl*) poorly cared for, dirty or ugly place (e g a village or town): *I should hate to live in a* ~ *like this*. □ *vt* **1** put on or into a dump(1); put or throw down carelessly; let fall with a bump or thud: *Where can I* ~ *this rubbish? They* ~*ed the coal outside the shed instead of putting it inside*. **2** (*commerce*) sell abroad at low prices goods which are unwanted in the home market.

dumper, (also '~ **truck**) vehicle with a bin that can be tilted, for carrying and emptying soil, rubble, etc (e g for road building).

dump·ling /'dʌmplɪŋ/ *n* [C] **1** small round mass of dough steamed or boiled with meat and vegetables. **2** baked pudding made of dough with an apple or other fruit inside it.

dumps /dʌmps/ *n pl* (**down**) **in the dumps**, (*informal*) depressed; feeling gloomy.

dumpy /'dʌmpɪ/ *adj* (-ier, -iest) short and fat.

dunce /dʌns/ *n* [C] slow learner (esp a child at school); stupid person.

'dunce's cap, pointed cap formerly given to wear in class as a punishment.

dune /djun/ *US:* dun/ *n* [C] low stretch of loose, dry sand formed by the wind, esp near the coast.

dung /dʌŋ/ *n* [U] waste matter dropped by animals (esp cattle), used as manure.

dunga·rees /'dʌŋgə'riz/ *n pl* **1** overalls or trousers (usually) of coarse cotton. **2** similar garment worn by babies.

dun·geon /'dʌndʒən/ *n* [C] dark underground cell used (in olden times) as a prison.

duo·denal /'djuə'dinəl *US:* 'duə-/ *adj* of the duodenum: *a* ~ *ulcer*.

duo·denum /'djuə'dinəm *US:* 'duə-/ *n* [C] (*pl* ~s) first part of the small intestine immediately below the stomach.

duo·logue /'djuəlog *US:* 'duələg/ *n* [C] conversation between two persons.

dupe /djup *US:* dup/ *vt* cheat; make a fool of. □ *n* [C] person who is duped.

du·pli·cate[1] /'djuplɪkət *US:* 'du-/ *adj* **1** exactly like: ~ *keys*. **2** with two corresponding parts; doubled; twofold. □ *n* [C] thing that is exactly like another. **in duplicate,** (of documents, etc) with a copy.

du·pli·cate[2] /'djuplɪkeɪt *US:* 'du-/ *vt* **1** make an exact copy of (a letter, etc); produce copies of. **2** multiply by two.

du·pli·ca·tion /'djuplɪ'keɪʃən *US:* 'du-/ *n* [U] duplicating or being duplicated; [C] copy.

du·pli·ca·tor /-tə(r)/, machine, etc that copies something written or typed.

du·plic·ity /dju'plɪsətɪ *US:* du-/ *n* [U] (*formal*) deliberate deception.

dur·able /'djʊərəbəl *US:* 'dʊə-/ *adj* likely to last for a long time: *a* ~ *pair of shoes*. □ *n pl* goods bought and expected to last a long time (e g vacuum cleaners).

dura·bil·ity /'djʊərə'bɪlətɪ *US:* 'dʊə-/ *n* [U]

dur·ation /dju'reɪʃən *US:* dʊ-/ *n* [U] time during which something lasts or exists: *for the* ~ *of the war; of short* ~.

dur·ess (also **-esse**) /djʊ'res *US:* dʊ-/ *n* [U] threats, imprisonment, or violence, used to compel a person to do something: *signed under* ~.

dur·ing /'djʊərɪŋ *US:* 'dʊə-/ *prep* **1** throughout the continuance of: *The sun gives us light* ~ *the day*. **2** at some point of time in the continuance of: *He called to see me* ~ *my absence*.

dusk /dʌsk/ *n* [U] time just before it is dark.

dusky /'dʌskɪ/ *adj* (-ier, -iest) rather dark; dark-coloured; dim.

dust[1] /dʌst/ *n* [U] dry earth or other matter in the form of fine powder, lying on the ground or the surface of objects, or blown about by the wind: *The* ~ *was blowing in the streets*.

'dust-bin, receptacle for household rubbish.

'dust-bowl, area that has no vegetation because of drought, unwise farming methods, etc.

'dust-cart, cart into which dustbins are emptied.

'dust-jacket/wrapper, removable paper cover to protect the binding of a book.

'dust-man, man employed (by city authorities, etc) to empty dustbins and take away refuse.

'dust-pan, pan into which dust is swept from the floor.

dust-sheet, one for covering furniture not in use.

dust[2] /dʌst/ *vt* **1** remove dust from by wiping, brushing, etc. **2** sprinkle with powder: *to* ~ *a cake with sugar*.

duster, cloth for removing dust from furniture, etc.

'dust-up, (*informal*) fight; noisy argument.

dusty /'dʌstɪ/ *adj* (-ier, -iest) covered with dust; full of dust; like dust; dry as dust.

Dutch /dʌtʃ/ *adj* **go Dutch (with sb)**, share expenses. ⇨ **double Dutch**.

Dutch auction, sale at which the price is reduced by the auctioneer until a buyer is found.

Dutch courage, that obtained by drinking (spirits, etc).

Dutch·man, native of Holland.

duti·able /ˈdjuːtɪəbəl *US:* ˈduː-/ *adj* on which customs duties must be paid: ~ *goods.* ⇨ duty(3).

duti·ful /ˈdjuːtɪfʊl *US:* ˈduː-/ *adj* doing one's duty well; showing respect and obedience (to): *a* ~ *son.*

duti·fully /-fəlɪ/ *adv*

duty /ˈdjuːtɪ *US:* ˈduːtɪ/ *n* (*pl* -ies) **1** [C,U] what one is obliged to do by morality, law, a trade, calling, conscience, etc: *Do not forget your* ~ *to your parents. His sense of* ~ *is strong.* **on/off duty,** engaged/not engaged in one's regular work: *He goes on* ~ *at 8 a m and comes off* ~ *at 5 p m.* **2** (as an *adjective*) moral obligation: *a* ˈ~ *call,* a visit one makes from a sense of duty, not because one expects to enjoy it. **3** [C,U] payment demanded by the government *on* certain goods exported or imported (ˈcustoms *duties*), or manufactured in the country (ˈexcise *duties*), or when property, etc is transferred to a new owner by sale (ˈstamp *duties*) or death (*e*ˈstate ~).

ˈduty-ˈfree, (of goods) allowed to enter without the payment of customs duties.

duvet /ˈdjuːveɪ *US:* duːˈveɪ/ *n* [C] bed quilt (filled with feathers or an artificial substitute) used in place of blankets.

dwarf /dwɔːf/ *n* [C] (*pl* ~s) **1** person, animal or plant much below the usual size. **2** (in fairy tales) small being with magic powers. □ *vt* **1** prevent from growing to full size. **2** cause to appear small by contrast or distance: *The big steamer* ~*ed our little launch.*

dwell /dwel/ *vt* (*pt* dwelt /dwelt/) **1** live, have as one's home. **2** think, speak or write at length about: *She* ~*s too much on her past.*

dwel·ler, (in compounds) inhabitant: ˈcity-~*ers.*

dwel·ling, place of residence (a house, flat, etc).

dwindle /ˈdwɪndəl/ *vt* become less or smaller by degrees.

dye¹ /daɪ/ *vt,vi* (3rd person sing, present tense, ~s, *pt,pp* ~d, present participle ~ing) **1** colour, usually by dipping in a liquid: *to* ~ *a white dress blue; to have a dress* ~*d.* **2** give colour to: *Deep blushes* ~*d her cheeks.* **3** take colour from dyeing: *This material does not* ~ *well.*

ˈdyed-in-the-ˈwool, (*fig*) complete, deep-rooted: *a* ~*d-in-the-wool Tory.*

dye² /daɪ/ *n* [C,U] substance used for dyeing cloth; colour given by dyeing.

dyer, person who dyes cloth.

dy·ing ⇨ die².

dyke ⇨ dike.

dy·namic /daɪˈnæmɪk/ *adj* **1** of physical power and forces producing motion. ⇨

static. **2** (of a person) having great energy, force of character. □ *n* **1** (*pl*) (used with a *sing verb*) branch of physics dealing with matter in motion. **2** moral force that produces activity or change: *driven by an inner* ~.

dy·nami·cally /-klɪ/ *adv*

dyna·mite /ˈdaɪnəmaɪt/ *n* [U] powerful explosive (as used in mining and quarrying). □ *vt* blow up with dynamite.

dy·namo /ˈdaɪnəməʊ/ *n* [C] (*pl* ~s) machine for changing steam-power, water-power, etc into electrical energy.

dyn·astic /dɪˈnæstɪk *US:* daɪ-/ *adj* of a dynasty.

dyn·asty /ˈdɪnəstɪ *US:* ˈdaɪ-/ *n* [C] (*pl*-ies) succession of rulers belonging to one family: *the Tudor* ~*y* (in England).

dys·en·tery /ˈdɪsəntrɪ *US:* -terɪ/ *n* [U] painful disease of the bowels, with discharge of mucus and blood.

dys·pep·sia /dɪsˈpepsɪə/ *n* [U] indigestion (the usual word).

dys·pep·tic /dɪsˈpeptɪk/ *adj* of indigestion. □ *n* [C] person suffering from indigestion.

Ee

E, e /iː/ (*pl* E's, e's /iz/), fifth letter of the English alphabet.

each /iːtʃ/ *adj* (of two or more) every one, thing, group, person, etc taken separately or individually: *He was sitting with a child on* ~ *side of him.* □ *pron* **1** every thing, person, group, etc: *E*~ *of them wants to try.* **2** all; both: *We* ~ *took a big risk. Tom, Dick and Harry* ~ *put forward a different scheme.* **3** to, for, every one of a group: *He gave the boys 50p* ~. **4 each other.** *We see* ~ *other* (= each of us sees the other) *at the office every day.* (*Note: one another* is often used when referring to more than one.)

eager /ˈiːgə(r)/ *adj* full of, showing, strong desire: ~ *for success/to succeed.*

eager·ly *adv*

eager·ness *n* [U]

eagle /ˈiːgəl/ *n* [C] **1** large, strong bird of prey of the falcon family with keen sight. **2** score in golf that is two below the number of strokes allowed as the average for the hole (except where the number allowed is three).

eag·let, young eagle(1).

ear¹ /ɪə(r)/ *n* [C] **1** organ of hearing. *be all ears,* be listening eagerly. *fall on deaf ears,* pass unnoticed; be ignored. *go in (at) one ear and out (at) the other,* said of something that makes no impression. *have an ear to the ground,* be well informed about what is or may be happening. *in secret. (have) a word in sb's ear,* say something in confidence. *lend an ear (to),* listen. *turn a deaf ear (to),* refuse to listen or help. *up to one's ears in work,* extremely busy. *walls have ears,* someone may be listening. *wet behind the ears,* naïve; immature. **2** sense of hearing. *have a good ear for music,* be able to discriminate sound. *(play sth) by ear,* (a) (play) without printed music, or without having memorized it. (b) *(fig)* do something without planning or preparing in advance.

`ear·ache, pain in the inner ear.

`ear·drum, thin membrane (in the inner ear) which vibrates when sound-waves strike it.

`ear·mark *vt (fig)* set aside for a special purpose: ~*mark a sum of money for research.*

`ear·ring, ornament worn in or on the lobe of the ear.

`ear·shot, hearing distance: *within/out of ~shot.*

-eared /ɪəd/ *prefix:* 'long-`eared, having long ears.

ear² /ɪə(r)/ *n* [C] seed-bearing part of corn, barley, etc.

earl /ɜːl/ *n* [C] title of a British nobleman of high rank (feminine = *countess*).

`earl·dom /-dəm/, rank, lands, of an earl.

early /ˈɜːlɪ/ (-ier, -iest) *adj, adv* near to the beginning of a period of time, sooner than usual or than others: *in the ~ part of this century; in ~ spring;* '~-`closing day, on which shops, etc are closed during the afternoon. *He's an ~ riser,* gets up early. *earlier on,* at an earlier time. ⇨ *later on* at late²(1).

early bird, person who gets up earlier or who arrives before others.

'early-`warning *adj* (of radar) giving early indication of the approach of enemy aircraft, missiles, etc: *an ~-warning system.*

earn /ɜːn/ *vt* get in return for work, as a reward for one's qualities or in payment for a loan: *to ~ £3000 a year. His achievements ~ed him respect and admiration. I had a* `well-~ed *rest.*

earn·ings *n pl* money earned: *He has spent all his ~ings.*

ear·nest /ˈɜːnɪst/ *adj* serious; determined: *an ~ worker/pupil.* □ *n in earnest,* in a determined manner; serious(ly): *I'm perfectly in ~,* am not joking.

earn·est·ly *adv* in an earnest manner: *We ~ly hope that...*

earn·est·ness *n* [U]

earth /ɜːθ/ *n* **1** this world; the planet on which we live: *The ~ goes round the sun. Who do you think was the greatest man on ~?* **2** [U] land surface of the world; land contrasted with the sky. *come down/back to earth,* return to practical realities. *move heaven and earth (to do sth),* make every possible effort. **3** [U] soil: *to cover the roots of a plant with ~.* **4** [C] hole of a fox, badger or other wild animal. *run sth/sb to earth,* (fig) discover by searching. **5** [C,U] (means of) electrical contact with the ground as the

completion of a circuit. □ *vt* **1** cover with earth: *to ~ up the roots of a newly-planted shrub.* **2** connect (an apparatus, etc) with the earth(5).

earth·ling, inhabitant of earth; mortal.

earth satellite, one which orbits the earth.

`earth·worm, common kind of worm that lives in the soil.

earthy *adj* (-ier, -iest) (a) of or like soil: *an ~y smell.* (b) *(fig)* coarse, unrefined; strong and healthy.

earthen·ware /ˈɜːθənweə(r)/ *n* [U] dish, etc made of baked clay: *an ~ casserole.*

earth·ly /ˈɜːθlɪ/ *adj* **1** of this world, not of heaven: *~ joys/possessions.* **2** *(informal)* possible; conceivable: *You haven't an ~ (chance),* no chance at all. *no earthly use,* quite useless, pointless.

earth·quake /ˈɜːθkweɪk/ *n* [C] sudden, violent movements of the earth's surface.

ear·wig /ˈɪəwɪg/ *n* [C] small insect with pincers at the rear end.

ease¹ /iːz/ *n* [U] freedom from work, discomfort, trouble, difficulty, anxiety: *a life of ~; to do something with ~,* without difficulty. *(be/feel) ill at ease,* anxious or embarrassed. *stand at ease,* (as a military command) with the legs apart and the hands behind the back.

ease² /iːz/ *vt, vi* **1** give relief to (the body or mind) from pain, discomfort, anxiety: *~ his anxiety; ~ him of his pain/trouble.* **2** make looser, less tight; lessen speed, efforts: *~ a coat under the armpits. E~ off a bit (= slow down), we're going too fast.* **3** become less tense or troublesome: *the easing of tension between the two countries. The situation has ~d (off).*

easel /ˈiːzl/ *n* [C] wooden frame to support a blackboard or a picture (while the artist is working at it).

east /iːst/ *n* **1** the ~, point of the horizon where the sun rises. **2** that part of a country, the world, etc in this direction: *living in the ~ of France.* **3** (as an *adjective*): *an ~ wind,* one blowing from the east; towards, at, in the direction of the east: *on the ~ coast.* □ *adv* towards the east: *to travel/face ~. east of,* farther east than. ⇨ also the Far East, Middle East, Near East.

the East, (a) the Orient. (b) the eastern side of the USA.

the 'East `End, the eastern part of London.

east·ward /ˈiːstwəd/ *adj* towards the east: *in an ~ direction.*

east·ward(s) *adv:* *to travel ~(s).*

Easter /ˈiːstə(r)/ *n* anniversary of the Resurrection of Christ, observed on the first Sunday (~ Day/Sunday) after a full moon on or after 21 Mar: *the ~ holidays.*

`Easter egg, egg with a painted or dyed shell, or an egg made of chocolate, used as a gift.

east·er·ly /ˈiːstəlɪ/ *adj, adv* in an eastern direction of position; (of the wind) coming from the east.

east·ern /ˈistən/ adj of, from, living in, the east part of the world: ~ religions.

the Eastern Church, the Greek Orthodox Church.

the Eastern Hemisphere, part of the world, east of London.

Eastern time, one of 4 standard time zones in USA.

east·ern·most /-məʊst/ adj farthest east.

easy /ˈizɪ/ (-ier, -iest) adj 1 not difficult: an ~ book. The place is ~ to reach. 2 free, from pain, discomfort, anxiety, trouble, etc: to lead an ~ life; an ~ chair, one that is soft and restful. She is ~ to get on with, relaxed, informal, pleasant. □ adv in an easy manner. **take it/things easy,** don't work too hard or too energetically. **go easy on,** (informal) be careful or moderate with: Go ~ on the wine—it's the last bottle! **Easier said than done,** It is easier to say one will do it than to do it.

'easy-'going, (of persons) pleasant; tolerant; casual.

eas·ily /ˈizəlɪ/ adv 1 with ease. 2 without doubt: ~ the best T V programme. 3 possibly: That may ~ be the case.

eat /it/ vt,vi (pt ate /et, eɪt/ pp ~en /ˈitən/) 1 take (solid food, also soup) into the mouth and swallow it: to ~ one's dinner; to ~ up (= finish eating) one's food. **eat one's heart out,** suffer in silence; be very sad. **eat one's words,** say in a humble way that one was wrong. 2 destroy as if by eating: Acids ~ into metals. He is ~en up with pride. The river had ~en away the banks.

eat·able /-əbəl/ adj edible (the usual word). □ n (usually pl) food.

eater, (a) person who eats: He's a big ~er, eats large quantities. (b) apple, pear, etc for dessert, good when eaten uncooked.

eats n pl (sl) food: There were plenty of ~, but not enough drinks.

eau de Cologne /ˈəʊ də kəˈləʊn/ n [U] (Fr) perfumed toilet water.

eaves /ivz/ n pl overhanging edges of a roof: icicles hanging from the ~.

'eaves·drop vi (-pp-) listen secretly to private conversation.

'eaves·drop·per, person who eavesdrops.

ebb /eb/ vi 1 (of the tide) flow back from the land to the sea. 2 (fig) grow less; become weak or faint: His fortune's beginning to ~. □ n [C] (usually sing only) 1 the flowing out of the tide: the ~ and flow of the sea/the tide. 2 (fig) low state; decline or decay: at a low ~.

'ebb-'tide n = ebb.

eb·ony /ˈebənɪ/ n [U] hard, black wood. □ adj made of, black as, ebony.

ebul·lience /ɪˈbʌlɪəns/ n [U] (formal) (outburst of) excitement, enthusiasm.

ebul·lient /ɪˈbʌlɪənt/ adj (formal) very excited, enthusiastic.

ec·cen·tric /ɪkˈsentrɪk/ adj 1 (of a person,

his behaviour) odd; not normal. 2 (of circles) not having the same centre; (of orbits) not circular; (of planets, etc) moving in an eccentric orbit. □ n [C] (esp) eccentric person.

ec·cen·tric·ity /ˌeksənˈtrɪsətɪ/ n (pl -ies) 1 [U] quality of being eccentric; strangeness of behaviour, etc: ~ in dress. 2 [C] instance of this; strange or unusual act or habit: One of his eccentricities is wearing bright red socks with his black suit.

ec·clesi·as·tic /ɪˌklizɪˈæstɪk/ n [C] clergyman.

ec·clesi·as·ti·cal /-kəl/ adj of the Christian Church; of clergymen.

ec·clesi·as·ti·cally -klɪ/ adv

eche·lon /ˈeʃəlɒn/ n [C] formation of troops, aircraft, ships, etc in lines to the side of the one in front, like steps: flying in ~.

echo[1] /ˈekəʊ/ n (pl ~es) 1 [C,U] sound reflected or sent back (e g from a wall of rock).

echo[2] /ˈekəʊ/ vi,vt 1 (of places) send back an echo: The valley ~ed as he sang. 2 (of sounds) be sent back as an echo: The shot ~ed through the woods. 3 repeat the words, actions etc of another: They ~ed every word of their leader.

éclair /eɪˈkleə(r)/ n [C] pastry iced on top and filled with cream: chocolate ~s.

eclipse /ɪˈklɪps/ n [C] 1 total or partial cutting off of the light of the sun (when the moon is between it and the earth), or of the reflected light of the moon (when the earth's shadow falls on it). 2 (fig) loss of brilliance, power, reputation, etc: After suffering an ~ he is famous again. □ vt 1 (of a planet, etc) cause an eclipse; cut off the light from. 2 (fig) make (a person or thing) appear dull by comparison: She was so beautiful that she ~d every other woman in the room.

eco·logi·cal /ˌikəˈlɒdʒɪkəl/ adj of ecology: the ~ effects of industry, e g the pollution of the atmosphere, of rivers, etc.

eco·logi·cally /-klɪ/ adv

ecol·ogy /ɪˈkɒlədʒɪ/ n [U] branch of biology that deals with the habits of living things, esp their relation to their environment.

econ·omic /ˌikəˈnɒmɪk/ adj 1 of economics (⇨ below): the government's ~ policy. 2 connected with commerce, systems of production, etc: ~ geography, studied chiefly in connection with industry. 3 designed to give a profit. 4 (informal) cheap: an ~ rent. 5 (informal) = economical.

econ·omi·cal /ˌikəˈnɒmɪkəl/ adj careful in the spending of money, time, etc and in the use of goods: an ~ fire, one that does not waste fuel.

econ·omi·cally /-klɪ/ adv

econ·omics /ˌikəˈnɒmɪks/ n [U] (used with a sing verb) science of the production, distribution and using up of goods; condition of a country's material prosperity.

econ·om·ist /ɪˈkɒnəmɪst/ n [C] 1 expert in, student of, economics or political economy. **2** person who is economical.

econ·om·ize /ɪ`konəmaɪz/ *vt,vi* use or spend less than before: *He ~d by using buses instead of taking taxis.*

econ·omy /ɪ`konəmɪ/ *n* (*pl* -ies) **1** [C,U] (instance of) avoidance of waste of money, strength or anything else of value: *By various little economies, she managed to save enough money for a holiday.* **2** [U] control and management of the money, goods and other resources of a community, society or household. **3** [C] system for the management and use of economic resources.

e'conomy class, cheapest class of travel (esp by air).

ec·static /ɪk`stætɪk/ *adj* of, in, causing ecstasy.

ec·stati·cally /-klɪ/ *adv*

ec·stasy /`ekstəsɪ/ *n* [C,U] (*pl* -ies) (feeling of) great joy and emotional uplift: *in an ~ of delight; to be in/go into ecstasies (over something).*

ecu·meni·cal /ˌikjʊ`menɪkəl/ *adj* **1** of or representing the whole Christian world or universal Church: *an ~ Council,* e g as summoned by the Pope. **2** seeking to reunite the Christian churches: *the ~ movement.*

ec·zema /`eksɪmə/ *n* [U] itching skin disease.

eddy /`edɪ/ *n* [C] (*pl* -ies) (of wind, smoke, fog, mist, dust, water) circular or spiral movement: *Eddies of mist rose from the valleys.* □ *vi* (*pt,pp* -ied) move in small circles; whirl.

edge¹ /edʒ/ *n* [C] **1** sharp, cutting part of a knife, sword or other tool or weapon: *a knife with a sharp ~.* **be on edge,** be excited or worried because unsure. **have the edge on sb,** (*informal*) have an advantage over him. **set sb's/one's `teeth on edge,** upset his/ one's nerves (as when hearing a scraping sound). **2** (line marking the) outer limit or boundary of a (flat) surface: *a cottage on the ~ of a forest/a lake. He fell off the ~ of the cliff.*

edgy /`edʒɪ/ *adj* (-ier, -iest) excited; nervous.

edge² /edʒ/ *vt,vi* **1** supply with a border: *to ~ a garden path with plants;* form a border to: *a road ~d with grass.* **2** (cause to) move slowly forward or along: *edging one's way through a crowd.*

edge·ways, edge·wise /`edʒweɪz, -waɪz/ *adv* with the edge outwards or forwards. **not get a word in edgeways,** be unable to say anything when a very talkative person is speaking.

edg·ing /`edʒɪŋ/ *n* [C] narrow border: *an ~ of lace on a dress.*

ed·ible /`edəbəl/ *adj* fit to be eaten. □ *n* [C] (usually *pl*) things fit to be eaten.

edict /`idɪkt/ *n* [C] order or proclamation issued by authority; decree.

edi·fi·ca·tion /ˌedɪfɪ`keɪʃən/ *n* [U] (*formal*) mental or moral improvement.

edi·fice /`edɪfɪs/ *n* [C] (*formal*) **1** building (esp a large or imposing one). **2** (*fig*) something built up in the mind: *The whole ~ of his hopes was destroyed.*

edify /`edɪfaɪ/ *vt* (*pt,pp* -ied) improve in morals or mind: *~ing books.*

edit /`edɪt/ *vt* **1** prepare (another person's writing) for publication: *~ a newspaper.* **2** do the work of planning and directing the publication of a newspaper, magazine, book, encyclopaedia, etc. **3** prepare a film, tape recording, etc by putting together parts in a suitable order.

edi·tion /ɪ`dɪʃən/ *n* [C] **1** form in which a book is published: *a paperback ~.* **2** total number of copies (of a book, newspaper, etc) issued from the same types: *the first/a revised ~.* ⇨ impression(2).

edi·tor /`edɪtə(r)/ *n* [C] person who edits (e g a newspaper, a manuscript or a T V or radio programme) or who is in charge of part of a newspaper: *the `sports/fi`nancial ~.*

edi·tor·ial /ˌedɪ`tɔːrɪəl/ *adj* of an editor: *~ work.* □ *n* [C] special article in a newspaper, etc usually written by the editor.

edu·cate /`edʒʊkeɪt/ *vt* give intellectual and moral training to: *You should ~ your children to behave well.*

edu·ca·tion /ˌedʒʊ`keɪʃən/ *n* [U] **1** systematic training and instruction: *No country can afford to neglect ~.* **2** knowledge and abilities, development of character and mental powers, resulting from such training.

edu·ca·tional /-nəl/ *adj* of, connected with, education: *~al books.*

eel /il/ *n* [C] long, snake-like fish.

eerie, eery /`ɪərɪ/ *adj* (-ier, -iest) causing a feeling of mystery and fear: *an ~ shriek.*

eer·ily /-əlɪ/ *adv*

eeri·ness *n* [U]

ef·face /ɪ`feɪs/ *vt* **1** rub or wipe out; make indistinct: *~ an inscription.* **2** (*fig*) obliterate: *~ unpleasant memories of the past.* **3** **efface oneself,** keep in the background in order to escape being noticed; make oneself appear to be unimportant. ⇨ self-effacing.

ef·face·ment *n* [U]

ef·fect /ɪ`fekt/ *n* **1** [C,U] result; outcome: *the ~ of heat on metals. The children were suffering from the ~s of the hot weather. Did the medicine have any ~/a good ~? of no effect,* not doing what was intended or hoped for. **In effect,** (a) in fact, really. (b) in operation: *The rule/law is still in ~.* **take effect,** (a) produce the result intended or required. (b) come into force; operate; become active. **2** [C] impression produced on the mind of a spectator, hearer, reader, etc: *`sound ~s,* (in broadcasting, etc) sounds characteristic of a scene, or incidental to an event, e g the noise of a train. *Everything he says and does is calculated for ~,* done to impress. **3** [U] meaning: *That is what he said, or words to that ~,* words with the same general meaning. **4** (*pl*) goods; property: *The hotel-keeper seized her personal ~s because she could not pay her bill.* □ *vt* bring about: ~ *a cure.*

ef·fec·tive /ɪˈfektɪv/ *adj* **1** having an effect; able to bring about the result intended: ~ *measures to reduce unemployment.* **2** making a striking impression: *an* ~ *scheme of decoration.* **3** actual or existing: *the* ~ *strength of the army.*
ef·fec·tive·ly *adv*
ef·fec·tive·ness *n*

ef·fec·tual /ɪˈfektʃʊəl/ *adj* (not used of persons) bringing about the result required; answering its purpose: *an* ~ *remedy/punishment.*
ef·fec·tually /-ʃʊələ/ *adv*

ef·fem·i·nate /ɪˈfemɪnət/ *adj* like, of, a woman.

ef·fer·vesce /ˌefəˈves/ *vi* **1** give off bubbles of gas; (of gas) issue in bubbles. **2** (*fig*) (of persons) be gay and excited.
ef·fer·vescence /-səns/ *n* [U]
ef·fer·vescent /-sənt/ *adj*

ef·fi·ciency /ɪˈfɪʃənsɪ/ *n* [U] state or quality of being efficient.

ef·fi·cient /ɪˈfɪʃənt/ *adj* **1** (of persons) capable; able to perform duties well: *an* ~ *secretary/staff of teachers.* **2** producing a desired or satisfactory result: ~ *methods of teaching.*
ef·fi·cient·ly *adv*

ef·figy /ˈefɪdʒɪ/ *n* [C] (*pl* -ies) representation of a person (in wood, stone, etc).

ef·flu·ent /ˈeflʊənt/ *n* [C] **1** stream flowing from a larger stream or from a lake. **2** discharge of waste liquid matter, sewage, etc, e g from a factory.

ef·fort /ˈefət/ *n* **1** [C,U] (attempt at) trying hard; use of strength and energy (to do something): *Please make an* ~ *to arrive early. I will make every* ~ (= do all I can) *to help you.* **2** [C] result of, something done with, effort: *That's a pretty good* ~.
ef·fort·less *adj* making no effort; easy: *done with* ~*less skill.*

ef·front·ery /ɪˈfrʌntərɪ/ *n* (*pl* -ies) **1** [U] shameless boldness. **2** [C] instance of this: *How can you have the* ~ *to ask for another loan?*

ef·fu·sion /ɪˈfjuːʒən/ *n* (*formal*) **1** [U] sending or pouring out (of liquid, e g blood); [C] quantity poured out. **2** [C] (esp unrestrained) outpouring of thought or feeling: ~*s in love letters.*

ef·fu·sive /ɪˈfjuːsɪv/ *adj* (of the feelings, signs of pleasure, gratitude, etc) expressed (too) freely: ~ *thanks.*
ef·fu·sive·ly *adv*
ef·fu·sive·ness *n* [U]

egali·tar·ian /ɪˌɡælɪˈteərɪən/ *n* [C], *adj* (person) favouring equal rights, benefits and opportunities for all citizens. ⇨ **elite**, **elitist**.

egg[1] /eɡ/ *n* **1** [C] embryo enclosed in a shell, e g of a hen, used as food: *Birds, reptiles and insects come from* ~*s. Will you have*

your ~ *boiled or fried?* [U] *You've got some* ~ (i e a bit of a cooked egg) *on your chin.*
put all one's eggs in one basket, risk everything one has in a single venture, e g by investing all one's money in one business.
teach one's grandmother to suck eggs, give advice to a person who has much more experience than oneself. **2** [C] female reproducing cell.
`**egg-cup,** small cup for a boiled egg.
`**egg-head,** intellectual person.
`**egg-plant,** (esp *US*) = aubergine.
`**egg-shell,** shell of an egg.
`**egg-whisk,** utensil for beating eggs.

egg[2] /eɡ/ *vt* **egg sb on,** urge him (to do something, usually bad).

ego /ˈeɡəʊ *US*: ˈiːɡəʊ/ *n* [C] self; individual's perception or experience of himself; individual's capacity to think, feel and act.

ego·cen·tric /ˌeɡəʊˈsentrɪk *US*: ˌiːɡ-/ *adj* interested chiefly in oneself.

ego·ism /ˈeɡəʊɪzm *US*: ˈiːɡ-/ *n* [U] **1** theory that our actions are always caused by the desire to benefit ourselves. **2** state of mind in which one is always thinking of oneself.

ego·ist /ˈeɡəʊɪst *US*: ˈiːɡ-/ *n* [C] believer, practicer, in egoism.
ego·istic /ˌeɡəʊˈɪstɪk *US*: ˈiːɡ-/, **ego·isti·cal** /-kəl/ *adj* of egoism or an egoist.

ego·tism /ˈeɡətɪzm *US*: ˈiːɡ-/ *n* [U] practice of talking too often or too much about oneself; selfishness.

ego·tist /ˈeɡəʊtɪst *US*: ˈiːɡ-/ *n* [C] selfish person
ego·tis·tic /ˌeɡəʊˈtɪstɪk *US*: ˈiːɡ-/ *adj* of egotism or an egotist.

egret /ˈiːɡret/ *n* [C] kind of heron with beautiful long feathers in the tail and on the back.

eh /eɪ/ *int* (used to express surprise or doubt, or to invite agreement).

eider·down /ˈaɪdədaʊn/ *n* [C] (quilted bed-covering filled with) soft feathers of a large, wild duck (called an `**eider**).

eight /eɪt/ *adj, n* [C] **1** (of) 8. **2** crew of eight in a rowing-boat; race between these.
eight·een /ˌeɪˈtiːn/ *adj, n* [C] (of) 18.
eight·eenth /-ˈtiːnθ/ *adj, n* [C] (abbr *18th*) (of) one of 18 parts or the next after 17.
eighth /eɪtθ/ *adj, n* [C] (abbr *8th*) (of) one of 8 parts or the next after 7.
eight·ieth /ˈeɪtɪθ/ *adj, n* [C] (abbr *80th*) (of) one of 80 parts or the next after 79.
eighty /ˈeɪtɪ/ *adj, n* [C] (of) 80: *during the eighties,* during the years '80 to '89 of the century.

eis·tedd·fod /ˈaɪˈsteðvɒd/ *n* [C] (in Wales) annual gathering of poets and musicians for competitions.

either /ˈaɪðə(r) *US*: ˈiːðər/ *adj, pron* **1** one or the other (of): *Take* ~ *half; they're exactly the same. E~ of them/E~ one will be satisfactory.* (*Note: any (one of)* is used when the number is greater than two.) **2** one and the other (of two): *There was an armchair at* ~ *end of the long table.* (*Note: both and* *each* are more usual.) □ adv, conj **1** (used in statements after *not*): *I don't like the red one, and I don't like the pink one,* ~. ⇨ **neither. 2** (used to introduce the first of two or more alternatives, followed by *or*): *He must be* ~ *mad or drunk.*

ejacu·late /ɪˈdʒækjʊleɪt/ vt **1** (*formal*) say suddenly and briefly. **2** eject (fluid, e g semen) from the body.

ejacu·la·tion /ɪˈdʒækjʊˈleɪʃən/ n [C,U]

eject /ɪˈdʒekt/ vt **1** compel (a person) to leave (a place); expel: *They were* ~ed *because they had not paid their rent for a year.* **2** send out (liquid, etc): *lava* ~ed *from a volcano.* **3** make an emergency exit, e g with a parachute from an aircraft.

ejec·tion /ɪˈdʒekʃən/ n [C,U]

ejec·tor /-tə(r)/, person who, that which, ejects.

eˈjector-seat, one in an aircraft for ejecting a pilot so that he may descend by parachute.

eke[1] /iːk/ vt make (supplies) enough for one's needs by adding what is lacking; make a living or something last in this way: *eking out one's grant by walking to college.*

elab·or·ate /ɪˈlæbərət/ adj **1** worked out with much care and in great detail: ~ *designs.* **2** carefully prepared and finished: ~ *plans.* □ vt /ɪˈlæbəreɪt/ work out, describe, in detail: *Please* ~ *your proposals a little.*

elab·or·ation /ɪˈlæbəˈreɪʃən/ n [C,U]

elapse /ɪˈlæps/ vi (of time) pass.

elas·tic /ɪˈlæstɪk/ adj **1** having the tendency to go back to the normal or previous size or shape after being pulled or pressed: ~ *bands. Rubber is* ~. **2** (*fig*) not firm, fixed or unalterable; able to be adapted: ~ *rules.* □ n [U] cord or material made elastic by weaving rubber into it: *a piece of* ~.

elas·tic·ity /ˈelæˈstɪsətɪ US: ɪˈlæ-/ n [U] the quality of being elastic.

elate /ɪˈleɪt/ vt stimulate; make happy, pleased, etc: *He was* ~d *at the news/by his success.*

ela·tion /ɪˈleɪʃən/ n [U] great happiness, etc: *be filled with elation.*

el·bow /ˈelbəʊ/ n [C] **1** (outer part of the) joint between the two parts of the arm; corresponding part of a sleeve (in a jacket, etc). **at one's elbow**, close to; near by. **2** elbow bend; corner or joint (e g in a pipe or chimney) shaped like an elbow. □ vt push or force (one's way through, forward, etc): *to* ~ *one's way through a crowd.*

ˈelbow room, space to move freely.

el·der[1] /ˈeldə(r)/ adj **1** (of members of a family, esp closely related members, or of two named persons) senior: *My* ~ *brother is in India.* ⇨ **older. 2** (used before or after a person's name to distinguish that person from another of the same name): *the* ~ *Pitt.* □ n [C] **1** (*pl*) persons of greater age: *Should we always follow the advice of our* ~s? **2** official in some Christian churches. **3** older

of two persons: *He is my* ~ *by several years.*

ˈelder ˈstatesman, one whose unofficial advice is sought and valued because of his long experience.

el·der[2] /ˈeldə(r)/ n [C] (kinds of) bush or small tree with clusters of white flowers and red or black berries.

el·der·ly /ˈeldəlɪ/ adj getting old; rather old.

el·dest /ˈeldɪst/ adj first-born or oldest surviving (member of a family): *my* ~ *son/ brother.*

elect[1] /ɪˈlekt/ adj (used after the *noun*) chosen, selected: *the bishop* ~, not yet in office. □ n **the** ~, those persons specially chosen, or considered to be the best.

elect[2] /ɪˈlekt/ vt **1** choose by vote: *to* ~ *a president.* **2** choose; decide: *He had* ~ed *to become a lawyer.*

elec·tion /ɪˈlekʃən/ n [U] choosing or selection (of candidates for an office, etc) by vote; [C] instance of this: ~ *results.* ~ by(e)-**election**; general **election**; local **election**.

elec·tion·eer·ing /ɪˈlekʃənˈɪərɪŋ/ n [U] working in elections, e g by canvassing, making speeches.

elec·tive /ɪˈlektɪv/ adj **1** having the power to elect: *an* ~ *assembly.* **2** chosen or filled by election: *an* ~ *office.* **3** (*US*) not compulsory: ~ *subjects in college.* ⇨ optional.

elec·tor /ɪˈlektə(r)/ n [C] person having the right to elect (esp by voting at a parliamentary election).

elec·toral /ɪˈlektrəl/ adj of an election: *the* ~al *register*, the list of electors.

elec·tor·ate /-ət/, whole body of qualified electors.

elec·tric /ɪˈlektrɪk/ adj **1** of, worked by, charged with, capable of developing, electricity: *an* ~ *current/torch/iron/shock; an* ~ *guitar*, one that has amplifiers for the sound. **2** (*fig*) (e g of news) causing strong and sudden emotion.

elec·tri·cal /ɪˈlektrɪkəl/ adj relating to electricity: ~ *engineering.*

elec·tri·cally /-klɪ/ adv

elec·tri·cian /ɪˈlekˈtrɪʃən/ n [C] expert in setting up, repairing and operating electrical apparatus.

elec·tri·city /ɪˈlekˈtrɪsətɪ/ n [U] **1** all the phenomena associated with electrons (negative charge) and protons (positive charge); the study of these phenomena. **2** supply of electric current (for heating, lighting, etc).

elec·trify /ɪˈlektrɪfaɪ/ vt (pt,pp -ied) **1** charge with electricity. **2** equip (a railway, etc) for the use of electric power. **3** (*fig*) excite, shock, as if by electricity: *to* ~ *an audience by an unexpected announcement.*

elec·tri·fi·ca·tion /ɪˈlektrɪfɪˈkeɪʃən/ n [U] electrifying, e g of a steam railway to an electric railway.

elec·tro- /ɪˈlektrəʊ/ prefix concerned with, caused by, electricity: *electro-magnet.*

ˈelec·tro·ˈcar·dio·gram /-ˈkɑːdɪəʊɡræm/,

graphic pictures from an electrocardiograph, used in the diagnosis of heart disease.

'elec·tro·'car·dio·graph, apparatus which detects and records activity in the muscles of the heart.

'elec·tro·'mag·net, piece of soft iron that becomes magnetic when an electric current is passed through wire coiled round it.

elec·tro·cute /ɪˈlektrəkjuːt/ *vt* kill accidentally, put to death, by means of an electrical current.

elec·tro·cu·tion /ɪˌlektrəˈkjuːʃən/ *n* [C,U]

elec·trode /ɪˈlektrəʊd/ *n* [C] solid conductor by which an electric current enters or leaves a vacuum tube, etc. ⇨ **anode**, **cathode**.

elec·tron /ɪˈlektrɒn/ *n* [C] particle of matter, smaller than an atom, having a negative electric charge.

elec·tron·ic /ɪˌlekˈtrɒnɪk/ *adj* (a) of electrons. (b) operated by, based on, electrons: ∼ic *music,* produced by changing natural sounds using electric currents, etc.

elec·tron·ics *n* (used with a *sing verb*) the science and technology of electrons and electronic devices and systems, as in radio, TV, tape recorders, computers, etc.

el·e·gance /ˈelɪɡəns/ *n* [U] elegant quality or style.

el·e·gant /ˈelɪɡənt/ *adj* showing, having, done with, good taste; graceful: *looking* ∼ *in a long dress;* ∼ *manners.*
el·e·gant·ly *adv*

el·e·gy /ˈelədʒɪ/ *n* [C] (*pl* -ies) poem or song of sorrow, esp for the dead.

el·e·ment /ˈelɪmənt/ *n* [C] 1 (*science*) substance which has not so far been split up into a simpler form by ordinary chemical methods: *Water is a compound containing the* ∼s *hydrogen and oxygen.* 2 (according to the ancient philosophers): *the four* ∼s, earth, air, fire and water (out of which the material universe was thought to be composed). *In/out of one's element,* in/not in suitable or satisfying surroundings: *He's in his* ∼ *when they start talking about economics.* 3 **the** ∼s, the forces of nature, the weather, etc: *exposed to the* ∼s, to the winds, storms, etc. 4 (*pl*) beginnings or outlines of a subject of study; parts that must be learnt first: *the* ∼s *of geometry.* 5 necessary or characteristic feature: *Justice is an important* ∼ *in good government.* 6 suggestion, indication, trace: *There's an* ∼ *of truth in his statement.* ⇨ **atom**(2). 7 resistance wire in an electrical appliance (e g a heater).

el·e·men·tal /ˌelɪˈmentəl/ *adj* of the elements(2,3).

ele·men·tary /ˌelɪˈmentrɪ US: -terɪ/ *adj* of or in the beginning stage(s); not developed; simple: *an* ∼ *course;* ∼ *arithmetic.*
ele·men·tar·ily /ˌeləˈmentrəlɪ/ *adv*

el·e·phant /ˈelɪfənt/ *n* [C] largest four-footed animal now living, with curved ivory tusks and a long trunk. ⇨ **white elephant**.

el·ev·ate /ˈelɪveɪt/ *vt* 1 lift up; raise: ∼*d to the House of Lords.* 2 (*fig*) make (the mind, morals) higher and better: *an elevating book/sermon.*

el·ev·ation /ˌelɪˈveɪʃən/ *n* 1 [U] elevating or being elevated: ∼ *to the House of Lords;* [C] instance of this. 2 [U] (*formal*) nobility or dignity: ∼ *of thought/style/language.* 3 [C] height (esp above sea-level); hill or high place: *an* ∼ *of 2000 metres.* 4 [C] plan (drawn to scale) of one side of a building. ⇨ **plan**.

el·ev·ator /ˈelɪveɪtə(r)/ *n* [C] 1 machine like a continuous belt with buckets at intervals, used for raising grain, etc. 2 store-house for grain. 3 person or thing that elevates, e g part of an aircraft that is used to gain or lose altitude. 4 (*US*) = **lift**(2).

eleven /ɪˈlevən/ *adj, n* [C] 1 (of) the number 11. 2 team of eleven players for football, hockey or cricket.

elev·enth /ɪˈlevnθ/ *adj, n* [C] (abbr *11th*) (of) one of 11 parts or the next after 10. *at the eleventh hour,* at the latest possible time.

elf /elf/ *n* [C] (*pl* elves /elvz/) small fairy; mischievous little creature.

elfin /ˈelfɪn/ *adj* of elves: ∼*in dances/laughter.*

elf·ish /ˈelfɪʃ/ *adj* mischievous.

elicit /ɪˈlɪsɪt/ *vt* cause to come out: *to* ∼ *the truth/a reply.*

eli·gible /ˈelɪdʒəbəl/ *adj* fit, suitable, to be chosen; having the right qualifications: ∼ *for promotion/a pension/membership in a society; an* ∼ *young man,* e g one who would be a satisfactory choice as a husband.
el·igi·bil·ity /ˌelɪdʒəˈbɪlətɪ/ *n* [U]

elim·in·ate /ɪˈlɪmɪneɪt/ *vt* remove; take or put away, get rid of (because unnecessary or unwanted): ∼ *suspects by interviewing them.*
elim·in·ation /ɪˌlɪmɪˈneɪʃən/ *n* [U]

elite /eɪˈliːt/ *n* [C] group in society considered to be superior because of the power, privileges, etc of its members: *the diplomatic* ∼. ⇨ **egalitarian**.

elit·ist /ɪˈliːtɪst/ *adj* supporting, relying on, superiority or dominance of a group.

elixir /ɪˈlɪksə(r)/ *n* [C] 1 preparation by which medieval scientists hoped to change metals into gold or (∼ *of life*) to prolong life indefinitely. 2 remedy that cures all ills.

Eliza·bethan /ɪˌlɪzəˈbiːθən/ *adj* of the time of Queen Elizabeth I of England: *the* ∼ *age;* ∼ *drama.* □ *n* [C] person who lived during her reign, e g Shakespeare.

elk /elk/ *n* [C] one of the largest kinds of living deer, found in the Rocky Mountains, N America (where it is called a 'moose').

el·lipse /ɪˈlɪps/ *n* [C] regular oval.

el·lip·tic /ɪˈlɪptɪk/, **el·lip·ti·cal** /-kəl/ *adj* shaped like an ellipse.

elm /elm/ *n* [C] common deciduous tree that grows to a great size and height; [U] its hard, heavy wood.

elo·cu·tion /ˈeləˈkjuʃən/ n [U] art or style of speaking well, esp in public.

elo·cu·tion·ist /-ɪst/, expert in elocution; person who recites, e g poetry.

elon·gate /ˈiːlɒŋgeɪt US: ɪˈlɔːŋ-/ vt,vi make or become long(er).

elope /ɪˈləʊp/ vi (of a woman) run away from home or a husband (with a lover).

elope·ment n [C,U]

elo·quence /ˈeləkwəns/ n [U] skilful use of language to persuade or to appeal; fluent speaking.

elo·quent /-ənt/ adj

elo·quent·ly adv

else /els/ adv 1 besides; in addition: Did you see anybody ∼, any other person(s)? Have you anything ∼ to do? Ask somebody ∼ to help you. Nothing ∼ (= Nothing more), thank you. We went nowhere ∼, to no other place. How ∼ (= In what other way) would you do it? 2 otherwise; if not: Run or ∼ you'll be late.

else·where /ˈelsˈweə(r) US: -ˈhweər/ adv somewhere else; in, at or to some other place.

eluci·date /ɪˈluːsɪdeɪt/ vt (formal) make clear; explain (a problem, difficulty).

eluci·da·tion /ɪˈluːsɪˈdeɪʃən/ n [C,U]

elude /ɪˈluːd/ vt (formal) escape capture (esp by means of a trick); avoid: ∼ one's enemies.

elu·sive /ɪˈluːsɪv/ adj 1 tending to elude: an ∼ criminal. 2 not easy to recall: an ∼ word.

elves /elvz/ pl of elf.

'em /əm/ pron (informal) = them.

em·aci·ate /ɪˈmeɪʃɪeɪt/ vt (formal) make thin or lean: ∼d by long illness.

emaci·ation /ɪˈmeɪʃɪˈeɪʃən/ n [U]

ema·nate /ˈeməneɪt/ vi (formal) come, flow, proceed from.

ema·na·tion /ˈeməˈneɪʃən/ n [C,U]

eman·ci·pate /ɪˈmænsɪpeɪt/ vt set free (esp from legal, political or moral restraint): an ∼d young woman, one who has freed herself from the conventions or restrictions of the community to which she belongs.

eman·ci·pa·tion /ɪˈmænsɪˈpeɪʃən/ n [U] emancipating or being emancipated: ∼ from the authority of one's parents.

em·balm /ɪmˈbɑːm/ vt preserve (a dead body) from decay by using spices or chemicals; preserve from oblivion; fill with fragrance.

em·balmer, person who embalms.

em·bank·ment /ɪmˈbæŋkmənt/ n [C] wall or mound of earth, stone, etc to hold back water or support a raised road or railway; roadway supported by such a wall: the Thames E∼.

em·bargo /ɪmˈbɑːgəʊ/ n [C] (pl ∼es) order that forbids trade, movement of ships, etc; stoppage of commerce, or of a branch of commerce: lift/raise/remove an ∼ (from something). □ vt (pt,pp ∼ed) seize (ships or

goods) by government authority, for the service of the State.

em·bark /ɪmˈbɑːk/ vi,vt 1 go, put or take on board a ship: The soldiers ∼ed for Malta. The ship ∼ed passengers and cargo. 2 start, take part in: ∼ on/upon a new business undertaking.

em·bar·ka·tion /ˈembɑːˈkeɪʃən/ n [C,U]

em·bar·rass /ɪmˈbærəs/ vt disconcert, cause mental discomfort or anxiety to: ∼ing questions; ∼ed by lack of money.

em·bar·rass·ing·ly adv

em·bar·rass·ment n [C,U]

em·bassy /ˈembəsɪ/ n [C] (pl -ies) duty and mission of an ambassador; his official residence; ambassador and his staff: the French ∼ in London; ∼ officials.

em·bed /ɪmˈbed/ vt (-dd-) 1 fix firmly (in a surrounding mass): stones ∼ded in rock. 2 (fig) fix: facts ∼ded in one's memory.

em·bel·lish /ɪmˈbelɪʃ/ vt make beautiful; add ornaments or details to: ∼ a story, e g by adding amusing but perhaps untrue details.

em·bel·lish·ment n [C,U]

em·ber /ˈembə(r)/ n [C] (usually pl) small piece of burning wood or coal in a dying fire; ashes of a dying fire.

em·bezzle /ɪmˈbezəl/ vt use (money or property placed in one's care) deceitfully and illegally for one's own benefit.

em·bezzle·ment n [C,U]

em·bit·ter /ɪmˈbɪtə(r)/ vt make (even more) bitter(2): ∼ed by repeated failures.

em·bit·ter·ment n

em·blem /ˈembləm/ n [C] symbol; device that represents something: an ∼ of peace, e g a dove.

em·blem·atic /ˈembləˈmætɪk/ adj

em·body /ɪmˈbodɪ/ vt (pt,pp -ied) (formal) 1 give form to ideas, feelings, etc: ∼ one's ideas in a speech. 2 include: The latest cameras ∼ many new features.

em·bodi·ment /ɪmˈbodɪmənt/ n [C] that which forms something or is formed: She is the embodiment of kindness.

em·boss /ɪmˈbos US: -ˈbɔs/ vt cause a pattern, writing, etc to stand out on (the surface of something); raise the surface of something into a pattern: ∼ed notepaper; a silver vase ∼ed with a design of flowers.

em·brace /ɪmˈbreɪs/ vt,vi 1 take (a person, etc) into one's arms, as a sign of affection: embracing a child. They ∼d. 2 (formal) accept; make use of: ∼ an offer/ opportunity. 3 (formal) (of things) include: ∼ many colours in a single design. □ n [C] act of embracing: He held her to him in a warm ∼.

em·bro·ca·tion /ˈembrəˈkeɪʃən/ n [U] oily liquid (a liniment) for rubbing a bruised or aching part of the body.

em·broider /ɪmˈbrɔɪdə(r)/ vt,vi 1 ornament (cloth) with needlework: a design ∼ed in gold thread. 2 (fig) add untrue details to a story for a better effect.

em·broid·ery *n* [U] embroidered needle-work; art of embroidering.

em·bryo /'embrɪəʊ/ *n* [C] (*pl* ~s) **1** off-spring of an animal in the early stage of its development before birth (or before coming out of an egg). **2** (*fig*) something in its very early stage of development.

em·bry·on·ic /'embrɪ'ɒnɪk/ *adj*

emend /ɪ'mend/ *vt* take out errors from: ~ *a passage in a book.*

em·er·ald /'emrəld/ *n* **1** [C] bright green precious stone. **2** [U] colour of this.

emerge /ɪ'mɜːdʒ/ *vi* **1** come into view; (esp) come out (from water, etc): *The moon ~d from behind the clouds.* **2** (of facts, ideas) appear; become known: *No new ideas ~d during the talks.*

emerg·ence /-dʒəns/ *n* [U] emerging.

emerg·ent /-dʒənt/ *adj*

emerg·ency /ɪ'mɜːdʒənsɪ/ *n* (*pl* -ies) **1** [C] serious happening or situation needing quick action: *This fire-extinguisher is to be used only in an ~.* **2** (used as an *adjective*): *an ~ exit.*

em·ery /'eмərɪ/ *n* [U] hard metal used (esp in powdered form) for grinding and polishing: `~-paper.`

emi·grant /'emɪɡrənt/ *n* [C] person who emigrates: ~ *to Canada.*

emi·grate /'emɪɡreɪt/ *vi* go away (from one's own country to another to settle there).

emi·gra·tion /'emɪ'ɡreɪʃən/ *n* [C,U]

émi·gré /'emɪɡreɪ US: 'emɪ'ɡreɪ/ *n* [C] person who has left his own country, usually for political reasons.

emi·nence /'emɪnəns/ *n* **1** [U] state of being famous or distinguished; superiority of position; *win ~ as a scientist.* **2** [C] area of high or rising ground. **3** *His/Your E~,* title used of (or to) a cardinal.

emi·nent /'emɪnənt/ *adj* (*formal*) **1** (of a person) distinguished: ~ *as a sculptor.* **2** (of qualities) remarkable in degree: *a man of ~ goodness.*

emi·nent·ly *adv*

emir /e'mɪə(r)/ *n* [C] Arab prince or governor; male descendant of Muhammad.

emir·ate /e'mɪəreɪt/ *n* [C] rank, lands, etc of an emir: *the great Muslim ~ates of Northern Nigeria.*

emis·sion /ɪ'mɪʃən/ *n* **1** [U] sending out or giving off: *an ~ of light/heat.* **2** [C] that which is sent out or given off.

emit /ɪ'mɪt/ *vt* (-tt-) give or send out: *A volcano ~s smoke and ashes.*

emo·tion /ɪ'məʊʃən/ *n* **1** [U] stirring up, excitement, of the mind or (more usually) the feelings; excited state of the mind or feelings: *He thought of his dead child with deep ~.* **2** [C] strong feeling of any kind: *Love, joy, hate, fear and grief are ~s.*

emo·tional /-ʃənəl/ *adj* (**a**) of, directed to, the emotions: *an ~al appeal.* (**b**) easily excited; capable of expressing strong feelings: *an ~al woman/actor/nature.*

emo·tion·ally /-əlɪ/ *adv*

emo·tion·less *adj* without (showing) emotion.

emot·ive /ɪ'məʊtɪv/ *adj* of, tending to excite, the emotions: ~ *language.*

em·pale /ɪm'peɪl/ *vt* = impale.

em·pa·thy /'empəθɪ/ *n* [U] (power of) entering into (and so fully understanding, and losing one's identity in) the spirit of a person, a work of art, etc.

em·peror /'empərə(r)/ *n* [C] ruler of an empire.

em·pha·sis /'emfəsɪs/ *n* [C,U] (*pl* ~es) **1** force or stress laid on a word or words to make the significance clear, or to show importance. **2** (the placing of) special value or importance: *Some schools lay/put special ~ on language study.*

em·pha·size /'emfəsaɪz/ *vt* give emphasis to: *He ~d the importance of careful driving.*

em·phatic /ɪm'fætɪk/ *adj* having, showing, using, emphasis: *an ~ opinion/person.*

em·phati·cally /-klɪ/ *adv*

em·pire /'empaɪə(r)/ *n* **1** [C] group of countries under a single supreme authority: *the Roman E~.* **2** [U] supreme political power: *the responsibilities of ~.*

em·piric, em·piri·cal /ɪm'pɪrɪk(əl)/ *n* [C], *adj* (person) relying on observation and experiment, not on theory.

em·piri·cally /-klɪ/ *adv*

em·piri·cism /ɪm'pɪrɪsɪzm/ *n* [U] (theory which supports the) use of empirical evidence to decide the truth of something.

em·piri·cist /-sɪst/ *n* [C] supporters of empiricism.

em·ploy /ɪm'plɔɪ/ *vt* **1** give work to, usually for payment: *He is ~ed in a bank.* **2** (*formal*) make use of: *How do you ~ your spare time?*

em·ploy·able /-əbəl/ *adj* that can be employed.

em·ployer, person who employs others.

em·ployee /'emplɔɪ'i/, person who is employed.

em·ploy·ment /ɪm'plɔɪmənt/ *n* [U] employing or being employed; one's regular work or occupation.

em`ployment agency, business establishment which helps a person (for a fee) to find a job.

em·por·ium /ɪm'pɔrɪəm/ *n* [C] (*pl* ~s) centre of commerce; market; large retail store.

em·power /ɪm'paʊə(r)/ *vt* give power or authority to act.

em·press /'emprəs/ *n* [C] woman governing an empire; wife of or widow of an emperor.

empty[1] /'emptɪ/ *adj* (-ier, -iest) having nothing inside; containing nothing: *an ~ box;* ~ *promises/words,* not meaning anything, not giving satisfaction. □ *n* [C] *pl* -ies) (usually *pl*) box, bottle, crate, etc that has been emptied.

'empty-'handed *adj* bringing back nothing; carrying nothing away.

'empty-'headed *adj* lacking in common sense

emp·ti·ness /'emptɪnəs/ *n* [U]

empty² /'emptɪ/ *vt,vi* (*pt,pp* -ied) make or become empty, remove what is inside: ~ one's glass, drink everything in it; ~ (out) a drawer; ~ the rubbish into the dustbin; ~ one's pockets. The cistern empties (= becomes empty) in five minutes.

emu /'iːmju/ *n* [C] large flightless Australian bird that runs well.

emu·late /'emjʊleɪt/ *vt* try to do as well as or better than.

emu·la·tion /'emjʊ'leɪʃən/ *n* [U] emulating: in ~ of each other.

emul·sion /ɪ'mʌlʃən/ *n* [C,U] (kinds of) creamy liquid in which particles of oil or fat are suspended: ~ paint.

en- /ɪn, en-/ (also **em-**) *prefix* **1** (~ + noun/verb = verb) put in or on: encase. **2** (~ + noun/adjective = verb) make into, cause to be: enlarge; empower.

-en /-ən/ *suffix* **1** (used to form the *pp* of some verbs): broken; hidden. **2** (used to form an adjective): wooden. **3** (used to form a verb): sadden.

en·able /ɪ'neɪbl/ *vt* make able, give authority or means: The collapse of the strike ~d the company to resume normal bus services.

en·abling /ɪ'neɪblɪŋ/ *adj* making possible: enabling them to get to work.

en·act /ɪ'nækt/ *vt* **1** make (a law); decree; ordain. **2** perform on, or as though on, the stage of a theatre (*act* is more usual).

en·act·ment *n* [U] enacting or being enacted; [C] law.

en·amel /ɪ'næml/ *n* [U] **1** glass-like substance used for coating metal, porcelain, etc, for decoration or as a protection: ~ paint, paint which dries to make a hard, glossy surface. **2** hard outer covering of teeth. □ *vt* (-ll-, US also -l-) cover, decorate, with enamel (esp with designs or decorations).

en·amour (US = **-amor**) /ɪ'næmə(r)/ *vt* (usually passive) **be enamoured of,** fond of, delighted with and inclined to use: ~ed of one's own voice.

en·case /ɪn'keɪs/ *vt* **1** put into a case. **2** surround or cover as with a case: a knight ~d in armour.

-ence /-əns/ *suffix* ⇨ -ance.

en·chant /ɪn'tʃɑːnt US: -'tʃænt/ *vt* **1** charm; delight: She was ~ed with/by the flowers you sent her. **2** use magic on; put under a magic spell: the ~ed palace, e g in a fairy tale.

en·chanter, man who enchants.

en·chant·ress, woman who enchants.

en·chant·ing *adj* charming; bewitching.

en·chant·ing·ly *adv*

en·chant·ment, (a) being enchanted. **(b)** [C] something which enchants; magic spell. **(c)** [U] charm; delight: the ~ment of moonlight.

en·circle /ɪn'sɜːkəl/ *vt* surround; form a circle round: a lake ~d by trees.

en·circle·ment [C,U]

en·clave /'enkleɪv/ *n* [C] territory wholly within the boundaries of another.

en·close /ɪn'kləʊz/ *vt* **1** put a wall, fence, etc round; shut in on all sides: ~ a garden with a wall. **2** put in an envelope, parcel, etc: A cheque for £5 is ~d.

en·clos·ure /ɪn'kləʊʒə(r)/ *n* **1** [U] enclosing: ~ of common land; [C] instance of this. **2** [C] something enclosed (esp with a letter).

en·com·pass /ɪn'kʌmpəs/ *vt* encircle; envelope; consist of.

en·core /'ɒŋkɔː(r)/ *int* Repeat! Again! □ *vt, n* [C] (call for a) repetition (of a song, etc) or further performance by the same person(s): The singer gave three ~s.

en·coun·ter /ɪn'kaʊntə(r)/ *vt* find oneself faced by (danger, difficulties, etc); meet (an enemy or enemies); meet (a friend, etc) unexpectedly. □ *n* [C] sudden or unexpected (esp hostile) meeting: an ~ with the bank manager.

en·cour·age /ɪn'kʌrɪdʒ US: -'kɜːr-/ *vt* give hope, courage or confidence to; support: ~ a man to work harder; ~ a boy in his studies.

en·cour·age·ment, (a) [U] encouraging: words of ~ment. **(b)** [C] something that encourages: Praise acts as an ~ment to the young.

en·croach /ɪn'krəʊtʃ/ *vi* go beyond what is right or natural: ~ on/upon his rights/time/land.

en·croach·ment *n* [C,U]

en·crust /ɪn'krʌst/ *vt,vi* **1** cover with a crust; put on (a surface) a layer of ornamental or costly material: a gold vase ~ed with precious stones. **2** form into a crust.

en·cum·ber /ɪn'kʌmbə(r)/ *vt* **1** get in the way of, be a burden to: be ~ed with a large family. **2** crowd; fill up: a room ~ed with old and useless furniture.

en·cum·brance /ɪn'kʌmbrəns/ *n* [C] thing that encumbers; burden: An idle grown-up daughter may be an ~ to her parents.

en·cyc·li·cal /en'sɪklɪkəl/ *n* [C], *adj* (letter written by the Pope) for wide circulation.

en·cy·clo·pedia (also **-paedia**) /ɪn'saɪklə'piːdɪə/ *n* [C] (*pl* ~s) book, or set of books, giving information about every branch of knowledge, or on one subject, with articles in ABC order.

en·cy·clo·pedic, -paedic /ɪn'saɪklə'piːdɪk/ *adj*

end¹ /end/ *n* [C] **1** farthest or last part: the ~ of a road/stick/line; the house at the ~ of the street; the west/east ~ of a town, the parts in the west/east. **begin/start at the wrong end,** in the wrong way, at a wrong point. **get/have hold of the 'wrong end of the 'stick,** have a completely mistaken idea of what is intended or meant. **go off the 'deep end,** express uncontrolled anger.

make (both) ends `meet*, live within one's income. *at a loose `end, having nothing important or interesting to do. *on end*, (a) upright: *Place the barrel/box on* (*its*) ~. *His hair stood on* ~. (b) continuously: *for two hours on* ~. *end `on*, with the ends meeting: *The two ships collided* ~ *on*, the stern (or bows) of one struck the stern (or bows) of the other. *`end to `end*, in a line with the ends touching: *Arrange the tables* ~ *to* ~. **2** small piece that remains: *a* '*ciga`rette* ~; *odds and* ~*s*. **3** finish; conclusion: *at the* ~ *of the day/the century. We shall never hear the* ~ *of it/the matter*, It will be talked about for a long time to come. (*be*) *at an end*, finished: *The war was at an* ~. (*be*) *at the end of*, have no: *She was at the* ~ *of her patience. come to an end*, finish: *The meeting came to an* ~ *at last. put an end to sth*, finish it, get rid of it (according to context): *You must put an* ~ *to your bad behaviour. in the end*, finally, at last: *He tried many ways of earning a living; in the* ~ *he became a farm labourer. no end of*, (*informal*) very many or much, very great, etc: *We met no* ~ *of interesting people. without end*, never reaching an end: *We had trouble without* ~. **4** death: *He's nearing his* ~, is dying. **5** purpose, aim: *gain/win/achieve one's* ~(*s*); *with this* ~ *in view; for/to this* ~.

end² /end/ *vt* (cause to) come to an end; reach an end: *The road* ~*s here*, goes no farther. *How does the story* ~? *end up*, finish: *If you continue to steal, you'll* ~ *up in prison*, will one day be sent to prison. *We started with soup, and had fruit to* ~ *up with*.

end·ing, last part, esp of a word or a story.

en·dan·ger /ɪnˈdeɪndʒə(r)/ *vt* put in danger; cause danger to: ~ *one's chances of success*.

en·dear /ɪnˈdɪə(r)/ *vt* make dear or precious: ~ *oneself to everyone; an* ~*ing smile*.

en·dear·ing·ly *adv*

en·dear·ment *n* [C,U] act, word, expression, of affection: *a term of* ~*ment*, e g *darling*.

en·deav·our (*US* = -**vor**) /ɪnˈdevə(r)/ *n* [C] (*formal*) effort (the usual word): *Please make every* ~ *to be early*. □ *vi* try (the usual word): ~ *to please one's wife*.

en·dem·ic /enˈdemɪk/ *n, adj* (disease) often recurring in a country or area, or among a particular class of people, e g miners. ⇨ epidemic.

en·dive /ˈendɪv *US*: -daɪv/ *n* [C] kind of curly-leaved chicory, used as salad.

end·less /ˈendləs/ *adj* having no end; never stopping: *a woman with* ~ *patience*.

end·less·ly *adv*

en·dorse /ɪnˈdɔːs/ *vt* **1** write one's name on the back of (a cheque). **2** write comments, etc in, on the back of, (a document): *His driving licence has been* ~*d*, a record of a

motoring offence has been entered in it. **3** approve, support a claim, statement, etc.

en·dorse·ment *n* [C,U]

en·dow /ɪnˈdaʊ/ *vt* **1** give money, property, etc to provide a regular income for (e g a college). **2** *be endowed with*, be born with (qualities, etc): *be* ~*ed by nature with great talents*.

en·dow·ment /ɪnˈdaʊmənt/ *n* **1** [U] endowing. **2** [C] money, property, etc given to (a college, etc) provide an income. **3** [C] (*formal*) talent.

en·dur·ance /ɪnˈdjʊərəns *US*: -ˈdʊə-/ *n* [U] ability to endure: *He showed remarkable powers of* ~. *past/beyond endurance*, to an extent that can no longer be endured.

en`durance test, test of how long a person or thing can put up with suffering, working hard, loneliness, etc.

en·dure /ɪnˈdjʊə(r) *US*: -ˈdʊər/ *vt,vi* **1** suffer pain, hardship, etc: *If help does not come, we must* ~ *to the end*, suffer until death comes. **2** = bear²(8) (which is more usual.) **3** last; continue in existence: *fame that will* ~ *for ever*.

en·dur·able /-əbəl/ *adj* able to endure.

en·dur·ing *adj* lasting: *an enduring peace*.

en·dur·ing·ly *adv*

end·ways /ˈendweɪz/ (also **end·wise** /-waɪz/) *adv* with the end towards the spectator; end forward; end to end.

en·ema /ˈenəmə/ *n* [C] (syringe used for an) injection of liquid into the rectum.

en·emy /ˈenəmɪ/ *n* [C] (*pl* -ies) **1** person who feels hatred and tries or wishes to harm or attack: *A successful man often has many enemies*. **2** *the* ~, armed forces of a nation with which one's country is at war; *The* ~ *were forced to retreat*. **3** (used as an *adjective*) of the enemy: ~ *aircraft/ships*. **4** anything that harms or injures: *Laziness is his chief* ~.

en·er·getic /ˌenəˈdʒetɪk/ *adj* full of, done with, energy(1).

en·er·geti·cally /-klɪ/ *adv*

en·ergy /ˈenədʒɪ/ *n* (*pl* -ies) **1** [U] force, strength; capacity to do things and get things done: *He had so much* ~ *that he did the work of three men. He's full of* ~. **2** (*pl*) (person's) powers available for working, or as used in working: *apply/devote all one's energies to a task*. **3** [U] capacity for, power of, doing work: *electrical* ~.

en·er·vate /ˈenəveɪt/ *vt* (*formal*) cause to lose physical, moral strength: *a country with an enervating climate*.

en·fold /ɪnˈfəʊld/ *vt* enclose in one's arms).

en·force /ɪnˈfɔːs/ *vt* **1** compel obedience to; impose: ~ *discipline/silence*. **2** give strength to: *Have you any statistics that would* ~ *your argument?*

en·force·able /-əbəl/ *adj* that can be enforced.

en·force·ment *n* [U]

en·fran·chise /ɪnˈfræntʃaɪz/ *vt* **1** give political rights to (esp, the right to vote at parliamentary elections): *In Great Britain women were ~d in 1918.* **2** set free (slaves).

en·gage /ɪnˈgeɪdʒ/ *vt, vi* **1** obtain the right to employ: *~ him as a guide/an interpreter.* **2** (*dated*) get the right to occupy: *~ a taxi* (*hire* is the usual word). **2 engage in,** take part in; busy oneself with: *~ in politics.* **3 be engaged (in),** be busy (with), be occupied; take part in: *be ~d in business/in writing a novel. The line/number is ~d,* (when telephoning) Someone else is using the line. **4** promise, agree, to marry: *Tom and Anne are ~d. Tom is ~d to Anne.* **5** (*formal*) attract: *Nothing ~s his attention for long.* **6** attack; begin fighting with: *The general did not ~ the enemy.* **7** (of parts of a machine) lock together; (cause to) fit into: *The teeth of one wheel ~ with those of the other.*

en·gag·ing *adj* attractive; charming: *an engaging smile/manner.*

en·gag·ing·ly *adv*

en·gage·ment /ɪnˈgeɪdʒmənt/ *n* [C] **1** agreement to marry: *Their ~ was announced in the papers.* **2** arrangement to go somewhere, meet someone or do something, at a fixed time: *I can't come because of another ~.* **3** battle: *The admiral tried to bring about an ~,* to make the enemy fight. **4** [C,U] engaging (of part of a machine, etc): *~ of first gear.*

en·gagement ring, one given by a man to a woman when they agree to marry.

en·gen·der /ɪnˈdʒendə(r)/ *vt* (*formal*) be the cause of: *Crime is often ~ed by poverty.*

en·gine /ˈendʒɪn/ *n* [C] machine that converts energy into power or motion: *a ˈsteam-~; a new ~ for a motor-vehicle.*

ˈengine-driver, (esp) man who drives a railway engine.

en·gin·eer /ˌendʒɪˈnɪə(r)/ *n* [C] **1** person who designs machines, bridges, railways, docks, etc: *a civil/electrical ~.* **2** skilled and trained person in control of an engine or engines: *the chief ~ of a ship.* **3** member of the branch of an army (called the E~s) that builds roads and bridges, controls communications, etc. □ *vt, vi* **1** act, construct or control as an engineer. **2** (*formal*) arrange or bring about skilfully: *~ a scheme/plot.*

en·gin·eer·ing, the technology, work or profession of an engineer.

Eng·lish /ˈɪŋglɪʃ/ *n* the English language. **the ~,** English people. □ *adj* **1** of England. **2** of, written in, spoken in, the English language.

Eng·lish·man, man born in England.

Eng·lish·woman, woman born in England.

en·grave /ɪnˈgreɪv/ *vt* **1** cut or carve (lines, words, designs, on) a hard surface: *a name ~d on a tombstone.* **2 engrave with,** mark such surfaces with (an inscription, etc). **3** (*fig*) impress deeply (on the memory or mind).

en·graver, person who engraves designs,

etc on stone, metal, etc.

en·grav·ing, [U] art of cutting or carving designs on metal, stone, etc; [C] copy of a picture, design, etc printed from an engraved plate.

en·gross /ɪnˈgrəʊs/ *vt* take up all the time or attention of: *He's ~ed in his work/a book.*

en·gulf /ɪnˈgʌlf/ *vt* swallow up (as in a gulf): *a boat ~ed in the sea/waves.*

en·hance /ɪnˈhɒns US: -ˈhæns/ *vt* add to (the value, attraction, powers, price, etc).

enigma /ɪˈnɪgmə/ *n* [C] (*pl ~s*) question, person, thing, circumstance, that is puzzling.

enig·matic /ˈenɪgˈmætɪk/ *adj* difficult to understand; mysterious.

enig·mati·cally /-klɪ/ *adv*

en·join /ɪnˈdʒɔɪn/ *vt* (*formal*) give an order for; urge; command: *~ silence/obedience.*

en·joy /ɪnˈdʒɔɪ/ *vt* **1** get pleasure from; take delight in: *~ one's dinner.* **2** have as an advantage or benefit: *~ good health/a good income.* **3 enjoy oneself,** experience pleasure; be happy.

en·joy·able /-əbəl/ *adj* giving joy; pleasant.

en·joy·ably /-əblɪ/ *adv*

en·joy·ment /ɪnˈdʒɔɪmənt/ *n* **1** [U] pleasure; joy; satisfaction: *to think only of/ live for ~.* **2** [U] (*formal*) possession and use: *be in the ~ of good health.* **3** [C] something that gives joy and pleasure.

en·large /ɪnˈlɑːdʒ/ *vt* **1** make or become larger: *~ a photograph/one's house.* **2** (*formal*) say or write more about: *I need not ~ on this matter; you all know my views.*

en·large·ment *n* [C,U]

en·lighten /ɪnˈlaɪtən/ *vt* give more knowledge to; free from ignorance, misunderstanding or false beliefs: *Can you ~ me on this subject,* help me to understand it better?

en·light·ened *adj* free from ignorance, prejudice, superstition, etc: *in these ~ed days.*

en·lighten·ment *n* [U] enlightening or being enlightened: *for the ~ment of mankind.*

en·list /ɪnˈlɪst/ *vt, vi* **1** take into, enter, the armed forces: *~ a recruit; ~ as a volunteer in the army.* **2** (*formal*) obtain; get the support of: *Can I ~ your sympathy in a charitable cause?*

en·list·ment *n* [C,U]

en·liven /ɪnˈlaɪvən/ *vt* make (more) lively: *How can we ~ the party?*

en·mity /ˈenmətɪ/ *n* (*pl -ies*) **1** [U] hatred. **2** [C] particular feeling of hatred.

enor·mity /ɪˈnɔːmətɪ/ *n* (*pl -ies*) (*formal*) **1** [U] great wickedness: *Does he realize the ~ of his offence?* **2** [C] serious crime. **3** immense size: *the ~ of the problem of feeding the world's population in 2 000 A D.*

enor·mous /ɪˈnɔːməs/ *adj* very great; immense: *an ~ sum of money.*

enor·mous·ly *adv* to a great extent: *The town has changed ~ly. I'm ~ly grateful.*

enough /ɪˈnʌf/ *adj, n, adv* (quantity or numbers) as great as is needed; as much or as many as necessary: *There's ~ food/food ~ for everbody. Will £5 be ~ for you/~ to meet your needs?* (*Note:* as an *adjective* **enough** may either precede or follow a *noun;* as a *noun* it occurs in the pattern: *~ (of the/ this/that/his, etc + noun).*) □ *adj* **1** to the right or necessary degree; sufficiently: *The meat is not cooked ~. You're old ~ to know better.* **2** adequate (but sometimes used to suggest something could be better, etc): *She sings well ~, but...* **3** *oddly/curiously/ strangely ~,* in a way that is odd, etc; *sure ~,* as expected, believed, etc.

en·quire, en·quiry /ɪnˈkwaɪə(r), ɪnˈkwaɪərɪ/ *v, n* ⇨ inquire, inquiry.

en·rage /ɪnˈreɪdʒ/ *vt* fill with rage: *~d at/by his stupidity.*

en·rap·ture /ɪnˈræptʃə(r)/ *vt* (*formal*) fill with great delight or joy.

en·rich /ɪnˈrɪtʃ/ *vt* make rich; improve in quality, flavour, etc: *~ the mind* (*with knowledge*); *soil ~ed with manure.*
en·rich·ment *n* [C,U]

en·roll, en·rol /ɪnˈrəʊl/ *vt, vi* (cause to) become a member of a society or institute: *to ~ in evening classes; to ~* (*a person*) *as a member of a society/club.*
en·roll·ment *n* [C,U]: *a school with an ~ment of 800 pupils.*

en route /ˌɒn ˈruːt *US:* ˈɒn ˈruːt/ *adv* on the way: *We stopped at Paris ~ from Rome to London.*

en·sem·ble /ɒnˈsɒmbəl *US:* ɒnˈsɒmbəl/ *n* [C] **1** something viewed as a whole; general effect. **2** (*music*) passage of music in which all the performers unite; group of musicians who play together regularly (smaller than an orchestra).

en·shrine /ɪnˈʃraɪn/ *vt* (*formal*) place or keep in, or as in, a shrine; serve as a shrine for: *basic human rights ~d in the constitution.*

en·sign /ˈensaɪn/ *n* [C] **1** naval flag or banner. **2** badge or symbol (showing office, authority, etc).

en·slave /ɪnˈsleɪv/ *vt* make a slave of.
en·slave·ment *n* [U]

en·snare /ɪnˈsneə(r)/ *vt* catch in, or as in, a snare or trap.

en·sue /ɪnˈsjuː *US:* -ˈsuː/ *vi* happen later; follow, happen as a result: *in the ensuing* (= next) *year.*

en·sure (*US* = **in·sure**) /ɪnˈʃʊə(r)/ *vt, vi* make sure; guarantee: *I can't ~ that he will be there in time.* **2** make safe: *We ~d* (*ourselves*) *against possible disappointment.* **3** secure; assure: *These documents ~ to you the authority you need.*
-ent /-ənt/ *suffix* ⇨ **-ant.**

en·tail /ɪnˈteɪl/ *vt* **1** make necessary: *That will ~ an early start.* **2** (*legal*) leave, settle, (land) to a line of heirs so that none of them can give it away or sell it. □ *n* [U] settlement of landed property in this way; [C] the property so settled.

en·tangle /ɪnˈtæŋgəl/ *vt* **1** catch in a snare or among obstacles: *My fishing line got ~d in weeds.* **2** (*fig*) put or get into difficulties, in unfavourable circumstances: *~ oneself with money-lenders.*
en·tangle·ment, (**a**) [U] entangling or being entangled; [C] situation that entangles: *emotional ~ments.* (**b**) (*pl*) barrier of stakes and barbed wire to prevent an enemy's advance.

en·tente /ɒnˈtɒnt *US:* ɒnˈtɒnt/ *n* [C] (group of States with a) friendly understanding.
'entente cordiale /ˈkɔːdɪˈɑːl/, one between two governments.

en·ter /ˈentə(r)/ *vt, vi* **1** come or go into: *The train ~ed a tunnel.* **2** become a member of; join: *~ university.* **3** *enter into sth* (*with sb*), begin, open: *~ into negotiations with a business firm.* **4** (*esp*) make a start on: *~ on/upon a new career/another term of office.* **5** write, record names, details, etc in a book, etc: *~* (*up*) *an item in the accounts.* **6** give the name of a person, etc for a competition, race, etc: *~ oneself for an examination;* *~ a horse for the Derby.*

en·ter·prise /ˈentəpraɪz/ *n* **1** [C] undertaking, esp one that needs courage or boldness or that offers difficulty. **2** [U] courage and willingness to engage in such projects: *He is a man of great ~.* **3** [U] carrying on of commercial projects: *Do you prefer private ~ to nationalization?*
en·ter·pris·ing *adj* having, showing, enterprise(2).

en·ter·tain /ˌentəˈteɪn/ *vt* **1** receive (people) as guests; give food and drink to: *The Smiths ~ a great deal/do a great deal of ~ing,* often give parties, etc. **2** amuse, interest: *We were all ~ed by his tricks.* **3** be ready to consider: *~ a proposal;* have in the mind: *~ ideas/doubts, etc.*
en·ter·tain·ing *adj* pleasing; amusing.
en·ter·tainer, person who entertains(2), e g a singer, comedian.
en·ter·tain·ment /ˌentəˈteɪnmənt/ *n* **1** [U] entertaining or being entertained(1,2): *a hotel famous for its ~. He fell into the water, much to the ~ of the onlookers.* **2** [C] public performance (at a theatre, circus, etc).

en·thral (also, esp *US* **en·thrall**) /ɪnˈθrɔːl/ *vt* (-ll-) **1** take the whole attention of; please greatly: *~led by an exciting story.* **2** greatly attracted: *~led by a woman's beauty.*

en·throne /ɪnˈθrəʊn/ *vt* place a king, bishop on a throne.
en·throne·ment *n* [C,U]

en·thuse /ɪnˈθjuːz *US:* -θuːz/ *vi* (*informal*) show great enthusiasm for: *~ over the new carpets.*

en·thusi·asm /ɪnˈθjuːzɪæzəm *US:* -ˈθuː-/ *n* [U] strong feeling of admiration or interest: *arouse ~ in him; feel no ~ for/about the play; an outburst of ~.*

en·thusi·ast /ɪnˈθjuːzɪæst *US:* -ˈθuː-/ *n* [C] person filled with enthusiasm: *a `sports* *enthusiast.*

en·thu·si·as·tic /ɪnˌθjuːzɪˈæstɪk US: -ˈθu-/ *adj* full of enthusiasm: ~ *admirers of a film star.*

en·thu·si·as·ti·cal·ly /-klɪ/ *adv*

en·tice /ɪnˈtaɪs/ *vt* tempt or persuade: ~ *her into doing something/to do something wrong.*

en·tice·ment *n* [C,U]

en·tire /ɪnˈtaɪə(r)/ *adj* whole, complete; unbroken: *She was in* ~ *ignorance of what was being done.*

en·tire·ly *adv* completely: ~*ly wrong/ different.*

en·tire·ty /ɪnˈtaɪərətɪ/ *n* [U] completeness: *We must examine the question in its* ~*ty, as a whole, not in parts only.*

en·title /ɪnˈtaɪtl/ *vt* **1** have as a title: *a book* ~*d 'Adam Bede'.* **2** (of conditions, circumstances, qualities, etc) give a right (to): *If you fail three times, you are not* ~*d to try anymore.*

en·title·ment *n* [U]

en·tity /ˈentɪtɪ/ *n* (*pl* -ies) **1** [C] something that has real existence; a thing's existence (contrasted with its qualities, relations, etc). **2** [U] being; existence.

en·to·mo·logi·cal /ˌentəməˈlɒdʒɪkəl/ *adj* of entomology.

en·to·mol·ogist /ˌentəˈmɒlədʒɪst/ *n* [C] student of, expert in, entomology.

ento·mol·ogy /ˌentəˈmɒlədʒɪ/ *n* [U] the study of insects.

en·tour·age /ˈɒntʊˌrɑːʒ/ *n* [C] all those accompanying and attending on an important or high-ranking person: *the President and his* ~.

en·trails /ˈentreɪlz/ *n pl* bowels; intestines.

en·trance¹ /ˈentrəns/ *n* **1** [C] opening, gate, door, passage, etc by which one enters: *The* ~ *to the cave had been blocked up.* **2** [U] coming or going in; coming of an actor on to the stage: *the university* ~ *examination. Actors must learn their* ~*s and exits,* when to come on and leave the stage. **3** [C,U] right of entering: *to be refused* ~.

en·trance² /ɪnˈtrɑːns US: -ˈtræns/ *vt* overcome, carry away as in a dream, with pleasure: ~*d with the music. She stood* ~*d at the sight.*

en·trant /ˈentrənt/ *n* [C] person who enters *to* a profession, *for* a competition, race, etc.

en·treat /ɪnˈtriːt/ *vt* ask earnestly: *I* ~ *you to show mercy.*

en·treaty /ɪnˈtriːtɪ/ *n* [C,U] (*pl* -ies) earnest request(ing): *He was deaf to all entreaties.*

en·trée /ˈɒntreɪ US: ˈɒntreɪ/ *n* **1** [U] right or privilege of admission. **2** [C] dish served between the fish and the meat course.

en·trench /ɪnˈtrentʃ/ *vt* **1** surround or protect with a trench or trenches. **2** establish firmly: *customs* ~*ed by tradition.*

entre·pre·neur /ˌɒntrəprəˈnɜː(r)/ *n* [C] person who organizes and manages a commercial undertaking.

en·trust /ɪnˈtrʌst/ *vt* (*formal*) trust a person to complete or look after something: *Can I* ~ *the task to you/* ~ *you with the task?*

en·try /ˈentrɪ/ *n* [C] (*pl* -ies) **1** coming or going in: *Thieves had forced an* ~ *into the building.* **2** (place of) entrance; right of entering. **3** item, section of, in a list; item noted in an account book: *dictionary entries; make an* ~ *in the accounts.* **4** (list, number, of) persons, etc entering for a competition: *a large* ~ *for the examination/for the race.*

enu·mer·ate /ɪˈnjuːməreɪt US: ɪˈnuː-/ *vt* count, mention (a list of articles) naming them one by one.

enu·mer·ation /ɪˌnjuːməˈreɪʃən US: ɪˈnuː-/ *n* [U] enumerating; [C] list.

enun·ci·ate /ɪˈnʌnsɪeɪt/ *vt,vi* **1** say, pronounce (words): *He* ~*s (his words) clearly.* **2** express a theory, etc clearly or definitely.

enun·ci·ation /ɪˌnʌnsɪˈeɪʃən/ *n* [U]

en·velop /ɪnˈveləp/ *vt* wrap up, cover, on all sides: *hills* ~*ed in mist.*

en·velop·ment *n* [U]

en·vel·ope /ˈenvələʊp/ *n* [C] paper wrapper or covering for a letter, etc.

en·vi·able /ˈenvɪəbəl/ *adj* likely to cause envy (used both of the object and the person, etc, possessing it): *an* ~ *school record,* one of great success, etc.

en·vi·ous /ˈenvɪəs/ *adj* full of, feeling, expressing, envy: ~ *of her success;* ~ *looks; looking at it with* ~ *eyes.*

en·vi·ous·ly *adv*

en·vi·ron·ment /ɪnˈvaɪərnmənt/ *n* (collective *sing*) surroundings, circumstances, influences: *suffer from a bad home* ~.

'Department of the En'vironment, (in GB) department responsible for land planning, construction industries, transport, preservation of public amenities, control of air and water pollution, the protection of the coast and the countryside.

en·vi·ron·mental /ɪnˌvaɪrənˈmentəl/ *adj*

en·virons /ˈenvɪrɒnz/ *n pl* districts surrounding a town, etc: *Berlin and its* ~.

en·vis·age /ɪnˈvɪzɪdʒ/ *vt* face danger, facts, etc; picture in the mind (esp under a particular aspect): *He had not* ~*d seeing her again.*

en·voy /ˈenvɔɪ/ *n* [C] **1** messenger, esp one sent on a special mission. **2** diplomatic agent next in rank below an ambassador.

envy¹ /ˈenvɪ/ *n* [U] **1** feeling of disappointment and ill will (at another's better fortune): *He was filled with* ~ *at my success.* **2** object of such feeling: *His splendid new car was the* ~ *of all his friends/an object of* ~ *to all his friends.*

envy² /ˈenvɪ/ *vt* (*pt,pp* -ied) feel envy of: *I* ~ *you. I* ~ *your good fortune.*

en·zyme /ˈenzaɪm/ *n* [C] organic chemical substance formed in living cells, able to cause changes in other substances without being changed itself.

ep·aulet (also **ep·aul·ette**) /ˈepəlet/ *n* [C]

shoulder ornament on a military officer's uniform.

épée /ˈeɪpeɪ/ n [C] sharp-pointed slender sword used in fencing.

ephem·er·al /ɪˈfemərəl/ adj living, lasting, for a very short time.

epic /ˈepɪk/ n [C], adj 1 (poetic account) of the deeds of one or more great heroes, or of a nation's past history, e g Homer's *Iliad*. 2 (of a) film made using large crowds and many locations.

epi·demic /ˌepɪˈdemɪk/ n, adj (disease) spreading rapidly among many people in the same place for a time: *an influenza ~*. ⟹ **endemic**.

epi·der·mis /ˌepɪˈdɜːmɪs/ n [U] (anat) outer layer of the skin.

epi·glot·tis /ˌepɪˈɡlɒtɪs/ n [C] (anat) structure of tissue at the root of the tongue, lowered during swallowing to prevent food, etc from entering the windpipe.

epi·gram /ˈepɪɡræm/ n [C] short poem or saying expressing an idea in a clever and amusing way.

epi·gram·matic /ˌepɪɡrəˈmætɪk/ adj

epi·lepsy /ˈepɪlepsi/ n [U] nervous disease causing a person to fall unconscious (often with violent involuntary movements).

epi·lep·tic /ˌepɪˈleptɪk/ adj of epilepsy: *an ~ fit*. □ n [C] person suffering from epilepsy.

epi·logue (US = -log) /ˈepɪlɒɡ US: -lɔːɡ/ n [C] last part of a literary work, esp a poem spoken by an actor at the end of a play.

epi·sode /ˈepɪsəʊd/ n [C] (description of) one event in a chain of events.

epi·sodic /ˌepɪˈsɒdɪk/ adj

epistle /ɪˈpɪsəl/ n [C] (old use) letter. **the E~s**, letters included in the New Testament, written by the Apostles.

epi·taph /ˈepɪtɑːf US: -tæf/ n [C] words (describing a dead person), usually cut on a tombstone.

epi·thet /ˈepɪθet/ n [C] adjective or phrase used to describe the character of a person or thing, as in 'Alfred the *Great*'.

epit·ome /ɪˈpɪtəmi/ n [C] 1 short summary of a book, speech, etc. 2 something which shows, on a small scale, the characteristics of a much larger thing.

epit·om·ize /ɪˈpɪtəmaɪz/ vt make or be an epitome of.

ep·och /ˈiːpɒk US: ˈepək/ n [C] (beginning of a) period of time in history, life, etc marked by special events or characteristics: *Einstein's theory marked a new ~ in mathematics*.

equal /ˈiːkwəl/ adj 1 the same in size, amount, number, degree, value, etc: *~ pay for ~ work; ~ opportunity; divide it into two ~ parts; two boys of ~ height*. 2 **equal to**, having strength, courage, ability, etc for: *He was ~ to the occasion*, was able to deal with it. □ n [C] person or thing ~ to another: *Is he your ~ in strength?* □ vt (-ll-, US also

-l-) be equal to: *He ~s me in strength but not in intelligence*.

equally /ˈiːkwəli/ adv in an equal manner; in equal shares: *~ly clever. Divide it ~ly*.

equal·ity /ɪˈkwɒləti/ n [U] the state of being equal: *sex ~ity*.

equal·ize /ˈiːkwəlaɪz/ vt make equal: *~ize incomes*.

equal·iz·ation /ˌiːkwəlaɪˈzeɪʃən US: -lɪˈz-/ n [U]

equa·nim·ity /ˌekwəˈnɪməti/ n [U] (formal) calmness of mind or temper: *bear misfortune with ~*.

equate /ɪˈkweɪt/ vt consider, treat (one thing as being equal): *I ~ happiness with health*.

equa·tion /ɪˈkweɪʒən/ n 1 [C] statement of equality between two expressions by the sign (=) as in: $2x + 5 = 11$. 2 [U] making equal, balancing, e g of demand and supply.

equa·tor /ɪˈkweɪtə(r)/ n [C] (often E~) imaginary line round the earth; line drawn on maps to represent points at an equal distance from the north and south poles.

equa·tor·ial /ˌekwəˈtɔːrɪəl/ adj of or near the equator: *equatorial Africa*.

equerry /ɪˈkwerɪ/ n [C] (pl -ies) officer in the court of a ruler; officer in attendance on a member of the royal family.

eques·trian /ɪˈkwestrɪən/ adj of horse-riding: *~ skill*. □ n [C] person clever at horse-riding: *an ~ performer*.

equi- /ˈiːkwɪ-/ prefix equal, the same: *equivalent*.

equi·dis·tant /ˌiːkwɪˈdɪstənt/ adj separated by equal distance(s) (*from*).

equi·lat·eral /ˌiːkwɪˈlætrəl/ adj having all sides equal: *an ~ triangle*.

equi·lib·rium /ˌiːkwɪˈlɪbrɪəm/ n [U] state of being balanced: *maintain/lose one's ~*.

equine /ˈekwaɪn/ adj of, like, a horse; of horses.

equi·nox /ˈiːkwɪnɒks/ n [C] time of the year at which the sun crosses the equator and when day and night are of equal length: *the spring* (= vernal) *~, 20 Mar; the autumnal ~, 22 or 23 Sept*.

equip /ɪˈkwɪp/ vt (-pp-) supply (a person, oneself, a ship, etc) (with what is needed, for a purpose): *~ oneself for a task; ~ a ship for a voyage; ~ soldiers with uniforms and weapons*.

equip·ment, (a) equipping or being equipped: *The ~ment of his laboratory took time and money*. **(b)** (collective noun) things needed for a particular purpose: *'radar ~ment*.

equi·table /ˈekwɪtəbəl/ adj fair; just; reasonable.

equi·tably /-əblɪ/ adv

equity /ˈekwətɪ/ n 1 [U] fairness; right judgement. 2 [U] (esp, English law) principles of justice outside common law or Statute law, used to correct laws when these would apply unfairly in special circumstances. **3** (pl) (-ies) ordinary stocks and shares not bearing fixed interest.

equiv·al·ent /ɪˈkwɪvələnt/ adj equal in value, amount, meaning: *What is $5 ~ to in French francs?* □ n [C] thing that is equivalent: *Is there a French word that is the exact ~ of the English word 'home'?*

equivo·cal /ɪˈkwɪvəkəl/ adj having a double or doubtful meaning; open to doubt: *an ~ reply.*

-er /-ə(r)/ suffix **1** (verb + ~ = noun) person carrying out the action: *runner.* **2** (noun + ~ = noun) practiser of: *philosopher.* **3** (also **-r**) (used to form a comparative): *stronger; rarer.*

era /ˈɪərə/ n [C] period in history, starting from a particular time or event: *the Christian ~.*

eradi·cate /ɪˈrædɪkeɪt/ vt **1** pull up by the roots. **2** destroy or put an end to: *~ crime/typhoid fever.*
eradi·ca·tion /ɪˈrædɪˈkeɪʃən/ n [U]

erase /ɪˈreɪz US: ɪˈreɪs/ vt rub or scrape out: *~ pencil marks.*
eraser, thing, usually of rubber, used to erase.

erect[1] /ɪˈrekt/ adj upright; standing on end: *stand ~.*
erect·ly adv
erect·ness n [U]

erect[2] /ɪˈrekt/ vt **1** build, set up; establish: *~ a statue (to somebody); ~ a tent.* **2** set upright: *~ a flagstaff/a mast.*

erec·tion /ɪˈrekʃən/ n **1** [U] act of erecting; state of being erected. **2** [C] building or other structure erected.

er·mine /ˈɜːmɪn/ n **1** [C] small animal whose fur is brown in summer and white (except for its black-pointed tail) in winter. **2** [U] its fur; garment made of this fur: *dressed in ~; a gown trimmed with ~.*

erode /ɪˈrəʊd/ vt (of acids, rain, etc) wear away; eat into: *Metals are ~d by acids.*
ero·sion /ɪˈrəʊʒən/, eroding or being eroded: *soil erosion,* by wind and rain.
ero·sive /ɪˈrəʊsɪv/ adj

erotic /ɪˈrɒtɪk/ adj of sexual love or desire.

err /ɜː(r) US: eər/ vi make mistakes; do or be wrong: *It is better to ~ on the side of mercy,* be too merciful than too severe.

er·rand /ˈerənd/ n [C] **1** short journey to take or get something, e g a message, goods from a shop: *to go on/run ~s for him.* **2** purpose of such a journey.

er·ratic /ɪˈrætɪk/ adj **1** (of a person or his behaviour) likely to do unusual or unexpected things. **2** (of things) uncertain in movement; irregular.
er·rati·cally /-klɪ/ adv

er·roneous /ɪˈrəʊnɪəs/ adj incorrect; mistaken.
er·roneous·ly adv

er·ror /ˈerə(r)/ n **1** [C] mistake: *spelling ~s; an ~ of judgement.* **2** [U] condition of being wrong in belief or conduct: *do something in*

~, by mistake.

eru·dite /ˈerʊdaɪt/ adj (formal) having, showing, great learning; scholarly.
eru·dite·ly adv

erupt /ɪˈrʌpt/ vi **1** (of a volcano) burst or break out (suddenly) (with hot lava, etc). **2** break out suddenly or violently: *~ with anger/cheering/into a painful rash.*
erup·tion /ɪˈrʌpʃən/, **(a)** outbreak of a volcano: *~ions of ashes and lava.* **(b)** (fig) outbreak (of war, disease, anger, etc).

es·ca·late /ˈeskəleɪt/ vt,vi increase in intensity or extent (e g a war).
es·ca·la·tion /ˈeskəˈleɪʃən/ n [U]

es·ca·la·tor /ˈeskəleɪtə(r)/ n [C] moving stairway carrying people up or down between floors or different levels.

es·ca·pade /ˈeskəˈpeɪd/ n [C] daring, mischievous or adventurous act, often one causing gossip or trouble.

es·cape[1] /ɪˈskeɪp/ n **1** [C,U] (act of) escaping; fact of having escaped: *There have been very few successful ~s from this prison.* **2** [C] means of escape: *a `fire-~.* **3** [C] (something that provides) temporary distraction from reality or dull routine (e g through music, reading).

es·cap·ism /-ɪzm/ n [U] avoidance of unpleasant realities by escaping into a more pleasant world of imagination.

es·cap·ist /-ɪst/, person, thing, doing this: *escapist literature.*

es·cape[2] /ɪˈskeɪp/ vi,vt **1** get free; get away; (of steam, fluids, etc) find a way out: *Two of the prisoners have ~d. Gas is escaping from this hole.* **2** avoid; keep free or safe from: *You were lucky to ~ punishment/being punished.* **3** be forgotten or unnoticed by: *His name ~s me for the moment.*

es·carp·ment /ɪˈskɑːpmənt/ n [C] steep slope or cliff separating two areas of different levels.

es·chew /ɪˈstʃuː/ vt (formal) avoid (the usual word): *~ wine/evil.*

es·cort[1] /ˈeskɔːt/ n [C] **1** one or more persons going with another or others, or with valuable goods, to protect them, or as an honour: *an ~ of soldiers; under police ~.* **2** one or more ships, aircraft, etc giving protection or honour: *an ~ of ten destroyers and fifty aircraft.*

es·cort[2] /ɪˈskɔːt/ vt go with as an escort: *a convoy of merchant ships ~ed by destroyers. Who will ~ this young lady home?*

esopha·gus (also **oesopha·gus**) /ɪˈsɒfəgəs/ n [C] passage from the pharynx to the stomach; gullet.

eso·teric /ˈesəˈterɪk/ adj understood by, intended for, only a small circle of disciples or followers.

es·pec·ially /ɪˈspeʃlɪ/ adv to an exceptional degree; in particular: *She likes the country, ~ in spring.*

espion·age /ˈesprɪənaːʒ/ n [U] practice of spying or using spies.

213

es·pouse /ɪˈspaʊz/ vt (formal) **1** give one's support to (a cause, theory, etc). **2** (old use) (of a man) marry.

Es·quire /ɪˈskwaɪə(r) US: ˈes-/ n [C] (dated) title of courtesy (used in GB and written *Esq*, esp in the address of a letter after a man's family name instead of *Mr* before it).

-ess /-əs, -es/ suffix female: *lioness; actress.*

es·say[1] /ˈeseɪ/ n [C] **1** piece of writing on any one subject. **2** testing or trial of the value or nature of something. **3** (formal) attempt.
es·say·ist, writer of essays(1).

es·say[2] /ɪˈseɪ/ vt, vi (formal) try; attempt: ∼ *a task.*

es·sence /ˈesəns/ n **1** [U] that which makes a thing what it is; the inner nature or most important quality of a thing: *Caution is the ∼ of that man's character.* **2** [C,U] extract obtained from a substance by taking out as much of the mass as possible, leaving all its important qualities in concentrated form: *meat ∼s.*

es·sen·tial /ɪˈsenʃəl/ adj **1** necessary; most important: *Is wealth ∼ to happiness?* **2** of an essence(2): *∼ oils.* **3** fundamental: *Being reserved is said to be an ∼ part of the English character.* □ n [C] fundamental element: *the ∼s of English grammar.*
es·sen·tially /ɪˈsenʃəlɪ/ adv in an essential(3) manner: *We are an ∼ly peace-loving people.*

-est /-ɪst/ suffix (also **-st**) (used to form a superlative): *fastest; bravest.*

es·tab·lish /ɪˈstæblɪʃ/ vt **1** set up, put on a firm foundation: *∼ a new state/government/business.* **2** settle, place a person, oneself in a position, office, place, etc: *We are now comfortably ∼ed in our new house.* **3** cause people to accept a belief, claim, custom, etc: *He succeeded in ∼ing a claim to the title.* **4** make (a church) national by law.

es·tab·lish·ment /ɪˈstæblɪʃmənt/ n **1** [U] establishing or being established: *the ∼ of a new state.* **2** [C] that which is established, e g a large organized body of persons (in the army or navy, a civil service, a business firm, with many employees, a hotel and the staff in it). **3** *Church E∼,* the *E∼,* church system established by law. **4 the E∼,** (GB) those persons in positions of power and authority, whose opinions, way of life, influence public life, etc.

es·tate /ɪˈsteɪt/ n **1** [C] piece of property in the form of land, esp in the country: *He owns large ∼s in Scotland.* ⇨ council estate, housing estate, industrial estate. **2** [U] (legal) a person's whole property. **3** [C] political or social group or class. **4** (old use) condition; stage in life: *the ∼ of matrimony.* ⇨ real estate.

e`state agent, person who buys and sells buildings and land for others.

e`state car, saloon-type motor-vehicle with removable or collapsible rear seats and door(s) at the back, for easy loading of luggage, etc.

es·teem /ɪˈstim/ vt (formal) **1** have a high opinion of; respect greatly: *No one can ∼ your father more than I do.* **2** consider; regard: *I shall ∼ it a favour if...* □ n [U] (high) regard: *We all hold him in great ∼,* have a high opinion of him.

es·thetic /esˈθetɪk/ ⇨ aesthetic.

es·ti·mable /ˈestɪməbəl/ adj (formal) worthy of esteem.

es·ti·mate[1] /ˈestɪmət/ n [C] judgement; approximate calculation (of size, cost, etc): *I hope the builders don't exceed their ∼. I don't know enough about him to form an ∼ of his abilities.*

es·ti·mate[2] /ˈestɪmeɪt/ vt, vi form a judgement about; calculate the cost, value, size, etc of: *They ∼d the cost at £8 000. We ∼ that it would take three months to finish the work.*

es·ti·ma·tion /ˌestɪˈmeɪʃən/ n [U] judgement; regard; opinion: *in my ∼; in the ∼ of most people.*

es·trange /ɪˈstreɪndʒ/ vt (formal) bring about a separation in feeling and sympathy: *foolish behaviour that ∼d all his friends.*
es·trange·ment n [C,U]

es·tu·ary /ˈestʃʊərɪ US: -ʊerɪ/ n [C] (pl -ies) (usually long) mouth of a river into which the tide flows: *the Thames ∼.*

et cet·era /ɪt ˈsetrə US: et/ (Latin) (usually shortened to **etc**) and other things; and so on.

etch /etʃ/ vt, vi use a needle and acid to make a picture, etc on a metal plate from which copies may be printed; make (pictures, etc) in this way.
etch·er, person who etches.
etch·ing n [U] the art of the etcher; [C] etched picture.

eter·nal /ɪˈtɜnəl/ adj **1** without beginning or end; lasting for ever: *The Christian religion promises ∼ life.* **2** (informal) too frequent: *Stop this ∼ chatter.*
eter·nally adv (a) throughout all time; for ever. (b) (informal) (too) frequently.

eter·nity /ɪˈtɜnətɪ/ n (pl -ies) **1** [U] time without end; the future life: *send a man to ∼,* to his death. **2** [U] (with a, an) period of time that seems endless: *It seemed an ∼ before news of his safety reached her.* **3** (pl) eternal truths.

ethic /ˈeθɪk/ n (with a, an) system of moral principles, rules of conduct: *Is the idea of thinking only of oneself a good ∼ for living?*
ethi·cal /-kəl/ adj
ethi·cally /-klɪ/ adv
eth·ics n pl (a) (used with a sing verb) science of morals: *E∼s is a branch of philosophy.* (b) (used with a pl verb) moral soundness: *The ∼s of his decision are doubtful.*

eth·nic /ˈeθnɪk/, **eth·ni·cal** /-kəl/ *adj* of race or the races of mankind.
eth·ni·cal·ly /-ɪklɪ/ *adv*
eth·nog·ra·pher /eθˈnɒɡrəfə(r)/ *n* [C] student of, expert in, ethnography.
eth·no·graphic /ˈeθnəˈɡræfɪk/ *adj* of ethnography.
eth·nog·ra·phy /eθˈnɒɡrəfɪ/ *n* [U] scientific description of the races of mankind.
eth·nol·o·gist /eθˈnɒlədʒɪst/ *n* [C] student of, expert in, ethnology.
eth·no·logi·cal /ˈeθnəˈlɒdʒɪkəl/ *adj* of ethnology.
eth·nol·ogy /eθˈnɒlədʒɪ/ *n* [U] science of the races of mankind, their relations to one another, etc.
eti·quette /ˈetɪket/ *n* [U] rules for formal relations or of behaviour among people, or in a class of society or a profession: *medical/legal* ~.
-ette /-et/ *suffix* 1 small: *kitchenette*. 2 female: *usherette*. 3 imitation: *leatherette*.
eyt·mol·ogi·cal /ˈetɪməˈlɒdʒɪkəl/ *adj* of etymology.
ety·mol·ogist /ˈetɪˈmɒlədʒɪst/ *n* [C] student of, expert in, etymology.
ety·mol·ogy /ˈetɪˈmɒlədʒɪ/ *n* 1 [U] science of the origin and history of words .2 [C] account of the origin and history of a word.
euca·lyptus /ˌjuːkəˈlɪptəs/ *n* [C] (*pl* ~es) sorts of tall evergreen tree (including the Australlian gum tree) from which an oil, used for colds, is obtained.
Eu·char·ist /ˈjuːkərɪst/ *n* the E~, Holy Communion; the bread and wine taken at this.
eu·logize /ˈjuːlədʒaɪz/ *vt* (*formal*) praise highly in speech or writing.
eu·logy /ˈjuːlədʒɪ/ *n* [C,U] (*pl* -ies) (speech or writing full of) high praise.
eu·phem·ism /ˈjuːfəmɪzm/ *n* [C,U] (example of the) use of usually less exact but less harsh words or phrases in place of words required by truth or accuracy: *'Pass away' is a* ~ *for 'die'*.
eu·phem·is·tic /ˈjuːfəˈmɪstɪk/ *adj*
eu·phe·mis·ti·cal·ly /-klɪ/ *adv*
eu·phoria /juːˈfɔːrɪə/ *n* [U] state of well-being and pleasant excitement.
eu·phoric /juːˈfɒrɪk US: -ˈfɔr-/ *adj*
Euro·pean /ˈjʊərəˈpɪən/ *n, adj* (native) of Europe; happening in, extending over, Europe: ~ *countries*.
Eu·sta·chian tube /juːˈsteɪʃən ˈtjuːb US: ˈtuːb/ *n* [C] tube connecting the middle ear with the pharynx.
eu·tha·nasia /ˈjuːθəˈneɪzɪə US: -ˈneɪʒə/ *n* [U] (bringing about of an) easy and painless death (for persons suffering from an incurable and painful disease).
evacu·ate /ɪˈvækjʊeɪt/ *vt* 1 (esp of soldiers) withdraw from: ~ *a fort/town*. 2 remove (a person) from a place or district, e g one considered to be dangerous in time of war: *The women and children were* ~d *to the country*.

3 empty (a vessel, bowels, etc.)
evacu·ation /ɪˈvækjʊˈeɪʃən/ *n* [U] evacuating or being evacuated; [C] instance of this.
evacuee /ɪˈvækjuˈiː/ *n* [C] person who is evacuated(2).
evade /ɪˈveɪd/ *vt* 1 get or keep out of the way of; ~ *a blow/one's enemies/an attack*. 2 find a way of not doing something: ~ *income tax*. 3 avoid answering (fully or honestly): ~ *a question*.
evalu·ate /ɪˈvæljʊeɪt/ *vt* find out, decide, the amount or value of.
evalu·ation /ɪˈvæljʊˈeɪʃən/ *n* [C,U]
evan·gelic /ˈiːvænˈdʒelɪk/, **evan·geli·cal** /-kəl/ *adj* 1 of, according to, the teachings of the Gospel: ~ *preaching*. 2 (usually *evangelical*) of the beliefs and teachings of those Protestants who stress the importance of the atoning death of Jesus Christ.
evan·geli·cal·ism /-ɪzm/ *n* [U]
evan·gel·ist /ɪˈvændʒəlɪst/ *n* [C] 1 one of the writers (Matthew, Mark, Luke or John) of the Gospels. 2 preacher of the Gospel, esp one who travels and holds religious meetings.
evan·gel·is·tic /ɪˈvændʒəˈlɪstɪk/ *adj*
evap·or·ate /ɪˈvæpəreɪt/ *vt,vi* 1 (cause to) change into vapour: *Heat* ~s *water*. 2 remove liquid from a substance, e g by heating: ~d *milk*. 3 disappear; die: *His hopes* ~d.
evap·or·ation /ɪˈvæpəˈreɪʃən/ *n* [U]
evas·ion /ɪˈveɪʒən/ *n* 1 [U] evading: ~ *of responsibility*. 2 [C] statement, excuse, etc made to evade something; act of evading: *His answers to my questions were all* ~s.
evas·ive /ɪˈveɪsɪv/ *adj* tending, trying, to evade: *an* ~ *answer; take* ~ *action*, do something in order to evade danger, etc.
evas·ive·ly *adv*
evas·ive·ness *n* [U]
eve /iːv/ *n* [C] day or evening before a Church festival or any date or event; time just before anything: *Christmas E~*, 24 Dec; *New Year's E~*, 31 Dec.
even[1] /ˈiːvən/ *adj* 1 level; smooth: *The best lawns are perfectly* ~. 2 regular; steady; of unchanging quality: *His* ~ *breathing showed that he had got over his excitement. The quality of work is not very* ~. 3 (of amounts, distances, values) equal: *Our scores are now* ~. **be/get even with somebody**, have one's revenge on him. **break even**, (*informal*) make neither a profit nor a loss. 4 (of numbers) that can be divided by two: *The pages on the left side of a book have* ~ *numbers*. 5 equally balanced. 6 (of temper, etc) not easily disturbed or made angry: *an* ~-*tempered wife*. □ *vt* make even or equal.
even·ly *adv*
even·ness *n* [U]
even[2] /ˈiːvən/ *adv* 1 (used to show a comparison between what is stated and what might have happened, been done, etc): *He*

never ∼ *opened the letter* (so he certainly did not read it). *It was cold there* ∼ *in July* (so you may imagine how cold it was in winter). *E*∼ *a child can understand the book* (so adults certainly can). **2 even if/though,** (used to stress the extreme case of what follows): *She won't leave the TV set,* ∼ *though her husband is waiting for his dinner.* **3** (used with comparatives) still, yet: *You know* ∼ *less about it than I do. You seem* ∼ *busier than usual today.* **4 even as,** just at the time when: *E*∼ *as I gave the warning the car skidded.* **even now/then,** in spite of these or those circumstances, etc: *E*∼ *now he won't believe me. E*∼ *then he would not admit his mistake.* **even `so,** though that is the case: *It has many omissions—*∼ *so, it is quite a useful reference book.*

even·ing /ˈivnɪŋ/ *n* [C] **1** that part of the day between afternoon and nightfall: *two* ∼*s ago; this/tomorrow/yesterday* ∼*; in the* ∼*; on Sunday* ∼. **2** (used as an *adjective*): *an* ∼ *paper,* published after the morning papers.

`evening `dress, dress as worn for formal occasions in the evening.

'Evening `prayer, church service in the evening.

even·song /ˈivənsɒŋ *US:* -sɔŋ/ *n* Evening prayer in the Church of England.

event /ɪˈvent/ *n* [C] **1** something (usually important) that happens or has happened: *the chief* ∼*s of 1901. It was quite an* ∼ (often used to suggest that what happened was unusual, memorable, etc). **2** fact of a thing happening: *in the* ∼ *of his death,* if he dies; *in that* ∼, if that happens. **in any event,** whatever happens. **3** outcome; result. **4** one of the races, competitions, etc in a sports programme: *Which* ∼*s have you entered for?*

event·ful /-fəl/ *adj* full of notable events: *He had an* ∼*ful life.*

event·ual /ɪˈventʃʊəl/ *adj* coming at last as a result: *his foolish behaviour and* ∼ *failure.*

event·ual·ly /-tʃʊlɪ/ *adv* in the end: *After several attempts he* ∼*ly swam across.*

event·ual·ity /ɪˈventʃʊˈælətɪ/ *n* [C] (*pl* -ies) possible event.

ever /ˈevə(r)/ *adv* **1** (usually in *negative* sentences and *questions,* and in sentences expressing doubt or conditions) at any time: *Nothing* ∼ *happens in this village. If you* ∼ *visit London....* **2** (used in questions) at any time up to the present: *Have you* ∼ *been in an aeroplane?* (*Note: ever* is not used in the answer; use either 'Yes, I have' or 'No, never', etc.) **3** (used after a comparative or superlative): *It is raining harder than* ∼, than it has been doing so far. *This is the best work you have* ∼ *done.* **4** continuously; at all times: ∼ *after; for* ∼ (*and* ∼); ∼ *since I was a boy.* **5** (used to stress surprise, uncertainty, etc): *When/Where/How* ∼ *did you lose it? What* ∼ *do you mean?* **6 Yours**

ever, (used at the end of a letter, informal or familiar style).

ever·green /ˈevəgrin/ *n* [C], *adj* (tree, shrub) having green leaves throughout the year: *The pine, cedar and spruce are* ∼*s.* ⇨ deciduous.

ever·last·ing /ˈevəˈlɑstɪŋ *US:* -ˈlæst-/ *adj* **1** going on for ever: ∼ *fame/glory.* **2** (*informal*) repeated too often: *I'm tired of his* ∼ *complaints.*

the Everlasting, God.

ever·more /ˈevəˈmɔ(r)/ *adv* for ever.

every /ˈevrɪ/ *adj* **1** all or each one of: *I have read* ∼ *book* (= all the books) *on that shelf. Not* ∼ *horse* (= Not all horses) *can run fast.* ⇨ all[1](1). (*Note:* when *every* is used attention is directed to the whole; when *each* is used, attention is directed to the unit or individual: *E*∼ *boy in the class* (= All the boys) *passed the examination.* Compare *Each boy may have three tries.*) **2** each one of an indefinite number (the emphasis being on the unit, not on the total or whole): *Such things do not happen* ∼ *day.* (*Note:* not replaceable by *all.*) **3** all possible: *You have* ∼ *reason to be satisfied.* **4** (used with numbers and with *other* and *few,* to indicate recurrence, or intervals in time or space): *Write on* ∼ *other line,* on alternate lines. *There are buses to the station* ∼ *ten minutes. I go there* ∼ *other day/*∼ *three days/*∼ *few days.* **every now and then/ again,** from time to time. **every time, (a)** always: *Our football team wins* ∼ *time.* **(b)** whenever: *E*∼ *time I meet him, he tries to borrow money from me.* **in every way,** in all respects: *This is in* ∼ *way better than that.*

every·body /ˈevrɪbɒdɪ/, **every·one** /ˈevrɪwʌn/ *pron* every person: *In a small village* ∼ *knows* ∼ *else.*

every·day /ˈevrɪˈdeɪ/ *adj* happening or used daily; common and familiar: *an* ∼ *occurrence; in his* ∼ *clothes.*

every·thing /ˈevrɪθɪŋ/ *pron* **1** all things: *Tell me* ∼ *about it.* **2** thing of the greatest importance: *Money means* ∼ *to him.*

every·where /ˈevrɪweə(r) *US:* -hweər/ *adv* in, at, to, every place: *I've looked* ∼ *for it.*

evict /ɪˈvɪkt/ *vt* expel (a tenant) (from a house or land) by authority of the law: *They were* ∼*ed for not paying the rent.*

evic·tion /ɪˈvɪkʃən/ *n* [C,U]

evi·dence /ˈevɪdəns/ *n* **1** [U] anything that gives a reason for believing, that makes clear or proves, something: *There wasn't enough* ∼ *to prove him guilty. The scientist must produce* ∼ *in support of his theories.* **2** [U or *pl*] indication, mark, trace: *There was* ∼/ *were* ∼*s of glacial action on the rocks.* **(be) in evidence,** conspicuous, clearly seen: *He was very much in* ∼ *at the party.*

evi·dent /ˈevɪdənt/ *adj* plain and clear to the eyes or mind): *It must be* ∼ *to all of you that...*

evi·dent·ly *adv*

evil /ˈiːvəl/ adj **1** wicked, sinful, bad, harmful: ~ men/thoughts. **2** likely to cause trouble; bringing trouble or misfortune: an ~ tongue. □ n **1** [U] sin; doing wrong. the spirit of ~. **2** [C] evil thing; disaster: War, famine and flood are terrible ~s. be/choose the lesser of two evils, the less harmful of two bad choices.

ˈevil-doer /-duə(r)/, person who does evil.
ˈevil-minded /-ˈmaɪndɪd/, having evil thoughts and desires.
evilly adv in an evil way: He eyed her ~ly.

evince /ɪˈvɪns/ vt (formal) show that one has a feeling, quality, etc: a child who ~s great intelligence.

evoca·tive /ɪˈvɒkətɪv/ adj that evokes, or is able to evoke: ~ words, that call up memories, emotions.

evoke /ɪˈvəʊk/ vt call up, bring out: ~ admiration/surprise/memories of the past.
evo·ca·tion /ˈiːvəʊˈkeɪʃən/ n [C,U]

evol·ution /ˈiːvəˈluːʃən US: ˈev-/ n **1** [U] process of opening out or developing: the ~ of a plant from a seed. The ~ of modern society. **2** [U] (theory of the) development of more complicated forms of life (plants, animals) from earlier and simpler forms.

evolve /ɪˈvɒlv/ vi,vt (cause to) unfold; develop; be developed, naturally and (usually) gradually: The American constitution was planned; the British constitution ~d.

ewe /juː/ n [C] female sheep. ⇨ ram.

ewer /ˈjuːə(r)/ n [C] large wide-mouthed pitcher or jug for holding water.

ex- /ɪks-, eks-, ɪgz-/ prefix **1** out (of): extract. **2** former: ex-president.

ex·acer·bate /ɪgˈzæsəbeɪt/ vt (formal) irritate (a person); make pain, disease, a problem, worse.
ex·acer·ba·tion /ɪgˈzæsəˈbeɪʃən/ n [U]

exact[1] /ɪgˈzækt/ adj **1** correct in every detail; free from error: Give me his ~ words. What is the ~ size of the room? **2** capable of being precise: ~ sciences; an ~ memory.
exact·ly adv (a) completely: Your answer is ~ly right. That's ~ly (= just) what I expected. (b) (as an answer or confirmation) quite so; just as you say.
exact·ness (also exacti·tude /ɪgˈzæktɪtjuːd US: -tuːd/) n [U]

exact[2] /ɪgˈzækt/ vt **1** demand and get payment of: ~ taxes (from people). **2** (formal) insist on: ~ obedience. **3** (formal) (of circumstances) require urgently; make necessary: work that ~s care and attention.
exact·ing adj making great demands; severe; strict: an ~ing piece of work.

exag·ger·ate /ɪgˈzædʒəreɪt/ vt,vi make something seem larger, better, worse, etc than it really is: You ~ the difficulties. If you always ~, people will no longer believe you.
exag·ger·ation /ɪgˈzædʒəˈreɪʃən/ n [U] exaggerating or being exaggerated; [C] such

a statement: a story full of exaggerations.

exalt /ɪgˈzɔːlt/ vt **1** make high(er) in rank, great(er) in power or dignity. **2** praise highly.
exalted adj dignified; ennobled: a person of ~ed rank.
exal·ta·tion /ˈegzɔːlˈteɪʃən/ n [U] (fig) elation; state of spiritual delight.

exam /ɪgˈzæm/ n (informal abbr of) examination(2).

exam·in·ation /ɪgˈzæmɪˈneɪʃən/ n **1** [U] examining or being examined: On ~, it was found that the signature was not genuine. The prisoner is still under ~, being questioned. **2** [C] testing of knowledge or ability: take an ~ (= be tested) in mathematics; ~ questions/papers; an oral ~. **3** inquiry into or inspection of something: an ~ of business accounts; an ~ of one's eyes. **4** questioning by a lawyer in a law court: an ~ of a witness.

exam·ine /ɪgˈzæmɪn/ vt **1** look at carefully in order to learn about or from: ~ old records; have one's teeth/eyes ~d. **2** put questions to in order to test knowledge or get information: ~ pupils in grammar; ~ a witness in a law court.
exam·iner, person who examines.

example /ɪgˈzɑːmpəl US: -ˈzæmpəl/ n [C] **1** fact, thing, etc which represents a general rule: This dictionary has many ~s of how words are used in sentences. for example, using this or these as typical: Many great men have risen from poverty—Lincoln and Edison, for ~. **2** specimen showing the quality of others in the same group or of the same kind: This is a good ~ of Shakespeare's sense of humour. **3** thing or person, person's conduct, to be copied or imitated: follow her ~; set him a good ~. **4** acting as a warning: Let her sorrow be an ~ to you. make an example of sb, punish him as a warning to others.

exas·per·ate /ɪgˈzɑːspəreɪt US: -ˈzæs-/ vt irritate; produce anger, etc in: ~d by/at his stupidity. It is exasperating to miss a train by half a minute.
exas·per·ation /ɪgˈzɑːspəˈreɪʃən US: -ˈzæs-/ n [U] state of being irritated: 'Stop that noise!', he cried out in exasperation.

ex·ca·vate /ˈekskəveɪt/ vt make, uncover, by digging: ~ a trench/a buried city.
ex·ca·va·tion /ˈekskəˈveɪʃən/ n [C,U]
ex·ca·vator, person engaged in, machine used for, excavating.

ex·ceed /ɪkˈsiːd/ vt **1** be greater than: Their success ~ed all expectations. **2** go beyond what is allowed, necessary or advisable: ~ the speed limit, drive faster than is allowed.
exceed·ing·ly adv extremely; to an unusual degree: an ~ingly difficult problem.

ex·cel /ɪkˈsel/ vi,vt (-ll-) **1** do better than others, be very good: He ~s in courage/as a writer. **2** do better than: He ~s all of us in/at tennis.

ex·cel·lence /ˈeksələns/ n 1 [U] the quality of being excellent: *a prize for ~ in French.* 2 [C] thing or quality in which a person excels: *They do not recognize her many ~s.*

Ex·cel·lency /ˈeksələnsɪ/ n [C] (pl -ies) title of ambassadors, governors and their wives, and some other officers and officials: *Your/His/Her ~.*

ex·cel·lent /ˈeksələnt/ adj very good; of the highest quality.
ex·cel·lent·ly adv

ex·cept¹ /ɪkˈsept/ prep 1 not including; but not: *He gets up early every day ~ Sunday. Nobody was late ~ me.* (*Note:* compare *Five others were late besides me*). 2 *except for,* (used when what is excluded is different from what is included): *Your essay is good ~ for the spelling.* 3 *except that,* apart from the fact that: *She knew nothing ~ that he was likely to be late.*

ex·cept² /ɪkˈsept/ vt exclude (from); set apart (from a list, statement, etc): *When I say that the boys are lazy, I ~ Tom.*

ex·cept·ing prep, conj (used after *not, always* and *without*) leaving out; excluding: *the whole staff, not ~ing the heads of departments.*

ex·cep·tion /ɪkˈsepʃən/ n 1 [C] person or thing that is excepted (not included): *You must all be here at 8 a m; I can make no ~s. I enjoyed all his novels with the ~ of his last.* 2 [C] something that does not follow the rule: *~s to a rule of grammar.* 3 [U] objection. *take exception to,* object to, protest against; be offended by: *He took great ~ to what I said.*

ex·cep·tional /ɪkˈsepʃənəl/ adj unusual: *weather that is ~ for June.*
ex·cep·tion·ally adv unusually: *an ~ly clever boy.*

ex·cerpt /ˈeksɜpt/ n [C] extract from a book, etc.

ex·cess /ɪkˈses/ n 1 [U] (and in *sing* with *a, an*) fact of being, amount by which something is, more than something else, or more than is expected or proper: *an ~ of enthusiasm. In excess of,* more than. *to excess,* to an extreme degree: *She is generous to ~.* 2 [U] an amount beyond usual limits (in eating and drinking): *drink to ~.* 3 (*pl*) personal acts which go beyond the limits of good behaviour, morality or humanity: *The ~es (= acts of cruelty, etc) committed by the troops when they occupied the capital will never be forgotten.* □ adj /ˈekses/ extra; additional: *~ fare/luggage/postage.*
ex·cess·ive /ɪkˈsesɪv/ adj too much; too great; extreme: *~ive charges.*
ex·cess·ive·ly adv

ex·change¹ /ɪksˈtʃeɪndʒ/ n 1 [C,U] (act of) exchanging: *He is giving her French lessons in ~ for English lessons.* 2 [U] the giving and receiving of the money of one country for that of another; relation in value between kinds of money used in different countries: *the rate of ~ between the dollar and the pound.* 3 [C] place where merchants or financiers meet for business.
the ˈStock Exchange, for the buying and selling of shares, etc.
ˈtelephone exchange, control office where lines are connected.

ex·change² /ɪksˈtʃeɪndʒ/ vt,vi give, receive (one thing) in place of another: *~ glances/ greetings. Mary ~d seats with Anne.*
ex·change·able /-əbəl/ adj that may be exchanged (*for*).

ex·chequer /ɪksˈtʃekə(r)/ n [C] 1 the E~, (GB) government department in charge of public money: *ˈChancellor of the Exˈchequer,* minister at the head of this department (= Minister of Finance in other countries). 2 supply of money (public or private); treasury.

ex·cise¹ /ˈeksaɪz/ n [U] government tax on certain goods manufactured, sold or used within a country: *the ~ on beer/tobacco; ˈ~ duties.*

ex·cise² /ɪkˈsaɪz/ vt (*formal*) remove by, or as if by cutting (a part of the body, a passage from a book, etc).
ex·ci·sion /ɪkˈsɪʒən/ n [C,U]

ex·cite /ɪkˈsaɪt/ vt 1 stir up the feelings (often of great pleasure) of: *Everybody was ~d by the news of the victory. It's nothing to get ~d about. Extremists were exciting the people to rebellion/to rebel.* 2 bring about: *~ admiration/envy/affection; ~ a riot.*
ex·cit·able /ɪkˈsaɪtəbəl/ adj easily excited.
ex·cite·ment /ɪkˈsaɪtmənt/ n 1 [U] state of being excited: *news that caused great ~.* 2 [C] exciting incident, etc: *He kept calm amid all these ~s.*

ex·claim /ɪkˈskleɪm/ vt,vi cry out suddenly and loudly from pain, anger, surprise, etc; say (the words quoted): *'What!' he ~ed, 'Are you leaving without me?'*

ex·cla·mation /ˌekskləˈmeɪʃən/ n 1 [U] crying out or exclaiming. 2 [C] sudden short cry, expressing surprise, pain, etc: *'Oh!' 'Look out!',* and *'Hurrah!' are ~s.*
excla'mation mark, the mark (!) used in writing.

ex·clama·tory /ɪkˈsklæmətərɪ US: -tɔrɪ/ adj using, containing, in the nature of, an exclamation: *an ~ sentence.*

ex·clude /ɪkˈsklud/ vt 1 prevent (a person from getting in somewhere): *~ him from membership.* 2 prevent (the chance of something arising): *~ all possibility of doubt.* 3 ignore as irrelevant: *We can ~ (from the reckoning) the possibility that the money won't arrive.*
ex·clu·sion /ɪkˈskluʒən/ n [U] excluding or being excluded (*from*).

ex·clus·ive /ɪkˈsklusɪv/ adj 1 (of a person) not willing to mix with others (esp those considered to be inferior in social position, education, etc). 2 (of a group or society) not readily admitting new members: *He belongs* *to the most* ~ *clubs.* **3** (of a shop, goods sold in it, etc) of the sort not to be found elsewhere; expensive. **4** reserved to the person(s) concerned; *have* ~ *rights/an* ~ *agency for the sale of Ford cars in a town; an* ~ *story/interview,* e g given to only one newspaper. **5** *exclusive of,* not including: *The ship had a crew of 57* ~ *of officers.* **6** excluding all but what is mentioned: *Teaching has not been his* ~ *employment.* □ *n* [C] article, report etc, published by only one newspaper.

ex·clus·ive·ly *adv*

ex·com·muni·cate /'ekskə'mjunɪkeɪt/ *vt* exclude (as a punishment) from the privileges of a member of the Christian Church.
ex·com·muni·ca·tion /'ekskə'mjunɪ'keɪʃən/ *n* [C,U]

excre·ment /'ekskrəmənt/ *n* [U] solid waste matter discharged from the bowels.

ex·creta /ɪk'skriːtə(r)/ *n pl* waste (excrement, urine, sweat) expelled from the body.

ex·crete /ɪk'skriːt/ *vt* (of an animal or plant) discharge from the system, e g waste matter, sweat.

ex·cre·tion /ɪk'skriːʃən/ *n* [U] excreting; [C,U] that which is excreted.

ex·cru·ciat·ing /ɪk'skruːʃɪeɪtɪŋ/ *adj* (of pain, bodily or mental) extreme.

ex·cru·ciat·ing·ly *adv*

ex·cur·sion /ɪk'skɜːʃən US: -ɜːʒən/ *n* [C] short (return) journey, esp one made by a number of people together for pleasure: *go on/make an* ~ *to the mountains; an* ~ *train.*

ex·cuse[1] /ɪk'skjuːs/ *n* [C] reason given (true or invented) to explain or defend one's conduct: *He's always making* ~*s for being late.* *without excuse:* *Those who are absent without (good)* ~ *will be punished.*

ex·cuse[2] /ɪk'skjuːz/ *vt* **1** give reasons showing, or intended to show, that a person or his action is not to be blamed: *Please* ~ *my coming late/*~ *me for being late/*~ *my late arrival.* **2** set free from a duty, punishment, etc: *He was* ~*d (from) attendance at the lecture.* **3** justify, be a reason for: *His lack of experience does not* ~ *his bad behaviour.* **4** *Excuse me,* (used as an apology when one interrupts, asks, disagrees, has to behave impolitely or disapprove): *E*~ *me, but is this seat vacant?*

ex·cus·able /ɪk'skjuːzəbəl/ *adj* that may be excused: *an excusable mistake.*

execu·tant /ɪg'zekjʊtənt/ *n* [C] person who executes or performs music, etc.

ex·ecute /'eksɪkjuːt/ *vt* **1** carry out (what one is asked or told to do): ~ *a plan/a command/a manoeuvre.* **2** give effect to: ~ *a will.* **3** make legally binding: ~ *a legal document,* by having it signed, witnessed, sealed and delivered. **4** carry out punishment by death: ~ *a murderer.* **5** perform on the stage, at a concert, etc: *The piano sonata was badly* ~*d.*

ex·ecu·tion /'eksɪ'kjuːʃən/ *n* **1** [U] the carry-

ing out or performance of a piece of work, etc: *His* ~ *of the plan was unsatisfactory.* **2** [U] skill in performing music: *a pianist with marvellous* ~. **3** [U] infliction of punishment by death; [C] instance of this: ~ *by hanging.*

ex·ecu·tioner, public official who executes criminals.

execu·tive /ɪg'zekjʊtɪv/ *adj* **1** having to do with managing or executing(1): ~ *duties.* **2** having authority to carry out decisions, laws, decrees, etc: *the* ~ *branch of the government.* □ *n* [C] **1 the E**~, the executive branch of a government. **2** (in the Civil Service) person who carries out what has been planned or decided. **3** person or group in a business or commercial organization with administrative or managerial powers.

execu·tor /ɪg'zekjʊtə(r)/ *n* [C] person who is appointed to carry out the terms of a will.

execu·trix /ɪg'zekjʊtrɪks/ *n* [C] woman executor.

exemp·lary /ɪg'zemplərɪ/ *adj* serving as an example or a warning: ~ *conduct/ punishment.*

exemp·lify /ɪg'zemplɪfaɪ/ *vt* (*pt,pp* -ied) illustrate by example; be an example of.
exemp·lifi·ca·tion /ɪg'zemplɪfɪ'keɪʃən/ *n* [C,U]

exempt /ɪg'zempt/ *vt* free from (an obligation): *Poor eyesight will* ~ *you from military service* □ *adj* not liable to; free (*from*): ~ *from tax.*

exemp·tion /ɪg'zempʃən/ *n* [C,U]

ex·er·cise[1] /'eksəsaɪz/ *n* **1** [U] use or practice (of mental or physical powers, of rights): *Walking, running, rowing and cycling are all healthy forms of* ~. *The* ~ *of patience is essential in diplomatic negotiations.* **2** [C] activity, drill, etc designed for bodily, mental or spiritual training: *vocal/ gymnastic* ~*s;* ~ *for the harp/flute, etc;* ~*s in English composition.* **3** (*pl*) series of movements for training troops, crews of warships, etc: *military* ~*s.*

ex·er·cise[2] /'eksəsaɪz/ *vt,vi* **1** take exercise; give exercise to, ⇨ exercise[1](1): *We get fat and lazy if we don't* ~ *enough.* **2** employ; make use of: ~ *patience/one's rights.* **3** trouble; worry the mind of: *The problem that is exercising our minds...*

exert /ɪg'zɜːt/ *vt* **1** put forth; bring into use: ~ *all one's energy/influence, etc.* **2** make an effort: ~ *oneself to arrive early.*

exer·tion /ɪg'zɜːʃən/ *n* [U] exerting; [C] instance of this.

ex·hale /eks'heɪl/ *vt,vi* **1** breathe out. **2** give off gas, vapour; be given off (as gas or vapour).

ex·ha·la·tion /'ekshə'leɪʃən/ *n* [C,U]

ex·haust[1] /ɪg'zɔːst/ *n* [C,U] (outlet, in an engine or machine, for) steam, vapour, etc that has done its work.

ex·haust-pipe, for releasing gases from a motor-vehicle engine.

ex·haust² /ɪgˈzɔːst/ vt **1** use up completely: ~ one's patience/strength; ~ oneself by hard work; feeling ~ed, tired out. **2** make empty: ~ a well; ~ a tube of air. **3** say, find out, all there is to say about (something): ~ a subject.

ex·haus·tion /ɪgˈzɔːstʃən/ n [U] exhausting or being exhausted; total loss of strength: They were in a state of ~ after climbing the mountain.

ex·haus·tive /ɪgˈzɔːstɪv/ adj thorough; complete: an ~ inquiry.

ex·hi·bit¹ /ɪgˈzɪbɪt/ n [C] **1** object or collection of objects, shown publicly, e g in a museum: Do not touch the ~s. **2** document, object, etc produced in a law court and referred to in evidence, e g a weapon said to have been used by the accused person.

ex·hi·bit² /ɪgˈzɪbɪt/ vt **1** show publicly for sale, in a competition, etc: ~ paintings. Mr X ~s in several galleries. **2** give clear evidence of (a quality): The girls ~ed great courage during the climb.

ex·hi·bi·tor, person who exhibits at an art show, flower show, etc.

ex·hi·bi·tion /ˌeksɪˈbɪʃən/ n **1** [C] collection of things shown publicly (e g of works of art); display of commercial or industrial goods for advertisement; public display of animals, plants, flowers, etc (often shown in competition). **2** (sing with the or a, an) act of showing: an ~ of bad manners; an opportunity for the ~ of one's knowledge.

ex·hi·bi·tion·ism /ˌeksɪˈbɪʃənɪzm/ n [U] tendency towards extravagant behaviour designed to attract attention to oneself.

ex·hi·bi·tion·ist, person who is given to exhibitionism.

ex·hil·ar·ate /ɪgˈzɪləreɪt/ vt fill with high spirits; make lively or glad: exhilarating news.

ex·hil·ar·ation /ɪgˌzɪləˈreɪʃən/ n [U]

ex·hort /ɪgˈzɔːt/ vt (formal) urge: ~ her to do good.

ex·hor·ta·tion /ˌeksɔːˈteɪʃən/ n [U] exhorting; [C] earnest request, sermon, etc.

ex·hume /ɪgˈzjuːm/ US: -ˈzuːm/ vt take out (a dead body) from the earth (for examination).

ex·hum·ation /ˌeksjuːˈmeɪʃən/ n [C,U]

ex·ile /ˈegzaɪl/ n **1** [U] being sent away from one's country or home, esp as a punishment: be/live in ~; go/be sent into ~; after an ~ of ten years. **2** [C] person who is banished in this way. □ vt send into exile.

ex·ist /ɪgˈzɪst/ vi **1** be; have being; be real: The idea ~s only in the minds of poets. Does life ~ on Mars? **2** continue living: We cannot ~ without food and water.

ex·ist·ence /-əns/ n **1** [U] the state of being: Do you believe in the ~ of ghosts? This is the oldest skull in ~ence. **2** (with a, an) manner of living: lead a happy ~ence. **3** all that exists.

ex·ist·ent /-ənt/ adj living; being real; actual.

exit /ˈeksɪt/ n [C] **1** departure of an actor from the stage: make one's ~, go out or away. **2** way out, e g from a theatre or cinema. □ vi (as a stage direction) E~ Macbeth, Macbeth goes off the stage.

ex·on·er·ate /ɪgˈzonəreɪt/ vt free, release: ~ him from blame/responsibility.

ex·on·er·ation /ɪgˌzonəˈreɪʃən/ n [U]

ex·or·bi·tant /ɪgˈzɔːbɪtənt/ adj (of a price, charge or demand) much too high or great.

ex·or·bi·tant·ly adv

ex·or·cize, -cise /ˈeksɔːsaɪz/ vt drive out, e g an evil spirit, by prayers or magic.

ex·or·cism /-sɪzm/ n [C,U] instance of, belief in, exorcizing.

ex·or·cist /-sɪst/, person who performs an exorcism.

ex·otic /ɪgˈzotɪk/ adj **1** (of plants, fashions, words, ideas) introduced from another country. **2** foreign or unusual in style; striking or pleasing because colourful, unusual: ~ birds.

ex·pand /ɪkˈspænd/ vt,vi **1** make or become larger: Metals ~ when they are heated. ⇨ contract³(1). Our foreign trade has ~ed during recent years. He ~ed his short story into a novel. **2** unfold or spread out: The petals of many flowers ~ in the sunshine. **3** (of a person) become good-humoured or genial.

ex·panse /ɪkˈspæns/ n [C] wide and open area: the broad ~ of the Pacific; the blue ~ of the sky.

ex·pan·sion /ɪkˈspænʃən/ n **1** [U] expanding or being expanded(1): the ~ of gases when heated. **2** [C] enlargement: The novel was an ~ of his short story.

ex·pan·sive /ɪkˈspænsɪv/ adj **1** able, tending, to expand. **2** (of persons, speech) unreserved, good-humoured.

ex·patri·ate /eksˈpætrɪeɪt US: -ˈpeɪt-/ vt leave one's own country to live abroad; renounce one's citizenship. □ n /-rɪət/ [C] person living outside his own country: American ~s in Paris.

ex·pect /ɪkˈspekt/ vt **1** think or believe that something will happen or come, that a person will come: We ~ed you yesterday. 'Will he be late?'—'I ~ so.' They ~ (= require) me to work on Saturdays. **2** be expecting, be pregnant.

ex·pect·ancy /-ənsɪ/ n [U] the state of expecting: with a look/an air of ~ancy; life ~ancy.

ex·pect·ant /-ənt/ adj expecting: an ~ant mother, woman who is pregnant. ⇨ expect(2).

ex·pec·ta·tion /ˌekspekˈteɪʃən/ n **1** [U] expecting; awaiting: He ate a light lunch in ~ of a good dinner. **2** (often pl) thing that is expected. **3** (pl) future prospects, esp something to be inherited: a young man with great ~s. **4** [C] years a person is expected to live: An insurance company can tell you the ~ of life of a man who is 40 years old.

ex·pedi·ent /ɪk'spidɪənt/ adj likely to be useful or helpful for a purpose; advantageous though contrary to principle: *In times of war governments do things because they are* ~. □ *n* [C] necessary plan, action, device, etc.
ex·pedi·ently adv
ex·pedi·ence /-əns/, **ex·pedi·ency** /-ənsɪ/ *n* [U] suitability for a purpose; self-interest: *act from expediency, not from principle.*
ex·pedite /'ekspɪdaɪt/ vt (formal) help the progress of; speed up (business, etc).
ex·pedi·tion /'ekspɪ'dɪʃən/ *n* **1** [C] (men, ships, etc making a) journey or voyage for a definite purpose: *send a party of men/go on an* ~ *to the Antarctic.* **2** [U] (formal) promptness; speed.
ex·pedi·tion·ary /-ʃənrɪ US: -ʃənerɪ/ adj of, making up, an expedition.
ex·pedi·tious /'ekspɪ'dɪʃəs/ adj (formal) acting quickly; prompt and efficient.
ex·pedi·tious·ly adv
ex·pel /ɪk'spel/ vt (-ll-) **1** send out or away by force: ~ *a boy from school.* **2** force out: ~ *air from the lungs.*
ex·pend /ɪk'spend/ vt **1** spend: ~ *time and care in doing something.* **2** use up: *They had* ~*ed all their ammunition.*
ex·pend·able /-əbəl/ adj (esp) that may be sacrificed to achieve a purpose: *The general considered that these troops were* ~*able.*
ex·pen·di·ture /ɪk'spendɪtʃə(r)/ *n* **1** [U] spending or using: *the* ~ *of money on armaments.* **2** [C,U] amount expended: *an* ~ *of £500 on new furniture.*
ex·pense /ɪk'spens/ *n* **1** [U] spending (of money, time, energy, etc); cost: *I want the best you can supply; you need spare no* ~, *you need not try to economize.* **at the expense of,** at the cost of: *He became a brilliant scholar, but only at the* ~ *of his health.* **2** (usually pl) money used or needed: *travelling* ~*s. Illness, holidays and other* ~*s reduced his bank balance to almost nothing.*
ex·pens·ive /ɪk'spensɪv/ adj causing expense; costing a great deal: *an* ~ *dress; too* ~ *for me to buy.*
ex·pens·ive·ly adv
ex·peri·ence /ɪk'spɪərɪəns/ *n* **1** [U] process of gaining knowledge or skill by doing and seeing things; knowledge or skill so gained: *We all learn by* ~. *Has he had much* ~ *in work of this sort?* **2** [C] event, activity, which has given one experience(1). **3** [C] event that affects one in some way: *an unpleasant/unusual/delightful* ~. **by/from experience:** *learn from* ~. □ *vt* have experience of: ~ *pleasure/pain/difficulty.*
ex·peri·enced adj having knowledge or skill as the result of experience: *an* ~*d nurse/teacher.*
ex·peri·ment /ɪk'sperɪmənt/ *n* **1** [C] test or trial carried out carefully in order to study what happens and gain new knowledge: *per-*

form/carry out an ~ *in chemistry.* **2** [U] experimenting: *learn by* ~. □ *vi* conduct experiments: ~ *with new methods.*
ex·peri·men·ta·tion /ɪk'sperɪmen'teɪʃən/ *n* [U]
ex·peri·men·tal /ɪk'sperɪ'mentəl/ adj of, used for, based on, experiments: ~ *methods; an* ~ *farm.*
ex·pert /'ekspɜːt/ *n* [C] person with special knowledge, skill or training: *an agricultural* ~; *an* ~ *in economics.* □ adj trained, skilled, by practice: *according to* ~ *advice/opinions.*
ex·pert·ly adv
ex·pert·ise /'ekspɜː'tiz/ *n* [U] **1** expert opinion. **2** expert knowledge and skill.
ex·pir·ation /'ekspɪ'reɪʃən/ *n* [U] **1** ending (of a period of time): *at the* ~ *of the lease.* **2** breathing out (of air).
ex·pire /ɪk'spaɪə(r)/ vi **1** (of a period of time) come to an end: *When does your driving licence* ~? **2** (literary) die.
ex·piry /ɪk'spaɪərɪ/ *n* [U] end, termination, esp of a contract or agreement: *the* ~ *of a driving licence.*
ex·plain /ɪk'spleɪn/ vt **1** make plain or clear; show the meaning of: *A dictionary tries to* ~ *the meanings of words. He* ~*ed that he had been delayed by the weather.* **2** account for: *Can you* ~ *his behaviour? That* ~*s his absence.*
ex·pla·na·tion /'eksplə'neɪʃən/ *n* **1** [U] (process of) explaining: *The plan needs* ~ *to make it clear.* **2** [C] statement, fact, circumstance, etc that explains: *an* ~ *of his conduct/of a mystery.*
ex·plana·tory /ɪk'splænətrɪ US: -tɔːrɪ/ adj serving or intended to explain.
ex·ple·tive /ɪk'splitɪv US: 'eksplətɪv/ *n* [C] (often meaningless) exclamation, e g 'My goodness', or an oath such as 'Damn'.
ex·plic·able /ek'splɪkəbəl/ adj that can be explained.
ex·pli·cit /ɪk'splɪsɪt/ adj (of a statement) clearly and fully expressed: *He was quite* ~ *about it,* left no doubt about what he meant.
ex·pli·cit·ly adv
ex·pli·cit·ness *n* [U]
ex·plode /ɪk'spləʊd/ vt, vi **1** (cause to) burst with a loud noise: ~ *a bomb/a charge of gunpowder. The bomb* ~*d.* **2** (of feelings) burst out; (of persons) show violent emotion: *At last his anger* ~*d. He* ~*d with rage.* **3** destroy, expose (the incorrectness of) an idea, a theory, etc: ~ *a superstition: an* ~*d idea.*
ex·ploit[1] /'eksplɔɪt/ *n* [C] bold or adventurous act.
ex·ploit[2] /ɪk'splɔɪt/ vt **1** use, work or develop mines and other natural resources of a country. **2** use selfishly, or for one's own profit: ~ *child labour.*
ex·ploi·ta·tion /'eksplɔɪ'teɪʃən/ *n* [U]
ex·plore /ɪk'splɔː(r)/ vt **1** travel into or through (a country, etc) for the purpose of

learning about it: ~ *the Arctic regions.* **2** examine thoroughly problems, possibilities, etc in order to test, learn about, them.

ex·plor·er, person who explores.

ex·plo·ra·tion /ˌeksplə`reɪʃən/ n [U] exploring: *the exploration of the ocean depths;* [C] instance of this.

ex·plora·tory /ɪk`splɔrətrɪ US: -tɔrɪ/ adj for the purpose of exploring.

ex·plo·sion /ɪk`spləʊʒən/ n [C] **1** (loud noise caused by a) sudden and violent bursting: *a* `bomb ~. *The* ~ *was heard a mile away.* **2** outburst or outbreak of anger, laughter, etc. **3** great and sudden increase: *the population* ~.

ex·plos·ive /ɪk`spləʊsɪv/ n, adj (substance) tending to or likely to explode: *a shell filled with high* ~. *An* ~ *charge. That's an* ~ *issue,* one likely to cause anger, etc.

ex·plos·ive·ly adv

ex·po·nent /ɪk`spəʊnənt/ n [C] person or thing that explains or interprets, or is a representative or example: *Huxley was an* ~ *of Darwin's theory of evolution.*

ex·port[1] /`ekspɔt/ n **1** [C] (business of) exporting: *a ban on the* ~ *of gold; the* `~ *trade;* `~ *duties.* **2** [C] thing exported: *Last year* ~*s exceeded imports in value.*

ex·port[2] /ɪk`spɔt/ vt,vi send (goods) to another country: ~ *cotton goods.*

ex·porter, person who exports goods.

ex·port·able /-əbəl/ adj

ex·pose /ɪk`spəʊz/ vt **1** uncover; leave uncovered or unprotected: ~ *one's body to the sunlight;* ~ *soldiers to unnecessary risks.* **2** display: ~ *goods in a shopwindow.* **3** disclose, make known: ~ *a plot/liar.* **4** (in photography) allow light to reach (film, etc): ~ *30 metres of cinema film.*

ex·po·si·tion /ˌekspə`zɪʃən/ n **1** [U] expounding or explaining. **2** [C] instance of this; explanation or interpretation of a theory, plan, etc. **3** [C] (abbr **expo**) /`ekspəʊ/ exhibition of goods, etc: *an industrial* ~.

ex·po·sure /ɪk`spəʊʒə(r)/ n **1** [U] exposing or being exposed (all senses): *The climbers lost their way on the mountain and died of* ~. *The* ~ *of the plot against the President probably saved his life.* **2** [C] instance of exposing or being exposed (all senses): *How many* ~*s have you taken,* How many pictures have you taken on the film? **3** aspect: *a house with a southern* ~, one that faces south.

ex·pound /ɪk`spaʊnd/ vt (*formal*) explain, make clear, by giving details: ~ *a theory.*

ex·press[1] /ɪk`spres/ adj **1** clearly and openly stated, not suggested or implied: *It was his* ~ *wish that you should remarry.* **2** going, sent, quickly; designed for high speed: *an* ~ *train.* □ adv by express delivery.

ex·press[2] /ɪk`spres/ n [C] **1** express train: *the 8.00 am* ~ *to Edinburgh.* **2** service rendered by the post office, railways, road ser-

vices, ing goods: *send goods by* ~.

ex·press[3] /ɪk`spres/ vt **1** make known, show by words, looks, actions: *I find it difficult to* ~ *my meaning. A smile* ~*ed her joy at the good news.* **2** send a letter, goods, etc fast by special delivery: *The letter is urgent; you had better* ~ *it.* **3** press or squeeze out juices/oil *from/out of: juice* ~*ed* (*pressed* is more usual) *from grapes.*

ex·pres·sion /ɪk`spreʃən/ n **1** [U] process of expressing(1): *read* (aloud) *with* ~, in a way that shows feeling for the meaning. **find expression in,** be expressed by means of: *Her feelings at last found* ~ *in tears.* **2** [C] word or phrase: *'Shut up'* (= Stop talking) *is not a polite* ~. **3** outward sign (on the face, in the voice, etc) of an emotion: *He had an angry* ~ *on his face.* **4** (in maths) symbols expressing a quantity, e g $3xy^2$.

ex·pres·sion·less adj without expression: *an* ~*less face.*

ex·press·ive /ɪk`spresɪv/ adj, serving to express: *looks* ~ *of despair; an* ~ *smile.*

ex·press·ive·ly adv

ex·press·ly /ɪk`spreslɪ/ adv plainly; definitely: *You were* ~*ly forbidden to touch my papers.*

ex·pro·pri·ate /eks`prəʊprɪeɪt/ vt take away (property); dispossess (a person of an estate, etc).

ex·pro·pri·ation /ˌeks`prəʊprɪ`eɪʃən/ n [U]

ex·pul·sion /ɪk`spʌlʃən/ n [U] expelling or being expelled; [C] instance of this: *the* ~ *of a student from college.*

ex·pur·gate /`ekspəgeɪt/ vt take out (from a book, etc what are considered to be) improper or objectionable parts: *an* ~*d edition of a novel.*

ex·pur·ga·tion /ˌekspə`geɪʃən/ n [U]

ex·quis·ite /ek`skwɪzɪt/ adj excellent, of a high state of perfection: ~ *workmanship.*

ex·quis·ite·ly adv

ex-ser·vice /eks `sɜvɪs/ adj having formerly served in the armed forces.

ex-ser·vice·man, (*GB*): *an* ~*men's organization.*

ex·tant /`ek`stænt/ adj (esp of documents, etc) still in existence: *the earliest* ~ *manuscript of this poem.*

ex·tem·por·ary /ɪk`stempərərɪ US: -pəreɪ/ adj = extempore.

ex·tem·pore /ek`stempərɪ/ adv, adj (spoken or done) without previous thought or preparation: *speak* ~, without notes.

ex·tem·por·aneous·(ly) /ˌek`stempə`reɪnɪəs(lɪ)/ adj, adv

ex·tend /ɪk`stend/ vt,vi **1** make longer (in space or time); enlarge: ~ *a railway/the city boundaries.* **2** lay or stretch out the body, a limb, or limbs at full length: ~ *one's hand to her.* **3** offer, grant: ~ *an invitation/a warm welcome to him.* **4** (of space, land, etc) reach, stretch: *a road that* ~*s for miles and miles.* **5** cause to reach or stretch: ~ *a cable between two posts.* **6** (usually passive) use the powers of a person, horse, etc to the utmost: *The horse was fully ~ed.*

ex·ten·sion /ɪk`stenʃən/ *n* **1** [U] extending or being extended: *the ~ of useful knowledge.* **2** [C] additional part; enlargement: *an ~ of one's summer holidays; build an ~ to a hospital; get an ~ of time,* eg for paying a debt: *telephone No 01—629—8494, ~ 15,* i e an internal telephone in one of the offices.

ex·ten·sive /ɪk`stensɪv/ *adj* extending far; far-reaching: *~ repairs/inquiries.*

ex·ten·sive·ly *adv*

ex·tent /ɪk`stent/ *n* [U] **1** length; area; range: *I was amazed at the ~ of his knowledge.* **2** degree: *to a certain extent,* partly; *to some ~.*

ex·tenu·ate /ɪk`stenjʊeɪt/ *vt* make (wrongdoing) seem less serious (by finding an excuse): *There are extenuating circumstances in this case.*

ex·tenu·ation /ɪk`stenjʊ`eɪʃən/ *n* [C,U]

ex·ter·ior /ek`stɪərɪə(r)/ *adj* outer; situated on or coming from outside: *the ~ of a building.* ⇨ interior. □ *n* [C] outside; outward appearance: *a good man with a friendly ~.*

ex·ter·mi·nate /ɪk`stɜːmɪneɪt/ *vt* make an end of (disease, ideas, a race, etc); destroy completely.

ex·ter·mi·na·tion /ɪk`stɜːmɪ`neɪʃən/ *n* [C,U]

ex·ter·nal /ek`stɜːnəl/ *adj* outside; situated on the outside; of or for the outside: *~ evidence,* obtained from independent sources, not from what is being examined. □ *n* [C] (usually *pl*) (*formal*) external circumstances: *the ~s of religion,* acts and ceremonies (contrasted with inner and spiritual aspects).

ex·ter·nally *adv*

ex·tinct /ɪk`stɪŋkt/ *adj* **1** no longer burning; no longer active: *an ~ volcano.* **2** (of feelings, passions) dead. **3** no longer in existence; having died out: *an ~ species; become ~.*

ex·tinc·tion /ɪk`stɪŋkʃən/ *n* [U] **1** making, being, becoming, extinct: *a race threatened by ~.* **2** act of extinguishing: *the ~ of a fire.*

ex·tin·guish /ɪk`stɪŋgwɪʃ/ *vt* **1** put out a light, fire. **2** end the existence of hope, love, passion, etc.

ex·tin·guisher, (kinds of) apparatus for discharging a jet of liquid chemicals for putting out a fire.

ex·tol /ɪk`stəʊl/ *vt* (-ll-) praise highly: *~ him as a hero.*

ex·tort /ɪk`stɔːt/ *vt* obtain by violence, threats, etc: *~ money from him.*

ex·tor·tion /ɪk`stɔːʃən/ *n* [C,U]

ex·tor·tion·ate /ɪk`stɔːʃənət/ *adj* **1** in the nature of extortion. **2** (of demands, prices) exorbitant.

ex·tor·tion·ate·ly *adv*

ex·tra /`ekstrə/ *adj* additional; beyond what is usual, expected or arranged for: *~ pay for ~ work.* □ *adv* **1** more than usually: *~ fine quality.* **2** in addition: *price £1.30, packing*

and postage ~. □ *n* [C] **1** additional thing; something for which an extra charge is made: *The bike costs £30; the pump and saddlebag are ~s.* **2** (in the cinema, TV, etc) person employed for a minor part, e g in a crowd scene. **3** special edition of a newspaper.

extra- /ekstrə-/ *prefix* outside, beyond, especially; *extramural; extraordinary.*

ex·tract /ɪk`strækt/ *vt* **1** take or get out (usually with effort): *have a tooth ~ed; ~ a bullet from a wound.* **2** (*fig*) obtain by force: *~ money/information from a person,* who is unwilling to give it. **3** obtain juices, etc) by pressing, crushing, boiling, etc: *~ oil from olives.* **4** select and copy out words, examples, passages, etc (from a book). □ *n* /`ekstrækt/ [C,U] **1** that which has been extracted(3): *beef ~.* **2** [C] passage extracted(4): *~s from a long poem.*

ex·trac·tion /ɪk`strækʃən/ *n* [C,U] (a) extracting or being extracted(1): *the ~ion of a tooth.* (b) descent: *Is he of French ~ion?*

extra·cur·ricu·lar /`ektrəkə`rɪkjʊlə(r)/ *adj* outside the regular course of academic work or studies: *~ activities,* e g a dramatic society.

ex·tra·dite /`ekstrədaɪt/ *vt* **1** give up, hand over (a person) from the State where he is a fugitive to the State where he is alleged to have committed, or has been convicted of, a crime. **2** obtain (such a person) for trial.

ex·tra·di·tion /`ekstrə`dɪʃən/ *n* [U]

ex·traneous /ɪk`streɪnɪəs/ *adj* **1** not related (to the object to which it is attached). **2** not belonging (to what is being dealt with); coming from outside: *~ interference.*

extra·ordi·nary /ɪk`strɔːdənərɪ *US:* -dənerɪ/ *adj* **1** beyond what is usual or ordinary; remarkable: *a man of ~ genius; ~ weather.* **2** (of officials) additional, specially employed: *envoy ~.*

ex·tra·ordi·nar·ily /ɪk`strɔːdənərəlɪ *US:* -dənerəlɪ/ *adv*

ex·trapo·late /ek`stræpəleɪt/ *vt,vi* estimate from known data, information, the unknown factors.

ex·trapo·la·tion /ek`stræp ə`leɪʃən/ *n* [C,U]

ex·trava·gance /ɪk`strævəgəns/ *n* **1** [U] being extravagant: *His ~ explains why he is always in debt.* **2** [C] something excessively expensive: *His new car was an ~ he could not afford.* **3** [C] absurd statement, act, etc.

ex·trava·gant /ɪk`strævəgənt/ *adj* **1** (in the habit of) wasting (money, etc); wasteful: *an ~ man; ~ tastes and habits.* **2** (of ideas, speech, behaviour) going beyond what is reasonable; not properly controlled: *~ praise/behaviour.*

ex·trava·gant·ly *adv*

ex·treme /ɪk`striːm/ *n* [C] **1** highest degree: *annoying in the ~,* very annoying. **2** (*pl*) qualities, etc as wide apart, as widely different, as possible: *the ~s of heat and cold. Love and hate are ~s.* **go/be driven to**

extremes, to do more than is usually considered right or desirable. □ *adj* **1** at the end(s); farthest possible: *in ~ old age.* **2** reaching the highest degree: *~ patience/ kindness.* **3** (of persons, their ideas) going to great lengths in views or actions: *the ~ left,* (in politics) those who are farthest to the left.
ex·treme·ly *adv*
ex·trem·ist /-ɪst/ *n* [C] person who holds extreme views (esp in politics). □ *adj* (of political views) extreme.
ex·trem·ity /ɪkˈstremətɪ/ *n* [C] (*pl* -ies) **1** extreme point, end or limit; (*pl*) hands and feet. **2** (*sing* only) extreme degree (of joy, misery, esp of misfortune): *an ~ of pain.* **3** (usually *pl*) extreme measures, e g for punishing, taking revenge: *Both armies were guilty of extremities.*
ex·tri·cate /ˈekstrɪkeɪt/ *vt* set free, get a person, oneself free: *~ oneself from a difficulty.*
ex·tri·cable /ekˈstrɪkəbəl/ *adj* that can be freed.
ex·tri·ca·tion /ˈekstrɪˈkeɪʃən/ *n* [U]
ex·trin·sic /ekˈstrɪnsɪk/ *adj* operating or originating from the outside; not essential.
ex·tro·vert /ˈekstrəvɜt/ *n* [C] **1** person more interested in what goes on around him than in his own thoughts and feelings. **2** (*informal*) lively, cheerful person. ⇨ introvert.
ex·tro·ver·sion /ˈekstrəˈvɜʃən US: -ˈvɜʒən/ *n* [U]
ex·uber·ant /ɪgˈzjubərənt US: -ˈzu-/ *adj* **1** growing vigorously; luxuriant: *plants with ~ foliage.* **2** full of life and vigour; high-spirited: *an ~ imagination.*
ex·uber·ant·ly *adv*
ex·uber·ance /-rəns/ *n* [U] state or quality of being exuberant: *The speaker's exuberance won over an apathetic audience.*
ex·ude /ɪgˈzjud US: -ˈzud/ *vt,vi* (*formal*) (of drops of liquid) come or pass out slowly: *Sweat ~s through the pores.*
ex·ult /ɪgˈzʌlt/ *vi* rejoice greatly: *~ at/in a success; ~* (= triumph) *over a defeated rival.*
ex·ult·ant /-ənt/ *adj* triumphant.
ex·ul·ta·tion /ˈegzʌlˈteɪʃən/ *n* [U] great joy (*at*); triumph (*over*).
eye¹ /ɑɪ/ *n* **1** organ of sight: *We see with our ~s.* **an eye for an eye,** punishment as severe as the injury suffered. **in the eyes of the law,** from the point of view of the law. **under/before one's very eyes,** (a) in one's presence, in front of one. (b) with no attempt at concealment. **up to one's eyes in** (*work, etc*), very busy with. **with an eye to,** with a view to, hoping for. **be in the public eye,** be often seen in public. **close one's eyes to,** refuse to see or take notice of. **have an eye for,** be a good judge of. **keep an eye on,** (*literary, fig*) keep a watch on. **make eyes at,** look amorously at. **open sb's eyes to,** cause him to realize. **see eye to eye (with),** agree entirely (with), have identical

views. **set/clap eyes on,** meet, see: *I hope I shall never set ~s on her again.* **2** thing like an eye: *the ~ of a needle,* the hole for the thread; *a hook and ~,* fastening with a hook and loop for a dress, etc.
ˈeye-ball, the eye within the lids and socket.
ˈeye-brow, arch of hair above the eye. **raise one's eyebrows,** express surprise, doubt, etc.
ˈeye-lash, hair, row of hairs, on the edge of the eyelid.
ˈeye-lid, upper or lower skin covering of the eye when blinking.
ˈeye-opener, circumstance, etc (often surprising) that makes one realize, understand something.
ˈeye-sight, power, faculty, of seeing: *to have good/poor ~sight.*
ˈeye-sore, something unpleasant to look at.
ˈeye-strain, tired condition of the eyes (as caused, for example, by reading very small print).
ˈeye-tooth, canine tooth.
ˈeye-witness, person who can give evidence of what he has himself seen: *an ~-witness account of a crime.*
eye² /ɑɪ/ *vt* observe, watch: *He ~d me with suspicion. They were ~ing us jealously.*
-eyed /ɑɪd/ *suffix:* *a ˈblue-~ girl,* girl having blue eyes; *ˈstarry-eyed* (*informal*), idealistic.
eye·let /ˈæɪlət/ *n* [C] small hole in cloth, etc for a rope, etc to go through; metal ring round such a hole, to strengthen it.

Ff

F, f /ef/ (*pl* F's, f's /efs/) the sixth letter of the English alphabet.
fa /fɑ/ *n* (in music) fourth of the syllables used in the scale *do, re, mi, fa, sol, la, ti, do.*
fab /fæb/ *adj* (*informal* abbr of) **fabulous(3)**.
fable /ˈfeɪbəl/ *n* **1** [C] short tale, not based on fact, esp one with animals in it, e g *Aesop's ~s,* and intended to give moral teaching. **2** [U] (*collective sing*) myths; legends: *sort out fact from ~.* **3** [C] false statement or account.
fabled /ˈfeɪbəld/ *adj* legendary.
fab·ric /ˈfæbrɪk/ *n* [C,U] **1** kind, length, of textile material; *woollen/silk ~s.* **2** structure: *the ~ of society; the ~ of the building.*
fab·ri·cate /ˈfæbrɪkeɪt/ *vt* **1** construct; put together. **2** make up (something false); forge (a document): *a ~d account of adventures.*
fab·ri·ca·tion /ˈfæbrɪˈkeɪʃən/ *n* [U] fabricating; [C] something fabricated (both senses).
fabu·lous /ˈfæbjʊləs/ *adj* **1** celebrated in

fable(2): ~ *heroes*. **2** incredible or absurd: ~ *wealth*. **3** (*informal*) wonderful; marvellous.

fabu·lous·ly *adv* extremely: ~*ly rich*.

fa·çade /fə'sɑd/ *n* [C] **1** front or face of a building (towards a street or open place). **2** (*fig*) false appearance: *a* ~ *of indifference*.

face[1] /feɪs/ *n* [C] **1** the front part of the head (eyes, nose, mouth, cheeks, chin): *He fell on his* ~. **face to face,** (of persons) together so that they look at each other: *The two politicians were brought* ~ *to* ~ *in a TV interview*. **in one's face,** (a) straight against: *The sun was shining in our* ~*s*. (b) with no attempt at concealment: *Death stared him in the* ~. *She'll only laugh in your* ~. **to one's face,** openly, in one's hearing: *I'll tell him so to his* ~, i e I'm not afraid to tell him. (*Note:* compare *behind one's back*). **fly in the face of sth,** openly defy, disregard. **show one's face,** appear, let oneself be seen: *How can you show your* ~ *here after the way you behaved last time?* **2** look; expression: *a sad* ~; *smiling* ~*s*. **on the face of it,** judging by appearances, when first seen or heard: *On the* ~ *of it, his story seems unconvincing*. **keep a straight face,** hide one's amusement (by not smiling or laughing). **lose face,** suffer loss of credit or reputation. **pull a face/faces,** distort the face, make grimaces. **put a good/bold face on sth,** make it look well; show courage in dealing with it. **save (one's) face,** avoid losing one's dignity or suffering loss of credit or reputation. Hence, **face-saver** *n*, **face-saving** *n, adj*: ~*-saving moves*. **3** surface; façade (of a building); front: *the* ~ *of a clock. He laid the cards* ~ *down on the table. The team climbed the north* ~ *of the mountain*.

face-ache, (*fig*) irritating, annoying, person.

face-card, king, queen, or knave.

face-cloth, (*esp*) small square towel for washing the face and hands.

face-cream, cosmetic cream for the face.

face-lift(ing), (a) operation of tightening the skin to smooth out wrinkles and make the face look younger. (b) (*fig*) improvement to the appearance (of a building etc).

face-powder, cosmetic powder for the face.

face value, (a) value shown on a coin or banknote. (b) (*fig*) apparent value of something: *accept a promise at* ~ *value*.

face-less *adj* (*fig*) unknown to the general public: *the* ~*less men who have power in commerce and industry*.

face[2] /feɪs/ *vt,vi* **1** have or turn the face to, or in a certain direction; be opposite to: *Turn round and* ~ *me. Who's the man facing us?* **2** meet confidently or defiantly: ~ *the enemy;* ~ *dangers*. **face the music,** show no fear at a time of trial, danger, difficulty. **face up to (sth),** recognize and deal with,

honestly and bravely: *F*~ *up to the fact that you are no longer young*. **3** recognize the existence of: ~ *facts*, be realistic. **4** present itself to: *the problem that* ~*s us*. **5** cover with a layer of different material: ~ *a wall with concrete*.

facet /'fæsɪt/ *n* [C] **1** one of the many sides of a cut stone or jewel. **2** view, aspect, e g of a problem.

fa·ce·tious /fə'siːʃəs/ *adj* (intended to be, trying to be) humorous; fond of, marked by, joking: *a* ~ *remark/young man*.

fa·ce·tious·ly *adv*

fa·ce·tious·ness *n* [U]

facia /'feɪʃə/ *n* = **fascia**.

fa·cial /'feɪʃəl/ *adj* of or for the face: *a* ~ *massage*. □ *n* [C] facial massage.

facile /'fæsaɪl *US:* -səl/ *adj* **1** easily done or obtained: *a* ~ *victory*. **2** (of a person) able to do things easily. **3** (of speech or writing) done easily but without attention to quality: *a* ~ *remark*.

fa·cil·i·tate /fə'sɪlɪteɪt/ *vt* make easy; lessen the difficulty of: *Modern inventions have* ~*d housework*. (*Note:* never used when the subject is a word for a person.)

fa·cil·ity /fə'sɪlətɪ/ *n* (*pl* -ies) **1** [U] quality which makes learning or doing things easy; aptitude: *have great* ~ *in learning languages*. **2** (*pl*) aids, circumstances, which make it easy to do things: *facilities for travel*, e g buses, trains, air services; `*sports facilities*, e g running tracks, swimming pools.

fac·ing /'feɪsɪŋ/ *n* **1** coating of different material, e g on a wall. **2** (*pl*) material of a different colour on a garment, e g on the cuffs, collar: *a purple jacket with green* ~*s*. ⇨ **face**[2](5).

fac·sim·ile /fæk'sɪməlɪ/ *n* [C] exact copy or reproduction of writing, printing, a picture, etc.

fact /fækt/ *n* **1** [C] something that has happened or been done. **accessary before the fact,** accessary who is not present when a crime is committed. **accessary after the fact,** person who knowingly helps another who has committed a crime. **2** [C] something known to be true or accepted as true: *No one can deny the* ~ *that fire burns*. **3** (*sing* without *a*) reality; what is true; what exists: *It is important to distinguish* ~ *from fiction*. **in fact; as a matter of fact, in point of fact,** really: *I think so; in* ~, *I'm certain*.

fact-finding *adj* designed to discover what is true: *a* ~*-finding tour/committee*.

fac·tion /'fækʃən/ *n* **1** [C] discontented, often unscrupulous and self-interested group of persons within a party (esp political): *The party split into petty* ~*s*. **2** [U] quarrelling among such groups; party strife.

fac·tious /'fækʃəs/ *adj* of, caused by, fond of faction: *a factious spirit*.

fac·tor /'fæktə(r)/ *n* [C] **1** (*maths*) whole number (except 1) by which a larger number can be divided exactly: *2, 3, 4 and 6 are ~s of 12*. **2** fact, circumstance, etc helping to bring about a result: *evolutionary ~s*, environmental influences, etc; *an unknown ~*, something unknown, likely to influence a result. **3** agent; person who buys and sells on commission.

fac·tory /ˈfæktərɪ/ *n* [C] (*pl* -ies) building(s) where goods are made (esp by machinery); workshop: *~ workers*.

fac·tual /ˈfæktʃʊəl/ *adj* concerned with fact.

fac·ulty /ˈfæktʃʊəl/ *n* [C] (*pl* -ies) **1** power of mind; power of doing things: *the mental faculties, reason; have a great ~ for learning languages*. **2** (in a university) department or grouping of related departments: *the F~ of Law/Science*; all the teachers, lecturers, professors, etc in one of these: *a member of (the) ~*.

fad /fæd/ *n* [C] fashion, interest, trend, unlikely to last: *Will Tom continue to collect foreign stamps or is it only a passing ~?*

fade /feɪd/ *vt,vi* **1** (cause to) lose colour, freshness or vigour: *The strong sunlight had ~d the curtains. Flowers soon ~ when cut*. **2** go slowly out of view, hearing or the memory: *Daylight ~d away. His hopes ~d*. **3** (in filming, broadcasting) (cause to) decrease or increase in strength: *~ one scene into another; ~ a conversation out/in*.

faeces (*US* = **feces**) /ˈfiːsiːz/ *n pl* waste matter excreted from the bowels.

fag[1] /fæg/ *n* **1** (*sing* only) tiring job: *What a ~! It's too much (of a) ~*. **2** [C] (*sl*) cigarette.

fag[2] /fæg/ *vi,vt* (-gg-) **1** do very tiring work: *~ (away) at a task*. **2** (of work) make very tired: *Doesn't that sort of work ~ you out?*

fag·got (*US* also **fagot**) /ˈfægət/ *n* [C] **1** bundle of sticks or twigs tied together for burning as fuel. **2** meat ball for frying.

Fahr·en·heit /ˈfærənhaɪt/ *n* name of a thermometer scale with freezing-point at 32° and boiling-point at 212°.

fail[1] /feɪl/ *n* (only in) **without fail**, for certain, no matter what difficulties, etc there may be: *I'll be there at two o'clock without ~*.

fail[2] /feɪl/ *vi,vt* **1** be unsuccessful: *~ (in) an examination; ~ to pass an examination. All our plans/attempts ~ed*. **2** (of examiners) decide that (a candidate) has been unsuccessful. **3** be not enough; come to an end while still needed or expected: *The crops ~ed because of drought. Words ~ me*, I cannot find words (to describe my feelings, etc). **4** (of health, eyesight, etc) become weak: *His eyesight is ~ing*. **5** omit; neglect; not remember: *He never ~s to write* (= always writes) *to his mother every week*. **6** become bankrupt: *Several of the biggest banks ~ed during the depression*. **7 fail in**, be lacking in: *He's a clever man, but ~s in plain sense*.

fail·ing[1] /ˈfeɪlɪŋ/ *n* [C] weakness or fault (of character): *We all have our little ~s*.

fail·ing[2] /ˈfeɪlɪŋ/ *prep* in the absence of: *~ this*, if this does not happen; *~ an answer*, if no answer is received.

fail·ure /ˈfeɪljə(r)/ *n* **1** [U] lack of success: *All his efforts ended in ~, were unsuccessful*. **2** [C] instance of failing; person, attempt, or thing that fails: *Success came after many ~s*. **3** [U] state of not being adequate; [C] instance of this: *`heart ~. F~ of crops often results in famine*. **4** [C] bankruptcy: *many bank ~s*. **5** [C,U] neglect, omission, inability: *His ~ to help us was disappointing*. **6** breakdown (of machinery, power etc): *`engine ~*.

faint[1] /feɪnt/ *adj* (-er, -est) **1** (of things known by the senses) weak; indistinct; not clear: *The sounds of the music grew ~er in the distance. There was a ~ smell of burning*. **2** (of things in the mind) weak; vague: *There is a ~ hope that she may be cured. I haven't the ~est idea what you mean*. **3** (of the body's movements and functions) weak; failing: *His breathing became ~*. **4** (of persons) likely to lose consciousness: *She looks/feels ~*. **5** (of persons) weak, exhausted: *~ with hunger and cold*. **6** (of actions, etc) unlikely to have much effect: *make a ~ attempt to do something*. **7** timid: *F~ heart never won fair lady*.

faint-'hearted *adj* lacking in courage.

faint·ly *adv*

faint[2] /feɪnt/ *vi* **1** lose consciousness (because of loss of blood, the heat, shock, etc): *He ~ed from hunger*. **2** become weak: *He was ~ing with hunger*. □ *n* [C] act, state, of fainting(1): *She collapsed in a ~*.

fair[1] /feə(r)/ *adj* (-er, -est) **1** just; acting in a just and honourable manner; in accordance with justice or the rules (of a game, etc): *Everyone must have a ~ share; a ~ fight/tackle*. **give get a fair hearing**, an opportunity to defend his conduct, etc, e g in a law court. **2** average; quite good: *a ~ chance of success*. **3** (of the weather) good; dry and fine; (of winds) favourable: *hoping for ~ weather*. **4** satisfactory; promising: *be in a ~ way to succeed*. **5** (of the skin, hair) pale; blond: *a `~-haired girl; a ~ complexion*. **6** (of speeches, promises, etc) carefully chosen to seem polite and gentle in order to please and persuade: *put sb off with ~ words/promises*. **7** clean; clear; without blemish: *Please make a ~ copy of this letter*, a new one without the errors, corrections, etc. **8** (*old use*) beautiful: *the ~ sex*, women.

fair `play, (*fig*) justice; equally just treatment for all.

fair·ish /ˈfeərɪʃ/ *adj* of average size, weight or quality.

fair[2] /feə(r)/ *adv* in a fair(1) manner: *play ~*. **fair enough**, (*informal*) used to indicate that a person has acted reasonably, made a reasonable suggestion, etc.

fair[3] /feə(r)/ *n* [C] **1** market (esp for cattle, sheep, farm products, etc) held periodically

in a particular place. **2** group of entertainments, side-shows, etc travelling from place to place. **3** large-scale exhibition of commercial and industrial goods: *a world* ~.
'fair-ground, open space for fairs(2).
fair-ly[1] /'feəlɪ/ *adv* **1** justly; honestly: *treat him* ~. **2** (*informal*) utterly; completely: *He was* ~ *beside himself with rage.*
fair-ly /'feəlɪ/ *adv of degree* moderately: *This is a* ~ *easy book.*
fair-way /'feəweɪ/ *n* [C] **1** navigable channel for ships. **2** part of a golf-links, between a tee and a green, free from hazards.
fairy /'feərɪ/ *n* [C] (*pl* -ies) small imaginary being with supernatural powers, able to help or harm human beings.
'fairy-land, home of fairies; enchanted place.
'fairy-tale, (**a**) tale about fairies. (**b**) untrue account, esp by a child.
faith /feɪθ/ *n* **1** [U] trust; unquestioning confidence: *have/put one's* ~ *in God. I haven't much* ~ *in this medicine.* **2** [C] belief in divine truth without proof; religion: *the Christian, Jewish and Muslim* ~*s.* **3** [U] promise; engagement. *keep/break faith with somebody,* be loyal/disloyal. **4** [U] loyalty; sincerity. *in bad/good faith,* with/ without the intention of deceiving.
'faith-healing, (belief in) healing (of disease, etc) by prayer, etc.
faith-ful /'feɪθfʊl/ *adj* **1** loyal and true: *a* ~ *friend;* ~ *to one's promise.* **2** true to the facts: *a* ~ *copy/description/account.* **3** *the* ~, (*pl*) the true believers, esp of Islam and Christianity.
faith-fully *adv* in a faithful manner: *He promised* ~ *that he would come. Yours faithfully,* formula for closing a letter (esp in formal or business style).
faith-less /'feɪθləs/ *adj* false; disloyal.
faith-less-ly *adv*
fake /feɪk/ *n* [C] **1** story, work of art, etc that looks genuine but is not. **2** person who tries to deceive by claiming falsely to be or have something. □ *vt* make (e g a work of art, a story) in order to deceive: ~ *an oil-painting.*
fakir /'feɪkɪə(r) *US:* fə'kɪər/ *n* [C] Muslim or Hindu religious mendicant who is regarded as a holy man.
fal-con /'fɔlkən *US:* 'fælkən/ *n* [C] small bird of prey trained to hunt and kill other birds and small animals.
fal-con-ry *n* [U] hunting with, art of training, falcons.
fall[1] /fɔl/ *n* [C] **1** act of falling: *a* ~ *from a horse; a* ~ *in temperature; a* ~ *in prices.* **2** amount of rain that falls; distance by which something falls or comes down: *The* ~ *of the river here is six feet.* **3** (often *pl*) place where a river falls over cliffs, etc: *Niagara F*~*s.* **4** (*US*) autumn: *in the* ~ *of 1970.*
fall[2] /fɔl/ *vi,vt* (*pt* fell /fel/, *pp* ~en /'fɔlən/) (For special uses with *adverbial*

particles and *prepositions,* ⇨ 14 below.) **1** come or go down freely (by force of weight, loss of balance, etc): *He fell into the water. The rain was* ~*ing steadily. fall on one's feet,* (*fig*) be fortunate; get out of a difficulty successfully. *fall short of,* fail to equal; be inferior to: *Your work* ~*s short of my expectations.* **2** no longer stand; come to the ground; collapse; be overthrown: *He fell over and broke his left leg. He fell on his knees* (= knelt down) *and begged for mercy. He fell in battle,* was killed. *fall flat (on one's face),* (*fig*) fail to have the intended effect: *His best jokes all fell flat, did not amuse his listeners. fall over oneself,* (**a**) fall because one is awkward, clumsy, or in too much of a hurry. (**b**) (*fig*) be very eager: *The big teams were* ~*ing over themselves/each other for this brilliant player.* **3** hang down: *Her hair/cloak fell over her shoulders.* **4** come or go to a lower level or point; become lower or less: *The barometer is* ~*ing. The temperature fell rapidly.* **5** become: *His horse fell lame. He fell silent. The old man fell asleep. fall in love (with),* become filled with love: *He fell in love with an actress. fall out of love (with),* cease to feel love (for). **6** descend on/upon: *Darkness fell on/upon the scene,* it became dark. **7** sin; give way to doing wrong: *Eve tempted Adam and he fell.* **8** be overcome or defeated; (of a city, fort, etc) be captured: *The Government has* ~*en again.* **9** *fall on,* take a direction or position: *A shadow fell on the wall. His eye fell on* (= He suddenly saw) *a curious object. In 'formidable' the stress may* ~ *on either the first or the second syllable.* **10** *fall on/among,* come by chance, design, or right: *All the expenses fell on me,* I had to pay them. *He has* ~*en on evil days,* is suffering misfortune. *fall foul of,* ⇨ foul[1](b). **11** (of land) slope: *The ground* ~*s towards the river.* **12** occur, have as date: *Easter* ~*s early next year.* **13** be spoken: *Not a word fell from his lips.*

14 (special uses with *adverbial particles* and prepositions):
fall about (laughing/with laughter), (*informal*) laugh uncontrollably.
fall among, get mixed up with: ~ *among thieves.*
fall astern, drop behind; not keep up with.
fall away, (**a**) desert: *His supporters began to* ~ *away.* (**b**) disappear, vanish.
fall back, move or turn back: *Our attack was so successful that the enemy fell back. fall back on,* turn to for support: *It's always useful to have savings to* ~ *back on.*
fall behind (with), fail to keep level with: *He always* ~*s behind when we're going uphill. Don't* ~ *behind with your rent, or you'll be evicted.*
fall for, (*informal*) be attracted by the merits of (esp when deceived): *He* ~*s for every*

pretty face he sees.

fall in, (a) collapse; give way: *The roof fell in.* **(b)** (*mil*) take, cause to take, places in the ranks: *The sergeant ordered the men to ~ in.* **(c)** (of a single soldier) take his place in the ranks. **(d)** (of a lease) expire. **(e)** (of a debt) become due. **fall in with, (a)** happen to meet. **(b)** agree to: *He fell in with my plans.*

fall into line (with), agree to (what others are doing or wish to do).

fall off, become smaller, fewer or less: *Attendance at church has ~en off.*

fall on, attack; assault (the enemy).

fall out, (a) (*mil*) leave one's place in the rank or file. **(b)** discontinue; give up: *the `~-out rate,* e g of students who give up a course of study. ⇨ *drop-out* at *drop²* (12).

fall out (with), quarrel (with): *He has ~en out with the girl he was going to marry.*

fall through, fail; come to nothing: *His scheme fell through.*

fall to, begin to eat, fight, attack, etc: *They fell to with a good appetite.*

fall under, be classifiable under: *The results ~ under three headings.*

fal·lacy /ˈfæləsɪ/ *n* (*pl* -ies) **1** [C] false or mistaken belief. **2** [U] false reasoning or argument: *a statement based on ~.*

fal·la·cious /fəˈleɪʃəs/ *adj* misleading; based on error.

fallen *pp* of *fall².*

fal·lible /ˈfæləbəl/ *adj* liable to error.

fal·li·bil·ity /ˌfæləˈbɪlətɪ/ *n* [U] (state of) being fallible.

Fal·lo·pian tube /fəˈləʊpɪən ˈtjub *US:* -ˈtub/ *n* = oviduct.

fall-out /ˈfɔl aʊt/ *n* [U] radioactive dust in the atmosphere, after a nuclear explosion.

fal·low /ˈfæləʊ/ *adj, n* [U] (land) ploughed but not sown or planted: *allow land to lie ~.*

fal·low-deer /ˈfæləʊ dɪə(r)/ *n* [C] (*pl* unchanged) small deer with a reddish-yellow coat with, in the summer, white spots.

false /fɔls/ *adj* **1** wrong; incorrect: *a ~ alarm; a ~ arrest.* **make a false start,** (*athletics*) start before the signal has been given. **2** deceitful; lying: *give a ~ impression; give ~ witness,* tell lies or deceive (e g in a law court). **3** not genuine; artificial: *~ teeth.*

false·ly *adv*

false·hood /ˈfɔlshʊd/ *n* **1** [C] lie (the usual word); untrue statement: *How can you utter such ~s?* **2** [U] telling lies; lying: *guilty of ~.*

fal·setto /fɔlˈsetəʊ/ *n* [C] (*pl ~s*) unnaturally high-pitched voice in men.

fals·ify /ˈfɔlsɪfaɪ/ *vt* (*pt,pp* -ied) **1** make false: *~ records/accounts.* **2** misrepresent: *~ an issue.*

falsi·fi·ca·tion /ˌfɔlsɪfɪˈkeɪʃən/ *n* [C,U]

fals·ity /ˈfɔlsətɪ/ *n* (*pl* -ies) **1** [U] falsehood (the usual word). **2** [C] false act, statement, etc: *several falsities in the witness's statement.*

fal·ter /ˈfɔltə(r)/ *vi,vt* **1** move, walk or act in an uncertain or hesitating manner, from either weakness or fear. **2** (of the voice) waver; (of a person) speak in a hesitating way or with a broken voice: *His voice ~ed as he tried to speak.*

fal·ter·ing·ly *adv*

fame /feɪm/ *n* [U] (condition of) being known or talked about by all; what people say (esp good) about a person: *His ~ as a poet did not come until after his death.*

famed *adj* famous: *~d for their courage.*

fam·il·iar /fəˈmɪlɪə(r)/ *adj* **1 familiar with,** having a good knowledge of: *I am not very ~ with European history.* **2 familiar to,** well known to: *facts that are ~ to every European.* **3** common; usual; often seen or heard: *the ~ voices of one's friends.* **4** close; personal: *Are you on ~ terms with Mr Green?* **5** claiming or showing a greater degree of friendship than is proper: *He made himself much too ~ with my wife.*

fam·il·iar·ly *adv*

fam·ili·ar·ity /fəˌmɪlɪˈærətɪ/ *n* (*pl* -ies) **1** [U] (the state of) being familiar: *His ~ with the languages used in Nigeria surprised me. You should not treat her with such ~.* ⇨ familiar(4,5). **2** (*pl*) instance of familiar behaviour such as the use of a pet name.

fam·il·iar·ize /fəˈmɪlɪəraɪz/ *vt* **1** make well acquainted (with): *~ oneself with the rules of a game.* **2** make well known: *Television has ~d the word 'newscast'.*

fam·ily /ˈfæmlɪ/ *n* (*pl* -ies) **1** [C] parents and children. (*Note:* used with a *sing verb* when *family* is a *collective noun: Almost every ~ in the village has a man in the army,* and used with a *pl verb* when *family* means members of my family: *My ~ are early risers.*) **2** (as a *collective noun*) children: *He has a large ~.* **3** [C] all those persons descended from a common ancestor: *families that have been in the US for two hundred years.* **4** [C] group of living things (plants, animals, etc) or of languages, with common characteristics and a common source: *animals of the cat ~,* e g lions and tigers. **5** (used as an *adjective*) of or for a family: *~ life; a ~ man,* one who is fond of home life with his family.

family name, = surname.

'family `planning, (use of birth control, contraceptives, for) planning the number of children, intervals between births, etc in a family.

'family `tree, genealogical chart.

fam·ine /ˈfæmɪn/ *n* **1** [U] extreme scarcity (esp of food) in a region: *Parts of India have often suffered from ~.* **2** [C] particular occasion when there is such scarcity: *a rice/coal ~.*

fam·ish /ˈfæmɪʃ/ *vi,vt* **1** suffer from extreme hunger: *They were ~ing for food.* **2** cause (a person) to suffer from hunger: *The child* *looked half ~ed.* (*Note:* usually passive.)

fa·mous /ˈfeɪməs/ *adj* known widely; having fame: *a ~ scientist.*

fa·mous·ly *adv* excellently: *getting on ~ly.*

fan¹ /fæn/ *n* [C] **1** object (waved in the hand, or operated mechanically, e g by an electric motor) for making a current of air (e g to cool a room). **2** something that is or can be spread out flat, e g the tail of a peacock.

'fan belt, rubber belt used to turn the cooling-fan of an engine.

'fan·light, fan-shaped window over a door.

fan² /fæn/ *vt,vi* (-nn-) **1** send a current of air on to: *~ oneself.* **2** (of a breeze) blow gently on: *The breeze ~ned our faces.* **3** open in fan-shaped formation: *The troops ~ned out across the fields.*

fan³ /fæn/ *n* [C] (*informal*) fanatical supporter: *'football ~s.*

'fan mail, letters from fans, e g to a pop singer.

fa·natic /fəˈnætɪk/ *n* [C] person with excessive enthusiasm: *food ~s,* willing to eat only certain kinds of food. □ *adj* (also **fa·nati·cal** /-kəl/) excessively enthusiastic: *~(al) beliefs.*

fa·nati·cally /-klɪ/ *adv*

fa·nati·cism /-sɪzm/ *n* [U] excessive enthusiasm; [C] instance of this.

fan·cier /ˈfænsɪə(r)/ *n* [C] person with special knowledge of and love for some article, animal, etc: *a 'rose ~.*

fan·ci·ful /ˈfænsɪfəl/ *adj* (*formal*) **1** (of persons) led by imagination instead of reason and experience: *a ~ writer.* **2** unreal; curiously designed: *~ drawings.*

fan·ci·fully /-fəlɪ/ *adv*

fancy¹ /ˈfænsɪ/ *adj* **1** (esp of small things) brightly coloured; made to please the eye: *~ cakes.* **2** not plain or ordinary: *~ dress,* i e unusual costume, often historical or exotic, as worn at parties. **3** (of goods) superior in quality: *'F~ Crab'* (on a label, etc).

fancy² /ˈfænsɪ/ *n* (*pl* -ies) **1** [U] power of creating images in the mind. (*Note: imagination* suggests a more active power.) **2** [C] something imagined; vague opinion or belief: *I have a ~* (= a vague idea) *that she will be late.* **3** [C] fondness, liking, desire (*for*): *I* (*have a*) *~* (*for*) *some wine with my dinner.* **take a 'fancy to,** become fond of: *The children have taken quite a ~ to you.*

'fancy-'free *adj* not in love; not taking things seriously.

fancy³ /ˈfænsɪ/ *vt* (*pt,pp* -ied) **1** picture in the mind; imagine: *Can you ~ me as a mother?* **2** be under the impression that (without being certain, or without enough reason): *I rather ~* (*that*) *he won't come.* **3** have a desire for: *What do you ~ for dinner?* **4** **fancy oneself,** be conceited: *He fancies himself as an orator.* **5** (used to express surprise): *F~ her saying such unkind things about you! F~ that!*

fan·fare /ˈfænfeə(r)/ *n* [C] short series of notes played loudly on trumpets or bugles.

fang /fæŋ/ *n* [C] **1** long, sharp tooth (esp of dogs and wolves). **2** snake's tooth.

fan·tas·tic /fænˈtæstɪk/ *adj* **1** wild and strange: *~ dreams/shapes/fashions.* **2** (of ideas, plans) impossible to carry out; absurd. **3** (*informal*) marvellous; wonderful: *She's a really ~ girl!*

fan·tas·ti·cally /-klɪ/ *adv*

fan·tasy /ˈfæntəsɪ/ *n* (*pl* -ies) **1** [U] imagination, esp when extravagant. **2** [C] wild or strange product of the imagination.

far¹ /fɑː(r)/ *adj* ⇨ farther, farthest, further, furthest. **1** (usually in literary style) distant: *a ~ country.* **a far cry,** ⇨ cry²(1). **2** (= farther) more remote: *on the ~ bank of the river.*

the 'Far 'East, countries of E and SE Asia.

far² /fɑː(r)/ *adv* ⇨ farther, farthest, further, furthest. **1** (suggesting distance in space or time): *How ~ did you go? We didn't go ~.* (*Note:* usually used in questions and in the *negative;* compare *We went a long way.*) **2** (used with other adverbs and prepositions): *~ beyond the bridge/above the clouds/into the night/back in history.* **few and far between,** ⇨ between¹. **far from,** (a) not at all: *Your work is ~ from* (*being*) *satisfactory.* (b) instead of: *F~ from admiring his paintings, I dislike them intensely.* **go far,** (a) (of persons) be successful; do much: *He's clever and intelligent, and will go ~.* (b) (of money) buy many goods, services, etc: *A pound doesn't go ~ nowadays.* **go/carry sth too far,** go beyond the limits of what is considered reasonable: *You've gone too ~ this time!* **far and near/wide,** everywhere: *They searched ~ and wide for the missing child.* **so far,** until now: *So ~ the work has been easy.* **So 'far, so 'good,** up to now everything has gone well. **as/so far as,** (a) to the place mentioned: *He walked as ~ as the post office.* (b) the same distance: *We didn't go as/so ~ as the others.* (c) to the extent that (suggesting a limit of advance or progress): *So ~ as I know he will be away for four months.* **3** (by) much; considerably; to a great extent: *It fell ~ short of our expectations.*

'far·away *adj* (a) distant, remote: *~away places/times.* (b) (of a look in a person's eyes) dreamy: *a ~away look in his eyes.*

'far-'fetched *adj* (of an idea, excuse, etc) difficult to believe because only remotely possible.

'far-'flung *adj* widely spread or extended.

'far 'gone, very ill, mad, drunk, etc.

'far-'reaching *adj* likely to have many consequences; having a wide application: *~reaching proposals.*

'far-'sighted *adj* (a) able to see distant objects more clearly than near objects. (b) (*fig*) having good judgement of future needs, etc.

farce /fɑs/ n 1 [C] play for the theatre, full of ridiculous situations intended to make people laugh; [U] this style of drama. 2 [C] series of actual absurd events like a farce: *The trial was a ~.*
far·ci·cal /ˈfɑsɪkəl/ adj
far·ci·cally /-klɪ/ adv

fare¹ /feə(r)/ n [C] 1 money charged for a journey by bus, ship, taxi, etc. 2 passenger in a hired vehicle: *The taxi-driver had only six ~s all day.*

fare² /feə(r)/ n [U] (*dated*) food provided at table: *simple/homely ~.*

fare³ /feə(r)/ vi progress; get on: *How did you ~ at the interview?* Were you successful or not?

fare·well /ˈfeəˈwel/ int (*literary*) goodbye. □ n 1 [C] leave-taking: *make one's ~s.* 2 (used as an *adjective*): *a ~ speech.*

farm¹ /fɑm/ n [C] 1 area of land and buildings for growing crops, raising animals, etc: *working on the ~.* 2 farmer's house on a farm.
farm·yard, space enclosed by farm buildings (sheds, barns, etc).

farm² /fɑm/ vt,vi 1 use (land) for growing crops, raising animals, etc: *He ~s 200 acres.* 2 **farm out**, send work out to be done by others.

farmer /ˈfɑmə(r)/ n [C] man who owns or manages a farm.

far·ther /ˈfɑðə(r)/ adv (*comparative* of *far*): *We can't go any ~ without a rest. They went ~ into the forest.* (*Note:* usually used to refer to distance but *further* is now often used.) □ adj more distant: *on the ~ bank of the river.*

far·thest /ˈfɑðɪst/ adv, adj (*superlative* of *far*): *Which village in England is ~ from London?* (*Note:* ⟹ farther.)

far·thing /ˈfɑðɪŋ/ n [C] (former GB coin worth) one-quarter of a penny.

fas·cia (also **fa·cia**) /ˈfeɪʃə/ n [C] = dashboard.

fas·ci·nate /ˈfæsɪneɪt US: -sən-/ vt 1 charm or attract greatly: *The children were ~d by the exhibition.* 2 take away power of movement by a fixed look, as a snake does.
fas·ci·nat·ing adj having strong charm or attraction: *a fascinating smile/idea/girl.*
fas·ci·nat·ing·ly adv
fas·ci·na·tion /ˈfæsɪˈneɪʃən US: -sə-/ n [C,U]

Fas·cism /ˈfæʃɪzm/ n [U] philosophy, principles and organization of the aggressive, nationalist and highly centralized governmental system started in Italy in 1922 and dissolved in 1943.
Fas·cist /ˈfæʃɪst/ n [C] supporter of Fascism. □ adj of Fascism; extreme right-wing; reactionary.

fashion /ˈfæʃən/ n 1 (*sing* with *the* or *a, an*) manner of doing or making something: *He was behaving in a strange ~.* **after a fashion,** not particularly well: *He can speak and write English, after a ~.* 2 [C,U] (of clothes, behaviour, thought, custom, etc) that which is considered most to be admired and imitated during a period or at a place: *dressed in the latest ~.* **in fashion,** fashionable. **come into/go out of fashion,** become/no longer be in fashion: *When did mini-skirts come into/go out of ~?* □ vt give form or shape to: *~ a lump of clay into a bowl.*
fashion·able /ˈfæʃənəbəl/ adj 1 following the fashion(2). 2 used by, visited by, many people: *a ~ summer resort.*
fashion·ably /-əblɪ/ adv

fast¹ /fɑst US: fæst/ adj 1 firmly fixed; not easily moved: *Make the boat ~,* Make it secure. **hard and fast rule,** that cannot be changed. 2 steady; loyal: *a ~ friend.* 3 (of colours) that will not fade. □ adv firmly, securely, tightly: *hold ~ to a rope.* **fast asleep,** ⟹ asleep. **play fast and loose with,** repeatedly change one's attitude towards: *play ~ and loose with a girl's affections.* **stand fast,** ⟹ stand²(3).

fast² /fɑst US: fæst/ adj (-er, -est) 1 quick; rapid: *a ~ train/horse.* 2 (of a watch or clock) showing time later than the true time: *My watch is five minutes ~,* eg showing 2.05 at 2.00. 3 (of a surface) producing quick motion: *a ~ cricket pitch.* 4 (of photographic film) suitable for very brief exposures.

fast³ /fɑst US: fæst/ adv quickly: *Don't speak so ~.*

fast⁴ /fɑst US: fæst/ vi go without food, or without certain kinds of food, esp as a religious duty: *days devoted to ~ing,* eg in Lent. □ n [C] (period of) going without food: *a ~ of three days.*

fas·ten /ˈfɑsən US: ˈfæsən/ vt,vi 1 fix firmly; tie or join together: *Have you ~ed all the doors and windows?* 2 become fast¹ or secure: *This dress ~s down the back,* has buttons, etc down the back. 3 (*formal*) direct one's looks, thoughts, attention, etc on: *He ~ed his eyes on/upon me.* 4 seize; select (a person) for attack: *He ~ed on/upon the idea.*
fas·tener /ˈfɑsnə(r)/, something that fastens things together: *a paper ~er;* a `zip-~er.*
fas·ten·ing, thing that fastens, e g a bolt.

fas·tid·ious /fəˈstɪdɪəs US: fæ-/ adj hard to please; quick to find fault: *He is ~ about his food.*
fa·stid·ious·ly adv

fast·ness /ˈfɑstnəs US: ˈfæs-/ n [U] the quality of being fast¹(3): *We guarantee the ~ of these dyes.*

fat¹ /fæt/ adj (-ter, -test) 1 covered with, having much, fat: *~ meat; a ~ man.* 2 thick; well filled: *a ~ wallet,* one full of banknotes. 3 rich; fertile: *~ lands.*
fat·head, dull, stupid person.
fat·tish adj rather fat.
fat·ness n [U]

fat² /fæt/ n [C,U] (kinds of) white or yellow substance, oily or greasy, found in animal bodies; oily substance in seeds, etc; this substance purified for cooking purposes: *Fried potatoes are cooked in deep ∼.* **live off the fat of the land,** have the best of everything.

fa·tal /ˈfeɪtəl/ adj **1** causing, ending in, death or disaster: *a ∼ accident.* **2** like fate; of, appointed by, destiny: *the ∼ day.*
fa·tally /ˈfeɪtəlɪ/ adv: *∼ly injured/wounded.*

fa·tal·ism /ˈfeɪtəlɪzm/ n [U] belief that events are decided by fate(1).

fa·tal·ist /ˈfeɪtəlɪst/ n [C] believer in fatalism.

fa·tal·is·tic /ˌfeɪtəˈlɪstɪk/ adj believing that all that happens is inevitable: *a ∼ic attitude.*

fa·tal·ity /fəˈtælətɪ/ n (pl -ies) **1** [C] misfortune, disaster, esp one that causes death and destruction: *floods, earthquakes and other fatalities.* **2** [C] death by accident, in war, etc. **3** [U] state of being subject to fate(1) or destiny. **4** [U] fatal influence; deadliness: *the ∼ of certain diseases,* e g cancer.

fate /feɪt/ n **1** [U] power looked on as controlling all events in a way that cannot be opposed: *He had hoped to live to 80 but ∼ decided otherwise.* **as sure as fate,** certain(ly). **2** [C] the future as decided by fate: *They abandoned the men to their ∼.* **3** (*sing*) death; destruction; person's ultimate condition: *decide a person's ∼,* e g whether he shall live or die. □ vt **be fated to/that,** destined (the usual word) to/that.

fate·ful /ˈfeɪtfəl/ adj **1** controlled by, showing the power of, fate(1); important and decisive: *a ∼ decision; on this ∼ day.* **2** prophetic.
fate·fully /-fəlɪ/ adv

fa·ther¹ /ˈfɑðə(r)/ n [C] **1** male parent: *You have been like a ∼ to me. The property had been handed down from ∼ to son for many generations.* **2** (usually *pl*) ancestor(s). **3** founder or first leader: *the F∼ of English poetry,* Chaucer. **4** priest, esp one belonging to a religious order; head of a monastic house. **5** title used in personifications: *F∼ Christmas; F∼ Time.*
Our (Heavenly) Father, God.
the Holy Father, the Pope.
'father figure, older man respected because of his concern for one's welfare.
'father·hood /-hʊd/ n [U] state of being a father.
'father-in-law /ˈfɑðər ɪn lɔ/ n [C] (pl ∼s-in-law) father of one's wife or husband.
'father·land /-lænd/ n [C] one's native country (*mother country* is more usual).
father·less adj without a living or known father.
father·ly adj of or like a father: *∼ly love/ smiles.*

fa·ther² /ˈfɑðə(r)/ vt **1** be the originator of an idea, plan, etc. **2** be (or admit to being) the father (of a child), the author (of a book).

fathom /ˈfæðəm/ n [C] measure (six feet or 1·8 metres) of depth of water: *The ship sank in six ∼s.* □ vt **1** find the depth of. **2** understand fully: *I cannot ∼ his meaning.*
fathom·less adj too deep to fathom, esp (2).

fa·tigue /fəˈtiːg/ n **1** [U] condition of being very tired: *Several men dropped with ∼ during the long march.* **2** [U] weakness in metals caused by prolonged stress. **3** [C] tiring task; non-military duty of soldiers, such as cleaning, cooking, etc. □ vt cause fatigue to: *fatiguing work.*

fat·ten /ˈfætən/ vt,vi make or become fat: *∼ cattle.*

fatty /ˈfætɪ/ adj (-ier, -iest) like, consisting of, fat: *∼ bacon.*

fa·tu·ity /fəˈtjuːətɪ US: -ˈtuː-/ n (pl -ies) **1** [U] state of being fatuous. **2** [C] fatuous remark, act, etc.

fatu·ous /ˈfætʃʊəs/ adj showing foolish self-satisfaction: *a ∼ smile/young man.*
fatu·ous·ly adv

fau·cet /ˈfɔːsɪt/ n [C] (US) = tap¹(1).

fault /fɔːlt/ n **1** [C] something that makes a person, thing, etc imperfect; defect: *She loves me in spite of all my ∼s. There is a ∼ in the electrical connections.* **at fault,** in the wrong; in a puzzled or ignorant state: *My memory was at ∼.* **find fault with,** complain about: *I have no ∼ to find with your work.* Hence, **'fault-finder, 'fault-finding.** **2** (*sing* only) responsibility for being wrong: *It's your own ∼.* **3** [C] place where there is a break in the continuity of layers of rock, etc. □ vt find fault with: *No one could ∼ his performance.*
fault·less adj
fault·less·ly adv
faulty adj (-ier, -iest) having a fault or faults.

faun /fɔːn/ n [C] (in Roman mythology) one of a class of gods of the woods and fields, a man with a goat's horns, legs and tail.

fauna /ˈfɔːnə/ n [U] all the animals of an area or an epoch: *the ∼ of E Africa.*

faux pas /ˌfəʊ ˈpɑː/ n [C] (pl unchanged) indiscreet action, remark, etc esp a social blunder.

fa·vour¹ (US = **fa·vor**) /ˈfeɪvə(r)/ n **1** [U] friendly regard; willingness to help, protect, be kind to: *look with ∼ on a plan,* approve of it. **2** [U] aid; support: *He obtained his position more by ∼ than by merit or ability.* **in favour of,** (**a**) in sympathy with; on the side of: *Are you in ∼ of women's lib?* (**b**) on behalf of; to the account of: *Cheques should be drawn in ∼ of the Society.* **be in/out of favour (with sb),** have/not have his friendship, support, etc. **in sb's favour,** to the advantage of: *The exchange rate is in our ∼.* **3** [C] act of kindness: *May I ask you a ∼? Would you do me a ∼?*

fa·vour² (US = **fa·vor**) /ˈfeɪvə(r)/ vt **1** show favour to; support: *Fortune ∼s the brave.* **2** give more support, help, to one person, group, etc than to another: *A teacher should not ~ any of his pupils.* **3** (*formal*) do something for: *Will you ~ me with an interview?* **4** (*formal*) (of circumstances) make possible or easy: *The weather ~ed our voyage.*

fa·vour·able (*US* = **-vor-**) /ˈfeɪvərəbəl/ *adj* giving or showing approval; helpful: *a ~ report on one's work.*

fa·vour·ably /-əblɪ/ *adv* in a favourable manner: *speak favourably of a plan.*

fa·vour·ite (*US* = **-vor-**) /ˈfeɪvrɪt/ *n* [C] **1** person or thing preferred above all others: *He is a ~ with his uncle/a ~ of his uncle's/ his uncle's ~.* **2** the ~, (racing) the horse, etc generally expected to win: *The ~ came in third.* **3** person who is given unfair preference. □ *adj* preferred above all others.

fa·vour·it·ism (*US* = **-vor-**) /-ɪzm/ *n* [U] (practice of) having favourites(3).

fawn¹ /fɔn/ *n* **1** [C] young fallow-deer less than one year old. **2** [U] light yellowish-brown colour. □ *adj* light yellowish-brown.

fawn² /fɔn/ *vi* **1** (of dogs) show pleasure and affection by jumping about, tail-wagging, etc. **2** *fawn on sb,* try to win his favour by flattery, etc.

fear¹ /fɪə(r)/ *n* **1** [C,U] feeling caused by the nearness or possibility of danger or evil; alarm: *They stood there trembling with ~,* frightened and shaking. *for fear of,* because of anxiety about: *She asked us not to be noisy, for ~ of waking the baby.* **2** [U] anxiety for the safety (*of*): *He is in ~ of his life.* **3** [U] likelihood: *There's not much ~ of my losing the money. No fear!* (*informal*) Certainly not!

fear·ful /-fəl/ *adj* (**a**) causing fear; terrible: *a ~ful railway accident.* (**b**) (*informal*) annoying; very great: *What a ~ful mess!* (**c**) frightened; apprehensive: *~ful of waking the baby.*

fear·fully /-fəlɪ/ *adv*

fear·less *adj* without fear.

fear·less·ly *adv*

fear·less·ness *n* [U]

fear² /fɪə(r)/ *vt,vi* **1** feel fear (of), be afraid (of): *~ death.* **2** *fear for,* feel anxiety about: *We ~ed for his life/safety.* **3** have an uneasy feeling or anticipation of: *~ the worst,* be afraid that the worst has happened or will happen.

feas·ible /ˈfizəbəl/ *adj* **1** that can be done: *A counter-revolution is ~.* **2** (*informal*) that can be managed or that is convenient or plausible; that can be believed: *His story sounds ~,* may be true.

feasi·bil·ity /ˌfizəˈbɪlətɪ/ *n* [U]

feast /fist/ *n* [C] **1** religious anniversary or festival, e g Christmas or Easter. **2** splendid meal. □ *vt,vi* **1** take part in, give, a feast: *~ one's friends; ~ all evening.* **2** give pleasure to: *~ one's eyes on beautiful scenes.*

feat /fit/ *n* [C] something difficult well done, esp showing skill, strength or daring: *bril-*

liant *~s of engineering.*

feather¹ /ˈfeðə(r)/ *n* [C] one of the light coverings that grow from a bird's skin. *as light as a feather,* very light. *birds of a feather,* people of the same sort. *a feather in one's cap,* something one can be proud of.

\feather·weight, (esp) boxer weighing between 118 and 126 lb or (53·5 to 57 kg)

feath·ery *adj* light and soft like feathers: *~y snow.*

feather² /ˈfeðə(r)/ *vt* supply with feathers: *~ an arrow. feather one's nest,* make things comfortable for oneself.

fea·ture /ˈfitʃə(r)/ *n* [C] **1** one of the named parts of the face: *Her eyes are her best ~.* **2** (*pl*) the face as a whole: *a man of handsome ~s.* **3** characteristic or striking part: *geographical ~s.* **4** prominent article or subject in a newspaper. **5** full-length film in a cinema programme, etc. □ *vt* be or make a feature(3,4) of: *a film that ~s a new French actress.*

fea·ture·less *adj* uninteresting.

Feb·ru·ary /ˈfebrʊərɪ *US:* -rʊerɪ/ *n* the second month of the year.

feces ⇨ faeces.

fed /fed/ *pt,pp* of feed².

fed·eral /ˈfedrəl/ *adj* **1** of, based on, federation: *In the USA foreign policy is decided by the ~* (i e central) *government, and ~ laws are made by Congress.* **2** relating to, supporting, central (as distinct from State) government.

Federal Bureau of Investigation, (*US*) (abbr **FBI**) department which is responsible for investigating violations of federal law and safeguarding national security. ⇨ State¹(2).

fed·er·al·ism /-ɪzm/ *n* [U]

fed·er·al·ist, supporter of federal union or power.

fed·er·ate /ˈfedəreɪt/ *vt,vi* (of States, societies, organizations) combine, unite, into a federation.

fed·er·ation /ˌfedəˈreɪʃən/ *n* **1** [C] political system in which a union of States leave foreign affairs, defence, etc to the central (Federal) government but keep powers of government over some internal affairs. **2** [C] such a union of States, e g the USA; similar union of societies, trade unions, etc. **3** [U] act of federating.

fee /fi/ *n* **1** [C] charge or payment for professional advice or services, e g doctors, lawyers, surveyors. **2** entrance money for an examination, club, etc. □ *vt* engage for a fee: *~ a barrister.*

feeble /ˈfibəl/ *adj* (-r, -st) weak; faint; without energy, force or decision: *a ~ old man; a ~ cry/argument/joke.*

\feeble-\minded *adj* (**a**) subnormal in intelligence. (**b**) (*informal*) lacking firmness or decision.

feebly /ˈfiblɪ/ *adv*

feed¹ /fid/ n 1 [C] (chiefly of animals and babies) meal: *We stopped to let the horses have a ~.* 2 [U] food for animals: *There isn't enough ~ left for the hens.* 3 [C] pipe, channel, etc through which material is carried to a machine; [U] material supplied.

feed-back n [U] (a) return of part of the output of a system to its source (e g to correct it). (b) (*informal*) information, etc (about a product) given by the user to the supplier, maker, etc: *interesting ~back via the market research department.* ⇨ feed back below.

feed² /fid/ vt,vi (pt,pp fed /fed/) 1 give food to: *Have the pigs been fed yet?* **be fed up (with),** (*sl*) have had enough of and therefore feel angry or discontented: *I'm fed up with your grumbling.* 2 (chiefly of animals) eat: *The cows were ~ing in the meadows.* 3 **feed on,** take as food: *Cattle ~ chiefly on grass.* 4 supply with material; supply (material) to: *This moving belt ~s the machine with raw material* 5 put information into (a computer). 6 **feed back,** send information, etc back, e g, from the marketing staff to the supplier. Hence, **feed-back** n

feeder /ˈfidə(r)/ n [C] 1 (of plants and animals, used with *adjectives*) one that feeds. 2 feeding-bottle or bib. 3 (often as an *adjective*) branch railway line, airline, canal, etc linking outlying areas with the main line, etc.

feeding-bottle, bottle from which a baby is given milk.

feel¹ /fil/ n (*sing* only) 1 sensation characteristic of something when touching or being touched: *You can tell it's wool by the ~.* 2 act of feeling; being touched: *Let me have a ~.*

feel² /fil/ vt,vi (pt,pp felt /felt/) 1 (try to) learn about, explore, by touching, holding in the hands, etc: *Blind persons can often recognize objects by ~ing them.* **feel one's way,** (a) go forward carefully, as in the dark, or as a blind man does. (b) be cautious: *They were ~ing their way towards an agreement.* 2 search (about) with the hand(s) (or the feet, a stick, etc): *He felt in his pocket for a penny.* 3 be aware of (through contact): *I can ~ a nail in my shoe.* 4 be aware of (not through contact): *He felt his heart beating wildly. She felt concern for them all.* 5 be in a certain physical, moral or emotional state: *~ cold/hungry/happy, etc. How are you ~ing today? Please ~ free* (= consider yourself welcome) *to come whenever you like.* 6 be capable of sensation: *The dead cannot ~.* 7 **feel for,** have sympathy, compassion: *I ~ for you in your sorrow.* 8 **feel as if/though,** have, give, the impression that: *She felt as if her head were splitting.* 9 give or produce an impression: *This new suit doesn't ~ right.* 10 **feel like,** (of persons) be in the mood for: *I don't ~ like* (*eating*) *a big meal now.* 11 be sensitive to; suffer because

of: *He doesn't ~ the heat at all.* 12 have the idea; be of the opinion: *He felt sure that he would succeed.* **feel in one's bones (that),** ⇨ bone(1). 13 appreciate; understand properly: *We all felt the force of his arguments.*

feeler /ˈfilə(r)/ n [C] 1 part of an animal used for testing things by touch, e g whiskers, antennae. 2 proposal, suggestion, made to test the opinions or feelings of others: *put out ~s.*

feel-ing /ˈfilɪŋ/ n 1 [U] power and capacity to feel: *He had lost all ~ in his legs.* 2 [C] physical or mental awareness; emotion: *a ~ of hunger/gratitude/joy.* 3 [C] idea or belief not based wholly on reason: *a ~ of danger.* 4 (usually *sing*) general opinion: *The ~ of the meeting was against the proposal.* 5 (*pl*) emotional side of a person's nature (contrasted with the intellect): *Have I hurt your ~s,* offended you? 6 [U] sympathy; understanding: *He doesn't show much ~ for the sufferings of others.* 7 [C,U] excitement of mind, esp of hatred or resentment: *F~ over the election ran high,* There was much bitterness, etc. 8 [U] taste and understanding; sensibility: *She plays the piano with ~.* □ adj (*formal*) sympathetic; showing emotion: *a ~ remark.*

feet /fit/ n pl of foot¹.

feint /feɪnt/ n [C] pretence (the more usual word). □ vi pretend.

fel-ic-ity /fəˈlɪsəti/ n (pl -ies) (*formal*) [U] great happiness or contentment.

fe-line /ˈfilaɪn/ adj of or like a cat: *walk with ~ grace.*

fell¹ /fel/ pt of fall².

fell² /fel/ n [C] stretch of rocky, bare moorland or bare hilly land (esp in N England): *the Derbyshire F~s.*

fell³ /fel/ vt cause to fall; strike down; cut down (a tree): *He ~ed his enemy with a single blow.*

fel-low /ˈfeləʊ/ n [C] 1 (*dated informal*) man or boy: *He's a pleasant ~.* 2 (usually *pl*) friend, companion: *~school ~s.* 3 (used as an *adjective*) of the same class, kind, etc: *~~citizens.* 4 member of a learned society: *F~ of the British Academy.* 5 member of the governing body of some university colleges; incorporated graduate member of a college.

fellow-feeling, sympathy.

fel-low-ship /ˈfeləʊʃɪp/ n 1 [U] friendly association; companionship: *enjoy ~ with people.* 2 [C] number of persons associated together; group or society. 3 [U] membership in such a group: *admitted to ~.* 4 [C] position of a college fellow(5).

felon /ˈfelən/ n [C] person guilty of felony.

fel-oni-ous /fɪˈləʊnɪəs/ adj criminal (the more usual word).

fel-ony /ˈfeləni/ n [C,U] (pl -ies) major serious crime, e g murder, armed robbery, arson.

felt¹ /felt/ pt,pp of feel²

felt[2] /felt/ n [U] wool, hair or fur, compressed and rolled flat into a kind of cloth: (as an *adjective*) ~ *hats/slippers*.

fe·male /ˈfiːmeɪl/ *adj* **1** of the sex that produces offspring: *a ~ child/dog*. **2** (of plants or their parts) fruit-bearing. **3** of women: ~ *suffrage*. **4** (of machines, tools) having a hollow part designed to receive an inserted part, e g a plug. □ n [C] female animal.

fem·i·nine /ˈfemɪnɪn/ *adj* **1** of, like, suitable for, women: ~ *curiosity*, said to be typical of women. **2** (*gram*) of the gender proper to the names of females: ~ *nouns and pronouns*, e g actress, lioness, she, her.

fem·i·nin·ity /ˈfemɪ`nɪnətɪ/, quality of being feminine.

fem·in·ism /ˈfemɪnɪzm/, movement for recognition of the claims of women for rights (legal, political, etc) equal to those possessed by men. ⇨ lib.

fem·in·ist /-ɪst/, supporter of feminism.

fe·mur /ˈfiːmə(r)/ n [C] (*anat*) thigh-bone.

fen /fen/ n [C] area of low marshy land.

fence[1] /fens/ n [C] barrier made of wood or metal, e g one put round a field, garden, etc.

sit/be on the fence, not commit oneself; wait to see where one can win most advantage. □ *vt* surround, divide, provide with a fence: *The land is ~d off/in/round.*

fenc·ing /ˈfensɪŋ/, material for making fences.

fence[2] /fens/ *vt* **1** practise the art of fighting with long slender swords or foils. **2** (*fig*) avoid giving a direct answer to a question(er): ~ (*with*) *a question*.

fencer, person who fences.

fenc·ing /ˈfensɪŋ/ n [U] art, sport, of fighting with swords.

fence[3] /fens/ n [C] receiver of stolen goods; his place of business. □ *vt, vi* receive stolen goods.

fend /fend/ *vt, vi* **1** *fend off,* defend oneself from: ~ *off a blow*. **2** *fend for oneself,* look after oneself: *When his father died, Tom had to ~ for himself.*

fender /ˈfendə(r)/ n [C] **1** metal frame bordering an open fireplace (to prevent burning coal, etc from rolling on to the floor). **2** something used to lessen shock or damage in a collision, e g on a ship's side. **3** (*US*) guard over the wheel of a motor-vehicle.

fer·ment[1] /ˈfɜːment/ n [C] substance, e g yeast, that causes other substances to ferment. **2** *in a ferment,* (*fig*) in a state of, e g social, political, excitement.

fer·ment[2] /fə`ment/ *vt, vi* **1** (cause to) undergo chemical changes through the action of organic bodies (esp yeast) which change glucose into alcohol, e g in beer, wine. **2** (*fig*) (cause to) become excited.

fer·men·ta·tion /ˈfɜːmenˈteɪʃən/ n [U]

fern /fɜːn/ n [C,U] sorts of feathery, green-leaved flowerless plant.

ferny *adj*

fer·ocious /fə`rəʊʃəs/ *adj* fierce, cruel, savage: *a ~ temper.*

fer·ocious·ly *adv*

fer·oc·ity /fə`rɒsətɪ/ n (*formal*) [U] fierceness; savage cruelty; [C] (*pl* -ies) fierce, savage or cruel act.

fer·ret /ˈferɪt/ n [C] small animal of the weasel family, used for driving rabbits from their burrows, killing rats, etc. □ *vt, vi* **1** hunt with ferrets. **2** discover by searching; search: ~ *about for a lost book.*

ferry /ˈferɪ/ n [C] (*pl* -ies) (place where there is a) boat, hovercraft or aircraft that carries people and goods across a river, channel, etc. □ *vt, vi* take, go, across in a ferry: ~ *people/a boat across a river.*

ferry-boat, one used for ferrying.

ferry-man, person who owns or runs a ferry.

fer·tile /ˈfɜːtaɪl US: ˈfɜːtəl/ *adj* **1** (of land, plants, etc) producing much: ~ *soil*. **2** (of a person, his mind, etc) full of ideas, plans, etc: *a ~ imagination*. **3** able to produce fruit, young; capable of developing: ~ *seeds/eggs*. ⇨ sterile.

fer·til·ity /fə`tɪlətɪ/, state of being fertile.

fer·til·ize /ˈfɜːtəlaɪz/ *vt* make fertile or productive: ~ *the soil* (by using manure).

fer·til·izer, n [U] chemical plant food; artificial manure; [C] substance of this kind.

fer·til·iz·ation /ˈfɜːtəlaɪˈzeɪʃən US: -lɪˈz-/ n [U]

fer·vent /ˈfɜːvənt/ *adj* **1** hot, glowing. **2** showing warmth of feeling; passionate: ~ *love/hatred.*

fer·vent·ly *adv*

fer·vour (*US* = **-vor**) /ˈfɜːvə(r)/ n [U] strength or warmth of feeling.

fes·tal /ˈfestəl/ *adj* festive (the usual word).

fes·ter /ˈfestə(r)/ *vi* **1** (of a cut or wound) (cause to) fill with poisonous matter (*pus*): *If the cut gets dirty, it will probably ~*. **2** (*fig*) act like poison in the mind: *The insult ~ed in his mind.*

fes·ti·val /ˈfestɪvəl/ n [C] **1** (day or season for) rejoicing; public celebration: *Christmas and Easter are Church ~s*. **2** series of performances (of music, ballet, drama, etc) given periodically, e g once a year): *a ~ of music*. □ *adj* of a feast or feast-day: ~ *music.*

fes·tive /ˈfestɪv/ *adj* of a feast or festival; joyous: *a ~ season*, e g Christmas.

fes·tiv·ity /fe`stɪvətɪ/ n (*pl* -ies) **1** [U] rejoicing; being merry and gay. **2** (*pl*) joyful events: *wedding festivities.*

fes·toon /fe`stuːn/ n [C] chain of flowers, leaves, ribbons, etc hanging in a curve or loop between two points, as a decoration. □ *vt* decorate (the usual word): ~ *ed with Christmas decorations.*

fetch /fetʃ/ *vt, vi* **1** go for and bring back: *F~ a doctor at once. Shall I ~ your coat (for you)?* **2** cause to come out: ~ *a deep sigh*. **3** (of goods) bring in; sell for (a price): *These old books won't ~ (you) much.* **4**

(*informal*) give (a blow) to: *She ~ed me a slap across the face.*

fête /feɪt/ *n* [C] festival or entertainment: *the village ~*, often one at which funds are raised, e g for a charity. □ *vt* honour by entertaining; make a fuss of: *The hero was ~d wherever he went.*

fetid /ˈfetɪd/ *adj* stinking.

fet·ish, fe·tich /ˈfetɪʃ/ *n* [C] (*pl ~es*) 1 object worshipped by pagan people because they believe a spirit lives in it. 2 anything to which foolishly excessive respect or attention is given: *Some women make a ~ of clothes.*

fet·lock /ˈfetlɒk/ *n* [C] (tuft of hair on a) horse's leg above and behind the hoof.

fet·ter /ˈfetə(r)/ *n* [C] 1 chain for the ankles of a prisoner or the leg of a horse. 2 (*fig*) (usually *pl*) something that hinders progress. □ *vt* 1 put in chains. 2 (*fig*) restrain.

feud /fjuːd/ *n* [C] bitter quarrel between two persons, families or groups, over a long period of time. □ *vt* quarrel; fight: *~ over a will.*

feu·dal /ˈfjuːdəl/ *adj* of the method of holding land (by giving services to the owner) during the Middle Ages in Europe.

feu·dal·ism /-ɪzm/ *n* [U] the feudal system.

fe·ver /ˈfiːvə(r)/ *n* 1 [U] condition of the human body with temperature higher than usual, esp as a sign of illness: *He has a high ~.* 2 [U] one of a number of diseases in which there is a high fever: *yellow/rheumatic ~.* 3 (usually *sing* with *a*) excited state; nervous agitation: *in a ~ of impatience. at/to `fever pitch,* at/to a high level of excitement.

fe·vered *adj* affected by a fever: *a ~ed imagination,* highly excited.

fe·ver·ish *adj* having symptoms of, caused by, causing fever.

fe·ver·ish·ly *adv*

few /fjuː/ *adj* (-er, -est), *pron* (contrasted with *many*; ⇨ *little*, *much*) 1 (used with a *pl noun*) not many: *F~ people live to be 100 and ~er still live to be 110. Such occasions are ~.* **no fewer than,** as many as: *No ~er than twenty workers were absent through illness.* 2 (with *a*) a small number (of): *I know a ~ of them.* 3 *every few minutes/days,* etc, ⇨ every(4). 4 **the ~,** the minority.

fez /fez/ *n* [C] red felt head-dress with a flat top and no brim, worn by some Muslim men.

fi·ancé /fɪˈɒnseɪ *US:* ˌfiːɑːnˈseɪ/ *n* [C] man to whom one is engaged to be married.

fi·ancée /fɪˈɒnseɪ *US:* ˌfiːɑːnˈseɪ/ *n* [C] woman to whom one is engaged to be married.

fi·asco /fɪˈæskəʊ/ *n* [C] (*pl ~s*, *US* also *~es*) complete failure, breakdown: *The new play was a ~.*

fib /fɪb/ *n* [C] (*informal*) untrue statement (esp about something unimportant). □ *vi* (-bb-) tell a fib.

fib·ber, person who tells fibs.

fib·bing, telling fibs.

fibre (*US* = **fiber**) /ˈfaɪbə(r)/ *n* 1 [C] one of the very thin threads of which many animal and vegetable growths are formed, e g cotton, wool, nerves, muscles. 2 [U] substance formed of a mass of fibres, for manufacture into various materials. 3 [U] structure; texture: *material of tough, coarse ~.* 4 [U] (*fig*) character: *a person of strong moral ~.* `**fibre-glass,** material of glass fibres in resin, used as an insulating material, and made into structural materials.

fi·brous /ˈfaɪbrəs/ *adj* made of, like, fibres.

fib·ula /ˈfɪbjʊlə/ *n* [C] (*pl ~s*) (*anat*) outer and smaller of the two bones from the knee to the ankle.

fickle /ˈfɪkəl/ *adj* (of moods, the weather, etc) often changing; not constant.

fic·tion /ˈfɪkʃən/ *n* 1 [C] something invented or imagined (contrasted with truth). 2 [U] (branch of literature concerned with) stories, novels and romances.

fic·ti·tious /fɪkˈtɪʃəs/ *adj* untrue; imagined or invented: *The account he gives of his movements is quite ~.*

fiddle /ˈfɪdəl/ *n* [C] 1 violin; any instrument of the violin family, e g a cello or viola. **fit as a fiddle,** very well; in good health. **play second fiddle (to),** take a less important part (than). 2 instance of fiddling; ⇨ 3 below. □ *vt* 1 play a tune, etc on the fiddle. 2 make aimless movements; play aimlessly (*with* something in one's fingers): *He was fiddling (about) with a piece of string.* 3 (*sl*) make or keep dishonestly inaccurate records of figures (in business accounts, etc): *~ the expenses.*

fid·dler, (a) person who plays a fiddle(1). **(b)** person who fiddles(3).

fid·dling *adj* (*informal*) trivial: *fiddling little jobs.*

fi·del·ity /fɪˈdelətɪ/ *n* [U] 1 loyalty, faithfulness: *~ to one's principles/wife.* 2 accuracy; exactness: *translate with the greatest ~.* ⇨ **high fidelity.**

fidget /ˈfɪdʒɪt/ *vi, vt* (cause to) move the body (or part of it) about restlessly; make nervous: *The boy was ~ing with his knife and fork.* □ *n* [C] 1 **the ~s,** fidgeting movements: *Having to sit still for a long time often gives small children the ~s.* 2 person who fidgets.

fidgety *adj*

field[1] /fiːld/ *n* [C] 1 area of land, usually enclosed by means of hedges, fences, etc: *working in the ~s.* 2 area or expanse; open space: *an `ice-~,* e g round the North Pole; *a `cricket/`football ~.* 3 area of land from which minerals, etc are obtained: *a new `oil-~;* `coal-~s.* 4 place, area, where a battle or war is or was fought: *the ~ of battle* (`battle-~). 5 area or department of study or activity: *the ~ of politics/medical research. That is outside my ~,* is not something that I have studied. **6** range (of operation, activity, use); area or space in which forces can be felt: *a magnetic ~*, round a magnet: *a wide ~ of vision*. **7** (in sports and athletics) all those taking part; (in cricket and baseball) team that is not batting.

'field day, (a) day on which military operations are practised or for exploration, etc by a society. **(b)** (*fig*) great or special occasion: *having a ~ day*, having great fun, success, etc.

'field event, athletic event such as jumping or throwing which does not take place on a track.

'field glasses, binoculars for outdoor use.

'field hockey, ⇨ hockey.

'field hospital, temporary one near the scene of fighting.

'field 'marshal, army officer of highest rank.

'field-officer, major, lieutenant colonel or colonel.

'field study, planned study of first-hand observations, interviews, etc.

'field work, (a) research done in the field, e g by a geologist. **(b)** = field study. **(c)** = spadework.

field² /fiːld/ *vt,vi* **1** (in cricket and baseball) (stand ready to) catch or stop (the ball): *He ~s well.* **2** (of football teams, etc) put into the field: *The school is ~ing a strong team in their next match.*

fielder, 'fields-man, (in cricket, etc) person who fields.

fiend /fiːnd/ *n* [C] **1** devil. **2** very wicked or cruel person. **3** (*informal*) person devoted to or addicted to something: *a 'fresh-'air ~.*

fiend-ish *adj* savage and cruel.

fiend-ish-ly *adv*

fierce /fɪəs/ *adj* (-r, -st) **1** violent; cruel; angry: *~ dogs/winds; look ~; have a ~ look.* **2** (of heat, desire, etc) intense, strong: *~ hatred.*

fierce-ly *adv*

fierce-ness *n* [U]

fiery /ˈfaɪərɪ/ *adj* (-ier, -iest) **1** flaming; looking like, hot as, fire: *a ~ sky; ~ eyes*, angry and glaring. **2** (of a person, his actions, etc) quickly or easily made angry; passionate: *a ~ temper/speech.*

fier-ily /-ɪlɪ/ *adv*

fi-esta /fɪˈestə/ *n* [C] (*pl ~s*) **1** religious festival; saint's day. **2** holiday, festival.

fif-teen /fɪˈtiːn/ *adj, n* [C] (of) 15.

fif-teenth /ˈfɪfˈtiːnθ/ *adj, n* [C] (abbr *15th*) (of) one of 15 parts or the next after 14.

fifth /fɪfθ/ *adj, n* [C] (abbr *5th*) (of) one of 5 parts or the next after 4.

'fifth 'column, organized body of persons sympathizing with and working for the enemy within a country at war.

fifth-ly *adv*

fifty /ˈfɪftɪ/ *adj, n* [C] (of) 50. **go fifty-fifty (with); on a fifty-fifty basis,** have equal shares. **a fifty-fifty chance,** equal chance.

the fifties, the years between 49 and 60 (in a century, a person's life).

fif-ti-eth /ˈfɪftɪəθ/ *adj, n* [C] (abbr *50th*) (of) one of 50 parts or the next after 49.

fig /fɪg/ *n* [C] (broad-leaved tree having a) soft, sweet, pear-shaped fruit full of small seeds. **not care/give a fig (for),** not care or value in the least.

'fig-leaf, conventional device for concealing male genital organs in drawings, statues, etc.

fight¹ /faɪt/ *n* **1** [C] act of fighting; struggle: *a ~ between two dogs; the ~ against poverty.* **2** [U] desire, spirit or ability to fight: *The news that their leader had surrendered took all the ~ out of them.*

fighter, (a) person who fights professionally: *a prize ~.* **(b)** thing used in fighting, e g aircraft: *a jet-~.* **(c)** (used as an *adjective*): *a '~er pilot/squadron.*

fight² /faɪt/ *vi,vt* (*pt,pp* fought /fɔːt/) struggle with the hands or with weapons; use physical force (as in war): *~ a battle. The dogs were ~ing over a bone. Britain has often fought against/with* (= against) *her enemies. Britain fought with* (= on the side of) *France.* **fight to the finish,** until there is a decision. **fight shy of,** keep away from, not get mixed up with. **fight back, (a)** use force to resist an attack. **(b)** (*fig*) make an effort to resist something: *~ back a cold.* **fight sth down,** repress: *~ down a feeling of jealousy.* **fight sb/sth off,** drive away; struggle against: *~ off a cold*, e g by taking aspirin. **fight it out,** fight until a dispute is settled.

fight-ing *n* [U]: *'street ~ing.* □ *adj* **a fighting chance,** a possibility of success if great effort is made. **fighting fit,** very healthy.

fig-ment /ˈfɪgmənt/ *n* [C] something invented or imagined: *~s of the imagination.*

fig-ura-tive /ˈfɪgjʊrətɪv/ *adj* (abbr *fig* used in this dictionary) (of words and language) used not in the literal sense but in an imaginative way e g bait¹(2).

fig-ura-tive-ly *adv*

fig-ure /ˈfɪgə(r) *US:* ˈfɪgjər/ *n* [C] **1** symbol for a number, esp 0 to 9: *He has an easy income of six figures, £100 000 or more.* ⇨ double figures. **2** (*pl*) arithmetic: *Are you good at ~s?* **3** diagram; illustration: *The blackboard was covered with geometrical ~s*, i e squares, triangles, etc. **4** person's, animal's, form drawn, painted or carved. **5** human form, esp the appearance and what it suggests: *I'm dieting to keep my ~*, in order not to grow fat. **6** person, esp his influence: *Russell, the greatest ~ of his era.* □ *vt,vi* **1** imagine; picture mentally. **2** appear; have a part; be prominent: *~ in history/in a play.* **3** **figure sth/sb out,** calculate; think about until one understands: *I can't ~ that man out*, I do not understand him.

'figure-head, (a) carved image (either bust

or full-length) placed for ornament at the prow of a ship. (b) person in high position but with no real authority.

'**figure of `speech,** expression, e g a simile or metaphor, that gives variety or force, using words out of their literal meaning.

fila·ment /ˈfɪləmənt/ n [C] slender thread, e g of wire in an electric light bulb.

filch /fɪltʃ/ vt steal (something of small value).

file [1] /faɪl/ n [C] metal tool with roughened surface(s) for cutting or smoothing hard substances. ◻ vt use a file on; make smooth, remove, cut through, with a file: *filing one's fingernails.*

file [2] /faɪl/ n [C] 1 holder, cover, case, box, drawer etc for keeping papers, etc together and in order for reference purposes. *on file,* on or in a file. 2 set of papers so kept. ◻ vt place on or in a file: *Please ～ (away) these letters.*

file [3] /faɪl/ n [C] line of persons or things one behind the other: *in single ～. the rank and file,* (a) common soldiers (not officers). (b) (*fig*) ordinary, undistinguished persons. ◻ vi march in file: *The men ～d in/out,* came or went in/out.

fil·ial /ˈfɪlɪəl/ adj of a son or daughter: *～ duty.*

fil·ings /ˈfaɪlɪŋz/ n pl bits removed by filing.

fill [1] /fɪl/ n [U] full supply; as much as is wanted: *eat/drink one's ～. have (had) one's fill of sth,* (*informal*) have had as much as one can bear.

fill·ing, something put in to fill something: *a ～ing in a tooth.*

fill [2] /fɪl/ vt,vi 1 make or become full; occupy all the space in: *～ a tank with petrol. Tears ～ed her eyes. I was ～ed with admiration.* 2 hold a position and do the necessary work; put a person in a position: *The vacancy has already been ～ed. fill the bill,* (*informal*) do or be what is wanted.

3 (uses with *adverbial particles* and *prepositions*):

fill in, add what is necessary to make complete: *～ in an application form,* write one's name, and other particulars required; *～ in an outline,* add details, etc.

fill out, (a) make or become larger, rounder or fatter: *Her cheeks began to ～ out.* (b) (esp *US*) = fill in.

fill up, make or become full: *～ up a petrol tank.*

fil·let /ˈfɪlɪt/ n [C] slice of fish or meat without bones. ◻ vt cut into fillets: *～ed plaice.*

fil·lip /ˈfɪlɪp/ n [C] 1 quick blow or stroke with a finger. 2 (*fig*) incentive or stimulus: *an advertising campaign that gave a fresh ～ to sales.*

filly /ˈfɪlɪ/ n [C] (*pl*-ies) female foal.

film [1] /fɪlm/ n 1 [C] thin coating or covering: *a ～ of dust/mist.* 2 [C,U] roll or sheet of thin flexible material for use in photography: *a roll (US = spool) of ～.* 3 [C] series or strip

of photographs projected onto a screen one after the other so quickly that the people, objects, etc appear to be moving; such a strip representing a story, drama, etc.

'**film star,** well-known cinema actor or actress.

'**film test,** photographic test of a person who wishes to act in films.

filmy adj (-ier, -iest) like a film(1): *～y clouds.*

film [2] /fɪlm/ vt,vi 1 cover, become covered, with a film(1): *The scene ～ed over.* 2 take a film (3) of: *～ a play.* 3 be well, badly suited for filming: *She ～s well.*

fil·ter /ˈfɪltə(r)/ n [C] 1 apparatus (sometimes containing, e g sand) for holding back solid substances in a liquid passed through it: *a `coffee ～.* 2 coloured glass (as used on a camera lens) which allows light of certain wave-lengths to pass through. 3 (in radio) device which separates alternating current of one frequency from others. ◻ vt,vi 1 (cause to) flow through a filter. 2 (*fig*) (of a crowd, road traffic, news, ideas, etc) make a way, pass or flow: *new ideas ～ing into people's minds.* 3 (of traffic in GB) be allowed to move when traffic going in other directions is held up by a red light.

'**filter tip,** cigarette end containing material that acts as a filter (for nicotine, etc). Hence, '**filter-`tipped** adj

filth /fɪlθ/ n [U] 1 disgusting dirt. 2 obscenity.

filthy adj (-ier, -iest).

fin /fɪn/ n [C] 1 part (like a wing) attached to a fish used in swimming. 2 thing shaped like or used in the same way as a fin, e g the `tail-～ of an aircraft.

fi·nal /ˈfaɪnəl/ adj 1 coming at the end: *the ～ chapter of a book.* 2 putting an end to doubt or argument: *a ～ decision/judgement.* ◻ n [C] (often *pl*) last of a series: *take one's ～s,* last examinations; *the tennis ～s,* at the end of a tournament; *the Cup F～,* football match between the last teams in a competition.

fi·nal·ist, (a) player who takes part in the last of a series of contests. (b) undergraduate in his last year.

fi·nally /-nəlɪ/ adv (a) lastly; in conclusion. (b) once and for all: *settle a matter ～ly.*

fi·nal·ity /faɪˈnælɪtɪ/ n [U] state or quality of being final: *speak with an air of ～,* as if there is nothing more to be said or done.

fi·nal·ize /ˈfaɪnəlaɪz/ vt give a final form to.

fi·nance /ˈfaɪnæns/ n 1 [U] (science of) the management of (esp public) money: *an expert in ～.* 2 (*pl*) money (esp of a government or a business company): *Are the country's ～s sound?.* ◻ vt provide money for (a scheme, etc).

fi·nan·cial /ˈfaɪˈnænʃəl/ adj of finance: *in ～ difficulties,* short of money; *the ～ year,* the annual period for which accounts are made up.

fi·nan·cial·ly /-ʃəlɪ/ adv

fin·an·cier /faɪˈnænsɪə(r) US: ˈfɪnənˈsɪər/ n [C] person skilled in finance.

finch /fɪntʃ/ n [C] kinds of small bird (usually with a *prefix*, e g `chaffinch`).

find¹ /faɪnd/ n [C] act of finding; something (esp valuable or pleasing) found: *I made a great ~ in a secondhand bookshop yesterday.*

finder, (a) person who finds something: *Lost, a diamond ring: ~er will be rewarded.* **(b)** lens in a camera (`view-~er`) or telescope used to find the object to be examined, etc.

find·ing, (usually pl) (a) what has been learnt as the result of inquiry: *the ~ings of the Commission.* **(b)** what is decided by a jury, etc. ⇨ find²(9).

find² /faɪnd/ vt (*pt,pp* found /faʊnd/) **1** get back, after a search: *Did you ever ~ that pen you lost? The missing child has not been found yet.* **2** get or discover after research, experience or effort: *~ a cure/remedy (for something); ~ a solution/an answer (to a problem). They couldn't ~ the way in/out/back.* **find fault (with),** ⇨ fault. **find one's feet, (a)** be able to stand and walk, e g as a baby does. **(b)** (*fig*) become able to act independently, without the help and guidance of others. **3** arrive at naturally: *Rivers ~ their way to the sea.* **4** discover by chance; come across: *He was found dead at the foot of a cliff.* **5** become informed or aware of, by experience or trial: *We found the beds quite comfortable. I ~ it difficult to understand him/~ him difficult to understand.* **6** (often **find out**) learn by study, calculation, inquiry: *Please ~ out when the train leaves.* **7** (= there is/are, the subject being *one* or *you*): *One doesn't/You don't find (= There isn't) much sunshine in this area.* **8** supply; furnish; provide: *Who will ~ the money for the expedition?* **all found,** everything provided: *Wanted, a waitress, £100 a month and all found*, board, lodging, etc provided in addition to wages. **9** (*legal*) decide and declare; give as a verdict: *How do you ~ the accused? The jury found the accused man guilty.*

fine¹ /faɪn/ adj (-r, -st) **1** (of weather) bright; clear; not raining: *It rained all morning, but turned ~ later.* **2** in good health: *I'm feeling ~.* **3** enjoyable; pleasing; splendid: *a ~ view; have a ~ time; ~ clothes.* **4** delicate; carefully made and easily injured: *~ silk.* **5** of very small particles: *Sand is ~r than gravel.* **6** slender; thin; sharp: *a pencil with a ~ point.* **not to put too fine a point on it,** to express it plainly. **7** (of metals) refined; pure: *~ gold.* **7** (able to be) seen only with difficulty or effort: *a ~ distinction.* **8** able to make delicate distinctions: *a ~ taste in art.*

fine art; the fine arts, the visual arts that appeal to the sense of beauty, esp painting

and sculpture.

fine·ly adv **(a)** splendidly: *~ly dressed.* **(b)** into small particles or pieces: *carrots ~ly chopped.*

fine·ness n [U]

fine² /faɪn/ adv (*informal*) very well: *That will suit me ~.*

fine³ /faɪn/ n [C] sum of money (to be) paid as a penalty for breaking a law or rule. □ vt punish by a fine: *~ him £5.*

fine·able (also **fin·able**) /ˈfaɪnəbl/ adj liable to a fine.

fin·ery /ˈfaɪnərɪ/ n [U] gay and elegant dress or appearance: *the garden in its summer ~,* with its flowers, etc.

fi·nesse /fɪˈnes/ n [U] artful or delicate way of dealing with a situation: *show ~ in dealing with people.*

fin·ger /ˈfɪŋɡə(r)/ n [C] one of the end parts of the hand or a glove: *There are five ~s (or four ~s and one thumb) on each hand.* **have a finger in every/the pie,** ⇨ pie. **keep one's fingers crossed,** (*fig*) hope that nothing will prevent success. **lay one's finger on,** show exactly (where something is wrong). **not lift a finger (to help sb),** do nothing to help when help is needed. **slip through one's fingers,** ⇨ slip²(3). □ vt touch with the fingers: *~ a piece of cloth.*

ˈfin·ger-nail, nail at the tip of the finger.

ˈfin·ger-print, mark made by a finger when pressed on a surface, used for identifying criminals.

ˈfin·ger-tip, top of a finger. **have sth at one's fingertips,** be thoroughly familiar with it.

fin·ish /ˈfɪnɪʃ/ vt,vi **1** bring or come to an end; complete: *~ one's work; ~ reading a book. Have you ~ed with that dictionary? Are you still using it?* **2** make complete or perfect: *He gave the picture a few ~ing touches.* □ n (*sing* only) **1** last part: *the ~ of a race.* **a fight to the finish,** until one side is defeated or exhausted. **2** the state, manner, of being finished: *His manners lack ~.* **3** shining surface (after polishing).

fi·nite /ˈfaɪnaɪt/ adj **1** limited: *Human understanding is ~.* **2** (*gram*) agreeing with a subject in number and person: *'Am', 'is', 'are', 'was', and 'were' are the ~ forms of 'be', and 'be', 'being' and 'been' are the 'non-~ forms.*

fiord, fjord /fɪˈɔːd/ n [C] long, narrow arm of the sea, between high cliffs (as in Norway).

fir /fɜː(r)/ n [C] conifer with leaves like needles; [U] wood of this tree.

ˈfir-cone, ⇨ cone(3).

fire¹ /ˈfaɪə(r)/ n **1** [U] condition of burning: *F~ burns.* **on fire,** burning: *The house was on ~.* **catch fire,** begin to burn: *Paper catches ~ easily.* **set sth on fire; set fire to sth,** cause it to begin burning: *He set his hair on ~.* **2** [U] destructive burning: *Have you insured your house against ~?* **3** [C] instance of destructive burning: *forest ~s.* **4** [C] burning fuel in a grate, etc to heat a building, for cooking, etc: *There's a ~ in the next room.* **5** [U] shooting (from guns). **open/cease fire,** start/stop shooting. **under fire, (a)** being shot at. **(b)** (*fig*) being criticised. **6** [U] strong emotion; angry or excited feeling; enthusiasm: *a speech that lacks ~, is uninspiring.*

ˈfire alarm, apparatus (bell, etc) for making known the outbreak of a fire.

ˈfire-arm, rifle, gun, pistol or revolver.

ˈfire brigade, organized team of men who put out fires.

ˈfire drill, practice of routine to be followed when fire breaks out.

ˈfire-engine, (motor-vehicle with a) machine for putting out a fire.

ˈfire-escape, outside staircase for leaving a burning building; apparatus, kind of extending ladder, used to save people from a burning building.

ˈfire-extinguisher, portable cylinder with a chemical substance, etc inside, for putting out a small fire.

ˈfire-guard, protective metal framework or grating round a fire in a room.

ˈfire-man (a) man who looks after the fire in a furnace, etc. **(b)** member of a fire brigade.

ˈfire-place, place for a fire in a room.

ˈfire-proof adj that does not burn; that does not crack or break when heated.

ˈfire-raising, arson.

ˈfire service, fire brigade(s).

ˈfire-side, (sing with *the*) part of a room round the fireplace: *sitting at/by the ~side;* (as an *adjective*): *a ~side chair.*

ˈfire station, building for a fire brigade.

ˈfire-wood, wood prepared for lighting fires or as fuel.

ˈfire-work, device containing gunpowder and chemicals, used for making a display at night, or as a signal.

fire² /faɪə(r)/ *vt,vi* **1** set fire to with the intention of destroying; cause to begin burning: *~ a heap of leaves.* **2** use heat on something in order to change it in some way: *~* (= bake to harden) *pottery in a kiln.* **3** supply (a furnace) with fuel: *an ˈoil~d furnace.* **4** excite or stimulate. **fire sb with sth,** fill with (enthusiasm, etc). **5** send (a bullet, etc) from a gun; explode (a charge of explosive); shoot: *~ a gun/six rounds of ammunition. The police ~d into the crowd.* **fire away, (a)** continue firing: *They were firing away at the enemy.* **(b)** (*fig*) go ahead; begin: *I'm ready to answer questions; ~ away.* **6** (*informal*) dismiss (an employee).

ˈfir-ing-line, front line where soldiers fire at the enemy. **in the firing-line,** exposed to attack, criticism, etc.

ˈfiring-party/-squad, number of soldiers ordered to fire volleys at a military funeral or to carry out a military execution.

firm¹ /fɜːm/ *adj* (-er, -est) **1** solid; hard; not yielding when pressed: *~ flesh/muscles.* **2** not easily changed or influenced; showing strength of character and purpose: *be ~ with children,* insist on obedience and discipline; *a ~ promise.* **3** (of a person, his body, its movements, characteristics, etc) steady, stable: *walk with ~ steps. He spoke in a ~ voice.* □ *vt,vi* make or become firm. □ *adv* = firmly: *stand ~; hold ~ to one's beliefs.*

firm-ly adv in a firm manner.

firm-ness *n* [U]

firm² /fɜːm/ *n* [C] (two or more) persons carrying on a business.

fir-ma-ment /ˈfɜːməmənt/ *n* the ~, the heavens and all that is in them.

first¹ /fɜːst/ *adj* (abbr *1st*) coming before all others in time or order: *January is the ~ month of the year; at the ~* (= earliest) *opportunity.* **first thing,** at the earliest opportunity: *I'll be here ~ thing in the morning.* **not know the first thing about sth,** not even one thing. **at first sight,** initially: *It seemed easy at ~ sight, but...*

ˈfirst ˈaid, treatment given at once to a sick or injured person before a doctor comes.

ˈfirst ˈclass, *n* [U] best accommodation in a train, steamer, aircraft, etc. □ **ˈfirst-class** adj of the best class: *~-class hotels; a ~-class* (university) *degree.* □ adv by the best class: *travel ˈ~-ˈclass.*

ˈfirst ˈfloor, (*GB*) floor immediately above the ground floor; (*US*) ground floor.

ˈfirst-ˈhand adj, adv (obtained) directly from the source: *~-hand information; learn something ~-hand.* **at first hand,** directly.

ˈfirst name, given name (contrasted with family name).

ˈfirst ˈnight, evening on which a play, etc is presented for the first time.

ˈfirst ˈmate, ⇒ mate¹(2).

ˈfirst ofˈfender, one against whom no previous conviction has been recorded.

ˈfirst ˈperson, (*gram*) the pronouns *I, me, we, us* (and the *verb* forms used with them).

ˈfirst-ˈrate adj of the best class; excellent: *~-rate acting.* □ adv (*informal*) very well: *getting on ~-rate.*

first-ly adv in the first place.

first² /fɜːst/ *adv* **1** before anyone or anything else (often, for emphasis, *~ of all; ~ and foremost*): *Which horse came in ~,* won the race? **2** for the first time: *When did you ~ see him/see him ~?* **3** before some other (specified or implied) time: *I must finish this work ~,* i e before starting something else. **4** in preference: *He said he would resign ~.*

ˈfirst-born adj, *n* [C] eldest (child).

first³ /fɜːst/ *n* **1** at first, at the beginning. **from the first,** from the start. **from first to last,** from beginning to end; throughout. **2** [C] (in examinations, competitions) place in the first class; person who takes this: *He got a ~ in Modern Languages.*

firth /fɜːθ/ *n* [C] (esp in Scotland) river estuary or sea inlet.

fis·cal /ˈfɪskəl/ adj of public revenue.

fish[1] /fɪʃ/ n (pl ~ or ~es) **1** [C] cold-blooded animal living wholly in water and breathing through gills: catch a ~/two ~es/a lot of ~. **have `other fish to fry**, more important business to attend to. **2** [U] fish as food: ~ and chips.

`fish·cake, fried rissole of fish.

`fish-hook, metal hook used for catching fish.

`fish-knife, knife with which fish is eaten.

`fish·monger, tradesman who sells fish.

`fish·paste, paste of fish or shellfish (spread on bread, etc).

`fish-slice, implement for serving fish at table.

fishy adj (-ier, -iest) **(a)** smelling or tasting like fish: a ~y smell. **(b)** (informal) causing a feeling of doubt: a ~y story.

fish[2] /fɪʃ/ vi,vt **1** try to catch fish: go ~ing. **2** (fig) try to get, by indirect methods: ~ for information/compliments. **3** draw or pull: ~ out a coin from one's pocket.

fish·ing, catching fish for a living or for pleasure.

`fish·ing-line, line[1](1) with a fish-hook attached for fishing.

`fish·ing-rod, rod to which a fishing-line is fastened.

`fish·ing-tackle, things needed for fishing.

fisher·man /ˈfɪʃəmən/ n [C] (pl -men) man who earns a living by fishing. ⇨ angler.

fish·ery /ˈfɪʃərɪ/ n [C] (pl -ies) part of the sea where fishing is carried on: in-shore fisheries, near the coast.

fis·sion /ˈfɪʃən/ n [C,U] splitting or division, e g of an atom.

fis·sure /ˈfɪʃə(r)/ n [C] narrow opening made by the splitting or separation of parts.

fist /fɪst/ n [C] hand when tightly closed (as in boxing): He struck me with his ~.

fit[1] /fɪt/ adj (-ter, -test) **1** suitable or suited; well adapted; good enough: The food was not ~ to eat. That man is not ~ for the job. **2** right and proper. **think/see fit (to do sth)**, decide to: Do as you think ~. **3** ready; in a suitable condition; (informal) (as an adverb): He was laughing ~ to burst. **4** in good athletic condition; in good health: I hope you're keeping ~. ⇨ keep[1](14).

fit·ness n [U] **(a)** suitability (for). **(b)** the state of being physically fit.

fit[2] /fɪt/ n [C] **1** sudden (usually short) attack of illness: a ~ of coughing. **2** sudden attack of hysteria, paralysis, e g with loss of consciousness and violent movements: fall down in a ~. **give sb a fit**, (informal) do something that greatly shocks or outrages him. **have a fit**, (informal) be greatly surprised or outraged: She almost had a ~ when she saw the bill. **3** sudden outburst lasting for a short time: a ~ of energy/enthusiasm/temper.

fit·ful /-fəl/ adj occurring, coming and going, irregularly.

fit·fully /-fəlɪ/ adv

fit[3] /fɪt/ vt,vi (-tt-) **1** be the right measure, shape and size for: shoes that ~ well. **2** put on (esp clothing) to see that it is the right size, shape, etc: have a new coat ~ted. **3** put into place: ~ a new lock on a door. **4** make (a person, oneself, something) suitable or competent: Can we make the punishment ~ the crime? **5** **fit in (with)**, (cause to) be in a suitable or harmonious relation (with); find, be in, the right or a suitable time or place for: I must ~ my holidays in with yours. **fit sb/sth out**, supply with what is needed; equip: ~ out a ship for a long voyage. **fit sb/sth up**, supply: a hotel ~ted up with modern comforts. □ n (usually sing with a or an and an adjective) style, manner, in which something, e g a garment, fits: The coat is a tight/an excellent ~.

fit·ment /ˈfɪtmənt/ n [C] piece of furniture or equipment: kitchen ~s.

fit·ter /ˈfɪtə(r)/ n [C] **1** person who cuts out, fits and alters garments. **2** workman who fits and adjusts parts of an engine, machine, etc.

fit·ting /ˈfɪtɪŋ/ adj proper; right; suitable. □ n [C] **1** act of fitting: go to the tailor's for a ~. **2** fixture in a building, esp (pl) things permanently fixed: gas and electric light ~s. **3** furnishing: office ~s, e g desks, filing cabinets.

five /faɪv/ adj, n [C] (of) 5. ⇨ fifth.

`five-fold adj with 5 parts; 5 times as much.

five·pence /ˈfaɪfpəns US: ˈfaɪvpens/ n [C] (pl~ pieces) (coin with a) value of 5 pence.

five·penny /ˈfaɪfpənɪ/ adj costing fivepence.

fiver /ˈfaɪvə(r)/, (informal) £5 note; $5 bill.

fix[1] /fɪks/ n [C] (pl ~es) **1** **be in/get oneself into a fix**, a dilemma, an awkward situation. **2** finding of a position, position found, by taking bearings, observing the stars, etc. **3** (sl) injection of a drug, e g heroin.

fix[2] /fɪks/ vt,vi **1** make firm or fast; fasten (something) so that it cannot be moved: ~ shelves to a wall. **2** **fix on**, direct (the eyes, one's attention, etc) steadily on or to: ~ one's attention on what one is doing. **3** (of objects) attract and hold (the attention): This unusual sight kept his attention ~ed. **4** determine or decide: ~ the rent/a date for a meeting; ~ed prices, prices with no discount, with no possibility of bargaining; a man with ~ed (= definite and decided) principles. **5** treat (photographic films, colours used in dyeing, etc) so that light does not affect them. **6** arrange; organize; provide for: ~ her up with a job. **7** settle one's choice, decide to have: They've ~ed on a villa near Rome. **8** (sl) **(a)** use bribery or deception, improper influence: Can you ~ a judge in Britain? **(b)** get even with; deal with: I'll ~ him! **9** (informal) put in order: ~ one's hair, brush and comb it. **10** (informal) repair: ~ a watch/car.

fixed /fɪkst/ adj unchanging: a ~ed idea, one which a person will not change and which tends to occupy his thoughts too much.

fix·ed·ly /ˈfɪksɪdlɪ/ adv

fix·a·tion /fɪkˈseɪʃən/ n [C] 1 fixing or being fixed: the ~ of a photographic film. 2 obsession: She has a ~ about bathing daily.

fixa·tive /ˈfɪksətɪv/ n [C] 1 substance which makes specimens firm for study under a microscope. 2 substance for keeping paint, etc in position.

fix·ture /ˈfɪkstʃə(r)/ n [C] 1 something fixed in place, esp (pl) built-in cupboards, etc which are bought with a building: We were charged for ~s and fittings. 2 (day fixed or decided for a) sporting event: football and racing ~s. 3 (informal) person or thing that appears unlikely to move from or leave a place: Professor Green seems to be a permanent ~ in the college.

fizz /fɪz/ vi make a hissing sound (as when gas escapes from a liquid). □ n [U] this sound.

fizzy adj (-ier, -iest).

fizzle /ˈfɪzəl/ vi hiss or splutter feebly. **fizzle out**, come to a weak, unsatisfactory end.

fjord /fiˈɔːd/ ⇨ fiord.

flabby /ˈflæbɪ/ adj (-ier, -iest) 1 (of the muscles, flesh) soft; not firm: A man who never takes exercise is likely to have ~ muscles. 2 (fig) weak; without moral force: a ~ will/character.

flab·bi·ness n [U]

flag[1] /flæg/ n [C] 1 (usually oblong) piece of cloth, attached by one edge to a rope, used as the distinctive symbol of a country, or as a signal: the national ~ of Great Britain, the Union Jack. 2 = flagstone. □ vt (-gg-) 1 place a flag on; decorate with flags: streets ~ged to celebrate a victory. 2 signal to stop a train, car, etc by moving one's outstretched arm up and down or waving a flag: ~ down the next car.

flag-pole, pole on which a flag is shown.

flag-ship, warship having an admiral on board.

flag-staff, pole on which a flag is flown.

flag[2] /flæg/ vi (-gg-) 1 (of plants, etc) droop, hang down, become limp. 2 (fig) become tired or weak: His strength/interest in his work was ~ging.

flagel·lant /ˈflædʒɪlənt/ n [C] person who practises whipping (as a religious penance).

flagel·late /ˈflædʒɪleɪt/ vt whip (esp as a religious penance).

flagel·la·tion /ˌflædʒɪˈleɪʃən/ n [U]

flagon /ˈflægən/ n [C] 1 large, round bottle in which wine, cider, etc is sold. 2 vessel with a handle, lip and lid for serving wine at table.

fla·grant /ˈfleɪgrənt/ adj (of a criminal or crime, etc) openly and obviously wicked: ~ offences/sinners.

fla·grant·ly adv

flag·stone /ˈflægstəʊn/ n [C] flat, square or oblong piece of stone for a floor, path or pavement.

flail /fleɪl/ n [C] old-fashioned tool for threshing grain. □ vt beat (as) with a flail.

flair /fleə(r)/ n [C] (usually sing) natural or instinctive ability (to do something well, to select or recognize what is best, most useful, etc): have a ~ for languages, be quick at learning them.

flake /fleɪk/ n [C] small, light, leaf-like piece: ~snow~s; ~soap-~s. □ vi fall off in flakes.

flaky adj (-ier, -iest) made up of flakes: flaky pastry.

flam·boy·ance /flæmˈbɔɪəns/ n [U] being flamboyant.

flam·boy·ant /flæmˈbɔɪənt/ adj 1 brightly coloured and decorated. 2 (of a person, his character) very energetic, lively, etc in order to attract attention.

flam·boy·ant·ly adv

flame[1] /fleɪm/ n 1 [C,U] (portion of) burning gas: He put a match to the papers and they burst into ~(s). 2 [C] blaze of light; brilliant colour: the ~s of sunset. 3 [C] passion: a ~ of anger/indignation/enthusiasm. 4 [C] (informal) sweetheart: She's an old ~ of his.

flame[2] /fleɪm/ vi 1 burn with, send out, flames. 2 be or become like flames in colour: hillsides flaming with the colours of autumn.

flam·ing adj

fla·mingo /fləˈmɪŋgəʊ/ n [C] (pl ~s, ~es) large long-legged, long-necked wading bird with pink feathers.

flam·mable /ˈflæməbəl/ adj (= inflammable, but preferred in US and in technical contexts) having a tendency to burst into flames and to burn rapidly.

flan /flæn/ n [C] tart containing fruit, etc not covered with pastry.

flange /flændʒ/ n [C] projecting or outside rim, e g of a wheel.

flank /flæŋk/ n [C] 1 fleshy part of the side of a human being or animal between the last rib and the hip. 2 side of a building or mountain. 3 right or left side of an army or body of troops: attack the left ~. □ vt 1 be situated at or on the flank of. 2 go round the flank of (the enemy).

flan·nel /ˈflænəl/ n 1 [U] loosely woven woollen cloth. 2 (pl) flannel trousers used for sports. 3 [C] piece of flannel for cleaning, etc: a ~face-~.

flap[1] /flæp/ n [C] 1 (sound of a) flapping blow or movement. 2 piece of material that hangs down or covers an opening: the ~ of a pocket/an envelope. 3 part of the wing of an aircraft that can be lifted in flight to alter its upward direction and speed. 4 **be in/get into a flap**, (sl) a state of nervous excitement or confusion.

flap[2] /flæp/ vt,vi (-pp-) 1 (cause to) move

up and down or from side to side: *The sails were ∼ping against the mast. The bird was ∼ping its wings.* **2** give a light blow to with something soft and flat: *∼ the flies off/ away.* **3** (*sl*) be in, get into, a flap¹(4).

flap·per /ˈflæpə(r)/ *n* [C] **1** something broad and flat (e g as used to swat flies, etc). **2** (fish's) broad fin.

flare¹ /fleə(r)/ *vi* **1** burn with a bright, unsteady flame: *flaring torches.* **2 flare up,** (a) burst into bright flame. (b) (*fig*) (of violence, anger) suddenly break out: *She ∼s up at the least thing. Rioting ∼d up again later.* Hence, **ˈflare-up** *n*. □ *n* **1** [U] flaring flame: *the ∼ of torches.* **2** [C] device for producing a flaring light, used as a signal, etc: *The crew of the sinking ship used ∼s to attract attention.*

flare² /fleə(r)/ *vi,vt* (of trousers, skirt, the sides of a ship) (cause to) spread gradually outwards. □ *n* [C] gradual widening.

flash¹ /flæʃ/ *n* [C] **1** sudden burst of flame or light: *a ∼ of lightning.* **2** (*fig*) sudden outburst of wit etc; sudden idea, realisation, etc: inspiration. **in a flash,** instantly, at once. **a flash in the pan,** an effort that is quickly over or at once ends in failure. **2** (also **ˈnews-flash**) brief item of news received by telephone, cable, etc. **4** (*informal*) (used as an *adjective*) showy; smart: *a ∼ sports car.*

ˈflash-back, part of a film, etc that shows a scene earlier in time than the rest.

ˈflash-bulb, bulb used in photography giving a momentary bright light.

ˈflash-gun, device to syncronize the actions of a flashbulb and the shutter in a camera.

ˈflash-light *n* (a) light used for signals, in lighthouses, etc. (b) device for producing a brilliant flash of light for taking a photograph indoors or when natural light is too weak. (c) small electric torch.

flash² /flæʃ/ *vi,vt* **1** send, give out, a sudden bright light: *Lightning ∼ed across the sky.* **2** come suddenly (into view, into the mind): *The idea ∼ed into/through his mind.* **3** send instantly: *∼ news across the world* (by radio or TV). **4** send or reflect like a flash: *Her eyes ∼ed defiance.* **5** show briefly: *∼ a light/a document at him.* **6** move quickly: *The train flashed past us.*

flashy /ˈflæʃɪ/ *adj* (-ier, -iest) brilliant and attractive but rather vulgar: *∼ clothes/ jewellery/men.*

flash·ily /-əlɪ/ *adv*

flask /flɑːsk *US*: flæsk/ *n* [C] **1** narrow-necked bottle used in laboratories, etc. **2** narrow-necked bottle for oil or wine. **3** (also **ˈhip-flask**) flat-sided bottle of metal or (often leather-covered) glass for carrying spirits in the pocket. **4** = thermos/vacuum flask.

flat¹ /flæt/ *n* [C] (*GB*) set of rooms on one floor of a building as a residence: *an old house divided into ∼s; a new block of ∼s.*

flat·let /-lət/ *n* [C] small flat.

flat² /flæt/ *adj* (-ter, -test) **1** smooth and level; even; having an unbroken surface: *The top of a table is ∼.* **2** spread out; (lying) at full length: *He fell ∼ on his back.* **3** with a broad level surface and little depth: *∼ plates/dishes/pans. The omelette was ∼, had failed to rise while cooking.* **4** dull; uninteresting; monotonous: *The party/ conversation/scenery was rather ∼.* **fall flat,** ⇨fall². **5** (*music*) below the true pitch: *sing ∼; a ∼ note; A ∼ (A♭), a note half a tone lower than A.* ⇨ sharp(9). **6** absolute; downright; unqualified: *give her a ∼ denial/refusal.* **7** (of colours, coloured surfaces) uniform, without relief: *His paintings all seem rather ∼.* **8** (of a battery) run down; needing to be recharged. **9** (of a tyre having no or not enough air in it. □ *adv* **1** in a flat manner: *sing ∼.* **2** positively: *He told me ∼ that… flat broke,* (*informal*) with no money at all. **3 flat out,** (a) (*informal*) with all one's strength and resources: *He was working/running ∼ out.* (b) exhausted.

ˈflat-fish, fish (*sole, plaice, etc*) having a flat body and swimming on one side.

ˈflat-ˈfooted *adj* (a) having feet with flat soles. (b) (*informal*) (of behaviour) clumsy. (c) (*informal*) determined.

ˈflat racing; the Flat, horse-racing over level ground with no obstacles.

ˈflat rate, (*business*) common price paid for each (different) thing or service.

ˈflat ˈspin, (a) (uncontrollable) descent of a spinning aircraft. (b) (*informal*) mental state of great confusion: *be in a ∼ spin.*

flat·ly *adv* in a flat(6) manner: *He ∼ly refused to join us.*

flat·ness *n* [U]

flat³ /flæt/ *n* **1** flat part of anything: *the ∼ of his sword.* **2** stretch of low level land, esp near water: *ˈmud ∼s.* **3** (*music*) flat note; the sign ♭. **4** deflated tyre, e g after a puncture. **5** piece of stage scenery on a movable frame.

flat·ten /ˈflætən/ *vt,vi* make or become flat: *a field of wheat ∼ed by storms; ∼ oneself against a wall.*

flat·ter /ˈflætə(r)/ *vt* **1** praise too much or insincerely (in order to please). **flatter oneself that…,** be pleased with one's belief that… **2** give a feeling of pleasure to: *I'm ∼ed by your invitation.* **3** (of a picture, artist, etc) show (a person) as better looking than he is: *This photograph ∼s you.*

flat·terer, person who flatters.

flat·tery, insincere praise: *Don't be deceived by her flatteries.*

flatu·lence /ˈflætʃʊləns/ *n* [U] (discomfort caused by) gas in the alimentary canal.

flaunt /flɔːnt/ *vt,vi* **1** show off in order to attract attention to: *∼ oneself/one's riches, etc.* **2** (*poetic*) wave proudly: *flags and banners ∼ing in the breeze.*

flau·tist /ˈflɔːtɪst/ *n* [C] flute-player.

fla·vour (*US* = **-vor**) /ˈfleɪvə(r)/ *n* **1** [U] sensation of taste and smell: *Some food has very little* ~. **2** [C] distinctive taste: *various* ~*s in ice-cream.* **3** [C] special quality: *a newspaper story with a* ~ *of romance.* □ *vt* give a flavour to: ~ *a sauce with onions.*

fla·vour·ing, (*US* = **-vor-**) something used to give flavour to (food, etc).

fla·vour·less (*US* = **-vor-**) *adj* having no flavour.

flaw /flɔː/ *n* [C] something that lessens the value, beauty or perfection of a thing: ~*s in a jewel/an argument/a person's character.*
flaw·less *adj* perfect.
flaw·less·ly *adv*

flax /flæks/ *n* [U] plant cultivated for the fibres obtained from its stems; these fibres (for making linen).
flaxen /ˈflæksən/ *adj* (of hair) pale yellow.

flay /fleɪ/ *vt* **1** take the skin or hide off (an animal). **2** (*fig*) criticize severely or pitilessly: *The tutor* ~*ed the idle students.*

flea /fliː/ *n* [C] small wingless jumping insect that feeds on the blood of human beings and some animals.
ˈflea-bite, (*fig*) small inconvenience.
ˈflea-bitten *adj* (*informal*) dirty; shabby.
ˈflea market, open-air market selling cheap and second-hand goods.

fleck /flek/ *n* [C] **1** small spot or patch: ~*s of colour on a bird's breast.* **2** small particle (of dust, etc). □ *vt* mark with flecks: *a sky* ~*ed with clouds.*

fled /fled/ *pt,pp* of flee.

fledged /fledʒd/ *adj* (of birds) with fully-grown wing feathers; able to fly.
ˈfully-ˈfledged *adj* (*fig*) trained and experienced: *a fully-* ~ *engineer.*
fledg(e)·ling, (a) young bird just able to fly. (b) (*fig*) young inexperienced person.

flee /fliː/ *vi,vt* (*pt,pp* fled /fled/) run or hurry away (from): *He killed his enemy and fled the country.*

fleece /fliːs/ *n* [C,U] woolly covering of a sheep or similar animal; quantity of wool cut from a sheep in one operation: *a coat lined with* ~. □ *vt* rob (a person) by trickery: *He was* ~*d of his money.*
fleecy *adj* (-ier, -iest) like fleece: *fleecy snow.*

fleet[1] /fliːt/ *n* [C] **1** number of warships under one commander; all the warships of a country. **2** number of ships, aircraft, buses, etc moving or working under one command or ownership.
fleet[2] /fliːt/ *adj* (*poet*) quick-moving.
fleet·ing /ˈfliːtɪŋ/ *adj* lasting for a short time: *a* ~ *visit;* ~ *happiness.*

flesh /fleʃ/ *n* [U] **1** soft substance, esp muscle, between the skin and bones of animal bodies: *Tigers are* ~*-eating animals.* **flesh and blood,** human nature with its emotions, weaknesses, etc: *more than* ~ *and blood can stand,* more than human nature can bear. **one's own flesh and blood,** one's near rel-

atives. **in the flesh,** in bodily form. **3** *the* ~, physical or bodily desires; sensual appetites: *the sins of the* ~. **4** the body (contrasted with the *mind* and *soul*): *The spirit is willing but the* ~ *is weak.* **5** pulpy part of fruits and vegetables.

ˈflesh-wound, one that does not reach the bone or vital organs.

fleshy *adj* (-ier, -iest) fat; of flesh.

fleur-de-lis, -lys /ˌflɜː də ˈliː/ *n* [C] (*pl* fleurs-de-lis, -lys with the pronunciation unchanged) heraldic lily; royal arms of France.

flew /fluː/ *pt* of fly[2].

flex[1] /fleks/ *n* [C,U] (*pl* -es) (length of) flexible insulated cord for electric current.

flex[2] /fleks/ *vt* bend, stretch, e g a limb, one's muscles.

flex·ible /ˈfleksəbəl/ *adj.* **1** easily bent without breaking. **2** (*fig*) easily changed to suit new conditions; (of persons) adaptable.
flexi·bil·ity /ˌfleksəˈbɪlətɪ/ *n* [U]

flick /flɪk/ *n* [C] **1** quick light blow, e g with a whip or the tip of a finger. **2** short sudden movement; jerk. □ *vt* strike with a flick, give a flick with (a whip, etc); touch lightly: *He* ~*ed his whip at the horse. He* ~*ed the switch,* e g for electric light. **flick sth away/off,** remove with a flick: *She* ~*ed the crumbs off the tablecloth.* **flick through,** turn over (cards, pages) quickly with the fingers.

ˈflick-knife, knife with a blade (inside the handle) which can be brought into position with a flick.

the flicks, (*GB sl*) cinema (films).

flicker /ˈflɪkə(r)/ *vi* **1** (of a light) burn or shine unsteadily: *The candle* ~*ed and then went out.* **2** (*fig*) (of hopes, etc) appear briefly: *A faint hope still* ~*ed in her heart.* **3** move back and forth, wave to and fro: ~*ing shadows.* □ *n* [C] (usually *sing*) flickering movement: *a* ~ *of hope.*

flier /ˈflaɪə(r)/ *⇨* flyer.

flight[1] /flaɪt/ *n* **1** [U] flying through the air: *study the* ~ *of birds,* how they fly. **in flight,** while flying. **2** [C] journey made by air; distance covered: *a non-stop* ~ *from Paris to New York.* **3** [C] group of aircraft in a country's Air Force. **4** [U] movement (and path) through the air: *the* ~ *of an arrow.* **5** [C] number of birds or objects moving together through the air: *a* ~ *of swallows.* **6** [U] swift passing: *the* ~ *of time.* **7** [C] going beyond the ordinary: *a* ~ *of the imagination/fancy.* **8** [C] series (*of* stairs, etc without change of direction); stairs between two landings: *My bedroom is two* ~*s up.*

ˈflight deck, (a) (on an aircraft-carrier) deck for taking off from and landing on. (b) (in an airliner) compartment used by the pilot, navigator, engineer, etc.

ˈflight lieutenant, (officer with a) commissioned rank in the Air Force.

ˈflight path, *n* [C] *n* planned course of aircraft or spacecraft.

flight·less *adj* (of birds) unable to fly.

flight² /flaɪt/ *n* [C,U] (act, instance, of) running away or fleeing (from danger, etc): *seek safety in ~.* **take (to) flight,** run away.

flight³ /flaɪt/ *vt* vary the speed and course of (arrow, cricket ball, etc).

flimsy /ˈflɪmzɪ/ *adj* (-ier, -iest) **1** (of material) light and thin. **2** (of objects) easily destroyed. **3** (*fig*) easily opposed: *a ~ excuse/argument.* □ *n* [C] (*pl* -ies) thin sheet of paper.

flims·ily /-əlɪ/ *adv*

flim·si·ness *n* [U]

flinch /flɪntʃ/ *vi* draw or move back: *have a tooth pulled out without ~ing.*

fling /flɪŋ/ *vt,vi* (*pt,pp* flung /flʌŋ/) **1** throw, move, quickly and with force: *~ a stone; ~ the doors and windows open; be flung into prison.* **2** move oneself, one's arms, etc, violently, quickly or angrily: *~ one's arms up/about; ~ one's clothes on,* dress quickly. **3** go angrily or violently: *She flung out of the room.* **4** (*fig*) work at with enthusiasm, *~ oneself into an enterprise.* □ *n* [C] **1** act, movement, of flinging. **2** kind of lively dance: *the Highland ~,* as danced in Scotland. **3** **have one's fling,** have a time of unrestricted pleasure.

flint /flɪnt/ *n* **1** [U] hard kind of stone; [C] piece of this used with steel to produce sparks. **2** [C] piece of hard alloy used in a cigarette-lighter to produce sparks.

flip /flɪp/ *vt,vi* (-pp-) put (something) into motion by a snap of the finger and thumb: *~ a coin (down) on the counter.* **flip through,** ⇨ flick through. □ *n* [C] quick, light blow.

flip side, (*informal*) the reverse side (of a gramophone record).

flip·pancy /ˈflɪpənsɪ/ *n* [U] being flippant; [C] flippant remark, etc.

flip·pant /ˈflɪpənt/ *adj* not showing deserved respect or seriousness: *a ~ answer/remark.*

flip·pant·ly *adv*

flip·per /ˈflɪpə(r)/ *n* [C] **1** limb of certain sea-animals (not fish) used in swimming: *Seals, turtles and penguins have ~s.* **2** similar device, usually of rubber, worn on the feet to aid swimming.

flirt /flɜːt/ *vi* **1** try to attract a person; show affection without serious intentions: *She ~s with every handsome man she meets.* **2** (*informal*) think about, but not seriously: *He's been ~ing with the idea of going to Moscow.* □ *n* [C] man or girl who flirts(1).

flir·ta·tion /flɜːˈteɪʃən/ *n* [U] flirting; [C] instance of this: *carry on a ~ation.*

flir·ta·tious /flɜːˈteɪʃəs/ *adj* (fond) of flirting.

flit /flɪt/ *vi* (-tt-) **1** fly or move lightly and quickly: *bees ~ting from flower to flower.* **2** (*fig*) pass quickly: *fancies that ~ through one's mind.* **3** (*informal*) remove from one house to another, e g secretly, to avoid paying debts. □ *n* [C] (*informal*) act of flit-

ting(3): *do a moonlight ~.*

float¹ /fləʊt/ *n* [C] **1** piece of cork or other light material used on a fishing-line (to show when the bait has been taken) or to support the edge of a fishing-net. **2** hollow ball, etc e g to regulate the level of water in a cistern. **3** low platform on wheels, as used for showing things in a procession. **4** money used, e g by shopkeepers, to provide change at the start of business dealings.

float² /fləʊt/ *vi,vt* **1** be held on the surface of a liquid, or up in air, gas: *Wood ~s on water. A balloon ~ed across the sky.* **2** cause to float: *There wasn't enough water to ~ the ship.* **3** (*business*) get (esp financial) support in order to start (something): *~ a new business company.* **4** allow the foreign exchange value (of a currency) to vary: *~ the pound/dollar.*

float·ing *adj* free from attachment; not fixed or settled; variable: *the ~ing population.*

flock¹ /flɒk/ *n* [C] **1** number of birds or animals (usually sheep, goats) of one kind, either kept together or feeding and travelling together. **2** crowd of people: *Visitors came in ~s to see the new bridge.* **3** Christian congregation: *a priest and his ~.* □ *vi* gather, come or go together in great numbers: *The children ~ed round their teacher.*

flock² /flɒk/ *n* [C] tuft of wool or hair; (*pl*) wool or cotton waste for stuffing mattresses, etc.

floe /fləʊ/ *n* [C] sheet of floating ice.

flog /flɒg/ *vt* (-gg-) **1** beat severely with a rod or whip. **flog a dead horse,** waste one's efforts. **flog** (e g an idea, a joke) **to death,** try to persuade people to accept something so persistently that they lose interest. **2** (*sl*) (try to) sell: *~ one's old car.*

flog·ging *n* [C,U]

flood¹ /flʌd/ *n* [C] **1** (coming of a) great quantity of water in a place that is usually dry: *The rainstorms caused ~s in the low-lying areas.* **2** great outpouring or outburst: *~s of rain/tears; a ~ of anger/letters.* **3** flowing in at the tide.

flood gate, gate opened and closed to admit or keep out water, esp the lower gate of a lock²(3).

flood·light, artificial lighting thrown in a bright and broad beam. □ *vt* (*pt,pp* -lit /-lɪt/) light up by this method: *The cathedral was ~lit.*

flood tide, rising tide. ⇨ ebb.

flood² /flʌd/ *vt,vi* **1** cover or fill (as) with a flood: *The meadows were ~ed. The soldiers ~ed the countryside. We have been ~ed with requests. Thousands of people were ~ed out,* forced to leave their homes. **2** (of rain) fill (a river) to overflowing.

floor¹ /flɔː(r)/ *n* [C] **1** lower surface of a room; part on which one walks: *a bare ~,* one with no carpet, etc. **wipe the floor with sb,** utterly defeat him, e g in a fight or argument. **2** number of rooms, etc on the same level in a building. ⇨ first floor. **3** bottom of the sea, of a cave, etc. **4** part of an assembly hall, e g the Houses of Parliament, Congress, where members sit. **take the floor,** speak in a debate. **5** lower limit (of prices).

ˈfloor-board, plank of a wooden floor.

ˈfloor-cloth, piece of rough cloth for wiping or washing floors.

ˈfloor show, cabaret, entertainment.

ˈfloor-walker, (= *shop-walker*) person employed in a large shop or store to direct customers, detect shop-lifters, etc.

floor-ing, material, e g boards, used for making floors.

floor² /flɔ(r)/ *vt* **1** put (a floor) in a building. **2** knock down: ~ *a man in a boxing match.* **3** (of a problem, argument, etc) puzzle, defeat: *Tom was* ~ed *by two questions in the examination.*

flop /flɒp/ *vi,vt* (-pp-) **1** move, fall, clumsily or helplessly: *The fish were* ~ping *about in the boat. He* ~ped *down on his knees.* **2** put down or drop clumsily or roughly: ~ *down a heavy bag.* **3** (*informal*) (of a book, a film, a play) fail. □ *n* [C] **1** act or sound of flopping. **3** (*informal*) failure of a book, play, etc. □ *adv* with a flop: *fall* ~ *into the water.*

floppy *adj* (-ier, -iest) hanging down loosely: *a* ~py *hat.*

flora /ˈflɔːrə/ *n* [U] all the plants of an area or epoch.

floral /ˈflɔːrəl/ *adj* of flowers: ~ *designs.*

florid /ˈflɒrɪd *US:* ˈflɔː-/ *adj* **1** (too) rich in ornament and colour: *a* ~ *style,* e g of writing. **2** (of a person's face) naturally red: *a* ~ *complexion.*

flor-id-ly *adv*

florin /ˈflɒrɪn *US:* ˈflɔː-/ *n* [C] name of a former British coin worth one tenth of £1.

flor-ist /ˈflɒrɪst *US:* ˈflɔː-/ *n* [C] person who grows or sells flowers.

flo-tilla /fləˈtɪlə/ *n* [C] (*pl* ~s) fleet of small warships, e g destroyers.

flot-sam /ˈflɒtsəm/ *n* [U] (*legal*) parts of a wrecked ship or its cargo floating in the sea. ⇨ jetsam.

flounce /flaʊns/ *vi* move, go, with quick, troubled or impatient movements: ~ *out of/about the room.* □ *n* [C] sudden impatient movement of the body.

floun-der /ˈflaʊndə(r)/ *vi* **1** make wild and usually useless efforts (as when one is in deep water and unable to swim). **2** (*fig*) hesitate, make mistakes.

flour /ˈflaʊə(r)/ *n* [U] fine powder, made from grain, used for making bread, cakes, pastry, etc. □ *vt* cover or sprinkle with flour.

flour-ish /ˈflʌrɪʃ *US:* ˈflɜː-/ *vi,vt* **1** grow in a healthy manner; be well and active; prosper: *His business is* ~ing. *I hope you are all* ~ing, *keeping well.* **2** wave about and show: ~ *a sword.* **3** (of famous writers, etc) be alive and active (at the time indicated):

Socrates ~ed *about* 400 B C. □ *n* [C] **1** flourishing movement. **2** curve or decoration, ornament in handwriting, e g to a signature. **3** loud, exciting passage of music; fanfare: *a* ~ *of trumpets.*

flout /flaʊt/ *vt* oppose; treat with contempt: ~ *his wishes/authority.*

flow /fləʊ/ *vi* (*pt, pp* ~ed) **1** move along or over as a river does; move smoothly: *Rivers* ~ *into the sea. The tears* ~ed *from her eyes.* **2** (of hair, clothes, etc) hang down loosely: ~ing *robes; hair* ~ing *down her back.* **3** come from; be the result of: *Wealth* ~s *from industry and economy.* **4** (of the tide) come in; rise: *The tide began to* ~. ⇨ ebb. □ *n* (*sing* only) flowing movement; quantity that flows: *a good* ~ *of water; a* ~ *of angry words; the ebb and* ~ *of the sea.*

flower /ˈflaʊə(r)/ *n* [C] **1** that part of a plant that produces seeds. **in flower,** with the flowers out. **2** (*sing* only) (*fig*) finest part: *in the* ~ *of one's youth.* □ *vi* produce flowers: ~ing *plants.*

ˈflower-bed, small area of land in which flowers are grown.

ˈflower-pot, pot in which a plant may be grown.

ˈflower show, exhibition of flowers.

flow-ered *adj* decorated with floral patterns: ~ed *cloth.*

flower-less *adj* not having, not producing, flowers: ~*less plants.*

flow-ery *adj* (-ier, -iest) **(a)** having many flowers: ~y *fields.* **(b)** (*fig*) having an elaborate style: ~y *language.*

flown /fləʊn/ *pp* of fly².

flu /fluː/ *n* [U] (*informal* abbr of) influenza.

fluc-tu-ate /ˈflʌktʃʊeɪt/ *vi* (of levels, prices, etc) move up and down; be irregular: *fluctuating prices.*

fluc-tu-ation /ˌflʌktʃʊˈeɪʃən/ *n* [U] fluctuating; [C] fluctuating movement: *fluctuations of temperature.*

flue /fluː/ *n* [C] pipe or tube for carrying heat, hot air or smoke to, from or through a boiler, oven, etc.

flu-ency /ˈfluːənsɪ/ *n* [U] the quality of being fluent (of movement, speech) smooth easy flow.

flu-ent /ˈfluːənt/ *adj* (of a person) able to speak smoothly and easily: *a* ~ *speaker;* (of speech, movement) coming smoothly and easily: *speak* ~ *French.*

flu-ent-ly *adv*

fluff /flʌf/ *n* **1** [U] soft, feathery stuff that comes from blankets or other soft woolly material. **2** [C] small error when doing something. □ *vt* **1** shake, puff or spread out: ~ *out a pillow. The bird* ~ed (*out*) *its feathers.* **2** make an error (in games, in speaking one's lines in a play, etc).

fluffy *adj* (-ier, -iest) of or like, covered with, fluff.

fluid /ˈfluːɪd/ *adj* **1** able to flow (as gases and liquids do). **2** (of ideas, etc) not fixed; capable of being changed: ∼ *opinions/plans.* □ *n* [C,U] liquid substance.

'fluid 'ounce, one twentieth of a pint.

flu·id·ity /fluˈɪdətɪ/ *n* [U] quality of being fluid.

fluke¹ /fluːk/ *n* [C] something resulting from a fortunate accident; instance of luck.

fluke² /fluːk/ *n* [C] 1 broad, triangular flat end of each arm of an anchor. 2 (lobe of a) whale's tail.

fluke³ /fluːk/ *n* [C] parasite, a kind of flat worm, found in a sheep's liver.

flung /flʌŋ/ *pt,pp* of fling.

flu·or·escence /fluəˈresəns/ *n* [U] emission of radiation, esp visible light; light so produced.

flu·or·escent /fluəˈresənt/ *adj* (of substances) taking in radiations and sending them out in the form of light: ∼ *lamps/ lighting.*

flurry /ˈflʌrɪ *US:* ˈflɜ-/ *n* [C] (*pl* -ies) 1 short, sudden rush of wind or fall of rain or snow. 2 (*fig*) nervous hurry: *in a* ∼ *of excitement.* □ *vt* cause to be confused, in a nervous hurry, etc.

flush¹ /flʌʃ/ *adj* 1 even; level: *doors* ∼ *with the walls.* 2 having plenty; well supplied: ∼ *with money.*

flush² /flʌʃ/ *n* 1 [C] rush of water; (reddening from a) rush of blood to the face; rush of emotion, excitement caused by this: *in the first* ∼ *of victory.* 2 [U] fresh growth, etc; first sign or part of something pleasant: *the first* ∼ *of spring; in the first* ∼ *of youth.*

flush³ /flʌʃ/ *n* [C] (in card games) hand in which all the cards are of the same suit.

'royal flush, ⇨ royal.

flush⁴ /flʌʃ/ *vi,vt* 1 (of a person, his face) become red because of a rush of blood to the skin: *She* ∼*ed when he spoke to her.* 2 (of health, heat, emotions, etc) cause (the face) to become red in this way: *She was* ∼*ed with exercise.* 3 (*fig*) fill with pride; encourage: *The men were* ∼*ed with success.* 3 clean or wash with a rush of water: ∼ *the drains.* 4 (of water) rush out in a flood.

flus·ter /ˈflʌstə(r)/ *vt* make nervous or confused. □ *n* [U] nervous state: *be all in a* ∼.

flute /fluːt/ *n* [C] wooden musical wind-instrument with holes to be stopped by keys.

flut·ist /ˈfluːtɪst/, (chiefly *US*) = flautist.

flut·ter /ˈflʌtə(r)/ *vt,vi* 1 (of birds) move the wings hurriedly or irregularly without flying, or in short flights only; cause (the wings) to move in this way: *The wounded bird* ∼*ed to the ground.* 2 (cause to) move about in a quick, irregular way: *curtains* ∼*ing in the breeze.* 3 (of the heart) beat irregularly. □ *n* 1 (usually *sing*) fluttering movement. 2 (*sing* with *a*) state of nervous excitement: *in a* ∼. 3 [U] vibration; distortion in sound reproduced from a disc or tape caused by faulty recording or reproduction. 4 [C] (*informal*) small bet: *have a* ∼.

flu·vial /ˈfluːvɪəl/ *adj* of, found in, rivers.

flux /flʌks/ *n* 1 [U] continuous succession of changes: *in a state of* ∼. 2 (*sing* only) flowing; flowing out.

fly¹ /flaɪ/ *n* [C] (*pl* flies) 1 two-winged insect, esp the common ˈhousefly. 2 natural or artificial fly, used as a bait in fishing for trout, etc.

ˈfly-weight, (boxer) weighing 112 lb (50·8 kg) or less.

fly² /flaɪ/ *vi,vt* (*pt* flew /fluː/, *pp* flown /fləʊn/) 1 move through the air as a bird does, or in an aircraft: *birds* ∼*ing in the air;* ∼ *from London to Paris.* 2 direct or control the flight of (aircraft); transport goods/ passengers in aircraft: *Five thousand passengers were flown to Paris during Easter weekend.* 3 go or move quickly; rush along; pass quickly: *He flew down the road. The door flew open. fly off the handle,* ⇨ handle(1). *fly into a rage/temper,* become suddenly angry. *send sb flying,* strike him so that he falls over or backwards. 4 cause (a kite) to rise and stay high in the air; raise (a flag) so that it waves in the air. 5 flee from: ∼ *the country.*

fly³ /flaɪ/ *n* [C] (*pl* flies) 1 (usually *pl*) flap of cloth to contain or cover a zip-fastener or buttonholes, e g down the front of a pair of trousers. 2 flap of canvas at the entrance to a tent or covered wagon. 3 outer edge of a flag farthest from the flagpole.

fly-leaf /ˈflaɪliːf/ *n* [C] blank page at the beginning or end of a book.

fly-over /ˈflaɪəʊvə(r)/ *n* [C] (*US* = *over-pass*) roadway, bridge, etc which crosses above another roadway, etc (as on a motor-way).

fly-past /ˈflaɪpɑːst *US:* -pæst/ *n* [C] flight of aircraft in formation as part of a military display.

fly-wheel /ˈflaɪwiːl *US:* -hwil/ *n* [C] heavy wheel revolving on a shaft to regulate machinery.

flyer, flier /ˈflaɪə(r)/ *n* [C] 1 animal, vehicle, etc going with exceptional speed. 2 pilot. 3 (*informal*) successful professional person.

fly·ing /ˈflaɪɪŋ/ *adj* that flies, flutters or waves swiftly.

ˈflying ˈcolours, flags on display (as during a ceremony). *come off with flying colours,* ⇨ colour¹(8).

ˈflying ˈdoctor, one visiting patients in an aircraft, as in Australia.

ˈflying field, (*old use*) airfield.

ˈflying-fish, (kinds of) tropical fish able to rise out of the water and move forward.

ˈflying officer, rank in the Royal Air Force.

ˈflying ˈjump, one made with a running start.

ˈflying machine, (*old use*) aircraft.

ˈflying ˈsaucer, unidentified flying object (abbr **U F O**) seen, or thought to have been seen, moving across the sky, e g one said to have come from another planet.

'**flying-squad,** part of a police force organized (with fast cars) for pursuit of (suspected) criminals.

'**flying 'visit,** short visit made while passing.

foal /fəʊl/ *n* [C] young horse (colt or filly). □ *vi* give birth to a foal.

foam /fəʊm/ *n* [U] white mass of small air bubbles as formed in or on a liquid. □ *vi* form, break into, foam; send out foam (at the mouth): *waves ~ing along the beach; ~ing beer.*
foamy *adj* (-ier, -iest)

'**foam-'rubber,** spongy rubber used in upholstery.

fob /fob/ *vt* (-bb-) get a person to accept something of little or no value by deceit or trickery: *He ~bed me off with promises that he never intended to keep.*

fo-cal /ˈfəʊkəl/ *adj* of or at a focus: *the ~ length/distance of a lens,* from the surface of a lens to its focus; *the ~ point of a discussion, exhibition.*

fo-cus /ˈfəʊkəs/ *n* [C] (*pl ~es* or *foci* /ˈfəʊsaɪ/) 1 meeting-point of rays of light, heat, etc; point, distance, where the sharpest outline is given (to the eye, through a telescope, through a lens on a camera, etc): *The image is out of/in ~.* 2 point at which interests, tendencies, etc meet: *the ~ of attention.* □ *vt,vi* (-s- or -ss-) 1 (cause to) come together at a focus; adjust (an instrument, etc) so that it is in focus: *~ the lens of a microscope.* 2 concentrate: *~ one's attention/efforts on a problem.*

fod-der /ˈfodə(r)/ *n* [U] dried food, hay, etc for farm animals, horses, etc.

foe /fəʊ/ *n* [C] (*poet*) enemy.

foe-tal, fe-tal /ˈfiːtəl/ *adj* of, like, a foetus: *the ~ position* (in the womb).

foe-tus, fe-tus /ˈfiːtəs/ *n* [C] (*pl ~es*) fully developed embryo in the womb or in an egg.

fog /fog *US:* fɔːg/ *n* 1 [U] vapour suspended in the atmosphere at or near the earth's surface, thicker than mist and difficult to see through. 2 [C] period of fog: *London used to have bad ~s in winter.* 3 [C,U] (area of) cloudiness on a photograph. □ *vt* (-gg-) 1 cover with, as with, fog; bewilder: *I'm a bit ~ged,* puzzled. 2 make (a photographic negative) cloudy.

'**fog-bound** *adj* unable to proceed safely because of fog.

'**fog-horn,** instrument used for warning ships in fog.

'**fog-lamp,** headlamp (on a motor-vehicle) providing a strong beam of light for use in foggy weather.

foggy *adj* (-ier, -iest) (a) dense, not clear, because of fog: *a ~gy evening.* (b) obscure, confused: *have a ~gy idea.*

foible /ˈfɔɪbəl/ *n* [C] slight peculiarity or defect of character, often one of which a person is wrongly proud.

foil [1] /fɔɪl/ *n* 1 [U] thin, flexible metal sheet: *aluminium ~,* eg as wrapped round chocolate. 2 [C] person or thing that contrasts with, and sets off, the qualities of another: *A plain old woman acts as a ~ to her beautiful daughter.*

foil [2] /fɔɪl/ *n* [C] light sword with a button on the point, for fencing.

foil [3] /fɔɪl/ *vt* frustrate or prevent from carrying out plans: *He was ~ed in his attempt to deceive the girl.*

foist /fɔɪst/ *vt* trick a person into accepting (a useless article, etc). *~ a broken bike on a buyer.*

fold [1] /fəʊld/ *vt,vi* 1 bend one part of a thing back on itself: *~ up a newspaper; ~ back the sheets.* 2 become, be able to be, folded: *~ing doors.* **fold up,** (a) collapse; come to an end: *The business finally ~ed up last week.* (b) (*informal*) burst into laughter. 3 **fold one's arms,** across them over the chest. 4 cover, wrap: *hills ~ed in mist.* 5 (in cooking) gently mix (an ingredient, eg beaten eggs) into another. □ *n* [C] 1 part that is folded. 2 hollow among hills.
folder *n* [C] (a) holder (made of cardboard, etc) for loose papers. (b) folded card or paper with railway timetables, etc; folded container, eg for matches.

fold [2] /fəʊld/ *n* [C] 1 enclosure for sheep. 2 (*fig*) body of religious believers; members of a Church. **return to the fold,** come or go back home (eg rejoin a body of believers). □ *vt* enclose (sheep) in a fold.

-fold /-fəʊld/ *suffix* (used to make an *adjective*) 1 multiplied by: *tenfold.* 2 of (the stated parts: *twofold.*

fo-li-age /ˈfəʊlɪɪdʒ/ *n* [U] all the leaves of a tree or plant.

fo-lio /ˈfəʊlɪəʊ/ *n* [C] (*pl ~s*) sheet of paper numbered on one side only (as in a book); page number of a printed book; volume made of such sheets: *the first ~,* first edition.

folk /fəʊk/ *n* 1 (used with a *pl verb*) people in general: *Some ~ are never satisfied.* 2 (in compounds) the common people of a country. 3 (*pl*) (*informal*) relatives: *the old ~s at home.* 4 folk music.

'**folk-dance,** (music for a) traditional popular dance.

'**folk-lore,** (study of the) traditional beliefs, tales, etc of a community.

'**folk music/song,** popular music/song handed down from the past.

fol-low /ˈfoləʊ/ *vt,vi* 1 come, go, have a place, after (in space, time or order): *You go first and I'll ~ (you). Monday ~s Sunday.* **as follows,** as now to be stated. **follow through,** (a) (in tennis, golf, etc) complete a stroke by moving the racket, club, etc after hitting the ball. Hence, '**follow-through** *n.* (b) complete a task, carry out a promise. 2 go along, keep to (a road, etc): *F~ this road for six miles.* 3 understand: *He spoke so fast that I couldn't ~ him/~ what he said.* 4 engage in as a business, trade, etc: *~ the* *sea,* be a seaman. **5** take or accept as a guide, an example, etc: ~ *sb's advice/the latest fashion.* **follow suit,** do what has just been done by somebody else. **6** be necessarily true: *It ~s from what you say that...* **7** *follow sth up,* pursue, work at further: ~ *up an enquiry.* Hence, **'follow-up** *n.*

fol·lower *n* **(a)** supporter; disciple: *the football team and their ~ers.* **(b)** pursuer.

fol·low·ing *adj* **(a)** the one/ones coming next: *the ~ Monday.* **(b)** (esp as a *pronoun*) *the ~ing,* the one or ones about to be mentioned. □ *n* [C] body of supporters: *a political leader with a large ~ing.*

folly /'fɒlɪ/ *n* (*pl* -ies) **1** [U] foolishness. **2** [C] foolish act, idea or practice; ridiculous thing.

fo·ment /fəʊ'ment/ *vt* **1** put warm water, lotions, etc on (a part of the body, to lessen pain, etc). **2** (*fig*) cause or increase (disorder, discontent, ill-feeling, etc).

fo·men·ta·tion /'fəʊmen'teɪʃən/ *n* [C,U]

fond /fɒnd/ *adj* **1 be fond of,** like, be full of love for, take pleasure in: ~ *of music.* **2** loving and kind: ~ *embraces.*

fond·ly *adv* **(a)** lovingly: *look ~ly at her.* **2** in a foolishly optimistic manner: *He ~ly imagined that he could learn French in six weeks.*

fond·ness *n* [U]

fondle /'fɒndəl/ *vt* touch or stroke lovingly: *fondling a kitten.*

font /fɒnt/ *n* [C] basin or vessel (often in carved stone) to hold water for baptism; basin for holy water.

food /fuːd/ *n* **1** [U] that which can be eaten by people or animals, or used by plants, to keep them living and for growth: (used as an *adjective*) ~ *poisoning.* **2** [C] *a kind of ~,* particular example. **food for thought,** something to think about.

'food-stuff, material used as food.

fool¹ /fuːl/ *n* [C] **1** person without much sense; person whose conduct one considers silly: *What ~s we were not to see the joke! She was ~ enough* (= enough of a fool) *to believe him.* **make a fool of sb,** cause him to seem like a fool. **play the fool,** behave stupidly. □ *adj* (*informal*) foolish; silly: *a scheme devised by some ~ politician.* □ *vi,vt* **1** behave like a fool; be idle and silly: *If you go on ~ing with that gun, there'll be an accident. Stop ~ing (about)!* **2** cheat; deceive: *You can't/don't ~ me!* ⇨ April.

'fool's 'paradise, happiness that is only an illusion.

fool² /fuːl/ *n* [U] creamy liquid of stewed fruit mixed with cream or custard.

fool·ery /'fuːlərɪ/ *n* (*pl* -ies) **1** [U] foolish behaviour. **2** [C] foolish acts, ideas or words.

fool·hardy /'fuːlhɑːdɪ/ *adj* taking unnecessary risks.

fool·hardi·ness *n* [U]

fool·ish /'fuːlɪʃ/ *adj* without reason, sense or

good judgement; silly: *It would be ~ for us to quarrel.*

fool·ish·ly *adv*

fool·ish·ness *n* [U]

fool-proof /'fuːlpruːf/ *adj* incapable of failure, involving no risk.

foot¹ /fʊt/ *n* (*pl* feet /fiːt/) **1** part forming the lower end of the leg, beginning at the ankle. **be caught on the wrong foot,** have to do something when one is not ready. **2** part of a sock, etc covering the foot. **on foot,** **(a)** walking, not riding. **(b)** active: *A project is on ~ to build a new tunnel here.* **be on one's feet, (a)** be standing: *I've been on my feet all day.* **(b)** rise (to speak): *The Minister was on his feet at once to answer the charge.* **(c)** (*fig*) be in good health after an illness: *It's nice to see you on your feet again.* **be rushed off one's feet,** be extremely busy. **be caught on the wrong foot,** be surprised when unprepared. **fall on one's feet,** (*informal*) have good luck. **put one's foot down,** (*informal*) object; protest; be firm. **put one's foot in it,** (*informal*) say or do something wrong or stupid. **put one's feet up,** (*informal*) rest with the legs in a horizontal position. **put one's best foot forward,** walk, do something as fast as possible. **sweep sb off his feet,** fill him with strong enthusiasm. **2** step, way of walking: *light of ~.* **3** lowest part; bottom: *at the ~ of the page/ladder/wall/mountain.* **4** lower end of a bed or grave. **5** measure of length, 12 inches: *George is very tall—he's six ~/feet two (6´ 2˝).* **6** division or unit of verse, each with one strong stress and one or more weak stresses, as in: *for mén/may cóme/and mén/may gó.*

'foot·ball *n* [C] inflated leather ball used in games; [U] game played with it.

'football pools, organized gambling on the results of professional football matches.

'foot·bridge, one for the use of persons on foot, not vehicles.

'foot·fall, sound of a footstep.

'foot-hills, hills lying at the foot of a mountain or a range of mountains.

'foot·hold, (a) support for the foot, e g when climbing on rocks or ice. **(b)** (*fig*) secure position.

'foot·light, screened light at the front of the stage of a theatre.

'foot·man, servant who admits visitors, waits at table, etc.

'foot·mark *n* = footprint.

'foot-and-'mouth disease, disease of cattle and other cloven-hoofed animals.

'foot·note, one at the foot of a page.

'foot·path, path for the use of persons on foot.

'foot·print, impression left on a soft surface by a foot.

'foot rule, ruler 12 inches long.

'foot·sore *adj* having sore feet, esp because of walking.

foot-step, (sound of a) step of a person walking. **follow in sb's footsteps,** do as he did.

foot-stool, low stool for resting the feet on.

foot-wear, (tradesmen's term for) boots, shoes, etc.

foot-work, manner of using the feet, e g in boxing, dancing.

foot² /fʊt/ vt,vi (informal) **foot it,** walk: We've missed the last bus, so we'll have to ~ it. **foot the bill,** (agree to) pay it.

-footed /-'fʊtɪd/ suffix having the (kind of) feet indicated: 'flat-'~; 'four-'~.

foot-age /'fʊtɪdʒ/ n [C] length measured in feet.

foot-ing /'fʊtɪŋ/ n [C] 1 placing of the feet; surface for standing on: He lost his ~ and fell. 2 (sing only) position in society; relationships (with people): be on a friendly ~ with them. 3 conditions; state: on a peace/war ~.

fop /fɒp/ n [C] (dated) man who pays too much attention to his clothes and personal appearance.

fop-pish /-ɪʃ/ adj or like a fop.

for¹ /fə(r)/ strong form: fɔ(r)/ prep 1 (showing destination, or progress towards) (a) after verbs: set out ~ home. The ship was making ~ (= sailing towards) the open sea. (b) after nouns: the train ~ Glasgow. 2 (showing what is or was aimed at): He felt that he was destined ~ something great. 3 (showing eventual possession): Here's a letter ~ you. **be 'for it,** (informal) be likely to be punished, get into trouble, etc. 4 (showing preparation): prepare ~ an examination; get ready ~ school. 5 (showing purpose) in order to be, have, obtain, etc: go ~ a walk/ride/swim. What's this tool ~? What did you do that ~? It's a machine ~ cutting steel. 6 (as (if): They left him ~ dead. They chose him ~ (= as, to be) their leader. **take sb/sth for,** mistakenly think that he or it is: He took me ~ my brother. **for certain,** as being certain: I cannot hold it ~ certain that... 7 (followed by an object of hope, wish, search, inquiry, etc): hope ~ the best; pray ~ peace; a cry ~ help. 8 (showing liking, affection, etc): a taste ~ art; no regret ~ the past. 9 (showing ability): a good ear ~ music. 10 (showing suitability): bad/good ~ your health. 11 (with too and enough): too beautiful ~ words; quite risky enough ~ me. 12 considering (the circumstances, etc); in view of: It's quite warm ~ January. She's tall ~ her age. 13 representing; in place of: B ~ Benjamin. **stand for,** represent: The letters MP stand ~ Member of Parliament. 14 in favour or support of; in favour of: Are you ~ or against the proposal? Three cheers ~ the President! 15 with regard to; so far as concerns: anxious ~ his safety. You may take my word ~ it, believe me. 16 because of; on account of: ~ this reason; ~ my sake; win a medal ~

bravery. 17 (after a comparative) as the result of; because of: Are you any the better ~ your long sleep? 18 in spite of: F~ all his wealth, he is unhappy. 19 to the amount or extent of: Put my name down ~ £5. 20 in exchange for: I paid 60p ~ the book. He did the job ~ nothing. 21 in contrast with: ~ one enemy he has fifty friends. 22 (showing extent in time): I'm going away ~ a few days. **for good,** ⇨ good²(2). 23 (showing extent in space): We walked (~) three miles. The road is lined with trees ~ ten miles. (Note: for may be omitted if it comes immediately after the verb.) 24 (used in the pattern for + noun or pronoun + to inf): I am anxious ~ you and my sister to become acquainted. There's no need ~ anyone to know. 25 (showing purpose, design, determination, etc): I have brought the books ~ you to examine. I'd have given anything ~ this not to have happened.

for² /fə(r) strong form: fɔ(r)/ conj (dated formal) (rare in spoken English; not used at the beginning of a sentence) the reason, proof, etc being that: I asked her to stay to tea, ~ I had something to tell her.

for-age /'fɒrɪdʒ US: 'fɔr-/ n [U] food for horses and cattle. □ vi search (for food, etc).

foray /'fɒreɪ US: 'fɔreɪ/ n [C] raid; sudden attack (esp to get food, animals, etc): make/go on a ~. □ vi make a foray.

for-bad, for-bade /fə'bæd US: -'beɪd/ pt of forbid.

for-bear¹ /fɔ'beə(r)/ vt,vi (pt forbore /fɔ'bɔ(r)/, pp forborne /fɔ'bɔn/) (formal) refrain (from); not use or mention: I cannot ~ from going into details.

for-bear-ance /-rəns/ n [U] patience; self-control: show ~ance in dealing with people.

for-bear² (US = **fore-bear**) /'fɔbeə(r)/ n [C] (usually pl) ancestor.

for-bid /fə'bɪd/ vt (pt forbade or forbad /fə'bæd US: -'beɪd/, pp ~den /fə'bɪdən/ or ~) order (a person) not to do something; order that something shall not be done: I ~ you to use that word.

for-bid-ding adj stern; uninviting; threatening: a ~ding appearance.

for-bore, for-borne ⇨ forbear¹.

force¹ /fɔs/ n 1 [U] strength; power of body or mind: the ~ of a blow/an explosion/argument. The enemy attacked in (great) ~. 2 [C] person or thing that makes great changes: the ~s of nature, e g storms, earthquakes. Communism has become a powerful ~ in world affairs. 3 [C] organized body of armed or disciplined men: the armed ~s of a country, the Army, Navy, Air F~; the po'lice ~. **join forces (with),** unite (with). 4 [C,U] (intensity of, measurement of) pressure or influence. 5 authority: When does the new law come into ~? It is no longer in ~.

force² /fɔs/ vt 1 compel, oblige; use force to (make somebody) get or do something: ~

one's way through a crowd. **2** break open by using force: ~ (*open*) *a door.* **3** cause plants, etc to mature earlier than is normal, e g by giving them extra warmth. **4** produce under stress: ~ *a smile*, e g when one is unhappy.

force·ful /'fɔsfəl/ *adj* (of a person, his character, of an argument, etc) convincing, believable: *a* ~ *speaker/style of writing.*
force·fully /-fəlɪ/ *adv*

for·ceps /'fɔseps/ *n* [C] (*pl* unchanged) (*a pair of* ~) pincers or tongs used by dentists (when pulling out teeth) and by doctors for gripping things: (used as an *adjective*) *a* ~ *delivery* (of a child).

forc·ible /'fɔsəbəl/ *adj* **1** done by, involving the use of, physical force: *a* ~ *entry into a building.* **2** (of a person) = forceful.
forc·ibly /-əblɪ/ *adj*

ford /fɔd/ *n* [C] shallow place in a river where it is possible to walk or drive across. □ *vt* cross (a ford).

fore /fɔ(r)/ *adj* situated in the front: *in the* ~ *part of the train.* □ *n* (*sing* only) **1** front part (of a ship). **2** *to the fore*, in or into a position of importance, prominence. □ *adv* (*naut*) in front. *fore and aft*, at the bow and stern of a ship; lengthwise in a ship.

fore- /fɔ(r)-/ *prefix* before, in front of: *foretell; foreground.*

fore·arm[1] /'fɔrɑm/ *n* [C] part of the arm from the elbow to the wrist or finger-tips.

fore·arm[2] /'fɔr`ɑm/ *vt* arm, prepare for trouble, in advance: *To be forewarned is to be* ~*ed.*

fore·bear *n* = forbear[2].

fore·bode /fɔ`bəʊd/ *vt* (*formal*) **1** be a sign of warning of: *These black clouds* ~ *a storm.* **2** have a feeling of, foresee, (something evil).
fore·bod·ing *n* [C,U] feeling that trouble is coming.

fore·cast /'fɔkɑst US: -kæst/ *vt* (*pt,pp* ~ or ~ed) say in advance what is likely to happen. □ *n* [C] such a statement: *inaccurate weather* ~*s.*

fore·court /'fɔkɔt/ *n* [C] enclosed space in front of a building.

fore·doom /'fɔ`dum/ *vt* destine (to): ~*ed to failure.*

fore·fathers /'fɔfɑðəz/ *n pl* = ancestors.

fore·fin·ger /'fɔfɪŋgə(r)/ *n* [C] index finger, next to the thumb.

fore·front /'fɔfrʌnt/ *n* the ~, most forward part: *in the* ~ *of the battle.*

fore·gather *vt* = forgather.

forego = forgo.

fore·going /fe`gəʊɪŋ/ *adj* preceding, already mentioned.

fore·gone /'fɔgɒn US: -gɔn/ *adj*: *a* ~ *conclusion*, ending that can be seen or could have been seen from the start.

fore·ground /'fɔgraʊnd/ *n* [C] **1** part of a view nearest to the observer. **2** (*fig*) most noticeable position: *keep oneself in the* ~.

fore·hand /'fɔhænd/ *adj* (of a stroke at tennis, etc) made with the palm turned forward. □ *n* [C] such a stroke.

fore·head /'fɔrɪd US: 'fɔrɪd/ *n* [C] part of the face above the eyes.

foreign /'fɒrən US: 'fɔr-/ *adj* **1** of, in, from, another country, not one's own: ~ *languages/countries.* **2** *foreign to*, not natural to, unconnected with: *Lying is* ~ *to his nature.* **3** coming or introduced from outside: *a* ~ *body in the eye*, e g a bit of dirt.
foreigner, person born in, from, a foreign country.

fore·leg /'fɔleg/ *n* [C] one of the front legs of a four-footed animal.

fore·lock /'fɔlɒk/ *n* [C] lock of hair growing just above the forehead.

fore·man /'fɔmən/ *n* [C] (*pl* -men /-mən/) **1** workman in authority over others. **2** chief member and spokesman of a jury.

fore·most /'fɔməʊst/ *adj* first; most notable; chief: *the* ~ *painter of his period.* □ *adv* first in position. '*first and* `*foremost*, in the first place.

fore·name /'fɔneɪm/ *n* [C] (as used, e g on forms) first name.

for·en·sic /fə`rensɪk/ *adj* of, used in, courts of law: ~ *medicine*, medical knowledge as needed in legal matters, e g about poisoning.

fore·part /'fɔpɑt/ *n* [C] part in front.

fore·run·ner /'fɔrʌnə(r)/ *n* [C] **1** sign of what is to follow: *swallows, the* ~*s of spring.* **2** person who foretells and prepares for the coming of another.

fore·see /fɔ`si/ *vt* (*pt* foresaw /fɔ`sɔ/, *pp* foreseen /fɔ`sin/) see in advance: ~ *trouble.*
fore·see·able *adj* which can be described, known, in advance: *the* ~*able future.*

fore·shadow /fɔ`ʃædəʊ/ *vt* be a sign or warning of.

fore·shore /'fɔʃɔ(r)/ *n* [C] part of the shore between the sea and land that is cultivated, built on, etc.

fore·shorten /fɔ`ʃɔtən/ *vt* draw (an object) with some lines shortened to give it perspective.

fore·sight /'fɔsaɪt/ *n* [U] ability to see future needs; care in preparing for these.

fore·skin /'fɔskɪn/ *n* [C] fold of skin covering the end of the penis.

for·est /'fɒrɪst US: 'fɔr-/ *n* **1** [C,U] (large area of) land covered with trees; the trees growing there: (used as an *adjective*) ~ *fires.* **2** area where game (e g deer) is or was hunted: *the deer* ~*s in Scotland.* **3** (*fig*) something like a forest: *a* ~ *of masts*, e g in a harbour.
for·ester, officer in charge of a forest (protecting wild animals, watching for fires, etc); man who works in a forest.
for·estry *n* [U] (science of) planting and caring for forests.

fore·stall /fɔ`stɔl/ *vt* do something first and so prevent another from doing it.

fore-swear /fɔˈsweə(r)/ v = forswear.

fore-taste /ˈfɔteɪst/ n [C] partial experience of enjoyment or suffering (*of* something) in advance.

fore-tell /fɔˈtel/ vt (*pt, pp* foretold /fɔˈtould/) tell beforehand; predict: ~ *her future*.

fore-thought /ˈfɔθɔt/ n [U] careful thought or planning for the future.

fore-told *pt, pp* of foretell.

for-ever /fəˈrevə(r)/ adv always; at all times; endlessly.

fore-warn /fɔˈwɔn/ vt warn in advance.

fore-woman /ˈfɔwumən/ n [C] (*pl* -women /-wɪmɪn/) woman in authority over other women workers.

fore-word /ˈfɔwəd/ n [C] introductory remarks to a book, printed in it.

for-feit /ˈfɔfɪt/ vt (have to) suffer the loss of something as a punishment or because of rules. □ n [C] something (to be) forfeited: *His health was the ~ he paid for over-working.*

for-feit-ure /ˈfɔfɪtʃə(r)/ n [U]

for-gather /fɔˈgæðə(r)/ vi come together.

for-gave /fɔˈgeɪv/ pt of forgive.

forge[1] /fɔdʒ/ n [C] **1** workshop with a fire and anvil where metals are heated and shaped, esp one used by a smith for making shoes for horses, etc. **2** (workshop with a) furnace or hearth for melting or refining metal.

forge[2] /fɔdʒ/ vt **1** shape by heating and hammering. **2** (*fig*) form or make: *Their friendship was ~d by poverty.* **3** make a copy of, e g a signature, a banknote, a will, in order to deceive.

forger, person who forges(2).

forg-ery /ˈfɔdʒərɪ/ n (*pl* -ies) **(a)** [U] forging(3) of a document, signature, etc. **(b)** [C] forged document, signature, etc.

forge[3] /fɔdʒ/ vi **forge ahead,** make steady progress; take the lead (in a race, etc).

for-get /fəˈget/ vt, vi (*pt* forgot /fəˈgot/, *pp* forgotten /fəˈgotən/) **1** fail to keep in the memory; fail to recall: *I ~/I've forgotten her name. I shall never ~ your kindness to me. I forgot all about it.* **2** neglect or fail (to do something): *Don't ~ to post the letters.* **3** put out of the mind; stop thinking about: *Let's ~ our quarrels.*

for-get-ful /-fəl/ adj in the habit of forgetting: *Old people are sometimes ~ful.*

for-get-fully /-fəlɪ/ adv

for-get-ful-ness n [U]

forget-me-not /fəˈgetmɪnɒt/ n [C] small plant with blue flowers.

for-give /fəˈgɪv/ vt, vi (*pt* forgave /fəˈgeɪv/, *pp* ~n /fəˈgɪvən/) excuse, pardon, a sin; pardon or show mercy to (a person): ~ *him for being rude/his rudeness.*

for-giv-able /-əbəl/ adj

for-giv-ing adj ready, willing, to forgive: *a forgiving nature.*

for-give-ness n [U] forgiving or being forgiven: *ask for/receive ~ness.*

for-go /fɔˈgəu/ vt (*pt* forwent /fɔˈwent/, *pp* forgone /fɔˈgon US: -ˈgɔn/) do without; give up: ~ *pleasures in order to study hard.*

for-got, for-got-ten ⇨ forget.

fork /fɔk/ n [C] **1** implement with two or more points (prongs), used for lifting food to the mouth, etc. **2** farm or gardening tool like a fork(1). **3** place where a road, tree-trunk, etc divides or branches; one such branch: *take the left ~.* **4** part of a bicycle frame to which a wheel is fixed. ⇨ also tuning-fork. □ vt, vi **1** lift, move, carry, with a fork: ~ *the ground over,* turn the soil over with a fork. **2** (of a road, river, etc) divide into branches. **3** (of persons) turn (left or right): *We ~ed right at the church.* **4** **fork out,** (*informal*) hand over, pay: *I've got to ~ out a lot in taxes this year.*

'fork-lift truck, powered trolley with a platform for lifting and lowering goods.

forked adj branching; divided into two or more parts: *the ~ed tongue of a snake.*

for-lorn /fəˈlɔn/ adj (*literary*) unhappy; uncared for.

for-lorn-ly adv

form[1] /fɔm/ n **1** [U] shape; outward or visible appearance: *without shape or ~. take form,* begin to have a (recognizable) shape. **2** [C] person or animal as it can be seen or touched: *A dark ~ could be seen in the distance.* **3** [U] general arrangement or structure; way in which parts are put together to make a whole or a group: *literary ~* (contrasted with subject-matter). **4** [C] particular kind of arrangement or structure; manner in which a thing exists; species, kind or variety: *~s of government. Ice, snow and steam are ~s of water.* **5** (*gram*) [U] shape taken by a word: *different in ~ but identical in meaning;* [C] one of the shapes taken by a word (in sound or spelling): *The word 'brother' has two plural ~s, 'brothers' and 'brethren'.* **6** [U] manner of behaving or speaking fixed, required or expected by custom or etiquette: *say 'Good morning' only as a matter of ~,* i e not because one is really pleased to see the person to whom the words are spoken. **7** [C] particular way of behaving, etc greeting, utterance, act, as required by custom: *accepted ~s of behaviour.* **8** [C] printed paper with space to be filled in: *appli'cation ~s.* **9** [U] condition of health and training (e g of horses, athletes): *Smith is out of ~/is not on ~ and is unlikely to race tomorrow.* **10** [U] spirits(9): *Jack was in great ~ at the dinner party,* in high spirits, lively. **11** [C] long wooden bench, usually without a back, for several persons to sit on. **12** [C] (*GB*) class(4).

'form of ad'dress, way of referring to or of a person.

form-less adj without shape.

form[2] /fɔm/ vt, vi **1** give shape or form to; make, produce: ~ *the plural of a noun by adding -s or -es.* **2** develop, build up, con-

ceive: ~ *good habits;* ~ *ideas/conclusions.*
3 organize: *They* ~*ed themselves into a committee.* **4** be (the material of): *This series of lectures* ~*s part of a complete course on French history.* **5** (*mil*) (cause to) move into a particular order: ~ *into line.* **6** come into existence; become solid; take shape: *The idea* ~*ed in his mind.*

-form /-fɔm/ *suffix* having the shape, character, of: *uniform.*

for·mal /ˈfɔməl/ *adj* **1** strictly in accordance with established rules, customs and convention: *pay a* ~ *call on the Ambassador.* **2** (of style, vocabulary, etc) chosen and used in formal(1) situations. **3** regular or geometric in design. **4** of the outward shape or appearance (not the reality or substance): *a* ~ *resemblance between two things.*
for·mal·ly /-məlɪ/ *adv*

for·mal·ity /fɔˈmælətɪ/ *n* (*pl* -ies) **1** [U] strict attention to rules, forms and convention: *There was too much* ~ *in the University.* **2** [C] action required by custom or rules: *legal formalities.* **a mere formality,** something one is required or expected to do, but which has little meaning or importance.

for·ma·tion /fɔˈmeɪʃən/ *n* **1** [U] forming or shaping: *the* ~ *of character/of ideas in the mind.* **2** [C] that which is formed: *Clouds are* ~*s of condensed water vapour.* **3** [C,U] structure or arrangement: *troops/warships in* `*battle* ~; *rock* ~*s.*

for·ma·tive /ˈfɔmətɪv/ *adj* giving, or tending to give, shape to: *the* ~ *years of a child's life.*

for·mer /ˈfɔmə(r)/ *adj* **1** of an earlier period: *in* ~ *times; my* ~ *students.* **2** (as a *pronoun*) the first (mentioned) of two: *I prefer the* ~ *alternative to the latter.*
for·mer·ly *adv* in earlier times.

for·mi·dable /ˈfɔmɪdəbəl/ *adj* **1** causing fear or dread: *a man with a* ~ *appearance.* **2** requiring great effort to deal with or overcome: ~ *obstacles/opposition/enemies/debts.*
for·mi·dably /-əblɪ/ *adv*

for·mula /ˈfɔmjʊlə/ *n* [C] (*pl* ~s, or, in scientific usage, ~e /-li/) **1** fixed form of words used regularly (as 'How d'you do?', 'Excuse me', 'Thank you') or used in legal documents, etc. **2** statement of a rule, fact, etc esp one in signs or numbers, e g 'Water = H_2O'. **3** set of directions, usually in symbols, as for a medical preparation.

for·mu·late /ˈfɔmjʊleɪt/ *vt* express clearly and exactly: ~ *one's thoughts/a doctrine.*
for·mu·la·tion /ˈfɔmjʊˈleɪʃən/ *n* [U] formulating; [C] exact and clear statement.

for·ni·cate /ˈfɔnɪkeɪt/ *vi* commit adultery.

for·ni·ca·tion /ˈfɔnɪˈkeɪʃən/ *n* [U] voluntary sexual intercourse between persons not married to one another. ⇨ **adultery.**

for·sake /fəˈseɪk/ *vt* (*pt* forsook /fəˈsʊk/, *pp* ~n /fəˈseɪkən/) give up; break away from; desert: ~ *one's wife and children.*

for·swear /fɔˈsweə(r)/ *vt* (*pt* forswore /fɔˈswɔ(r)/, *pp* forsworn /fɔˈswɔn/) give up doing or using (something): ~ *bad habits.*

fort /fɔt/ *n* [C] building or group of buildings specially erected or strengthened for military defence.

forte /ˈfɔteɪ *US:* fɔrt/ *n* [C] something a person does particularly well: *Singing is not my* ~.

forth /fɔθ/ *adv* **1** out (which is more usual): *set forth,* begin a journey. **2** onwards; forwards: *from this day* ~. **and** `*so forth* and so on. **back and forth,** to and fro (which is more usual). **3** *hold forth,* ⇨ hold³(14).

forth·com·ing /fɔθˈkʌmɪŋ/ *adj* **1** about to appear: ~ *books.* **2** ready for use when needed: *The money/help we hoped for was not* ~, We did not receive it. **3** (*informal*) ready to be helpful, give information, etc: *The girl at the reception desk was not very* ~.

forth·right /ˈfɔθraɪt/ *adj* outspoken; straightforward.

forth·with /fɔθˈwɪθ *US:* -ˈwɪð/ *adv* at once; without losing time.

for·ti·eth /ˈfɔtɪəθ/ *adj, n* [C] (abbr *40th*) (of) one of 40 parts or the next after 39.

for·tify /ˈfɔtɪfaɪ/ *vt* (*pt,pp* -ied) strengthen (a place) against attack (with walls, trenches, guns, etc); support or strengthen oneself, one's courage, etc: ~ *a town against the enemy;* ~ *oneself against the cold.*

for·ti·fi·ca·tion /ˈfɔtɪfɪˈkeɪʃən/ *n* [U] fortifying; [C] (often *pl*) defensive wall(s), tower(s), etc.

for·ti·tude /ˈfɔtɪtjud *US:* -tud/ *n* [U] (*formal*) calm courage, self-control, in the face of pain, danger or difficulty.

fort·night /ˈfɔtnaɪt/ *n* [C] period of two weeks.
fort·night·ly *adj, adv* happening or occurring every fortnight.

for·tress /ˈfɔtrəs/ *n* [C] fortified building or town.

for·tu·itous /fɔˈtjuɪtəs *US:* -ˈtu-/ *adj* happening by chance: *a* ~ *meeting.*
for·tu·itous·ly *adv*

for·tu·nate /ˈfɔtʃənət/ *adj* favoured by fortune; lucky; prosperous; having, bringing, brought by, good fortune: *You were* ~ *to escape being injured.*
for·tu·nate·ly *adv* in a fortunate manner; luckily: ~*ly for everybody.*

for·tune /ˈfɔtʃun/ *n* **1** [C,U] chance; chance looked on as a power deciding or influencing; fate; good or bad luck coming to a person or undertaking: *have* ~ *on one's side,* be lucky. **tell sb's fortune,** say, e g as gypsies do, from a reading of playing cards or the lines on his palm, what will happen to him. **2** [C,U] prosperity; success; great sum of money: *a man of* ~. **come into a fortune,** inherit a lot of money. **make a fortune,** make a lot of money.

'fortune hunter, man seeking a rich woman to marry.

'fortune teller, person who claims to be able to tell a person's fortune.

for·ty /ˈfɔːtɪ/ *adj, n* [C] (of) 40: *under/over* ~.

the forties, years of life or of a century between 39 and 50.

fo·rum /ˈfɔːrəm/ *n* [C] (*pl* ~s) **1** (in ancient Rome) public place for meetings. **2** any place for public discussion: *TV is an accepted* ~ *for the discussion of public affairs.*

for·ward¹ /ˈfɔːwəd/ *adj* **1** directed towards the front; situated in front; moving on, advancing: *a* ~ *march/movement;* ~ *planning,* for future needs, etc. **2** (of plants, crops, seasons, children) well advanced; making progress towards maturity: *a* ~ *spring.* **3** eager or impatient; ready and willing; too eager: *a* ~ *young girl.* **4** too advanced, extreme: ~ *opinions.* □ *n* [C] one of the attacking players in football (now often called a *striker*), hockey, etc.
for·ward·ness *n* [U]

for·ward² /ˈfɔːwəd/ *vt* **1** help or send forward; help to advance: ~ *his plans.* **2** send, dispatch: *We have* ~*ed you our new catalogue.* **3** send a letter, parcel, etc after a person to a new address: *Please* ~ *my letters to this address.*

for·ward(s) /ˈfɔːwəd(z)/ *adv* (*Note:* ~*s* is not much used except as in 4 below.) **1** onward so as to make progress: *rush/step* ~; *go* ~. **2** towards the future; onwards in time: *from this time* ~; *look* ~, think ahead, think about the future. **3** to the front; into prominence. **bring forward,** ⇨ bring(6). **come forward,** ⇨ come(15). **4 backward(s) and forward(s),** to and fro.

fos·sil /ˈfɒsəl/ *n* [C] recognizable (part, trace or imprint of a) prehistoric animal or plant once buried in earth, now hardened like rock.

fos·sil·ize /ˈfɒsəlaɪz/ *vt,vi* change or turn into stone.

fos·ter /ˈfɒstə(r) *US:* ˈfɔː-/ *vt* **1** help the growth and development of: ~ *good relations/evil thoughts.* **2** take into one's home and care for but without legal guardianship: ~ *a child.* ⇨ adopt(1).

'foster-brother/-child/-parent, etc, ⇨ **2** above

fought /fɔːt/ *pt,pp* of fight².

foul¹ /faʊl/ *adj* (-er, -est) **1** causing disgust; having a bad smell or taste; filthy: *a* ~ *taste;* 'ˈ~-smelling drains.* **2** wicked; evil; (of language) full of oaths; obscene. **3** (of the weather) stormy; rough. **fall foul of,** (a) (of a ship) run against, collide with. (b) (*fig*) get into trouble with: *fall* ~ *of the law.* □ *n* **1** [C] (in sport) something contrary to the rules. **2** [U] **through fair and foul,** through good and bad fortune.

'foul play, (a) (in sport) something contrary to the rules. (b) violent crime, esp murder: *Is* ~ *play suspected?*
foul·ly /ˈfaʊlɪ/ *adv*

foul² /faʊl/ *vt,vi* **1** make or become foul: *chimneys that* ~ *the air with smoke.* **2** collide (with); (cause to) become entangled: *The rope* ~*ed the anchor chain.* **3** (in sport) commit a foul(1) against: ~ *an opponent.*

found¹ /faʊnd/ *pt,pp* of find².

found² /faʊnd/ *vt* **1** start the building of; lay the base of; establish: *The Methodist Church was* ~*ed by John Wesley.* **2** get something started by providing money: ~ *a new school.* **3** base on: *arguments* ~*ed on facts.*

foun·da·tion /faʊnˈdeɪʃən/ *n* **1** [U] founding or establishing (of a town, school, church, etc). **2** [C] something that is founded, e g a college. **3** [C] fund of money for charity, research, etc: *the Ford F*~. **3** [C] (often *pl*) strong base of a building, on which it is built up: *the* ~(*s*) *of a block of flats.* **4** [C,U] that on which an idea, belief, etc is based; starting-point: *the* ~*s of religious beliefs; a story that has no* ~ *in fact/is without* ~, is untrue.

foun·'dation-stone stone laid at a ceremony to celebrate the founding of a building.

founder¹ /ˈfaʊndə(r)/ *n* [C] person who founds or establishes a school, etc.

foun·der² /ˈfaʊndə(r)/ *vi,vt* **1** (of a ship) (cause to) fill with water and sink. **2** (of a horse) fall or stumble (esp in mud) or from overwork.

found·ling /ˈfaʊndlɪŋ/ *n* [C] (*dated*) deserted or abandoned child of unknown parents.

foun·dry /ˈfaʊndrɪ/ *n* [C] (*pl* -ies) place where metal or glass is melted and moulded.

foun·tain /ˈfaʊntɪn *US:* -tən/ *n* [C] **1** spring of water, esp one made artificially with water forced through holes in a pipe or pipes for ornamental purposes. **2** (*fig*) source or origin: *the* ~ *of honour.*

'fountain-head, original source.

'fountain-pen, pen with a supply of ink inside the holder.

four /fɔː(r)/ *adj, n* [C] (of) 4: *a child of* ~, ~ *years old; an income of* ~ *figures.* **on all fours,** on the hands and knees.

'four·fold *adj* having 4 parts. □ *adv* 4 times as much or as many.

'four·pence, the sum of 4p.

'four·penny /-pənɪ/ *adj* costing 4p.

'four-ply *adj* (of wool, etc) having 4 strands or thicknesses.

'four·score *adj, n* (*old use*) (of) 80.

'four-square *adj* (a) square-shaped. (b) (*fig*) steady; firm.

four·teen /ˈfɔːˈtiːn/ *adj, n* [C] (of) 14.

four·teenth /ˈfɔːˈtiːnθ/ *adj, n* [C] (abbr *14th*) (of) one of 14 parts or the next after 13.

fourth /fɔːθ/ *adj, n* [C] (abbr *4th*) (of) one of 4 parts or the next after 3.

'fourth·ly *adv* in the 4th place.

fowl /faʊl/ *n* [C] **1** (*old use*) any bird: *the*

~s of the air. 2 (with a prefix) one of the larger birds: `wild~. 3 domestic cock or hen: keep ~s. 4 [U] flesh of fowls as food. □ vi catch, hunt, wildfowl: go ~ing.

fox /foks/ n [C] (feminine = vixen /ˈvɪk-sən/) wild animal of the dog family, with red fur and a bushy tail: **as cunning as a fox,** very cunning. □ vt deceive by cunning; confuse; puzzle: He was completely ~ed.

ˈfox·hound, kind of dog bred and trained to hunt foxes.

ˈfox·hunt n chasing of foxes with hounds. □ vi chase foxes.

ˈfox-ˈterrier, small and lively short-haired dog.

ˈfoxy adj (-ier, iest) crafty.

foyer /ˈfɔɪ-eɪ US: ˈfɔɪ-ər/ n [C] large hall, e g an entrance hall in a hotel, cinema, etc.

frac·tion /ˈfrækʃn/ n [C] 1 small part or bit. 2 number that is not a whole number (e g ½, 0.76).

frac·tional /-nəl/ adj of or in fractions.

frac·tious /ˈfrækʃəs/ adj (formal) irritable; bad-tempered.

frac·ture /ˈfræktʃə(r)/ n 1 [U] breaking or being broken, e g of a bone, a pipeline. 2 [C] instance of this: compound/simple ~s, with/without skin wounds. □ vt, vi break; crack: ~ one's leg.

frag·ile /ˈfrædʒaɪl US: -dʒəl/ adj easily injured, broken or destroyed: ~ china/ health/happiness.

fra·gil·ity /frəˈdʒɪlətɪ/ n [U]

frag·ment /ˈfrægmənt/ n [C] part broken off; separate or incomplete part: overhear ~s of conversation; ~s of a broken vase. □ vi /frægˈment/ break into pieces.

frag·men·tary /ˈfrægməntrɪ US: -terɪ/ adj incomplete; disconnected: a ~ary report of an event.

frag·men·ta·tion /ˈfrægmənˈteɪʃən/ n [U]

fra·grance /ˈfreɪgrəns/ n [U] sweet smell.

fra·grant /ˈfreɪgrənt/ adj sweet-smelling: ~ flowers.

frail /freɪl/ adj (-er, -est) weak; fragile: a ~ child.

frailty /ˈfreɪltɪ/ n 1 [U] the quality of being frail: the ~ of human life. 2 [C] (pl -ies) fault; moral weakness: He loved her in spite of her little frailties.

frame¹ /freɪm/ n [C] 1 skeleton or main structure, e g steel girders, pieces of wood, of a ship, building, aircraft, etc which makes its shape, esp in the process of building. 2 border in which a picture, photograph, window or door is enclosed or set. 3 structure that holds the lenses of a pair of spectacles. 4 human or animal body: a girl of slender ~. 5 box-like structure of wood and glass for protecting plants from the cold: a cold/ heated ~. 6 **frame of mind,** temporary state or condition of mind: in a cheerful ~ of mind. 7 single exposure on a roll of photographic film.

ˈframe·work, that part of a structure that gives shape and support: a bridge with a steel ~work; the ~work of a government.

frame² /freɪm/ vt, vi 1 put together; shape; build up: ~ a plan/theory/sentence. 2 put a frame(2) round; enclose in a frame: have a painting ~d. 3 develop: plans that are framing well/badly. 4 (sl) make (a person) appear guilty of something: The accused man said he had been ~d.

ˈframe-up, (sl) scheme to make an innocent person appear guilty.

fran·chise /ˈfræntʃaɪz/ n [C] 1 (usually sing with the) full rights of citizenship given by a country or town, esp the right to vote at elections. 2 (chiefly US) special right given by public authorities to a person or company: a ~ for a bus service.

Franco- /ˈfræŋkəʊ/ prefix French: the `~–German War of 1870—71.

Franco·phile /ˈfræŋkəʊfaɪl/ adj, n [C] person) loving France and French things to excess.

Franco·phobe /ˈfræŋkəʊfəʊb/ adj, n [C] (person) hating France and French things to excess.

Franco·phone /ˈfræŋkəfəʊn/ adj (of persons, countries) French speaking.

frank¹ /fræŋk/ adj (-er, -est) showing clearly the thoughts and feelings: a ~ look; make a ~ confession of one's guilt; be quite ~ with him (about something).

frank·ly adv

frank·ness n [U]

frank² /fræŋk/ vt stamp (letters, parcels, with a `~ing-machine which shows the charge for sending).

frank·furter /ˈfræŋkfɜtə(r)/ n [C] seasoned and smoked sausage made of beef and pork.

frank·in·cense /ˈfræŋkɪnsens/ n [U] kind of resin from trees, giving a sweet smell when burnt.

fran·tic /ˈfræntɪk/ adj wildly excited with joy, pain, anxiety, etc: ~ cries for help.

fran·ti·cally /-klɪ/ adv

fra·ter·nal /frəˈtɜnəl/ adj brotherly: ~ love.

fra·ter·nally /-nəlɪ/ adv

fra·ter·nity /frəˈtɜnətɪ/ n (pl -ies) 1 [U] brotherly feeling. 2 [C] society of men, e g monks, who treat each other as equals; men who are joined together by common interests. 3 [C] (US) society of students, with branches in various colleges, usually with names made up of Greek letters.

frat·er·nize /ˈfrætənaɪz/ vi become friendly (with).

frat·er·niz·ation /ˈfrætənaɪˈzeɪʃən US: -nɪˈz-/ n [U]

frat·ri·cide /ˈfrætrɪsaɪd/ n [C,U] (person guilty of) intentional killing of one's brother or sister.

fraud /frɔd/ n 1 [U] criminal deception; [C] act of this kind: get money by ~. 2 [C] person or thing that deceives.

fraudu·lent /ˈfrɔdjʊlənt US: -dʒʊ-/ adj acting with, obtained by, fraud; deceitful.

fraudu·lent·ly adv

fraught /frɔːt/ adj 1 involving; attended by; threatening (unpleasant consequences): an expedition ∼ with danger. 2 filled with: ∼ with meaning.

fray[1] /freɪ/ n [C] fight; contest.

fray[2] /freɪ/ vt,vi 1 (of cloth, rope, etc) become worn, make worn, by rubbing so that there are loose threads. 2 (fig) strain[1](3).

freak /friːk/ n [C] 1 absurd or very unusual idea, act or happening: (as an adjective) a ∼ storm. 2 person, animal or plant that is abnormal in form or behaviour. □ vi freak (out), (sl) react with an intense emotion as from hallucinatory drugs. Hence, `freak-out n

freak·ish /-ɪʃ/ adj abnormal: ∼ish behaviour.

freak·ish·ly adv

freaky adj (-ier, -iest) = freakish.

freckle /`frekl/ n [C] one of the small light-brown spots on the human skin. □ vt,vi (cause to) become covered with freckles: ∼ more easily than others.

free[1] /friː/ adj (-r, -st) 1 (of a person) not a slave; not in the power of another person. 2 not in prison; having personal rights and social and political liberty: The prisoners were set ∼. 3 (of a State, its citizens, and institutions) not controlled by a foreign government; having representative government: the land of the ∼. 4 not fixed or held back; able to move about; not controlled by rules, regulations or conventions: You are ∼ to go or stay as you please. Leave one end of the rope free , not tied or held. **have/give sb a free hand,** permission to act without consulting others. 5 **free from,** without: ∼ from blame/error/anxiety; released or exempt from: ∼ from the ordinary regulations. **free of,** (a) away from: as soon as the ship was ∼ of the harbour. At last I am ∼ of her, have got away from her. (b) without: ∼ of charge. 6 without payment; costing nothing: ∼ tickets for the theatre; give it away ∼; admission ∼. 7 (of place or time) not occupied or engaged; (of persons) not having time occupied; not doing anything: Her afternoons are usually ∼. She is usually ∼ in the afternoon(s). 8 coming or given readily: a ∼ flow of water; ∼ with his money/advice. 9 without constraint: He is somewhat ∼ in his conversation, not as proper or decent as he ought to be.

`free-and-`easy adj informal, casual.

`free-for-all, dispute, quarrel, etc in which all (are allowed to) express their views.

`free-hand adj (of drawings) done by hand, no compasses or other instrument being used: a ∼hand sketch.

`free-hold, (legal) (holding of) land in absolute ownership. ⇨ leasehold.

`free-holder, person who owns freehold property.

`free-lance /-lɑːns US: -læns/ n [C] independent journalist, writer, etc who sells his services wherever he can. □ vi work this way.

`free `speech, right to speak in public without interference from the authorities.

`free-style, (in swimming) race where the competitors choose their own stroke, usually the crawl.

`free-`trade n trade not hindered by customs duties to restrict imports.

`free `verse, without regular metre and rhyme.

`free-way, (US) highway with several lanes; motorway.

`free `will, individual's power of guiding and choosing his actions: do it of one's own ∼ will, without being required or compelled.

free·ly adv in a free manner; readily.

free[2] /friː/ vt (pt,pp ∼d /friːd/) make free (from): ∼ an animal (from a trap); ∼ oneself from debt.

free·dom /`friːdəm/ n 1 [U] condition of being free (all senses). 2 [C] particular kind of freedom.

freeze /friːz/ vt,vi (pt froze /frəʊz/, pp frozen /`frəʊzən/) 1 be so cold that water turns into ice: It was freezing last night. 2 (of water) become ice; (of other substances) become hard or stiff from cold: The lake froze over, became covered with ice. 3 be or feel very cold: I'm freezing. 4 make cold; make hard; cover with ice: frozen food, preserved by being kept very cold. ⇨ deep-freeze. 5 stop dealings in assets, credits, etc temporarily or permanently; fix or set prices, wages: `price-/`wage-`freezing. 6 become motionless, e g of an animal that stands still to avoid attracting attention. □ n [C] 1 period of freezing weather. 2 severe control of prices, wages, etc: a `wage-∼.

`freeze-`dry vt preserve (food) by rapid freezing and drying in a vacuum. Hence, **`freeze-`dry·ing** n.

freezer, machine, room, for freezing food.

`freezing-point, temperature at which a liquid (esp water) freezes.

freight /freɪt/ n [C] (money charged for) the carrying of goods from place to place by water (in US also by land); the goods carried. □ vt load (a ship) with cargo; send or carry (goods): ∼ a boat with fruit.

freighter, ship or aircraft that carries cargo.

French /frentʃ/ adj, n (of) France or the language or the people of France.

`French `horn, brass wind instrument.

French·man, man who is of French birth or nationality.

`French `window, one that serves as both a window and a door, opening on to a garden or balcony.

fren·etic /frə`netɪk/ adj = frantic.

frenzy /`frenzɪ/ n [U] violent excitement: in a ∼ of despair/enthusiasm.

fren·zied *adj* wildly excited.

fre·quency /ˈfriːkwənsɪ/ *n* (*pl* -ies) 1 [U] frequent occurrence: *the ~ of earthquakes in Italy.* 2 [C] rate of occurrence; number of repetitions (in a given time): *a ~ of 25 per second,* e g of an alternating electric current.

fre·quent¹ /ˈfriːkwənt/ *adj* often happening; numerous: *Hurricanes are ~ here in autumn. He's a ~ visitor.*
fre·quent·ly *adv*

fre·quent² /frɪˈkwent/ *vt* go often to (a place); be often found in or at: *Frogs ~ wet places.*

fresco /ˈfreskəʊ/ *n* [C] (*pl* ~s, ~es) 1 [U] pigment applied to moist plaster surfaces and allowed to dry; method of painting with this pigment: *painting in ~.* 2 [C] picture painted in this way. □ *vt* paint in fresco.

fresh /freʃ/ *adj* (-er, -est) 1 newly made, produced, gathered, grown, arrived, etc: *~ paint* (= still wet). 2 (of food) not stale or bad; not salted, tinned or frozen; *~ butter/ meat.* 3 new or different: *Is there any ~ news?* **make a fresh start,** begin again. 4 (of the air, wind, weather) cool; refreshing: *go out for some ~ air.* 5 bright and pure: *~ colours.* 6 not sea-water: *~-water fish.*
freshen /ˈfreʃən/ *vt,vi* make or become fresh. **freshen up,** make (oneself) feel fresh by washing.
fresher, ˈfresh·man, first-year student.
fresh·ly *adv* (only with a *pp*) recently: *~ly gathered fruit.*
fresh·ness *n* [U]

fret¹ /fret/ *vi,vt* (-tt-) 1 (cause to) be worried or bad-tempered: *What are you ~ting about?* 2 wear away by rubbing or biting at: *a horse ~ting its bit.* □ *n* [U] irritated state of mind: *in a ~.*
fret·ful /-fəl/ *adj* irritable; *a ~ful baby.*
fret·fully /-fəlɪ/ *adv*

fret² /fret/ *vt* (-tt-) decorate (wood) with patterns made by cutting or sawing.
ˈfret·saw, very narrow saw, fixed in a frame, for cutting designs in thin sheets of wood.
ˈfret·work *n* [U] (a) work in decorative patterns. (b) wood cut with such patterns by using a fretsaw.

fret³ /fret/ *n* [C] one of the metal ridges across the neck of a guitar, banjo, etc.

friar /ˈfraɪə(r)/ *n* [C] man who is a member of one of certain religious orders, esp one who has vowed to live in poverty.

fric·tion /ˈfrɪkʃən/ *n* 1 [U] the rubbing of one thing against another. 2 [C,U] (instance of a) difference of opinion leading to argument and quarrelling: *political ~ between two countries.*

Fri·day /ˈfraɪdɪ/ *n* sixth day of the week.
ˈGood ˈFriday, the one before Easter Sunday.

fridge /frɪdʒ/ *n* [C] (common abbr of) refrigerator.

fried /fraɪd/ *pt,pp* of fry.

friend /frend/ *n* [C] 1 person, not a relation, whom one knows and likes well: *He has been a good ~ to me.* 2 helpful thing or quality: *Among gossips silence can be your best ~.* 3 helper or sympathizer: *a good ~ of the poor.* ⇨ also Quaker.
friend·less·ness *n* [U]

friend·ly /ˈfrendlɪ/ *adj* (-ier, -iest) acting, or ready to act, as a friend; showing or expressing kindness: *be ~ with/be on ~ terms with her.*
friend·li·ness *n* [U]

friend·ship /ˈfrendʃɪp/ *n* 1 [U] being friends; the feeling or relationship that exists between friends: *my ~ for her.* 2 [C] instance or period of this feeling: *a ~ of twenty years.*

frieze /friːz/ *n* [C] ornamental band or strip along (usually the top of) a wall.

frig·ate /ˈfrɪgət/ *n* [C] 1 fast sailing-ship formerly used in war. 2 (*modern use*) fast escort vessel.

fright /fraɪt/ *n* [U] great and sudden fear: *die of ~;* [C] instance of this.

frighten /ˈfraɪtən/ *vt* fill with fright; alarm suddenly: *Did the noise ~ you?*
fright·ened *adj* (a) afraid: *be ~ed of him or it.* (b) alarmed: *~ed at the idea of something happening.*
fright·en·ing *adj* causing fright: *a ~ing experience.*

fright·ful /ˈfraɪtfəl/ *adj* 1 causing fear; dreadful: *a ~ accident.* 2 (*informal*) very great, unpleasant.
fright·fully /-fəlɪ/ *adv* (a) in an unpleasant or frightening way. (b) (*informal*) very: *I'm ~ly sorry!*

frigid /ˈfrɪdʒɪd/ *adj* 1 cold: *a ~ climate.* 2 unfriendly: *a ~ manner.* 3 (of women) having no sexual desire.
frigid·ly *adv*
frigid·ity /frɪˈdʒɪdətɪ/ *n* [U]

frill /frɪl/ *n* [C] 1 ornamental border on a dress, etc. 2 (*pl*) unnecessary adornments, e g to speech or writing.
frilly *adj*

fringe /frɪndʒ/ *n* [C] 1 ornamental border of loose threads, e g on a rug. 2 edge (of a crowd, forest, etc): *on the ~(s) of the desert.* 3 part of the hair cut short and allowed to hang over the forehead. □ *vt* put on, serve as, a fringe: *fringing a roadside with trees.*

frisk /frɪsk/ *vi,vt* 1 jump and run about playfully. 2 pass the hands over (a person) to search for concealed weapons.
frisky *adj* (-ier, -iest) lively.

frit·ter¹ /ˈfrɪtə(r)/ *vt* waste on useless aims: *~ away one's time/energy/money.*

frit·ter² /ˈfrɪtə(r)/ *n* [C] piece of fried batter with sliced fruit, meat, in it.

friv·ol·ous /ˈfrɪvələs/ *adj* 1 not serious or important: *~ remarks/behaviour.* 2 (of persons) not serious; enjoying pleasure.
friv·ol·ous·ly *adv*

friv·ol·ity /frɪ'vɒlətɪ/ n (pl -ies) **1** [U] frivolous behaviour or character. **2** [C] frivolous act or statement.

frizz /frɪz/ vt (of hair) form into masses of small curls.

frizzy adj (-ier, -iest) (of hair) frizzed.

frizzle¹ /'frɪzl/ vt, vi cook, be cooked, with a spluttering noise: *bacon frizzling in the pan.*

frizzle² /'frɪzl/ vt, vi (of hair) twist in small, crisp curls.

fro /frəʊ/ adv (only in) **to and fro,** backwards and forwards: *to and ~ between London and Paris.*

frock /frɒk/ n [C] **1** woman's or girl's dress (the usual word). **2** monk's long gown with loose sleeves.

frog /frɒg US: frɔg/ n [C] small, cold-blooded, jumping animal living in water and on land.

frog·man, person skilled in swimming under water with the aid of flippers on the feet and breathing apparatus.

frog·march vt carry (a prisoner) away, face downwards, by four men holding his arms and legs.

frolic /'frɒlɪk/ vi (pt,pp ~ked) play about in a gay, lively way. □ n [C] outburst of gaiety or merrymaking.

frolic·some /-səm/ adj

from /frəm strong form: from/ prep **1** (introducing the place, person, etc that is the starting-point): *jump (down) ~ a wall; travel ~ London to Rome.* **2** (showing the starting of a period of time): *~ the first of May; ~ childhood; ~ beginning to end.* **3** (showing the place, object, etc from which distance, absence, etc is stated): *ten miles ~ the coast; stay away ~ school.* **4** (showing the giver, sender, etc): *a letter ~ my brother.* **5** (showing the model, etc): *painted ~ life.* **6** (showing the limit): *There were ~ ten to fifteen boys absent.* **7** (showing the source from which something is taken): *some quotations ~ Shakespeare; ~ this point of view.* **8** (showing the material, etc used in a process, the material being changed as a result): *Wine is made ~ grapes.* **9** (showing separation, removal, prevention, escape, avoidance, etc): *When were you released ~ prison?* **10** (showing change): *Things are going ~ bad to worse.* **11** (showing reason, cause or motive): *suffer ~ starvation and disease.* **12** (showing distinction or difference): *How would you know an Englishman ~ an American?* **13** (used in adverbial and prepositional phrases): *seen ~ above/below.*

frond /frɒnd/ n [C] part of a fern or palm-tree that is like a leaf.

front /frʌnt/ n **1** (usually sing with the; used as an adjective) foremost or most important side: *the ~ of a building; sitting in the ~ of the class; the ~ page of a newspaper,* page 1. **In front,** adv: *Please go in ~.* **In front of,** prep: *There are some trees in ~ of the*

house. **2** [C] (in war) part where the fighting is taking place: *at the ~; go/be sent to the ~.* **3** [C] road, etc bordering the part of a town facing the sea: *have a walk along the ~.* **4** [U] **put on/show/present a bold front,** face a situation with (apparent) boldness. **5** boundary between masses of cold and warm air: *a cold ~/warm ~.* □ vt, vi face: *hotels that ~ the sea; windows ~ing the street.* ⇨ also seafront, shirt-front.

front bench, seat in the House of Commons reserved for ministers or ex-ministers.

front door, main door of a building to the street or road.

front·age /'frʌntɪdʒ/ n [C] extent of a piece of land or a building along its front: *a building site with a road ~ of 500 metres.*

frontal /'frʌntəl/ adj of, on or to, the front: *a ~ attack.*

fron·tier /'frʌntɪə(r) US: frʌn'tɪər/ n [C] **1** part of a country bordering on another country; (land on each side of a) boundary. **2** (fig) extreme limit: *the ~s of knowledge.* **3** (fig) underdeveloped area (e g of scientific research).

frost /frɒst US: frɔst/ n **1** [U] weather condition with temperature below the freezing-point of water; [C] occasion or period of such weather: *ten degrees of ~.* ⇨ Jack frost. **2** [U] frozen coating of vapour on the ground, roofs, plants, etc: *white ~.* □ vt, vi **1** cover with frost(2): *~ed window-panes.* **2** injure or kill (plants, etc) with frost(1). **3** give a roughened surface to (glass) to make it opaque: *~ed glass.* **4** become covered with frost(2): *The windscreen of my car ~ed over during the night.* **5** cover (a cake, etc) with finely powdered sugar.

frost·bite, injury to tissue in the body from freezing.

frost·bitten adj having, suffering from, frost-bite.

frost·bound adj (of the ground) made hard by frost.

frosty /'frɒstɪ US: 'frɔstɪ/ adj (-ier, -iest) **1** cold with frost: *~ weather.* **2** (fig) unfriendly; without warmth of feeling: *a ~ welcome.*

froth /frɒθ/ n [U] mass of small bubbles; foam: *a glass of beer with a lot of ~ on it.* □ vi have, give off, froth: *A mad dog may ~ at the mouth.*

frothy adj (-ier, -iest) of, like, covered with, froth: *~y beer.*

frown /fraʊn/ vi draw the eyebrows together causing lines on the forehead, (to express displeasure, puzzlement, deep thought, etc). **frown on/upon** disapprove of: *Gambling is ~ed on here.* □ n [C] frowning look: *There was a deep ~ on his brow.*

froze, frozen ⇨ freeze.

fru·gal /'frʊgəl/ adj careful, economical (esp of food, expenditure); costing little: *a ~ meal.*

fru·gal·ly /-gəlɪ/ adv

fru·gal·ity /fruˈgælətɪ/ n [C,U]

fruit /fruːt/ n 1 (usually sing as a collective noun) that part of a plant or tree that contains the seeds and is used as food, e g apples, bananas: *Do you eat much ~?* 2 [C] that part of any plant in which the seed is formed. 3 (pl) any plant or vegetable products used for food: *the ~s of the earth.* 4 (fig) (often pl) profit, result or reward (of labour, study, etc): *the ~s of industry.* □ vi (of trees, bushes, etc) bear fruit.

'fruit-fly, (kinds of a) common small fly that feeds on fermenting fruit.

'fruit 'salad, various kinds of fruit cut up and mixed in a bowl.

fruit·erer, person who sells fruit.

fruit·ful /-fəl/ adj (a) producing fruit. (b) (fig) producing good results: *a ~ful career.*

fruit·ful·ness n [U]

fruit·less adj (a) without fruit. (b) (fig) without results or success: *~less efforts.*

fruit·less·ly adv

fruity adj (-ier, -iest) (a) of or like fruit. (b) (informal) full of rough (often suggesting something indecent) humour: *a ~y novel* (c) (informal) rich; mellow: *a ~y voice.*

fru·ition /fruˈɪʃən/ n [U] achievement of what was wanted or hoped for: *aims brought/that come to ~.*

frus·trate /frʌˈstreɪt US: ˈfrʌstreɪt/ vt prevent (a person) from doing something; prevent (plans) from being carried out: *~ an enemy in his plans.*

frus·tra·tion /frʌˈstreɪʃən/ n [C,U]

fry /fraɪ/ vt,vi (3rd person sing pres tense fries, pt,pp fried) cook, be cooked, in boiling fat: *fried chicken.*

'fry·ing-pan, shallow pan used for frying.

fudge /fʌdʒ/ n [U] sort of soft sweet made with milk, sugar, chocolate, etc.

fuel /fjuəl/ n [U] (pl = kinds of ~) 1 material for producing heat or energy, e g coal, oil. 2 (fig) something that inflames the passions. □ vt,vi (-ll-, US also -l-) supply with or obtain fuel: *a power station ~led by uranium.*

fugi·tive /ˈfjuːdʒətɪv/ n [C] person running away from the police, danger, etc. □ adj of a fugitive.

-ful /-fəl/ suffix 1 full of, having the quality of: *eventful; peaceful.* 2 /-fʊl/ amount that fills: *handful.*

ful·crum /ˈfʌlkrəm/ n [C] (pl ~s) point on which a lever turns.

ful·fil (US also **ful·fill**) /fʊlˈfɪl/ vt (-ll-) perform or carry out a task, duty, promise, etc: *~ one's duties/an obligation/his hopes.*

ful·fil·ment n [U]

full /fʊl/ adj (-er, -est) 1 holding or having plenty (of); completely filled: *The room was ~ of people.* 2 full of, completely occupied with thinking of: *She was ~ of the news.* 3 plump; rounded: *a ~ figure; rather ~ in the face.* 4 (of clothes) having material arranged in wide folds: *a ~ skirt.* 5 reaching the usual or the specified extent, limit, length, etc: *wait a ~ hour,* not less than an hour. **in full,** without omitting or shortening anything: *paid in ~; write one's name in ~,* e g John Henry Smith, *not* J H Smith. **at full speed,** at the highest possible speed. **to the full,** to the utmost extent: *enjoy oneself to the ~.* 6 (with comp and superl) complete: *A ~er account will be given later. This is the ~est account yet received.*

'full-back, player (defender) placed farthest from the centre line (in football, etc)

'full-'length adj (a) (of a portrait) showing the whole figure. (b) of standard or usual length: *a ~-length novel.*

'full 'moon, moon seen as a complete disc.

'full-page adj filling a whole page: *a ~-page advertisement in a newspaper.*

'full 'point, (US) = full stop.

'full 'stop, the punctuation mark (.) **come to a full stop,** stop completely.

'full-'scale adj (of drawings, plans, etc) of the same size, area, etc as the object itself.

'full-time adj, adv occupying all normal working hours: *a ~-time worker; working ~-time.*

fully /ˈfʊlɪ/ adv (a) to the full; completely: *~y satisfied.* (b) altogether; at least: *The journey will take ~y two hours.*

'fully-'grown adj mature.

full·ness n [U]

fumble /ˈfʌmbəl/ vi,vt 1 feel about uncertainly with the hands; use the hands awkwardly: *~ in one's pockets for a key.* 2 handle or deal with nervously or incompetently: *~ a ball,* e g in cricket.

fume /fjuːm/ n [C] 1 (often pl) strong-smelling smoke, gas or vapour: *petrol ~s.* 2 (formal) excited state of mind: *in a ~ of anxiety.* □ vi,vt 1 give off fumes. 2 (fig) burst with anger or irritation: *fuming at her incompetence.*

fu·mi·gate /ˈfjuːmɪgeɪt/ vt disinfect by means of fumes: *~ a room.*

fu·mi·ga·tion /ˈfjuːmɪˈgeɪʃən/ n [U]

fun /fʌn/ n [U] 1 amusement, sport; playfulness: *What ~ the children had!* **make fun of; poke fun at,** ridicule; cause people to laugh at: *It is wrong to make ~ of a cripple.* **for/in fun,** as a joke, for amusement; not seriously: *He did it for ~.* 2 that which causes merriment or amusement: *Paul is great ~,* is very amusing. *Sailing is good ~.* 3 (informal) (as an adjective): *a 'fun car/fur,* used, worn, for amusement.

'fun-fair, = fair³(4).

func·tion /ˈfʌŋkʃən/ n [C] 1 special activity or purpose of a person or thing: *the ~s of a judge/of education.* 2 public or formal ceremony or event: *the numerous ~s that the Queen must attend.* □ vi fulfill a function(1); operate; act: *The telephone was not ~ing,* was out of order.

func·tional /-nəl/ adj (a) having, designed to have, functions(1) (b) in working order: *the* *lift isn't ∼al.*

fund /fʌnd/ n [C] **1** store or supply (of non-material things): *a ∼ of amusing stories.* **2** (often *pl*) sum of money available for a purpose: *a re`lief ∼*, e g to help in a disaster. **3** (*pl*) resources in the form of money: *run off with the ∼s.* □ *vt* provide a sum of money in return for the payment of interest.

fun·da·men·tal /ˌfʌndə`mentəl/ *adj* of or forming a foundation; serving as a starting point; of great importance: *∼ changes in education.* □ *n* [C] (usually *pl*) basic or most important rule or principle; essential part: *the ∼s of mathematics.*
fun·da·men·tally /-təlɪ/ *adv*

fu·neral /ˈfjuːnərəl/ n [C] burial or cremation of a dead person with the usual ceremonies.
funeral march, sad and solemn piece of music.
fu·ner·eal /fjuˈnɪərɪəl/ *adj* **(a)** of a funeral. **(b)** (*fig*) = gloomy; dark.

fun·gus /ˈfʌŋgəs/ n [C,U] (*pl* -gi /-gaɪ/) plant without leaves, flowers or green colouring matter, growing on other plants or on decaying matter, e g old wood: *A mushroom is a ∼.*
fun·gi·cide /ˈfʌŋgɪsaɪd/ n [U] substance that destroys fungi.
fun·goid /ˈfʌŋgɔɪd/ *adj* of or like fungi.
fun·gous /ˈfʌŋgəs/ *adj* of or like, caused by, fungi.

funk /fʌŋk/ *vi,vt* (*informal*) (try to) escape (doing something) because of fear.

funnel /ˈfʌnəl/ n [C] **1** tube or pipe wide at the top and narrowing at the bottom, for pouring liquids or powders through small openings. **2** outlet for smoke of a steamer, railway engine, etc. □ *vt,vi* (-ll-, *US* -l-) (cause to) move (as if) through, a funnel.

fun·nily /ˈfʌnɪlɪ/ *adv* in an odd or an amusing way: *∼*(= strangely) *enough*

funny /ˈfʌnɪ/ *adj* (-ier, -iest) **1** causing fun or laughter: *∼ stories.* **2** strange; queer; causing surprise: *There's something ∼ about him/the affair*, perhaps not quite honest or straightforward.
funny-bone, part of the elbow over which a very sensitive nerve passes.

fur /fɜː(r)/ n **1** [U] soft thick hair covering certain animals, e g cats, rabbits. **2** [C] animal skin with the fur on it, esp when made into garments: (as an *adjective*) *a ∼ coat.* **3** [U] coating on a person's tongue when ill; crust on the inside of a kettle, boiler, etc. □ *vt,vi* cover, become covered, with fur(3): *a ∼red tongue/kettle.*
furry /ˈfɜːrɪ/ *adj* (-ier, -iest) of or like fur; covered with fur.

furi·ous /ˈfjʊərɪəs/ *adj* violent; full of fury: *a ∼ struggle/storm/quarrel.*
furi·ous·ly *adv*

furl /fɜːl/ *vt,vi* (of sails, flags, umbrellas, etc) roll up: *∼ the sails of a yacht.*

fur·long /ˈfɜːlɒŋ *US*: -lɔːŋ/ n [C] measure of 220 yards (= 201 metres); eighth of a mile.

fur·lough /ˈfɜːləʊ/ n [C,U] (permission for) absence from duty (esp civil officials, the armed forces, missionaries, living abroad): *a ∼ every three years.* ⇨ **leave**[2].

fur·nace /ˈfɜːnɪs/ n [C] **1** enclosed fireplace for heating buildings with hot water or steam in pipes. **2** enclosed space for heating metals, making glass, etc.

fur·nish /ˈfɜːnɪʃ/ *vt* supply or provide; put furniture in: *∼ a library with books; ∼ a room/an office.*
fur·nish·ings n *pl* furniture and equipment.

fur·ni·ture /ˈfɜːnɪtʃə(r)/ n [U] all those movable things such as chairs, beds, desks, etc needed in a house, office, etc.

fu·rore (*US* = **fu·ror**) /fjuˈrɔːrɪ *US*: fjuˈrɔː(r)/ n [C] state of enthusiastic admiration; uproar: *The new play at the National Theatre created a ∼.*

fur·rier /ˈfʌrɪə(r) *US*: ˈfɜr-/ n [C] person who prepares, or who deals in, furs.

fur·row /ˈfʌrəʊ *US*: ˈfɜr-/ n [C] **1** long cut in the ground made by a plough: *newly turned ∼s.* **2** wrinkle, esp on the forehead. □ *vt* make furrows in: *a forehead ∼ed by old age/anxiety, etc.*

furry /ˈfɜːrɪ/ ⇨ **fur.**

fur·ther /ˈfɜːðə(r)/ *adv, adj* **1** (often used for *farther*): *It's not safe to go any ∼.* **2** (not interchangeable in this sense with *farther*) more; in addition; additional: *We must get ∼ information. We need go no ∼ into the matter,* need make no more inquiries. **3** (= furthermore) moreover; also; besides: *He said that the key was lost and, ∼, that there was no hope of its being found.* □ *vt* help forward; promote: *∼ the cause of peace.*
fur·ther·ance /ˈfɜːðərəns/ n [U] (*formal*) advancement: *in ∼ance of your aims.*
fur·ther·more /ˌfɜːðəˈmɔː(r)/ *adv* moreover; in addition.
fur·ther·most /-məʊst/ *adj* most distant; furthest.
fur·thest /ˈfɜːðɪst/ *adj, adv* = farthest.

fur·tive /ˈfɜːtɪv/ *adj* done secretly so as not to attract attention: *a ∼ glance; ∼ behaviour.*
fur·tive·ly *adv*
fur·tive·ness n [U]

fury /ˈfjʊərɪ/ n (*pl* -ies) **1** [U] violent excitement, esp anger; *filled with ∼.* **2** [C] outburst of wild feelings: *He flew into a ∼.*

furze /fɜːz/ n [U] = gorse.

fuse[1] /fjuːz/ n [C] **1** tube, cord, etc for carrying a spark to explode powder, etc, e g in a firework, bomb. **2** (*US* = **fuze**) part of a shell or mine that detonates the explosive charge.

fuse[2] /fjuːz/ *vt,vi* **1** make or become liquid as the result of great heat; join, become joined, as the result of melting: *∼ two pieces of wire together.* **2** (of an electric circuit, or part of it) be broken through melting of the fuse: *The light has ∼d.* □ n [C] short piece of wire which causes a fuse(2).

fu·sel·age /ˈfjuːzəlɑːʒ/ n [C] body of an aircraft (to which the engine(s), wings and tail are fitted).

fus·il·lade /ˈfjuːzɪˈleɪd/ n [C] continuous discharge of firearms.

fu·sion /ˈfjuːʒən/ n [C,U] mixing or uniting of different things into one: *the ~ of copper and tin; a ~ of races/political parties.*

fuss /fʌs/ n [U] **1** unnecessary nervous excitement, esp about unimportant things; (with *a, an*) nervous state: *Don't make so much ~.* **2** excessive or needless show of anxiety, concern. **make a fuss of,** treat with excessive affection: *Don't make so much ~ of the children.* □ vt,vi get into, (cause to) be in a fuss; *Stop ~ing. Don't ~ over the children so much.*

fuss·ily /-əlɪ/ adv

fus·si·ness n [U]

fussy adj (-ier, -iest) **(a)** full of, showing, nervous excitement. **(b)** too concerned with unimportant details: *be too ~y about one's clothes.* **(c)** (of dress, style, etc) too elaborate.

fu·tile /ˈfjuːtaɪl US: -təl/ adj **1** (of actions) of no use; without result: *a ~ attempt.* **2** (of persons) unlikely to accomplish much.

fu·til·ity /fjuˈtɪlətɪ/ n [C,U]

fu·ture /ˈfjuːtʃə(r)/ adj **1** coming after the present. **2** of or in the future: *the ~ life,* after death of the body; *his ~ wife,* the woman he will marry. □ n [C] time, event, coming after the present: *I hope you have a happy ~ before you.* **in future,** from this time onwards: *Try to live a better life in ~.*

future tense, (*gram*) with 'shall' and 'will'.

fu·ture·less adj

fuzz /fʌz/ n [U] **1** fluff (1), fluffy or frizzed hair. **2** the ~, (*sl*) police.

fuzzy /ˈfʌzɪ/ adj (-ier, -iest) **1** blurred; indistinct (in shape or outline). **2** frayed or fluffy.

Gg

G, g /dʒiː/ (*pl* G's, g's /dʒiːz/) the seventh letter of the English alphabet.

gab·ar·dine /ˈɡæbəˈdiːn/ n [U] material of cotton or silk with wool lining (as used for raincoats).

gabble /ˈɡæbəl/ vt,vi speak, say, sing, things, quickly and indistinctly: *The little girl ~d her prayers and jumped into bed. Listen to those children gabbling away.* □ n [U] fast, confused, unintelligible talk.

gab·er·dine /ˈɡæbəˈdiːn/ n = gabardine.

gable /ˈɡeɪbəl/ n [C] three-cornered part of an outside wall between sloping roofs.

gabled /ˈɡeɪbəld/ adj

gad /ɡæd/ vi (-dd-) (*informal*) go from place to place for excitement or pleasure.

ˈgad·about, person who does this.

gadget /ˈɡædʒɪt/ [C] n (*informal*) small (usually mechanical) device: *a new ~ for opening tin cans.*

gadgetry n [U] gadgets collectively.

gaffe /ɡæf/ n [C] indiscreet act or remark.

gag /ɡæɡ/ n [C] **1** something put in or over a person's mouth to prevent him from speaking or crying out. **2** words or action added to his part by an actor in a play; joke, funny story, esp as part of a comedian's act. □ vt,vi (-gg-) **1** put a gag(1) into or over the mouth of. **2** (*fig*) prevent (a person) from speaking freely. **3** (of an actor, etc) use gags(2).

gaga /ˈɡɑːɡɑ US: ˈɡɑːɡɑ/ adj (*sl*) senile.

gage /ɡeɪdʒ/ ⇨ gauge.

gaggle /ˈɡæɡəl/ n [C] flock (of geese).

gai·ety /ˈɡeɪətɪ/ n (*pl* -ies) **1** [U] being gay; cheerfulness; bright appearance: *flags and scarves that added to the ~ of the Cup Final scene.* **2** (*pl*) merrymaking; joyful, festive occasions: *the gaieties of the Christmas season.*

gaily /ˈɡeɪlɪ/ adv in a gay manner.

gain[1] /ɡeɪn/ n **1** [U] increase of possessions; acquiring of wealth: *interested only in ~,* in becoming rich. **2** [C] increase in amount or power: *a ~ in weight/health.*

gain·ful /-fəl/ adj providing wealth: *~ful occupations.*

gain·fully /-fəlɪ/ adv in order to earn money: *~fully employed.*

gain[2] /ɡeɪn/ vt,vi **1** obtain (something wanted or needed): *~ experience; ~ an advantage over a competitor.* **gain time,** improve one's chances by delaying something, making excuses, etc. **gain the upper hand,** be victorious. **2** make progress; be improved; benefit: *The baby ~ed five pounds (in weight).* **3** (of a watch or clock) become fast, ahead of the correct time: *The clock ~s three minutes a day.* **4** **gain on/upon (a)** get closer to (the person or thing pursued): *~ on the other runners in a race.* **(b)** go faster than; get farther in advance of: *~ on one's pursuers.* **5** reach, arrive at (a desired place, esp with effort): *The swimmer ~ed the shore.*

gait /ɡeɪt/ n [C] manner of walking or running: *an awkward ~.*

gai·ter /ˈɡeɪtə(r)/ n [C] cloth or leather covering for the leg from knee to ankle, or for the ankle: *a pair of ~s.*

gal /ɡæl/ n (*dated informal*) = girl.

gala /ˈɡɑːlə US: ˈɡeɪlə/ n [C] festive occasion: (as an *adjective*) *a ~ performance,* e g at a theatre, with special guests.

ga·lac·tic /ɡəˈlæktɪk/ adj of the Galaxy.

gal·axy /ˈɡæləksɪ/ n (*pl* -ies) **1** any of the large-scale clusters of stars in outer space. **2** company of persons: *a ~ of beautiful women.*

the Galaxy, that which includes our solar system, visible as a luminous band known as *the Milky Way.*

gale /geɪl/ n [C] **1** strong and violent wind: *The ship lost her masts in the ~*. **2** noisy outburst: *~s of laughter*.

gall¹ /gɔːl/ n [U] **1** bitter liquid (*bile*) produced by the liver. **2** bitter feeling. **3** (*informal*) impudence: *Of all the ~!*

`gall-bladder, vessel attached to the liver containing and discharging gall.

`gall-stone, hard mass that forms in the gall-bladder.

gall² /gɔːl/ n [C] painful swelling on an animal caused by rubbing. □ vt **1** rub sore. **2** (*fig*) hurt the feelings of; humiliate: *It was ~ing to have to ask for a loan.*

gal-lant /ˈɡælənt/ adj **1** brave (now the usual word): *~ deeds*. **2** (*dated*) fine; stately: *a ~-looking ship*. **3** (also /ɡəˈlænt/) showing special respect and courtesy to women: *He was very ~ at the ball*.

gal-lant-ly adv

gal-lantry n [U] **(a)** bravery. **(b)** [U] devotion, chivalrous attention, to women.

gal-leon /ˈɡælɪən/ n [C] Spanish sailing-ship (15th to 17th centuries).

gal-lery /ˈɡælərɪ/ n [C] (pl -ies) **1** room or building for the display of works of art. **2** (people in the) highest and cheapest seats in a theatre. **3** raised floor or platform extending from an inner wall of a hall, church, etc: *the `press ~ of the House of Commons*, used by newspaper reporters. **4** covered walk or corridor, partly open at one side. **5** long, narrow room: *a `shooting-~*, for indoor target practice. **6** horizontal underground passage in a mine. ⇨ shaft.

gal-ley /ˈɡælɪ/ n [C] (pl ~s) **1** low, flat ship, using sails and oars, rowed by slaves or criminals. **2** ancient Greek or Roman warship. **3** ship's kitchen.

gal-li-vant /ˈɡælɪˌvænt/ vi = gad.

gal-lon /ˈɡælən/ n [C] measure for liquids, four quarts.

gal-lop /ˈɡæləp/ n [C] (of a horse, etc) fastest pace with all four feet off the ground at each stride; period of riding at such a pace: *He rode away at a ~/at full ~*. □ vi,vt **1** (cause to) go at a gallop: *He ~ed across the field*. **2** hurry: *~ through one's work/lecture*.

gal-lows /ˈɡæləʊz/ n pl (usually used with a *sing verb*) wooden framework on which to put criminals to death by hanging: *send a man to the ~*, condemn him to be hanged.

ga-lore /ɡəˈlɔː(r)/ adv in plenty: *a meal with beef and beer ~*.

ga-loshes /ɡəˈlɒʃɪz/ n pl (often *a pair of ~*) rubber overshoes worn in wet weather.

gam-bit /ˈɡæmbɪt/ n [C] **1** kinds of opening move in chess. **2** (*fig*) any initial move: *His opening ~ at the debate was a direct attack on Government policy.*

gamble /ˈɡæmbəl/ vi,vt **1** play games of chance for money; take great risks for the chance of winning something or making a profit: *He lost his money gambling at cards.*

2 gamble sth away, lose by gambling: *He has ~d away half his fortune.* □ n [C] undertaking or attempt with risk of loss and chance of profit or advantage. **take a gamble (on sth),** do it knowing it is risky.

gam-bler, person who gambles.

gam-bling n [U] playing games for money; taking risks for possible advantage: *fond of gambling.*

gam-bol /ˈɡæmbəl/ n [C] (usually *pl*) quick, playful, jumping or skipping movements, e g of lambs, children. □ vi (-ll-, *US* also -l-) make such movements.

game¹ /ɡeɪm/ adj **1** brave; ready to go on fighting. **2** spirited, willing: *Are you ~ for a 10-mile walk?*

game² /ɡeɪm/ n **1** [C] form of play, sport, esp with rules, e g tennis, football, cards: *play ~s*. **be off one's game,** be not playing well. **play the game,** (a) obey the rules. (b) (*fig*) be straightforward and honest. **2** [C] apparatus, etc needed for a game, e g one played by children with a board and dice and counters. **3** (*pl*) athletic contests: *the Highland G~s* (in Scotland, today); (in Greece and Rome, ancient times) athletic and dramatic contests; (modern times) (international) athletic contests: *the Olympic/Commonwealth G~s*. **4** single round in some contests, e g tennis: *win four ~s in the first set; ~, set and match*. **5** [C] scheme, plan or undertaking; dodge or trick: *I wish I knew what his ~ is*, what he is trying to do. *None of your little ~s!* **'give the `game away,** reveal a secret trick, scheme, etc. **play games,** (a) (of children) be naughty. (b) (of adults) act without sincerity. **6** [U] (flesh of) animals and birds hunted for sport and food.

`big game, the larger animals (elephants, lions, tigers).

`fair game, (a) what may be lawfully hunted or shot. (b) (*fig*) person or institution that may with reason be attacked or criticized.

`game-keeper, man employed to breed and protect game, e g pheasants, grouse, on a country estate.

gamma /ˈɡæmə/ n [C] third letter of the Greek alphabet.

`gamma ray, ray of very short wavelength from radioactive substances.

gam-mon /ˈɡæmən/ n [U] smoked or cured ham.

gammy /ˈɡæmɪ/ adj (*informal*) (of a limb) lame.

gamut /ˈɡæmət/ n [C] **1** whole range of musical notes. **2** (*fig*) complete extent or scope of anything: *the whole ~ of feeling*, e g from the greatest joy to the depths of despair or misery.

gan-der /ˈɡændə(r)/ n [C] male goose.

gang /ɡæŋ/ n [C] **1** number of workmen, slaves or prisoners working together. **2** group of persons going about or working together, esp for criminal purposes. ⇨

gangster. □ *vi* act together as a gang(2): *They ∼ed up on/up against me.*

gan·gling /ˈgæŋglɪŋ/ *adj* (of a person) tall, thin and awkward.

gang·plank /ˈgæŋplæŋk/ *n* [C] movable plank placed between a ship or boat and the land, or between two boats or ships.

gan·grene /ˈgæŋgriːn/ *n* [U] death and decay of a part of the body, e g because the supply of blood to it has been stopped. □ *vt, vi* affect, become affected, with gangrene.
gan·gren·ous /ˈgæŋgrɪnəs/ *adj*

gang·ster /ˈgæŋstə(r)/ *n* [C] member of a gang of armed criminals.

gang·way /ˈgæŋweɪ/ *n* [C] 1 opening in a ship's side; movable bridge from this to the land. 2 passage between rows of seats, e g in a theatre, or between rows of people.

gan·try /ˈgæntrɪ/ *n* [C] (*pl* -ies) structure of steel bars to support a travelling crane, etc.

gaol, jail /dʒeɪl/ *n* 1 [C] public prison. 2 (without *the* or *a, an*) confinement in prison: *three years in ∼; be sent to ∼.* □ *vt* put in prison.
gaoler, jailer, jailor /ˈdʒeɪlə(r)/ *n* [C] man in charge of a prison or the prisoners.

gap /gæp/ *n* [C] 1 break or opening in a wall, hedge, etc: *The sheep got out of the field through a ∼ in the hedge.* 2 unfilled space; interval; wide separation (of ideas, etc): *a ∼ in a conversation.* 3 gorge or pass between mountains.
ˈgeneˈration gap, failure or inability of the younger and older generations to communicate, understand one another.

gape /geɪp/ *vi* 1 open the mouth wide; stare open-mouthed and in surprise: *country visitors gaping at the neon lights.* 2 open or be open wide: *a gaping hole,* an obvious one. □ *n* [C] open-mouthed stare.

garage /ˈgærɑːʒ US: gəˈrɑːʒ/ *n* [C] 1 building in which to keep a car or cars. 2 roadside petrol and service station. □ *vt* put (a motor-vehicle) in a garage.

garb /gɑːb/ *n* [U] (style of) dress (esp as worn by a particular kind of person): *a man in clerical ∼.* □ *vt* (*dated*) dress: *∼ed in black.*

gar·bage /ˈgɑːbɪdʒ/ *n* [U] 1 waste food thrown out, or fed to pigs, etc. 2 (*US*) rubbish, refuse (of any kind).
ˈgarbage-can *n* (*US*) = dustbin.

garble /ˈgɑːbl/ *vt* make an incomplete or unfair selection from statements, facts, etc esp in order to give false ideas: *a ∼d report of a speech.*

gar·den /ˈgɑːdn/ *n* 1 [C,U] (piece of) ground used for growing flowers, fruit, vegetables, etc: *a ∼ suburb,* housing area with large gardens. 2 (usually *pl*) public park: *zoological ∼s.* 3 (*pl*) (with name prefixed) row(s) of houses with open spaces planted with bushes and trees: *Spring G∼s.* □ *vi* cultivate a garden: *He's been ∼ing all day.*
gardener, person who works in a garden.

gar·den·ing, cultivating of gardens: *fond of ∼ing;* (as an *adjective*) *∼ing tools.*

gargle /ˈgɑːgl/ *vt, vi* wash the throat with liquid kept in motion by a stream of breath. □ *n* [C] 1 liquid used for this purpose. 2 act of gargling.

gar·goyle /ˈgɑːgɔɪl/ *n* [C] stone or metal spout, usually in the form of a grotesque human or animal creature, to carry off rain-water from the roof of a building.

gar·ish /ˈgeərɪʃ/ *adj* unpleasantly coloured, over-decorated: *∼ clothes.*
gar·ish·ly *adv*

gar·land /ˈgɑːlənd/ *n* [C] circle of flowers or leaves as an ornament or decoration; this as a prize for victory, etc. □ *vt* decorate, crown, with a garland.

gar·lic /ˈgɑːlɪk/ *n* [U] plant like an onion with strong taste and smell, used in cooking.

gar·ment /ˈgɑːmənt/ *n* [C] article of clothing.

gar·net /ˈgɑːnɪt/ *n* [C] semi-precious gem of deep transparent red.

gar·nish /ˈgɑːnɪʃ/ *vt* decorate, esp food for the table: *fish ∼ed with slices of lemon.* □ *n* [C] something used to garnish.

gar·ret /ˈgærət/ *n* [C] room on the top floor of a house, esp in the roof.

gar·ri·son /ˈgærɪsən/ *n* [C] military force stationed in a town or fort. □ *vt* 1 supply a town, etc with a garrison. 2 place, troops, etc on garrison duty.

gar·rotte, ga·rotte /gəˈrɒt/ *vt* execute (a person condemned to death), murder, by strangling or throttling. □ *n* [C] (apparatus for) this method of capital punishment.

gar·ru·lous /ˈgærələs/ *adj* (*formal*) talking too much about unimportant things.
gar·ru·lity /gəˈruːlətɪ/ *n* [U]

gar·ter /ˈgɑːtə(r)/ *n* [C] (elastic) band worn round the leg to keep a stocking in place.
the Garter, (badge of) the highest order of English knighthood.

gas /gæs/ *n* [C, but used with *a, an* or in *pl* meaning 'kind(s) of gas'] (*pl* ∼es) 1 any air-like substance (used chiefly of those that do not become liquid or solid at ordinary temperatures): *Air is a mixture of ∼es.* 2 [U] one of the gases or mixtures of gases used for lighting and heating: *ˈcoal-∼.* 3 (*US*) = petrol. □ *vt, vi* (-ss-) 1 poison or overcome by gas. 2 (*informal*) talk for a long time without saying much that is useful.
ˈgas-cooker, stove (with gas-rings and an oven) for cooking by gas.
ˈgas-mask, breathing apparatus to protect the wearer against harmful gases.
ˈgas-meter, one for registering the amount of gas that passes through it.
ˈgas-oven, oven in a gas-cooker.
ˈgas-ring, metal ring with numerous small holes and supplied with gas for cooking, etc
ˈgas-stove = gas-cooker.
ˈgas-station, (*US*) = petrol station.
ˈgas-works, place where coal-gas is manu

factured.

gas·eous /ˈgæsɪəs/ adj of or like gas: a ~
mixture.

gash /gæʃ/ n [C] long deep cut or wound. □
vt make a gash in.

gas·ify /ˈgæsɪfaɪ/ vt, vi (pt, pp -ied) (cause
to) change into gas.

gas·ket /ˈgæskɪt/ n [C] strip of soft, flat
piece of material used for packing a piston,
etc to prevent steam, gas, etc from escaping.

gaso·line (also **-lene**) /ˈgæsəlin/ n [U]
(US) = petrol.

gas·ometer /gəˈsɒmɪtə(r)/ n [C] large
round tank in which gas is stored, measured
and distributed.

gasp /gɑsp US: gæsp/ vi, vt 1 struggle for
breath; take short, quick breaths: ~ing for
breath; ~ing (= breathless) with rage/
surprise. 2 utter in a breathless way: He
~ed out a few words. □ n [C] catching of the
breath through pain, surprise, etc.

gassy /ˈgæsɪ/ adj of or like gas; full of gas.

gas·tric /ˈgæstrɪk/ adj of the stomach: a ~
ulcer; ~ juices.

gas·tron·omy /gæˈstrɒnəmɪ/ n [U] (formal) art and science of choosing, preparing
and eating good food.

gas·tron·omic /ˈgæstrəˈnɒmɪk/ adj.

gate /geɪt/ n [C] 1 opening in the wall of a
city, hedge, fence or other enclosure,
capable of being closed by a barrier. 2 barrier that closes such an opening; barrier used
to control the passage of water, e g into or
out of a lock on a canal.

`gate-crash` vt enter (a building at which
there is a private social occasion of some
sort) without invitation or payment. Hence,
`gate-crasher` n [C]

`gate-post`, post on which a gate is hung or
against which it is closed. *between you
(and) me and the gate-post*, in strict confidence.

`gate-way`, (a) way in or out that can be
closed by a gate. (b) (fig) means of
approach: a ~way to fame/knowledge.

ga·teau /ˈgætəʊ US: gɑˈtəʊ/ n [C] (pl ~x
/-təʊz/) (Fr) rich fancy cake.

gather /ˈgæðə(r)/ vt, vi 1 get, come or bring
together: A crowd soon ~ed round him. 2
pick (flowers, etc); collect: ~ one's papers
and books together. 3 obtain gradually; gain
little by little: ~ information. 4 understand;
conclude: What did you ~ from his statement? 5 (in sewing) pull together into small
folds by putting a thread through: a skirt
~ed at the waist. 6 (of an abscess or boil)
form pus and swell up.

gather·ing n [C] coming together of people;
meeting.

gauche /ɡəʊʃ/ adj socially awkward, tactless.

gaudy /ˈgɔdɪ/ adj (-ier, -iest) too bright and
showy; gay or bright in a tasteless way:
cheap and ~ jewels.

gaud·ily /-əlɪ/ adv

gauge (US also **gage**) /geɪdʒ/ n [C] 1 standard measure; extent: take the ~ of his character, judge. 2 distance between rails (or
between opposite wheels of a vehicle that
runs on rails). 3 (instrument for measuring
the) thickness of wire, sheet-metal, etc;
diameter of a bullet, etc. 4 instrument for
measuring, e g rainfall, strength of wind. □
vt 1 measure accurately: ~ the diameter of
wire/the strength of the wind. 2 (fig) make
an estimate, form a judgement, of: ~ a person's character.

gaunt /gɔnt/ adj 1 (of a person) lean as from
hunger, ill-health or suffering. 2 (of a place)
barren, desolate: a ~ hillside.

gaunt·ness n [U]

gaunt·let /ˈgɔntlət/ n [C] 1 glove with metal
plates worn by soldiers in the Middle Ages.
*throw down/pick up/take up the gaunt-
let*, give/accept a challenge to a fight. 2
strong glove used for driving, fencing, etc.

gauze /gɔz/ n [U] 1 thin, net-like material
of cotton, etc (for medical use). 2 similar
material of wire (for screening windows
against insects, etc).

gave /geɪv/ pt of give.

gavel /ˈgævəl/ n [C] hammer used by an
auctioneer or a chairman as a signal for order
or attention.

gawky /ˈgɔkɪ/ adj (-ier, -iest) (of persons)
awkward, shy.

gawp /gɔp/ vi stare at in a foolish way:
What are they all ~ing at?

gay /geɪ/ adj (-er, -est) 1 light-hearted;
cheerful; happy and full of fun: ~ voices/
looks/laughter. 2 suggesting happiness and
joy: ~ colours. 3 (informal) homosexual.

gay·ness n [U]

gaze /geɪz/ n (sing only) long, steady look:
with a bewildered ~. □ vi look long and
steadily: What are you gazing at?

ga·zelle /gəˈzel/ n [C] small, graceful kind
of antelope.

ga·zette /gəˈzet/ n [C] 1 government
periodical with legal notices, news of
appointments, promotions, etc of officers
and officials. 2 (as part of a title) newspaper:
the Marlowe G~.

ga·zet·teer /ˈgæzəˈtɪə(r)/ n [C] index of
geographical names, e g at the end of an
atlas.

gear /gɪə(r)/ n 1 [C] set of toothed wheels
working together in a machine, e g to connect the engine of a motor-vehicle with the
road wheels: change ~. 2 [C] apparatus,
appliance, mechanism, arrangement, of
wheels, levers, etc for a special purpose: the
`landing-~` of an aircraft. 3 [U] equipment
in general: `hunting-~`. 4 [U] (modern
informal) clothes: Carnaby Street ~. □ vt, vi
adjust one thing to the working of another:
The country's economics must be ~ed to
wartime requirements.

`gear-box`, case enclosing the gears in a
machine or engine.

263

`gear-lever/-shift/-stick, device for engaging or disengaging gears.

gecko /ˈgekəʊ/ n [C] (pl ~s, ~es) kind of small house lizard, found in warm countries.

geese /gis/ n pl of goose.

geisha /ˈgeɪʃə/ n [C] Japanese girl or woman trained to entertain men by singing and dancing at parties, etc.

gel /dʒel/ n [C,U] semisolid like a jelly. □ vi (-ll-) 1 set into a jelly. 2 (informal) succeed: That new idea has really ~led.

gela-tine /ˈdʒelətin US: ˈdʒelətɪn/ (also gela-tin /ˈdʒelətɪn/) n [U] clear, tasteless substance, made by boiling bones, etc, dissolved in water to make jelly.

gel-ati-nous /dʒɪˈlætməs US: -tənəs/ adj of or like gelatine; jelly-like in consistency, etc.

geld /geld/ vt castrate.

geld-ing, gelded animal, esp a horse.

gel-ig-nite /ˈdʒelɪgnaɪt/ n [U] explosive made from nitric acid and glycerine.

gem /dʒem/ n [C] 1 precious stone or jewel, esp cut or polished. 2 something valued, e g because of great beauty: the ~ of the collection. □ vt (-mm-) adorn with, or as with, gems: the night sky ~med with stars.

Gemini /ˈdʒemɪnɪ/ n third sign of the zodiac.

gen-der /ˈdʒendə(r)/ n [C] grammatical grouping of words (nouns and pronouns) into classes (masculine, feminine and neuter).

gene /dʒin/ n [C] one of the biological factors controlling heredity.

genea-logi-cal /ˌdʒiːnɪəˈlodʒɪkəl/ adj of genealogy: a ~ tree, a diagram (like a tree) showing the descent of a family or species.
genea-logi-cally /-klɪ/ adv

gen-eal-ogy /ˌdʒiːnɪˈælədʒɪ/ n (pl -ies) 1 [U] science of the development of plants and animals from earlier forms. 2 [C] (diagram illustrating the) descent or line of development of a plant or animal from earlier forms, or of a family from ancestors.

gen-era /ˈdʒenərə/ n pl of genus.

gen-eral /ˈdʒenrəl/ adj 1 of, affecting, all or nearly all; not special, local or particular: a matter of ~ interest, one in which all or most people are likely to be interested; a ~ meeting, one to which all members (of a society, etc) are invited; a good ~ education, in all the chief subjects; a word that is in ~ use, used by all people. as a general rule; in general, in most cases; usually. 2 not in detail; not definite: a ~ outline of a scheme; have a ~ idea of what a book is about. 3 (after an official title) chief: 'postmaster-'~; 'inspector-'~. □ n [C] army officer with the highest rank below Field Marshal (and also, by courtesy, of 'Lieutenant-'~ and 'Major-'~).

'general anaes'thetic, one affecting the whole body, causing sleep.

'general e'lection, one for representatives in the House of Commons from the whole country. ⟹ by-election.

'general 'knowledge, of a wide variety of subjects.

'general prac'titioner, (GB) doctor who is not a specialist or consultant and treats his patients in his surgery or in their homes.

'general 'strike, of all trade unionists.

gen-er-al-ity /ˌdʒenəˈrælətɪ/ n (pl -ies) 1 [C] general rule or statement; vague or indefinite remark, etc: I wish you would come down from generalities to particularities. 2 [U] quality of being general: a rule of great ~, one with few exceptions.

gen-er-al-iz-ation /ˌdʒenərəlaɪˈzeɪʃən US: -lɪˈz-/ n 1 [U] generalizing: It is unwise to be hasty in ~. 2 [C] statement or proposition obtained by generalizing, esp one based on too few examples.

gen-er-al-ize /ˈdʒenərəlaɪz/ vi,vt 1 draw a general conclusion; make a general statement. 2 state in general terms or principles: ~ a conclusion from a collection of instances or facts. 3 bring into general use: ~ the use of a new invention.

gen-er-ally /ˈdʒenrəlɪ/ adv 1 usually; as a general rule: I ~ get up at six o'clock. 2 widely; for the most part: The new plan was ~ welcomed, was welcomed by most people. 3 in a general sense; without paying attention to details: ~ speaking.

gen-er-ate /ˈdʒenəreɪt/ vt cause to exist or occur; produce: ~ heat/electricity; hatred ~d by racial differences.

gen-er-ation /ˌdʒenəˈreɪʃən/ n 1 [U] generating; bringing into existence: the ~ of electricity by steam or water-power. 2 [C] single stage or step in family descent: three ~s, children, parents and grandparents. 3 [C] average period (regarded as 30 years) in which children grow up, marry, and have children: a ~ ago. 4 [C] all persons born about the same time, and, therefore, of about the same age: the young ~.

'gene'ration gap, ⟹ gap(2).

gen-er-at-ive /ˈdʒenərətɪv/ adj able to produce; productive.

gen-er-ator /ˈdʒenəreɪtə(r)/ n [C] machine or apparatus that generates (electricity, gas, etc).

gen-eric /dʒɪˈnerɪk/ adj 1 of a genus. 2 common to a whole group or class.
gen-eri-cally /-klɪ/ adv

gen-er-os-ity /ˌdʒenəˈrosətɪ/ n (pl -ies) 1 [U] the quality of being generous; greatness of heart: show ~ in dealing with a defeated enemy. 2 [C] generous act, etc.

gen-er-ous /ˈdʒenrəs/ adj 1 giving, ready to give, given, freely: He is ~ with his money/~ in giving help. 2 plentiful: a ~ helping of meat and vegetables.
gen-er-ous-ly adv

gen-esis /ˈdʒenəsɪs/ n 1 [C] (pl -eses /-əsiz/) beginning; starting-point: the ~ of civilization. 2 G~, the first book of the Old

Testament.

gen·etic /dʒɪˈnetɪk/ adj of genes or genetics.

gen·etics n pl (used with a sing verb) science (branch of biology) dealing with heredity, the ways in which characteristics are passed on from parents to offspring.

gen·eti·cist /dʒɪˈnetɪsɪst/ n [C] specialist in genetics.

ge·nial /ˈdʒiːnɪəl/ adj 1 kindly, sympathetic; sociable: a ~ old man; ~ smiles. 2 favourable to growth; mild; warm: a ~ climate.

ge·ni·ally adv

ge·nial·ity /ˌdʒiːnɪˈælətɪ/ n [C,U]

ge·nie /ˈdʒiːnɪ/ n [C] (pl ~s or genii /ˈdʒiːnɪaɪ/) (in Arabic stories) spirit or goblin with strange powers.

geni·tal /ˈdʒenɪtəl/ adj of animal reproductive organs.

geni·tals n pl external sex organs.

geni·tive /ˈdʒenətɪv/ adj (gram) (also ~ case) showing source or possession.

gen·ius /ˈdʒiːnɪəs/ n [C] (pl ~es, but ⇨ 5 below) 1 [U] great and exceptional capacity of the mind or imagination: men of ~. 2 [C] person having this capacity: Einstein was a mathematical ~. 3 (usually sing with a, an, followed by for) natural ability: have a ~ for languages/acting/making friends. 4 (usually sing with the) guardian spirit of a person, place or institution, (hence, by extension) special and inborn character, spirit or principles of a language, a period of time, etc: the ~ of the Renaissance period in Italy. 5 (pl genii /ˈdʒiːnɪaɪ/) demon; supernatural being. ⇨ genie.

geno·cide /ˈdʒenəsaɪd/ n [U] extermination of a race or community by mass murder, or by imposing conditions that make survival impossible.

gent /dʒent/ n [C] (informal abbr of) gentleman.

gents, (GB informal) public toilet for men.

gen·tile /ˈdʒentaɪl/ n [C], adj (person) not of the Jewish race.

gentle /ˈdʒentəl/ adj (-r, -st) kind, friendly; not rough or violent: a ~ nature/heart/look/voice/call/touch; a ~ breeze; a ~ slope, i e not steep.

gentle·ness n [U]

gentle·man /ˈdʒentəlmən/ n [C] (pl -men /-mən/) 1 man who shows consideration for the feelings of others, who is honourable and well-bred: a fine old ~; a true ~. 2 (old use) man of a family attached to a court or the household of a great noble: one of the king's gentlemen. 3 (dated use) man of wealth and social position, esp one who does not work for a living: 'What does he do for a living?' 'Nothing; he's a ~.' 4 any man of any social position: A ~ has called to see you. 5 (pl) polite form of address to male members of an audience: Gentlemen! Ladies and Gentlemen! 6 (dated) used instead of Sirs or Dear Sirs when writing to a business

firm, etc.

gentle·man·ly adj suiting, feeling, behaving, or looking like a gentleman: a ~ly appearance.

gen·tly /ˈdʒentlɪ/ adv in a gentle manner: Hold it ~, carefully. The road slopes ~ (= gradually) to the sea.

gen·try /ˈdʒentrɪ/ n (collective pl, usually with the) people of good social position next below the nobility.

genu·flect /ˈdʒenjʊflekt/ vi bend the knee, esp in worship.

genu·flec·tion, /ˌdʒenjʊˈflekʃən/ n [C]

genu·ine /ˈdʒenjʊɪn/ adj true; really what it is said to be: a ~ picture by Rubens; ~ pearls; a ~ signature.

genu·ine·ly adv

genu·ine·ness n [U]

ge·nus /ˈdʒiːnəs/ n [C] (pl genera /ˈdʒenərə/) 1 (science) division of animals or plants within a family. 2 sort; kind; class.

ge·ogra·pher /dʒɪˈɒɡrəfə(r)/ n [C] student, expert, in geography.

geo·graphi·cal /ˌdʒɪəˈɡræfɪkəl/ adj of geography.

geo·graphi·cally /-klɪ/ adv

ge·ogra·phy /dʒɪˈɒɡrəfɪ/ n [U] 1 science of the earth's surface, physical features, divisions, climate, products, population, etc. 2 arrangement, location of features of an area: the ~ of a house/a region.

geo·logi·cal /ˌdʒɪəˈlɒdʒɪkəl/ adj of geology.

geo·logi·cally /-klɪ/ adv

ge·ologist /dʒɪˈɒlədʒɪst/ n [C] expert in, student of, geology.

ge·ol·ogy /dʒɪˈɒlədʒɪ/ n [U] 1 science of the earth's history as shown by its rocks, etc. 2 rock structure of a specific region.

geo·met·ric, geo·met·rical /ˌdʒɪəˈmetrɪk(əl)/ adj of geometry; of or like the lines, figures, etc used: ~ patterns.

geo·met·ri·cally /-klɪ/ adv

ge·ometry /dʒɪˈɒmətrɪ/ n [U] science of the properties and relations of lines, angles, surfaces and solids.

Geor·gian /ˈdʒɔːdʒən/ adj 1 of the time of any of the first four Georges, Kings of England (18th century). 2 of (the period of) George V (20th century): ~ architecture.

ger·anium /dʒəˈreɪnɪəm/ n [C] (pl ~s) kind of garden plant with red, pink or white flowers.

geri·atrics /ˌdʒerɪˈætrɪks/ n pl (with a sing verb) medical care of old people.

geri·atric adj

germ /dʒɜːm/ n [C] 1 portion of a living organism capable of becoming a new organism. 2 (fig) beginning or starting-point (of an idea, etc). 3 microbe or bacillus, esp one causing disease: ~ warfare, use of bacteria as a weapon in war.

Ger·man /ˈdʒɜːmən/ adj, n [C] (of) Germany, its language and its people.

Ger·manic /dʒɜːˈmænɪk/ adj of the group of

languages now including German, English and Dutch.

ger·mi·nate /ˈdʒɜːmɪneɪt/ *vi,vt* (of seeds) (cause to) start growth.

ger·mi·na·tion /ˌdʒɜːmɪˈneɪʃən/ *n* [U]

ger·und /ˈdʒerənd/ *n* [C] the *-ing* form of an English verb when used as a noun (as in 'fond of *swimming*').

ges·ta·tion /dʒeˈsteɪʃən/ *n* [U] carrying or being carried in the womb between conception and birth; this period.

ges·ticu·late /dʒɪˈstɪkjʊleɪt/ *vi* use movements of the hands, arms or head instead of, or to accompany, speaking.

ges·ticu·la·tion /dʒɪˌstɪkjʊˈleɪʃən/ *n* [C,U]

ges·ture /ˈdʒestʃə(r)/ *n* **1** [C] movement of the hand or head to show or illustrate an idea, feeling, etc: *a ∼ of refusal.* **2** [C] something done to show friendship, etc: *give money as a ∼ of support.* **3** [U] use of expressive movements: *an actor who is a master of the art of ∼.* □ *vi* gesticulate.

get /get/ *vt,vi* (*pt* got /gɒt/, *pp* got or, in older English and in US gotten /ˈgɒtən/) (For uses with *adverbial particles* and *prepositions* ⇨ **15, 16, 17**, below.) **1** (cause oneself to) become: *∼ wet/tired/drunk. You'll soon ∼ used to the climate here.* **2** bring to a certain condition; cause to be or become: *She soon got the children ready for school.* **3** reach the stage where one is doing something: *It's time we got going,* started. **4** bring a person or thing to the point where he/it is doing something: *Can you really ∼ that old car going again,* restart or repair it? **5** reach the stage where one knows, feels, etc something: *When you ∼ to know him you'll like him.* **6** bring, persuade, cause to do or act in a certain way: *You'll never ∼ him to understand.* **7** receive; have; obtain; acquire: *I got* (= now have) *your telegram. I'll come as soon as I ∼ time. If we divide 12 by 4, we ∼ 3.* **get the sack,** ⇨ **sack²**. **get one's own way,** ⇨ **way.** **get wind of,** ⇨ **wind¹(4). get the worst of,** ⇨ **worst.** **8** catch (an illness): *∼ the measles.* **9** receive as a punishment: *∼ six months,* be sentenced to six months' imprisonment. **get told off,** (*informal*) be warned about having done wrong: *I daren't be late home again or I'll ∼ told off.* **10** (*informal*) understand: *I don't ∼ you/your meaning. She didn't ∼ my jokes.* **11** puzzle: *Ah! That's got him!* **12** **has/have/had got,** e g as a possession or characteristic: *What ugly teeth he's got!* **13** **has/have/had got to,** must, be compelled or obliged: *It has got to* (= must) *be done today.* ⇨ **have³(1). 14** be able: *Do you ever ∼ to see him,* have opportunities of seeing him? **15** (non-idiomatic uses with *adverbial particles* and *prepositions;* for idiomatic uses, ⇨ **17** below) move to or from a specified point or in a particular direction: *When did you ∼ here,* arrive? *A car makes it easier to ∼ about. Did you manage to ∼*

away (= have a holiday) *this Easter? She got back into bed. I'm ∼ting off* (= leaving the train) *at the next station.* **get somewhere/anywhere/nowhere,** have, obtain, achieve, some/any/no result; make some/any/no progress. **16** (non-idiomatic uses with *adverbial particles* and *prepositions;* for idiomatic uses, ⇨ **17** below) cause to move to or from a point, or in a particular direction: *It was nailed to the wall and I couldn't ∼ it off. ∼* (= Put) *your hat and coat on. I can't ∼ the lid on/off.*

17 (idiomatic uses with *adverbial particles* and *prepositions*):

get (sth) across (to sb), (*informal*) (cause something to) be understood: *I spoke slowly, but my meaning didn't ∼ across.*

get ahead (of sb), go forward and pass others; make progress: *Tom has got ahead of all the other boys in the class.*

get along, (a) manage: *We can't ∼ along without money.* **(b)** make progress: *How is he ∼ting along with his French?*

get at sb/sth, reach; gain access to: *The books are locked up and I can't ∼ at them.* **get at sb, (a)** bribe, corrupt: *One of the witnesses had been got at.* **(b)** taunt; criticize: *He's always ∼ting at his wife.* **be getting at,** (*informal*) (be trying to) say or suggest: *What are you ∼ting at?*

get away, manage to leave; escape: *Two of the prisoners got away.* Hence, **`get-away** *n:* **make one's get-away,** escape; (as an adjective): *The get-away car had been stolen.* **get away with sth,** pursue successfully a course of action which might usually be expected to result in blame, punishment or misfortune: *The thieves got away with the contents of the safe. If I cheat in the examination, do you think I might ∼ away with it?*

get back, return to power or prominence after losing it for a time: *The Democrats hope to ∼ back at the next election.* **get one's `own back (on sb),** have one's revenge: *He tricked me this time but I'll ∼ my own back one day.*

get by, (a) (*fig*) pass; be accepted, without comment or criticism: *I have no formal clothes for this occasion; perhaps I can ∼ by in a dark suit.* **(b)** manage; survive: *She can't ∼ by without him.*

get sb down, (*informal*) depress: *Don't let this wretched weather ∼ you down.* **get sth down, (a)** swallow: *The medicine was horrid, and she couldn't ∼ it down.* **(b)** write down: *Did you ∼ that telephone message down?* **get down to sth,** deal (seriously) with: *∼ down to one's work after the holidays.* **get down to business,** ⇨ **business(3).**

get in, (a) arrive: *The train got in five minutes early.* **(b)** be elected: *He got in* (= was elected M P) *for Islington.* **get sb in,** call a person to one's house, etc to perform a service: *We must ∼ someone in to repair the*

TV. **get sth in, (a)** collect, gather: ~ *in the crops/the harvest*. **(b)** obtain a supply: ~ *coal in for the winter*.

get into, (a) put on: *I can't ~ into these shoes*. **(b)** have, develop, a particular condition: ~ *into trouble/a rage/a temper*; ~ *into debt*. **(c)** acquire: ~ *into bad habits*. **(d)** learn by experience or experiment: ~ *into the habit/routine of doing something*. **(e)** become interested: *I can't ~ into the book I'm reading*.

get off, start: *We got off immediately after breakfast*. **get off lightly/cheaply,** escape severe punishment, suffering, etc. **tell sb where to get off/where he gets off,** (*informal*) tell that his misbehaviour, impudence, etc will no longer be tolerated. **get sb off,** save from punishment or a penalty: *His youth and inexperience got him off*. **get off with sth,** escape more severe punishment or misfortune: *He got off with only a fine*, e g instead of possible imprisonment.

get on, make progress; advance: *He's sure to ~ on in life. Time is ~ting on*, is passing. **get on sth,** mount: *He got on his bike/horse/the train*. **get on one's nerves,** ⇨ nerve(2). **be getting on for,** be approaching: *He's ~ting on for seventy. It's ~ting on for midnight*. **get on to sb,** get in touch with, e g by telephone: *If you're not satisfied with the firm's service ~ on to the manager*. **get on (with sb),** work or live in a sociable way: *The new manager is easy to ~ on with*. **get on (with sth),** continue: *Please ~ on with your work*.

get out, become known: *The secret got out. If the news ~s out there'll be trouble*. **get out of (sth/doing sth), (a)** (*fig*) avoid; escape (from): *I wish I could ~ out of going to that wedding*. **(b)** (*fig*) abandon gradually: ~ *out of bad habits*. **get sth out of sb,** extract by force: *The police will ~ a confession out of him*.

get over sb, (*informal*) forget: *He never got over Jane, you know, She stayed in his memory*. **get over sth, (a)** recover from, e g illness, surprise, a loss: *I can't ~ over his rudeness*. **(b)** overcome: *She can't ~ over her shyness*.

get round sb, persuade somebody to do or to agree to something to which he was at first opposed or indifferent: *Alice knows how to ~ round her father*. **get round sth,** evade, e g a law or regulation, but without committing a legal offence: *A clever lawyer might find ways of ~ting round that clause*. **get round to sth/to doing sth,** deal with it (when more important matters have been dealt with): *I'm very busy this week but I hope to ~ round to your request next week*.

get through, reach a person; arrive: *I rang you several times yesterday but couldn't ~ through*. **get through (sth),** pass, e g an examination: *Tom failed but his sister got*

through. **get through sth,** reach the end of: *He has got through* (= spent) *all his money*. **get to,** reach a particular state. **get to grips with sth,** ⇨ grip(1). **get to the point,** ⇨ point[1](9). **get to work,** ⇨ work[1](1).

get together, come or meet together, e g for discussion or social purposes: *Let's ~ together one evening and talk about old times*. Hence, `**get-together** *n* [C] e g a social reunion of old friends. **get people/things together,** collect; organise, put in order: *The rebel leader couldn't ~ an army together*.

get under control, ⇨ control. **get under way,** ⇨ way(7).

get up, (a) rise: *What time do you ~ up*, i e from bed? *He got up* (= stood up) *to ask a question*. **(b)** mount: ~ *up behind me*, e g on a horse. **get sb/oneself up, (a)** cause to rise, be out of bed: ~ *the children up and dressed for school*. **(b)** put on cosmetics, fine clothes: *She was got up like a film star*. **(c)** dress in a certain style: ~ *oneself up as a sailor*. Hence, `**get-up** *n* [C] (unusual) style of dress. **get up to sth, (a)** reach: *We got up to page seventy-two last lesson*. **(b)** become involved in; plan: *What will they ~ up to next?*

gey·ser /ˈgiːzə(r) *US:* ˈgaɪzə(r)/ *n* [C] **1** natural spring[1](2) sending up at intervals a column of hot water or steam. **2** /*US:* ˈgiːzə(r)/ apparatus for heating water, e g by gas, in a bathroom, etc.

ghast·ly /ˈgɑːstlɪ *US:* ˈgæs-/ *adj* (-ier, -iest) **1** as if dead; pale and ill: *looking ~*; (also as an *adverb*): ~ *pale*. **2** causing horror or fear: *a ~ accident*. **3** (*informal*) very unsatisfactory or unpleasant: *a ~ dinner*. **4** (of a smile) painfully forced.

gher·kin /ˈgɜːkɪn/ *n* [C] small, green cucumber for pickling.

ghet·to /ˈgetəʊ/ *n* [C] (*pl* ~s) **1** (formerly, in some countries) Jewish quarter of a town. **2** section of a town, lived in by underprivileged classes, or people who are discriminated against, e g because of race or religion.

ghost /gəʊst/ *n* [C] **1** spirit of a dead person appearing to a person still living: *He looked as if he had seen a ~*, looked frightened. **2** (*old use*) spirit of life. **give up the ghost,** die. **3** something shadowy or without substance. **not have the ghost of a chance,** no chance at all.
the Holy Ghost, the Third Person of the Trinity.
`**ghost town,** one now abandoned, e g an area where gold was once mined.
`**ghost-writer,** person who does literary or artistic work for another person who takes the credit.
ghost·ly *adj* of, like, suggesting, a ghost.

gi·ant /ˈdʒaɪənt/ *n* [C] **1** (in fairy tales) man of very great height and size. **2** man, animal or plant much larger than normal. **3** (*fig*) person of extraordinary ability or genius. **4**

(as an *adjective*) of great size or force: ~ *strength; a ~ cabbage.*

gi·ant·ess /ˈdʒaɪəntˈes/ *n* [C] female giant.

gib·ber·ish /ˈdʒɪbərɪʃ/ *n* [U] unintelligible talk.

gib·bet /ˈdʒɪbɪt/ *n* **1** [C] wooden post on which corpses of executed criminals were formerly exposed as a warning. **2** [U] death by hanging. □ *vt* put to death by hanging.

gib·bon /ˈgɪbən/ *n* [C] kinds of long-armed ape.

gib·bous /ˈdʒɪbəs/ *adj* (of the moon) having the bright part greater than a semicircle and less than a circle.

gibe, jibe /dʒaɪb/ *vi* make fun of: ~ *at a boy's mistakes.*

gib·lets /ˈdʒɪbləts/ *n pl* heart, liver, gizzard, etc of a goose, hen, etc taken out before the bird is cooked.

giddy /ˈgɪdɪ/ *adj* (-ier, -iest) **1** causing, having, the feeling that everything is turning round so that one cannot stand firm. **2** too fond of pleasure; not serious: *a ~ young girl.*
gid·di·ly *adv*
gid·di·ness *n* [U]

gift /gɪft/ *n* **1** [C] something given: ~*s to charities.* (*Note:* compare *birthday* and *Christmas presents.*) **2** [C] natural ability or talent: *have a ~ for art/languages.* **3** [U] right or power to give: *The property came to me by free ~, was given to me.* □ *vt* bestow, e g land, as a gift.
`**gift-voucher,** document supplied with certain articles when bought, to be collected and exchanged for gifts.
gifted *adj* talented.

gig /gɪg/ *n* [C] **1** small, light two-wheeled carriage pulled by one horse. **2** ship's small boat.

gi·gan·tic /dʒaɪˈgæntɪk/ *adj* of immense size.

giggle /ˈgɪgəl/ *vi* laugh in a nervous and silly way. □ *n* [C] laugh of this kind.

gild[1] /gɪld/ *vt* (*pp* usually ~ed, but ⇨ **gilt** below) cover with gold leaf or gold-coloured paint: ~ *a picture-frame.*
gilder, person who gilds (picture-frames, etc).
gild·ing *n* [U] material with which things are gilded.

gild[2] ⇨ **guild.**

gill[1] /gɪl/ *n* [C] (*usually pl*) organ with which a fish breathes.

gill[2] /dʒɪl/ *n* [C] liquid measure, one-quarter of a pint.

gilt /gɪlt/ *n* [U] = gilding.

gim·let /ˈgɪmlət/ *n* [C] small tool for boring holes in wood, etc.

gim·mick /ˈgɪmɪk/ *n* [C] (esp of actors, advertisers) trick, catchword, article of clothing, etc used to attract attention, customers, etc.

gin /dʒɪn/ *n* [U] colourless alcoholic drink.

gin·ger /ˈdʒɪndʒə(r)/ *n* [U] **1** (plant with a) hot-tasting root used in cooking and for making a kind of wine. **2** liveliness; energy: *a `~ group,* (in Parliament) group of M P's that urges the Government to be more active. **3** (as an *adjective*) light reddish-yellow colour: ~ *hair.* □ *vt* make more vigorous or lively: ~ *the supporters up.*
'ginger `ale/`beer, non-alcoholic drink flavoured with ginger.

gin·ger·ly /ˈdʒɪndʒəlɪ/ *adv* with great care to avoid harming oneself, what one touches, making a noise, etc. □ *adj* cautious; careful: *in a ~ fashion.*

ging·ham /ˈgɪŋəm/ *n* [U] printed cotton or linen cloth, usually with designs in stripes or checks.

gipsy, gypsy /ˈdʒɪpsɪ/ *n* [C] (*pl* -ies) member of a wandering Asiatic race, now living in many parts of Europe.

gi·raffe /dʒɪˈrɑːf US: -ˈræf/ *n* [C] African animal with a very long neck and legs.

girder /ˈgɜːdə(r)/ *n* [C] **1** wood, iron or steel beam to support the joists of a floor. **2** structure of steel forming the span of a bridge, roof, etc.

girdle /ˈgɜːdəl/ *n* [C] **1** cord or belt fastened round the waist to keep clothes in position. **2** = corset. **3** something that encircles like a girdle: *a ~ of green fields round a town.* □ *vt* encircle: *a lake ~d with trees.*

girl /gɜːl/ *n* [C] **1** female child; daughter; young unmarried woman. **2** girl or woman working in a shop, office, etc (irrespective of age): `*office ~s.*
`**girl-friend,** regular female companion with whom one may or may not be in love.
'Girl `Guide, (*GB*) member of an organization for girls similar to the Boy Scouts.
`**girl-hood,** state or time of being a girl.
girl·ish *adj* of, for, like, a girl.
girl·ish·ly *adv*
girl·ish·ness *n* [U]

girth /gɜːθ/ *n* [C] **1** leather or cloth band tightened round the body of a horse to keep the saddle in place. **2** measurement round anything like a cylinder in shape: *a tree 10 metres in ~.*

gist /dʒɪst/ *n* **the ~,** real or main points or substance, general sense: *Tell me the ~ of what he said.*

give[1] /gɪv/ *vt,vi* (*pt* gave /geɪv/, *pp* ~n /ˈgɪvən/) (For uses with *adverbial particles* and *prepositions*, ⇨ **13** below.) **1** hand over (to a person) without payment or exchange, e g as a present or gift: *I gave David a book.* *G~ one to me.* **2** *give for; give to + inf,* cause (a person) to have (something) in exchange for something else, for payment, as compensation, etc: *How much will you ~ me for my old car? I would ~ a lot to know where she is.* **3** allow (a person or thing) to pass into the care or custody of: *G~ the porter your bags.* **4** allow, e g time; agree to; grant: *You'd better ~ yourself half an hour for the journey. They gave me a week to*

make up my mind. 'The car has a good engine' 'OK, I'll ~ you that (= agree) but the body's very rusty'. **5** furnish; supply; provide: The sun ~s us warmth and light. **6** be the source or origin of: You've ~n me your cold. **7** devote; dedicate: He gave his life to the cause of peace. **8** (used in the imperative to show preference): G~ me liberty or ~ me death, if I cannot have liberty, I prefer to die. **9** (used with a noun in a pattern that may be replaced by a verb): ~ a groan/yell, groan, yell; ~ him a kick, kick him; ~ her a ring, phone her. **10** (in fixed phrases) **give or take...**, plus or minus: She'll be here at 4 o'clock, ~ or take a few minutes. **give sb to understand that**, inform, assure him, that: I was ~n to understand that you might help me to find employment. **give way**, (a) retire, retreat: Our troops had to ~ way. (b) fail to support: The rope gave way, broke. **give way (to sth/sb)**, (a) allow priority to: G~ way to traffic coming in from the right. (b) be replaced by: Sorrow gave way to smiles. (c) abandon oneself to: Don't ~ way to despair. (d) make concessions (to): We mustn't ~ way to these impudent demands. **11** lose firmness; bend; yield to pressure: The branch gave (e g bent) but did not break. His knees seemed to ~, to feel weak (so that he fell down). **12 given** (a) (in formal documents) delivered: ~n under my hand and seal in this fifth day of May, 1705. (b) granting or assuming that one has, e g as a basis for reasoning: G~n good health, I hope to finish the work this year. (c) agreed on: They were to meet at a ~n time and place. ⇨ given name below. **given to (doing) sth**, devoted or addicted to; having a habit or inclination: He's ~n to boasting.
13 (Uses with adverbial particles and prepositions):
give sb away, (esp) hand over (the bride) to the bridegroom at a wedding. **give sth away**, (a) allow somebody else to have; sacrifice: You've ~n away a good chance of winning the match. (b) distribute: The Mayor gave away the prizes. (c) give freely, not expecting anything in return: He gave away all his money. (d) reveal, intentionally or unintentionally: His accent gave him away. Hence, **`give-away** n [C] (a) something given without charge, expected returns: The last question on the exam paper was a ~-away, so easy that it needed no effort, etc. (b) something revealed, intentionally or unintentionally: The expression on the thief's face was a ~-away, showed his guilt. **`give the `game away**, ⇨ game²(5).
give sth back (to sb); give sb back sth, restore; return: ~ it back to its rightful owner.
give in (to sb), surrender; submit: The rebels were forced to ~ in. **give sth in**,

hand over (papers, etc) to the proper authorities: Please ~ in your examination papers now.
give sth off, send out, e g smoke, vapour, etc: This chemical ~s off a horrid smell!
give out, come to an end; be exhausted: Our food supplies began to ~ out. His strength gave out. **give sth out**, distribute; send out: ~ out books.
give up, abandon the attempt to do something, find the answer: I can do nothing more; I ~ up. I can't answer that puzzle; I ~ up. **give sb up**, (a) say that one regards him as hopeless: The doctors have ~n him up, say that they cannot cure him. (b) (informal) stop keeping company with him/her: She was tired of Tom's nagging so she gave him up. (c) no longer expect a person: She was so late that we had ~n her up. **give sb up for lost**, no longer expect him to be found or saved. **give sb/oneself/sth up**, surrender; part with: ~ up one's seat to sb, e g in a crowded bus. The escaped prisoner gave himself up. **give sth up**, stop (doing sth): I wish I could ~ up smoking.

give² /gɪv/ n [U] **1** quality of being elastic, of yielding to pressure: A stone floor has no ~ in it. **2** (fig) (of a person) quality of yielding. **give and take**, compromise; willingness on both sides to give way: There must be ~ and take on both sides if the negotiations are to succeed.

given /ˈgɪvən/ pp of give¹.
`given name, = first name.

giver /ˈgɪvə(r)/ n [C] one who gives.

giz·zard /ˈgɪzəd/ n [C] bird's second stomach for grinding food.

glacé /ˈglæseɪ US: glæˈseɪ/ adj **1** (of fruits) iced, sugared. **2** (of leather, cloth) smooth, polished.

gla·cial /ˈgleɪʃəl/ adj of ice or the Ice Age.

gla·cier /ˈglæsɪə(r) US: ˈgleɪʃər/ n [C] mass of ice, formed by snow on mountains, moving slowly along a valley.

glad /glæd/ adj (-der, -dest) **1** pleased: be/look/feel ~ about something. I'm ~ to see you. **2** causing or bringing joy; joyful: Have you heard the ~ news?
glad·den /ˈglædən/ vt make glad.
glad·ly adv
glad·ness n [U]

glade /gleɪd/ n [C] clear, open space in a forest.

gladi·ator /ˈglædɪeɪtə(r)/ n [C] (in ancient Rome) man trained to fight with weapons at public shows in an arena.

gladi·olus /ˌglædɪˈəʊləs/ n (pl -li /-laɪ/ or ~es) plant with sword-shaped leaves and spikes of brightly coloured flowers.

glam·our (US also **glamor**) /ˈglæmə(r)/ n [U] **1** charm or enchantment; power of beauty to move the feelings: a scene full of ~. **2** attractive feminine beauty or charm.
glam·our·ous (US also **-or-**) /-əs/ adj full of glamour: glamorous film stars.

glam·our·ize (*US* also **-or-**) /-aɪz/ *vt* make glamorous: *newspapers that glamorize the lives of pop stars.*

glance /ɡlɑns *US:* ˈɡlæns/ *vi,vt* **1** take a quick look: ~ *at the clock;* ~ *over/through a letter;* ~ *round a room. He* ~*d his eye down the classified advertisements.* **2** *glance off,* (of a weapon or a blow) strike and bounce off: *The bullet* ~*d off his helmet.* **3** (of bright objects, light) flash: *Their helmets* ~*d in the sunlight.* □ *n* [C] **1** quick look: *take a* ~ *at the newspaper headlines; see something at a* ~, at once. **2** quick turning of the eyes: *loving* ~*s.* **3** (sudden movement producing a) flash of light: *a* ~ *of spears in the sunlight.*

gland /ɡlænd/ *n* [C] simple or complex organ that separates from the blood substances that are to be used by or expelled from the body: *sweat* ~*s.*

glandu·lar /ˈɡlændjʊlə(r) *US:* -dʒʊ-/ *adj* of or like a gland: ~*ular fever.*

glare[1] /ɡleə(r)/ *n* **1** [U] strong, fierce, unpleasant light: *the* ~ *of the sun on the water.* **2** (*fig*) *in the full* ~ *of publicity,* with public attention directed towards one. **3** [C] angry or fierce stare: *look at someone with a* ~.

glare[2] /ɡleə(r)/ *vi,vt* **1** shine in a dazzling or disagreeable way: *The tropical sun* ~*d down on us all the day.* **2** stare angrily or fiercely: *They stood glaring at each other.*

glar·ing *adj* (a) dazzling: *a car with glaring headlights.* (b) angry; fierce; *glaring eyes.* (c) gross; conspicuous: *a glaring mistake; glaring injustice.* (d) (of colours) too bright and showy.

glass /ɡlɑs *US:* ɡlæs/ *n* **1** [U] hard, brittle substance (as used in windows): *made of* ~. **2** [C] article made of this substance. (a) drinking vessel or its contents: *a* ~ *of milk.* (b) mirror. (c) telescope: *The sailor looked through his* ~. (d) barometer: *The* ~ *is falling.* (e) (*pl*) spectacles: *She can't read without* ~*es.* (f) (*pl*) binoculars. ⇨ looking-glass, magnifying-glass. □ *vt* fit with glass; glaze.

`**glass·blower**, workman who blows molten glass to shape it into bottles, etc.

`**glass·cutter**, (a) workman who cuts designs on glass. (b) tool for cutting glass.

`**glass·house**, building with glass sides and roof (for growing plants).

`**glass·ware**, articles made of glass.

`**glass·wool**, fine glass fibres used for filtering and in man-made fibres.

`**glass·works**, factory where glass is manufactured.

glass·ful /-fʊl/ *n* as much as a drinking glass will hold.

glassy *adj* (-ier, -iest) like glass in appearance: *a* ~*y stare/look/eye,* lifeless, expressionless, fixed.

glaze /ɡleɪz/ *vt,vi* **1** fit glass into: ~ *a window/house.* **2** cover with a glass-like surface: ~ *pottery.* **3** (of the eyes) become glassy: *His eyes* ~*d over.* □ *n* [C,U] (substance used for, surface obtained by giving, a) thin glassy coating.

glaz·ier /ˈɡleɪzɪə(r) *US:* -ʒə(r)/ *n* [C] workman who fits glass into the frames of windows, etc.

gleam /ɡliːm/ *n* [C] **1** beam or ray of soft light, esp one that comes and goes: *the* ~*s of the morning sun.* **2** (*fig*) brief show of some quality or emotion: *an essay with an occasional* ~ *of intelligence; a* ~ *of hope.* □ *vi* send out gleams: *reflector studs* ~*ing in the roadway.*

glean /ɡliːn/ *vi,vt* **1** pick up grain left in a harvest field by the workers. **2** (*fig*) gather news, facts in small quantities.

gleaner, person who gleans.

glean·ings *n pl* (usually *fig*) small items of knowledge from various sources.

glee /ɡliː/ *n* [U] feeling of joy caused by success or triumph: *shout with* ~.

glee·ful /-fəl/ *adj* full of glee; joyous.

glee·fully /-fəlɪ/ *adv*

glen /ɡlen/ *n* [C] narrow valley.

glib /ɡlɪb/ *adj* (-ber, -best) (of a person, what he says or how he says it) ready and fluent, but not sincere: *a* ~ *talker;* ~ *excuses.*

glib·ly *adv*

glib·ness *n* [U]

glide /ɡlaɪd/ *vi* move along smoothly and continuously: *The pilot* ~*d skilfully down to the landing-field.* □ *n* [C] gliding movement: *The dance consists of a series of glides.*

glider, aircraft without an engine, e g the kind towed behind a powered aircraft.

glid·ing *n* [U] sport of flying in gliders.

glim·mer /ˈɡlɪmə(r)/ *vi* send out a weak, uncertain light: *lights* ~*ing in the distance.* □ *n* [C] **1** faint, unsteady light: *a* ~ *of light through the curtains.* **2** (*fig*) *a* ~ *of hope.*

glimpse /ɡlɪmps/ *n* [C] **1** quick, imperfect view: *get/catch a* ~ *of something from the window of a train.* **2** short look (*at*). □ *vt* catch a glimpse of.

glint /ɡlɪnt/ *vi* gleam. □ *n* [C] gleam or flash: ~*s of gold in her hair.*

glis·ten /ˈɡlɪsən/ *vi* (esp of wet or polished surfaces) shine brightly; sparkle: *eyes* ~*ing with tears; snow* ~*ing in the sunlight.*

glit·ter /ˈɡlɪtə(r)/ *vi* shine brightly with flashes of light: ~*ing with jewels.* □ *n* [U] brilliant light: *the* ~ *of the decorations.*

glit·ter·ing *adj* brilliant; attractive: ~*ing jewels;* ~*ing prizes.*

gloat /ɡləʊt/ *vi* look at with selfish delight: ~ *over one's wealth.*

gloat·ing·ly *adv*

glo·bal /ˈɡləʊbəl/ *adj* **1** world-wide: ~ *war.* **2** of the whole of a group of items, etc.

globe /ɡləʊb/ *n* [C] **1** object shaped like a ball, esp a model of the earth. **2** (with *the*) the Earth. **3** spherical glass vessel, esp a lampshade or a fishbowl

glob·ule /ˈglɒbjuːl/ n [C] tiny drop.

globu·lar /ˈglɒbjʊlə(r)/ adj (a) globe-shaped (b) made of globules.

glock·en·spiel /ˈglɒkənspiːl/ n [C] musical instrument consisting of metal bars which are struck with two light hammers.

gloom /gluːm/ n [C] 1 semi-darkness. 2 feeling of sadness and hopelessness: *The news cast a ∼ over the village.*

gloomy /ˈgluːmɪ/ adj (-ier, -iest) 1 dark, unlit. 2 depressed; depressing: *feeling ∼ about the future.*

gloom·ily /-ɪlɪ/ adv

glor·ify /ˈglɔːrɪfaɪ/ vt (pt,pp -ied) 1 give adoration and thanksgiving to (God); worship. 2 give honour and glory to (a hero). 3 invest (something common or simple) with charm or beauty; make (a person or thing) seem more imposing: *His weekend cottage is only a glorified barn.*

glori·fi·ca·tion /ˌglɔːrɪfɪˈkeɪʃn/ n [U]

glori·ous /ˈglɔːrɪəs/ adj 1 splendid; magnificent: *a ∼ sunset/view.* 2 illustrious; honourable; possessing or conferring glory: *a ∼ victory.* 3 (informal) very enjoyable: *have a ∼ time; ∼ fun.* 4 (ironic) dreadful: *What a ∼ mess!*

glori·ous·ly adv

glory /ˈglɔːrɪ/ n [U] 1 high fame and honour won by great achievements. 2 adoration and thanksgiving offered to God: *'G∼ to God in the highest.'* 3 quality of being beautiful or magnificent: *the ∼ of a sunset.* 4 (sometimes [C] pl -ies) reason for pride; something deserving respect and honour: *the glories of ancient Rome.* □ vi (pt,pp -ied) **glory in**, rejoice in, take great pride in: *∼ in one's strength/in her success.*

gloss¹ /glɒs/ n 1 [U] smooth, bright surface: *the ∼ of silk and satin.* 2 (fig) (usually sing with a, an) deceptive appearance: *a ∼ of respectability.* □ vt **gloss over** 1 give a bright surface to. 2 cover up or explain away (an error, etc): *∼ over a person's faults.*

`gloss paint, paint which, when dry, leaves a glossy surface.

glossy adj (-ier, -iest) smooth and shiny: *a ∼ surface; a ∼ magazine,* one with colour photographs of e g clothes, fashions, etc.

gloss² /glɒs/ n [C] explanation (in a footnote, etc) of a word in the text; comment. □ vt write glosses on; make comments on. **gloss over,** avoid explaining fully: *∼ over a subject.*

gloss·ary /ˈglɒsərɪ/ n [C] (pl -ies) 1 collection of glosses. 2 list and explanations of special, e g technical, commercial vocabulary.

glove /glʌv/ n [C] covering of leather, knitted wool, etc for the hand. **fit like a glove,** fit perfectly. **be hand in glove (with...),** be in close relations (with...).

glow /gləʊ/ vi 1 send out brightness or warmth without flame: *∼ing logs/coal/charcoal.* 2 (fig) be, look, feel, warm or

flushed (as after exercise or when excited): *∼ing with enthusiasm/health/pride.* 3 show strong or warm colours: *trees ∼ing with autumn tints.* □ n (sing only, with the, a or an) glowing state; warm or flushed look; warm feeling: *in a ∼ of enthusiasm; the ∼ of the sky at sunset.*

`glow-worm, insect of which the wingless female gives out a green light at its tail.

glow·ing adj showing warm colour or (fig) enthusiasm: *give a ∼ing account of what happened.*

glow·ing·ly adv

glower /ˈglaʊə(r)/ vi look in an angry or threatening way: *∼ at her.*

glower·ing·ly adv

glu·cose /ˈgluːkəʊs/ n [U] grape sugar.

glue /gluː/ n [U] adhesive substance used for joining (esp wooden) things. □ vt (pt,pp ∼d; gluing) 1 stick, make fast, with glue: *∼ two pieces of wood together; ∼ a piece of wood on to something.* 2 put tightly or closely: *His eyes were/His ear was ∼d to the keyhole. Why must you always be ∼d to the TV,* Why do you always watch it?

gluey /ˈgluːɪ/ adj sticky, like glue.

glum /glʌm/ adj (-mer, -mest) gloomy; sad.

glum·ly adv

glum·ness n [U]

glut /glʌt/ vt (-tt-) 1 supply too much to: *∼ the market (with fruit, etc).* 2 overeat; satisfy to the full; fill to excess: *∼ one's appetite; ∼ted with pleasure.* □ n [C] supply in excess of demand: *a ∼ of pears in the market.*

glut·ton /ˈglʌtən/ n [C] person who eats too much: *You've eaten the whole pie, you ∼! He's a ∼ for work,* (fig) is always willing and ready to work.

glut·ton·ous /ˈglʌtənəs/ adj very greedy.

glut·ton·ous·ly adv

glut·tony /-ənɪ/ n [U] habit or practice of eating too much.

gly·cer·ine (US = **gly·cer·in**) /ˈglɪsəˈriːn US: ˈglɪsərɪn/ n [U] thick, sweet, colourless liquid made from fats and oils, used in medical and toilet preparations and explosives.

gnarled /nɑːld/ adj (of tree trunks) twisted and rough; covered with knobs: *a ∼ old oak; ∼(= knotty, deformed) fingers.*

gnash /næʃ/ vi,vt 1 (of the teeth) strike or grind together, e g in rage. 2 (of a person) cause (the teeth) to do this.

gnat /næt/ n [C] small two-winged fly that bites.

gnaw /nɔː/ vt,vi 1 bite steadily at: *The dog was ∼ing (at) a bone.* 2 torment; waste away: *fear and anxiety ∼ing (at) the heart.*

gnome /nəʊm/ n [C] (in tales) small goblin living under the ground.

gnu /nuː/ n [C] kind of antelope like an ox (= wildebeest).

go¹ /gəʊ/ vi (3rd person, present tense goes /gəʊz/, pt went /went/, pp gone /gɒn US:

271

gɔn/) (For idiomatic uses with *adverbial particles* and *prepositions*, ⇨ 24 below.) **1** (with a *preposition* or *adverb* of place or direction; ⇨ **come**) move, pass, from one point to another and away from the speaker, etc: *He has gone to see his sister. G~ and get your hat. Let's ~ to the cinema. They came at six and went* (= left) *at nine. I wish this pain would ~ (away).* `go places,` be successful. **2** (a) be placed; have as a usual or proper position: *Where do you want your piano to ~?* Where shall we put it? (b) be fitted or contained in: *My clothes won't ~ into this small suitcase. 7 into 15 won't ~,* 15 does not contain exact multiples of 7. **3** reach, extend; last; (of a person's behaviour, remarks, achievements, etc) reach certain limits: *This road ~es to London.* **go a long way,** last: *She makes a little money ~ a long way.* **go a long way/far towards doing sth,** make a considerable contribution towards: *The Prime Minister's statement went a long way towards reassuring the nation.* **go (very) far,** (a) last: *A pound doesn't ~ far nowadays.* (b) (used in the future tense) (of a person) succeed: *He will ~ far in the diplomatic service,* will win promotion, etc. **go too far,** go beyond acceptable limits: *That's ~ing too far,* saying or doing more than is right. **go to great lengths/trouble/pains (to do sth),** take care to do something well: *He went to great trouble to make his guests comfortable.* **go to one's head,** ⇨ head[1](20). **4** **go on a journey/trip/an outing,** make a journey, take a trip, have an outing, etc. **go for a walk, etc,** go out in order to walk, etc. **go swimming/shopping, etc,** swim/shop, etc. **5** (in the pattern, *go + prep + noun*) (a) pass into/from the state described by the noun: *~ from bad to worse; ~ out of fashion; ~ to pieces; ~ to sleep.* ⇨ the noun entries. (b) go to the place, etc described by the noun for the purpose associated with it: *~ to church,* attend a church service; *~ to school/college/university,* attend school, etc in order to learn or study. **6** **go to sb,** pass into somebody's possession; be allotted to: *The first prize went to Mr Hill.* **7** become; pass into a specific condition: *~ blind/mad,* etc. *He went grey with worry.* **go bad,** ⇨ bad[1](4). **8** be moving, working, etc: *This clock doesn't ~. Is your watch ~ing?* **go like a bomb,** ⇨ bomb. **9** be or live habitually in a specific state or manner: *Refugees often ~ hungry.* **10** (showing manner of progress; sometimes after 'How'): *How's everything ~ing* (= progressing)? *How's your work ~ing?* Things went better than had been expected. **go slow,** (of workers in factories, etc) work slowly esp to reduce output, as a protest or to draw attention to demands: (as an *adjective*) *a ~-slow (policy).* **be going strong,** be proceeding vigorously; be still flourishing: *He's ninety and/but still ~ing strong.* **11** work; operate: *This machine ~es on electricity.* **12** **go (to sb) for,** be sold (to a person) for: *The house went cheap. I shan't let mine ~* (= sell it) *for less than £8 000.* **13** **go on/in,** (of money) be spent on: *All his spare money ~es on books. Half the money he inherited went in debts.* **14** be given up, abandoned, lost: *I'm afraid the car must ~. My sight is ~ing,* I'm losing my ability to see. **15 as men/things, etc go,** considering the average men, etc: *They're good workers, as workers ~ nowadays.* **16** fail; collapse; give way; break off: *First the sails and then the mast went in the storm.* **let oneself go,** relax, enjoy oneself, etc. **17** (*gone* and phrases) die: *He's dead and gone,* dead and buried. **18** be decided: *The case* (i e in a law court) *went against him,* he lost. *How did the election ~ at Hull,* Who was elected? **19** (various phrases) **go bail (for sb),** ⇨ bail[1]. **go shares/halves (in sth with sb),** ⇨ share[1](1), half. **go sick,** ⇨ sick[1](2). **go it alone,** act by oneself, without support. **20** have a certain wording or tune: *I'm not quite sure how the tune ~es.* **21** make a specific sound: *The clock ~es 'tick-tock, tick-tock'. 'Bang! went the gun'.* **22** begin an activity: *One, two, three, ~!* or *Ready, steady, ~!* (e g as a signal for competitors in a race to start). *Well, here ~es!* (used to call attention to the fact that one is about to start to do something). **23** **be going to do sth,** (a) (showing what is intended, determined or planned): *We're ~ing to spend our holidays in Wales this year. We're ~ing to buy a house.* (b) (showing what is considered likely or probable): *Look at those black clouds—we're ~ing to have/there's ~ing to be a storm.* (c) about to: *I'm ~ing to tell you a story. I'm ~ing to be twenty next month.* **24** (idiomatic uses with *adverbial particles* and *prepositions*):

go about, (a) move from place to place; pay visits: *He's ~ing about with that Polish girl now,* is often seen with her in public. (b) (of rumours, stories, etc) pass from person to person: *A rumour is ~ing about that... There's a flu virus ~ing about.* (c) (of a ship) change course. **go about sth,** set to work at: *You're not ~ing about that job in the right way.*

go after sb/sth, try to win or obtain: *He's ~ne after a job in the City.*

go against sb, (a) oppose: *Don't ~ against your father.* (b) have an unsatisfactory outcome: *The war is ~ing against them,* They seem likely to be defeated. ⇨ also **18** above.

go against sth, be contrary to: *It ~es against my principles/interests.*

go ahead, proceed without hesitation: *'May I start now?' 'Yes, ~ ahead.'* Hence, `go-ahead n` permission to proceed: *give them the ~-ahead.*

go along, proceed: *You may have some dif-*

ficulty first but you'll find it easier as you ~ along. **go along with sb,** (a) accompany: *I'll ~ along with you as far as the corner.* (b) agree with: *I can't ~ along with you on that point.*

go at sb/sth, (a) rush at; attack: *They went at each other for nearly an hour.* (b) deal with something energetically: *They were ~ing at the job for all they were worth,* making the greatest effort.

go away, leave.

go back, (a) return. (b) extend backwards in space or time: *His family ~es back for hundreds of years.* **go back on,** fail to keep; break or withdraw from, e g a promise: *He's not the sort of man who would/to ~ back on his word.*

go behind sb's back, do or say something without their knowledge.

go beyond sth, exceed: *You've ~ne beyond your instructions. That's ~ing beyond a joke,* is too serious to be amusing.

go by, pass: *Time went by slowly. We waited for the procession to ~ by.* `**go by sth,** be guided or directed by: *That's a good rule to ~ by. Have we enough evidence to ~ by?* **go by/under the name of,** be called: *My dog ~es by the name of Rover.*

go down, (a) (of a ship, etc) sink. (b) (of the sun, moon, etc) set. (c) (of food and drink) be swallowed. (d) leave a university for the vacation, having graduated, etc. (e) (of the sea, wind, etc) become calm. (f) (of prices) go lower: *The price of eggs/The cost of living has ~ne down.* **go down (in sth),** be written, recorded or remembered in: *It all ~es down in his notebook. He'll ~ down in history as a great statesman.* **go down to,** be continued or extended as far as: *This 'History of Europe' ~es down to 1970.* **go down with sb,** (a) (of an explanation or excuse, of a story, play, etc) be accepted or approved: *The new teacher doesn't ~ down well with his pupils.* (b) fall ill with: *Poor Peter—he's ~ne down with 'flu.*

go for sb, (a) fetch: *Shall I ~ for a doctor?* (b) attack: *The dog went for the postman as soon as he opened the garden gate.* (c) be applicable to: *What I have said about Smith ~es for you, too.* (d) (informal) like, enjoy: *I ~ for his new sports car.*

go in, (a) enter: *The key won't ~ in (the lock). She went in (the house, kitchen) to cook the dinner.* (b) (of the sun, moon, etc) be obscured by clouds: *The sun has ~ne in and it is rather cold.* **go in for sth,** (a) take, sit for: *~ in for an examination.* (b) enter a competition: *~ in for the hurdles.* (c) have an interest in, etc: *~ in for golf.*

go into sth, (a) enter: *~ into the Army/the Church/Parliament. When did Britain ~ into Europe,* join the EEC? (b) busy or occupy oneself with: *~ into (the) details/ particulars; ~ into the evidence. This problem will need a lot of ~ing into,* will need

thorough investigation. (c) (allow oneself to) pass into (a certain state): *~ into fits of laughter.*

go off, (a) explode; be fired: *The gun went off by accident.* (b) = go bad. ⇨ bad[1](4). (c) become unconscious, either in sleep or in a faint: *Hasn't the baby ~ne off yet?* (d) (of events) proceed well, etc: *The concert/performance went off well.* (e) (as a stage direction in a printed play) leave the stage: *Hamlet ~es off.* **go off sb/sth,** lose interest in any one's taste for: *Jane seems to have ~ne off Peter. I've ~ne off beer.* **go off one's head,** ⇨ head[1](20). **go off with sb/sth,** go away with: *He's ~ne off to Edinburgh with Paul/ with the college silver.*

go on, (a) (of time) pass: *As the months went on, he became impatient.* (b) behave, esp in a wrong, shameful or excited way: *If you ~ on like this you'll be expelled.* (c) happen; take place; be in progress: *What's ~ing on here?* (d) appear on the stage: *She doesn't ~ on until Act Two.* (e) take one's turn at doing something; (e g cricket) begin bowling: *The captain told Snow to ~ on next.* `**go on sth,** take or accept, e g as evidence: *What have we got to ~ on?* **go on about sth,** talk persistently and often irritatingly about: *I wish you'd stop ~ing on about your problems.* **go on (at sb),** nag; scold: *She ~es on at her husband terribly.* **be going on for,** be approaching: *He's ~ing on for seventy.* **go on to sth/to do sth,** do or say next: *Let's now ~ on to the next item on the agenda.* **go on (with sth/doing sth),** continue, persevere, with: *G~ on with your work. That's enough to be ~ing on with,* enough for our immediate needs.

go out, (a) leave the room, building, etc: *She was (all) dressed to ~ out. Out you ~!* (b) attend social functions, go to parties, dances, etc: *She still ~es out a great deal, even at seventy-five.* (c) be extinguished: *The fire/lights went out.* (d) become unfashionable: *Have mini-skirts ~ne out?* **go out to,** leave, e g one's own country, and go to: *He couldn't get work at home* (e g in England) *so went out to Australia.* **go out to sth,** (of the heart, feelings) be extended to: *Our hearts/sympathies ~ out to those poor children orphaned by war.* **go out with sb,** (informal) be regularly in a person's company: *How long has Jane been ~ing out with David? How long have Jane and David been ~ing out together?*

go over sth, (a) examine the details of: *We must ~ over the accounts carefully before we settle them.* (b) look at; inspect: *We should like to ~ over the house before deciding whether we want to buy it.* (c) rehearse; study or review carefully: *Let's ~ over this chapter/lesson/the main facts/ Scene 2 again.* Hence, '**going-'over** n (pl goings-over) (a) (informal) process of examining or putting in good working order:

The document will need a careful ~ing-over before we can make a decision. (b) (*sl*): *The thugs gave him a thorough ~ing-over,* struck him repeatedly. **go over to sb/sth,** change one's political party, side, a preference, etc: *He has ~ne over to the Democrats.*

go round, (a) be enough, in number or amount, for everyone to have a share: *There aren't enough apples/isn't enough whisky to ~ round.* (b) reach one's destination by using a route other than the usual or nearest way: *The main road to Worcester was flooded and we had to ~ (the long way) round.* **go round (to a place/to do sth):** *We're ~ing round to my mother's/to see my mother at the weekend.* **go round the bend,** (*informal*) become enraged, mad, etc.

go through, (a) (= get through) be passed or approved: *The Bill* (i e in Parliament) *did not ~ through.* (b) be concluded: *The deal did not ~ through.* **go through sth,** (a) discuss in detail: *Let's ~ through the arguments again.* (b) search: *The police went through his pockets.* (c) perform; take part in: *She made him ~ through both a civil and religious wedding.* (d) undergo; suffer: *If you only knew what she has to ~ through with that husband of hers!* (e) reach the end of; spend: *~ through a fortune/all one's money.* **go through with sth,** do it: *He's determined to ~ through with the marriage in spite of his parents' opposition.*

go to/towards sth, contribute to, be contributed to: *What qualities ~ to the making of a statesman? This money can ~ towards the motor-bike you're saving up for.*

go together, ⇨ go with.

go under, (a) sink. (b) (*fig*) fail; become bankrupt: *The firm will ~ under unless business improves.*

go up, (a) rise: *The temperature is ~ing up. Everything went up in the budget except pensions.* (b) be erected: *New office blocks are ~ing up everywhere.* (c) be destroyed by explosion or fire: *The whole building went up in flames.* (d) enter a university or travel to a town, esp the capital: *~ up to London/to town. When will you ~ up* (e g to Cambridge university)? **go up sth,** climb: *~ up a tree/ladder/wall/hill.* **go up the wall,** ⇨ wall.

go with sb/sth, (a) accompany: *I'll ~ with you.* or, *Let's ~ together.* (b) be a normal accompaniment of: *Five acres of land ~* (*together*) *with the house,* become the property of the buyers or are for the use of the tenant. (c) match; be fitting and suitable with: *These new curtains don't ~ well with your rugs,* don't suit them. or, *These curtains and rugs don't ~ together.*

go without (sth), endure the lack of: *There's no money for a holiday this year—we'll just have to ~ without.* **go without saying,** be understood without actually

being stated: *It ~es without saying that she's a good cook.*

go-between /ˈgəʊ bɪtwiːn/ *n* [C] person who makes arrangements for two persons who do not meet at first: *In some countries marriages are arranged by ~s.*

go² /gəʊ/ *n* [C] (*pl* goes /gəʊz/) (*informal*) **all the go,** very popular, fashionable: *Pop festivals were all the ~ last year.* **be full of go; have plenty of go,** be full of energy, enthusiasm. **be on the go,** be very busy, active: *She's been on the ~ all day.* **have a go (at sth),** make an attempt: *He had several ~es at the high jump before he succeeded in clearing it. The police warned the public not to have a ~ because the bank raiders were armed,* not to try to intercept, catch them. **at one go,** at one attempt: *He blew out all the candles on his birthday cake at one ~.*

goad /gəʊd/ *n* [C] **1** pointed stick for urging cattle on. **2** (*fig*) something urging a person to action. ◻ *vt* urge; incite: *~ him on; ~ him into stealing.*

goal /gəʊl/ *n* [C] **1** point marking the end of a race; (in games such as football) posts between which the ball is to be driven in order to score; point(s) made by doing this: *score/kick a ~; win by three ~s to one.* **2** (*fig*) object of efforts or ambition: *one's ~ in life.*

ˈgoal-keeper, player whose duty is to keep the ball out of the goal.

goat /gəʊt/ *n* [C] small horned animal: `*she-~* (or `*nanny-~*) being kept for its milk; `*he-~* (or `*billy-~*), male goat. ⇨ kid¹(1).

ˈgoat-herd, person who looks after a flock of goats.

ˈgoat-skin, skin of a goat.

gobble¹ /ˈgɒbl/ *vt,vi* eat fast, noisily and greedily: *~ up an ice-cream.*

gobble² /ˈgɒbl/ *vi* (of a male turkey) make the characteristic sound in the throat ◻ *n* [U] this sound.

gob-let /ˈgɒblət/ *n* [C] glass or pottery drinking-vessel with a stem and base and no handle.

gob-lin /ˈgɒblɪn/ *n* [C] mischievous demon; ugly evil spirit.

god /gɒd/ *n* [C] **1** being regarded or worshipped as having power over nature and control over human affairs; image in wood, stone, etc to represent such a being. **2** God, the Supreme Being, creator and ruler of the universe. **God willing,** if circumstances permit. **3** person greatly adored or admired; very influential person; something to which excessive attention is paid.

ˈgod-child, `god-daughter, `god-son, person for whom a godparent acts as sponsor at baptism.

ˈgod-father, `god-mother, `god-parent, person who undertakes, when a child is baptized, to take an active interest in its welfare.

ˈgod-fearing *adj* living a good life and sincerely religious.

`god-for-saken` adj (of places) dismal; wretched.

god-send, something (unexpected and) welcome because it is a great help in time of need.

god-dess /ˈgɒdɪs/ n [C] female god, esp in Greek and Latin mythology: *Venus, the ~ of love.*

god-less /ˈgɒdləs/ adj wicked; not having belief in God; not recognizing God.

god-like /ˈgɒdlaɪk/ adj like God or a god in some quality; suitable for a god.

god-ly /ˈgɒdlɪ/ adj (-ier, -iest) loving and obeying God; deeply religious.

god-li-ness n [U]

goggle /ˈgɒgl/ vi roll the eyes about (or *at* something): *He ~d at her in surprise.*

goggles /ˈgɒglz/ n pl large round glasses with special rims to protect the eyes from the wind, dust, etc (worn by motor-cyclists, etc).

go-ing /ˈgəʊɪŋ/ n ⇨ also go¹. **1** [U] condition of the ground, a road, a race-course, etc, for walking, riding, etc: *The ~ is hard over this mountain road.* **2** [U] method or speed of working or travelling: *For a car this old, 50 miles an hour is good ~.* **3** (usually pl) **comings and goings,** (literally or fig) arrivals and departures: *the comings and ~s in the corridors of power.* □ adj **the going rate,** the current price, value. **a going concern,** ⇨ concern²(2).

goitre (US = **goi-ter**) /ˈgɔɪtə(r)/ n [C] swelling of the thyroid gland (in the neck).

go-kart /ˈgəʊ kɑːt/ n [C] very small open racing-car with a petrol engine.

gold /gəʊld/ n [U] **1** precious yellow metal used for making coins, ornaments, jewellery, etc: *£500 in ~,* in gold coins; (used as an *adjective*) *a ~ watch/bracelet.* **2** money in large sums; wealth. **3** (fig) brilliant or precious things or qualities: *a heart of ~.* **4** (also used as an *adjective*) colour of the metal, yellow.

`gold-field,` area in which gold is found.

`gold-finch,` bright-coloured songbird with yellow feathers in the wings.

`gold-fish,` small red carp kept in bowls or ponds.

`gold-leaf,` gold beaten into thin sheets.

`gold-mine,` (a) place where gold is mined. (b) (fig) source of wealth, e g a shop that is very successful in making money.

`gold-smith,` smith who makes articles of gold.

`gold standard,` system by which the value of money is based on gold.

golden /ˈgəʊldən/ adj **1** of gold or like gold in value or colour: *~ hair.* **2** precious; excellent; important: *a ~ opportunity.*

`golden `handshake,` sum of money given to a high-ranking member of a company when he retires (in recognition of good work and loss of continuation of salary).

the `golden `rule,` any important rule of conduct.

golf /gɒlf/ n [U] game played by two or four persons with small, hard balls, driven with `golf-clubs` into a series of 9 or 18 holes on smooth greens²(3) over a stretch of land called a `golf-course` or `golf-links.` □ vi play golf.

golfer, person who plays golf.

golly /ˈgɒlɪ/ int (sl) used to express surprise.

-gon /-gən/ suffix angle, corner: *polygon.*

gon-dola /ˈgɒndələ/ n [C] long, flat-bottomed boat with high peaks at each end, used on canals in Venice.

gon-do-lier /ˌgɒndəˈlɪə(r)/ n [C] man who propels a gondola.

gone /gɒn/ pp of go¹.

goner /ˈgɒnə(r)/ US: `gɔn-/ n [C] (sl) person or thing in desperate straits, ruined or doomed.

gong /gɒŋ/ n [C] metal disc with a turned rim giving a resonant note when struck with a stick. □ vt strike a gong.

gon-or-rhea (also **-rhœa**) /ˌgɒnəˈrɪə/ n [U] contagious venereal disease which causes an inflammatory discharge from the genital organs.

good¹ /gʊd/ adj (better, best) **1** having the right or desired qualities; giving satisfaction: *a ~* (e g sharp) *knife; ~* (= fertile) *soil; a woman of ~ family,* of a family with high social position; well born. **2** beneficial; wholesome: *Milk is ~ for children. Exercise is ~ for you.* **3** efficient; competent; able to do satisfactorily what is required: *a ~ teacher/driver/worker; ~ at mathematics/ languages.* **4** pleasing; agreeable; advantageous: *~ news. It's ~ to be home again.* **be a good thing,** be something that one approves, enjoys: *Do you think lower taxes are a ~ thing?* **put in/say a good word for sb,** say something in his favour. **have a good time,** enjoy oneself. **(all) in good time,** at a suitable or advantageous time. **in good time,** early. **5** kind; benevolent; willing to help others: *It was ~ of you to help them. Will you be ~ enough to/ be so ~ as to come early? so far, so `good,* ⇨ far(2). **6** (in exclamations of surprise, shock, etc): *'G~ `God! 'G~ `Gracious! 'G~ `Heavens!* **7** thorough; sound; complete: *give her a ~ beating/scolding; find a ~ excuse.* **have a good mind (to do sth),** feel a strong desire to: *I've a ~ mind to report you to the police.* **8** strong; vigorous: *His eyesight is still ~.* **9** fresh; eatable: *Fish does not stay ~ in hot weather.* **10** reliable; safe; sure: *a car with ~ brakes.* **good for, (a)** safely to be trusted for (the amount stated): *His credit is ~ for £5 000.* **(b)** having the necessary strength, inclination, etc: *My car is ~ for another five years.* **(c)** valid: *The return half of the ticket is ~ for three months.* **11** (esp of a child) well behaved; not giving trouble. *Try to be a ~ boy.* **as**

good as gold, well-behaved. **12** morally excellent; virtuous: *live a ~ life*. **13** (used in forms of greeting and farewell): *G~ morning/afternoon/evening/night.* **14** considerable in number, quantity, etc: *a ~ deal of money; a ~ many people; a ~ few,* a considerable number. *We've come a ~ way,* quite a long way. **15** not less than; rather more than: *We waited for a ~ hour.* **16 as good as,** practically, almost: *He as ~ as said I was a liar,* suggested that I was a liar without actually using the word 'liar'. *My car is as ~ as new,* even though I've had it a year. **17 make good,** accomplish what one attempts; prosper: *He went to Canada, where he soon made ~.*

'**good-for-nothing** *adj, n* [C] worthless (person).

'**good 'humour,** cheerful mood; happy state of mind. Hence, '**good-'humoured** *adj*

'**good-'looking** *adj* beautiful, handsome.

'**good-'natured** *adj* kind; ready and willing to help others.

'**good 'sense,** soundness of judgement.

'**good-'tempered** *adj* not easily irritated or made angry.

good² /gʊd/ *n* [U] **1** that which is good; what is morally right, beneficial, advantageous, profitable, etc; what has use, worth, value: *It's no ~ (my) talking to him. Was his advice ever any ~? What ~ was it? This gadget isn't much ~.* **do good,** help (through charitable works, etc). **(do sth) for the good of,** in order to benefit: *He works for the ~ of the country. G~ and bad alike respected the parson.* **4** (*pl*) movable property; merchandise: *He buys and sells leather ~s.* **deliver the goods,** (*informal*) produce what is expected; fulfil a promise. **5** (*pl*) things carried by rail, etc (contrasted with passengers): *a ~s agent/station/train.*

good-bye /'gʊd'baɪ/ *int, n* [C] (saying of) farewell.

good-ish /'gʊdɪʃ/ *adj* rather large, extensive, etc: *It's a ~ walk from here,* quite a long way.

good-ness /'gʊdnəs/ *n* [U] **1** quality of being good; virtue: *~ of heart.* **have the goodness to,** be kind enough to: *Have the ~ to come this way, please.* **2** strength or essence: *meat with all the ~ boiled out.* **3** (in exclamations) used instead of *God!*: *G~ Gracious! G~ me! For ~' sake! Thank ~!*

goods /gʊdz/ *n pl* ⇨ good² (4,5).

good-will /'gʊd'wɪl/ *n* [U] **1** friendly feeling: *a policy of ~ in international relations.* **2** good relationship of a business with its customers: *The ~ is to be sold with the business.*

goody-goody /'gʊdɪ 'gʊdɪ/ *adj, n* [C] (*pl -ies*) (person who is) pretentiously virtuous.

goofy /'gʊfɪ/ *adj* (-ier, -iest) (*sl*) **1** having long, protruding top teeth. **2** silly.

goose /gus/ *n* (*pl* geese /gis/) **1** [C] water bird larger than a duck; female of this, ⇨ gander. **2** [U] its flesh as food. **3** [C] (*informal*) mildly foolish person.

'**goose-flesh,** rough bristling skin caused by cold or fear.

'**goose-step,** way of marching without bending the knees.

goose-berry /'gʊzbrɪ *US:* 'gusberɪ/ *n* [C] (*pl -ies*) (bush with a) green, hairy berry. **play gooseberry,** be present with two persons, e g lovers, who prefer to be alone.

gore /gɔ(r)/ *vt* pierce, wound, with the horns or tusks: *~d to death by a bull.*

gorge /gɔdʒ/ *n* [C] **1** narrow opening, usually with a stream, between hills or mountains. **2** gullet; contents of the stomach: *His ~ rose at the sight/It made his ~ rise,* He was disgusted. □ *vi,vt* eat greedily: *~ on rich food; ~ oneself with meat.*

gorg-eous /'gɔdʒəs/ *adj* **1** richly coloured; magnificent: *a ~ sunset.* **2** (*informal*) giving pleasure and satisfaction: *~ weather; a ~ dress.*

gorg-eous-ly *adv*

gor-illa /gə'rɪlə/ *n* [C] (*pl ~s*) man-sized, tree-climbing African ape.

gor-man-dize /'gɔməndaɪz/ *vi* (*formal*) eat, devour, greedily for pleasure.

gorse /gɔs/ *n* [U] evergreen shrub with sharp thorns and yellow flowers growing on waste land.

gory /'gɔrɪ/ *adj* (-ier, -iest) covered with blood.

gosh /gɒʃ/ *int* (*sl*) exclamation of surprise.

gos-ling /'gɒzlɪŋ/ *n* [C] young goose.

gos-pel /'gɒspəl/ *n* **1** G~, (the life and teachings of Jesus Christ as recorded in the) first four books of the New Testament; any one of these four books. **2** [C] thing that may be believed with confidence; principle or set of principles that one acts upon or believes in. *the ~ of health.*

'**Gospel 'oath,** oath sworn on the Gospels.

'**Gospel 'truth,** truth contained in the Gospels or as true as the Gospels.

gos-sa-mer /'gɒsəmə(r)/ *n* **1** [C,U] (thread of) fine silky substance of webs made by small spiders. **2** [U] soft, light, delicate material: *a ~ veil.*

gos-sip /'gɒsɪp/ *n* **1** [U] idle, often critical, talk about the affairs of other people: *Don't believe all the ~ you hear.* **2** [U] informal writing about persons and social happenings, e g in letters or in newspapers: (as an *adjective*) *the ~ column,* of a newspaper; *a ~ writer.* **3** [C] instance of gossip: *have a good ~ with a neighbour over the garden fence.* **4** [C] person who is fond of gossip(1): *She's* an old ~. □ *vi* (-pp-) talk or write gossip.

got *pt,pp* of get.

Gothic /ˈgɒθɪk/ *adj* 1 of the style of architecture common in Western Europe in the 12th to 16th centuries, characterized by pointed arches, clusters of columns, etc. 2 of the 18th century style of romantic literature: ~ *novels*. □ *n* [U] Gothic language or architecture.

got·ten *pp* (in US) of get.

gouache /gʊˈɒʃ/ *n* 1 [U] opaque watercolour paint. 2 [U] method of painting using this material. 3 [C] picture painted by this method.

gouge /gaʊdʒ/ *n* [C] tool with a sharp semicircular edge for cutting grooves in wood. □ *vt* cut, shape, force out (as) with a gouge: ~ *out a person's eye with one's thumb.*

gou·lash /ˈguːlæʃ/ *n* [C,U] (dish of) stew of steak and vegetables, seasoned with paprika.

gourd /gʊəd/ *n* [C] 1 (large, hard-skinned fleshy fruit of) kinds of climbing or trailing plant. 2 bottle or bowl consisting of the dried skin of this fruit.

gour·mand /ˈgʊəmənd/ *n* [C] lover of food.

gour·met /ˈgʊəmeɪ/ *n* [C] person who enjoys, and is expert in the choice of, delicate food, wines, etc.

gout /gaʊt/ *n* [U] disease causing painful swellings in joints, esp toes, knees and fingers.

gov·ern /ˈgʌvən/ *vt,vi* 1 rule (a country, etc). 2 control or direct the public affairs of (a city, country, etc). 3 control: ~ *one's temper*. 3 (usually passive) determine; influence: *be* ~*ed by the opinions of others*. 4 (*gram*) (esp of a *verb* or *preposition*) require, make necessary (a certain case or form of another word).

gov·ern·ing *adj* having the power or right to govern: *the* ~*ing body of a school/college, etc*.

gov·ern·ess /ˈgʌvənɪs/ *n* [C] woman who is employed to teach young children in a private family.

gov·ern·ment /ˈgʌvəmənt/ *n* 1 [U] governing; power to govern: *What the country needs is strong* ~. 2 [U] method or system of governing: *We prefer democratic* ~. 3 [C] ministry; body of persons governing a State: *The Prime Minister has formed a G*~, *has selected Ministers for the Cabinet*.

gov·ern·mental /ˈgʌvənˈmentəl/ *adj* connected with government.

gov·ernor /ˈgʌvənə(r)/ *n* [C] 1 person who governs a province or colony or (US) a State: *the G*~ *of New York State*. 2 member of the governing body of an institution (e g a school in England, a college, a hospital).

'governor-'general, (in the British Commonwealth) representative of the Crown, having no special powers: *the G*~*-General of Canada*.

gown /gaʊn/ *n* [C] 1 woman's dress, esp one for special occasions: *a* '*dressing*~'/

'*night*~. 2 loose, flowing robe worn by members of a university, judges, etc.

grab /græb/ *vt,vi* (-bb-) take roughly, selfishly or eagerly: *The dog* ~*bed the bone and ran off with it. He* ~*bed at the opportunity of going abroad*. □ *n* [C] 1 sudden snatch: *make a* ~ *at something*. 2 mechanical device for taking up and holding something to be lifted or moved. **up for grabs,** available for anyone to take, buy, etc: *the old house is up for grabs*.

grab·ber, person who grabs or whose chief aim in life appears to be making money.

grace /greɪs/ *n* 1 [U] quality of being pleasing, attractive or beautiful, esp in structure or movement: *She danced with* ~/*with a* ~ *that surprised us*. 2 (usu *pl*) pleasing accomplishment; elegance of manner. **airs and graces,** ways of speaking and behaving that are intended to impress and attract people. 3 [U] favour; goodwill. **give sb a week's, etc grace,** allow him an extra week, etc before requiring him to fulfil an obligation. 4 **do sth with a good/bad grace,** do it willingly/reluctantly. 5 short prayer of thanks before or after a meal: *say* (*a*) ~. 6 [U] God's mercy and favour towards mankind; influence and result of this. **in a state of grace,** being influenced by the strength and inspiring power of God; having received the Sacraments. **fall from grace,** fall to a lower moral state. 7 as a title, used when speaking of or to an archbishop, duke or duchess: *His/Her/Your G*~. □ *vt* add grace to; confer honour or dignity on; be an ornament to: *The occasion was* ~*d by the presence of the Queen*.

grace·ful /ˈgreɪsfʊl/ *adj* having or showing grace(1,4): *a* ~ *dancer; a* ~ *letter of thanks*.

grace·fully /-fəlɪ/ *adv*

grace·less /ˈgreɪsləs/ *adj* without grace(1,4); without a sense of what is right and proper: ~ *behaviour*.

grace·less·ly *adv*

gra·cious /ˈgreɪʃəs/ *adj* 1 (of persons and their behaviour) pleasant; kind; agreeable: *her* ~ *Majesty the Queen. It was* ~ *of her to come*. 2 (of God) merciful. 3 (in exclamations) expressing surprise: *Good(ness) G*~! **gra·cious·ly** *adv*

gra·cious·ness *n* [U]

gra·da·tion /grəˈdeɪʃən/ *n* 1 [C] step, stage, degree in development. 2 [U] gradual change from one thing to another or from one state to another.

grade[1] /greɪd/ *n* [C] 1 step, stage or degree in rank, quality, value, etc; number or class of things of the same kind: *The rank of major is one* ~ *higher than that of captain. This pupil has a high* ~ *of intelligence*. 2 (*US*) division of the school course; one year's work; pupils in such a division. 3 the mark, e g 80%, or rating, e g 'Excellent' or 'Fair', given to a pupil for his work in school. **make the grade,** (*informal*) reach a good standard; do as well as is required. **4** (*US*) = gradient.

grade[2] /greɪd/ *vt* **1** arrange in order in grade or class: ~*d by size.* **2** make land (esp for roads) more level by reducing the slope.

gradi·ent /ˈɡreɪdɪənt/ *n* [C] degree of slope.

grad·ual /ˈɡrædʒʊəl/ *adj* **1** taking place by degrees. **2** (of a slope) not steep.

grad·ually /-dʒʊlɪ/ *adv* by degrees.

grad·uate[1] /ˈɡrædʒʊət/ *n* [C] **1** (*GB*) person who holds a university degree, esp the first, or Bachelor's, degree: *London* ~*s; a* ~ *student; post-*~ *studies.* **2** (*US*) person who has completed a course at an educational institution: *high school* ~*s.*

grad·uate[2] /ˈɡrædʒʊət/ *vt, vi* **1** mark with degrees for measuring: *a ruler* ~*d in both inches and centimetres.* **2** arrange according to grade. **3** successfully complete an academic course.

gradu·ation /ˌɡrædʒʊˈeɪʃən/ *n* [C,U] **1** graduating or being graduated. **2** ceremony at which degrees are conferred.

graf·fiti /ɡrəˈfiːtɪ/ *n pl* (*It*) drawing, words, scratched or written on a hard surface, esp a wall.

graft[1] /ɡrɑːft *US:* ɡræft/ *n* [C] **1** shoot from a branch or twig of a living tree, fixed in another tree to form a new growth. **2** (in surgery) piece of skin, bone, etc from a living person or animal, transplanted on another body or another part of the same body. □ *vt, vi* put a graft in or on: ~ *one variety on/ upon/in/into another;* ~ *new skin.*

graft[2] /ɡrɑːft *US:* ɡræft/ *n* [C,U] (instance of) getting business advantages, profit-making, etc by taking wrong advantage of connections in politics, municipal business, etc. □ *vi* practise graft.

grain /ɡreɪn/ *n* **1** [U] (collective *sing*) small, hard seed of food plants such as wheat and rice: *a cargo of* ~. **2** [C] single seed of such a plant: *eat up every* ~ *of rice.* **3** [C] tiny, hard bit: ~*s of sand/sugar.* **4** (*fig*) small amount: *a boy without a* ~ *of intelligence.* **5** smallest unit of weight, 1/7 000 lb or 0·065 gr. **6** [U] natural arrangement or pattern of the lines of fibre in wood, etc as seen on a surface that has been sawn or cut: *woods of fine/coarse* ~. **be/go against the grain,** (*fig*) be undesirable, unpleasant.

gram /ɡræm/ ⇨ gramme.

-gram /-ɡræm/ *suffix* something written down or drawn: *telegram; diagram.*

gram·mar /ˈɡræmə(r)/ *n* [U] study or science of, rules for, the combination of words into sentences (*syntax*), and the forms of words (*morphology*).

gram·mar·ian /ɡrəˈmeərɪən/ *n* [C] expert in grammar.

gram·mati·cal /ɡrəˈmætɪkəl/ *adj* of, conforming to, the rules of grammar: *a* ~ *error.*

gram·mati·cally /-klɪ/ *adv*

gramme /ɡræm/ *n* (also **gram**) [C] metric unit of weight; weight of one cubic cen-

timetre of water at maximum density.

gramo·phone /ˈɡræməfəʊn/ *n* [C] (*dated*) = record-player.

gran·ary /ˈɡrænərɪ/ *n* [C] (*pl* -ies) **1** storehouse for grain. **2** region producing large amounts of grain.

grand /ɡrænd/ *adj* (-er, -est) **1** (in official titles) chief; most important: *G*~ *Master,* e g of some orders of knighthood; *a* ~ *master,* chess champion. **2** of most or greatest importance: *the* ~ *finale.* **3** magnificent; splendid: *living in* ~ *style.* **4** self-important; proud: *He puts on a very* ~ *manner/air.* **5** (*informal*) very fine or enjoyable: *We had a* ~ *time. What* ~ *weather!* **6** full; complete: *a* ~ *orchestra,* one with all kinds of instruments (not strings only); *the* ~ *total,* including everything. □ *n* [C] (*informal*) **1** a grand piano. **2** a thousand pounds or dollars.

'grand pi'ano, large piano with horizontal strings.

'Grand 'Prix /ˌɡrɒn ˈpriː/, (in motor-racing) one of several international races.

'grand·stand, rows of roofed seats for spectators at races, sports meetings, etc.

grand·ly *adv*

grand- *prefix* one generation more remote.

'grand-aunt/-uncle, aunt/uncle of either of one's parents.

'grand·child/-daughter/-son, daughter/son of one's son or daughter.

'grand-father/-mother/, father/mother of one's father or mother.

'grand-father('s) 'clock, clock worked by weights in a tall wooden case.

'grand-nephew/-niece, son/daughter of one's nephew or niece.

grandad, grand·dad /ˈɡrændæd/ *n* [C] (*informal*) grandfather.

gran·deur /ˈɡrændʒə(r)/ *n* [U] greatness; magnificence: *the* ~ *of the Swiss Alps; a man with delusions of* ~.

gran·di·ose /ˈɡrændɪəʊs/ *adj* planned on an impressive scale; imposing.

grand·ma /ˈɡrænmɑː/ *n* [C] (*informal*) grandmother.

grand·pa /ˈɡrænpɑː/ *n* [C] (*informal*) grandfather.

grange /ɡreɪndʒ/ *n* [C] country house with farm buildings attached.

gran·ite /ˈɡrænɪt/ *n* [U] hard, usually grey, stone used for building.

granny, grannie /ˈɡrænɪ/ *n* [C] (*informal*) grandmother.

grant /ɡrɑːnt *US:* ɡrænt/ *vt* **1** consent to give or allow (what is asked for): ~ *a favour/ request.* **2** agree (that something is true): *He's a nice person, I'll* ~ *you that.* **take sth for granted,** accept it as true or as certain without discussion. □ *n* [C] something granted, e g money from a government: ~*s towards the cost of a university education.*

granu·lar /ˈɡrænjʊlə(r)/ *adj* of or like grains.

granu·late /ˈɡrænjʊleɪt/ *vt, vi* form into

grains; roughen the surface of.

'granulated 'sugar, sugar in the form of small crystals.

gran·ule /ˈgrænjul/ n [C] small grain.

grape /greɪp/ n [C] green or purple berry growing in clusters on vines, used for making wine: a bunch of ~s.

'grape-vine n [C] (a) kind of vine on which grapes grow. (b) means by which news gets about, e g in an office, school or a group of friends: I heard on the ~-vine that Jill is to be promoted.

grape-fruit /ˈgreɪpfruːt/ n [C] (pl with or without -s) (usually yellow) fruit like a large orange but with an acid taste.

graph /græf/ n [C] diagram consisting of a line or lines showing the variation of two quantities, e g the temperature at each hour.

'graph paper, paper with small squares of equal size.

-graph /-græf US: græf/ suffix something written down: autograph.

-graphic /-ˈgræfɪk/: telegraphic.

-graphy /-grəfɪ/: calligraphy.

graphic /ˈgræfɪk/ adj 1 of visual symbols (e g lettering, diagrams, drawings): a ~ artist. 2 (of descriptions) giving a clear and easily understood image: a ~ account of the battle. □ n (pl) lettering, drawings, etc.

graphi·cally /-klɪ/ adv (a) by writing or diagrams. (b) vividly.

graph·ite /ˈgræfaɪt/ n [U] soft, black substance (a form of carbon) as used in making lead pencils.

grap·nel /ˈgræpnəl/ n [C] 1 anchor with many hooks. 2 instrument like this formerly used in sea battles for holding enemy ships.

grapple /ˈgræpəl/ vi 1 seize firmly; struggle with at close quarters: ~ with an enemy. 2 (fig) try to deal with (a problem, etc): grappling with staff problems.

'grappling-iron, grapnel.

grasp /grɑːsp US: græsp/ vt,vi 1 seize firmly with the hand(s) or arm(s): ~ sb's hand/a rope. 2 understand: ~ an argument/her meaning. 3 grasp at, try to seize; accept eagerly: ~ at an opportunity. □ n [C] (usually sing) firm hold or grip; (power of) grasping: in the ~ of a wicked enemy; have a thorough ~ of the problem; a problem within/beyond my ~, that I can/cannot understand.

grasp·ing adj greedy (for money, etc): a ~ing rascal.

grass /grɑːs US: græs/ n 1 [U] kinds of common, wild, low-growing, green plant. 2 [C] (with pl ~es) any species of this plant (including, in botanical use, cereals, reeds and bamboos). 3 [U] grazing land; pasture.

'grass-land, area of land covered with grass where there are few trees.

'grass-'roots n pl (often used as an adjective) ordinary people remote from political decisions, but who are affected by these decisions: a ~roots rebellion.

'grass 'widow, wife whose husband is temporarily not living with her.

grassy adj (-ier, -iest) covered with grass.

grass-hopper /ˈgrɑːshɒpə(r) US: ˈgræs-/ n [C] jumping insect which makes a shrill, chirping noise.

grate¹ /greɪt/ n [C] (metal frame for holding coal, etc in a) fireplace.

grate² /greɪt/ vt,vi 1 rub into small pieces, usually against a rough surface; rub small bits off: ~ cheese. 2 make a harsh noise by rubbing: The gate ~s on its hinges. 3 (fig) have an irritating effect (on a person, his nerves): His bad manners ~d on everyone. □ n [C] (usually sing) harsh noise made by rubbing: the ~ of a door on its hinges.

grater, device with a rough surface for grating food, etc.

grat·ing·ly adv

grate·ful /ˈgreɪtfəl/ adj feeling or showing thanks: We are ~ to you for your help.

grate·fully /-fəlɪ/ adv

grat·ify /ˈgrætɪfaɪ/ vt (pt,pp -ied) 1 give pleasure or satisfaction to: It's gratifying to know that you have been successful. 2 give what is desired to: ~ a child's curiosity.

grat·ify·ing adj pleasing: It is very ~ing to learn that.

grati·fi·ca·tion /ˌgrætɪfɪˈkeɪʃən/ n [C,U]

grat·ing /ˈgreɪtɪŋ/ n [C] framework of wooden or metal bars, either parallel or crossing one another, placed across an opening, e g a window, to keep out burglars or to allow air to flow through.

gra·tis /ˈgrætɪs/ adv, adj free of charge: be admitted ~.

grati·tude /ˈgrætɪtjuːd US: -tud/ n [U] being grateful: We showed our ~ for his help by buying him a present.

gra·tu·itous /grəˈtjuːɪtəs US: -ˈtuː-/ adj 1 given, obtained or done, without payment: ~ service/information/help/advice. 2 done or given, acting, without good reason: a ~ insult.

gra·tu·itous·ly adv

gra·tu·ity /grəˈtjuːɪtɪ US: -ˈtuː-/ n [C] (pl -ies) 1 gift (of money in addition to pay or pension) to a retiring employee for services. 2 money given to a member of the armed forces at the end of his period of service. 3 tip (for service).

grave¹ /greɪv/ adj (-r, -st) serious; requiring careful consideration: ~ news.

grave·ly adv

grave² /greɪv/ n [C] hole dug in the ground for a corpse; the mound of earth or the monument over it. have one foot in the grave, be nearing death, be very old.

'grave-stone, stone over a grave, with the name, etc of the person buried there.

'grave-yard burial ground; cemetery.

grave³ /grɑːv/ n [C] (also ~ accent) mark (`) placed over a vowel to indicate how it is to be sounded (as in French mère).

graven /ˈgreɪvən/ adj carved: a ~ image, an

idol.

gravel /ˈgrævəl/ n [U] small stones with coarse sand, as used for roads and paths. □ vt (-ll-, US also -l-) cover with gravel.

grav·ing dock /ˈgreɪvɪŋ dok/ n [C] dry dock in which the outside of a ship's hull may be cleaned.

gravi·tate /ˈgrævɪteɪt/ vi move or be attracted: ~ towards the cities.

gravi·ta·tion /ˌgrævɪˈteɪʃən/ n [U] (a) process of gravitating. (b) gravity(1).

grav·ity /ˈgrævətɪ/ n [U] 1 force of attraction between any two objects, esp that force which attracts objects towards the centre of the earth. 2 weight: centre of ~. 3 quality of being serious or solemn: the ~ of the international situation.

gravy /ˈgreɪvɪ/ n [U] juice which comes from meat while it is cooking; sauce made from this.

`gravy-boat, vessel in which gravy is served at table.

gray /greɪ/ adj, n ⇨ grey.

graze[1] /greɪz/ vi, vt 1 (of cattle, sheep, etc) eat growing grass: cattle grazing in the fields. 2 put (cattle, etc) in fields to graze.

graze[2] /greɪz/ vt, vi touch or scrape lightly in passing; rub the skin from: The bullet ~d his cheek; the boy ~d his knees when he fell. □ n [C] place where the skin is grazed.

grease /griːs/ n [U] 1 animal fat, esp when soft. 2 any thick, semi-solid oily substance. □ vt put or rub grease on or in (esp parts of a machine). grease sb's palm, bribe him.

`grease-gun, device for forcing grease into the parts of an engine, machine, etc.

`grease-paint n [U] make-up used by actors.

greasy /ˈgriːsɪ/ adj (-ier, -iest) covered with grease; slippery: ~ fingers; a ~ road.

greas·ily /-əlɪ/ adv

greasi·ness n [U]

great /greɪt/ adj (-er, -est) 1 well above the average in size, quantity or degree: take ~ care of; a ~ friend of mine, one for whom I feel more than ordinary friendship; a ~ work of art. 2 of remarkable ability or character: ~ men; a ~ painter/musician. 3 important; noted; of high rank or position: a ~ occasion; Alexander the G~. 4 (informal) implying surprise, indignation, contempt, etc according to context: Take your ~ big head out of my light! 5 the larger of two. 6 (used with words showing quantity, etc): a ~ deal, very much; a ~ number. 7 (informal) splendid: We had a ~ time in Paris. great at, clever or skilful at.

Great Bear, a constellation.

Great ˈBritain, England, Wales and Scotland, excluding Northern Ireland.

Great ˈLakes, series of five large lakes in N America along the boundary between Canada and the US.

the Great War, that of 1914—18.

great·ly adv much; by much: ~ly amused.

great·ness n [U]

great- /greɪt/ prefix showing one more generation remote than grand-: ˈ~-ˈgrandfather, one's mother's or father's grandfather; ˈ~-ˈ~-ˈgrandfather, one's grandmother's or grandfather's grandfather.

greaves /griːvz/ n pl pieces of armour to protect the shins.

grebe /griːb/ n [C] kinds of diving bird.

Gre·cian /ˈgriːʃən/ adj (eg of architecture, pottery, culture and features of the face) Greek.

greed /griːd/ n [U] strong desire for more food, wealth, etc, esp for more than is right or reasonable.

greedy /ˈgriːdɪ/ adj (-ier, -iest) filled with greed: I'm not hungry, just ~. He's ~ for gain/honours.

greed·ily /-əlɪ/ adv

greedi·ness n [U]

Greek /griːk/ n member of the Greek race, either of ancient Greece or modern Greece; the Greek language. be Greek to sb, be beyond his understanding. □ adj of Greece, its people, or the Greek language.

green[1] /griːn/ adj (-er, -est) 1 of the colour between blue and yellow, the colour of growing grass. 2 (of fruit) not yet ripe: ~ apples; (of wood) not yet dry enough for use: G~ wood does not burn well. 3 (a) inexperienced; untrained: a boy who is still ~ at his job. (b) gullible, easily deceived: I'm not so ~ as to believe that. 4 (fig) flourishing; full of vigour: keep a person's memory ~, not allow it to fade. 5 (of the complexion) pale; sickly looking. green with envy, jealous.

'green `belt, wide area of land round a town, where building is controlled (by town-planning) so that there are fields, woods, etc.

`green fingers, (informal) skill in gardening.

`green-fly, kinds of small insect.

`green-gage /-geɪdʒ/, kind of plum with greenish-yellow skin and flesh.

`green-grocer, shopkeeper selling vegetables and fruit.

`green-grocery, business of, things sold by, a greengrocer.

`green-house, building with sides and roof of glass, used for growing plants that need protection from the weather.

'green `light, give sb/get the green light, permission to go ahead with a project, etc.

`green room, room in a theatre for actors and actresses when they are not on the stage.

`green-stuffs, vegetables.

`green `tea, tea made from steam-dried leaves.

`green-wood, woodlands, esp in summer; forest in full leaf, esp as the home of outlaws in olden times.

green[2] /griːn/ n 1 [C,U] green colour: a girl dressed in ~; a picture in ~s and blues. 2

(*pl*) green leaf vegetables, e g cabbage, before or after cooking. **3** area of land with growing grass. **(a)** public or common land: *the village* ~. **(b)** for the game of bowls: *a `bowling-*~. **(c)** surrounding a hole on a golf course: *a `putting* ~.

green·ery /ˈgriːnəri/ *n* [U] green foliage: *the* ~ *of the woods in spring.*

green·ish /ˈgriːnɪʃ/ *adj* somewhat green: (used in compounds) '~*-`yellow.*

Green·wich /ˈgrenɪtʃ/ *n* suburb of London east and west of which longitude is measured.

Greenwich (Mean) Time, (abbr **GMT**), mean² time for the meridian of Greenwich, used as a basis for calculating time in most parts of the world (now called *Universal time*).

greet /griːt/ *vt* **1** welcome; express one's feelings on receiving (news, etc); write (in a letter) words expressing respect, friendship, etc: ~ *a friend by saying 'Good morning!';* ~ *someone with a smile.* **2** (*formal*) (of sights and sounds) meet the eyes and ears: *the view that* ~*ed us at the hill-top.*

greet·ing, first words or act used on seeing a person or in writing to a person; this expression or act: *'Good morning' and 'Dear Sir' are* ~*ings; a '*~*ings telegram,* one sent with, e g birthday greetings.

greg·ari·ous /grɪˈgeərɪəs/ *adj* **1** living in groups or societies. **2** liking the company of others.

greg·ari·ous·ly *adv*

greg·ari·ous·ness *n* [U]

Greg·or·ian /grɪˈgɔːrɪən/ *adj* of the kind of church music named after Pope Gregory I (540—604): ~ *chant.*

Gregorian `calendar, the calendar introduced by Pope Gregory XIII (1502—85), with the days and months arranged as now.

grem·lin /ˈgremlɪn/ *n* [C] goblin said to trouble airmen during World War II (by causing mechanical trouble).

gre·nade /grɪˈneɪd/ *n* [C] small bomb thrown by hand.

grena·dier /ˌgrenəˈdɪə(r)/ *n* [C] **1** (formerly) soldier who threw grenades. **2** soldier in *the* G~*s, the* G~ *Guards,* British infantry regiment.

grew /gruː/ *pt* of grow.

grey, (also **gray**) /greɪ/ *adj* (-er, -est) between black and white, coloured like ashes: *His hair has turned* ~. □ *n* grey colour: *dressed in* ~, grey clothes. □ *vt, vi* make or become grey.

`grey matter, (a) nervous tissue of the brain. **(b)** intellect.

grey·hound /ˈgreɪhaʊnd/ *n* [C] slender, long-legged dog, able to run fast, used in chasing live hares and in racing.

grey·ish /ˈgreɪɪʃ/ *adj* somewhat grey.

grid /grɪd/ *n* [C] **1** system of overhead cables carried on pylons, for distributing electric current over a large area. **2** network of

squares on maps, numbered for reference. **3** grating: *a `cattle* ~, one placed on the ground at a gate, etc to prevent cattle from straying.

griddle /ˈgrɪdəl/ *n* [C] circular iron plate used for cooking cakes.

grid·iron /ˈgrɪdaɪən/ *n* [C] **1** framework of metal bars used for cooking meat or fish over a clear fire. **2** field for American football.

grief /griːf/ *n* **1** [U] deep or violent sorrow: *die of* ~. **2** [C] something causing grief: *His failure was a great* ~ *to his parents.* **3** *bring sb/come to grief,* cause a person to/meet with misfortune, injury or ruin.

griev·ance /ˈgriːvəns/ *n* [C] real or imagined cause for complaint or protest (*against*).

grieve /griːv/ *vt, vi* cause grief to; feel grief: ~ *for the dead/over his death.*

griev·ous /ˈgriːvəs/ *adj* **1** causing grief or suffering: *a* ~ *railway accident;* ~ *wrongs.* **2** severe: ~ *pain.*

griev·ous·ly *adv*

grif·fin /ˈgrɪfɪn/ (also **grif·fon, gry·phon** /ˈgrɪfən/) *n* (in Greek myth) creature with the head and wings of an eagle and a lion's body.

grill /grɪl/ *n* [C] **1** = grating; grille; gridiron. **2** dish of meat, etc cooked directly over or under great heat. □ *vt, vi* **1** cook, be cooked, under or over great heat. **2** (*fig*) expose oneself to great heat: *lie* ~*ing in the hot sun.* **3** (e g of the police) question relentlessly and severely.

grille /grɪl/ *n* [C] **1** screen of parallel bars used to close an open space, e g in a convent. **2** similar screen over a counter, e g in a post office or bank as a protection.

grim /grɪm/ *adj* (-mer, -mest) stern; severe; without mercy: *a* ~ *struggle; a* ~ *smile/expression. hold on like grim death,* very firmly.

grim·ly *adv*

grim·ness *n* [U]

gri·mace /grɪˈmeɪs US: ˈgrɪmɪs/ *n* [C] ugly, twisted expression of pain, disgust, etc or intended to cause laughter: *Only rude children make* ~*s.* □ *vi* make grimaces.

grime /graɪm/ *n* [U] dirt, esp a coating on the surface of something or on the body: *a face covered with* ~ *and sweat.* □ *vt* make dirty with grime: ~*d with dust.*

grimy /ˈgraɪmɪ/ *adj* (-ier, -iest) covered with grime.

grin /grɪn/ *vi, vt* (-nn-) **1** smile broadly so as to show the teeth, expressing amusement, foolish satisfaction, contempt, etc: ~*ning with delight;* ~ *from ear to ear. grin and bear it,* endure pain, disappointment, etc, uncomplainingly. **2** express by grinning: *He* ~*ned his approval.* □ *n* [C] act of grinning.

grind /graɪnd/ *vt, vi* (*pt, pp* **ground** /graʊnd/) **1** crush to grains or powder between millstones, the teeth, etc: ~ *coffee beans;* ~ *corn into flour.* **2** be capable of grinding: *This wheat* ~*s well.* **3** (*fig*) oppress or crush: *people who were ground (down) by poverty.* 4 polish, shape or sharpen by rubbing on or with a rough, hard surface: ∼ *a knife/lens.* 5 rub harshly together, esp with a circular motion: ∼ *one's teeth (together);* ∼ *one's heel into the ground.* 6 work by turning; produce by turning: ∼ *a barrel-organ.* **grind to a halt,** (a) (of a vehicle) stop noisily. (b) (*fig*) (of a process) stop slowly: *The strikes brought industry* ∼*ing to a halt.* 7 (cause to) work or study hard and long: ∼ *away at one's studies.* □ *n* 1 [C] act, noise of grinding. 2 [U] (*informal*) long, monotonous task: *Do you find learning English a* ∼?

grinder /ˈgraɪndə(r)/ *n* [C] thing or person that grinds, e g an apparatus for grinding coffee: *a* `*coffee-*∼; *an* `*organ-*∼, person who produces tunes by turning the handle of a barrel-organ.

grind·stone /ˈgraɪndstəʊn/ *n* [C] stone shaped like a wheel, turned on an axle, used for sharpening tools. **keep sb's nose to the grindstone,** force him to work hard without rest.

grip /grɪp/ *vt,vi* (-pp-) 1 take and keep a firm hold of; seize firmly: *The frightened child* ∼*ped its mother's hand. The brakes failed to* ∼ *and the car ran into a wall.* 2 hold the attention of: *The speaker* ∼*ped the attention of his audience. The film is a* ∼*ping story of love and hate.* □ *n* 1 (*sing* only except as shown) act, manner, or power of gripping: *let go one's* ∼ *of a rope; have a good* ∼ (*fig* = understanding) *of a problem; have a good* ∼ *on an audience,* hold their attention and interest. **be at/come/get to grips with,** be attacking, begin to attack: *get to* ∼*s with a problem.* 2 [C] (in a machine, etc) part that grips or clips. 3 [C] small bag for travelling: *a leather* ∼.

gripes /graɪps/ *n pl* **the** ∼, (*informal*) violent pains in the abdomen.

gris·ly /ˈgrɪzlɪ/ *adj* causing horror or terror.

gristle /ˈgrɪsəl/ *n* [U] tough, elastic tissue in animal bodies, esp in meat.

grit /grɪt/ *n* [U] 1 (collective *sing*) tiny, hard bits of stone, sand, etc: *spread* ∼ *on icy roads.* 2 quality of courage and endurance: *have plenty of* ∼. □ *vt* (-tt-) spread grit on, ∼ *the road when it snows.* **grit one's teeth,** keep the jaws tight together.
gritty *adj* (-ier, -iest)

grizzle /ˈgrɪzəl/ *vi* (*informal*) (esp of children) cry irritably.

groan /grəʊn/ *vi,vt* 1 make a deep sound forced out by pain, or expressing despair or distress: *The wounded men lay there* ∼*ing. The teacher* ∼*ed with dismay.* 2 (of things) make a noise like that of groaning: *The ship's timbers* ∼*ed during the storm.* 3 express with groaning: *He* ∼*ed out a sad story.* □ *n* [C] deep sound of groaning: ∼*s of disapproval.*

grocer /ˈgrəʊsə(r)/ *n* [C] shopkeeper who

sells food in packets, tins and bottles, and household requirements such as polish, soap-powders, etc.

grocery /*n* (*pl* -ies) (a) [U] grocer's trade: *a* `∼*y business.* (b) (*pl*) things sold by a grocer.

groggy /ˈgrɒgɪ/ *adj* (-ier, -iest) unsteady; likely to collapse or fall: *You look rather* ∼.

groin /grɔɪn/ *n* [C] 1 part of the body at the top of the thigh. 2 curved edge where two vaults meet (in a roof). □ *vt* build with groins.

groom /grum/ *n* [C] 1 person in charge of horses. 2 = bridegroom. □ *vt* 1 feed, brush and in other ways look after (horses). 2 (of apes, monkeys) clean the fur and skin of: *a female ape* ∼*ing her mate.* 3 (in the *pp*) (of persons): *well/badly* ∼*ed,* looking clean and smart, with the hair tidy. 4 (*informal*) prepare (for a career, etc).

groove /gruv/ *n* [C] 1 long, hollow channel in the surface of hard material, esp one made to guide the motion of something that slides along it, e g a sliding door or window. 2 spiral cut on a gramophone record (in which the needle or stylus moves). 3 way of living that has become a habit. **get into/be stuck in a groove,** become set in one's ways. □ *vt* make grooves in: *a* ∼*d shelf.*
groovy *adj* (*sl*) up-to-date (esp of young people): *groovy clothes/people.*

grope /grəʊp/ *vi,vt* feel about, search, as one does in the dark: *He* ∼*d for the door-handle.*

gross¹ /grəʊs/ *n* [C] (*pl* unchanged) twelve dozen; 144

gross² /grəʊs/ *adj* 1 vulgar; coarse in mind or morals: ∼ *morals.* 2 (of the senses) heavy and dull. 3 glaring; clearly seen: ∼ *injustice/negligence.* 4 (of vegetation) luxuriant: *the* ∼ *vegetation of the tropical rain-forest.* 5 (of persons) extremely fat. 6 (opposite of *net*) total, whole: *his* ∼ *income;* ∼ *profit.* □ *vt* make or earn as a total amount: *His last film* ∼*ed five million pounds.*
gross·ly *adv*
gross·ness *n* [U]

gro·tesque /grəʊˈtesk/ *adj* 1 absurd; laughable because strange and incongruous: *a* ∼ *appearance;* ∼ *manners.* 2 (in art) combining human, animal and plant forms in a fantastic way; made up of comically distorted figures and designs. □ *n* [C] grotesque person, animal, style or design.
gro·tesque·ly *adv*

grotto /ˈgrɒtəʊ/ *n* (*pl* ∼es, ∼s) cave, esp one made artificially as a garden shelter.

grotty /ˈgrɒtɪ/ *adj* (*sl*) (-ier, -iest) dirty; useless; bad.

grouch /graʊtʃ/ *vi* (*informal*) complain. □ *n* [C] fit of ill temper.

ground¹ /graʊnd/ *n* 1 (*sing* with *the*) solid surface of the earth: *lie on/sit on/fall to the* ∼. **get off the ground,** (a) (of an aircraft) rise into the air. (b) (*fig*) (of an undertaking or scheme) pass from the planning stage and make a start. *above ground,* alive. *below ground,* dead and buried. **2** [U] position, area or distance on the earth's surface. *cover (much, etc) ground,* (a) travel: *We've covered a great deal of ~ today,* have come a long way. (b) *(fig)* (of a lecture, report, inquiry, etc) deal with a variety of subjects: *The committee's report covers much new ~,* deals with many new matters. *gain ground,* (a) make progress. (b) win a success or an advantage. *give/lose ground,* fail to keep one's position or advantage. *hold/stand/keep one's ground,* stand firm; not yield; maintain one's claim, intention, argument, etc. *common ground,* subject on which two or more persons or parties are in agreement or on which they have similar views. **3** [U] soil; earth: *The frost has made the ~ hard.* **4** [C] area or piece of land for a special purpose or a particular use: *a `football/ `cricket/`sports ~; a pa`rade/`recre`ation ~; a `play~.* **5** (always *pl*) land, gardens, round a building, often enclosed with walls, hedges or fences: *the Palace ~s.* **6** (*pl*) particles of solid matter that sink to the bottom of a liquid: *`coffee~s.* **7** (*pl* or [U]) reason(s) for saying, doing or believing something: *On what ~s do you suspect him? be/have/give grounds for,* be, have, give a cause or reason for: *I have good ~s for believing him. What are the ~s for the divorce?* **8** [C] surface on which a design is painted, printed, cut, etc: *a design on a white ~.*

`ground-nut,` kind of pea with pods ripening under the ground (also called *peanut*).

`ground-sheet,` waterproof sheet spread on the ground, e g in a tent.

'ground `floor, the floor of a building level with the ground.

`ground rule, basic principle.

`ground-work, (usually *fig*) foundation; basis.

ground² /graʊnd/ *vt,vi* **1** (of a ship) (cause to) touch the sea bottom. **2** (of aircraft, airmen) compel to stay on the ground: *All aircraft at London Airport were ~ed by fog yesterday.* **3** base (the more usual word) on a belief, etc) on: *a well-~ed theory.* **4** give good teaching or basic training in: *The teacher ~ed his pupils in arithmetic.*

ground³ /graʊnd/ *pt,pp* of grind.

ground-ing, thorough teaching of the elements of a subject: *a good ~ing in grammar.*

ground-less /ˈgraʊndləs/ *adj* without foundation or good reason: *~ fears.* ⇨ ground¹(7).

group /gruːp/ *n* [C] number of persons or things gathered or placed together, or naturally associated; number of jointly-controlled business companies: *a ~ of islands/trees/houses/girls; the Germanic ~ of languages.* □ *vt,vi* form into, gather in, a

group or groups.

grouse¹ /graʊs/ *n* [C] (*pl* unchanged) (sorts of) bird with feathered feet, shot for sport and food.

grouse² /graʊs/ *vi* (*informal*) grumble; complain. □ *n* [C] complaint.

grove /grəʊv/ *n* [C] group of trees; small wood.

grov-el /ˈgrɒvəl/ *vi* (-ll-; *US* also -l-) **1** lie down on one's face, crawl, in fear, (as if) begging for mercy. **2** (*fig*) humble oneself; behave in a way that shows one has no self-respect.

grov-el-ler, person who grovels.

grow /grəʊ/ *vi,vt* (*pt* grew /gruː/, *pp* ~n /grəʊn/) **1** develop; increase in size, height, length, etc: *Rice ~s in warm climates. How tall you've ~n! grow out of,* (a) become too big for: *~ out of one's clothes.* (b) become too old for; cease to practise: *He has ~n out of playing with toys.* (c) have as a source: *His troubles grew out of his bad temper. grow up,* (a) (of persons, animals) become adult or mature: *When the boys ~ up,....* (b) develop: *A warm friendship grew up between them.* **2** become: *~ older. It began to ~ dark.* **3** *grow to be/like, etc,* reach the point or stage where one is/likes, etc: *He grew to like his mother-in-law.* **4** cause or allow to grow: *~ roses. He's ~ing a beard.* **5** *grow on,* (a) become more deeply rooted: *a habit that ~s on you.* (b) become more attractive to: *a book/a piece of music that ~s on you.*

`grown-up, adult person (contrasted with children).

grower, (a) person who grows things: *a `fruit-~er; `rose-~ers.* (b) plant, etc that grows in a certain way: *a fast ~er.*

growl /graʊl/ *vi,vt* **1** (of animals, men, thunder) make a low, threatening sound: *The dog ~ed at me. We heard thunder ~ing in the distance.* **2** say in a growling manner: *He ~ed (out) his answer.* □ *n* [C] low threatening sound; angry complaint.

growl-ing-ly *adv*

grown /grəʊn/ *pp* of grow: *a ~ man,* a mature man.

growth /grəʊθ/ *n* **1** [U] growing; development; process of growing: *the rapid ~ of our economy.* **2** [U] cultivation: *apples of foreign ~,* grown abroad. **3** [C] something that grows or has grown: *a three-days' ~ of beard.* **4** [C] diseased formation in the body, e g a cancer.

grub¹ /grʌb/ *n* **1** [C] larva of insect. **2** [U] (*sl*) food.

grub² /grʌb/ *vt,vi* (-bb-) turn over the soil, esp in order to get something: *~bing about among the bushes.*

grubby /ˈgrʌbɪ/ *adj* (-ier, -iest) **1** dirty; unwashed. **2** having grubs in it.

grudge /grʌdʒ/ *vt* be unwilling to give or allow: *I don't ~ him his success.* □ *n* [C] feeling of ill-will, resentment, envy or spite:

I bear him no ~. *He has a* ~ *against me.*

grudg·ing·ly *adv*

gruel /ˈgruəl/ *n* [U] liquid food of oatmeal, etc boiled in milk or water.

gruel·ling, (*US* **gruel·ing**) *adj* severe; exhausting: *a* ~*ling race.*

grue·some /ˈgrusəm/ *adj* horrible, repulsive.

grue·some·ly *adv*

gruff /grʌf/ *adj* (of a person, his voice, behaviour) rough and abrupt.

gruff·ly *adv*

grumble /ˈgrʌmbəl/ *vi,vt* **1** complain or protest, say, in a bad-tempered way: *He's always grumbling. He* ~*d (out) a reply.* **2** make a low, growling sound: *hear thunder grumbling in the distance.* □ *n* [C] complaint or protest: *That fellow is full of* ~*s.*

grum·bler, person who grumbles.

grumpy /ˈgrʌmpɪ/ *adj* (-ier, -iest) bad-tempered.

grump·ily *adv*

grumpi·ness *n* [U]

grunt /grʌnt/ *vi,vt* **1** (of animals, esp pigs) make a low, rough sound. **2** (of persons) make a similar sound expressing disagreement, boredom, irritation, etc: ~ *one's approval.* □ *n* [C] low, rough sound.

gry·phon /ˈgrɪfən/ *n* = griffin.

guar·an·tee[1] /ˌgærənˈti/ *n* [C] **1** (*legal* = **guaranty**) promise or undertaking that certain conditions agreed to in a transaction will be fulfilled: *under* ~; *a watch with a year's* ~. **2** (*legal* = **guaranty**) undertaking given by one person to another that he will be responsible for something e g payment of a debt, by a third person. **3** (*legal* = **guarantor**) person who gives such an undertaking: *be* ~ *for a friend's good behaviour.* **4** (*legal* = **guaranty**) something offered, as security for the fulfilling of conditions in a guarantee(1,2): *'What* ~ *can you offer?'* **5** (*informal*) something that seems to make an occurrence likely: *Blue skies are not always a* ~ *of fine weather.*

guar·an·tee[2] /ˌgærənˈti/ *vt* **1** give a guarantee(1,2,3) for: ~ *a man's debts;* ~ *to pay a man's debts. We can't* ~ *our workers regular employment.* **2** (*informal*) promise (without legal obligation): *Many shopkeepers* ~ *satisfaction to customers.*

guar·an·tor /ˈgærənˌtɔ(r)/ *n* ⇨ guarantee[1](3).

guar·an·ty /ˈgærəntɪ/ *n* ⇨ guarantee[1](1,2,4).

guard[1] /gɑd/ *n* **1** [U] state of alertness or watchfulness against attack, danger or surprise: *The sentry/soldier is on* ~*/was ordered to keep* ~. **2** [U] position of readiness to defend oneself, e g in fencing, boxing. **3** [C] soldier or party of soldiers keeping guard; sentry. **4** (*GB*) official in charge of a railway train (and formerly a stage-coach). **5** (*pl*) (in GB and some other countries) troops employed to protect the sovereign: *the G*~*s;* *the Royal Horse G*~*s.* **6** [C] body of soldiers with the duty of protecting, honouring or escorting a person: *The Duke, on his arrival, inspected the* ~ *of honour at the station.* **7** person (also called *warder*) or body of people in charge of a prison. **8** (esp in compounds) (part of) an article or apparatus designed to prevent injury or loss: *a* ˈfire-~, in front of a fireplace; *a* ˈmud-~, over the wheel of a bicycle, etc. **9** part of a sword that protects the hand.

ˈguard·house, building for a military guard or one in which soldiers who are prisoners are kept.

ˈguard·room, room for soldiers on guard.

ˈguards·man, soldier of the Guards.

guard[2] /gɑd/ *vt,vi* **1** protect; keep from danger: ~ *a camp;* ~ *one's life/one's reputation.* **2** watch over (sb) to prevent escape: ~ *prisoners.* **3** use care and caution to prevent: ~ *against disease.*

guarded *adj* (of statements, etc) cautious: *a* ~*ed answer.*

guard·ian /ˈgɑdɪən/ *n* [C] (official or private) person who guards, esp (legal use) one who is responsible for the care of a young or incapable person and his property.

ˈguardian ˈangel, spirit watching over a person or place.

guard·ian·ship /-ʃɪp/, position of a guardian.

guava /ˈgwɑvə/ *n* [C] (tropical tree with) acid fruit used for making jelly.

guer·rilla, guer·illa /gəˈrɪlə/ *n* [C] (*pl* ~s) man engaged in a guerrilla war.

guerˈrilla ˈwar, fighting by small groups of civilians, usually for a political cause.

guess /ges/ *vt,vi* form an opinion, give an answer, make a statement, based on supposition, not on careful thought, calculation or definite knowledge: *Can you* ~ *my weight/ what my weight is/how much I weigh?* □ *n* [C] opinion formed by guessing: *make/have a* ~ *at who took the money.*

ˈguess·work, (result of) guessing.

guest /gest/ *n* [C] person staying at or paying a visit to another's house or being entertained at a meal: *We're having* ~*s to dinner.*

ˈguest·room, bedroom kept for guests.

ˈguest·house, superior boarding-house.

guf·faw /gəˈfɔ/ *vi, n* [C] (give a) noisy laugh.

guid·ance /ˈgaɪdəns/ *n* [U] (a) act of guiding; leadership. (b) advice, counsel.

guide /gaɪd/ *n* [C] **1** person who shows others the way, esp a person employed to point out interesting sights on a journey or visit. **2** something that directs or influences (conduct, etc): *Instinct is not always a good* ~. **3** (also **ˈguide-book**) book for travellers, tourists, etc with information about a place: *a* ~ *to the British Museum.* **4** book of information; manual: *a* ~ *to growing roses.* □ *vt* act as guide to: ~ *a person to a place. You must be* ~*ed by common sense.*

'Girl 'Guide, ⇨ girl(5).

'guided 'missile, rocket (for use in war) which can be directed while in flight by electronic devices.

guild /gɪld/ n [C] (older spelling gild) society of persons for helping one another, forwarding common interests, e g trade, social welfare.

guile /gaɪl/ n [U] deceit; cunning: full of ~.
guile-less adj

guille-mot /ˈgɪlɪmɒt/ n [C] kinds of arctic seabird.

guillo-tine /ˈgɪləˈtiːn/ n [C] 1 machine for beheading (criminals) with a heavy blade sliding in grooves dropped from a height. 2 machine for cutting the edges of books, trimming sheets of paper, etc. 3 (in Parliament) method of stopping obstruction of a bill (by excessive debate) by fixing times for taking votes. □ vt use the guillotine on.

guilt /gɪlt/ n [U] feeling or condition of having done wrong; responsibility for wrongdoing: The ~ of the accused man was in doubt.
guilt-less adj innocent.
guilt-i-ly /-əlɪ/ adv
guilty adj (-ier, -iest) (a) having done wrong: plead ~y to a crime; be ~y of a crime. (b) showing or feeling guilt: a ~y conscience.

guinea /ˈgɪnɪ/ n (abbr gns) (money of account) formerly the sum of twenty-one shillings, for which there was neither coin nor banknote, used in stating prices, fees, charges, etc.

guinea-fowl /ˈgɪnɪ faʊl/ n [C] domestic fowl of the pheasant family.

guinea-pig /ˈgɪnɪ pɪg/ n [C] 1 short-eared animal like a big rat, often used in experiments. 2 person allowing himself to be used in medical or other experiments.

guitar /gɪˈtɑː(r)/ n [C] stringed musical instrument, plucked with the fingers or a plectrum.
guitar-ist, guitar-player.

gulf /gʌlf/ n 1 part of the sea almost surrounded by land: the G~ of Mexico. 2 deep hollow; chasm; abyss. 3 (fig) dividing line, division (between opinions, etc).

gull¹ /gʌl/ n [C] (kind of) large, long-winged seabird.

gull² /gʌl/ vt cheat; deceive: ~ a fool out of his money. □ n [C] person easily gulled.
gull-ible /-əbəl/ adj easily deceived.
gulli-bil-ity /ˈgʌləˈbɪlətɪ/ n

gul-let /ˈgʌlɪt/ n [C] food passage from the mouth to the stomach; throat.

gully /ˈgʌlɪ/ n [C] (pl -ies) narrow channel cut or formed by rainwater, e g on a hillside, or made for carrying water away from a building.

gulp /gʌlp/ vt,vi 1 swallow (food or drink) quickly or greedily: ~ down a cup of tea. 2 hold back or suppress (as if swallowing); make a gulping motion. □ n [C] act of gulp-

ing; amount that is gulped.

gum¹ /gʌm/ n [C] (usually pl) firm, pink flesh round the teeth.
gum-boil /ˈgʌmbɔɪl/ n [C] boil or abscess on the gums.

gum² /gʌm/ n 1 [U] sticky substance obtained from some trees, used for sticking things together. 2 [U] gum that has been specially prepared for chewing: `chewing-~. 3 (also `gum-tree) (kinds of) eucalyptus tree. up a gum-tree, (sl) in difficulties. 4 [U] rubber. □ vt (-mm-) stick together with gum; spread gum on the surface of: ~ two things together.
`gum boots, high rubber boots.
gummy adj (-ier, -iest) sticky.

gump-tion /ˈgʌmpʃən/ n [U] (informal) common sense and initiative; qualities likely to bring success.

gun /gʌn/ n [C] 1 general name for any kind of firearm that sends shells or bullets from a metal tube: ma`chine-~. stick to one's guns, maintain one's position against attack or argument. 2 person using a sporting gun, as a member of a shooting party. □ vt gun sb (down), shoot with a gun. gun for sb, seek to harm, destroy.
`gun-boat, small warship carrying heavy guns, or long-range missiles.
`gun-carriage, wheeled support of a big gun, or part on which a gun slides when it recoils.
`gun dog, dog trained to retrieve killed birds.
gun-man, man who uses a gun to rob or kill people.
`gun-metal, alloy of copper and tin or zinc.
`gun-powder, explosive powder used in guns, fireworks, blasting, etc.
`gun-room, (in a warship) room for junior officers.
`gun-running, introduction of firearms, secretly and illegally, into a country, e g to help a revolt.
`gun-runner, person engaged in gun-running.
`gun-shot, range of a gun: be out of/within ~shot.
`gun-smith, person who makes and repairs small firearms.

gun-ner /ˈgʌnə(r)/ n [C] (in the army) officer or man in the artillery; (official term) private soldier in an artillery regiment; (in the navy) warrant officer in charge of a battery of guns.
gun-nery, construction and management or firing of large guns.

gun-wale /ˈgʌnəl/ n [C] upper edge of the side of a boat or a small ship.

gurgle /ˈgɜːgəl/ n [C,U] bubbling sound as of water flowing from a narrow-necked bottle: ~s of delight. □ vi make this sound: The baby was gurgling happily.

guru /ˈgʊruː/ n [C] Hindu spiritual teacher.

gush /gʌʃ/ vi 1 burst, flow, out suddenly: oil

~*ing from a new well; blood* ~*ing from a wound.* **2** talk with excessive enthusiasm: *girls who* ~ *over handsome pop stars.* □ *n* [C] sudden outburst or outflow: *a* ~ *of oil/ anger/enthusiasm.*

gush·ing *adj:* ~*ing compliments.* ⇨ **2** above.

gus·set /ˈɡʌsɪt/ *n* [C] (usually triangular or diamond-shaped) piece of cloth inserted in a garment to strengthen or enlarge it.

gust /ɡʌst/ *n* [C] **1** sudden, violent rush of wind; burst of rain, hail, fire or smoke: *The wind was blowing in* ~*s.* **2** (*fig*) outburst of feeling: *a* ~ *of rage.*

gusty *adj* (-ier, -iest) stormy.

gut /ɡʌt/ *n* [C] **1** (*pl*) intestines; bowels. *hate sb's guts,* (*sl*) hate him intensely. **2** (*pl*) (*informal*) courage and determination: *a man with plenty of* ~*s.* **3** [U] strong cord made from the intestines of animals, used for the strings of violins, etc. ⇨ *catgut.* **4** (*informal*) important parts of something: *the* ~*s of a car.* □ *vt* (-tt-) **1** take the guts(1) out of (a fish, etc). **2** destroy the inside of or the contents of: *a building* ~*ted by fire.*

gut·ter /ˈɡʌtə(r)/ *n* [C] **1** channel or trough fixed under the edge of a roof to carry away rainwater; channel at the side of a road for the same purpose. **2** (*fig*) streets, esp of a poor district: *the language of the* ~, low and vulgar language.

gut·ter·snipe poor, badly-dressed child.

gut·tural /ˈɡʌtərəl/ *n* [C] *adj* (sound) produced in the throat.

guy¹ /ɡaɪ/ *n* [C] rope or chain used to keep sth steady or secured, e g to hold a tent in place.

guy² /ɡaɪ/ *n* [C] **1** figure in the form of a man, dressed in old clothes (e g as burned on 5 Nov in Britain.) **2** (*sl*) man. □ *vt* (*pt,pp* ~ed) ridicule.

guzzle /ˈɡʌzəl/ *vi,vt* (*informal*) eat or drink greedily: *guzzling beer.*

gym /dʒɪm/ *n* [C] (*sl*) (short for) gymnasium, gymnastics.

ˈgym-shoes, = plimsolls.

ˈgym-slip, sleeveless tunic worn by girls in GB as part of school uniform.

gym·khana /dʒɪmˈkɑːnə/ *n* [C] public display of athletics and sports competitions.

gym·nasium /dʒɪmˈneɪzɪəm/ *n* [C] (*pl* ~s) room or hall with apparatus for gymnastics and sports.

gym·nast /ˈdʒɪmnæst/ *n* [C] expert in gymnastics.

gym·nas·tic /dʒɪmˈnæstɪk/ *adj* of bodily training.

gym·nas·tics *n pl* (forms of) exercises for physical training.

gynae·col·ogy (*US* = **gyne-**) /ˈɡaɪnɪˈkolədʒɪ/ *n* [U] science of the diseases of women and pregnancies.

gynae·co·logi·cal (*US* = **gyne-**) /ˈɡaɪnɪkəˈlodʒɪkəl/ *adj*

gynae·colo·gist (*US* = **gyne-**) *n* [C] expert

in gynaecology.

gypsy /ˈdʒɪpsɪ/ *n* [C] = gipsy.

gy·rate /ˈdʒaɪˈreɪt *US:* ˈdʒaɪreɪt/ *vi* move round in circles or spirals; revolve.

gy·ra·tion /ˈdʒaɪˈreɪʃən/ *n* [C,U] revolving; revolution.

gyro·scope /ˈdʒaɪrəskəʊp/ *n* heavy wheel which, when spinning fast, keeps steady the object in which it is fixed.

Hh

H, h /eɪtʃ/ (*pl* H's, h's /ˈeɪtʃɪz/), the eighth letter of the English alphabet. *drop one's h's,* omit the sound /h/, e g by saying *'ot* for *hot.*

ha /hɑ/ *int* used to express surprise, joy, triumph, suspicion, etc. When repeated in print (*'Ha! Ha! Ha!'*) it indicates laughter.

hab·er·dasher /ˈhæbədæʃə(r)/ *n* [C] shopkeeper who sells clothing, pins, cotton, etc.

hab·er·dash·ery *n* [U] haberdasher's trade or goods.

habit /ˈhæbɪt/ *n* **1** [C] person's usual or normal practice, esp one that cannot easily be given up: *the* ~ *of smoking. fall/get into bad habits,* acquire them. *get out of a habit,* abandon it. **2** [U] usual behaviour: *Are we all creatures of* ~, Do we do things because of habit? **3** [C] dress worn by members of a religious order: *a monk's* ~.

hab·it·able /ˈhæbɪtəbəl/ *adj* fit to be lived in: *The old house is no longer* ~.

habi·tat /ˈhæbɪtæt/ *n* [C] (of plants, animals) usual natural place and conditions of growth.

habi·ta·tion /ˈhæbɪˈteɪʃən/ *n* [U] living in: *houses that were not fit for* ~.

ha·bit·ual /həˈbɪtʃʊəl/ *adj* **1** regular, usual: *He took his* ~ *seat in the train.* **2** acting by habit; having a regular habit: *a* ~ *liar.*

ha·bit·ually /-tʃʊlɪ/ *adv* as a habit: ~*ly late for school.*

ha·bitu·ate /həˈbɪtʃʊeɪt/ *vt* accustom: ~ *oneself to hard work.*

habi·tude /ˈhæbɪtjud *US:* -tud/ *n* [U] custom; tendency; habitual way of acting or doing things.

haci·enda /ˈhæsɪˈendə/ *n* (*pl* ~s) (in Latin American countries) large landed estate with a dwelling house.

hack¹ /hæk/ *vt,vi* cut roughly or clumsily; chop: *He* ~*ed at the branch until it fell to the ground.*

ˈhack-saw, one with a replaceable blade in a frame, for cutting through metal.

hack² /hæk/ *n* [C] **1** horse that may be hired. **2** person paid to do hard and uninteresting work as a writer.

hackles /ˈhækəlz/ *n pl* long feathers on the

neck of the domestic cock. **have one's/get sb's hackles up,** be, make angry, ready to fight.

hack·ney /ˈhæknɪ/ n [C] kind of horse for riding or driving.

`hackney-carriage,` vehicle, e g a taxi, that may be hired.

hack·neyed adj (esp of sayings) too common; repeated too often.

had /hæd/ ⇨ have¹.

had·dock /ˈhædək/ n [C] (pl unchanged) seafish much used for food.

Hades /ˈheɪdiːz/ n (in Greek myth) place where the spirits of the dead go.

Hadji /ˈhædʒɪ/ n (title of a) Muslim pilgrim who has been to Mecca.

hæ·mo·glo·bin /ˈhiːməˈɡləʊbɪn/ n [U] = hemoglobin.

hæ·mo·philia /ˈhiːməˈfɪliə/ n [U] = hemophilia.

hæm·or·rhage /ˈhemərɪdʒ/ n pl = hemorrhage.

hæm·or·rhoids /ˈhemərɔɪdz/ n [C] = hemorrhoids.

haft /hɑft US: hæft/ n [C] handle of an axe, knife, dagger, etc.

hag /hæg/ n [C] witch; ugly old woman, esp one who does, or is thought to do, evil.

hag·gard /ˈhæɡəd/ adj (of a person, his face) looking tired and lined, esp from worry, lack of sleep.

hag·gis /ˈhæɡɪs/ n [C,U] Scottish dish of parts of a sheep, mixed with oatmeal, and cooked in a sheep's stomach.

haggle /ˈhæɡəl/ vi argue, dispute: *haggling with the Manager over/about an increase in salary.*

hail¹ /heɪl/ n 1 [U] frozen rain-drops falling from the sky. 2 (usually with a, an) something coming in great numbers and force: a ∼ of blows. □ vi,vt 1 (of hail) come down: It ∼ed during the morning. 2 (of blows, etc) come, send down: They ∼ed curses down on us.

`hail-stone,` small piece of hail.

`hail-storm,` storm with fall of hail.

hail² /heɪl/ vt,vi 1 greet; call out to (so as to attract attention): He was ∼ed as a hero. Let's ∼ a taxi, shall we? 2 come from: Where does the ship ∼ from. □ n [C] greeting.

hair /heə(r)/ n 1 [U] (collective sing) all the growths like threads on the skin of animals, esp on the human head; growth like a thread as on the stems and leaves of some plants: brush one's `∼; have one's `∼ cut. **keep your `hair on,** (sl) don't lose your temper. **let one's `hair down,** (fig) relax after a period of being formal. **make one's `hair stand on end,** fill one with fright or horror. 2 [C] single thread of hair: find a ∼ in the soup. **split hairs,** make or pretend to see differences of meaning, distinctions, etc, so small as to be unimportant. **not turn a hair,** give no sign of being troubled.

`hair('s)-breadth,` very small distance: escape by a ∼'s breadth.

`hair-brush,` brush for the hair.

`hair-cut,` act or style of cutting the hair.

`hair-do,` (informal) style of a woman's hair.

`hair-dresser,` person who styles, esp a woman's, hair. ⇨ barber.

`hair-line,` (a) area where the roots of hair join the forehead. (b) width of a hair: (as an adjective) a ∼line fracture.

`hair-net,` net for keeping the hair in place.

`hair-pin,` (woman's) bent pin for keeping the hair in place.

'hairpin `bend,` sharp bend on a road.

`hair-raising` adj terrifying.

`hair-slide,` ornamental clip for keeping hair in place.

`hair-spring,` very delicate spring in a watch, controlling the balance-wheel.

hair·less adj bald.

hairy adj (-ier, -iest) of or like, covered with, hair: a ∼y chest.

hale /heɪl/ adj (only in) **hale and hearty,** strong and healthy.

half /hɑf US: hæf/ n (pl halves /hɑvz US: hævz/) adj, adv 1 one of two equal or corresponding parts into which a thing is divided: H∼ of 6 is 3. Two halves make a whole. Two pounds and a ∼/Two and a ∼ pounds; ∼ an hour. **go halves (with sb) (in sth),** share equally. **too clever, etc by half,** far too clever, etc. 2 (as an adv) to the extent of a half; to a considerable degree: meat that is only ∼ cooked. **Half-dead,** (informal) exhausted, very tired. **not half `bad,** (informal) not at all bad; quite good. '**half a `dozen, 'half-`dozen,** six.

`half-back,` (in football/hockey, etc) (position of a) player (defender) between the forwards and the backs.

'half-`baked adj (informal) foolish; crude and inexperienced: a ∼-baked idea/young man.

`half-breed,` (a) person with parents of different races (half-caste is preferred). (b) offspring of two animals or plants of different species.

`half-brother/-sister,` brother/sister by one parent only.

`half-caste,` half-breed (a).

`half-hearted adj done with, showing, little interest or enthusiasm: a ∼-hearted attempt. Hence, '**half-`heartedly** adv

'**half-`holiday,** day of which half is free from work or duty.

'**half-`hourly** adj, adv (done, occurring) every half hour.

'**half-`mast,** (of a flag) the position, near the middle of a mast, to indicate mourning: Flags were at ∼-mast for the President's funeral.

'**half-`measures** n pl compromise, ineffective policy.

halfpenny /ˈheɪpənɪ US: `hæfpenɪ/ n [C]

British coin worth half a penny.

'half-'price adv adj (at) half the usual price: Children admitted ~-price.

'half-'time, (a) work and pay for half the usual time: The workers are on ~-time this month. **(b)** interval between the two halves of a game of football, etc: The score at ~-time was 2—2.

'half-truth, statement that conveys only a part of the truth.

'half-'way adj **(a)** (of a house, etc) at an equal distance from two towns, etc. **(b)** going half the way; not thorough: In an emergency ~-way measures are usually unsatisfactory. □ adv to or at half the distance: meet a person ~-way, be ready to make a compromise.

'half-'witted adj having low intelligence. Hence, **'half-wit** n [C]

'half-'yearly adj, adv (done, occurring) every half year.

hall /hɔːl/ n [C] **1** (building with a) large room for meetings, concerts, public business, etc: the Festival H~, for concerts, in London; `dance-~s. **2** (in castles, universities) large room for meals. **3** building for university students: a ~ of residence. **4** (in England) large country house, usually one that belongs to the chief landowner in the district. **5** passage, space, into which the main entrance or front door of a building opens: Leave your hat and coat in the ~.

'hall-mark n [C] **1** mark used at Goldsmiths' Hall for marking the standard of gold and silver in articles (as a guarantee of quality). **2** any indication of quality or excellence. □ vt stamp a hallmark on.

hal-le-lu-jah /ˌhælɪˈluːjə/ n, [C] int praise to God.

hallo /həˈləʊ/ int, n [C] cry to attract attention; greeting.

hal-low /ˈhæləʊ/ vt (usually passive) make holy; regard as holy: ~ed ground.

Hal-low-e'en /ˌhæləʊˈiːn/ 31 Oct, eve of All Saints' Day.

hal-luci-na-tion /həˈluːsɪˈneɪʃən/ n [C,U] (instance of) seeming to see something not actually present: Drugs sometimes cause ~s.

hal-luci-na-tory /həˈluːsɪnətərɪ/ adj

halo /ˈheɪləʊ/ n [C] (pl ~es, ~s) **1** circle of light round the sun or moon. **2** (in paintings) ring round or above the heads of Christ or sacred figures.

halt¹ /hɔːlt/ n [C] **1** call a halt (to), **(a)** order a short stop on a march or journey. **(b)** (fig) order an end: It's time to call a ~ to vandalism. **2** stop or pause: The train came to a ~. □ vi, vt **1** stop marching. **2** bring to an end.

halt² /hɔːlt/ vi hesitate; act in a hesitating way: speak in a ~ing voice.

halt-ing-ly adv in a hesitating way.

hal-ter /ˈhɔːltə(r)/ n [C] **1** rope or leather strap put round a horse's head (for leading or fastening the horse). **2** rope used for hanging

a person.

halve /hɑːv US: hæv/ vt **1** divide into two equal parts: ~ an apple. **2** lessen by one half: The supersonic plane has ~d the time needed for crossing the Atlantic.

halves /hɑːvz US: hævz/ plof half.

hal-yard /ˈhæljəd/ n [C] rope for raising or lowering a sail or flag.

ham /hæm/ n **1** [C] upper part of a pig's leg, salted and dried or smoked; [U] this as meat: a ~ sandwich. **2** [C] (of animals) back of the thigh, thigh and buttock. **3** [C] (sl) poor actor or performer. **4** amateur operator who sends and receives radio messages: a radio ~. □ vt, vi (-mm-) (informal) overact.

'ham-'handed/-'fisted adj clumsy in using the hands.

ham-burger /ˈhæmbɜːgə(r)/ n [C] **1** minced or chopped beef made into round flat cakes and fried. **2** sandwich or bread roll filled with this.

ham-let /ˈhæmlət/ n [C] group of houses in the country; small village, esp one without a church.

ham-mer /ˈhæmə(r)/ n [C] **1** tool with a heavy metal head used for driving in nails, etc. be/go at it 'hammer and `tongs, fight, argue, etc with great energy and noise. **2** athletic competition in which a heavy metal ball fixed to a long wire is thrown as far as possible. **3** (in a piano, etc) part like a hammer that strikes the strings. **4** part of a gun that strikes and explodes the charge. **5** wooden mallet used by an auctioneer. be/come under the hammer, be sold by auction. **6** bone in the ear. □ vt, vi **1** strike or beat (as if) with a hammer: ~ in a nail/~ a nail in; ~ at the door, eg with a stick or one's fists; ~ at the keys, play the piano loudly, without feeling. **2** (fig) work hard: ~ away at a problem/a solution. **3** (fig) force: ~ an idea into his head. **4** (informal) heavily defeat (a person) in war or in games.

ham-mock /ˈhæmək/ n [C] hanging bed of canvas or rope network.

ham-per¹ /ˈhæmpə(r)/ n [C] basket, etc with a lid, esp one used for carrying food: a picnic ~.

ham-per² /ˈhæmpə(r)/ vt prevent free movement or activity: ~ed by heavy boots.

ham-ster /ˈhæmstə(r)/ n [C] rodent like a large rat, kept as a pet.

ham-string /ˈhæmstrɪŋ/ vt (pt, pp -strung /-strʌŋ/) **1** cripple (a person or animal) by cutting the tendon(s) at the back of the knee(s). **2** (fig) destroy the power or efficiency of. □ n [C] tendon at the back of the knee.

hand¹ /hænd/ n [C] **1** part of the human arm beyond the wrist. at/to hand, near; within reach: He lives close at ~. by hand, **(a)** without the use of machinery: Are your socks knitted by ~/~-knitted? **(b)** without the use of a post office: a letter delivered by ~, brought by a messenger. from hand to

hand, from one person to another: *pass buckets of water from ~ to ~.* **in hand,** (a) reserved; ready for use: *have money in ~ for paying the bill.* (b) receiving attention: *the work is in ~.* **hand in hand,** (a) holding hands: *walk ~ in hand.* (b) in cooperation: *work ~ in ~ with the police.* **go hand in hand,** be connected: *War and misery go ~ in ~.* **in the hands of,** being looked after, managed by: *evidence in the ~s of the police.* **in good hands,** being well cared for. **Hands off!** Don't touch/interfere! **off one's hands,** free from one's responsibility. **on hand,** available: *have new designs on ~ in the shops.* **on one's hands,** being one's responsibility or burden: *I've too many children on my ~s.* **out of hand,** out of control: *He has got out of ~.* **Hands up!** Raise your hands! **give/lend a hand,** help with, take part in, doing something: *Please give me a ~ with this suitcase.* **have/take a hand in sth,** be involved: *Did he have a ~ in the burglary?* **have sth (well) in hand,** be dealing with something (well). **eat/feed out of sb's hand,** (a) (of an animal) be tame. (b) (*fig*) be ready to obey without hesitation. **have one's hands full,** be very busy. **have/get the upper hand,** have/get control, an advantage, over. **lay (one's) hands on,** ⇨ lay²(2). **not lift a hand,** make no attempt (to help). **live from hand to mouth,** poorly, spending money as soon as it is earned. **(rule) with a heavy hand,** with great force, discipline. **shake hands (with sb),** grasp his hand as a greeting, to show agreement, etc. **take a hand (in),** accept an involvement in. **take sb/sth in hand,** accept control of: *These noisy children must be taken in hand.* **wait on sb hand and foot,** do whatever he asks. **wash one's hands of,** refuse to be involved, responsible, any longer. **win hands down,** win easily and convincingly. **2** (*pl*) power; possession; responsibility: *The matter is in your ~s, you must decide how to deal with it.* **change hands,** pass to another owner. **3** (*sing* only) influence or agency: *The ~ of an enemy has been at work here.* **play into sb's hands,** give him the advantage. **4 at first/ second, etc hand,** directly/indirectly. **'second-'hand** (*adj*) ⇨ second³. **5** (*sing* only) skill in using one's hands: *Why don't you try your ~ at embroidery?* **keep one's hand in,** practise in order to be skilled: *practise the piano every day to keep one's ~ in.* **try one's hand at,** attempt something to see if you can do it. **6** person who does what is indicated by the context; performer: *He's an old ~ at this sort of work,* has long experience of it. **7** workman; member of a ship's crew: *The factory has taken on 200 extra ~s. All ~s on deck!* All seamen are needed on deck! **8** pointer or indicator on the dial of a watch, clock or other instrument: *the `hour/`minute/`second ~ of a watch.* **9**

position or direction (to right or left). **on the `one hand (and) on the `other hand,** (used to indicate contrasted points of view, arguments, etc). **10** (*sing* only) handwriting: *He writes a good/legible ~.* **11** (in card games, e g bridge) (a) (number of) cards dealt to, held by, a player at one time: *a good/bad/poor ~; take a ~ at whist/ bridge,* join in and play. (b) player at cards: *We have only three players—we need a fourth ~.* (c) one round in a game of cards: *Let's play one more ~.* **12** [C] unit of measurement, about four inches (10·16 cm), used for the height of a horse (from the ground to the top of the shoulder). **13** (*informal*) applause by clapping; *give a performer a good ~.*

`hand-bag, woman's bag for money, keys, etc.

`hand-ball, game played by hitting a ball with the hand against a wall or between two goals.

`hand-brake, brake in a motor-vehicle, used when the vehicle is stationary.

`hand-cart, small cart pushed or pulled by hand.

`hand-clap, clapping.

`hand-cuff, one of a pair of metal rings joined by a chain, fastened round a prisoner's wrists. □ *vt* put handcuffs on.

hand-ful, (a) as much or as many as can be held in one hand. (b) small number: *Only a ~ful of people came to the meeting.* (c) (*informal*) person or animal difficult to control: *That young boy of hers is quite a ~ful.*

'hand-'made *adj* made by hand (contrasted with *machine-made*).

'hand-'picked *adj* carefully selected.

`hand-rail, railing along the edge of a staircase, etc.

`hand-shake, greeting given by grasping a person's hand with one's own.

`hand-stand acrobatic feat of supporting oneself in an upright position on the hands: *do a ~stand.*

`hand-writing, (person's style of) writing by hand.

hand² /hænd/ *vt* give or pass (to a person); help with the hand(s): *Please ~ me that book/~ that book to me.* **hand sth down (to sb),** pass by tradition, inheritance, etc: *We cannot always observe the traditions ~ed down to us from the past.* **hand sth on (to sb),** send, give, to another: *Please ~ on the magazine to your friends.* **hand sth out,** distribute. **hand sb over,** deliver a person to authority: *~ him over to the police.* **hand sth over (to sb),** transfer: *H~ over that knife at once.* **hand it to sb,** (*informal*) give him the credit that is his due: *He's done well! You've got to ~ it to him.*

`hand-out, (a) printed statement, leaflet, e g political, distributed free of charge. (b) something given free of charge, e g money, clothes.

handi-cap /ˈhændɪkæp/ n [C] **1** (competition, race, in which there is a) disadvantage imposed on a competitor to make the chances of success more equal for all. **2** anything likely to lessen one's chance of success: *Poor eyesight is a ～ to a student.* □ vt (-pp-) give or be a handicap to: *～ped children,* suffering from a disability.

handi-craft /ˈhændɪkrɑft US: -kræft/ n [C] art or craft needing skill with the hands, e g needlework, pottery.

handi-work /ˈhændɪwɜːk/ n **1** [U] work done by hand. **2** [C] thing made, by hand. **3** [U] something done by a named person: *That's some of Smith's ～.*

hand-ker-chief /ˈhæŋkətʃɪf/ n [C] square piece of cotton, etc for blowing the nose into or wiping the face; similar square worn, e g round the neck.

handle /ˈhændl/ n [C] part of a tool, cup, bucket, door, drawer, etc by which it may be held in the hand. *fly off the handle,* (informal) get into a rage and lose self-control. □ vt **1** touch with, take up in, the hands: *Gelignite is dangerous stuff to ～.* **2** manage; deal with; control: *Can you ～ the situation?* **3** treat; behave towards: *The speaker was roughly ～d by the crowd.* **4** buy and sell: *This shop does not ～ imported goods.*
`handle-bar, (often pl) bar with a handle at each end, for steering a bicycle, etc.

han-dler, person who trains and controls an animal, e g a police dog.

hand-some /ˈhænsəm/ adj **1** of fine appearance; (of men) good-looking; (of women) having a fine figure and dignity: *What a ～ old building it is! He's so ～.* **2** (of gifts, behaviour) generous: *He said some very ～ things about you.*

hand-some-ly adv in a generous manner.

handy /ˈhændɪ/ adj (-ier, -iest) **1** (of persons) clever with the hands. **2** (of things) convenient to handle; easily used: *A good toolbox is a ～ thing to have in the house. come in handy,* be useful at some time or other: *Don't throw that plastic bag away; it may come in ～.* **3** (of things, places) not far away; available for use: *Always keep a first-aid kit ～.*

handy-man, person clever at doing odd jobs of various kinds.

hand-ily /-əlɪ/ adv

hang¹ /hæŋ/ n (sing only) **1** way in which a thing hangs: *the ～ of a coat/skirt.* **2** get the hang of sth, (a) see how something works or is managed: *I've been trying to get the ～ of this new typewriter.* (b) see the meaning or significance of what is said or written: *I don't quite get the ～ of your argument.*

hang² /hæŋ/ vt,vi (pt,pp hung /hʌŋ/ or, for 2 below, ～ed) (For uses with adverbial particles and prepositions, ⇨ 5 below.) **1** support, be supported, from above so that the lower end is free: *～ a lamp from the ceiling. H～ your coat on that hook.* **2** (pt,pp

～ed) put, be put, to death by hanging with a rope around the neck: *He was ～ed for murder.* **3** (various uses) *～ wallpaper,* attach it to a wall with paste: *～ a door,* fasten it on hinges. *hang by a hair/a single thread,* (of a persons's fate, etc) be in a delicate or critical state. *hang fire,* (of events) be slow in developing. **4** leave, e g meat, birds, hanging until in the right condition for eating: *How long has this meat hung for?*

5 (uses with adverbial particles and prepositions):

hang about/(a)round, stand, doing nothing definite, loiter: *boys ～ing about at street corners.*

hang back, show unwillingness to act or advance: *When volunteers were asked for, not one man hung back.*

hang on, (a) hold tight: *He hung on until the rope broke.* (b) persevere: *It's hard work, but if you ～ on long enough you'll succeed.* (c) (informal) wait.

hang sth out, (a) hang (wet clothes, etc) from a line to dry. (b) display: *～ out flags for the Queen's visit.*

hang together, (a) (of persons) support one another; act in unison: *If we all ～ together, our plan will succeed.* (b) fit well together: *Their accounts don't ～ together,* are inconsistent.

hang up, replace the receiver at the end of a telephone conversation. *be hung up,* (informal) be frustrated; feel inhibited: *Everything seems to have gone wrong—I feel really hung up about things.*

hang-man, executioner who hangs criminals.
`hang-over, (a) unpleasant after-effects of excessive drinking. (b) survival of out-of-date news, rules, etc.
`hang-up, (feeling of) frustration, etc. ⇨ 5 above.

han-gar /ˈhæŋə(r)/ n [C] building for keeping aircraft.

hang-er /ˈhæŋə(r)/ n [C] device, loop, etc to, on or by which something is hung: *a `coat-～.*

'hanger-`on, (pl ～s-on) person who forces his company on another or others in the hope of profit or advantage.

hang-ing /ˈhæŋɪŋ/ n **1** [C] death by hanging: *There were three ～s here last month.* **2** (usually pl) curtains, etc with which walls are hung.

hank /hæŋk/ n [C] (twisted) coil of wool, silk, etc.

han-ker /ˈhæŋkə(r)/ vi have a strong desire: *～ for sympathy/after wealth.*

han-ker-ing n: *have a ～ing for/after fame.*

hanky /ˈhæŋkɪ/ n [C] (pl -ies) (informal) = handkerchief.

hap-haz-ard /ˌhæpˈhæzəd/ adj, adv accidental; (by) chance.

hap-pen /ˈhæpən/ vi **1** take place; come

about: *How did it ~? If anything ~s to him* (= *If he meets with an accident*), *let me know.* 2 chance; have the fortune: *I ~ed to be out when he called.* 3 find by chance: *I ~ed on just the thing I'd been looking for.*

hap·pen·ing, (a) (often *pl*) event: *There have been strange ~ings here lately.* (b) (*sl*) spontaneous entertainment involving frenzied outbursts of excitement.

happy /ˈhæpɪ/ *adj* (-ier, -iest) 1 fortunate; lucky; feeling or expressing pleasure, contentment, satisfaction, etc: *Their marriage has been a ~ one.* 2 (in polite formulas) pleased: *We shall be ~ to accept your kind invitation.* 3 (of language, conduct, suggestions) well suited to the situation: *a ~ thought/idea, etc.*

'happy-go-'lucky *adj* carefree.

hap·pily /-pəlɪ/ *adv*

hap·pi·ness *n* [U]

hara-kiri /ˈhærə ˈkɪrɪ/ *n* [C] suicide by disembowelment as practised in the past by Japanese men when they believed they had failed in their duty.

har·angue /həˈræŋ/ *n* [C] long, loud (often scolding) talk or speech. □ *vt, vi* make such a speech (to).

har·ass /ˈhærəs *US*: həˈræs/ *vt* 1 trouble; worry: *~ed by the cares of a large family.* 2 make repeated attacks on: *Long ago England was ~ed by the Vikings.*

har·ass·ment *n* [U]

harbour (*US* = **-bor**) /ˈhɑːbə(r)/ *n* [C] 1 place of shelter for ships: *a natural ~,* e g an inlet of the sea. 2 (*fig*) any place of safety or shelter. □ *vt, vi* 1 give lodging or shelter to; protect; conceal: *~ an escaped criminal.* 2 hold in the mind: *~ thoughts of revenge.* 3 come to anchor (in a harbour).

har·bour·age /-ɪdʒ/ *n* (place of) shelter.

hard[1] /hɑːd/ *adj* (-er, -est) 1 (contrasted with *soft*) firm; not yielding to the touch; not easily cut; solid: *as ~ as rock.* 2 (contrasted with *easy*) difficult (to understand or explain): *She found it ~ to make up her mind. That man is ~ to please/He is a ~ man to please.* 3 causing unhappiness, discomfort, or pain; difficult to bear: *have/be given a ~ time,* experience difficulties, misfortunes, etc. **learn sth the hard way,** by suffering, making a tiring effort, etc. 4 severe; harsh: *a ~ father; ~ words,* showing lack of sympathy. **take a hard line,** be uncompromising. 5 (of the body) having hard muscles and not much fat: *Exercises soon made the boys ~.* 6 done, doing (something), with much effort or force; strenuous: *a ~ worker.* 7 (of the weather) severe: *a ~ winter/frost.* 8 (of sounds) *The letter 'c' is hard in 'cat'. The letter 'g' is ~ in 'gun' and soft in 'gin'.* 9 (various uses) **hard and fast (rules, etc),** that cannot be altered. **hard of hearing,** rather deaf.

'hard-back, book bound in a hard (= stiff) cover (contrasted with paperback).

hard·board, kind of material like plywood in appearance and use.

'hard 'cash, coins and notes, not a cheque or a promise to pay.

'hard court, tennis court with a hard surface, not of grass.

'hard 'currency, one which, because of an adverse balance of trade, a country has difficulty in getting enough of.

'hard 'drugs, those likely to lead to addiction, e g *heroin.*

'hard 'facts, reliable, certain facts.

'hard-'headed *adj* not sentimental; business-like.

'hard-'hearted *adj* lacking in sympathy.

'hard 'labour, hard physical work (done by criminals as a punishment).

'hard 'luck/'lines, worse fortune than is deserved.

'hard 'liquor/'drink, with high alcoholic content e g *whisky.*

'hard 'shoulder, hard surface at the side of a motorway, to be used in an emergency.

'hard·ware, (a) metal goods for domestic use, e g *pans, locks.* (b) (*computers*) mechanical equipment (contrasted with information and programmes, called *software*).

'hard·wood, heavy wood, e g *oak, teak.*

'hard-working, working hard(6).

hard[2] /hɑːd/ *adv* 1 with great energy; strenuously; with all one's force: *try ~ to succeed.* 2 severely; heavily: *freezing/raining ~.* 3 with difficulty; with a struggle; painfully: *my '~-earned money.* **be hard up,** be short of money. 4 so as to be hard(1), solid: *'~-boiled eggs.* 5 closely; immediately: *follow ~ after/upon/behind someone.*

harden /ˈhɑːdən/ *vt, vi* make or become hard, strong, hardy, etc: *a ~ed criminal,* one who shows no signs of shame or repentance.

hard·ly /ˈhɑːdlɪ/ *adv* 1 only just; not quite; scarcely: *I ~ know her. I'm so tired I can ~ walk.* 2 (used to suggest that something is improbable, unlikely or unreasonable): *You can ~ expect me to lend you money again. I need ~ say* (= It is almost unnecessary for me to say) *that I am innocent.* 3 (negative in meaning) almost no, not, never: *He ~ ever goes to bed before midnight. There's ~ any coal left. H~ anybody* (= Very few people) *came to the meeting.*

hard·ship /ˈhɑːdʃɪp/ *n* 1 [C] circumstance that causes discomfort or suffering: *the ~s of war.* 2 [U] severe suffering: *bear ~ without complaining.*

hardy /ˈhɑːdɪ/ *adj* (-ier, -iest) 1 strong; able to endure suffering or hardship: *A few ~ men broke the ice on the lake and had a swim.* 2 (of plants) able to survive frost: *~ annuals.* 3 bold; ready to face danger.

har·di·ness *n* [U]

hare /heə(r)/ *n* [C] fast-running field animal with long ears and a divided upper lip, like but larger than a rabbit. **mad as a (March)**

hare, very mad. □ *vi* run fast: *They ～d off.*

'hare-'brained *adj* rash; wild.

'hare-'lip, person's upper lip divided (from birth) like that of a hare.

harem /ˈheərəm/ *n* [C] women's part of a Muslim household: women living in it.

hari-cot /ˈhærɪkəʊ/ *n* [C] (also ～ *bean*) kidney bean; French bean.

hark /hɑk/ *vi* 1 (*informal*) listen to: *Just ～ at him!* 2 **hark back (to),** refer to something done or said earlier.

har-le-quin /ˈhɑləkwɪn/ *n* [C] character as in Italian comedy or English pantomime.

har-lot /ˈhɑlət/ *n* [C] (*archaic*, or *abusive*) prostitute.

harm /hɑm/ *n* [U] damage; injury: *It will do you no ～. He meant no ～.* **out of harm's `way,** safe. □ *vt* cause harm to.

harm-ful *adj* causing harm (*to*).

harm-fully *adv*

harm-less *adj* (a) not doing harm (to): *～less snakes.* (b) innocent; inoffensive: *Several ～less spectators were hurt.*

harm-less-ly *adv*

har-mon-ica /hɑˈmɒnɪkə/ *n* [C] kinds of musical instruments using metal bars, e g the mouth-organ.

har-moni-ous /hɑˈməʊnɪəs/ *adj* 1 pleasingly or satisfactorily arranged: *a ～ group of buildings.* 2 in agreement; free from ill feeling: *～ neighbours.* 3 tuneful.

har-moni-ous-ly *adv*

har-mo-nium /hɑˈməʊnɪəm/ *n* [C] (*pl ～s*) musical instrument with a keyboard and metal reeds, supplied with wind by means of bellows.

har-mon-ize /ˈhɑmənaɪz/ *vt,vi* 1 bring (one thing) into, be in, harmony (with another). 2 (in music) add notes (to a melody) to make chords. 3 (in music) sing or play an instrument in harmony.

har-mon-iz-ation /ˌhɑmənaɪˈzeɪʃən/ *n* [U]

har-mony /ˈhɑmənɪ/ *n* (*pl* -ies) 1 [U] agreement (of feeling, interests, opinions, etc): *racial ～.* 2 [C,U] (instance or example of) pleasing combination of related things: *the ～ of colour in nature.* 3 [C,U] pleasing combination of musical notes sounded together to make chords.

har-ness /ˈhɑnɪs/ *n* [U] 1 (collective *sing*) all the leatherwork and metalwork by which a horse is controlled and fastened to the cart, waggon, plough, etc, that it pulls. 2 arrangement of straps, etc for fastening sth to the body, e g a parachute. □ *vt* 1 put harness on (a horse). 2 use (a river, waterfall, etc) to produce (esp electric) power.

harp /hɑp/ *n* [C] upright musical instrument with vertical strings played with the fingers. □ *vi* 1 play the harp. 2 (*fig*) talk repeatedly or tediously about: *She is always ～ing on about her misfortunes.*

harp-ist /-ɪst/ *n* [C] person who plays the harp.

har-poon /hɑˈpun/ *n* [C] spear on a rope, thrown by hand or fired from a gun, for catching whales and other large sea-animals. □ *vt* strike with a harpoon.

harp-si-chord /ˈhɑpsɪkɔd/ *n* [C] instrument like a piano from the 16th to the 18th centuries.

har-rier /ˈhærɪə(r)/ *n* [C] 1 hound used for hunting hares. 2 cross-country runner.

har-row /ˈhærəʊ/ *n* [C] heavy frame with metal teeth or discs for breaking up ground after ploughing. □ *vt* use a harrow. 2 (*fig*) distress (the feelings): *a ～ing tale of misfortunes.*

harry /ˈhærɪ/ *vt* (*pt,pp* -ied) 1 attack frequently: *The Vikings used to ～ the English coast.* 2 annoy or worry: *money-lenders ～ing their debtors.*

harsh /hɑʃ/ *adj* (-er, -est) 1 rough and disagreeable, esp to the senses: *a ～ voice.* 2 stern, cruel, severe: *a ～ judge/punishment.*

harsh-ly *adv*

harsh-ness *n* [U]

hart /hɑt/ *n* [C] adult male of (esp red) deer.

har-vest /ˈhɑvɪst/ *n* [C] 1 (season for) cutting and gathering in of grain and other food crops; quantity obtained. 2 (*fig*) result of action or behaviour: *reap the ～ of one's hard work.* □ *vt* cut, gather, dig up, a crop: *～ rice.*

'harvest 'festival, service of thanksgiving in Christian churches after the harvest has been gathered.

har-ves-ter (a) person who harvests. (b) machine for cutting and gathering grain, esp the kind that also binds the grain into sheaves or (**'combine-'harvester**) threshes the grain.

has ⇨ have[1].

hash /hæʃ/ *vt* chop (meat) into small pieces. □ *n* 1 [U] (dish of) cooked chopped meat. 2 **make a hash of sth,** (*fig*) do it very badly, make a mess of it.

hash-ish, hash-eesh /ˈhæʃɪʃ/ *n* [U] = cannabis.

hasn't /ˈhæzənt/ = has not. ⇨ have[1].

hasp /hæsp/ *n* [C] metal fastening of a padlock used with a staple.

has-sock /ˈhæsək/ *n* [C] cushion for kneeling on, e g in church.

haste /heɪst/ *n* [U] quickness of movement; hurry: *Why all this ～?*

hasten /ˈheɪsən/ *vi,vt* 1 move or act with speed: *～ to tell sb the good news.* 2 cause to or to be done, to happen quickly or earlier: *Artificial heating ～s the growth of plants.*

hasty /ˈheɪstɪ/ *adj* (-ier, -iest) said, made or done (too) quickly: *～ preparations.*

hast-ily /-əlɪ/ *adv*

hasti-ness *n* [U]

hat /hæt/ *n* [C] covering for the head worn out of doors. **old hat,** rubbish. **take one's hat off to,** (*fig*) express admiration for. **talk through one's hat,** (*informal*) talk foolishly.

hat-ter, man who makes or sells hats. **as**

mad as a hatter, very mad.

hatch¹ /hætʃ/ n [C] **1** (movable covering over an) opening in a door or floor, esp (**'hatch·way**) one in a ship's deck through which cargo is lowered and raised. **2** opening in a wall between two rooms, esp a kitchen and a dining room, through which dishes, etc, are passed. **3** lower half of a divided door.

hatch² /hætʃ/ vt, vi **1** (cause to) break out (of an egg): ∼ chickens. **2** think out and produce (a plan, etc).

hatch·ery, place for hatching (esp fish): a `trout-∼ery.

hatchet /ˈhætʃɪt/ n [C] light, short-handled axe. **bury the hatchet,** stop quarrelling or fighting.

hatch·way /ˈhætʃweɪ/ n ⇨ hatch¹.

hate /heɪt/ vt **1** have a great dislike of or for: My cat ∼s dogs. **2** regret: I ∼ to trouble you. □ n [U] extreme dislike.

hate·ful /ˈheɪtfəl/ adj causing hatred or strong dislike: The bloodshed was ∼.

hate·fully adv

hatred /ˈheɪtrɪd/ n [U] hate: He looked at me with ∼.

hat·ter /ˈhætə(r)/ n ⇨ hat.

haughty /ˈhɔːtɪ/ adj (-ier, -iest) having or showing a high opinion of oneself; arrogant: treating staff with ∼ contempt.

haught·ily /-əlɪ/ adv

haugh·ti·ness n [U]

haul /hɔːl/ vt, vi pull (with effort or force): They ∼ed the boat up the beach. □ n [C] **1** act of hauling. **2** distance along which something is hauled. **3** amount gained, esp of fish hauled up in a net. **4** (fig) catch: The thief made a good ∼, What he stole was valuable.

haul·age /ˈhɔːlɪdʒ/ n [U] transport (of goods).

haul·ier /ˈhɔːlɪə(r)/ n [C] person or firm that contracts to carry goods by road.

haunch /hɔːntʃ/ n [C] (in man and animals) part of the body between the ribs and the thighs: a dog sitting on its ∼es.

haunt /hɔːnt/ vt **1** visit, be with, habitually or repeatedly. **2** (esp of ghosts and spirits) appear repeatedly in. **3** return to the mind repeatedly: constantly ∼ed by fear of discovery. □ n [C] place frequently visited by the person(s) named: a ∼ of criminals.

have¹ /usual form həv; strong form hæv/ auxiliary verb (3rd person sing **has** strong form hæz/, pp **had** /usual form həd; strong form hæd/; negative forms **haven't** /ˈhævənt/, **hasn't** /ˈhæzənt/, **hadn't** /ˈhædənt/) **1** (used in forming the perfect tenses and the perfect infinitive): I ∼/I've finished. He has/He's gone. H∼ you done it? Yes, I ∼. No, I ∼n't. I shall ∼ done it by next week. **2** (used to form an equivalent of an if-clause): Had I (= If I had) known, ... ⇨ if(1).

have² /hæv/ verb (3rd person sing **has** /hæz/, pp **had** /hæd/; negative forms

haven't /ˈhævənt/, **hasn't** /ˈhæzənt/, **hadn't** /ˈhædənt/) (used in the negative and interrogative) without 'do' in GB usage, but not always in US usage; in informal style often replaced by have got, e g I've got for I ∼) **1** (in sentences that can be replaced using the verb 'be'); I ∼ no doubt (= There is no doubt in my mind) that .... **2** possess; own: He's (got) a house in the country/five pounds. Has she blue eyes or brown eyes? Are her eyes blue or brown? (Note: In US usage do is common: Does she ∼ blue eyes? In GB informal style, the pp got is common: Has she got blue eyes?) **3** (used to show various connections): How many children ∼ they? ⇨ the Note above. **4** equivalent to be + adj + inf): Will you ∼ the kindness/goodness, etc (= Please be kind or good enough) to hand me that book. **5** (informal) (often with got) hold or keep in the mind; exercise some quality of the mind; experience (some emotion): H∼ you (got) any idea where he lives? **6** (in the inf only and always stressed) allow; endure: I won't `∼ such conduct.

have³ (for pronunciations ⇨ have²) vt (used in the negative and interrogative with or without 'do'.) **1** (expressing obligation or necessity): You ∼n't (got) to go to school today, ∼ you? We had to leave early. **2** (in various senses as shown in these examples): Do you often ∼ (= suffer from) colds? H∼ you (got) (= Are you suffering from) a cold now? How often does your dog ∼ (i e give birth to) puppies? Can you ∼ (= take and look after) the children for a few days? **have⁴** (for pronunciations ⇨ have²) verb (always used in the negative and interrogative with 'do') **1** take; receive; accept; obtain: What shall we ∼ for dinner? **2** (used with a noun where the meaning is the same as the use of the noun as a verb: ∼ a swim/walk. Let me ∼ a try/look. **3** experience; undergo: We didn't ∼ much difficulty. Did you ∼ a good holiday? let sb `have it, (sl) shoot, punish etc him. **4** cause (a person to do something): I must ∼ these shoes repaired. ⇨ get(2). ⇨ also 6 below. **5** want: I would ∼ you know that..., I want you to know that... **6** be effected in some way; experience or suffer: He had his pocket picked, something stolen from his pocket. **7** (a) trick; deceive: I'm afraid you've been had. (b) beat; win an advantage over: You had me there! **8** express; maintain: Rumour has it (= There is a rumour) that the Prime Minister is going to resign.

9 (uses with adverbial particles and prepositions):

have sth back, have it returned: You shall ∼ it back next month.

have sb in, have him in the room, house, etc: We shall be having the decorators in next month. **have sth in,** have in the house, etc: Do we ∼ enough coal in for winter?

have sb on, (*informal*) play a trick on him, deceive him. ⇨ 7 above. **have sth on, (a)** be wearing: *He had nothing on,* was naked. **(b)** be busy, engaged: *I ~ nothing on tomorrow evening,* I am free.

have sth out, cause to be out: *~ a tooth out.* **have it out with sb,** reach an understanding about something by discussion, argument.

have sb up, (a) have a visitor (up from the country, etc). **(b)** (*informal*) cause him to appear before a magistrate, etc: *He was had up* (= was prosecuted) *for exceeding the speed limit.*

ha·ven /ˈheɪvən/ *n* [C] (*fig*) place of safety or rest.

hav·er·sack /ˈhævəsæk/ *n* [C] canvas bag carried by soldiers, hikers, etc on the back.

havoc /ˈhævək/ *n* [U] widespread damage; destruction: *The floods caused terrible ~.*

hawk¹ /hɔːk/ *n* [C] **1** strong, swift, keen-sighted bird of prey. **2** person who favours the use of military force in foreign policy. ⇨ dove.

hawk² /hɔːk/ *vt* **1** go from house to house, street to street, with goods for sale. **2** (*fig*) spread about: *~ news about.*

hawker *n* [C] person who hawks goods from a barrow or cart.

haw·ser /ˈhɔːzə(r)/ *n* [C] **1** thick, heavy rope. **2** thin steel cable (used on ships).

haw·thorn /ˈhɔːθɔːn/ *n* [C] thorny shrub or tree with white, red or pink blossom and small red berries.

hay /heɪ/ *n* [U] grass cut and dried for use as animal food. **make hay while the sun shines,** (*prov*) make the earliest use of one's opportunities.

ˈhay fever, disease affecting the nose and throat, caused by pollen (dust) from various plants.

ˈhay-fork, long-handled two-pronged fork for turning and lifting hay.

ˈhay-rick/stack, large pile of hay firmly packed for storing.

ˈhay·wire *n* [U] wire for tying up bales of hay. □ (*informal*) *adj* out of order; excited or distracted. **go haywire, (a)** (of persons) become distraught. **(b)** (of something, e g a plan) become badly disorganised.

haz·ard /ˈhæzəd/ *n* [C] risk; danger: *ˈhealth ~s,* e g smoking cigarettes. □ *vt* **1** take the risk of; expose to danger: *Rock-climbers sometimes ~ their lives.* **2** try to make: *~ a guess.*

haz·ard·ous /-əs/ *adj* risky: *a ~ous climb.*

haze /heɪz/ *n* [U] **1** thin mist. **2** (*fig*) mental confusion or uncertainty.

hazel /ˈheɪzəl/ *n* **1** [C] bush with edible nuts. **2** [U] (esp of eyes) colour of the shell of the nut, reddish brown. □ *adj* reddish-brown.

hazy /ˈheɪzɪ/ *adj* (-ier, -iest) **1** misty: *~ weather.* **2** (*fig*) vague; slightly confused; uncertain: *~ about what to do next.*

haz·ily /-əlɪ/ *adv*

hazi·ness *n* [U]

H-bomb /ˈeɪtʃ bom/ *n* [C] hydrogen bomb.

he /hiː/ *pron* **1** male person or animal previously referred to: *Where's your brother? H~'s in Paris.* **2** (often as a *prefix*) male: *a ˈ~-goat. Is it a ~ or a she?*

head¹ /hed/ *n* [C] **1** that part of the body which contains the eyes, nose, mouth and brain: *They cut his ~ off.* **2** (as a measure) head's length: *The Queen's horse won by a ~.* **3** that side of a coin on which the head of a ruler appears, the other side being the *tail.* **be unable to make ˈhead or ˈtail of sth,** be unable to understand it in the least. **4** per son: *50 dinners at £1.50 a ~.* **5** (*pl* unchanged) one animal in a flock or herd: *50 ~ of cattle.* **6** intellect; imagination; power to reason: *He made the story up out of his own ~.* **7** natural aptitude or talent: *He has a good ~ for business.* **8** something like a head in form or position, e g the part that is pressed (*the ~ of a pin*), struck (*the ~ of a nail*), used for striking (*the ~ of a hammer*). **9** top: *at the ~ of the page/staircase.* **10** upper end: *the ~ (waters) of the Nile,* its sources and upper streams; *the ~ of a bed,* where a person's head rests. **11** (of plants) mass of leaves or flowers at the top of a stem or stalk: *a fine ~ of cabbage.* **12** (often as an *adjective*) ruler; chief; position of command: *~s of government,* e g the President of the US, the Prime Minister of GB; *at the ~ of the class,* having gained the highest marks; *the ~ office,* the chief or most important office; *the ~master/ mistress of the school.* **13** front; front part: *at the ~ of the procession.* **14** (chiefly in proper names) projecting part, cape: *Beachy H~.* ⇨ headland. **15** body of water kept at a certain height (e g for a hydro–electric power station). **16** pressure or force of a confined body of steam, etc: *They kept up a good ~ of steam.* **17** main division in a discourse, essay, etc: *a speech arranged under five ~s.* ⇨ heading. **18** foam on a liquid that has been poured out, esp liquor: *the ~ on a glass of beer.* **19** point rising from a boil or other swelling on the flesh: *The boil came to a ~.* **20** (various phrases) **bite sb's head off,** scold them angrily. **come to a head,** (*fig*) reach a cri sis: *Affairs have come to a ~.* **eat one's head off,** eat a great deal. **give sb his head,** (*fig*) leave him to act freely. **go to one's head, (a)** (of liquor) intoxicate: *The whisky went to his ~.* **(b)** excite: *His successes have gone to his ~,* made him conceited, etc. **have a ˈgood ˈhead on one's shoulders,** have practical ability, common sense, etc. **head over heels, (a)** headlong: *fall ~ over heels.* **(b)** (*fig*) deeply or completely: *~ over heels in debt/in love.* **keep one's head,** keep calm in a crisis. **laugh/scream one's head off,** laugh/scream loudly. **lose one's head,** become confused or excited. **(go) off one's head, (a)** (become) crazy;

mad. (b) (become) wildly excited. *put our/ your, etc heads together,* consult together. *put sth into a person's head,* suggest it to him. *put sth out of one's head,* stop thinking about it. *talk one's head off,* talk a great deal. *turn sb's head,* make them conceited. *(be) weak in the head,* (be) not very intelligent.

`head-ache *n* [C,U] (a) continuous pain in the head: *have a bad ~ache.* (b) (*informal*) troublesome problem: *more ~aches for the Government.*

`head-dress, (ornamental) covering for the head.

`head-hunter, savage who cuts heads off and keeps them as trophies.

`head-lamp, powerful lamp fixed to the front of a motor-vehicle, etc.

`head-land, = head(14).

`head-light, large lamp on the front of a motor-vehicle, etc.

`head-line, newspaper heading.

`head-man, chief man of a tribe, etc.

`head-`master/·`mistress, principal master/mistress of a school.

`head-on *adj, adv* (of collisions) with the front parts (of vehicles) meeting: *a ~-on collision.*

`head-phones, receivers fitting over the head (for radio, etc).

`head-`quarters *n* (*sing* or *pl*) place from which (e g police, army) operations are controlled.

`head-rest, something that supports the head.

`head-room, = clearance(2).

`head-set, = headphones.

`head-stone, stone set up at the head of a grave.

`head-way, progress.

`head-wind, one that blows directly into one's face, or against the course of a ship, etc.

`head-word, word used as a heading, e g the first word of a dictionary entry.

head-less *adj* having no head.

head² /hed/ *vt,vi* 1 be at the head or top of: *~ a procession; Smith's name ~ed the list.* 2 strike, touch, with the head (e g the ball in football). 3 *head sth/sb off,* get in front of, so as to turn back or aside: *~ off a flock of sheep* (to prevent them from going the wrong way). 4 move in the direction indicated: *~ south; ~ straight for home;* (*fig*) *be ~ing for disaster.*

-headed /-hedɪd/ *suffix* having the type or number of heads mentioned: *three-`headed.*

header /`hedə(r)/ *n* [C] 1 fall, dive or jump with the head first: *take a ~ into a swimming pool.* 2 (football) act of striking the ball with the head.

head-ing /`hedɪŋ/ *n* [C] word or words printed at the top of a section (to show the subject of what follows).

head-long /`hedlɒŋ US: -lɔːŋ/ *adv, adj* 1 with the head first: *fall ~.* 2 thoughtless(ly) and hurried(ly): *rush ~ into a decision.*

head-strong /`hedstrɒŋ US: -strɔːŋ/ *adj* self-willed; obstinate.

heady /`hedɪ/ *adj* (-ier, -iest) 1 acting, done, on impulse; headstrong. 2 (of alcoholic drink) having a quick effect on the senses. 3 (*fig*) (e g of sudden success) having an exciting effect.

heal /hiːl/ *vt,vi* 1 (esp of wounds) (cause to) become healthy and sound: *The wound soon ~ed up/over.* ⇨ also faith-healing. 2 (*fig*) *~ a quarrel,* end it.

healer, person or thing that heals: *Time is a great ~er.*

health /helθ/ *n* [U] 1 condition of the body or the mind; (used in names of organizations, etc): *the 'World `H~ Organisation* (abbr **W H O**). 2 (esp) state of being well and free from illness.

healthy /`helθɪ/ *adj* (-ier, -iest) 1 having good health; well, strong and able to resist disease: *The children look very ~.* (*Note: well* is the usual word in polite references, e g *I hope you're quite well.*) 2 likely to produce good health: *a ~ climate.* 3 showing good health: *a ~ appetite.*

health-ily /-əlɪ/ *adj*

heap /hiːp/ *n* [C] 1 number of things, mass of material, piled up: *a ~ of sand.* 2 (*informal*) large number; plenty: *We have ~s of books/time.* □ *vt* 1 put in a heap: *~ (up) stones.* 2 fill; load: *heap a plate with food; a ~ed spoonful,* more than a level spoonful.

hear /hɪə(r)/ *vt,vi* (*pt,pp* ~d /hɜːd/) 1 become aware of (sound, etc) with the ears: *I ~d someone laughing.* 2 be told or informed: *Have you ~d the news? I've just ~d about his dismissal/illness. hear from sb,* receive a letter, news, etc: *How often do you ~ from your sister? hear of sb/sth,* have knowledge of: *I've never ~d of her/the place,* know nothing of her/the place. 3 listen to; pay attention to: *You'd better ~ what they have to say. hear sb out,* listen to the end: *Don't judge me before I've finished my explanation: ~ me out, please.* 4 (of a judge in a law court) try (a case): *The court ~d the evidence.*

'Hear! `Hear! (used as a form of cheering).

hearer, person who hears.

hear-ing /`hɪərɪŋ/ *n* 1 [U] ability to hear; perception of sound: *Her ~ is poor,* she is rather deaf. *be hard of hearing,* deaf. 2 [U] distance within which one can hear: *in the ~ of strangers,* where strangers may hear. *within/out of hearing,* near enough/not near enough to hear or be heard. 3 [C] opportunity of being heard (esp in self-defence). *a fair hearing,* an opportunity of being listened to impartially. 4 (legal) trial of a case at law, esp before a judge without a jury.

`hearing-aid, electronic device to improve hearing.

hearken /ˈhɑkən/ vi (literary) listen (to).

hear·say /ˈhɪəseɪ/ n [U] rumour; what one has heard another person or other persons say: I don't believe it; it's merely ~.

hearse /hɜs/ n [C] vehicle for carrying a coffin at a funeral.

heart /hɑt/ n [C] 1 that part of the body which pumps blood: When a man's ~ stops beating, he dies. 2 centre of the emotions, esp love; deepest part of one's nature: a man with a kind ~. at heart, deep down; basic-ally. from (the bottom of) one's heart, sincerely. to one's heart's content, as much as, for as long as, etc one wishes. with all one's heart, completely and will-ingly: I love you with all my ~. heart and soul, completely: I'm yours ~ and soul. break a person's heart, make him very sad. (learn/know sth) by heart, from memory. (have) a change of heart, change that makes one a better person. have one's heart in one's mouth, be anxious, badly frightened. have one's heart in the right place, have true or kind feelings. have one's heart set on sth, desire greatly. lose heart, be discouraged. set one's heart on sth/having sth/doing sth, etc, desire greatly, be very anxious (to have, to do, etc). take heart (from) gain courage (from). take sth to heart, be much affected by it. 3 central part: in the ~ of the forest. the heart of the matter, the essence. 4 (of a vegetable, etc) the central part: a cabbage ~. 5 heart-shaped thing, esp the red design used on some playing-cards: the ten/queen/etc of ~s. 6 (as a term of endearment to a person): `sweet~.

`heart-ache, deep sorrow.

`heart attack, sudden irregular working of the heart, often causing death.

`heart-beat, movement of the heart (about 70 beats a minute).

`heart-break, overwhelming sorrow.

`heart-break-ing adj causing deep sorrow.

`heart-broken, overwhelmed by sorrow.

`heart-burn, burning sensation in the lower part of the chest, caused by indigestion.

`heart-felt adj sincere: ~felt emotion/thanks.

`heart-strings, deepest feelings of love.

`heart-throb, person, e g a pop star, who is fanatically admired.

heart-less adj unkind; without pity.

heart-less-ly adv

-hearted /hɑtɪd/ suffix having the heart(2) mentioned: 'kind-`~; 'broken-'~, heart-broken.

hearten /ˈhɑtən/ vt give courage to; cheer: ~ing news.

hearth /hɑθ/ n [C] 1 (floor of a) fireplace. 2 (fig) fireside as representing the home.

heart·ily /ˈhɑtɪlɪ/ adv 1 with goodwill, courage or appetite: eat ~. 2 very: ~ sick of this wet weather.

heart·land /ˈhɑtlænd/ n [C] central, most important region in a country.

hearty /ˈhɑtɪ/ adj (-ier, -iest) 1 (of feelings) sincere: give a person a ~ welcome. 2 strong; in good health: still hale and ~ at eighty-five. 3 (of meals, appetites) big: a ~ meal.

heat¹ /hit/ n 1 [U] hotness: the ~ of the sun's rays. 2 [U] (fig) intense feeling: in the ~ of the debate/argument. 3 [C] competi-tion the winners of which take part in (further competitions leading to) the finals: trial/preliminary ~s. 4 [U] be on heat, (of female mammals) in a period or condition of sexual excitement.

`heat-stroke, sudden illness, caused by excessive heat.

`heat-wave, unbroken period of unusually hot weather.

heat² /hit/ vt,vi 1 make or become hot: ~ (up) some water. 2 (fig) become excited: a ~ed discussion, one during which feelings are roused.

heat·ed·ly adv in an excited manner.

heater, device for supplying warmth to a room, or for heating water, etc: an `oil-~er.

heath /hiθ/ n 1 [C] area of waste land, esp if covered with the shrubs called heath. 2 [C,U] (kinds of) low evergreen shrub with small purple, pink or white flowers, e g heather.

hea·then /ˈhiðən/ n 1 [C] (pl without s when used with the) believer in a religion other than the chief world religions: The Saxons who invaded England in olden times were ~s. 2 [C] person whose morals, etc are disapproved of: a young ~, wild, ill-mannered youth.

hea·then·ish /-ɪʃ/ adj

heather /ˈheðə(r)/ n [U] shrub with small light-purple or white flowers.

heave /hiv/ vt,vi (pt,pp ~d or 6 hove /həʊv/) 1 raise, lift up (something heavy): ~ the anchor. 2 utter: ~ a sigh/groan. 3 (informal) lift and throw: ~ a brick through a window. 4 pull (at a rope, etc). 5 rise and fall regularly; move up and down. 6 (of a sailing-ship) (cause to) come to a standstill (without anchoring or mooring): The barque hove to. □ n [C] act of heaving: with a mighty ~.

heaven /ˈhevən/ n [C] 1 home of God and the saints: die and go to ~. 2 (usually H~) God, Providence: Thank H~ you were not killed. 3 (as an exclamation): Good H~s! 4 place, state, of supreme happiness. 4 (often pl) the sky. move heaven and earth, do one's utmost.

'heaven-'sent adj opportune, fortunate: a ~sent opportunity.

heaven·ward(s) /-wəd(z)/ adj, adv.

heav·en·ly /ˈhevənlɪ/ adj 1 of, from, like, heaven: a ~ angel/vision. 2 of more than earthly excellence. 3 (informal) very pleas-ing: What a ~ dress!

'heavenly `body, sun, moon, planet, etc.

heavy /'hevɪ/ adj (-ier, -iest) **1** having (esp great) weight; difficult to lift, carry or move: *It's too ~ for me to lift.* **2** of more than usual size, amount, force, etc: *~ rain/work; a ~ heart*, made sad; *a ~ smoker; ~ food*, rich, difficult to digest. **heavy going,** difficult or boring. **3** (of persons) slow in speech or thought; (of writing or painting) dull, tedious. **4** (of bodily states) inactive: *~ with sleep/wine.* □ *adv* heavily: *The crime lies ~ on his conscience.*
'**heavy-'hearted** adj sad.
'**heavy-'laden** adj (a) carrying a heavy load. (b) (fig) having a sad heart.
'**heavy-weight,** boxer weighing 175 lb (79·3 kg) or more.
heav·ily /'hevɪlɪ/ adv
heavi·ness n [U]
He·bra·ic /hi'breɪk/ adj Hebrew.
He·brew /'hibru/ n [C] **1** Jew; Israelite. **2** (a) language used by the ancient Hebrews (as in the Old Testament). (b) language now spoken by the people of Israel. □ adj of the Hebrew language or people.
heck /hek/ n (sl) (used in exclamations) hell: *Oh! What the ~!*
heckle /'hekəl/ vt interrupt and ask questions at a meeting: *~ the Socialist candidate.*
heck·ler /'heklə(r)/ n [C]
hec·tare /'hektɑ(r)/ US: -teər/ n [C] metric measure of area, 10 000 sq metres (= 2·471 acres).
hec·tic /'hektɪk/ adj **1** unnaturally red; feverish: *~ cheeks.* **2** full of excitement and without rest: *lead a ~ life.*
hecto- /'hektəʊ/ prefix hundred: '~gram(me), 100 grammes.
he'd /hid/ = he had; he would.
hedge /hedʒ/ n [C] **1** row of bushes, shrubs or tall plants, etc forming a boundary for a field, garden, etc. **2** (fig) means of defence against possible loss: *buy gold/diamonds as a ~ against inflation.* □ vt,vi **1** put a hedge or (fig) barrier round: *~ a field; ~ a person in/round with rules and regulations.* **2** avoid giving a direct answer to a question: *Answer 'yes' or 'no'—don't ~!* **3** (informal) protect a bet, investment, by compensating transactions: *~ one's bets.*
'**hedge-row,** row of bushes forming a hedge.
hedge·hog /'hedʒhog US: -hɔg/ n [C] insect-eating animal covered with spines.
he·don·ism /'hidənɪzm/ n [U] belief that pleasure is the chief good.
he·don·ist /-ɪst/ n [C] believer in hedonism.
he·don·is·tic /'hidə'nɪstɪk/ adv
heed /hid/ vt pay attention to: *~ a warning.* □ n [U] attention, notice: *pay/take no ~ to a warning.*
heed·ful adj: *be more ~ful of advice.*
heed·less adj: *~less of danger.*
hee·haw /'hihɔ/ n [U] **1** noise made by an ass. **2** rude laugh.

heel[1] /hil/ n [C] **1** back part of the human foot; part of a sock, stocking, etc covering this; part of a shoe, boot, etc supporting this. **at/(up)on sb's heel(s),** close behind: *Famine often follows on the ~s of war.* **down at heel,** (of a person) untidy and poor. **head over heels,** ⇨ head[1](20). **come to heel, (a)** (of a dog) come, walk, close behind its master. **(b)** (fig) submit to discipline and control. **take to one's heels,** run away. **turn on one's heel,** turn sharply round. **2** (sl) worthless person. □ vt put a heel on.
'**well-'heeled** adj (sl) very rich; drunk.
heel[2] /hil/ vi,vt **heel over,** (of a ship) (cause to) lean over to one side.
hef·ty /'heftɪ/ adj (-ier, -iest) (informal) big, strong: *a ~ increase/farm worker.*
he·gem·ony /hɪ'geməni US: hɪ'dʒeməni/ n [C] (pl -ies) (formal) leadership, esp of one state in a group of states.
He·gira, He·jira /'hɪdʒɑrərə/ n Muhammad's flight from Mecca to Medina; Muslim era reckoned from this (A D 622).
heifer /'hefə(r)/ n [C] young cow that has not yet had a calf.
height /haɪt/ n [C] **1** measurement from bottom to top; distance to the top of something, esp from sea-level: *the ~ of a mountain. What is your ~?* How tall are you? **2** high place: *on the mountain ~s.* **3** utmost degree: *the ~ of his ambition/of fashion/of a storm.*
heighten /'haɪtn/ vt,vi make or become high(er); make greater in degree: *~ a person's anger.*
hei·nous /'heɪnəs/ adj (of crime) extremely bad; atrocious.
hei·nous·ly adv
heir /eə(r)/ n [C] person with the legal right to receive a title, property, etc when the owner dies: *He is ~ to a large fortune.*
heir·ess /'eəres/ n [C] female heir.
heir·loom /'eəlum/ n [C] something handed down in a family for several generations.
He·jira /'hɪdʒɑrərə/ n = Hegira.
held /held/ pt,pp of hold[2].
heli·cop·ter /'helɪkoptə(r)/ n [C] kind of aircraft with horizontal revolving blades (rotors).
heli·port /'helɪpot/ n [C] airport for helicopters.
he·lium /'hiliəm/ n [C] light, colourless gas (symbol He) that does not burn, used in balloons and airships.
hell /hel/ n [C] **1** (in some religions) place of punishment after death. **2** place, condition, of great suffering or misery: *suffer ~ on earth.* **play hell with sb,** become very angry with him. **3** (informal) (used in exclamations, to express anger, or to intensify a meaning): *What the ~ do you want? He ran like ~*, very fast. *I like him a ~ of a lot.* **for the hell of it,** for no particular reason.
hell·ish /-ɪʃ/ adj horrible.
he'll /hil/ = he will, he shall.

hello /heˈləʊ/ int = hallo.

helm /helm/ n [C] handle (also called *tiller*) or wheel for moving the rudder of a boat or ship. *at the helm,* in control.

helms·man, man at the helm.

hel·met /ˈhelmɪt/ n [C] protective covering for the head as worn by soldiers, police, motorbike riders, etc.

helmeted adj wearing, provided with, a helmet.

helot /ˈhelət/ n [C] **1** one of a class of slaves in ancient Sparta. **2** (*fig*) member of a low social class.

help[1] /help/ n **1** [U] act of helping: *Thank you for your kind* ∼. **2** (*sing* with *a, an*) person or thing that helps: *Your advice was a great* ∼. **3** [U] remedy: *There's no* ∼ *for it.* **4** [C] girl or woman paid to do the house-work. ⇨ also home help.

helper, person who helps.

help·ful /-fəl/ adj giving help.

help·fully /-fəlɪ/ adv

help·ing, (esp) portion of food served at a meal: *three* ∼*ings of pie.*

help·ful·ness n [U]

help·less adj **(a)** not receiving ∼. **(b)** dependent on others: *a* ∼*less invalid.*

help·less·ly adv

help[2] /help/ vt,vi **1** do part of the work of another person; make it easier for (a person) to do something or for (something) to happen: *I can't lift this box by myself, please* ∼ *me. We* ∼*ed the old man out of the car. Would it* ∼ *you to know that...,* if I told you that... *help out,* give help (esp in a crisis). **2** serve with food, drink, etc: *H*∼ *yourself to the fruit.* **3** (with *can/cannot/can't*) avoid; refrain; prevent: *I can't* ∼ *thinking he's still alive. She burst out crying; she couldn't* ∼ *herself. It can't be* ∼*ed,* is inevitable.

hel·ter-skel·ter /ˈheltə ˈskeltə(r)/ adv in disorderly haste. □ n [C] spiral slide[1](2) in a fairground, etc.

hem[1] /hem/ n [C] border or edge of cloth, esp one on an article of clothing, when turned and sewn down. □ vt (-mm-) **1** make a hem on. **2** enclose; confine; surround: ∼*med in by the enemy.*

hemline, (esp) lower edge of a skirt or dress.

hem[2] (also **h'm**) /hem, həm/ int used to indicate doubt, etc or to call attention.

hemi·sphere /ˈhemɪsfɪə(r)/ n [C] **1** half a sphere. **2** half the earth.

the Eastern hemisphere, Europe, Asia, Africa and Australia.

the Northern/Southern hemisphere, north/south of the equator.

the Western hemisphere, N and S America.

hem·lock /ˈhemlɒk/ n [C,U] (small, white plant which produces a) poison.

he·mo·glo·bin (also **hæ-**) /ˈhiːməˈgləʊbɪn/ n [U] colouring matter of the red corpuscles of the blood.

he·mo·philia (also **hæ-**) /ˈhiːməˈfɪlɪə/ n [U] (usually hereditary) tendency of blood (from a wound, etc) not to clot, so that bleeding continues.

he·mo·phil·iac (also **hæ-**) /ˈhiːməˈfɪlɪæk/ n [C] person having hemophilia.

hem·or·rhage (also **hæm-**) /ˈhemərɪdʒ/ n [U] (*med*) bleeding; [C] instance of this.

hem·or·rhoids (also **hæm-**) /ˈhemərɔɪdz/ n pl (*med*) swelling of a vein or veins, esp at or near the anus.

hemp /hemp/ n [U] **1** (kinds of) plant from which coarse fibres are obtained for the manufacture of rope and cloth. **2** (also *Indian* ∼) narcotic from the flowering tops, seed and resin of such plants, e g *cannabis, marijuana.*

hempen /ˈhempən/ adj made of, like, hemp: *a* ∼*en rope.*

hem·stitch /ˈhemstɪtʃ/ vt, n [C] (ornament the hem of a dress, etc with a) decorative stitch made by pulling out some of the threads and tying the cross-threads in groups.

hen /hen/ n [C] **1** female of the common domestic fowl. ⇨ cock[1](1). **2** female (of the bird named): `guinea-∼, `pea-∼.

hen-coop, hut for keeping poultry in.

hen-house, building for poultry.

hen-party, (*informal*) party for women only. ⇨ stag party.

hen-pecked adj (of a man) ruled by his wife.

hence /hens/ adv **1** from here; from now: *a week* ∼, in a week's time. **2** for this reason.

hence·forth, hence·forward, adv from this time on; in future.

hench·man /ˈhentʃmən/ n [C] (pl -men) faithful supporter, esp one who obeys without question the orders of his leader.

henna /ˈhenə/ n [U] (plant, kind of Egyptian privet, producing) reddish-brown dye stuff for colouring leather, the hair, etc.

hen·naed /ˈhenəd/ adj dyed with henna.

hepa·titis /ˈhepəˈtaɪtɪs/ n [U] inflammation of the liver.

hep·ta·gon /ˈheptəgən US: -gɒn/ n [C] plane figure with 7 (esp equal) sides.

hep·tag·onal /hepˈtægənəl/ adj seven-sided.

her /hə(r) strong form: hɜː(r)/ personal pron (used as object form of *she*): *Give* ∼ *the book.* □ adj belonging to her: *That's* ∼ *hat, not yours.*

hers /hɜːz/ possessive pron belonging to her: *Is that his or* ∼?

her·ald /ˈherəld/ n [C] **1** person (formerly) making public announcements for, and carrying messages from, a ruler. **2** person or thing foretelling the coming of a person or thing: *In England the cuckoo is a* ∼ *of spring.* **3** official who keeps records of families that have coats of arms. □ vt proclaim the approach of.

her·al·dic /heˈrældɪk/ adj of heralds or heraldry.

her·aldry n [U] science dealing with the coats of arms, descent, and history of old families.

herb /hɜb US: ɜb/ n [C] **1** small, soft-stemmed flowering plant. **2** plant of this kind whose leaves or seeds, because of their scent or flavour, are used in medicine or for flavouring food, e g sage, mint.

herb·age /-ɪdʒ/ n [U] grass and other field plants.

herbal /-əl/ adj of (esp) medicinal herbs: ~al remedies.

herb·al·ist /-ɪst/, person who grows or sells herbs.

her·ba·ceous /hɜ`beɪʃəs/ adj (of plants) having stems that are not woody: a ~ border, border with plants which grow and flower year after year.

her·bivor·ous /hɜ`bɪvərəs/ adj (of animals) feeding on grass, etc. ⇨ **carnivorous**.

her·cu·lean /`hɜkju`liən/ adj having, needing, great powers of body or mind: a ~ task.

herd /hɜd/ n [C] **1** number of animals, esp cattle, feeding or going about together: a ~ of cattle/deer/elephants. **2** (used chiefly in compounds) keeper of a herd: a `cow~. **3** the common ~, the mass of common people. □ vi,vt (cause to) gather (as) into a herd; look after a herd: We were ~ed together like cattle.

herds·man, keeper of a herd.

here /hɪə(r)/ adv of place or direction **1** in, at, to, towards, this point of place: Come ~. I live ~. H~ comes the bus! H~ you are/it is! Do you live near ~? **2** at this point (in a series of events, in a process, etc): H~ the speaker paused to have a drink. **Here goes!** Now I'm going to make a start, have a go. **3** **here and there**, in various places. **here, there and everywhere**, in all parts; all round. **neither here nor there**, (informal) irrelevant. **4** (used to call attention, or for emphasis): My friend ~ was a witness of the accident. **5** (when answering a roll-call) present. **6** (used when drinking to a person's health, etc): H~'s to the bride and bride-groom!

here·a·bouts adv near or about here.

here·'after adv, n [U] (in the) future; the life after death.

here·by adv (legal) by reason of this.

here·'in adv (legal) in this.

here·'of adv (legal) of or about this.

here·to·'(fore adv (legal, archaic) until now; formerly.

here·'with adv with this.

her·ed·itary /hɪ`redɪtrɪ US: -terɪ/ adj passed on from parent to child, from one generation to following generations: ~ rulers/diseases.

her·ed·ity /hɪ`redətɪ/ n [U] **1** tendency to pass characteristics on to offspring, etc. **2** characteristics, etc so passed on.

her·esy /`herəsɪ/ n [C,U] (pl -ies) (holding

of a) belief or opinion contrary to what is generally accepted, esp in religion: be guilty of ~.

her·etic /`herətɪk/ n [C] person guilty of, supporting, heresy; person who holds an unorthodox opinion.

her·eti·cal /hɪ`retɪkəl/ adj of heresy of heretics: ~al beliefs.

heri·tage /`herɪtɪdʒ/ n [C] that which has been or may be inherited.

her·maph·ro·dite /hɜ`mæfrədaɪt/ n [C] animal or other creature, e g an earthworm, which has both male and female sexual organs or characteristics.

her·metic /hɜ`metɪk/ adj completely air-tight.

her·meti·cally adv: ~ally sealed.

her·mit /`hɜmɪt/ n [C] person living in isolation from others.

her·mit·age /-ɪdʒ/ n [C] living-place of a hermit.

her·nia /`hɜnɪə/ n [U] rupture, esp part of the bowel through the muscle wall of the abdomen.

hero /`hɪərəʊ/ n [C] (pl ~es) **1** boy or man respected for bravery or noble qualities. **2** chief man in a poem, story, play, etc.

hero·ism /-ɪzm/ n [U] quality of being a hero; courage.

her·oic /hɪ`rəʊɪk/ adj **1** of, like, fit for, a hero: ~ deeds/tasks. **2** of a size larger than life: a statue on a ~ scale. **3** (of poetry) dealing with heroes. **4** (of language) grand; attempting great things.

her·oics n pl (a) grand talk or sentiments. (b) bravery; brave actions.

he·roi·cally /-klɪ/ adv

her·oin /`herəʊɪn/ n [U] narcotic drug prepared from morphine.

her·oine /`herəʊɪn/ n [C] female hero.

heron /`herən/ n [C] long-legged water-bird living in marshy places.

her·ring /`herɪŋ/ n [C] (pl often unchanged) seafish valued as food (fresh, salted, or dried).

her·ring·bone adj n [U] pattern for stitching (like the spine and bones of a herring).

red `herring, ⇨ red.

hers /hɜz/ ⇨ her.

her·self /hɜ`self strong form: hɜ-/ pron **1** (reflexive): She hurt ~. She ought to be ashamed of ~. **(all) by herself**, (a) alone. (b) without help. **2** (used for emphasis): She told me the news ~. **3** She's not quite ~ today, not in her normal state of health or mind.

hertz /hɜts/ n [C] (symbol **Hz**) unit of frequency equal to one cycle per second.

he's /hiz/ = he is, he has.

hesi·tant /`hezɪtənt/ adj tending to hesitate.

hesi·tant·ly adv

hes·i·tance /-əns/, **hes·i·tancy** /-ənsɪ/ n [U]

hesi·tate /`hezɪteɪt/ vi show signs of uncertainty or unwillingness in speech or action:

He's still hesitating about joining.
hesi·tat·ing·ly adv
hesi·ta·tion /ˌhezɪˈteɪʃən/ n 1 [U] state of hesitating. 2 [C] instance of this: *His doubts and ~s were tedious.*
hes·sian /ˈhesɪən US: ˈheʃən/ n [U] strong, coarse cloth of hemp or jute.
het·ero·dox /ˈhetərədoks/ adj not normal, accepted, established.
het·ero·doxy, heterodox state, activity.
het·ero·gen·eous /ˌhetərəˈdʒiːnɪəs/ adj different; made up of different kinds: *the ~ population of the USA,* of many different races. ⇨ **homogeneous.**
het·ero·sex·ual /ˌhetərəˈseksʊəl/ adj attracted to/by the opposite sex.
het·up /ˈhet ˈʌp/ adj (informal) worried.
hew /hjuː/ vt,vi (pt ~ed, pp ~ed or ~n) 1 cut (by striking or chopping); aim cutting blows (at, among): *~ down a branch.* 2 shape by chopping: *~n timber.* 3 make by hard work: *~ out a career for oneself.*
hewer, person who hews: *~s of coal.*
hexa·gon /ˈheksəgən US: -gon/ n [C] plane figure with 6 (esp equal) sides.
hex·ag·onal /heksˈægənəl/ adj six-sided.
hey /heɪ/ int used to call attention, to express surprise, etc.
hey·day /ˈheɪ deɪ/ n (sing only) time of greatest prosperity or power: *in the ~ of steam railways.*
hi /haɪ/ int 1 = hey. 2 (esp US) = hallo.
hi·atus /haɪˈeɪtəs/ n [C] (pl ~es) gap in a series, making it incomplete.
hi·ber·nate /ˈhaɪbəneɪt/ vi (of some animals) pass the whole of the winter in a state like sleep.
hi·ber·na·tion /ˌhaɪbəˈneɪʃən/ n [U]
Hi·ber·nian /haɪˈbɜːnɪən/ adj of Ireland; Irish.
hi·bis·cus /hɪˈbɪskəs/ n [C,U] (usually tropical) plant or shrub with brightly coloured flowers.
hic·cup, hic·cough /ˈhɪkʌp/ vt, n [C] (have a) sudden stopping of the breath with a sound like a cough.
hick·ory /ˈhɪkərɪ/ n [C,U] (pl -ies) (hard wood of a) N American tree with edible nuts.
hid, hidden ⇨ hide¹.
hide¹ /haɪd/ vt,vi (pt hid /hɪd/, pp hidden /ˈhɪdən/ or hid) 1 put or keep out of sight; prevent from being seen, found or known: *Quick, ~ yourself! The sun was hidden by the clouds. His words had a hidden meaning.* 2 be or become hidden: *Where is he hiding?* □ n [C] (US = blind) place where wild animals, birds, etc may be observed, e g by photographers, without alarming them.
ˋhide-out/-away, (informal) hiding-place: *a guerrilla ~-out in the mountains.*
hid·ing n be in/go into hiding, be hidden/ hide oneself. **come out of hiding,** show oneself.

ˋhiding-place, place where a person or thing is or could be hidden.
hide² /haɪd/ n [C] 1 animal's skin. 2 (informal) human skin.
hid·ing n [C] beating: *give/get a good hiding.*
hide·bound /ˈhaɪdbaʊnd/ adj having, showing, too much respect for rules and traditions.
hid·eous /ˈhɪdɪəs/ adj very ugly; filling the mind with horror: *a ~ crime/noise.*
hid·eous·ly adv
hi·er·archy /ˈhaɪərɑːkɪ/ n [C] (pl -ies) organization with grades of authority from lowest to highest.
hi·ero·glyph /ˈhaɪərəglɪf/ n [C] 1 picture or figure of an object, representing a word, syllable or sound, as used in the writing of the ancient Egyptians and Mexicans. 2 other secret or unintelligible written symbol.
hi·ero·glyphic /ˌhaɪərəˈglɪfɪk/ adj of hieroglyphs. □ n [C] = hieroglyph.
hi-fi /ˈhaɪ ˈfaɪ/ adj (informal abbr of) high fidelity.
high¹ /haɪ/ adj (-er, -est) 1 extending far upwards; measuring (the distance given) from the base to the top: *There was an aeroplane ~ in the sky. How ~ is Mt Everest?* (Note: *tall* is used for human beings and for a few things which have great height in relation to breadth, e g *a tall building/tower.*) *high and dry,* stranded; abandoned. 2 chief; important: *a ~ official; the ~ altar,* in a church. 3 (of sounds) at or near the top of the scale; shrill; sharp: *speak in a ~ tone/key.* 4 extreme; great: *~ prices/temperatures; have a ~ opinion of her; in ~ spirits; have a ~ (= joyous) time; ~ (= luxurious) living; ~ noon/summer,* at or near its peak. 5 *high time,* time when something should be done at once: *It's ~ time you started.* 6 noble; virtuous: *~ aims/ideals; a ~ calling,* e g that of a priest, doctor or nurse. 7 (of food, esp meat and fish) slightly tainted. 8 (informal) intoxicated; under the influence of hallucinatory drugs.
ˋhigh-born adj of noble birth.
ˋhigh-brow n, adj (person) with intellectual tastes and interests considered to be superior.
ˋhigh-chair, one on high legs for an infant.
ˈHigh ˋChurch, section of the Anglican Church which gives great importance to church authority, ritual, etc.
ˋhigh-class adj first-class.
ˈHigh Comˋmissioner, representative of one Commonwealth country in another, equivalent to an ambassador.
ˋHigh Court, supreme court of justice.
ˋhigh-fiˋdelity adj (informal abbr **hi-fi**) (of radios, records, tapes and equipment for reproducing sound) giving faithful reproduction by the use of a wide range of sound waves. □ n [C] equipment producing this sound.

'**high-'filer/·'flyer** ambitious person.
'**high-'flown** adj pompous; pretentious
'**high-'flying** adj ambitious.
'**high-'frequency,** (abbr **h f**) radio frequency between 3 and 30 megacycles per second.
high gear, (in the engine of a motor-vehicle) used when driving fast.
'**high-grade** adj of superior quality.
'**high-'handed** adj using power or authority without consideration for the feelings of another.
'**high-jack** vt = hijack.
'**high jump** athletic contest for jumping over an adjustable horizontal bar.
'**high-land,** mountainous region; (pl) any mountainous parts of a country.
'**high-level** adj (of conferences, etc) of persons in high positions.
'**high life,** (a) fashionable and luxurious style of living. (b) (in W Africa) popular kind of music and dance.
'**high-light,** (a) (usually pl) luminous area on a photograph, picture, etc which shows reflected light; reflection or contrast of light, colour. (b) (fig) most conspicuous or prominent part: the ~lights of the week's events. □ vt give prominence or emphasis to.
'**High 'Mass,** (R C Church) according to the complete rite.
'**high-'minded** adj having high morals, ideals or principles.
'**high-'powered** adj (a) having, using, great power: a ~powered engine. (b) (of optical instruments) giving great magnitude. (c) (of persons) important; energetic.
'**high 'priest,** chief priest.
'**high-rise** adj (of tall buildings) with many storeys or levels: ~-rise flats.
'**high-road,** main road.
'**High School,** secondary school like a grammar school.
'**high 'seas** n pl (with the) all parts of the seas and oceans beyond territorial waters.
'**high-sounding** adj (of style) pretentious.
'**high so'ciety,** upper classes; aristocracy.
'**high-'spirited** adj bold; lively.
'**high spot,** outstanding feature, memory, event, etc.
'**high street,** (esp in proper names) main street of a town.
'**high 'tea,** (GB) early evening meal (or late tea) in homes where dinner is not eaten in the evening.
'**high 'tide,** (time at which the) tide is at its highest level.
'**high treason,** treason against the State or a sovereign.
'**high-up,** (informal) person of high rank or great importance.
'**high 'water,** = high tide.
'**high-way,** (a) main public road; main route (by air, sea or land). (b) (fig) easiest or most direct way.
'**high-way-man,** (formerly) man, often

masked, who robbed travellers on highways by using, threatening, violence.
high² /haɪ/ adv in or to a high degree: climb ~. **hold one's head high,** proudly. **run high,** (a) (of the sea) have a strong current with a high tide. (b) (of the feelings) be very excited. **search/hunt/look high and low (for sth),** look everywhere (for it).
high³ /haɪ/ n high level: from (on) ~, from Heaven; reach a new ~, highest known level.
high-ly /'haɪlɪ/ adv in or to a high degree: a ~ paid official; a ~ amusing film. **think highly of sb,** have a high opinion of them.
high-ness /'haɪnəs/ n 1 [U] (opposite of lowness) state or quality of being high. 2 [C] title used of and to British and various foreign princes: His/Her/Your/Royal H~.
hi-jack (also **high-jack**) /'haɪdʒæk/ vt 1 steal goods from, e g a lorry, by stopping it in transit. 2 rob (a vehicle of goods) in this way. 3 use, threaten, force against those in control of (an aircraft or vehicle) in order to achieve certain aims or to reach a desired destination.
hi-jacker (also **high-jacker**) n [C]
hike /haɪk/ vi, n [C] (informal) (go for a) long walk in the country, taken for pleasure or exercise. ⇨ hitch-hike.
hiker, person who hikes.
hil-ari-ous /hɪ'leərɪəs/ adj (making a person) noisily merry.
hil-ari-ous-ly adv
hil-ar-ity /hɪ'lærətɪ/ n [U] cheerfulness; loud laughter.
hill /hɪl/ n [C] 1 mass of high land, lower than a mountain. 2 slope, e g on a road: drive up a steep ~. 3 heap of earth: 'ant~s.
'**hill-side,** side, slope, of a hill.
'**hill-top,** summit of a hill.
hilly adj (-ier, -iest) having many hills.
hill-ock /'hɪlək/ n [C] small hill(1).
hilt /hɪlt/ n [C] handle of a sword or dagger. **(up) to the hilt,** completely: His guilt was proved to the ~.
him /hɪm/ personal pron (used as object form of he): Give ~ the money.
him-self /hɪm'self/ pron 1 (reflexive): He cut ~. He ought to be ashamed of ~. **(all) by himself,** (a) alone. (b) without help. 2 (used for emphasis): Did you see the manager ~? 3 He's not quite ~ today, not in his normal state of health or mind.
hind¹ /haɪnd/ adj (of things in pairs, front and back) at the back: the ~ legs of a horse. ⇨ fore.
'**hind-'quarters** n pl back part of the halved carcass of lamb, beef, etc.
'**hind-most** adj farthest behind or back.
'**hind-sight** n [U] becoming aware of the characteristics, etc of an event after its occurrence.
hind² /haɪnd/ n [C] female of (esp the red) deer.
hin-der /'hɪndə(r)/ vt obstruct; get in the

way of: *Don't ∼ me in my work.*

hin·drance /ˈhɪndrəns/ *n* [C] person or thing that hinders: *You are more of a ∼ than a help.*

Hindi /ˈhɪndɪ/ *n, adj* of one of the official languages of N India.

Hindu /ˈhɪnˈduː US: ˈhɪnduː/ *n* [C] person, esp of N India, whose religion is Hinduism. □ *adj* of the Hindus.

Hin·du·ism /-ɪzm/ *n* [U] religion involving religious, social and philosophical beliefs with elaborate ritual, a belief in reincarnation, and a divinely ordained caste system.

hinge /hɪndʒ/ *n* [C] 1 joint on which a lid, door or gate turns or swings. 2 (*fig*) central principle on which something depends. □ *vt, vi* 1 support, attach with, a hinge or hinges. 2 *hinge on/upon*, depend on.

hint /hɪnt/ *n* [C] slight or indirect indication or suggestion: *I know how to take a ∼,* realize and will do what is suggested. □ *vt, vi* 1 suggest; give a hint: *I ∼ed that he ought to work harder.* 2 refer indirectly to: *He ∼ed at my indiscretion.*

hin·ter·land /ˈhɪntəlænd/ *n* [C] 1 area of land supplying goods to a port. 2 coastal areas of a country.

hip[1] /hɪp/ *n* [C] part on either side where the bone of a person's leg is joined to the trunk: *He stood there with his hands on his ∼s.* ˈ**hip-flask**, small flask (for brandy, etc).

hip[2] /hɪp/ *n* [C] fruit (red when ripe) of the wild rose.

hip[3] /hɪp/ *int* '**Hip, hip, hurˋrah!** exclamation of satisfaction or approval.

hippy, hip·pie /ˈhɪpɪ/ *n* [C] (*pl* -ies) person who rejects social values.

hippo /ˈhɪpəʊ/ *n* [C] (*pl* ∼s) (*informal* abbr of) hippopotamus.

hip·po·pota·mus /ˌhɪpəˈpɒtəməs/ *n* [C] (*pl* ∼es or -mi /maɪ/) large, thick-skinned African river animal.

hip·ster /ˈhɪpstə(r)/ *adj* held at the hips (not at the waist): ∼ *trousers.*

hire /ˈhaɪə(r)/ *vt* obtain or allow the use or services of in return for fixed payment: *∼ a horse/car.* □ *n* [U] (money paid for) hiring: *bicycles on ∼, 50p an hour.*
'**hire-ˋpurchase,** (abbr **H P**) contract to pay for something by instalments, and having the use of it after the first payment.

his /hɪz/ *adj, pron* belonging to him: *He hurt ∼ hand. Are you a friend of ∼?*

hiss /hɪs/ *vi, vt* 1 make the sound /s/, or the noise heard when water falls on a very hot surface: *The steam escaped with a ∼ing sound.* 2 show disapproval by making this sound: *∼ (at) an actor.* □ *n* [C] hissing sound: *The speaker ignored the ∼es.*

his·tor·ian /hɪˈstɔːrɪən/ *n* [C] writer, student of, expert in, history.

his·toric /hɪˈstɒrɪk US: -ˋstɔːr-/ *adj* notable or memorable in history; associated with past times: *a(n) ∼ event.*

historic present, (*gram*) simple present

tense used for events in the past (to make the description more vivid).

his·tori·cal /hɪˈstɒrɪkl US: -ˋstɔːr-/ *adj* 1 belonging to history (as contrasted with legend and fiction): *a(n) ∼ novel/play/film, etc,* one dealing with real events in history. 2 having to do with history: *∼ studies.*
his·tori·cally /-klɪ/ *adv*

his·tory /ˈhɪstərɪ/ *n* (*pl* -ies) 1 [U] branch of knowledge dealing with past events of a country, continent or the world. *make history,* do something which will be recorded in history 2 [C] description of past events: *a new ∼ of Europe.* 3 [C] events connected with a person or thing: *a house with a strange ∼; a person's medical ∼.*
ancient history, to A D 476, when the Western Roman Empire was destroyed.
medieval history, to 1453, when Constantinople was taken by the Turks.
modern history, since 1453.
'**natural ˋhistory,** science, study, of all objects in nature.

his·tri·onic /ˌhɪstrɪˈɒnɪk/ *adj* 1 of drama, the theatre or acting. 2 artificial; insincere.
his·tri·on·ics *n pl* 1 (*formal*) theatrical performances. 2 exaggerated manners, behaviour, etc, to create an effect.

hit /hɪt/ *vt, vi* (-tt-; *pt, pp* ∼) 1 give a blow or stroke to; strike (a target, an object aimed at); come against (something) with force: *∼ a man on the head; be ∼ by a falling stone. hit the nail on the head,* guess, say or do exactly the right thing. *hit it off (with sb/together),* get on well. 2 *hit sb hard,* cause him to suffer: *He was hard ∼/∼ hard by his financial losses.* 3 go to; find; reach: *∼ the right path,* find it during a journey. *∼ town,* arrive. *Prices ∼ a new low.* 4 *hit out (against),* (*fig*) attack strongly: *The Minister ∼ out against trade union leaders.* 5 *hit on/upon,* find by chance or unexpectedly: *∼ on an idea.* 6 (in cricket) score: *He quickly ∼ 60 runs.* □ *n* [C] 1 blow; stroke: *three ∼s and five misses.* 2 successful attempt or performance: *The new play is quite a ∼.* 3 stroke of sarcasm, etc: *That was a ∼ at me,* the words were directed against me.
'**hit parade,** list of top selling popular records.
'**hit song/ˋsong hit,** song that is very popular.

hitch /hɪtʃ/ *vt, vi* 1 pull up with a quick movement: *∼ up one's trousers.* 2 fasten, become fastened, on or to a hook, etc: *∼ a horse to a fence.* 3 (*informal*) = hitchhike. □ *n* [C] 1 sudden pull or push. 2 kind of noose or knot used by sailors. 3 temporary stoppage or difficulty: *a technical ∼. go off without a hitch,* without difficulty.

hitch·hike /ˈhɪtʃhaɪk/ *vi* get a free ride by asking for one (from the driver of a car, lorry, etc).
hitch·hiker *n* [C]

hither /ˈhɪðə(r)/ adv (old use) here
'**hither·to** adv until now.

hive /haɪv/ n [C] **1** box (of wood, straw, etc)
for bees to live in; the bees living in a hive. **2**
(fig) place full of busy people: What a ~ of
industry! □ vt,vi **1** cause (bees) to go into a
hive; (of bees) store (honey) in a hive. **2** live
close together as bees do. **hive off (from)**,
(fig) become a separate (and perhaps self-
governing) body; separate and make
independent (a part of an organization).

h'm /həm/ ⇨ hem².

ho /həʊ/ int expressing surprise, admiration,
etc.

hoard /hɔːd/ n [C] carefully saved and
guarded store or collection of money, coins,
food or other treasured or valuable objects. □
vt,vi save and store: ~ (up) gold.
hoarder, person who hoards.

hoard·ing /ˈhɔːdɪŋ/ n [C] (often temporary)
fence of boards round waste land, etc, frequently used for advertisements.

hoar·frost US: -frost/ n [U] white
frost; frozen dew on grass, leaves, etc.

hoarse /hɔːs/ adj (-r, -st) (of the voice)
rough and harsh; (of a person) having a
hoarse voice: He shouted himself ~.
hoarse·ly adv
hoarse·ness n [U]

hoary /ˈhɔːrɪ/ adj (-ier, -iest) grey or white
with age.
hoari·ness n [U]

hoax /həʊks/ n [C] mischievous trick
intended to deceive. □ vt deceive in this way.
hoaxer n [C]

hob /hɒb/ n [C] flat metal shelf at the side of
a fireplace where pots and pans can be kept
warm or a kettle boiled.

hobble /ˈhɒbəl/ vi,vt **1** walk as when lame:
The old man ~d along with the aid of his
stick. **2** tie two legs of a horse or donkey to
prevent it from going far away. □ n [C]
stumbling or limping way of walking.

hobby /ˈhɒbɪ/ n [C] (pl -ies) occupation,
not one's regular business, for one's leisure
time, eg stamp-collecting.

hobby·horse /ˈhɒbɪhɔːs/ n [C] **1** wooden
horse on rockers as a child's toy. **2** long stick
with a horse's head. **3** favourite topic: Now
he's started on his ~.

hob·gob·lin /hɒbˈɡɒblɪn/ n [C] mischievous
imp; ugly and evil spirit.

hob·nail /ˈhɒbneɪl/ n [C] short nail with a
heavy head used for the soles of heavy shoes
and boots, eg for mountain-climbing.
hob-nailed adj

hob·nob /hɒbˈnɒb/ vi (-bb-) have a friendly
talk, drink: Mrs Green, happily ~bing with
the Manager.

hock¹ /hɒk/ n [C] middle joint of an animal's hind leg.

hock² /hɒk/ n [U] (kinds of) German white
wine.

hock³ /hɒk/ vt (sl) = pawn. □ n in hock,
pawned.

hockey /ˈhɒkɪ/ n [U] **field hockey**, game
played with sticks on a field by two teams of
eleven players each and a ball. **ice hockey**,
game played on ice by two teams of six
players each wearing skates and with sticks
and a rubber disc (a puck).
hockey stick, long curved or angled stick
used to hit the ball or puck.

ho·cus-po·cus /ˌhəʊkəs ˈpəʊkəs/ n [U]
talk, behaviour, used to take one's attention
away from something.

hod /hɒd/ n [C] box with a long handle used
by workmen for carrying bricks, etc on the
shoulder.

hoe /həʊ/ n [C] implement for loosening
soil, etc. □ vt,vi (pt,pp ~d) work with a
hoe: ~ing up weeds.

hog /hɒɡ US: hɔːɡ/ n [C] **1** castrated male pig
reared for meat. **2** (fig) greedy, dirty, selfish
person. **go the whole hog**, do something
thoroughly. □ vt (-gg-) take or keep greedily
and selfishly.
hog·gish /-ɪʃ/ adj greedy and selfish.

Hog·ma·nay /ˈhɒɡməneɪ/ n (Scotland) New
Year's Eve (and its festivities).

hogs·head /ˈhɒɡzhed US: ˈhɔːɡ-/ n [C] **1**
large barrel for beer. **2** liquid measure (52¼
gallons in GB or about 238·5 litres, 62 gallons in US or about 234·5 litres).

hoi pol·loi /ˌhɔɪ pəˈlɔɪ/ n the ~, (used to
discredit) the masses; the common people.

hoist /hɔɪst/ vt lift with an apparatus of
ropes and pulleys or a kind of elevator: ~ a
flag/sail; ~ crates aboard. □ n [C] **1** apparatus for hoisting. **2** (informal) push up:
give him a ~, eg when he is climbing a
wall.

hoity-toity /ˌhɔɪtɪ ˈtɔɪtɪ/ adj (informal)
snobbish and haughty.

hold¹ /həʊld/ n **1** [C,U] act, manner, power
of holding: Take ~ of the wheel. Keep ~ of
my hand. He has a great ~ (= influence)
over his younger brother. **2** [C] something
that may be used for holding on to: The rock
face provides few ~s to climbers. ⇨ foot-
hold. **3** (in boxing and wrestling) (kinds of)
grip: all-in wrestling, with no ~s barred.

hold² /həʊld/ n [C] part of a ship below
deck, where cargo is stored.

hold³ /həʊld/ vt,vi (pt,pp held /held/) (For
uses with adverbial particles and prepositions, ⇨ 14 below.) **1** have or keep in one's
possession, keep fast or steady, in or with
the hand(s), arm(s) or other part of the body,
eg the teeth, or with a tool: The girl was
~ing her father's hand. He held the knife in
his teeth as he climbed the tree. **hold the
line**, keep a telephone connection (eg whilst
the person at the other end goes away temporarily). **2** restrain; keep back; control: The
police held back the crowd. **hold one's
breath**, eg from excitement or fear: The
watchers held their breath as the acrobat
crossed the tightrope. **hold one's tongue/
peace**, be quiet. **There is no holding (sb)**,

It is impossible to restrain or control (him). **3** keep or maintain in a specified position, manner, attitude or relationship: *H~ your head up.* **4** maintain a grip of: *This new car ~s the road well,* is stable, e g when cornering at speed. **5** support; bear the weight of: *Come down—that branch won't ~ you!* **6** be filled by; have the capacity to contain or accommodate: *Will this suitcase ~ all your clothes? What does the future ~ for us? He ~s (= has) strange views on this question.* **(not) hold water,** (not) be sensible, valid, logical: *Your argument doesn't ~ water.* **7** keep the interest or attention of: *The speaker held his audience spellbound.* **8** consider; regard; believe; affirm: *He does not ~ himself responsible for his wife's debts.* **9** defend; keep possession of: *They held the fort against all attacks.* **hold the fort,** (*fig*) be in charge during a person's absence. **hold one's ground/own,** not give way: *The patient is still ~ing his own,* maintaining his strength. *Our soldiers held their ground bravely.* **10** be the legal owner or possessor of: *~ shares/stock.* **11** occupy; have the position of: *The Social Democrats held office then.* **12** have; conduct; cause to take place: *~ a meeting. We ~ a General Election every four or five years.* **13** remain unbroken, unchanged, secure, when under strain, pressure, etc. ⇨ 5 above: *How long will this fine weather ~,* continue? *The argument/theory still ~s.*
14 (uses with *adverbial particles* and *prepositions*):
hold sth against sb, allow something to influence one's opinions unfavourably: *Don't ~ his criminal convictions against him.*
hold back, hesitate; show unwillingness: *Buyers are ~ing back,* making few or no offers. **hold sb/sth back,** (a) ⇨ 2 above. (b) hinder the progress of: *His poor education is ~ing him back.* (c) keep secret or to oneself: *~ back information.*
hold sb/sth down, (a) keep or maintain in a low position. (b) keep down; suppress: *We must ~ (= keep) prices down.* **hold a job down,** (*informal*) keep it by proving one's capabilities.
hold forth, speak rather pompously, as if in public.
hold in, check, restrain; control one's feelings.
hold off, (a) remain at a distance: *The storm held off.* (b) delay action: *H~ off firing for a minute.*
hold on, (a) stand firm when there is danger, difficulty, etc: *How much longer do they think we can ~ on?* (b) (usually imperative) stop: *H~ on a minute!* **hold on to,** (a) keep one's grip on; not let go: *~ on to one's hat on a windy day.* (b) not give up the ownership of: *You should ~ on to your oil shares.* **hold sth on,** keep in position: *These*

bolts and nuts ~ the wheels on.
hold out, (a) not give way: *How long can we ~ out against these attacks?* (b) last: *How long will our food supplies ~ out?* **hold out for,** refuse to compromise: *The workers are still ~ing out for higher wages.* **hold out on,** refuse to deal with: *He's still ~ing out on me,* still opposing my wishes, refusing to share information.
hold sth over, defer; postpone: *The matter was held over until the next meeting.*
hold to sth, (a) remain loyal or steadfast to: *He held to his convictions.* (b) keep to: *The ship held to a southerly course.* **hold sb to sth,** make him keep, e g a promise: *We must ~ the contractors to their estimates,* not allow them to exceed them.
hold together, (a) be and continue whole: *an old car that hardly ~s together,* is falling apart. (b) remain united: *~ together in times of crisis.* **hold sb/sth together,** cause to remain together: *a leader who will ~ the nation together.*
hold sb/sth up, (a) ⇨ 1,2 above. (b) delay: *They were held up by fog.* (c) stop by the use or threat of force, for the purpose of robbery: *The travellers were held up by bandits.* Hence, **'hold-up** *n* a ~*-up on the Underground,* e g by a power failure; *a bank ~-up,* e g one by armed robbers. (d) put forward as an example: *Don't ~ me up as a model husband.*
hold with sth, approve of: *Do you ~ with nudity on the stage?*

hold-all /ˈhəʊld ɔl/ *n* [C] portable bag or case to hold clothes, etc when travelling.
holder /ˈhəʊldə(r)/ *n* [C] person or thing that holds: *a `cigarette-~; the ~ of the contract.*
hold-ing /ˈhəʊldɪŋ/ *n* [C] something held or owned; land or the owning of land.
hold-up /ˈhəʊld ʌp/ *n* ⇨ hold²(14).
hole /həʊl/ *n* [C] **1** opening or hollow place in a solid body: *a ~ in a tooth; roads full of ~s.* **make a hole in,** use a large amount of: *The hospital bills made a large ~ in his savings.* **pick holes in,** find fault with, e g an argument. **a square peg in a round hole,** person not fitted for the position he occupies. **2** (*informal*) awkward situation: *I'm in rather a ~.* **3** animal's burrow: *a mouse's ~.* **4** (*fig*) small, dark, wretched place: *What a wretched little ~ he lives in!* **5** (in golf) hollow into which the ball must be hit; point scored by a player who does this with the fewest strokes: *win the first ~.* □ *vt,vi* **1** make a hole in or through: *~ a ship,* e g by striking a rock. **2** (in golf) get (a ball) into a hole.
holi-day /ˈhɒlədɪ *US:* -deɪ/ *n* [C] **1** day of rest from work: *Sunday is a ~ in Christian countries.* ⇨ **bank holiday. 2** (often *pl*) (*US* = *vacation*) period of rest from work: *take a month's ~ in summer.* **on holiday,** having a holiday.
'holiday-maker, person on holiday.

holi·ness /ˈhəʊlɪnəs/ n 1 [U] being holy or sacred. 2 **His/Your H~**, title used of or to the Pope.

hol·ler /ˈhɒlə(r)/ vi,vt (sl) yell: *Stop ~ing!*

hol·low /ˈhɒləʊ/ adj 1 not solid; with a hole or empty space inside: *a ~ tree.* 2 (of sounds) as if coming from something hollow: *a ~ groan.* 3 (fig) unreal; false; insincere: *a ~ laugh; a ~ victory*, one without real value. 4 sunken: *~ cheeks.* □ n [C] hole: *a ~ in the ground*; small valley: *a wooded ~.* □ vt make a hollow in: *river banks ~ed out by rushing water.*

holly /ˈhɒlɪ/ n [U] evergreen shrub with shiny, spiny leaves and, in winter, with red berries.

holo·caust /ˈhɒləkɔːst/ n [C] large-scale destruction, esp of human lives: *a nuclear ~.*

hol·ster /ˈhəʊlstə(r)/ n [C] leather case for a gun.

holy /ˈhəʊlɪ/ adj (-ier, -iest) 1 of God; associated with God or with religion: *the H~ Bible; the H~ Land*, where Jesus lived; *the H~ City*, Jerusalem; *H~ Week*, the week before Easter Sunday; *H~ Communion; the H~ Father*, the Pope. 2 devoted to religion: *live a ~ life.* □ n **the 'H~ of 'Holies, (a)** most sacred inner chamber in a Jewish temple, entered by the High Priest once a year. (b) (fig) any sacred place.

hom·age /ˈhɒmɪdʒ/ n [U] expression of respect. *do/pay homage (to sb): Many came to do the dead man ~.*

home¹ /həʊm/ adv 1 at, in or to one's home or country: *Is he ~ yet?* 2 to the point aimed at; so as to be in the right place: *drive a nail ~*, strike it so that it is completely in. **bring sth/come home to sb**, (cause sb to) realize (an unpleasant truth). *drive a point/an argument home*, cause its full force to be understood.

home² /həʊm/ n [C] 1 place where one lives, esp with one's family: *He left ~ at the age of 16.* **at home, (a)** in the house: *I've left my books at ~.* (b) (football, etc) in the town, etc to which the team belongs: *Is our next match at ~ or away? at home in*, familiar with, confident: *Is it difficult to feel at ~ in a foreign language? not at home (to)*, not receiving visitors: *Mrs Hill is not at ~ to anyone except relatives. make oneself/ be/feel at home*, as if in one's own house; at ease: *The boy did not feel at ~ in such a splendid house. nothing to write home about,* (informal) nothing remarkable. 2 institution or place (for the care of children, old or sick people, etc): *a 'nursing ~.* 3 (often as an adjective) family or domestic life: *the pleasures of ~; ~ life.* 4 place where an animal or plant is native or most common: *the ~ of the tiger and the elephant*, e g the jungle. 5 (in sport and in various games) goal; place where a player is safe and cannot be caught, etc. 6 (as an adjective)

of one's own country (= domestic, inland, contrasted with foreign): *~ industries.* □ vt (of missiles, aircraft) be guided to (a target): *the rocket ~d (in) on its target.*

'home-coming, arrival at home.

the 'home front, the civilians (in a country at war).

'home-'grown adj (of food, etc) produced in the country (contrasted with what is imported).

'home 'help, woman trained to do domestic work.

'home-land, native land; country from which one's ancestors came.

'Home 'Rule, government of a country by its own citizens.

'home-'made adj made at home (not bought from shops).

'Home Office, government department controlling local government, police, prisons, etc in England and Wales.

'home-sick adj sad because away from home. Hence, **'home-sick-ness** n [U]

'home-stead, house with the land and outbuildings round it.

'home 'team, local team.

'home 'town, where a person lives or was born.

'home 'truth, unpleasant and obvious fact.

'home-work, work which a pupil is required to do at home. *do one's homework*, prepare for a meeting or discussion.

home·less adj having no home.

home·like adj like home: *a hotel with a ~like atmosphere.*

home·ward /-wəd/ adj going towards home.

home·wards /-wədz/ adv towards home.

home·ly /ˈhəʊmlɪ/ adj (-ier, -iest) 1 simple and plain; of the sort used every day. 2 causing one to think of home or feel at home: *a ~ atmosphere.*

home·li·ness n [U]

ho·meo·path n = homoeopath.

homi·cide /ˈhɒmɪsaɪd/ n 1 [U] killing of a human being. 2 [C] person who kills a human being.

homi·cidal /ˈhɒmɪˈsaɪdəl/ adj of homicide: *~ tendencies.*

hom·ily /ˈhɒmɪlɪ/ n [C] (pl -ies) sermon; long and tedious moralizing talk.

hom·ing /ˈhəʊmɪŋ/ adj 1 (of pigeons) having the instinct to fly home (when released a long way from home). 2 (of torpedoes, missiles) fitted with electronic devices that enable them to reach a target.

ho·moeo·path (US = **ho·meo·path**) /ˈhəʊmɪəpæθ/ n [C] person who practises homeopathy.

ho·moeo·pathy (US = **ho·meo·pathy**) /ˌhəʊmɪˈɒpəθɪ/ n [U] treatment of disease by very small doses of drugs that, if given to a healthy person, would produce symptoms like those of the disease.

ho·mo·gene·ous /ˌhɒməˈdʒiːnɪəs/ adj

(formed of parts) of the same kind. ⇨ hete-rogeneous.

hom·ogen·ize /həˈmɒdʒɪnaɪz/ vt **1** make homogeneous. **2** (esp) make milk more uniform in consistency by breaking down and blending the particles of fat.

homo·graph /ˈhɒməgrɑːf US: -græf/ n [C] word spelt like another but with a different meaning.

homo·nym /ˈhɒmənɪm/ n [C] word that is the same in form and sound as another but different in meaning, e g bow (front end of a ship) and bow (bending of the head).

homo·phone /ˈhɒməfəʊn/ n [C] word pronounced like another but different in meaning, spelling or origin, e g sum/some, new/knew.

homo·sex·ual /ˌhəʊməˈseksjʊəl/ adj sexually attracted to persons of one's own sex. ◻ n [C] homosexual person.

homo·sex·ual·ity /ˌhəʊməˌseksjʊˈælətɪ/ n [U]

hone /həʊn/ n [C] stone used for sharpening tools. ◻ vt sharpen on a hone.

hon·est /ˈɒnɪst/ adj **1** not telling lies; not cheating or stealing: an ~ man; ~ in business; give an ~ opinion. **2** showing, resulting from, an honest person: an ~ face; an ~ piece of work.

hon·est·ly adv in an honest manner; truthfully: ~ly, that's all the money I have.

hon·esty n [U] the quality of being honest.

honey /ˈhʌnɪ/ n **1** [U] sweet, sticky yellowish substance made by bees from nectar. **2** [C] (pl ~s) (informal) sweetheart; darling.

ˈhoney-bee, ordinary kind of bee that lives in hives.

ˈhoney-suckle n [U] climbing shrub with sweet-smelling yellow or red flowers.

hon-eyed /ˈhʌnɪd/ adj sweet as honey.

honey·comb /ˈhʌnɪkəʊm/ n [C] **1** (container with) wax structure of six-sided cells made by bees for honey and eggs. **2** (piece of) ornamental work in a honeycomb pattern. ◻ vt fill with holes, tunnels, etc.

honey·moon /ˈhʌnɪmuːn/ n [C] **1** holiday taken by a newly married couple. **2** (fig) period of harmony at the start of an undertaking, etc. ◻ vi go on a honeymoon: They will ~ in Paris.

honk /hɒŋk/ n [C] **1** cry of the wild goose. **2** sound made by (the old style of) motor horn. ◻ vi make a honk.

hon·or·ary /ˈɒnərɪ US: ˈɒnəreri/ adj **1** (shortened in writing to Hon) [C,U] unpaid: the ~ secretary. **2** (of a degree, rank) given as an honour: an ~ degree/doctorate; an ~ vice-president.

hon·our¹ (US = honor) /ˈɒnə(r)/ n **1** [U] great respect; high public regard: win ~ in war; Statues in ~ of those killed in battle. **2** [U] good personal character; reputation for good behaviour, loyalty, truthfulness, etc. **be/feel in honour bound to do sth,** required to do it as a moral duty, but not by

law. **give/on one's word of honour,** guarantee to fulfil an obligation, keep a promise, etc. **3** (in polite formulas): May I have the ~ of your company at dinner? I have the ~ to inform you that.... **4** Your/His H~, title of respect used to or of some judges. **5** (with a, an) person or thing bringing credit: He is an ~ to his school/family. **6** (pl) marks of respect, distinction, etc; titles: birthday ~s, (in GB) list of titles, decorations, etc conferred by the Sovereign on her or his birthday; full military ~s, ceremonies by soldiers at the burial of a soldier, to distinguished visitors, e g Presidents. **7** (pl) (in universities) (place in the) top division of marks in degree examinations; special distinction for extra proficiency. **pass with honours,** obtain a high standard.

ˈguard of ˈhonour, number of soldiers chosen to escort or welcome a distinguished person as a mark of respect.

ˈmaid of ˈhonour, lady attending a queen, princess, etc.

hon·our² (US = honor) /ˈɒnə(r)/ vt **1** respect highly, feel honour for; confer honour on: I feel highly ~ed by the kind things you say about me. **2** accept and pay when due: ~ a bill/cheque/draft, etc.

hon·our·able (US = hon·or-) /ˈɒnrəbəl/ adj **1** possessing or showing the principles of honour; consistent with honour(1,2): ~ conduct. **2** (shortened to Hon) title given to judges and some other officials, to the children of peers below the rank of Marquis, and (during debates) to members of the House of Commons: my H~ friend the member for Chester.

ˈRight ˈHonourable, title given to judges and peers below the rank of Marquis.

hon·our·ably /-əblɪ/ adv

hood /hʊd/ n [C] **1** covering like a bag for the head and neck, often fastened to a coat, etc so that it can hang down at the back when not in use. **2** anything like a hood in shape or use, e g a folding roof over a sports car. **3** (US) = bonnet(3). ◻ vt (chiefly in pp) cover with, or as with, a hood.

-hood /-hʊd/ suffix (noun + ~ = noun) status, rank, condition of life: boyhood; motherhood.

hood·lum /ˈhuːdləm/ n [C] (sl) dangerous criminal.

hood·wink /ˈhʊdwɪŋk/ vt deceive; trick.

hoof /huːf/ n [C] (pl ~s or hooves /huːvz/) horny part of the foot of a horse, ox or deer.

hook¹ /hʊk/ n [C] **1** curved or bent piece of metal or other material, for catching hold, or for hanging something on: a ˈfish-~; a ˈclothes-~. **get/be let off the hook,** get out of a difficult situation, of punishment. **2** curved tool for cutting (grain, etc) or for chopping (branches, etc): a ˈreaping-~. **3** (boxing) short blow with the elbow bent: a left ~. ◻ vt,vi **1** fasten, be fastened, hold with a hook: a dress that ~s/is ~ed at the

back; ~ *a fish*. **2** make into the form of a
hook: ~ *one's finger*. **3** (in golf) hit the ball
in a curve.

`hook-nosed *adj* having a nose shaped like
a hook.

`hook-worm,* worm that infests the intes-
tines of men and animals.

hooked *adj* (a) hook-shaped: *a ~ed nose.*
(b) (*sl*) addicted to; completely committed
to: *be/get ~ed on heroin. My aunt is ~ed on
package holidays in Spain.*

hookah /ˈhʊkə/ *n* [C] tobacco pipe (also
called a *hubble-bubble*) with a long flexible
tube through which smoke is drawn through
water in a vase and so cooled.

hooky /ˈhʊkɪ/ *n* **play hooky,** (*sl*) = play
truant.

hoo-li-gan /ˈhuːlɪɡən/ *n* [C] person making
disturbances in the streets or other public
places.

hoo-li-gan-ism /-ɪzm/ *n* [U]

hoop /huːp/ *n* [C] **1** circular band of wood or
metal as put around a barrel, etc. **2** large ring
with paper stretched over it through which
circus riders and animals jump. □ *vt* bind (a
barrel, etc) with hoops.

hoop-la /ˈhuːp lɑː/ *n* [C] game in which rings
are thrown at small objects which are won if
the rings encircle them.

hoo-ray /huːˈreɪ/ = hurrah.

hoot /huːt/ *n* [C] **1** cry of an owl. **2** sound
made by a motor-car horn, foghorn, etc. **3**
shout or cry expressing disapproval or scorn.
not care a hoot/two hoots, (sl) not care at
all. □ *vi,vt* **1** make a hoot (at): *an owl ~ing
in the garden; ~ an actor; ~ a speaker
down.*

hooter, (a) siren, etc, esp as a signal for
work to start or stop. (b) similar device in a
motor-vehicle to attract attention. (c) (*GB
sl*) nose.

hooves /huːvz/ *pl* of hoof.

hop¹ /hɒp/ *n* [C] tall climbing plant, the ripe
cones (seed-vessels) of it being dried and
used for giving a bitter flavour to beer, etc. □
vi (-pp-) gather hops: *go ~ping in Kent.*

hop² /hɒp/ *vi,vt* (-pp-) **1** (of persons) jump
on one foot; (of other living creatures, eg
birds, frogs, grasshoppers) jump with both
or all feet together: *Sparrows were ~ping
about on the lawn.* **ˈhopping ˈmad,** (*informal*) very angry. **2** make a quick journey,
esp in an aircraft: *~ over to France.* □ *n* [C]
1 the action of hopping. **2** short jump. **hop,
skip/step and jump,** athletic exercise consisting of these three movements one after
the other. **3** (*dated informal*) party and
dance, with popular music. **4** one stage in a
long-distance flight: *from Berlin to Tokyo in
three ~s.*

`hop-scotch,* children's game of throwing a
stone into numbered squares marked on the
ground, and hopping from square to square
to collect it.

hope¹ /həʊp/ *n* **1** [C,U] feeling of desire,

trust, confidence: *There is not much ~ that
they are alive.* **hold out some/no/little/
not much hope (of sth),** give some, etc
encouragement or expectation: *The doctors
could hold out no ~ of recovery.* **(be)
beyond/past hope,** without possibility of
success, recovery, etc. **raise sb's hopes,**
encourage him to expect better fortune, etc:
Don't raise his ~s too much. **2** [C] person,
thing, circumstance, etc on which hope is
based: *You are my last ~; if you can't help,
I'm ruined.*

hope² /həʊp/ *vt,vi* expect and desire: *We ~
to see you soon. We've had no news from
him but we're still hoping.*

hope-ful /ˈhəʊpfəl/ *adj* **1** having hope: *be/
feel ~ about the future.* **2** giving hope; promising: *The future does not seem very ~.* □
n [C]: *a young ~,* boy or girl who seems
likely to succeed.

hope-fully *adv*

hope-ful-ness *n* [U]

hope-less /ˈhəʊpləs/ *adj* **1** feeling, giving
or promising no hope: *a ~ case.* **2** incurable: *a ~ idiot.*

hope-less-ly *adv*

hop-per¹ /ˈhɒpə(r)/ *n* [C] person or machine
employed to pick hops. ⇨ hop¹.

hop-per² /ˈhɒpə(r)/ *n* [C] **1** structure like an
inverted cone or pyramid through which
grain passes to a mill, coal or coke to a furnace, etc. **2** any hopping insect, eg a flea, a
young locust. **3** (in Australia) kangaroo.

horde /hɔːd/ *n* [C] **1** wandering tribe (of
nomads). **2** crowd; great number: *~s of
people/locusts.*

hor-izon /həˈraɪzən/ *n* [C] **1** line at which
the earth or sea and sky seem to meet: *The
sun sank below the ~.* **2** (*fig*) limit of one's
knowledge, experience, thinking, etc.

hori-zon-tal /ˈhɒrɪˈzɒntəl *US:* ˈhɔːr-/ *adj*
parallel to the horizon; flat or level. ⇨ vertical. □ *n* [C] horizontal line, bar, etc.

hori-zon-tally *adv*

hor-mone /ˈhɔːməʊn/ *n* [C] (kinds of) internal secretion that passes into the blood and
stimulates the bodily organs.

horn /hɔːn/ *n* **1** [C] one of the hard, pointed,
usually curved, outgrowths on the heads of
cattle, deer, and some other animals. **2** [U]
substance made of this: *a ~ spoon.* **3** [C]
article made from this substance (or a
modern substitute): *a ˈshoe-~.* **4** [C] kinds
of musical instrument: *a French ~* (like a
trumpet): *an English ~,* cor anglais. **5** device for making warning sounds: *a ˈfog~; a
ˈmotor-~.* **6** horn-like part, eg on the head
of a snail. □ *vi* **horn in (on),** (sl) join in
without being invited.

horned *adj* having horns(1): *~ed cattle.*

horny *adj* (-ier, -iest) made of, like, horn:
hands ~y from hard work.

hor-net /ˈhɔːnɪt/ *n* [C] large insect of the
wasp family.

horn-pipe /ˈhɔːnpaɪp/ *n* [C] (music for a)

lively dance (usually for one person, esp a sailor).

hor·ol·ogy /hɒˈrɒlədʒɪ/ n [U] art of designing and constructing clocks.

hor·o·scope /ˈhɒrəskəʊp US: ˈhɔr-/ n [C] diagram of, observation of, positions of planets at a certain time, e g a person's birth, for the purpose of forecasting future events; such a forecast.

hor·rible /ˈhɒrəbəl US: ˈhɔr-/ adj **1** causing horror: ~ cruelty/crimes. **2** (informal) unpleasant: ~ weather.
hor·ribly /-əblɪ/ adv

hor·rid /ˈhɒrɪd US: ˈhɔrɪd/ adj **1** frightful; terrible. **2** (informal) unpleasant: ~ weather.
hor·rid·ly adv

hor·rific /həˈrɪfɪk/ adj (informal) horrifying.

hor·rify /ˈhɒrəfaɪ US: ˈhɔr-/ vt (pt,pp -ied) fill with horror; shock: We were horrified by what we saw.

hor·ror /ˈhɒrə(r) US: ˈhɔr-/ n [C,U] (something that causes a) feeling of extreme fear or dislike: To her ~ she saw her husband knocked down by a bus. We have all read about the ~s of modern warfare.
ˈhorror fiction/comics/films, in which the subject-matter and treatment are intended to cause horror.
ˈhorror-struck/-stricken adj (of persons) filled with horror.

hors d'œuvres /ˈɔː ˈdəvr US: ˈdəv/ n pl dishes of food served at the beginning of a meal.

horse /hɒs/ n **1** [C] four-legged animal with solid hooves used from early times to carry loads, for riding, etc. ⇨ colt¹, filly, foal, mare, stallion. **back the wrong horse**, support the loser in a contest. **be/get on one's high horse**, insist on being treated with proper respect. **hold one's horses**, hesitate; hold back. **look a gift horse in the mouth**, accept something ungratefully esp by examining it critically for faults. **(straight) from the horse's mouth**, (of tips, advice, information) from a first–hand source. **2** (collective sing) cavalry: the H~ Guards, ⇨ guard¹(6). **3** [C] framework, often with legs, on which something is supported: a ˈclothes-~, on which clothes may be dried; a ˈvaulting-~, block used in a gymnasium for vaulting over.
ˈhorse-back n (only in) **on horseback**, on a horse.
ˈhorse-fly, large insect which troubles horses and cattle.
ˈhorse-man, (skilled) horse rider.
ˈhorse-play, rough, noisy fun or play.
ˈhorse-power, (shortened to h p) unit for measuring the power of an engine, etc (550 foot-pounds per second).
ˈhorse-sense, practical common sense.
ˈhorse-shoe, U-shaped metal shoe for a horse.

ˈhorse-whip vt (-pp-), n [C] (thrash with a) whip for horses.
ˈhorse-woman, (skilled) woman who rides a horse.

hor·ti·cul·tural /ˈhɔːtɪˈkʌltʃərəl/ adj of horticulture: a ~ show.

hor·ti·cul·ture /ˈhɔːtɪkʌltʃə(r)/ n [U] (art of) growing flowers, fruit and vegetables.

hose¹ /həʊz/ n [C,U] (length of) flexible tubing (of rubber, plastic, etc) for directing water on to fires, gardens, etc. □ vt water (a garden, etc) with a hose; wash (a car, etc) by using a hose.
ˈhose-pipe, length of hose.

hose² /həʊz/ n **1** (collective, as pl) (trade name for) stockings and socks: six pair of ~. **2** garment from the waist to the knees or feet formerly worn by men.

ho·sier /ˈhəʊzɪə(r) US: -ʒə(r)/ n [C] shop keeper who sells knitted clothes such as socks, underwear.

ho·siery /ˈhəʊzɪərɪ US: ˈhəʊʒərɪ/ n [U] goods sold by a hosier.

hos·pit·able /həˈspɪtəbəl/ adj giving, liking to give, hospitality: a ~ man.
hos·pit·ably /-əblɪ/ adv

hos·pi·tal /ˈhɒspɪtəl/ n [C] place where people are treated for, nursed through, illness or injuries.

hos·pi·tal·ity /ˈhɒspɪˈtælətɪ/ n [U] friendly and generous reception and entertainment of guests, esp in one's own home.

host¹ /həʊst/ n [C] **1** great number: He has ~s of friends.

host² /həʊst/ n [C] **1** person who entertains guests. **2** inn-keeper; hotel-keeper. **3** (in biology) animal, plant from which a parasite feeds.

hos·tage /ˈhɒstɪdʒ/ n [C] person given or left as a guarantee that demands will be satisfied: The hijackers demanded that one of the travellers should stay with them as a ~.

hos·tel /ˈhɒstəl/ n [C] building in which board and lodging are provided for students, workmen in training, etc: a ˈYMCA ~.
ˈyouth hostel, one for young people on walking, riding or cycling holidays.
ˈhos·telry, (archaic) inn.
ˈhos·tel·ler, person travelling from one hostel to another: youth ~lers.

host·ess /ˈhəʊstɪs/ n **1** woman who entertains guests; wife of one's host. **2** woman inn-keeper. ⇨ air hostess.

hos·tile /ˈhɒstaɪl US: -təl/ adj **1** of an enemy: a ~ army. **2** being or appearing unfriendly: a ~ crowd/look.
hos·tile·ly adv

hos·til·ity /hɒˈstɪlətɪ/ n (pl -ies) **1** [U] unfriendly feeling; hatred: feelings of ~. **2** (pl) (acts of) war.

hot /hɒt/ adj (-ter, -test) **1** having great heat or a high temperature: ~ weather; feel ~. **2** producing a burning sensation on the taste: Pepper and mustard are ~. **3** intense; violent; excited: a man with a ~ temper. **4**

(of music, esp jazz) performed with strong rhythms, improvisation, etc. **5** (*sl*) (of stolen goods) difficult to dispose of (because of determined efforts made by the police to trace them). **6** (as an *adverb*) (a) recently: ~ *off the press*, recently published, announced. ⇨ hot news below. (b) *blow hot and cold*, (*fig*) be by turns favourable and unfavourable. □ *vt,vi* (-tt-) *hot* (*sth*) *up*, (*informal*) make or become hotter or (*fig*) more exciting: *Things are* ~*ting up*.

'hot `air, meaningless talk, promises, etc.

'hot-bed, (*fig*) place favourable to growth, esp of something evil: *a* ~*bed of vice/crime*.

'hot-`blooded *adj* passionate.

'hot dog, sausage served with onions and mustard in a sandwich or bread roll.

'hot-foot *adv* eagerly; in great haste: *follow the enemy* ~*foot*. □ *vi* go hastily: ~*foot it down to the library*.

'hot-head, person acting on impulse

'hot-`headed *adj* violent; rash.

'hot-house, heated building, usually made of glass, for growing plants.

'hot line, direct line of communication (telephone or teleprinter) between heads of governments.

hot news, recent (esp sensational) news.

'hot-plate, flat surface, e g of a cooking-stove, that can be heated.

'hot spring, naturally heated spring[1](2).

'hot-`tempered *adj* easily angered.

'hot `water, (*informal*) trouble: *be/get into hot water*.

'hot-`water bottle, container (often of rubber) to be filled with hot water for warmth in bed.

hot-ly *adv* (a) passionately: *a* ~*ly contested match*. (b) closely: ~*ly pursued by the police*.

ho-tel /həʊˈtel/ *n* [C] (either *a* ~ or (*dated*) *an* ~) building where meals and rooms are provided for travellers.

ho-tel-ier /həʊˈtelɪeɪ *US*: ˈhəʊtelˈjeɪ/ *n* [C] person who manages a hotel.

hound /haʊnd/ *n* [C] (kinds of) dog used for hunting and racing: `fox~; `blood~; `grey~. □ *vt* **1** chase or hunt with hounds. **2** trouble; worry: *be* ~*ed by one's creditors*.

hour /aʊə(r)/ *n* [C] **1** twenty-fourth part of a day; 60 minutes: *walk for* ~*s* (*and* ~*s*); *a three* ~*s' journey*. *at the eleventh hour*, when almost too late. **2** time of day; point or period of time: *They disturb me at all* ~*s of the day and night*, constantly. **3** (*pl*) fixed periods of time, esp for work: `*Office* ~*s*, *9 a m to 5 p m*. **4** particular, or the present, point in time: *in the* ~ *of danger*.

'hour hand, small hand on a clock or watch, pointing to the hour.

hour-ly /ˈaʊəlɪ/ *adv* **1** every hour; once every hour: *This medicine is to be taken* ~. **2** at any hour: *We're expecting news* ~. **3** by the hour: *paid* ~*/*~ *rates of pay*. □ *adj* **1** done or occurring every hour: *an* ~ *bus ser-*

vice. **2** continual: *live in* ~ *fear of discovery*.

house[1] /haʊs/ *n* [C] (*pl* ~s /ˈhaʊzɪz/) **1** building made for people to live in: *New* ~*s are going up everywhere*. ⇨ home[1](1). *get on like a `house on fire*, (of people) quickly become friendly. *under `house arrest*, forbidden (by persons in authority) to leave one's house or receive visitors. **2** (usually with a *prefix*) building made or used for some particular purpose or occupation: *a `hen*~; *a `ware*~. **3** (building used by an) assembly: *the H*~ *of Commons/Lords*; *the H*~*s of Parliament*. **4** household; family line; dynasty: *the H*~ *of Windsor*, the British Royal family. **5** spectators, audience, in a theatre: *a full* ~, every seat occupied. *bring the `house down*, win very great applause and approval.

'house agent, (*GB*) person who, firm which, sells or lets houses.

'house-boat, boat fitted up as a place to live in.

'house-bound *adj* having to stay at home.

'house-breaker, (a) burglar. (b) man employed to pull down old houses.

'house-craft, theory and practice of running a home[1](1).

'house-father, man in charge of children in an institution.

'house-fly, ⇨ fly[1].

'house-ful, as much as a house can accommodate.

'house-hold, all persons (family, lodgers, etc) living in a house.

'house-hold `cavalry, employed to guard the Sovereign.

'house-holder, person leasing or owning and occupying a house.

'house-keeper, woman employed to look after a household.

'house-man, (*GB*) doctor who is an assistant to a physician or surgeon in a hospital.

'house-master, teacher in charge of a school boarding-house.

'house-mother, woman in charge of children in an institution.

'house-proud *adj* very much concerned with the care and appearance of one's home.

'house physician/surgeon, one who resides in a hospital.

'house-trained *adj* (of domestic pets) trained not to defecate and urinate inside buildings.

'house-wife, woman head of a family, who runs the home, brings up the family, etc.

'house-work, work done in a house, cleaning, sweeping, etc. ⇨ homework

house[2] /haʊz/ *vt* provide a home, room or shelter for: *We can* ~ *you and your friends if the hotels are full*.

hous-ing /ˈhaʊzɪŋ/ *n* **1** [U] accommodation in houses, etc: *More* ~ *is needed for old people*. **2** [C] solid cover to protect a machine.

'**housing estate,** area of houses planned and built either by a local authority or other organization, to be let or sold.

hove /həʊv/ *pt,pp* of heave.

hovel /ˈhɒvəl *US:* ˈhʌvəl/ *n* [C] small, wretched house or hut.

hover /ˈhɒvə(r) *US:* ˈhʌvər/ *vi* **1** (of birds) remain in the air at one place: *a hawk ∼ing overhead.* **2** (of persons) wait about. **3** (*fig*) remain at or near: *∼ between life and death.*

'**hover-craft,** craft capable of moving over land or water while supported on a cushion of air made by jet engines.

how /haʊ/ *adv* **1** in what way or manner; by what means: *H∼ is the word spelt? Tell me ∼ to spell the word.* **2** (in questions and exclamations) to what extent; in what degree: *∼ old is he? H∼ kind you are!* **3** in what state of health: *H∼ are you? How do you do?* (formula used as a conventional greeting, esp when persons are formally introduced.) **4** (used in asking for an opinion, decision, explanation, etc) *How's that?* **(a)** What's the explanation of that? **(b)** What's your opinion of that? e g an object pointed to. *How about...,* What do you think about...; Would you like to...: *H∼ about coming for a walk?*

how-ever /haʊˈevə(r)/ *adv* in whatever way or degree: *He will never succeed, ∼ hard he tries.* □ *conj* all the same; nevertheless: *Later, ∼, he decided to go.*

howl /haʊl/ *n* [C] **1** long, loud cry, e g of a wolf. **2** long cry of a person in pain, or expressing scorn, amusement, etc: *∼s of derision.* **3** noise of a strong wind, gale. □ *vi,vt* make such noises (at): *The wind ∼ed through the trees. They ∼ed with laughter/ ∼ defiance at the enemy.*

howl-ing *adj* **(a)** making such a noise: *a ∼ling gale.* **(b)** (*informal*) extreme; glaring: *a ∼ing error.*

how-so-ever /ˈhaʊ səʊˈevə(r)/ *adv* (*old use*) = however.

hub /hʌb/ *n* [C] **1** central part of a wheel from which the spokes radiate. **2** (*fig*) central point of activity or importance: *a ∼ of industry/commerce.*

hubble-bubble /ˈhʌbəl bʌbəl/ *n* [C] = hookah.

hub-bub /ˈhʌbʌb/ *n* [U] confused noise, e g of voices.

hubby /ˈhʌbɪ/ *n* [C] (*GB informal*) husband.

huddle /ˈhʌdəl/ *vt,vi* **1** crowd together: *sheep huddling together for warmth.* **2** curl or coil up against: *Tom was cold, so he ∼d up against his brother in bed.* **3** heap up in a confused mass: *∼ things together.* □ *n* [C] number of things or persons close together without order or arrangement.

hue[1] /hju/ *n* [C] (shade of) colour: *the dark ∼ of the ocean.*

hue[2] /hju/ *n* [C] (only in) *hue and cry,* /ˈhju ən ˈkraɪ/ general outcry of alarm as when a

criminal is being pursued or to express opposition: *raise a ∼ and cry against new tax proposals.*

huff /hʌf/ *n be in/get into a huff,* be/ become bad-tempered.

hug /hʌg/ *vt* (-gg-) **1** put the arms round tightly, esp to show love: *The child was ∼ging her doll.* **2** cling to: *∼ cherished beliefs.* **3** *hug the shore,* (of a ship) keep close to it. □ *n* [C] tight embrace: *She gave her mother a big ∼.*

huge /hjuʤ/ *adj* very great.

huge-ly *adv* enormously; very much.

hulk /hʌlk/ *n* [C] **1** old ship no longer in use or used only as a storehouse. **2** big, clumsy person or object.

hulk-ing *adj* clumsy; awkward: *Get out of my way, you big ∼ing creature!*

hull[1] /hʌl/ *n* [C] body or frame of a ship.

hull[2] /hʌl/ *n* [C] outer covering of some fruits and seeds, esp the pods of peas and beans. □ *vt* remove the hulls of.

hul-la-ba-loo /ˈhʌləbəˈlu/ *n* [C] uproar; disturbance: *What's all this ∼ about?*

hullo /ˈhʌˈləʊ/ *int* = hallo.

hum /hʌm/ *vi,vt* (-mm-) **1** make a continuous sound like that made by bees. **2** sing with closed lips: *She was ∼ming a song to herself.* **3** be in a state of activity: *a factory ∼ming with activity.* **4** (*informal*) make sounds expressing hesitation or doubt. □ *n* [C] humming noise: *the ∼ of bees/of distant traffic/of voices.*

'**hum-ming-bird,** name used of several species, usually small and brightly coloured, that make a humming sound by vibration of the wings.

hu-man /ˈhjumən/ *adj* **1** of man or mankind (contrasted with animals, God): *a ∼ being; ∼ nature.* **2** having, showing, moral qualities that distinguish man: *His cruelty shows that he is less than ∼.*

hu-man-ly *adv* (esp) by human means; without divine help: *The doctors have done all that is ∼ly possible.*

hu-mane /hjuˈmeɪn/ *adj* caring about the feelings of another; sympathetic: *a man of ∼ character.*

hu-mane-ly *adv.*

hu-mani-tar-ian /hjuˈmænɪˈteərɪən/ *adj, n* [C] (of, holding the views of, a) person who works for the welfare of all human beings by reducing suffering, reforming laws about punishment, etc.

hu-man-ity /hjuˈmænətɪ/ *n* [U] **1** the human race; mankind: *crimes against ∼.* **2** human nature. **3** quality of being humane: *treat people and animals with ∼.*

the humanities, the branches of learning concerned with ancient Greek and Latin culture or art, literature, history, philosophy.

hu-man-ize /ˈhjumənaɪz/ *vt,vi* make or become human or humane.

humble /ˈhʌmbəl/ *adj* (-r, -st) **1** having or showing a modest opinion of oneself, one's position, etc: *He is very ~ towards his superiors.* **2** (of persons) low in rank or position; obscure and unimportant. **3** (of things) poor in appearance. □ *vt* make lower in rank or self-opinion: *~ one's enemies.*

hum·bly *adv* in a humble way: *beg most humbly for forgiveness.*

hum·bug /ˈhʌmbʌɡ/ *n* **1** [C,U] (instance of) dishonest and deceiving behaviour or talk. **2** [C] (*dated*) dishonest, deceitful person. **2** (*GB*) hard-boiled sweet flavoured with peppermint. □ *vt* (-gg-) deceive or trick: *Don't try to ~ me!* □ *int* (*dated*) Nonsense!

hum·drum /ˈhʌmdrʌm/ *adj* dull; ordinary: *live a ~ life.*

hu·merus /ˈhjuːmərəs/ *n* [C] bone of the upper arm in man.

hu·mid /ˈhjuːmɪd/ *adj* (esp of air, climate) damp.

hu·mid·ify /hjuːˈmɪdɪfaɪ/ *vt* (*pt,pp* -ied) make humid.

hu·mid·ity /hjuːˈmɪdətɪ/ *n* [U] (degree of) moisture (in the air).

hu·mili·ate /hjuːˈmɪlɪeɪt/ *vt* cause to feel ashamed; lower the dignity or self-respect of: *humiliating peace terms.*

hu·mili·ation /hjuːˌmɪlɪˈeɪʃən/ *n* [C,U]

hu·mil·ity /hjuːˈmɪlətɪ/ *n* [U] humble condition or state of mind.

hum·ming-bird /ˈhʌmɪŋbɜːd/ *n* ⇨ hum.

hum·mock /ˈhʌmək/ *n* [C] hillock; rising ground in a marsh, an ice-field.

hu·mor·ist /ˈhjuːmərɪst/ *n* [C] humorous talker or writer.

hu·mor·ous /ˈhjuːmərəs/ *adj* having or showing a sense of humour; funny: *~ remarks.*

hu·mor·ous·ly *adv*

hu·mour (*US* = **hu·mor**) /ˈhjuːmə(r)/ *n* **1** [U] (capacity to cause or feel) amusement: *a good sense of ~.* **2** [U] person's state of mind (esp at a particular time); temper: *not in the ~ for work*, not feeling inclined to work. □ *vt* give way to: *Is it wise to always ~ a child?*

hump /hʌmp/ *n* [C] **1** round lump, e g on a camel's back or (as a deformity) on a person's back. **2** (*sl*) fit of depression: *It gives me the ~.* □ *vt* make hump-shaped: *The cat ~ed (up) her back when she saw the dog.*

hu·mus /ˈhjuːməs/ *n* [U] earth formed by the decay of vegetable matter (dead leaves, plants).

hunch /hʌntʃ/ *n* [C] **1** thick piece; hunk; hump. **2** *have a hunch that*, (*sl*) have a vague feeling, idea, that. □ *vt* arch to form a hump: *with his shoulders ~ed up.*

hunch-back, (person having a) back with a hump. Hence, **hunch-backed** *adj*

hun·dred /ˈhʌndrəd/ *adj n* [C] (of) the number 100: *two ~ and five*, 205; *~s of people.*

hundred·weight, (often written **cwt**) (*GB*) twentieth of one ton.

hundred·fold *adv* one hundred times as much or as many.

hun·dredth /ˈhʌndrədθ/ *adj, n* [C] (abbr *100th*) (of) one of a hundred equal parts or the next after 99.

hung /hʌŋ/ *pt,pp* of hang².

hun·ger /ˈhʌŋɡə(r)/ *n* **1** [U] need, desire for food: *die of ~.* **2** (*fig*) any strong desire: *a ~ for excitement.* □ *vi* **1** feel, suffer from, hunger. **2** have a strong desire: *~ for news.*

hunger-strike, refusal to take food as a protest.

hun·gry /ˈhʌŋɡrɪ/ *adj* (-ier, -iest) feeling, showing signs of, causing, hunger: *be/go ~. The orphan child was ~ for affection.*

hun·grily /ˈhʌŋɡrəlɪ/ *adv*

hunk /hʌŋk/ *n* [C] thick piece cut off: *a ~ of bread.*

hunt¹ /hʌnt/ *n* **1** (*sing* with *the*, *a* or *an*) act of hunting; search: *find something after a long ~.* **2** group of persons who regularly hunt foxes and stags with horses and hounds; the area in which they do this.

hunter, (**a**) person who hunts; *~ers of big game in Africa.* (**b**) horse used in fox-hunting.

hunting, the act of chasing wild animals, esp foxes for sport, food: *He's fond of ~ing.*

hunt² /hʌnt/ *vi,vt* **1** go after (wild animals) for food or sport: *~ deer/elephants.* **2** *hunt down*, look for, track and find: *~ down a criminal/an escaped prisoner.* *hunt for*, search; try to find: *~ for a lost book.* *hunt high and low*, search everywhere.

hurdle /ˈhɜːdəl/ *n* [C] **1** light frame to be jumped over in a *hurdle-race* on a race-track. **2** (*fig*) difficulty to be overcome. □ *vt* take part in a hurdle-race.

hurdler *n* person who runs in hurdle-races.

hurl /hɜːl/ *vt* throw with force: *~ a spear at a tiger.* □ *n* [C] violent throw.

hurly-burly /ˈhɜːlɪ ˈbɜːlɪ/ *n* [U] noisy commotion.

hur·rah /huˈrɑː/ *int* expressing joy, approval, etc. □ *vi* cheer (the usual word).

hur·ri·cane /ˈhʌrɪkən *US:* ˈhɜːrəkeɪn/ *n* [C] violent windstorm, esp a W Indian cyclone.

hurricane lamp/lantern, lamp with the light protected from the wind.

hurry /ˈhʌrɪ *US:* ˈhɜːrɪ/ *n* [U] eager haste; wish to get something done quickly: *Why all this ~? in a hurry*, (**a**) impatient; acting, anxious to act, quickly: *He was in a ~ to leave.* (**b**) (*informal*) soon, willingly: *I shan't ask that rude man to dinner again in a ~.* (**c**) (*informal*) easily: *You won't find a better one than that in a ~.* □ *vt,vi* (*pt,pp* -ied) (cause to) move or do something (too) quickly: *It's no use ~ing her/trying to make her ~. Hurry up!* Be quick!.

hur·ried *adj* done, etc in a hurry; showing haste: *a hurried meal.*

hur·ried·ly *adv*

hurt /hɜːt/ *vt,vi* (*pt,pp* ~) **1** cause bodily injury or pain to; damage: *He ~ his back when he fell.* **2** affect a person's feelings unfavourably: *He was rather ~ by their*

criticisms. **3** suffer injury; have a bad effect (on): *It won't ~ to wait for a few days.* □ *n* [U] (or with *a, an*) harm; injury: *I intended no ~ to his feelings.*
hurt·ful *adj*

hurtle /ˈhɜtəl/ *vi* (cause to) fall or be flung violently: *During the gale the tiles came hurtling down.*

hus·band /ˈhʌzbənd/ *n* [C] man to whom a woman is married.

hush /hʌʃ/ *vt, vi* make or become silent or quiet: *H~! Be silent!* **hush sth up**, prevent it from becoming public knowledge: *She tried to ~ up the fact that her husband was an ex-convict.* □ *n* [U] silence; stillness: *in the ~ of night.*

husk /hʌsk/ *n* [C] dry outer covering of seeds, esp of grain: *rice in the ~.* □ *vt* remove husks from.

husky /ˈhʌskɪ/ *adj* (-ier, -iest) **1** (dry) like husks. **2** (of a person, his voice) hoarse; with a dry and almost whispering voice: *a ~ voice/cough.* □ *n* [C] (*pl* -ies) thick-coated dog of N American Eskimos.
husk·ily /-əlɪ/ *adv*
huski·ness *n* [U]

hus·sar /hʊˈzɑ(r)/ *n* [C] soldier of a light cavalry regiment.

hussy /ˈhʌzɪ/ *n* [C] (*pl* -ies) worthless, ill-mannered, girl or woman.

hus·tings /ˈhʌstɪŋz/ *n pl* proceedings (canvassing, speech-making, etc) leading up to a parliamentary election.

hustle /ˈhʌsəl/ *vt, vi* **1** push or jostle roughly: *The police ~d the thief into their van.* **2** (make a person) act quickly and with energy: *I don't want to ~ you into a decision.* **3** (esp *US*) (*informal*) sell or obtain something by energetic (esp deceitful) activity. □ *n* (*sing* only) quick and energetic activity: *The railway station was a scene of ~ and bustle.*
hus·tler, person who hustles.

hut /hʌt/ *n* [C] **1** small, roughly made house or shelter. **2** temporary wooden building for soldiers.

hutch /hʌtʃ/ *n* [C] box or cage, esp one used for rabbits.

hya·cinth /ˈhaɪəsɪnθ/ *n* [C] plant growing from a bulb with spikes of coloured flowers; its sweet-smelling flowers.

hy·aena /haɪˈinə/ ⇨ hyena.

hy·drangea /haɪˈdreɪndʒə/ *n* [C] (sorts of) shrub with large heads of white, blue or pink flowers.

hy·drant /ˈhaɪdrənt/ *n* [C] pipe from a water-main (esp in a street) with a nozzle to which a hose can be attached for putting out fires, etc.

hy·drau·lic /haɪˈdrɒlɪk/ *adj* of water moving through pipes; worked by the pressure of a fluid, esp water: *~ brakes,* in which the braking force is transmitted by compressed fluid.

hy·drau·lics *n pl* science of using water to produce power.

hy·dro·chloric acid /ˈhaɪdrəˈklɔrɪk ˈæsɪd *US*: -ˈklɔr-/ *n* [U] acid (symbol **HCl**) containing hydrogen and chlorine, used widely in industrial processes.

hy·dro·elec·tric /ˈhaɪdrəʊɪˈlektrɪk/ *adj* of electricity produced by water-power.

hy·dro·foil /ˈhaɪdrəfɔɪl/ *n* [C] boat with plates or fins which, when the boat is in motion, raise the hull out of the water.

hy·dro·gen /ˈhaɪdrədʒən/ *n* [U] gas (symbol **H**) without colour, taste or smell, that combines with oxygen to form water.
`hydrogen bomb, bomb with a force much greater than an atomic bomb.

hy·dro·pho·bia /ˈhaɪdrəˈfəʊbɪə/ *n* [U] **1** rabies. **2** (illness marked by a) great fear of water.

hy·ena, hy·aena /haɪˈinə/ *n* [C] carnivorous wild animal, like a wolf, with a laughing cry.

hy·giene /ˈhaɪdʒin/ *n* [U] science of, rules for, healthy living; cleanliness.

hy·gienic /ˈhaɪˈdʒinɪk *US*: ˈhaɪdʒɪˈenɪk/ *adj* of hygiene; free from disease germs: *hygienic conditions.*
hy·gieni·cally /-klɪ/ *adv*

hymen /ˈhaɪmən/ *n* [C] (*anat*) membrane over part or all of the opening of the vagina.

hymn /hɪm/ *n* [C] song of praise to God, as used in a religious service. □ *vt* praise in hymns.
hym·nal /ˈhɪmnəl/ *n* [C] book of hymns.

hyper- /ˈhaɪpə(r)-/ *prefix* to a large, extreme, extent: *hypercritical.*

hy·per·bole /haɪˈpɜbəlɪ/ *n* **1** [U] (use of) exaggerated statement(s) made for effect and not to be taken literally. **2** [C] instance of this, e g *waves as high as Everest.*

hy·per·criti·cal /ˈhaɪpəˈkrɪtɪkəl/ *adj* too critical, esp of small faults.

hy·per·market /ˈhaɪpəmɑkɪt/ *n* [C] very large supermarket occupying an extensive area outside a town, selling all varieties of goods.

hy·phen /ˈhaɪfən/ *n* [C] the mark (-) used to join two words together (as in *Anglo-French*), or between syllables (as in *co-operate*). □ *vt* join (words) with a hyphen.
hy·phen·ate /-eɪt/ *vt* = hyphen.

hyp·no·sis /hɪpˈnəʊsɪs/ *n* [C] (*pl* -ses /-sɪz/) (artificially produced) state like deep sleep in which a person's acts may be controlled by another person.

hyp·notic /hɪpˈnotɪk/ *adj* of hypnosis: *in a ~ state.*

hyp·not·ism /ˈhɪpnətɪzm/ *n* [U] (production of) hypnosis.

hyp·not·ist /-ɪst/, person able to produce hypnosis.

hyp·not·ize /-aɪz/ *vt* produce hypnosis in (a person).

hy·po·chon·dria /ˈhaɪpəˈkondrɪə/ *n* [U] mental depression due to unnecessary anxiety about one's health.

hy·po·chon·driac /-æk/ adj of, affected by, hypochondria. □ n [C] sufferer from hypochondria.

hy·poc·risy /hɪˈpɒkrəsɪ/ n [C,U] (pl -ies) (instance of) falsely making oneself appear to be virtuous or good.

hyp·o·crite /ˈhɪpəkrɪt/ n [C] person guilty of hypocrisy.

hy·po·criti·cal /ˈhɪpəˈkrɪtɪkəl/ adj of hypocrisy or a hypocrite.

hy·po·criti·cally /-klɪ/ adv

hy·po·der·mic /ˈhaɪpəˈdɜmɪk/ adj (of drugs, etc) injected beneath the skin: ~ injections.

hy·pot·en·use /ˈhaɪˈpɒtənjuz US: -tənus/ n [C] side of a right-angled triangle opposite the right angle.

hy·poth·esis /ˈhaɪˈpɒθəsɪs/ n [C] (pl -ses /-sɪz/) idea, suggestion, put forward as a starting-point for reasoning or explanation.

hy·po·theti·cal /ˈhaɪpəˈθetɪkəl/ adj of, based on, a hypothesis.

hys·teria /hɪˈstɪərɪə/ n [U] 1 disturbance of the nervous system, with outbursts of uncontrollable emotion. 2 uncontrolled excitement, e g in a crowd round a pop star.

hys·teri·cal /hɪˈsterɪkəl/ adj caused by, suffering from, hysteria: ~ laughter.

hys·teri·cally /-klɪ/ adv

hys·ter·ics /hɪˈsterɪks/ n pl attack(s) of hysteria: go into ~.

Ii

I¹ i /aɪ/ (pl I's i's /aɪz/) 1 the ninth letter of the English alphabet. 2 Roman numeral, as I (= 1), iii (= 3), IX (= 9).

I² /aɪ/ personal pron (used by a speaker or writer to refer to himself. (Note: compare me, object form, and we, us, plural forms.)

-ial /-ɪəl/ suffix characteristic of: dictatorial.

-ian /-ɪən/ suffix 1 (proper noun + ~ = noun/adjective): Brazilian. 2 specialist in: optician.

ibi·dem /ɪˈbaɪdəm/ adv (Latin) in the same book, chapter, etc (previously quoted).

ibis /ˈaɪbɪs/ n [C] large bird (like a stork or heron) found in lakes and swamps in warm climates.

-ible /-əbəl/ suffix ⇨ -able.

-ic /-ɪk/ suffix (used to form an adjective): poetic.

-ical /-ɪkəl/ (sometimes an alternative to -ic.

-ically /-ɪklɪ/ (used to form an adverb): poetically.

ice¹ /aɪs/ n 1 [U] frozen water; water made solid by cold: Is the ~ thick enough for skating? 2 [C] frozen sweet of various kinds: `water-~; ~-cream; two strawberry ~s.

`Ice Age, time when much of the N hemisphere was covered with glaciers.

`ice-berg, mass of ice moving in the sea.

`ice-bound adj (of harbours, etc) obstructed by ice.

`ice-box, box in which ice is used to keep food cool.

'ice-`cream n [C,U] (portion of) cream or custard, flavoured and frozen.

`ice-field, large area of ice in the Polar regions.

`ice hockey, ⇨ hockey.

`ice-lolly, flavoured ice on a stick.

`ice-rink, indoor skating-rink with a floor of artificial ice.

`ice-skate, thin metal runner or blade on a boot for skating on ice. □ vi skate on ice.

`ice-tray, one in a refrigerator, for making cubes of ice.

ice² /aɪs/ vt,vi 1 make very cold: ~d water. 2 cover, become covered, with a coating of ice: The pond is icing over. 3 cover (a cake) with icing. ⇨ icing.

icicle /ˈaɪsɪkəl/ n [C] pointed piece of ice formed by the freezing of dripping water.

icing /ˈaɪsɪŋ/ n [U] 1 mixture of sugar, white of egg, flavouring, etc for covering cake(s). 2 formation of ice on the wings of an aircraft.

icon /ˈaɪkɒn/ n [C] (in the Eastern Church) painting, mosaic, etc of a sacred person, itself regarded as sacred.

icy /ˈaɪsɪ/ adj (-ier, -iest) 1 very cold, like ice: ~ winds. 2 covered with ice: ~ roads. 3 (fig) unfriendly: an ~ welcome.

icily /ˈaɪsɪlɪ/ adv

-ics /-ɪks/ suffix science or specific activity: physics; athletics.

I'd /aɪd/ = I had or I would.

idea /aɪˈdɪə/ n [C] 1 thought; picture in the mind: have a good ~ of life in ancient Greece. 2 plan; scheme; design; purpose: He's full of new ~s. 3 opinion: You shouldn't force your ~s on other people. 4 vague belief, feeling that something is probable: I have an ~ that she will be late. 5 conception: You have no ~ (of) how anxious we have been. 6 (in exclamations): What an ~! (what has been suggested is unrealistic, outrageous, etc).

-ide /-aɪd/ suffix chemical compound: chloride.

ideal /aɪˈdɪəl/ adj 1 satisfying one's idea of what is perfect: ~ weather for a holiday. 2 existing only in the imagination; not likely to be achieved: ~ happiness. □ n [C] idea, example, looked on as perfect: She's looking for a husband but hasn't found her ~ yet.

ideal·ist /-ɪst/, person who pursues (often impractical) ideals.

ideal·istic /aɪˈdɪəˈlɪstɪk/ adj

ideally /aɪˈdɪəlɪ/ adv

ideal·ize /aɪˈdɪəlaɪz/ vt see, think of, as perfect.

ideal·iz·ation /aɪˈdɪəlaɪˈzeɪʃən US: -lɪˈz-/ n

[U]

idem /ˈaɪdem/ *adj, n* [C] (*Latin*) (by) the same author, etc; the same book, etc (already mentioned).

ident·i·cal /aɪˈdentɪkəl/ *adj* 1 the same: *This is the ~ knife with which the murder was committed.* 2 exactly alike: *Our views of what should be done are ~.*

i'dentical `twins, twins from one single fertilized ovum.

ident·i·cally /-klɪ/ *adv*

ident·ify /aɪˈdentɪfaɪ/ *vt* (*pt,pp* -ied) 1 say, show, prove, who or what a person or thing is: *Could you ~ your umbrella among a hundred others?* 2 **identify with,** treat (something) as identical (with another). **identify oneself with,** be associated with: *He refused to ~ himself with the new political party.*

identi·fi·ca·tion /aɪˌdentɪfɪˈkeɪʃən/ *n* (a) [U] act of identifying. (b) [C] proof of who a person is, e g a passport.

iden·ti·kit /aɪˈdentɪkɪt/ *n* [C] composite drawing of the face of an unidentified person (esp a suspected criminal), from features recalled by those who saw him.

ident·ity /aɪˈdentətɪ/ *n* (*pl* -ies) 1 [U] state of being identical; exact likeness. 2 [C,U] who a person is; what something is: *He was arrested because of mistaken ~.*

ideo·gram /ˈɪdɪəgræm/ *n* [C] written or printed character that symbolizes the idea of a thing, e g as used in Chinese writing.

ideo·graph /ˈɪdɪəgrɑf US: -græf/ *n* = ideogram.

ideo·lect /ˈɪdɪəʊlekt/ *n* [C] form of a language used by one particular person: *Is the word 'corny' part of your ~?* ⇨ **dialect.**

ideol·ogy /ˌaɪdɪˈɒlədʒɪ/ *n* (*pl* -ies) 1 [C] manner of thinking, ideas, characteristic of a person, group, etc, esp as forming the basis of an economic or political system. 2 [U] producing of impractical theories.

ideo·logi·cal /ˌaɪdɪəˈlɒdʒɪkəl/ *adj*
ideo·logi·cally /-klɪ/ *adv*

id est /ˈɪd `est/ (*abbr* **i e**) (*Latin*) that is to say.

idi·ocy /ˈɪdɪəsɪ/ *n* (*pl* -ies) 1 [U] state of being an idiot; extreme stupidity. 2 [C] extremely stupid act, remark, etc.

id·iom /ˈɪdɪəm/ *n* [C] 1 specific character of the language of a people or country, e g one peculiar to a district, group of people, or to one individual: *the ~ of the Northern England countryside,* i e the kind of English used there. 2 succession of words whose meaning is not obvious through knowledge of the individual words but must be learnt as a whole (especially when not used literally), e g *give up, in order to, be all ears.*

idio·matic /ˌɪdɪəˈmætɪk/ *adj*
idi·om·ati·cally /ˌɪdɪəˈmætɪklɪ/ *adv*

idio·syn·crasy /ˌɪdɪəˈsɪŋkrəsɪ/ *n* [C] (*pl* -ies) way of thinking or behaving that is peculiar to a person.

idio·syn·cratic /ˌɪdɪəsɪŋˈkrætɪk/ *adj*

id·iot /ˈɪdɪət/ *n* [C] 1 person suffering severe mental handicap and incapable of rational conduct. 2 (*informal*) fool: *'I've left my umbrella in the train. What an ~ I am!'*

idi·otic /ˌɪdɪˈɒtɪk/ *adj* very stupid.

idi·oti·cally /-klɪ/ *adv*

idle /ˈaɪdəl/ *adj* (-r, -st) 1 doing no work; not active or in use: *When men cannot find employment thay are ~* (though not necessarily lazy). 2 (of time) not spent in doing something: *We spent many ~ hours during the holidays.* 3 (of persons) lazy (the more usual word for this sense): *an ~, worthless girl.* 4 useless; worthless: *Don't listen to ~ gossip.* □ *vi,vt* 1 be idle: *Don't ~* (*about*). 2 spend in a lazy manner: *idling away your time.* 3 (of a car engine) run slowly in neutral gear.

idler, person who is idle.

idly /ˈaɪdlɪ/ *adv*

idol /ˈaɪdəl/ *n* [C] 1 image in wood, stone, etc of a god; such an image used as an object of worship. 2 person or thing greatly loved or admired: *He was an only child, and the ~ of his parents.*

idol·ater /aɪˈdɒlətə(r)/ *n* [C] 1 worshipper of idols. 2 devoted admirer (*of...*).

idol·atress /-trəs/ *n* [C] woman idolater.

idol·atrous /aɪˈdɒlətrəs/ *adj* (of a person) worshipping idols; of the worship of idols.

idol·atrous·ly *adv*

idol·atry /aɪˈdɒlətrɪ/ *n* (*pl* -ies) 1 [U] the worship of idols; excessive devotion to or admiration of (a person or thing). 2 [C] instance of this.

idol·ize /ˈaɪdəlaɪz/ *vt* 1 make an idol of. 2 love or admire to excess.

idol·iz·ation /ˌaɪdəlaɪˈzeɪʃən US: -lɪˈz-/ *n* [U]

idyll /ˈɪdəl US: `aɪdəl/ *n* [C] 1 short description, usually in verse, of a simple scene or event. 2 scene, etc suitable for this.

idyl·lic /ɪˈdɪlɪk US: aɪˈd-/ *adj* suitable for, like, an idyll.

if /ɪf/ *conj* 1 on the condition that; supposing that: (**a**) (of something that is possible, probable, or likely): *I~ you ask him, he will help you.* (**b**) (if an event is unlikely or improbable). *I~ anyone should call, please let me know.* (**c**) (of a condition that cannot be, or is unlikely to be realized, or is one put forward for consideration): *I~ I asked him/I~ I were to ask him for a loan, would he agree?* (**d**) (if a condition was not fulfilled, e g because it was an impossible one, or through failure to act): *I~ they had started earlier, they would have arrived in time.* 2 when; whenever: *I~ you mix yellow and blue you get green. I~ she wants the steward she rings the bell.* 3 granting or admitting that: *Even ~ he did say that, I'm sure he didn't intend to hurt your feelings.* 4 (**even**) **if,** (may mean 'although'): *I'll do it, even ~ it takes me all the afternoon.* 5 (*informal*) whether: *Do you know* ~ *Mr Smith is at home?* **6 as if**, as it would be if. (*It isn't as* ~ suggests that the contrary of what follows is true): *It isn't as* ~ *we were rich*, i e We are *not* rich. ⇨ **as**²(11). **7 if only**, (often introducing a wish, or of an unfulfilled condition, especially in exclamations): *I*~ *only he had arrived in time!*

-ify (also **-fy**) /-(ɪ)faɪ/ *suffix* (*noun/adjective* + ~ = *verb*) make into, cause to be: *terrify; solidify*.

ig·loo /ˈɪglu/ *n* [C] (*pl* ~s) winter hut of blocks of hard snow, used by the Eskimos.

ig·neous /ˈɪgnɪəs/ *adj* (of rocks) formed by volcanic action.

ig·nite /ɪgˈnaɪt/ *vt, vi* set on fire.

ig·ni·tion /ɪgˈnɪʃən/ *n* **1** [U] igniting or being ignited. **2** [C] (in a petrol engine) electrical mechanism for igniting the mixture of explosive gases.

ig·nom·in·ious /ˌɪgnəˈmɪnɪəs/ *adj* bringing contempt, disgrace, shame: *an* ~ *defeat*.
ig·nom·in·ious·ly *adv*

ig·nom·iny /ˈɪgnəmɪnɪ/ *n* (*pl* -ies) **1** [U] public dishonour or shame. **2** [C] dishonourable or disgraceful act. **3** [U] dishonourable behaviour.

ig·nor·amus /ˌɪgnəˈreɪməs/ *n* [U] (*pl* ~es) ignorant person.

ig·nor·ance /ˈɪgnərəns/ *n* [U] the state of being ignorant; want of knowledge: *We are in complete* ~ *of his plans*.

ig·nor·ant /ˈɪgnərənt/ *adj* **1** (of persons) knowing little or nothing; not aware: *I am quite* ~ *of his plans*. **2** showing ignorance; resulting from ignorance: ~ *conduct*.
ig·nor·ant·ly *adv*

ig·nore /ɪgˈnɔː(r)/ *vt* take no notice of; refuse to take notice of: ~ *rude remarks*.

I'll /aɪl/ = *I will* or *I shall*.

ill /ɪl/ *adj* **1** in bad health; sick: *She was* ~ *with anxiety*. **fall/be taken ill**, become ill. **2** bad: *in an* ~ *temper/humour; in* ~ *health*. □ *n* **1** [U] evil; injury; *do* ~. **2** [C] misfortune; trouble: *the various* ~*s of life*. □ *adv* badly; imperfectly; unfavourably: *We could* ~ (= not well, not easily) *afford the time and money*. **be/feel ill at ease**, uncomfortable, embarrassed.

ill-adˈvised *adj* unwise; imprudent.
ill-ˈbred *adj* badly brought up; rude.
ill-disˈposed (towards) *adj* (a) wishing to do harm (to). (b) unfavourable (towards a plan, etc).
ill-ˈfeeling, feeling of being angry, jealous, etc.
ill-ˈjudged *adj* done at an unsuitable time; showing poor judgement: *an* ~-*judged attempt*.
ill-ˈmannered *adj* having bad manners; rude.
ill-ˈnatured *adj* bad-tempered, unkind, etc.
ill-ˈtimed *adj* done at a wrong or unsuitable time.
ill-ˈtreat/-ˈuse *vt* treat badly or cruelly.

ill-ˈwill, enmity; unkind feeling.

il·legal /ɪˈliːgəl/ *adj* not legal.
il·legally *adv*
il·legal·ity /ˌɪlɪˈgælətɪ/ *n* [C,U]

il·leg·ible /ɪˈledʒəbəl/ *adj* difficult or impossible to read.
il·leg·ibly /-əblɪ/ *adv*
il·leg·ibil·ity /ɪˌledʒəˈbɪlətɪ/ *n* [U]

il·legit·imate /ˌɪlɪˈdʒɪtɪmət/ *adj* **1** not authorized by law; contrary to law. **2** born of parents who were not married to each other: *an* ~ *child*. **3** (of a conclusion in an argument, etc) not logical. □ *n* [C] illegitimate person.
il·legit·imate·ly *adv*

il·lib·eral /ɪˈlɪbərəl/ *adj* narrow-minded; intolerant; ungenerous; mean.
il·lib·erally /-rəlɪ/ *adv*

il·licit /ɪˈlɪsɪt/ *adj* unlawful; forbidden: *the* ~ *use of drugs*.
il·licit·ly *adv*

il·lit·er·ate /ɪˈlɪtərət/ *adj* with little or no education; unable to read or write. □ *n* [C] illiterate person.
il·lit·er·acy /-rəsɪ/ *n* [U]

ill·ness /ˈɪlnəs/ *n* **1** [U] state of being ill: *no/not much/a great deal of* ~ *this winter*. **2** [C] specific kind of, occasion of, illness: *She had one* ~ *after another*.

il·logi·cal /ɪˈlɒdʒɪkəl/ *adj* without, contrary to, logic.
il·logi·cally /-klɪ/ *adv*
il·logi·cal·ity /ɪˌlɒdʒɪˈkælətɪ/ *n* [C,U]

il·lumi·nate /ɪˈluːmɪneɪt/ *vt* **1** give light to: *a street* ~*d by street lamps*. **2** decorate (streets, etc) with bright lights as a sign of rejoicing. **3** make clear, help to explain: ~ *a difficult passage in a book*.

il·lumi·na·tion /ɪˌluːmɪˈneɪʃən/ *n* **(a)** [U] lighting or being lit. **(b)** bright lights, e g used for a special occasion.

il·lu·sion /ɪˈluːʒən/ *n* **1** [C] (the seeing of) something that does not really exist; false idea or belief: *an optical* ~. **2** [U] state of mind in which one is deceived in this way.

il·lu·sive /ɪˈluːsɪv/ *adj* = **illusory**.
il·lu·sive·ly *adv*

il·lu·sory /ɪˈluːsərɪ/ *adj* unreal; deceptive.

il·lus·trate /ˈɪləstreɪt/ *vt* **1** explain by examples, pictures, etc. **2** supply a book, article, lecture, etc with pictures, diagrams, etc: *a well-*~*d textbook*.
il·lus·tra·tor /-tə(r)/, person who illustrates books, etc.

il·lus·tra·tion /ˌɪləˈstreɪʃən/ *n* **1** [U] illustrating or being illustrated: ~ *is often more useful than definition for giving the meanings of words*. **2** [C] something that illustrates, e g a picture, diagram, etc.

il·lus·tra·tive /ˈɪləstrətɪv US: ɪˈlʌs-/ *adj* serving to explain, as an explanation or example (*of*).

il·lus·tri·ous /ɪˈlʌstrɪəs/ *adj* celebrated, famous.
il·lus·tri·ous·ly *adv*

I'm /aɪm/ = *I am.* ⇨ **be.**

im·age /ˈɪmɪdʒ/ *n* [C] **1** likeness or copy of something, esp made in wood, stone, etc: an ∼ *of the Virgin Mary.* **2** close likeness; counterpart: *Did man create God in his own* ∼? **3** mental picture or idea, e g of a politician, political party, commercial firm, product: *How can we improve our* ∼? **speak in images,** use figures of speech that bring pictures to the mind. **4** reflection seen in a mirror or through the lens of a camera. □ *vt* **1** make an image of, portray. **2** reflect.
imag·ery /ˈɪmɪdʒrɪ/ *n* [U]

im·agin·able /ɪˈmædʒənəbəl/ *adj* that can be imagined: *We had every* ∼ *difficulty getting here in time.*

im·agin·ary /ɪˈmædʒənərɪ US: -dʒənerɪ/ *adj* existing only in the mind; unreal.

im·agin·ation /ɪˌmædʒɪˈneɪʃən/ *n* [C,U] **1** power of the mind to imagine: *He hasn't much* ∼. **2** what is imagined: *You didn't really see a ghost—it was only* ∼.
im·agin·ative /ɪˈmædʒənətɪv US: -əneɪtɪv/ *adj* of, having, using, imagination: *an imaginative child/idea.*

im·ag·ine /ɪˈmædʒɪn/ *vt* **1** form a picture of in the mind: *Can you* ∼ *life without electricity?* **2** think of as probable: *Don't* ∼ *that I can lend you money every time you ask!*

imam /ɪˈmɑm/ *n* [C] title of various Muslim leaders; prayer leader in a mosque; scholar on Islamic law.

im·bal·ance /ˈɪmˈbæləns/ *n* [C] absence of balance between two totals, e g payments: *the increasing* ∼ *between rich and poor countries.*

im·be·cile /ˈɪmbəsil US: -səl/ *adj* mentally weak; stupid: ∼ *remarks.* □ *n* [C] fool.
im·be·cil·ity /ˌɪmbəˈsɪlətɪ/ *n* [C,U]

im·bue /ɪmˈbju/ *vt* (*pt,pp* ∼d) (*formal*) fill, inspire: ∼d *with patriotism/hatred.*

imi·tate /ˈɪmɪteɪt/ *vt* **1** copy the behaviour of; take as an example: *You should* ∼ *great and good men.* **2** mimic (consciously or not): *Parrots imitating human speech.* **3** be like; make a likeness of: *wood painted to* ∼ *marble.*
imi·ta·tor /-tə(r)/ *n* [C]

imi·ta·tion /ˌɪmɪˈteɪʃən/ *n* **1** [U] imitating: *I* ∼ *is the sincerest form of flattery.* **2** [C] something made or done like something else. **3** (as an *adjective*) not real: ∼ *leather/ jewellery.*
imi·tat·ive /ˈɪmɪtətɪv US: -teɪtɪv/ *adj* following the model or example of: *as* ∼ *as a monkey.*

im·macu·late /ɪˈmækjʊlət/ *adj* pure; faultless: ∼ *conduct.*
im·macu·late·ly *adv*: ∼*ly dressed.*

im·ma·terial /ˌɪməˈtɪərɪəl/ *adj* **1** unimportant: *That's quite* ∼ *to me.* **2** not having physical substance: *as* ∼ *as a ghost.*

im·ma·ture /ˌɪməˈtjʊə(r) US: -ˈtʊər/ *adj* not yet fully developed: *an* ∼ *girl.*
im·ma·tur·ity /ˌɪməˈtjʊərətɪ US: -ˈtʊər-/ *n*

[U] being immature or underdeveloped.

im·measur·able /ɪˈmeʒərəbəl/ *adj* that cannot be measured; without limits.

im·medi·ate /ɪˈmidɪət/ *adj* **1** without anything coming between; nearest: *my* ∼ *neighbours.* **2** occurring, done, at once: *take* ∼ *action.*
im·medi·ate·ly *adv* **(a)** at once; without delay. **(b)** directly or closely. □ *conj* as soon as: *You can go* ∼*ly he comes.*

im·mem·or·ial /ˌɪməˈmɔrɪəl/ *adj* (esp) **from time immemorial,** going back beyond memory.

im·mense /ɪˈmens/ *adj* very large.
im·mense·ly *adv* **(a)** to a very large degree: ∼*ly popular.* **(b)** (*informal*) very much: *They enjoyed themselves* ∼*ly.*
im·men·sity /ɪˈmensətɪ/ *n* [C,U]

im·merse /ɪˈmɜs/ *vt* **1** put under the surface of (water or other liquid): ∼ *one's head in the water.* **2** absorb (2): *be* ∼d *in one's work.*
im·mer·sion /ɪˈmɜʃən US: -ˈɜrʒən/ *n* [C,U]
im`mersion heater, electric heater (fixed in a tank).

im·mi·grant /ˈɪmɪgrənt/ *n* [C] person who immigrates: *European immigrants in Australia.*

im·mi·grate /ˈɪmɪgreɪt/ *vi* come as a settler (into another country), not as a tourist or visitor.
im·mi·gra·tion /ˌɪmɪˈgreɪʃən/ *n* [C,U]

im·mi·nent /ˈɪmɪnənt/ *adj* (of events, esp dangers) likely to come or happen soon: *A storm is* ∼.
im·mi·nent·ly *adv*
im·mi·nence /-əns/ *n* [U] the state of being imminent.

im·mo·bile /ɪˈməʊbaɪl US: -bəl/ *adj* not able to move or be moved; motionless.
im·mo·bi·lize /ɪˈməʊbəlaɪz/ *vt* make immobile
im·mo·bil·ity /ˌɪməˈbɪlətɪ/ *n* [U] state of being immobile.
im·mo·bil·iz·ation /ɪˌməʊbəlaɪˈzeɪʃən US: -əlɪˈz-/ *n* [U]

im·mod·er·ate /ɪˈmɒdərət/ *adj* excessive: ∼ *eating and drinking.*
im·mod·er·ate·ly *adv*

im·mod·est /ɪˈmɒdɪst/ *adj* **1** lacking in modesty; indecent or indelicate: ∼ *behaviour.* **2** impudent: ∼ *boasts.*
im·mod·est·ly *adv*
im·mod·esty *n* [C,U]

im·moral /ɪˈmɒrəl US: ɪˈmɔrəl/ *adj* not moral; wicked and evil: ∼ *conduct.*
im·mor·ally *adv*
im·mor·al·ity /ˌɪməˈrælətɪ/ *n* [C,U]

im·mor·tal /ɪˈmɔtəl/ *adj* **1** living for ever: *the* ∼ *gods.* **2** never forgotten: ∼ *fame.* □ *n* [C] immortal being. **the** ∼**s,** the gods of ancient Greece and Rome.
im·mor·tal·ity /ˌɪmɔˈtælətɪ/ *n* [U] endless life or fame.
im·mor·tal·ize /ɪˈmɔtəlaɪz/ *vt* give endless

life or fame to.

im·mov·able /ɪˈmuːvəbəl/ adj **1** that cannot be moved: ∼ property, e g buildings, land. **2** incapable of being affected or changed.

im·mov·ably /-əblɪ/ adv

im·mune /ɪˈmjuːn/ adj free, secure, protected: ∼ from smallpox.

im·mun·ity /ɪˈmjuːnətɪ/ n [U] **(a)** safety, security: immunity from disease. **(b)** exemption (from taxation, etc): diplomatic immunity.

im·mu·nize /ˈɪmjʊnaɪz/ vt make immune (against).

im·mu·niz·ation /ˈɪmjʊnaɪˈzeɪʃən US: -nɪˈz-/ n [C,U].

imp /ɪmp/ n [C] **1** little devil or demon. **2** (informal) mischievous child.

im·pact /ˈɪmpækt/ n **1** [C] collision. **2** [U] force exerted by one object when striking against another: The car body collapses on ∼. **3** strong influence or effect: the ∼ of his speech on the audience. □ vt /ɪmˈpækt/ pack, drive or wedge firmly together.

im·pair /ɪmˈpeə(r)/ vt weaken; damage: ∼ one's health by overwork.

im·pair·ment n [U]

im·pale /ɪmˈpeɪl/ vt pierce through, pin down, with a spear, etc.

im·pale·ment n [U]

im·pal·pable /ɪmˈpælpəbəl/ adj **1** that cannot be touched or felt. **2** not easily grasped by the mind.

im·part /ɪmˈpɑːt/ vt (formal) give, pass on, a secret, news, etc.

im·par·tial /ɪmˈpɑːʃəl/ adj just; not favouring one more than another: an ∼ decision.

im·par·tially adv

im·par·tial·ity /ˈɪmˈpɑːʃɪˈælətɪ/ n [U]

im·pass·able /ɪmˈpɑːsəbəl US: -ˈpæs-/ adj (of roads, etc) impossible to travel through or on.

im·passe /ˈæmpɑːs US: ˈɪmpæs/ n [C] **1** position from which there is no way out: the talks reached an ∼. **2** road, alley, etc with no exit.

im·pas·sioned /ɪmˈpæʃənd/ adj full of, showing, deep feeling: an ∼ speech.

im·pass·ive /ɪmˈpæsɪv/ adj showing no sign of feeling; unmoved.

im·pass·ive·ly adv

im·pa·tience /ɪmˈpeɪʃəns/ n [U] lack of patience; intolerance.

im·pa·tient /ɪmˈpeɪʃənt/ adj not patient: The children were ∼ to start.

im·pa·tient·ly adv

im·peach /ɪmˈpiːtʃ/ vt **1** (formal) question, raise doubts about (a person's character, etc). **2** (legal) accuse a person of doing wrong, (esp) of a crime against the State: ∼ a judge for taking bribes.

im·peach·ment n [U]

im·pec·cable /ɪmˈpekəbəl/ adj (formal) faultless; incapable of doing wrong: an ∼ character/record.

im·pe·cuni·ous /ˈɪmpɪˈkjuːnɪəs/ adj (for-

mal) having little or no money.

im·pede /ɪmˈpiːd/ vt get in the way of: What is impeding an early start?

im·pedi·ment /ɪmˈpedɪmənt/ n [C] **1** physical defect esp in speech, e g a stammer. **2** something that hinders; obstacle.

im·pel /ɪmˈpel/ vt (-ll-) force, urge: He said he had been ∼led to crime by poverty.

im·pend /ɪmˈpend/ vi (formal) be about to come or happen: her ∼ing arrival.

im·pen·etrable /ɪmˈpenɪtrəbəl/ adj that cannot be penetrated: ∼ forests.

im·pera·tive /ɪmˈperətɪv/ adj **1** urgent; essential: Is it ∼ that they should have/for them to have two cars? **2** not to be disobeyed; done, given with, authority: The colonel's orders were ∼. **3** (gram) form of a verb and sentence expressing commands: Listen! Go away!

im·pera·tive·ly adv

im·per·cep·tible /ˈɪmpəˈseptəbəl/ adj that cannot be perceived; unnoticeable; very slight or gradual.

im·per·cep·tibly /-əblɪ/ adv

im·per·fect /ɪmˈpɜːfɪkt/ adj not perfect or complete.

imperfect tense, (gram) denoting action still in progress (also called progressive or continuous tenses), e g I am thinking about it.

im·per·fect·ly adv

im·per·fec·tion /ˈɪmpəˈfekʃən/ n **1** [U] state of being imperfect. **2** [C] fault: the little ∼s in her character.

im·per·ial /ɪmˈpɪərɪəl/ adj **1** of an empire or its ruler(s): ∼ trade. **2** (formal) majestic; magnificent: with ∼ generosity. **3** (of weights and measures) used by law in the United Kingdom: an ∼ pint/gallon.

im·per·ially /-rɪəlɪ/ adv

im·per·ial·ism /ɪmˈpɪərɪəlɪzm/ n [U] (political system using a) policy of extending a country's empire and influence, of having colonies.

im·per·ial·ist /-ɪst/ adj of, like, imperialism: imperialist policy. □ n [C] supporter of, believer in, imperialism.

im·per·ial·is·tic /ɪmˈpɪərɪəˈlɪstɪk/ adj

im·peril /ɪmˈperəl/ vt (-ll-, US also -l-) put or bring into danger.

im·peri·ous /ɪmˈpɪərɪəs/ adj (formal) **1** dictatorial; arrogant: ∼ gestures/looks. **2** urgent; imperative.

im·peri·ous·ly adv

im·peri·ous·ness n [U]

im·per·ish·able /ɪmˈperɪʃəbəl/ adj (formal) **1** that cannot perish. **2** that will never pass away: ∼ fame/glory.

im·per·ma·nent /ɪmˈpɜːmənənt/ adj (formal) not permanent.

im·per·ma·nence /-əns/ n [U]

im·per·sonal /ɪmˈpɜːsənəl/ adj **1** not influenced by personal feeling; not referring to any particular person: an ∼ discussion. **2** having no existence as a person: ∼ forces,

e g those of nature. **3** (of *verbs*) used after 'it' to make general statements such as *'It is raining.'*
im·per·son·al·ly /-nəlɪ/ *adv*

im·per·son·ate /ɪm`pɜːsəneɪt/ *vt* **1** act the part of (in a play, etc); pretend to be. **2** personify.
im·per·son·ation /ɪm`pɜːsən`eɪʃən/ *n* [C,U]

im·per·ti·nent /ɪm`pɜːtɪnənt/ *US:* -tənənt/ *adj* **1** not showing proper respect; impudent: ~ *remarks.* **2** not pertinent; irrelevant.
im·per·ti·nent·ly *adv*
im·per·ti·nence /-əns/ *n* [C,U]

im·per·turb·able /`ɪmpə`tɜːbəbəl/ *adj* (*formal*) not easily excited; calm.

im·per·vi·ous /ɪm`pɜːvɪəs/ *adj* **1** (of materials) not allowing (water, etc) to pass through. **2** (*fig*) not moved or influenced by: ~ *to criticism.*

im·pet·u·ous /ɪm`petʃʊəs/ *adj* **1** acting, inclined to act, on impulse, with insufficient thought or care: ~ *remarks.* **2** moving quickly or violently.
im·pet·u·ous·ly *adv*
im·pet·u·os·ity /ɪm`petʃʊ`ɒsətɪ/ *n* [C,U]

im·pe·tus /`ɪmpɪtəs/ *n* (*pl* -es) **1** [U] force with which a body moves. **2** [C] stimulus; driving force: *The treaty will give an* ~ *to trade between the two countries.*

im·pinge /ɪm`pɪndʒ/ *vi* (*formal*) **1** make an impact (*on/upon*). **2** encroach (*on/upon*): ~ *on a person's time.*
im·pinge·ment *n* [U]

im·pi·ous /`ɪmpɪəs/ *adj* (*formal*) not pious; wicked (the more usual word).
im·pi·ous·ly *adv*

imp·ish /`ɪmpɪʃ/ *adj* of or like an imp.
imp·ish·ly *adv*

im·plac·able /ɪm`plækəbəl/ *adj* (*formal*) that cannot be appeased; relentless: *an* ~ *enemy.*

im·plant /ɪm`plɑːnt *US:* -`plænt/ *vt* fix or put ideas, feelings, etc (in).

im·ple·ment[1] /`ɪmpləmənt/ *n* [C] tool or instrument for working with: *farm* ~*s.*
im·ple·ment[2] /`ɪmpləmənt/ *vt* carry out an undertaking, agreement, promise: ~ *a scheme.*
im·ple·men·ta·tion /`ɪmpləmen`teɪʃən/ *n* [U]

im·pli·cate /`ɪmplɪkeɪt/ *vt* show or imply that (a person) is or was involved (*in* a crime, etc).

im·pli·ca·tion /`ɪmplɪ`keɪʃən/ *n* **1** [U] implicating or being implicated (in a crime, etc). **2** [C] what is implied: *What are the* ~*s of this statement?*

im·pli·cit /ɪm`plɪsɪt/ *adj* (*formal*) **1** implied though not plainly expressed: *an* ~ *threat.* **2** unquestioning: ~ *belief.*
im·pli·cit·ly *adv*

im·plore /ɪm`plɔː(r)/ *vt* request earnestly: *imploring a judge for mercy.*
im·plor·ing·ly *adv*

im·ply /ɪm`plaɪ/ *vt* (*pt,pp* -ied) **1** give or

make a suggestion (*that*): *Are you* ~*ing that I am not telling the truth?* **2** involve as necessary: *A fever implies an illness.*

im·po·lite /`ɪmpə`laɪt/ *adj* not polite.
im·po·lite·ly *adv*
im·po·lite·ness *n* [U]

im·poli·tic /ɪm`pɒlətɪk/ *adj* (*formal*) not judged well; not likely to be useful.

im·pon·der·able /ɪm`pɒndərəbəl/ *adj* (*fig*) of which the effect cannot be estimated. □ *n* [C] imponderable thing.

im·port /ɪm`pɔːt/ *vt* **1** bring in, introduce, from a foreign country: ~ *coffee from Brazil.* **2** (*formal*) mean; make known (that): *What does this* ~*?* □ *n* /`ɪmpɔːt/ **1** [C] (often *pl*) goods imported: *food* ~*s.* **2** [U] act of importing goods. **3** [U] (*formal*) meaning: *What is the* ~ *of his statement?* **4** [U] (*formal*) importance: *questions of great* ~.
im·porter, person who imports goods.
im·por·ta·tion /`ɪmpɔː`teɪʃən/ *n* [C,U]

im·port·ance /ɪm`pɔːtəns/ *n* [U] being important: *The matter is of great/no/not much/little* ~ *to us.*

im·port·ant /ɪm`pɔːtənt/ *adj* **1** of great influence; to be treated seriously; having a great effect: ~ *decisions/books.* **2** (of a person) having a position of authority.
im·port·ant·ly *adv*

im·por·tu·nate /ɪm`pɔːtʃʊnət/ *adj* (*formal*) **1** (of persons) making repeated and inconvenient requests: *an* ~ *beggar.* **2** (of affairs, etc) urgent: ~ *demands.*
im·por·tun·ity /`ɪmpə`tjuːnɪtɪ *US:* -`tuː-/ *n* [C,U]

im·por·tune /ɪm`pɔːtʃuːn/ *vt* (*formal*) beg urgently and repeatedly: *importuning for more money.*

im·pose /ɪm`pəʊz/ *vt,vi* **1** lay or place a tax, duty, etc on: *New duties were* ~*d on wines and spirits.* **2** force (something, oneself, one's company) on others. **3** take advantage of: ~ *on/upon a person's good nature.*
im·pos·ing *adj* making a strong impression because of size, character, appearance: *an imposing old lady.*
im·pos·ing·ly *adv*

im·po·si·tion /`ɪmpə`zɪʃən/ *n* **1** [U] the act of imposing(1): *the* ~ *of new taxes.* **2** [C] something imposed, e g tax, burden, punishment. **3** [C] fraud; trick; extra charge.

im·poss·ible /ɪm`pɒsəbəl/ *adj* **1** not possible: *Don't ask me to do the* ~. **2** that cannot be endured: *It's an* ~ *situation!*
im·poss·ibil·ity /ɪm`pɒsə`bɪlətɪ/ *n* [C,U]
im·poss·ibly /-əblɪ/ *adv*

im·pos·tor /ɪm`pɒstə(r)/ *n* [C] person pretending to be somebody else.

im·pos·ture /ɪm`pɒstʃə(r)/ *n* [C,U] (act of) deception by an impostor.

im·po·tence /`ɪmpətəns/ *n* [U] state of being impotent.

im·po·tent /`ɪmpətənt/ *adj* **1** lacking sufficient strength (to do something). **2** (of men) incapable of sexual intercourse.

im·po·tent·ly adv

im·pound /ɪmˈpaʊnd/ vt take possession of by law or by authority.

im·pov·er·ish /ɪmˈpɒvərɪʃ/ vt (formal) cause to become poor; take away good qualities: ~ed by doctors' fees.

im·prac·ti·cable /ɪmˈpræktɪkəbəl/ adj that cannot be put into practice or used: an ~ scheme.

im·prac·ti·cably /-əblɪ/ adv

im·prac·ti·cal /ɪmˈpræktɪkəl/ adj not practical.

im·preg·nable /ɪmˈpregnəbəl/ adj that cannot be overcome or taken by force: ~ defences/arguments.

im·preg·nably /-əblɪ/ adv

im·preg·nate /ˈɪmpregneɪt US: ɪmˈpreg-/ vt 1 make pregnant; fertilize, e g an ovum. 2 fill, saturate: paper ~d with water. 3 (formal) fill with feelings, moral qualities, etc.

im·pre·sario /ˌɪmprɪˈsɑːrɪəʊ/ n [C] (pl ~s) manager of an operatic or concert company.

im·press /ɪmˈpres/ vt 1 press (one thing on or with another); make (a mark, etc) by doing this: ~ a design on cloth. 2 have a strong influence on; fix deeply (on the mind, memory): The book/He did not ~ me at all. □ n /ˈɪmpres/ [C] mark made by a seal, etc.

im·pres·sion /ɪmˈpreʃən/ n 1 [C] mark made by pressing: the ~ of a seal on wax. 2 [C] (product of) any one printing operation: a first ~ of 5 000 copies. 3 [C,U] effect produced on the mind or feelings: It's my ~ that he doesn't want to come. **be under the impression that,** have a vague idea, think, that.

im·pres·sion·ism /-ɪzm/ n [U] method of painting or writing so as to give the general effect without elaborate detail.

im·pres·sion·ist /-ɪst/ adj, n [C] (of a) person who uses this method.

im·pres·sion·is·tic /ɪmˌpreʃənˈɪstɪk/ adj (a) of, characteristic of, impressionism. (b) producing only a general effect.

im·pres·sion·able /ɪmˈpreʃənəbəl/ adj easily influenced: the ~ age, adolescence.

im·pres·sive /ɪmˈpresɪv/ adj making a deep impression on the mind and feelings: an ~ ceremony.

im·pres·sive·ly adv

im·print /ɪmˈprɪnt/ vt print; stamp; produce an effect: ideas ~ed on the mind. □ n /ˈɪmprɪnt/ [C] that which is imprinted: the ~ of suffering on her face.

im·prison /ɪmˈprɪzən/ vt put or keep in a-prison.

im·prison·ment n [U]

im·prob·able /ɪmˈprɒbəbəl/ adj not likely to be true or to happen: an ~ story/result.

im·prob·ably /-əblɪ/ adv

im·prob·abil·ity /ˈɪmˌprɒbəˈbɪlətɪ/ n [C,U]

im·promptu /ɪmˈprɒmptju US: -tu/ adj, adv without preparation: an ~ speech. □ n [C] musical composition that seems to have

been improvised.

im·proper /ɪmˈprɒpə(r)/ adj 1 not suited for the purpose, situation, circumstances, etc: Laughing is ~ at a funeral. 2 incorrect: an ~ diagnosis of disease. 3 indecent: ~ stories.

im·proper·ly adv

im·pro·pri·ety /ˌɪmprəˈpraɪətɪ/ n (pl -ies) (formal) 1 [U] incorrectness; unsuitability. 2 [C] improper act, remark, etc.

im·prove /ɪmˈpruːv/ vt,vi make or become better: His health is improving.

im·prove·ment n 1 [U] improving or being improved: There is need for ~ment in your handwriting. 2 [C] something which adds to beauty, usefulness, value, etc: an ~ment in the weather.

im·pro·vi·dent /ɪmˈprɒvɪdənt/ adj (formal) wasteful; not looking to future needs.

im·pro·vise /ˈɪmprəvaɪz/ vt,vi 1 compose music while playing, compose verse while reciting, etc: If an actor forgets his words, he has to ~. 2 provide, make or do something quickly, using whatever happens to be available: an ~d meal.

im·pro·vis·ation /ˌɪmprəvaɪˈzeɪʃən US: -vɪˈz-/ n [C,U]

im·prud·ent /ɪmˈpruːdənt/ adj rash; indiscreet: an ~ act/remark.

im·pru·dent·ly adv

im·prud·ence /-əns/ n [C,U]

im·pu·dence /ˈɪmpjʊdəns/ n [U] (act of) being impudent: None of your ~!

im·pu·dent /ˈɪmpjʊdənt/ adj shamelessly rude, disrespectful: What an ~ rascal he is!

im·pu·dent·ly adv

im·pulse /ˈɪmpʌls/ n 1 [C] push or thrust: give an ~ to trade/education. 2 [C] sudden inclination to act without thought about the consequences: feel an irresistible ~ to jump out of a window. 3 [U] state of mind in which such inclinations occur: a man who acts on ~.

im·pul·sive /ɪmˈpʌlsɪv/ adj 1 (of persons, their conduct) acting on impulse; resulting from impulse: a girl with an ~ nature. 2 (of a force) tending to impel.

im·pul·sive·ly adv

im·pul·sive·ness n [U]

im·pun·ity /ɪmˈpjuːnətɪ/ n [U] (esp) **with impunity,** without risk of injury or punishment.

im·pure /ɪmˈpjʊə(r)/ adj not pure: ~ motives.

im·pur·ity /-ətɪ/ n [C,U]

im·pute /ɪmˈpjuːt/ vt (formal) attribute an act, quality, or outcome to: He was innocent of the crime ~d to him.

im·pu·ta·tion /ˈɪmpjʊˈteɪʃən/ n [C,U]

in[1] /ɪn/ adverbial particle (contrasted with **out**) (for special uses with **verbs,** e g give in, ⇨ the **verb** entries.) 1 **be in,** (a) at home: Is there anyone ~? (b) arrive: Is the train ~ yet? (c) (of crops) harvested: The wheat crop is safely ~. (d) in season; obtainable:

Strawberries are ~ now. (e) in fashion: *Long skirts are ~ again.* (f) elected; in power; in office: *The Democrats are ~.* (g) (in cricket, baseball) batting: *Which side is ~? be in on,* (informal) participate in; have a share in: *I'd like to be ~ on this scheme.* 2 *in for,* (a) likely to have or experience (often something unpleasant): *I'm afraid we're ~ for a storm.* (b) committed to; having agreed to take part in: *I'm ~ for the competition,* shall be a competitor. *have it in for sb,* be waiting ready to punish him when a chance occurs.

in² /ɪn/ *prep* **1** (of place; ⇨ at): ~ *Africa; children playing ~ the street; not a cloud ~ the sky; lying ~ bed. He was wounded ~ the leg. I read about it ~ the newspapers.* **2** (of direction): ~ *this/that direction;* ~ *all directions.* **3** (of direction of motion or activity) into: *He put his hands ~ his pockets. Cut/break it ~ two.* **4** (of time when): ~ *1970;* ~ *spring/summer.* ⇨ at¹(2). ⇨ on²(2). *in the end,* finally. **5** (of time) in the course of; within the space of: *I shall be back ~ a few days. I'll be ready ~ a moment.* **6** (indicating inclusion): *seven days ~ a week; a man ~ his thirties,* i e between 29 and 40 years of age. **7** (of ratio): *He paid 25p ~ the pound. Not one ~ ten of the boys could spell well.* **8** (of dress, etc): *dressed ~ white,* wearing white clothes; ~ *uniform.* **9** (of physical surroundings, circumstances, etc): *go out ~ the rain.* **10** (of a state or condition): ~ *good order;* ~ *poor health;* ~ *a hurry;* ~ *love;* ~ *public.* **11** (of form, shape, arrangement): *words ~ alphabetical order; dancing ~ a ring.* **12** (of the method of expression, means, material, etc): *speaking/writing ~ English; payment ~ cash.* **13** (of degree or extent): ~ *large/small quantities.* **14** (of identity): *We have lost a first-rate teacher ~ Hill,* Hill, who has left us, was a first-rate teacher. **15** (of relation, reference, respect): ~ *every way; blind ~ the left eye; my equal ~ strength.* **16** (of occupation, activity, etc): *He's ~ the army/~ the Civil Service. How much time do you spend ~ reading.* **17** (used in numerous prepositional phrases of the pattern *in + n + prep;* ⇨ the noun entries, e g): ~ *defence of;* ~ *exchange for.* **18** *in that,* since, because: *High income tax is harmful ~ that it may discourage people from trying to earn more. in as/so far as,* to the extent that: *He is a Russian ~ so far as he was born there. in itself,* considered apart from other things: *Playing cards is not harmful ~ itself, but gambling may be.*

in³ /ɪn/ *n* (only in) **the ins and (the) outs,** (a) the different parts; the full details: *know all the ~s and outs of a problem.* (b) those in office and those out of office.

in-¹ (also **il-, im-, ir-**) /ɪn-, ɪl-, ɪm-, ɪr-/ *prefix* **1** in, on: *intake, imprint.* **2** not: *in-*

finite, illicit, immoral, irrelevant.

in-² /ɪn/ *prefix* (before a *noun*): `in-patient, one who lives in hospital while being treated (contrasted with *out-patient*).

-in /ɪn/ *suffix* used (usually with a *verb*) to show participation in a group activity, etc: `sit-in, `teach-in.

in·abil·ity /ˌɪnəˈbɪlɪtɪ/ *n* [U] being unable; lack of power or means: *an ~ to pay one's debts.*

in·ac·cess·ible /ˌɪnəkˈsesəbəl/ *adj* (formal) not accessible.

in·ac·cessi·bil·ity /ˌɪnəkˈsesəˈbɪlɪtɪ/ *n* [U]

in·ac·cur·acy /ɪnˈækjʊrəsɪ/ *n* **1** [U] being inaccurate. **2** [C] (*pl* -**ies**) inaccurate statement, etc.

in·ac·cur·ate /ɪnˈækjʊrət/ *adj* not accurate.
in·ac·cur·ate·ly *adv*

in·ac·tive /ɪnˈæktɪv/ *adj* not active.
in·ac·tiv·ity /ˌɪnækˈtɪvətɪ/ *n* [U]

in·ad·equate /ɪnˈædɪkwət/ *adj* not adequate; insufficient.
in·ad·equate·ly *adv*
in·ad·equacy /ɪnˈædɪkwəsɪ/ *n* [C,U]

in·ad·miss·ible /ˌɪnədˈmɪsəbəl/ *adj* that cannot be admitted or allowed: ~ *evidence;* ~ *in evidence.*

in·ad·ver·tent /ˌɪnədˈvɜːtənt/ *adj* (formal) **1** not paying or showing proper attention. **2** (of actions) done thoughtlessly or not on purpose.
in·ad·ver·tent·ly *adv*

in·alien·able /ɪnˈeɪlɪənəbəl/ *adj* (formal) (of rights, etc) that cannot be given away or taken away.

in·ane /ɪˈneɪn/ *adj* silly; senseless: *an ~ remark.*
in·ane·ly *adv*
in·an·ity /ɪˈnænətɪ/ *n* [C,U]

in·ani·mate /ɪnˈænɪmət/ *adj* **1** lifeless: ~ *rocks and stones.* **2** without animal life: *Is the moon ~? 3* spiritless; dull: ~ *conversation.*

in·ap·pli·cable /ɪnˈæplɪkəbəl/ *adj* **inapplicable (to),** not applicable.

in·ap·preci·able /ˌɪnəˈpriːʃəbəl/ *adj* not worth reckoning; too small or slight to be perceived: *an ~ difference.*

in·ap·proach·able /ˌɪnəˈprəʊtʃəbəl/ *adj* not approachable.

in·ap·pro·pri·ate /ˌɪnəˈprəʊprɪət/ *adj* not appropriate or suitable.

in·apt /ɪnˈæpt/ *adj* unskilful; not relevant: ~ *remarks.*

in·ap·ti·tude /ɪnˈæptɪtjuːd *US:* -tuːd/ *n* [U] being inapt.

in·ar·ticu·late /ˌɪnɑːˈtɪkjʊlət/ *adj* **1** (of speech) not clear or distinct; (of a person) not speaking distinctly, clearly or fluently: ~ *rage.* **2** not jointed: *an ~ body,* e g a jelly-fish.

in·ar·tis·tic /ˌɪnɑːˈtɪstɪk/ *adj* not artistic.

in·as·much as /ˌɪnəzˈmʌtʃ əz/ *adv* since; because.

in·at·ten·tion /ˌɪnəˈtenʃən/ *n* lack of, failure to pay, attention.

in·at·ten·tive /ˈɪnəˈtentɪv/ *adj* not attentive.

in·aud·ible /ɪnˈɔːdəbəl/ *adj* that cannot be heard.

in·audi·bil·ity /ɪnˈɔːdəˈbɪlətɪ/ *n* [U]

in·aug·ural /ɪˈnɔːɡjʊrəl/ *adj* of or for an inauguration: *an ~ lecture.* □ *n* [C] inaugural speech.

in·aug·ur·ate /ɪˈnɔːɡjʊreɪt/ *vt* **1** introduce a new official, professor, etc at a special ceremony: *~ a president.* **2** open an exhibition/a new public building with formalities. **3** be the beginning of: *The invention of the internal combustion engine ~d a new era in travel.*

in·aug·ur·ation /ɪˈnɔːɡjʊˈreɪʃən/ *n* [C,U]

in·aus·pi·cious·ly *adv*

in·board /ˈɪnˈbɔːd/ *adj* within the hull of a ship: *an ~ motor.*

in·born /ˈɪnˈbɔːn/ *adj* (of a quality) possessed (by a person or animal) at birth: *an ~ talent.*

in·bred /ˈɪnˈbred/ *adj* **1** inborn: *~ courtesy.* **2** bred for several generations from ancestors closely related.

in·breed·ing /ˈɪnˈbriːdɪŋ/ *n* [U] breeding from closely related ancestors, stocks, etc.

in·built /ˈɪnbɪlt/ *adj* = built-in.

in·cal·cu·lable /ɪnˈkælkjʊləbəl/ *adj* too great to be calculated: *This has done ~ harm to our reputation.*

in·can·descent /ˈɪnkænˈdesənt/ *adj* giving out, able to give out, light when heated.

in·can·ta·tion /ˈɪnkænˈteɪʃən/ *n* [C,U] (the use of) (a form of) words used in magic; spell.

in·ca·pable /ɪnˈkeɪpəbəl/ *adj* not capable: *~ of telling a lie.*

in·capa·bil·ity /ˈɪnˈkeɪpəˈbɪlətɪ/ *n* [U]

in·ca·paci·tate /ˈɪnkəˈpæsəteɪt/ *vt* make unfit (for work, etc).

in·ca·pac·ity /ˈɪnkəˈpæsətɪ/ *n* [U] inability; powerlessness.

in·car·cer·ate /ɪnˈkɑːsəreɪt/ *vt* (*formal*) imprison.

in·car·cer·ation /ˈɪnˈkɑːsəˈreɪʃən/ *n* [U]

in·car·nate /ɪnˈkɑːnət/ *adj* **1** having a body; (esp) in human form: *That prison officer is a devil ~.* **2** (of an idea, ideal, etc) appearing in human form: *Liberty ~.* □ *vt* /ɪnˈkɑːneɪt/ **1** make (an idea, etc) incarnate. **2** (of a person) be a living form of (a quality): *a wife who ~s all the virtues.*

in·car·na·tion /ˈɪnkɑːˈneɪʃən/ *n* the I**~**, the taking of bodily form by Jesus.

in·cen·di·ary /ɪnˈsendɪərɪ/ *US*: -dɪerɪ/ *n* [C] (*pl* -ies), *adj* **1** (person) setting fire to property unlawfully and with an evil purpose. **2** (person) tending to stir up violence: *an ~ speech.* **3** (bomb) causing fire.

in·cense¹ /ˈɪnsens/ *n* [U] (smoke of a) substance producing a sweet smell when burning.

in·cense² /ɪnˈsens/ *vt* make angry: *~d by his conduct/at her remarks.*

in·cen·tive /ɪnˈsentɪv/ *n* [C,U] that which

incites or encourages a person: *He hasn't much ~ to work hard; an ~ scheme.*

in·cep·tion /ɪnˈsepʃən/ *n* [C] (*formal*) start.

in·cess·ant /ɪnˈsesənt/ *adj* continual; often repeated: *a week of ~ rain.*

in·cess·ant·ly *adv*

in·cest /ˈɪnsest/ *n* [U] sexual intercourse between near relations, e g brother and sister.

in·ces·tuous /ɪnˈsestʃʊəs/ *adj*

inch /ɪntʃ/ *n* [C] **1** measure of length, one-twelfth of a foot. **2** small amount. □ *vt,vi* make one's way gradually: *~ along a ledge on a cliff.*

in·ci·dence /ˈɪnsɪdəns/ *n* [C] way in which something occurs or affects things: *the ~ of a disease,* the range or extent of its effect.

in·ci·dent¹ /ˈɪnsɪdənt/ *adj* forming a natural or expected part of; naturally connected with: *the risks ~ to the life of a racing driver.*

in·ci·dent² /ˈɪnsɪdənt/ *n* [C] **1** event, esp one of less importance than others: *frontier ~s,* e g disputes between forces on a frontier. **2** happening which attracts general attention. **3** separate piece of action in a play or poem.

in·ci·den·tal /ˈɪnsɪˈdentəl/ *adj* **1** accompanying but not forming a necessary part: *~ music to a film.* **2** small and comparatively unimportant: *~ expenses.*

in·ci·den·tally /-təlɪ/ *adv* by chance; by the way.

in·cin·er·ate /ɪnˈsɪnəreɪt/ *vt* burn to ashes.

in·cin·er·ation /ɪnˈsɪnəˈreɪʃən/ *n* [U]

in·cin·er·ator /-tə(r)/ *n* [C] furnace, etc for burning rubbish, etc.

in·cipi·ent /ɪnˈsɪpɪənt/ *adj* in an early stage: *~ decay of the teeth.*

in·cise /ɪnˈsaɪz/ *vt* make a cut in; engrave.

in·ci·sion /ɪnˈsɪʒən/ *n* **1** [U] cutting (into something). **2** [C] cut, e g in surgery.

in·cis·ive /ɪnˈsaɪsɪv/ *adj* **1** sharp and cutting. **2** (of a person's mind, remarks) clear-cut: *~ criticism.*

in·cis·ive·ly *adv*

in·cisor /ɪnˈsaɪzə(r)/ *n* [C] (in human beings) any one of the front cutting teeth with sharp edges.

in·cite /ɪnˈsaɪt/ *vt* stir up, provoke: *insults inciting resentment.*

in·cite·ment *n* [C,U]

in·clem·ent /ɪnˈklemənt/ *adj* (*formal*) (of weather or climate) severe; cold and stormy.

in·clem·ency /-ənsɪ/ *n* [U]

in·cli·na·tion /ˈɪnklɪˈneɪʃən/ *n* **1** [C] bending; bowing; slope; slant: *the ~ of a roof,* its degree of slope. **2** [C,U] liking or desire: *He showed no ~ to leave.*

in·cline¹ /ɪnˈklaɪn/ *vt,vi* **1** (cause to) lean, slope or slant. **2** bend (the head, body, oneself) forward or downward: *~ the head in prayer.* **3** (usually passive) direct the mind on a certain path; cause to have a tendency or wish: *I am ~d to think* (= I have a feeling or idea) *that he is opposed to the plan.*

He's ~*d to be lazy.* **4** tend: *I* ~ *to believe in his innocence.* **5** have a physical tendency: *He* ~*s to leanness.*

in·cline² /ɪnˈklaɪn/ *n* [C] slope; sloping surface: *a steep* ~.

in·close, **in·clos·ure** /ɪnˈkləʊz, ɪnˈkləʊʒə(r)/ = enclose, enclosure.

in·clude /ɪnˈkluːd/ *vt* bring in, reckon, as part of the whole: *ten competitors, including six from America.*

in·clu·sion /ɪnˈkluːʒn/ *n* [U]

in·clus·ive /ɪnˈkluːsɪv/ *adj* **1** including: *from 1 May to 3 June* ~, 1 May and 3 June being included. **2** including much or all: *a price* ~ *of tax.*

in·clus·ive·ly *adv*

in·cog·nito /ˌɪnkɒɡˈniːtəʊ/ *adj* disguised; with an assumed name. □ *adv* with one's name, character, etc concealed: *travel* ~.

in·co·her·ent /ˌɪnkəʊˈhɪərənt/ *adj* not coherent.

in·co·her·ent·ly *adv*
in·co·her·ence /-əns/ *n* [U]

in·come /ˈɪnkʌm/ *n* [C] money received during a given period (as salary, receipts from trade, interest from investments, etc): *live within/beyond one's* ~, spend less/more than one receives.

'income-tax, tax imposed on income.

in·com·ing /ˈɪnkʌmɪŋ/ *adj* coming in: *the* ~ *tide/tenant.* ⇨ outgoing.

in·com·men·sur·ate /ˌɪnkəˈmenʃərət/ *adj* not comparable (*to*) in respect of size; not worthy to be measured (*with*).

in·com·par·able /ɪnˈkɒmprəbəl/ *adj* not to be compared; without equal: ~ *beauty.*

in·com·pat·ible /ˌɪnkəmˈpætəbəl/ *adj* opposed in character; unable to exist in harmony: *Excessive drinking is* ~ *with good health.*

in·com·pati·bil·ity /ˈɪnkəmˌpætəˈbɪlətɪ/ *n* [U]

in·com·pe·tent /ɪnˈkɒmpətənt/ *adj* not qualified or able: *an* ~ *teacher.*

in·com·pe·tent·ly *adv*
in·com·pe·tence /-əns/ (also **in·com·pe·tency** /-ənsɪ/) *n* [U] being incompetent.

in·com·plete /ˌɪnkəmˈpliːt/ *adj* not complete.

in·com·plete·ly *adv*

in·com·pre·hen·sible /ɪnˌkɒmprɪˈhensəbəl/ *adj* (*formal*) that cannot be understood.

in·com·pre·hen·si·bil·ity /ɪnˌkɒmprɪˈhensɪˈbɪlətɪ/ *n* [U]

in·com·pre·hen·sion /ˌɪnkɒmprɪˈhenʃən/ *n* [U] failure to understand.

in·con·ceiv·able /ˌɪnkənˈsiːvəbəl/ *adj* **1** that cannot be imagined. **2** (*informal*) hard to believe; very remarkable.

in·con·clus·ive /ˌɪnkənˈkluːsɪv/ *adj* (of evidence, arguments, discussions, actions) not decisive or convincing.

in·con·clus·ive·ly *adv*
in·con·gru·ous /ɪnˈkɒŋɡruəs/ *adj* not in

harmony or agreement; out of place.

in·con·gru·ous·ly *adv*
in·con·gru·ity /ˌɪnkɒŋˈɡruːətɪ/ *n* [C,U]

in·con·sequent /ɪnˈkɒnsɪkwənt/ *adj* not following naturally what has been said or done before: *an* ~ *remark.*

in·con·sequent·ly *adv*
in·con·sequen·tial /ˌɪnkɒnsɪˈkwenʃəl/ *adj* (esp) unimportant.

in·con·sid·er·able /ˌɪnkənˈsɪdrəbəl/ *adj* not worth considering; of small size, value, etc.

in·con·sid·er·ate /ˌɪnkənˈsɪdrət/ *adj* (of a person, his actions) thoughtless: ~ *children/remarks.*

in·con·sid·er·ate·ly *adv*

in·con·sist·ent /ˌɪnkənˈsɪstənt/ *adj* not in harmony; contradictory; having parts that do not agree: *Their accounts of what happened were* ~.

in·con·sist·ent·ly *adv*
in·con·sist·ency /-ənsɪ/ *n* [C,U]

in·con·sol·able /ˌɪnkənˈsəʊləbəl/ *adj* that cannot be consoled: ~ *grief.*

in·con·spicu·ous /ˌɪnkənˈspɪkjuəs/ *adj* not striking or obvious: *dressed in* ~ *colours.*

in·con·spicu·ous·ly *adv*

in·con·stant /ɪnˈkɒnstənt/ *adj* (*formal*) (of persons) changeable in feelings, intentions, purpose, etc: *an* ~ *lover.*

in·con·stancy /-ənsɪ/ *n* [C,U]

in·con·test·able /ˌɪnkənˈtestəbəl/ *adj* that cannot be disputed.

in·con·ti·nent /ɪnˈkɒntɪnənt/ *adj* **1** lacking self-control or self-restraint. **2** unable to control excretion.

in·con·ti·nence /-əns/ *n* [U]

in·con·tro·vert·ible /ɪnˌkɒntrəˈvɜːtəbəl/ *adj* that cannot be disputed.

in·con·ven·ience /ˌɪnkənˈviːnɪəns/ *n* [C,U] (cause or instance of) discomfort or trouble: *I suffered great* ~. □ *vt* cause inconvenience to.

in·con·ven·ient /ˌɪnkənˈviːnɪənt/ *adj* causing discomfort, trouble or annoyance.

in·con·ven·ient·ly *adv*
in·con·vert·ible /ˌɪnkənˈvɜːtəbəl/ *adj* that cannot be converted.

in·cor·por·ate¹ /ɪnˈkɔːpərət/ *adj* formed into, united in, a corporation.

in·cor·por·ate² /ɪnˈkɔːpəreɪt/ *vt,vi* **1** make, become, united in one body or group: *Hanover was* ~*d into Prussia in 1886.* **2** (*legal*) form into, become, a corporation(2): *The firm* ~*d with others.*

in·cor·por·ation /ɪnˌkɔːpəˈreɪʃən/ *n* [U]

in·cor·rect /ˌɪnkəˈrekt/ *adj* not correct.

in·cor·rect·ly *adv*
in·cor·rect·ness *n* [U]

in·cor·ri·gible /ɪnˈkɒrɪdʒəbəl/ *US*: -ˈkɔːr-/ *adj* (of a person, his faults, etc) that cannot be corrected: *an* ~ *liar.*

in·cor·rupt·ible /ˌɪnkəˈrʌptəbəl/ *adj* **1** that cannot decay or be destroyed. **2** that cannot be corrupted, esp by being bribed.

in·cor·rupti·bil·ity /ˈɪnkəˌrʌptəˈbɪlətɪ/ *n* [U]

in·crease[1] /ˈɪnkriːs/ n **1** [U] increasing; growth. **2** [C] amount by which something increases.

in·crease[2] /ɪnˈkriːs/ vt,vi make or become greater in size, number, degree, etc: *Our difficulties are increasing.*

in·creas·ing·ly /ɪnˈkriːsɪŋlɪ/ adv more and more.

in·cred·ible /ɪnˈkredəbəl/ adj **1** that cannot be believed. **2** (*informal*) difficult to believe; very surprising.

in·cred·ibly /-əblɪ/ adv

in·credi·bil·ity /ɪnˈkredəˈbɪlətɪ/ n [U]

in·credu·lous /ɪnˈkredjʊləs US: -dʒʊ-/ adj unbelieving; showing disbelief: ∼ *looks.*

in·credu·lous·ly adv

in·cred·ul·ity /ˈɪnkrɪˈdjuːlətɪ US: -ˈduː-/ n [U]

in·cre·ment /ˈɪnkrəmənt/ n **1** [U] profits; increase. **2** [C] amount of increase: *'Salary £5 000 per annum, with yearly ∼s of £500'.*

in·crimi·nate /ɪnˈkrɪmɪneɪt/ vt say, be a sign, that (a person) is guilty of doing wrong: *incriminating evidence.*

in·cu·bate /ˈɪnkjʊbeɪt/ vt,vi hatch (eggs) by sitting on them or by artificial warmth.

in·cu·ba·tion /ˈɪnkjʊˈbeɪʃən/ n [U]

in·cu·ba·tor /-tə(r)/ n [C] **1** apparatus for hatching eggs by artificial warmth. **2** apparatus for rearing small, weak babies.

in·cum·bent /ɪnˈkʌmbənt/ adj (*formal*) rest upon a person as a duty: *It is ∼ on you to warn him not to smoke.* □ n [C] **1** person holding a church benefice; rector or vicar. **2** (*informal*) holder of any position or appointment.

in·cum·bency /-ənsɪ/ n [C] (*pl* -ies) position of an incumbent.

in·cur /ɪnˈkɜː(r)/ vt (-rr-) bring on oneself: ∼ *debts/hatred/great expense.*

in·cur·able /ɪnˈkjʊərəbəl/ adj that cannot be cured: ∼ *diseases/habits.* □ n [C] person who is incurable.

in·cur·ably /-əblɪ/ adv

in·cur·sion /ɪnˈkɜːʃən US: -ˈkɜːrʒən/ n [C] sudden attack or invasion: ∼s *into enemy territory;* (*fig*) ∼s *on my leisure time.*

in·debted /ɪnˈdetɪd/ adj owing money or gratitude: *I am ∼ to you for your help.*

in·de·cent /ɪnˈdiːsənt/ adj **1** (of behaviour, talk, etc) not decent(2); obscene. **2** (*informal*) improper.

in·de·cent·ly adv

in·de·cency /-ənsɪ/ n [C,U]

in·de·cipher·able /ˈɪndɪˈsaɪfrəbəl/ adj that cannot be deciphered.

in·de·cision /ˈɪndɪˈsɪʒən/ n [U] the state of being unable to decide; hesitation.

in·de·cis·ive /ˈɪndɪˈsaɪsɪv/ adj not decisive.

in·de·cis·ive·ly adv

in·deed /ɪnˈdiːd/ adv **1** really; as you say; as you may imagine: *'Are you pleased at your son's success?'—'Yes, ∼.'* **2** (used to intensify): *Thank you very much ∼.* **3** (used as a comment to show interest, surprise, etc): *'He spoke to me about you.'—'Oh, ∼!'*

in·de·fens·ible /ˈɪndɪˈfensəbəl/ adj that cannot be defended, justified or excused.

in·de·fin·able /ˈɪndɪˈfaɪnəbəl/ adj that cannot be defined.

in·defi·nite /ɪnˈdefənɪt/ adj **1** vague: *an ∼ answer,* neither 'Yes' nor 'No'. **2** having no precise limit: *an ∼ period of time.*

the ˈindefinite ˈarticle, n the word *a* or *an.*

in·defi·nite·ly adv

in·del·ible /ɪnˈdeləbəl/ adj that cannot be rubbed out or removed ∼ *ink.*

in·del·ibly /-əblɪ/ adv

in·deli·cate /ɪnˈdelɪkət/ adj (of a person, his speech, behaviour, etc) lacking in refinement: ∼ *remarks.*

in·deli·cacy /-kəsɪ/ n [C,U]

in·dem·nify /ɪnˈdemnɪfaɪ/ vt (*pt,pp* -ied) **1** (*legal, comm*) make safe: ∼ *a person against harm/loss.* **2** pay (a person) back: *I will ∼ you for any expenses.*

in·dem·nity /ɪnˈdemnətɪ/ n (*pl* -ies) **1** [U] security against damage or loss; compensation for loss. **2** [C] something giving security against damage or loss or given, received, as compensation.

in·dent /ɪnˈdent/ vt,vi **1** break into the edge or surface of. **2** start (a line of print or writing) farther from the margin than the others: *You must ∼ the first line of each paragraph.*

in·den·ta·tion /ˈɪndenˈteɪʃən/ n (a) [U] indenting or being indented. (b) [C] deep recess in a coastline; space left at the beginning of a line of print or writing.

in·de·pen·dence /ˈɪndɪˈpendəns/ n [U] state of being independent: *colonies given ∼ from European countries.*

ˈInde·pendence Day, 4 July, celebrated in the US as the anniversary of the day, in 1776, on which the *Declaration of I∼* (that the American colonies were free and independent of GB) was made.

in·de·pen·dent /ˈɪndɪˈpendənt/ adj **1** not dependent on or controlled by (other persons or things): *Campers are ∼ of hotels, etc.* **2** not needing to work for a living: ∼ *means,* private wealth. **3** self-governing: *when the colony became ∼.* **4** acting or thinking freely: *an ∼ witness.* □ n [C] (esp) M P, candidate, etc who does not belong to a political party.

in·de·pen·dent·ly adv

in·de·scrib·able /ˈɪndɪˈskraɪbəbəl/ adj that cannot be described.

in·de·struct·ible /ˈɪndɪˈstrʌktəbəl/ adj that cannot be destroyed: ∼ *concrete buildings.*

in·de·ter·mi·nate /ˈɪndɪˈtɜːmɪnət/ adj not fixed; vague or indefinite.

in·de·ter·min·able /ˈɪndɪˈtɜːmɪnəbəl/ adj that cannot be determined, decided or (esp of an industrial dispute) settled.

in·de·ter·min·ably /-əblɪ/ adv

in·dex /ˈɪndeks/ n [C] (*pl* ∼es or, in science, indices /ˈɪndɪsiːz/) **1** something that points to or indicates; pointer (on an instrument) showing measurements: *increasing* *unemployment was an ~ of the country's poverty.* **2** list of names, subjects, references, etc in ABC order, at the end of a book, or on cards (*a 'card ~*) in a library, etc. □ *vt* make an index for a book, collection of books, etc.

the 'index finger, the forefinger, used for pointing.

in·dexer, person who prepares an index.

In·dian /ˈɪndɪən/ *n, adj* **1** (native) of the Republic of India. **2** (one) of the original inhabitants of America.

'Indian 'summer, (a) period of calm, dry weather in late autumn. **(b)** (*fig*) revival of the feelings of youth in old age.

A'merican/'Red 'Indian, = Indian(2).

'West 'Indian, (native) of the West Indies.

in·di·cate /ˈɪndɪkeɪt/ *vt* point to; make known; be a sign of: *He ~d that the interview was over. The sudden rise in temperature ~d pneumonia.*

in·di·ca·tion /ˌɪndɪˈkeɪʃən/ *n* **1** [U] indicating or being indicated. **2** [C,U] sign or suggestion: *I had no indication of his decision.*

in·dica·tive /ɪnˈdɪkətɪv/ *adj* (*gram*) stating a fact or asking questions of fact: *the ~ mood.* **2** giving indications: *Is a high forehead ~ of intelligence?*

in·di·ca·tor /ˈɪndɪkeɪtə(r)/ *n* [C] person, thing, that points out or gives information: *a 'traffic-~* (on a motor-vehicle) flashing light or other device to indicate a change of direction.

in·di·ces /ˈɪndɪsiːz/ *pl* of index.

in·dict /ɪnˈdaɪt/ *vt* (*legal*) accuse (a person): *~ sb on a charge of murder/for murder.*

in·dict·able /-əbəl/ *adj*

in·dict·ment *n* [C,U]

in·dif·fer·ence /ɪnˈdɪfrəns/ *n* [U] absence of interest or feeling: *his ~ towards the needs of other people.*

in·dif·fer·ent /ɪnˈdɪfrənt/ *adj* **1** having no interest; neither for nor against: *It is quite ~ to me whether you go or stay,* I don't care which you do. **2** not of good quality or ability: *an ~ footballer.*

in·dif·fer·ent·ly *adv*

in·di·gen·ous /ɪnˈdɪdʒɪnəs/ *adj* native, belonging naturally to: *Kangaroos are ~ to Australia.*

in·di·gest·ible /ˈɪndɪˈdʒestəbəl/ *adj* difficult or impossible to digest.

in·di·ges·tion /ˈɪndɪˈdʒestʃən/ *n* [U] (pain from) difficulty in digesting food: *an attack of ~.*

in·dig·nant /ɪnˈdɪɡnənt/ *adj* angry. esp at injustice or because of undeserved blame, etc.

in·dig·nant·ly *adv*

in·dig·na·tion /ˈɪndɪɡˈneɪʃən/ *n* [U] anger caused by injustice, misconduct, etc.

in·dig·nity /ɪnˈdɪɡnəti/ *n* (*pl* -ies) **1** [U] rude or unworthy treatment causing shame or loss of respect. **2** [C] something said or done that humiliates a person: *subjected to all sorts of indignities.*

in·digo /ˈɪndɪɡəʊ/ *n* [U] deep blue dye (obtained from plants).

'indigo 'blue, blue-violet (colour).

in·di·rect /ˈɪndɪˈrekt/ *adj* **1** not straight or direct: *an ~ answer to a question.* **2** (of taxes) not paid direct to a tax-collector, but in the form of higher prices for taxed goods: *the ~ taxes on tobacco, wines, etc.*

'indirect 'object, (*gram*) referring to the person, etc affected by the *verb,* e g *him* in *Give him the money.*

'indirect 'speech, (*gram*) speech as it is reported with the necessary changes of pronouns, tenses, etc, e g *He said he would come.* for *He said 'I will come'.*

in·di·rect·ly *adv*

in·dis·cern·ible /ˈɪndɪˈsɜːnəbəl/ *adj* that cannot be discerned.

in·dis·ci·pline /ɪnˈdɪsəplɪn/ *n* [U] absence of discipline.

in·dis·creet /ˈɪndɪˈskriːt/ *adj* not wary, cautious or careful.

in·dis·creet·ly *adv*

in·dis·crete /ˈɪndɪˈskriːt/ *adj* not formed of distinct or separate parts.

in·dis·cre·tion /ˈɪndɪˈskreʃən/ *n* **1** [U] indiscreet conduct. **2** [C] indiscreet remark or act.

in·dis·crimi·nate /ˈɪndɪˈskrɪmɪnət/ *adj* acting, given, without care: *~ praise; ~ bombing.*

in·dis·crimi·nate·ly *adv*

in·dis·pens·able /ˈɪndɪˈspensəbəl/ *adj* absolutely essential: *Air, food and water are ~ to life.*

in·dis·posed /ˈɪndɪˈspəʊzd/ *adj* (*formal*) **1** unwell. **2** unwilling: *He seems ~ to help us.*

in·dis·put·able /ˈɪndɪˈspjuːtəbəl/ *adj* that cannot be disputed.

in·dis·sol·uble /ˈɪndɪˈsɒljʊbəl/ *adj* (*formal*) that cannot be dissolved or broken up; firm and lasting: *The Roman Catholic Church regards marriage as ~.*

in·dis·tinct /ˈɪndɪˈstɪŋkt/ *adj* not distinct: *~ sounds/memories.*

in·dis·tinct·ly *adv*

in·dis·tinct·ness *n* [U]

in·dis·tin·guish·able /ˈɪndɪˈstɪŋgwɪʃəbəl/ *adj* that cannot be distinguished.

in·di·vid·ual /ˈɪndɪˈvɪdʒʊəl/ *adj* **1** (opposite of *general*) specially for one person or thing: *~ attention.* **2** characteristic of a single person, animal, plant or thing: *an ~ style of speaking.* □ *n* [C] any one human being (contrasted with *society*): *the rights of the ~.*

in·di·vid·ually *adv* separately; one by one: *be interviewed ~ly.*

in·di·vidu·al·ity /ˈɪndɪˈvɪdʒʊˈæləti/ *n* (*pl* -ies) **1** [U] all the characteristics that belong to an individual and that distinguish him from others. **2** [C] state of separate existence.

in·di·vis·ible /ˈɪndɪˈvɪzəbəl/ *adj* that cannot be divided.

in·doc·tri·nate /ɪnˈdɒktrɪneɪt/ vt fill the mind of (a person) (with ideas or beliefs).
in·doc·tri·na·tion /ɪnˈdɒktrɪˈneɪʃən/ n [U]

in·do·lent /ˈɪndələnt/ adj (formal) lazy; inactive.
in·do·lent·ly adv
in·dol·ence /-əns/ n [U]

in·dom·i·table /ɪnˈdɒmɪtəbəl/ adj that cannot be subdued or conquered; unyielding: ∼ courage.

in·door /ˈɪnˈdɔ(r)/ adj belonging to, carried on, situated, inside a building: ∼ games.

in·doors /ˈɪnˈdɔːz/ adv in or into a building: go/stay ∼; kept ∼ all week by bad weather.

in·dorse /ɪnˈdɔːs/ = endorse.

in·du·bi·table /ɪnˈdjuːbɪtəbəl US: -ˈduː-/ adj (formal) that cannot be doubted.

in·duce /ɪnˈdjuːs US: -ˈduːs/ vt 1 persuade or influence; cause: What ∼d you to do such a thing? 2 bring about: illness ∼d by overwork.
in·duce·ment n [C,U] that which induces; incentive: He hasn't much ∼ment to study English.

in·duct /ɪnˈdʌkt/ vt 1 introduce, install, formally in a position or appointment. 2 introduce knowledge or experience (to).

in·duc·tion /ɪnˈdʌkʃən/ n 1 [U] inducting or being inducted: an ∼ course, designed to provide general background knowledge. 2 method of reasoning which obtains general laws from particular facts or examples; production of facts to prove a general statement. ⇨ deduction.

in·duc·tive /ɪnˈdʌktɪv/ adj (of reasoning) based on induction(2).

in·dulge /ɪnˈdʌldʒ/ vt,vi 1 give way to and satisfy (desires, etc): ∼ a sick child. 2 indulge in, allow oneself the pleasure of: He occasionally ∼s in the luxury of a good cigar.
in·dul·gent /-ənt/ adj inclined to indulge; indulgent parents.
in·dul·gent·ly adv

in·dul·gence /ɪnˈdʌldʒəns/ n 1 [U] indulging; the state of being indulged: Constant ∼ in gambling brought about his ruin. 2 [C] something in which a person indulges: Wine and cigarettes are his only ∼s. 3 [U] (in the R C Church) granting of freedom from punishment for sin after being forgiven; [C] instance of this.

in·dus·trial /ɪnˈdʌstrɪəl/ adj of industries: an ∼ dispute, one between workers and management.
in'dustrial e`state, area of land planned and used for factories.
the in'dustrial 'revo`lution, the social changes brought about by mechanical inventions in the 18th and early 19th centuries.
in·dus·trial·ism /-ɪzm/ n [U] social system in which large-scale industries have an important part.
in·dus·trial·ist /-ɪst/ n [C] (a) owner of a large-scale industrial undertaking. (b) sup-

porter of industrialism.

in·dus·tri·ous /ɪnˈdʌstrɪəs/ adj hardworking.

in·dus·try /ˈɪndəstrɪ/ n (pl -ies) 1 [U] quality of being hard-working; being always employed usefully: a man admired for his ∼. 2 [C,U] (branch of) trade or manufacture (contrasted with distribution and commerce): the cotton and woollen industries.

in·ebri·ate /ɪˈniːbrɪeɪt/ vt make drunk. □ n [C], adj /ɪˈniːbrɪət/ (person who is habitually) drunk.

in·ed·ible /ɪnˈedəbəl/ adj (of a kind) not suitable to be eaten.

in·ef·fable /ɪnˈefəbəl/ adj too great to be described in words: ∼ joy/beauty.
in·ef·fably /-əblɪ/ adv

in·ef·fec·tive /ˈɪnɪˈfektɪv/ adj not producing the effect(s) desired.
in·ef·fec·tive·ly adv
in·ef·fec·tive·ness n [U]

in·ef·fec·tual /ˈɪnɪˈfektʃuəl/ adj without effect; lacking confidence and unable to get things done: an ∼ teacher/leader.
in·ef·fec·tually /-tʃuəlɪ/ adv

in·ef·fi·cient /ˈɪnɪˈfɪʃənt/ adj 1 (of persons) wasting time, energy, etc in their work or duties: an ∼ management/administration. 2 (of machines, processes, etc) wasteful; not producing adequate results.
in·ef·fi·cient·ly adv
in·ef·fi·ciency /-ənsɪ/ n [U]

in·el·egant /ɪnˈelɪgənt/ adj not graceful or refined.
in·el·egant·ly adv
in·el·egance /-əns/ n [U]

in·eli·gible /ɪnˈelɪdʒəbəl/ adj not suitable or qualified: ∼ for the position.
in·eli·gi·bil·ity /ˈɪnˈelɪdʒəˈbɪlətɪ/ n [U]

in·ept /ɪˈnept/ adj unsuitable, said or done at the wrong time: ∼ remarks.
in·ept·ly adv
in·ep·ti·tude /ɪˈneptɪtjuːd US: -tuːd/ n [C,U]

in·e·qual·ity /ˈɪnɪˈkwɒlətɪ/ n (pl -ies) 1 [U] want of, absence of, equality in size, degree, circumstances, etc. 2 [C] instance of this; difference in size, rank, wealth, etc: Great inequalities in wealth cause social unrest.

in·equi·table /ɪnˈekwɪtəbəl/ adj (formal) unjust; unfair: an ∼ division of the profits.

in·equity /ɪnˈekwətɪ/ n [C,U] (pl -ies) (instance of) injustice or unfairness.

in·ert /ɪˈnɜːt/ adj 1 without power to move or act: ∼ matter. 2 without active chemical properties: ∼ gases. 3 heavy and slow in (mind or body).

in·er·tia /ɪˈnɜːʃə/ n [U] 1 state of being inert(3). 2 property of matter by which it remains in a state of rest or, if it is in motion, continues in the same direction and in a straight line unless it is acted on by an external force.

in·es·cap·able /ˈɪnɪˈskeɪpəbəl/ adj that cannot be escaped, unavoidable: an ∼ conclusion that he is a thief.

in·es·ti·mable /ɪnˈestɪməbəl/ *adj* too great, precious, etc to be estimated.

in·evi·table /ɪnˈevɪtəbəl/ *adj* **1** that cannot be avoided, that is sure to happen. **2** (*informal*) so frequently seen, heard, etc that it is familiar and expected: *a Japanese tourist with his ∼ camera.*
in·evi·ta·bil·ity /ɪnˈevɪtəˈbɪlətɪ/ *n* [U]

in·ex·act /ˈɪnɪɡˈzækt/ *adj* not exact.

in·ex·acti·tude /ˈɪnɪɡˈzæktɪtjud US: -tud/ *n* [C,U]

in·ex·cus·able /ˈɪnɪkˈskjuzəbəl/ *adj* that cannot be excused: ∼ *conduct/delays.*

in·ex·haust·ible /ˈɪnɪɡˈzɔstəbəl/ *adj* that cannot be exhausted: *My patience is not ∼.*

in·exor·able /ɪnˈeksərəbəl/ *adj* (*formal*) relentless; unyielding: ∼ *demands.*
in·exor·ably /-əblɪ/ *adv*

in·ex·ped·ient /ˈɪnɪkˈspidɪənt/ *adj* not expedient.
in·ex·ped·iency /-ənsɪ/ *n* [U]

in·ex·pen·sive /ˈɪnɪkˈspensɪv/ *adj* not expensive; low priced.
in·ex·pen·sive·ly *adv*

in·ex·pe·ri·ence /ˈɪnɪkˈspɪərɪəns/ *n* [U] lack of experience.
in·ex·pe·ri·enced *adj*

in·ex·plic·able /ˈɪnɪkˈsplɪkəbəl/ *adj* that cannot be explained.

in·ex·press·ible /ˈɪnɪkˈspresəbəl/ *adj* that cannot be expressed in words: ∼ *sorrow/ anguish.*

in·ex·tri·cable /ɪnˈekstrɪkəbəl/ *adj* that cannot be solved or escaped from: ∼ *confusion.*

in·fal·lible /ɪnˈfæləbəl/ *adj* **1** incapable of making mistakes or doing wrong: *None of us is ∼.* **2** never failing: ∼ *cures.*
in·fal·li·bil·ity /ˈɪnˈfæləˈbɪlətɪ/ *n* [U] complete freedom from the possibility of being in error: *the infallibility of the Pope.*

in·fa·mous /ˈɪnfəməs/ *adj* wicked; shameful; disgraceful: ∼ *behaviour; an ∼ plot/ traitor.*

in·famy /ˈɪnfəmɪ/ *n* (*pl* -ies) **1** [U] being infamous; public dishonour. **2** [C] infamous act.

in·fancy /ˈɪnfənsɪ/ *n* [U] **1** state of being, period when one is, an infant. **2** (*legal*) (in GB) minority(1). **3** early stage of development or growth: *when space-travel was still in its ∼.*

in·fant /ˈɪnfənt/ *n* [C] **1** child during the first few years of its life. **2** (as an *adjective*): ∼ *voices.*
'infant school, part of a primary school for children under 7.

in·fan·ti·cide /ɪnˈfæntɪsaɪd/ *n* [U] crime of killing an infant.

in·fan·tile /ˈɪnfəntaɪl/ *adj* characteristic of infants: ∼ *behaviour.*

'infantile pa'ralysis, name formerly used for poliomyelitis.

in·fan·try /ˈɪnfəntrɪ/ *n* (collective *sing*) foot-soldiers: *an ∼ regiment.*

in·fatu·ate /ɪnˈfætʃʊeɪt/ *vt* **be infatuated**

with/by sb, be filled with a wild and foolish love for: *He's ∼d with that girl.*
in·fatu·ation /ɪnˈfætʃʊˈeɪʃən/ *n* [C,U]

in·fect /ɪnˈfekt/ *vt* **1** contaminate; affect with disease. **2** (*fig*) influence feelings, ideas, etc: *Mary's high spirits ∼ed the whole class.*

in·fec·tion /ɪnˈfekʃən/ *n* **1** [U] infecting or being infected; communication of disease, esp through the atmosphere or water, ⇨ contagion. **2** [C] an infectious disease. **3** (*fig*) influence that infects.

in·fec·tious /ɪnˈfekʃəs/ *adj* **1** causing infection, disease; (of disease) that can be spread by means of bacteria carried in the atmosphere or in water. ⇨ **contagious. 2** (*fig*) quickly influencing others; likely to spread to others: ∼ *humour.*

in·fer /ɪnˈfɜ(r)/ *vt* (-rr-) reach an opinion (from facts or reasoning): *Am I to ∼ from your remarks that you think I am a liar?*
in·fer·ence /ˈɪnfərəns/ *n* **1** [U] process of inferring. **by inference,** as the result of drawing a conclusion. **2** [C] that which is inferred.

in·fer·ior /ɪnˈfɪərɪə(r)/ *adj* low(er) in rank, social position, importance, quality, etc: *make a person feel ∼.* □ *n* [C] person who is low(er) (in rank, ability, etc).
in·fer·ior·ity /ɪnˈfɪərɪˈɒrətɪ US: -ˈɔr-/ *n* [U] state of being inferior.

in'feri'ority complex, feeling of being inferior producing behaviour such as boasting and aggression.

in·fer·nal /ɪnˈfɜnəl/ *adj* of hell; devilish; abominable: *the ∼ regions; ∼ cruelty.*

in·ferno /ɪnˈfɜnəʊ/ *n* [C] (*pl* ∼s) hell; scene of horror, e g a blazing building in which people are trapped.

in·fer·tile /ɪnˈfɜtaɪl US: -təl/ *adj* not fertile.
in·fer·til·ity /ˈɪnfɜˈtɪlətɪ/ *n* [U]

in·fest /ɪnˈfest/ *vt* (of rats, insects, robbers, etc) be present in large numbers: *warehouses ∼ed with rats.*
in·fes·ta·tion /ˈɪnfeˈsteɪʃən/ *n* [C,U]

in·fi·del /ˈɪnfɪdəl/ *n* [C] person with no belief in an accepted religion.

in·fi·del·ity /ˈɪnfɪˈdelətɪ/ *n* [C,U] (*pl* -ties) (formal act of) disloyalty or unfaithfulness.

in·fight·ing /ˈɪnfaɪtɪŋ/ *n* [U] (*informal*) often ruthless competition between colleagues or rivals (esp in commerce and industry).

in·fil·trate /ˈɪnfɪltreɪt/ *vt,vi* **1** (cause to) pass through or into by filtering. **2** (of troops) pass through defences without attracting notice. **3** (of ideas) pass into people's minds.
in·fil·tra·tion /ˈɪnfɪlˈtreɪʃən/ *n* [U]

in·fi·nite /ˈɪnfɪnɪt/ *adj* endless; without limits; that cannot be measured, calculated, or imagined: ∼ *space. Such ideas may do ∼ harm.*
in·fi·nite·ly *adv* in an infinite degree: *Atoms and molecules are ∼ly small.*

in·fini·tesi·mal /ˈɪnˈfɪnɪˈtesɪməl/ *adj* infinitely small.

in·fini·tive /ɪnˈfɪnətɪv/ adj, n [C] (gram) (in English) the non-finite form of a verb used with or without to, eg let him go; allow him to go.

in·fin·ity /ɪnˈfɪnətɪ/ n [U] 1 (maths) infinite quantity (expressed by the symbol ∞). 2 infinite space, time.

in·firm /ɪnˈfɜːm/ adj 1 physically weak (esp through age): walk with ~ steps. 2 mentally or morally weak.

in·firm·ity /ɪnˈfɜːmətɪ/ n [C,U] (pl -ties) (particular form of) weakness.

in·firm·ary /ɪnˈfɜːmərɪ/ n [C] (pl -ies) 1 hospital. 2 (in an institution, etc) room used for people who are ill or injured.

in·flame /ɪnˈfleɪm/ vt,vi (cause to) become red, angry, overheated: ~d eyes; ~d with passion.

in·flam·mable /ɪnˈflæməbəl/ adj 1 easily set on fire. 2 (fig) easily excited.

in·flam·ma·tion /ˌɪnfləˈmeɪʃən/ n 1 [U] inflamed condition (esp of some part of the body): ~ of the eyes. 2 [C] instance, place, of this.

in·flam·ma·tory /ɪnˈflæmətrɪ US: -tɔːrɪ/ adj 1 tending to inflame: ~ speeches. 2 of, tending to produce, inflammation(1).

in·flate /ɪnˈfleɪt/ vt 1 fill a tyre, balloon, etc (with air or gas); (cause to) swell. 2 (fig) puff up: ~d with pride. 3 (finance) take action to increase the amount of money in circulation so that prices rise. ⇨ deflate.

in·flat·able /-əbəl/ adj that can be inflated: an inflatable rubber dinghy.

in·fla·tion /ɪnˈfleɪʃən/ n [U] (a) act of inflating; state of being inflated. (b) (esp) (rise in prices brought about by the) expansion of the supply of money, credit, etc.

in·fla·tion·ary /ɪnˈfleɪʃənrɪ US: -əneri/ adj of, caused by, inflation.

in·flect /ɪnˈflekt/ vt 1 (gram) change the ending or form of (a word) to show its relationship to other words in a sentence. 2 adapt, regulate (the voice). 3 bend inwards; curve.

in·flec·tion /ɪnˈflekʃən/ n 1 [U] inflecting. 2 [C] inflected form of a word; suffix used to inflect, eg -ed, -ing. 3 [U] rise and fall of the voice in speaking.

in·flec·tional /-ʃənəl/ adj

in·flex·ible /ɪnˈfleksəbəl/ adj 1 that cannot be bent or turned. 2 (fig) unyielding: an ~ will.

in·flex·ibly /-əblɪ/ adv

in·flexi·bil·ity /ɪnˈfleksɪˈbɪlətɪ/ n [U]

in·flex·ion /ɪnˈflekʃən/ n = inflection.

in·flict /ɪnˈflɪkt/ vt 1 give (a blow, etc); cause to suffer: ~ a blow/a severe wound on him. 2 impose: I'm sorry to have to ~ my company upon you.

in·flic·tion /ɪnˈflɪkʃən/ n [C,U]

in·flow /ˈɪnfləʊ/ n 1 [U] flowing in. 2 [C,U] that which flows in.

in·flu·ence /ˈɪnfluəns/ n 1 [U] (use of the)

power to affect a person's character, beliefs or actions through example, fear, admiration, etc. 2 [C] person, fact, etc that exercises such power. He's an ~ for good in the town. 3 [U] action of natural forces: the ~ of climate (on vegetation). 4 [U] power due to wealth, position, etc: Will you use your ~ to get me a job? □ vt exert an influence on; having an effect on: Don't be ~d by what she says.

in·flu·en·tial /ˌɪnfluˈenʃəl/ adj having influence.

in·flu·en·tially /-ʃəlɪ/ adv

in·flu·enza /ˌɪnfluˈenzə/ n [U] infectious disease with fever, muscular pain and catarrh.

in·flux /ˈɪnflʌks/ n (pl ~es) 1 [U] flowing in. 2 [C] constant inflow of large numbers or quantities: an ~ of wealth.

in·form /ɪnˈfɔːm/ vt,vi 1 give knowledge to: Keep me ~ed of fresh developments. He's a `well-~ed man. 2 bring evidence or an accusation (against a person) (to the police).

in·form·ant /-ənt/ n [C] person who gives information.

in·former n [C] person who informs(2), esp against a criminal.

in·for·mal /ɪnˈfɔːməl/ adj not formal(1,2); without ceremony or formality: an ~ visit; ~ dress.

in·for·mally /-məlɪ/ adv

in·for·mal·ity /ˌɪnfɔːˈmælətɪ/ n [C,U]

in·for·ma·tion /ˌɪnfəˈmeɪʃən/ n [U] 1 informing or being informed. 2 news or knowledge given: That's a useful piece/bit of ~.

in·for·ma·tive /ɪnˈfɔːmətɪv/ adj giving information; instructive: ~ books; an ~ talk.

in·for·ma·tive·ly adv

in·fre·quent /ɪnˈfriːkwənt/ adj not frequent; rare.

in·fre·quent·ly adv

in·fre·quency /ɪnˈfriːkwənsɪ/ n [U]

in·fringe /ɪnˈfrɪndʒ/ vt,vi 1 break (a rule, etc). 2 go beyond what is right or natural: Be careful not to ~ on/upon the rights of other people.

in·fringe·ment n [C,U]

in·furi·ate /ɪnˈfjʊərɪeɪt/ vt fill with fury or rage: infuriating delays.

in·fuse /ɪnˈfjuːz/ vt,vi (formal) 1 put, pour (a quality, etc into); fill (a person with): ~ fresh courage/new life into soldiers. 2 pour (hot) liquid on (leaves, herbs, etc) to flavour it or to extract its constituents: ~ herbs. 3 undergo infusion: Let the tea ~ for three minutes.

in·fu·sion /ɪnˈfjuːʒən/ n 1 [U] infusing or being infused. 2 [C] liquid made by infusing. 3 [U] pouring in; mixing: the ~ of new breeds into old stock.

-ing /-ɪŋ/ suffix (verb + ' ~ = present participle or gerund): talking; stopping.

in·geni·ous /ɪnˈdʒiːnɪəs/ adj 1 (of a person)

very clever and skilful (at making or inventing). **2** (of things) skilfully made: *an ~ tool.*

in·geni·ous·ly *adv*

in·gen·uity /ˌɪndʒɪˈnjuːɪti US: -ˈnuː-/ *n* [U] **(a)** (of a person) cleverness and skill. **(b)** (of things) originality in design.

in·got /ˈɪŋgət/ *n* [C] (usually brick-shaped) lump of metal (esp gold and silver), cast in a mould.

in·grained /ˈɪnˈgreɪnd/ *adj* **1** (of habits, tendencies, etc) deeply fixed: *~ prejudices.* **2** going deep: *~ dirt.*

in·grati·ate /ɪnˈgreɪʃɪeɪt/ *vt* bring oneself into favour, esp in order to gain an advantage: *an ingratiating smile.*

in·grati·at·ing·ly *adv*

in·grati·tude /ɪnˈgrætɪtjuːd US: -tuːd/ *n* [U] lack of gratitude.

in·gredi·ent /ɪnˈgriːdɪənt/ *n* [C] one of the parts of a mixture: *the ~s of a cake.*

in·habit /ɪnˈhæbɪt/ *vt* live in; occupy.

in·hab·it·able /-əbəl/ *adj* that can be lived in.

in·habit·ant /-ənt/, person living in a place.

in·hale /ɪnˈheɪl/ *vt, vi* draw into the lungs: *~ air.*

in·haler, device for producing a chemical vapour to make breathing easier.

in·her·ent /ɪnˈhɪərənt/ *adj* existing as a natural and permanent part or quality of: *He has an ~ love of beauty.*

in·herit /ɪnˈherɪt/ *vt, vi* **1** receive property, a title, etc as heir: *The eldest son will ~ the title.* **2** derive (qualities, etc) from ancestors: *She ~ed her mother's good looks.*

in·herit·ance /-əns/ *n* [U] **(a)** inheriting: *receive money by ~ance.* **(b)** [C] (*literally*, *fig*) what is inherited: *an ~ance of ill-feeling.*

in·hibit /ɪnˈhɪbɪt/ *vt* hinder, restrain: *an ~ed person*, one who is unable or unwilling to express his feelings.

in·hi·bi·tion /ˌɪnɪˈbɪʃən/ *n* [U] habitual shrinking from an action for which there is an impulse or desire; [C] instance of this.

in·hibi·tory /ɪnˈhɪbɪtrɪ US: -tɔːrɪ/ *adj* tending to inhibit; of an inhibition.

in·hos·pi·table /ˌɪnhɒˈspɪtəbəl/ *adj* not hospitable.

in·hu·man /ɪnˈhjuːmən/ *adj* cruel; without feeling: *~ treatment.*

in·hu·man·ity /ˌɪnhjuːˈmænɪti/ *n* [C,U] lack of pity; cruelty: *man's ~ity to man.*

in·hu·mane /ˌɪnhjuːˈmeɪn/ *adj* not humane; cruel; without pity.

in·hu·mane·ly *adv*

in·iqui·tous /ɪˈnɪkwɪtəs/ *adj* (*formal*) very wicked or unjust.

in·iqui·tous·ly *adv*

in·iquity /ɪˈnɪkwətɪ/ *n* [C,U]

in·itial /ɪˈnɪʃəl/ *adj* of or at the beginning: *the ~ letter of a word.* □ *n* [C] first letter, esp (*pl*) first letters of a person's names, as *GBS* (for *George Bernard Shaw*). □ *vt* (-ll-, *US* also -l-) mark, sign, with one's initials.

in·itially /-ʃəlɪ/ *adv* at the beginning.

in·iti·ate /ɪˈnɪʃɪeɪt/ *vt* **1** set (a scheme, etc) working: *~ a plan.* **2** admit or introduce a person (to membership of a group, etc). **3** give a person elementary instruction, or secret knowledge of, instruct. □ *n* [C], *adj* /ɪˈnɪʃɪət/ (person) who has been initiated(2,3).

in·iti·ation /ɪˌnɪʃɪˈeɪʃən/ *n* [U]

in·iti·at·ive /ɪˈnɪʃɪətɪv/ *n* **1** first or introductory step or move. *act/do sth on one's own initiative*, without an order or suggestion from others. *have/take the initiative*, (be in the position to) make the first move, e g in war. **2** [U] capacity to see what needs to be done and the will to do it: *A statesman must show ~.*

in·ject /ɪnˈdʒekt/ *vt* **1** drive or force a liquid, drug, etc (into something) with, or as with, a syringe; fill by injecting: *~ penicillin into the blood-stream.* **2** (*fig informal*) fill: *His appointment may ~ some new life into the committee.*

in·jec·tion /ɪnˈdʒekʃən/ *n* [C,U]

in·ju·di·cious /ˌɪndʒuːˈdɪʃəs/ *adj* (*formal*) not well-judged: *~ remarks.*

in·junc·tion /ɪnˈdʒʌŋkʃən/ *n* [C] authoritative order, esp a written order from a law court, demanding that something shall or shall not be done.

in·jure /ˈɪndʒər/ *vt* hurt; damage.

in·jured *adj* wounded; wronged; offended: *~d looks.* □ *n* (collective *noun* used with *the*) people hurt: *The ~ are in hospital.*

in·juri·ous /ɪnˈdʒʊərɪəs/ *adj* (*formal*) causing, likely to cause, injury: *habits that are ~ to health.*

in·jury /ˈɪndʒərɪ/ *n* (*pl* -ies) **1** [U] harm; damage; wrongful treatment. **2** [C] place (in the body) that is hurt or wounded; act that hurts; insult: *a ~ back ~; a severe ~ to his reputation.*

in·jus·tice /ˈɪnˈdʒʌstɪs/ *n* [U] lack of justice; [C] unjust act, etc.

ink /ɪŋk/ *n* **1** (kinds of) coloured liquid used for writing and printing. **2** black liquid ejected by cuttlefish, etc. □ *vt* mark with ink: *~ one's fingers. ink in: ~ in a drawing*, mark with ink something drawn in pencil.

inky *adj* (-ier, -iest)

ink·ling /ˈɪŋklɪŋ/ *n* vague idea: *have/get/give an ~ (of the truth).*

in·land /ˈɪnlənd/ *adj* **1** situated in the interior of a country, far from the sea or border: *~ towns.* **2** carried on, obtained, within the limits of a country: *~ (= domestic) trade.* □ *adv* /ɪnˈlænd/ in or towards the interior.

'Inland `Revenue, government department that collects taxes.

in-laws /ˈɪnlɔːz/ *n pl* (*informal*) relatives by marriage.

in·lay /ɪnˈleɪ/ *vt* (*pt, pp* inlaid /-leɪd/) set pieces of (designs in) wood, metal, etc in the surface of another kind. □ *n* /ˈɪnleɪ/ **1** [U] inlaid work; materials used for this. **2** [C] design, pattern, made by inlaying.

in·let /ˈɪnlet/ n [C] **1** strip of water extending into the land from a larger body of water (the sea, a lake), or between islands. **2** something let in or inserted, e g a piece of material inserted into a garment.

in·mate /ˈɪnmeɪt/ n [C] one of a number of persons living in a prison or other institution.

in mem·or·iam /ˌɪn məˈmɔːrɪəm/ (*Latin*) (used in epitaphs, etc) in memory of; as a memorial to.

in·most /ˈɪnməʊst/ adj **1** farthest from the surface. **2** (*fig*) most private or secret: *my ∼ feelings.*

inn /ɪn/ n [C] **1** public house where lodgings, drink and meals may be had. **2** '**Inn of 'Court,** (building of) four law societies in London having the exclusive right of admitting persons to the bar. ⇨ bar ¹ (12).

'**inn-keeper,** person who keeps an inn.

in·nards /ˈɪnədz/ n pl (*informal*) **1** stomach and bowels. **2** (*informal*) any inner parts: *the ∼ of a motor car.*

in·nate /ɪˈneɪt/ adj (of a quality, etc) in one's nature; possessed from birth: *her ∼ courtesy.*

in·nate·ly adv

in·ner /ˈɪnə(r)/ adj inside; of the inside: *an ∼ room.*

in·ner·most /-məʊst/ adj = inmost.

in·ning /ˈɪnɪŋ/ n [C] **1** (baseball) division of a game in which each team bats. **2** (cricket, always pl) time during which a player or team is batting. **3** (*fig*) period of power, e g of a political party, or of opportunity to show one's ability; period of active life: *have a good ∼s.*

in·no·cence /ˈɪnəsəns/ n [U] quality or state of being innocent.

in·no·cent /ˈɪnəsənt/ adj **1** (*legal*) not guilty: *∼ of the charge.* **2** harmless: *∼ amusements.* **3** knowing nothing of evil or wrong: *as ∼ as a new-born babe.* **4** foolishly trusting: *Don't be so ∼ as to believe everything he says.* □ n [C] innocent person, esp a young child.

in·no·cent·ly adv

in·nocu·ous /ɪˈnɒkjʊəs/ adj causing no harm.

in·no·vate /ˈɪnəveɪt/ vi introduce new things.

in·no·va·tor /-tə(r)/ person who innovates.

in·no·va·tion /ˌɪnəˈveɪʃən/ n [U] innovating; [C] instance of this; something new that is introduced: *technical innovations in industry.*

in·nu·endo /ˌɪnjʊˈendəʊ/ n [C] (pl ∼es) indirect reference (usually unfavourable to a person's reputation).

in·numer·able /ɪˈnjuːmrəbl US: ɪˈnuː-/ adj too many to be counted.

in·ocu·late /ɪˈnɒkjʊleɪt/ vt inject a serum or vaccine into (a person or animal) to give (him, it) a mild form of the disease to safeguard him against it: *inoculating against*

cholera.

in·ocu·la·tion /ɪˌnɒkjʊˈleɪʃən/ n [C,U]

in·of·fen·sive /ˌɪnəˈfensɪv/ adj not giving offence; not objectionable: *an ∼ remark/ person.*

in·op·er·at·ive /ɪnˈɒpərətɪv/ adj (of laws, rules, etc) not working or taking effect; invalid.

in·op·por·tune /ɪnˈɒpətʃuːn US: -tuːn/ adj not suitable or appropriate: *at an ∼ time.*

in·op·por·tune·ly adv

in·or·di·nate /ɪˈnɔːdənət/ adj (*formal*) not properly restrained or controlled; excessive: *∼ tax demands.*

in·or·di·nate·ly adv

in·or·ganic /ˌɪnɔːˈɡænɪk/ adj **1** not having an organized physical structure, as plants and animals have: *Rocks and metals are ∼ substances.* **2** not the result of natural growth: *an ∼ form of society.*

in·or·gani·cally /-klɪ/ adv

in·pa·tient /ˈɪn peɪʃənt/ n ⇨ in-.

in·quest /ˈɪnkwest/ n [C] official inquiry to learn facts, esp concerning a death which may not be the result of natural causes.

in·quire /ɪnˈkwaɪə(r)/ vt, vi **1** ask to be told: *∼ what a person wants/where to stay.* **2** ask for information (about): *∼ about trains to London.* **inquire after sb,** ask about (his health, welfare). **inquire into,** investigate.

in·quirer, person who inquires.

in·quir·ing adj in the habit of asking for information: *an inquiring mind.*

in·quir·ing·ly adv

in·quiry /ɪnˈkwaɪərɪ US: ˈɪnkwərɪ/ n (pl -ies) **1** [U] asking; inquiring. **on inquiry,** when one has asked. **2** [C] question; investigation: *hold an official ∼ into the incident.*

in·qui·si·tion /ˌɪnkwɪˈzɪʃən/ n **1** [C] thorough search or investigation; [C] instance of this, esp a judicial or official inquiry. **2 the I∼,** (also called *the Holy Office*) court appointed by the Church of Rome to suppress heresy.

in·quisi·tive /ɪnˈkwɪzətɪv/ adj fond of, showing a fondness for, inquiring into other people's affairs.

in·quisi·tive·ly adv

in·quisi·tive·ness n [U]

in·road /ˈɪnrəʊd/ n [C] **1** sudden attack (into a country, etc), esp to steal supplies. **2** (*fig*) something that gradually trespasses on or uses up: *make ∼s on one's savings.*

in·rush /ˈɪnrʌʃ/ n [C] rushing in: *an ∼ of water/tourists.*

in·sane /ɪnˈseɪn/ adj **1** mad. **2** (*informal*) senseless(1).

in·sane·ly adv

in·san·ity /ɪnˈsænətɪ/ n [U] madness.

in·sani·tary /ɪnˈsænɪtrɪ US: -terɪ/ adj not sanitary: *living under ∼ conditions.*

in·sa·tiable /ɪnˈseɪʃəbl/ adj (*formal*) that cannot be satisfied; very greedy: *∼ appetites.*

in·sa·tiably /-ʃəblɪ/ adv

in·scribe /ɪnˈskraɪb/ vt mark, write (words, one's name, etc in or on).

in·scrip·tion /ɪnˈskrɪpʃən/ n [C] (esp) words cut on a stone, e g a monument, or stamped on a coin or medal.

in·scru·table /ɪnˈskruːtəbl/ adj that cannot be understood or known: *the ~ ways of fate.*

in·sect /ˈɪnsekt/ n [C] sorts of small animal, e g ant, fly, wasp, having six legs and no backbone and a body divided into three parts (head, thorax, abdomen).

in·sec·ti·cide /ɪnˈsektɪsaɪd/ n [C,U] preparation used for killing insects, e g DDT.

in·sec·tiv·or·ous /ˈɪnsekˈtɪvərəs/ adj eating insects as food: *Swallows are ~.*

in·se·cure /ˈɪnsɪˈkjʊə(r)/ adj 1 not safe; not providing good support; not to be relied on: *an ~ job.* 2 feeling unsafe; without protection; lacking confidence.
in·se·cure·ly adv
in·se·cur·ity /ˈɪnsɪˈkjʊərətɪ/ n [U]: *suffer from feelings of insecurity.*

in·sen·si·bil·ity /ɪnˈsensəˈbɪlətɪ/ n [U] (*formal*) lack of mental feeling or emotion; inability to know, recognize, understand or appreciate: *~ to pain/beauty.*

in·sen·sible /ɪnˈsensəbl/ adj 1 unconscious as the result of injury, illness, etc. 2 unaware (of): *~ of danger.* 3 unsympathetic; emotionless. 4 (of changes) too small or gradual to be perceived: *by ~ degrees.*
in·sen·sibly /-əblɪ/ adv

in·sen·si·tive /ɪnˈsensɪtɪv/ adj not sensitive (to touch, light, a person's feelings).
in·sen·si·tive·ly adv
in·sen·si·tiv·ity /ɪnˈsensəˈtɪvətɪ/ n [U]

in·sep·ar·able /ɪnˈseprəbl/ adj that cannot be separated: *~ friends.*

in·sert /ɪnˈsɜːt/ vt put, fit, place (*in, into, between*, etc): *~ a key in a lock.* □ n /ˈɪnsɜːt/ [C] something inserted, e g in a book.
in·ser·tion /ɪnˈsɜːʃən/ n [C,U]

in·set /ˈɪnset/ n [C] 1 extra page(s) inserted in a book, etc; small map, diagram, etc within the border of a printed page or of a larger map. 2 piece of material let into a dress. □ vt /ˈɪnˈset/ put in; insert.

in·shore /ˈɪnʃɔː(r)/ adj, adv close to the shore: *an ~ current; ~ fisheries.*

in·side /ˈɪnˈsaɪd/ n [C] 1 inner side or surface; part(s) within: *the ~ of a box.* **'inside 'out,** (a) with the inner side out: *He put his socks on ~ out.* (b) thoroughly: *He knows the subject ~ out.* 2 part of a road, track, etc on the inner edge of a curve; part of a pavement or footpath farthest from the road. 3 (*informal*) (often *pl*) stomach and bowels: *a pain in his ~.* □ adj /ˈɪnsaɪd/ situated on or in, coming from the inside: *the ~ pages of a newspaper.* □ adv 1 on or in the inside: *Look ~. There's nothing ~.* 2 (*GB sl*) in prison: *Jones is ~ for three years.* □ prep on the inner side of: *Don't let him come ~ the house.*

'inside 'left/'right, (in football, etc) player in the forward (attacking) line immediately to the left/right of the centre-forward.

in·sider, person who, because he is a member of some society, organization, etc can obtain facts and information, or has advantages over others. ⇨ outsider.

in·sidi·ous /ɪnˈsɪdɪəs/ adj doing harm secretly, unseen: *an ~ enemy/disease.*
in·sidi·ous·ly adv

in·sight /ˈɪnsaɪt/ n 1 [U] understanding; power of understanding something; [C] instance of this: *show ~ into human character.* 2 [C] (often sudden) glimpse or understanding: *On holiday, she had a good ~ into what life would be like as his wife.*

in·sig·nia /ɪnˈsɪgnɪə/ n pl symbols of authority, dignity, or honour.

in·sig·nifi·cant /ˈɪnsɪgˈnɪfɪkənt/ adj having little or no value, use, meaning or importance.
in·sig·nifi·cant·ly adv
in·sig·nifi·cance /-əns/ n [U]

in·sin·cere /ˈɪnsɪnˈsɪə(r)/ adj not sincere.
in·sin·cere·ly adv
in·sin·cer·ity /ˈɪnsɪnˈserətɪ/ n [U]

in·sinu·ate /ɪnˈsɪnjʊeɪt/ vt 1 make a way for (oneself/something) gently and craftily: *~ oneself into a person's favour.* 2 suggest unpleasantly and indirectly: *~ (to her) that a man is a liar.*
in·sinu·ation /ɪnˈsɪnjʊˈeɪʃən/ n [C,U]

in·sipid /ɪnˈsɪpɪd/ adj 1 without taste or flavour: *~ food.* 2 (*fig*) without interest, spirit: *~ conversation.*
in·sip·id·ly adv

in·sip·ient /ɪnˈsɪpɪənt/ adj foolish.

in·sist /ɪnˈsɪst/ vi, vt 1 urge strongly against opposition or disbelief: *~ on one's innocence/that one is innocent.* 2 declare that a purpose cannot be changed: *I ~ed that he should come with us/~ed on his coming with us.*
in·sist·ent /-ənt/ adj urgent; compelling attention: *~ent requests for more staff.*
in·sist·ence /-əns/ n [U]

in·so·lent /ˈɪnsələnt/ adj insulting; offensive; rude.
in·so·lent·ly adv
in·so·lence /-əns/ n [U]

in·sol·uble /ɪnˈsɒljʊbl/ adj 1 (of substances) that cannot be dissolved. 2 (of problems, etc) that cannot be solved or explained.

in·sol·vable /ɪnˈsɒlvəbl/ adj = insoluble(2).

in·sol·vent /ɪnˈsɒlvənt/ n [C], adj (person) unable to pay debts; bankrupt.
in·sol·vency /-ənsɪ/ n [U]

in·som·nia /ɪnˈsɒmnɪə/ n [U] inability to sleep.

in·som·niac /ɪnˈsɒmnɪæk/, person suffering from insomnia.

in·so·much /ˈɪnsəʊˈmʌtʃ/ adv to such a degree or extent (*as/that*).

in·spect /ɪnˈspekt/ vt 1 examine carefully. 2

visit officially to see that work is done properly, etc.

in·spec·tion /ɪnˈspekʃən/ n [C,U]

in·spec·tor /ɪnˈspektə(r)/ n [C] **1** official who inspects, e g schools, factories, mines. **2** (GB) police officer who is, in rank, below a superintendent and above a sergeant.

in·spec·tor·ate /ɪnˈspektərət/ n [C] group of inspectors: the Ministry of Education ~ate.

in·spi·ra·tion /ˌɪnspəˈreɪʃən/ n **1** [U] influence(s) producing creative activity in literature, music, art, etc: draw ~ from nature. **2** [C] person or thing that inspires: His wife was a constant ~ to him. **3** [C] (informal) good thought or idea that comes to the mind. **4** [U] divine guidance held to have been given to those who wrote the Bible.

in·spire /ɪnˈspaɪə(r)/ vt **1** put uplifting thoughts, feelings or aims into: ~ confidence in her. What ~d him to give such a brilliant performance? **2** fill with creative power: ~d poets/artists.

in·sta·bil·ity /ˌɪnstəˈbɪlətɪ/ n [U] lack of stability (of character).

in·stall (US also **in·stal**) /ɪnˈstɔːl/ vt **1** place (a person) in a new position of authority with the usual ceremony: ~ a dean. **2** place, fix (apparatus) in position for use: ~ central heating. **3** settle in a place: ~ed in a new home.

in·stal·la·tion /ˌɪnstəˈleɪʃən/ n [C,U]

in·stal·ment (US also **in·stall·ment**) /ɪnˈstɔːlmənt/ n [C] **1** any one of the parts in which something is presented over a period of time: a story that will appear in ~s, e g in a periodical. **2** any one of the parts of a payment spread over a period of time: pay by monthly ~s.

in·stance /ˈɪnstəns/ n [C] example; fact, etc supporting a general truth: This is only one ~ out of many. **for instance,** by way of example. □ vt give as an example.

in·stant¹ /ˈɪnstənt/ adj **1** coming or happening at once: an ~ success; ~ relief. **2** urgent: in ~ need of help. **3** (of food, drink) hatt can be prepared quickly and easily: ~ coffee.

in·stant·ly adv at once.

in·stant² /ˈɪnstənt/ n [C] **1** precise point of time: Come here this ~! at once! I sent you the news the ~ (that) (= as soon as) I heard it. **2** moment: Help arrived not an ~ too soon.

in·stan·taneous·ly adv

in·stead /ɪnˈsted/ adv as an alternative or substitute: If Harry is not well enough to go with you, take me ~. **instead of,** in place of; as an alternative or substitute for: I will go ~ of you.

in·step /ˈɪnstep/ n [C] upper surface of the human foot between the toes and the ankle; part of a shoe, etc covering this.

in·sti·gate /ˈɪnstɪgeɪt/ vt incite; cause (something) by doing this: ~ a strike.

in·sti·ga·tor /-tə(r)/ person who instigates.

in·sti·ga·tion /ˌɪnstɪˈgeɪʃən/ n [U]

in·stil (US = **in·still**) /ɪnˈstɪl/ vt (-ll-) introduce (ideas, etc) gradually.

in·stil·la·tion /ˌɪnstɪˈleɪʃən/ n [U]

in·stinct /ˈɪnstɪŋkt/ n **1** [U] natural tendency to behave in a certain way without reasoning or training: Birds learn to fly by ~. **2** [C] instance of this: an ~ for always saying the right thing. □ adj **instinct with,** filled with: a picture ~ with life.

in·stinc·tive /ɪnˈstɪŋktɪv/ adj based on instinct, not from training or teaching.

in·stinc·tive·ly adv

in·sti·tute¹ /ˈɪnstɪtjuːt US: -tuːt/ n [C] society or organization for a special (usually a social or educational) purpose; its office(s) or building(s).

in·sti·tute² /ˈɪnstɪtjuːt US: -tuːt/ vt **1** establish, get started an inquiry, custom, rule, etc: ~ legal proceedings. **2** appoint (a person to, into, a benefice).

in·sti·tu·tion /ˌɪnstɪˈtjuːʃən US: -ˈtuːʃən/ n **1** [U] instituting or being instituted: the ~ of customs/rules, etc. **2** [C] established law, custom or practice, e g a club or society. **3** [C] person who has become known to everyone because of long service. **4** [C] (building of) organization with charitable purposes or for social welfare, e g an orphanage, a home for old people.

in·sti·tu·tional /-ʃənəl/ adj

in·struct /ɪnˈstrʌkt/ vt **1** teach a school subject, a skill: ~ a class in history. **2** give orders or directions to: ~ him to start early. **3** inform: I have been ~ed by my bank to pay the deposit.

in·struc·tor /-tə(r)/, person who teaches; trainer.

in·struc·tress /-trəs/, woman who teaches or trains.

in·struc·tion /ɪnˈstrʌkʃən/ n **1** [U] instructing or being instructed: ~ in chemistry. **2** (pl) directions; orders: give ~s to arrive early.

in·struc·tional /-ʃənəl/ adj educational: ~al films.

in·struc·tive /ɪnˈstrʌktɪv/ adj giving or containing instruction: ~ books.

in·stru·ment /ˈɪnstrəmənt/ n [C] **1** implement, apparatus, used in performing an action, esp for delicate or scientific work: optical ~s, e g a microscope. **2** apparatus for producing musical sounds, e g a piano, violin, flute or drum: musical ~s. **3** person used by another for his own purposes: be made the ~ of another's crime. **4** formal (esp legal) document: The King signed the ~ of abdication.

in·stru·men·tal /ˌɪnstrəˈmentəl/ adj **1** serving as an instrument or means: be ~ in finding well-paid work for a friend. **2** of or for musical instruments: ~ music.

in·stru·men·tal·ist /-təlɪst/ player of a musical instrument.

in·stru·men·ta·tion /ˌɪnstrəmenˈteɪʃən/ n

[U] **1** arrangement of music for instruments. **2** development and manufacture of instruments(1).

in·sub·or·di·nate /ˌɪnsəˈbɔːdɪnət US: -dənət/ adj disobedient; rebellious.

in·sub·or·di·na·tion /ˌɪnsəˌbɔːdɪˈneɪʃən US: -dnˈeɪʃən/ n [U] being disobedient; [C] instance of this.

in·sub·stan·tial /ˌɪnsəbˈstænʃəl/ adj **1** not solid or real; lacking substance: an ∼ vision. **2** without good foundation or proof: an ∼ accusation.

in·suf·fer·able /ɪnˈsʌfrəbəl/ adj unbearably conceited; unbearable: ∼ insolence.

in·suf·fi·cient /ˌɪnsəˈfɪʃənt/ adj not sufficient: ∼ evidence.

in·suf·fi·cient·ly adv

in·suf·fi·ciency /-ʃənsɪ/ n [U]

in·su·lar /ˈɪnsjʊlə(r) US: -səl-/ adj **1** of an island. **2** of or like islanders. **3** narrow-minded: ∼ habits and prejudices.

in·su·lar·ity /ˌɪnsjʊˈlærətɪ US: -səˈl-/ n [U] state of being insular (esp 3).

in·su·late /ˈɪnsjʊleɪt US: -səl-/ vt **1** cover or separate (something) with non-conducting materials to prevent loss of heat, passage of electricity, etc: ˈinsulating tape. **2** separate; isolate: children carefully ∼d from harmful experiences.

in·su·la·tor /-tə(r)/ n [C] substance, device, for insulating.

in·su·la·tion /ˌɪnsjʊˈleɪʃən US: -səˈl-/ n [U] insulating or being insulated; materials used for this.

in·sult /ɪnˈsʌlt/ vt speak or act in a way that hurts or is intended to hurt a person's feelings or dignity. □ n /ˈɪnsʌlt/ [C,U] remark or action that insults.

in·sult·ing adj

in·sup·er·able /ɪnˈsjuːprəbəl US: -ˈsuː-/ adj (of difficulties, etc) that cannot be overcome: ∼ barriers.

in·sup·port·able /ˌɪnsəˈpɔːtəbəl/ adj unbearable.

in·sur·ance /ɪnˈʃʊərəns/ n **1** [U] (undertaking, by a company, society, or the State, to provide) safeguard against loss, provision against sickness, death, etc in return for regular payments. **2** [U] payment made to or by such a company, etc: When her husband died, she received £20 000 ∼. **3** [C] insurance policy: How many ∼s have you? **4** any measure taken as a safeguard against loss, failure, etc: try for a place at Leeds University as an ∼ against failure to obtain a place at York.

in·sure /ɪnˈʃʊə(r)/ vt make a contract that promises to pay, secures payment of, a sum of money in case of accident, damage, loss, death, etc: ∼ one's house against fire.

the insured, the person to whom payment will be made.

the insurer, the person or company undertaking to make payment in case of loss, etc.

in·sur·gent /ɪnˈsɜːdʒənt/ adj rebellious: ∼

troops. □ n [C] rebel soldier.

in·sur·mount·able /ˌɪnsəˈmaʊntəbəl/ adj (of obstacles, etc) that cannot be surmounted or overcome.

in·sur·rec·tion /ˌɪnsəˈrekʃən/ n [U] rising of people in open resistance to the government; [C] instance of this.

in·tact /ɪnˈtækt/ adj untouched; undamaged; complete.

in·take /ˈɪnteɪk/ n **1** [C] place where water, gas, etc is taken into a pipe, channel, etc. **2** [C,U] quantity, number, etc entering or taken in (during a given period): an annual ∼ of 200 students. **3** (area of) land reclaimed from a moor, marsh or the sea.

in·tan·gible /ɪnˈtændʒəbəl/ adj that cannot be touched or grasped by the mind: ∼ ideas.

in·tan·gi·bil·ity /ɪnˌtændʒəˈbɪlətɪ/ n [U]

in·te·ger /ˈɪntɪdʒə(r)/ n [C] whole number (contrasted with fractions).

in·te·gral /ˈɪntɪgrəl/ adj **1** necessary for completeness: The arms and legs are ∼ parts of a human being. **2** whole; having or containing all parts that are necessary for completeness. **3** (maths) (made up) of integers.

in·te·grally /-grəlɪ/ adv

in·te·grate /ˈɪntɪgreɪt/ vt **1** combine (parts) into a whole; complete by adding parts. **2** join with other groups or different race(s): The schools have ∼, joined together.

in·te·gra·tion /ˌɪntɪˈgreɪʃən/ n [U]

in·teg·rity /ɪnˈtegrətɪ/ n [U] **1** quality of being honest and upright in character: commercial ∼. **2** state or condition of being complete: Wasn't this Treaty supposed to guarantee our territorial ∼?

in·tel·lect /ˈɪntəlekt/ n **1** [U] power of the mind to reason (contrasted with feeling and instinct): I∼ distinguishes man from other animals. **2** (collective sing, or in pl) person of good understanding, reasoning power, etc: the ∼(s) of the age.

in·tel·lec·tual /ˌɪntəˈlektʃʊəl/ adj **1** of the intellect: ∼ pursuits. **2** having or showing good reasoning power: ∼ people/interests. □ n [C] intellectual person.

in·tel·lec·tual·ly /-tʃʊəlɪ/ adv

in·tel·li·gence /ɪnˈtelɪdʒəns/ n [U] **1** the power of seeing, learning, understanding and knowing; mental ability: The children were given an ∼ test. **2** news; information, esp with reference to important events: have secret ∼ of the enemy's plans. **3** government department that secretly collects information on enemies.

in·tel·li·gent /-ənt/ adj having, showing, intelligence.

in·tel·li·gent·ly adv

in·tel·li·gible /ɪnˈtelɪdʒəbəl/ adj that can be easily understood.

in·tel·li·gibly /-əblɪ/ adv

in·tel·li·gi·bil·ity /ɪnˌtelɪdʒəˈbɪlətɪ/ n [U]

in·tend /ɪnˈtend/ vt **1** have in mind as a purpose or plan: What do you ∼ to do/∼ doing today? **2** (*old use*) mean: *What do you ~ by this word?*

in·tense /ɪnˈtens/ *adj* **1** (of qualities) high in degree: *~ heat.* **2** (of feelings, etc) ardent; violent; (of persons) highly emotional: *an ~ young lady.*
in·tense·ly *adv*

in·ten·si·fy /ɪnˈtensɪfaɪ/ *vt,vi* (*pt,pp* -ied) make or become more intense.

in·ten·si·ty /ɪnˈtensətɪ/ *n* [U] state or quality of being intense; strength or depth (of feeling, etc).

in·ten·sive /ɪnˈtensɪv/ *adj* **1** deep and thorough: *make an ~ study of a subject.* **2** (*gram*) giving force and emphasis: *In 'a terribly hot day' 'terribly' is used as an ~ word.*
in·ten·sive·ly *adv*

in·tent¹ /ɪnˈtent/ *adj* **1** (of looks) eager; earnest. **2** (of persons) with earnest desire or attention: *He was ~ on his work.*
in·tent·ly *adv*

intent² /ɪnˈtent/ *n* **1** [U] purpose; intention: *shoot with ~ to kill.* **2** (*pl*) **to all intents and purposes,** in all essential points.

in·ten·tion /ɪnˈtenʃən/ *n* [C,U] intending; thing intended; aim; purpose: *He hasn't the least ~ of marrying yet.*
'well-in·ten·tioned, *adj* having good intentions.

in·ten·tional /ɪnˈtenʃənəl/ *adj* done on purpose: *If I hurt your feelings, it was not ~.*
in·ten·tion·al·ly /-ʃənəlɪ/ *adv* on purpose.

in·ter /ɪnˈtɜ(r)/ *vt* (-rr-) (*formal*) bury.

inter- /ˈɪntə(r)-/ *prefix* between, from one to another: *international; interplanetary.*

in·ter·act /ˈɪntərˈækt/ *vi* act on each other.
in·ter·ac·tion /-ˈækʃən/ *n* [C,U]
in·ter·ac·tive /-ˈæktɪv/ *adj*

in·ter·cede /ˈɪntəˈsid/ *vi* plead (as a peacemaker, or to obtain a favour): *~ with the father for/on behalf of the daughter.*
in·ter·ces·sion /ˈɪntəˈseʃən/ *n* [C,U]

in·ter·cept /ˈɪntəˈsept/ *vt* stop, catch (a person or thing) between the starting-point and destination: *~ a letter/a messenger.*
in·ter·cep·tion /ˈɪntəˈsepʃən/ *n* [U]
in·ter·cep·tor /-tə(r)/, person or thing that intercepts.

in·ter·change /ˈɪntəˈtʃeɪndʒ/ *vt* **1** (of two persons, etc) give and receive: *~ views.* **2** put (each of two things) in the other's place. □ *n* [C] act of interchanging.
in·ter·change·able /-əbəl/ *adj* that can be ~d: *True synonyms are ~able.*

in·ter·col·legi·ate /ˈɪntəkəˈlidʒɪət/ *adj* carried on, etc between colleges: *~ games/ debates.*

in·ter·con·ti·nen·tal /ˈɪntəˈkontɪˈnentəl/ *adj* carried on, etc between continents: *~ ballistic missiles,* that can be fired from one continent to another.

in·ter·course /ˈɪntəkɔːs/ *n* [U] **1** social conversation, dealings, between individuals. **2** exchanges of trade, ideas, etc between persons, societies, nations, etc.
sexual intercourse, = coitus.

in·ter·de·nomi·na·tional /ˈɪntədɪˈnomɪˈneɪʃənəl/ *adj* common to, shared by, different religious denominations, e g Methodist, C of E.

in·ter·de·pen·dent /ˈɪntədɪˈpendənt/ *adj* depending on each other.
in·ter·de·pen·dence /-əns/ *n* [U]

in·ter·dict /ˈɪntəˈdɪkt/ *vt* (*formal*) prohibit (an action). □ *n* /ˈɪntədɪkt/ [C] formal or authoritative prohibition, esp (R C Church) an order debarring a person or place from church services, etc: *lay a priest/a town under an ~.*

in·ter·est¹ /ˈɪntrəst/ *n* **1** [U] condition of wanting to know or learn about a person or thing: *feel/take no/not much/a great ~ in politics.* **2** [U] quality that causes concern or curiosity: *of considerable/not much ~.* **3** [C] something with which one concerns oneself: *His two great ~s in life are music and painting.* **4** [C] (often *pl*) advantage; profit; wellbeing: *It is in your ~(s) to work hard.* **5** [C] legal right to a share in something, esp in its profits: *have an ~ in a brewery.* **6** [U] money charged or paid for the use of money: *rate of ~/~ rate,* payment made by a borrower for a loan, expressed as a percentage, e g 5%. **7** (often *pl*) group of persons engaged in a trade, etc: *business ~s,* large business firms collectively. **in the interest(s) of** on behalf of, for the benefit of: *in the interests of truth.*

in·ter·est² /ˈɪntrəst/ *vt* cause (a person) to give his attention to: *He is ~ed in shipping,* **(a)** likes to know and learn about ships. **(b)** has money invested in the shipping industry.
in·ter·ested *adj* **(a)** having an interest(6) in; not impartial. **(b)** showing interest(1): *an ~ed look.*
in·ter·est·ing *adj* holding the attention; causing interest(1): *an ~ing conversation.*

in·ter·fere /ˈɪntəˈfɪə(r)/ *vi* **1** (of persons) break in on (other person's affairs) without right or invitation: *Please don't ~ in my business.* **2** (of persons) meddle; tamper (with): *Do not ~ with this machine.* **3** (of events, circumstances, etc) come into opposition; hinder or prevent: *Do you ever allow pleasure to ~ with duty?*
in·ter·fer·ence /ˈɪntəˈfɪərəns/ *n* [U]

in·terim /ˈɪntərɪm/ *n* **1 in the interim,** meanwhile; during the time that comes between. **2** (as an *adjective*) as an instalment: *an ~ report,* one that precedes the final report.

in·ter·ior /ɪnˈtɪərɪə(r)/ *adj* **1** situated inside; of the inside. **2** inland; away from the coast. **3** home or domestic (contrasted with *foreign*). □ *n* [C] **1** the inside: *~ decorators,* those who decorate the inside of a building. **2** inland areas. **3** (department dealing with the) domestic affairs of a country.

in·ter·ject /ˈɪntəˈdʒekt/ *vt* put in suddenly (a

333

remark, etc) between statements, etc made by another.

in·ter·jec·tion /ˌɪntəˈdʒekʃən/ n [C] word or phrase used as an exclamation, e g *Oh! Good! Indeed!*

in·ter·lace /ˌɪntəˈleɪs/ vt,vi join, be joined, (as if) by weaving or lacing together: *interlacing branches.*

in·ter·linear /ˌɪntəˈlɪnɪə(r)/ adj written, printed, between the lines.

in·ter·link /ˌɪntəˈlɪŋk/ vt,vi link together.

in·ter·lock /ˌɪntəˈlɒk/ vt,vi lock or join together; clasp firmly together.

in·ter·lop·er /ˌɪntələʊpə(r)/ n [C] person who, esp for profit or personal advantage, pushes himself in where he has no right.

in·ter·lude /ˈɪntəluːd/ n [C] 1 interval between two events or two periods of time of different character: ～s *of bright weather.* 2 interval between two parts of a play, etc; music played during such an interval.

in·ter·marry /ˌɪntəˈmærɪ/ vi (pt,pp -ied) (of tribes, races, etc) become connected by marriage with other tribes, etc.

in·ter·mar·riage /ˌɪntəˈmærɪdʒ/ n [U]

in·ter·medi·ary /ˌɪntəˈmiːdɪərɪ US: -dɪerɪ/ n [C] (pl -ies), adj 1 (person or thing) acting as a link between (persons and groups). 2 (something) intermediate.

in·ter·medi·ate /ˌɪntəˈmiːdɪət/ adj situated or coming between in time, space, degree, etc: *at an* ～ *stage.* □ n [C] something that is intermediate.

in·ter·medi·ate·ly adv

in·ter·ment /ɪnˈtɜːmənt/ n [U] being buried; [C] burial.

in·ter·mi·nable /ɪnˈtɜːmɪnəbəl/ adj endless; tedious because too long: *an* ～ *debate.*

in·ter·mi·nably /-əblɪ/ adv

in·ter·mingle /ˌɪntəˈmɪŋɡəl/ vt,vi mix together (two things, one with the other)

in·ter·mis·sion /ˌɪntəˈmɪʃən/ n [C] pause; interval: *without* ～/*with a short* ～.

in·ter·mit·tent /ˌɪntəˈmɪtənt/ adj pausing or stopping at intervals: ～ *fever.*

in·ter·mit·tent·ly adv

in·tern[1] /ɪnˈtɜːn/ vt compel (persons, esp aliens during a war) to live within certain limits or in a special building, camp, etc.

in·tern·ment n [U]

in·tern[2] (US also **in·terne**) /ˈɪntɜːn/ n [C] (US) young doctor who is completing his training by residing in a hospital and acting as an assistant physician or surgeon there. (GB = *house physician/surgeon*).

in·ter·nal /ɪnˈtɜːnəl/ adj 1 of or in the inside: *suffer* ～ *injuries.* 2 domestic; of the home affairs of a country: ～ *trade.*

in·ter·nally adv

in·ter·na·tional /ˌɪntəˈnæʃənəl/ adj existing, carried on, between nations: ～ *trade.*

in·ter·na·tion·al·ize /-aɪz/ vt make international; bring under the control or protection of all or many nations: *Should the Suez Canal be* ～*ized?*

in·terne /ˈɪntɜːn/ n ⇨ intern[2].

in·ter·necine /ˌɪntəˈniːsaɪn/ adj (of war) causing destruction to both sides.

in·ter·plan·etary /ˌɪntəˈplænɪtrɪ US: -terɪ/ adj between planets: *an* ～ *journey in a spacecraft.*

in·ter·play /ˈɪntəpleɪ/ n [U] operation, effect, of two things on each other: *the* ～ *of colours.*

in·ter·po·late /ɪnˈtɜːpəleɪt/ vt make (sometimes misleading) additions to a book.

in·ter·po·la·tion /ɪnˌtɜːpəˈleɪʃən/ n [C,U]

in·ter·pose /ˌɪntəˈpəʊz/ vt,vi 1 put forward an objection, etc as an interference: *Will they* ～ *their veto yet again?* 2 make an interruption. 3 step in; mediate: ～ *between two persons who are quarrelling.*

in·ter·pret /ɪnˈtɜːprɪt/ vt,vi 1 show, explain, the meaning of (either in words or by artistic performance): ～ *a difficult passage in a book/the role of Hamlet.* 2 consider to be the meaning of: *We* ～*ed his silence as a refusal.* 3 act as interpreter (esp when translating(1)).

in·ter·preter, person who gives an immediate oral translation of words spoken in another language.

in·ter·pre·ta·tion /ɪnˌtɜːprɪˈteɪʃən/ n [C,U]

in·ter·racial /ˌɪntəˈreɪʃəl/ adj between, involving, different races.

in·ter·reg·num /ˌɪntəˈreɡnəm/ n [C] (pl ～s, -na /-nə/) 1 period between the end of a Sovereign's reign and the beginning of his normal or legitimate successor's reign. 2 pause or interval.

in·ter·re·late /ˌɪntərɪˈleɪt/ vt,vi come together in mutual relationship: ～*d studies,* of separate but related subjects.

in·ter·ro·gate /ɪnˈterəɡeɪt/ vt question thoroughly or formally: ～ *a prisoner.*

in·ter·ro·ga·tion /ɪnˌterəˈɡeɪʃən/ n (a) [U] asking questions. (b) [C,U] oral examination; inquiry: ～*s by the police.*

in·ter·ro·ga·tor /-tə(r)/, person who interrogates.

in·ter·roga·tive /ˌɪntəˈrɒɡətɪv/ adj 1 showing or having the form of a question; of inquiry: *an* ～ *look/glance; in an* ～ *tone.* 2 (gram) used in questions: ～ *pronouns/ adverbs,* e g who, why. □ n [C] interrogative word or construction.

in·ter·roga·tive·ly adv

in·ter·roga·tory /ˌɪntəˈrɒɡətrɪ US: -tɔːrɪ/ adj of inquiry: *in an* ～ *tone.*

in·ter·rupt /ˌɪntəˈrʌpt/ vt,vi 1 break the continuity of: *The war* ～*ed trade between the two countries.* 2 break in on (a person speaking, doing something, etc): *Don't* ～ (me) *while I'm busy.*

in·ter·rup·tion /ˌɪntəˈrʌpʃən/ n [C,U]

in·ter·sect /ˌɪntəˈsekt/ vt,vi 1 divide by cutting, passing or lying across. 2 (of lines) cross each other.

in·ter·sec·tion /ˌɪntəˈsekʃən/ n [C,U]

in·ter·sperse /ˌɪntəˈspɜːs/ vt place, scatter,

here and there.

in·ter·stel·lar /ˌɪntəˈstelə(r)/ adj between the stars: ~ communications.

in·ter·tri·bal /ˌɪntəˈtraɪbəl/ adj between tribes.

in·ter·twine /ˌɪntəˈtwaɪn/ vt, vi twine or twist together: a lattice ~d with vines.

in·ter·ur·ban /ˌɪntərˈɜːbən/ adj between towns.

in·ter·val /ˈɪntəvəl/ n [C] 1 time between two events or two parts of an action (esp time between two acts of a play, two parts of a concert, etc). 2 space between (two objects or points): arranged at ~s of two metres. 3 (music) difference of pitch between two notes on a given scale.

in·ter·vene /ˌɪntəˈviːn/ vi 1 (of events, circumstances) come between (others) in time: I shall leave on Sunday if nothing ~s. 2 (of persons) interfere (so as to try to stop something): ~ in a dispute; ~ between people who are quarrelling. 3 (of time) come or be between: during the years that ~d. **in·ter·ven·tion** /ˌɪntəˈvenʃən/ n [C,U]

in·ter·view /ˈɪntəvjuː/ n [C] 1 meeting for discussion or conference, e g between employers and applicants for posts. 2 meeting (of a reporter, etc) with a person whose views are requested: He refused to give any newspaper ~. □ vt have an interview with.

in·ter·weave /ˌɪntəˈwiːv/ vt (pt -wove /-ˈwəʊv/, pp -woven /-ˈwəʊvən/) weave together (one with another).

in·tes·tate /ɪnˈtesteɪt/ adj not having made a will before death occurs: die ~.

in·tes·tine /ɪnˈtestɪn/ n [C] (usually pl) lower part of the food canal from below the stomach to the anus: the small/large ~, parts of this. **in·tes·ti·nal** /ɪnˈtestɪnəl/ adj

in·ti·macy /ˈɪntɪməsɪ/ n (pl -ies) 1 [U] the state of being intimate; close friendship or relationship. 2 (pl) caresses, kisses, etc. 3 sexual intercourse.

in·ti·mate[1] /ˈɪntɪmət/ adj 1 close and familiar: ~ friends. 2 innermost; private and personal: the ~ details of one's life. 3 resulting from close study or great familiarity: an ~ knowledge of Greek. □ n [C] close friend. **in·ti·mate·ly** adv

in·ti·mate[2] /ˈɪntɪmeɪt/ vt make known; show clearly; suggest: ~ one's approval. **in·ti·ma·tion** /ˌɪntɪˈmeɪʃən/ n [C,U]

in·timi·date /ɪnˈtɪmɪdeɪt/ vt frighten, esp in order to force (a person into doing something): ~ a witness, e g by threatening him. **in·timi·da·tion** /ɪnˌtɪmɪˈdeɪʃən/ n [U]

into /ˈɪntə strong form: ˈɪntuː/ prep 1 (showing motion or direction to a point within): Come ~ the house/garden. 2 (showing change of condition, result): She burst ~ tears. The rain changed ~ snow. 3 against: crash ~ a tree. 4 (maths): 5 ~ 25 (= 25 divided by 5).

in·tol·er·able /ɪnˈtɒlərəbəl/ adj that cannot be tolerated or endured: ~ heat/insolence. **in·tol·er·ably** /-əblɪ/ adv

in·tol·er·ant /ɪnˈtɒlərənt/ adj not tolerant. **in·tol·er·ant·ly** adv **in·tol·er·ance** /-əns/ n [U]

in·ton·ation /ˌɪntəˈneɪʃən/ n [U] the rise and fall of the pitch of the voice in speaking.

in·toxi·cant /ɪnˈtɒksɪkənt/ adj, n [C] intoxicating (liquor).

in·toxi·cate /ɪnˈtɒksɪkeɪt/ vt 1 cause to lose self-control as the result of taking alcoholic drink. 2 (fig) excite greatly: be ~d with joy. **in·toxi·ca·tion** /ɪnˌtɒksɪˈkeɪʃən/ n [U]

intra- (also **intro-**) /ɪntrə-/ prefix inside: intravenous; introspection.

in·tran·si·gent /ɪnˈtrænsɪdʒənt/ adj (formal) uncompromising, esp in politics.

in·tran·si·tive /ɪnˈtrænsətɪv/ adj (gram) (of verbs) used without a direct object. **in·tran·si·tive·ly** adv

in·tra·venous /ˌɪntrəˈviːnəs/ adj within a vein or veins: ~ injections.

in·trepid /ɪnˈtrepɪd/ adj (formal) fearless. **in·trep·id·ly** adv

in·tri·cacy /ˈɪntrɪkəsɪ/ n [C,U] pl -ies) (instance of) being intricate.

in·tri·cate /ˈɪntrɪkət/ adj complicated; difficult to follow or understand: an ~ piece of machinery. **in·tri·cate·ly** adv

in·trigue /ɪnˈtriːg/ vi, vt 1 make and carry out secret plans or plots: intriguing with Smith against Robinson. 2 bring out the interest or curiosity of: The news ~d all of us. □ n /ˈɪntriːg/ 1 [U] secret plotting. 2 [C] secret plan, plot.

in·trin·sic /ɪnˈtrɪnsɪk/ adj (of value, quality) belonging naturally; existing within, not coming from outside: a man's ~ worth. **in·trin·si·cally** /-klɪ/ adv

in·tro·duce /ˌɪntrəˈdjuːs US: -ˈduːs/ vt 1 bring in or forward: ~ a Bill before Parliament. 2 bring into use or operation for the first time: ~ new ideas into a business. 3 make (persons) known by name (to one another): He ~d me to his parents. 4 insert: ~ a new subject into a conversation.

in·tro·duc·tion /ˌɪntrəˈdʌkʃən/ n 1 [U] introducing or being introduced. 2 [C] introducing of persons to one another. 3 [C] opening paragraph of a letter, essay, speech, etc; explanatory article at or before the beginning of a book. 4 [C] elementary textbook: 'An I~ to Greek Grammar.'

in·tro·duc·tory /ˌɪntrəˈdʌktərɪ/ adj serving to introduce: an ~ chapter.

in·tro·spect /ˌɪntrəˈspekt/ vi (formal) think about oneself, one's feelings. **in·tro·spec·tion** /ˌɪntrəˈspekʃən/ n [U] **in·tro·spec·tive** /-tɪv/ adj

in·tro·vert /ˈɪntrəvɜːt/ vt turn (one's mind, thought) inward on itself. □ n /ˈɪntrəvɜːt/ [C] person who is more interested in his own thoughts and feelings than in things outside himself. ⇨ **extrovert.**

in·trude /ɪnˈtruːd/ *vt,vi* force (something, oneself, on a person, into a place); enter without invitation: *I hope I'm not intruding.*
in·truder, person or thing that intrudes.

in·tru·sion /ɪnˈtruːʒən/ *n* [U] intruding; [C] instance of this.

in·tru·sive /ɪnˈtruːsɪv/ *adj* (a) intruding. (b) (of rocks) forced between layers of other rock.

intrusive 'r', one with no grammatical or spelling justification, eg the r-sound often heard after *law* in *law and order.*

in·tu·ition /ˌɪntjuˈɪʃən/ *n* **1** [U] (power of) the immediate understanding of something without conscious reasoning or study. **2** [C] piece of knowledge gained by this power.
in·tu·itive /ɪnˈtjuːɪtɪv/ *US:* -ˈtuː-/ *adj*
in·tu·itive·ly *adv*

in·un·date /ˈɪnʌndeɪt/ *vt* **1** flood; cover (with water) by overflowing. **2** (*fig*) (esp passive) be overwhelmed: *be ∼d with requests for help.*
in·un·da·tion /ˌɪnʌnˈdeɪʃən/ *n* [C,U]

in·vade /ɪnˈveɪd/ *vt* **1** enter (a country) with armed forces in order to attack. **2** (*fig*) crowd into; enter: *a city ∼d by tourists.* **3** violate; interfere with: *∼ a person's rights.*
in·vader, person, thing, that invades.

in·valid[1] /ɪnˈvælɪd/ *adj* not valid.
in·vali·date /ɪnˈvælɪdeɪt/ *vt* make invalid.
in·vali·da·tion /ɪnˌvælɪˈdeɪʃən/ *n* [C,U]

in·va·lid[2] /ˈɪnvəlɪd/ *US:* -lɪd/ *adj* **1** weak or disabled through illness or injury: *∼ soldiers.* **2** suitable for invalid persons: *an ∼ chair/diet.* □ *n* [C] invalid person. □ *vt* (esp of members of the armed forces) remove from active service as an invalid: *be ∼ed home.*

in·valu·able /ɪnˈvæljʊbəl/ *adj* of value too high to be measured: *Her services are ∼ to me.*

in·vari·able /ɪnˈveərɪəbəl/ *adj* unchangeable; constant: *an ∼ temperature.*
in·vari·ably /-əblɪ/ *adv*

in·va·sion /ɪnˈveɪʒən/ *n* [U] invading or being invaded; [C] instance of this: *an ∼ of privacy.*

in·vec·tive /ɪnˈvektɪv/ *n* [U] abusive language: *speeches filled with ∼.*

in·vent /ɪnˈvent/ *vt* **1** create or design (something not existing before): *When was television ∼ed?* **2** make up, think of: *∼ an excuse.*
in·ven·tor /-tə(r)/, person who invents things.

in·ven·tion /ɪnˈvenʃən/ *n* **1** [U] inventing: *the ∼ of the telephone.* **2** [C] something invented: *the many ∼s of Edison.*

in·ven·tive /ɪnˈventɪv/ *adj* able to invent easily; imaginative: *an ∼ive mind.*

in·ven·tory /ˈɪnvəntrɪ *US:* -tɔːrɪ/ *n* [C] (*pl* -ies) detailed list, eg of household goods, furniture, etc.

in·verse /ɪnˈvɜːs/ *adj* inverted; reversed in position, direction or relations.
in·verse·ly *adv*

in·ver·sion /ɪnˈvɜːʃən *US:* -ˈvɜːrʒən/ *n* [U] inverting or being inverted; [C] instance of this; something inverted.

in·vert /ɪnˈvɜːt/ *vt* put upside down or in the opposite order, position or arrangement.
in'verted 'commas, quotation marks ('' '' or ' ').

in·vert·ebrate /ɪnˈvɜːtəbreɪt/ *adj* not having a backbone or spinal column, eg insects, worms. □ *n* [C] invertebrate animal.

in·vest /ɪnˈvest/ *vt,vi* **1** put (money in): *∼ £1 000 in a business.* **2** (*informal*) buy: *∼ in a new hat.* **3** clothe; give (authority); decorate; surround (with qualities): *∼ed with full military power.* **4** surround (a fort, town, etc) with armed forces.
in·ves·tor /-tə(r)/, person who invests money.

in·ves·ti·gate /ɪnˈvestɪgeɪt/ *vt* examine, inquire into; make a careful study of: *∼ a crime/the market for sales of a product.*
in·ves·ti·ga·tion /ɪnˌvestɪˈgeɪʃən/ *n* [C,U]
in·ves·ti·ga·tor /-tə(r)/, person who investigates.

in·ves·ti·ture /ɪnˈvestɪtʃə(r) *US:* -tʃʊə(r)/ *n* [C] (from **invest**(3)) ceremony of investing a person (*with* a rank, power, etc).

in·vest·ment /ɪnˈvestmənt/ *n* **1** [U] investing money: *careful ∼ of capital.* **2** [C] sum of money that is invested; that in which money is invested: *profitable ∼s.* **3** [U] act of surrounding a town, fort, etc. **4** = investiture.

in·vet·er·ate /ɪnˈvetərət/ *adj* (esp of habits, feelings) long-established: *an ∼ liar.*

in·vi·able /ɪnˈvaɪəbəl/ *adj* not viable.

in·vidi·ous /ɪnˈvɪdɪəs/ *adj* likely to cause anger, resentment, (because of real or apparent injustice).
in·vidi·ous·ly *adv*

in·vigi·late /ɪnˈvɪdʒɪleɪt/ *vi* watch over students during examinations.
in·vigi·la·tion /ɪnˌvɪdʒɪˈleɪʃən/ *n* [U]
in·vigi·la·tor /-tə(r)/, person who invigilates.

in·vig·or·ate /ɪnˈvɪgəreɪt/ *vt* give strength, energy or courage to: *an invigorating climate.*

in·vin·cible /ɪnˈvɪnsəbəl/ *adj* too strong to be overcome or defeated: *an ∼ will.*
in·vin·cibly /-əblɪ/ *adv*

in·viol·able /ɪnˈvaɪələbəl/ *adj* not to be violated, dishonoured: *an ∼ oath.*

in·viol·ate /ɪnˈvaɪələt/ *adj* kept sacred; held in respect; not violated.

in·vis·ible /ɪnˈvɪzəbəl/ *adj* that cannot be seen: *stars that are ∼ to the naked eye.*
in·visi·bil·ity /ɪnˌvɪzəˈbɪlətɪ/ *n* [U]
in·visi·bly /-əblɪ/ *adv*

in·vite /ɪnˈvaɪt/ *vt* **1** ask (a person to do something, come somewhere, etc): *∼ a friend to one's house.* **2** ask for: *∼ questions.* **3** encourage: *Don't leave the windows*

open—it's inviting thieves to enter.
in·vit·ing *adj* tempting; attractive.
in·vit·ing·ly *adv*
in·vi·ta·tion /ˌɪnvɪˈteɪʃən/ *n* **1** [U] inviting or being invited: *admission by ~ only.* **2** [C] request to come or go somewhere, or do something: *send out ~s to a party.*
in·vo·ca·tion /ˌɪnvəˈkeɪʃən/ *n* [U] invoking or being invoked; [C] prayer or appeal that invokes.
in·voice /ˈɪnvɔɪs/ *vt, n* [C] (make a) list of goods sold with the price(s) charged.
in·voke /ɪnˈvəʊk/ *vt* **1** call on God, the power of the law, etc for help or protection. **2** request earnestly: *~ vengeance on one's enemies.* **3** summon up (by magic): *~ evil spirits.*
in·vol·un·tary /ɪnˈvɒləntrɪ *US:* -terɪ/ *adj* done without intention; done unconsciously: *an ~ movement of fear.*
in·vol·un·tar·ily /ɪnˈvɒləntrəlɪ *US:* mˈvɒlən-ˈterəlɪ/ *adv*
in·volve /ɪnˈvɒlv/ *vt* **1** cause (a person or thing) to take part or be mixed up (in trouble, a difficult condition, etc): *They are deeply ~d in debt.* **2** have as a necessary consequence: *It is involving me in a lot of extra work.*
in·volved *adj* complicated in form, etc: *an ~d sentence/style.*
in·volve·ment *n* [C,U]
in·vul·ner·able /ɪnˈvʌlnrəbəl/ *adj* that cannot be wounded, hurt, attacked.
in·ward /ˈɪnwəd/ *adj* **1** situated within; inner: *one's ~* (ie mental or spiritual) *nature.* **2** turned towards the inside: *an ~ curve.*
in·ward·ly *adv* in mind or spirit: *suffer ~ly,* i e so as not to show one's grief.
in·ward·ness *n* [U] (person's) inner nature.
in·ward(s) *adv* (a) towards the inside. (b) into or towards the mind or soul.
iod·ine /ˈaɪədiːn *US:* -daɪn/ *n* [U] chemical substance widely used as an antiseptic, in photography and in the manufacture of some dyes.
ion /ˈaɪən/ *n* [C] electrically charged particle formed by losing or gaining electrons.
ion·ize /ˈaɪənaɪz/ *vt* convert into ions.
iono·sphere /aɪˈɒnəsfɪə(r)/ *n* the ~, (also known as the *Heaviside Layer*) set of layers of the earth's atmosphere, which reflect radio waves and cause them to follow the earth's shape.
iota /aɪˈəʊtə/ *n* [C] (*pl* ~s) **1** the Greek letter (ι). **2** extremely small part: *not an ~ of truth in the story,* no truth at all.
ipso facto /ˌɪpsəʊ ˈfæktəʊ/ *adverbial phrase* (*Latin*) by that very fact.
irate /aɪˈreɪt/ *adj* angry.
irate·ly *adv*
ire /ˈaɪə(r)/ *n* [U] (*poetic* or *formal*) anger.
iri·descent /ˌɪrɪˈdesənt/ *adj* (*formal*) showing colours like those of the rainbow; changing colour as light falls from different direc-

tions.
iri·descence /-ˈdesəns/ *n* [U]
iris /ˈaɪərɪs/ *n* [C] **1** coloured part round the pupil of the eye. **2** kinds of flowering plant with sword-shaped leaves.
irk /ɜːk/ *vt* trouble; annoy.
irk·some /-səm/ *adj* tiresome; annoying.
iron¹ /ˈaɪən *US:* aɪərn/ *n* **1** [U] commonest of all metallic elements (symbol **Fe**), used in various forms. **2** [C] tool, etc made of iron, esp a flat-bottomed implement heated and used for smoothing clothes, etc. **3** (*pl*) fetters: *put him in ~s.*
the ˈIron Age, prehistoric period when iron came into use for tools and weapons.
ˈiron ˈcurtain, frontier(s) dividing U S S R and allied countries from other countries; this as a barrier to information and trade.
ˈiron ˈlung, apparatus fitted over the whole body, except the head, to provide artificial respiration.
ˈiron·monger, dealer in metal goods.
ˈiron·mongery, business of an ironmonger.
ˈiron ˈrations, store of food for use in an emergency as for troops or explorers.
iron² /ˈaɪən *US:* aɪərn/ *vt, vi* smooth cloth/ clothes with an iron: *She's been ~ing all afternoon. iron out,* (a) remove by ironing: *~ out wrinkles.* (b) (*fig*) remove: *~ out misunderstandings.*
ˈiron·ing-board, padded board on which to iron clothes, etc.
ironic /aɪˈrɒnɪk/ (also **ironi·cal** /aɪˈrɒnɪkəl/) *adj* of, using, expressing, irony: *an ~ smile.*
ironi·cally /-klɪ/ *adv*
irony /ˈaɪərənɪ/ *n* (*pl* -ies) **1** [U] saying something which is the direct opposite of one's thoughts in order to make one's remarks forceful. **2** [C] event, situation, etc which is itself desirable, but which, because of the circumstances, is of little or no value, and appears to be directed by evil fate: *Inheriting a large fortune and dying a month later might be called one of life's ironies.*
ir·ra·tional /ɪˈræʃənəl/ *adj* **1** not being able to reason: *an ~ animal.* **2** absurd; illogical: *~ fears/behaviour.*
ir·ra·tion·ally *adv*
ir·rec·on·cil·able /ɪˈrekənˈsaɪləbəl/ *adj* **1** (of persons) that cannot be reconciled. **2** (of ideas, actions) that cannot be brought into harmony.
ir·re·cover·able /ˌɪrɪˈkʌvərəbəl/ *adj* that cannot be recovered: *~ losses.*
ir·re·fut·able /ˈɪrɪfjuːtəbəl/ *adj* that cannot be proved false: *an ~ argument.*
ir·regu·lar /ɪˈregjələ(r)/ *adj* **1** contrary to rules, to what is normal and established: *~ attendance.* **2** uneven; not regular in shape, arrangement, etc: *a coast with an ~ outline.* **3** (*gram*) (of words), not having the usual endings or forms in a sentence: *'Child' has an ~ plural.*
ir·regu·lar·ly *adv*
ir·regu·lar·ity /ˌɪˈregjʊˈlærətɪ/ *n* [C,U]

ir·rel·e·vant /ɪˈreləvənt/ adj not to the point; having nothing to do with: ~ remarks.

ir·re·li·gious /ˌɪrɪˈlɪdʒəs/ adj opposed to, showing no interest in, religion: ~ acts/persons.

ir·re·mov·able /ˌɪrɪˈmuːvəbəl/ adj that cannot be removed (esp from an appointment).

ir·rep·ar·able /ɪˈrepərəbəl/ adj (of a loss, injury, etc) that cannot be put right or restored: ~ damage.

ir·re·place·able /ˌɪrɪˈpleɪsəbəl/ adj of which the loss cannot be supplied.

ir·re·proach·able /ˌɪrɪˈprəʊtʃəbəl/ adj free from blame or fault: ~ conduct.

ir·re·sist·ible /ˌɪrɪˈzɪstəbəl/ adj too strong, convincing, delightful, etc to be resisted: ~ temptations.

ir·re·spec·tive /ˌɪrɪˈspektɪv/ adj not taking into account: ~ of the danger.

ir·re·spon·sible /ˌɪrɪˈspɒnsəbəl/ adj (esp) (doing things, done) without a proper sense of responsibility: ~ behaviour.

ir·re·spon·si·bil·ity /ˌɪrɪˈspɒnsəˈbɪlətɪ/ n [U]

ir·re·triev·able /ˌɪrɪˈtriːvəbəl/ adj that cannot be retrieved or remedied: an ~ loss.

ir·rev·er·ence /ɪˈrevərəns/ n [U] being irreverent.

ir·rev·er·ent /ɪˈrevərənt/ adj feeling or showing no respect for sacred things.

ir·rev·er·ent·ly adv

ir·re·vers·ible /ˌɪrɪˈvɜːsəbəl/ adj that cannot be reversed or revoked: an ~ decision.

ir·revo·cable /ɪˈrevəkəbəl/ adj final and unalterable: an ~ legal decision.

ir·ri·gate /ˈɪrɪɡeɪt/ vt 1 supply (land, crops) with water (by means of rivers, pipes, etc): ~ desert areas to make them fertile. 2 construct reservoirs, canals, etc for the distribution of water (to fields).

ir·ri·ga·tion /ˌɪrɪˈɡeɪʃən/ [U]

ir·ri·table /ˈɪrɪtəbəl/ adj easily annoyed or made angry.

ir·ri·tably /-əblɪ/ adv

ir·ri·ta·bil·ity /ˌɪrɪtəˈbɪlətɪ/ n [U]

ir·ri·tant /ˈɪrɪtənt/ adj causing irritation. □ n [C] irritating substance.

ir·ri·tate /ˈɪrɪteɪt/ vt 1 make angry or annoyed: irritating delays. 2 cause discomfort to (part of the body); make sore or inflamed: The smoke ~d her eyes.

ir·ri·ta·tion /ˌɪrɪˈteɪʃən/ n [C,U]

ir·rup·tion /ɪˈrʌpʃən/ n [C] sudden and violent entry; bursting in.

is ⇨ be¹.

-ise /-aɪz/ suffix ⇨ -ize.

-ish /-ɪʃ/ suffix 1 (national name + ~ = adjective): Spanish. 2 resembling: childish. 3 a little like, near to: reddish; twentyish.

Is·lam /ɪzˈlɑːm/ n faith, religion, proclaimed by the Prophet Muhammad; all Muslims; all the Muslim world.

Is·lamic /ɪzˈlæmɪk/ adj

is·land /ˈaɪlənd/ n [C] 1 piece of land surrounded by water. 2 something like an island because it is detached or isolated. ⇨ traffic island.

is·lander, person born on or living on an island.

isle /aɪl/ n [C] island (not much used, except in proper names): the British I~s.

is·let /ˈaɪlət/ n [C] small island.

-ism /-ɪzm/ suffix (used to form a noun) 1 showing quantities typical of: Americanism. 2 doctrine, principle, cause: Communism.

isn't /ˈɪznt/ ⇨ be¹.

iso·bar /ˈaɪsəbɑː(r)/ n [C] line on a map, esp a weather chart, joining places with the same atmospheric pressure at a particular time.

iso·late /ˈaɪsəleɪt/ vt separate, put or keep apart from others: isolating the infected children

iso·la·tion /ˌaɪsəˈleɪʃən/ n [U] isolating or being isolated: an ~ ward, one for persons with infectious diseases.

isos·celes /aɪˈsɒsəliːz/ adj (of a triangle) having two sides equal.

iso·therm /ˈaɪsəθɜːm/ n [C] line on a map joining places having the same mean temperature.

iso·tope /ˈaɪsətəʊp/ n [C] form of a chemical element having a nuclear mass different from other forms of the same element: radio-active ~s, unstable forms used in medicine and industry.

issue /ˈɪʃuː/ vi,vt 1 come, go, flow, out: blood issuing from a wound. 2 distribute for use or consumption: ~ travel tickets to the passengers. 3 publish (books, etc). 4 put stamps, banknotes, shares ¹(3), etc into circulation. □ n 1 [U] outgoing; outflowing; [C] the act of flowing out; that which flows out: an ~ of blood. 2 [C,U] publication: the ~ of a newspaper; the most recent ~s of a periodical. 3 [C] question that arises for discussion: argue political ~s. 4 [C] result; outcome; consequence: await the ~. 5 [U] (legal) children: die without ~, ie without children.

-ist /-ɪst/ suffix ⇨ -ism: dramatist.

isth·mus /ˈɪsməs/ n (pl ~es) strip of land joining two larger bodies of land: the I~ of Panama.

it /ɪt/ pron (pl they /ðeɪ/, them /ðem/) 1 (used of lifeless things, animals and of a baby or small child when the sex is unknown or unimportant): Where's my book?—Have you seen ~? Where's the cat?—I~'s in the garden. She's expecting another baby and hopes ~ will be a boy. 2 (used to refer to a group of words which follows, this being the grammatical subject): Is ~ difficult to learn Chinese? I~ was hard for him to live on his pension. I~'s no use trying to do that. Does ~ matter what you do next? 3 (used to identify a person or thing): 'Who's that at the door?'—'I~'s the postman.' 4 (used as a subject with be, etc): I~ is raining. I~'s six o'clock. I~'s ten miles to Oxford. Whose turn is ~ next? 5 (used to bring into prominence one part of a sentence): I~ was work that exhausted him. I∼ was John I gave the book to, not Harry.

italic /ɪ'tælɪk/ adj (of printed letters) sloping: This is ∼ type. □ n (pl) italic letters.

itch /ɪtʃ/ n [C] **1** (rarely pl) feeling of irritation on the skin, causing a desire to scratch: have an ∼. **2** restless desire or longing: an ∼ to travel. □ vi **1** have an itch(1): scratch where it ∼es. **2** have a strong desire: ∼ing to go on holiday.

itchy adj (-ier, -iest)

item /'aɪtəm/ n [C] **1** single article or unit in a list, etc: the first ∼ on the programme. **2** detail or paragraph (of news): interesting 'news ∼s/∼s of news in the paper. □ adv also (used to introduce successive articles in a list).

item-ize /-aɪz/ vt give, write, every item of: an ∼ized account.

it-er-ate /'ɪtəreɪt/ vt say again and again.

it-er-ation /ɪtə'reɪʃən/ n [C,U]

i-tin-er-ant /aɪ'tɪnərənt/ adj (formal) travelling from place to place: ∼ circus performers.

i-tin-er-ary /aɪ'tɪnərərɪ US: -rerɪ/ n [C] (pl -ies) plan for, details of, a journey.

it'll /'ɪtəl/ = it will.

it's /ɪts/ = it is or it has.

its /ɪts/ adj of it: The dog wagged ∼ tail.

itself /ɪt'self/ pron **1** (reflex): The dog got up and stretched ∼. **by itself,** (a) automatically: The machine works by ∼. (b) alone. **2** (emphatic): The thing ∼ is not valuable.

I've /aɪv/ = I have.

-ive /-ɪv/ suffix having a tendency, quality: active; productive.

ivory /'aɪvərɪ/ adj, n [U] **1** (of the) white, bone-like substance forming the tusks of elephants, used for ornaments, piano-keys, etc. **2** (of the) colour of ivory.

ivy /'aɪvɪ/ n [U] climbing, clinging, evergreen plant with dark, shiny leaves.

-ize (also **-ise** which is not used in this dictionary but is equally acceptable) /-aɪz/ suffix (used to form a verb) **1** cause to be, make like: dramatize; computerize. **2** act with the qualities of: criticize.

Jj

J, j /dʒeɪ/ (pl J's, j's /dʒeɪz/) the tenth letter of the English alphabet.

jab /dʒæb/ vt, vi (-bb-) **1** poke or push (at, into): He ∼bed at the lid with a knife. He ∼bed his elbow into my side. **2** force or push out by jabbing: Don't ∼ my eye out with your umbrella! □ n [C] **1** sudden blow or thrust. **2** (informal) injection or inoculation: smallpox ∼s.

jab-ber /'dʒæbə(r)/ vi, vt talk excitedly or in

a confused manner: Listen to those children ∼ing away! □ n [U] chatter: the ∼ of monkeys.

jack¹ /dʒæk/ n [C] **1** (usually portable) device for raising heavy weights off the ground, esp one for raising the axle of a car so that a wheel may be changed. **2** (in a pack of playing-cards) knave.

'Jack 'Frost, frost personified.

'Jack of 'all trades, person who has many skills.

the 'Union 'Jack, flag of the United Kingdom.

jack² /dʒæk/ vt lift with a jack(1): J∼ (up) the car and change the wheel.

jackal /'dʒækɔl/ n [C] wild animal like a dog.

jack-ass /'dʒækæs/ n [C] **1** male ass. **2** foolish person.

jack-boot /'dʒæk but/ n [C] large boot coming above the knee (as formerly worn by cavalrymen).

jack-daw /'dʒækdɔ/ n [C] bird of the crow family (noted for flying off with small bright objects).

jacket /'dʒækɪt/ n [C] **1** short coat with sleeves. **2** outer covering round a tank, pipe, etc. **3** skin (of a potato): baked in their ∼s. **4** (also 'dust ∼) loose paper cover in which a hardback book is issued.

jack-knife /'dʒæk næf/ n [C] large pocketknife with a folding blade. □ vi (esp of an articulated truck) fold and double back.

jack-pot /'dʒækpɒt/ n [C] accumulated stake(3) in various games increasing in value until won.

jade /dʒeɪd/ adj, n [U] **1** (of a) hard, usually green stone, carved into ornaments, etc. **2** (of) its colour.

jaded /'dʒeɪdɪd/ adj worn out; over-worked: She looks ∼d.

jag¹ /dʒæg/ n [C] sharp projection, e g of rock.

jaggy adj (-ier, -iest) having jags.

jag² /dʒæg/ vt (-gg-) cut or tear unevenly.

jag-ged /'dʒægɪd/ adj with rough, uneven edges: ∼ged rocks.

jag-uar /'dʒægjʊə(r)/ n [C] large, fierce, flesh-eating animal of Central and South America.

jail /dʒeɪl/ ⇨ gaol.

jam¹ /dʒæm/ n [U] fruit boiled with sugar until it is thick, and preserved in jars, pots, tins, etc.

'jam-jar/-pot, one for jam.

jam² /dʒæm/ vt, vi (-mm-) **1** crush, be crushed, between two surfaces or masses; squeeze, be squeezed: a piano ∼med in the doorway. **2** (of parts of a machine, etc) (cause to) become fixed so that movement or action is prevented: ∼ the brakes on/∼ on the brakes. **3** push (things) together tightly: ∼ clothes into a suitcase. **4** make the reception of a broadcast programme impossible or difficult by broadcasting that deliberately interferes: ∼ the enemy's stations during a *war*. □ *n* [C] **1** number of things or people crowded together so that movement is difficult or impossible: `traffic~s in our big towns.` **2** stoppage of a machine due to jamming(2). **3** (*sl*) awkward position; difficult situation: *be in/get into a ~.*

jam·bo·ree /ˌdʒæmbəˈriː/ *n* [C] **1** merry meeting. **2** large rally or gathering, esp of Boy Scouts.

jam-pack /ˌdʒæmˈpæk/ *vt* (*informal*) crowd to capacity: *a stadium ~ed with spectators.*

jan·gle /ˈdʒæŋgəl/ *vt,vi* (cause to) give out a harsh metallic noise. □ *n* [U] harsh noise.

jani·tor /ˈdʒænɪtə(r)/ *n* [C] **1** doorkeeper. **2** (*US*) person hired to take care of a building, offices, etc, e g by cleaning, etc.

Jan·uary /ˈdʒænjʊərɪ *US*: -jʊerɪ/ *n* the first month of the year.

ja·pan /dʒəˈpæn/ *vt* (-nn-), *n* [U] (cover with a) hard, shiny black enamel.

jape /dʒeɪp/ *vi* (*archaic*) jest. □ *n* [C] jest; joke.

jar¹ /dʒɑː(r)/ *n* [C] **1** (usually harsh) sound or vibration: *We felt a ~ when the train started to move.* **2** shock; thrill to the nerves; discord: *an unpleasant ~ to my nerves.*

jar² /dʒɑː(r)/ *n* [C] tall vessel, usually round, with a wide mouth of glass, stone or earthenware; its contents: *a ~ of jam.*

jar·ful /-fʊl/ *n* [C] amount a jar holds.

jar³ /dʒɑː(r)/ *vi,vt* (-rr-) **1** strike with a harsh unpleasant sound. **2** have an unpleasant effect: *The way he laughs ~s on my nerves.* **3** send a shock through (the nerves): *He was badly ~red by the blow.* **4** be out of harmony: *His opinions ~ with mine.*

jar·ring *adj* causing disharmony; harsh: *a ~ring note.*

jar·ring·ly *adv*

jar·gon /ˈdʒɑːgən/ *n* [U] **1** language difficult to understand, because it is a bad form or spoken badly: *a baby's ~.* **2** language full of technical or special words: *scientific ~.*

jas·mine /ˈdʒæzmɪn/ *n* [C] kinds of shrub with white or yellow and fragrant flowers.

jas·per /ˈdʒæspə(r)/ *n* [U] semi-precious stone, red, yellow or brown.

jaun·dice /ˈdʒɔːndɪs/ *n* [U] **1** disease, caused by stoppage of the flow of bile, marked by yellowness of the skin and the whites of the eyes. **2** (*fig*) state of mind in which one is jealous, spiteful, envious and suspicious. □ *vt* (usually passive) affect with jaundice: *take a ~d view*, one influenced by jealousy, etc.

jaunt /dʒɔːnt/ *n* [C] short journey for pleasure. □ *vi* make such a journey.

jaunty /ˈdʒɔːntɪ/ *adj* (-ier, iest) feeling or showing self-confidence and self-satisfaction.

jaunt·ily /-əlɪ/ *adv*

jav·elin /ˈdʒævəlɪn/ *n* [C] light spear for throwing (in sport).

jaw /dʒɔː/ *n* [C] **1 lower/upper jaw**, either

of the bone structures containing the teeth. **2** (*pl*) framework of the mouth, including the teeth; (*sing*) lower part of the face: *a man with a strong ~.* **3** (*pl*) narrow mouth of a valley, channel, etc. **4** (*fig*) something like jaws(2): *the ~ of death.* **5** (*pl*) parts of a tool, machine, etc, e g a vice, between which things are gripped or crushed. □ *vi* talk, esp at tedious length.

jaw-bone, one in which the teeth are set.

jay /dʒeɪ/ *n* [C] **1** (sorts of) noisy European bird with brightly coloured feathers. **2** (*fig*) impertinent person who chatters too much.

jay-walker, person who walks across or along streets without paying attention to traffic.

jazz /dʒæz/ *n* [U] popular music first played by Negro groups in Southern USA in the early 20th century, characterized by improvisation and strong rhythms, called *traditional ~*; similar music played by large bands for dancing; a later variation much influenced by the *blues* to produce an unhurried emotive style, called *modern ~.* □ *vt* **1** play or arrange in the style of jazz. **2** *jazz up*, (*fig*) liven up: *~ up a party.*

jazzy *adj* (-ier, -iest) (*informal*) **(a)** of or like jazz. **(b)** showy: *a ~y sports car.*

jeal·ous /ˈdʒeləs/ *adj* **1** feeling or showing fear or unkind feeling because of possible or actual loss of rights or love: *a ~ husband; ~ looks.* **2** feeling or showing unhappiness because of the better fortune, etc of others: *~ of her success.* **3** taking watchful care (*of*): *~ of one's rights.*

jeal·ous·ly *adv*

jeal·ousy *n* (*pl* -ies) **(a)** [U] being jealous: *a lover's ~y.* **(b)** [C] instance of this; jealous act or utterance.

jeans /dʒiːnz/ *n pl* trousers (usually of denim) worn informally by men, women and children.

jeep /dʒiːp/ *n* [C] small, light, military motor-vehicle with great freedom of movement.

jeer /dʒɪə(r)/ *vi,vt* mock, laugh rudely: *a ~ing crowd.* □ *n* [C] jeering remark.

jeer·ing·ly *adv*

Je·ho·vah /dʒɪˈhəʊvə/ *n* name of God used in the Old Testament.

jell /dʒel/ *vi,vt* (*informal*) take shape: *My ideas are beginning to ~.*

jelly /ˈdʒelɪ/ *n* (*pl* -ies) **1** [U] soft, semi-solid food substance made from gelatin, animal fat or fruit juice and sugar. **2** [C,U] (portion of) fruit jelly prepared in a mould, flavoured and coloured, as a sweet dish. **3** [U] substance like jelly. □ *vt,vi* (*pt,pp* -ied) (cause to) become like jelly.

jelly-fish, kinds of fish like jelly with long tentacles.

jeop·ard·ize /ˈdʒepədaɪz/ *vt* put in danger.

jeop·ardy /ˈdʒepədɪ/ *n* [U] danger. *be in jeopardy* (*of* one's life, etc).

jer·boa /dʒɜːˈbəʊə/ *n* [C] small rat-like animal of Asia and the N African deserts with long hind legs and the ability to jump well.

jere·miad /ˈdʒerɪˈmaɪæd/ n [C] long, sad and complaining story of troubles, misfortunes, etc.

jerk /dʒɜːk/ n [C] **1** sudden push, pull, start, stop, twist, lift or throw: *The train stopped with a ~.* **2** sudden involuntary twitch of a muscle or muscles. □ vt,vi move with a jerk: *He ~ed the fish out of the water.*

jerky adj (-ier, -iest) with jerks: *a ~y ride in an old bus.*

jer·kin /ˈdʒɜːkɪn/ n [C] short, close-fitting jacket (as worn by men in olden times).

jerry /ˈdʒerɪ/ n [C] (pl -ies) (sl) chamberpot.

ˈjerry-builder/-building, builder/building of houses of poor quality with bad materials. Hence, **ˈjerry-built** adj.

ˈjerry-can, army-style metal container used for carrying water or petrol.

jer·sey /ˈdʒɜːzɪ/ n (pl ~s) **1** [U] (ˈ~-wool) soft, fine knitted fabric used for clothes. **2** [C] close-fitting knitted woollen garment with sleeves. **3** J~, cow of the breed that originally came from Jersey, one of the Channel Islands (near the French coast).

jest /dʒest/ n [C] joke. **in jest,** as a joke. □ vi make jokes: *He's not a man to ~ with.*

jes·ter /ˈdʒestə(r)/ n [C] person who jests, esp (in olden times) a man whose duty it was to make jokes to amuse the court or noble household in which he was employed.

Jesus /ˈdʒiːzəs/ n the founder of the Christian religion.

jet¹ /dʒet/ n [C] **1** fast, strong stream of gas, liquid, steam or flame, forced out of a small opening: *a ~ of water.* **2** narrow opening from which a jet comes out: *a ˈgas-~.* **3** = jet plane. □ vi,vt (-tt-) **1** come, send out, in a jet or jets. **2** travel by jet plane.

jet engine, one that is used to propel an aircraft by sending out gases in jets at the back.

jet plane/aircraft, one operated by jet engines.

jet propulsion, method of producing movement using jets of air or water.

jet set, wealthy persons who often travel in jet aircraft for holidays.

jet stream, exhaust of a jet engine.

jet² /dʒet/ adj, n [U] (made of a) hard, black mineral that takes a brilliant polish.

ˈjet ˈblack, deep, glossy black.

jet·sam /ˈdʒetsəm/ n [U] goods thrown overboard from a ship at sea to lighten it, e g in a storm.

jet·ti·son /ˈdʒetɪsən/ vt **1** throw (goods) overboard in order to lighten a ship, e g during a storm. **2** abandon, discard (what is unwanted): *~ part of a spacecraft.*

jetty /ˈdʒetɪ/ n [C] (pl -ies) structure built out into a body of water as a breakwater or as a landing-place for ships and boats.

jewel /ˈdʒuːəl/ n [C] **1** precious stone, e g a diamond or a ruby; ornament with jewels set

in it. **2** artificial diamond: *This watch has 15 ~s.* **3** (fig) highly valued person or thing: *His wife is a ~.* □ vt (-ll-, US -l-) adorn with jewels: (usually in pp) *a ~led ring.*

jew·el·ler, (US = **jew·eler**) /ˈdʒuːələ(r)/, trader in jewels.

jew·elry, jew·el·lery /ˈdʒuːəlrɪ/ n [U] jewels collectively.

jib¹ /dʒɪb/ n [C] **1** small triangular sail (in front of the mainsail). **2** projecting arm of a crane or derrick.

jib² /dʒɪb/ vi (-bb-) **1** (of a horse, etc) stop suddenly; refuse to go forwards. **2** (fig) refuse to proceed. **jib at,** (fig) show unwillingness or dislike: *He ~bed at working overtime.*

jibe /dʒaɪb/ vi = gibe.

jiffy /ˈdʒɪfɪ/ n [C] (pl -ies) (informal) moment: *I won't be a ~.* **in a jiffy,** soon.

jig¹ /dʒɪg/ n [C] **1** (music for a) quick, lively dance. **2** appliance that holds a piece of work and guides the tools that are used on it. □ vi,vt (-gg-) **1** dance a jig. **2** move up and down in a quick, jerky way: *~ging up and down in excitement.*

jig·saw /ˈdʒɪgsɔː/ n [C] (also ˈ~ puzzle) picture, map, etc pasted on cardboard or wood and cut in irregularly shaped pieces which are to be fitted together again.

ji·had /dʒɪˈhɑːd/ n [C] religious war by Muslims against unbelievers.

jilt /dʒɪlt/ vt give up, send away, a man after giving him encouragement or a promise to marry: *When he lost his job, she ~ed him.* □ n [C] person who jilts.

jingle /ˈdʒɪŋgəl/ n [C] **1** metallic clinking or ringing sound (as of coins, keys or small bells). **2** series of the same or similar sounds in words, esp when designed to attract the attention: *advertising ~s.* □ vt,vi **1** (cause to) make a light, ringing sound: *He ~d his keys.* **2** (of verse) be full of repetition and rhymes that make it easy to remember.

jinks /dʒɪŋks/ n (only in) **high jinks,** noisy merrymaking; uncontrolled fun.

jinx /dʒɪŋks/ n [C] (sl) person or thing that brings bad luck.

jit·ters /ˈdʒɪtəz/ n pl (sl) extreme nervousness: *give her/have/get the ~.*

jit·tery /ˈdʒɪtərɪ/ adj nervous; frightened.

jiu-jitsu /ˈdʒuːˈdʒɪtsu/ n = judo (the usual word).

jive /dʒaɪv/ n [C] style of popular music with a strong beat; dancing to this. □ vi dance to jive music.

job /dʒɒb/ n [C] **1** piece of work, either to be done, or completed. **on the job,** (informal) at work; busy. **make a good/fine job of** sth, do it well. **odd jobs,** bits of work not connected with one another. **an odd-ˈjob man,** one who makes a living by doing any bits of work he is asked to do. **2** (informal) employment; position: *He has lost his ~.* **3** **a good job,** a fortunate state of affairs: *He lost his seat in Parliament, and a good ~,* *too!* **make the best of a bad job,** do what one can to remedy an unfortunate state of affairs. **4** be/have a (hard) job doing/to do sth, be/have (great) difficulty. **5** a 'job `lot,** collection of miscellaneous articles, bought together. **6** (*informal*) **just the job,** exactly what is wanted. **7** (*sl*) something done dishonestly for private profit or advantage. **8** (*sl*) criminal act, esp theft.

jockey /ˈdʒɒkɪ/ n [C] (*pl* ~s) professional rider in horse-races. ⇨ also disc jockey. □ vt,vi trick; cheat: *He ~ed Green out of his job.*

jo·cose /dʒəʊˈkəʊs/ adj (*formal*) humorous.

jocu·lar /ˈdʒɒkjʊlə(r)/ adj (*formal*) humorous.

jocu·lar·ly adv

jocu·lar·ity /ˌdʒɒkjʊˈlærətɪ/ n [C,U]

joc·und /ˈdʒɒkənd/ adj (*formal*) merry; cheerful.

joc·und·ity /dʒəʊˈkʌndətɪ/ n [C,U]

jodh·purs /ˈdʒɒdpəz/ n pl breeches for horse-riding, close-fitting from the knee to the ankle.

jog /dʒɒg/ vt,vi (-gg-) **1** give a slight knock or push to: ~ *up and down on a horse. He ~ged my elbow,* touched it, e g to attract my attention. **jog sb's memory,** (try to) make him remember something. **2 jog along/on,** make slow, patient progress: *We ~ged along the bad roads. We must ~ on somehow until business conditions improve.* **3** (of a horse) trot. **4** (of a person) run slowly (esp for exercise). □ n [C] **1** slight push, shake or nudge. **2** (also ˈjog-trot) slow trot. **3** slow run.

joggle /ˈdʒɒgəl/ vt,vi shake, move, by or as if by repeated jerks. □ n [C] slight shake.

joie de vivre /ˌʒwɑː də ˈviːvr/ n (*Fr*) carefree enjoyment of life.

join /dʒɔɪn/ vt,vi **1** unite; connect (two points, things) with a line, rope, bridge, etc: ~ *one thing to another;* ~ *two things together.* **join hands,** clasp each other's hands. **join forces (with),** unite in action; work together. **2** come together: *Parallel lines never ~.* **3** become a member of: ~ *the army.* **join up,** (*informal*) join the army. **4** come into the company of; associate with: *I'll ~ you in a few minutes. May I ~ in (the game)?* □ n [C] place or line where two things are joined.

joiner /ˈdʒɔɪnə(r)/ n [C] skilled workman who makes the inside woodwork of buildings, etc.

join·ery, work of a joiner.

joint [1] /dʒɔɪnt/ adj held or done by, belonging to, two or more persons together: ~ *responsibility.*

joint account, bank account in the name of more than one person, e g a husband and wife.

ˈjoint-ˈstock company, group of persons who carry on a business with capital contributed by all.

joint·ly adv

joint [2] /dʒɔɪnt/ n [C] **1** place, line or surface at which two or more things are joined: *Can you see the ~s?* **2** device or structure by which things, e g lengths of pipe, bones, are joined together: *finger ~s.* **put sb's nose out of joint,** frustrate him. **3** limb (shoulder, leg) or other division of an ox, a sheep, etc which a butcher supplies to customers: *a ~ of beef/lamb.* **4** (*sl*) place for gambling, drinking or drug-taking. **5** (*sl*) cigarette containing a drug.

joint [3] /dʒɔɪnt/ vt **1** provide with a joint or joints(2): *a ~ed doll.* **2** divide into joints(3).

joist /dʒɔɪst/ n [C] **1** one of the pieces of timber (from wall to wall) to which floorboards are fastened. **2** steel beam supporting a floor or ceiling.

joke /dʒəʊk/ n [C] something said or done to cause amusement. **play a joke on sb,** cause him to be the victim of a joke. **It's no joke,** It's serious. □ vi make jokes: *I was only joking when I said that.*

jok·ing·ly adv in a joking manner.

joker /ˈdʒəʊkə(r)/ n [C] **1** person who is fond of making jokes. **2** extra playing card which is used in some games as the highest trump.

jolly /ˈdʒɒlɪ/ adj (-ier, -iest) joyful; gay; merry. □ adv (*GB dated informal*) very: *Take ~ good care of it!* □ vt (pt,pp -ied) **jolly sb along,** keep him in a good humour (esp in order to win his co-operation).

ˈJolly ˈRoger, pirate's black flag (with skull and crossbones).

jolt /dʒəʊlt/ vt,vi give a jerk or jerks to; shake up; (of a vehicle) move along by jerks: *The old bus ~ed along.* □ n [C] sudden bump or shake.

jostle /ˈdʒɒsəl/ vt,vi push roughly (against): *We were ~d by the crowd.*

jot [1] /dʒɒt/ n [C] small amount: *not a ~ of truth in it,* no truth at all.

jot [2] /dʒɒt/ vt (-tt-) **jot sth down,** make a quick written note of: ~ *down my name and address.*

ˈjot·ter, notebook or pad for rough notes.

ˈjot·tings, notes jotted down.

jour·nal /ˈdʒɜːnəl/ n [C] **1** newspaper; periodical: *the Economic J~.* **2** daily record of news, events, business accounts, etc.

jour·nal·ese /ˌdʒɜːnəlˈiːz/, style of English used in some journalists.

jour·nal·ism /-ɪzm/, work of writing for, editing or publishing journals.

jour·nal·ist /-ɪst/, person engaged in journalism.

jour·nal·is·tic /ˌdʒɜːnəlˈɪstɪk/ adj

jour·ney /ˈdʒɜːnɪ/ n [C] (*pl* ~s) (distance travelled in) going to a place, esp a distant place: *go on a ~ round the world.* □ vi travel.

jour·ney·man /ˈdʒɜːnɪmən/ n [C] (*pl* -men /-mən/) skilled workman who works for a master (contrasted with an **apprentice**).

joust /dʒaʊst/ vi, n [C] (engage in a) fight on

horseback with lances (as between knights in the Middle Ages).

jov·ial /ˈdʒəʊvɪəl/ adj full of fun and good humour; merry: in a ~ mood.
jov·ially /-ɪəlɪ/ adv
jov·ial·ity /ˌdʒəʊvɪˈælətɪ/ n [C,U]

jowl /dʒaʊl/ n [C] jaw; lower part of the face: a man with a heavy ~.

joy /dʒɔɪ/ n 1 [U] deep pleasure; great gladness: I wish you ~. 2 [C] something that gives joy: the ~s and sorrows of life. □ vi (poet) rejoice: ~ in a friend's success.

ˈjoy-ride, (sl) ride in a motor-car, esp for fun and thrills.

ˈjoy-stick, (sl) control lever on an aircraft.

joy·ful /-fəl/ adj filled with, showing, causing, joy.
joy·fully /-fəlɪ/ adj
joy·ful·ness n [U]
joy·less adj without joy; gloomy; sad.
joy·ous /ˈdʒɔɪəs/ adj full of joy.
joy·ous·ly adv

ju·bi·lant /ˈdʒuːbɪlənt/ adj triumphant.
ju·bi·lant·ly adv

ju·bi·la·tion /ˌdʒuːbɪˈleɪʃən/ n [C,U] (instance of) expressing triumph.

ju·bi·lee /ˈdʒuːbɪliː/ n [C] celebration of a special anniversary of some event, e g a wedding.
ˈdiamond jubilee, 60th anniversary.
ˈgolden jubilee, 50th anniversary.
ˈsilver jubilee, 25th anniversary.

Ju·da·ism /ˈdʒuːdeɪɪzm/ US: -dɪɪzm/ n the religion of the Jewish people; their culture and social way of life.

judge¹ /dʒʌdʒ/ n [C] 1 public officer with authority to hear and decide cases in a law court. 2 person who decides in a contest, competition, dispute, etc. 3 person qualified and able to give opinions on merits and values: a good ~ of horses.

judge² /dʒʌdʒ/ vt,vi (present participle judging) 1 act as a judge(1). 2 give a decision (in a competition, etc): Who is going to ~ the long-jump competition? 3 estimate; consider; form an opinion about: Judging from what you say, he ought to succeed.

judge·ment (US, and GB legal judg·ment) /ˈdʒʌdʒmənt/ n 1 [U] judging or being judged: sit in ~ on a case, (in a law court); pass ~ on a prisoner, give a decision after trial. 2 [C] decision of a judge or court: The ~ was in his favour. 3 [U] process of judging: an error of ~. 4 [U] good sense; ability to judge(2,3): He showed excellent ~ in choosing a wife. 5 [C] misfortune considered to be a punishment from God: Your failure is a ~ on you for being so lazy. 6 [C,U] opinion: in the ~ of most people.
ˈjudgement Day, the ˈDay of ˈJudgement, the day when God will judge all men.

ju·di·ca·ture /ˈdʒuːdɪkətʃə(r)/ n 1 [U] administration of justice: the Supreme Court of J~, full title of the English Courts of Justice. 2 [C] body of judges.

ju·di·cial /dʒuːˈdɪʃl/ adj 1 of or by a court of justice; of a judge or of judgement: the ~ bench, the judges. 2 critical; impartial: a ~ mind.
ju·di·cially /-ʃəlɪ/ adv

ju·dici·ary /dʒuːˈdɪʃərɪ US: -ʃɪerɪ/ n [C] (pl -ies) 1 the judges of a State collectively. 2 the system of law courts in a country.

ju·di·cious /dʒuːˈdɪʃəs/ adj (formal) showing or having good sense.
ju·di·cious·ly adv

judo /ˈdʒuːdəʊ/ n [U] Japanese art of wrestling and self-defence in which an opponent's own weight and strength are used against him.

jug /dʒʌɡ/ n [C] 1 deep vessel with a handle and lip: a ˈmilk-~. 2 the contents of such a vessel: a ~ of milk. 3 (sl) prison.
jug·ful /-fʊl/, amount a jug holds.

jug·ger·naut /ˈdʒʌɡənɔːt/ n [C] 1 (fig) cause or belief to which persons sacrifice themselves: the ~ of war. 2 (informal) huge long-distance transport vehicle.

juggle /ˈdʒʌɡl/ vi,vt 1 do tricks, perform (with balls, plates, etc thrown into the air) to amuse people. 2 play tricks (with facts, figures, etc) to deceive people.
jug·gler, person who juggles.

jugu·lar /ˈdʒʌɡjʊlə(r)/ adj of the neck or throat: ~ veins. □ n [C] jugular vein.

juice /dʒuːs/ n [C,U] 1 fluid part of fruits, vegetables and meat: a glass of ˈorange ~. 2 fluid in organs of the body: gastric ~s. 3 (informal) electricity, petrol or other source of power.

juicy /ˈdʒuːsɪ/ adj (-ier, -iest) 1 containing much juice: ~ oranges. 2 (informal) interesting (esp because scandalous, etc).
juici·ness n [U]

juju /ˈdʒuːdʒuː/ n [C] West African charm or fetish; its magic power.

juke·box /ˈdʒuːk bɒks/ n [C] coin-operated record-player in pubs, cafés, etc.

July /dʒuːˈlaɪ/ n seventh month of the year.

jumble /ˈdʒʌmbl/ vi,vt mix, be mixed, in a confused way: toys ~d up together in the cupboard. □ n [C] muddle; confused mixture.
ˈjumble-sale, sale of a mixed collection of old or second-hand articles, usually for charity.

jumbo /ˈdʒʌmbəʊ/ adj unusually large: ~ jets.

jump¹ /dʒʌmp/ n [C] 1 act of jumping. 2 sudden movement caused by fear. 3 sudden rise in amount, price, value, etc: a ~ in car exports.
jumpy adj (-ier, -iest) excited and nervous.

jump² /dʒʌmp/ vi,vt 1 move quickly by the sudden use of the muscles of the legs or (of fish) the tail: ~ to one's feet/over a fence. 2 pass over by moving in this way: ~ a ditch; cause (a horse, etc) to move in this way: ~ a horse over a fence. 3 (fig) move, act, suddenly or aimlessly· ~ from one subject to *another in a speech.* **jump down sb's throat,** answer, interrupt, him with sudden anger. **4** move with a jerk or jerks from excitement, joy, etc; start suddenly: $\sim$ *for joy;* $\sim$ *up and down in excitement.* **5** rise suddenly in price: *Gold shares* $\sim$*ed on the Stock Exchange yesterday.* **6** spring on, attack: *the thieves* $\sim$*d him and stole his money.* **7** *jump at,* accept eagerly: $\sim$ *at an offer.* **jump to conclusions,** reach them hastily. **8** *jump (one's) bail,* fail to surrender to one's bail. *jump the gun,* start too soon. *jump the queue,* (*fig*) obtain something without waiting one's turn.

jumper /ˈdʒʌmpə(r)/ *n* [C] **1** outer loose-fitting garment pulled on over the head and coming down to the hips. **2** person, animal or insect, that jumps.

junc·tion /ˈdʒʌŋkʃən/ *n* **1** [U] joining or being joined; [C] instance of this. **2** [C] place where roads, railway lines or sections of an electrical circuit meet or diverge.

junc·ture /ˈdʒʌŋktʃə(r)/ *n* [C] (*formal*) **1** junction(1). **2** state of affairs, esp the phrase: *at this juncture,* at this time.

June /dʒuːn/ *n* sixth month of the year.

jungle /ˈdʒʌŋɡəl/ *n* [C] (land covered with) thickly growing undergrowth and tangled vegetation: *cut a path through the* $\sim$. *the law of the jungle,* (*fig*) ruthless competition or exploitation.

jun·gly /ˈdʒʌŋɡlɪ/ *adj*

jun·ior /ˈdʒuːnɪə(r)/ *n* [C], *adj* **1** (person) younger, lower in rank, than another: *He is my* $\sim$ *by two years. Tom Brown, Junior* (or abbr to *Jun, Jnr* or *Jr*), used of a son having the same first name as his father, or the younger of two boys of the same surname in a school, etc. **2** (*US*) student in his third year (of four) at school or college.

junk[1] /dʒʌŋk/ *n* [U] old, discarded things of little or no value: *a* $\sim$ *shop.*

junk[2] /dʒʌŋk/ *n* [C] flat-bottomed Chinese sailing-vessel.

junkie, junky /ˈdʒʌŋkɪ/ *n* [C] (*pl* -ies) (*sl*) drug (esp heroin) addict.

junta /ˈdʒʌntə *US:* ˈhʊntə/ *n* [C] (*pl* -s) **1** (in Spain and Italy) deliberative or administrative council. **2** group of army officers who have seized power by a coup d'état.

Jupi·ter /ˈdʒuːpɪtə(r)/ *n* **1** (ancient Rome) ruler of gods and men. **2** largest planet of the solar system.

ju·ridi·cal /dʒʊˈrɪdɪkəl/ *adj* of law or legal proceedings.

ju·ris·dic·tion /ˌdʒʊərɪsˈdɪkʃən/ *n* [U] administration of justice; legal authority; right to exercise this; extent of this: *This matter does not come/fall within our* $\sim$, *We have no authority to deal with it.*

ju·ris·pru·dence /ˌdʒʊərɪsˈpruːdəns/ *n* [U] science and philosophy of human law.

jur·ist /ˈdʒʊərɪst/ *n* [C] expert in law.

juror /ˈdʒʊərə(r)/ *n* [C] member of a jury.

jury /ˈdʒʊərɪ/ *n* [C] (*pl* -ies) **1** body of persons (in US and GB twelve) who swear to give a true decision (*a verdict*) on issues of fact in a case in a court of justice: *The* $\sim$ *found the prisoner not guilty.* **2** body of persons chosen to give a decision or make an award in a competition.

'jury-box, enclosure for a jury in court.

jury·man, = juror.

just[1] /dʒʌst/ *adj* **1** fair; in accordance with what is right: *a* $\sim$ *man; be* $\sim$ *to a person.* **2** well deserved; fairly earned: *get/receive one's* $\sim$ *rewards.* **3** reasonable; based on reasonable grounds: $\sim$ *suspicions.*

just·ly *adv*

just[2] /dʒʌst/ *adv* **1** (of an immediate past): (*GB*) *I've* $\sim$ *had dinner.* (*US*) *I* $\sim$ *had dinner.* **2** exactly; precisely: *It's* $\sim$ *two o'clock. This is* $\sim$ *what I wanted. J*$\sim$ *my luck!* **3** *just as* (*adj*) *as,* (a) exactly as: *Leave everything* $\sim$ *as* (*tidy as*) *you find it.* (b) when: *He arrived* $\sim$ *as I was leaving.* (c) in the same way as: *J*$\sim$ *as you hate Mr Green, so I dislike his wife.* **4** exactly: $\sim$ *here/there.* **5** more or less: *Put it* $\sim$ *over there,* near that place. **6** at this, that very moment: *We're* $\sim$ *off/going/about to start. just now,* (a) at this moment: *I'm busy* $\sim$ *now.* (b) a short time ago: *Tom came in* $\sim$ *now.* **7** barely: *We* (*only*) $\sim$ *caught the train,* almost missed it. **8** (used informally, esp with imperatives, to call attention to something): *J*$\sim$ *listen to him! J*$\sim$ *a moment, please.* Please wait a moment. **9** only; merely: *He's* $\sim$ *an ordinary man. Would you walk five miles* $\sim$ *to see a film? I* $\sim$ *meant that...* **10** (*informal*) absolutely: *The concert was* $\sim$ *splendid.*

jus·tice /ˈdʒʌstɪs/ *n* **1** [U] just conduct; the quality of being right and fair: *treat all men with* $\sim$. **2** [U] the law and its administration: *a court of* $\sim$. **3** [C] judge of the Supreme Courts: *the Lord Chief J*$\sim$.

'Justice of the 'Peace, magistrate.

De'partment of 'Justice, (*US*) executive department, headed by the Attorney General, supervising internal security, naturalization, immigration, etc.

jus·tify /ˈdʒʌstɪfaɪ/ *vt* (*pt,pp* -ied) **1** show that (a person, statement, act, etc) is right, reasonable or proper: *You can hardly* $\sim$ *such conduct.* **2** be a good reason for: *Your wish to go for a walk cannot* $\sim$ *leaving the baby alone in the house.*

jus·ti·fi·able /ˈdʒʌstɪˈfaɪəbəl/ *adj* that can be justified.

jus·ti·fi·ably /-əblɪ/ *adv*

jus·ti·fi·ca·tion /ˌdʒʌstɪfɪˈkeɪʃən/ *n* [U]

jut /dʒʌt/ *vi* (-tt-) *jut out,* stand out from; be out of line (from what is around): *The balcony* $\sim$ *out over the garden.*

jute /dʒuːt/ *n* [U] fibre from the outer skin of certain plants, used for making canvas, rope, etc.

ju·ven·ile /ˈdʒuːvənaɪl/ *n* [C] young person. □ *adj* of, characteristic of, suitable for, juveniles: *a* $\sim$ *court.*

'juvenile de'linquency, law-breaking by young people.

'juvenile de'linquent, young offender.

jux·ta·pose /'dʒʌkstə'pəʊz/ *vt* place side by side.

jux·ta·po·si·tion /'dʒʌkstəpə'zɪʃən/ *n* [U]

Kk

K, k /keɪ/ (*pl* K's, k's /keɪz/) the 11th letter of the English alphabet.

kale, kail /keɪl/ *n* [C,U] kind of curly-leaved cabbage.

ka·leido·scope /kə'laɪdəskəʊp/ *n* [C] **1** tube containing mirrors and small, loose pieces of coloured glass, turned to produce changing patterns. **2** (*fig*) frequently changing pattern of bright scenes: *a ~ of colour in the landscape.*

ka·leido·scopic /kə'laɪdə'skopɪk/ *adj*

kan·ga·roo /'kæŋgə'ru/ *n* [C] Australian animal that jumps along on its strong hind legs. The female has a pouch in which its young are carried.

kangaroo court, one set up without authority by workers, prisoners, etc to try someone whom they consider to have acted against their interests.

kao·lin /'keɪəlɪn/ *n* [U] fine white clay used in making porcelain, etc.

ka·pok /'keɪpok/ *n* [U] soft cotton-like material (from seeds of a tropical tree) used for filling cushions, etc.

karat /'kærət/ = carat.

ka·rate /kə'rɑtɪ/ *n* [U] Japanese method of unarmed combat using blows made with the sides of the hands, foot, head or elbow.

karma /'kɑmə/ *n* [C] (in Buddhism) person's acts in one of his successive existences, looked on as deciding his fate in his next existence.

kayak /'kaɪæk/ *n* [C] **1** Eskimo canoe of light wood covered with sealskins. **2** any rigid, canvas-covered canoe.

ke·bab /kə'bæb/ *n* [C] dish of small pieces of meat, seasoned and roasted on skewers.

ked·geree /'kedʒərɪ/ *n* [U] rice cooked with fish, eggs, etc.

keel /kil/ *n* [C] timber or steel structure on which the framework of a ship is built up. **on an even keel,** steady. □ *vt,vi* **1** turn (a ship) over on one side to repair it, etc. **2** *keel over,* capsize; upset; (of persons) collapse.

keen /kin/ *adj* (-er, -est) **1** (of points and edges) sharp: *a knife with a ~ edge.* **2** (*fig*) sharp: *a ~ (= cutting) wind.* **3** (of interest, the feelings) strong; deep: *He has a ~ interest in his work.* **4** (of the mind, the senses) active; sensitive: *~ eyesight.* **5** (of persons, their character, etc) eager; anxious

to do things: *a ~ sportsman.* **keen on,** (*informal*) enthusiastic about: *~ on going abroad.*

keen·ly *adv*

keen·ness *n* [U]

keep¹ /kip/ *vt,vi* (*pt,pp* kept /kept/) (For idiomatic uses with *adverbial particles* and *prepositions*, ⇨ 18 below. For *keep* and *nouns* not given here, ⇨ the *noun* entries, e g *~ pace/step (with) sb, ~ time, ~ watch, ~ good/early hours.*) **1** cause to remain in a specified state or position: *~ the children quiet/happy. The cold weather kept us indoors.* **keep an eye on,** (*informal*) watch over closely: *Please ~ an eye on the baby.* **keep sth in mind,** remember it. **2** cause a process or state to continue: *~ a person waiting. Please ~ the fire burning.* **3** *keep sb/sth from doing sth,* prevent, hold back: *What kept you (from joining me)?* **4** *keep sth (back) from,* (a) not let others know about it: *She can ~ nothing (back) from her friends.* (b) hold back; withhold: *They ~ back £3 a month from my salary for National Insurance.* **keep sth to oneself,** (a) not express, e g comments, views, etc: *K~/You may ~ your remarks to yourself,* I don't want to hear them. (b) refuse to share: *He kept the good news to himself.* **keep a secret,** ⇨ secret. **5** pay proper respect to; be faithful to; observe; fulfil: *~ a promise/a treaty/an appointment/the law.* **6** celebrate: *~ Christmas/one's birthday.* **7** guard; protect: *~ goal.* ⇨ goalkeeper. **8** continue to have; have in one's possession and not give away: *K~ the change,* i e from money offered in payment. *Please ~ these things for me while I'm away.* **9** support; take care of; provide what is needed for; maintain: *Does he earn enough to ~ himself and his family?* **10** have habitually on sale or in stock: *'Do you sell batteries for transister sets?'—'Sorry, but we don't ~ them'.* **11** *keep house,* be responsible for the housework, cooking, shopping, etc. ⇨ housekeeper. **12** own or manage, esp for profit: *~ hens; ~ a shop.* **13** make entries in, records of: *~ a diary.* ⇨ book-keeper. **14** continue to be, remain, in a specified condition: *Please ~ quiet! I hope you're ~ing well.* **keep fit,** (do physical exercise to) remain in good health. **15** continue in a particular direction; remain in a particular relationship to a place, etc: *K~ straight on until you get to the church. Traffic in Britain ~s (to the) left.* **16** continue doing something: *K~ smiling! Why does she ~ (on) giggling?* **keep going,** not stop; not give up: *This is exhausting work, but I manage to ~ going.* **17** (of food) remain in good condition: *Will this meat ~ till tomorrow?*

18 (uses with *adverbial particles* and *prepositions*):

keep at sth, continue to work at it: *K~ at it,* don't give up!

keep away (from), avoid, prevent coming or going near (to): *K~ away from the edge.*

keep back (from), remain in the rear, at the back. **keep sb back,** prevent him from advancing.

keep sth back, ⇨ 4 above.

keep sb down, hold in subjection; oppress: *~ down subject races.* **keep sth down,** (a) control: *He couldn't ~ down his anger.* (b) limit: *We must ~ down expenses.*

keep from, refuse to share: *He kept the news from his friends.* ⇨ also 3 above.

keep in with sb, remain on good terms with, continue to be friendly with: *You must ~ in with your customers,* retain their good will.

keep off, remain at a distance; not come: *if the rain ~s off, if it doesn't start to rain.* **keep off sth,** refrain from: *Please ~ off that subject,* say nothing about it. **keep sb/sth off,** hold, cause to remain, at a distance: *K~ your hands off,* Don't touch it, me, etc.

keep on (doing sth), continue; persist: *~ on (working) although one is tired.* ⇨ also 16 above. **keep sth on,** continue to wear: *~ one's hat on.* **keep sb on,** continue to employ him/her. **keep on at sb,** worry with repeated complaints, questions, etc.

keep out (of), remain outside: *Danger! K~ out! K~ out of their quarrels,* Don't get involved in them. **keep sb/sth out (of),** prevent from entering: *K~ that dog out of the kitchen.*

keep to sth, (a) do what one has agreed to do: *He always ~s to his promises.* (b) limit oneself to: *keep to the subject.* **keep (oneself) to oneself,** avoid meeting people.

keep up (with), go at the same pace or speed as: *Harry couldn't ~ up with the class. I can't ~ up with you,* walk as fast as you. **keep sb up,** delay a person from going to bed. **keep sth up,** (a) prevent from sinking or getting low: *K~ your chin up!* Cheer up, have courage, etc. (b) observe: *~ up old customs.* (c) continue: *They kept up the attack all day.* (d) maintain in proper condition: *How much does it cost you to ~ up your large house and garden?* **keep it up,** continue without slowing down: *He works far too hard; he'll never be able to ~ it up.*

keep² /kip/ *n* **1** [U] (food needed for) support: *The dog doesn't earn his ~,* is not worth the cost of keeping him. **2** [C] (in olden times) tower of a fortress, etc: *the castle ~.* **3 for keeps,** (*sl*) permanently.

keeper /ˈkipə(r)/ *n* [C] **1** guard, e g a person who looks after animals in a zoo. **2** (in compounds) person with special duties: `park~; `goal~; `shop~; `house~.

keep·ing /ˈkipɪŋ/ *n* [U] **1** care. **in safe keeping,** being kept carefully. **2** (in verbal senses of keep(12)): *the ~ of bees;* `bee-~. **3** agreement: *His actions are not in ~ with his promises.*

keep·sake /ˈkipseɪk/ *n* [C] something kept in memory of the giver.

keg /keg/ *n* [C] small barrel, usually of less than 10 gallons: *a ~ of brandy.*

ken·nel /ˈkenəl/ *n* [C] **1** hut to shelter a dog. **2** (establishment for a) pack of hounds. **3** place where dogs are cared for, e g during quarantine. □ *vt,vi* (-ll-, *US* also -l-) put, keep, live, in a kennel.

kept /kept/ ⇨ keep¹.

kerb (also **curb**) /kɜb/ *n* [C] stone edging to a raised path or pavement.

`**kerb-stone,** stone forming a part of this.

ker·chief /ˈkɜtʃɪf/ *n* [C] square piece of cloth or lace used by women as a head covering.

ker·nel /ˈkɜnəl/ *n* [C] **1** softer, inner part of a nut or fruit-stone. **2** part of a seed, e g a grain of wheat, within the husk. **3** (*fig*) central or important part of a subject, problem, etc.

kero·sene /ˈkerəsin/ *n* [U] paraffin oil.

kes·trel /ˈkestrəl/ *n* [C] kind of small hawk.

ketch·up /ˈketʃəp/ *n* [U] sauce made from tomato juice.

kettle /ˈketəl/ *n* [C] metal vessel with lid, spout and handle, for boiling water.

kettle·drum /ˈketəldrʌm/ *n* [C] drum shaped like a hemisphere with parchment over the top.

key¹ /ki/ *n* [C] **1** metal instrument for moving the bolt of a lock. **2** instrument for winding a clock or a watch by tightening the spring. **3** (*fig*) something that provides an answer (to a problem or mystery). **4** set of answers to exercises or problems; translation from a foreign language. **5** operating part (lever or button) of a typewriter, piano, organ, flute, etc pressed down by a finger. **6** winged fruit of some trees, e g the ash and elm. **7** (*music*) scale of notes definitely related to each other and based on a particular note called the `key-note: *the ~ of C major.* **8** (*fig*) tone or style of thought or expression: *in a minor ~.* sadly. **in a low key,** = low-keyed. **9** (also used as an *adjective*) place which, from its position, gives control of a route or area: *a ~ position.* **10** (as an *adjective*) *~ industry,* one essential to the carrying on of others; *a ~ man,* one essential to the work of others.

`**key·board,** row of keys(5) (on a piano, organ, typewriter).

`**key·note,** (a) note on which a key(7) is based. (b) (*fig*) most important attitude or idea: *The ~note of the Minister's speech was the need for higher productivity.*

`**key-ring,** ring on which to keep keys.

key·less *adj* not having or needing a key.

key² /ki/ *vt* **key up,** (*fig*) stimulate or raise the standard of (a person, his activity, etc): *The crowd was ~ed up for the football match.*

key³ /ki/ *n* [C] low island or reef, esp off the coasts of Florida, W Indies.

key·stone /ˈkistəʊn/ *n* [C] **1** stone at the top of an arch locking the others into position. **2**

(*fig*) central principle on which everything depends.

khaki /ˈkɑːkɪ/ *n* [U], *adj* (cloth, military uniform, of a) dull yellowish-brown.

kha·lif /ˈkeɪlɪf/ *n* = caliph.

kha·lif·ate /ˈkeɪlɪfeɪt/ *n* = caliphate.

kick[1] /kɪk/ *n* [C] **1** act of kicking: *The bruise was caused by a* ∼. *The* ∼ *of an old rifle*. **2** (*informal*) thrill of pleasure or excitement: *He gets a big* ∼ *out of motor-racing.* **3** [U] strength: *He has no* ∼ *left in him, is exhausted.*

`kick-back, (*sl*) payment made to a person who has helped one to make money.

'kick-'start(er), lever on a motorcycle, etc used to start the engine.

kick[2] /kɪk/ *vt,vi* **1** hit with the foot; move the foot: ∼ *a ball;* ∼ *a hole in the door.* **kick the bucket,** (*sl*) die. **2** (of a gun) jolt, recoil when fired: *This old rifle* ∼*s badly.* **3 kick against/at,** show annoyance; protest: *He* ∼*ed at/against the treatment he was receiving.* **kick off,** (in football) start the game. Hence, `kick-off *n* [C]. **kick up a fuss/row, etc,** (*informal*) cause a disturbance, e g by protesting strongly.

kid[1] /kɪd/ *n* **1** [C] young goat. **2** [U] leather made from skin of this: ∼ *gloves.* **handle sb with kid gloves,** (*fig*) deal with him gently. **3** (*sl*) child. **4** (*US sl*) young person: *college* ∼*s.*

kiddy *n* [C] (*pl* -dies) (*sl*) child.

kid[2] /kɪd/ *vt* (-dd-) (*sl*) deceive: *You're* ∼*ding (me)!*

kid·nap /ˈkɪdnæp/ *vt* (-pp-, *US* -p-) steal (a child) (esp in order to obtain a ransom).

kid·nap·per, person who kidnaps.

kid·ney /ˈkɪdnɪ/ *n* [C] (*pl* ∼s) one of a pair of organs in the abdomen that separate urine from the blood; kidney of sheep, cattle, etc as food.

'kidney `bean, (plant with pod containing) reddish-brown kidney-shaped bean.

`kidney machine, one which does the work of diseased kidneys.

kill /kɪl/ *vt,vi* **1** put to death; cause the death of: ∼ *animals for food.* **kill sb/sth off,** get rid of: *The frost* ∼*ed off most of the insect pests.* **kill time,** find ways of passing the time without being bored, e g when waiting for a train. **2** neutralize, make ineffective, by contrast: *That scarlet carpet* ∼*s the effect of your curtains.* **3** cause the failure or defeat of: ∼ *a proposal.* **4** overwhelm with admiration; impress deeply: ∼ *her with kindness.* □ *n* (*sing* only) act of killing, esp in hunting.

`kill-joy, person who makes sad those who are enjoying themselves.

killer, person who, that which, kills; murderer.

kill·ing *adj* (*dated informal*) (a) amusing: *a* ∼*ing joke.* (b) exhausting: *a* ∼*ing experience.* □ *n* **make a killing,** be extraordinarily successful.

kill·ing·ly *adv*

kiln /kɪln/ *n* [C] furnace or oven for burning, baking or drying, esp `brick-∼, for baking bricks; `hop-∼, for drying hops.

kilo /ˈkiːləʊ/ *n* [C] (*pl* ∼s) abbr of kilogram.

kilo- *prefix* 1 000.

kilo·cycle /ˈkɪləsaɪkəl/ *n* [C] unit of frequency of vibration, used of radio waves.

kilo·gram(me) /ˈkɪləgræm/ *n* [C] 1 000 grammes.

kilo·litre /ˈkɪləliːtə(r)/ *n* [C] 1 000 litres.

kilo·metre (*US* = **-meter**) /ˈkɪləmiːtə(r) *US*: kɪˈlɒmɪtər/ *n* [C] 1 000 metres.

kilo·watt /ˈkɪləwɒt/ *n* [C] 1 000 watts.

kilt /kɪlt/ *n* [C] pleated skirt, usually of tartan cloth, worn as part of male dress in the Scottish Highlands; similar skirt worn by women and children.

kim·ono /kɪˈməʊnəʊ *US*: -nə/ *n* [C] (*pl* ∼s) **1** wide-sleeved long flowing gown, characteristic of Japanese traditional costume. **2** style of loose garment worn as a dressing-gown.

kin /kɪn/ *n* (collectively) family; relations. **next of kin,** nearest relation(s).

kind[1] /kaɪnd/ *adj* (-er, -est) having, showing, thoughtfulness, sympathy or love for others: *be* ∼ *to animals. It was* ∼ *of you to help us.*

'kind-'hearted *adj* being kind.

kind·ly *adv* (a) in a kind manner: *speak/treat her* ∼*ly.* (b) (used in polite formulas) *Will you* ∼*ly tell me the time?* (c) naturally; easily: *He doesn't take* ∼*ly to being cheated.*

kind·ness *n* (a) [U] kind nature; being kind: *do something out of* ∼*ness.* (b) [C] **do sb a kindness,** perform a kind act: *He has done/shown me many* ∼*nesses.*

kind[2] /kaɪnd/ *n* [C] **1** race, natural group, of animals, plants, etc: *man*∼. **2** class, sort or variety: *What* ∼ *of tree is this? nothing of the kind,* not at all like it. **of a kind, (a)** of the same kind: *two of a* ∼. **(b)** scarcely deserving the name: *They gave us coffee of a* ∼. **a kind of...,** (used when there is uncertainty): *I had a* ∼ *of suspicion* (= I vaguely suspected) *that he was cheating.* **3** [U] nature; character: *They differ in degree but not in* ∼. **4 in kind, (a)** (of payment) in goods or natural produce, not in money: *benefits in* ∼, benefits other than wages or salary, e g the right to buy articles at cost price. **(b)** (*fig*) in the same manner: *repay insolence in* ∼.

kin·der·gar·ten /ˈkɪndəgɑːtən/ *n* [C] school for children too young to begin formal education.

kindle /ˈkɪndəl/ *vt,vi* **1** (cause to) catch fire or burst into flames or flaming colour: *The sparks* ∼*d the dry wood.* **2** rouse, be roused, to a state of strong feeling, interest, etc: ∼ *the interest of an audience.*

kind·ly[1] /ˈkaɪndlɪ/ *adj* (-ier, -iest) friendly: *give* ∼ *advice.*

kind·ly[2] /ˈkaɪndlɪ/ *adv* ⇨ kind[1].

kin·dred /ˈkɪndrəd/ n (*sing* only) **1** [U] relationship by birth between persons: *claim* ~ *with a person.* **2** (used with a *pl verb*) (*rare*) all one's relatives. □*adj* **1** related; having a common source: ~ *languages,* e g English and Dutch. **2** similar: *a* ~ *spirit,* person whom one feels to be congenial, sympathetic.

kin·etic /kɪˈnetɪk/ *adj* of, relating to, produced by, motion.
ˈkinetic ˈenergy, energy of a moving body because of its motion.
kin·etics n [U] (used with a *sing verb*) science of the relations between the motions of bodies and the forces acting on them.

king /kɪŋ/ n [C] **1** male sovereign ruler. **turn King's/Queen's evidence,** (of one who has shared in a crime) give evidence against accomplices (often in order to escape punishment). **2** person of great influence: *an* ˋ*oil* ~. **3** principal piece in the game of chess. **4** (playing-cards) court-card with a picture of a king: *the* ~ *of spades.* **5** largest variety of a species; most prominent member of a group, category, etc: *the* ~ *of beasts,* the lion; *the* ~ *of the forest,* the oak.
King's/Queen's Bench, ⇨ bench.
King's/Queen's Counsel, (abbr **KC, QC**) barrister appointed to act for the State.
ˋking·fisher, small brightly-coloured bird feeding on fish in rivers, etc.
ˋking-pin, (a) vertical bolt used as a pivot. **(b)** (*fig*) indispensable or essential person or thing.
ˋking-size *adj* extra large: *I perfer* ~*-size cigarettes.*
ˋking·like, king·ly *adj* of, like, suitable for, a king.
king·ship, state, office, of a king.

king·dom /ˈkɪŋdəm/ n [C] **1** country ruled by a king or a queen. **2** the spiritual reign of God: *Thy K*~ *come,* May the rule of God be established. **3** any one of the three divisions of the natural world: *the animal, vegetable and mineral* ~*s.* **4** realm or province: *the* ~ *of thought,* the mind.
the Uˋnited ˋKingdom, Great Britain and Northern Ireland.

kink /kɪŋk/ n [C] **1** twist in a length of wire, pipe, cord, etc such as may cause a break or obstruction. **2** (*fig*) something abnormal in a person's way of thinking. □ *vt,vi* make, form, kink: *This hosepipe* ~*s easily.*
kinky *adj* (ier, -iest) (*informal*) eccentric; perverted.

kins·folk /ˈkɪnzfəʊk/ n *pl* relations by blood.

kin·ship /ˈkɪn-ʃɪp/ n [U] relationship by blood; similarity in character.

kins·man /ˈkɪnzmən/ n [C] (*pl* -men) (*old use*) male relative.

kins·woman /ˈkɪnzwʊmən/ n [C] (*pl* -women) (*old use*) female relative.

kiosk /ˈkiosk/ n [C] **1** small open-fronted structure for the sale of newspapers, sweets, cigarettes, etc. **2** small booth for a public telephone.

kip /kɪp/ n (*GB sl*) sleep. □ *vi* (-pp-) go to bed; sleep: *time to* ~ *down.*

kip·per /ˈkɪpə(r)/ n [C] salted herring, dried or smoked.

kirk /kɜk/ n [C] (*Scot*) church.

kiss /kɪs/ *vt,vi* touch with the lips to show affection or as a greeting: ~ *the children goodnight.* □ n [C] touch, caress, given with the lips. **kiss of life,** method of mouth-to-mouth resuscitation, e g for a person rescued from drowning.
kisser, (*sl*)

kit /kɪt/ n **1** (collective) all the equipment (esp clothing) of a soldier, sailor or traveller: ˋ~ *inspection,* examination of kit by an officer to see that it is complete, etc. **2** [C] equipment needed by a workman for his trade: *a plumber's* ~. **3** [C,U] outfit or equipment needed for sport or some other special purpose: ˋ*skiing* ~; *a sur*ˋ*vival* ~, articles to be used by a person in distress, e g a pilot who has come down in a desert or jungle. □ *vt* (-tt-) **kit out/up (with sth),** fit out, be fitted out, with a kit.
ˋkit-bag, long canvas bag in which kit(1) is carried.

kit·chen /ˈkɪtʃɪn/ n [C] room in which meals are cooked or prepared, and for other forms of housework.
ˈkitchen-ˋsink, ⇨ sink¹(1).
ˋkitchen-maid, employed to help in a kitchen, usually to help the cook.
ˈkitchen unit, unit combining articles of kitchen equipment, e g a sink and a storage cabinet.

kit·chen·ette /ˈkɪtʃɪˋnet/ n [C] tiny room or alcove used as a kitchen (esp in a small flat).

kite /kaɪt/ n [C] **1** bird of prey of the hawk family. **2** framework of wood, etc covered with paper or cloth, made to fly in the wind at the end of a long string or wire.

kith /kɪθ/ n (only in) **kith and kin,** friends and relations.

kit·ten /ˈkɪtən/ n [C] young cat.

kitty¹ /ˈkɪtɪ/ n [C] (*pl* -ies) playful name for a kitten.

kitty² /ˈkɪtɪ/ n [C] (*pl* -ies) **1** (in some card games) pool of stakes (money) to be played for. **2** (*informal*) any joint pool or fund, e g of savings.

kiwi /ˈkiwi/ n [C] New Zealand bird with undeveloped wings.

klaxon /ˈklæksən/ n [C] powerful electric horn for a motor-car.

kleenex /ˈklineks/ n [U] (*P*) tissue paper. ⇨ tissue(2).

klep·to·mania /ˈkleptəˋmeɪnɪə/ n [U] irresistible wish to steal, not necessarily from poverty.

klep·to·maniac /-nɪæk/, person with kleptomania.

knack /næk/ n [C] (rarely *pl*) cleverness (intuitive or acquired through practice) enabling one to do something skilfully: *It's quite easy when you have/get the ~ of it.*

knacker /ˈnækə(r)/ *n* [C] **1** person who buys and slaughters useless horses (to sell the meat and hides). **2** person who buys and breaks up old houses, ships, etc for the materials in them.

knap·sack /ˈnæpsæk/ *n* [C] canvas or leather bag, strapped to the back and used (by soldiers, travellers) for carrying clothing, food, etc.

knave /neɪv/ *n* [C] **1** (*old use*) dishonest man. **2** (playing-cards) court-card between 10 and Queen in value: *the ~ of hearts.* ⇨ Jack.

knav·ery /ˈneɪvərɪ/ *n* [C,U]

knead /niːd/ *vt* **1** make (flour and water) into a firm paste (*dough*) by working with the hands; do this with wet clay; make (bread, pots) in this way. **2** massage (muscles, etc) as if making dough.

knee /niː/ *n* [C] **1** joint between the thigh and the lower part of the leg in man; corresponding part in animals. ***be on/go (down) on one's knees,*** be kneeling/kneel down (to pray, or in submission). ***bring sb to his knees,*** force him to submit. **2** part of a garment covering the knees: *the ~s of a pair of trousers.*

`**knee-breeches** /ˈbrɪtʃɪz/ *n pl* breeches reaching down to or just below the knees.

`**knee-cap,** flat, movable bone at the front of the knee.

`**knee-ˈdeep** *adj, adv* so deep as to reach the knees: *The water was ~-deep.*

kneel /niːl/ *vi* (*pt,pp* knelt /nelt/) go down on the knees; rest on the knees: *Everyone knelt in prayer.*

knell /nel/ *n* (*sing* with *a* or *the*) sound of a bell, esp for a death or at a funeral.

knelt /nelt/ ⇨ kneel.

knew /njuː *US:* nuː/ ⇨ know[1].

knicker·bock·ers /ˈnɪkəbɒkəz/ *n pl* loose wide breeches gathered in below the knees.

knickers /ˈnɪkəz/ *n pl* **1** (*informal*) knicker-bockers. **2** (*dated*) = panties.

knick-knack /ˈnɪk næk/ *n* [C] small ornament, piece of jewellery, article of dress, etc.

knife /naɪf/ *n* [C] (*pl* knives /naɪvz/) sharp blade with a handle, used as a cutting instrument or as a weapon: *a* `*table ~,* used for food at table; *a* `*pocket ~,* one with hinged blade(s). ***get one's knife into sb,*** have the wish to harm him. □ *vt* stab (a person) with a knife.

`**knife-edge,** cutting edge of a knife. ***on a knife-edge,*** (of an important outcome, result, etc) extremely uncertain.

knight /naɪt/ *n* [C] **1** (in the Middle Ages) man, usually of noble birth, raised to honourable military rank. **2** (*modern use*) man on whom a title or honour is conferred (lower than that of baronet) as a reward for services to the State or to a political party.

(*Note:* The title *Sir* is used before Christian name and surname, as *Sir James Hill*). **3** piece in the game of chess with a horse's head. □ *vt* make (a person) a knight(2).

`**knight·hood** *n* (a) [U] rank, character or dignity of a knight; [C] (used after *confer*): *The Queen conferred ~hoods on two bankers.* (b) [U] knights collectively: *the ~hood of France.*

knight·ly *adj* chivalrous; brave and gentle.

knit /nɪt/ *vt,vi* (*pt,pp* ~ted or knit; -tt-) **1** make (an article of clothing, etc) by looping wool, etc on long needles: *She often ~s while reading.* **2** unite firmly or closely: *The two families are ~ together by common interests.* **knit the brows,** frown.

knit·ter, person who knits.

knit·ting, (a) action of one who knits. (b) material being knitted.

`**knit·ting-machine,** machine that knits.

`**knit·ting-needle,** long slender rod of steel, wood, etc used to knit.

`**knit·wear,** /-weə(r)/, (trade use) knitted garments.

knives /naɪvz/ ⇨ knife.

knob /nɒb/ *n* [C] **1** round handle of a door, drawer, etc. **2** (*informal*) control, e g of a radio, television set, etc. **3** round swelling or mass on the surface of e g a tree trunk.

knob·bly /ˈnɒblɪ/ *adj* (-ier, -iest) having knobs(3): *~bly legs.*

knock[1] /nɒk/ *n* [C] **1** (short, sharp sound of a) blow: *He got a nasty ~ on the head when he fell. I heard a ~ at the door.* ⇨ knock[2](3). **2** sound of knocking in a petrol engine. ⇨ knock[2](3). **3** (*sl*) criticism; insult; financial loss: *He's taken a bad ~,* had an unfortunate experience.

knocker, person or thing that knocks, esp a hinged metal device on a door.

knock[2] /nɒk/ *vt,vi* **1** hit; strike; cause to be (in a certain state) by hitting; make by hitting: *Someone is ~ing at the door. He ~ed the bottom out of the box. He ~ed (= accidently hit) his head on/against the wall.* **2** (*sl*) surprise; shock: *I was ~ed flat by her news.* **3** (of a petrol engine) make a tapping or thumping noise. **4** (*sl*) criticize unfavourably: *Why must you always ~ British products?*

5 (uses with *adverbial particles* and *prepositions*):

knock sth back, (*sl*) drink: *~ back a pint of beer.*

knock sb down, strike to the ground or floor: *He was ~ed down by a bus.* **knock sth down,** (a) demolish: *These old houses are to be ~ed down.* (b) take to pieces: *The machines will be ~ed down before being packed for shipment.* (c) lower (a price): *He ~ed down the price by ten per cent.*

knock sth in, strike so that it goes in: *~ in a nail.*

knock off (work), stop work. **knock sth off,** (a) deduct: *I'll ~ 50p off the price.* (b)

compose or finish rapidly: ~ *off an article.*
(c) (*sl*) break into, rob: ~ *off a bank.*

knock sb out, (a) (in boxing) strike (an
opponent) so that he cannot rise to his feet
for the count. **(b)** (*fig*) shock: *She was* ~*ed
out by the news.*

knock (things) together, make roughly or
hastily: *The bookshelves had obviously been*
~*ed together.*

knock sb up, (*GB informal*) waken him by
knocking at his door, etc. **knock sth up, (a)**
drive upwards with a blow: *K*~ *his arm up!*
(b) arrange, put together quickly: ~ *up a
meal.* **(c)** score (runs) at cricket.

`**knock-down** *adj* (of prices, e g at an auc-
tion) lowest at which goods are to be sold.

'**knock-'kneed** *adj* having legs curved so
that the knees touch when walking.

`**knock out** *adj, n* [C] **(a)** (abbr **K O**) (blow)
that knocks a boxer out. **(b)** (in a tournament
or competition) round for eliminating
weaker competitors. **(c)** (person, thing)
impressive or attractive: *Isn't she a* ~ *out!*
(d) (*sl*) drug, etc which induces sleep or
unconsciousness: ~ *out pills.*

knoll /nəʊl/ *n* [C] small hill.

knot /nɒt/ *n* [C] **1** parts of one or more
pieces of string, rope, etc twisted together to
make a fastening: *tie/make a* ~. **2** (*fig*)
something that ties together: *the* `*marriage-*
~. **3** piece of ribbon, etc twisted and tied as
an ornament. **4** difficulty; hard problem. **5**
hard lump in wood where a branch grew out
from a bough or trunk. **6** group of persons or
things: *People were standing about in* ~*s,
anxiously waiting for news.* **7** measure of
speed for ships, one nautical mile per hour.
□ *vt,vi* (-tt-) make a knot in; tie with knots:
~ *two ropes together.*

`**knot-hole,** hole (in a board) from which a
knot(5) has come out.

knotty *adj* (-ier, -iest) full of knots. *a
knotty problem,* one that is difficult to
solve.

know[1] /nəʊ/ *vt,vi* (*pt* knew /njuː *US*: nuː/,
pp ~n /nəʊn/) **1** have in the mind as the
result of experience or of being informed, or
because one has learned: *Every child* ~*s that
two and two make four. Do you* ~ *how to
play chess? There's no* ~*ing* (= It is impossible to know) *when we shall meet again. At
your age you should* ~ *better,* be more sensible. **2** be acquainted with (a person): *Do
you* ~ *Mr Hill? I* ~ *Mr White by sight but
have never spoken to him. They're twins and
it's almost impossible to* ~ *one from the
other.* **not know sb from Adam,** have no
idea who he is. **3** have personal experience
of: *He's* ~*n better days,* has not always
been so poor, etc. **4** be able to recognize: *He*
~*s a good drama when he sees one.* **know
the ropes/a thing or two,** have practical
experience. **5** *know about/of,* have information concerning; be aware of: *I knew
about that last week.*

`**know-all,** person who knows, or (claims
to) know, everything.

`**know-how,** knowledge of methods;prac-
tical ability through experience.

know[2] /nəʊ/ *n* (only in) **in the know,**
(*informal*) having information not shared by
all or not available to all.

know·ing /ˈnəʊɪŋ/ *adj* cunning; having,
showing that one has, intelligence, sharp
wits, etc: ~ *looks.*

know·ing·ly *adv* **(a)** intentionally: *I didn't
hurt her* ~*ly.* **(b)** in a knowing way: *look
*~*ly at somebody.*

knowl·edge /ˈnɒlɪdʒ/ *n* [U] **1** understanding: *A baby has no* ~ *of good and evil.* **2**
familiarity gained by experience; range of
information: *My* ~ *of French is poor. It has
come to my* ~ (= I have been informed) *that
you have been spreading gossip about me.
To the best of my* ~ (= As far as I know) *he
is honest and reliable.*

knowl·edge·able /-əbəl/ *adj* having much
knowledge.

knuckle /ˈnʌkəl/ *n* [C] **1** bone at a finger-
joint. **2** (in animals) knee-joint, or part joining leg to foot (esp as food). □ *vi* **knuckle
down to,** (of a task, etc) apply oneself
earnestly. **knuckle under,** submit, yield.

ko·ala /kəʊˈɑːlə/ *n* [C] Australian tree-
climbing mammal, like a small bear.

Ko·ran /kəˈrɑːn *US*: kɔːˈræn/ *n* sacred book
containing the Prophet Muhammad's oral
revelations.

Ko·ranic *adj*

ko·sher /ˈkəʊʃə(r)/ *adj* fulfilling the
requirements of Jewish dietary law.

kow·tow /ˈkaʊˈtaʊ/ *vi* show great humility.

Ll

L, l /el/ (*pl* L's l's /elz/) **1** the 12th letter of the
English alphabet. **2** the Roman numeral 50.

la /lɑː/ *n* [C] sixth note of the musical scale.

lab /læb/ *n* [C] (*informal*) (abbr of) laboratory.

label /ˈleɪbəl/ *n* [C] **1** piece of paper, cloth,
metal, wood or other material used for describing what something is, where it is to go,
etc: *put* ~*s on one's luggage.* **2** short word
or phrase describing a person or thing: *the* ~
of thief. **3** (*informal*) trade name (esp of a
record company). □ *vt* (-ll-, *US* -l-) **1** put a
label on: *properly* ~*led luggage.* **2** give a
label(2) to: ~*led as untrustworthy.*

la·bial /ˈleɪbɪəl/ *adj* of, made with, the lips:
~ *sounds,* e g m, p, b.

la·bor /ˈleɪbə(r)/ *n* (*US*) = labour.

lab·ora·tory /ləˈbɒrətrɪ *US*: ˈlæbrətɔːrɪ/ *n*
[C] (*pl* -ies) room, building, for scientific

experiments, research, etc. ⇨ **language laboratory**.

la·bo·ri·ous /lə`bɔːrɪəs/ adj **1** (of work, etc) requiring great effort: a ~ *task*. **2** showing signs of great effort: a ~ *style of writing*. **3** (of persons) hard-working.
la·bo·ri·ous·ly adv

la·bour (US = **la·bor**) /`leɪbə(r)/ n **1** [U] bodily or mental work: *manual* ~. **2** [C] task; piece of work. *a labour of love*, task gladly undertaken (e g one for the good of a person one loves). **3** [U] workers as a class (contrasted with the owners of capital, etc): *skilled and unskilled* ~. **4** [U] process of childbirth: *a woman in* ~. □ vi,vt **1** work; try hard: ~ *in the cause of peace*. **2** move, breathe, slowly and with difficulty: *The old man* ~*ed up the hillside*. **3 labour under**, be the victim of, suffer because of: ~ *under a disadvantage*. **4** work out in detail; treat at great length: *There's no need to* ~ *the point*. **'hard 'labour**, hard physical work (done by criminals as a punishment).

labour leader, top official of the Labour Party or a Trade Union.

'Labour Party, one of the principal British political parties, representing socialist opinion.

'Labour re'lations, relations(3) between labour(3) and employers.

'labour-saving adj reducing the amount of physical work needed.

la·boured (US = **la·bored**) adj (a) slow and troublesome: ~*ed breathing*. (b) not easy or natural; showing too much effort: *a* ~*ed style of writing*.

la·bourer (US = **la·borer**), man who performs heavy unskilled work: `farm ~*ers*.

la·bur·num /lə`bɜːnəm/ n [C] (pl ~s) small tree with yellow flowers that hang down.

lab·yr·inth /`læbərɪnθ/ n [C] **1** network of winding paths, roads, etc which it is difficult to get through. **2** (fig) any similar confused state.
lab·yr·in·thine /ˌlæbə`rɪnθaɪn US: -θiːn/ adj

lace /leɪs/ n **1** [U] delicate material with the threads making patterns: a ~ *collar*. **2** [C] string or cord put through small holes in shoes, etc to fasten edges together: `shoe~s. □ vt,vi **1** fasten or tighten with laces(2): ~ (up) *one's shoes*. **2** put (a lace) (through holes). **3 lace with**, flavour or strengthen (a drink) (with an alcoholic spirit): *milk* ~*d with rum*.

lac·er·ate /`læsəreɪt/ vt **1** tear (the flesh). **2** (fig) hurt the feelings.
lac·er·ation /ˌlæsə`reɪʃən/ n [C,U]

lack /læk/ vt,vi **1** be without; not have; have less than enough of: *He's* ~*ing in*/*He* ~*s courage*. **2 be lacking**, be in short supply, not be available: *Money was* ~*ing to complete the building*. **3 lack for**, (formal) need: *They* ~*ed for nothing*, had everything they wanted. □ n [U] want, need, shortage: ~ *of water*.

lacka·daisi·cal /ˌlækə`deɪzɪkəl/ adj appearing tired, unenthusiastic.
lacka·daisi·cally /-klɪ/ adv

la·conic /lə`kɒnɪk/ adj (formal) using, expressed in, few words: a ~ *person/reply*.
la·coni·cally /-klɪ/ adv

lac·quer /`lækə(r)/ n [C,U] **1** (sorts of) varnish used to give a hard, bright coating to metal (esp brass). **2** kind of varnish used for wood. □ vt coat with lacquer.

la·crosse /lə`krɒs US: -`krɔːs/ n [U] outdoor game, played with a ball which is caught in, carried in, and thrown from, a racket (called a *crosse*).

lac·tic /`læktɪk/ adj of milk.

lacy /`leɪsɪ/ adj (-ier, -iest) of or like lace(1).

lad /læd/ n [C] (informal) boy; young man.

lad·der /`lædə(r)/ n [C] **1** two lengths of wood, metal or rope, with crosspieces (*rungs*), used in climbing up and down. **2** fault which looks like a ladder in a stocking. **3** (fig) scale; means of progressing: *the social* ~; ~ *of success*. □ vi (of stockings, etc) develop ladders: *Have you any tights that won't* ~?
'ladder-proof adj impossible, difficult, to ladder.

lad·die /`lædɪ/ n [C] = lad.

laden /`leɪdən/ adj weighted or burdened (with): *trees* ~ *with apples*.

la-di-da /ˌlɑː dɪ `dɑː/ adj (informal) showing unjustified social importance (esp by using affected pronunciation).

lad·ing /`leɪdɪŋ/ n [U] cargo; freight.
'bill of 'lading, details of a ship's cargo.

ladle /`leɪdəl/ n [C] large, deep, spoon for serving liquids: *a* `soup ~. □ vt serve with a ladel: ~ *out soup*. **2** (fig) distribute: ~ *out honours*.

lady /`leɪdɪ/ n [C] (pl -dies) **1** (corresponding to *gentleman*) woman belonging to the upper classes. **2** woman who has good manners. **3** (used courteously for any) woman. **4** (pl only) form of address(4), esp '*Ladies and Gentlemen*'. **5** (as an adjective) female: ~ *doctor*. **6 L~**, (title in GB) used of and to the wives of some nobles; (prefixed to Christian names) titles used of and to the daughters of some nobles. **7 Ladies** (as a sing noun) women's public lavatory: *Is there a Ladies near here?*
Our 'Lady, the Virgin Mary.
'Lady-chapel, one dedicated to the Virgin Mary.
'lady-bird, reddish-brown (sometimes yellow) flying beetle with black spots
'Lady Day, 25th March, a quarter-day.
'lady-killer, man with the reputation of being successful with women.
'lady-like adj behaving as a lady(1,2).
'Lady·ship /-ʃɪp/, used in speaking to or of a lady(6): *Your/Her L~ship*.

lag¹ /læg/ vi (-gg-) go too slow, not keep up with: ~ *behind*. □ n `time lag, period of time by which something is slower or later.

lag[2] /læg/ n [C] (sl) person convicted of crime: an old ~, one who has often been imprisoned.

lag[3] /læg/ vt (-gg-) wrap (waterpipes, cisterns, etc) with material that will prevent heat or cold from escaping.
  lag·ging; material used for this.

la·ger /ˈlɑːgə(r)/ n 1 [U] sort of light beer. 2 [C] bottle or glass of this.

lag·gard /ˈlægəd/ n [C] 1 person who lags behind. 2 person who lacks energy, enthusiasm, etc.

la·goon /ləˈguːn/ n [C] (usually shallow) lake separated from the sea by a sandbank or coral reef.

laid /leɪd/ pt,pp of lay[1].

lain /leɪn/ pp of lie[2].

lair /leə(r)/ n [C] house, sleeping-place, of a wild animal.

laird /leəd/ n (Scot) landowner.

laity /ˈleɪətɪ/ n [C] (usually with the and a pl verb) 1 all laymen. 2 those outside a particular profession, e g used by a doctor of those not trained for the medical profession.

lake /leɪk/ n [C] large area of water enclosed by land. ⇨ great lakes.
  the ˈLake District, part of N W England with many lakes.
  ˈLake Poet, poet who lived in the Lake District, e g Coleridge, Wordsworth.

lama /ˈlɑːmə/ n [C] (pl ~s) Buddhist priest in Tibet or Mongolia.
  lama·sery /ˈlɑːməsərɪ US: -serɪ/ n [C] (pl -ies) monastery of lamas.

lamb /læm/ n 1 [C] young of the sheep; [U] its flesh as food: roast ~. 2 [C] innocent, mild-mannered person. **like a lamb,** without resistance or protest. □ vi give birth to lambs: the ~ing season.
  ˈlamb·kin, newborn lamb.
  ˈlamb-skin, [C] skin of a lamb with the wool on it; [U] leather made from this.

lam·baste /ˈlæmˈbeɪst/ vt (sl) beat; scold.

lame /leɪm/ adj (-r, -st) 1 not able to walk normally because of an injury or defect. 2 (of an excuse, argument, etc) unconvincing; unsatisfactory. 3 (of the rhythm of verse) irregular, unattractive. □ vt make lame.
  lame duck, (a) disabled person on a ship. (b) business or commercial organization in financial difficulties.
  lame·ly adv
  lame·ness n [U]

lamé /ˈlɑːmeɪ US: lɑːˈmeɪ/ n [U] fabric of metal threads.

la·ment /ləˈment/ vt,vi show, feel, express, great sorrow or regret: ~ (over) the death of a friend. □ n [C] 1 expression of grief. 2 song or poem expressing grief: a funeral ~.
  lam·en·table /ˈlæməntəbəl/ adj regrettable: a ~able (= poor, unsatisfying) performance.
  lam·en·tably /-əblɪ/ adv
  lam·en·ta·tion /ˈlæmenˈteɪʃən/ n [C,U]

lami·nate /ˈlæmɪneɪt/ vt,vi 1 beat or roll

(metal, wood, etc) into thin layers. 2 make material strong by putting these layers together.

lamp /læmp/ n [C] 1 apparatus for giving light (from gas, electricity, etc). 2 apparatus for heating: a ˈspirit ~. 3 apparatus for giving a particular kind of light: an infra-red ~. 4 container with oil and a wick, used to give light.
  ˈlamp-light, light from a lamp: read by ~light.
  ˈlamp-post, post for a street light.
  ˈlamp-shade, globe of glass, plastic, etc placed round or over a lamp.

lam·poon /læmˈpuːn/ n [C] piece of writing attacking and ridiculing someone. □ vt write a lampoon.

lance[1] /lɑːns US: læns/ n [C] 1 weapon with a long wooden shaft and a pointed steel head used by a horseman. 2 similar instrument used for spearing fish.
  ˈlance-ˈcorporal, lowest grade of non-commissioned officer in the army.
  lancer, soldier of a cavalry regiment originally armed with lances.

lance[2] /lɑːns US: læns/ vt cut open with a lancet: ~ an abscess.

lan·cet /ˈlɑːnsɪt US: ˈlæn-/ n [C] 1 pointed, two-edged knife used by surgeons. 2 high, narrow, pointed arch or window.

land[1] /lænd/ n 1 [U] solid part of the earth's surface (contrasted with sea, water): travel over ~ and sea. **by land,** (travelling) by train, car, etc not by plane, ship, etc. **make land,** see, reach the shore. 2 [U] surface of the moon, a planet, etc. 3 [U] ground, earth, as used for farming, etc: working on the ~. 4 [U] (sometimes pl) property in the form of land: Do you own much ~ here? 5 [C] country (which is the usual word) and its people: my native ~. **the land of the living,** this present existence.
  ˈland-agent, person employed to look after, buy or sell land(4).
  ˈland-holder, owner or tenant of land(4).
  ˈland-lady, woman who leases property to a tenant.
  ˈland-locked, adj (a) (of a country) with no frontier at the sea. (b) (of a bay, harbour, etc) almost or completely surrounded by land.
  ˈland-lord, (a) man who leases property to a tenant. (b) owner, manager, of a public house, lodging-house, etc.
  ˈland-lubber, (used by sailors) person not used to the sea and ships.
  ˈland-mark, (a) object that marks the boundary of a piece of land. (b) object, etc easily seen by travellers and helpful to them. (c) (fig) event, change, discovery, etc that marks a stage or turning-point: ~marks in the course of social history.
  ˈland-mine, explosive put in the ground and exploded by vehicles, footsteps, etc.
  ˈland-owner, owner of land(4).

ˋland·slide, (a) sliding down of a mass of earth, rock, etc from the side of a cliff, hillside, etc. (b) sudden change in political opinion resulting in an overwhelming majority of votes for one side in an election; *a Democratic ∼slide.*

land² /lænd/ *vt,vi* 1 go, come, put, on land (from a ship, aircraft, etc): *The airliner ∼ed safely. The pilot ∼ed the airliner safely. land on one's feet,* (*fig*) be lucky; escape injury. 2 *land in,* get into (trouble, difficulties, etc): *What a mess you've ∼ed us all in! land up,* (*informal*) find oneself: *You'll ∼ up in prison one day.* 3 (*informal*) obtain: *∼ a good job.* 4 (*sl*) hit: *She ∼ed him one in the eye.*

landed *adj* (a) consisting of land: *∼ed property.* (b) owning land: *the ∼ed classes.* ˋland·less *adj*

land·ing /ˈlændɪŋ/ *n* [C] 1 act of coming or bringing to land: *The pilot made an emergency ∼.* 2 place where people and goods may be landed from a ship, etc. 3 area at the top of a flight of stairs on to which doors can open.

ˋlanding·craft, ship with an end that opens up to allow soldiers, vehicles, etc to go ashore without being lifted out.

ˋlanding·field/-strip, place for aircraft to take off from and land on.

ˋlanding·gear, undercarriage and wheels of an aircraft.

ˋlanding·stage, platform where passengers and goods from ships are landed.

land·scape /ˈlændskeɪp/ *n* 1 [C] (picture of) inland scenery. 2 [U] branch of art dealing with this.

ˋlandscape ˋgardening / ˋarchitecture, planning of parks, gardens, etc.

lane /leɪn/ *n* [C] 1 narrow country road. 2 narrow street: *Drury L∼.* 3 marked division of a road to guide motorists; line of vehicles within such a division: *the inside/outside ∼.* 4 marked division to guide competitors in a race (e g on a running track or a swimming pool). 5 passage made or left between lines of persons. 6 route regularly used by liners or aircraft.

lan·guage /ˈlæŋgwɪdʒ/ *n* 1 [U] human communication of knowledge, ideas, feelings, etc using a system of sound symbols. 2 [C] form of this used by a nation or race: *foreign ∼s.* 3 [U] words, phrases, etc used by a profession or class: *medical/legal ∼.* 4 [C] system of signs used as language: `finger ∼, as used by the deaf. 5 (*fig*) expression of feelings, etc: *the ∼ of flowers.*

ˋlanguage laboratory, place where languages are taught using tape-recorders, etc.

lan·guid /ˈlæŋgwɪd/ *adj* having no energy; slow.

lan·guid·ly *adv*

lan·guish /ˈlæŋgwɪʃ/ *vi* 1 lose health and strength: *∼ in prison.* 2 be unhappy because of a desire: *∼ for love and sympathy.*

lan·guor /ˈlæŋgə(r)/ *n* (*formal*) 1 [U] loss of strength, energy, happiness. 2 [U] stillness or heaviness: *the ∼ of a summer day.* 3 (often *pl*) loving, affectionate mood.

lan·gor·ous /-əs/ *adj*

lan·gor·ous·ly *adv*

lank /læŋk/ *adj* 1 (of hair) straight and limp. 2 (of persons) tall and lean.

lanky /ˈlæŋkɪ/ *adj* (-ier, -iest) tall and thin (and unattractive): *a ∼ girl.*

lano·lin /ˈlænəlɪn/ *n* [U] fat from sheep's wool used as a basis of ointments for the skin.

lan·tern /ˈlæntən/ *n* [C] apparatus for giving light enclosing a flame to protect it from the wind.

lan·yard /ˈlænjəd/ *n* [C] 1 cord (worn by sailors and soldiers) for a whistle or knife. 2 short rope used on a ship for fastening.

lap¹ /læp/ *n* [C] one complete journey round a track or race-course. □ *vt* (-pp-) overtake another competitor who is a lap behind.

lap² /læp/ *n* [C] front part of a person from the waist to the knees, when sitting: *The mother had the baby on her ∼. the lap of luxury,* fortunate, wealthy, state or condition.

lap³ /læp/ *vi,vt* (-pp-) 1 drink by taking up with the tongue, as a cat does. 2 (*fig*) (of human beings) take quickly or eagerly: *∼ up compliments.* 3 (of water) move with a sound like the lapping up of liquid: *waves ∼ping on the shore.* □ *n* [C] 1 act of lapping up. 2 sound of lapping: *the ∼ of the waves against the side of the boat.*

la·pel /ləˈpel/ *n* [C] part of the breast of a coat or jacket folded back and forming a continuation of the collar.

lapse /læps/ *n* [C] 1 small error in speech, behaviour, memory, etc. 2 disappearance of what is right: *a moral ∼.* 3 (of time) passing away; interval: *a long ∼ of time.* 4 (*legal*) ending of a right, etc because of failure to use it or renew it. □ *vi* 1 make a lapse(1). 2 fall (from good ways into bad ways): *lapsing into bad habits.* 3 (of time) pass: *several hours ∼d before he woke up.* 4 (*legal*) (of rights and privileges) be lost because not used or renewed.

lap·wing /ˈlæpwɪŋ/ *n* [C] bird of the plover family; pewit.

lar·ceny /ˈlɑsənɪ/ *n* (*pl* -ies) 1 [U] stealing; theft. 2 [C] instance of this.

larch /lɑtʃ/ *n* 1 [C] deciduous tree with small cones and light-green leaves. 2 [C] its wood.

lard /lɑd/ *n* [U] fat of pigs used in cooking. □ *vt* put lard on. *lard with,* (often used disapprovingly) fill with: *a speech ∼ed with boring quotations.*

lar·der /ˈlɑdə(r)/ *n* [C] room, cupboard, for storing meat and other kinds of food

large /lɑdʒ/ *adj* (-r, -st) 1 of considerable size; taking up much space; able to contain much: *A man with a ∼ family needs a ∼ house.* (*Note: large* is less informal than *big* and not so emotive as *great*. 'A great city' is large, but the use of 'great' suggests that it is also important or famous. *Large* is not often used of a person's size.) **2** generous; unprejudiced: *He has a ~ heart.* **3** not confined or restricted: *give an official ~ powers; ~ ideas.* □ *n* (only in) **at large, (a)** free: *The escaped prisoner is still at ~.* **(b)** in general: *Did the people at ~ approve of the government's policy?* **(c)** at full length; with details: *to talk/write at ~* (at *length* is more usual). □ *adv* **by and large,** ⇨ **by** [1] (2).

`large-scale *adj* **(a)** extensive: *~-scale operations.* **(b)** made or drawn to a large scale: *a ~-scale map.*

large-ish /-ɪʃ/ *adj* rather large.

large-ly *adv* to a great extent: *His success was ~ly due to luck.*

large-ness *n* [U]

lark [1] /lɑːk/ *n* [C] (kinds of) small songbird: *the sky~.*

lark [2] /lɑːk/ *n* [C] bit of fun: *He did it for a ~,* in fun. *What a ~!* How amusing! □ *vi* fool about: *Stop ~ing about and get on with your work.*

larva /ˈlɑːvə/ *n* [C] (*pl* ~e /-viː/) insect in the first stage of its development after coming out of the egg.

lar-val /ˈlɑːvəl/ *adj*.

lar-yn-gi-tis /ˌlærɪnˈdʒaɪtɪs/ *n* [U] inflammation of the larynx.

lar-ynx /ˈlærɪŋks/ *n* [C] upper part of the windpipe where the vocal cords are.

las-civ-ious /ləˈsɪvɪəs/ *adj* (*formal*) feeling, causing, showing, lust.

las-civ-ious-ly *adv*

laser /ˈleɪzə(r)/ *n* [C] device for generating, amplifying and concentrating light waves into an intense, highly directional beam.

lash [1] /læʃ/ *n* [C] **1** flexible part of a whip; blow or stroke given with a lash: *twenty ~es.* **2** = eyelash.

lash [2] /læʃ/ *vt,vi* **1** whip; strike violently; make a sudden movement of (a limb, etc): *The rain was ~ing (against) the windows. The tiger ~ed its tail angrily. He ~ed the horse across the back with his whip.* **2** **lash out (against/at) sb/sth,** attack violently (with blows or words): *He ~ed out against the government.* **3** fasten tightly (together) (with ropes, etc).

lash-ing /ˈlæʃɪŋ/ *n* **1** [C] cord or rope used for binding or fastening. **2** [C] whipping or beating. **3** (*pl*) (*informal*) plenty: *~s of cream.*

lass /læs/ *n* [C] (*informal*) girl; young woman.

las-sie /ˈlæsɪ/ *n* [C] = lass.

lassi-tude /ˈlæsɪtjuːd US: -tuːd/ *n* [U] (*formal*) tiredness; state of being uninterested.

lasso /læˈsuː/ *n* [C] (*pl* ~s, ~es) looped rope with a slipknot, used for catching horses and cattle, esp in America. □ *vt* catch with a lasso

last [1] /lɑːst US: læst/ *adj* **1** (contrasted with

first; ⇨ **late** [1]) coming after all others in time or order: *the ~ Sunday in June; the ~ time I saw you.* **'last but not `least,** coming at the end, but not least in importance. **be on one's last legs,** ⇨ **leg**(1). **have the last word,** ⇨ **word.** **2** (contrasted with *next*) coming immediately before the present: *~ night/year; on Tuesday ~.* **3** only remaining: *This is our ~ hope. I wouldn't marry you if you were the ~ person on earth.* **4** least likely, suitable, willing, desirable, etc: *That's the ~ thing I should expect him to do.* **5** final; leaving nothing more to be said or done: *That's my ~ word on the subject.* **6** latest, most up-to-date: *This is the ~ thing in labour-saving devices.* □ *adv* **1** (contrasted with *first*) after all others: *I am to speak ~ at the meeting.* **2** (contrasted with *next*) on the last occasion before the present time: *She was quite well when I saw her.* | *when I ~ saw her.* □ *n* **the ~,** that which comes at the end: *These are the ~ of our apples. I hope we've seen the ~ of her,* that we shall never see her again. **at (long) last,** in the end; after (much) delay: *At (long) ~ we reached London.*

last-ly *adv* (as in making a list) finally: *L~ly I must explain that...*

last [2] /lɑːst US: læst/ *vi* go on; be enough (for): *How long will the fine weather ~?*

last-ing *adj* continuing for a long time.

last [3] /lɑːst US: læst/ *n* [C] block of wood shaped like a foot for making shoes on.

latch /lætʃ/ *n* [C] **1** fastening for a door or gate, the bar falling into a catch and being lifted by a small lever. **2** small spring lock for a door, opened from outside. □ *vt,vi* **1** fasten with a latch. **2** **latch on (to),** (*informal*) cling to; get possession of; understand.

late [1] /leɪt/ *adj* (-r, st) ⇨ **last** [1], latter. **1** (contrasted with *early*) after the right, fixed or usual time: *Am I ~?* **2** far on in the day or night, in time, in a period or season: *in the ~ afternoon.* **3** recent; that recently was: *the ~st news/fashions.* **4** former, recent (and still living): *the ~ prime minister.* **5** former, recent (and now dead): *her ~ husband.* **6 of late,** recently. **at the latest,** before or not later than: *Be here by Monday at the ~st.*

late [2] /leɪt/ *adv* **1** (contrasted with *early*) after the usual, right, fixed or expected time: *get up/go to bed/arrive home ~.* **later on,** at a later time; afterwards. **sooner or later,** some time or other. **2** recently: *I saw him as ~ as/no ~r than yesterday.*

lat-ish /ˈleɪtɪʃ/ *adj* rather late.

late-ly /ˈleɪtlɪ/ *adv* in recent times; recently: *Have you been to the cinema ~? I saw her as ~ as last Sunday. It is only ~ that she has been well enough to go out.*

latent /ˈleɪtənt/ *adj* present but not yet active, developed or visible: *~ energy.*

lat-eral /ˈlætərəl/ *adj* of, at, from, to, the side(s).

lat-erite /ˈlætəraɪt/ *n* [U] kind of red soil

formed in the tropics.

latex /ˈleɪteks/ n [U] white liquid of (esp rubber) plants; emulsion of rubber used in paints etc.

lath /lɑːθ US: læθ/ n [C] (pl ~s /lɑːðz US: /læðz/) long, thin strip of wood, esp as used for plaster walls and ceilings.

lathe /leɪð/ n [C] **1** machine for holding and turning pieces of wood or metal while they are being shaped, etc. **2** potter's wheel.

lather /ˈlɑːðə(r) US: ˈlæð-/ n [U] **1** soft mass of white froth from soap and water. **2** frothy sweat on a horse. □ vt,vi **1** make foam on: ~ one's chin before shaving. **2** form foam.

Latin /ˈlætɪn US: ˈlætən/ adj, n (of the) language, peoples, of ancient Rome.

Latin Aˈmerica, countries of S and Central America in which Spanish and Portuguese are spoken.

the Latin Church, the Roman Catholic Church.

the Latin races/peoples, those of Italy, France, Spain, Portugal, etc.

lati-tude /ˈlætɪtjuːd US: -tuːd/ n **1** [C] distance north or south of the equator measured in degrees. **2** (pl) geographical regions or districts: warm ~s. **3** [U] (measure of) freedom in action or opinion: ~ in political belief.

lati-tudi-nal /ˈlætɪˈtjuːdməl US: -ˈtuːd-/ adj

la-trine /ləˈtriːn/ n [C] (in places where there are no sewers, e g camps) pit or ditch for human urine and excrement.

lat-ter /ˈlætə(r)/ adj **1** recent; belonging to the end (of a period): the ~ half of the year. **2** the ~, (contrasted with the former) the second of two things or persons already mentioned: Of these two men the former is dead, but the ~ is still alive.

ˈlatter-ˈday adj modern.

lat-ter-ly adv of late; nowadays.

lat-tice /ˈlætɪs/ n [C] framework of crossed laths or metal strips as a screen, fence or door, or for climbing plants to grow over: a ~ window.

lat-ticed adj

laud /lɔːd/ vt (rare except in hymns) praise; glorify.

laud-able /-əbəl/ adj deserving praise.

laud-ably /-əblɪ/ adv

lauda-tory /ˈlɔːdətərɪ US: -tɔːrɪ/ adj expressing or giving praise.

laugh /lɑːf US: læf/ vi,vt **1** make sounds and movements of the face and body, showing amusement, joy, contempt, etc: The jokes made everyone ~. **laugh at,** (a) be amused by: ~ at a joke. (b) make fun of: It's unkind to ~ at a person who is in trouble. (c) disregard; treat with indifference: ~ at difficulties. **laugh in sb's face,** show contempt for; defy. **laugh one's head off,** laugh heartily. **laugh up one's sleeve,** be secretly amused. **2** arrive at a state, obtain a result, by laughing: ~ oneself silly/helpless. □ n [C] sound, act, of laughing: We've had a good many

~s over his foolishness. **have the last laugh,** win after an earlier defeat. ⇨ belly-laugh.

laugh-able /-əbəl/ adj amusing; ridiculous: a ~able mistake.

laugh-ably /-əblɪ/ adv

laugh-ing adj showing happiness, amusement, etc: ~ing faces. □ n [U] laughter.

laugh-ter n [U] laughing: burst into ~ter.

launch[1] /lɔːntʃ/ vt,vi **1** set (a ship, esp one newly built) afloat: ~ a new passenger liner. **2** set in motion; send; aim: ~ an attack; ~ a missile/spacecraft. **3** (fig) get started; set going: ~ a new business enterprise. **4** launch (out) into, make or start (on): ~ into a new career. □ n [C] act of launching (a ship or spacecraft).

ˈlaunching-pad, base or platform from which spacecraft, etc are launched.

ˈlaunching-site, place for launching-pads.

launch[2] /lɔːntʃ/ n [C] mechanically-propelled boat (used on rivers and lakes, in harbours).

laun-der /ˈlɔːndə(r)/ vt,vi wash and press (clothes): Send these sheets to be ~ed.

laun-der-ette /ˈlɔːndəˈret/ n [C] place with coin-operated automatic washing-machines and dryers.

laun-dress /ˈlɔːndrəs/ n [C] woman who earns money by washing and ironing clothes.

laun-dry /ˈlɔːndrɪ/ n (pl -ies) **1** [C] place where clothes, sheets, etc are sent to be laundered. **2** the ~, clothes (to be) laundered: Has the ~ come back yet?

laur-eate /ˈlɔːrɪət US: ˈlɒr-/ adj crowned with a laurel wreath. ⇨ Poet Laureate.

laurel /ˈlɒrəl US: ˈlɔːrəl/ n [C] evergreen shrub with smooth, shiny leaves, used by ancient Romans and Greeks as an emblem of victory, success and distinction. **look to one's laurels,** be on the look out for possible successes among rivals. **rest on one's laurels,** be content with present achievements.

lav /læv/ n [C] (informal) (abbr of) lavatory.

lava /ˈlɑːvə/ n [U] hot liquid material flowing from a volcano: a stream of ~.

lava-tory /ˈlævətrɪ US: -tɔːrɪ/ n [C] (pl -ies) **1** toilet. **2** room for washing the hands and face in.

lav-en-der /ˈlævɪndə(r)/ adj, n [U] (of the) plant with pale purple scented flowers; (of) its colour.

ˈlavender water, scent from lavender.

lav-ish /ˈlævɪʃ/ adj **1** giving or producing freely, liberally or generously: ~ in giving money to charity. **2** (of what is given) given abundantly; excessive: ~ praise. □ vt give generously: ~ care on an only child.

lav-ish-ly adv

law /lɔː/ n **1** [C] rule made by authority for the proper regulation of a community or society or for correct conduct in life. **2** the

~, the whole body of laws considered collectively: *If a man breaks the ~ he can be punished*. **lay down the law**, talk as if one is certain of being right. **3** [U] controlling influence of the laws. **law and order**, state of respect for, keeping of, laws: ~ *and order must be maintained*. **4** [U] the laws as a system or science; the legal profession: *study* ~; `~s *students*. **5** (with a defining word) one of the branches of the study of law: *commercial/international* ~. **6** [U] operation of the law (as providing a remedy for wrongs). **take the 'law into one's own `hands**, try to get justice without legal help or disregarding the law(2). **7** [C] rule of action or procedure, esp in art or life, or a game: *the* ~s *of perspective/of tennis*. **be a law unto oneself**, disregard rules and conventions. **8** (also **law of nature** or **natural law**) factual statement of what always happens in certain circumstances; regularity in nature, e g the order of the seasons: *Newton's* ~; *the* ~ *of supply and demand*.

`**law-abiding** *adj* obeying the law(2).

`**law-breaker**, person who disobeys the law(2).

`**law court**, court of justice.

`**law list**, published list of barristers and solicitors.

`**law-maker**, legislator.

`**law report**, account of legal proceedings of a lawsuit.

`**Law Society**, one which controls the legal profession and sets examinations for law students.

`**law-suit**, case in a law court.

law-ful /-fəl/ *adj* (a) allowed by law; according to law: ~*ful acts*. (b) (of offspring) legitimate: *the* ~*ful heir*.

law-fully /-fəlɪ/ *adv*

law-less *adj* not according to, not conforming to, the law.

law-less-ly *adv*

law-less-ness *n* [U]

lawn[1] /lɔːn/ *n* [C] **1** area of grass cut short and smooth, e g in a garden or park. **2** such an area of grass used for a game: *a* `*tennis* ~.

`**lawn-mower**, machine for cutting grass.

`**lawn 'tennis**, played on a grass court.

lawn[2] /lɔːn/ *n* [U] kind of fine linen.

law-yer /'lɔːjə(r)/ *n* [C] person who practises law, esp an attorney or solicitor.

lax /læks/ *adj* **1** negligent; inattentive; not strict or severe: ~ *in morals*. **2** (of the bowels) free in action.

lax-ity /'læksətɪ/ *n* [C,U]

lax-ly *adv*

laxa-tive /'læksətɪv/ *n* [C], *adj* (medicine, drug) causing the bowels to empty.

lay[1] /leɪ/ *adj* **1** of, for, done by, persons who are not priests: *a* ~ *brother/sister*, one who has taken religious vows but who does manual work and is excused other duties. ⇨ **laity**. **2** non-professional; not expert (esp

with reference to the law and medicine): ~ *opinion*, what non-professional people think

`**lay-man**, lay person.

lay[2] /leɪ/ *vt,vi* (*pt,pp* laid /leɪd/) For uses with *adverbial particles* and *prepositions* ⇨ **11** below. **1** put on a surface; put in a certain position: *He laid his hand on my shoulder*. **2** (of non-material things, and *fig*) place; put. **lay (one's) hands on sth/sb**, (a) seize; get possession of: *He keeps everything he can* ~ (*his*) *hands on*. (b) do violence to: *How dare you* ~ *hands on me?* (c) find: *The book is somewhere, but I can't* ~ *my hands on it just now*. (d) confirm; ordain (a person) as a deacon or priest by the laying on of hands (as a bishop does) or consecrate (a person) as a bishop (as an archbishop does). **lay the blame (for sth) on sb**, say that he is responsible for what is wrong, etc. **3** cause to be in a certain state, condition, or situation. **lay sb to rest**, bury him. **lay claim to sth**, ⇨ **claim**. **lay sth at sb's door**, ⇨ **door**. **lay one's finger on**, ⇨ **finger**. **lay siege to**, ⇨ **siege**. **4** cause to be in a specified condition. **lay sth bare**, show; reveal: ~ *bare one's heart*, reveal one's inmost feelings, etc. **lay sth flat**, cause to be flat: *crops laid flat by heavy rainstorms*. **be laid low**, be ill in bed: *I've been laid low by influenza*. **lay sth open**, (esp) expose, reveal: ~ *open a plot*. **lay oneself open to sth**, expose oneself to criticism, etc. **lay sth waste**, ravage, destroy: *a countryside laid waste by invading armies*. **5** cause to be down, settle: *sprinkle water on the roads to* ~ *the dust*. **6** place or arrange (ready for use, etc): ~ *a carpet*; ~ *the table* (*for breakfast*), put out plates, knives, etc; *lay a fire*, make it ready for lighting. **7** put down (a sum of money) as a bet: *I'll* ~ *you a hundred to one that...* **8** (of birds and insects) produce (an egg): *Are your hens* ~*ing yet?* **9** (usually passive) set (a story, etc) in time and place: *The scene is laid in Athens, in the third century, B* C. **10** cover; coat: ~ *colours on canvas*. ⇨ **lay on** below.

11 (uses with *adverbial particles* and *prepositions*):

lay sth aside, (a) save; keep for future use: ~ *aside money for one's old age*. (b) put down: *He laid his book aside to listen to me*.

lay sth by, = lay sth aside(a).

lay sb/oneself down, place in a lying position. **lay sth down**, (a) pay or wager: *How much are you ready to* ~ *down?* (b) (begin to) build: ~ *down a new ship*. (c) convert (land) to pasture: ~ *down land to grass*. (d) store (wine) in a cellar: ~ *down claret and port*. **lay down one's arms**, put one's weapons down as a sign of surrender. **lay down the law**, say with (or as if with) authority what must be done. **lay down one's life**, sacrifice it: *He laid down his life for his country*.

lay sth in, provide oneself with a stock of:

~ in provisions/stores.

lay into sb, (a) assault, attack. (b) criticize.

lay off, (informal) (a) discontinue: The doctor told me to ~ off work for a week. (b) stop doing something which annoys: You've been seeing my sister again—Well, you can just ~ off. **lay sb off,** dismiss temporarily: ~ off workmen, e g because of a shortage of materials. Hence, ᐟlay-off n period during which men are laid off.

lay sth on, (a) supply services to a building: Are gas and water laid on? (b) (informal) provide: A party was laid on for the visitors. **lay it on (thick/with a trowel),** use exaggerated praise, flattery, etc.

lay sth out, (a) spread out ready for use or so as to be seen easily: ~ out one's evening clothes. (b) prepare for burial: ~ out a corpse. (c) spend (money): ~ out on a new suit. (d) make a plan for; arrange well: well-laid out streets and avenues. Hence, ᐟlay-out n arrangement, plan of a printed page, a factory etc.

lay sth up, (a) save; store: ~ up provisions. (b) ensure by what one does or fails to do that one will have trouble, etc in future: ~ing up trouble for yourself. (c) put (a ship) out of commission: ~ a ship up for repairs. **be laid up,** forced to stay in bed: He's laid up with a broken leg.

lay·about /ˈleɪəbaʊt/ n [C] (GB sl) person who avoids working for a living.

lay·by /ˈleɪbaɪ/ n [C] (GB modern use) area at the side of a road where vehicles may park.

layer /ˈleɪə(r)/ n [C] 1 thickness of material (esp one of several) laid or lying on or spread over a surface, or forming one horizontal division: a ~ of clay. 2 (of hens): good/bad ~s, laying eggs in large/small numbers. 3 person who bets against and on a horse, etc.

lay·ette /leɪˈet/ n [C] outfit for a newborn baby.

lay·man ⇨ lay¹.

laze /leɪz/ vi,vt be lazy: lazing away the afternoon.

lazy /ˈleɪzɪ/ adj (-ier, -iest) unwilling to work; doing little work; suitable for, causing, inactivity: a ~ girl; a ~ afternoon. ⇨ idle.

ᐟlazy-bones, lazy person.

lazi·ly adv

lazi·ness n [U]

lea /li/ n [C] (poetic) stretch of open grassland.

lead¹ /led/ n 1 [U] soft, heavy, easily melted metal (symbol Pb) used for pipes, etc; its colour, dull blue-grey. 2 [U] (stick of) graphite as used in a lead-pencil. 3 [C] lump of lead(1) on a line marked in fathoms for measuring the depth of the sea from ships. ᐟlead ᐟpoisoning, diseased condition caused by taking lead(1) into the body.

lead shot, ⇨ shot¹ (5).

leaded adj secured with strips of lead: ~ed windows.

leaden /ˈledən/ adj (a) made of lead. (b) having the colour or appearance of lead: ~en clouds. (c) dull and heavy: a ~en heart.

lead² /lid/ n 1 (sing with the or a, an) action of guiding or giving an example; direction given by going in front; something that helps or hints. **take the lead,** take the leading place; give an example. 2 (with the) first place or position: have/gain the ~ in a race. (with a, an) distance by which one leads: an actual ~ of ten feet. 3 [C] cord, leather strap, for leading a dog. 4 [C] principal part in a play; actor or actress who plays such a part. 5 [C] (in card games) act or right of playing first: Whose ~ is it? 6 [C] conductor conveying electricity current.

lead³ /lid/ vt,vi (pt,pp led /led/) 1 guide or take, esp by going in front. **lead the way (to),** go first; show the way. 2 guide the movement of (a person, etc) by the hand, by touching him, or by a rope, etc: ~ a blind man/a horse. **lead sb astray,** (fig) tempt him to do wrong. 3 act as chief; direct by example or persuasion; direct the movements of: ~ an army/an expedition/the Conservative Party. 4 have the first place in; go first: Which horse is ~ing, e g in a race? 5 guide the actions and opinions of; influence; persuade: What led you to think that? 6 be a path, way or road to: Where does this road ~? (fig) have as a result: The change of plan led to great confusion. **lead up to,** be a preparation for or an introduction to: That's just what I was ~ing up to. 8 (cause a person to) pass, spend (his life, etc): ~ a miserable existence. 9 (in card games) put down, as first player (a certain card or kind of card): ~ trumps. 10 have as the main article of news: We'll ~ with the dock strike.

leader /ˈlidə(r)/ n [C] 1 person who leads: the ~ of an army/an expedition/the Labour Party. 2 principal counsel in a law court case: the ~ for the defence. 3 (GB) leading article (in a newspaper).

leader·less adj

leader·ship, being a leader; power of, qualities of, a leader.

lead·ing /ˈlidɪŋ/ adj chief; most important: the ~ men of the day; the ~ lady, the actress with the chief part in a play. ▫ n [U] act of leading.

ᐟleading ᐟarticle, (in a newspaper) one giving editorial opinions on events, policies, etc.

ᐟleading ᐟlight, (informal) prominent or outstanding person.

ᐟleading ᐟquestion, one formed to suggest the answer that is hoped for.

leaf /lif/ n [C] (pl leaves /livz/) 1 one of the parts (usually green and flat) growing from the side of a stem or branch or direct from the root of a tree, bush, plant, etc: The trees *will soon be in* ~. **2** single sheet of paper forming two pages of a book. *turn over a new leaf,* (*fig*) make a new and better start. **3** hinged flap, etc of a table (used to make it larger). **4** [U] very thin sheet of metal, esp of gold or silver: *gold* ~. □ *vi: leaf through* (*a book, etc*), turn over the pages quickly; glance through.

leafy *adj* (-ier, -iest) covered with, having, made by, leaves: *a* ~*y shade*.

leaf·let /'liflət/ *n* [C] printed sheet (sometimes folded) with announcements, etc esp one for free distribution.

league¹ /liːg/ *n* [C] former measure of distance (about three miles or 4·8 kms).

league² /liːg/ *n* [C] **1** agreement made between persons, groups or nations for their common welfare, e g to work for peace; the parties that make such an agreement. *in league with,* having made an agreement with. **2** group of sports clubs or teams playing matches among themselves: *the* `*football* ~. □ *vt,vi* form into, become, a league: *countries that are* ~*d together.*

the League of Nations, that formed in 1919 after the First World War, dissolved in 1946. ⇨ United Nations.

leak /liːk/ *n* [C] **1** hole, crack, etc caused by wear, injury, etc through which a liquid, gas, etc may wrongly get in or out: *a* ~ *in the roof.* **2** (*fig*) instance of leaking(2): *a* ~ *of secret information.* **3** the liquid, gas, etc that gets out or in. □ *vi,vt* **1** (allow to) pass out or in through a leak: *The rain is* ~*ing in.* **2** (of news, secrets, etc) (cause to) become known by chance or deliberately: *Who* ~*ed the news to the press?*

leak·age /-ɪdʒ/ *n* [C,U]

leaky *adj* (-ier, -iest) having a leak.

lean¹ /liːn/ *adj* (-er, -est) **1** (of persons and animals) having less than the usual proportion of fat; (of meat) containing little or no fat. **2** not productive; of poor quality: *a* ~ *harvest.* □ *n* [U] meat with little or no fat.

lean·ness *n* [U]

lean² /liːn/ *vi,vt* (*pt,pp* ~ed or ~ /lent/) **1** be or put in a sloping position: ~ *backwards;* ~ *out of a window. lean over backward(s) (to do sth),* (*informal*) make too great an effort. **2** rest in a sloping position for support: ~ *on one's elbows.* **3** cause to rest against and be supported by: ⇨ *a ladder against a wall.* **4** *lean towards,* have a tendency: *Does the Labour Party* ~ *towards socialism?* **5** depend: ~ *on a friend's advice.*

lean·ing *n* [C] tendency (of mind *towards*): *He has pacifist* ~*ings.*

leap /liːp/ *vi,vt* (*pt,pp* ~ed /lept/ or ~t /lept/) **1** = jump (the usual word): *He* ~*t at the opportunity,* seized it eagerly. *Look before you leap,* ⇨ look²(1). **2** (cause to) jump over: ~ *a wall.* □ *n* [C] sudden upward or forward movement: *a great* ~ *forward,* (*fig*) a great advance. *by leaps and*

bounds, very rapidly.

`**leap-frog** *n* [U] game in which players jump with parted legs over others who stand with bent backs. □ *vt* (-gg-) jump over in this way.

`**leap-year,** in which February has 29 days.

learn /lɜːn/ *vt,vi* (*pt,pp* ~t /lɜːnt/, ~ed) **1** gain knowledge of or skill in, by study, practice or being taught: ~ *a foreign language;* ~ *to swim/how to ride a horse. learn sth by heart,* memorize it. **2** be told or informed: *We haven't yet* ~*ed if he arrived safely.*

learned /'lɜːnɪd/ *adj* having or showing much knowledge: ~*ed men/books/ members/societies.*

learn·ed·ly *adv*

learner, person who is learning.

learn·ing *n* [U] (knowledge gained by) study.

lease /liːs/ *n* [C] contract by which the owner of land or a building (*the lessor*) agrees to let another (*the lessee*) have the use of it for a certain time for a fixed money payment (*rent*); the rights given under such a contract: *When does the* ~ *expire? get/give sb a new* '*lease of* '*life,* a better chance of living longer, or of being happier, etc. □ *vt* give, take possession of (land, etc), by lease.

`**lease·hold** *n* [U], *adj* (land) (to be) held on lease. ⇨ freehold.

`**lease·holder,** person who has a lease.

leash /liːʃ/ *n* [C] leather strap or thong for holding or controlling an animal.

least /liːst/ *adj, n* [U] (contrasted with *most;* ⇨ less, little) smallest in size, amount extent, etc: *A has little, B has less, and C has* (*the*) ~. *That's the* ~ *of my anxieties. at least:* It will cost at ~ five pounds, five pounds and perhaps more. *(not) in the least:* It doesn't matter in the ~. *to say the least (of it),* without saying more: *It's not a very good record, to say the* ~ *of it.* □ *adv* to the smallest extent: *This is the* ~ *useful of the four books. least of all:* None of you can complain, *Charles* ~ *of all,* Charles has the least reason for complaining.

`**least-wise** /-waɪz/, `**least-ways** /-weɪz/ *adv* (or) at least.

leather /'leðə(r)/ *n* [U] material from animal skins, used for making shoes, bags, etc.

leathery *adj* like leather: ~*y meat,* hard, tough.

leave¹ /liːv/ *vt,vi* (*pt,pp* left /left/) **1** go away from: *It's time for us to* ~/*time we left. leave for,* go away to: *We're leaving for Rome next week.* **2** go away finally or permanently; no longer live (in a place); cease to belong to a school, society, etc; give up working for (an employer, etc): *When did you* ~ *school?* **3** neglect or fail to take, bring or do something: *Leave my books on the table. leave sb/sth behind,* (deliberately) forget to bring or take: *Don't* ~ *me behind!* **4** allow or cause to remain in a certain place or condition: *Who left that window open? Don't ~ her waiting outside in the rain.* **leave sb/sth alone,** not touch, spoil or interfere with: *L~ me alone.* **leave off,** stop: *Has the rain left off yet?* **leave sth off,** (a) stop: *It's time to ~ off work.* (b) no longer wear: *They left off their vests when the weather got warm.* **leave sth/sb out,** omit; fail to consider: *Don't ~ me out, please!* **leave sth over,** postpone: *That matter can be left over until the committee meets next week.* **5** (cause to) remain; allow to remain: *Three from seven ~s four (7 − 3 = 4). When I've paid all my debts, there'll be nothing left/I'll have nothing left.* **6** hand over (before going away): *Did the postman ~ anything for me?* **7** entrust; commit; hand over: *I'll ~ the matter in your hands/~ it to you. He left his assistant in charge of the shop.* **8** bequeath by will; have at the time of one's death: *He left me £500. He ~s a widow and two sons.* **9** pass beyond (a place, etc) so that it is in the direction or relation shown: *L~ the church on your right and go on up the hill.*

leave² /liːv/ *n* **1** [U] permission; consent; authority, esp to be absent from duty: *You have my ~ to stay away from the office tomorrow.* **on leave,** absent with permission: *He went home on ~.* **2** [C] period, occasion, of such absence: *a six months' ~.* **3** (*sing* only) departure. **take (one's) leave (of sb),** (*formal*) say goodbye. **take leave of one's senses,** behave as if mad. **'leave of 'absence,** permission to be absent.

leaven /ˈlevən/ *n* [U] substance, e g yeast, used to make dough rise before it is baked to make bread. □ *vt* add leaven to: act like leaven on.

leaves /liːvz/ *pl* of **leaf**.

leavings /ˈliːvɪŋz/ *n pl* what is left, esp something unwanted such as unwanted food.

lech·er·ous /ˈletʃərəs/ *adj* having, giving way to, strong sexual desires.

lecher /ˈletʃə(r)/, lecherous man.

lech·ery /ˈletʃəri/ *n* [C,U]

lec·tern /ˈlektən/ *n* [C] tall, sloping reading-desk.

lec·ture /ˈlektʃə(r)/ *n* [C] talk for the purpose of teaching: *a course of philosophy ~s.* **give sb a lecture,** scold or reprove him. □ *vi,vt* give a lecture (course): *~ on modern drama.* **lecture sb (for),** scold; reprove: *~d for being lazy.*

lec·turer, person, lower in rank than a professor, who gives lectures, esp at a college or university.

lec·ture·ship, position as a lecturer.

led /led/ *pt,pp* of **lead³**.

ledge /ledʒ/ *n* [C] **1** narrow shelf coming out from a wall, cliff or other upright surface: *a 'window ~.* **2** ridge of rocks under water, esp near the shore.

ledger /ˈledʒə(r)/ *n* [C] **1** book in which a business firm's accounts are kept. **2** (*music*)

'~ (or '*leger*) *line,* short line added above or below the stave to increase its range.

lee /liː/ *n* [C,U] (place giving) protection against wind. □ *adj* of or on the side away from the wind.

leech /liːtʃ/ *n* [C] **1** small blood-sucking worm living in wet places of which one kind was formerly used by doctors for bleeding patients. **2** (*fig*) person who sucks profit out of others.

leek /liːk/ *n* [C] vegetable like an onion with a long, slender white bulb.

leer /lɪə(r)/ *n* [U] sly, unpleasant look that suggests evil desire. □ *vi* look with a leer: *~ing at his neighbour's wife.*

lee·ward /ˈliːwəd (among sailors) ˈluːəd/ *adj, adv, n* [U] (on or to the) sheltered side (contrasted with *windward*).

lee·way /ˈliːweɪ/ *n* [U] **1** sideways drift (of a ship) in the direction towards which the wind is blowing. **2** small amount of freedom of action, expenditure, etc. **make up leeway,** (*fig*) make up for lost time; get back into position.

left¹ *pt,pp* of **leave**.

left² /left/ *adj, adv, n* [U] (opposite of *right*) (of, in, on, the) side of a person's body which is towards the west when he faces north: *The ~ bank of a river is on your ~ as you face the direction in which it flows.*

'left-'hand *adj* of, situated on, the left side: *a house on the ~-hand side of the street.*

'left-'handed *adj* (of a person) using the left hand more easily or with more skill than the right. **a left-handed compliment,** one that is of doubtful sincerity.

the Left (Wing), more radical group(s), party or parties, e g socialists, communists: (as an *adjective*): *~-wing militants.*

'left·ist /-ɪst/ *n* [C], *adj* (supporter) of socialism or radicalism.

leg /leg/ *n* [C] **1** one of the parts of an animal's or a person's body used for walking, esp (of a human body) the part above the foot. **be on one's last legs,** exhausted; near one's death or end. **pull sb's leg,** deceive him for fun. **show a leg,** (*informal*) (a) get out of bed. (b) make more effort. **not have a leg to stand on,** have nothing to support one's opinion, defence, etc. **stretch one's legs,** go for a walk. **2** that part of a garment that closely covers a leg: *the ~s of a pair of trousers; a 'trouser-~.* **3** support of a chair, table, etc: *a chair with four ~. on its last legs,* weak and likely to collapse. **4** one section of a journey, esp by air: *the first ~ of a round-the-world flight.* **5** one of a series of games in a competition.

leg·less *adj* having no legs.

leg·acy /ˈlegəsi/ *n* [C] (*pl* -ies) **1** money, etc (to be) received by a person under the will of and at the death of another person. **2** (*fig*) something handed down from ancestors or predecessors: *a ~ of firm government.*

legal /ˈliːgəl/ *adj* connected with, in accordance with, authorized or required by, the law. ~ *affairs*. **take legal action,** ⇨ action.

ˈlegal ˈtender, form of money which must be accepted as payment.

legally /ˈliːgəlɪ/ *adv*

legal·ity /lɪˈgælɪtɪ/ *n* [C,U] state or quality of being legal: *the ~ of an act*.

legal·ize /ˈliːgəlaɪz/ *vt* make legal: ~ *the sale of alcoholic drinks*.
legal·iz·ation /ˈliːgəlaɪˈzeɪʃn US: -lɪˈz-/ *n* [U]

leg·ation /lɪˈgeɪʃn/ *n* [C] (house, offices, etc, of a) diplomatic minister below the rank of ambassador, with those under him, representing his government in a foreign country.

leg·end /ˈledʒənd/ *n* **1** [C] old story handed down from the past, esp one of doubtful truth: *the Greek ~s*. **2** [U] literature of such stories: *heroes who are famous in ~*. **3** [C] inscription on a coin or medal; explanatory words on a map, a picture, etc.

leg·end·ary /ˈledʒəndrɪ US: -derɪ/ *adj* famous, known only, in legends: ~*ary heroes*.

leger /ˈledʒə(r)/ ⇨ ledger(2).

leg·gings /ˈleɡɪŋz/ *n pl* outer covering, of leather or strong cloth, for the leg up to the knee, or (for small children) for the whole of the leg: *a pair of ~s*.

leggy /ˈleɡɪ/ *adj* (-ier, -iest) (esp of young children, colts, etc) having long legs.

leg·ible /ˈledʒəbl/ *adj* (of handwriting, print) that can be read easily.
leg·ibly /-əblɪ/ *adv*
legi·bil·ity /ˈledʒəˈbɪlətɪ/ *n* [U]

legion /ˈliːdʒən/ *n* [C] **1** division of several thousand men in the armies of ancient Rome. **2** great number (of armed men). **3** any great number or number
British Legion, national association of ex-servicemen formed in 1921.
(French) Foreign Legion, body of non-French volunteers who serve in the French army, usually overseas.
Legion of Honour, high French decoration (civilian and military).
legion·ary /ˈliːdʒənərɪ US: -nerɪ/ *n* [C] (*pl* -ies), *adj* (member) of a legion, esp the (French) Foreign Legion.

legis·late /ˈledʒɪsleɪt/ *vi* make laws: ~ *against gambling*.
legis·la·tion /ˈledʒɪsˈleɪʃn/ *n* [U].

legis·la·tive /ˈledʒɪslətɪv US: -leɪtɪv/ *adj* of, having the function of, making laws: ~ *reforms/assemblies*.

legis·la·tor /ˈledʒɪsleɪtə(r)/ *n* [C] member of a legislative body.

legis·la·ture /ˈledʒɪsleɪtʃə(r)/ *n* [C] assembly which makes laws, e g Parliament in GB.

le·git·imacy /lɪˈdʒɪtɪməsɪ/ *n* [U] being legitimate.

le·git·imate /lɪˈdʒɪtɪmət/ *adj* **1** lawful, regular: *the ~ king*. **2** reasonable; that can be justified: *a ~ reason for being absent from work*. **3** born of persons married to one another; the result of lawful marriage: *of ~ birth*.
le·git·imate·ly *adv*
le·git·ima·tize /lɪˈdʒɪtɪmətaɪz/ *vt* make legitimate.

leg·umin·ous /lɪˈgjuːmɪnəs/ *adj* of, like, the botanical family that includes peas and beans (and other seeds in pods).

lei·sure /ˈleʒə(r) US: ˈliːʒər/ *n* [U] spare time; time free from work.
lei·sure·ly *adv* without hurrying: *work ~ly*. □ *adj* unhurried: ~*ly movements*.

lemon /ˈlemən/ *n* [C] (tree with a) pale yellow fruit with acid juice used for drinks and flavouring: [U] colour of this fruit.
ˈlemon ˈcurd, jam made from lemons boiled with sugar.
ˈlemon ˈsquash, drink of lemon-juice and water or soda-water.
ˈlemon squeezer, device for pressing juice out of a lemon.

lem·on·ade /ˈleməˈneɪd/ *n* [C,U] drink made from lemon-juice, sugar and water.

lemur /ˈliːmə(r)/ *n* [C] (kinds of) nocturnal animal similar to a monkey but with a face like a fox.

lend /lend/ *vt* (*pt,pp* lent /lent/) **1** give (a person) the use of (something) on the understanding that it or its equivalent will be returned: *I will ~ you £100*. **lend a hand (with sth),** help. **2** contribute: *facts that ~ probability to a theory*. **3** help or serve: *This hot weather ~s itself to* (= is favourable for) *sleeping*.
lender, person who lends.

length /leŋθ/ *n* [C] **1** measurement from end to end (space or time): *a river 300 miles in ~; the ~ of time needed for the work*. **at length, (a)** at last; finally. **(b)** for a long time: *speak at (great) ~*. **(c)** in detail; thoroughly: *treat a subject at ~*. **2** measurement of a particular thing from end to end: *The horse won by a ~*, by its own length, this being used as a unit of measurement. **3** extent; extreme. **go to any length(s),** do anything necessary to get what one wants. **4** piece of cloth, etc long enough for a purpose: *a ˈdress ~; a ~ of tubing/pipe*.

lengthen /ˈleŋθən/ *vt,vi* make or become longer: ~*en a skirt. The days ~en in March*.

ˈlength·wise /-waɪz/, **ˈlength·ways** /-weɪz/ *adv, adj* in the direction from end to end.

lengthy *adj* (-ier, -iest) (of speech, writing) very long; too long.

leni·ent /ˈliːnɪənt/ *adj* not severe (esp in punishing people): ~ *towards juvenile offenders*.
leni·ence /-əns/, **leni·ency** /-ənsɪ/ *n* [U] being lenient.

leni·ent·ly adv

lens /lenz/ n [C] (pl ∼es) **1** piece of glass or substance like glass with one or both sides curved, for use in spectacles, cameras, telescopes and other optical instruments. **2** transparent part of the eye through which light is refracted.

lent /lent/ pt,pp of lend.

Lent /lent/ n (in Christian Churches) annual period of forty days before Easter, observed by devout persons as a period of fasting and penitence.

Lenten /ˈlentən/ adj of Lent: ∼en services.

len·til /ˈlentəl/ n [C] kind of bean plant; edible seed of this: ∼ soup.

Leo /ˈliːəʊ/ n the lion, the fifth sign of the zodiac.

leop·ard /ˈlepəd/ n [C] large African and South Asian flesh-eating animal of the cat family with a yellow coat and dark spots.

leop·ard·ess /ˈlepəˈdes/ n [C] female leopard.

leper /ˈlepə(r)/ n [C] person suffering from leprosy.

lep·rosy /ˈleprəsɪ/ n [U] skin disease that forms scales on the skin, causes local insensibility to pain, etc and the loss of fingers and toes.

lep·rous /ˈleprəs/ adj of, having, leprosy.

les·bian /ˈlezbɪən/ n [C] homosexual woman.

lesion /ˈliːʒən/ n [C] **1** wound. **2** harmful change in the tissues of a bodily organ, caused by injury or disease.

less /les/ adj (contrasted with more) **1** not so much; a smaller quantity of: ∼ butter/ food/speed. **2** less than, I have ∼ money than you. □ adv **1** to a smaller extent; not so much: Eat ∼, drink ∼, and sleep more. **2** not so: Tom is ∼ clever than his brother. **3** the less, (as in): The ∼ you worry about it the better it will be. ⇨ the. no less, (as in): He won no ∼ than £50 (expressing surprise at the amount). even/still less, (as in): I don't suspect him of robbery, still ∼ of robbery with violence. none the less, all the same: Though he cannot leave the house, he is none the ∼ busy and active. □ n smaller amount, quantity, time, etc: in ∼ than an hour; ∼ than £50. □ prep minus; without: £50 a week ∼ £10 for the rent.

-less /-ləs/ suffix (noun + ∼ = adjective) without: priceless.

-lessly /-ləslɪ/ adv

-lessness /-ləsnəs/ n

les·see /leˈsiː/ n [C] ⇨ lease.

les·sen /ˈlesən/ vt,vi **1** make or become less: to ∼ the impact/effect. **2** cause (something) to appear smaller, less important: ∼ a person's contribution.

les·ser /ˈlesə(r)/ adj not so great as the other: choose the ∼ evil. to a lesser extent, lower, smaller, in range, importance, value, etc.

les·son /ˈlesən/ n [C] **1** something to be learnt or taught; period of time given to learning or teaching: `English ∼s. **2** (pl) children's education in general: Tom is very fond of his ∼s. **3** something serving as an example or a warning: Let his fate be a ∼ to you all! **4** passage from the Bible read aloud during a church service.

les·sor /lesˈɔ(r)/ n [C] ⇨ lease.

lest /lest/ conj (dated) **1** for fear that; in order that... not: He ran away ∼ he should be seen. **2** (after fear, be afraid, anxious) that: We were afraid ∼ he arrive too late.

let [1] /let/ vt,vi (pt,pp ∼) (-tt-) (For uses with adverbial particles and prepositions ⇨ **6** below.) **1** allow (to): Her father will not ∼ her go to the dance. Her father won't let her (go). **let alone**, (informal) not to mention: There were five people in the car, ∼ alone the luggage and the two dogs! **let oneself go**, no longer hold back one's feelings, desires, etc. **let it go at that**, say or do no more about it: I disagree but we'll ∼ it go at that. **let sb know**, inform him. **live and let live**, ⇨ live [2] (2). **let sb/sth loose**, release him/it. **let sth pass**, disregard it. **2** (used in imperatives or to order): ∼'s go! Don't ∼'s start yet! ∼ her do it at once. ∼ me be! Stop annoying/holding me! **3** (of permission or an assumption): L∼ A B be equal to C D. L∼ them all come! **4** give the use of (buildings, land) in return for regular money payments: This house is to be ∼. **5** (in surgery) **let blood**, cause it to flow. Hence, `blood-letting n

6 (uses with adverbial particles and prepositions):

let sth down, lower; put or take down: Please ∼ the window down. This skirt needs ∼ting down, lengthening by lowering the hemline. **let sb down**, (fig) disappoint; fail to help: Harry will never ∼ you down. Hence, `let-down, n disappointment. **let the side down**, ⇨ side [1] (10).

let sb/sth in/into sth, allow to enter: Windows ∼ in the light and air. Who ∼ you into the building? **let sb in for**, involve in loss, difficulty, hard work, etc: He didn't realise how much work he was ∼ting himself in for when he became secretary of the society.

let sb into/in on, allow to share (a secret): She has been ∼ into (= told) the secret.

let sb off, excuse; not punish (severely): He was ∼ off with a fine instead of being sent to prison. Hence, `let-off, n escape (from punishment). **let sth off**, explode: The boys were ∼ting off fireworks.

let `on (that), (informal) reveal a secret: He knew where the boy was but he didn't ∼ on.

let sb/sth out, allow to go (flow, etc) out: He ∼ the air out of the tyres. **let sth out**, make (a garment, etc) looser, larger, etc: He's getting so fat that his trousers need to be ∼ out round the waist.

let sb/sth through, allow to pass (an

examination, etc): *He got only 40%, so the examiners couldn't possibly ~ him through.*
let up, become less strong, etc: *Will the rain never ~ up? Hence,* **'let-up,** (*informal*): *There has been no ~-up in the rain yet.*

let² /let/ *n* [C] (from let ¹(4)) lease: *I can't find a ~ for my house,* can find no one willing to rent it from me.
let·ting, property that is let: *a furnished ~ting.*

let³ /let/ *vt* (*archaic*) hinder; obstruct. □ *n* [C] **1** hindrance, esp in the legal phrase: *without ~ or hindrance.* **2** (*tennis*) ball which when served, hits the net before dropping into the opponent's court.

-let /-lət/ *suffix* small: *booklet; piglet.*

lethal /'liːθəl/ *adj* causing, designed to cause, death: *a ~ dose of poison.*

leth·argy /'leθədʒɪ/ *n* [U] (state of) being tired, uninterested.
leth·ar·gic /lɪ'θɑːdʒɪk/ *adj*
leth·ar·gi·cally /-klɪ/ *adv*

let's /lets/ = *let us.* ⇨ **let ¹**(2).

let·ter /'letə(r)/ *n* [C] **1** character or sign representing a sound, of which words in writing are formed: *capital ~s* (A, B, C, etc) *and small ~s*(a, b, c, etc). *Do you have any ~s* (e g B A) *after your name?* **2** written message, request, account of events, etc sent by one person to another: *I have some ~s to write.* **to the letter,** paying strict attention to the actual wording, to every detail: *carry out an order to the ~.* **3** (*pl*) literature and learning: *a man of ~s.*
'letter-box, (a) slot in a door for letters. **(b)** box (in the street, at a post office) in which letters are posted. **(c)** box (in a building) for receiving letters from the post.
'letter·head, (sheet of paper with a) printed name and address, e g of a business firm.
let·ter·ing /'letərɪŋ/ *n* [U] letters, words, esp with reference to their style and size: *the ~ing on a book cover.*

let·tuce /'letɪs/ *n* [C] garden plant with crisp green leaves used in salads; [U] these leaves as food.

leu·ke·mia /luːˈkiːmɪə/ *n* [U] (usually fatal) disease in which there are too many white blood-cells causing anaemia.

level¹ /'levəl/ *adj* **1** having a horizontal surface: *~ ground.* **2** on an equality: *draw ~ with the other runners.* **3 have a level head,** be well-balanced, able to judge well. Hence, **'level-'headed** *adj.* **do one's level best,** do everything possible.
level crossing, place where a road and a railway cross on the same level.

level² /'levəl/ *n* **1** [C] line or surface parallel with the horizon; such a surface with reference to its height: *1 000 metres above sea ~.* **2** natural or right position, stage, social standing, etc: *He has found his own ~,* (*fig*) has found the kind of people with whom he is morally, socially or intellectually equal. **3** [U] (group of persons having) equal position

or rank: *top-~ talks,* talks between persons in the highest positions (in government, etc). **4 on the level,** (*informal*) honest(ly); straightforward(ly): *Is he on the ~?*

O-/A-level (examination), level of achievement (Ordinary/Advanced) in school-leaving examinations in England and Wales.

level³ /'levəl/ *vt,vi* (-ll-, *US* -l-) **1** make or become level or flat: *~ a building with the ground.* **level off/out,** (*fig*) reach a point beyond which no further increase or progress is likely: *Inflation seems to have ~ed off at 20%.* **2** make (two or more things, persons) equal in status, etc. **3** aim (a weapon, criticism, at): *~ a gun at a tiger.* **level sth against sb,** put forward (a charge, an accusation, etc). **4 level with sb,** (*informal*) be honest, give him information.

lever /'liːvə(r)* *US:* 'levər/ *n* [C] **1** bar or other tool used to lift something or to force something open. **2** (*fig*) means by which moral force may be exerted. □ *vt* move (something up, along, into/out of position, etc) with a lever.
lever·age /-ɪdʒ/ *n* [U] action of, power or advantage gained by, using, a lever.

lev·eret /'levərɪt/ *n* [C] young (esp first-year) hare.

levi·tate /'levɪteɪt/ *vt,vi* (with reference to powers claimed by spiritualists) (cause to) rise and float in the air in defiance of gravity.
levi·ta·tion /ˌlevɪ'teɪʃən/ *n* [C,U]

lev·ity /'levɪtɪ/ *n* [C,U] (*pl* -ies) (*formal*) (instance of a) tendency to treat serious matters without respect; lack of seriousness.

levy /'levɪ/ *vt,vi* (*pt,pp* -ied) **1** impose; collect by authority or force: *~ a tax/a fine.* **2 levy war on/upon/against,** declare, make, war on. **3 levy on,** seize by law: *~ on a person's property.* □ *n* [C] (*pl* -ies) act, amount, of levying.

lewd /luːd/ *adj* indecent; lustful.
lewd·ly *adv*
lewd·ness *n* [U]

lexi·cal /'leksɪkəl/ *adj* of the vocabulary of a language.
lexi·cally /-klɪ/ *adv*

lexi·cogra·phy /ˌleksɪ'kɒgrəfɪ/ *n* [U] dictionary compiling.
lexi·cogra·pher /ˌleksɪ'kɒgrəfə(r)/ *n* [C] person who compiles a dictionary.

lexi·con /'leksɪkən* *US:* -kɒn/ *n* [C] dictionary (esp of Greek, Latin or Hebrew).

lia·bil·ity /ˌlaɪə'bɪlətɪ/ *n* **1** [U] the state of being liable: *~ to pay taxes.* **2** (*pl*) obligations; sums of money that must be paid (contrasted with *assets*). **3** [C] (*informal*) handicap: *His wife is more of a ~ than an asset.*

liable /'laɪəbəl/ *adj* **1** responsible according to law: *Is a man ~ for his wife's debts in your country?* **2 be liable to sth,** be subject to: *be ~ to a heavy fine.* **3 be liable to do sth,** have a tendency to, be likely to: *We are* *all* ~ *to make mistakes occasionally.*

li·aison /lɪˈeɪzən US: ˈlɪəzɒn/ n 1 [U] connection between two separated parts of an army, a committee, etc or two different armies, committees, etc. 2 [C] illicit sexual relationship.

li·aise /lɪˈeɪz/ vi act as a link (*with, between*).

liar /ˈlaɪə(r)/ n [C] person who tells, or who has told, a lie.

lib /lɪb/ n (*informal* abbr for) liberation.

women's lib, movement (early 1970's) for the liberation of women from social and economic inequalities.

li·ba·tion /laɪˈbeɪʃən/ n [C] (pouring out of an) offering of wine, etc to honour a god: *make a* ~ *to Jupiter.*

li·bel /ˈlaɪbəl/ n 1 [U,C] (the publishing of a) written or printed statement that damages a person's reputation: *sue for* ~. 2 [C] (*informal*) anything that brings discredit on or fails to do justice to: *The portrait is a* ~ *on me.* □ vt (-ll-, US -l-) publish a libel against; fail to do full justice to.

li·bel·lous (*US* = **li·bel·ous**) /ˈlaɪbələs/ adj (a) containing, in the nature of, a libel: ~*lous reports.* (b) in the habit of uttering ~s: *a* ~*lous person/periodical.*

lib·eral /ˈlɪbərəl/ adj 1 giving or given freely; generous: *a* ~ *supply of food and drink.* 2 having, showing, a broad mind, free from prejudice. 3 (of education) directed chiefly towards the broadening of the mind, not specially to professional or technical needs: *the* ~ *arts,* eg philosophy, history, languages. 4 L~, of the British political party □ n [C] 1 person in favour of progress and reform and opposed to privilege. 2 L~, member of the Liberal party.

`Liberal Party, (*GB*) political party representing moderate democratic views.

lib·er·al·ism /-ɪzm/ n [U] liberal views, opinions and principles.

lib·er·al·ize /ˈlɪbərəlaɪz/ vt make liberal.

lib·er·al·iz·ation /ˈlɪbrəlaɪˈzeɪʃən US: -lɪˈz-/ n [U]

lib·er·al·ity /ˈlɪbəˈrælətɪ/ n (*formal*) (pl -ies) 1 [U] generosity; freedom from prejudice. 2 (pl) instances of generosity.

lib·er·ate /ˈlɪbəreɪt/ vt set free: ~ *the mind from prejudice.*

lib·er·ator /-tə(r)/ n [C] person who liberates.

lib·er·ation /ˈlɪbəˈreɪʃən/ n [U]. liberating or being liberated. ⇨ **lib.**

lib·erty /ˈlɪbətɪ/ n (pl -ies) 1 [U] state of being free (from captivity, slavery, imprisonment, despotic control, government by others); right or power to decide for oneself what to do, how to live, etc: *They fought to defend their* ~. **at liberty,** (of a person) free; not imprisoned: *You are now at* ~ *to leave any time,* may do so. 2 [U] ungranted and sometimes improper familiarity. **take the liberty of doing sth/to do sth:** *I took*

the ~ *of borrowing your lawn-mower while you were away on holiday.* **take liberties with:** *You must stop taking liberties with the young woman, stop treating her with too much familiarity.* 3 (*pl*) privileges or rights granted by authority: *the liberties of the City of London.*

Libra /ˈlibrə/ n the Scales or Balance, the seventh sign of the zodiac.

li·brary /ˈlaɪbrərɪ US: -brerɪ/ n [C] (pl -ies) 1 room or building for a collection of books kept there for reading; the books in such a room or building: *a public* ~; *a* `reference ~, one in which books may be consulted but not taken away. 2 (as an *adjective*): *a* `~ *book.* 3 writing and reading room in a private house.

li·brar·ian /laɪˈbreərɪən/ n [C] person in charge of a library(1).

li·brar·ian·ship n [C] profession, duties, of a librarian.

li·bretto /lɪˈbretəʊ/ n [C] (pl ~s or -ti /-tɪ/) book of words of **lice** /laɪs/ n pl of louse.

li·cence (*US* = **li·cense**) /ˈlaɪsəns/ n 1 [C,U] (written or printed statement giving) permission from someone in authority to do something: *a* ~ *to drive a car/a* `driving ~. 2 [U] excessive or wrong use of freedom: *The* ~ *shown by the troops when they entered enemy territory disgusted everyone.* ⇨ also poetic licence.

`off-licence, (place) for the sale of liquor to be taken away.

li·cense (also **li·cence**) /ˈlaɪsəns/ vt give a licence to: *shops* ~*d to sell tobacco.*

li·cen·see /ˈlaɪsənˈsiː/ n 6œCæ person holding a licence (esp to sell alcohol).

li·cen·tiate /laɪˈsenʃɪət/ n [C] person who has a licence or certificate showing that he is competent to practice a profession.

li·cen·tious /laɪˈsenʃəs/ adj immoral (esp in sexual matters).

li·cen·tious·ly adv

li·cen·tious·ness n [U]

li·chee, li·chi /ˈlaɪtʃiː/ variant spellings of lychee.

lich·gate, lych·gate /ˈlɪtʃgeɪt/ n [C] roofed gateway of a churchyard, where, at a funeral, the coffin used to await the arrival of the clergyman.

licit /ˈlɪsɪt/ adj lawful; permitted.

lick /lɪk/ vt,vi 1 pass the tongue over or under: *The cat was* ~*ing its paws.* **lick sb's boots,** (*informal*) be abject, servile. **lick one's lips,** show eagerness or satisfaction. 2 (esp of waves, flames) touch lightly: *The flames* ~*ed up the dry grass.* 3 (*informal*) overcome; triumph over. □ n [C] 1 act of licking with the tongue. **give sth a lick and a promise,** a feeble attempt to clean, polish, etc. 2 (also `salt-lick) place to which animals go for salt.

lick·ing n [C] (*informal*) beating; defeat: *Our football team got a* ~*ing yesterday.*

licor·ice /ˈlɪkərɪs/ n = liquorice.

lid /lɪd/ *n* [C] **1** movable cover (hinged or detachable) for an opening, esp at the top of a container: *the* `teapot ~. **2** = eyelid.
lid-less *adj*

lido /ˈliːdəʊ/ *n* [C] (*pl* ~s) open-air swimming pool.

lie[1] /laɪ/ *vi* (*pt,pp* ~d, *present participle* **lying**), *n* [C] (make a) statement that one knows to be untrue: *tell* ~*s. He* ~*d to me. What a pack of* ~*s!*
`lie de**tector**, device which records heart beats, etc caused by emotional stresses while a person is being questioned.

lie[2] /laɪ/ *vi* (*pt* **lay** /leɪ/, *pp* **lain** /leɪn/, *present participle* **lying**) **1** be, put oneself, flat on a horizontal surface or in a resting position; be at rest: ~ *on one's back/side. He lay on the grass enjoying the sunshine.* *(not) take sth lying down*, (not) submit to a challenge, an insult without protest. *lie in*, **(a)** stay in bed after one's usual time. Hence, *'lie-'in n: have a nice* ~*-in on Sunday morning.* **(b)** (*dated*) remain in bed to give birth to a child: *The time had come for her to* ~ *in. lie low*, (*informal*) ⇨ **low**[1] (1). **2** (of things) be resting flat on something: *The book lay open on the table.* **3** be kept, remain, in a certain state or position: *money lying idle in the bank. The snow lay thick on the ground. lie heavy on sth*, cause discomfort, trouble, distress: *The theft lay heavy on his conscience.* **4** be spread out to view; extend: *The valley lay before us. If you are young, your life still* ~*s before you. see/find out how the* `land lies, (fig) learn how matters stand. **5** be situated: *ships lying at anchor. The fleet lay off the headland. lie to*, (of a ship) come almost to a stop, facing the wind. **6** (of abstract things) exist: *The trouble* ~*s* (= is) *in the engine. He knows where his interest* ~*s*, where he may win an advantage, make a profit. **7** (*legal*) be admissible: *The appeal will not* ~, is not according to law, cannot be admitted. □ *n* (*sing* only) the way something lies. *the lie of the land*, **(a)** the natural features of an area. **(b)** (*fig*) the state of affairs.

lieu /luː/ *n* (only in) *in lieu (of)*, instead (of).

lieu·ten·ancy /lefˈtenənsɪ *US*: /luː-/ *n* [C] rank, position, of a lieutenant.

lieu·ten·ant /lefˈtenənt *US*: luˈt-/ *n* [C] **1** army officer below a captain; junior officer in the Navy. **2** (in compounds) officer with the highest rank under: `~-`colonel; `~-com`mander. **3** deputy or substitute; one who acts for a superior.

life /laɪf/ *n* (*pl* lives /laɪvz/) **1** [U] condition that distinguishes animals and plants from earth, rock, etc: *How did* ~ *begin?* **2** [U] living things collectively, in general; plants, animals, people: *Is there any* ~ *on the planet Mars?* **3** [U] state of existence as a human being: *great loss of* ~ *in war. bring to life*, cause to live; cause to recover from a faint, an illness thought to be fatal, etc

come to life, recover consciousness. *run for one's/for dear life*, in order, or as if to, save oneself from death. *a matter of 'life or `death*, one on which continued existence depends. *the kiss of life*, ⇨ **kiss**. *a new lease of life*, ⇨ **lease**. **4** [C] state of existence, as an individual living being: *How many lives were lost in the disaster? take sb's life*, kill him. *take one's own life*, commit suicide. *cannot for the life of...*, however hard I try (= even if my ~ depended on it): *For the* ~ *of me I couldn't recall her name. Not on your life!* (*informal int*) Definitely not! **5** [C] period between birth and death, or between birth and the present, or between the present and death: *He lived all his* ~ *in London. The murderer received a* ~ *sentence/was sentenced to imprisonment for* ~. *early/late in life*, during the early/late part of one's life. *have the 'time of one's `life*, enjoy oneself immensely. **6** [U] human relations; the business, pleasures, social activities, etc, of the world: *There is not much* ~ (eg social activity) *in our small village. true to life*, (of a story, drama, etc) giving a true description of how people live. **7** [C,U] (way of) living; career: *Which do you prefer, town* ~ *or country* ~*?* ⇨ also **highlife**. **8** [C] biography: *He has written a new* ~ *of Newton.* **9** [U] activity, liveliness, interest: *The children are full of* ~, are active and cheerful. *the life and soul of the party*, person who is the most lively and amusing member of a social gathering. **10** [U] living form or model: *a* `~ *drawing; a* `~ *class*, (in an art school) one in which students draw or paint from living models. **11** [C] fresh start or opportunity after a narrow escape from death, disaster, etc: *They say a cat has nine lives.* **12** [C] period during which something is active or useful: *the* ~ *of a ship.*
`life-belt, belt of cork or other buoyant material to keep a person afloat in water.
`life-blood, **(a)** blood necessary to life. **(b)** (*fig*) something that gives strength and energy.
`life-boat, **(a)** boat specially built for going to the help of persons in danger at sea along the coast. **(b)** boat carried on a ship for use in case the ship is in danger of sinking, etc.
`life-buoy, device to keep a person afloat in water.
`life cycle progression through different stages of development: *the* ~ *cycle of a frog*, from the egg to the tadpole to the final stage.
life force, vital energy thought of as working for the survival of the human race and the individual.
`life-giving *adj* that strengthens or restores physical or spiritual life.
`life-guard, **(a)** expert swimmer on duty at dangerous places where people swim. **(b)** (*pl* `Life Guards) cavalry regiment in the

British army. (**c**) bodyguard of soldiers.

`life history, record of the life cycle of an organism.

`life-jacket, one of cork or other buoyant material or that can be inflated to keep a person afloat in water.

`life-like adj resembling real life; looking like the person represented: a ~like portrait.

`life-line, (**a**) rope used for saving life. (**b**) (fig) anything on which one's life depends. (**c**) line across the palm of the hand, alleged to show one's length of life, major events in one's life, etc.

`life-long adj continuing for a long time; lasting throughout life.

life peer, member of the House of Lords whose title cannot be inherited.

`life-raft, structure of wood, etc used instead of a boat, e g by swimmers.

`life-size(d) adj (of pictures, statues, etc) having the same size, proportions, etc, as the person represented.

`life-span, longest period of life of an organism known from the study of it.

`life-time, duration of a person's life. **the chance of a lifetime,** an opportunity that comes only once.

`life-work, task to which one devotes all one's life.

life-less adj (**a**) never having had life: ~less stones. (**b**) having lost life; dead. (**c**) dull; not lively: answer in a ~less manner.

`life-less-ly adv

lifer /ˈlaɪfə(r)/ n [C] (sl) person sentenced to life imprisonment.

lift /lɪft/ vt,vi **1** raise, be raised to a higher level or position: ~ a child out of his cot. This box is too heavy for me to ~. **not lift a finger,** ⇨ finger. **lift off,** (of a spacecraft) rise from the launching site. Hence, `lift-off n: We have ~-off. **2** make louder: ~ (up) one's voice. **3** make more hopeful, cheerful, etc: The good news ~ed her spirits. **4** (of clouds, fog, etc) rise; pass away: The mist began to ~. **5** remove (plants, shrubs, etc) from the ground: ~ potatoes. **6** (informal) steal: ~ articles in a supermarket. Hence, `shoplifter, `shoplifting. **7** take without permission or proper acknowledgement: long passages ~ed from other authors. **8** end (a ban, prohibition, blockade, siege). □ n [C] **1** act of lifting. **get/give sb a lift,** be offered/offer a free ride in a motor-vehicle: Can you give me a ~ to the station? (**b**) (of a person's spirits) become/make more cheerful, contented: The salary increase gave me a tremendous ~. **2** (US = elevator) moving cage for taking people up or down to another floor.

`lift-boy/-man, one who operates a lift.

liga-ment /ˈlɪɡəmənt/ n [C] band of tough, strong tissues that holds two or more bones together.

light¹ /laɪt/ adj (-er, -est) (opposite of dark) **1** (of a place) well provided with light³(1):

It's beginning to get ~. A ~ room. **2** pale-coloured: ~ blue/green/brown.

`light-coloured adj

light² /laɪt/ adj (-er, -est) **1** not heavy; not having much weight (for its size): as ~ as air/as a feather; ~ fall of snow; ~ clothes for the summer. **2** gentle; delicate: give her a ~ touch on the shoulder. **3** below the correct weight, amount, etc: give ~ weight. We're about 50p ~ on the petty cash, 50p short. **4** (of beer, wines) not very strong; (of food) easily digested; (of meals) small in quantity: a ~ supper. **5** (of sleep) not deep; easily disturbed; (of sleepers) easily waked. **6** (of books, plays, music) primarily for amusement, not for serious entertainment or study: ~ reading/music. **7** (of soil) easily broken up. **8** (of taxes, punishment) not difficult to bear. **9** (of work) easily done. **make light work of sth,** do it without much effort. **10** not serious or important: a ~ attack of flu. **make light of,** treat as of no or little importance. □ adv in a light manner: tread/sleep ~; travel ~, with little luggage.

`light-`fingered adj skilful in using the fingers, esp as a pickpocket.

`light-`footed adj moving with light(2), easy steps.

`light-`handed adj (**a**) having a light(2) hand. (**b**) not carrying much.

`light-`headed adj (**a**) dizzy; delirious. (**b**) frivolous.

`light-`hearted adj cheerful; gay.

`light-`heavyweight n [C], adj (boxer) weighing between 160 and 175 lbs (or 72·5 to 79·3 kg).

`light-weight n [C], adj (**a**) (person, animal, thing) light in weight. (**b**) (boxer) weighing between 126 and 135 lbs (or 57 to 61 kg). (**c**) (informal) person of little influence or importance.

light-ly adv (esp) **get off lightly,** (informal) avoid having to pay a lot, be punished severely, etc.

`light-ness n [U]

light³ /laɪt/ n (opposite of darkness) **1** [U] that which makes things visible: the ~ of the sun/a lamp/the fire; `moon~; `sun~. **in a good/bad light,** (**a**) so as to be seen well/badly: The picture has been hung in a bad ~. (**b**) (fig) so as to make a good/bad impression: Press reports always make him appear in a bad ~. **see the light,** (esp) realize the truth of something that one has been obstinate about. **2** [C] something that gives light, e g a candle or lamp: `traffic ~s. Turn/switch the ~s on/off. **3** [C] (something used for producing a) spark or flame: Can you give me a ~, please? **4** [U] expression of brightness or liveliness in a person's face (esp in the eyes), suggesting happiness or other emotion. **5** [U] knowledge or information that helps understanding; [C] fact or discovery that explains. **come/bring sth to light,** become/cause something to be visible

or known: *Much new evidence has come to
∼/has been brought to ∼ in recent years*.
shed/throw (a new) light on sth, make
something clearer, provide new information.
in the light of, with the help given by or
gained from. **6** [C] way in which something
appears: *I've never viewed the matter in that
∼*. **7** [C] famous person; person (to be)
regarded as an example or model: *one of the
shining ∼s of our age*. **8** [C] window or
opening, in a roof, for the admission of
light: *a `sky∼*. **9** part of a painting or photo-
graph shown as lighted up: *∼ and shade*,
contrasts. ⇨ **highlight**.
`light-house, tower or other tall structure
containing a strong, flashing light for warning or guiding ships at sea.
`light-ship, ship provided with a light, for
the same purpose as those in a lighthouse.
`light year, unit of measurement, the dis-
tance travelled by light in one year (about 6
million million miles).
light⁴ /laɪt/ *vt,vi* (*pt,pp* lit /lɪt/) **1** cause to
begin burning or to give out light: *∼ a
cigarette/fire*. **2** provide lights(2) to or for:
Our streets are lit by electricity. **3** cause to
become bright: *The burning building lit up
the whole district*. **4 light up**, (a) switch on
(electric) light, etc: *It's getting dark—time
to ∼ up*. Hence, **'lighting-`up time**, when,
according to regulations, lamps in the roads
and on vehicles must be lit. **(b)** (*informal*)
begin to smoke a pipe or cigarette: *He struck
a match and lit up*. **5 light up (with)**, (of a
person's face or expression) (cause to)
become bright: *Her face lit up with pleasure*.
light⁵ /laɪt/ *vi* (*pt,pp* lit /lɪt/) (*literary*) find
by chance: *∼ on/upon a rare book*.
lighten¹ /ˈlaɪtən/ *vt,vi* make or become less
heavy; reduce the weight of: *∼ a ship's
cargo. Her heart ∼ed when she heard the
news*.
lighten² /ˈlaɪtən/ *vt,vi* **1** make (more) light
or bright: *A solitary candle ∼ed the darkness of the cellar*. **2** become light or bright:
The eastern sky ∼ed. **3** send out lightning:
It's thundering and ∼ing.
lighter¹ /ˈlaɪtə(r)/ *n* [C] **1** device for lighting
cigarettes or cigars. **2** (chiefly in compounds) person or thing that lights: *a `lamp-
∼, man* who lit gas-lamps.
lighter² /ˈlaɪtə(r)/ *n* [C] shallow boat used
for loading and unloading ships not brought
to a wharf, and for carrying goods in a harbour or river.
`lighter-age /-ɪdʒ/, fees charged for carry-
ing goods in lighters.
light-ning /ˈlaɪtnɪŋ/ *n* [U] flash of bright
light produced by natural electricity between
clouds in the sky or clouds and the ground,
with thunder: *be struck/killed by ∼*. **like
lightning; with lightning speed**, very
fast.
`lightning-rod/-conductor, metal rod
fixed on the top of a high building, etc and

connected to the earth, to prevent damage by
lightning.
lightning strike, strike¹(1) started without
warning.
lights /laɪts/ *n pl* lungs of sheep, pigs, bullocks, etc used as food for pet animals.
lik-able, like-able /ˈlaɪkəbl/ *adj* of a kind
that is, or deserves to be, liked: *He's a very
∼ fellow*.
like¹ /laɪk/ *adj* similar; having the same or
similar qualities, etc; having a resemblance:
The two girls are very ∼. ⇨ **alike**. **Like
father, like son**, As the one is, so the other
will be. □ *conj* as: *She can't cook ∼ her
mother (does)*. □ *n* **1** similar person or
things; that which is equal or similar to
something else: *Music, painting and the ∼*,
and similar branches of the arts. **2** (*pl*)
(*informal*) similar persons, things, etc:
Have you ever seen the ∼s of this? □ *prep* **1**
such as; resembling: *What is he ∼?* What
sort of person is he—in looks, behaviour,
etc, according to the situation? *This is nothing ∼ as good*, not nearly so good. **nothing
like**, nothing to be compared with: *There's
nothing ∼ walking as a means of keeping fit*.
something like, nearly; about: *The cost
will be something ∼ five pounds*. **2 `feel
like**, be in a suitable state or mood for: *She
felt ∼ crying. We'll go for a walk if you feel
∼ it*. **`look like**, look as if a person or thing
might (used to show probability or in likelihood): *It looks ∼ rain*. **3** characteristic of:
Isn't that just ∼ a woman! **4** in the manner
of; to the same degree as: *Don't talk ∼ that*,
in that way. *It fits him ∼ a glove*, closely,
tightly. *He drinks ∼ a fish*. **5 like anything**,
(*sl*) as hard, etc as can be expected or imagined: *She works ∼ anything when she's
interested*. **like mad/crazy**, as if crazy: *He
complains ∼ mad when things go wrong*.
like hell, (a) furiously; energetically: *He
moans ∼ hell when he loses a bet*. **(b)** (used
as an *int*): *'But you were there, weren't
you?' 'L∼ hell, I was!'* I certainly wasn't!
'like-`minded *adj* having the same tastes,
aims, etc.
like² /laɪk/ *vt,vi* **1** be fond of; have a taste
for; find satisfactory or agreeable: *Do you ∼
fish? She ∼s him but she doesn't love him.
Well, I ∼ that!* (what has been said or done
is surprising, unexpected, unacceptable etc).
2 (in *negative* sentences) be unwilling or
reluctant: *I didn't ∼ to disturb you*. **3
would/should like**, (of a wish): *She would
∼ a cup of tea. I should ∼ to know/to see…*,
often ironic, meaning that it would be difficult to explain, show, etc. **4** prefer; choose;
wish: *I ∼ people to tell the truth. How do
you ∼ your tea?* **if you like**, (used to express
consent to a request or suggestion): *I'll come
if you ∼*. **5** suit the health of: *I ∼ lobster but
it doesn't ∼ me*, ie it gives me indigestion.
□ *n* (*pl*) (only in) **'likes and `dislikes**, things
one prefers or hates.

-like /-laɪk/ *suffix* resembling: *childlike.*

like-li-hood /-hʊd/ *n* [U] probability: *There is a strong likelihood of rain tomorrow.*

like-ly /ˈlaɪklɪ/ *adj* (-ier, -iest) **1** that seems reasonable or suitable for a purpose: *What do you think is the likeliest/the most ∼ time to find him at home? That's a ∼ story/ excuse* (often used ironically). **2** to be expected (to...): *He is not ∼ to succeed. It's highly* (= very) *∼ that he will succeed.* □ *adv* **most/very likely,** probably: *I shall very ∼ be here again next month.* **as likely as not,** with greater probability: *He will succeed as ∼ as not.* **not likely,** (used as an *int*): *'Will you come to the theatre?' 'Not ∼!'* I certainly will not!

liken /ˈlaɪkən/ *vt* **liken sth to sth,** point out the likeness of one thing (to another): *∼ the heart to a pump.*

like-ness /ˈlaɪknəs/ *n* **1** [U] resemblance; being like: *I can't see much ∼ between the two boys.* **2** [C] detail, instance, of being like: *There's a family ∼ in all of them.* **3** [C] copy, portrait, picture, photograph: *The portrait is a good ∼.*

like-wise /ˈlaɪkwaɪz/ *adv* in the same or a similar way: *Watch him and do ∼.* □ *conj* also; moreover.

lik-ing /ˈlaɪkɪŋ/ *n* [U] **1** being fond of: *L∼ is not the same as loving.* **2** (with *a,* but not *pl*) fondness. **have a liking for,** be fond of. **to one's liking,** as one likes it; satisfactory: *Is everything to your ∼?* **take a liking to,** become fond of.

li-lac /ˈlaɪlək/ *n* **1** [C] shrub with sweet-smelling pale purple or white blossom. **2** [U] pale purple or pinkish-purple: (as an *adjective*) *a ∼ dress.*

lilt /lɪlt/ *n* [C] (lively song or tune with a) well-marked rhythm. □ *vt,vi* go, sing with a lilt: *a ∼ing waltz.*

lily /ˈlɪlɪ/ *n* [C] (*pl* -ies) (kinds of) plant growing from a bulb, of many sizes, shapes and colours: *∼ water lilies.*
'lily-livered *adj* cowardly.
'lily-'white *adj* pure white.

limb /lɪm/ *n* [C] **1** leg, arm or wing: *escape with life and ∼,* without serious injury. **2** bough (of a tree). **leave sb/be/go out on a limb,** (*informal*) leave a person/be/put oneself in a vulnerable position, e g because separated from supporters.

-limbed /lɪmd/ *suffix*: *'long-/'strong-'∼,* having long/strong limbs.

lim-ber /ˈlɪmbə(r)/ *vt,vi* **limber (oneself) up,** make oneself (one's muscles) pliant, flexible.

limbo /ˈlɪmbəʊ/ *n* [C] (*pl* ∼s) **1** [U] condition of being forgotten and unwanted. **in limbo,** (*informal*) put to one side: *the idea is in ∼ until the new Manager is appointed.* **2** [C] place for forgotten and unwanted things.

lime¹ /laɪm/ *n* [U] white substance (calcium oxide, **CaO**) used in making cement and mortar. □ *vt* put lime on (fields, etc) (to control acidity).

'lime-light, intense white light produced by heating a rod of lime in a very hot flame, formerly used for lighting the stage in theatres. **fond of/in the limelight,** liking/ receiving great publicity.

'lime-stone, (kinds of) rock containing lime quarried for industrial use.

lime² /laɪm/ *n* [C] (also *linden*) tree with smooth heart-shaped leaves and sweet-smelling yellow blossoms.

lime³ /laɪm/ *n* [C] (tree with) round juicy fruit like, but more acid than, a lemon.

'lime-juice, juice of this fruit used for flavouring and as a drink.

lim-er-ick /ˈlɪmərɪk/ *n* [C] humorous or nonsense poem of five lines.

limit¹ /ˈlɪmɪt/ *n* [C] line or point that may not or cannot be passed; greatest or smallest amount, degree, etc of what is possible: *within a ∼ of five miles/a five-mile ∼. We must set a ∼ to the expense of the trip. She has reached the ∼ of her patience.* ⇨ **age** limit. **within limits,** in moderation: *I'm willing to help you, within ∼s.* **off limits,** (*US*) = out of bounds, ⇨ **bound¹.**

limit² /ˈlɪmɪt/ *vt* put a limit or limits to; be the limit of: *We must ∼ our spending to what we can afford.*

lim-ited *pp* small; restricted; narrow: *Accommodation is very ∼ed. He seems to have only a ∼ed intelligence.*

'limited 'lia'bility company, (abbr **Ltd** placed after the name) business company whose members are liable for its debts only to the extent of the capital sum they have provided.

lim-it-less *adj* without limit: *∼less ambitions.*

limi-ta-tion /ˌlɪmɪˈteɪʃən/ *n* **1** [U] limiting; condition of being limited. **2** [C] condition, fact or circumstance that limits; disability or inability: *He knows his ∼s,* knows the extent of his ability.

limou-sine /ˈlɪməzɪn/ *n* [C] car with the front seats separated from the back seats by means of a partition (as in a London taxi).

limp¹ /lɪmp/ *adj* not stiff or firm; lacking strength: *The flowers looked ∼ in the heat.*
limp-ly *adv*
limp-ness *n* [U]

limp² /lɪmp/ *vt* walk lamely or unevenly as when one leg or foot is hurt or stiff: *The wounded soldier ∼ed off the battlefield. The damaged ship ∼ed* (= managed with difficulty to get) *back to port.* □ *n* [U] (usually with *a, an*) lame walk: *have/walk with a bad ∼.*

lim-pet /ˈlɪmpɪt/ *n* [C] **1** small shellfish that fastens itself tightly to rocks. **2** (*fig*) person who sticks tightly to an office, a position or another person.

lim-pid /ˈlɪmpɪd/ *adj* (of liquids, the atmosphere, the eyes) clear; transparent.

lim·pid·ly adv

lim·pid·ity /lɪmˈpɪdətɪ/ n [U]

linch·pin /ˈlɪntʃpɪn/ n [C] **1** iron pin passed through the end of an axle to keep the wheel in position. **2** (fig) vital part; person who, because of his work, etc, keeps an organization, etc together.

lin·den /ˈlɪndən/ n ⇨ lime².

line¹ /laɪn/ n [C] **1** piece or length of thread, string, rope or wire for various purposes: many `fishing/`telephone/`washing ~s. L~ engaged! (US = L~ busy) used of a telephone line already in use. ⇨ hotline. **2** [C] long, narrow mark made on a surface: Draw a ~ from A to B. **3** [U] the use of lines(2) in art, etc: a `~ drawing, eg with a pen or pencil. **4** (in games) mark made to limit a court or ground, or special parts of them: Did the ball cross the ~? **5** crease on the skin of the face; furrow or wrinkle; one of the marks on the palm of the hand. **6** (pl) contour; outline: a dress with flattering ~s. **7** row of persons or things: a ~ of trees/chairs/people; manufactured goods on the as`sembly ~. **in line for,** next in order for: He's in ~ for promotion. **stand in line,** form a queue. **8** edge, boundary, that divides: cross the ~ into Canada (i̯e from US). **draw the line (at),** ⇨ draw²(13). **9** railway; single track of railway lines: the main ~; a `branch ~. **reach the end of the line,** (fig) (of a relationship) reach the point where it breaks down, ends. **10** organized system of transport under one management and giving a regular service: an `air~. **11** direction; course; track; way of behaviour, dealing with a situation, etc: `communi`cation ~s. Don't stand in the ~ of fire! **choose/follow/take the line of least resistance,** the easiest way of doing things. **take a strong/firm line (over sth),** deal with a problem, etc in a firm(2) manner: Should the government take a stronger ~ over inflation? **(be/get) in/out of line (with),** in agreement/disagreement (with). **come/fall into line (with),** accept views, conform, agree. **follow the party line,** vote, speak, in agreement with established political party policy. **toe the line,** (fig) ⇨ toe v. **12** connected series of persons following one another in time, esp of the same ancestry: a long ~ of great kings. **13** row of words on a page of writing or in print: page 5, ~ 10. The leading actor was not sure of his ~s. **drop sb a line,** (informal) write a short letter to somebody. **read between the lines,** (fig) find more meaning than the words suggest. **14** series of connected military defence posts, trenches, etc: the front/enemy ~(s). **15** (mil) row of tents, huts, etc in a camp: inspect the ~s; the `horse ~s. **16** business; occupation: He's in the `grocery ~. That's not much in my ~, (fig) I don't know/care much about it. **17** class of commercial goods: a cheap ~ in denim jeans.

18 (pl) conditions of life; fate. **Hard lines!** Bad luck!

line² /laɪn/ vt,vi **1** mark with lines: ~d paper, with lines printed on it. **2** cover with lines: a face ~d with anxiety. **3** **line up,** (cause to) be in a line, get into a line: The soldiers quickly ~d up. ⇨ line-up below. **4** form, be placed, in a line or lines along: a road ~d with trees/spectators.

line³ /laɪn/ vt ⇨ lining below. **1** add a layer of material to the inside of (bags, boxes, articles of clothing): fur~d gloves. **2** (fig) fill (one's purse, pocket, stomach, etc): He has ~d his pockets with bribes.

lin·eage /ˈlɪnɪɪdʒ/ n [U] (formal) = ancestry.

lin·eal /ˈlɪnɪəl/ adj in the direct line of descent (from father to son, etc): a ~ descendant/heir.

lin·eal·ly /-rəlɪ/ adv

lin·ear /ˈlɪnɪə(r)/ adj **1** of or in lines: a ~ design. **2** of length: ~ measurement.

linen /ˈlɪnɪn/ n [U] cloth made of flax; articles made from this cloth, esp sheets, tablecloths, etc. **wash one's dirty linen in public,** discuss family quarrels, unpleasant personal affairs, etc in the presence of other people.

line-out /ˈlaɪnaʊt/ n = throw-in.

liner /ˈlaɪnə(r)/ n [C] **1** ship or aircraft of a line(10) a jet `air~. **2** (also `freight ~) long distance express goods train between industrial centres and seaports, with facilities for fast (un)loading of goods. **3** cosmetic for drawing lines round the eyes: an `eye-~.

lines·man /ˈlaɪnzmən/ n [C] (in sport) person who helps the umpire or referee by saying whether or where the ball touches or crosses one of the lines.

line-up /ˈlaɪn ʌp/ n [C] **1** way in which persons, states, etc are arranged or allied: a new ~ of Afro-Asian powers; a ~ of men in an identification parade. **2** formation of players ready for action (in a game such as baseball or football). **3** arrangements of items (esp in a radio or TV programme): This evening's ~ includes an interview with the Chairman of British Rail.

lin·ger /ˈlɪŋgə(r)/ vi be late or slow in going away; stay at or near a place: ~ about/around.

`ling·er·er, person who lingers.

ling·er·ing adj long; prolonged: a ~ing illness; a ~ing look, one showing unwillingness to leave or give up something: a few ~ing (= remaining) doubts.

ling·er·ing·ly adv

linge·rie /ˈlænʒərɪ US: -reɪ/ n [U] (Fr) (trade name for) women's underwear.

lingo /ˈlɪŋgəʊ/ n [C] (pl ~es) language, esp one that one does not know; way of talking, vocabulary, of a special subject or class of people: the strange ~ used by disc jockeys.

lin·gua franca /ˌlɪŋgwə ˈfræŋkə(r)/ n [C] language adopted for local communication over an area in which several languages are spoken, e g Swahili in E Africa.

lin·gual /ˈlɪŋgwəl/ *adj* of the tongue, speech or languages: *bi*~.

lin·guist /ˈlɪŋgwɪst/ *n* [C] **1** person skilled in foreign languages: *She's a good* ~. **2** person who makes a scientific study of language(s).

lin·guis·tic /lɪŋˈgwɪstɪk/ *adj* of (the scientific study of) languages.

lin·guis·tics *n* (used with a *sing verb*) the science of language, e g of its structure, relationship to other forms of communication, etc. **ap'plied lin'guistics,** this study put to practical uses, esp in the teaching of languages.

lini·ment /ˈlɪnɪmənt/ *n* [C,U] (kind of) liquid for rubbing on stiff or aching parts of the body.

lin·ing /ˈlaɪnɪŋ/ *n* **1** [C] layer of material added to the inside of something: *a fur* ~. **Every cloud has a silver lining,** (*proverb*) There is a possibility of good out of every evil. **2** [U] material used for this purpose.

link /lɪŋk/ *n* [C] **1** one ring or loop of a chain. **2** one of a pair of fasteners for the cuffs of a shirt: `*cuff*-~*s*. **3** person or thing that unites or connects two others: *the* ~ *between the past and the future*. **4** measure of length, one hundredth of a chain; 7·92 inches or about 20 centimetres. □ *vt,vi* join, be joined, with, or as with, a link: ~ *things together; two towns* ~*ed by a canal. Where shall we* ~ *up, meet?*

links /lɪŋks/ *n* **1** (used with a *pl verb*) grassy land, esp sand-hills, near the sea. **2** (often used with *a, an* and a *sing verb*) golf-course.

lin·net /ˈlɪnɪt/ *n* [C] small brown songbird, common in Europe.

lino /ˈlaɪnəʊ/ *n* [U] (abbr for) linoleum.

lin·oleum /lɪˈnəʊliəm/ *n* [U] strong floor-covering of canvas treated with powdered cork and oil.

lin·seed /ˈlɪnsiːd/ *n* [U] seed of flax: `~*-oil*, used in making printing ink, linoleum, etc.

lint /lɪnt/ *n* [U] soft cotton material, used for dressing wounds.

lin·tel /ˈlɪntəl/ *n* [C] horizontal piece of wood or stone forming the top of the frame of a door or window.

lion /ˈlaɪən/ *n* [C] large, strong, flesh-eating animal of the cat family found in Africa and S Asia. **the lion's share,** the larger or largest part.

lion·ess /-es/ *n* [C] female lion.

`**lion·ize** /-aɪz/ *vt* treat (a person) as a celebrity.

lip /lɪp/ *n* [C] **1** one or other of the fleshy edges of the mouth: *the lower/upper* ~. **bite one's lip,** hide one's feelings. **curl one's lip,** show scorn. **give/pay `lip-service to sth,** make insincere promises, express insincere regret. **keep a stiff upper lip,** show no emotion, sign of fear, anxiety, etc. **lick/ smack one's lips,** show (anticipation of) enjoyment. **2** edge of a hollow vessel or

opening: *the* ~ *of a bowl/crater*. **3** [U] (*sl*) impudence: *That's enough of your* ~*!*

`**lip-reading,** method (taught to deaf people) of understanding speech from lip movements. Hence, `**lip-read** *vt*

`**lip·stick,** (stick of) cosmetic material for reddening the lips.

liquefy /ˈlɪkwɪfaɪ/ *vt,vi* (*pt,pp* -ied) make or become liquid.

li·queur /lɪˈkjʊə(r) *US:* -ˈkɜː/ *n* [C,U] (kinds of) strong-flavoured alcoholic drink for taking in small quantities: *a* ~ *glass*, a very small one for liqueurs.

liquid /ˈlɪkwɪd/ *n* [C,U] substance like water or oil that flows freely and is neither a solid nor a gas. □ *adj* **1** in the form of a liquid: ~ *food*, soft, easily swallowed, suitable for sick people. **2** clear, bright and moist-looking: ~ *eyes*, bright and shining. **3** (of sounds) clear; pure: *the* ~ *notes of a black-bird*. **4** easily changed: ~ *opinions*. **5** (in finance) easily sold or changed into cash: ~ *assets*.

liqui·date /ˈlɪkwɪdeɪt/ *vt,vi* **1** pay or settle (a debt). **2** bring (esp an unsuccessful business company) to an end by dividing up its property to pay debts; (of a company) go through this process. **3** (*informal*) get rid of, put an end to; kill: *gangsters who* ~ *their rivals*.

liqui·da·tion /ˌlɪkwɪˈdeɪʃən/ *n* [U] liquidating or being liquidated. **go into liquidation,** become bankrupt.

liq·ui·da·tor /-tə(r)/, official who liquidates (2).

liq·uid·ity /lɪˈkwɪdətɪ/ *n* [U] **1** state of being ~(5). **2** state of being able to raise funds easily by selling assets.

liquid·ize /ˈlɪkwɪdaɪz/ *vt* crush, e g fruit, vegetables, to a liquid pulp.

liquid·izer, device for liquidizing fruit, etc.

liquor /ˈlɪkə(r)/ *n* **1** [C,U] (*GB*) (kind of) alcoholic drink. **2** (*US*) distilled alcoholic drinks: *a* `~ *store*. **3** [U] liquid produced by boiling or fermenting a food substance.

liquor·ice (*US* = **licor·ice**) /ˈlɪkərɪs/ *n* [U] (plant from whose root is obtained a) black substance used in medicine and in sweets.

lisp /lɪsp/ *vi,vt* fail to use the sounds /s/ and /z/ correctly, e g by saying /θɪkˈθtɪn/ for *sixteen;* say in a lisping manner: *She* ~*s*. □ *n* [C] lisping way of speaking: *The child has a bad* ~.

lis·som, lis·some /ˈlɪsəm/ *adj* quick and graceful in movement.

list¹ /lɪst/ *n* [C] number of names (of persons, items, things, etc) written or printed: *a* `*shopping* ~. □ *vt* make a list of; put on a list.

`**list price,** published or advertised price.

list² /lɪst/ *vi* (esp of a ship) lean over to one side, e g because the cargo has shifted: *The ship* ~*ed to starboard*. □ *n* [C] listing (of a ship)

list³ /lɪst/ *vt,vi* (*old use*) listen (*to*).

369

lis·ten /ˈlɪsən/ vi 1 try to hear; pay attention: *We ~ed but heard nothing. The boys were not ~ing to me.* **listen in (to), (a)** listen to a radio programme: *Did you ~ in to the Prime Minister yesterday evening?* (b) listen secretly to a conversation, e g by using an extension telephone receiver. 2 take (a person's) advice: *Don't ~ to him; he wants to get you into trouble.*
lis·tener, person who listens.

list·less /ˈlɪstləs/ adj too tired to show interest or do anything.
list·less·ly adv
list·less·ness n [U]

lists /lɪsts/ n pl area of ground for fights (in former times) between men on horseback wearing armour and using lances. **enter the lists,** (fig) send out, accept, a challenge to a contest.

lit /lɪt/ pt,pp of light [4].

lit·any /ˈlɪtənɪ/ n [C] (pl -ies) form of prayer for use in church services, recited by a priest with responses from the congregation.
the Litany, that in the Book of Common Prayer of the Church of England.

lit·chi /ˈlaɪtʃɪ/ variant spelling of lychee.

liter /ˈliːtə(r)/ n (US) ⇨ litre.

lit·er·acy /ˈlɪtərəsɪ/ n [U] ability to read and write.

lit·eral /ˈlɪtərəl/ adj 1 connected with, expressed in, letters of an alphabet. 2 corresponding exactly to the original: *a ~ translation.* 3 taking words in their usual and obvious sense, without exaggeration, etc: *the ~ sense of a word.* 4 (of a person) lacking in imagination: *He has a rather ~ mind.* □ n [C] misprint.
lit·er·ally /ˈlɪtrəlɪ/ adv (a) word for word; strictly: *carry out orders too ~ly.* (b) (informal) without exaggeration: *The children were ~ly starving.*

lit·er·ary /ˈlɪtərərɪ US: ˈlɪtərerɪ/ adj of literature or authors: *a ~ man,* either an author or a man interested in literature; *a ~ style,* as used in literature.

lit·er·ate /ˈlɪtərət/ adj 1 able to read and write. 2 cultured; well-read: *Ben's a remarkably ~ young man.* □ n [C] literate person.

lit·era·ture /ˈlɪtrətʃə(r) US: -tʃʊər/ n [U] 1 (the writing or the study of) books, etc valued as works of art (drama, fiction, essays, poetry, biography, contrasted with technical books and journalism). 2 (also with a, an) all the writings of a country (French ~) or a period (18th century English ~); books dealing with a special subject: *travel ~; an extensive ~ dealing with the First World War.* 3 [U] printed material describing or advertising something, e g brochures: *We shall be glad to send you some ~ about our package holidays.*

lithe /laɪð/ adj (of a person, etc) bending, twisting or turning easily: *~ movements.*

liti·gant /ˈlɪtɪɡənt/ n [C] person engaged in a lawsuit.

liti·gate /ˈlɪtɪɡeɪt/ vi,vt 1 go to law; make a claim at a law court. 2 contest at a court of law.
liti·ga·tion /ˈlɪtɪˈɡeɪʃən/ n [U]

lit·mus /ˈlɪtməs/ n [U] blue colouring-matter that is turned red by acid and can then be restored to blue by alkali: *~-paper,* used as a test for acids and alkalis.

li·totes /ˈlaɪtəʊtiːz/ n [C] (pl unchanged) understatement used ironically, esp using a negative to express the contrary, as 'I shan't be sorry when it's over' meaning 'I shall be very glad'.

litre (US = liter) /ˈliːtə(r)/ n [C] unit of capacity in the metric system. (1 litre = about 1¾ pints).

lit·ter[1] /ˈlɪtə(r)/ n [C] 1 couch or bed (often with a covering and curtains) in which a person may be carried about, e g on men's shoulders, and as used in ancient Rome. 2 sort of stretcher for carrying a sick or wounded person.

lit·ter[2] /ˈlɪtə(r)/ n 1 [U] bits of paper, wrappings, bottles, etc left lying about in a room or public place: *Pick up your ~ after a picnic.* 2 [U] straw and similar material, e g dry bracken, used as bedding for animals or for protecting plants from frost. 3 [C] all the newly born young ones of an animal: *a ~ of puppies.* □ vt,vi 1 make untidy with litter(1): *~ a desk with papers; ~ up one's room.* 2 supply (a horse, etc) with straw; make a bed for an animal: *~ down a horse/a stable.* 3 (of animals, esp dogs and pigs) bring forth a litter(3).
litter-basket/-bin, bin/basket for litter(1).

little[1] /ˈlɪtl/ adj (Note: In senses 1, 2 and 3 little has no real comparative and superlative; ~r and ~st are occasionally used but are better avoided. ⇨ less and least for senses 5 and 6.) 1 small, or small in comparison: *the ~ finger/toe.* 2 (suggesting affection, tenderness, regard, admiration, or the contrary, depending on the preceding adjective): *What a pretty ~ house! That poor ~ girl!* 3 short (in time, distance, stature): *Won't you stay a ~ time with me?* 4 young: *How are the ~ ones,* the children? 5 not much: *I have very ~ time for reading.* 6 (with a) some but not much; a small quantity of: *He knows a ~ French. Will you have a ~ cake?* □ adv 1 not much; hardly at all; only slightly: *He is ~ known. She slept very ~ last night. I see him very ~* (= rarely) *nowadays. He left ~ more than an hour ago. He is ~ better than* (= is almost as bad as) *a thief.* **a little,** rather; somewhat: *a ~ afraid; a ~ too big.* **not a little,** very: *not a ~ annoyed.* 2 (with such verbs as know, think, imagine, guess, suspect, realize, and always placed before the verb) not at all: *He ~ knows/L~ does he know that the police are about to arrest him.*
Little Bear, a constellation.

little·ness n [U] the quality of being little.
little /ˈlɪtəl/ n [U] (⇨ less, least) **1** not much; only a small amount: *You have done very ~ for us. I see very ~ of him. I got ~ out of it*, not much advantage or profit. *He did what ~ he could.* **little by little,** gradually; by degrees. **little or nothing,** hardly anything. **2** (with *a*) a small quantity; something (*a ~* is positive; *~* is negative): *He knows a ~ of everything. Please give me a ~.* **after/for a little,** after/for a short time or distance.
lit·urgy /ˈlɪtədʒɪ/ n [C] (*pl* -ies) [C] fixed form of public worship used in a church.
li·tur·gi·cal /lɪˈtɜːdʒɪkəl/ adj
liv·able /ˈlɪvəbəl/ adj **1** (of a house, room, climate, etc) fit to live in. **2** (of life) tolerable. **livable with,** (of persons) easy to live with.
live /laɪv/ adj **1** having life: *~ fish.* **2** burning or glowing: *~ coals;* unexploded: *a ~ bomb;* not used: *a ~ match;* charged with electricity: *a ~ rail,* carrying current for trains. **3** (of a broadcast) not recorded in advance (on tape or records). **4** full of energy, activity, interest, importance, etc: *a ~ question/issue,* one in which there is great interest. □ adv (from 3 above): *The concert will be broadcast ~.*
live-birth, baby born alive (in contrast to a *still-birth,* baby born dead).
live,wire, (*fig*) lively, energetic person.
live /lɪv/ vi, vt **1** exist(1); be alive (the more usual words). **2** continue to be, remain, alive: *She's very ill—the doctors don't think she will ~.* **live `on,** continue to live: *The old people died but the young people ~d on in the village.* **live through,** experience and survive: *He has ~d through two wars and three revolutions.* **live and let live,** be tolerant. **3** *live on,* (**a**) have as food or diet: *~ on fruit;* (**b**) depend on for support, etc: *~ on one's salary.* **live off the land,** use its agricultural products for one's food needs. **4** make one's home: *~ in England/abroad. Where do you ~?* **live together,** (**a**) live in the same house, etc. (**b**) live as if married: *I hear that Jane and Bill are living together.* **5** spend, pass, experience: *He ~d and died a bachelor.* **6** conduct oneself; pass one's life in a specified way: *~ honestly/happily; ~ like a saint.* **7** **live sth down,** live in such a way that (past guilt, scandal, foolishness, etc) is forgotten: *He hopes to ~ down the scandal caused by the divorce proceedings.* **live up to sth,** put (one's faith, principles, etc) into practice; reach the standard that may be expected: *He didn't ~ up to his reputation.* **live with sth,** accept and endure it: *I don't like commuting, but I've learnt to ~ with it.* **8** (of things without life) remain in existence; survive: *No ship could ~ in such a rough sea.* **9** enjoy life intensely: *'I want to ~', she said, 'I don't want to spend my days looking after babies.'* **live it up,** have

great fun: *Let's go into town and ~ it up a little.*
live·li·hood /ˈlaɪvlɪhʊd/ n [C] means of living; way in which one earns money: *earn/ gain one's ~ by teaching.*
live·long /ˈlɪvlɒŋ US: ˈlaɪvlɒŋ/ adj (only in) **the livelong day/night,** all day/night.
live·ly /ˈlaɪvlɪ/ adj (-ier, -iest) **1** full of life and spirit; gay and cheerful: *The patient seems a little livelier/a little more ~ this morning. He has a ~ imagination.* **2** (of colour) bright; gay. **3** (of non-living things) moving quickly or causing quick movement: *a ~ ball.* **4** lifelike; realistic: *a ~ description of a football game.*
live·li·ness n [U]
liven /ˈlaɪvən/ vt, vi make or become lively: *How can we ~ things up?*
liver¹ /ˈlɪvə(r)/ n **1** [C] large, reddish-brown organ in the body which secretes bile and cleans the blood. **2** [U] animal's liver as food.
liv·er·ish /-ɪʃ/, **liv·ery** adj (*informal*) bilious.
liver² /ˈlɪvə(r)/ n [C] person who lives in a specified way: *a clean/loose ~.*
liv·ery /ˈlɪvərɪ/ n [C] (*pl* -ies) **1** special dress or uniform worn by male staff in a great household (esp of a king or noble) or by members of one of the city companies of London (trade or craft guilds). **2** (*poetic*) dress; covering: *birds in their winter ~.* **3** (also *~-stable*) stable where horses are fed and looked after for payment; stable from which horses may be hired.
liv·er·ied /ˈlɪvərɪd/ adj wearing livery(1).
liv·ery·man, (**a**) member of a livery company. (**b**) keeper of, worker in, a livery-stable.
lives /laɪvz/ *pl* of **life.**
live·stock /ˈlaɪvstɒk/ n [U] (esp) farm animals kept for use or profit, e g cattle, sheep, pigs.
livid /ˈlɪvɪd/ adj **1** of the colour of lead, blue-grey. **2** (of a person or his looks) furiously angry: *~ with rage.*
liv·id·ly adv
liv·ing¹ /ˈlɪvɪŋ/ adj **1** alive, esp now existent: *~ languages.* **within/in living memory,** within the memory of people now alive. **2** (of a likeness) true to life: *He's the ~ image of* (= is exactly like) *his father.* **3** strong; active; lively: *a ~ hope/faith.* **4** (as an intensifier): *scare the ~ daylight out of him.* □ **n the ~,** (used with a *pl verb*) those now alive: *He's still in the land of the ~.*
liv·ing² /ˈlɪvɪŋ/ n **1** [C] means of keeping alive, of earning what is needed for life: *earn/gain/get/make a ~ as a car salesman* **2** [U] manner of life: *good ~,* having good food, etc; *a poor standard of ~.* **3** [C] (Church of England) benefice.
`living-room, room for general use such as relaxing, entertaining.
liz·ard /ˈlɪzəd/ n [C] (kinds of) small, creep-

ing, long-tailed four-legged reptile.

llama /ˈlɑːmə/ n [C] S American animal with a thick woolly coat, used as a beast of burden.

lo /ləʊ/ int (old use) Look! See!

load[1] /ləʊd/ n [C] **1** that which is (to be) carried or supported, esp if heavy. **loads of,** (informal) a large amount. **2** (fig) weight of care, responsibility, etc: a heavy ∼ on one's shoulders. **take a load off sb's mind,** relieve him of anxiety, etc. **3** amount which a cart, etc can take: a ˋbus-∼ of passengers. **4** amount of work that a motor, engine, etc is required to do; amount of current supplied by a generating station or carried by an electric circuit.

load[2] /ləʊd/ vt, vi **1** put a load in or on: ∼ sacks on to a lorry; a poor old woman ∼ed (down) with her shopping. **load (sth) up,** fill with goods, materials, etc: Have you finished ∼ing up (the van) yet? **2** put a cartridge or shell into (a gun). **3** put a length of film into (a camera). **4** weight with lead; add extra weight to: ∼ed dice, so weighted as to give an unfair advantage.

a loaded question, one that is intended to trap a person into making an admission which may be harmful.

loaded adj (sl) having a lot of money.

loaf[1] /ləʊf/ n [C] (pl loaves /ləʊvz/) **1** bread cooked as a separate quantity; a two-pound ∼. **Half a loaf is better than none,** It is better to take what one can get or is offered than to run the risk of having nothing. **2** [C,U] (quantity of) food shaped and cooked: (a) meat ∼, made of minced meat, eggs, etc. **3** (sl) **use one's loaf,** think intelligently.

loaf[2] /ləʊf/ vi, vt waste time; spend time idly: Don't ∼ about while there's so much work to be done.

loafer, person who loafs.

loam /ləʊm/ n [U] fertile soil of sand and clay, often with much decayed vegetable matter in it.

loamy adj of or like loam: ∼y land.

loan /ləʊn/ n [C] **1** something lent, esp a sum of money: a ˋbank-∼. **2** [U] lending or being lent: I have the book out on ∼ from the library. □ vt (formal) = lend.

ˋloan-word, word taken from another language.

loath, loth /ləʊθ/ adj loath to do sth, unwilling.

loathe /ləʊð/ vt **1** feel disgust for; dislike greatly: She was seasick, and ∼d the smell of greasy food. **2** (informal) dislike: He ∼s travelling by air.

loathing, disgust.

loathsome /-səm/ adj disgusting; causing one to feel shocked: a loathsome disease.

loaves /ləʊvz/ pl of loaf[1].

lob /lɒb/ vi, vt (-bb-) strike or send (a ball) in a high arc (as in tennis). □ n [C] ball that is lobbed

lobby /ˈlɒbɪ/ n [C] (pl -ies) **1** porch, entrance-hall, corridor: the ∼ of a hotel/theatre. **2** (in the House of Commons, etc) large hall used for interviews between members and the public; group of people who try to influence members, e g of the House of Commons, the Senate in Washington, DC, to support or oppose proposed legislation. **3** (also diˋvision) (in the House of Commons) one of two corridors to which members go when a vote is taken in the House. □ vt, vi (try to) influence the members of a lawmaking body; get (a bill) passed or rejected in this way: ∼ a bill through the Senate; the Miners' Union ∼ing their M P's.

ˋlobby·ist /-ɪst/, person who lobbies.

lobe /ləʊb/ n [C] **1** lower rounded part of the external ear. **2** subdivision of the lungs or the brain.

lobed adj having lobes.

lob·ster /ˈlɒbstə(r)/ n **1** [C] shellfish with eight legs and two claws, bluish-black before and scarlet after being boiled. **2** [U] its flesh as food.

lo·cal /ˈləʊkəl/ adj **1** of, special to, a place or district: the ∼ doctor, working nearby; ∼ customs; ∼ government. **2** affecting a part, not the whole: a ∼ pain/injury/anaesthetic. □ n [C] **1** (usually pl) inhabitant(s) of a particular district. **2** item of local news in a newspaper. **3** (informal) local public house: pop into the ∼ for a pint.

ˋlocal anaesˋthetic, affecting only a part of the body.

ˋlocal auˋthority, officers elected to administer local government.

ˋlocal ˋcolour, details of the scenes and period described in a story, added to make the story more real.

ˋlocal eˋlection, of representatives for local government.

ˋlocal ˋgovernment, administration of the affairs of a district (roads, education, etc) by representatives elected by the residents.

ˋlocal ˋtime, time at any place in the world as calculated from the position of the sun.

lo·cally /-kəlɪ/ adv

lo·cale /ləʊˈkɑːl/ n [C] scene of an event; scene of a novel, etc.

lo·cal·ity /ləʊˈkælətɪ/ n (pl -ies) **1** [C] position of something; place in which an event occurs; place, district, neighbourhood. **2** [U] faculty of remembering and recognizing places, esp as a help in finding one's way: She has a good sense of ∼.

lo·cal·ize /ˈləʊkəlaɪz/ vt **1** make local, not general; confine within a particular part or area: There is little hope of localizing the disease. **2** invest with local characteristics.

lo·cal·iz·ation /ˌləʊkəlaɪˈzeɪʃən US: -lɪˈz-/ n [U]

lo·cate /ləʊˈkeɪt US: ˈləʊkeɪt/ vt **1** discover, show, the locality of: ∼ a town on a map. **2** establish in a place: Where is the new factory to be ∼d?

lo·ca·tion /ləʊˈkeɪʃən/ n 1 [U] locating or being located. 2 [C] position or place: *suitable ~s for new factories.* 3 place, not a film studio, where (part of) a cinema film is photographed. **on location,** shooting film in this way.

loch /lɒk/ n [C] (*Scot*) 1 long, narrow arm of the sea almost enclosed by land. 2 lake.

lock¹ /lɒk/ n [C] portion of hair that naturally hangs or clings together.

lock² /lɒk/ n [C] 1 appliance, mechanism, by which a door, lid, etc may be fastened with a bolt that needs a key to work it. **be/ put/keep sth under 'lock and 'key,** locked in something. 2 mechanism by which a gun is fired. **'lock, 'stock and 'barrel,** completely. 3 enclosed section of a canal or river at a point where the water level changes, for raising or lowering boats by the use of gates fitted with sluices. 4 [U] condition of being fixed or jammed so that movement is impossible. 5 extent of the turning arc of a steering wheel: *full ~,* with the steering wheel turned (right or left) as far as it will go.

'lock-'gate, gate on a lock(3).

'lock-keeper, keeper of a canal or river lock(3).

'lock-jaw, form of disease (tetanus) that causes the jaws to be firmly locked together.

'lock-smith, maker and mender of locks.

lock³ /lɒk/ vt,vi 1 fasten a door, box, etc with a lock. **lock sth away, (a)** put it away in a locked box, drawer, etc. **(b)** (*fig*) keep securely: *have a secret safely ~ed (away) in one's heart.* **lock sb in,** put him in a room of which the door is locked on the outside. **lock sb out,** keep him outside, prevent him from entering, by locking the gate or door on the inside. **lock sth/sb up, (a)** make safe by locking it/him away: *L~ up your jewellery before you go away.* **(b)** shut up a house, etc by locking all the doors. **(c)** put (a person) in prison, a mental home, etc. 2 have a lock; become locked: *This door doesn't ~,* has no lock or has a lock that does not work. 3 (cause to) become fixed, unable to move: *He ~ed the wheels of the car to prevent its being stolen. They were ~ed in each other's arms.* 4 **lock on to,** (of a missile, etc) find and automatically follow (a target) by radar.

'lock-out, refusal of employers to allow workmen to enter their place of work until certain conditions are agreed to or demands given up. ⇨ **strike**¹.

'lock-up, (*informal*) prison. □ *adj* that can be locked: *a ~-up garage,* one, e g at a hotel, with door(s) that can be ~ed.

lock·er /ˈlɒkə(r)/ n [C] 1 small cupboard, esp one for storing one's clothes, e g at a swimming-pool. 2 box or compartment used for clothes, stores, ammunition, etc.

lock·et /ˈlɒkɪt/ n [C] small (often gold or silver) case for a portrait, a lock of hair, etc, worn round the neck on a chain.

loco /ˈləʊkəʊ/ adj (*dated sl*) mad.

loco·mo·tion /ˌləʊkəˈməʊʃən/ n [U] moving, ability to move, from place to place.

loco·mo·tive /ˌləʊkəˈməʊtɪv/ adj of, having, causing, locomotion. □ n [C] self-propelled engine for use on railways.

lo·cust /ˈləʊkəst/ n [C] 1 (kinds of) migratory African and Asian winged insect which flies in great swarms and destroys crops and vegetables. 2 (kind of) thorny American tree.

locu·tion /ləˈkjuːʃən/ n [U] (*formal*) style of speech; way of using words; [C] particular phrase or expression.

lode /ləʊd/ n [C] vein of metal ore.

lode·star /ˈləʊdstɑː(r)/ n [C] star by which a ship may be steered.

lode·stone /ˈləʊdstəʊn/ n [U] magnetized iron ore.

lodge¹ /lɒdʒ/ n [C] 1 small house, esp one at the entrance to the grounds of a large house, occupied by a gatekeeper, gardener or other staff. 2 country house for temporary use: *a 'hunting ~ in the Highlands; a 'skiing ~.* 3 = porter's lodge. 4 (place of meeting for) members of a branch of a society such as the Freemasons. 5 beaver's den.

lodge² /lɒdʒ/ vt,vi 1 supply (a person) with a room or place to sleep in for a time: *The shipwrecked sailors were ~d in the school.* 2 live as a paying guest: *Where are you lodging now?* 3 **lodge in,** (cause to) enter and become fixed: *The bullet ~d in his jaw.* 4 put (money, etc) for safety: *~ one's valuables in the bank.* 5 place (a statement, etc) with the proper authorities: *~ a complaint against one's neighbours with the authorities.*

lodg·er, person lodging(2) in a house: *Taking in lodgers.*

lodg·ing /ˈlɒdʒɪŋ/ n [C] (usually *pl*) room or rooms (not in a hotel) rented to live in: *Where can we find (a) ~ for the night?*

lodge·ment (*US* also **lodgment**) /ˈlɒdʒmənt/ n 1 [U] act or process of lodging: the *~ of a complaint.* ⇨ **lodge**¹(5). 2 [C] something that has been deposited: *a ~ of dirt in a pipe.*

loft¹ /lɒft *US:* lɔːft/ n [C] 1 room, place, used for storing things, in the highest part of a house, under the roof. 2 space under the roof of a stable or barn, where hay or straw is stored. 3 gallery in a church or hall: *the 'organ-~.*

loft² /lɒft *US:* lɔːft/ vt (in golf, cricket) hit (a ball) high: *~ a ball over the fielders' heads.*

lofty /ˈlɒftɪ *US:* ˈlɔːftɪ/ adj (-ier, -iest) 1 (not used of persons) of great height: *a ~ mountain/tower.* 2 (of thoughts, aims, feelings, etc) distinguished; noble: *~ sentiments; a ~ style.* 3 haughty; proud; consciously superior: *in a ~ manner.*

loft·ily /-əlɪ/ adv

lofti·ness n [U]

log¹ /lɒg US: lɔg/ n [C] rough length of tree-trunk that has fallen or been cut down; short piece of this for a fire. *sleep like a log*, sleep soundly and with little or no movement.

'log 'cabin, cabin made of logs.

log-ging, work of cutting down forest trees for timber: *a ~-ging camp.*

log² /lɒg US: lɔg/ n [C] **1** device attached to a knotted line, trailed from a ship, to measure its speed through the water. **2** = log-book(a). □ vt (-gg-) enter (facts) in the log-book of a ship or aircraft.

'log-book, (a) book with a permanent daily record of events during a ship's voyage (esp the weather, ship's position, speed, and distance). **(b)** any record of performance, e g of a car or aircraft. **(c)** (*informal*) Registration Book (of a motor-vehicle).

log³ /lɒg US: lɔg/ n [C] (abbr of) logarithm.

lo-gan-berry /ˈləʊɡənberɪ/ n [C] (pl -ies) (large dark-red berry from a) plant that is a cross between a blackberry and a raspberry.

log-ar-ithm /ˈlɒɡərɪθm US: ˈlɔg-/ n [C] one of a series of numbers set out in tables which make it possible to work out problems in multiplication and division by adding and subtracting.

log-ger-heads /ˈlɒgəhedz/ n (only in) *at loggerheads*, disagreeing or disputing: *He's constantly at ~ with his wife.*

log-gia /ˈlɒdʒɪə/ n [C] (*It*) open-sided gallery or arcade; part of a house with one side open to the garden.

logic /ˈlɒdʒɪk/ n [U] **1** science, method, of reasoning. **2** (person's) ability to argue and convince: *argue with ~.*

logi-cal /-kəl/ adj **(a)** in accordance with the rules of logic. **(b)** able to reason correctly: *~al behaviour.*

logi-cally /-klɪ/ adv

lo-gician /ləˈdʒɪʃən/, person skilled in logic.

loin /lɔɪn/ n **1** (pl) the lower part of the body on both sides of the spine between the ribs and the hip-bones. **2** [C] joint of meat which includes the loins: *~ of mutton.*

'loin-cloth, piece of cloth covering the body, folded between the legs, and fastened round the loins.

loi-ter /ˈlɔɪtə(r)/ vi, vt go slowly and stop frequently on the way somewhere; stand about; pass (time) in this way: *~ on one's way home.*

loi-terer, person who loiters.

loll /lɒl/ vi, vt **1** rest, sit or stand (*about/around*) in a lazy way. **2** (of the tongue) (allow to) hang (the usual word): *The dog's tongue was ~ing out.*

lol-li-pop /ˈlɒlɪpɒp/ n [C] large sweet of boiled sugar on a stick, held in the hand and sucked.

'ice-lollipop, quantity of frozen fruit juice on a stick.

lolly /ˈlɒlɪ/ n (pl -ies) **1** [C] (*informal*) lollipop: *iced lollies.* **2** [U] (*sl*) money.

lone /ləʊn/ adj solitary; without companions; unfrequented. (*Note: alone* and *lonely* are more usual.)

lone-ly /ˈləʊnlɪ/ adj (-ier, -iest) **1** without companions: *a ~ traveller.* **2** sad or melancholy because one lacks companions, sympathy, friendship: *feel ~.* **3** (of places) not often visited; far from inhabited places or towns: *a ~ mountain village.*

lone-li-ness n [U] state of being lonely.

lone-some /ˈləʊnsəm/ adj **1** = lonely(2). **2** unvisited: *a ~ valley.*

long¹ /lɒŋ US: lɔŋ/ adj (-er, -est) **1** (of extent in space; measuring much from end to end): *How ~ is the River Nile? What ~ hair men have nowadays!* *put on a long face,* ⇨ face¹(3). **2** (in phrases: of (great) extent) *have a long arm,* be able to make one's power felt far. *the long arm of the law,* its far-reaching power. **3** (of duration or extent in time): *the ~ vacation,* the summer vacation of law courts and universities. *He was ill for a ~ time. He won't be ~* (*in*) *making up his mind,* will soon do so. **4** (of vowel sounds) taking more time to utter than others: *'Fit' has a short vowel and 'feel' has a ~ vowel.* **5** (in phrases concerned with extent in time) *take a long, cool/hard look at sth,* consider facts, problems seriously and for a long time. *take the long view,* consider events, situations, etc a long time ahead, rather than the present situation, etc. *in the 'long run,* ⇨ run¹(6). *in the long term,* looking ahead for a long time. Hence, **'long-term** adj: *~-term agreements.*

'long-boat, sailing-ship's largest boat.

'long-'distance adj covering a long distance: *a ~-distance race/telephone call/lorry driver.*

'long-hand, ordinary handwriting (contrasted with shorthand *and* typing).

the 'long jump, athletic contest for jumping along the ground. ⇨ high jump.

long odds, (in betting) that are very risky, e g 50 to 1.

'long-play(ing) 'record, (abbr **LP**) with many tracks(6).

'long-range adj of long periods, distances: *a ~-range weather forecast,* e g for one month ahead.

long shot, ⇨ shot¹(2).

'long 'sighted adj **(a)** able to see things a great distance away. **(b)** (*fig*) having foresight.

'long-'standing adj of long duration: *a ~-standing promise,* made a time ago.

long suit, many playing-cards of the same suit(5).

'long wave, (radio telegraphy) wave o. 1 000 metres or over.

'long-'winded adj (*fig*) boring: tedious; *a ~-winded lecturer.*

long² /lɒŋ US: lɔŋ/ adv **1** for a long time: *Stay* (*for*) *as ~ as you like. as/so long as,* on condition that, provided that: *You may* borrow the book so ∼ as you return it. **2** at a long time (from a point of time): ∼ ago/ before/after/since. **3** (of duration) throughout the specified time: all day ∼, throughout the whole day. **4** no/any/much longer, after a certain point of time: I can't wait any/much ∼er. He's no ∼er living here.

'long-drawn-'out adj extended; unduly prolonged: a ∼-drawn-out visit from my mother-in-law.

'long-suffering adj patient and uncomplaining: his ∼-suffering wife.

long³ /loŋ US: loŋ/ n (sing only) **1** long time or interval: The work won't take ∼. **before long,** soon. **the long and the short of it,** all that need be said; the general effect or result. **2** long syllable, esp in Latin verse: four ∼s and six shorts.

long⁴ /loŋ US: loŋ/ vi desire earnestly; wish for very much: She ∼ed for him to say something. I'm ∼ing to see you.

long·ing n [C,U] (an) earnest desire: a ∼ing to be home. □ adj having or showing a keen desire: with ∼ing eyes.

long·ing·ly adv

lon·gev·ity /lon'dʒevətɪ/ n [U] long life.

longi·tude /'londʒɪtjud US: -tud/ n [C] distance east or west (measured in degrees) from a meridian(1), esp that of Greenwich, in London.

longi·tudi·nal /'londʒɪ'tjudməl US: -'tudənəl/ adj (a) of longitude. (b) of or in length. (c) running lengthwise: longitudinal stripes.

long·ways /'loŋweɪz US: 'loŋ-/, **long·wise** /'loŋwaɪz US: 'loŋ-/ adv = lengthways.

loo /lu/ n [C] (GB informal) = lavatory; toilet.

look¹ /lʊk/ n [C] **1** act of looking: Let me have a ∼ at your new car. **take a look at,** examine (briefly). **2** appearance; what something suggests when seen: There were angry ∼s from the neighbours. The town has a European ∼. **3** (pl) person's appearance: She's beginning to lose her ∼s, her beauty.

look² /lʊk/ vi,vt (For uses with adverbial particles and prepositions⇨ **5** below.) **1** use one's sight; turn the eyes in some direction; try to see: ∼ (up) at the ceiling; ∼ (down) at the floor. We ∼ed but saw nothing. **Look before you leap,** (proverb) Do not act without considering the possible consequences. **2** seem to be, have a certain appearance: ∼ sad/ill/tired. **(not) look oneself,** (not) have one's normal appearance, health etc. **look one's age,** have an appearance that conforms to one's age: You don't ∼ your age, look younger than you are. **look one's best,** appear most attractive, to the greatest advantage: She ∼s her best in black. **look blue,** appear sad or discontented. **Look here!** (often used to call or demand attention). **Look sharp!** Hurry up!

look well, (a) (of persons) be healthy in appearance: He's ∼ing very well. **(b)** (of things, a person) be attractive, pleasing: Does this hat ∼ well on me? He ∼s well in naval uniform. **3 look like/as if,** appear, seem (to be); probably will: It ∼s like rain. You ∼ as if you've seen a ghost! **4** pay attention; learn by seeing: L∼ where you're going!

5 (uses with adverbial particles and prepositions):

look about (for sth), be on the watch, in search of; examine one's surroundings, the state of affairs, etc: Are you still ∼ing about for a job?

look after sb/sth, (a) take care of; attend to: He needs a wife to ∼ after him. **(b)** follow with the eyes: They ∼ed after the train as it left the station.

look at sth, (special uses) **(a)** (in negative sentences) refuse; reject: They wouldn't ∼ at my proposal. **(b)** examine: We must ∼ at the question from all sides. Doctor, will you ∼ at my ankle? **good/bad, etc to look at,** of good, etc appearance: The hotel/She is not much to ∼ at.

look away (from sth), turn the eyes away.

look back (on sth), (fig) think about something in the past.

look down on sb, consider oneself superior to. **look down one's nose at sb,** (informal) consider him to be inferior.

look for sb/sth, search for; try to find: Are you still ∼ing for a job? **be looking for trouble,** behave in a way that will get one into trouble.

look forward to sth, think about something which will happen in the future (usually with pleasure): We're ∼ing forward to seeing you again.

look in (on sb), make a short visit: Won't you ∼ in (on me) next time you're in town? **get/give sb a 'look-in,** (informal) get/give him chance (of winning, etc).

look into sth, (a) investigate; examine: ∼ into a question. **(b)** look at (the inside of): He ∼ed into the box/the mirror/her eyes.

look on, watch: Why don't you play football instead of just ∼ing on? **look on sb as,** consider as. **look on sb with,** consider in the way specified: He seems to ∼ on me with distrust. **look on to,** (of a place, room, etc) overlook: My bedroom ∼s on to the garden. **look out (of sth) (at sth):** He stood at the window and ∼ed out (at the view). **look out (for sb/sth),** be prepared (for), be on the watch for: Will you go to the station and ∼ out for Mr Hill? Hence, **'look-out,** n **(a)** (sing only) state of being watchful: keep a good ∼-out; be on the ∼-out for bargains. **(b)** [C] place from which to watch; person who has the duty of watching. **(c)** (sing only) prospect; what seems likely to come or happen: That's your own ∼-out, something you yourself must deal with. **look sth out**

(for sb), select by making an inspection: ~ *out some old toys for the school jumble sale.*

look over sth, inspect; examine: ~ *over a house before buying it.*

look round, (a) examine before deciding: *Don't make a hurried decision; ~ round first.* **(b)** turn the head (to see): *When I ~ed round for her, she was leaving the hall.* **look round sth,** (go and) visit: *Have we time to ~ round (the town/cathedral) before lunch?*

look through, study; examine: *L~ through your notes before the examination.*

look to sth, be careful of or about: *The country must ~ to its defences.* **look to sb for sth/to do sth,** rely on: *They are all ~ing to you for help.* **look to/towards,** face: *a house ~ing towards the river/to the south.*

look up, (a) raise the eyes: *Don't ~ up.* **(b)** improve in price or prosperity: *Business is ~ing up.* **look sth up,** search for (a word in a dictionary, facts in a guide, etc): *Please ~ up a fast train to Leeds.* **look sb up,** visit: *Do ~ me up next time you're in London.*

look sb up and down, look at him with contempt.

look upon sb as/with, = look on sb as/ with.

look·ing glass /ˈlʊkɪŋ glɑs US: glæs/ *n* [C] *(dated)* mirror.

loom¹ /lum/ *n* [C] machine for weaving cloth.

loom² /lum/ *vi* **1** appear indistinctly and in a threatening way: *The dark outline of another ship ~ed (up) through the fog.* **2** *(fig)* appear great and fill the mind: *The threat of the H-bomb ~ed large in their minds.*

loon /lun/ *n* [C] **1** large diving-bird that lives on fish and has a loud, wild cry. **2** *(informal)* silly person.

loony /ˈlunɪ/ *n* [C], *adj (sl)* = lunatic. **ˈloony-bin,** *n (sl)* = mental home.

loop /lup/ *n* [C] **1** (shape produced by a) curve crossing itself. **2** part of a length of string, wire, ribbon, metal, etc in such a shape, eg as a knot, fastening, or handle. □ *vt,vi* **1** form or bend into a loop; supply with a loop: ~ *things together.* **2** make a loop.

loop·hole /ˈluphəʊl/ *n* [C] **1** narrow vertical opening in a wall (as in old forts, stockades, etc). **2** *(fig)* way of escape from control, esp one provided by inexact wording of a rule: *find a ~ in the law.*

loopy /ˈlupɪ/ *adj* (-ier, -iest) *(dated sl)* = crazy.

loose¹ /lus/ *adj* (-r, -st) **1** not held, tied up, fastened, packed, or contained in something: *That dog is too dangerous to be left ~.* **break/get loose,** escape confinement: *One of the tigers in the zoo has broken/got ~.* **2** not close-fitting; not tight or tense: ~*-fitting clothes.* **3** moving more freely than is right or usual: *a ~ tooth.* **come/work loose,** (of a fastening, bolt, etc) come unfastened or insecure. **4** not firmly or properly tied: *a ~*

knot. **at a loose end,** *(fig)* (of a person) having nothing to do. **5** (of talk, behaviour, etc) not controlled: *a ~* (= immoral) *woman.* **6** inexact; indefinite; (of translations) not close to the original: *a ~ argument.* **7** not compact; not closely packed: ~ *soil; cloth with a ~ weave.* **8** (of the human body) rather awkward, ungainly in appearance. **9** (of bodily actions) careless, inaccurate: ~ *passes* (in football).

loose·ly *adv* in a loose manner.

loose² /lus/ *vt* loosen (which is more usual): *Wine ~d his tongue,* made him talk freely.

loosen /ˈlusən/ *vt,vi* make or become loose or looser: *L~ the screw. I must exercise and ~ up my muscles.*

loot /lut/ *n* [U] goods (esp private property) taken away unlawfully and by force, e g by thieves, or by soldiers in time of war. □ *vt,vi* carry off loot from.

looter, person who loots.

lop /lɒp/ *vt* (-pp-) cut, chop (branches, etc from a tree).

lope /ləʊp/ *vi* move along with long, easy steps or strides. □ *n* [C] loping step, stride.

lop-eared /ˈlɒp ɪəd/ *adj* having drooping ears: *a ~ rabbit.*

lop-sided /ˈlɒp ˈsaɪdɪd/ *adj* with one side lower than the other.

lord /lɔd/ *n* [C] **1** supreme male ruler: *our sovereign ~ the King.* **2** L~, God; Christ: *the ˈL~'s Day,* Sunday; *the ˈL~'s ˈPrayer,* that given by Jesus to his followers. **3** (used in exclamations of surprise, etc): *Good L~!* **3** peer; nobleman. **as drunk as a lord,** very drunk. **4** title prefixed to names of peers and barons: *L~ Derby.* **5** person in a position of authority: *the First L~ of the Admiralty,* the president of the Admiralty **6** first word in many official titles: *the L~ Mayor of London.* **7 My ~,** respectful formula for addressing certain noblemen and judges and bishops. **8** (in feudal times) socially superior man: *the ~ of the manor,* man from whom men held land and to whom they owed service. **9** (*pl*) = the House of Lords.

the ˈHouse of ˈLords, *(GB)* upper division of Parliament.

lord·ly /ˈlɔdlɪ/ *adj* (-ier, -iest) **1** arrogant; feeling superior. **2** like, suitable for, a lord.

lord·ship /ˈlɔdʃɪp/ *n* **1** [U] rule, authority (*over*). **2 His/Your L~,** (used when speaking of (to) a lord).

lore /lɔ(r)/ *n* [U] learning or knowledge, esp handed down from past times, or possessed by a class of people: ˈfolk~.

lor·gnette /lɔˈnjet/ *n* [C] pair of framed lenses formerly held to the eyes on a long handle.

lorry /ˈlɒrɪ US: ˈlɔrɪ/ *n* [C] (*pl* -ies) (*US* = truck) strong, usually roofless, motor-vehicle, used for carrying goods by road.

lose /luz/ *vt,vi* (*pt,pp* lost /lost US: lɔst/) **1** no longer have; have taken away from one by accident, carelessness, misfortune, death, etc: ∼ one's money; She has lost her husband, He is dead. He has lost his job, has been dismissed. He's losing patience, is becoming impatient. **lose one's balance,** fall over. **lose one's head,** ⇨ head¹(19). **lose interest (in sb/sth),** cease to be interested in, attracted by. **lose one's temper,** become angry. **2 be lost,** disappear; die; be dead: Is letter-writing a ∼ art? Has the art of writing (social) letters died, e g because of the use of the telephone? **be/get lost,** not know where one is: The climbers were lost for three days on the mountain. **be lost in sth,** be deeply occupied or filled with, e g thought, wonder, admiration. **3** be unable to find: I've lost the keys of my car. We lost our way in the dark. **lose one's place,** (in a book, etc) be unable to find the page, paragraph, etc where one stopped reading. **lose sight of sth,** (a) fail to take account of: We mustn't ∼ sight of the fact that.... (b) no longer be able to see: We lost sight of him in the crowd. **lose track of sth,** ⇨ track. **4** be too late for: ∼ one's train (miss is more usual). **5** be, become; unable to be heard, seen, etc. What he said was lost in the applause that greeted him. **6** cause (a person) the loss of: Lateness will ∼ you your job. **7** fail to win, be defeated: ∼ a game/a battle/a lawsuit. **a lost cause,** one that has already been defeated or is sure to be defeated. **8** be, become, worse: You will ∼ nothing by waiting, will not suffer any loss. **9** (of a watch or clock) go too slowly; fail to keep correct time because of this: My watch ∼s two minutes a day. **10** spend time, opportunity, efforts to no purpose; waste: There's not a moment to ∼. He lost no time in doing it, did it at once. **11 lose oneself in sth,** become deeply interested in it so that one is unaware of other things: She lost herself in a book. **lose out,** be unsuccessful, fail to win something.

loser, person who loses or is defeated: He's a good/bad ∼r, is cheerful/discontented when he loses.

loss /lɒs US: lɔs/ n **1** [U] act or fact or process of losing: L∼ of health is more serious than ∼ of money. **2** [U] (with a, an) failure to keep, maintain or use: an enormous ∼. There was a temporary ∼ of power. **3** [U] failure to win or obtain: the ∼ of a game/contract. **4** [C] that which is lost: suffer heavy ∼es in war, men killed, wounded, captured; ships and aircraft put out of action. **a total loss,** from which nothing can be saved: The ship was wrecked and became a total ∼. **5** (sing only) disadvantage or deprivation: Such a man is no great ∼, We need not regret losing his services. **a dead loss,** (informal) (of a person) worthless. **6 (be) at a loss for sth/to do sth,** be uncertain: He was at a ∼ for words/to know what to say, did not know how to express himself.

lost /lɒst US: lɔst/ pt,pp of lose.

lot¹ /lɒt/ n [C] (informal) **1 the ∼,** the whole number or quantity: That's the ∼, That's all or everything. Take the (whole) ∼. **2 a lot (of)/lots (and lots) (of),** a great amount or number (of): What a ∼ of time you take to dress! I saw quite a ∼ of her (= saw her often) when I was in London last month. **3** (used as an adverb) very much: He's feeling a ∼ better today.

lot² /lɒt/ n **1** (one of a set of objects used in) the making of a selection or decision by methods depending on chance: divide property by ∼. **draw/cast lots,** e g by taking pieces of paper marked in some way from a box: They drew ∼s to decide who should begin. **2** [C] decision or choice resulting from this: The ∼ came to/fell on me. **3** [C] person's fortune or destiny: His ∼ has been a hard one. **cast/throw in one's lot with sb,** decide to share work, interests, money, etc. **4** item, or number of items, (to be) sold at an auction sale: L∼ 46, six chairs. **5** collection of objects of the same kind: We have received a new ∼ of coats from Paris. **6 a bad lot,** (informal) a bad person. **7** plot of land: a vacant ∼, a building site.

loth /ləʊθ/ adj ⇨ loath.

lotion /ˈləʊʃən/ n [C,U] (kind of) medicinal liquid for use on the skin: ∼ for the face; soothing ∼s for insect bites.

lottery /ˈlɒtərɪ/ n [C] (pl -ies) **1** arrangement to give prizes to holders of numbered tickets previously bought by them and drawn by lot. **2** (fig) something considered to be uncertain: Is marriage a ∼?

lotus /ˈləʊtəs/ n [C] (pl -ses) (kinds of) water-lily, esp the Egyptian and Asiatic kinds.

'lotus-eater, lazy person who is only interested in pleasure.

loud /laʊd/ adj (-er, -est) **1** not quiet or soft; easily heard: ∼ voices/cries/laughs. **2** (of a person's behaviour; of colours) of the obvious kind that forces itself on the attention; conspicuous. □ adv in a loud manner: Don't talk so ∼.

loud·ly adv in a loud manner: Someone knocked ∼ly at the door.

loud·ness n [U]

'loud-'speaker, (often shortened to speaker) part of a radio receiving apparatus that converts electric impulses into audible sounds.

lounge /laʊndʒ/ vi sit, stand about (leaning against something) in a lazy way: lounging at street corners. □ n [C] **1** act of lounging. **2** comfortable sitting-room, esp in a club or hotel. **3** best bar in a public house.

'lounge-chair, comfortable armchair.

'lounge-suit, (dated) man's suit for informal wear.

lour, lower /ˈlaʊə(r)/ vi **1** frown; look bad-tempered: **2** (of the sky, clouds) look dark, stormy.

377

lour·ing·ly adv

louse /laʊs/ n [C] (pl lice /laɪs/) **1** (kinds of) small insect living on the bodies of animals and human beings; similar insect living on plants. **2** (sl) contemptible person: He's an absolute ~.

lousy /ˈlaʊzɪ/ adj (-ier, -iest) **1** infested with lice. **2** (informal) bad: a ~ film. **3** (sl) well provided (with): He's ~ with money.

lout /laʊt/ n [C] clumsy, ill-mannered man. `**lout·ish** /-ɪʃ/ adj

lov·able /ˈlʌvəbəl/ adj deserving, inspiring, worthy of love: a ~ child; a child's ~ ways.

love[1] /lʌv/ n **1** [U] warm, kind feeling; fondness; affectionate and tender devotion: a mother's ~ for her children; a ~ of adventure; ~ of (one's) country, patriotism; show ~ towards one's neighbours. **not to be had for love or money,** impossible to get by any means. **There's no love lost between them,** They dislike each other. **a labour of love,** (a) done for the enjoyment of doing it. (b) done out of love of somebody. **for the love of,** (in appeals, etc) for the sake of; in the name of: Put that gun down, for the ~ of God! **2** [U] warm, kind feeling between two persons of opposite sex; sexual passion or desire; this as a literary subject: My ~ for you is deeper than the sea. **be/fall in love (with sb),** have/begin to have love and desire (for). **make love (to sb),** show that one is in love; do the things that lovers do, e g kiss, caress, have sexual intercourse: Make ~, not war! **3** form of address between lovers, husband and wife, or to a child: Come here, my ~. **4** personification of love, i e a Cupid. **5** (in games) no score, nothing, nil: ~ all, no score for either side.

`**love-affair,** relationship between people in love, (now implying a sexual relationship).

`**love-bird,** (a) small brightly coloured parrot which stays very near its mate. (b) (young) lover very much in love.

`**love-knot,** bow of ribbon, tied in a special way, formerly given or worn as a pledge of love.

`**love-letter,** letter between persons in love and about their love.

`**love-lorn** /-lɔːn/ adj unhappy because one's love is not returned.

`**love-match,** marriage made for love's sake, not an arranged marriage.

`**love-sick** adj suffering because of (unreturned) love.

`**love-song,** song about love.

`**love-story,** novel or story of which the main theme is love.

`**love-token,** something given as a symbol of love.

love-less adj unloved; without love: a ~less marriage.

love[2] /lʌv/ vt **1** have strong affection or deep tender feelings for: loving one's parents/ one's country. **2** worship: ~ God. **3** have

kind feelings towards: ~ your neighbours. **4** be very fond of; like; find pleasure in: ~ ice-cream / new clothes / going to parties. 'Will you come with me?'—'I'd ~ to'.

love·ly /ˈlʌvlɪ/ adj **1** beautiful; attractive; pleasant: a ~ view; a ~ woman; a ~ hair/ weather. **2** (informal) pleasant; amusing: We had a ~ holiday. It's ~ and warm here, pleasant because warm. **3** lovable: Oh, she's a ~ person.

love·li·ness n [U]

lover /ˈlʌvə(r)/ n [C] **1** person who is fond of or devoted to (something): a ~ of music/ horses/good wine. **2** (pl) man and woman in love: happy ~s. **3** man who deeply admires a woman, esp, now, a man who loves a woman and has a sexual relationship with her.

lov·ing /ˈlʌvɪŋ/ adj feeling or showing love: a ~ friend; ~ parents.

lov·ing·ly adv in a loving way.

low[1] /ləʊ/ adj (-er, -est) **1** not extending far upwards; not high: a ~ wall/ceiling/shelf/ hills. She was wearing a dress cut ~ in the neck/a ~-necked dress, one leaving part of the shoulders and breasts visible. **lie low,** (fig) keep hidden or quiet (and wait): The escaped prisoners had to lie ~ for months. **2** below the usual or normal level or intensity: ~ pressure, e g of the atmosphere, of gas or water. The rivers were ~ during the dry summer. **3** (of sounds) not loud; not high in pitch: speak in a ~ voice; the ~ notes of a cello. **4** of or in inferior rank or social class: men of ~ birth. **5** commonplace; coarse; vulgar: ~ manners/tastes. **bring sb/sth low,** reduce in position, wealth, etc. **6** feeble; lacking in strength of body or mind: in a ~ state of health; feel ~/in ~ spirits, unhappy, depressed. **7** of small amount as measured by a scale or by degrees: a ~ temperature; ~ prices/wages/rates of pay. **have a low opinion of sb/sth,** think very little of him, his work, etc. **8** (of a supply of anything) **be/run low,** be/become nearly exhausted: The sugar is running ~. **9** not highly developed: ~ forms of life.

`**low-'born** adj of humble birth.

`**low-'bred** adj having coarse manners.

`**low-brow** n [C], adj (person) showing little interest in or taste for intellectual things.

lower case, (in printing) small letters, not capitals.

Lower Chamber/House, lower branch of a legislative assembly, e g the House of Commons in GB, the House of Representatives in US.

Low Church, group in the Church of England giving a low place to the authority of bishops and priests, ecclesiastical organization, ritual, etc (contrasted with High Church). Hence, **Low Churchman,** supporter of this.

`**low-down** adj (informal) dishonourable: ~-down behaviour/tricks. □ n get/give sb *the low-down (on sth/sb),* (*informal*) the true facts, inside information which is not generally known.

'**low `key(ed),** *adj* (*fig*) in a restrained, reserved, manner.

Low Mass, celebration of the Eucharist without a choir.

'**low-rise** *adj* (of buildings) having only one or two storeys.

'**low-`spirited** *adj* depressed; sad.

Low Sunday, Low Week, coming after Easter Day and Easter Week.

low tide/water, time when the tide is far from the shore or river bank.

low·ness *n* [U]

low² /ləʊ/ *adv* (-er, -est) in or to a low position; in a low manner; *aim/shoot ∼; bow ∼ to the Queen; buy ∼* (= at low prices) *and sell high.*

low³ /ləʊ/ *n* [C] low level or figure: *Several industrial shares reached new ∼s yesterday.*

low⁴ /ləʊ/ *n* [U] sound made by cows. □ *vt* (of cows) make this sound.

lower¹ /'ləʊə(r)/ *vt,vi* **1** let or bring down; cause to be down: *∼ the sails/a flag.* **2** make or become less high: *∼ the rent of a house. He ∼ed his voice to a whisper.* **3** *lower oneself,* degrade, disgrace: *He would never ∼ himself by taking bribes.* **4** weaken: *Poor diet ∼s resistance to illness.*

lower² /'laʊə(r)/ *vi* = lour.

lower·most /'ləʊəməʊst/ *adj* = lowest.

low·ly /'ləʊlɪ/ *adj* (-ier, -iest) humble; modest.

low·li·ness *n* [U]

loyal /'lɔɪəl/ *adj* true and faithful (*to*): *∼ supporters; ∼ to one's country.*

'**loyal·ist** /-ɪst/, person who is loyal to his ruler and government, esp one who supports the head of an established government during a revolt.

loy·ally /'lɔɪəlɪ/ *adv*

loy·alty *n* (*pl* -ies) **(a)** [U] being loyal; loyal conduct. **(b)** (*pl*) faithful attachment: *tribal loyalties.*

loz·enge /'lozɪndʒ/ *n* [C] **1** four-sided, diamond-shaped figure. **2** sweet of this shape, esp one containing medicine: `*cough ∼s.*

L-plate /'el pleɪt/ *n* [C] plate with a large capital L, fixed to a motor-vehicle for a person learning to drive.

lu·bri·cant /'lubrɪkənt/ *n* [U] substance that lubricates.

lu·bri·cate /'lubrɪkeɪt/ *vt* **1** put oil or grease into (machine parts) to make (them) work easily. **2** (*fig*) do something that makes action, etc easier.

lu·bri·ca·tion /lubrɪ'keɪʃən/ *n* [U]

lu·cid /'lusɪd/ *adj* **1** clear; easy to understand: *a ∼ mind; a ∼ explanation.* **2** mentally sound: *∼ intervals,* periods of sanity between periods of insanity. **3** (*poetry*) bright, clear.

lu·cid·ly *adv*

lu·cid·ity /lu'sɪdətɪ/ *n* [U]

luck /lʌk/ *n* [U] chance; fortune (good or bad); something considered to come by chance: *have good/bad ∼. As ∼ would have it,...* Fortunately,... (or Unfortunately,.... according to context). *It was hard ∼ on you that...,* It was unfortunate for you that.... *Bad luck!* (used to show sympathy). *Good Luck!* (used to encourage, express hopes of good fortune, etc).

luck·less *adj* unfortunate; turning out badly: *a ∼less day/attempt.*

lucky /'lʌkɪ/ *adj* (-ier, -iest) having, bringing, resulting from, good luck: *a ∼ man/ guess/escape. You are ∼ to be alive after being in that accident.*

luck·ily /'lʌkəlɪ/ *adv* fortunately: *Luckily for me the train was late, so I just caught it.*

lu·cra·tive /'lukrətɪv/ *adj* profitable.

lu·di·crous /'ludɪkrəs/ *adj* ridiculous.

lu·di·crous·ly *adv*

lug /lʌg/ *vt* (-gg-) pull or drag roughly and with much effort: *∼ging two heavy suitcases up the stairs.* □ *n* [C] hard or rough pull.

lug·gage /'lʌgɪdʒ/ *n* [U] bags, trunks, etc and their contents taken on a journey: *six pieces of ∼.* (*US* = baggage.)

'**luggage-rack,** rack (above the seats) in a train, coach, etc for luggage.

'**luggage-van,** carriage for luggage on a train.

lu·gu·bri·ous /lu'gubrɪəs/ *adj* (*formal*) dismal; mournful.

lu·gu·bri·ous·ly *adv*

luke·warm /'luk`wɔm/ *adj* **1** (of liquids, etc) neither very warm nor cold. **2** (*fig*) not eager either in supporting or opposing: *give only ∼ support to a cause.*

lull /lʌl/ *vt,vi* make or become quiet or less active: *∼ a baby to sleep,* e g by rocking it and singing to it. □ *n* [C] interval of quiet or calm: *a ∼ in the storm/in the conversation.*

lull·aby /'lʌləbaɪ/ *n* [C] (*pl* -ies) **1** song for lulling a baby to sleep. **2** gentle, soft sound, e g made by wind in trees or by the running water of a brook.

lum·bago /lʌm'beɪgəʊ/ *n* [U] muscular pain in the lumbar regions.

lum·bar /'lʌmbə(r)/ *adj* of the loins: *the ∼ regions,* the lower part of the back.

lum·ber¹ /'lʌmbə(r)/ *n* [U] **1** roughly prepared wood; wood that has been sawn into planks, boards, etc. **2** (chiefly *GB*) useless or unwanted articles stored away or taking up space (e g old furniture, pictures). □ *vt* **1** fill with lumber: *a room ∼ed up with useless articles.* **2** (*fig*) fill: *a mind that is ∼ed (up) with useless bits of information.* **3** (*informal*) leave (something or somebody unpleasant or unwanted) with: *be ∼ed with one's in-laws for the weekend.*

'**lum·ber·jack,** person who fells trees, saws or transports lumber.

'**lum·ber·room,** for storing lumber(2).

lum·ber² /'lʌmbə(r)/ *vi* move in a heavy,

clumsy, noisy way: *The tanks ~ed along/ by/past.*

lu·min·ary /ˈluːmɪnərɪ *US*: -nerɪ/ *n* [C] (*pl* -ies) **1** star; the sun or moon. **2** (*fig*) great moral or intellectual leader.

lu·mi·nous /ˈluːmɪnəs/ *adj* **1** giving out light; bright: *~ paint*, as used on road signs, clocks and watches, visible in the dark. **2** (*fig*) easily understood: *a ~ speaker/ explanation.*

lu·min·os·ity /ˌluːmɪˈnɒsətɪ/ *n* [U].

lump¹ /lʌmp/ *n* [C] **1** hard or compact mass, usually without a regular shape: *a ~ of coal/ sugar. a 'lump ˋsum,* one payment for a number of separate sums that are owed. **2** swelling or bump; bruise: *He has a bad ~ on the forehead. have a lump in one's throat,* a feeling of pressure (as caused by strong emotion). **3** (*informal*) heavy, dull person. □ *vt* **1** *lump together,* put together: *Can we ~ all these items together under the heading 'costs'?* **2** form into lumps.
lumpy *adj* (-ier, -iest) full of, covered with, lumps; *~y soup.*

lump² /lʌmp/ *vt* (only on) *lump it,* put up with something unpleasant or unwanted: *If you don't like it you can ~ it.*

lu·nacy /ˈluːnəsɪ/ *n* [U] madness.

lu·nar /ˈluːnə(r)/ *adj* of the moon.
lunar module, detachable section of a spacecraft that orbits the moon and may descend to its surface.
lunar month, average time between successive new moons, about 29½ days.

lu·na·tic /ˈluːnətɪk/ *n* [C] mental patient (the preferred term). □ *adj* mad; extremely foolish: *a ~ proposal.*
ˋlunatic asylum, (*dated*) mental home or hospital.
ˈlunatic ˈfringe, minority group with extreme views, or engaged in eccentric activities.

lunch /lʌntʃ/ *n* [C] meal taken in the middle of the day: *They were at ~ when I called.* □ *vi, vt* eat/provide lunch.
lunch·eon /ˈlʌntʃən/ *n* (*formal*) = lunch.

lung /lʌŋ/ *n* [C] either of the two breathing organs in the chest of man and other animals.
ˋlung-power, power of voice.

lunge /lʌndʒ/ *n* [C] sudden forward movement, e g with a sword, or forward movement of the body (e g when aiming a blow). □ *vi* make a lunge: *lunging out suddenly.*

lu·pin, lu·pine /ˈluːpɪn/ *n* [C] garden plant with tall spikes of flowers.

lurch¹ /lɜːtʃ/ *n* (only in) *leave sb in the lurch,* leave him when he is in difficulties and needing help.

lurch² /lɜːtʃ/ *n* [C] sudden change of weight to one side; sudden roll or pitch: *The ship gave a ~ to starboard.* □ *vi* move along with a lurch: *The drunken man ~ed across the street.*

lure /lʊə(r)/ *n* [C] **1** bunch of brightly col-

oured feathers used to attract and recall a trained hawk; bait or decoy to attract wild animals or fish. **2** (*fig*) something that attracts or invites; attraction: *the ~ of the sea; the ~s used by a pretty woman.* □ *vt* attract, tempt: *~ him away from his duty.*

lu·rid /ˈlʊərɪd/ *adj* **1** highly coloured, esp suggesting flame and smoke: *a ~ sky/ sunset; ~ thunder-clouds.* **2** (*fig*) sensational; shocking: *~ details of a railway accident.*
lu·rid·ly *adv*
lu·rid·ness *n* [U]

lurk /lɜːk/ *vi* be, keep, out of view, lying in wait or ready to attack: *a man ~ing in the shadows. Some suspicion still ~ed in his mind.*

luscious /ˈlʌʃəs/ *adj* **1** rich and sweet in taste and smell, attractive: *~ peaches/lips.* **2** (of art, music, writing) very rich in ornament; suggesting sensual delights.

lush /lʌʃ/ *adj* **1** (esp of grass and vegetation) growing luxuriantly: *~ meadows.* **2** (*fig*) luxuriously comfortable.

lust /lʌst/ *n* **1** [U] great desire to possess something, esp strong sexual desire (*for*); passionate enjoyment (*of*): *filled with ~.* **2** [C] instance of this: *a ~ for power/gold; the ~s of the flesh.* □ *vi* have lust for: *~ for/ after gold.*
ˋlust·ful /-fəl/ *adj* full of lust.
ˋlust·fully /-fəlɪ/ *adv*

lustre (*US* = **lus·ter**) /ˈlʌstə(r)/ *n* [U] **1** brightness, esp of a smooth or polished surface: *the ~ of pearls.* **2** (*fig*) glory; distinction: *add ~ to one's name.*
lus·trous /ˈlʌstrəs/ *adj* having lustre: *~ pearls/eyes.*

lusty /ˈlʌstɪ/ *adj* (-ier, -iest) healthy and strong; vigorous: *a ~ girl; ~ cheers.*
ˋlust·ily /-əlɪ/ *adv: work/fight/shout lustily.*

lute /luːt/ *n* [C] stringed musical instrument (14th to 17th centuries) associated with poets and poetry.
lu·ten·ist /ˈluːtənɪst/, player of the lute.

lux·uri·ant /lʌɡˈʒʊərɪənt/ *adj* **1** strong in growth; abundant: *the ~ vegetation of the tropics.* **2** (of literary and artistic style) richly ornamented; very elaborate.
lux·uri·ant·ly *adv*
lux·uri·ance /-əns/ *n* [U]

lux·uri·ate /lʌɡˈʒʊərɪeɪt/ *vi* (*formal*) take great delight (in): *~ in the warm spring sunshine.*

lux·uri·ous /lʌɡˈʒʊərɪəs/ *adj* **1** supplied with luxuries; very comfortable: *a ~ hotel.* **2** choice and costly: *~ food.* **3** fond of luxuries: *~ habits.*
lux·uri·ous·ly *adv*

lux·ury /ˈlʌkʃərɪ/ *n* (*pl* -ies) **1** [U] state of life in which one has and uses things that please the senses (good food and drink, clothes, comfort, beautiful surroundings): *live in ~; a life of ~.* **2** (as an *adjective*) enabling people to live this kind of life: *a ~*

hotel/ocean liner. **3** [C] something not essential but which gives enjoyment and pleasure, esp something expensive: *His salary is low and he gets few luxuries.*

-ly /-lɪ/ *suffix* **1** (*noun* + ∼ = *adjective*) having the qualities of: *cowardly.* **2** (*adjective* + ∼ = *adverb*) in the manner of the *adjective*: *quickly.*

ly·chee /ˈlaɪtʃi/ *n* (also **li·chee, li·tchee, li·tchi**) fruit-tree, originally from China; its fruit consisting of a thin brown shell containing a white pulp round a single seed.

ly·ing /ˈlaɪɪŋ/ *pres p* of **lie**¹, **lie**².

lymph /lɪmf/ *n* [U] colourless fluid in animal matter, like blood but without colouring matter.

lym·phatic /lɪmˈfætɪk/ *adj* of or carrying lymph.

lynch /lɪntʃ/ *vt* put to death (usually by hanging) without a lawful trial.

lynch·pin /ˈlɪntʃpɪn/ variant spelling of **linchpin**.

lynx /lɪŋks/ *n* [C] short-tailed wild animal of the cat family, noted for its keen sight. **ˈlynx-ˈeyed** *adj* keen-sighted.

lyre /ˈlaɪə(r)/ *n* [C] kind of harp with strings fixed in a U-shaped frame, used by the ancient Greeks.

lyric /ˈlɪrɪk/ *adj* **1** of, composed for, singing. **2** of poetry written on the theme of love, death, etc. □ *n* [C] **1** lyric poem. **2** (*pl*) verses of a song, e g in a musical play.

lyri·cal /ˈlɪrɪkəl/ *adj* **1** = **lyric**. **2** full of emotion: enthusiastic. **lyri·cally** /-klɪ/ *adv*

Mm

M, m /em/ (*pl* **M's, m's** /emz/) **1** the 13th letter of the English alphabet. **2** the Roman numeral 1 000.

ma /mɑ/ *n* [C] short for **mamma**, mother.

ma'am /mæm/ *n* [C] **1** madam, e g as used in addressing the Queen and other royal ladies. **2** (*informal*) madam.

mac /mæk/ *n* (*GB informal* abbr for) **mackintosh**.

ma·cabre /məˈkɑbr/ *adj* gruesome; suggesting death.

ma·cadam /məˈkædəm/ *n* [C,U] (road with a) surface of several layers of crushed rock or stone, each rolled hard before the next is put down.

maca·roni /ˈmækəˈrəʊnɪ/ *n* [U] flour paste made in the form of hollow tubes (often chopped into short pieces), cooked by boiling.

maca·roon /ˈmækəˈrun/ *n* [C] small, hard, flat, sweet cake or biscuit made of sugar, white of egg, and almonds or coconut.

ma·caw /məˈkɔ/ *n* large, long-tailed parrot of tropical America.

mace¹ /meɪs/ *n* [C] **1** large, heavy club, usually with a metal head covered with spikes, used as a weapon in the Middle Ages. **2** ceremonial rod or staff carried or placed before an official, e g a Mayor. **ˈmace-bearer,** official who carries a mace(2).

mace² /meɪs/ *n* [U] dried outer covering of nutmegs, used as spice.

Mach /mɑk/ *n* (also `∼ number`) ratio of the air speed of an aircraft to the speed of sound: ∼ *two,* twice the speed of sound.

ma·chete /məˈtʃeɪti US: -ˈtʃetɪ/ *n* [C] broad, heavy knife used in Latin America as a tool and weapon.

mach·ia·vel·lian /ˈmækɪəˈveliən/ *adj* showing or having no scruples in gaining what is wanted.

machi·na·tion /ˈmækɪˈneɪʃən/ *n* [C] evil plot or scheme; evil scheming.

ma·chine /məˈʃin/ *n* [C] **1** appliance or mechanical device with parts working together to apply power: *the* ∼ *age,* the age in which machines replace human labour more and more. **2** persons organized to control a political group: *the party* ∼. □ *vt* operate on, make (something) with, a machine (esp of sewing and printing).

ma·ˈchine-gun, gun that fires continuously while the trigger is pressed.

ma·ˈchine-ˈmade *adj* made by machine (contrasted with *hand-made*).

ma·ˈchine tool, tool, mechanically operated, for cutting or shaping materials.

ma·chin·ist /məˈʃinɪst/, **(a)** person who makes, repairs or controls machine tools. **(b)** person who works a machine, esp a sewing-machine.

ma·chin·ery /məˈʃinərɪ/ *n* (*pl* -ies) [U] **1** moving parts of a machine; machines collectively: *How much new* ∼ *has been installed?* **2** methods, organization (e g of government): *the* ∼ *of state.*

mack·erel /ˈmækrəl/ *n* [C] (*pl* unchanged) kind of sea-fish used as food.

mack·in·tosh /ˈmækɪntoʃ/ *n* (*GB*) rainproof coat made of cloth treated with rubber.

mac·ro·biotic /ˈmækrəʊbaɪˈotɪk/ *adj* prolonging life: ∼ *food,* without chemicals added.

mac·ro·cosm /ˈmækrəʊkozm/ *n* the great world or universe. ⇨ **microcosm**.

mad /mæd/ *adj* (-der, -dest) **1** mentally ill. *drive/send sb mad,* cause him to be mad. *as 'mad as a 'March `hare/as a `hatter,* very mad. **2** (*informal*) very excited; filled with great enthusiasm: ∼ *about pop music. be/go mad,* be/become wildly excited, angry, upset, etc. **3** (*informal*) angry: *They were* ∼ *about/at missing the train. Dad was* ∼ *with me for coming home late.* **4** (of a dog, etc) rabid.

`mad-man/-woman, who is mad(1).

mad·ly *adv* (a) in a mad manner. (b) (*informal*) extremely: ~*ly excited/in love*.

mad·ness *n* [U] the state of being mad; mad behaviour.

madam /ˈmædəm/ *n* **1** respectful form of address to a woman (whether married or unmarried) e g by a shop-assistant: *Can I help you,* ~? **2** (used in formal letters): *Dear M*~. **3** (*informal*) woman or girl who likes to order people about: *She's a bit of a* ~.

mad·den /ˈmædən/ *vt* make mad; irritate; annoy: ~*dening delays*.

made /meɪd/ *pt,pp* of make[1].

Ma·donna /məˈdɒnə/ *n* **the** ~, (picture or statue of) Mary, Mother of Jesus Christ.

mad·ri·gal /ˈmædrɪɡl/ *n* [C] song for several voices without instrumental accompaniment.

mael·strom /ˈmeɪlstrəm/ *n* [C] **1** great whirlpool. **2** (*fig*) violent or destructive force or series of events: *the* ~ *of war*.

maes·tro /ˈmaɪstrəʊ/ *n* [C] (*pl* maestri /ˈmaɪstri/) (*It*) distinguished musical composer, teacher, or conductor.

mag /mæɡ/ *n* [C] (*informal* abbr of) magazine(4): *the colour* ~*s*.

maga·zine /ˈmæɡəˈzin US:* ˈmæɡəzin/ *n* [C] **1** store for arms, ammunition, explosives, etc. **2** chamber for holding cartridges to be fed into the breech of a rifle or gun. **3** place for rolls or cartiges of film in a camera. **4** (weekly or monthly) periodical, with stories, articles, etc by various writers.

ma·genta /məˈdʒentə/ *adj*, *n* [U] bright crimson (substance used as a dye).

mag·got /ˈmæɡət/ *n* [C] larva or grub, e g of the house-fly.

mag·goty *adj* having maggots: ~*y cheese*.

Magi /ˈmeɪdʒaɪ/ *n pl* **the M**~, the three wise men from the East who brought offerings to the infant Jesus.

magic /ˈmædʒɪk/ *adj* done by, or as if by, magic; possessing magic; used in magic: ~ *arts/words; a* ~ *touch*. □ *n* [U] **1** art of controlling events by the pretended use of supernatural forces; superstitious practices based on a belief in supernatural agencies. *as if by/like magic*, in a mysterious manner. **2** art of obtaining mysterious results by tricks: *use* ~ *to produce a rabbit*. **3** (*fig*) mysterious charm; quality produced as if by magic: *the* ~ *of poetry*.

ˈblack ˈmagic, witchcraft.

magi·cal /-kəl/ *adj* = magic.

magi·cally /-klɪ/ *adv*

ma·gician /məˈdʒɪʃən/ *n* [C] person skilled in magic(2); wizard.

magis·ter·ial /ˌmædʒɪˈstɪərɪəl/ *adj* **1** of, conducted by, a magistrate. **2** having or showing authority: *a* ~ *manner*.

magis·ter·ially /-rəlɪ/ *adv*

magis·tracy /ˈmædʒɪstrəsɪ/ *n* [C] (*pl* -ies) **1** position of a magistrate. **2** (with *the*) magistrates collectively.

magis·trate /ˈmædʒɪstreɪt/ *n* [C] civil officer acting as a judge in the lowest courts (Police Courts); Justice of the Peace.

mag·nani·mous /mæɡˈnænɪməs/ *adj* having, showing, generosity.

mag·nani·mous·ly *adv*

mag·na·nim·ity /ˌmæɡnəˈnɪmətɪ/ *n* [C,U]

mag·nate /ˈmæɡneɪt/ *n* [C] wealthy and powerful leader of business or industry.

mag·nesia /mæɡˈniʃə/ *n* [U] white, tasteless powder (**MgO**) used medicinally and in industry.

mag·nesium /mæɡˈniziəm/ *n* [U] silver-white metal (symbol **Mg**) used in the manufacture of aluminium and other alloys, and in photography: ~ *light*, bright light obtained by burning magnesium.

mag·net /ˈmæɡnɪt/ *n* [C] **1** piece of iron able to attract iron, either natural (as in lodestone) or by means of an electric current. **2** (*fig*) person or thing that attracts.

mag·net·ic /mæɡˈnetɪk/ *adj* **1** of magnetism. **2** having the properties of a magnet: *the* ~ *field*, area in which a magnetic force may be detected; *a* ~ *smile/personality*, attracting the attention of people.

magnetic needle, magnetized steel rod which, when horizontal, indicates north and south.

magnetic north, the point indicated by a magnetic needle.

magnetic pole, point near the North or South Pole to which the compass needle points.

magnetic tape, kind of tape coated with iron oxide used for recording sound and vision.

mag·neti·cally /-klɪ/ *adv*

mag·net·ism /ˈmæɡnɪtɪzm/ *n* [U] **1** (the science of) magnetic phenomena and properties. **2** (*fig*) personal charm and attraction.

mag·net·ize /ˈmæɡnɪtaɪz/ *vt* **1** give magnetic properties to. **2** (*fig*) attract as a magnet does.

mag·nifi·cent /mæɡˈnɪfɪsənt/ *adj* splendid; remarkable: *a* ~ *house; his* ~ *generosity*.

mag·nifi·cent·ly *adv*

mag·nifi·cence /-səns/ *n* [U]

mag·nify /ˈmæɡnɪfaɪ/ *vt* (*pt,pp* -ied) **1** make (a person or thing) appear larger (as with a lens or microscope). **2** exaggerate: ~ *dangers*. **3** give praise to (God): ~ *the Lord*.

ˈmagnifying-glass, lens for making objects appear larger.

mag·ni·fier /-faɪə(r)/ *n* [C] instrument, etc that magnifies.

mag·ni·fi·ca·tion /ˌmæɡnɪfɪˈkeɪʃən/ *n* [U] (esp) power of magnifying, e g of a lens, a pair of binoculars.

mag·nil·oquent /mæɡˈnɪləkwənt/ *adj* (*formal*) (of a person, speech) pompous.

mag·nil·oquence /-əns/ *n* [U]

mag·ni·tude /ˈmæɡnɪtjud US:* -tud/ *n* [C] (*formal*) **1** size. **2** (degree of) importance. **3**

comparative brightness of stars.

mag·num /ˈmægnəm/ n [C] (pl ~s) (bottle containing) two quarts (of wine or spirit).

mag·num opus /ˈmægnəm ˈəupəs/ n [C] **1** great literary work. **2** person's chief (literary) work.

mag·pie /ˈmægpaɪ/ n [C] **1** noisy black-and-white bird which is attracted by, and often takes away, small, bright objects. **2** (fig) person who chatters very much. **3** (fig) petty thief.

ma·hog·any /məˈhɒgənɪ/ n [C,U] (tropical tree with) dark-brown wood much used for furniture.

maid /meɪd/ n [C] **1** (literary) girl. **2** (old use) young, unmarried woman. **3** (modern use) woman servant: It's the ~'s day off. **4** (in compounds): a `nurse~. ⇨ old maid.

'maid of `honour, unmarried woman attending a queen or princess.

maiden /ˈmeɪdən/ n [C] (literary) girl; young unmarried woman. □ adj **1** of a girl or woman. **2** first or earliest: a ship's ~ voyage. **3** (also maiden over) (in cricket) one in which no runs are scored. **4** (of an older woman) unmarried: my ~ aunt.

`maiden-head, virginity.

`maiden·hood, state, period, of being a maiden.

maiden name, woman's family name before marriage.

maiden speech, first speech in Parliament of a new member.

`maiden·like, maiden·ly adj gentle; modest; of or like a maiden.

mail¹ /meɪl/ n [U] body armour of metal rings or plates: a coat of ~; `chain~.

mail² /meɪl/ n **1** [U] government system of collecting, carrying and delivering letters and parcels: send a letter by air~. **2** [C,U] letters, parcels, etc, sent or delivered by post; the letters, etc, sent collected or delivered at one time: Is there any ~ this morning? □ vt (chiefly US; in GB post is more usual) send by post.

`mail-bag, strong bag in which mail is carried.

`mail-boat, one that transports mail.

`mail-box, (US) letter-box.

`mail-man, (US) postman.

`mail `order, order for goods to be delivered by post.

`mail-train, train that carries mail.

`mail·ing-card, (US) postcard.

`mail·ing-list, list of names of persons to whom something, eg a catalogue is regularly sent.

maim /meɪm/ vt wound or injure so that some part of the body is useless: He was seriously ~ed in the war.

main¹ /meɪn/ adj chief; most important: the ~ thing to remember; the ~ street of a town; the ~ point of my argument; the ~ course of a meal.

`main deck, upper deck.

`main-land /-lænd/, country, continent or land mass, without its islands.

`main-spring, (a) principal spring of a clock or watch. **(b)** (fig) driving force or motive.

`main-stay /-steɪ/, (fig) chief support.

`main-stream, (a) dominant trend, tendency, etc: the ~stream of political thought. **(b)** style of jazz between traditional and modern.

main·ly adv chiefly; for the most part: You are ~ly to blame.

main² /meɪn/ n **1** [C] principal pipe bringing water or gas, principal wire transmitting electric current, from the source of supply into a building: My new house is not yet connected to the ~s. **2** in the main, for the most part; on the whole. **3** (only in) with might and main, physical force; strength. **4** (poetry) sea, esp a wide expanse of sea.

main·tain /meɪnˈteɪn/ vt **1** keep up; retain; continue: ~ friendly relations (with…); ~ prices, keep them stable; ~ law and order; ~ a speed of 60 miles an hour. **2** support: ~ a son at the university. **3** assert as true: ~ one's innocence/that one is innocent. **4** keep in good repair or working order: ~ the roads. **5** defend: ~ one's rights.

main·tain·able /-əbəl/ adj that can be maintained.

main·ten·ance /ˈmeɪntənəns/ n [U] maintaining or being maintained; (esp) what is needed to support life.

mai·son·ette /ˈmeɪzənˈet/ n [C] small house; part of a house let or used separately as a self-contained dwelling.

maize /meɪz/ n [U] (also called Indian corn) sort of grain plant.

ma·jes·tic /məˈdʒestɪk/ adj having, showing, majesty.

ma·jes·ti·cally /-klɪ/ adv

maj·esty /ˈmædʒəstɪ/ n (pl -ies) **1** [U] impressive appearance; conduct, speech, causing respect; royal power. **2** His/Her/Your ~; Their/Your Majesties, (form used when speaking of or to a sovereign ruler or rulers).

ma·jor¹ /ˈmeɪdʒə(r)/ adj **1** (contrasted with minor) greater or more important: ~ roads; a ~ operation, (in surgery) one that may be dangerous to the person's life. **2** (placed after a name) elder or first of two persons of the same name, eg in a school: Smith ~. ⇨ minor, senior. □ vi major in sth, specialize in (a certain subject, at college or university): Brian ~ed in economics.

ma·jor² /ˈmeɪdʒə(r)/ n [C] army officer between a captain and a colonel.

'major-'general, army officer next above a brigadier and under a lieutenant-general.

ma·jor·ity /məˈdʒɒrətɪ US: -ˈdʒɔːr-/ n [C] (pl -ies) **1** (used with a sing or pl verb) greater number or part (of): The ~ were/ was in favour of the proposal. **2** number by which votes for one side exceed those for the other side: *He was elected by a large ~/by a ~ of 3 749.* **be in (the) majority,** have the majority. **3** legal age of reaching manhood or womanhood: *He will reach his ~ next month.*

ma'jority `verdict, verdict by the majority (of a jury, etc).

make¹ /meɪk/ *vt,vi* (*pt,pp* made /meɪd/) (For uses with *nouns,* ⇨ 24,25 below; for uses with *adjectives,* ⇨ 26 below; for uses with *adverbial particles* and *prepositions,* ⇨ 27 below.) **1** construct or produce by combining parts or putting materials together; form or shape from material; bring into existence (esp by effort): *~ bread. She made (= prepared) coffee for all of us. Cloth is made of cotton, wool, nylon and other materials. God made man.* **2** cause to appear by breaking, tearing, removing material: *~ a hole in the ground/a gap in a hedge.* **3** enact; establish: *Who made this ridiculous rule?* **4** draft; draw up: *A treaty has been made with our former enemies.* **5** eat, have (a meal): *He made a hasty lunch.* **6** cause: *I don't want to ~ any trouble for you.* **7** (passive only) be meant or intended: *John and Mary seem to have been made for each other,* e g because they get on so well together. **8** cause to be or become: *The news made her happy. He soon made himself understood.* **make it worth sb's while (to do sth),** pay or reward him: *If you will help me with this job, I'll ~ it worth your while.* **9** earn; win; gain; acquire: *~ a profit/loss of £100. He first made his name/reputation as a junior Minister.* **make or break/mar,** be successful or be ruined. **make one's living (as/at/by/from),** have as one's work or livelihood: *He ~s his living as a teacher/ from teaching/by giving piano lessons.* **make a pile/packet,** (*informal*) acquire a great deal of money. **10** (in card-games): *Six tricks bid and made,* won. **11** score (at cricket): *~ a century in a test match.* **12** (of the tide) begin to flow or ebb: *The tide is making fast.* **13** compel; force; persuade; cause (something) to happen: *Can you ~ this old car start? What ~s the grass grow? His jokes made us all laugh.* **'make one's `blood boil/one's `hackles rise,** make one furious. **'make sb's `hair stand on end,** shock or frighten him. **make sth do; make do with sth,** manage with it although it may not be really adequate or satisfactory: *You'll have to ~ do with cold meat for dinner.* **make sth go round,** make it last or be enough: *I don't know how she ~s the money go round.* **make believe (that),** pretend: *Let's ~ believe that we're soldiers.* Hence, **'make-believe** *n* [U] pretending; [C] pretence. **14** represent as; cause to appear as: *In the play the author ~s the villain commit suicide,* describe him as doing this. *You've made my nose too big,* e g in a drawing or painting. **15** estimate or reckon (to

be); put (a total, etc) at: *What time do you ~ it? What do you ~ the time? I ~ the distance about 70 miles.* **16** come to, equal; add up to; amount to (in significance): *A hundred pence ~s one pound. 5 and 7 and 3 is 15, and 4 more ~s 19. His adventures ~ excellent reading.* **make (good/much/ little) sense,** seem to have (plenty of/little) sense: *His arguments have never made much sense.* **17** be (in a series); count as: *This ~s the fifth time you've failed this examination.* **18** turn into; turn out to be; prove to be: *She will ~ him a good wife,* will be one. **19** (*informal*) travel over (a distance); reach, maintain (a speed); be in time for, catch; reach (a place); gain the rank of or place of: *We've made 80 miles since noon. The train leaves at 7.13; can we ~ it,* reach the station in time? *He'll never ~ (= win a place on) the team.* **20** elect; appoint; nominate; raise to the rank of: *~ him King/an earl/a peer.* **21** offer, propose: *M~ me an offer,* suggest a price! *The Chairman of British Rail has made a new offer to the men,* e g of a rise in wages during a strike. *I made her a present of the vase.* **22** **make + noun + of (sth/ sb); make sth/sb sth,** cause a person or thing to be or become: *His parents want to ~ a doctor of him,* want him to be educated for the medical profession. *Don't ~ a habit of it/~ it a habit,* don't let it become a habit. *Don't ~ an ass/fool of yourself,* behave stupidly. ⇨ 24 and 25 below for other examples. **23** **make as if,** behave as if about to (do something): *He made as if to hit me.* **24** (used with many *nouns* where *make* and the *noun* together have the same meaning as a *verb* related in form to the *noun*). **make allowances (for),** ⇨ allowance(3). **make an application (to sb) (for sth),** apply (to sb) (for sth). **make arrangements for,** arrange for. **make a decision,** decide. **make a success of (sth),** succeed in/with. For other phrases of this kind, ⇨ the *noun* entries. **25** (used with *nouns* in special senses; the examples below are a selection only; for definitions ⇨ the entry for the *noun* in the example): *~ an* attempt; *~ an* appointment; *~ a* bid (*for*); *~ the* bed(s); *~ the* best *of*; *~ a* break *for it*; *~ a* change; *~ one's* day; *~* demands (*of/ on*); *~ an* effort; *~ an* excuse; *~* eyes *at*; *~ a* face/faces (*at*); *~* fun *of*; *~ a* fuss (*of*); *~ a* go *of sth*; *~* head *or tail of*; *~ a* good/poor job *of*; *~ a* man *of*; *~ the* most *of*; *~* much *of*; *~* room *for oneself*; *~ a* night of it; *~ a* pass *at*; *~ one's* peace (*with*); *~ a* point (*of*); *~* room (*for*); *~* war (*on*); *~ one's* way *in the world*; *~* heavy weather *of*. **26** (used with *adjectives* in special senses; for definitions ⇨ the entry for the *adjective* in the example): *~ so* bold (*as to*); *~* certain (*of/that*); *~ sth* good; *~* light *of*; *~* sure. **27** (uses with *adverbial particles* and *prep-*

ositions):

make for sb/sth, (a) move in the direction of: *It's late; we'd better ~ for home.* (b) charge at, rush towards: *When the interval came everyone made for the bar,* i e to buy drinks. (c) contribute to, tend towards: *Does early rising ~ for good health?*

make sth/sb into sth, change or convert to: *The huts can be made into temporary houses.*

make sth of, understand, interpret: *What are we to ~ of his behaviour? I can ~ nothing of all this scribble.*

make off, hurry away (esp in order to escape): *The get-away car made off at top speed.* **make off with sth,** steal and hurry away: *The cashier made off with the firm's money.*

make sth out, (a) write out; complete or fill in: *~ out a cheque for £10.* (b) manage to see, read: *We made out a figure in the darkness.* **make sb out to be,** claim; assert; maintain: *He ~s himself out to be cleverer than he really is.* **make sb/sth out,** understand him/it: *What a queer fellow he is! I can't ~ him out at all. I can't ~ out what he wants. I couldn't ~ it out.* **make out (with sb),** progress, get on: *How are you making out with Lucy? How's your friendship progressing?* **make out a case for/against/ that,** ⇨ case¹ (2).

make sth/sb over, transfer the possession or ownership of: *He has made over his property to the National Trust.*

make sth up, (a) complete: *We still need £5 to ~ up the sum we asked for. There's a lot of time to ~ up.* (b) invent; compose (esp to deceive): *It's all a made-up story. Stop making things up!* (c) form; compose; constitute: *Are all animal bodies made up of cells? I object to the way the committee is made up/to the make-up of the committee.* (d) prepare, e g medicine, by mixing ingredients: *Ask the chemist to ~ this up for you.* (e) make (material, cloth, etc) into a garment: *This material will ~ up into two dresses.* (f) add fuel to, e g a fire: *The fire needs making up,* needs to have more coal put on it. (g) prepare (a bed): *They made up a bed on the sofa for the unexpected visitor.*

make sb/oneself up, prepare (an actor/ oneself) by applying cosmetics to the face: *It takes him more than an hour to ~ up for the part of Othello.* Hence, `**make-up** n. **make up one's/sb's mind,** come/cause him to come to a decision: *I've made up my mind. My mind's made up.* **make up for sth,** compensate for: *Hard work can often ~ up for a lack of intelligence.* **make up for lost time,** hurry, work hard, etc after losing time, starting late, etc. **make it up to sb,** give or do something in payment for something, he has lost, missed: *I'm sorry you can't come to the party but I'll ~ it up to you.* **make it up (with sb),** end a quarrel,

dispute or misunderstanding: *Why don't you ~ it up with her?*

`**make-believe,** ⇨ 13 above.

`**make.shift,** something used for a time until something better is obtainable: *use an empty crate as a ~shift for a table/as a ~shift table.*

`**make-up,** (a) ⇨ up in make 27 above. (b) character, temperament: *men of that ~-up.*

`**make-weight,** (a) small quantity added to get the weight required. (b) (*fig*) person or thing of small value that fills a gap, supplies a deficiency.

make² /meɪk/ *n* [C,U] way a thing is made; method or style of manufacture: *cars of all ~s. Is this your own ~, made by you?* **on the make,** (*sl*) concerned with making a profit, gaining an advantage.

maker /ˈmeɪkə(r)/ *n* [C] 1 the/our M~, the Creator; God. 2 (esp in compounds) person or thing that makes: `**dress~.**

mak·ing /ˈmeɪkɪŋ/ *n* **be the making of,** cause the well-being of; cause to develop well: *The two years he served in the Army were the ~ of him.* **have the makings of,** have the necessary qualities for becoming: *He has in him the ~s of a great man.*

mal- /mæl-/ *prefix* bad, wrong, not: *mal-adjusted.*

mala·chite /ˈmæləkaɪt/ *n* [U] green mineral, a kind of stone used for ornaments, decoration, etc.

mal·adjusted /ˈmæləˈdʒʌstɪd/ *adj* (esp of a person) unable to adapt himself properly to his environment, e g social or occupational. **mal·adjust·ment** *n* [U].

mal·ady /ˈmælədɪ/ *n* [C] (*pl* -ies) [C] (*formal*) (chronic) disease; illness; disorder.

mal·aise /mæˈleɪz/ *n* (*sing* with *a, an*) (*formal*) feeling of bodily discomfort, but without clear signs of a particular illness.

ma·laria /məˈleərɪə/ *n* [U] kinds of disease with chills, sweating and fever, conveyed by mosquitoes. **ma·lar·ial** /-rəl/ *adj*

male /meɪl/ *adj* of the sex that does not give birth to offspring: *a '~ voice `choir,* of men and/or boys. □ *n* [C] male person, animal, etc.

mal·for·ma·tion /ˈmælfɔˈmeɪʃən/ *n* 1 [U] state of being badly formed or shaped. 2 [C] badly formed part: *a ~ of the spine.*

mal·formed /ˈmælˈfɔmd/ *adj* badly formed or shaped.

mal·ice /ˈmælɪs/ *n* [U] active hatred; desire to harm others. **bear sb malice,** feel hatred for him.

ma·li·cious /məˈlɪʃəs/ *adj* feeling, showing, caused by, malice: *~ gossip.* **ma·li·cious·ly** *adv*

ma·lig·nancy /-nənsɪ/ *n* [U] the state of being malignant.

ma·lig·nant /məˈlɪgnənt/ *adj* 1 (of persons, their actions) filled with, showing, a desire to hurt: *~ glances.* 2 (of diseases) harmful

to life: ~ *cancer.*
ma·lig·nant·ly *adv*
ma·lig·nity /məˈlɪgnətɪ/ *n* (*pl* -ies) **1** [U]
deep-rooted hatred; [C] instance of this;
hateful act, remark, etc. **2** [U] (of diseases)
harmful character.
ma·lin·ger /məˈlɪŋgə(r)/ *vi* pretend to be ill,
extend the period of being ill, in order to
escape duty or work.
ma·lin·ger·er, person who malingers.
mal·lard /ˈmælɑd/ *n* [C] kind of wild duck.
mal·leable /ˈmælɪəbəl/ *adj* **1** (of metals)
that can be hammered or pressed into new
shapes. **2** (*fig*) (e g of a person's character)
easily trained or adapted.
mal·lea·bil·ity /ˌmælɪəˈbɪlətɪ/ *n* [U]
mal·let /ˈmælɪt/ *n* [C] **1** hammer with a
wooden head. **2** hammer with a long handle
and wooden head for striking a croquet or
polo ball.
mal·nu·tri·tion /ˌmælnjuˈtrɪʃən US: -nu-/
n [U] condition caused by not getting
(enough of) (the right kind(s) of) food.
mal·prac·tice /ˌmælˈpræktɪs/ *n* (*legal*) **1**
[U] doing wrong; neglect of duty. **2** [C]
instance of this.
malt /mɔlt/ *n* [U] grain (usually barley)
allowed to sprout, prepared for brewing or
distilling. □ *vt,vi* **1** make (grain) into malt;
(of grain) become malt. **2** prepare with malt:
~*ed milk.*
mal·treat /mælˈtrit/ *vt* (*formal*) treat
roughly or cruelly.
mal·treat·ment *n* [U]
mama /məˈmɑ US:* ˈmæmə/ *n* [C] (*dated*)
= mummy, mother.
mamba /ˈmæmbə/ *n* [C] (*pl* ~s) black or
green poisonous African tree snake.
mam·mal /ˈmæməl/ *n* [C] any of the class
of animals which feed their young with milk
from the breast.
mam·moth /ˈmæməθ/ *n* [C] large kind of
elephant now extinct. □ *adj* (*informal*) huge:
a ~ *task.*
man /mæn/ *n* [C] (*pl* men /men/) **1** adult
male human being: *a* ˈpost~/ˈclergy~.
man and boy, from boyhood onwards: *He
has worked for the firm,* ~ *and boy, for
thirty years. a man of letters,* a writer and
scholar. *a man about town,* one who
spends much time at parties, theatres, in
clubs, etc. *a man of the world,* one with
wide experience of business and society. *the
man in the street,* person regarded as representing the interests and opinions of ordinary people. **2** human being; person: *All
men must die.* **3** (*sing* only, without *the, a* or
an) the human race; all mankind: *M~ is
mortal.* **4** male person under the authority of
another: *officers and men,* e g in the army. **5**
male person having the qualities (e g
strength, confidence) associated with men:
How can we make a ~ *of him?* **6** husband:
~ *and wife.* **7** piece in chess, etc. **8** (with
possessive adjectives): *If you want a good*

teacher, here's your ~, here's someone
suitable.
ˈ**man-eater,** cannibal; tiger or shark that
eats human beings.
ˈ**man-handle** *vt* (a) move by physical
strength. (b) (*sl*) handle roughly: *Be
*~*handled by the police.*
ˈ**man-hole,** opening through which a man
may enter (an underground sewer, boiler,
tank, etc).
ˈ**man-hood,** (a) state of being a man. (b)
male qualities, e g virility, courage. (c) (collective) men in general.
ˈ**man-hour,** work done by one man in one
hour.
man-ˈmade, made by humans; produced
artificially or from synthetic materials.
ˈ**man-power,** number of men available for
military service, work, etc: *a shortage of
*~*power in the coalmines.*
ˈ**man-servant,** male servant.
ˈ**man-sized** *adj* of a size right for a man; *a
~-sized steak.*
ˈ**man-slaughter,** (act of) killing a human
being unlawfully but not wilfully.
man-to-ˈman *adj* frank, not holding back:
a ~-*to-*~ *discussion.*
man[2] /mæn/ *vt* (-nn-) supply with men for
service or defence: ~ *a fort/a ship/*~ *the
barricades.*
-man /-mən, -mæn/ *suffix* **1** dweller in:
countryman. **2** person occupied in a specific
activity: *businessman; doorman.*
man·acle /ˈmænəkəl/ *n* [C] (usually *pl*)
chains for the hands or feet. □ *vt* **1** put in
chains. **2** (*fig*) restrain.
man·age /ˈmænɪdʒ/ *vt,vi* **1** control: *managing a business/one's wife; the managing
director.* **2** succeed: *I shan't be able to* ~
without help. We can't ~ *with these poor
tools.* **3** (*informal*) (with can, could, be able
to) make use of; eat: *Can you* ~ *another
slice of cake?*
ˈ**man·age·able** /-əbəl/ *adj* that can be dealt
with; easily controlled.
man·age·abil·ity /ˌmænɪdʒəˈbɪlətɪ/ *n* [U]
man·age·ment /ˈmænɪdʒmənt/ *n* **1** [U]
managing or being managed: *under new* ~.
2 [U] skilful treatment or handling: *It needed
a good deal of* ~ *to persuade them to give
me the job.* **3** [C,U] (collective) all those
concerned in managing an industry, enterprise, etc: *joint consultation between workers and* ~.
man·ager /ˈmænɪdʒə(r)/ *n* [C] **1** person
who controls a business, a hotel, etc. **2** (usually with an *adjective*) person who manages
a business, household affairs, etc, in a certain way: *My wife is an excellent* ~.
man·ager·ess /ˌmænɪdʒəˈres/ *n* [C] woman
manager(1).
mana·ger·ial /ˌmænɪˈdʒɪərɪəl/ *adj* of
managers.
man·date /ˈmændeɪt/ *n* [C] **1** order from a
superior; command given with authority. **2**

authority to administer a territory authorized by the League of Nations after the First World War. **3** authority given to representatives by voters, members of a trade union, etc: *the ~ given to us by the electors.* □ *vt* put (a territory) under a mandate(2): *the ~d territories.*

man·da·tory /ˈmændətrɪ *US:* -tɔːrɪ/ *adj* of, conveying, a command: *the mandatory power.*

man·dible /ˈmændəbəl/ *n* [C] **1** lower jaw in mammals and fishes. **2** either part of a bird's beak. **3** (in insects) either half of the upper pair of jaws, used for biting, etc.

man·do·lin /ˈmændəlɪn/ *n* [C] musical instrument with 6 or 8 metal strings stretched in pairs on a rounded body.

mane /meɪn/ *n* [C] long hair on the neck of a horse, lion, etc.

ma·neu·ver /məˈnuːvə(r)/ *n, v* (*US*) = manoeuvre.

man·ful /ˈmænfəl/ *adj* brave; determined.
man·fully /-fəlɪ/ *adv*

man·ga·nese /ˈmæŋɡəniːz *US:* ˈmæŋɡəniːz/ *n* [U] hard, brittle, light-grey metal (symbol **Mn**) used in making steel, glass, etc.

mange /meɪndʒ/ *n* [U] contagious skin disease, esp of dogs and cats.

mangy /ˈmeɪndʒɪ/ *adj* (-ier, -iest)

manger /ˈmeɪndʒə(r)/ *n* [C] long open box or trough for horses or cattle to feed from.

mangle[1] /ˈmæŋɡəl/ *n* [C] machine with rollers for pressing out water from and for smoothing clothes, etc, that have been washed. □ *vt* put (clothes, etc) through a mangle.

mangle[2] /ˈmæŋɡəl/ *vt* cut up, tear, damage, badly: *be badly ~d in a car accident.*

mango /ˈmæŋɡəʊ/ *n* [C] (*pl* ~es or ~s) (tropical tree bearing) pear-shaped fruit with yellow flesh.

man·grove /ˈmæŋɡrəʊv/ *n* [C] tropical tree growing in swamps and sending down new roots from its branches.

mangy /ˈmeɪndʒɪ/ ⇨ mange.

man·handle ⇨ man[1].

mania /ˈmeɪnɪə/ *n* **1** [U] madness shown by great excitement, delusions, violence. **2** extreme enthusiasm, excitement: *a ~ for powerful motorbikes.*

maniac /ˈmeɪnɪæk/ *n* [C] **1** raving madman. **2** (*fig*) extreme enthusiast.

ma·niacal /məˈnaɪəkəl/ *adj* (a) violently mad. (b) (*fig*) extremely enthusiastic.
ma·niacally /-klɪ/ *adv*

manic-depressive /ˈmænɪk dɪˈpresɪv/ *adj, n* [C] (person) suffering from alternating periods of excitement and melancholic depression.

mani·cure /ˈmænɪkjʊə(r)/ *n* [U] care of the hands and finger-nails. □ *vt* cut, clean and polish the finger-nails.

`mani·cur·ist` /-ɪst/, person who manicures

as a profession.

mani·fest[1] /ˈmænɪfest/ *adj* clear and obvious: *a ~ truth.* □ *vt* **1** show clearly: *~ the truth of a statement.* **2** give signs of: *She doesn't ~ much desire to marry him.* **3** (reflexive) appear: *No disease ~ed itself during the long voyage.*
mani·fest·ly *adv*
mani·fes·ta·tion /ˈmænɪfeˈsteɪʃən/ *n* [C,U]

mani·festo /ˈmænɪˈfestəʊ/ *n* [C] (*pl* ~s or ~es) public declaration of principles, policy, purposes, etc by a ruler, political party, etc or of the character, qualifications of a person or group.

mani·fold /ˈmænɪfəʊld/ *adj* having or providing for many uses, copies, etc. □ *n* [C] pipe or chamber with several openings or connections.

mani·kin /ˈmænɪkɪn/ *n* [C] **1** pygmy; dwarf. **2** anatomical model of the human body. **3** figure of the human body used by artists. **4** = mannequin.

ma·nipu·late /məˈnɪpjʊleɪt/ *vt* **1** operate, handle, with skill: *~ machinery.* **2** manage or control skilfully or craftily, esp by using one's influence or unfair methods: *A clever politician knows how to ~ his supporters/ public opinion.*
ma·nipu·la·tion /məˈnɪpjʊˈleɪʃən/ *n* [C,U]

man·kind *n* [U] **1** /ˈmænˈkaɪnd/ the human species. **2** /ˈmænkaɪnd/ the male sex; all men (contrasted with `womankind`).

man·like /ˈmænlaɪk/ *adj* having the qualities (good or bad) of a man.

man·ly /ˈmænlɪ/ *adj* (-ier, -iest) **1** having the strong qualities expected of a man. **2** (of a woman) having a man's qualities. **3** (of things, qualities, etc) right for a man.
man·li·ness *n* [U]

manna /ˈmænə/ *n* [U] **1** (in the Bible) food provided by God for the Israelites during their forty years in the desert. **2** (*fig*) something unexpectedly supplied or that gives spiritual refreshment.

man·ne·quin /ˈmænəkɪn/ *n* [C] **1** = model(5) (the usual word). **2** life-size dummy of a human body, as used in shop-windows for the display of clothes.

man·ner /ˈmænə(r)/ *n* [C] **1** way in which a thing is done or happens: *Do it in this ~.* **(as) to the 'manner 'born**, as if naturally suitable; knowing how to deal with a situation, practice, custom, etc from birth. **2** (*sing* only) person's way of behaving towards others: *I don't like his ~.* **3** (*pl*) habits and customs. **4** (*pl*) social behaviour: *good/bad ~s.* **5** style in literature or art: *a painting in the ~ of Raphael.* **6** kind, sort: *What ~ of man is he?* **all manner of,** every kind of.

man·nered *adj* (a) (used in compounds): `ill-~ed`, having bad manners(4). (b) showing mannerisms.

man·ner·ism /ˈmænərɪzm/ *n* [C] **1** peculiarity of behaviour, speech, etc, esp one that is habitual. **2** excessive use of a distinctive manner in art or literature.

man·ner·ly /ˈmænəlɪ/ *adj* courteous, polite.

man·nish /ˈmænɪʃ/ *adj* **1** (of a woman) like a man. **2** more suitable for a man than for a woman: *a ~ style of dress.*

ma·noeuvre (US = **ma·neu·ver**) /məˈnuːvə(r)/ *n* [C] **1** planned movement (of armed forces); (*pl*) series of such movements, e g as training exercises: *army ~s.* **2** movement or plan, made to deceive, or to escape, or to win or do something: *the desperate ~s of some politicians.* □ *vi,vt* (cause to) perform manoeuvres: *manoeuvring a car into a difficult space.*

ma·noeuvrer (US = **ma·neu·verer**), person who manoeuvres.

ma·noeuvr·able (US = **ma·neu·ver·able**) /-vrəbəl/ *adj* that can be manoeuvred.

ma·noeuvr·abil·ity (US = **-neu·ver-**) /məˈnuːvrəˈbɪlətɪ/ *n* [U]

manor /ˈmænə(r)/ *n* [C] **1** unit of land under the feudal system, part of which was used directly by the *lord of the ~* and the rest occupied and farmed by tenants who paid rent in crops and service. **2** (*modern use*) area of land with a principal residence (called the *~-house*).

ma·nor·ial /məˈnɔːrɪəl/ *adj* of a manor.

man·sion /ˈmænʃən/ *n* [C] **1** large and stately house. **2** (*pl*) (*in proper names*) block of flats: *Victoria M~s.*

the ˈMansion-house, the official residence of the Lord Mayor of London.

man·tel /ˈmæntəl/ *n* [C] structure of wood, marble, etc above and around a fireplace.

ˈmantel·piece, shelf projecting from the wall above a fireplace.

man·tilla /mænˈtɪlə/ *n* [C] (*pl* ~s) large veil or scarf worn by Spanish women to cover the hair and shoulders.

man·tis /ˈmæntɪs/ *n* [C] (kinds of) long-legged insect.

mantle¹ /ˈmæntəl/ *n* [C] **1** loose, sleeveless cloak. **2** (*fig*) covering: *hills with a ~ of snow.* **3** metal cover like lace fixed round the flame of a gas-light.

mantle² /ˈmæntəl/ *vt,vi* cover in, or as in, a mantle: *an ˈivy-~d wall.*

man·ual /ˈmænjʊəl/ *adj* of, done with, the hands: *~ labour.* □ *n* [C] **1** handbook or textbook: *a technical ~.* **2** keyboard of an organ, played with the hands.

man·ually /-jʊəlɪ/ *adv*

manu·fac·ture /ˌmænjʊˈfæktʃə(r)/ *vt* **1** make, produce (goods, etc) on a large scale by machinery: *manufacturing industries; ~d goods.* **2** invent (a story, an excuse, etc). □ *n* [U] **1** the making or production of goods and materials: *the ~ of plastic.* **2** (*pl*) manufactured goods and articles.

manu·fac·turer, person, firm, etc that manufactures things.

ma·nure /məˈnjʊə(r)/ *n* [U] animal waste, e g from stables, cow barns; other material,

natural or artificial, spread over or mixed with the soil to make it fertile. □ *vt* put manure in or on (land/soil).

manu·script /ˈmænjʊskrɪpt/ *n* [C] (abbr to **M S,** *pl* **M SS**) book, etc as first written out or typed: *poems still in ~.*

many /ˈmenɪ/ *adj, n* (contrasted with *few;* ⇨ **more, most**) **1** (used with *pl nouns*) a large number (*of*), plenty (*of*): *I have some, but not ~. M~ people think so. How ~ do you want? Do you need so ~?* **as many again,** the same number, quantity, again. **one too many,** one more than the correct or needed number. **2** (used with a *sing noun*): *M~ a man* (= Many men) *would welcome the opportunity.*

ˈmany-ˈsided *adj* (a) having many sides. (b) (*fig*) having many aspects, capabilities, etc: *a ~-sided problem.*

map /mæp/ *n* [C] representation on paper, etc of the earth's surface or a part of it, showing countries, oceans, rivers, mountains, etc; representation of the sky showing positions of the stars, etc. **put sth on the map,** (*fig*) cause it to be considered important, to be reckoned with. **off the map,** (*informal*) (of a place) inaccessible. **wipe sth off the map,** destroy it. □ *vt* (-pp-) **1** make a map of; show on a map. **2 map out,** plan, arrange: *~ out one's time.*

ˈmap-reader, person able to get information from maps: *He's a good/poor ~-reader.*

maple /ˈmeɪpəl/ *n* **1** [C] (sorts of) tree of the northern hemisphere, grown for timber and ornament. **2** [U] wood of this tree.

ˈmaple-leaf, emblem of Canada.

ˈmaple-sugar/-syrup, sugar/syrup that is obtained from the sap of one kind of maple.

mar /mɑː(r)/ *vt* (-rr-) injure; spoil; damage: *Nothing ~red their happiness.* **make or mar,** make a great success of or ruin completely.

mara·thon /ˈmærəθən US: -θɒn/ *n* [C] **1 the M~,** long-distance race on foot (about 26 miles (or 41·8 kilometres) at modern sports meetings). **2** (*fig*) test of endurance.

ma·raud /məˈrɔːd/ *vi* go about in search of loot or prey.

ma·rauder, person, animal that marauds.

marble /ˈmɑːbəl/ *n* **1** [U] (sorts of) hard limestone used, when cut and polished, for building and sculpture: (as an *adjective*) *a ~ statue/tomb.* **2** (*pl*) works of art in marble. **3** [C] small ball of glass, clay or stone used in games played by children.

March /mɑːtʃ/ *n* the third month of the year.

march¹ /mɑːtʃ/ *n* **1** [U] act of marching (by soldiers, etc). **2** [C] instance of marching; distance travelled: *a ~ of ten miles.* **steal a march on sb,** win an advantage by doing something earlier than expected by him. **3 the ~,** progress: *the ~ of events/time.* **4** [C] piece of music for marching to: *military ~es.*

dead march, one in slow time for a funeral.

forced march, one made more quickly than usual, or for a greater distance, in an emergency.

marcher, person who marches.

march² /mɑtʃ/ vi,vt (cause to) walk as soldiers do, with regular and measured steps: *The troops ⁓ed by/past/in/out/off/away. He was ⁓ed off to prison.*

'marching orders, orders for troops to leave for war, etc.

mar·chion·ess /'mɑʃə'nes/ n [C] **1** wife or widow of a marquis. **2** woman who holds in her own right a position equal to that of a marquis.

mare /'meə(r)/ n [C] female horse or donkey.

mare's nest, a discovery thought valuable that turns out to be false or worthless.

mar·gar·ine /'mɑdʒə'rin US: 'mɑdʒərɪn/ n [U] food substance, used like butter, made from animal or vegetable fats.

marge /mɑdʒ/ n [U] (*informal abbr for*) margarine.

mar·gin /'mɑdʒɪn/ n [C] **1** blank space round the printed or written matter on a page. **2** edge or border: *the ⁓ of a lake.* **3** amount (of time, money, etc) above what is estimated as necessary. **4** condition near the limit or borderline, below or beyond which something is impossible: *He escaped defeat by a narrow ⁓.*

mar·gin·al /-nəl/ adj (a) of or in a margin(1): *⁓al notes.* (b) of a margin(4): *a ⁓al seat/constituency,* one where the MP has been elected by a small majority.

mar·gin·ally /-nəlɪ/ adv

mari·juana, mari·huana /'mærɪ'wɑnə/ n [U] (also called *hashish, cannabis, pot*) dried leaves and flowers of Indian hemp smoked in cigarettes (called *reefers* or *joints*) to induce euphoria.

ma·rina /məˈriːnə/ n [C] (pl ⁓s) harbour designed for pleasure boats (small yachts, cabin cruisers, etc) often with hotels, etc.

mari·nade /'mærɪ'neɪd/ n [C,U] (kinds of) pickle of wine, vinegar and spice; fish or meat pickled in this. □ vt (also **mari·nate** /'mærɪneɪt/) soak in (a) marinade.

mar·ine /məˈriːn/ adj **1** of, by, found in, produced by, the sea: *⁓ fishing.* **2** of ships, sea-trade, the navy, etc: *⁓ insurance,* of ships and cargo. □ n **1** [U] shipping in general. **2** [C] soldier serving on a warship.

mari·ner /'mærɪnə(r)/ n [C] sailor, esp one who assists in navigating a ship: *a ⁓'s compass.*

master mariner, captain of a merchant ship.

mari·on·ette /'mærɪə'net/ n [C] jointed doll or puppet moved by strings.

mari·tal /'mærɪtəl/ adj of a husband, of marriage.

mari·time /'mærɪtaɪm/ adj **1** connected with the sea or navigation: *⁓ law.* **2** situated or found near the sea: *the ⁓ provinces of the* USSR.

mark¹ /mɑk/ n [C] **1** line, scratch, cut, stain, etc that spoils the appearance of something: *Who made these dirty ⁓s on my new book?* **2** noticeable spot on the body by which a person or animal may be recognized: *a 'birth⁓.* **3** visible trace; sign or indication (of a quality, etc): *⁓s of old age/ suffering.* **4** figure, design, line, etc, made as a sign or indication: *'punctu'ation ⁓s; 'trade⁓s.* **5** numerical or alphabetical symbol, eg A+, to indicate an award in an examination, or for conduct: *He got the best ⁓s of his year.* **6** target. **be/fall wide of the mark,** be inaccurate, imprecise: *Your guess/calculation is wide of the ⁓.* **beside the mark,** irrelevant. **7** [U] distinction; fame. **make one's mark,** become distinguished. **8** (*sing* only) standard. **up to/ below the mark,** equal to/below the required or normal standard. **not be/feel (quite) up to the mark,** not in one's usual health. **9** (in athletics) line showing the starting-point of a race: *On your ⁓s, get set, go!* (words used by the starter). **10** (with numbers) model or type: *Meteor M⁓ III,* eg of an aircraft.

mark² /mɑk/ vt **1** put or have a mark on something by writing, stamping, etc: *All our stock has been ⁓ed down/up,* reduced/ increased in price. Hence, **'mark-up,** amount by which a price is increased. **2** (passive) have natural marks or visible signs: *A zebra is ⁓ed with stripes.* **3** give marks(5) to: *⁓ examination papers.* **4** indicate something by putting a mark, eg a tick or a cross, on or against: *⁓ an answer wrong.* **5** pay attention (to): *M⁓ carefully how it is done. (You) mark my words,* Note what I say (and you will find, later, that I am right). **6** be a distinguishing feature of: *What are the qualities that ⁓ a great leader?* **7** signal; denote: *His death ⁓ed the end of an era. Ceremonies ⁓ing an anniversary.* **mark time,** (a) stamp the feet as when marching but without moving forward. (b) (*fig*) wait until further progress becomes possible.

8 (uses with *adverbial particles*):

mark sth off, put marks on (to show boundary lines, measurements, etc).

mark sth out, put lines on (to show limits, etc): *⁓ out a tennis-court.*

marked adj clear; obvious: *a ⁓ed difference/improvement.*

a marked man, one whose conduct is watched with suspicion or hatred.

mark·ed·ly /'mɑkɪdlɪ/ adv

mark·ing, (esp) pattern of different colours of feathers, skin, etc: *a tiger's ⁓ings.*

marker /'mɑkə(r)/ n [C] **1** person or tool that marks, esp a person who marks the score at games. **2** thing that marks or indicates, eg a flag or post on a playing field, a post showing distances. **3** person who marks examination papers.

mar·ket¹ /ˈmɑːkɪt/ n [C] **1** public place (an open space or a building) where people meet to buy and sell goods: *She went to (the) ∼ to buy food for the family.* **2** time during which such a meeting takes place: *The next ∼ is on Monday.* **3** trade in a class of goods: *the ˋcoffee ∼.* **4** state of trade as shown by prices: *The ∼ rose/fell/was steady, Prices rose/fell/did not change much. **play the market,** buy and sell to make the most profit. **5** demand: *There's no/not much/only a poor ∼ for these goods.* **6** (*sing* only) buying and selling. **be in the market for sth,** be ready to buy something. **be on/come on (to)/put on the market,** be offered/offer for sale: *This house will probably come on the market next month.* **7** [C] area, country, in which goods may be sold: *We must find new ∼s for our manufacturers.*
ˈCommon ˋMarket, ⇨ common¹.

ˋmarket-day, day on which a market is regularly held.

ˈmarket-ˋgarden, one where vegetables are grown for market. Hence, ˈmarket-ˋgardening n [U]

ˋmarket-place open place in a town where a market is held.

market price, price for which something, e g securities, is sold in the open market.

ˈmarket reˋsearch, study of the reasons why people buy, or do not buy, certain goods, the effect of advertising, etc.

ˋmarket town, one where a market (esp one for cattle and sheep) is held.

mar·ket² /ˈmɑːkɪt/ vi,vt **1** buy or sell in a market. **2** take or send to market; prepare and offer for sale.
ˋmar·ket·able /-əbl/ adj that can be, fit to be, sold.
ˋmar·ket·ing, theory and practice of (large-scale) selling.

marks·man /ˈmɑːksmən/ n [C] (pl -men /-mən/) person skilled in aiming at a mark, esp with a rifle.

mar·ma·lade /ˈmɑːməleɪd/ n [U] (bitter) jam made from citrus fruit (usually oranges).

mar·mo·set /ˈmɑːməzet/ n [C] small, tropical American monkey with soft, thick hair and a bushy tail.

mar·mot /ˈmɑːmət/ n [C] small animal of the squirrel family.

ma·roon¹ /məˈruːn/ adj, n [U] brownish-red (colour).

ma·roon² /məˈruːn/ vt put (a person) on a desert island, uninhabited coast, etc, and abandon him there.

mar·quee /mɑːˈkiː/ n [C] large tent (as used for flower shows, a circus, etc).

mar·quis, mar·quess /ˈmɑːkwɪs/ n **1** (*GB*) nobleman next in rank above an earl and below a duke. **2** (in other countries) nobleman next in rank above a count. ⇨ marchioness.

mar·riage /ˈmærɪdʒ/ n **1** [C,U] (instance of a) legal union of a man and woman as husband and wife; state of being married: *A ∼ has been arranged between... and....* **2** = wedding (the usual word).
ˋmar·riage·able /-əbl/ adj old enough, fit for, marriage: *a girl of ∼able age.*

mar·ried /ˈmærɪd/ adj united in marriage; of marriage: *∼ couples; ∼ life.*

mar·row /ˈmærəʊ/ n **1** [U] soft, fatty substance that fills the hollow parts of bones. **chill/chilled to the marrow,** (make) cold through and through. **2** [U] (*fig*) essence; essential part. **3** [C] (*GB*) (also ˋvegetable ∼) vegetable of the gourd family like a large fat cucumber (*US* = squash); [U] this as food.

marry /ˈmærɪ/ vt,vi (pt,pp -ied) **1** take as a husband or wife; have a husband or wife. **2** (of a priest, a civil official) join as husband or wife: *Which priest is going to ∼ them?* **3** give in marriage: *He married both his daughters to rich directors.* **4** obtain by marrying: *∼ money/wealth.*

Mars /mɑːz/ n **1** (Roman myth) the god of war. **2** (*astron*) planet fourth in order from the sun.

marsh /mɑːʃ/ n [C,U] (area of) low-lying, wet land.
marshy adj (-ier, -iest) of or like a marsh.

mar·shal¹ /ˈmɑːʃəl/ n [C] **1** officer of highest rank: ˈField-ˋM∼, Army; ˈAir-ˋM∼, Air Force. **2** official responsible for important public events or ceremonies, e g one who accompanies a High Court judge; an officer of the royal household. **3** (*US*) official with the functions of a sheriff; head of a fire or police department.

mar·shal² /ˈmɑːʃəl/ vt (-ll-, *US* -l-) **1** arrange in proper order: *∼ facts/military forces.* **2** guide or lead (a person) with ceremony: *∼ persons into the presence of the Queen.*
ˋmarshalling-yard, railway yard in which goods wagons, etc are made up into trains.

mar·su·pial /mɑːˈsuːpɪəl/ adj, n [C] (animal) of the class of mammals the females of which have a pouch to carry their young, e g kangaroos.

mar·tial /ˈmɑːʃəl/ adj **1** of, associated with, war: *∼ music.* **2** brave; fond of fighting: *∼ spirit.*
ˈmartial ˋlaw, military government, by which ordinary law is suspended, e g during a rebellion.
ˋmar·tial·ly /-ʃəlɪ/ adv

mar·tin /ˈmɑːtɪn *US*: -tən/ n [C] (also ˋhouse-∼), bird of the swallow family that builds a mud nest on walls, etc.

mar·ti·net /ˌmɑːtɪˈnet *US*: -təˈnet/ n [C] person who requires and enforces strict discipline.

mar·tyr /ˈmɑːtə(r)/ n [C] person who is put to death or caused to suffer greatly for his religious beliefs or for the sake of a great cause or principle: *the early Christian ∼s in Rome.* **be a martyr to sth,** suffer greatly

from: *He's a ~ to rheumatism.* **make a martyr of oneself,** sacrifice one's own wishes or advantage (or pretend to do so) in order to get credit or reputation. □ *vt* put to death, cause to suffer, as a martyr.
`mar·tyr·dom` /-dəm/ *n* [U] martyr's suffering or death: *His wife's never-ending complaints made his life one long ~dom.*

mar·vel /ˈmɑvəl/ *n* [C] **1** something causing great surprise, wonder, astonishment: *the ~s of modern science.* **work marvels,** produce a highly successful result. **2** wonderful example: *She's a ~ of patience.* □ *vi* (-ll-, US -l-) **1** be greatly surprised (at): *~ at her patience.* **2** wonder: *I ~ that she should agree to marry him.*

mar·vel·lous, (US = **mar·vel·ous**) /ˈmɑvələs/ *adj* astonishing; wonderful.
mar·vel·lous·ly (US = **mar·vel·ous·ly**) *adv*

Marx·ism /ˈmɑksɪzm/ *n* (esp) economic theory that class struggle has been the major force behind historical change, that the dominant class has exploited the masses and that capitalism will inevitably be superseded by socialism and a classless society.

Marx·ist /ˈmɑksɪst/ *n* follower of Karl Marx /mɑks/, (1818—83) the German economist and socialist.

mar·zi·pan /ˈmɑzɪpæn/ *n* [U] thick paste of ground almonds, sugar, etc, made up into small cakes.

mas·cara /mæˈskɑrə/ *n* [U] cosmetic preparation for darkening the eyelashes.

mas·cot /ˈmæskət/ *n* [C] person, animal or object thought to bring good fortune.

mas·cu·line /ˈmæskjʊlɪn/ *adj* **1** of, like, men: *a ~ style.* **2** of male gender: *'He' and 'him' are ~ pronouns.*
mas·cu·lin·ity /ˈmæskjʊˈlɪnətɪ/ *n* [U] quality of being masculine. ⇨ **feminine.**

mash /mæʃ/ *n* [U] **1** grain, bran, etc cooked in water as food for poultry, cattle or pigs. **2** any substance softened and crushed, e g boiled potatoes beaten and crushed: *sausage and ~.* **3** mixture of malt and hot water used in brewing. □ *vt* beat or crush into a mash: *~ed potato.*

mask[1] /mɑsk US: mæsk/ *n* [C] **1** covering for the face, or part of it, e g a piece of silk or velvet. **2** replica of the face carved in wood, ivory, etc; disguise. **throw off one's mask,** (*fig*) show one's true character and intentions. **3** pad of sterile gauze worn over the mouth and nose by doctors and nurses. **4** replica of the face worn by an actor or actress. **5** likeness of a face made by taking a mould in wax, etc.
`death mask,` one made by taking a mould of the face of a dead person.
`gas-mask,` breathing apparatus, in some cases for the whole of the head, worn as a protection against poisonous gas, smoke, etc.

mask[2] /mɑsk US: mæsk/ *vt* **1** cover (the face) with a mask: *a ~ed ball,* one at which masks are worn. **2** conceal: *~ one's hatred under an appearance of friendliness.*

maso·chism /ˈmæsəkɪzm/ *n* [U] mental disorder of getting satisfaction (esp sexual) from (self-inflicted) pain or humiliation.
maso·chist /-kɪst/, person suffering from masochism.
maso·chis·tic /ˈmæsəˈkɪstɪk/ *adj*

ma·son /ˈmeɪsən/ *n* [C] **1** worker who builds or works with stone. **2** = freemason.
ma·sonic /məˈsɒnɪk/ *adj* of freemasons.
ma·sonry /ˈmeɪsnrɪ/ **(a)** stonework; that part of a building made of stone and mortar. **(b)** = freemasonry.

mas·quer·ade /ˈmɑskəˈreɪd US: ˈmæsk-/ *n* [C] **1** ball[1] at which masks and other disguises are worn. **2** (*fig*) false show or pretence. □ *vi* appear, be, in disguise: *a prince masquerading as a peasant.*

mass /mæs/ *n* **1** [C] lump, quantity of matter, without regular shape; large number, quantity or heap: *~es of dark clouds in the sky; a ~ of colour in the garden.* **2** the ~es, the proletariat; (manual) workers. **3** [U] (science) quantity of material in a body measured by its resistance to change of motion. ⇨ **size**[1] (1). □ *vt, vi* form or collect into a mass: *Troops are ~ing/are being ~ed on the frontier.*
`mass com·muni·cations/media,` means (esp newspapers, radio, TV) of supplying information to, influencing the ideas of, enormous numbers of people.
`mass pro·duction,` manufacture of large numbers of identical articles by standardized processes. Hence, `mass-pro·duce` *vt*

Mass /mæs/ *n* [C] celebration (esp R C) of the Eucharist.

mass·acre /ˈmæsəkə(r)/ *n* [C] cruel killing of large numbers of (esp defenceless) people (occasionally used of animals). □ *vt* make a massacre of.

mass·age /ˈmæsɑʒ/ *n* [C,U] (instance of) pressing and rubbing the body with the hands, esp the muscles and joints, in order to lessen pain, stiffness, etc. □ *vt* apply a massage to.

mass·eur /mæˈsɜ(r)/ *n* [C] man who practises massage.

mass·euse /mæˈsɜz/ *n* [C] woman who practises massage.

mass·ive /ˈmæsɪv/ *adj* **1** large, heavy and solid: *a ~ monument.* **2** (of the features) heavy-looking: *a ~ forehead.* **3** (*fig*) substantial; impressive.
mass·ive·ly *adv*
mass·ive·ness *n* [U]

mast /mɑst US: mæst/ *n* [C] **1** upright support (of wood or metal) for a ship's sails. **2** tall pole (for a flag). **3** tall steel structure for aerials of a radio or television transmitter.
`mast·head,` highest part of a mast, used as a look-out post.

mas·ter /ˈmɑstə(r) US: ˈmæs-/ *n* [C] **1** man who has others working for him or under him. *be one's own master,* be free and independent. **2** male head of a household: *the ~ of the house.* *be master in one's own house,* manage one's affairs without interference from others. **3** captain of a merchant ship: *a ~ mariner.* **4** male owner of a dog, horse, etc. **5** male teacher: *the ˈmatheˈmatics ~; a ˈschool~.* **6** *master of,* person who has control: *He is ~ of the situation,* has it under control. **7** (with a boy's name) young Mr: *M~ Charles Smith,* sometimes used when speaking of or to a boy up to about the age of 14. **8** title of the heads of certain colleges: *the M~ of Balliol,* Oxford. **9** great artist. ⇨ old master. **10** title of various officials. **11** original (recording tape, etc) from which copies are made. □ *adj* **1** having or showing professional skill: *a ~ builder/carpenter.* **2** superior: *a ~ hand at diplomacy.* **3** original: *a ~ tape.*

ˈMaster of ˈArts/ˈScience, holder of the second university degree.

ˈMaster of ˈCeremonies, (abbr **M C**) person who controls the procedure on various social occasions, e g a public banquet.

ˈmaster-key, one that will open many different locks.

ˈmaster-mind, person with superior intelligence (esp one who plans work to be carried out by others). Hence, ˈmastermind *vt* plan, direct, a scheme.

ˈmaster-piece, something made or done with very great skill.

ˈmaster-stroke, highly skilful act (of policy, etc).

mas-ter² /ˈmɑstə(r) US: ˈmæs-/ *vt* become the master(6) of: *~ one's feelings; ~ a foreign language.*

mas-ter-ful /ˈmɑstəfəl US: ˈmæs-/ *adj* **1** fond of controlling others: *speak in a ~ manner.* **2** = masterly.
mas-ter-fully /-fəlɪ/ *adv*

mas-ter-ly /ˈmɑstəlɪ US: ˈmæs-/ *adj* **1** worthy of a great master. **2** very skilful: *with a few ~ strokes of the brush.*

mas-tery /ˈmɑstərɪ US: ˈmæs-/ *n* [U] **1** complete control or knowledge: *his ~ of the violin.* **2** supremacy: *Which side will get the ~ (over us)?*

mas-ti-cate /ˈmæstɪkeɪt/ *vt* (*formal*) chew; soften, grind up (food) with the teeth.
mas-ti-ca-tion /ˈmæstɪˈkeɪʃən/ *n* [U]

mas-tiff /ˈmæstɪf/ *n* [C] large, strong dog much used as a watchdog.

mas-toid /ˈmæstɔɪd/ *n* [C] bone at the back of the ear.

mas-tur-bate /ˈmæstəbeɪt/ *vi* procure sexual excitement by manual or other stimulation of the genital organs.
mas-tur-ba-tion /ˈmæstəˈbeɪʃən/ *n* [U]

mat¹ /mæt/ *n* [C] **1** piece of material used for a floor covering, for sleeping on, or (a `door~) for wiping dirty shoes on. **2** small piece of material placed under vases, ornaments, etc, or (a `table-~) under hot dishes

on a table. **3** anything thickly tangled or twisted together: *a ~ of weeds.* □ *vt,vi* (-tt-) **1** cover or supply with mats. **2** (cause to) be or become tangled or knotted: *matted hair.*

mat², matt (US = matte) /mæt/ *adj* (of surfaces) dull; not shiny or glossy: *paint that dries with a ~ finish.* ⇨ gloss¹(1).

mata-dor /ˈmætədɔ(r)/ *n* [C] man whose task is to kill the bull in a bull-fight.

match¹ /mætʃ/ *n* [C] short piece of wood, waxed paper, etc, with a top made of material that bursts into flame when rubbed on a rough or specially prepared surface.
`match-box, box for holding matches.

match² /mætʃ/ *n* [C] **1** contest; game: *a `football ~.* **2** person able to meet another as his equal in strength, skill, etc: *You are no ~ for him,* are not strong, clever, etc enough to compete with him. **3** marriage: *They decided to make a ~ of it,* (of two persons) They decided to marry. **4** person considered from the point of view of marriage: *He's a good ~,* is considered satisfactory or desirable as a possible husband. **5** person or thing exactly like, or corresponding to, or combining well with, another: *colours/materials that are a good ~.*
`match-maker, (esp) person who is fond of arranging matches(3) for others.
`match `point, final point needed to win a match(1).

match³ /mætʃ/ *vt,vi* **1** put in competition: *I'm ready to ~ my strength with/against yours.* **2** be equal to; be, obtain, a match(2) for: *a well-~ed pair,* e g boxers about equal in skill. **3** be equal to, correspond (with) (in quality, colour, design, etc): *The carpets should ~ the curtains.* ⇨ clash(4). **4** find a material, etc that matches(3) with (another): *Can you ~ this silk?* **5** join (one person *with* another) in marriage.
match-less *adj* unequalled: *~less beauty.*

match-et /ˈmætʃɪt/ *n* [C] = machete.

mate¹ /meɪt/ *n* **1** (*informal*) companion; fellow-workman: *Where are you going, ~?* ⇨ class-mate, playmate. **2** ship's officer (not an engineer) below the rank of captain. **3** helper: (in titles) *a plumber's ~.* **4** one of a pair of birds or animals: *the lioness and her ~.*

mate² /meɪt/ *vt,vi* (of birds or animals) (cause to) unite for the purpose of producing young.
the `mating season, spring, when birds make their nests.

mate³ /meɪt/ *n, v* = checkmate.

ma-terial¹ /məˈtɪərɪəl/ *adj* **1** (contrasted with *spiritual*) made of, connected with, matter or substance: *the ~ world.* **2** of the body; of physical needs: *~ needs,* e g food and warmth. **3** (*legal*) important; essential: *~ evidence/testimony.*
ma`terial noun, naming a material, e g stone, wood, wool.
ma-teri-ally /-ɪəlɪ/ *adv* essentially.

ma·te·rial[2] /məˈtɪərɪəl/ n 1 [C,U] that of which something is or can be made or with which something is or can be done: *raw* ∿s, not yet used in manufacture; `*dress* ∿s, cloth; `*writing* ∿s, pen, ink, paper, etc. 2 [U] (*fig*) facts, happenings, elements: *the* ∿ *from which history is made.*

ma·te·ri·al·ism /məˈtɪərɪəlɪzm/ n [U] 1 theory, belief, that only material things exist 2 tendency to value, valuation of material things (wealth, bodily comforts, etc) too much and spiritual and intellectual things too little.
ma·te·ri·al·ist /-ɪst/, n [C] believer in materialism; person who ignores religion, art, music, etc.
ma·te·ri·al·is·tic /məˌtɪərɪəˈlɪstɪk/ adj
ma·te·ri·al·is·ti·cally /-klɪ/ adv

ma·te·ri·al·ize /məˈtɪərɪəlaɪz/ vi take material form; (cause to) become fact: *Our plans did not* ∿, came to nothing, were not carried out.
ma·te·ri·al·iz·ation /məˌtɪərɪəlaɪˈzeɪʃən US: -lɪˈz-/ n [U]

ma·ter·nal /məˈtɜnəl/ adj of or like a mother: ∿ *care/instincts.*
ma·ter·nally /-nəlɪ/ adv

ma·tern·ity /məˈtɜnətɪ/ n [U] being a mother: (as an *adjective*) *a* ∿ *ward/ hospital*, for women who are about to become mothers.

matey /ˈmeɪtɪ/ adj (*informal*) sociable, familiar, friendly.

mathe·mat·ics /ˌmæθəˈmætɪks/ n [U] (used with a *sing* or *pl verb*) science of size and numbers (of which arithmetic, algebra, trigonometry and geometry are branches).
math·emat·ical /ˌmæθəˈmætɪkəl/ adj
math·emat·ically /-klɪ/ adv
math·ema·ti·cian /ˌmæθəməˈtɪʃən/ n [C] expert in mathematics.

maths (US = **math**) /mæθs US: mæθ/ n (abbr of) mathematics.

mati·née /ˈmætɪneɪ US: ˈmætənˈeɪ/ n [C] afternoon performance at a cinema or theatre.

mat·ins /ˈmætɪnz US: -tənz/ n pl 1 service for Morning Prayer in the Church of England. 2 prayers recited at daybreak in the R C Church.

ma·tri·arch /ˈmeɪtrɪɑk/ n [C] woman head of a family or tribe.
ma·tri·archy /-ɑkɪ/ n [C] social organization in which mothers are the heads of families.
ma·tri·ar·chal /ˌmeɪtrɪˈɑkəl/ adj

ma·trices /ˈmeɪtrɪsɪz/ pl of matrix.

mat·ri·cide /ˈmætrɪsaɪd/ n [U] killing of one's own mother; [C] instance of this; [C] person guilty of this.

ma·tricu·late /məˈtrɪkjʊleɪt/ vt,vi (allow to) enter a university as a student, usually after passing an examination.
ma·tricu·la·tion /məˌtrɪkjʊˈleɪʃən/ n [C,U]

mat·ri·mony /ˈmætrɪmənɪ US: -məʊnɪ/ n [U] state of being married

mat·ri·mo·nial /ˌmætrɪˈməʊnɪəl/ adj

ma·trix /ˈmeɪtrɪks/ n (pl matrices /ˈmeɪtrɪsɪz/, or ∿es) 1 mould into which hot metal, or other material in a soft or liquid condition, is poured to be shaped. 2 substance in which a mineral, etc is found embedded in the ground.

ma·tron /ˈmeɪtrən/ n [C] 1 woman housekeeper in a school or other institution. 2 woman who manages the domestic affairs and nursing staff of a hospital. 3 married woman or widow often used with a suggestion of dignity and social position).
ma·tronly adj

matt /mæt/ adj variant spelling of mat[2].

mat·ter[1] /ˈmætə(r)/ n 1 [U] substance(s) of which a physical thing is made (contrasted with *mind, spirit, etc*): *organic/inorganic* ∿. 2 material for thought or expression, substance of a book, speech, etc contrasted with the form or style. 3 [U] something printed or written: `*reading* ∿, books, periodicals, etc. 4 [C] something to which attention is given; piece of business; affair: `*money* ∿s. *That's a* ∿ *of opinion*, about which opinions may differ. *a matter of course*, expected in the natural course of events. *as a matter of fact*, although you may not know it or may be surprised. *for* `*that matter*, so far as that is concerned. *no laughing matter*, serious. 5 [U] importance. *(make/be) no matter*, (be) of no importance: *It's no* ∿*/makes no* ∿ *whether you arrive early or late. no matter* `*who/* `*what/*`*where, etc*, whoever (it is), whatever (happens, etc). 6 [U] the ∿, wrong (*with*): *What's the* ∿ *with it?* 7 [U] pus. *8 a matter of*, about: *a* ∿ *of 20 weeks /10 miles /£50; within a* ∿ *of hours.*
'matter-of-'course adj to be expected.
'matter-of-'fact adj (of a person, his manner) unimaginative; keeping to the facts.

mat·ter[2] /ˈmætə(r)/ vi be of importance: *It doesn't* ∿ *much, does it?*

mat·ting /ˈmætɪŋ/ n [U] rough woven material used for floor covering and for packing goods: *coconut-*∿.

mat·tins /ˈmætɪnz US: -tənz/ n pl = mat·ins.

mat·tock /ˈmætək/ n [C] tool used for breaking up hard ground, etc, with an iron bar at a right angle to the handle.

mat·tress /ˈmætrəs/ n [C] thick, flat, oblong pad of wool, hair, feathers foam rubber, etc on which to sleep.
spring mattress, one with coiled wires fitted inside a padded cover.

matu·rate /ˈmætʃʊreɪt/ vi (*formal*) become mature.
matu·ra·tion /ˌmætʃʊˈreɪʃən/ n [U]

ma·ture /məˈtʃʊə(r) US: -ˈtʊər/ vt,vi 1 come or bring to full development or to a state ready for use: *His character* ∿*d during these years* 2 (of bills) become due. □ adj 1 fully grown or developed; ripe with fully developed powers: *persons of* ~ *years.* **2** careful; perfected: ~ *plans.* **3** (of bills) due for payment.

ma·ture·ly *adv*

ma·tur·ity /məˈtjʊərətɪ/ *n* [U] the state of being mature.

maud·lin /ˈmɔdlɪn/ *adj* sentimental or self-pitying in a silly or tearful way.

maul /mɔl/ *vt* hurt or injure by rough or brutal handling: ~*ed by a tiger.*

Maundy Thurs·day /ˈmɔndɪ ˈθɜzdɪ/ *n* Thursday before Easter, commemorating Jesus' Last Supper.

mau·so·leum /ˌmɔsəˈliəm/ *n* [C] magnificent and monumental tomb.

mauve /məʊv/ *adj, n* [U] bright but delicate pale purple (colour).

maxi /ˈmæksɪ/ *n* [C] (*informal*) woman's ankle-length skirt, coat, etc. ⇨ mini.

maxim /ˈmæksɪm/ *n* [C] widely accepted rule of conduct or general truth briefly expressed, e g '*Waste not, want not*'.

maxi·mal /ˈmæksɪməl/ *adj* greatest in amount or degree.

maxi·mize /ˈmæksɪmaɪz/ *vt* increase to a maximum: ~ *educational opportunities.*

maxi·mi·za·tion /ˌmæksɪmaɪˈzeɪʃən US: -mɪˈz-/ *n* [U]

maxi·mum /ˈmæksɪməm/ *n* (*pl* ~s or -ma /-mə/) (opp of *minimum*) greatest possible or recorded degree, quantity, etc: *the* ~ *temperature recorded in London. The* ~ *load is one ton.*

may /meɪ/ *auxiliary verb* (*pt* might /maɪt/) (*negative* may not, shortened to **mayn't** /meɪnt/ and might not, shortened to **mightn't** /ˈmaɪtnt/) **1** (used of possibility or probability): *That* ~ *or* ~ *not be true. He* ~ *have* (= Perhaps he has) *missed his train. This might have cured your cough,* if you had taken it. **2** (used of permission or request for permission): *M*~ *I come in? Might I make a suggestion?* **3** (used of uncertainty, and asking for information, or expressing wonder): *Well, who* ~ *you be?* **4** (used to suggest 'There is good reason'): *We* ~ *as well stay where we are,* It seems reasonable to do so. **5** (used to express wishes and hopes): *M*~ *you both be happy!* **6** (used to express requests): *I think you might at least offer to help.* **7** (in clauses) (used to express purpose, and after *wish, fear, be afraid,* etc): *He died so that others might live. I'm afraid the news* ~ *be true.*

May /meɪ/ *n* the fifth month of the year.

'May Day, 1st of May, celebrated as a spring festival and also a day for socialist and labour demonstrations.

may·be /ˈmeɪbɪ/ *adv* perhaps; possibly.

may·on·naise /ˈmeɪəneɪz US: ˈmeɪəneɪz/ *n* [U] thick dressing of eggs, cream, oil, vinegar, etc used on cold foods, esp salads.

mayor /meə(r) US: ˈmeɪə(r)/ *n* [C] head of a local authority of a city or borough.

mayor·ess /ˌmeəˈres US: ˈmeɪərəs/ *n* [C] **1** woman mayor. **2** wife of a mayor.

maze /meɪz/ *n* [C] **1** network of lines, paths, etc; labyrinth: *a* ~ *of narrow roads.* **2** state of confusion or bewilderment (when faced by a confused mass of facts, etc).

ma·zurka /məˈzɜkə/ *n* [C] (piece of music for a) lively Polish dance for four or eight couples.

me /mi/ *personal pron* used as the object form of *I: He saw* ~. *Give* ~ *one. It's* ~, (*informal*) It is I.

mead[1] /mid/ *n* [U] alcoholic drink made from fermented honey and water.

mead[2] /mid/ *n* [C] (*poetry*) meadow.

meadow /ˈmedəʊ/ *n* [C,U] (area, field, of) grassland, esp kept for hay.

meagre (*US* = **mea·ger**) /ˈmiɡə(r)/ *adj* **1** thin; lacking in flesh: *a* ~ *face.* **2** insufficient; poor; scanty: *a* ~ *meal/attendance.*

meagre·ly (*US* = **mea·ger·ly**) *adv*

meager·ness (*US* = **mea·ger-**) *n* [U]

meal[1] /mil/ *n* [C] **1** occasion of eating: *three* ~*s a day.* **2** food that is eaten: *have a good* ~; *I hope you enjoy your* ~.

'meal·time, usual time for taking a meal.

meal[2] /mil/ *n* [U] grain coarsely ground: *'oat*~.

mealy /ˈmilɪ/ *adj* (-ier, -iest) of, like, containing, covered with, meal[2].

'mealy-bug, insect that infests vines, etc.

'mealy-'mouthed *adj* tending to avoid straightforward, frank, language because of shyness, hypocrisy, etc.

mean[1] /min/ *adj* (-er, -est) **1** poor in appearance; shabby: *a* ~ *house in a* ~ *street.* **2** (of behaviour) unworthy: *That was a* ~ *trick! It was* ~ *of you to take all the oranges.* **3** (of persons, their character, etc) cruel, malicious: *Don't be so* ~ *to your little brother,* Don't tease him, treat him unkindly, etc. **4** of low rank or humble birth: *We offer justice even to the* ~*est citizens.* **5** (of the understanding, the natural powers) inferior; poor: *This should be clear even to the* ~*est intelligence.* **6** lacking in generosity; selfish: *Her husband is so* ~ *about money.* **7** (*informal*) ashamed: *feel rather* ~ *for not helping more.* **8** (*US*) nasty; vicious: *He's* ~—*he likes to see people suffer.*

mean·ly *adv*

mean·ness *n* [U]

mean[2] /min/ *adj* occupying the middle position between two extremes: *the* ~ *annual temperature in Malta.*

Greenwich Mean Time, ⇨ Greenwich.

mean[3] /min/ *n* **1** [C] condition, quality, course of action, etc that is halfway between two extremes. **2** (in maths) term between the first and the last of a series: *The* ~ *of 3, 5 and 7 is 5* (because 3 + 5 + 7 = 15 and 15 ÷ 3 = 5).

mean[4] /min/ *vi* (*pt, pp* ~t /ment/) **1** (of words, sentences, etc) have as an explanation: *A dictionary tries to tell you what* *words* ~. **2** be a sign of; be likely to result in: *These new orders will ~ working overtime.* **3** have as a purpose; intend; refer to: *What do you ~ by saying that? Do you ~* (= refer to) *Miss Ann Smith or Miss Angela Smith? Is this figure ~t to be a 1 or a 7? I'm sorry if I hurt your feelings—I didn't ~ to.* **mean business,** (*informal*) be in earnest, ready to act (not merely to talk). **4** intend; be determined: *a building ~t for offices. He ~s you no harm,* does not intend to hurt you. *He ~s to succeed.* **5** be of importance or value to: *Your friendship ~s a great deal to me. £20 ~s a lot to her.* **6** **mean well,** have good intentions (though perhaps not the will or capacity to carry them out): *His plans never work but he ~s well.*

mean-ing *n* [C,U] what is meant or intended: *a word with many distinct ~ings. What's the ~ing of this?* (asked, for example, by a person who thinks he has been badly treated, etc). □ *adj* full of meaning: *well ~ing,* having good intentions.

mean-ing-ful /-fəl/ *adj* significant; full of meaning.

mean-ing-fully /-flɪ/ *adv*

mean-ing-less *adj* without meaning or motive.

me-ander /mɪˈændə(r)/ *vi* **1** (of a stream) follow a winding course, flowing slowly and gently. **2** wander here and there. **3** (*fig*) speak in an aimless way.

me-ander-ings /mɪˈændrɪŋz/ *n pl* winding path, etc.

means¹ /miːnz/ *n pl* (often used as a *sing*, as in examples) method, process, by which a result may be obtained: *There is/are no ~ of learning what is happening. Does the end always justify the ~,* If the aim or purpose is good, may any methods, even if bad, be employed? **by means of,** through; with the help of: *Thoughts are expressed by ~ of words.* **by all means,** certainly. **by no means,** not at all.

ways and means, methods, esp of providing money by taxation for government needs: *a ways and ~ committee.*

means² /miːnz/ *n pl* money; wealth; resources: *a man of ~,* a rich man; *have private ~,* an income from property, investments, etc (not earned as salary, etc). **live beyond/within one's means,** spend more/less than one's income.

`**means test,** inquiry into a person's financial resources who is seeking help from the State, e g for a student's grant.

meant /ment/ *pt,pp* of mean⁴.

mean-time /ˈmiːntaɪm/ *adv, n* (*sing*) (in the) interval between.

mean-while /ˈmiːnwaɪl* US: -ˈhwaɪl/ *adv* in or during the time between.

measles /ˈmiːzəlz/ *n* [U] (used with a *sing verb*) infectious disease, marked by fever and small red sports that cover the whole body.

measly /ˈmiːzlɪ/ *adj* (-ier, iest) (*informal*) of little value; of poor quality; of small size or amount; *What a ~ helping of ice-cream!*

measure¹ /ˈmeʒə(r)/ *n* **1** [U] size, quantity, degree, weight, etc as found by a standard or unit. **made to measure,** (of clothing) specially made for a person after taking measurements. **get the measure of sb,** (fig) form an estimate of his character, abilities, etc. **2** [C] unit, standard or system used in stating size, quantity, or degree: *liquid/dry ~.* **for good measure,** in addition to the necessary amount. **3** [C] something with which to test size, quantity, etc: *a pint ~.* `**tape-measure,** ⇨ tape. `**greatest** `**common** `**measure,** (abbr G C M) largest number that will divide each of several given numbers exactly. **4** extent, (esp in) *beyond measure,* very great(ly): *Her joy was beyond ~.* **in great/large measure,** to a large extent: *Their success was in some ~/in great ~ the result of thorough preparation.* **5** [C] (proposed) law: *~s to halt inflation.* **6** [C] proceeding; step: *They took strong ~s against dangerous drivers.* **7** [U] (kinds of) short rhythm or arrangement of music or poetry.

measure² /ˈmeʒə(r)/ *vt,vi* **1** find the size, extent, volume, degree, etc of: *~ an area of ground/the strength of an electric current/the speed of a car/the length of my arm.* **2** be (a certain length, etc): *This room ~s 10 metres across.* **3** give or mark a measured quantity: *~ out a dose of medicine; ~ off 2 metres of cloth.*

meas-ured *adj* (a) (of language) carefully chosen or considered: *~d words.* (b) in slow and regular rhythm: *with a ~d tread.*

measur-able /ˈmeʒrəbəl/ *adj*

measur-ably /-əblɪ/ *adv*

measure-less *adj* limitless.

measure-ment *n* (a) [U] measuring: *the metric system of ~ment.* (b) (*pl*) figures about length, breadth, depth, etc: *the ~ments of a room.*

meat /miːt/ *n* **1** [U] flesh of animals used as food, excluding fish and birds. **2** (*fig*) substance: *There's not much ~ in his argument.* `**meat-ball,** small ball of minced meat.

meaty *adj* (-ier, -iest) (*fig*) full of substance.

mech-anic /mɪˈkænɪk/ *n* [C] skilled workman, esp one who repairs or adjusts machinery and tools: *a* `*motor-~.*

mech-an-ical /mɪˈkænɪkəl/ *adj* **1** of, connected with, produced by, machines: *~ engineering.* **2** (of persons, their actions) like machines; automatic; as if done without thought: *~ movements.*

mech-an-ically /-klɪ/ *adv*

mech-an-ics /mɪˈkænɪks/ *n* **1** (usually used with a *sing verb*) science of motion and force; science of machinery: *M~ is taught by Mr Hill.* **2** (*pl*) (method of) construction: *the ~ of producing plays.*

mech·an·ism /ˈmekənɪzm/ n [C] 1 working parts of a machine collectively. 2 structure or arrangement of parts that work together as the parts of a machine do: *the ~ of government*. 3 way in which something works or is constructed.

mech·an·ize /ˈmekənaɪz/ vt use machines in or for; give a mechanical character to.

mech·an·iz·ation /ˌmekənaɪˈzeɪʃən US: -nɪˈz-/ n [U]

medal /ˈmedəl/ n [C] flat piece of metal, usually shaped like a coin, with words and a design stamped on it, given as an award, for bravery to commemorate something or for distinction in scholarship.

med·al·list (US = **med·alist**) /ˈmedəlɪst/ person who has been awarded a medal, e g for distinction in sport, literature, art.

me·dal·lion /mɪˈdælɪən/ n [C] large medal; large, flat circular ornamental design.

meddle /ˈmedəl/ vi become involved without being asked to do so; interfere: *Don't ~ in my affairs. Who's been meddling with my papers?*

med·dler, person who meddles.

ˈmeddle·some /-səm/ adj fond of, in the habit of, meddling.

me·dia /ˈmiːdɪə/ n ⇨ **mass(2)**, medium.

the media, (usually used with a *sing* verb) mass communications, e g television, radio, the press.

medi·aeval /ˈmedɪˈiːvəl US: ˈmiːd-/ = medieval.

me·dial /ˈmiːdɪəl/ adj 1 situated, placed, in the middle. 2 of average size.

me·di·ally /-rəlɪ/ adv

me·di·ate /ˈmiːdɪeɪt/ vi,vt 1 act as go-between or peacemaker: *~ between employers and their workers*. 2 bring about by doing this: *~ a settlement/a peace*.

me·dia·tion /ˌmiːdɪˈeɪʃən/ n [U]

me·dia·tor /-tə(r)/ person who mediates.

medic /ˈmedɪk/ n (*informal* abbr for) medical student.

medi·cal /ˈmedɪkəl/ adj 1 of the art of medicine (the treatment of disease): *a ~ practitioner*, a qualified doctor; *a ~ school*. 2 of the art of medicine (contrasted with *surgery*): *The hospital has a ~ ward and a surgical ward*. □ n [C] medical examination.

medi·cally /-klɪ/ adv

medi·cate /ˈmedɪkeɪt/ vt treat medically; fill with a medicinal substance: *~d soap*.

medi·ca·tion /ˌmedɪˈkeɪʃən/ n [CU]

med·ici·nal /mɪˈdɪsənəl/ adj able to heal or cure: *~ preparations; for ~ use*.

medi·cine /ˈmedəsən US: ˈmedɪsən/ n 1 [U] the art and science of the prevention and cure of disease: *study ~ and surgery*. 2 [C,U] (kind of) substance, esp one taken through the mouth, used to treat disease: *He's always taking ~s*. 3 (fig) deserved punishment. 4 [U] (among primitive peoples) spell; charm; fetish; magic.

ˈmedicine-man /-mæn/, = witch-doctor.

medi·eval (also **medi·aeval**) /ˈmedɪˈiːvəl US: ˈmiːd-/ adj of the Middle Ages (about A D 1100—1500).

me·di·ocre /ˈmiːdɪˈəʊkə(r)/ adj not very good; neither very good nor very bad; second-rate.

me·di·oc·rity /ˌmiːdɪˈɒkrətɪ/ n [C,U] (pl -ies) quality of being mediocre.

medi·tate /ˈmedɪteɪt/ vt,vi 1 think about; consider: *~ revenge/mischief*. 2 give oneself up to serious thought: *He sat there meditating on his misfortunes*. 3 think deeply about a moral, religious or philosophical topic: *~ on world peace*.

medi·ta·tion /ˌmedɪˈteɪʃən/ n 1 [U] meditating: *deep in ~*. 2 [C] instance of this.

medi·tat·ive /ˈmedɪtətɪv US: -teɪt-/ adj

medi·tat·ive·ly adv

Medi·ter·ra·nean /ˌmedɪtəˈreɪnɪən/ adj of, characteristic of, the Mediterranean Sea or the countries, etc bordering it: *a ~ climate*.

me·dium /ˈmiːdɪəm/ n [C] (pl ~s or media /ˈmiːdɪə/) 1 that by which something is expressed: *Commercial television is a ~ for advertising*. 2 middle quality or degree. 3 (pl often **media**) substance, surroundings, in which something exists or moves: *Air is the ~ of sound*. 4 person who acts as a go-between, esp in spiritualism; person who claims to be able to receive messages from the spirits of the dead. □ adj coming halfway between; not extreme: *a man of ~ height; a ~-sized firm*.

the happy medium, satisfaction by avoiding extremes, e g by being neither very lax nor very severe in maintaining discipline.

ˈmedium wave, (radio telegraphy) wave between long and short (200 to 1000 metres).

med·ley /ˈmedlɪ/ n [C] (pl ~s) mixture of things or persons of different sorts: *the ~ of races in Hawaii*.

meek /miːk/ adj (-er, -est) mild and patient; unprotesting: *She's as ~ as a lamb*.

meek·ly adv

meek·ness n [U]

meet /miːt/ vt,vi (pt,pp met /met/) 1 come face to face with from the opposite or a different direction; come together from different points or directions: *We met (each other) quite by chance. The Debating Society ~s every Friday at 8 p m*. **meet with**, (a) experience: *~ with misfortune/an accident*. (b) encounter by chance: *~ with obstacles; ~ with an old friend at a party*. 2 make the acquaintance of; be introduced to: *I know Mrs Hill by sight, but have never met her/we've never met. Pleased to ~ you*, as a formal introduction. 3 go to a place and await the arrival of: *I'll ~ you at the station/~ your train*. 4 satisfy (a demand, etc): *~ his wishes*, do what he wants; *~ all the expenses*, pay them. **meet sb halfway**, (fig) give way to some extent in order to satisfy him or reach agreement. 5 come into contact; touch: *Their hands met. The roads should ~ about a mile away.* **make both ends meet,** make one's income and one's expenditure equal. **6 meet the eye/ear, our eyes/ears,** be visible/audible: *There's more to that man than ~s the eye,* (fig) he has qualities, characteristics, etc that are not obvious.

meet² /miːt/ *n* [C] **1** (*GB*) gathering of riders and hounds at a fixed place (for foxhunting). **2** coming together of a number of people for a purpose: *an ath`letic ~.*

meet·ing /ˈmiːtɪŋ/ *n* [C] **1** coming together of a number of persons at a certain time and place, esp for discussion: *political ~s.* **2** any coming together: *a `race—~; a `sports—~.*

`meeting-house,` building for meetings, esp those held by Quakers.

`meeting-place,` place fixed for a meeting.

mega- /megə-/ *prefix* **1** large: *megalith.* **2** one million: *megacycle.*

mega·cycle /ˈmegəsaɪkəl/ *n* [C] million cycles (of changes of radio current, esp per second).

mega·lith /ˈmegəlɪθ/ *n* [C] large stone, esp an ancient one used as a monument.

mega·lith·ic /ˈmegəˈlɪθɪk/ *adj* made of, marked by, the use of megaliths.

mega·lo·ma·nia /ˈmegələˈmeɪnɪə/ *n* [U] mental illness in which a person has exaggerated ideas of his importance of power, wealth, etc: *The dictator was obviously suffering from ~.*

mega·lo·ma·niac /-nɪæk/ person suffering from megalomania.

mega·phone /ˈmegəfəʊn/ *n* [C] device for magnifying sound, for carrying the voice to a distance.

mega·ton /ˈmegətʌn/ *n* [C] explosive force equal to one million tons of TNT.

mel·an·cholic /ˈmelənˈkɒlɪk/ *adj* (with a tendency to) melancholy.

mel·an·choly /ˈmelənkəlɪ *US:* -kɒlɪ/ *n* [U] sadness, esp often or for long periods. □ *adj* sad; depressed; causing sadness or depression: *a ~ occasion,* e g a funeral.

mel·an·cholia /ˈmelənˈkəʊlɪə/ *n* [U] mental illness marked by melancholy.

meli·or·ate /ˈmiːlɪəreɪt/ *vt,vi* (*formal*) make or become better.

meli·or·ation /ˈmiːlɪəˈreɪʃən/ *n* [U]

mel·low /ˈmeləʊ/ *adj* (-er, -est) **1** soft and sweet in taste. **2** soft, pure and rich in colour or sound. **3** made wise and sympathetic by age or experience: *~ judgement.* **4** (*informal*) kindly; sympathetic. □ *vt,vi* make or become mellow.

mel·low·ly *adv*

mel·low·ness *n* [U]

mel·odic /məˈlɒdɪk/ *adj* of melody; melodious.

mel·odi·ous /məˈləʊdɪəs/ *adj* of, producing, melody; sounding tuneful.

mel·odi·ous·ly *adv*

mel·odi·ous·ness *n* [U]

melo·drama /ˈmelədrɑːmə/ *n* **1** [C] exciting and emotional (often sensational, exaggerated) drama, usually with a happy ending. **2** [C] event or series of events, behaviour or writing, which suggests a stage melodrama. **3** [U] language, behaviour, suggestive of plays of this kind.

melo·dram·atic /ˈmelədrəˈmætɪk/ *adj*

melo·dram·ati·cally /-klɪ/ *adv*

mel·ody /ˈmelədɪ/ *n* (*pl* -ies) **1** [U] sweet music; tunefulness; musical arrangement of words. **2** [C] song or tune: *old Irish melodies.* **3** [C] principal part or theme in harmonized music: *The ~ is next taken up by the flutes.*

melon /ˈmelən/ *n* [C] (kinds of) large, juicy round fruit growing on a plant that trails along the ground.

melt /melt/ *vt,vi* (*pt,pp ~ed*; *pp* used as an *adj*, of metal **molten** /ˈməʊltən/) **1** (cause to) become liquid through heating: *The ice will ~ when the sun shines on it.* **melt away,** become less, disappear, (as) by melting: *The snow soon ~ed away when the sun came out. Her money seemed to ~ away in Paris.* **melt sth down,** melt metals (e g articles of gold and silver) in order to use the metal as raw material. **2** (of soft food) dissolve, be softened, easily: *This cake/pear ~s in the mouth.* **3** (of a solid in a liquid) dissolve (the usual word). **4** (of a person, heart, feelings) soften, be softened: *Her heart ~ed with pity.* **5** fade; go (slowly) away: *One colour ~ed into another,* e g in the sky at sunset.

melt·ing *adj* (*fig*) tender; sentimental: *in a ~ing voice/mood.*

`melt·ing-point,` temperature at which a solid melts.

`melting-pot,` (a) pot in which metals, etc are melted. (b) any situation in which there is a mixture of ideas, differences, etc.

mem·ber /ˈmembə(r)/ *n* [C] **1** person belonging to a group, society, etc: *Every ~ of her family came to her wedding.* **2** (*old use*) part of a human or animal body.

'Member of `Parliament, (abbr **MP**) elected representative in the House of Commons.

`mem·ber·ship,` (a) [U] the state of being a member (of a society, etc). (b) [C] number of members: *a ~ship of 80.*

mem·brane /ˈmembreɪn/ *n* [C] (soft, thin, pliable layer of) animal, vegetable or synthetic tissue.

mem·bra·nous /ˈmembrənəs/ *adj*

mem·ento /məˈmentəʊ/ *n* [C] (*pl ~s, ~es*) something that serves to remind one of a person or event.

memo /ˈmeməʊ/ *n* [C] (*pl ~s*) (abbr for) memorandum.

mem·oir /ˈmemwɑː(r)/ *n* [C] **1** short life-history, esp by someone with first-hand knowledge. **2** essay on a academic subject specially studied by the writer. **3** (*pl*) person's written account of his own life or experiences: *war ~s.*

mem·or·able /ˈmemrəbl/ *adj* deserving to be remembered; remarkable.

mem·or·ably /-əblɪ/ *adv*

mem·or·an·dum /ˌmeməˈrændəm/ *n* [C] (*pl* -da /-də/ or ~s) **1** note or record for future use. **2** informal business communication, usually without a personal signature. **3** report of an agreement that has been reached but not yet formally drawn up and signed: *M~ and articles of association,* legal document for this.

mem·or·ial /məˈmɔːrɪəl/ *n* [C] **1** something made or done to remind people of an event, person, etc: *a* ~*war* ~. **2** (as an *adjective*) serving to commemorate: *a* ~ *service.* **3** (usually *pl*) historical records or chronicles.

mem·or·ize /ˈmeməraɪz/ *vt* commit to memory.

mem·ory /ˈmemərɪ/ *n* (*pl* -ies) **1** [U] power of keeping facts in the conscious mind and of being able to recall them at will; preservation of past experience for future use. *commit sth to memory,* learn it by heart. *to the best of my memory,* as far as I can remember. **2** [C] this power in an individual (also used, by extension, of the unit of a computer which stores data for future use): *He has a bad ~ for dates.* **3** [U] period over which the memory can go back. *within living memory,* within the years that people now alive can remember. **4** [C] something remembered or stored in the memory: *memories of childhood.* **5** [U] reputation after death: *the late pope, of blessed ~.*

memory bank, part of a computer in which data and instructions are stored.

men /men/ *n pl* of man [1] (1).

men·ace /ˈmenəs/ *n* [C,U] danger; threat: *a* ~ *to world peace. That woman is a* ~, is a nuisance. □ *vt* threaten: *countries ~d by/ with war.*

men·ac·ing·ly *adv*

men·ag·er·ie /məˈnædʒərɪ/ *n* [C] collection of wild animals in captivity, esp for a travelling circus.

mend /mend/ *vt,vi* **1** remake, repair (something broken, worn out or torn); restore to good condition or working order: ~ *shoes/a broken window.* **2** (= *amend*) free from faults or errors: *That won't ~* (= *improve*) *matters. mend one's ways,* ⇨ way(10). **3** regain health; heal. □ *n* [C] damage or torn part, that has been mended: *The ~s were almost invisible. on the mend,* improving in health or condition.

mend·ing, (esp) work of repairing (clothes, etc).

men·da·cious /menˈdeɪʃəs/ *adj* (*formal*) false; untruthful: ~ *newspaper reports.*

men·dac·ity /ˈmenˈdæsətɪ/ *n* (*formal*) **1** [U] untruthfulness. **2** [C] (*pl* -ties) untrue statement.

men·di·cant /ˈmendɪkənt/ *n, adj* (person)

getting a living as a beggar: ~ *friars.*

men·folk /ˈmenfəʊk/ *n pl* (*informal*) men, esp the men of a family: *The* ~ *have all gone out fishing.*

me·nial /ˈmiːnɪəl/ *adj* suitable for, to be done by, a household servant: ~ *tasks such as washing pots and pans.*

me·ni·ally /-ɪəlɪ/ *adv*

men·in·gi·tis /ˌmenɪnˈdʒaɪtɪs/ *n* [U] (serious illness caused by) inflammation of any or all of the membranes enclosing the brain and spinal cord.

meno·pause /ˈmenəpɔːz/ *n* [C] final stopping of the menses at the age of about 50 (*informally* called 'the change of life').

men·ses /ˈmensiz/ *n pl* monthly bleeding from the uterus.

men·strual /ˈmenstrʊəl/ *adj* of the menses.

men·stru·ate /ˈmenstrʊeɪt/ *vi* discharge the menses.

men·stru·ation /ˌmenstrʊˈeɪʃən/ *n* [U]

-ment /-ment/ *suffix* (*verb* + ~ = *noun*) result or means of an action: *development.*

-men·tal /ˈmentəl/ *adj*

-men·tally /-ˈmentəlɪ/ *adv*

men·tal /ˈmentəl/ *adj* **1** of or in the mind. **2** mentally ill. **3** (*informal*) mad.

'mental a'rithmetic, done in the mind without using written figures or a mechanical device.

'mental de'ficiency, subnormal development of intellectual powers.

'mental 'health, general condition of the mind.

'mental home/hospital, one for mental patients.

'mental 'illness, illness of the mind.

men·tally /ˈmentəlɪ/ *adv.* ~*ly deficient/ defective,* suffering from mental illness.

men·tal·ity /menˈtælətɪ/ *n* (*pl* -ies) **1** [U] general intellectual character; degree of intellectual power: *persons of average* ~. **2** [C] characteristic attitude of mind: *a war* ~.

men·thol /ˈmenθɒl/ *n* [U] solid white substance obtained from oil of peppermint, used medically and as a flavouring.

men·tho·lated /ˈmenθəleɪtɪd/ *adj*

men·tion /ˈmenʃən/ *vt* speak or write something about; say the name of; refer to: *I'll* ~ *it to him. Did I hear my name ~ed,* Was somebody talking about me? *Don't mention it,* phrase used to show that thanks, an apology, etc are unnecessary. □ *n* **1** [U] mentioning or naming: *He made no ~ of your request.* **2** [C] brief notice or reference: *several honourable ~s in dispatches.*

-men·tioned *adj* (with an *adverb* prefixed): *a'bove-/be'low-'mentioned,* referred to above/below.

men·tor /ˈmentɔː(r)/ *n* [C] wise and trusted adviser and helper.

menu /ˈmenjuː/ *n* [C] list of courses or dishes that are available in a restaurant.

mer·can·tile /ˈmɜːkəntaɪl/ *adj* of trade, commerce and merchants.

'**mercantile ma`rine,** country's merchant ships and seamen.

mer·cen·ary /ˈmɜːsənrɪ US: -ənerɪ/ adj working only for money or other reward; inspired by love of money: ∼ politicians; act from ∼ motives. □ n[C] (pl -ies) soldier hired for pay to serve in a foreign army.

mer·chan·dise /ˈmɜːtʃəndaɪz/ n [U] goods bought and sold; trade goods. □ vt,vi buy and sell (goods).

mer·chant /ˈmɜːtʃənt/ n [C] **1** (usually wholesale) trader, esp one doing business with foreign countries. **2** (chiefly as an adjective) of overseas trade and the carriage of goods by sea: ∼ ships. **3** (with a prefix) person trading inside a country in the goods mentioned: a `coal-∼/`wine-∼.

mer·ci·ful /ˈmɜːsɪfəl/ adj having, showing, feeling mercy (to).

mer·ci·fully /-flɪ/ adv

mer·ci·less /ˈmɜːsɪləs/ adj showing no mercy.

mer·ci·less·ly adv

mer·cur·ial /mɜːˈkjʊərɪəl/ adj **1** of, like, caused by, containing, mercury: ∼ poisoning. **2** (fig) lively; quickwitted. **3** (of persons) changeable; inconstant.

mer·cury /ˈmɜːkjʊrɪ/ n [U] (also called quicksilver) heavy, silver-coloured metal (symbol **Hg**) usually liquid, as used in thermometers and barometers.

Mer·cury /ˈmɜːkjʊrɪ/ n planet nearest the sun.

mercy /ˈmɜːsɪ/ n (pl -ies) **1** [U] (capacity for) holding oneself back from punishment, or from causing suffering to, a person whom one has the right or power to punish; We were given no ∼. He threw himself on my ∼, begged me not to punish him, etc. **at the mercy of,** in the power of; without defence against: The ship was at the ∼ of the waves. **2** [C] piece of good fortune; something to be thankful for; relief: We must be thankful for small mercies.

'**mercy killing,** (informal) euthanasia.

mere¹ /mɪə(r)/ adj (-r, -st) not more than: She's a ∼ child. It's a ∼/the ∼st trifle, nothing at all important, nothing of any value, etc.

mere·ly adv only; simply: I ∼ly asked his name, I said it ∼ly as a joke.

mere² /mɪə(r)/ n [C] pond; small lake.

mer·etri·cious /ˌmerəˈtrɪʃəs/ adj (formal) attractive on the surface but of little value: ∼ jewellery.

merge /mɜːdʒ/ vt,vi **1** (of business companies) (cause to) become one: The small banks ∼d/were ∼d into one large organization. **2** **merge into,** fade or change gradually into: Twilight ∼d into darkness.

merger, n [U] merging; [C] instance of this.

mer·id·ian /məˈrɪdɪən/ n [C] **1** (either half of) circle round the globe, passing through a given place and the north and south poles: the ∼ of Greenwich (of longitude 0° on Brit-

ish maps). **2** highest point reached by the sun or other star as viewed from a point on the earth's surface; 12 noon.

me·ringue /məˈræŋ/ n [U] whites of egg and sugar baked and used as a covering over pies, tarts, etc; [C] small cake made of this mixture.

merit /ˈmerɪt/ n **1** [U] quality or fact of deserving approval; worth; excellence: A certificate of ∼; Do men of ∼ always win recognition? **2** [C] quality, fact, action, etc that deserves reward (or, less often, punishment): We must decide the case on its ∼s, according to the rights and wrongs of the case, without being influenced by personal feelings. □ vt deserve; be worthy of: ∼ reward.

meri·toc·racy /ˌmerɪˈtɒkrəsɪ/ n [C] (pl -ies) (system of government or control by) persons of practical or intellectual ability.

meri·tori·ous /ˌmerɪˈtɔːrɪəs/ adj (formal) praiseworthy; deserving reward: a prize for ∼ conduct.

meri·tori·ous·ly adv

mer·maid /ˈmɜːmeɪd/ n [C] (in children's stories, etc) woman with a fish's tail in place of legs.

merry /ˈmerɪ/ adj (-ier, -iest) **1** happy; cheerful; bright and gay: a ∼ laugh. I wish you a ∼ Christmas. **2** (old use) pleasant: M∼ England.

'**merry-go-round** revolving machine with horses, cars, etc on which children ride at fun fairs.

mer·rily /ˈmerəlɪ/ adv

mer·ri·ment /ˈmerɪmənt/ n[U]

mesh /meʃ/ n [C] **1** one of the spaces in material such as a net or wire screen: a net with half-inch ∼es. ⇨ micromesh. **2** (pl) network: the ∼es of a spider's web. **3** (fig) complex system: the ∼es of political intrigue. □ vt,vi **1** catch (e g fish) in a net. **2** (of toothed wheels) be engaged (with others). **3** (fig) harmonize: Our ways of looking at these problems don't ∼.

mess¹ /mes/ n (with a, an, but rarely pl) state of confusion, dirt or disorder: The workmen cleaned up the ∼ before they left. He has got into another ∼, is in trouble again. □ vt,vi **1** put into disorder or confusion: The late arrival of the train ∼ed up all our plans. Hence, '**mess-up** n (informal). **2** **mess about,** (a) do things with no very definite plan; behave foolishly. (b) make a mess or muddle; treat roughly or inconsiderately: Stop ∼ing me about!

messy adj (-ier, -iest) dirty; in a state of disorder: a ∼y job; look ∼y.

mess² /mes/ n [C] company of persons taking meals together (esp in the Armed Forces); these meals; the room, etc in which the meals are eaten.

mess·age /ˈmesɪdʒ/ n [C] **1** piece of news, or a request, sent to a person: Will you take this ∼ to my brother? **2** something announced by a prophet and said to be inspired social or moral teaching.

mess·en·ger /'mesɪndʒə(r)/, person carrying a message.

Mess·iah /mə'saɪə/ n 1 person expected by the Jews to come and set them free. 2 the Saviour, Jesus Christ.

met /met/ pt, pp of meet[1].

me·tab·olism /mɪ'tæbəlɪzm/ n [U] process by which food is built up into living matter or by which living matter is broken down into simple substances.

meta·bolic /metə'bolɪk/ adj.

meta·car·pal /'metə'kɑpəl/ adj, n [C] (of a) bone in the hand.

metal /'metəl/ n 1 [C] any of a class of mineral substances such as tin, iron, gold and copper. 2 [U] one of these (as a material noun): Is it made of wood or ~?

me·tal·lic /mə'tælɪk/ adj of or like metal: ~ sounds, e g as made by brass objects struck together.

meta·mor·pho·sis /'metə'mɔfəsɪs/ n [C] (pl -ses /-siz/) change of form or character, e g by natural growth or development: the ~ in the life of an insect, from the egg, etc.

meta·phor /'metəfə(r)/ n [C,U] (example of) the use of words to indicate something different from the literal meaning, as in 'I'll make him eat his words'.

meta·phori·cal /'metə'forɪkəl US: -'fɔr-/ adj of, like, containing or using a metaphor.

meta·phori·cally /-klɪ/ adv

meta·tar·sal /'metə'tɑsəl/ adj, n [C] (of a) bone in the foot.

mete /mit/ vt mete out, portion or measure: Justice was ~d out to them.

me·teor /'mitɪə(r)/ n [C] small body rushing from outer space into the earth's atmosphere and becoming bright (as a 'shooting star' or 'falling star') as it is burnt up.

me·teoric /'mitɪ'orɪk US: -'ɔr-/ adj 1 of the atmosphere or of atmospheric conditions; of meteors. 2 (fig) swift and dazzling; brilliant: a ~ career; a ~ rise to fame.

me·teor·ite /'mitɪəraɪt/ n [C] fallen meteor.

me·teoro·logi·cal /'mitrə'lodʒɪkəl US: 'mitɪɔr-/ adj of meteorology.

me·teor·ol·ogist /'mitɪə'rolədʒɪst/ n [C] expert in meteorology.

me·teor·ol·ogy /'mitɪə'rolədʒɪ/ n [U] science of the weather; study of the earth's atmosphere and its changes.

me·ter[1] /'mitə(r)/ n [C] apparatus which measures, esp one that records the amount of whatever passes through it, or the distance travelled, fare payable, etc: a `parking-~, one that measures the time during which a car is parked in a public place.

me·ter[2] /'mitə(r)/ n (US) = metre.

-meter /-mitə(r)/ suffix means of measuring: thermometer.

method /'meθəd/ n 1 [U] system, order: He's a man of ~. 2 [C] way of doing something: modern ~s of teaching arithmetic.

meth·odi·cal /mə'θodɪkəl/ adj (a) done, carried out, with order or method: ~ical work. (b) having orderly habits: a ~ical worker.

meth·odi·cally /-klɪ/ adv

Meth·od·ism /'meθədɪzm/ n [U] teaching, organization and manner of worship in the Christian denomination started by John Wesley.

Meth·od·ist /-ɪst/ n [C], adj (member) of this denomination.

meth·od·ol·ogy /'meθə'dolədʒɪ/ n [U] science or study of methods(2), esp in academic subjects.

meth·yl·ated spirit /'meθəleɪtɪd 'spɪrɪt/ n [U] form of alcohol used for lighting and heating.

me·ticu·lous /mɪ'tɪkjʊləs/ adj giving, showing, great attention to detail; careful and exact.

me·ticu·lous·ly adv

mé·tier /'meɪtɪeɪ US: meɪ'tjeɪ/ n [C] one's trade or profession.

metre[1] (US = me·ter) /'mitə(r)/ n [C] unit of length in the metric system.

metre[2] (US = me·ter) /'mitə(r)/ n [U] rhythm in verse; [C] particular form of this.

-metre (US -meter) /-mitə(r)/ suffix part of a metre: centimetre.

met·ric /'metrɪk/ adj of metre[1].

'metric system, the decimal measuring system based on the metre as the unit of length, the kilogram as the unit of mass and the litre as the unit of capacity.

met·ri·cal /'metrɪkəl/ adj 1 of, composed in, metre[2] (contrasted with ordinary prose): a ~ translation of the Iliad. 2 connected with measurement: ~ geometry.

met·ri·cally /-klɪ/ adv

metri·ca·tion /'metrɪ'keɪʃən/ n [U] conversion to the metric system.

met·ro·nome /'metrənəum/ n [C] (music) graduated inverted pendulum for sounding an adjustable number of beats per minute.

me·trop·olis /mə'tropəlɪs/ n [C] (pl ~es) 1 chief city of a country; capital. 2 archbishop's see.

metro·poli·tan /'metrə'polɪtən/ adj 1 of or in a capital city: the ~ police. 2 of an ecclesiastical province: a ~ bishop, one having authority over the bishops in his province □ n [C] 1 person who lives in a metropolis. 2 M~, metropolitan bishop.

mettle /'metəl/ n [U] quality, e g in persons, horses, of endurance and courage: a man of ~. be/put sb on his mettle, rouse him to do his best, put him in a position that tests him.

mew /mju/ n, vi = miaow.

mews /mjuz/ n pl (used with a sing verb) (formerly a) square or street of stables behind a residential street; such stables rebuilt as garages or flats, etc: a South Kensington ~.

mezza·nine /'metsənin US: 'mezə-/ n [C],

adj (floor) between the ground floor and first floor.

mi·aow /miˋaʊ/ *n* [C] sound made by a cat. □ *vi* make this sound.

mice /maɪs/ *n pl* of mouse.

mickey /ˈmɪkɪ/ *n* **take the mickey (out of sb),** (*sl*) mock or tease him.

micro- /maɪkrəʊ/ *prefix* **1** relatively small: *microwave*. **2** of examining or reproducing small quantities: *microscope; microphone*.

mi·crobe /ˈmaɪkrəʊb/ *n* [C] tiny living creature that can be seen only with the help of a microscope, esp kinds of bacteria causing diseases and fermentation.

micro·cosm /ˈmaɪkrəʊkozm/ *n* [C] **1** something considered as representing (on a small scale) mankind or the universe. **2** miniature representation (*of* a system, etc). ⇨ macrocosm.

micro·dot /ˈmaɪkrəʊdɒt/ *n* [C] photograph reduced to the size of a very small dot.

micro·fiche /ˈmaɪkrəʊfiːʃ/ *n* [C] piece of microfilm.

micro·film /ˈmaɪkrəʊfilm/ *n* [C,U] (roll, section, of) photographic film for small-scale reproduction of documentary material, etc. □ *vt* photograph in this way.

micro·mesh /ˈmaɪkrəʊmeʃ/ *adj* of very small mesh: ∼ *tights*.

mi·crom·eter /maɪˈkrɒmɪtə(r)/ *n* [C] device for measuring very small objects.

mi·cron /ˈmaɪkrɒn/ *n* [C] unit of length (symbol *μ*) equal to one millionth of a metre.

micro·or·gan·ism /ˈmaɪkrəʊ ˈɔːgənɪzm/ *n* [C] organism that can only be seen under a microscope.

micro·phone /ˈmaɪkrəfəʊn/ *n* [C] instrument for changing sound waves into electrical waves, used to increase the volume of sound, as in telephones, radio, etc.

micro·scope /ˈmaɪkrəskəʊp/ *n* [C] instrument with lenses for making very small objects appear larger.
micro·scopic /ˈmaɪkrəˋskɒpɪk/
micro·scopi·cally /-klɪ/ *adj*

micro·wave /ˈmaɪkrəʊweɪv/ *n* [C] very short wave (as used in radio and radar).

mid¹ /mɪd/ *adj* **1** in the middle of; middle: *from* ∼ *June to* ∼ *August; in* ∼ *winter*. **2** (used in compounds): *mid-*∼*-morning coffee*.
'mid-ˋoff, 'mid-ˋon, (in cricket) fielder near the bowler on the off, on, side.

the 'Midˋwest, (also known as the **Middle West**) that part of the US which is the Mississippi basin as far south as Kansas, Missouri and the Ohio River.

mid² /mɪd/ *prep* (*poetry*) among.

mid·day /ˈmɪdˋdeɪ/ *n* noon: (as an *adjective*) *the* ∼ *meal*.

middle /ˈmɪdəl/ *n* **1** the ∼, point, position or part, which is at an equal distance from two or more points, etc or between the beginning and the end: *the* ∼ *of a room*. *They were in the* ∼ *of dinner* (= were having dinner) *when I called*. **2** [C] (*informal*) waist. □ *adj* in the middle: *the* ∼ *house in the row*.

'middle ˋage, the period between youth and old age. Hence, **'middle-ˋaged** *adj*.

the 'Middle ˋAges, the period (in European history) from about AD 1100 to 1400 (or, in a wider sense, AD 600—1500).

'middle ˋclass, class of society between the lower and upper classes (e g business men, professional workers). Hence, **'middle-ˋclass** *adj*

'middle course, compromise between two extreme courses (of action).

the 'Middle ˋEast, countries from Egypt to Iran.

'middle·man, any trader who buys goods from a producer and sells them.

middle name, second of two given names, e g *Bernard* in *George Bernard Shaw*.

'middle school, (*GB*) type of school between primary school and high school.

the middle watch, (on ships) period of duty between midnight and 4 a m.

'middle·weight, (esp) boxer weighing between 147 and 160 lb or (66·6 to 72·5 kg).

the 'Middle ˋWest, = Midwest.

mid·dling /ˈmɪdlɪŋ/ *adj* of middle or medium size, quality, grade, etc: *a town of* ∼ *size*. **fair to middling,** (*informal*) in fairly good but not very good health.

midge /mɪdʒ/ *n* [C] small winged insect like a gnat.

midget /ˈmɪdʒɪt/ *n* [C] extremely short person. □ *adj* very small: *a* ∼ *submarine*.

mid·land /ˈmɪdlənd/ *adj*, *n* (of the) middle part of a country.

the Midlands, the middle counties of England.

mid·night /ˈmɪdnaɪt/ *n* [C] 12 o'clock at night: *at/before/after* ∼. □ *adj* during the middle of the night; at midnight.

mid·riff /ˈmɪdrɪf/ *n* [C] **1** diaphragm. **2** abdomen, belly.

mid·ship·man /ˈmɪdʃɪpmən/ *n* [C] (*pl* -men) **1** non-commissioned officer ranking below a sublieutenant in the Royal Navy. **2** student training to be commissioned as an officer in the US Navy.

mid·ships /ˈmɪdʃɪps/ *adv* = amidships.

midst /mɪdst/ *n*, *adv* (*literary* or *archaic*) (in the) middle part.

mid·sum·mer /ˈmɪdˋsʌmə(r)/ *n* [U] the middle of summer.

'midsummer ˋmadness, (*informal*) temporary foolishness, esp in summer.

mid·way /ˈmɪdˋweɪ/ *adj*, *adv* **midway between,** halfway.

mid·wife /ˈmɪdwaɪf/ *n* [C] (*pl* midwives /-waɪvz/) woman trained to help women in childbirth.

mid·wifery /ˈmɪdwɪfrɪ/ *n* [U] profession and work of a midwife.

might¹ /maɪt/ *pt* of may.

might² /maɪt/ *n* [U] great power; strength:

work with all one's ~.

mighty /ˈmaɪtɪ/ *adj* (-ier, -iest) **1** powerful: *a* ~ *nation.* **2** great; massive: *the* ~ *ocean.* **3** (*informal*) great. **high and mighty,** very proud. □ *adv* (*informal*) very: *think oneself* ~ *clever.*

might·i·ly /-əlɪ/ *adv*

mi·graine /ˈmiːgreɪn/ *n* [C] severe, frequently recurring, headache.

mi·grant /ˈmaɪgrənt/ *n* [C] person, bird which migrates.

mi·grate /maɪˈgreɪt US: ˈmaɪgreɪt/ *vi* **1** move from one place to another (to live there). **2** (of birds and fishes) come and go to a region with the season.

mi·gra·tion /maɪˈgreɪʃn/ *n* [C,U]

mi·gra·tory /ˈmaɪgrətərɪ US: -tɔːrɪ/ *adj* having the habit of migrating: *migratory birds.*

mike /maɪk/ *n* [C] (*informal* abbr for) microphone.

mi·lage /ˈmaɪlɪdʒ/ *n* = mileage.

mild /maɪld/ *adj* (-er, -est) **1** soft; gentle; not severe: ~ *weather; a* ~ *answer.* **2** (of food, drink, tobacco) not sharp or strong in taste or flavour: ~ *cheese; a* ~ *cigar.*

mild·ly *adv* in a mild manner. **to put it mildly,** to speak without exaggeration.

mild·ness *n* [U]

mil·dew /ˈmɪldjuː US: -duː/ *n* [U] (usually destructive) growth of tiny fungi forming on plants, leather, food, etc in warm and damp conditions: *roses ruined by* ~. □ *vt,vi* affect, become affected, with mildew.

mile /maɪl/ *n* [C] **1** unit of distance (*statute* ~, (of land) 1760 yards; *nautical* ~, (of sea) about 6076 feet) *He ran the* ~ *in 4 minutes/a 4-minute* ~. *My car can do 40* ~*s to the gallon.* **2** (*pl*) (*informal*) any long distance: *walk for* ~*s (and* ~*s). There's no one within* ~*s of him as a tennis player,* no one who can rival him. **3** (*informal*) a great deal: *She's feeling* ~*s better today.*

mile·om·eter /maɪˈlɒmɪtə(r)/ *device* (in a motor-vehicle) recording the number of miles travelled.

ˈmile·stone, (a) stone at the side of a road showing places and distances. **(b)** (*fig*) (important) stage or event in history, research, etc.

mile·age /ˈmaɪlɪdʒ/ *n* [C] **1** distance travelled, measured in miles: *a used car with a small* ~. **2** allowance for travelling expenses at a fixed rate a mile. **3** = miles per gallon.

miler /ˈmaɪlə(r)/ *n* [C] (*informal*) runner specializing in one mile races.

mili·tancy /-ənsɪ/ *n* [U] state of being militant.

mili·tant /ˈmɪlɪtənt/ *adj* ready for fighting; actively engaged in or supporting the use of force: ~ *students/workers.* □ *n* [C] militant person.

mili·tary /ˈmɪlɪtərɪ US: -terɪ/ *adj* of or for soldiers, an army, war on land: ~ *training;* ~ *government.* □ *n* **the** ~, soldiers; the army.

mili·tate /ˈmɪlɪteɪt/ *vi* (of evidence, facts) have force, operate: *Several factors combined to* ~ *against the success of our plan.*

mil·itia /mɪˈlɪʃə/ *n* [C] (usually **the** ~) force of civilians trained as soldiers but not part of the regular army.

milk[1] /mɪlk/ *n* [U] **1** white liquid produced by female mammals as food for their young, esp that of cows, drunk by human beings and made into butter and cheese. **the milk of human kindness,** the kindness that should be natural to human beings. **It's no use crying over spilt milk,** over a loss or error for which there is no remedy. **2** juice like milk of some plants and trees, e g of a coconut. **3** preparation like milk made from herbs, drugs, etc: ~ *of magnesia.*

ˈmilk loaf, sweet-tasting white bread.

ˈmilk·maid, woman who milks cows and works in a dairy.

ˈmilk ˈpudding, hot or cold dish of rice, etc boiled or baked in milk.

ˈmilk round, milkman's route from house to house, street to street.

ˈmilk·shake, beverage of milk with ice-cream or flavouring mixed into it and beaten up.

ˈmilk·sop, (*dated*) *n* man or youth who is lacking in spirit, who is too soft and gentle.

ˈmilk-tooth, one of the first (temporary) teeth in young mammals.

milk[2] /mɪlk/ *vt,vi* **1** draw milk from a cow/ ewe/goat, etc. **2** (*fig*) extract money, information, etc (by deceit or dishonesty) from a person or institution. **3** yield milk: *The cows are* ~*ing well.*

milky /ˈmɪlkɪ/ *adj* (-ier, -iest) **1** of or like milk; mixed with milk. **2** (of a liquid) cloudy, not clear.

the ˈMilky ˈWay, = the Galaxy.

mill[1] /mɪl/ *n* **1** (building (e g a ˈflour-~) with machinery or apparatus for grinding grain into flour. **go/put sb through the mill,** (cause to) undergo hard training or experience. ⇨ also run-of-the-mill. **2** building, factory, workshop, for industry: a ˈcotton/ˈpaper-~. **3** small machine for grinding: a ˈcoffee-/ˈpepper-~.

ˈmill-stone, (a) one of a pair of circular stones between which grain is ground. **(b)** (*fig*) heavy burden: *That mortgage has been like a* ~*stone round my neck.*

mill[2] /mɪl/ *vt,vi* **1** put through a machine for grinding; produce by doing this: ~ *grain/ flour.* **2** produce regular markings on the edge of (coin): *silver coins with a* ~*ed edge.* **3** **mill about/around,** (of cattle, crowds of people) move in a disorganised group.

mil·len·nium /mɪˈlenɪəm/ *n* [C] (*pl* -nia /-nɪə/, ~s) **1** period of 1000 years. **2** (*fig*) future time of great happiness and prosperity for everyone.

mil·le·pede /ˈmɪlɪpiːd/ *n* [C] = millipede.

mil·ler /ˈmɪlə(r)/ *n* [C] owner or tenant of a

mill, esp the old-fashioned flour-mill worked by wind or water.

mil·let /ˈmɪlɪt/ n [U] cereal plant growing 3 to 4 feet high and producing a large crop of small seeds (as food).

milli- /ˈmɪlɪ-/ prefix one-thousandth part of: `millimetre.

mil·li·bar /ˈmɪlɪbɑː(r)/ n [C] unit of atmospheric pressure.

mil·liner /ˈmɪlɪnə(r)/ n [C] person who makes and sells women's hats, and sells lace, trimmings, etc for hats.

mil·len·ery /-nərɪ US: -nerɪ/ n [U] (the business of making and selling) women's hats.

mil·lion /ˈmɪlɪən/ adj, n [C] **1** (of) one thousand thousand (1 000 000). (Note: the pl is rarely used after a number: six ∼ people.) **make a million,** earn, gain, a million pounds/dollars, etc. **2** (informal) great number: ∼s of people were at the party.

mil·lion·aire /ˈmɪlɪəˈneə(r)/ person who has a million dollars, pounds, etc; extremely rich man.

mil·lionth /-lɪənθ/ adj, n [C] (of) the next after 999 999 or one part of a million.

mil·li·pede /ˈmɪlɪpiːd/ n [C] small creature like a worm with many legs usually in double pairs.

mime /maɪm/ n [C] **1** (in ancient Greece and Rome) simple kind of drama in which real persons and events were made fun of and in which mimicry and dancing were important. **2** (in the theatre, etc) use of only facial expressions and gestures to tell a story; actor in such drama. □ vi, vt act (as) in a mime.

mimic /ˈmɪmɪk/ adj imitated or pretended: ∼ warfare, as in peacetime manoeuvres. □ n [C] person who is clever at imitating others, esp in order to make fun of their habits, appearance, etc. □ vt (pt, pp ∼ked) **1** ridicule by imitating: He was ∼king his uncle's voice. **2** (of things) resemble closely: wood painted to ∼ marble.

`mim·icry n [U]

min·aret /ˈmɪnəˈret/ n [C] tall, slender spire, connected with a mosque, from the balconies of which people are called to prayer.

mince /mɪns/ vt, vi **1** cut or chop (meat, etc) into small pieces (with a knife, or a machine with revolving blades, called a `mincing machine or mincer). **2** (dated) say (words) with affected delicacy; try to appear elegant when speaking or walking. □ n [U] minced meat.

`mince·meat, mixture of currants, raisins, sugar, candied peel, apples, suet, etc. **make mincemeat of,** (informal) destroy a person, an argument, etc.

mincer, device for mincing food.

mind /maɪnd/ n **1** [U] memory; remembrance. **bear/keep sth in mind,** not forget it. **bring/call sth to mind,** remember it. **2** [U] (but with a, an or pl in some phrases, as

shown below) what a person thinks or feels; way of thinking; conscious thoughts; feeling, opinion; intention: Nothing was further from his ∼. **absence of mind,** failure to think of what one is doing. ⇨ absentminded. **presence of mind,** ability to act or decide quickly when this is needed. **be in two minds about sth,** feel doubtful, hesitate, about something. **blow one's mind,** (informal) (of drugs, extraordinary or sensational sights, sounds, etc) cause mental excitement, state of ecstasy, etc. Hence, `mind-blowing adj. **change one's mind,** change one's decision, purpose or intention. **give sb a piece of one's mind,** ⇨ piece¹ (2). **have a good mind to `do sth,** be strongly determined or ready to do it. **have half a mind to `do sth,** be almost decided to do it. **have sth/sb on one's mind,** be troubled about a thing or person which, one feels, one ought to deal with. **keep one's mind on sth,** continue to pay attention to: Keep your ∼ on what you're doing. **know one's own mind,** know what one wants, have no doubts. **make up one's mind,** come to a decision: I've made up my ∼ to be a doctor. **speak one's mind,** say plainly what one thinks. **take one's/sb's mind off sth,** turn one's/a person's attention away from something (disagreeable). **in the 'mind's `eye,** in imagination. **to one's mind,** according to one's way of thinking: To my ∼, this is all nonsense. **3** [C,U] (person with) mental ability; intellect: He has a very good ∼. No two ∼s think alike.

`mind reading, knowing by intuition what a person is thinking. Hence, `mind-reader n.

mind² /maɪnd/ vt, vi **1** take care of; attend to: Who's ∼ing the baby? M∼ the dog, Beware of it. M∼ (out), there's a bus coming! mind one's 'P's and `Q's, be careful what one says or does. 'mind your 'own `business, do not interfere in the affairs of others. **2** be troubled by; feel objection to: He doesn't ∼ the cold weather at all. Do you ∼ if I smoke? Would you ∼ opening the window, Will you please do this? I wouldn't ∼ a glass of iced beer, I would like one. **Never mind,** (a) It doesn't matter. (b) Don't worry about it.

minder, person whose duty it is to look after something or somebody: a ma`chine-∼er; a `baby-∼er.

minded /ˈmaɪndɪd/ adj having the kind of mind mentioned (by an adj or adv prefixed): a `strong-∼ man; `high-∼ leaders.

mind·ful /ˈmaɪndfəl/ adj **mindful of,** giving thought and attention to: ∼ of one's duties/ the nation's welfare.

mind·less /ˈmaɪndləs/ adj **1 mindless of,** paying no attention to; forgetful of: ∼ of danger. **2** lacking in or not requiring intelligence: ∼ layabouts.

mind·less·ly adv.

mind·less·ness n [U]

mine[1] /maɪn/ *possessive pron* of or belonging to me: *Is this book yours or ~? He's an old `friend of ~*, one of my old friends.

mine[2] /maɪn/ *n* [C] **1** excavation with shafts/galleries, etc made in the earth from which coal, mineral ores, etc, are extracted: *a `coal~*. **2** (*fig*) rich or abundant source: *A good encyclopaedia/My grandmother is a ~ of information*. **3** (tunnel for a) charge of high explosive exploded by electricity or contact with a vehicle, or a time fuse, etc: *The lorry was destroyed by a `land ~*.
`mine-detector, electro-magnetic device for finding mines(3).
`mine-field, (a) area of land or sea where mines(3) have been laid. **(b)** area of land where there are many mines(3).
`mine-sweeper, naval vessel employed for clearing the sea of mines.

mine[3] /maɪn/ *vt, vi* **1** dig (for coal, ores, etc) from the ground; obtain (coal, etc) from mines. **2** lay mines(3) in; destroy by means of these: *~ the entrance to a harbour*.

miner /ˈmaɪnə(r)/ *n* [C] **1** man who works in a mine underground: *`coal~s*. **2** soldier trained to dig tunnels and lay mines under enemy trenches, etc.

min·eral /ˈmɪnərəl/ *n* [C] natural substance (not vegetable or animal) got from the earth by mining. □ *adj* of, containing, mixed with, minerals: *~ ores*.
the `mineral kingdom, natural substances of inorganic matter.
`mineral water, (a) water that naturally contains a mineral substance, esp one said to have medicinal value. **(b)** (*GB*) non-alcoholic flavoured drink containing soda-water.

min·er·al·ogy /ˌmɪnəˈrælədʒɪ/ *n* [U] the study and science of minerals.
min·er·al·ogist /ˌmɪnəˈrælədʒɪst/ *n* [C] expert in, student of, mineralogy.

mingle /ˈmɪŋgəl/ *vt, vi* mix: *~ with* (= go about among) *the crowds*.

mingy /ˈmɪndʒɪ/ *adj* (-ier, -iest) (*GB informal*) mean, ungenerous: *a ~ fellow*.

mini /ˈmɪnɪ/ *prefix* of small size, length, etc: *`~bus; a `~skirt*.

minia·ture /ˈmɪnɪtʃə(r)/ *US*: -tʃuər/ *n* **1** [C] very small painting of a person, esp one on ivory or vellum; [U] this branch of painting. *in miniature*, on a small scale. **2** [C] small-scale copy or model of any object. **3** (as an *adjective*) on a small scale: *a ~ railway*.

minia·tur·ize /ˈmɪnɪtʃəraɪz/ *vt* make on a very small scale.

minim /ˈmɪnɪm/ *n* [C] (in music) note half the value of a semibreve.

mini·mal /ˈmɪnɪməl/ *adj* smallest in amount or degree: *On these cliffs vegetation is ~*.

mini·mize /ˈmɪnɪmaɪz/ *vt* reduce to, estimate at, the smallest possible amount or degree: *~ an error*, try to reduce its importance, say that it is not serious.

mini·mum /ˈmɪnɪmən/ *n* [C] (*pl* ~s or -ma

/-mə/) (opposite of *maximum*) **1** least possible or recorded amount, degree, etc: *reduce something to a ~*. **2** (as an *adjective*) *the ~ temperature; a ~ wage*, lowest wage that regulations allow to be paid.

min·ing /ˈmaɪnɪŋ/ *n* [U] the process of getting minerals, etc from mines.

min·ion /ˈmɪnɪən/ *n* [C] (usually contemptuous) employee who, in order to win favour, obeys orders slavishly.

min·is·ter[1] /ˈmɪnɪstə(r)/ *n* **1** person at the head of a Department of State (and often a member of the Cabinet): *the Prime M~*. **2** person representing his Government in a foreign country of lower rank than an ambassador. **3** Christian priest or clergyman, esp one in the Presbyterian and Non-comformist Churches.

min·is·ter[2] /ˈmɪnɪstə(r)/ *vi* give help or service: *~ to the wants of a sick man*.

min·is·ter·ial /ˌmɪnɪˈstɪərɪəl/ *adj* **1** of a Minister of State, his position, duties, etc: *~ functions/duties*. **2** of or for the Ministry (or Cabinet): *the ~ benches*.
min·is·ter·ially /-rɪlɪ/ *adv*

min·is·tra·tion /ˌmɪnɪˈstreɪʃən/ *n* **1** [U] ministering or serving, e g in performing a religious service. **2** [C] act of this kind.

min·is·try /ˈmɪnɪstrɪ/ *n* [C] (*pl* -ies) **1** Department of State under a Minister: *`M~ of `Defence*. **2** office, duties, term of service, of a minister. **3** **the ~**, the ministers of religion as a body. *enter the ministry*, become a minister of religion.

mink /mɪŋk/ *n* [C,U] (valuable brown fur skin of a) small animal like a stoat: (as an *adjective*) *a ~ coat*.

min·now /ˈmɪnəʊ/ *n* [C] (sorts of) very small fresh-water fish.

mi·nor /ˈmaɪnə(r)/ *adj* ⇨ major. **1** smaller, less important: *~ repairs/alteration*. **2** comparatively unimportant: *the ~ poets; play only a ~ part in the play*. **3** second or younger of two boys (esp in the same school): *Smith ~*. **4** (in music): *a ~ third*, an interval of three semi-tones; *a ~ key*, in which the scale has a minor third. □ *n* (*legal*) person not yet legally of age.

mi·nor·ity /maɪˈnɒrətɪ *US*: -ˈnɔːr-/ *n* (*pl* -ies) **1** [U] (*legal*) the state of being under age (in GB under 18). **2** the smaller number or part, esp of a total of votes. *be in the minority*, be in the smaller of two groups. **3** [C] small racial, religious, etc group in a community, nation, etc.
a minority government, one which has a minority of the total number of seats in a legislative assembly.

Mino·taur /ˈmaɪnətɔː(r)/ *n* [C] (Greek myth) monster, half man and half bull, kept in the labyrinth in Crete.

min·ster /ˈmɪnstə(r)/ *n* [C] large or important church, esp one that once belonged to a monastery: *York ~*.

min·strel /ˈmɪnstrəl/ *n* [C] **1** (in the Middle

Ages) travelling composer, player and singer of songs and ballads. **2** one of a company of public entertainers at fairs, race-meetings and on the seashore at holiday resorts.

mint[1] /mɪnt/ *n* [U] (sorts of) plant whose leaves are used for flavouring: ∼ *sauce*, chopped mint leaves, in vinegar and sugar, as eaten with lamb.

mint[2] /mɪnt/ *n* [C] **1** place where coins are made. **make/earn a mint (of money)**, (*informal*) a large amount. **2** (as an *adjective*) of medals, stamps, prints, books, etc). **in mint condition**, as if new; unsoiled; perfect. □ *vt* **1** make (a coin) by stamping metal: ∼ *coins of 50p.* **2** (*fig*) invent a word, phrase, etc.

min·uet /ˌmɪnjʊˈet/ *n* [C] (piece of music for a) slow, graceful 17th century dance.

minus /ˈmaɪnəs/ *adj* **1** the '∼ sign, the sign −. **2** negative: *a* ∼ *quantity*, a quantity less than zero (e g − 2x). □ *prep* **1** less; with the deduction of: 7 ∼ 3 *is* 4. **2** (*informal*) without: *He came back from the war* ∼ *a leg.* □ *n* [C] minus sign or quantity.

min·us·cule /ˈmɪnəskjul/ *adj* tiny; small.

min·ute[1] /ˈmɪnɪt/ *n* [C] **1** the sixtieth part of one hour: *seven* ∼s *to six; arrive ten* ∼s *early.* **in a minute**, soon: *I'll come in a* ∼. **the minute (that)**, as soon as: *I'll give him your message the* ∼ (*that*) *he arrives.* **2** the sixtieth part of a degree (in an angle): 37° 30′, 37 degrees 30 minutes. **3** official record giving authority, advice or making comments. **4** (*pl*) summary, records, of what is said and decided at a meeting, esp of a society or committee. □ *vt* **1** record in the minutes(4). **2** make a record of something.

`minute-hand`, long hand on a watch or clock pointing to the minute.

`minute-man`, (*US*) (period of the revolution) member of the militia ready to fight at a minute's notice.

'up-to-the-`minute *adj* most recent: *up-to-the-*∼ *information.*

mi·nute[2] /maɪˈnjut *US:* -ˈnut/ *adj* (-r, -st) **1** very small: ∼ *particles of dust.* **2** giving small details; careful and exact: *the* ∼st *details.*

mi·nute·ly *adv*

mi·nute·ness *n* [U]

mir·acle /ˈmɪrəkəl/ *n* [C] act or event (good or welcome) which does not follow the known laws of nature; remarkable and surprising event: *work/accomplish* ∼s. **a miracle of,** exceptional example or specimen: *It's a* ∼ *of technology.*

mir·acu·lous /mɪˈrækjʊləs/ *adj*

mir·acu·lous·ly *adv*

mi·rage /ˈmɪrɑʒ *US:* mɪˈrɑʒ/ *n* [C] **1** effect, produced by air conditions, causing something distant to become visible (or usable down), esp the illusive appearance of a sheet of water in the desert. **2** (*fig*) any illusion or hope that cannot be realized.

mire /ˈmaɪə(r)/ *n* [U] **1** swampy ground;

soft, deep mud. **2** *be in the mire,* (fig) be in difficulties. □ *vt,vi* **1** cover with mud; cause to be, sink, in mud.

mir·ror /ˈmɪrə(r)/ *n* [C] **1** polished surface (usually of glass) that reflects images. **2** (*fig*) something that reflects or gives a likeness: *Pepys's 'Diary' is a* ∼ *of the times he lived in.* □ *vt* reflect as in a mirror: *The still water of the lake* ∼ed *the hillside.*

'mirror `image, reflection or copy with the right and left sides reversed.

mirth /mɜθ/ *n* [U] (*formal*) being merry, happy and bright; laughter.

mis- /mɪs-/ *prefix* bad, wrong, not: *misbehave.*

mis·ad·ven·ture /ˌmɪsədˈventʃə(r)/ *n* [C,U] (event caused by) bad luck; misfortune. **death by misadventure,** by accident.

mis·al·liance /ˌmɪsəˈlaɪəns/ *n* [C] unsuitable alliance, esp marriage.

mis·an·thrope /ˈmɪsənθrəʊp/ *n* [C] person who hates mankind; person who avoids society.

mis·an·thropic /ˌmɪsənˈθrɒpɪk/ *adj*

mis·an·thropy /mɪsˈænθrəpɪ/ *n* [U] hatred of mankind.

mis·apply /ˌmɪsəˈplaɪ/ *vt* (*pt,pp* -ied) apply wrongly; use for a wrong purpose, e g public funds.

mis·ap·pli·ca·tion /ˌmɪsˌæplɪˈkeɪʃən/ *n* [C,U]

mis·ap·pre·hend /ˌmɪsˌæprɪˈhend/ *vt* (*formal*) misunderstand.

mis·ap·pre·hen·sion /ˌmɪsˌæprɪˈhenʃən/ *n* [C,U]

mis·ap·pro·pri·ate /ˌmɪsəˈprəʊprɪeɪt/ *vt* take and use wrongly; apply (a person's money) to a wrong (esp one's own) use: *The treasurer* ∼d *the society's funds.*

mis·ap·pro·pri·ation /ˌmɪsəˈprəʊprɪˈeɪʃən/ *n* [C,U]

mis·be·got·ten /ˌmɪsbɪˈɡɒtən/ *adj* **1** illegitimate. **2** (*informal*) worthless: ∼ *plans.*

mis·be·have /ˌmɪsbɪˈheɪv/ *vt,vi* behave improperly.

mis·be·hav·iour (*US* = **-ior**) /ˌmɪsbɪˈheɪvɪə(r)/ *n* [U]

mis·be·liever /ˌmɪsbɪˈlivə(r)/ *n* [C] person having, or thought to have, false beliefs, e g about religion.

mis·cal·cu·late /ˌmɪsˈkælkjʊleɪt/ *vt,vi* calculate (amounts, etc) wrongly.

mis·cal·cu·la·tion /ˌmɪsˈkælkjʊˈleɪʃən/ *n* [C,U]

mis·car·riage /ˈmɪskærɪdʒ/ *n* **1** [U] ∼ *of justice,* failure of a court to administer justice properly; mistake in judgement or in punishment; [C] instance of this. **2** [C] failure to deliver to, or arrive at, the destination: ∼ *of goods;* [C] instance of this. **3** [U] premature expulsion of a foetus from the womb; [C] instance of this: *have a* ∼.

mis·carry /ˈmɪsˈkærɪ/ *vi* (*pt,pp* -ied) **1** (of plans, etc) fail; have a result different from what was hoped for. **2** (of letters, etc) fail to reach the right destination. **3** (of a woman) have a miscarriage(3).

mis·cast /ˈmɪsˈkɑːst US: -ˈkæst/ vt (pt,pp ~) (usually passive) (of an actor, a play) be cast unsuitably: *She was badly ~ as Juliet.*

mis·cel·laneous /ˌmɪsəˈleɪnɪəs/ adj of mixed sorts; having various qualities and characteristics: *a ~ collection of goods.*

mis·cel·lany /mɪˈselənɪ US: ˈmɪsəleɪnɪ/ n [C] (pl -ies) collection, e g of writings on various subjects by various authors.

mis·chance /ˈmɪsˈtʃɑːns US: -ˈtʃæns/ n [C,U] (piece of) bad luck: *by ~.*

mis·chief /ˈmɪstʃɪf/ n **1** [U] injury or damage done by a person or other agent, esp on purpose. **do sb a mischief,** hurt him. **2** [U] moral harm or injury: *Such wild speeches may work great ~.* **make mischief (between...),** cause discord or ill feeling. Hence, **ˈmischief-maker/-making.** **3** [U] foolish or thoughtless behaviour likely to cause trouble: *Boys are fond of ~,* of playing tricks, etc. *Tell the children to keep out of ~.* **4** light-hearted, innocent desire to tease: *Her eyes were full of ~.* **5** [C] person who is fond of mischief(4).

mis·chiev·ous /ˈmɪstʃɪvəs/ adj **1** causing mischief; harmful: *a ~ letter/rumour.* **2** filled with, fond of, engaged in, mischief: *~ looks/tricks; as ~ as a monkey.*

mis·con·ceive /ˌmɪskənˈsiːv/ vt,vi **1** understand wrongly. **2** (formal) have a wrong conception: *~ of one's duty.*

mis·con·cep·tion /ˌmɪskənˈsepʃən/ n [C,U]

mis·con·duct /ˌmɪsˈkɒndʌkt/ n [U] **1** improper behaviour, e g adultery. **2** bad management. □ vt /ˌmɪskənˈdʌkt/ **1** behave badly; be guilty of adultery (with...). **2** manage badly: *~ one's business affairs.*

mis·con·struc·tion /ˌmɪskənˈstrʌkʃən/ n [U] false or inaccurate interpretation or understanding; [C] instance of this.

mis·con·strue /ˌmɪskənˈstruː/ vt get a wrong idea of: *You have ~d my words/meaning.*

mis·count /ˈmɪsˈkaʊnt/ vt,vi count wrongly. □ n [C] /ˈmɪskaʊnt/ wrong count, esp of votes at an election.

mis·cre·ant /ˈmɪskrɪənt/ n [C] (dated) scoundrel.

mis·date /ˈmɪsˈdeɪt/ vt give a wrong date to an event, etc; put a wrong date on a letter, cheque, etc.

mis·deal /ˈmɪsˈdiːl/ vt,vi (pt,pp ~t /-ˈdelt/) deal (playing-cards) wrongly. □ n [C] error in dealing cards.

mis·deed /ˈmɪsˈdiːd/ n [C] wicked act; crime: *be punished for one's ~s.*

mis·de·mean·our (US = **-meanor**) /ˌmɪsdɪˈmiːnə(r)/ n [C] (legal) offence less serious than a felony.

mis·di·rect /ˌmɪsdɪˈrekt/ vt direct wrongly: *~ a letter,* by failing to put the full or correct address on it; *~ one's energies or abilities,* e g by using them for a bad purpose.

mis·di·rec·tion /ˌmɪsdɪˈrekʃən/ n [C,U]

mis·doings /ˈmɪsˈduːɪŋz/ n pl misdeeds.

miser /ˈmaɪzə(r)/ n [C] person who loves wealth for its own sake and spends as little as possible.

mi·ser·ly adj

mis·er·able /ˈmɪzrəbəl/ adj **1** wretched; very unhappy: *feeling ~; the ~ lives of refugees.* **2** causing wretchedness and unhappiness: *~ weather.* **3** poor in quality: *a ~ attempt/meal.*

mis·er·ably /-əblɪ/ adv

mis·ery /ˈmɪzərɪ/ n (pl -ies) **1** [U] state of being miserable; great suffering (of mind or body): *be in a ~/suffer ~ from toothache.* **2** (pl) painful happenings; great misfortunes: *the miseries of mankind.* **3** [C] (informal) person who is always miserable and complaining.

mis·fire /ˈmɪsˈfaɪə(r)/ vi **1** (of a gun) fail to go off. **2** (informal) (of a joke, etc) fail to have the intended effect. □ n /ˈmɪsfaɪə(r)/ [C] such a failure.

mis·fit /ˈmɪsfɪt/ n [C] **1** article of clothing which does not fit well. **2** (fig) person not fitting in with his position or his associates.

mis·for·tune /ˈmɪsˈfɔːtʃən/ n **1** [U] bad luck: *suffer ~.* **2** [C] instance of bad luck: *He bore his ~s bravely.*

mis·giv·ing /ˈmɪsˈgɪvɪŋ/ n [C,U] (feeling of) doubt, suspicion, distrust: *a heart/mind full of ~(s).*

mis·gov·ern /ˈmɪsˈgʌvən/ vt govern (the State, etc) badly.

mis·gov·ernment n [U]

mis·guide /ˈmɪsˈgaɪd/ vt give wrong or misleading information or directions to.

mis·guided adj (of behaviour) foolish and wrong (because of bad or wrong guidance or influence).

mis·handle /ˈmɪsˈhændəl/ vt deal with roughly, rudely or inefficiently.

mis·hap /ˈmɪshæp/ n **1** [C] unlucky accident: *meet with a slight ~.* **2** [U] bad luck; accident: *arrive without ~.*

mis·in·form /ˌmɪsɪnˈfɔːm/ vt give wrong information to.

mis·in·ter·pret /ˌmɪsɪnˈtɜːprɪt/ vt give a wrong interpretation to: *He ~ed her silence as giving consent.*

mis·judge /ˈmɪsˈdʒʌdʒ/ vt,vi judge or estimate wrongly; form a wrong opinion of: *He ~d the distance and fell into the stream.*

mis·lay /ˈmɪsˈleɪ/ vt (pt,pp mislaid /-ˈleɪd/) put something where it cannot easily be found: *I've mislaid my passport.*

mis·lead /ˈmɪsˈliːd/ vt (pt,pp misled /-ˈled/) lead wrongly; cause to be or do wrong: *This information is rather ~ing,* gives a wrong impression.

mis·man·age /ˈmɪsˈmænɪdʒ/ vt manage badly or wrongly.

mis·man·agement n [U]

mis·nomer /ˈmɪsˈnəʊmə(r)/ n [C] wrong use of a name or word: *It's a ~ to call this* *place a first-class hotel.*

mis·ogyn·ist /mɪˈsɒdʒɪnɪst/ n [C] hater of women.

mis·place /ˌmɪsˈpleɪs/ vt **1** put in a wrong place. **2** (usually passive) give wrongly or unwisely: ~d confidence. **3** lose; mislay.

mis·pro·nounce /ˌmɪsprəˈnaʊns/ vt pronounce wrongly.

mis·pro·nun·ci·ation /ˌmɪsprəˈnʌnsɪˈeɪʃən/ n [C,U]

mis·quote /ˌmɪsˈkwəʊt/ vt quote wrongly.

mis·quo·ta·tion /ˌmɪskwəʊˈteɪʃən/ n [C,U]

mis·read /ˌmɪsˈriːd/ vt (pt,pp ~ /-ˈred/) read or interpret wrongly: ~ one's instructions.

mis·rep·re·sent /ˌmɪsˈreprɪˈzent/ vt represent wrongly; give a false account of.

mis·rep·re·sen·ta·tion /ˌmɪsˈreprɪzenˈteɪʃən/ n [C,U]

mis·rule /ˌmɪsˈruːl/ n [U] **1** bad government. **2** lawlessness; confusion.

miss¹ /mɪs/ n [C] failure to hit, catch, reach, etc: *ten hits and one* ~. **give sth a miss,** (*informal*) decide not to do it, take it, eat it, etc.

miss² /mɪs/ n [C] **1** M~, title for an unmarried woman or girl who has no other title: *M~ Smith*. **2** (e g by schoolchildren to a woman teacher, also to shopkeepers, etc): *Good morning,* ~! *Two cups of coffee,* ~.

miss³ /mɪs/ vt,vi **1** fail to hit, hold, catch, reach, see, etc: ~ *the target. He* ~ed *the 9.30 train* (= was too late and did not catch it), *and therefore* ~ed (= escaped) *the accident. The house is at the next corner; you can't* ~ *it,* you'll certainly see it. *He* ~ed (= failed to understand) *the point of my joke.* **miss the boat,** (be too late and) lose an opportunity. **2** realize, learn, feel regret at, the absence of: *He's so rich that he wouldn't* ~ *£100. She'd* ~ *her husband if he died. When did you* ~ *your purse,* realize you didn't have it? **3** *miss out* (*on sth*), lose an opportunity to benefit, enjoy oneself: *If you don't come, you'll be* ~ing *out on the fun.* **miss sth out,** omit; fail to put in or say: *The printers have* ~ed *out a word/line.*

miss·ing adj not to be found; not in the place where it ought to be: *a book with two pages* ~ing; ~ing *persons.*

mis·sal /ˈmɪsəl/ n [C] **1** book containing the order of service for Mass in the R C Church. **2** book of prayers and devotions.

mis·shapen /ˌmɪsˈʃeɪpən/ adj (esp of the body or a limb) deformed.

mis·sile /ˈmɪsaɪl US: ˈmɪsəl/ n [C] object or weapon that is thrown (e g a stone), shot (e g an arrow) or projected (e g a rocket).

guided missiles, e g from ground to air, for destroying aircraft, directed by electronic devices.

mis·sion /ˈmɪʃən/ n [C] **1** (the sending out of a) number of persons to perform a special task, usually abroad: *a* `trade ~ *to S America.* **2** (esp) the sending out of mission-

aries to convert people by preaching, teaching, etc. **3** place where the work of missionaries is carried on; settlement where charitable or medical work is carried on, esp among poor people. **4** *one's mission in life,* that work which a person feels called on to do by God: *She thinks her* ~ *in life is to reform juvenile delinquents.* **5** special task, assigned to an individual or a unit of the armed forces: *The group has flown twenty* ~s.

mis·sion·ary /ˈmɪʃənərɪ US: -nerɪ/ n [C] (pl -ies) person sent to preach his religion, esp among people who are ignorant of it. □ adj of missions(2) or missionaries.

mis·sive /ˈmɪsɪv/ n [C] (used humorously for) (esp) a long, serious-looking letter.

mis·spell /ˌmɪsˈspel/ vt (pt,pp ~ed or mis-spelt /ˈspelt/) spell wrongly.

mis·spell·ing n [C,U]

mis·spent /ˌmɪsˈspent/ adj used wrongly or foolishly: *a mis-spent youth.*

mist /mɪst/ n **1** [C,U] (occasion when there is, an area with) water vapour in the air, at or near the earth's surface, less thick than fog: *Hills hidden/shrouded in* ~. **2** [C] filmy appearance before the eyes (caused by tears, etc). **3** (*fig*) something which dims, obscures, etc: *the* ~s *of time.* □ vi,vt cover, be covered, with mist: *The scene* ~ed *over.*

misty adj (-ier, iest) (a) with mist: *a* ~y *evening;* ~y *weather.* (b) not clear: *have only a* ~y *idea.*

mist·ily /-əlɪ/ adv

misti·ness n

mis·take¹ /mɪˈsteɪk/ n [C] wrong opinion, idea or act: *spelling* ~s. *We all make* ~s *occasionally.* **by mistake,** as the result of carelessness, forgetfulness, etc; in error: *I took your umbrella by* ~.

mis·take² /mɪˈsteɪk/ vt,vi (pt mistook /mɪˈstʊk/, pp ~n /mɪˈsteɪkən/) **1** be wrong, have a wrong idea, about: *We've* ~n *the house,* come to the wrong house. **2** *mistake sb/sth for,* identify wrongly: *She is often* ~n *for her twin sister.*

mis·taken adj (a) in error; wrong in opinion: *a case of* ~n *identity;* ~n *ideas.* **be mistaken (about sth),** be wrong: *If I'm not* ~n, *there's the man we met on the train.* (b) ill-judged: ~n *kindness/zeal.*

mis·tak·en·ly adv

mis·ter /ˈmɪstə(r)/ n [C] **1** (always written *Mr*) title prefixed to a man's name when he has no other title: *Mr Green.* **2** (*sl*) (used by children): *Please,* ~, *can I have my ball back?*

mis·timed /ˌmɪsˈtaɪmd/ adj said or done at an unsuitable time: *a* ~d *intervention.*

mistle·toe /ˈmɪsəltəʊ/ n [U] evergreen plant (growing on fruit and other trees) with small white sticky berries (used as a Christmas decoration).

mis·took /mɪˈstʊk/ pt of mistake.

mis·tress /ˈmɪstrəs/ n [C] **1** woman at the

head of a household or family: *Is your ~ at home?* ⇨ master(2). **2** woman school teacher: *the `games ~.* **3** woman with a good knowledge or control of something: *She is ~ of the situation.* **4** (in stories, plays, etc dealing with periods before the 18th century) title equivalent to the modern *Mrs* or *Miss.* **5** (*poetry*) woman loved and courted by a man: *'O ~ mine!'* **6** woman having regular sexual intercourse with a man to whom she is not married.

mis-trial /ˈmɪsˈtraɪl/ *n* [C] (*legal*) trial which is made invalid because of some error in the proceedings.

mis-trust /ˈmɪsˈtrʌst/ *vt* feel no confidence in: *~ one's own powers.* □ *n* [U] (or with *the*) lack of confidence or trust: *a strong ~ of anything new.*
mis-trust-ful /-fəl/ *adj*

misty /ˈmɪstɪ/ ⇨ mist.

mis-un-der-stand /ˈmɪsˌʌndəˈstænd/ *vt,vi* (*pt,pp* -stood /-ˈstʊd/) take a wrong meaning from (instructions, messages, etc); form a wrong opinion of: *She had always felt misunderstood.*

mis-un-der-stand-ing *n* [C,U] failure to understand rightly, esp when this has led or may lead to ill feelings: *clear up ~ings between nations that may lead to war.*

mis-use /ˌmɪsˈjuz/ *vt* **1** use wrongly; use for a wrong purpose. **2** treat badly. □ *n* /ˌmɪsˈjus/ [U] using wrongly; [C] instance of this: *the ~ of power.*

mite[1] /maɪt/ *n* [C] **1** very small or modest contribution or offering: *offer a ~ of comfort.* **2** tiny object, esp a small child: *Poor little ~!*

mite[2] /maɪt/ *n* [C] small parasitic creature that may be found in food and carry disease.

mi-ter /ˈmaɪtə(r)/ *n* (*US*) = mitre.

miti-gate /ˈmɪtɪgeɪt/ *vt* make less severe, violent or painful.
mitigating circumstance, that may make a mistake, crime, etc seem less serious.
miti-ga-tion /ˌmɪtɪˈgeɪʃən/ *n* [U]

mitre (*US* = **mi-ter**) /ˈmaɪtə(r)/ *n* [C] tall headdress worn by bishops.

mitt /mɪt/ *n* [C] **1** mitten. **2** baseball glove. **3** (*sl*) hand; fist.

mit-ten /ˈmɪtən/ *n* [C] **1** kind of glove covering four fingers together and the thumb separately. **2** covering for the back and palm of the hand only, leaving the thumb and fingers bare.

mix[1] /mɪks/ *vt,vi* **1** (of different substances, people, etc) put, bring or come together so that the substances, etc are no longer distinct; make or prepare by doing this: *~ flour and water. We can sometimes ~ business with pleasure. Many races are ~ed in Hawaii.* **2** (of persons) come or be together in society: *He doesn't ~ well,* doesn't get on well with people. **3** *be/get mixed up (in sth),* be involved or confused: *Don't get ~ed up in politics. He feels very ~ed up (= confused) about life.* Hence, `**mix-up** *n* [C]

mix[2] /mɪks/ *n* [C] (used chiefly in trade) ingredients, mixed or to be mixed, for a purpose, e g for plaster, mortar, concrete or kinds of food: *a `cake ~.*

mixed /mɪkst/ *adj* of different sorts: *a ~ school,* for boys and girls. **have mixed feelings (about sth),** be undecided.

'**mixed `doubles,** (in tennis, etc) with two players, one man and one woman, on each side.

'**mixed `farming,** e g dairy farming and cereals.

mixer /ˈmɪksə(r)/ *n* [C] **1** person or thing that mixes: *a ce`ment/`food ~.* **2** (in T V, films) person who combines shots on to one length of film or video-tape. **3** (*informal*) one who is at ease with others on social occasions. ⇨ mix[1] (2).

mix-ture /ˈmɪkstʃə(r)/ *n* **1** [U] mixing or being mixed. **2** [C] something made by mixing: *a `cough ~. Air is a ~ of gases.*

moan /məʊn/ *n* [C] low sound (as) of pain, suffering or regret: *the ~s of the wounded; the ~ of the wind on a winter evening.* □ *vi,vt* utter moans: *What's she ~ing (= complaining) about now?*

moat /məʊt/ *n* [C] deep, wide ditch filled with water, round a castle, etc as a defence.

mob /mɒb/ *n* [C] **1** disorderly crowd, esp one that has gathered for mischief or attack. **2 the ~,** (*dated*) the common people. **3** gang of criminals. □ *vt* (-bb-) (of people) crowd round in great numbers, either to attack or to admire: *The pop singer was ~bed by teenagers.*

mo-bile /ˈməʊbaɪl *US:* -bəl/ *adj* **1** moving, able to be moved, easily and quickly from place to place: *~ troops/artillery.* **2** easily and often changing. □ *n* [C] ornamental structure with parts that move in currents of air.

mo-bil-ity /məʊˈbɪlətɪ/ *n* [U] being mobile.

mo-bi-lize /ˈməʊbəlaɪz/ *vt,vi* collect together for service or use, esp in war.

mo-bi-liz-ation /ˌməʊbəlaɪˈzeɪʃən *US:* -lɪˈz-/ *n* [U]

moc-ca-sin /ˈmɒkəsɪn/ *n* **1** [U] soft leather made from deerskin. **2** (*pl*) style of shoes made from this.

mock /mɒk/ *vt,vi* **1** make fun (of) (esp by copying in a funny or contemptuous way): *The naughty boys ~ed the blind man.* **2** defy: *The heavy steel doors ~ed the attempts of the thieves to open the safe* □ *adj* not real or genuine: *a ~ battle.*

mock-ing-ly *adv*

mock-ery /ˈmɒkərɪ/ *n* (*pl* -ies) **1** [U] contempt; ridicule: *hold a person up to ~.* **2** [C] person or thing that is mocked; mocking occasion. **3** [C] very bad example: *His trial was a ~ of justice.* **make a mockery of,** ridicule.

mock-ing bird /ˈmɒkɪŋ bɜd/ *n* [C] American bird of the thrush family that mimics other birds.

mo·dal /ˈməʊdəl/ adj 1 relating to mode, manner or form (contrasted with substance). 2 (gram) related to the mood of a verb: ∼ auxiliaries, e g can, may.

mode /məʊd/ n [C] 1 way in which something is done; way of speaking or behaving. 2 (music) one of the two chief scale systems in modern music (the major and the minor modes).

model[1] /ˈmɒdəl/ n [C] 1 small-scale reproduction or representation; design to be copied: ∼ of an ocean liner; (as an adjective) ∼ aircraft/trains. 2 person or thing to be copied: He's a ∼ of kindness. 3 (informal) person or thing exactly like another: She's the ∼/a perfect ∼ of her mother. 4 person who poses for sculptors, painters or photographers. 5 person employed to wear clothes, hats, etc so that prospective buyers may see them. 6 article of clothing, hat, etc shown by models(5): the latest Paris ∼s. 7 design or structure of which many copies or reproductions are (to be) made: the latest ∼s of Ford cars. 8 (as an adjective) perfect; deserving to be imitated: ∼ behaviour; a ∼ wife.

model[2] /ˈmɒdəl/ vt,vi (-ll-, US -l-) 1 shape (in some soft substance): ∼ her head in clay. 2 work as a model(4,5): She earns a living by ∼ling clothes/hats. 3 **model oneself on/upon sb,** take as a copy or example: ∼ oneself on one's father.

mod·el·ler (US = -eler), person who models(1).

mod·el·ling (US = -eling), (a) art, method, of making models(1). (b) working as a model(5).

mod·er·ate[1] /ˈmɒdrət/ adj 1 not extreme; limited; having reasonable limits: a ∼ appetite. 2 midway; keeping or kept within reasonable limits: a ∼ political party; be ∼ in one's demands. □ n [C] person who holds moderate opinions, e g in politics.

mod·er·ate·ly adv

mod·er·ate[2] /ˈmɒdəreɪt/ vt,vi 1 make or become less violent or extreme: ∼ one's enthusiasm/demands. 2 act as a moderator.

mod·er·ation /ˌmɒdəˈreɪʃən/ n [U] quality of being moderate. **In moderation,** in a moderate manner or degree: Will alcoholic drinks be harmful if taken in ∼?

mod·er·ator /ˈmɒdəreɪtə(r)/ n [C] 1 Presbyterian minister presiding over a church court. 2 presiding examiner at some university examinations. 3 material in which neutrons are slowed down in an atomic pile.

mod·ern /ˈmɒdən/ adj 1 of the present or recent times: ∼ technical achievements. 2 new and up-to-date: ∼ methods and ideas; a house with all ∼ conveniences. □ n [C] person living in modern times.

modern English, since 1475.

modern history, ⇨history.

modern language, near the form now spoken and written.

mo·dern·ity /məˈdɜːnətɪ/ n [U] being modern.

mod·ern·ize /ˈmɒdənaɪz/ vt make suitable for present-day needs; bring up to date: Ought we to ∼ our spelling?

mod·ern·iz·ation /ˌmɒdənaɪˈzeɪʃən/ US: -nɪˈz-/ n [U]

mod·est /ˈmɒdɪst/ adj 1 having, showing, a not too high opinion of one's merits, abilities, etc: be ∼ about one's achievements. 2 moderate; not large in size or amount: a ∼ house. My needs are quite ∼. 3 taking, showing, care not to do or say anything indecent or improper: ∼ in speech, dress and behaviour.

mod·est·ly adv

mod·esty /ˈmɒdɪstɪ/ n [U] state of being modest (all senses).

modi·cum /ˈmɒdɪkəm/ n (sing only) small or moderate amount: a ∼ of effort.

modi·fier /ˈmɒdɪfaɪə(r)/ (gram) word that modifies, e g an adj or adv.

mod·ify /ˈmɒdɪfaɪ/ vt (pt,pp -ied) 1 make changes in; make different: The industrial revolution modified the whole structure of English society. 2 make less severe, violent, etc: You'd better ∼ your tone, e g be less rude. 3 (gram) make the sense of (a word) less general; limit the meaning of: In 'red shoes' 'red' modifies 'shoes'.

modi·fi·ca·tion /ˌmɒdɪfɪˈkeɪʃən/ n [C,U]

mod·ish /ˈməʊdɪʃ/ adj fashionable.

mod·ish·ly adv

modu·late /ˈmɒdjʊleɪt US: -dʒʊ-/ vt,vi 1 regulate; adjust; adapt. 2 (music) make a change in the pitch intensity or key of. 3 change or pass from one key to another. 4 vary the frequency, amplitude or other characteristics of sound waves.

modu·la·tion /ˌmɒdjʊˈleɪʃən/ US: -dʒʊˈl-/ n 1 [U] process of modulating; state of being modulated; [C] change resulting from this. 2 [U] (in music) changing of key; [C] particular change of key. 3 variation in the amplitude, frequency or phase of a sound wave so that it is suitable for the radio or telephone.

mod·ule /ˈmɒdjuːl US: -dʒəl/ n [C] 1 standard or unit of measurement as used in building. 2 standard uniform component used in the structure of a building; unit of electronic components as used in the assembly of a computer. 3 independent and self-contained unit of a spacecraft.

com'mand module, for the astronaut in command.

'lunar module, to be separated for a moon landing.

modu·lar /ˈmɒdjʊlə(r) US: -dʒʊ-/ adj

mo·hair /ˈməʊheə(r)/ n [U] (thread, cloth, made from the) fine, silky hair of the Angora goat.

Mo·ham·medan /məˈhɒmɪdən US: məʊˈhæmɪdən/ n ⇨ Muhammad.

moist /mɔɪst/ adj (esp of surfaces) slightly wet: eyes ~ with tears.

mois·ten /ˈmɔɪsən/ vt,vi make or become moist: ~en the lips.

mois·ture /ˈmɔɪstʃə(r)/ n [U] condensed vapour on a surface; liquid in the form of vapour.

mo·lar /ˈməʊlə(r)/ n [C], adj (one) of the back teeth used for grinding food.

mo·las·ses /məˈlæsɪz/ n pl (used with a sing verb) thick, dark syrup drained from raw sugar during the refining process.

mold, molder, mold·ing, moldy, ⇨ mould, etc.

mole[1] /məʊl/ n [C] permanent, small dark spot on the human skin.

mole[2] /məʊl/ n [C] small, dark-grey fur-covered animal living in tunnels (or burrows).

`mole-hill, pile of earth thrown up by a mole while burrowing. **make a mountain out of a mole-hill,** treat a trivial matter as important.

mole[3] /məʊl/ n [C] stone wall built in the sea as a breakwater or causeway.

mol·ecule /ˈmɒlɪkjul/ n [C] smallest unit (usually of a group of atoms) into which a substance could be divided without a change in its chemical nature.

mol·ecu·lar /məˈlekjʊlə(r)/ adj.

mo·lest /məˈlest/ vt trouble or annoy intentionally.

mol·lify /ˈmɒlɪfaɪ/ vt (pt,pp -ied) make (a person, his feelings) calmer or quieter: ~ing remarks; ~ his anger.

mol·li·fi·ca·tion /ˌmɒlɪfɪˈkeɪʃən/ n [U]

mol·lusc (US also **mol·lusk**) /ˈmɒləsk/ n [C] one of a class of animals with soft bodies (and often hard shells), e g oysters, mussels, cuttlefish, snails, slugs.

molt /molt/ ⇨ moult.

mol·ten /ˈməʊltən/ adj (pp of melt). **1** (of metals) melted: ~ steel. **2** made of metal that has been melted and cast.

mo·ment /ˈməʊmənt/ n [C] point or very brief period of time: It was all over in a few ~s. Just a ~, please. □ conj as soon as; at the time when: The ~ I saw you I knew you were angry with me.

mo·men·tary /ˈməʊməntrɪ US: -terɪ/ adj **1** lasting for, done in, a moment. **2** at every moment: in ~ expectation of an accident.

mo·men·tar·ily /ˈməʊmənˈterəlɪ/ adv

mo·men·tous /məˈmentəs/ adj important; serious.

mo·men·tum /məˈmentəm/ n [U] **1** (science) quantity of motion of a moving body (the product of its mass and velocity): Do falling objects gain ~? **2** (fig) (of events) force (as) gained by movement; impetus: lose/gain ~.

mon·arch /ˈmɒnək/ n [C] supreme ruler (a king, queen, emperor or empress).

mon·ar·chic /məˈnɑkɪk/ adj

mon·ar·chism /-ɪzm/ n [U] system of

government by a monarch.

mon·ar·chist /-ɪst/ n [C] supporter of monarchism.

mon·archy /ˈmɒnəkɪ/ n [U] government by a monarch; [C] (pl -ies) state ruled by a monarch.

mon·as·tery /ˈmɒnəstrɪ US: -sterɪ/ n [C] (pl -ies) building in which monks live as a secluded community under religious vows.

mon·as·tic /məˈnæstɪk/ adj of monks or monasteries: ~ vows, i e of poverty, chastity, and obedience.

mon·as·ti·cism /məˈnæstɪsɪzm/ n [U] monastic system and way of life.

mon·aural /ˈmɒnˈɔrəl/ adj **1** for one ear. **2** (abbr **mono**) (of sound-reproducing equipment and recordings) not stereophonic.

Mon·day /ˈmʌndɪ/ n second day of the week.

mon·et·ary /ˈmʌnɪtrɪ US: -terɪ/ adj of money or coins: The ~ unit in the US is the dollar.

money /ˈmʌnɪ/ n [U] coins stamped from metal or printed on paper and accepted when buying and selling, etc: Do you know any easy ways of making ~?

`money-box, closed box into which coins are dropped through a slit, used for savings or for collecting.

`money-lender, one whose business is to lend money at interest.

`money-maker, (a) person who is successful in making a profit. (b) profitable item.

the `money-market, bankers, financiers, etc whose operations decide the rates of interest on borrowed capital.

`money-order, official order bought from a post office for payment at another post office to a named person.

`money-spinner, (informal) book, play, etc that makes a lot of money.

moneyed /ˈmʌnɪd/ adj having much money: the ~ed classes.

money-less adj having no money.

-mon·ger /-ˈmʌŋgə(r)/ suffix person who deals in: `ironmonger.

mon·gol /ˈmɒŋgəl/ n [C], adj person suffering from mongolism.

mon·gol·ism /ˈmɒŋgəlɪzm/ n [U] congenital condition in which a child is born with mental deficiency and a flattened broad skull and slanting eyes.

mon·goose /ˈmɒŋgus/ n [C] (pl ~s) small Indian animal clever at destroying venomous snakes.

mon·grel /ˈmʌŋgrəl/ n [C] **1** dog of mixed breed. **2** any plant or animal of mixed origin. □ adj of mixed breed, race or origin: a ~ dog.

moni·tor /ˈmɒnɪtə(r)/ n [C] **1** pupil given authority over his fellows. **2** person employed to listen to and report on foreign broadcasts; apparatus for testing transmissions by radio, for detecting radioactivity, etc. □ vt,vi act as a monitor(2).

monk /mʌŋk/ n [C] member of a community of men living together under religious vows in a monastery.
monk·ish /-ɪʃ/ adj.

mon·key /mʌŋkɪ/ n [C] (pl ~s) 1 animals of the group of animals most closely resembling man. 2 person, esp a child, who is fond of mischief: *You little ~!* □ vi **monkey about (with)**, play mischievously: *Stop ~ing about with those tools!*
'monkey-nut, groundnut.
'monkey wrench, wrench (spanner) with a jaw that can be adjusted to various lengths.

mono /ˈmɒnəʊ/ (abbr of) monaural.

mono- /mɒnə-, etc/ prefix one, a single: *monosyllable*.

mono·chrome /ˈmɒnəkrəʊm/ n [C] painting in (different tints of) one colour. □ adj having only one colour.

mon·ocle /ˈmɒnəkəl/ n [C] framed lens for one eye, kept in position by the muscles round the eye.

mon·og·amist /məˈnɒɡəmɪst/ n [C] person who practises monogamy.
mon·og·amous /məˈnɒɡəməs/ adj practising monogamy.
mon·og·amy /məˈnɒɡəmɪ/ n [U] practice of being married to only one person at a time. ⇨ polygamy.

mono·gram /ˈmɒnəɡræm/ n [C] two or more letters (esp a person's initials) combined in one design (used on notepaper, etc).

mono·graph /ˈmɒnəɡrɑːf US: -ɡræf/ n [C] detailed (scientific) account, esp a published report on one particular subject.

mono·lith /ˈmɒnəlɪθ/ n [C] single upright block of stone (as a pillar or monument).
mono·lithic /ˈmɒnəˈlɪθɪk/ adj

mono·logue /ˈmɒnəlɒɡ US: -lɔːɡ/ n [C] 1 scene in a play or a complete play in which only one person speaks. 2 any long talk by one person in a conversation.

mono·mania /ˈmɒnəʊˈmeɪnɪə/ n [U] state of mind, sometimes amounting to madness, caused by the attention being occupied exclusively by one idea or subject; [C] instance of this.
mono·maniac /ˈmɒnəʊˈmeɪnɪæk/ n [C] person suffering from monomania.

mono·plane /ˈmɒnəpleɪn/ n [C] aircraft with one wing on each side of the fuselage.

mon·op·ol·ize /məˈnɒpəlaɪz/ vt get or keep control of the whole of, so that others cannot share: *Don't let me ~ the conversation.*
mon·op·ol·iz·ation /məˈnɒpəlaɪˈzeɪʃən US: -lɪˈz-/ n [U]

mon·op·oly /məˈnɒpəlɪ/ n [C] (pl -ies) 1 (possession of the) sole right to supply; the supply or service thus controlled. 2 complete possession of trade, talk, etc: *a government ~*. 3 anything over which one person or group has control and which is not or cannot be shared by others.
mon·op·ol·ist /-lɪst/, person who has a monopoly.

mon·op·ol·is·tic /məˈnɒpəˈlɪstɪk/ adj

mono·rail /ˈmɒnəʊreɪl/ n [C] single rail serving as a track for vehicles; railway system for vehicles using such a rail.

mono·syl·lable /ˈmɒnəsɪləbəl/ n [C] word of one syllable.
mono·syl·labic /ˈmɒnəsɪˈlæbɪk/ adj having only one syllable.

mon·ot·on·ous /məˈnɒtənəs/ adj (uninteresting because) unchanging, without variety: *a ~ voice; ~ work*.
mon·ot·on·ous·ly adv

mon·ot·ony /məˈnɒtənɪ/ n [U] the state of being monotonous.

Mon·si·gnor /mɒnˈsiːnjə(r)/ n (title given to) certain officials in the R C Church.

mon·soon /mɒnˈsuːn/ n [C] seasonal wind blowing in the Indian Ocean from S W from April to October (wet ~) and from N E during the other months (dry ~); the rainy season that comes with the wet monsoon.

mon·ster /ˈmɒnstə(r)/ n [C] 1 abnormally shaped animal or plant. 2 person or thing of extraordinary size, shape or qualities. 3 (in stories) imaginary creature (e g half animal, half bird): *dragons are ~s*. 4 person who is remarkable for some bad or evil quality: *a ~ of cruelty*. 5 (as an adjective) huge: *a ~ ship*.

mon·stros·ity /mɒnˈstrɒsətɪ/ n (pl -ies) 1 [U] state of being monstrous. 2 [C] monster; hideous object, building, etc.

mon·strous /ˈmɒnstrəs/ adj 1 of or like a monster; of great size. 2 causing horror and disgust: *~ crimes*. 3 (informal) absurd; incredible; scandalous: *It's perfectly ~ that men should be paid more than women for the same job*.
mon·strous·ly adv

mon·tage /ˈmɒntɑːʒ/ n [C,U] (Fr) 1 selection, cutting and arrangement of photographic film, etc to make a consecutive whole. 2 process of using many pictures, designs, sometimes superimposed, to make a composite picture.

month /mʌnθ/ n [C] approximately a twelfth of a year: *a baby of three ~s; a three-~ old baby*. *a month of Sundays*, a very long time.
calendar month, any of the twelve parts into which the year is divided; period of time from a day in one month to the corresponding day in the next (e g 2 Jan to 2 Feb).
lunar month, period in which the moon makes a complete revolution; period of 28 days.
month·ly adj, adv done, happening, etc, once a month; valid for one month: *a ~ly season ticket*, for railway travel. □ n [C] (pl -ies) periodical issued once a month.

monu·ment /ˈmɒnjʊmənt/ n [C] 1 building, column, statue, etc in memory of a person or event: *a ~ in the church to the late rector*. 2 piece of scholarship or research that deserves to be remembered; work of literature or science of lasting value: *a* ~ *of learning*.

monu·men·tal /ˌmɒnjʊˈmentəl/ *adj* **1** of, serving for, a monument: *a* ~ *inscription*. **2** (of books, studies, etc) of lasting value: *a* ~ *production*, e g *the Oxford English Dictionary*. **3** (of qualities, buildings, tasks) very great: ~ *ignorance*.

moo /muː/ *n* [C] sound made by a cow or ox. □ *vi* make the sound moo.

`moo-cow`, (child's word for a) cow.

mood ¹ /muːd/ *n* [C] state of mind or spirits: *not in the* ~ *for serious music*.

moody *adj* (-ier, -iest) having moods that often change, esp being bad-tempered.

mood·ily /-əlɪ/ *adv*

mood·iness *n* [U]

mood ² /muːd/ *n* [C] (*gram*) one of the groups of forms that a verb may take to show whether things are regarded as certain, possible, doubtful, etc: *the indicative/ imperative* ~.

moon ¹ /muːn/ *n* [C] **1 the** ~, the body which moves round the earth once in a month and shines at night by light reflected from the sun. **2** (with *a, an*) this body regarded as an object distinct from that visible in other months: *Is it a new* ~ *or a full* ~? **promise sb the moon,** make extravagant promises. **3** satellite of other planets: *How many* ~*s has the planet Jupiter?* **4** (*poetry*) month. **once in a blue moon,** (*informal*) rarely or never.

`moon-beam`, ray of moonlight.

`moon-light`, light of the moon: (often as an *adjective*) *a* ~*light night*.

`moon-shine`, **(a)** light of the moon. **(b)** foolish or idle talk, ideas, etc.

`moon-stone`, semi-precious felspar.

`moon-struck` *adj* wild and mad (supposedly as the result of the moon's influence).

moon·less *adj* without a visible moon: *a dark,* ~*less night*.

moon ² /muːn/ *vi,vt* **moon about/around,** move or look listlessly.

moor ¹ /mʊə(r)/ *n* [C,U] (area of) open, uncultivated land, esp if covered with heather.

`moor-land` /-lənd/ land consisting of open moor and covered with heather.

moor ² /mʊə(r)/ *vt,vi* make (a boat, ship, etc) secure (to land or buoys) by means of cables, etc.

moor·ings /ˈmʊərɪŋz/ *n pl* **(a)** cables, anchors and chains, etc, by which a ship or boat is moored. **(b)** place where a ship is moored.

Moor /mʊə(r)/ *n* **1** member of the Muslim peoples of mixed Arab and Berber who now live in N W Africa. **2** one of the Muslim Arabs who invaded Spain in the 8th century.

moose /muːs/ *n* [C] (*pl* ~ or ~s /-sɪz/) large sort of deer with coarse fleece and large, flat antlers, found in the forests of N America, and in northern Europe (where it is called an *elk*).

moot /muːt/ *adj* (only in) **a moot point/ question,** one about which there is uncertainty. □ *vt* raise or bring forward for discussion: *This question has been* ~*ed before*.

mop /mɒp/ *n* [C] **1** bundle of coarse strings, cloth, etc fastened to a long handle for cleaning floors, etc; similar material on a short handle for cleaning dishes, etc. **2** mass of thick, untidy hair. □ *vt* (-pp-) **1** clean with a mop: ~ *the floor*. **2** wipe with, or as with, a mop: ~ *one's brow*; ~ *up a mess*.

mope /məʊp/ *vi* pity oneself, feel sad or in low spirits: ~ (*about*) *in the house all day*. □ *n pi* the ~s, low spirits.

mo·ped /ˈməʊped/ *n* [C] (*GB*) pedal bicycle fitted with a small petrol engine (under 50 cc).

mo·raine /məˈreɪn *US:* mɔ-/ *n* [U] heap or mass of earth, gravel, rock, etc carried down and deposited by a glacier.

moral ¹ /ˈmɒrəl *US:* ˈmɔːrəl/ *adj* **1** concerning principles of right and wrong: ~ *standards/law*. **2** good and virtuous: *a* ~ *life/ man*. **3** able to understand the difference between right and wrong: *At what age do we become* ~ *beings?* **4** teaching or illustrating good behaviour: *a* ~ *talk*. **5** (contrasted with *physical* or *practical*) connected with the sense of what is right and just: *a* ~ *victory*, outcome of a struggle in which the weaker side is comforted because it has established the righteousness of its cause. **give sb moral support,** help by saying that he has justice and right on his side.

`moral phi'losophy`, ethics, the study of right and wrong in human behaviour.

mor·ally /-rəlɪ/ *adv* **(a)** in a moral manner: *M~ly he is all that can be desired*. **(b)** according to what is most probable: ~*ly bound to fail*.

moral ² /ˈmɒrəl *US:* ˈmɔːrəl/ *n* [C] **1** that which a story, event or experience teaches; lesson: *And the* ~ *is that a young girl should not speak to strange men*. **2** (*pl*) moral habits; standards of behaviour; principles of right and wrong: *a man without* ~*s*.

mo·rale /məˈrɑːl *US:* -ˈræl/ *n* [U] state of discipline and spirit (in a person, an army, a nation, etc); attitude, state of mind, as expressed in action: *The army recovered its* ~ *and fighting power*.

mor·al·ist /ˈmɒrəlɪst *US:* ˈmɔːr-/ *n* [C] person who points out morals(1) or who practises or teaches morality.

mor·al·is·tic /ˌmɒrəlˈɪstɪk *US:* ˈmɔːr-/ *adj* concerned with morals(2).

mor·al·ity /məˈrælətɪ/ *n* (*pl* -ies) **1** [U] (standards, principles, of) good behaviour: *standards of commercial* ~. **2** [C] particular system of morals: *Christian* ~.

mor·al·ize /ˈmɒrəlaɪz *US:* ˈmɔːr-/ *vt,vi* talk or write on questions of duty, right and wrong, etc: ~ *about/on the failings of the young generation*.

mo·rass /məˈræs/ n [C] 1 stretch of low, soft, wet land; marsh. 2 (fig) difficult, complicated situation: a ~ of problems.

mora·tor·ium /ˌmɒrəˈtɔːrɪəm US: ˈmɔː-/ n [C] (pl ~s or -ria /-rɪə/) [C] 1 (period of) legal authorization to delay payment of debts. 2 temporary deferment or delay, esp when agreed.

mor·bid /ˈmɔːbɪd/ adj 1 diseased: ~ anatomy, the study of diseased organs in the body. 2 (of the mind or ideas) unhealthy: a ~ imagination, one that dwells on horrible or nasty things.
mor·bid·ly adv

more /mɔː(r)/ (contrasted with less and fewer; ⇨ many, most ¹, much ¹) adj greater in number, quantity, quality, degree, size, etc; additional: We need ~ men/help, etc. □ n [U] a greater amount, number, etc; an additional amount: What ~ do you want? There are still a few ~. □ adv 1 (forming the comparative degree of most adjectives and adverbs): ~ beautiful/useful/interesting/serious (than...). 2 to a greater extent; in a greater degree: You need to sleep ~, ie more than you sleep now. 3 again: I shall not go there any ~, ever again. once more, one more time. 4 more and more, increasingly: Life is becoming ~ and ~ expensive. more or less, about: It's an hour's journey, ~ or less. 5 (with a noun, = an adjective): The ~ fool you to believe him, You are foolish to believe him.
more·over /mɔːrˈəʊvə(r)/ adv further; besides; in addition (to this).

morgue /mɔːg/ n [C] building in which bodies of persons found dead are kept until they are identified and claimed by members of their families. ⇨ mortuary.

mori·bund /ˈmɒrɪbənd US: ˈmɔːrɪbʌnd/ adj at the point of death; about to come to an end: ~ civilizations.

morn /mɔːn/ n [C] (poetry) morning.

morn·ing /ˈmɔːnɪŋ/ n [C] 1 early part of the day between dawn and noon (or, more generally, before the midday meal): in/during the ~; this ~; yesterday/tomorrow ~; every ~; on Sunday/Monday, etc ~; a few ~s ago. 2 (as an adjective): a ~ walk; an early ~ swim.
'morning coat, black formal coat with tails.
'morning dress, as worn on formal occasions such as weddings.
'Morning 'Prayer, service used in the Church of England at morning service.
'morning-room, room for the morning, esp for breakfast.
'morning 'sickness, (feeling of) nausea early in the morning, often during the first few months of pregnancy.
the 'morning 'star, Venus, or other bright star seen about dawn.

mo·rocco /məˈrɒkəʊ/ n [U] soft leather made from goatskins.

mo·ron /ˈmɔːrɒn/ n [C] 1 person with low intelligence (not so low as imbeciles or idiots). 2 (informal) stupid person.
mo·ronic /məˈrɒnɪk/ adj

mo·rose /məˈrəʊs/ adj gloomy; bad-tempered.
mo·rose·ly adv
mo·rose·ness n [U]

mor·pheme /ˈmɔːfiːm/ n [C] smallest meaningful part into which a word can be divided: 'Run-s' contains two ~s and 'un-man-ly' contains three.

mor·phia /ˈmɔːfɪə/, **mor·phine** /ˈmɔːfiːn/ n [U] drug made from opium and used for relieving pain.

mor·phol·ogy /mɔːˈfɒlədʒɪ/ n [U] 1 branch of biology dealing with the form and structure of animals and plants. 2 (gram) study of the morphemes of a language and of how they are combined to make words.

mor·ris dance /ˈmɒrɪs dɑːns US: ˈmɒrɪs dæns/ n [C] old English folk-dance for men.

mor·row /ˈmɒrəʊ US: ˈmɔː-/ n 1 (literary) the next day after the present or after any given day. 2 (archaic) morning: Good ~!

Morse /mɔːs/ n (also the ~ code) system of dots and dashes or short and long sounds, flashes of light, representing letters of the alphabet and numbers.

mor·sel /ˈmɔːsəl/ n [C] tiny piece (esp of food); mouthful: not a ~ of food anywhere.

mor·tal /ˈmɔːtəl/ adj 1 (contrasted with immortal) which must die; which cannot live for ever: Man is ~. 2 causing death: a ~ wound. 3 lasting until death: ~ hatred. 4 accompanying death: in ~ agony. 5 (informal) extreme; very great or long: in ~ fear. □ n [C] (literary) human being.
mor·tally /-təlɪ/ adv (a) so as to cause death: ~ly wounded. (b) extremely: ~ly offended.
'mortal 'combat, only ended by the death of one of the fighters.
'mortal 'enemy, whose hatred will not end until death.
'mortal 'sin, one causing spiritual death.

mor·tal·ity /mɔːˈtælətɪ/ n [U] 1 state of being mortal. 2 number of deaths caused (e g by a disaster or disease): an epidemic with a heavy ~. 3 death-rate.

mor·tar¹ /ˈmɔːtə(r)/ n [U] mixture of lime, sand and water used to hold bricks, stones, etc together in building. □ vt join (bricks, etc) with mortar.
'mortar-board, (a) small board with a short handle underneath, used for holding mortar. (b) square cap sometimes worn as part of academic costume.

mor·tar² /ˈmɔːtə(r)/ n [C] 1 bowl of hard material in which substances are crushed with a pestle. 2 cannon for firing shells at high angles.

mort·gage /ˈmɔːgɪdʒ/ vt give a person a claim on (property) as a security for payment of a debt or loan. □ n [C] act of mortgaging; agreement about this.

mort·ga·gee /'mɔːgɪ`dʒiː/, person to whom property is mortgaged.

mort·ga·gor /'mɔːgɪ`dʒɔ(r) US: `mɔːgɪdʒər/, person who mortgages his property.

mor·tice /'mɔːtɪs/ n ⇨ mortise.

mor·tify /'mɔːtɪfaɪ/ vt,vi (pt,pp -ied) **1** cause to be ashamed, humiliated, or hurt: a ~ing defeat. **2** mortify the flesh, discipline bodily passions, overcome bodily desires. **3** (of flesh, e g round a wound) decay, be affected with gangrene.

mor·ti·fi·ca·tion /'mɔːtɪfɪ`keɪʃən/ n [U].

mor·tise, mor·tice /'mɔːtɪs/ n [C] hole cut in a piece of wood, etc to receive the end of another piece (the tenon). □ vt join or fasten in this way: ~ two beams together.

mor·tu·ary /'mɔːtʃʊrɪ US: -tʃʊerɪ/ n [C] (pl -ies) room or building (e g part of a hospital) to which dead bodies are taken to be kept until burial.

mo·saic /məʊ`zeɪɪk/ n [C], adj (form or work of art) in which designs, pictures, etc are made by fitting together differently coloured bits of stone, etc.

Mos·lem /'mɒzləm/ n, adj (variant of) Muslim.

mosque /mɒsk/ n [C] building in which Muslims worship Allah.

mos·quito /məˈskiːtəʊ/ n [C] (pl ~es) small, flying, blood-sucking insect, esp the sort that spreads malaria.

moss /mɒs US: mɔːs/ n [U] sorts of small green or yellow plant growing in thick masses on wet surfaces. A rolling stone gathers no moss, A person who too frequently changes his occupation or who never settles in one place will not succeed in life.
mossy adj (-ier, -iest) covered with, like, moss: ~y green.

most[1] /məʊst/ (contrasted with least and fewest; ⇨ many, more, much[1]) adj, n **1** (the) greatest possible number, quantity, degree, etc: Which of you has made (the) ~ mistakes? **at the (very) most**, not more than: I can pay only £10 at the ~. **make the most of**, use to the best advantage: We have only a few hours so we must make the ~ of it. **for the `most part**, usually; on the whole: Japanese cameras are, for the ~ part, of excellent quality. **2** (without the) the majority of; the greater part of: M~ people think so. He was ill ~ of the summer.

most[2] /məʊst/ adv **1** (forming the superlative degree of nearly all adjectives and adverbs): the ~ beautiful/interesting/useful. **2** to the greatest extent; in the greatest degree: What is troubling you ~? **3** very; exceedingly: This is a ~ useful book. He was ~ polite to me.

-most /-məʊst/ suffix (used to form a superlative): innermost.

most·ly /'məʊstlɪ/ adv chiefly; almost all; generally: The medicine was ~ sugar and water. We are ~ out on Sundays.

mote /məʊt/ n [C] particle (of dust, etc).

mo·tel /məʊ`tel/ n [C] motorists' hotel (with rooms, a parking area, service station, etc).

moth /mɒθ US: mɔːθ/ n [C] sorts of winged insect flying chiefly at night, attracted by lights.

`moth-ball, small ball (of camphor, etc) used to discourage clothes-moths.

`moth-eaten, adj (a) eaten or destroyed by clothes-moths. (b) (fig) shabby; out-of-date.

mother /'mʌðə(r)/ n [C] **1** female parent; woman who has adopted a child; woman (often `house~) who is in charge of children in a boarding-school or home [2]. **2** quality or condition that causes something (as in the proverb, **Necessity is the mother of invention**). **3** head of a female religious community. □ vt take care of (as a mother does).
the `mother country, (a) one's native land. **(b)** country in relation to dominions (e g Great Britain for Canada).
mother-in-law /'mʌðər ɪn lɔ/ n [C] (pl ~s-in-law) mother of one's wife or one's husband.
'mother-of-`pearl, hard, shiny rainbow-coloured lining of some shells, esp the pearl-oyster, used for ornaments, etc.
`mother ship, one from which other ships (e g submarines) get supplies.
'mother `tongue, one's native language.
`mother·hood /-hʊd/, state of being a mother.
mother·less adj having no (living) mother.
mother·ly adj having, showing, the tender, kind qualities of a mother.
mother·li·ness n [U]

mo·tif /məʊ`tiːf/ n [C] **1** theme in music for treatment and development, often one which recurs. **2** main feature in a work of art.

mo·tion /'məʊʃən/ n **1** [U] (manner of) moving. **put/set sth in motion,** cause it to start moving or working. **'time and `motion study,** analysis of the movements of workers (in industry, etc) undertaken by experts, who aim at improving efficiency. **2** [C] gesture; particular movement: All her ~s were graceful. **go through the motions,** (informal) do something in a disinterested or insincere manner. **3** [C] proposal to be discussed and voted on at a meeting: The ~ was adopted/carried/rejected/lost, etc by a majority of six. **4** [C] = movement(6). □ vt,vi **1** direct by a motion or gesture: He ~ed (to) me to enter.
'motion `picture, film shown in a cinema.
mo·tion·less adj not moving; still.

mo·ti·vate /'məʊtɪveɪt/ vt be the motive of; give a motive or encouragement to; encourage.
mo·tiv·ation /'məʊtɪ`veɪʃən/ n [C,U]

mo·tive /'məʊtɪv/ adj causing motion: ~ power/force, e g steam, electricity. □ n [C] that which causes action: do it from ~s of kindness.

mo·tive·less *adj*

mot·ley /ˈmɒtlɪ/ *adj* **1** of various colours. **2** of varied character or various sorts: *a ~ crowd*, e g people of many different occupations, social classes, etc.

mo·tor /ˈməʊtə(r)/ *n* [C] **1** device which produces or uses power (esp electric power) to produce motion, but not used of a steam engine: *electric ~s.* **2** (often as an *adjective*) self-powered (by an internal combustion engine) vehicle: `~-vehicles.` **3** (*dated*) (*car* is more usual) (abbr for) motor-car: *the* `M~ Show.` □ *vi,vt* travel by motor-car: *~ from London to Brighton.*

`motor-bike/cycle,` motor vehicle like a bike, for 1 or 2 people.

`motor-boat,` boat with a motor.

`motor-cade,` (*US*) procession of motor-vehicles.

`motor-car,` enclosed motor-vehicle with space for passengers.

`motor nerve,` nerve that excites movements of a muscle or muscles.

`motor scooter,` ⇨ scooter.

`motor-way,` wide road designed for fast traffic, with separate carriageways and going over or under other roads.

`mo·tor·ist` /-ɪst/, person who drives a car.

`motor-ize` /-aɪz/ *vt* equip with a motor-vehicle.

mot·tled /ˈmɒtld/ *adj* marked with spots or areas of different colours without a regular pattern.

motto /ˈmɒtəʊ/ *n* [C] (*pl* ~es or ~s) **1** short sentence or phrase used as a guide or rule of behaviour (e g 'Every man for himself'). **2** short sentence or phrase written or inscribed (e g on a coat of arms) expressing a suitable sentiment.

mould¹ (*US* = **mold**) /məʊld/ *n* [C] **1** container, hollow form, into which molten metal or a soft substance is poured to cool into a desired shape; the shape or form given by this container. **2** jelly, pudding, etc made in such a container. □ *vt* **1** make something in, or as in, a mould: *~ a head out of/in clay.* **2** (*fig*) guide or control the growth of; influence: *~ a person's character.*

mould² (*US* = **mold**) /məʊld/ *n* [U] woolly or furry growth of fungi appearing on damp surfaces. □ *vi* (*US*) become covered with mould: *Cheese ~s in warm, wet weather.*

mouldy *adj* (-ier, -iest) (a) covered with, smelling of, mould: *~y bread.* (b) (*fig*) (of a person) mean and obstructive; worthless.

mould³ (*US* = **mold**) /məʊld/ *n* [U] soft, fine loose earth: `leaf ~,` from decayed leaves.

moul·der (*US* = **mol·der**) /ˈməʊldə(r)/ *vi* crumble to dust by natural decay: *~ing away in his grave.*

mould·ing (*US* = **mold-**) /ˈməʊldɪŋ/ *n* **1** [U] act, way, of moulding or shaping. **2** line of ornamental plaster, carved woodwork, etc round a wall or window etc.

moult (*US* = **molt**) /məʊlt/ *vt,vi* **1** (of birds) lose (feathers) before a new growth. **2** (of dogs and cats) lose hair.

mound /maʊnd/ *n* [C] mass of piled up earth; small hill: *a `burial-~,` of earth over a grave.*

mount¹ /maʊnt/ *n* [C] **1** (*literary*) mountain, hill: *Christ's sermon on the ~.* **2** (abbr **Mt**) (before proper names) mountain: *Mt. Everest.*

mount² /maʊnt/ *vt,vi* **1** go up (a hill, a ladder, etc). **2** get on to (a horse, etc); supply with a horse; put on a horse: *He ~ed (his horse) and rode away.* **3** *mount the throne*, become king/queen/emperor, etc. **4** become greater in amount: *Our expenses are ~ing (up).* **5** put and fix in position: *~ pictures*, e g fix them in an album; *~ insects*, e g for display or preservation in a museum. **6** (*mil* uses): *mount guard (at/over)*, act as a guard or sentry. *mount an offensive*, take the offensive, attack. **7** put (a play) on the stage or TV. **8** (esp of large animals, e g a stallion) get up on (a female animal) in order to copulate. □ *n* [C] that on which a person or thing is or may be mounted (e g a card for a drawing or photograph, a horse for riding on, a gun-carriage).

moun·tain /ˈmaʊntɪn US: -tən/ *n* [C] **1** mass of very high land going up to a peak: *Everest is the highest ~ in the world.* **2** (*fig*) very large thing: *a ~ of debt/letters.*

moun·tain·eer /ˌmaʊntɪˈnɪə(r) US: -tənˈɪər/ *n* [C] climber, inhabitant, of mountains.

moun·tain·eer·ing *n* [C] climbing mountains (as a sport).

moun·tain·ous /ˈmaʊntɪnəs US: -tənəs/ *adj* (a) having mountains: *~ous country.* (b) huge: *~ous waves.*

mourn /mɔːn/ *vi,vt* feel or show sorrow or regret: *~ for a dead child; ~ over the child's death.*

mourner, person who mourns, esp at a funeral.

mourn·ful /-fəl/ *adj* sad.

mourn·fully /-fəlɪ/ *adv*

mourn·ing /ˈmɔːnɪŋ/ *n* [U] **1** grief. **2** (the wearing of) black clothes as a sign of grief: *go into ~ for three weeks.*

mouse /maʊs/ *n* [C] (*pl* mice /maɪs/) **1** sorts of small rodent (`house ~, `field-~, `harvest-~).` **2** (*fig*) shy, timid person. □ *vi* (of cats) hunt for, catch, mice.

`mousetrap,` trap for catching mice.

mousse /muːs/ *n* [C,U] (dish of) flavoured cream beaten and frozen: *chocolate ~.*

mous·tache (*US* = **mus-**) /məˈstɑːʃ US: `mʌstæʃ/ *n* [C] hair allowed to grow on the upper lip.

mousy /ˈmaʊsɪ/ *adj* (-ier, -iest) **1** (esp of hair) dull brown. **2** (of a person) timid, shy.

mouth¹ /maʊθ/ *n* [C] (*pl* ~s /maʊðz/) **1** opening through which animals take in food; space behind this containing the teeth, tongue, etc. **by word of mouth,** (of news, etc) orally (not in writing, etc). **down in the mouth,** sad, dejected. **look a gift-horse in the mouth,** accept something ungratefully esp by examining it critically for faults. **put words into sb's mouth,** (a) tell him what to say. (b) suggest or claim that he has said something. **take the words out of sb's mouth,** say what he was about to say. **2** opening or outlet (of a bag, bottle, tunnel cave, river, etc).

`mouth-organ,` small musical wind-instrument with metal reeds, played by passing it along the lips.

`mouth-piece,` (a) that part of a tobacco pipe, a musical instrument, etc placed at or between the lips. (b) person, newspaper, etc that expresses the opinions of others: *Which newspaper is the ~piece of the Socialists?*

mouth-ful /-fʊl/ *n* [C] (*pl* ~s) as much as can be put into the mouth comfortably at one time: *have only a ~ful of food.*

mouth² /maʊð/ *vt, vi* speak (words) too distinctly or pompously: *An actor who ~s his words is a poor actor.*

mov-able /ˈmuːvəbəl/ *adj* **1** that can be moved; (of property) that can be taken from place to place (e g furniture). ⇨ **portable. 2** varying in date: *Christmas is fixed but Easter is a ~ feast.* □ *n* (*pl*) personal property; articles that can be removed from a house (contrasted with *fixtures*).

move¹ /muːv/ *n* [C] **1** change of place or position, esp of a piece in chess or other games played on boards; player's turn to do this: *Do you know all the ~s in chess? Whose ~ is it?* **2** something (to be) done to achieve a purpose: *What's our next ~?* **3 on the move,** moving about: *Large enemy forces are on the ~.* **get a move on,** (*sl*) hurry up. **make a move,** (a) move to a different place. (b) begin to act: *Unless we make a ~ soon, we shall never get to the top of the mountain.*

move² /muːv/ *vt, vi* **1** (cause to) change position; put, cause to be, in a different place or attitude; (cause to) be in motion: *M~ your chair nearer to the fire. It was calm and not a leaf ~d.* **move 'heaven and 'earth,** use every possible means (*to do* something). **2** **move house,** take one's furniture, etc to another house, flat, etc. **move in,** take possession of a new dwelling-place. **move out,** give up a dwelling-place: *We ~d out on Monday and the new tenants ~d in on Tuesday.* **3** **move (sb) on,** move (a person) to another place or position: *'M~ on, please'.* **move along/down/up,** move farther in the direction indicated so as to make space for others. *'M~ along, please', said the bus conductor.* **4** affect the feelings of with pity, etc: *be ~d to tears. The story of their sufferings ~d us deeply.* **5** cause to do something: *If the spirit ~s him,* (= if he feels like doing so,) *he'll come and help us.* **6** put forward for discussion and decision (at a meeting): *Mr Chairman, I ~ that the money be used for library books.* ⇨ **motion(3). 7** make progress; go forward: *Time is moving on.* **8** take action: *Nobody seems willing to ~.* **9** be socially active in: *They ~ in the best society.* **10** cause (the bowels) to act, to empty; (of the bowels) be emptied.

`moving 'staircase,` = escalator.

move-ment /ˈmuːvmənt/ *n* **1** [U] moving or being moved; activity (contrasted with quiet and rest): *He lay there without ~.* **2** [C] act of changing position: *an opening ~ in chess; ~s of troops in the far East.* **3** [C] moving part of a machine or mechanism or a particular group of such parts: *the ~ of a clock or a watch.* **4** [C] united actions and efforts of a group of people for a special purpose: *the ~ to abolish nuclear armaments.* **5** [C] (*music*) principal division of a musical work with a distinctive structure of its own: *the final ~ of the Ninth Symphony.* **6** [C] emptying of the bowels. **7** [U] activity (in a stock market, etc): *not much ~ in oil shares.*

mover /ˈmuːvə(r)/ *n* [C] (*esp*) person who moves(6) a proposal.

movie /ˈmuːvɪ/ *n* [C] (*informal or US*) **1** motion picture. **2** **the ~s,** the cinema.

mow /məʊ/ *vt* (*pt* ~ed *pp* ~n /məʊn/ or ~ed) **1** cut (grass, etc) (with a `lawn-~er`). **2** **mow down,** destroy, kill, as if by mowing: *Our men were ~n down by the enemy's machine-gun fire.*

mower, person or machine that mows.

Mr /ˈmɪstə(r)/ ⇨ **mister.**

Mrs /ˈmɪsɪz/ title prefixed to the surname of a married woman who has no title.

much¹ /mʌtʃ/ (**more, most.** ⇨ **little**) *adj, n* [U] (used with *sing* nouns; compare *many* which is used with *pl* nouns. *Much* can often be replaced by *plenty* (*of*), *a lot* (*of*), *a large quantity* (*of*), *a good/great deal* (*of*). *Much* is often used with *how, too, so,* or *as*): *There isn't ~ food in the house. M~ of what you say is true. You have given me too ~.* **a bit much,** (*informal*) excessive: *I don't mind taking you but it's a bit ~ to expect me to pay for you. I thought as ~,* That is what I thought. *It is as ~ your responsibility as mine,* You and I are equally responsible. *It was as ~ as he could do to* (= He could do no more than) *pay his way.* **be too much,** more than can be endured: *Your insolence really is too ~!* **(with) not/without so much as,** not even: *He left without so ~ as saying 'Thank you'.* **how much,** (a) what quantity: *Tell me how ~ flour* (= what weight) *you want.* (b) what price: *How ~ is that dress?* **not much of a,** not a good: *He's not ~ of a singer.* **(not) up to much,** (not) worth much: *I don't think his work is up to ~,* ie it is not good. `so much,` (a) an unspecified (often large) quantity: *so ~ money; four meals at `so ~ a head.* (b) nothing but: *His essays are `so ~ rubbish.*

not so much as, (a) not even: *He didn't so ~ as ask me to sit down!* (b) less...than: *He's not so ~ rude as forgetful.* `**so much for,** that is all that needs to be said, done, etc about: `*So ~ for the organising; now what about the cost?* **so much so that,** to such an extent that: *He's ill— so ~ so that he can't get out of bed.* **this/that much,** the quantity, extent etc indicated: *I will say this ~..., I will admit, agree, that....* **make much of,** (a) understand: *I didn't make ~ of that lecture.* (b) attach importance to; exaggerate: *He makes (too) ~ of his connections with rich people.* **not think much of,** have a poor opinion of: *I don't think ~ of the new teacher.*

much² /mʌtʃ/ *adv* 1 (modifying comparatives and superlatives, sometimes preceding *the*): *You must work ~ harder.* (= by far) *the best.* **much more/less,** (used to show that what has been stated applies with greater force to the following statement): *It is difficult to understand him, ~ more his wife. I didn't even speak to him, ~ less discuss your problems.* 2 (modifying participles and adjectives such as *afraid*): *I am very ~ afraid that... I was ~ annoyed.* 3 (modifying a *verbal phrase*): *It doesn't ~ matter. I enjoyed it very ~. He doesn't like beef ~.* 4 (in phrases) **much as,** although: *M~ as I should like to go, I can't.* **how much,** to what extent: *How ~ does losing your job really matter?* **much the same,** about the same: *The patient's condition is ~ the same.* **much to,** to my/his, her, etc great...: *M~ to her surprise/regret... too much,** too highly: *He thinks too ~ of himself.*

much·ness /mʌtʃnəs/ *n* (only in) `**much of a `muchness,** (almost) alike.

muck /mʌk/ *n* [U] 1 dung; farmyard manure (the droppings of animals). 2 dirt; filth. **make a muck of sth,** (*informal*) make a mess of it. □ *vt, vi* 1 **muck sth up,** (*informal*) make it dirty; make a mess of it. 2 **muck about,** (*sl*) do useless or unnecessary things: *'What's he up to?'—'Oh, just ~ing about.'* 3 **muck out,** clean out (stables, etc) by removing dung: *She ~s out (the stables) every morning.*

mucky *adj* (-ier, -iest) dirty.

mu·cous /mjukəs/ *adj* of, like, covered with, mucus. **the mucous membrane,** the moist skin that lines the nose, mouth and food canal.

mu·cus /mjukəs/ *n* [U] sticky, slimy substance (as) produced by the mucous membrane: *Snails and slugs leave a trail of ~.*

mud /mʌd/ *n* [U] soft, wet earth: *Rain turns soil into ~.* **his/her/your, etc name is mud,** he/she/you, etc are in disgrace. ⇨ **stick-in-the-mud.** `**mud-guard,** guard (curved cover) over a wheel (of a bicycle, etc).

muddle /mʌdəl/ *vt, vi* 1 bring into a state of confusion and disorder; make a mess of: *You've ~d the scheme completely. A glass of whisky soon ~s him. Don't ~ (= mix) things up (together).* 2 **muddle along/on,** progress with no clear purpose or plan: *He's still muddling on/along.* **muddle through,** reach the end of an undertaking in spite of inefficiency, obstacles of one's own making, etc. □ *n* (usually sing with *a, an*) confused state; confusion of ideas: *Everything was in a ~ and I couldn't find what I wanted. You have made a ~ of it,* mismanaged it, bungled it.

`**muddle-headed** *adj* confused in mind; stupid.

muddy /mʌdɪ/ *adj* (-ier, -iest) 1 full of, covered with, mud: *~ roads/shoes.* 2 mud-coloured; like mud because thick: *~ coffee.* □ *vt* (*pt,pp* -ied) fill, cover, stain, with mud: *You've muddied the carpet.*

mu·ez·zin /mu`ezɪn US: mju-/ *n* [C] man who calls the hours of prayers from the minaret of a mosque.

muff¹ /mʌf/ *n* [C] person who is awkward or clumsy, esp in games (e g by failing to catch the ball). □ *vt* fail to catch; miss: *~ an easy catch; ~ an opportunity.*

muff² /mʌf/ *n* [C] covering, open at both ends, (formally) used by a woman to keep the hands warm; similar covering for the foot.

muf·fin /mʌfɪn/ *n* [C] light, flat, round cake, usually eaten hot with butter.

muffle /mʌfəl/ *vt* 1 wrap or cover for warmth or protection: *~d up in a heavy overcoat.* 2 decrease the sound of something (e g a bell or a drum) by covering it in cloth, etc: *~d voices,* e g from persons whose mouths are covered.

muf·fler /mʌflə(r)/ *n* [C] 1 cloth, scarf, worn round the neck for warmth. 2 something used to muffle sound: *the ~ in the engine of a motor-vehicle.*

mufti /mʌftɪ/ *n* [C] official expounder of Muslim law.

mug¹ /mʌg/ *n* [C] 1 drinking vessel with a handle, for use without a saucer; its contents: *a `beer-~; a ~ of coffee.* 2 (*sl*) face; mouth: *What an ugly ~ you have!*

mug² /mʌg/ *n* [C] (*sl*) fool; easily deceived person.

mug³ /mʌg/ *vt* (-gg-) **mug sth up,** (*informal*) (try to) become familiar with information, etc on which one is to be tested.

mug⁴ /mʌg/ *vt* (-gg-) (*sl*) attack (a person) violently and rob (e g in a dark street, a lift, an empty corridor, etc). **mug·ger,** person who mugs⁴. **mug·ging,** such an attack.

mug·gins /mʌgɪnz/ *n* [C] (*sl*) (*pl* ~es) fool, esp one who is outwitted.

muggy /mʌgɪ/ *adj* (-ier, -iest) (of the weather, etc) damp and warm; close and sticky. **muggi·ness** *n* [U]

Mu·ham·mad /məˈhæmɪd/ n Prophet and Founder of Islam.

Mu·ham·madan /-ən/ adj, n (of a) believer in Islam.

Mu·ham·ma·dan·ism /məˈhæmɪdənɪzm/ n Islam (the preferred name).

mu·latto /mjuˈlætəʊ US: məˈl-/ n [C] (pl ~s, ~es) person who has one parent of a white race and one Negroid parent.

mul·berry /ˈmʌlbrɪ US: -berɪ/ n [C] (pl -ies) tree with broad, dark-green leaves on which silkworms feed; its fruit (dark purple or white).

mulch /mʌltʃ/ n [U] covering of peat, spread to protect the roots of trees and bushes. □ vt cover (ground) with a mulch.

mule[1] /mjul/ n [C] animal that is the offspring of an ass and a mare. **as obstinate/ stubborn as a mule,** very obstinate/ stubborn.

mu·lish /-ɪʃ/ adj stubborn; obstinate.

mu·lish·ly adv

mu·lish·ness n [U]

mule[2] /mjul/ n [C] slipper without a heel.

mull[1] /mʌl/ vt make (wine, beer) into a hot drink with sugar, spices, etc: ~ed claret.

mull[2] /mʌl/ vt **mull sth over; mull over sth,** think about it carefully.

mul·lah /ˈmʌlə/ n [C] Muslim expert in Islamic theology and sacred law.

mul·let /ˈmʌlɪt/ n [C] (pl unchanged) kinds of seafish used as food: red/grey ~.

mul·li·ga·tawny /ˈmʌlɪɡəˈtɔːnɪ/ n [U] (~ soup) highly seasoned soup with curry powder in it.

mul·lion /ˈmʌlɪən/ n [C] vertical stone division between parts of a window.

multi- /ˈmʌltɪ/ prefix many: multi-coloured.

multi·far·ious /ˌmʌltɪˈfeərɪəs/ adj (formal) many and various: his ~ duties.

multi·form /ˈmʌltɪfɔːm/ adj having many forms or shapes.

multi·lat·eral /ˌmʌltɪˈlætərəl/ adj involving two or more participants: ~ disarmament, after agreement between two or more countries.

multiple /ˈmʌltɪpəl/ adj having many parts or elements: a ~-storey carpark. □ n [C] quantity which contains another quantity an exact number of times: 28 is a ~ of 7. **'least/'lowest common `multiple,** (abbr LCM) least quantity that contains two or more given quantities exactly: 12 is the LCM of 3 and 4.

multi·plex /ˈmʌltɪpleks/ adj having many parts or forms; of many elements.

multi·pli·ca·tion /ˌmʌltɪplɪˈkeɪʃən/ n 1 [U] multiplying or being multiplied: The symbol × stands for ~. 2 [C] instance of this: 3 × 11 is an easy ~.

multi·plic·ity /ˌmʌltɪˈplɪsətɪ/ n [U] (formal) being great in number: a ~ of duties.

multi·ply /ˈmʌltɪplaɪ/ vt,vi (pt,pp -ied) 1 take (a given quantity or number) a given

number of times: ~ 3 by 5. 6 multiplied by 5 is 30, 6 × 5 = 30. 2 produce a large number of; make greater in number. 3 increase in number by procreation: Rabbits ~ rapidly.

multi·tude /ˈmʌltɪtjud US: -tud/ n 1 [C] great number (esp of people gathered together). 2 (with the) the common people; the masses: policies which appeal to the ~. 3 [U] greatness of number: like the stars in ~.

multi·tud·in·ous /ˌmʌltɪˈtjudɪnəs US: -ˈtudənəs/ adj great in number.

mum[1] /mʌm/ n **Mum's the word!** Say nothing about this!

mum[2] /mʌm/ n [C] (informal) mother.

mumble /ˈmʌmbəl/ vt,vi say something indistinctly: The old man was mumbling away to himself.

mumbo-jumbo /ˈmʌmbəʊ ˈdʒʌmbəʊ/ n [U] (fig) meaningless language.

mum·mify /ˈmʌmɪfaɪ/ vt (pt,pp -ied) preserve (a corpse) by embalming.

mum·mi·fi·ca·tion /ˌmʌmɪfɪˈkeɪʃən/ n [C,U]

mummy[1] /ˈmʌmɪ/ n [C] (pl -ies) 1 body of a human being or animal embalmed for burial. 2 dried-up body preserved from decay (as in early Egypt).

mummy[2] /ˈmʌmɪ/ n [C] (pl -ies) (informal) mother.

mumps /mʌmps/ n [U] (with sing verb) contagious disease with painful swellings in the neck.

munch /mʌntʃ/ vt,vi chew with much movement of the jaw: ~ing (away at) a hard apple.

mun·dane /ˈmʌndeɪn/ adj 1 worldly (contrasted with spiritual or heavenly). 2 dull, routine: ~ jobs in factories.

mun·dane·ly adv

mu·nici·pal /mjuˈnɪsɪpəl/ adj of a town or city having self-government: ~ buildings, eg the town hall, public library.

mu·ni·ci·pally /-plɪ/ adv

mu·ni·ci·pal·ity /mjuˈnɪsɪˈpælətɪ/ n [C] (pl -ies) town, city, district, with local self-government; governing body of such a town, etc.

mu·nifi·cence /mjuˈnɪfɪsəns/ n [U] (formal) great generosity.

mu·nifi·cent /mjuˈnɪfɪsənt/ adj (formal) extremely generous; (of a gift) large in amount or splendid in quality.

mu·ni·tion /mjuˈnɪʃən/ n [C] (pl except when used as an adjective) military supplies, esp guns, shells, bombs, etc: The war was lost because of a shortage of ~s/a ~(s) shortage. □ vt provide with munitions: ~ a fort.

mural /ˈmjʊərəl/ adj of, like, on, a wall: a ~ painting. □ n [C] wall-painting.

mur·der /ˈmɜːdə(r)/ n [U] unlawful killing of a human being on purpose; [C] instance of this: commit ~; guilty of ~. **get away with murder,** (informal) do whatever one wishes. □ vt 1 kill (a human being) unlawfully and on purpose. **2** spoil by lack of skill or knowledge: ∼ *a piece of music,* play it very badly.

mur·derer, person guilty of murder.

mur·der·ess /-əs/ woman murderer.

mur·der·ous /-əs/ *adj* planning, suggesting, designed for, murder: *a* ∼*ous-looking villain.*

mur·der·ous·ly *adv*

murk /mɜk/ *n* [U] darkness; gloom.

murky *adj* (-ier, -iest) dark; gloomy: *a* ∼*y night;* ∼*y coffee.*

murk·ily /-əlɪ/ *adv*

mur·mur /ˈmɜːmə(r)/ *n* [C] **1** low, continuous, indistinct sound: *the* ∼ *of bees in the garden; the* ∼ *of distant traffic/conversation from the next room.* **2** subdued expression of feeling: *They paid the higher taxes without a* ∼, i e without complaining. □ *vi,vt* **1** make a murmur(1): *a* ∼*ing brook.* **2** complain in a murmur(2): ∼ *against new taxes.* **3** say in a low voice: ∼ *a prayer.*

muscle /ˈmʌsəl/ *n* **1** [C,U] (band or bundle of) elastic substance in an animal body that can be tightened or loosened to produce movement: *Don't move a* ∼, stay perfectly still. **2** (*fig*) authority, power: *modern weapons added more* ∼ *to the attack.* □ *vi* **muscle** ˈ**in** (**on**), (*sl*) use force to get a share of something advantageous.

ˈ**muscle-bound** *adj* having stiff muscles as the result of excessive exercise.

ˈ**muscle-man** /-mæn/ *n* [C] (*pl* -men) man of great muscular development.

mus·cu·lar /ˈmʌskjʊlə(r)/ *adj* **1** of the muscles: ∼ *rheumatism.* **2** having strong muscles: *a* ∼ *man.*

muse¹ /mjuz/ *n* [C] **1** (in Greek myth) any one of the nine goddesses, daughters of Zeus, who protected and encouraged poetry, music, dancing, history and other branches of art and learning. **2** the ∼, spirit that inspires a poet.

muse² /mjuz/ *vi* **muse over/on/upon,** think deeply or dreamily, ignoring what is happening around one: *musing over memories of the past.*

mu·seum /mjuˈzɪəm/ *n* [C] building in which objects illustrating art, history, science, etc are displayed.

mush /mʌʃ/ *n* [U] soft, thick mixture or mass.

mushy *adj* like mush.

mush·room /ˈmʌʃrʊm US: -rum/ *n* [C] **1** fast-growing fungus of which some kinds can be eaten. **2** sudden, rapid, development: *the* ∼ *growth of London suburbs.* □ *vi* **1** gather mushrooms. **2** spread or grow rapidly: *English language schools are* ∼*ing in Bournemouth.*

mu·sic /ˈmjuzɪk/ *n* [U] art of making pleasing combinations of sounds in rhythm and harmony; the sounds and composition so made; written or printed signs representing these sounds: (as an *adjective*) *a* ∼ *lesson/*

teacher. **face the music,** face one's critics, difficulties, boldly. **set/put sth to music,** provide words, e g of a poem, with music.

ˈ**music-hall,** (*GB*) place for variety entertainment (e g songs, acrobatic performances, comedians).

ˈ**music-stand,** framework for holding sheets of printed music.

ˈ**music-stool,** adjustable seat without a back used when playing a piano.

mu·si·cal /ˈmjuzɪkəl/ *adj* of, fond of, skilled in, music: *She's not at all* ∼, does not enjoy or understand music. □ *n* [C] **1** musical comedy. **2** cinema film in which music and singing have an essential part.

ˈ**musical** ˈ**comedy,** light, amusing play with songs and dancing.

ˈ**musical** ˈ**instrument,** used to play music e g the piano, violin, flute.

mu·si·cally /-klɪ/ *adv*

mu·si·cian /mjuˈzɪʃn/ *n* [C] person skilled in playing music; composer of music.

musk /mʌsk/ *n* [U] **1** strong-smelling substance produced in glands by male deer, used in the manufacture of perfumes. **2** kinds of plant with a musky smell.

ˈ**musk-rat,** (also *musquash*) large water animal like a rat of N America, valuable for its fur.

ˈ**musk-rose,** rambling rose with large, sweet-smelling flowers.

musky *adj* (-ier, -iest) having the smell of musk.

mus·ket /ˈmʌskɪt/ *n* [C] light gun used by foot-soldiers (16th to 19th centuries) now replaced by the rifle.

mus·ket·eer /ˌmʌskɪˈtɪə(r)/, soldier armed with a musket.

Mus·lim /ˈmʊzlɪm/ *n* believer in Islam; (used as an *adjective*) of Islam: ∼ *holidays.*

mus·lin /ˈmʌzlɪn/ *n* [U] thin, fine, cotton cloth, used for dresses, curtains, etc.

mus·quash /ˈmʌskwɒʃ/ *n* [C,U] (fur of the) musk-rat.

mus·sel /ˈmʌsəl/ *n* [C] (sorts of) mollusc with a black shell in two parts.

must¹ /mʌst/ *n* [U] grape-juice before fermentation has changed it into wine.

must² /məst *strong form:* mʌst/ *auxiliary verb* (No infinitive, no participles, no inflected forms; *must not* may be contracted to **mustn't** /ˈmʌsnt/.) **1** (expressing an immediate or future obligation or necessity; *must not* expresses a prohibition): *You* ∼ *do as you're told. Cars* ∼ *not be parked in front of the entrance. We* ∼*n't be late.* (*Note:* compare the use of *may* to express permission and of *need not* to express non-obligation. Compare the use of *had to* for a past obligation and *shall/will have to* for a future obligation.) **2** (used to show what was necessary or obligatory at a time in the past): *As he had broken it, he agreed that he* ∼ *buy a new one.* **3** (with less emphasis on necessity; stressing what is desirable or

advisable): *I ~ ask you not to do that again.*
4 (expressing certainty): *If you try hard, you
~ win* (= will certainly win) *eventually.* **5**
(expressing strong probability): *You ~ be
hungry after your long walk. You ~ be joking!* You can't be serious! **6** (indicating
something unwelcome): *M~ you worry her
with questions, just when she is busy cooking
the dinner!* □ *n* [C] (*informal*) something
that must be done, seen, heard, etc: *Stop-
pard's new play is a ~.*

mus·tache *n* ⇨ moustache.

mus·tard /ˈmʌstəd/ *n* [U] **1** plant with yellow flowers and seeds (black or white) in
long, slender pods. **2** fine, yellow powder
made from the seeds of this plant; this
powder made into hot sauce. *as keen as
mustard,* very keen.

mus·ter /ˈmʌstə(r)/ *n* [C] assembly or gathering of persons, esp for review or inspection. *pass muster,* be considered satisfactory. □ *vt, vi* call, collect or gather together:
*Go and ~ all the men you can find. They
~ed (up) all their courage.*

musty /ˈmʌstɪ/ *adj* (-ier, -iest) **1** stale;
smelling or tasting mouldy: *a ~ room/book.*
2 (*fig*) out-of-date: *a professor with ~
ideas.*

musti·ness /ˈmʌstɪnəs/ *n* [U]

mu·table /ˈmjuːtəbəl/ *adj* (*formal*) liable to
change; likely to change.

mu·ta·bil·ity /ˈmjuːtəˈbɪlətɪ/ *n* [U]

mu·ta·tion /mjuːˈteɪʃən/ *n* [U] change; alteration; [C] instance of this: *Are ~s in plants
caused by cosmic rays?*

mute /mjuːt/ *adj* **1** silent; making no sound:
staring at me in ~ amazement. **2** (of a person) dumb. **3** (of a letter in a word) not
sounded: *The 'b' in 'dumb' is ~.* □ *n* [C] **1**
dumb person. **2** piece of bone or metal used
to soften the sounds produced from a
stringed instrument; pad placed in the mouth
of a wind instrument for the same purpose. □
vt muffle the sound of (esp a musical instrument).

mute·ly *adv*

mu·ti·late /ˈmjuːtɪleɪt US: -təl-/ *vt* damage
by breaking, tearing or cutting off a necessary part; destroy the use of (a limb, etc).

mu·ti·la·tion /ˈmjuːtɪˈleɪʃən US: -təlˈeɪʃən/ *n*
[U] mutilating or being mutilated; [C] injury
or loss caused by this.

mu·ti·nous /ˈmjuːtɪnəs US: -tənəs/ *adj*
guilty of mutiny; rebellious: *~ sailors.*

mu·tiny /ˈmjuːtɪnɪ US: -tənɪ/ *n* (*pl* -ies) [U]
(esp of soldiers and sailors) open rebellion
against lawful authority; [C] instance of this.
□ *vi* be guilty of mutiny.

mu·tin·eer /ˈmjuːtɪˈnɪə(r) US: -tənˈɪə(r)/ *n*
person guilty of mutiny.

mut·ter /ˈmʌtə(r)/ *vt, vi* speak in a low voice
not meant to be heard; grumble in a indistinct voice: *He was ~ing away to himself.* □
n [C] muttered utterance or sound.

mutterer, person who mutters.

mut·ton /ˈmʌtən/ *n* [U] flesh of fully grown
sheep: eaten as food.

mu·tual /ˈmjuːtʃʊəl/ *adj* **1** (of love, friendship, respect, etc) shared; (of feelings, opinions, etc) held in common with others: *~
suspicion/affection.* **2** each to the other(s);
reciprocal: *~ aid.* **3** common to two or more
persons: *our ~ friend Smith,* i e a friend of
both of us.

mu·tual·ly /-tʃəlɪ/ *adv*

muzzle /ˈmʌzəl/ *n* [C] **1** nose and mouth of
an animal (e g dog or fox). **2** guard of straps
or wires placed over this to prevent biting,
etc. **3** open end or mouth of a firearm: *a
~-loading gun.* □ *vt* **1** put a muzzle on (a
dog, etc). **2** (*fig*) prevent (a person, society,
newspaper, etc) from expressing opinions
freely.

muzzy /ˈmʌzɪ/ *adj* (-ier, -iest) (of a person,
thoughts) confused; stupid from drinking.

my /maɪ/ *possessive adj* **1** belonging to me:
Where's ~ hat? **2** (as a part of a form of
address): *Yes, ~ dear. M~ dear Anne,...!*
3 (used in exclamations): *M~ goodness!*

my·col·ogy /maɪˈkɒlədʒɪ/ *n* [U] science or
study of fungi.

my·nah (also **my·na**) /ˈmaɪnə/ *n* [C] (kinds
of) starling of S E Asia, known for their ability to mimic human speech.

my·opia /maɪˈəʊpɪə/ *n* [U] short-sight.

my·opic /maɪˈɒpɪk/ *adj* short-sighted.

myr·iad /ˈmɪrɪəd/ *n* [C] very great number
(*of*).

myrrh /mɜː(r)/ *n* [U] sweet-smelling, bitter-
tasting kind of gum or resin obtained from
shrubs, used for making incense and perfumes.

myrtle /ˈmɜːtəl/ *n* [C] (kinds of) evergreen
shrub with shiny leaves and sweet-smelling
white flowers.

my·self /maɪˈself/ *pron* **1** (reflexive): *I hurt
~.* *(all) by myself,* (a) alone. (b) without
help. **2** (used for emphasis); *I said so ~.* **3**
I'm not ~ today, am not in my normal state
of health or mind.

mys·teri·ous /mɪˈstɪərɪəs/ *adj* full of, suggesting, mystery: *a ~ visitor; a ~-looking
parcel.*

mys·teri·ous·ly *adv*

mys·tery /ˈmɪstərɪ/ *n* (*pl* -ies) **1** [C] something of which the cause or origin is hidden
or impossible to understand: *The murder
remained an unsolved ~.* **2** [U] condition of
being secret or obscure: *The origin of this
tribe is lost in ~,* It has been impossible to
learn anything about it. **3** (*pl*) secret religious rites and ceremonies.

`mystery (play),` medieval drama based on
episodes in the life of Jesus.

mys·tic /ˈmɪstɪk/ *adj* of hidden meaning or
spiritual power; causing feelings of awe and
wonder: *~ rites and ceremonies.* □ *n* [C]
person who seeks union with God and,
through that, realization of truth beyond
men's understanding.

mys·ti·cal /ˈmɪstɪkəl/ *adj* = mystic.

mys·ti·cism /ˈmɪstɪsɪzm/ *n* [U] beliefs, experiences, of a mystic; teaching and belief that knowledge of God and of real truth may be obtained through meditation.

mys·tify /ˈmɪstɪfaɪ/ *vt* (*pt,pp* -ied) puzzle; bewilder.

mys·ti·fi·ca·tion /ˌmɪstɪfɪˈkeɪʃən/ *n* [U] mystifying or being mystified; [C] something that mystifies.

mys·tique /mɪˈstik/ *n* [C] **1** puzzling atmosphere, impressive character of a person, institution, etc caused by devotion and veneration: *the ～ of the monarchy in Great Britain.* **2** secret skill, etc known only to the practitioner (of an art, etc).

myth /mɪθ/ *n* **1** [C] story, handed down from olden times, e g ideas or beliefs about the early history of a race, explanations of natural events, etc. **2** [U] such stories collectively: *famous in ～ and legend.* **3** [C] persons, thing, etc that is imaginary or invented: *That rich uncle of whom he boasts is only a ～.*

mythi·cal /ˈmɪθɪkəl/ *adj* (a) of, existing only in, myth: *～ical heroes.* (b) imaginary: *～ical wealth.*

myth·ol·ogy /mɪˈθɒlədʒɪ/ *n* (*pl* -ies) **1** [U] study or science of myths. **2** [U] myths collectively: *Greek ～;* [C] body or collection of myths: *the mythologies of primitive races.*

mytho·logi·cal /ˌmɪθəˈlɒdʒɪkəl/ *adj* of mythology.

myxo·ma·to·sis /ˌmɪksəməˈtəʊsɪs/ *n* [U] infectious fatal disease of rabbits.

Nn

N, n /en/ (*pl* N's, n's /enz/) **1** the 14th letter of the English alphabet. **2** (*maths*) indefinite number.

nab /næb/ *vt* (-bb-) (*informal*) catch (e g a thief, etc): *be ～bed by the police.*

na·celle /næˈsel/ *n* [C] outer casing for an engine of an aircraft or airship.

na·dir /ˈneɪdɪə(r) *US:* ˈneɪd-/ *n* [C] (*fig*) lowest, weakest, point: *at the ～ of one's hopes.* ⇨ zenith.

nag¹ /næg/ *n* [C] (*informal*) small horse.

nag² /næg/ *vt,vi* (-gg-) find fault with continuously: *She ～ged (at) him all day long.*

nag·ger, person who nags.

nail /neɪl/ *n* [C] **1** layer of hard substance over the outer tip of a finger (ˈfinger-nail) or toe (ˈtoe-nail). *fight tooth and nail*, making every possible effort to win. **2** piece of metal, pointed at one end and with a head at the other, (to be) hammered into articles to hold them together, or into a wall, etc. *as hard as nails*, (of a person) (a) in a first-rate

physical condition (b) pitiless; unsympathetic. *hit the nail on the head*, pick out the real point at issue. □ *vt* **1** make fast with a nail: *～ a lid on a box; ～ down a carpet.* *nail sb down (to sth),* make him say clearly what he intends to do. **2** keep fixed (a person, his attention, etc): *He ～ed me in the corridor.*

`nail-brush, for cleaning the nails.

`nail-file, small, flat file for shaping the nails.

`nail-scissors, for trimming the nails.

`nail-varnish/-polish, for giving a shiny tint, colour, to the nails.

naive, (also **naïve**) /naɪˈiv/ *adj* natural and innocent in speech and behaviour (e g because young or inexperienced): *a ～ girl; ～ remarks.*

naive·ly *adv*

naiveté, naivety /naɪˈivteɪ/ *n* [U] being naive; [C] naive remark, etc.

naked /ˈneɪkɪd/ *adj* **1** without clothes on: *as ～ as the day he was born.* **2** without the usual covering: *a ～ sword*, without its sheath; *a ～ light*, without a lampshade, etc. *see sth with the naked eye,* without using a microscope, telescope or other aid. *the naked truth,* not disguised.

naked·ly *adv*

naked·ness *n* [U]

name¹ /neɪm/ *n* **1** [C] word(s) by which a person, animal, place, thing, etc is known and spoken to or of: *The teacher knows all the pupils in his class by ～.* *in the name of,* (a) with the authority of: *Stop! in the ～ of the law!* (b) in the cause of (used when making an appeal): *In the ～ of common sense, what are you doing?* *call sb names,* call him insulting names (e g liar, coward). *not have a penny to one's name,* be without money. *take sb's 'name in 'vain,* use a name disrespectfully. **2** (*sing* only) reputation; fame: *have a ～ for being honest.* *make/win a name for oneself,* become well-known. **3** [C] famous person: *the great ～s of history.*

`name-day, day of the Saint whose name one was given at christening; Saint's Day (in the R C Church).

`name-dropping, the practice of casually mentioning the names of important people (as if they were friends) to impress people. Hence, `name-drop *vi*

`name-sake, person or thing with the same name as another.

name² /neɪm/ *vt* **1** give a name to: *They ～d the child John.* ⇨ Christian/first name. **2** say the names(s) of: *Can you ～ all the plants and trees in this garden?* **3** make an offer of (price, etc): *N～ your price,* Say what price you want. **4** state (what is desired, etc): *Please ～ the day,* say on what date you will be willing to (e g marry). **5** nominate for, appoint to, a position: *Mr X has been ～d for the directorship.*

name·less /ˈneɪmləs/ adj 1 not having a name; having an unknown name: a ∼ grave; a well-known person who shall be ∼, whose name I shall not mention. 2 too bad to be named: ∼ vices.

name·ly /ˈneɪmlɪ/ adv that is to say: Only one boy was absent, ∼ Harry.

nanny /ˈnænɪ/ n [C] (pl -ies) woman employed by rich people to look after their babies and young children below school age.

nanny-goat /ˈnænɪ gəʊt/ n [C] female goat, ⇨ billy-goat.

nap¹ /næp/ n [C] short sleep (esp during the day, not necessarily in bed): have/take a ∼ after lunch. □ vi (-pp-) (rare, except in) **catch sb napping**, (a) find him asleep. (b) catch him unawares.

nap² /næp/ n [U] surface of cloth, felt, etc made of soft, short hairs or fibres.

na·palm /ˈneɪpɑːm/ n [U] jellied petroleum used in making fire-bombs.

nape /neɪp/ n [C] back of the neck.

nap·kin /ˈnæpkɪn/ n [C] 1 (ˈtable) ∼, piece of cloth used at meals for protecting clothing, for wiping the lips, etc. 2 = nappy (the usual word).
ˈnapkin-ring, ring for a person's napkin(1).

nappy /ˈnæpɪ/ n [C] (pl -ies) towel folded round a baby's bottom and between its legs, to absorb excreta.

nar·cissus /nɑːˈsɪsəs/ n [C] (pl ∼es or -cissi /-ˈsɪsaɪ/) sorts of bulb plant (daffodil, etc), esp the kind having heavily scented white or yellow flowers in the spring.

nar·cotic /nɑːˈkɒtɪk/ n [C], adj 1 (kinds of drug) producing sleep, often dulling the senses and, in large doses, producing complete insensibility: Opium is a ∼ (drug). 2 (person) addicted to narcotics.

nar·rate /nəˈreɪt/ vt tell (a story); give an account of: ∼ one's adventures.
nar·rator /-tə(r)/ person who narrates.
nar·ra·tion /nəˈreɪʃən/ n [U] the telling of a story, etc; [C] story; account of events, etc.

nar·ra·tive /ˈnærətɪv/ n 1 [C] story or tale; orderly account of events; [U] (composition that consists of) story-telling. 2 (used as an adjective) in the form of, concerned with, story-telling: ∼ literature, stories and novels; ∼ poems.

nar·row /ˈnærəʊ/ adj (-er, -est) (contrary to wide) 1 measuring little across in comparison with length: a ∼ bridge. 2 small, limited: a ∼ circle of friends. 3 with a small margin: a ∼ escape from death; elected by a ∼ majority. 4 strict; exact: What does the word mean in the ∼est sense? 5 limited in outlook; having little sympathy for the ideas, etc, of others. □ n (usu pl) narrow strait or channel between two larger bodies of water; narrow place in a river or pass. □ vt,vi (cause to) become narrow.
ˈnarrow-ˈminded /-ˈmaɪndɪd/ adj not sympathizing with the ideas of others.
ˈnarrow-ˈmindedly adv

ˈnarrow-ˈmindedness n [U]
nar·row·ly adv only just; with little to spare: He ∼ly escaped drowning.
nar·row·ness n [U]

na·sal /ˈneɪzəl/ adj of, for, in the nose: ∼ sounds, e g /m, n, ŋ/. □ n [C] nasal sound.
na·sal·ize /ˈneɪzəlaɪz/ vt make (a sound) with the air stream, or part of it, passing through the nose.

nas·tur·tium /nəˈstɜːʃəm US: næ-/ n [C] (pl ∼s) garden plant with red, orange or yellow flowers, round leaves, and seeds that may be pickled and eaten.

nasty /ˈnɑːstɪ US: ˈnæ-/ adj (-ier, -iest) 1 dirty; disgusting; unpleasant; medicine with a ∼ smell and a nastier taste. 2 immoral: a man with a ∼ mind. 3 unpleasant: a ∼ temper/look in his eye. a nasty piece of work, (informal) unpleasant person. 4 causing difficulty or danger; awkward: That's a ∼ question, an awkward one.
nas·tily /-əlɪ/ adv
nas·ti·ness n [U]

na·tal /ˈneɪtəl/ adj of, from, one's birth.

na·tion /ˈneɪʃən/ n [C] large community of people associated with a particular territory usually speaking a single language and having a society under one government: the United N∼s Organization.
ˈnation-wide adj (a) throughout a nation. (b) concerning, expressed by, all citizens.

nation·al /ˈnæʃnəl/ adj of the (whole) nation; of a particular nation: a ∼ theatre, one supported by the State; ∼ pride, expressed by all citizens. □ n [C] citizen of a particular nation: British ∼s in Spain.
ˈnational ˈanthem, song or hymn of a nation (e g 'God Save the Queen' in GB).
ˈnational ˈpark, public area of land for the use and enjoyment of the people.
ˈnational ˈservice, period of compulsory service in the armed forces.
National ˈTrust, (in GB) society founded in 1895 to preserve places of natural beauty or historic interest for the nation.
na·tion·ally /ˈnæʃnəlɪ/ adv

nation·al·ism /ˈnæʃnəlɪzm/ n [U] 1 patriotic feelings, efforts, principles. 2 movement for political (economic, etc) independence (in a country controlled by another).

nation·al·ist /ˈnæʃnəlɪst/ n [C] supporter of nationalism(2): Scottish ∼s. □ adj (also **nation·al·ist·ic** /ˈnæʃnəlˈɪstɪk/) favouring, supporting, nationalism.

nation·al·ity /ˈnæʃənˈælətɪ/ n [C,U] (pl -ies) being a member of a nation: What is your ∼?

nation·al·ize /ˈnæʃnəlaɪz/ vt 1 transfer from private to State ownership: ∼ the railways. 2 make (a person) a national: ∼d Poles and Greeks in the US. 3 make into a nation: The Poles were ∼d after the war of 1914—18, They became an independent nation.
nation·al·iz·ation /ˈnæʃnəlaɪˈzeɪʃən US:

-lɪˋz/ *n* [U]

na·tive /ˋneɪtɪv/ *n* [C] **1** person born in a place, country, etc and associated with it by right of birth: *a ~ of London/Wales/India/ Kenya.* **2** animal or plant natural to and having its origin in a certain area: *The kangaroo is a ~ of Australia.* □ *adj* **1** associated with the place and circumstances of one's birth: *my ~ land.* **2** of the natives of a place, esp non-European: *~ customs.* **3** (of qualities) belonging to a person by nature, not acquired through training, by education, etc: *~ ability/charm.* **4** **native to,** (of plants, animals, etc) having their origin in: *One of the animals ~ to India is the tiger.* **5** (of metals) found in a pure state, uncombined with other substances: *~ gold.*

na·tiv·ity /nəˋtɪvətɪ/ *n* [C] (*pl* -ies) birth, esp (**the N~**) of Jesus Christ.

ˋ**Nativity Play,** one about the Nativity.

nat·ter /ˋnætə(r)/ *vi* (*informal*) chatter, grumble (esp to oneself): *What's she ~ing (on) about now?*

natu·ral /ˋnætʃərəl/ *adj* **1** of, concerned with, produced, by nature: *animals living in their ~ (=wild) state; a country's ~ resources,* its minerals, forests, etc. **2** of, in agreement with, the nature(4) of a living thing: *~ gifts/abilities.* **3** (of persons) born with qualities or powers: *He's a ~ orator,* makes speeches easily. *It comes ~ to her.* **4** ordinary; normal; to be expected: *It is ~ for a bird to fly.* **5** not cultivated, exaggerated or self-conscious: *speak in a ~ voice.* **6** (*music*) of the normal scale of C; neither sharp nor flat. **7** (of offspring) illegitimate: *a ~ child/son/daughter.* □ *n* [C] **1** (*music*) natural(6) note. **2** **a natural (for sth),** (*informal*) person naturally expert or qualified: *He's a ~ for the job/the part.*

ˋ**natural ˋchildbirth,** without anaesthesia.

ˋ**natural ˋdeath,** from age or disease, not as the result of an accident, murder, etc.

ˋ**natural ˋforces/pheˋnomena,** the forces of nature, such as storms, thunder and lightning.

ˋ**natural ˋgas,** gas occurring with petroleum deposits, e g North Sea gas.

ˋ**natural ˋhistory,** botany and zoology.

ˋ**natural ˋlife,** duration one's life on earth.

ˋ**natural ˋscience,** botany, zoology, etc.

ˋ**natural seˋlection,** evolutionary theory that animals and plants survive or become extinct in accordance with their ability to adapt themselves to their environment.

natu·ral·ism /ˋnætʃərəlɪzm/ *n* [U] **1** accurate representation of nature in literature and art; drawing and painting of things in a way true to nature. **2** system of thought which rejects the supernatural and divine revelation and holds that natural causes and laws explain all phenomena.

natu·ral·ist /ˋnætʃərəlɪst/ *n* [C] **1** person who makes a special study of animals or plants. **2** believe in naturalism.

natu·ral·is·tic /ˌnætʃərəlˋɪstɪk/ *adj* of naturalism: *a ~ painter.* ➪ abstract (1), cubism, surrealism.

natu·ral·ize /ˋnætʃərəlaɪz/ *vt,vi* **1** give (a person from another country) rights of citizenship: *~ immigrants into the US.* **2** take (a word) from one language into another: *English sporting terms have been ~d in many languages.* **3** introduce and acclimatize (an animal or plant) into another (part of a) country.

natu·ral·iz·ation /ˌnætʃərəlaɪˋzeɪʃən US: -lɪˋz-/ *n* [U]

nat·ur·ally /ˋnætʃərəlɪ/ *adv* **1** by nature(4): *She's ~ musical.* **2** of course; as might be expected: *'Did you answer her letter?'—'N~!'* **3** without artificial help, special cultivation, etc: *Her hair curls ~.* **4** without exaggeration, pretence, etc: *She speaks and behaves ~.*

na·ture /ˋneɪtʃə(r)/ *n* **1** [U] the whole universe and every created thing: *Is ~ at its best in spring?* **2** [U] force(s) controlling the phenomena of the physical world: *Miracles are contrary to ~.* **in the course of nature,** according to the ordinary course of things. **3** [U] simple life without civilization: *a return to ~,* to the simple and primitive life before mankind became civilized. **4** [C,U] qualities and characteristics, physical, mental and spiritual, which naturally belong to a person or thing: *It is the ~ of a dog to bark.* ➪ human nature; good/ill-natured. **5** essential qualities of things: *Chemists study the ~ of gases. The ~ of his beliefs.* **6** sort; kind: *Things of this ~ do not interest me.*

ˋ**nature cure,** treatment of disease relying on natural remedies (sunlight, diet, exercise).

ˋ**nature study,** (at school) the study of animals, plants, etc.

na·tur·ism /ˋneɪtʃərɪzm/ *n* [U] = nudism.

na·tur·ist /-ɪst/ *n* [C] = nudist.

naught /nɔt/ *n* nothing, esp in the phrases: *care naught for,* have no interest in; consider worthless. *come to naught,* fail.

naughty /ˋnɔtɪ/ *adj* (-ier, -iest) **1** (of children, their behaviour, etc) bad; wrong; disobedient; causing trouble. **2** taking pleasure in shocking, intended to shock, people: *~ stories.*

naught·ily /-əlɪ/ *adv*

naughti·ness *n* [U]

nausea /ˋnɔsɪə US: ˋnɔʃə/ *n* [U] feeling of sickness or disgust: *be overcome by/filled with ~ after eating octopus/at the sight of cruelty to animals.*

naus·eate /ˋnɔsɪeɪt US: ˋnɔʒ-/ *vt* cause nausea: *a nauseating sight.*

naus·eous /ˋnɔsɪəs US: ˋnɔʃəs/ *adj*

nauti·cal /ˋnɔtɪkəl/ *adj* of ships, sailors or navigation: *~ terms,* used by sailors.

nautical mile, sixtieth of a degree (1), 2 025 yds (= 1 852 metres).

na·val /ˋneɪvəl/ *adj* of a navy; of warships:

~ officers/battles.

nave /neɪv/ n [C] central part of a church where the people sit.

na·vel /ˈneɪvəl/ n [C] depression in the surface of the belly (left by the detachment of the umbilical cord).

navi·ga·ble /ˈnævɪgəbəl/ adj **1** (of rivers, seas, etc) suitable for ships: The Rhine is ~ from Strasbourg to the sea. **2** (of ships, etc) that can be steered and sailed: not in a ~ condition.

navi·ga·bil·ity /ˈnævɪgəˈbɪlətɪ/ n [U]

navi·gate /ˈnævɪgeɪt/ vt,vi **1** plot the course, find the position, etc of a ship or aircraft, using charts and instruments. **2** steer (a ship); pilot (an aircraft). **3** sail over (a sea); sail up or down (a river). **4** (fig) direct: ~ a Bill through the House of Commons.

navi·ga·tor /-tə(r)/, (a) person who navigates(1). (b) sailor with skill and experience who has taken part in many voyages.

navi·ga·tion /ˈnævɪˈgeɪʃən/ n [U] **1** the act, science of navigating. **2** the making of voyages on water or of journeys through the air.

navy /ˈneɪvɪ/ n [C] (pl -ies) **1** a country's warships. **2** the officers and men of a country's warships: join the ~. ~ ice-cream.

'navy 'blue, dark blue.

neap /niːp/ n [C] (also ~-tide) tide when high water is at its lowest level of the year.

Ne·an·der·thal /nɪˈændətɑːl/ adj (also ~ man), extinct type of man of the stone age.

Nea·poli·tan /nɪəˈpɒlɪtən/ n, adj **1** (inhabitant) of Naples. **2** (small n) with many flavours and colours: ~ ice-cream.

near[1] /nɪə(r)/ adj (-er, -est) **1** not far from; close in space or time: The post office is quite ~. **near to,** close to; almost: She was ~ to tears. **a near miss,** eg of a bomb or shell, not a direct hit, but close enough to the target to cause damage. **a near thing,** a narrow escape. **2** close in relation or affection: a ~ relation, eg a mother, a son; friends who are ~ and dear to us. **3** (contrasted with off) (of parts of animals and vehicles, etc) the left side: the ~ foreleg; the ~ front wheel of a car. □ vt,vi come or draw near (to); approach: The ship was ~ing land. He's ~ing his end, is dying.

nearness n [U]

near[2] /nɪə(r)/ adv not far; to or at a short distance in space or time: We searched far and ~ (= everywhere) for the missing child. **as near as,** as closely as: As ~ as I can guess there were forty people present. **as near as makes no difference,** with no difference worth considering: They're the same height, or as ~ as makes no difference. **near at hand,** (a) within easy reach: Always have your dictionary/books ~ at hand. (b) not far distant in the future: The examinations are ~ at hand. **nowhere near,** far from: She's nowhere ~ as old as her husband. **near by,** not far off.

'Near 'East, Turkey, etc.

'near·side, side nearest the kerb: the ~ side lane of traffic.

'near·sighted adj = short-sighted.

near[3] /nɪə(r)/ prep (= near to) close to (in space, time, relationship, etc): Come and sit ~ me.

near·by /nɪəˈbaɪ/ adj not far away: a ~ restaurant.

near·ly /ˈnɪəlɪ/ adv **1** almost: It's ~ one o'clock. I'm ~ ready. ⇨ hardly, scarcely. **2** closely: We're ~ related, are near relations. **3** not nearly, nowhere near: I have £20, but that isn't ~ enough for my fare.

neat /niːt/ adj (-er, -est except **5** below) **1** (liking to have everything) tidy; done carefully: a ~ worker; ~ writing. **2** simple and pleasant: a ~ dress. **3** pleasing in appearance: a woman with a ~ figure. **4** cleverly said or done: a ~ reply/conjuring trick. **5** (of wines and spirits) undiluted: drink one's whisky ~.

neat·ly adv

neat·ness n [U]

'neath /niːθ/ prep (poetic) beneath.

neb·ula /ˈnebjʊlə/ n [C] (pl ~e /-li/) group of very distant stars, mass of gas, seen in the night sky as a patch of light.

nebu·lar /-lə(r)/ adj of nebulae.

nebu·lous /ˈnebjʊləs/ adj **1** = nebular. **2** like clouds; hazy. **3** (fig) without form; vague: a ~ argument.

necess·ari·ly /ˈnesəˈserəlɪ/ adv as a necessary result: Big men are not ~ strong men.

necess·ary /ˈnesəsrɪ US: -serɪ/ adj which has to be done; which must be; which cannot be avoided: Sleep is ~ to health. Is that really ~? Is it ~ for you to play your records so loudly?

necessi·tate /nɪˈsesɪteɪt/ vt (formal) make necessary: The increase in population ~s a greater food supply.

necess·ity /nɪˈsesətɪ/ n (pl -ies) **1** [U] urgent need; circumstances that make a person do something: He was driven by ~ to steal food for his starving children. **of necessity,** unavoidably. **2** (obligation regarded as a) natural law that directs human life, the universe, etc. **3** [C] something that is indispensable: The necessities of life, food, clothing and shelter. **4** [C] something which must be or happen: Is it a logical ~ that prices go up if wages go up?

neck /nek/ n [C] **1** part of the body that connects the head and the shoulders: wrap a scarf round one's ~. **neck and neck,** side by side, level, in a race or struggle. **a pain in the neck,** (informal) annoying person. **break one's neck,** (a) be killed as the result of breaking the bones in the neck. (b) work extremely hard (to achieve something). ⇨ breakneck. **risk one's neck,** (informal) do something dangerous. **stick one's neck out,** (informal) do or say something at the risk of severe criticism, pain, etc. **talk**

through (the back of) one's neck, talk, argue, foolishly. **2** flesh of an animal's neck as used for food; ∼ *of lamb.* **3** something like a neck in shape or position: *the ∼ of a bottle; a narrow ∼ of land; the ∼ of a guitar.*

`neck·lace /-ləs/ string of beads, pearls, etc worn round the neck as an ornament.

`neck·let /-lət/ ornament (e g of beads) for the neck.

`neck·line, (of fashions for women's clothes) line of a garment at or near the neck.

`neck·tie, (*tie* is the usual word) band of material worn round the neck and knotted in front.

neck² /nek/ *vi* (*sl*) (of young couples of opposite sex) exchange kisses, caresses and hugs: ∼*ing in the dark.*

nec·tar /ˈnektə(r)/ *n* [U] **1** (in Greek myth) the drink of the gods. ⇨ **ambrosia. 2** sweet liquid in flowers, collected by bees; any delicious drink.

nec·tar·ine /ˈnektərɪn/ *n* [C] kind of peach with thin, smooth skin and firm flesh.

née /neɪ/ *adj* (*Fr*) born (put after the name of a married woman and before her father's family name): *Mrs J Smith, ∼ Brown.*

need¹ /niːd/ *n* **1** [U] circumstances in which something is lacking or necessary, or requiring some course of action: *There's no ∼ (for you) to start yet. There's a great ∼ for a book on this subject. If need be,* if necessary. **2** (*pl*) something felt to be necessary: *My ∼s are few.* **3** [U] poverty; misfortune; adversity: *He helped me in my hour of ∼.*

needy *adj* (-ier, -iest) very poor: *help the poor and ∼y.*

need² /niːd/ *auxiliary verb* (No infinitive, no participles, *3rd person sing* present tense is need, not *needs;* need *not* may be contracted to needn't /ˈniːdənt/) **1** be obliged; be necessary: *N∼ you go yet? No, I ∼n't.* **2** indicating that although something may have occurred or been done in the past, it was or may have been unnecessary): *N∼ it have happened? We ∼n't have hurried,* We hurried but now we see that this was unnecessary.

need·ful /-fəl/ *adj* necessary: *do what is ∼ful.*

need·fully /-fəlɪ/ *adv*

need·less *adj* unnecessary: *∼less work/ trouble. Needless to say...,* It is unnecessary to say....

need·less·ly *adv*

need³ /niːd/ *vt* **1** want; require: *Does he ∼ any help? I'm here if you ∼ me.* **2** be under a necessity or obligation: *I agree that they ∼ to be told about the arrangement.* **3** deserve; ought to have: *What he ∼s is a slap!*

needle /ˈniːdl/ *n* [C] **1** small, thin piece of polished steel, pointed at one end and with a small hole at the other end for thread, used in sewing and darning. *look for a needle in a haystack,* search hopelessly. *as sharp as a*

needle, very observant. ⇨ **pins and needles. 2** long, thin piece of polished wood, bone or metal (without an eye), with a pointed end (for knitting) or a hook (for crocheting). **3** thin steel pointer in a compass, showing magnetic north; similar pointer in a telegraphic instrument. **4** something like a needle(1) in shape, appearance or use (e g the thin, pointed leaves of pine-trees; a sharp, pointed peak or rocky summit; the long, sharp, end of a syringe used for giving injections). **5** stylus used in recording and playing records. **6** obelisk: *Cleopatra's ∼,* in London. □ *vt* **1** sew, pierce, operate on, with a needle. **2** (*informal*) annoy, make angry.

`needle·craft/·work, sewing; embroidery.

needs /niːdz/ *adv* (now used only with *must*) needs `must, circumstances may compel us (to do something). *must* `needs, foolishly insists or insisted: *He must ∼ go away just when I want his help.*

ne'er /neə(r)/ *adv* (*poetic*) never.

ne'er-do-well /ˈneə du wel/ *n* [C] useless person.

ne·gate /nɪˈɡeɪt/ *vt* (*formal*) deny; make null and void.

ne·ga·tion /nɪˈɡeɪʃən/ *n* [U] **1** act of denying, refusing: *Shaking the head is a sign of ∼.* ⇨ **affirmation(1). 2** absence of any positive or real quality or meaning.

nega·tive /ˈneɡətɪv/ *adj* **1** (of words and answers) showing *no* or *not:* *give a ∼ answer.* ⇨ **affirmative. 2** expressing the absence of any positive character; that stops, hinders or makes powerless: *∼ criticism,* that does not help by making constructive suggestions. ⇨ **positive(3). 3** (*maths*) (of a number or quantity) less than zero, to be subtracted from others (e g $-x^2$). **4** of that kind of electricity carried by electrons: *the ∼ plate in a battery.* ⇨ **positive(6). 5** (in photography) having lights and shades of the actual scene reversed. □ *n* [C] **1** word or statement that denies: *'No', 'not' and 'neither' are ∼s. The answer is in the ∼,* is 'No'. **2** (*maths*) minus quantity (e g $-5x$). **3** developed film etc on which lights and shades are reversed. □ *vt* **1** prove (a theory, etc) to be untrue: *Experiments ∼d his theory.* **2** reject; refuse to accept; neutralize (an effect).

nega·tive·ly *adv*

ne·glect /nɪˈɡlekt/ *vt* **1** pay no attention to; give no or not enough care to: *∼ing one's studies/children/health.* **2** omit or fail (*to do* something): *He ∼ed to say 'Thank you'.* □ *n* [U] neglecting or being neglected: *∼ of duty. The garden was in a state of ∼.*

ne·glect·ful /-fəl/ *adj* in the habit of neglecting things: *∼ful of her appearance.*

ne·glect·fully /-fəlɪ/ *adv*

ne·glect·ful·ness *n* [U]: *He has a tendency to ∼fulness.*

nég·ligé, neg·li·gee /ˈneɡlɪʒeɪ *US:* ˈneɡlɪ`ʒeɪ/ n [C,U] loose, informal, often transparent, dress.

neg·li·gence /`neglɪdʒəns/ n [U] 1 carelessness; failure to take proper care or precautions: *The accident was due to* ∼. 2 neglected condition or appearance.

neg·li·gent /`neglɪdʒənt/ adj taking too little care; guilty of neglect: *He was* ∼ *in his work/of his duties.*

neg·li·gent·ly adv

neg·li·gible /`neglɪdʒəbəl/ adj of little or no importance or size: *a* ∼ *quantity.*

ne·go·ti·able /nɪ`gəʊʃəbəl/ adj 1 that can be negotiated(2): *Is the dispute* ∼? 2 that can be changed into cash, or passed from person to person instead of cash: ∼ *securities,* e g cheques. 3 (of roads, rivers, etc) that can be passed over or along.

ne·go·ti·ate /nɪ`gəʊʃɪeɪt/ vi,vt 1 discuss, confer, in order to come to an agreement: *We've decided to* ∼ *with the employers about our wage claims.* 2 arrange by discussion: ∼ *a sale/a loan/a treaty/peace.* 3 get or give money for (cheques, bonds, etc). 4 get past or over: *This is a difficult corner for a large car to* ∼.

ne·go·ti·ator /-tə(r)/ person who negotiates.

ne·go·ti·ation /nɪ`gəʊʃɪeɪʃən/ n [C,U] negotiating: *enter into/start/carry on* ∼s *with him. Price is a matter of* ∼.

Ne·gress /`nigrəs/ n [C] Negro woman or girl.

Ne·gro /`nigrəʊ/ n [C] (pl ∼es) member (or, outside Africa, descendant) of one of the black African races south of the Sahara.

Ne·groid /`nigrɔɪd/ adj of Negroes or the Negro race. □ n [C] = Negro (the usual word).

neigh /neɪ/ vi, n [C] (make) cry of a horse.

neigh·bour (US = -bor) /`neɪbə(r)/ n [C] person living in a house, street, etc near another; person, thing or country that is near(est) another: *We're nextdoor* ∼s, *Our houses are side by side. Britain's nearest* ∼ *is France.* □ vt,vi (chiefly in the form ∼ing) be near to: ∼ing *countries; in the* ∼ing *village.*

neigh·bour·ly (US = -bor-) adj kind; friendly.

neigh·bour·li·ness (US = -bor-) n [U] friendly feeling, help.

neigh·bour·hood (US = -bor-) /-hʊd/ n [C] 1 (people living in a) district; area near the place, etc referred to: *There's some beautiful scenery in our* ∼hood. *He lives in the* ∼hood *of London.* 2 condition of being near: *He lost a sum in the* ∼hood *of £500.*

nei·ther /`naɪðə(r) US:* `niθ-/ adj, pron (used with a sing noun or pron) not one nor the other (of two): N∼ *statement is true. In* ∼ *case can I agree.* ⇨ either. □ adv, conj 1 **neither... nor,** not one or the other: *He* ∼ *knows nor cares what happened. N*∼ *you nor I could do it.* 2 (after a negative if-

clause, etc): *If you don't go,* ∼ *shall I. A: 'I don't like it.'*—B: 'N∼ *do I.'*

neo- /`niəʊ/ prefix new; revived, later: *neo-classical.*

neo·col·onial·ism /`niəɪt kə`ləʊnɪəlɪzm/ n [U] control by powerful countries of less developed countries by economic pressure.

neo·lithic /`niə`lɪθɪk/ adj of the new or later stone age: ∼ *man.*

neon /`niɒn/ n [U] colourless gas occuring in small proportions in the earth's atmosphere.

neon light, orange-red light produced when an electric current passes through this gas.

neon sign, advertisement, etc in which neon light is used.

nephew /`nevju US:* `nefju/ n [C] son of one's brother(-in-law) or sister(in-law).

nep·ot·ism /`nepətɪzm/ n [U] the giving of special favour (esp employment) by a person in high position to his relatives.

Nep·tune /`neptjun US:* -tun/ n 1 (Roman god of) the sea. 2 one of the farthest planets of the solar system.

nerve /nɜv/ n 1 [C] fibre or bundle of fibres carrying impulses of feeling and motion between the brain and all parts of the body. 2 (pl) condition of being easily excited, worried, irritated: *He is suffering from* ∼s. *a bundle of nerves,* very nervous person. **get on one's nerves,** worry or annoy: *That noise/man gets on my* ∼s. 3 [U] quality of being bold, courage: *A test pilot needs plenty of* ∼. **have the nerve to do sth,** (a) have the necessary courage etc. (b) (*informal*) be impudent enough: *He had the* ∼ *to suggest that I was cheating.* **have a nerve,** (*informal*) be self-assured or impudent: *He's got a* ∼, *going to work dressed like that!* **lose/regain one's nerve,** lose/recover one's courage, etc. □ vt summon up (one's strength) (physical or moral): ∼ *oneself for a task.*

`nerve-cell,` cell that transmits impulses in nerves(1).

`nerve-centre,` (a) group of nerve-cells. (b) (*fig*) centre of power or control.

`nerve-gas,` poisonous gas that affects the nervous system.

`nerve-racking,` greatly affecting the nerves(2).

nerve·less adj (a) confident, not nervous. (b) lacking in vigour or spirit; without energy: *The knife fell from his* ∼less *hand.*

nerve·less·ly adv

nerv·ous /`nɜvəs/ adj 1 of the nerves(1): *the* ∼ *system.* 2 easily excited, afraid, timid: *Are you* ∼ *in the dark?*

`nervous `breakdown, exhaustion, ill-health, severe loss of self-control and confidence.

`nervous `energy, (*informal*) energy produced in an excitable sometimes uncontrolled, state.

`nervous system, nerves(1) and nerve-centres as a whole.

ner·vous·ly *adv*

ner·vous·ness *n* [U]

nervy /ˈnɜːvɪ/ *adj* (*informal*) suffering from nervous (2) strain.

ness /nes/ *n* [C] (usually in place names) headland.

-ness /-nəs/ *suffix* (*adjective* + ~ = *noun*) a quality, state, character: *dryness; silliness*.

nest /nest/ *n* [C] **1** place made or chosen by a bird for its eggs. **2** place in which certain living things have and keep their young: *a ˈwasps' ~*. **3** comfortable place: *make oneself a ~ of cushions*. **4** number of like things (esp boxes, tables) fitting one inside another. **5** (*fig*) shelter; hiding-place; secluded retreat: *a ~ of crime/vice/pirates*. □ *vi* make and use a nest: *The swallows are ~ing in the woodshed*.

ˈnest-egg, (*fig*) sum of money saved for future use.

nestle /ˈnesəl/ *vt,vi* **1** settle comfortably and warmly: *~ (down) among the cushions*. **2** press oneself lovingly to: *The child was nestling closely against/~d up to her mother*.

nest·ling /ˈnestlɪŋ/ *n* [C] bird too young to leave the nest.

net¹ /net/ *n* [U] open material of knotted string, hair, wire, etc; [C] such material made up for a special purpose: *a ˈhair~; mosˈquito~, for use over a bed; ˈfishing ~s; ˈtennis ~s*. □ *vt* (-tt-) **1** catch (fish, animals, etc) with or in a net. **2** cover with a net or nets: *~ strawberries* **3** put nets in place in: *~ a river*.

ˈnet-ball, game for women in which a ball has to be thrown so that it falls through a net fastened to a ring on the top of a post.

ˈnet·work (a) complex system of lines that cross: *a ~work of railways/canals*. (b) connected system: *An intelligence/spy ~work*.

net², **nett** /net/ *adj* remaining when nothing more is to be taken away: *~ price*, off which discount is not to be allowed; *~ profit*, when working expenses have been deducted. □ *vt* (-tt-) gain as a net profit: *He ~ted £5 from the deal*.

nether /ˈneðə(r)/ *adj* (*archaic*) lower: *the ~ regions/world*, the world of the dead; hell.

nether·most /-məʊst/ *adj* lowest.

nett ⇨ **net²**.

net·ting /ˈnetɪŋ/ *n* [U] **1** making or using nets. **2** net of string, thread or wire.

nettle /ˈnetəl/ *n* [C] common wild plant which has on its leaves hairs that sting and redden the skin when touched. □ *vt* **1** sting (oneself) with nettles. **2** (*fig*) make angry; annoy: *She looked ~d by my remarks*.

net·work ⇨ **net¹**.

ˈnettle-rash, eruption on the skin with red patches (like those) caused by nettles.

neu·ral /ˈnjʊərəl/ *US: ˈnʊə-/ adj* of the nerves(1).

neur·al·gia /njʊˈrældʒə *US:* nʊ-/ *n* [U] sharp, nervous pain, esp of the face and head.

neur·al·gic /-dʒɪk/ *adj*

neu·rologist /njʊəˈrɒlədʒɪst *US:* nʊ-/ *n* [C] expert in neurology.

neur·ol·ogy /njʊəˈrɒlədʒɪ *US:* nʊ-/ *n* [U] branch of medical science that is concerned with nerves.

neur·osis /njʊˈrəʊsɪs *US:* nʊ-/ *n* [C] (*pl -ses* /-siːz/) disturbance in behaviour, bodily activity, etc caused by disorders of the nervous system or by something in the subconscious mind.

neur·otic /njʊˈrɒtɪk *US:* nʊ-/ *adj* **1** (of a person) suffering from a neurosis; abnormally sensitive, excited. **2** (of a drug) affecting the nervous system. □ *n* [C] neurotic person or drug.

neu·ter /ˈnjuːtə(r) *US:* ˈnuː-/ *adj* **1** (*gram*) (of gender) neither feminine nor masculine. **2** (of plants) without male or female parts. **3** (of insects, eg worker ants) sexually undeveloped; sterile. □ *n* [C] **1** neuter noun or gender. **2** sexually undeveloped insect; castrated animal: *My cat is an enormous ginger ~*. □ *vt* castrate: *a ~ed cat*.

neu·tral /ˈnjuːtrəl *US:* ˈnuː-/ *adj* **1** taking neither side in a war or quarrel: *~ nations*. **2** belonging to a country that remains neutral in war: *~ territory/ships*. **3** having no definite characteristics; not clearly one (colour, etc) or another: *~ tints*. **4** (*chemistry*) neither acid nor alkaline. **5** (of gear mechanism) of the position in which no power is transmitted: *leave a car in ~ gear*. □ *n* [C] **1** neutral person, country, etc. **2** neutral position of gears: *slip the gears into ~*.

neu·tral·ity /njuːˈtrælətɪ *US:* nuː-/ *n* [U] state of being neutral, esp in war.

neu·tral·ize /-aɪz/ *vt* **1** make neutral; declare by agreement that (a place) shall be treated as neutral in war. **2** take away the effect or special quality of, by using something with an opposite effect or quality: *~ize a poison*.

neu·tral·iz·ation /ˌnjuːtrəlaɪˈzeɪʃən *US:* -lɪˈz-/ *n* [U]

neu·tron /ˈnjuːtrɒn *US:* ˈnuː-/ *n* [C] particle carrying no electric charge, of about the same mass as a proton, and forming part of the nucleus of an atom.

never /ˈnevə(r)/ *adv* **1** at no time; on no occasion: *He has ~ been abroad. N~ in all my life have I heard such nonsense! Such a display has ~ been seen before*. **2** (used as an emphatic substitute for *not*): *That will ~ do*, isn't good enough at all. *Never mind!* Don't worry!

never·more /ˈnevəˈmɔː(r)/ *adv* never again.

never·the·less /ˌnevəðəˈles/ *adv, conj* however; in spite of that; still: *There was no news; ~, she went on hoping*.

new /njuː *US:* nuː/ *adj* (-er, -est) **1** not existing before; seen, heard of, introduced, for the first time; of recent origin, growth, manufacture, etc: *a ~ invention/film/novel/idea; the newest* (= latest) *fashions*. **as good as new,** in very good condition. **2** already in existence, but only now seen, discovered, etc: *learn ~ words in a foreign language.* **3 new to,** unfamiliar with; not yet accustomed to: *I am ~ to this town.* **new from,** recently arrived from: *a typist ~ from school.* **4** (with *the*) later, modern, having a different character. **5** beginning again: *a ~ life after a divorce.* □ *adv* (preceding, joined or hyphened to. the word it qualifies) recently: *a `~-born baby; `~-laid eggs.*

`**new-comer,** person who has recently arrived in a place.

`**new-fangled,** recently in use or fashion (and, for this reason, disliked by some): *~-fangled ideas.*

new mathematics, recent system of teaching using related sequences or sets.

'**new `Moon,** (period of the) moon seen as a crescent after being invisible.

new pence, (used to distinguish British decimal pence from those used up to 1971).

'**New `Testament,** second part of the Bible, containing the life and teachings of Christ.

`**new town,** one for the population from overcrowded cities.

the 'New `World, N and S America.

new year, coming or recently begun year.

'**New Year's `Day,** 1 January.

'**New Year's `Eve,** 31 December.

new-ness *n* [U]

new-ly /`njulɪ *US:* `nu/ *adv* **1** recently: *a ~ married couple.* **2** in a new, different way: *~ arranged furniture.*

`**newly-weds** *n pl* newly married couple(s).

news /njuz *US:* nuz/ *n pl* (used with a *sing verb*) new or fresh information; report(s) of what has most recently happened: *What's the latest ~? Here are the ~ headlines. Here are some interesting pieces/bits of ~. That's two ~ to me,* I already know that. '**No news is `good news,** Absence of information means we/you, etc can continue to be optimistic.

`**news-agent,** shopkeeper who sells newspapers, periodicals, etc.

`**news-flash,** important piece of news broadcast on radio or television.

`**news-letter,** letter or circular sent out to members of a society, etc.

`**news-paper,** printed publication, usually issued daily, with news, advertisements, etc.

`**news-print,** paper for printing newspapers on.

`**news-stand,** stall for the sale of newspapers, etc.

`**news-worthy** *adj* sufficiently interesting for reporting, e g in a newspaper.

newt /njut *US:* nut/ *n* [C] (kinds of) small animal like a lizard which spends most of its time in the water.

next /nekst/ *adj, n* **1** coming immediately after, in order or space: *Take the ~ turning to the right. Miss Green was the ~* (person) *to arrive.* **the next best (thing),** that which is chosen or accepted if the first choice fails: *There are no tickets for the Circus: the ~ best thing is the Zoo.* **2** close to; at the side of: *the chair ~ to mine; sit ~ to the fire.* **next to nothing,** scarcely anything; almost nothing: *She earns ~ to nothing.* **next door,** the next house: *He lives ~ door* (to me). *We are `~-door neighbours.* **next of kin,** nearest relations. **3** (of time; *the* is needed if the reference is to a time that is future in relation to a time already mentioned): *I shall go there ~ Friday/week/year. We arrived in Turin on a Monday; the ~ day we left for Rome. Is he coming this weekend* (i e the coming weekend) *or ~ weekend* (i e the following weekend)? □ *adv* **1** after this/that; then: *What are you going to do ~? When I ~ saw her she was dressed in green.* **come next,** follow: *What comes ~? What's the next thing (to do, etc)?* **2** (used to express surprise or wonder): *Whatever will he be saying ~?*

nib /nɪb/ *n* [C] split pen-point (to be) inserted in a pen-holder.

nibble /`nɪbəl/ *vt, vi* **1** take tiny bites: *rabbits nibbling carrots.* **2** (*fig*) show some willingness to accept (an offer), agree (to a suggestion, etc), but without being definite. □ *n* [C] act of nibbling: *I felt a ~ at the bait.*

nice /naɪs/ *adj* (-r, -st) **1** (contrary to *nasty*) pleasant; agreeable; kind; friendly; fine: *a ~ day; ~ weather; a ~ little girl; medicine that is not very ~ to take.* **nice and...,** pleasant because...: *~ and warm by the fire.* **2** needing care and exactness; sensitive; subtle: *~ shades of meaning.* **3** (*ironic*) difficult; bad: *You've got us into a ~ mess.* **4** scrupulous: *He's not too ~ in his business methods.*

nice-ly *adv* **(a)** in a nice manner. **(b)** (*informal*) very well: *The patient is doing ~ly,* is making good progress.

nice-ness *n* [U]

nicety /`naɪsətɪ/ *n* (*pl* -ies) **1** [U] accuracy; exactness: *~ of judgement.* **2** [C] delicate distinction: *the niceties of criticism.*

niche /nɪtʃ/ *n* [C] **1** (usually shallow) recess (often with a shelf) in a wall, e g for a statue or ornament. **2** (*fig*) suitable or fitting position: *He found the right ~ for himself in the Civil Service.*

nick[1] /nɪk/ *n* [C] **1** small V-shaped cut. **2 in the nick of time,** only just in time. **3** (*sl*) prison. □ *vt* make a nick(1) in.

nick[2] /nɪk/ *n* (*sl*) (only in) **in good/poor nick,** in good health or condition.

nickel /`nɪkəl/ *n* **1** [U] hard, silver-white metal (symbol **Ni**) used in alloys. **2** [C] coin used in the US, value 5 cents. □ *vt* (-ll-, *US* = -l-) coat with nickel.

nick-nack /`nɪknæk/ *n* [C] = knick-knack.

nick-name /`nɪkneɪm/ *n* [C] name given in

addition, altered from or used instead of the real name (e g *Fatty* for a fat boy). □ *vt* give a nickname to: *They ∼d him Hurry.*

nic·o·tine /ˈnɪkətiːn/ *n* [U] poisonous, oily substance in tobacco leaves.

niece /niːs/ *n* [C] daughter of one's brother(-in-law) or sister(-in-law).

nig·ger /ˈnɪgə(r)/ *n* [C] ⚠ (impolite and offensive word for) Negro.

niggle /ˈnɪgəl/ *vi, vt* **1** give too much time or attention to unimportant details; complain about trivial matters. **2** irritate: *bad manners ∼ me.*
nig·gling *adj.*

nigh /naɪ/ *adv, prep* (-er, -est) (*archaic* and *poetic*) near (to).

night /naɪt/ *n* [C] dark hours between sunset and sunrise or twilight and dawn: *in/during the ∼; on Sunday ∼; on the ∼ of Friday, the 13th of June.* **night after night,** for many nights in succession. **all night (long),** throughout the whole night. **night and day,** continuously: *travel ∼ and day for a week.* **at night, (a)** when night comes. **(b)** during the night: *6 o'clock at ∼,* 6 p m. **by night,** during the night: *travel by ∼.* **have a good/ bad night,** sleep well/badly. **make a night of it,** spend all night in pleasure-making, e g at a party. **spend the night with, (a)** stay as a guest during the night. **(b)** sleep with.

`night-club,` club open until the early hours of the morning to members for dancing, supper, entertainment, etc.

`night-dress,` long, loose garment worn by a woman or child in bed.

`night-fall,` the coming of night; evening.

`night-gown,` = nightdress.

`nightie,` `nighty,` (*informal*) = nightdress.

`night life,` entertainment, e g cabaret, nightclubs, available in a town late at night: *the ∼ life of London.*

`night-long` *adj* lasting the whole night.

`night-mare` /-meə(r)/, **(a)** frightening dream. **(b)** haunting fear; memory of a horrible experience: *Travelling on those bad mountain roads was a ∼mare.*

`night-time,` time of darkness.

`night-ˈwatch,` (person or group keeping) watch by night.

`night-ˈwatchman` /-mən/, man employed to keep watch (e g in a factory) at night.

night·ly *adj, adv* (taking place, happening, existing) in the night or every night

night·in·gale /ˈnaɪtɪŋgeɪl US: -təŋ-/ *n* [C] small, reddish-brown migratory bird that sings sweetly by night as well as by day.

nil /nɪl/ *n* nothing: *The result of the game was 3—0 (read 'three-∼').*

nimble /ˈnɪmbəl/ *adj* (-r, -st) **1** quick-moving; agile: *as ∼ as a goat.* **2** (of the mind) sharp; quick to understand.
nim·bly /ˈnɪmblɪ/ *adv*

nim·bus /ˈnɪmbəs/ *n* [C] (*pl* -∼es or -bi /-baɪ/) **1** bright disc round or over the head

of a saint (in a painting, etc). **2** rain cloud.

nin·com·poop /ˈnɪŋkəmpuːp/ *n* [C] foolish, unintelligent person.

nine /naɪn/ *adj, n* [C] (of) 9: *He's ∼ (years old).*

`nine-pence,` the sum of 9p.

`nine-penny` /-pənɪ US: -penɪ/ *adj* costing 9p.

nine·teen /ˈnaɪnˈtiːn/ *adj, n* [C] (of)19. **(talk) nineteen to the dozen,** (talk) continually.

nine·teenth /ˈnaɪnˈtiːnθ/ *adj, n* [C] (*abbr* *19th*) (of) one of 19 parts or the next after 18.

nine·ti·eth /ˈnaɪntɪəθ/ *adj, n* [C] (*abbr* *90th*) (of) one of 90 parts or the next after 89.

ninety /ˈnaɪntɪ/ *adj, n* [C] (*pl* -ies) (of) 90. **ninety-nine times out of a hundred,** almost always.

the nineties, between 89 and 100, e g of a person's age, or of the years -90 to -99 of a century (esp the 19th century), or the temperature (in the Fahrenheit scale).

ninth /naɪnθ/ *adj, n* [C] (*abbr* *9th*) (of) one of 9 parts or the next after 8.

nine-pins /ˈnaɪnpɪnz/ *n pl* (used with a *sing* verb) **1** game in which a ball is rolled along the floor at nine bottle-shaped pieces of wood. **2** (*sing*) one of these pins.

ninny /ˈnɪnɪ/ *n* [C] (*pl* -ies) fool.

nip¹ /nɪp/ *vt, vi* (-pp-) **1** pinch; press hard (e g between finger and thumb, or with the claws as a crab does, or with the teeth as a dog or horse does): *He ∼ped his finger in the door.* **2** (of frost, wind, etc) stop the growth of; damage. **nip sth in the bud,** stop its (bad) development. **3** perform the action of biting or pinching. **4** (*informal*) hurry: *I'll ∼ on ahead and open the door.* □ *n* [C] **1** sharp pinch or bite. **a cold nip in the air,** sharp feeling of frost. **2** small drink (esp of spirits): *a ∼ of brandy.*

nip·ping *adj* (of the air or wind) sharp; biting cold. ⇨ nippy.

nip·per /ˈnɪpə(r)/ *n* [C] **1** (*pl*) (*informal*) pincers, forceps or other tool for gripping. **2** claw of a crab, etc. **3** (*informal*) small child.

nipple /ˈnɪpəl/ *n* [C] **1** part of the breast through which a baby gets its mother's milk; similar small projection on the breast of a human male. (*Note:* teat is used for other mammals.) **2** something like a nipple: *greasing ∼s in an engine.*

nippy /ˈnɪpɪ/ *adj* (-ier, -iest) (*informal*) biting cold.

nir·vana /nɪəˈvɑːnə/ *n* [U] (in Buddhism) state in which individuality becomes extinct by being absorbed into the supreme spirit.

nisi /ˈnaɪsaɪ/ *conj* (*Latin, legal*) unless.

de·cree ˈnisi, decree (of divorce, etc) valid unless cause is shown for rescinding it before the time when it is made absolute.

nit¹ /nɪt/ *n* [C] egg of a louse or other parasitic insect (e g as found in the human hair).

nit² /nɪt/ *n* [C] = nitwit.

ni·trate /ˈnaɪtreɪt/ n [C,U] salt formed by the chemical reaction of nitric acid with an alkali, esp *potassium* ～ and *sodium* ～, used as fertilizers.

ni·tric /ˈnaɪtrɪk/ adj of, containing, nitrogen. **'nitric `acid,** (symbol HNO₃), clear colourless, powerful acid that eats into and destroys most substances.

ni·tro·gen /ˈnaɪtrədʒən/ n [U] gas (symbol N) without colour, taste or smell, forming about four-fifths of the earth's atmosphere.

ni·tro·glycer·ine, –glycerin /ˌnaɪtrəˈglɪsəriːn US: -ˈglɪsərɪn/ n [U] powerful explosive made by adding glycerine to a mixture of nitric and sulphuric acids.

nit·wit /ˈnɪtwɪt/ n [C] (*informal*) unintelligent person.
nit·wit·ted /ˈnɪtˈwɪtɪd/ adj unintelligent.

nix /nɪks/ n [U] (*sl*) nothing.

no /nəʊ/ adj 1 not one; not any: *She had* ～ *money. N*～ *two men think alike. N*～ *other man could do the work.* **no end of,** (*informal*) a large number or quantity of; very great: *He spends* ～ *end of money on clothes.* 2 (implying the opposite of the following word): *He's* ～ *friend of mine.* 3 (in the pattern: *there + to be + no + ...ing*): *There's* ～ *saying* (= It is impossible to say) *what he'll be doing next.* 4 (in commands, etc): *N*～ *smoking,* Smoking is not allowed. **be no good/use,** useless: *It's* ～ *good worrying about her now.* **by `no means,** ▷ **means¹. in `no time (at all),** very soon, quickly.
'no-`go, (*informal*) impossible to do (successfully).
'no-`go area, (*informal*) (usually urban) area barricaded to prevent the police or security force from entering.
`no-man's-land, (in war) ground between the fronts of two opposing armies.
`no-one, `no one, pron = nobody.

no² /nəʊ/ adv (used with comparatives): *We went* ～ *farther than* (= only as far as) *the bridge. I have* ～ *more money.* **no more... than,** ▷ **more(5). no such,** ▷ such. □ *particle* 1 (opposite of 'Yes'): *Is it Monday today?* ～ *it isn't.* 2 (used with *not* or *nor* to emphasize a negative): *One man couldn't lift it;* ～ *not even half a dozen.* □ n [C] word or answer no; refusal; negative vote. **not take no for an answer,** persist. **The noes** nəʊz/ **have it,** Those voting 'no' are in the majority.

nob /nɒb/ n [C] (*sl*) member of the upper classes; person of high rank.

nobble /ˈnɒbəl/ vt (*sl*) 1 tamper with (a race-horse) to lessen its chance of winning. 2 (*informal*) get the attention of (in order to gain an advantage, etc). 3 (*informal*) get something dishonestly or by devious means.

no·bil·ity /nəʊˈbɪlətɪ/ n [U] 1 quality of being noble; noble character, mind, birth, rank. 2 (usually with *the*) the nobles as a class: *a member of the* ～.

noble /ˈnəʊbəl/ adj (-r, -st) 1 of high rank, title or birth: *a man of* ～ *rank/birth.* 2 having, showing, impressive character and qualities: *a* ～ *leader;* ～ *sentiments.* 3 splendid; that excites admiration: *a building planned on a* ～ *scale.* □ n [C] person of noble birth.
`noble·man, peer; peeress.

nobly /ˈnəʊblɪ/ adv in a noble manner; splendidly.

no·body /ˈnəʊbədɪ/ pron [C] (*pl* -ies) 1 not anybody; no person: *We saw* ～ *we knew. He said he would marry me or* ～. *N*～ *could find their luggage nobody else,* no other person. 2 (used in the *sing* with *a* or *an,* and in the *pl*) unimportant or unimpressive person: *Don't marry a* ～ *like James.*

noc·tur·nal /nɒkˈtɜːnəl/ adj of, in or done, active, or happening in, the night: ～ *birds,* e g owls.

noc·turne /ˈnɒktɜːn/ n [C] 1 (*art*) night-scene. 2 dreamy piece of music.

nod /nɒd/ vi,vt (-dd-) 1 bow (the head) slightly and quickly as a sign of agreement or as a familiar greeting: *He* ～*ded to me as he passed.* **have a nodding acquaintance with,** ▷ acquaintance. 2 let the head fall forward as if sleepy or falling asleep: *She sat* ～*ding by the fire.* **nod off,** fall asleep. 3 indicate by nodding: *He* ～*ded his approval.*

node /nəʊd/ n [C] point on the stem of a plant where a leaf or bud grows out.

nod·ule /ˈnɒdjuːl US: ˈnɒdʒuːl/ n [C] small rounded lump, knob or swelling.
nod·u·lar /-lə(r)/, **nodu·lat·ed** /-leɪtɪd/ adj.

Noel /nəʊˈel/ n = Christmas.

nog·gin /ˈnɒgɪn/ n [C] small measure, usually a quarter of a pint, of liquor.

no·how /ˈnəʊhaʊ/ adv (*informal*) 1 in no way; not at all. 2 out of order; unwell: *feel/ look* ～.

noise /nɔɪz/ n [C,U] loud and unpleasant sound, esp when confused and undesired: *the* ～ *of jet aircraft. Don't make so much* ～*/such a loud* ～*!* **make a noise (about sth),** talk or complain in order to get attention. □ vt make public: *It was* ～*d abroad that he had been arrested.*
noise·less adj making little or no noise: *with* ～*less footsteps.*
noise·less·ly adv
noise·less·ness n [U]

noi·some /ˈnɔɪsəm/ adj (esp of smell) disgusting.

noisy /ˈnɔɪzɪ/ adj (-ier, -iest) 1 making, accompanied by, much noise: ～ *children/ games.* 2 full of noise: *a* ～ *classroom.*
nois·ily /-əlɪ/ adv
noisi·ness n [U]

no·mad /ˈnəʊmæd/ n [C] member of a tribe that wanders from place to place, with no fixed home.
no·madic /nəʊˈmædɪk/ adj of nomads: *a* ～*ic society.*

nom de plume /ˈnɒm də ˈpluːm/ n [C] (*pl*

noms de plume) (*Fr*) pen-name.

no·men·cla·ture /nəʊˈmenklətʃə(r)/ *n* [C] (*formal*) system of naming: *botanical* ~.

nom·inal /ˈnɒmɪnl/ *adj* **1** existing, etc, in name or word only, not in fact: *the* ~ *ruler of the country.* **2** inconsiderable: *a* ~ *rent,* one very much below the actual value of the property. **3** (*gram*) of a noun or nouns. **4** of, bearing, a name: ~ *shares.*
nom·inal·ly /-nəlɪ/ *adv*

nomi·nate /ˈnɒmɪneɪt/ *vt* **1** put forward for election to a position: ~ *a man for the Presidency.* **2** appoint to office: *a committee of five* ~*d members and eight elected members.*

nomi·na·tion /ˌnɒmɪˈneɪʃən/ *n* **1** [U] nominating; [C] instance of this: *How many* ~*s have there been so far?* **2** [U] right of nominating.

nomi·na·tive /ˈnɒmɪnətɪv/ *adj, n* [C] (*gram*) (of the) form of a word when it is the grammatical subject; *the* ~ *case,* eg the pronoun *we.*

nomi·nee /ˌnɒmɪˈniː/ *n* [C] person who is nominated for an office or appointment.

non- /ˈnɒn/ *prefix* who or which is not, does not, etc:

ˈnon-aˈlignment, principle or practice of not joining a large group of world powers.

ˈnon-agˈgression, not attacking; not starting hostilities: *a* ~ *pact.*

ˈnon-ˈcombatant, person (esp in the armed forces, eg a surgeon or chaplain) who does not take part in the fighting.

ˈnon-comˈmissioned *adj* (esp of army officers such as sergeants and corporals) not holding commissions(4).

ˈnon-comˈmittal *adj* not committing oneself to a definite course or to either side (in a dispute, etc): *give a* ~ *answer.*

ˈnon-conˈductor, substance that does not conduct heat or electric current.

ˈnonconˈformist, (a) person, esp a Protestant, who does not conform to the ritual, etc of an established Church. **(b) N**~, (in England) member of a sect that has separated from the Church of England.

ˈnonconˈformity, (beliefs and practices of) nonconformists as a body; failure to conform.

ˈnon-conˈtributory *adj* not involving contributions: *a* ~ *pension scheme.*

ˈnon-eˈvent, planned event which turns out to be unworthy of what it was declared to be.

ˈnon-ˈfiction *n* [U] literature based on fact (not novels, stories, plays which deal with fictitious events and persons).

ˈnon-ˈflammable *adj* not inflammable.

ˈnon-ˈinterˈference, ˈnon-ˈinterˈvention, principle or practice, esp in international affairs, of keeping out of disputes.

ˈnon-ˈpayment, failure or neglect to pay (a debt, etc).

ˈnon-ˈresident *adj* who does not reside in: *a* ~ *landlord.* □ *n* [C] person not staying at a

hotel, etc: *Meals served to* ~.

ˈnon-ˈsmoker, (a) person who does not smoke tobacco. **(b)** place, eg a train compartment, where smoking is forbidden.

ˈnon-ˈstarter, (a) horse which, although entered for a race, does not run. **(b)** (*fig*) person who has no chance of success in sth he undertakes to do.

ˈnon-ˈstick *adj* (eg of a pan) made so that food, etc will not stick to its surface during cooking.

ˈnon-ˈstop *adj, adv* without a stop: *a* ~ *train from London to Brighton; fly* ~ *from New York to Paris.*

ˈnon-ˈU *adj* **(a)** not (of the) upper class. **(b)** not fashionable.

ˈnon-ˈunion *adj* not belonging to, not of, a trade union: ~ *labour.*

ˈnon-ˈviolence, policy of rejecting violent means (but using peaceful protest, etc) to gain a political or social objective.

nona·gen·ar·ian /ˌnɒnədʒəˈneərɪən/ *n* [C], *adj* (person who is) between 90 and 99 years old.

non·cha·lance /ˈnɒnʃələns/ *n* [U] indifference; unconcern.

non·cha·lant /ˈnɒnʃələnt/ *adj* not having, not showing, interest or enthusiasm.
non·cha·lant·ly *adv*

non com·pos men·tis /ˌnɒn ˈkɒmpəs ˈmentɪs/ (*Latin*) (*legal*) not legally responsible because not of sound mind.

non-de·script /ˈnɒndɪskrɪpt/ *n* [C], *adj* (person or thing) not easily classed, not having a definite character.

none /nʌn/ *pron* **1** not any, not one: *I wanted some string but there was* ~ *in the house. 'Is there any petrol left?' 'No,* ~ *at all.' N*~ *of them has/have come back yet.* **none but,** only: *They chose* ~ *but the best.* **none the less,** ⇨ **less. none other than:** *The new arrival was* ~ *other than the President* (= the President himself). **2** (in constructions equal to an imperative): *N*~ *of that! Stop that! N*~ *of your impudence! Don't be impudent!* **3** (*literature*): *Answer came there* ~. □ *adv* by no means; in no degree; not at all: *I hope you're* ~ *the worse for that accident.*

non·en·tity /nɒnˈentətɪ/ *n* [C] (*pl* -ties) **1** unimportant person. **2** thing that does not really exist or that exists only in the imagination.

none·such, non·such /ˈnʌnsʌtʃ, ˈnɒn-/ *n* [C] person or thing without equal.

non-pareil /ˈnɒn pəˈreɪl *US:* -ˈrel/ *adj, n* [C] (*formal*) unique or unrivalled (person or thing).

non-plus /nɒnˈplʌs/ *vt* (-ss-, *US:* -s-) (usually passive) surprise or puzzle (a person) so much that he does not know what to do or say: *I was completely* ~*sed when she said 'No' to my proposal of marriage.*

non·sense /ˈnɒnsəns *US:* -sens/ *n* (with or without *a, an* but not usually *pl* meaningless words; foolish talk, ideas, behaviour: *N~! I don't believe a word of it. What (a) ~!*

non·sen·si·cal /nɒnˈsensɪkəl/ *adj* not making sense: *~ remarks.*

non·such ⇨ nonesuch.

non se·qui·tur /ˌnɒn ˈsekwɪtə(r)/ *n* [C] (*Latin*) (in logic) conclusion which does not follow from the premises.

noodle /ˈnuːdl/ *n* (usually *pl* paste of flour and water or flour and eggs prepared in long, narrow strips and used in soups, etc: *chicken-~ soup.*

nook /nʊk/ *n* [C] out-of-the-way place; hidden corner: *search every ~ and cranny,* everywhere.

noon /nuːn/ *n* midday; 12 o'clock in the middle of the day; *at ~.*

ˈnoon·day /-deɪ/, **ˈnoon·tide** /-taɪd/, = noon.

no-one, no one /ˈnəʊ wʌn/ *pron* = nobody(1).

noose /nuːs/ *n* [C] loop of rope (with a slip-knot) that becomes tighter when the rope is pulled: *the hangman's ~.* **put one's head in the noose,** (*fig*) allow oneself to be caught, defeated. □ *vt* catch with a noose; make a noose.

nope /nəʊp/ *int* (*sl*) No!

nor /nɔː(r)/ *conj* **1** (after *neither* or *not*) and not: *I have neither time ~ money for pop festivals.* **2** and... not: *He can't do it; ~ can I, ~ can you, ~ can anybody.*

nor'- /nɔː(r)/ *prefix* ⇨ north.

norm /nɔːm/ *n* **1** standard; pattern; type (as representative of a group when judging other examples). **2** (in some industries, etc) amount of work required or expected in a working day: *fulfil one's ~.*

nor·mal /ˈnɔːml/ *adj* in agreement with what is representative, usual, or regular: *the ~ temperature of the human body.* □ *n* (*sing* only) usual state, level, etc: *above/below ~.*

nor·mally /ˈnɔːməlɪ/ *adv*

north /nɔːθ/ *n* **1 the ~,** one of the four cardinal points of the compass, to the left of a person facing the sunrise; part of any country farther in this direction than other parts: *the ~ of England; cold winds from the ~.* **2** (as an *adjective*) situated in, living in, of, coming from, the north: *a ~ wind.* □ *adv* to or towards the north: *sailing ~.*

the North, northern area (of England, Wales, etc).

ˈnorth-ˈeast, ˈnorth-ˈwest (abbr **NE, NW**) *n, adj adv* (sometimes, esp *naut*, **nor'-east** /ˈnɔː ˈiːst/, **nor'-west** /ˈnɔː ˈwest/) (regions) midway between north and east or north and west.

ˈnorth-north-ˈeast, ˈnorth-north-ˈwest (abbr **NNE, NNW**) *n, adj, adv* (sometimes, esp *naut*, **nor'-nor'-east, nor'-nor'-west**) (regions) midway between north and northeast or northwest.

ˈnorth-ˈeaster·ly *adj* (a) (of wind) blowing from the northeast. (b) (of direction) towards the northeast.

ˈnorth-ˈeastern /-ˈiːstən/ *adj* of, from, situated in, the northeast.

ˈnorth-ˈwester·ly *adj* (a) (of wind) from the northwest. (b) (of direction) towards the northwest.

ˈnorth-ˈwestern /-ˈwestən/ *adj* of, from, situated in the northwest.

north·er·ly /ˈnɔːðəlɪ/ *adj, adv* (a) (of winds) from the north. (b) (of direction) towards the north; in or to the north.

north·ern /ˈnɔːðən/ *adj* of, from, in, the north part of the world, a country, etc: *the ~ hemisphere.*

the northern lights, bands of light appearing in the sky; the aurora borealis.

north·erner, person born in or living in the north regions of a country.

ˈnorth·ern·most /-məʊst/ *adj* farthest north.

north·ward /ˈnɔːθwəd/ *adj* towards the north: *in a ~ direction.*

north·wards *adv: to travel ~s.*

nose¹ /nəʊz/ *n* [C] **1** part of the face above the mouth, through which breath passes, and serving as the organ of smell: *hit a man on the ~.* **as plain as the nose on one's face,** obvious. **(right) under one's very nose,** (a) directly in front of one. (b) in one's presence, and regardless of one's disapproval. **cut off one's nose to spite one's face,** damage one's own interests in a fit of bad temper. **follow one's nose,** (a) go straight forward. (b) be guided by instinct. **keep one's nose clean,** avoid trouble. **lead sb by the nose,** ⇨ lead³(2). **look down one's nose at sb,** act as if superior to him. **pay through the nose,** pay an excessive price. **poke/stick one's nose into** (*sb else's business*), ask questions, etc without being asked to do so. **put sb's nose out of joint,** ⇨ joint²(2). **turn one's nose up at,** show contempt for. **2** sense of smell: *a dog with a good ~.* **3** (*fig*) good sense for finding out: *a reporter with a ~ for news/scandal/a story.* ⇨ nose². **4** something like a nose in shape or position, eg the open end of a pipe or the most forward part of the fuselage of an aircraft.

ˈnose-bag, bag for food (oats, etc) fastened on a horse's head.

ˈnose-bleed, bleeding from the nose.

ˈnose-cone, most forward section of a rocket or guided missile, usually separable.

ˈnose-dive, sharp vertical descent made by an aircraft. □ *vi* (of an aircraft) come down steeply with the nose pointing to earth.

ˈnose-gay, bunch of cut (esp sweet-scented) flowers.

ˈnose-ring, ring fixed in the nose of a bull etc, for leading it.

ˈnose-wheel, the front landing-wheel under the fuselage of an aircraft.

nose² /nəʊz/ *vt, vi* **1** go forward carefully, push (one's way): *The ship ~d its way* *slowly through the ice.* **2 nose sth out,** discover by smelling: *The dog ~d out a rat.* **3** *(fig)* pry or search for: *~ out a scandal; nosing into other people's affairs/nosing about for information.*

-nosed *suffix* (in compounds) having the kind of nose indicated: *red-/long-~ed.*

nosey, nosy /ˈnəʊzɪ/ *adj* (-ier, -iest), *n* [C] *(sl)* inquisitive (person).

`**nosey-parker,** *(informal)* inquisitive person.

nos·tal·gia /noˈstældʒə/ *n* [U] longing for something one has known in the past; homesickness: *full of ~.*

nos·tal·gic /noˈstældʒɪk/ *adj* of, feeling or causing, nostalgia.

nos·tal·gi·cally /-klɪ/ *adv*

nos·tril /ˈnostrɪl/ *n* [C] either of the two external openings into the nose.

not /not/ *adv* (often contracted to -n't /-ənt/, as in *hasn't* /ˈhæznt/, *needn't* /ˈniːdnt/) Used to make a negative. **1** (used with non-finite *verbs*): *He warned me ~ to be late.* **2** (used after certain *verbs*, esp *think, suppose, believe, expect, fear, fancy, trust, hope, seem, appear,* and the phrase *be afraid* equivalent to a *that*-clause): *'Can you come next week?'—'I'm afraid ~.'* I'm afraid that I cannot come. *'Will it rain this afternoon?'—'I hope ~'.* **as likely as not,** probably: *He'll be at home now, as likely as ~.* **as soon as not,** ⇨ soon(5). **not at all,** /ˈnot əˈtɔl/ (used as a polite response to thanks, enquiries after a person's health, etc): *'Thank you very much'.—'N~ at all.'* *'Are you tired?'—'N~ at all.'* Not in the least. **3** (used in understatements): *~ a few,* = many; *~ seldom,* = often; *~ without reason,* = with good reason. **not that,** it is not suggested that: *if he ever said so—~ that I ever heard him say so—he told a lie.*

nota bene /ˈnəʊtə ˈbeneɪ/ *v imperative* (*Latin*) (abbr **NB, nb** /ˈen ˈbiː/) observe, note, carefully.

no·table /ˈnəʊtəbəl/ *adj* deserving to be noticed; remarkable: *~ events/speakers.* □ *n* [C] eminent person.

no·tably /-əblɪ/ *adv*

no·tary /ˈnəʊtərɪ/ *n* [C] (*pl* -ies) (often '~ ˈpublic*) official with authority to do certain kinds of legal business, such as witnessing the signing of legal documents.

no·ta·tion /nəʊˈteɪʃən/ *n* **1** [C] system of signs or symbols representing numbers, amounts, musical notes, etc. **2** [U] representing of numbers, etc by such signs or symbols.

notch /notʃ/ *n* [C] V-shaped cut (*in* or *on* something). □ *vt* make or cut a notch in or on.

note[1] /nəʊt/ *n* [C] **1** short record (of facts, etc) made to help the memory: *He spoke for an hour without ~s.* **2** short letter: *a ~ of thanks.* **3** short comment on or explanation of a word or passage in a book, etc: *a new*

edition of 'Hamlet', with ~s at the back. ⇨ footnote. **4** observation (not necessarily written): *He was comparing ~s with a friend,* exchanging views, comparing experiences, etc. **5** written or printed promise to pay money: `bank~s; a £5 ~.` **6** single sound of a certain pitch and duration: *play ~s on the piano.* **strike the right note,** (*fig*) speak in such a way that one wins the approval or sympathy of one's listeners. **7** sign used to represent such a sound in manuscript or printed music. **8** (usually *sing* with *a, an*) quality or tone (esp of voice) showing feelings, attitude, etc: *There was a ~ of pleasure in his speech.* **9** [U] distinction; importance: *a family of ~.* **10** [U] notice; attention: *worthy of ~. Take ~ of what he says,* Pay attention to it.

`**note-book,** pad(2) in which to write notes.

`**note-case,** wallet for banknotes.

`**note-paper,** kinds of paper for writing, esp private, letters.

note[2] /nəʊt/ *vt* **1** notice; pay attention to: *N~ how I did it.* **2** make a note of; write (*down*) in order to remember: *The policeman ~d down every word I said.*

noted /ˈnəʊtɪd/ *adj* celebrated; well known (*for, as*): *a town ~ for its pottery/as a health resort.*

note·worthy /ˈnəʊtwɜðɪ/ *adj* deserving to be noted; remarkable.

noth·ing[1] /ˈnʌθɪŋ/ *adv* not at all; in no way: *It is ~ near as large/as good.*

noth·ing[2] /ˈnʌθɪŋ/ *n* not anything: *He's had ~ to eat yet. N~ ever pleases her. There's ~ like leather* (= Nothing is so good as leather) *for shoes.* **for nothing,** **(a)** free: without payment. **(b)** without a reward or result; to no purpose: *it was not for ~ that he spent three years studying the subject.* **next to nothing,** ⇨ next. **be nothing to,** **(a)** not be of interest to: *She's ~ to him.* **(b)** not to be compared to: *My losses are ~ to yours.* **come to nothing,** fail; be without result. **have nothing to do with,** **(a)** avoid; have no dealings with: *Have ~ to do with that man.* **(b)** not to be the business or concern of: *This has ~ to do with you.* **mean nothing to,** **(a)** have no meaning for: *These technical words mean ~ to me.* **(b)** be of no concern or interest to: *He used to like Jane but she means ~ to him now.* **think nothing of,** consider as ordinary, usual or unremarkable: *He thinks ~ of a twenty-mile walk.* **to say nothing of,** without mentioning: *He owns houses, cars and shops, to say ~ of his land abroad.*

no·tice /ˈnəʊtɪs/ *n* **1** [C] (written or printed) news of something about to happen or that has happened: *put up a ~.* **2** [U] warning, suggestion (of what will happen): *give the typist a month's ~,* tell her that she must leave her job at the end of one month. **(do sth) at short notice,** with little warning, time for preparation, etc. **3** [U] attention.

bring sth/come to sb's notice, call a person's attention/have one's attention called to something: *It has come to my ~ that...,* I have learnt that... *take no notice (of),* pay no attention: *Take no ~ of them/of what they're saying about you.* **4** [C] short particulars of a new book, play, etc in a periodical. □ *vt,vi* pay attention; observe: *I wasn't noticing. I didn't ~ you.*

`no·tice·able /-əbəl/ adj easily seen or noticed.

`no·tice·ably /-əblɪ/ adv

no·ti·fi·able /'nəʊtɪˌfaɪəbəl/ adj that must be reported (esp of certain diseases that must be reported to public health authorities).

no·tify /'nəʊtɪfaɪ/ vt (pt,pp -ied) give notice of; report: *~ the police of a loss; ~ the authorities that....*

no·ti·fi·ca·tion /ˌnəʊtɪfɪ'keɪʃən/ n [CU]

no·tion /'nəʊʃən/ n [C] idea; opinion: *I have no ~ of what he means.*

no·tional /-nəl/ adj **1** (of knowledge, etc) not based on experiment or demonstration. **2** existing only in thought.

no·tor·iety /ˌnəʊtə'raɪətɪ/ n [U] state of being notorious.

no·tori·ous /nəʊ'tɔːrɪəs/ adj widely known (esp for something bad): *a ~ criminal.*

no·tori·ous·ly adv

not·with·stand·ing /ˌnɒtwɪð'stændɪŋ/ adv nevertheless; all the same. □ *conj* although. □ *prep* in spite of.

nou·gat /'nuːgɑː US: 'nuːgət/ n [U] sort of hard sweet made of sugar, nuts, etc.

nought /nɔːt/ n [C] nothing; the figure 0: *point ~ one,* i e ·01. *come to nought,* fail.

noun /naʊn/ n [C] (*gram*) word (not a *pronoun*) which can function as the subject or object of a *verb,* or the object of a *preposition* (marked *n* in this dictionary).

nour·ish /'nʌrɪʃ US: 'nɜr-/ vt **1** keep (a person) alive and well with food: *~ing food.* **2** improve (land) with manure, etc: *~ the soil.* **3** have or encourage (hope, fear, etc): *~ hope in one's heart.*

nour·ish·ment n [U] (*formal*) food.

nova /'nəʊvə/ n [C] (*pl* ~s or ~e /-vɪ/) star that suddenly increases its brilliance and then dims again.

novel¹ /'nɒvəl/ adj strange; new; of a kind not previously known: *~ ideas.*

novel² /'nɒvəl/ n [C] story in prose, long enough to fill one or more volumes, about either imaginary or historical people: *the ~s of Dickens.*

'novel·`ette /-'et/, short novel.

`novel·ist /-ɪst/, writer of novels.

nov·elty /'nɒvəltɪ/ n (*pl* -ies) **1** [U] newness; strangeness; quality of being novel: *the ~ of his surroundings.* **2** [C] previously unknown or unfamiliar thing, idea, etc. **3** (*pl*) miscellaneous manufactured goods of low cost, e g toys, decorations.

No·vem·ber /nəʊ'vembə(r)/ n the eleventh month of the year.

nov·ice /'nɒvɪs/ n [C] **1** person who is still learning and who is without experience. **2** person who is training to become a monk or a nun.

no·vi·ci·ate, no·vi·ti·ate /nəʊ'vɪʃɪət/, novice; period of being a novice.

now /naʊ/ adv **1** at the present time; in the present circumstances: *Where are you ~ living/living ~? N~ is the best time to visit Devon.* **2** (used after a preposition): *Up to/Till/Until ~ we have been lucky.* (*every*) *now and then/again,* occasionally; from time to time: *We go to the opera ~ and then.* *now... now; now... then,* at one time, at another time: *N~ you see me, ~ you don't.* **3** at once; immediately: *Do it* (*right*) *~! just now,* ⇨ just² (6). **4** (used without reference to time, to indicate the mood of the speaker, to explain, warn, comfort, etc): *N~ stop quarrelling and listen to me.* 'now, `now; `now then, (used at the beginning of a sentence, often as a protest or warning, or simply to call attention): *N~ then, what have you been up to?* □ *conj* as a consequence of the fact (that): *N~ (that) you're grown up, you must stop this childish behaviour.*

now·adays /'naʊədeɪz/ adv at the present time (and often used in contrasts between present day manners, customs, etc and those of past times): *N~ children are much healthier.*

no·where /'nəʊweə(r) US: -hweər/ adv not anywhere: *The boy was ~ to be found. £50 is ~ near enough,* not nearly enough.

nox·ious /'nɒkʃəs/ adj harmful: *~ gases.*

nox·ious·ly adv

nox·ious·ness n

nozzle /'nɒzəl/ n [C] metal end of a hose, etc through which a stream of liquid or air is directed.

nu·ance /'njuːɑːns US: nuː'æns/ n [C] small difference in or of shade of meaning, opinion, colour, etc.

nu·bile /'njuːbaɪl US: 'nuːbəl/ adj (of girls) marriageable; old enough to marry.

nu·clear /'njuːklɪə(r) US: 'nuː-/ adj of a nucleus; using nuclear energy.

'nuclear `bomb, using nuclear energy to provide its destructive power.

`nuclear dis`armament, agreement not to develop, stock or use nuclear weapons.

'nuclear `energy, great energy produced during reactions on atomic nuclei.

'nuclear `power, (a) power from nuclear energy. (b) country having nuclear weapons.

'nuclear-powered adj using nuclear energy: *a ~-powered submarine.*

'nuclear re`actor, device that generates power by atomic fission.

'nuclear `warfare, warfare using nuclear bombs, etc.

nu·cleus /'njuːklɪəs US: 'nuː-/ n [C] (*pl* nuclei /-klɪaɪ/) **1** central part of an atom, consisting of protons and neutrons. **2** central part, round which other parts are grouped or round which other things collect.

nude /njud US: nud/ adj naked. □ n [C] nude human figure (esp in art). *In the nude*, naked.

nu·dist /-ıst/ person who lives unclothed and believes that sun and air is good for the health.

`nudist camp/colony, place where nudists practise their beliefs.

nu·dity /-ətı/, nakedness.

nudge /nʌdʒ/ vt touch or push slightly with the elbow in order to attract a person's attention. □ n [C] push given in this way.

nug·get /ˈnʌgıt/ n [C] lump of metal, esp gold, as found in the earth.

nui·sance /ˈnjusəns US: ˈnu-/ n [C] thing, person, act, etc that causes trouble or offence: *These flies are a* ~.

null /nʌl/ adj of no effect or force. *null and void*, (*legal*) without legal effect; invalid.

nul·li·fi·ca·tion /ˌnʌlıfıˈkeıʃən/ n [U]

nul·lify /ˈnʌlıfaı/ vt (pt,pp -ied) make null and void.

numb /nʌm/ adj without ability to feel or move: ~ *with cold/shock*. □ vt make numb: ~*ed with grief*.

numb·ly adv

numb·ness n [U]

num·ber /ˈnʌmbə(r)/ n [C] **1** *3, 13, 33 and 103 are* ~*s*. **2** quantity or amount: *a large* ~ *of people. A* ~ *of books* (= Some books) *are missing from the library. In number*: *They were fifteen in* ~, There were fifteen of them. *without number*, too many to be counted. **3** (usually shortened to **No**, with *pl* **Nos**, before a figure): *Room No 145*, e g in a hotel. **4** one issue of a periodical, esp for one day, week, etc: *the current* ~ *of 'Punch'*. *back numbers*, earlier issues (of a periodical, etc). *a back number*, (*fig*) out-of-date or old-fashioned person. **5** dance, song, music etc for the stage. **6** (*pl*) numerical superiority: *The enemy won by force of* ~*s*. **7** (*pl*) arithmetic: *He's not good at* ~*s*. □ vt **1** give a number to: *Let's* ~ *them from 1 to 10*. **2** amount to; add up to: *We* ~*ed 20 in all*. **3** include; place: ~ *her among one's friends*. **4** (passive) be restricted in number: *His days are* ~*ed*, He has not long to live. **5** (*mil*) call out one's number in a rank of soldiers: *The company* ~*ed off from the right*.

`number-plate, plate showing the index-mark and number of motor vehicles, the number of a house, etc.

No 10 (Downing Street), official residence of the British Prime Minister.

nu·mer·able /ˈnjumərəbəl US: ˈnu-/ adj that can be numbered or counted.

nu·meral /ˈnjumərəl US: ˈnu-/ n [C], adj (word, figure or sign) standing for a number; of number.

Arabic numerals, 1, 2, 3, etc.

Roman numerals, I, II, IV, etc.

nu·mer·ate /ˈnjumərət US: ˈnu-/ adj (of a

person) having a good basic competence in mathematics and science. ⇨ literate.

nu·mer·ation /ˌnjuməˈreıʃən US: ˈnu-/ n [C] **1** method or process of numbering or calculating. **2** expression in words of numbers written in figures.

nu·mer·ator /ˈnjuməreıtə(r) US: ˈnu-/ n [C] number above the line in a vulgar fraction, e g 3 in ⅜. ⇨ denominator.

nu·meri·cal /njuˈmerıkəl US: nu-/ adj of, in, denoting, numbers: ~ *symbols*.

nu·meri·cally /-klı/ adv: *The enemy were* ~*ly superior*.

nu·mer·ous /ˈnjumərəs US: ˈnu-/ adj great in number; very many: *her* ~ *friends*.

num·skull /ˈnʌmskʌl/ n [C] foolish person.

nun /nʌn/ n [C] woman who, after taking religious vows, lives, with other women in a convent, a secluded life in the service of God.

nun·nery /ˈnʌnərı/, convent.

nup·tial /ˈnʌpʃəl/ adj (formal) of marriage or weddings.

nup·tials n pl (formal) wedding.

nurse¹ /nɜs/ n [C] **1** person who cares for people who are ill or injured (in a hospital, etc). **2** (`nurse-)maid, woman or girl employed to look after babies and small children. ⇨ nanny. **3** (`wet-)nurse, woman (formerly) employed to suckle the infant of another. **4** [U] nursing or being nursed: *put a child to* ~. **5** country, college, institution, etc which protects or encourages a certain quality: *England, the* ~ *of liberty*.

nurse² /nɜs/ vt **1** take charge of and look after (persons who are ill, injured, etc). **2** feed (a baby) at the breast. **3** hold (a baby, a child, a pet dog) on the knees; clasp carefully. **4** give special care to: ~ *young plants*. *nurse a cold*, stay at home, keep warm, in order to cure it. *nurse a constituency*, keep in touch with the voters (to obtain or retain their support). **5** have in the mind, think about a great deal: ~ *feelings of revenge*.

nurs·ery /ˈnɜsərı/ n [C] (pl -ies) **1** room (in a house, passenger liner, etc) for the special use of small children. **2** place where young plants and trees are raised (for transplanting later).

`day nursery, (a) room (in a wealthy home) where small children play, have their meals, etc. (b) building where mothers who go out to work may leave babies and young children.

`nurs·ery·man /-mən/, man who owns a nursery(2).

`nursery rhyme, poem or song (usually traditional) for young children.

`nursery school, for children of 2 to 5.

`nursery slope, skiing slope suitable for learners.

nurs·ing /ˈnɜsıŋ/ n [U] the profession or duties of a nurse(1): *Careful* ~ *will be needed*.

`nursing-home, building, usually privately

435

owned, smaller than a hospital, for the sick or aged.

nur·ture /ˈnɜːtʃə(r)/ n [U] (formal) care, training; education (of children). □ vt bring up; train: a delicately ~d girl.

nut /nʌt/ n [C] 1 fruit consisting of a hard shell enclosing a kernel that can be eaten. *a hard nut to crack,* a difficult problem to solve. 2 small piece of metal with a threaded hole for screwing on to a bolt. 3 (sl) head (of a human being). *off one's nut,* (sl) insane. 4 (pl) small lumps of coal.

`nutcrackers n pl device for cracking nuts open.

`nut house, (sl) mental hospital.

`nut·shell, hard outside covering of a nut. *(put sth) in a nutshell,* (fig) in the fewest possible words; in the smallest possible space.

nut·meg /ˈnʌtmeg/ n 1 [C] hard, small, round, sweet-smelling seed of an E Indian evergreen. 2 [U] this seed grated to powder, used as a flavouring.

nu·tri·ent /ˈnjuːtrɪənt US: ˈnuː-/ adj (formal) serving as or providing nourishment.

nu·tri·ment /ˈnjuːtrɪmənt US: ˈnuː-/ n [C,U] (formal) nourishing food.

nu·tri·tion /njuːˈtrɪʃən US: nuː-/ n [U] (formal) the process of supplying and receiving nourishment; the science of food values: the care and ~ of children.

nu·tri·tious /njuːˈtrɪʃəs US: nuː-/ adj (formal) having high value as food.

nu·tri·tive /ˈnjuːtrɪtɪv US: ˈnuː-/ adj (formal) serving as food; of nutrition.

nuts /nʌts/ adj (sl) crazy; mad. *be nuts about/over sb/sth,* be very much in love with, infatuated with.

nutty /ˈnʌtɪ/ adj (-ier, -iest) 1 tasting like nuts. 2 (sl) crazy. 3 containing, made up of, nuts(4): ~ coal.

nuzzle /ˈnʌzəl/ vt,vi press, rub or push the nose against: The horse ~d (up against) my shoulder.

ny·lon /ˈnaɪlɒn/ n 1 [U] (P) synthetic fibre used for hosiery, rope, brushes, etc: ~ tights/blouses, etc. 2 (pl) nylon stockings; tights.

nymph /nɪmf/ n [C] 1 (in Greek and Roman stories) one of the lesser goddesses, living in rivers, trees, hills, etc. 2 (literary) beautiful young woman. 3 pupa; chrysalis.

Oo

O, o /əʊ/ (pl O's, o's /əʊz/) 1 the 15th letter of the English alphabet. 2 O-shaped sign or mark. 3 zero (esp when saying telephone numbers).

O, oh /əʊ/ int cry of surprise, fear, pain, sudden pleasure, etc.

oak /əʊk/ n [C] sorts of large tree with tough, hard wood, common in many parts of the world; [U] the wood of this tree: a forest of ~(s)/~-trees.

oaken /ˈəʊkən/ adj made of oak.

oar /ɔː(r)/ n [C] pole with a flat blade, pulled by hand against a pin, rowlock or other support on the side of a boat, in order to propel the boat through the water. *put/shove one's oar in,* (informal) interfere. *rest on one's oars,* relax one's efforts.

`oars·man, `oars·woman, rower.

oasis /əʊˈeɪsɪs/ n [C] (pl -ses /-siːz/) 1 fertile place, with water, in a desert. 2 (fig) experience, place, etc which is pleasant in the midst of what is dull, unpleasant, etc.

oast /əʊst/ n [C] kiln for drying hops.

`oast-house, building containing an oast.

oat /əʊt/ n [C] (usually pl) 1 (grain from a) cereal plant grown in cool climates as food (oats for horses, oatmeal for human beings). *sow one's wild oats,* lead a life of pleasure and gaiety while young before settling down seriously. 2 (used with a sing verb) oatmeal porridge: Is Scotch ~s on the breakfast menu?

`oat·meal, oats in porridge, etc.

oath /əʊθ/ n (pl ~s /əʊðz/) 1 solemn undertaking with God's help to do something. 2 solemn declaration that something is true. *be on/under oath,* (legal) having sworn to tell the truth. *swear/take an oath,* promise solemnly to give (one's loyalty, allegiance, etc). 3 wrongful use of God's name or of sacred words to express strong feeling; swear-word.

ob·du·racy /ˈɒbdjʊərəsɪ US: -dər-/ n [U] (formal) stubbornness.

ob·du·rate /ˈɒbdjʊərət US: -dər-/ adj (formal) stubborn; not showing regret.

ob·du·rate·ly adv

obedi·ence /əˈbiːdɪəns/ n [U] being, showing obedience: Soldiers act in ~ to the orders of their superior officers.

obedi·ent /əˈbiːdɪənt/ adj doing, willing to do, what one is told to do: ~ children.

obedi·ent·ly adv

ob·elisk /ˈɒbəlɪsk/ n [C] pointed, tapering, four-sided stone pillar, set up as a monument or landmark.

obese /əʊˈbiːs/ adj (formal) (of persons) very fat.

obes·ity /əʊˈbiːsətɪ/ n [U] (formal) being obese.

obey /əˈbeɪ/ vt,vi do what one is told to do; carry out (a command): ~ an officer/orders.

obitu·ary /əˈbɪtʃʊərɪ US: -tʃʊerɪ/ n [C] (pl -ies) 1 printed notice of a person's death, often with a short account of his life. 2 (used as an adjective): ~ notices, e g in a newspaper.

ob·ject[1] /ˈɒbdʒɪkt/ n [C] 1 something that can be seen or touched; material thing: Tell me the names of the ~s in this room. 2 person or thing to which action or feeling or thought is directed: *an ~ of pity/admiration*. **3** purpose; end: *with no ~ in life; fail/succeed in one's ~*. **4** (*gram*) noun, clause, etc towards which the action of the verb is directed, or to which a preposition indicates some relation, as in:

direct object, 'He took *the money*' or 'He took *what he wanted*'.

indirect object, 'I gave *him* the money'.

prepositional object, 'I gave the money to *the treasurer*'.

ob·ject² /əb'dʒekt/ say that one is not in favour of something; be opposed (to); make a protest against: *I ~ to all this noise/to being treated like a child. He stood up and ~ed in strong language*.

ob·jec·tor /-tə(r)/, person who objects. ⇨ conscientious objector.

ob·jec·tion /əb'dʒekʃən/ *n* **1** [C,U] statement or feeling of dislike, disapproval or opposition: *He has a strong ~ to getting up early. He took ~ to what I said*. **2** [C] that which is objected to; defect.

ob·jec·tion·able /-əbəl/ *adj* likely to be objected to; unpleasant: *~able smell/~able remarks*.

ob·jec·tion·ably /-əblı/ *adv*

ob·jec·tive /əb'dʒektıv/ *adj* **1** (in philosophy) having existence outside the mind; real. ⇨ **subjective**. **2** (of persons, writings, pictures) not influenced by personal thought or feeling; dealing with things, actual facts, etc. **3** (*gram*) of the object(4): *the ~ case*. ⇨ **case**¹ (3). □ *n* [C] **1** object aimed at; purpose. **2** position to which armed forces are moving to capture it; military aim: *All our ~s were won*.

ob·ject·ive·ly *adv* in an objective(2) manner.

ob·jec·tiv·ity /'ɒbdʒek'tıvətı/ *n* [U] state of being objective; impartial or unprejudiced judgement.

ob·la·tion /ə'bleıʃən/ *n* [C] offering made to God or a god.

ob·li·gate /'ɒblıgeıt/ *vt* (usually passive) bind (a person, esp legally) (to do something): *He felt ~d to help*.

ob·li·ga·tion /'ɒblı'geıʃən/ *n* [C] promise, duty or condition that show what action ought to be taken (e g the power of the law, duty, a sense of what is right): *the ~s of conscience*. **be/place sb under an obligation**, be/make him indebted to another.

ob·li·ga·tory /ə'blıgətrı US: -tɔrı/ *adj* that is required by law, rule or custom: *Is attendance at the meeting ~ or optional?*

ob·lige /ə'blaıdʒ/ *vt* **1** require, bind, by a promise, oath, etc: *The law ~s parents to send their children to school*. **be obliged to do sth**, compelled: *They were ~d to (= had to) sell their house in order to pay their debts*. ⇨ **have**³(1). **2** do something as a favour or in answer to a request: *Please ~ me by closing the door. I'm much ~d to you*, I'm grateful for what you've done.

oblig·ing *adj* willing to help: *obliging neighbours*.

oblig·ing·ly *adv*

ob·lique /ə'blik/ *adj* sloping; slanting.

oblique angle, angle that is not a right angle (i e not 90°).

ob·lique·ly *adv*

ob·lit·er·ate /ə'blıtəreıt/ *vt* rub or blot out; remove all signs of; destroy.

ob·lit·er·ation /ə'blıtə'reıʃən/ *n* [U]

ob·liv·ion /ə'blıvıən/ *n* [U] state of being completely forgotten. **sink/fall into oblivion**, be forgotten.

ob·livi·ous /ə'blıvıəs/ *adj* unaware, having no memory: *~ of one's surroundings/of what was happening*.

ob·long /'ɒblɒŋ US: -lɔŋ/ *n* [C], *adj* (figure) having four straight sides and angles at 90°, longer than it is wide.

ob·nox·ious /əb'nɒkʃəs/ *adj* (of, e g smell) nasty; very disagreeable (to).

ob·nox·ious·ly *adv*

oboe /'əubəu/ *n* [C] woodwind instrument of treble pitch with a double-reed mouthpiece.

'obo·ist /-ıst/, player of the oboe.

ob·scene /əb'sin/ *adj* (of words, thoughts, books, pictures, etc) morally disgusting; offensive; likely to corrupt (esp by regarding or describing sex indecently).

ob·scene·ly *adv*

ob·scen·ity /əb'senətı/ *n* (*pl* -ies) [U] being obscene; offensive language, etc; [C] instance of this.

ob·scure /əb'skjuə(r)/ *adj* **1** dark; hidden; not clearly seen or understood: *an ~ view/corner. Is the meaning still ~ to you?* **2** not well known: *an ~ village/poet*. □ *vt* make obscure: *The moon was ~d by clouds*.

ob·scure·ly *adv*

ob·scur·ity /əb'skjuərətı/ *n* (*pl* -ies) **1** [U] state of being obscure: *content to live in ~*. **2** [C] something that is obscure: *a philosophical essay full of obscurities*.

ob·sequi·ous /əb'sikwıəs/ *adj* too eager to obey or serve; showing excessive respect (esp from hope of reward or advantage): *~ to the Manager*.

ob·sequi·ous·ly *adv*

ob·sequi·ous·ness *n* [U]

ob·serv·able /əb'zɜvəbəl/ *adj* **1** that can be seen or noticed. **2** deserving to be observed.

ob·serv·ably /-əblı/ *adv*

ob·serv·ance /əb'zɜvəns/ *n* **1** [U] the keeping or observing(2) of a law, custom, festival, etc: *the ~ of the Queen's birthday*. **2** [C] act performed as part of a ceremony, or as a sign of respect or worship.

ob·serv·ant /əb'zɜvənt/ *adj* **1** quick at noticing things: *an ~ boy*. **2** careful to observe(2) laws, customs, etc: *~ of the rules*.

ob·serv·ant·ly *adv*

ob·ser·va·tion /'ɒbzə'veıʃən/ *n* **1** [U] observing or being observed: *~ of the stars*.

437

be/come/keep under observation, be watched/watch carefully: *under medical ~.* **2** [U] power of taking notice: *a man of little ~.* **3** (usually *pl*) collected and recorded information: *~s on bird life in the Antarctic.* **4** [C] taking of the altitude of the sun or other heavenly body in order to find the latitude and longitude of one's position.

'obser`vation post (*mil*) post as near to the enemy's lines as possible, from which reports of the enemy's movements may be obtained.

ob·serv·atory /əbˈzɜːvətrɪ *US:* -tɔːrɪ/ *n* [C] (*pl* -ies) building from which natural things (e g the sun and the stars, marine life) may be observed.

ob·serve /əbˈzɜːv/ *vt,vi* **1** see and notice; watch carefully: *~ the behaviour of birds. The accused man was ~d entering the bank.* **2** pay attention to (rules, etc); celebrate (festivals, birthdays, anniversaries, etc): *Do they ~ Christmas Day in that country?* **3** say by way of comment: *He ~d that the house seemed to be too small.* **4** attend (e g a conference) to listen but not to take an active part.

ob·server, (**a**) person who observes(1): *an ~r of nature.* (**b**) person who observes(2): *an ~r of the Sabbath.* (**c**) person who observes(4).

ob·serv·ing *adj* quick to notice.
ob·serv·ing·ly *adv*

ob·sess /əbˈses/ *vt* (usually passive) (of a fear, etc) occupy the mind of; continually distress: *~ed by fear of unemployment.*

ob·ses·sion /əbˈseʃən/ *n* **1** [U] state of being obsessed. **2** [C] thing, fixed idea, etc that occupies one's mind.

ob·sess·ive /əbˈsesɪv/ *adj* of or like an obsession.

ob·sol·es·cence /ˌɒbsəˈlesəns/ *n* [U] being obsolescent.

ob·sol·es·cent /ˌɒbsəˈlesənt/ *adj* becoming out of date; passing out of use.

ob·sol·ete /ˈɒbsəliːt/ *adj* no longer used; out-of-date.

ob·stacle /ˈɒbstəkəl/ *n* [C] something that stops progress or makes it difficult: *~s to world peace.*

'obstacle race, (**a**) one in which obstacles, e g ditches, hedges, have to be crossed. (**b**) (*fig*) aim, etc with many difficulties to be overcome.

ob·ste·tri·cian /ˌɒbstəˈtrɪʃən/ *n* [C] expert in obstetrics.

ob·stet·rics /əbˈstetrɪks/ *n pl* branch of medicine and surgery connected with childbirth.

ob·sti·nacy /ˈɒbstɪnəsɪ/ *n* [U] being obstinate; stubbornness.

ob·sti·nate /ˈɒbstɪnət/ *adj* **1** not easily giving way to argument or persuasion: *~ children.* **2** not easily overcome: *an ~ disease.*
ob·sti·nate·ly *adv*

ob·struct /əbˈstrʌkt/ *vt* **1** be, get, put,

something in the way of; block up (a road, passage, etc): *Trees ~ed the view.* **2** make (the development, etc of something) difficult: *~ justice in the magistrate's court.*

ob·struc·tion /əbˈstrʌkʃən/ *n* **1** [U] obstructing or being obstructed: *The Opposition adopted a policy of ~.* **2** [C] something that obstructs: *~s on the road,* e g trees blown down in a gale.

ob·struc·tive /əbˈstrʌktɪv/ *adj* causing, likely or intended to cause, obstruction: *a policy ~ to our plans.*
ob·struc·tive·ly *adv*

ob·tain /əbˈteɪn/ *vt,vi* **1** get; secure for oneself; buy; have lent or granted to oneself: *~ what one wants. Where can I ~ the book?* **2** (*formal*) (of rules, customs) be established or in use: *The custom still ~s in some districts.*

ob·tain·able /-əbəl/ *adj* that can be obtained.

ob·trude /əbˈtruːd/ *vt,vi* push (oneself, one's opinions, etc) forward, esp when unwanted.

ob·trus·ive /əbˈtruːsɪv/ *adj* (making oneself) unduly noticeable.
ob·trus·ive·ly *adv*

ob·tuse /əbˈtjuːs *US:* -ˈtuːs/ *adj* **1** blunt: *an ~ remark.* **2** slow in understanding; unintelligent. **3** (of an angle) between 90° and 180°.
obtuse·ly *adv*
ob·tuse·ness *n* [U]

ob·vi·ate /ˈɒbvɪeɪt/ *vt* (*formal*) get rid of, clear away (dangers, difficulties, needs etc).

ob·vi·ous /ˈɒbvɪəs/ *adj* easily seen or understood; clear; plain.
ob·vi·ous·ly *adv*

oc·ca·sion /əˈkeɪʒən/ *n* **1** [C] time at which a particular event takes place or should take place: *on this/that ~...; on the present/last ~...; on rare ~s. He has had few ~s to speak French.* **on occasion,** now and then; whenever the need arises. **rise to the occasion,** show that one is capable of doing what needs to be done. **2** [U] reason; cause; need: *I've had no ~ to visit him recently.* **3** [C] immediate, subsidiary or incidental cause of something: *The real causes of the strike are not clear, but the ~ was the dismissal of two workmen.* □ *vt* (*formal*) be the cause of: *The boy's behaviour ~ed his parents much anxiety.*

oc·ca·sional /əˈkeɪʒənəl/ *adj* **1** happening, coming, seen, etc from time to time, but not regularly: *He pays me ~ visits.* **2** used or meant for a special event, time, purpose, etc: *~ verses,* e g written to celebrate an anniversary.

oc·ca·sion·ally *adv* now and then; at times.

oc·cu·pancy /ˈɒkjʊpənsɪ/ *n* [C] (*pl* -ies) act, fact, period of occupying a house, land, etc by being in possession.

oc·cu·pant /ˈɒkjʊpənt/ *n* [C] person who occupies a house, room or office; person in actual possession of land, etc.

oc·cu·pa·tion /ˈɒkjʊˈpeɪʃən/ n 1 [U] act of occupying(1,2); taking and holding possession of: *the ~ of a house by a family.* 2 [U] period during which land, a building, etc is occupied. 3 [C] business, trade, etc; that which occupies one's time, either permanently or as a hobby, etc.

oc·cu·pa·tional /-nəl/ adj arising from, connected with, a person's job.

ˈoccuˈpational ˈhazards, risks that arise from a person's work (eg explosions in coalmines).

ˈoccuˈpational ˈtherapy, treatment of illness, etc by mental or physical activity.

oc·cu·pier /ˈɒkjʊpaɪə(r)/ n [C] occupant; person in (esp temporary or subordinate) possession of land or a building (contrasted with the owner or tenant).

oc·cu·py /ˈɒkjʊpaɪ/ vt (pt,pp -ied) 1 live in, be in possession of (a house, farm, etc). 2 take and keep possession of (towns, countries, etc) in war: *~ the enemy's capital.* 3 take up, fill (space, time, attention, the mind): *Many anxieties ~ my mind.* 4 hold, fill: *She occupies an important position in the Department of the Environment.*

oc·cur /əˈkɜː(r)/ vi (-rr-) 1 take place; happen: *When did the accident ~?* 2 **occur to,** come to mind: *Did it ever ~ to you that...,* Did you ever have the idea that...? 3 exist; be found: *Misprints ~ on every page.*

oc·cur·rence /əˈkʌrəns US: əˈkɜːrəns/ n 1 [C] happening; event: *an unfortunate ~.* 2 [U] fact or process of occurring: *of frequent/rare ~.*

ocean /ˈəʊʃən/ n [C] 1 the great body of water that surrounds the land masses of the earth. 2 one of the main divisions of this: *the Atlantic/Pacific O~.* 3 (informal) great number or quantity: *~s of time.*

oceanic /ˈəʊʃɪˈænɪk/ adj of, like, living in, the ocean.

ochre (US also **ocher**) /ˈəʊkə(r)/ n [U] 1 sorts of earth used for making pigments varying from light yellow to brown. 2 pale yellowish-brown colour.

o'clock /əˈklɒk/ particle (used in asking and telling the time) (ie an hour): *He left at five ~/between five and six ~.*

oc·ta·gon /ˈɒktəgən US: -gɒn/ n [C] flat figure with eight sides and angles.

oc·tag·onal /ɒkˈtægənəl/ adj eight-sided.

oc·tane /ˈɒkteɪn/ n [C,U] hydrocarbon paraffin (as in fuels such as petrol).

oc·tave /ˈɒktɪv/ n [C] 1 (music) note that is six whole tones above or below a given note; the interval of five whole tones and two semi-tones; note and its octave sounded together. 2 (poetry) first eight lines of a sonnet; stanza of eight lines.

oc·tet, oc·tette /ɒkˈtet/ n [C] 1 (piece of music for) eight singers or players. 2 = octave(2).

Oc·to·ber /ɒkˈtəʊbə(r)/ n the tenth month of the year, with 31 days.

oc·to·gen·arian /ˈɒktədʒɪˈneərɪən/ n [C], adj (person) of an age from 80 to 89.

oc·to·pus /ˈɒktəpəs/ n [C] (pl ~es) sea-animal with a soft body and eight arms (tentacles) provided with suckers.

ocu·lar /ˈɒkjʊlə(r)/ adj (formal) of, for, by, the eyes; of seeing: *~ proof/demonstration.*

ocu·list /ˈɒkjʊlɪst/ n [C] specialist in diseases of the eye.

odd /ɒd/ adj 1 (of numbers) not even; not exactly divisible by two: *1, 3, 5 and 7 are ~ numbers.* 2 of one of a pair when the other is missing: *an ~ shoe/glove.* 3 of one or more of a set or series when not with the rest: *two ~ volumes of an encyclopaedia.* **ˈodd man ˈout, (a)** person or thing left when the others have been arranged in pairs. **(b)** (informal) person who keeps away from, or cannot fit himself into, the society, community, etc, of which he is a member. 4 with a little extra: *ˈthirty-~ years,* between 30 and 40; *twelve ˈpounds ~,* £12 and some pence extra. 5 not regular, habitual or fixed; occasional: *make a living by doing ~ jobs; knit at ~ times/moments.* 6 (-er, -est) strange; peculiar: *He's an ~/~-looking old man. How ~!*

odd·ly adv in an odd manner: *Oddly enough,* As strange as it may seem.

odd·ity /ˈɒdətɪ/ n (pl -ies) 1 [U] quality of being odd(6); strangeness: *~ of behaviour/dress.* 2 [C] queer act, thing or person.

odd·ment /ˈɒdmənt/ n [C] something left over; spare piece: *The chair was sold as an ~ at the end of the auction.* ⇨ odds and ends, below.

odds /ɒdz/ n pl 1 the chances in favour of or against something happening: *The ~ are in our favour/against us,* We are likely/unlikely to succeed. 2 difference in amount between the money betted and the money that will be paid if the bet is successful: *~ of ten to one.* 3 **be at odds (with sb) (over sth),** be quarrelling or disagreeing.

odds and ends, small articles, bits and pieces, of various sorts and usually of small value.

ode /əʊd/ n [C] poem, usually in irregular metre, rhyming and expressing noble feelings.

odi·ous /ˈəʊdɪəs/ adj hateful; repulsive.

odi·ous·ly adv

odium /ˈəʊdɪəm/ n [U] (formal) general or widespread hatred; strong feeling against something: *behaviour that exposed him to ~.*

odour (US = **odor**) /ˈəʊdə(r)/ n [C] pleasant or unpleasant smell.

odour·less (US = **odor-**) adj

od·ys·sey /ˈɒdɪsɪ/ n [C] (pl ~s) long, adventurous journey or series of adventures (from the voyage of Odysseus after the siege of Troy, in Homer's epic).

oecu·meni·cal /ˈiːkjuˈmenɪkəl/ adj = ecumenical.

439

o'er /ɔ(r)/ adv, prep (poetic) = over.

oe·soph·agus /iˈsofəgəs/ n = esophagus.

of /usual form: əv strong form: ov/ prep **1** (showing separation in space or time): five miles south ~ Leeds. **2** (showing origin, authorship): ~ royal descent; the works ~ Shakespeare. **3** (showing cause): die ~ grief/hunger. **4** (showing relief, removal, separation, etc): cure her ~ a disease/a bad habit; rid a warehouse ~ rats; free ~ customs duty; independent ~ help; short ~ money. **5** (showing material, substance or identity): a dress ~ silk; built ~ brick; an inch ~ rain; your letter ~ 2 June. **6** (description, quality, etc): a girl ~ ten years, ten years old; a case ~ measles; cameras ~ Japanese manufacture; the countries ~ Europe. **7** (in the pattern noun + of + noun): Where's that fool ~ an assistant, that foolish assistant? We had a whale ~ a good time. ⇨ whale(2). **8** (showing objective relation): the writer ~ this letter; loss ~ power/appetite; the fear ~ being killed. **9** (showing subjective relation): the love ~ God, God's love for mankind; with the help ~ my family. **10** (showing connection, reference or belonging): the cause ~ the accident; a topic ~ conversation; the leg ~ the table, the table leg; the opposite ~ what I intended; a Doctor ~ Medicine; be accused/suspected/convicted ~ a crime; What ~ (= about) the risk? **11** (showing sharing, inclusion, measure, selection): a pint ~ milk; one/a few/all ~ us. He's the most dangerous ~ enemies. It surprises me that you, ~ all men (= most or least of all), should be so foolish. **12** (in the pattern noun + of + possessive) from among the number of: a friend ~ mine; a volume ~ Keat's poetry; that foolish young wife ~ yours. **13** (in the pattern adj + of + pronoun/noun): How kind ~ you to help! **14** (showing time): In days ~ old, in the past. of late, recently. **15** by: beloved ~ all.

off¹ /ɔf US: ɔf/ adj **1** (contrasted with near) (of horses, vehicles) on the right-hand side: the ~ front wheel; the `~-side lane of the motorway. **2** (remotely) possible or likely. on the `off chance, ⇨ chance¹(2). **3** inactive; dull: the `~ season.

off² /ɔf US: ɔf/ adverbial particle (For special uses with off as an adverbial particle such as go off; turn sth off, ⇨ the verb entries.) **1** (showing distance in space or time) departure, removal, separation at or to a distance; away: The town is five miles ~. The holidays are not far ~. He's ~ to London. It's time I was ~/I must be ~ now, I must leave now. Take your coat ~. O~ with his head! Cut his head off! **2** (contrasted with on) (showing the ending of something arranged, planned, etc): Their engagement (ie to marry) is (broken) ~, ended. The miners' strike is ~. I've paid ~ the loan. **3** (contrasted with on) disconnected; no longer available: The water/gas/electricity/brake is ~. **4** (showing absence or freedom from work or duty): The manager gave the staff a day ~, a day's holiday. **5** (of food) no longer fresh: This meat/fish is/has gone ~. a bit `off, (sl) (slightly) annoying: It's a bit ~, making me work over the weekend! **6** (in a theatre) behind or at the side(s) of the stage: Noises ~. on and off; off and on, from time to time; now and again; irregularly: It rained on and ~ all day. better/worse off, ⇨ better²(1), worse adv(1). badly/comfortably/well off, ⇨ these adverbs. right/straight off, at once.

off³ /ɔf US: ɔf/ prep **1** not on; down or up from; away from: fall ~ a ladder/a tree/a horse. Keep ~ the grass. Can you take something ~ (ie reduce) the price? She is wearing an ~ the shoulder dress, with no neckline, straps, etc. **2** (of a road or street) extending or branching from: a narrow lane ~ the main road. **3** at some distance from: an island ~ the coast. **4** (informal) not taking or indulging in: I'm ~ my food, have no appetite, don't enjoy it. She's ~ smoking/drugs, does not smoke/take drugs any more. **5** not quite: `~white. (look) off colour, ⇨ colour¹(2). off duty, ⇨ duty. be rushed off one's feet, ⇨ foot¹(1). (go) off one's head, ⇨ head¹(20). off the map, ⇨ map. (wander) off the point, ⇨ point¹(9). off side, ⇨ offside.

off- /ɔf US: ɔf/ prefix (used in numerous compounds) ⇨ the entries below.

of·fal /ˈofəl US: ˈɔfəl/ n [U] those parts of an animal, e g heart, head, kidneys, but not the flesh, used for food.

off-beat /ˈof ˈbit US: ˈɔf/ adj (informal) unusual; unconventional: an ~ boutique.

off-day /ˈof dei US: ˈɔf/ n [C] (informal) day when one is unlucky, when one does things badly; etc: I'm afraid this is one of my ~s.

of·fence (US = **of·fense**) /əˈfens/ n **1** [C] crime, sin, breaking of a rule: an ~ against God/the law/good manners; be charged with a serious ~. **2** [U] the hurting of a person's feelings; condition of being hurt in one's feelings: He is quick to take ~, is easily offended. No ~ meant! (phrase used to say) I did not intend to hurt your feelings. **3** [U] attacking: They say that the most effective defence is ~. **4** [C] that which annoys or causes anger: That dirty house is an ~ to the neighbourhood.

of·fence·less (US = **of·fense-**) adj without, not giving offence.

of·fend /əˈfend/ vi,vt **1** do wrong; commit an offence: ~ against good manners/the law/traditions, etc. **2** hurt the feelings of: I'm sorry if I've ~ed you/if you were ~ed by my remarks. **3** displease; annoy: ugly buildings that ~ the eye.

of·fender, person who offends, esp by breaking a law.

of·fense /ə'fens/ ⇨ offence.

of·fen·sive /ə'fensɪv/ adj **1** causing offence to the mind or senses; disagreeable: *fish with an ~ smell; ~ language.* **2** used for, connected with, attacking: *~ weapons/wars.* ⇨ defensive. □ n [C] attacking; an attitude of attack: *launch an ~ against the enemy.* **take the offensive,** attack.

of·fen·sive·ly adv

of·fen·sive·ness n [U]

of·fer /'ɒfə(r) US: 'ɔːf-/ vt,vi **1** hold out, put forward, to be accepted or refused; say what one is willing to pay, give or exchange: *They ~ed a reward. I have been ~ed a job in Spain. He ~ed to help me. He ~ed me his help.* **2** present (to God): *~ (up) prayers to God.* **3** attempt; give signs of: *~ no resistance to the enemy.* **4** occur; arise: *Take the first opportunity that ~s,* that there is. □ n [C] statement offering to do or give; that which is offered: *an ~ of help. I've had an ~ of £9000 for the house.* **be open to offers,** be willing to consider a price to be named by a buyer.

of·fer·ing /'ɒfərɪŋ US: 'ɔːf-/ n **1** [U] act of offering: *the ~ing of bribes.* **2** [C] something offered or presented, e g the money collected during a church service. **a `peace offering,** something offered in the hope of restoring friendship after a quarrel, etc.

of·fer·tory /'ɒfətrɪ US: -tɔːrɪ/ n [C] (pl -ies) money collected in church during, or at the end of, a service.

off-hand /'ɒf 'hænd US: 'ɔːf/ adj **1** without previous thought or preparation: *~ remarks.* **2** (of behaviour, etc) casual; impolite: *in an ~ way.* □ adv without previous thought or preparation: *I can't say ~ whether I agree.*

of·fice /'ɒfɪs US: 'ɔːf-/ n [C] **1** (often pl room(s) used as a place of business, for clerical work: *a lawyer's/business ~.* ⇨ booking-office, box-office. **2** (buildings of a) government department, including the staff, their work and duties: *the `Foreign O~.* **3** duty, esp in a public position of trust or authority: *Which party will be in ~ after the next general election?* **4** duty: *the ~ of host/chairman.* **5** (pl) attentions, services, help: *through the good ~s (= kind help) of a friend.*

`office-bearer, official, officer.

`office-block, large building containing business offices.

`office-boy, boy employed to do minor jobs.

`office hours, period during the day when a business is active.

`office-worker, employee in a business office.

of·fi·cer /'ɒfɪsə(r) US: 'ɔːf-/ n [C] **1** person appointed to command others in the armed forces, in merchant ships, aircraft, the police force, etc usually wearing special uniform with indications of rank: *~s and men/crew.* **2** person with a position of authority or trust,

engaged in active duties, e g in the government: *executive/clerical ~s; a customs ~.* **3** form of address to a policeman.

of·fi·cial /ə'fɪʃəl/ adj **1** of a position of trust or authority; said, done, etc with authority: *~ responsibilities/records; in his ~ uniform; ~ statements. The news is not ~.* **2** characteristic of, suitable for, persons holding office: *written in ~ style.* □ n [C] person holding public office (e g in national or local government).

of·fi·cial·ly /-ʃəlɪ/ adv in an official manner; with authority.

of·fi·ci·ate /ə'fɪʃɪeɪt/ vi perform the duties of an office or position: *~ as chairman; ~ at a marriage ceremony,* (of a priest) perform the ceremony.

of·fi·cious /ə'fɪʃəs/ adj (formal) too eager or ready to help, offer advice, use authority, etc.

of·fi·cious·ly adv

of·fi·cious·ness n [U]

off·ing /'ɒfɪŋ US: 'ɔːf-/ n **1** [C] part of the sea distant from the point of observation but visible: *a steamer in the ~.* **2 in the offing,** (fig) likely: *promotion is in the ~.*

off·ish /'ɒfɪʃ US: 'ɔːf-/ adj (informal) distant in manner. ⇨ stand-offish.

off-licence /'ɒf laɪsəns US: 'ɔːf/ n [C] **1** licence to sell beer and other alcoholic drinks for consumption off the premises. **2** shop, part of a public house, where such drinks may be bought and taken away.

off-load /'ɒf 'ləʊd US: 'ɔːf/ vt unload: *~ a cargo; ~ shares onto the market.*

off-peak /'ɒf piːk US: 'ɔːf/ adj ⇨ peak¹.

off-putting /'ɒf 'pʊtɪŋ US: 'ɔːf/ adj (informal) disconcerting. ⇨ put off at put¹ (10).

off·set /'ɒfset US: 'ɔːf-/ vt (-tt-) balance, compensate for: *He has to ~ his small salary by freelance work.* □ n [C] method of printing in which the ink is transferred from a plate to a rubber surface and then on to paper.

off·shoot /'ɒfʃuːt US: 'ɔːf-/ n [C] **1** stem or branch growing from a main stem. **2** (fig) branch (of a family, mountain range, etc).

off-shore /'ɒf ʃɔː(r) US: 'ɔːf/ adj **1** in a direction away from the shore or land: *~ breezes.* **2** at a short way out to sea: *~ islands/fisheries.*

off·side /'ɒf 'saɪd US: 'ɔːf/ adj, adv (in football, hockey) (of a player) in a position in front of the ball which is against the rules: *be ~; the ~ rule.*

off·spring /'ɒfsprɪŋ US: 'ɔːf-/ n [C] (pl unchanged) child; children; young of animals: *He is the ~ of a scientist and a ballet dancer.*

off-white /'ɒf 'waɪt US: 'ɔːf 'hwaɪt/ adj not pure white, with a pale greyish or yellowish tinge.

oft /ɒft US: ɔːft/ adv (poetry) = often: *many a time and ~,* very often.

`oft-times adv (archaic) = often.

of·ten /ˈɒftən, ˈɒfən US: ˈɔːfən/ adv of frequency (more ~, most ~ is more usual than -er, -est). many times; in a large number of instances: We ~ go there. We've been there quite ~. **as often as not; more often than not,** very frequently: During foggy weather the trains are late more ~ than not. **every so often,** from time to time. **how often:** How ~ do the buses run? **once too often,** once more than is wise, safe, etc: You've let me down once too ~ and I shall not trust you again..

ogle /ˈəʊgəl/ vi,vt stare at; make eyes at (suggesting love or longing): ogling all the pretty girls.

ogre /ˈəʊgə(r)/ n [C] (in fables) cruel man-eating giant.

ogress /ˈəʊgres/, female ogre.

oh /əʊ/ int exclamation of surprise, fear, etc.

ohm /əʊm/ n [C] (symbol Ω) unit of electrical resistance.

oho /əʊˈhəʊ/ int exclamation of surprise or triumph.

oil /ɔɪl/ n [C,U] **1** (sorts of) liquid which does not mix with water, obtained from animals (e g ˈcod-liver ˈoil) plants (e g ˈolive-ˈoil), or found in rock underground (mineral oil, petroleum). **burn the midnight oil,** sit up late at night to study, etc. **paint in oils,** paint with oil colours (⇨ below). **strike oil, (a)** find petroleum in the ground. **(b)** (fig) become very prosperous or successful. **2** (pl) oil colours. □ vt put oil on or into (e g to make a machine run smoothly).

`oil-bearing adj (e g of rock) containing mineral oil.

`oil-can, can with a long nozzle, used for oiling machinery.

`oil-cloth, waterproofed cotton material.

`oil colours n pl paints made by mixing colouring matter in oil.

`oil-field, area where petroleum is found.

`oil-fired adj burning oil as fuel: oil-fired central heating.

`oil-painting, (a) [U] art of painting in oil colours. (b) [C] picture painted in oil colours.

`oil-rig, structure for drilling (e g in the seabed) for oil.

`oil-skin, (a) [C,U] (coat etc, made of) cloth treated with oil to make it waterproof. (b) (pl) suit of clothes made of this material, as worn by sailors, etc.

`oil slick, film of oil covering the sea, etc (e g from an oil-tanker after a collision).

`oil-tanker, ship, large vehicle, for carrying oil (esp petroleum).

`oil-well, well from which petroleum is obtained.

oiled /ɔɪld/ adj (usually well-oiled) (sl) intoxicated.

oily /ˈɔɪlɪ/ adj (-ier, -iest) **1** of or like oil: an ~ liquid. **2** covered or soaked with oil: ~ fingers. **3** (of speech or manner) fawning, flattering (to win favour).

oint·ment /ˈɔɪntmənt/ n [C,U] (sorts of) medicinal paste made from oil or fat and used on the skin (to heal injuries or roughness, or as a cosmetic).

okay /ˈəʊˈkeɪ/ adj, adv (common abbr **O K**) (informal) all right; correct; approved. □ vt agree to; approve of. □ n [C] agreement; sanction: Have they given you their O K?

okra /ˈəʊkrə/ n [C] (tropical and semi-tropical plant with) edible green seed pods used as a vegetable.

old /əʊld/ adj (-er, -est) ⇨ also elder [1], eldest. **1** (with a period of time, and with how) of age: He's forty years ~/a forty-year-~. How ~ are you? He's ~ enough to know better. **2** (contrasted with young) having lived a long time; no longer young or middle-aged: He's far too ~ for the job. What will he do when he grows/is/gets ~? **(the) young and old,** everyone. **3** (contrasted with new, modern, up-to-date) belonging to past times; having been in existence or use for a long time: ~ clothes; ~ customs/families/civilizations/times. **one of the old school,** conservative; old-fashioned. **4** long known or familiar: an ~ friend of mine, one who has been a friend for a long time (but not necessarily old in years). **5** former; previous (but not necessarily old in years): ~ boys, former pupils. **6** having much experience or practice: He's an ~ supporter of the club/member of the committee. **7** (informal) (used in addressing persons): 'Good ~ John!' 'Hullo, ~ thing!' **8** (informal) (used to intensify): Any ~ thing (= Anything whatever) will do. □ n [U] **1** the ~, old people. **2** of old, in, from, the past: in days of ~; the men of ~.

`old-ish /-ɪʃ/ adj rather old.

old age, period of life from about 60 years: ~ age ˈpensioner, = senior citizen.

`old country, person's country of origin.

`old-ˈfashioned (a) out-of-date. (b) keeping to older ways, etc: an ~-fashioned child. (c) critical: an ~-fashioned look.

the old guard, faithful members, supporters.

old hand, person with long experience: an ~ hand at negotiating.

old hat, (informal) boringly familiar thing or person.

old maid, elderly woman thought unlikely to marry.

old man, (informal) (a) husband; father. (b) employer, headmaster, ship's captain, etc. (c) male friend. ⇨ 4,7 above.

old master, great painter or painting, esp of the 13th to 17th centuries.

Old Nick, the devil.

old offender, person often convicted of crimes.

`old school, (a) the school attended as a pupil. (b) conservative, old-fashioned (person).

old soldier, (fig) experienced person.

old-time *adj* belonging to former times: ~-time dancing.

old-timer, person having a long association with a place, job, group, etc.

old woman, (*informal*) (a) wife; mother. (b) fussy or timid man. Hence, **'old- 'womanish** *adj*.

old-world, *adj* belonging to former times. **the Old World**, Europe, Asia and Africa.

old year, year just ended or about to end.

olden /ˈəʊldən/ *adj* (*literary*) of a former age: times/days.

oleagi-nous /ˌəʊlɪˈædʒɪnəs/ *adj* having properties of oil; producing oil; greasy.

oli-garchy /ˈɒlɪɡɑːkɪ/ *n* [C,U] (*pl* -ies) (country with) government by a small group of powerful persons; such a group.

ol-ive /ˈɒlɪv/ *n* 1 [C] (evergreen tree common in S Europe bearing a) small oval fruit with a hard seed like a stone and a bitter taste, yellowish-green when unripe and bluish-black when ripe; used for pickling, eaten raw or used to make an oil, (`~-`oil), which is used for cooking, in salads, etc. 2 [C] leaf, branch or wreath of olive branches as an emblem of peace. 3 [U] (also as an *adjective*) the colour of the unripe fruit, yellowish-green or yellowish-brown.

Olym-pic /əˈlɪmpɪk/ *adj* **the ~ Games** (*informal* **the ~s**), 1 the contests held at Olympia in Greece in ancient times. 2 the international athletic and sports competitions held in modern times every four years in a different country.

om-buds-man /ˈɒmbʊdzmæn/ *n* [C] **the O~**, (in GB officially called *Parliamentary Commissioner*) experienced person having authority to inquire into and judge grievances of citizens (against the executive branch of Government).

omega /ˈəʊmɪɡə *US:* əʊˈmegə/ *n* [C] 1 the last letter (Ω) of the Greek alphabet. 2 (*fig*) final development; last of a series.

om-elette, (also **om-elet**) /ˈɒmlət/ *n* [C] eggs beaten together and fried, often flavoured with cheese, onion, herbs, etc or jam, sugar.

omen /ˈəʊmen/ *n* [C,U] (thing, happening, regarded as a) sign of something good or warning of evil fortune: *an event of good/bad ~.* □ *vt* be an omen of.

om-in-ous /ˈɒmɪnəs/ *adj* threatening: *an ~ silence; ~ of disaster.*

om-in-ous-ly *adv*

omis-sion /əˈmɪʃən/ *n* 1 [U] act of omitting, leaving out; neglect. 2 [C] something that is omitted.

omit /əˈmɪt/ *vt* (-tt-) 1 fail: *~ to say/~ saying who wrote it.* 2 fail to include; leave out: *This cost may be ~ted from the accounts.*

om-ni-bus /ˈɒmnɪbəs/ *n* [C] (*pl* ~es) 1 (former name for a) bus (sometimes used in names): *The 'Midland `O~ Co.* 2 (as an *adjective*) for, including, many purposes: *an ~ volume,* in which a number of books, e g

by the same author, are reprinted.

om-nip-otence /ɒmˈnɪpətəns/ *n* [U] infinite power: *the ~ of God.*

om-nip-otent /-ənt/ *adj* having infinite power. **the O~,** God.

on[1] /ɒn/ *adverbial particle* (For special uses with *on* as an *adverbial particle* such as *go on; go on sth,* ⇨ the *verb* entries.) 1 (expressing the idea of progress, advance, continued activity; ⇨ *verb* entries for special uses): *Come ~! I'll follow ~,* come after you. *He's getting ~ in years,* growing old. *~ with the show!* Let the show begin/continue! **and `so on,** ⇨ so[2](6). **later on,** ⇨ late[2](1). **'on and `on,** without stopping: *We walked ~ and ~.* **off and on,** ⇨ off[2]. 2 (corresponding in meaning to on[2](1): *Your hat is not ~ straight. He climbed ~ to the table.* **have nothing on,** be naked. ⇨ 4 below. 3 (contrasted with off[2](3)) in action; in use; available; functioning; flowing, running, etc: *The lights were all ~. Someone has left the bathroom tap ~,* running. *The film is ~,* has begun. *Is the strike ~? Is the hot water ~ yet?* 4 (combined with *be* and *have* in various meanings): *What's ~?* What's the programme/happening? *Have you anything ~ this evening,* any engagements, plans, etc? *I've nothing ~ until 9 o'clock.* **be `on to,** (a) be aware of a person's intentions activities, etc. (b) be aware of the importance, etc of something. 5 towards: *end/head ~,* i e with the end/front forward.

on[2] /ɒn/ *prep* 1 supported by; fastened or attached to; covering or forming part of (a surface); lying against; in contact with: *a carpet ~ the floor; the jug ~ the table; the words (written) ~ the poster; sit ~ the grass; write ~ paper; stick a stamp ~ the envelope; live ~ the Continent; have lunch ~ the train. Have you a match/any money ~ you,* i e in your pockets, etc? 2 (of time) (a) during; exactly at: *~ Sunday(s)/the 1st of May; ~ that day; ~ this occasion.* (b) at the time of: *~ my arrival home; ~ (my) asking for information.* **on time,** punctual(ly). 3 about; concerning: *a lecture ~ Shakespeare.* 4 (of membership): *He is ~ the committee/the jury/the staff.* 5 (of direction) towards: *marching ~ the enemy's capital; turn one's back ~ her.* 6 (expressing the basis, ground or reason for something): *a story based ~ fact; act ~ your lawyer's advice; arrested ~ a charge of theft; be ~ one's oath/one's honour.* 7 (of a charge or imposition): *put a tax ~ tobacco.* 8 close to; against: *a town ~ the coast; ~ both sides of the river; ~ my right/left; just ~ (= almost) 2 o'clock/£10.* 9 (concerning, about, affecting) an activity, action, manner, state): *~ business/holiday; ~ the way; ~ fire,* burning; *~ sale/loan.* 10 added to: *suffer disaster ~ disaster.*

once /wʌns/ *adv* 1 for one time, on one

occasion, only: *I have been there* ~. *He goes to see his parents* ~ (*in*) *every six months.* **once more,** again; another time. **once or twice; (every) once in a while,** occasionally; a few times. *(just) for once,* on this one occasion only, as an exception. **'once and for `all,** ⇨ all ⁵(5). **5.** 2 at some indefinite time in the past; formerly. (**a**) *He* ~ *lived in Munich.* (**b**) (in story-telling style): *O*~ *upon a time there was a giant with two heads. There* ~ *lived a king who had twelve beautiful daughters.* **3** ever; at all; even for one time: *He didn't* ~/*He never* ~ *offered to help.* **4 at once,** (**a**) without delay; immediately: *I'm leaving for Rome at* ~. *Come here at* ~! (**b**) at the same time: *Don't all speak at* ~! *I can't do two things at* ~. □ *conj* as soon as; when: *O*~ *you understand this rule, you will have no further difficulty.*

on·com·ing /ˈɒnˈkʌmɪŋ/ *adj* advancing; approaching: ~ *traffic.* □ *n* [C] approach: *the* ~ *of winter.*

one ¹ /wʌn/ *adj, n* [C] **1** (of) 1: ~ *pen, two pencils and three books;* ~ *from twenty leaves nineteen;* ~ *o'clock;* '*twenty-*'~ ~ *thousand;* ~ *half.* **one and all,** everyone. **one or two,** a few: *I shall be away only* ~ *or two days.* **by ones and twos,** one or two at a time: *People began to leave the meeting by* ~*s and twos.* **be one up (on sb),** have an advantage over him, be one step ahead of him. **2** (similar in function to *a* and *an*): ~ *day/morning.* (*Note:* Compare *one summer evening* and *on a summer evening.*) **3** (used to show a contrast with *the other,* *another* or *other(s)*): *It is difficult for strangers to tell (the)* ~ *from the other. Well, that's* ~ *way of doing it, but there is another way. He did not know which to admire more, the* ~*'s courage or the other's determination.* **for** `**one thing,** for one reason (out of several or many): *I can't help you. For* ~ *thing, I've no money.* **4** (always stressed; used for emphasis): *That's the* '~ *thing needed.* **5** (*dated*) (used before a family name, with or without a title) a certain: *I heard the news from* ~ *Mr Smith.* **6** (used as an *adjective*) the same: *They all went off in* ~ *direction.* **in one,** combined: *He is President, Chairman and Secretary in* ~. **7 one of...,** single person or thing of the sort indicated: or supplied: *O*~ *of my friends* (*pl Some* of my friends) *arrived late. If* ~ *of them* (*pl any* of them) *should need help...; I borrowed* ~ *of your books* (= a book of yours; *pl some* of your books) *last week.*

'one-`sided *adj* (**a**) having one side only; occurring on one side only. (**b**) unfair; prejudiced: *a* ~*-sided argument.*

`one-time *adj* former: *a* ~*-time politician.*

`one-way, in which traffic may proceed in one direction only: *a* ~*-way street.*

one ² /wʌn/ *indefinite pron* (used in place of a *noun* standing for a member of a class) **1 one of,** (showing inclusion; equivalent to

among): *Mr Smith is not* ~ *my customers. We have always treated her as* ~ (= as a member) *of the family.* **2** (replacing a noun used with *a, an; any, some*): *I haven't a pen. Can you lend me* ~? *I haven't any stamps. Will you please give me* ~? Compare: *I like that pen. Can I borrow it?* **3** (equivalent to *that, those*): *I drew my chair nearer to the* ~ (= to that) *on which Mary was sitting. The children who do best in examinations are not always the ones* (= those) *with the best brains.* **4** (used after *the, that, etc* or after an *adjective* as in): *a better* ~; *that* ~. *He collects stamps and he has some very rare* ~*s. My cheap camera seems to be just as good as John's expensive* ~. **this/that one:** *Will you have this* (~) *or that* (~)? (*Note: pl* = Will you have these or those? With an *adjective 'one'* is, of course, necessary: *Will you have this green one/these green* ~*s?*) **which one:** *Here are some books on European history. Which* ~(ṣ) *do you want?*

one ³ /wʌn/ *personal pron* **1** a particular person or creature: *the* `*Holy O*~, God; *the* `*Evil O*~, Satan, the Devil; *the little* ~*s,* the children. *He's not* ~ *to be* (= not a man who is) *easily frightened.* **2 one another('s),** (used, like *each other,* to show mutual action or relation): *They don't like* ~ *another. They were throwing stones and trying to break* ~ *another's heads.*

one ⁴ /wʌn/ *impersonal pron* (*possessive* = one's; *reflexive* = oneself) any person, including the speaker or writer: *O*~ *cannot always find time for reading. O*~ *doesn't like to have* ~*'s word doubted.*

on·er·ous /ˈɒnərəs/ *adj* (*formal*) needing effort; burdensome (*to*): ~ *duties.*

on·er·ous·ly *adv*

one·self /wʌnˈself/ *pron* **1** (reflexive) one's own self: *wash/dress* ~. **(all) by oneself,** (**a**) alone. (**b**) without help. **2** (used for emphasis): *To be really sure one ought to look at it* ~.

on·go·ing /ˈɒnˈɡəʊɪŋ/ *adj* progressing; continuing: ~ *research.*

onion /ˈʌnɪən/ *n* [C] vegetable plant which is a (usually) round bulb with a strong smell and flavour, used in cooking and pickled; [U] this plant as food.

on·looker /ˈɒnlʊkə(r)/ *n* [C] person who looks on at something happening.

only ¹ /ˈəʊnlɪ/ *adj* **1** (used with a *sing noun*) that is the one specimen of its class; single: *Smith was the* ~ *person able to do it. Harry is an* ~ *child,* has no brothers or sisters. **2** (used with a *pl noun*) that are all the specimens or examples: *We were the* ~ *people wearing hats.* **3** best; most worth consideration: *He's the* ~ *man for me.*

only ² /ˈəʊnlɪ/ *adv* solely; and no, no one, nothing, more: *I'* ~ *saw* `*Mary,* I saw Mary and no one else. Compare: *I'* ~ `*saw Mary,* I saw her but didn't speak to her. *We've* ~

half an hour to wait now. **if only,** ⇨ if(8).
only too, (+ *adj* or *pp*) very: *I shall be ~ too pleased to get home.*

only³ /ˈəʊnlɪ/ *conj* but then; it must, however, be added that: *The book is likely to be useful, ~ it's rather expensive.*

ono·mato·poeia /əˈnɒmətəˈpɪə *US:* ˈɒnəˈmætəˈpɪə/ *n* [U] (formation of) words or names from sounds of the thing concerned (e g *cuckoo* for the bird that utters this cry).

on·rush /ˈɒnrʌʃ/ *n* [C] strong, onward rush or flow.

on·set /ˈɒnset/ *n* [C] attack; vigorous start: *at the first ~ of the disease.*

on·shore /ˈɒnʃɔː(r)/ *adj, adv* toward the shore.

on·slaught /ˈɒnslɔt/ *n* [C] furious attack (*on*).

onto /ˈɒntə *strong form:* ˈɒntu/ *prep* = on; on to; upon. ⇨ on¹ (2).

onus /ˈəʊnəs/ *n* (*sing* only) responsibility for, duty of, doing something: *The ~ of proof rests with you.*

on·ward /ˈɒnwəd/ *adj, adv* forward: *an ~ march/movement.* □ *adv* (also **on·wards**) towards the front; forward: *move ~(s).*

onyx /ˈɒnɪks/ *n* [U] (sorts of) quartz in layers of different colours, used for ornaments, in jewellery, etc.

oodles /ˈuːdəlz/ *n pl* (*sl*) great amounts: *~ of money.*

ooze /uːz/ *n* [U] soft liquid mud, esp on a river-bed, the bottom of a pond, lake, etc. □ *vi,vt* **1** (of moisture, thick liquids) pass slowly through small openings: *Blood was still oozing from the wound.* **2** emit (moisture, confidence, etc): *He was oozing sweat.* **3** (*fig*) slowly go away: *Their courage was oozing away.*

opac·ity /əʊˈpæsətɪ/ *n* [U] (quality of) being opaque.

opal /ˈəʊpəl/ *n* [C] semi-precious stone some of which slowly change colour.

opaque /əʊˈpeɪk/ *adj* not allowing light to pass through; that cannot be seen through.
opaque·ly *adv*
opaque·ness *n* [U]

op art /ˈɒp ɑːt/ *n* [U] form of modern abstract art using geometrical patterns which produce optical illusions of movement.

open¹ /ˈəʊpən/ *adj* **1** not closed; allowing (things, persons) to go in, out, through: *sleep with ~ windows; leave the door ~.* **2** not enclosed, fenced in, barred or blocked: *~ country; the ~ sea.* **3** not covered in or over: *an ~ boat,* one without a deck; *an ~ carriage/car,* with no roof, or a roof that is folded back. *in the open air,* outside (a building, etc). **4** spread out; unfolded: *The flowers were all ~. The book lay ~ on the table. with open arms,* with affection or enthusiasm. **5** public; free to all; not limited to any special persons, but for anyone to enter: *an ~ competition/championship/scholarship. The position is still ~,* No one

has yet been chosen to fill it. *keep open house,* offer hospitality to all comers. **6** not settled or decided: *leave a matter ~. have/keep an open mind (on sth),* be ready to consider further, to listen to new evidence, etc. **7** ready for business or for the admission of the public: *Are the shops ~ yet?* **8** known to all; not secret or disguised; frank: *an ~ quarrel/scandal. Let me be quite ~* (= frank) *with you.* **9** unprotected; unguarded; vulnerable: *~ to ridicule/attack.* **10** not settled, finished or closed: *keep one's account ~ at a bank; be ~ to offers,* willing to consider one. □ *n the ~,* the open air. *come out into the open,* (*fig*) come into public view; make one's ideas, plans, etc, known.

ˈopen-air *adj* taking place out of doors; not covered: *an ~-air swimming-pool.* ⇨ 3 above.

ˈopen-cast *adj* (of mines or mining) on the surface.

open cheque, one that is not crossed and may be cashed at the bank named.

open court, one to which the public are admitted.

ˈopen-ˈended *adj* (a) with no limit or boundary. (b) (of a debate, etc) with many possible solutions or where no agreement is expected, reached, etc.

ˈopen-ˈhanded *adj* generous.

ˈopen-ˈhearted *adj* kind, generous.

open market, with free competition for sellers and buyers.

ˈopen-ˈminded *adj* without prejudice.

ˈopen-ˈmouthed *adj* amazed; surprised.

open prison, one with fewer physical restrictions.

open sandwich, single slice of bread, etc with meat, cheese, etc on top.

open season, (fishing and shooting) when there are no restrictions.

open secret, something meant to be secret, but known to all.

open society, without a rigid class structure, religiously free, etc.

Open University, British university (founded in 1971) whose students live at home and are taught by correspondence, textbooks and special radio and TV programmes.

open verdict, jury's agreement that a crime was committed but not naming the criminal, not giving the cause of death, etc.

open vowel, one made with the roof of the mouth and the tongue wide apart, e g /e, æ, ɒ/.

ˈopen-work, work (in lace, metal) with spaces.

open·ly *adv* without secrecy; frankly; publicly: *speak ~ly.*

open·ness *n* [U] frankness.

open² /ˈəʊpən/ *vt,vi* **1** make, cause to be, open; unfasten: *~ a box. O~ up!* Open the door! **2** cut or make an opening in or a passage through: ∼ *a new road through a forest.* O∼ *up!* **3** make accessible; make possible the development of: ∼ *up a mine/undeveloped land/a new territory to trade.* **4** spread out; unfold: ∼ *one's hand/a book/a newspaper/an envelope/a map.* **open one's mind/heart to sb,** make known one's ideas/feelings. **5** start: ∼ *an account,* e g at a bank, shop; ∼ *a debate/a public meeting.* **open fire (at/on),** start shooting. **open with,** start: *The story ∼s with a murder.* **6** declare, show, that business, etc may now start: ∼ *a shop/an office;* ∼ *Parliament.* **7** become open; be opened: *The flowers are ∼ing. The door ∼ed and a man came in.*

opener, person or thing that opens: (used chiefly in compounds): *a `tin-/`bottle-∼er.* ⇨ eye-opener.

open·ing /ˈəʊpnɪŋ/ *n* [C] **1** open space; way in or out: *an ∼ in a hedge.* **2** beginning: *the ∼ of a book/speech.* **3** process of becoming open: *the ∼ of a flower.* **4** position (in a business firm) which is open or vacant; opportunity: *an ∼ in an advertising section.* **5** (in chess) known system of early moves in a game. □ *adj* first: *his ∼ remarks.* **`opening time,** when public houses, bars, etc begin to serve customers.

op·era /ˈɒprə/ *n* (*pl* ∼s) **1** [C] dramatic composition with music, in which the words are sung. **2** [U] dramatic works of this kind as entertainment: *fond of ∼; the ∼ season.*

comic opera, with spoken dialogue and a happy ending.

grand opera, with no spoken dialogue.

light opera, with a humorous subject.

`opera-glasses, small binoculars for use in a theatre.

`opera-house, theatre for operas.

op·er·atic /ɒpəˈrætɪk/ *adj*

op·er·ate /ˈɒpəreɪt/ *vt,vi* **1** (cause to) work, be in action, have an effect; manage: ∼ *a machine. The lift was not operating properly. The company ∼s two factories.* **2** perform a surgical operation: *The doctors decided to ∼ at once.* **3** (of an army) carry out various movements: *operating on a large scale.*

`operating-table/-theatre, for use in surgical operations.

op·er·able /ˈɒpərəbəl/ *adj* that can be treated by means of a surgical operation.

op·er·ation /ɒpəˈreɪʃən/ *n* **1** [U] working; way in which something works: *Is this rule in ∼ yet?* **2** [C] piece of work; something (to be) done. **3** (usu *pl*) movements of troops, ships, aircraft, etc in warfare or during manoeuvres. **4** [C] planned campaigns in industry, etc: *building/banking ∼s.* **5** [C] act performed by a surgeon on any part of the body, esp by cutting to take away or deal with a diseased part: *an ∼ for appendicitis.*

op·er·ational /-nəl/ *adj* **1** of, for, used in, operations. **2** ready for use: *When will the new airliner be ∼al?*

op·er·at·ive /ˈɒprətɪv US: -əreɪt-/ *adj* **1** operating; having an effect: *This law became ∼ on 1 May.* **2** of surgical operations: ∼ *treatment.* □ *n* [C] worker; mechanic: *cotton ∼s.*

op·er·ator /ˈɒpəreɪtə(r)/ *n* [C] **1** person who operates or works something: *telephone ∼s; airline ∼s.* **2** (*sl*) confident, efficient man (in business, love affairs, etc): *He's a smooth ∼.*

op·er·etta /ˈɒpəˈretə/ *n* [C] (*pl* ∼s) one-act, or short, light musical comedy.

oph·thal·mic /ɒfˈθælmɪk/ *adj* of the eyes.

opin·ion /əˈpɪnɪən/ *n* **1** [C] belief or judgement not founded on complete knowledge: *political ∼s. What's your ∼* (= view) *of the new President? In my ∼/In the ∼ of most people, the scheme is unsound.* **be of the opinion that,** feel, believe, that. **2** [U] views, beliefs, of a group: *O∼ is shifting in favour of stiffer penalties for armed robbery.* **3** [C] professional estimate or advice: *get a lawyer's ∼ on the question.*

opin·ion·ated /-eɪtɪd/ *adj* obstinate; dogmatic.

public opinion, what the majority of people think: *Public ∼ is against the proposed change.*

o`pinion poll, survey of public opinion by questioning a section of the community.

opium /ˈəʊpɪəm/ *n* [U] substance prepared from poppy seeds, used to relieve pain, cause sleep, and as a narcotic drug.

opos·sum /əˈposəm/ (also **pos·sum** /ˈposəm/) *n* [C] kinds of small American animal that lives in trees.

op·po·nent /əˈpəʊnənt/ *n* [C] person against whom one fights, struggles, plays games or argues.

op·por·tune /ˈopətjuːn US: -tuːn/ *adj* (*formal*) **1** (of time) suitable, favourable; good for a purpose: *arrive at an ∼ moment.* **2** (of an action or event) done, coming, at a favourable time: *an ∼ remark/speech.*

op·por·tune·ly *adv*

op·por·tun·ism /ˈopəˈtjuːnɪzm US: -ˈtuːn-/ *n* [U] being guided by what seems possible, preferring what can be done to what should be done.

op·por·tun·ist /ˈopətjuːnɪst/ *n* [C] **1** believer in opportunism. **2** person who is more anxious to gain an advantage for himself than to consider whether he is trying to get it fairly.

op·por·tun·ity /ˈopəˈtjuːnɪt US: -ˈtuːn-/ *n* [C,U] (*pl* -ies) favourable time or chance: *to make/find/get an ∼; have no/little/not much ∼ for hearing good music.* **take the opportunity of doing/to do sth,** make use of a favourable moment to act.

op·pose /əˈpəʊz/ *vt* **1** place oneself, fight, against: ∼ *the Government/a scheme.* **2** put forward as a contrast or opposite; set up against: ∼ *your will against mine/your views to mine.* **as opposed to,** in contrast with.

op·po·site /'opəzɪt/ *adj* **1** facing; front to front or back to back (with): *the house* ~ *(to) mine; on the* ~ *side of the road.* **2** entirely different; contrary: *in the* ~ *direction.* **3** similarly placed elsewhere. **one's opposite number,** person or thing occupying the same or a similar position in another group, etc. □ *prep* facing: *stop* ~ *the house.* □ *n* [C] word or thing that is entirely different: *Black and white are* ~s. *I think the* ~.

op·po·si·tion /ˌopə'zɪʃən/ *n* **1** [U] the state of being opposite or opposed: *The Socialist Party was in* ~. **2 the O**~, (*sing*) M P's of the political party or parties opposing the Government: *the leader of the O*~; *the O*~ *benches.* **3** [U] resistance: *Our forces met with strong* ~.

op·press /ə'pres/ *vt* **1** rule unjustly or cruelly; keep down by unjust or cruel government. **2** (*fig*) cause to feel troubled, uncomfortable: ~ed *with anxiety; feel* ~ed *with the heat.*

op·pres·sion /ə'preʃən/ *n* (**a**) [U] the condition of being oppressed: *a feeling of* ~ion. (**b**) [U] oppressing or being oppressed: *victims of* ~ion; [C] instance of this.

op·pres·sive /ə'presɪv/ *adj* (**a**) unjust: ~ive *laws/rules.* (**b**) hard to endure: ~ive *weather/heat/taxes.*

op·pres·sive·ly *adv*

op·pres·sor /-sə(r)/, cruel or unjust ruler, leader, etc.

opt /opt/ *vi* exercise a choice; decide: *Fewer students are* ~ing *for science courses nowadays.* **opt out of,** choose to take no part in: *young people who have* ~ed *out of society,* chosen not to be conventional members of society.

op·tic /'optɪk/ *adj* of the eye or the sense of sight.

optic nerve, from the eye to the brain.

op·tics *n* (used with a *sing verb*) science of light and the laws of light.

op·ti·cal /'optɪkəl/ *adj* **1** of the sense of sight. **2** for looking through; to help eyesight.

optical illusion, something by which the eye is deceived: *A mirage is an* ~ *illusion.*

optical instrument, e g a microscope, telescope.

op·ti·cal·ly /-klɪ/ *adv*

op·ti·cian /op'tɪʃən/ *n* [C] person who makes or supplies optical instruments, esp lenses and spectacles.

op·ti·mism /'optɪmɪzm/ *n* [U] **1** belief that in the end good will triumph over evil. **2** tendency to feel confidence in success.

op·ti·mist /-mɪst/, person who believes that all things happen for the best.

op·ti·mis·tic /ˌoptɪ'mɪstɪk/ *adj* expecting the best; confident: *an optimistic view of events.*

op·ti·mis·ti·cally /-klɪ/ *adv*

op·ti·mum /'optɪməm/ *adj* best or most favourable: *the* ~ *temperature for the growth of plants.*

op·tion /'opʃən/ *n* **1** [U] right or power of choosing: *I haven't much* ~ *in the matter,* cannot choose. **2** [C] thing that is or may be chosen: *None of the* ~s *is satisfactory.* **leave one's options `open,** not commit oneself. **3** [C] (*commerce*) right to buy or sell at a certain price within a certain period of time: *have an* ~ *on a piece of land.*

op·tional /'opʃənəl/ *adj* which may be chosen or not as one wishes; not compulsory: ~ *subjects at school.*

opus /'əʊpəs/ *n* [C] (*pl* opera /'opərə/, rarely used) separate musical composition (abbr **op,** used in citing a composition by number, as *Beethoven, Op 112*).

'magnum 'opus, great literary undertaking, completed or in course of being written.

-or /-ə(r)/ *suffix* person or thing performing the action: *governor; actor.*

or /ɔ(r)/ *conj* **1** (introducing an alternative): *Is it green* ~ *blue? Are you coming* ~ *not?* **either... or,** ⇨ either. **or (else),** otherwise; if not: *Hurry up* ~ *(else) you'll be late.* **2** (introducing all but the first of a series): *I'd like it to be black,* (~) *white* ~ *grey.* **3** (introducing a word that explains, ~ means the same as, another): *an English pound,* ~ *one hundred new pence.* **4 or so,** (often equivalent to *about*) suggesting vagueness or uncertainty: *I'd like twenty* ~ *so.*

or·acle /'orəkəl *US:* 'ɔr-/ *n* [C] **1** (in ancient Greece) (answer given at a) place where questions about the future were asked of the gods; priest(ess) giving the answers: *consult the* ~. **2** person considered able to give reliable guidance.

oracu·lar /ə'rækjʊlə(r)/ *adj*

oral /'ɔrəl/ *adj* **1** using the spoken, not the written, word: *an* ~ *examination.* **2** (*anat*) of, by, for, the mouth: ~ *medicine.* □ *n* [C] (*informal*) oral examination.

orally /'ɔrəlɪ/ *adv* by spoken words; by the mouth.

or·ange /'orɪndʒ *US:* 'ɔr-/ *n, adj* [C] (evergreen tree with a) round, thick-skinned juicy fruit, green and usually changing to a colour between yellow and red; [U] colour of this fully-ripened fruit.

orange·ade /'orɪndʒ'eɪd *US:* 'ɔr-/, drink made of orange juice.

orang-outang /ɔ'ræŋ u'tæŋ *US:* ə'ræŋ ə'tæŋ/ (also **-utan, -outan** /-'tæn/) *n* [C] large ape with long arms of Borneo and Sumatra.

orate /ə'reɪt/ *vi* (*formal*) speak publicly.

ora·tion /ɔ'reɪʃən/ *n* **1** [C] formal speech made on a public occasion: *a funeral* ~. **2** [U] (*gram*) way of speaking: *direct/indirect* ~, direct/reported speech.

ora·tor /'orətə(r) *US:* 'ɔr-/ *n* [C] person who makes speeches (esp a good speaker).

ora·tori·cal /ˌorə'torɪkəl *US:* 'ɔrə-'tɔr-/ *adj* of speech-making and orators.

ora·tory[1] /'orətrɪ *US:* 'ɔrətɔrɪ/ *n* [U] (art of) making speeches.

ora·tory² /ˈɒrətrɪ US: ˈɔrətɔrɪ/ n [C] (pl -ies) small chapel for private worship or prayer.

orb /ɔb/ n [C] **1** globe, esp the sun, moon or one of the stars. **2** jewelled globe with a cross on top, part of a sovereign's regalia.

or·bit /ˈɔbɪt/ n [C] path followed by a heavenly body, e g a planet, or a man-made object, e g a spacecraft, round another body: *the earth's* ∼ *round the sun. How many satellites have been put in* ∼ *round the earth?* □ *vt,vi* put into, (cause to) move, in orbit: *When was the first satellite* ∼*ed?*
or·bi·tal /ˈɔbɪtəl/ adj

or·chard /ˈɔtʃəd/ n [C] piece of ground (usually enclosed) with fruit-trees.

or·ches·tra /ˈɔkɪstrə/ n [C] (pl ∼s) **1** band of persons playing musical instruments (including stringed instruments) together: *a* `dance ∼; *a* `symphony ∼. **2** (also `∼ *pit*) place in a theatre for an orchestra.
or·ches·tral /ɔˈkestrəl/ adj of, for, by, an orchestra: ∼ *instruments/performances.*

or·ches·trate /ˈɔkɪstreɪt/ vt compose, arrange, score, for orchestral performances.
or·ches·tra·tion /ˌɔkɪˈstreɪʃən/ n [C,U]

or·chid /ˈɔkɪd/ n [C] sorts of plant of which the tropical kinds have flowers of brilliant colours and fantastic shapes.

or·dain /ɔˈdeɪn/ vt **1** make (a person) a priest or minister: *He was* ∼*ed priest.* **2** (of God, law, authority) decide; give orders (*that*): *God has* ∼*ed that all men shall die.*

or·deal /ɔˈdil/ n **1** [U] (in former times) method of deciding a person's guilt or innocence by a physical test, such as passing through fire unharmed or fighting his accuser: *trial by* ∼; ∼ *by fire.* **2** [C] any severe test of character or endurance: *pass through terrible* ∼*s.*

or·der¹ /ˈɔdə(r)/ n **1** [U] way in which things are placed in relation to one another: *put names in alphabetical* ∼. **in order of,** arranged according to: *in* ∼ *of size/ importance.* **2** [U] condition in which everything is carefully arranged; working condition. **(not) in order,** (not) as it should be: *Is your passport in* ∼, Is it valid? **in good/ bad, etc running/working order,** (esp of machines) working well/badly: *The engine has been tuned and is now in perfect running* ∼. **out of order,** (of a machine, etc) not functioning properly: *The lift/phone is out of* ∼. **3** [U] (condition brought about by) good and firm government, obedience to law, rules, authority: *It is the business of the police to keep* ∼. ⇨ disorder. **law and order,** ⇨ law(3). **4** [U] rules usual at a public meeting; rules accepted, e g in Parliament, committee meetings, by members and enforced by a president, chairman, or other officer: *Is it in* ∼ *to interrupt?* **on a point of order,** on a point (= question) of procedure. **5** [C] command given with authority: *Soldiers must obey* ∼*s.* **by order of,** according

to directions given by proper authority of: *by* ∼ *of the Governor.* **under starters' orders,** ⇨ starter. **6** [C] request to supply goods; the goods (to be) supplied: *an* ∼ *worth £50.* **on order,** requested but not yet supplied. **7** [C] written instruction (esp to a bank or post office) to pay money, or giving authority: *a* `postal ∼ *for thirty new pence.* **8** [U] purpose, intention. **in order to do sth,** with the purpose of, with a view to, doing something: *in* ∼ *(for you) to see clearly.* **in order that,** with the intention that; so that: *in* ∼ *that he can be here in time.* **9** [C] rank or class in society: *the* ∼ *of knights/baronets.* **10** [C] group of people belonging to or appointed to a special class (as an honour or reward): *the O*∼ *of Merit/of the Bath.* **11** [C] badge, sign, etc worn by members of an order(10): *wearing all his* ∼*s and decorations.* **12** (*pl*) authority given by a bishop to perform church duties. **be in/take (holy) orders,** be/become a priest. **13** [C] class of persons on whom holy orders have been conferred: *the O*∼ *of Deacons/Priests/Bishops.* **14** [C] group of persons living under religious rules, esp a brotherhood of monks: *the monastic* ∼*s.* **15** [C] style of architectural forms, esp of columns (pillars) and capitals, esp the classical orders (*Doric, Ionic, Corinthian,* etc). **16** [C] (*biol*) highest division in the grouping of animals, plants, etc: *The rose and the bean families belong to the same* ∼. **17** [C] kind; sort: *intellectual ability of a high* ∼. **18** [C] arrangement of military forces: *in open/close* ∼, with wide/with only slight spaces between the men, etc.

or·der² /ˈɔdə(r)/ vt **1** give an order(5,6,7): *The doctor* ∼*ed me to (stay in) bed. The judge* ∼*ed that the prisoner should be remanded. I've* ∼*ed lunch for 1.30.* **order sb about,** keep on telling him to do things. **2** arrange; direct: ∼ *one's life according to strict rules.*
or·der·ing, (from 2 above) arrangement: *the* ∼*ing of words in an index.*

or·der·ly /ˈɔdəlɪ/ adj **1** well arranged; in good order; tidy: *an* ∼ *room/desk.* **2** methodical: *a man with an* ∼ *mind.* **3** well behaved; obedient to discipline: *an* ∼ *crowd.* □ n [C] (pl -ies) (army) officer's messenger; attendant in a (military) hospital.
or·der·li·ness n [U]

or·di·nal /ˈɔdɪnəl US: -dənəl/ adj, n [C] (number) showing order or position in a series: *first, second, third.* ⇨ cardinal.

or·di·nance /ˈɔdɪnəns/ n [C] order, rule, statute, made by authority or decree: *the* ∼*s of the City Council.*

or·di·nary /ˈɔdənrɪ US: ˈɔdənerɪ/ adj normal; usual; average: *an* ∼ *day's work; in* ∼ *dress.* **in the ordinary way,** in the usual or customary way.
or·di·nar·ily /ˈɔdənərəlɪ US: ˈɔdənerəlɪ/ adv in the usual or normal way: *behave quite ordinarily.*

or·di·na·tion /ˌɔːdɪˈneɪʃən US: -dənˈeɪʃən/ n [U] ceremony of ordaining (a priest or minister); [C] instance of this.

ord·nance /ˈɔːdnəns/ n [U] artillery; munitions.

'Ord·nance 'Sur·vey, (the preparation of) accurate and detailed maps of Britain and Ireland.

ore /ɔː(r)/ n [C,U] (kinds of) rock, earth, mineral, etc from which metal can be mined or extracted: iron ~.

or·gan[1] /ˈɔːgən/ n [C] 1 any part of an animal body or plant serving an essential purpose: the ~s of speech, the tongue, teeth, lips, etc; the reproductive ~s. 2 means of getting work done; organization: Parliament is the chief ~ of government. 3 means for making known what people think: ~s of public opinion, newspapers, radios, TV, etc.

or·gan[2] /ˈɔːgən/ musical instrument from which sounds are produced by air forced through pipes, played by keys pressed with the fingers and pedals pressed with the feet.

'or·gan·ist /-ɪst/, person who plays an organ.

or·gan·ic /ɔːˈgænɪk/ adj 1 of an organ or organs of the body: ~ diseases. 2 (opposite = inorganic) having bodily organs: ~ life. 3 made of related parts; arranged as a system: an ~ (i e organized) structure.

or·gan·i·cally /-klɪ/ adv

or·gan·ism /ˈɔːgənɪzm/ n [C] 1 living being (plant or animal) with parts which work together. 2 any system with parts dependent upon each other: the social ~.

or·gan·i·za·tion /ˌɔːgənaɪˈzeɪʃən US: -nɪˈz-/ n 1 [U] act of organizing; condition of being organized: He is engaged in the ~ of a new club. 2 [C] organized body of persons; organized system: The human body has a very complex ~.

or·gan·ize /ˈɔːgənaɪz/ vt put into working order; arrange in a system; make preparations for: ~ an army/a government/a trade union/one's work/oneself.

or·gan·ized adj 1 furnished with organs; made into a living organism: highly ~d forms of life. 2 (of a business, etc) with a recognized trade union representation.

or·gan·izer, person who organizes things.

or·gi·as·tic /ˌɔːdʒɪˈæstɪk/ adj of the nature of an orgy.

orgy /ˈɔːdʒɪ/ n [C] (pl -ies) 1 occasion of wild merry-making. 2 (pl) drunken or immoral revels. 3 (informal) succession of innocent, pleasant activities: an ~ of concerts/spending.

orient[1] /ˈɔːrɪənt/ n the O~, (poetical name for) countries east of the Mediterranean, esp the Far East. □ adj (poetic) Eastern; (of the sun) rising: the ~ sun.

orient[2] /ˈɔːrɪənt/ vt (US) = orientate.

orien·tal /ˌɔːrɪˈentəl/ adj of the Orient: ~ civilization/art/rugs. □ n [C] O~, inhabitant of the Orient, esp China and Japan.

orien·tate /ˈɔːrɪənteɪt/ (US = orient) vt 1 place (a building, etc) so as to face east; build (a church) with the chancel end facing east. 2 place or exactly determine the position of (something) with regard to the points of the compass. 3 (fig) bring into clearly understood relations: ~ oneself, make oneself familiar with a situation, one's surroundings, etc.

orien·ta·tion /ˌɔːrɪənˈteɪʃən/ n [U]

ori·fice /ˈɔːrɪfɪs US: ˈɔːr-/ n [C] outer opening; mouth (of a cave, etc).

ori·gin /ˈɔːrədʒɪn US: ˈɔːrədʒɪn/ n [C,U] starting-point: the ~ of a quarrel; the ~(s) of civilization; words of Latin ~.

orig·inal /əˈrɪdʒənəl/ adj 1 first or earliest: the ~ inhabitants of the country. 2 newly created; not copied or imitated: an ~ design. 3 able to produce new ideas, etc: an ~ thinker/mind. □ n 1 [C] original(2) thing: This is a copy; the ~ is in Madrid. 2 (sing with the) language in which something was first written: study Don Quixote in the ~, in Spanish.

o'riginal 'sin, tendency to commit sin which, some Christians believe, is inherited.

orig·in·ally /-nəlɪ/ adv (a) in an original (2) manner: write ~ly. (b) from or in the beginning: The school was ~ly quite small.

orig·in·al·ity /əˌrɪdʒəˈnælətɪ/ n [U] state or quality of being original(2): work that lacks ~ity.

orig·in·ate /əˈrɪdʒɪneɪt/ vi,vt 1 have as a cause or beginning: With whom did the scheme ~? 2 be the author or creator of: ~ a new style of dancing.

orig·in·ator /-tə(r)/, person who originates something.

or·na·ment /ˈɔːnəmənt/ n 1 [U] adorning or being adorned; that which is added for decoration: embroider by way of ~. 2 [C] something designed or used to add beauty or to decorate: a shelf crowded with ~, e g pieces of china. 3 [C] person, act, quality, etc that adds beauty, charm, etc: He is an ~ to his profession. □ vt /ˈɔːnəment/ decorate; make beautiful: ~ a dress with lace.

or·na·men·tal /ˌɔːnəˈmentəl/ adj decorative.

or·nate /ɔːˈneɪt/ adj 1 richly ornamented. 2 (of literary style) not simple in style or vocabulary.

or·nate·ly adv

or·nate·ness n [U]

or·ni·tho·logi·cal /ˌɔːnɪθəˈlɒdʒɪkəl/ adj of ornithology.

or·ni·thol·ogist /ˌɔːnɪˈθɒlədʒɪst/ n [C] expert in ornithology.

or·ni·thol·ogy /ˌɔːnɪˈθɒlədʒɪ/ n [U] scientific study of birds.

or·phan /ˈɔːfən/ n [C] child who has lost one or both of its parents by death: (as an adjective) an ~ child. □ vt cause to be an orphan: ~ed by war.

'or·phan·age /-ɪdʒ/, charitable home for orphans.

or·tho·dox /ˈɔːθədɒks/ adj (having opinions, beliefs, etc which are) generally accepted or approved: an ~ member of the Church; ~ behaviour. ⇨ heterodox.

the Orthodox Church, the Eastern or Greek Church, recognizing the Patriarch of Istanbul (Constantinople) as its head, and the national churches of Russia, Rumania, etc.

or·tho·doxy /ˈɔːθədɒksɪ/ n (pl -ies) [U] being orthodox; [C] orthodox belief, character, practice.

or·thog·ra·phy /ɔːˈθɒgrəfɪ/ n [U] (system of) spelling; correct or conventional spelling.

or·tho·paedic (also **-pedic**) /ˌɔːθəˈpiːdɪk/ adj of the curing of deformities and diseases of bones: ~ surgery.

or·tho·paed·ics (also **-ped·ics**) n (used with a sing verb) branch of surgery dealing with bone deformities and diseases.

os·cil·late /ˈɒsɪleɪt/ vi,vt 1 swing backwards and forwards as the pendulum of a clock does. 2 (fig) change between extremes of opinion, etc. 3 cause to swing to and fro. 4 (of electric current) undergo high frequency alternations; (of radio receivers) radiate electro-magnetic waves; experience interference (in reception) from this.

os·cil·la·tion /ˌɒsɪˈleɪʃən/ n [C,U]

os·cil·la·tor /-tə(r)/, (esp) device for producing electric oscillations.

os·prey /ˈɒspreɪ US: -prɪ/ n [C] (pl ~s) large kind of hawk that preys on fish.

oss·ify /ˈɒsɪfaɪ/ vt,vi (pt,pp -ied) 1 (formal) make or become hard like bone; change into bone. 2 (fig) make or become rigid, unprogressive.

ossi·fi·ca·tion /ˌɒsɪfɪˈkeɪʃən/ n [U]

os·ten·sible /ɒˈstensəbəl/ adj (formal) (of reasons, etc) put forward in an attempt to hide the real reason; apparent.

os·ten·sibly /-əblɪ/ adv apparently; seemingly.

os·ten·ta·tion /ˌɒstenˈteɪʃən/ n [U] display (of wealth, learning, skill, etc) made to obtain admiration or envy.

os·ten·ta·tious /ˌɒstenˈteɪʃəs/ adj showing ostentation: ~ jewellery/manners/people.

os·ten·ta·tious·ly adv

os·tra·cize /ˈɒstrəsaɪz/ vt shut out from society: refuse to meet, talk to, etc: She was ~ed by her neighbours after her imprisonment.

os·trich /ˈɒstrɪtʃ/ n [C] (pl ~es) fast-running desert bird, the largest in existence, unable to fly, bred for its valuable tail feathers.

other /ˈʌðə(r)/ adj, pron (person or thing) not already named or implied. 1 **the** ~, (sing) the second of two: The twins are so much alike that people find it difficult to know (the) one from the ~. The post office is on the ~ side of the street. **on the `other hand,** (used to introduce something in contrast to an earlier statement, etc): It's cheap, but on the ~ hand the quality is poor. 2 **the ~s,** (pl) (used when the reference is to two

or more): Six of them are mine; the ~s are John's. 3 **another** (always written as one word) an additional (one); a different one: Will you have an~ cup of tea? I don't like this one; can you show me an~ (one)? (Note: the pl of another is some/any others or some/any more: I don't like these. Have you any ~s/any more?) 4 (used when one member of a group is compared with other members): Green is far better as a striker than any ~ member of the team. **each other,** ⇨ each(4). **every other,** (a) all the rest: John is stupid; every ~ boy in the class knows the answer. (b) alternate: Write only on every ~ line. **one another,** ⇨ one³(2). **one after the other/another,** in succession, not together. **...or other,** (used to suggest absence of certainty or precision): I shall be coming again some day or ~, one of these days. **the other day,** a few days ago. 6 different: I do not wish her to be ~ than she is. □ adv (= otherwise) in a different way: I can't do it ~ than slowly.

other·wise /ˈʌðəwaɪz/ adv 1 in another or different way: You evidently think ~. 2 in other or different respects or conditions: The rent is high, but ~ the house is satisfactory. □ conj if not; or else: Do what you've been told; ~ you will be punished.

ot·ter /ˈɒtə(r)/ n [C] fur-covered, fish-eating aquatic animal with four webbed feet and a flat tail; [U] its fur.

ouch /aʊtʃ/ int (used to express sudden pain).

ought /ɔːt/ auxiliary verb (No infinitive, no participles, no inflected forms; ought not may be contracted to oughtn't /ˈɔːtənt/.) 1 (showing duty or obligation): Such things ~ not to be allowed. You ~ to have done that earlier. ⇨ shall(2). 2 (showing what is advisable, desirable or right): There ~ to be more buses during the rush hours. You ~ (i e I advise you) to see that new film at the Odeon. 3 (showing probability): That ~ to be enough fish for three people. Harry ~ to win the race.

ounce /aʊns/ n [C] (abbr oz) unit of weight, one sixteenth of a pound avoirdupois or one twelfth of a pound troy.

our /usual form: ɑ(r) strong form: aʊə(r)/ adj of or belonging to us, that we are concerned with, etc: We have done ~ share.

Our Father, God.

Our Lady, the Virgin Mary.

ours /ˈaʊəz/ possessive pron (the one or ones) belonging to us: This house is ~. O~ is larger than theirs.

our·selves /ɑːˈselvz/ pron 1 (reflexive): It's no use worrying ~ about that. (all) **by ourselves,** (a) alone. (b) without help. 2 (used for emphasis): We've often made that mistake ~.

-ous /-əs/ suffix having the qualities of: poisonous.

oust /aʊst/ vt cause (a person) to leave (his

job, position, etc): ~ *him from being the secretary of the committee.*

out[1] /aʊt/ *adverbial particle* (contrasted with *in*) (For special uses with *verbs*, e g *go out*, ⇨ the *verb* entries.) **1** away from, not in or at, a place, the usual or normal condition, etc: *go* ~; *order him* ~; *find one's way* ~. **2 be out:** *Mrs White is* ~, not at home. *The dockers are* ~ *again*, on strike. *The book I wanted was* ~, was not in the library. *The tide is* ~, low. *The Socialist party was* ~, not in power. *Short skirts are* ~, not fashionable. **be out and about,** (of a person who has been in bed through illness or injury) able to get up, go outdoors, etc. **be out to** + *inf*, trying or hoping to: *I'm not* ~ (= It is not my aim) *to reform the world.* **3** (used in various phrases to show absence from home): *We don't go* ~ *much. We're dining* ~ *this evening.* **4** (used to emphasize the idea of distance): *He lives* ~ *in the country. The fishing boats are all* ~ *at sea. What are you doing* ~ *there?* **5** available; free from confinement or restraint; discovered: *The secret is* ~, discovered, known. *The apple blossom is* ~, open. *The sun is* ~, not hidden by cloud. *His new book is* ~, published. **6** exhausted, extinct: *The fire/gas/ light is* ~, not burning. *Put that cigarette* ~! **7** to or at an end; completely: *I'm tired/worn* ~. **have it 'out with sb,** ⇨ have[4] (9). **all out,** exerting the maximum power or effort: *His car does 100 miles an hour when it's going all* ~. *What is needed is an all-*~ *effort.* **8** (showing error): *I'm* ~ *in my calculations. We're ten pounds* ~ *in our accounts.* **a long way/not far out,** badly/ not much in error. **9** (showing clearness or loudness): *call/cry/shout* ~. **out loud,** in a loud voice. **straight/right out,** without hesitating, without avoiding the truth. **10** (in cricket) (of a batsman) no longer batting; having been bowled, caught, etc: *The captain was* ~ *for three.*

out[2] *prep* **out of,** (contrasted with *in* and *into;* ⇨ the *noun* and *verb* entries for special uses, e g *out of date, out of the way.*) **1** (of place): *Fish cannot live* ~ *of water. Mr Green is* ~ *of town this week.* **2** (of movement): *He walked* ~ *of the shop.* **3** (of motive or cause): *They helped us* ~ *of pity/ kindness.* **4** from among: *It happens in nine cases* ~ *of ten.* **5** by the use of; from: *The hut was made* ~ *of old planks. Can good ever come* ~ *of evil?* **6** without: ~ *of breath/stock/work/petrol.* **7** (of condition): ~ *of fashion/control/order/danger.* ⇨ the *noun* entries. **8** (of origin or source): *a scene* ~ *of a play; drink* ~ *of a cup/a bottle.* **9** (of result): *talk him* ~ *of doing it*, talk to him with the result that he does not do it; *cheat him* ~ *of his money; frighten her* ~ *of her wits.* **10** at a certain distance from: *The ship struck a mine ten miles* ~ *of Hull.* **out of it,** (a) not invited to be a member of a party,

etc; sad for this reason: *She felt* ~ *of it as she watched the others leave for the cinema.* (b) not concerned or involved: *It's a dishonest scheme and I'm glad to be* ~ *of it.*

out /aʊt/ *n* (only in) **the ins and (the) outs,** ⇨ in[3].

out-back /'aʊtbæk/ *adj, n* **the** ~, (e g in Australia) (of) the more remote and sparsely populated areas.

out-bid /aʊt'bɪd/ *vt* (-dd-) bid higher than (another person) at an auction, etc.

out-board /'aʊtbɔːd/ *adj* placed on or near the outside of a ship or boat.
  outboard motor, detachable engine that is mounted at the stern, outside the boat.

out-brave /aʊt'breɪv/ *vt* endure bravely: ~ *the storm.*

out-break /'aʊtbreɪk/ *n* [C] breaking out: *an* ~ *of fever/hostilities.*

out-build-ing /'aʊtbɪldɪŋ/ *n* [C] building, e g a shed or stable, separate from the main building.

out-burst /'aʊtbɜːst/ *n* [C] bursting out (of steam, energy, laughter, anger, etc).

out-cast /'aʊtkɑːst *US:* -kæst/ *n* [C], *adj* (person or animal) driven out from home or society.

out-caste /'aʊtkɑːst *US:* -kæst/ *n* [C], *adj* (e g in India) (person) having lost, or been expelled from, or not belonging to, a caste.

out-class /aʊt'klɑːs *US:* -'klæs/ *vt* be, do much better than: *He was* ~*ed from the start of the race.*

out-come /'aʊtkʌm/ *n* [C] effect or result of an event, or of circumstances.

out-crop /'aʊtkrɒp/ *n* [C] that part of a layer or vein (of rock, etc) which can be seen above the surface of the ground.

out-cry /'aʊtkraɪ/ *n* (*pl* -ies) **1** [C] loud shout or scream (of fear, alarm, etc). **2** [C,U] public protest (*against* something).

out-dated /aʊt'deɪtɪd/ *adj* made out-of-date (by the passing of time).

out-dis-tance /aʊt'dɪstəns/ *vt* travel faster than, and leave behind.

out-do /aʊt'duː/ *vt* (*3rd person sing pres* -does /-'dʌz/, *pt* -did /-'dɪd/, *pp* -done /-'dʌn/) do more or better than: *Not to be outdone he tried again.*

out-door /aʊt'dɔː(r)/ *adj* done, existing, used, outside a house or building: *leading an* ~ *life;* ~ *sports.*

out-doors /aʊt'dɔːz/ *adv* in the open air; outside: *It's cold* ~.

outer /'aʊtə(r)/ *adj* **1** of or for the outside. ⇨ inner. **2** farther from the middle or inside.
  'outer 'space, the universe beyond the earth's atmosphere.
  'outer-most /-məʊst/ *adj* farthest from the inside or centre.

out-fight /aʊt'faɪt/ *vt* (*pt, pp* -fought) fight better than.

out-fit /'aʊtfɪt/ *n* [C] all the clothing or articles needed for a purpose: *a camping* ~, tent, etc. □ *vt* (-tt-) equip (chiefly in the *pp*

~ted).

out·fitter, shopkeeper, shop selling clothes: *a school ~ter.*

out·flank /ʊʊtˈflæŋk/ *vt* go or pass round the side of (the enemy): *an ~ing movement.*

out·fox /aʊtˈfɒks/ *vt* defeat by being cunning.

out·go·ing /ˈaʊtgəʊɪŋ/ *adj* going out; leaving: *the ~ tenant/tide.* ⇨ incoming.

out·go·ings *n pl* expenditure.

out·grow /aʊtˈgrəʊ/ *vt* (*pt* –grew /-ˈgruː/, *pp* –grown /-ˈgrəʊn/) **1** grow too large or too tall for, e g one's clothes. **2** grow faster or taller than, e g one's brother. **3** leave behind, as one grows older (bad habits, childish interests, opinions, etc).

out·growth /ˈaʊtgrəʊθ/ *n* [C] **1** natural development or product. **2** that which grows out of something: *an ~ on a tree.*

out·house /ˈaʊthaʊs/ *n* [C] (*pl* ~s /-haʊzɪz/) small building adjoining the main building (e g a shed, barn, or stable).

out·ing /ˈaʊtɪŋ/ *n* [C] **1** holiday away from home; pleasure trip: *go for an ~ to the seaside.* **2** practice (e g by a race-horse).

out·land·ish /aʊtˈlændɪʃ/ *adj* looking or sounding odd, strange or foreign: *~ dress/ behaviour/ideas.*

out·land·ish·ly *adv*

out·last /aʊtˈlɑːst/ *US*: -ˈlæst/ *vt* last or live longer than.

out·law /ˈaʊtlɔː/ *n* [C] (in olden times) person punished by being placed outside the protection of the law. □ *vt* make (a person) an outlaw.

out·lay /ˈaʊtleɪ/ *n* [U] spending; providing money; [C] sum of money that is spent: *a large ~ on/for scientific research.*

out·let /ˈaʊtlet/ *n* [C] **1** way out for water, steam, etc: *an ~ for water.* **2** (*fig*) means of or occasion for releasing (one's feelings, energies, etc).

out·line /ˈaʊtlaɪn/ *n* [C] **1** line(s) showing shape or boundary: *an ~ map of Great Britain; draw it in ~.* **2** statement of the chief facts, points, etc: *an ~ for an essay/a lecture.* □ *vt* draw, give, in outline.

out·live /aʊtˈlɪv/ *vt* **1** live longer than: *~ one's wife.* **2** live until something is forgotten: *~ a disgrace.*

out·look /ˈaʊtlʊk/ *n* [C] **1** view on which one looks out: *a pleasant ~ over the valley.* **2** what seems likely to happen: *a bright ~ for trade; further ~, dry and sunny* (weather forecast). **3** person's way of looking at something: *a narrow ~ on life.*

out·lying /ˈaʊtlaɪɪŋ/ *adj* far from the centre: *~ villages.*

out·man-oeuvre (*US* = **-ma·neu·ver**) /ˈaʊtməˈnuːvə(r)/ *vt* overcome, defeat, by being superior in manoeuvring.

out·match /aʊtˈmætʃ/ *vt* be more than equal to: *be ~ed in skill and endurance.*

out·moded /aʊtˈməʊdɪd/ *adj* out of fashion.

out·most /ˈaʊtməʊst/ *adj* = outermost.

out·num·ber /aʊtˈnʌmbə(r)/ *vt* be greater in number than.

out-of-date /ˈaʊt əv ˈdeɪt/ *adj* (hyphens are used when the use is *attrib*). = out of date *an ~ set of figures.* ⇨ date[1].

out-of-the-way /ˈaʊt əv ðə ˈweɪ/ *adj* **1** remote; secluded: *an ~ cottage.* **2** not commonly known: *~ items of knowledge.*

out·patient /ˈaʊtpeɪʃnt/ *n* [C] person visiting a hospital for treatment but not living there.

out·play /aʊtˈpleɪ/ *vt* play better than: *The English were ~ed by the Brazilians.*

out·point /aʊtˈpɔɪnt/ *vt* (in boxing, etc) score more points than; defeat on points.

out·post /ˈaʊtpəʊst/ *n* [C] **1** (soldiers in an) observation post at a distance from the main body of troops. **2** any distant settlement: *an ~ of the Roman Empire.*

out·put /ˈaʊtpʊt/ *n* [C] **1** quantity of goods, etc produced: *the ~ of a gold mine/a factory.* **2** power, energy, etc produced. **3** information produced from a computer. ⇨ input.

out·rage /ˈaʊtreɪdʒ/ *n* [C,U] **1** (act of) extreme violence or cruelty: *The use of H-bombs would be an ~ against humanity.* **2** act that shocks public opinion: *an ~ on decency.* □ *vt* treat violently; violate; assault sexually: *~ public opinion/one's sense of justice.*

out·rage·ous /aʊtˈreɪdʒəs/ *adj* shocking; very cruel, shameless, immoral: *~ behaviour; an ~ price/remark.*

out·rage·ous·ly *adv*

out·rider /ˈaʊtraɪdə(r)/ *n* [C] person, e g policeman on a motorcycle accompanying a vehicle as an attendant or guard.

out·rig·ger /ˈaʊtrɪgə(r)/ *n* [C] beam or structure projecting from or over the side of a boat for various purposes (e g for the rowlock in a racing shell, or to give stability to a canoe or yacht).

out·right /ˈaʊtraɪt/ *adj* **1** thorough; positive: *an ~ denial; ~ wickedness.* **2** clear; unmistakable: *On the voting for secretary, Smith was the ~ winner.* □ *adv* **1** openly, with nothing held back: *tell a man ~ what one thinks of his behaviour.* **2** completely; at one time: *buy a house ~,* i e not by instalments; *be killed ~,* quickly, e g by a single blow.

out·rival /aʊtˈraɪvl/ *vt* (-ll-, *US* also -l-) be or do better than a rival.

out·run /aʊtˈrʌn/ *vt* (*pt* -ran /-ˈræn/, *pp* -run) (-nn-) run faster or better than.

out·set /ˈaʊtset/ *n* **at/from the outset,** at/ from the beginning.

out·shine /aʊtˈʃaɪn/ *vt* (*pt,pp* -shone /-ˈʃɒn/) **1** shine more brightly than. **2** (*fig*) be more successful than.

out·side /aʊt`saɪd/ *n* (contrasted with *inside*) **1** [C] the other side or surface; the outer part(s): *The ∼ of the house needs painting.* **2 at the (very) outside,** at the most; at the highest reckoning: *There were only fifty people there at the ∼,* certainly not more than fifty. □ *adj* **1** of or on, nearer, the outside: *∼ measurements,* e g of a box; *an ∼ broadcast,* from a place away from the studios. **2** greatest possible or probable: *an ∼ estimate.* **3** not connected with or included in a group, organization, etc: *We shall need ∼ help* (= extra workers) *for this job.* **4** unlikely, small; *an ∼ chance/ possibility.* □ *adv* on or to the outside: *The car is waiting ∼.* □ *prep* **1** at or on the outer side of: *∼ the house.* **2** beyond the limits of: *He has no occupation ∼ his office work.*

out·sider /aʊt`saɪdə(r)/ *n* [C] **1** person who is not, or who is not considered to be, a member of a group, society, etc. **2** horse that is thought to have little chance of winning a race.

out·size /aʊt`saɪz/ *adj* (esp of articles of clothing, etc) larger than the usual size.

out·skirts /`aʊtskɜːts/ *n pl* borders or outly-ing parts (esp of a town): *on the ∼ of Lille.*

out·smart /aʊt`smɑːt/ *vt* (*informal*) be cleverer, more cunning than.

out·spoken /aʊt`spəʊkən/ *adj* saying freely what one thinks: *∼ comments/delegates.*
out·spoken·ly *adv*

out·spread /aʊt`spred/ *adj* spread or stretched out: *with '∼ `arms/'arms `∼.*

out·stand·ing /aʊt`stændɪŋ/ *adj* **1** in a position to be easily noticed; attracting no-tice: *an ∼ landmark. The boy who won the scholarship was quite ∼.* **2** (of problem, work, payments, etc) still to be attended to: *∼ debts; work that is still ∼.* **3** /`aʊtstændɪŋ/ sticking out: *a boy with big, ∼ ears.*
out·stand·ing·ly *adv*

out·stay /aʊt`steɪ/ *vt* stay longer than: *∼ the other guests.* **outstay one's welcome,** stay until one is no longer a welcome guest.

out·stretched /aʊt`stretʃt/ *adj* stretched or spread out: *lie ∼ on the grass.*

out·strip /aʊt`strɪp/ *vt* (-pp-) do better than.

out·ward /`aʊtwəd/ *adj* **1** of or on the out-side: *the ∼ appearance of things.* **2** going out: *during the ∼ voyage.* □ *adv* (also **out-wards**) towards the outside; away from home or the centre: *The two ends must be bent ∼s. The ship is ∼ bound,* sailing away from its home port.
out·ward·ly *adv* on the surface; apparently: *Though badly frightened she appeared ∼ly calm.*

out·wear /aʊt`weə(r)/ *vt* (*pt* -wore /-`wɔː(r)/ *pp* -worn /-`wɔːn/) **1** last longer than: *Leather shoes will ∼ cheaper ones.* **2** wear out; use up; exhaust: *outworn* (= out-of-date) *practices in industry.*

out·weigh /aʊt`weɪ/ *vt* be greater in weight, value or importance than: *Do the*

disadvantages ∼ the advantages?

out·wit /aʊt`wɪt/ *vt* (-tt-) defeat by being cleverer or more cunning than.

out·wore /aʊt`wɔː(r)/, **out·worn** /aʊt`wɔːn/ ⇨ outwear.

ova /`əʊvə/ *n pl* of ovum.

oval /`əʊvəl/ *n* [C], *adj* (plane figure or out-line that is) shaped like an egg or ellipse.

ovary /`əʊvərɪ/ *n* [C] (*pl* -ies) (*anat*) **1** either of the two reproductive organs in which ova are produced in female animals. **2** seed-vessel in a plant. ⇨ ovum.

ova·tion /əʊ`veɪʃən/ *n* [C] enthusiastic expression (clapping, cheering) of welcome or approval: *a standing ∼,* standing up to clap, etc.

oven /`ʌvən/ *n* [C] **1** enclosed space (in a cooker) heated for baking, roasting, etc: *Bread is baked in an ∼.* **2** small furnace or kiln used in chemistry, etc.
`oven·ware /-weə(r)/, heat-proof dishes for use in an oven.

over¹ /`əʊvə(r)/ *adv* (⇨ the *verb* entries for special combinations, e g *give over.*) **1** (sug-gesting movement from an upright position, from one side to the other side, or so that a different side is seen, etc): *Don't knock that vase ∼. He turned ∼ in bed.* **2** (suggesting motion upwards and outwards): *The milk boiled ∼.* (*fig*) *He was boiling ∼ with rage.* **3** from beginning to end; through: *You should think it ∼,* consider the matter care-fully. **4** (suggesting repetition). **(all) over again,** again completely: *He did it so badly that I had to do it all ∼ again myself.* **over and over (again),** repeatedly; many times: *I've warned you ∼ and ∼ again not to do that.* **5** across (a street, an open space, a dis-tance, etc): *Take these letters ∼ to the post office. Come ∼ and see me some time.* **6** remaining; not used after part has been taken or used: *Seven into thirty goes four times and two ∼. If there's any meat (left) ∼,* give it to the dog. **7** in addition; in excess; more: *children of fourteen and ∼; 10 metres and a little ∼.* **8** ended; finished; done with: *The meeting/The storm is ∼. His sufferings will soon be ∼.* **9** more than is right, usual, wise, etc: *'∼(-)`anxious; '∼(-)`taxed.* ⇨ over- below. **10** (suggesting transference or change from one person, party, etc to another): *He has gone ∼ to the enemy,* joined them. **11** on the whole surface; in all parts: *He was aching all ∼. Paint the old name ∼,* cover it with paint. *That's Smith all ∼,* It's typical of him.

over² /`əʊvə(r)/ *prep* **1** resting on the sur-face of and covering, partly or completely: *He spread his handkerchief ∼ his face to keep the flies off. I knocked the man's hat ∼ his eyes,* so that he couldn't see. at a level higher than, but not touching: *The sky is ∼ our heads. I leant ∼ the table.* **3** of superior-ity in rank, authority, etc): *He reigns ∼ a great empire. He has no command ∼ his* students. *Mr White is* ∼ *me in the office.* **4** in or across every part of: *Snow is falling* ∼ *the north of England. He has travelled all* ∼ *Europe.* **5** from one side to the other of; to or at the other side of: *He escaped* ∼ *the frontier. She spoke to me* ∼ *her shoulder. Look* ∼ *the hedge.* **6** so as to be over and on the other side of: *climb* ∼ *a wall; jump* ∼ *a brook.* **7** (of time): *Can you stay* ∼ *Sunday, until Monday?* **8** (opposite = *under*) more than: *He spoke for* ∼ *an hour. He stayed in London (for)* ∼ *a month. The river is* ∼ *fifty miles long. He's* ∼ *fifty years old.* **over and above**, in addition to: *The waiters get good tips* ∼ *and above their wages.* **9** in connection with; while engaged in; concerning: *an argument* ∼ *methods; He went to sleep* ∼ *his work,* while doing it. *How long will he be* ∼ *it?* How long will it take him to do it, get there, etc?

over³ /'əʊvə(r)/ *n* [C] (in cricket) number of balls bowled in succession by each bowler in turn.

over- /'əʊvə(r)/ *prefix* **1** across, above: *overland; overhead.* **2** too (much): *'over-po'lite.*
The meanings of the *adjectives* below may be obtained by putting *too* in place of *over*:

'over-a'bundant	'over-ex'cited
'over-'active	'over-fa'miliar
'over-am'bitious	'over-'fond
'over-'anxious	'over-'full
'over-'bold	'over-'generous
'over-'busy	'over-'greedy
'over-'careful	'over-'hasty
'over-'cautious	'over-'jealous
'over-'confident	'over-'nervous
'over-'critical	'over-'proud
'over-'curious	'over-'ripe
'over-'delicate	'over-'sensitive
'over-'eager	'over-'serious
'over-e'motional	'over-sus'picious
'over-en'thusi'astic	'over-'zealous

The meanings of the *nouns* below may be obtained by putting *too much* in place of *over*:

'over-a'bundance	'over-'payment
'over-an'xiety	'over-popu'lation
'over-'confidence	'over-pro'duction
'over-ex'posure	'over-'strain
'over-in'dulgence	'over-'valu'ation

The meaning of the *verbs* below may be obtained by putting *too much* after the *verb* in place of *over*:

'over-'burden	'over-'heat
'over-'cook	'over-in'dulge
'over-'eat	'over-'praise
'over-'emphasize	'over-pro'duce
'over-'estimate	'over-'simplify
'over-ex'ert	'over-'strain
'over-ex'pose	'over-'value

over·act /'əʊvər'ækt/ *vi,vt* act in an exaggerated way.

over·all¹ /'əʊvər'ɔl/ *adj* including everything; containing all: *the* ∼ *measurements of a room.*

over·all² /'əʊvərɔl/ *n* **1** [C] loose-fitting garment that covers other garments (e g as worn by housewives). **2** (*pl*) loose-fitting trousers, with the front extended above the waist and of heavy, strong material, worn to protect other clothes from dirt, etc.

over·arm /'əʊvərɑm/ *adv* (in sport, e g cricket) with the arm swung over the shoulder: *bowl* ∼; *an* ∼ *bowler;* ∼ *bowling.*

over·awe /'əʊvər'ɔ/ *vt* gain complete reverence, respect, obedience, etc.

over·bal·ance /'əʊvə'bæləns/ *vt,vi* **1** (cause to) fall over: *He* ∼*d and fell into the water.* **2** weigh, be, more than: *The gains* ∼ *the losses.*

over·bear /'əʊvə'beə(r)/ *vt* (*pt* -bore /-'bɔ(r)/, *pp* -borne /-'bɔn/) overcome (by strong arguments, force or authority).
over·bear·ing *adj* forcing others to one's will: *an* ∼*ing manner.*
over·bear·ing·ly *adv*

over·bid /'əʊvə'bɪd/ *vt,vi* (*pt,pp* ∼) (-dd-) **1** (at an auction) bid higher than (another person). **2** bid more than the value of (something offered for sale). □ *n* [C,U] act of overbidding.

over·board /'əʊvəbɔd/ *adv* over the side of a ship or boat into the water: *fall/jump* ∼.

over·bore /'əʊvə'bɔ(r)/, **over·borne** /'əʊvə'bɔn/ ⇨ overbear.

over·bur·den /'əʊvə'bɜdən/ *vt* burden too heavily: ∼*ed with grief.*

over·cast /'əʊvə'kɑst *US*: -'kæst/ *adj* **1** (of the sky) darkened (as) by clouds. **2** (*fig*) gloomy; sad. □ *n* [C] cloud-covered sky.

over·charge /'əʊvə'tʃɑdʒ/ *vt,vi* **1** charge too high a price: *We were* ∼*d for the eggs.* **2** fill or load too much: ∼ *an electric circuit.* □ *n* /'əʊvətʃɑdʒ/ [C] load, price, etc that is too high or great.

over·cloud /'əʊvə'klaʊd/ *vt,vi* cover, become covered, with clouds or shadows.

over·coat /'əʊvəkəʊt/ *n* [C] long coat worn out of doors over other clothes in cold weather.

over·come /'əʊvə'kʌm/ *vt* (*pt* -came /-'keɪm/, *pp* -come) **1** defeat; be too strong for: ∼ *the enemy/a bad habit/temptation.* **2** make weak: *be* ∼ *by tiredness/sadness/whisky/fumes.*

over·crowd /'əʊvə'kraʊd/ *vt* crowd too much: ∼*ed buses and trains; the* ∼*ing of large cities.*

over·do /'əʊvə'du/ *vt* (*pt* -did /-'dɪd/, *pp* -done /-'dʌn/) **1** do too much; exaggerate; overact: *He overdid his part in the play.* **overdo it**, (a) work, etc too hard: *You should work hard, but don't* ∼ *it and make yourself ill.* (b) exaggerate; go too far in order to achieve one's object: *He tried to show sympathy for us, but didn't he* ∼ *it?* **2** cook too much: *overdone beef.*

over·dose /ˈəʊvədəʊs/ n [C] excessive dose of a drug.

over·draft /ˈəʊvədrɑːft US: -dræft/ n [C] amount of money by which a bank account is overdrawn.

over·draw /ˌəʊvəˈdrɔː/ vt,vi (pt -drew /-ˈdruː/, pp -drawn /-ˈdrɔːn/) 1 draw a cheque for a sum in excess of (one's credit balance in a bank): an ~n account. 2 exaggerate: The characters in this novel are rather ~n, are not true to life.

over·dress /ˌəʊvəˈdres/ vt,vi dress (oneself, etc) too richly or too formally.

over·due /ˌəʊvəˈdjuː US: -ˈduː/ adj beyond the time fixed (for arrival, payment, etc): The train is ~, is late. These bills are all ~, ought to have been paid before now. The baby is two weeks ~, still not born two weeks after the expected date of birth.

over·flow /ˌəʊvəˈfləʊ/ vt,vi (pt,pp ~ed) 1 flow over; flow over the edges or limits; spread beyond the ordinary or usual area: The river ~ed its banks. The crowds were so big that they ~ed into the street. 2 be more than filled: a heart ~ing with love. □ n /ˈəʊvəfləʊ/ [C] flowing over of liquid; that which flows over or is too much for the space, area, etc available: an ~ meeting, one held for those unable to find room in the hall, etc where the principal meeting is held.

over·grown /ˌəʊvəˈɡrəʊn/ adj 1 having grown too fast: an ~ boy. 2 covered with something that has grown over: a garden ~ with weeds.

over·growth /ˈəʊvəɡrəʊθ/ n [C] 1 that which has grown over: an ~ of weeds. 2 growth that is too fast or excessive: weakness due to ~.

over·hand /ˈəʊvəhænd/ adj (in swimming) with the hand and arm raised out of the water: the ~ stroke.

over·hang /ˌəʊvəˈhæŋ/ vt,vi (pt,pp -hung /-ˈhʌŋ/) hang, project, over, like a shelf: The cliffs ~ the stream. The ledge ~s several feet. □ n /ˈəʊvəhæŋ/ [C] part that overhangs: the ~ of a roof.

over·haul /ˈəʊvəˈhɔːl/ vt 1 examine thoroughly in order to learn about the condition of: have the engine of a car ~ed. 2 overtake; catch up with: The fast cruiser soon ~ed the old cargo boat. □ n /ˈəʊvəhɔːl/ [C] examination for the purpose of repairing, cleaning, etc.

over·head /ˌəʊvəˈhed/ adv above one's head; in the sky: the people in the room ~; the stars ~. □ adj /ˈəʊvəhed/ raised above the ground: ~ wires/cables. □ n pl /ˈəʊvəhedz/ those expenses, etc needed for carrying on a business, e g rent, advertising, salaries, light, not manufacturing costs.

over·hear /ˌəʊvəˈhɪə(r)/ vt (pt,pp ~d /-ˈhɜːd/) 1 hear without the knowledge of the speaker(s). 2 hear what one is not intended to hear, deliberately or by chance.

over·joyed /ˌəʊvəˈdʒɔɪd/ adj very delighted

(at one's success, etc).

over·kill /ˈəʊvəkɪl/ n [U] nuclear capacity greatly exceeding what is needed to exterminate the enemy.

over·land adj /ˈəʊvəlænd/, adv /ˈəʊvəˈlænd/ across the land (contrasted with the sea): take the ~ route; travel ~.

over·lap /ˈəʊvəˈlæp/ vt,vi (-pp-) 1 partly cover by extending beyond one edge: tiles that ~ one another; ~ping boards. 2 (fig) partly coincide; involve duplication: His duties/authority and mine ~. □ n /ˈəʊvəlæp/ [C,U]

over·leaf /ˈəʊvəˈliːf/ adv on the other side of the leaf (of a book, etc).

over·load /ˈəʊvəˈləʊd/ vt put too great a load (of electric current, weight) on.

over·look /ˌəʊvəˈlʊk/ vt 1 have a view of from above: Our garden is ~ed from the neighbours' windows, They can look down on to our garden from their windows. 2 fail to see or notice; pay no attention to: His services have been ~ed by his employers, They have not properly rewarded him. 3 pass over without punishing: ~ a fault.

over·mas·ter /ˌəʊvəˈmɑːstə(r) US: -mæs-/ vt overcome, overpower: an ~ing desire.

over·much /ˈəʊvəˈmʌtʃ/ adj, adv too great(ly): an author who has been praised ~.

over·night /ˌəʊvəˈnaɪt/ adv 1 on the night before: get everything ready for the journey ~. 2 for, during, the night: stay ~ at a friend's house, sleep there for the night. □ adj /ˈəʊvənaɪt/, during or for the night: an ~ journey.

over·pass /ˈəʊvəpɑːs US: -pæs/ n [C] bridge that carries a road over a highway or motorway. ⇨ flyover, underpass.

over·pay /ˈəʊvəˈpeɪ/ vt (pt,pp -paid /-ˈpeɪd/) pay too much or too highly: Has Jack been overpaid for his work?

over·power /ˈəʊvəˈpaʊə(r)/ vt defeat by greater strength or numbers: The criminals were easily ~ed by the police. He was ~ed by the heat.

over·power·ing adj too strong; very powerful: an ~ing stink; ~ing grief.

over·rate /ˈəʊvəˈreɪt/ vt put too high a value on: ~ her abilities; an ~d book.

over·reach /ˈəʊvəˈriːtʃ/ vt **overreach oneself,** fail, damage one's own interests, by being too ambitious.

over·ride /ˌəʊvəˈraɪd/ vt (pt -rode /-ˈrəʊd/, pp -ridden /-ˈrɪdn/) refuse to agree with, accept, (a person's opinions, decisions, wishes, claims, etc): They overrode my wishes.

over·rule /ˈəʊvəˈruːl/ vt decide against (esp by using one's higher authority): The judge ~d the previous decision.

over·run /ˌəʊvəˈrʌn/ vt (pt -ran /-ˈræn/, pp ~) 1 spread over and occupy or injure: a country ~ by enemy troops; a garden ~ with weeds. 2 go beyond (a limit): speakers

Ω

who ~ the time allowed them.

over·seas /ˈəʊvəˈsiːz/ *adj* (at, to, from, for, places) across the sea: *~ trade.* □ *adv:* go/ live *~s,* abroad.

over·see /ˈəʊvəˈsiː/ *vt* (*pt* -saw /-ˈsɔː/, *pp* -seen /-ˈsiːn/) look after, control (work, workmen).

over·seer /ˈəʊvəsɪə(r)/, person whose duty it is to take charge of work and see that it is properly done.

over·shadow /ˈəʊvəˈʃædəʊ/ *vt* **1** throw a shade over. **2** (*fig*) cause to seem less important or obvious.

over·shoe /ˈəʊvəʃuː/ *n* [C] rubber shoe worn over an ordinary one in wet weather ⇨ galosh.

over·shoot /ˈəʊvəˈʃuːt/ *vt* (*pt,pp* -shot /-ˈʃɒt/) **1** shoot or travel over or beyond (a mark or limit): *The aircraft overshot the runway.* **2** (*literary, fig*) go too far.

over·sight /ˈəʊvəsaɪt/ *n* **1** [U] failure to notice; [C] instance of this: *Through an unfortunate ~ your letter was left unanswered.* **2** [U] supervision: *under the ~ of a nurse.*

over-simplification /ˈəʊvə ˌsɪmplɪfɪˈkeɪʃən/ *n* [C,U] (instance of) making something (a process, explanation, etc) seem too easy.

over·sleep /ˈəʊvəˈsliːp/ *vi* (*pt,pp* -slept /-ˈslept/) sleep too long or after the intended time for waking: *He overslept and was late for work.*

over·spill /ˈəʊvəspɪl/ *n* [C] **1** what has overflowed. **2** (*fig*) surplus population (leaving a town to live elsewhere): *new towns for London's ~.*

over·state /ˈəʊvəˈsteɪt/ *vt* **1** express or state too strongly. **2** state more than is true about: *Don't ~ your case.*

over·state·ment /ˈəʊvəsteɪtmənt/ *n* [U] exaggeration; [C] exaggerated statement.

over·stay /ˈəʊvəˈsteɪ/ *vt* = outstay.

over·step /ˈəʊvəˈstep/ *vt* (-pp-) go beyond: *~ one's authority.*

over·stock /ˈəʊvəˈstɒk/ *vt* supply, fill, with too much stock.

over·strung /ˈəʊvəˈstrʌŋ/ *adj* (of a person, his nerves) intensely nervous; easily excited; too sensitive.

over·sub·scribed /ˈəʊvəsəbˈskraɪbd/ *adj* (*finance*) (of an issue of shares, etc) with applications in excess of what is offered.

overt /ˈəʊvɜːt US: əʊˈvɜːt/ *adj* done or shown openly, publicly: *~ hostility.*
overt·ly *adv*

over·take /ˈəʊvəˈteɪk/ *vt* (*pt* -took /-ˈtʊk/, *pp* -taken /-ˈteɪkən/) **1** catch up with and pass: *~ other cars on the road.* **2** (of storms, troubles, etc) happen suddenly, by surprise: *be ~n by/with fear/surprise.*

over·tax /ˈəʊvəˈtæks/ *vt* **1** tax too heavily. **2** put too heavy a burden or strain on: *~ one's strength/her patience.*

over·throw /ˈəʊvəˈθrəʊ/ *vt* (*pt* -threw

/-ˈθruː/, *pp* -thrown /-ˈθrəʊn/) defeat; put an end to; cause to fall or fail: *~ the government.* □ *n* /ˈəʊvəθrəʊ/ [C] ruin; defeat; fall.

over·time /ˈəʊvətaɪm/ *n* [U], *adv* (time spent at work) after the usual hours: *working ~; be on ~; ~ pay.*

over·ture /ˈəʊvətʃə(r)/ *n* [C] **1** (often pl) approach made (*to* a person) with the aim of starting discussions: *peace ~s; make ~s to strikers.* **2** musical composition played as an introduction to an opera, or as a separate item at a concert.

over·turn /ˈəʊvəˈtɜːn/ *vt,vi* (cause to) turn over; upset: *He ~ed the boat. The car ~ed.*

over·weight /ˈəʊvəweɪt/ *n* [U] excess of weight above what is usual or legal. □ *adj* /ˈəʊvəˈweɪt/ exceeding the weight allowed or normal: *If your luggage is ~ you'll have to pay extra.*

over·whelm /ˈəʊvəˈwelm US: -ˈhwelm/ *vt* weigh down; cover, completely by pouring down on; crush; cause to feel confused or embarrassed: *be ~ed by the enemy/by superior forces; ~ing sorrow*

over·work /ˈəʊvəˈwɜːk/ *vt,vi* (cause to) work too hard or too long: *~ a horse. It's foolish to ~.* □ *n* /ˈəʊvəwɜːk/ [U] working too much or too long: *ill through ~.*

over·wrought /ˈəʊvəˈrɔːt/ *adj* tired out by too much work or excitement.

ovi·duct /ˈəʊvɪdʌkt/ *n* [C] (*anat*) (also called *Fallopian tube*) either of two tubes through which ova pass from the ovary to the uterus.

ovum /ˈəʊvəm/ *n* [C] (*pl* ova /ˈəʊvə/) female germ or sex cell in animals, capable of developing into a new individual when fertilized by male sperm.

owe /əʊ/ *vt,vi* **1** be in debt to (a person) (for something): *He ~s his father £50.* **2** be under an obligation to, feel the necessity of gratitude to: *We ~ a great deal to our parents and teachers.* **3** be bound to give as a duty: *~ reverence and obedience to the Pope.* **4** be indebted to as the source of: *He ~ his success to good luck more than to ability. To whom do we ~ the discovery of penicillin?*

ow·ing /ˈəʊɪŋ/ *adj* still to be paid: *large sums still ~.* **owing to,** *prep* because of; on account of: *O~ to the rain they could not come.*

owl /aʊl/ *n* [C] night-flying bird that lives on small birds and animals, e g mice.

own[1] /əʊn/ *adj, pron* **1** (used with possessive adjectives) for emphasis in possession, individual, and not another's: *I saw it with my ~ eyes. It's my ~,* belongs to me. *This fruit has a flavour all its ~.* **(all) on one's own, (a)** alone: *I'm (all) on my ~ today.* **(b)** independently of an employer: *He's (working) on his ~,* self-employed. **(c)** without help: *I did it on my ~.* **(d)** outstanding; excellent: *For craftsmanship, Smith is on his ~,* has no equal. **come into one's**

own, receive the credit, fame, etc that is deserved. **get one's `own back,** have one's revenge. **hold one's own, (a)** maintain one's position against attack. **(b)** not lose strength: *The patient is holding her* ~. **2** done or produced by and for oneself: *She makes all her* ~ *clothes.*

own² /əʊn/ *vt, vi* **1** possess; have as property; *This house is mine; I* ~ *it.* **2** agree; confess; recognize: ~ *that a claim is justified.* **own up (to sth),** confess fully and frankly.

owner /ˈəʊnə(r)/ *n* [C] person who owns something: *Who's the* ~ *of this house?*

`own·er·ship /-ʃɪp/, state of being an owner; right of possession.

ox /ɒks/ *n* [C] (*pl* oxen /ˈɒksən/) **1** general name for domestic cattle. **2** (esp) fully grown castrated bullock.

`ox-cart, cart drawn by oxen.

`oxtail, tail of ox, used for soup, etc.

oxi·dize /ˈɒksɪdaɪz/ *vt, vi* (cause to) combine with oxygen; make or become rusty.

oxy·acety·lene /ˌɒksɪəˈsetəliːn/ *adj, n* [U] (of a) mixture of oxygen and acetylene: ~ *welding,* using a hot flame of oxyacetylene.

oxy·gen /ˈɒksɪdʒən/ *n* [U] chemical element (symbol O), gas without colour, taste or smell, present in the air and necessary to the existence of all forms of life.

`oxygen mask, mask placed over the nose and mouth to supply oxygen.

`oxygen tent, enclosure to allow a patient to breathe air with a greater oxygen content.

oy·ster /ˈɔɪstə(r)/ *n* [C] kinds of shellfish used as food, usually eaten uncooked.

`oyster-bed/-bank, where oysters breed or are bred.

`oyster-catcher, wading seabird.

Pp

P, p /piː/ (*pl* P's, p's /piːz/) the 16th letter of the English alphabet. **mind one's ¹P's and `Q's,** be careful not to offend either through speech or behaviour.

pa /pɑː/ *n* [C] (*informal*) short for papa.

pace /peɪs/ *n* [C] **1** (distance covered by the foot in a) single step in walking or running. **2** rate of walking or running: *go at a good* ~, go fast. **set the pace (for),** set a speed for (e g runners in a race). **keep pace (with)** (*literary, fig*) progress at the same rate: *He finds it hard to keep* ~ *with all the developments in nuclear physics.* **3** (esp of horses) way of walking, running, etc. □ *vi, vt* **1** walk, trot, etc with slow or regular steps: ~ *up and down,* (often suggesting restlessness, impatience). **2** move across in this way: *pacing the room.* **3** measure by taking paces: ~ *off*

30 *metres;* ~ *out a room.* **4** set the pace(2) for (a rider or runner in a race).

`pace-maker, (a)** (also **`pace-setter) rider, runner, etc who sets the pace for another in a race. **(b)** electronic device to correct weak or irregular heartbeats.

pa·cific /pəˈsɪfɪk/ *adj* peaceful; making or loving peace.

pa·cifi·cally /-klɪ/ *adv*

paci·fi·ca·tion /ˌpæsɪfɪˈkeɪʃən/ *n* [U] making or becoming peaceful.

paci·fism /ˈpæsɪfɪzm/ *n* [U] principle that war should and could be abolished.

paci·fist /ˈpæsɪfɪst/ *n* [C] believer in pacifism.

pac·ify /ˈpæsɪfaɪ/ *vt* (*pt, pp* -ied) **1** calm (a person's anger, excitement, etc). **2** end violence in (a country).

pack¹ /pæk/ *n* [C] **1** bundle of things tied or wrapped up together for carrying. **2** number of dogs kept for hunting (*a* ~ *of hounds*) or of wild animals that go about together: *Wolves hunt in* ~*s.* **3** (used contemptuously) number of things or persons: *a* ~ *of thieves/liars/lies.* **4** complete set (usually 52) of playing-cards. **5** quantity of fish, meat, fruit, etc packed in a season: *this year's* ~ *of salmon.* ⇨ pack²(5). **6** (*US*) = packet: *a* ~ *of cigarettes.*

`pack-horse/-animal, one used for carrying packs(1).

`pack-ice, mass of large blocks of ice in the sea.

`pack-thread *n* [U] strong thread for sewing or tying up packs or canvas bags.

pack² /pæk/ *vt, vi* **1** put things, into, fill, a box, bundle, bag, etc; get ready for a journey by doing this: ~ *clothes into a trunk. Have you* ~*ed (up) your things? You must begin* ~*ing at once. Her husband takes a* ~*ed lunch* (e g sandwiches, etc in a container) *to work every day.* **pack up, (***informal***) (a)** put one's tools, etc away; stop working: *It's time to* ~ *up.* **(b)** fail: *One of the aircraft's engines* ~*ed up.* **2** crush or crowd together (into a place or period of time): ~*ing people into a bus. She managed to* ~ *a lot of sightseeing into the short time she had in London.* **3** put soft material into or round (something) to keep it safe, or to prevent loss or leakage: *glass* ~*ed in straw.* **4** **pack sb off; send sb packing,** send him away quickly and roughly (because he is troublesome, etc). **5** prepare and put (meat, fruit, etc) in tins for preservation. ⇨ pack¹(5). **6** choose (the members of a committee, etc) so that their decisions are likely to be in one's favour.

pack·age /ˈpækɪdʒ/ *n* [C] parcel, bundle of things, packed together. □ *vt* place in, make, a package.

`package `deal, (*informal*) number of proposals put forward for discussion.

`package `holiday/`tour, (*informal*) holiday including travel, accomodation, etc arranged in advance by travel agents and sold at a fixed price.

packer /ˈpækə(r)/ n [C] person or machine that packs(1).

packet /ˈpækɪt/ n [C] **1** small parcel or bundle: a ~ of letters; a ~ of 20 cigarettes. **2** (sl) large sum of money: make/cost a ~.
`packet-boat`, mailboat.

pack·ing /ˈpækɪŋ/ n [U] **1** process of packing (goods). **2** materials used in packing(3), e g for closing a leaking joint.
`packing-case`, crate of rough boards in which goods are packed for shipment.

pact /pækt/ n [C] compact; agreement: a new Peace P~.

pad [1] /pæd/ n [C] **1** mass of, container filled with, soft material, used to prevent damage, give comfort or improve the shape of something. **2** number of sheets of writing-paper fastened together along one edge. **3** = launching pad. **4** guard for the leg or other parts of the body (in cricket and other games). **5** (also `inking-pad`) absorbent material used for inking rubber stamps. **6** soft, fleshy underpart of the foot (of a dog, fox, etc). **7** (sl) bed; room to sleep in. □ vt (-dd-) **1** put pads(1) in or on (to prevent injury, to give comfort, or to fill out hollow spaces, etc): a ~ded cell, one with padded walls (in a mental hospital). **2** pad sth out, make (a sentence, essay, book, etc) longer by using unnecessary material.

pad·ding /ˈpædɪŋ/ n [U] material used for padding(1,2).

pad [2] /pæd/ vi,vt (-dd-) travel on foot: ~ding qlong.

paddle [1] /ˈpædəl/ n **1** short oar with a broad blade at one or at both ends, used (without a rowlock) to propel a canoe through the water. **2** (in rowing) act or period of propelling a boat with light, easy strokes. **3** instrument shaped like a paddle (e g one used for beating, stirring or mixing things). □ vt,vi use a paddle; row with light, easy strokes. **paddle one's own canoe,** depend on oneself alone.
`paddle-steamer`, steam vessel propelled by paddle-wheels.
`paddle-wheel`, one of a pair of wheels, each with boards round the circumference which press backwards against the water and propel a paddle-steamer.

paddle [2] /ˈpædəl/ vi walk with bare feet in shallow water (as children do at the seaside): a `paddling pool`, shallow pool (e g in a public park) where children paddle. □ n [C] act or period of paddling.

pad·dock /ˈpædək/ n [C] **1** small grass field, esp one used for exercising horses. **2** (at a race-course) enclosed area where horses are assembled and paraded before a race.

paddy /ˈpædɪ/ n [U] rice that is still growing; rice in the husk.
`paddy-field`, field where rice is grown.

pad·lock /ˈpædlɒk/ n [C] detachable lock hung by a hook to the object fastened. □ vt fasten with a padlock.

padre /ˈpɑːdreɪ/ n [C] **1** (army and navy) chaplain. **2** (GB informal) priest; parson.

paedi·at·rics /ˈpiːdɪˈætrɪks/ ⇨ pediatrics.

pa·gan /ˈpeɪɡən/ n [C], adj (person who is) not a believer in any of the chief religions of the world.

page [1] /peɪdʒ/ n [C] **1** one side of a leaf of paper in a book, periodical, etc. **2** entire leaf of a book, etc: Several ~s have been torn out. □ vt number the pages of.

page [2] /peɪdʒ/ n [C] **1** (also `~ boy`) boy servant, usually in uniform, in a hotel, club, etc. **2** (in the Middle Ages) boy in training for knighthood and living in a knight's household. **3** boy acting as a personal attendant of a person of high rank. □ vt summon or call the name of (a person) in a hotel, club, etc: paging Mr Green.

pag·eant /ˈpædʒənt/ n [C] **1** public entertainment, often outdoors, in which historical events are acted in the costume of the period. **2** public celebration, esp one in which there is a procession of persons in fine costumes (e g a coronation).

pag·eantry /ˈpædʒəntrɪ/ n [U] rich and splendid ceremony or display.

pagi·na·tion /ˈpædʒɪˈneɪʃən/ n [C] (figures used for the) numbering of the pages of a book.

pa·goda /pəˈɡəʊdə/ n [C] (pl ~s) (in India, Ceylon, Burma, China, Japan) religious building, typically a sacred tower shaped like a pyramid (Hindu temple), or of several storeys (Buddhist tower).

pah /pɑː/ int used to express disgust.

paid /peɪd/ ⇨ pay [2].

pail /peɪl/ n [C] vessel, usually round, of metal or wood, for carrying liquid: a ~ of milk.
`pail·ful` /-fʊl/ n [C] as much as a pail holds.

pain /peɪn/ n **1** [U] suffering of mind or body: be in (great) ~; cry with ~; feel some/no/not much/a great deal of ~. **2** [C] particular or localized kind of bodily suffering: a ~ in the knee; stomach ~s. **a pain in the neck,** (sl) irritating person. □ vt cause pain to: My foot is still ~ing me.
`pain-killer`, medicine for lessening pain(1).
`pained` adj distressed: She had a ~ed look.
`pain·ful` /-fəl/ adj causing pain: This duty is ~ful to me.
`pain·fully` /-fəlɪ/ adv
`pain·less` adj without, causing no, pain: ~less methods of killing animals.
`pain·less·ly` adv

pains /peɪnz/ n pl trouble; effort: work hard and get very little for all one's ~. **be at/ take (great) pains to do sth,** make a great effort, work hard, to do it. **spare no pains,** do everything possible.

pains·taking /ˈpeɪnsteɪkɪŋ/ adj very careful; industrious.

paint /peɪnt/ n 1 [U] solid colouring matter (to be) mixed with oil or other liquid and used to give colour to a surface: *give the doors two coats of* ~. 2 (*pl*) collection of tubes or cakes of colouring materials. □ *vt,vi* 1 coat with paint: ~ *a door.* **paint the town red,** (*informal*) go out and have a lively, exciting time esp when celebrating. 2 make a picture (of) with paint: ~ *flowers;* ~ *in oils/in water-colours.* **paint sth in,** add to a picture: ~ *in the foreground.* 3 (*fig*) describe vividly in words. **not so black as one is painted,** not so bad as one is represented to be.
  `paint-box,` box with a collection of paints(2).
  `paint-brush,` brush for applying paint.
  paint-ing, (a) [U] using paint; occupation of a painter, **(b)** [C] painted picture.
painter /ˈpeɪntə(r)/ n [C] 1 person who paints pictures. 2 workman who paints woodwork, buildings, ships, etc.
painter /ˈpeɪntə(r)/ n [C] rope fastened to the bow of a boat by which it may be tied to a ship, pier, etc.
pair /peə(r)/ n [C] 1 two things of the same kind (to be) used together: *a* ~ *of shoes/gloves.* 2 single article with two parts always joined: *a* ~ *of trousers/tights/scissors/tongs.* 3 two persons closely associated, e g an engaged or married couple. **in pairs,** in twos. 4 two animals of opposite sex; two horses harnessed together. 5 (in Parliament) two persons of opposite political parties who are absent from voting by mutual agreement; one member willing to do this: *The member for Lewisham couldn't find a* ~. □ *vi,vi* 1 form a pair; join, go off, in pairs. 2 (in Parliament) make a pair(5).
pa-ja-mas /pəˈdʒɑːməz/ n *pl* ⇨ pyjamas.
pal /pæl/ n [C] (*informal*) comrade; friend. □ *vi* (-ll-) **pal up (with sb),** become friendly.
  pally /ˈpælɪ/ adj (*informal*) friendly.
pal-ace /ˈpælɪs/ n [C] 1 official residence of a sovereign, archbishop or bishop. 2 any large and splendid house; large, splendid building for entertainment. 3 **the** ~, influential persons at the palace of a sovereign ruler.
pal-at-able /ˈpælətəbəl/ adj 1 agreeable to the taste. 2 (*fig*) pleasing.
pal-ate /ˈpælət/ n [C] 1 roof of the mouth: *the hard/soft* ~, its front/back part. ⇨ **cleft palate.** 2 sense of taste: *have a good* ~ *for wines.*
pa-la-tial /pəˈleɪʃəl/ adj of or like a palace: *a* ~ *residence.*
pale /peɪl/ adj (-r, -st) 1 (of a person's face) having little colour: *He turned* ~ *at the news.* 2 (of colours) not bright; faintly coloured: ~ *blue.* □ *vi* grow pale; lose colour.
  pale-ly /ˈpeɪllɪ/ adv
  pale-ness n [U]
pale /peɪl/ n [C] pointed piece of wood

used for fences; stake. ⇨ **paling.**
paleo-lithic (also **palaeo-**) /ˌpælɪəʊˈlɪθɪk US: ˈpeɪl-/ adj of the period marked by the use of primitive stone implements.
pale-on-tol-ogist (also **palæ-**) /ˌpælɪɒnˈtɒlədʒɪst US: ˈpeɪl-/ n [C] expert in paleontology.
pale-on-tol-ogy (also **palæ-**) /ˌpælɪɒnˈtɒlədʒɪ US: ˈpeɪl-/ n [U] study of fossils as a guide to the history of life on earth.
pal-ette /ˈpælɪt/ n [C] board (with a hole for the thumb) on which an artist mixes his colours.
  `palette-knife,` wide flat knife, used (by artists) for mixing (and sometimes spreading) oil colours, by potters for moulding clay and in cookery.
pal-ing /ˈpeɪlɪŋ/ n [C,U] fence made of pales ².
pal-ish /ˈpeɪlɪʃ/ adj somewhat pale.
pall /pɔːl/ n [C] 1 heavy cloth spread over a coffin. 2 (*fig*) any dark, heavy covering: *a* ~ *of smoke.*
  `pall-bearer,` person who walks alongside a coffin at a funeral.
pall /pɔːl/ vi become distasteful or boring because done, used, etc for too long a time: *pleasures that* ~ *after a time.*
pal-let /ˈpælɪt/ n [C] 1 straw-filled mattress for sleeping on. 2 portable platform for carrying and storing loads.
pal-lid /ˈpælɪd/ adj pale; looking ill.
  pal-lid-ly adv
pal-lor /ˈpælə(r)/ n [U] paleness, esp of the face.
pally ⇨ pal.
palm /pɑːm/ n [C] inner surface of the hand between the wrist and the fingers. □ *vt* hide (a coin, card, etc) in the hand when performing a trick. **palm sth off (on sb),** get him to accept it by fraud, deceit, etc.
palm /pɑːm/ n [C] 1 sorts of tree growing in warm climates, with no branches and a mass of large wide leaves at the top: `date-~; `coconut ~. 2 leaf of a palm as a symbol of victory.
palm-ist /ˈpɑːmɪst/ n [C] person who claims to tell a person's future by examining the lines on his palm.
palm-is-try /ˈpɑːmɪstrɪ/ n [U] art of doing this.
pal-pable /ˈpælpəbəl/ adj 1 that can be felt or touched. 2 clear to the senses or mind: *a* ~ *error.*
  pal-pably /-əblɪ/ adv
pal-pi-tate /ˈpælpɪteɪt/ vi 1 (of the heart) beat rapidly and irregularly. 2 (of a person, his body) tremble (with terror, etc).
pal-pi-ta-tion /ˌpælpɪˈteɪʃən/ n [C,U] (instance of) palpitating of the heart (from disease, great efforts, etc).
palsy /ˈpɔːlzɪ/ n [U] (*old use*) paralysis: *cerebral* ~. □ *vt* paralyse.
pal-try /ˈpɔːltrɪ/ adj (-ier, -iest) worthless; of no importance; contemptible.

pam·pas /ˈpæmpəs US: -əz/ n pl extensive, treeless plains of S America. Compare: *prairie* in N America and *savannah* in tropical America and W Africa.

pam·per /ˈpæmpə(r)/ vt indulge too much; be unduly kind to: a ～ed child/dog.

pamph·let /ˈpæmflət/ n [C] small paper-covered book, esp on a question of current interest.

pamph·let·eer /ˌpæmfləˈtɪə(r)/ n [C] writer of pamphlets.

pan[1] /pæn/ n [C] 1 flat dish, usually shallow and without a cover, used for cooking and other domestic purposes. 2 receptacle with various uses: the ～ (= bowl) of a lavatory; a ˋbed～. 3 (natural or artificial) depression in the ground: a ˋsalt-～, where salt water is evaporated. 4 either of the dishes on a pair of scales. 5 open dish for washing gravel, etc to separate gold ore or other metals. □ vt,vi (-nn-) 1 wash (gold-bearing gravel, etc) in a pan. *pan out,* (a) yield gold. (b) (fig) succeed; turn out: How did things ～ out? 2 (informal) criticize harshly.

ˋpan·cake, (a) batter fried on both sides until brown. (b) **pancake landing,** emergency landing in which the aircraft drops flat to the ground. (c) cosmetic face-powder pressed into a flat cake, used without a foundation cream.

pan[2] /pæn/ vi,vt (cinema and TV) turn a camera right or left to follow a moving object or get a panoramic effect. ⇨ zoom(2).

pan- prefix all, throughout: *Pan-African.*

pana·cea /ˌpænəˈsɪə/ n [C] (pl ～s) remedy for all troubles, diseases, etc.

pa·nache /pæˈnæʃ US: pə-/ n [U] (air of) confidence: He does everything with ～.

pana·tella /ˌpænəˈtelə/ n [C] (pl ～s) long slender cigar.

pan·chro·matic /ˌpænkrəˈmætɪk/ adj (in photography) equally sensitive to all colours: ～ film.

pan·creas /ˈpæŋkrɪəs/ n [C] gland near the stomach, discharging a juice which helps digestion.

pan·cre·atic /ˌpæŋkrɪˈætɪk/ adj of the pancreas.

panda /ˈpændə/ n [C] (pl ～s) mammal like a bear of Tibet and China, with black legs and a black and white body.

ˋPanda car, (GB) police patrol car.

ˋPanda crossing, (GB) pedestrian crossing controlled by traffic lights

pan·de·mo·nium /ˌpændɪˈməʊnɪəm/ n [C,U] (pl ～s) (scene of) wild and noisy disorder.

pan·der /ˈpændə(r)/ vi give help or encouragement (to): newspapers that ～ to the public interest in crime; ～ to low tastes.

pane /peɪn/ n [C] sheet of glass in (a division of) a window.

panel /ˈpænəl/ n [C] 1 separate part of the surface of a door, wall, ceiling, etc, raised above or sunk below the surrounding area. 2 large piece of material of a different kind or colour inserted in a dress. 3 board or other surface for controls and instruments: the ˋinstrument ～, of an aircraft or motor-vehicle; the conˋtrol ～, on a radio or TV set. 4 list of names, e g of doctors who (in GB) have agreed to attend persons under the National Health Service. 5 group of speakers, esp one chosen to speak, answer questions, take part in a game, before an audience, e g of listeners to a broadcast: (as an adjective) a ˋ～ discussion/game. □ vt (-ll-, US -l-) furnish or decorate with panels(1,2): a ～led room/skirt.

pan·el·ling, series of panels on a wall, etc.

pang /pæŋ/ n [C] sudden, sharp feeling of pain, guilt, etc.

panic /ˈpænɪk/ n [C,U] unreasoning, uncontrolled, quickly spreading fear: There is always danger of (a) ～ when a building catches fire. □ vi (-ck-) be affected with panic: Stop ～king!

pan·icky /ˈpænɪkɪ/ adj (informal) easily affected by, in a state of, panic.

ˋpanic-stricken adj terrified; overcome by panic.

pan·nier /ˈpænɪə(r)/ n [C] 1 one of a pair of baskets placed across the back of a horse or ass. 2 one of a pair of bags on either side of the back of a (motor-)bike.

pan·or·ama /ˌpænəˈrɑːmə US: -ˈræmə/ n [C] (pl ～s) wide, uninterrupted view; constantly changing scene: the ～ of London life.

pan·or·amic /ˌpænəˈræmɪk/ adj

pan·pipes /ˈpæn paɪps/ n pl musical instrument made of a series of reeds or pipes, played by blowing across the open ends.

pansy /ˈpænzɪ/ n [C] (pl -ies) flowering herbaceous plant.

pant /pænt/ vi,vt 1 take short, quick breaths; gasp: The dog ～ed along behind its master's horse. 2 say while panting: He₂～ed out his message. 3 (old use) = pine[2](2). □ n [C] short, quick breath; gasp.

pan·ta·loon /ˈpæntəˈluːn/ n 1 [C] (in pantomime) foolish character on whom the clown plays tricks. 2 (pl) (old use) = pants(2).

pan·tech·ni·con /pænˈteknɪkən/ n [C] (GB) large van for removing furniture.

pan·the·ism /ˈpænθɪɪzm/ n [U] belief that God is in everything and that everything is God; belief in and worship of all gods.

pan·the·ist /-ɪst/, believer in pantheism.

pan·the·is·tic /ˌpænθɪˈɪstɪk/ adj.

pan·ther /ˈpænθə(r)/ n [C] leopard; (US) puma.

pan·ties /ˈpæntɪz/ n pl (informal) (woman's or girl's) close-fitting short knickers.

panto /ˈpæntəʊ/ n [C] (pl ～s) (informal) (abbr of) pantomime.

pan·to·mime /ˈpæntəmaɪm/ n 1 [C,U]

(example of a) kind of English drama based on a fairy tale or traditional story, with music, dancing and clowning. **2** [C] acting without words.

pan·try /ˈpæntrɪ/ n [C] (pl -ies) **1** room (in a large house, hotel, ship, etc) in which silver, glass, table-linen, etc are kept. **2** larder; room (in a house) in which food is kept.

pants /pænts/ n pl **1** trousers. **2** (in trade use) drawers(2).

pantyhose /ˈpæntɪhəʊz/ n (collective, as pl) tights fitting below the waistline.

papa /pəˈpɑ US: ˈpɑpə/ n [C] (child's word for) father.

pa·pacy /ˈpeɪpəsɪ/ n [C] (pl -ies) position of, authority of, the Pope; system of government by Popes.

pa·pal /ˈpeɪpəl/ adj of the Pope or a papacy.

pa·paw (also **paw·paw**) /pəˈpɔ US: ˈpɔpɔ/ n [C] **1** tropical tree like a palm; its large edible fruit with a yellow pulp inside (also called papaya). **2** small N American evergreen tree with small fleshy edible fruit (also called custard apple).

pa·per /ˈpeɪpə(r)/ n **1** [U] substance manufactured from wood, rags, etc in the form of sheets, used for writing, printing, drawing, wrapping, packing, etc: a sheet of ~; a ~ bag. **(be) good on paper**, (be) good when judged from written or printed evidence: It's a good scheme on ~ (but has not yet been tested). **2** [C] = newspaper: the evening ~s. **3** (pl) documents showing who a person is, what authority he has, etc: identification ~s; ship's ~s. **4** [C] set of printed examination questions on a given subject: The biology ~ was difficult. **5** [C] essay, esp one to be read to a learned society: a ~ on currency reform. □ vt paste paper on (walls, etc): ~ the dining-room.

ˈpaper·back, book in paper covers.

ˈpaper-clip, ⇨ clip¹(1).

ˈpaper-mill, factory where paper is made.

ˈpaper ˈtiger, person, group of persons, etc which seems to be, but is not, powerful.

ˈpaperwork, written work (in an office, etc, e g filling in forms, correspondence, contrasted with practical affairs, dealing with people): He's good at ~work.

pa·poose /pæˈpus US: pəˈpus/ n [C] **1** (word used by Indians of N America for a) baby. **2** framed bag (like a rucksack) for carrying a young baby on one's back.

pap·rika /ˈpæprɪkə US: pəˈprikə/ n [U] sweet red pepper used in cooking.

pa·py·rus /pəˈpaɪərəs/ n **1** [U] (kind of paper made in ancient Egypt from) tall water plant or reed. **2** [C] (pl papyri /pəˈpaɪəraɪ/) manuscript written on this paper.

par¹ /pɑ(r)/ n [C] **1** average, normal amount, degree, value, etc. **above/below/at par**, (of shares, bonds, etc), above/below/at the original price or face value. **on a par (with)**, equal (to). **2** (in golf) number of strokes considered necessary for a player to complete a hole or course.

par·able /ˈpærəbəl/ n [C] simple story designed to teach a moral lesson.

para·bol·i·cal /ˈpærəˈbɒlɪkəl/ adj

par·ab·ola /pəˈræbələ/ n [C] (pl ~s) plane curve formed by cutting a cone on a plane parallel to its side.

para·bolic /ˈpærəˈbɒlɪk/ adj

para·chute /ˈpærəʃut/ n [C] apparatus used for a jump from an aircraft or for dropping supplies, etc. □ vt, vi drop, descend, from an aircraft by means of a parachute.

para·chut·ist /-ɪst/, person who jumps with a parachute.

par·ade /pəˈreɪd/ vt, vi **1** (of troops) (cause to) gather together for drilling, inspection, etc; march in procession. **2** make a display of; try to attract attention to: ~ one's wealth. □ n **1** [U] parading of troops: be on ~; [C] instance of this: a church ~. **2** [C] display or exhibition: a ˈfashion ~. **3** wide, pavement on a seafront.

paˈrade-ground, area on which parades (1) are held.

para·dise /ˈpærədaɪs/ n **1** the Garden of Eden, home of Adam and Eve. **2** Heaven. **3** (with a, an) any place of perfect happiness; [U] condition of perfect happiness. ⇨ fool's paradise.

para·dox /ˈpærədɒks/ n [C] statement that seems to say something opposite to common sense or the truth, but which may contain a truth (e g 'More haste, less speed'). **para·doxi·cal** /ˈpærəˈdɒksɪkəl/ adj

para·doxi·cally /-klɪ/ adv

par·af·fin /ˈpærəfɪn/ n [U] **1** (GB) oil obtained from petroleum, coal, etc used as a fuel. (US = kerosene). **2** substance like wax used for making candles. **3** odourless, tasteless form of paraffin used as a laxative.

para·gon /ˈpærəgən US: -gɒn/ n [C] model (of excellence); apparently perfect person or thing: a ~ of virtue.

para·graph /ˈpærəgrɑf US: -græf/ n [C] **1** division (usually a group of several sentences dealing with one main idea) of a piece of writing, started on a new line. **2** small item of news in a newspaper. □ vt divide into paragraphs.

para·keet /ˈpærəkit/ n [C] small, long-tailed parrot of various kinds.

par·al·lel /ˈpærəlel/ adj **1** (of lines) always at the same distance from one another. **2** (of one line) having this relation (to or with another): in a ~ direction (with/to...). **3** (fig) similar; corresponding: a ~ job in another company. □ n [C] **1 in parallel**, (of the components of an electrical circuit) with the supply of current taken to each component independently. ⇨ series. **2** person, event, etc precisely similar: a brilliant career without (a) ~ in modern times. **3** comparison: draw a ~ between.... □ vt (-l- or (GB) -ll-) **1** quote, produce or mention a

461

comparison. **2** be the same as: *His experiences ~ mine in many instances.*

par·al·lel·o·gram /ˌpærəˈleləgræm/ n [C] four-sided plane figure whose opposite sides are parallel.

par·al·ysis /pəˈræləsɪs/ n [U] **1** loss of feeling or power to move in any or every part of the body. **2** (*fig*) state of total powerlessness.

para·lyt·ic /ˌpærəˈlɪtɪk/ adj **(a)** suffering from paralysis(1). **(b)** (*fig*) helpless: *paralytic laughter.* **(c)** (*informal*) very drunk. □ n [C] paralytic person.

para·lyse (*US* = **-lyze**) /ˈpærəlaɪz/ vt **1** affect with paralysis. **2** (*fig*) make helpless: *paralysed with fear.*

para·meter /pəˈræmɪtə(r)/ n [C] variable factor in an analysis, experiment.

para·mili·tary /ˌpærəˈmɪlɪtrɪ US: -terɪ/ adj having a status or function subordinate to regular military forces.

para·mount /ˈpærəmaʊnt/ adj (*formal*) **1** supreme, superior in power: ~ *chiefs.* **2** pre-eminent, superior: *of ~ importance.*

para·noia /ˌpærəˈnɔɪə/ n [U] mental disorder marked by fixed delusions, e g of persecution or grandeur.

para·noid /ˈpærənɔɪd/, (also **para·noiac** /ˌpærəˈnɔɪæk/) n [C], adj (person) suffering from paranoia.

para·pet /ˈpærəpɪt/ n [C] **1** protective wall at the edge of a flat roof, side of a bridge, etc. **2** defensive bank of earth, stone, etc along the front edge of a trench (in war).

para·pher·nalia /ˌpærəfəˈneɪlɪə/ n [U] numerous small possessions, tools, instruments, etc.

para·phrase /ˈpærəfreɪz/ vt, n [C] (give a) restatement of the meaning of (a piece of writing) in other words.

para·ple·gia /ˌpærəˈpliːdʒə/ n [U] paralysis of the lower part of the body, including both legs, caused by injury to the spinal cord.

para·plegic /ˌpærəˈpliːdʒɪk/ n [C], adj (person) suffering from paraplegia.

para·site /ˈpærəsaɪt/ n [C] **1** animal (e g *louse, hookworm*) or plant (e g *mistletoe*) living on or in another and getting its food from it. **2** person supported by another and giving him nothing in return.

para·sitic /ˌpærəˈsɪtɪk/, **para·siti·cal** /ˌpærəˈsɪtɪkəl/ adj

para·sol /ˈpærəsɒl US: -sɔl/ n [C] umbrella used to give shade from the sun.

para·troops /ˈpærətruːps/ n pl troops trained for being dropped by parachute.

para·trooper /ˈpærətruːpə(r)/ n [C] one of these.

par·boil /ˈpɑːbɔɪl/ vt boil (food) until partially cooked.

par·cel /ˈpɑːsəl/ n [C] thing or things wrapped and tied up for carrying, sending by post, etc. *part and parcel of,* an essential part of. □ vt (-ll-, *US* also -l-) **1** divide into portions: ~ *out the food.* **2** make into a

parcel: ~ *up the books.*

parch /pɑːtʃ/ vt (of heat, the sun, etc) make hot and dry: *the ~ed deserts of N Africa.*

parch·ment /ˈpɑːtʃmənt/ n **1** [C,U] (manuscript on) writing material prepared from the skin of a sheep or goat. **2** [U] kind of paper resembling parchment.

par·don /ˈpɑːdən/ n **1** [U] forgiveness: *ask for ~*; [C] instance of this. **2** (used to show politeness). *beg sb's pardon,* excuse oneself, e g for disagreeing with somebody, or apologize, e g for not hearing or understanding somebody. **3** = indulgence(3). □ vt forgive; excuse: ~ *her for doing wrong.*

par·don·able /-əbəl/ adj that can be forgiven, etc.

pare /peə(r)/ vt **1** cut away the outer part, edge or skin of: ~ *the claws of an animal.* **2** (*fig*) reduce little by little: ~ *down one's expenses.*

par·ent /ˈpeərənt/ n [C] **1** father or mother; ancestor. **2** (*fig*) source, origin: ~*s of evil.*

par·ent·age /-ɪdʒ/ n [U] fatherhood or motherhood; origin.

par·ental /pəˈrentəl/ adj of a parent: *showing ~al care.*

par·enth·esis /pəˈrenθəsɪs/ n [C] (*pl* -eses /-əsiːz/) **1** sentence or phrase within another sentence, marked off by commas, dashes or brackets. **2** (*sing* or *pl*) round brackets ( ) for this: *a comment in ~.*

par·en·thetic /ˌpærənˈθetɪk/, **par·en·theti·cal** /-ɪkəl/ adj

par·en·theti·cally /-klɪ/ adv

par·ish /ˈpærɪʃ/ n [C] **1** division of a county with its own church and clergymen. **2** (*civil* ~) (*GB*) division of a county for local government: *the ~ council.*

par·ish·ioner /pəˈrɪʃənə(r)/ n [C] inhabitant of a parish.

par·ity /ˈpærətɪ/ n [U] equality; being equal; being at par: *The two currencies have now reached ~,* are equivalent.

park /pɑːk/ n [C] **1** public garden or public recreation ground in a town. **2** area of grassland, trees, etc round a large country house or mansion. ⇨ also car park, national park. □ vt, vi **1** place or leave (a motor-vehicle) in a car park, a drive (2), etc: *Where can we ~ (the car)?* **2** (*informal*) put (a person or thing) somewhere: *Where can I ~ my luggage?*

parka /ˈpɑːkə/ n [C] = anorak.

parking /ˈpɑːkɪŋ/ n [U] (area for the) parking of motor-vehicles: *No ~ between 9 a m and 6 p m.*

parking lot, (*US*) = car park.

parking meter, coin-operated meter beside which a car may be parked in a public place, e g a street.

Parkinson's disease /ˈpɑːkɪnsənz dɪziːz/ n [U] chronic progressive disease of old people, with muscular tremors, muscular rigidity and general weakness.

par·lia·ment /ˈpɑːləmənt/ n [C] (in countries with representative government) supreme law-making council or assembly (in GB formed of the House of Commons and the House of Lords): *enter P~*; '*Members of* `P~.`

par·lia·men·tar·ian /ˌpɑːləmənˈteərɪən/, person skilled in the rules and procedures of parliament.

par·lia·men·tary /ˌpɑːləˈmentrɪ/ *adj*

par·lour (*US* = -**lor**) /ˈpɑːlə(r)/ *n* [C] **1** (*dated*) ordinary sitting-room for the family in a private house (now called sitting-room or living-room). **2** private sitting-room at an inn; room for the reception of visitors. **3** (*esp US*) room for customers and clients: *a* `beauty ~`.

par·ochial /pəˈrəʊkɪəl/ *adj* **1** of a parish. **2** (*fig*) limited, narrow: *a ~ mind/attitude*.

par·ochi·al·ly /-kɪəlɪ/ *adv*

par·ody /ˈpærədɪ/ *n* (*pl* -**ies**) **1** [C,U] (piece of) writing intended to amuse by imitating the style of writing used by somebody else. **2** [C] feeble imitation: *a ~ of justice.* □ *vt* (*pt, pp* -**ied**) make a parody of.

pa·role /pəˈrəʊl/ *n* [U] prisoner's solemn promise, on being given certain privileges, that he will not try to escape. **on parole**, freed after making such a promise. □ *vt* set (a prisoner) free on parole.

paro·quet /ˈpærəkɪt/ *n* = parakeet.

par·ox·ysm /ˈpærəksɪzm/ *n* [C] sudden attack or outburst (of pain, anger, laughter, etc).

par·quet /ˈpɑːkeɪ *US:* pɑːˈkeɪ/ *n* [C] flooring of wooden blocks fitted together to make a pattern.

par·ri·cide /ˈpærɪsaɪd/ *n* [C,U] (person guilty of the) murder of one's father or near relation.

par·rot /ˈpærət/ *n* [C] **1** sorts of bird with a short hooked bill and (often) brightly coloured feathers of which some kinds can be trained to imitate human speech. **2** person who repeats, often without understanding, what others say.

parry /ˈpærɪ/ *vt* (*pt,pp* -**ied**) **1** turn aside, avoid (a blow). **2** (*fig*) evade (a question). □ *n* [C] act of parrying, esp in fencing and boxing.

parse /pɑːz *US:* pɑːrs/ *vt* **1** describe (a word) grammatically. **2** point out how the words of a sentence are related.

Par·see /pɑːˈsiː/ *n* [C] supporter of a religious system in India, the members being descended from Persians who settled in India in the 8th century.

par·si·moni·ous /ˌpɑːsɪˈməʊnɪəs/ *adj* too economical: mean `1(6)`.

pars·ley /ˈpɑːslɪ/ *n* [U] garden plant with aromatic leaves, used in seasoning, sauces.

pars·nip /ˈpɑːsnɪp/ *n* [C] long, white or pale-yellow root, cooked as a vegetable.

par·son /ˈpɑːsən/ *n* [C] parish priest; clergyman.

parson's nose, (*informal*) tail-end of a

cooked fowl.

`par·son·age` /-ɪdʒ/, parson's house.

part /pɑːt/ *n* [C] **1** (often *sing* without *a, an*) some but not all of a thing or a number of things; something less than the whole: *We spent* (*a*) *~ of our holiday in France. P~s of the book are interesting.* **for the** `most part`, in most cases; generally. **In part**, to some degree. **2** (*pl*) region; district: *in these/those ~s.* **3** any one of a number of equal divisions: *A minute is the sixtieth ~ of an hour.* **4** person's share in some activity; his duty or responsibility; what an actor in a play, film, etc says and does: *a man with an important ~ in a play/in a conference.* **play one's part**, be involved, do what is expected. **take part (in)**, have a share (in); help: *Are you going to take ~ in the discussion*, Do you intend to speak? **5** side in a dispute, transaction, agreement, mutual arrangement, etc. **take sb's part**, support him: *He always takes his brother's ~.* **for** `my part`, as far as I am concerned: *For my ~ I am quite happy about the division of the money.* **6 take sth in good part**, not be offended by it. **7** each issue of a work published in instalments: *a new encyclopaedia to be issued in monthly ~s.* **8** essential piece or section (e g a *spare ~*), extra piece, etc to be used when needed, when something breaks or wears: *When can I get a ~ for my pump?* **9** (*music*) each of the melodies that make up a harmony; the melody for a particular voice or instrument. □ *adv* partly: *made ~ of iron and ~ of wood.*

'part-`time` *adj, adv* for only a part of the working day or week: *be employed ~-time; ~-time teaching.* Hence, '**part-`timer** *n* [C]

'**part of** `speech`, one of the classes of words, e g *noun, verb, adjective.*

part² /pɑːt/ *vt,vi* **1** (cause to) separate or divide: *We tried to ~ the two fighters. Let's ~ friends.* **part company (with),** (**a**) end a relationship. (**b**) leave and travel in a different direction. (**c**) disagree: *On that question I am afraid I must ~ company with you.* **2** give up, give away: *He hates to ~ with his money.* **3** divide one's hair by combing it in opposite ways.

part·ing *n* (**a**) [C] line where the hair is combed in opposite ways. (**b**) [C,U] departure. **at the parting of the ways,** (*fig*) at the point when one has to choose between courses of action.

part·ly *adv* to some extent.

par·take /pɑːˈteɪk/ *vi,vt* (*pt* -**took** /-ˈtʊk/, *pp* -**taken** /-ˈteɪkən/) (*formal*) **1** take a share in: *They partook* (*of*) *our simple meal.* **2** have some of (the nature or characteristics of): *His manner ~s of insolence.*

par·tial /ˈpɑːʃəl/ *adj* **1** forming only a part; not complete: *a ~ success; a ~ eclipse of the sun.* **2** showing too much favour to one person or side: *examiners who are ~ towards pretty women students.* **3** having a liking for: ~ *to French wines.*

par·ti·sai·ly /ˈpɑʃəlɪ/ *adv* (a) partly; not completely. (b) in a partial(2) manner.

par·ti·al·i·ty /ˌpɑʃɪˈælətɪ/ *n* (a) [U] being partial(2) in treatment of people, etc. (b) [C] fondness: *a ~ity for moonlight walks.*

par·tici·pant /pɑˈtɪsɪpənt/ *n* [C] person who takes part in something.

par·tici·pate /pɑˈtɪsɪpeɪt/ *vi* have a share, be involved: ~ *in a plot.*

par·ti·ciple /ˈpɑtəsɪpəl/ *n* [C] (verbal adjective qualifying nouns but retaining some characteristics of a verb, e g): *'Hurrying' and 'hurried' are the present and past ~s of 'hurry'.* (*Note:* past participle is abbreviated to *pp* in this dictionary.)

par·ti·cip·ial /ˌpɑtɪˈsɪpɪəl/ *adj*

par·ticle /ˈpɑtɪkəl/ *n* [C] **1** very small bit: ~s *of dust.* **2** (*gram*) minor part of speech, e g an article (*a, an, the*), or an affix (*un-, in-, -ness, -ly*).

par·ticu·lar /pɑˈtɪkjʊlə(r)/ *adj* **1** relating to one as distinct from others: *in this ~ case.* **2** special; worth notice; outstanding: *for no ~ reason. He took ~ trouble to get it right. in particular,* especially: *I remember the colour in ~.* **3** very exact: *a full and ~ account of what we saw.* **4** difficult to satisfy: *She's very ~ about what she wears.* □ *n* [C] detail. *go into particulars,* give details.

par·ticu·lar·ly *adv* especially: *He was ~ly noticeable.*

part·ing /ˈpɑtɪŋ/ ⇨ part².

par·ti·san /ˈpɑtɪzæn *US:* ˈpɑtɪzən/ *n* [C] **1** person devoted to a party, group or cause. **2** (esp) member of an armed resistance movement in a country occupied by enemy forces: ~ *troops.* □ *adj* uncritically devoted to a cause: *His loyalties are too ~.*

par·ti·tion /pɑˈtɪʃən/ *n* **1** [U] division into parts: *the ~ of India in 1947.* **2** [C] that which divides, e g a thin wall between rooms. **3** [C] part formed by dividing; section. □ *vt* divide into sections, e g using a partition (2): ~ *off a room.*

par·ti·tive /ˈpɑtɪtɪv/ *n* [C], *adj* (*gram*) (word) denoting part of a collective whole: *'Some' and 'any' are ~s.*

part·ner /ˈpɑtnə(r)/ *n* [C] **1** person who takes part with another or others in some activity, esp one of the owners of a business: ~s *in crime;* `business ~s. ⇨sleeping partner.* **2** one of two persons dancing together, playing tennis, cards, etc together. **3** husband or wife. □ *vt* **1** be a partner to. **2** bring (people) together as partners.

`part·ner·ship /-ʃɪp/, (a) [U] state of being a partner. (b) [C] joint business: *enter/go into ~ship (with her).*

par·took /pɑˈtʊk/ ⇨ partake.

par·tridge /ˈpɑtrɪdʒ/ *n* [C] sorts of bird of the same family as the pheasant; [U] its flesh eaten as food.

party /ˈpɑtɪ/ *n* (*pl* -ies) **1** [C] group of persons united in policy and opinion, in support of a cause, esp in politics: *the Conservative, Labour and Liberal parties.* **2** [U] (esp used as an *adjective*) government based on political parties: ~ *politics,* politics of and within a political party: *Our best men put public interest before ~. follow the party line,* ⇨ line¹ (11). **3** [C] one of the persons or sides in a legal agreement or dispute. **4** [C] group of persons travelling or working together, or on duty together: *a ~ of tourists; a `firing-~,* of soldiers, at a military funeral or execution. **5** [C] gathering of persons, by invitation, for pleasure: *a `dinner/`birthday ~.* **6** [C] person taking part in and approving of or being aware of what is going on: *be ~ to a decision.*

`party line, (a) telephone line shared by two or more persons. (b) agreed or established policy of a political party.

`party-`wall, one that divides two properties and is the responsiblity of both owners.

pass¹ /pɑs *US:* pæs/ *n* **1** [C] act of passing. **2** [C] success in an examination, esp (in university degree examinations) success in satisfying the examiners but without distinction or honours¹ (7): *get a ~ in History; a `~ degree.* **3** (*sing* only) **bring to pass,** accomplish, carry out. **come to pass,** happen. **reach/come to (such) a fine/sad/ pretty pass,** reach such a state or condition. **4** [C] (paper, ticket, etc giving) permission or authority to travel, enter a building, occupy a seat in a cinema, etc: *No admittance without a ~.* **5** [C] act of kicking, throwing, or hitting the ball from one player to another player (of the same team). **6** [C] narrow way over or through mountains; such a way viewed as the entrance to a country. **7 make a pass at (a woman),** (*sl*) make (possibly unwelcome) friendly or amorous approach. **8** [C] (in card-games) act of passing(16).

`pass-key, (a) private key to a gate, etc. (b) key which opens a number of locks.

`pass-mark, minimum mark needed to pass an examination.

`pass-word, secret word or phrase which enables a person to be recognized as a friend and not an enemy.

pass² /pɑs *US:* pæs/ *vi,vt* (Compare past¹) (For special uses with *adverbial particles* and *prepositions,* ⇨ 19 below.) **1** move towards and beyond, proceed (*along, through, down, etc*): ~ *through a village. Please let me ~. The road was too narrow for cars to ~. The two ships ~ed by/~ed each other during the night.* **2** leave (a person, place, object, etc) on one side or behind as one goes forward: *Turn right after ~ing the post office. I ~ed Miss Green in the street.* **3** go through, across, over or between: *The ship ~ed the channel. No complaints ~ed her lips.* **4** give by handing: *Please ~ (me) the butter. The letter was ~ed on/round to all the members of the* *family*. **5** (of time) go by; be spent: *Six months ~ed and still we had no news of them*. **6** spend (time): *How shall we ~ the evening?* **pass the time,** do something during a period of spare time, e g while waiting for a person, a train. **7** change from one state of things to another; change into another state of things: *Water ~es from a liquid to a solid state when it freezes*. (*Note: change* is the usual word.) **8** say (something): *~ a remark*. **pass the 'time of `day with sb,** have an unimportant conversation with him. **9** (cause to) circulate: *He was imprisoned for ~ing forged banknotes*. **10** be known by or recognised as: *He can easily ~ for an officer. She ~es under the name of Mrs Green*. **11** examine and accept; be examined and accepted: *Parliament ~ed the Bill. The Bill ~ed and became law. The examiners ~ed most of the candidates. The candidates ~ed (the examination). We have to ~ the Customs before we leave*. **12** take place; be said or done (between persons): *Tell me everything that ~ed between you*. **13** be beyond the range of: *a story that ~es belief. It ~es my comprehension*. **14** give (an opinion, judgement, etc): *~ sentence on an accused man. I can't ~ an opinion on your work without seeing it*. **15** be accepted without criticism or blame: *His rude remarks ~ed without comment. I don't like it, but I'll let it ~*, will not make objections, etc. **16** (in card games) let one's turn go by without playing a card or making a bid. **17** move; cause to go: *He ~ed his fingers through his hair*. **pass an eye over,** look quickly at. **pass water,** urinate. **18** (in football, hockey, etc) kick, hand or hit (the ball) to a player of one's own side.

19 (special uses with *adverbial particles* and *prepositions*):

pass away, die: *He ~ed away peacefully*.

pass between, be exchanged by: *Don't tell anyone about what has ~ed between us*, about what we have discussed.

pass sb/sth by, pay no attention to: *I can't ~ the matter by without a protest*.

pass down, hand over. ⇨ hand[2].

pass for sb/sth, be accepted as: *Do I speak French well enough to ~ for a Frenchman?*

pass in/into, gain admission to: *He ~ed into Sandhurst* (Royal Military College).

pass off, (a) (of events) take place, be carried through: *The meeting of the strikers ~ed off quietly*. (b) (of pain, a crisis) end gradually: *Has your toothache ~ed off yet?* **pass sth off,** turn attention from (to avoid embarrassment): *~ off an awkward situation*. **pass sth/sb off as,** represent falsely to be: *He tried to ~ himself off as a qualified doctor*.

pass on, (of a person) die. **pass sth on (to),** hand or give it (to another person or others).

pass out, (*informal*) = faint. **pass out**

(*of*), leave college, etc having passed one's examinations.

pass over, fail to notice or include: *~ over an important mistake and hope it will not be noticed*. **pass sb over,** fail to consider for promotion, etc: *They ~ed me over in favour of a younger man*.

pass through, experience; suffer: *~ through a difficult period after a divorce*.

pass sth up, (*informal*) not take advantage of something: *~ up an opportunity*.

pass-able /ˈpɑːsəbəl US: ˈpæs-/ *adj* **1** (of roads, etc) that can be passed over or crossed: *Are the Alpine roads ~ yet?* **2** that can be accepted as fairly good but not excellent: *a ~ knowledge of German*.

pass-ably /-əblɪ/ *adv*

pas-sage /ˈpæsɪdʒ/ *n* **1** [U] passing; act of going past, through or across; right to go through: *the ~ of time*. **2** [C] journey from point to point by sea or air: *book one's ~ to New York*. **work one's passage,** ⇨ work[2](4). **3** [C] way through: *force a ~ through a crowd*. **4** [C] corridor in a building: *She has to keep her bicycle in the ~*. **5** [C] short extract from a speech or piece of writing, quoted or considered separately. **6** [U] (in Parliament) passing of a Bill so that it becomes law. **7** (*pl*) what passes between two persons in conversation: *have angry ~s with an opponent during a debate*.

`pass-age-way,` = passage(4).

passé /ˈpɑːseɪ US: pæˈseɪ/ *adj* (*feminine* **passée**) **1** no longer in use. **2** (esp, of a woman) past the period of greatest beauty.

pas-sen-ger /ˈpæsəndʒə(r)/ *n* [C] **1** person being conveyed by bus, taxi, tram, train, ship, aircraft, etc. **2** (*informal*) member of a team, crew, etc who does no effective work.

passer-by /ˈpɑːsə ˈbaɪ US: ˈpæsər/ *n* [C] (*pl* passers-by) person who passes a person or a thing by chance.

pas-sing /ˈpɑːsɪŋ US: ˈpæs-/ *adj* going by; not lasting: *the ~ years*. □ *n* [U] the act of going by: *the ~ of the old year*, i e on New Year's Eve.

passion /ˈpæʃən/ *n* **1** [U] strong feeling or enthusiasm, esp of love, hate or anger. **2** (with *a*, *an*) outburst of strong feeling: *be in a ~ about the news*.

the Passion, the suffering and death of Jesus.

`Passion play,` drama about the Passion.

`Passion `Sunday,` the fifth Sunday in Lent. `Passion Week,` the week between Passion Sunday and Palm Sunday.

passion-less *adj*

passion-ate /ˈpæʃənət/ *adj* filled with, showing, love or anger: *a ~ nature; ~ language*.

passion-ate-ly *adv*

pass-ive /ˈpæsɪv/ *adj* acted upon but not acting; not offering active resistance: *In spite of my efforts the boy remained ~*, showed no signs of interest, activity, etc. □ *n*

[U] = passive voice.

the passive voice, (*gram*) the form in italic type in the sentence 'The letter *was written* yesterday.'

pass·ive·ly *adv*

pass·ive·ness *n* [U]

pass·key ⇨ pass¹(9).

Pass·over /ˈpɑːsəʊvə(r) *US*: ˈpæs-/ *n* Jewish religious festival commemorating the liberation of the Jews from slavery in Egypt.

pass·port /ˈpɑːspɔːt *US*: ˈpæs-/ *n* [C] 1 official document to be carried by a traveller abroad, certifying identity and citizenship. 2 (*fig*) something that enables one to win or obtain something: *Is flattery a ∼ to success with that teacher?*

pass·word ⇨ pass¹(9).

past¹ /pɑːst *US*: pæst/ *adj* of the time before the present; gone by in time: *during the ∼ week; in times ∼; ∼ generations.* (*Note:* compare *passed* in pass².) □ *n* 1 (with *the*) past time: *We cannot change the ∼. In the ∼ trains were pulled by steam-engines.* 2 person's past life or experiences: *We know nothing of his ∼.*

past participle, (*gram*) ⇨ participle.

past tense, (*gram*) ⇨ tense².

past² /pɑːst *US*: pæst/ *prep* 1 beyond in time; after: *half ∼ two; a woman ∼ middle age.* 2 beyond in space; up to and farther than: *He walked ∼ the house.* 3 beyond the limits, power or range of: *The old man is ∼ work,* is too old, weak, etc. *The pain was almost ∼ bearing,* too severe to be endured. **be past caring,** have reached the stage of complete indifference (after a long period of suffering, etc). **would not put sth past sb,** consider him capable of doing something disreputable, unusual, etc: *I wouldn't put it ∼ him to run off with the money.* □ *adv* (in the sense of 2 above: *go/run/hurry ∼.*

pasta /ˈpæstə/ *n* [U] (*It*) (dish of food prepared from a dough of) flour, eggs and water mixed and dried, e g macaroni, spaghetti, ravioli.

paste /peɪst/ *n* [U] 1 soft mixture of flour, fat, etc for making pastry. 2 preparation of fish, meat, etc, made into a soft, moist mass: `anchovy ∼; `fish-∼. 3 mixture used for sticking things together, e g paper on walls. 4 substance like glass used in making artificial diamonds, etc. □ *vi* stick with paste(3).

pas·tel /ˈpæstəl *US*: pæˈstel/ *n* [C] 1 (picture drawn with) dried paste made into coloured crayons. 2 (as an *adjective*) soft, light, delicate shades of colour.

pas·tern /ˈpæstən/ *n* [C] part of a horse's foot between the fetlock and the hoof.

pas·teur·ize /ˈpæstʃəraɪz/ *vt* rid (milk, etc) of disease-producing bacteria by heating.

pas·teur·iz·ation /ˌpæstʃəraɪˈzeɪʃən *US*: -rɪˈz-/ *n* [U]

pas·tille /ˈpæstɪl *US*: pæˈstil/ *n* [C] small flavoured tablet to be sucked, e g one containing medicine for the throat.

pas·time /ˈpɑːstaɪm *US*: ˈpæs-/ *n* [C] anything done to pass time pleasantly: *Flirting was her favourite ∼.*

pas·tor /ˈpɑːstə(r) *US*: ˈpæs-/ *n* [C] minister(3), esp of a nonconformist church.

pas·toral /ˈpɑːstərəl *US*: ˈpæs-/ *adj* 1 of shepherds and country life: *∼ poetry.* 2 of a pastor; (esp) of a bishop: *a ∼ letter,* one to the members of a bishop's diocese. 3 of (duties towards) the spiritual welfare of Christians: *∼ care/responsibilities.* □ *n* [C] pastoral(1) poem, play, letter, etc.

pas·try /ˈpeɪstrɪ/ *n* (*pl* -ies) 1 [U] paste of flour, fat, etc baked in an oven. 2 [C] article of food made wholly or partly of this, e g a pie or tart.

pas·ture /ˈpɑːstʃə(r) *US*: ˈpæs-/ *n* [U] grassland for cattle; grass on such land. ⇨ meadow; [C] piece of land of this kind. □ *vt,vi* 1 (of persons) put (cattle, sheep, etc) to graze. 2 (of cattle, etc) eat grass.

pasty¹ /ˈpeɪstɪ/ *adj* like paste(1): *a ∼ complexion,* white and unhealthy.

pasty² /ˈpæstɪ/ *n* [C] (*pl* -ies) pie of meat or jam, etc enclosed in paste and baked without a dish: *a Cornish ∼.*

pat /pæt/ *vt,vi* (-tt-) 1 tap gently with the open hand or with something flat: *∼ a dog.* **pat sb/oneself on the back,** (*fig*) show approval, congratulate, etc. 2 carry out the action of patting. □ *n* [C] 1 tap with the open hand, e g as a caress or to show sympathy. 2 small mass of something, esp butter, formed by patting. 3 light sound made by hitting something with a flat object.

patch¹ /pætʃ/ *n* [C] 1 small piece of material put over a hole or a damaged or worn place: *a coat with ∼es on the elbows; a ∼ on the inner tube of a tyre.* 2 piece of plaster put over a cut or wound. 3 pad worn to protect an injured eye. 4 small, irregular, differently coloured part of a surface: *a dog with a white ∼ on its neck.* 5 small area: *a ∼ of ground; ∼es of fog.* **not a patch on,** not nearly so good as. **a bad patch,** a period of bad luck, difficulty, unhappiness.

patch² /pætʃ/ *vt* put a patch on; (of material) serve as a patch for. **patch up,** repair; make roughly ready for use. **patch up a quarrel,** end it.

patchy *adj* (-ier, -iest) made up of patches; uneven in quality: *∼y work/fog.*

patch·work /ˈpætʃwɜːk/ *n* [U] 1 piece of material made up of bits of cloth of various sizes, shapes and colours: (as an *adjective*) *a ∼ quilt.* 2 (*fig*) piece of work made up of odds and ends.

pâté /ˈpæteɪ *US*: pɑˈteɪ/ *n* [U] 1 small pie. 2 paste(2).

pa·tel·la /pəˈtelə/ *n* [C] (*anat*) = kneecap.

pat·ent /ˈpeɪtənt *US*: ˈpætənt/ *adj* 1 evident, easily seen: *It was ∼ to everyone that he disliked the idea.* 2 protected by a patent(1): *∼ medicines,* made by one firm or person only.

'patent leather, leather with a smooth, shiny surface.

pa·tent·ly adv clearly; obviously.

pat·ent² /ˈpeɪtənt US: ˈpætənt/ n [C] **1** government authority giving exclusive right to make or sell a new invention. **2** that which is protected by a patent; invention or process. □ vt obtain a patent for (an invention or process).

Patent (usually /ˈpætənt/) **Office,** government department which issues patents.

pa·ter·nal /pəˈtɜːnəl/ adj **1** of or like a father: ~ care. **2** related through the father: my ~ grandfather.

pa·ter·nal·ism /-ɪzm/ n [U] (practice of) governing or controlling people in a paternal way (limiting their freedom or responsibility by well-intentioned rules).

pa·ter·nally /-nəlɪ/ adv

pa·ter·nity /pəˈtɜːnɪtɪ/ n [U] **1** fatherhood; being a father; origin on the father's side: ~ unknown. **2** (fig) source; authorship.

pater·nos·ter /ˈpætəˈnɒstə(r)/ n [C] (Latin for 'Our Father') **1** (recital of) the Lord's Prayer. **2** bead in a rosary at which the Lord's Prayer is repeated. **3** lift(2) with a series of doorless cars(3) moving on a continuous belt so that passengers can step on or off at each floor.

path /pɑːθ/ n [C] (pl ~s /pɑːðz US: pæðz/) **1** way made (across fields, through woods, etc) by people walking: Keep to the ~ or you may lose your way. ⇨ footpath. **2** line along which something or somebody moves: the ˈflight ~ of a spacecraft. **3** = track(4) (the usual word).

ˈpath·finder, explorer; person sent in advance to find a route, etc.

ˈpath·way, = path(1).

path·less adj having no paths.

pa·thetic /pəˈθetɪk/ adj **1** sad; pitiful: a ~ sight; ~ ignorance. **2** of the emotions.

pa·theti·cally /-klɪ/ adv

path·o·logical /ˈpæθəˈlɒdʒɪkəl/ adj of the nature of disease.

path·o·logi·cally /-klɪ/ adv

path·ol·ogist /pəˈθɒlədʒɪst/ n [C] student of, expert in, pathology.

pa·thol·ogy /pəˈθɒlədʒɪ/ n [U] science of diseases.

pa·thos /ˈpeɪθɒs/ n [U] quality in speech, writing, etc which arouses a feeling of pity, sympathy or tenderness.

pa·tience /ˈpeɪʃəns/ n [U] **1** (power of) enduring trouble, suffering, inconvenience, without complaining: She has no ~ with people who are always grumbling. **2** ability to wait for results, to deal with problems, calmly and without haste. **3** (GB) kind of card game, usually for one player (US = solitaire).

pa·tient¹ /ˈpeɪʃənt/ adj having, showing, patience: be ~ with a child.

pa·tient·ly adv

pa·tient² /ˈpeɪʃənt/ n [C] person who has

received, is receiving, or is on a doctor's list for, medical treatment: an old ~ of mine.

patio /ˈpætɪəʊ/ n [C] (pl ~s) **1** courtyard, open to the sky, within the walls of a Spanish or Spanish American house. **2** (modern use) paved area near a house, used for recreation.

pa·tis·serie /pəˈtiːsərɪ/ n [C] (Fr) shop, bakery, specializing in (French) pastry and cakes.

pa·trial /ˈpeɪtrɪəl/ n [C], adj (person) having the right to be considered legally a British citizen, eg an Asian in E Africa who has a British passport.

pa·tri·arch /ˈpeɪtrɪɑːk US: ˈpæt-/ n [C] **1** venerable old man. **2** male head of a family or tribe. **3** bishop among the early Christians; (in the RC Church) high-ranking bishop; (in Eastern Churches) bishop of highest honour: the P~ of Antioch/Jerusalem.

pa·tri·archal /ˈpeɪtrɪˈɑːkəl US: ˈpæt-/ adj

pat·ri·cide /ˈpætrɪsaɪd/ n [U] killing of one's own father; [C] instance of this; [C] person guilty of this.

pat·ri·mony /ˈpætrɪmənɪ US: -məʊnɪ/ n [C] (pl -ies) **1** property inherited from one's father or ancestors. **2** endowment of a church, etc.

pat·ri·mo·nial /ˈpætrɪˈməʊnɪəl/ adj

pa·triot /ˈpeɪtrɪət US: ˈpæt-/ n [C] person who loves and is ready to defend his country.

pa·tri·otic /ˈpeɪtrɪˈɒtɪk US: ˈpæt-/ adj having, showing, the qualities of a patriot.

pa·tri·oti·cally /-klɪ/ adv

ˈpa·triot·ism /-ɪzm/ n [U] the feelings and qualities of a patriot.

pa·trol /pəˈtrəʊl/ vt,vi (-ll-) go round (a camp, town, the streets, etc) to see that all is well, to look out (for persons doing wrong, in need of help, etc). □ n **1** [U] the act of patrolling: soldiers on ~; (as an adjective) a police ˈ~ car, eg on a motorway. **2** [C] person(s), ship(s) or aircraft on patrol.

pa·trol·man /-mən/, policeman who patrols an area.

pa·tron /ˈpeɪtrən/ n [C] **1** person who gives encouragement, moral or financial support, to a person, cause, the arts, etc: Modern artists have difficulty in finding wealthy ~s. **2** regular customer at a shop.

ˈpatron ˈsaint, saint regarded as the special protector (of a church, town, travellers, etc).

ˈpa·tron·ess /-ɪs/ n [C] woman patron(1).

pa·tron·age /ˈpætrənɪdʒ/ n [C] **1** support, encouragement, given by a patron: with/under the ~ of the Duke of X. **2** right of appointing a person to an office, to grant privileges, etc: He's an influential man, with a great deal of ~ in his hands. **3** customer's support (to a shopkeeper, etc): take away one's ~ because of poor service. **4** patronizing manner. ⇨ patronize(2).

pa·tron·ize /ˈpætrənaɪz US: ˈpeɪt-/ vt **1** act

as patron towards: ~ *a young musician/the corner shop.* **2** treat (a person in need, etc) as if he were an inferior person.

pat·ron·iz·ing *adj*

pat·ron·iz·ing·ly *adv*

pat·ter[1] /ˈpætə(r)/ *n* [U] **1** kind of talk used by a particular class of people: *thieves' ~.* **2** rapid talk of a conjuror or comedian. □ *vt,vi* recite, say, repeat very quickly or in a mechanical way.

pat·ter[2] /ˈpætə(r)/ *n* [U] sound of quick, light taps or footsteps: *the ~ of rain on a roof; the ~ of tiny feet.* □ *vi* make this sound.

pat·tern /ˈpætən/ *n* [C] **1** excellent example: *She's a ~ of all the virtues.* **2** something used as a model, e g shape of a garment cut out in paper and used as a guide in dressmaking, etc, model for a cast and from which a mould is made (in a foundry, etc). **3** sample, esp a small piece of cloth: *~s from the tailor.* **4** ornamental design, e g on a carpet, on wallpaper, or cloth: *a ~ of roses; geometrical ~s.* **5** way in which something happens, develops, is arranged, etc: *new ~s of family life.* □ *vt* **1** model: *He ~s himself on his father.* **2** decorate with a pattern(4).

pau·city /ˈpɔːsətɪ/ *n* [U] (*formal*) smallness of number or quantity.

paunch /pɔːntʃ/ *n* [C] belly, esp if fat: *He was getting quite a ~,* getting wide round the waist.

paunchy *adj* having a large paunch.

pau·per /ˈpɔːpə(r)/ *n* [C] very poor person, esp one who is supported by charity.

pause /pɔːz/ *n* [C] **1** short interval or stop (while doing or saying something): *during a ~ in the conversation.* **2** (*music*) sign (⌢ or ⌣) over or under a note or rest to show that it is to be lengthened. □ *vi* stop for a short time: *~ to look round.*

pave /peɪv/ *vt* put flat stones, bricks, etc on (a path, etc): *a path ~d with brick.* **pave the way for,** make conditions easy or ready for.

ˈpaving-stone, slab of stone for paving.

pave·ment /ˈpeɪvmənt/ *n* [C] (*GB*) paved way at the side of a street for people on foot (*US* = **sidewalk**). ⇨ **crazy paving.**

pa·vil·ion /pəˈvɪlɪən/ *n* [C] **1** building on a sports ground for the use of players, spectators, etc. **2** ornamental building for concerts, dancing, etc. **3** large tent, e g as used for an exhibition.

paw /pɔː/ *n* [C] animal's foot that has claws or nails. □ *vt* **1** (of animals) feel or scratch with the paw(s); (of a horse) strike (the ground) with a hoof. **2** (of persons) touch with the hands, awkwardly, rudely or with improper familiarity: *No girl likes being ~ed (about) by men.*

pawn[1] /pɔːn/ *n* [C] **1** least valuable piece in the game of chess. **2** person made use of by others for their own advantage.

pawn[2] /pɔːn/ *vt* deposit (clothing, jewellery,

etc) as security for money borrowed: *The medical student ~ed his microscope to pay his rent.* □ *n* [U] state of being pawned: *My watch is in ~.*

ˈpawn-broker, person licensed to lend money at interest on the security of goods left with him.

ˈpawn-shop, pawnbroker's place of business.

paw-paw /pəˈpɔː *US:* ˈpɔːpɔː/ *n* = **papaw.**

pay[1] /peɪ/ *n* [U] money paid for regular work or services, esp in the armed forces: *get an increase in ~.* **in the pay of,** employed by (often with a suggestion of dishonour, e g *in the ~ of the enemy*).

ˈpay-day, (a) day on which wages, salaries, etc are (to be) paid. (b) day (on the Stock Exchange) on which transfer of stock has to be paid for.

ˈpay load, (a) that part of the load (of a ship, aircraft, etc) for which payment is received, e g passengers and cargo, but not fuel. **(b)** warhead of a missile.

ˈpay-master, official responsible for paying troops, workers, etc.

ˈpay-master ˈgeneral, officer at the head of a department of the Treasury.

ˈpay-off, (*informal*) (time of) full and final settlement of accounts or of revenge.

ˈpay-packet, envelope or packet containing pay.

ˈpay-phone, (*US*) coin-operated telephone.

ˈpay-roll/-sheet, (a) list of persons to be paid and the amounts due to each. **(b)** total amount of wages, salaries, etc to be paid.

ˈpay-slip, piece of paper showing how pay has been calculated, deductions for tax, etc.

pay[2] /peɪ/ *vt,vi* (*pt,pp* paid /peɪd/ (For special uses with *adverbial particles* and *prepositions,* ⇨ **5** below.) **1** give (a person) money for goods, services, etc: *You must ~ me what you owe. I paid you the money last week. He paid £600 to a dealer for that car.* **2** give (a person) reward or recompense: *He says that sheep farming doesn't ~,* that it isn't profitable. **3** settle (debts, etc): *Have you paid all your taxes?* **put ˈpaid to sth,** (*informal*) settle; end it so that it gives no more trouble. **4** give, e g attention, respect, etc to: *Please ~ more attention to your work. He seldom ~s his wife any compliments.* **pay one's way,** not get into debt. **pay through the nose,** ⇨ nose[1](1). **pay a visit,** visit.

5 (uses with *adverbial particles* and *prepositions*):

pay sth back, return (money, etc) that has been borrowed. **pay sb back/out (for sth),** punish him; have one's revenge: *I've paid him out for the trick he played on me.*

pay for, (a) give money owed: *~ for the use of the room.* **(b)** suffer pain or punishment for: *He'll be made to ~ for his stupidity.*

pay in/into, deposit (money) with a bank to

one's own or another's account: *Please ~ this sum into my/my wife's account.*

pay off, (a) pay a person his wages and discharge him. **(b)** pay in full and no longer owe: *~ off one's debts.* ⇨ pay-off.

pay sth out, (a) give money, e g in settlement of expenses: *~ing out (money) on rent.* **(b)** allow (rope) to run out freely through the hands; slacken (rope) so that it runs freely.

pay up, pay in full what is owing: *If you don't ~ up, I'll take legal action.*

pay·able /ˈpeɪəbəl/ *adj* which must or may be paid.

payee /peɪˈiː/ *n* [C] person to whom something is (to be) paid.

payer /ˈpeɪə(r)/ *n* [C] person who pays or is to pay.

pay·ment /ˈpeɪmənt/ *n* **1** [U] paying or being paid: *demand prompt ~; a cheque in ~ for services rendered.* **2** [C] sum of money (to be) paid: *£50 now and ten monthly ~s of £5.* **3** [C,U] (*fig*) reward; punishment.

pea /piː/ *n* [C] plant with seeds in pods, used for food. *as like as two peas (in a pod),* exactly alike.

`pea-green *adj*, *n* [U] (of) bright light-green colour of young peas.

`pea-fowl,** **`pea-hen, ⇨ peacock.

peace /piːs/ *n* [U] (not used in *pl*, but see examples for uses with *a, an*) **1** state of freedom from war: *be at ~ with neighbouring countries.* *After a brief ~* (= a brief period of *~*) *war broke out again.* **2** (often P*~*) treaty of peace: *P~/A P~ was signed between the two countries.* **3** freedom from civil disorder. *keep the peace,* obey the laws. *a breach of the peace,* a disturbance or riot. ⇨ Justice of the Peace. **4** rest; quiet; calm: *the ~ of the countryside.* *at peace (with),* in a state of friendship or harmony: *He's never at ~ with himself,* is always restless. *In peace,* peacefully: live in *~* with one's neighbours. *make one's peace (with sb),* settle a quarrel. *peace of mind,* calm, contented mental state.

`peace-maker, person who restores friendly relations.

`peace-offering, something offered to show that one is willing to make peace.

peace·ful /ˈpiːsfəl/ *adj* **1** loving peace: *~ nations.* **2** calm; quiet: *a ~ evening.*

peace·ful·ly /-fəlɪ/ *adv*

peace·ful·ness *n* [U]

peach /piːtʃ/ *n* [C] **1** (tree with) juicy, round fruit with delicate yellowish-red skin and a rough seed; yellowish-red colour. **2** (*sl*) person or thing greatly admired, e g a very attractive girl: *Isn't she/it a ~!*

pea·cock /ˈpiːkɒk/ *n* [C] large male bird noted for its fine tail feathers.

`peacock-`blue *adj*, *n* [U] bright blue (colour).

pea-hen /ˈpiːhen/ *n* [C] female of the peacock.

peak /piːk/ *n* [C] **1** pointed top of a mountain. **2** pointed front part of a cap; projecting brim (to shade the eyes). **3** highest point in a record of figures that fluctuate: *~ hours of traffic,* times when the traffic is heaviest; *the ~ period of selling as shown on this graph.* *off peak,* when traffic, electricity consumption is lightest. **4** point of a beard.

peaked *adj* having a peak: *a ~ed cap/roof.*

peal /piːl/ *n* [C] **1** loud ringing of a bell or of a set of bells with different notes; changes rung on a set of bells; set of bells tuned to each other. **2** loud echoing noise: *a ~ of thunder; ~s of laughter.* □ *vi, vt* (cause to) ring or sound loudly.

pea-nut /ˈpiːnʌt/ *n* [C] = groundnut.

`peanut `butter, paste of roasted ground peanuts.

pear /peə(r)/ *n* [C] (tree with) sweet, juicy fruit, usually narrower towards the stalk.

pearl /pɜːl/ *n* [C] **1** silvery-white or bluish-white round deposit found inside the shells of some oysters, valued as a gem: *a necklace of ~s; a ~ necklace.* **2** small round fragment of various substances such as barley. **3** something that looks like a pearl, e g a dew drop. **4** very precious person or thing: *~s of wisdom. She's a ~ among women.* □ *vi* fish for pearls: *go ~ing.*

peas·ant /ˈpezənt/ *n* [C] (not current in GB, Australia, Canada, New Zealand, US) man working on the land, either for wages or on a very small farm which he either rents or owns.

peas·antry /ˈpezəntrɪ/ *n* [U] (usually with *the*) the peasants of a country or as a class.

peat /piːt/ *n* [U] plant material partly decomposed by the action of water, used as a fuel: *a ~-bog,* a marshy place where peat is found.

peaty *adj* of, like, smelling of, peat.

pebble /ˈpebəl/ *n* [C] small stone made smooth and round by water, e g in a stream.

peb·bly /ˈpeblɪ/ *adj* having pebbles: *a pebbly beach.*

pe-can /prˈkæn US: ˈpiːkən/ *n* [C] (nut of a) kind of hickory tree growing in the Mississippi region of the USA.

peck¹ /pek/ *n* [C] (before metrication) measure for grain or fruit (= 2 gallons).

peck² /pek/ *vi, vt* **1** (try to) get, make, strike with the beak: *hens ~ing at the corn/each other; ~ing a hole in the sack.* **2** *peck (at),* (*informal*) (of a person) eat only small amounts: *~ at one's food.* **3** (*informal*) kiss (a person) hurriedly from habit or a sense of duty. □ *n* [C] **1** strike with the beak; mark made by this. **2** (*informal*) hurried kiss.

`peck-ing order, (a) order (within a flock of poultry) in which a bird is dominated by stronger birds and itself dominates weaker birds. **(b)** any similar arrangement in a group of human beings: *Poor Tom! He's at the bottom of the ~ing order.*

ˋpeck·ish /-ɪʃ/ adj (informal) hungry.

pec·toral /ˈpektərəl/ adj of, for, the chest or breast: a ~ muscle/fin.

pe·cu·liar /prɪˈkjuːlɪə(r)/ adj 1 owned, used, adopted, practised, only by: customs ~ to these tribes. 2 strange; unusual; odd: I can smell something ~ in the bathroom. 3 particular; special: a matter of ~ interest.

pe·cu·liar·ly adv in a strange or special way: ~ly annoying, more than usually annoying.

pe·cu·liar·ity /prɪˌkjuːlɪˈærətɪ/ n (pl -ies) 1 [U] the quality of being peculiar. 2 [C] something distinctive or characteristic. 3 [C] something odd or strange.

pe·cuni·ary /prɪˈkjuːnɪərɪ US: -ɪerɪ/ adj (formal) of money: ~ reward.

peda·gog·ic /ˌpedəˈɡɒdʒɪk/ (also peda·gogi·cal /-ɪkəl/) adj of pedagogy.

peda·gogue (US also -gog) /ˈpedəɡɒɡ/ n [C] pedantic teacher.

peda·gogy /ˈpedəɡɒdʒɪ/ n [U] (formal) science of teaching.

pedal /ˈpedəl/ n [C] lever (e g on a bicycle, sewing-machine, organ or piano) worked by the foot or feet. □ vi,vt (-ll-, US also -l-) use, work by using, a pedal or pedals (for playing an organ, riding a bicycle, etc).

ped·ant /ˈpedənt/ n [C] person who values book-learning, technical knowledge, formal rules too highly.

pe·dan·tic /prɪˈdæntɪk/ adj of or like a pedant.

pe·danti·cally /-klɪ/ adv

ped·antry /ˈpedəntrɪ/ n [U] tiresome and unnecessary display of knowledge; too much insistence on formality; [C] instance of this.

peddle /ˈpedəl/ vi,vt 1 go from house to house trying to sell small articles. 2 (fig) give out in small quantities: She loves to ~ gossip round the village.

ped·estal /ˈpedɪstəl/ n [C] base of a column, for a statue or for other works of art. put/set sb on a pedestal, treat him as very important or special.

pe·des·trian /prɪˈdestrɪən/ n [C] person walking in a street, etc: ~s killed in traffic accidents. □ adj 1 connected with walking. 2 (of writing, a person's way of making speeches, etc) uninteresting, ordinary.

pedestrian crossing, place marked on a road where pedestrians may walk across.

pedia·tri·cian /ˌpiːdɪəˈtrɪʃən/ n [C] physician who specializes in pediatrics.

pedi·at·rics /ˌpiːdɪˈætrɪks/ n pl (used with a sing verb) branch of medicine concerned with children and their illness.

pedi·cure /ˈpedɪkjʊə(r)/ n [C] treatment of the feet, toe-nails, corns, bunions, etc.

pedi·gree /ˈpedɪɡriː/ n [C] line of ancestors: proud of their long ~s; [U] ancestry, esp ancient descent. □ adj having a known line of descent: ~ cattle/dogs.

ped·lar /ˈpedlə(r)/ n [C] person who goes from house to house selling small articles.

pee /piː/ vi, n [C,U] (sl) (pass) urine.

peek /piːk/ vi peek at, peep at. □ n [C] quick look: have a ~ at the answers before doing the exercises.

peel /piːl/ vt,vi 1 take the skin off (fruit, etc): ~ a banana; ~ potatoes. 2 come off in strips or flakes: The wallpaper is ~ing off. After a day in the hot sun my skin began to ~/my face ~ed. □ n [U] skin of fruit, some vegetables, etc.

peeler n [C] device used for peeling fruit and vegetables.

peep¹ /piːp/ n [C] short, quick look, often secret or cautious: have a ~ at her through the keyhole. □ vi take a peep (at): neighbours ~ing at us from behind curtains.

peep² /piːp/ n [C] weak, shrill sound made by mice, young birds, etc □ vi make this sound.

peer¹ /pɪə(r)/ n [C] 1 person equal in rank, merit or quality: It will not be very easy to find his ~. 2 (in GB) member of one of the nobility, e g duke, marquis, earl, viscount. ˈpeer of the ˈrealm, person with the right to sit in the House of Lords.

ˋlife peer, one elected to the House of Lords for life only.

peeress /ˈpɪəres/, (a) woman peer(2). (b) wife of a peer(2).

peer² /pɪə(r)/ vi look closely, as if unable to see well: ~ into dark corners; ~ing at her over his spectacles.

peer·age /ˈpɪərɪdʒ/ n [C,U] 1 the whole body of peers; rank of peer(2). 2 book containing a list of peers with their ancestry.

pee·wit /ˈpiːwɪt/ n = pewit.

peg¹ /peɡ/ n [C] 1 wooden or metal pin or bolt, used to fasten parts of woodwork together. a square peg in a round hole, a person unsuited to the work he is doing. 2 pin driven into the ground to hold a rope (a ˈtent-~); hook fastened to a wall or door. (buy sth) off the peg, (informal) (buy clothes) ready-made. ⇨ clothes-peg. 3 wooden screw for tightening or loosening the string of a violin, etc. ˈtake sb ˈdown a peg (or two), make him feel less important. 4 piece of wood for stopping the hole in a cask, etc. 5 (fig) theme, excuse: a ~ on which to hang a sermon.

peg² /peɡ/ vt,vi (-gg-) 1 fasten with pegs: ~ a tent down. peg sb down, (fig) make him keep to a certain line of action, to the rules, etc. 2 mark, e g by means of pegs fixed in the ground. 3 (commerce) keep (prices, wages, etc) steady. 4 peg away at, keep on working at. 5 peg out, (informal) die.

pe·jor·at·ive /prɪˈdʒɒrətɪv US: -ˈdʒɔr-/ adj having or giving an idea of being unimportant or valueless; discrediting.

pe·jor·at·ive·ly adv

pe·kin·ese /ˌpiːkɪˈniːz/ n [C] small breed of Chinese dog with long, silky hair.

peli·can /ˈpelɪkən/ n [C] large waterbird with a large bill under which hangs a pouch for storing food.

pel·let /ˈpelɪt/ n [C] **1** small ball of something soft, e g wet paper, bread, made, for example, by rolling between the fingers. **2** small shot, e g as used from an air gun.

pell-mell /ˈpel ˈmel/ adv in a hurrying, disorderly manner.

pel·met /ˈpelmɪt/ n [C] ornamental strip above a window or door to hide a curtain rod.

pelt[1] /pelt/ n [C] animal's skin with the fur or hair on it.

pelt[2] /pelt/ vt,vi **1** attack by throwing things at: *pelt them with stones/snowballs/mud.* **2** (of rain, etc) fall heavily: *It was ∼ing with rain. The rain was ∼ing down.* □ n [C] pelting. **at full pelt,** (running) as fast as possible.

pel·vic /ˈpelvɪk/ adj of the pelvis.

pel·vis /ˈpelvɪs/ n [C] (pl pelves /ˈpelviːz/) (anat) bony frame with the hip-bones and the lower part of the backbone, holding the kidneys, rectum, bladder, etc.

pen[1] /pen/ n [C] **1** instrument for writing with ink, with a pointed piece of split metal (a nib) fixed into a holder of wood or other material. ⇨ ballpoint-pen and fountain-pen. **2** (formerly) quill, pointed and split at the end, for writing with ink. **3** (style of) writing: *make a living with one's ∼.* □ vt (-nn-) write (a letter, etc).

'pen-and-'ink adj drawn with these: *a ∼-and-ink sketch.*

'pen-friend, person (e g in another country) with whom one has a friendship through exchanges of letters.

'pen-knife, small knife with one or more folding blades.

'pen-name, name used by a writer instead of his real name.

pen[2] /pen/ n [C] **1** small enclosure, e g for cattle, sheep, poultry, etc. **2** = play-pen. □ vt (-nn-) **pen up/in,** shut up (as) in a pen

penal /ˈpiːnəl/ adj connected with punishment: *∼ laws; a ∼ offence,* one for which there is legal punishment. **penal servitude,** imprisonment with hard labour.

pe·nal·ize /ˈpiːnəlaɪz/ vt **1** declare to be punishable by law. **2** give a penalty(3) to (a player, competitor, etc).

pe·nal·iz·ation /ˌpiːnəlaɪˈzeɪʃən US: -əlɪˈz-/ n [U]

pen·alty /ˈpenəltɪ/ n (pl -ies) **1** [U] punishment for doing wrong, for failure to obey rules or to keep an agreement; [C] what is imposed (imprisonment, payment of a fine, etc) as punishment: *forbidden under ∼ of death.* **2** (fig) disadvantage, suffering, caused by a person to himself or others: *The ∼ for not working will be failing the exams.* **3** (in sport, competitions, etc) disadvantage to a player or team for breaking a rule: *The referee awarded a ∼.* **4** handicap imposed on a player or team for winning a previous contest.

'penalty area, (football) area in front of the goal where a free kick at goal is given as a penalty if a defender breaks a rule.

'penalty kick, (football) free kick at goal by the attackers as a penalty against the opposing team.

'penalty spot, (football) mark in the penalty area where a penalty kick is taken.

pen·ance /ˈpenəns/ n [U] punishment which one imposes on oneself to show repentance.

pence /pens/ n pl ⇨ penny.

pen·cil /ˈpensəl/ n [C] instrument for drawing or writing, esp of graphite or coloured chalk in wood or fixed in a metal holder. □ vt (-ll-, US also -l-) write, draw, mark, with a pencil: *∼led sketches/eyebrows.*

pen·dant /ˈpendənt/ n [C] **1** ornament which hangs down, esp one attached to a necklace, bracelet, etc. **2** (naut) pennant.

pend·ing /ˈpendɪŋ/ adj waiting to be decided or settled: *The lawsuit was still ∼.* □ prep **1** during: *∼ these discussions.* **2** until: *∼ his acceptance of the offer.*

pen·du·lous /ˈpendjʊləs US: -dʒʊləs/ adj (formal) (of nests, breasts, etc) hanging down loosely so as to swing freely.

pen·du·lum /ˈpendjʊləm US: -dʒʊləm/ n [C] (pl ∼s) weighted rod hung from a fixed point so that it swings freely, esp one to regulate the movement of a clock. **the swing of the pendulum,** (fig) the movement of public opinion from one extreme to the other.

pen·etrable /ˈpenɪtrəbəl/ adj (formal) that can be penetrated.

pen·etrate /ˈpenɪtreɪt/ vt,vi **1** make a way into or through: *The cat's sharp claws ∼d my skin. The smell ∼d (into) the room.* **2** (fig) see into or through: *Our eyes could not ∼ the darkness.*

pen·etrat·ing adj **(a)** (of a person, his mind) able to see and understand quickly and well. **(b)** (voices, cries, etc) piercing; loud and clear.

pen·etrat·ing·ly adv

pen·etra·tion /ˌpenɪˈtreɪʃən/ n [U] **1** penetrating. **2** ability to grasp ideas quickly and well.

pen-friend /ˈpen frend/ ⇨ pen[1].

pen·guin /ˈpengwɪn/ n [C] seabird of the Antarctic with wings like flippers used for swimming.

peni·cil·lin /ˌpenɪˈsɪlɪn/ n [U] antibiotic drug that, by changing the chemical environment of germs, prevents them from surviving or multiplying.

pen·in·sula /pəˈnɪnsjʊlə US: -nsələ/ n [C] (pl ∼s) area of land, e g Italy, almost surrounded by water or projecting into the sea

pen·in·su·lar /-lə(r)/ adj

pe·nis /ˈpiːnɪs/ n [C] organ of copulation of a male animal.

peni·tence /ˈpenɪtəns/ n [U] sorrow and regret (for doing wrong, sin)

peni·tent /ˈpenɪtənt/ adj feeling or showing

regret or remorse.
peni·tent·ly adv

peni·ten·tiary /ˌpenɪˈtenʃərɪ/ n [C] (pl -ies) prison for persons guilty of serious crimes, esp one in which reform of the prisoners is the main aim. □ adj of reformatory treatment.

pen-knife /ˈpen naɪf/ ⇨pen¹.

pen-name /ˈpen neɪm/ ⇨ pen¹.

pen·nant /ˈpenənt/ n [C] flag (usually long and narrow) used on a ship for signalling, identification, etc.

pen·ni·less /ˈpenɪləs/ adj without any money: I'm ~ until pay-day.

pen·non /ˈpenən/ n [C] 1 long, narrow (usually triangular) flag, as used by a knight, by soldiers and on ships, e g in signalling. 2 (US) flag of this shape as a school or team banner.

penn'orth /ˈpenəθ/ n = pennyworth.

penny /ˈpenɪ/ n [C] (pl pence /pens/ when combined with numbers, as in `sixpence, `tenpence, `eighteen-pence; pl pennies /ˈpenɪz/ when used of individual coins: Please give me ten pennies for this tenpence piece.) 1 (since 1971) British bronze coin (abbr p) worth one hundredth of an English pound: These cigarettes are 30 new pence/30p /pi/ a packet. (cost) a pretty penny, a lot of money. spend a penny, (informal) use a W C. the penny (has) dropped, the desired result was achieved, the meaning of a remark, etc was understood. 2 (until 1971) British coin worth one-twelfth of a shilling. 3 coin of the US and Canada, the cent.
`penny pinching adj (informal) miserly.
`penny-weight, 24 grains, one-twentieth of an ounce Troy.
`penny-worth (also penn'orth /ˈpenəθ/), as much as can be bought for a penny.

pen·sion¹ /ˈpenʃən/ n [C] regular payment made by the State to a person who is old (re`tirement ~), disabled (e g `war ~) or widowed, or by a former employer to an employee after long service: retire on a ~. draw one's pension, obtain it: go to the Post Office to draw one's ~. □ vt pension sb off, grant or pay a ~ to: dismiss or allow to retire with a pension.
`pen·sion·able /-əbəl/ adj (of services, posts, age, work, etc) entitling one to a pension.
pen·sioner, person receiving a pension.

pen·sion² /ˈpɒnsɪɒn/ n [C] boarding-house at which fixed rates are charged (by the week or month).

pen·sive /ˈpensɪv/ adj seriously thoughtful: ~ looks; looking ~.
pen·sive·ly adv
pen·sive·ness n [U]

pen·ta·gon /ˈpentəgən/ US: -gɒn/ n [C] plane figure with five sides and five angles.
the Pentagon, building in Arlington, Virginia, headquarters of the US Armed Forces.
pen·tag·onal /penˈtægənəl/ adj

pen·tath·lon /penˈtæθlən/ n [C] (modern Olympic Games) contest in which each competitor takes part in five events (running, horseback riding, swimming, fencing and shooting with a pistol).

Pente·cost /ˈpentɪkɒst US: -kɔst/ n 1 Jewish harvest festival, fifty days after the Passover. 2 (esp US) Whitsunday, the seventh Sunday after Easter.

pent·house /ˈpenthaʊs/ n [C] 1 sloping roof supported against a wall, esp one for a shelter or shed. 2 apartment or flat built on the roof of a tall building.

pent-in /ˈpent ˈɪn/ adj closely confined: feel ~.

pent-up /ˈpent ˈʌp/ adj shut-in; not expressed: ~ feelings/anger.

pen·ul·ti·mate /penˈʌltɪmət/ n [C] adj (word, syllable, event, etc which is) last but one.

pen·ury /ˈpenjʊərɪ/ n [U] (formal) poverty·living in ~.

peony /ˈpiːənɪ/ n [C] (pl -ies) garden plant with large round pink, red or white flowers.

people /ˈpiːpəl/ n (1 to 4 below collective, never pl in form but used with a pl verb. For one human being use man, woman, boy, girl and not person, which, although useful in definitions, may seem to be discrediting or formal.) 1 persons in general: streets crowded with ~. 2 those persons belonging to a place, or forming a social class: The ~ in the village like the new doctor. 3 all the persons forming a State: government of the ~, by the ~, for the ~. 4 those persons who are not nobles, not high in rank, position, etc: live like ordinary ~. 5 (used with a sing or pl verb and in pl) race, tribe, nation: the ~s of Asia; a brave and intelligent ~. □ vt fill with people: a thickly ~d district.

pep /pep/ n [U] (sl) vigour; spirit. □ vt (-pp-) give energy or life to.
`pep pill, one that stimulates the nervous system.
`pep talk, one intended to fill the listener(s) with spirit and energy

pep·per /ˈpepə(r)/ n 1 [U] hot-tasting powder made from the dried berries of certain plants, used to season food. 2 [C] (garden plant with a) red or green seed-pod which is used as a vegetable: stuffed ~s. □ vt put pepper(1) on (food).
pep·pery adj (a) tasting of pepper. (b) (fig) hot-tempered: a ~y old colonel.
`pep·per·corn, (a) the dried, black berry of the pepper(1) plant. (b) (fig) nominal: a ~corn rent.
`pep·per·mint, (a) kind of mint grown for its oil, used in medicine and confectionery. (b) sweet of boiled sugar flavoured with this mint.

per /pɜː(r)/ prep for each: ~ pound; 15 rounds of ammunition ~ man; 30 miles ~ gallon, (abbr m p g). as per, according to: as ~ instructions. per usual, (informal) as usual.

'per 'annum /ˈænəm/, for each year.

'per 'cent, (abbr %) for, in, each hundred: *40% income tax.*

per·am·bu·la·tor /pəˈræmbjʊleɪtə(r)/ *n* [C] (more usually **pram**) four-wheeled carriage, pushed by hand, for a baby.

per·ceive /pəˈsiːv/ *vt* (*formal*) become aware of, esp through the eyes or the mind.

per·cen·tage /pəˈsentɪdʒ/ *n* [C] **1** rate or number per cent (= for each hundred). **2** proportion: *What ~ of his income is paid in income tax?*

per·cep·tible /pəˈseptəbəl/ *adj* (*formal*) that can be seen or noticed.

per·cep·tibly /-əblɪ/ *adv*

per·cep·tion /pəˈsepʃən/ *n* [U] (*formal*) process, act, by which we become aware of changes (through seeing, hearing, etc).

per·cep·tive /pəˈseptɪv/ *adj* (*formal*) **1** having, connected with, perception. **2** showing that one has seen or noticed: *~ remarks.*

per·cep·tive·ly *adv*

perch[1] /pɜːtʃ/ *n* [C] (*pl* unchanged) kinds of freshwater fish with spiny fins, used as food.

perch[2] /pɜːtʃ/ *n* [C] **1** bird's resting-place, e g a branch, bar or rod. **2** (*informal*) high position occupied by a person: *come off your ~,* (*informal*) stop being so superior (in manner, etc). **3** (also **pole, rod**) measure of length, esp for land, 5 and a half yards. □ *vi,vt* **1** settle: *The birds ~ed on the television aerial.* **2** (of a person) sit on a tall seat: *~ed on stools at the bar.* **3** (chiefly in *pp*) (of buildings) be situated high up: *a castle ~ed on a rock.*

per·co·late /ˈpɜːkəleɪt/ *vi,vt* **1** (of liquid) (cause to) pass slowly (*through*): *Has the water ~d through the coffee yet?* **2** (*fig*) filter (2): *Has the news ~d through?*

per·co·lator /-tə(r)/, (esp) kind of coffee pot in which boiling water percolates through coffee.

per·cus·sion /pəˈkʌʃən/ *n* [U] **1** the striking together of two (usually hard) objects; sound or shock produced by this. **2** the '~ (*section*), musical instruments played by percussion, e g drums, cymbals.

per·cus·sion·ist /-ɪst/, player of a percussion instrument.

per·emp·tory /pəˈremptərɪ *US:* ˈperəmptɔːrɪ/ *adj* (*formal*) **1** (of commands) not to be disobeyed or questioned. **2** (of a person, his manner) (too) commanding; insisting on obedience.

per·emp·tor·ily /-trɪlɪ *US:* -tɔːrəlɪ/ *adv*

per·en·nial /pəˈrenɪəl/ *adj* **1** continuing throughout the whole year. **2** lasting for a very long time. **3** (of plants) living for more than two years. □ *n* [C] perenn¹al plant.

per·en·nial·ly /-nɪəlɪ/ *adv*

per·fect[1] /ˈpɜːfɪkt/ *adj* **1** complete with everything needed. **2** without fault; excellent: *a ~ wife.* **3** exact; accurate: *a ~ circle.*

4 having reached the highest point in training, skill, etc: *a ~ shot* (6). **5** complete: *a ~ stranger/fool; ~ nonsense.*

perfect tense, (*gram*) tense composed of the finites of *have* and a *past participle,* e g *He has/had/will have written the letter.*

per·fect·ly *adv* completely: *~ly happy.*

per·fect[2] /pəˈfekt/ *vt* make perfect: *~ oneself in a foreign language.*

per·fect·ible /-əbəl/ *adj* that can be perfected.

per·fec·tion /pəˈfekʃən/ *n* [U] **1** perfecting or being perfected: *busy with the ~ of detail.* **2** perfect quality or example: *It was the very ~ of beauty.* **3** best possible state or quality: *beef roasted/done to ~.*

per·fec·tion·ist /-ɪst/ *n* [C] **1** person who believes that it is possible to live without sinning. **2** (*informal*) person who is satisfied with nothing less than what he thinks to be perfect.

per·fidi·ous /pəˈfɪdɪəs/ *adj* (*formal*) treacherous; faithless (*to*).

per·fidi·ous·ly *adv*

per·for·ate /ˈpɜːfəreɪt/ *vt,vi* make a hole or holes in; make rows of tiny holes (in paper) so that part may be torn off easily: *a ~d sheet of postage stamps.*

per·for·ation /ˈpɜːfəˈreɪʃən/ *n* [C,U]

per·form /pəˈfɔːm/ *vt,vi* **1** do (a piece of work, something one is ordered or has promised to do): *~ a task.* **2** act (a play); play (music); sing, do tricks, etc before an audience: *~ 'Hamlet'. Do you enjoy seeing ~ing animals?*

per·former, one who performs, esp at a concert or other entertainment.

per·form·ance /pəˈfɔːməns/ *n* **1** [U] performing: *faithful in the ~ of his duties.* **2** [C] notable action; achievement: *The orchestra/musicians gave a fine ~.* **3** [C] performing of a play at the theatre; public exhibition; concert: *two ~s a day. What a ~! What shocking behaviour!*

per·fume /ˈpɜːfjuːm/ *n* [C,U] (kinds of prepared liquid with a) sweet smell, esp from an essence of flowers. □ *vt* /pəˈfjuːm/ give a perfume to; put perfume on.

per·func·tory /pəˈfʌŋktərɪ/ *adj* (*formal*) **1** done as a duty or routine but without care or interest: *a ~ inspection.* **2** (of persons) doing things in this way.

per·func·tor·ily /-trɪlɪ *US:* -tərəlɪ/ *adv*

per·gola /ˈpɜːgələ/ *n* [C] (*pl* ~s) structure of posts (forming an arbour, or over a garden path) for climbing plants.

per·haps /pəˈhæps/ *adv* possibly; it may be.

peril /ˈperəl/ *n* **1** [U] serious danger: *in ~ of one's life.* **do sth at one's peril,** at one's own risk. **2** [C] something that causes danger: *the ~s of the ocean,* storm, shipwreck, etc.

peril·ous /ˈperələs/ *adj* dangerous: *a ~ous journey.*

peril·ous·ly adv

per·imeter /pə`rɪmɪtə(r)/ n [C] (length of the) outer boundary of a closed figure or area, e g an airfield, etc.

period /`pɪərɪəd/ n [C] **1** length or portion of time, e g hours, days, months and years: ~s of sunny weather; the ~ when the disease is contagious; 20 teaching ~s a week. **2** portion of time in the life of a person, a nation, a stage of civilization, etc; division of geological time: the ~ of the French Revolution. The actors will wear costumes of the ~/~ costumes, i e of the time when the events of the play took place. **3** full pause at the end of a sentence; full stop (.) marking this in writing and print. **4** (astron) time taken to complete one revolution. **5** (informal) occurrence of menstruation.

peri·odic /ˌpɪərɪ`ɒdɪk/ adj occurring or appearing at regular intervals: ~ headaches.

periodic table, (chem) chart of the elements(1) according to their atomic weights.

peri·od·ical /-kəl/ adj = periodic. □ n [C] magazine or other publication which appears at regular intervals, e g monthly, quarterly.

peri·od·ically /-klɪ/ adv (a) at regular intervals. (b) occasionally.

peri·pa·tetic /ˌperɪpə`tetɪk/ adj going about from place to place; wandering: the ~ religious teachers of India.

pe·riph·eral /pə`rɪfərəl/ adj of, on, forming, a periphery.

pe·riph·ery /pə`rɪfərɪ/ n [C] (pl -ies) external boundary or surface.

peri·scope /`perɪskəup/ n [C] instrument, as used in submarines, with mirrors and lenses arranged to reflect a view down a tube, etc so that the user may see things from a level above normal eyesight.

per·ish /`perɪʃ/ vi,vt **1** be destroyed, come to an end, die: Hundreds of people ~ed in the earthquake. **2** (of cold or exposure) reduce to distress or inefficiency: We were ~ed with cold/hunger. **3** (esp of rubber) (cause to) lose natural qualities; decay: Oil on your car tyres will ~ them.

per·ish·able /-əbəl/ adj (esp of food) quickly or easily going bad.

per·ish·ables n pl (esp) goods that go bad if delayed in transit, e g fish, fresh fruit.

per·ito·ni·tis /ˌperɪtə`naɪtɪs/ n [U] inflammation of the membrane lining the walls of the abdomen.

per·jure /`pɜːdʒə(r)/ vt (reflex) **perjure oneself**, knowingly make a false statement after taking an oath to tell the truth.

per·jurer /`pɜːdʒərə(r)/, person who has perjured himself.

per·jury /`pɜːdʒərɪ/ n [C,U]

perk /pɜːk/ vi,vt **1 perk up,** (of a person) become lively and active (after depression, illness, etc). **2 perk sb/sth up,** smarten; show interest, liveliness: The horse ~ed up its head, lifted its head as a sign of interest.

perky adj (-ier, -iest) lively; showing interest or confidence.

perks /pɜːks/ n pl (informal) perquisite: an executive's salary with the usual ~.

perm /pɜːm/ n [C] (informal abbr for) permanent wave: go to the hairdresser's for a ~. □ vt give a perm to.

per·ma·nence /`pɜːmənəns/ n [U] state of being permanent.

per·ma·nent /`pɜːmənənt/ adj not expected to change; going on for a long time; intended to last: my ~ address. ⇨ temporary.

'permanent `secretary, senior civil servant.

permanent (wave), artificial curls put in the hair so that they last several months.

per·ma·nent·ly adv

per·meate /`pɜːmɪeɪt/ vt,vi pass, flow or spread into every part of: water permeating (through) the soil; new ideas that have ~d (through/among) the people.

per·me·ation /ˌpɜːmɪ`eɪʃən/ n [U]

per·mis·sible /pə`mɪsəbəl/ adj that may be permitted.

per·mis·sibly /-əblɪ/ adv

per·mis·sion /pə`mɪʃən/ n [U] act of allowing or permitting; consent: with your ~, if you will allow me. Has he given you ~ to leave?

per·miss·ive /pə`mɪsɪv/ adj giving permission.

the per'missive so`ciety, (in GB, 1967 onwards) term used for social changes, including greater sexual freedom, homosexual law reform, abolition of censorship in the theatre, frank discussion of taboo subjects, increased drug-taking, etc.

per·miss·ive·ness n [U]

per·mit [1] /`pɜːmɪt/ n [C] written authority to go somewhere, do something, etc: You won't get into the atomic research station without a ~.

per·mit [2] /pə`mɪt/ vt,vi (-tt-) **1** allow: We'll play football, weather ~ting. Smoking is not ~ted in this cinema. **2** (formal) admit (of): The situation does not ~ of any delay, There must be no delay.

per·mu·ta·tion /ˌpɜːmjʊ`teɪʃən/ n [C] (maths) change in the order of a set of things arranged in a group; any one such arrangement: The ~s of x, y and z are xyz, xzy, yxz, yzx, zxy, zyx.

per·mute /pə`mjuːt/ vt (formal) change the order of.

per·ni·cious /pə`nɪʃəs/ adj (formal) harmful, injurious: ~ gossip.

per·ni·cious·ly adv

per·ox·ide /pə`rɒksaɪd/ n [U] (esp) ~ of hydrogen, (H_2O_2) colourless liquid used as an antiseptic and to bleach hair.

per·pen·dicu·lar /ˌpɜːpən`dɪkjʊlə(r)/ adj **1** at an angle of 90° (to another line or surface). **2** upright; crossing the horizontal at an angle of 90°. □ n [C] perpendicular line.

per·pe·trate /`pɜːpɪtreɪt/ vt commit (a crime, an error).

per·pe·tra·tor /-tə(r)/. person who perpetrates a crime, etc.

per·pe·tra·tion /ˌpɜːpɪˈtreɪʃən/ n [U]

per·pet·ual /pəˈpetʃʊəl/ adj going on for a long time or without stopping.

per'petual `motion, the motion of a machine, if it could be invented, which would go on for ever without a continuing source of energy.

per·pet·ually /-ʃʊəlɪ/ adv

per·petu·ate /pəˈpetʃʊeɪt/ vt preserve from being forgotten or from going out of use: ~ his memory by erecting a statue of him.

per·petu·ation /pəˈpetʃʊˈeɪʃən/ n [U]

per·petu·ity /ˌpɜːpɪˈtjuətɪ US: -ˈtuː-/ n (pl -ies) 1 [U] state of being perpetual. **In perpetuity,** for ever. 2 [C] (legal) perpetual annuity or possession.

per·plex /pəˈpleks/ vt 1 puzzle; bewilder: ~ her with questions. 2 make more complicated: Don't ~ the issue.

per·plexed adj puzzled; complicated.

per·plex·ed·ly /-ɪdlɪ/ adv

per·plex·ity /-ətɪ/ n (pl -ies) (a) [U] state of being confused, e g because of doubt: He looked at us in ~ity. (b) [C] perplexing thing.

per·qui·site /ˈpɜːkwɪzɪt/ n [C] (formal) profit, allowance, etc given or looked on as one's right, in addition to regular wages or salary: The salesman's ~s include the use of his firm's car out of business hours. ⇨ perks.

per·se·cute /ˈpɜːsɪkjuːt/ vt 1 punish, treat cruelly, esp because of religious beliefs. 2 cause repeated trouble to: ~ a man with questions.

per·se·cu·tor /-tə(r)/. person who persecutes.

per·se·cu·tion /ˌpɜːsɪˈkjuːʃən/ n [C,U]

per·se·ver·ance /ˌpɜːsɪˈvɪərəns/ n [U] constant effort to achieve something.

per·se·vere /ˌpɜːsɪˈvɪə(r)/ vi continue with (esp something difficult or tiring)· ~ with/in one's studies.

per·se·ver·ing adj

per·se·ver·ing·ly adv

per·sist /pəˈsɪst/ vi 1 refuse, in spite of argument, opposition, failure, etc to make any change in (what one is doing, one's beliefs, etc): She ~s in wearing that old coat. 2 **persist with,** continue to work hard at. 3 continue to exist: The fog is likely to ~ in most areas.

per·sist·ence /-əns/ n [U]

per·sist·ent /-ənt/ adj continuing (to refuse); occurring again and again: ~ent denials/attacks of malaria.

per·sist·ent·ly adv

per·son /ˈpɜːsən/ n [C] (Note: people is the usual plural, not ~s.) 1 man, woman (the usual words): Who is this ~? 2 living body of a human being. **In person,** physically present: He'll collect his certificate in ~, will be there himself. 3 (gram) each of three

classes of personal pronouns: the first ~ (I, we), the second ~ (you) and the third ~ (he, she, it, they).

per·son·able /ˈpɜːsənəbəl/ adj good-looking and pleasant.

per·son·age /ˈpɜːsənɪdʒ/ n [C] (important) person.

per·sonal /ˈpɜːsnəl/ adj 1 private; individual; of a particular person: My ~ affairs/needs/opinions; your ~ rights. 2 done or made by a person himself: The Prime Minister made a ~ appearance at the meeting. 3 done or made for a particular person: give him one's ~ attention. He did me a ~ favour, one directed to me and by him. 4 of the body: P~ cleanliness is important to health. 5 of the nature of a human being: Do you believe in a ~ God? 6 of or about a person in a critical or hostile way: I object to such ~ remarks.

'personal as`sistant, one who helps an official, e g by making travel arrangements, organising meetings, etc.

`personal column, one (in a newspaper, etc) in which private messages or advertisements appear.

'personal `pronoun, of the three persons(3).

per·son·ally /-nəlɪ/ adv 1 in person, not through a representative: He showed me round the exhibition ~. 2 speaking for oneself: P~ly I have no objection to your joining us.

per·son·al·ize /ˈpɜːsnəlaɪz/ vt 1 personify. 2 have (something) printed with one's address (~d stationery) or sewn with one's initials (~d shirts, handkerchiefs).

per·son·al·ity /ˌpɜːsəˈnælətɪ/ n (pl -ies) 1 [U] state of being a person; existence as an individual: respect the ~ of a child. 2 [C,U] qualities that make up a person's character: a man with little ~; a woman with a strong ~. 3 [C] (modern use) person who is well known in a particular context: a TV ~, known to television viewers. 4 (pl) impolite remarks about a person's looks, habits, etc: Let's avoid personalities, avoid such remarks.

per·son·ify /pəˈsɒnɪfaɪ/ vt (pt,pp -ied) 1 regard or represent (something) as a person: ~ the sun and moon, by using 'he' and 'she'. 2 be an example of (a quality): That man is greed personified.

per·soni·fi·ca·tion /pəˌsɒnɪfɪˈkeɪʃən/ n (a) [U] personifying or being personified; [C] instance of this. (b) (usually sing with the) excellent example of a quality: He's the personification of every virtue.

per·son·nel /ˌpɜːsəˈnel/ n [U] (used with a sing or pl verb) staff, esp in large companies and the armed forces: Five airline ~ died in the plane crash. He's a `~ officer/manager, one employed to deal with employees, their personal problems, etc.

per·spec·tive /pəˈspektɪv/ n 1 [U] the art of

drawing solid objects on a flat surface so as to give the right impression of their relative height, width, depth, distance, etc; [C] drawing so made. **2** [U] apparent relation between different aspects of a problem: *He sees things in their right ~.* **3** [C] (*literary, fig*) view; prospect: *a ~ of the nation's history.*

per·spex /ˈpɜːspeks/ *n* [U] (P) tough plastic material used as a substitute for glass (e g in the windscreens of cars).

per·spi·ca·cious /ˌpɜːspɪˈkeɪʃəs/ *adj* (*formal*) quick to judge and understand.
per·spi·cac·ity /ˌpɜːspɪˈkæsətɪ/ *n* [U]

per·spire /pəˈspaɪə(r)/ *vi* sweat.
per·spir·ation /ˌpɜːspəˈreɪʃən/ *n* [U] sweat; sweating.

per·suade /pəˈsweɪd/ *vt* **1** convince (a person): *How can I ~ you of my sincerity/that I am sincere?* **2** cause (a person) by reasoning (not) (to do something): *We ~d him/He was ~d to try again. Can you ~ her out of her foolish plans?*
per·suad·able /-əbəl/ *adj*

per·sua·sion /pəˈsweɪʒən/ *n* **1** [U] persuading or being persuaded; power of persuading. **2** [U] belief (the usual word): *It is my ~ that...* **3** [C] group of people holding a particular belief: *various political ~s.*

per·sua·sive /pəˈsweɪsɪv/ *adj* able to persuade: *She has a ~ manner/voice.*
per·sua·sive·ly *adv*
per·sua·sive·ness *n* [U]

pert /pɜːt/ *adj* cheeky; not showing proper respect: *a ~ child/answer.*
pert·ly *adv*
pert·ness *n* [U]

per·tain /pəˈteɪn/ *vi* (*formal*) belong as a part or accessory; have reference; be appropriate: *the farm and the lands ~ing to it.*

per·ti·na·cious /ˌpɜːtɪˈneɪʃəs US: -təˈneɪʃəs/ *adj* (*formal*) determined.
per·ti·na·cious·ly *adv*
per·ti·nac·ity /ˌpɜːtɪˈnæsətɪ US: -təˈnæ-/ *n* [U] (*formal*) determination.

per·ti·nent /ˈpɜːtɪnənt US: -tənənt/ *adj* (*formal*) referring directly; relevant: *a ~ reply.*
per·ti·nent·ly *adv*

per·turb /pəˈtɜːb/ *vt* (*formal*) cause concern to; make anxious: *~ing rumours; a man who is never ~ed.*
per·tur·ba·tion /ˌpɜːtəˈbeɪʃən/ *n* [U]

pe·rusal /pəˈruːzəl/ *n* [C,U] act of reading carefully.
pe·ruse /pəˈruːz/ *vt* (*formal*) read carefully.

per·vade /pəˈveɪd/ *vt* (*formal*) spread through every part of: *The ideas that ~ all these periodicals may do great harm.*
per·va·sion /pəˈveɪʒən/ *n* [U]

per·va·sive /pəˈveɪsɪv/ *adj* tending to pervade: *~ influences.*
per·va·sive·ly *adv*
per·va·sive·ness *n* [U]

per·verse /pəˈvɜːs/ *adj* **1** (of persons) deliberately continuing in doing wrong. **2** (of circumstances) contrary (to one's wishes). **3** (of behaviour) unreasonable.
per·verse·ly *adv*
per·verse·ness *n* [U]

per·ver·sion /pəˈvɜːʃən US: -ʒən/ *n* **1** [U] perverting or being perverted. **2** [C] turning from right to wrong; change to something abnormal, unnatural, etc: *a ~ of justice; sexual ~s.*

per·ver·sity /pəˈvɜːsətɪ/ *n* (*pl* -ies) [U] being perverse; [C] perverse act.

per·vert[1] /ˈpɜːvət/ *n* [C] person whose (sexual) behaviour is abnormal.

per·vert[2] /pəˈvɜːt/ *vt* **1** turn (something) to a wrong use. **2** cause (a person, his mind) to turn away from right behaviour, beliefs, etc: *~ (the mind of) a child.*

pes·si·mism /ˈpesɪmɪzm/ *n* [U] tendency to believe that the worst thing is most likely to happen, that everything is fundamentally evil.
pes·si·mist /-ɪst/, believer in pessimism.
pes·si·mis·tic /ˌpesɪˈmɪstɪk/ *adj*
pessi·mis·ti·cally /-klɪ/ *adv*

pest /pest/ *n* [C] **1** troublesome or destructive thing, animal, etc: *garden ~s,* e g insects, mice, snails; *`~ control,* the use of various methods to get rid of ~s. **2** (*informal*) child who is a nuisance: *You little ~!*

pes·ter /ˈpestə(r)/ *vt* annoy; trouble: *be ~ed with flies/by requests for help.*

pes·ti·cide /ˈpestɪsaɪd/ *n* [C,U] substance used to destroy pests.

pes·ti·lence /ˈpestɪləns/ *n* [C,U] (any kind of) fatal epidemic disease, esp bubonic plague.

pestle /ˈpesəl/ *n* [C] stick with a thick end used in a mortar for pounding or crushing things. □ *vt* crush in (or as in) a mortar.

pet /pet/ *n* **1** (often as an *adjective*) animal, etc kept as a companion, treated with care and affection, e g a cat or a dog: *`~ food/shops.* **2** person treated as a favourite: *Mary is the teacher's ~.* **3** person specially loved or lovable: *make a ~ of a child.* □ *vt* (-tt-) treat with affection; kiss and caress.
pet aversion, person or thing disliked most: *Cowboy films are her ~ aversion.*
`pet name, name other than the real name, used affectionately.

petal /ˈpetəl/ *n* [C] one of the divisions of a flower: *`rose ~s.*

peter /ˈpiːtə(r)/ *vi* **peter out,** (of supplies, etc) come gradually to an end.

pe·ti·tion /pɪˈtɪʃən/ *n* [C] **1** prayer; earnest request; appeal (esp a written document signed by a large number of people). **2** formal application made to a court of law. □ *vt,vi* **1** make an appeal to, e g the authorities: *~ Parliament to stop unemployment.* **2** **petition for,** ask earnestly or humbly: *~ for a retrial.*
pe·ti·tioner, one who petitions, esp the plaintiff in a divorce suit.

pet·rel /ˈpetrəl/ n [C] long-winged black and white seabird.

pet·rify /ˈpetrɪfaɪ/ vt,vi (pt,pp -ied) **1** (cause to) change into stone. **2** (fig) take away power to think, feel, act, etc (through fear, surprise, etc).

pet·rol /ˈpetrəl/ n [U] refined petroleum used as a fuel in internal combustion engines (US = gasoline): fill up with ~. `petrol station, place where motor-vehicles can be filled with petrol.

pe·tro·leum /pɪˈtrəʊlɪəm/ n [U] mineral oil found underground and used in various forms (petrol, paraffin, etc) for lighting, heating and driving machines. pe`troleum `jelly n [U] semi-solid substance obtained from petroleum, used as a lubricant and in ointments.

pet·ti·coat /ˈpetɪkəʊt/ n [C] woman's underskirt.

petty /ˈpetɪ/ adj (-ier, -iest) **1** small; unimportant: ~ regulations enforced by ~ officials. **2** on a small scale: ~ farmers/ shopkeepers. **3** having or showing a narrow mind; mean: ~ spite. petty cash, (business) money for or from small payments. petty larceny, theft of articles of little value. `petty `officer, naval officer below commissioned rank. pet·tily /ˈpetəlɪ/ adv pet·ti·ness n [U]

petu·lance /ˈpetjʊləns/ n [U] petulant behaviour.

petu·lant /ˈpetjʊlənt/ US: -tʃʊ-/ adj unreasonably impatient or irritable. petu·lant·ly adv

pe·tu·nia /pɪˈtjuːnɪə/ US: -ˈtuː-/ n [C] (pl ~s) garden plant with funnel-shaped flowers of various colours.

pew /pjuː/ n [C] bench with a back in a church.

pe·wit, pee·wit /ˈpiːwɪt/ n [C] lapwing.

pew·ter /ˈpjuːtə(r)/ n [U] (objects made of a) grey alloy of lead and tin.

phal·anx /ˈfælæŋks/ n [C] (pl ~es or phalanges /fəˈlændʒiːz/) **1** (in ancient Greece) body of soldiers in close formation for fighting. **2** number of persons banded together for a common purpose. **3** (anat) bone in a finger or toe.

phal·lic /ˈfælɪk/ adj of a phallus: ~ symbols/emblems.

phal·lus /ˈfæləs/ n [C] (pl ~s or phalli /ˈfælaɪ/) image of the penis, as a symbol of generative power.

phan·tasy /ˈfæntəsɪ/ n = fantasy.

phan·tom /ˈfæntəm/ n [C] ghost; something seen as in a dream or vision: (as an adjective) ~ ships.

Phar·aoh /ˈfeərəʊ/ n [C] title of the kings of ancient Egypt.

Phari·see /ˈfærɪsɪ/ n [C] **1** member of an ancient Jewish sect known for strict obedience to written laws and for claiming reverance. **2** (small p) hypocritical and self-righteous person.

phar·ma·ceuti·cal /ˈfɑːməˈsjuːtɪkəl US: -ˈsuː-/ adj of, engaged in, pharmacy; of the use or sale of medicinal drugs.

phar·ma·cist /ˈfɑːməsɪst/ n [C] person skilled in preparing medicines. ⇨ chemist, druggist.

phar·ma·col·ogist /ˈfɑːməˈkɒlədʒɪst/ n [C] expert in, student of, pharmacology.

phar·ma·col·ogy /ˈfɑːməˈkɒlədʒɪ/ n [U] science of pharmacy.

phar·macy /ˈfɑːməsɪ/ n (pl -ies) **1** [U] preparation and dispensing of medicines and drugs. **2** [C] (part of a) shop where medical goods are sold. (US = drug-store).

phar·yn·gi·tis /ˈfærɪnˈdʒaɪtɪs/ n [U] inflammation of the mucous membrane of the pharynx.

phar·ynx /ˈfærɪŋks/ n [C] cavity (with the muscles, etc that enclose it) at the back of the mouth, where the passages to the nose, mouth and larynx begin.

phase /feɪz/ n [C] **1** stage of development: the critical ~ of an illness. **2** (of the moon) amount of bright surface visible from the earth (new moon, full moon, etc). □ vt plan, carry out, by phases: a well-~d withdrawal, one made by stages. phase in/out, introduce/withdraw one stage at a time.

pheas·ant /ˈfezənt/ n [C] long-tailed game bird; [U] its flesh as food.

phe·nom·enal /fɪˈnɒmɪnəl/ adj **1** that is known only through the senses. **2** concerned with phenomena. **3** enormous; extraordinary. phe·nom·enally /-nəlɪ/ adv

phe·nom·enon /fɪˈnɒmɪnən US: -nɒn/ n [C] (pl -ena /-nə/) **1** thing that is known to exist by the senses: the phenomena of nature. **2** remarkable or unusual person, thing, happening, etc.

phew /fjuː/ int suggesting astonishment, impatience, discomfort, disgust, etc according to context.

phial /ˈfaɪəl/ n [C] small bottle, esp one for liquid medicine; vial.

phil·an·thropic /ˈfɪlənˈθrɒpɪk/ adj benevolent; kind and helpful. phil·an·thropi·cally /-klɪ/ adv

phil·an·thro·pist /fɪˈlænθrəpɪst/ n [C] person who helps others, esp those who are poor or in trouble.

phil·an·thropy /fɪˈlænθrəpɪ/ n [U] love of mankind; practical sympathy and benevolence.

Phi·lis·tine /ˈfɪlɪstaɪn US: -stɪn/ n **1** (Biblical) one of the warlike people in Palestine who were the enemies of the Israelites. **2** (small p) (modern use) uncultured person; person whose interests are material and commonplace.

philo·logi·cal /ˈfɪləˈlɒdʒɪkəl/ adj of philology.

phil·ol·ogist /fɪˈlɒlədʒɪst/ n [C] student of, expert in, philology.

phil·ol·ogy /fɪˈlɒlədʒɪ/ n [U] study of the development of language, or of particular languages. ⇨ linguistics.

phil·os·opher /fɪˈlɒsəfə(r)/ n [C] 1 person studying or teaching philosophy, or having a system of philosophy. 2 (informal) person whose mind is untroubled by stormy feelings or hardships; person who lets reason govern his life.

philo·sophi·cal /ˌfɪləˈsɒfɪkəl/ adj 1 of, devoted to, guided by, philosophy. 2 (informal) (of a person, his behaviour) guided by reason and not feelings: take a ~ view of a personal situation.

philo·sophi·cally /-klɪ/ adv

phil·os·ophize /fɪˈlɒsəfaɪz/ vi think, discuss, like a philosopher.

phil·os·ophy /fɪˈlɒsəfɪ/ n (pl -ies) 1 [U] the search for knowledge, esp the nature and meaning of existence. 2 [C] system of thought resulting from such a search for knowledge: a man with a practical ~. 3 [U] calm, quiet attitude towards life, even in the face of unhappiness, danger, difficulty, etc. **moral philosophy,** the study of the principles underlying the actions and behaviour of men.

phleb·itis /flɪˈbaɪtɪs/ n [U] inflammation of a vein.

phlegm /flem/ n [U] 1 thick, semi-fluid substance forming on the skin of the throat and in the nose, and expelled by coughing. 2 quality of being phlegmatic.

phleg·matic /flegˈmætɪk/ adj being slow to act or to show feeling or interest.

phleg·mat·i·cally /-klɪ/ adv

pho·bia /ˈfəʊbɪə/ n [C] (pl ~s) unhealthy, strong, fear or dislike.

phone[1] /fəʊn/ n, vt, vi (informal abbr for) telephone.

`phone–booth/-box, telephone kiosk; callbox.

phone[2] /fəʊn/ n [C] (linguistics) single speech-sound (vowel or consonant).

pho·neme /ˈfəʊniːm/ n [C] (linguistics) unit of the system of sounds that distinguish words of a language as represented ideally by single letters of the alphabet.

pho·nemic /fəˈniːmɪk/ adj

pho·netic /fəˈnetɪk/ adj 1 concerned with the sounds of human speech. 2 (of transcriptions) providing a symbol for each phoneme of the language transcribed. 3 (of a language) having a system of spelling that approximates closely to the sounds represented by the letters: Spanish spelling is ~.

pho·neti·cally /-klɪ/ adv

pho·net·ics n (used with a sing verb) (a) study and science of speech sounds, their production, and the signs used to represent them. (b) sound–system of a language.

pho·neti·cian /ˌfəʊnɪˈtɪʃən/ n [C] expert in phonetics

pho·ney, phony /ˈfəʊnɪ/ adj (-ier, -iest) (sl) fake; not genuine. □ n [C] phony person: He's a complete ~.

pho·nic /ˈfɒnɪk/ adj of (vocal) sounds.

pho·nol·ogy /fəˈnɒlədʒɪ/ n [U] (linguistics) scientific study of the organization of speech sounds (including phonemes), esp in particular languages.

phooey /ˈfuːɪ/ int exclamation of disgust, disbelief, etc.

phos·pho·res·cence /ˌfɒsfəˈresəns/ n [U] the giving out of light without burning or heat that can be felt.

phos·pho·rescent /-sənt/ adj

phos·phorus /ˈfɒsfərəs/ n [U] yellowish, non-metallic, poisonous element like wax (symbol P) which catches fire easily and gives out a faint light in the dark.

photo /ˈfəʊtəʊ/ n [C] (informal abbr for) photograph.

photo– /ˈfəʊtəʊ/ prefix 1 of light: photoelectric. 2 of photography: photogenic.

photo·copy /ˈfəʊtəʊkɒpɪ/ vt (pt, pp -ied) make a copy of (a document, etc) by a photographic method. □ n [C] (pl -ies) such a copy.

photo·electric /ˌfəʊtəʊɪˈlektrɪk/ adj: ~ cell, device which gives out an electric current when light falls on it, used for many purposes, e g to cause a door to open when someone approaches it.

photo·finish /ˈfəʊtəʊ ˈfɪnɪʃ/ n [C] finish of a horse-race so close that a photograph is needed to decide the winner.

photo·genic /ˌfəʊtəʊˈdʒenɪk/ adj that is photographed well or effectively.

photo·graph /ˈfəʊtəgrɑːf US: -græf/ n [C] picture recorded by means of the chemical action of light on a specially prepared film in a camera, etc which is transferred to specially prepared paper. □ vt take a photograph of.

photographer /fəˈtɒgrəfə(r)/ n [C] person (esp professional) who takes photographs.

pho·to·graphic /ˌfəʊtəˈgræfɪk/ adj of, related to, used in, taking photographs.

photo·graphi·cally /-klɪ/ adv

pho·tog·ra·phy /fəˈtɒgrəfɪ/ n [U] art or process of taking photographs.

phrasal /ˈfreɪzəl/ adj in the form of a phrase.

phrasal verb, idiomatic use of a verb with an adverb and/or a preposition, e g go in for, blow up.

phrase /freɪz/ n [C] 1 group of words forming part of a sentence, e g in the garden, in order to. 2 short, clever expression. 3 (music) short, independent passage forming part of a longer passage. □ vt express in words: a neatly ~d compliment.

`phrase book, one listing expressions with equivalents in another language, e g for tourists.

phras·eol·ogy /ˌfreɪzɪˈɒlədʒɪ/ n [U] choice

of words; wording.

phren-etic /frəˈnetɪk/ *adj* (*formal*) frantic; fanatic.

physic /ˈfɪzɪk/ *n* [U] (*old use*) medicine.

physi-cal /ˈfɪzɪkəl/ *adj* 1 of things that are known through the senses (contrasted with moral and spiritual things): *the ~ world.* 2 of the body: *~ exercise,* e g running. 3 of the laws of nature: *a ~ impossibility.* 4 of the natural features of the world: *~ geography.*

physical ˈscience, e g physics, chemistry.

physi-cally /-klɪ/ *adv*

phys-ician /fɪˈzɪʃən/ *n* [C] doctor of medicine and surgery.

physi-cist /ˈfɪzɪsɪst/ *n* [C] expert on physics.

phys-ics /ˈfɪzɪks/ *n pl* (used with a *sing verb*) group of sciences dealing with matter and energy (e g heat, light, sound), but usually excluding chemistry and biology.

physi(o)- /ˈfɪzɪ(ə)-, *etc/ prefix* of the body or living things: *physiology.*

physio-logi-cal /ˈfɪzɪəˈlɒdʒɪkəl/ *adj* of physiology.

physi-ol-ogist /ˈfɪzɪˈɒlədʒɪst/ *n* [C] expert in, student of, physiology.

physi-ol-ogy /ˈfɪzɪˈɒlədʒɪ/ *n* [U] science of the normal functions of living things, esp animals.

physio-thera-pist /ˈfɪzɪəˈθerəpɪst/ *n* [C] person trained to give physiotherapy.

physio-ther-apy /ˈfɪzɪəˈθerəpɪ/ *n* [U] treatment of disease by means of exercise, massage, the use of light, heat, electricity and other natural forces.

phy-sique /fɪˈziːk/ *n* [U] structure and development of the body: *a strong ~.*

pia-nist /ˈpɪənɪst/ *n* [C] person who plays the piano.

pi-ano /pɪˈænəʊ/ *n* [C] (*pl ~s*) musical instrument in which metal strings are struck by hammers operated from a keyboard.

grand piano, one with horizontal strings.

upright piano, one with vertical strings.

piano-forte /pɪˈænəʊˈfɔːtɪ *US:* pɪˈænəfɔrt/ *n* [C] (*formal*) piano.

pica-dor /ˈpɪkədɔː(r)/ *n* [C] man (on a horse) who uses a lance to anger and weaken bulls in the sport of bull-fighting.

pic-ca-lilli /ˈpɪkəˈlɪlɪ/ *n* [U] kind of hot-tasting pickle made of chopped vegetables, spices in mustard, vinegar, etc.

pic-colo /ˈpɪkələʊ/ *n* [C] (*pl ~s*) small flute.

pick[1] /pɪk/ *n* [C] picking; selection: *the ~ of the bunch,* the best of all of them.

pick[2] /pɪk/ *n* [C] 1 (also **ˈpick(-axe)**), heavy tool with an iron head having two pointed ends, used for breaking up hard surfaces (e g roads, brickwork). 2 small, sharp-pointed instrument: *a ˈtooth~.*

pick[3] /pɪk/ *vt,vi* (For special uses with *adverbial particles* and *prepositions,* ⇨ 7 below.) 1 take up, remove, pull away, with the fingers: *~ flowers/fruit; ~ one's nose,*

remove bits of dried mucus from the nostrils. *pick sb's brains,* get ideas and information. *pick sb's pocket,* steal from it. 2 tear or separate; use a pointed instrument to clean, etc: *~ one's teeth,* get bits of food from the spaces between them, etc by using a ˈtooth-pick. *pick a lock,* use a pointed tool, a piece of wire, etc to unlock it without a key. *have a ˈbone to pick with sb,* ⇨ bone(1). 3 choose; select: *~ a team,* choose players; *~ the winning horse/~ the winner,* make a successful guess at the winner (before the race). *pick a quarrel with sb,* cause a quarrel intentionally. 4 make by picking. *pick holes in an argument,* (*fig*) find its weak points. 5 (of birds) take up (grain, etc) in the bill; (of persons) eat (food, etc) in small amounts: *She only ~ed at her food.* 6 (*US*) pluck (the strings of): *~ a banjo.*

7 (special uses with *adverbial particles* and *prepositions*):

pick at sb, (*informal*) find fault with: *Why are you always ~ing at the poor child?*

pick on sb, select for punishment, criticism, etc: *You're always ~ing on me.*

pick sb/sth out, (a) choose. (b) distinguish from surrounding persons, objects, etc: *~ out a friend in a crowd.*

pick sth over, examine and make a selection from: *~ over a basket of grapes,* e g to throw out any that are bad.

pick sth up, (a) take hold of and lift: *~ up one's hat/parcels, etc.* (b) gain; get: *~ up a foreign language,* learn it without taking lessons or studying; *~ up bits of information; ~ up a bargain at a sale.* (c) succeed in seeing or hearing (by means of apparatus): *enemy planes ~ed up by our searchlights/ radar, etc.* (d) recover; regain: *You'll soon ~ up health when you get to the seaside.* *pick sb up,* (a) make the acquaintance of casually: *a girl he ~ed up on the street.* (b) take (persons) along with one: *He stopped the car to ~ up a young girl who was hitch-hiking across Europe. The escaped prisoner was ~ed up* (= seen and arrested) *by the police at Hull. pick oneself up,* raise (oneself) after a fall: *She slipped and fell, but quickly ~ed herself up.*

picker /ˈpɪkə(r)/ *n* [C] person or thing that picks (chiefly in compounds): ˈhop-~s.

picket /ˈpɪkɪt/ *n* [C] 1 pointed stick, etc set upright in the ground (as part of a fence, etc). 2 small group of men on police duty, or sent out to watch the enemy. 3 worker, or group of workers, stationed at the gates of a factory, dockyard, etc during a strike, to try to persuade others not to go to work. ▫ *vt,vi* 1 put pickets(1) round. 2 station (men) as pickets (2). 3 place/be a picket(3) at: *~ a factory.*

pick-ings /ˈpɪkɪŋz/ *n pl* odds and ends left over from which profits may be made; these profits.

pickle /ˈpɪkəl/ *n* 1 [U] salt water, vinegar,

etc for keeping meat, vegetables, etc in good condition. **2** (often *pl*) vegetables kept in pickle: *onion ~s*. **3** *in a (sad/sorry) pickle,* in a sad, etc plight. □ *vt* preserve in pickle: *~d onions.*

pickled *adj* (*sl*) intoxicated.

pick-me-up /ˈpɪk mɪ ʌp/ *n* [C] drink, etc that gives new strength, cheerfulness.

pick-pocket /ˈpɪk pɒkɪt/ *n* [C] person who steals from pockets. ⇨ **pick³**(1).

pick-up /ˈpɪk ʌp/ *n* [C] (*pl ~s*) **1** that part of a record-player that holds the stylus. **2** small general-purpose van or truck, open and with low sides. **3** (*sl*) person of the opposite sex who a person meets deliberately, e g at a party, in the street. **4** acceleration: *an engine/car with a good ~-up.*

pic·nic /ˈpɪknɪk/ *n* [C] **1** pleasure trip on which food is carried to be eaten outdoors. **2** (*informal*) something easy and enjoyable: *It's no ~,* is not an easy job. □ *vi* (-ck-) take part in a picnic: *~king in the woods.*

pic·tor·ial /pɪkˈtɔːrɪəl/ *adj* of, having, represented in, pictures: *a ~ record of the wedding.* □ *n* [C] periodical of which pictures are the main feature.

pic·ture /ˈpɪktʃə(r)/ *n* [C] **1** painting, drawing, sketch, photograph, esp as a work of art. **2** beautiful scene, object, person, etc. **3** type or example. *be the picture of health,* appear to be very healthy. **4** (*fig*) account or description that enables somebody to see in his mind an event, etc. *be/put sb in the picture,* be/cause him to be aware of all the facts of a situation. **5** film (to be) shown in a cinema. **6** what is seen on a television screen. □ *vt* **1** make a picture of; paint. **2** imagine: *P~ me upon your knee.*

the pictures, (*informal*) the cinema.

`picture-book,` book with many illustrations, esp one for children.

`picture-card,` (in playing cards) one with a king, queen or knave on it.

pic·tur·esque /ˌpɪktʃəˈresk/ *adj* **1** having the quality of being like, or of being fit to be, the subject of a painting: *a ~ village.* **2** vivid; graphic: *~ language.* **3** (of a person, his character) attractive; original.

pic·tur·esque·ly *adv*

piddle /ˈpɪdəl/ *vi, n* [C,U] (*sl*) (pass) urine.

pid·dling /ˈpɪdlɪŋ/ *adj* (*informal*) insignificant: *~ jobs.*

pidgin /ˈpɪdʒɪn/ *n* [C] **1** any of several languages resulting from contact between European traders and local peoples, e g in West Africa and the Far East, containing elements of the local language(s) and English, French or Dutch. **2** (*informal*) (only in) *(not) one's pidgin,* not one's job or concern.

pie /paɪ/ *n* [C,U] meat or fruit covered with pastry and baked in a deep dish: *fruit/meat ~s. have a finger in every pie,* be (too) concerned in all that is going on. *as easy as pie,* (*sl*) very easy. *pie in the sky,* unrealis-

tic hopes.

pie-bald /ˈpaɪbɔːld/ *adj* (of a horse) having white and dark patches of irregular shape.

piece¹ /piːs/ *n* [C] **1** part or bit of a solid substance (complete in itself, but broken, separated or made from a larger portion): *a ~ of paper/string. Will you have another ~* (= slice) *of cake? The vase is in ~s. The teapot fell and was broken to ~s. come/take (sth) to pieces,* divide (it) into the parts which make it up: *Does this machine come/take to ~s?* *go (all) to pieces,* (*informal*) (of a person) break up physically, mentally or morally. *a piece of cake,* (*sl*) very easy. **2** separate instance or example: *a ~ of news/ luck/advice/information/furniture. give sb a piece of one's mind,* criticize him strongly. **3** single composition (in art, music, etc): *a fine ~ of work/music/poetry.* **4** single thing out of a set: *a dinner service of 50 ~s.* **5** one of the objects moved on a board in such games as chess. **6** coin: *a ten-pence.~.*

piece² /piːs/ *vt* put (parts, etc together); make by joining or adding (pieces) together: *~ together odds and ends of cloth.*

piece-meal /ˈpiːsmiːl/ *adv* one (part) at a time: *work done ~.* □ *adj* coming, done, etc piecemeal.

pier /pɪə(r)/ *n* [C] **1** structure of wood, iron, etc built out into the sea as a landing-stage; similar structure for walking on for pleasure (often with a pavilion, restaurant, etc). **2** pillar supporting a span of a bridge, etc.

pierce /pɪəs/ *vt,vi* **1** (of sharp-pointed instruments) go into or through; make (a hole) by doing this: *The arrow ~d his shoulder.* **2** (*fig*) (of cold, pain, sounds, etc) force a way into or through: *Her screams ~d the air.* **3** go (through, into, etc): *Our forces ~d through the enemy's lines.*

pierc·ing *adj* (esp of cold, voices) sharp: *a piercing wind.*

pierc·ing·ly *adv*: *a piercingly cold wind.*

piety /ˈpaɪətɪ/ *n* (*pl* -ies) (*formal*) **1** [U] devotion to God and good actions. **2** [C] act, etc that shows piety.

pig /pɪg/ *n* **1** [C] domestic and wild animal without fur that does not chew grass; [U] its flesh as meat. ⇨ **bacon, ham, pork.** *pigs might fly,* the impossible might happen. **2** (*informal*) dirty, greedy or ill-mannered person. *make a pig of oneself,* eat or drink too much.

`pig-headed` *adj* stubborn.

`pig-skin,` [U] (leather made of a) pig's skin.

`pig-sty` /-staɪ/, (a) small building for pigs. (b) (*informal*) dirty home.

`pig-tail,` plait of hair hanging down over the back of the neck and shoulders.

`pig-gish` /-ɪʃ/ *adj* dirty, greedy.

piggy /ˈpɪgɪ/ *n* [C] (*pl* -ies) little pig. □ *adj* (*informal*) greedy.

`piggy bank,` model of a pig used by a child for saving coin money.

pigeon /ˈpɪdʒən/ n [C] **1** bird, wild or tame, of the dove family. **2** clay pigeon, disc thrown up into the air as a target for shooting. **3** easily deceived person. **4** ⇨ stool-pigeon.

\`pigeon-breasted adj (of a human being) having a bulging, large, chest.

\`pigeon-hole n [C] one of a number of small open boxes (e g above a desk) for keeping papers in. □ vt put (papers, etc) in a ~hole and ignore or forget them; postpone consideration of: The scheme was ~holed.

\`pigeon-toed adj having the toes turned inwards.

pig-let /ˈpɪɡlət/ n [C] young pig.

pig·ment /ˈpɪɡmənt/ n **1** [U] colouring matter for making dyes, paint, etc; [C] particular substance used for this. **2** [U] the natural colouring matter in the skin, hair, etc of living beings.

pigmy /ˈpɪɡmɪ/ n [C] = pygmy.

pike¹ /paɪk/ n [C] long wooden shaft with a spearhead, formerly used by soldiers fighting on foot.

pike² /paɪk/ n [C] large, fierce, freshwater fish.

pil-chard /ˈpɪltʃəd/ n [C] small seafish resembling the herring.

pile¹ /paɪl/ n [C] **1** number of things lying one on another: a ~ of books. **2** \`funeral pile, heap of wood, etc on which a corpse is burnt. **3** (informal) large amount of money. make a/one's pile, earn a lot of money.

pile² /paɪl/ n [C] heavy beam of timber, steel, concrete, etc driven into the ground, as a foundation for a building, a support for a bridge, etc.

\`pile-driver, machine for driving piles into the ground.

pile³ /paɪl/ n [U] soft, thick, surface like hair of velvet, carpets, etc.

pile⁴ /paɪl/ vt,vi **1** make into a pile(1); put on or in a pile(1): ~ up dishes on a table; ~ more coal on (the fire). **pile it on**, (informal) exaggerate. **2** pile up, (a) accumulate: My work keeps piling up, There is more and more for me to do. (b) (of a number of vehicles) crash into each other. Hence, \`pile-up n: another bad ~-up on the motorway. **3** pile into/out of sth, enter/leave in a disorderly way: They all ~d into/out of the car/cinema.

piles /paɪlz/ n [U] hemorrhoids.

pil-fer /ˈpɪlfə(r)/ vt,vi steal, esp in small quantities.

pil-grim /ˈpɪlɡrɪm/ n [C] person who travels to a sacred place as an act of religious devotion: ~s to Mecca.

the Pilgrim Fathers, English Puritans who went to America in 1620 and founded the colony of Plymouth, Massachusetts.

\`pil-grim-age /-ɪdʒ/, journey of a pilgrim.

pill /pɪl/ n [C] **1** small ball or tablet of medicine for swallowing whole. **2** the ~, oral contraceptive. **be/go on the pill**, be taking/ start to take such pills regularly.

pil-lar /ˈpɪlə(r)/ n [C] **1** upright column, of stone, wood, metal, etc as a support or ornament. (driven) from pillar to post, (fig) (forced to go) to and fro. **2** pillar of, (fig) strong supporter: a ~ of the Church. **3** something in the shape of a pillar, e g a column of fire, smoke.

\`pillar-box, cylindrical container (in GB, scarlet) in which letters are posted.

pil-lion /ˈpɪlɪən/ n [C] **1** saddle for a passenger behind the driver of a motor bike: a ~ passenger. **2** seat for a second rider behind the rider of a horse.

pil-low /ˈpɪləʊ/ n [C] soft cushion for the head, esp while lying in bed. □ vt rest, support, on or as on a pillow.

\`pillow-case/-slip, washable cover for a pillow.

pi-lot /ˈpaɪlət/ n [C] **1** person trained and licensed to take ships into or out of a harbour, along a river, through a canal, etc. **2** person trained to operate the controls of an aircraft. **3** (used as an adjective) experimental; used to test how something will work, how it may be improved, etc: a ~ census/ survey/scheme. □ vt act as a pilot.

\`pilot fish, small fish which often swims in company with larger fish, e g sharks, or sometimes ships.

\`pilot light, small flame in a gas cooker, which lights large burners, etc when the gas is turned on.

pi-mento /pɪˈmentəʊ/ n (pl ~s) **1** [U] dried aromatic berries of a West Indian tree, also called Jamaica pepper and allspice. **2** [C] tree that produces the berries.

pimp /pɪmp/ n [C] man who solicits for a prostitute. □ vt act as a pimp.

pimple /ˈpɪmpəl/ n [C] small, hard, inflamed spot on the skin.

pim-pled adj having pimples.

pim-ply /ˈpɪmplɪ/ adj (-ier, -iest)

pin¹ /pɪn/ n [C] **1** short, thin piece of stiff wire with a sharp point and a round head, used for fastening together parts of a dress, papers, etc. **2** similar piece of wire with an ornamental head for special purposes: a \`hat-~. ⇨ safety pin. **3** peg of wood or metal for various purposes. ⇨ drawing pin, hairpin, ninepins, rolling pin. **4** each of the pegs round which the strings of a musical instrument are fastened.

\`pins and \`needles, tingling sensation in a part of the body caused by blood flowing again when its circulation has been slowed down.

\`pin-cushion, pad for pins(1).

\`pin-money, money earned by a woman to buy small personal necessities, etc.

\`pin-point n [C] something very small. □ vt find, hit, a target with the required accuracy: Our planes ~pointed the target.

\`pin-prick, (fig) small act, remark, etc causing annoyance.

`pin-stripe, (of dress material) with many very narrow stripes.

pin² /pɪn/ vt (-nn-) 1 fasten with a pin or pins: ∼ papers together; ∼ up a notice, e g with drawing pins on a notice board. pin sth on sb, make him appear responsible or deserving blame. pin one's hopes on, rely completely on a person, a decision, etc. 2 make unable to move: He was ∼ned under the wrecked car. He ∼ned me against the wall, held me there and prevented me from moving. pin sb down, (fig) get him to commit himself, to decide, etc.

pina-fore /ˈpɪnəfɔː(r)/ n [C] loose article of clothing worn over a dress to keep it clean.

pince-nez /ˈpæns.neɪ/ n [C] (pl unchanged) pair of spectacles which clip on the nose (not a frame that fits round the ears).

pin-cers /ˈpɪnsəz/ n pl (also a pair of ∼s) 1 instrument for gripping things, pulling nails out of wood, etc. 2 pincer-shaped claws of certain shellfish.

pinch /pɪntʃ/ vt, vi 1 squeeze between the thumb and finger; have in a tight grip between two hard things which are pressed together: He ∼ed the boy's cheek. 2 be too tight; hurt by being too tight: These shoes ∼ (me). 3 (informal) take without permission: Who's ∼ed my dictionary? 4 live economically: ∼ and scrape in order to save money. 5 (sl) (of the police) arrest: be ∼ed for stealing. □ n [C] 1 painful squeeze: He gave her a spiteful ∼. 2 (fig) stress: feel the ∼ of poverty. 3 amount which can be taken up with the thumb and finger: a ∼ of tobacco. take sth with a pinch of salt, ⇨ salt. 4 at a pinch, if there is need and if there is no other way: We can get six people round the table at a ∼.

pine¹ /paɪn/ n [C] kinds of evergreen tree with needle-shaped leaves (`pine-needles) and cones (`pine-cones); [U] the wood of this tree.

pine² /paɪn/ vi 1 waste away through sorrow or illness: pining from hunger. 2 pine for sth/to do sth, have a strong desire: exiles pining for home/to return home.

pine-apple /ˈpaɪnæpəl/ n [C] (tropical plant with spiny leaves above a) sweet, juicy fruit; [U] this as food: ∼ juice; tinned ∼.

ping /pɪŋ/ n [C] short, sharp, ringing sound as of a small bell being hit □ vi make this sound.

ping-pong /ˈpɪŋpɒŋ/ n [C] = table tennis.

pin-ion¹ /ˈpɪnɪən/ n [C] bird's wing, esp the outer joint; flight-feather of a bird. □ vt 1 cut off a pinion of (a bird) to hamper flight. 2 bind the arms of (a person).

pin-ion² /ˈpɪnɪən/ n [C] small cog-wheel with teeth fitting into those of a larger cog-wheel.

pink¹ /pɪŋk/ n 1 [U] pale red colour of various kinds (rose ∼, salmon ∼). 2 [C] garden plant with sweet-smelling white, pink, crimson or variegated flowers. 3 in the pink, (informal) very well. □ adj of pale red colour.

`pink-ish /-ɪʃ/ adj rather pink.

pink² /pɪŋk/ vt 1 pierce with a sword. 2 decorate (leather, cloth) with small holes, etc.

`pink-ing scissors/shears, sewing scissors with serrated edges, used to prevent edges of cloth from fraying.

pin-money /ˈpɪn mʌnɪ/ n ⇨ pin¹.

pin-nacle /ˈpɪnəkəl/ n [C] 1 tall, pointed part of buttress. 2 high, slender mountain peak. 3 (fig) highest point: at the ∼ of his fame. □ vt put (as) on a pinnacle.

pinny /ˈpɪnɪ/ n [C] (pl -ies) (child's name for a) pinafore.

pinpoint /ˈpɪn pɔɪnt/ ⇨ pin¹.

pin-prick /ˈpɪn prɪk/ ⇨ pin¹.

pinstripe /ˈpɪn straɪp/ ⇨ pin¹.

pint /paɪnt/ n [C] unit of measure for liquids and certain dry goods, one-eighth of a gallon or about ·57 of a litre: a ∼ of milk/beer.

pin-up /ˈpɪn ʌp/ n [C] picture of an attractive person, esp a woman.

pion-eer /ˌpaɪəˈnɪə(r)/ n [C] 1 person who goes into a new or undeveloped country to settle or work there. 2 first student of a new branch of study, method etc; explorer. 3 (mil) one of an advance party of soldiers (e g clearing or making roads). □ vi, vt act as a pioneer.

pi-ous /ˈpaɪəs/ adj having, showing, deep devotion to religion.

pi-ous-ly adv

pip¹ /pɪp/ n seed, esp of a lemon, orange, apple or pear.

pip² /pɪp/ n 1 the ∼, disease of poultry. 2 give one the pip, (sl) fit of depression, disgust, etc.

pip³ /pɪp/ n [C] note of a time-signal on the telephone or radio.

pip⁴ /pɪp/ n [C] 1 each spot on playing-cards, dice and dominoes. 2 (GB informal) star on an army officer's shoulder-strap.

pipe¹ /paɪp/ n [C] 1 tube through which liquids or gases can flow: `water-∼s; `gas-∼s; `drain-∼s. 2 musical wind-instrument (a single tube with holes stopped by the fingers); each of the tubes from which sound is produced in an organ; (pl) = bagpipes. 3 (sound of the) whistle used by a sailor. 4 song or note of some birds. 5 tubular organ in the body: the `wind∼. 6 (also to`bacco ∼), tube with a bowl, used for smoking tobacco; quantity of tobacco held in the bowl. Put `that in your pipe and smoke it, (informal) Think about that and accept it whether you want to or not.

`pipe-dream, plan, idea, etc that is impracticable.

`pipe-line, (esp) pipes, often underground, for conveying petroleum to distant places. in the pipeline, (modern use) (of any kind of goods or proposals) on the way; about to be delivered, to receive attention.

`pipe-rack,` for tobacco pipes.

`pipe-ful` /-fʊl/ *n* as much as a pipe(6) holds.

pipe² /paɪp/ *vi,vt* **1** convey (water, etc) through pipes: ~ *water into a house*. **2** play as on a pipe. **pipe down,** (*informal*) be less noisy. **3** (*naut*) summon (sailors), welcome on board, with a pipe: ~ *the captain on board*. **4** trim (a dress), ornament (a cake, etc) with piping. ⇨ piping(2).

pipe-line /paɪplaɪn/ *n* ⇨ pipe¹.

piper /paɪpə(r)/ *n* [C] one who plays on a pipe or bagpipes.

pip-ette /pɪ'pet/ *n* [C] slender tube for transferring small quantities of liquid, esp in chemistry.

pip-ing /paɪpɪŋ/ *n* [U] **1** length of pipe(1), esp for water and drains: *ten metres of lead* ~. **2** narrow cord used to decorate the edges of some garments; lines of icing sugar used to decorate cakes, etc. **3** action of playing on a pipe; sound produced from a pipe. □ *adj* like the sound from a pipe(2): *in a* ~ *voice*. □ *adv* **piping hot,** (of liquids, food) very hot.

pip-squeak /pɪpskwiːk/ *n* [C] (*dated sl*) annoying, conceited, person or thing.

pi-quancy /piːkənsɪ/ *n* [U] the quality of being piquant.

pi-quant /piːkənt/ *adj* pleasantly sharp to the taste: *a* ~ *sauce*.
pi-quant-ly *adv*

pique /piːk/ *vt* hurt the pride or self-respect of. □ *n* [U] resentment: *go away in a fit of* ~.

pi-qué /piːkeɪ *US:* pɪ'keɪ/ *n* [U] stiff cotton fabric.

pi-racy /paɪərəsɪ/ *n* (*pl* -ies) **1** [U] robbery on the high seas. **2** [U] pirating of books, etc. **3** [C] instance of either of these.

pi-ranha /pɪ'rɑːnjə/ *n* [C] (kind of) tropical American freshwater fish, noted for attacking and eating live animals.

pi-rate /paɪərət/ *n* [C] **1** person who commits piracy(1). **2** person who uses something, eg another's copyright, without authorization. □ *vt* use, reproduce (a book, a recording, etc) without authority.
pi-rati-cal /paɪə'rætɪkəl/ *adj*
pi-rati-cally /-klɪ/ *adv*

pir-ou-ette /pɪrʊ'et/ *n* [C] ballet-dancer's rapid turn on the ball or the toe of the foot. □ *vi* dance a pirouette.

Pis-ces /paɪsiːz/ *n* the Fish, twelfth sign of the zodiac.

piss /pɪs/ *vt,vi* ⚠ (*vulgar sl*) pass urine. □ *n* [U] urine.
pissed *adj* ⚠ (*vulgar sl*) very drunk.

pis-ta-chio /pɪ'stɑːtʃɪəʊ *US:* -tæʃɪəʊ/ *n* [C] (*pl* ~s) (tree with) nut with a green edible kernel; colour of this kernel.

pis-til /pɪstɪl/ *n* [C] seed-producing part of a flower.

pis-tol /pɪstəl/ *n* [C] small firearm held and fired in one hand.

pis-ton /pɪstən/ *n* [C] round plate or short cylinder fitting closely inside another cylinder or tube in which it moves, used in engines, pumps, etc to impart motion.

pit¹ /pɪt/ *n* [C] **1** large hole in the earth, esp one from which material is dug out (*a* `coal-~`) or for industrial purposes (*a* `saw-~`). **2** covered hole as a trap for wild animals, etc. **3** hollow in an animal or plant body, esp *the* ~ *of the stomach,* the depression in the belly between the ribs. ⇨ also armpit. **4** scar left on the body after smallpox. **5** (*GB*) (people in the) seats on the ground floor of a theatre. **6** hole in the floor (of a garage, workshop) from which the underside of a motor vehicle can be examined and repaired. **7** place at which cars stop (at race-courses) for fuel, new tyres, etc. **8** =I cockpit(1). □ *vt* (-tt-) mark with pits(4) or with hollows in the ground: *The moon is* ~*ted with craters*.
`pit-fall,` (a) covered pit as a trap for animals. (b) (*fig*) unsuspected snare or danger.
`pit-head,` entrance of a coalmine.
`pit pony,` pony kept underground in coalmines for pulling wagons.
`pit-prop,` prop used to support the roof of a gallery in a mine.

pit² /pɪt/ *n* [C] (*US*) hard seed like a stone (of such fruits as cherries, plums, peaches, dates). □ *vt* (-tt-) (*US*) remove pits from.

pit-a-pat /'pɪt ə 'pæt/ *adv* with (the sound of) light, quick taps or steps: *Her heart/feet went* ~.

pitch¹ /pɪtʃ/ *n* [C] **1** place where a person (esp a street trader) usually does business. **queer sb's pitch,** upset his plans. **2** area for playing football, etc. **3** (*cricket*) part of the ground between the wickets; manner in which the ball is delivered in bowling. **4** act of pitching or throwing anything. **5** (in music and speech) degree of highness or lowness: *the* ~ *of a voice*. **6** degree: *the noise reached such a* ~ *that...* ⇨ fever pitch. **7** amount of slope (esp of a roof). **8** (of a ship) process of pitching(5).

pitch² /pɪtʃ/ *n* [U] black substance made from coal-tar, turpentine or petroleum, sticky and semi-liquid when hot, hard when cold, used eg between planks forming a floor, to make roofs waterproof, etc.
`pitch-black/-dark` *adj* very black or dark.

pitch³ /pɪtʃ/ *vt,vi* **1** set up, erect (a tent, camp). **2** throw (a ball, etc). **3** (*music*) set in a certain key: *This song is* ~*ed too low for me*. **4** (cause to) fall heavily forwards or outwards: *The boat overturned and the passengers were* ~*ed out*. **5** (of a ship) move up and down as the bows rise and fall. ⇨ roll²(6). **6** *pitch in,* set to work with energy. **pitch into,** (a) attack violently. (b) get busy with: *We* ~*ed into the work/the food*. **7** (*cricket*) (cause the ball to) strike the ground near or around the wicket. **8** (*baseball*) throw (the ball) to the batter.
□ *vt* (a) lift or move with a fork. (b) (*fig*) force (a person) (*into* a job, etc).
`pitch-fork,` long-handled fork with sharp

prongs for lifting hay, etc.

pitcher[1] /'pɪtʃə(r)/ n [C] large jug.

pitcher[2] /'pɪtʃə(r)/ n [C] (*baseball*) player who throws the ball.

pit·eous /'pɪtɪəs/ adj arousing pity.

pit·eous·ly adv

pit·fall /'pɪtfɔːl/ ⇨ pit[1].

pith /pɪθ/ n [U] 1 soft substance that fills the stems of some plants (e g reeds). 2 similar substance lining the rind of oranges, etc. 3 (*fig*) essential part: *the ~ of his argument/speech, etc.*

`**pith hat/helmet**, light sun hat made of dried pith of marrow.

pithy adj (-ier, -iest) (a) of, like, full of, pith. (b) full of meaning: *~y remarks.*

`**pith·ily** /-əlɪ/ adv

piti·able /'pɪtɪəbəl/ adj arousing pity; deserving only contempt: *a ~ attempt.*

piti·ably /-əblɪ/ adv

piti·ful /'pɪtɪfəl/ adj 1 feeling, showing pity. 2 causing pity: *a ~ sight.* 3 arousing contempt.

piti·fully /-fəlɪ/ adv

piti·less /'pɪtɪləs/ adj showing no pity.

piti·less·ly adv

pi·ton /'piton/ n [C] (*Fr*) metal spike driven into rock, with a hole for rope, used as a hold in mountain climbing.

pit·tance /'pɪtəns/ n [C] low, insufficient amount, payment: *work all day for a ~.*

pitter-patter /'pɪtə pætə(r)/ n [U] rapid succession of light sounds: *the ~ of rain.*

pi·tu·itary /pɪ'tjuɪtərɪ US: -'tuətərɪ/ n [C] (*pl* -ies) (also *~ gland*) small ductless gland at the base of the brain, secreting hormones that influence growth, etc.

pity /'pɪtɪ/ n (*pl* -ies) 1 [U] feeling of sorrow for the troubles, sufferings, etc of another person: *be filled with/feel ~ for her.* **have/take pity on sb**, help a person in trouble, etc. **for pity's sake**, (used when asking for urgent action, a decision, etc): *For ~'s sake try to stop this persecution.* **out of pity**, because of a feeling of pity. 2 (with *a, an*, but not in *pl* (event which gives) cause for regret or sorrow: *What a ~* (= How unfortunate) (*that*) *you can't come with us!* **more's the pity**, so much the worse. □ *vt* (*pt, pp* -ied) feel genuine (but often used with scorn) pity for: *I ~ you having such an ugly wife.*

pivot /'pɪvət/ n [C] 1 central pin or point on which something turns. 2 (*fig*) something on which an argument or discussion depends. □ *vt, vi* turn (as) on a pivot.

pi·votal /-təl/ adj

pixy, pixie /'pɪksɪ/ n [C] (*pl* -ies) small elf or fairy.

pizza /'piːtsə/ n [C,U] (*It*) (food made by baking a) layer of dough covered with a mixture of tomatoes, cheese, etc.

plac·ard /'plækɑːd/ n [C] written or printed announcement (to be) publicly displayed; poster. □ *vt* make known using a placard.

pla·cate /plə'keɪt US: 'pleɪkeɪt/ vt = pacify.

place[1] /pleɪs/ n [C] 1 particular part of space (to be) occupied by a person or thing: *I can't be in two ~s at once.* **all over the place**, in disorder. **in/out of place**, (a) in/not in the right or proper place: *I like to have everything in ~.* (b) (*fig*) suitable/unsuitable: *his remarks were out of ~.* **in place of**, instead of. **give place**, yield. **give place to**, be succeeded by. **put sb in his (proper) place; put oneself in sb's/sb else's place**, ⇨ put (2). **take the place of**, be substituted for: *Plastics have taken the ~ of many natural materials.* **take place**, happen. 2 city, town, village, etc: *go to ~s and see things*, travel as a tourist. `**go places**, (*informal*) have increasing success. 3 building or area of land used for some particular purpose that is specified: *a ~ of worship*, a church, mosque etc; *a ~ of business.* 4 particular area on a surface: *a sore ~ on my neck.* 5 passage, part, in a book, etc: *I've lost my ~.* 6 rank or station (in society, etc). **keep sb in his place**, not allow him to be too familiar. 7 (in a race) position among those competitors who are winners: *Whose horse got the first ~?* 8 (in sport) position in a team. 9 (*maths*) position of a figure in a series: *calculated to two decimal ~s*, e g 6·57. 10 single step or stage in an argument, etc: *in the first/second, etc ~.* 11 office, employment, e g a government appointment; duties of an office-holder. 12 position as an undergraduate: *get a ~ at Cambridge.* 13 (*informal*) house or other residence, e g a flat: *He has a nice little ~ in the country. Come round to my ~ one evening.* 14 (in proper names) alternative name for *Street, Square*, etc in a town: *St James's P~.* 15 setting for one person at a table.

place[2] /pleɪs/ vt 1 put in a certain place; arrange (things) in their proper places: *P~ them in the right order.* 2 appoint to a position: *He was ~d in command of the Second Army.* 3 invest (money): *~ £500 in Saving Bonds.* 4 put (an order for goods, etc) with a business firm: *~ an order for books with the bookshop.* 5 dispose of (goods) to a customer: *How can we ~ all this surplus stock?* 6 have: *~ confidence in a leader.* 7 recognize by connecting a person with past experience: *I know that man's face, but I can't ~ him.* 8 (*racing*) state the position of runners, athletes, team members. **be placed**, be among the first three: *The Duke's horse wasn't ~d.*

pla·centa /plə'sentə/ n [C] (*pl* -s) (*med*) organ lining the womb during pregnancy, by which the foetus is nourished.

pla·cid /'plæsɪd/ adj calm; untroubled; (of a person) not easily irritated.

pla·cid·ly adv

pla·giar·ism /'pleɪdʒərɪzm/ n [U] plagiarizing; [C] instance of this.

pla·glar·ist /-ɪst/ n [C] person who plagiarizes.

pla·giar·ize /ˈpleɪdʒəraɪz/ vt take and use somebody else's ideas, words, etc as if they were one's own.

plague /pleɪg/ n [C,U] 1 kind of fatal disease which spreads quickly: *bubonic ~*. 2 (*fig*) cause of serious trouble or disaster: *a ~ of locusts/flies*. □ vt annoy (*with* repeated requests or questions).

plaice /pleɪs/ n [C] (*pl* unchanged) edible flatfish.

plaid /plæd/ n 1 [C] long piece of woollen cloth worn over the shoulders by Scottish Highlanders. 2 [U] cloth with a chequered or tartan pattern, as used for this article of dress.

plain /pleɪn/ adj (-er, -est) 1 easy to see, hear or understand: *~ English; The meaning is quite ~*. 2 simple; ordinary; without luxury or ornament: *~ cooking; a ~ blue dress*, without a pattern on it, or without trimmings, etc. *In plain clothes*, (esp of policemen) in ordinary clothes, not in uniform. 3 (of persons, their thoughts, actions, etc) straightforward; frank. *In plain words*, frankly. 4 (of a person's appearance) not pretty or handsome: *It's a pity his wife is so ~*. □ adv clearly: *learn to speak ~*.

plain 'sailing, (*fig*) course of action that is simple and free from difficulties: *After we engaged a guide, everything was ~ sailing*.

'plain-'spoken adj frank in speech.

'plain-song/-chant, music for a number of voices together, used in the Anglican and Roman Catholic Church services.

plain·ly adv: *It was ~ly visible*.

plain·ness n [U]

plain² /pleɪn/ n [C] area of level land: *the wide ~s of Canada*.

plain³ /pleɪn/ n [C] simple stitch in knitting. ⇨ purl. □ vt,vi knit this stitch.

plain·tiff /ˈpleɪntɪf/ n [C] person who brings an action at law. ⇨ defendant.

plain·tive /ˈpleɪntɪv/ adj sounding sad.

plain·tive·ly adv

plait /plæt/ vt weave or twist (lengths of hair, straw, etc) under and over one another into one rope-like length. □ n [C] something made by plaiting: *wearing her hair in a ~*.

plan /plæn/ n [C] 1 outline drawing (of or for a building) showing the relative size, positions, etc of the parts, esp as if seen from above: *~s for a new school*. ⇨ eleva·tion(5). 2 diagram (of the parts of a machine). 3 diagram showing how a garden, park, town or other area of land has been, or is to be, laid out. (*Note:* map is used for a large area of land.) 4 arrangement for doing or using something, considered in advance: *make ~s for the holidays; go according to plan*, happen as planned. □ vt (-nn-) make a plan (of, for, to): *~ a house/holiday/a military campaign. We're ~ning to visit London this summer*.

plan·ner, one who makes plans, esp (3).

plane¹ /pleɪn/ n [C] one of several kinds of tree (a *~-tree*) with spreading branches, broad leaves and thin bark.

plane² /pleɪn/ n [C] tool for trimming the surface of wood by taking shavings from it. □ vt,vi use a plane.

plane³ /pleɪn/ n [C] 1 flat or level surface; surface such that the straight line joining any points on it is touching it at all points. 2 wing or supporting surface of an aeroplane. 3 (*informal*) = aeroplane. 4 (*fig*) level or stage (of development, etc): *on a higher social ~*. □ adj perfectly level; lying in a plane: *a ~ curve*. □ vi plane (down), (of aeroplanes) travel, glide.

planet /ˈplænɪt/ n [C] one of the heavenly bodies (e g *Mars, Venus*) which move round a star such as the sun and is illuminated by it.

plan·et·ary /ˈplænɪtrɪ US: -terɪ/ adj

plank /plæŋk/ n [C] 1 long, flat piece of timber. *walk the plank*, (of a person captured by pirates in former times) be forced to walk blindfolded into the sea along a plank laid over the ship's side. 2 basic principle in a political platform. □ vt cover (a floor, etc) with planks.

'plank·ing n [U] planks put down to form a floor.

plank·ton /ˈplæŋktən/ n [U] the minute forms of organic life that drift in or float on the water of the oceans, lakes, rivers, etc.

plant¹ /plɑːnt US: plænt/ n [C] 1 living organism which is not an animal, esp the kind smaller than trees and shrubs: *'garden ~s; a to'bacco ~*. 2 apparatus, fixtures, machinery, etc used in an industrial or manufacturing process: *We get our tractors and bulldozers from a '~-hire firm*. 3 (*US*) factory; buildings and equipment of an institution. 4 (*sl*) planned swindle; person who joins a gang of criminals to get evidence against them.

plant² /plɑːnt US: plænt/ vt 1 put plants, bushes, trees, etc in (a garden, etc): *~ a garden with rose-bushes*. 2 (*fig*) cause (an idea) to form in the mind: *~ the idea of organizing a demonstration among the members*. 3 place firmly in position; take up a position or attitude: *He ~ed his feet firmly on the ground*. 4 establish, found (a community, colony, etc). 5 deliver (a blow, etc) with deliberate aim: *~ a blow on his ear*. 6 (*sl*) hide (esp in order to deceive sb, or to cause an innocent person to seem guilty, etc): *He ~ed the stolen pen in my room*.

planter, (a) person who grows crops on a plantation: *'tea-~ers; 'rubber-~ers*. (b) machine for planting: *po'tato-~er*.

plan·tain¹ /ˈplæntɪn/ n [C] tropical plant bearing fruit similar to that of the banana-palm; its fruit.

plan·tain² /ˈplæntɪn/ n [C] common wild plant with broad leaves and seeds.

plan·ta·tion /plænˈteɪʃən/ n [C] 1 area of

land planted with trees: ∼s of fir and pine. 2 estate on which a cash crop is cultivated.

plaque /plɑk US: plæk/ n [C] flat metal or porcelain plate fixed on a wall as an ornament or memorial.

plasma /ˈplæzmə/ n [U] clear, yellowish fluid in which the blood-cells are carried.

plas·ter /ˈplɑstə(r) US: ˈplæs-/ n 1 [U] soft mixture of lime, sand, water, etc used for coating walls and ceilings. 2 [C] piece of fabric spread with a medicinal substance, used to cover a wound, etc. □ vt 1 cover (a wall, etc) with plaster(1). 2 put a plaster(2) on (the body). 3 cover thickly: hair ∼ed with oil.

'**plaster of ˈParis,** white paste that becomes very hard when dry, used for covering broken limbs etc.

'**plaster cast, (a)** mould made with gauze and plaster of Paris to hold a broken or dislocated bone in place. **(b)** mould (e g for a small statue) made of plaster of Paris.

'**plaster-board,** board made of plaster and cardboard, used for inside walls and ceilings.

plas·tered adj (informal) drunk.

plas·terer, workman who uses plaster(1).

plas·tic /ˈplæstɪk/ adj 1 (of materials) easily shaped or moulded: Clay is a ∼ substance. 2 (of goods) made of plastic: ∼ raincoats/ curtains. 3 of the art of modelling: the ∼ arts. 4 (fig) easily influenced or changed: the ∼ mind of a child. □ n [C,U] (kinds of) man-made material which can be shaped or moulded and which keeps its shape when hard.

'**plastic ˈsurgery,** for the restoration of deformed or diseased parts of the body (by grafting skin, etc).

plas·tics n pl (used with a sing verb) (science of) plastic substances, esp man-made materials.

plas·tic·ity /plæˈstɪsətɪ/ n [U] state or quality of being plastic(1).

plas·ti·cine /ˈplæstɪsin/ n [U] (P) substance like clay used for modelling in schools.

plate /pleɪt/ n 1 [C] shallow, almost flat dish from which food is served or eaten: a ˈdinner/ˈsoup/desˈsert ∼; contents of this: a ∼ of beef and vegetables. **hand/give sb sth on a plate,** (informal) give him something without his having to make any effort. 2 [U] (collective) gold or silver articles, e g spoons, dishes, bowls. ⇔ plate²(2). 3 [C] flat, thin sheet of metal, glass, etc e g for building ships: 'boiler ∼s. 4 [C] sheet of glass coated with sensitive film for photography: 'whole-∼, 'half-∼, 'quarter-∼, the usual sizes. 5 [C] oblong piece of metal with a person's name, etc on it (as used by professional persons). 6 sheet of metal, plastic, rubber, etc from which the pages of a book are printed; book illustration printed separately from the text. 7 thin piece of plastic material, moulded to the shape of the

gums, with artificial teeth attached to it. 8 (in baseball) (also home ∼) home base of the batting side.

plate·ful /-fʊl/, amount that a plate holds.

plate² /pleɪt/ vt 1 cover (esp a ship) with metal plates(3). 2 cover (another metal) with gold, silver, copper or tin: silver-∼d spoons.

pla·teau /ˈplætəʊ US: plæˈtəʊ/ n [C] (pl ∼s or ∼x /-təʊz/) expanse of level land high above sea-level.

plat·form /ˈplætfɔm/ n [C] 1 flat surface built at a higher level than the track in a railway station, where travellers wait: Which ∼ does your train leave from? 2 flat structure raised above floor-level for speakers, teachers in a classroom, etc; space at the entrance of a bus or tram (for the conductor). 3 programme of a political party, esp as stated before an election.

plat·ing /ˈpleɪtɪŋ/ n [U] (esp) thin coating of gold, silver, etc. ⇔ plate²(2).

plati·num /ˈplætənəm/ n [U] grey metal (symbol Pt) used for jewellery and mixed with other metals for use in industry.

plati·tude /ˈplætɪtjud US: -tud/ n 1 [C] statement that is obviously true, esp one often heard before, but made as if it were new. 2 [U] quality of being dull and ordinary.

plati·tudi·nous /ˈplætɪˈtjudɪnəs US: -ˈtudənəs/ adj dull and ordinary: ∼ remarks.

Pla·tonic /pləˈtɒnɪk/ adj of Plato or his teachings: ∼ love/friendship, between a man and a woman without a desire for physical love.

pla·toon /pləˈtun/ n [C] body of soldiers, subdivision of a company, acting as a unit and commanded by a lieutenant.

plat·ter /ˈplætə(r)/ n [C] (US) large, shallow dish for serving food, esp meat and fish.

platy·pus /ˈplætɪpəs/ n [C] (pl ∼es /-pəsɪz/) 'duck-billed ˈplatypus, small aquatic Australian animal which suckles its young but lays eggs (called duckbill because it has a bill like that of a duck).

plau·dit /ˈplɔdɪt/ n [C] (usually pl) (formal) cry, clapping or other sign of approval: gratified at the ∼s of the audience.

plaus·ible /ˈplɔzəbəl/ adj seeming to be right or reasonable: a ∼ excuse/explanation.

plaus·ibly /-əblɪ/ adv

play /pleɪ/ n 1 [C] (performance of a) representation, acting, of a story, etc on a stage, TV, etc. 2 [U] (what is done for) amusement; recreation: The children are at ∼, playing. **a play on words,** = pun. 3 [U] (the manner of) playing of a game; rough ∼ in a football match. **In/out of play,** (of the ball in football, cricket, etc) in/not in a position where the rules of the game allow it to be played. ⇔ **fair play.** 4 (sing only) turn or move in sport or in a game (e g chess): It's your ∼. 5 [U] gambling: lose £50 in one evening's ∼;

6 [U] light, quick, movement: *the ~ of sunlight on water.* **7** [U] (space for) free and easy movement; scope for activity: *give free ~ to one's emotions; a knot with too much ~,* one that is not tight enough. **8** [U] activity; operation: *the ~ of natural forces.* **be in full play/come into play,** begin to operate or be active. **bring sth into play,** make use of it; bring it into action. **9** [C] pretence: *My tears were a ~ to get your sympathy.*

`play-acting,` (*fig*) pretence.

`play-boy,` rich pleasure-loving man.

`play-goer,` person who often goes to the theatre.

`play-group,` school for children under 5.

`play-ground,` area of ground at a school, etc for children to play.

`play-house,` = theatre.

`play-mate,` (of children) friend one plays with.

`play-pen,` portable enclosure for a baby to be left to play.

`play-reading,` recital of the text of a play by a group.

`play-room,` one in a house for children to play in.

`play-school,` = play group.

`play-suit,` garment (trousers and bib) for children.

`play-thing,` (**a**) toy. (**b**) (*fig*) person treated like a toy.

`play-time,` period for play.

`play-wright,` person who writes plays.

play² /pleɪ/ *vt,vi* (*pt,pp* ~ed /pleɪd/) (For special uses with *adverbial particles and prepositions,* ⇨ 14 below.) **1** (contrasted with *work*) have fun; do things to pass the time pleasantly, as children do: *Let's go out and ~. She was ~ing with the kitten.* **2** pretend, for fun, to be or do: *Let's ~ (at being) pirates.* **3** practice, do: *He has played a trick on me.* **play it cool,** ⇨ cool¹ (5). **play with fire,** ⇨ fire¹ (1). **play into sb's hands,** ⇨ hand¹ (3). **play hell with,** ⇨ hell(2). **play the market,** ⇨ market¹ (4). **play for time,** ⇨ time¹ (3). **play truant,** ⇨ truant. **4** (be able to) take part in a game, e g of cricket, football, golf, cards: *He ~s (football) for Stoke/England. On Saturday France ~ (Rugby) against Wales/~ Wales at Rugby.* **5** fill a particular position in a team: *Who's ~ing in goal? Who shall we ~ as goalkeeper?* **6** (cricket, football, etc) strike (the ball) in a specified way: *In soccer only the goalkeeper may ~ the ball with his hands.* **play ball (with),** (*informal*) co-operate. **7** move (a chesspiece); lay a card on the table: *~ the ace of hearts.* **play one's cards well/right/badly,** (*fig*) make good/bad use of opportunities. **play fair,** fairly; in accordance with the rules. **play the game,** (**a**) observe the rules of the game. (**b**) (*fig*) be fair and honest. **8** perform on (a musical instrument), perform (a musical composition): *~ the piano; ~ a Beethoven sonata.*

play sth back, reproduce (music, speech, etc) from a tape or disc after it has been recorded. Hence, `play-back` *n* (**a**) the device on a tape-recorder which ~s back recorded material. (**b**) occasion when this is done. **play second fiddle (to),** ⇨ fiddle. **play sth by ear,** ⇨ ear¹ (2). **9** perform (a drama on the stage); act (a part in a drama); (of a drama) be performed: *~ 'Twelfth Night'; ~ Shylock; the National Theatre, where 'Hamlet' is now ~ing,* = being played. **play the fool,** act foolishly. **10** move about in a gentle, lively manner; direct (light) (*on, over, along,* etc): *sunlight ~ing on the water. They ~ed coloured lights over the dance floor.* **11** operate continuously; discharge in a steady stream: *The firemen ~ed their hoses on the burning building.* **12** fire: *We ~ed our guns on the enemy's lines.* **13** *play a fish,* (when angling with a rod and line) allow a fish to exhaust itself by pulling against the line.

14 (special uses with *adverbial particles and prepositions*):

play at sth, (**a**) ⇨ 2 above. (**b**) do in a half-hearted way, or merely for pleasure: *fight properly—you're only ~ing at boxing!*

play sth back, ⇨ 8 above.

play down to sb, deliberately talk to or behave towards him so that he does do not feel inferior, in order to win support or favour. **play sth down,** deliberately treat it as unimportant.

play off, play again (e g a football) match that was drawn: *~ off a draw/tie.* Hence, `play-off` *n* such a match. **play one person off against another,** encourage rivalry, esp for one's own advantage.

play on sth, try to make use of (a person's feelings, trust, etc) for one's own advantage: *He tried to ~ on her sympathies.*

play sth out, (*fig*) play it to the finish: *The long struggle between the strikers and their employers is not yet ~ed out.* **be played out,** be exhausted, used up; be out of date: *Isn't that theory ~ed out,* no longer worth considering?

play up, (**a**) (esp in the *imperative*) (*sport*) play vigorously, energetically. (**b**) (*informal*) behave mischievously: *Don't let the children ~ up.* **play sth up,** deliberately treat it with too much importance: *Don't let him ~ up his illness,* e g by making it an excuse for doing nothing. **play sb up,** (*informal*) give trouble to: *This wretched car has been ~ing me up again.* **play up to sb,** (*informal*) flatter (to win favour for oneself): *He always ~s up to his political bosses.*

play with sb, (**a**) ⇨ 1 above. (**b**) treat, think about, casually: *It's wrong for a man to ~ with a woman's affections. He's ~ing with the idea of emigrating to Canada.*

player /ˈpleɪə(r)/ *n* [C] **1** person who plays a game. **2** actor. **3** person who plays a musical instrument. **4** mechanical device for producing musical sounds: *a `record-~*.

play·ful /ˈpleɪfəl/ *adj* in a mood for play; not serious: *as ~ as a kitten; in a ~ manner*.
play·ful·ly /-fəlɪ/ *adv*
play·ful·ness *n* [U]

play·ing field /ˈpleɪɪŋ fild/ *n* [C] field for such games as football and cricket.

play·let /ˈpleɪlət/ *n* [C] short dramatic piece.

plaza /ˈplɑːzə *US:* ˈplæzə/ *n* [C] (*pl ~s*) market-place; open square (esp in a Spanish town).

plea /pliː/ *n* [C] **1** (*legal*) statement made by or for a person charged in a law court. **2** request: *~s for mercy*. **3** reason or excuse offered for doing wrong or failing to do something, etc.

plead /pliːd/ *vt,vi* (*pt,pp ~ed*, or, *US pled*, /pled/) **1** (*legal*) address a court of law on behalf of either the plaintiff or the defendant: *~ for/against her*. **2** admit or deny that one is guilty: *'How do you ~?' Did you ~ not guilty?* **3** offer as an explanation or excuse: *The thief ~ed poverty*. **4** ask earnestly: *He ~ed with his son to be less trouble to his mother*. **5** argue in favour of; give reasons for (a cause, etc): *~ the cause of political freedom*.

plead·ings *n pl* (*legal*) statements, replies to accusations, etc, made by the parties in a legal action.

pleas·ant /ˈplezənt/ *adj* giving pleasure; agreeable; friendly: *a ~ afternoon/taste/wine/surprise/companion*.
pleas·ant·ly *adv*
pleas·ant·ness *n* [U].

pleas·ant·ry /ˈplezəntrɪ/ *n* (*pl -ies*) (*formal*) **1** [U] humour. **2** [C] humorous or casual remark.

please /pliːz/ *vi,vt* **1** (used as a polite form of request): *Come in, ~. P~ come in. Two coffees, ~. P~ don't do that.* **2** give satisfaction to: *It's difficult to ~ everybody. Are you ~d with your new clothes?* **3** think fit; choose; prefer: *I shall do as I ~. Take as many as you ~.*

pleased /pliːzd/ *adj* glad; feeling or showing satisfaction: *He looked ~d with himself. I'm very ~d with what he has done.*

pleas·ing /ˈpliːzɪŋ/ *adj* **1** giving pleasure (*to*). **2** attractive.
pleas·ing·ly *adv*

pleas·ure /ˈpleʒə(r)/ *n* **1** [U] feeling of enjoyment, of being happy or satisfied: *It gave me much ~ to hear of your success. May we have the ~ of your company for lunch? Some boys take great ~ in teasing their little sisters.* **2** [U] (*formal*) will; desire: *You may go or stay at your ~, as you wish.* **3** [C] something that gives happiness: *the ~s of friendship*.
`**pleasure-boat/-craft**, one used for enjoyment only.

pleas·ur·able /ˈpleʒərəbəl/ *adj* giving enjoyment.

pleat /pliːt/ *n* [C] fold made by doubling cloth on itself. □ *vt* make pleats in: *a ~ed skirt.*

pleb /pleb/ *n* [C] (*informal*) (abbr for) plebeian.

pleb·eian /plɪˈbiːən/ *n* [C], *adj* (person who is) of the lower social classes.

plebi·scite /ˈplebɪsɪt *US:* -saɪt/ *n* [C] (decision made about a political question by) the votes of all qualified citizens.

plec·trum /ˈplektrəm/ *n* [C] small piece of metal, plastic, etc attached to the finger for plucking the strings of some instruments, e g the guitar.

pled /pled/ ⇨ plead.

pledge /pledʒ/ *n* **1** [C] something left with a person to be kept until the giver has done whatever he has to do. **2** [U] state of being left on these conditions: *put/hold goods in ~.* **3** [C] something given as a sign of love, approval, etc. **4** [U] agreement; promise: *under ~ of secrecy.* **take/sign the pledge**, (esp) make a written promise not to take alcoholic drink. □ *vt* **1** give as security; put in pawn. **2** make an undertaking: *be ~d to secrecy; ~ one's word/honour.*

ple·nary /ˈpliːnərɪ/ *adj* **1** (of powers, authority) unlimited; absolute. **2** (of meetings) attended by all who have a right to attend: *a ~ session.*

pleni·po·ten·tiary /ˈplenɪpəˈtenʃərɪ/ *n* [C] (*pl -ries*), *adj* (person, e g a representative, an ambassador) having full power to act, make decisions, etc (on behalf of his government, etc).

plen·teous /ˈplentɪəs/ *adj* (chiefly *poetic*) plentiful.

plen·ti·ful /ˈplentɪfəl/ *adj* in large quantities or numbers.
plen·ti·fully /-fəlɪ/ *adv*

plenty /ˈplentɪ/ *n* [U] as much as or more than is needed or desired; a large number or quantity: *There are ~ of eggs. We must get to the station in ~ of time. Six will be ~, as many as I need.*

pleth·ora /ˈpleθərə/ *n* [C] (*pl ~s*) (*formal*) **1** (unhealthy) state of being too much or too many; excess. **2** (*med*) state of having too many red corpuscles in the blood.

pleur·isy /ˈplʊərɪsɪ/ *n* [U] serious illness with inflammation of the delicate membrane of the thorax and the lungs.

plexus /ˈpleksəs/ *n* [C] (*pl ~es* /-səsɪz/ or ~) (*anat*) network of fibres or vessels in the body: *the solar ~*, in the abdomen.

pli·able /ˈplaɪəbəl/ *adj* **1** easily bent, shaped or twisted. **2** (of the mind) easily influenced.
pli·abil·ity /ˌplaɪəˈbɪlətɪ/ *n* [U]

pli·ant /ˈplaɪənt/ *adj* = pliable.

pli·ers /ˈplaɪəz/ *n pl* (also *a pair of ~*) kind of pincers with long, flat jaws, used for holding, bending or cutting wire, etc

plight[1] /plaɪt/ *n* [C] serious and difficult condition: *His affairs were in a terrible ~.*

plight² /plaɪt/ vt 1 (formal) promise: one's ∼ed word. 2 (archaic) engage oneself to be married: ∼ed lovers.

plim·soll /ˈplɪmsəl/ n [C] (also a pair of ∼s) rubber-soled canvas shoe (US = sneaker).

Plim·soll line /ˈplɪmsəl laɪn/ n [C] line on the hull of a ship to mark how far it may legally go down in the water when loaded.

plinth /plɪnθ/ n [C] square base or block on which a column or statue stands.

plod /plod/ vi,vt (-dd-) 1 walk slowly with a heavy step. 2 continue working, etc slowly and without resting: ∼ away at a dull task.
plod·der, (a) person who plods(1). (b) slow but earnest person.
plod·ding adj

plonk¹ /plɒŋk/ n [C] dull sound of something dropping: the ∼ of a shoe falling down the stairs. □ adv with this sound. □ vt put down with a plonking sound: ∼ the book down on the table.

plonk² /plɒŋk/ n [U] (sl) cheap wine.

plop /plɒp/ n [C] sound (as) of a small smooth object dropping into water without a splash. □ adv with a plop. □ vi (-pp-) make, fall with, a plop.

plot¹ /plɒt/ n [C] piece of ground (usually small): a `building ∼; a ∼ of vegetables. □ vt,vi (-tt-) 1 make a plan, map or diagram of. 2 mark (the position of something) on a diagram by connecting points on a graph. 3 divide into plots: ∼ out a vegetable garden.

plot² /plɒt/ n [C] 1 secret plan (good or bad): a ∼ to overthrow the government. 2 plan or outline (of the events of a story, esp of a novel or drama). □ vt,vi (-tt-) form, take part in, a plot.
plot·ter, person who plots.

plough (US = **plow**) /plaʊ/ n [C] 1 implement for cutting furrows in soil and turning it up, drawn by animals or (more usually) a tractor. 2 any kind of implement resembling a plough. 3 [U] ploughed land: 100 acres of ∼. 4 the P∼, (astron) the group of stars called Charles's Wain, the Dipper or the Great Bear. □ vt,vi 1 break up (land) with a plough; ∼ a field. 2 (fig) reinvest: ∼ back the profits of a business. 3 force a way through: ∼ (one's way) through the mud/a dull textbook. 4 (informal) reject (a candidate) in an examination.
`**plough·man** /-mən/ n (pl -men) man who guides a plough.
`**plough·share** broad blade of a plough.
`**snow·plough** n one for clearing away snow from roads and railways.

plover /ˈplʌvə(r)/ n [C] sort of long-legged, short-tailed bird living near marshes.

plow /plaʊ/ (US) = plough.

ploy /plɔɪ/ n [C] (informal) something said or done to gain an advantage over a person: crying as a ∼ to gain sympathy.

pluck /plʌk/ vt,vi 1 pull the feathers off (a hen, goose, etc): Has this goose been ∼ed? 2 pick (flowers, fruit, etc) 3 take hold of and pull: He was ∼ing at his mother's skirt. 4 **pluck up courage,** overcome one's fears. □ n 1 [U] courage; spirit: a boy with plenty of ∼. 2 [C] short, sharp pull.
plucky adj (-ier, -iest) brave.

plug /plʌg/ n [C] 1 piece of wood, metal, etc used to stop up a hole (e g in a wash-basin, bath, etc). 2 device for making a connection with a supply of electric current: put the ∼ in the socket. ⇨ also sparking-plug. 3 cake of pressed or twisted tobacco; piece of this cut off for chewing. 4 (sl) favourable publicity (e g in a radio or T V programme) for a commercial product. ⇨ 4 below. □ vt,vi (-gg-) 1 stop or fill (up) with a plug: ∼ a leak. 2 **plug (sth) in,** make a connection with a plug(2): ∼ in the T V set. 3 (informal) **plug away at,** work hard at. 4 (sl) advertise (something) repeatedly: ∼ a new song, e g on radio or T V.

plum /plʌm/ n [C] 1 (tree having) soft round, smooth-skinned fruit with a seed like a stone. 2 (informal) (usually as an adjective) considered good and desirable: a ∼ job in the Civil Service.

plum·age /ˈpluːmɪdʒ/ n [U] bird's feathers: brightly coloured ∼.

plumb /plʌm/ n [C] ball or piece of lead tied to the end of a cord or rope (a `∼-line) for finding the depth of water or testing whether a wall is vertical. □ adv 1 exactly: ∼ straight. 2 (US) (informal) very: ∼ crazy. □ vt (fig) get to the root of: ∼ the depths of a mystery.

plumber /ˈplʌmə(r)/ n [C] workman who fits and repairs pipes.

plumb·ing /ˈplʌmɪŋ/ n [U] 1 the work of a plumber. 2 the pipes, water-tanks, cisterns, etc in a building.

plume /pluːm/ n [C] 1 feather, esp a large one used as a decoration. 2 something suggesting a feather by its shape: a ∼ of smoke. □ vt (of a bird) smooth (its feathers).

plum·met /ˈplʌmɪt/ n [C] (weight attached to a) plumb-line or to a fishing-line to keep the float upright. □ vi (-tt-) fall steeply: Share prices have ∼ted.

plump¹ /plʌmp/ adj (of an animal, a person, parts of the body) fat in a pleasant-looking way: a baby with ∼ cheeks. □ vt,vi make or become rounded: She ∼ed up the pillows.

plump² /plʌmp/ vi,vt 1 (cause to) fall or drop, suddenly and heavily: ∼ (oneself) down in a chair; ∼ down a heavy bag. 2 vote for, choose, with confidence: ∼ for the Liberal candidate. □ adv suddenly, abruptly: fall ∼ into the hole. □ n [C] abrupt, heavy fall.

plun·der /ˈplʌndə(r)/ vt,vi rob, esp during war or civil disorder: ∼ (the citizens of) a conquered town. □ n [U] goods taken.

plunge /plʌndʒ/ vt,vi 1 put (something), or go suddenly and with force, into: ∼ one's hand into cold water/a hole; ∼ a country *into war.* **2** (of a horse) move forward and downward quickly; (of a ship) thrust its bows into the water. □ *n* [C] act of plunging (e g from a diving-board into water). **take the plunge,** (*fig*) do something decisive, e g marry.

plunger, (**a**) part of a mechanism that moves with a plunging motion, e g the piston of a pump. (**b**) suction device for clearing a blocked pipe.

plunk /plʌŋk/ = plonk¹.

plu·per·fect /ˈpluːˈpɜːfɪkt/ *n* [C], *adj* (*gram*) (tense) expressing action completed before some past time, stated or implied. (*Note:* shown by *had* and a *pp*, as in 'As he *had* not *received* my letter, he did not come'.)

plu·ral /ˈplʊərəl/ *n* [C], *adj* (form of word) used with reference to more than one: 'The ~ of *child* is *children*'.

plus /plʌs/ *prep* with the addition of: *Two ~ five is seven,* 2 + 5 = 7. □ *adj:* *a ~ quantity,* one greater than zero. ⇨ minus. □ *n* [C] (-ss-) the sign +.

plush /plʌʃ/ *adj* (also **plushy** (-ier, -iest)) (*sl*) smart, rich: *a ~(y) restaurant.*

Pluto /ˈpluːtəʊ/ *n* (*astron*) planet farthest from the sun.

plu·to·cracy /pluːˈtɒkrəsɪ/ *n* [C,U] (*pl* -ies) (government by a) rich and powerful class.

plu·to·crat /ˈpluːtəkræt/ *n* [C] person who is powerful because of his wealth.

plu·to·cratic /ˈpluːtəˈkrætɪk/ *adj*

plu·to·nium /pluːˈtəʊnɪəm/ *n* [U] (artificially produced) radioactive element (symbol **Pu**) used in nuclear reactors and weapons.

ply¹ /plaɪ/ *n* [C] **1** layer of wood or thickness of cloth: `three-~ wood,` made by sticking together three layers with the grain of each at a right angle to that of the next. **2** one strand in wool, rope, etc: `four-~ wool for knitting socks.`

`ply·wood,` board(s) made by gluing together thin layers of wood.

ply² /plaɪ/ *vt,vi* (*pt,pp* plied, *present part* plying) **1** (*formal*) work with (an instrument, e g a needle). **2** (of ships, buses, etc) go regularly to and from: *ships that ~ between Glasgow and New York.* **3** *ply sb with sth,* keep him constantly supplied with (food and drink); attack him constantly with (questions, arguments, etc).

pneu·matic /njuːˈmætɪk *US:* nu-/ *adj* **1** worked or driven by compressed air: *~ drills.* **2** filled with compressed air: *~ tyres.*

pneu·mati·cally /-klɪ/ *adv*

pneu·monia /njuːˈməʊnɪə *US:* nu-/ *n* [U] serious illness with inflammation of one or both lungs.

poach¹ /pəʊtʃ/ *vt* cook (an egg) by cracking the shell and dropping the contents into boiling water.

poach² /pəʊtʃ/ *vt,vi* **1** (go on a person's property and) take (hares, pheasants, salmon, etc) illegally. **2** (*fig*) be active in some

kind of work that another person believes is his own responsibility.

poacher, person who poaches.

pock /pɒk/ *n* [C] spot on the skin caused by smallpox.

`pock-marked,` with marks (as) left after smallpox.

pocket /ˈpɒkɪt/ *n* [C] **1** small bag forming part of an article of clothing, for carrying things in. *pick sb's pocket,* steal from his pocket. ⇨ pickpocket. **2** (as an *adjective*) of a size suitable for a pocket: *a ~ dictionary.* **3** money. *in/out of pocket,* rich(er)/poor(er). **4** bag, hollow, e g a small cavity in the ground or in rock, containing gold or ore. **5** partial vacuum in the atmosphere (*an* `air-~`) affecting the flight of an aircraft; cavity of air (*an* `air-~`) in a mine ²(1). **6** (isolated area occupied by) enemy forces, etc: *~s of resistance; ~s of unemployment in the Midlands.* □ *vt* **1** put into one's pocket: *He ~ed the money.* **2** keep for oneself (often dishonestly): *He ~ed half the profits.*

`pocket-money,` small sum given to children to spend on sweets, etc.

pocket·ful /-fʊl/ *n* [C] amount which a pocket holds.

pod /pɒd/ *n* [C] long, green container for seeds of various plants, esp peas and beans. □ *vt,vi* (-dd-) **1** take (peas, etc) out of pods. **2** *pod (up),* form pods.

podgy /ˈpɒdʒɪ/ *adj* (-ier, -iest) (of a person) short and fat.

poem /ˈpəʊɪm/ *n* [C] piece of creative writing (often in verse form), e g one expressing deep feeling in beautiful language, one written to describe an experience, etc.

poet /ˈpəʊɪt/ *n* [C] writer of poems.

`poet laureate,` poet appointed to write poems on great state or royal occasions.

poet·ess /ˈpəʊɪtes/ *n* [C] (*rare*) woman poet.

po·etic /pəʊˈetɪk/ (also **po·eti·cal** /-ɪkəl/) *adj* of poets and poetry: *~ genius.*

po'etic 'justice, ideal justice, with proper distribution of rewards and punishments.

po'etic 'licence, freedom from the normal rules of language (as in poetry).

po·eti·cally /-klɪ/ *adv*

po·etry /ˈpəʊɪtrɪ/ *n* [U] **1** the art of a poet; poems. **2** quality that produces feelings as produced by poems: *the ~ of motion,* e g in some kinds of athletics.

po·grom /ˈpɒɡrəm *US:* pəˈɡrɒm/ *n* [C] organized persecution or killing (of a group or class of people).

poig·nancy /ˈpɔɪnjənsɪ/ *n* [U] (*formal*) state or quality of being poignant.

poign·ant /ˈpɔɪnjənt/ *adj* (*formal*) causing sad feelings: *~ memories.*

poign·ant·ly *adv*

point¹ /pɔɪnt/ *n* **1** [C] sharp tip (of a pin, pencil, knife, etc). *not to put too fine a point on it,* to speak bluntly, to tell the plain truth. **2** [C] tapering piece of land that stretches out into the sea, a lake, etc. **3** dot (as) made by the point of a pen, etc. ⇨ decimal point; full point. **4** [C] real or imaginary mark of position, in space or time: *on the ~ of learning; a `turning-~ in my career.* **at this point,** at this place or moment. **a point of view,** (a) position from which something is viewed. (b) *(fig)* way of looking at a question. **be at the point of death,** be dying. **be on the point of doing sth,** be about to do it. **if/when it comes to the point,** if/when the moment for action or decision comes: *When it came to the ~, he refused to help.* **5** [C] mark on a scale; unit of measuring: *the `boiling-~ of water.* **possession is nine points of the law,** is strong evidence in favour of the person in possession of something. **6** [C] unit of scoring in some games, sports and competitions. **7** [C] one of the thirty-two marks or divisions on the circumference of a compass. **8** [C] single item, detail, idea, etc: *There are ~s on which we've agreed to differ.* **stretch a point,** do what is not normal, e g when deciding something. **9** [C] chief idea or thought. **come to/get to/reach the point,** give the essential, relevant fact. **get/see/miss the point of sth,** see/fail to understand: *She missed the ~ of the joke.* **make a point of doing sth,** regard or treat it as important or necessary. **take sb's point,** (during a discussion) understand what a person is proposing, etc. **(wander) off/away from the point,** say something irrelevant. **on a point of order,** ⇨ order ¹(4). **to the point,** apt, relevant. **10** [U] **no/not much point in doing sth,** little reason for doing it: *There's very little ~ in protesting,* It won't help much. **11** [C] characteristic: *What are her best ~s as a secretary?* **12** *(GB)* socket or outlet for electric current. **13** *(pl)* tapering movable rails by which a train can move from one track to another. **14** [U] effectiveness: *His remarks lack ~.* **15** (of a dog) act of pointing(6): *make/come to a ~.*

point² /pɔɪnt/ *vt,vi* **1** direct attention to; show the position or direction of; be a sign of: *He ~ed to the door. All the evidence ~s to his guilt.* **2** aim or direct (something): *~ing a gun at him.* **3** **point sth out,** show; call or direct attention to: *~ out a mistake. Can you ~ (me) out the man you suspect? I must ~ out that the price is too high.* **4** make a point(1) on (a pencil). **5** fill in the joints of (brickwork, etc) with mortar or cement, using a trowel to smooth the material. **6** (of a dog) take up a position with the body steady and the head pointing in the direction of game. ⇨ pointer(3).

pointed *adj* **1** *(fig)* directed definitely against a person or his behaviour: *Jack was making ~ed comments to the glamorous teacher.* **2** (of humour, etc) apt, relevant.
point·ed·ly *adv*

point-blank /ˌpɔɪnt ˈblæŋk/ *adj* **1** (of a shot aimed, fired) at very close range: *fired at ~ range.* **2** *(fig)* (something said) in a manner that leaves no room for doubt: *a ~ refusal.* □ *adv* in such a manner: *ask him ~ whether he intends to help.*

pointer /ˈpɔɪntə(r)/ *n* [C] **1** stick used to point to things on a map, etc. **2** indicator on a dial or balance. **3** short-haired hunting dog, **4** indication; piece of advice.

point·less /ˈpɔɪntləs/ *adj* **1** *(fig)* with little or no sense, aim or purpose: *It seemed ~ to argue.* **2** without points scored: *a ~ draw.*
point·less·ly *adv*

poise /pɔɪz/ *vt,vi* **1** be or keep balanced: *~d in mid-air.* **2** balance; support in a particular place or manner: *Note the way the dancer ~s his head.* □ *n* **1** [U] balance, equilibrium. **2** [C] way in which one carries oneself, holds one's head, etc. **3** [U] self-confidence.

poi·son /ˈpɔɪzən/ *n* [C,U] **1** substance causing death or harm if absorbed by a living thing (animal or plant): *~ for killing weeds; commit suicide by taking ~.* **2** *(fig)* evil principle, teaching, etc considered harmful to society. □ *vt* **1** put poison on or in: *~ the rats.* **2** *(fig)* injure morally: *~ somebody's mind against another person.*

pois·on·er, (esp) person who murders by using poison.

pois·on·ous /ˈpɔɪzənəs/ *adj* (a) causing death or injury: *~ous plants.* (b) hurting the feelings, a reputation, etc: *a man with a ~ous tongue.*
pois·on·ous·ly *adv*

poke /pəʊk/ *vt,vi* **1** push sharply, jab (with a stick, one's finger, etc): *~ a man in the ribs; ~ the fire,* move the coals to make the fire burn better. **2** put, move (something) with a sharp push: *Don't let him ~ his head out of the (train) window—it's dangerous!* **poke fun at sb,** try to make him look foolish. **3** search: *Who's that poking about in the garden?* **4** make (a hole) by poking. □ *n* [C] act of poking.

poker¹ /ˈpəʊkə(r)/ *n* [C] strong metal rod or bar for moving or breaking up the coal in a fire.

poker² /ˈpəʊkə(r)/ *n* [U] card game for two or more persons in which the players gamble on the value of the cards they hold.

poky /ˈpəʊkɪ/ *adj* (-ier, -iest) (of a place) too small: *a ~ little room.*

po·lar /ˈpəʊlə(r)/ *adj* **1** of or near the North or South Pole. **2** directly opposite.

polar bear, the white kind living in the north polar regions.

po·lar·ity /pəˈlærətɪ/ *n* [U] possession of two contrasted or opposite qualities, principles or tendencies.

po·lar·ize /ˈpəʊləraɪz/ *vt* cause to centre on two opposite, conflicting or contrasting positions.

po·lar·iz·ation /ˌpəʊləraɪˈzeɪʃən US: -rɪˈz-/ *n* [U]

po·lar·oid /ˈpəʊlərɔɪd/ n [U] thin transparent film used in sun-glasses, etc to lessen sun glare.

pole¹ /pəʊl/ n [C] **1** either of the two ends of the earth's axis: *the North P~; the South P~*. **2** = magnetic pole. **3** *North P~, South P~*, (*astron*) two points in the night sky about which the stars appear to turn. **4** either of the two ends of a magnet or the terminal points of an electric battery: *the negative/positive ~*. **5** (*fig*) each of two opposed principles, etc. *be poles apart*, be opposite: *The employers and the trade union leaders are still ~s apart*, are far from reaching an agreement, etc.
ˈpole star, the North Star almost coinciding with true north.

pole² /pəʊl/ n [C] **1** long, slender, rounded piece of wood or metal, e g as a support for a tent, as a handle for a broom, etc. *up the pole*, (*sl*) (a) in difficulty. (b) slightly mad; eccentric. **2** measure of length (also called *rod* or *perch*), 5½ yds or about 5 metres.
ˈpole-jumping, (athletic contest) jumping with the help of a long pole held in the hands.
ˈpole-vault, jump of this kind over a bar which can be raised or lowered.

pole-cat /ˈpəʊlkæt/ n [C] small, dark-brown, fur-covered European animal which gives off an unpleasant smell.

pol·emic /pəˈlemɪk/ n **1** [C] (*formal*) dispute; argument. **2** (*pl*) art or practice of arguing, esp in theology. □ *adj* of polemics.
pol·emi·cally /-klɪ/ *adv*

po·lice /pəˈliːs/ n (always *sing* in form, used with *the* and a *pl verb*) department, body of men, concerned with the keeping of public order: *the ~*, the members of this body; *Several hundred ~ were on duty at the demonstration. The ~ have not made any arrests*. □ *vt* keep order in (a place) (as) with police: *United Nations forces ~d the Gaza Strip for a long time.*
po·lice·man /-mən/, member of a police force.
poˈlice constable, policeman of ordinary rank.
ˈpolice court, court in which minor offences can be dealt with by a magistrate.
poˈlice force, the police of a country or region.
poˈlice officer, policeman.
poˈlice State, country controlled by political police.
poˈlice station, office of a local police force: *I was taken to the ~-station.*
poˈlice-woman, woman police officer.

pol·icy¹ /ˈpɒləsɪ/ n (pl -ies) **1** [C] plan of action, statement of aims and ideals, e g one made by a government, political party, business company, etc: *Is honesty the best ~?* **2** [U] wise, sensible conduct; art of government.

pol·icy² /ˈpɒləsɪ/ n [C] written statement of the terms of a contract of insurance: *an in'surance ~; a ~-holder*.

po·lio /ˈpəʊlɪəʊ/ n [U] (*informal* abbr for) poliomyelitis.

po·lio·mye·litis /ˈpəʊlɪəʊˌmaɪəˈlaɪtɪs/ n [U] infectious disease with inflammation of the grey matter of the spinal cord, often resulting in physical disablement.

polish /ˈpɒlɪʃ/ *vt,vi* **1** make or become smooth and shiny by rubbing (with or without a chemical substance): *~ furniture/ shoes*. **2** improve in behaviour, intellectual interests, etc. **3** (*pp*) make refined or elegant: *a ~ed speech*. **4** finish quickly: *~ off a large meal*. □ n **1** [U] (surface, etc obtained by) polishing: *shoes/tables with a good ~*. **2** substance used for polishing: *ˈshoe/ ˈfurniture ~*. **3** (*fig*) refinement; elegance.

pol·it·buro /pəˈlɪtbjʊərəʊ/ n [C] (*pl ~s*) chief executive committee of a (Communist) party.

pol·ite /pəˈlaɪt/ *adj* having, showing the possession of, good manners and consideration for other people: *a ~ boy; a ~ remark*.
pol·ite·ly *adv*
pol·ite·ness n [U]

poli·tic /ˈpɒlətɪk/ *adj* **1** (of persons) acting or judging wisely. **2** (of actions) well judged: *a ~ remark at the conference*.
the ˈbody ˈpolitic, the state as an organized group of citizens.

pol·iti·cal /pəˈlɪtɪkəl/ *adj* **1** of the State; of government; of public affairs in general: *for ~ reasons*. **2** because of politics: *a ~ crisis; ~ prisoners*.
poˈlitical aˈsylum, protection given by a Government to a person who has left his own country for political reasons.
poˈlitical eˈconomy, science of economics.
poˈlitical ˈprisoner, one who is imprisoned because he opposes the (system of) government.
po·liti·cally /-klɪ/ *adv*

poli·ti·cian /ˈpɒləˈtɪʃən/ n [C] person taking part in politics or very interested in politics: *party ~s*.

poli·tics /ˈpɒlətɪks/ n pl (used with a *sing* or *pl verb*) the science or art of government; political views, affairs, questions, etc: *study ~ at University.*

pol·ity /ˈpɒlətɪ/ n (pl -ies) **1** [U] form or process of government. **2** [C] society as an organized State.

polka /ˈpɒlkə US: ˈpəʊlkə/ n [C] (piece of music, of E European origin, for a) lively kind of dance.

poll¹ /pəʊl/ n [C] **1** voting at an election; list of voters; counting of the votes; place where voting takes place: *a light/heavy ~*, voting by a small/large number of voters. *go to the polls*, vote (in a general election). **2** survey of public opinion by putting questions to a representative selection of persons. ⇨ opinion poll.

poll² /pəʊl/ *vt,vi* **1** vote at an election **2**

receive (a certain number of) votes: *Mr Hill ~ed over 3 000 votes.*

`poll·ing-booth/-station,` place where voters go to vote.

`poll·ing-day,` day appointed for a poll.

pol·len /ˈpɒlən/ n [U] fine powder (usually yellow) formed on flowers which fertilizes other flowers when carried to them by the wind, insects, etc.

`pollen count,` figure of the amount of pollen in the atmosphere.

pol·lin·ate /ˈpɒlɪneɪt/ vt make fertile with pollen.

pol·li·na·tion /ˌpɒlɪˈneɪʃən/ n [U]

poll·ster /ˈpəʊlstə(r)/ n [C] person who conducts public opinion polls.

pol·lute /pəˈluːt/ vt make dirty, impure: *rivers ~d with waste from factories.* 2 (fig) make immoral: *~ young minds.*

pol·lu·tant /-ənt/, anything that pollutes, e g exhaust fumes from motor-vehicles.

pol·lu·tion /pəˈluːʃən/ n [C,U]

polo /ˈpəʊləʊ/ n [U] ball game played on horseback with mallets. ⇨water-polo.

`polo-neck,` (having) a rolled collar: *~-neck sweaters.*

poly- /ˈpɒlɪ-/ prefix many: polygamy.

poly·ga·mist /pəˈlɪɡəmɪst/ n [C] man who practises polygamy.

poly·ga·mous /pəˈlɪɡəməs/ adj of, practising, polygamy.

poly·gamy /pəˈlɪɡəmɪ/ n [U] custom of having more than one wife at the same time.

poly·glot /ˈpɒlɪɡlɒt/ adj knowing, using, written in, many languages. □ n [C] polyglot person or book.

poly·gon /ˈpɒlɪɡən US: -ɡɒn/ n [C] plane figure or shape with five or more straight sides.

poly·mor·phous /ˌpɒlɪˈmɔːfəs/, (also poly·mor·phic /-fɪk/) adj having, passing through many stages (of development, growth, etc).

poly·tech·nic /ˌpɒlɪˈteknɪk/ n [C] institution for advanced full-time and part-time education, esp of scientific and technical subjects: *Manchester P~.*

poly·theism /ˈpɒlɪθiːɪzm/ n [C] belief in, worship of, more than one god.

poly·theis·tic /ˌpɒlɪˈθiːɪstɪk/ adj

poly·thene /ˈpɒlɪθiːn/ n [U] plastic material widely used for waterproof packaging, insulation, etc.

pom·egran·ate /ˈpɒmɪɡrænət/ n [C] (tree with) thick-skinned round fruit which, when ripe, has a reddish centre full of seeds.

pom·mel /ˈpʌməl/ n [C] 1 the tall part at the front of a saddle. 2 rounded knob on the hilt of a sword. □ vt (-ll-, US also -l-) = pummel.

pomp /pɒmp/ n [U] splendid display, magnificence, esp at a public event: *the ~ and ceremony of the State Opening of Parliament.*

pom·pos·ity /pɒmˈpɒsətɪ/ n (pl -ies) 1 [U] being pompous. 2 [C] instance of this.

pom·pous /ˈpɒmpəs/ adj full of, showing, (too much) self-importance: *a ~ official.*

pon·cho /ˈpɒntʃəʊ/ n [C] (pl ~s) large piece of cloth with a slit in the middle for the head, worn as a cloak.

pond /pɒnd/ n [C] small area of water, e g for ducks, children's boats, etc.

pon·der /ˈpɒndə(r)/ vt, vi (over), think about: *He ~ed over the incident.*

pon·der·ous /ˈpɒndərəs/ adj 1 heavy; bulky: *~ movements,* e g of a fat man. 2 (of style) dull; laboured.

pon·der·ous·ly adv

pon·tiff /ˈpɒntɪf/ n [C] 1 the Pope. 2 (old use) bishop; chief priest.

pon·tifi·cal /pɒnˈtɪfɪkəl/ adj 1 of or relating to the Pope; papal. 2 authoritative (in a pompous way). □ n pl vestments and insignia used by bishops and cardinals at some church functions and ceremonies.

pon·tifi·cate /pɒnˈtɪfɪkeɪt/ n [C] office of a pontiff, esp of the Pope; period of this. □ vi speak, act, pompously.

pon·toon¹ /pɒnˈtuːn/ n [C] 1 flat-bottomed boat. 2 many of these or a similar metal structure, supporting a roadway over a river: *a ~ bridge.* 3 either of two supports shaped like boats that enable a sea-plane to come down on, and take off from, water.

pon·toon² /pɒnˈtuːn/ n [U] kind of card game.

pony /ˈpəʊnɪ/ n [C] (pl -ies) horse of small breed, used by children for riding.

`pony-trekking,` the making of a journey for pleasure on ponies.

poodle /ˈpuːdəl/ n [C] kind of dog with thick curling hair, often clipped and shaved into patterns.

pooh /puː/ int expressing impatience or contempt or a bad smell.

pool¹ /puːl/ n [C] 1 small area of water (smaller than a pond). 2 quantity of water or other liquid lying on a surface: *He was lying in a ~ of blood.* 3 = swimming pool.

pool² /puːl/ n [C] 1 total of money staked by a number of gamblers. 2 = football pools: *win a fortune on the ~s.* 3 arrangement by business firms to share business and divide profits, to avoid competition and agree on prices. 4 common fund, supply or service, provided by or shared among many: *a `typing ~.* 5 [U] (US) = snooker. □ vt put (money, resources, etc) together for the use of all who contribute: *They ~ed their savings and bought a car.*

poop /puːp/ n [C] (raised deck at the) stern of a ship.

poor /pʊə(r)/ adj (-er, -est) 1 having little money; not having and not able to get the necessities of life. 2 deserving or needing help or sympathy: *The ~ little puppy had been abandoned.* 3 small in quantity: *a ~ supply of well-qualified science teachers; a country ~ in minerals.* 4 low in quality: *~*

soil; in ~ health.
the poor *n pl* poor people.
poor·ly /'pʊəlɪ/ *adj* (*informal*) unwell: *He's rather ~ this morning.* □ *adv* **1** in a poor manner; badly: *~ lit streets.* **2** *poorly off,* having very little money: *She's been ~ off since her husband died.*
poor·ness /'pʊənəs/ *n* [U] lack of some necessary quality or element: *the ~ of the soil.* (*Note: poverty* is used for having little or no money.)
pop¹ /pɒp/ *n* [C] **1** short, sharp, explosive sound: *the ~ of a cork.* **2** (*informal*) bottled drink with gas in it: *a bottle of pop.* □ *adv* with the sound of popping: *I heard it go ~.*
pop² /pɒp/ *n* [C] (*informal*) = father.
pop³ /pɒp/ *adj* (*informal*) (abbr for) popular: '~ *music;* '~ *singers;* '~ *groups,* (singers and players) (esp) those whose records sell in large numbers and who are most popular on radio, TV and in discotheques. □ *n* (*informal*) [U] pop music, etc; [C] pop song: *top of the ~s,* most popular record, etc during a given period of time.
'**pop concert,** of popular music.
'**pop festival,** large outdoor gathering of people to hear pop singers and musicians.
'**pop star,** famous pop singer or musician.
pop⁴ /pɒp/ *vt,vi* (-pp-) **1** (cause to) make a sharp, quick sound (as when a cork comes out of a bottle). **2** *pop the question,* (*sl*) propose marriage. **3** (*sl*) shoot: *They were ~ping away at the wood-pigeons.* **4** (uses with *adverbial particles* and *prepositions*):
pop across to, ⇨ pop over below.
pop in/out, (cause to) go or come in/out quickly (giving the idea of rapid or unexpected movement or activity): *He ~ped his head in at the door. The neighbours' children are always ~ping in and out,* are very frequent visitors.
pop sth into sth, quickly put it there: *She ~ped the gin bottle into the cupboard as the vicar entered the room.*
pop off, (a) go away. (b) (*sl*) die.
pop out of: *His eyes almost ~ped out of his head when he saw that he had won.*
pop over/across to, make a quick, short visit to: *She's just ~ped over/across to the grocer's.*
'**pop-corn,** dried maize heated until it bursts open (eaten with honey, salt, etc.
'**pop-eyed** *adj* having eyes wide open (with surprise, etc).
pope /pəʊp/ *n* **the P~,** Bishop of Rome as head of the Roman Catholic Church.
pop·lar /'pɒplə(r)/ *n* [C] tall, straight, fast-growing tree; [U] its wood.
poppa /'pɒpə/ *n* (*US*) = papa.
poppy /'pɒpɪ/ *n* [C] (*pl* -pies) sorts of plant, wild and cultivated, with large flowers, esp red: '**opium ~,** kind from which opium is obtained.
poppy-cock /'pɒpɪkɒk/ *n* [U] (*GB sl*) = nonsense.

popu·lace /'pɒpjʊləs/ *n* [C] (*formal*) the general public.
popu·lar /'pɒpjʊlə(r)/ *adj* **1** of or for the people: *~ government,* by the elected majority of all those who have votes. **2** suited to the tastes, needs, educational level, etc of the general public: *food at ~* (= low) *prices.* **3** liked and admired: *~ film stars; a man who is ~ with his neighbours.* ⇨ pop³.
'**popular 'front,** (in politics) coalition of parties opposed to reaction and fascism.
popu·lar·ly *adv*
popu·lar·ity /'pɒpjʊ'lærətɪ/ *n* [U] quality of being popular(3).
popu·lar·ize /'pɒpjʊləraɪz/ *vt* make popular: *~ a new book.*
popu·lar·iz·ation /'pɒpjʊləraɪ'zeɪʃən US. -rɪ'z-/ *n* [U]
popu·late /'pɒpjʊleɪt/ *vt* supply with people; inhabit; form the population of: *the thickly ~d parts of India.*
popu·la·tion /'pɒpjʊ'leɪʃən/ *n* [C] (number of) people living in a place, country, etc or a special section of them: *the ~ of London; the working-class ~.*
por·ce·lain /'pɔːsəlɪn/ *n* [U] (articles, e g cups and plates, made of a) fine china with a coating of translucent material called *glaze.*
porch /pɔːtʃ/ *n* [C] **1** built-out roofed doorway or entrance to a building. **2** (*US, also*) veranda.
por·cu·pine /'pɔːkjʊpaɪn/ *n* [C] small animal covered with spines that the animal can stick out if attacked.
pore¹ /pɔː(r)/ *n* [C] tiny opening (in the skin) through which fluids (e g sweat) may pass.
pore² /pɔː(r)/ *vi* study something with close attention: *~ over a letter/book.*
pork /pɔːk/ *n* [U] flesh of a pig (usually fresh, not salted or cured) used as food: *a leg of ~; a ~ chop; roast ~.* ⇨ bacon, ham(1).
porker, pig raised for food.
porn /pɔːn/ *n* [U] (*informal*) (abbr of) pornography.
'**porn shop,** where pornographic books, etc are sold.
por·nogra·phy /pɔː'nɒgrəfɪ/ *n* [U] treatment of obscene subjects, esp sexual perversions, in writing, pictures, etc; such writings, etc.
por·nogra·pher /pɔː'nɒgrəfə(r)/ *n* [U] writer of pornography.
por·no·graphic /'pɔːnə'græfɪk/ *adj*
po·rous /'pɔːrəs/ *adj* **1** having pores. **2** allowing liquid to pass through: *Sandy soil is ~.*
por·poise /'pɔːpəs/ *n* [C] sea-animal rather like a dolphin or small whale.
por·ridge /'pɒrɪdʒ US: 'pɔːr-/ *n* [U] soft food made by boiling oatmeal in water or milk; *a bowl/plate of ~.*
port¹ /pɔːt/ *n* [C] **1** harbour: *a naval ~, reach ~.* **2** town or city with a harbour, esp one where customs officers are stationed.
free port, one open for the merchandise of all countries to load and unload in; one

where there is exemption of duties for imports or exports. **3** (*fig*) refuge.

port² /pɔt/ *n* [C] (*naut*) opening in the side of a ship for entrance, or for loading and unloading cargo.

ˋport‧hole, (a) opening in a ship's side for admission of light and air. (b) small glass window in the side of a ship or aircraft.

port³ /pɔt/ *n* [U] (*naut*) **1** left-hand side of a ship or aircraft as one faces forward: *put the helm to* ~. **2** (as an *adjective*): *on the* ~ *bow/quarter.* ⇨ **starboard.** □ *vt* turn (the ship's helm) to port.

port⁴ /pɔt/ *n* [U] strong (usually sweet) dark-red wine of Portugal.

port‧able /ˈpɔtəbəl/ *adj* that can be carried about: ~ *radios/typewriters.*

port‧abil‧ity /ˈpɔtəˈbɪlətɪ/ *n* [U] being portable.

port‧age /ˈpɔtɪdʒ/ *n* [C,U] (cost of) carrying goods, esp when (e g in forest country in Canada) goods have to be carried overland between two rivers or parts of a river; place where this is done.

por‧tal /ˈpɔtəl/ *n* [C] doorway, esp a large, elaborate one of a large building.

port‧cul‧lis /ˈpɔtˈkʌlɪs/ *n* [C] (*pl* ~es) iron grating that was raised or lowered to protect the gateway of a castle.

por‧tend /pɔˈtend/ *vt* (formal) be a sign or warning of (a future event, etc): *This* ~s *war.*

por‧tent /ˈpɔtent/ *n* [C] (*formal*) omen.

por‧ten‧tous /pɔˈtentəs/ *adj* (*formal*) (a) ominous; threatening. (b) marvellous; extraordinary.

por‧ten‧tous‧ly *adv*

por‧ter¹ /ˈpɔtə(r)/ *n* [C] **1** person whose work is to carry luggage, etc at stations, airports, hotels, etc. **2** person carrying a load on his back or head (usually in country where there are no roads for motorvehicles). **3** (*US*) attendant on a train.

por‧ter² /ˈpɔtə(r)/ *n* [C] doorkeeper (at a hotel, public building, etc).

ˋporter's lodge, (rooms in a) small house at the entrance to a college, etc.

por‧ter³ /ˈpɔtə(r)/ *n* [U] dark-brown bitter beer.

por‧ter‧house /ˈpɔtəhaʊs/ *n* [C] (~ *steak*), superior cut of beefsteak.

port‧folio /pɔtˈfəʊlɪəʊ/ *n* [C] (*pl* ~s) **1** flat case for keeping papers, documents, drawings, etc. **2** position and duties of a minister of state: *He is minister without* ~, not in charge of any particular department. **3** list of securities and investments (stocks, shares, etc) owned by an individual, a bank, etc.

port‧hole *n* ⇨ **port².**

port‧ico /ˈpɔtɪkəʊ/ *n* [C] (*pl* ~es or ~s) roof on columns, esp at the entrance of a building.

por‧tion /ˈpɔʃən/ *n* [C] **1** part, esp a share, (to be) given when something is distributed. **2** quantity of any kind of food served in a

restaurant: *a generous* ~ *of roast duck.* **3** (*formal, poetic*) (*sing*) one's lot or fate: *Brief life is here our* ~. □ *vt* **portion sth out (among/between),** share out (which is more usual).

port‧ly /ˈpɔtlɪ/ *adj* stout; round and fat (person): *a* ~ *city councillor.*

port‧man‧teau /pɔtˈmæntəʊ/ *n* [C] (*pl* ~s or ~x /-təʊz/) oblong, leather case for clothes, opening on a hinge into two equal parts.

por‧trait /ˈpɔtrɪt/ *n* [C] **1** painted picture, drawing, photograph, of a person or animal. **2** vivid description in words.

ˋpor‧trait‧ist /-ɪst/, maker of portraits.

ˋpor‧trait‧ure /-tʃə(r) *US:* -tʃʊə(r)/ *n* [U] art of making portraits.

por‧tray /pɔˈtreɪ/ *vt* **1** make a picture of. **2** describe vividly in words. **3** act the part of (in a play).

por‧tray‧al /pɔˈtreɪəl/ *n* [U] portraying; [C] act at portraying.

pose /pəʊz/ *vt, vi* **1** put (a person) in a position before making a portrait, taking a photograph, etc: *All the subjects are well* ~d. **2** **pose for,** take up a position (for a photograph, etc): *Will you* ~ *for me?* **3** put forward for discussion; create; cause: *The increase in student numbers* ~s *many problems for the universities.* **4** **pose as,** claim to be (esp deliberately): ~ *as an expert on old coins.* **5** behave in an affected way hoping to impress people: *She's always posing.* □ *n* [C] **1** position taken up for a portrait, photograph, etc: *an unusual* ~. **2** unnatural way of behaving, intended to impress people: *That rich man's socialism is a mere* ~.

poser *n* [C] awkward or difficult question or problem.

posh /pɒʃ/ *adj* (*informal*) smart; first-class: *a* ~ *hotel;* ~ *clothes; her* ~ *friends.*

po‧si‧tion /pəˈzɪʃən/ *n* **1** [C] place where a person or thing is or stands, esp in relation to others: *find a* ~ *where one will get a good view of the procession.* **In/out of position,** in/not in the right place. **2** [U] state of being well placed (in war or any kind of struggle): *They were manoeuvring for* ~. **3** [C] attitude or posture: *sit/lie in a comfortable* ~. **4** [C] person's place or rank in relation to others, in employment, in society, etc: *a pupil's* ~ *in class; a high/low* ~ *in society.* **5** [C] job; employment: *apply for the* ~ *of assistant manager.* **6** [C] condition; circumstances: *I'm sorry but I am not in a* ~ (= am unable) *to help you.* **7** [C] opinion: *What's your* ~ *on this problem?* □ *vt* **1** place in position. **2** find the position of.

posi‧tive /ˈpɒzətɪv/ *adj* **1** definite; sure; leaving no room for doubt: *I gave you* ~ *instructions.* **2** (of persons) quite certain, esp about opinions: *Are you* ~ (*that*) *it was after midnight?* **3** practical and constructive; that definitely helps: *a* ~ *suggestion;* ~ *help;* ~ *criticism.* **4** (*informal*) complete:

That man is a ~ *fool.* **5** (*maths*) greater than zero. **6** (of electricity) of the sort caused by deficiency of electrons: *a* ~ *charge.* **7** (*photography*) showing light and shadows as in nature, not reversed (as in a *negative*). **8** (*gram*) (of *adjectives* and *adverbs*) of the simple form, not the comparative or superlative. **9** (*med*) showing presence of a disease, etc: *the blood tests were* ~. □ *n* [C] **1** positive degree, adjective, quantity, etc. **2** positive photograph.

positive sign, the sign (+).

pos·i·tive·ly *adv* definitely; certainly.

pos·sess /pəˈzes/ *vt* **1** own, have: ~ *nothing; lose all that one* ~*es.* **2** occupy (the mind); dominate: *What* ~*ed you to do that?* What influenced or caused you to do that?

pos·ses·sor /-sə(r)/ *n* [C] owner.

pos·ses·sion /pəˈzeʃən/ *n* **1** [U] possessing; ownership: *How did it come into your* ~? *How did you get* ~ *of it? The information in my* ~ *is strictly confidential. Is she in full* ~ *of her senses?* Is she sane? **2** [C] (often *pl*) property: *lose all one's* ~*s.*

pos·sess·ive /pəˈzesɪv/ *adj* **1** of possession or ownership: *She has a* ~ *nature,* is eager to own things or wants the whole of (someone's) love or attention. **2** (*gram*) showing possession.

possessive case, e g *Tom's, the boy's, the boys'.*

possessive pronoun, e g *yours, his.*

pos·sess·ive·ly *adv*

pos·si·bil·ity /ˌpɒsəˈbɪlətɪ/ *n* (*pl* -ies) **1** [U] state, degree, of being possible: *Is there any/much* ~ *of your getting to London this week? Help is still within the bounds of* ~, is possible. **2** [C] something that is possible: *I see great possibilities for this scheme.*

poss·ible /ˈpɒsəbl/ *adj* **1** that can be done; that can exist or happen: *Come as quickly as* ~. *Frost is* ~, *though not probable.* **2** that is reasonable or satisfactory: *He is the only* ~ *man for the position.* □ *n* [C] possible(2) person or thing.

poss·ibly /-əblɪ/ *adv* (a) (used to emphasise effort, etc): *I will come as soon as I possibly can.* (b) perhaps: *'Will they put your salary up?'—'Possibly.'*

post[1] /pəʊst/ *n* [C] **1** place where a soldier is on duty: *The sentries are all at their* ~*s.* **2** place occupied by soldiers, esp a frontier fort; the soldiers there. ⇨ outpost. **3** position or appointment; job: *be given the* ~ *as general manager.* □ *vt* **1** send to a post(1,2): ~ *an officer to a unit; be* ~*ed at the gates.* **2** be appointed, appoint to a job (overseas): *be* ~*ed to Brussels.*

post[2] /pəʊst/ *n* [C] (mil) bugle-call sounded at sunset: *the first/last* ~. (*Note: the last* ~ is also sounded at military funerals.)

post[3] /pəʊst/ *n* [C] **1** (*GB*) (*US = mail*) public corporation which transports and delivers letters, parcels, etc; one collection of letters, parcels, etc; one delivery or distri-

bution of letters, etc: *I will send you the book by* ~. *Please reply by return of* ~, in the next collection. **2** box (into which letters are dropped for collection): *take letters to the* ~. **3** letters, parcel, etc posted: *Has the* ~ *arrived yet?* **4** (formerly) one of a number of men placed with horses at intervals, the duty of each being to ride with letters, etc to the next stage.

post-box, = post(2).

post-card, oblong card (usually with a picture on one side) used for sending short messages.

post-code, (*US = zipcode*) group of letters and numbers, written on the envelope, used to make the sorting and delivery of mail easier (by use of a computer).

post-free *adj, adv* carried free of charge by post, or with postage prepaid.

post-man /-mən/, (*US = mailman*) man employed to deliver letters, etc.

post-mark, official mark stamped on letters, cancelling postage stamp(s) and giving the place, date, and time of collection. □ *vt* mark (an envelope, etc) with this.

post-master/mistress, official in charge of a post office.

post office, building, etc where postal business is carried on, together with the telegrams and telephones, payment of state pensions, etc.

post office box, (abbr **P O Box**) numbered box in a post office where letters are kept for collection by an individual or company.

post-paid *adj, adv* with postage already paid.

post[4] /pəʊst/ *vt, vi* **1** (*US = mail*) put (letters, etc) into a post box or take (them) to a post office to be forwarded. **2** (formerly) travel by stages, using relays of horses: ~ *from London to Bristol.* **3** *keep sb posted,* (fig) keep him supplied with news.

post-haste *adv* with great speed.

post[5] /pəʊst/ *n* [C] upright piece of wood, metal, etc supporting or marking something: *gate*~*s; the* ~*starting/*~*winning-*~, marking the starting and finishing points in a race. ⇨ lamp-post. □ *vt* **1** display in a public place by means of a paper, placard, etc: *The announcement was* ~*ed up on the wall of the town hall.* **2** make known by means of a posted notice: *a ship* ~*ed as missing.*

post- /pəʊst/ *prefix* after: *postscript.*

post·age /ˈpəʊstɪdʒ/ *n* [U] payment for the carrying of letters, etc: *What is the* ~ *for an air-letter?*

postage stamp, stamp (to be) stuck on letters, etc showing the amount of postage paid.

postal /ˈpəʊstəl/ *adj* of the post[3](1): ~ *rates;* ~ *workers; a* ~ *vote,* e g of trade union members, sent by post to decide a ballot.

postal order, written form for money (to be) cashed at a post office.

post·date /ˈpəʊstˈdeɪt/ vt **1** put (on a letter, cheque, etc) a date later than the date of writing. **2** give to (an event) a date later than its actual date.

poster /ˈpəʊstə(r)/ n [C] **1** placard displayed in a public place (announcing or advertising something). **2** large printed picture, e g of a pop star.

pos·ter·ior /pɒˈstɪərɪə(r)/ adj **1** later in time or order. ⇨ prior¹. **2** placed behind; at the back.

pos·ter·ity /pɒˈsterətɪ/ n [U] **1** person's descendants (his children, their children, etc). **2** future generations: plant trees for the benefit of ~.

post·gradu·ate /ˈpəʊst ˈgrædʒʊət/ adj (of studies, etc) done after taking a first academic degree. □ n [C] person engaged in such studies.

post·hum·ous /ˈpɒstʃʊməs/ adj **1** (of a child) born after the death of its father. **2** coming or happening after death: ~ fame.
post·hum·ous·ly adv

post mer·idiem /ˈpəʊst məˈrɪdɪəm/ adv (abbr **p m** which is more usual) after midday.

post-mor·tem /ˈpəʊst ˈmɔːtəm/ n [C], adj **1** (medical examination) made after death: A ~ showed that the man had been poisoned. **2** (informal) review of an event, etc in the past.

post·pone /pəˈspəʊn/ vt change to a later time: ~ a meeting.
post·pone·ment n [C,U]

post·script /ˈpəʊskrɪpt/ n [C] (abbr **P S**) sentence(s) added (to a letter) after the signature.

pos·tu·lant /ˈpɒstjʊlənt US: -tʃʊ-/ n [C] candidate for admission to a religious order. ⇨ novice.

pos·tu·late /ˈpɒstjʊleɪt US: -tʃʊ-/ vt put forward, defend, as a necessary fact, as a basis for reasoning. □ n [C] something (that may be) considered undeniably true.

pos·ture /ˈpɒstʃə(r)/ n [C] **1** attitude of, way of holding, the body: Good ~ helps you to keep well. **2** attitude: Will the Government alter its ~ over aid to the railways? □ vt, vi **1** put or arrange in a position: ~ a model. **2** be vain, etc: She was posturing before a tall mirror.

posy /ˈpəʊzɪ/ n [C] (pl -ies) small bunch of cut flowers.

pot¹ /pɒt/ n [C] **1** round vessel of earthenware, metal or glass, for holding liquids or solids, for cooking things in, etc; contents of such a vessel: a ˈjam-~/ˈtea-~/ˈcoffee-~/ˈflower-~ **2** (phrases and proverbs) **go to pot,** (sl) be ruined or (mentally) destroyed. **keep the pot boiling,** earn enough money to buy one's food, etc. **take pot luck,** whatever is available (without choice). **the pot calling the kettle black,** the accuser having the same fault as the accused. **3** (informal) large sum: make a ~/~s of

money. **4** (sl) marijuana.
ˈpot-ˈbellied adj (of a person) having a large, round belly.
ˈpot-boiler, book, picture, etc produced merely to bring in money.
ˈpot-bound, (of a plant) having roots that have filled its pot.
ˈpot-head, (sl) habitual user of marijuana.
ˈpothole, (a) hole in a road made by rain and traffic. **(b)** deep cylindrical hole worn in rock (e g in limestone caves) by water
ˈpotholer, person who explores potholes in caves.
ˈpot ˈluck, ⇨ 2 above.
ˈpot plant one grown (indoors).
pot roast, beef, etc browned in a pot and cooked slowly with very little water.
ˈpot-shot, shot aimed at a bird or animal that is near, so that careful aim is not needed.

pot² /pɒt/ vt, vi (-tt-) **1** put (meat, fish paste, etc) in a glass jar to preserve it: ~ted shrimps. **2** plant in a flower-pot. **3** (informal) put (a baby) on a chamber-pot.

po·tass·ium /pəˈtæsɪəm/ n [U] (symbol **K**) soft, shining, white metallic element.

po·tato /pəˈteɪtəʊ/ n [C,U] (pl ~es) plant with rounded tubers eaten as a vegetable; one of the tubers: baked ~es. May I have some more ~? ⇨ sweet potato.

po·tency /ˈpəʊtənsɪ/ n [U] (formal) strength (e g of drugs, etc.)

po·tent /ˈpəʊtənt/ adj (of arguments, charms, drugs, etc) powerful.
po·tent·ly adv

po·ten·tial /pəˈtenʃəl/ adj that can or may come into existence or action: ~ wealth; the ~ sales of a new book. □ n **1** [C] possibility. **2** [U] what a person or thing is capable of: He/It hasn't much ~.
po·ten·tially /-ʃəlɪ/ adv: a ~ly rich country, e g one with rich but undeveloped natural resources.

po·ten·ti·al·ity /pəˈtenʃɪˈælətɪ/ n [C] (pl -ies) power or quality which is possible, and needs development: a country with great potentialities.

po·tion /ˈpəʊʃən/ n [C] dose of liquid medicine, poison, etc.

potted /ˈpɒtɪd/ adj **1** ⇨ pot². **2** (of a book, etc) inadequately abridged: a ~ version of a classical novel.

pot·ter¹ /ˈpɒtə(r)/ (US also **put·ter** /ˈpʌtə(r)/) vi, vt **1** move about from one little job to another: ~ing about in the garden. **2** waste (time) in this way: ~ away a whole afternoon.

pot·ter² /ˈpɒtə(r)/ n [C] maker of (clay, stone, etc) pots.
potter's wheel, horizontal revolving disc on which pots are shaped.
pot·tery n (pl -ies) **(a)** [U] earthenware; pots. **(b)** [C] potter's workshop.

potty /ˈpɒtɪ/ adj (-ier, -iest) (GB informal) **1** unimportant; insignificant: ~ little *jobs.* **2** (of a person) mad. **3** (of a person) in love with: *He's ~ about his new girl friend.*

potty² /ˈpɒtɪ/ *n* [C] (*pl* -ies) child's chamber-pot.

pouch /paʊtʃ/ *n* [C] **1** small bag carried in the pocket (*a `tobacco~*) or fastened to the belt. **2** formation like a bag, e g that in which a female kangaroo carries her young. □ *vt* put into a pouch.

pouf, pouffe /puf/ *n* [C] large, thick cushion used as a seat.

poul-tice /ˈpəʊltɪs/ *n* [C] soft heated mass of e g linseed, mustard, spread on a cloth, and put on the skin to relieve pain, etc. □ *vt* put a poultice on.

poul-try /ˈpəʊltrɪ/ *n* (*collective*) **1** (used with a *pl verb*) hens, ducks, geese, etc: *The ~ are being fed.* **2** (used with a *sing verb*) these considered as food: *P~ is expensive this Christmas.*

pounce /paʊns/ *vi* **1** make a sudden attack (downward) or swoop on: *Someone was ~ing at the door with his fist. She could feel her heart ~ing as she finished the 100 metres race.* **2** (*fig*) seize: *He ~d at the first chance of a holiday.* □ *n* [C] such an attack.

pound¹ /paʊnd/ *n* [C] **1** unit of weight, 16 ounces avoirdupois, 12 ounces troy. **2** British unit of money: *five ~s,* written £5; *a five-~ note,* banknote for £5. **3** monetary unit of various other countries, esp former British dependencies, and Israel.

pound² /paʊnd/ *n* [C] (*modern use*) place where stray dogs and cats, and motor-vehicles left in unauthorized places, are kept until claimed.

pound³ /paʊnd/ *vt,vi* **1** strike heavily and repeatedly: *Someone was ~ing at the door with his fist. She could feel her heart ~ing as she finished the 100 metres race.* **2** crush to powder; break to pieces: *~ crystals in a mortar; a ship ~ing/being ~ed to pieces on the rocks.* **3** ride, run, walk, heavily: *He ~ed along the road.*

a fish. **2** gun that fires a shot of so many pounds: *an eighteen-~.*

pour /pɔ(r)/ *vt,vi* **1** cause (a liquid or a substance like a liquid) to flow in a continuous stream: *P~ yourself another cup of tea. The sweat was ~ing off him.* **2** (*fig*) flow in a continuous stream: *Tourists ~ into London during the summer months. The crowds were ~ing out of the football ground. Letters of complaint ~ed in.* **3** (of rain) come down heavily: *The rain ~ed down.* **4** tell, describe, in a long speech: *He ~ed out his story of the road crash.*

pout /paʊt/ *vt,vi* push out the lips (as a sign of displeasure): *~ n* such an act.

pov-erty /ˈpɒvətɪ/ *n* [U] **1** state of being poor: *live in ~.* **2** state of being low in quality: *an essay which shows ~ of ideas.*

`poverty-stricken *adj* affected by poverty: *~-stricken homes.*

pow-der /ˈpaʊdə(r)/ *n* [C,U] (kind of) substance that has been crushed, rubbed or worn to dust, for use on the skin (`*face~*), for

---

cleaning things (`*soap~*), or for cooking (`*baking~*) ⇨ gunpowder. □ *vt,vi* use face-powder or talcum-powder.

`powder-puff, soft, pad used for applying face-powder to the skin.

`powder-room, (esp *US*) ladies' cloakroom in an hotel, restaurant, cinema, etc with wash-basins and lavatories.

pow-dered *adj* reduced to powder: *~ed milk/eggs.*

pow-dery *adj* of, like, covered with, powder: *~y snow.*

power /ˈpaʊə(r)/ *n* **1** [U] (in living things, persons) ability to do or act: *It is not within/ It is beyond/It is outside my ~ to help you,* I am unable to do so. *I will do everything in my ~ to help.* **2** (*pl*) faculty of the body or mind: *His ~s are failing,* He is becoming weak. *He's a man of great intellectual ~s.* **3** [U] strength; force: *the ~ of a blow.* **4** [U] energy of force that can be used to do work: *e`lectric ~.* ⇨ horse power. **5** [U] right; control; authority: *the ~ of the law; the ~ of Congress. **have power over sb,** be in authority, control. **in power,** (of a ministry or political party) in office. **6** [C] right possessed by, or granted to, a person or group of persons: *The President has exceeded his ~s,* has done more than he has authority to do. **7** [C] person or organization having great authority or influence: *Is the press a great ~ in your country?* **8** [C] State having great authority and influence in international affairs. **9** [C] (*maths*) result obtained by multiplying a number or quantity by itself a certain number of times: *the second, third, fourth, etc ~ of x* $(= x^2, x^3, x^4, etc)$; *the fourth ~ of 3* $(= 3 \times 3 \times 3 \times 3 = 81)$. **10** [U] capacity to magnify: *the ~ of a lens; a telescope of high ~.* **11** [U] (*informal*) large number or amount: *This beer does me a ~ of good.*

`power-boat, motorboat (esp one used for racing; or towing water-skiers).

`power-house/-station, building where electric power is generated for distribution.

`power-point, socket on a wall, etc for a plug to connect an electric circuit.

power politics, diplomacy backed by force.

pow-ered *adj* (a) having, able to exert or produce, mechanical energy: *a high-~ed car.* (b) (*fig*) having great energy: *a high-~ed salesman.*

power-ful /ˈpaʊəfəl/ *adj* having or producing great power: *a ~ enemy; a ~ drug.*

power-fully /-flɪ/ *adv*

power-less /ˈpaʊələs/ *adj* without power; unable: *be ~ to resist.*

power-less-ly *adv*

prac-ti-cable /ˈpræktɪkəbəl/ *adj* that can be done or used or put into practice: *ideas that are not ~.*

prac-ti-cably /-əblɪ/ *adv*

prac-ti-cal /ˈpræktɪkəl/ *adj* **1** concerned with practice (contrasted with *theory*): *a* *suggestion/proposal with little* ~ *value.* **2** (of persons, their character. etc) clever at and liking doing and making things: *a* ~ *husband/mind.* **3** doing well what it is intended to do: *Your invention is clever, but not very* ~.

'practical 'joke, trick in which a person does something or has something done to him, so that he appears ridiculous.

prac·ti·cally /-klɪ/ *adv* (**a**) in a practical manner. (**b**) almost: *We've had* ~*ly no sunshine this month.*

prac·ti·cal·ity /ˌpræktɪˈkælətɪ/ *n* [C] (*pl* -ies): *Let's get down to* ~*ities,* to considering the things to be done.

prac·tice (*US* also **prac·tise**) /ˈpræktɪs/ *n* **1** [U] performance; the doing of something (contrasted with *theory*): *put a plan into* ~, do what has been planned. *The idea would never work in* ~, may seem good theoretically, but would be useless if carried out. **2** [C] something done regularly: *the* ~ *of closing shops on Sundays.* **make a practice of** (*sth*), do it habitually: *boys who make a* ~ *of cheating at examinations.* **3** [U] frequent or systematic repetition, repeated exercise: *Piano-playing needs a lot of* ~. *It takes years of* ~ *to become an expert.* **in/out of practice,** having/not having given enough time recently to practice. **4** [U] work of a doctor or lawyer; [C] (number of) persons who regularly consult a doctor or lawyer: *a doctor with a large* ~. ⇨ general practitioner.

prac·tise (*US* also **prac·tice**) /ˈpræktɪs/ *vt,vi* **1** do something repeatedly or regularly in order to become skilful: ~ *the piano;* ~ *two hours every day.* **2** make a habit of: ~ *getting up early.* **practise what one preaches,** make a habit of doing what one advises others to do. **3** be employed in (a profession, etc): ~ *medicine/the law,* work as a doctor/lawyer.

prac·tised (*US* also **-ticed**) *adj* skilled; having had much practice.

prac·ti·tioner /prækˈtɪʃənə(r)/ *n* [C] **1** one who practices a skill or art. **2** professional man, esp in medicine and the law. ⇨ general practitioner.

prag·matic /prægˈmætɪk/ *adj* concerned with practical results, reasons and values.
prag·mati·cally /-klɪ/ *adv*

prag·ma·tism /ˈprægmətɪzm/ *n* [U] philosophical belief that the truth or value of a theory depends on its practical use.

prag·ma·tist /-tɪst/ *n* [C] believer in pragmatism.

prairie /ˈpreərɪ/ *n* [C] wide area of level land with grass but no trees, esp in N America. ⇨ pampas, savanna.

praise /preɪz/ *vt* **1** say that one admires or approves: ~ *a man for his courage/the meal as the best of its kind.* **2** give honour and glory to (God). □ *n* **1** [U] act of praising: *His heroism is worthy of great* ~*/is beyond* (=

too great for) ~. **2** [U] worship; glory: *P*~ *be to God.*

'praise·worthy /-wɜːðɪ/ *adj* deserving praise.

pram /præm/ *n* [C] (*GB*) (abbr for, and the usual word for) perambulator.

prance /prɑːns *US:* præns/ *vi* **1** (of a horse) move forwards jerkily, by raising the forelegs and jumping from the hind legs. **2** (*fig*) move in an arrogant manner; dance or jump happily and gaily. □ *n* [C] prancing movement.

prank /præŋk/ *n* [C] playful or mischievous trick: *play* ~*s on her.*

prattle /ˈprætəl/ *vi* talk in a simple, childish way. □ *n* [U] such talk.

prawn /prɔːn/ *n* [C] edible shellfish like a large shrimp. □ *vi* fish for prawns: *go* ~*ing.*

pray /preɪ/ *vt,vi* commune with God; offer thanks, make requests known: ~ *to God for help. They knelt down and* ~*ed.*

prayer /preə(r)/ *n* **1** [U] act of praying to God: *He knelt down in* ~. **2** [U] form of church worship: *Morning/Evening P*~. **3** [C] form of words used in praying: *the Lord's P*~.

'prayer-book, containing prayers for use in church services, etc.

'prayer-rug/-mat, small rug used by Muslims to kneel on when they pray.

'prayer-wheel, revolving cylinder inscribed with or containing prayers, used by the Buddhists of Tibet.

pre- /prɪ, pre-/ *prefix* before; beforehand: *pre-war; premature.*

preach /priːtʃ/ *vt,vi* **1** deliver (a sermon); give a talk (in church) about religion or morals: ~ *the gospel;* ~ *Buddhism.* **2** give moral advice (*to*): *The headmaster was* ~*ing to his boys about being lazy.* **3** urge; recommend (as right or desirable): *The Dictator* ~*ed war as a means of making the country great.*

preacher, one who delivers sermons.

pre·amble /prɪˈæmbəl/ *n* [C] introduction or preliminary statement (esp to a formal document).

pre·arrange /ˌpriːəˈreɪndʒ/ *vt* arrange in advance.
pre·arrange·ment *n* [C,U]

pre·cari·ous /prɪˈkeərɪəs/ *adj* (*formal*) uncertain; unsafe; depending on chance: *make a* ~ *living as an author.*
pre·cari·ous·ly *adv*

pre·cast /ˌpriːˈkɑːst *US:* -ˈkæst/ *adj* (of concrete) in blocks ready for use in building.

pre·caution /prɪˈkɔːʃən/ *n* **1** [U] care taken in advance to avoid a risk. **2** [C] instance of this: *take an umbrella as a* ~.
pre·cau·tion·ary /ˈprɪkɔːʃənərɪ *US:* -ʃənerɪ/ *adj*

pre·cede /prɪˈsiːd/ *vt,vi* come or go before (in time, place or order): *The singer who is preceding the pop group in the programme is very good.*

pre-ced-ing *adj* existing or coming before.

pre-ced-ence /ˈpresɪdəns/ *n* [U] (*formal*) (right to a) priority, or to a senior place. *have/take* **precedence** *(over)*, must be considered first.

pre-ced-ent /ˈpresɪdənt/ *n* [C] (*formal*) earlier happening, decision, etc taken as an example or rule for what comes later: *set/ create/establish a* ~.

pre-cen-tor /prɪˈsentə(r)/ *n* [C] (in English cathedrals) member of the clergy in general control of the singing.

pre-cept /ˈprisept/ *n* (*formal*) 1 [U] moral instruction: *Example is better than* ~. 2 [C] rule or guide, esp for behaviour.

pre-cinct /ˈprisɪŋkt/ *n* [C] 1 space enclosed by outer walls or boundaries, esp of a cathedral or church: *within the sacred* ~s. 2 (*US*) subdivision of a county or city or ward: *an e`lection* ~; *a po`lice* ~. 3 (*pl*) neighbourhood (of a town). 4 boundary: *within the city* ~s. 5 (*modern use*) area of which the use is in some way restricted: *a `shopping* ~, for shops only.

pre-cious /ˈpreʃəs/ *adj* 1 of great value and beauty: *my* ~ *possessions*. 2 highly valued; dear: *Her children are very* ~ *to her*. 3 (of language) affected. □ *adv* (*informal*) very: *I have* ~ *little* (= hardly any) *money left*.
precious `metal, gold, platinum.
precious `stone, diamond, ruby, emerald etc.
pre-cious-ly *adv*
pre-cious-ness *n* [C]

preci-pice /ˈpresəpɪs/ *n* [C] perpendicular or very steep face of a rock, cliff or mountain.

pre-cipi-tate /prəˈsɪpɪteɪt/ *vt* (*formal*) 1 throw or send violently down from a height. 2 cause (an event) to happen suddenly, quickly, or in haste: ~ *a crisis*. 3 (*chem*) separate (solid matter) from a solution. 4 condense (vapour) into drops which fall as rain, dew, etc. □ *n* [C] that which is precipitated(3,4). □ *adj* /prəˈsɪpɪtət/ (doing things, done) without enough thought.
pre-cipi-tate-ly *adv*

pre-cipi-ta-tion /prəˌsɪpɪˈteɪʃən/ *n* 1 [C] (esp) fall of rain, sleet, snow or hail; amount of this: *the annual* ~ *in Scotland*. 2 [U] being hurried: *act with* ~, without enough thought or consideration of the consequences. 3 act of precipitating.

pre-cipi-tous /prəˈsɪpɪtəs/ *adj* (*formal*) very steep.
pre-cipi-tous-ly *adv*

pré-cis /ˈpreɪsi US: preɪˈsi/ *n* [C] (*pl* unchanged in spelling but with usual change in pronunciation to /-siz/) restatement in shortened form of the chief ideas, points, etc of a speech or piece of writing. □ *vt* make a précis of.

pre-cise /prɪˈsaɪs/ *adj* 1 exact; correctly and clearly stated; free from error: ~ *measurements; at the* ~ *moment when she sat down*. 2 taking care to be exact, not to make errors:

a very ~ *man*. 3 too careful, fussy, about details: *prim and* ~ *in his manner*.
pre-cise-ly *adv* (a) exactly: *at 2 o'clock* ~ly. (b) (as a response) I agree.
pre-cise-ness *n* [U]

pre-ci-sion /prɪˈsɪʒən/ *n* [U] accuracy; freedom from error: (as an *adjective*) ~ *instrument/tool*, used in technical work, very precise (for measuring, etc).

pre-clude /prɪˈkluːd/ *vt* (*formal*) prevent; make impossible: ~ *all doubts*.
pre-clu-sion /prɪˈkluːʒən/ *n* [U]

pre-co-cious /prɪˈkəʊʃəs/ *adj* 1 (of a person) having developed intelligence earlier than is normal. 2 (of actions, knowledge, etc) showing such development.
pre-co-cious-ly *adv*
pre-co-cious-ness *n* [U]

pre-con-ceive /ˌpriːkənˈsiːv/ *vt* form (ideas, opinions) in advance (before getting knowledge or experience): *visit a foreign country with* ~d *ideas*.
pre-con-cep-tion /ˌpriːkənˈsepʃən/ *n* [C] preconceived idea, opinion.

pre-cur-sor /ˌpriːˈkɜːsə(r)/ *n* [C] (*formal*) person or thing coming before, as a sign of what is to follow.
pre-cur-sory /-sərɪ/ *adj* preliminary; anticipating.

pred-ator /ˈpredətə(r)/ *n* [C] predatory animal.

preda-tory /ˈpredətərɪ US: -tɔːrɪ/ *adj* (*formal*) 1 of plundering and robbery: ~ *tribesmen*. 2 (of animals) preying on others.

pre-de-ces-sor /ˈpriːdɪsesə(r) US: ˈpredɪ-/ *n* [C] 1 former holder of any office or position: *Mr Green's* ~ *on the Board*. 2 thing to which another has succeeded: *Is the new proposal any better than its* ~?

pre-des-ti-na-tion /ˌpriːdestɪˈneɪʃən/ *n* [U] 1 theory or doctrine that God has decreed from eternity that part of mankind shall have eternal life and part eternal punishment. 2 destiny; doctrine that God has decreed everything that comes to pass.

pre-des-tine /ˌpriːˈdestɪn/ *vt* 1 (often passive) (of God, fate) decide, ordain, beforehand. 2 decide or make inevitable: *Everything took place as if he was* ~d *to succeed*.

pre-de-ter-mine /ˌpriːdɪˈtɜːmɪn/ *vt* (*formal*) 1 decide in advance: *Does social class* ~ *a man's career?* 2 persuade or force a person in advance to do something: *Did an unhappy childhood* ~ *him to behave as he did?*
pre-de-ter-mi-na-tion /ˌpriːdɪˌtɜːmɪˈneɪʃən/ *n* [U]

pre-dica-ment /prɪˈdɪkəmənt/ *n* [C] unpleasant situation from which escape seems difficult: *be in an awkward* ~.

predi-cate[1] /ˈpredɪkət/ *n* [C] (*gram*) part of a statement which says something about the subject, e g *'is short'* in *'Life is short'*.

predi-cate[2] /ˈpredɪkeɪt/ *vt* (*formal*) 1 declare to be true or real: ~ *a motive to be good*. 2 make necessary as a consequence:

These policies were ~d by Britain's deci-sion to join the Common Market.

predi·cat·ive /prɪ`dɪkətɪv US: `predɪkeɪt-/ *adj* (*gram*) (of an *adjective* or *noun*) forming part or the whole of the predicate.

predicative adjective, one used in the predicate, e g *asleep, alive.*

pre·dict /prɪ`dɪkt/ *vt* say, tell in advance: ~ *a good harvest/that there will be an earth-quake.*

pre·dict·able /-əbəl/ *adj* that can be pre-dicted.

pre·dic·tion /prɪ`dɪkʃən/ *n* [U] predicting; [C] something predicted.

pre·dis·pose /ˈpriːdɪ`spəʊz/ *vt* (*formal*) cause (somebody) to be interested, liable, etc before the event: *His early training ~d him to travel widely.*

pre·dis·posi·tion /ˈpriːdɪspə`zɪʃən/ *n* [C] state of mind or body favourable to: *a ~ to arthritis/to going on safari.*

pre·domi·nance /prɪ`dɒmɪnəns US: -`dɑːmɪ-/ *n* [U] superiority in strength, num-bers, etc; state of being predominant.

pre·domi·nant /prɪ`dɒmɪnənt US: -`dɑːmɪ-/ *adj* (*formal*) having more power, attraction or influence than others: *Her ~ characteristic is her friendliness.*

pre·domi·nant·ly *adv* for the most part: *a ~ly brown-eyed race.*

pre·domi·nate /prɪ`dɒmɪneɪt/ *vi* (*formal*) have control (over); be superior in numbers, strength, influence, etc: *a forest in which oak-trees ~.*

pre·emi·nence /priː`emɪnəns/ *n* [U] being best.

pre·emi·nent /priː`emɪnənt/ *adj* best of all: *~ above all his rivals.*

pre·emi·nent·ly *adv*

pre·empt /priː`empt/ *vt* (*formal*) **1** obtain by pre-emption(a). **2** (*US*) occupy (public land) so as to have the right of pre-emption. **3** take for oneself (and exclude others).

pre·emp·tion /priː`empʃən/ *n* [U] (*formal*) **(a)** purchase by one person, etc before others are offered the chance to buy; right to pur-chase in this way. **(b)** pre-empting(2).

pre·emp·tive /-tɪv/ *adj*

preen /priːn/ *vt* **1** (of a bird) smooth (itself, its feathers) with its beak. **2** (*fig*) (of a per-son) tidy (oneself).

pre·exist /ˈpriːɪg`zɪst/ *vi* exist beforehand; live a life before this life.

pre·exist·ence /-əns/, life of the soul before entering its present body or this world.

pre·fab·ri·cate /priː`fæbrɪkeɪt/ *vt* manufac-ture the parts, e g roofs, walls, of a building for putting together on the site: *~d houses.*

pre·fab·ri·ca·tion /ˈpriːfæbrɪ`keɪʃən/ *n* [U]

pref·ace /`prefɪs/ *n* [C] author's explanatory remarks at the beginning of a book. □ *vt* pro-vide with a preface; begin (a talk, etc, with...): *He ~d his remarks with some sharp knocks on the table.*

prefa·tory /`prefətərɪ US: -tɔrɪ/ *adj*: *after a few prefatory remarks.*

prefect /`priːfekt/ *n* **1** (in some English schools) one of a number of senior pupils given responsibility, e g for keeping order. **2** (in France) title of the chief administrative officer of a department; head of the Paris police.

pre·fer /prɪ`fɜː(r)/ *vt* (-rr-) **1** choose (from several); like better: *Which would you ~ tea or coffee? I ~ walking to cycling.* **2** put forward: *~ charges against a motorist,* i e accuse him of dangerous driving.

pre·fer·able /`prefərəbəl/ *adj* superior: *Your idea is ~ to mine.* (*Note:* not used with *more.*)

pre·fer·ably /-əblɪ/ *adv*

pref·er·ence /`prefərəns/ *n* **1** [C,U] act of preferring: *have a ~ for modern jazz.* **2** [C] that which is preferred: *What are your ~s?* **3** [U] the favouring of one person, country, etc more than another; [C] instance of this.

pref·er·en·tial /ˈprefə`renʃəl/ *adj* of, giv-ing, receiving, preference: *get ~ treatment.*

pre·fix /`priːfɪks/ *n* **1** word or syllable, e g *pre-, co-,* placed in front of a word to add to or change its meaning. **2** word used before a person's name, e g Mr, Dr. □ *vt* /priː`fɪks/ add a prefix to or in front of.

preg·nancy /`pregnənsɪ/ *n* [U] the state of being pregnant (both senses); [C] (*pl* -ies) instance of this.

preg·nant /`pregnənt/ *adj* **1** (of a woman or female animal) having in the uterus offspring in a stage of development before birth. **2** (*fig*) (of words, actions) significant: *words ~ with meaning.*

pre·hen·sile /prɪ`hensaɪl/ *adj* (of a foot or tail, e g a monkey's) able to seize and hold.

pre·his·toric /ˈpriːhɪ`stɒrɪk US: -tɔrɪk/ (also -tori·cal /-kəl/) *adj* of the time before recorded history.

pre·his·tory /priː`hɪstərɪ/ *n* [U]

pre·judge /ˈpriː`dʒʌdʒ/ *vt* make a decision, form an opinion, about a person, cause, action, etc before hearing the evidence, making a proper inquiry, etc.

pre·judge·ment *n* [C,U]

preju·dice /`predʒədɪs/ *n* **1** [U] opinion, like or dislike, formed before one has adequate knowledge or experience; [C] instance of this: *racial ~,* against members of other races. **2** [U] (*legal*) injury that may or does arise from some action or judgement. □ *vt* **1** cause a person to have a prejudice(1). **2** injure or weaken (a person's interests, etc): *He ~d his claim by asking too much.*

preju·di·cial /ˈpredʒʊ`dɪʃəl/ *adj* causing pre-judice or injury.

prel·ate /`prelət/ *n* [C] bishop or other churchman of equal or higher rank.

pre·limi·nary /prɪ`lɪmɪnərɪ US: -nerɪ/ *adj* coming first and preparing for what follows: *a ~ examination; after a few ~ remarks.* □ *n* [C] (*pl* -ries) (usually *pl*) preliminary actions, measures, etc.

prel·ude /ˈpreljud/ n [C] **1** action, event, etc that serves as an introduction to (another). **2** (in music) introductory movement (e g as part of a suite). □ vt serve as, be, a prelude to.

pre·mari·tal /ˌpriˈmærɪtəl/ adj before marriage.

pre·ma·ture /ˈpremətʃə(r) US: ˈprimətʊər/ adj done, happening, doing something, before the right or usual time: ~ birth.
pre·ma·ture·ly adv

pre·medi·tate /priˈmedɪteɪt/ vt consider, plan, (something) in advance: a ~d murder.
pre·medi·ta·tion /priˈmedɪˈteɪʃən/ n [U]

pre·mier /ˈpremɪə(r) US: ˈpri-/ adj first in position, importance, etc. □ n [C] prime minister; head of the government.
ˈpre·mier·ship /-ʃɪp/ n [C]

pre·mière /ˈpremɪeə(r) US: prɪˈmɪər/ n [C] first performance of a play or (ˈfilm-~) first public showing of a cinema film.

prem·ise, prem·iss /ˈpremɪs/ n [C] **1** statement on which reasoning is based. **2** (pl) house or building with its sheds, land, etc: business ~s, the building(s), offices, etc where a business is carried on. **3** (pl) details of property, names of persons, etc in the first part of a legal agreement. □ vt make a statement (that) or a statement of (fact) by way of introduction.

pre·mium /ˈprimɪəm/ n [C] (pl ~s) **1** amount or instalment paid for an insurance policy. **2** reward; bonus: a ~ for good conduct. **3** addition to ordinary charges, rent, etc: He had to pay the agent a ~ before he could rent the house. **4** fee (to be) paid by a pupil to a professional man, e g an accountant or architect, for instruction and training.

pre·mon·ition /ˌpreməˈnɪʃən/ n [C] feeling of uneasiness considered as a warning (of approaching danger, etc): have a ~ of failure.
pre·moni·tory /prɪˈmɒnɪtərɪ US: -tɔrɪ/ adj

pre·natal /priˈneɪtəl/ adj before birth.

pre·oc·cu·pa·tion /priˈɒkjʊˈpeɪʃən/ n [U] state of mind in which something takes up all a person's thoughts; [C] the subject, etc that takes up all his thoughts: His greatest ~ was saving money for a holiday in Europe.

pre·oc·cupy /priˈɒkjʊpaɪ/ vt (pt,pp -ied) take all the attention of a person so that attention is not given to other matters: preoccupied with thoughts of a holiday.

pre·or·dain /ˌpriɔˈdeɪn/ vt determine in advance.

pre·pack·aged /priˈpækɪdʒd/ (also **pre·packed** /priˈpækt/) adj (of products) cut, wrapped, packed, before being supplied to shops.

prep·ara·tion /ˌprepəˈreɪʃən/ n **1** [U] preparing or being prepared: The book is in ~. **2** [C] (usually pl) things done to get ready: ~s for war; make ~s for a voyage. **3** [C] kind of medicine, food, etc specially prepared:

chemical ~s.

pre·para·tory /prɪˈpærətərɪ US: -tɔrɪ/ adj introductory; needed for preparing: ~ measures/training.

pre·pare /prɪˈpeə(r)/ vt,vi **1** prepare (for), get or make ready: ~ a meal; ~ pupils for an examination, teach them; be ~d for anything to happen. **2** be prepared to, be able and willing to: I'm prepared to help you if you want me to.

pre·pay /priˈpeɪ/ vt (pt,pp -paid /-ˈpeɪd/) pay in advance: postage prepaid.

pre·pon·der·ance /prɪˈpɒndərəns/ n [U] greater amount, weight, etc.

pre·pon·der·ant /prɪˈpɒndərənt/ adj (formal) greater in weight, number, strength, etc.
pre·pon·der·ant·ly adv

prep·osi·tion /ˌprepəˈzɪʃən/ n [C] (abbr prep used in this dictionary) word or group of words (e g in, from, to) often placed before a noun or pronoun to show place, direction, source, method, etc.

prep·osi·tional /-ʃənəl/ adj of, containing, a preposition.

prepositional phrase, (a) phrase made up of a group of words, e g in front of, on top of. **(b)** preposition and the noun following it, e g in the night; on the beach.

pre·pos·sess /ˈpriˈpəˈzes/ vt (formal) give (a person) a feeling (about something), or an idea: I was ~ed by his manners, They made a favourable impression upon me.

pre·pos·sess·ing adj attractive; making a good impression: a girl of ~ing appearance.

pre·pos·ses·sion /ˈpriˈpəˈzeʃən/ n [C] favourable feeling experienced in advance.

pre·pos·ter·ous /prɪˈpɒstərəs/ adj completely unreasonable or senseless; ridiculous.
pre·pos·ter·ous·ly adv

pre·re·cord /ˈpriˈkɔd/ vt record, e g a radio or T V programme, in advance on tape or record.

pre·requi·site /ˈpriˈrekwɪzɪt/ n [C], adj (thing) required as a condition for something else: Three passes at 'A' level are a ~ for university entrance.

pre·roga·tive /prɪˈrɒgətɪv/ n [C] special right(s) or privilege(s), esp of a ruler.
the Royal Prerogative, (GB) the (theoretical) right of the sovereign to act independently of Parliament.

Pres·by·ter·ian /ˌprezbɪˈtɪərɪən/ adj (also ~ Church) church governed by elders, all of equal rank. □ n [C] member of this Church.

pres·by·tery /ˈprezbɪtərɪ US: -terɪ/ n [C] (pl -ies) **1** (in a church) eastern part of the chancel beyond the choir; sanctuary. **2** (regional) administrative court of the Presbyterian Church. **3** residence of a Roman Catholic parish priest.

pre·scribe /prɪˈskraɪb/ vt,vi **1** advise or order the use of: ~d textbooks, books which pupils are required to use. **2** say, with authority, what course of action is to be followed: *penalties ~d by the law.*

pre·scrip·tion /prɪˈskrɪpʃən/ n **1** [U] act of prescribing; [C] that which is prescribed. **2** (esp) doctor's written order or direction for the making up and use of a medicine; the medicine itself.

pre·scrip·tive /prɪˈskrɪptɪv/ adj giving orders or directions. ⇨ descriptive.

pres·ence /ˈprezəns/ n [U] **1** being present in a place, etc: *in the ~ of his friends,* with his friends there. *presence of mind,* ⇨ mind ¹(2). **2** person's way of standing, moving, etc: *a man of noble ~.*

pres·ent ¹ /ˈprezənt/ adj **1** being in this/that place: *The Smiths were ~ at the ceremony.* ⇨ absent ¹(1). **2** being discussed or dealt with; now being considered: *the ~ government.* □ n **1** the ~, now; the time now passing: *the past, the ~, and the future.* **at present,** now: *We don't need any more at ~.* **2** (gram) = present tense.

present participle, (gram) verb form used to show the present tense, e g *coming.*

present tense, (gram) tense showing action now, descriptions existing now, etc.

pres·ent ² /ˈprezənt/ n [C] something given for pleasure: *`birthday ~s.*

pre·sent ³ /prɪˈzent/ vt **1** give; offer: *the clock that was ~ed to me when I retired.* **2** introduce (a person, esp to a Sovereign): *be ~ed at Court.* **3** (reflex) appear; attend: *~ oneself for trial/for examination.* **4** show; reveal: *A good opportunity has ~ed itself for doing what you suggested.* **5** (of a theatrical manager or company) produce (a play); cause (an actor) to take part in a play: *The Mermaid Company will ~ 'Hamlet' next week.* **6** introduce a programme on TV or radio.

pre·sent·able /prɪˈzentəbəl/ adj fit to appear, be shown, in public: *Is the girl he wants to marry ~,* the sort of girl he can introduce to his friends and family?

pre·sent·ably /-əblɪ/ adv: *presentably dressed.*

pres·en·ta·tion /ˌprezənˈteɪʃən US: ˈprizən-/ n [U] presenting or being presented; [C] something presented: *the ~ of a new play.*

pre·sen·ti·ment /prɪˈzentɪmənt/ n [C] (formal) vague feeling that something (esp unpleasant or undesirable) is about to happen.

pres·ent·ly /ˈprezəntlɪ/ adv **1** soon: *I'll be with you ~.* **2** (US) at the present time: *The Secretary of State is ~ in Africa.*

pres·er·va·tion /ˌprezəˈveɪʃən/ n [U] **1** act of preserving: *the ~ of food/one's health/wild life.* **2** condition of something preserved: *old paintings in an excellent state of ~.*

pre·serv·ative /prɪˈzɜːvətɪv/ n [C], adj (substance) used for preserving: *free from*

~s.

pre·serve /prɪˈzɜːv/ vt **1** keep safe from harm or danger: *preserving old people from the loneliness of old age.* **2** keep from decay, risk of going bad, etc (by pickling, making into jam, etc): *~ fruit.* **3** keep from loss; retain (health, etc): *~ one's eyesight.* **4** care for and protect land, rivers, lakes, etc with the animals, birds and fish: *The fishing in this stream is strictly ~d.* **5** keep alive (a name or memory): *Few of his early poems are ~d.* □ n [C] **1** (usually pl) jam (the usual word). **2** woods, streams, etc where animals, birds and fish are preserved: *a `game ~.*

pre·serv·able /-əbəl/ adj that can be preserved.

pre·server, person or thing that preserves.

pre·side /prɪˈzaɪd/ vi **preside at,** be chairman, be the head of: *The Prime Minister ~s at meetings of the Cabinet. The city council is ~d over by the mayor.*

presi·dency /ˈprezɪdənsɪ/ n [C] (pl -ies) **1** the ~, the office and functions of president. **2** term of office as a president: *during the ~ of Lincoln.*

presi·dent /ˈprezɪdənt/ n [C] **1** elected head of the government in the US and other modern republics. **2** head of some government departments (*P~ of the Board of Trade*). **3** head of some business companies, colleges, societies, etc.

presi·den·tial /ˌprezɪˈdenʃəl/ adj of a president or his duties: *the ~ial election.*

press ¹ /pres/ n [C] **1** act of pressing: *give something a light ~.* **2** machine or apparatus for pressing: *a `wine-~.* **3** the ~, printed periodicals; the newspapers generally; journalists: *The book was favourably noticed by the ~/had a good ~,* was favourably reviewed by the literary critics. *The liberty/freedom of the ~* (= The right of newspapers to report events, express opinions, etc freely) *is a feature of democratic countries.* **4** business for printing (and sometimes publishing) books or periodicals; (also `printing-~*) machine for printing: *in the ~,* being printed; *go to ~,* start printing. **5** pressure (the usual word): *the ~ of modern life.*

`press conference, one of newspaper reporters, organized by a government official, for a well-known person, etc who talks about policy, achievements, etc.

`press-cutting/-clipping, story, paragraph, article, etc cut out from a newspaper or other periodical.

`press photographer, newspaper photographer.

`press-up, exercise in which one stretches out face down on the floor, the arms being straightened and bent by pressing against the floor with the palms of one's hands to raise and lower one's body.

press ² /pres/ vt,vi **1** push steadily against:

~ *the trigger of a gun;* ~ (*down*) *the accelerator pedal* (of a car); ~ *the button,* e g *of an electric bell.* **2** use force or weight to get something smooth or flat, to get juice out of fruit, etc: ~ *a suit/skirt, etc,* with an iron, to remove creases, etc; ~ *the juice out of an orange.* **3** keep close to and attack: ~ *home an attack,* carry it out with determination. **4** (*fig*) obtain support, agreement, etc using a determined, organized effort: ~ *one's point home in the debate.* **5** make repeated requests: demand urgently: ~ *for an inquiry into a question;* ~ *the Government for support.* **6 be pressed for,** have barely enough of: ~*ed for time/money/space.* **7** push, crowd, with weight or force: *crowds* ~*ing against the barriers.* **8** urge; insist on: ~ *him for an answer.* **9** demand action or attention: *The matter is* ~*ing,* is urgent. **10** squeeze (a person's hand, arm, etc) as a sign of affection or sympathy: *He* ~*ed her to his side.* **11** weigh heavily on: *The new taxes* ~*ed down heavily on the people.* **12** hurry, continue in a determined way: ~ *on with one's work/journey.*

press·ing /ˈpresɪŋ/ *adj* **1** urgent; requiring immediate attention: ~*ing business.* **2** (of persons, their requests, etc) insistent: *as you are so* ~*ing.*

press·ure /ˈpreʃə(r)/ *n* [C,U] **1** pressing; (amount of) force on or against something: *I hope that the tyre* ~ *is right.* ⇨ blood-pressure. **2** force or influence: *He pleaded* ~ *of work and resigned his place on the committee.* **be/come under pressure,** feel/be caused to feel forced (to act): *He's under strong* ~ *to vote with the government on this issue.* **bring pressure to bear on sb (to do sth); put pressure on sb (to do sth),** use force or influence. **3** something that is difficult to bear: *the* ~ *of taxation.*

ˈpressure-cooker, airtight saucepan for cooking quickly with steam under pressure.

ˈpressure group, organized group, e g a union, which tries to use influence for the benefit of its members.

press·ur·ize /ˈpreʃəraɪz/ *vt* **1** maintain normal air-pressure, e g in an aircraft. **2** (*informal*) use pressure(2).

press·ur·ized /ˈpreʃəraɪzd/ *adj* (of an aircraft, a submarine, etc) built so that its internal air-pressure can be controlled and made normal.

pres·tige /preˈstiːʒ/ *n* [U] **1** respect that results from the good reputation (of a person, nation, etc); power or influence coming from this. **2** distinction, glamour, that comes from achievements, success, possessions, etc: (as an *adjective*) *the* ~ *value of living in a fashionable street.*

pres·ti·gious /preˈstɪdʒəs/ *adj* producing respect, influence, etc.

pre·stressed /ˈpriːˈstrest/ *adj* (of concrete) strengthened by being compressed.

pre·sum·able /prɪˈzjuːməbəl *US:* -ˈzuː-/ *adj*

that may be presumed.

pre·sum·ably /-əblɪ/ *adv*

pre·sume /prɪˈzjuːm *US:* -ˈzuːm/ *vt,vi* **1** suppose (to be true): *In Britain an accused man is* ~*d* (*to be*) *innocent until he is proved guilty.* **2** (*formal*) take the liberty: *I won't* ~ *to disturb you.*

pre·sum·ing *adj* having, showing, a tendency to presume, to take an unfair advantage of.

pre·sump·tion /prɪˈzʌmpʃən/ *n* **1** [C] something which seems likely although there is no proof: *on the* ~ *that he was drowned.* **2** [U] arrogance: *What* ~ *to say that he is better than me!*

pre·sump·tive /prɪˈzʌmptɪv/ *adj* based on presumption(1): *the heir* ~, person who is heir (to the throne, etc) until a person with a stronger claim is born.

pre·sump·tu·ous /prɪˈzʌmptʃʊəs/ *adj* (of behaviour, etc) too self-confident.

pre·sump·tu·ous·ly *adv*

pre·sup·pose /ˈpriːsəˈpəʊz/ *vt* **1** assume beforehand. **2** require as a condition: *Sound sleep* ~*s a peaceful mind.*

pre·sup·po·si·tion /ˈpriːsʌpəˈzɪʃən/ *n* [C] something presupposed; [U] presupposing.

pre·tence (*US* also **pre·tense**) /prɪˈtens/ *n* **1** [U] pretending: *under the* ~ *of friendship. It's all* ~. **2** [C] pretext or excuse; false claim or reason: *It is only a* ~ *of friendship.* **false pretences,** (*legal*) acts intended to deceive: *get money by/on/under false* ~*s.*

pre·tend /prɪˈtend/ *vt,vi* **1** make oneself appear (to be doing) something, either in play or to deceive others: ~ *to be asleep. They* ~*ed not to see us.* **2** say falsely that one has (as an excuse or reason, or to avoid danger, difficulty, etc): ~ *sickness.*

pre·ten·der, person who has a claim (to a throne, etc) that not everyone agrees to.

pre·tense /prɪˈtens/ ⇨ pretence.

pre·ten·sion /prɪˈtenʃən/ *n* **1** [C] (often *pl*) (statement of a) claim: *He makes no* ~*s to expert knowledge of the subject.* **2** [U] being pretentious: ~ *is his worst fault.*

pre·ten·tious /prɪˈtenʃəs/ *adj* claiming (without justification) great merit or importance: *a* ~ *student/speech; use* ~ *language.*

pre·ten·tious·ly *adv*

pre·ten·tious·ness *n* [U]

pre·text /ˈpriːtekst/ *n* [C] reason that is not true (*for* an action, etc): *find a* ~ *for refusal/refusing the invitation.*

pretty /ˈprɪtɪ/ *adj* (-ier, -iest) **1** pleasing and attractive without being beautiful or magnificent: *a* ~ *girl/garden/picture/piece of music.* **2** fine; good: *A* ~ *mess you've made of it!* **3** (*informal*) large in amount or extent: *a* ~ *big fine for such a minor offence.* **a** ˈ**pretty kettle of fish,** ⇨ fish [1] (1). **a pretty penny,** ⇨ penny(1). □ *adv* to a certain extent: *The situation seems* ~ *hopeless. It's* ~ *cold outdoors today.* **pretty much,** very nearly: *The result of the ballot is* ~ *much* what we expected. **pretty nearly,** almost: *The car is new, or ~ nearly so.* **pretty well,** almost: *We've ~ well finished the work.* **sitting pretty,** (*informal*) rich; favourably placed for future developments, etc. □ *n* [C] (*pl* -ies) (used of a child): *my ~.*

pret·ti·ly /ˈprɪtɪlɪ/ *adv*

pret·ti·ness *n* [U]

pre·vail /prɪˈveɪl/ *vi* **1** gain victory (over); fight successfully (against): *Truth will ~.* **2** be generally seen, done, etc: *the conditions now ~ing in Africa.* **3** persuade (a person to do): *~ on/upon a friend to lend you £10.*

pre·vail·ing *adj* most frequent or usual: *the ~ing winds/fashions.*

pre·va·lence /ˈprevələns/ *n* [U] being general: *~ of bribery among officials.*

pre·va·lent /ˈprevələnt/ *adj* (*formal*) common, seen or done everywhere (at the time in question): *Is malaria still ~ in that country?*

pre·vari·cate /prɪˈværɪkeɪt/ *vi* (*formal*) make untrue or partly untrue statements; (to avoid telling the (whole) truth).

pre·vari·ca·tion /prɪˌværɪˈkeɪʃən/ *n* [C,U].

pre·vent /prɪˈvent/ *vt* stop or hinder: *Who can ~ us from getting married/~ our getting married?*

pre·vent·able /-əbəl/ *adj* that can be prevented.

pre·ven·tion /prɪˈvenʃən/ *n* [U] act of preventing: *P~ is better than cure.*

pre·ven·tive /prɪˈventɪv/ *adj* serving or designed to prevent.

preventive custody, imprisonment of a person unlikely to be reformed, so that he may not commit further crimes.

preventive detention, detention without trial because a person is thought likely to commit crime or (in some countries) oppose the government.

preventive medicine, research into means of avoiding disease, illness.

pre·view /ˈpriːvjuː/ *n* [C] view of a film, play, etc before it is shown to the general public. □ *vt* have/give a preview of.

pre·vi·ous /ˈpriːvɪəs/ *adj* coming earlier in time or order: *on a ~ occasion.* **previous to,** before.

pre·vi·ous·ly *adv*

prey /preɪ/ *n* (*sing* only) animal, bird, etc hunted for food: *The eagle was devouring its ~.* □ *vi* **1** take, hunt, as prey: *hawks ~ing on small birds.* **2** steal from; plunder: *Our ships were ~ed on/upon by pirates.* **3** (of fears, etc) produce great trouble: *anxieties/ losses that ~ on my mind.*

'beast/bird of 'prey, one that kills and eats others, e g tigers, eagles.

price /praɪs/ *n* **1** [C] sum of money for which something is (to be) sold or bought: *What ~ are you asking?* **put a 'price on sb's head,** offer a reward for his capture (dead or alive). **2** [U] value; worth: *a pearl of great ~.* **3** [C] that which must be done, given or experienced to obtain or keep something:

Loss of independence is a high ~ to pay for peace! □ *vt* fix, ask about, the price; mark (goods) with a price. **price oneself/one's goods out of the market,** (of manufacturers, producers) fix prices so high that sales decline or stop.

'asking price, (for a house, etc) price stated by the seller: *accept £200 below the asking ~.*

'list-price, price recommended by the manufacturer, etc but not always compulsory.

'price-control, control or fixing of prices by authorities, manufacturers, etc.

price·less *adj* too valuable to be priced: *~less paintings.*

pricey /ˈpraɪsɪ/ *adj* (*informal*) expensive.

prick¹ /prɪk/ *n* [C] **1** small mark or hole caused by the act of pricking: *~s made by a needle.* **2** pain caused by pricking: *I can still feel the ~.* **a prick of conscience,** mental uneasiness.

'pin-prick, (*fig*) something small that irritates.

prick² /prɪk/ *vt,vi* **1** make a hole or a mark in (something) with a sharp point: *~ a blister, on the skin.* **2** hurt, cause pain to, with a sharp point or points: *~ one's finger with/on a needle.* **3** feel sharp pain: *My fingers ~.* **4** **prick sth out/off,** put (seedlings) in the earth (in holes made with a pointed stick, etc). **5** (*fig*) cause uneasy feeling: *His conscience ~ed him.* **6** **prick up one's ears,** (a) (of dogs, horses) raise the ears. (b) (*fig*) (of persons) pay sharp attention.

prickle /ˈprɪkəl/ *n* [C] pointed growth on the stem, etc of a plant, or on the skin of some animals, e g hedgehogs. □ *vt,vi* give or have a pricking sensation.

prick·ly /ˈprɪklɪ/ *adj* (a) having prickles. (b) (*informal*) easily irritated or annoyed: *you're a bit ~ today!*

prickly heat, inflammation of the sweat glands, marked by a prickling sensation, common in the tropics during the hot-weather season.

prickly pear, cactus covered with prickles and having pear-shaped fruit.

pride /praɪd/ *n* **1** [U] feeling of satisfaction arising from what one has done, or from persons, things, etc one is concerned with: *look with ~ at one's garden.* **take a great/no/ little pride in,** have some/much/no/little pride about: *take (a) great ~ in one's achievements.* **pride of place,** a position of superiority. **2** [U] self-respect: knowledge of one's worth and character: *Don't say anything that may wound his ~.* **3** [U] object of pride(1): *a girl who is her mother's ~ and joy.* **4** [U] too high an opinion of oneself, one's position, possessions, etc: *be puffed up with ~.* **Pride comes/goes before a fall,** (*proverb*) such a high opinion comes before a personal disaster (and may cause it). **5** (*sing* with *the*) prime: *in the full ~ of youth.* **6** [C] group: (esp) *a ~ of lions/*

peacocks. □ *vt* (*reflex*) be pleased and satisfied about: *He ~s himself on his skill as a pianist.*

priest /priːst/ *n* [C] **1** clergyman of a Christian Church, esp one who is between a deacon and a bishop in the Church of England or Roman Catholic Church. (*Note:* clergyman is usual in the Church of England, except in official use.) ⇨ minister for Methodist, Baptist, etc Churches. **2** (of non-Christian religions) person trained to perform special acts of religion, give advice, etc.

priest·ess /priˈstes *US:* ˈpriːstɪs/, woman priest(2).

`priest·hood /-hʊd/, the whole body of priests of a Church: *the Irish ~hood.*

priest·ly, `priest·like *adj* of, for or like a priest.

prig /prɪg/ *n* [C] (*dated*) smug, self-satisfied, proud person.

prim /prɪm/ *adj* (-mer, -mest) neat; formal: *a ~ garden;* (of persons, their manner, speech, etc) showing a dislike of, anything rough, rude, improper: *a very ~ and proper old lady.*
prim·ly *adv*
prim·ness *n* [U]

prima /priːmə/ *adj* (*It*) first.
`prima `balle`rina leading woman performer in ballet.
`prima `donna /ˈdɒnə/, (**a**) leading woman singer in opera. (**b**) (*informal*) tempramental and conceited person.

pri·macy /ˈpraɪməsɪ/ *n* [U] (esp) position of an archbishop.

pri·mae·val /praɪˈmiːvəl/ *adj* ⇨ primeval.

prima facie /ˌpraɪmə ˈfeɪʃɪ/ *adv, adj* (*Latin*) (based) on the first impression: *have ~ a good case.*
prima facie evidence, (*legal*) sufficient to prove something (unless proved wrong).

pri·mal /ˈpraɪməl/ *adj* (*formal*) **1** primeval. **2** first in importance.

pri·mar·ily /ˈpraɪmərəlɪ *US:* praɪˈmerəlɪ/ *adv* in the first place; above all.

pri·mary /ˈpraɪmərɪ *US:* -merɪ/ *adj* leading in time, order or development: *of ~* (= chief) *importance; a `~ school,* (*GB*) for young pupils (5 to 11 years). □ *n* [C] (*pl* -ies) (*US*) meeting of electors to name candidates for a coming election.
primary colours, red, blue or yellow, from which all other colours can be obtained by mixing two or more.
primary stress, (marked ` in this dictionary) strongest stress(3) used in a word.

pri·mate¹ /ˈpraɪmeɪt/ *n* [C] archbishop.

pri·mate² /ˈpraɪmeɪt/ *n* [C] one of the highest order of mammals (including men, apes, monkeys and lemurs).

prime¹ /praɪm/ *adj* **1** chief; most important: *his ~ motive.* **2** excellent; first-rate: *~ (cuts of) beef.* **3** fundamental; primary.
the `Prime `Minister, head of the British Government.

prime number, one which cannot be divided exactly except by itself and the number 1 (*eg* 7, 17, 41).

prime² /praɪm/ *n* **1** [U] state of highest perfection; the best part: *in the ~ of life.* **2** [U] first or earliest part: *the ~ of the year,* spring.

prime³ /praɪm/ *vt* **1** get ready for use or action: *~ a gun,* (the old-fashioned kind) put in gunpowder, etc. **2** supply with facts, etc: *The witness had been ~d by a lawyer.* **3** (*informal*) fill (a person) with (esp) alcoholic drink. **4** cover (a surface) with the first coat of paint, oil, varnish, etc.

primer /ˈpraɪmə(r)/ *n* [C] **1** small quantity of explosive, contained in a cap or cylinder, for igniting the powder in a cartridge, bomb, etc. **2** special paint for priming(4).

pri·meval (also **-mae·val**) /praɪˈmiːvəl/ *adj* **1** of the earliest time in the world's history. **2** very ancient: *~ forests.*

prim·ing /ˈpraɪmɪŋ/ *n* [U] **1** gunpowder used to fire the charge of a gun, bomb, mine, etc. **2** mixture used by painters for a first coat.

primi·tive /ˈprɪmətɪv/ *adj* **1** of the earliest times; of an early stage of social development: *~ man; ~ culture.* **2** simple; old-fashioned; having undergone little development: *~ weapons,* eg bows and arrows, spears. □ *n* [C] primitive man.
primi·tive·ly *adv*
primi·tive·ness *n* [U]

pri·mor·dial /praɪˈmɔːdɪəl/ *adj* in existence at or from the beginning: *~ forests.*

prim·rose /ˈprɪmrəʊz/ *n* [C] common wild plant with pale yellow flowers; the flower; [U] its colour. □ *adj* pale-yellow.

prim·ula /ˈprɪmjʊlə/ *n* [C] (*pl ~s*) kinds of perennial herbaceous plants with flowers of various colours and sizes (including the primrose and polyanthus).

prince /prɪns/ *n* [C] **1** ruler, esp of a small state. **2** male member of a royal family, esp (in GB) a son or grandson of the Sovereign.
`Prince `Consort, husband of a reigning queen.
`prince·dom /-dəm/ *n* [C] rank or dignity of, area ruled by, a prince(1).
prince·ly *adj* (-ier, -iest) (worthy) of a prince; splendid; generous: *a ~ly gift.*

prin·cess /prɪnˈses/ *n* [C] wife of a prince; daughter or granddaughter of a sovereign.

prin·ci·pal /ˈprɪnsəpəl/ *adj* highest in order of importance: *the ~ rivers of Europe.* □ *n* [C] **1** title of some heads of colleges and of some other organizations. **2** person for whom another acts as agent in business: *I must consult my ~.* **3** money lent, put into a business, etc on which interest is payable. **4** (*legal*) person directly responsible for a crime.
prin·ci·pally /-plɪ/ *adv* for the most part; chiefly.

prin·ci·pal·ity /ˈprɪnsəˈpælətɪ/ *n* [C] (*pl* -ies) country ruled by a prince.

prin·ciple /ˈprɪnsəpəl/ *n* [C] **1** basic truth; general law of cause and effect: *the* (*first*) ~*s of geometry.* **2** guiding rule for behaviour: *moral* ~*s.* **in principle,** (contrasted with **in detail**) in general. **on principle,** from a moral motive: *He refuses on* ~ *to avoid paying taxes.* **3** general law shown in the working of a machine, etc: *These machines work on the same* ~.

-prin·cipled *suffix* following, having, the kind of principle(2) shown: *a high-~d woman,* very moral.

print[1] /prɪnt/ *n* **1** [U] mark(s), letters, etc in printed form. **in print,** (of a book) on sale. **out of print,** all copies sold, no longer available. **2** [C] mark left on a surface preserving the shape, pattern, left by the pressure of something: ˈfinger-~s; ˈfoot-~s.* **3** [C] picture, design, etc made by printing on paper, etc: *old Japanese* ~*s.* **4** photograph printed from a negative. ⇨ blueprint.

print[2] /prɪnt/ *vt, vi* **1** make marks on (paper), etc by pressing it with inked type, etc; make books/pictures, etc in this way; (of a publisher, an editor, an author) cause to be printed: ~ *6 000 copies of a novel.* **2** shape (one's letters), write (words), like printed characters (instead of ordinary handwriting). **3** make (a photograph) from a negative film or plate: *How many copies shall I* ~ (*off*) *for you?* **4** (of a plate or film) be produced as the result of printing(3): *This film/plate/picture hasn't* ~*ed very well.* **5** mark (a textile fabric) with a coloured design. **6** (*fig*) make an impression: *The accident* ~*ed itself on her memory.*

ˈprint-out, printed output of a computer.

ˈprint·able /-əbəl/ *adj* that can be printed, suitable to be printed.

printer, workman who prints books, etc; (owner of a) printing business.

prior[1] /ˈpraɪə(r)/ *adj* earlier in time, order or importance: *have a* ~ *claim* (*to the money*). **prior to,** *prep* before: *The house was sold* ~ *to auction,* before the day of the auction.

prior[2] /ˈpraɪə(r)/ *n* [C] head of a religious order or house; (in an abbey) next below an abbot.

prioress /ˈpraɪərəs/ *n* [C] woman prior.

pri·or·ity /praɪˈɒrətɪ US: -ˈɔːr-/ *n* (*pl* -ies) **1** [U] right to have or do something before others: *I have* ~ *over you in my claim.* **2** [C] high place among competing claims: *Road building is a first/top* ~.

priory /ˈpraɪərɪ/ *n* [C] (*pl* -ies) religious house governed by a prior or prioress.

prise /praɪz/ *vt* = prize[2].

prism /ˈprɪzm/ *n* [C] **1** solid figure with similar, equal and parallel ends, and with sides which are parallelograms. **2** solid of this form, usually triangular and made of glass, which breaks up white light into the colours of the rainbow.

pris·matic /prɪzˈmætɪk/ *adj* **1** like, having the shape of, a prism. **2** (of colours) brilliant and varied.

prison /ˈprɪzən/ *n* [C] **1** building in which a person who commits a crime is kept locked up. **2** place where a person is shut up against his will. **3** [U] confinement in such a place: *escape/be released from* ~.

pris·oner, (a) person kept in prison for crime or until tried in a law court. **(b)** person, animal, kept in confinement: *political* ~*s.*

priv·acy /ˈprɪvəsɪ US: ˈpraɪv-/ *n* [U] **1** state of being away from others, alone and undisturbed: *I don't want my* ~ *disturbed.* **2** secrecy (opposite to *publicity*): *They were married in strict* ~.

pri·vate /ˈpraɪvɪt/ *adj* **1** (opposite of *public*) of, for the use of, concerning, one person or group of persons, not people in general: *a* ~ *letter; for* ~ *reasons,* not to be explained to everybody; ~ *means,* income not earned as a salary, etc but coming from personal property, investments, etc. **2** secret; kept secret: *have* ~ *information about it.* **3** having no official position; not holding any public office: *do sth in one's* ~ *capacity,* not as an official, etc. **4** (of a soldier) without rank: *P~ Dodd.* □ *n* **1** [C] private soldier. **2** **in private,** not in public.

ˈprivate acˈcount, bank account opened by and drawn on by one person: *My wife and I have a joint account, and in addition we each have a* ~ *account.*

ˈprivate ˈenterprise, the management of industry, etc by private individuals, companies, etc (contrasted with State ownership or control).

private member, (of the House of Commons) not a member with a position in the Government.

private parts, external sex organs.

private school, one at which fees are paid (contrasted with a State school).

pri·vate·ly *adv*

pri·va·tion /praɪˈveɪʃən/ *n* (*formal*) **1** [C,U,] lack of the necessities of life; destitution: *fall ill through* ~; *suffering many* ~*s.* **2** [C] state of being deprived of something: *He found it a great* ~ *not being allowed to smoke in prison.*

privet /ˈprɪvɪt/ *n* [U] evergreen shrub used for garden hedges.

pri·vi·lege /ˈprɪvəlɪdʒ/ *n* **1** [C] right or advantage available only to a person, class or rank, or the holder of a certain position, etc: *the* ~*s of birth,* e g that come because one is born into a wealthy family. **2** [C] special favour or benefit: *It was a* ~ *to hear her sing.* **3** [C,U] right to do or say things without risk of punishment, etc (as when Members of Parliament may say things in the House which might result in a libel case if said outside Parliament).

privi·leged *adj* having, granted, a privilege.

priv·y /ˈprɪvɪ/ adj (old use or legal) secret; private. **privy to,** having secret knowledge of: ~ to the plot against the President.

the 'Privy `Council, committee of persons appointed by the Sovereign, advising on some State affairs, but membership now being chiefly a personal dignity.

'Privy `Councillor/`Counsellor, member of the Privy Council.

prize[1] /praɪz/ n [C] **1** something (to be) awarded to one who succeeds in a competition, etc: win first ~. **2** (fig) anything struggled for or worth struggling for: the ~s of life. □ vt value highly: my most ~d possessions.

prize[2] (also **prise**) /praɪz/ vt use force to get something, e g a box, lid, open/up/off.

pro /prəʊ/ n [C] (pl ~s) (informal) (short for) professional (player): a `tennis ~.

pro- /ˈprəʊ/ prefix **1** supporting; in favour of: pro-Chinese. **2** acting for: pro-vice-chancellor.

the pros and cons, the arguments for and against.

prob·abil·ity /ˌprɒbəˈbɪlətɪ/ n (pl -ies) **1** [U] quality of being probable. **In all probability,** most probably. **2** [U] likelihood: There is not much ~ of his succeeding. **3** [C] (most) probable event or outcome: What are the probabilities?

prob·able /ˈprɒbəbəl/ adj likely to happen or to prove true or correct: the ~ result; a ~ winner. □ n [C] person who will most likely be chosen, e g for a team.

prob·ably /-əblɪ/ adj

pro·bate /ˈprəʊbeɪt/ n (legal) **1** [U] the official process of proving the validity of a will: take out/grant ~ of a will. **2** [C] copy of a will with a certificate showing that it is correct. □ vt (US) establish the validity of a will (GB = prove).

pro·ba·tion /prəˈbeɪʃən US: prəʊ-/ n [U] **1** testing of a person's conduct, abilities, qualities, etc before he is finally accepted for a position, admitted into a society, etc: an officer on ~. **2** system by which (esp young) offenders are allowed to go unpunished for their first offence while they continue to live without further breaking of the law: on three years' ~.

pro`bation officer, official who watches over the behaviour of offenders who are on probation.

probationer, (a) hospital nurse receiving training and still on probation(1). (b) offender who is on probation(2).

probe /prəʊb/ n [C] **1** slender instrument with a blunt end, used by doctors for learning about the depth and direction of a wound, etc. **2** (journalism) investigation (into a scandal, etc). **3** object used to investigate an unknown area: a `space-~ to the moon. □ vt **1** examine with a probe. **2** investigate or examine thoroughly (e g the causes of something).

prob·lem /ˈprɒbləm/ n [C] question to be solved or decided, esp something difficult: mathematical ~s.

prob·lem·atic /ˌprɒbləˈmætɪk/ adj (esp of a result) doubtful; that cannot be foreseen.

prob·lem·ati·cally /-klɪ/ adv

pro·bos·cis /prəˈbɒsɪs/ n [C] (pl ~es) **1** elephant's trunk. **2** long part of the mouth of some insects.

pro·cedure /prəˈsiːdʒə(r)/ n [C,U] (the regular) order of doing things, esp legal and political: the usual ~ at committee meetings.

pro·cedural /prəˈsiːdʒərəl/ adj

pro·ceed /prəˈsiːd/ vi **1** go forward; continue, go on: Let us ~ to business/to the next item on the agenda. **2** come, arise (from): famine, plague and other evils ~ing from war. **3** take legal action (against).

pro·ceed·ing /prəˈsiːdɪŋ/ n **1** [U] course of action; (way of) behaving: What is our best way of ~? **2** [C] something done: There have been suspicious ~s in committee meetings. **3** (pl) legal action (against): start legal ~s against a person. **4** (pl) records (of the activities of a society, etc): the P~s of the Archaeological Society.

pro·ceeds /ˈprəʊsiːdz/ n pl financial results, profits, of an undertaking: All the ~ go to Oxfam.

pro·cess[1] /ˈprəʊses US: ˈprɒses/ n **1** [C] connected series of actions, changes, etc esp such as are involuntary or unconscious: the ~es of digestion, reproduction and growth. **2** [C] series of operations deliberately undertaken: Unloading the cargo was a slow ~. **3** [C] method, esp one used in manufacture or industry: the ~ of melting iron. **4** [U] forward movement; progress: a building in ~ of construction. **5** [C] (legal) action at law; formal start of this. □ vt **1** treat (material, food) in order to preserve it: ~ leather; ~ed cheese. **2** (photo): ~ film, develop it, etc. **3** (computers): ~ tape/information, put it through the system in order to obtain the information.

pro·cess[2] /prəˈses/ vi walk in or as if in procession.

pro·ces·sion /prəˈseʃən/ n **1** [C] number of persons, vehicles, etc moving forward and following each other in an orderly way: a `funeral ~. **2** [U] act of moving forward in this way: walking in ~ through the streets.

pro·ces·sional /-nəl/ adj of, for, used in, processions: ~al music.

pro·claim /prəˈkleɪm/ vt **1** make known publicly or officially; declare: ~ war/peace; ~ a man (to be) a traitor/that he is a traitor. **2** show (the usual word): His accent ~ed that he was a Scot.

proc·la·ma·tion /ˌprɒkləˈmeɪʃən/ n **1** [U] proclaiming: by public ~. **2** [C] that which is proclaimed: issue/make a ~.

pro·con·sul /ˈprəʊkɒnsəl/ n [C] (modern use) governor of a colony or dominion.

pro·con·su·lar /ˈprəʊˈkɒnsjʊlə(r) US: -səl-/ adj

pro·con·su·late /-lət/ n [C] position of a proconsul; his term of office.

pro·cras·ti·nate /prəʊˈkræstɪneɪt/ vi (formal) delay action: He ~d until it was too late.

pro·cras·ti·na·tion /prəʊˈkræstɪˈneɪʃən/ n [U]

pro·create /ˈprəʊkrɪeɪt/ vt (formal) give birth to.

pro·cre·ation /ˈprəʊkrɪˈeɪʃən/ n [C,U]

pro·cure /prəˈkjʊə/ vt (formal) 1 obtain, esp with care or effort: ~ an abortion. 2 (old use) bring about; cause: ~ his death by poison.

prod /prɒd/ vt, vi (-dd-) 1 push or poke with something pointed: ~ding (at) the bear through the bars of the cage. 2 (fig) urge an action: I was always ~ding her to see her doctor. □ n [C] prodding action: She gave him a ~ with her umbrella.

prodi·gal /ˈprɒdɪgəl/ adj (formal) spending or using too much: a ~ administration, spending public funds too freely.

pro·di·gious /prəˈdɪdʒəs/ adj enormous; surprisingly great; wonderful: a ~ sum of money.

pro·di·gious·ly adv

prod·igy /ˈprɒdɪdʒɪ/ n [C] (pl -ies) something wonderful because it seems to be contrary to the laws of nature; person who has unusual or remarkable abilities or who is a remarkable example of something.

pro·duce¹ /ˈprɒdjus US: -dus/ n [U] that which is procued, esp by farming: garden/ farm/agricultural ~.

pro·duce² /prəˈdjus US: -ˈdus/ vt, vi 1 put or bring forward to be looked at or examined: ~ one's railway ticket when asked to do so. 2 manufacture; make; grow; create: We must ~ more food and import less. 3 give birth to; lay (eggs). 4 cause; bring about: success ~d by hard work and enthusiasm; a film that ~d a sensation. 5 organize (a play, film) for the stage, TV, etc.

pro·ducer /prəˈdjusə(r) US: -ˈdu-/ n [C] 1 person who manufactures goods (contrasted with the consumer). 2 person responsible for presenting a play in the theatre or for the production of a film or a radio or TV programme ⇨ director.

prod·uct /ˈprɒdʌkt/ n [C] 1 thing produced (by nature or by man): metal ~s from Germany. 2 result; outcome: The plan was the ~ of many hours of careful thought. 3 (maths) quantity obtained by multiplication. 4 (chem) substance obtained by chemical reaction.

pro·duc·tion /prəˈdʌkʃən/ n 1 [U] process of producing: the ~ of crops/manufactured goods, etc. ⇨ mass production. 2 [U] quantity produced: a fall/increase in ~. 3 [C] thing produced: his early ~s as a writer, his first novels, plays, etc.

pro·duc·tive /prəˈdʌktɪv/ adj 1 able to produce; fertile: ~ land. 2 resulting in: ~ of happiness. 3 producing things economic ally: ~ methods.

pro·duc·tive·ly adv

pro·duc·tiv·ity /ˈprɒdʌkˈtɪvətɪ/ n [U] being productive; power of being productive: a ~ bonus for workers.

'produc·tivity agreement, (as part of a wage settlement) better pay and conditions for an increased output.

pro·fane /prəˈfeɪn US: prəʊ-/ adj 1 (formal) (contrasted with sacred, holy) worldly: ~ literature. 2 having or showing contempt for God and sacred things: ~ language. □ vt treat (sacred or holy places, things) with contempt, without proper reverence: ~ the name of God.

pro·fane·ly adv

pro·fan·ity /prəˈfænɪtɪ US: prəʊ-/ n (pl -ies) 1 [U] use of profane conduct, speech or language. 2 (pl) profane language.

pro·fess /prəˈfes/ vt, vi 1 declare that one has (beliefs, likes, ignorance, interests, etc): He ~ed a great interest in my welfare. 2 declare one's faith in (a religion, Christ): ~ Islam. 3 claim; represent oneself: I don't ~ to be an expert on that subject.

pro·fessed adj (a) self-confessed: a ~ed Christian. (b) having taken religious vows: a ~ed nun.

pro·fes·sion /prəˈfeʃən/ n [C] 1 occupation, esp one needing advanced education and special training, e g the law, teaching, medicine. 2 statement or declaration (of belief, feeling, etc): ~s of faith/loyalty.

pro·fes·sional /prəˈfeʃənəl/ adj 1 of a profession(1): ~ skill; ~ men, e g doctors, lawyers. 2 doing or practising something for payment or to make a living: ~ football. ⇨ amateur. □ n [C] 1 (abbr = pro) person who teaches or engages in some kind of sport for money. 2 person who does something for payment that others do (without payment) for pleasure: ~ musicians. turn professional, become a professional.

pro·fes·sion·ally /-nəlɪ/ adv

pro·fes·sion·al·ism /-ɪzm/ n [U] (a) high standard of a profession(1). (b) the practice of employing professionals (2) to play games.

pro·fes·sor /prəˈfesə(r)/ n [C] university teacher at the highest level, holding a chair of some branch of learning; (US also) teacher or instructor.

prof·es·sor·ial /ˈprɒfɪˈsɔrɪəl/ adj

pro·fes·sor·ship /-ʃɪp/ n [C] professor's post.

prof·fer /ˈprɒfə(r)/ vt (formal) offer.

pro·fi·ciency /prəˈfɪʃnsɪ/ n [U] being skilled: a certificate of ~ in English.

pro·fi·cient /prəˈfɪʃnt/ adj skilled: ~ in using a calculator.

pro·fi·cient·ly adv

pro·file /ˈprəʊfaɪl/ n 1 side view, esp of the

head. **2** edge or outline of something seen against a background. **3** brief biography, as given in a periodical or on TV. □ *vt* draw, show, in profile.

profit[1] /ˈprɒfɪt/ *n* **1** [U] advantage or good obtained from something: *gain ~ from one's studies.* **2** [C,U] money gained in business, etc: *sell a bike at a ~; gross/net ~.*
ˈprofit-margin, difference between the cost of purchase or production and the selling price.
ˈprofit-sharing, the sharing of profits between employers and employees.
ˈprofit-less *adj*

profit[2] /ˈprɒfɪt/ *vt,vi* (of persons) gain or be helped: *I have ~ed by your advice.*

prof-it-able /ˈprɒfɪtəbəl/ *adj* **1** bringing profit: *~ investments.* **2** (*fig*) useful: *a deal that was ~ to all of us.*
ˈprof-it-ably /-əblɪ/ *adv*

profi-teer /ˌprɒfɪˈtɪə(r)/ *vi* make large profits, esp by taking advantage in times of difficulty, e g in war. □ *n* [C] person who does this.

prof-li-gate /ˈprɒflɪɡət/ *adj* (*formal*) **1** (of a person, his behaviour) shamelessly immoral. **2** (of the spending of money) very extravagant: *~ of one's inheritance.* □ *n* [C] such a person.

pro-found /prəˈfaʊnd/ *adj* **1** (*formal*) deep: *a ~ sleep.* **2** needing, showing, having, great knowledge: *a man of ~ learning.* **3** needing much thought to understand: *~ mysteries.*
pro-found-ly *adv* deeply: *~ly grateful.*

pro-fun-dity /prəˈfʌndətɪ/ *n* (*formal*) [U] depth: *the ~ of his knowledge.*

pro-fuse /prəˈfjuːs/ *adj* (*formal*) **1** very plentiful: *~ gratitude.* **2** extravagant: *He was ~ in his apologies,* apologized almost too much.
pro-fuse-ly *adv*

pro-fu-sion /prəˈfjuːʒən/ *n* [U] (*formal*) great supply: *flowers in ~.*

pro-geni-tor /prəʊˈdʒenɪtə(r)/ *n* [C] (*formal*) = ancestor.

progeny /ˈprɒdʒɪnɪ/ *n* (*collective sing*) (*formal*) offspring; descendants.

prog-no-sis /prɒɡˈnəʊsɪs/ *n* [C] (*pl ~es*) (*med*) forecast of the probable course of a disease or illness. ⇨ **diagnosis.**

prog-nos-tic /prɒɡˈnɒstɪk/ *adj* (*formal*) predictive (*of*). □ *n* [C] indication (*of*): *a ~ of failure.*

prog-nos-ti-cate /prɒɡˈnɒstɪkeɪt/ *vt* (*formal*) predict: *~ trouble.*

prog-nos-ti-ca-tion /ˌprɒɡnɒstɪˈkeɪʃən/ *n* [C,U]

pro-gramme (also and *US* **-gram**) /ˈprəʊɡræm/ *n* [C] **1** list of items, events, etc, e g for a concert, for radio or TV or for a sports meeting; list of names of singers at a pop concert, actors in a play, etc. **2** plan of what is to be done: *a political ~. What's the ~ for tomorrow?* What are we/you going to

do? **3** coded collection of information, data, etc fed into a computer. □ *vt* make a programme of or for; plan.
pro-gram-mer, person who prepares a computer programme.

prog-ress[1] /ˈprəʊɡres *US*: ˈprɒɡ-/ *n* **1** [U] forward movement; improvement; development: *making fast ~.* **In progress,** being made, done. **make good progress,** (a) (of health) improve satisfactorily. (b) (of a task) do it well.

pro-gress[2] /prəˈɡres/ make progress: *The work is ~ing steadily. She is ~ing in her studies.*

pro-gres-sion /prəˈɡreʃən/ *n* [U] moving forward; improvement.

pro-gres-sive /prəˈɡresɪv/ *adj* **1** making continuous forward movement. **2** increasing by regular amounts: *~ taxation.* **3** improving; supporting or favouring improvement, modernization: *a ~ political party.* □ *n* [C] person supporting a progressive (political) policy.
pro-gres-sive-ly *adv*

pro-hibit /prəˈhɪbɪt *US*: prəʊ-/ *vt* say that something must not be done, that somebody must not do something: *Smoking is strictly ~ed in libraries.*

pro-hi-bi-tion /ˌprəʊɪˈbɪʃən/ *n* **1** [U] prohibiting. **2** [C] law or order that forbids: *a ~ against smoking.*

pro-hibi-tive /prəˈhɪbətɪv *US*: prəʊ-/ *adj* **1** intended to prevent use or abuse: *laws to stop racialism.* **2** (*informal*) have the effect of prohibiting: *~ prices.*

pro-ject[1] /ˈprɒdʒekt/ *n* [C] (plan for a) scheme or undertaking: *a ~ to study community welfare.*

pro-ject[2] /prəˈdʒekt/ *vt,vi* **1** make plans for: *~ a new dam/waterworks.* **2** cause a shadow, an outline, a picture from a film, slide, etc to fall on a surface, etc: *~ a beam of light on to a wall.* **3** say a person has feelings (usually unpleasant ones such as guilt, inferiority) that one has oneself: *She always ~s her own bad temper onto her colleagues.* **4** make known the characteristics of: *Does the BBC World Service adequately ~ Great Britain,* give listeners right ideas about British life, etc? **5** throw; send: *to ~ missiles into space.* **6** draw (a solid thing) on a plane surface using straight lines through every point of it from a centre; make (a map) in this way. **7** stand out beyond the surface nearby: *a balcony that ~s over the street.*

pro-jec-tile /prəˈdʒektaɪl *US*: -təl/ *n* [C] something (to be) sent forward, esp from a gun or launching-pad.

pro-jec-tion /prəˈdʒekʃən/ *n* [C] the act of projecting (all senses); [C] something that projects or has been projected.
pro-jection room, (in a cinema) room from which pictures are projected on to the screen.

pro-jec-tion-ist /-ɪst/, person who, in a

cinema, projects the films on to the screen.

pro·jec·tor /prə`dʒektə(r)/ *n* [C] apparatus for projecting pictures by rays of light on to a screen: *a `cinema/`slide ~*.

pro·let·ar·iat /ˌprəʊlɪ`teərɪət/ *n* [C] (*modern use*) the wage-earners contrasted with the owners of industry and capital (the bourgeoisie).

pro·let·ar·ian /-ɪən/ *n* [C], *adj* (member) of the proletariat.

pro·lif·er·ate /prə`lɪfəreɪt US: prəʊ-/ *vi,vt* (*formal*) **1** reproduce, by rapid multiplication of cells, new parts, etc. **2** (*fig*) reproduce; exist in large numbers: *guerillas proliferating in the hills.*

pro·lif·er·ation /prəˌlɪfə`reɪʃən US: prəʊ-/ *n* [U]

pro·lific /prə`lɪfɪk/ *adj* (*formal*) producing much or many: *a ~ author.*

pro·logue /`prəʊlɒg US: -lɔg/ *n* [C] **1** introductory (part of a) poem: *the 'P~' to the 'Canterbury Tales'.* **2** (*fig*) first of a series of events.

pro·long /prə`lɒŋ US: -`lɔŋ/ *vt* make longer: *~ a visit.*

pro·longed *adj* continuing for a long time: *a ~ed discussion.*

pro·lon·ga·tion /ˌprəʊlɒŋ`geɪʃən US: -lɔŋ-/ *n* [C,U]

prom·en·ade /ˌprɒmə`nɑːd US: -`neɪd/ *n* [C] **1** (place suitable for, made for, a) walk or ride taken in public, for exercise or pleasure, esp along the water-front at a seaside resort. **2** (*US*) formal dance or ball (for a class in a high-school or college). □ *vi,vt* go, take, up and down a promenade.

promi·nence /`prɒmɪnəns/ *n* **1** [U] the state of being prominent. **2** [C] prominent(1) part or place: *a ~ in the middle of a plain.*

promi·nent /`prɒmɪnənt/ *adj* **1** standing out; easily seen: *~ cheek-bones; the most ~ feature in the landscape.* **2** (of persons) distinguished: *~ politicians.* **3** important: *play a ~ part in public life.*

promi·nent·ly *adv*

prom·is·cu·ity /ˌprɒmɪ`skjuːətɪ/ *n* [U] (state of) being promiscuous.

pro·mis·cu·ous /prə`mɪskjʊəs/ *adj* (esp) indiscriminate; casual (esp in sexual relationships): *~ teenagers.*

pro·mis·cu·ous·ly *adv*

prom·ise¹ /`prɒmɪs/ *n* **1** [C] written or spoken undertaking to do, or not to do, give, something, etc: *make/give/keep/carry out/break a ~.* **2** [C] that which one undertakes to do, etc: *It was a ~ so I'm doing it.* **3** [U] (something that gives) hope of success or good results: *a writer who shows much ~, seems likely to succeed.*

prom·ise² /`prɒmɪs/ *vt,vi* **1** make a promise(1) to: *He ~d (me) to be here/that he would be here at 6 o'clock.* **2** give cause for expecting: *The clouds ~ rain.*

prom·is·ing *adj* likely to succeed, have good results etc.

prom·on·tory /`prɒməntrɪ US: -tɔrɪ/ *n* [C] (*pl* -ies) high point of land standing out from the coastline.

pro·mote /prə`məʊt/ *vt* **1** give (a person) higher position or rank: *He was ~d sergeant/to sergeant/to the rank of sergeant.* **2** help to organize and start; help the progress of: *try to ~ good feelings (between...).*

pro·mo·ter, (esp) person who supports with money, etc new trading companies, professional sports, etc.

pro·mo·tion /prə`məʊʃən/ *n* **1** [U] promoting or being promoted; *He has got/gained ~.* **2** [C] instance of promoting or being promoted: *He resigned because ~s were few.* **3** advertising using publicity, etc: *sales ~,* advertising, publicizing one's products.

prompt¹ /prɒmpt/ *adj* acting, done, sent, given, without delay: *a ~ reply; at 6 pm ~*

prompt·ly *adv*

prompt·ness *n* [U]

prompt² /prɒmpt/ *vt* **1** be the reason causing (a person to do something): *He was ~ed by patriotism.* **2** follow the text of a play and tell (an actor) what to say if he forgets. □ *n* [C] action of prompting(2).

promp·ter, person who prompts actors.

prom·ul·gate /`prɒməlgeɪt/ *vt* (*formal*) **1** make public, announce officially (a decree, a new law, etc). **2** make known beliefs, knowledge.

prom·ul·ga·tion /ˌprɒməl`geɪʃən/ *n* [U]

prone /prəʊn/ *adj* **1** (stretched out, lying) face downwards: *in a ~ position.* **2** prone to, have a tendency: *~ to accidents* (and other generally undesirable things). *Some people seem to be `accident ~.*

prong /prɒŋ US: prɔŋ/ *n* [C] (something like) one of the long, pointed parts of a fork.

pro·noun /`prəʊnaʊn/ *n* [C] (abbr *pron* used in this dictionary) word used in place of a noun or noun phrase, e g *he, it, hers, me, them.*

pro·nounce /prə`naʊns/ *vt,vi* **1** make the sound of (a word, etc): *The 'b' in 'debt' is not ~d.* **2** declare, announce (esp formally, solemnly or officially): *Has judgement been ~d yet?* **3** (*formal*) declare as one's opinion: *He ~d himself in favour of the plan.* **4** (*legal*) pass judgement (in a law court): *~ for/against him.*

pro·nounce·able /-əbəl/ *adj* (of sounds, words) that can be pronounced.

pro·nounced *adj* definite; easy to notice: *a man of ~d opinions.*

pro·nounce·ment *n* [C] formal statement or declaration.

pro·nun·ci·ation /prəˌnʌnsɪ`eɪʃən/ *n* **1** [U] way in which a language is spoken: *the ~ of English.* **2** [U] person's way of speaking a language, or words of a language: *His ~ is improving.* **3** [C] way in which a word is pronounced: *Which of these three ~s do you recommend?*

proof[1] /pruf/ adj proof (against), giving safety or protection; able to resist: ~ against bullets; `bullet-~; `water-~; `sound-~. `splinter-~; (fig) ~ against temptation. ⇨ foolproof. □ vt make safe or resistant (esp make a fabric waterproof).

proof[2] /pruf/ n 1 [U] evidence (in general), or [C] a particular piece of evidence, that is sufficient to show that something is a fact: Is there any ~ that the accused man was at the scene of the crime? 2 [U] demonstrating; testing of whether something is true, a fact, etc: He produced documents in ~ of his claim. 3 [C] test, trial, examination. 4 [C] trial copy of something printed or engraved, for approval before other copies are printed. 5 [U] standard of strength of distilled alcoholic liquors: This rum is 30 per cent ~.

prop[1] /prop/ n 1 support used to keep something up: a `clothes-~, holding up a line on which laundered clothes are drying. 2 (fig) person who supports another person: He is the ~ of his parents in their old age. □ vt (-pp-) 1 support; keep in position: Use this box to ~ the door open. 2 (fig) support: He can't always expect his colleagues to ~ him up.

prop[2] /prop/ n (usually pl) (abbr of) (stage) property.

propa·gan·da /ˌpropəˈgændə/ n [U] (means of, methods for the) spreading of information, doctrines, ideas, etc: political ~; (as an adjective) ~ plays/films.
propa·gan·dize /-daɪz/ vi engage in propaganda.

propa·gate /ˈpropəgeɪt/ vt,vi (formal) 1 increase the number of (plants, animals, diseases) by natural process from the parent stock: Trees ~ themselves by seeds. 2 spread more widely: ~ news/knowledge. 3 (of animals and plants) reproduce.
propa·ga·tion /ˌpropəˈgeɪʃən/ n [U] propagating: the propagation of disease by insects.

pro·pel /prəˈpel/ vt (-ll-) drive forward: a boat ~led by oars.
pro·pel·lant, (or -lent) /-ənt/ adj, n [C] something used to produce forward motion, e g fuel that burns to fire a rocket, etc.
pro·pel·ler, two or more blades which turn to move a ship, helicopter, etc.

pro·pen·sity /prəˈpensətɪ/ n [C] (pl -ies) (formal) natural tendency: a ~ to exaggerate.

proper /ˈpropə(r)/ adj 1 right, correct, fitting, suitable: Are you doing it the ~ way? Is this the ~ tool for the job? 2 in conformity with, paying regard to, the conventions of society: ~ behaviour. 3 (placed after the noun) strictly so called; genuine: architecture ~, excluding, for example, the question of water-supply, electric current, etc. 4 (informal) great: We're in a ~ mess.
proper fraction, (e g ½, ¾) one in which the number above the line is smaller than that below the line.
proper noun/name, (gram) name used for an individual person, town, etc e g Mary, Prague.
proper·ly adv (a) in a correct manner: behave ~ly. (b) (informal) thoroughly: He was ~ly beaten by the champion.

prop·erty /ˈpropətɪ/ n (pl -ies) 1 [U] (collectively) things owned; possessions: Don't take my bike—it's not your ~. 2 [C] area of land or land and buildings: He has a small ~ (i e land and a house) in Kent. 3 [U] ownership; the fact of owning or being owned: P~ has its obligations, e g you must look after it. 4 [C] special quality that belongs to something: the chemical properties of iron. 5 (in the theatre) (abbr prop) article of dress or furniture or other thing (except scenery) used on the stage in the performance of a play.
prop·er·tied /ˈpropətɪd/ adj owning property, esp land.

proph·ecy /ˈprofɪsɪ/ n (pl -ies) 1 [U] power of telling what will happen in the future: have the gift of ~. 2 [C] statement that tells what will happen: His ~ came true.

proph·esy /ˈprofɪsaɪ/ vt,vi (pt,pp -ied) 1 say what will happen: ~ war/that war will break out. 2 speak as a prophet.

prophet /ˈprofɪt/ n [C] 1 person who teaches religion and claims that his teaching comes to him directly from God: the ~ Isaiah. 2 pioneer of a new theory, cause, etc: William Morris, one of the early ~s of socialism. 3 person who tells, or claims to tell, what will happen in the future: I'm not a good weather-~.
prophet·ess /ˈprofɪtes US: -ɪs/ n [C] woman prophet.
pro·phetic /prəˈfetɪk/ adj of a prophet or prophecy: Her dreams were ~.
pro·pheti·cally /-klɪ/ adv

pro·pi·ti·ate /prəˈpɪʃɪeɪt/ vt (formal) do something to take away the anger of; win the favour or support of; offer a sacrifice to ~ the gods.
pro·pi·ti·ation /prəˌpɪʃɪˈeɪʃən/ n [U]
pro·pi·ti·atory /prəˈpɪʃɪətərɪ US: -tɔrɪ/ adj
pro·pi·tious /prəˈpɪʃəs/ adj (formal) favourable: ~ weather.
pro·pi·tious·ly adv

pro·por·tion /prəˈpɔʃən/ n 1 [U] relation of one thing to another in quantity, size, etc; relation of a part to the whole: The ~ of imports to exports is worrying the government. **in proportion to**, relative to: payment in ~ to work done. **get sth/be out of proportion (to)**, (make it) bear no relation (to): When you're angry, you often get things out of ~, have an exaggerated view of things. 2 [C] part; share: You have not done your ~ of the work. 3 (often pl) the correct relation of parts or of the sizes of the several parts: a room of good ~s. 4 (pl) size; measurements: export trade of substantial ~s. 5 (maths) equality of relationship between two sets of numbers; statement that two ratios are equal (e g 4 is to 8 as 6 is to 12). □ *vt* (*formal*) put into a correct relationship: *Do you ~ your expenditure to your income?*

pro·por·tion·able /-ʃənəbəl/ *adj* = proportional.

pro·por·tional /prə'pɔʃənəl/ *adj* (*formal*) corresponding in degree or amount (to): *payment ~ to the work done.*

pro'portional 'represen'tation, system of voting so that parties have a number of representatives corresponding to the size of their success in the election.

pro·por·tion·ally /-nəlɪ/ *adv*

pro·por·tion·ate /prə'pɔʃənət/ *adj* (*formal*) = proportional.

pro·por·tion·ate·ly *adv*

pro·po·sal /prə'pəʊzəl/ *n* **1** [U] proposing. **2** [C] plan or scheme: *a ~ for peace.* **3** [C] offer (esp of marriage): *five ~s in one week.*

pro·pose /prə'pəʊz/ *vt, vi* **1** offer or put forward for consideration, as a suggestion, plan or purpose: *I ~ starting early/an early start/that we should start early.* **2** offer (marriage). **3** put forward (a person's name) for an office; nominate: *I ~ Mr Smith for chairman.*

pro·poser, person who proposes

prop·osi·tion /ˌprɒpə'zɪʃən/ *n* [C] **1** statement; assertion: *a ~ stated so well that it needs no explanation.* **2** question or problem (with or without the answer or solution): *Tunnelling under the English Channel is a big ~.* **3** (*informal*) matter to be dealt with, esp something immoral or illegal, e g an indecent suggestion made to a girl. □ *vt* (*sl*) make a proposition(3) to.

pro·pound /prə'paʊnd/ *vt* (*formal*) offer for consideration or solution: *~ a theory.*

pro·pri·etary /prə'praɪətərɪ US: -terɪ/ *adj* owned or controlled by somebody; held as property: *a ~ name,* e g Kodak for cameras and films.

pro·pri·etor /prə'praɪətə(r)/ *n* [C] owner, esp of a hotel, store, land or patent.

pro·pri·e·tress /prə'praɪətrəs/ *n* [C] woman proprietor.

pro·pri·ety /prə'praɪətɪ/ *n* (*pl* -ies) (*formal*) **1** [U] state of being correct in behaviour and morals: *a breach of ~.* **2** (*pl*) details of correct social behaviour: *observe the proprieties.* **3** [U] reasonableness; fitness: *I question the ~ of granting such a request,* doubt whether it is right to do so.

pro·pul·sion /prə'pʌlʃən/ *n* [U] propelling force.

pro rata /ˌprəʊ 'rɑːtə/ *adv* (*Latin*) according to the share, etc of each.

pro·rogue /prəʊ'rəʊg/ *vt* bring (a session of Parliament) to an end without dissolving it (so that unfinished business may be taken up again in the next session).

pro·ro·ga·tion /ˌprəʊrə'geɪʃən/ *n* [C,U]

pro·saic /prəʊ'zeɪɪk/ *adj* (*formal*) dull; uninteresting; commonplace: *a ~ husband.*

pro·sai·cally /-klɪ/ *adv*

pro·scenium /prə'siːnɪəm/ *n* [C] (*pl* ~s) (in a theatre) that part of the stage between the curtain and the orchestra; an enclosing arch.

pro·scribe /prəʊ'skraɪb/ *vt* **1** denounce (a person, practice, etc) as dangerous. **2** (*old use*) publicly put (a person) out of the protection of the law.

pro·scrip·tion /prə'skrɪpʃən US: prəʊ-/ *n* [U] proscribing or being proscribed; [C] instance of this.

prose /prəʊz/ *n* [U] language not in verse form. ⇨ poetry.

pros·ecute /ˈprɒsɪkjuːt/ *vt* start legal proceedings against: *Trespassers will be ~d.*

pros·ecu·tion /ˌprɒsɪ'kjuːʃən/ *n* **1** [U] prosecuting or being prosecuted: *make oneself liable to ~;* [C] instance of this: *start a ~ against him.* **2** (*collective*) person who prosecutes together with his advisers: *the case for the ~.* ⇨ defence(3).

pros·ecutor /ˈprɒsɪkjuːtə(r)/ *n* [C] person who prosecutes.

pros·pect[1] /ˈprɒspekt/ *n* **1** [C] wide view over land or sea. **2** (*fig*) broad view before the mind, in the imagination. **3** (*pl*) something expected, hoped for, looked forward to: *There are bright ~s for me if I accept the position.* **4** [U] expectation; hope: *I see no/little/not much ~ of his recovery.* **5** [C] possible customer or client: *He's a good ~.*

pros·pect[2] /prə'spekt US: 'prɒspekt/ *vi* search (for): *~ing for gold.*

pros·pec·tive /prə'spektɪv/ *adj* hoped for; looked forward to: *a ~ buyer; the ~ Labour candidate.*

pros·pec·tor /prə'spektə(r)/ *n* [C] person who explores a region looking for gold or other valuable ores, etc.

pros·pec·tus /prə'spektəs/ *n* [C] (*pl* ~es) printed account giving details of and advertising something, e g a book about to be published.

pros·per /ˈprɒspə(r)/ *vi, vt* succeed; do well: *The business ~ed.*

pros·per·ity /prɒ'sperətɪ/ *n* [U] state of being successful; good fortune: *a life of happiness and ~; live in ~.*

pros·per·ous /ˈprɒspərəs/ *adj* successful; rich: *a ~ business; ~ years.*

pros·per·ous·ly *adv*

pros·ti·tute /ˈprɒstɪtjuːt US: -tuːt/ *n* [C] person who offers herself/himself for sexual intercourse for payment. □ *vt* **1** (*reflexive*) make a prostitute of (oneself). **2** put to wrong or unworthy uses: *~ one's reputation,* lose it; *~ one's talents,* use in an unworthy cause.

pros·ti·tu·tion /ˌprɒstɪ'tjuːʃən US: -'tuːʃən/ *n* [U] practice of prostituting.

pros·trate /ˈprɒstreɪt/ *adj* **1** lying stretched out on the ground, usually face downward, e g because exhausted, or to show submission or deep respect. **2** (*fig*) overcome (with grief, etc); conquered. □ *vt* /prɒ'streɪt US

ˋprostreɪt/ **1** make oneself, cause to be, prostrate: *trees ~d by the gale.* **2** make helpless: *She is ~d with grief.*

pros·tra·tion /proˈstreɪʃən/ *n* [C,U]

pro·tag·on·ist /prəʊˈtægənɪst/ *n* [C] (*formal*) chief person in a drama; (by extension) chief person in a story or factual event.

pro·tect /prəˈtekt/ *vt* keep safe (from danger, enemies; against attack): *well ~ed from the cold/against the weather.*

pro·tec·tion /prəˈtekʃən/ *n* [U] **1** protecting or being protected: *These plants need ~ against the sun.* **2** [U] system of protecting home industry against foreign competition. **3** [C] person or thing that protects: *wearing a heavy coat as a ~ against the cold.*

pro·tec·tive /prəˈtektɪv/ *adj* **1** giving protection: *a ~ covering.* **2** *protective (towards),* (of persons) with a wish to protect: *A mother naturally feels ~ towards her children.*

pro·tec·tive·ly *adv*

pro·tec·tor /prəˈtektə(r)/ *n* [C] person who protects; something made or designed to give protection.

pro·tec·tor·ate /prəˈtektərət/ *n* [C] country which is under the protection of one of the great powers.

pro·té·gé (feminine = **-gée**) /ˈprotɪʒeɪ US: ˈprəʊtɪˈʒeɪ/ *n* [C] person to whom another gives protection and help (usually over a long period).

pro·tein /ˈprəʊtiːn/ *n* [C,U] body-building substance essential to good health, in such foods as milk, eggs, meat.

pro·test¹ /ˈprəʊtest/ *n* **1** [C,U] statement of disapproval or objection: *He paid without ~, without making any objection.* **2** (as an *adjective*) expressing protest: *a ~ march.*

pro·test² /prəˈtest/ *vt,vi* **1** affirm strongly; assert against opposition: *He ~ed his innocence.* **2** raise an objection, say something (*against*): *I ~ against being called an old fool.*

pro·tester, person who protests.

pro·test·ing·ly *adv*

Prot·es·tant /ˈprotɪstənt/ *n* [C], *adj* (member) of any of the Christian bodies that separated from the Church of Rome at the time of the Reformation (16th century), or their later branches.

prot·esta·tion /ˌprotɪˈsteɪʃən/ *n* [C] (*formal*) serious declaration: *~s of innocence.*

pro·to·col /ˈprəʊtəkol/ *n* **1** [C] first or original draft of an agreement (esp between States), signed by those making it, in preparation for a treaty. **2** [U] code of behaviour as practised on diplomatic occasions: *Was the seating arranged according to ~?*

pro·ton /ˈprəʊton/ *n* [C] positively charged particle forming part of an atomic nucleus. ⇨ electron.

pro·to·type /ˈprəʊtətaɪp/ *n* [C] first or original example, e g of an aircraft, from which others have been or will be copied or developed.

pro·to·zoa /ˌprəʊtəˈzəʊə/ *n pl* (division of the animal kingdom consisting of) animals of the simplest type formed of a single cell.

pro·tract /prəˈtrækt US: prəʊ-/ *vt* lengthen the time taken by: *a ~ed visit/argument.*

pro·trac·tion /prəˈtrækʃən US: prəʊ-/ *n* [U] lengthening out.

pro·trac·tor /prəˈtræktə(r) US: prəʊ-/ *n* [C] instrument, usually a semicircle, marked (0° to 180°) for measuring and drawing angles.

pro·trude /prəˈtruːd US: prəʊ-/ *vi,vt* (cause to) stick out or project: *protruding eyes/teeth.*

pro·tru·sion /prəˈtruːʒən US: prəʊ-/ *n* [U] protruding; [C] something that protrudes.

pro·trus·ive /prəˈtruːsɪv US: prəʊ-/ *adj* protruding.

pro·tu·ber·ance /prəˈtjuːbərəns US: prəʊ-/ *n* (*formal*) [U] bulging; [C] bulge or swelling.

pro·tu·ber·ant /prəˈtjuːbərənt US: prəʊ-/ *adj* (*formal*) curving or swelling outwards; bulging.

proud /praʊd/ *adj* (-er, -est) **1** (in a good sense) having or showing a proper pride or dignity: *~ of their success/of being so successful.* **2** (in a bad sense) having or showing too much pride: *He was too ~ to join our party.* **3** of which one is or may be properly proud; splendid: *It was a ~ day for the school when its team won the championship.* ⇨ houseproud.

proud·ly *adv*

prov·able /ˈpruːvəbəl/ *adj* that can be proved.

prove /pruːv/ *vt,vi* (*pp ~d,* or, as below, 1, *~n* /ˈpruːvən/) **1** supply proof of; show beyond doubt to be true: *~ that he is guilty. Can you ~ it (to me)? The exception proves the rule,* shows that the rule is valid in most cases. **2** establish the genuineness, quality or accuracy of: *~ a man's worth.* **3** be seen or found (to be): *The new typist ~d (to be) useless. Our wood supply ~d (to be) insufficient.*

prov·erb /ˈprovɜːb/ *n* [C] popular short saying, with words of advice or warning, e g 'It takes two to make a quarrel'.

prov·erb·ial /prəˈvɜːbɪəl/ *adj* widely known and talked about: *His stupidity is ~ial.*

prov·erb·ial·ly /-əlɪ/ *adv*

pro·vide /prəˈvaɪd/ *vi,vt* **1** do what is necessary: *We have had many visitors to ~ food for.* **2** give, supply (what is needed, esp what a person needs in order to live): *~ one's children with food and clothes/food and clothes for one's family.* **3** state: *The agreement ~s that the tenant shall pay for repairs to the building.*

pro·vider, person who provides.

pro·vided /prəˈvaɪdɪd/ *conj* on condition (that): *I'll come ~ that he stays away.*

provi·dence /ˈprovɪdəns/ *n* **1** P~, God; God's care for human beings and all He has created. **2** [U] (small *p*) particular instance of this care: *the mysterious working of* ~.

provi·dent /ˈprovɪdənt/ *adj* (*formal*) (careful in) providing for future needs or events, esp in old age.
provi·dent·ly *adv*

pro·vid·ing /prəˈvaɪdɪŋ/ *conj* = provided.

prov·ince /ˈprovɪns/ *n* [C] **1** large administrative division of a country. **2** the ~s, all the country outside the capital: *The pop group is now touring the* ~s. **3** district under an archbishop. **4** area of learning or knowledge; department of activity: *That is outside my* ~, not something with which I can or need deal.

pro·vin·cial /prəˈvɪnʃəl/ *adj* **1** of a province(1): ~ *government*. **2** of the provinces(2): ~ *roads*. **3** having, typical of, the speech, manners, views, etc of a person living in the provinces (esp in former times when communications were poor): *a* ~ *accent*. □ *n* [C] person from the provinces(2).
prov·in·cial·ly /-ʃəlɪ/ *adv*

pro·vi·sion /prəˈvɪʒən/ *n* **1** [U] providing, preparation (esp for future needs): *make* ~ *for one's old age*, e g by saving money. **2** [C] amount provided: *issue a* ~ *of meat to the troops*. **3** (*pl*) food; food supplies: *have a good store of* ~s. **4** [C] condition in a legal document, e g a clause in a will: *Have you made* ~s *for your children?* □ *vt* supply with food and stores.

pro·vi·sional /prəˈvɪʒənəl/ *adj* **1** of the present time only, and to be changed or replaced later: *a* ~ *government/chairman, etc*. **2** (of an appointment or acceptance e g as an undergraduate) to be confirmed if certain conditions are met.
pro·vi·sional·ly /-nəlɪ/ *adv*

pro·vo·ca·tion /ˌprovəˈkeɪʃən/ *n* **1** [U] provoking or being provoked: *She shouts at/on the slightest* ~. **2** [C] something that provokes or annoys.

pro·voca·tive /prəˈvokətɪv/ *adj* causing, likely to cause, anger, argument, interest, etc: ~ *remarks; a* ~ *dress*.
pro·voca·tive·ly *adv*

pro·voke /prəˈvəʊk/ *vt* **1** make angry: *If you* ~ *the dog, it will attack you*. **2** cause: ~ *laughter/a smile/a riot. His suggestion* ~d *her into slapping his face*.
pro·vok·ing *adj* annoying.
pro·vok·ing·ly *adv*

prow /prau/ *n* [C] pointed front of a ship or boat.

prow·ess /ˈprauɪs/ *n* [U] (*formal*) bravery; valour; unusual skill or ability.

prowl /praul/ *vi,vt* go about quietly looking for a chance to get food (as wild animals do), or to steal, etc. □ *n* **be on the prowl**, be prowling.
prowl·er, animal or person that prowls.

prox·im·ity /prokˈsɪmətɪ/ *n* [U] nearness: *in* (*close*) ~ *to*, (very) near to (the more usual phrase).

proxy /ˈproksɪ/ *n* (*pl* -ies) **1** [C,U] (document giving) authority to represent or act for another (esp in voting at an election). **2** [C] person given a proxy: *vote by* ~.

prude /prud/ *n* [C] person who is extremely moral (often exaggerated or affected) in behaviour or speech.
pru·dery /ˈprudərɪ/ *n* (*pl* -ies) [U] prudish behaviour; [C] prudish act or remark.
pru·dence /ˈprudəns/ *n* [U] careful forethought.
pru·dent /ˈprudənt/ *adj* acting only after careful thought or planning: *a* ~ *housewife*.
pru·dent·ly *adv*
pru·den·tial /pruˈdenʃəl/ *adj* relating to, marked by, prudence (often used in names of insurance companies).
prud·ish /ˈprudɪʃ/ *adj* easily shocked; extremely moral.
prud·ish·ly *adv*

prune² /prun/ *n* [C] dried plum.

prune² /prun/ *vt* **1** cut away parts of (trees, bushes, etc) in order to control growth or shape: ~ *the rose-bushes*. **2** (*fig*) take out unnecessary parts from: ~ *a report of unnecessary detail*.

pry¹ /praɪ/ *vi* (*pt,pp* pried /praɪd/) **1** *pry into*, inquire too curiously (into other people's affairs). **2** *pry about*, look (about) for.
pry·ing·ly *adv*

pry² /praɪ/ *vt* = prize².

psalm /sam/ *n* [C] sacred song or hymn, esp (the P~s) in the Bible.

pseud(o)- /ˈsjudəʊ US: ˈsu-/ *prefix* false; fake: *pseudonym*.

pseu·do·nym /ˈsjudənɪm US: ˈsud-/ *n* [C] name taken, esp by an author, instead of his real name.
pseud·ony·mous /sjuˈdonɪməs US: su-/ *adj*

psyche /ˈsaɪkɪ/ *n* [C] **1** human soul or spirit. **2** human mind.

psyche·delic /ˌsaɪkəˈdelɪk/ *adj* **1** (of drugs) of, causing, hallucinations, ecstasy, terror, etc. **2** (of visual and sound effects) acting on the mind like psychedelic drugs: ~ *music*.

psy·chi·atric /ˌsaɪkɪˈætrɪk/ *adj* of psychiatry: *a psychiatric ward*.

psy·chia·trist /saɪˈkaɪətrɪst/ *n* [C] expert in psychiatry.

psy·chia·try /saɪˈkaɪətrɪ US: sɪ-/ *n* [U] the study and treatment of mental illness.

psy·chic /ˈsaɪkɪk/, **psy·chi·cal** /ˈsaɪkɪkəl/ *adj* **1** of the soul or mind. **2** of phenomena and conditions which appear to be outside physical or natural laws, e g telepathy.

psy·cho /ˈsaɪkəʊ,-etc/ *prefix* of the mind: *psychosis*.

psy·cho·an·al·yse (*US* = **-lyze**) /ˈsaɪkəʊ ˈænəlaɪz/ *vt* treat (a person) by psychoanalysis.

psy·cho·an·aly·sis /ˌsaɪkəʊ əˈnæləsɪs/ *n* [U] **1** method of healing mental illnesses by tracing them, through interviews, to events in the patient's early life, and bringing those events to light. **2** body of doctrine based on this method concerned with the investigation and treatment of emotional disturbances.

psy·cho·anal·yst /ˈsaɪkəʊ ˈænəlɪst/ *n* [C] person who practises psycho-analysis.

psy·cho·an·a·lytic(al) /ˈsaɪkəʊ ˌænəˈlɪtɪk(əl)/ *adj* relating to psycho-analysis.

psy·cho·logi·cal /ˈsaɪkəˈlɒdʒɪkəl/ *adj* of psychology.

'**psycho'logical `warfare,** attempt at winning a struggle by affecting the opponent's mind.

psy·cho·logi·cally /-klɪ/ *adv*

psy·chol·ogist /saɪˈkɒlədʒɪst/ *n* [C] student of, expert in, psychology.

psy·chol·ogy /saɪˈkɒlədʒɪ/ *n* [U] science, study, of the mind and its processes.

psy·cho·path /ˈsaɪkəʊpæθ/ *n* [C] person suffering from severe emotional derangement, esp one who is aggressive and anti-social.

psy·cho·pathic /ˈsaɪkəʊˈpæθɪk/ *adj*

psy·cho·sis /saɪˈkəʊsɪs/ *n* [C] (*pl* -choses /-ˈkəʊsiːz/) abnormal or diseased mental state.

psy·cho·therapy /ˈsaɪkəʊˈθerəpɪ/ *n* [U] treatment by psychological methods of mental, emotional and nervous disorders.

pub /pʌb/ *n* [C] (common abbr for) public house.

pu·berty /ˈpjuːbətɪ/ *n* [U] stage at which a person becomes physically able to become a parent.

pu·bic /ˈpjuːbɪk/ *adj* of the lower part of the abdomen: ∼ *hair.*

pub·lic /ˈpʌblɪk/ *adj* (opposite of *private*) of, for, connected with, owned by, done for or done by, known to, people in general: *a* ∼ *library/park.* **in the public eye,** having much publicity. □ *n* **1** the ∼, members of the community in general: *The* ∼ *are not admitted.* **in public,** openly, not in private. **2** particular section of the community: *the reading* ∼.

'**public `house** *n* [C] (*GB*) (*formal*) place (not a club, hotel, etc) licensed to sell alcoholic drinks to be drunk on the premises.

'**public o'pinion poll,** ⇨ poll¹ (2).

'**public `ownership,** ownership by the State, e g of the railways.

'**Public `Prosecutor,** State official who prosecutes.

'**public re'lations** *n pl* (esp) relations between a government department or authority, business organization, etc and ordinary people.

'**public school, (a)** (*GB*) private school for fee-paying pupils. **(b)** (*US* and *Scot*) school providing free education from public funds.

'**public `spirit,** readiness to do things that are for the good of the community. Hence, '**public-'spirited** *adj*

pub·lic·ly /-klɪ/ *adv*

pub·li·ca·tion /ˌpʌblɪˈkeɪʃən/ *n* **1** [U] act of

making known to the public, of publishing something. **2** [C] something published, e g a book or a periodical.

pub·lic·ity /pʌbˈlɪsətɪ/ *n* [U] **1** the state of being known to, seen by, everyone: *an actress who seeks/avoids* ∼. **2** (business of) providing information to interest people in general: *a `*∼ *campaign.*

pub·li·cize /ˈpʌblɪsaɪz/ *vt* bring to the attention of the public.

pub·lish /ˈpʌblɪʃ/ *vt* **1** have (a book, periodical, etc) printed and announce that it is for sale. **2** make known to the public: ∼ *the news.*

pub·lisher, person, company, whose business is publishing books.

puck /pʌk/ *n* [C] hard rubber disc used like a ball in ice-hockey.

pucker /ˈpʌkə(r)/ *vt,vi* draw or come together into small folds or wrinkles: ∼ *up one's lips.*

pudding /ˈpʊdɪŋ/ *n* **1** [C,U] (dish of) food, usually a soft, sweet mixture, served as part of a meal, eaten after the meat or fish course. **2** kind of sausage: *black* ∼.

puddle /ˈpʌdəl/ *n* [C] small, dirty pool of rain-water, esp on a road.

pudgy /ˈpʌdʒɪ/ *adj* (-ier, -iest) short, thick and fat: ∼ *fingers.*

puer·ile /ˈpjʊəraɪl *US:* -rəl/ *adj* trivial, childish: *ask* ∼ *questions.*

puff¹ /pʌf/ *n* [C] **1** (sound of a) short, quick sending out of breath, air, etc: *have a* ∼ *at a pipe.* **2** = powder-puff. **3** mass of material on a dress, etc: ∼ *sleeves,* swelling out like balloons.

'**puff-adder,** poisonous African viper which inflates the upper part of its body when excited.

puffy *adj* (-ier, -iest) **(a)** short of breath (by running, climbing, etc). **(b)** swollen: ∼*y under the eyes.*

puff² /pʌf/ *vi,vt* **1** breathe quickly (as after running); (of smoke, steam, etc) come out in puffs: *He was* ∼*ing hard when he jumped on to the bus. He was* ∼*ing (away) at his cigar.* **2** send out in puffs: *he* ∼*ed smoke into my face.* **3** *puff sth out,* cause to swell with air: *He* ∼*ed out his chest with pride.*

puf·fin /ˈpʌfɪn/ *n* [C] North Atlantic seabird with a large bill.

pug /pʌg/ *n* [C] breed of small dog with a flat nose.

pug·na·cious /pʌgˈneɪʃəs/ *adj* (*formal*) fond of, in the habit of, fighting.

puke /pjuːk/ *vi,vt n* [U] (*sl*) vomit.

pull¹ /pʊl/ *n* **1** [C] act of pulling: *give a* ∼ *at a rope.* **2** [U] force or effort: *It was a long* ∼ (= a long, hard climb) *to the top of the mountain.* **3** [C,U] (*informal*) power to get help or attention through influence, e g with people in high positions: *He has strong* ∼*/a great deal of* ∼ *with the Managing Director.*

pull² /pʊl/ *vt,vi* (For special uses with *adverbial particles and prepositions,* ⇨ **6**

below.) **1** (contrasted with *push*) use force on (a person or thing) so as to draw towards or after one, or in the direction shown: *The horse was ~ing a heavy cart. Would you rather push the barrow or ~ it? pull sth to pieces,* (a) use force to separate its parts or to break it up into parts. (b) (*fig*) criticize severely by pointing out the weak points or faults: *He ~ed my theory to pieces.* **2** row²; (of a boat) be rowed (by): *The men ~ed for the shore. pull together,* (*fig*) work together; co-operate. *do a fair share of the work.* **3** *pull at/on sth,* (a) give a tug: *~ at/on a rope.* (b) draw or suck: *~ing at his pipe.* **4** *pull a muscle,* strain it. For other uses with *nouns,* ⇨ the *noun* entries, e g at face, leg, string, wool. **5** (*sl*) raid; rob; steal.

6 (special uses with *adverbial particles* and *prepositions*):

pull sb/sth about, treat roughly.

pull sth apart, tear or pull into its parts.

pull sth down, destroy or demolish, e g an old building.

pull in, (a) (of a train) enter a station: *The express from Rome ~ed in on time.* (b) (of a motor vehicle or boat) move in towards: *The lorry driver ~ed in to the side of the road.* Hence, `*pull-in* n place to stop at the side of the road. *pull sb in,* (a) attract, draw: *The new play at the National Theatre is ~ing in large audiences.* (b) (*informal* of the police) arrest. *pull oneself in,* draw in the stomach muscles (so as to be less fat).

pull sth off, (a) drive a motor vehicle off the road into a lay-by or hard shoulder. (b) succeed in a plan, in winning: *~ off a deal,* be successful in getting agreement.

pull out (of), (a) move out (in order to pass or go round): *The driver of the car ~ed out from behind the lorry. The train ~ed out of Euston on time.* (b) detach, e g from a magazine. *pull (sb) out (of),* leave a place or situation which is too difficult to manage: *Troops are being ~ed out/are ~ing out of these troubled areas.*

pull (sth) over, (cause a vehicle, boat, etc to) move or steer to one side, e g to let another vehicle or boat pass: *P~ (your car) over and let me pass!*

pull (sb) round, (help to) recover from illness, weakness, a faint, etc: *Have this brandy; it will ~ you round.*

pull through, (a) = pull round. (b) succeed in avoiding difficulties, dangers, etc. *pull sb through,* (a) help to recover from illness, etc. (b) help to avoid failure, help to pass an examination, etc.

pull together, ⇨ 2 above. *pull oneself together,* get control of oneself, of one's feelings, etc.

pull (sth) up, bring or come to a stop: *The driver ~ed up when he came to the traffic lights. pull sb up,* reprimand: *He was ~ed up by the chairman. pull up to/with sb/*

sth, improve one's relative position (in a race, etc): *The favourite soon ~ed up with the other horses.*

pul·let /ˈpʊlɪt/ n [C] young hen, esp at the time she begins to lay eggs.

pul·ley /ˈpʊlɪ/ n [C] (pl ~s) grooved wheel(s) for ropes or chains, used for lifting things.

pull·over /ˈpʊləʊvə(r)/ n [C] knitted garment pulled on over the head.

pul·mon·ary /ˈpʌlmənərɪ US: -nerɪ/ adj (*anat*) of, in, connected with, the lungs: ~ *diseases; the* ~ *arteries,* conveying blood to the lungs.

pulp /pʌlp/ n [U] **1** soft, fleshy part of fruit. **2** soft mass of other material, esp of wood fibre as used for making paper. □ vt,vi make into, become like, pulp: ~ *old books.*

pul·pit /ˈpʊlpɪt/ n [C] raised and enclosed structure in a church, used by a clergyman, esp when preaching.

pul·sate /pʌlˈseɪt US: ˈpʌlseɪt/ vt,vi (cause to) beat or throb; expand and contract rhythmically.

pul·sa·tion /pʌlˈseɪʃən/ n [C,U]

pulse /pʌls/ n [C] **1** the regular beat of the arteries, e g as felt at the wrist, as the blood is pumped through them by the heart. **2** (*fig*) activities or thrill of life or emotion: *the* ~ *of life in a big city.* □ vi beat; throb; *news that sent the blood pulsing through his veins.*

pul·ver·ize /ˈpʌlvəraɪz/ vt,vi **1** grind to a powder; smash completely. **2** become powder or dust.

puma /ˈpjuːmə/ n [C] (pl ~s) large brown American animal of the cat family (also called a *cougar* and *mountain lion*).

pum·ice /ˈpʌmɪs/ n [U] (also `~-*stone*), light, porous stone (from lava) used for cleaning and polishing.

pum·mel /ˈpʌməl/ vt (-ll-, US also -l-) beat repeatedly with the fists.

pump /pʌmp/ n [C] machine or device for forcing liquid, gas or air into, out of or through something, e g water from a well, air into a tyre: *a* `*bicycle* ~. □ vt,vi **1** force, e g water, etc into, from, something using a pump: ~ *petrol into a car;* ~ *up a tyre.* **2** (*fig*) obtain, explain, something using repetition, etc: ~ *information out of her;* ~ *facts into the heads of dull pupils.*

pump·kin /ˈpʌmpkɪn/ n [C,U] (plant, a trailing vine, with a) large, round orange-yellow fruit, used as a vegetable and (*US*) as a filling for pies.

pun /pʌn/ n [C] (also *a play on words*) humorous use of words which sound the same or of two meanings of the same word, e g 'The soldier laid down his *arms.*' □ vi (-nn-) make a pun or puns.

punch¹ /pʌntʃ/ n [C] **1** tool or machine for cutting holes in leather, metal, paper, etc. **2** tool for stamping designs on surfaces. □ vt **1** make a hole (in something) with a punch: ~ *a train ticket.* **2** force (nails, etc) in or out with a punch.

punch[2] /pʌntʃ/ n [U] drink made of wine or spirits mixed with hot water, sugar, lemons, spice, etc.

`punch-bowl, bowl in which punch is mixed.

punch[3] /pʌntʃ/ vt hit hard with the fist: ~ a man on the chin. □ n 1 [C] blow given with the fist: a ~ on the nose. 2 [U] (fig) energy: a speech with plenty of ~ in it.

`punch-up, fight with the fists: The quarrel ended in a ~-up.

punc·tili·ous /pʌŋk`tɪlɪəs/ adj (formal) very careful to carry out duties correctly, etc.

punc·tili·ous·ly adv

punc·tual /pʌŋktʃʊəl/ adj neither early nor late; coming, doing something, at the time fixed: be ~ for the lecture/in the payment of one's rent.

punc·tu·ally /-ʊəlɪ/ adv

punc·tu·al·ity /ˌpʌŋktʃʊˈælətɪ/ n [U] being punctual.

punc·tu·ate /pʌŋktʃʊeɪt/ vt 1 put stops, commas, etc, e g .,;:?!, into a piece of writing. 2 interrupt from time to time: a speech ~d with cheers.

punc·tu·ation /ˌpʌŋktʃʊˈeɪʃən/ n [U] (use of) stops, commas, etc in writing: ~ mark.

punc·ture /pʌŋktʃə(r)/ n [C] small hole, esp one made accidentally in a tyre. □ vt,vi 1 make a puncture in: ~ an abscess. 2 experience a puncture: Two of my tyres ~ed while I was on that stony road.

pun·dit /pʌndɪt/ n [C] 1 very learned Hindu; authority on a subject. 2 (informal) learned teacher; pedant.

pun·gent /pʌndʒənt/ adj (formal) 1 (of smells, tastes) sharp; stinging: a ~ sauce. 2 (fig) (of remarks) hurting: ~ criticism.

pun·ish /pʌnɪʃ/ vt 1 cause (a person) suffering or discomfort for doing wrong: ~ a man with/by a fine. 2 treat roughly; hit: The champion ~ed his opponent severely.

`pun·ish·able /-əbəl/ adj that can be punished (by law).

pun·ish·ment n [U] punishing or being punished: Does the ~ment fit the crime? [C] penalty for doing wrong: severe ~ment for murder.

pu·ni·tive /pjuːnɪtɪv/ adj (intended for) punishing.

pun·net /pʌnɪt/ n [C] small basket, made of very thin wood, plastic, etc esp as a measure for fruit: strawberries, 20p a ~.

pun·ster /pʌnstə(r)/ n [C] person who has the habit of making puns.

punt[1] /pʌnt/ n [C] flat-bottomed, shallow boat with square ends, moved by pushing the end of a long pole against the river-bed. □ vt,vi move, carry in, a punt.

punt[2] /pʌnt/ vi bet on a horse.

pun·ter /pʌntə(r)/ n [C] 1 person using a punt. 2 person who bets on a horse.

puny /pjuːnɪ/ adj (-ier, -iest) small and weak: What a ~ little man!

pun·ily /pjuːnəlɪ/ adv

pup /pʌp/ n [C] = puppy.

pupa /pjuːpə/ n [C] (pl ~s, or ~e /-piː/) = chrysalis.

pu·pil[1] /pjuːpəl/ n [C] young person at school.

pu·pil[2] /pjuːpəl/ n [C] (anat) round opening in the centre of the iris of the eye, regulating the passage of light.

pup·pet /pʌpɪt/ n [C] 1 doll, small figure of an animal, etc with jointed limbs moved by wires or strings, used in plays or shows called `~-plays/-shows. 2 (`glove-~) doll of which the body can be put on the hand like a glove, moved by the fingers. 3 person, group of persons, whose acts are completely controlled by another: (as an adjective) a ~ government/State.

puppy /pʌpɪ/ n [C] (pl -ies) young dog.

`puppy love, love by young people.

pur·chase[1] /pɜːtʃəs/ n 1 [U] buying. 2 [C] (formal) something bought: I have some ~s to make.

pur·chase[2] /pɜːtʃəs/ vt buy (which is much more usual): a dearly ~d victory, e g a battle in which many lives are lost.

pur·chaser, = buyer (the usual word).

pur·dah /pɜːdə/ n [U] (esp in Muslim communities) curtain for, convention of, keeping women from the sight of strangers, esp men: live/be in ~.

pure /pjʊə(r)/ adj (-r, -st except 5,6 below) 1 unmixed with any other substance, etc: ~ air, free from smoke, fumes, etc. 2 of unmixed race or breed: a ~ poodle. 3 without evil or sin: ~ in body and mind. 4 (of sounds) clear and distinct: a ~ note. 5 dealing with, studied for the sake of, theory only (not applied): ~ mathematics/science. 6 nothing but: a ~ waste of time.

pure·ly adv (esp) entirely; completely; merely: ~ly by accident.

pu·rée /pjʊəreɪ US: pjʊəˈreɪ/ n [C,U,] soup of vegetables, etc boiled to a pulp and pressed through a sieve; fruit similarly treated: apple ~.

pur·ga·tive /pɜːgətɪv/ n [C], adj (substance) having the power to empty or cleanse the bowels.

pur·ga·tory /pɜːgətrɪ US: -tɔːrɪ/ n [C] (pl -ies) 1 (esp in R C doctrine) condition after death in which the soul requires to be purified by temporary suffering; place where souls are so purified. 2 (fig) any place of temporary suffering.

pur·ga·tor·ial /ˌpɜːgəˈtɔːrɪəl/ adj

purge /pɜːdʒ/ vt 1 make clean or free (of physical or moral impurity): be ~d of/from sin; purging away one's sins. 2 empty (the bowels) of waste matter by means of medicine. 3 clear (oneself, a person, of a charge, of suspicion). 4 rid (e g a political party, etc) of members who are considered undesirable. □ n [C] clearing out or away: the political ~s *that followed the counter-revolution.*

pu·ri·fy /ˈpjʊərɪfaɪ/ *vt* (*pt,pp* -ied) make pure; cleanse: ∼*ing the air in a factory.*

pu·ri·fi·ca·tion /ˈpjʊərɪfɪˈkeɪʃən/ *n* [U]

pu·rist /ˈpjʊərɪst/ *n* [C] person who pays great attention to the correct use of words, grammar, style, etc.

puri·tan /ˈpjʊərɪtən/ *n* [C] **1 P∼,** (16th and 17th centuries, in England) member of a division of the Protestant Church which wanted simpler forms of church ceremony. **2** person who is strict in morals and religion, who considers some kinds of fun and pleasure as sinful: *Don't marry a ∼.* □ *adj* of or like a Puritan or a puritan.

puri·tani·cal /ˈpjʊərɪˈtænɪkəl/ *adj*

puri·tani·cally /ˈpjʊərɪˈtænɪklɪ/ *adv*

pu·rity /ˈpjʊərətɪ/ *n* [U] state or quality of being pure.

purl /pɜːl/ *n* [C] (in knitting) inverted stitch, which produces a ribbed appearance (the opposite of *plain*). □ *vt, vi* knit in this way.

pur·loin /pɜːˈlɔɪn/ *vt* (*formal*) steal.

purple /ˈpɜːpəl/ *n* [U], *adj* (colour) of red and blue mixed together.

pur·port /ˈpɜːpət US:* -pɔrt/ *n* [C] (*formal*) general meaning or intention of something said or written; likely explanation of a person's actions: *the ∼ of what he said.* □ *vt* /pəˈpɔt/ **1** seem to mean: *The statement ∼s that....* **2** claim: *It's ∼ed to be an original but it is really a fake.*

pur·pose /ˈpɜːpəs/ *n* [C] **1** that which one means to do, get, be, etc; plan; design; intention: *This van is used for various ∼s.* **2** [U] (*formal*) determination; power of forming plans and keeping to them: *weak of ∼.* **3** **on purpose,** by intention, not by chance: *She sometimes does things on ∼ just to annoy me.* □ *vt* (*formal*) have as one's purpose: *They ∼ a further attempt/∼ to make/ ∼ making a further attempt.*

'purpose-'built *adj* made to serve a particular function.

pur·pose·ful /-fəl/ *adj*

pur·pose·fully /-fəlɪ/ *adv*

pur·pose·less *adj* having no plan, design, reason.

purr /pɜː(r)/ *vi, vt* **1** (of a cat) make a low, continuous vibrating sound expressing pleasure. **2** (of a car engine) make a similar vibrating sound. □ *n* [C] purring sound.

purse¹ /pɜːs/ *n* [C] **1** small bag for money. **2** money; funds. ⇨ privy purse. **3** (*US*) = handbag.

purse² /pɜːs/ *vt* draw (the lips) together in tiny folds or wrinkles.

the purse-strings, control of expenditure.

purser /ˈpɜːsə(r)/ *n* [C] officer responsible for a ship's accounts and stores, esp in a passenger liner.

pur·su·ance /pəˈsjuəns US:* -su-/ *n* **in pursuance of,** (*formal*) in the carrying out or performance of (one's duties, a plan, etc).

pur·su·ant /-ənt/ *adj* **pursuant to,** (*for-*

mal) in accordance with: *pursuant to your instructions.*

pur·sue /pəˈsju US:* -ˈsu/ *vt* **1** go after in order to catch up with, capture or kill: *pursuing a robber/a bear; make sure that you are not being ∼d.* **2** (*fig*) (of consequences, penalties, etc) persistently attend: *His record as a criminal ∼d him wherever he went.* **3** go on with: *∼ one's studies after leaving school.* **4** have as an aim or purpose: *∼ pleasure.*

pur·suer, person who pursues(1).

pur·suit /pəˈsjut US:* -ˈsut/ *n* **1** [U] act of pursuing: *a dog in ∼ of rabbits.* **2** [C] something at which one works or to which one gives one's time: *scientific/literary ∼s.*

pur·vey /pɜːˈveɪ/ *vt, vi* **1** (*formal*) provide, supply (food, as a trader). **2** supply provisions (for): *a firm that ∼s for the Navy.*

pur·veyor /-ə(r)/, supplier (the usual word).

pus /pʌs/ *n* [U] thick yellowish-white liquid formed in and coming out from a poisoned place in the body.

push¹ /pʊʃ/ *n* **1** [C] act of pushing: *Give the door a hard ∼.* **2** [C] vigorous effort: *We must make a ∼ to finish the job this week.* **3** **get the push,** (*sl*) be dismissed (from one's employment, etc). **give sb the push,** (*sl*) dismiss him. **4** [U] confidence to put oneself forward, to attract attention, etc: *He hasn't enough ∼ to succeed as a salesman.*

push² /pʊʃ/ *vt, vi* (For special uses with *adverbial particles* and *prepositions*, ⇨ **8** below.) **1** (contrasted with *pull*) use force on (a person or thing) to cause forward movement: *Please ∼ the table nearer to the wall. We had to ∼ our way* (= go forward by pushing) *through the crowd.* **2** persuade others to recognize, eg claims, or buy, eg goods: *Unless you ∼ your claim you'll get no satisfaction.* ⇨ also *∼ oneself forward* in **8** below. **3** sell (illicit drugs) by acting as a link between large suppliers and the drug addicts. ⇨ **pusher** below. **4** insist, put pressure on: *We're ∼ing them for payment/an answer.* **5** urge: *She'll ∼ him to the verge of suicide.* **6** press: *∼ a button,* eg to ring a bell. **7 be pushing fifty, etc,** (*informal*) be nearing the age mentioned: *She wouldn't like you to think so, but she's ∼ing thirty.*

8 (special uses with *adverbial particles* and *prepositions*):

push along, (*informal*) leave: *I'm afraid it's time I was ∼ing along.*

push sb around, (*informal*) bully him; order him about: *I'm not going to be ∼ed around by you or anybody!*

push forward/on (to), go on resolutely with a journey, one's work, etc: *We must ∼ on with our work,* hurry and finish it. **push oneself forward,** ambitiously draw attention to oneself, eg at work, in society: *He never ∼es himself forward.*

push off, (*informal*) leave; go away: *I told him to ∼ off!*

s

push sb/sth over, cause to fall: *Several children were ~ed over by the crowd.*

`push-over,** (*sl*) something very easy to do; person who is easily defeated, converted, etc.

push sb through (sth), enable a person to succeed: *~ a weak student through an exam.* **push sth through,** do something by making a special effort: *~ the bill through the Commons.*

push sth up, force, e g prices, to rise. **push up the daisies,** (*informal*) die, be buried in a grave.

`push-bike,** one that is worked by pedalling (not a *moped* or *motor bike*).

`push-cart,** small cart pushed by a man.

`push-chair,** chair on wheels (used when a child is old enough to sit up).

pusher, (a) (said of someone who takes every opportunity of gaining an advantage for herself). (b) (*sl*) seller of illicit drugs.

push-ing *adj* having a tendency to be a pusher(a).

puss /pʊs/ *n* [C] cat; word used to call a cat.

pussy /'pʊsɪ/ *n* [C] (*pl* -ies) (also `~y-cat) (child's word for a cat.

put /pʊt/ *vi,vt* (*pt,pp* put, *present part* putting) (For special uses with *adverbial particles* and *prepositions*, ⇨ 10 below.) 1 move (something) so as to be in a certain place or position: *He ~ the book on the table. He ~ his hands in(to) his pockets. Did you ~ milk in my tea? It's time to ~ the baby to bed. They've ~ men on the moon.* **put one's foot in it,** ⇨ foot [1](1). 2 cause to be in some relationship, e g as an employee, client, with a person. **put sb in his (proper) place,** make him humble. **put oneself in sb's/sb else's place/position,** imagine oneself in his position. 3 make a person bear (the particular nervous or moral strain shown). **put the blame on sb**: *Don't ~ all the blame on me.* **put pressure on sb (to do sth)**: *They're ~ting great pressure on him to resign.* 4 affect the progress of. **put an end/a stop to sth,** end or abolish it. 5 cause to pass into or suffer the emotional, physical etc state shown by the phrase that follows. **put oneself to death,** commit suicide. **put sb to death,** kill him. **put sb at his ease,** cause him to feel relaxed. **put sb/sth to the test,** test him/it. 6 cause (a person or thing) to become (what is shown by the *adjective*): *That picture on the wall is crooked—I must ~ it straight.* **put sth right,** correct it: *A short note ~ the matter right,* ended any misunderstanding. 7 write; indicate; mark: *~ a tick against a name/a price on an article/one's signature to a will.* 8 **put sth (to sb); put it to sb (that),** offer; express: *~ a proposal to the Board of Directors; ~ a question to the vote/a resolution to the meeting. I ~ it to you that...,* invite you to agree with me that... *How can I ~ it,* express it? *How would you ~ (= *

express, translate) *this in Danish? That can all be ~ in a few words.* 9 set a value (on): *The experts refused to ~ a price on the Rubens painting.*

10 (special uses with *adverbial particles* and *prepositions*):

put sth about, spread, e g rumours: *Don't believe all these stories that are being ~ about.*

put sth across (to sb), communicate something successfully: *a teacher who quickly ~s his ideas across to his students.* **put sth across sb,** deceive; trick: *You can't ~ that across me,* make me believe or accept it.

put sth aside, (a) lay down: *~ one's work aside.* (b) save: *He has ~ aside a good sum of money.* (c) ignore: *P~ aside for a moment the fact that the man's been in prison.*

put sth away, (a) put in the usual place of storage, e g a drawer, box: *P~ your books/ toys away.* (b) save: *~ money away for one's old age.* **put sb away,** (*informal*) put into confinement, e g in a mental home: *He acted so strangely that he had to be ~ away.*

put back, (*naut*) return: *The ship/We ~ back to harbour.* **put sth back,** (a) replace: *P~ the dictionary back on the shelf.* (b) move backwards: *That clock is fast; I'd better ~ it back five minutes,* move the minute hand back. (c) (*fig*) stop the advance of, cause delay to: *The strike ~ back production by two months.*

put sth by, save for future use: *Has she any money ~ by/~ any money by?*

put (sth) down, (a) land: *He ~ down (his glider) in a field.* (b) set or place down: *P~ down your hands!* (c) press down: *When you get on the motorway, you can really ~ your foot down,* press the accelerator pedal down and go fast. **put one's foot down,** ⇨ foot [1](1). (d) place in storage: *~ down wine.* (e) suppress by force or authority: *~ down a rebellion.* (f) write down; make a note of: *Here's my address—~ it down before you forget it.* (g) (of animals, e g sick or old pets) kill. **put sb down,** (a) allow to alight: *The bus stopped to ~ down passengers.* (b) reduce to silence: *~ down hecklers at a political meeting.* **put sb down as,** consider that he is: *They ~ me down as a fool.* **put sb down for,** (a) write his name on a list as willing to give, e g to a charity or other fund: *You can ~ me down for £5.* (b) put a person's name down as an applicant, participant, etc: *They ~ him down for the school football team.* **put sth down to sth,** (a) charge to an account: *You can ~ the cost of the petrol down to business expenses.* (b) attribute to: *Can we ~ it down to his ignorance?*

put sth forward, (a) suggest for consideration: *~ forward a new theory.* (b) move on: *~ forward the hands of a clock,* e g when it is stopped or slow. **put sb forward,** propose: *~ oneself/a friend forward as a can-*

didate.

put in/into, (*naut*) (of a boat, its crew) enter: *The boat ~ in at Malta/~ into Malta for repairs.* **put in for sth,** apply formally for: *~ in for the position of manager.* **put in for leave,** request permission to be absent from duty, work, etc. **put sth in,** (a) cause to be in: *He ~ his head in at the window.* (b) present formally: *~ in a claim for damages.* (c) manage to hint or say: *~ in a blow.* (d) do, perform: *~ in an hour's work before breakfast.* (e) pass (time): *There's still an hour of work to ~ in before the pubs open.* **put in a good word for sb,** say something good about him to help him. **put sb in,** elect to office: *Which party will be ~ in at the next general election?* **put sb in mind of sb/sth,** remind him. ⇨ the noun entries for **put in** an appearance; **put the** boot **in**; **put one's** oar **in**. **put sth in/into sth,** devote; give: *~ a lot of work into improving one's French.*

put sth off, (a) postpone: *~ off going to the dentist.* (b) get rid of: *You must ~ off your doubts and fears.* (*Note: take off clothes.*) **put sb off (sth),** (a) do something with somebody at a later date: *We shall have to ~ the Smiths off till next week.* (b) make excuses and try to avoid, e g a duty: *I won't be ~ off with such silly excuses,* won't accept them. (c) hinder or dissuade: *~ a man off his game,* e g distract him when he is about to play.

put sth on, (a) (opposite = *take off*) clothe oneself with: *~ one's hat/shoes, etc on.* (b) pretend to have: *Her modesty is all ~ on,* she's only pretending to be modest. (c) increase; add to: *~ on more steam/ pressure/speed.* (d) add to: *He's ~ting on weight,* is getting heavier/fatter. (e) arrange for; make available: *~ on extra trains during the rush hours.* **put a play on,** arrange for it to be shown at a theatre. (f) advance: *~ the clock on one hour,* move the hands forward, e g for Summer Time. (g) (*informal*) exaggerate; pretend to be more important, etc than is justified: *Stop ~ting it on!* (h) turn on: *~ the light/T V on.* **put money on sb/sth,** gamble (in horse-racing, etc): *I've ~ a pound on the favourite.*

put sth out, (a) extinguish; cause to stop burning: *~ out the lights/the gas/the fire.* (b) dislocate: *She fell off a horse and ~ her shoulder out.* (c) produce: *The firm ~s out 1 000 bales of cotton sheeting every week.* ⇨ output. (d) issue; broadcast: *The Health Department has ~ out a warning about dangerous drugs.* **put one's tongue out,** show it, e g for a doctor, or as a rude act. **put sb out,** (a) cause to be confused or worried: *She was very much ~ out by your rudeness.* (b) inconvenience: *He was ~ out by the late arrival of his guests.* **put sb out (of),** expel: *Don't get drunk—you'll be ~ out!* e g of the bar

put sth through, carry it out: *~ through a business deal.* **put sb/sth through,** connect (by telephone): *Please ~ me/this call through to the Manager.* **put sb through sth,** cause him to undergo, e g an ordeal, a test: *The police ~ him through a severe examination.* **put sb through it,** (*informal*) test or examine him thoroughly, e g by inflicting suffering on him to get a confession.

put sth to sb, ⇨ 8 above. **be hard put to it (to do sth),** find difficulty in doing it: *I'd be hard ~ to say exactly why I disliked him.*

put sth together, construct (a whole) by combining parts: *It's easier to take a machine to pieces than to ~ it together again.* **put our / your / their heads together,** consult one another. **put two and two together,** ⇨ two.

put up (for sth), offer oneself for election: *Are you going to ~ up for Finchley again,* i e as a prospective member of Parliament? **put sb up,** provide lodging and food (for): *We can ~ you up for the weekend.* **put sb up (for sth),** propose, nominate him for a position.

put sb up to sth, urge him to do something naughty or wrong: *Who ~ you up to all these tricks?* **put sth up,** (a) raise; hold up: *~ up one's hands,* e g over one's head, as a sign that one is ready to answer, surrender; *~ up a flag/a sail.* (b) build: *~ up a shed/a tent.* (c) place so as to be seen: *~ up a notice.* (d) raise, increase: *~ up the rent by 50p (a week).* (e) offer, make: *~ up a good fight.* (f) supply (a sum of money for an undertaking): *I will supply the skill and knowledge if you will ~ up the £2 000 capital.* **put sb's back up,** ⇨ back¹ (1). **put sth up for auction/sale,** offer it to be auctioned/sold. **put up with sb/sth,** endure without protest; bear patiently: *There are many inconveniences that have to be ~ up with when you are camping.*

pu·ta·tive /ˈpjuːtətɪv/ *adj* generally considered to be: *his ~ father.*

pu·trefy /ˈpjuːtrɪfaɪ/ *vt,vi* (*pt,pp* -ied) (cause to) decay.

pu·tre·fac·tion /ˌpjuːtrɪˈfækʃən/ *n* [C,U]

pu·tres·cent /pjuˈtresənt/ *adj* in the process of decaying.

pu·trid /ˈpjuːtrɪd/ *adj* having become decayed; decomposed and smelling bad: *~ fish.*

putt /pʌt/ *vi,vt* strike (a golf ball) gently with a club so that it rolls across the ground towards or into a hole.

putty /ˈpʌtɪ/ *n* [U] soft paste of white powder and oil used for fixing glass in window frames, etc. □ *vt* (*pt,pp* -ied) fill or fix with putty: *~ up a hole.*

puzzle /ˈpʌzəl/ *n* [C] **1** question or problem difficult to understand or answer. **2** problem (e g *a `crossword-~*) or toy (e g *a `jig- saw-~*) designed to test a person's knowledge, skill, patience. **3** (*sing* only) state of feeling confused, thinking hard about a problem: *be in a ~ about this refusal.* □ *vt, vi* **1** cause (a person) to be confused, worried, (about the solution to a problem): *This letter ~s me.* **2** *puzzle over sth,* think very much about it. *puzzle sth out,* (try to) find the answer or solution by thinking hard.

puz·zler, difficult problem.

puz·zle·ment *n* [U] state of being puzzled.

pygmy, pigmy /ˈpɪgmɪ/ *n* [C] (*pl* -ies) **1** P~, dwarf race in Equatorial Africa. **2** very small person; dwarf.

py·ja·mas (*US* = **pa·ja·mas**) /pəˈdʒɑːməz *US:* -ˈdʒæm-/ *n pl* (also *a pair of ~*) loose-fitting jacket and trousers for sleeping in. (*Note: singular* when used as an *adjective: py`jama tops/bottoms.*)

py·lon /ˈpaɪlən *US:* -lɒn/ *n* [C] tower (steel framework) for carrying overhead high-voltage electric cables.

py·or·rhoea (also **-rhea**) /ˌpaɪəˈrɪə/ *n* [U] inflammation of the gums causing them to shrink, with loosening of the teeth.

pyra·mid /ˈpɪrəmɪd/ *n* [C] **1** structure with a triangular or square base and sloping sides meeting at a point, esp one of those built of stone in ancient Egypt. **2** pile of objects in the shape of a pyramid.

pyre /ˈpaɪə(r)/ *n* [C] large pile of wood for burning, esp a funeral pile for a corpse.

py·thon /ˈpaɪθən/ *n* [C] large snake that kills its prey by twisting itself round it and crushing it.

Qq

Q, q /kjuː/ (*pl* Q's, q's /kjuːz/) the seventeenth letter of the English alphabet. *mind one's P's and Q's,* ⇨ P,p.

quack[1] /kwæk/ *vi, n* (make the) cry of a duck.

quack[2] /kwæk/ *n* [C] person dishonestly claiming to have medical knowledge and skill: (as an *adjective*) ~ *remedies.*

quad /kwɒd/ *n* [C] (abbr of) **1** = quadrangle. **2** = quadruplet (but *quad* is more usual).

quad·rangle /ˈkwɒdræŋgəl/ *n* [C] **1** flat shape with four sides, esp a square or a rectangle. **2** (abbr **quad**) space in the form of a rectangle, (nearly) surrounded by buildings.

quad·ran·gu·lar /kwɒˈdræŋgjʊlə(r)/ *adj*

quad·rant /ˈkwɒdrənt/ *n* [C] **1** quarter of a circle or its circumference. **2** graduated strip of metal, etc shaped like a quarter of a circle, for use in measuring angles (of altitude) in astronomy and navigation.

quad·ri·lat·eral /ˌkwɒdrɪˈlætrəl/ *adj, n* [C] (of a) quadrangle(1).

quad·ru·ped /ˈkwɒdrʊped/ *n* [C] (*formal*) four-footed animal.

quad·ruple /ˈkwɒdrʊpəl *US:* kwɒˈdrʊpəl/ *adj* **1** made up of four parts. **2** agreed to by four persons, parties, etc: *a ~ alliance,* of four Powers. □ *n* [C] number or amount four times as great as another: *20 is the ~ of 5.* □ *vt, vi* multiply by four: *He has ~d his income/His income has ~d in the last four years.*

quad·ru·plet /ˈkwɒdrʊplɪt *US:* kwɒˈdruː-/ *n* [C] (abbr **quad** which is more usual) one of four babies at a birth. (*Note:* usually *pl: one of the ~s,* not *a ~*).

quad·ru·pli·cate /kwɒˈdrʊplɪkət/ *adj* repeated or copied four times. □ *n: in ~,* in four exactly similar examples or copies. □ *vt* /kwɒˈdrʊplɪkeɪt/ make four specimens of.

quag·mire /ˈkwɒgmaɪə(r)/ *n* [C] area of soft, wet land.

quail[1] /kweɪl/ *n* [C] small bird, similar to a partridge, valued as food.

quail[2] /kweɪl/ *vi* feel or show fear: *He ~ed at the prospect before him.*

quaint /kweɪnt/ *adj* (-er, -est) attractive or pleasing because unusual or old-fashioned: *American visitors to England admire our ~ villages/customs.*

quaint·ly *adv*

quaint·ness *n* [U]

quake /kweɪk/ *vi* **1** (of the earth) shake: *The ground ~d under his feet.* **2** (of persons) tremble: *quaking with fear/cold.*

Quaker /ˈkweɪkə(r)/ *n* member of the Society of Friends, a Christian group that holds informal meetings instead of formal church services and is opposed to the use of violence or resort to war under any circumstances.

quali·fi·ca·tion /ˌkwɒlɪfɪˈkeɪʃən/ *n* **1** [U] act of restricting, modifying or limiting; [C] something which restricts, modifies or limits: *You can accept his statement without ~/with certain ~s.* **2** [C] training, test, diploma, degree, etc that qualifies(1) a person.

qual·ify /ˈkwɒlɪfaɪ/ *vt, vi* (*pt, pp* -ied) **1** be trained, educated and approved as having the required standard: *He's qualified/His training qualifies him as a teacher of English/for this post.* **2** have the necessary experience, ability, age, etc: *He's the manager's son but that does not ~ him to criticize my work. Do you ~ for the vote/to vote?* **3** limit; make less general: *The statement 'Boys are lazy' needs to be qualified,* e g by saying 'Some boys' or 'Many boys'. **4** (*gram*) limit the meaning of: *Adjectives ~ nouns.*

quali·fied /-faɪd/ *adj* (a) having the necessary qualifications: *a qualified doctor.* (b) limited: *give a scheme one's qualified approval.*

`**quali·fier** /-faɪə(r)/ *n* [C] (*gram*) qualifying word, e g an adjective or adverb.

quali·ta·tive /ˈkwɒlɪtətɪv *US:* -teɪt-/ *adj*

relating to quality: ~ *analysis.* ⇨ quantitative.

qual·ity /ˈkwolətɪ/ n (pl -ies) **1** [C,U] (esp high standard, of) goodness or worth: *We aim at ~ rather than quantity,* aim to produce superior goods, not large quantities. **2** [C] something that is special in or that distinguishes a person or thing: *One ~ of pinewood is that it can be sawn easily.*

qualm /ˈkwɑm/ n [C] **1** feeling of doubt (esp about whether one is doing or has done right): *He felt no ~s about borrowing money from friends.* **2** temporary feeling of sickness in the stomach: *~s which spoilt his appetite.*

quan·dary /ˈkwondərɪ/ n [C] (pl -ies) state of doubt or confusion: *be in a ~ about what to do next.*

quan·ti·tat·ive /ˈkwontɪtətɪv US: -teɪt-/ adj relating to quantity: *~ analysis.* ⇨ qualitative.

quan·tity /ˈkwontətɪ/ n (pl -ies) **1** [U] the property of things which can be measured, e g size, weight, number: *I prefer quality to ~.* **2** [C] amount, total or number: *There's only a small ~* (i e not much or not many) *left.* **3** (often pl) large amount or number; *He buys things in large quantities.* **4 an unknown quantity, (a)** (maths) symbol (usually *x*) representing an unknown value in an equation. **(b)** (fig) person or thing whose ability, etc is not known.

'quantity sur'veyor, expert who estimates quantities of materials needed in building, their cost, etc.

quar·an·tine /ˈkworəntin US: ˈkwɔr-/ n [C,U] (esp of imported animals) (period of) separation from others until it is known that there is no danger of spreading disease: *be in/out of ~.* □ vt put in quarantine.

quar·rel /ˈkworəl US: ˈkwɔrəl/ n [C] **1** angry argument; strong disagreement: *have a ~ with him about the weather.* **2** cause for being angry; reason for protest or complaint: *I have no ~ with/against him.* **pick a quarrel (with sb),** find or invent some occasion or excuse for disagreement, etc. □ vi (-ll-, US also -l-) **1** have, take part in, a quarrel: *The thieves ~led with one another about how to divide the loot.* **2** disagree (with); complain about: *It's not the fact of examinations I'm ~ling with; it's the way they're conducted.*

'quar·rel·some /-səm/ adj quickly made to argue.

quarry[1] /ˈkworɪ US: ˈkwɔrɪ/ n [C] (pl -ies) (usually sing) animal, bird, etc which is hunted.

quarry[2] /ˈkworɪ US: ˈkwɔrɪ/ n [C] (pl -ies) place (not underground like a mine) where stone, slate, etc is obtained (for building, road-making, etc). □ vt,vi (pt,pp -ied) get from a quarry: *~ limestone.*

quart /ˈkwɔt/ n [C] measure of capacity equal to two pints or about 1·14 litre.

quar·ter /ˈkwɔtə(r)/ n [C] **1** fourth part (¼);

one of four equal or corresponding parts: *a ~ of a mile; a mile and a ~; a ~ of an hour,* 15 minutes; *an hour and a ~; the first ~ of this century,* i e 1901—25. **2** point of time 15 minutes before or after any hour: *a ~ to* (US = of) *two; a ~ past six.* **3** three months, esp as a period for which rent and other payments are made. **4** (US) (coin worth) 25 cents. **5** (used of animals in compounds) section including a leg: `*fore-~s;* `*hind-~s.* **6** direction; district; source of supply. help, information, etc: *travel in every ~ of the globe,* everywhere. *As his father was penniless, he could expect no help from that ~.* **7** division of a town, esp one of a particular group of people: *the Chinese ~ of San Francisco.* **8** one-fourth of a lunar month: *the moon at the first ~/in its last ~.* **9** (pl) place to stay in: *married ~s. All troops must return to ~s at once,* return to barracks. ⇨ headquarters. **10 at close quarters,** close together. **11** place for duty by sailors on a ship, esp for fighting: *Officers and men at once took up their ~s.* **12** back part of a ship's side: *on the port/ starboard ~.* **13** (GB) fourth part of a hundredweight, 28 lb; (US) 25 lb; measure of grain of eight bushels. □ vt **1** divide into quarters. **2** place (troops) in lodgings: *~ troops on the villagers.*

'quarter-'final, (sport) one of four competitions or matches, the winners of which play in the semi-finals.

`quarter·master, **(a)** (army) (abbr QM) officer in charge of the stores, etc of a battalion. **(b)** (navy) petty officer in charge of steering the ship, signals, etc.

'quarter·master-'general, (abbr QMG) staff officer in charge of supplies for a whole army.

quar·ter·ly /ˈkwɔtəlɪ/ adj, adv (happening) once in each three months: *~ payments; to be paid ~.*

quar·tet, quar·tette /kwɔˈtet/ n [C] (piece of music for) four players or singers: *a string ~,* for (usually) two violins, viola and cello; *a piano ~,* for piano and three stringed instruments.

quartz /ˈkwɔts/ n [U] sorts of hard mineral (esp crystallized silica), including agate and other semi-precious stones.

quash /ˈkwoʃ/ vt put an end to, annul, reject as not valid (by legal procedure): *~ a verdict/decision.*

quasi- /ˈkweɪsaɪ/ prefix almost, partly: *a quasi-official position.*

quat·er·cen·ten·ary /ˌkwotəˈsenˈtinərɪ US: ˌkwotərˈsentənerɪ/ adj, n [C] (pl -ies) (of the) 400th anniversary: *the ~ celebrations in 1964 of Shakespeare's birth.*

qua·ver /ˈkweɪvə(r)/ vt,vi **1** (of the voice or a sound) shake; tremble: *in a ~ing voice; in a voice that ~ed.* **2** say or sing in a shaking voice. □ n [C] **1** trembling sound. **2** (music) note with one-half the value of a crotchet.

quay /kiː/ n [C] landing-place usually built of stone or iron, alongside which ships can be tied up for loading and unloading.

queasy /ˈkwiːzɪ/ adj (-ier, -iest) 1 (of food) causing a feeling of sickness in the stomach. 2 (of the stomach) easily upset. 3 (of a person) easily made sick.
`queas·ily` /-əlɪ/ adv

queen /kwiːn/ n [C] 1 woman ruler in her own right: the Q∼ of England; Q∼ Elizabeth II. 2 wife of a king. 3 woman regarded as first of a group: a `beauty-∼. 4 (chess) most powerful piece for attack or defence. 5 (playing-cards) one with the picture of a queen: the ∼ of spades/hearts. 6 fertile, egg-producing, female of bees, ants, etc.
queen mother, mother of a reigning sovereign.
`Queen's `Counsel, (abbr Q C) ⇨ King's Counsel.
queen·ly adj like, fit for, a queen.

queer /kwɪə(r)/ adj (-er, -est) 1 strange; unusual: a ∼ way of talking. 2 causing doubt or suspicion: ∼ noises in the attic. 3 (informal) unwell: feel very ∼.

quell /kwel/ vt suppress (a rebellion, rebels, opposition).

quench /kwentʃ/ vt 1 put out (flames, fire). 2 satisfy (thirst). 3 put an end to (hope).

queru·lous /ˈkwerjələs/ adj (formal) full of complaints: in a ∼ tone.

query /ˈkwɪərɪ/ n [C] (pl -ies) 1 question, esp one raising a doubt about the truth of something: raise a ∼. 2 mark (eg ?) put against something, eg in the margin of a document, as a sign of doubt. □ vt 1 inquire: I ∼ whether/if his word can be relied on. 2 express doubt about: ∼ a person's instructions. 3 put a mark (eg ?) against.

quest /kwest/ n [C] (formal) search: the ∼ for gold. □ vt (formal) search (for): ∼ing for further evidence.

ques·tion[1] /ˈkwestʃən/ n [C] 1 sentence which by word-order, use of words such as who, why, etc written with ? at the end, or by intonation, asks for information, an answer, etc. 2 something which needs to be decided; inquiry; problem: economic ∼s. Success is only a ∼ of time, will certainly come sooner or later. The ∼ is..., What we want to know, What we must decide, is.... In question, being talked about: Where's the man in ∼? out of the question, impossible: We can't go out in this weather; it's out of the ∼. 3 [U] (the putting forward of) doubt; objection: There is no ∼ about/some ∼ as to his honesty. beyond (all)/without question, certain(ly); without doubt: His honesty is beyond all ∼. Without ∼, he's the best man for the job.
`question-mark, the mark (?) at the end of a written question.
`question time, (in the House of Commons) period when ministers answer questions put by Members.

ques·tion[2] /ˈkwestʃən/ vt 1 ask a question; examine: He was ∼ed by the police. 2 express or feel doubt about: ∼ her honesty; ∼ the value/importance of games at school.
`ques·tion·able` /-əbəl/ adj doubtful: a ∼able assertion.
`ques·tion·ably` /-əblɪ/ adv
ques·tioner, person who questions.

ques·tion·naire /ˌkwestʃəˈneə(r)/ n [C] printed list of questions to be answered by a group of people, esp to get facts or information, or for a survey.

queue /kjuː/ n [C] 1 line of people waiting for their turn (eg to enter a cinema, get on a bus, buy something): form a/stand in a ∼. jump the queue, ⇨ jump[2](8). 2 line of vehicles waiting to proceed: a ∼ of cars held up by the traffic lights. □ vi get into, be in, a queue: ∼ up for tickets/to buy tickets for the pop festival.

quibble /ˈkwɪbəl/ n [C] attempt to escape giving an honest answer (in an argument), by using a secondary or doubtful meaning of a word or phrase. □ vi argue about small points or differences: ∼ over nothing of importance.

quick /kwɪk/ adj (-er, -est) 1 moving fast; able to move fast and do things in a short time; done in a short time: a ∼ train/ worker; have a ∼ meal. Be ∼ about it! Hurry up! 2 lively; bright; active; prompt: ∼ to seize an opportunity; ∼ at figures; a ∼ (= intelligent) child; a ∼ temper, easily angered. □ n [U] tender or sensitive flesh below the skin, esp the nails: bite one's nails to the ∼. cut/touch sb to the quick, hurt his feelings deeply. □ adv (-er, -est) (informal, = quickly and always placed after the verb): Can't you run ∼er? He wants to get rich ∼.
`quick-step, kind of ballroom dancing step.
quick·ly adv
quick·ness n [U]

quicken /ˈkwɪkən/ vt,vi 1 make or become quick(er): We ∼ed our pace. Our pace ∼ed. 2 make or become more lively, vigorous or active: His pulse ∼ed.

quick·sand /ˈkwɪksænd/ n [C] (area of) loose, wet, deep sand which sucks down men, animals, vehicles, etc that try to cross it.

quick·sil·ver /ˈkwɪksɪlvə(r)/ n [U] = mercury.

quick·step /ˈkwɪkstep/ n ⇨ quick.

quid /kwɪd/ n [C] (GB sl; pl unchanged) = pound[2](2): earning twenty ∼ (= £20) a week.

quiet /ˈkwaɪət/ adj (-er, -est) 1 with little or no movement or sound: a ∼ sea/evening. 2 free from excitement, trouble, anxiety: live a ∼ life in the country. 3 gentle; not rough (in disposition, etc): ∼ children. 4 (of colours) not bright. 5 not open or revealed: harbouring ∼ resentment. keep sth quiet, keep it secret. **on the quiet**, (or, *informal*, **on the q t** /ˈkjuː ti/), secretly: *have a whisky on the ~*. □ *n* [U] state of being quiet (all senses): *live in peace and ~*.

quieten /ˈkwaɪətən/ *vt, vi* make or become quiet: *~ children/fears/suspicions. The city ~ed down after the political disturbances.*

quiff /kwɪf/ *n* [C] lock of hair brushed up above the forehead.

quill /kwɪl/ *n* [C] 1 (also `~-feather`) large wing or tail feather; (hollow stem of) such a feather formerly used for writing with: *a ~ pen.* 2 long, sharp, stiff spine of a porcupine.

quilt /kwɪlt/ *n* [C] thick bed-covering of two layers of cloth padded with soft material kept in place by cross lines of stitches. ⇨ continental quilt, duvet. □ *vt* make in the form of a quilt, ie with soft material between layers of cloth: *a ~ed dressing-gown.*

quin /kwɪn/ *n* [C] quintuplet (but *quin* is more usual).

quin·cen·ten·ary /ˌkwɪnsənˈtiːnərɪ *US:* -ˈsentənerɪ/ *adj, n* [C] (*pl* -ies) (of) (the celebration of the) 500th anniversary of an event.

quin·ine /kwɪˈniːn *US:* ˈkwaɪnaɪn/ *n* [U] bitter medicine used for fevers such as malaria.

Quin·qua·ges·ima /ˌkwɪŋkwəˈdʒesɪmə/ *n* the Sunday before Lent.

quin·tes·sence /kwɪnˈtesəns/ *n* [C] (*formal*) perfect example: *the ~ of virtue/ politeness.*

quin·tet, quin·tette /kwɪnˈtet/ *n* [C] (piece of music for) five players or singers: *a string ~*, string quartet and an additional cello or viola; *a piano ~*, string quartet and piano; *a wind ~*, bassoon, clarinet, flute, horn and oboe.

quin·tu·plet /ˈkwɪntjʊplɪt *US:* kwɪnˈtuplɪt/ *n* [C] (abbr *quin* which is more usual) one of five babies at a birth. (*Note:* usually *pl*, one of the *~s*, not *a ~*.)

quip /kwɪp/ *n* [C] clever, witty or sarcastic remark or saying. □ *vi* (-pp-) make quips.

quire /ˈkwaɪə(r)/ *n* [C] twenty-four sheets of writing-paper.

quirk /kwɜːk/ *n* [C] 1 quip. 2 odd action or behaviour.

quis·ling /ˈkwɪzlɪŋ/ *n* [C] person who cooperates with the authorities of an enemy country which are occupying his country.

quit[1] /kwɪt/ *adj* free, clear: *We are well ~ of him*, fortunate to be rid of him.

quit[2] /kwɪt/ *vt* (*pt* ~ted or ~) (-tt-, *US* also -t-) 1 go away from; leave: *I ~ted him in disgust. We've had notice to ~*, a warning that we must give up the house we rent. 2 stop: *~ work when the bell rings.*

quit·ter, (*informal*) person who does not finish what he has started.

quite /kwaɪt/ *adv* 1 completely; altogether: *I ~ agree/understand. She was ~ alone. That's ~ another* (ie a completely different) *story.* 2 to a certain extent; more or less: *~ a*

good player. *It's ~ warm today. She ~ likes him.* (*Note:* used before an *adjective.*) 3 really; truly: *She's ~ a beauty.* 4 (used to show agreement, understanding, etc): A: *'It's a difficult situation'.* B: *'Q~ (so)!'* A: *'I'm so sorry; I'm afraid I'm late'.* B: *'Oh, that's ~ all right'.*

quits /kwɪts/ *adj* **be quits (with sb)**, be on even terms (by repaying a debt of money, punishment, etc): *We're ~ now.* **call it quits**, agree that things are even, that a dispute or quarrel is over. **double or quits**, ⇨ double[3](1).

quiver[1] /ˈkwɪvə(r)/ *n* [C] sheath for carrying arrows.

quiver[2] /ˈkwɪvə(r)/ *vt, vi* (cause to) tremble slightly or vibrate: *a ~ing leaf.* □ *n* [C] quivering sound or movement.

quix·otic /kwɪkˈsɒtɪk/ *adj* (*formal*) generous, unselfish, imaginative, in a way that disregards one's own welfare.

quiz /kwɪz/ *vt* (-zz-) ask questions of, as a test of knowledge. □ *n* [C] (-zz-) (*modern use*) general knowledge test or contest.

quiz·zi·cal /ˈkwɪzɪkəl/ *adj* (*formal*) 1 causing amusement. 2 teasing: *a ~ smile.* 3 expressing disbelief, puzzlement; questioning: *a ~ look.*

quiz·zi·cally /-klɪ/ *adv*

quoit /kɔɪt *US:* kwɔɪt/ *n* [C] ring (of metal, rubber, rope) to be thrown at a peg so as to encircle it; (*pl*) this game (often played on the deck of a ship).

quo·rum /ˈkwɔːrəm/ *n* [C] (*pl* ~s) number of persons who must, by the rules, be present at a meeting (of a committee, etc) before its proceedings can have authority: *have/form a ~.*

quota /ˈkwəʊtə/ *n* [C] (*pl* ~s) limited share, amount or number, esp a quantity of goods allowed to be manufactured, sold, etc or number, e g of immigrants allowed to enter a country: *The ~ of trainees for this year has already been filled.*

quo·ta·tion /kwəʊˈteɪʃən/ *n* 1 [U] quoting(1). 2 [C] something quoted(1): *~s from Shakespeare.* 3 [C] statement of the current price of an article, etc: *the latest ~s from the Stock Exchange.* 4 [C] estimate of the cost of a piece of work: *Can you give me a ~ for building a garage?*

quotation marks, the marks ' ' or ' ' enclosing words quoted.

quote /kwəʊt/ *vt* 1 repeat, write (words used by another, from a book, an author, etc): *~ from the newspaper; ~ the Chairman.* 2 give (a reference, etc) to support a statement: *Can you ~ (me) a recent instance?* 3 name, mention (a price): *This is the best price I can ~ you.*

quot·able /-əbəl/ *adj* that can be, or deserves to be, quoted.

quoth /kwəʊθ/ *vt* (*archaic*) (1st and 3rd person *sing*, *pt* only) said: *~ I/he/she.*

quo·tient /ˈkwəʊʃənt/ *n* [C] (*maths*) number obtained by dividing one number by another.

Rr

R, r /ɑ(r)/ (pl R's, r's /ɑz/) the eighteenth letter of the English alphabet. **the three R's**, reading, (w)riting and (a)rithmetic as the basis of an elementary education.

rabbi /ˈræbaɪ/ n [C] (pl ~s) teacher of the Jewish law; (title of a) spiritual leader of a Jewish congregation.

rab·bin·i·cal /rəˈbɪnɪkəl/ adj

rab·bit /ˈræbɪt/ n [C] small burrowing animal with long ears of the hare family, brownish-grey in its natural state, black or white or bluish-grey in domestic varieties. □ vt (-tt-) hunt rabbits: go ~ting.

`rabbit-hutch, wooden cage for domestic rabbits.

`rabbit-punch, punch on the back of the neck with the side of the hand.

`rabbit-warren, area of land full of rabbit-burrows.

rabble /ˈræbəl/ n [C] disorderly crowd; mob.

`rabble-rousing adj inciting the passions of the mob: ~-rousing speeches/speakers.

rabid /ˈræbɪd/ adj 1 affected with rabies. 2 (fig) furious; fanatical: ~ hate of Socialism.

ra·bies /ˈreɪbiz/ n [U] infectious fatal disease causing madness in dogs and other animals.

rac·coon = racoon.

race[1] /reɪs/ n [C] 1 contest or competition in speed, e g in running, swimming or to see who can finish a piece of work, or get to a certain place, first: a `horse-~; run a ~ with the other school. **a race against time**, an effort to finish something before a certain time. 2 strong, fast current of water in the sea, a river, etc. □ vi, vt 1 compete in speed, have a race; move at full speed: boys racing home from school; ~ with/against somebody for a prize. 2 own or train horses for racing and take part in horse-races: He ~s at all the big meetings. 3 cause (a person or thing) to move at full speed: He ~d me to the station in his car.

rac·ing n [U] (esp) the hobby, sport or profession of running horses or driving motor-cars in races.

`race-course, ground where horse-races are run.

`race-horse, special breed for running in races.

`race-meeting, occasion when a number of horse-races are held at a certain place.

`race-track, path prepared for races, e g in a stadium.

race[2] /reɪs/ n 1 [C,U] any of several subdivisions of mankind sharing certain physical characteristics, esp colour of skin, colour and type of hair, shape of eyes and nose: people of the same ~ but of different culture. 2 [C] (used loosely for) group of people having a common culture, history or language: the `German ~. 3 (as an adjective): Can ~ relations be improved by legislation? 4 [U] ancestry (the usual word). 5 [C] main division of any living creatures: the human ~, mankind.

ra·cial /ˈreɪʃəl/ adj relating to race[2](1,2): ~ conflict/minorities/discrimination.

ra·cially /-ʃəlɪ/ adv

ra·cial·ism /-ɪzm/ n [U] conflict between different races; belief that one's own race is superior.

ra·cial·ist /-ɪst/, person who believes that some races are superior to others.

ra·cily, raci·ness ⇨ racy₁

ra·cing /ˈreɪsɪŋ/ n ⇨ race[1].

ra·cism /ˈreɪsɪzm/ n [U] = racialism.

ra·cist /-ɪst/ n [C] = racialist.

rack[1] /ræk/ n [C] 1 wooden or metal framework for holding food for animals (in a stable or in the fields). 2 framework with bars, pegs, etc for holding things, hanging things on, etc: a `plate-~; a tool-`~. 3 shelf over the seats of a train, plane, bus, etc for light luggage: a `luggage-~. 4 rod, bar or rail with teeth or cogs into which the teeth on a wheel (or pinion) fit (as used on special railways up a steep hill-side).

rack[2] /ræk/ n [C] (usually the ~) instrument of torture consisting of a frame with rollers to which a person's wrists and ankles were tied so that his joints were stretched when the rollers were turned. □ vt 1 torture by placing on the rack. 2 (of a disease or mental agony) inflict torture on: ~ed with pain. 3 **rack one's brains (for),** make great mental efforts (for, in order to find, an answer, method, etc).

rack[3] /ræk/ n (only in) **go to rack and ruin,** fall into a ruined state.

racket[1] /ˈrækɪt/ n 1 (sing only, with a, an or [U]) loud noise: The drunken men in the street kicked up such a ~, were very noisy. 2 [U] (time of) great social activity: I hate the ~ of living in London. 3 [C] (informal) dishonest way of getting money (by deceiving or threatening people, selling worthless goods, etc). 4 [C] ordeal.

rack·et·eer /ˈrækɪˈtɪə(r)/ n [C] person who is engaged in a racket(3).

racket[2], **rac·quet** /ˈrækɪt/ n [C] 1 light, stringed bat used for hitting the ball in tennis, badminton, etc. 2 (pl) ball-game for two or four players in a court with four walls.

rac·on·teur /ˈrækonˈtɜ(r)/ n [C] person who tells stories with skill and wit.

rac·oon, rac·coon /rəˈkun US: ræ-/ n [C] small, flesh-eating animal of N America with a bushy, ringed tail; [U] its fur.

rac·quet /ˈrækɪt/ n = racket².

racy /ˈreɪsɪ/ adj (-ier, -iest) **1** (of speech or writing) full of activity; spirited; vigorous: a ~ style/novel. **2** having strongly marked qualities: a ~ flavour
ra·ci·ly /-əlɪ/ adv
ra·ci·ness n [U]

ra·dar /ˈreɪdɑ(r)/ n [U] (the use of) apparatus that shows on a screen (by means of radio echoes) solid objects that come within its range, used (e g by pilots of ships, aircraft or spacecraft) in fog or darkness and which gives information about their position, movement, speed, etc: follow an aircraft by ~; (as an adjective): a ~ screen.

ra·dial /ˈreɪdɪəl/ adj **1** relating to a ray, rays or a radius. **2** (of spokes in a bicycle wheel, etc) from a centre; arranged like rays or radii. □ n [C] (also ~ tyre) tyre designed (by having the material inside the tyre wrapped in a direction radial to the hub of the wheel) to give more grip on road surfaces, esp when cornering or when roads are wet.
ra·di·al·ly /-ɪəlɪ/ adv

radi·ance /ˈreɪdɪəns/ n [U] radiant quality.

ra·di·ant /ˈreɪdɪənt/ adj **1** sending out rays of light; shining: the ~ sun. **2** (of a person, his looks, eyes) showing great joy or love: a ~ face. **3** (physics) transmitted by radiation: ~ heat/energy.
ra·di·ant·ly adv

ra·di·ate /ˈreɪdɪeɪt/ vt,vi **1** send out rays of (light or heat). **2** (fig) send out: a bride who ~s happiness. **3** come or go out in rays; show: heat that ~s from a fireplace; the happiness that ~s from her eyes. **4** spread out like radii: the avenues that ~ from the Arc de Triomphe in Paris.

ra·di·ation /ˌreɪdɪˈeɪʃən/ n **1** [U] radiating. **2** [U] (physics) the sending out of energy, heat, light, etc in rays. **3** [C] something radiated: ~s emitted by an X-ray apparatus.

ra·di·ator /ˈreɪdɪeɪtə(r)/ n [C] **1** apparatus (in a room) for radiating heat, esp heat from hot water supplied through pipes or from electric current. **2** device for cooling the cylinders of the engine of a motor vehicle: This car has a fan-cooled ~.
`radiator grill, grill in front of the engine of a motor vehicle.

rad·ical /ˈrædɪkəl/ adj **1** of or from the root or base: ~ (= thorough and complete) changes. **2** (in politics) favouring complete reform; advanced (and usually left-wing) in opinions and policies: a member of the R~ Party. □ n [C] person with radical(2) opinions.
radi·cal·ly /-klɪ/ adv

ra·dii /ˈreɪdɪaɪ/ n pl ▷ radius.

ra·dio /ˈreɪdɪəʊ/ n (pl ~s) **1** [U] (communication by) electromagnetic waves or by telephone: send a message by ~. **2** [U] broadcasting by this means: hear something on the ~; (as an adjective) a ~ programme. **3** [C] apparatus (e g on ships, aircraft) for transmitting and receiving radio messages or (e g in the home) for receiving sound broadcast programmes: a transistor ~.
`radio frequency, frequency(2) between 10 kilocycles per second and 300 000 megacycles per second.

radio- /ˈreɪdɪəʊ/ prefix (esp) of rays.
'radio `telescope, apparatus that detects stars by means of radio waves from outer space and tracks spacecraft.
'radio `therapist, expert in radio therapy.
'radio-`therapy, treatment of disease by means of X-rays or other forms of radiation, e g of heat.

radio-active /ˌreɪdɪəʊ ˈæktɪv/ adj (of such metals as uranium) having atoms that break up and, in so doing, send out rays in the form of electrically charged particles capable of passing through material that cannot be seen through and of producing electrical effects: ~active dust, dust (e g as carried by winds) from explosions of nuclear bombs, etc.
'radio-ac·tiv·ity n [U]

radi·ogra·phy /ˌreɪdɪˈɒɡrəfɪ/ n [U] production of X-ray photographs.
'radi·`ogra·pher, person trained in radiography.

radio-iso·tope /ˈreɪdɪəʊ ˈaɪsətəʊp/ n [C] radioactive form of an element, used in medicine, industry, etc.

rad·ish /ˈrædɪʃ/ n [C] salad plant with a white or red edible root.

ra·dius /ˈreɪdɪəs/ n [C] (pl radii /-dɪaɪ/) **1** (length of a) straight line from the centre of a circle or sphere to any point on the circumference or surface. **2** circular area measured by its radius: The police searched all the fields and woods within a ~ of two miles. **3** (anat) outer of the two bones in the forearm.

raf·fia /ˈræfɪə/ n [U] fibre from the leafstalks of a kind of palm-tree, used for making baskets, hats, mats, etc.

raffle /ˈræfəl/ n [C] sale of an article by a lottery, often for a charitable purpose. □ vt sell in a raffle: ~ (off) a television.

raft /rɑft US: ræft/ n [C] **1** number of logs fastened together to be floated down a river. **2** = life-raft: The sailors got away from the wrecked ship on a ~. □ vt,vi carry, move, go, on a raft.

raf·ter /ˈrɑftə(r) US: ˈræf-/ n [C] one of the sloping beams of the framework on which the tiles or slates of a roof are supported.

rag¹ /ræg/ n [C] **1** odd bit of cloth: a ~ to polish the car with. **2** (used contemptuously for a) newspaper: Why do you read that worthless ~?

rag² /ræg/ vt (-gg-) (informal) play practical jokes on. □ n [C] procession of amusing floats (3), e g as held by college students.
`rag-day, day on which students hold a rag, and often collect money for charity.

raga·muf·fin /ˈrægəmʌfɪn/ n [C] (dated)

527

dirty, disreputable person, esp a small boy dressed in rags.

rage /reɪdʒ/ n 1 [C,U] (outburst of) furious anger: *shouting with ~; the ~ of the sea*, its violence during a storm. *be in/fly into a rage*, be, become, very angry. 2 [C] strong desire: *He has a ~ for collecting butterflies.* 3 *be (all) the rage*, (*informal*) something for which there is temporary enthusiasm: *Long hair on men is all the ~ this summer.* □ *vi* be very angry; (of storms, etc) be violent: *He ~d and fumed against me for not letting him have his own way. The storm/battle ~d all day.*

rag·ged /ˈrægɪd/ adj 1 (with clothes) badly torn or in rags: *a ~ coat/old man.* 2 having rough or irregular edges or outlines or surfaces: *a dog with a ~ coat of hair; a sleeve with ~ edges.* 3 (of work, etc) lacking smoothness or uniformity: *a ~ performance*, e g of an actor, a piece of music.
rag·ged·ly adv

rag-time /ˈrægtaɪm/ n [U] (1920's) popular music and dance of US Negro origin, the accent of the melody falling just before the regular beat of the accompaniment.

raid /reɪd/ n [C] 1 surprise attack made by troops, ship(s) or aircraft: *make a ~ on the enemy's camp; killed in an `air~* (attack by aircraft). 2 sudden visit by police to make arrests: *a ~ on a casino.* 3 sudden attack for the purpose of taking money: *a ~ on a bank by armed men.* □ *vt,vi* carry out a raid: *Boys have been ~ing my orchard*, visiting it to steal fruit.
raider, person, ship, aircraft, etc that makes a raid.

rail¹ /reɪl/ n [C] 1 horizontal or sloping bar or rod or continuous series of bars or rods, of wood or metal, as part of a fence, as a protection against contact or falling over: *metal ~s round a monument. He was leaning over the (ship's) ~.* 2 similar bar or rod placed for things to hang on: *a `towel-~*, e g at the side of a wash-basin. 3 steel bar or continuous line of such bars, laid on the ground as one side of a track for trains or trams: *a `~ strike*, of railway workers. *off the rails*, (a) (of a train) off the track. (b) (*fig*) out of order, out of control. (c) (*informal*) mad. □ *vt rail off/in*, put rails(1) round: *fields that are ~ed off from the road.*
`rail-road, (*US*) = railway.
**`rail-way**, (a) track on which trains run: *build a new ~way.* (b) system of such tracks, with the locomotives, wagons, etc and the organization controlling the system: *work on/nationalize the ~way.* (c) (as an adjective): *a `~way station/bridge.*
rail·ing n [C] (often *pl*) fence made with rails.
rail² /reɪl/ *vi* find fault; criticize.
rai·ment /ˈreɪmənt/ n [U] (*literary*) clothing.
rain¹ /reɪn/ n 1 [U] condensed moisture of the atmosphere falling in separate drops; fall of such drops: *It looks like ~*, as if there will be a fall of ~. *Don't go out in the ~.* *(come) rain or shine*, whether the weather is wet or sunny. 2 (with *a* and an *adjective*) fall or shower of rain: *There was a heavy ~ last night.* 3 (usually *sing* with *a*) fall of something like rain: *a ~ of arrows/bullets.*
the rains, the season in tropical countries when there is heavy and continuous rain.
rain-bow /ˈreɪnbəʊ/, arch containing the colours of the spectrum, formed in the sky opposite the sun when rain is falling or when the sun shines on mist or spray.
`rain-coat, light coat of waterproof or tightly-woven material.
`rain-drop, single drop of rain.
`rain-fall, amount of rain falling within a given area in a given time.
`rain forest, hot, wet forest in tropical areas, where rainfall is heavy and there is no dry season.
`rain-gauge, instrument for measuring rainfall.
`rain-proof adj able to keep rain out.
`rain-water, water that has fallen as rain and has been collected.

rain² /reɪn/ *vi,vt* 1 fall as rain: *It was ~ing. It never rains but it pours*, (*proverb*) Things, usually unwelcome, do not come singly but in numbers, e g if one disaster happens, another will follow. 2 fall in a stream: *Tears ~ed down her cheeks.* 3 send or come down (on): *The people ~ed gifts on/upon the heroes returning from the war.*

rainy /ˈreɪni/ adj (-ier, -iest) having much rain: *~ weather; a ~ day/climate; the `~ season. save/put away/keep sth for a rainy day*, save money for a time when one may need it.

raise /reɪz/ *vt* 1 lift up; move from a low(er) to a high(er) level; cause to rise: *~ a sunken ship to the surface of the sea; ~ one's glass to one's lips; ~ prices; ~* (= build, erect) *a monument. raise sb's hopes*, make him more hopeful. *raise one's voice*, speak more loudly or in a higher tone: *voices ~d in anger.* 2 cause to be upright: *~ a man from his knees; ~ the standard of revolt.* 3 cause to rise or appear: *~ a cloud of dust; shoes that ~ blisters on my feet; a long, hot walk that ~d a good thirst*, caused the walker to be thirsty. *raise sb from the dead*, restore him to life. *raise a laugh*, do something to cause laughter. *raise Cain/hell/the devil/the roof*, (*sl*) become very angry; start a big row. 4 bring up for discussion or attention: *~ a new point/a question/a protest/an objection.* 5 grow or produce (crops); breed (sheep, etc); rear, bring up (a family). 6 get or bring together; manage to get: *~ an army; ~ a loan; ~ money for a new swimming-pool.* □ n [C] (*US*) = rise² (2).

raisin /ˈreɪzən/ n [C] dried sweet grape, as used in cakes, etc.

ra·jah /ˈrɑːdʒə/ n Indian prince; Malayan chief.

rake[1] /reɪk/ n [C] long-handled tool with prongs used for drawing together straw, dead leaves, etc, for smoothing soil or gravel, etc. □ vt,vi **1** use a rake (on); make smooth with a rake: ~ garden paths; ~ together dead leaves; ~ the soil smooth for a seedbed. **2** get (something together, up, out, etc) with or as with a rake: ~ out a fire, get the ashes or cinders out from the bottom of a grate, etc. **rake sth in**, (fig) earn, make, much money: The firm is very successful—they're raking it in/raking in the money. **rake over/through sth**, search for facts, etc: ~ through old manuscripts for information. **rake sth up**, (esp) bring to people's knowledge (something which it is better not to remember): ~ up old quarrels/the past. **3** fire with guns at, from end to end: ~ a ship.

`**rake-off**, (sl) (usually dishonest) share of profits: If I put this bit of business your way, I expect a ~-off.

rake[2] /reɪk/ n [C] (dated) immoral man.

rake[3] /reɪk/ vi,vt **1** (of a ship, or its bow or stern) project beyond the keel; (of the funnel, masts) (cause to) slope towards the stern. **2** (of the stage of a theatre, cinema) slope down (towards the audience). □ n [C] degree of slope.

rak·ish /ˈreɪkɪʃ/ adj **1** of or like a rake[2]: a ~ appearance. **2** on one side: set one's hat at a ~ angle (from rake[3]).
rak·ish·ly adv

rally /ˈrælɪ/ vt,vi (pt,pp -lied) **1** (cause to) come together, esp after defeat or confusion, or in the face of threats or danger, to make new efforts: The troops rallied round their leader. The leader rallied his men. They rallied to the support of the Prime Minister. **2** give new strength to; (cause to) recover health, strength, firmness: ~ one's strength/spirits; ~ from an illness. The boy rallied his exchange of several strokes before a point was scored. **3** gathering or assembly, esp to encourage fresh effort: a po`litical ~: a `peace ~, one to urge the ending or avoiding of war. **4** meeting of a number of car drivers or motor-cyclists for a competition, etc.

ram /ræm/ n [C] **1** uncastrated male sheep. **2** one of various implements or devices for striking or pushing with great force. **3** = battering ram. □ vt (-mm-) strike and push heavily: ~ piles into a river bed.
`**ram-rod**, iron bar for ramming the charge into old (muzzle-loading) guns.

Rama·dan /ˈræməˈdɑːn US: -ˈdæn/ n ninth month of the Muslim year, when Muslims fast between sunrise and sunset.

ramble /ˈræmbəl/ vi **1** walk for pleasure, with no special destination. **2** (fig) wander in one's talk, not keeping to the subject. **3** (of plants) grow with long shoots that trail or

straggle: rambling roses. □ n [C] rambling walk: go for a country ~.
ram·bler, person or thing that rambles.
ram·bling adj (a) (esp of buildings, streets, towns), extending in various directions as if built without planning. (b) (of a speech, essay, etc) disconnected.

ramp /ræmp/ n [C] sloping way from one level to another, e g instead of stairs or steps.

ram·page /ræmˈpeɪdʒ/ vi rush about in excitement or rage. □ n be/go on the ram-page, be/go rampaging.

ram·pa·geous /ræmˈpeɪdʒəs/ adj (formal) excited and noisy.

ram·pant /ˈræmpənt/ adj **1** (of plants, etc) luxuriant: Rich soil makes some plants too ~, causes them to spread too thickly, to have too much foliage, etc. **2** (of diseases, social evils, physical activity etc) beyond control: Revenge was ~ in the village. **3** (of animals, esp of a lion in heraldry) on the hind legs.
ram·pant·ly adv

ram·part /ˈræmpɑːt/ n [C] wide bank of earth, often with a wall, built to defend a fort, etc.

ram·rod /ˈræmrɒd/ ⇨ ram.

ram·shackle /ˈræmʃækəl/ adj almost collapsing: a ~ house/old bus.

ran /ræn/ pt of run[2].

ranch /rɑːntʃ US: ræn-/ n [C] (in N America) large farm, esp one with extensive lands for cattle, but also for fruit, chickens, etc.
`**ranch house**, (US) rectangular bungalow type of house.
rancher, person who owns, manages or works on, a ranch.

ran·cid /ˈrænsɪd/ adj with the smell or taste of stale, decaying fat or butter.

ran·cour (US = -cor) /ˈræŋkə(r)/ n [U] (formal) deep and long-lasting feeling that one has been ignored, injured or insulted: full of ~ (against him).
ran·cor·ous /ˈræŋkərəs/ adj

ran·dom /ˈrændəm/ n **1** at random, without reason, aim or purpose: choosing children at ~ to help in the class. **2** (as an adjective) done, made, taken, at random: a ~ remark/sample/selection.

rang /ræŋ/ pt of ring[2].

range[1] /reɪndʒ/ n [C] **1** row, line or series of things: a magnificent ~ of mountains; a `mountain-~. **2** area of ground with targets for shooting at: a `rifle-~. **3** area in which rockets and missiles are fired. **4** distance to which a gun will shoot or to which a missile, etc can be fired: in/within/out of/beyond ~. **5** distance at which one can see or hear, or to which sound will carry. **6** extent; distance between limits: the range of an aircraft, how far it can travel without refuelling; the annual ~ of temperature, e g from −10°C to 40°C; a long-~ weather forecast, for a long period; cotton in a wide ~ of colours. **7** (fig) extent: a subject that is outside my ~, one that I have not studied; *a wide ~ of interests*. **8** (*US*) area of grazing or hunting ground. **9** area over which plants are found growing or in which animals are found living: *What is the ~ of the elephant in Africa?* **10** type of stove, with ovens, a coal boiler, and a surface for pans, kettles, etc: *a `kitchen ~*.

range² /reɪndʒ/ *vt,vi* **1** place or arrange in a row or rows; put, take one's place, in a specified situation, order, class or group: *The general ~d his men along the river bank.* **2** go, move, wander: *animals ranging through the forests/over the hills.* **3** (*fig*) be extensive: *researches that ~d over a wide field; a wide-ranging discussion.* **4** extend, run in a line: *a boundary that ~s north and south/ from A to B.* **5** vary between limits: *prices ranging from £7 to £10/between £7 and £10.* **6** (of guns, projectiles) carry: *This gun ~s over six miles*, can fire to this distance.

ranger /reɪndʒə(r)/ *n* [C] **1** (N America) forest guard. **2** (esp in Canada) one of a body of mounted troops employed as police (e g in thinly populated areas). **3** (*GB*) keeper of a royal park, who sees that the forest laws are observed.

rank /ræŋk/ *n* **1** [C] line of persons or things: *Take the taxi at the head of the ~*, the first one in the line. **2** number of soldiers placed side by side. **3** the **~s**, ordinary soldiers, i e privates and corporals, contrasted with officers. **4** [C,U] position in a scale, distinct grade in the armed forces; category or class: *promoted to the ~ of captain; be in the ~s of the unemployed*. □ *vt,vi* **1** put or arrange in a rank; put in a class: *Would you ~ him among the world's great statesmen?* **2** have a place: *Does he ~ among/with the failures? A major ~s above a captain.*

rankle /ræŋkəl/ *vi* continue to be a painful or annoying memory: *The insult ~d in his mind.*

ran·sack /rænsæk US: ræn`sæk/ *vt* **1** search (a place) thoroughly: *~ a drawer for money/to find money.* **2** rob: *The house had been ~ed of all that was worth anything.*

ran·som /rænsəm/ *n* [U] freeing of a person who has been kidnapped on payment; [C] sum of money, etc, paid for this. *hold a man to ransom*, keep him as a prisoner and ask for money. *worth a king's ransom*, a very large sum of money. □ *vt* obtain the freedom of (a person), set (a person) free, in exchange for ransom: *~ a kidnapped diplomat.*

rant /rænt/ *vi,vt* use extravagant, boasting, loud language: *ranting and raving on the stage.*

rap /ræp/ *n* [C] **1** (sound of a) light, quick blow: *I heard a ~ on the door.* **2** (*informal*) blame; consequences. *take the rap (for sth),* be punished, etc (esp when innocent). □ *vt,vi* (-pp-) hit, strike quickly; make the sound of a rap: *~ (at) the door.*

ra·pa·cious /rə`peɪʃəs/ *adj* (*formal*) greedy (esp for money).
ra·pa·cious·ly *adv*

rape /reɪp/ *vt* commit the crime of forcing sexual intercourse on. □ *n* [C] act of raping.
rap·ist /reɪpɪst/ *n* [C] person who rapes.

rapid /ræpɪd/ *adj* **1** quick; moving, happening, with great speed: *a ~ decline in sales; ~-fire questions*, in quick succession. **2** (of a slope) steep; descending steeply.
ra·pid·ity /rə`pɪdətɪ/ *n* [U]
rap·id·ly *adv*

rap·ids /ræpɪdz/ *n pl* part of a river where a steep slope causes the water to flow fast.

rapier /reɪpɪə(r)/ *n* [C] light sword used for thrusting in duels and the sport of fencing.

rapt /ræpt/ *adj* so deep in thought, so carried away by feelings, that one is unaware of other things: *listening to the pop singer with ~ attention; ~ in a book.*

rap·ture /ræptʃə(r)/ *n* **1** [U] state of being ecstatic: *gazing with ~ at the face of the girl he loved.* **2** (*pl*) extremely happy, full of joy and enthusiasm: *She went into ~s over the dresses they showed her.*
rap·tur·ous /ræptʃərəs/ *adj*
rap·tur·ous·ly *adv*

rare¹ /reə(r)/ *adj* (-r, -st) unusual; uncommon; not often happening, seen, etc: *a ~ animal. It is very ~ for her to arrive late.*
rare·ly *adv* not often: *~ly seen.*
rare·ness *n* [U]

rare² /reə(r)/ *adj* (of meat) cooked so that the redness and juices are kept: *a ~ steak.*

rarefy /reərɪfaɪ/ *vt,vi* (*pt,pp* -ied) make or become less dense; purify: *the rarefied air on the mountain.*

rar·ing /reərɪŋ/ *adj* (*informal*) full of eagerness: *They're ~ to go.*

rar·ity /reərətɪ/ *n* (*pl* -ies) **1** [U] rareness. **2** [C] something uncommon or unusual (and so valuable): *The person who is always happy is a ~.*

ras·cal /rɑskəl US: `ræskəl/ *n* [C] **1** dishonest person. **2** (playfully) naughty child.

rash¹ /ræʃ/ *n* [C] **1** (appearance, patch, of) tiny red spots on the skin: *a `heat-~.* **2** (*fig*) sudden spread: *a ~ of new bungalows on a country road.*

rash² /ræʃ/ *adj* too hasty; done, doing things, without enough thought of the possible result: *a ~ act/statement/man*
rash·ly *adv*
rash·ness *n* [U]

rasher /ræʃə(r)/ *n* [C] slice of bacon or ham (to be) fried.

rasp /rɑsp US: ræsp/ *n* [C] **1** metal tool like a coarse file with a surface or surfaces having sharp points, used for scraping. **2** rough, grating sound produced by this tool. □ *vt,vi* **1** scrape with a rasp. **2** (*fig*) have an irritating effect on: *~ing my nerves.* **3** say in a way that grates or sounds like the noise of a rasp: *~ out orders/insults.* **4** make a harsh, grating sound: *a learner ~ing (away) on his* *violin.*

rasp·ing·ly *adv*

rasp·berry /ˈrɑːzbərɪ *US:* ˈræzberɪ/ *n* [C] (*pl* -ies) **1** (bush with a) small, sweet yellow or red berry: (as an *adjective*) ~ *jam.* **2** (*sl*) noise made with the tongue and lips or by wind passing out of the anus, or a gesture to show dislike or disapproval.

rat /ræt/ *n* [C] **1** animal like, but larger than, a mouse. **2** person who deserts a cause that he thinks is about to fail. **smell a rat**, suspect that something wrong is being done. **3** (*fig*) cowardly traitor, e g a strike-breaker. □ *vt* (-tt-) **1** hunt rats: *go* ~*ting.* **2 rat (on sb)**, (*sl*) break a promise, withdraw from an undertaking.

the ˈrat race, endless and undignified competition for success in one's career, social status, etc.

rat·ty *adj* (-ier, -iest) (*informal*) irritable.

rate[1] /reɪt/ *n* **1** [C] standard or reckoning, obtained by bringing two numbers or amounts into relationship: *the* ˈbirth-/ ˈdeath-~; *walk at the* ~ *of 3 miles an hour. What is the letter postage* ~ *to foreign countries?* **2** **at ˈthis/ˈthat rate**, if this/that is true, if this/that state of affairs continues. **at ˈany rate**, in any case; whatever happens. **3** (*GB*) tax on property (land and buildings), paid to local authorities for local purposes. **4** (with ordinal numbers) class or grade: *first* ~, excellent; *second* ~, fairly good; *third* ~, (rather) poor; (as an *adjective*, with a hyphen): *a* ˈfirst-~ *teacher.*

the rates, payments of rates(3) collectively.

ˈrate of exˈchange, relationship between two currencies (e g US dollars and Fr francs).

ˈrate-payer, person liable to have rates(3) exacted from him.

rate[2] /reɪt/ *vt,vi* **1** judge or estimate the value or qualities of: *What do you* ~ *his wealth at? He was* ~*d as kind and hospitable.* **2** (*GB*) value (property) for the purpose of assessing rates(3) on: *My property was* ~*d at £100 per annum.*

rat·able (also **rate·able**) /ˈreɪtəbəl/ *adj* having to pay rates(3): *the* ~ *value of a house*, its value as assessed for the levying of rates.

rat·abil·ity (also **rate-**) /ˈreɪtəˈbɪlətɪ/ *n* [U]

rather /ˈrɑːðə(r) *US:* ˈræ-/ *adv* **1** more willingly; by preference or choice: *I would* ~ *you came tomorrow than today. A: 'Will you join us in a game of cards?'—B: 'Thank you, but I'd* ~ *not.'*, prefer not to. **2** more truly, accurately or precisely: *He arrived very late last night or* ~ *in the early hours this morning.* **3** (to be distinguished from *fairly*[2]) in a certain degree or measure; more (so) than not; (a) (with *adjectives*, preceding *a*, following *the*): *a* ~ *surprising result/*~ *a surprising result.* (b) (with *comparatives*): *My brother is* ~ *better today.* (c) (with *nouns*): *It's* ~ *a pity.* (d) (with *verbs*): *We were all* ~ *exhausted when*

we got to the top of the mountain.

rat·ify /ˈrætɪfaɪ/ *vt* (*pt,pp* -ied) confirm (an agreement) by signature or other formality.

rati·fi·ca·tion /ˌrætɪfɪˈkeɪʃən/ *n* [U]

rat·ing /ˈreɪtɪŋ/ *n* **1** [C] act of valuing property for the purpose of assessing rates(3); amount or sum fixed. **2** [C] class, classification, e g motor cars by engine capacity or horse-power. **3** [C] popularity of radio or T V programmes as estimated by asking a selected group. **4** (*navy*) person's position or class as recorded in the ship's books; non-commissioned sailor: *officers and* ~*s.*

ratio /ˈreɪʃɪəʊ/ *n* [C] (*pl* ~s) relation between two amounts determined by the number of times one contains the other: *The* ~*s of 1 to 5 and 20 to 100 are the same.*

ra·tion /ˈræʃən/ *n* **1** [C] fixed quantity, esp of food, allowed to one person. **2** (*pl*) fixed allowance served out to, e g members of the armed forces: *go and draw* ~*s.* □ *vt* **1** limit (a person) to a fixed ration. **2** limit (food, water, etc): *We'll have to* ~ *the water.*

ra·tional /ˈræʃnəl/ *adj* **1** of reason or reasoning. **2** able to reason; having the faculty of reasoning. **3** sensible; that can be tested by reasoning: ~ *conduct/ explanations.*

ra·tion·ally /-nəlɪ/ *adv*

ra·tion·al·ity /ˌræʃəˈnælətɪ/ *n* [U]

ra·tion·ale /ˌræʃəˈnɑːl/ *n* [C] fundamental reason, logical basis of something.

ration·al·is·tic /ˌræʃnəlˈɪstɪk/ *adj* sensible, accepting a reasonable argument.

ra·tion·al·ize /ˈræʃnəlaɪz/ *vt* **1** make reasonable; treat or explain in a rational manner: ~ *one's fears/behaviour.* **2** reorganize (an industry, etc) so as to lessen or get rid of waste (in time, labour, expense, etc).

ration·al·iz·ation /ˌræʃnəlaɪˈzeɪʃən *US:* -lɪˈz-/ *n* [U]

rattle /ˈrætəl/ *vt,vi* **1** (cause to) make short, sharp sounds quickly, one after the other: *The windows were rattling in the wind. The hailstones* ~*d the tin roof.* ⇨ death-rattle. **2** talk, say or repeat (something) quickly and in a thoughtless way: *The boy* ~*d off the poem he had learnt.* **3** (*informal*) frighten; make nervous: *He was* ~*d by the accident.* □ *n* **1** [U] rattling sound: *the* ~ *of bottles from a milkman's van.* **2** [C] toy for producing a rattling sound.

ˈrattle-snake, poisonous American snake that makes a rattling noise with its tail.

ratty ⇨ rat.

rau·cous /ˈrɔːkəs/ *adj* (of sounds) harsh; rough; hoarse: *the* ~ *cries of the crows.*

rau·cous·ly *adv*

rav·age /ˈrævɪdʒ/ *vt,vi* **1** destroy; damage badly: *forests* ~*d by fire.* **2** (of armies, etc) rob, plunder, with violence: *They had* ~*d the countryside.* □ *n* **1** [U] destruction. **2** (*pl*) destructive effects: *the* ~*s of time*, e g on a woman's looks.

rave /reɪv/ *vi* **1** talk wildly, violently, angrily: *The patient* (eg someone with a high fever) *began to* ~. **2** (of the sea, wind, etc) roar; rage. **3** talk or act with (often) excessive enthusiasm: *She* ~d *about the food she had had in France.* □ *n* [C] **1** (*informal*) (often as an *adjective*) enthusiastic praise: *a* ~ *review*, eg of a book. **2** (*sl*) wild, exciting party, dance, outing, etc. **3** (*sl*) great enthusiasm: *be in a* ~ *about him.*
raver (*informal*) person who raves(3).
rav·ing *adj* talking wildly: *a raving lunatic.* □ *adv* to the point of talking wildly: *You're raving mad!*

ravel /ˈrævəl/ *vt,vi* (-ll-, *US* also -l-) **1** (of knitted or woven things) separate into threads. **2** (*fig*) make confused.

raven /ˈreɪvən/ *n* [C] **1** large, black bird like a crow. **2** (as an *adjective*) glossy, shining black: ~ *black hair.*

rav·en·ous /ˈrævənəs/ *adj* **1** very hungry. **2** greedy: *a* ~ *appetite.*
rav·en·ous·ly *adv* hungrily; greedily: *eat* ~*ly.*

ra·vine /rəˈviːn/ *n* [C] deep, narrow valley.

ravi·oli /ˌrævɪˈəʊlɪ/ *n* [U] (*It*) (dish of) small pieces of pasta containing chopped meat, etc.

rav·ish /ˈrævɪʃ/ *vt* fill with delight: ~*ed by the view.*
rav·ish·ing·ly *adv*

raw /rɔː/ *adj* **1** uncooked: ~ *meat.* **2** in the natural state, not manufactured or prepared for use: *the* ~ *materials of industry,* eg coal, ores. **in the raw,** (a) in the natural state. (b) (*fig*) naked. **3** (of persons) untrained; unskilled; inexperienced: ~ *recruits,* for the army, etc. **4** (of the weather) damp and cold: *a* ~ *February morning.* **5** (of a place on the flesh) with the skin rubbed off; sore and painful. **6** (*informal*) unjust (esp) *a raw deal,* harsh or cruel treatment. □ *n* [C] raw place on the skin, esp on a horse's skin.
ˈraw·hide, (of) untanned hide.

ray[1] /reɪ/ *n* [C] **1** line, beam, of radiant light, heat, energy: *the* ~*s of the sun;* `*X-rays.* **2** (*fig*) small sign: *a* ~ *of hope.* **3** any one of a number of lines coming out from a centre. □ *vi, vt* send out or come out in rays.

ray[2] /reɪ/ *n* [C] (*pl* often unchanged) kinds of large sea-fish with a broad, flat body, eg skate.

rayon /ˈreɪɒn/ *n* [U] material like silk made from cellulose.

raze, rase /reɪz/ *vt* destroy (towns, buildings) completely, esp by making them level with the ground: *a city* ~*d by an earthquake.*

razor /ˈreɪzə(r)/ *n* [C] instrument with a sharp blade or cutters used for shaving hair from the skin.

re[2] /reɪ/ *n* [C] second note in the musical octave

re- /riː-/ *prefix* **1** again: *reappear.* **2** in a different way: *rearrange.*

reach /riːtʃ/ *vt,vi* **1** stretch (out): *He* ~*ed* (*out his hand*) *for the knife.* **2** stretch out the hand for and take; get and give (something) to: *Can you* ~ *that book for your brother?* **3** get to, go as far as: ~ *London;* ~ *the end of the chapter. When did the news* ~ *you?* **as far as the eye can reach,** to the horizon. **4** extend; go; pass: *My land* ~*es as far as the river.* □ *n* **1** (*sing* only) act of stretching out (a hand, etc): *a long* ~. **2** [U] extent to which a hand, etc can be reached out: *This boxer has a long* ~. *I like to have my reference books within my* ~/*within easy* ~, *so near that I can get them quickly and easily.* **3** [C] continuous extent, esp of a river or canal, that can be seen between two bends or locks(3).

re·act /rɪˈækt/ *vi* **1** have an effect (on the person or thing): *Applause* ~*s on/upon a speaker,* eg has the effect of giving him confidence. **2** behave differently, be changed, as the result of being acted on: *Do children* ~ *to kind treatment by becoming more self-confident?* **3** respond to something with a feeling: *The people will* ~ *against the political system that oppresses them.* **4** (*chem*) (of one substance applied to another) have an effect: *How do acids* ~ *on metals?*

re·ac·tion /rɪˈækʃən/ *n* [C,U] **1** action or state resulting from, in response to, something, esp a return to an earlier condition after a period of the opposite condition: *After these days of excitement there was a* ~, eg a period when life seemed dull. **2** opposition to progress: *The forces of* ~ *made reform difficult.* **3** response; opinion: *What was his* ~ *to your proposal?* **4** (*science*) action set up by one substance in another; change within the nucleus of an atom.
re·ac·tion·ary /rɪˈækʃənərɪ *US:* -nerɪ/ *n* [C] (*pl* -ies), *adj* (person) opposing progress or reform.
re·ac·tor /rɪˈæktə(r)/ *n* = nuclear reactor.

read /riːd/ *vt,vi* (*pt,pp* read /red/) **1** (used in the simple tenses or with *can/be able*) look at and (be able to) understand (something written or printed): *Can you* ~ *French/a musical score?* **2** reproduce mentally or vocally the words of (an author, book, etc): *She was* ~*ing the letter aloud/to herself/to the children. She* ~ *out the letter to all of us.* **3** study (a subject, esp at a university): *He's* ~*ing physics/*~*ing for a degree in physics/*~*ing for a physics degree.* **4** interpret mentally; learn the significance of: ~ *a person's thoughts.* **5** give a certain impression; seem (good, etc) when read: *The play* ~*s better than it acts,* is better for ~*ing than for performing.* **6** find implications in (what is read, etc): *Silence mustn't always be* ~ *as consent.* **read between the lines,** look for or discover meanings that are not actually expressed. **read into sth,** add more than is justified: *You have* ~ *into her letter more sympathy than she probably feels.* **7** (of instruments) show: *What does the thermometer* ~? **8** bring into a specified state by reading: *She* ~ *herself to sleep.* **9** (*pp* with an *adverb*) having knowledge gained from books, etc: *a well-*~ *man.* □ *n* [C] period of time given to reading: *have a good* ~ *in the train.*

read·able /ˈriːdəbəl/ *adj* that is easy or pleasant to read.

read·abil·ity /ˌriːdəˈbɪlətɪ/ *n* [U]

re·ad·dress /ˌriː əˈdres/ *vt* change the address on (a letter, etc).

reader /ˈriːdə(r)/ *n* [C] **1** person who reads, esp one who spends much time in reading. **2** (*GB*) university teacher of a rank immediately below a professor: *R*~ *in English Literature.* **3** textbook for reading in class; book with selections for reading by students of a language: *a German R*~. **4** person who can interpret what is hidden or obscure, esp *a* `mind/`thought-~.

`reader·ship /-ʃɪp/, **(a)** position of a reader(2). **(b)** (of a periodical) number of persons who read it.

read·ily, readi·ness ⇨ ready.

read·ing /ˈriːdɪŋ/ *n* **1** [U] act of one who reads. ⇨ play-reading. **2** [U] knowledge, esp of books: *a man of wide* ~. **3** [C] way in which something is interpreted or understood: *My* ~ *of the situation is…* **4** [C] figure of measurement, etc as shown on a dial, scale, etc: *The* ~s *on my thermometer last month were well above the average.*

`reading-lamp, shaded table-lamp used to read by.

`reading-room, room (eg in a public library) set apart for reading.

re·ad·just /ˌriːəˈdʒʌst/ *vt* adjust again: *It's sometimes difficult to* ~ (*oneself*) *to life in England after working abroad.*

re·ad·just·ment *n* [C,U]

ready /ˈredɪ/ *adj* (-ier, -iest) **1** in the condition needed for use; willing: ~ *for work. He's always* ~ *to help his friends.* **make ready,** prepare. **2** quick; prompt: *He always has a* ~ *answer.* **3** within reach; easily obtained: *keep a revolver* ~, near at hand. **4** (*adverbial* use, with *pp*) prepared beforehand: *buy food* ~-*cooked.* □ *n* (only in) **at the ready, (a)** (of a rifle) in the position for aiming and firing. **(b)** in the correct position, condition.

`ready-`made *adj* ready to wear or use: ~-*made clothes.*

`ready `money, money in the form of coins or notes, which can be used for payment at the time when goods are bought (contrasted with *credit*).

`ready `reckoner, book of answers to various common calculations needed in business, etc.

read·ily *adv* **(a)** without showing hesitation

or unwillingness. **(b)** without difficulty.

readi·ness /ˈredɪnəs/ *n* [U] **(a) in readiness (for),** in a ready or prepared state: *have everything in readiness for an early start.* **(b)** willingness: *a surprising readiness to accept the proposal.*

re·af·firm /ˌriːəˈfɜːm/ *vt* affirm again: ~ *one's loyalty.*

real /rɪəl/ *adj* **1** existing in fact; not imagined or supposed; not made up or artificial: *Was it a* ~ *man you saw or a ghost? Things that happen in* ~ *life are sometimes stranger than in stories. Who is the* ~ *manager of the business? Tell me the* ~ (= true) *reason for your absence from work.*

`real estate, (*legal*) immovable property consisting of land, any natural resources, and buildings (contrasted with *personal estate*).

real·ism /ˈrɪəlɪzm/ *n* [U] **1** (in art and literature) showing of real life, facts, etc in a true way, omitting nothing that is ugly or painful, and idealizing nothing. **2** behaviour based on the facing of facts and disregard of sentiment and convention.

real·ist /-ɪst/ *n* [C] (esp) person who believes himself to be without illusions.

real·is·tic /ˌrɪəˈlɪstɪk/ *adj* **(a)** showing the true form. **(b)** practical: *realistic politics.*

real·is·ti·cally /-klɪ/ *adv*

re·al·ity /rɪˈælətɪ/ *n* (*pl* -ies) **1** [U] the quality of being real; real existence: *belief in the* ~ *of miracles.* **in reality,** in actual fact. **2** [C] something actually seen or experienced: *the grim realities of war.* **3** [U] (in art, etc) truth; lifelike resemblance to the original: *The TV broadcast described what was happening with extraordinary* ~.

real·ize /ˈrɪəlaɪz/ *vt* **1** be fully conscious of; understand: *Does he* ~ *his mistake yet?* **2** convert (a hope, plan, etc) into a fact: ~ *one's hopes/ambitions.* **3** exchange (property, business shares, etc) for money: *Can these shares/bonds, etc, be* ~d *at short notice?* **4** (of property, etc) obtain as a price for or as a profit: *How much did you* ~ *on the paintings you sent to the sale?*

real·iz·able /-əbəl/ *adj*

real·iz·ation /ˌrɪəlaɪˈzeɪʃən US: -lɪˈz-/ *n* **(a)** [U] realizing (of a plan, one's ambitions or hopes). **(b)** [C] act of exchanging property for money.

really /ˈrɪəlɪ/ *adv* **1** in fact; without doubt; truly: *What do you* ~ *think about it? I'm* ~*ly sorry.* **2** (as an expression of interest, surprise, mild protest, doubt, etc according to context): *'We're going to Mexico next month.' —'Oh,* ~!'

realm /relm/ *n* [C] **1** (*poetic* or *legal*) = kingdom: *the defence of the R*~. **2** (*fig*) region: *the* ~ *of the imagination.*

ream /riːm/ *n* [C] **1** measure for paper, 480 (or US 500) sheets or 20 quires. **2** (*pl*) (*informal*) great quantity (of writing): *She has written* ~s *of verse.*

re·ani·mate /ˈriːˈænɪmeɪt/ vt fill with new strength, courage or energy.

reap /riːp/ vt, vi 1 cut (grain, etc); gather in a crop of grain from (a field, etc): ~ *a field of barley;* ~ *the corn.* 2 (fig) gain: ~ *the reward of virtue.*

reaper, person who, machine which, reaps.

re·appear /ˈriːəˈpɪə(r)/ vi appear again (after disappearing).

re·appear·ance /-rəns/ n [C,U]

re·apprais·al /ˈriːəˈpreɪzəl/ n [C] new examination and judgement: *a* ~ *of our relations with China.*

rear[1] /rɪə(r)/ n [C] 1 back part: *The kitchen is in the* ~ *of the house.* 2 (as an *adjective*) in or at the rear: *the* ~ *wheels/mirror,* of a car, etc. 3 last part of any army, fleet, etc: *attack the enemy in the* ~. **bring up the rear,** come/be last.

'**rear-`admiral,** naval officer below a vice-admiral.

'**rear-guard,** body of soldiers given the duty of guarding the rear of an army.

rearguard action, fight between an army in retreat and the enemy.

rear·most /ˈrɪəməʊst/ adj farthest back.

rear[2] /rɪə(r)/ vt, vi 1 cause or help to grow; bring up: ~ *poultry/cattle;* ~ *children.* ⇨ raise(5). 2 (esp of a horse) rise on the hind legs. 3 lift up: *The snake* ~ed *its head.*

re·arm /ˈriːˈɑːm/ vt, vi supply (an army, etc) with weapons again, or with weapons of new types, etc.

re·arma·ment /ˈriːˈɑːməmənt/ n [U]

re·ar·range /ˈriːəˈreɪdʒ/ vt arrange in a different way.

rea·son[1] /ˈriːzən/ n 1 [C,U] (fact put forward or serving as a) cause of or justification for something: *Is there any* ~ *why you are late? The* ~ *why he's late is that/because there was a breakdown on the railway. He complains with* ~ (= rightly) *that he has been punished unfairly.* **by reason of,** because of: *He was excused by* ~ *of his age.* 2 [U] power of the mind to understand, form opinions, etc: *Only man has* ~. **lose one's reason,** go mad. 3 [U] what is right or practicable; common sense; sensible conduct. **do anything (with)in reason,** anything sensible or reasonable. **listen to reason,** pay attention to common sense, sensible advice, etc. **without rhyme or reason,** ⇨ rhyme(1). **It stands to reason (that),** is obvious to sensible people; most people will agree....

rea·son[2] /ˈriːzən/ vi, vt 1 make use of one's reason(2); exercise the power of thought: *Man's ability to* ~ *makes him different from animals.* 2 **reason with sb,** argue in order to convince him: *She* ~ed *with me for an hour.* 3 say by way of argument: *He* ~ed *that if we started at dawn, we could arrive before noon.* 4 express logically or in the form of an argument: *a well* ~ed *statement/ manifesto.* **reason sth out,** find an answer

by considering successive arguments, etc. 5 persuade by argument (not) to do something: ~ *a person out of his fears.*

reason·ing n [U] process of reaching conclusions by using one's reason: *There's no* ~ing *with that woman,* She won't listen to sensible advice, arguments.

rea·son·able /ˈriːznəbəl/ adj 1 having ordinary common sense; able to reason; acting, done, in accordance with reason; willing to listen to reason: *Is the accused guilty beyond* ~ *doubt?* 2 neither more or less than seems right or acceptable: *a* ~ *price/offer.* 3 not absurd: *a* ~ *excuse; be* ~ *in one's demands.*

rea·son·ably /-əblɪ/ adv

re·as·sure /ˈriːəˈʃʊə(r)/ vt remove the fears or doubts of: *She felt* ~d *after her teacher told her she would pass the examination.*

re·as·sur·ance /-rəns/ n [U]

re·as·sur·ing·ly adv

re·bate /ˈriːbeɪt/ n [C] sum of money by which a debt, tax, etc may be reduced: *There is a* ~ *of £1.50 if the account is settled before 31 Dec.*

rebel[1] /ˈrebəl/ n [C] 1 person who takes up arms against, or refuses to accept, the established government; person who resists authority or control. 2 (as an *adjective*) of the nature of a rebellion: *the* ~ *forces.*

re·bel[2] /rɪˈbel/ vi (-ll-) 1 take up arms to fight (against the government). 2 show resistance; protest strongly: *The children* ~led *against having to do three hours' homework each evening.*

re·bel·lion /rɪˈbeljən/ n 1 [U] rebelling, e g against a government: *rise in* ~ (*against the Union*). 2 [C] instance of this: *a* ~ *against the dictator.*

re·bel·li·ous /rɪˈbeljəs/ adj 1 acting like a rebel; taking part in a rebellion: ~ *members/behaviour.* 2 not easily controlled: *a child with a* ~ *temper.*

re·bel·li·ous·ly adv

re·bind /ˈriːˈbaɪnd/ vt (pt, pp -bound /-ˈbaʊnd/) put a new binding on (a book, etc).

re·birth /ˈriːˈbɜːθ/ n [C] 1 change in moral attitude, e g by religious conversion, causing a person to lead a new kind of life. 2 revival: *the* ~ *of learning.*

re·born /ˈriːˈbɔːn/ adj changed in spirit.

re·bound /rɪˈbaʊnd/ vi 1 spring or bounce back after hitting something: *The ball* ~ed *from the wall.* 2 happen as the consequence of one's own action: *The nasty things you say could* ~ *on yourselves.* **on the rebound, (a)** while bouncing back: *hit a ball on the* ~. **(b)** (fig) while still reacting to depression or disappointment: *She quarrelled with Paul and then married Peter on the* ~. 3 ⇨ rebind.

re·buff /rɪˈbʌf/ n [C] unkind or offensive refusal of, or show of indifference to (an offer of or request for help, friendship, etc). □ vt give a rebuff to.

re·build /ˈriːˈbɪld/ vt (pt,pp -built /-ˈbɪlt/) build or put together again: *a rebuilt engine*.

re·buke /rɪˈbjuːk/ vt (formal) blame, speak severely to (e g officially): ∼ *an employee for being rude*. □ n [C] blame (the usual word).

re·buk·ing·ly adv

re·but /rɪˈbʌt/ vt (-tt-) prove (a charge, piece of evidence, etc) to be false.

re·but·tal /-təl/ n [C] act of rebutting; evidence that proves a charge, etc to be false.

re·cal·ci·trance /rɪˈkælsɪtrəns/ n [U] (formal) being disobedient.

re·cal·ci·trant /rɪˈkælsɪtrənt/ adj (formal) disobedient; resisting authority or discipline.

re·call /rɪˈkɔːl/ vt 1 ask to come back: ∼ *an ambassador (from his post/to his own country)*. 2 bring back to the mind; remember: *I don't ∼ his name/face/meeting him/where I met him*. 3 take back; cancel (an order, a decision). □ n 1 [C] request to return (esp to an ambassador): *letters of ∼*. 2 [U] ability to remember: *instant ∼*, able to remember quickly. *beyond/past recall*, that cannot be taken back or cancelled. 3 [C] signal, e g a bugle call, to troops, etc to return.

re·cant /rɪˈkænt/ vt,vi give up (an opinion, a belief); take back (a statement) as being false: *The torturers could not make him ∼*.

re·can·ta·tion /ˈriːkænˈteɪʃən/ n [C,U]

re·cap /ˈriːkæp/ vt,vi, n (informal = abbr of) recapitulate, recapitulation.

re·cap·itu·late /ˈriːkəˈpɪtjʊleɪt/ vt,vi repeat, go through again, the chief points of (something that has been said, discussed, argued about, etc).

re·cap·itu·la·tion /ˈriːkəˈpɪtjʊˈleɪʃən/ n [C,U]

re·cap·ture /rɪˈkæptʃə(r)/ vt 1 capture again. 2 recall: *try to ∼ the past*.

re·cast /ˈriːˈkɑːst US: -ˈkæst/ vt 1 cast or fashion again: ∼ *a gun/a bell*; ∼ (= rewrite) *a sentence/paragraph/chapter*. 2 change the cast of a play, i e find different actors or give actors different parts.

re·cede /rɪˈsiːd/ vi 1 (appear to) go back (from an earlier position): *As the tide ∼d we were able to explore the beach. As our ship steamed out to sea the coast slowly ∼d.* 2 slope away from the front or from the observer: *a receding chin.* 3 withdraw (from an opinion, etc).

re·ceipt /rɪˈsiːt/ n 1 [U] receiving or being received: *on ∼ of the news.* 2 (pl) money received (in a business, etc) (contrasted with *expenditure*). 3 [C] written statement that something (money or goods) has been received: *get a ∼ for money spent; sign a ∼.* □ vt (rare) write out and sign or stamp a receipt(3): ∼ *a hotel bill*.

re·ceiv·able /rɪˈsiːvəbl/ adj 1 that can be, fit to be, received. 2 (commerce) (of bills, accounts, etc) on which money is to be received.

re·ceive /rɪˈsiːv/ vt,vi 1 accept, take, get

(something offered, sent, etc): *When did you ∼ the letter/news/telegram, etc? He ∼d a good education.* 2 take possession of stolen property: *caught receiving soon after his release from prison.* 3 allow to enter: *He was ∼d into the Church*, admitted as a member.

re·ceiver /rɪˈsiːvə(r)/ n [C] 1 person who receives, esp who knowingly receives stolen goods. 2 R∼, official appointed to take charge of the property and affairs of a bankrupt, or to administer property in dispute. 3 part of an apparatus for receiving something, e g that part of a telephone that is held to the ear; apparatus for receiving broadcast signals: *a ˈradio-∼*.

re·cent /ˈriːsnt/ adj (having existed, been made, happened) not long before; begun not long ago: ∼ *news; a ∼ event; within ∼ memory*.

re·cent·ly adv not long ago: *until quite ∼ly*.

re·cep·tacle /rɪˈseptəkəl/ n [C] container or holder in which things may be put (away).

re·cep·tion /rɪˈsepʃən/ n 1 [U] receiving or being received: *prepare rooms for the ∼ of guests; a ˈ∼ area/camp/centre*, one where persons, e g evacuees, refugees, are received and accommodated. 2 [C] formal occasion on which guests are received: *There was a ∼ after the wedding ceremony.* 3 [C] welcome or greeting of a specified kind; demonstration of feeling: *The new book/minister had a favourable ∼*, was welcomed by the public, etc. 4 [U] receiving of radio, etc signals; degree of efficiency of this: *Is radio ∼ good in your district?*

re·ception desk, (in a hotel) counter where guests are received, where they ask for rooms, etc.

re·cep·tion·ist /-ɪst/, person employed in a hotel, or by a hairdresser, dentist or other professional person, to receive clients.

re·cep·tive /rɪˈseptɪv/ adj quick or ready to receive suggestions, new ideas, etc: ∼ *to new ideas*.

re·cep·tive·ly adv

re·cess /rɪˈses US: ˈriːses/ n [C] 1 (US = vacation) period of time when work or business is stopped, e g when Parliament, the law courts, are not in session. 2 part of a room where the wall is set back from the main part. 3 secret place; place difficult to get in: *the dark ∼es of a cave.* 4 (fig) deep, inner part: *in the ∼es of the mind.* □ vt place in, provide with, a recess(2).

re·ces·sion /rɪˈseʃən/ n 1 [U] withdrawal; act of receding. 2 [C] slowing down of business and industrial activity: *Did the recent ∼ in Europe cause a lot of unemployment?*

re·ces·sional /rɪˈseʃənəl/ n [C] hymn sung while the clergy and choir withdraw after a church service. □ adj 1 of a recession: ∼ *music.* 2 relating to a Parliamentary recess.

re·ces·sive /rɪˈsesɪv/ adj 1 tending to recede or go back. 2 (biology) showing weak characteristics (the stronger ones are called *dominant*) which are passed on by means of genes to later generations, e g blue eyes and blond hair.

recipe /'resəpɪ/ *n* [C] direction for preparing (a cake, a dish of food, a medical remedy) or for getting (any result): *a ~ for a fruit cake. Have you a ~ for happiness?*

re·cipi·ent /rɪ'sɪpɪənt/ *n* [C] (*formal*) person who receives something.

re·cip·ro·cal /rɪ'sɪprəkəl/ *adj* 1 given and received in return: *~ affection/help.* 2 corresponding, but the other way round: *a ~ mistake,* e g I thought he was a waiter and he thought I was a guest, but I was a waiter and he was a guest.

re·cip·ro·cal·ly /-klɪ/ *adv*

re·cip·ro·cate /rɪ'sɪprəkeɪt/ *vt,vi* 1 give in return; give and receive, each to and from each: *He ~d by wishing her a pleasant journey.* 2 (of parts of a machine) (cause to) move backwards and forwards in a straight line (e g the piston of an engine): *a reciprocating engine/saw.*

re·cip·ro·ca·tion /rɪ'sɪprə'keɪʃən/ *n* [U]

reci·proc·ity /'resɪ'prosətɪ/ *n* [U] (*formal*) principle or practice of give and take, of making mutual concessions; the granting of privileges in return for similar privileges: *~ in trade (between two countries).*

re·cital /rɪ'saɪtl/ *n* [C] 1 detailed account of a number of connected events, etc: *We were bored by the long ~ of his adventures.* 2 performance of music by a soloist or small group, or of the works of one composer: *a pi'ano ~.*

reci·ta·tion /'resɪ'teɪʃən/ *n* 1 [U] the act of reciting(2): *a boring ~ of his grievances.* 2 [U] public delivery of passages of prose or poetry learnt by heart; [C] instance of this: *a `Dickens ~,* of dramatic extracts from the novels. 3 [C] piece of poetry or prose (to be) learnt by heart and recited.

re·cite /rɪ'saɪt/ *vt,vi* 1 say (esp poems) aloud from memory: *The little girl refused to ~ at the party.* 2 give a list of, tell one by one (names, facts, etc): *~ the names of all the capital cities of Europe.*

reck·less /'rekləs/ *adj* not thinking or caring about the consequences: *a ~ spender/ driver.*

reck·less·ly *adv*

reck·less·ness *n* [U]

reckon /'rekən/ *vt,vi* 1 find out (the quantity, number, cost, etc) by working with numbers: *~ the cost of a holiday.* 2 **reckon with sb,** (a) deal with; settle with: *When the fighting is over, we'll ~ with the enemy's sympathizers.* (b) take into account; consider: *He is certainly a man to be ~ed with,* a man who cannot be ignored. 3 depend (on): *I am ~ing on your help.* 4 be of the opinion, suppose; consider: *One-fourth of the country is ~ed as unproductive. Do you still ~ him among/as one of your friends?* 5

(*US* (*informal*) assume: *I ~ we'll go next week.*

reck·oner /'rekənə(r)/, person or thing that counts.

reck·on·ing /'rekənɪŋ/ *n* (a) [C] (*old use*) (totalled) account of items to be paid for: *pay the ~ing.* **day of reckoning,** time when one must be punished for doing something. (b) [U] calculation.

re·claim /rɪ'kleɪm/ *vt* 1 return (waste land, etc) to a useful condition, a state of cultivation, etc. 2 (*formal*) reform (a person): *a ~ed drunkard.* 3 demand that something be given back.

rec·la·ma·tion /'reklə'meɪʃən/ *n* [U]

re·cline /rɪ'klaɪn/ *vi,vt* place oneself, be, in a position of rest; lie back or down: *~ on a couch/in a chair.*

re·cluse /rɪ'kluːs/ *n* [C] person who lives alone and avoids other people.

rec·og·ni·tion /'rekəg'nɪʃən/ *n* [U] recognizing or being recognized: *He was given a cheque for £25 in ~ of his services. R~ of the new State is unlikely,* It is unlikely that diplomatic relations will be established with it. **alter/change beyond/out of (all) recognition,** completely: *The town has changed out of all ~ since I was there ten years ago.*

re·cog·ni·zance /rɪ'kognɪzəns/ *n* [C] (*legal*) 1 bond by which a person is bound to appear before a court of law at a certain time, or to observe certain conditions, and to forfeit a certain sum if he fails to do so. 2 sum of money (to be) paid as security for observing such a bond.

rec·og·nize /'rekəgnaɪz/ *vt* 1 know, (be able to) identify again (a person or thing) that one has seen, heard, etc before: *~ a tune/an old friend.* 2 be willing to accept (a person or something) as what he or it claims to be or has been in the past: *refuse to ~ a new government. The Browns no longer ~ the Smiths,* do not accept them as friends. 3 be prepared to admit; be aware: *He ~d that he was not qualified for the post/~d his lack of qualifications.* 4 acknowledge: *Everyone ~d him to be the greatest living poet.*

rec·og·niz·able /-əbəl/ *adj* that can be identified.

rec·og·niz·ably /-əblɪ/ *adv*

re·coil /rɪ'kɔɪl/ 1 draw or jump back: *~ from doing something* (in fear, horror, disgust, etc). 2 (of a gun) kick back (when fired); (of a spring) close again. 3 (*fig*) react: *Revenge may ~ on the person who takes it.* □ *n* [C] act of recoiling.

rec·ol·lect /'rekə'lekt/ *vt,vi* succeed in remembering: *~ childhood days.*

rec·ol·lec·tion /'rekə'lekʃən/ *n* 1 [U] act or power of over which the memory goes back: *Such a problem has never arisen within my ~.* 2 [C] that which is remembered: *The old letters brought many ~s of my father.*

rec·om·mend /'rekə'mend/ *vt* 1 speak favourably of; say that one thinks something is good (for a purpose) or that a person is suitable (for a post, etc as...): *I can ~ this soap. He has been ~ed for first class honours. Can you ~ Miss Hill as a good typist?* **2** suggest as wise or suitable; advise: *Do you ~ raising the school-leaving age?* **3** (of a quality, etc) cause to be or appear pleasing, satisfactory; make acceptable: *Behaviour of that sort will not ~ you.* **4** commend (the more usual word): *~ oneself/one's soul to God.*

rec·om·men·da·tion /ˌrekəmen`deɪʃən/ n (**a**) [U] recommending: *speak in ~ation of my secretary/the plan; buy it on the ~ation of a friend.* (**b**) [C] statement that is favourable: *The jury brought in a verdict of guilty, with a ~ to mercy.* (**c**) [C] something which causes a person to be well thought of: *Is good cooking a ~ation in a wife?*

rec·om·pense /`rekəmpens/ vt reward or punish; make payment to: *~ a person for losing his pen.* □ n [C,U] reward; payment; satisfaction given for injury: *work hard without ~. Here is £1 in ~ for your help.*

rec·on·cile /`rekənsaɪl/ vt **1** cause (persons) to become friends after they have quarrelled: *He refused to become ~d with his brother.* **2** settle, end (a quarrel, difference of opinion, etc). **3** cause to agree with: *I can't ~ what you say with the facts of the case.* **4** overcome one's objections to; resign oneself to: *You must ~ yourself to a life of hardship and poverty.*

rec·on·cil·able /-əbəl/ adj

rec·on·cili·ation /ˌrekən`sɪlɪ`eɪʃən/ n [U] reconciling or being reconciled; [C] instance of this: *bring about a reconciliation between friends who have quarrelled.*

re·con·di·tion /ˌrikən`dɪʃən/ vt put into good condition again: *a car with a ~ed engine.*

re·con·nais·sance /rɪ`konɪsəns/ n **1** [U] act of getting information (about an enemy): *~ in force,* with many soldiers. **2** [C] survey, made by troops or a group of scouting vessels or aircraft, of an enemy's position or whereabouts. **3** (*fig*) survey of any kind of work before it is started: *make a ~ of the campaign to be organized.*

re·con·noitre (*US* = **-ter**) /ˌrekə`nɔɪtə(r)/ vt,vi go to or near (a place or area occupied by enemy forces) to learn about their position, strength, etc: *~ the ground.*

re·con·struct /ˌrikən`strʌkt/ vt **1** construct again. **2** build up a complete structure or description of (something of which one has only a few parts or only partial evidence): *~ a ruined abbey. The detective tried to ~ the crime,* picture to himself how it had been committed.

re·con·struc·tion /ˌrikən`strʌkʃən/ n [C,U]

rec·ord¹ /`rekɔd US: `rekərd/ n **1** [C] written account of facts, events, etc: *a ~ of school attendances/of road accidents.* **2** [U] state of

being recorded or preserved in writing, esp as authentic evidence: *I don't want to go on ~/dont want you to put me on ~ as saying that I think the Prime Minister a fool.* **off the record,** (*informal*) not for publication or for recording: *What the President said at his press conference was off the ~,* not to be repeated by the newspaper men there. **put the record straight,** ⇨ straight¹ (3). **3** [C] facts known about the past of a person or something: *He has an honourable ~ of service/a good ~. That airline has had a bad ~,* e g has had many accidents to its aircraft. **4** [C] something that provides evidence or information: *Our museums are full of ~s of past history.* **5** [C] disc on which sound has been registered; what is recorded on such a disc: *`gramophone ~s.* ⇨ recording. **6** [C] limit, score, point, mark, etc (high or low), not reached before; (esp in sport) the best yet done: *Which country holds the ~ for the 5 000 metres race?* (as an *adjective*) *There was a ~ rice crop in Thailand that year.* **break/beat the record,** do better than has been done before. Hence, `record-breaking adj.

`record-player, instrument for reproducing sound from discs.

re·cord² /rɪ`kɔd/ vt **1** preserve for use or for reference, by writing or in other ways, e g on a disc, magnetic tape, video-tape, film, etc: *This volume ~s the history of the regiment. The programme was ~ed.* **2** (of an instrument) mark or show on a scale: *The thermometer ~ed 40°C.*

re·corder /rɪ`kɔdə(r)/ n [C] **1** judge who has criminal and civil responsibility in a borough or city. **2** apparatus that records. ⇨ taperecorder, video tape-recorder. **3** wooden musical instrument resembling a flute.

re·cord·ing /rɪ`kɔdɪŋ/ n [C] (esp for radio, T V and for record-players, etc) programme, piece of music, etc registered on a disc, magnetic tape, film, etc for reproduction: *It wasn't a 'live' performance but a B B C ~.*

re·count¹ /rɪ`kaʊnt/ vt (*formal*) give a description of; tell: *He ~ed to them the story of his adventures in Mexico.*

re·count² /ˌri`kaʊnt/ vt count again: *~ the votes.* □ n [C] /ˌri kaʊnt/ another count: *One of the candidates demanded a ~.*

re·coup /rɪ`kup/ vt pay (a person, oneself, for a loss, etc); *~ one's losses.*

re·course /rɪ`kɔs/ n (*formal*) [U] **1** act of seeking help from: *I still have ~ to the money-lenders.* **2** something turned to for help: *Your only ~ is legal action against them.*

re·cover¹ /rɪ`kʌvə(r)/ vt,vi **1** get back (something lost, etc); get back the use of: *~ what was lost; ~ consciousness* (after fainting); *~ one's sight/hearing.* **2** **recover from,** become well; get back to a former position of prosperity, state of health, mental condition, etc: *He is slowly ~ing from his* illness. *Has the country ~ed from the effects of the war yet?* **3** get control of oneself again; become calm or normal: *He almost fell, but quickly ~ed (himself).*

re-cover·able /-əbəl/ *adj* that can be recovered(1): *Is the deposit I've paid ~able?*

re-cov·ery *n* [U] recovering: *make a quick recovery, get well again quickly or quickly regain one's position.*

re-cover² /ˌriːˈkʌvə(r)/ *vt* supply with a new cover: *This chair needs to be ~ed.*

rec·re·ation /ˌrekrɪˈeɪʃən/ *n* [C,U] (form of) play or amusement; refreshment of body and mind; something that pleasantly occupies one's time after work is done: *walk and climb mountains for ~.*

'recre'ation ground, land, e g in a public park, set aside for games, etc.

rec·re·ational /-nəl/ *adj*

re-crimi·nate /rɪˈkrɪmɪneɪt/ *vi* accuse (a person) in return: *~ against my sister.*

re-crimi·na·tory /rɪˈkrɪmɪnətərɪ US: -tɔːrɪ/ *adj* of recrimination.

re-crimi·na·tion /rɪˌkrɪmɪˈneɪʃən/ *n* [C,U] accusation made in return for one already made; (act of) doing this.

re-cruit /rɪˈkruːt/ *n* [C] new member of a society, group, etc esp a soldier in the early days of his training: *gain a few ~s to one's political party.* □ *vt,vi* get new members for; *a ~ing officer.*

rec·tal /ˈrektəl/ *adj* (anat) of the rectum.

rec·tangle /ˈrektæŋɡəl/ *n* [C] four-sided shape with four right angles, esp one with adjacent sides unequal.

rec·tangu·lar /rekˈtæŋɡjʊlə(r)/ *adj*

rec·tify /ˈrektɪfaɪ/ *vt* (pt,pp -ied) **1** put right; take out mistakes from: *mistakes that cannot be rectified.* **2** purify or refine by repeated distillation or other process: *rectified spirits.*

rec·ti·lin·ear /ˌrektɪˈlɪnɪə(r)/ *adj* in or forming a straight line; bounded by, characterized by, straight lines.

rec·tor /ˈrektə(r)/ *n* [C] **1** (Church of England) clergyman in charge of a parish the taxes of which were not withdrawn, e g to a monastery or university, at or after the time when the English Church separated from the Church of Rome. ⇨ vicar. **2** head of certain universities, colleges, schools or religious institutions.

rec·tory /ˈrektərɪ/ *n* [C] (pl -ies) rector's residence.

rec·tum /ˈrektəm/ *n* [C] (pl ~s) (anat) lower and final part of the large intestine.

re·cum·bent /rɪˈkʌmbənt/ *adj* (formal) (esp of a person) lying down: *a ~ figure on a tomb.*

re·cu·per·ate /rɪˈkjuːpəreɪt/ *vt,vi* make or become strong again after illness, exhaustion or loss: *~ one's health; go to the seaside to ~.*

re·cu·per·ation /rɪˌkjuːpəˈreɪʃən/ *n* [U]

recuperating.

re·cu·per·at·ive /rɪˈkjuːpərətɪv US: -reɪtɪv/ *adj* helping, relating to, recuperation.

re·cur /rɪˈkɜː(r)/ *vi* (-rr-) **1** come, happen, again; be repeated: *a problem which ~s frequently.* **2** (of ideas, events etc) come back: *My first meeting with her often ~s to me/my memory.*

re·cur·rence /rɪˈkʌrəns US: -ˈkɜːrəns/ *n* [C,U] repetition: *Let there be no ~rence of this error.*

re·cur·rent /-ənt/ *adj* (of events, fevers etc) happening again frequently or regularly.

re·cycle /ˌriːˈsaɪkəl/ *vt* treat (substances already used for industry, etc) so that further use is possible: *~ waste paper.*

red /red/ *adj* (-der, -dest) **1** of the colour of fresh blood, rubies, human lips, the tongue, of shades varying from crimson to bright brown (as of iron rust): *~ with anger/embarrassment,* flushed in the face; *with red eyes,* eyes red with weeping. **paint the town `red,** go on a spree and indulge in noisy, rough behaviour. **see red,** lose control of oneself through anger, or indignation. **2** Russian; Soviet; Communist: *The R~ Army/Air Force.* □ *n* **1** [C,U] (shade of) red colour: *the ~s and browns of the woods in autumn.* **2** red clothes: *dressed in ~.* **3** person favouring or supporting Communism or the Soviet system. **4** debtor side of business accounts. **be/get into/out of the red,** have/get liabilities that (no longer) exceed assets.

'red·breast, (also *robin redbreast*) robin.

'red `carpet, one laid out for the reception of an important visitor.

'Red `Crescent, (emblem of an) organization in Muslim countries corresponding to the Red Cross.

'Red `Cross, (emblem of the) international organization concerned with the relief of suffering caused by natural disasters, etc and for helping the sick and wounded and those taken prisoner in war.

red deer, kind of deer native to the forests of Europe and Asia.

'red `ensign, red flag with the Union Jack in one corner, used by British merchant ships.

'red `flag, (a) flag used a a symbol of danger (e g on railways, by workers on the roads). **(b)** symbol of left wing revolution. **(c)** (*the Red Flag*) revolutionary song.

'red·head, person having red hair.

'red `herring, (esp) something doubtful or irrelevant to take attention from the subject being discussed.

'red-`hot *adj* (fig) highly excited, furious: *~-hot enthusiasm.*

'Red `Indian, N American Indian.

'red-`letter day, (fig) memorable because something good happened.

'red meat, beef and mutton (contrasted with *white* meat, i e veal, pork, poultry).

'red `pepper, red fruit of the capsicum

plant.

`red·skin, (informal) (old name for) Red Indian.

the Red Star, symbol of the USSR and other Communist States.

red tape, excessive use of formalities in public business; too much attention to rules and regulations: ∼ tape in government offices.

red·den /ˈredən/ vt,vi make or become red; blush.

red·dish /ˈredɪʃ/ adj rather red.

re·deem /rɪˈdiːm/ vt 1 get (something) back by payment or by doing something: ∼ a mortgage; ∼ one's honour. 2 perform (a promise or obligation). 3 set free by payment: ∼ a slave/prisoner. 4 compensate: his ∼ing feature, the feature or quality that balances his faults, etc.

re·deem·able /-əbəl/ adj

the Re·dee·mer, Jesus Christ.

re·demp·tion /rɪˈdempʃən/ n [U] (formal) redeeming or being redeemed: the ∼ of a promise; past/beyond ∼, too bad to be rescued from being evil.

re·de·ploy /ˈriːdɪˈplɔɪ/ vt withdraw and rearrange (troops, workers) so as to use more efficiently.

re·de·ploy·ment n: the ∼ment of labour.

re·do /ˈriːˈduː/ vt (pt -did /-ˈdɪd/, pp -done /-ˈdʌn/) do again: We must have the house redone, redecorated, etc.

redo·lent /ˈredələnt/ adj (formal) having a strong smell, esp one that recalls something: bed sheets ∼ of lavender.

re·double /riːˈdʌbəl/ vt,vi make or become greater or stronger: They ∼d their efforts.

re·dress /rɪˈdres/ vt 1 dress again. 2 set (a wrong) right again; make up for, do something that compensates for (a wrong): You should confess and ∼ your errors. redress the balance, make things equal again. □ n [U] redressing.

re·duce /rɪˈdjuːs US: -ˈduːs/ vt,vi 1 make less; make smaller in size, number, degree, price, etc: ∼ speed/pressure/costs, etc; ∼ one's expenses/weight. 2 bring or get to a certain condition, way of living, etc: ∼ a class of noisy children to order; ∼ him to silence, cause him to stop talking. They were ∼d to begging or starving, They became so poor that they had either to beg or starve. 3 change to another form): ∼ an equation/argument/statement to its simplest form.

re·duc·ible /-əbəl/ adj

re·duc·tion /rɪˈdʌkʃən/ n 1 [U] reducing or being reduced; [C] instance of this: a ∼ in/of numbers; great ∼s in prices; price ∼s. 2 [C] copy, on a smaller scale, of a picture, map, etc.

re·dun·dancy /rɪˈdʌndənsɪ/ n [U] being redundant: ∼ among clerks caused by the increasing use of computers; [C] (pl -ies) instance of this: more redundancies in the docks.

re·dun·dant /rɪˈdʌndənt/ adj not needed: With the decreasing demand for coal many thousands of miners may become ∼.

re-echo /riˈekəʊ/ vt,vi echo again and again. □ n [C] (pl ∼s) echo of an echo.

reed /riːd/ n 1 [C] (tall, firm stem or stalk of) kinds of coarse grasses growing in or near water; [U] (collective) mass of such grasses growing together. a broken reed, (fig) an unreliable person or thing. 2 [C] (in some wind-instruments, eg the oboe, bassoon, clarinet and in some organ-pipes) strip of metal, etc that vibrates to produce sound.

reef¹ /riːf/ n [C] that part of a sail which can be rolled up or folded so as to reduce its area. □ vt reduce the area of (a sail) by rolling up or folding a part.

`reef-knot, ordinary double knot (= US square knot).

reef² /riːf/ n [C] ridge of rock, shingle etc just below or above the surface of the sea: a coral ∼.

reek /riːk/ n [U] strong, bad smell: the ∼ of stale tobacco smoke. □ vi reek of, smell unpleasantly of: He ∼s of whisky/garlic.

reel¹ /riːl/ n [C] 1 cylinder, roller or similar device on which cotton, thread, wire, photographic film, magnetic tape, hose (for water, etc), etc is wound. 2 length of film rolled on one reel. □ vt roll or wind (thread, a fishing-line etc) on to, or with the help of, a reel: ∼ in the fish. reel sth off, tell, say or repeat something without pause or apparent effort: ∼ off a list of names.

reel² /riːl/ vi 1 be shaken (physically or mentally) by a blow, a shock, rough treatment, etc: His mind ∼ed when he heard the news. 2 walk or stand unsteadily, moving from side to side; sway: He ∼ed like a drunken man. 3 appear to move, sway or shake: The street ∼ed before his eyes when the bike hit him.

reel³ /riːl/ n [C] (music for a) lively Scottish dance, usually for two couples.

re-en·try /ˈriːˈentrɪ/ n [C] (pl -ies) act of re-entering, eg return of a spacecraft into the earth's atmosphere.

re·face /ˈriːˈfeɪs/ vt put a new surface on.

re·fec·tion /rɪˈfekʃən/ n [U] (formal) refreshment in the form of food and drink.

re·fec·tory /rɪˈfektərɪ/ n [C] (pl -ies) dining-hall (in a monastery, convent or college).

re·fer /rɪˈfɜː(r)/ vt,vi (-rr-) 1 send, take, hand over (to, back to, a person or thing) to be dealt with, decided etc: The dispute was ∼red to the United Nations. I was ∼red to the Manager/to the Inquiry Office. 2 (of a speaker, what is said, etc) speak about; apply to: When I said that some people are stupid I wasn't ∼ring to you. Does that remark ∼ to me? 3 turn to, go to, for information, etc: The speaker often ∼red to his notes. 4 credit, attribute (the more usual words): He ∼red his success to the good *teaching he'd had.*

ref·er·able /rɪ'fərəbəl/ *adj* that can be referred(4): *Lung cancer is ∼able to smoking cigarettes.*

ref·eree /ˌrefə'riː/ *n* [C] **1** person to whom disputes, e g in industry, between workers and employers, are referred for decision. **2** (in football, boxing, etc) person who controls matches, judges points in dispute, etc. ⇨ **umpire**. □ *vt,vi* act as a referee: *∼ a football match.*

ref·er·ence /ˈrefrəns/ *n* **1** [C,U] (instance of) referring: *The book is full of ∼s to places that I know well.* **terms of reference,** (of a commission, etc) scope or range given to an authority: *Is this question outside our terms of ∼,* one that we are not required to investigate? **2** [C] (person willing to make a) statement about a person's character or abilities: *The clerk has excellent ∼s from former employers.* **3** [C] note, direction, etc telling where certain information may be found: *He dislikes history books that are crowded with ∼s to earlier authorities.* **4** [U] **in/with reference to,** concerning; about.

ˈreference book, one that is not read through but consulted for information, e g a dictionary or encyclopaedia.

ˈreference library, one containing reference books.

ˈreference marks, mark, e g *, †, ‡, §, used to refer the reader to the place, e g a footnote, where information may be found. ⇨ **cross-reference.**

ref·er·en·tial /ˌrefə'renʃəl/ *adj* (*formal*) having reference to.

ref·er·en·dum /ˌrefə'rendəm/ *n* [C] (*pl* ∼s, -da /-də/) the referring of a political question to a direct vote of the electorate.

re·fill /ˌriː'fɪl/ *vt* fill again. □ *n* [C] /ˈriːfɪl/ amount used to refill; a container: *two ∼s for a ball-point pen.*

re·fine /rɪ'faɪn/ *vt,vi* **1** free from other substances; make or become pure: *∼ sugar/oil/ores.* **2** cause to become more cultured, polished in manners: *∼d language/manners/speech/taste.*

re·fine·ment /rɪ'faɪnmənt/ *n* **1** [U] refining or being refined. **2** [U] purity of feeling, taste, language, etc: *lack of ∼,* i e vulgarity. **3** [C] clever or remarkable example of such purity of tastes, etc: *∼s of meaning.*

re·finer /rɪ'faɪnə(r)/ *n* [C] **1** person whose business is to refine something: *sugar ∼s.* **2** machine for refining metals, sugar, etc.

re·finery /-nərɪ/ *n* [C] place, building, etc where something is refined: *a `sugar ∼y.*

re·fit /ˈriː'fɪt/ *vt,vi* (-tt-) (of a ship, etc) make, be made, ready for use again by renewing or repairing parts. □ *n* /ˈriːfɪt/ [C] refitting.

re·fla·tion /riː'fleɪʃən/ *n* [U] inflation of currency after a deflation, to restore the system to its previous condition.

re·flate /riː'fleɪt/ *vt* restore to a former economic or currency state: *plans to ∼ the eco-*

nomy.

re·flect /rɪ'flekt/ *vt,vi* **1** (of a surface) throw back (light, heat, sound); (of a mirror) send back an image of: *Look at the trees ∼ed in the lake. The sight of my face ∼ed in the mirror never pleases me.* **2** show the nature of: *Her sad looks ∼ed the thoughts passing through her mind.* **3** (of actions, results) bring (credit or discredit on): *The results ∼ the greatest credit on all concerned.* **4** injure the good reputation of: *Your rude behaviour ∼s only on yourself,* You are the only person whose reputation is hurt by it. **5** consider; think: *I must ∼ on/upon what answer to give/how to answer that question.*

re·flec·tion (*GB* also **re·flexion**) /rɪ'flekʃən/ *n* **1** [U] reflecting or being reflected: *the ∼ of heat.* **2** [C] something reflected, esp an image reflected in a mirror or in water. **3** [U] thought (the usual word): *be lost in ∼.* **on reflection,** after reconsidering the matter. **4** [C] expression of a thought in speech or writing: *∼s on the pleasures of being idle.* **5** [C] something that brings discredit: *This is a ∼ on your honour.*

re·flec·tor /rɪ'flektə(r)/ *n* [C] something that reflects heat, light or sound, esp a piece of glass or metal for reflecting light, etc in a required direction.

re·flex /ˈriːfleks/ *adj* **1** bent backwards. **2** (of thought) directed back on itself or its own action. □ *n* [C] reflex action: *test one's ∼es.*

ˈreflex action, one that is an involuntary response to a stimulation of the nerves, e g sneezing.

ˈreflex angle, one that is bigger than 180°.

ˈreflex camera, in which, by using a mirror, the image to be photographed can be focused up to the moment of exposure.

re·flexion /rɪ'flekʃən/ *n* = reflection.

re·flex·ive /rɪ'fleksɪv/ *adj, n* [C] (*gram*) (of a) word or form showing that the subject's action is on himself or itself.

reflexive pronoun, e g *myself, themselves.*

reflexive verb, showing that the subject and object are the same: *He cut himself.*

re·float /riː'fləʊt/ *vt,vi* cause (something) to float again after it has gone aground, been sunk, etc.

re·form[1] /rɪ'fɔːm/ *vt,vi* make or become better by removing or putting right what is bad or wrong: *∼ a sinner/one's character/the world.* □ *n* **1** [U] reforming; removal of vices, imperfections, etc: *demonstrate for social or political ∼.* **2** [C] instance of reform: *a ∼ in teaching methods.*

re·former, person active in trying to get or carrying out reforms.

re·form[2] /ˌriː'fɔːm/ *vt,vi* form again; (of soldiers) get into ranks, etc again.

re·for·ma·tion /ˌriː fɔː'meɪʃən/ *n* [C,U]

ref·or·ma·tion /ˌrefə'meɪʃən/ *n* **1** [U] reforming or being reformed; [C] radical change for the better in social, political or religious affairs. **2 the Reformation,** the 16th-century movement for reform of the Roman Catholic Church, resulting in the establishment of the Protestant Churches.

re·fract /rɪˈfrækt/ vt cause (a ray of light) to bend aside where it enters, e g water, glass: *Light is ～ed when it passes through a prism.*
re·frac·tion /rɪˈfrækʃən/ n [U]
re·frain[1] /rɪˈfreɪn/ n [C] (*formal*) = chorus(2).
re·frain[2] /rɪˈfreɪn/ vi (*formal*) not do something: *Please ～ from smoking/swearing.*
re·fresh /rɪˈfreʃ/ vt 1 give new strength to; make fresh: *～ oneself with a warm bath.* 2 *refresh one's memory,* remember by referring to notes, etc. 3 (*formal*) take something to eat or drink: *They stopped at a pub to ～ themselves.*
re·fresh·ing adj (a) strengthening; giving rest and relief: *a ～ing breeze/sleep.* (b) welcome and interesting because rare or unexpected: *the news that the children were doing things to help the old man was ～ing.*
re·fresher /rɪˈfreʃə(r)/ n [C] (*informal*) refreshing drink.
re·fresher course, course providing instructions, e g to teachers already in service, on modern methods, newer professional techniques, etc.
re·fresh·ment /rɪˈfreʃmənt/ n 1 [U] refreshing or being refreshed: *feel ～ of mind and body.* 2 (*pl*) food and drink: *R～s were provided during the interval.*
re·frig·er·ate /rɪˈfrɪdʒəreɪt/ vt make cool or cold; keep (food) in good condition by making and keeping it cold.
re·frig·er·ation /rɪˌfrɪdʒəˈreɪʃən/ n [U] (esp) the cooling or freezing of food in order to preserve it: *the refrigeration industry.*
re·frig·er·ator /rɪˈfrɪdʒəreɪtə(r)/ n [C] (common abbr *fridge*) apparatus in which food is kept cold.
re·fuel /ˌriːˈfjuːəl/ vt (-ll-, *US* also -l-) supply with, take on, more fuel.
ref·uge /ˈrefjuːdʒ/ n [C,U] (place giving) shelter or protection from trouble, danger, pursuit, etc: *seek ～ from the floods.*
refu·gee /ˌrefjʊˈdʒiː *US:* ˈrefjʊdʒiː/ n [C] person who has been forced to flee from danger, e g from floods, war, political persecution: (as an *adjective*) *～ camps.*
re·fund /rɪˈfʌnd/ vt pay back (money): *～ the cost of postage.* □ n /ˈriːfʌnd/ [C,U] repayment: *obtain a ～ of a deposit.*
re·fur·bish /ˈriːˈfɜːbɪʃ/ vt make clean or bright again, (as if) like new.
re·fusal /rɪˈfjuːzəl/ n 1 [U] act of refusing; [C] instance of this: *his ～ to do what I asked.* 2 (with *the*) right of deciding whether to accept or refuse something before it is offered to others: *If you ever decide to sell your car, please give me (the) first ～.*
ref·use[1] /ˈrefjuːs/ n [U] waste or worthless material (to be burnt, etc).
ˈrefuse-collector, = dustman.

re·fuse[2] /rɪˈfjuːz/ vt,vi 1 say 'no' to (a request or offer): *～ permission.* 2 show unwillingness to accept (something offered), to do (something that one is asked to do): *～ a gift; ～ to help.*
re·fute /rɪˈfjuːt/ vt prove (a person, statements, opinions, etc) to be wrong or mistaken: *～ an argument/an opponent.*
re·fut·able /ˈrefjʊtəbəl *US:* rɪˈfjuː-/ adj that can be proved wrong.
refu·ta·tion /ˌrefjʊˈteɪʃən/ n [U] (*formal*) refuting; [C] argument against.
re·gain /rɪˈgeɪn/ vt 1 get possession of again: *～ consciousness; ～ one's freedom.* 2 get back to (a place or position): *～ one's footing,* recover one's balance after slipping or falling.
re·gal /ˈriːgəl/ adj of, for, fit for, by, a monarch: *～ dignity/splendour/power.*
re·gally /-gəlɪ/ adv
re·gale /rɪˈgeɪl/ vt (*formal*) give pleasure or delight to: *regaling themselves on caviar.*
re·galia /rɪˈgeɪlɪə/ n pl (often used with a *sing verb*) 1 emblems (crown, orb, sceptre, etc) of royalty, as used at coronations. 2 emblems or decorations of an order(10), e g of the freemasons.
re·gard[1] /rɪˈgɑːd/ n 1 [U] attention; concern; consideration: *He has very little ～ for the feelings of others. More ～ must be paid to safety on the roads.* 2 [U] consideration; respect: *hold a person in high/low ～.* 3 (*pl*) kindly thoughts and wishes: *Please give my kind ～s to your brother,* (e g at the end of a letter). 4 (*old use*) long, steady or significant look: *He turned his ～ on the accused man.* 5 *in/with regard to,* with respect to; concerning.
re·gard·less adj paying no attention: *～less of expense.*
re·gard[2] /rɪˈgɑːd/ vt 1 be of the opinion: *～ her as a hero; ～ political persecution as a crime.* 2 consider (a person, his behaviour) to be: *How is he ～ed locally? He is ～ed with disfavour/unfavourably.* 3 pay attention to: *He never ～s my advice.* (*Note:* usually *negative* or a question.) *as regards; regarding,* with reference to; about.
re·gatta /rɪˈgætə/ n [C] (*pl ～s*) meeting for boat races (rowing boats or yachts).
re·gency /ˈriːdʒənsɪ/ n [C] (*pl -ies*) (the period of) office of a regent.
re·gen·er·ate /rɪˈdʒenəreɪt/ vt,vi 1 reform spiritually or morally. 2 give new strength or life to. 3 grow again. □ adj /rɪˈdʒenərət/ spiritually reborn: *a ～ society.*
re·gen·er·ation /rɪˌdʒenəˈreɪʃən/ n [U]
re·gent /ˈriːdʒənt/ n [C] 1 person appointed to perform the duties of a ruler who is too young, old, ill, etc or who is absent. 2 (*US*) member of a governing board (e g of a State university). □ adj (used after the *noun*) performing the duties of a regent: *the Prince R～.*
regi·cide /ˈredʒɪsaɪd/ n [C,U] (person taking

541

part in the) crime of killing a king.

re·gime, ré·gime /reɪˈʒiːm/ n [C] **1** method or system of government or of administration; usual system of things: *under the old ~, before the changes were made,* etc. **2** = regimen(2).

regi·men /ˈredʒɪmən/ n [C] **1** (old use) = regime(1). **2** set of rules for diet, exercise, etc for improving one's health and physical well-being.

regi·ment /ˈredʒɪmənt/ n [C] **1** (cavalry and artillery) unit divided into squadrons or batteries and commanded by a colonel; (*GB* infantry) organization usually based on a city or county, with special traditions and dress, represented in the field by battalions: *the 1st battalion of the Manchester R~.* **2** *regiment of,* (*informal*) large number: *a ~ of children.* □ vt organize; discipline: *~ the members of a Trade Union.*

regi·men·tal /ˌredʒɪˈmentəl/ adj of a regiment: *a ~ badge.* □ n (pl) military uniform.

Re·gina /rɪˈdʒaɪnə/ n [C] (pl ~s) (abbr **R**) reigning queen: *Elizabeth ~,* (*legal*) (used in titles of lawsuits): *~ v Hay,* the Crown against Hay.

re·gion /ˈriːdʒən/ n **1** [C] area or division with or without definite boundaries or characteristics: *the `Arctic ~s; the densely populated ~s of Europe.* **2** (pl) areas away from the capital: *live in the ~s.*

re·gional /-nəl/ adj of a region or regions.

re·gion·al·ly /-nəlɪ/ adv

reg·is·ter /ˈredʒɪstə(r)/ n [C] **1** (book containing a) record or list: *the R~ of voters, the Parliamentary R~,* of persons qualified to vote at elections. **2** range of the human voice or of a musical instrument; part of this range: *the lower ~ of the clarinet.* **3** mechanical device for indicating and recording speed, figures, numbers, etc. ⇨ **cash register.** **4** = registry. **5** vocabulary, etc used by a particular group, in a particular situation, etc e g legal, sports.

reg·is·ter /ˈredʒɪstə(r)/ vt, vi **1** make a written and formal record of, in a list: *~ one's car. I am a foreigner here; must I ~ (myself) with the police?* **2** put or get a person's name, one's own name, on a register, e g at a hotel. **3** (of instruments) indicate; record: *The thermometer ~ed only two degrees above freezing-point.* **4** show (emotion, etc): *Her face ~ed surprise.* **5** send (a letter or parcel) by special post, paying an extra charge which promises compensation if it is lost: *Send your money by ~ed post.*

reg·is·trar /ˈredʒɪstrɑː(r)/ n [C] person whose duty is to keep records or registers, e g for a town council or a university.

reg·is·tra·tion /ˌredʒɪˈstreɪʃən/ n **1** [U] registering; recording: *~ of letters; ~ of students for an examination/an academic course.* **2** [C] entry; record of facts.

'regis·tration mark, numbers and letters on the front and back of a motor vehicle used to identify it.

reg·is·try /ˈredʒɪstrɪ/ n [C] (pl -ies) **1** (sometimes *register*) place where registers are kept: *a ship's port of ~.* **2** [U] = registration.

'registry office, (esp) where a marriage is conducted without a religious ceremony.

re·gress /rɪˈgres/ vi return to an earlier or more primitive form or state: *~ mentally/culturally.*

re·gres·sion /rɪˈgreʃən/ n [C,U] regressing.

re·gres·sive adj tending to regress.

re·gret /rɪˈgret/ n **1** [U] feeling of being sorry or sadness at the loss of something, or of annoyance or disappointment because something has or has not or cannot be done: *hear with ~ that a friend is ill. Much to my ~ I am unable to accept your kind invitation.* **2** (pl) (in polite expressions of refusal, etc): *I have no ~s,* do not feel sorry (about what I did, etc).

re·gret·ful /-fəl/ adj sad; sorry.

re·gret·fully /-fəlɪ/ adv sadly; with regret.

re·gret /rɪˈgret/ vt (-tt-) **1** be sorry for the loss of; wish to have again: *~ lost opportunities.* **2** feel sorry for; be sorry (*to say, etc that...*): *I ~ that I cannot help.*

re·gret·table /-əbəl/ adj to be regretted: *~table failures.*

re·gret·tably /-əblɪ/ adv

re·group /ˈriːˈgruːp/ vt, vi form again into groups; form into new groups.

regu·lar /ˈregjʊlə(r)/ adj **1** evenly arranged; symmetrical; systematic: *~ teeth; a ~ wallpaper design.* **2** coming, happening, done, again and again at even intervals: *keep ~ hours,* e g leaving and returning home, getting up and going to bed, at the same times every day. *He has no ~ work,* no continuous occupation. **3** properly qualified; recognized; trained; full-time or professional: *~ soldiers,* not volunteers; *the ~ army,* made up of professional soldiers. **4** in agreement with what is considered correct procedure or behaviour: *I doubt whether your methods would be considered ~ by the Customs officials.* **5** (gram) (of verbs, nouns, etc) having normal inflections: *The verb 'go' is not ~.* **6** (*informal*) thorough; complete: *He's a ~ nuisance.* **7** (*US*) normal: *Do you want king size cigarettes or ~ size?* □ n [C] **1** soldier of the regular army. **2** (*informal*) frequent customer or client, e g at a pub.

regu·lar·ity /ˌregjʊˈlærətɪ/ n [U] state of being systematic, on time, etc: *win a prize for ~ity of attendance at school.*

regu·lar·ly adv in a proper manner; at frequent intervals or times: *as ~ly as clockwork,* always at the same time.

regu·lar·ize /ˈregjʊləraɪz/ vt make lawful or correct: *~ the proceedings.*

regu·lar·iz·ation /ˌregjʊləraɪˈzeɪʃən/ *US:* -rɪˈz-/ n [U]

regu·late /ˈregjʊleɪt/ vt **1** control systematically; cause to obey a rule or standard: *~*

one's expenditure; ∼ *the traffic.* **2** adjust (an apparatus, mechanism) to get the desired result: ∼ *the speed of a machine.*

reg·u·la·tion /ˈreɡjʊˈleɪʃən/ *n* **1** [U] regulating or being regulated: *the* ∼ *of affairs/of a clock.* **2** [C] rule; order; authoritative direction: `safety` ∼s, e g in factories; `traffic` ∼s, made by the police for drivers of vehicles. **3** (as an *adjective*) as required by rules: ∼ *dress/size.*

re·gur·gi·tate /rɪˈɡɜːdʒɪteɪt/ *vi,vt* **1** (of liquid, etc) rush back. **2** bring (swallowed food) up again to the mouth.

re·ha·bili·tate /ˈriəˈbɪlɪteɪt/ *vt* **1** restore (e g old buildings) to a good condition. **2** restore (a person) to former rank, position or reputation: *He has been* ∼d *in public esteem.* **3** bring back (a person who is physically or mentally disabled) to a (more) normal life by special treatment.

re·ha·bili·ta·tion /ˈriəˈbɪlɪˈteɪʃən/ *n* [U]

re·hearsal /rɪˈhɜːsəl/ *n* **1** [U] rehearsing: *put a play into* ∼. **2** [C] trial of a play or other entertainment: *a* `dress` ∼, one in which the actors wear the costumes and use the props as for public performances.

re·hearse /rɪˈhɜːs/ *vt,vi* practise (a play, music, programme, etc) for public performance: ∼ (*the parts in) a play.*

re·house /ˈriːˈhaʊz/ *vt* provide with a new house: *be* ∼d *after the fire.*

reign /reɪn/ *n* (C) (period of) sovereignty, rule: *during five successive* ∼s; *in the* ∼ *of King George.* □ *vi* **1** hold office as a monarch: *The king* ∼ed *but he did not rule or govern. He* ∼ed *over the country for ten years.* **2** exist at the present time: *the* ∼ing *beauty among the students. Silence* ∼ed *everywhere.*

re·im·burse /ˈriːɪmˈbɜːs/ *vt* pay back (to a person who has spent money, the money spent): *You will be* ∼d *for your expenses.*

re·im·burse·ment *n* [C,U] repayment (of expenses).

rein /reɪn/ *n* (often *pl* in the same sense as the *sing*) long, narrow strap fastened to the bit of a bridle for controlling a horse. **give free rein to sb/sth,** allow freedom to: *give free* ∼ *to one's imagination.* **hold/take the reins,** (*fig*) have/take control: *hold the* ∼s *of government.* **keep a tight rein on sb/ sth,** allow little freedom to. □ *vt* control (as) with reins: ∼ *in a horse,* restrain it.

re·in·car·nate /ˈriːɪmkɑˈneɪt/ *vt* give a new body to (a soul). □ *adj* /ˈriːmˈkɑnət/ born again in a new body.

re·in·car·na·tion /ˈriːɪmkɑˈneɪʃən/ *n* [U] religious doctrine that the soul enters, after death, into another (human or animal) body; [C] instance of this.

rein·deer /ˈreɪndɪə(r)/ *n* [C] (*pl* unchanged) kind of large deer with branched antlers, used in Lapland for transport and kept in herds for its milk, flesh and hide.

re·in·force /ˈriːɪnˈfɔːs/ *vt* make stronger by

adding or supplying more men or material: ∼ *an army/a fleet.* **2** increase the size, thickness, of something so that it supports more weight, etc: ∼ *a bridge.*

re·in·forced concrete, concrete which is strengthened with steel bars or metal netting.

re·in·force·ment *n* [U] **(a)** reinforcing or being reinforced. **(b)** (esp *pl*) (esp) soldiers, ships, etc sent to reinforce.

re·in·state /ˈriːɪmˈsteɪt/ *vt* replace (a person) (in a former position or condition): ∼ *the chairman.*

re·in·state·ment *n* [C,U]

re·in·sure /ˈriːɪmˈʃʊə(r)/ *vt* insure again.

re·in·sur·ance /-rəns/ *n* [U]

re·is·sue /ˈriːˈɪʃuː/ *vt* issue **(2)** again after temporary discontinuance: ∼ *stamps/books.* □ *n* [C] something reissued.

re·iter·ate /rɪˈɪtəreɪt/ *vt* say or do again several times: ∼ *a command.*

re·iter·ation /ˈriːˈɪtəˈreɪʃən/ *n* [C,U]

re·ject[1] /ˈriːdʒekt/ *n* [C] something rejected: *export* ∼s, made for export but rejected because of an imperfection.

re·ject[2] /rɪˈdʒekt/ *vt* **1** put aside, throw away, as not good enough to be kept: ∼ *fruit that is overripe.* **2** refuse to accept: ∼ *an offer of help/of marriage. The army doctors* ∼ed *him,* would not accept him as medically fit.

re·jec·tion /rɪˈdʒekʃən/ *n* [U] rejecting or being rejected: [C] instance of this; something rejected.

re·joice /rɪˈdʒɔɪs/ *vt,vi* **1** feel great joy; show signs of great happiness: ∼ *over a victory;* ∼ *at her success.* **2** make glad; cause to be happy: *The boy's success* ∼d *his mother's heart.* (*Note:* **be glad** and **be pleased** are more common than *rejoice*).

re·joic·ing *n* [U] happiness; joy.

re·join[1] /rɪˈdʒɔɪn/ *vt,vi* answer; reply

re·join·der /-də(r)/ *n* [C] what is said in reply.

re·join[2] /rɪˈdʒɔɪn/ *vt* join the company of again: ∼ *one's regiment/ship.*

re·join[3] /ˈriːˈdʒɔɪn/ *vt* join (together) again.

re·ju·ven·ate /rɪˈdʒuːvəneɪt/ *vt,vi* make or become young or active again in nature or appearance.

re·ju·ven·ation /rɪˈdʒuːvəˈneɪʃən/ *n* [U]

re·kindle /ˈriːˈkɪndəl/ *vt,vi* **1** kindle again: ∼ *a fire.* **2** (*fig*) (cause to) be active again: *Our hopes* ∼d.

re·laid /ˈriːˈleɪd/ ⇨ relay[2].

re·lapse /rɪˈlæps/ *vi* fall back again (into bad ways, error, heresy, illness, silence etc). □ *n* [C] falling back, esp after recovering from illness: *The patient has had a major* ∼.

re·late /rɪˈleɪt/ *vt,vi* **1** (*formal*) tell (a story); give an account of (facts, adventures etc): *He* ∼d *to his wife some amusing stories about his employer.* **2** connect in thought or meaning: *It is difficult to* ∼ *these results with/to any known cause.* **3 relate to,** have reference (to): *She is a girl who notices* *nothing except what ∼s to herself.* **4 be related (to),** be connected by family (to): *She says she is ∼d to the royal family.*

re·la·tion /rɪˈleɪʃn/ n **1** [U] the act of relating(1,2)or telling: *the ∼ of his adventures.* **2** [C] that which is told; tale or narrative. **3** [U] = relationship(3): *The effort and expense needed for this project bore no ∼/were out of all ∼ to the results. In/with relation to,* as regards; concerning. **4** (usually *pl*) dealings; affairs; what one person, group, country etc, has to do with another: *have business ∼s with a firm in Stockholm; the friendly ∼s between my country and yours; diplomatic ∼s.* ⇨ public relations officer. **5** [C] relative(2): *All his poor ∼s came to spend their holidays at his home.*

re·la·tion·ship /-ʃɪp/ n **(a)** [C] what there is between one thing, person, idea, etc and another or others: *He admitted his affair with Susan could never develop into a lasting ∼ship.* **(b)** [U] condition of belonging to the same family; being connected by birth or marriage. **(c)** [C] instance of being related: *the ∼ship between oil and water/of oil to water.*

rela·tive /ˈrelətɪv/ adj **1** comparative: *the ∼ advantages of gas and electricity for cooking. They are living in ∼ comfort,* ie compared with other people or with themselves at an earlier time. **2** relative to, referring to; having a connection with: *the facts ∼ to this problem.* □ n [C] **1** relative word, esp a pronoun. **2** person to whom one is related, eg an uncle or aunt, a cousin, a nephew or niece.

relative adverb, eg *where* in 'the place where the accident occurred'.

relative clause, one joined by a relative pronoun or adverb.

relative pronoun, eg *whom* in 'the man whom we saw'.

rela·tive·ly adv comparatively; in proportion to: *The matter is ∼ly unimportant.*

re·lax /rɪˈlæks/ vt,vi **1** cause or allow to become less tight, stiff, strict or rigid: *∼ one's grip/hold on something; ∼ the muscles.* **2** become less tense, rigid, energetic, strict: *His face ∼ed in a smile. Let's stop working and ∼ for an hour.*

re·lax·ation /ˌriːlækˈseɪʃn/ n **(a)** [U] relaxing or being relaxed: *∼ation of the muscles.* **(b)** [C,U] (something done for) recreation: *Fishing is his favourite ∼ation.*

re·lay¹ /ˈriːleɪ/ n [C] **1** gang or group of men, supply of material, to replace tired or worn ones: *working in/by ∼s.* **2** (in telegraphy, broadcasting) device which receives messages, radio programmes, etc and transmits them with greater strength to increase the distance over which they are carried. **3** (short for a) relay race; relayed broadcast. □ vt /rɪˈleɪ/ (pt,pp ∼ed) send out (a broadcast programme received from another station).

ˈrelay race, one between two teams, each member of the team running one section of the total distance.

ˈrelay station, place from which radio programmes are broadcast after being received from another station.

re·lay² /ˈriːleɪ/ vt (pt,pp -laid /-ˈleɪd/) lay (a cable, carpet, etc) again.

re·lease /rɪˈliːs/ vt **1** allow to go; set free; unfasten: *∼ one's grip/a man from prison; ∼ a bomb (from an aircraft),* allow it to fall. **2** allow (news) to be known or published; allow (a film) to be exhibited or (goods) to be placed on sale: *recently ∼d films/records.* **3** (legal) give up or surrender (a right, debt, property) to another. □ n **1** [U] releasing or being released; [C] instance of this: *an order for his ∼ from prison; a ˈpress ∼,* ie of a news item to the newspapers; *the newest ∼es,* eg films/records. **on general release,** (of cinema films) available for seeing at the usual network of local cinemas. **2** [C] handle, lever, catch, etc that releases part of a machine: *the ˈcarriage ∼ (on a typewriter).*

rel·egate /ˈrelɪɡeɪt/ vt **1** delegate. **2** dismiss to a lower position or condition: *Will our team be ∼d to the second division?*

rel·ega·tion /ˌrelɪˈɡeɪʃn/ n [U].

re·lent /rɪˈlent/ vi become less severe; give up unkind or cruel intentions: *At last mother ∼ed and let us to stay up and watch TV.*

re·lent·less adj without pity: *∼less persecution.*

re·lent·less·ly adv

rel·evance /ˈreləvəns/ n [U] state of being relevant: *What ∼ does your theory have to the facts?*

rel·evant /ˈreləvənt/ adj connected with what is being discussed: *have all the ∼ documents; supply the facts ∼ to the case.*

rel·evant·ly adv

re·li·able /rɪˈlaɪəbl/ adj that may be relied or depended on: *∼ tools/assistants/ information/witnesses.*

re·li·ably /-əblɪ/ adv

re·lia·bil·ity /rɪˌlaɪəˈbɪlətɪ/ n [U]

re·li·ance /rɪˈlaɪəns/ n **1** [U] trust; confidence: *Do you place much ∼ on/upon your doctor?* **2** person or thing depended on.

re·li·ant /-ənt/ adj trusting.

relic /ˈrelɪk/ n [C] **1** something that belonged to a saint or was connected with him, kept after his death, as an object of reverence, and in some cases said to have miraculous powers. **2** something from the past that serves to keep memories alive: *a ∼ of early civilization.* **3** (pl) person's dead body or bones; what has survived destruction or decay.

re·lief¹ /rɪˈliːf/ n [U] (used with the *a, an* as in examples, but not normally in the *pl*) **1** lessening, ending or removal of pain, distress, anxiety, etc: *The doctor's treatment gave/brought some/not much ∼. It was a great ∼ to find the children safe.* **2** help given to those in need; food, clothes, money, etc for persons in trouble: *send ~ to people made homeless by floods; provide ~ for refugees; a '~ fund*. **3** something that makes a change from monotony or that relaxes tension: *Shakespeare introduced comic scenes into his tragedies by way of ~.* **4** help given to a beseiged town; raising (of a siege): *The general hastened to the ~ of the fortress.* **5** (replacing of a person, persons, on duty by a) person or persons appointed to go on duty: (as an *adjective*) *a ~ driver*.

re·lief /rɪˈliːf/ *n* **1** [U] method of carving or moulding in which a design stands out from a flat surface: *a profile of Mao Tse-Tung in ~.* **2** [C] design or carving made in this way. **3** [U] (in drawing, etc) appearance of being done in relief by the use of shading, colour, etc. **4** [U] vividness; distinctness of outline. `re'lief map`, one showing hills, valleys, etc by shading or other means, not only by contour lines.

re·lieve /rɪˈliːv/ *vt* **1** give or bring relief [1] to; lessen or remove (pain or distress): *We were ~d to hear that you had arrived safely. The fund is for relieving distress among the flood victims.* **2** take one's turn on duty: *~ the guard/the watch/a sentry.* **3** take something from somebody: *Let me ~ you of your suit-case*, carry it (which is more usual). **4** dismiss from: *He was ~d of his duties.*

re·lig·ion /rɪˈlɪdʒən/ *n* **1** [U] belief in the existence of a supernatural ruling power, the creator and controller of the universe. **2** [C] one of the various systems of faith and worship based on such belief: *the great ~s of the world*, e g Christianity, Islam, Buddhism. **3** [U] life as lived under the rules of a monastic order: *Her name in ~ is Sister Mary*, This is her name as a nun.

re·lig·ious /rɪˈlɪdʒəs/ *adj* **1** of religion. **2** (of a person) devout; having faith. **3** of a monastic order: *a ~ house*, a monastery or convent. **4** conscientious: *do one's work with ~ care.*

re·lig·ious·ly *adv*

re·line /ˈriːˈlaɪn/ *vt* put a new lining in, e g a coat.

re·lin·quish /rɪˈlɪŋkwɪʃ/ *vt* **1** give up: *~ a hope/a habit/a belief.* **2** surrender: *~ one's rights/shares to a partner.*

rel·ish /ˈrelɪʃ/ *n* **1** [C,U] (something used to give, or which has, a) special flavour or attractive quality: *Olives and sardines are ~es. Some pastimes lose their ~ when one grows old.* **2** [U] liking (*for*): *I have no further ~ for active pursuits now that I am 90.* □ *vt* enjoy; get pleasure out of: *She won't ~ having to get up before dawn to catch that train.*

re·live /ˈriːˈlɪv/ *vt* live through, undergo, again: *It's an experience I don't want to ~.*

re·lo·cate /ˈriːləʊˈkeɪt/ *US:* ˈriːˈləʊkeɪt/ *vt,vi* establish, become established, in a new place or area.

re·lo·ca·tion /ˈriːləʊˈkeɪʃən/ *n* [U]

re·luc·tance /rɪˈlʌktəns/ *n* [U] being reluctant.

re·luc·tant /rɪˈlʌktənt/ *adj* (slow to act because) unwilling or not wanting to: *He seemed ~ to join us.*

re·luc·tant·ly *adv*

rely /rɪˈlaɪ/ *vi* (*pt,pp* -lied) depend (on) with confidence, look to for help: *He can always be relied on/upon for help.*

re·main /rɪˈmeɪn/ *vi* **1** be still present after a part has gone or has been away: *After the fire, very little ~ed of my house. If you take 3 from 8, 5 ~s.* **2** continue in some place or condition; continue to be: *How many weeks will you ~ (= stay) here? He ~ed silent.*

re·main·der /rɪˈmeɪndə(r)/ *n* [C,U] that which remains; persons or things that are left over: *Twenty people came in and the ~ (= the rest, the others) stayed outside.*

re·mains /rɪˈmeɪnz/ *n pl* **1** what is left: *the ~s of a meal; ancient ~s of Rome.* **2** dead body; corpse: *His mortal ~s are buried in the churchyard.*

re·make /ˈriːˈmeɪk/ *vt* (*pt,pp* -made /-ˈmeɪd/) make again. □ *n* /ˈriːmeɪk/ [C] something made again: *a ~ of a film.*

re·mand /rɪˈmɑːnd *US:* -ˈmænd/ *vt* send (an accused person) back (from a court of law) into custody so that more evidence may be obtained: *~ed for a week.* □ *n* [U] remanding or being remanded: *detention on ~.*

re·mark /rɪˈmɑːk/ *vt,vi* **1** (*formal*) notice; see: *Did you ~ the similarity between them?* **2** say (*that*): *He ~ed that he would be absent the next day.* **3** say something by way of comment: *It would be rude to ~ on/upon her appearance.* □ *n* **1** [U] notice; looking at: *There was nothing worthy of ~ at the Flower Show.* **2** [C] comment: *pass rude ~s about her; make a few ~s*, give a short talk.

re·mark·able /-əbəl/ *adj* out of the ordinary; deserving or attracting attention: *a ~able event/boy.*

re·mark·ably /-əblɪ/ *adv*

re·marry /ˈriːˈmærɪ/ *vt,vi* (*pt,pp* -ied) marry again.

re·medial /rɪˈmiːdɪəl/ *adj* providing, or intended to provide, a remedy: *~ education/classes*, e g for backward children.

re·medi·able /rɪˈmiːdɪəbəl/ *adj* that can be remedied.

rem·edy /ˈremədɪ/ *n* [C,U] (*pl* -ies) cure (for a disease, evil, etc), method of, something used for, putting something right: *a good ~ for colds. Your only ~ (= way to get satisfaction) is to go to law.* □ *vt* (*pt,pp* -ied) put right; provide a cure for (evils, defects): *Your faults of pronunciation can be remedied.*

re·mem·ber /rɪˈmembə(r)/ *vt,vi* **1** call back to mind the memory of: *Can you ~ where you were? I ~ed (= did not forget) to post your letters.* **2** have, keenp in the mind: *I shall always ~ her (= picture her in my*

545

mind) *as a slim young girl*. **3** make a present to: *I hope you'll ~ me in your will*, leave me something. **4** convey greetings: *Please ~ me to your brother*.

re·mem·brance /rɪˈmembrəns/ n **1** [U] remembering or being remembered; memory: *have no ~ of something; a service in ~ of those killed in the war*. **2** [C] something given or kept in memory of a person or thing: *He sent us a small ~ of his visit*. **3** (*pl*) regards; greetings (the usual words): *Give my kind ~s to your parents*.

re·mind /rɪˈmaɪnd/ vt cause (a person) to remember (to do something, etc); cause (a person) to think (of something): *Please ~ me to answer that letter. He ~s me of his brother. That ~s me,..., What you have just said makes me remember..., I've just remembered..., etc*.

re·mind·er, something (e g a letter) that helps a person to remember something: *He hasn't paid the money yet—I must send him a ~er*.

remi·nisce /ˈremɪˈnɪs/ vi think or talk (about past events and experiences).

remi·nis·cence /ˈremɪˈnɪsəns/ n **1** [U] recalling of past experiences. **2** (*pl*) remembered experiences (thought, spoken or written): *~s of my days in the Navy*. **3** something that reminds one (*of* something, somebody else): *There is a ~ of his father in the way he walks*.

remi·nis·cent /ˈremɪˈnɪsənt/ adj reminding one of; recalling past experiences.

remi·nis·cent·ly adv

re·miss /rɪˈmɪs/ adj (formal) **1** careless: *You have been ~ in your duties*. **2** negligent: *That was very ~ of you*.

re·mis·sion /rɪˈmɪʃən/ n **1** [U] pardon or forgiveness (of sins, by God). **2** [U] freeing (from debt, punishment, etc): *~ of a claim*; [C] instance of this: *~ (from a prison sentence) for good conduct*. **3** [U] lessening or weakening (of pain, efforts, etc): *~ of a fever*.

re·mit /rɪˈmɪt/ vt,vi (-tt-) **1** (of God) forgive (sins). **2** excuse payment (of a debt, a punishment): *Your fees cannot be ~ted*. **3** send (money, etc) by post: *Kindly ~ by cheque*, send a cheque for the sum owing. **4** make or become less: *~ one's efforts*. **5** take or send (a question to be decided) (to some authority): *The matter has been ~ted to a higher tribunal*.

re·mit·tance /-təns/ n [U] the sending of money; [C] sum of money sent.

re·mit·tent /rɪˈmɪtənt/ adj (esp of a fever) that is less severe at intervals.

rem·nant /ˈremnənt/ n [C] **1** small part that remains: *~s of a banquet; ~s of former glory*. **2** (esp) length of cloth offered at a reduced price after the greater part has been sold.

re·mon·strate /ˈremənstreɪt/ vi (formal) make a protest; argue in protest: *~ against cruelty to children*.

re·morse /rɪˈmɔːs/ n [U] deep, bitter regret for doing wrong: *feel/be filled with ~ for one's failure to help her; in a fit of ~; without ~*, mercilessly(ly).

re·morse·ful /-fəl/ adj feeling remorse.

re·morse·fully /-fəlɪ/ adv

re·morse·less adj without remorse.

re·morse·less·ly adv

re·mote /rɪˈməʊt/ adj (-r, -st) **1** far away in space or time: *in the ~st parts of Asia; live in a house ~ from any town or village*. **2** widely separated (in feeling, interests, etc *from*): *Some of your statements are too ~ from the subject we are discussing*. **3** distant in manner. **4** (often in the superlative) slight: *a ~ possibility. I haven't the ~st idea of what you mean*.

remote control, control of apparatus, e g an aircraft, a rocket, from a distance by means of radio signals.

re·mote·ly adv distantly: *We're ~ly related*.

re·mote·ness n [U]

re·mount[1] /ˈriːˈmaʊnt/ vt,vi (esp) get on a (horse, bicycle, etc) again.

re·mount[2] /ˈriːˈmaʊnt/ vt **1** supply (a man, a regiment) with a fresh horse or horses. **2** put (a photograph, etc) on a new mount. □ n [C] /ˈriːmaʊnt/ fresh horse; supply of fresh horses.

re·moval /rɪˈmuːvəl/ n [U] act of removing: *the ~ of furniture*; (as an adjective) *a ~ van* (for furniture); [C] instance of removal.

re·move /rɪˈmuːv/ vt,vi **1** take off or away (from the place occupied): *~ the cloth from the table*. **2** get rid of: *~ doubts/fears. What do you advise for removing grease/ink stains from clothes?* **3** dismiss: *~ a Civil Servant*. **4** go to live in another place (*move* is more usual): *We're removing from London to the country*. **5** *removed from*, distant or remote from: *an explanation far ~d from the truth*.

removed, (of cousins) different by a generation: *first cousin once ~d*, first cousin's child.

re·mov·able /-əbəl/ adj that can be removed.

re·mover /rɪˈmuːvə(r)/ n **1** [C] (esp) person who follows the business of moving furniture when people move house. **2** (in compounds) something that removes(2): *`stain ~r*.

re·mun·er·ate /rɪˈmjuːnəreɪt/ vt (formal) pay (a person) (for work or services); reward.

re·mun·er·ation /rɪˈmjuːnəˈreɪʃən/ n [C,U] payment; reward.

re·mun·er·ative /rɪˈmjuːnərətɪv US: -reɪt-/ adj profitable.

re·nais·sance /rɪˈneɪsəns US: ˈrenəsɒns/ n **1** the R~, (period of) revival of art and literature in Europe in the 14th, 15th and 16th centuries, based on ancient Greek learning; (as an adjective) *~ art*. **2** [C] any similar revival.

re·nal /ˈriːnəl/ adj (anat) of or in the (region of the) kidneys: ~ artery.

re·name /riːˈneɪm/ vt give a new name to; name again.

re·nas·cence /rɪˈnæsəns/ = renaissance(2).

re·nas·cent /-sənt/ adj reviving; being reborn.

rend /rend/ vt (pt,pp rent /rent/) (literary) 1 pull or divide forcibly; penetrate: a country rent (in two) by civil war. Loud cries rent the air. 2 tear or pull (off, away) violently: Children were rent away from their mothers' arms by the brutal soldiers.

ren·der /ˈrendə(r)/ vt 1 give in return or exchange, or as something due: ~ thanks to God; ~ good for evil; ~ help to those in need; ~ a service to him/~ him a service; a reward for services ~ed. 2 present; offer; send in (an account for payment): You will have to ~ an account of your expenditure. 3 cause to be (in some condition): be ~ed helpless by an accident. 4 give a performance of; express in another language: The piano solo was well ~ed. There are many English idioms that cannot be ~ed into other languages. 5 melt and make clear: ~ down fat/lard.

ren·der·ing /ˈrendərɪŋ/ n [C] way of performing, playing, translating, something. ⇨ 4 above: clever ~ings of Chaucer.

ren·dez·vous /ˈrɒndɪvuː/ n [C] (pl unchanged) 1 (place decided on for a) meeting at a time agreed on. 2 place where people often meet: This café is a ~ for writers and artists. □ vi meet at a rendezvous.

ren·di·tion /renˈdɪʃn/ n [C] (formal) interpretation or performance (of a song, etc).

ren·egade /ˈrenɪɡeɪd/ n [C] person who changes his religious beliefs, esp from Christianity; person who deserts his political party; traitor: (as an adjective) a ~ priest. □ vi become a renegade.

re·new /rɪˈnjuː US: -ˈnuː/ vt 1 make (as good as) new; put new life and vigour into; restore to the original condition: ~ acquaintance with an old friend; with ~ed enthusiasm. 2 get, make, say or give, again: ~ a lease/contract; ~ one's subscription to a periodical. 3 replace (with the same sort of thing, etc): We must ~ our supplies of coal.

re·new·able /-əbəl/ adj that can be renewed.

re·newal /-əl/ n [U] renewing or being renewed: urban ~al, e g the provision of better housing; [C] something renewed, e g an insurance premium.

re·nounce /rɪˈnaʊns/ vt 1 declare formally that one will no longer have anything to do with, that one no longer recognizes (a person or thing): ~ one's faith/one's family; ~ the world, give up meeting people socially, etc. 2 consent formally to give up (a claim, right, possession): ~ one's claim to an inheritance. 3 refuse to recognize: He ~d his sons because they were criminals.

reno·vate /ˈrenəveɪt/ vt restore, e g old buildings, oil paintings, to a good or strong condition.

reno·va·tion /ˈrenəˈveɪʃn/ n [U] renovating; (pl) instances of this.

re·nown /rɪˈnaʊn/ n [U] fame: win ~; a man of high ~.

re·nowned adj famous; celebrated: He was ~ed for his skill.

rent¹ /rent/ n [C,U] regular payment for the use of land, a building, a room or rooms, machinery, etc; sum of money paid in this way: You owe me three weeks' ~. □ vt,vi 1 occupy or use (land, buildings, etc) for rent: We don't own our house, we ~ it from Mr Gay. 2 allow (land, buildings, etc) to be used or occupied in return for rent: Mr Hill ~s this land to us at £50 a year.

ˈrent-collector, person who goes from house to house to collect rents.

ˈrent-ˈfree adj, adv. a ~-free house, for which no rent is charged to the tenant.

ˈrent-rebate, rebate, based on earnings and the amount of rent payable, given by a local government authority to the lower paid, esp council tenants.

rent·able /-əbəl/ adj

ren·tal /ˈrentəl/ n [C] amount of rent paid or received.

rent² /rent/ n [C] 1 torn place in cloth, etc: a ~ in the balloon. 2 (fig) division or split (in a political party, etc).

rent³ /rent/ pt,pp of rend.

re·nunci·ation /rɪˌnʌnsɪˈeɪʃn/ n [U] renouncing; self-denial.

re·open /riːˈəʊpən/ vt,vi open again after closing or being closed: ~ a shop; ~ a discussion. School ~s on Monday.

re·or·gan·ize /riːˈɔːɡənaɪz/ vt,vi organize again or in a new way.

re·orien·tate /riːˈɔːrɪənteɪt/ (also **re·orient** /riːˈɔːrɪənt/) vt,vi orient(ate) again or anew.

rep /rep/ n [C] (informal) (abbr of) repertory (company).

re·pair¹ /rɪˈpeə(r)/ vt 1 restore (something worn or damaged) to good condition: ~ the roads/a watch. 2 put right again: ~ an error. □ n 1 [U] repairing or being repaired: road under ~. 2 (sing or pl but not with a, an) work or process of repairing: The shop will be closed during ~s. 3 [U] condition for using or being used: The machine is in a bad state of ~/in good ~.

re·pair·able /-əbəl/ adj that can be repaired.

re·pairer, person who repairs things: ˈshoe ~ers.

re·pair² /rɪˈpeə(r)/ vi (formal) (esp) go frequently, go in large numbers to: ~ to the seaside for the summer.

rep·ar·able /ˈrepərəbəl/ adj (of a loss, etc) that can be made good.

rep·ar·ation /ˈrepəˈreɪʃn/ n [U] act of compensating for loss or damage; (pl) compen-

547

sation for war damages demanded from a defeated enemy.

rep·ar·tee /ˌrepɑˈti/ n [C] witty, clever reply; [U] the making of such remarks.

re·past /rɪˈpɑst US: -ˈpæst/ n [C] (formal) meal: a luxurious ~ in the banqueting hall.

re·pat·ri·ate /riˈpætrɪeɪt US: -ˈpeɪt-/ vt send or bring (a person) back to his own country: ~ refugees after a war. □ n [C] repatriated person.

re·pat·ri·ation /ˈriˈpætrɪˈeɪʃən US: -ˈpeɪt-/ n [U]

re·pay /rɪˈpeɪ/ vt,vi (pt,pp -paid /-ˈpeɪd/) 1 pay back (money): If you'll lend me 75p, I'll ~ you next week. 2 give in return: How can I ~ Jim for his kindness.

re·pay·able /-əbəl/ adj that can or must be repaid.

re·pay·ment n [U] repaying; [C] instance of this.

re·peal /rɪˈpil/ vt cancel, annul (a law, etc). □ n [C,U] repealing.

re·peat /rɪˈpit/ vt,vi 1 say or do again: ~ word/a mistake. 2 say (what somebody else has said or what one learnt by heart): You must not ~ what I've told you; it's very confidential. 3 (of food) continue to be tasted after being eaten: Do you find that onions ~? 4 (of numbers, e g decimals) recur: The last two figures are ~ed. 5 supply a further amount, order, etc: We regret that we cannot ~ this article. □ n [C] another supply, performance, etc: a ~ performance. There will be a ~ (= another broadcast) of this talk on Friday.

re·peat·ed·ly adv again and again.

re·pel /rɪˈpel/ vt (-ll-) 1 drive back or away; refuse to accept: ~ the enemy/temptation. 2 cause a feeling of dislike in: His long, rough beard ~led her.

re·pel·lent /-ənt/ adj unattractive; uninviting: ~lent work/food/manners. □ n [C] something that causes something to go or stay away, esp a preparation that repels insects.

re·pent /rɪˈpent/ vi,vt think with regret or sorrow of; be full of regret; wish one had not done (something): Don't you ~ (of) having wasted your money so foolishly?

re·pent·ance /-əns/ n [U] regret for doing wrong: show ~ance (for ...).

re·pent·ant /-ənt/ adj feeling or showing regret.

re·pent·ant·ly adv

re·per·cus·sion /ˌripəˈkʌʃən/ n 1 [U] springing back; driving or throwing back. 2 [C] something that comes back; echoing sound: the ~ of the waves from the rocks. 3 [C] (usually pl) far-reaching and indirect effect (of an event, etc): The assassination of the President was followed by ~s throughout the whole country.

rep·er·toire /ˈrepətwɑ(r)/ n [C] all the plays, songs, pieces, etc which a company, actor, musician, etc is prepared to perform:

She has a large ~ of songs.

rep·er·tory /ˈrepətəri US: -tɔri/ n [C] (pl -ies) = repertoire.

ˈrepetory company/theatre, (common abbr rep) one in which the actors/plays are changed regularly (instead of having long runs as in most London theatres).

rep·eti·tion /ˌrepɪˈtɪʃən/ n 1 [U] repeating or being repeated; [C] instance of this: after numerous ~s. 2 [C] another repeat: Let there be no ~ of this, Don't do it again. 3 [C] piece (of poetry, etc) set to be learnt by heart and repeated.

re·peti·tive /rɪˈpetətɪv/ (also **rep·eti·tious** /ˌrepəˈtɪʃəs/) adj characterized by repeated action: the repetitive work typical of modern industry.

re·phrase /ˌriˈfreɪz/ vt say again, using different words: ~ a question.

re·place /rɪˈpleɪs/ vt 1 put back in its place: replacing a dictionary on the shelf; ~ the receiver, i e after telephoning. 2 take the place of: Can anything ~ a mother's love and care? 3 supply as a substitute for: ~ coal by/with oil.

re·place·able /-əbəl/ adj that can be replaced.

re·place·ment n [U] replacing or being replaced; [C] person or thing that replaces: get a ~ment while one is away on holiday.

re·play /ˈriˈpleɪ/ vt play (e g a football match that was drawn) again. □ n /ˈri:pleɪ/ [C] replaying of a record, a football match etc.

re·plen·ish /rɪˈplenɪʃ/ vt (formal) fill up again; get a new supply of or for.

re·plete /rɪˈplit/ adj (formal) filled with; holding as much as possible: ~ with food; feeling ~.

re·ple·tion /rɪˈpliʃən/ n [U] (formal) state of being replete.

rep·lica /ˈreplɪkə/ n [C] (pl ~s) exact copy (esp one made by an artist of one of his own pictures).

re·ply /rɪˈplaɪ/ vi,vt (pt,pp -ied) give as an answer to, in words or action: He failed to ~ (to my question). 'Certainly, sir', he replied. □ n [C] act of replying; what is replied: He made no ~. What was said in ~?

re·port[1] /rɪˈpɔt/ n 1 [C] account of, statement about, something heard, seen, done, etc: the annual ~ of a business company; ˈlaw ~s, i e of trials, etc in the law courts; a school ~, e g by teachers about a pupil, with his examination marks, etc; newspaper ~s. 2 [U] rumour; [C] piece of gossip: R~ has it that..., People are saying that.... 3 [C] sound of an explosion: the loud ~ of a gun.

re·port[2] /rɪˈpɔt/ vt,vi 1 give an account of (something seen, heard, done, etc); give as news: The discovery of a new planet has been ~ed. 2 write down (e g in shorthand) the words of speeches, etc for newspapers, etc: ~ a speech/a Parliamentary debate. 3 give news or information concerning: ~

on/upon a meeting. **4** go (somewhere), and announce that one has come, that one is ready for work, duty, etc: ~ *for duty at the office;* ~ *to the Manager.* **5** make a complaint against a person (to authorities): ~ *an official for insolence. I shall have to ~ your lateness.*

reported speech, = indirect speech.

re·porter, person who supplies news to a newspaper, for radio or TV.

re·pose¹ /rɪˈpəʊz/ *vt* (*formal*) place (trust, confidence, etc) in: *Don't ~ too much confidence in his honesty.*

re·pose² /rɪˈpəʊz/ *vt, vi* (*formal*) **1** rest; give rest or support to: *a girl reposing on a cushion.* **2** be based or supported (*on*). □ *n* [U] (*formal*) **1** rest; sleep: *Her face is beautiful in ~.* **2** peaceful, restful or quiet behaviour or appearance: *His attitude lacked ~,* ease of manner.

re·pose·ful /-fəl/ *adj* calm, quiet (the usual words).

re·posi·tory /rɪˈpɒzɪtrɪ US: -tɔrɪ/ *n* [C] (*pl* -ies) (*formal*) place where things are or may be stored: *Desks are repositories for all sorts of useless papers.*

rep·re·hend /ˌreprɪˈhend/ *vt* (*formal*) disapprove of strongly: ~ *his conduct.*

rep·re·hen·sible /ˌreprɪˈhensəbəl/ *adj* deserving to be disapproved of.

rep·re·sent¹ /ˌreprɪˈzent/ *vt* **1** be, give, make, a picture, sign, symbol or example of: *Phonetic symbols ~ sounds. This painting ~s a hunting scene.* **2** declare to be; describe (*as*): *He ~ed himself as an expert.* **3** explain; make clear: *Let me try to ~ my ideas to you in another way.* **4** express: *They ~ed their grievances to the headmaster.* **5** act or speak for; be MP for; be an agent for: *members* (ie MP's) ~*ing Welsh constituencies.*

rep·re·sen·ta·tion /ˌreprɪzenˈteɪʃən/ *n* (**a**) [U] representing or being represented; [C] that which is represented: *no taxation without ~ation,* ie citizens should not be taxed without being represented (in Parliament, etc).⊳proportional representation. (**b**) [C] (esp) polite protest: *make ~ations to the Inspector of Taxes about an excessive assessment.*

re·pre·sent² /ˌriːprɪˈzent/ *vt* submit again: *Please ~ your cheque when you have funds in your account.*

rep·re·sen·ta·tive /ˌreprɪˈzentətɪv/ *adj* serving to show; serving as an example of a class or group; containing examples of a number of classes or groups: *a ~ collection of French impressionist paintings.* **2** consisting of elected deputies; based on representation by such elected deputies: ~ *government/institutions.* □ *n* [C] **1** example; typical specimen (*of*). **2** person elected or appointed to represent or act for others: *send a ~ to a conference; our ~* (= MP) *in the House of Commons.*

the House of Representatives, the lower house of the US Congress or of a state legislature.

re·press /rɪˈpres/ *vt* keep or put down or under; prevent from finding an outlet: ~ *a revolt;* ~ed *emotions.*

re·pres·sion /rɪˈpreʃən/ *n* [U]

re·pres·sive /rɪˈpresɪv/ *adj* serving or tending to repress: ~*ive legislation.*

re·prieve /rɪˈpriːv/ *vt* **1** postpone or delay punishment (esp the execution of a person condemned to death). **2** (*fig*) give relief for a short time (from danger, trouble, etc). □ *n* [C] (order giving authority for the) postponement or cancelling of punishment (esp by death): *grant a prisoner a ~.*

re·pri·mand /ˈreprɪmɑːnd US: -ˈmænd/ *vt* express disapproval to (a person) severely and officially (because of a fault, etc). □ *n* /ˈreprɪmænd US: -mænd/ [C] official expression of disapproval.

re·print /riːˈprɪnt/ *vt* print again. □ *n* /ˈriːprɪnt/ [C] book, etc printed again.

re·prisal /rɪˈpraɪzəl/ *n* **1** [U] paying back injury with injury: *do something by way of ~.* **2** (*pl*) such acts, esp of one country on another during a war.

re·proach /rɪˈprəʊtʃ/ *vt* find fault with (a person, usually with a feeling of sorrow, or suggesting the need for sorrow): ~ *one's wife for being late with the dinner* □ *n* **1** [U] reproaching: *a term/look of ~.* **2** [C] instance, word, phrase, etc of reproach. *above/beyond reproach,* perfect, blameless: *She/Her behaviour is beyond ~.* **3** [C] something that brings disgrace or discredit (*to*): *slums that are a ~ to the city council.*

re·proach·ful /-fəl/ *adj* full of, expressing, reproach: *a ~ful look.*

re·proach·fully /-fəlɪ/ *adv*

re·pro·duce /ˌriːprəˈdjuːs US: -ˈduːs/ *vt, vi* **1** cause to be seen, heard, exist, act again: ~ *music from magnetic tape;* ~ *copies of an original painting.* **2** bring forth as offspring; bring about a natural increase: ~ *one's kind; plants that ~ easily.* **3** grow anew (a part that is lost, etc): *Can lizards ~ their tails?*

re·pro·ducer, person who, that which, reproduces.

re·pro·duc·ible /-əbəl/ *adj* that can be reproduced.

re·pro·duc·tion /ˌriːprəˈdʌkʃən/ *n* [U] process of reproducing; [C] something reproduced, esp a work of art.

re·pro·duc·tive /ˌriːprəˈdʌktɪv/ *adj* reproducing; for, relating to, reproduction (esp (2)): *reproductive organs.*

re·proof¹ /rɪˈpruːf/ *n* **1** [U] blame (the more usual word); disapproval: *a glance of ~; conduct deserving of ~.* **2** [C] expression of blame or disapproval.

re·proof² /ˈriːˈpruːf/ *vt* make (a coat, etc) waterproof again.

re·prove /rɪˈpruːv/ *vt* find fault with; disapprove of strongly: *The priest ~d the people*

for not attending church services.
re·prov·ing·ly *adv*

rep·tile /ˈreptaɪl US: -təl/ *n* [C] cold-blooded animal that creeps or crawls and lays eggs e g *a lizard, tortoise, crocodile, snake.*

rep·til·ian /repˈtɪlɪən/ *adj* of, like, a reptile.

re·pub·lic /rɪˈpʌblɪk/ *n* [C] (country with a) system of government in which the elected representatives of the people are supreme, and with an elected head (the President): *a constitutional ~,* e g the US.

re·pub·li·can /rɪˈpʌblɪkən/ *adj* of, relating to, supporting the principles of, a republic. □ *n* [C] **1** person who favours republican government. **2** R~, member of one of the two main political parties in the US (the other is *Democrat*).

re·pu·di·ate /rɪˈpjuːdɪeɪt/ *vt* (*formal*) **1** say that one will have nothing more to do with: *~ a wicked son.* **2** refuse to accept or acknowledge: *~ the authorship of an article,* declare that one did not write it. **3** refuse to pay (a debt).

re·pu·di·ation /rɪˌpjuːdɪˈeɪʃən/ *n* [U]

re·pug·nance /rɪˈpʌgnəns/ *n* [U] (*formal*) strong dislike or distaste: *a great ~ to accept charity.*

re·pug·nant /rɪˈpʌgnənt/ *adj* (*formal*) causing a feeling of dislike or opposition: *I find his views/proposals ~.*

re·pulse /rɪˈpʌls/ *vt* **1** drive back (the enemy); resist (an attack) successfully. **2** refuse to accept (a person's help, friendly offers, etc); discourage (a person) by unfriendly treatment. □ *n* [U] repulsing or being repulsed.

re·pul·sion /rɪˈpʌlʃən/ *n* [U] (a) feeling of dislike or distaste: *feel repulsion for him.* (b) (*physics*) (opp of *attraction*) tendency of bodies to repel each other.

re·pul·sive /rɪˈpʌlsɪv/ *adj* **1** causing a feeling of disgust: *a ~ sight.* **2** (*physics*) showing repulsion(b): *~ forces.*

re·pul·sive·ly *adv*

repu·table /ˈrepjʊtəbəl/ *adj* respected; of good reputation: *~ occupations.*

repu·tably /-əblɪ/ *adv*

repu·ta·tion /ˌrepjʊˈteɪʃən/ *n* [U] (used with *a, an* as in examples) the general opinion about the character, qualities, etc of a person or thing: *have a good ~ as a doctor; make a ~ for oneself.* **live up to one's reputation,** live, act, in the way that people expect.

re·pute /rɪˈpjuːt/ *vt* **1** **be reputed as/to be,** be generally considered or reported (to be), be thought of as: *He is ~ed (to be) very wealthy. He is ~d (as/to be) the best surgeon in Paris.* **2** (as an *adjective*) generally considered to be (but with some element of doubt): *the ~d father of the child.* □ *n* [U] **1** reputation (good or bad): *know a man by ~.* **2** good reputation: *a doctor of ~.*

re·put·ed·ly /-ədlɪ/ *adv*

re·quest /rɪˈkwest/ *n* **1** [U] asking or being

asked: *We came at your ~/at the ~ of Mr Brown. Buses stop here by ~,* if signalled to do so. *This is a ~ stop. Catalogues of our books will be sent on ~.* **2** [C] expression of desire for something: *repeated ~s for help.* **3** [C] thing asked for: *All my ~s were granted.* □ *vt* make a request: *Visitors are ~ed not to touch the paintings.*

requiem /ˈrekwɪəm/ *n* [C] (musical setting for a) special mass for the repose of the souls of the dead.

re·quire /rɪˈkwaɪə(r)/ *vt* **1** need (the usual word); depend on for success, etc: *We ~ extra help.* **2** (*formal*) order; demand; insist on as a right or by authority: *Students are ~d to take three papers in English literature. I have done all that is ~d by law.*

re·quire·ment *n* [C] (*formal*) something needed: *meet his ~ments,* do what he wants done.

requi·site /ˈrekwɪzɪt/ *n* [C], *adj* (thing) needed or required by circumstances or for success: *We supply every ~ for travel/all travelling ~s.*

requi·si·tion /ˌrekwɪˈzɪʃən/ *n* **1** [U] act of requiring or demanding. **2** [C] formal, written demand: *a ~ for supplies/that the cheques should be sent to him.* □ *vt* make a demand for: *~ a cheque to pay the translator.*

re·run /ˈriːrʌn/ *n* [C] (cinema and TV) reshowing of a film or recorded programme. □ *vt* (-nn-) show a film, etc again.

re·scind /rɪˈsɪnd/ *vt* (*legal*) repeal, cancel (a law, contract, etc).

res·cue /ˈreskjuː/ *vt* make safe (from danger, etc); set free: *~ a child (from drowning).* □ *n* **1** [U] rescuing or being rescued: *John came to my ~.* **2** [C] instance of this: *three ~s from drowning in one afternoon.*

res·cuer, person who rescues a person or thing.

re·search /rɪˈsɜːtʃ US: ˈriːsɜːtʃ/ *n* [U] (and with *a, an,* and in the *pl,* but not usually with *many* or numerals) investigation undertaken in order to discover new facts, get additional information, etc: *be engaged in ~; much ~ work; carry out a ~/~es into the causes of cancer. His ~es have been successful.* □ *vi* (a problem, etc): *~ into the causes of cancer.*

re·searcher, person engaged in research.

re·seat /ˈriːsiːt/ *vt* supply with a new seat: *~ an old pair of trousers/a cane chair.*

re·sem·blance /rɪˈzembləns/ *n* [C,U] (point of) likeness, similarity: *There's very little ~ between them.*

re·semble /rɪˈzembəl/ *vt* be like; be similar to: *She ~s her mother.*

re·sent /rɪˈzent/ *vt* feel bitter, indignant or angry at: *~ criticism. Does he ~ my being here?*

re·sent·ful /-fəl/ *adj* feeling or showing resentment.

re·sent·fully /-fəlɪ/ *adv*

re·sent·ment *n* [U] feeling that one has when insulted, ignored, injured, etc: *bear/ feel no ~ment against anyone.*

res·er·va·tion /ˌrezəˈveɪʃən/ *n* 1 [U] keeping or holding back; failure or refusal to express something that is in one's mind; [C] that which is kept or held back: *accept a plan without ~,* wholeheartedly, completely: *accept a plan with ~s,* with limiting conditions. 2 [C] *the central ~ of a motorway,* land dividing the two carriageways. 3 [C] (*US*) area of land reserved for a special purpose: *the Indian ~s,* land for the exclusive use of the Indians. 4 [C] arrangement to keep something for somebody, e g a seat in a train, a room in a hotel: *My travel agents have made all the ~s for my journey.*

re·serve¹ /rɪˈzɜːv/ *n* 1 [C] something that is being or has been stored (for later use): *a ~ of food; the bank's ~s,* i e of money. 2 (*sing* or *pl*) (*mil*) military forces kept back for use when needed. 3 [U] **in reserve,** kept back unused, but available if needed: *have/hold a little money in ~.* 4 [C] place or area reserved for some special use or purpose: *a `game ~,* e g in Africa, for the preservation of wild animals. 5 [C,U] (instance of) limitation or restriction; condition that limits or restricts: *We accept your statement without ~,* believe it completely. 6 [U] self-control in speech and behaviour: *break through his ~,* get him to talk and be sociable. 7 [C] person who replaces an injured member of a team, e g in football.

re·serve² /rɪˈzɜːv/ *vt* 1 store, keep back, for a later occasion: *R~ your strength for the climb. The judge ~d his judgement,* deferred announcing it until a future time. 2 keep for the special use of, or for a special purpose: *These seats are ~d for special guests.* 3 secure possession of, or the right to use, e g by advance payment: *~ rooms at a hotel.*

re·served *adj* (of a person, his character) slow to reveal feelings or opinions: *He is too ~d to be popular.*

re·serv·ed·ly /-ədlɪ/ *adv*

res·er·voir /ˈrezəvwɑː(r)/ *n* [C] 1 place (often an artificial lake) where water is stored, e g for supplying a town. 2 (*fig*) supply (of facts, knowledge, etc).

re·set /ˌriːˈset/ *vt* (*pt,pp* reset; -tt-) 1 sharpen again: *~ a saw.* 2 place in position again: *~ a diamond in a ring; ~ a broken bone.* 3 (of a book, etc) set the type again. ⇨ set ²(9).

re·settle /ˌriːˈsetəl/ *vt,vi* (esp of refugees) (help to) settle again in a new country: *~ European refugees in Canada.*

re·settle·ment *n* [C,U]

re·shuffle /ˌriːˈʃʌfəl/ *vt* 1 shuffle (playing-cards) again. 2 redistribution (of Cabinet responsibilities). □ *n* [C] shuffling again: *a Cabinet ~,* a redistribution of Cabinet posts.

re·side /rɪˈzaɪd/ *vi* (*formal*) 1 live (the more

usual word), have one's home: *~ abroad.* 2 (of power, rights, etc) be the property of, be present in: *The supreme authority ~s in the President.*

resi·dence /ˈrezɪdəns/ *n* 1 [U] residing: *take up ~ in a new house.* **in residence,** (a) (of an official, etc) living in the house officially provided for him. (b) (of members of a university) living in a college or other part of a university. 2 place where one lives: *this desirable family ~ for sale.*

resi·dent /ˈrezɪdənt/ *adj* residing: *the ~ population of the town* (contrasted with visitors, tourists, etc); *a ~ physician,* one who lives in the hospital, etc where he works. □ *n* [C] 1 person who resides in a place (contrasted with a visitor). 2 **R~,** resident physician.

resi·den·tial /ˌrezɪˈdenʃəl/ *adj* 1 of residence: *the ~ qualifications for voters,* i e requiring that they should live in the constituency. 2 of, with, private houses: *~ parts of the town* (contrasted with business or industrial parts).

re·sid·ual /rɪˈzɪdjʊəl US: -dʒʊ-/ *adj* remaining: *~ income after tax.*

resi·due /ˈrezɪdjuː US: -duː/ *n* [C] that which remains after a part is taken or used.

re·sign /rɪˈzaɪn/ *vt,vi* 1 give up (a post, claim, etc): *~ one's job; ~ from the Committee.* 2 (*formal*) hand over: *I ~ my children to your care.* 3 be ready to accept or endure without complaining: *be ~ed to one's fate.*

re·signed *adj* having or showing patient acceptance: *with a ~ed look.*

re·sign·ed·ly /-ədlɪ/ *adv*

res·ig·na·tion /ˌrezɪgˈneɪʃən/ *n* 1 [U] resigning(1); [C] instance of this; letter (to one's employers, superior, etc) stating this: *offer/send in/hand in one's ~.* 2 [U] state of being resigned to, accepting, conditions, etc: *accept failure with ~.*

re·sil·ience /rɪˈzɪlɪəns/ *n* (also **re·sil·iency** /-nsɪ/) 1 [U] quality or property of quickly recovering the original shape or condition after being pulled, pressed, crushed, etc: *the ~ of rubber.* 2 (*fig*) power of recovering quickly: *the ~ of the human body.*

re·sil·ient /-ənt/ *adj* having or showing resilience.

resin /ˈrezɪn US: ˈrezən/ *n* [C,U] 1 sticky substance that flows out from most plants when cut or injured, esp from fir and pine trees, hardening in air, used in making varnish, lacquer, etc. 2 kind of similar substance (plastics) made chemically, widely used in industry.

re·sist /rɪˈzɪst/ *vt,vi* 1 oppose; use force against in order to prevent the advance of: *~ the enemy/an attack/authority/the police.* 2 be undamaged or unaffected by: *a kind of glass that ~s heat,* e g that does not break or crack in a hot oven. 3 try not to yield to: *~ temptation. She can't ~ chocolates.*

re·sis·ter, person who resists: *passive ~ers.*

re·sis·tance /rɪˈzɪstəns/ *n* **1** [U] (power of) resisting: *make/offer no/not much ~ to the enemy's advance.* **2 the ~**, (in a country occupied by an enemy) group of people organized to oppose the invaders. **3** [U] opposing force: *An aircraft has to overcome the ~ of the air.* **line of least resistance,** (a) direction in which a force meets least opposition. (b) (*fig*) easiest way or method. **4** [C,U] desire to oppose: `*sales ~,* unwillingness of the public to buy goods offered for sale.

re·sis·tant /rɪˈzɪstənt/ *adj* offering resistance: *insects that have become ~ to DDT.*

re·sis·tor /rɪˈzɪstə(r)/ *n* [C] device to reduce the power in an electric circuit.

re·sole /ˈriːˈsəʊl/ *vt* put a new sole on (a shoe).

res·o·lute /ˈrezəlut/ *adj* (*formal*) determined; firm: *a ~ man.*

re·sol·ute·ly *adv*

re·sol·ute·ness *n* [U]

res·o·lu·tion /ˌrezəˈluːʃən/ *n* **1** [U] quality of being determined: *show great ~; a man who lacks ~.* **2** [C] something that is decided; formal expression of opinion by a legislative body or a public meeting; proposal for this: *pass/carry/adopt/reject a ~ (for/against/in favour of/that...).* **3** [C] something one makes up one's mind to do: *a New Year ~,* something one resolves to do in a new year, e g to give up smoking. **4** [U] resolving, solution (of a doubt, question, etc). ⇨ resolve(3).

re·solve /rɪˈzɒlv/ *vt,vi* **1** decide; determine: *He ~d that nothing should prevent him from succeeding. He ~d to succeed.* **2** (of a committee, public meeting, legislative body) pass by formal vote the decision (*that*): *The House of Commons ~d that...* **3** put an end to (doubts, difficulties, etc) by supplying an answer. **4** break up, separate (into parts); convert, be converted: *~ a problem into its elements.* □ *n* [C] something that has been decided: *keep one's ~.*

re·solv·able /-əbəl/ *adj* that may be resolved.

res·on·ance /ˈrezənəns/ *n* [U] quality of being resonant.

res·on·ant /ˈrezənənt/ *adj* **1** (of sound) resounding; continuing to resound: *a deep, ~ voice.* **2** (of places) resounding: *Alpine valleys ~ with the sound of church bells.*

res·on·ate /ˈrezəneɪt/ *vt,vi* produce or show resonance.

re·sort /rɪˈzɔːt/ *vi* **1** make use of for help or to gain one's purpose, etc: *If other means fail, we shall ~ to force.* **2** frequently visit: *The police watched the cafés to which the wanted man was known to ~.* □ *n* **1** [U] resorting(1): *Can we do it without ~ to force?* **in the/as a last resort,** when all else has failed, as a last means of finding help or relief. **2** [C] person or thing that is

resorted(1) to: *an expensive taxi was the only ~ left.* **3** [C] place often visited for a particular purpose: *a `seaside/`holiday/`health ~.*

re·sound /rɪˈzaʊnd/ *vi,vt* **1** (of a voice, instrument, sound, place) echo and re-echo: *The organ ~ed. The hall ~ed with the fans' screaming.* **2** (*fig*) (of fame, an event) be much talked of; spread far and wide: *The film was a ~ing success.*

re·sound·ing·ly *adv*

re·source /rɪˈsɔːs/ *US:* `riːsɔrs/ *n* **1** (*pl*) wealth, supplies of goods, raw materials, etc which a person, country, etc has or can use: *the natural ~s of our country,* its mineral wealth, potential water power, etc. **2** [C] something which helps in doing something, that can be turned to for support, help, consolation: *Leave him to his own ~s,* to amuse himself, find his own way of passing the time. **3** [U] skill in finding resources(2): *a man of ~.*

re·source·ful /-fəl/ *adj* good or quick at finding resources(2).

re·source·ful·ly /-fəlɪ/ *adv*

re·spect¹ /rɪˈspekt/ *n* **1** [U] honour; high opinion or regard; esteem for a person or quality: *The Prime Minister is held in the greatest ~. Children should show ~ for their teachers.* **2** [U] consideration; attention: *We must have ~ for/pay ~ to the needs of the general reader,* think about his requirements or preferences. **3** [U] reference; relation. **with/without respect to,** concerning/paying no attention to. **4** [C] detail; particular aspect. **in respect of,** as regards: *Your action was admirable in ~ of the courage you showed.* **in some/any/no, etc respects,** with regard to some aspect(s), detail(s): *They resemble one another in some/a few ~s.* **5** (*pl*) regards; polite greetings: *My father sends you his ~s.*

re·spect² /rɪˈspekt/ *vt* show respect for; treat with consideration: *He is ~ed by everyone. We must ~ his wishes. Do you ~ the laws of your country?*

re·spec·ter *n* (only in) **no respecter of persons,** person or thing paying little or no attention to wealth, social rank, etc: *Death is no ~ of persons.*

re·spect·able /rɪˈspektəbəl/ *adj* **1** deserving respect: *act from ~ motives.* **2** (of persons) of good character and fair social position; having the qualities associated with such social position. **3** (of clothes, appearance, behaviour, etc) suitable for such persons: *Is she/her appearance ~?* **4** of considerable size, merit, importance, etc: *He earns a ~ income.*

re·spect·ably /-əblɪ/ *adv* in a respectable manner: *respectably dressed.*

re·spect·ful /rɪˈspektfəl/ *adj* (*formal*) showing respect: *They stood at a ~ distance from the President.*

re·spect·fully /-fəlɪ/ *adv* (*dated*) (at the

close of a letter to a much senior person): *I remain, yours ~ly,...*

re·spect·ive /rɪˈspektɪv/ *adj* for, belonging to, each of those in question: *The three men were given work according to their ~ abilities.*

re·spect·ive·ly *adv* separately or in turn, and in the order mentioned: *Rooms for men and women are on the first and second floors ~ly,* i e for men on the first floor and for women on the second.

res·pir·ation /ˌrespəˈreɪʃən/ *n* [U] breathing; [C] single act of breathing in and breathing out.

res·pir·ator /ˈrespəreɪtə(r)/ *n* [C] apparatus for breathing through, e g by firemen, to filter the air of smoke and fumes.

res·pir·at·ory /rɪˈspɪrətrɪ US: ˈrespərətɔrɪ/ *adj* of breathing: *~ diseases,* e g bronchitis, asthma.

re·spire /rɪˈspaɪə(r)/ *vi* (*formal*) breathe (the usual word).

res·pite /ˈrespaɪt US: ˈrespɪt/ *n* [C] **1** time of relief or rest (from toil, suffering, anything unpleasant): *work without (a) ~.* **2** permitted postponement or delay in punishment, having to do something, etc.

re·splen·dent /rɪˈsplendənt/ *adj* very bright; looking rich and colourful: *a ~ display by the Household Cavalry.*

re·splen·dent·ly *adv*

re·spond /rɪˈspond/ *vi* **1** answer: *~ to a speech of welcome.* **2** act in answer to, or because of, the action of another: *When Tom insulted the referee, he ~ed by ordering him off the field.* **3** react (to); be affected (by): *The illness/patient quickly ~ed to treatment.*

re·sponse /rɪˈspons/ *n* **1** [C] answer: *My letter of inquiry brought no ~.* **2** [C,U] reaction: *My appeal to her pity met with no ~.* **3** [C] (in a church service) part of the liturgy said or sung by the congregation alternately with the priest.

re·spon·si·bil·ity /rɪˌsponsəˈbɪlətɪ/ *n* (*pl* -ies) **1** [U] being responsible; being accountable: *I'll lend you my camera if you will take full ~ for it.* **2** [C] something for which a person is responsible; duty: *the heavy responsibilities of the Prime Minister.*

re·spon·sible /rɪˈsponsəbəl/ *adj* **1** (of a person) legally or morally having to carry out a duty, care for a person or thing; in a position where one may be blamed for loss, failure, etc: *The pilot of an airliner is ~ for the safety of the passengers. Who is ~ to the parents for the education of children?* **2** involving the obligation to make decisions for others and bear the blame for their mistakes: *I've made you ~ and you must decide what to do.* **3** to be relied on: *Give the task to a ~ man.* **4** be responsible for sth, be the cause or source of: *Who's ~ for this mess in the kitchen?*

re·spon·sibly /-əblɪ/ *adv*

re·spon·sive /rɪˈsponsɪv/ *adj* **1** answering: *a ~ gesture.* **2** answering easily or quickly: *~ to affection/treatment.*

re·spon·sive·ly *adv*

rest¹ /rest/ *n* **1** [U] condition of being free from activity, movement, disturbance; quiet; sleep: *R~ is necessary after hard work. She had a good night's ~,* sleep. **at rest, (a)** free from movement. **(b)** dead. **be laid to rest,** be buried. **come to rest,** (of a moving body) stop moving. **set sb's mind at rest,** relieve him of doubt, anxiety, etc. **2** [C] that on which something is supported: *an ˈarm-~.* **3** [C] (*music*) (sign marking an) interval of silence. **4** (as an *adjective*) place where people may recuperate from illness, etc: *a ˈ~ home/centre.*

ˈrest-cure, course of treatment for persons suffering from nervous disorders.

ˈrest-house, house or bungalow for the use of travellers (esp in areas where there are no hotels).

ˈrest room, public lavatory; cloakroom.

rest·ful /-fəl/ *adj* quiet; peaceful; giving (a feeling of) rest: *a ~ful scene; colours that are ~ful to the eyes.*

rest·less *adj* never still or quiet; unable to rest: *the ~less waves; spend a ~less night.*

rest·less·ly *adv*

rest·less·ness *n* [U]

rest² /rest/ *n* (always) **the ~. 1** what remains; the remainder: *Take what you want and throw the ~ away. Her hat was red, like the ~ of her clothes. for the rest...,* as regards other matters... **2** (used with a *pl verb*) the others: *John and I are going to play tennis; what are the ~ of you going to do?*

rest³ /rest/ *vi,vt* **1** be still or quiet; be free from activity, movement, disturbance, etc: *We ~ed (for) an hour after lunch. He ~s* (= is buried) *in the churchyard. He will not ~* (= will have no peace of mind) *until he knows the truth.* **2** give rest or relief to: *He stopped to ~ his horse. These dark glasses ~ my eyes.* **3** (cause to) be supported (*on/against* something): *She ~ed her elbows/Her elbows were ~ing on the table. R~ the ladder against the wall.*

ˈrest·ing-place, (esp) place of burial.

rest⁴ /rest/ *vi* **1** continue to be in a specified state: *You may ~ assured that everything possible will be done.* **2** rest with, be left in the hands or charge of: *It ~s with you to decide,* It is your responsibility. **3** depend, rely: *His fame ~s on/upon his plays more than upon his novels.*

re·state /ˌriˈsteɪt/ *vt* state again or in a different way.

re·state·ment *n* [C,U] (instance of) restating.

res·taur·ant /ˈrestront US: -tərənt/ *n* [C] place where meals can be bought and eaten.

res·ti·tu·tion /ˌrestɪˈtjuːʃən US: -ˈtuː-/ *n* [U] **1** restoring (of something stolen, etc) to its owner: *~ of property.* **2** = reparation.

res·tive /ˈrestɪv/ adj 1 (of a horse or other animal) refusing to move forward; moving backwards or sideways. 2 (of a person) reluctant to be controlled or disciplined; unable to lie still (and sleep).
res·tive·ly adv
res·tive·ness n [U]

re·stock /ˌriˈstok/ vt put fresh stock into: ~ the shelves in a shop.

res·to·ra·tion /ˌrestəˈreɪʃən/ n 1 [U] restoring or being restored: ~ to health and strength; ~ of stolen property. 2 the R~, (the period of) the re-establishment of the monarchy in England in 1660, when Charles II became king: R~ poetry/comedy. 3 [C] model representing the supposed original form of an extinct animal, ruined building, etc; building formerly ruined and now rebuilt.

re·stora·tive /rɪˈstɔːrətɪv/ adj tending to restore health and strength. □ n [C,U] restorative food, medicine, etc.

re·store /rɪˈstɔː(r)/ vt 1 give back: ~ stolen property/borrowed books. 2 bring back into use; reintroduce: ~ old customs. 3 make well or normal again; bring back (to a former condition): quite ~d to health; feel completely ~d. Law and order have been ~d. 4 repair; rebuild as before: ~ a ruined abbey. 5 place in or bring back to the former position, etc: ~ an employee to his old post/an officer to his command.

re·storer, someone who, something which, restores, e g an expert who cleans old oil paintings.

re·strain /rɪˈstreɪn/ vt hold back; keep under control; prevent (a person or thing from doing something): ~ a child from (doing) mischief; ~ one's anger.

re·strained adj (esp) not emotional or wild; kept under control.

re·straint /rɪˈstreɪnt/ n 1 [U] restraining or being restrained. without restraint, freely; without control. 2 [U] (in art, literature, etc) avoidance of excess or exaggeration. 3 [C] that which restrains; check; controlling influence: the ~s of poverty.

re·strict /rɪˈstrɪkt/ vt limit; keep within limits: Discussion at the meeting was ~ed to the agenda. We are ~ed to 30 miles an hour in built-up areas.

re·stric·tion /rɪˈstrɪkʃən/ n (a) [U] restricting or being restricted: ~ion of expenditure. (b) [C] instance of this; something that restricts: currency ~ions, e g on the sums that a person may use for foreign travel.

re·stric·tive /rɪˈstrɪktɪv/ adj tending to restrict: ~ive practices (in industry), practices that hinder the most effective use of labour, etc.
re·stric·tive·ly adv

re·style /ˌriˈstaɪl/ vt 1 give a new name to: The chairman has been ~ed 'the President'. 2 redesign: ~ the seats for a new model of a car.

re·sult /rɪˈzʌlt/ vi 1 come about, happen, as a natural consequence: Any damage ~ing from negligence must be paid for by the borrower. 2 bring about; have as a consequence: Their diplomacy ~ed in war. 3 end in a specified manner: Their efforts ~ed badly. □ n 1 [C,U] that which is produced by an activity or cause; outcome; effect: work without (much) ~; announce the ~s of a competition, the names of prize-winners, etc. 2 [C] answer (to a mathematical problem, etc).

re·sult·ant /-ənt/ adj coming as a result, esp as the total outcome of forces or tendencies from different directions. □ n [C] product or outcome (of something).

re·sume /rɪˈzjuːm US: -ˈzuːm/ vt 1 go on after stopping for a time: ~ one's work/a story. 2 take or occupy again: ~ one's seat.

ré·sumé /ˈrezʊmeɪ US: ˈrezʊˈmeɪ/ n [C] summary.

re·sump·tion /rɪˈzʌmpʃən/ n [U] resuming; [C] instance of this.

re·sur·face /ˌriˈsɜːfɪs/ vt,vi 1 put a new surface on (a road, etc). 2 (of a submarine) come to the surface again. 3 (fig) (of persons, ideas, etc) reappear, come back.

re·sur·gence /rɪˈsɜːdʒəns/ n [U] revival; return of energy, etc.

re·sur·gent /rɪˈsɜːdʒənt/ adj (formal) reviving, coming back to activity, vigour, etc (after defeat, destruction, etc): ~ hopes.

res·ur·rect /ˈrezəˈrekt/ vt,vi bring back into use; revive the practice of: ~ an old word/custom.

res·ur·rec·tion /ˈrezəˈrekʃən/ n [U] 1 the R~, (a) the rising of Jesus from the tomb; anniversary of this. (b) the rising of all the dead on the Last Day. 2 revival from disuse, inactivity, etc: the ~ of hope.

re·sus·ci·tate /rɪˈsʌsɪteɪt/ vt,vi bring or come back to consciousness: ~ a person who has been nearly drowned.
re·sus·ci·ta·tion /rɪˈsʌsɪˈteɪʃən/ n [U]

re·tail /ˈriːteɪl/ n [C] sale of goods to the general public, not for resale: sell goods (by) ~; (as an adjective) ~ prices. ⇨ wholesale. □ adv by retail: Do you buy wholesale or ~? □ vt,vi 1 sell (goods) by retail; (of goods) be sold retail: an article that is ~ed at/that ~s at seventy pence. 2 repeat (what one has heard, esp gossip) bit by bit or to several persons in turn: ~ a criticism to the person affected.

re·tailer, tradesman who sells by retail; shopkeeper.

re·tain /rɪˈteɪn/ vt 1 keep; continue to have or hold; keep in place: This dyke was built to ~ the flood waters. She ~s a clear memory of her schooldays. 2 get the services of (esp a barrister) by payment (a ~ing fee).

re·tainer n [C] (a) (legal) fee paid to retain the services of, e g a barrister. (b) (old use) servant of somebody of high rank: the duke and his ~ers.

re·take /ˈriːteɪk/ vt (pt -took /-ˈtʊk/, pp -taken /-ˈteɪkən/) take, capture, photograph, again. □ n /ˈriːteɪk/ [C] (esp, cinema, TV) rephotographed scene.

re·tal·i·ate /rɪˈtælɪeɪt/ vi return the same sort of ill treatment that one has received: He ∼d by kicking the other fellow on the ankle. If we raise our import duties on their goods, they may ∼ against us.

re·tal·i·ation /rɪˌtælɪˈeɪʃn/ n [U] retaliating: in retaliation for being critical.

re·tal·i·at·ive /rɪˈtælɪətɪv US: -eɪt-/, **re·tal·i·at·ory** /rɪˈtælɪətrɪ US: -tɔrɪ/ adj returning ill treatment for ill treatment; of or for retaliation: retaliatory punches.

re·tard /rɪˈtɑːd/ vt check; hinder: ∼ progress/development; a mentally ∼ed child, one whose mental or emotional development has been slowed down or stopped.

retch /retʃ/ vi make (involuntarily) the sound and physical movements of vomiting but without bringing up anything from the stomach.

re·tell /ˈriːtel/ vt (pt,pp -told /-ˈtəʊld/) tell again; tell in a different way or in a different language: old Greek tales retold for children.

re·ten·tion /rɪˈtenʃn/ n [U] retaining or being retained: the ∼ of funds for emergency use.

re·ten·tive /rɪˈtentɪv/ adj having the power of retaining(1) things: a ∼ memory.
re·ten·tive·ly adv
re·ten·tive·ness n [U]

re·think /ˈriːˈθɪŋk/ vt,vi (pt,pp -thought /-ˈθɔːt/) think about again; reconsider: They will have to ∼ their policy towards China.

reti·cence /ˈretɪsəns/ n [U] being reticent; [C] instance of this.

reti·cent /ˈretɪsənt/ adj in the habit of saying little; not saying all that is known or felt: She was ∼ about/on what Tom had said to her.
re·ti·cent·ly adv

ret·ina /ˈretɪnə US: ˈretənə/ n [C] (pl ∼s or -nae /-niː/) layer of membrane at the back of the eyeball, sensitive to light.

reti·nue /ˈretɪnjuː US: ˈretənuː/ n [C] number of persons (staff, officers, etc) travelling with a person of high rank.

re·tire /rɪˈtaɪə(r)/ vi,vt 1 withdraw; go away: He ∼d to his cabin. 2 (formal) go to bed: My wife usually ∼s at 10 o'clock. 3 (of an army) withdraw; go back: Our forces ∼d to prepared positions. 4 give up one's work, position, business, etc: He will ∼ on a pension at 65. 5 cause (a person) to retire(3,4): ∼ the head clerk. 6 ∼ from the world, enter a monastery or become a hermit. **retire into onself**, become unfriendly. □ n signal to troops to withdraw: sound the ∼, i e on the bugle.

re·tired adj having retired(4): a ∼d civil servant.

re·tir·ing adj (of persons, their way of life,

etc) avoiding society: a girl of a retiring nature.

re·tire·ment n (a) [U] retiring or being retired; seclusion: ∼ment from the world, e g in a convent. (b) [U] condition of being retired(4): be/live in ∼ment. **go into retirement**, retire (esp 4 and 6 above). (c) [C] instance of this: There have been several ∼ments in my office recently.
`retirement pension, ⇨ pension.

re·tort /rɪˈtɔːt/ vt,vi answer back quickly, cleverly or angrily (esp to an accusation or challenge): 'It's entirely your fault,' he ∼ed. □ n [U] retorting: say something in ∼; [C] retorting answer: make an insolent ∼.

re·touch /ˈriːˈtʌtʃ/ vt improve (a photograph, painting, etc) by a few touches of a brush, etc.

re·trace /rɪˈtreɪs/ vt 1 go back over or along: ∼ one's steps. 2 go over (past actions, etc) in the mind.

re·tract /rɪˈtrækt/ vt,vi 1 take back or withdraw (a statement, offer, opinion, etc): Even when confronted with proof the accused man refused to ∼ his statement. 2 draw in or back; move back or in; be capable of doing this: A cat can ∼ its claws.

re·tract·able /-əbəl/ adj that can be retracted: a ∼able undercarriage, (in an aircraft) wheels, etc which can be drawn up into the body of the aircraft during flight.

re·trac·tion /rɪˈtrækʃən/ n [C,U]

re·tread /ˈriːˈtred/ vt (pt,pp ∼ed) put a new tread(3) on (an old tyre). □ n /ˈriːtred/ [C] tyre that has been retreaded.

re·treat /rɪˈtriːt/ vi (esp of an army) go back; withdraw: force the enemy to ∼; ∼ on (ie towards) the capital. □ n 1 [U] act of retreating: The army was in full ∼. We made good our ∼, withdrew safely. 2 [C] signal for this: sound the ∼, e g on a bugle. 3 [C] instance of retreating: after many advances and ∼s. **beat a (hasty) retreat**, (fig) abandon an undertaking. 4 [C,U] (place for a) period of quiet and rest: a quiet country ∼. **go into retreat**, e g temporary retirement for religious purposes.

re·trial /ˈriːˈtraɪəl/ n [C] act of trying again in a law court.

ret·ri·bu·tion /ˌretrɪˈbjuːʃən/ n [U] deserved punishment: R∼ for loose living does not always come in this life.

re·tri·bu·tive /rɪˈtrɪbjʊtɪv/ adj inflicted or coming as a penalty for doing wrong.

re·triev·able /rɪˈtriːvəbl/ adj that may be retrieved.

re·trieval /rɪˈtriːvəl/ n [U] 1 act of retrieving: the ∼ of one's fortunes. 2 possibility of recovery: beyond/past ∼.

re·trieve /rɪˈtriːv/ vt,vi 1 get possession of again: ∼ a lost umbrella; ∼ information from a computer. 2 put or set right; make amends for: ∼ an error/a loss/disaster/defeat. 3 rescue (from); restore: ∼ a person from ruin; ∼ one's honour/fortunes. 4 (of specially trained dogs) find and bring in (killed or wounded birds, etc).

re·triev·er breed of dog used for retrieving(4).

retro·ac·tive /'retrəʊ`æktɪv/ adj (of laws, etc) = retrospective(b).
retro·ac·tive·ly adv

retro·grade /'retrəgreɪd/ adj 1 directed backwards: ∼ motion. 2 deteriorating; likely to cause worse conditions: a ∼ policy. □ vi decline; grow worse.

retro·gress /'retrə`gres/ vi (formal) go or move backwards.
retro·gres·sion /'retrə`greʃən/ n [U] return to a less advanced state.
retro·gres·sive /'retrə`gresɪv/ adj returning, tending to return, to a less advanced state; becoming worse.

retro·rocket /'retrəʊrɒkɪt/ n [C] jet engine fired to slow down or alter the course of a missile, spacecraft, etc.

retro·spect /'retrəspekt/ n **in retrospect,** looking back at past events, etc.
retro·spec·tion /'retrə`spekʃən/ n (formal) [U] action of looking back at past events, scenes, etc; [C] instance of this: indulge in dreamy ∼ions.
retro·spec·tive /'retrə`spektɪv/ adj (a) looking back on past events, etc. (b) (of laws, payments, etc) applying to the past: ∼ive legislation; a ∼ive (= backdated) wage increase.
retro·spec·tive·ly adv

ret·ro·ver·sion /'retrəʊ`vəʃən US: -`vɜrʒən/ n [U] state of being turned backwards; turning backward.

re·turn¹ /rɪ`tɜn/ n 1 [C,U] coming, going, giving, sending, putting, back: on my ∼, when I got/get back; the ∼ of spring. **by return,** by the next post out: Please send a reply by ∼. **in return (for),** as repayment (for). **Many happy returns (of the day),** phrase used as a greeting on somebody's birthday. **point of no return,** (fig) stage of an activity, etc at which withdrawal, stopping, is not possible. 2 (as an adjective) involving going back or coming back, etc: the ∼ voyage. 3 [C] (often pl) profit on an investment or undertaking: small profits and quick ∼s, large sales and quick turnover. 4 [C] official report or statement: make one's ∼ of income (to the Inspector of Taxes).
return fare, needed for the journey back.
return half, the ticket for the journey back.
return match, one played between teams which have already played one match.
return ticket, one giving a traveller the right to go to a place and back to his starting-point (two-way ticket in US).

re·turn² /rɪ`tɜn/ vi,vt 1 come or go back: ∼ home; ∼ to Paris from London. I shall ∼ to this point later in my lecture. 2 pass or go back (to a former state): He has ∼ed to his old habits. 3 give, put, send, pay, carry, back: When will you ∼ the book I lent you?

She ∼ed the compliment, said something pleasant after a compliment had been paid to her. 4 (of a constituency) elect (a person) as representative to Parliament. 5 state or describe officially, esp in answer to a demand: ∼ the details of one's income (for taxation purposes). The jury ∼ed a verdict of guilty.
returning officer, official in charge of a Parliamentary election and announcing the name of the person elected.

re·turn·able /-əbəl/ adj that may be sent, given back.

re·un·ion /ri`junɪən/ n 1 [U] reuniting or being reunited. 2 [C] (esp) meeting of old friends, former colleagues, etc after separation: a family ∼ at Christmas.
re·unite /'riju`naɪt/ vt,vi bring or come together again: ∼d after long years of separation.

rev /rev/ vt,vi (-vv-) (informal) increase the speed of revolutions in (an internal-combustion engine): Don't rev up (the engine) so hard.

re·value /ri`væljuː/ vt 1 value again or anew. 2 increase the value of: ∼ the currency.
re·valu·ation /'ri`vælju`eɪʃən/ n [C,U].

re·vamp /'ri`væmp/ vt (informal) reconstruct; renew; revise: ∼ an old book with new illustrations.

re·veal /rɪ`viːl/ vt 1 allow or cause to be seen; display: Bikinis ∼ more than swimming-costumes. 2 make known: One day the truth about these events will be ∼ed. The doctor did not ∼ to him his hopeless condition.

re·veille /rɪ`vælɪ US: `revəlɪ/ n [C] (in the armed forces) bugle signal to men to get up in the morning: sound (the) ∼.

revel /`revəl/ vi (-ll-; US also -l-) 1 have a gay, lively time: They ∼led until dawn. 2 **revel in,** take great delight in: ∼ in one's success; people who ∼ in gossip. □ n [C,U] (occasion of) joyous festivity.
rev·el·ler, (US = rev·eler) /`revələ(r)/, person who revels.

rev·el·ation /'revə`leɪʃən/ n 1 [U] making known of something secret or hidden. 2 [C] that which is revealed, esp something that causes surprise: It was a ∼ to John when Mary said she had married him only for his money.

rev·elry /`revəlrɪ/ n [U] (or pl; -ies) noisy, joyous festivity and merrymaking: when the ∼/revelries ended.

re·venge /rɪ`vendʒ/ vt 1 do something to get satisfaction for (an offence, etc to oneself or another): ∼ an injustice/insult. 2 get satisfaction by deliberately inflicting injury in return for injury inflicted on a person or oneself: ∼ a friend; be ∼ed on a persecutor. ⇨ avenge. □ n [U] 1 deliberate infliction of injury on the person(s) from whom injury has been received: thirsting for ∼; take ∼ on; have/get one's ∼ (on a person); do it out of/in ∼ (for). 2 [U] revenging.

re·venge·ful /-fəl/ *adj* feeling or showing a desire for revenge.

re·venge·fully /-fəlɪ/ *adv*

rev·enue /ˈrevənjuː *US:* -ənuː/ *n* **1** [U] income, esp the total annual income of the State; government department which collects money for public funds. ⇨ **Inland Revenue.** **2** (*pl*) separate items of revenue put together: *the ~s of the City Council.*

re·ver·ber·ate /rɪˈvɜːbəreɪt/ *vt,vi* (esp of sound) send or throw back, be sent back, again and again: *The roar of the train ~d/ was ~d in the tunnel.*

re·ver·ber·ation /rɪˈvɜːbəˈreɪʃn/ *n* [U] reverberating or being reverberated; (*pl*) echoes; effects (of an event).

re·vere /rɪˈvɪə(r)/ *vt* have deep respect for; regard as sacred: *my ~d grandfather.*

rev·er·ence /ˈrevərəns/ *n* [U] deep respect; feeling of wonder and awe: *a bishop who was held in ~ by everyone.* □ *vt* treat with reverence.

rev·er·end /ˈrevərənd/ *adj* deserving to be treated with respect (because of age, character, etc). □ *n* the R~, (usual **Revd**) used as a title of a clergyman: *the Revd John Smith.*

Reverend Mother, Mother Superior of a convent.

rev·er·ent /ˈrevərənt/ *adj* feeling or showing reverence.

rev·er·ent·ly *adv*

rev·er·en·tial /ˈrevəˈrenʃəl/ *adj* caused by or marked by reverence.

rev·erie /ˈrevərɪ/ *n* [C,U] (instance of, occasion of a) condition of being lost in dreamy, pleasant thoughts.

re·vers /rɪˈvɪə(r)/ *n* [C] (*pl ~*) turned-back edge of a coat, etc showing the reverse side, as on a lapel.

re·ver·sal /rɪˈvɜːsəl/ *n* **1** [U] reversing or being reversed. **2** [C] instance of this: *a ~ of procedure.*

re·verse¹ /rɪˈvɜːs/ *adj* contrary or opposite in character or order; inverted: *the ~ side of a coin.* **in reverse order,** from the end to the start, or in the opposite order.

re·verse² /rɪˈvɜːs/ *n* **1** [U] (with *the*) opposite; contrary: *do the ~ of what one is expected to do.* **2** [C] reverse side (of a coin, medal, disc, etc): *The Queen's head is on this side, what is on the ~?* **3** [C] mechanism or device that reverses: *Most cars have three forward gears and (a) ~. Put the car into ~.* **4** [C] defeat; change to bad fortune: *Our forces/My finances have suffered a slight ~.*

re·verse³ /rɪˈvɜːs/ *vt,vi* turn (something) the other way round or up or inside out: *~ a procedure; ~ one's policy.* **2** (cause to) go in the opposite direction: *~ one's car into the garage.* **3** change the order or position of: *Their positions are now ~d; Tom is poor and Ben is rich.* **4** cancel, annul: *~ the decision of a lower court; ~ a decree.* **5** make (the charge for a telephone call) payable by

the person who receives it: *~ charges.*

re·vers·ible /-əbəl/ *adj* that can be reversed, e g of a coat, either side of which can be used on the outside.

re·ver·sion /rɪˈvɜːʃən *US:* -ˈvɜːrʒən/ *n* **1** [U] reverting (of property, etc). ⇨ **revert(2).** **2** [C] right to possess property in certain circumstances.

re·vert /rɪˈvɜːt/ *vi* **1** return (to a former state, condition, topic, etc): *The fields have ~ed to moorland,* have gone out of cultivation, etc. *R~ing to your original statement, I think....* **2** (*legal*) (of property, rights, etc) return at some named time or under certain conditions (*to* the original owner, the State, etc): *If he dies without an heir, his property will ~ to the state.*

re·view /rɪˈvjuː/ *vt,vi* **1** consider or examine again; go over again in the mind: *~ the past; ~ last week's lesson.* **2** inspect formally (troops, a fleet, etc). **3** write an account of (new books, etc) for newspapers and other periodicals: *His new novel has been favourably ~ed.* □ *n* **1** [U] act of reviewing(1). *come under review,* be considered or examined; [C] instance of this: *a ~ of the year's sporting events.* **2** [C] inspection of military, naval, etc forces: *hold a ~.* **3** [C] article that critically examines a new book, etc: *write ~s for the monthly magazines.* **4** [C] periodical with articles on current events, reviews of new books, etc.

re·viewer, person who writes reviews(3).

re·vile /rɪˈvaɪl/ *vt,vi* (*formal*) swear at; use abusive language: *~ one's persecutors.*

re·vise /rɪˈvaɪz/ *vt* reconsider; read carefully through, esp in order to correct and improve: *~ one's estimates; ~ one's opinions of her.*

re·viser, person who revises.

re·vi·sion /rɪˈvɪʒən/ *n* (a) [U] revising or being revised; [C] instance of this: *Several more revisions have been made.* (b) [C] that which has been revised; corrected version.

re·vi·sion·ist /rɪˈvɪʒənɪst/ *n* [C] person who supports a review of the basic principles and beliefs of a political ideology.

re·vital·ize /rɪˈvaɪtəlaɪz/ *vt* put new life into; restore power, strength, etc.

re·vital·iz·ation /ˈriːvaɪtəlaɪˈzeɪʃən *US:* -lɪˈz-/ *n* [U]

re·vival /rɪˈvaɪvəl/ *n* **1** [U] reviving or being revived; bringing or coming back into use or knowledge; [C] instance of this: *a ~ of trade.* **2** [C] (series of meetings intended to produce an) increase of interest in religion: *a religious ~; ~ meetings.*

re·vival·ist /rɪˈvaɪvəlɪst/ *n* [C] person who organizes or conducts revival meetings.

re·vive /rɪˈvaɪv/ *vi,vt* **1** come or bring back to consciousness, health or an earlier state: *~ a person who has fainted; ~ an old play,* produce it for the theatre after many years. **2** come or bring into use again: *customs which have been ~d.*

re·viv·ify /rɪˈvɪvɪfaɪ/ *vt* (*pt,pp* -ied) (*for-*

mal) give new life or liveliness to.

revo·ca·ble /ˈrevəkəbəl/ *adj* that can be revoked.

revo·ca·tion /ˈrevəˈkeɪʃən/ *n* [U] revoking or being revoked; [C] instance of this.

re·voke /rɪˈvəʊk/ *vt, vi* **1** repeal; cancel; withdraw (a decree, consent, permission, etc): ~ *a driving licence*. **2** (of a player at such card games as whist and bridge) fail to follow suit (i e not play a card of the same suit as that led by another player although he could do so). □ *n* [C] failure of this kind.

re·volt /rɪˈvəʊlt/ *vi, vt* **1** rise in rebellion: *The people ~ed against their rulers.* **2** be filled with disgust or horror: *Human nature ~s at/from/against rape.* **3** fill with disgust or horror: *scenes that ~ed all who saw them.* □ *n* **1** [U] act of revolting; state of having revolted(1): *a period of ~; stir the people to ~.* **2** [C] rebellion or rising: *~s against authority.*

re·volt·ing /rɪˈvəʊltɪŋ/ *adj* disgusting.

re·volt·ing·ly *adv* in a way that disgusts: *a ~ly dirty child.*

rev·ol·ution /ˈrevəˈluːʃən/ *n* **1** [C] act of revolving or going round: *the ~ of the earth round the sun*; [C] complete turn of a wheel, etc: *sixty-five ~s (or, informally revs) a minute.* **2** [C,U] (instance of a) complete change (in conditions, ways of doing things, esp in methods of government when caused by the overthrow of one system by force): *the Russian R~* (in 1917); *~s in our ways of travelling*, e g the development of supersonic aircraft.

re·vol·ution·ary /ˈrevəˈluːʃənrɪ US: -ənerɪ/ *adj* **1** of a revolution(2). **2** bringing, causing, favouring, great (and perhaps violent) changes: ~ *ideas*. □ *n* [C] supporter of a (political) revolution.

re·vol·ution·ize /ˈrevəˈluːʃənaɪz/ *vt* **1** fill with revolutionary principles. **2** make a complete change in; cause to be entirely different: *The use of nuclear energy will ~ the lives of coming generations.*

re·volve /rɪˈvolv/ *vt, vi* **1** (cause to) go round in a circle: *The earth ~s round/about the sun. The life of the home ~s around the mother,* is centered on her. **2** think about all sides of (a problem, etc): *revolving a problem in one's mind.*

re·volver /rɪˈvolvə(r)/ *n* [C] pistol with a revolving mechanism that makes it possible to fire it a number of times without reloading.

re·vue /rɪˈvjuː/ *n* [C] theatrical entertainment which consists of dialogue, dance and song, usually making fun of current events, fashions, etc; [U] this form of entertainment: *to appear/perform in ~.*

re·vul·sion /rɪˈvʌlʃən/ *n* [U] (often with *a, an*) sudden and complete change of feeling to hatred or opposition: *a ~ against slavery.*

re·ward /rɪˈwɔːd/ *n* **1** [U] recompense for service or merit: *work without hope of any*

~. **2** [C] that which is offered, given or obtained in return for work or services, or the restoration of lost or stolen property, the capture of a criminal, etc: *offer a ~ of £10 for information about a stolen necklace.* □ *vt* give a reward to: ~ *a man for his honesty.*

re·wire /rɪˈwaɪə(r)/ *vt* provide, e g a building, with new wiring (for electric current).

re·word /rɪˈwɜːd/ *vt* express again in different words: *If we ~ the telegram we can save one-third of the cost.*

re·write /rɪˈraɪt/ *vt* write again in a different style, etc.

rex /reks/ *n* (abbr **R**) reigning king. ⇨ **Regina**.

rhap·so·dize /ˈræpsədaɪz/ *vi* talk or write with great enthusiasm: ~ *over Previn's conducting.*

rhap·sody /ˈræpsədɪ/ *n* [C] (*pl* -ies) **1** enthusiastic expression of delight (in speech, poetry, etc): *Everyone went into rhapsodies over Olivier's performance as Othello.* **2** (*music*) composition in irregular form: *Liszt's Hungarian Rhapsodies.*

rhet·oric /ˈretərɪk/ *n* [U] **1** (art of) using words impressively in speech and writing. **2** language with much ornamentation (often with the implication of insincerity and exaggeration): *the ~ of politicians.*

rhe·tori·cal /rɪˈtorɪkəl US: -ˈtɔr-/ *adj* in a style designed to impress or persuade; artificial or exaggerated in language.

rhetorical question, one asked for the sake of effect, to impress people, no answer being needed or expected.

rhe·tori·cally /-klɪ/ *adv*

rheu·matic /ruˈmætɪk/ *adj* relating to, causing, caused by, suffering from, rheumatism: ~ *fever*, serious form of rheumatism, chiefly in children. □ *n* [C] person who suffers from rheumatism.

rheu·ma·tism /ˈruːmətɪzm/ *n* [U] (kinds of) painful disease with stiffness and inflammation of the muscles and joints.

rheu·ma·toid /ˈruːmətɔɪd/ *adj* of rheumatism.

rhinal /ˈraɪnəl/ *adj* (*anat*) of the nose or nostrils.

rhino /ˈraɪnəʊ/ *n* [C] (*pl* ~) (*informal*) (abbr of) rhinoceros.

rhi·noc·eros /raɪˈnosərəs/ *n* [C] (*pl* ~es or, collectively, ~) thick-skinned, heavy animal of Africa and Asia with one or two horns on the nose.

rhom·boid /ˈromboɪd/ *adj* of the shape of a rhombus. □ *n* [C] rhombus with only its opposite sides equal.

rhom·bus /ˈrombəs/ *n* [C] four-sided figure with equal sides, and angles which are not right angles (e g diamond or lozenge shape).

rhu·barb /ˈruːbɑːb/ *n* [U] **1** (garden plant with) thick, juicy stalks which are cooked and eaten like fruit. **2** (*informal*) noisy talk of many speakers; confused discussion.

rhyme (*US* also **rime**) /raɪm/ *n* **1** [U] sameness of sound of the endings of two or more words at the ends of lines of verse, e g *say, play; measure, pleasure; puff, rough.* **without rhyme or reason,** without meaning. **2** [C] word which provides a rhyme: *Is there a ~ to/for 'hiccups'?* **3** [C] verse or verses with rhyme. ⇨ nursery rhyme. **4** [U] the use of rhyme: *The story should be written in ~.* □ *vt,vi* **1** put together to form a rhyme: *Can we ~ 'hiccups' with 'pick-ups'?* **2** (of words or lines of verse) be in rhyme: *'Ship' doesn't ~ with 'sheep'.* **3** (*dated*) write verse(s) with rhyme.

rhythm /ˈrɪðəm/ *n* **1** [U] regular succession of weak and strong stresses, accents, sounds or movements (in speech, music, dancing, etc). **2** [U] regular recurrence of events, processes, etc: *the ~ of the tides,* their regular rise and fall. **3** [C] particular kind of such regular succession or recurrence.

rhyth-mic /ˈrɪðmɪk/, **rhyth-mi-cal** /ˈrɪðmɪkəl/ *adj* marked by, having, rhythm: *the ~ical noise of a typewriter.*

rib /rɪb/ *n* [C] **1** any one of the 12 pairs of curved bones extending from the backbone round the chest to the front of the body in man; corresponding bone in an animal. **2** (of various things like ribs) vein of a leaf; mark left on sand on the sea-shore by waves. **3** (pattern of a) raised line in a piece of knitting. □ *vt* (-bb-) **1** supply with, mark off in, ribs: *~bed patterns.* **2** (*US*) (*informal*) tease.

rib-ald /ˈrɪbəld/ *adj* (*dated*) (of a person) using indecent or irreverent language or humour; (of language, laughter, etc) coarse: *~ jests/songs.* □ *n* [C] (*dated*) person who uses such language.

ri-baldry /-drɪ/ *n* [U] such language.

rib-bon /ˈrɪbən/ *n* **1** [C,U] (piece or length of) cotton or other material woven in a long, narrow strip or band, used for ornamenting, for tying things, etc: *She had a ~ in her hair. Typewriter ~s may be all black or black and red.* **2** [C] piece of ribbon of a special design, colour, etc worn to show membership of an order, as a military decoration (when medals are not worn). **3** [C] long, narrow strip: *His clothes were hanging in ~s,* were very torn or worn.

ˈribbon-deˈvelopment, (the building of) long lines of houses along main roads leading out of a town.

rice /raɪs/ *n* [U] (plant with) pearl-white grain used as food.

rich /rɪtʃ/ *adj* (-er, -est) **1** having much money or property: *~ people.* **2** (of clothes, jewels, furniture, etc) costly; splendid; luxurious. **3** **rich in,** producing or having much or many: *a country ~ in minerals.* **4** (of food) containing a large proportion of fat, oil, butter, eggs, etc: *a ~ fruit cake.* **5** (of colours, sounds, etc) full; deep; mellow; strong: *the ~ colours of the national flags; the ~ voice of the baritone.* □ *n* **the ~,** rich

people.

rich-ly *adv* (a) in a rich manner: *~ly dressed.* (b) thoroughly; fully: *He ~ly deserved the punishment he received.*

rich-ness, quality or state of being rich (but not in the sense of **1** above).

riches /ˈrɪtʃɪz/ *n pl* wealth; being rich: *from rags to ~,* from poverty to being rich.

rick /rɪk/ *n* [C] regular stack of hay, straw, corn, etc (in a field). □ *vt* make (hay, etc) into a rick.

rick-ets /ˈrɪkɪts/ *n pl* (used with a *sing* or *pl verb*) disease of childhood, marked by softening and malformation of the bones, caused by deficiency of vitamin D as found in fresh food, e g milk, butter.

rick-ety /ˈrɪkɪtɪ/ *adj* likely to break and collapse: *~ furniture.*

rick-shaw /ˈrɪkʃɔː/ *n* [C] two-wheeled carriage for one or two passengers, pulled by a man.

rico-chet /ˈrɪkəʃeɪ US: ˈrɪkəˈʃeɪ/ *n* [U] movement (of a stone, bullet, etc) after hitting the ground, a solid substance or the surface of water; [C] hit made in this way. □ *vi,vt* (-t- or -tt-) (of a shot, etc) (cause to) rebound or move away sharply: *The bullet ~ed off his helmet.*

rid /rɪd/ *vt* (*pt, pp* rid) make free: *~ oneself of debt/a country of bandits.* **be/get rid of,** be/become free of: *We were glad to be ~ of our overcoats. They are difficult to get ~ of,* e g of articles in a shop, difficult to sell.

rid-dance /ˈrɪdəns/ *n* [U] (usually **good riddance)** state of being rid of something unwanted or undesirable: *Good ~ to bad rubbish,* (said of something or somebody undesirable which is now finished, gone, etc).

rid-den /ˈrɪdən/ (esp in compounds) oppressed or dominated by: *poˈlice-~.*

riddle[1] /ˈrɪdəl/ *n* [C] **1** question, statement or description, intended to make a person think hard in order to know the answer or meaning: *know the answer to a ~.* **2** mysterious person, thing, situation, etc: *the ~ of the universe.*

riddle[2] /ˈrɪdəl/ *n* [C] coarse sieve (for stones, earth, gravel, cinders etc). □ *vt* **1** pass (soil, ashes, etc) through a riddle. **2** make many holes in (something), e g by firing bullets into it: *~ a man with bullets.*

ride[1] /raɪd/ *n* [C] **1** period of riding; journey on horseback, on a bicycle, bus, etc: *It's a fivepenny ~ on the bus.* **take sb for a ride,** (*informal*) deceive, or humiliate him. **2** road or track for the use of persons on horseback and not for vehicles.

ride[2] /raɪd/ *vi,vt* (*pl* rode /rəʊd/, *pp* ridden /ˈrɪdən/) **1** sit on a horse, etc and be carried along; sit on a bicycle, etc and cause it to go forward: *He jumped on his horse and rode off/away. He was riding fast.* **2** sit on and control: *~ a horse/pony/bicycle.* **3** be in, be carried in, a bus or other (public) vehicle: *~*

in a bus/taxi. **4** compete in, on horseback, etc: ~ *a race.* **5** (allow to) sit or be on something as if on a horse: *The boy was riding on his father's shoulders.* **6** go out regularly on horseback (as a pastime, for exercise, etc): *I've given up riding.* **7** go through or over on horseback, etc: ~ *the desert.* **8** float on: *a ship riding the waves;* float on water: *a ship riding at anchor;* be supported by: *an albatross riding (on) the wind.* **ride out a storm,** (*fig*) come safely through trouble, attack, controversy, etc. **let sth ride,** (*informal*) take no action on it. **9** *ride up,* e g of an article of clothing, shift or move upwards.

rider /ˈraɪdə(r)/ *n* [C] **1** person who rides, esp one who rides a horse: *Miss White is no* ~. **2** additional observation following a statement, verdict, etc: *The jury added a* ~ *to their verdict recommending mercy.*
rider-less *adj* without a rider.

ridge /rɪdʒ/ *n* [C] **1** raised line where two sloping surfaces meet: *the* ~ *of a roof.* **2** long mountain range. **3** long, narrow stretch of high land between the tops of a line of hills: *a* ~ *walk,* along this high land. **4** (in ploughed land) raised part between two furrows.

ridi-cule /ˈrɪdɪkjuːl/ *n* [U] being made fun of; derision: *She has become an object of* ~. **hold a man up to ridicule,** make fun of him. □ *vt* make fun of; cause to appear foolish: *Why do you* ~ *my proposal?*

rid-icu-lous /rɪˈdɪkjʊləs/ *adj* deserving to be laughed at; absurd: *You look* ~ *in that old hat. What a* ~ *idea/old man!*
rid-icu-lous-ly *adv*

rid-ing-breeches /ˈraɪdɪŋ brɪtʃɪz/ *n pl* short trousers fastened below the knee, worn for riding on horseback.

rife /raɪf/ *adj* widespread; common: *Is superstition still* ~ *in the country?*

riffle /ˈrɪfəl/ *vt,vi* **1** shuffle playing cards quickly. **2** turn over (the pages of a book, etc) quickly.

rifle¹ /ˈraɪfəl/ *vt* cut spiral grooves in (a gun, its barrel or bore). □ *n* [C] gun with a long barrel, to be fired from the shoulder.
rifle-range, (a) place where men practise shooting with rifles. (b) distance that a bullet from a rifle will travel: *within/out of* ~-*range.*
rifle-man /-mən/, soldier of a rifle regiment.

rifle² /ˈraɪfəl/ *vt* search thoroughly in order to steal from: *The thief* ~*d every drawer in the room.*

rift /rɪft/ *n* [C] **1** split or crack: *a* ~ *in the clouds.* **2** (*fig*) disagreement, quarrel, (e g between two friends or friendly groups, etc).
rift-valley, steep-sided valley caused by sinking of the earth's crust.

rig¹ /rɪg/ *vt* (-gg-) **1** supply (a ship) with masts, rigging, sails, etc; (of a ship) be supplied with these things; prepare for sea in this way. **2** provide (a person) with necessary clothes, equipment, etc: ~ *the children out with rainwear.* **3** *rig sth up,* (a) assemble or adjust parts (of an aircraft, etc). (b) make, put together, quickly or with any materials that may be available: *They* ~*ged up some scaffolding for the workmen.* □ *n* [C] **1** way in which a ship's masts, sails, etc, are arranged. **2** equipment put together for a special purpose. ⇨ oil-rig.
rig-out, (*informal*) person's clothes, etc: *What a queer* ~-*out!*
rig-ging *n* [U] all the ropes, etc which support a ship's masts and sails.
rig-ger, (a) person who rigs ships, etc. (b) person whose work is to assemble and adjust the parts of aircraft, etc.

rig² /rɪg/ *vt* (-gg-) manage fraudulently for private profit or gain: ~ *an election,* use dishonest methods to be successful.

right¹ /raɪt/ *adj* (**1** to **3** contrasted with *wrong*) **1** (of conduct, etc) just; morally good; required by law or duty: *Always do what is* ~ *and honourable. You were quite* ~ *to refuse.* **2** true; correct; satisfactory: *What's the* ~ *time? Have you got the* ~ (= exact) *fare?* **put sth right,** restore to order, good health, a good condition, etc: *put a watch* ~, i e to the correct time. *This medicine will put you* ~. **All right,** ⇨ all²(**1**) and **4** below. **3** most suitable; best in view of the circumstances, etc: *Are we on the* ~ *road? He is the* ~ *man for the job. Which is the* ~ *side* (i e the side meant to be seen or used) *of this cloth? get on the right side of sb,* win his favour. **4** in healthy condition; sane: *Do you feel all* ~? *not in one's right mind,* in an abnormal mental state. **right as rain,** (*informal*) perfectly sound or healthy. **5** (of an angle) of 90° (i e neither acute nor obtuse): *at* ~ *angles/at a* ~ *angle.*
right-minded *adj* having opinions or principles based on what is right: *All* ~-*minded people will agree with me when I say....*
right-ly *adv* justly; justifiably; correctly; truly: *She has been sacked, and* ~*ly so.*
right-ness *n* [U]

right² /raɪt/ *adv* **1** straight; directly: *Put it* ~ *in the middle. right away/now,* at once, without any delay. **2** all the way (*to/round, etc*); completely (*off/out, etc*): *Go* ~ *to the end of this road, and then turn left. There's a fence* ~ *round the building. The pear was rotten* ~ *through. The prisoner got* ~ *away. He turned* ~ *round. right, left and centre,* on all sides. **3** justly; correctly, satisfactorily; properly: *if I remember* ~. **Right on!** (*informal*) (used to show approval). **It serves him right,** It is what he deserves, etc.
Right Honourable, title of certain peers, Privy Councillors, Justices, etc.

right³ /raɪt/ *n* **1** [U] that which is good, just, honourable, true, etc: *know the difference between* ~ *and wrong.* **be in the right,**

have justice and truth on one's side. **2** [U] proper authority or claim; the state of being justly entitled to something. **3** [C] something one may do or have by law, authority, social acceptance, etc: *human* ~*s,* means to live, freedom, etc justly claimed by all men. *What gives you the* ~ *to say that?* **by right(s),** if justice were done: *The property is not mine by* ~(*s*)*.* **in one's own right,** because of a personal claim, qualification, etc: *She's a peeress in her own* ~, i e not by marriage. **right of way, (a)** right of the general public to use a path, road, etc: *Is there a* ~ *of way across these fields?* **(b)** (in road traffic) right to procede before others: *It's my* ~ *of way, so that lorry must stop or slow down until I've passed it.* **assert one's rights,** say what one's rights are and declare that they will not be surrendered. **4** (*pl*) true state: **set/put things to rights,** put them in order.

right⁴ /raɪt/ *vt* put, bring or come back, into the right or an upright condition: *The ship* ~*ed herself after the big wave had passed.*

right⁵ /raɪt/ *adj* (contrasted with *left*) of the side of the body which is toward the east when a person faces north: *my* ~ *hand/leg. In Great Britain traffic keeps to the left, not the* ~, *side of the road.* □ *adv* to the right hand or side: *He looked neither* ~ *nor left. Eyes* ~*!* as a military command. *He owes money* ~ *and left,* everywhere. □ *n* [U] **1** side or direction on one's right hand: *Take the first turning to the* ~. **2** (*politics*) the R~, ⇨ Right Wing: *members of the R~.*

'right-about ('turn/'face), right turn continued until one is faced in the opposite direction.

'right-'handed *adj* **(a)** (of a person) using the right hand more, or with more ease, than the left. **(b)** (of a blow, etc) given with the right hand.

'right-'turn, turn into a position at right angles (90°) with the original one.

the Right (Wing), more conservative or reactionary political group(s), party or parties: (as an *adjective*) ~*-wing demonstrators.*

right-ist /-ɪst/, member of a right wing political party. □ adj of such a party: ~*ist sympathizers.*

right-eous /ˈraɪtʃəs/ *adj* **1** doing what is morally right; obeying the law. **2** morally justifiable: ~ *anger.*

right-eous-ly *adv*

right-eous-ness *n* [U]

right-ful /ˈraɪtful/ *adj* **1** according to law and justice: *the* ~ *owner of the land.* **2** (of actions, etc) fair; justifiable.

right-ful-ly /-fəlɪ/ *adv*

right-ness *n* [U]

rigid /ˈrɪdʒɪd/ *adj* **1** stiff; that cannot be bent: *a* ~ *support for a tent.* **2** firm; strict; not changing; not to be changed: *a* ~ *disciplinarian; practise* ~ *economy.*

rigid-ly *adv*

ri-gid-ity /rɪˈdʒɪdətɪ/ *n* [U] **1** inflexibility: *the* ~ *of his religious beliefs.* **2** strictness.

rig-ma-role /ˈrɪgmərəʊl/ *n* [C] long, incoherent account or description.

rigor mor-tis /ˈraɪgɔ ˈmɔːtɪs US: ˈrɪgɔr/ *n* (*Latin*) the stiffening of the muscles after death.

rig-or-ous /ˈrɪgərəs/ *adj* **1** stern; strict; determined: *a* ~ *search for drugs.* **2** harsh; severe: *a* ~ *climate.*

rig-or-ous-ly *adv*

rig-our (*US* = **rigor**) /ˈrɪgə(r)/ *n* **1** [U] sternness; strict enforcement (of rules, etc): *use the* ~ *of the law.* **2** (often *pl*) severe conditions: *the* ~*s of prison life.*

rile /raɪl/ *vt* (*informal*) annoy; cause anger in: *It* ~*d him that no one would believe his story.*

rim /rɪm/ *n* [C] circular edge of the framework of a wheel, round the lenses of spectacles, etc; edge, border or margin of something circular: *the* ~ *of a cup/bowl.* □ *vt* (-mm-) provide with a rim; be a rim for.

rind /raɪnd/ *n* [U] hard, outside skin or covering (of some fruits, e g melons, or of bacon and cheese); [C] piece or strip of this skin.

ring¹ /rɪŋ/ *n* [C] **1** circular band worn round a finger as an ornament, or as a token: *an* en`gagement ~; *a* `wedding ~; similar band for other parts of the body: *an* `ear~. **2** circular band of any kind of material, e g metal, wood, ivory: *a* `key~, one of split metal, for carrying keys on. **3** circle: *a* ~ *of light round the moon; the* ~*s of a tree,* seen in wood when the trunk is cut across, showing the tree's age. **make/run `rings round sb,** argue, do things, better than he does. **4** combination of persons (traders, politicians, etc) working together for their own advantage, e g to keep prices up or down, to control policy: *a* ~ *of dealers at a public auction.* **5** (also `circus-~), circular enclosure or space for circus performances. **6** roped area for a boxing-match. □ *vt,vi* (*pt,pp* ~ed) **1** surround: ~*ed about with enemies.* **2** put a ring in the nose of (a bull, etc) or on the leg of (a bird, e g a homing pigeon). **3** make a ring round (something), e g with a pencil, or by shooting holes round a target.

`ring-finger, third finger of the left hand.

`ring-leader, person who leads others in a rising against authority.

`ring-master, man who directs performances in a circus.

`ring road, road round, and through the outskirts of, a large town, for the use of through traffic.

`ring-side, place near to the ring of a circus, a boxing-ring, etc: *have a* ~*side seat,* be favourably placed for seeing an event, etc.

`ring-worm, contagious skin disease, esp of children, producing round, red patches.

ring² /rɪŋ/ *vt,vi* (*pt* rang /ræŋ/, *pp* rung /rʌŋ/) **1** give out a clear, musical sound as when metal vibrates: *How long has that telephone* (*bell*) *been ~ing? A shot rang out*, The noise of a shot was heard. **2** produce a certain effect when heard: *His words rang true*, seemed sincere. **3** cause a bell to sound, as a summons, warning, etc: *She rang for the porter*. **4** cause something, esp a bell, to ring: *~ the church bells; ~ the bell for the steward*. **ring a bell**, (*informal*) bring something vaguely back to mind: *Ah! That name ~s a bell!* **5** resound; echo: *The children's playground rang with happy shouts.* **6** linger in one's hearing or memory: *His last words are still ~ing in my ears.* **7** get into communication by telephone: *I'll ~ you* (*up*) *this evening.* (US = *call* (*up*).) **ring off**, end a telephone conversation. **8** (of a chime of bells) announce (the hour, etc); strike the hours. **9** give a signal by ringing a bell, etc: *Did the cyclist ~ his bell?* **ring the alarm**, give one by ringing. **ring the changes** (**on**), (*fig*) put or arrange things, do things, in as many different ways as possible. **ring the curtain up/down**, (in a theatre) give the signal for it to be raised/lowered. **ring out the Old** (*year*) **and ring in the New**, (using bells). □ *n* **1** (*sing* only) sound produced by a bell or piece of metal when it is struck: *This coin has a good ~.* **2** (*sing* only) loud and clear sound: *the ~ of happy voices.* **3** (*sing* only) effect of sincerity, etc: *There was a ~ of truth in his statement.* **4** [C] act of ringing; sound of a bell: *There was a ~ at the door. I'll give you a ~ this evening*, will telephone you.

ring·let /ˈrɪŋlət/ *n* [C] small curl of hair: *She arranged her hair in ~s.*

rink /rɪŋk/ *n* [C] specially prepared area of ice for skating or hockey, or floor for roller-skating.

rinse /rɪns/ *vt* **1** wash with clean water in order to remove unwanted substances, etc: *~ soap out of the clothes; ~ the clothes; (out) the mouth*, e g while being treated by a dentist. **2 rinse sth down**, help (food) down with a drink: *R~ it down with a glass of beer.* □ *n* [C] **1** act of rinsing: *Give your hair a good ~ after you've had your shampoo.* **2** solution for tinting the hair: *the blue ~ used by some elderly women.*

riot /ˈraɪət/ *n* **1** [C] violent outburst of lawlessness: *R~s during the election were dealt with/put down by the police.* **2** [U] noisy, uncontrolled behaviour, e g by students celebrating, etc. **run riot**, (a) lose all discipline. (b) (of plants) be out of control by growing fast and in wrong places. **3** (*sing* only, with *a, an*) profusion: *The flowerbeds in the park were a ~ of colour.* **4** (*sing* only) unrestrained indulgence in or display of something: *a ~ of emotion.* □ *vi* **1** take part in a riot(1,2): *They were ~ing all night after the elections.* **2 riot in**, indulge or revel (in): *The tyrant ~ed in cruelty.*

rioter, person who riots.

riot·ous /-əs/ *adj* likely to cause a riot; disorderly; running wild: *a ~ous assembly; ~ous behaviour.*
riot·ous·ly *adv*

rip /rɪp/ *vt,vi* (-pp-) **1** pull, tear or cut (something) quickly and with force (to get it off, out, open, etc): *~ open a letter; ~ the cover off; ~ the seams of a dress.* **2** saw (wood, etc) with the grain. **3** (of material) tear; be ripped. **4** go forward, rush along. **Let her/it rip**, (*informal*) (of a boat, car, machine, etc) allow it to go at its maximum speed. **let things rip**, let things take their natural course. □ *n* [C] torn place; long cut: *bad ~s in my tent.*
ˋrip-cord, cord which, when pulled during a descent, releases a parachute from its pack.
ˋrip-saw, saw used for ripping(2).

ripe /raɪp/ *adj* (-r, -st) **1** (of fruit, grain, etc) ready to be gathered and used: *~ fruit; cherries not ~ enough to eat.* **2** matured and ready to be eaten or drunk: *~ cheese/wine.* **3** fully developed: *a person of ~(r) years*, past the stage of youth. **4 ripe for**, ready, fit, prepared: *land that is ~ for development*, e g for building houses or factories. **when the time is ripe**, at the most suitable moment.
ripe·ly *adv*
ripe·ness [U]

ripen /ˈraɪpən/ *vt,vi* make or become ripe.

ri·poste /rɪˈpəʊst/ *n* [C] **1** quick return or thrust in fencing. **2** quick, sharp reply or retort. □ *vi* deliver a riposte.

ripple /ˈrɪpəl/ *n* [C] (sound of) small movement(s) on the surface of water, etc, e g made by a gentle wind, or of the rise and fall of soft voices or laughter: *A long ~ of laughter passed through the audience.* □ *vt,vi* (cause to) move in ripples; (cause to) rise and fall gently: *The wheat ~d in the breeze.*

rip-tide /ˈrɪp taɪd/ *n* [C] tide causing strong currents and rough water.

rise¹ /raɪz/ *n* [C] **1** small hill; upward slope: *on the ~ of a hill; a ~ in the ground.* **2** increase (in value, temperature, etc): *a ~ in prices; have a ~ in wages* (US = *raise*). **3** upward progress: *a ~ in social position; the ~ and fall of the tide.* **4** (*literary*) coming up (of the sun, etc): *at ~ of the sun/day*, (more usually *sunrise*). **5** movement of fish to the surface of water: *I fished two hours without getting a ~.* **take the rise out of sb**, tease him. **6** origin; start: *The river has/takes its ~ among the hills*, **give rise to**, be the cause of; suggest: *Such conduct might give ~ to misunderstandings.*

riser, (a) *an early/late ~r*, person who gets up early/late. (b) vertical part of a step, connecting two treads of a staircase.

rise² /raɪz/ *vi* (*pt* rose /rəʊz/, *pp* risen /ˈrɪzən/) **1** (of the sun, moon, stars) appear above the horizon: *The sun ~s in the East.* ⇨ **set¹**(1). **2** get up from a lying, sitting or kneeling position: *The wounded man fell* *and was too weak to* ∼. *The horse rose on its hind legs.* **3** get out of bed; get up (which is more usual): *He* ∼*s very early.* **4** come to life (again): *Jesus Christ rose (again) from the dead. He looked as though he had* ∼*n from the grave.* **5** go, come, up or higher; reach a high(er) level or position: *The river/ flood, etc has* ∼*n two feet. His voice rose in anger/excitement, etc,* became high, louder. *Prices continue to* ∼. *The temperature is rising. New office blocks are rising in our town.* ⇨ **high-rise.** **6** come to the surface: *Bubbles rose from the bottom of the lake.* **7** slope upwards: *rising ground.* **8** have as a starting-point: *Where does the Nile* ∼? **9** become or be visible above the surroundings: *A range of hills rose on our left.* **10** develop greater intensity: *The wind is rising.* **11** reach a higher position in society; make progress (in one's profession, etc): ∼ *in the world;* ∼ *from the ranks,* i e to be an officer; *a rising young politician/lawyer.* **12** (of meetings, etc) cease to be held: *Parliament will* ∼ *on Thursday next,* will stop for a recess. **13** *rise to the occasion,* prove oneself able to deal with an unexpected problem, a difficult task, etc. **14** *rise against,* rebel (against the government, etc).

ris·ing, (esp) armed rebellion. ⇨ **uprising.**

risk /rɪsk/ *n* **1** [C,U] (instance of a) possibility or chance of meeting danger, suffering loss, injury, etc: *There's no/not much* ∼ *of injury if you obey the rules. at risk,* threatened by uncertainties (such as failure, loss, etc): *Is the Government's income policy seriously at* ∼? *at one's own risk,* accepting responsibility, agreeing to make no claims, for loss, injury, etc. *at the risk of; at risk to,* with the possibility of loss, etc: *He was determined to get there even at the* ∼ *of his life. run a/the risk of; take risks,* put oneself in a position where there is risk: *She's too sensible to take* ∼*s when she's driving. He was ready to run the* ∼ *of being taken prisoner by the enemy.* **2** [C] amount for which a person or thing is insured; the person or thing insured: *He's a good/poor* ∼. □ *vt* **1** expose to risk: ∼ *one's health in the jungle. risk one's neck,* ⇨ neck(1). **2** take the chances of: *We mustn't* ∼ *getting caught in a storm.*

risky *adj* (-ier, -iest) full of danger: *a* ∼*y undertaking.*

ri·sotto /rɪˈzɒtəʊ/ *n* [U] dish of rice cooked with butter, cheese, onions, etc.

ris·qué /ˈrɪskeɪ *US:* rɪˈskeɪ/ *adj* (of a story, remark, situation in a drama, etc) likely to be considered indecent.

ris·sole /ˈrɪsəʊl/ *n* [C] small, fried, ball of minced meat, fish, etc.

rite /raɪt/ *n* [C] ceremony (esp in religious services): `*burial* ∼*s.*

rit·ual /ˈrɪtjʊəl/ *n* **1** [U] all the rites or forms connected with a ceremony; way of con-

ducting a religious service: *the* ∼ *of the Catholic Church;* [C] particular form of ritual. **2** [C] any procedure regularly followed, as if it were a ritual: *He went through his usual* ∼ *of cutting and lighting his cigar.* **3** (*pl*) ceremonial observances. □ *adj* of religious rites; done as a rite: *the* ∼ *dances of an African tribe.*

ri·val /ˈraɪvl/ *n* [C] person who competes with another (because he wants the same thing, or to be or do better than the other): `*business* ∼*s;* ∼*s in love;* (as an *adjective*) ∼ *business firms.* □ *vt* (-ll-, *US* also -l-) be a rival of; claim to be (almost) as good as: *Can cricket* ∼ *football in excitement?*

ri·valry /ˈraɪvlrɪ/ *n* [C,U] (*pl* -ies) (instance of) being rivals: *the* ∼*ries between political parties.*

river /ˈrɪvə(r)/ *n* [C] **1** natural stream of water flowing in a channel to the sea or to a lake, etc or joining another river: *the R*∼ *Thames. sell sb down the river,* (*fig*) betray him. **2** great flow: *a* ∼ *of lava;* ∼*s of blood,* great bloodshed (as in war).

`**river-basin,** area drained by a river and its tributaries.

`**river-bed,** ground over which a river flows.

`**river-side,** ground along a river bank: *a* ∼*side walk.*

rivet /ˈrɪvɪt/ *n* [C] metal pin or bolt for fixing metal plates (e g in a ship's sides), the plain end being hammered flat to prevent slipping. □ *vt* **1** fasten with rivets; flatten (the end of a bolt) to make it secure. **2** (*fig*) fix or concentrate (one's eyes, attention) on: *He* ∼*ed his eyes on the scene.* **3** take up, secure (attention, etc): *Some television documentaries are* ∼*ing.*

rivu·let /ˈrɪvjʊlət/ *n* [C] small stream.

road /rəʊd/ *n* [C] **1** specially prepared way between places for the use of vehicles, pedestrians, etc: *travel by* ∼; (as an *adjective*) *a* `∼ *map of Great Britain;* `∼ *accidents. R*∼ *works in progress,* the road is under construction or repair. **2** (in proper names) (**a**) (with *the*) name of a road leading to the town, etc named: *the Oxford R*∼, leading to Oxford. (**b**) (without *the,* usually abbr to **Rd**) street of buildings: *35 York Rd, London, S W.* **3** one's way or route: *You're in the/my* ∼, obstructing me. **4** *road to,* way of getting: *Is excessive drinking the* ∼ *to ruin?*

`**road-block,** barricade built across a road to stop or slow down traffic (e g by police to catch an escaped prisoner.

`**road-hog,** motorist who is inconsiderate of others.

`**road-house,** building(s) on a main road, often with facilities for meals, etc used by people who travel by car.

`**road `safety,** safety from road accidents.

`**road-sense,** capacity for intelligent behaviour on roads: *Harry/Harry's dog has no* ∼ *sense.*

ˋ**road·side,** ground along the side of a road.

ˋ**road·way,** (usually with *the*) central part used by wheeled traffic (contrasted with the footpath, etc): *Dogs should be kept off the* ∼*way.*

ˋ**road·worthy** *adj* (of a motor-vehicle, etc) fit for use on the roads.

roam /rəʊm/ *vi, vt* walk or travel without any definite aim or destination over or through (a country, etc): ∼ *about the world/*∼ *the seas.*

roar /rɔː(r)/ *n* [C] loud, deep sound as of a lion, of thunder, of a person in pain, etc: *the* ∼*s of a tiger; the* ∼ *of London's traffic;* ∼*s of laughter.* □ *vt, vi* **1** make such loud, deep sounds: *lions* ∼*ing in the distance. Several lorries* ∼*ed past;* ∼ *with laughter/pain.* **2** say, sing, loudly: ∼ *out an order/a drinking song;* ∼ *oneself hoarse,* make oneself hoarse by roaring.

roar·ing *adj* (a) noisy; rough. (b) stormy: *the* ∼*ing forties,* part of the Atlantic between 40° and 50° N latitude, often very stormy. (c) lively; healthy: *do a* ∼*ing trade.* □ *adv* extremely: ∼*ing drunk.*

roast /rəʊst/ *vt, vi* **1** (of meat, potatoes, etc) cook, be cooked, in a hot oven, or over or in front of a hot fire: ∼ *a joint. The meat was* ∼*ing in the oven.* **2** expose for warmth to heat of some kind: ∼ *oneself in front of the fire; lie in the sun and* ∼. □ *adj* that has been ∼*ed:* ∼ *beef/pork.* □ *n* **1** [C] joint of roasted meat; [U] slices from such a joint: ∼ *and vegetables.* **2** [C] operation of roasting.

roaster, kind of oven for roasting; chicken, etc suitable for roasting.

roast·ing, *give sb a good roasting,* criticize or scold him harshly.

rob /rɒb/ *vt* (-bb-) **1** deprive (a person) of his property; take property from (a place) unlawfully (and often by force): *The bank was* ∼*bed last night. I was* ∼*bed of my watch.* (*Note:* compare - *I had my watch stolen.*) **2** deprive a person of (what is due to him, etc): *be* ∼*bed of the rewards of one's labour.*

rob·ber, person who robs: *a* ˋ*bank-*∼*ber.*

rob·bery /ˈrɒbərɪ/ *n* [C,U] (*pl* -ries) (instance of) robbing: ∼*bery with violence.* ˈ**daylight** ˋ**robbery,** (*informal*) obvious charging of excessive prices.

robe /rəʊb/ *n* [C] **1** long, loose outer garment: *a* ˋ*bath-*∼. **2** (*US*) = dressing-gown. **3** (often *pl*) long, loose garment worn as a sign of rank or office: *magistrates/judges in their black* ∼*s.* □ *vt* put a robe on: *professors* ∼*d in their academic gowns.*

robin /ˈrɒbɪn/ *n* [C] small, brownish bird with red breast-feathers.

ro·bot /ˈrəʊbɒt/ *n* [C] machine made to act like a man.

ro·bust /rəʊˈbʌst/ *adj* strong, active; fit, healthy: *a* ∼ *young man; a* ∼ *appetite.*

ro·bust·ly *adv*

ro·bust·ness *n* [U]

rock[1] /rɒk/ *n* **1** [U] solid stony part of the earth's crust: *a house built on* ∼. **2** [C,U] mass of rock standing out from the earth's surface or from the sea. *as firm/solid as a rock,* (a) that cannot be moved. (b) (*fig*) (of persons) reliable; dependable. *on the rocks,* (*fig*) (of a person) very short of money; (of a marriage) likely to end in divorce or separation. **3** [C] large stone or boulder: ∼*s rolling down the side of a mountain;* (*US*) = stone[1] (2). **4** [U] (*GB*) length of hard, sticky sweet. **5** *on the rocks,* (*US*) (*of spirits* (13)) with ice-cubes.

ˈ**rock-**ˋ**bottom,** lowest point: *His morale has reached* ∼*-bottom;* (as an *adjective*) ∼*-bottom prices.*

ˋ**rock-cake,** small cake or bun with a hard, rough surface.

ˋ**rock-climbing,** the climbing of rocky mountain-sides (with the help of ropes, etc).

ˋ**rock-crystal,** pure natural transparent quartz.

ˋ**rock-garden,** area of ground with rocks and stones and rock-plants growing among them.

ˋ**rock-plant,** kinds of small plant found growing among rocks, esp in rock-gardens.

ˈ**rock-**ˋ**salmon,** (trade name for) dogfish.

ˋ**rock-salt,** common salt as found in mines in crystal form.

rock·ery, = rock-garden.

rock[2] /rɒk/ *vt, vi* (cause to) sway or swing backwards and forwards, or from side to side: ∼ *a baby to sleep. The town was* ∼*ed by an earthquake. rock the boat,* (*fig*) do something that upsets the smooth progress of an undertaking, etc.

rocker, (a) one of the curved pieces of wood on which a rocking-chair or rocking-horse rests. (b) = rocking-chair. (c) (*GB*) (1960's) member of a teenage gang, wearing leather jackets and riding motor-bikes. (d) *off one's rocker,* (*sl*) crazy; mad.

ˋ**rock·ing-chair,** one fitted with rockers on which it rests.

ˋ**rock·ing-horse,** wooden horse with rockers for a child to ride on.

rock[3] /rɒk/ *n* [U] highly rhythmic popular music for dancing, played on electric guitars. □ *vi* dance to this music.

rock-'n-roll /ˈrɒk ən ˈrəʊl/ *n* [U] (also *rock and roll*) = rock[3].

rocket /ˈrɒkɪt/ *n* **1** [C] tube-shaped case filled with fast-burning material, which launches itself into the air (as a firework, as a signal of distress, or as a self-propelled projectile or missile (as used to launch an aircraft or spacecraft, or attached to an aircraft, to give it higher speed and range): ∼ *propulsion;* ∼*-propelled.* **2** (*informal*) severe scolding: *get/give him a* ∼. □ *vi* go up fast like a rocket: (*informal*) *Prices are* ∼*ing.*

ˋ**rocket-base,** military base for missiles.

ˋ**rocket-range,** area used for experiments

with missiles.

rock·et·ry /-trɪ/ n [U] (art or science of) using rockets for space missiles, etc.

rocky /ˈrokɪ/ adj (-ier, -iest) **1** of rock, full of rocks; hard like rock: a ∿ road; ∿ soil. **2** (informal) shaky; informal: The table is rather ∿. His business is very ∿.

rod /rod/ n **1** thin, straight piece of wood or metal: a ˋfishing-∿. **2** stick used for punishing. **make a rod for one's own back,** prepare trouble for oneself. **3** (US) (sl) = revolver. **4** measure of length equal to 5½ yds. **5** metal bar; shaft, etc: ˋpiston-∿.

rode /rəʊd/ pt of ride².

ro·dent /ˈrəʊdənt/ n [C] animal, e g a rat, rabbit, squirrel or beaver, which gnaws things with its strong teeth specially adapted for this purpose.

ro·deo /ˈrəʊdeɪəʊ US: ˈrəʊdɪəʊ/ n [C] (pl ∿s) **1** (on the plains of Western US) rounding up of cattle. **2** contest of skill in lassoing cattle, riding untamed horses, etc.

roe¹ /rəʊ/ n [C,U] (hard ∿) (mass of) eggs in a female fish; (soft ∿) sperm-filled gland of a male fish.

roe² /rəʊ/ n [C] (pl ∿s or, collectively, ∿) small kind of European and Asiatic deer. **ˋroe-buck,** male roe.

Roent·gen /ˈrontjən US: ˈrentgən/ ⇨ X-rays.

ro·ga·tion /rəʊˈgeɪʃən/ n [C] (usually pl) litany of the saints chanted on the three days before Ascension Day.

rogue /rəʊg/ n [C] **1** (old use) vagabond. **2** scoundrel; rascal. **3** wild animal living apart from the herd: (as an adjective) a ∿ elephant.

ro·guery /ˈrəʊgərɪ/ n (pl -ies) **(a)** [C,U] (instance of the) conduct of a rogue. **(b)** [U] playful mischief; (pl) mischievous acts.

ro·guish /ˈrəʊgɪʃ/ adj

role, rôle /rəʊl/ n [C] **1** actor's part in a play: play the ˋtitle-∿ in 'Hamlet', play the part of Hamlet. **2** person's task or duty in an undertaking: What is your ∿ on the Committee?

roll¹ /rəʊl/ n [C] **1** something made into the shape of a cylinder by being rolled: a ∿ of carpet/photographic film; a man with ∿s of fat on his neck; a sausage ∿, a sausage rolled in pastry and then baked; a bread ∿, small loaf of bread. **2** turned-back edge: a ˋ∿-ˋcollar, large collar made by turning back the edge of the material. **3** rolling movement: The slow, steady ∿ of the ship made us sick. **4** official list or record, esp of names. **call the roll,** read the names (to check who is present and who absent). Hence, ˋroll-call n. **5** rolling sound: the distant ∿ of thunder/drums.

roll² /rəʊl/ vt,vi (For special uses with adverbial particles and prepositions, ⇨ 11 below.) **1** (cause to) move along on wheels or by turning over and over: The brakes failed and the car ∿ed down the hill. The coin fell and ∿ed under the table. The bicycle hit me and sent me ∿ing/∿ed me over. He ∿ed (= wrapped by turning over) himself (up) in the blanket. **2** make into the shape of a ball or a cylinder: R∿ the string/wool into a ball. **rolled into one,** combined in one person: She's mother and father ∿ed into one, e g of a widow. **3** come or go in a wavy or rolling motion: The clouds ∿ed away as the sun rose higher. The years ∿ed on/by, passed. The smoke ∿ed up the chimney. The tears were ∿ing (= flowing) down her cheeks. **4** turn about in various directions: a dog ∿ing on the ground. **5** make or become flat, level or smooth by pressing with a rolling cylinder of wood, metal, etc or by passing between two such cylinders: ∿ a lawn; ∿ a road flat. **roll sth out,** flatten it by rolling: ∿ out pastry. **6** (cause to) sway or move from side to side: The ship was ∿ing heavily. The drunken man ∿ed up to me. **7** (of surfaces) have long slopes that rise and fall: miles and miles of ∿ing country. **8** (of furniture, etc) move, be moved, on wheels. **9** make, utter, be uttered with, long, deep, vibrating or echoing sounds: The thunder ∿ed in the distance. **roll one's r's,** utter them with the tongue making a rapid succession of taps against the palate. **10** (of the eyes) (cause to) change direction with a rotary motion: His eyes ∿ed strangely at me. Don't ∿ your eyes at me, woman!

11 (special uses with adverbial particles and prepositions):

roll sth back, cause to retreat, e g enemy forces.

roll in, come, arrive, in large numbers or quantities: Offers of help are ∿ing in. **be ˋrolling in,** **(a)** have large quantities of: He's ∿ing in money. **(b)** be living in: ∿ing in luxury.

roll into, form into by rolling: Hedgehogs can ∿ into balls. ⇨ roll up.

roll on, (a) be capable of being put on by rolling. **(b)** (of time) pass steadily: Time ∿ed on. **(c)** (of time, chiefly imperative) come soon: R∿ on the day when I retire! **roll sth on,** put on by rolling over a part of the body: She ∿ed her stockings on.

roll up, (a) form into a cylinder or ball: the cat ∿ed up into a ball. He ∿ed up his sleeves. **(b)** arrive (in a vehicle); join a group: Two or three latecomers ∿ed up. R∿ up! R∿ up!, used e g to call possible customers to a street stall.

roller /ˈrəʊlə(r)/ n [C] **1** cylinder-shaped object of wood, metal, rubber, etc, usually part of a machine, for pressing, smoothing, crushing, printing, etc: a ˋgarden-∿, for use on a lawn; a ˋroad-∿, used for making roads even by crushing rock, etc. **2** cylinder of wood, metal, etc placed beneath an object to make movement easy, or round which something may be rolled easily: a ˋ∿-blind, on which a window blind is rolled; a ˋ∿-

towel, an endless towel on a roller. **3** long, rolling wave.

`**roller-skate,** (also *a pair of skates*) skate with small wheels for use on a smooth surface.

rolling /ˈrəʊlɪŋ/ *prefix* (using rotatory motion).

`**rolling-pin,** cylinder of wood for rolling pastry, etc.

`**rolling-stock,** all the carriages and wagons belonging to a railway.

`**rolling-stone,** person who is unsettled, uncommitted.

roly-poly /ˈrəʊlɪ ˈpəʊlɪ/ *n* [C] (*pl* -ies) (*GB*) (also ~ *pudding*) pudding made of paste spread with jam, etc formed into a roll and boiled.

Ro·man /ˈrəʊmən/ *adj* **1** of Rome, esp ancient Rome: *the* ~ *Empire.* **2** R~, (esp) = Roman Catholic. □ *n* **1** citizen of ancient Rome; (*pl*) Christians of ancient Rome. **2** Roman Catholic.

'**roman 'numeral,** I, IV, XL, M, etc.

'**roman 'letter/'type,** upright kind, not italic.

ro·mance /rəˈmæns/ *n* **1** [C] story or novel of adventure; love story. **2** [U] class of literature consisting of love stories. **3** [C] R~, medieval story, usually in verse, relating the adventures of some hero of chivalry. **4** [C] experience, esp a love-affair, considered to be remarkable or worth description: *My first meeting with her was quite a* ~. **5** [U] mental tendency which welcomes stories of the marvellous, etc; the qualities characteristic of stories of life and adventure: *travel abroad in search of* ~.

Ro·mance /rəˈmæns/ *adj* **Romance language,** French, Italian, Spanish, Portuguese, Rumanian, etc developed from Latin.

ro·man·tic /rəˈmæntɪk/ *adj* **1** (of persons) having ideas, feelings, etc remote from experience and real life given to romance(1, 4, 5): *a* ~ *girl.* **2** of, like, suggesting, romance: ~ *music/scenes/adventures/tales/situations; a* ~ *old castle.* **3** (in art, literature and music) marked by feeling rather than by intellect; preferring passion, beauty, to order and proportion (opp of *classic* and *classical*): *the* ~ *poets,* e g Shelley, Keats. □ *n* [C] person with romantic(1, 4) ideals.

ro·man·ti·cally /-klɪ/ *adv*

ro·man·ti·cism /-tɪsɪzm/ *n* [U] romantic or imaginative tendency in literature, art and music (contrasted with *realism* and *classicism*).

ro·man·ti·cist /-tɪsɪst/ *n* [C] follower of romanticism.

ro·man·ti·cize /-tɪsaɪz/ *vt,vi* treat in a romantic way; use a romantic style in writing, etc.

romp /romp/ *vi* **1** (esp of children) play about, esp running, jumping and being rather rough. **2** win, succeed, quickly or without apparent effort: *The favourite* (*horse*) ~*ed home,* won easily. *John just* ~*s through his examinations,* passes them easily. □ *n* [C] period of romping: *have a* ~.

rom·pers, loose-fitting garment with legs worn by a child: *a pair of* ~*ers; a* `~*er suit.*

roof /ruːf/ *n* (*pl* ~s) **1** top covering of a building, tent, bus, car, etc: *How can you live under the same* ~ *as that woman,* in the same building? **raise the roof,** (*informal*) ⇨ raise(3). **2** *the* ~ *of heaven,* the sky: *the* ~ *of the world,* a high mountain range; *the* ~ *of the mouth,* the palate. □ *vt* (*pp* ~ed /ruːft/) supply with a roof; be a roof for: *a shed* ~*ed over with strips of bark.*

roof·ing, material used for roofs (e g slates, tiles).

rook[1] /rʊk/ *n* [C] large black bird like a crow.

rook·ery /-ərɪ/, (**a**) place (a group of trees) where many rooks have their nests. (**b**) colony of penguins or seals.

rook[2] /rʊk/ *n* [C] person who makes money by cheating when gambling. □ *vt* **1** win money from (a person) at cards, etc by cheating. **2** charge (a customer) a ridiculously high price.

rook[3] /rʊk/ *n* [C] chess piece (also called a *castle*).

room /rʊm *US:* ruːm/ *n* **1** [C] part of a house or other buildings enclosed by walls and a ceiling. **2** (*pl*) apartment: *Come and see me in my* ~*s one evening.* **3** [U] space that is or might be occupied, or that is enough for a purpose: *Is there* ~ *for me in the car? This table takes up too much* ~. *Can you make* ~ *on that shelf for some more books?* **4** [U] scope; opportunity: *There's* ~ *for improvement in your work,* It is not as good as it could be. *There's no* ~ *for doubt.* □ *vi* (*US*) occupy a room or rooms: *He's* ~*ing with my friend Smith.*

`**room-mate,** one of two or more persons sharing a room or apartment.

room·ful /-fʊl/, amount (of furniture, etc), number of persons, that fills a room.

roomy *adj* (-ier, -iest) having plenty of space: *a* ~*y cabin.*

-roomed /rʊmd *US:* ruːmd/ *suffix: a six-* ~*ed house,* having six rooms.

roost /ruːst/ *n* [C] branch, pole, etc on which a bird rests, esp one for hens to sleep or rest on; hen-house. **come home to roost,** (*proverb*) effect the person responsible: *Her extravagance came home to* ~ *a month later.* **rule the roost,** be the leader or master. □ *vi* (of birds or persons) settle down for the night's sleep.

rooster /ˈruːstə(r)/ *n* [C] domestic cock.

root[1] /ruːt/ *n* [C] **1** that part of a plant, tree, etc which is normally in the soil and which takes water and food from it: *pull up a plant by the* ~*s.* **take/strike roots,** (**a**) (e g of a cutting) send out. (**b**) (*fig*) become established. **root and branch**, (*fig*) thoroughly; completely: *These evil practices must be destroyed ∼ and branch.* **2** (*pl*) = root crop. **3** that part of a hair, tooth, the tongue, a finger-nail, etc that is like a root in position, function, etc. **4** (*fig*) basis; source: *He has no ∼s in society*, is not settled, does not belong to any particular group or place. *Is money the ∼ of all evil?* **get at/to the root of sth**, tackle it at its source. **pull up one's roots**, (*fig*) move from a settled home, job, etc to start a new life elsewhere. **put down new roots,** (*fig*) establish oneself in another place after leaving a place where one has been established. **5** (*gram*) (also *base form*) form of a word on which other forms of that word are based: *'Walk' is the ∼ of 'walks', 'walked', 'walking', and 'walker'.* **6** (*maths*) quantity which, when multiplied by itself a certain number of times, produces another quantity: *4 is the square ∼ of 16 and the cube ∼ of 64.*

'**root beer,** (*US*) non-alcoholic drink made from roots.

the root cause, fundamental, basic cause.

'**root crop,** plant with a root used as food.

'**root sign,** (*maths*) the symbol √.

root·less *adj* having no roots; (of a person) without roots in society.

root² /ruːt/ *vt,vi* **1** (of plants, cuttings, etc) (cause to) send out roots and begin to grow: *Some cuttings ∼ easily.* **2** cause to stand fixed and unmoving: *He stood there ∼ed to the spot.* **3** (chiefly in *pp*) (of ideas, principles, etc) establish firmly: *She has a ∼ed objection to cold baths. Her affection for him is deeply ∼ed.* **4 root sth out,** get rid of (an evil, etc).

root³ /ruːt/ *vi,vt* **1 root about (for),** (**a**) (of pigs) turn up the ground with the snout in search of food. (**b**) (of persons) search for; turn things over when searching: *∼ing about among piles of papers for a missing document.* **root sth out,** find by searching: *I managed to ∼ out a copy of the document.* **2** (*US sl*) cheer: *∼ing for the college baseball team.*

rope /rəʊp/ *n* **1** [C,U] (piece or length of) thick strong cord or wire cable made by twisting finer cords or wires together. **give sb (plenty of) rope,** (*fig*) freedom of action. **give sb enough rope to hang himself,** leave him to bring about his own ruin. **the ∼s**, those that enclose the prize-ring or other place used for sport or games. **know/learn/show sb the ropes,** the conditions, the rules, the procedure (in some sphere of action). **3** [C] number of things twisted, strung or threaded together: *a ∼ of onions.* □ *vt* **1** fasten or bind with rope: *∼ climbers together,* connect them with a rope for safety. **2 rope sth off,** enclose with a rope: *Part of the field was ∼d off.* **3 rope sb in,** persuade him to help in some activity.

'**rope-'ladder,** ladder made of two long

ropes connected by rungs of rope.

ropey /ˈrəʊpɪ/ *adj* (*sl*) very poor in quality.

ro·sary /ˈrəʊzərɪ/ *n* [C] (*pl* -ies) **1** form of prayer used in the R C Church; book containing this. **2** string of beads for keeping count of these prayers; such beads used by a person of another religion.

rose¹ /rəʊz/ *pt* ⇨ rise².

rose² /rəʊz/ *n* **1** [C] (shrub or bush with prickles or thorns on its stems and bearing a) colourful and usually sweet-smelling flower. **a bed of roses,** a pleasant, easy condition of life. (**be**) **not all roses,** not perfect; having some discomfort and disadvantages. **no rose without a thorn,** complete, pure happiness cannot be found. **2** [U] pinkish-red colour. **see things through rose-coloured/-tinted spectacles,** be very optimistic. **3** (of various things thought to be like a rose in shape) (**a**) sprinkling nozzle of a watering can or hose. (**b**) rosette. (**c**) the national emblem of England.

'**rose-bed,** bed in which rose bushes are grown.

'**rose-bud,** bud of a rose.

'**rose-'red** *adj* red as a rose.

'**rose-water,** perfume made from roses.

'**rose window,** ornamental circular window (usually in a church).

'**rose-wood,** hard, dark red wood obtained from several varieties of tropical tree.

rose·mary /ˈrəʊzmərɪ *US:* -merɪ/ *n* [U] evergreen shrub with fragrant leaves used as a herb and in making perfumes.

ro·sette /rəʊˈzet/ *n* [C] small rose-shaped badge, ornament or carving in stone.

rosin /ˈrɒzɪn *US:* ˈrɒzən/ *n* [U] resin, esp in solid form, as used on the strings of violins, etc and on the bow with which violins are played. □ *vt* rub with rosin.

ros·ter /ˈrɒstə(r)/ *n* [C] list of names of persons showing duties to be performed by each in turn.

ros·trum /ˈrɒstrəm/ *n* [C] (*pl* ∼s or -tra /-trə/) platform or pulpit for public speaking.

rosy /ˈrəʊzɪ/ *adj* (-ier, -iest) **1** of the colour of red roses: *∼ cheeks.* **2** (*fig*) good, bright, cheerful: *∼ prospects.*

rot /rɒt/ *n* [U] **1** decay; condition of being bad: *R∼ has set in*, decay has begun. ⇨ dry rot. **2** (also '*tommy-'rot*) (*sl*) nonsense: *Don't talk ∼!* **3** (in sport, war, etc) succession of failures: *A ∼ set in. How can we stop the ∼?* □ *vi,vt* (-tt-) **1** decay by processes of nature: *The shed had fallen in, and the wood was ∼ting away.* **2** (*fig*) (of a club, etc) gradually become inactive; (of prisoners, etc) waste away: *left to ∼ in a deep dungeon.* **3** cause to decay or become useless: *Oil and grease will ∼ your tyres.*

rota /ˈrəʊtə/ *n* [C] (*pl* ∼s) (*GB*) list of persons who are to do things in turn; list of duties to be performed in turn.

ro·tary /ˈrəʊtərɪ/ *adj* **1** (of motion) moving

round a central point. **2** (of an engine, machine) moved by rotary motion.

Rotary Club, (branch of an) international association of professional and business men in a town for the purpose of serving the community.

ro·tate /rəʊˈteɪt US: ˈrəʊteɪt/ *vi,vt* **1** (cause to) move round a central point. **2** (cause to) take turns or come in succession: ∼ *crops*, ⇨ rotation(2). *The office of Chairman* ∼*s*.

ro·ta·tion /rəʊˈteɪʃən/ *n* **1** [U] rotating or being rotated: *the* ∼ *of the earth*; [C] complete turning: *five* ∼*s an hour*. **2** [C,U] regular coming round of things or events in succession: `*crop*-∼, ∼ *of crops*, varying the crops grown each year on the same land to avoid exhausting the soil. *In rotation,* in turn; in regular succession.

ro·ta·tory /ˈrəʊtətərɪ US: -tɔrɪ/ *adj* relating to, causing, moving in, rotation: ∼ *movement*.

ro·tor /ˈrəʊtə(r)/ *n* [C] assembly of horizontally rotating blades of a helicopter propellor.

rot·ten /ˈrɒtən/ *adj* **1** decayed; having gone bad: ∼ *eggs*. **2** (*sl*) very unpleasant and undesirable: *What* ∼ *luck! I'm feeling* ∼ *today*, unwell, tired.

ro·tund /rəʊˈtʌnd/ *adj* **1** (of a person, his face) round and plump. **2** (of the voice) rich and deep. **3** (of speech, style) grand.

rouge /ruːʒ/ *n* [U] **1** fine red powder or other cosmetic substance for colouring the cheeks. **2** powder for cleaning silver plate. ▢ *vt* use rouge.

rough[1] /rʌf/ *adj* (-er, -est) **1** (of surfaces) not level, smooth or polished; (of roads) of irregular surface, not easy to walk or ride on: ∼ *paper*; *a* ∼ *skin*. **2** not calm or gentle; moving or acting violently: ∼ *children*; ∼ *behaviour*; *a* ∼ (= stormy) *sea*. *a rough tongue*, habit of speaking rudely or sharply. *give sb/have a rough time,* (cause him to) experience hardship, to be treated severely, etc (according to context). **3** made or done without attention to detail, esp as a first attempt: *a* ∼ *sketch/translation*; *a* ∼ *draft*, e g of a letter. *rough and ready,* good enough for ordinary or general purposes, occasions, etc; not particularly efficient, etc: ∼ *and ready methods*. **4** (of sounds) harsh: *a* ∼ *voice*.

rough luck, worse luck than is deserved.

rough house, (*sl*) disturbance, row.

rough-neck, (*informal*) noisy, ill-mannered person.

rough·ly *adv* **(a)** in a rough manner: *treat him* ∼*ly*. **(b)** approximately: *at a cost of* ∼*ly £5*. **(c)** *roughly speaking,* with no claim to accuracy.

rough·ness *n* [U] quality or state of being rough.

rough[2] /rʌf/ *adv* in a rough manner: *play* ∼, be (rather) violent (in games, etc). *live rough,* live in the open (as a homeless per-

son may do). *sleep rough,* (of homeless persons) sleep wherever there is some shelter, e g under a bridge, in the open air.

rough[3] /rʌf/ *n* **1** [U] rough state, ground or surface; unpleasantness; hardship. *take the rough with the smooth,* accept what is unpleasant with what is pleasant. **2** [U] unfinished state: *My notes are only in* ∼. ⇨ rough[1] (3). **3** [U] *the* ∼, part of a golf-course where the ground is uneven and the grass uncut. **4** [C] hooligan: *A gang of* ∼*s knocked him down and took all his money.*

rough[4] /rʌf/ *vt* **1** make untidy or uneven: *Don't* ∼ (*up*) *my hair*. **2** *rough sb up,* (*sl*) treat him roughly, with physical violence: *He was* ∼*ed up by hooligans*. **3** *rough it,* live without the usual comforts of life: *Some students have to* ∼ *it*.

rough·age /ˈrʌfɪdʒ/ *n* [U] coarse foodstuff, esp husks of cereals, eaten to stimulate bowel movements.

roughen /ˈrʌfən/ *vt,vi* make or become rough.

rou·lette /ruːˈlet/ *n* [U] gambling game in which a small ball falls by chance into one of the numbered compartments of a revolving wheel.

round[1] /raʊnd/ *adj* **1** shaped like a circle or a ball: *a* ∼ *plate/window/table*. **2** *a* ∼*-table conference,* at which there is no position of importance at the head of the table, everyone being apparently of equal importance. **3** done with, involving, a circular motion; going and returning: ∼ *trip/tour/voyage*. **4** entire; continuous; full: *a* ∼ *dozen/score,* that number and not less. *In round figures/numbers,* given in 10's, 100's, 1000's, etc (and so roughly correct).

round-shouldered *adj* having the shoulders bent forward.

round·ness *n* [U]

round[2] /raʊnd/ *adv* part (For special uses with *verb,* ⇨ the *verb* entries. Specimens only are given here.) **1** in a circle or curve to face the opposite way: *Turn your chair* ∼ *and face me*. **2** with a return to the starting-point: *The hour hand of a clock goes right* ∼ *in twelve hours. Christmas will soon be* ∼ *again. round and round,* with repeated revolutions. *all/right round,* completely round: *We walked right* ∼ *the lake. all the year round,* at all seasons of the year. **3** in circumference: *Her hips are a metre* ∼. **4** (so as to be) in a circle: *A crowd soon gathered* ∼. *The garden has a high wall all* ∼. **5** from one (place, point, person, etc) to another: *Please hand these papers* ∼, i e distribute them. *The news was soon passed* ∼. *go round,* supply everybody: *Have we enough food to go* ∼? **6** by a longer way or route; not by the direct route: *The taxi-driver brought us a long way* ∼. **7** to a place where a person is or will be: *Come* ∼ *and see me this evening.* **8** in the neighbourhood: *in all the villages* ∼ *about.*

round³ /raʊnd/ n 1 something round in shape: a ~ of toast, a slice. 2 **in the round,** so as to be viewed from all sides: a statue in the ~. **theatre in the round,** with the audience on (nearly) all sides of the stage. 3 regular series or succession or distribution: the daily ~, the ordinary occupations of the day; the doctor's ~ of visits (to the homes of his patients); the postman's ~, the route he takes to deliver letters. **make one's rounds,** make one's usual visits: The doctor makes his ~s of the wards every evening. 4 (in games, contests, etc) one stage: a boxing-match of ten ~s; the sixth ~ of the F A Cup, the quarter-finals of this soccer contest; have a ~ of cards; a ~ of golf, to all the 9 or 18 holes of the course. 5 allowance of something distributed or measured out; one of a set or series: pay for a ~ of drinks, drinks for every member of the group; another ~ of wage claims, by trade unions for higher wages for their members; have only three ~s of ammunition left, enough to fire three times. 6 song for several persons or groups, the second singing the first line while the first is singing the second line, etc. 7 dance in which the dancers move in a circle.

round⁴ /raʊnd/ prep 1 (of movement) in a path that passes on all sides of and comes back to the starting-point: The earth moves ~ the sun. Drake sailed ~ the world. **round the clock,** all day and all night. 2 (of movement) in a path changing direction: walk/ follow her ~ a corner. **round the bend,** (sl) mad. 3 (of position) so as to be on all sides of: They were sitting ~ the table. He had a scarf ~ his neck. 4 in various or all directions: He looked ~ the room. Can I show you ~ the house, i e take you to the various rooms, etc? 5 to or at various points away from the point or person mentioned: The players stood ~ the goal. 6 approximate(ly): Come ~ about 2 o'clock. He paid ~ £20 for it.

round⁵ /raʊnd/ vt,vi 1 make or become round: stones ~ed by the action of water. 2 go round: a ~ a corner. 3 **round sth off,** bring it to a satisfactory conclusion, add a suitable finish: ~ off a sentence; ~ off one's career by being made a Minister. **round on sb,** attack him (in words or action). **round sb up,** drive, bring or collect, together: He ~ed up the tourists and took them back to the coach. **round sth up,** collect (it, them) together: The cowboy ~ed up the cattle. Hence, `round-up, a bringing together: a ~-up of criminals/cattle. **round up** (a figure/price), bring it to a whole number: The price had been ~ed up from £647.50 to £650.

round-about /ˈraʊndəbaʊt/ adj not going or coming by, or using, the shortest or most direct route: I heard the news in a ~ way. What a ~ way of doing things! □ n [C] 1 (= merry-go-round) revolving circular plat-

form with wooden horses, etc on which children ride for fun (at fairs, etc). 2 circular area at a road junction causing traffic to go round instead of directly across.

roun-ders /ˈraʊndəz/ n pl game for two teams, played with bat and ball, the players running through four bases arranged in a square.

rouse /raʊz/ vt,vi (usually formal) 1 wake up: I was ~ed by the ringing of a bell. 2 cause (a person) to be more active, interested, etc: politicians rousing the masses; be ~d to anger by insults.

rout¹ /raʊt/ n [C] utter defeat and disorderly retreat: The defeat became a ~. □ vt defeat completely: ~ the enemy.

rout² /raʊt/ vt, get a person up, out of bed, etc: We were ~ed out of our cabins before breakfast.

route /ruːt/ n [C] way taken or planned from one place to another: The climbers tried to find a new ~ to the top of the mountain. **en route** /ˈɒn ˈruːt/, on the way. □ vt plan a route for; send by a specific route: We were ~d through Dover.

rou-tine /ruːˈtiːn/ n [C,U] fixed and regular way of doing things: the ~ (= usual, ordinary) procedure; my ~ duties, those performed regularly.

rove /raʊv/ vi,vt 1 wander (the more usual word): ~ over sea and land. 2 (of the eyes, one's affections) be directed first one way, then another.

rover, (a) wanderer. (b) (old use) pirate. (c) senior boy scout.

row¹ /raʊ/ n [C] number of persons or things in a line: a ~ of books/houses/desks/ cabbages; sitting in a ~/in ~s.

row² /raʊ/ vt,vi propel (a boat) by using oars; carry or take in a boat with oars: Shall I ~ you up/down/across the river? □ n [C] journey or outing in a boat moved by oars; period of this; distance rowed: go for a ~.

rower, person who rows a boat.

`rowing-boat, one moved by the use of oars.

`rowing-club, one for persons who row.

row³ /raʊ/ n 1 [U] uproar; noisy disturbance: How can I study with all this ~ going on outside my windows? 2 [C] noisy or violent argument or quarrel: have a ~ with the neighbours. 3 [C] instance of being in trouble, scolded, etc: get into a ~ for being late at the office. □ vt,vi 1 scold. 2 quarrel noisily: He's always ~ing with his neighbours.

rowdy /ˈraʊdɪ/ adj (-ier, -iest) rough and noisy: There were ~ scenes at the elections. □ n [C] (pl -ies) rowdy person.

row-dily /-əlɪ/ adv

row-di-ness n [U].

row-lock /ˈrɒlək US: ˈraʊlɒk/ n [C] pivot for an oar or scull on the side (gunwale) of a boat (US = oarlock).

royal /ˈrɔɪəl/ adj of, like, suitable for, supported by, belonging to the family of, a king or queen: *His R~ Highness; the ~ family; the R~ Navy/Air Force.*

roy·ally /ˈrɔɪəlɪ/ *adv* in a splendid manner: *We were ~ly entertained.*

roy·al·ist /-ɪst/ *n* [C] supporter of a king or queen; supporter of the royal side in a civil war.

roy·alty /ˈrɔɪəltɪ/ *n* (*pl* -ies) **1** [U] royal persons: *The play was performed in the presence of ~.* **2** [U] position, rank, dignity, power, etc of a royal person. **3** [C] payment of money by a mining or oil company to the owner of the land, to the owner of a copyright or patent: *a ~ of 10 per cent.*

rub¹ /rʌb/ *n* [C] period of rubbing: *give the bruise a good ~ with this cream.*

rub² /rʌb/ *vt,vi* (-bb-) (For special uses with *adverbial particles* and *prepositions*, ⇨ 3 below.) **1** move (one thing) backwards and forwards on the surface of (another); make (something *clean, dry*, etc) by doing this: *He was ~bing his hands together. R~ this oil on your skin. The dog ~bed itself/its head against my legs.* **2** come into, or be in, contact with, by a sliding or up and down movement: *What is the wheel ~bing on/against?* **3** (special uses with *adverbial particles* and *prepositions*):

rub sb/oneself/a horse down, rub thoroughly, vigorously, e g with a towel, to make dry and clean: *He ~bed himself down after his bath. rub sth down,* make it smooth or level by rubbing: *R~ the walls down well before applying new paint.* Hence, `rub-down *n*: *Give the horse/the walls a good ~-down.*

rub sth in/into sth, (a) force (ointment, etc) into e g the skin, by rubbing: *R~ the ointment well in/into the skin.* (b) force (a humiliating or unpleasant fact) into a person's mind. *rub it in,* remind a person repeatedly of a fault, failure, etc: *I know I behaved foolishly but you needn't ~ it in.*

rub sth off, remove it (from a surface) by rubbing.

rub sth out, remove (marks, writing, etc) by rubbing: *~ out a word/pencil marks/ mistakes.*

rub sth up, polish by rubbing: *~ up the silver spoons. rub sb (up) the wrong way,* irritate him.

rub-ber¹ /ˈrʌbə(r)/ *n* **1** [U] tough elastic substance made from the milky liquid that flows from certain trees when the bark is cut, used for making tyres, tennis balls, etc: (as an *adjective*) `~ trees; ~ bands,* elastic bands for keeping things together. **2** [C] piece of rubber material for rubbing out pencil marks, etc.

rub-ber-ize /-aɪz/ *vt* cover or treat with rubber.

rub-ber² /ˈrʌbə(r)/ *n* [C] (in such card games as whist and bridge) **1** three successive games between the same sides or per-

sons. **2** the winning of two games out of three; the third game when each side has won one.

rub-bing /ˈrʌbɪŋ/ *n* [C] impression of something, e g an engraving, by rubbing paper laid over it with wax, etc: `brass-~s.

rub-bish /ˈrʌbɪʃ/ *n* [U] **1** waste material; that which is, or is to be, thrown away as worthless. **2** nonsense; worthless ideas: *This book is ~.* **3** (used as an exclamation) Nonsense!

rub-bishy *adj* worthless.

rubble /ˈrʌbəl/ *n* [U] bits of broken stone, rock or brickwork: *build roads with a foundation of ~.*

ruby /ˈrubɪ/ *n* [C] (*pl* -ies) red precious stone. □ *adj, n* [U] deep red (colour).

ruck /rʌk/ *n* [C] irregular fold or crease (esp in cloth). □ *vi,vt* be pulled, make, into rucks: *The sheets have ~ed up.*

ruck·sack /ˈrʌksæk/ *n* [C] canvas bag strapped on the back from the shoulders, used by people on a walking holiday, etc.

ruc·tions /ˈrʌkʃənz/ *n* (*pl*) angry words or protests: *There'll be ~ if you don't do what you're told.*

rud·der /ˈrʌdə(r)/ *n* [C] **1** flat, broad piece of wood or metal hinged vertically at the stern of a boat or ship for steering. **2** similar structure on an aircraft.

ruddy /ˈrʌdɪ/ *adj* (-ier, -iest) **1** (of the face) red, as showing good health: *~ cheeks.* **2** red or reddish: *a ~ glow in the sky.* **3** (euphemism for) bloody(3).

rude /rud/ *adj* (-r, -st) **1** (of a person, his speech, behaviour) impolite; not showing respect or consideration: *It's ~ to interrupt/to point at people. Don't be ~ to your teacher.* **2** startling; violent; rough: *get a ~ shock.* **3** roughly made; simple: *the ~ prehistoric implements.*

rude·ly *adv* in a rude manner.

rude·ness *n* [U]

ru·di·ment /ˈrudɪmənt/ *n* **1** (*pl*) first steps or stages (of an art or science): *learn the ~s of chemistry/grammar.* **2** [C] earliest form on which a later development is or might have developed: *A new-born chick has only the ~s of wings.*

ru·di·men·tary /ˈrudɪˈmentrɪ/ *adj* **1** elementary: *a ~ knowledge of mechanics.* **2** undeveloped: *~ wings.*

rue /ru/ *vt* (*old use* or *literary*) think of with sadness or regret: *You'll ~ the day when…*

rue·ful /ˈrufəl/ *adj* showing, feeling, expressing, regret.

rue·fully /ˈrufəlɪ/ *adv*

ruff /rʌf/ *n* [C] **1** ring of differently coloured or marked feathers round a bird's neck, or of hair round an animal's neck. **2** wide, stiff frill worn as a collar in the 16th century.

ruf·fian /ˈrʌfɪən/ *n* [C] violent, cruel young man.

ruffle /ˈrʌfəl/ *vt,vi* disturb the peace, calm or smoothness of; become annoyed: *The bird ~d up its feathers. Who's been ruffling your*

hair? *Anne is easily* ~*d, easily annoyed.* □ n
1 [C] frill used to ornament a garment at the
wrist or neck. **2** [U] ruffling or being
ruffled(1).

rug /rʌg/ n [C] **1** mat of thick material (usually smaller than a carpet): *a `hearth-~.* **2**
thick covering or blanket: *a `travelling-~*
(in a car, etc).

Rugby /rʌgbɪ/ n [U] kind of football using
an oval-shaped ball which may be handled:
~ *League,* form of Rugby with thirteen
players and allowing professionalism;
Rugby Union, with fifteen players and having amateur teams only.

rug·ged /rʌgɪd/ adj **1** rough; uneven;
rocky: *a ~ coast.* **2** having furrows or
wrinkles: *a ~ face.*

rug·ged·ly adv

rug·ged·ness n [U]

ruin /ruɪn/ n **1** [U] destruction; overthrow;
serious damage: *the ~ of her hopes; brought
to ~ by gambling and drink.* **2** [U] state of
being decayed, destroyed, collapsed: *The
castle has fallen into ~.* **go to rack and
ruin,** ⇨ rack³. **3** [C] something which has
decayed, been destroyed, etc: *The building
is in ~s.* **4** (*sing* only) cause of ruin: *Gambling was his ~.* □ vt cause the ruin of: *The
storm ~ed the crops.*

ruin·ation /ruɪ`neɪʃən/ n [U] being ruined;
bringing to ruin: *These debts will be the
~ation of him.*

ruin·ous /-əs/ adj causing ruin: ~*ous
expenditure.*

ruin·ous·ly adv. ~*ously expensive.*

rule /rul/ n **1** [C] law or custom which guides
or controls behaviour or action: *obey the ~s
of the game. It's against the ~s to handle
the ball in soccer.* **by/according to rule,**
according to regulations: *He does everything
by ~,* never uses his own judgement. **work
to rule,** pay exaggerated attention (deliberately) to regulations and so slow down
output: *Instead of coming out on strike, the
men decided to work to ~.* **rule of thumb,**
⇨ thumb. **2** [C] habit: *He makes it a ~ to
do an hour's work in the garden every day.*
as a rule, usually; more often than not. **3**
[U] government; authority: *countries that
were once under French ~.* **4** [C] strip of
wood, metal, etc, used to measure: *a `foot-
~; a `slide-~.* □ vi,vt **1** govern; have
authority (over): *King Charles I ~d
(England) for eleven years without a parliament. Is it true that Mrs Jones ~s her husband?* **2** be guided or influenced by; have
power or influence over: *Don't be ~d by
your passions/by hatred.* (*Note:* usually
passive.) **3** give as a decision: *The chairman
~d the motion out of order/that the motion
was out of order.* **rule sth out,** declare that
it cannot be considered, that it is out of the
question: *That's a possibility that can't be
~d out,* It is something we must consider. **4**
make (a line or lines) on paper (with a ruler):

~*d notepaper.* **rule sth off,** separate it, end
it, by ruling a line.

ruler /rulə(r)/ n [C] **1** person who rules or
governs. **2** straight length of wood, plastic,
metal, etc used in drawing straight lines or
for measuring.

rul·ing /rulɪŋ/ adj that rules: *his ~ passion,*
that which governs his actions. □ n [C] (esp)
decision made by a person in authority, e g a
judge.

rum¹ /rʌm/ n [C,U] (portion of) alcoholic
drink made from sugar-cane juice.

rum² /rʌm/ adj (-mer, -mest) (*dated informal*) odd: *What a ~ person he is!*

rumble /rʌmbl/ vi,vt **1** make, move with,
a deep, heavy, continuous sound: *thunder/
gun-fire rumbling in the distance.* **2** utter,
say, in a deep voice: ~ *out a few comments.*
□ n [U] deep, heavy, continuous sound: *the
~ of juggernauts through the village.*

ru·mi·nant /ruːmɪnənt/ n [C], adj (animal)
which chews the cud, e g cows, deer.

ru·mi·nate /ruːmɪneɪt/ vi **1** meditate: ~
over/about/on recent events. **2** (of animals)
chew the cud.

ru·mi·na·tive /ruːmɪnətɪv/ adj inclined to
meditate.

ru·mi·na·tion /ruːmɪ`neɪʃən/ n [U]

rum·mage /rʌmɪdʒ/ vi,vt **1** turn things
over, move things about, while looking for
something: ~ (*about*) *in a desk drawer.* **2**
search thoroughly: ~ *a ship,* e g by Customs
officers. □ n [U] **1** search (esp of a ship by
Customs officers). **2** things found by rum-
maging.

ru·mour (*US* = **ru·mor**) /ruːmə(r)/ n **1** [U]
general talk, gossip: *R~ has it that she will
be promoted.* **2** [C] (statement, report, story)
which cannot be verified and is of doubtful
accuracy: *There is a ~ that there will be a
General Election in the autumn.* □ vt report
by way of rumour: *He is ~ed to have
escaped to Dublin.* (*Note:* usually *passive.*)

rump /rʌmp/ n [C] **1** animal's buttocks. **2**
contemptible remnant of a parliament or
similar body.

'rump-'steak, beefsteak cut from near the
rump.

rumple /rʌmpəl/ vt crease; crumple; make
rough: *Don't sit on my lap or you'll ~ my
dress.*

rum·pus /rʌmpəs/ n (*sing* only) (*informal*)
disturbance; noise: *What's all this ~ about?*
kick up/make a rumpus, cause a rumpus.

run¹ /rʌn/ n [C] **1** act of running on foot: *go
for a short ~ across the fields.* **at a run,**
running: *He started off at a ~ but soon tired
and began to walk.* **on the run,** (**a**) running
away: *He's on the ~ from the police.* (**b**)
continuously active and moving about: *I've
been on the ~ all day.* **get/give sb a
(good) run for his money,** provide him
with strong competition: *We must give him a
good ~ for his money.* **2** [C] outing or journey in a car, train, etc: *Can we have a trial*

~ in the new car? 3 [C] distance travelled by a ship in a specified time: make bets on the day's ~, on the distance travelled in 24 hours. 4 route taken by vehicles, ships, etc: The bus was taken off its usual ~. 5 series of performances: The play had a long ~/a ~ of six months. 6 period; succession: a ~ of bad luck, a series of misfortunes. **a run on a bank,** a demand by many customers together for immediate repayment. **In the `long run,** in the end: It pays in the long ~ to buy goods of high quality. 7 (enclosed) space for domestic animals, fowls, etc: a `chicken-~. **8** (cricket and baseball) unit of scoring, made by running over a certain course. 9 common, average or ordinary type or class: the common ~ of mankind, ordinary, average people; an hotel out of the common run, different from, and better than, the kind one usually finds. 10 (informal) permission to make free use (of). **get/give sb the run of sth,** the permission to use it: I have the ~ of his library. 11 way in which things tend to move; general direction or trend: The ~ of events is rather puzzling. 12 (music) series of notes sung or played quickly and in the order of the scale. 13 shoal of fish in motion: a ~ of salmon, e g on their way upstream. 14 long hole in cloth where a thread has broken: a ~ in a sock/stocking. ⊃²(26).

'run-of-the-`mill, ordinary; average.

run² /rʌn/ vi, vt (pt ran /ræn/, pp ~; -nn-) (For special uses with adverbial particles and prepositions, ⊃ 27 below; ⊃ also running.) 1 (of men and animals) move with quick steps, faster than when walking: ~ three miles; ~ fast; ~ upstairs. We ran to help him. Don't ~ across the road until you're sure it's safe. 2 escape or avoid by going away; As soon as we appeared the boys ran off. 3 practice running for exercise or as a sport; compete in races on foot: Is he ~ning in the 100 metres? Is your horse likely to ~ in the Derby? **run a race,** take part in one. `also ran, (as a noun) person or animal unsuccessful in a race or other form of competition. 4 **run for,** compete for (an elected office): ~ for President. 5 present or nominate (for an office): How many candidates is the Liberal Party ~ning in the General Election? 6 (cause to) reach a certain condition or place as the result of running: He ran second in the race. **run oneself/sb into the ground,** exhaust oneself/a person by hard work or exercise. 7 make one's way quickly to the end of, or through or over (something). **run its course,** develop in the usual or normal way: The disease ran its course. 8 expose oneself to; be open to. **run the chance/danger of sth:** You ~ the chance of being suspected of theft. **run risks/a risk/the risk of sth,** ⊃ risk. 9 chase; compete with: It was a close run thing, (of competition, etc) The result was very close. 10 (of ships, etc) sail or

steer; (of fish) swim: a ship ran aground/on the rocks/ashore. The salmon are ~ning, swimming upstream from the sea. 11 go forward with a sliding, smooth or continuous motion: Sledges ~ well over frozen snow. The train ran past the signal. 12 be in action; work freely; be in working order: Don't leave the engine of your car ~ning. 13 (of buses, ferry-boats, etc) journey to and fro: The buses ~ every ten minutes. 14 organize; manage; cause to be in operation: ~ a business/a theatre. I can't afford to ~ a car (= own and use one) on my small salary. Who ~s his house for him now that his wife has divorced him? 15 convey; transport: I'll ~ you back home, drive you there in my car. **run arms,** convey them into a country unlawfully. **run errands/ messages (for sb),** make journeys to do things, carry messages, etc. **run liquor,** smuggle it into a country. 16 cause to move quickly (in a certain direction or into a certain place): ~ one's fingers/a comb through one's hair; ~ one's eyes over a page. 17 (of thoughts, feelings, eyes, exciting news, etc) pass or move briefly or quickly: The thought kept ~ning through my head. The pain ran up my arm. A shiver ran down his spine. The news ran like wildfire. A whisper ran through the crowd. 18 cause (something) to penetrate (intentionally or by accident) or come into contact with: ~ a splinter into one's finger. The drunken driver ran his car into a tree. 19 (of liquids, grain, sand, etc) flow, drip; The tears ran down my cheeks. Who has left the tap/water ~ning? His legs were covered with ~ning sores. Your nose is ~ning. 20 (of colours, dyes) spread: Will the colours ~ if the dress is washed? 21 cause (a liquid, molten metal, etc) to flow: ~ some hot water into the bowl. 22 become; pass into (a specified condition): Supplies are ~ning short/low. I have ~ short of money. Feelings/Passions ran high, became stormy or violent. My blood ran cold, I was filled with horror. **run riot, (a)** behave in a wild and lawless way. **(b)** (of plants, etc) grow unchecked. **run wild,** be without control, discipline, etc: The garden is ~ning wild. She lets her children ~ wild. **run a temperature,** become feverish. 23 extend; have a certain course or order; be continued or continuous; shelves ~ning round the walls; a scar that ~s across his left cheek; a road that ~s across the fields. It happened several days ~ning, several days in succession. The play ran (for) six months, was kept on the stage, was performed, during this period of time. The lease of my house has only a year to ~. ⊃ running. 24 have a tendency or common characteristic; have as an average price or level: Yellow hair ~s in the family. Inflation is ~ning high. 25 be told or written: So the story ran, that is what was told or said. 26 (of woven or knitted material) become unwoven or unravelled; drop stitches through several rows: *Nylon tights sometimes* ~.

27 (special uses with *adverbial particles* and *prepositions*):

run across sb/sth, meet or find by chance; *I ran across her in Paris last week.*

run after sb/sth, (a) try to catch: *The dog was ~ning after a rabbit.* (b) go after in order to get the attention of: *She ~s after every man in the village.*

run against sb, compete with him in a race or for an elected office.

run along, (*informal*) go away: *Now, children*, ~ *along!*

run away, leave: *The boy ran away to sea*, left home and became a sailor. **run away with sb**, (a) elope with: *The butler ran away with the duke's daughter.* (b) go at a speed too high for control: *Don't let your car* ~ *away with you.* (c) destroy the self-control of: *Don't let your temper* ~ *away with you.* **run away with sth**, (a) steal: *The maid ran away with the duchess's jewels.* (b) get a clear win over: *The girl from Peru ran away with the first set*, e g in a tennis tournament. **run away with the idea/notion that**, assume (too quickly that something is the case): *Don't* ~ *away with the idea that I can lend you money every time you need help.*

run sth back, rewind (film, tape, etc).

run down, (a) (of a clock or other mechanism worked by weights) stop because it needs winding up. (b) (of a battery) become weak or exhausted: *The battery is/has* ~ *down.* **run down**, (of a person, his health) exhausted or weak from overwork, mental strain, etc. **run sb/sth down**, knock down or collide with: *The cyclist was* ~ *down by a big lorry.* **run sb down**, (a) say unkind things about: *That man doesn't like me; he's always* ~*ning me down.* (b) chase and overtake: ~ *down an escaped prisoner.* **run sth down**, allow to become less active or occupied: ~ *down a factory*, do less work and employ fewer workers. Hence, `**run-down**, reduction: *the* ~*-down of the coal industry.*

run for sth, ⇨ 4 above. **run for it**, avoid something by running: *It's raining; lets* ~ *for it*, i e run for shelter.

run sb in, (*informal*) (of the police) arrest and take to a police station. **run sth in**, bring (esp the engine of a car) into good condition by running it carefully for a time or distance: *He's still* ~*ning in his new car and doesn't do more than thirty miles an hour.*

run into sb, meet unexpectedly: ~ *into an old friend in the street.* **run into sth**, (a) collide with: *The bus got out of control and ran into a wall.* (b) reach (a condition): ~ *into debt/danger/difficulties.* (c) reach (a level or figure): *His income* ~*s into five figures*, is now ten thousand (pounds, dollars, etc) or more. **run sth into sth**, cause

(sth) to be in collision: ~ *one's car into a wall.*

run off with sb/sth, go away with; steal and take away: *His daughter has* ~ *off with a married man/with all the funds.* **run sth off**, (a) cause to flow away: ~ *off the water from a tank*, empty the tank. (b) write or recite fluently, e g a list of names: ~ *off an article for the local (news)paper.* (c) print; produce: ~ *off a hundred copies on the duplicating machine.* (d) decide (a race) after a tie, or trial heats: *When will the race be* ~ *off?* Hence, `**run-off**, deciding race, etc after a dead heat or tie.

run on, (a) talk continuously: *He will* ~ *on for an hour if you don't stop him.* (b) elapse: *Time ran on.* (c) (of a disease) continue its course. **run (sth) on**, (of written letters of the alphabet) join, be joined, together: *When children are learning to write, they should* ~ *the letters on.* **run on sth**, be concerned with: *Our talk ran on recent events in India.*

run out, (a) go out: *The tide is* ~*ning out.* (b) (of a period of time) come to an end: *When does the lease of the house* ~ *out?* (c) (of stocks, supplies) come to an end, be exhausted; (of persons) become short of (supplies, etc): *Our provisions are* ~*ning out. We're* ~*ning out of milk. Her patience is* ~*ning out.* (d) jut out; project: *a pier* ~*ning out into the sea.* **run (sth) out**, (of rope) pass out: *The rope ran out smoothly.* **be run out**, (*cricket*) (of a batsman) have his innings ended because, while trying to make a run, he fails to reach the crease before the ball hits the bails or stump(s). **run `out on sb**, (*sl*) abandon, desert: *Poor Jane! Her husband has* ~ *out on her.*

run over, (a) (of a vessel or its contents) overflow. (b) pay a short or quick visit to: ~ *over to a neighbour's house.* **run over sth**, (a) review: *Let's* ~ *over our parts again*, e g when learning and rehearsing parts in a play. (b) read through quickly: *He ran over his notes before starting his lecture.* **run over sb/run sb over**, (of a vehicle) (knock down and) pass over (a person, etc lying on the ground): *He was* ~ *over and had to be taken to hospital.*

run round, = run over(b).

run through sth, (a) use up (a fortune, etc) esp by foolish spending: *He soon ran through the money he had inherited.* (b) examine quickly; deal with in rapid succession: ~ *through one's post during breakfast.* **run to sth**, (a) reach (an amount, number, etc): *That will run to $50.* (b) have money for; (of money) be enough for: *We can't/ Our funds won't* ~ *to a holiday abroad this year.* (c) extend to: *His new novel has already* ~ *to three impressions.*

run sth up, (a) raise; hoist: ~ *up a flag on the mast.* (b) erect, make, quickly: ~ *up a dress.* (c) add up (a column of figures). (d) cause to grow quickly in amount: ~ *up a big* bill at a hotel. **run up against sth,** meet by chance or unexpectedly: *run up against difficulties.* **run up to,** amount, extend to (a figure): *Prices ran up to £5 a ton.*

rung¹ /rʌŋ/ *n* [C] **1** crosspiece forming a step in a ladder. **2** (*fig*) particular level in society, one's employment, etc: *start on the lowest/reach the highest* ~ (*of the ladder*).

rung² /rʌŋ/ *pp* of ring².

run·ner /ˈrʌnə(r)/ *n* [C] **1** person, animal, etc that runs: *How many* ~*s were there in the Derby?* **2** messenger, scout, etc. **3** (as a *suffix*) smuggler: `gun-~s; `rum-~s. **4** part on which something slides or moves along: *the* ~*s of a sledge.* **5** long piece of cloth; long piece of carpet, e g for stairs. **6** kinds of twining bean-plant, esp `scarlet ~s; (as an *adjective*) ~ *beans.*

'**runner-`up,** person, animal, taking second place in a race.

run·ning /ˈrʌnɪŋ/ *n* [U] act of a person or animal that runs, esp in racing. **make the running,** (literally and *fig*) set the pace. **take up the running,** take the lead. **in/out of the running,** (of competitors) having some/no chance of winning. □ *adj* **1** done, made, carried on, while or immediately after running: *a* ~ *kick/jump/fight.* **2** continuous; uninterrupted: *a* ~ *fire of questions,* coming in a continuous stream. **3** in succession: *win three times* ~. **4** (of water) flowing; coming from a mains supply: *All bedrooms in this hotel have hot and cold* ~ *water.* **5** (of sores, etc) with liquid or pus coming out.

'**running `commentary,** commentary as the event occurs.

`**running costs,** costs incurred in production (not preparation, planning).

runny /ˈrʌnɪ/ *adj* (-ier, -iest) (*informal*) semi-liquid; tending to run(19) or flow: *a* ~ *nose.*

run·way /ˈrʌnweɪ/ *n* [C] **1** specially prepared surface along which aircraft take off and land. **2** way made for rolling felled trees and logs down a hill-side.

rup·ture /ˈrʌptʃə(r)/ *n* **1** [U] breaking apart or bursting; [C] instance of this. **2** [C,U] (instance of) ending of friendly relations. **3** [C] hernia. □ *vt,vi* break or burst, e g a blood-vessel or membrane; end (a connection, etc).

ru·ral /ˈrʊərəl/ *adj* in, of, characteristic of, suitable for, the countryside: ~ *scenery* ⇨ urban.

ruse /ruːz/ *n* [C] deceitful way of doing something; trick.

rush¹ /rʌʃ/ *n* **1** [U] rapid movement toward; sudden advance; [C] instance of this: *I don't like the* ~ *of city life. Why all this* ~, *this hurry and excitement?* **2** [C] sudden demand: *the Christmas* ~, the period before Christmas when crowds of people go shopping.

the `rush-hour, when crowds of people are travelling to or from work in a large town: (as an *adjective*) *We were caught in the* ~*-hour traffic.*

rush² /rʌʃ/ *n* [C] (tall stem of one of numerous varieties of) marsh plant with slender leafless stems, often dried and used for weaving into mats, baskets, etc.

rush³ /rʌʃ/ *vi,vt* **1** (cause to) go or come, do something, with violence or speed: *The children* ~*ed out of the school gates. They* ~*ed more soldiers to the front.* **rush to conclusions,** form them (too) hastily. **rush sth through,** do it at high speed: *The new Bill was* ~*ed through Parliament.* **2** get through, over, into, etc by pressing eagerly or violently forward: ~ *the gates of the football ground.* **3** force into hasty action: *I must think things over, so don't* ~ *me.* **rush sb off his feet,** exhaust him. **4** (*sl*) charge an exorbitant price: *How much did they* ~ *you for this?*

rusk /rʌsk/ *n* [C] piece of bread or biscuit baked hard and crisp.

rus·set /ˈrʌsɪt/ *n* **1** [U] yellowish or reddish brown. **2** [C] kind of apple. □ *adj* reddish brown.

rust /rʌst/ *n* [U] **1** reddish-brown coating formed on iron by the action of water and air; similar coating on other metals. **2** (plant-disease with rust-coloured spots caused by) kinds of fungus. □ *vt,vi* (cause to) become covered with rust.

rusti·ness *n* [U]

rusty *adj* (-ier, -iest) (a) covered with rust: ~*y needles.* (b) in need of being polished or revised: *My German is rather* ~*y,* needs to be practised. (c) (of persons) behind the times.

rus·tic /ˈrʌstɪk/ *adj* **1** (in a good sense) characteristic of country people: ~ *simplicity.* **2** rough; unrefined: ~ *speech/manners.* **3** of rough workmanship: *a* ~ *seat,* made of rough wood. □ *n* [C] countryman; peasant.

rus·ti·cate /ˈrʌstɪkeɪt/ *vi,vt* **1** lead a rural life. **2** (*GB*) send (a student) temporarily away from the university as a punishment.

rustle /ˈrʌsəl/ *vi,vt* **1** make a gentle, light sound (like dry leaves blown by the wind); move along making such a sound: *Did you hear something rustling in the hedge?* **2** cause to make this sound: *I wish people wouldn't* ~ *their programmes while the band is playing.* **3** get together, provide: ~ *up some food for an unexpected guest.* □ *n* [U] gentle light sound as of dry leaves blown by the wind: *the* ~ *of paper.*

rust·ling /ˈrʌslɪŋ/, sound made by something that rustles: *the rustling of dry leaves.*

rut /rʌt/ *n* [C] **1** line or track made by wheel(s) in soft ground. **2** (*fig*) way of doing something, behaving, living, etc that has become established. **be in/get into a rut,** a fixed (and boring) way of living so that it becomes difficult to change. □ *vt* (-tt-) (usually in *pp*) mark with ruts: *a deeply* ~*ted road.*

ruth·less /ˈruːθləs/ *adj* cruel; without pity;

showing no mercy.
ruth·less·ly adv
ruth·less·ness n [U]
rye /raɪ/ n [U] **1** (plant with) grain used for making flour, and as a food for cattle. **2** kind of whisky made from rye.

Ss

S, s /es/ (pl **S's, s's** /ˈesɪz/) the nineteenth letter of the English alphabet.
Sab·bath /ˈsæbəθ/ n day of rest, Saturday for Jews, Sunday for Christians: break/keep the ~.
sab·bati·cal /səˈbætɪkəl/ adj of or like the Sabbath: After this uproar there came a ~ calm.
sabbatical year, year of freedom from routine duties given to some university teachers to enable them to travel or study.
sa·ber /ˈseɪbə(r)/ ⇨ sabre.
sable /ˈseɪbəl/ n [C] small animal valued for its beautiful dark fur; [U] fur of this animal.
sa·bot /ˈsæbəʊ US: sæˈbəʊ/ n [C] shoe hollowed out of a single piece of wood.
sab·otage /ˈsæbətɑːʒ/ n [U] the wilful damaging of machinery, materials, etc or the hindering of an opponent's activity, during an industrial or political dispute, or during war. □ vt perform an act of sabotage against.
sab·oteur /ˈsæbəˈtɜː(r)/ n [C] person who commits sabotage.
sabre (US = **sa·ber**) /ˈseɪbə(r)/ n [C] heavy cavalry sword with a curved blade.
`sabre-toothed adj having teeth like sabres: a ~-toothed tiger.
sac /sæk/ n [C] skin enclosing a cavity in an animal or plant.
sac·er·do·tal /ˈsæsəˈdəʊtəl/ adj connected with priests.
sachet /ˈsæʃeɪ US: sæˈʃeɪ/ n [C] **1** small perfumed bag. **2** small plastic, etc bag for shampoo, etc.
sack¹ /sæk/ n [C] (quantity held by a) large bag of strong material (e g coarse flax, rushes, stiffened paper) for storing and carrying heavy goods: two ~s of potatoes.
`sack-cloth, coarse material made of flax or hemp.
sack·ing, = sackcloth.
sack² /sæk/ n (sing with the) (informal) dismissal from employment: He got the ~ for petty thieving. □ vt dismiss from employment.
sack³ /sæk/ vt (of a victorious army) steal from, destroy (a captured city, etc). □ n (usually sing with the) sacking of a captured town, etc: The citizens lost everything they had during the ~ of the town.
sack⁴ /sæk/ n [U] (sl) bed. **hit the sack**, go

to bed.
sac·ra·ment /ˈsækrəmənt/ n [C] solemn religious ceremony in the Christian Church, e g Baptism, Confirmation, Matrimony, believed to be accompanied by great spiritual benefits.
sac·ra·men·tal /ˈsækrəˈmentəl/ adj
sacred /ˈseɪkrəd/ adj **1** of God; connected with religion: a ~ building, e g a church, mosque, synagogue or temple. **2** solemn: hold a promise ~. **3** (to be) treated with great respect or reverence: In India the cow is a ~ animal.
sacred·ly adv
sacred·ness m [U]
sac·ri·fice /ˈsækrɪfaɪs/ n **1** [U] the offering of something precious to a god; [C] instance of this; [C] the thing offered: the ~ of an ox to Jupiter; kill a sheep as a ~. **2** [C,U] the giving up of something of great value to oneself for a special purpose, or to benefit another person; [C] something given up in this way: Parents often make ~s (e g go without things) for their children. □ vt,vi **1** make a sacrifice(1): ~ a lamb to the gods. **2** give up as a sacrifice(2): He ~d his life to save the drowning child.
sac·ri·fi·cial /ˈsækrɪˈfɪʃəl/ adj of or like a sacrifice.
sac·ri·lege /ˈsækrɪlɪdʒ/ n [U] disrespectful treatment of, injury to, what should be sacred: It would be a ~ to steal a crucifix from a church altar.
sac·ri·legious /ˈsækrɪˈlɪdʒəs/ adj
sac·ro·sanct /ˈsækrəʊsæŋkt/ adj **1** (to be) protected from all harm, because sacred or holy. **2** (fig) not to be violated: He regards his privileges as ~.
sad /sæd/ adj (-der, -dest) **1** unhappy; causing unhappy feelings: It was a ~ day for Mary when her mother died. Why is he looking so ~? **2** (of colours) dull.
sad·ly adv
sad·ness n [U]
sad·den /ˈsædən/ vt,vi make or become sad.
saddle /ˈsædəl/ n [C] **1** leather seat for a rider on a horse, donkey or bicycle; part of a horse's back on which the seat is placed: a ~ of lamb. **in the saddle**, (a) on horseback. (b) (fig) in a position of control or power. **2** line or ridge of high land rising at each end to a high point. □ vt **1** put a saddle on (a horse). **2 saddle sb with sth**, put a heavy responsibility or burden on: be ~d with a wife and ten children.
`saddle-bag, (a) one of pair over the back of a horse or donkey. (b) bag at the back of a bicycle saddle.
`saddle-sore, (of a rider) having sores because of horse-riding.
sad·dler /ˈsædlə(r)/, maker of saddles and leather goods for horses.
sa·dism /ˈseɪdɪzm/ n [C] **1** kind of sexual perversion marked by getting pleasure from

cruelty to other persons of either sex. **2** (loosely) (delight in) excessive cruelty.

sa·dist /-ɪst/, person guilty of sadism.

sa·dis·tic /səˈdɪstɪk/ adj of sadism.

sa·fari /səˈfɑːrɪ/ n [C,U] **1** hunting expedition, overland journey, esp in E and Central Africa. **2** organized tour (for people on holiday) to game reserves, etc. **on safari,** hunting or visiting game.

safe[1] /seɪf/ adj (-r, -st) **1** free from, protected from, danger: ∼ from attack. **2** unhurt and undamaged: a ∼ journey. **safe and sound,** secure and unharmed: return ∼ and sound from a dangerous expedition. **3** not causing or likely to cause harm or danger: Is 120 kilometres an hour ∼ on this road? Are these toys ∼ for small children? **4** (of a place, etc) giving security: Keep it in a ∼ place. **5** (in Parliament) that can be depended on: Is this a ∼ seat for the Tories? Is it certain that the Tory candidate will be elected? **6** cautious; not taking risks: They appointed a ∼ man as Headmaster. **it is safe to say...,** it can be said without risk of being proved wrong, etc. **be on the `safe side,** take more precautions than may be necessary: He took his umbrella to be on the ∼ side. **better safe than sorry,** it is better to be cautious than to take risks.

'safe-`conduct, (document giving the) right to visit or pass through a district without the risk of being arrested or harmed (esp in time of war).

`safe-deposit, building containing strongrooms and safes which persons may rent separately for storing valuables.

`safe·guard n [C] condition, circumstance, etc that tends to prevent harm, give protection: a ∼guard against death. □ vt protect, guard.

'safe-`keeping, care; custody: Leave your jewels in the bank for ∼-keeping while you are on holiday.

`safe period, (in the menstrual cycle) when conception is least likely.

safe seat, ⇨ 5 above.

safe·ly adv

safe[2] /seɪf/ n [C] **1** fireproof and burglarproof box in which money and other valuables are kept. **2** cool cupboard used to protect food from flies, etc: a `meat-∼.

safety /ˈseɪftɪ/ n [U] being safe; freedom from danger: do nothing that might endanger the ∼ of other people. **play for safety,** avoid taking risks. ⇨ road safety.

`safety belt, = seat belt.

`safety catch/ lock, device that gives safety against a possible danger (e g to prevent a gun from being fired by accident or a door being opened without the proper key).

`safety curtain, fireproof screen that can be lowered between the stage and auditorium of a theatre.

'safety `first, motto used to warn that safety is important.

`safety glass, glass that does not splinter.

`safety match, one that lights only when rubbed on the side of a match-box.

`safety pin, one with a guard for the point which is bent back to the head.

`safety razor, razor with a guard to prevent the blade from cutting the skin.

`safety valve, (a) valve which releases pressure (in a steam boiler, etc) when it becomes too great. **(b)** (fig) way of releasing feelings of anger, excitement, etc harmlessly.

`safety net, used to catch an acrobat, etc if he falls.

saf·fron /ˈsæfrən/ n [U], adj orange colouring obtained from flowers of the autumn crocus, used as a dye and for flavouring.

sag /sæg/ vi (-gg-) sink or curve down under weight or pressure: a ∼ging roof. Sales are ∼ging, falling (as shown on a graph). □ n [C] (degree of) sagging: There is a bad ∼ in the seat of this chair.

saga /ˈsɑːgə/ n [C] (pl ∼s) **1** old story of heroic deeds, esp of Icelandic or Norwegian heroes. **2** long narrative, e g a number of connected books (esp novels) about a family, social group, etc: the Forsyte S∼. **3** (modern use) long account (of troubles, bad experiences, etc): listen to boring ∼s about her holiday.

sa·ga·cious /səˈgeɪʃəs/ adj (formal) showing good judgement, common sense or (of animals) intelligence.

sa·ga·cious·ly adv

sa·gac·ity /səˈgæsɪtɪ/ n [U] (formal) wisdom of a practical kind.

sage[1] /seɪdʒ/ n [C] wise man; man who is believed to be wise. □ adj wise; having the wisdom of experience.

sage[2] /seɪdʒ/ n [U] herb with dull greyishgreen leaves, used to flavour food: ∼ and onions, stuffing used for a goose, duck, etc.

'sage-`green n [U], adj colour of sage leaves.

Sag·it·ta·rius /ˈsædʒɪˈteərɪəs/ n the Archer, ninth sign of the zodiac.

sago /ˈseɪgəʊ/ n [U] starchy food, in the form of hard, white grains, used to make a milk pudding.

said /sed/ pt,pp of say.

sail[1] /seɪl/ n **1** [C,U] sheet of canvas spread to catch the wind and move a boat or ship forward: hoist/lower the ∼s. **under sail,** (moving) with sails spread. **set sail (from/ to/for),** begin a voyage. **2** [C] set of boards attached to the arm of a windmill to catch the wind. **3** (pl unchanged) ship: a fleet of twenty ∼. **4** [C] (rarely pl) voyage or excursion on water for pleasure: go for a ∼; voyage of a specified duration: How many days' ∼ is it from Hull to Oslo?

`sail-plane, aircraft that uses air currents, etc instead of engines.

sail[2] /seɪl/ vi,vt **1** move forward across the sea, a lake, etc by using sails or engine-power, move forward (in sport) across ice or a sandy beach, by means of a sail or sails: ∼ up/along the coast; ∼ into harbour; go ∼ing. **2** (of a ship or persons on board) begin a voyage; travel on water by use of sails or engines: When does the ship ∼? He has ∼ed for New York. **3** travel across or on: ∼ the sea/the Pacific. **4** (be able to) control (a boat): He ∼s his own yacht. Do you ∼? **5** move smoothly like a ship with sails: The moon/clouds ∼ed across the sky.

`sail·ing-boat/-ship/-vessel, boat, etc moved by sails.

sailor /ˈseɪlə(r)/ n [C] seaman; member of a ship's crew.

saint /seɪnt GB weak form immediately before names: sənt/ n [C] **1** holy person. **2** person who, having died, is among the blessed in Heaven. **3** (abbr **St**) person who has been declared by the Church to have won by holy living on earth a place in Heaven and veneration on earth. **4** unselfish or patient person: What a ∼ my wife is!

St Bernard /ˈbɜːnəd US: bərˈnɑːrd/, large, powerful breed of dog, originally bred by monks in the Swiss Alps, trained to rescue travellers lost in snowstorms.

St `Andrew's Day, 30th November (patron saint of Scotland).

St `David's Day, 1st March (patron saint of Wales).

St `George's Day, 23rd April (patron saint of England).

St `Patrick's Day, 17th March (patron saint of Ireland).

St `Valentine's Day, ⇨ Valentine.

saint·ly adj (also **saint-like**) very holy or good; like, of, a saint: a ∼ly expression on his face.

sake /seɪk/ n **for the sake of sb/sth; for `my/`your/the `country's, etc sake**, for the welfare or benefit of; because of an interest in or desire for: We must be patient for the ∼ of peace. He argues for the ∼ of arguing, only because he likes arguing.

sa-laam /səˈlɑːm/ n **1** Muslim greeting (from an Arabic word) meaning 'Peace'. **2** [C] low bow. □ vi make a low bow.

sal·able, sale-able /ˈseɪləbəl/ adj fit for sale; likely to find buyers.

sa-la-cious /səˈleɪʃəs/ adj (formal) (of speech, books, pictures, etc) obscene; indecent.

sa-la-cious-ly adv

sa-la-cious-ness n [U]

salad /ˈsæləd/ n **1** [C,U] (cold dish of) sliced (and usually uncooked) vegetables such as lettuce, cucumber, tomatoes, seasoned with oil, vinegar, etc eaten with, or including, cheese, cold meat, etc: a chicken ∼; cold beef and ∼. ⇨ fruit salad. **2** lettuce or other green vegetables for eating raw.

`salad-days n pl period of inexperienced youth.

`salad-dressing, mixture of oil, vinegar, cream, etc used with salad.

`salad-oil, superior quality of olive oil.

sa-lami /səˈlɑːmɪ/ n [U] sausage salted and flavoured with garlic.

sal·ary /ˈsælərɪ/ n [C] (pl -ies) (weekly, monthly) payment for regular employment on a yearly basis: a ∼ of £6000 per annum. ⇨ wage.

sal·ar·ied adj receiving a salary; (of employment) paid for by means of a salary; the salaried staff; salaried posts.

sale /seɪl/ n **1** [U] exchange of goods or property for money; act of selling: The ∼ of his old home made him sad. **for sale**, intended to be sold: Is the house for ∼? **on sale**, (of goods in shops, etc) offered for purchase. **put sth up for sale**, announce that it may be bought. **2** [C] instance of selling something: S∼s are up/down this month, more/fewer goods have been sold. **3** [C] the offering of goods at low prices for a period (to get rid of old stock, etc): the winter/summer ∼s; `∼ price, low price at a sale. **4** occasion when goods, property, etc are put up for sale by auction: for ∼ to the highest bidder; get bargains at ∼s.

`sale-room, room where goods, etc are sold by public auction.

`sales department, that part of a business company that is concerned with selling goods (contrasted with manufacture, dispatch, etc).

`sales-man, `sales-woman, person selling goods in a shop or (on behalf of wholesalers) to shopkeepers.

`sales-man-ship /-mənʃɪp/, skill in selling goods.

`sales talk, talk (to a prospective customer) to sell goods.

`sales tax, tax payable on the sum received for articles sold by retail.

sa-li-ent /ˈseɪlɪənt/ adj (formal) **1** most significant; easily noticed: the ∼ points of a speech. **2** (of an angle) pointing outwards.

sa-line /ˈseɪlaɪn US: -liːn/ adj containing salt; salty: a ∼ solution, e g as used for gargling. □ n [U] solution of salt and water.

sal·iva /səˈlaɪvə/ n [U] the natural liquid present in the mouth.

sali-vary /ˈsælɪvərɪ US: -verɪ/ adj of or producing saliva: the `∼ry glands.

sali-vate /ˈsælɪveɪt/ vi secrete (too much) saliva.

sal·low /ˈsæləʊ/ adj (-er, -est) (of the human skin or complexion) of an unhealthy yellow colour. □ vt,vi make or become sallow: a face ∼ed by years of living in the tropics.

sally /ˈsælɪ/ n [C] (pl -ies) **1** sudden breaking out by soldiers who are surrounded by the enemy. **2** lively, witty remark. □ vi **1** make a sally(1). **2** **sally forth**, go out on a journey or for a walk.

salmon /ˈsæmən/ n [C] (pl unchanged) large fish, valued for food and the sport of catching it with rod and line; [U] its flesh as food; the colour of its flesh, orange-pink.

salon /ˈsælɒn/ n [C] **1** assembly, as a regular event, of notable persons at the house of a lady of fashion (esp in Paris); reception room used for this purpose. **2** business offering services connected with fashion, etc: *a* `beauty-~`.

sa·loon /səˈluːn/ n [C] **1** room for social use in a ship, hotel, etc: *the ship's* `dining-~`. **2** (*US*) = **pub**. **3** (*GB*) (also ~*-car*) motor-car with wholly enclosed seating space for 4 or 5 passengers.

sa`loon bar, where drinks are served in a public house or inn.

salt /sɔːlt/ n **1** [U] white substance obtained from mines, present in sea-water and obtained from it by evaporation, used to flavour and preserve food: `table ~`, powdered for convenient use at table. **rub salt in the wound,** (*fig*) make humiliation, suffering, worse. **take (a statement, etc) with a grain/pinch of salt,** feel some doubt whether it is altogether true. **the salt of the earth,** person(s) with very high qualities. **2** [C] (*chem*) chemical compound of a metal and an acid. **3** [C] experienced sailor. **4** (*pl*) medicine used to empty the bowels: *take a dose of* (*Epsom*) ~*s*. **5** (*fig*) something that gives flavour or appeal: *Adventure is the ~ of life to some men.* □ *vt* put salt on or in (food) to season it or preserve it: ~*ed meat.* □ *adj* **1** (opp of *fresh*) containing, tasting of, preserved with, salt: ~ *water.* **2** (of land) containing salt: ~ *marshes.*

`salt-cellar, small container for salt at table.

`salt-`water, of the sea: ~*-water fish.*

salti·ness n [U]

salty adj (-ier, -iest) containing, tasting of, salt.

salt·petre (*US* = *-peter*) /sɔːltˈpiːtə(r)/ n [U] salty white powder used in making gunpowder, for preserving food and as medicine.

sa·lu·bri·ous /səˈluːbrɪəs/ adj (*formal*) (esp of climate) health-giving: *the ~ air of Switzerland.*

salu·tary /ˈsæljʊtrɪ *US:* -terɪ/ adj having a good effect (on body or mind): ~ *exercise/ advice.*

salu·ta·tion /ˌsæljuːˈteɪʃən/ n [C,U] (*formal*) (act or expression of) greeting or good-will (e g a bow or a kiss): *He raised his hat in* ~.

sa·lute /səˈluːt/ n [C] **1** something done to welcome a person or to show respect or honour, esp (e g in the armed forces) the raising of the hand to the forehead, the firing of guns, the lowering and raising of a flag: *give a* ~; *fire a* ~ *of ten guns.* **2** friendly greeting such as a bow or wave. □ *vt,vi* **1** give a salute (to): *The soldier* ~*d smartly.* **2** greet.

sal·vage /ˈsælvɪdʒ/ n [U] **1** the saving of property from loss (by fire or other disaster, e g a wrecked ship): *a* `~ *company,* one whose business is to bring wrecked ships to port, raise valuables from a ship that has sunk, etc. **2** property so saved. **3** payment given to those who save property. **4** (saving of) waste material that can be used again after being processed. □ *vt* save from loss, fire, wreck, etc.

sal·va·tion /sælˈveɪʃən/ n [U] **1** the act of saving, the state of having been saved, from sin and its consequences. **2** that which saves a person from loss, disaster, etc: *Government loans have been the ~ of several shaky business companies.*

Sal`vation `Army, religious and missionary organization on a semi-military model for the revival of religion among the masses and for helping the poor everywhere.

salve /sɑv *US:* sæv/ n **1** [C,U] (kinds of) oily medicinal substance used on wounds, sores or burns: `lip-~`. **2** (*fig*) something that comforts wounded feelings or soothes an uneasy conscience. □ *vt* soothe: ~ *one's conscience by giving stolen money to charity.*

sal·ver /ˈsælvə(r)/ n [C] (usually silver) tray on which servants hand letters, drinks, etc.

salvo /ˈsælvəʊ/ n [C] (*pl* ~s, ~es) the firing of a number of guns together as a salute.

Sa·mari·tan /səˈmærɪtən/ n [C] person who pities and gives practical help to persons in trouble.

same /seɪm/ adj, pron (*Note:* always with *the* except as noted in 5 below.) **1** identical; unchanged; not different: *He is the ~ age as his wife. We have lived in the ~ house for fifty years.* **2** *the same… that/as: He uses the ~ books that you do/the ~ books as you.* **3** (used with a clause introduced by *that, where, who,* etc): *Put the book back in the ~ place where you found it.* **4** (used as a *pronoun*) the same thing: *We must all say the ~. I would do the ~ again.* **Same here,** the same applies to me. **And the same to you,** I hope you experience the same thing. **at the same time, (a)** together: *Don't all speak at the ~ time.* **(b)** (introducing a fact, etc that is to be borne in mind) still; nevertheless: *At the ~ time you must not forget that… one and the same,* absolutely the same: *Jekyll and Hyde were one and the ~ person.* **be all/just the same to,** make no difference to: *You can do it now or leave it till later; it's all the ~ to me.* **come/amount to the same thing,** have the same result, meaning, etc: *You may pay in cash or by cheque; it comes to the ~ thing.* **5** (with *this, that, these, those*) already thought of, mentioned or referred to: *On the Monday I didn't go to work. On that ~ day, the office was bombed.* □ *adv* in the same way: *Old people do not feel the ~ about these things as the younger generation.* **all the same,** ⇨ all².

same·ness, the condition of being the same, (and so being uninteresting through lack of variety).

samo·var /ˈsæməvɑ(r)/ n [C] metal urn used in Russia for boiling water for tea.

sam·pan /ˈsæmpæn/ n [C] small, flat-bottomed boat used in the Far East.

sample /ˈsɑmpəl US: ˈsæm-/ n [C] specimen; one of a number, part of a whole, taken to show what the rest is like. □ vt take a sample of; test a part of: *sampling the quality of the wine.*

sam·urai /ˈsæmʊraɪ/ n (pl unchanged) 1 the ∼, the military caste in feudal Japan. 2 [C] member of this caste.

sana·tor·ium /ˌsænəˈtɔrɪəm/ n [C] (pl ∼s) establishment for the treatment of people who are ill, esp convalescents.

sanc·tify /ˈsæŋktɪfɪ/ vt (pt,pp -ied) make holy; observe as sacred.
  sanc·ti·fi·ca·tion /ˌsæŋktɪfɪˈkeɪʃən/ n [U]

sanc·ti·moni·ous /ˌsæŋktɪˈməʊnɪəs/ adj making a show (often insincere) of sanctity.
  sanc·ti·moni·ous·ly adv

sanc·tion /ˈsæŋkʃən/ n 1 [U] right or permission given by authority to do something: *translate a book without the ∼ of the author.* 2 [U] approval, encouragement (of behaviour, etc), by general custom or tradition. 3 [C] penalty esp as adopted by several States together against a country violating international law: *apply economic ∼s against a country.* 4 [C] reason for obeying a rule, etc: *The best moral ∼ is that of conscience.* □ vt give a sanction to: *Torture should never be ∼ed.*

sanc·tity /ˈsæŋktətɪ/ n (pl -ies) 1 [U] holiness; sacredness; saintliness: *violate the ∼ of an oath.* 2 (pl) sacred obligations, feelings, etc.

sanc·tu·ary /ˈsæŋktʃʊərɪ US: -ʊerɪ/ n (pl -ies) 1 [C] holy or sacred place, esp a church, temple or mosque. 2 [C] sacred place (eg the altar of a church) where, in former times, a person running away from the law, etc could by Church law, take refuge: *Great Britain has always been a ∼ of political refugees from many parts of the world.* 3 [U] (right of offering such) freedom from arrest: *to seek/be offered ∼.* 4 [C] area where by law it is forbidden to kill birds, rob their nests, etc to shoot animals, etc: *a ˋbird-∼.*

sand /sænd/ n 1 [U] (mass of) finely crushed rock as seen on the sea-shore, in river-beds, deserts, etc. 2 (often pl) expanse of sand (on the sea-shore or a desert). □ vt 1 cover, sprinkle, with sand. 2 make smooth by using sand paper.
  ˋsand-bag, bag filled with sand used in groups as a defensive wall (in war, against rising flood-water, etc).
  ˋsand-bank, bank of sand in a river or the sea.
  ˋsand-bar, bank of sand at the mouth of a river or harbour.
  ˋsand-blast, vt send a jet of sand against e g stonework, to clean it, or against glass to

make a design on it.
  ˋsand dune, hill of sand (as in the desert).
  ˋsand-fly, kind of fly common on sea-shores.
  ˋsand-glass, glass with two bulbs containing enough sand to take a definite time in passing from one bulb to the other.
  ˋsand-paper, strong paper with sand glued to it, used for rubbing rough surfaces smooth. □ vt make smooth with sandpaper.
  ˋsand-piper, small bird living in wet, sandy places near streams.
  ˋsand-pit, enclosure with sand for children to play in.
  ˋsand-stone, type of rock formed of sand.
  ˋsand-storm, storm in a sandy desert with clouds of sand raised by the wind.

sandy adj (-ier, -iest) (a) covered with, of, sand: *a ∼y beach.* (b) (of hair, etc) yellowish-red.

san·dal /ˈsændəl/ n [C] (often *a pair of ∼s*) kind of shoe made of a sole with straps to hold it on the foot.

san·dal·wood /ˈsændəlwʊd/ n [U] hard, sweet-smelling wood; its perfume.

sand·wich /ˈsænwɪdʒ US: -wɪtʃ/ n [C] two slices of bread with meat, etc between: *ham/chicken/cheese, etc ∼es.* □ vt put (one thing or person) between two others, esp when there is little space: *I was ∼ed between two fat men on the bus.*
  ˋsandwich course, course of study, e g at a polytechnic, between periods of practical work in industry.
  ˋsandwich-board, structure with two boards hung over the shoulders displaying advertisements.

sane /seɪn/ adj (-r, -st) 1 mentally healthy; not mad. 2 sensible: *a ∼ policy; ∼ judgement.*
  sane·ly adv

sang /sæŋ/ pt of sing.

san·gui·nary /ˈsæŋgwɪnərɪ US: -nerɪ/ adj (formal) 1 with much killing or wounding: *a ∼ battle.* 2 delighting in cruel acts: *a ∼ ruler.*

san·guine /ˈsæŋgwɪn/ adj (formal) 1 hopeful; optimistic: *∼ of success.* 2 having a red complexion.

sani·tar·ium /ˌsænɪˈteərɪəm/ n [C] (pl ∼s) (US) sanatorium; health resort.

sani·tary /ˈsænɪtrɪ US: -terɪ/ adj 1 clean; free from dirt which might cause disease: *∼ conditions.* 2 of, concerned with, the protection of (public) health: *a ˋ∼ inspector.*
  ˋsanitary towel/napkin, absorbent pad used during menstruation.

sani·ta·tion /ˌsænɪˈteɪʃən/ n [U] arrangements to protect public health, esp the disposal of sewage.

san·ity /ˈsænətɪ/ n [U] 1 health of mind. 2 soundness of judgement.

sank /sæŋk/ pt of sink².

Santa Claus /ˈsæntə ˈklɔz US: ˈsæntə klɔz/ n the person who, small children are told, gives them toys by night at Christmas.

sap¹ /sæp/ n [C] tunnel or covered trench made to get nearer to the enemy. □ vt,vi (-pp-) **1** make a sap or saps. **2** (fig) destroy or weaken (a person's health, strength, energy, faith, confidence, etc): *the climate ∼ped his health. The criticism ∼ped his determination.*

sap² /sæp/ n [U] **1** liquid in a plant, carrying food to all parts. **2** (fig) (anything that provides) strength or energy.
sap·less adj without sap or energy.
sap·ling, young tree.

sap·phire /'sæfaɪə(r)/ n **1** [C] bright blue precious stone. **2** [U] (often as an *adjective*) bright blue colour.

sar·casm /'sɑːkæzm/ n [U] (use of) remarks intended to hurt the feelings; [C] such a remark.
sar·cas·tic /sɑː'kæstɪk/ adj of, using, sarcasm.
sar·cas·ti·cally /-klɪ/ adv

sar·copha·gus /sɑː'kɒfəgəs/ n [C] (pl -gi /-gaɪ/, ∼es) stone coffin.

sar·dine /sɑː'diːn/ n [C] small fish (usually preserved and tinned in oil or tomato sauce). *packed like sardines,* closely crowded together.

sar·donic /sɑː'dɒnɪk/ adj scornful; cynical: *a ∼ smile.*
sar·doni·cally /-klɪ/ adv

sari /'sɑːrɪ/ n [C] (pl ∼s) length of cotton or silk cloth draped round the body, worn by Hindu women.

sa·rong /sə'rɒŋ US: -'rɔːŋ/ n [C] long strip of cotton or silk material worn round the middle of the body by Malays and Javanese.

sash¹ /sæʃ/ n [C] long strip of cloth worn round the waist or over one shoulder for ornament or as part of a uniform.
sash window, one with a frame that slides up and down on ropes.

sat /sæt/ pt,pp of sit.

Satan /'seɪtən/ n the Devil.
Sa·tanic /sə'tænɪk US: seɪ-/ adj of, like, the Devil.

satchel /'sætʃəl/ n [C] bag with a long strap for carrying school books.

sate /seɪt/ vt = satiate.

sat·el·lite /'sætəlaɪt/ n [C] **1** small body moving in orbit round a planet; moon. **2** artificial object, e g a spacecraft put in orbit round a celestial body: *com'muni'cations ∼,* for sending back to the earth telephone messages, radio and T V signals. **3** (fig) (often as an *adjective*) person, state, depending on and taking the lead from another.

sati·able /'seɪʃəbl/ adj (formal) that can be fully satisfied.

sati·ate /'seɪʃɪeɪt/ vt (formal) satisfy fully or too much: *be ∼d with food/pleasure.*

sat·iety /sə'taɪətɪ/ n [U] (formal) condition of being satiated.

satin /'sætɪn US: 'sætən/ n [U] silk material shiny on one side: (as an *adjective*) ∼ ribbons. □ adj smooth like satin.

sat·ire /'sætaɪə(r)/ n **1** [U] form of writing, drama, etc making a person, idea, appear foolish or absurd. **2** [C] piece of writing that does this.
sa·tiri·cal /sə'tɪrɪkəl/ adj
sa·tiri·cally /-klɪ/ adv
sat·ir·ist /'sætərɪst/ n [C] person who writes or uses satire.
sat·ir·ize /'sætəraɪz/ vt attack with satire; describe satirically.

sat·is·fac·tion /'sætɪs'fækʃən/ n **1** [U] the state of being satisfied, pleased or contented; act of satisfying: *have the ∼ of being successful in life.* **2** [C] (with a, an, but rarely pl) something that satisfies: *It is a great ∼ to know that he is well again.* **3** [U] (opportunity of getting) revenge or compensation for an injury or insult: *The angry man demanded ∼ but the other refused it,* would neither apologize nor fight.

sat·is·fac·tory /'sætɪs'fæktərɪ/ adj **1** giving pleasure or satisfaction: *a ∼ holiday.* **2** good enough for a purpose: *Will these shoes be ∼ for a long walk?*
sat·is·fac·tor·ily /-əlɪ/ adv

sat·isfy /'sætɪsfaɪ/ vt,vi (pt,pp -ied) **1** make contented; give (a person) what he wants or needs: *Nothing satisfies him; he's always complaining.* **2** be enough for (one's wants); be equal to (what one hopes for or desires): *∼ one's hunger.* **3** make free from doubt: *He satisfied me that he could do the work well.*
sat·is·fy·ing adj giving satisfaction: *a ∼ing meal.*

satu·rate /'sætʃəreɪt/ vt **1** make thoroughly wet; soak with moisture: *We were caught in the rain and came home ∼d.* **2** cause to absorb like water: *be ∼d with sunshine.* **3** be unable to take any more: *The market for used cars is ∼d.* **4** (chem) cause (one substance) to absorb the greatest possible amount of another: *a ∼d solution of salt.*
satu·ra·tion /'sætʃə'reɪʃən/ n [U] state of being saturated.
'satu'ration point, the stage beyond which no more can be absorbed.

Sat·ur·day /'sætədɪ/ n the seventh and last day of the week.

Sat·urn /'sætən/ n **1** (astron) large planet encircled by rings. **2** (Roman myth) god of agriculture.

satyr /'sætə(r)/ n (Greek and Roman myth) god of the woods, half man and half animal.

sauce /sɔːs/ n **1** [C,U] (kind of) (semi-)liquid preparation served with food to give flavour: *spaghetti and tomato ∼.* **2** [U] (informal) impudence (usually amusing rather than annoying): *What ∼! How impudent!*
sauc·ily adv impudently.
saucy adj (-ier, -iest) impudent.

sauce·pan /'sɔːspən US: -pæn/ n [C] deep metal cooking pot with a lid and a handle.

saucer /'sɔːsə(r)/ n [C] small curved dish on

which a cup stands. ⇨ flying saucer.

sauer·kraut /ˈsaʊəkraʊt/ n [U] (Ger) chopped, pickled cabbage.

sauna /ˈsaʊnə/ n [C] (pl ~s) (building for a) steam bath.

saun·ter /ˈsɔːntə(r)/ vi walk in a leisurely way: ~ along Oxford Street window-shopping. □ n [C] quiet, unhurried walk or pace.

saus·age /ˈsɒsɪdʒ US: ˈsɔːs-/ n [U] chopped up meat, etc flavoured and stuffed into a casing or tube of thin skin; [C] one section of such a tube.
`sausage-dog, (GB informal) = dachshund.
`sausage-meat, meat minced for making sausages.

sauté /ˈsəʊteɪ US: səʊˈteɪ/ adj (Fr) (of food) quickly fried in a little fat: ~ potatoes. □ vt fry food in this way.

sav·age /ˈsævɪdʒ/ adj 1 in a primitive or uncivilized state: ~ people/tribes/countries. 2 fierce; cruel: a ~ dog/attack; ~ criticism. □ n [C] member of a primitive tribe living by hunting and fishing. □ vt attack, bite, etc: a lion savaging its trainer.
sav·age·ly adv
sav·agery /ˈsævɪdʒrɪ/ n [U] the state of being savage; savage behaviour.

sa·vanna(h) /səˈvænə/ n [C] treeless plain, e g in tropical America and parts of W Africa. (Note: compare prairie, N America, and pampas, S America.)

save¹ /seɪv/ vt, vi 1 make or keep safe (from loss, injury, etc): ~ her from drowning; ~ his life. save one's face, ⇨ face¹ (2). save one's skin, ⇨ skin(1). 2 keep for future use: ~ (up) money for a holiday; ~ some of the meat for tomorrow. He is saving himself/ saving his strength for the heavy work he'll have to do this afternoon. save for a rainy day, ⇨ rainy. 3 free (a person) from the need of using: That will ~ you 50 pence a week/a lot of trouble. 4 (in the Christian religion) set free from the power of (or the eternal punishment for) sin: Jesus Christ came into the world to ~ sinners. □ n (in football, etc) act of preventing the scoring of a goal: Banks made a brilliant ~ in Brazil.
saver, (a) person who saves (money) (b) means of saving: This device is a useful `time-~r.
sav·ing adj (esp) that compensates. **saving grace,** good quality in a person whose other qualities are not all good. □ n 1 [C] way of saving; amount saved: a useful saving of time and money. 2 (pl) money saved up: keep one's savings in the Post Office.
`savings account, (with a bank) on which interest is paid.
`savings-bank, bank which holds, and gives interest on, small savings.

save² /seɪv/ (also **sav·ing** /ˈseɪvɪŋ/) prep (dated) except: all ~ him.

sav·iour (US = **-ior**) /ˈseɪvɪə(r)/ n [C] 1 person who rescues or saves a person from danger. 2 **The S~, Our S~,** Jesus Christ.

sa·vour (US = **-vor**) /ˈseɪvə(r)/ n [C,U] 1 taste or flavour (of something): soup with a ~ of garlic. 2 (fig) quality (of): His political views have a ~ of facism. □ vi have the quality (of): His speech ~s of a humane approach.

sa·voury (US = **-vory**) /ˈseɪvərɪ/ adj 1 having an appetizing taste or smell. 2 having a salt or sharp, not a sweet, taste: a ~ omelette. □ n [C] (pl -ies) savoury dish, biscuit, etc.

sa·voy /səˈvɔɪ/ n [C,U] (kind of) winter cabbage with wrinkled leaves.

saw¹ /sɔː/ pt of see¹.

saw² /sɔː/ n [C] (kinds of) tool with a sharp-toothed edge, for cutting wood, metal, □ vt, vi (pt ~ed, pp ~n /sɔːn/ and (US) ~ed) 1 cut with, use, a saw: ~ wood; ~ a log in two. **saw sth off,** cut off with a saw: ~ a branch off a tree. **saw sth up,** cut into pieces with a saw: This wood saws easily. 3 move backward and forward: ~ing at his violin, using his bow as if it were a saw.
`saw-dust, tiny bits of wood falling off when wood is being sawn.
`saw-mill, factory with power-operated saws.
saw·yer /ˈsɔːjə(r)/, man whose work is sawing wood.

saxo·phone /ˈsæksəfəʊn/ n [C] musical wind-instrument with a reed in the mouthpiece and keys for the fingers, made of brass.
sax·ophon·ist /sækˈsɒfənɪst US: ˈsæksəfəʊnɪst/, saxophone player.

say /seɪ/ vt, vi (3rd person, present tense ~s /sez/, pt, pp said /sed/) 1 make (a word or remark); use one's ordinary voice (not singing, etc) to produce (words, sentences): Did you ~ anything? He said that his friend's name was Smith. The boy was ~ing his prayers. **that is to say,** or to use other words: He's 15, that is to ~, he's very young. **to say nothing of,** ⇨ nothing. **What do you say to...?** What do you think about...: What do you ~ to a walk/to playing tennis? **When all is said and done,** after all (the effort to convince a person): He thinks he is brilliant but when all is said and done, he's only an ordinary student. **You can say `that again!** (informal) I agree. **You don't say!** (informal) (used to express surprise when hearing news, etc). **go without saying,** ⇨ go (28) go without. **say no more,** you need not add anything because I agree. **say so,** say what you think, feel: If you think I have lied to you, ~ so. **say the word; say a good word for,** ⇨ word(2). 2 state: It ~s here that he was killed. **They say/It is said (that),** (used to introduce rumours): They ~/It's said that he's a thief. 3 make known information: She spoke for *an hour but didn't ~ much.* **4** form and give an opinion concerning: *There is no ~ing when peace will be achieved. and so say all of us,* that is the opinion of us all. **5** estimate: *You could speak English in, let's ~, six weeks. be hard to say,* be difficult to estimate. □ *n* (only in the following) *have/ say one's say,* express one's opinion; state one's views: *Let him have his ~. have/be allowed a/no/not much, etc say in the matter,* have some/no/not much right or opportunity to share in a discussion, express one's opinions, etc: *He wasn't allowed much ~ in choosing his holiday.*

say-ing /ˈseɪɪŋ/ *n* [C] remark often made; well-known phrase, proverb, etc: *'More haste, less speed', as the ~ goes.*

scab /skæb/ *n* [C] **1** dry crust formed over a wound or sore. **2** (*informal*) workman who refuses to join a strike, or his trade union, or who takes a striker's place.

scabby *adj* (-ier, -iest) covered with scabs(1).

scab-bard /ˈskæbəd/ *n* [C] sheath for the blade of a sword, etc.

sca-bies /ˈskeɪbɪz/ *n* [U] kind of skin disease causing itching.

scaf-fold /ˈskæfəʊld/ *n* [C] **1** structure put up for workmen and materials around a building which is being erected or repaired. **2** platform on which criminals are executed: *go to the ~,* be executed.

scaf-fold-ing /ˈskæfəldɪŋ/ *n* [U] (materials for a) scaffold(1) (e g poles and planks).

scald /skɔːld/ *vt* **1** burn with hot liquid or steam: *~ one's hand with hot fat.* **2** clean (instruments, etc) with boiling water or steam. □ *n* [C] injury to the skin from hot liquid or steam.

scale¹ /skeɪl/ *n* **1** [C] one of the thin overlapping pieces of hard material that cover the skin of many fish, etc: *scrape the ~s off a herring.* **2** [C] piece like a scale, e g a flake of skin that loosens and comes off the body in some diseases, a flake of rust on iron. **3** [U] chalky deposit inside boilers, kettles, waterpipes, etc (from the lime in hard water). **4** [U] deposit of tartar on teeth. □ *vt,vi* **1** cut or scrape scales from (e g fish). **2** *scale off,* come off in flakes: *paint/plaster scaling off a wall.*

scaly *adj* (-ier, -iest) covered with, coming off in, scales: *a kettle scaly with rust.*

scale² /skeɪl/ *n* [C] **1** series of marks at regular intervals for the purpose of measuring (as on a ruler or a thermometer): *This ruler has one ~ in centimetres and another in inches.* **2** ruler or other tool or instrument marked in this way. **3** system of units for measuring: *the `decimal ~.* **4** arrangement in steps or degrees: *a ~ of wages; a person who is high in the social ~.* ⇨ **sliding scale.** **5** proportion between the size of something and the map, diagram, etc which represents it: *a map on the ~ of ten*

kilometres to the centimetre. drawn to scale, with a uniform reduction or enlargement. **6** relative size, extent, etc: *They are preparing for war on a large ~.* **7** (*music*) series of tones arranged in order of pitch, esp a series of eight starting on a keynote: *practise ~s on the piano.* □ *vt* **1** make a copy or representation of, according to a certain scale: *~ a map/building.* **2** *scale up/down,* increase/decrease by a certain proportion: *All wages/marks were ~d up by 10 per cent.*

scale³ /skeɪl/ *n* [C] **1** one of the two pans on a balance. **2** (*pl,* or *a pair of ~s*) simple balance or instrument for weighing. **3** any machine for weighing: *bathroom ~s,* for measuring one's weight. □ *vi* weigh: *~ 10 pounds/stone.*

scale⁴ /skeɪl/ *vt* climb up (a wall, cliff, etc).

scal-lop /ˈskɒləp/ *n* [C] kind of water animal with a hinged double shell divided into grooves.

scalp /skælp/ *n* [C] **1** skin and hair of the head, excluding the face. **2** this skin, etc from an enemy's head as a trophy of victory. □ *vt* cut the scalp off.

scal-pel /ˈskælpəl/ *n* [C] small, light knife used by surgeons.

scamp /skæmp/ *n* [C] (used playfully of a child) rascal.

scam-per /ˈskæmpə(r)/ *vi* (of small animals, e g mice, rabbits, when frightened, or of children and dogs at play) run quickly. □ *n* [C] short, quick run.

scampi /ˈskæmpɪ/ *n pl* (used with a *sing verb*) large prawns.

scan /skæn/ *vt,vi* (-nn-) **1** look attentively or over every part of: *The shipwrecked sailor ~ned the horizon anxiously every morning.* **2** (*modern usage*) glance at quickly but not very thoroughly: *He ~ned the newspaper while having his breakfast.* **3** test the rhythm of (a line of verse). **4** (of verse) be composed so that it can be scanned: *This line does not/will not ~. The verses ~ well.* **5** (T V) prepare (a picture) for transmission (by separating its elements of light and shade. **6** (*radar*) traverse an area with electronic beams in search of something.

scan-sion /ˈskænʃən/ *n* [U] scanning of verse; the way verse scans.

scan-dal /ˈskændəl/ *n* **1** [C,U] (action, behaviour, etc that causes) general shock, anger, opposition; [C] shameful or disgraceful action: *The way they treat the poor is a ~.* **2** [U] careless or unkind talk which damages a person's reputation: *Most of us enjoy a bit of ~.*

`scandal-monger /-mʌŋɡə(r)/, person who gossips.

`scan-dal-ize /-aɪz/ *vt* offend the moral feelings of: *~ize the neighbours by sunbathing in the nude.*

`scan-dal-ous /-əs/ *adj* (a) disgraceful; shocking. (b) (of reports, rumours) containing scandal. **(c)** (of persons) fond of gossiping.

scan·dal·ous·ly *adv* in a scandalous way.

scan·sion /ˈskænʃən/ ⇨ scan.

scant /skænt/ *adj* (having) hardly enough: *pay ~ attention to her advice.* □ *vt* provide hardly enough: *Don't ~ the butter when you make a cake.*

scant·i·ly /-əlɪ/ *adv* in a scanty manner: *~ily dressed.*

scanty *adj* (-ier, -iest) (opposite of *ample*) small in size or amount; barely large enough: *a ~y bikini.*

scape·goat /ˈskeɪpɡəʊt/ *n* [C] person blamed or punished for the mistake(s) or wrong acts of another or others.

scap·ula /ˈskæpjʊlə/ *n* [C] (*pl ~s*) (*anat*) = shoulder-blade.

scar /skɑ(r)/ *n* [C] **1** mark remaining on the surface (of skin, furniture, etc) as the result of injury or damage. **2** (*fig*) mark or effect of suffering, bad planning, etc: *Mining that leaves a ~ on the countryside.* □ *vt, vi* (-rr-) **1** mark with a scar: *a face ~red by small-pox.* **2** (*fig*) mark with effects of suffering, etc: *the ~s of war in many European towns.* **3** form scars: *The cut on his forehead ~red over.*

scarab /ˈskærəb/ *n* [C] **1** kinds of beetle, esp one regarded as sacred in ancient Egypt. **2** ornament, etc in the shape of a scarab.

scarce /skeəs/ *adj* (-r, -st) **1** (opposite of *plentiful*) not available in sufficient quantity; not equal to the demand: *Jobs are ~ this month.* **2** rare; seldom met with: *a ~ book.*

scar·city /ˈskeəsətɪ/ *n* [C,U] (*pl* -ies) occasion, state of being scarce; smallness of supply compared with demand: *The scarcity of fruit was caused by the drought.*

scarce·ly /ˈskeəslɪ/ *adv* barely; not quite; almost not: *There were ~ a hundred people present. I ~ know him.*

scare /skeə(r)/ *vt, vi* frighten; become frightened: *The dogs ~d the thief away. He was ~d by the thunder. He ~s easily/is easily ~d.* **scare sb stiff,** (*informal*) make him very afraid, nervous: *He's ~d stiff of women.* **scare sb out of his wits,** make him extremely frightened: *The sound of footsteps outside ~d her out of her wits.* □ *n* [C] feeling, state, of alarm: *The news caused a war ~,* a fear that war might break out.

ˈscare-crow, figure of a man dressed in old clothes, set up to scare birds away from crops.

ˈscare-monger /-mʌŋɡə(r)/, person who spreads alarming news.

scary /ˈskeərɪ/ *adj* (-ier, -iest) (*informal*) causing alarm.

scarf /skɑf/ *n* [C] (*pl* scarves /skɑvz/ or ~s) long strip of material (silk, wool, etc) worn over the shoulders, round the neck or (by women) over the hair.

scar·ify /ˈskærəfaɪ/ *vt* (*pt, pp* -ied) (in surgery) make small cuts in, cut off skin, from.

scar·let /ˈskɑlət/ *n* [U], *adj* bright red **go scarlet,** blush.

ˈscarlet ˈfever, infectious disease with red marks on the skin.

ˈscarlet ˈrunner, kind of bean plant.

ˈscarlet ˈwoman, (*old use*) prostitute.

scarp /skɑp/ *n* [C] steep slope.

scat /skæt/ *int* (*sl*) Go away!

scath·ing /ˈskeɪðɪŋ/ *adj* (of criticism, etc) severe; harsh: *a ~ review of a new book.*

scath·ing·ly *adv*

scat·ter /ˈskætə(r)/ *vt, vi* **1** send, go, in different directions: *The police ~ed the crowd. The crowd ~ed.* **2** throw or put in various directions: *~ seed.* □ *n* [C] that which is scattered; sprinkling: *a ~ of hailstones.*

ˈscatter-brain, person who cannot keep his thoughts on one subject for long. Hence, **ˈscatter-brained** *adj*

scat·tered *adj* not situated together: *a few ~ed villages.*

scatty /ˈskætɪ/ *adj* (-ier, -iest) (*informal*) behaving as if mad: *a ~ woman.* **drive sb scatty,** cause him to become mad.

scav·enge /ˈskævɪndʒ/ *vt, vi* act as a scavenger.

scav·en·ger /ˈskævɪndʒə(r)/ *n* [C] **1** animal or bird, e g a vulture, that lives on decaying flesh. **2** person who looks among rubbish for food, useful things.

scen·ario /sɪˈnɑːriəʊ US: -ˈnær-/ *n* [C] (*pl ~s*) written outline of a play, an opera, a film, with details of the scenes, etc.

scene /sin/ *n* [C] **1** place of an actual or imagined event: *the ~ of a great battle. The ~ of the novel is set in Scotland.* **2** description of an incident, or of part of a person's life; incident in real life suitable for such a description: *There were distressing ~s when the earthquake occurred.* **3** (incident characterized by an) emotional outburst: *She made a ~/We had a ~ when I arrived late.* **4** view; something seen: *The boats in the harbour make a beautiful ~.* **change of scene,** new surroundings. **5** (abbr **Sc**) one of the parts, shorter than an act, into which some plays and operas are divided; episode within such a part: *'Macbeth', Act* II, *Sc 1.* **6** place represented on the stage of a theatre; the painted background, woodwork, canvas, etc representing such a place: *The ~s are changed during the intervals.* **behind the scenes,** **(a)** out of sight of the audience; behind the stage. **(b)** (*fig*) (of a person) influencing events secretly; having private or secret information and influence. **come on the scene,** (usually *fig*) appear. **7** (*informal*) area of what is currently fashionable or notable: *the ˈdrug ~ in big cities.*

ˈscene-painter, person who paints scenery(2).

ˈscene-shifter, person who changes the scenes(6).

scen·ery /ˈsinərɪ/ *n* [U] **1** general natural features of a district, e g mountains, plains, valleys, forests: *mountain* ∼; *stop to admire the* ∼. **2** the furnishings, painted canvas, etc used on the stage of a theatre.

scenic /ˈsiːnɪk/ *adj* of scenery: *a* ∼ *highway across the Alps*; ∼ *effects*, e g in a film.
sceni‧cal‧ly /-klɪ/ *adv*

scent /sent/ *n* **1** [U] smell, esp of something pleasant: *a rose that has no* ∼. **2** [C] particular kind of smell: ∼*s of lavender and rosemary*. **3** [U] perfume: *a bottle of* ∼; *a* `∼-*bottle*. **4** [C] (usually *sing*) smell left by (the track of) an animal: *follow/lose/recover the* ∼. *off/on the scent*, not having/having the right clue. *put/throw sb off the scent*, (*fig*) mislead him by giving false information. **5** [U] sense of smell (in dogs): *hunt by* ∼. □ *vt* **1** learn the presence of by smell: *The dog* ∼*ed a rat*. **2** begin to suspect the presence or existence of: ∼ *a crime*; ∼ *treachery/trouble*. **3** put scent on; make fragrant: ∼ *a handkerchief*; *roses that* ∼ *the air*.
scent‧less *adj* having no scent: ∼*less flowers*.

scep‧ter /ˈseptə(r)/ *n* = sceptre.

scep‧tic (*US* = **skep‧tik**) /ˈskeptɪk/ *n* [C] **1** person who doubts the truth of a particular claim, theory, etc. **2** person who doubts the truth of the Christian religion or of all religions.
scep‧ti‧cal (*US* = **skep-**) /-kəl/ *adj* in the habit of not believing, of questioning the truth of claims, statements, etc.
scep‧ti‧cally (*US* = **skep-**) /-klɪ/ *adv*
scep‧ti‧cism (*US* = **skep-**) /ˈskeptɪsɪzm/ *n* [U] doubting state of mind, attitude.

sceptre (*US* = **scep‧ter**) /ˈseptə(r)/ *n* [C] rod or staff carried by a ruler as a symbol of power or authority.

sched‧ule /ˈʃedjul *US:* ˈskedʒəl/ *n* [C] list or statement of details, esp of times for doing things; programme or timetable for work: *a* pro`duction ∼, e g in a factory; *a full* ∼, *a busy programme*. *on/behind schedule*, on/not on time: *The train arrived on* ∼. *(according) to schedule*, as planned. □ *vt* **1** make, put in, a schedule: ∼*d flights*, (e g of aircraft) flying according to announced timetables. ⇨ **charter(2)**. **2** enter in a list of arrangements: *The President is* ∼*d to make a speech tomorrow*.

sche‧matic /skiˈmætɪk/ *adj* **1** of the nature of a scheme or plan. **2** (shown) in a diagram or chart.
sche‧mati‧cally /-klɪ/ *adv*

scheme /skim/ *n* [C] **1** arrangement, ordered system: *a* `colour ∼, e g for a room, so that colours of walls, rugs, curtains, etc match. **2** plan or design (for work or activity): *a* ∼ *for manufacturing paper from straw*. **3** secret and dishonest plan: *a* ∼ *to avoid paying taxes*. □ *vi,vt* **1** make a (esp dishonest) scheme: *They* ∼*d to defeat/for the overthrow of the government*. **2** make plans for (esp something dishonest): *a scheming* (= crafty) *young man*.

schemer, person who schemes.

schism /ˈsɪzm *or* ˈskɪzm/ *n* [U] (offence of causing the) division of an organization (esp a Church) into two or more groups; [C] instance of such separation.
schis‧matic /sɪzˈmætɪk *or* skɪzˈmætɪk/ *adj*

schizo‧phre‧nia /ˈskɪtsəʊˈfriːnɪə/ *n* [U] type of mental disorder marked by lack of association between the intellectual processes and actions.
schizo‧phrenic /ˈskɪtsəʊˈfrenɪk/ *adj* of, suffering from, schizophrenia. □ *n* [C] person suffering from schizophrenia.

schnor‧kel /ˈsnɔːkəl/ *n* = snorkel.

scholar /ˈskɒlə(r)/ *n* [C] **1** (*dated*) boy or girl at school. **2** student who, after a competitive examination or other means of selection, is awarded money or other help so that he may attend school or college: *British Council* ∼*s*. **3** person with much knowledge (usually of a particular subject): *Professor X, the famous Greek* ∼. **4** (*informal*) person able to read and write: *I'm not much of a* ∼.
schol‧ar‧ly *adj* having or showing much learning; of or suitable for a scholar(3); fond of learning: *a* ∼*ly translation*; *a* ∼*ly young woman*.
schol‧ar‧ship /ˈskɒləʃɪp/ *n* **1** [U] learning or knowledge obtained by study; proper concern for scholarly methods. **2** [C] payment of money, e g a yearly grant to a scholar(2) so that he may continue his studies: *win a* ∼ *to the university*.
schol‧as‧tic /skəˈlæstɪk/ *adj* **1** (*dated*) of schools and education: *the* ∼ *profession*, teaching. **2** connected with the learning of the Middle Ages, esp when men argued over small points of dogma.

school[1] /skul/ *n* **1** [C] institution for educating children: `*primary and* `*secondary* ∼*s*. **2** (not with *the,a* or *an*) process of being educated in a school: `∼ *age*, between the ages of starting and finishing school. *Is he old enough for* ∼*/to go to* ∼? *He left* ∼ *when he was fifteen*. **3** (not with *the, a* or *an*) time when teaching is given; lessons: *S*∼ *begins at 9a m. There will be no* ∼ (= no lessons) *tomorrow*. **4** (with *the*) all the pupils in a school: *The whole* ∼ *hopes that its football team will win the match*. **5** [C] department or division of a university for the study of a particular subject: *the* `*Law/* `*Medical S*∼; *the S*∼ *of Dentistry*. **6** [C] (*GB*) branch of study for which separate examinations are given in a university: *the* `*History* ∼. **7** [C] (*fig*) circumstances or occupation that provides discipline or instruction: *the hard* ∼ *of experience/adversity*. **8** [C] group of persons who are followers or imitators of an artist, a philosopher, etc: *the* `*Dutch/Ve*`*netian, etc* ∼ *of painting*; *from the same* ∼ *of thought*, thinking the same way. **9** [C] group of persons having the same characteristics, principles: *of the* `*old* ∼, having traditional attitudes. □ *vt* train; control; discipline: ∼ *a* *horse;* ∼ *one's temper.*

`school-bag,` for carrying school books, equipment.

`school-book,` (*dated*) textbook.

`school-boy,` boy at school: (as an *adjective*) ∼*boy* slang.

`school-days,` time of being at school: *look back on one's* ∼*-days with pleasure.*

`school-fellow,` boy, past or present, of the same school.

`school-girl,` girl at school.

`school-house,` building of a school in a village.

`school-ing,` education (the usual word): *He had very little* ∼*ing.*

`school-master/-mistress,` teacher (esp in a private school or old-fashioned grammar school).

`school-mate,` boy, girl, of the same school.

`school teacher,` person who teaches in a school.

`school-time,` lesson time at school.

school[2] /skuːl/ *n* [C] large number (*of fish*) swimming together.

schoo·ner /ˈskuːnə(r)/ *n* [C] **1** kind of sailing-ship with two or more masts. **2** tall drinking-glass.

schwa /ʃwɑː/ *n* [C] (*pl* ∼s) the symbol /ə/ as used in the phonetic notation for *ago* /əˈgəʊ/.

science /ˈsaɪəns/ *n* **1** [U] knowledge arranged in an orderly manner, esp knowledge obtained by observation and the testing of facts; effort to find such knowledge: *S*∼ *is an exact discipline.* **2** [C,U] branch of such knowledge, eg physics. *study* ∼*/the* ∼*s at school.* ⇨ applied/natural/physical/social science. ⇨ also art [1](2).

`science fiction,` fiction dealing with recent or imagined scientific discoveries and advances.

scien-tist /ˈsaɪəntɪst/, student of, expert in, one of the natural or physical sciences.

scien-ti-fic /ˌsaɪənˈtɪfɪk/ *adj* of, for, connected with, used in, science; guided by the rules of science: ∼ *methods;* ∼ *instruments.*

scien-ti-fi-cally /-klɪ/ *adv*

scimi-tar /ˈsɪmɪtə(r)/ *n* [C] oriental, curved sword.

scin-til-late /ˈsɪntɪleɪt US: -təleɪt/ *vi* **1** sparkle. **2** (*fig*) talk cleverly: *scintillating conversation.*

scin-til-la-tion /ˌsɪntɪˈleɪʃən/ *n* [U]

scis-sors /ˈsɪzəz/ *n pl* (often *a pair of* ∼s) instrument with two blades which cut as they come together: *Where are my* ∼?

scoff[1] /skɒf US: skɔːf/ *vi* say disrespectful things, eg about religion. □ *n* [C] **1** scoffing remark. **2** object of ridicule.

scoffer, person who scoffs.

scoff[2] /skɒf US: skɔːf/ *vt* (*sl*) eat greedily: *Who's* ∼*ed all the pastries?* □ *n* [C] act of scoffing: *have a good* ∼.

scold /skəʊld/ *vt,vi* **1** blame with angry words: ∼ *a child for being lazy.* **2** complain:

She's always ∼*ing.* □ *n* [C] woman who scolds.

scold-ing *n* [C] complaint using angry words: *get/give her a* ∼*ing for being late.*

scol-lop /ˈskɒləp/ *n* = scallop.

scone /skɒn US: skəʊn/ *n* [C] soft, flat cake of oatmeal or flour, etc baked quickly.

scoop /skuːp/ *n* [C] **1** (sorts of) short-handled tool like a shovel for taking up and moving quantities of grain, flour, sugar, etc. **2** motion of, or as of, using a scoop: *at one* ∼, in one single movement of a scoop. **3** (*informal*) piece of news obtained and published by one newspaper before its competitors. **4** (*commerce*) large profit from sudden luck. □ *vt* **1** *scoop sth out/up,* lift with, or as with, a scoop. **2** make (a hole, groove, etc) with, or as with, a scoop: ∼ *out a hole in the sand.* **3** (*informal*) get (news, a profit, etc) as a scoop(3).

scoop-ful /-fʊl/, as much as a scoop holds.

scoot /skuːt/ *vi* (*informal*) = scram.

scooter /ˈskuːtə(r)/ *n* [C] **1** (also `motor-`∼) motor-bike with a low seat and a small engine. **2** child's toy, an L-shaped vehicle with small wheels, one foot being used to steer it and the other to move it by pushing against the ground.

scope /skəʊp/ *n* [U] **1** opportunity: *work that gives* ∼ *for one's abilities.* **2** range of action or observation: *Economics is beyond the* ∼ *of a child's mind.*

scorch /skɔːtʃ/ *vt,vi* **1** burn or discolour the surface of (something) by dry heat; cause to dry up (and die): *You* ∼*ed my shirt when you ironed it. The long, hot summer* ∼*ed the grass.* **2** become discoloured, etc with heat. □ *n* [C] brown mark on the surface of something (esp cloth) made by dry heat.

scorcher, something that scorches: *Yesterday was a* ∼*er,* a very hot day.

scorch-ing *adj* very hot. □ *adv:* ∼*ing hot,* extremely hot.

score[1] /skɔː(r)/ *n* [C] **1** cut, scratch or notch made on a surface: ∼*s on rock.* **2** mark made by whipping. **3** *pay/settle an old score,* get even with a person for past offences; have one's revenge: *I have some old* ∼*s to settle with him.* **4** (record of) points, goals, runs, etc made by a player or team in sport: *The* ∼ *in the tennis final was 6—4, 3—6, 7—5. The half-time* ∼ (eg football) *was 2—1.* *keep the score,* keep a record of the score as it is made. **5** reason; account. *on that score,* as far as that point is concerned: *You need have no anxiety on that* ∼. **6** copy of orchestral, etc music showing what each instrument is to play. each voice to sing: *follow the* ∼ *while listening to music.* **7** twenty; set of twenty: *a* ∼ *of people; three* ∼ *and ten,* 70, the normal length of human life according to the Bible *scores of times,* very often. **8** (*sl*) remark or act by which a person gains an advantage for himself in an argument, etc: *a politician* *who is clever at making ~s off opponents.*

'**score-board/-book/-card,** one on which the score (eg cricket) is recorded (during play).

score² /skɔː(r)/ *vt,vi* **1** mark with scratches, cuts, lines, etc: *Don't ~ the floor by pushing heavy furniture about. The composition was ~d with corrections in red ink. score out,* draw a line or lines through: *Three words had been ~d out.* ⇨ score¹ (1). **2** make or keep a record (esp for games): *Who's scoring?* **3** make as points in a game: *~ a goal; ~ a century,* 100 runs at cricket; *~ tricks,* when playing card games. *score an advantage over,* win one. *score a point (over sb),* = score off sb(4). **4** *score off sb,* (*informal*) defeat him in an argument; make a clever response. **5** enter as a record: *That remark will be ~d up against you,* will be remembered (and, perhaps, be revenged). **6** write instrumental or vocal parts for a musical composition: *~d for violin, viola and cello.* ⇨ score¹ (6).

scorer, (a) person who keeps a record of points, goals, runs, etc scored in a game. (b) player who scores runs, goals, etc.

scorn /skɔːn/ *n* [U] **1** feeling that a person or thing deserves no respect: *be filled with ~ for her; dismiss a suggestion with ~. laugh sb/sth to scorn,* laugh in a manner showing that he/it is inferior, worthless. **2** object of scorn: *He was the ~ of the village.* □ *vt* feel or show disrespect, disregard, for; refuse (to do something because it is unworthy): *He ~ed my advice. She ~s lying/telling lies/to tell a lie.*

scorn·ful /-fəl/ *adj* showing or feeling scorn: *a ~ful smile.*

scorn·fully /-fəlɪ/ *adv*

Scor·pio /ˈskɔːpɪəʊ/ *n* the Scorpion, eighth sign of the zodiac.

scor·pion /ˈskɔːpɪən/ *n* [C] small animal of the spider group with a poisonous sting in its long, jointed tail.

Scot /skɒt/ *n* [C] native of Scotland.

scot-free /ˈskɒt ˈfriː/ *adj* unharmed, unpunished: *He went/got off ~.*

Scotch /skɒtʃ/ *adj* of Scotland: *~ whisky,* the kind distilled in Scotland. □ *n* [C,U] (portion of) Scotch whisky.

Scots /skɒts/ *n* [C], *adj* ⇨ Scot.

'**Scots·man** /-mən/, '**Scots·woman** /-wʊmən/, native of Scotland.

Scot·tish /ˈskɒtɪʃ/ *adj* of, from, Scotland: *~ music.*

scoun·drel /ˈskaʊndrəl/ *n* [C] person who does wicked things.

scour¹ /ˈskaʊə(r)/ *vt,vi* **1** make (a dirty surface) clean or bright by using a rough cloth, pad of wire, with soap, sand, etc: *~ the pots and pans; ~ out a saucepan,* clean the inside. **2** get rid of (rust, marks, etc) by rubbing, etc: *~ the rust off/away.* **3** clear out (a channel, etc) by flowing over or through it: *The torrent ~ed a channel down the hill-*

side. □ *n* [C] act of scouring.

scourer, pad of stiff nylon or wire for cleaning pots and pans.

scour² /ˈskaʊə(r)/ *vt,vi* look everywhere for: *The police ~ed London for the thief/ were ~ing about.*

scourge /skɜːdʒ/ *n* [C] **1** (*old use*) whip. **2** (*modern use*) (*fig*) cause of suffering: *After the ~ of war came the ~ of disease.* □ *vt* **1** (*old use*) whip. **2** (*fig*) cause suffering to.

scout /skaʊt/ *n* [C] **1** person, ship or small, fast aircraft, sent out to get information of the enemy's movements, strength, etc. **2** = Boy Scout. **3** patrolman on the roads, helping motorists who are members of a motoring organization. **4** person employed to look out for talented performers (in sport, the theatre, etc) and recruit them for his employer(s): *a talent ~.* □ *vi* *scout about/around (for sb/sth),* go about looking for.

'**scout·master,** officer who leads a troop of Boy Scouts.

scowl /skaʊl/ *n* [C] bad-tempered look (on the face). □ *vi* look in a bad-tempered way: *The prisoner ~ed at the judge.*

scrabble /ˈskræbəl/ *vi* *scrabble about (for sth),* grope about to find ●r collect: *scrabbling about for a fork dropped under the table.* □ *n* [C] act of scrabbling.

scrag /skræg/ *n* [C] **1** lean, skinny person or animal. **2** (also '~-end) bony part of a sheep's neck, used for making soup and stews.

scraggy *adj* (-ier, -iest) thin and bony.

scram /skræm/ *vi* (-mm-) (*sl*) (used as an *imperative*) Go away quickly!

scramble /ˈskræmbəl/ *vi,vt* **1** climb (with difficulty) or crawl (over steep or rough ground): *~ up the side of a cliff/over a rocky hillside.* **2** struggle with others to get something: *The players were scrambling for possession of the ball.* **3** cook (eggs) by beating them and then heating them in a saucepan with butter and milk. **4** make a message sent by telephone, etc unintelligible. □ *n* [C] **1** walk, motor-bike competition or trial, over or through obstacles, rough ground, etc. **2** rough struggle: *There was a ~ for the best seats.*

scrap¹ /skræp/ *n* **1** [C] small (usually unwanted) piece: *~s of paper/broken glass.* **2** (*fig*) small amount: *not a ~ of truth in her statement.* **3** [U] waste or unwanted articles, esp those of value only for the material they contain: *He offers good prices for ~.* **4** (*pl*) bits of uneaten food: *Give the ~s to the dog.* **5** [C] picture or paragraph cut out from a periodical, etc for a collection. □ *vt* (-pp-) **1** throw away as useless or worn-out: *You ought to ~ that old bicycle and buy a new one.* **2** reject a plan, idea, etc: *This idea won't work, let's ~ it.*

'**scrapbook,** book of blank pages on which to paste scraps (5).

'**scrap heap,** pile of waste or unwanted

material or articles. ***throw sth/sb on the
scrap heap,*** reject it/them as no longer
wanted.

`scrap-iron`, things made of iron to be sold
for scrap(3).

scrappy *adj* (-ier, -iest) (a) made up of bits
or scraps. (b) not complete or properly
organized: *a ~ idea.*

scrap² /skræp/ *n* [C] (*dated informal*) fight,
quarrel (between children). □ *vi* (-pp-) fight;
quarrel.

scrape /skreɪp/ *vt,vi* **1** make clean, smooth
or level by drawing or pushing the hard edge
of a tool, or something rough, along the surface; remove (mud, grease, paint, etc) in this
way: *~ the rust off a nail; ~ paint from a
door.* **2** injure or damage by rubbing, etc:
*The boy fell and ~d (the skin off) his knee.
He ~d the side of his car.* **3** make by scraping: *~ (out) a hole.* **4** go, get, pass along,
touching or almost touching: *branches that
~ against the window.* **scrape through
(sth),** only just pass: *The boy just ~d
through (his exams).* ***bow and scrape,***
(*fig*) behave with exaggerated respect. **5**
obtain by being careful, or with effort: *We
managed to ~ together an audience of fifty
people/enough money for a short holiday.*
scrape a living, with difficulty make
enough money for a living. □ *n* [C] **1** act or
sound of scraping: *the ~ of a fork across a
plate.* **2** place that is scraped: *a bad ~ on the
elbow,* e g as the result of a fall. **3** awkward
situation resulting from foolish or thoughtless behaviour: *That boy is always getting
into ~s.*

scraper, tool used for scraping, e g for
scraping paint from woodwork.

scrappy /ˈskræpɪ/ *adj* ⇨ scrap¹.

scratch¹ /skrætʃ/ *n* **1** [C] mark, cut, injury,
sound, made by scratching(1): *It's only a ~,*
a very slight injury. *He escaped without a
~,* quite unhurt. **2** (*sing* only) act or period
of scratching(5): *The dog enjoys having a
good ~.* **3** (*sing* only without *the, a* or *an*)
starting line for a race. ***start from scratch,***
(*fig*) (a) start without being allowed any
advantage(s). (b) begin (something) without
preparation. ***be/come/bring sb up to
scratch,*** (*fig*) be ready/get him ready to do
what is expected or required: *Will you be up
to ~ for the examination?* **4** (as an *adjective*)
brought together, done, made, with
whatever or whoever is available: *a ~ team.*

scratchy *adj* (-ier, -iest) (a) (of writing,
drawings) done carelessly. (b) (of a pen)
making a scratching noise.

scratch² /skrætʃ/ *vt,vi* **1** make lines on or in
a surface with something pointed or sharp,
e g fingernails, claws: *This cat ~es. Who
has ~ed the paint? **scratch the surface,**
(fig) deal with a subject without getting
deeply into it: *The teacher merely ~ed the
surface of the subject.* **2** get (oneself, a part
of the body) scratched by accident: *He ~ed*

his hands badly on a rose-bush. **3** draw a
line or lines through a word or words, a
name, etc: *~ out his name from the list.* **4**
withdraw (a horse, a candidate, oneself)
from a competition: *The horse was ~ed.* **5**
scrape or rub (the skin), esp to stop itching:
~ mosquito bites. Stop ~ing (yourself).
scratch one's head, show signs of being
puzzled. **6** make by scratching: *~ (out) a
hole.* **7** make a scraping noise: *This pen
~es.* **8** tear or dig with the claws, finger-
nails, etc in search of something: *The chickens were ~ing about in the yard.*

scrawl /skrɔːl/ *vi,vt* write or draw quickly or
carelessly; make meaningless marks: *He
~ed a few words on a postcard to his wife.
Who has ~ed all over this wall?* □ *n* **1** [C]
piece of bad writing; hurried note or letter. **2**
(*sing* only) shapeless, untidy handwriting:
His signature was an illegible ~.

scrawny /ˈskrɔːnɪ/ *adj* (-ier, -iest) thin and
bony.

scream /skriːm/ *vi,vt* **1** (of humans, birds,
animals) give a loud, sharp cry or cries of, or
as of, fear or pain: *The baby has been ~ing
for an hour.* **2** shout in a high voice: *She
~ed out that there was a burglar under the
bed.* ***scream with laughter,*** laugh noisily.
3 (of the wind, machines, etc) make a loud,
high noise: *The wind ~ed through the trees.*
□ *n* [C] **1** loud, high, cry or noise: *~s of
pain/laughter.* **2** (*informal*) person or thing
that causes screams of laughter: *He/It was a
perfect ~.*

scree /skriː/ *n* [C,U] (part of a mountain-side
covered with) small loose stones.

screech /skriːtʃ/ *vi,vt* **1** make a harsh, piercing sound: *The brakes ~ed as the car
stopped.* **2** scream (as) in anger or pain:
monkeys ~ing in the trees. □ *n* [C] screech-
ing cry or noise: *the ~ of tyres on wet roads.*

screed /skriːd/ *n* [C] long, dull letter or
speech.

screen /skriːn/ *n* [C] **1** (often movable)
upright framework (some made so as to
fold), used to divide a room, protect from
draughts, etc. **2** (in a church) structure of
wood or stone separating (but not completely) the main part of the church and the
altar, or the nave of a cathedral and the
choir. **3** anything that is or can be used to
give shelter or protection from observation,
the weather, etc: *a ~ of trees,* hiding a
house from the road; *a `smoke-~,* used in
war to hide ships, etc from the enemy. **4**
white or silver surface on to which film
transparencies, cinema films, T V pictures,
etc are projected. **5** surface on which an
image is seen on a cathode ray tube (as in a
television set). **6** frame with fine wire netting (`window ~, `door ~) to keep out
flies, mosquitoes, etc. □ *vt,vi* **1** shelter, hide,
protect, with a screen: *The trees ~ our
house from public view.* **2** (*fig*) protect from
blame, discovery, punishment: *I'm not wil-*

ling to ~ *you from blame.* **3** investigate (a person's) past history, e g of a person applying for a position in government service, in order to judge his loyalty, dependability, etc. **4** show (an object, a scene) on a screen(4, 5).

`screen-play`, script of a film.

`screen-test`, test of a person's suitability for acting in films.

`screen-ing`, **(a)** wire netting for a screen(6). **(b)** process of screening(3).

screw /skru/ *n* [C] **1** metal peg with slotted head and a spiral groove cut round its length, driven into wood, metal, etc by twisting under pressure, for fastening and holding things together. **2** something that is turned like a screw and is used for producing pressure, tightening, etc. **3** action of turning; turn: *This isn't tight enough yet; give it another* ~. **4** (also `~-propeller`) propeller of a ship: *a twin-~ steamer.* ⇨airscrew. □ *vt,vi* **1** fasten or tighten with a screw: ~ *a lock on a door;* ~ *down the lid of a coffin.* **have one's head screwed on (the right way)**, be sensible, have good judgement. **2** twist round; make tight, tense or more efficient: ~ *a lid on/off a jar;* ~ *up one's face/features/eyes,* contract the muscles, e g when going out into bright sunshine from a dark room. **screw up one's courage**, overcome one's fears. **3** (esp *fig*) force (out of): ~ *water out of a sponge/more taxes out of the people.*

`screw-driver`, tool for turning a screw(1).

screwy *adj* (-ier, -iest) (*informal*) crazy; absurd.

scribble /'skrɪbəl/ *vt,vi* **1** write quickly or carelessly. **2** make meaningless marks on paper, etc. □ *n* [U] careless handwriting; [C] something scribbled.

scrib-bler /'skrɪblə(r)/, person who scribbles.

scribe /skraɪb/ *n* [C] **1** person who, before the invention of printing, made copies of writings, e g in monasteries. **2** (among the Jews in olden times) maker and keeper of records; teacher of Jewish law (at the time of Jesus Christ).

script /skrɪpt/ *n* **1** [U] handwriting; printed characters in imitation of handwriting. **2** [C] (short for) manuscript or typescript.

`script-writer`, person who writes scripts for radio, TV, films.

scrip-ture /'skrɪptʃə(r)/ *n* **1 The (Holy) S~s**, the Bible; (as an *adjective*) taken from, relating to, the Bible: *a* `~ *lesson.* **2** sacred book of a religion other than Christianity.

scrip-tural /'skrɪptʃərəl/ *adj* based on the Bible.

scroll /skrəʊl/ *n* [C] **1** roll of paper or parchment for writing on; ancient book written on a scroll **2** ornamental design cut in stone like the curves of a scroll.

scro-tum /'skrəʊtəm/ *n* [C] (*pl* ~s) pouch of skin enclosing the testicles in mammals.

scrounge /skraʊndʒ/ *vi,vt* (*informal*) get what one wants by taking it without permission, borrowing or by trickery.

scrounger, person who scrounges.

scrub[1] /skrʌb/ *n* [U] (land covered with) trees and bushes of poor quality.

scrub[2] /skrʌb/ *vt,vi* (-bb-) **1** clean by rubbing hard, esp with a stiff brush, soap and water: ~ *the floor.* **2** cancel; ignore: ~ (*out*) *an order.* □ *n* [C] act of scrubbing: *The floor needs a good* ~.

`scrub-bing-brush`, stiff brush for scrubbing floors, etc.

scruff /skrʌf/ *n* (only in) **the scruff of the neck**, the back of the neck when used for grasping.

scruffy /'skrʌfɪ/ *adj* (-ier, -iest) (*informal*) dirty, untended and untidy looking.

scrum /skrʌm/ *n* [C] (abbr of) **scrummage**.
`scrum` `half`, (Rugby) the half-back who puts the ball into the scrum.

scrum-mage /'skrʌmɪdʒ/ *n* [C] (*Rugby*) the play when the forwards of both sides pack together with their heads down while the ball is thrown into the middle of them; all those forwards when such play occurs.

scruple /'skrupəl/ *n* [C,U] (feeling of doubt caused by a) troubled conscience: *Have you no* ~*s about borrowing things without permission?* □ *vi* hesitate owing to scruples: *He doesn't* ~ *to tell a lie if he thinks it useful.* (*Note:* usually negative.)

scru-pu-lous /'skrupjʊləs/ *adj* careful to do nothing morally wrong; paying great attention to small points (esp of conscience): *A solicitor must act with* ~ *honesty.*

scru-pu-lous-ly *adv* in a scrupulous manner.

scru-ti-nize /'skrutɪnaɪz/ *US*: -tənaɪz/ *vt* make a detailed examination of.

scru-tiny /'skrutɪnɪ/ *US*: -tənɪ/ *n* (*pl* -ies) **1** [U] thorough and detailed examination; [C] instance of this. **2** [C] official examination of votes, esp a re-count: *demand a* ~.

scuff /skʌf/ *vi,vt* **1** walk without properly lifting the feet from the ground. **2** wear out or scrape (shoes, etc) by walking in this way: ~ *one's shoes.*

scuffle /'skʌfəl/ *vi, n* [C] (take part in a) rough fight or struggle: *scuffling police and demonstrators.*

scull /skʌl/ *n* [C] **1** one of a pair of oars used together by a rower, one in each hand. **2** oar worked at the stern of a boat with twisting strokes. □ *vt,vi* propel, row, (a boat) with sculls.

scul-ler, person who sculls.

scul-lery /'skʌlərɪ/ *n* [C] (*pl* -ies) room in a large house next to the kitchen, where dishes, pots, etc are washed up.

`scullery-maid`, servant who helps the cook by washing up dishes, etc.

sculpt /skʌlpt/ *vt,vi* = sculpture.

sculp-tor /'skʌlptə(r)/ *n* [C] artist who sculptures.

sculp·tress /ˈskʌlptrəs/ n [C] woman who sculptures.

sculp·ture /ˈskʌlptʃə(r)/ n 1 [U] art of making representations in stone, wood, metal, etc by carving or modelling. 2 [C,U] (piece of) such work. □ vt,vi 1 represent in, decorate with, sculpture: ~ a statue out of stone; ~d columns. 2 be a sculptor.

scum /skʌm/ n [U] 1 froth which forms on the surface of some boiling liquids; dirt on the surface of a pond or other area of still water. 2 the ~, (fig) the worst, or seemingly worthless, section (of the population, etc).

scup·per /ˈskʌpə(r)/ n [C] opening in a ship's side to allow water to run off the deck. □ vt 1 sink a ship deliberately. 2 (informal) (usually passive) ruin; disable: We're ~ed!

scurf /skɜːf/ n [U] small bits of dead skin, esp on the scalp.

scurfy adj having, covered with, scurf.

scur·ri·lous /ˈskʌrɪləs US: ˈskɜːrələs/ adj using, full of, violent words of abuse: ~ attacks on the Prime Minister.

scurry /ˈskʌrɪ US: ˈskɜːrɪ/ vi (pt,pp -ied) run with short, quick steps; hurry: The rain sent everyone ~ing about/~ing for shelter. □ n 1 [U] act or sound of scurrying: There was a ~ towards the bar. 2 [C] windy shower (of snow); cloud (of dust).

scurvy /ˈskɜːvɪ/ n [U] diseased state of the blood caused by eating too much salt meat and not enough fresh vegetables and fruit.

scuttle¹ /ˈskʌtəl/ n [C] (also ˈcoal-~) container for a supply of coal at the fireside.

scuttle² /ˈskʌtəl/ vi scuttle off/away, = scurry.□ n [C] hurried departure.

scuttle³ /ˈskʌtəl/ n [C] small opening with a lid, in a ship's side or on deck or in a roof or wall. □ vt cut holes in, open valves in, a ship's sides or bottom to sink it: The captain ~d his ship to avoid its being captured by the enemy.

scythe /saɪð/ n [C] tool with a curved blade on a long wooden pole and two short handles, for cutting long grass, grain, etc. □ vt use a scythe.

sea /siː/ n 1 the ~, expanse of salt water that covers most of the earth's surface; any part of this (in contrast to areas of fresh water and dry land): Ships sail on the ~. The ~ covers nearly three-quarters of the world's surface. **on the sea**, on the coast: Brighton is on the ~. 2 (pl) same sense as 1 above. **the high seas**, ⇨ high¹. **the freedom of the seas**, the right to carry on sea-trade without interference. 3 (in proper names) particular area of sea which is smaller than an ocean: the Caspian S~; the S~ of Galilee. 4 (in various phrases without the, a or an) **at sea**, away from, out of sight of, the land: He was buried at ~. **all/completely at sea**, (fig) puzzled: He was all at ~ when he began his new job. **by sea**, in a ship: travel by ~ and land. **go to sea**, become a sailor. **put to**

sea, leave port or land. 5 (with a, an or in pl) local state of the sea swell of the ocean· big wave or billow: There was a heavy ~. large waves. **half seas over**, having drunk too much. 6 large quantity or expanse (of): a ~ of up-turned faces, e g crowds of people looking upwards.

ˈsea ˈair, air at the seaside, considered to be good for health.

ˈsea-anemone, popular name for a sea-creature like a flower.

ˈsea-animal, animal living in the sea, e g fish, mammals, molluscs, etc.

ˈsea-bathing, bathing in the sea.

ˈsea·bed, floor of the sea

ˈsea-bird, any bird which lives close to the sea, i e on cliffs, islands, etc.

ˈsea·board, coastal region.

ˈsea-borne adj (of trade) carried in ships.

ˈsea-breeze, breeze blowing inland from the sea.

ˈsea·faring /-feərɪŋ/ adj of work or voyages on the sea: a ˈseafaring man, a sailor.

ˈsea-fish, fish living in the sea.

ˈsea-food, edible fish or shellfish from the sea.

ˈsea-front, part of a town facing the sea.

ˈsea-god, god living in or having power over the sea, e g Neptune.

ˈsea-going adj (a) (of ships) built for crossing the sea, not for coastal voyages only. (b) (of a person) seafaring.

ˈsea-ˈgreen adj, n [U] bluish-green as of the sea.

ˈsea·gull, common sea-bird with long wings.

ˈsea-horse, small fish with a head like a horse.

ˈsea-legs, ability to walk on the deck of a rolling ship: get/find one's ~-legs.

ˈsea-level, level of sea halfway between high and low tide as the basis for measuring height of land and depth of sea: 100 metres above/below ~-level.

ˈsea-lion, large seal of the N Pacific Ocean.

ˈsea·man /-mən/, (a) (in the Navy) rating, not an officer. (b) person expert in nautical matters.

ˈsea·man·ship, skill in managing a boat or ship.

ˈsea mile, nautical mile.

ˈsea·plane, aircraft constructed so that it can come down on and rise from water.

ˈsea·port, town with a harbour used by sea-going ships.

ˈsea-power, ability to control and use the seas (by means of naval strength).

ˈsea·scape, picture of a scene at sea. ⇨ landscape.

ˈsea-shell, shell of any shellfish inhabiting the sea.

ˈsea-shore, land close to the shore.

ˈsea-sick adj (feeling) sick from the motion of a ship.

ˈsea·side, (often as an adjective) place,

town, etc by the sea, esp a holiday resort: *go to the ~side; a ~side town.*

`sea-urchin,` small sea-animal with a shell covered with sharp points.

'sea-'wall, wall built to stop the sea from approaching the land.

`sea-water,` water from the sea.

`sea-weed,` kinds of plant growing in the sea, esp on rocks washed by the sea.

`sea-ward` /-wəd/ *adj* towards the sea; in the direction of the sea.

`sea-wards` /-wədz/ *adv*

`sea-worthy` *adj* (of a ship) fit for a voyage.

seal¹ /sil/ *n* [C] kinds of round sea-animal with flippers. □ *vi* hunt seals.

`seal-skin,` skin of a seal.

seal² /sil/ *n* [C] 1 piece of wax, lead, etc stamped with a design, attached to a document to show that it is genuine, or to a letter, packet, box, bottle, door, etc to guard against its being opened by unauthorized persons. 2 something used instead of a seal(1), e g a paper disc stuck to, or an impression stamped on, a document. 3 piece of metal, etc with a design used to stamp the seal on wax, etc. 4 *seal of,* (*fig*) act, event, etc regarded as a confirmation or guarantee or giving approval (of something): *the ~ of approval for spending the money.* 5 something that closes a thing tight to prevent leaks: *an airtight ~.* □ *vt* 1 put a seal(1) on: *~ a letter.* 2 fasten or close tightly: *~ an envelope; ~ up a drawer so that it cannot be opened.* 3 seal off, enclose to prevent entry or exit: *~ off an area of land.* 4 decide: *His fate is ~ed!*

`seal-ing-wax,` kind of wax used to seal letters, etc.

seam /sim/ *n* [C] 1 line where two edges, e g of cloth, are turned back and sewn together. 2 line where two edges, e g of boards forming a ship's deck, meet. 3 layer of coal, etc between layers of other materials, e g rock, clay. 4 line or mark like a seam(1) (e g of folded paper).

seam-stress /ˈsimstrəs/, (also semp-stress /ˈsempstrəs/) *n* [C] woman who makes a living by sewing.

sé-ance /ˈseɪəns US: ˈseɪæns/ *n* [C] meeting for communicating with the spirits of the dead through a medium(4).

sear /sɪə(r)/ *vt* 1 burn or scorch the surface of, esp with a heated iron. 2 (*fig*) make (a person, his conscience, etc) hard and without feeling: *His soul had been ~ed by injustice.*

search /sɜtʃ/ *vt,vi* examine, look carefully at, through, or into (in order to find a person or thing): *He ~ed through all the drawers for the missing papers. I've ~ed my memory but can't remember that man's name.* □ *n* [C,U] 1 act of searching: *go in ~ of a missing child; a ~ for a missing aircraft.* 2 (*legal*) investigation (e g by lawyers) into possible reasons (e g planned demolition)

why one should not buy land or property.

`search-light,` powerful light with a beam that can be turned in any direction to search for the enemy, escaped prisoners, etc.

`search-party,` number of persons looking for a person or thing that is lost.

`search-warrant,` official authority to enter and search a building (e g for stolen property).

searcher, person who searches.

search-ing *adj* (a) (of a look) taking in all details. (b) (of a test, etc) thorough.

search-ing-ly *adv*

sea-son /ˈsizən/ *n* [C] 1 one of the divisions of the year according to the weather, e g spring, summer, etc: *the `dry ~; the `rainy ~.* 2 period suitable or normal for something, or closely associated with it: *the `football ~; the `holiday/`tourist ~. in/out of season,* available/not available: *Oysters/ Strawberries are out of ~ now.* □ *vt,vi* 1 make or become suitable for use: *Has this wood been well ~ed,* dried and hardened? *The soldiers were not yet ~ed to the rigorous climate.* 2 flavour (food) (with salt, pepper, etc): *highly ~ed dishes.*

places as often as he wishes during a stated period of time. (b) ticket that gives the owner the right to attend a concert hall, etc (for the concerts, etc specified) during a certain period.

sea-son-ing, something used to season food: *Salt and pepper are ~ings.*

sea-son-able /ˈsizənəbəl/ *adj* 1 (of the weather) of the kind to be expected at the time of year. 2 (of help, advice, gifts, etc) coming at the right time.

sea-sonal /ˈsizənəl/ *adj* depending on a particular season; changing with the seasons: *~ occupations,* e g fruit-picking.

sea-son-ally /-əlɪ/ *adv*

seat /sit/ *n* [C] 1 something used or made for sitting on, e g a chair, box, bench: *The back ~ of the car is wide enough for three persons. take a seat,* sit: *Won't you take a seat? take one's seat,* sit down in one's place, e g in a hall or theatre. *take a back seat,* ⇨ back⁴(2). 2 that part of a chair, stool, bench, etc on which one sits (contrasted with the back, legs, etc): *a `chair-~.* 3 part of the body (the buttocks) on which one sits; part of a garment covering this: *He tore the ~ of his pants.* 4 place to sit in a cinema, theatre, etc or in which one has a right to sit: *Mr Smith has a ~ in the House of Commons,* is a member. *win a seat/lose one's seat,* win/be defeated in a Parliamentary election. 5 place where something is, or where something is carried on: *In the US, Washington is the ~ of government. A university is a ~ of learning.* 6 large house in the country: *He has a country ~ as well as a large house in London.* □ *vt* 1 (*formal*) *be seated,* sit down: *Please be ~ed, gentlemen.* 2 have seats for: *Our community* *hall* ~s 500.

`seat-belt, strap for fastening across a seated passenger in a car or aircraft.

seca·teurs /ˈsekətɜz/ n pl pair of clippers used by gardeners for pruning bushes, etc.

se·cede /sɪˈsid/ vi (of a group) withdraw (*from* membership of a state, federation, organization, etc).

se·ces·sion /sɪˈseʃən/ n [U] seceding; [C] instance of this (as in the US when eleven Southern States withdrew from the Federal Union in 1810—11).

se·ces·sion·ist /-ɪst/ n [C] supporter of secession.

se·clude /sɪˈklud/ vt keep (a person, oneself) apart from the company of others: ~ *oneself from society; keep a wife ~d in the kitchen.*

se·cluded adj (esp of a place) quiet; solitary.

se·clu·sion /sɪˈkluʒən/ n [U] secluding or being secluded; solitary place: *live in ~; in the ~ of one's own home.*

sec·ond¹ /ˈsekənd/ adj (abbr 2nd) 1 next after the first (in place, time, order, importance, etc): *February is the ~ month of the year. Tom is the ~ son—he has an elder brother.* **second to none,** no other person, idea, etc is better. **In the `second place...,** = secondly. 2 additional; extra: *You will need a ~ pair of shoes.* **play second fiddle (to),** ⇨ fiddle. 3 of the same kind as one that has gone before: *This man seems to think he's a ~ Napoleon!* □ adv in the second place (in importance or in a race): *The English swimmer came (in) ~.*

'second-`Advent/`Coming, return of Jesus Christ at the Last Judgement.

'second-`best adj next after the best: *my ~-best suit.* □ n, adv: *I won't accept/put up with ~-best.* **come off second-best,** get the worst of it.

'second `chamber, upper house in a legislature: *The House of Lords is the ~ chamber of Parliament in Great Britain.*

'second-`class adj, n (a) (of the) class next after the first: *a ~-class hotel;* (b) class below the first in examination results: *take a ~-class degree in law.* (c) (regarded or treated as) inferior: *~-class citizens.* □ adv: *go/travel ~-class.*

'second `childhood, period of old age when a person shows a weakening of mental powers.

'second `cousin, child of a first cousin of either of one's parents.

'second `floor, the one above the first (*GB* two floors up, in *US* one floor above the ground: (as an *adjective*) *a ~-floor apartment*).

'second `gene`ration, having parents who were immigrants, members, etc.

'second-`hand adj (a) previously owned by someone else: *~-hand furniture/books.* (b) (of news, knowledge) obtained from others,

not based on personal observation, etc: *get news ~-hand.*

'second `home, (a) another home. (b) (*fig*) like one's house (because friendly, comfortable, etc).

'second lieu`tenant, lowest commissioned rank in the Army.

'second `name, = surname.

'second `nature, acquired habit that has become instinctive: *kindness is ~ nature to him.*

'second-`rate adj not of the best quality; inferior: *a man with ~-rate ideas.*

'second `sight, power to see future events, or events happening at a distance, as if present. Hence, **'second-`sighted** adj having this power.

'second `teeth, those which grow after a child's first teeth are out.

`second thoughts, opinion or resolution reached after reconsideration: *On ~ thoughts I will accept the offer. I'm having ~ thoughts* (= am not so sure) *about buying that house.*

'second `wind, renewed strength, energy.

second·ly adv in the next place; furthermore.

sec·ond² /ˈsekənd/ n [C] 1 person or thing that comes next to the first: *the ~ of May; Queen Elizabeth the S~* (or II). **get a second,** get a second-class degree. 2 another person or thing besides the person or thing previously mentioned: *You are the ~ to ask me that question.* 3 (*pl*) goods below the best in quality. 4 supporter of a boxer or wrestler in a match; supporter in a duel.

sec·ond³ /ˈsekənd/ n [C] 1 sixtieth part of a minute or a degree (indicated by the mark ″): *The winner's time was 1 minute and 5 ~s. 1° 6′ 10″ means one degree, six minutes, and ten ~s.* 2 moment; short time: *I shall be ready in a ~ or two/in a few ~s.*

`second-hand, extra hand in some watches and clocks recording seconds. ⇨ also second-hand at second¹.

se·cond⁴ /ˈsekənd/ vt 1 support (esp a boxer, wrestler or dueller). 2 (a debate, etc) rise or speak formally in support of a motion to show that the proposer is not the only person in favour of it: *Mr Smith proposed, and Mr Green ~ed, a vote of thanks to the lecturer.*

se·conder, person who supports a proposal at a meeting.

se·cond⁵ /sɪˈkond US: ˈsekənd/ vt take (a person) from his ordinary duty and give him special duty: *be ~ed by the BBC to work for another radio station.*

se·cond·ment n [U]

sec·ond·ary /ˈsekəndrɪ US: -derɪ/ adj 1 coming after: *~ education/schools,* for children over eleven. 2 less important or less strong: *~symptoms.*

secondary stress, (marked /ˈ/ in this dictionary) e g on the second syllable of 'pro-nunciation' /prəˌnʌnsɪˈeɪʃən/.

sec·ond·ar·ily /-dərɪlɪ US: -der-/ adv

se·crecy /ˈsiːkrəsɪ/ n [U] keeping of secrets; ability to keep secrets; habit of keeping secrets; state of being kept secret: I depend on your ~; prepare an escape in ~, secretly; do it with great ~. **be sworn to secrecy,** ⇨ swear(2).

se·cret /ˈsiːkrɪt/ adj 1 (to be) kept from the knowledge or view of others; of which others have no knowledge: a ~ marriage. **keep sth secret, (from),** not tell it. 2 (of places) quiet and unknown. □ n 1 [C] something that is secret. **keep a secret,** not tell anyone else: Can you keep a ~? **(be) an open secret,** (of something thought to be secret) be (in fact) widely known. 2 [C] hidden cause; explanation; way of doing or getting something, that is not known to some or most people: What is the ~ of his success? 3 [U] **in secret,** secretly: I was told about it in ~. 4 [C] mystery: the ~s of nature.
'secret `agent, member of the secret service.
'secret `ballot, when voters' choices are secret.
'secret po`lice, operating in secret (against political opposition).
the 'secret `service, government department concerned with spying.
se·cret·ly adv

sec·re·tary /ˈsekrətrɪ US: -rəterɪ/ n [C] (pl -ies) 1 employee in an office, who deals with correspondence, keeps records, makes arrangements and appointments for a particular member of staff. 2 official who has charge of the correspondence, records, and other business affairs of a society, club or other organization.
Secretary of State, (a) (GB) minister in charge of a Government office: the S~ of State for Foreign and Commonwealth Affairs. **(b)** (US) chief and foreign minister.
'Secretary-`General, principal administrator (e g of UNO).
sec·re·tar·ial /ˌsekrəˈteərɪəl/ adj of (the work of) secretaries: ~ duties/training/ colleges.

se·crete /sɪˈkriːt/ vt 1 produce by secretion(1). 2 put or keep in a secret place.

se·cre·tion /sɪˈkriːʃən/ n 1 [U] process by which certain substances in a plant or animal body are separated (from sap, blood, etc); [C] substance so produced, e g saliva, bile. 2 [C] (formal) act of hiding: the ~ of stolen goods.

se·cret·ive /ˈsiːkrətɪv/ adj having the habit of hiding one's thoughts, feelings, intentions, etc.
se·cre·tive·ly adv

sect /sekt/ n [C] group of people united by (esp religious) beliefs or opinions.

sec·tar·ian /sekˈteərɪən/ n [C], adj (member, supporter) of a sect or sects: ~ politics, in which the advantage of a sect is considered more important than the public wel-fare.

sec·tion /ˈsekʃən/ n [C] 1 part cut off; one of the parts into which something may be divided: the ~s of an orange. 2 one of a number of parts which can be put together to make a structure: glue the ~s of the model together. 3 subdivision of an organized body of persons (the `Postal S~), or of a piece of writing or of a town or community: 'resi`dential/ˈshopping ~s (area is the usual word). 4 view or representation of something seen as if cut straight through; thin slice suitable for examination under a microscope.
sec·tional /-əl/ adj **(a)** made or supplied in sections(2): a ~al fishing-rod. **(b)** of one or more sections of a community, etc: ~al interests, the different and often conflicting interests of various sections of a community.
sec·tion·al·ism /-ɪzm/ n [U] concern about sectional interests, not the community as a whole.

sec·tor /ˈsektə(r)/ n [C] 1 part of a circle lying between two straight lines drawn from the centre to the circumference. 2 one of the parts into which an area is divided for the purpose of controlling (esp military) operations. 3 branch (of industry, etc): the public and private ~s of industry, those parts publicly owned and those privately owned.

secu·lar /ˈsekjʊlə(r)/ adj 1 worldly or material, not religious or spiritual: the ~ power, the State contrasted with the Church. 2 living outside monasteries: the ~ clergy, parish priests, etc.

se·cure /sɪˈkjʊə(r)/ adj (rarely -r, -st) 1 free from anxiety: feel ~ about the future. 2 certain; guaranteed: He has a ~ position as a university lecturer. 3 unlikely to involve risk; firm: Are you sure the doors and windows are ~? Is that ladder ~? 4 safe: Are we ~ from attack? □ vt 1 lock: ~ all the doors and windows before leaving the house. 2 make secure: By strengthening the embankments they ~d the village against/ from floods. 3 succeed in getting (something for which there is a great demand): She has ~d a good teaching job.
se·cure·ly adv

se·cur·ity /sɪˈkjʊərətɪ/ n (pl -ies) 1 [C,U] (something that provides) safety, freedom from danger or anxiety: children who lack the ~ of parental care. 2 [C,U] something valuable, e g a life-insurance policy, given as a guarantee for the repayment of a loan or the fulfilment of a promise or undertaking: lend money on ~; offer a house as (a) ~ for a loan. 3 [C] document, certificate, etc showing ownership of property (esp bonds, stocks and shares): government securities, for money lent to a government.

se·date /sɪˈdeɪt/ adj (of a person, his behaviour) calm; serious.
se·date·ly adv

se·da·tion /sɪˈdeɪʃən/ n [U] treatment using

sedatives; condition resulting from this. **be under sedation,** have taken sedatives.

seda·tive /ˈsedətɪv/ *n* [C], *adj* (medicine, drug) tending to calm the nerves and reduce stress: *After taking a ∼ she was able to get to sleep.*

sed·en·tary /ˈsedəntrɪ US: -terɪ/ *adj* **1** (of work) done sitting down (at a desk, etc). **2** (of persons) spending much of their time seated: *lead a ∼ life.*

sedi·ment /ˈsedɪmənt/ *n* [U] matter (e g sand, dirt, gravel) that settles to the bottom of a liquid.

sedi·men·tary /ˈsedɪˈmentrɪ/ *adj* of the nature of, formed from, sediment: *∼ary rocks,* e g sandstone.

se·di·tion /sɪˈdɪʃən/ *n* [U] words or actions intended to make people rebel against authority, disobey the government, etc.

se·di·tious /sɪˈdɪʃəs/ *adj* of the nature of sedition: *seditious speeches/writings.*

se·duce /sɪˈdjuːs US: -ˈduːs/ *vt* **1** persuade (a person) to do wrong, to commit a crime or to sin: *be ∼d by the offer of money into betraying one's country.* **2** persuade a person less experienced to have sexual intercourse: *How many women did Don Juan ∼?*

se·ducer, person who seduces, esp (2).

se·duc·tion /sɪˈdʌkʃən/ *n* **1** [U] seducing or being seduced; [C] instance of this. **2** something attractive that may lead a person to do something (but often with no implication of immorality): *surrender to the ∼s of country life.*

se·duc·tive /sɪˈdʌktɪv/ *adj* attractive; captivating: *seductive smiles; a seductive offer.*

se·duc·tive·ly *adv*

sedu·lous /ˈsedjʊləs US: ˈsedʒʊləs/ *adj* (*formal*) persevering; done with perseverance: *He paid her ∼ attention.*

see¹ /siː/ *vi,vt* (*pt* saw /sɔː/, *pp* ∼n /siːn/) (For special uses with *adverbial particles* and *prepositions*, ⇒ 11 below.) **1** (often with *can*, *could*; not usually in the progressive tenses) have or use the power of sight: *If you shut your eyes you can't ∼. It was getting dark and I couldn't ∼ to read. On a clear day we can ∼ (for) miles.* **seeing is believing,** (*proverb*) What we ourselves see is the most satisfactory evidence. **be ˋseeing things,** imagine that one can see things that are not there or that do not exist: *You're ∼ing things—there's nobody there!* **2** (often with *can*, *could*, esp when effort is needed; not in the progressive tenses) be aware of by using the power of sight: *I saw him put the key in the lock, turn it and open the door. The suspected man was ∼n to enter the building. If you watch carefully you will ∼ how to do it/how I do it/how it is done.* **see the back of sb,** get rid of him; see him for the last time: *That man's a nuisance; I shall be glad to see the back of him.* **see the last of sb/sth,** have done with; see for the last time: *I'll be glad to see the last of*

this *job*, get to the end of it. **see the sights,** visit notable places, etc as a tourist. **see stars,** have dancing lights before the eyes, e g as the result of a blow on the head. **see one's way (clear) to doing sth,** understand how to manage to do it, feel willing to do it: *He didn't ∼ his way to lending me the money I needed.* **3** (in the *imperative*) look (at): *S∼, here he comes! S∼ page 4.* **4** (not in the progressive tenses) understand; learn by search or inquiry or thinking: *He didn't ∼ the joke/the point of the story. Do you ∼ what I mean?* **as ˋI see it,** in my opinion. **see for oneself,** find out in order to be convinced or satisfied: *If you don't believe me, go and ∼ for yourself!* **5** learn from the newspaper or other printed sources: *I ∼ that the Prime Minister is in China.* **6** have knowledge or experience of: *He has ∼n a good deal in his long life. I never saw such rudeness.* **have seen better days,** have now declined, lost former prosperity, etc. **7** give an interview to; visit; receive a call from: *The manager can ∼ you for five minutes. You ought to ∼ a doctor about that cough.* **8** allow; look on without protest or action: *You can't ∼ people starve without trying to help them, can you?* **9** attend to; take care; make provision: *S∼ that the windows and doors are locked/that the children have enough food.* **10** imagine: *He saw himself as the saviour of his country.*

11 (special uses with *adverbial particles* and *prepositions*):

see about sth, deal with: *He promised to ∼ about my broken window.* **see sb about sth,** take advice: *I must ∼ a builder about my roof.*

see sb across sth, guide, help, him across (a road, etc): *That man's blind—I'd better ∼ him across the street.*

see sb back/home, accompany him: *May I ∼ you home?*

see sb off, go to a railway station, an airport, etc with a person about to start on a journey: *I was ∼n off by many of my friends*

see sb out, accompany a person until he is out of a building: *My secretary will ∼ you out.*

see over sth, visit and examine or inspect carefully: *We saw over a house that we wanted to buy.*

see through sb/sth, not be deceived by: *We all saw through him,* knew what kind of man he really was. **see sb through (sth),** give him support, encouragement during (it). **ˋsee sth ˋthrough,** not give up an undertaking until the end is reached: *Whatever happens, we'll ∼ the struggle through.*

see to sth, attend to it: *The break won't work; get a mechanic to ∼ to it.*

see² /siː/ *n* [C] district under a bishop; bishop's position, office, jurisdiction: *the S∼ of Canterbury.*

seed /siːd/ *n* [C] (*pl* ~s or unchanged) **1** flowering plant's element of life, from which another plant can grow: *a packet of* ~(*s*). **run/go to seed,** (a) stop flowering as seed is produced. (b) (*fig*) become careless of one's appearance and manners. **2** cause, origin (*of a tendency, development, etc*): *sow the ~s of virtue in young children.* **3** = semen. **4** (*sport*) seeded player: *England's No. 1* ~, e g in a tennis championship. ⇨ **4** below. □ *vi, vt* **1** (of a plant) produce seed when full grown. **2** sow with seed: ~ *a field with wheat.* **3** remove seed from: ~ *raisins.* **4** (esp in tennis) separate the best players from the rest when organizing competitions (in order to make good matches later in a tournament): ~*ed players.*
`**seed-bed,** area of fine soil in which to sow seed.
`**seeds·man,** dealer in seeds.
seed·less *adj* having no seed: ~*less raisins.*
seed·ling /ˈsiːdlɪŋ/, young plant grown from a seed.
seedy /ˈsiːdɪ/ *adj* (-ier, -iest) **1** full of seed: *as ~ as a dried fig.* **2** (*informal*) looking worn, neglected, etc: *a ~ hotel; a ~-looking person.* **3** (*informal*) unwell: *feel ~.*
seed·ily /-əlɪ/ *adv*

seek /siːk/ *vt* (*pt, pp* sought /sɔːt/) **1** look for; try to find: ~ *shelter from the rain.* **seek one's fortune,** to try to become rich: *He's gone to Canada to ~ his fortune.* **2** ask for: *I will ~ my doctor's advice.* **3 seek for,** try to win: ~*ing for glory in football.* **(much) sought after,** (much) in demand.

seem /siːm/ *vi* have or give the impression or appearance of being or doing; appear to be: *What ~s easy to some people ~s difficult to others. He ~s to think so. The book ~s (to be) quite interesting.*
seem·ing *adj* apparent but perhaps not real or genuine: *In spite of his ~ing friendship he gave me no help.*
seem·ing·ly *adv* apparently.
seem·ly /ˈsiːmlɪ/ *adj* (-ier, -iest) (of behaviour) proper or correct (for the occasion or circumstances): *It isn't ~ to praise oneself.*
seen /siːn/ *pp* of see

seep /siːp/ *vi* (of liquids) come out or through: *water ~ing through the roof.*
seep·age /-ɪdʒ/ *n* [U] slow leaking through.
seer /sɪə(r)/ *n* [C] person claiming to see into the future.
see·saw /ˈsiːsɔː/ *n* [C,U] **1** (game played on a) long plank with a person sitting on each end which can rise and fall alternately. **2** (*fig*) up-and-down or to-and-fro movement: *the ~ of bank interest charges.* □ *vi* **1** play on a seesaw. **2** move up and down or to and fro. **3** be uncertain: ~ *between two opinions/points of view.*
seethe /siːð/ *vi, vt* be very excited or agitated: ~ *with anger; a country seething with discontent; streets seething with people.*

seg·ment /ˈsegmənt/ *n* [C] **1** part cut off or marked off by a line: *a ~ of a circle.* **2** section: *a ~ of an orange.* □ *vt, vi* /segˈment/ divide, become divided, into segments.
seg·men·ta·tion /ˌsegmenˈteɪʃən/ *n* [U]
seg·re·gate /ˈsegrɪgeɪt/ *vt* put apart from the rest; isolate: ~ *the boys from the girls.*
seg·re·ga·tion /ˌsegrɪˈgeɪʃən/ *n* [U]
seis·mic /ˈsaɪzmɪk/ *adj* of earthquakes.
seis·mo·graph /ˈsaɪzməgrɑːf *US*: -græf/ *n* [C] instrument which records the strength, duration and distance away of earthquakes.
seis·mol·ogist /saɪzˈmɒlədʒɪst/ *n* [C] scientist studying earthquakes.
seis·mol·ogy /saɪzˈmɒlədʒɪ/ *n* [U] science of earthquakes.

seize /siːz/ *vt, vi* **1** take possession of (property, etc) by law: ~ *her house for payment of a debt.* **2** take hold of, suddenly and with force: ~ *a thief by the collar.* **3** see clearly and use: ~ (*on*) *an idea/a chance/ an opportunity.* **4** (of moving parts of machinery) become stuck or jammed, e g because of too much heat or friction: *the engine has ~ed (up).*
seiz·ure /ˈsiːʒə(r)/ *n* **1** [U] act of seizing or taking possession of by force or the authority of the law; [C] instance of this: ~ *of drugs by Customs officials.* **2** [C] heart attack.
sel·dom /ˈseldəm/ *adv* not often; rarely: *She ~ goes out. She goes out very ~.*
se·lect /sɪˈlekt/ *vt* choose (as being the most suitable, etc): ~ *a book/a present for a child. Who has been ~ed to speak at the meeting?* □ *adj* **1** carefully chosen: ~ *passages from 'Hamlet'.* **2** of or for a particular group of persons, not for all: *shown to a ~ audience.*
se·lec·tion /sɪˈlekʃən/ *n* **1** [U] choosing. ⇨ natural selection. **2** [C] collection or group of selected things or examples; number of things from which to select: *That shop has a good ~ of handbags.*
se·lec·tive /sɪˈlektɪv/ *adj* **1** having the power to select; characterized by selection. **2** choosing only the best: *a ~ school,* that chooses its pupils.
se·lec·tive·ly *adv*
se·lec·tor /sɪˈlektə(r)/ *n* [C] person who, that which, selects, e g a member of a committee choosing a national sports team, etc.
self /self/ *n* (*pl* selves /selvz/) **1** [U] person's nature, special qualities; one's own personality: *my former ~,* myself as I used to be. **2** one's own interests or pleasure: *She has no thought of ~ (herself* is more usual), thinks only of others.
self– /self/ *prefix* of oneself or itself alone, independent: '~-`taught,* taught by oneself.
`**self-a`basement,** degrading of oneself.
`**self-ab`sorbed** *adj* thinking of one's own interests only, unaware of other people.
`**self-as`sertion,** *n* [U] the putting forward of oneself or one's ideas in an effort to be noticed by everyone.

'self-as'surance, confidence in oneself. Hence. **'self-as'sured** *adj*

'self-'centred *adj* interested chiefly in oneself and one's own affairs.

'self-con'fessed *adj* admitted by oneself: *a ~-confessed thief.*

'self-'confidence, belief in one's own abilities. Hence, **'self-'confident** *adj*

'self-'conscious *adj* (a) aware of one's own existence, thoughts and actions. (b) shy; embarrassed. Hence, **'self-'consciousness** *n* [U]

'self-con'tained *adj* (a) (of a person) not dependent on others. (b) (esp of a flat ¹,) complete in itself (not sharing the kitchen, bathroom, etc with occupants of other flats).

'self-con'trol, control of one's own feelings, behaviour, etc: *exercise ~-control; lose one's ~-control.*

'self-de'fence, defence of one's own body, property, rights, etc: *kill a person in ~-defence,* while defending oneself against attack.

'self-de'nial, going without things in order to help others: *~-denial to help the children.*

'self-ef'facing *adj* keeping oneself in the background (and avoiding praise, attention).

'self-em'ployed *adj* working, e g as a shop-keeper, as an owner of a business.

'self-e'steem, good opinion (sometimes exaggerated) of oneself.

'self-'evident *adj* clear without proof or more evidence. Hence, **'self-'evidently** *adv*

'self-ex'planatory *adj* clear without (further) explanation.

'self-'generating, produced from the thing itself or the person himself.

'self-'government, independent government (not a colony).

'self-im'portant *adj* having too high an opinion of oneself. Hence, **'self-im'portance** *n* [U]

'self-im'posed *adj* (of a duty, task, etc) imposed on oneself.

'self-in'dulgent *adj* giving way too easily to one's preferred comfort, pleasures, etc. Hence, **'self-in'dulgence** *n* [U]

'self-'interest, one's own interests and personal advantage.

'self-'pity, (exaggerated) pity for oneself.

'self-pos'sessed *adj* calm, confident: *a ~-possessed young woman.*

'self-'preser'vation, keeping oneself from harm or destruction: *the instinct of ~-preservation.*

'self-'raising *adj* (of flour) not needing the addition of baking-powder for cakes, etc to rise.

'self-re'liant *adj* having or showing confidence in one's own powers, judgement, etc. Hence, **'self-re'liance** *n* [U]

'self-re'spect, feeling that one is behaving and thinking in ways that will not cause one to be ashamed of oneself: *lose all ~-respect.*

'self-re'specting *adj* having self-respect: *No ~-respecting man could agree to do such a thing.*

'self-'righteous *adj* convinced of one's own goodness and that one is better than others.

'self-'rule, = self-government.

'self-'sacrifice, the giving up of one's own interests and wishes for the sake of other people. Hence, **'self-'sacrificing** *adj*

'self-same *adj* very same; identical: *Tom and I reached Paris on the ~-same day.*

'self-'service, (a) (of a canteen, restaurant,) one at which persons collect their own food and drink from counters and carry it to tables. (b) (of a shop) one at which customers collect what they want from counters or shelves (in wire baskets) and pay as they leave. (c) (of a garage) one at which customers fill their cars with petrol.

'self-'styled *adj* using a name, title, etc which one has given oneself and to which one has no right: *a ~-styled expert on music.*

'self-suf'ficient *adj* needing no help from others: *The country is now ~-sufficient in oil,* no longer has to import it.

'self-sup'porting *adj* (a) (of a person) earning enough money to keep oneself: *now that my children are ~-supporting.* (b) (of a business, etc) paying its way; not needing a subsidy.

'self-'taught *adj* not taught or educated by others.

'self-'will, determination to do as one wishes and not be guided by others.

'self-'willed *adj* obstinate; refusing advice or guidance.

self-ish /ˈselfɪʃ/ *adj* chiefly thinking of one's self and one's own affairs: *act from ~ motives.*

self-ish-ly *adv*

self-ish-ness *n* [U]

sell /sel/ *vt, vi* (*pt, pp* sold /səʊld/) **1** give in exchange for money: *~ books; ~ a car at a good price; ~ oranges at fivepence each. Will you ~ me your bike? I'll ~ it to you for £5.* **sell sth off,** sell (goods, etc) cheaply. **sell sth out,** sell all of one's stock of something: *We are sold out of small sizes.* **sell (sb) short,** ⇨ short ²(3). **2** keep stocks for sale; be a dealer in: *Do you ~ needles?* **3** (of goods) be sold; find buyers: *Your house ought to ~ for at least £12 000.* **4** cause to be sold: *It's the low prices which ~ our goods.* **5** ` **sell oneself,** (a) present oneself to others in a convincing way (e g when applying for a job). (b) do something dishonourable for money or reward. **6** cheat; disappoint by failure to keep an agreement, etc: *I've been sold!* **sell sb down the river,** ⇨ river(1). **7 be sold on sth,** (*informal*) agree with it, believe that it is good, etc: *Are they sold on (the idea of socialism?)*

sel-ler, person who sells: *a `book~er.* ⇨

bestseller.

'sell-out, (a) event (a football match, concert, etc) for which all tickets have been sold. **(b)** (*informal*) betrayal: *government policies which are ∼-out of their manifesto.*

sel·vage, sel·vedge /'selvɪdʒ/ *n* [C] edge of cloth woven so that threads do not come apart.

selves /selvz/ *pl* of self.

sem·an·tic /sɪ'mæntɪk/ *adj* relating to meaning in language.

se·man·tics *n pl* (used with a *sing verb*) branch of linguistics concerned with studying the meanings of words and sentences.

sema·phore /'seməfɔ(r)/ *n* [U] system (code) for sending signals, e g by using arms on a post or flags held in the hands, with various positions for the letters of the alphabet. □ *vt,vi* send (messages) by semaphore.

sem·blance /'sembləns/ *n* [C] appearance: *put on a ∼ of gaiety.*

se·men /'siːmən/ *n* [U] fertilizing fluid of male animals.

semi- /'semɪ/ *prefix* half of; partly; midway: *semi-circle, semi-literate, semi-final.*

'semi-circle, half a circle.

'semi-'circular *adj* (having the shape of a) half a circle.

'semi-'colon (*US* = **'semi·colon**), the punctuation mark (;) used in writing and printing, between a comma and a full stop in value.

'semi-'conscious *adj* partly conscious.

'semi-de'tached *adj* (of a house) joined to another on one side.

'semi-'final, match or round before the final (e g in football competitions). Hence, **'semi-'finalist** *n* [C] player, team, in the semi-finals.

'semi-of'ficial *adj* (esp of announcements, etc made to newspapers) with the condition that they must not be considered as coming from an official source.

'semi-'skilled, having or needing some skill from training but less than skilled.

sem·inar /'seminɑ(r)/ *n* [C] group studying a problem and meeting for discussion with a tutor or professor.

sem·inary /'seminəri *US:* -neri/ *n* [C] (*pl* -ies) Roman Catholic training college for priests.

semo·lina /'semə'liːnə/ *n* [U] hard grains from wheat, used for making pasta, in milk puddings, etc.

semp·stress /'sempstrəs/ ⇨ seamstress.

sen·ate /'senət/ *n* [C] **1** (in ancient Rome) highest council of state. **2** (*modern use*) Upper House of the legislative assembly in various countries, e g France, US. **3** governing council of some universities.

sena·tor /-tə(r)/, member of senate(1,2).

sena·tor·ial /'senə'tɔːrɪəl/ *adj* of a senate or senator: *a senatorial district*, (*US*) one entitled to elect a senator.

send /send/ *vt,vi* (*pt,pp* sent) (For special uses with *adverbial particles* and *prepositions*, ⇨ 4 below.) **1** cause a person or thing to go or be carried without going oneself: ∼ *a telegram*; ∼ *a message to her/*∼ *her a message. The children were sent to bed.* ⇨ take. **2** use force to cause a person or thing to move rapidly: *The wind sent the vase crashing to the ground.* **3** cause to become: *This noise is* ∼*ing me crazy.*

4 (special uses with *adverbial particles* and *prepositions*):

send sb away, dismiss, e g an employee.

send away for sth, order (goods) to be delivered by rail, post, etc: *Shall we* ∼ *away for this bargain in the newspaper?*

send sb down, (esp) expel a student from a university (for misconduct, etc). **send sth down,** cause to fall: *The excellent weather sent the price of food down. The clouds sent the temperature down.*

send for sb/sth (to do sth), ask or order a person/thing to come, for something to be delivered: ∼ *for a doctor/taxi.*

send sth in (for e g a competition, exhibition): ∼ *in one's entry for a competition.*

send sth on, (a) send it (e g luggage) in advance. **(b)** (of letters) readdress and repost (e g when on holiday).

send sth out, (a) give out: *The sun* ∼*s out light and warmth.* **(b)** produce: *The trees* ∼ *out new leaves in spring.* **(c)** circularize.

send sb/sth up, show that he/it is ridiculous or false. Hence, **'send-up** *n.* **send sth up,** cause to rise: *The heavy demand for beef sent the price up.*

sender /'sendə(r)/ *n* [C] person or thing that sends: *Who was the* ∼ *of the telegram?.*

se·nile /'siːnaɪl/ *adj* suffering from bodily or mental weakness because of old age; caused by old age: ∼ *decay.*

sen·il·ity /sɪ'nɪlətɪ/ *n* [U] weakness (of body or mind) in old age.

sen·ior /'siːnɪə(r)/ *adj* (opp of *junior*) **1** older in years; higher in rank, authority, etc: *He is ten years* ∼ *to me. Smith is the* ∼ *partner in* (= the head of) *the firm.* **2** (abbr **Snr, Sen** or **Sr**) the father (used after a person's name esp when a father and his son have the same Christian name). □ *n* [C] **1** senior person: *He is my* ∼ *by ten years.* **2** (*US*) student in his/her fourth year at high school or college.

'senior 'citizen, person over the age of retirement.

sen·ior·ity /'siːnɪ'ɒrətɪ *US:* -'ɔːr-/ *n* [U] condition of being senior (in age, rank, etc): *Should promotion be through merit or through* ∼*?*

senna /'senə/ *n* [U] dried leaves of the cassia plant, used as a laxative.

sen·sa·tion /sen'seɪʃən/ *n* **1** [C,U] ability to feel; feeling: *lose all* ∼ *in one's legs; have a* ∼ *of warmth/dizziness/falling.* **2** [C,U] (instance of, something that causes, a) quick and excited reaction: *The news created a* *great* ~.

sen·sa·tional /-nəl/ *adj* (a) causing a sensation(2): *a* ~*al murder*. (b) (of newspapers, etc) presenting news in a manner designed to cause sensation(2): *a* ~*al writer/ newspaper*.

sen·sa·tion·al·ly /-nəlɪ/ *adv*

sen·sa·tion·al·ism /-ɪzm/ *n* [U] the deliberate causing of sensation: *avoid* ~*ism during an election campaign*.

sen·sa·tion·al·ist /-ɪst/ *n* [C] person causing sensation.

sense /sens/ *n* [C] **1** any one of the special powers of the body by which a person is conscious of things (i e sight, hearing, smell, taste and touch): *have a keen* ~ *of hearing*. ⇨ sixth sense. **2** (*pl*) normal state of mind: *in one's* (*right*) ~*s*, sane; *out of one's* ~*s*, insane. **bring sb to his senses,** cause him to stop behaving foolishly or wildly: *Perhaps a month in prison will bring you to your* ~*s*. **come to one's senses,** stop behaving foolishly or wildly. **have taken leave of one's senses,** have become mad. **3** (with *a, an* or a *possessive pronoun* but not *pl*) appreciation or understanding of the value or worth (of): *a* ~ *of humour; my* ~ *of duty*. ⇨ direction(2). **4** (not *pl*) consciousness: *have no* ~ *of shame*. **5** [U] power of judging; good, practical, judgement: *Haven't you any* ~? *There's a lot of* ~ *in what he says. There's no* ~ *in doing that,* It's pointless. ⇨ common sense. **6** [C] meaning: *In what* ~ *are you using the word? Using the widest* ~ *of the word...,* the meaning which is the most general or the fullest... **make sense,** have a meaning that can be understood: *It just doesn't make* ~, means nothing. **7** [U] general feeling or opinion among a number of people: *take the* ~ *of a public meeting*. ⇨ consensus. □ *vt* have the opinion; be vaguely aware of; realize: *He* ~*d that his proposals were unwelcome*.

`sense-organ`, part of the body, e g ear, eye, used to experience a sense(1).

sense·less /senslǝs/ *adj* **1** foolish: *a* ~ *idea. What a* ~ *person he is!* **2** unconscious: *fall* ~ *to the ground*.

sense·less·ly *adv*

sense·less·ness *n* [U]

sen·si·bil·ity /ˌsensəˈbɪlətɪ/ *n* (*pl* -ies) **1** [U] power of feeling, esp delicate emotional impressions: *the* ~ *of an artist or poet*. **2** (*pl*) sensitive(2) impressions (of what is right, in good taste, etc): *Her sensibilities are quickly injured*.

sen·sible /ˈsensǝbǝl/ *adj* **1** having or showing good sense(5); reasonable; practical: *a* ~ *woman;* ~ *clothes,* practical, not for only appearance or fashion. *That was* ~ *of you*. **2** (*science*) that can be known by the senses(1): ~ *phenomena*.

sen·sibly /-ǝblɪ/ *adv* in a sensible way: *sensibly dressed for hot weather*.

sen·si·tive /ˈsensǝtɪv/ *adj* **1** quickly or easily receiving impressions: *The eyes are* ~ *to light*. **2** (of feelings) easily hurt or offended: *He is very* ~ *about his ugly appearance*. **3** (of instruments, and institutions thought of as measuring things) able to record or reproduce small changes: *a* ~ *record-player. The Government is* ~ *to political opinion*. **4** (of photographic film, etc) affected by light.

sen·si·tiv·ity /ˌsensǝˈtɪvǝtɪ/ *n* [U] quality, degree, of being sensitive: *an injection to reduce the sensitivity of the pain*.

sen·si·tize /ˈsensǝtaɪz/ *vt* make (photographic film, etc) sensitive to light.

sen·sory /ˈsensǝrɪ/ *adj* of the senses(1) or sensation: ~ *nerves*.

sen·sual /ˈsenʃʊǝl/ *adj* **1** of, engaged in, the pleasures of the senses: ~ *perception*. **2** enjoy physical pleasures such as eating and drinking and sex: ~ *enjoyment*.

sen·su·al·ity /ˌsenʃʊˈælǝtɪ/ *n* [U] love of, pleasure in, sensual pleasures.

sen·su·ous /ˈsenʃʊǝs/ *adj* affecting, noticed by, appealing to, the senses(1): ~ *music/ painting*.

sent /sent/ *pt,pp* of send.

sen·tence /ˈsentǝns/ *n* [C] **1** (statement by a judge, etc, of) punishment: *pass* ~ (*on him*), declare what the punishment is to be; *be under* ~ *of death*. **2** (*gram*) set of words complete in itself, used to express a statement, question, command, etc. □ *vt* state that (a person) is to have a certain punishment: ~ *a thief to six months' imprisonment*.

sen·ti·ment /ˈsentɪmǝnt/ *n* **1** [C] mental feeling, the total of what one thinks and feels on a subject; [U] such feelings collectively as an influence: *The* ~ *of pity includes a feeling of sympathy and of a desire to help. What are your* ~*s towards my sister?* What do you feel towards her? **2** [U] (tendency to be affected by a) (display of) emotional feeling (contrasted with reason): *There's no place for* ~ *in business*. **3** expression of feeling; opinions or point of view: *The ambassador explained the* ~*s of his government*.

sen·ti·men·tal /ˌsentɪˈmentǝl/ *adj* **1** having to do with the feelings; emotional: *have a* ~ *attachment to one's birthplace. The bracelet had only* ~ *value,* e g because it belonged to one's mother. **2** (of things) producing, expressing, (often excessive) feelings: ~ *music;* (of persons) having such excessive feelings: *She's far too* ~ *about her cats*.

sen·ti·men·tal·ity /ˌsentɪmenˈtælǝtɪ/ *n* [U] the quality of being very sentimental

sen·ti·men·tally /-tǝlɪ/ *adv*

sen·try /ˈsentrɪ/ *n* [C] (*pl* -ies) soldier keeping watch or guard.

`sentry-box`, hut for a sentry.

sep·ar·able /ˈsepǝrǝbǝl/ *adj* that can be separated.

sep·ar·ate¹ /ˈseprǝt/ *adj* **1** divided, not

joined or united: *Cut it into three ~ parts.* **2** not physically united but forming a distinct unit: *The children sleep in ~ beds.* Each of them has his own bed. *Mr Green and his wife are living ~* (= apart) *now.* □ *n* (*pl*) garments which may be worn in a variety of combinations, e g jerseys, blouses and skirts.

sep·ar·ate·ly *adv* in a separate manner: *Tie them up ~ly.*

sep·ar·ate² /ˈsepəreɪt/ *vt,vi* **1** make, be, separate: *~ the boys from the girls. England is ~d from France by the Channel.* **2** (of a number of people) leave each other: *We talked until midnight and then ~d.*

sep·ar·ation /ˌsepəˈreɪʃən/ *n* **1** [U] (state of) being separated or separate; act of separating: *S~ from his friends made him sad.* **2** [C] instance of, period of not being together: *after a ~ of five years.*

se·pia /ˈsiːpiə/ *n* [U], *adj* dark brown (ink or paint).

Sep·tem·ber /sepˈtembə(r)/ *n* the ninth month of the year.

sep·tet /sepˈtet/ *n* [C] (musical composition for a) group of seven voices or instruments.

sep·tic /ˈseptɪk/ *adj* causing, caused by, infection (with disease germs): *A dirty wound may become/turn ~.*

'septic 'tank, tank outside a building in which sewage is disposed of and purified.

sep·ul·chral /sɪˈpʌlkrəl/ *adj* of a burial (in a tomb).

sep·ulchre (US = **-ul·cher**) /ˈsepəlkə(r)/ *n* [C] tomb, esp one cut in rock or built of stone.

se·quel /ˈsiːkwəl/ *n* [C] **1** that which follows or arises out of (an earlier happening): *Famine has often been the ~ of war.* **2** story, film, etc continuing the plot, etc of an earlier one or having the same director, actor, etc.

se·quence /ˈsiːkwəns/ *n* [U] succession; [C] connected line of events, ideas, etc: *the ~ of events,* the order in which they occur.

se·quin /ˈsiːkwɪn/ *n* [C] tiny shining disc sewn on to cloth as an ornament

sere /sɪə(r)/ *n* = **sear²**.

ser·en·ade /ˌserəˈneɪd/ *n* [C] (piece of) music (to be) sung or played outdoors at night. □ *vt* sing or play a serenade to (a person).

se·rene /sɪˈriːn/ *adj* clear and calm: *a ~ sky/ look/smile.*
se·rene·ly *adv*
ser·en·ity /sɪˈrenətɪ/ *n* [U]

serf /sɜːf/ *n* [C] (in olden times) person who worked on the land and was sold with it like a slave.

serf·dom /-dəm/ *n* [U] **(a)** economic and social system using serfs. **(b)** serf's condition of life.

ser·geant /ˈsɑːdʒənt/ *n* [C] **1** non-commissioned army officer above a corporal. **2** police-officer with rank below that of an inspector.

'sergeant-'major, warrant officer, between commissioned and non-commissioned army officer.

ser·ial /ˈsɪərɪəl/ *adj* **1** of, in or forming a series: *the `~ number of a banknote or cheque.* **2** (of a story, etc) appearing in parts (on radio, TV, in a magazine etc). □ *n* [C] serialized play, story, etc.

ser·ial·ize /-laɪz/ *vt* publish or produce in serial form.

series /ˈsɪəriːz/ *n* [C] (*pl* unchanged) number of things, events, etc each of which is related in some way to the others, esp to the one before it: *a ~ of stamps,* e g of different values, but issued at one time; *a `television ~,* a number of programmes, each complete in itself, linked by cast, theme, etc. **in series, (a)** in an orderly arrangement. **(b)** (of the parts of an electrical circuit) with the supply of current fed directly through each component.

seri·ous /ˈsɪərɪəs/ *adj* **1** thoughtful; not funny, silly or for pleasure: *a ~ attempt/ appearance/face; look ~. Stop laughing and be ~ for a moment.* **2** important because of possible danger: *a ~ illness/mistake. The international situation looks ~.* **3** in earnest; sincere: *a ~ worker. Please be ~ about your work.*

seri·ous·ly *adv* in a serious manner: *be ~ly ill.*

seri·ous·ness *n* [U] state of being serious: *the ~ness of inflation.* **in all seriousness,** very seriously: *I tell you this in all ~ness,* I am not joking, being insincere, etc.

ser·mon /ˈsɜːmən/ *n* [C] spoken or written speech on a religious or moral subject, esp one given from a pulpit in a church.

ser·mon·ize /-aɪz/ *vt,vi* (*fig*) preach or talk seriously to: *Stop ~izing,* lecturing to me on my faults, etc.

ser·ous /ˈsɪərəs/ *adj* of or like serum.

ser·pent /ˈsɜːpənt/ *n* [C] **1** snake (the more usual word). **2** (*fig*) sly, deceptive person.

ser·rated /seˈreɪtɪd *US:* ˈsereɪtɪd/ *adj* having notches on the edge like a saw.

ser·ried /ˈserɪd/ *adj* (of lines or ranks of persons) close together, shoulder to shoulder: *in ~ ranks.*

serum /ˈsɪərəm/ *n* (*pl ~s*) **1** [U] watery fluid in animal bodies; thin, transparent part of blood. **2** [C,U] (dose of) such a fluid taken from the blood of an animal and used for inoculations.

ser·vant /ˈsɜːvənt/ *n* [C] **1** person who works in a household for wages, food and lodging. **2** public servant, person who works for the public, e g a police officer, member of the Fire Service. ⇨ civil servant. **3** person devoted to a person or thing: *a ~ of Jesus Christ,* e g a Christian priest.

serve /sɜːv/ *vt,vi* **1** be a servant to, work for, (a person): *He ~s as gardener and also as chauffeur.* **2** perform duties (for): *~ one's country,* e g in Parliament or in the armed forces. **serve on sth,** be a member of: ∼ *on a committee.* **serve under sb,** be in the armed forces (esp the Navy) under the command of: *My great-grandfather* ∼*d under Nelson.* **3** attend to (customers in a shop, etc); supply (with goods and services); place (food, etc) on the table for a meal; give (food, etc) to people at a meal: *There was no one in the shop to* ∼ *me. Mint sauce is often* ∼*d with lamb.* **4** be satisfactory for a need or purpose: *This box will* ∼ *for a seat.* **5** act towards, treat (a person in a certain way): *I hope I'll never be* ∼*d such a trick again,* have such a trick played on me. **serve one right,** experience failure, misfortune, etc which is deserved. **6** pass the usual or normal number of years (learning a trade, etc): *He's* ∼*d his apprenticeship.* **7** go through a term of office: *He* ∼*d his time as manager for five years.* **8** undergo a period of imprisonment: *He has* ∼*d five years of his sentence.* **9** (*legal*) deliver (a summons, etc) to the person named in it. **10** (in tennis, etc) put the ball into play by batting it to an opponent: ∼ *a ball;* ∼ *well/badly.* □ *n* [C] (in tennis, etc) (turn for) striking and putting the ball into play: *Whose* ∼ *is it?*

server, (a) person who serves, e g a tennis-player. (b) tray for dishes of food.

serv·ing *n* [C] quantity of food (to be) served to one person: *four servings of soup.*

ser·vice /ˈsɜːvɪs/ *n* **1** [U] being a servant; position as a servant: *Miss White has been in our* ∼ *for five years.* **2** [C] department or branch of public work, government employment, etc: *the* ˈ*Diploˈmatic S*∼. ⇨ civil service. **on active service,** performing duties as a member of the armed forces in time of war. **3** [C] something done to help or benefit another or others: *His* ∼*s to the State have been immense. Do you need the* ∼*s of a doctor/lawyer?* **4** [U] benefit, use, advantage: *Can I be of* ∼ *to you,* help you in any way? *I am/My car is at your* ∼, ready to help you. **5** [C] system or arrangement that supplies public needs, etc for communications: *a* ˈ*bus/*ˈ*train* ∼; *the* ˈ*telephone* ∼; *a good* ˈ*postal* ∼. **6** [C] form of worship and prayer to God: *three* ∼*s every Sunday; the* ˈ*marriage* ∼. **7** [C] complete set of plates, dishes, etc for use at table: *a* ˈ*tea/*ˈ*dinner* ∼. **8** [U] serving of food and drink (in hotels, etc); work done by hotel staff, etc: *The food is good at this hotel, but the* ∼ *is poor.* **9** [U] maintenance given after the sale of an article: *send the car in for* ∼ *every 3 000 miles,* eg for greasing, checking of brakes, etc. **10** (*legal*) serving of a writ, summons, etc. **11** (in tennis, etc) act of serving the ball; manner of doing this; person's turn to serve: *Her* ∼ *is weak. Whose* ∼ *is it?* □ *vt* maintain or repair (a car, radio, machine, etc) after sale (⇨ 9 above): *have the car* ∼*d regularly.*

ˈ**service charge,** additional charge for ser-

vice(8).

ˈ**service flat,** in which domestic help is provided.

ˈ**service industry,** providing services, not making things.

ˈ**service-line,** (in tennis, etc) from which the ball is served(10).

ˈ**service road,** branch off a main road giving access to houses, etc.

ˈ**service station,** petrol station with servicing facilities.

ser·vice·able /-əbəl/ *adj* (a) suited for ordinary wear and use; strong and durable: ∼*able clothes for children.* (b) capable of giving good service.

ser·vi·ette /ˌsɜːvɪˈet/ *n* [C] = napkin.

ser·vile /ˈsɜːvaɪl *US:* -vəl/ *adj* **1** of or like slaves: ∼ *work.* **2** characteristic of a slave; not showing the spirit of independence: ∼ *to public opinion,* giving too much attention to it.

ser·vi·tude /ˈsɜːvɪtjuːd *US:* -tuːd/ *n* [U] condition of being forced to work for others and having no freedom. ⇨ penal.

ses·ame /ˈsesəmɪ/ *n* [C] **1** plant with seeds used in various ways as food and giving an oil used in salads. **2** **Open sesame!** magic words used to cause a door to open.

ses·sion /ˈseʃən/ *n* [C] **1** (meeting of a) law court, law-making body, etc; time occupied by discussions at such a meeting: *the autumn* ∼ (= sitting) *of Parliament; go into secret* ∼. **in session,** meeting, active (not on holiday). **2** (*Scot* and *US*) university term. **3** single, uninterrupted meeting for a purpose: *a re*ˈ*cording* ∼, e g of music (on records or tapes).

set¹ /set/ *n* **1** [C] number of things of the same kind, that belong together because they are similar or complementary to each other: *a* ˈ*tea-*∼, cups, saucers, etc. *a new* ∼ *of false teeth.* **2** [C] number of persons who associate, or who have similar or identical tastes and interests: *the* ˈ*racing/*ˈ*literary/* ˈ*golfing* ∼; *the* ˈ*smart* ∼, those who consider themselves leaders in society; *the* ˈ*fast* ∼, those who gamble, etc; *the* ˈ*jet* ∼, rich people flying from one holiday resort to another. **3** [C] radio receiving apparatus: *a transistor* ∼. **4** (not *pl*) direction (of current, wind, etc); tendency (of opinion): *the* ∼ *of the tide.* **5** (not *pl*) position or angle: *I recognize him by the* ∼ *of his head/shoulders.* **6** [C] way in which a garment conforms to the shape of the body: *the* ∼ *of a coat.* ⇨ set²(14). **7** [C] (in tennis, etc) group of games counting as a unit to the side that wins more than half the games in it. **8** setting of the hair: *have a shampoo and* ∼. **9** [C] scenery on the stage of a theatre or in a studio or outside for filming: *everyone to be on the* ∼ *by 7 a m.* **10** [C] young plant, cutting, bulb, etc ready to be planted: *onion* ∼*s.* **11** (*maths*) collection of things of a similar type.

set² /set/ *vt,vi* (-tt-, *pt,pp* ~) (For special uses with *adverbial particles* and *prepositions*, ⇨ 17 below.) **1** (of the sun, moon, stars) go down below the horizon: *It will be cooler when the sun has ~.* **2** move or place something so that it is near to or touching something else: *~ a glass to one's lips; ~ pen to paper,* begin to write. **set a match/ (a) light/fire to sth,** cause it to begin burning. **3** cause (a person or thing) to be in, or reach, a specified state or relation. **set sb/ sth on his/its feet,** (a) help him to get to his feet after a fall. (b) help him/it to gain strength, financial stability, etc: *Foreign aid ~ the country on its feet after the war.* **set sb free,** free (prisoners, etc). **set sb's mind at ease/rest,** help him to be free from worry, free him from anxiety. **be all set (for sth/to do sth),** be ready (for the start of a race, etc). **4** cause a person or thing to begin to do something: *It's time we ~ the machinery going,* start operations. *The news ~ me thinking.* **set sth on fire,** cause it to begin burning. **5** (usually with an *adverb* or *adverbial phrase;* ⇨ 17 below for combinations of *set* and *adverbial particles* with special meanings) put, place, lay, stand: *She ~ the food on the table.* **6** put forward as (material to be dealt with as a task, a pattern, etc): *I have ~ myself a difficult task. Who will ~ the papers for the examination,* prepare the examination questions? **set (sb) an example/a good example,** offer a good standard for others to follow. **set the fashion,** start a fashion to be copied by others. **set the pace,** fix it by leading (in a race, etc). **7** give something (to a person/ oneself) as a task: *He ~ the farm labourer to chop wood.* **8** (used with various grammatical objects, the *nouns* in alphabetical order) **set one's cap at sb,** ⇨ cap. **set eyes on sb,** see him. **set one's heart/hopes/mind on sth,** be filled with strong desire for; direct one's hopes towards: *The boy has ~ his heart on becoming an engineer.* **set a price on sth,** declare what it will be sold for. **set much/great/little/no store by sth,** value it highly/little/not at all. **9** put in a certain state or condition for a particular purpose: *~ a (broken) bone,* bring the parts together so that they may unite. **set a clock/ watch,** put the hands to the correct time (or, for an alarm clock, to sound at the desired time). **set one's hair,** arrange it (when damp) so that when it is dried, it is waved: *She's having her hair ~ for the party.* **set the scene,** describe a place and the people taking part in an activity, e g in a play, novel or sporting event: *Our commentator will now ~ the scene in the stadium.* **set sail (from/to/for),** begin a voyage. **set the table,** lay it ready with plates, cutlery, etc. **10** put, fix, one thing firmly in another: *~ a diamond in gold; a gold ring ~ with gems* **11** (of tides, winds) move or flow

along; gather force: *The current is ~ting in towards the shore. The wind ~s from the west. The tide has ~ in his favour,* (fig) He is winning public support and approval **12** **set sth (to sth):** *~ words/a poem to music,* provide with music **13** (of plants, fruit trees, their blossom) form or develop fruit as the result of fertilization: *The apple-blossom hasn't/The apples haven't ~ well this year.* **14** (of a garment) adapt itself to the shape of the body. **15** (cause to) become firm, solid, rigid (from a liquid or soft state): *The jelly is/has not ~ yet.* **16** (*pp*) (a) unmoving, fixed: *a ~ smile/look/purpose.* (b) prearranged; *at a ~ time.* (c) unchanging: *~ in one's ways,* having fixed habits; *a man of ~ opinions,* unable or unwilling to change them. (d) planned, learned; regular: *~ phrases; a ~ speech; ~ forms of prayers* (e) **set fair,** (of the weather) fine and with no signs of change.

17 (special uses with *adverbial particles* and *prepositions*):

set about sth, start it: *I don't know how to ~ about this job,* how to make a start on it. **set about sb,** (*informal*) attack: *They ~ about each other in the park.*

set sb against sb, cause him to compete with, fight, him. **set one thing against another,** regard it as compensating for, balancing, another.

set sth apart/aside, (a) put on one side for future use. (b) disregard: *Let's ~ aside our personal feelings.* (c) (*legal*) reject: *~ a claim aside.*

set sth back, (a) move back: *The horse ~ back its ears.* (b) be placed at a distance from: *The house is ~ back from the road* **set sb/sth back,** (a) stop or reverse the progress of: *All our efforts at reform have been ~ back.* Hence, `set-back *n* (*pl* setbacks). (b) (*sl*) cost: *That dinner party ~ me back £20.*

set sth down, (a) put down: *~ down a load.* (b) write down on paper: *~ it down for all to read.* **set sb down,** (of a vehicle, its driver) allow (a passenger) to get down or out: *The bus stopped to ~ down an old lady.* **set forth,** (a) = set out (which is more usual). **set sth forth,** (*formal*) make known: *~ forth one's political views.*

set in, (a) start and seem likely to continue: *The rainy season has ~ in.* (b) (of tides, winds; ⇨ 11 above) begin to flow: *The tide is ~ting in,* flowing towards the shore.

set off, start (a journey, race, etc): *They've ~ off on a trip round the world.* **set sth off,** (a) explode a mine, firework, etc. (b) make more striking by comparison: *This gold frame ~s off your painting very well.* (c) balance; compensate: *~ off gains against losses.* (d) mark off: *~ off a clause by a comma.* **set sb off (doing sth),** cause to start: *Don't ~ him off talking about football or he'll go on all evening.*

set on sb, attack: *She had been ~ on by muggers.* **be set on sth**, be determined to be or get: *His heart* (= He) *is ~ on being a doctor.*

set out, begin (a journey, etc): *They ~ out at dawn.* **set out to do sth**, have it as an aim or intention: *He ~ out to break the world record.* **set sth out**, (a) declare; make known: *~ out one's reasons.* (b) arrange: *He ~s out his ideas clearly in this essay.* (c) plant out.

set sb over sb, put him in control/ command: *A younger man has been ~ over me.*

set `to`, begin doing something: *The engineers ~ to and repaired the bridge.*

set sth up, (a) place something in position: *~ up a statue.* (b) establish (an institution, business, argument, etc): *~ up an office.* Hence, **`set-up** n *(informal)* arrangement of an organization: *What's the ~-up here?* **set (oneself) up as**, (a) go into business as: *He has ~ (himself) up as a bookseller.* (b) believe oneself to be: *I've never ~ myself up as perfect.* **set sb up (as sth)**, get him started or established; by supplying money: *His father ~ him up in business.* **set up house**, start living in one. **set up house with sb/together**, (of two persons) begin living together (as husband and wife).

be set upon sth, = be set on sth.

set-square /'set skweər/ n [C] triangular plate of wood, plastic, metal, etc with angles of 90°, 60° and 30° (or 90°, 45°, 45°), used for drawing lines at these angles

set-tee /se'ti/ n [C] seat like a sofa, with sides and back, for two or more persons.

set-ter /'setə(r)/ n [C] **1** (breeds of) long-haired dog trained to stand motionless on scenting game **2** (as a *suffix*) person who, thing which, sets (various meanings): *a* `bone-~.*

set-ting /'setɪŋ/ n [C] **1** framework in which something is fixed or fastened: *the ~ of a jewel.* **2** surroundings: *a beautiful ~ for a picnic.* **3** music composed for a poem, etc. ⇨ set²(12). **3** descent (of the sun, moon, etc) below the horizon.

settle¹ /'setəl/ n [C] long, wooden seat with a high back and arms, the seat often being the lid of a chest.

settle² /'setəl/ vt, vi (For special uses with *adverbial particles* and *prepositions*, ⇨ **8** below.) **1** make one's home in (permanently): *~ in London/in Canada/in the country.* **2** come to rest (on); stay for some time (on): *The bird ~d on a branch. The dust ~d on everything.* **3** cause (a person) to become used to, or comfortable in, a new position (after a period of movement or activity): *The nurse ~d her patient for the night,* made him/her comfortable, etc **4** make or become calm, untroubled: *We want a period of ~d weather for the harvest. Wait until the excitement has ~d.* **5** make an

agreement about; decide: *It's time you ~d the dispute/argument. Nothing is ~d yet. The lawsuit was ~d out of court,* a decision was reached by the parties themselves (and their lawyers) instead of by the court. **6** pay ~ a bill. **7** (of dust, etc in the air, particles of solid substances in a liquid, etc) (cause to) sink; (of a liquid) become clear as solid particles sink: *We need a shower to ~ the dust.* **8** (special uses with *adverbial particles* and *prepositions*):

settle down, sit or lie comfortably (after a period of movement or activity): *He ~d down in his armchair to read.* **settle (sb) down**, make or become calm and peaceful: *Wait until the children have ~d down before you start your lesson.* **settle (down) to sth**, give one's attention to: *It's terrible—I can't ~ (down) to anything today,* am too restless to do my work, etc **settle down (to sth)**, become established (in a new way of life, new work, etc): *~ down well in a new career/job.*

settle for sth, accept, although not altogether satisfactory: *I had hoped to get £200 for my old car but had to ~ for £180*

settle (sb) in, (help him to) move into a new house, flat, job, etc and put things in order. *You must come and see our new house when we're/we've ~d in.*

settle sth on/upon sb, *(legal)* give him (property, etc) for use during his lifetime: *~ part of one's estate on one's son.* ⇨ settlement(2). **settle on/upon sth**, decide to have: *Which of the hats have you ~d on?*

settle (up) (with sb), pay what one owes: *I shall ~ (up) with you at the end of the month.*

settled /'setəld/ adj **1** fixed; unchanging, permanent: *~ weather; a man of ~ opinions.* **2** (of a bill) paid.

settle-ment /'setəlmənt/ n **1** [U] the act of settling (a dispute, debt, etc); [C] instance of this: *The strikers have reached a ~ with the employers. I enclose a cheque in ~ of your account.* **2** [C] (statement of) property settled(8) on a person: *a `marriage ~,* one made by a man in favour of his wife. **3** [U] process of settling people in a colony; [C] new colony: *empty lands awaiting ~; Dutch and English ~s in America.*

set-tler /'setlə(r)/ n [C] person who has settled in a newly developed country: *white ~s in Kenya.*

seven /'sevən/ adj, n [C] (of) 7.

`seven-fold /-fəʊld/ adj, adv seven times as much, as great or as many

sev-enth /'sevənθ/ adj, n [C] (abbr 7th) (of) one of 7 parts or the next after 6.

sev-enth-ly adv in the 7th place.

seven-teen /'sevən'tin/ adj, n [C] (of) 17

seven-teenth /'sevən'tinθ/ adj, n [C] (abbr 17th) (of) one of 17 parts or the next after 16.

seven-ti-eth adj, n [C] (abbr 70th) (of) one

of 70 parts or the next after 69

sev·enty /ˈsevəntɪ/ adj, n [C] (of) 70. **the seventies, (a)** (of a person's age, temperature, etc) between 69 and 80 **(b)** (of a period) the years from 70 to 79 inclusive in a century.

sever /ˈsevə(r)/ vt, vi **1** cut (the usual word): ~ a rope. **2** (fig) break off: ~ one's connections with her. **3** break (the usual word): The rope ~ed under the strain.

sev·er·ance /ˈsevərəns/ n [U]

sev·eral /ˈsevrəl/ adj **1** three or more; some but not many: You will need ~ more I've read it ~ times. **2** separate; individual· They went their ~ ways. Each went his own way □ pron a few; some: S~ of us decided to walk home.

sev·er·ally /ˈsevrəlɪ/ adv separately (the usual word).

se·vere /səˈvɪə(r)/ adj **1** stern, strict: ~ looks; be ~ with one's children. **2** (of the weather, attacks of disease, etc) strong, extreme: a ~ storm; ~ pain. **3** making great demands on skill, ability, patience and other qualities The pace was too ~ to be kept up for long.

sev·ere·ly adv

se·ver·ity /səˈverətɪ/ n (pl -ies) **1** [U] quality of being severe: the ~ (= extreme cold) of the winter in Canada. **2** (pl) severe treatment or experiences: the severities of the winter campaign.

sew /səʊ/ vt, vi (pt ~ed, pp ~n /səʊn/) work with a needle and thread; fasten with stitches; make (a garment) by stitching: ~ a button on. This dress is hand-ˈ~n/~n by hand. **sew sth up, (a)** join (at the edges) with stitches. **(b)** (informal) arrange; complete· All the details of the project have been ~n up.

sewer /ˈsəʊə(r)/ n [C] person who sews.

sew·ing n [U] work (clothes, etc) being sewn

`**sewing-machine**, machine for sewing

sew·age /ˈsjuːɪdʒ US· ˈsuː-/ n [U] waste organic matter, etc carried off in sewers.

sewer[1] /ˈsjuːə(r) US: ˈsuː-/ n [C] underground channel (pipeline, etc) to carry off sewage and rainwater

sewer[2] /ˈsəʊə(r)/ n ⇨ sew.

sewn /səʊn/ pp of sew.

sex /seks/ n **1** [U] being male or female: What is the cat's ~? Help them all, without distinction of race. age or ~ **2** [C] males or females as a group· the ˈfair ~, women. **3** [U] differences between males and females consciousness of these differences: ˈ~ appeal, attractiveness of a person of one sex to the other **4** [U] sexual activity and everything connected with it

sex·less adj neither male nor female

sexy adj (-ier, -iest) sexually attractive

sex·ist /ˈseksɪst/ n [C], adj (person who) considers women to be inferior to men

sex·tant /ˈsekstənt/ n [C] instrument used for measuring the altitude of the sun, etc (in order to determine a ship's position, etc)

sex·ton /ˈsekstən/ n [C] man who takes care of a church buildings, digs graves in the churchyard, etc

sex·ual /ˈseksjʊəl/ adj of sex or the sexes· ~ intercourse = coitus.

sexu·al·ity /ˈseksjʊˈælətɪ/ n [U] sex characteristics or appeal

shabby /ˈʃæbɪ/ adj (-ier, -iest) **1** in bad repair or condition; poorly dressed: wearing a ~ hat. You look rather ~ in those clothes **2** (of behaviour) mean; unfair

shab·bily /ˈʃæbəlɪ/ adv

shab·bi·ness n [U]

shack /ʃæk/ n [C] small, wooden shed, hut or house

shackle /ˈʃækəl/ n [C] **1** one of a pair of iron rings joined by a chain for fastening a prisoner's wrists or ankles **2** (fig) something that prevents freedom of action: the ~s of convention. □ vt put shackles on; prevent from acting freely.

shade /ʃeɪd/ n **1** [U; with adj, verb and a or an] **1** comparative darkness caused by the cutting off of direct rays of light: a temperature of 35°C in the ~. The trees give a pleasant ~. **2** (fig) comparative obscurity. **put sb/sth in the shade,** cause to appear small, unimportant, etc by contrast: You are so clever and brilliant that my poor efforts are put in the ~. **3** [U] darker part(s) of a picture, etc; reproduction of the darker part of a picture· There is not enough light and ~ in your drawing. **4** [C] degree or depth of colour: dress materials in several ~s of blue. **5** [C] degree of difference. a word with many ~s of meaning. **6** something that reduces light; a ˈlamp~ □ vt, vi **1** keep direct light from: He ~d his eyes with his hands **2** screen (a light, lamp, etc) to reduce brightness. **3** darken (parts of a drawing, etc) to give the appearance of light and dark. **4** change by degrees: scarlet shading off into pink.

shad·ing n (a) [U] use of black, etc to give light and shade to a drawing. (b) [C] slight difference or variation

shadow /ˈʃædəʊ/ n **1** [C] area of shade, dark shape, thrown on the ground, a wall, floor. etc by something which cuts off the direct rays of light. **2** [C] something unsubstantial or unreal: He is only the ~ of his former self, is very thin and weak. **3** (pl) partial darkness: the ~s of evening. **4** [C] dark patch or area: have ~s under/round the eyes, such areas thought to be caused by lack of sleep, illness, etc. **5** (sing only) very small amount or degree: without/beyond a ~ of doubt. **6** person's inseparable friend or determined follower □ vt **1** darken. **2** follow closely and watch the movements of· The suspected spy was ~ed by detectives.

ˈ**Shadow ˈCabinet,** members of the Opposition in Parliament who would form a Cabinet if they were in power

shad·owy adj

shady /ˈʃeɪdɪ/ adj (-ier, -iest) 1 giving shade from sunlight; situated in shade: *the ~ side of the street.* 2 of doubtful honesty: *a ~ deal.*

shaft /ʃɑːft US: ʃæft/ n [C] 1 (long, slender stem of an) arrow or spear 2 long handle of an axe or other tool 3 one of the pair of bars (wooden poles) between which a horse is harnessed to pull a cart, etc 4 long part of a column (between the base and the top) 5 long, narrow space, usually vertical, e g for descending into a coalmine, for a lift in a building, or for ventilation. 6 bar or rod joining parts of a machine, or transmitting power. 7 ray (of light).

shag /ʃæg/ n [U] coarse kind of cut tobacco.

shaggy /ˈʃægɪ/ adj (-ier, -iest) 1 (of hair) rough, coarse and untidy. 2 covered with rough, coarse hair: *a ~ dog; ~ eyebrows.*

shake[1] /ʃeɪk/ n [C] shaking or being shaken: *a ~ of the head,* to indicate 'no'.

shake[2] /ʃeɪk/ vt, vi (pt shook /ʃʊk/, pp ~n /ˈʃeɪkən/) 1 (cause to) move from side to side, up and down etc: *~ a rug; ~ a man by the hand; ~ one's head,* to indicate 'No', or doubt, disapproval, etc; *~ one's fist at him,* to show anger, defiance. *His sides were shaking with laughter. He was shaking with cold.* 2 shock; trouble; weaken: *They were badly ~n by the news.* 3 (of a person's voice) tremble; become weak: *Her voice shook with emotion.*

4 (special uses with *adverbial particles* and *prepositions*):

shake down, become adjusted to a new environment, new conditions, etc: *The new teaching staff is shaking down nicely.* The members are getting used to their duties, to one another, etc.

shake sth from/out of sth, get from/out of by shaking: *~ apples from a tree; ~ sand out of one's shoes.*

shake sb off, free oneself from: *The thief ran fast and soon shook off the police.*

shake sth off, get rid of: *~ off a cold/a fit of depression.*

shake sth out, spread so as to be out by shaking: *~ out a tablecloth.*

shake sth up, (a) mix well by shaking: *~ up a bottle of medicine.* (b) restore something to shape by shaking: *~ up a cushion*

shake sb up, restore from apathy or laziness: *Some of these managers need shaking up—they're asleep on the job.* Hence, `shake-up n: *We need a good ~-up in our office.*

shak·ing /ˈʃeɪkɪŋ/ n = shake: *give a pillow a good shaking,* shake it well.

shaky /ˈʃeɪkɪ/ adj (-ier, -iest) 1 (of a person, his movements, etc) weak; unsteady: *~ hands, speak in a ~ voice; feel very ~.* 2 unsafe, unreliable. *a ~ table. My French is rather ~*

shak·ily /-əlɪ/ adv

shale /ʃeɪl/ n [U] soft rock that splits easily into layers.

shall /ʃəl strong form: ʃæl/ auxiliary verb (I shall, he shall, we shall, often shortened to **I'll** /aɪl/, **he'll** /hil/, **we'll** /wil/, shall not is often shortened to **shan't** /ʃɑːnt/ US: ʃænt/; pt **should** /ʃʊd weak form: ʃəd/; should not is often shortened to **shouldn't** /ˈʃʊdənt/) 1 (used to express the future tense): *We ~/We'll arrive tomorrow. I'll see you soon* (*Note*: will is often used in informal style.) 2 (used to form a future or conditional statement expressing the speaker's will or intention; with stress on *shall, should,* it expresses obligation or compulsion; without special stress on *shall, should,* it expresses a promise or a threat): *You say you will not do it, but I say you ~ do it. You shan't catch me so easily next time. If you work well, you ~ have higher wages.* 3 (used to form statements or questions expressing the ideas of duty, command, obligation, conditional duty, and (in the *neg*) prohibition): *S~ I(= Do you want me to) open the window? I asked the man whether the boy should wait. You should (= ought to) have been more careful.* 4 (used in clauses expressing *may* or *might*): *I lent him the book so that he should study the subject.* 5 (should is used after *how, why*): *How should I know? Why should you/he think that?* 8 (should is used to express probability or expectation): *They should be there by now.*

shal·lot /ʃəˈlɒt/ n [C] sort of small onion

shal·low /ˈʃæləʊ/ adj (-er, -est) 1 of little depth: *~ water.* 2 (fig) not reasonable or serious: *a ~ argument; ~ talk.* □ n [C] (often *pl*) shallow place in a river or in the sea

sham /ʃæm/ vi, vt (-mm-) pretend to be: *He ~med dead/death. He's only ~ming.* □ n [C] 1 person who shams; something intended to deceive: *His love was only a ~.* 2 [U] pretence: *What he says is all ~.* □ adj false; pretended: *~ pity.*

shamble /ˈʃæmbəl/ vi walk unsteadily as if unable to lift the feet properly. *The old man ~d up to me.* □ n [C] shambling walk.

shambles /ˈʃæmbəlz/ n (used with a *sing* verb) 1 scene of bloodshed: *The place became a ~.* 2 scene of muddle or confusion: *His flat is a complete ~.*

shame /ʃeɪm/ n [U] 1 sad feeling, loss of self-respect, caused by wrong, dishonourable or foolish behaviour, failure, etc (of oneself, one's family, etc): *feel ~ at having told a lie; hang one's head for/in ~* 2 capacity for experiencing shame: *He has no ~/is without ~.* 3 [U] dishonour **bring shame on sb/oneself,** dishonour him/oneself. 4 (with *a, an* but not *pl*) something unworthy; something that causes shame; a person or thing that is wrong: *It's a ~ to* take the money for doing such easy work He's a ~ to his family. □ vt **1** cause shame to; cause a person to feel shame; bring disgrace on: ~ one's family. **2** frighten or force (a person to do/not to do something): ~ a man into apologizing.

'**shame-faced** adj looking unhappy through shame.

shame-ful /-fəl/ adj causing or bringing shame: ~ful conduct.

shame-fully /-fəlɪ/ adv

shame-less adj without shame: The ~less girl had no clothes on.

sham-poo /ʃæm'pu/ n [C,U] (special liquid, powder, etc for a) washing of the hair: give her a ~ and set. □ vt wash (the hair of the head): Have you finished ~ing her hair?

sham-rock /'ʃæmrok/ n [C] plant with (usually) three leaves on each stem (the national emblem of Ireland).

shandy /'ʃændɪ/ n [C,U] drink of beer and lemonade.

shank /ʃæŋk/ n [C] **1** leg, esp the part between the knee and the ankle. **2** straight part of an anchor, etc.

shan't /ʃɑnt US: ʃænt/ = shall not. ⇨ shall.

shanty /'ʃæntɪ/ n [C] (pl -ies) poorly made hut or house.

'**shanty-town**, area of a town with shanties.

shape /ʃeɪp/ n **1** [C,U] outer form; total effect produced by the outlines of something: There were clouds of different ~s. What's the ~ of his nose? **knock sth into/ out of shape**, put it into/out of the right shape. **take shape**, become definite in form or outline: The new building/His plan is beginning to take ~. **2** sort, description: I've had no help from him in any ~ or form, none of any sort. **3** condition: He is in good ~, is physically fit. Her affairs are in good ~, are satisfactory. **4** [C] vague form: I could see a ~ in the darkness.

shape /ʃeɪp/ vt,vi **1** give a shape or form to: ~ a pot on a wheel. **2** (pp): ~d like a pear/'pear-~d, having the shape of a pear. **3** give signs of future shape or development: Our plans are shaping well, giving promise of success.

shape-less adj with no definite shape.

shape-ly /'ʃeɪplɪ/ adj (-ier, -iest) (esp of a person) having a pleasing shape: a ~ pair of legs.

share /ʃeə(r)/ n **1** [C] part or division which a person has in, receives from, or gives to, a stock held by several or many persons, or which he contributes to a fund, expenses, etc: We shall all have a ~ in the profits. **go shares (with sb) (in sth)**, divide (profits, costs, etc) with others; become part owner (with others); pay (a part of an expense): Let me go ~s with you in the taxi fare. **2** [U] part taken or received by a person in an action, etc, eg of responsibility, blame: You must

take your ~ of the blame. **3** [C] one of the equal parts into which the capital of a company is divided with which the holder can have a part of the profits. □ vt,vi **1** give a share of to others; divide and distribute: ~ (out) £100 among/between five men, eg by giving them £20 each. **share sth with sb**, give a part to somebody else: He would ~ his last pound with me. **2** have or use (with): He hated having to ~ the hotel bedroom with a stranger. **3** have a share: I will ~ (in) the cost with you. '**share and 'share a'like**, have equal shares with others in the use, enjoyment, expense, etc of something.

'**share-holder**, owner of shares(3).

'**share-out**, distribution.

share /ʃeə(r)/ n [C] blade of a plough.

shark /ʃɑk/ n [C] **1** sea-fish, often large and dangerous. **2** (fig) person who cheats to gain money.

sharp /ʃɑp/ adj (-er, -est) **1** with a fine cutting edge: a ~ knife; with a fine point: a ~ pin/needle. ⇨ blunt. **2** well-defined; distinct: a ~ outline; a ~ image, (in photography) one with clear contrasts between light and shade. **3** (of curves, slopes, bends) changing direction quickly: a ~ bend in the road. **4** (of sounds) shrill; piercing: a ~ cry of distress. **5** quickly aware of things: a ~ intelligence/sense of smell. **keep a sharp look-out**, look very carefully (for): keep a ~ look-out for thieves. **6** (of feelings, taste) producing a physical sensation like cutting or pricking: a ~ pain. **7** harsh, severe: ~ words; a ~ tongue, of a person who criticizes, is easily angry, etc. **8** quick to take advantage: a ~ lawyer. **9** (music) (of a note) raised half a tone in pitch: C ~. ⇨ flat (5). □ n [C] (music) sharp note; the symbol # used to show this. □ adv **1** punctually: at seven (o'clock) ~. **2** suddenly, abruptly: turn ~ to the left.

sharpen /'ʃɑpən/ vt,vi make or become sharp: ~en a pencil.

sharp-ener /'ʃɑpənə(r)/, thing that sharpens: a 'pencil-~ener.

sharp-ly adv

sharp-ness n [U]

shat-ter /'ʃætə(r)/ vt,vi **1** break suddenly into small pieces: The explosion ~ed every window in the building. **2** (fig) destroy; be destroyed: Our hopes were ~ed.

shave /ʃeɪv/ vt,vi (pt,pp ~d or, as in (4) below, ~n /'ʃeɪvən/) **1** cut (hair) off the chin, etc with a razor: He is shaving off his beard. **2** take off (a thin layer, etc): ~ off a piece of wood. **3** pass very close to, almost but not touching: The bus ~d by me. **4** (pp) (as an adjective): '**clean-'~n**, without a beard. □ n [C] **1** shaving (of the face): A sharp razor gives a good ~. **2 a close/ narrow shave**, a narrow escape from injury, danger, etc.

shaver, razor with an electric motor.

'**shaving-brush**, brush for spreading lather

over the face before shaving.

shav·ings n pl thin pieces of wood shaved (2) off.

shawl /ʃɔl/ n [C] large (usually square or oblong) piece of material worn about the shoulders or head of a woman, or wrapped round a baby.

she /ʃi/ pron (⇨ her; they) 1 female person, animal, etc already referred: *My sister says ～ is going for a walk.* 2 (often as a prefix) female: *Is it a he or a ～? a `～-goat*

sheaf /ʃif/ n [C] (pl sheaves /ʃivz/) 1 corn barley, etc tied together after reaping 2 arrows, etc tied together

shear /ʃɪə(r)/ vt (pt, ～ed, pp shorn /ʃɔn/ or ～ed) 1 cut the wool off (a sheep) with shears. 2 (fig) take away completely from. **shorn of**, having lost completely: *The gambler came home shorn of his money*

shears /ʃɪəz/ n pl (also a pair of ～) large cutting instrument shaped like scissors.

sheath /ʃiθ/ n [C] (pl ～s /ʃiðz/) cover for the blade of a weapon or tool: *Put the dagger back in its ～.*
`**sheath-knife,** knife, with a blade, that fits into a sheath.

sheathe /ʃið/ vt put into a sheath

sheaves /ʃivz/ ⇨ sheaf.

shed¹ /ʃed/ n [C] small building, usually of wood, used for storing things (`tool-～, `wood-～, `coal-～), for sheltering animals (`cattle-～), for vehicles (`engine-～ `bicycle-～).

shed² /ʃed/ vt (pt,pp ～) (-dd-) 1 let (leaves, etc) fall; let come off: *Some trees ～ their leaves in autumn.* **shed blood,** (a) be wounded or killed. (b) cause the blood of others to flow: *The wicked ruler ～ rivers of blood.* ⇨ bloodshed. **shed tears,** = cry. 2 throw or take off; get rid of: *People on the beach began to ～ their clothes as it got hotter and hotter.* 3 spread or send out: *a fire that ～s warmth; a woman who ～s happiness.* **shed light on,** (fig) ⇨ light³(5).

she'd /ʃid/ = she had; she would.

sheen /ʃin/ n [U] brightness: *the ～ of silk*

sheep /ʃip/ n [C] (pl unchanged) grass-eating animal kept for its flesh as food (mutton) and its wool. ⇨ ewe, lamb and ram.
`**sheep-dog,** dog trained to help a shepherd to look after sheep.
`**sheep-fold,** enclosure for sheep.
`**sheep-skin,** rug of a sheep's skin with the wool on it; garment made of two or more such skins.
`**sheep-ish** /-ɪʃ/ adj (a) awkwardly self-conscious: *a ～ish-looking boy.* (b) (feeling) foolish or embarrassed because of a fault.
sheep·ish·ly adv
sheep·ish·ness n [U]

sheer /ʃɪə(r)/ adj 1 complete; thorough; absolute: *～ nonsense; a ～ waste of time; by ～ chance.* 2 (of textiles, etc) finely woven and almost transparent: *～ nylon* 3 (almost)

without a slope, *a ～ drop of 50 metres.* □ adv straight up or down: *He fell 500 feet ～*

sheet¹ /ʃit/ n [C] 1 rectangular piece of cotton, etc cloth, used in pairs for sleeping between: *put clean ～s on the bed.* 2 flat thin piece (of a material): *a ～ of glass/ notepaper.* 3 wide expanse (of water, ice, snow, flame, etc): *The rain came down in ～s, very heavily.*
`**sheet-lightning,** lightning that comes in wide flashes of brightness (not in zigzags, etc).
`**sheet music,** published on sheets of paper not in a book.
sheet-ing n [U] material used for making sheets(1).

sheet² /ʃit/ n [C] rope fastened at the lower corner of a sail to hold it and control the angle at which it is set.

sheik(h) /ʃeɪk US: ʃik/ n [C] Arab chieftain. head of an Arab village, tribe, etc.
sheik(h)·dom /-dəm/ n [C]

shelf /ʃelf/ n [C] (pl shelves /ʃelvz/) 1 flat piece of wood, metal, etc, fastened at right angles to a wall or in a cupboard, etc used to stand things on. **on the shelf,** (informal) (a) put aside as done with, e g of a person too old to continue working. (b) (of a woman) unmarried and considered as being unlikely to be asked to marry. 2 piece of rock on a cliff face, etc like a shelf (as used by rock-climbers).

shell /ʃel/ n [C] 1 hard outer covering of eggs, nuts, some seeds (e g peas) and fruits, and of some animals (e g snails) or parts of them. **go/retire into/come out of one's shell,** become/cease to be shy, reserved, quiet. 2 outside walls etc, of an unfinished building ship, etc or of one of which the contents have been destroyed (e g by fire). 3 (US = cartridge) metal case filled with explosive, to be fired from a large gun □ vt,vi 1 take out of a shell(1): *～ing peas.* 2 fire shells(3) at: *～ the enemy's trenches.* 3 **shell out,** (informal) pay up (money, a required sum): *Must I ～ out (the money) for the party?*
`**shellfish,** kinds of sea-animal (crabs, lobsters, etc) with shells(1).
`**shell-proof** adj built so that a shell(3) cannot break it.
`**shell-shock,** nervous or mental disorder caused by the noise of shells(3).

she'll /ʃil/ = she will, she shall.

shel·ter /ʃeltə(r)/ n 1 [U] condition of being kept safe, e g from rain, danger: *take ～ from the storm.* 2 [C] something that gives safety or protection: *a `bus ～,* in which people wait for buses. □ vt,vi 1 give shelter to; protect: *trees that ～ a house from cold winds;* (= hide, protect) *an escaped prisoner.* 2 take shelter: *～ under the trees.*

shelve¹ /ʃelv/ vt 1 put (books, etc) on a shelf. 2 (fig) (or problems, plans. etc) postpone dealing with: *～ a problem*

shelve[2] /ʃelv/ vi (of land) slope gently: *The shore ~s down to the sea*

shelves /ʃelvz/ pl of shelf.

shep·herd /ʃepəd/ n [C] man who takes care of sheep. □ vt **1** take care of. **2** guide or direct (people) like sheep: *The passengers were ~ed across the tarmac to the airliner.*

shep·herd·ess /'ʃepə'des/ n [C] woman shepherd.

sher·iff /ʃerif/ n [C] **1** (also *High ~*) chief officer of the Crown in counties and certain cities, with legal and ceremonial duties. **2** (*US*) chief law-enforcing officer of a county.

sherry /ʃeri/ n [U] yellow or brown wine from S Spain, Cyprus, etc.

shied /ʃaid/ ⇨ shy[2].

shield /ʃild/ n [C] **1** piece of metal, leather, etc carried to protect the body when fighting **2** representation of a shield showing a coat of arms. **3** (*fig*) person or thing that protects. **4** (in machinery, etc) piece of metal, etc designed to keep out dust, wind, etc. □ vt **1** protect; keep safe: *~ one's eyes with one's hand.* **2** protect (a person) from suffering, etc: *~ a friend from criticism.*

shift[1] /ʃift/ n [C] **1** change of place or character: *a ~ in emphasis* **2** change of one thing for another: *a ~ from cars to bicycles* **3** [C] group of workmen who start work as another group finishes; period for which such a group works: *on the `day/`night ~* **4** trick, way of avoiding a difficulty; clever way of getting something: *use clever ~s to get some money.* **5** woman's narrow dress without a waistline. **6** (*motoring*) mechanism for changing gear.

shift·less adj without ability to find ways of doing things

shift[2] /ʃift/ vt,vi **1** change position or direction; transfer: *~ luggage from one hand to the other. Don't try to ~ the blame (on) to somebody else.* **2** (*motoring*) change (gears): *~ into second/third gear.* **3** **shift for oneself**, manage as best one can (to make a living, etc) without help: *When their father died the children had to ~ for themselves.*

shifty adj (-ier, -iest) not to be trusted: *a ~y customer; ~y behaviour.*

shil·ling /ʃilɪŋ/ n [C] (until 1971) British coin with the value of twelve pennies, one-twentieth of a pound

shim·mer /ʃimə(r)/ vi, n [U] (have a shine with a) wavering soft or faint light: *moonlight ~ing on the water.*

shin /ʃin/ n [C] front part of the leg below the knee. □ vi (-nn-) **shin up**, climb up (using arms and legs to grip something): *~ up a tree.*

`shin-bone, inner and thicker of the two bones below the knee.

shine /ʃain/ vi,vt (*pt,pp* shone /ʃon *US* ʃəʊn/ but ⇨ below) **1** give out or reflect light; be bright: *The moon is shining. His face shone with excitement.* **2** (*fig*) show particular ability or intelligence: *He didn't ~ in the exams. I don't ~ at tennis.* **3** (*informal*) (*pp ~d*) polish (which is more usual): *~ shoes.* □ n **1** (*sing* only) polish (which is more usual): *Give your shoes a good ~.* **2** [U] **come rain or shine,** (a) whatever the weather may be (b) (*fig*) whatever may happen.

shiny adj (-ier, -iest) polished; bright: *shiny shoes.*

shingle /ʃiŋgəl/ n [U] small rounded pebbles on the seashore.

shin·gly /ʃiŋgli/ adj

shingles /ʃiŋgəlz/ n (used with a *sing verb*) skin disease forming a band of inflamed, irritating spots (often round the waist)

ship[1] /ʃip/ n [C] **1** large boat with an engine that can travel on a sea: *a `sailing-~; a `merchant-~; a `war~* **2** (*informal*) = spacecraft. **3** (*US informal*) = aircraft.

`ship-breaker, contractor who buys and breaks up old ships (for scrap).

`ship-broker, agent of a shipping company; one who buys, sells and charters ships; agent for marine insurance.

`ship-builder,** person whose business is building ships. Hence, **`ship-building n [U]

`ship's-chandler, dealer in equipment for ships.

`ship-load, as much cargo, or as many passengers, as a ship can carry.

`ship-mate, person belonging to the same crew: *Harry and I were ~mates in 1972.*

`ship-owner, person who owns a ship or ships.

`ship-shape adj tidy; in good order.

`ship-wreck n [U] loss or destruction of a ship at sea; [C] instance of this. □ vi destroy by shipwreck.

`ship-wright, shipbuilder.

`ship-yard, place where ships are built.

ship[2] /ʃip/ vt,vi **1** put, take, send, in a ship: *~ oil to Europe.* **2** take, send, by train, road, etc: *~ goods by express train.* **3** **ship oars,** take them out of the water into the boat. **4** **ship water,** be flooded with water during a storm or through a hole in the side.

ship·ment n [U] putting of goods, etc on a ship; [C] quantity of goods shipped.

ship·per, person who arranges for goods to be shipped

ship·ping n [U] all the ships of a country, part, etc.

`ship-ping-agent, shipowner's representative at a port.

-ship /-ʃip/ suffix **1** state of being; status, office: *friendship; professorship.* **2** skill: *musicianship.*

shire /ʃaiə(r)/ n [C] = county (the usual word). □ suffix /-ʃə(r)/ (used in the names of certain counties): *Hamp~, York~.*

shirk /ʃɜk/ vt,vi try to avoid (doing something, responsibility, duty, etc): *He's ~ing (his duty)*

shirker, person who shirks.

shirt /ʃɜːt/ n [C] man's garment for the upper part of the body (of cotton, nylon, etc) with sleeves. *keep one's shirt on,* (*sl*) keep one's temper.

shirty adj (-ier, -iest) (*sl*) easily annoyed; bad-tempered.

shiver /ˈʃɪvə(r)/ vi tremble, esp from cold or fear: ~ing like a leaf. □ n [C] trembling that cannot be controlled: *The sight sent cold ~s down my back.*

shoal¹ /ʃəʊl/ n [C] great number of fish swimming together: *a ~ of herring.* □ vi form shoals.

shoal² /ʃəʊl/ n [C] shallow place in the sea, esp where there are sandbanks. □ vi become shallow(er).

shock /ʃɒk/ n 1 [C] violent blow or shaking (e g as caused by a collision or explosion): *the ~ of a fall.* 2 [C] effect caused by the passage of an electric current through the body: *If you touch that live wire you'll get a ~.* 3 [C] sudden and strong disturbance of the feelings or the nervous system (caused by bad news, severe injury, etc); [U] condition caused by such a disturbance: *The news of her mother's death was a terrible ~ to her. She died of ~ following an operation on the brain.* □ vt cause shock(3) to: *I was ~ed at the news of her death.*

`shock tactics,` (a) sudden use of many troops to attack (in war). (b) (*fig*) similar show of force to attack.

`shock treatment/therapy,` use of electric shocks to cure mental illness.

`shock wave,` sudden change in air-pressure in a region, e g behind a supersonic aircraft or a nuclear bomb.

shocker, person or thing that shocks.

shock·ing adj (a) very bad or wrong: ~ing behaviour. (b) causing shock(3): ~ing news, e g of a flood that causes great loss of life. (c) (*informal*) bad: ~ing handwriting.
shock·ing·ly adv

shod /ʃɒd/ ⇨ shoe verb.

shoddy /ˈʃɒdɪ/ adj (-ier, -iest) of poor quality: *a ~ piece of work.*

shoe /ʃuː/ n [C] 1 (often *a pair of ~s*) outer covering of leather, etc for the foot, esp one which does not reach above the ankle. 2 = horseshoe. 3 part of a brake that presses against the wheel or drum (of a bicycle, motor-vehicle, etc). □ vt (*pt,pp* shod /ʃɒd/) fit with shoes: *well shod for wet weather.*

`shoe-horn,` device with a curved blade for getting the heel easily into a shoe.

`shoe-lace,` cord for fastening a shoe.

`shoe-string,` (*US*) = shoelace. *do sth on a shoestring,* do it (e g start a business) with a very small amount of money.

`shoe·maker,` person who makes shoes and boots.

shone /ʃɒn *US:* ʃəʊn/ *pt,pp* of shine.

shoo /ʃuː/ int cry used for telling children, pets, birds, etc to go away □ vt (*pt,pp* ~ed) make them go away by making this cry

shook /ʃʊk/ *pt* of shake.

shoot¹ /ʃuːt/ n [C] 1 new, young growth on a plant or bush. 2 party of people shooting for sport.

shoot² /ʃuːt/ vi,vt (*pt, pp* shot /ʃɒt/) 1 move, come, go, send, suddenly or quickly (*out, in, up,* etc): *Flames were ~ing up from the burning house. The meteor shot across the sky. Rents have shot up* (= risen suddenly) *in the last few months. Tom is ~ing up fast,* quickly growing tall. *She shot an angry look at him/shot him an angry look.* 2 (of plants, bushes) send out new twigs or branches from a stem. 3 (of pain) happen suddenly and go quickly: *The pain shot up his arm.* 4 (of boats) move, be moved, rapidly over, through, etc: *~ a bridge,* pass under it quickly. 5 aim and fire with a gun or revolver; aim with a bow and send an arrow at; hit with a shell, bullet, arrow, etc; wound or kill (a person, animal, etc) by doing this: *They were ~ing at a target. The soldier was shot* (= executed by ~ing) *for desertion. The bomber was shot down in flames. He had his arm shot off.* 6 photograph (a scene): *a ~ing script,* one to be used for a film (giving the order in which scenes are photographed, etc). 7 make an attempt to score a goal.

`shoot·ing-gallery,` place where shooting is practised with pistols or airguns

`shooting `star,` meteor seen as a moving star.

`shooting-stick,` stick with a spiked end (to be pushed into the ground) and a handle which unfolds to form a seat.

-shooter /ˈʃuːtə(r)/ suffix shooting implement: *a `six-~,`* revolver firing six shots without reloading.

shop /ʃɒp/ n [C] 1 (part of a) building where goods are shown and sold: *a butcher's ~.* (*US* = store). *set up shop,* set up in business as a retail trader. *all `over the shop,`* (a) in a great mess: *His clothes were all over the ~.* (b) in every direction: *We looked for him all over the ~.* 2 [U] a person's profession, etc and things connected with it. *talk shop,* talk about one's work, profession, etc. 4 = workshop: *a ma`chine-~; the men on the ~ floor,* the workers (not the management). ⇨ closed shop. □ vi (-pp-) 1 go to shops to buy things (usually *go shopping*). *shop around,* (*informal*) visit many shops, markets, etc to obtain the best value for one's money, etc. 2 inform against, esp to the police: *~ on an accomplice.*

`shop-assistant,` employee in a shop.

`shop-front,` front of a shop with its window display, etc.

`shop-keeper,` owner of (usually a small) shop.

`shop-lifter,` person who steals things from shops. Hence, `shop-lifting` n [U]

`shop-`steward,` member of a branch of a

trade union elected by the workers

'shop-'window, window used for the display of things on sale.

shop·per, person who is shopping.

shop·ping n [U]: *do one's ~ping; a `~ping bag/basket*, in which to carry purchases. **`shopping centre**, part of a town where there are shops, markets, etc close together and often where cars are not allowed. ⇨ window-shopping.

shore[1] /ʃɔ(r)/ n [C] stretch of land bordering on the sea or a large body of water. *a house on the ~(s) of a lake*.

shore[2] /ʃɔ(r)/ n [C] wooden support or prop (as set against the side of a ship while it is being built). □ *vt* **shore sth up**, support, prop up, (with a wooden beam, etc).

shore[3] /ʃɔ(r)/, **shorn** /ʃɔn/ ⇨ shear.

short[1] /ʃɔt/ adj (-er, -est) 1 (opp of *long*) measuring little from end to end in space or time: *a ~ stick; ~ hair; a ~ way off*, not far away; *a ~ journey*. **in the short run**, over a short period of time; during the present time. **short and sweet**, brief and (therefore) pleasant. 2 (opposite of *tall*) below the average height: *a ~ man/mountain*. 3 not reaching the usual, stated or required number, amount, distance, etc: *have a ~ temper*, be easily made angry. *These goods are in ~ supply*, only a few are available. *The factory is on ~ change*, less than the correct change. **short of** (a) not enough of: *~ of money/breath/time*. (b) distant from: *have no petrol left five miles ~ of the garage*. **little/nothing short of**, almost: *Our escape was nothing ~ of a miracle*. 4 (of a person) saying very little or saying much in a few words; (of what he says) using a few words: *He/His answer was ~ and to the point*. **for short; short for**, as an abbreviation: *Benjamin, called Ben for ~. Ben is ~ for Benjamin*. **in short**, briefly. **the long and the short of it**, ⇨ long[2](1). 5 (of cake, pastry) easily breaking or crumbling. 6 (of vowels or syllables) taking a short time: *There is a ~ vowel in 'slip' and a long vowel in 'sheep'*.

`short·bread, kind of dry cake or biscuit.

`short·comings, failure (to reach the standard, to develop properly, to do one's duty).

'short-'circuit n [C] fault in the wiring so that an electric current flows without going through the resistance of a complete circuit. □ *vt, vi* (a) cause, make or take a short-circuit in. (b) (*fig*) shorten or avoid by taking a more direct route.

`short cut, way of getting somewhere, doing something that is quicker than the usual way: *take a ~ cut across the fields*.

short drink, neat whisky, etc in small portions.

`short·fall, = deficit.

short·hand, system of writing quickly

using special symbols.

'short-'handed, having not enough workers or helpers.

`short list**, list of candidates (e g for a job) reduced to a small number from which which the final choice is to be made. Hence, **`short-list vt.

'short-'lived adj lasting for a short time: *a ~-lived success*.

`short-range adj (a) (of plans, etc) of use for a limited period, (b) (of missiles, etc) with a limited range[1](3).

short sight, (a) inability to see distant objects clearly. (b) (*fig*) inability to forecast the obvious (and act accordingly). Hence, **'short-'sighted** adj: *a ~-sighted economic policy*.

'short-'tempered adj easily made angry.

`short-term adj related to a short period of time: *~-term loans*.

`short·wave, radio wave of between 10 and 100 metres in length.

'short-'winded adj (a) quickly breathless after physical activity. (b) (*fig*) unable or unwilling to act or speak for a long time.

short·ly adv (a) soon; in a short time: *~ly after(wards); ~ly before noon*. (b) briefly; in a few words. (c) sharply: *answer ~ly*.

short·ness n [U]

short[2] /ʃɔt/ adv 1 abruptly; suddenly: *stop ~*. **short of**, except: *They would commit every crime ~ of murder*. 2 before the natural or expected time. **come/fall short of**, be insufficient, inadequate, disappointing (expectations, etc): *Your exam results fell ~ of my expectations*. **cut sth/sb short**, (a) interrupt; bring to an end before the usual or natural time: *The chairman had to cut ~ the discussion*. (b) make short(er). **go short (of)**, do without: *I don't want you to go ~* (of money, etc) *in order to lend me what I need*. **run short (of)**, reach the end: *We're running ~ of bread*. **sell sb short**, betray, cheat them.

short·age /ʃɔtɪdʒ/ n [C,U] (amount of) deficiency; condition of not having enough: *food ~s; a ~ of staff*.

short·en /ʃɔtən/ vt, vi make or become shorter: *Can you ~ my dress? The days are beginning to ~*, e g in autumn.

short·en·ing /ʃɔtənɪŋ/ n [U] fat used for making pastry light and flaky. ⇨ short[1](5).

shorts /ʃɔts/ n (pl) short trousers extending to or above the knees, as worn by children, by adults for games, etc.

shot /ʃɔt/ n 1 [C] (sound of the) firing of a gun, etc: *hear ~s in the distance*. **(do sth) like a shot**, at once; without hesitation. 2 [C] (attempt at) hitting of something; attempt to do something, answer a question, etc; throw stroke, hit, etc in certain games: *Good ~, Sir! That remark was a ~ at me*, was aimed at me. **a shot in the dark**, a guess. **have a shot (at sth)**, try to do it: *Have a ~ at solving the problem. Let me* have a ~ at it. **a** `**long shot,** an attempt to solve a problem, etc with little chance of success: *It's a long ~ but I think John must have stolen the bike.* **not by a** `**long shot,** not even if circumstances were most favourable. **3** [C] that which is fired from a gun. ⇨ shell(3). **4** [C] heavy iron ball thrown in athletic competition called the `~-*put: putting the* ~. **5** [U] (also *lead* ~) quantity of tiny balls of lead contained in the cartridge of a sporting gun (instead of a single bullet). **6** [C] person who shoots, with reference to his skill: *He's a first-class/good/poor, etc* ~. **7** [C] photograph, or one of a series of photographs, taken with a cine-camera: *The exterior* ~*s were taken in Bermuda.* **8** (esp US) = injection (of a drug). *have/get/ give sb a shot in the arm,* have/give something that revives or restores, e g the economy. **9 a** `**big shot,** (*sl*) an important person, esp a conceited one.

`**shot-gun,** sporting gun with a smooth bore firing cartridges containing shot(5).

`**shot-put,** ⇨ 4 above.

should /ʃʊd *weak form* ʃəd/ *v* ⇨ shall.

shoul-der /ˈʃəʊldə(r)/ *n* [C] **1** that part of the body of a human being or animal where an arm or foreleg is joined to the trunk, or where the wing of a bird joins its neck: *He has one* ~ *a little higher than the other. shoulder to shoulder,* (*fig*) united. *give sb the cold shoulder,* ⇨ cold¹(1). *stand head and shoulders above* (others), **(a)** be considerably taller than. **(b)** (*fig*) be mentally or morally better than. *straight from the shoulder,* frankly. **2** (*pl*) part of the back between the shoulders: *give a child a ride on one's* ~*s.* **3** part of a bottle, tool, mountain, etc like a shoulder. ⇨ hard shoulder. □ *vt* **1** take the weight of responsibility: ~ *a task/the responsibility for his debts.* **2** push with the shoulder: *be* ~*ed to one side.*

`**shoulder-blade,** either of the flat bones of the upper back, behind and below the neck.

`**shoulder-strap,** **(a)** narrow strap on the shoulders of a military uniform. **(b)** similar strap on woman's underwear or a dress.

shout /ʃaʊt/ *n* [C] loud call or cry: *They greeted him with* ~*s of 'Long live the President'.* □ *vi,vt* **1** speak or call out in a loud voice: *Don't* ~ *at me! He* ~*ed to attract attention.* **2** say in a loud voice: ~ (*out*) *one's orders. He* ~*ed to me/* ~*ed for me to come. 'Go back!' he* ~*ed. shout sb down,* shout to prevent him from being heard: *The crowd* ~*ed the speaker down.*

shout·ing *n* [U] shouts. *be all over bar the shouting,* (of a struggle, fight, etc) be finished except for the praise, cheers, etc to follow.

shove /ʃʌv/ *vt,vi* (*informal*) push: ~ *a boat into the water.* □ *n* [C] push: *Give it a* ~.

shovel /ˈʃʌvəl/ *n* [C] **1** spade-like tool, used for moving coal, sand, snow, etc. **2** large device used for the same purpose, mechanically operated from a crane in a vehicle. □ *vt* (-ll-, *US* -l-) lift, move, clear, using a shovel: ~ *the snow away from the garden path;* ~ *a path through the snow.*

shovel-ful /-fʊl/, as much as a shovel will hold.

show¹ /ʃəʊ/ *n* **1** [U] showing (chiefly in): *by* (*a*) ~ *of hands,* (voting) by the raising of hands for or against (a proposal). **2** [C] collection of things publicly displayed, esp for competition, or as a public entertainment: *a* `*flower/* `*horse/* `*cattle* ~. *on show,* exhibited. **3** [C] (*informal*) natural display: *Those trees make a fine* ~. **4** [C] kind of public entertainment, e g circus, theatre, on radio, TV, etc: *Have you seen any good* ~*s lately?* **5** [C] (*informal*) performance (not theatrical, etc): *put up a good/poor* ~, do something well/badly. *steal the show,* attract all the attention. **6** [C] (*informal*) organization; business; something that is happening: *Who's running this* ~? *Who controls or manages it?* **7** outward appearance; impression: *He didn't offer even a* ~ *of resistance.* **8** [U] something done to attract envy: *She does it for* ~, *to make others envious. They're fond of* ~.

`**show-boat,** river steam-boat on which theatrical performances were given (esp on the Mississippi, US).

`**show-business,** business of entertaining the public.

`**show-case,** case with glass sides and (or) top, for displaying articles in a shop, museum, etc.

`**show-down,** (*sl*) full and frank declaration of one's strength, intentions, etc.

`**show-girl,** girl who sings or dances in a musical play, revue, etc.

`**show-jumping,** display of skill in riding horses over fences, barriers, etc.

`**show-man,** **(a)** organizer of public entertainments (esp circuses). **(b)** person (esp in public life) who uses publicity, etc to attract attention to himself: *Some politicians are great* ~*men and very little else.*

`**show-place,** one that tourists go to see: *old palaces, castles and other* ~-*places.*

showy *adj* (-ier, -iest) likely to attract attention because (too much) decorated or ornamented, or (too) brightly coloured: *a* ~*y dress.*

show² /ʃəʊ/ *vt,vi* (*pt* ~ed, *pp* ~n /ʃəʊn/) **1** cause to be seen: *You must* ~ *your ticket at the barrier. What films are they* ~*ing this week?* **2** allow to be seen: *A dark suit will not* ~ *the dirt. My shoes are* ~*ing signs of wear.* **3** be visible or noticeable: *Does the mark of the wound still* ~? *His fear* ~*ed in his eyes.* **4** be visible: *His annoyance* ~*ed itself in his looks. show one's face,* appear before people: *He's ashamed to* ~ *his face at the tennis-club. have nothing to show for it/sth,* have nothing that is evidence of what one has achieved or tried to achieve. **5** give; grant: *He ~ed me great kindness.* **6** give evidence or proof of having or being: *She ~ed great courage. His new book ~s him to be a first-rate novelist.* **7** conduct a person into/out of a place: *Please ~ this gentleman out. We were ~n into the living-room.* **8** make clear; cause (a person) to understand: *He ~ed me how to do it/how he had done it. That ~s how little you know.* **show sb the way,** (*fig*) set an example. **9** **show sb/sth off,** display (him/it) to advantage: *a bikini that ~s off her figure well.* **show off,** make a display of one's wealth, learning, abilities, etc in order to impress people: *a man who is always ~ing off.* **show sb/sth up,** make the truth about (a dishonest, disreputable, etc person or thing) known: *~ up a fraud.* **show sb up,** attract criticism towards him: *Some children often ~ their mothers up by crying in the street.* **show up, (a)** be conspicuous, easily visible: *Her wrinkles ~ed up in the strong sunlight* **(b)** (*informal*) put in an appearance; be present (*at*): *Three of those we invited to the party didn't ~ up.*

`show-off, person who shows off: *He's a dreadful ~-off, is always trying to attract attention, etc.*

show·ing n(usually *sing*) (act of) displaying or pointing out; appearance: *a firm with a poor financial ~ing,* whose financial accounts do not appear to be good.

shower /ˈʃaʊə(r)/ n [C] **1** brief fall of rain, sleet or hail; sudden sprinkle of water (as from a fountain). **2** (washing by using a) device which sprays water from above. **3** large number of things arriving together: *a ~ of stones/blessings/insults.* □ *vt, vi* **1** send or give, in a shower: *They ~ed the hero with honours.* **2** fall in a shower: *Good wishes ~ed (down) on the bride.*

show·ery adj (of the weather) with frequent showers.

shown /ʃəʊn/ pp of show².

shrank /ʃræŋk/ pt of shrink.

shrap·nel /ˈʃræpnəl/ n [U] fragments of shell or bullets packed inside a shell.

shred /ʃred/ n [C] **1** strip or piece scraped, torn or broken off something. **2** (*fig*) very small amount: *not a ~ of truth in what she says; not a ~ of evidence against me.* □ *vt* (-dd-) tear into shreds.

shrew /ʃru/ n [C] **1** bad-tempered, scolding woman. **2** small animal like a mouse that feeds on insects.

shrew·ish /-ɪʃ/ adj scolding.

shrewd /ʃrud/ adj (-er, -est) **1** having, showing, sound judgement and common sense: *~ businessmen; ~ arguments.* **2** likely to be correct or effective: *make a ~ guess*

shrewd·ly adv

shrewd·ness n [U]

shriek /ʃrik/ vi,vt **1** scream **2** utter in a screaming voice: *~ out a warning ~ with laughter* □ n [C] scream *~s of girlish laughter; the ~ (= whistle) of a railway engine.*

shrift /ʃrɪft/ n [U] **get/give sb short shift,** give little attention to because not deserving: *They gave us/We got short ~.*

shrill /ʃrɪl/ adj (-er, -est) (of sounds, voices, etc) sharp; piercing; high-pitched: *a ~ voice/whistle.*

shrill·ness n [U]

shrimp /ʃrɪmp/ n [C] small shellfish used for food. □ *vi* catch shrimps: *go ~ing.*

shrine /ʃraɪn/ n [C] **1** tomb or casket containing holy relics; altar or chapel with special associations or memory. **2** building or place associated with a person deeply respected or venerated

shrink /ʃrɪŋk/ vi,vt (*pt* shrank /ʃræŋk/, or shrunk /ʃrʌŋk/, *pp* shrunk, or, as an *adj* shrunken /ˈʃrʌŋkən/) **1** make or become less, smaller (esp of cloth through wetting): *Will this soap ~ woollen clothes? They will ~ in the wash. Look at these shrunken jeans!* **2** **shrink from/back,** move back, show unwillingness to do something (from shame, dislike, etc): *A shy man ~s from meeting strangers.*

`shrink·age /-ɪdʒ/ n [U] process, degree, of shrinking: *The ~age in our export trade is serious.*

shrivel /ˈʃrɪvəl/ vt,vi (-ll-, US also -l-) (cause to) become dried or curled (through heat, frost, dryness or old age): *The heat ~led up the leaves. He has a ~led face,* with the skin wrinkled.

shroud /ʃraʊd/ n [C] **1** cloth or sheet (to be) wrapped round a corpse. **2** something which covers and hides: *a ~ of mist.* **3** (*pl*) ropes supporting a ship's masts; ropes linking a parachute and the harness which is strapped to the parachutist. □ *vt* **1** wrap (a corpse) in a shroud. **2** cover; hide: *~ed in darkness/ mist; a crime ~ed in mystery.*

shrove /ʃrəʊv/ ⇨ shrive.

Shrove Tues·day /ˌʃrəʊv ˈtjuːzdɪ US: ˈtuːz-/ n day before the beginning of Lent.

shrub /ʃrʌb/ n [C] plant with a woody stem, lower than a tree, and (usually) with several separate stems from the root.

shrub·bery /ˈʃrʌbərɪ/ n [C] (*pl* -ies) place, e g part of a garden, planted with shrubs.

shrug /ʃrʌg/ vt (-gg-) lift (the shoulders) slightly (to show indifference, doubt, etc) **shrug sth off,** dismiss it as not deserving attention. □ n [C] such a movement: *with a ~ of the shoulders/a ~ of despair.*

shrunk /ʃrʌŋk/, **shrunken** /ˈʃrʌŋkən/ ⇨ shrink.

shud·der /ˈʃʌdə(r)/ vi tremble as with fear or disgust: *~ with cold/horror; ~ at the sight of blood. He ~ed to think of it.* □ n [C] uncontrollable shaking: *a ~ went through her*

shuffle /ˈʃʌfəl/ vi,vt **1** walk without raising

the feet properly. **2** move (playing-cards, etc) one over the other to change their relative positions: *He ~d the papers together an put them in a drawer.* **3** do something in a careless way: *~ through one's work.* **4** (*fig*): *~ off responsibility onto others,* get rid of it by passing it to others. **5** keep shifting one's position; try to avoid giving an answer, a decision etc. □ *n* [C] **1** shuffling movement. **2** change of relative positions: *give the cards a ~; a Cabinet ~,* giving members different duties. **3** instance of dishonesty; misleading statement or action.

shun /ʃʌn/ *vt* (-nn-) avoid: *~ publicity/ society.*

'shun /ʃʌn/ *int* short for *Attention!* (as a word of command).

shunt /ʃʌnt/ *vt,vi* **1** send (railway wagons, coaches, etc) from one track to another, esp to keep a track clear: *~ a train on to a siding.* **2** (of a train) be moved to a siding. **3** (*fig*) put aside (a project); leave (a person) unoccupied, or inactive.

shun·ter, (esp) railway employee who shunts wagons, etc.

shush /ʃʊʃ/ *vi,vt* call for silence by saying 'Shush!'

shut /ʃʌt/ *vt,vi* (*pt,pp* shut) (-tt-) (For special uses with *adverbial particles and prepositions,* ⇨ 5 below.) **1** move (a door, one's lips, etc) into position to stop an opening: *~ the doors and windows; ~ a drawer; ~ one's mouth.* **shut/close one's ears/eyes to,** deliberately ignore: *He ~ his eyes to her faults. He ~ his ears to all appeals for help.* **shut the door on,** refuse to consider: *Why have you ~ the door on further negotiations?* **2** become closed: *The window ~s easily. The door won't ~.* **3** bring the folding parts of (something) together: *~ a book.* (*Note:* close is more usual.) **4** catch or pinch by shutting something: *~ one's fingers/ dress in the door.*

5 (special uses with *adverbial particles and prepositions*):

shut (sth) down, (of a factory, etc) stop working; end activity: *The workshop has ~ down and the workers are unemployed.* Hence, **'shut-down** *n* [C] (temporary or permanent) closing of a factory, etc.

shut sb in, keep or enclose: *We're ~ in by hills here,* surrounded by hills. *They ~ the boy in his bedroom,* kept him there.

shut sth off, stop the supply or flow of, e g gas, steam, water.

shut sb/sth out, keep out; exclude: *~ out immigrants/competitive goods.*

shut sth up, (a) close and secure all the doors and windows: *~ up a house before going away for a holiday.* **(b)** put away for safety: *~ up one's jewels in the safe.* **shut (sb) up,** (cause him to) stop talking: *Tell him to ~ up. Can't you ~ him up?*

shut·ter /ʃʌtə(r)/ *n* [C] **1** movable cover (usually of wood and hinged) for a window,

to keep out light or thieves. **put up the shutters,** (*fig*) stop doing business (for the day, or permanently). **2** device that opens to admit light through the lens of a camera. □ *vt* provide with, close with, shutters.

shuttle /ʃʌtl/ *n* [C] (in a loom) instrument with two pointed ends by which thread is carried between other threads; (in a sewing-machine) sliding holder which carries the lower thread. □ *vt,vi* (cause to) move backwards and forwards, to and fro, like a shuttle.

'shuttle-cock, cork with feathers in it, struck to and fro across a net in the games of shuttlecock and badminton.

'shuttle service, service (of trains, airlines, etc) to and fro between places not far apart.

shy¹ /ʃaɪ/ *adj* (-er, -est) **1** (of persons) self-conscious and uncomfortable in the presence of others; (of behaviour, etc) showing this: *He's not at all ~ with women. She gave him a ~ look/smile.* **2** (of animals, birds, fish, etc) easily frightened. **3** *shy of,* hesitating about: *Don't be ~ of telling me what you want.* **fight shy of,** ⇨ fight²(1).

shy·ly *adv*

shy·ness *n* [U]

shy² /ʃaɪ/ *vi* (*pt,pp* shied /ʃaɪd/) (of a horse) turn aside from in fear or alarm: *The horse was ~ing at a white object in the hedge.*

Sia·mese /ˌsaɪə'miːz/ *adj, n* [C] **1** (also *~ twin*) (of) one of two persons joined together from birth. **2** (of an) oriental breed of cat with blue eyes and short-haired coat of cream, fawn or light grey hair.

sib·ling /ˈsɪblɪŋ/ *n* [C] brother or sister (the usual words).

sic /sɪk/ *adv* (*Latin*) thus (placed in brackets to show that the preceding word statement, etc is correctly quoted, etc even though this seems unlikely or is incorrect).

sick /sɪk/ *adj* **1** be *~,* throw up food from the stomach; *feel ~,* feel that one is about to do this. ⇨ seasick. **2** unwell; ill: *He has been ~ for six weeks.* (*Note:* sick is normal US usage, *ill* or *unwell* are normal GB usage.) *~ at heart,* very sad, disappointed. **fall sick,** become ill. **3** *sick (and tired) of; sick to death of,* (*informal*) very tired of, disgusted with: *I'm ~ to death of being blamed for everything that goes wrong.* **4** **feel sick at/about,** (*informal*) unhappy, filled with regret: *feel ~ at failing the examination.* **5** *sick for,* filled with a longing for: *~ for home.* ⇨ homesick. **6** (*modern use*) perverted; basically sad: *~ humour/jokes.* □ *vt* **sick sth up,** (*informal*) throw up from the stomach.

'sick-bay, (a) (*Navy*) part of a ship for those who are ill. **(b)** medical centre on a university campus, etc.

'sick-bed, bed of a sick person.

'sick-leave, permission to be away from duty or work because of illness: *be/go on*

~-leave.

`sick-list,** list of those who are ill (in a regiment, on a warship, etc).

`sick-pay,** pay to an employee who is absent because ill.

sicken /ˈsɪkən/ vi,vt **1** be in the first stages of (an illness): *The child is ~ing for something*. **2** cause to feel disgusted: *Torture is ~ing*. **3** feel sick to see: *They ~ed at the sight of so much slaughter*. **4** become tired of, disgusted with: *He ~ed of trying to bring about reforms*.

sick·en·ing /ˈsɪkənɪŋ/ adj disgusting; unpleasant: *~ing smells/news*.

sick·ish /ˈsɪkɪʃ/ adj a little sick or sickening: *feel ~; a ~ smell*.

sickle /ˈsɪkəl/ n [C] short-handled tool with a curved blade for cutting grass, grain, etc.

sick·ly /ˈsɪklɪ/ adj (-ier, -iest) **1** often in poor health: *a ~ child*. **2** having the appearance of sickness or ill health: *These plants are/look rather ~*. **3** suggesting unhappiness: *a ~ smile*. **4** causing, or likely to cause, a feeling of sickness or distaste: *a ~ smell/taste*.

sick·ness /ˈsɪknəs/ n **1** [U] illness; ill health. **2** [C,U] (an) illness or disease: *suffering from `sea-~*. **3** [U] tendency to vomit.

`sickness benefit,** (State) payment to a person absent from work through illness.

side [1] /saɪd/ n [C] **1** one of the flat or fairly flat surfaces of a solid object: *the six ~s of a cube*. **2** one of the surfaces which is not the top or the bottom: *A box has a top, a bottom, and four ~s*. **3** one of the surfaces which is not the top, bottom, front or back: (as an *adjective*) *the ~ entrance of the house* (not the *front* or *back* entrance). **4** (*maths*) one of the lines of a figure such as a rectangle or triangle. **5** either of the two surfaces of a thin, flat object or of material such as paper: *Write on one ~ of the paper only Which is the right ~ of the cloth*, the side intended to be seen? **6** inner or outer surface of something vertical, sloping, round or curved: *the ~ of a mountain*. **7** one of the two halves of a person on his left or right, esp from armpit to hip: *Come and sit by/at my ~. **side by side,** close together*. **8** one of the two halves of an animal from foreleg to hindleg, esp as part of a carcass: *a ~ of beef/bacon*. **9** part of an object, area, space, etc away from, at a distance from, a central line real or imaginary: *the left/right/shady/sunny ~ of the street; the east ~ of the town; the debit/credit ~ of an account. **on/ from all sides; on/from every side,** in/ from all directions; everywhere. **put sth on one side,** (a) put it aside, apart. (b) postpone dealing with it. **10** one of two groups or parties of people who are opposed (in games, politics, war, etc) or who uphold beliefs, opinions, etc against the other: *be on the winning/losing ~; faults on both ~s; to

pick (= choose) ~s. The school has a strong ~, e g a good football team. **be on sb's side,** be a supporter. **let the side down,** give an inferior performance and disappoint one's colleagues, team-mates, etc. **take sides (with),** support (a person, a group) in a dispute. ⇨ side². **11** aspect or view that is not complete; aspect different from or opposed to other aspects: *look on the bright ~ of things/life, etc; study all ~s of a question; a man with many ~s to his character. There are two ~s to the story,* two points of view. **on the `high/ˈlow, etc side,** rather high/low, etc: *Prices are on the high ~. **12** line of descent through a parent: *a cousin on my father's ~*.

`side-arms** n pl (a) swords or bayonets, worn at the left side by soldiers. (b) pistol worn at the right side (usually in a holster).

`side-board,** table with drawers and cupboards, placed against the wall of a dining-room.

`side-burns/-boards** = side-whiskers.

`side effect,** secondary or indirect effect, e g an undesirable effect of a drug used for a specific purpose.

`side-glance,** look to or from one side.

`side issue,** question of less importance (in relation to the main one).

`side-line,** (a) class of goods sold in addition to the chief class of goods; occupation which is not one's main work. (b) (*pl*) (space immediately outside) lines round a football pitch, tennis-court, etc at the sides.

`side-long** adj, adv (directed) to or from one side: *a ~long glance*.

`side-road,** minor road branching off a main road.

`side-saddle** n [C] woman's saddle, made so that both feet may be on the same side of the horse. □ adv on a side-saddle: *Not all women ride ~-saddle*.

`side-show,** (a) small show at a fair or exhibition. (b) activity of small importance in relation to the main activity.

`side-step** n [C] step taken to one side (e g to avoid a blow in boxing). □ vt,vi (-pp-) (a) avoid (a blow, etc) by stepping to one side. (b) (*fig*) avoid answering (a question). (c) move, step, to one side

`side-street,** = side-road.

`side-stroke,** (kinds of) stroke used in swimming in which one side is above and the other below the water.

`side-track** n [C] railway siding. □ vt (a) turn (a train) into a siding. (b) (*fig*) turn (a person's attention) from his work.

`side-view,** view obtained from the side

`side-walk,** (*US*) = pavement.

`side-whiskers** n pl (of men) hair on the sides of the face near the ears

side·wards /-wədz/, **sideways** /-weɪz/ adv to, towards, from, the side; with the edge first: *look ~ways at her; walk/carry a chair ~ways through a narrow opening*

side² /saɪd/ vi **side with**, take part, be on the same side (as a person in an argument or quarrel): *It is safer to ~ with the stronger party.*

-sided /saɪdɪd/ suffix have a specified number of sides: *a `five-~ shape.*

sid·ing /ˈsaɪdɪŋ/ n [C] short railway track to and from which trains may be moved (from the main lines).

sidle /ˈsaɪdəl/ vi move (away from/up to a person) in a shy or nervous way: *The little girl ~d up to me.*

siege /siːdʒ/ n [C,U] (period of) operations of armed forces who surround and blockade a town or fortress in order to capture it: *a ~ of 50 days; lay ~ to a town.* **raise a seige,** end it by forcing the enemy's forces to withdraw.

si·enna /sɪˈenə/ n [U] kind of earth used as a colouring matter.

sieve /sɪv/ n [C] utensil with wire network for separating finer grains, etc from coarse grains, etc or solids from liquids. **have a head/memory like a sieve,** be incapable of remembering anything. □ vt put through, sift with, a sieve.

sift /sɪft/ vt,vi 1 put, separate by putting, through a sieve: *~ the cinders.* 2 shake through a sieve: *~ flour.* 3 fall, pass, come through, as from a sieve. 4 (fig) examine carefully: *~ the evidence.*

sifter, small sieve: *a `flour-~er.*

sigh /saɪ/ vi,vt 1 take a deep breath that can be heard (showing sadness, tiredness, relief, etc). 2 (of the wind) make a sound like sighing. 3 feel a longing (for): *~ for the return of a lost friend.* 4 express with sighs: *~ out a prayer.* □ n [C] act of, sound, of sighing: *with a ~ of relief.*

sight¹ /saɪt/ n 1 [U] power of seeing: *lose one's ~,* become blind; *have long/short or near ~,* be able to see things well only at long/short range; *have good/poor ~* (= eyesight). **know sb by sight,** know him by his appearance only. 2 [U] seeing or being seen: *Their first ~ of land came after three days at sea.* **catch sight of; have/get a sight of,** begin to see; succeed in seeing: *If ever I catch ~ of him again, I'll ask for the money he owes me.* **keep/lose sight of,** see/no longer see; (not) forget about: *I've lost ~ of Smith. We must not lose ~ of the fact that… at first sight,* when first seen; without examination, etc: *He fell in love with her at first ~. At first ~ the problem seemed insoluble.* **at (the) sight of,** on seeing: *They all laughed at the ~ of the old man dancing with a girl of sixteen.* 3 [U] range of seeing; distance within which seeing is possible: *in/within/out of (one's) ~,* (of objects, etc) visible/invisible; *The train was still in ~/was not yet out of ~. Victory was not yet in ~,* not yet probable. **in/within/out of sight of sth,** (of the viewer) where it can/cannot be seen: *We are*

not yet within ~ of land, can't see it. *We are now within ~ of finishing this job,* are near to the end. **come into/go out of sight,** come near enough/go too far away to be visible. **keep out of sight,** stay where one cannot be seen. 4 [U] opinion: *All men are equal in the ~ of God.* 5 [C] something seen or worth seeing; (pl) noteworthy buildings, places, features, etc of a place or district: *Come and see the ~s of London.* **a sight for sore eyes,** person or thing one enjoys seeing. 6 (sing with a, an) (informal) person or thing that produces unfavourable comment: *What a ~ you are! She `does look a ~!* 7 [C] device that helps to aim or observe when using a rifle, telescope, etc.

`sight-seeing, visiting sights(5) as a tourist.

`sight-seer, person who visits sights(5).

sight² /saɪt/ vt 1 get sight of, esp by coming near: *After many months at sea, Columbus ~ed land.* 2 observe (a star, etc) by using sights(7); adjust the sights(7) of a gun.

sight·ing, occasion on which something is seen: *~ings of a new star.*

-sighted /saɪtɪd/ suffix have the kind of sight(1) mentioned: *`far-/`long-~.*

sight·less /ˈsaɪtləs/ adj blind (the usual word).

sign¹ /saɪn/ n [C] 1 mark, object, symbol, used to represent something: *mathematical ~s,* eg +, −, ×, ÷. 2 word or words, design, etc on a board or plate to give a warning, or to give directions: *`traffic ~s,* eg for a speed limit, a bend in the road. 3 something that gives evidence, points to the existence or probability of something: *the ~s of suffering on his face. Are dark clouds a ~ of rain?* 4 movement of the hand, head, etc used with or instead of words; signal. 5 symbol and name (often painted on a board) displayed by traders and shopkeepers (`shop-~s), and (`pub-~) by many public houses to advertise their business.

`sign-board, = sign(5).

`sign-language, used by deaf and dumb persons.

`sign-painter, person who paints signboards.

`sign-post, post placed at a crossroads or road junction with signs on its arms giving directions to different places.

sign² /saɪn/ vt,vi 1 write one's name on (a letter, document, etc) to show that one is the writer or that one accepts or agrees with the contents: *~ a letter/a cheque; ~ one's name,* write it for this purpose. **sign sth away,** give up (rights, property, etc) by signing one's name. **sign off,** (a) end (a letter, etc) with a signature. (b) (radio, TV) end broadcasting (by saying goodnight, etc). **sign sb on/up,** (of an employer, etc) employ: *The firm ~ed on fifty more workers last week.* 2 write one's name on a document, etc: *Please ~ on the dotted line.* **sign on/up,** (of a worker, etc), sign an agreement about employment **3** make known (to a person) an order or request by making signs(4): *He ~ed to me to be quiet* (*Note: signal is more usual.*)

sig·nal /ˈsɪgnəl/ *n* [C] **1** (making of a) movement, (showing of a) light, (sending of a) message, device used, to give a warning, an order or information; order, warning, etc given in this way: `traffic ~s`, for cars, etc in the streets; `hand ~s`, made with the hand by the driver of a motor-vehicle to show which way it will turn, etc. **2** event which is the immediate cause of general activity, etc: *The arrival of the President was the ~ for an outburst of cheering.* **3** electronic impulse in radio, TV, etc; sound or TV image, transmitted or received: *an area with a poor/excellent TV ~.* □ *vt,vi* (-ll-, *US* -l-) make a signal to; send by signal: *~ a message; ~ (to) the waiter to bring the menu; ~ that one is about to turn left.*

`signal-box`, building on a railway from which signals and movements of trains are controlled

`signal-man`, **(a)** person who operates signals on a railway. **(b)** man who sends and receives signals (in the army and navy).

sig·nal·ler (*US* = **sig·naler**) /ˈsɪgnələ(r)/ *n* [C] person who signals, esp a soldier.

sig·na·tory /ˈsɪgnətrɪ *US*: -tɔːrɪ/ *n* [C] (*pl* -ies) (person, country, etc) that has signed an agreement: *the signatories to the Treaty.*

sig·na·ture /ˈsɪgnətʃə(r)/ *n* [C] person's name signed by himself: *Can I have your ~ on these letters?*

`signature tune`, tune (a few bars of a piece of music) identifying a broadcasting station or a particular programme or performer.

sig·net /ˈsɪgnɪt/ *n* [C] private seal used with or instead of a signature.

`signet-ring`, finger ring with a signet set in it.

sig·ni·fi·cance /sɪgˈnɪfɪkəns/ *n* [U] meaning; importance: *a speech of great/little ~*

sig·ni·fi·cant /sɪgˈnɪfɪkənt/ *adj* having a special or important meaning: *a ~ speech*
sig·ni·fi·cant·ly *adv*

sig·ni·fi·ca·tion /ˌsɪgnɪfɪˈkeɪʃən/ *n* [C] (*formal*) (intended) meaning (of a word, etc).

sig·nify /ˈsɪgnɪfaɪ/ *vt,vi* (*pt,pp* -ied) (*formal*) **1** make known (one's views, intentions, purpose, etc); be a sign of; mean: *He signified his agreement/that he agreed by nodding. Does a high forehead ~ intelligence?* **2** (*formal*) be of importance: *It signifies much/little*

Sikh /siːk/ *n* member of an Indian sect believing in one God, founded in the 16th century in the Punjab.

si·lage /ˈsaɪlɪdʒ/ *n* [U] kind of dry, green cattle food

si·lence /ˈsaɪləns/ *n* [U] **1** condition of being quiet or silent; absence of sound: *the ~ of night/of the grave.* **2** condition of not speaking, answering (questions spoken or written), or making comments, etc; (with *a, an*) period (of saying nothing): *Your ~ on recent events surprises me. There was a short ~ and then uproar broke out.* **in silence**, silently: *listen in ~ to a speaker.* □ *vt* make (a person or thing) silent; cause to be quiet(er): *~ one's critics/the enemy's guns.*

si·lencer, device that reduces the noise made by the exhaust of a petrol engine, a gun, etc.

si·lent /ˈsaɪlənt/ *adj* **1** making no or little sound; not accompanied by any sound: *a ~ prayer; with ~ footsteps.* **2** saying little or nothing; giving no answer, views, etc: *You'd better be ~ about what happened. Her husband is the strong, ~ type.* **3** written but not pronounced: *a ~ letter,* e g *b* in *doubt, w* in *wrong.*

silent film, one without a sound track
si·lent·ly *adv*

sil·hou·ette /ˌsɪluˈet/ *n* [C] picture in solid black showing only the outline; outline of a person or object seen against a light background: *~s of famous authors.* **in silhouette**, produced as a silhouette □ *vt* (*passive*) shown, exhibited, in silhouette: *~ed against the sky.*

silk /sɪlk/ *n* **1** [U] fine, soft thread from the cocoons of certain insects; material made from this: (as an *adjective*) *~ scarves.* **2** [C] (in England) Queen's/King's Counsel (abbr **QC, KC**). **take silk**, become a QC/KC.

`silk-worm`, silk caterpillar that spins silk to form a cocoon.

silken /ˈsɪlkən/ *adj* soft and smooth; soft and shining: *a ~ voice; ~ hair.*

silky /ˈsɪlkɪ/ *adj* (-ier, -iest) soft, shiny, smooth, like silk: *a ~ voice*

sill /sɪl/ *n* [C] flat shelf at the base of a window: *a vase of flowers on the `window-~.`*

silly /ˈsɪlɪ/ *adj* (-ier, -iest) (appearing to be) foolish: *say ~ things. How ~ of you to do that!* □ *n* [C] (*pl* -ies) (chiefly used to or by children) silly person: *Don't be a ~!*

silt /sɪlt/ *n* [U] sand, mud, etc carried by moving water (and left at the mouth of a river, in a harbour, etc). □ *vt,vi* (cause to) become stopped with silt: *The sand has ~ed up the mouth of the river.*

sil·ver /ˈsɪlvə(r)/ *n* [U] **1** shining white metal (symbol **Ag**) used for ornaments, coins, utensils, etc: `table ~,` spoons, forks, teapots, dishes, etc. **2** silver vessels, dishes, articles, e g candlesticks, trays: *have all one's ~ taken by burglars.* **3** (as an *adjective*) the colour of silver: *the ~ moon.* **Every cloud has a silver lining,** We should remain hopeful during moments of bad luck. **4** (of sounds) soft and clear: *He has a ~ tongue.* **5** silver(3) coins: £20 *in notes and* £5 *in ~.* □ *vt,vi* **1** coat with (something that looks like) silver: *The years have ~ed her hair.* **2** become white or silver colour: *Her hair had ~ed.*

silver jubilee, 25th anniversary of a

sovereign s rule.

silver medal, medal of silver given as second prize.

silver paper, (*informal*) thin, light foil made of tin or aluminium (as used for packing cigarettes, etc).

`**silver·side,** best side of a round of beef.

`**silver·smith,** manufacturer of silver articles; merchant who sells these.

'**silver `wedding,** 25th anniversary.

sil·very *adj* like silver: *the ~y notes of a temple bell.*

simi·lar /ˈsɪmələ(r)/ *adj* like; of the same sort: *My wife and I have ~ tastes in music. Your guitar is ~ to mine. They are ~.*

simi·lar·ly *adv*

simi·lar·ity /ˌsɪməˈlærətɪ/ *n* (*pl* -ies) [U] likeness; state of being similar; [C] point or respect in which there is likeness: *many ~s between the two men.*

sim·ile /ˈsɪməlɪ/ *n* [C,U] (use of) comparison of one thing to another, e g He is as brave as a lion: *He uses interesting ~s. His style is rich in ~.*

sim·mer /ˈsɪmə(r)/ *vi, vt* **1** be, keep (something), almost at boiling-point: *S~ the stew for an hour.* **2** be filled with (anger, etc), which is only just kept under control: *~ with rage/annoyance.* **simmer down,** (*fig*) become calm (after being angry or excited).

sim·per /ˈsɪmpə(r)/ *vi, n* [C] (give a) silly, self-conscious smile.

simple /ˈsɪmpəl/ *adj* (-r, -st) **1** not mixed; not divided into parts; having only a small number of parts: *a ~ machine.* **2** plain; not much decorated or ornamented: *~ food/ cooking; a ~ design.* **3** not highly developed: *~ forms of life.* **4** easily done or understood; not needing great effort: *written in ~ English; a ~ task.* **5** innocent; straightforward: *as ~ as a child; ~ folk.* **6** inexperienced; easily deceived: *I'm not so ~ as to suppose you really like me.* **7** with nothing added; absolute: *a ~ fact.* **pure and simple,** (*informal*) absolute(ly), unquestionably: *It's a case of kill or be killed, pure and ~.*

'**simple-`minded** *adj* unsophisticated.

sim·ply /ˈsɪmplɪ/ *adv* (**a**) in a simple(2) manner: *dress simply; simply dressed.* (**b**) completely; absolutely: *His pronunciation is simply terrible,* is very bad indeed. *She looks simply lovely.* (**c**) nothing more nor less than: *He is simply a workman. It is simply a matter of working hard.*

simple·ton /ˈsɪmpəltən/ *n* [C] (*dated*) foolish person, esp one who is easily deceived.

sim·plic·ity /sɪmˈplɪsətɪ/ *n* [U] (*formal*) the state of being simple: *A small child often has a look of ~.* **be simplicity itself,** (*informal*) be extremely easy.

sim·plify /ˈsɪmplɪfaɪ/ *vt* (*pt,pp* -ied) make simple; make easy to do or understand: *a simplified reader/text.*

sim·pli·fi·ca·tion /ˌsɪmplɪfɪˈkeɪʃən/ *n* [U] act

or process of making simple; [C] instance of simplifying; thing simplified.

simu·late /ˈsɪmjʊleɪt/ *vt* (*formal*) pretend to be; pretend to have or feel: *~d innocence/ enthusiasm; insects that ~ dead leaves.*

simu·la·tion /ˌsɪmjʊˈleɪʃən/ *n* [U] pretence; imitation.

sim·ul·ta·neous /ˌsɪməlˈteɪnɪəs US: ˈsaɪm-/ *adj* happening or done at the same time: *~ signing of an agreement.*

sim·ul·ta·neous·ly *adv*

sin /sɪn/ *n* **1** [U] breaking of God's laws; behaviour that is against the principles of morality. **2** [C] instance of this; immoral act such as telling a lie, stealing, adultery: *confess one's ~s to a priest; ask for one's ~s to be forgiven.* ⇨ original sin. **the seven deadly sins,** pride, covetousness, lust, anger, gluttony, envy, sloth. **3** [C] (*informal*) offence against convention; something considered to be not common sense: *It's a ~ to give the children so many sweets. It's a ~ to stay indoors on such a fine day.* □ *vi* (-nn-) commit sin; do wrong: *We are all liable to sin.*

sin·ner /ˈsɪnə(r)/, person who sins/has sinned.

sin·ful /-fəl/ *adj* wrong; wicked.

sin·ful·ness *n* [U]

since /sɪns/ *adv* **1** (with the perfect tenses) after a date, event, etc in the past; before the present time; between some time in the past and the present time, or the time referred to: *The town was destroyed by an earthquake ten years ago and has ~ been rebuilt. He left home in 1970 and has not been heard of ~.* **ever since,** throughout the whole of a period of time referred to and up to the present: *He went to Italy in 1970 and has lived there ever ~.* **2** (*dated*) (used with the simple tenses) ago (the usual word): *He did it many years ~.* □ *prep* (with perfect tenses in the main clause) after; during a period of time after: *She hasn't been home ~ her marriage.* □ *conj* **1** from the past time when: *Where have you been ~ I last saw you? How long is it ~ you were in London?* **2** as: *S~ we've no money, we can't buy it.*

sin·cere /sɪnˈsɪə(r)/ *adj* **1** (of feelings, behaviour) genuine; not pretended: *It is my ~ belief that...* **2** (of persons) not expressing feelings that are pretended.

sin·cere·ly *adv* in a sincere manner. **yours sincerely,** (used before a signature at the end of a letter to a friend or informally in a business letter).

sin·cer·ity /sɪnˈserətɪ/ *n* [U] the quality of being sincere: *speaking in all ~,* very sincerely and honestly.

sinew /ˈsɪnjuː/ *n* [C] tendon (strong cord) joining a muscle to a bone.

sin·ewy *adj* tough; having strong sinews.

sing /sɪŋ/ *vi, vt* (*pt* sang /sæŋ/, *pp* sung /sʌŋ/) **1** make musical sounds with the voice, utter words one after the other to a tune: *She ~s well. He was ~ing a French song. He was ~ing to the guitar. She sang the baby to sleep.* **2** make a humming, buzzing or ringing sound: *The kettle was ~ing (away) on the cooker.* **3** celebrate in verse. **sing sb's praises,** praise him with enthusiasm. **4 sing out (for),** shout (for).

singer, person who sings, esp one who does this in public.

sing·ing, (esp) art of the singer: *teach ~ing; take `~ing lessons.*

singe /sɪndʒ/ *vt,vi* blacken the surface of by burning; burn slightly: *Careful! You're ~ing that dress!* □ *n* [C] slight burn (on cloth, etc).

single /ˈsɪŋgəl/ *adj* **1** one only; one and no more: *a ~ ticket,* for a journey to a place, not back. **in single file,** (moving, standing) one behind the other in a line. **2** not married: *~ men and women; remain ~.* **3** for the use of, used for, done by, one person: *a ~ bed; reserve* (at a hotel) *two ~ rooms and one double room.* □ *n* [C] **1** (in tennis and golf) game with one person on each side. **2** (in cricket) hit for which one run is scored: *run a quick ~.* **3** (short for a) single ticket: *two second-class ~s to Leeds.* □ *vt* **single sb/ sth out,** select from others (for special attention, etc): *Why have you ~d me out for criticism?*

'single-'breasted *adj* (of a coat) having only one row of buttons down the front.

'single-'handed *adj, adv* done by one person without help from others.

'single-'minded *adj* having, intent on, only one purpose.

sing·ly /ˈsɪŋglɪ/ *adv* one by one; by oneself.

sin·glet /ˈsɪŋglət/ *n* [C] (*GB*) sleeveless cotton T-shirt; vest.

sing·song /ˈsɪŋsɒŋ/ *n* [C] meeting of friends to sing songs together (esp unplanned)· *have a ~ round the piano.*

sin·gu·lar /ˈsɪŋgjʊlə(r)/ *adj* **1** (*dated*) uncommon; strange: *look ~ in a dress,* to be unconventional. **2** (*formal*) outstanding: *a man of ~ courage and honesty.* **3** (*gram*) of the form used in speaking or writing of one person or thing: *The ~ of 'children' is 'child'.* □ *n* [C] the singular name: *What is the ~ of 'parties'?*

sin·gu·lar·ly *adv* (*formal*) strangely; peculiarly.

sin·gu·lar·ity /ˌsɪŋgjʊˈlærətɪ/ *n* (*pl* -ies) (*formal*) [U] strangeness; [C] something unusual or strange.

sin·is·ter /ˈsɪnɪstə(r)/ *adj* **1** suggesting evil or the likelihood of coming misfortune: *a ~ beginning.* **2** showing a bad temper; unkind: *a ~ face; ~ looks.* **3** (in heraldry) on the left side of the shield.

sink¹ /sɪŋk/ *n* [C] **1** fixed basin (of china, steel, etc) with a drain for taking away water, usually in a kitchen. **2** = cesspool.

sink² /sɪŋk/ *vi,vt* (*pt* sank /sæŋk/, *pp* sunk /sʌŋk/, and, as an *adjective*, sunken /ˈsʌŋ-

kən/) **1** go down, esp below the horizon or the surface of water or other liquid or a soft substance, e g mud: *The sun was ~ing in the west. Wood does not ~ in water, it floats. The ship sank,* went to the bottom. **2** slope downwards; become lower or weaker: *The foundations have sunk.* **3** make by digging: *~ a well;* place (something) in a hole made by digging: *~ a post one foot deep in the ground.* **4 sink in/into,** (of liquids, and fig) go down deep: *The rain sank into the dry ground.* **5** (*fig*) lose faith, hope, etc: *His heart sank at the thought of failure; have a ~ing feeling,* feel all hope is lost. **6** (*fig*) (of warnings, information) be understood, learnt: *I've explained it to you often but nothing ~s in!* **7** come to a lower level or state (physical or moral): *~ into a deep sleep; ~ into crime. The old man has sunken cheeks. His voice sank to a whisper.* **6** cause or allow to sink: *~ a ship. He sank* (= lowered) *his voice to a whisper. Let us ~ our differences* (= put them out of our thoughts, forget them), *and work together.*

'sink·able /-əbəl/ *adj* (of a boat, etc) that can be sunk.

sinu·ous /ˈsɪnjʊəs/ *adj* (*formal*) full of curves and twists.

sinus /ˈsaɪnəs/ *n* [C] (*pl* ~es) [C] hollow in a bone, esp one of several air-filled cavities in the bones of the skull linked to the nostrils.

–sion *suffix* ⊳ -tion.

sip /sɪp/ *vt,vi* (-pp-) drink, taking a very small quantity at a time: *~ (up) one's coffee.* □ *n* [C] (quantity taken in a) sipping.

si·phon /ˈsaɪfən/ *n* [C] **1** bent or curved tube, pipe, etc so arranged (like an inverted U) that liquid will flow up through it and then down. **2** bottle from which soda-water can be forced out by the pressure of gas in it. □ *vt,vi* **syphon sth off/out,** draw (liquid) out or off through or as if through a syphon.

sir /sɜ(r)/ *n* **1** polite form used in addressing a man (esp a school teacher) to whom one wishes to show respect: *Yes, ~.* **2** (used in letters): *My dear S~; Dear S~.* **3** prefix to the name of a knight or baronet: *Sir 'Winston `Churchill.*

sire /saɪə(r)/ *n* [C] **1** (*old use*) father or male ancestor. **2** male parent of an animal: *race-horses with pedigree ~s.* □ *vt* (esp of horses) be the sire of: *a Derby winner ~d by Pegasus.*

si·ren /ˈsaɪərən/ *n* [C] **1** (Greek myth) one of a number of winged women whose songs charmed sailors and caused their destruction; (hence) woman who attracts and is dangerous to men. **2** ship's whistle for sending warnings and signals. **3** device for producing a loud shrill noise (as a warning, etc): *an ambulance racing along with its ~s wailing.*

sir·loin /ˈsɜlɔɪn/ *n* [C,U] best part of loin of beef.

si·sal /ˈsaɪzəl/ *n* [U] plant with leaves which

provide strong fibre used for making rope.

sis·ter /ˈsɪstə(r)/ *n* [C] **1** daughter of the same parents as oneself or another person: *my/your/his* ~. ⇨ half-sister, step-sister. **2** woman who behaves like a sister: *She was a* ~ *to him*. **3** (*GB*) senior hospital nurse. **4** member of a religious society; nun: *S~s of Mercy*. **5** woman of the same society, profession, trade union, socialist party, etc as another.

sis·ter·hood /-hʊd/ *n* (**a**) [U] feeling of a sister for a sister. (**b**) [C] society of women who live together in a religious order, belong to a socialist organization, do charitable works, etc.

`sister ship, of the same design, type, etc (as another).

sis·ter·ly *adj* of, like, a sister: ~*ly love*.

sit /sɪt/ *vi,vt* (*pt,pp* sat /sæt/) (-tt-) (For special uses with *adverbial particles* and *prepositions*, ⇨ **9** below.) **1** take or be in a position in which the body is upright and supported by the buttocks (resting on the ground or on a seat): ~ *on a chair/on the floor/in an armchair/at a table or desk/on a horse*. **sit tight, (a)** remain firmly in one's place, esp in the saddle. (**b**) (*informal*) hold firmly to one's opinions, not give in to opposition, etc. **2** cause to sit; place in a sitting position: *He lifted the child and sat* (= seated) *her at a little table*. **3** (of Parliament, a law court, a committee, etc) hold meetings: *The House of Commons was still* ~*ting at 3 a m*. **4** keep one's seat on (a horse, etc): *She* ~*s her horse well*. **5** (of birds) rest (on a branch, fence, etc) with the body close to it: ~*ting on a branch*. **6** (of domestic fowls) remain on the nest in order to hatch eggs: *That hen wants to* ~. **7** (of clothes) suit, fit, hang: *The coat* ~*s badly across the shoulders*. **8** act as a baby-sitter. **9** (special uses with *adverbial particles* and *prepositions*):

sit back, (a) settle oneself comfortably back, e g in a chair. (**b**) (*fig*) rest (after great activity, etc). (**c**) take no (further) action.

sit down, take a seat: *Please* ~ *down, all of you*. **a sit-down strike,** strike by workers who refuse to leave the factory, etc until their demands are considered or satisfied.

sit for, (a) take (an examination). (**b**) pose (for one's portrait).

sit in, (of workers, students, etc) demonstrate by occupying a building (or part of it) and staying there until their demands are met: *There are reports of students* ~*ting in at several universities*. Hence, `sit-in, such a demonstration. **sit in on sth,** attend (a discussion, etc) as an observer, not as a participant.

sit on sb, (*sl*) prevent him from interfering, opposing, etc. **sit on sth, (a)** be a member of (a jury, committee, etc). (**b**) (*informal*) neglect to deal with: *They've been* ~*ting on my application for a month*.

sit out, sit outside· ~*ting out in the garden*

sit sth out, (a) stay to the end of (a performance, etc): ~ *out a play*. (**b**) take no part in (esp a dance): *I think I'll* ~ *out the next dance*.

sit up, not go to bed (until later than the usual time): *The nurse sat up with her patient all night*. **sit (sb) up,** (cause to) take a sitting position: *The patient is well enough to* ~ *up in bed now. S~ up straight! Don't lean back!* **(make sb) sit up (and take notice),** (*informal*) alarm or frighten him; have one's interest (suddenly) stimulated.

sit upon, = sit on.

si·tar /ˈsɪtɑː(r)/ *US*: sɪˈtɑː(r)/ *n* [C] Indian stringed musical instrument with a long neck.

site /saɪt/ *n* [C] place where something was, is, or is to be: *a* ~ *for a new school; a* `building ~. □ *vt* position; place: *Where have they decided to* ~ *the new factory?*

sit·ter /ˈsɪtə(r)/ *n* [C] **1** person who is sitting for a portrait. **2** hen that sits(6): *a good/poor* ~. **3** bird or animal that is sitting and therefore easy to shoot. **4** = baby-sitter.

sit·ting /ˈsɪtɪŋ/ *n* [C] **1** time during which a court of law, Parliament, etc is in session: *during a long* ~. **2** period of time during which one is engaged continuously in a particular occupation: *finish reading a book at one* ~. **3** act of posing for a portrait **4** occasion of sitting down (for a meal, etc): *In this hotel 100 people can be served at one* ~, i e together. **5** collection of eggs on which a hen sits.

`sitting duck, an easy target or victim.

sitting member, candidate in a parliamentary election who held the seat before.

`sitting-room, room for general daytime use (contrasted with a *dining-room, bedroom, etc*).

sitting tenant, one already in occupation of a house, etc.

situ·ated /ˈsɪtʃʊeɪtɪd/ *adj* **1** (of a town, building, etc) placed: *The village is* ~ *in a valley*. **2** (of a person) in (certain) circumstances: *I'm badly* ~ *at the moment*, in difficult circumstances.

situ·ation /ˌsɪtʃʊˈeɪʃən/ *n* [C] **1** position (of a town, building, etc). **2** condition, state of affairs, esp at a certain time: *be in an embarrassing* ~. **3** work, employment, e g in domestic service: *S~s vacant, S~s wanted*, headings of newspaper advertisements of employment offered and asked for.

six /sɪks/ *adj, n* [C] (of) 6. **six of one and half a dozen of the other,** very little difference between the one and the other. **at sixes and sevens,** in confusion.

`six·pence, (a) (*GB*) coin worth (formerly) six pennies, or (since 1971) 2½p. (b) the sum of six pennies.

`six·penny *adj* costing sixpence.

`six·fold /-fəʊld/ *adj, adv* six times as much or as many or as great.

six·teen /ˌsɪkˈstiːn/ *adj, n* [C] (of) 16

six·teenth /sɪkˈstinθ/ adj, n [C] (abbr *16th*) (of) one of 16 parts or the next after 15.

sixth /sɪksθ/ adj, n, (C] (abbr *6th*) (of) one of 6 parts or the next after 5.

'sixth `sense, power to be aware of things independently of the five senses.

sixth·ly adv

six·ti·eth /ˈsɪkstɪə/ adj, n [C] (abbr *60th*) (of) one of 60 parts or the next after 59.

sixty /ˈsɪkstɪ/ adj, n [C] (of) 60: *in the six-ties,* between 59 and 70 years of age; the years between 59 and 70 of a century.

size¹ /saɪz/ n 1 [U] degree of largeness or smallness: *about the* ∼ *of* (= about as large as) *a duck's egg. They're both of a* ∼, are the same size. *cut sb down to size,* reduce him to his correct level of (un)importance. 2 [C] one of the degrees of size in which articles of clothing, etc are made: ∼ *five shoes; three* ∼s *too large. I take* ∼ *ten.* □ vt 1 arrange according to size. 2 *size sb/sth up,* (*informal*) form a judgement or opinion of.

'size·able /-əbəl/ adj fairly large.

size² /saɪz/ n [U] sticky substance used to glaze paper, stiffen cloth, etc. □ vt stiffen or treat with size.

-sized /-saɪzd/ suffix having a certain size· *medium-*∼.

sizzle /ˈsɪzəl/ vi, n [C] (*informal*) 1 (make the) hissing sound as of something cooking in fat: *sausages sizzling in the pan.* 2 (*fig*) be in a state of great heat: *a sizzling hot day.*

skate /skeɪt/ n [C] (also *a pair of* ∼s) a sharp-edged steel blade to be fastened to a boot for moving smoothly over ice ⇨ roller-skate. □ vi 1 move on skates. 2 (*fig*) *skate over/round a difficulty/problem,* make only passing and cautious reference to it.

skater, person who skates.

'skat·ing n [U] (sport of) moving on skates.

'skat·ing-rink, specially prepared surface for skating.

skein /skeɪn/ n [C] length of silk or wool or thread coiled loosely into a bundle.

skel·eton /ˈskelɪtən/ n [C] 1 bony frame-work of an animal body; bones of an animal body in the same relative positions as in life. *a skeleton in the cupboard,* something of which a person is ashamed and which he tries to keep secret. 2 framework of a build-ing, outline, plan, to which details are to be added.

'skeleton key, one that will open a number of different locks.

skeleton staff/crew/service, etc, one reduced to the smallest possible number needed.

sketch /sketʃ/ n [C] 1 rough, quickly made drawing: *make a* ∼ *of a harbour.* 2 short account or description; general outline, without details: *He gave me a* ∼ *of his plans for the expedition.* 3 short, humorous play or piece of writing. □ vt,vi 1 make a sketch of.

sketch sth out, give a rough plan of; indi-cate without detail: ∼ *out plans for a new road.* 2 practise the art of making sketches· *My sister often goes into the country to* ∼

sketcher, person who sketches(2).

sketchy adj (-ier, -iest) (a) done roughly and without detail or care. (b) incomplete: *He has a* ∼y *knowledge of geography.*

skew /skju/ adj twisted or turned to one side; not straight.

skewer /ˈskjuə(r)/ n [C] pointed stick of wood or metal for holding meat together while cooking. □ vt fasten with a skewer.

ski /ski/ n [C] (*pl* ∼ or ∼s) one of a pair of long, narrow strips of wood, etc strapped under the feet for moving over snow. □ vi (*pt,pp* ∼'d, *present participle* ∼ing) move over snow on skis: *go* ∼ing.

'ski-jump, steep slope before a sharp drop to let a skier leap through the air.

'ski-lift, seats on an overhead cable for car-rying skiers uphill.

'ski-plane, aircraft fitted with skis instead of wheels, to enable it to land on snow.

skier /ˈskiə(r)/, person using skis.

skid /skɪd/ n [C] 1 slipping movement, often sideways, of the wheels of a car, etc on a slippery or icy road, or while turning a corner: *How would you get out of/correct a* ∼? 2 piece of wood or metal fixed under the wheel of a cart, etc to prevent it from turn-ing, to control the speed when going down-hill. 3 log, plank, etc used to make a track over which heavy objects may be dragged or rolled. □ vi (-dd-) (of a car, etc) move or slip sideways, etc.

skies /skaɪz/ pl of sky.

skiff /skɪf/ n [C] small, light, rowing boat.

skil·ful (*US* = **skillful**) /ˈskɪlfəl/ adj having or showing skill.

skil·ful·ly /-fəlɪ/ adv

skill /skɪl/ n [U] 1 ability to do something well. 2 [C] particular kind of skill.

skilled adj (needing a person who is) trained; experienced: ∼ed *workmen;* ∼ed *work.*

skim /skɪm/ vt,vi (-mm-) 1 remove floating matter from (the surface of a liquid): ∼ *milk;* ∼ *off the grease from soup.* 2 move lightly over (a surface), not touching, or only lightly or occasionally touching (it): *The swallows were* ∼ming (*over*) *the water.* 3 *skim through sth,* read quickly, noting only the chief points: ∼ *through a news-paper.*

skimp /skɪmp/ vt,vi supply, use, the mini-mum of what is needed: *They are so poor that they have to* ∼.

skimpy adj (-ier, -iest)

skin /skɪn/ n 1 [U] (substance forming the) outer covering of the body of a person or animal: *We all got wet to the* ∼, thoroughly wet (e g in heavy rain). *by the skin of one's teeth,* by a narrow margin. *get under one's skin,* (*fig*) (a) cause irritation or anger. (b) cause infatuation. *have a thin/ thick skin*, (*fig*) be sensitive/insensitive; be easily hurt/not easily hurt by unkindness, criticism, swearing, etc. Hence, '**thin-/ 'thick-'skinned** *adj*. *save one's skin*, escape safely. **2** [C] animal's skin with or without the hair or fur: `rabbit—~s`. **3** [C,U] outer covering of a fruit, or plant: *slip on a ba`nana ~*. **4** [C,U] thin layer that forms on boiled milk: *the ~ on a milk pudding.* □ *vt,vi* (-nn-) take the skin off: *~ a rabbit.*

'**skin-'deep** *adj* (of beauty, feelings, etc) only on the surface; not deep or lasting.

`**skin-diving,** form of sport in which a person dives into and swims under the water without a diving-suit, with goggles to protect the eyes and a snorkel or aqualung to help breathing.

`**skin-flint,** = miser.

'**skin-'tight** *adj* (of a garment) fitting closely to the body.

skinny *adj* (-ier, -iest) having little flesh, not fat.

skint /skɪnt/ *adj* (*GB sl*) very poor.

skip[1] /skɪp/ *vi,vt* (-pp-) **1** jump lightly and quickly: *The lambs were ~ping about in the fields.* **2** jump over a rope which is turned over the head and under the feet as one jumps. **3** go from one place to another quickly: *~ over/across to Paris for the weekend. He ~ped off* (= *left*) *without saying anything to any of us.* **4** change from one subject to another when talking: *He ~s from one excuse to another.* **5** go from one part (of a book, etc) to another without reading, paying attention, etc: *We'll ~ the next chapter.* □ *n* [C] skipping movement: *a hop, a ~ and a jump.*

`**skip-ping-rope,** length of rope with handles, used in the children's game of skipping.

skip[2] /skɪp/ *n* [C] **1** cage or bucket in which men or materials are raised and lowered in mines and quarries. **2** large metal container for carrying away builders' refuse, etc.

skip-per /ˈskɪpə(r)/ *n* [C] **1** captain, esp of a small merchant ship or fishing-boat. **2** (*informal*) captain of a team in games such as football and cricket. □ *vt* act as captain: *~ a team.*

skir-mish /ˈskɜːmɪʃ/ *n* [C] fight between small parts of armies or fleets. □ *vi* engage in such a fight.

skirt /skɜːt/ *n* [C] **1** woman's garment that hangs from the waist. **2** part of a dress, etc that hangs from the waist. **3** (*pl*) = outskirts (which is more usual). □ *vt,vi* be on, pass along, the edge of: *Our road ~ed the forest.*

`**skirt-ing-board,** strip or line of boards fixed round the walls of a room close to the floor.

skit /skɪt/ *n* [C] short piece of humorous writing making fun of a person, idea, style, etc: *a ~ on Wagner/on 'Macbeth'.*

skit-tish /ˈskɪtɪʃ/ *adj* **1** (of horses) excitable; lively; difficult to control. **2** (*fig*) (of women) frivolous; excitable.
skit-tish-ly *adv*
skit-tish-ness *n* [U]

skittles /ˈskɪtlz/ *n pl* (used with a *sing verb*) (game in which a ball is thrown to knock down) a number of bottle-shaped pieces of wood.

skulk /skʌlk/ *vi* hide, move secretly, because afraid, or to avoid work or duty, or with an evil purpose: *~ing about in the corridors.*

skull /skʌl/ *n* [C] bony framework of the head: *have a thick ~*, be stupid.

skunk /skʌŋk/ *n* [C] small, bush-tailed N American animal able to send out a strong evil smell as a defence when attacked.

sky /skaɪ/ *n* [C] (*pl* skies /skaɪz/) the space we look up to from the earth, where we see the sun, moon and stars. (*Note:* usually *sing* with *the*, but with *a*, *an* when used with an *adj*: *a clear, blue ~*, and often *pl*: *The skies opened and the rain fell.*)

'**sky-'blue** *adj*, *n* [U] (of) the bright blue colour of the sky on a cloudless day.

'**sky-'high** *adv* so as to reach the sky: *When the bomb exploded, the bridge was blown ~-high.*

`**sky-light,** window in a sloping roof.

`**sky-line,** outline of hills, buildings, etc, defined against the sky: *the ~line of New York.*

`**sky-lark,** small bird that sings as it flies up into the sky. □ *vi* = lark[1].

`**sky-rocket** *vi* (of prices) rise quickly.

`**sky-scraper,** very tall building.

sky-ward(s) /ˈskaɪwəd(z)/ *adj,adv* toward(s) the sky; upward(s).

slab /slæb/ *n* [C] thick flat (usually square or rectangular) piece of stone, etc: *paved with ~s of stone; a ~ of chocolate.*

slack[1] /slæk/ *adj* (-er, -est) **1** giving little care or attention to one's work: *Don't get ~ at your work.* **2** inactive; with not much work to be done or business being done: *Trade/Business is ~ this week.* **3** loose, not tight: *a ~ rope.* **4** slow-moving: *periods of ~ water*, when the tide is neither ebbing nor flowing. □ *vi* **1** be lazy or careless in one's work: *Don't ~ off in your studies.* **2** reduce speed: *S~ up before you reach the crossroads.* **3** make (a rope, etc) loose.
slack-ly *adv*
slack-ness *n* [U]

slack[2] /slæk/ *n* **the ~**, that part of a rope, etc that hangs loosely.

slacken /ˈslækən/ *vt,vi* **1** make or become slower, less active, etc: *The ship's speed ~ed.* **2** make or become loose(r): *~ the ropes/reins.*

slacks /slæks/ *n pl* (*dated*) loose-fitting trousers, not part of a suit, worn as informal wear by men or women.

slag /slæg/ *n* [U] waste matter remaining

when metal has been extracted from ore.

`slag-heap`, hill of slag (dumped from a mine).

slain /sleɪn/ pp of slay.

slake /sleɪk/ vt **1** satisfy or make less strong (thirst, desire for revenge). **2** change the chemical nature of (lime) by adding water.

sla·lom /ˈslɑːləm/ n [C] ski-race along a zig-zag course marked out by poles with flags.

slam /slæm/ vt,vi (-mm-) **1** shut violently and noisily: ~ the door (to); ~ the door in his face. **2** be shut violently: The door ~med (to). **3** put, throw or knock with force: She ~med the box down on the table. □ n [C] **1** noise of something being slammed: the ~ of a car door. **2** (in whist, bridge): a grand ~, taking of 13 tricks; a small ~, taking of 12 tricks.

slan·der /ˈslɑːndə(r) US: ˈslæn-/ n [C,U] (offence of making a) false statement that damages a person's reputation. □ vt use slander.

slan·derer, person who uses slander.

slan·der·ous /-əs/ adj using or containing slander.

slang /slæŋ/ n [U] (abbr sl used in this dictionary) words, phrases, meanings of words, etc often used in conversation but not suitable for writing or for formal occasions. □ vt abuse: Stop ~ing me. **a slanging match**, a long exchange of insults and accusations.

slangy adj (-ier, -iest) using, slang.

slant /slɑːnt US: slænt/ vi,vt **1** slope: His handwriting ~s from right to left. **2** present information, etc so that it is seen from, and supports, a particular point of view, eg in a newspaper. □ n [C] **1** slope. **2** (informal) point of view (sometimes prejudiced or biassed) when thinking about something; a new ~ on the political situation.

slap /slæp/ vt (-pp-) **1** strike with the palm of the hand; smack: She ~ped his face/ ~ped him on the face. **2** put something down with a slapping noise: He ~ped the book down on the table. □ n [C] quick blow with the palm of the hand or with something flat. □ adv straight; directly: The car ran ~ into the wall.

`slap-dash` adj, adv careless(ly): a ~dash worker.

`slap-happy` adj carefree.

`slap-stick` n [U] comedy using violence.

`slap-up` adj (sl) first-class; extremely good: a ~-up dinner at a ~-up restaurant.

slash /slæʃ/ vt,vi **1** make a cut or cuts in (or at something) with sweeping strokes; strike with a whip: His face had been ~ed with a razor-blade. **2** condemn with force and energy: a ~ing attack on the government's policy. **3** (informal) cut, reduce greatly: ~ prices/taxes/salaries. □ n [C] act of slashing; long cut or gash.

slat /slæt/ n [C] thin narrow piece of wood, metal or plastic material, eg as in Venetian blinds or louvred doors.

slate /sleɪt/ n **1** [U] kind of blue-grey stone that splits easily into thin, flat layers; [C] one of these layers, square or oblong, used for making roofs: a ~ quarry. **2** [C] sheet of slate in a wooden frame for writing on (as formerly used by school-children). □ vt **1** cover (a roof, etc) with slates. **2** (informal) criticize severely (esp in a review of a book, play, etc).

slaty adj of or like slate.

slaugh·ter /ˈslɔːtə(r)/ n [U] **1** killing of animals (esp for food). **2** killing of many people at once: the ~ on the roads, the killing of people in road accidents. □ vt kill (animals, people) in large numbers.

`slaughter-house`, place where animals are butchered for food.

slaugh·ter·er, (a) person who kills animals for food. (b) person who kills many people.

slave /sleɪv/ n [C] **1** person who is the property of another and must serve him. **2** person compelled to work very hard for someone else: You mustn't make ~s of your workers. **3** person completely in the power of, under the control of, a habit, etc: a ~ to duty/passion/convention/drink. □ vi work hard: Poor Jane! She's been slaving away (at her cooking) for three hours!

`slave-driver`, overseer of slaves at work; person who makes those who are under him work very hard.

`slave ship`, ship used in the slave-trade.

`Slave States`, southern States of N America in which there was slavery before the Civil War.

`slave-trade/-traffic`, capturing, transportation, buying and selling, of slaves.

slav·ery /ˈsleɪvərɪ/ n [U] (a) condition of being a slave: sold into ~ry. (b) custom of having slaves: men who worked for the abolition of ~ry. (c) hard or badly paid work.

slav·ish /ˈsleɪvɪʃ/ adj like, fit for, a slave.

slaver /ˈslævə(r)/ vi let spit run from the mouth (over). □ n [U] saliva.

slay /sleɪ/ vt (pt slew /sluː/ pp slain /sleɪn/) (literary) kill, murder.

sleazy /ˈsliːzɪ/ adj (-ier, -iest) (informal) uncared-for, dirty, untidy: a ~ lodging house.

sled /sled/ n = sledge.

sledge /sledʒ/ n [C] vehicle with runners (long, narrow strips of wood or metal) instead of wheels, used on snow, larger types being pulled by horses or dogs and smaller types used in sport for travelling downhill at speed. □ vi,vt travel or carry by sledge: go sledging.

sledge-hammer /ˈsledʒ hæmə(r)/ n [C] heavy hammer with a long handle, used for driving posts into the ground, and by blacksmiths.

sleek /sliːk/ adj (-er,-est) **1** (of hair, an animal's fur, etc) soft, smooth and glossy. **2** (of a person) having such hair. □ vt make sleek: ~ a cat's fur.

sleep[1] /sliːp/ n **1** [U] condition of the body and mind at rest as happens regularly every night, in which the eyes are closed and the muscles, nervous system, etc are relaxed: *How many hours'* ~ *do you need?* **2** (with *a, an*) period of sleep: *have a short/good/ restful, etc* ~. **3 get to sleep**, manage to fall asleep: *I couldn't get to* ~ *last night*. **go to sleep**, fall asleep. **put sb to sleep**, cause him to fall asleep.

sleep[2] /sliːp/ *vi,vt* (*pp,pt* slept /slept/) **1** rest in the condition of sleep, be or fall asleep: *We go to bed to* ~. *She slept* (*for*) *eight hours*. **sleep like a top/log**, very deeply, well. **2** provide beds for: *This hotel* ~*s 300 guests*. **3** (uses with *adverbial particles* and *prepositions*):

sleep around, (*informal*) be promiscuous.

sleep sth off, recover from (a party, headache, etc) by sleeping: ~ *off a bad headache/a hangover.*

sleep on, continue to sleep: *Don't wake him up—let him* ~ *on for another hour*. **sleep on sth**, leave the answer, solution, to a problem, etc to the next day.

sleep through sth, not be woken up by (a noise, the alarm-clock, etc).

sleep with sb, have sexual intercourse with.

sleep·er /ˈsliːpə(r)/ n [C] **1** person who sleeps: *a heavy/light* ~, one who is hard/ easy to wake up. **2** heavy beam of wood (or similarly shaped piece of other material) on a railway track, etc supporting the rails. **3** (bed or berth in a) sleeping-car on a train.

sleep·ing /ˈsliːpɪŋ/ (in compounds): `sleeping-bag`, warmly lined and waterproof bag in which to sleep, e g in a tent.

`sleeping-car`, railway coach fitted with beds or berths.

`sleeping `partner`, person who owns a share in a business but does not do any work in it.

`sleeping-pill`, one that contains a drug to encourage sleep.

`sleeping-sickness`, disease caused by the tsetse-fly with a weakening of the mental powers and (usually) death.

sleep·less /ˈsliːpləs/ adj without sleep: *pass a* ~ *night*.

sleep·less·ly adv

sleep·less·ness n [U]

sleepy /ˈsliːpɪ/ adj (-ier, -iest) **1** needing, ready for, sleep: *feel/look* ~. **2** (of places, etc) quiet; inactive: *a* ~ *little village*. **3** (of some kinds of fruit) over-ripe: ~ *bananas*, soft and brown inside.

sleep·ily /-əlɪ/ adv

sleet /sliːt/ n [U] falling snow or hail mixed with rain. □ vi *It was* ~*ing*, Sleet was falling.

sleety adj (-ier, -iest)

sleeve /sliːv/ n [C] **1** part of a garment that covers all or part of the arm: *one's* `shirt-` ~*s*. **have sth up one's sleeve**, have an idea, plan, etc which one keeps secret for future use. *laugh up one's sleeve*, be secretly amused. **2** stiff envelope for a record.

sleeve·less adj without sleeves.

sleigh /sleɪ/ n [C] sledge, esp one drawn by a horse: *go for a* `~-ride/a ride in a* ~. □ *vi,vt* travel in a sleigh; carry (goods) by sleigh.

sleight /slaɪt/ n (usually in) **sleight of hand**, great skill in using the hand(s) in performing tricks, juggling, etc.

slen·der /ˈslendə(r)/ adj (-er, -est) **1** small in width or circumference compared with height or length: ~ *fingers; a* ~ *waist*. **2** (of persons) slim: *a woman with a* ~ *figure*. **3** slight; inadequate: *have* ~ *means/hopes*.

slen·der·ness n [U]

slept /slept/ pt,pp of sleep.

slew /sluː/ pt of slay.

slice /slaɪs/ n [C] **1** thin, wide, flat piece cut off something, esp bread or meat. **2** part, share or price: *Smith took too big a* ~ *of the credit for our success*. **3** utensil with a wide, flat blade for cutting, serving or lifting (e g cooked fish, fried eggs). **4** (in games such as golf, tennis) stroke that causes the ball to go spinning off in a different direction. □ *vt,vi* **1** cut into slices: ~ (*up*) *a loaf*. **2** (golf): ~ *the ball*, ⇨ 4 above.

slick /slɪk/ adj (*informal*) **1** smooth; slippery: *The roads were* ~ *with wet mud*. **2** done smoothly and efficiently, perhaps with a little deceit: *a* ~ *business deal*; (of a person) doing things in a slick way: *a* ~ *salesman*. ⇨ oil slick.

slide[1] /slaɪd/ n [C] **1** act of sliding(1); smooth stretch of ice, hard snow, etc on which to slide: *have a* ~ *on the ice*. **2** smooth slope down which persons or things can slide (e g a wooden or metal slope made for children to play on). **3** picture, diagram, etc on photographic film (and usually mounted in a frame). **4** glass plate on which is placed something to be examined under a microscope. **5** part of a machine, etc that slides (e g the U-shaped part of a trombone). **6** = landslide(a). **7** = hair-slide.

slide[2] /slaɪd/ *vi,vt* (*pt,pp* slid /slɪd/) **1** (cause to) move smoothly over, slip along, a polished surface: *children sliding on the ice*. *The drawers of this desk* ~ *in and out easily*. **let things slide**, not take care of, organize, do, them. **2** have, become, gradually, without being fully aware: ~ *into dishonesty/ bad habits*. **3** (cause to) move quickly, or so as to avoid observation: *The thief slid behind the curtains*. *She slid a coin into his hand*.

`slide-rule`, device of two rulers with logarithmic scales, one of which slides in a groove, used for calculating quickly.

slid·ing door, one that is pulled across an opening (instead of turning on hinges).

slid·ing scale, scale by which one thing, e g wages, goes up or down in relation to changes in something else, e g the cost of living.

slight¹ /slaɪt/ adj (-er, -est) **1** slim; slender; frail-looking: a ~ figure. **2** small; not serious or important: a ~ error; a ~ headache; without the ~est difficulty, with no difficulty at all. She takes offence at the ~est thing, is very easily offended.
slight·ly adv **(a)** slenderly: a ~ly built boy. **(b)** to a small degree: The patient is ~ly better today. I know her ~ly.
slight·ness n [U]

slight² /slaɪt/ vt treat without proper respect or courtesy: She felt ~ed because no one spoke to her. □ n [C] failure to show respect or courtesy: suffer ~s.

slim /slɪm/ adj (-mer, -mest) **1** slender: a ~-waisted girl. **2** (informal) small; insufficient: ~ hopes/chances of success. □ vi (-mm-) eat less, take exercise, etc in order to reduce one's weight and become thin: ~ming exercises.
slim·ness n [U]

slime /slaɪm/ n [U] **1** soft, thick, sticky mud. **2** sticky substance from snails, etc: a trail of ~.
slimy /ˈslaɪmɪ/ adj (-ier, -iest) **(a)** of, like, covered with, slime. **(b)** (fig) disgustingly dishonest, flattering, etc: That slimy boy gets everything he wants.

sling /slɪŋ/ n [C] **1** band of material, length of rope, chain, etc looped round an object, e g a barrel, a broken arm, to support or lift it. **2** strip of leather (held in the hand in a loop) used to throw stones to a distance. **3** act of throwing. □ vt, vi (pt, pp slung /slʌŋ/) **1** throw with force; naughty boys ~ing stones at girls. **sling sb out**, throw him out (of a room, party, etc). **2** support (something) so that it can swing, be lifted, etc: a ~ rope over the cliff; with his rifle slung over his shoulder.

slink /slɪŋk/ vi (pt, pp slunk /slʌŋk/) go or move (off, away, in, out, by) in a secret or sneaking way.

slip¹ /slɪp/ n [C] **1** act of slipping; false step; slight error caused by carelessness or inattention: make a ~. **a slip of the tongue/pen**, error in speaking/writing. **give sb the slip**, escape from, get away from him. **2** = pillow-slip. **3** loose sleeveless garment worn under a dress. **4** young, slender person: a (mere) ~ of a boy/girl, a slim boy/girl. **5** (usually pl) sloping way (of stone or timber) down to the water, on which ships are built, or pulled up out of the water for repairs. **6** (cricket) one of the fielders: first/second/third ~; (pl) part of the ground where these fielders stand. **7** [U] liquid clay for coating earthenware or making patterns on it
`slip-cover, detachable cover for a piece of furniture.
`slip-knot, **(a)** knot which slips along the cord round which it is made to tighten or loosen the loop. **(b)** knot which can be undone by a pull.
`slip-over, knitted garment to be slipped on (over a shirt, etc).
`slip-road, road for joining or leaving a motorway.
`slip-stream, stream of air from the propeller or jet engine of an aircraft.
`slip-up (informal) ⇨ slip²(5).
`slip-way, = slip(5).

slip² /slɪp/ vi, vt (-pp-) **1** fall or almost fall as the result of losing one's balance: He ~ped on the icy road and broke his leg. **2** go or move quietly or quickly, esp without attracting attention: She ~ped away/out/past without being seen. The years ~ped (= passed) by. **3** move, get away, escape, fall, by being difficult to hold, or by not being balanced, fastened: The fish ~ped out of my hand. The blanket ~ped off the bed. **let sth slip**, **(a)** allow it to fall from one's hands, escape, or be neglected: Don't let the opportunity ~. **(b)** accidentally reveal (a secret, etc). **slip through one's fingers**, (fig) fail to keep a hold on. **slip one's mind**, (of a name, address, message, etc) be forgotten (because one is in a hurry, busy, etc). **4** put, pull on or push off, with a quick, easy movement: ~ a coat on/off; ~ into/out of a dress. **5** allow (small mistakes etc) to enter, esp by carelessness: errors that have ~ped into the text. **slip up**, (informal) make a mistake. Hence, **`slip-up** n [C]. **6** move smoothly and effortlessly; go with a gliding motion: The ship ~ped through the water. **7** get free from; let go: ~ anchor, detach a ship from the anchor; ~ a stitch, (in knitting) move a stitch from one needle to the other without knitting it.

slip-per /ˈslɪpə(r)/ n [C] loose-fitting shoe worn in the house.

slip-pery /ˈslɪpərɪ/ adj (-ier, iest) **1** (of a surface) smooth, wet, polished, etc so that it is difficult to hold, to stand on, or to move on: ~ roads. **2** (fig) (of a subject) needing care: We're on ~ ground when dealing with this subject. **3** (fig) (of persons) unreliable; not to be trusted: He's as ~ as an eel.

slit /slɪt/ n [C] long, narrow cut, tear or opening. □ vt (pt, pp slit) **1** make a slit in; open (by slitting): ~ a man's throat; ~ an envelope open. **2** be cut or torn lengthwise: The shirt has ~ down the back.

slither /ˈslɪðə(r)/ vi slide or slip unsteadily: ~ down an ice-covered slope.

sliver /ˈslɪvə(r)/ n [C] **1** small, thin strip of wood; splinter. **2** thin piece cut off a large piece: a ~ of cheese. □ vt, vi break off, into slivers.

slob-ber /ˈslɒbə(r)/ vi, vt **1** let saliva run from the mouth (as a baby does). **2** make wet with saliva: The baby has ~ed its bib. □ n [U] saliva running from the mouth.

sloe /sləʊ/ n [C] small, bluish-black wild plum, fruit of the blackthorn.

slog /slɒg/ vi, vt (-gg-) **1** hit hard and wildly

esp in boxing and cricket: ∼ (*at*) *the ball.* **2** walk, work, etc long and hard: ∼*ing away at one's work;* ∼*ing along the road.*

slog·ger, person who slogs.

slo·gan /ˈsləʊgən/ n [C] striking and easily remembered phrase used to advertise something, or to make clear the aim(s) of a group, organization, campaign, etc: *political* ∼*s.*

sloop /sluːp/ n [C] **1** small one-masted sailing-ship. **2** (*modern use*) small warship used for anti-submarine escort duty.

slop /slɒp/ vi,vt (-pp-) **1** (of liquids) spill over the edge: *The tea* ∼*ped* (*over*) *into the saucer.* **2** cause to spill: ∼ *beer over the counter of a pub.* **3** empty buckets containing urine, etc: *The wretched men in prison have to* ∼ *out every morning.* **4** make a mess with: ∼ *paint all over the floor.* **5** splash: *Why do some children love* ∼*ping about in puddles?* □ n **1** (*pl*) dirty waste water from the kitchen or from bedrooms (where there are no basins with running water and drains). **2** (*pl*) urine, excrement (in buckets, as in a prison cell). **3** [U] liquid food, eg milk, soup, esp for people who are ill. **4** [U] swill (for pigs).

slope /sləʊp/ n **1** [C,U] slanting line; position or direction at an angle, less than 90°, to the earth's surface or to another flat surface: *the* ∼ *of a roof; a hill with a* ∼ *of 1 in 5.* **2** area of rising or falling ground: ˈmountain ∼*s;* ˈski ∼*s.* □ vi,vt **1** have a slope: *Our garden* ∼*s* (*down*) *to the river.* **2** cause to slope. **3** (*informal*) **slope off**, go off or away (to avoid somebody, or escape doing something).

sloppy /ˈslɒpɪ/ adj (-ier, -iest) **1** wet or dirty with rain, etc; full of puddles: *The melting snow made the roads* ∼. **2** (*informal*) not done with or using care and thoroughness: *a* ∼ *piece of work/workman.* **3** (*informal*) foolishly sentimental; weakly emotional: ∼ *talk about girlfriends and boyfriends.*

slop·pily /-əlɪ/ adv in a sloppy manner **sloppily** (= carelessly) *dressed*

slop·pi·ness n [U]

slosh /slɒʃ/ vt,vi **1** (*sl*) hit (somebody). ∼ *him on the chin.* **2** splash about in water or mud. **3** throw water or other liquid

sloshed adj (*informal*) drunk.

slot /slɒt/ n [C] **1** narrow opening through which something is to be put, eg for a coin in a machine to buy something, eg tickets, cigarettes, sweets. **2** slit, groove or channel into which something fits or along which it slides. **3** (*informal*) right or suitable place for something (in a broadcast programme, scheme, etc): *too many advertising* ∼*s.* □ vt (-tt-) make a slot in: ∼ *30 000 graduates a year into jobs,* find jobs for them.

sloth /sləʊθ/ n **1** [U] laziness; idleness **2** [C] S American mammal which lives in the branches of trees and moves very slowly

sloth·ful /-fəl/ adj inactive; lazy

slouch /slaʊtʃ/ vi stand, sit or move, in a lazy, tired way: *boys who* ∼ *about at street corners all day.* □ n [C] lazy attitude or way of walking: *walk with a* ∼.

sloven /ˈslʌvən/ n [C] person who is untidy, dirty.

sloven·ly /ˈslʌvənlɪ/ adj untidy, dirty, careless: *a* ∼ *appearance*

slow[1] /sləʊ/ adj (-er, -est) **1** not quick; taking a long time: *a* ∼ *runner; a* ∼ *journey.* **2** at less than the usual rate or speed. **in slow motion**, (of a cinema film) with the number of exposures per second greatly increased (so that when the film is shown at normal rate the action appears to be slow). **3** not quick to learn: *a* ∼ *child.* **4** not acting immediately; acting only after a time; ∼ *poison. He is* ∼ *to anger/*∼ *to make up his mind.* **5** (of watches and clocks) showing a time behind the correct time (eg 1.55 when it is 2.00): *That clock is five minutes* ∼. **6** not sufficiently interesting or lively: *We thought the party was rather* ∼. **7** (of a surface) of such a nature that what moves over it (esp a ball) tends to do so at a reduced speed: *a* ∼ *running track.*

ˈ**slow·coach**, person who is slow in action or who has out-of-date ideas.

slow[2] /sləʊ/ adv (-er, -est) **1** at a low speed; slowly: *Tell the driver to go* ∼*er.* **go slow**, (a) (of workers in a factory, etc) work slowly as a protest, or in order to get attention to demands, etc. Hence, ˈ**go-**ˈ**slow** n [C]. (b) be less active: *You ought to go* ∼ *until you feel really well again.* **2** ˈ∼**-**ˈ**going**/**-**ˈ**moving**/**-**ˈ**spoken**, going/moving/speaking slowly.

slow[3] /sləʊ/ vi,vt (cause to) go, work, etc at a slower speed: *S*∼ *up/down before you reach the crossroads. You should* ∼ *up a bit* (= stop working so hard) *if you want to avoid a breakdown.*

slow-worm /ˈsləʊ wɜːm/ n [C] small, legless European lizard.

sludge /slʌdʒ/ n [U] **1** thick, greasy mud. **2** thick, dirty oil or grease.

slug[1] /slʌg/ n [C] slow-moving creature like a snail but without a shell.

slug[2] /slʌg/ n [C] **1** bullet of irregular shape. **2** strip of metal with a line of type along one edge.

slug[3] /slʌg/ vt,vi (-gg-) (*US informal*) **1** shoot(5). **2** hit hard; punch.

slug·gish /ˈslʌgɪʃ/ adj inactive; slow-moving: *a* ∼ *river; feeling* ∼.

sluice /sluːs/ n [C] **1** apparatus, device, for regulating the level of water by controlling the flow into or out of (a canal, lake, etc). **2** artificial water channel, eg one made by gold-miners for rinsing gold from sand and dirt. **3** flow of water above, through or below a floodgate □ vt,vi **1** send a stream of water over; wash with a stream of water: ∼ *ore,* to separate it from gravel, etc. **2** **sluice out**, (of water) rush out as from a sluice.

`'sluice-gate/-valve,` = 1 above.

`'sluice-way,` = 2 above.

slum /slʌm/ *n* [C] street of dirty, crowded houses: *live in a* ~. □ *vi* (-mm-) (*informal*) live very cheaply: *They've been* ~*ming off me for years.*

slummy *adj* of slums: *a* ~*my part of the town.*

slum·ber /'slʌmbə(r)/ *vi, vt* (*literary*) **1** sleep peacefully or comfortably. **2** pass (time) in sleep: ~ *away a hot afternoon.* □ *n* (often *pl*) sleep.

slump /slʌmp/ *vi* **1** drop or fall heavily: *Tired from his walk, he* ~*ed into a chair.* **2** (of prices, trade, business activity) fall steeply or suddenly. □ *n* [C] general drop in prices, trade activity etc; business depression.

slung /slʌŋ/ *pt, pp* of sling.

slunk /slʌŋk/ *pt, pp* of slink.

slur /slɜ(r)/ *vt, vi* (-rr-) **1** join (sounds, letters, words) so that they are indistinct. **2** deal quickly with in an attempt to conceal: *He* ~*red over the dead man's faults and spoke chiefly of his virtues.* □ *n* [C] **1** suggestion of having done wrong: *cast a* ~ *on her reputation; keep one's reputation free from* (*all*) ~*s.* **2** act of slurring sounds.

slush /slʌʃ/ *n* [U] **1** melting, dirty snow. **2** (*fig*) foolish sentiment.

slut /slʌt/ *n* [C] slovenly or immoral woman.

slut·tish /-ɪʃ/ *adj*

sly /slaɪ/ *adj* (-er, -est) deceitful; keeping or doing things secretly; seeming to have, suggesting, secret knowledge: *a* ~ *look.* **on the sly,** secretly.

sly·ly *adv*

sly·ness *n* [U]

smack /smæk/ *n* [C] **1** (sound of a) blow given with the open hand on something with a flat surface; sound of the lips parted suddenly or of a whip: *with a* ~ *of the lips,* with this sound (suggesting enjoyment of food or drink). □ *vt* **1** strike with the open hand: *If you say that again, I'll* ~ *your face.* **2** part the lips with a smacking sound to show pleasure (at food or drink, etc). □ *adv* in a sudden and violent way: *It hit me* ~ *in the eye.*

smack·ing, act or occasion of hitting with the palm of the hand: *The child needs a good* ~*ing*

smack² /smæk/ *n* [C] small sailing-boat for fishing.

smack³ /smæk/ *vi* have a slight flavour or suggestion (*of*): *opinions that* ~ *of heresy.*

small /smɔl/ *adj* (-er, -est) (opposite of *large*) **1** not large in degree, size, etc: *a* ~ *town/room/audience/sum of money.* **on the `small side,** a little too small. **2** not doing things on a large scale: ~ *farmers/ businessmen/shopkeepers.* **3** unimportant, trifling. **4** morally mean; ungenerous: *Only a* ~ *man/a man with a* ~ *mind would behave so badly.* Hence, **'small-`minded**

adj. **5** of low social position: *great and* ~, all classes of people. **6** *in a* `small way, modestly, unpretentiously: *He contributed to scientific progress in a* ~ *way.* **7** little or no: *have* ~ *cause for gratitude. He failed, and* ~ *wonder,* It is not surprising. □ *n* **1** (with *the*) slenderest part: *the* ~ *of the back* **2** (*pl*) (*informal*) small articles of clothing (for laundering).

`'small-arms` *n pl* weapons light enough to be carried in the hand by a soldier.

small change, coins of small value: *Can you give me* ~ *change for this note?*

`'small-fry,` persons of no importance.

`'small-holder,` person owning a smallholding.

`'small-holding,` (in GB) piece of land under fifty acres in size.

the small hours *n pl* the three or four hours after midnight.

small letters *n pl* not capitals.

`'small-pox` *n* [U] serious contagious disease which leaves permanent marks on the skin.

small talk, about everyday and unimportant social matters.

`'small-time` *adj* (*informal*) of minor importance; third-rate.

small-ness *n* [U]

smart¹ /smɑt/ *adj* (-er, -est) **1** bright; new-looking; clean; well-dressed: *a* ~ *dress/ suit/car. You look very* ~. **2** fashionable; conspicuous in society: *the* `~ *set;* ~ *people.* **3** clever; skilful; having a good, quick brain: *a* ~ *student/officer.* **4** quick; brisk: *walk at a* ~ *pace.* **Look smart!** Hurry up! **5** severe: *a* ~ *rebuke; a* ~ *slap on the ear.*

smart·ly *adv*

smart·ness *n* [U]

smart² /smɑt/ *vt* feel or cause a sharp pain (of body or mind): *The smoke made my eyes* ~. *She was* ~*ing with anger.* □ *n* [U] sharp pain, bodily or mental: *The* ~ *of his wound kept him awake.*

smarten /'smɑtən/ *vt, vi* make or become smart(1,4): ~ *oneself up to see visitors.*

smash /smæʃ/ *vt, vi* **1** break, be broken, with force into small pieces: ~ *a window. The firemen* ~*ed in/down the doors.* **2** rush, force a way, (*into, through, etc*): *The car* ~*ed into a wall.* **3** defeat thoroughly: ~ *the enemy.* **smash a record,** (in sport, etc) set up a far better record. **4** (in tennis) hit (a ball) downwards over the net with a hard, overhand stroke. **5** (of a business firm) go bankrupt. □ *n* [C] **1** breaking to pieces. **2** (in tennis) stroke in which the ball is brought swiftly down. □ *adv* with a smash: *go/run* ~ *into a wall.*

`'smash-and-`grab raid,` one in which a thief breaks a shop-window, e g a jeweller's, and grabs valuables from behind it.

`'smash-up,` collision (of cars, trains, etc).

smasher /'smæʃə(r)/ *n* [C] **1** violent blow. **2** person or thing considered to be very fine: *That girl's a ~!*

smash·ing /ˈsmæʃɪŋ/ *adj* (*dated sl*) excellent.

smat·ter·ing /ˈsmætərɪŋ/ *n* (usually *sing* with *a*, *an*) slight knowledge (*of* a subject): *a ~ of French.*

smear /smɪə(r)/ *vt, vi* **1** cover or mark with something oily or sticky; spread (something oily, etc) on: *~ one's hands with grease; hands ~ed with blood.* **2** make dirty, greasy marks on. **3** (*fig*) defame (a person, his reputation): *a ~ of paint.* □ *n* [C] mark made by smearing: *a ~ of paint.*

smell¹ /smel/ *n* **1** [U] that one of the five senses special to the nose: *S~ is more acute in dogs than in men.* **2** [C,U] that which is noticed by means of the nose; quality that affects this sense: *What a nice/horrible/unusual ~!* **3** (used without an *adj*) bad or unpleasant quality that affects the nose: *What a ~!* **4** (usually *sing* with *a*, *an*) act of breathing in through the nose to get the smell(2) of: *Have a ~ of this egg and tell me whether it's good.*

smell² /smel/ *vt, vi* (*pt, pp* smelt /smelt/) **1** (not used in the progressive tenses; often used with *can*, *could*) be aware of through the sense of smell: *Can/Do you ~ anything unusual? I can ~ something burning.* **smell a rat,** ⇨ rat. **2** (use with progressive tenses possible) use one's sense of smell in order to learn something: *S~ this and tell me what it is.* **smell sth out, (a)** discover by means of the sense of smell. **(b)** (*fig*) discover by intuition. **3** (not used in the progressive tenses) have the sense of smell: *Do/Can fishes ~?* **4** give out a smell (of the kind specified by an *adj* or *adv*); suggest or recall the smell (of): *The flowers ~ sweet. Your breath ~s of brandy.* (*Note:* if there is no *adj*, the suggestion is usually something unpleasant): *His breath/He ~s.*

smell·ing-salts *n pl* sharp-smelling substances to be sniffed as a cure for faintness etc.

smelly *adj* (-ier, -iest) (*informal*) having a bad smell.

smelt¹ /smelt/ *vt* melt (ore); separate (metal) from ore by doing this.

smelt² *pp, pt* of smell².

smile /smaɪl/ *n* [C] pleased, happy, amused or other expression on the face, with (usually a parting of the lips and) loosening of the face muscles: *There was a pleasant/amused ~ on her face. He was all ~s, looked very happy.* □ *vi, vt* **1** give a smile; show pleasure, amusement, sympathy, contempt, etc by this means: *He never ~s. What are you smiling at?* **2** express by means of a smile: *Father ~d his approval.* **3** give the kind of smile indicated: *~ a bitter ~.*

smirch /smɜːtʃ/ *vt* **1** make dirty. **2** (*fig*) dishonour. □ *n* [C] (*fig*) blot or stain.

smirk /smɜːk/ *vi, n* [C] (give a) silly, self-satisfied smile.

smite /smaɪt/ *vt, vi* (*pt* smote /sməʊt/, *pp* smitten /ˈsmɪtən/) (*old use*) **1** strike; hit hard: *The sound of an explosion smote our ears.* **2** affect greatly: *He was smitten with guilt/smitten with that pretty girl.* **3** defeat utterly: *God will ~ our enemies.*

smith /smɪθ/ *n* [C] worker in iron or other metals: *a `black~.*

smithy /ˈsmɪðɪ/, blacksmith's workshop.

smith·er·eens /ˌsmɪðəˈriːnz/ *n pl* small fragments: *broken to/into ~.*

smit·ten /ˈsmɪtən/ ⇨ smite.

smock /smɒk/ *n* [C] loose shirt (with smocking on it) like an overall.

smock·ing, kind of ornamentation on a garment made by gathering the cloth tightly with stitched patterns.

smog /smɒg/ *n* [U] fog with smoke, exhaust fumes from motor-vehicles, etc.

smoke¹ /sməʊk/ *n* **1** [U] visible vapour with particles of carbon, etc coming from a burning substance: *~ pouring from factory chimneys; 'ciga`rette ~.* **go up in smoke, (a)** be burnt up. **(b)** (*fig*) be without result, leave nothing permanent or worth while behind. **2** [C] (act of smoking) a cigarette, etc: *stop working and have a ~.*

`smoke-screen, (a) clouds of smoke made to hide military operations. **(b)** (*fig*) explanation, etc designed to mislead people about one's real intentions, etc.

`smoke-stack, (a) outlet for smoke and steam from a steamship. **(b)** tall chimney.

smoke-less *adj* **(a)** that burns without smoke: *~less fuel.* **(b)** free from smoke: *a ~less zone,* where smoke is prohibited.

smoky *adj* (-ier, -iest) **(a)** full of smoke: *smoky chimneys/fires.* **(b)** like smoke in smell, taste or appearance.

smoke² /sməʊk/ *vi, vt* **1** give out smoke, or something thought to be like smoke, e g visible vapour or steam: *a smoking volcano.* **2** (of a fire or fireplace) send out smoke into the room (instead of up the chimney): *This fireplace ~s badly.* **3** draw in and let out the smoke of burning tobacco or other substance: *~ a pipe/cigar.* **4** bring (*oneself*) into a specific state by smoking tobacco: *He ~d himself sick.* **5** dry and preserve (meat, fish) with smoke (from wood fires). **6** stain, darken, dry, with smoke: *~d glass,* e g through which to look at the sun. **7** send smoke on to (plants, insects) (to kill pests). **smoke sth out,** force to leave by smoking: *~ out snakes from a hole.*

smoker, person who habitually smokes tobacco.

smol·der /ˈsməʊldə(r)/ ⇨ smoulder.

smooth¹ /smuːð/ *adj* (-er, -est) **1** having a surface like that of glass; free from roughness: *~ paper/skin; ~ to the touch; a ~ sea,* calm, free from waves. **take the rough with the smooth,** take things (both the ups and downs of life) as they come. **2** (of movement) free from shaking, bumping, etc: *a ~ ride in a car.* **3** (of a liquid mixture) free from lumps; well beaten or mixed: *mix to a ~ paste.* **4** free from harshness of sound or taste; flowing easily: *a ~ voice; ~ claret/whisky.* **5** (of a person, his manner) flattering, polite (often with a suggestion of insincerity): *~ manners.* □ *vt,vi* **1** make smooth: *~ away/over obstacles/difficulties,* get rid of them. **2** become calm: *The sea has ~ed down.* □ *n* [C] act of smoothing: *give one's hair a ~.*

smooth·ly *adv* in a smooth manner: *Things are not going very ~ly,* there are troubles, obstacles, interruptions, etc.

smooth·ness *n* [U]

smote /sməʊt/ *pt* of smite.

smother /ˈsmʌðə(r)/ *vt* **1** cause the death of, by stopping the breath of or by keeping air from. **2** put out (a fire); keep (a fire) down (so that it burns slowly) by covering *with* ashes, sand, etc. **3** cover, wrap up: *~ a grave with flowers/a child with kisses/one's wife with kindness; be ~ed with/in dust by passing cars.* **4** suppress; hold back: *~ a yawn/one's anger.* □ *n* (usually *sing* with *a, an*) cloud of dust, smoke, steam, spray, etc.

smoul·der (*US* = **smol-**) /ˈsməʊldə(r)/ *vi* **1** burn slowly without flame. **2** (*fig*) (of feelings, etc) exist but be unseen, undetected, suppressed, etc: *~ing discontent/hatred.* □ *n* [U] slow burning: *The ~ became a blaze.*

smudge /smʌdʒ/ *n* [C] dirty mark: *You've got a ~ on your cheek.* □ *vt,vi* **1** make a smudge on. **2** (of ink, paint, etc) become blurred or smeared: *Ink ~s easily.*

smug /smʌg/ *adj* (-ger, -gest) having, showing, a character that is easily satisfied and without imagination, kindness for others, etc: *a ~ smile/young man.*

smug·ly *adv*

smug·ness *n* [U]

smuggle /ˈsmʌgl/ *vt* **1** get (goods) secretly and illegally (*into, out of,* a country, *through* the customs, *across* a frontier): *~ drugs into England.* **2** take (a person or thing) secretly and in defiance of rules or regulations: *~ a letter into a prison.*

smug·gler /ˈsmʌglə(r)/, person who smuggles.

smut /smʌt/ *n* **1** [C] (mark or stain made by a) bit of soot, dirt, etc. **2** [U] disease of corn (wheat, etc) that causes the ears to turn black. **3** [U] indecent or obscene words, topics: *Don't talk ~* □ *vt* (-tt-) mark with smuts(1).

smutty *adj* (-ier, -iest) (**a**) dirty with smuts (**b**) containing smut(3): *~ty stories.*

snack /snæk/ *n* [C] light meal (sandwiches, pies, etc).

`snack-bar/-counter, where snacks may be eaten.

snag /snæg/ *n* [C] **1** rough or sharp object, root of a tree, hidden rock, which may be a source of danger. **2** (*informal*) hidden

unknown or unexpected difficulty or obstacle: *There's a ~ in this plan somewhere.*

snail /sneɪl/ *n* [C] kinds of animal with a soft body, no limbs and with a spiral shell. **at a `snail's pace,** very slowly.

snake /sneɪk/ *n* [C] **1** kinds of long, legless reptile, some of which are poisonous. **2** (*fig*) insincere, harmful person who pretends to be a friend. □ *vi* move in twists and glides: *The road ~s through the mountains.*

`snake-charmer, person who can control snakes with music.

snap /snæp/ *vt,vi* (-pp-) **1** (try to) catch with the teeth: *The dog ~ped at my leg.* **2** (*fig*) (try to) catch quickly: *They ~ped at the offer,* offered eagerly to accept it. **snap sth up,** buy eagerly: *The cheapest articles were quickly ~ped up.* **3** break with a sharp crack; open or close with, make a sudden, sharp sound: *The rope ~ped. He ~ped down the lid of the box.* **4** say (something) quickly, sharply: *The sergeant ~ped out his orders.* **snap at sb,** speak to him sharply: *Stop ~ping at me.* **5** take a photograph of. **6** **snap out of it,** get out of a mood, habit, etc. □ *n* **1** [C] act or sound of snapping: *The dog made a ~ at the meat. The lid shut with a ~.* **2** [C] ⇨ cold snap. **3** [C] kinds of small, crisp cake: `ginger-~s.* **4** [C] = snapshot. **5** (as an *adjective*) done quickly and with little or no warning: *a ~ election/decision.*

`snap-dragon, (= antirrhinum) kinds of plant with flowers that open when pressed.

`snap-shot, quickly taken photograph with a hand camera.

snappy *adj* (-ier, -iest) bright; lively: *Make it ~py!* Hurry up!

snare /sneə(r)/ *n* [C] **1** trap for catching small animals and birds. **2** (*fig*) something that tempts one to expose oneself to defeat, disgrace, loss, etc: *His promises are a ~ and a delusion.* □ *vt* catch in a snare: *~ a rabbit.*

snarl[1] /snɑl/ *vi,vt* **1** (of dogs) show the teeth and growl (at). **2** (of persons) speak in an angry voice. □ *n* [C] act, sound, of snarling.

snarl[2] /snɑl/ *n* [C] tangle; confused state: *the `traffic ~s in a big town.* □ *vt,vi* (cause to) become jammed: *The traffic (was) ~ed up.* Hence, `**snarl-up** *n* [C]

snatch /snætʃ/ *vt,vi* **1** put out the hand suddenly and take: *He ~ed the letter from me/ ~ed the letter out of my hand. He ~ed at* (i e tried to seize) *the letter but was not quick enough.* **2** get quickly or when a chance occurs: *~ an hour's sleep/a meal; ~ a kiss.* □ *n* [C] **1** act of snatching: *make a snatch at the letter.* **2** (as an *adjective*): *a ~ decision,* made quickly when the chance occurs. **3** short outburst or period: *overhear ~es of conversation.*

snatcher, person who snatches.

sneak /snik/ *vi,vt* go quietly and secretly (*in, out, away, back, past,* etc). □ *n* [C] (*informal*) cowardly, harmful person.

sneak·ing *adj* (a) secret, sly: *have a ~ing respect/sympathy for him*, respect, etc which is not shown openly. (b) *a ~ing suspicion*, a vague, puzzling one.

sneak·ers /ˈsniːkəz/ *n pl* (also *a pair of ~*) shoes soled with rope, rubber or some other substance; tennis shoes.

sneer /snɪə(r)/ *vi* show contempt by using a wrinkled nose and a derisive smile (and perhaps despising words): *~ at religion*. □ *n* [C] sneering look, smile, etc.
sneer·ing·ly *adv*

sneeze /sniːz/ *n* [C] sudden, uncontrollable outburst of air through the nose and mouth: *Coughs and ~s spread diseases*. □ *vi* make a sneeze: *sneezing into a handkerchief*. **not to be sneezed at**, (*informal*) not to be accepted lightly: *A prize of £50 is not to be ~d at*.

snick /snɪk/ *vt,vi, n* [C] (make a) small cut in something.

snicker /ˈsnɪkə(r)/ *vi, n* [C] = snigger.

snide /snaɪd/ *adj* sneering; slyly critical: *~ remarks*.

sniff /snɪf/ *vi,vt* 1 draw air in through the nose so that there is a sound: *~ing and sneezing*. 2 sniff(1) to show disapproval or contempt. 3 draw in through the nose as one breathes: *~ the sea-air; ~ (at) a rose. The dog was ~ing (at) the lamp-post*. □ *n* [C] act or sound of sniffing; breath (of air, etc): *One ~ of this stuff is enough to kill you*.

sniffle /ˈsnɪfəl/ *vi* = snuffle.

snig·ger /ˈsnɪgə(r)/ *n* [C] short giggle (esp at something improper, or in a cynical manner). □ *vi* laugh in this way.

snip /snɪp/ *vt,vi* (-pp-) cut with scissors or shears, esp in short, quick strokes: *~ off the ends of the string*. □ *n* [C] 1 cut made by snipping; thing cut off (something large). 2 (*informal*) profitable bargain: *Only 50p! It's a ~!*

snipe¹ /snaɪp/ *n* [C] (*pl* unchanged) bird with a long bill which lives in marshes.

snipe² /snaɪp/ *vi,vt* fire shots (at) from a hiding-place, usually at long range; kill or hit in this way
sniper, person who snipes.

snip·pet /ˈsnɪpɪt/ *n* [C] 1 small piece cut off. 2 (*pl*) bits (of information, news, etc): *~s of conversation*.

snitch /snɪtʃ/ *vt,vi* 1 (*sl*) steal (something of little or no value). 2 inform (*on a person*).

snivel /ˈsnɪvəl/ *vi* (*GB* -ll-; *US* -l-) cry from insincere grief, sorrow or fear; complain, cry, in a miserable way: *a harassed woman with six ~ling children*.

snob /snɒb/ *n* [C] person who pays too much respect to social position or wealth, or who dislikes persons who are of lower social position: `*~ appeal*, power to attract the interest of snobs.
snob·bish /-ɪʃ/ *adj* of or like a snob.
snob·bish·ly *adv*

snob·bery /ˈsnɒbərɪ/, state, quality, of being snobbish.

snooker /ˈsnuːkə(r)/ *n* [U] game played with 15 red balls and six balls of other colours on a billiard-table.

snoop /snuːp/ *vi* **snoop into,** enquire into matters one is not properly concerned with. **snoop around,** look for faults, breaking of laws, etc (to gain an advantage).

snooty /ˈsnuːtɪ/ *adj* (-ier, -iest) (*informal*) snobbish.
snoot·ily /-əlɪ/ *adv*

snooze /snuːz/ *vi, n* [C] (*informal*) (take a) short sleep (esp in the daytime): *have a ~ after lunch*.

snore /snɔː(r)/ *vi* breathe roughly and noisily while sleeping. □ *n* sound of snoring: *His ~s woke me up*.
snorer, person who snores.

snor·kel, schnor·kel /ˈsnɔːkəl, ˈʃn-/ *n* [C] 1 tube that enables a submarine to take in air while submerged. 2 tube from the mouth to the device for enabling a swimmer to take in air while under water.

snort /snɔːt/ *vi,vt* 1 force air violently out through the nose; do this to show impatience, contempt, etc: *~ with rage (at her/ the idea)*. 2 express by snorting: *~ out a reply. 'Never!', he ~ed*. □ *n* [C] 1 act or sound of snorting: *give a ~ of contempt*. 2 snorkel (of a submarine).
snorty *adj* having a bad temper.

snot /snɒt/ *n* [U] (*vulgar*) mucus of the nose.
snotty *adj* (*vulgar*) running with, wet with, mucus.
`**snotty-nosed,** *adj* superior; snobbish: *You ~-nosed little creep*.

snout¹ /snaʊt/ *n* [C] 1 nose (and sometimes the mouth or jaws) of an animal (esp a pig). 2 front of something, thought to be like a snout.

snout² /snaʊt/ *n* (*prison sl*) [U] tobacco; [C] cigarette.

snow¹ /snəʊ/ *n* 1 [U] frozen vapour falling from the sky in soft, white flakes; mass of such flakes on the ground, etc: *a heavy fall of ~*.
`**snow-ball, (a)** mass of snow pressed into a hard ball for throwing in play. **(b)** something that increases quickly in size as it moves forward. □ *vt,vi* **(a)** throw snowballs (at). **(b)** grow quickly in size, importance, etc: *Opposition to the war ~balled*.
`**snow-blind** *adj* (temporarily) unable to see because the eyes are tired by the glare of the sun on snow.
`**snow-bound** *adj* unable to travel because of heavy falls of snow.
`**snow-drift,** snow heaped up by the wind.
`**snow-drop,** bulb plant with small white flowers at the end of winter or in early spring.
`**snow-fall, (esp)** amount of snow that falls on one occasion or in a period of time.

'snow·flake, one of the collections of small crystals in which snow falls.

'snow·man, figure of a man made of snow by children.

'snow-plough (US -plow), device for pushing snow from roads and railways.

'snow-shoes n pl frames with leather straps for walking on deep snow without sinking in.

'snow·storm, heavy fall of snow, esp with strong wind.

'snow-'white adj as white as snow.

snow² /snəʊ/ vi,vt 1 (of snow) come down from the sky: It ~ed all day. be snowed in/up, be prevented by heavy snow from going out. 2 come in large numbers or quantities: Gifts and messages ~ed in on her birthday. She was ~ed under with work/ with invitations to dinner parties.

snowy adj (-ier, -iest) (a) covered with snow: ~y roofs. (b) characterized by snow: ~y weather.

snub /snʌb/ vt (-bb-) ignore, treat with contempt (esp a younger or less senior person); reject (an offer) in this way: be/get ~bed by a civil servant. □ n [C] snubbing words or behaviour: suffer a ~.

snub nose /ˌsnʌbˈnəʊz/ n [C] short, turned up nose.

'snub-nosed adj

snuff¹ /snʌf/ n [U] powdered tobacco to be taken up into the nose by sniffing: take a pinch of ~.

'snuff-box, box for snuff.

snuff³ /snʌf/ vt,vi cut or pinch off the burnt black end of the wick of (a candle).

snuffle /ˈsnʌfəl/ vi make sniffing sounds, breathe noisily (as when the nose is partly stopped up while one has catarrh). □ n [C] act or sound of snuffing.

snug /snʌɡ/ adj (-gg-) 1 sheltered from wind and cold; warm and comfortable: ~ in bed. 2 neat and tidy; rightly or conveniently placed or arranged: a ~ cabin, on a ship. 3 closely fitting: a ~ jacket.

snug·ly adv

snuggle /ˈsnʌɡəl/ vi,vt lie or get (close to a person) for warmth, comfort or affection: The child ~d up to its mother. She ~d down in bed, made herself comfortable.

so¹ /səʊ/ adv of degree to such an extent: It is not ~ big as I thought it would be. We didn't expect him to stay ~ long, as, in fact, he did stay. He is not ~ stupid as to do that. He was ~ ill that we had to send for a doctor. There were ~ many that we didn't know where to put them all. I'm `~ glad to see you! so far, so far, so good, ⇨ far² (2). so long as, ⇨ long² (1). ⇨ also much¹.

so² /səʊ/ adv of manner 1 in this (that) way, thus: Stand just ~. S~ it was (= That is how) I became a sailor. As you treat me, ~ I shall treat you. and `so on, and other things of the same kind. 2 so that, (a) in order that: Speak clearly, ~ that they may

understand you. (b) with the result that: Nothing more was heard of him, ~ that people thought that he was dead. so... that, (a) with the intent that: We have ~ arranged matters that one of us is always on duty. (b) with the result that; in a way that: It ~ happened that I couldn't attend the meeting. so as to, in order to; in such a way that: I'll have everything ready ~ as not to keep you waiting. 3 (used as a substitute for a word, phrase or situation): I told you ~! That is what I told you! 4 (used to express agreement): A: 'It was cold yesterday.' B: 'S~ it was.' 5 also: You are young and ~ am I, i e I also am young.

'so-called, called or named thus but perhaps wrongly or doubtfully: Your ~-called friends won't help you in your troubles.

'so-so adj (informal) not very good: 'How are you feeling?' 'Only ~-~.

so-and-so /ˈsəʊ n səʊ/, person not needing to be named: Don't worry about what old ~-and-~ says.

so³ /səʊ/ conj 1 therefore; that is why: The shops were closed ~ I couldn't get any. She asked me to go, ~ I went. 2 (used in exclamations) S~ there you are!

soak /səʊk/ vt,vi 1 become completely wet by being in liquid or by absorbing liquid: The clothes are ~ing in soapy water. 2 cause something to absorb as much liquid as possible: S~ the cloth in the dye for one hour. 3 absorb; take in (liquid): Blotting-paper ~s up ink. 4 soak oneself in sth, (fig) absorb: ~ oneself in the atmosphere of a place. 5 (of rain, etc) make very wet: We all got ~ed (through). be soaked to the skin, get wet right through one's clothes. 6 enter and pass through: The rain had ~ed through the roof/his overcoat. □ n [C] act of soaking: Give the sheets a good ~. in soak, being soaked: The sheets are in ~.

soap /səʊp/ n [U] substance made of fat or oil, etc, used for washing and cleaning: a bar/cake of ~; use plenty of ~ and water. ⇨ soft soap. □ vt 1 apply soap: ~ oneself down. 2 (informal) use flattery to try to please.

'soap-box, improvised stand for a speaker (in a street, park, etc).

'soap-bubble, filmy ball of soapy water, full of air.

'soap-flakes/-powder, used to wash clothes.

'soap-suds n pl bubbly lather of soap and water.

soapy adj (-ier, -iest) (a) of or like soap. This bread has a ~y taste. (b) (fig) over-anxious to please: He has a ~y voice.

soar /sɔː(r)/ vi 1 (of birds, aircraft) fly or go up high in the air. 2 (fig) rise high up: Prices ~ed when war broke out.

sob /sɒb/ vi,vt (-bb-) 1 draw in the breath sharply and irregularly from sorrow or pain, esp while crying: She ~bed her heart out, cried bitterly. **2** tell while sobbing: *She ~bed out the story of her son's death in a traffic accident.* □ *n* [C] act or sound of sobbing: *The child's ~s gradually died down.*

so·ber /ˈsəʊbə(r)/ *adj* **1** self-controlled; serious in thought, etc; calm: *make a ~ estimate of what is possible; ~ colours*, not bright. **2** avoiding drunkenness; not drunk: *Does he ever go to bed ~?* □ *vt, vi* **1** make or become sober(1): *The bad news ~ed all of us. I wish those noisy children would ~ down*, become less excited, etc. **2** make or become sober(2): *Put him to bed until he ~s up.*

so·ber·ly *adv* in a controlled, serious manner.

so·bri·ety /səˈbraɪətɪ/ *n* [U] (*formal*) quality or condition of being sober(1).

soc·cer /ˈsɒkə(r)/ *n* [U] association football.

so·ciable /ˈsəʊʃəbl/ *adj* friendly; liking company.

so·ciably /-əblɪ/ *adv*

so·cia·bil·ity /ˌsəʊʃəˈbɪlətɪ/ *n* [U]

so·cial /ˈsəʊʃl/ *adj* **1** living in groups, not separately: *~ ants. Man is a ~ animal.* **2** of people living in communities; of relations between persons and communities: *~ customs/reforms/welfare; `~ worker*, person who works for the improvement of social conditions. **3** of or in society: *one's ~ equals*, persons of the same class as oneself in society. **4** for companionship: *a `~ club.* **5** = sociable. □ *n* [C] social gathering, e g one organized by a club.

'Social 'Democrat, (in politics) person who wishes society to move, by peaceful changes, to a system of socialism.

'social se'curity, government provisions for helping people who are unemployed, ill, disabled, etc: *The family is on ~ security*, receiving such help.

'social science, e g psychology, politics.

so·cially /-ʃəlɪ/ *adv*

so·cial·ism /ˈsəʊʃəlɪzm/ *n* [U] philosophical, political and economic theory that land, transport, the chief industries, natural resources, e g coal, waterpower, etc should be owned and managed by the State and wealth equally distributed.

so·cial·ist /-ɪst/ *n* [C] supporter of, believer in socialism. □ *adj* of socialism.

so·cial·ize /-aɪz/ *vt* make socialist.

so·cial·ite /ˈsəʊʃəlaɪt/ *n* [C] person well-known in fashionable society.

so·ciety /səˈsaɪətɪ/ *n* (*pl* -ies) **1** [U] social way of living; system whereby people live together in organized communities: *a danger to ~*, person, idea, etc that endangers the bodily or moral welfare of the members of a community. **2** [C] social community: *modern industrial societies.* **3** [U] company; companionship: *spend an evening in the ~ of one's friends.* **4** [U] people of fashion or distinction in a place, district, country, etc; the upper classes: *leaders of ~.* ⇨ **high**

society. **5** [C] organization of persons formed with a purpose; club; association: *the school de`bating ~; a co-`operative ~; the S~ of Friends.*

so·cio·logi·cal /ˌsəʊsɪəˈlɒdʒɪkəl/ *adj* of sociology.

so·cio·logi·cally /-klɪ/ *adv*.

so·ci·ol·ogist /ˌsəʊsɪˈɒlədʒɪst/ *n* [C] student of, expert in sociology.

so·ci·ol·ogy /ˌsəʊsɪˈɒlədʒɪ/ *n* [U] science of the nature and growth of society and social behaviour.

sock¹ /sɒk/ *n* [C] (also *a pair of ~s*) **1** woollen, cotton, etc covering for the foot and ankle. **pull one's socks up**, improve, make a greater effort: *You won't pass the exam if you don't pull your ~s up!* **2** loose sole used inside a shoe.

sock² /sɒk/ *n* [C] (*sl*) blow given with the fist: *Give him a ~ on the jaw!* □ *vt* (*sl*) give (a person) such a blow: *S~ him on the jaw!* □ *adv* (*sl*) exactly: *It hit her ~ in the eye.*

socket /ˈsɒkɪt/ *n* [C] natural or artificial hollow into which something fits or in which something turns: *the `eye~s; a ~ for an electric light bulb.*

sod /sɒd/ *n* [U] upper layer of grassland including the grass with its roots and earth; [C] square or oblong piece of this pared off.

soda /ˈsəʊdə/ *n* [U] common chemical substance used to make soap, glass manufacture, etc: *baking~*, kind used in cooking.

'soda-water, water containing carbon dioxide gas to make it bubble.

sod·den /ˈsɒdn/ *adj* **1** soaked through: *clothes ~ with rain.* **2** (of bread, etc) moist or sticky because undercooked.

so·dium /ˈsəʊdɪəm/ *n* [U] silver-white metal (symbol **Na**) occurring naturally only in compounds: *~ chloride*, (NaCl) common salt.

sod·omy /ˈsɒdəmɪ/ *n* [U] anal sexual intercourse, esp between males.

-so·ever /ˌsəʊˈevə(r)/ *suffix* (used with *relative pronouns, adverbs* and *adjectives*): *`how~, `who~*, etc.

sofa /ˈsəʊfə/ *n* [C] long seat with raised ends and back, on which several persons can sit or one person can lie.

soft /sɒft *US:* sɔːft/ *adj* (-er, -est) **1** (opposite of *hard*) changing shape easily when pressed: *~ soil/ground/mud.* **a soft landing,** (e g of a spacecraft on the moon) one that avoids damage or destruction. **2** (of surfaces) smooth and delicate: *~ fur; ~ furnishings*, curtains, etc. **3** (of light, colours) restful to the eyes: *lampshades that give a ~ light.* **4** (of sounds) not loud: *~ music; in a ~ voice.* **5** (of outlines) indistinct. **6** (of answers, words, etc) mild; gentle; intended to please: *a ~ answer; have a ~ tongue.* **7** (of the air, weather) mild: *a ~ breeze/wind.* **8** (of water) free from mineral salts and therefore good for washing: *as ~ as rainwater.* **9** (of certain sounds)· *C is ~ in 'city`* and hard in 'cat'. G is ~ in 'gin' and hard in 'get' **10** easy: *have a ~ job*, an easy well-paid job. **11** feeble; lacking in strength and determination: *Are the young people today getting* ~? **12** sympathetic; considerate: *have a ~ heart*. **13** (*informal*) easily affected, fooled: *He's not as ~ as he looks. Jack is ~* (= sentimentally silly) *about Anne.*

'soft-'boiled *adj* (of eggs) boiled so that the yolk is liquid.

'soft 'currency, one that is not convertible to gold, or into certain other currencies which are more in demand.

'soft drink, non-alcoholic fruit juice.

'soft-'headed *adj* idiotic; foolish.

'soft-'hearted *adj* sympathetic; kind.

'soft 'option, alternative which is thought to involve little work.

'soft 'palate, back part of the roof of the mouth.

'soft-'pedal *vi,vt* (*fig*) make (a statement, etc) less definite or confident.

'soft soap, (a) semi-liquid soap. (b) (*fig*) flattery. □ **'soft-'soap** *vt* flatter.

'soft-'spoken *adj* having a gentle voice; saying pleasant, friendly things.

'soft·ware, data, programmes, etc not forming parts of a computer but used for its operation. ⇨ hardware.

soft·ly *adv*

soft·ness *n* [U]

sof·ten /ˈsofən US: ˈsofən/ *vt,vi* **1** make or become soft: *curtains that ~ the light; people who are ~ed by luxurious living.* **2** make (something) easier to bear: *Her gentle manner ~ed the effect of the news.*

soft·ener *n* [C] something used to soften water.

soggy /ˈsogɪ/ *adj* (-ier, -iest) (esp of ground) heavy with water.

sog·gi·ness *n* [U]

soil /sɔɪl/ *n* [C,U] ground; earth, esp the upper layer of earth in which plants, trees, etc grow: *good/poor/sandy ~; a man of the ~,* one who works on the land (and likes to do so). □ *vt,vi* **1** make dirty: *He refused to ~ his hands,* refused to do dirty work. **2** become soiled: *material that ~s easily.*

so·journ /ˈsodʒən US: səʊˈdʒɜːn/ *vi, n* [C] (*literary*) (make a) stay (*with a person, at* or *in*) for a time.

sol·ace /ˈsolɪs/ *n* [C,U] (*formal*) (that which gives) comfort or relief (when one is in trouble or pain): *The invalid found ~ in music.* □ *vt* give relief to: *The unhappy man ~d himself with whisky.*

so·lar /ˈsəʊlə(r)/ *adj* of the sun.

solar cell, device (as used in satellites) which converts the energy of sunlight into electric energy.

the 'solar system, the sun and the planets which revolve round it.

solar 'plexus /ˈpleksəs/, complex of nerves at the pit of the stomach.

the solar year, time taken by the earth to complete one revolution round the sun, about 365 days, 5 hours, 48 minutes and 46 seconds.

sold /səʊld/ *pt,pp* of sell.

sol·der /ˈsoldə(r) US: ˈsodər/ *n* [U] easily melted alloy used, when melted, to join harder metals, wires, etc. □ *vt* join with solder.

'solder·ing-iron, tool used for this work.

sol·dier /ˈsəʊldʒə(r)/ *n* [C] member of an army: *three ~s, two sailors and one civilian.* □ *vi* serve as a soldier: *be tired of ~ing.*

'soldier 'on, continue bravely with one's work, etc in the face of difficulties.

sol·dier·ly, 'soldier-like *adj* like a soldier; smart; brave.

sole [1] /səʊl/ *n* [C] flat sea-fish with a delicate flavour.

sole [2] /səʊl/ *n* [C] under surface of a human foot, or of a sock, shoe, etc. □ *vt* put a sole on (a shoe, etc): *send a pair of shoes to be ~d and heeled.*

-soled *suffix* (with the kind mentioned): *'rubber-~d boots.*

sole [3] /səʊl/ *adj* **1** one and only; single: *the ~ cause of the accident.* **2** restricted to one person, company, etc: *We have the ~ right of selling the article.*

sole·ly *adv* alone; only: *~ly responsible; ~ly because of you.*

sol·emn /ˈsoləm/ *adj* **1** done with religious or other ceremony; causing deep thought or respect: *a ~ silence as the coffin was carried out of the church; a ~ oath,* grave and important. **2** serious-looking: *~ faces; look as ~ as a judge.*

sol·emn·ly *adv*

sol·emn·ness *n* [U]

sol·em·nity /səˈlemnətɪ/ *n* (*pl* -ies) (*formal*) **1** [U] seriousness; gravity. **2** [U] (but also *pl*) solemn ceremony: *The Queen was crowned with all ~/with all the proper solemnities.*

sol·em·nize /ˈsoləmnaɪz/ *vt* perform (a religious ceremony, esp a wedding) with the usual rites; make solemn.

sol·em·niz·ation /ˌsoləmnaɪˈzeɪʃən US: -nɪˈz-/ *n* [U]

sol·icit /səˈlɪsɪt/ *vt,vi* **1** ask (for) seriously; make determined requests (for): *Both the candidates ~ed my vote.* **2** (of a prostitute) make an immoral sexual offer (to), esp in a public place.

sol·ici·tor /səˈlɪsɪtə(r)/ *n* [C] **1** (*GB*) lawyer who prepares legal documents, e g wills, sale of land or buildings, advises clients on legal matters, and speaks on their behalf in lower courts. ⇨ barrister. **2** (*US*) person who solicits trade, support, etc.

So·licitor-'General, one of the principal law officers in the British Government, advising on legal matters.

sol·ici·tous *adj* (*formal*) anxious, concerned about (a person's welfare, etc) or to

help somebody: ∼ *to please;* ∼ *for her comfort.*
sol·ici·tous·ly *adv*
sol·ici·tude /səˈlɪsɪtjud *US:* -tud/ *n* [U] (*formal*) concern or anxiety: *my deep* ∼ *for your welfare.*
solid /ˈsɒlɪd/ *adj* **1** not in the form of a liquid or gas: *When water freezes and becomes* ∼, *we call it ice.* **2** compact; substantial; heavy: *a man with good* ∼ *flesh on him;* ∼ *food.* **3** without holes or spaces; not hollow: *a* ∼ *sphere.* **4** of strong or firm material or construction; able to support weight or resist pressure: ∼ *buildings/furniture.* **5** that can be depended on: ∼ *arguments; a* ∼ (= financially sound) *business firm; a man of* ∼ *character.* **6** of the same substance throughout: *made of* ∼ *gold.* **7** unanimous; undivided: *There was a* ∼ *vote in favour of the proposal.* **8** continuous; without a break: *wait for a* ∼ *hour; sleep ten* ∼ *hours/ten hours* ∼. **9** (*maths*) having length, breadth and thickness: *a* ∼ *figure,* e g a cube. □ *n* [C] **1** body or substance which is solid, not a liquid or a gas. **2** (*maths*) figure of three dimensions.
solid·ly *adv*
sol·id·ity /səˈlɪdətɪ/, **solid·ness** *n* [U] quality of being solid: *the* ∼*ity of a building/ argument.*
soli·dar·ity /ˈsɒlɪˈdærətɪ/ *n* [U] unity because of common interests or feelings: *national* ∼ *in the face of danger.*
sol·id·ify /səˈlɪdɪfaɪ/ *vt,vi* (*pt,pp* -ied) make or become solid, hard or firm.
sol·idi·fi·cation /səˈlɪdɪfɪˈkeɪʃən/ *n* [U]
sol·il·oquy /səˈlɪləkwɪ/ *n* [C,U] (*pl* -ies) **1** (instance of) speaking one's thoughts aloud. **2** (in drama) speech in which a character speaks his thoughts without addressing a listener.
sol·il·oquize /səˈlɪləkwaɪz/ *vi* talk to oneself; think aloud.
soli·taire /ˈsɒlɪˈteə(r) *US:* ˈsɒlɪteə(r)/ *n* [C] **1** (ornament such as an earring having a) single gem or jewel. **2** (also called *patience*) kinds of game for one player.
soli·tary /ˈsɒlɪtrɪ *US:* -terɪ/ *adj* **1** (living) alone; without companions; lonely: *a* ∼ *life; a* ∼ *walk.* **2** only one: *not a* ∼ *one/instance.* **3** seldom visited: *a* ∼ *valley.*
ˈsolitary conˈfinement, prison punishment by which a person is isolated in a separate cell.
soli·tar·ily /ˈsɒlɪtrɪlɪ *US:* ˈsɒlɪˈterəlɪ/ *adv*
soli·tude /ˈsɒlɪtjud *US:* -tud/ *n* **1** [U] being without companions; solitary state: *live in* ∼; *not fond of* ∼. **2** [C] lonely place: *spend six months in the* ∼*s of the Antarctic.*
solo /ˈsəʊləʊ/ *n* [C] (*pl* ∼s) **1** piece of music (to be) performed by one person: *a violin/ piano* ∼. **2** any performance by one person: (as an *adverb*) *fly* ∼; (as an *adjective*) *his first* ∼ *flight.* **3** [U] kind of whist in which ⊃ne playeɪ opposes others.

ˈsolo·ist /-ɪst/, person who gives a solo(1).
sol·stice /ˈsɒlstɪs/ *n* [C] either time (*summer* ∼, about 21 June; *winter* ∼, about 22 December) at which the sun is farthest N or S of the equator.
sol·uble /ˈsɒljʊbəl/ *adj* **1** that can be dissolved. **2** = solvable.
solu·bil·ity /-nsɪ/ *n* [U]
sol·ution /səˈluʃən/ *n* **1** [C] answer (*to* a question, etc); way of dealing with a difficulty: *Perhaps economy is the* ∼ *to/of your financial troubles.* **2** [U] process of finding an answer or explanation: *problems that defy* ∼, *cannot be solved.* **3** [U] process of dissolving a solid or a gas in liquid: *the* ∼ *of sugar in tea.* **4** [C,U] liquid that results from this process: *a* ∼ *of salt in water.*
solv·able /ˈsɒlvəbəl/ *adj* that can be solved or explained.
solve /sɒlv/ *vt* find the answer to (a problem, etc); explain (a difficulty): ∼ *a crossword puzzle.*
sol·vent /ˈsɒlvənt/ *adj* **1** of the power of dissolving or forming a solution: *the* ∼ *action of water.* **2** having money enough to meet one's debts. □ *n* [C] substance (usually a liquid) able to dissolve another substance: *grease* ∼, e g petrol.
sol·vency /-nsɪ/ *n* [U] being solvent(2).
sombre (*US* = **som·ber**) /ˈsɒmbə(r)/ *adj* dark-coloured; gloomy: *a* ∼ *January day;* ∼ *clothes.*
sombre·ly (*US* = **som·ber·ly**) *adv*
sombre·ness (*US* = **som·ber-**) *n* [U]
som·brero /sɒmˈbreərəʊ/ *n* [C] (*pl* ∼s) hat with a wide brim (as worn in Latin American countries).
some¹ /sʌm *weak form* səm *used only in the adjectival sense consisting of an undefined amount or number of/ adj* **1** (used to show an amount or quantity, a certain degree or number (more than one): *Please give me* ∼ *milk. There are* ∼ *children outside. S*∼ (= some people) *say that...* (*Note: some* is used in affirmative sentences; usually replaced by *any* in questions and negative sentences; *Have you any milk? We haven't any milk;* used in sentences where doubt or negation is implied. *Some* and *any* are *pl* equivalents of the numeral article *a, an,* of numeral *one,* and the *indefinite pron 'one'.*) **2** (used in questions if the speaker expects, or wishes to suggest, an affirmative answer): *Aren't there* ∼ *stamps in that drawer?* **3** (used in questions which are really invitations or requests): *Will you have* ∼ *cake?* **4** (used after *if,* introducing something supposed): *If we had* ∼*/any money, we could buy it. If we find* ∼*/any, we'll share them with you.* (*Note: some* or *any* can be used.) **5** (used with *more*): *Give me* ∼ *more. Won't you have* ∼ *more? I haven't any more.* (*Note:* compare *Do you want any more? I haven't any more.*) **6** (always /sʌm/) (contrasted with *the rest, other*(*s*), and *all*): *S*∼ *children learn languages easily*

(*and others with difficulty*). *All work is not dull;* ~ *work is pleasant* **7** (always /sʌm/) (used to show that the person, place, object, etc is unknown, or when the speaker does not wish to be specific): *He's living at* ~ *place in East Africa. I've read that story before in* ~ *book or other.* **8** (always /sʌm/) about; approximately: *That was* ~ *twenty years ago.* **9** (always /sʌm/) considerable quantity or number of: *I shall be away for* ~ *time,* a fairly long time. *The railway station is* ~ *distance* (= quite a long way) *from the village.* **10** (always /sʌm/) (used suggest 'to a certain extent'): *That is* ~ *help* (i e It helps to a certain extent) *towards understanding the problem.*

some² /sʌm/ *pron* (*Some* as a *pron* is used in the same ways as some, *adj,* 1,2,3 and 4. *S*~ of and *any of* are equivalent to *a few of, a little of, part of*): *S*~ *of these books are quite useful.* (Compare: *I don't want any of these* (*books*).) *I don't want any of this* (*paper*).) *I agree with* ~ (= *part*) *of what you say. Scotland has* ~ *of the finest scenery in the world.* □ *adv* ▷ some *adj* 8 above.

-some /-səm/ *suffix* (used to form an *adjective*) likely to, productive of: *quarrelsome.*

some·body /ˈsʌmbədɪ/, **some·one** /ˈsʌmwʌn/ *pron* **1** a person (unknown or unnamed): *There's* ~ *at the door.* (*Note:* replaced by *anybody* or *anyone* in questions, negative sentences: *Is there anyone at home? There isn't anybody at home.*) **2** (often with *a;* also in the *pl*) a person of some importance: *If you had studied harder at college you might have become* ~. *He's nobody here but he's a* ~ *in his own village.*

some·how /ˈsʌmhaʊ/ *adv* **1** in some way (or other); by one means or another: *We must find money for the rent* ~ (*or other*). *We shall get there* ~. **2** for some (vague) reason (or other): *S*~ *I don't trust that man.*

some·one /ˈsʌmwʌn/ *n* = somebody.

some·place /ˈsʌmpleɪs/ *adv* (*US informal*) = somewhere: *I've left my bag* ~.

som·er·sault /ˈsʌməsɔlt/ *n* [C] leap or fall in which one turns over completely before landing on one's feet: *turn/throw a* ~. □ *vi* turn a somersault.

some·thing /ˈsʌmθɪŋ/ *pron* **1** a thing, object, event, etc (unknown, unnamed, etc): *There's* ~ *on the floor. I want* ~ *to eat. There's* ~ (= some truth, some point) *in what he says.* (*Note:* replaced by *anything* in questions, negative sentences: *Is there anything in that box? There isn't anything to eat.*) **2 or something,** (used to show absence of precise information): *I hear he has broken an arm or* ~, met with some sort of accident and has broken a limb, etc. ~ **something like, (a)** having a little resemblance to: *The noise sounded* ~ *like an explosion.* **(b)** approximately: *It cost* ~ *like ten pounds.*

some·time /ˈsʌmtaɪm/ *adv* **1** at a point in time: *I saw him* ~ *in May. It was* ~ *last summer. I will speak to him about it* ~. (*Note:* do not confuse with *some time* meaning 'for some period of time', as in: *I have been waiting some time.*) **2** former(ly): *Thomas Atkins,* ~ *professor at this University.*

some·times /ˈsʌmtaɪmz/ *adv* now and then; from time to time: *I* ~ *have letters from him. I have* ~ *had letters from him.*

some·way /ˈsʌmweɪ/ *adv* (*US informal*) = somehow.

some·what /ˈsʌmwɒt US:* -hwɒt/ *adv* to some extent; in some degree: *I was* ~ *surprised/disappointed, etc.*

some·where /ˈsʌmweə(r) US:* -hweər/ *adv* in, at, to, a place (unknown, unnamed, etc): *It must be* ~ *near here. He lost it* ~ *between his office and the station.* (*Note:* replaced by *anywhere* in questions, negative sentences: *Is it anywhere near here? I didn't go anywhere yesterday.*)

son /sʌn/ *n* [C] **1** male child of a parent. **2** (used as a form of address, e g by an older men to a young man, a confessor to a penitent): *my* ~. **3** person having the qualities, etc shown: ~*s of freedom,* those who have inherited freedom from their ancestors. **the Son of God/Man,** Jesus Christ.

`son-in-law *n* [C] (*pl* ~s-in-law) husband of one's daughter.

so·nata /sə'nɑtə/ *n* [C] (*pl* ~s) musical composition for one instrument (e g the piano), or two (e g piano and violin), normally with three or four movements.

song /sɒŋ US:* sɔŋ/ *n* **1** [U] singing; music for the voice: *burst into* ~*; the* ~ (= musical sound) *of the birds.* **2** [U] (*poetic*) poetry; verse. **3** [C] short poem or number of verses set to music and intended to be sung: *popular* ~*s.*

`song·bird, bird (e g blackbird, thrush) noted for its musical sound.

`song-book, collection of songs (with both words and music).

song·ster /-stə(r)/, **(a)** singer. **(b)** songbird.

sonic /ˈsɒnɪk/ *adj* relating to sound, soundwaves or the speed of sound: *a* ~ *bang/boom,* noise made when an aircraft exceeds the speed of sound ▷ supersonic, ultrasonic.

son·net /ˈsɒnɪt/ *n* [C] kind of poem containing 14 lines, each of 10 syllables, and with a formal pattern of rhymes.

sonny /ˈsʌnɪ/ *n* [C] (*pl* -ies) familiar form of address to a young boy.

son·or·ous /ˈsɒnərəs/ *adj* (*formal*) **1** having a full, deep sound: *the* ~ *note of a large bell.* **2** (of language, words, etc) making a deep impression: *a* ~ *style.*

son·or·ous·ly *adv*

soon /sun/ *adv* (-er, -est) **1** not long after the present time or the time in question; in a short time: *We shall* ~ *be home. We shall be home quite* ~ *now. He'll be here very* ~. *It will* ~ *be five years since we came to live* *in London.* **soon after,** a short time after: *He arrived* ~ *after three.* (*Note:* the opposite of ~ *after* is *a little before.*) **2** early: *How* ~ *can you be ready? Must you leave so* ~? **3 as/so soon as,** at the moment that; when; not later than: *He started as* ~ *as he received the news. We didn't arrive so/as* ~ *as we had hoped.* **no sooner... no sooner,** immediately when or after: *He had no* ~*er/ No* ~*er had he arrived home than he was asked to go out again. No* ~*er said than done,* i e done immediately. **4** (used to show comparatives): *The* ~*er you begin the* ~*er you'll finish. The* ~*er the better.* **as soon as not,** more willingly: *I'd go there as* ~ *as not.* **sooner or later,** one day whether now or (much) later. **sooner than,** rather than: *He would* ~*er resign than take part in such dishonest business deals.*

soot /sʊt/ *n* [U] black powder in smoke, or left by smoke on surfaces. □ *vt* cover with soot.

sooty *adj* (-ier, -iest) black with, like, soot.

sooth-sayer /ˈsuːθseɪə(r)/ *n* [C] (*old use*) fortune-teller.

soothe /suːð/ *vt* **1** make (a person, his nerves, passions) quiet or calm: ~ *a crying baby; a soothing voice.* **2** make (pains, aches) less sharp or severe: *a soothing lotion for the skin,* e g against sunburn.

sooth-ing-ly *adv*

sop /sɒp/ *n* [C] **1** piece of bread, etc soaked in milk, soup, etc. **2** something offered to prevent trouble or to give temporary satisfaction: *ask a tenant to leave and offer money as a* ~. □ *vt* (-pp-) **1** soak (bread, etc in soup, etc). **2** absorb (liquid): ~ *up the water with this towel.*

sop-ping *adj, adv* thoroughly (wet): ~*ping wet.*

soph-is-ti-cated /səˈfɪstɪkeɪtɪd/ *adj* **1** having lost natural simplicity through experience of the world; cultured: *a* ~ *girl; with* ~ *tastes.* **2** with the latest improvements and refinements: ~ *modern weapons.* **3** (of mental activity) cultured, elaborate: *a* ~ *discussion/argument.*

soph-is-ti-ca-tion /səˌfɪstɪˈkeɪʃən/ *n* [U]

sop-or-ific /ˌsɒpəˈrɪfɪk/ *n* [C], *adj* (substance, drink, etc) producing sleep.

sop-ping /ˈsɒpɪŋ/ *adj* ⇨ sop.

soppy /ˈsɒpɪ/ *adj* (-ier, -iest) **1** very wet. **2** (*informal*) foolishly sentimental: *be* ~ *on his sister.*

so-prano /səˈprɑːnəʊ *US:* -ˈpræn-/ *n* [C] (*pl* ~s), *adj* (person having the) highest singing voice of women and girls and boys.

sor-cerer /ˈsɔːsərə(r)/ *n* [C] man who practises magic with the help of evil spirits.

sor-cer-ess /ˈsɔːsərəs/ *n* [C] woman sorcerer.

sor-cery /ˈsɔːsərɪ/ *n* (*pl* -ies) [U] witchcraft (the usual word); (*pl*) evil acts done by sorcery.

sor-did /ˈsɔːdɪd/ *adj* **1** (of conditions) poor,

dirty, uncomfortable. *a* ~ *slum; living in* ~ *poverty.* **2** (of persons, behaviour, etc) without respect or honour

sor-did-ly *adv*

sor-did-ness *n* [U]

sore /sɔː(r)/ *adj* (-r, -st) **1** (of a part of the body) tender and painful; hurting when touched or used: *a* ~ *knee/throat.* **a sight for sore eyes,** welcome, pleasant, person or thing. **2** filled with sorrow; sad: *a* ~ *heart.* **3** causing sorrow or annoyance. **a sore point/subject,** one that hurts the feelings when talked about. **4** hurt in one's feelings: *feel* ~ *about not being invited to the party.* □ *n* [C] **1** sore place on the body (where the skin or flesh is injured). **2** (*fig*) painful subject or memory: *Let's not recall old* ~*s.*

sore-ly *adv* (a) (*formal*) severely: ~*ly afflicted.* (b) greatly: *More financial help is* ~*ly needed.*

sore-ness *n* [U]

sor-row /ˈsɒrəʊ/ *n* [C,U] (cause of) grief or sadness; regret: *express* ~ *for having done wrong; to my great* ~ □ *vi* feel grief (*at/ for/over*): ~*ing over her child's death.*

sor-row-ful /-fəl/ *adj* feeling, showing, causing, sorrow

sor-row-fully /-fəlɪ/ *adv*

sorry /ˈsɒrɪ/ *adj* **1** feeling regret or sadness: *We're* ~ *to hear of your father's death.* **be/feel sorry (about/for sth),** feel regret: *Aren't you* ~ *for/about what you've done?* **be/feel sorry for sb,** (a) feel sympathy: *I feel* ~ *for anyone who has to drive in weather like this.* (b) feel pity: *I'm* ~ *for you, but you've been rather foolish, haven't you?* **2** (used to express mild regret or an apology): '*Can you lend me a pound?*' —'*S*~, *but I can't.*' **3** (-ier, -iest) pitiful.

sort¹ /sɔːt/ *n* [C] **1** group or class of persons or things which are alike in some way: *Pop music is the* ~ *she likes most. We can't approve of this* ~ *of thing/these* ~ *of things/things of this* ~. **2 a good sort,** (*esp*) a person who is likable, who has good qualities. **3** '**out of** '**sorts,** (*informal*) feeling unwell, depressed.

sort² /sɔːt/ *vt,vi* arrange in groups; separate things of one sort from things of other sorts: *The boy was* ~*ing/*~*ing out/over the foreign stamps he had collected. We must* ~ *out the good apples from the bad.* **sort sth out,** (*informal*) (a) put in good order: ~ *out a drawer.* (b) solve: *I'll leave you to* ~ *that out,* find a solution. (c) clear up problems, misunderstandings: *Let's leave John and Ann to* ~ *themselves out.*

sor-ter, (*esp*) post office worker who sorts letters.

so-so /ˈsəʊ səʊ/ *adj, adv* ⇨ so²

souf-flé /ˈsuːfleɪ *US:* suːˈfleɪ/ *n* [C] (*Fr*) dish of eggs, milk, etc.

soul /səʊl/ *n* [C] **1** non-material part of a human, believed to exist for ever: *believe in the immortality of the* ~ *He eats hardly* *enough to keep body and* ∼ *together,* to keep himself alive. *That man has no* ∼, is unfeeling, selfish. **2** emotional and intellectual energy: *He put his heart and* ∼ *into the work.* **3** person regarded as the ideal or personification of some virtue or quality: *He is the* ∼ *of honour/discretion.* **4** departed spirit: *'All 'S*∼*s' Day,* 2 Nov. **5** person: *There wasn't a* ∼ *to be seen,* No one was in sight. **6** (expressing familiarity, pity, etc according to context): *She's lost all her money, poor* ∼. **7** (*informal*) all those qualities that enable a person to be in harmony with himself and others, used esp by Afro-Americans and expressed through their music and dancing.

`**soul brother/sister**, fellow Afro-American.

`**soul-destroying** *adj* killing the will-power or spirit: ∼*-destroying work.*

`**soul music**, modern popular blues with strong rhythm for dancing.

soul·ful /-fəl/ *adj* having, affecting, showing, deep feeling: ∼*ful eyes/music/glances.*

soul·fully /-fəlɪ/ *adv*

soul·less *adj* without pity or deeper feelings.

soul·less·ly *adv*

sound /saʊnd/ *adj* (-er, -est) **1** healthy; in good condition; not hurt, injured or decayed: ∼ *fruit/teeth.* **2** dependable; based on logic, facts: *a* ∼ *argument/policy;* ∼ *advice.* **3** capable, careful: *a* ∼ *tennis player.* **4** thorough; deep: *be a* ∼ *sleeper; give him a* ∼ *beating.* □ *adv* deeply: *be* ∼ *asleep.*

sound·ly *adv* in a deep, thorough manner: *sleep* ∼*ly; be* ∼*ly beaten at tennis.*

sound·ness *n* [U]

sound² /saʊnd/ *n* [C,U] **1** that which is or can be heard: *We heard the* ∼ *of voices/footsteps.* **2** (*sing* only) mental impression produced by something stated (or read): *I don't like the* ∼ *of it.*

`**sound barrier**, point at which an aircraft's speed equals that of sound-waves, causing sonic booms.

`**sound effects**, sound (recorded on tape, film, etc) for use in broadcasts, in studio.

`**sound-track**, music, etc used in a cinema film.

`**sound-wave**, vibrations made in the air or other medium by which sound is carried.

sound-less *adj* silent (the usual word).

sound·less·ly *adv*

sound³ /saʊnd/ *vt,vi* **1** produce sound from; make (something) produce sound: ∼ *a trumpet.* **2** produce: ∼ *a note of alarm/ danger.* **3** pronounce: *Don't* ∼ *the 'h' in 'hour' or the 'b' in 'dumb'.* **4** give notice of: ∼ *the alarm,* e g by ringing a bell. **5** give forth sound: *The trumpet* ∼*ed.* **6** test, examine (e g a person's lungs by tapping the chest). **7** give an impression when heard: *How sweet the music* ∼*s!* **8** (*fig*) give an impression: *His explanation* ∼*s all right,*

seems reasonable enough.

sound⁴ /saʊnd/ *vt,vi* **1** test the depth of (the sea, etc) by letting down a weighted line (called a `∼*ing-line* or ∼*ing apparatus*); find the depth of water in a ship's hold (with a `∼*ing-rod*). **2** get records of temperature, pressure, etc in (the upper atmosphere) (by sending up instruments in a `∼*ing-balloon*). **3** try (esp cautiously or in a reserved manner) to learn a person's views, sentiments, etc: *I will* ∼ *out the manager about/on the question of holidays.*

sound·ing, (a) (*pl*) place or area near enough to the shore to make it possible to sound(1). (b) measurement obtained by sounding(1).

sound⁵ /saʊnd/ *n* [C] narrow passage of water joining two larger areas of water: *Plymouth S*∼.

soup¹ /suːp/ *n* [U] liquid food made by cooking meat, vegetables, etc in water: *chicken/pea/tomato* ∼. *in the soup,* (*informal*) in trouble.

soup² /suːp/ *vt* **soup sth up,** (*sl*) fit a motor-vehicle, its engine) with a super-charger (to increase its power and so its speed): *a* ∼*ed-up car.*

sour /saʊə(r)/ *adj* **1** having a sharp taste (like that of vinegar, a lemon or an unripe plum, apple, etc). **2** having a taste of having gone bad: ∼ *milk.* **3** (*fig*) bad-tempered: *made* ∼ *by disappointments.* □ *vt,vi* turn or become sour (all uses): *The hot weather has* ∼*ed the milk. Her temper has* ∼*ed.*

sour·ly *adv*

sour·ness *n* [U]

source /sɔːs/ *n* [C] **1** starting-point of a river: *the* ∼*s of the Nile. Where does the Rhine have its* ∼? **2** place from which something comes or is got: *The news comes from a reliable* ∼. *Is that well the* ∼ *of infection?* **3** (*pl*) original documents, etc serving as material for a study, e g of a period of history: (as an *adjective*) ∼ *materials.*

souse /saʊs/ *vt* **1** throw into water; throw water on. **2** put (fish, etc) into salted water, vinegar, etc to preserve it: ∼*d herrings.*

south /saʊθ/ *n* **1 the** ∼, one of the four cardinal points of the compass, on the right of a person facing the sunrise; part of any place, country, etc lying farther in this direction than other parts: *the* ∼ *of London/England. Mexico is to the* ∼ *of the US.* **2** (as an *adjective*) situated in, living in, of, coming from, the south: *S*∼ *America; the S*∼ *Pacific* □ *adv* to or towards the south: *sailing* ∼.

`**south·'east, **south·'west** (abbr **S E, S W**), *n, adj, adv* (sometimes, esp *naut,* **sou'·'east** /'saʊ 'iːst/, **sou'·west** /'saʊ 'west/) (regions) midway between south and east or south and west.

`**south-south·'east, **south-south·'west** (abbr **S S E, S S W**) *n, adj, adv* (sometimes, esp *naut,* **'sou'-sou'-'east,** **'sou'-**

sou'-ˈwest (regions) midway between south and southeast or southwest.

ˈsouth-ˈeaster·ly adj (a) (of wind) from the southeast. (b) (of direction) towards the southeast.

ˈsouth-ˈeastern /-ˈistən/ adj of, from, situated in, the southeast.

ˈsouth-ˈwester·ly adj (a) (of wind) from the southwest. (b) (of direction) towards the southwest.

ˈsouth-ˈwestern /-ˈwestən/ adj of, from, situated in, the southwest.

south·er·ly /ˈsʌðəlɪ/ adj, adv from the south, towards the south, in or to the south.

south·ern /ˈsʌðən/ adj of, from, in the south part of the world, a country, etc: ~ Europe; the S~ States of the USA.

south·erner, person born or living in the south regions of the country.

ˈsouth·ern·most /-məʊst/ adj farthest south.

south·ward /ˈsaʊθwəd/ adj towards the south: in a ~ direction.

south·wards adv: to travel ~s.

sou·ve·nir /ˈsuvəˈnɪə(r) US: ˈsuvənɪər/ n [C] something taken, bought or received as a gift, and kept as a reminder of a person, place or event.

sou'-ˈwester /ˈsaʊwestə(r)/ n [C] (esp) waterproof hat with a flap at the back to protect the neck.

sov·er·eign /ˈsɒvrɪn/ adj (of power) highest; without limit; (of a nation, state, ruler) having sovereign power: become a ~ state, fully self-governing and independent in foreign affairs. □ n [C] 1 sovereign ruler, e g a king, queen or emperor. 2 former GB gold coin (face value one pound).

sov·er·eignty /ˈsɒvrəntɪ/, sovereign power.

so·viet /ˈsəʊvɪət/ n [C] one of the councils of workers, etc in any part of the USSR (the Union of S~ Socialist Republics); any of the higher groups to which these councils give authority, forming part of the system of government (the Supreme S~) of the whole of the USSR: S~ Russia; the S~ Union.

sow¹ /saʊ/ n [C] fully grown female pig.

sow² /səʊ/ vt,vi (pt ~ed, pp ~n /səʊn/ or ~ed) 1 put (seed) on or in the ground or in soil (in pots, seed-boxes, etc); plant (land with seed): ~ seeds; ~ a plot of land with grass. 2 (fig) start, introduce: ~ the seeds of hatred.

sower, person who sows.

soya /ˈsɔɪə/ n [U] (also ˈsoya-bean) plant grown as food and for the oil obtained from its seeds: ~ sauce, from soya beans in brine.

soz·zled /ˈsɒzəld/ adj (GB sl) very drunk.

spa /spɑ/ n [C] (pl ~s) (place where there is a) spring of mineral water having medicinal properties.

space /speɪs/ n 1 [U] that in which all objects exist and move: The universe exists in ~. Travel through ~ to other planets interests many people today. 2 [C,U] interval or distance between two or more objects: the ~s between printed words; separated by a ~ of ten metres. 3 [C,U] area or volume: open ~s, (esp) land, in or near a town, not built on. 4 [U] limited or unoccupied place or area; room(3): There isn't enough ~ in this classroom for thirty desks. 5 (sing only) period of time: a ~ of three years. □ vt space sth out, set out with regular spaces between: ~ out the posts three metres apart.

ˈspace-capsule/ ·craft/ -helmet/ -rocket/ -ship/ -suit/ -vehicle, of the kind needed for travel beyond the earth's atmosphere.

spa·cious /ˈspeɪʃəs/ adj having much space.

spa·cious·ly adv

spa·cious·ness n [U]

spade /speɪd/ n [C] 1 tool with flat blade having a sharp edge for digging. 2 (one of a) suit of playing-cards with black shape like inverted hearts: the five of ~s. □ vt dig with a spade.

ˈspade-work, (fig) hard, basic, work.

ˈspade-ful /-fʊl/, amount that spade holds.

spa·ghetti /spəˈgetɪ/ n [U] Italian pasta of narrow long rods, cooked by boiling.

span /spæn/ n [C] 1 distance between the tips of a persons's thumb and little finger when stretched out. 2 distance or part between the supports of an arch: The arch has a ~ of 60 metres. 3 length in time, from beginning to end: for a short ~ of time. □ vt (-nn-) 1 extend across (from side to side): The Thames is ~ned by many bridges. 2 (of time) from one period or point to another: His life ~ned almost all of the 19th century. 3 measure by spans(1).

spangle /ˈspæŋgəl/ n [C] tiny disc of shining metal, esp one of many, as used for ornament on a dress, etc. □ vt (esp as a pp) cover with, or as with, spangles.

span·iel /ˈspænɪəl/ n [C] sorts of dog with short legs and drooping ears.

spank /spæŋk/ vt,vi punish (a child) by slapping on the buttocks with the open hand or a slipper, etc.

spank·ing, slapping on the buttocks.

span·ner /ˈspænə(r)/ n [C] (US = wrench) tool for gripping and turning nuts on screws, bolts, etc.

spar¹ /spɑ(r)/ n [C] strong wooden or metal pole used as a mast, yard, boom, etc.

spar² /spɑ(r)/ vi (-rr-) 1 make the motions of attack and defence with the fists (as in boxing). 2 (fig) quarrel or argue.

ˈspar·ring-partner, man with whom a boxer spars as part of his training.

spare¹ /speə(r)/ adj 1 additional to what is usually needed or used; in reserve for use when needed; (of time) leisure; unoccupied: I have no/very little ~ time/money, no time/money that I cannot use. Is there a ~ wheel in your car? 2 (of persons) thin; lean: a tall, ~ man. □ n [C] spare part (for a machine, etc).

'spare `part, part to replace a broken or worn-out part of a machine, an engine, etc.

'spare-`rib, rib of pork with most of the meat cut off.

spare² /speə(r)/ *vt,vi* **1** (decide to) not hurt, damage or destroy; show mercy to: ~ *a prisoner's life. He doesn't* ~ *himself,* makes great demands on himself (his energies, time, etc). **spare sb's feelings,** avoid hurting his feelings. **2** afford to, be able to, give (time, money, etc) to a person, or for a purpose: *Can you* ~ *me an extra ticket for me? Can you* ~ *me a few minutes (of your time)? We haven't enough to* ~, are not able to give any more. **spare a thought for sb** consider a person when making a decision. **3** with no economy in money or effort: *I'm going to redecorate the house, no expense* ~d.

spar·ing *adj* **sparing of,** economical, careful (of): *You should be more sparing of your energy.*
spar·ing·ly *adv*

spark /spɑk/ *n* [C] **1** tiny glow from a burning substance or still present in ashes, etc or produced by hard metal and stone banging together, or by the breaking of an electric current: *The firework burst into a shower of* ~s. **2** (*fig*) sign of life, energy, etc: *He hasn't a* ~ *of generosity in him.* □ *vt,vi* **1** give out sparks. **2 spark sth off,** (*fig*) be the immediate cause of: *His statement* ~ed off a *quarrel between them.*

`spark·ing-plug, device for firing the mixture of air and petrol in an engine by means of an electric spark.

sparkle /spɑkəl/ *vi* **1** send out flashes of light: *Her diamonds* ~d *in the bright light.* **2** (*fig*) express brightly: *Her eyes* ~d *with excitement.* □ *n* [C] spark; glitter; gleam.

spark·ler, something that sparkles, e g a kind of firework.

spark·ling /spɑklɪŋ/ *adj*

spar·row /spærəʊ/ *n* [C] very common, small brownish-grey bird.

sparse /spɑs/ *adj* **1** not crowded: *a* ~ *population.* **2** not dense, thick: *a* ~ *beard.*

sparse·ly *adv*: *a* ~ly *furnished room,* one with little furniture
sparse·ness *n* [U]

spasm /spæzm/ *n* [C] **1** sudden and involuntary tightening of a muscle or muscles: *asthma* ~s. **2** sudden, convulsive movement: *in a* ~ *of pain/excitement; a coughing* ~. **3** sudden burst (of energy).

spas·modic /spæzˈmɒdɪk/ *adj* **1** taking place, done, at irregular intervals. **2** caused by, affected by, spasms: ~ *asthma.*
spas·modi·cally /-klɪ/ *adv*

spas·tic /spæstɪk/ *n* [C], *adj* (person) physically disabled because of faulty links between the brain and motor nerves, causing difficulty in controlling voluntary muscles.

spat /spæt/ *pt,pp* of spit.

spate /speɪt/ *n* [C,U] **1** strong current of water at abnormally high level (in a river). **2** sudden rush of business, etc: *a* ~ *of orders.*

spa·tial /speɪʃəl/ *adj* of, in relation to, existing in, space.
spa·tially /-ʃəlɪ/ *adv*

spat·ter /spætə(r)/ *vt,vi* **1** splash, scatter, in drips: ~ *grease on one's clothes/* ~ *one's clothes with grease.* **2** fall or spread out in drops: *rain* ~ing *down on the tent.* □ *n* [C] shower: *a* ~ *of rain/bullets.*

spat·ula /spætjʊlə *US:* spætʃʊlə/ *n* [C] (*pl* ~s) tool with a wide, flat, flexible blade used for mixing or spreading various substances.

spawn /spɔn/ *n* [U] eggs of fish and certain water animals, e g frogs. □ *vt,vi* **1** produce spawn. **2** (*fig*) produce in great numbers: *committees which* ~ *sub-committees.*

speak /spik/ *vi,vt* (*pt* spoke /spəʊk/, *pp* spoken /spəʊkən/) **1** use language in an ordinary, not a singing, voice: *Please* ~ *more slowly. I was* ~ing *to him about plans for the holidays.* **speak for sb,** (a) state the views, wishes, etc of. (b) give evidence on behalf of. **nothing to speak of,** nothing worth mentioning. **speak out/up,** (a) speak loud(er). (b) give one's opinions, etc without hesitation or fear. **be on `speaking terms with sb,** (a) know him well enough to speak to him. (b) continue to speak to him (because there has not been a quarrel). **so to speak,** if I may use this expression, etc. **2** give evidence (of), express ideas (not necessarily in words): *Actions* ~ *louder than words.* **3** know and be able to use (a language): *He* ~s *several languages.* **4** address an audience; make a speech: *He spoke for forty minutes.* **5** make known: ~ *the truth.* **speak one's mind,** express one's views. **6** **strictly / roughly / generally speaking,** using the word(s) in a strict/rough/general sense.

speaker, (a) person who makes speeches (in the manner shown): *He's a good/poor* ~er. (b) (short for) loudspeaker. (c) **the Speaker,** presiding officer of the House of Commons and other legislative assemblies.

spear /spɪə(r)/ *n* [C] weapon with a metal point on a long shaft, used in hunting, or (formerly) by men fighting on foot. □ *vt* pierce, wound, make (a hole) in, with a spear.

`spear·head, (*fig*) individual or group chosen to lead an attack. □ *vt* act as spearhead for: ~head *the campaign for human rights.*

spear·mint /spɪəmɪnt/ *n* [U] aromatic variety of mint used for flavouring; chewing-gum flavoured with this.

special /speʃəl/ *adj* **1** of a particular or certain sort; not common, usual or general; of or for a certain person, thing or purpose: *His painting is something* ~, particularly good. *He did it for her as a* ~ *favour. What are your* ~ *interests?* **2** exceptional in amount, degree, etc: *Why should we give you* ~

treatment? □ *n* [C] special train, edition of a newspaper, etc.

special delivery, delivery of mail (a letter, package, etc) by a special messenger instead of by the usual postal services.

specially /-ʃəlɪ/ *adv* particularly: *I came here ~ly to see you.*

special·ist /-ʃəlɪst/, person who is an expert in a profession, esp special ~ist.

spe·ci·al·ity /ˈspeʃɪˈælətɪ/ *n* [C] (*pl* -ies) 1 special quality or characteristic. 2 particular activity, product, operation, etc; thing to which a person (firm, etc) gives particular attention or for which a place is well known: *Embroidery is her ~.*

spe·cial·ize /ˈspeʃəlaɪz/ *vi,vt* 1 be or become a specialist; give special or particular attention to: *After his first degree he hopes to ~.* 2 (usually as a *pp*) for a particular purpose: *~d knowledge.*

spe·cial·iz·ation /ˈspeʃəlaɪˈzeɪʃən US: -lɪˈz-/ *n* [C,U]

spe·cial·ty /ˈspeʃəltɪ/ *n* [C] (*pl* -ies) = speciality(2).

spe·cies /ˈspiːʃiz/ *n* [C] (*pl* unchanged) 1 group of animals having some common characteristics able to breed with each other but not with other groups: *the human ~,* mankind. 2 sort: *He's a rare ~,* rare type of person.

spe·ci·fic /spəˈsɪfɪk/ *adj* 1 detailed and precise: *~ orders.* 2 relating to one particular thing, etc, not general: *The money is to be used for a ~ purpose.*

spe·cifi·cally /-klɪ/ *adv* in a specific manner: *You were ~ally warned by your doctor not to smoke.*

spec·ifi·ca·tion /ˈspesɪfɪˈkeɪʃən/ *n* 1 [U] specifying. 2 (often *pl*) details, instructions, etc for the design, materials, of something to be made or done: *~s for (building) a garage.*

spec·ify /ˈspesɪfaɪ/ *vt* (*pt,pp* -ied) name a particular one, type, etc: *~ which colours to use.*

speci·men /ˈspesɪmən/ *n* [C] 1 one as an example of a class: *~s of rocks and ores.* 2 part taken to represent the whole: *~ pages of books.* 3 something to be tested, etc for definite or special purposes: *supply the doctor with a ~ of urine.*

spe·cious /ˈspiːʃəs/ *adj* (*formal*) appearing right or true, but not really so: *a ~ argument/person.*

spe·cious·ly *adv*

spe·cious·ness *n* [U]

speck /spek/ *n* [C] 1 small spot or particle (of dirt, etc): *~s of dust.* 2 (*fig*) small spot: *The ship was a ~ on the horizon.*

specked *adj* marked with specks: *~ed apples.*

speckle /ˈspekəl/ *n* [C] small mark or spot, esp one of many, distinct in colour, on the skin, feathers, etc.

speckled *adj*

specs /speks/ *n pl* (*informal*) spectacles(3): *Where are my ~?*

spec·tacle /ˈspektəkəl/ *n* [C] 1 public display, procession, etc: *The Jubilee parade was a fine ~.* 2 something seen, esp something grand, remarkable: *The sunrise as seen from the top of the mountain was a tremendous ~.* 3 (*pl*) (also *a pair of ~s*) pair of lenses in a frame, resting on the nose and ears, to help the eyesight. (*Note: glasses* is more usual.)

spec·tacu·lar /spekˈtækjʊlə(r)/ *adj* making a fine spectacle(1,2).

spec·tacu·lar·ly *adv*

spec·ta·tor /spekˈteɪtə(r) US: ˈspekteɪtər/ *n* [C] person looking at (a show or game).

spectre (*US* = **spec·ter**) /ˈspektə(r)/ *n* [C] ghost; haunting fear of future trouble.

spec·tral /ˈspektrəl/ *adj* (a) of, like, a spectre. (b) of spectra or the spectrum: *spectral colours.*

spec·trum /ˈspektrəm/ *n* [C] (*pl* -tra /-trə/) 1 image of a band of colours (as seen in a rainbow and usually described as red, orange, yellow, green, blue, indigo and violet). 2 (*fig*) wide range or sequence: *the whole ~ of political opinion.*

specu·late /ˈspekjʊleɪt/ *vi* 1 consider, form opinions (without having complete knowledge): *~ about/upon/on the future of the human race.* 2 buy and sell goods, stocks and shares, etc with risk of loss and hope of profit through changes in their market value: *~ in oil shares.*

specu·la·tor /-tə(r)/, person who speculates(2).

specu·la·tion /ˈspekjʊˈleɪʃən/ *n* 1 [U] speculating(1); [C] opinion reached by this means. 2 [U] speculating(2): *~ in rice;* [C] *business deal of this kind.*

specu·la·tive /ˈspekjʊlətɪv US:-leɪtɪv/ *adj* 1 concerned with speculation(1): *~ philosophy.* 2 concerned with speculation(2): *~ purchase of grain.*

specu·la·tive·ly *adv*

sped /sped/ *pt,pp* of speed.

speech /spiːtʃ/ *n* 1 [U] power, act, manner, of speaking: *Man is the only animal that has the power of ~.* 2 [C] talk or address given in public: *make a ~ on/about human rights.*

'speech therapy, remedial treatment for defective speech, e g for stuttering.

speech·less *adj* (a) unable to speak, esp because of deep feeling: *Anger left him ~less.* (b) that causes a person to be unable to speak: *~less rage.*

speed /spiːd/ *n* 1 [U] quickness of movement. *More haste, less speed,* (*proverb*) Too much haste may result in delay. 2 [C,U] rate of motion or moving: *travelling at full/top ~;* *at a ~ of thirty miles an hour.* □ *vt,vi* (*pt,pp* sped but see 3 below) 1 move along, go quickly: *cars ~ing past the school.* 2 cause to move or go quickly: *~ an arrow from the bow.* 3 (*pt,pp* ~ed) increase the

speed (of): *They have* ∼*ed up production/
the train service.*

'**speed-boat,** motor-boat designed for high
speeds.

speed·ing *n* [U] (of motorists) travelling at
an illegal or dangerous speed: *fined £10 for*
∼*ing.*

'**speed-limit,** fastest speed allowed, e g in a
built-up area.

speedom·eter /spɪˈdɒmɪtə(r)/, instrument
showing the speed of a motor-vehicle, etc.

speed·way, (a) track, for fast driving and
racing, esp by motor bikes. **(b)** (*US*) road
for fast traffic.

speedy *adj* (-ier, -iest) quick; coming,
done, without delay: *I wish you a* ∼*y
recovery* (*from illness*).

spell [1] /spel/ *n* [C] **1** words used as a charm,
supposed to have magic power: *cast a* ∼
over him; put a ∼ *on him; be under a* ∼. **2**
attraction, fascination, exercised by a person, occupation, etc: *the* ∼ *of Mozart's
music.*

'**spell·bound** /-baʊnd/ *adj* with the attention held by a spell: *The speaker held his
audience* ∼*bound.*

spell [2] /spel/ *n* [C] **1** period of time: *a long* ∼
of warm weather; **2** period of activity or
duty, esp one at which two or more persons
take turns: *take* ∼*s at the wheel,* e g of two
persons making a long journey by car.

spell [3] /spel/ *vt,vi* (*pt,pp* ∼ed /speld/ or
spelt /spelt/) **1** name or write the letters of
(a word): *How do you* ∼ *your name? These
children can't* ∼. **2** (of letters) form when
put together in a particular order: *C-A-T* ∼*s
cat.* **3 spell sth out,** make clear and easy to
understand; explain in detail: *My request
seems simple enough—do you want me to* ∼
it out for you? **4** have as a consequence:
Does laziness always ∼ *failure?*

speller person who spells: *a good/poor*
∼*er.*

spell·ing, way a word is spelt: *Do you use
English or American* ∼*ing(s)?*

spelt ⇨ spell [3].

spend /spend/ *vt,vi* (*pt,pp* spent /spent/) **1**
pay out (money) for goods, services, etc: ∼
all one's money. **2** use up; consume: ∼ *a lot
of care/time cleaning the car. They went on
firing until all their ammunition was spent.* **3**
pass: ∼ *a weekend in London.*

spend·er, person who spends money (usually in the way shown by the *adjective*): *an
extravagant* ∼*er.*

'**spend-thrift,** person who spends money
extravagantly.

sperm /spɜːm/ *n* [U] fertilizing fluid of a
male animal.

spew /spjuː/ *vt,vi* = vomit.

sphere /sfɪə(r)/ *n* [C] **1** form of a globe;
star; planet. *music of the spheres,* (*myth*)
music produced by the movement of
heavenly bodies which men cannot hear. **2**
globe representing the earth or the night sky.

3 person's range of interests, activities, surroundings, etc: *gardening is outside the* ∼ *of
my activities.* **4** range, extent: *a* ∼ *of influence.*

spheri·cal /ˈsferɪkəl/ *adj* shaped like a
sphere.

sphe·roid /ˈsfɪərɔɪd/, solid that is almost
spherical.

spice /spaɪs/ *n* **1** [C,U] sorts of substance,
e g ginger, nutmeg, cinnamon, cloves, used
to flavour food. **2** [U] (and with *a, an*) (*fig*)
interesting flavour, suggestion, or trace of:
a story that lacks ∼. *She has a* ∼ *of malice
in her character.* □ *vt* add flavour to (something) with: ∼*d with humour.*

spicy *adj* (-ier, -iest) **(a)** of, flavoured with,
spice. **(b)** (*fig*) exciting or interesting
because a little immoral: *spicy gossip about
a pop star's love life.*

spick /spɪk/ *adj* (only in) **spick and span,**
bright, clean and tidy.

spi·der /ˈspaɪdə(r)/ *n* [C] sorts of creature
with eight legs, many species of which spin
webs for the capture of insects as food.

spid·ery *adj* (of handwriting) with long, thin
strokes.

spied /spaɪd/ *pt,pp* of spy.

spigot /ˈspɪgət/ *n* [C] **1** plug or peg for the
hole of a cask or barrel. **2** valve for controlling the flow of water, etc from a tank, etc.

spike /spaɪk/ *n* [C] **1** sharp point; pointed
piece of metal, e g on iron railings or on
running-shoes. **2** long, pointed cluster of
flowers or grain on a single stem: ∼*s of
lavender.* □ *vt* **1** put spikes (on shoes, etc):
∼*d running-shoes.* **2** pierce or injure with a
spike.

spiky *adj* (-ier, -iest) having sharp points.

spill /spɪl/ *vt,vi* (*pt,pp* spilt /spɪlt/ or ∼ed) **1**
(of liquid or powder) (allow to) run over
the side of the container: *Who has spilt/*∼*ed
the milk?* **2** (of a horse, etc) cause (the rider,
passenger, etc) to fall: *His horse spilt him.* □
n [C] fall from a horse, motor-bike: *have a
nasty* ∼.

'**spill-over,** (often as an *adjective*) (of population) extra: *new towns for London's* ∼*over*
(*population*).

spin /spɪn/ *vt,vi* (*pt* spun /spʌn/ or span
/spæn/, *pp* spun); (-nn-) **1** form (thread)
by twisting wool, cotton, silk, etc; draw out
and twist (wool, cotton, etc) into threads. **2**
form by means of threads: *spiders* ∼*ning
their webs; silkworms* ∼*ning cocoons.* **3**
(*fig*) produce, compose (a story). **spin sth
out,** make it last as long as possible: ∼ *out
the time by talking.* **4** cause (something) to
go round and round: ∼ *a coin,* send it up in
the air, revolving as it goes up, to decide
something (by 'heads or tails'). **5** move
round quickly: *The top was* ∼*ning merrily.
The collision sent the car* ∼*ning across the
road.* □ *n* **1** [U] turning or spinning motion,
esp as given to the ball in some games, e g
cricket, baseball: *The pitcher gave* (*a*) ∼ *to*

the ball. **2** [C] short ride in a motor-car, on a bicycle, etc; *have/go for a* ~. **3** [C] fast spinning movement of an aircraft during a diving descent: *get into/out of a* ~. **in a flat spin,** in a panic.

'spin-`drier, device that spins (clothes) to dry them.

'spin-`dry *vt* (*pt,pp* dried) dry in a spin-drier.

`spin·ning jenny, early kind of machine for spinning more than one thread at a time.

`spinning-wheel, machine for spinning thread continuously on a spindle turned by a large wheel.

`spin-off, incidental benefit or product (from a larger enterprise, or from research for such an enterprise).

spin·ach /'spɪnɪdʒ *US:* -ɪtʃ/ *n* [U] plant with small green leaves, cooked and eaten as a vegetable.

spi·nal /'spaɪnəl/ *adj* (*anat*) of or to the spine: *the* ~ *column,* the backbone.

spindle /'spɪndəl/ *n* [C] **1** (in spinning) thin rod for twisting and winding thread by hand. **2** bar or pin which turns round, or on which something turns (e g an axle or a shaft).

spin·dly /'spɪndlɪ/ *adj* (-ier, -iest) long and thin; (too) tall and thin.

spine /spaɪn/ *n* [C] **1** = backbone. **2** sharp, pointed part on some plants, e g a cactus, and animals, e g a porcupine. **3** part of a book's cover that can be seen when it is on a shelf, usually with the book's title on it.

spine·less *adj* (**a**) having no spine(1). (**b**) (*fig*) without power to make decisions.

spiny *adj*(-ier, -iest) having spines(2).

spinet /spɪ'net *US:* 'spɪnɪt/ *n* [C] old type of keyboard instrument like a harpsichord.

spin·na·ker /'skɪnəkə(r)/ *n* [C] large tri-angular sail on a racing yacht.

spin·ney /'spɪnɪ/ *n* [C] (*pl* ~s) small wood with thick bushes, etc.

spin·ster /'spɪnstə(r)/ *n* [C] (usually offical or legal use) unmarried woman, esp after the conventional age for marrying.

`spin·ster·hood /-hʊd/, being a spinster.

spi·ral /'spaɪərəl/ *adj, n* [C] (in the form of an) advancing or ascending continuous curve winding round a central point: *A snail's shell is* ~. □ *vi* (-ll-, *US* also -l-) move in a spiral: *The smoke* ~*led up.*

spire /'spaɪə(r)/ *n* [C] pointed structure rising above a tower (esp of a church).

spirit /'spɪrɪt/ *n* **1** [C,U] soul; immaterial, intellectual or moral part of man: *The* ~ *is willing but the flesh is weak,* One is willing to do it, but physically unable to do it. **2** [C] the soul thought of as separate from the body: *believe in* ~*s.* **3** [C] elf; goblin. **4** [U] life and consciousness not associated with a body: *God is pure* ~. **5** [C] (always with an *adjective*) person considered from the intellectual, moral or emotional point of view: *What a noble/generous, etc* ~ *he is!* **6** [U] quality of courage, strength, liveliness: *Put a*

little more ~ *into your work.* **7** (*sing* only) mental or moral attitude: *Whether it was unwise or not depends on the* ~ *in which it was done.* **8** [U] real meaning or purpose underlying a law, etc (contrasted with the apparent meaning of the words, etc): *obey the* ~, *not the letter, of the law.* **9** (*pl*) state of mind: *in high* ~*s,* cheerful; *in poor/low* ~*s, out of* ~*s,* depressed, unhappy. **10** (*sing* only) influence or tendency that causes development: *We cannot resist the* ~ *of the age.* **11** [U] industrial alcohol. **12** (usually *pl*) strong alcoholic drink (e g whisky, brandy, gin, rum). □ *vt* take a person or thing quickly, secretly or mysteriously: *She has disappeared as completely as if she had been* ~*ed away to another planet.*

`spirit-level, (piece of wood with a) glass tube partly filled with water or alcohol, with a bubble or air which, when centred, shows that a surface is horizontal.

spir·ited /'spɪrɪtɪd/ *adj* (**a**) full of spirit(6): *a* ~*ed attack/defence/reply.* (**b**) having the kind of spirits(9) shown: **'high-/`low-/ `~**ed, happy/depressed.

spiri·tual /'spɪrɪtʃʊəl/ *adj* **1** of the spirit(1) or soul; of religion, not of material things; of, from, God; *concerned about one's* ~ *welfare.* **2** of spirits(2); supernatural. **3** caring much for things of the spirit(1). **4** of the church. □ *n* [C] religious song as sung by Negroes in the US.

spiri·tu·al·ly /-tʃʊlɪ/ *adv*

spiri·tu·al·ism /'spɪrɪtʃʊlɪzm/ *n* [U] belief in the possibility of receiving messages from the spirits of the dead; practice of attempting to do this.

spiri·tu·al·ist /-ɪst/, believer in spiritualism

spiri·tu·al·is·tic /'spɪrɪtʃʊ'lɪstɪk/ *adj*

spirt /spɜt/ *vi n* [C] = spurt.

spit[1] /spɪt/ *n* [C] **1** long thin metal spike on which to fix meat, etc for roasting. **2** small, narrow point of land running out into a sea, lake, etc. □ *vt* (-pp-) put a spit through (a chicken, piece of meat, etc).

spit[2] /spɪt/ *vt,vi* (*pt,pp* spat /spæt/) (-tt-) **1** send liquid (saliva) out from the mouth; do this as a sign of contempt or hatred: *He spat in the man's face/spat at him. The cat spat* (= made an angry spitting noise) *at the dog.* **2** send (out) from the mouth: ~ *out a pip.* **3** (*fig*) say angrily or sharply: *She spat* (*out*) *curses at me.* **4** (of a fire, gun, etc) make the noise of spitting (while sending out something): *The frying-pan was* ~*ting.* **5** (of rain or snow) fall lightly: *It's not raining heavily, only* ~*ting.* □ *n* **1** [U] = spittle (the usual word). **2** act of spitting. **3** *the spit and/spitting image of,* exact replica or likeness of: *He's the* ~*ting image of his father.*

spit[3] /spɪt/ *n* [C] depth of a spade.

spite /spaɪt/ *n* **1** [U] desire to cause pain or damage: *do something out of/from* ~. *in spite of,* not to be prevented by; although: *They went out in* ~ *of the rain. In* ~ *of all*

his efforts (= Although he tried) *he failed.* □
vt injure or annoy because of spite: *The
neighbours let their radio blare every afternoon just to ∼ us.*

spite·ful /-fəl/ *adj* having, showing, spite.
spite·fully /-fəlɪ/ *adv*
spite·ful·ness *n* [U]

spittle /ˈspɪtəl/ *n* [U] liquid of the mouth.

splash /splæʃ/ *vt,vi* **1** cause (a liquid) to be
flung about in drops; make (a person or
thing) wet: *Children love to ∼ water over
one another.* **2** (of a liquid) be flung about
and fall in drops: *fountains ∼ing in the park.*
3 move, fall, so that there is splashing: *The
spacecraft ∼ed down in the Pacific.* Hence,
`**splash·down**, landing of a spacecraft in the
sea. □ *n* [C] **1** (sound, spot, mark, made by)
splashing: *He jumped into the swimming
pool with a ∼.* **2** patch of colour: *Her dog is
brown with white ∼es.*

splay /spleɪ/ *vt,vi* make the distance
between opposite sides (of an opening)
wider; cause to slant or slope □ *n* [C] sloping side (of a window opening, etc).

spleen /spliːn/ *n* [C] (*anat*) organ in the
abdomen which causes changes in the blood.

splen·did /ˈsplendɪd/ *adj* **1** magnificent: *a
∼ sunset/house/victory; ∼ jewellery.* **2**
(*informal*) excellent: *a ∼ dinner/idea.*
splen·did·ly *adv*

splen·dour (*US* = **-dor**) /ˈsplendə(r)/ *n*
[U] (sometimes *pl*) magnificence; brightness: *the ∼ of the moonlight over the sea.*

splice /splaɪs/ *vt* **1** join (two ends of rope)
by twisting the threads of one into those of
the other. **2** join (two pieces of wood, magnetic tape, film) by fastening them at the
ends. **3** *get spliced*, (*sl*) get married. □ *n*
[C] joint made by splicing.

splint /splɪnt/ *n* [C] strip of wood, etc
strapped to an arm, leg, etc to keep a broken
bone in the right position.

splin·ter /ˈsplɪntə(r)/ *n* [C] sharp piece of
hard material (wood, metal, glass, etc) split,
torn or broken off a larger piece: *have a ∼ in
one's finger.* □ *vt,vi* break into splinters.
`**splinter group/party**, (in politics) group of
persons who have broken away from their
party.

split /splɪt/ *vt,vi* (*pt,pp* split) (**-tt-**) **1** break,
cause to break, be broken, into two or more
parts, esp from end to end along the line of
natural division: *Some kinds of wood ∼
easily.* **2** break open by bursting: *His coat
has ∼ at the seams.* *a splitting headache,*
so severe that it feels that one's head may
break. **3** (cause to) break into parts; divide:
The party ∼ up into small groups. *split the
difference,* (when making a bargain) compromise (on the price, cost, etc). *split hairs,*
make very fine distinctions (in an argument,
etc). *split one's sides (with laughter),*
laugh with movements of the sides. **4** (*sl*)
give away a secret or information about a
person (to his disadvantage). □ *n* [C] **1** (crack

or tear made by splitting): *Will you sew up
this ∼ in my trousers?* **2** separation or division resulting from splitting: *a ∼ in the
Labour Party.* **3** *the splits,* acrobat's feat of
sitting on the floor with legs stretched out in
a line with the trunk upright: *do the ∼s.*

split mind/personality, = schizophrenia
split second, a brief moment.

splut·ter /ˈsplʌtə(r)/ *vi,vt* speak quickly,
confusedly (from excitement, etc): *∼ out a
few words/a threat.* □ *n* [U] spluttering
sound.

spoil /spɔɪl/ *vt,vi* (*pt,pp* ∼t or ∼ed) **1** make
useless or unsatisfactory: *fruit ∼t by insects;
holidays ∼t by bad weather.* **2** harm the
character or temperament of by too much
kindness or lack of discipline: *parents who
∼ their children.* **3** pay great attention to the
comfort and wishes of: *He likes having a
wife who ∼s him.* **4** (of food, etc) become
bad, unfit for use: *Some kinds of food soon
∼.* □ *n* **1** (either [U] or *pl*, not with numerals)
stolen goods: *The thieves divided up the
∼(s).* **2** (*pl*) profits, profitable positions,
gained from political power: *the ∼s of
office.* **3** [U] earth, unwanted material, etc
thrown or brought up in excavating, draining, etc.

`**spoil·sport**, person who does things that
interfere with the enjoyment of other people.

spoke[1] /spəʊk/ *n* [C] any one of the bars or
wire rods connecting the hub (centre) of a
wheel with the rim (outer edge).

spoke[2], **spoken** /spəʊk, ˈspəʊkən/ ⇨
speak.

spokes·man /ˈspəʊksmən/ *n* [C] (*pl*
-men) person speaking, chosen to speak on
behalf of a group.

sponge /spʌndʒ/ *n* **1** [C] kinds of simple
sea-animal; its body made of elastic material
full of holes and able to absorb water easily;
one of these, or something similar, used for
washing, cleaning, etc. **2** piece of absorbent
material, eg gauze, used in surgery. **3** =
sponge-cake. □ *vt,vi* **1** wash, wipe or clean
with a sponge: *∼ a wound/a child's face.* **2**
take up (liquid) with a sponge: *∼ up the
mess.* **3** (*informal*) obtain money from a
person, without giving, or intending to give,
anything in return: *∼ on one's friends.*
`**sponge-cake**, soft cake like a sponge
sponger, person who sponges(3).
spongy *adj* (**-ier, -iest**)

spon·sor /ˈsponsə(r)/ *n* [C] **1** person (e g a
godfather) making himself responsible for
another. **2** person who first puts forward or
guarantees a proposal. □ *vt* act as a sponsor
for.

spon·ta·neous /sponˈteɪnɪəs/ *adj* done,
happening, from natural impulse, not suggested: *He made a ∼ offer of help*
spon·ta·neous·ly *adv*
spon·ta·neity /ˌspontəˈneɪətɪ/ *n* [U]

spook /spuːk/ *n* [C] ghost.
spooky *adj* (**-ier, -iest**) of, suggesting,

ghosts: *a* ~y (= *haunted*) *house*.

spool /spuːl/ *n* [C] reel (for thread, wire, photographic film, magnetic tape, etc).

spoon¹ /spuːn/ *n* [C] utensil with a shallow bowl on a handle, used for stirring, serving and taking up food (named according to use) *a*: *des`sert-/`soup-/`table-/`tea*~. □ *vt* take with a spoon: ~ *up one's soup;* ~ *out the peas,* serve them.

`**spoon·feed** *vt* (a) feed (a baby, etc) from a spoon. (b) (*fig*) give (a person) much help or teaching: *Some teachers* ~*feed their pupils.*

`**spoon·ful** /-ful/ *n* [C] (*pl* ~fuls) as much as a spoon can hold.

spoon² /spuːn/ *vi* (*dated*) behave in a way that shows that one is in love: *young couples* ~*ing on park seats.*

spor·adic /spəˈrædɪk/ *adj* occurring, seen, only here and there or occasionally: ~ *raids/firing.*

spor·adi·cally /-klɪ/ *adv*

spore /spɔː(r)/ *n* [C] germ, single cell, by which a flowerless plant (e g moss, a fern) reproduces itself.

spor·ran /ˈspɔrən/ *n* [C] pouch worn in front of a kilt.

sport /spɔːt/ *n* **1** [U] activity engaged in, esp outdoors, for amusement and exercise; [C] particular form of such activity: *fond of* ~; *athletic* ~*s*, e g running, jumping; `~*s coverage/reporting on T V.* **2** (*pl*) meeting for athletic contests: *the school* ~*s.* **3** (*informal*) unselfish, kind person: *Be a* ~ *and help me with this suitcase.* □ *vi,vt* **1** play about, amuse oneself: *seals* ~*ing about in the water.* **2** (*informal*) have or wear proudly: ~ *a moustache/a diamond ring.*

`**sports·car,** small motor-car designed for high speeds.

`**sports·man, (a)** person who takes part in, is fond of, sport. (b) = sport(3). Hence, `**sports·man·ship** /-ʃɪp/ *n* [U]

sport·ing *adj* (a) connected with, interested in, sport: *a* ~*ing man.* (b) willing to take a risk of losing; involving a risk of losing: *give her a* ~*ing chance.*

sport·ing·ly *adv*

spot /spɒt/ *n* [C] **1** small (esp round) mark different in colour from what it is on. *Which has* ~*s, the leopard or the tiger?* **knock spots off sb,** do much better than him. **2** dirty mark or stain: ~*s of mud on your boots.* **3** small, red place on the skin: *This ointment won't clear your face of* ~*s.* **4** (*fig*) moral stain: *There isn't a* ~ *on her reputation.* **5** drop: *Did you feel a few* ~*s of rain?* **6** particular place or area: *the (very)* ~ *where he was murdered.* **on the spot, (a)** at the place where one is needed: *The police were on the* ~ *within a few minutes.* **(b)** immediately: *The bullet struck his head and he was killed on the* ~. **find/put one's finger on sb's `weak spot,** find the point (of character, etc) where he is most open to attack. **7** (*GB informal*) small quantity of

anything: *I need a* ~ *of brandy. He's having a* ~ *of bother with his brother,* a quarrel. □ *vt,vi* (-tt-) **1** mark, become marked, with spots: *a table* ~*ted with ink.* **2** pick out, recognize, see (one person or thing out of many): ~ *a friend in a crowd.*

spot check, sudden check without warning.

spot·ted *adj* marked with spots, e g of animals or material.

spot·less *adj* free from spots; clean: *a* ~*less kitchen/reputation.*

spot·less·ly *adv:* ~*lessly clean.*

spotty *adj* (-ier, -iest) **(a)** marked with spots (on the skin): *a* ~*ty complexion.* **(b)** of varying quality: *a* ~*ty piece of work,* done unevenly.

spot·light /ˈspɒtlaɪt/ *n* [C] (projector or lamp used for sending a) strong light directed on to a particular place or person, e g on the stage of a theatre. **be in/hold the spotlight,** (*fig*) be the centre of attention. □ *vt* direct a spotlight on to.

spouse /spaʊz *US:* spaʊs/ *n* [C] (*legal*) husband or wife.

spout /spaʊt/ *n* [C] **1** pipe through or from which liquid pours, e g for tea from a teapot. **2** stream of liquid coming out with great force. ⇨ waterspout. **3** *up the spout,* (*sl*) in difficulties, broken, etc according to context. □ *vt,vi* **1** (of liquid) come or send out with great force: *blood* ~*ing from a severed artery.* **2** (*informal*) speak, recite (verses, etc) pompously: ~*ing political slogans.*

sprain /spreɪn/ *vt* injure (a joint, e g in the wrist or ankle) by twisting violently so that there is pain and swelling: ~ *one's wrist.* □ *n* [C] injury so caused.

sprang /spræŋ/ *pt* of spring³.

sprat /spræt/ *n* [C] small European sea-fish used as food.

sprawl /sprɔːl/ *vi* **1** sit or lie with the arms and legs loosely spread out; fall so that one lies in this way: ~*ing on the sofa; be sent* ~*ing in the mud.* **2** (of plants, handwriting) spread out loosely and irregularly. **3** (*fig*) (of towns) spread over much space: *suburbs that* ~ *out into the countryside.* □ *n* [C] sprawling position, movement or area.

spray¹ /spreɪ/ *n* [C] small branch of a tree or plant, esp as an ornament; artificial ornament in a similar form: *a* ~ *of diamonds.*

spray² /spreɪ/ *n* **1** [U] liquid sent through the air in tiny drops (by the wind, or through an apparatus): `*sea-*~. **2** [C,U] kinds of liquid preparation, e g a perfume, disinfectant or insecticide, to be applied in the form of spray. **3** [C] device that sprays (perfume, etc). □ *vt* scatter spray on: ~ *fruit-trees.*

`**spray·gun,** apparatus using pressure to spread cellulose, paint, varnish, etc over surfaces.

sprayer, (a) person who sprays. **(b)** apparatus for spraying.

spread /spred/ *vt,vi* (*pt,pp* ~) **1** extend the surface or width of something by unfolding or unrolling it: ~ *out a map;* ~ *(out) one's arms. The bird* ~ *its wings.* **2** cover by spreading: ~ *a table with a cloth.* **3** put (a substance) on a surface and extend its area by flattening, etc; cover (a surface) by doing this: ~ *butter on bread/a slice of bread with butter.* **spread the table,** place dishes, glasses, food, etc on it ready for a meal. **4** (cause to) become more widely extended or distributed: ~ *knowledge. Flies* ~ *disease. The water* ~ *over the floor. The rumour quickly* ~ *through the village. The fire* ~ *from the factory to the houses near by.* **5** extend in space: *a desert* ~*ing for hundreds of miles.* **6** extend in time: *a course of studies* ~ *over three years; payments* ~ *over twelve months.* □ *n* [C] (rarely *pl*) **1** extent; breadth: *the* ~ *of a bird's wings.* **2** extension; spreading(4): *the* ~ *of disease/knowledge/education.* **3** (*informal*) table with good things to eat and drink on it: *What a* ~*!* **4** something that is spread(1) (usually in compounds): *a* `*bed*~, a cover spread over the bed-clothes. **5** name used for various kinds of paste (to be) spread on bread, etc.

`**spread-eagle** *vt* (*reflexive*) take up a lying position with arms and legs extended to form a cross: *sunbathers* ~*eagled on the grass.*

spreader, person who, that which, spreads, e g an implement used for spreading paste, etc on bread.

spree /spri/ *n* [C]: *have a* ~, have a lively, merry time; *a* `*spending/*`*buying* ~,· an occasion of (extravagant or unusual) spending of money. **be on the spree/go out on a spree,** be having/go out to enjoy, a spree.

sprig /sprɪg/ *n* [C] small twig (*of* a plant or bush) with leaves, etc: *a* ~ *of holly.*

spright·ly /ˈspraɪtlɪ/ *adj* (-ier, -iest) lively; brisk.

spright·li·ness *n* [U]

spring[1] /sprɪŋ/ *n* [C] **1** act of springing or jumping up. **2** (place where there is) water coming up from the ground: *a* `*hot-*~; `*mineral-*~. **3** device of twisted, bent or coiled metal or wire which tends to return to its shape or position when pulled or pushed or pressed: *the* ~ *of a watch.* **4** [U] elastic quality: *rubber bands that have lost their* ~. **5** (often *pl*) cause or origin: *the* ~*s of human conduct.*

'**spring-`balance,** device that measures weight by the tension of a spring.

`**spring-board,** board to give a springing motion to a person jumping from it.

springy *adj* (-ier, -iest) (of movement or substances) elastic; that springs: *walk with a youthful* ~*y step.*

spring[2] /sprɪŋ/ *n* [C] season of the year in which vegetation begins; season between winter and summer: *in* (*the*) ~; (as an *adjective*) ~ *flowers/weather.*

'**spring-`clean** *vt* clean (a house, a room) thoroughly. Hence, '**spring-`cleaning** *n*.

`**spring·time,** (also `**spring·tide**), season or spring.

`**spring·like** *adj:* ~*like weather.*

spring[3] /sprɪŋ/ *vi,vt* (*pt* sprang /spræŋ/, *pp* sprung /sprʌŋ/) **1** jump suddenly from the ground; move suddenly (*up, down, out,* etc) from rest, concealment, etc: *He sprang to his feet/sprang out of bed/sprang out from behind the bush/sprang up from his seat. The branch sprang back and hit me in the face.* **2** grow up quickly from the ground or from a stem: *Weeds were* ~*ing up everywhere.* **3** (*fig*) appear suddenly: *A suspicion/doubt sprang up in her mind.* **4** appear suddenly: *Where have you sprung from?* **5** bring forward suddenly: *He sprang a surprise on me.* **6** cause to operate by means of a mechanism: ~ *a trap,* cause it to go off. **7** **spring a leak,** (of a ship, etc) crack or burst so that water enters.

spring·bok /ˈsprɪŋbok/ *n* [C] small, Southern African gazelle.

sprinkle /ˈsprɪŋkəl/ *vt* direct, throw, a shower of (something) on to (a surface): ~ *water on a dusty path;* ~ *the floor with sand.*

sprink·ler /ˈsprɪŋklə(r)/, (esp) apparatus or device for sprinkling water (e g on to a lawn) or (permanently installed in buildings) for fighting fire.

sprink·ling, small quantity or number: *There was a sprinkling of young people in the audience.*

sprint /sprɪnt/ *vi* run a short distance at full speed: *He* ~*ed past his competitors just before reaching the tape.* □ *n* [C] such a run; (esp) a short race.

sprin·ter, person who sprints.

sprite /spraɪt/ *n* [C] fairy; elf.

sprout /spraʊt/ *vi,vt* **1** put out leaves; begin to grow: *Peter has really* ~*ed up in the past year.* **2** cause to grow: *The continuous wet weather has* ~*ed the wheat.* **3** develop, produce: *Tom has* ~*ed a moustache.* □ *n* [C] **1** new part of a plant. **2** = Brussels sprout.

spruce[1] /sprus/ *adj* neat and smart in dress and appearance. □ *vt,vi* make oneself smart: *Go and* ~ *yourself up.*

spruce·ly *adv*

spruce·ness *n* [U]

spruce[2] /sprus/ *n* [C,U] (also `~ *fir*) kinds of fir-tree grown in plantations for its wood, used for making paper.

sprung /sprʌŋ/ *pp* of spring[3].

spry /spraɪ/ *adj* (-er, -est) lively: *still* ~ *at eighty.* **look spry,** be quick.

spud /spʌd/ *n* [C] (*sl*) potato.

spue /spju/ *vt,vi* = spew.

spume /spjum/ *n* [U] foam; froth.

spun /spʌn/ *pp* of spin.

spunk /spʌŋk/ *n* [U] (*informal*) courage: *a boy with plenty of* ~.

spur /spɜ(r)/ *n* [C] **1** one of a pair of sharp-toothed wheels on the heels of a rider's boots and used to make the horse go faster **2** (*fig*) something that urges a person on to greater activity: *the ~ of poverty*. **act on the spur of the moment,** act on a sudden impulse. **3** ridge extending from a mountain or hill. □ *vt,vi* (-rr-) urge on with, or as with, spurs: *He was ~red on by ambition.*

spu·ri·ous /ˈspjʊərɪəs/ *adj* (*formal*) false; not genuine: *a ~ argument.*
spu·ri·ous·ly *adv*

spurn /spɜːn/ *vt* reject or refuse; have nothing to do with (an offer, a person or his advances).

spurt /spɜːt/ *vi* **1** (of liquids, flame, etc) come out in a sudden burst: *Blood ~ed (out) from the wound.* **2** make a sudden, short and violent effort, esp in a race or other contest: *The runner ~ed as he approached the winning-post.* □ *n* [C] sudden bursting forth; sudden burst of energy: *~s of water/ flame/energy; put on a ~* (= increase speed) *towards the end of a race.*

sput·ter /ˈspʌtə(r)/ *vi* **1** make a series of spitting sounds: *The sausages were ~ing in the frying-pan.* **2** = splutter(1,2).

spu·tum /ˈspjuːtəm/ *n* [U] matter coughed up from the throat.

spy /spaɪ/ *n* [C] (*pl* spies) **1** person who tries to get secret information, esp about the military affairs of other countries. **2** person who keeps a secret watch on the movements of others: *industrial spies,* employed to learn trade secrets, etc. □ *vi,vt* **1** act as a spy on, watch secretly: *~ on the enemy's movements; ~ out the land.* **2** observe; see; discover: *I ~ someone coming up the garden path.*
ˈspy-glass, small telescope.

squabble /ˈskwɒbəl/ *vi* engage in a petty or noisy quarrel: *Tom was squabbling with his sister about who should use the bicycle.* □ *n* [C] noisy small quarrel.

squad /skwɒd/ *n* [C] small group of persons, e g of soldiers, working or being trained together.
ˈsquad car, (*US*) police patrol car.

squad·ron /ˈskwɒdrən/ *n* [C] **1** sub-unit of a cavalry, armoured or engineer regiment (120—200 men). **2** number of warships or military aircraft forming a unit.

squalid /ˈskwɒlɪd/ *adj* dirty, poor, uncared for: *living in ~ conditions/houses.*
squalid·ly *adv*

squall /skwɔːl/ *n* [C] **1** loud cry of pain or fear (esp from a baby or child). **2** sudden violent wind, often with rain or snow. □ *vi* utter squalls(1): *~ing babies.*

squalor /ˈskwɒlə(r)/ *n* [U] squalid state: *born in ~; the ~ of the slums.*

squan·der /ˈskwɒndə(r)/ *vt* waste (time, money),

square¹ /skweə(r)/ *adj* **1** having the shape of a square(1): *a ~ table.* **2** having or forming (exactly or approximately) a right angle: *~ corners; a ~ jaw/chin,* with angular, not curved, outlines **3** level or parallel (*with*);

balanced; settled: *get one's accounts ~,* settled. **be (all) square,** neither in debt to the other: *Let's call it all ~, shall we?* **4** connected with a number multiplied by itself: *a ~ metre,* an area equal to that of a square surface which has sides of one metre: *nine ~ cm. The ~ root of x⁴ is x²/of 9 is 3* **5** thorough; uncompromising: *meet with a ~ refusal.* **a square meal,** one that is satisfactory because there is plenty of good food. **6** fair, honest: *~ dealings,* in business. **7** (*fig*) (of a person) formal, conventional, old-fashioned. □ *adv* **1** in a square(2) manner: *stand/sit ~; hit a man ~ on the jaw.* **2** fair and square, in a square(6) manner.
ˈsquare-ˈbuilt *adj* (of a person) of comparatively broad shape.
ˈsquare dance/game, one in which the dancers/players face inwards from four sides.
ˈsquare-ˈshouldered *adj* with the shoulders at right angles to the neck, not sloping.
ˈsquare-toed *adj* (of shoes) having a square toe-cap.
square·ly *adv* (a) so as to form a right angle. (b) fairly; honestly: *act ~ly.* (c) directly opposite: *He faced me ~ly across the table.*
square·ness *n* [U]

square² /skweə(r)/ *n* [C] **1** shape, area, with four equal sides and four right angles (□). **back to square one,** back to the starting-point and forced to start again. **2** anything having the shape of a square. **3** four-sided open area, e g in a town, used as a garden or for recreation, or one enclosed by streets and buildings: *listening to the band playing in the ~.* **4** buildings and streets surrounding a square(3): *He lives at No 95 Russell S~.* **5** block of buildings bounded by four streets; distance along one side. **6** result when a number or quantity is multiplied by itself: *The ~ of 7 is 49.* **7** L-shaped or (ˈT-**square**) T-shaped instrument for drawing or testing right angles. **8** (*sl*) person (considered to be) square(7).
ˈsquare-bashing, (*sl*) military drill.

square³ /skweə(r)/ *vt,vi* **1** make square; give a square shape to. **2** cause one line or side to make a right angle with another: *~ timber.* **3** make straight or level: *~ one's shoulders.* **4** multiply a number by itself: *Three ~d is nine.* **5** mark (*off*) in squares. **6** settle, balance (accounts): *~ up on Friday.* **7** (*fig*) have one's revenge: *~ accounts with an enemy.* **8** make or be consistent: *It would help if the facts ~d with the theory, but they do not.* **9** take up the attitude of a boxer (ready to begin fighting).

squash¹ /skwɒʃ/ *vt,vi* **1** press flat or into a small space: *~ too many people into a bus.* **2** become squashed or pressed out of shape: *Soft fruits ~ easily.* **3** squeeze or crowd: *Don't all try to ~ into the lift together.* **4** (*informal*) silence (a person) with a clever, sarcastic, etc reply, statement: *He was/felt* *completely* ∼ed. **5** (*informal*) defeat (a rebellion). □ *n* [C] (rarely *pl*) **1** crowd of persons squashed together: *There was a frightful* ∼ *at the gate.* **2** (sound of) something squashing or being squashed: *The ripe tomato hit the speaker in the face with a* ∼. **3** [C,U] drink made from fruit juice: `*orange*⌃*lemon* ∼.

squash² /skwoʃ/ *n* [U] (also `∼ *rackets*) game played with rackets and a rubber ball in a walled court.

squash³ /skwoʃ/ *n* [U] (*pl* unchanged) kinds of gourd, like a pumpkin, eaten as a vegetable.

squat /skwot/ *vi* (-tt-) **1** sit on one's heels, or on the ground with the legs drawn up under or close to the body: *The old man* ∼*ted in front of the fire.* **2** (of animals) crouch with the body close to the ground. **3** (*informal*) sit: *Find somewhere to* ∼. **4** settle on land without permission, esp publicly owned and unoccupied land (in order to acquire ownership); occupy empty (usually deserted, derelict) buildings without authority. □ *adj* short and thick: *a* ∼ *man*.

squat·ter, (**a**) person who squats(1). (**b**) person who squats(4).

squaw /skwɔ/ *n* [C] North American Indian woman or wife.

squawk /skwɔk/ *vi, n* [C] **1** *n* (chiefly of birds) (make a) loud, harsh cry, as when hurt or frightened. **2** (*informal*) (make a) loud complaint. **3** (*sl*) betray: *The old man* ∼ed (*to the police*).

squawker, person, bird, that squawks.

squeak /skwik/ *n* [C] **1** short, shrill cry, e g made by a mouse, or similar sound, e g from an unoiled hinge. **2** *a narrow squeak,* a narrow escape from danger or failure. □ *vi, vt* **1** make a squeak: *These new shoes* ∼. **2** (*informal*) become an informer.

squeaky *adj* (-ier, -iest) squeaking: ∼*y* shoes.

squeal /skwil/ *n* [C] shrill cry or sound, longer and louder than a squeak, often showing terror or pain: *the* ∼ *of brakes,* e g on lorries. □ *vi, vt* **1** make a squeal: *The pigs were* ∼*ing. He* ∼*ed like a pig.* **2** say in a squealing voice. **3** (*informal*) become an informer.

squealer, (**a**) animal that squeals. (**b**) (*sl*) informer.

squeam·ish /ˈskwimɪʃ/ *adj* **1** having a delicate stomach and easily made sick; feeling sick. **2** too easily disgusted or offended.

squeam·ish·ly *adv*

squeam·ish·ness *n*

squeeze /skwiz/ *vt, vi* **1** press on from the opposite side or from all sides; change the shape, size, etc of something by doing this: ∼ *her hand;* ∼ *a sponge;* ∼ *one's fingers,* e g by catching them in a doorway. **2** get (water, juice, etc) out of something by pressing hard: ∼ (*the juice out of*) *a lemon;* ∼ *the water out.* **3** force (a person, oneself)

into or through a narrow passage or small space: ∼ (*one's way*) *into a crowded bus;* ∼ (*oneself*) *through a gap in a hedge.* **4** get by force, entreaty, etc: ∼ *more money out of the public,* e g by increasing taxes. **5** give in to pressure: *Sponges* ∼ *easily.* □ *n* [C] **1** act of squeezing; condition of being squeezed; something obtained by squeezing: *give her a hug and a* ∼. *a tight squeeze,* (**a**) closely packed crowd. (**b**) a narrow victory, escape, etc. **2** [U] (*informal*) policy of high taxation, high interest rates, etc aimed at deflation; [U] money obtained by squeezing(4).

squeezer, person, thing, that squeezes, e g a device for squeezing out juice: *a* `*lemon-* ∼*r*.

squelch /skweltʃ/ *vi, vt* make a sucking sound as when feet are lifted from stiff, sticky mud: *cows* ∼*ing through the mud.* □ *n* [C] squelching sound or act.

squid /skwɪd/ *n* [C] kind of sea-animal with ten long arms round the mouth.

squiggle /ˈskwɪgəl/ *n* [C] small twisty line or scrawl: *Is this* ∼ *supposed to be his signature?*

squint /skwɪnt/ *vi* **1** have eyes that do not turn together but look in different directions at once. **2** look at sideways or with half-shut eyes or through a narrow opening. □ *n* [C] squinting position of the eyeballs: *a man with a* ∼.

squire /ˈskwaɪə(r)/ *n* [C] **1** (*dated*) (in England) chief landowner in a country parish. **2** (in olden times) young man who was a knight's attendant until he himself became a knight.

squirm /skwɜm/ *vi* twist the body, wriggle (from discomfort, shame or embarrassment). □ *n* [C] squirming movement.

squir·rel /ˈskwɪrəl US: ˈskwɜrəl/ *n* [C] (kinds of) small, tree-climbing, bushy-tailed animal with red or grey fur.

squirt /skwɜt/ *vt, vi* (of liquid, powder) force out, be forced out, in a thin stream or jet: *The water* ∼*ed all over me.* □ *n* [C] **1** thin stream or jet (of liquid, powder, etc). **2** something from which liquid, etc can be squirted, e g a syringe. **3** (*informal*) insignificant, nasty person.

stab /stæb/ *vt, vi* (-bb-) **1** pierce or wound with a sharp-pointed weapon or instrument: e g a knife: ∼ *a man in the back.* **2** produce a sensation of being stabbed: ∼*bing pains in the back.* □ *n* [C] **1** stabbing blow; pain caused by this. **2** (*informal*) try, attempt: *Let me have a* ∼ *at it,* try to do it.

stab·ber, person who stabs.

stable¹ /ˈsteɪbəl/ *adj* (-er, -est) firm; fixed; not likely to move or change: *What we need is a* ∼ *Government. He needs a* ∼ *job.*

sta·bil·ity /stəˈbɪlətɪ/ *n* [U] quality of being stable.

sta·bil·ize /ˈsteɪbəlaɪz/ *vt* make stable: ∼ *prices and wages.*

sta·bi·lizer, person or thing that stabilizes.

sta·bil·iz·ation /ˌsteɪbəlaɪˈzeɪʃən US: -lɪˈz-/ n [U] making, becoming, stable.

stable² /ˈsteɪbəl/ n [C] **1** building in which horses are kept and fed. **2** number of horses (esp race-horses) belonging to one particular owner and kept in one set of stables. □ vt put, keep, in a stable: *Where did you ~ your horse?*

stack /stæk/ n [C] **1** pile of hay, straw, grain, etc usually with a sloping top, for storage in the open. **2** group of rifles arranged in the form of a pyramid. **3** pile or heap (of books, papers, wood, etc). **4** (*informal*) large amount: *I have ~s of work waiting to be done.* **5** (brickwork or stonework enclosing a) number of chimneys. **6** rack with shelves for books (in a library or bookshop). **7** number of aircraft circling at different heights while waiting for instructions to land. □ vt make into a stack; pile up.

sta·dium /ˈsteɪdɪəm/ n [C] (pl ~s) enclosed area of land for games, athletic competitions, etc, with seats, etc for spectators: *a new Olympic ~.*

staff /stɑːf US: stæf/ n [C] **1** strong stick used as a support when walking or climbing, or as a weapon. **2** such a stick as a sign of office or authority: *a pastoral ~*, e g an ornamental one carried by or before a bishop, etc. **3** pole serving as a support: *a ˈflag~.* **4** group of assistants working together under a manager or head: *the headmaster and his ~*, i e the teachers; `office-~. **5** group of senior army officers engaged in planning and organization: *the General S~*; (as an adjective) `~ officers. **6** (*music*) (pl staves /ˈsteɪvz/) set of five parallel lines or on between which symbols for notes are placed. □ vt provide with, act as, a staff(4): *a well-~ed hotel/ hospital.*

stag /stæg/ n [C] male deer.

`**stag party**, (*informal*) party for men only, usually for a man about to get married.

stage /steɪdʒ/ n [C] **1** (in a theatre) raised platform or structure of boards on which the actors appear. **2** the ~, theatrical work; the profession of acting in theatres. *be/go on the stage*, be/become an actor or actress. **3** (*fig*) scene of action; place where events occur. **4** point, period or step in development: *at an early ~ in our history. The baby has reached the `talking ~*, is learning to talk. **5** any of two or more successive periods on the journey of a spacecraft: *a multi-~ rocket.* **6** journey, distance, between two stopping-places along a road or route; such a stopping-place: *travel by easy ~s*, for only a short distance at a time. **7** = stage-coach. ⇨ also landing-stage. □ vt,vi **1** put on the stage(1); put before the public: *~ 'Hamlet'.* *stage a come-back*, come back (to a sport, e g to the boxing ring) from retirement or after having failed. **2** *~ well/badly*, (of a drama) be well/badly suited for the theatre.

`**stage-coach**, horse-drawn vehicle formerly carrying passengers (and often mail) along a regular route.

`**stage-craft**, skill or experience in writing or directing plays.

`**stage direction**, printed direction in a play to actors about their positions, movements, etc.

'**stage `door**, entrance at the back of a theatre, used by actors, etc.

`**stage fright**, nervousness felt when facing an audience.

'**stage `manager**, person who organizes scenery and props, etc, supervises the rehearsals, etc.

`**stage-struck** adj having a strong desire to become an actor or actress.

'**stage-`whisper**, whisper that is meant to be overheard.

stag·ger /ˈstæɡə(r)/ vi,vt **1** walk or move unsteadily (from weakness, a heavy burden, drunkenness, etc): *The man ~ed along/to his feet/across the room/from side to side of the pavement.* **2** (of a blow or shock) cause to walk or move unsteadily. **3** (of news, etc) shock deeply; cause worry or confusion to: *I was ~ed to hear/on hearing/when I heard that the firm was bankrupt.* **4** arrange (times of events) so that they do not all occur together: *~ office hours*, so that employees are not all using buses, trains, etc at the same time. □ n (sing) staggering movement.

stag·ing /ˈsteɪdʒɪŋ/ n **1** [C,U] (platform or working area on) scaffolding for men on constructional work, e g building. **2** [U] (method of) presenting a play on the stage of a theatre.

stag·nant /ˈstæɡnənt/ adj **1** (of water) without current or tide: *water lying ~ in ponds and ditches.* **2** (*fig*) unchanging; inactive: *Business was ~ last week.*

stag·nancy /-nənsɪ/ n [U]

stag·nate /stæɡˈneɪt US: ˈstæɡneɪt/ vi **1** be stagnant. **2** (*fig*) be or become dull through disuse, inactivity, etc.

stag·na·tion /stæɡˈneɪʃən/ n [U]

staid /steɪd/ adj (of persons, their appearance, behaviour, etc) conservative, quiet and serious.

staid·ly adv

staid·ness n [U]

stain /steɪn/ vt,vi **1** (of liquids, other substances) change the colour of; make coloured patches or dirty marks on: *blood-~ed hands.* **2** colour (wood, fabrics, etc) with a substance that soaks into the material: *He ~ed the wood brown.* **3** (of material) become discoloured or soiled: *Does this material ~ easily?* □ n **1** [U] liquid used for staining wood, etc. **2** [C] stained place; dirty mark or patch of colour: `ink-/`blood-~s. **3** [C] (*fig*) blemish: *a ~ on your character.*

stain·less adj **(a)** without a blemish: *a ~less reputation.* **(b)** (esp of a kind of steel alloy) that resists rust and corrosion: *~less*

645

steel cutlery.

stained glass, glass made by mixing into it transparent colours during the process of manufacture: ~*ed glass windows in a church.*

stair /steə(r)/ n [C] (any one of a) series of fixed steps leading from one floor of a building to another; *The child was sitting on the bottom* ~. *She always runs up/down the* ~*s.* **a flight of stairs,** a set of stairs in a continuous line. ⇨ **downstairs, upstairs.**

`**stair-case,** series of stairs (often with banisters) inside a building.

`**stair-rod,** rod for keeping a carpet in the angle between two steps of a stair

`**stair-way,** = staircase.

`**stair-well,** space in a building surrounded by a staircase.

stake /steɪk/ n [C] **1** strong, pointed length of wood or metal (to be) driven into the ground as a post (e g for a fence) or as a support for something, e g plants, young trees. **2** post, as used in olden times, to which a person was tied before being burnt to death as a punishment: *condemned to the* ~; *suffer at the* ~. **3** sum of money risked when gambling. **at stake,** to be won or lost; risked, depending, on the result of something: *His reputation/His life itself was at* ~. **4** interest or concern (*in* something); sum of money invested in an enterprise. **5** (*pl*) money to be contended for, esp in a horse-race; such a race: *the trial* ~*s at Newmarket.* □ *vt* **1** support with a stake: ~ *newly planted trees.* **2** mark (an area) with stakes: ~ *out a claim* (to land in a new country, etc). **3** risk (money, one's hopes, etc): *I'd* ~ *my life on it,* am very confident about it.

`**stake-holder,** person who keeps the stakes(3) until the result (of a race, etc) is known.

stal·ac·tite /ˈstæləktaɪt US: stəˈlæk-/ n [C] length of lime hanging from the roof of a cave as water drips from it.

stal·ag·mite /ˈstæləgmaɪt US: stəˈlæg-/ n [C] length of lime mounting upwards from the floor of a cave as water containing lime drips from the roof.

stale /steɪl/ adj **1** (of food) dry and unappetizing because not fresh: ~ *bread.* **2** uninteresting because heard before: ~ *news/ jokes.* **3** (of athletes, musicians, etc) no longer able to perform really well because of too much playing, training, practice, etc: *become* ~. □ *vi* become stale: *Are there any kinds of pleasure that never* ~?

stale·ness n [U]

stale·mate /ˈsteɪlmeɪt/ n [C,U] **1** (*chess*) position of the pieces from which no further move is possible. **2** (*fig*) any stage of a dispute at which further action by either side seems to be impossible. □ *vt* **1** (*chess*) reduce a player to a stalemate. **2** (*fig*) bring to a standstill.

stalk[1] /stɔːk/ n [C] part of a plant that supports a flower or flowers, a leaf or leaves, or a fruit or fruits.

stalk[2] /stɔːk/ *vt,vi* **1** walk with slow, stiff strides, esp in a proud, self-important or serious way: ~ *out of the room.* **2** move quietly and cautiously towards (wild animals, etc) in order to get near: ~ *deer.*

stalker, person who stalks animals.

stall /stɔːl/ n [C] **1** compartment for one animal in a stable or cattle shed. **2** table, small, open shop, etc used by a trader in a market, on a street, in a railway-station, etc: *a* `*book-/*`*flower-/*`*coffee-*~. **3** (*pl*) seats in the part of a theatre nearest to the stage. **4** fixed seat for the special use of a clergyman (usually in the choir or chancel): *canon's/ dean's* ~. **5** condition of an aircraft when its speed has decreased to the point at which it no longer responds to the controls. □ *vt,vi* **1** place or keep (an animal) in a stall(1). **2** (e g of a car engine) fail to keep going through insufficient power or speed; (of a driver) cause an engine to stop from such a cause. **3** (of an aircraft) cause to be, become, out of control through loss of speed. **4** avoid giving a clear answer to a question (in order to get more time): ~ *for time.*

stal·lion /ˈstæliən/ n [C] uncastrated fully grown male horse, esp used for breeding.

stal·wart /ˈstɔːlwət/ adj (*formal*) **1** tall and muscular; solidly built. **2** firm and determined: ~ *supporters.* □ n [C] loyal supporter (of a political party, etc).

sta·men /ˈsteɪmən/ n [C] male part of a flower, bearing pollen.

stam·ina /ˈstæmɪnə/ n [U] energy and physical, mental and moral strength, enabling a person or animal to work hard for a long time, to survive a serious illness, to deal with serious problems, etc.

stam·mer /ˈstæmə(r)/ *vi,vt* **1** speak with a tendency to repeat rapidly the same sound or syllable, as in 'G-g-give me that b-b-book'. **2** say something in this confused or halting way: ~ *out a request.* □ n [C] (tendency to) stammering talk.

stam·merer, person who stammers.

stamp[1] /stæmp/ n [C] **1** act of stamping with the foot: *a* ~ *of impatience.* **2** that with which a mark or design is made on a surface: *a rubber* ~, one on which a design, words, etc are cut (used for printing dates, signatures, addresses, etc). **3** design, word(s), etc made by stamping on a surface. **4** piece of printed paper stuck on envelopes (also `*postage-stamp*), documents, etc to show the postage paid, the insurance contribution, duty paid, etc. **5** (usually *sing*) characteristic mark or quality: *He bears the* ~ *of genius.* **6** (usually *sing*) kind; class: *men of that* ~.

`**stamp-album,** one in which a collector of postage-stamps keeps his specimens.

`**stamp-collector,** person who collects postage-stamps.

`**stamp-duty,** tax imposed on certain kinds

of legal documents.

stamp² /stæmp/ *vt,vi* **1** put (one's foot) down with force (on something): ~ *one's foot*; ~ *on a spider*. **2** move (about, etc) doing this: ~ *about/out of the room.* **stamp sth out**, crush, destroy, end: ~ *out a fire in the grass/a rebellion/an epidemic disease.* **3** print (a design, lettering, the date, etc) on paper, cloth or other surface: *The girl forgot to ~ my library books*, stamp the date on which they were taken out (or should be returned). **4** put a stamp(4) on (a letter, etc): *I enclose a ~ed, addressed envelope for your reply.* **5** give shape to something (e g pieces of metal) with a die or cutter. **6** (*fig*) impress: *He ~ed his authority/personality on the game*, e g of a great footballer.

'**stamp-ing-ground, (a)** place where specified animals, e g elephants, may usually be found. **(b)** place where specified people often gather: *Soho, the ~ing-ground in London of those who enjoy exotic food and entertainment.*

stam-pede /stæm'piːd/ *n* [C] sudden rush of frightened people or animals. □ *vi,vt* **1** take part in a stampede; cause to do this. **2** force or frighten a person into action: *Don't be ~d into buying the house.*

stance /stæns/ *n* [C] **1** (in golf, cricket) position taken for a stroke. **2** person's intellectual attitude.

stand¹ /stænd/ *n* [C] **1** *make a stand*, be ready to resist or fight: *make a ~ against the enemy.* **2** position taken up: *He took his ~ near the window.* **3** small article of furniture, support, etc on or in which things may be placed: *a 'music-/'hat-/um'brella-~.* **4** structure from which things are sold or exhibited: *a 'news~; the British ~s at the Hanover Fair.* **5** place where vehicles may stand in line in a street, etc while waiting for passengers: *a 'taxi-~.* **6** structure, usually sloping, where people may stand or sit to watch races, sports-meetings, etc: *a seat in the ~s.* ⇨ grandstand. **7** engagement by a theatrical company when touring the country. *a one-night stand*, (*fig*) a social meeting between two people that will not be repeated. **8** (*US*) witness-box (in a law court): *take the ~.*

'**stand-point**, point of view: *from the ~point of the consumer.*

'**stand-still**, *be at/come to/bring sth to a standstill*, (of progress, motion) stop, be stopped.

stand² /stænd/ *vi,vt* (*pt,pp* stood /stʊd/) (For special uses with *adverbial particles and prepositions*, ⇨ **10** below.) **1** have, take, keep, an upright position; balance, support, the body on the feet: *He was too weak to ~. Standing room only*, all seats are occupied, e g in a bus or cinema. *His hair stood on end*, i e with terror. *He ~s six foot two*, is of this height when standing. ⇨ handstand. **2** rise to the feet: *S~ up*,

please. Everyone stood (up) as the President entered. **3** remain without change: *Let the words ~*, don't alter them or take them out. **stand firm/fast**, not give way, retreat, change one's views, etc. **4** be in a certain condition or situation: *As affairs now ~...,* As they are at present... *I ~ corrected*, accept that I was wrong, etc. *He ~s alone among his colleagues*, None of them equals him in ability, etc. *S~ clear of the gates*, e g as a warning when they are about to be closed. **5** have a certain place; be situated: *These dishes ~ on the top shelf. The house ~s on the hill. Where does Tom ~ in class*, What is his position (in order of ability, etc)? **6** cause to be placed in an upright position: *S~ the ladder against the wall. S~ the empty barrels on the floor.* **7** put up with; bear: *He can't ~ hot weather. I can't ~ that woman*, strongly dislike her. *stand one's ground*, (*fig*) not give way in an argument. *stand (one's) trial*, be tried (in a court of law). **8** provide at one's expense: ~ *a friend a good dinner.* **9** *stand on ceremony*, ⇨ ceremony. *stand a (good/poor, etc) chance*, ⇨ chance¹(3). *It stands to reason that*, ⇨ reason¹(3). *stand to win/gain/lose sth*, be in a position where one is likely to win, etc: *What do we ~ to gain by the treaty?*

10 (special uses with *adverbial particles and prepositions*):

stand aside, **(a)** be inactive, do nothing: *He's a man who never ~s aside when there's something that needs doing.* **(b)** move to one side: ~ *aside to let someone pass.*

stand at, be at a certain level (on a scale, etc): *The temperature stood at 30°C.*

stand back, **(a)** move back: *The policeman ordered us to ~ back.* **(b)** be situated away from: *The house ~s back from the road.*

stand by, **(a)** look on without doing anything: *How can you ~ by and see such cruelty?* ⇨ bystander. **(b)** be ready for action: *The troops are ~ing by.* *stand by sb*, support; show oneself to be a good friend: *I'll ~ by you whatever happens.* *stand by sth*, be faithful to (a promise, one's word, etc). Hence, '**stand-by, (a)** state of readiness: *The troops are on 24-hour ~by*, ready to move at 24 hours' notice. **(b)** person or thing that one may depend on: *Aspirin is a good ~by for headaches.*

stand down, **(a)** leave a witness-box or similar position. **(b)** (of a candidate) withdraw.

stand for sth, **(a)** represent: *P O ~s for Post Office or postal order.* **(b)** (*GB*) be a candidate for: ~ *for Parliament.* **(c)** (*informal*) tolerate: *She says she's not going to ~ for her children disobeying her.* ⇨ **7** above.

stand in (for sb), take the place of, e g a musician who is ill. Hence, '**stand-in**, person who does this.

stand off, remain at a distance; move away. **'stand-'off·ish** *adj* cold and distant in behaviour.

stand out, (a) be easily seen above or among others: *Does your work ~ out from that of others?* Is it obviously better? ⇨ outstanding. **stand out a mile,** be extremely obvious. **(b)** continue to resist: *The troops stood out against the enemy until their ammunition was exhausted.*

stand over sb, supervise, watch closely: *Unless I ~ over him he makes all sorts of mistakes.*

stand up, ⇨ 2 above. **'stand-up** *adj* **(a)** (of a meal) eaten while standing: *a ~-up buffet.* **(b)** (of a fight) violent and hard-hitting. **stand sb up,** (*informal*) not keep an appointment: *First she agreed to come out with me, then she stood me up.* **stand up for sb,** support; take the part of; defend. **stand up to sth,** (of materials) remain in good condition after long or hard use, etc: *metals that ~ up well to high temperatures.*

stan·dard /'stændəd/ *n* [C] **1** distinctive flag, esp one to which loyalty is given or asked: *the royal ~,* e g as flown to show that the Queen is in residence. **2** (often as an *adjective*) something used as a test or measure for weights, lengths, qualities or for the required degree of excellence: *~ weights and measures; set a high ~ for candidates in an examination; a high ~ of living,* one with plenty of material comforts, etc; *~ authors,* accepted as good. **be up to/below standard,** be equal to, not so good as, normal, etc: *Their work is not up to ~.* ⇨ gold standard. **3** (often as an *adjective*) upright support; pole or column.

'standard bearer, (a) person carrying a standard(1). **(b)** (*fig*) prominent leader.

'standard lamp, tall one with its base on the floor.

standard time, time officially adopted for (part of) a country.

stan·dard·ize /'stændədaɪz/ *vt* make of one size, shape, quality, etc according to fixed standards: *The parts of motor-vehicles are usually ~d.*

stan·dard·iz·ation /ˌstændədaɪ'zeɪʃən *US:* -dɪ'z-/ *n* [U]

stand·ing /'stændɪŋ/ *n* **1** [U] duration: *a debt of long ~.* **2** [C,U] position or reputation; (if there is no *adjective*) established position: *men of high ~; a member in full ~.* □ *adj* established and permanent; ready for use: *a ~ committee,* a permanent one that meets regularly; *a ~ order for newspapers and periodicals,* to be delivered regularly.

stank /stæŋk/ *pt* of stink.

stan·za /'stænzə/ *n* [C] (*pl* ~s) group of rhymed lines forming a division in some forms of poem.

staple [1] /'steɪpəl/ *n* [C] **1** U-shaped metal pin hammered into a surface, to hold something in position. **2** U-shaped part of a padlock. **3** piece of wire pushed through sheets of paper and bent to hold them together. □ *vt* fasten or fit with a staple.

sta·pler /'steɪplə(r)/, small device for fixing papers together with staples(3).

staple [2] /'steɪpəl/ *n* **1** [C] chief sort of article or goods produced or traded in: *Cotton is one of the ~s of Egypt.* **2** [U] fibre of cotton, wool, etc (as determining its quality): *cotton of short/fine ~.* **3** (as an *adjective*) forming the chief part: *Is coffee still the ~ product of Brazil?*

star /stɑ(r)/ *n* [C] **1** any one of the bodies seen in the sky at night as distant points of light. **see stars,** seem to see flashes of light, e g as the result of a hit on the head. **2** figure or design with points round it, suggesting a star by its shape; an asterick (*): *a five-~ hotel, of the highest grade.* **3** badge of rank (worn by officers on the shoulder-strap). **4** planet or heavenly body regarded as influencing a person's fortune, etc: *born under a lucky ~.* **5** person famous as a singer, actor, actress, etc: *the ~s of stage and screen; 'pop ~s.* □ *vi, vt* (-rr-) **1** mark or decorate with, or as with, stars. **2** mark with an asterisk, etc to direct attention to something; *I've ~red the important articles to read.* **3** be a star(5) (in a play, film, etc); present (a person) as a star(5).

'star·dom /-dəm/, status of being a star(5).

'star-fish, sea-animal shaped like a star.

'star·let /-lət/, young successful actress.

'star·light, light from the star. Hence, **'star·lit** *adj.*

star·less *adj* with no stars to be seen: *a ~less sky/night.*

starry /'stɑrɪ/ *adj* lighted by, shining like, stars: *a ~ry night; ~ry eyes.*

'starry-'eyed *adj* (*informal*) full of ideas but impractical: *~ry-eyed reformers.*

star·board /'stɑbəd/ *n* [U] right side of a ship or aircraft from the point of view of a person looking forward. ⇨ port.

starch /stɑtʃ/ *n* [U] **1** white, tasteless food substance, as in potatoes, grain, etc. **2** this substance prepared in powered form and used for stiffening cotton clothes, etc. **3** (*fig*) stiffness of manner; formality. □ *vt* make, e g shirt collars, stiff with starch.

starchy *adj* (-ier, -iest) of, like, containing, starch: *~y foods.*

stare /steə(r)/ *vi, vt* **1** look fixedly; (of eyes) be wide open: *Do you like being ~d at? She was staring into the distance. They all ~d with astonishment.* **2** **stare one in the face,** (*fig*) be obvious, be right in front of one: *The book I was looking for was staring me in the face.* □ *n* [C] staring look: *give him a rude ~.*

stark /stɑk/ *adj* **1** stiff, esp in death. **2** complete: *~ madness.* □ *adv* completely: *~ naked.*

star·ling /'stɑlɪŋ/ *n* [C] common small bird

(black with brown-spotted plumage)

starry /ˈstɑːrɪ/ ⇨ **star**.

start [1] /stɑːt/ n [C] **1** beginning of a journey, activity, etc: *make an early ~; the ~ of a race; from ~ to finish.* **2** (*sing* only) amount of time or distance by which one person starts in front of competitors: *They didn't give me much/any ~. He got a good ~* (= a position of advantage) *in life/business.* **3** sudden movement of surprise, fear, etc: *He sat up with a ~.* **by fits and starts,** ⇨ **fit** [2](3). **make a fresh start,** ⇨ **fresh**.

start [2] /stɑːt/ vi, vt (*Note: begin* may replace *start* only as in 2 below.) **1** leave; set out: *We must ~* (*out*) *early. We ~ed at six.* **2** begin: *~ work. It ~ed raining. It's ~ing to rain.* **3** make a beginning: *~* (*on*) *one's journey home.* **4** make a sudden movement (from pain, surprise, fear, etc) or change of position: *He ~ed at the sound of my voice.* **5** set going; originate, bring into existence; cause or make able to begin: *This news ~ed me thinking. The smoke ~ed her coughing. A rich uncle ~ed him in business,* helped him, e g by supplying capital. **6 to start with,** (**a**) in the first place: *To ~ with, we haven't enough money, and secondly we haven't enough time.* (**b**) at the beginning: *We had only six members to ~ with.*

7 (special uses with *adverbial particles* and *prepositions*):

start back, begin to return: *It's time we ~ed back.*

start off, begin to move: *The horse ~ed off at a steady trot.*

start out (to do sth), (*informal*) begin; take the first steps: *~ out to write a novel.*

start sth up, put (an engine, etc) in motion: *We couldn't ~ up the car.*

ˈstart·ing gate, barrier where horses start a race.

ˈstart·ing-point, place at which a start is made.

ˈstart·ing-post, place from which competitors start in a race.

ˈstart·ing-price, (in horse-racing) the odds just before the start of a race.

star·ter, (**a**) person, horse, etc that takes part in a race: *There were only five ~ers in the last race.* (**b**) person who gives the signal for a race to start. (**c**) device for causing an engine to start working. (**d**) (*informal*) first course of a meal.

startle /ˈstɑːtəl/ vt give a shock of surprise to; cause to move or jump: *be ~d out of one's sleep; be ~d out of one's wits,* suffer a sudden great shock. *What startling news!*

starve /stɑːv/ vi, vt **1** (cause to) suffer or die from hunger: *~ to death. They tried to ~ the soldiers out,* force them to surrender by preventing them from getting supplies of food. **be starved of,** (*fig*) be in great need of: *The motherless children were ~ed of affection.* **2** (*informal*) feel hungry: *What time's dinner? I'm starving!*

star·va·tion /stɑːˈveɪʃən/ n [U] suffering or death caused by lack of food; *die of starvation.*

state [1] /steɪt/ n [C] **1** (*sing* only) condition in which a person or thing is (in circumstances, appearance, mind, health, etc): *The house was in a dirty ~. She's in a poor ~ of health.* **state of play,** (**a**) (*sport*) score. (**b**) (*fig*) how parties in dispute stand in relation to one another (as likely to win or lose). **2** (often **S~**) organized political community with a government; territory in which this exists; such a community forming part of a federal republic: *Railways in Great Britain belong to the S~. How many S~s are there in the United States of America?* (as an *adjective*) of, for, concerned with, the State(2): *~ documents/records/archives.* **4** [U] civil government: *Church and S~; S~ schools,* contrasted with Church or private schools. **5** [U] rank; dignity: *persons in every ~ of life.* **6** [U] ceremonial formality: *The President was received in ~.* **7** (as an *adjective*) of or for ceremony and formality: *the ~ apartments at the palace.* **8 lie in state,** be placed on view in a public place before burial.

state coach, one used by a monarch on ceremonial occasions.

the ˈState Department, (*US*) of foreign Affairs.

ˈState-house, building in which a government of a State holds meetings.

ˈstate-room, private cabin (or sleeping-compartment) on a steamer (and, in US, in a railway-carriage).

state·less adj (of a person) not recognized as a citizen or national of any country: *~less persons,* e g some political refugees.

state·ly adj (-ier, -iest) impressive; dignified: *the ~ly homes of England,* those of the nobility, etc.

state [2] /steɪt/ vt express in words, esp carefully, fully and clearly: *~ one's views.*

stated adj made known; announced: *at ~d times/intervals.*

state·ment, (**a**) [U] expression in words. (**b**) [C] stating of facts, views, a problem, etc (spoken or written); report: *a ˈbank ~ment; make a ~ment* (*in court*), give a formal account in a law court setting out the cause of a legal action or its defence.

states·man /ˈsteɪtsmən/ n [C] (*pl* -men) person taking an important part in the management of State affairs.

ˈstates·man·like adj gifted with, showing, wisdom in public affairs.

ˈstates·man·ship /-ʃɪp/ n [U] skill and wisdom in managing public affairs.

static /ˈstætɪk/ adj at rest; in a state of balance: *Sales are ~,* not increasing or decreasing.

sta·tion /ˈsteɪʃən/ n [C] **1** place, building, etc where a service is organized and provided: *a ˈbus/poˈlice-~.* **2** position, or relative position, to be taken up or maintained by a person or thing: *One of the cruisers was out of* ∼, not in its correct position. **3** stopping-place for railway trains. **4** social position, rank: *people in all* ∼*s of life.* **5** military or naval base; those living there. □ *vt* put (a person, oneself, etc) at or in a certain place: *The detective* `ed himself among the bushes,* hid there.

`**station-master,** person in charge of a railway station.

`**station-wagon,** estate car.

sta·tion·ary /ˈsteɪʃənrɪ *US:* -ənerɪ/ *adj* **1** not intended to be moved from place to place: *a* ∼ *crane/engine.* ⇨ mobile(1). **2** not moving or changing: *remain* ∼.

sta·tion·er /ˈsteɪʃənə(r)/ *n* [C] dealer in stationery.

sta·tion·ery /ˈsteɪʃənrɪ *US:* -nerɪ/ *n* [U] paper, envelopes, etc for writing.

stat·is·tics /stəˈtɪstɪks/ *n* [U] **1** (used with a *pl verb*) collection of information shown in numbers: *S*∼ *suggest that the population of this country will be doubled in ten years' time.* **2** (used with a *sing verb*) the science of statistics.

stat·is·ti·cal /stəˈtɪstɪkəl/ *adj* of statistics: *statistical evidence.*

stat·is·ti·cally /-klɪ/ *adv*

stat·is·ti·cian /ˌstætɪˈstɪʃən/ *n* [C] expert in statistics.

statue /ˈstætʃu/ *n* [C] figure of a person, animal, etc in wood, stone, bronze, etc, usually of life size or more than life size.

statu·ette /ˈstætʃʊˈet/, small statue.

stat·ure /ˈstætʃə(r)/ *n* [U] **1** (person's) natural bodily height. **2** (*fig*) mental or moral quality.

status /ˈsteɪtəs/ *n* [U] person's legal, social or professional position in relation to others: *have no official* ∼, no official position.

`**status symbol,** something which is thought to be evidence of social rank, wealth, etc, e g a car.

stat·ute /ˈstætʃut/ *n* [C] (written) law passed by Parliament or other law-making body.

`**statute-book,** book(s) containing statutes.

statu·tory /ˈstætʃʊtrɪ *US:* -tɔrɪ/ *adj* fixed, done, required, by statute: *statutory control of incomes.*

staunch[1] /stɔntʃ/ (*US* also **stanch** /stɑntʃ *US:* stæntʃ/) *vt* stop the flow of (esp blood).

staunch[2] /stɔntʃ/ *adj* (of a friend, supporter, etc) loyal; firm.

staunch·ly *adv*

staunch·ness *n* [U]

stave[1] /steɪv/ *n* **1** one of the curved pieces of wood used for the side of a barrel or tub. **2** (*music*) = staff(6). **3** stanza; verse.

stave[2] /steɪv/ *vt,vi* (*pt,pp* ∼d or **stove** /stəʊv/) **1** break, smash, make a hole *in*: *The side of the yacht was* ∼*d in by the collision.* **2** **stave sth off,** keep off, delay (danger, disaster, bankruptcy, etc).

stay[1] /steɪ/ *vi,vt* **1** be, remain, in a place or condition: ∼ *in the house/at home/in bed;* ∼ (= be a guest) *at a hotel/with friends. I'm too busy to/I can't* ∼, *must leave now.* **stay in,** not go outdoors. **stay out, (a)** remain outdoors: *Tell the children they mustn't* ∼ *out after dark.* **(b)** remain on strike: *The miners* ∼*ed out for several weeks.* **stay up,** not go to bed: *I* ∼*ed up reading until midnight.* **come to stay,** (*informal*) become, or seem likely to be, permanent: *Has shoulder-length hair for men come to* ∼? **2** continue in a certain state: ∼ *single,* not marry. *That fellow never* ∼*s sober for long,* frequently gets drunk. **stay** `**put,** (*informal*) remain where placed. **3** stop, delay, postpone: ∼ *the progress of a disease.* **4** be able to continue (work, etc); show endurance: *The horse lacks* `∼*ing power.* **stay the course, (a)** be able to continue to the end of the course. **(b)** (*fig*) continue the struggle, etc. □ *n* [C] **1** period of staying(1): *make a short* ∼ *in Karachi.* **2** (*legal*) delay; postponement. *a stay of execution,* that an order of the court need not be carried out immediately.

stay[2] /steɪ/ *n* [C] **1** rope or wire supporting a mast, pole, etc. **2** (*pl*) (*dated* name for) kind of corset reinforced with strips of stiff material (bone or plastic). □ *vt* support by means of a wire, rope or prop.

stead·fast /ˈstedfast *US:* -fæst/ *adj* firm and unchanging; keeping firm (*to*): *a* ∼ *gaze.*

stead·fast·ly *adv*

steady /ˈstedɪ/ *adj* (-ier, -iest) **1** firmly fixed or supported; balanced; not likely to fall over: *make a table* ∼, e g by repairing a leg; *not very* ∼ *on one's legs,* e g of a person after a long illness. **2** regular in movement, speed, direction, etc: *a* ∼ *speed/rate of progress.* **3** regular in behaviour, habits, etc: *a* ∼ *worker.* **4** constant, unchanging: *a* ∼ *purpose.* □ *adv* = steadily. **go steady,** (*informal*) go about regularly with a person of the opposite sex, though not yet engaged to marry: *Are Tony and Jane going* ∼? □ *n* [C] (*pl* -ies) (*sl*) regular boyfriend or girlfriend. □ *vt,vi* make, become, keep, steady: ∼ *a boat;* ∼ *oneself by holding on to the rail,* e g on the deck of a ship that is rolling.

stead·ily /ˈstedəlɪ/ *adv* in a regular manner: *His health is getting steadily worse.*

steak /steɪk/ *n* [C,U] (thick slice of) meat or fish for frying, grilling, stewing, etc.

steal /stil/ *vt,vi* (*pt* **stole** /stəʊl/, *pp* **stolen** /ˈstəʊlən/) **1** take (a person's property) secretly, without right: *Someone has stolen my watch.* **2** obtain by surprise or a trick: ∼ *a glance at her in the mirror.* **3** move, come, go (*in, out, away, etc*) secretly and quietly: *He stole into the room.*

steam /stim/ *n* [U] **1** gas or vapour which rises from boiling water: ∼*-covered windows.* **2** power obtained from steam: *The ship was able to proceed under her own* ∼, using her own engines and not needing to be lowed. *Full steam ahead!* order to go forward at full speed. **3** (*fig*) (*informal*) energy. *let off steam*, release surplus energy or emotion; become less excited. *run out of steam*, become exhausted. *under one's own steam*, without help from others. □ *vi, vt* **1** give out steam or vapour: ~*ing hot coffee*. **2** move, work, etc under (or as if under) the power of steam: *a ship ~ing up the Red Sea*. **3** cook, soften, clean, by the use of steam: ~ *fish*. **4** *steam up*, become misty with condensed steam: *The windows ~ed up.*

`**steam-boat,** vessel propelled by steam.

`**steam-engine,** one worked or driven by pressure of steam.

`**steam-heat,** heat given out by steam from radiators, pipes, etc. □ *vt*: ~*-heated buildings,* kept warm by steam-heat.

`**steam-ship,** ship driven by steam.

steamer, (a) = steamship. (b) vessel in which food is steamed.

steamy *adj* (-ier, -iest) of, like, full of, steam: *the ~y heat of the tropics.*

steel /stiːl/ *n* [U] hard alloy of iron and carbon or other elements, used for knives, tools, machinery, etc. □ *vt* harden: ~ *oneself/one's heart* (*against pity*).

steel band, band of musicians who use old oil drums, etc as percussion instruments.

'**steel-plated** *adj* covered with steel plates.

steel wool, fine steel shavings (used for scouring and polishing).

`**steel-works,** (often used with a *sing·verb*) factory where steel is made.

steep [1] /stiːp/ *adj* (-er, -est) **1** (of a slope) rising or falling sharply: *a ~ gradient/path/descent.* **2** (*informal*) (of a demand) unreasonable; excessive: *It's a bit ~ that I should pay for all of you!*

steep-ly *adv*

steep-ness *n* [U]

steep [2] /stiːp/ *vt, vi* **1** soak or bathe in liquid: ~ *sheets in bleach.* **2** (*fig*) become full of; get a thorough knowledge of: ~*ed in ignorance; a scholar ~ed in Greek history.*

steeple /ˈstiːpl/ *n* [C] high tower with a spire, rising above the roof of a church.

`**steeple-chase,** race with obstacles such as fences, hedges and ditches.

`**steeple-jack,** man who climbs steeples, tall chimney-stacks, etc to do repairs.

steer [1] /stɪə(r)/ *n* [C] young male of the ox family, esp castrated and raised for beef.

steer [2] /stɪə(r)/ *vt, vi* direct the course of (a boat, ship, car, etc): ~ *north*; ~ *by the stars. steer clear of,* (*fig*) avoid.

`**steer-ing-wheel,** (a) (on a ship) wheel turned to control for rudder. (b) (on a motor-vehicle) wheel for steering.

stel-lar /ˈstelə(r)/ *adj* (*formal*) of stars: ~ *light.*

stem [1] /stem/ *n* [C] **1** part of a plant coming up from the roots; part of a leaf, flower or fruit that joins it to the main stalk or twig. **2** part like a stem, eg the narrow part of a wine-glass or a tobacco pipe. **3** (*gram*) root or main part of a noun or verb from which other words are made by additions. □ *vi* (-mm-) *stem from,* have as origin.

stem [2] /stem/ *vt* (-mm-) **1** check, stop, dam up (a stream, a flow of liquid, etc). **2** make progress against the resistance of: ~ *the tide.*

stench /stentʃ/ *n* [C] horrid smell.

sten-cil /ˈstensəl/ *n* [C] thin sheet of metal, cardboard, waxed paper, etc with letters or designs cut through it; lettering, design, etc printed through a stencil. □ *vt* (-ll-, US also -l-) produce (a pattern, wording, etc) by using a stencil.

step [1] /step/ *n* **1** act of stepping once; distance covered by doing this: *He was walking with slow ~s. step by step,* gradually. *watch one's step,* be careful or cautious. **2** sound made by somebody walking; way of walking (as seen or heard): *That's Lucy—I recognize her ~.* **3** *be/get in/out of step (with),* (a) put/not put the right foot to the ground at the same time as others (in marching, dancing). (b) conform/not conform with other members of a group: *He's out of ~ with the official view. keep step with,* march in step with. **4** one action in a series of actions with a view to effecting a purpose: *take ~s to prevent the spread of influenza; a false ~,* a mistaken action. *What's the next ~?* **5** place for the foot when going from one level to another: *The child was sitting on the bottom ~.* **6** grade, rank; promotion: *When do you get your next ~ up?* When will you be promoted? **7** (*pl*) (also *a pair of ~s*) = step-ladder.

`**step-ladder,** portable folding ladder with steps, not rungs.

step [2] /step/ *vi, vt* (-pp-) **1** move the foot, or one foot after the other (forward, or in the direction shown): ~ *across a stream*; ~*over a puddle*; ~ *into a boat.* **2** (uses with adverbial particles and prepositions):

step aside, (a) move to one side. (b) (*fig*) let another person take one's place.

step down, (*fig*) resign (to make way for another person).

step in, (*fig*) intervene (either to help or to obstruct).

step sth up, increase: ~ *up production*; ~ *up the campaign,* put more effort into it.

`**step-ping-stone,** (a) stones in a shallow stream, so that it can be crossed without getting wet. (b) (*fig*) means of getting something: *a first ~ping-stone to success.*

step- /step/ *prefix* (used to show a relationship not by blood but by a later marriage):

`**step-child/-son/-daughter,** child of an earlier marriage of one's wife or husband.

`**step-brother/-sister,** child of an earlier marriage of one's stepfather or stepmother.

`**step-father/-mother,** one's parent's later husband, wife.

stereo /ˈsterɪəʊ/ *n* **1** [U] (abbr of) stereophonic: *in* ∼, with stereophonic sound. **2** [C] stereophonic record-player.

stereo·phonic /ˈsterɪəˈfonɪk/ *adj* **1** (of broadcast and recorded sound, using two separately placed loudspeakers) giving the effect of naturally distributed sound. **2** (of apparatus) designed for recording or reproducing sound in this way: *a* ∼ *recording*.

stereo·type /ˈsterɪətaɪp/ *n* [C] (esp) fixed phrase, idea, belief. □ *vt* (of phrases, ideas, etc) used and repeated without change: ∼*d greetings*, e g 'Good morning', 'How d'you do'?

ster·ile /ˈsteraɪl US: ˈsterəl/ *adj* **1** not producing, not able to produce, seeds or offspring. **2** (of land) barren. **3** (*fig*) having no result; producing nothing: *a* ∼ *discussion*. **4** free from living germs.

ste·ril·ity /stəˈrɪlətɪ/ *n* [U] being sterile.

ster·il·iz·ation /ˈsterəlaɪˈzeɪʃən US: -lɪˈz-/ *n* [U]

ster·il·ize /ˈsterəlaɪz/ *vt* make sterile.

ster·ling /ˈstɜːlɪŋ/ *adj* **1** (of gold and silver) of standard value and purity. **2** (*fig*) of solid worth; genuine: ∼ *qualities*. □ *n* [U] British money: *payable in* ∼.

stern¹ /stɜːn/ *adj* (-er, -est) **1** demanding and enforcing obedience: *a* ∼ *teacher*. **2** severe; strict: *a* ∼ *face/look*.

stern·ly *adv*

stern·ness *n* [U]

stern² /stɜːn/ *n* [C] rear end of a ship or boat.

ster·num /ˈstɜːnəm/ *n* [C] (*pl* ∼s) (*anat*) narrow bone in the front of the chest (also called `breast-bone') connecting the collarbone and the top seven pairs of ribs.

stetho·scope /ˈsteθəskəʊp/ *n* [C] instrument for listening to the beating of the heart, sounds of breathing, etc.

stet·son /ˈstetsən/ *n* [C] man's hat with a high crown and a wide brim.

steve·dore /ˈstiːvədɔː(r)/ *n* [C] man whose work is loading and unloading ships.

stew /stjuː US: stuː/ *vt,vi* cook, be cooked, in water or juice, slowly in a closed dish, pan, etc: ∼*ed chicken/fruit*. **let a person `stew in his own `juice,** do nothing to help him (when he is in trouble for which he is himself responsible). □ *n* **1** [C,U] (dish of) stewed meat, etc: *lamb* ∼. **2 be in/get into/a stew (about sth),** (*informal*) a nervous, excited condition.

stew·ard /ˈstjuːəd US: ˈstuː-/ *n* [C] **1** man who attends to the needs of passengers in a ship or airliner. **2** man responsible for organizing details of a race-meeting, public meeting, show, etc: *The hecklers were thrown out by the* ∼*s*. **3** = shop steward.

stew·ard·ess /ˈstjuːəˈdes US: ˈstuːədɪs/ *n* [C] woman steward (esp 1).

stick¹ /stɪk/ *n* [C] **1** thin branch broken, cut or fallen, from a bush, tree, etc. **2** such a branch cut to a convenient length, piece of cane cut, shaped, etc for a special purpose:

The old man cannot walk without a (`walking-)∼. *We have only a few* ∼*s of furniture,* furniture of the simplest kind. ⇨ *hockey stick.* **have/get hold of the wrong end of the stick,** be confused; misunderstand things completely. **3** slender piece (of chalk, sealing-wax, celery, etc).

stick² /stɪk/ *vt,vi* (*pt,pp* stuck /stʌk/) (For special uses with *adverbial particles* and *prepositions,* ⇨ 7 below.) **1** push (something pointed) (*into, through,* etc): ∼ *a fork into a potato.* **2** (of something pointed) be, remain, in a position by the point: *The needle stuck in my finger.* **3** (cause to) be or become joined or fastened with, or as with, paste, glue or other substance: ∼ *a stamp on a letter.* **be/get stuck with (sb/sth),** (*sl*) permanently involved with; unable to escape from: *It looks as if I'm stuck with the job of clearing up this mess.* **4** (*informal*) put (in some position or place), esp quickly or carelessly: *He stuck his pen behind his ear/his hands in his pockets/the papers in a drawer.* **5** be or become fixed; fail to work properly: *The key stuck in the lock,* could not be turned or taken out. **6** (*informal*) put up with; bear: *I can't* ∼ *it any longer.* ⇨ 7, ∼ **it out,** below.

7 (special uses with *adverbial particles* and *prepositions*):

stick around, (*informal*) stay in or near a place: *S*∼ *around; we may need you.*

stick at sth, (a) stop short of, hesitate at: *He* ∼*s at nothing,* allows no feelings of doubt, etc to stop him. (b) keep on with: *He* ∼*s at his work ten hours a day.*

stick sth down, (a) (*informal*) put down: *S*∼ *it down anywhere you like.* (b) (*informal*) write down. (c) fasten with paste, etc· ∼ *down* (*the flap of*) *an envelope.*

stick sth on, fasten it with paste, etc: ∼ *on a label.*

stick sth out, (cause to) project, stand out: *with his chest stuck out; a rude boy* ∼*ing his tongue out at his sister. Don't* ∼ *your head out of the window.* **stick it out,** (*informal*) endure hardship, etc until the end. ⇨ 6 above. **stick one's neck out,** ⇨ neck(1).

stick out for sth, refuse to give way until one gets (something demanded): *They're* ∼*ing out for higher wages.*

stick to sb/sth, (a) be faithful to (one's ideals, a friend, etc). (b) remain determined: ∼ *to a resolution.* (c) continue at: ∼ *to a timetable,* make no changes in what has been agreed.

stick together, (*informal*) (of persons) remain loyal or friendly to one another.

stick up, project upwards (and out of): *The branch was* ∼*ing up out of the water.* **stick sb up,** (*sl*) threaten to shoot in order to rob: ∼ *up a bank.* Hence, `**stick-up** *n.* **stick up for sb/oneself/sth,** defend, support: ∼ *up for one's friends.*

stick with sb/sth, remain loyal to, continue

to support: ∼ *with a friend/an ideal.*

sticker /ˈstɪkə(r)/ *n* [C] adhesive label

stick·ing plas·ter /ˈstɪkɪŋ plɑːstə(r)/ *n* [C,U] ⇨ plaster(2).

stick-in-the-mud /ˈstɪk ɪn ðə mʌd/ *n* [C] conservative, stubborn person.

stick·ler /ˈstɪklə(r)/ *n* [C] **stickler for,** person who insists on the importance of something (e g discipline).

sticky /ˈstɪkɪ/ *adj* (-ier, -iest) **1** that sticks or tends to stick to anything that touches it: ∼ *fingers.* **2 come to a sticky end,** (*sl*) die in an unpleasant and painful way. **3** (*informal*) making, likely to make, objections, be unhelpful, etc: *be* ∼ *about an overdraft.*

stiff /stɪf/ *adj* (-er, -est) **1** not easily bent or changed in shape: *a sheet of* ∼ *cardboard; have a* ∼ *leg/back,* not easily bent. **keep a stiff upper lip,** not complain when in pain, or trouble, etc). **2** hard to stir, work, move, etc: *a* ∼ *paste.* **3** hard to do; difficult: *a* ∼ *climb/examination.* **4** (of manners, behaviour) formal, unfriendly: *be rather* ∼ *with one's neighbours.* **5** great in degree: *a* ∼ (= strong) *breeze; a* ∼ (= high) *price.* □ *adv* thoroughly: *It bored me* ∼, bored me very much. *She was scared* ∼. □ *n* [C] (*sl*) corpse.

stiff·ly *adv*

stiff·ness *n* [U]

stif·fen /ˈstɪfən/ *vt,vi* make or become stiff(1,2)

stiff·en·ing /ˈstɪfnɪŋ/ *n* [U] material used to stiffen a substance or object.

stiff·ener /ˈstɪfnə(r)/, something used to stiffen, e g starch.

stifle /ˈstaɪfl/ *vt,vi* **1** give or have the feeling that breathing is difficult: *They were* ∼*d by the heat. The heat was stifling.* **2** suppress; put down; keep back: ∼ *a yawn.*

stigma /ˈstɪgmə/ *n* [C] **1** (*pl* ∼s) (*fig*) mark of shame or disgrace: *the* ∼ *of imprisonment.* **2** (*pl* -mata /ˈstɪgˈmɑːtə/) marks resembling those made by the nails on the body of Jesus at His crucifixion. **3** (*pl* ∼s) that part of the pistil of a flower which receives the pollen.

stile /staɪl/ *n* [C] device to enable persons to climb over a fence, gate, etc.

still¹ /stɪl/ *adj, adv* **1** without movement or sound: *Please keep* ∼ *while I take your photograph.* **2** (of wines) not sparkling. □ *n* **1** (*poetic*) deep silence: *in the* ∼ *of the night.* **2** [C] one photograph from a motion picture film. □ *vt* cause to be still or at rest; make calm.

still·ness *n* [U]

ˈstill-birth, child or foetus dead at birth.

ˈstill-born *adj* (a) (of a child) dead at birth. (b) (*fig*) (of an idea, etc) never acted on.

ˈstill-ˈlife *n* [U] representation of non-living things (e g fruit, flowers, etc) in painting; [C] (*pl* ∼s) painting of this kind.

still² /stɪl/ *adv* **1** even to this or that time: *He is* ∼ *busy. Will he* ∼ *be here when I get back? In spite of his faults she* ∼ *loved him/ loved him* ∼. *Is your brother* ∼ *here. Hasn't he left?* (*Note:* compare *Is your brother here yet, Has he arrived?*) **2** (used with a *comparative*) even; yet; in a greater degree: *Tom is tall but Mary is* ∼ *taller/ taller* ∼. **3** nevertheless; admitting that: *He has treated you badly;* ∼, *he's your brother and you ought to help him.*

still³ /stɪl/ *n* [C] apparatus for making liquors (brandy, whisky, etc) by distilling.

stilt /stɪlt/ *n* [C] (also *a pair of* ∼s) poles with a support for the foot at some distance from the bottom, used to raise the user from the ground: *walk on* ∼s.

stilted /ˈstɪltɪd/ *adj* (of written style, talk, behaviour, etc) stiff and unnatural; too formal.

stimu·lant /ˈstɪmjʊlənt/ *n* [C] **1** drink (e g coffee, brandy), drug, etc that increases bodily or mental activity. **2** something that encourages a person (e g praise, hope of gain).

stimu·late /ˈstɪmjʊleɪt/ *vt* excite; increase; quicken thought or feeling: ∼ *him to make greater efforts.*

stimu·lat·ing *adj*

stimu·lus /ˈstɪmjʊləs/ *n* [C] (*pl* -li /-laɪ/) something that stimulates: *a* ∼ *to make extra efforts.*

sting¹ /stɪŋ/ *n* **1** [C] sharp, often poisonous, pointed organ of some insects (e g bees). **2** hairs projecting from the surface of the leaves of plants (esp 'ˈ∼ing-nettles), which cause pain to the fingers, etc when touched. **3** [C] sharp pain caused by the sting of an insect or plant; wound made by a sting. **4** [C,U] any sharp pain of body or mind: *the* ∼ *of a whip/of hunger.*

sting² /stɪŋ/ *vt,vi* (*pt,pp* stung /stʌŋ/) **1** (have the power to) prick or wound with a sting or as with a sting: *A hornet stung me on the cheek.* **2** cause sharp pain (to): *He was stung by his enemy's insults.* **3** (of parts of the body) feel sharp pain: *His fingers were still* ∼*ing from the caning he had had.* **4** (*informal*) charge (a person) an excessive price: *He was stung for £5,* had to pay this sum.

stingy /ˈstɪndʒɪ/ *adj* (-ier, -iest) spending, using or giving unwillingly: *Don't be so* ∼ *with the sugar!*

stin·gily /-əlɪ/ *adv*

stin·gi·ness *n* [U]

stink /stɪŋk/ *vi,vt* (*pt* stank /stæŋk/ or stunk /stʌŋk/, *pp* stunk) **1** have a horrid and offensive smell: *Her breath stank of garlic.* **2** fill a place with a stink: *You'll* ∼ *the place out with your cheap cigars!* □ *n* [C] horrid smell. **raise/kick up a stink (about sth),** (*informal*) cause trouble or annoyance, e g by complaining.

stinker, (*sl*) (a) letter intended to convey strong disapproval. (b) (*informal*) something difficult: *The biology paper* (i e in an examination) *was a* ~*er*.

stint /stɪnt/ *vt,vi* restrict (a person) to a small allowance: *Don't* ~ *yourself/the food.* □ n **1** (usually) *without stint*, without limit, without sparing any effort. **2** [C] fixed or allotted amount (of work): *do one's daily* ~.

stipple /ˈstɪpəl/ *vt* draw, paint, with dots.

stipu·late /ˈstɪpjʊleɪt/ *vt,vi* state as a necessary condition: *It was* ~d *that the goods should be delivered within three days.*

stipu·la·tion /ˌstɪpjʊˈleɪʃən/ *n* [C] condition: *on the stipulation that....*

stir¹ /stɜː(r)/ *vi,vt* (-rr-) **1** be moving; cause to move: *A breeze* ~*red the leaves. Nobody was* ~*ring in the house*, Everyone was resting, in bed. *not stir a finger*, make no effort to help. **2** move a spoon, etc round and round in liquid, etc in order to mix it thoroughly: ~ *one's tea*. **3**.excite: *The story* ~*red the boy's imagination.* □ n (usually *sing* with *a, an*) commotion; excitement: *The news caused quite a* ~ *in the village.*

stir·ring *adj* exciting: ~*ring tales of adventure.*

stir² /stɜː(r)/ *n* [C] (*sl*) prison: *in* ~ *for six months.*

stir·rup¹ /ˈstɪrəp US: ˈstɜːrəp/ *n* [C] footrest, hanging down from a saddle, for the rider of a horse.

stir·rup² /ˈstɪrəp US: ˈstɜːrəp/ *n* [C] (*anat*) bone in the ear.

stitch /stɪtʃ/ *n* **1** [C] (in sewing) the passing of a needle and thread in and out of cloth, etc to join or decorate; (in knitting) one complete turn of the wool, etc over the needle. **2** the thread, etc seen between two consecutive holes made by a needle; result of a single movement with a knitting-needle, etc: *drop a* ~, allow a loop to slip off the end of a knitting-needle; *put* ~*es into/take* ~*es out of a wound. A stitch in time saves nine,* (*proverb*) A small piece of work done now may save a lot of work later. **3** particular kind of stitch: *a* ˈ*chain-*~. **4** (*sing* only) sharp pain in the side (as caused sometimes when running). □ *vt,vi* put stitches in or on.

stoat /stəʊt/ *n* [C] small furry animal larger than a rat.

stock¹ /stɒk/ *n* **1** [C,U] store or goods available for sale, distribution or use, esp goods kept by a trader or shopkeeper. *(be) in/out of stock*, be available/not available. *take stock of*, (*fig*) review (a situation); estimate (a person's abilities, etc). **2** (as an *adjective*) usually in stock (and therefore usually obtainable): ~ *sizes; She's tired of her husband's* ~ *jokes.* **3** [C,U] supply of anything: *a good* ~ *of information; get in* ~*s of coal and coke for the winter.* **4** [U] = livestock. **5** [C,U] money lent to a government in return for interest; shares in the capital of a business company. **6** [U] line of ancestry: *a woman of Irish/farming* ~. **7** [U] raw material ready for manufacture: ˈ*paper* ~. **8** [U] liquid in which bones, etc have been

stewed, used for making soup, gravy, etc. **9** [C] base, support, or handle of an instrument, tool, etc: *the* ~ *of a rifle.* ˈ*lock,* ˈ*stock and* ˈ*barrel*, (*fig*) completely. **10** *on the stocks,* under construction; in preparation. **11** (*pl*) wooden framework with holes for the feet in which wrongdoers were formerly locked in a sitting position. **12** [C] sort of garden plant with single or double brightly coloured sweet-smelling flowers.

ˈ**stock-breeder/-farmer**, one who breeds, raises, cattle.

ˈ**stock-broker**, man who buys and sells stock(5).

ˈ**stock-car**, railway truck for cattle.

ˈ**stockcar racing**, racing of ordinary (not racing-) cars.

ˈ**stock-cube**, cube of dehydrated stock(8).

ˈ**stock exchange**, place where stocks(5) and shares are bought and sold.

ˈ**stock-holder**, (chiefly *US*) = shareholder.

ˈ**stock-in-**ˈ**trade**, everything needed for a trade or occupation.

ˈ**stock market**, (business at the) stock exchange.

ˈ**stock-pile** *vt* keep large quantities of materials, weapons, etc in reserve.

ˈ**stock-pot**, pot for stock(8).

ˈ**stock-room**, for storing stock(1).

ˈ**stock-**ˈ**still** *adv* motionless: *stand* ~*still.*

ˈ**stock-taking** examining and listing stock(1).

ˈ**stock-yard**, enclosure for cattle (e g at a market).

stock² /stɒk/ *vt* supply or equip with stock; have, keep, a stock of: ~ *a shop with goods. He is well* ~*ed with ideas.*

stock·ist /-ɪst/, person who stocks (goods) for sale.

stock·ade /stɒˈkeɪd/ *n* [C] wall of upright stakes, built as a defence.

stock·ing /ˈstɒkɪŋ/ *n* [C] (*dated*) = tights.

stocky /ˈstɒkɪ/ *adj* (-ier, -iest) (of persons, animals, plants) short, strong and stout.

stock·ily /-əlɪ/ *adv*. stockily built.

stodge /stɒdʒ/ *n* [U] (*sl*) heavy and solid food.

stodgy /ˈstɒdʒɪ/ *adj* (a) (of food) heavy and solid. (b) (of style) heavy, uninteresting. (c) (of persons) dull.

stoic /ˈstəʊɪk/ *n* [C] person who has great self-control.

sto·ical /-kəl/ *adj* of, like, a stoic.

sto·ically /-klɪ/ *adv*

sto·icism /ˈstəʊɪsɪzm/ *n* [U] patient and uncomplaining endurance of suffering, etc.

stoke /stəʊk/ *vt,vi* put (coal, etc) on the fire of (an engine, furnace, etc); attend to a furnace: ~ (*up*) *the furnace.*

stoker, workman who stokes a furnace, etc

stole¹ /stəʊl/ *n* [C] **1** strip of material worn (round the neck with the ends hanging down in front) by priests of some Christian Churches during services. **2** woman's wrap worn over the shoulders.

stole^2, **stolen** *pt,pp* of steal.

stolid /ˈstɒlɪd/ *adj* not easily excited.

stolid·ly *adv*

stom·ach /ˈstʌmək/ *n* **1** [C] part (bag) of the alimentary canal into which food passes to be digested: *work on an empty* ∼. **2** (*formal*) = abdomen. **3** [U] appetite. **have no stomach for sth,** dislike or disapprove of it: *have no* ∼ *for bull-fighting.* □ *vt* put up with: *How can you* ∼ *the violence in so many films today?*

ˈstomach-ache, pain in the belly.

stomp /stɒmp/ *vi* stamp, tread, heavily: ∼ *about the room in anger.*

stone /stəʊn/ *n* **1** [U] (often as an *adjective*) solid mineral matter which is not metallic; rock (often with a defining word as prefix, as `sand∼, `lime∼): *a wall made of* ∼; ∼ *walls/buildings.* **have a heart of `stone,** be unsympathetic, hard. **2** [C] piece of stone: *a fall of* ∼*s down a hillside.* **leave no stone unturned,** try every possible means. **throw stones at,** (*fig*) attack the character of. **within a `stone's throw (of),** very close (to). **3** [C] (also `precious ∼) = jewel. **4** [C] piece of stone of a definite shape, for a special purpose: *a `grave∼; `stepping-∼; `tomb∼.* **5** [C] something round and hard like a stone, esp **(a)** the hard shell and nut or seed of such fruits as the cherry. **(b)** hailstone. **(c)** small hard object that has formed in the gall-bladder, etc. ⇨ **gallstone. 6** (not *US*) (*pl* unchanged) unit of weight, 14 lb: *I weigh 10 stone.* □ *vt* **1** throw stones at: *be* ∼*d to death.* **2** take the stone(5(a)) out of (fruit): ∼*d dates.*

the `Stone Age, period of culture when weapons and tools were made of stone (before the use of metals was known).

`stone-`blind/-`cold/-`dead/-`deaf *adj* completely blind, etc.

`stone-fruit, kind with stones(5).

`stone-mason, man who cuts, prepares and builds with stone.

`stone-`wall *vt* (*fig*) (in Parliament) obstruct progress by making long speeches, etc.

`stone-ware, pottery made from clay and flint.

`stone-work, masonry; part(s) of a building made of stone.

stoned /stəʊnd/ *adj* (*informal*) **1** under the influence of drugs. **2** drunk.

stony /ˈstəʊnɪ/ *adj* (-ier, -iest) **1** having many stones: ∼ *soil/ground;* covered with stones: *a* ∼ *path/road.* **2** hard, cold and unsympathetic: *a* ∼ *stare.*

`stony-`broke, (*sl*) completely without money.

ston·i·ly /-əlɪ/ *adv* in a stony(2) manner.

stood /stʊd/ *pt,pp* of stand^4.

stool /stuːl/ *n* [C] **1** seat without a back or arms, usually for one person; *a piˈano-∼.* **fall between two stools,** lose an opportun-

ity through hesitating between two courses of action. **2** = footstool. **3** (*pl*) (*medical*) solid excrement.

`stool-pigeon, (*fig*) person acting as a decoy, eg one employed by the police to trap a criminal.

stoop /stuːp/ *vi,vt* **1** bend the body forwards and downwards: ∼*ing with old age.* **2** (*fig*) lower oneself morally: *He's a man who would* ∼ *to anything,* who would not hesitate to act immorally. □ *n* (usually *sing*) stooping position of the body.

stop^1 /stɒp/ *n* [C] **1** stopping or being stopped: *The train came to a sudden* ∼. **put a stop to sth,** cause it to stop or end: *I'll put a* ∼ *to this nonsense. Traffic was brought to a complete* ∼. **2** place at which buses, trams, etc stop regularly or (*re`quest* ∼) when requested to do so: *Where's the nearest `bus-∼?* **3** (*music*) key or lever (eg in a flute) for regulating pitch; in an organ, knob or lever regulating the flow of air to a row of pipes. **pull out all the stops,** (*fig*) make a great effort. **4** = full-stop.

`stop-cock, valve inserted in a pipe by which the flow of liquid or gas through the pipe can be regulated.

`stop-gap, temporary substitute.

`stop-press, (not *US*) latest news inserted in a newspaper already on the printing machines.

`stop-watch, watch with a hand that can be started and stopped when desired, used to time events such as races.

stop^2 /stɒp/ *vt,vi* (-pp-) **1** put an end to (the movement or progress of a person, thing, activity, etc): ∼ *a car/a train.* **2** prevent: *What can* ∼ *our going/∼ us from going if we want to go?* **3** discontinue (doing something): ∼ *work. We* ∼*ped talking.* **4** break off; discontinue: *The rain has* ∼*ped. It has* ∼*ped raining.* **5** halt: *Does this train* ∼ *at Rome?* **stop dead,** stop suddenly. **6** fill or close (a hole, opening, etc): ∼ *a leak in a pipe.* **7** cut off; keep back or refuse to give (something normally supplied): ∼ (*payment of*) *a cheque,* order the bank not to cash it. **stop sth out of sth,** deduct (a part) from (wages, salary, etc). **8** (*informal*) stay: ∼ *at home. Are you* ∼*ping at this hotel?* **stop off (at/in); stop over,** break a journey and stay for a short period: ∼ *off/over in Paris.* Hence, **`stop-over** *n.* **stop up (late),** stay up, not go to bed until late.

stop·page /ˈstɒpɪdʒ/ *n* [C] **1** obstruction. **2** stopping(7): ∼ *of leave/pay,* (esp in the armed forces, eg as a form of punishment). **3** interruption of work (in a factory, etc as the result of strike action).

stop·per /ˈstɒpə(r)/ *n* [C] object which fits into and closes an opening, esp the mouth of a bottle or pipe.

stor·age /ˈstɔːrɪdʒ/ *n* [U] (space used for, money paid for) the storing of goods: *put one's furniture in* ∼; (as an *adjective*) `∼

tanks.

`storage heater,` electric radiator which stores heat.

store /stɔː(r)/ *n* **1** [C] quantity or supply of something kept for use as needed: *have a good ~ of tinned food in the house.* **2** [U] *in store,* (a) kept ready for use; for future use: *That's a treat in ~,* a pleasure still to come. (b) destined (*for*); coming to: *Who knows what the future has in ~ (for us)?* **3** (*pl*) goods, etc of a particular kind, or for a special purpose: *naval and military ~s.* **4** [C] = store-house. **5** [C] (chiefly *US* but ⇨ 6 below) shop: *a `clothing ~.* **6** [C] shop selling many different goods: *the big de`partment ~s of London.* ⇨ also chain-store. **7** [U] *set great/little/no/not much store by,* consider of great/little, etc value or importance. □ *vt* **1** collect and keep for future use: *Do squirrels ~ up food for the winter?* **2** put (furniture, etc) in a warehouse, etc, for safe keeping. **3** equip, supply: *a mind well ~d with facts.*

`store-house,` place where goods are kept.

`store-room,` one in which household supplies are kept.

storey (*US* = **story**) /`stɔːrɪ/ *n* (*pl* ~s, (*US* -ies) floor or level in a building.

-storeyed (*US* = **stor·ied**) /-`stɔːrɪd/ *suffix* having the number of storeys shown: *a six-~ building.*

stork /stɔːk/ *n* [C] large, long-legged, usually white wading-bird.

storm /stɔːm/ *n* **1** [C] occasion of violent weather conditions: *a `thunder-/`rain/`dust/`sand-~. a 'storm in a `teacup,* much excitement about something unimportant. **2** violent outburst of feeling: *a ~ of protests/cheering/applause/abuse.* **3** *take by storm,* capture by a violent and sudden attack. □ *vi, vt* **1** give violent expression to anger; shout angrily. **2** force (a way) into a building, etc; capture (a place) by sudden and violent attack: *The men ~ed (their way) into the fort/~ed the fort.*

`storm-bound` *adj* unable to continue a journey, voyage, etc unable to go out, because of storms.

`storm-cloud,` heavy grey cloud accompanying, or showing the likelihood of, a storm.

`storm-lantern,` one made so that the light is well protected from wind.

`storm-proof` *adj* able to resist storms.

`storm-tossed` *adj* damaged or blown about by storms.

`storm-troops,` soldiers trained for violent attacks.

stormy *adj* (-ier, -iest) (a) marked by strong wind, heavy rain, snow or hail: *~y weather; a ~y night.* (b) marked by strong feelings of anger, etc: *a ~y discussion/ meeting.*

story /`stɔːrɪ/ *n* [C] (*pl* -ies) **1** account of past events: *stories of ancient Greece.* **2** account of imaginary events. **3** (esp by and to children) untrue statement: *Don't tell stories,* Tom.

`story-book,` child's book of stories. *a story-book ending,* a happy one.

`story-teller,` person who tells stories.

story[2] /`stɔːrɪ/ *n* (*US*) ⇨ storey.

stout /staʊt/ *adj* (-er, -est) **1** strong, thick, not easily broken or worn out: *~ boots for mountain-climbing.* **2** determined and brave: *a ~ heart.* Hence, `stout-`hearted *adj* courageous. **3** (of a person) fat: *She's growing too ~ to walk far.* □ *n* [U] strongest kind of dark beer.

stout·ly *adv*

stout·ness *n* [U]

stove[1] /staʊv/ *n* [C] closed apparatus burning wood, coal, gas, oil or other fuel, used for cooking, etc.

`stove-pipe,` pipe for taking away smoke from a stove.

stove[2] /staʊv/ ⇨ stave[2].

stow /staʊ/ *vt* pack, esp carefully and closely: *~ cargo in a ship's holds; ~ things away in the attic.*

`stow-away,` person who hides himself in a ship or aircraft (until after it starts) in order to make a journey without paying.

straddle /`strædəl/ *vt, vi* sit or stand across (something) with the legs on either side: *~ a horse.*

strafe /strɑːf/ *vt* (*informal*) = bombard.

straggle /`strægəl/ *vi* **1** grow, spread, in an irregular or untidy manner: *vines straggling over the fences.* **2** drop behind (a group) while moving forward.

strag·gler, person who straggles(2).

strag·gly /`strægəlɪ/ *adj* straggling(1).

straight[1] /streɪt/ *adj* **1** without a bend or curve; extending in one direction only: *a ~ line/road; ~ hair,* with no curls in it. **2** level (esp horizontal): *Put the picture ~.* **3** in good order; tidy: *put a room ~. put the record straight,* give a more accurate account of events, etc. **4** (of a person, his behaviour, etc) honest, frank, upright: *give a ~ answer to a question.* ⇨ straight[2](4). **5** *keep a straight face,* refrain from smiling or laughing. **6** (of alcoholic drinks) neat, i e without added (soda-)water: *Two ~ whiskies, please.*

straight fight, (in politics) one in which there are only two candidates.

straight play, an ordinary drama (contrasted with variety).

straight·ness *n* [U]

straight[2] /streɪt/ *adv* **1** directly; not in a curve or at an angle: *Keep ~ on. Look ~ ahead. Can you shoot ~,* aim accurately? **2** by a direct route; without going elsewhere; without delay: *Come ~ home. He went ~ to Rome without staying in Paris. come straight to the point,* make a prompt and clear statement of what is meant, wanted, etc. **3** *straight away,* immediately. **4** *go* *straight,* (*fig*) live an honest life (esp after imprisonment).

straight³ /streɪt/ *n* (usually *sing* with *the*) condition of being straight; straight part of something, esp the final part of a track or race-course: *The two horses were together as they entered the final ∼.*

straighten /ˈstreɪtən/ *vt, vi* make or become straight (1,2,3).

straight·for·ward /ˌstreɪtˈfɔːwəd/ *adj* 1 honest; without avoiding anything: *a ∼ explanation.* 2 easy to understand or do: *written in ∼ language.*
straight·forward·ly *adv*

straight·way /ˈstreɪtˈweɪ/ *adv* = straight away.

strain¹ /streɪn/ *n* 1 [C,U] condition of being stretched; the force used: *The rope broke under the ∼.* 2 [C,U] something that tests one's powers; severe demand on one's strength, etc: *Do you suffer from the ∼ of modern life? He has been under (a) severe ∼.* 3 [U] exhaustion; fatigue: *suffering from mental/nervous ∼.* 4 [C] = sprain. 5 (*pl*) (*poetic*) music, song, verse (of the kind shown): *the ∼s of a violin.* 6 [C] manner of speaking or writing: *in a cheerful ∼.* 7 tendency in a person's character: *There is a ∼ of insanity in the family.* 8 breed (of animals, insects, etc); line of descent: *∼s of mosquitoes that are resistant to insecticides.*

strain² /streɪn/ *vt,vi* 1 stretch tightly by pulling (*at*): *a dog ∼ing at its lead.* 2 make the greatest possible use of; use one's strength, etc: *∼ every nerve (to do it),* do all one can; *I had to ∼ my eyes to see it,* look with great effort. 3 injure or weaken by straining(2): *∼ a muscle; ∼ one's eyes,* by using them too much, or in poor light, etc. Hence, `eye-strain *n.* 4 make an intense effort: *The wrestlers ∼ed and struggled.* 5 (*fig*) force beyond a limit or what is right: *∼ the belief of one's listeners,* ask too much of it. 6 pass (liquid) through a cloth, or a network of fine wire, etc; separate solid matter in this way: *∼ the soup; ∼ off the water from the vegetables.* 8 (*pp*) (esp of feelings and behaviour) unnatural; (as if) forced: *a ∼ed laugh; ∼ed relations,* showing loss of patience, risk of quarrelling.
strainer, sieve or other device for straining(6) liquid: *a `tea-∼er.*

strait /streɪt/ *n* [C] 1 narrow passage of water connecting two seas or two large bodies of water: *the S∼s of Gibraltar; the Magellan S∼.* 2 (usually *pl*) trouble; difficulty: *be in financial ∼s.*

strait-jacket /ˈstreɪt dʒækɪt/ *n* [C] jacket with long sleeves used to bind a mentally ill or violent person. □ *vt* 1 use a straight-jacket on. 2 (*fig*) prevent growth or development.

strait-laced /ˈstreɪt ˈleɪsd/ *adj* strict, conservative, serious.

strand¹ /strænd/ *n* [C] (*poetic*) sandy shore □ *vi,vt* 1 (of a ship) (cause to) run aground. 2 *be (left) stranded,* (*fig*) (of a person) be left without means of transport, without money or friends, etc: *be ∼ed in a foreign country.*

strand² /strænd/ *n* [C] 1 any of the threads, hairs, wires, etc twisted together into a rope, cable or cloth. 2 hair. 3 (*fig*) line of development (in a story, etc).

strange /streɪndʒ/ *adj* (-r, -st) 1 not previously known, seen, felt or heard of; (for this reason) surprising: *hear a ∼ noise. Truth is ∼r than fiction.* 2 *strange to sth,* fresh or new to: *The village boy was ∼ to city life.*
strange·ly *adv: behave/act ∼ly; S∼ly (enough)...,* It's hard to believe but..
strange·ness *n* [U]

stran·ger /ˈstreɪndʒə(r)/ *n* [C] person one does not know; person in a place or in company that he does not know: *The dog always barks at ∼s.*

strangle /ˈstræŋɡəl/ *vt* kill by squeezing the throat of.
`strangle-hold, (usually *fig*) tight grip: *The new laws have put a ∼hold on our imports.*

strap /stræp/ *n* [C] strip of leather, cloth, plastic (usually with a buckle) to fasten things together or to keep something (e g a wrist-watch) in place. □ *vt* (-pp-) 1 fasten or hold in place with a strap: *∼ on a wrist-watch. Is the baby ∼ped in?* 2 beat with a belt.

strata /ˈstrɑːtə/ ⇨ stratum.

strat·agem /ˈstrætədʒəm/ *n* [C,U] (*pl* ∼s) (use of a) trick or device to deceive a person.

stra·tegic /strəˈtiːdʒɪk/, **stra·tegi·cal** /-kəl/ *adj* of, by, serving the purpose of strategy: *a ∼ retreat.*
stra·tegi·cally /-klɪ/ *adv*
stra·tegics *n* [U] science, art, of strategy.

strat·egy /ˈstrætədʒɪ/ *n* 1 [U] the art of planning operations or actions, esp of the movements of armies and navies. 2 [U] skill in organizing and doing something. 3 [C] general plan of action.
strat·egist, person skilled in strategy.

strat·ify /ˈstrætɪfaɪ/ *vt,vi* (*pt,pp* -ied) 1 arrange in strata: *stratified rock.* 2 form into strata.
strat·ifi·ca·tion /ˌstrætɪfɪˈkeɪʃən/ *n* [U]

strato·sphere /ˈstrætəsfɪə(r)/ *n* [C] layer of atmospheric air between about 10 and 60 km above the earth's surface.

stra·tum /ˈstrɑːtəm/ *n* [C] (*pl* -ta /-tə/) 1 horizontal layer of rock, etc in the earth's crust. 2 social class or division.

straw /strɔː/ *n* 1 [U] dry cut stalks of wheat, barley, rice and other grains, as material for making mats, etc or bedding for cattle, etc. 2 [C] single stalk or piece of straw. *not worth a straw,* worth nothing. *a straw in the wind,* a slight hint that shows which way things may develop. *the last straw,* addition to a task, burden, etc, that makes it intolerable. 3 [C] thin tube of other material for sucking up liquid: *suck lemonade* through a ~.

`**straw-coloured** adj pale yellow.

straw·berry /ˈstrɔːbrɪ US: -berɪ/ n [C] (pl -ies) (plant having) juicy red fruit with tiny yellow seeds on its surface.

stray /streɪ/ vi (pt, pp ~ed) **1** move away (without realizing) (from the right path, from one's friends, etc). **2** (fig) lose one's line of argument, story, etc: Don't ~ from the point. □ n **1** strayed animal or person (esp a child). **2** (as an adjective) without a home: ~ cats and dogs. **3** occasional: a few ~ taxis.

streak /striːk/ n [C] **1** long, thin, usually irregular line or band: like a ~ of lightning, very fast. **2** trace or touch (of): There's a ~ of cruelty in his character. **3** brief period: The gambler had a ~ of good luck. □ vt, vi **1** mark with streaks: white fur ~ed with brown. **2** (informal) move very fast (like a streak of lightning).

streaky adj (-ier, -iest) marked with, having, streaks: ~y bacon.

stream /striːm/ n [C] **1** small river or brook. **2** current: go up/down stream, move up/down the river. **3** steady flow (of liquid, persons, things, etc): a ~ of blood/abuse. S~s of people were coming out of the railway station. **3** (division of a) class of children in groups according to ability and intelligence: bright boys and girls in the `A-stream. □ vi **1** flow freely; move continuously and smoothly in one direction: Sweat was ~ing down his face. **2** float or wave (in the wind): Her long hair was ~ing in the wind. **3** place (children) in streams(3).

`**stream·line** vt make more efficient (by simplifying, getting rid of, wasteful methods, etc): ~line production, eg in a factory.

`**stream·lined** adj (a) having a shape that offers least resistance to the flow of air, water, etc: ~lined cars. (b) having nothing likely to obstruct progress: ~lined controls.

streamer, long narrow flag; long narrow ribbon of paper.

street /striːt/ n [C] town or village road with houses on one side or both: meet a friend in the ~; cross the ~; a `~-map/-plan of York. (Note: compare a road-map of York-shire.) **the man in the street**, typical citizen. **streets ahead of**, (informal) far ahead of. **(not) up my street**, (informal) (not) within my area of knowledge, interests, etc.

`**street-car**, (US) tram.

strength /streŋθ/ n [U] **1** quality of being strong: a man/horse of great ~. She hasn't the ~/hasn't ~ enough to walk upstairs. How is the ~ of alcoholic liquors measured? **on the strength of**, encouraged by, relying on: I employed the boy on the ~ of your recommendation. **2** that which helps to make a person or thing strong: God is our ~. **3** power measured by numbers of persons

present or persons who can be used: The police force is 500 below ~, needs 500 more men. **be/bring sth up to strength**, the required number: We must bring the police force up to ~.

strengthen /ˈstreŋθən/ vt, vi make or become strong(er).

strenu·ous /ˈstrenjʊəs/ adj using or needing great effort: ~ work; make ~ efforts; lead a ~ life.

strenu·ous·ly adv

strenu·ous·ness n [U]

stress /stres/ n **1** [U] condition causing depression, mental illness, trouble etc: times of ~, of trouble and danger; under the ~ of poverty/fear. **2** [U] (and with a, an) emphasis: a school that lays ~ on foreign languages. **3** [C,U] (result of) extra force, used in speaking, on a particular word or syllable: S~ and rhythm are important in speaking English. **4** [C,U] (in mechanics) force exerted between two bodies that touch, or between two parts of one body. □ vt put stress or emphasis on: He ~ed the point that...

`**stress-mark**, mark (e g `(principal or main stress) and ' (secondary stress) as used in this dictionary) that shows the stress(3) on a syllable.

stretch /stretʃ/ vt, vi **1** make wider, longer or tighter, by pulling; be or become wider, etc when pulled: ~ a rope tight; ~ a rope across a path; ~ out one's arm for a book. **stretch one's legs**, exercise by walking, e g after sitting. **2** lie on at full length: They were ~ed out on the lawn. **3** make (a word, law, etc) include or cover more than is strictly right: ~ the law/one's principles. ⇨ point '(8). **4** use, strain, fully; ~ one's powers, work very hard or too hard. **5** extend: forests ~ing for hundreds of miles. □ n [C] **1** act of stretching or being stretched: by a ~ of authority. The cat woke and gave a ~. **by** `any/`no **stretch of the imagination**, however much one may try to imagine something. **at full stretch;** fully stretched: The factory was/The workers were at full ~. ⇨ 4 above. **2** unbroken or continuous period of time or extent of country, etc; a beautiful ~ of land; working twelve hours at a ~.

stretcher, **(a)** framework of poles, canvas, etc for carrying a sick, injured or wounded person. **(b)** device for stretching things (e g gloves, shoes).

strew /struː/ vt (pt ~ed, pp ~ed or ~n /struːn/) scatter (things) over a surface; (partly) cover (a surface) (with things): ~ flowers over a path; ~ a path with flowers.

stricken /ˈstrɪkən/ adj affected or overcome: `terror-~, very frightened.

strict /strɪkt/ adj (-er, -est) **1** demanding obedience or exact observance: a ~ father; be ~ with children. **2** clearly and exactly defined; precisely limited: I told her in ~est confidence; in the ~ sense of the word.

strict·ly *adv* in a strict manner.

strict·ness *n* [U]

stride /straɪd/ *vi,vt* (*pt* strode /strəʊd/, *pp* (rare) stridden /ˈstrɪdən/) **1** walk with long steps: ~ *along the road;* ~ *off/away.* **2** pass over in one step: ~ *over a ditch.* □ *n* [C] (distance covered in) one long step. **get in to one's stride,** settle down to the task. **make great strides,** make good and rapid progress. **take sth in one's stride,** do it without effort.

strife /straɪf/ *n* [U] state of conflict: *industrial* ~ (between workers and employers).

strike¹ /straɪk/ *n* [C] **1** act of striking(5): *a* ~ *of bus-drivers;* (as an *adjective*) *take* ~ *action.* **be (out) on strike; come/go out on strike,** be engaged in, start, a strike. ⇨ **general strike. 2** act of finding (oil, etc) in the earth: *a lucky* ~, a fortunate discovery.

ˈstrike-bound *adj* unable to function because of a strike: *The docks were* ~*bound for a week.*

ˈstrike fund, special fund to supplement strike-pay.

ˈstrike-pay, money paid to strikers from trade-union funds.

strike² /straɪk/ *vt,vi* (*pt,pp* struck /strʌk/) (For special uses with *adverbial particles* and *prepositions,* ⇨ **16** below.) **1** hit; aim a blow at: *He struck me on the chin. He struck the table with a heavy blow. The ship struck a rock. That tree was struck by lightning.* **strike at the root of sth,** attack trouble, evil, etc at its source. **Strike while the ˈiron is ˈhot,** (*proverb*) Act promptly while action is likely to get results. **within ˈstriking distance,** near enough to reach or attack easily. **2** produce (a light) by striking or scraping: ~ *a match,* cause it to burst into flame by scraping it on a surface. **3** discover (by mining, drilling, etc): ~ *oil.* **strike it rich,** win wealth suddenly. **4** (cause to) sound: *The clock has struck* (*four*). **strike a note of,** give an impression (of the kind shown): *The Prime Minister struck a note of warning against over-optimism.* **5** (of workers, etc) stop working for an employer in order to get more pay, shorter hours, better conditions, etc or as a protest against something): ~ *for higher pay/against bad working conditions.* ⇨ **strike** (1). **6** impress; have an effect on the mind: *How does the idea/suggestion* ~ *you?* **7** have an effect on the body or mind: *The room* ~*s you as warm and comfortable when you enter.* **8** produce by stamping or punching: ~ *a coin/ medal.* **9** achieve, arrive at, by reckoning or weighing: ~ *a balance between freedom and repression.* **strike a bargain (with sb),** reach one by agreement. **10** set out, go (in a certain direction): *The boys struck out across the fields.* **11** cause (a person) to be, suddenly and as if by a single stroke: *be struck blind.* **12** fill, afflict, with fear, etc: *The bombing attack struck fear into their hearts.* **13** lower, take down, (sails, tents). **strike camp,** pack up tents, etc. **14** **strike root,** put out roots. **15** hold or put the body in a certain way to show something: ~ *an attitude of defiance.*

16 (special uses with *adverbial particles* and *prepositions*):

strike sb down, (a) hit so that he falls to the ground. (b) (*fig*) kill: *He was struck down in the prime of life.*

strike sth off, cut off with a blow, e g of an axe. **strike sth off (sth),** remove: ~ *his name off a list.*

strike out, (a) use the arms and legs vigorously in swimming: ~ *out for the shore.* (b) aim wild blows: *He lost his temper and struck out.* (c) follow a new or independent path, a new form of activity: ~ *out on one's own.* **strike sth out,** = cross sth out.

strike (sth) up, begin to play: *The band struck up* (*a tune*). **strike up sth (with sb),** begin (perhaps casually) a friendship or acquaintance: *She struck up an acquaintance with him during the flight.*

striker /ˈstraɪkə(r)/ *n* [C] **1** worker who strikes(5). **2** (in football) player in an attacking position.

strik·ing /ˈstraɪkɪŋ/ *adj* **1** attracting attention or great interest. **2** that strikes(4): *a* ~ *clock*

strik·ing·ly *adv*

string¹ /strɪŋ/ *n* **1** [C,U] (piece or length of) fine cord for tying things, keeping things in place, etc; *a ball of* ~; *a piece of* ~. **the first/second string,** the first/the alternative person or thing relied on for achieving one's purpose. **2** [C] tightly stretched length of cord, gut or wire, e g in a violin or guitar, for producing musical sounds. **3** [C] (usually *pl*) string used for causing puppets to move. **have/keep sb on a string,** have/keep him under control. **pull (the) strings,** control the actions of other people (as if they were puppets). **no strings (attached),** (*informal*) (of help, esp of money) without conditions about how the help is to be used. ⇨ heartstrings. **4** [C] series of things threaded on a string: *a* ~ *of beads.* **5** repetition of types of things: *a* ~ *of abuses/curses/lies.*

the strings, string instruments (in an orchestra).

string bean, kind of bean of which the long pod is used as a vegetable.

string instrument, musical instrument with strings(2), e g the violin, guitar, harp.

string orchestra, having only string instruments.

string quartet. for, with, four string instruments.

stringy *adj* (-ier, -iest) like string; having tough fibres: ~*y meat.*

string² /strɪŋ/ *vt,vi* (*pt,pp* strung /strʌŋ/) **1** put a string or strings on (a bow, violin, tennis racket, etc). **2** (*pp*) **strung (up),** (of a person, his senses, nerves) made tense, ready, excited, etc: *He is a very highly* *strung person,* is very sensitive, tense. **3** put (pearls, etc) on a string. **4** tie or hang on a string, etc: ∼ *(up) lamps across a street.* **5** (special uses with *adverbial particles* or *prepositions*):

string sb along, deliberately mislead a person into the belief that he/she will benefit, etc: *He doesn't intend to marry the girl —he's just* ∼*ing her along.* **string along with sb,** maintain a relationship with a person for as long as it suits one, without making genuine commitments.

string out, be, become, spread out at intervals in a line. **string sth out,** cause this to happen: *horses strung out towards the end of a long race.*

string sb up, (*sl*) put him to death by hanging. **string sth up,** ⇨ 4 above.

strin·gent /ˈstrɪndʒənt/ *adj* (*formal*) **1** (of rules) strict, severe; that must be obeyed: *take a* ∼ *measures against smoking.* **2** (of the money-market) difficult to operate because of scarcity of money.
strin·gent·ly *adv*

strip /strɪp/ *vt,vi* (-pp-) **1** take off (coverings, clothes, parts, etc): *They* ∼*ped the house of all its furnishings. They* ∼*ped off their clothes and jumped into the lake.* **strip sth down,** (e g of an engine) remove detachable parts (for servicing, etc). **2** deprive of property, etc: ∼ *a man of his possessions/titles, etc.* □ *n* [C] **1** long narrow piece (of material, land, etc): *a* ∼ *of garden behind the house; a* ∼ *of paper.* ⇨ airstrip, comic-strip. **2** (*modern informal*) clothes worn by players in a team: *the colourful* ∼ *of football teams.*

strip cartoon, cartoon (often one of a series) made up of a number of drawings in a row.

'strip-'tease, 'strip-show, cabaret or night club entertainment in which a woman takes off her clothes one by one.

stripe /straɪp/ *n* [C] **1** long, narrow band on a surface different in colour, material, texture, etc: *a tiger's* ∼*s.* **2** (often a V-shaped) badge worn on a uniform, showing rank, e g of a soldier: *How many* ∼*s are there on the sleeve of a sergeant?*
striped /straɪpt/ *adj* having stripes(1)
stripy *adj* having stripes: *a stripy tie.*

strip·per /ˈstrɪpə(r)/ *n* [C] woman who performs a strip-tease.

strive /straɪv/ *vi* (*pt* strove /strəʊv/, *pp* striven /ˈstrɪvən/) **1** struggle: ∼ *with/ against poverty/opposition/the enemy.* **2** make great efforts: ∼ *for power/to win.*

strode /strəʊd/ *pt of* stride.

stroke[1] /strəʊk/ *n* [C] **1** (act of striking or dealing a) blow: *the* ∼ *of a sword; 20* ∼*s of the whip.* **2** one of a series of regularly repeated movements, esp as a way of swimming or rowing: *swimming with a slow* ∼; *the* `*breast-/*`*side-/*`*back-*∼. **3** (in a rowing crew) oarsman nearest the boat's stern who

sets the rate of striking the oars. **4** single movement of the upper part of the body or arm(s), esp in games, e g cricket, golf. **5** single effort; result of this: *I haven't done a* ∼ *of work today.* **a stroke of luck,** a piece of good fortune. **at a/one stroke,** with one effort and immediately. **6** (mark made by a) single movement of a pen or brush: *cross a name out with one* ∼ *of the pen; thin/thick* ∼*s.* **7** sound made by a bell striking the hours: *on the* ∼ *of three,* at three o'clock. **8** sudden attack of illness in the brain, with loss of feeling, power to move, etc: *a paralytic* ∼[2], ⇨ also sunstroke.

stroke[2] /strəʊk/ *vt* pass the hand along a surface, usually again and again: ∼ *a cat/ one's beard.* □ *n* [C] act of stroking; stroking movement.

stroll /strəʊl/ *n* [C] quiet, unhurried walk: *have/go for a* ∼. □ *vi* go for a stroll.
strol·ler, person who strolls.

strong /strɒŋ US: strɔːŋ/ *adj* (-er, -est) **1** (opposite of *weak*) having power to resist; not easily hurt, injured, broken, captured, etc; having great power of body or mind: *a* ∼ *stick,* not easily broken; *a* ∼ *wind; a* ∼ *will/imagination; feel quite* ∼ *again,* in good health after an illness; *an army 500 000* ∼, numbering 500 000; *a* ∼ *candidate,* one likely to be well supported, etc; ∼ (= deeply held or rooted) *beliefs/convictions.* **as strong as a horse,** physically powerful. **one's** `**strong point,** that which one does well. **2** having a large proportion of the flavouring element: ∼ *tea/coffee.* **3** having a considerable effect on the mind or the senses: *a* ∼ *smell of gas.* **4** (*adverbial* uses) **going strong,** (*informal*) continuing (the race, activity, etc) with energy; continuing in good health: *aged 90 and still going* ∼. **5** (*commerce*) (of prices) rising steadily: *Prices/Markets are* ∼.

`**strong-arm,** (of methods tactics, etc) using physical force.

`**strong-box,** strongly built for keeping valuables.

strong drink, containing alcohol, e g rum.

`**strong-hold, (a)** fort. **(b)** (*fig*) place where a cause or idea has a strong support: *a* ∼*hold of Protestantism.*

strong language, with swear-words, abuses, etc.

`**strong-**`**minded** /ˈmaɪndɪd/ *adj* having a mind that is capable and energetic.

`**strong-room,** one built with thick walls (e g in a bank) for storing valuables.

strong verb, (*gram*) which forms the past tense with a vowel change, e g *sing, sang, sung.*

strong·ly *adv* in a strong manner: *I* ∼*ly advise you to go.*

strove /strəʊv/ *pt of* strive.
struck /strʌk/ *pt,pp of* strike[2].
struc·tural /ˈstrʌktʃərəl/ *adj* of a structure, esp the framework: *structural alterations to*

a building, e g combining two rooms into one.

struc·tur·ally /-rəlɪ/ *adv: The building is structurally sound.*

struc·ture /ˈstrʌktʃə(r)/ *n* **1** [U] way in which something is put together, organized, etc: *the ~ of the human body; sentence ~.* **2** [C] framework or essential parts of a building, etc: *The Parthenon was a magnificent marble ~.*

struggle /ˈstrʌgəl/ *vi* fight, make great efforts: *~ against difficulties/with the accounts; ~ for power. The thief ~d to get free.* □ *n* [C] struggling; contest: *the ~ for freedom.*

strum /strʌm/ *vi,vt* (-mm-) *strum (on)*, play music, (usually on a string instrument) (and esp without skill): *~ (on) the guitar.* □ *n* [C] sound of strumming.

strung /strʌŋ/ *pt,pp* of string².

strut¹ /strʌt/ *n* [C] piece of wood or metal in a framework to strengthen it.

strut² /strʌt/ *vi* (-tt-) walk (*about, along, in, out, into a room, etc*) in a stiff, thoughtful, anxious, etc way. □ *n* [C] such a way of walking.

strych·nine /ˈstrɪknɪn/ *n* [U] strong poison.

stub /stʌb/ *n* [C] **1** short remaining end of a pencil, cigarette or similar object: *a ~ of a tail*, a very short one. **2** counterfoil: *the ~s of a cheque-book.* □ *vt* (-bb-) **1** *~ one's toe*, hit it against something. **2** extinguish (esp a cigarette) by pressing it against something hard.

stubble /ˈstʌbəl/ *n* [U] **1** stalks of grain plants left in the ground after harvest. **2** something suggesting this, e g a short growth of beard.

stub·bly /ˈstʌblɪ/ *adj: a stubbly beard.*

stub·born /ˈstʌbən/ *adj* obstinate; determined: *~ soil*, difficult to plough, etc. *as stubborn as a mule*, extremely obstinate.

stub·born·ly *adv*

stub·born·ness *n* [U]

stubby /ˈstʌbɪ/ *adj* (-ier, -iest) short and thick: *~ fingers.*

stuck /stʌk/ *pt,pp* of stick².

stuck-up /ˈstʌk ˈʌp/ *adj* (*informal*) conceited; snobbish.

stud¹ /stʌd/ *n* [C] **1** small device put through button-holes to fasten a collar, cuff, etc. **2** *re`flector ~s*, used on roads to mark out lanes (and reflecting light from headlamps at night). □ *vt* (-dd-) (usually *pp*) having (something) set in or scattered on the surface: *a crown ~ded with jewels; a sea ~ded with islands.*

stud² /stʌd/ *n* [C] number of horses kept by one owner for a special purpose (esp breeding or racing).

`stud-farm, place where horses are bred.

stu·dent /ˈstjuːdənt US: ˈstuː-/ *n* [C] **1** (*GB*) (undergraduate or post graduate) person who is studying at a college, polytechnic or university: *`medical ~s.* **2** (*US*) boy or girl

attending school. **3** anyone who studies or who is devoted to learning: *a ~ of nature.*

stu·dio /ˈstjuːdɪəʊ US: ˈstuː-/ *n* [C] (*pl ~s*) **1** workroom of a painter, sculptor, photographer, etc. **2** room(s) where films/plays are acted and photographed. **3** room from which radio or TV programmes are broadcast or in which recordings are made.

`studio couch, couch that can be used as a bed.

stu·di·ous /ˈstjuːdɪəs US: ˈstuː-/ *adj* (*formal*) **1** having or showing the habit of learning. **2** painstaking: *with ~ politeness*

stu·di·ous·ly *adv*

study¹ /ˈstʌdɪ/ *n* (*pl* -ies) **1** [U and in *pl*] devotion of time and thought to getting knowledge of, close examination of, a subject, esp from books: *fond of ~; My studies show that...* **2** [C] something that attracts investigation; that which is (to be) investigated: *social studies.* **3** room used for reading, writing, etc: *You will find Mr Green in the/his ~.* **4** sketch, etc made for practice or experiment; piece of music played as a technical exercise.

study² /ˈstʌdɪ/ *vt,vi* (*pt,pp* -ied) **1** give time and attention to learning or discovering something: *~ medicine. He was ~ing to be a doctor.* **2** examine carefully: *~ the map.*

stuff¹ /stʌf/ *n* **1** [C,U] material or substance of which something is made or which may be used for some purpose: *What ~ will you use to fill the cushions?* **2** [U] (*fig*) quality, type: *He is not the ~ heroes are made of.* **3** [U] material of which the name is uncertain, unknown or unimportant; material of poor quality: *Do you call this ~ beer?* **4** (*sl*) *Do your stuff*, Show what you can do, etc. *know one's stuff*, be expert in what one claims to be able to do, etc.

stuff² /stʌf/ *vt* **1** fill tightly with; press tightly into: *~ feathers into a bag; ~ oneself with food*, eat too much; *a head ~ed with silly ideas.* **2** put chopped up and specially flavoured food into (a bird, etc) before cooking it: *a ~ed chicken.* **3** fill the carcass of (an animal, etc) with material to give it the original shape, e g for exhibition in a museum: *a ~ed tiger.*

stuff·ing *n* [U] material for stuffing, e g cushions, birds, ⇨ 2,3 above.

stuffy /ˈstʌfɪ/ *adj* (-ier, -iest) **1** (of a room) badly ventilated. **2** (*informal*) (of a person) easily shocked or offended. **3** dull; formal: *a ~ book.*

stuff·ily /-əlɪ/ *adv*

stuffi·ness *n* [U]

stul·tify /ˈstʌltɪfaɪ/ *vt* (*pt,pp* -ied) (*formal*) cause to seem foolish or to be useless: *~ efforts to reach agreement*

stumble /ˈstʌmbəl/ *vi* **1** hit the foot against something and (almost) fall: *~ over the root of a tree. The child ~d and fell. stumble across/on/upon sth*, (*fig*) find it unexpectedly or by accident. **2** move or walk in an unsteady way: *stumbling along.* **3** speak in a hesitating way, with pauses and mistakes: ∼ *over one's words.* ▢ *n* [C] act of stumbling.

`stum·bling block`, something that causes difficulties or prevents progress.

stump /stʌmp/ *n* [C] **1** part of a tree remaining in the ground when the trunk has fallen or has been cut down. **2** anything remaining after the main part has been cut or broken off or has worn off, eg an amputated limb, the end of a pencil, etc. **3** (*cricket*) one of the three upright pieces of wood at which the ball is bowled. ▢ *vi,vt* **1** walk (*along, about, etc*) with stiff, heavy movements. **2** (*informal*) be too difficult for: *All the candidates were* ∼*ed by the second question.* **3** (*cricket*) end the innings of (a batsman) by touching the stumps with the ball. **4** (*sl*) pay or give money required: *Mr Green has had to* ∼ *up (£50) for his son's debts.*

stumpy /stʌmpɪ/ *adj* (-ier, -iest) short and thick: *a* ∼ *little man; a* ∼ *umbrella.*

stun /stʌn/ *vt* (-nn-) **1** make unconscious by a blow, esp one on the head. **2** shock; confuse the mind of: *He was* ∼*ned by the news of his father's death.*

stun·ning *adj* (*informal*) splendid: *a* ∼*ning performance.*

stung /stʌŋ/ *pt,pp* of sting².

stunk /stʌŋk/ *pp* of stink.

stunt¹ /stʌnt/ *n* [C] (*informal*) something done to attract attention: ∼ *flying,* aerobatics.

`stunt man`, person employed to perform stunts (involving risk, etc) as a stand-in for an actor in films, etc.

stunt² /stʌnt/ *vt* halt or slow down the growth or development of: *a* ∼*ed mind.*

stu·pefy /stjuːpɪfaɪ US: `stu-/ *vt* (*pt,pp* -ied) (*formal*) make clear thought impossible: *stupefied with drink/amazement.*

stu·pen·dous /stjuːpendəs US: stu-/ *adj* amazing (in size, degree): *a* ∼ *achievement.*
stu·pen·dous·ly *adv*

stu·pid /stjuːpɪd US: `stu-/ *adj* **1** unintelligent; foolish: *Don't be* ∼ *enough to believe that.* **2** in a state of stupor. ▢ *n* [C] (*informal*) foolish person: *I was only teasing,* ∼*!*
stu·pid·ly *adv*
stu·pid·ity /stjuːpɪdətɪ US: stu-/ *n* [C,U]

stu·por /stjuːpə(r) US: `stu-/ *n* [C,U] almost unconscious condition caused by shock, drugs, drink, etc: *in a drunken* ∼.

sturdy /stɜːdɪ/ *adj* (-ier, -iest) strong and solid: ∼ *children; offer a* ∼ *resistance.*
stur·dily /-əlɪ/ *adv: a sturdily built bicycle*

stut·ter /stʌtə(r)/ *vi,vt n* = stammer.
stut·terer, person who stutters.

sty¹ /staɪ/ *n* [C] (*pl* sties) = pigsty.

sty² (also **stye**) /staɪ/ *n* [C] (*pl* sties, styes) inflamed swelling on the edge of the eyelid.

style /staɪl/ *n* **1** [C,U] manner of writing or speaking (contrasted with the subject matter); manner of doing anything, esp when it is characteristic of an artist or of a period of art: *written in a delightful* ∼. *What do you know about the* ∼*s of architecture?* **2** [U] quality that marks something done or made as superior, fashionable or distinctive: *live in* (*grand*) ∼, in a fashionable house, with luxuries, etc. *Did they live in European* ∼ *when they were in Japan?* **3** [C,U] (esp) fashion in dress, etc: *the latest* ∼*s in shoes/ in hair-dressing.* **4** [C] general appearance, form or design; kind or sort: *made in all sizes and* ∼*s.* **5** [C] right title (to be) used when addressing a person: *Has he any right to assume the* ∼ *of Colonel?* **6** [C] (*botany*) part of the seed-producing part of a flower. ▢ *vt* **1** describe by a specified title: *Should he be* ∼*d 'Right Honourable'?* **2** design: *new handbags* ∼*d by Italians.*

styl·ish /-ɪʃ/ *adj* having style(2,3); fashionable: *stylish clothes.*
styl·ish·ly *adv: stylishly dressed.*

sty·list /staɪlɪst/ *n* [C] **1** person, esp a writer, with a good literary style. **2** person who is concerned with creating styles(3): *a* `hair-∼.

sty·lis·tic /staɪˈlɪstɪk/ *adj* of style(1).
styl·is·ti·cally /-klɪ/ *adv*

sty·lize /staɪlaɪz/ *vt* represent or treat (art forms, etc) in the particular, conventional style.

sty·lus /staɪləs/ *n* [C] (*pl* ∼es) part like a needle used to cut grooves in records or to reproduce sound from records.

suave /swɑːv/ *adj* smooth and gracious (often superficially) in manner.
suave·ly *adv*

sub /sʌb/ *n* [C] (*informal*) (abbr of) **1** submarine. **2** substitute. **3** subscription.

sub- /sʌb-/ *prefix* **1** under: *subway.* **2** secondary, lower in rank: *sub-committee.* **3** not quite: *sub-tropical.*

sub·com·mit·tee /sʌb kəmɪtɪ/ *n* [C] committee formed from members of a main committee.

sub·con·scious /sʌbˈkɒnʃəs/ *adj* of those mental activites of which we are not (completely) aware: *the* ∼ *self.* ▢ *n* **the** ∼, subconscious thoughts, desires, etc.
sub·con·scious·ly *adv*
sub·con·scious·ness *n* [U]

sub·con·ti·nent /sʌbˈkɒntɪnənt US: -tən-/ *n* [C] mass of land large enough to be regarded as a separate continent but forming part of a larger mass.

sub·con·tract /sʌbˈkɒntrækt/ *n* [C] contract which is for carrying out a previous contract or a part of it. ▢ *vt,vi* /ˈsʌbkənˈtrækt US: -ˈkɒntrækt/ give or accept a subcontract.
sub·con·tractor /ˈsʌbkənˈtræktə(r) US: -ˈkɒntræk-/, person who accepts a subcontract.

sub·cu·taneous /ˈsʌbkjuːˈteɪnɪəs/ *adj* under the skin.

sub·di·vide /ˈsʌbdɪˈvaɪd/ *vt,vi* divide into

further divisions.

sub·di·vi·sion /ˈsʌbdɪˈvɪʒən/ n [U] subdividing; [C] something produced by subdividing.

sub·due /səbˈdjuː US: -ˈduː/ vt **1** bring under control: ~ one's hatred. **2** make quieter, softer, gentler: (esp pp) ~d voices/lights.

sub·hu·man /ˈsʌbˈhjuːmən/ adj more like an animal than a human being.

sub·ject[1] /ˈsʌbdʒɪkt/ adj **subject to**, **1** owing obedience (to): We are ~ to the law of the land. **2** having a tendency (to): Are you ~ to colds? **3** (adj, adv) conditional(ly) on: The plan is ~ to confirmation.

sub·ject[2] /ˈsʌbdʒɪkt/ n [C] **1** any member of a State except the supreme ruler: British ~s. **2** something (to be) talked or written about or studied: an interesting ~ of conversation. What ~ are you studying? **change the subject,** talk about something different. **3** person, animal or thing (to be) treated or dealt with, to be made to undergo or experience something: a ~ for experiment. **4** (gram) word(s) in a sentence which is described, which does, something, etc, e g book in 'The book is green' and they in 'Did they come early?' **5** (music) theme on which a composition is based.

`subject matter, plot, topic, etc of in a book or speech (contrasted with style).

sub·ject[3] /səbˈdʒekt/ vt **1** bring, get (a country, nation, person) under control: The Romans ~ed most of Europe to their rule. **2** cause to undergo or experience: ~ a man to torture.

sub·jec·tion /səbˈdʒekʃən/ n [U]

sub·jec·tive /səbˈdʒektɪv/ adj **1** (opposite of objective) (of ideas, feelings, etc) existing in the mind, not produced by things outside the mind: Did he really see a ghost or was it only a ~ impression? **2** (of art and artists, writing, etc) giving the personal or individual point of view or feeling (opposite of realistic). **3** (gram) of the subject.

sub·jec·tive·ly adv

sub·jec·tiv·ity /ˈsʌbdʒekˈtɪvətɪ/ n [U]

sub·ju·gate /ˈsʌbdʒʊɡeɪt/ vt (formal) subdue; conquer.

sub·ju·ga·tion /ˈsʌbdʒʊˈɡeɪʃən/ n [U]

sub·junc·tive /səbˈdʒʌŋktɪv/ adj (gram) expressing a condition, hypothesis, possibility, etc. □ n [C] the subjunctive mood; form of a verb in this mood.

sub·lease /ˈsʌbˈliːs/ vt, vi lease to another person. □ n [C] lease of this kind.

sub·let /ˈsʌbˈlet/ vt, vi (-tt-) rent (a room, house, etc of which one is a tenant) to somebody else.

sub·li·mate /ˈsʌblɪmeɪt/ vt **1** (psychology) direct (emotions, impulses) into higher or more desirable channels. **2** (informal) idealize.

sub·lime /səˈblaɪm/ adj **1** of the greatest and highest sort; causing wonder or reverence: ~ heroism. **2** extreme (as of a person

who does not fear the consequences): What ~ indifference! □ n the ~, that which fills one with wonder or reverence.

sub·lime·ly adv

sub·lim·inal /ˈsʌbˈlɪmɪnəl/ adj of which one is not consciously aware.

sub·mar·ine /ˈsʌbməˈriːn US: ˈsʌbməriːn/ adj existing, designed for use, under the surface of the sea: a ~ cable. □ n [C] ship which can operate under water.

sub·merge /səbˈmɜːdʒ/ vt, vi **1** put under water; cover with a liquid. **2** sink out of sight; (of a submarine) go down under the surface. **3** (fig) inundate.

sub·merged adj (a) under the surface of the sea, etc: ~d rocks. (b) (fig) overwhelmed.

sub·merg·ence /səbˈmɜːdʒəns/, **sub·mer·sion** /sæbˈmɜːʃən US: -ɜːrʒən/ n [U] submerging or being submerged.

sub·mis·sion /səbˈmɪʃən/ n **1** [U] act of submitting; acceptance of another's power or authority: The enemy were starved into ~. **2** [U] obedience; respect: with all due ~. **3** [C,U] (legal) theory, etc submitted to a judge or jury: My ~ is that…

sub·mis·sive /səbˈmɪsɪv/ adj yielding to the control or authority of another: Marian is not a ~ wife.

sub·mis·sive·ly adv

sub·mis·sive·ness n [U]

sub·mit /səbˈmɪt/ vt, vi (-tt-) **1** put (oneself) under the control of another: ~ oneself to discipline. **2** put forward for opinion, discussion, decision, etc: ~ plans/proposals, etc to a committee. **3** (legal) suggest: Counsel ~ted that there was no case against his client. **4** surrender: ~ to separation from one's family.

sub·nor·mal /ˈsʌbˈnɔːməl/ adj below normal (esp intelligence).

sub·or·di·nate /səˈbɔːdɪnət US: -dənət/ adj junior in rank or position; less important: in a ~ position. □ n [C] person in a junior position. □ vt /səˈbɔːdɪneɪt US: -dəneɪt/ treat as junior.

subordinate clause, (gram) dependent clause; clause which, introduced by a conjunction, serves as a noun, adj or adv.

sub·scribe /səbˈskraɪb/ vi, vt **1** (agree to) pay (a sum of money) with other persons (to a cause, for something): He ~s liberally to charities. **2** agree to take (a newspaper, periodical, etc) regularly. **3** agree with, share (an opinion, view, etc): ~ to the general view that …

sub·scriber, (a) person who subscribes (esp to funds). **(b)** person, business, etc paying for having a telephone.

sub·scrip·tion /səbˈskrɪpʃən/ n **(a)** [U] subscribing or being subscribed: paid for by public subscription. **(b)** [C] sum of money paid (to charity, for receiving a newspaper, magazine, etc, or for membership of a club).

sub·se·quent /ˈsʌbsɪkwənt/ adj later; following: ~ events; ~ to this event.

sub·se·quent·ly adv afterwards.

sub·ser·vi·ent /səb`sɜːvɪənt/ adj **1** giving too much respect to: ～ junior staff. **2** subordinate or subject to.

sub·ser·vi·ent·ly adv

sub·side /səb`saɪd/ vt **1** (of flood water) sink to a lower or to the normal level. **2** (of land) sink, e g because of mining operations. **3** (of buildings) settle lower down in the ground. **4** (of winds, passions, etc) become quiet(er).

sub·sid·ence /səb`saɪdəns/ n [C,U] act or process of subsiding(2,3); instance of this.

sub·sidi·ary /səb`sɪdɪərɪ US: -dɪerɪ/ adj serving as a help or support but not of first importance: a ～ company, one that is controlled by a larger one. □ n [C] (pl -ies) subsidiary company, thing or person.

sub·si·dize /`sʌbsɪdaɪz/ vt give a subsidy to.

sub·si·diz·ation /ˌsʌbsɪdaɪ`zeɪʃən US. -dɪ`z-/ n [U]

sub·sidy /`sʌbsədɪ/ n [C] (pl -ies) money granted, esp by a government or society, to an industry or other cause needing help, or (e g food subsidies) to keep prices at a desired level.

sub·sist /səb`sɪst/ vi (formal) exist; be kept in existence on: ～ on a vegetable diet.

sub·sis·tence /-təns/ n [U] (means of) existing: ～ence crops, those grown for consumption (contrasted with `cash crops, sold for money).

sub·soil /`sʌbsɔɪl/ n [U] layer of soil that lies immediately beneath the surface layer.

sub·sonic /`sʌb`sɒnɪk/ adj (at) less than the speed of sound.

sub·stance /`sʌbstəns/ n **1** [C,U] (particular kind of) matter: Water, ice and snow are the same ～ in different forms. **2** [U] most important part, chief or real meaning, of something: I agree in ～ with what you say, but differ on some small points. **3** [U] firmness; solidity: This material has some ～, is fairly solid or strong. **4** [U] money; property: a man of ～, e g a property owner.

sub·stan·dard /`sʌb`stændəd/ adj below average standard.

sub·stan·tial /səb`stænʃəl/ adj **1** solidly or strongly built or made. **2** large; considerable: a ～ meal/improvement/loan. **3** possessing considerable property: a ～ business firm. **4** in essentials: We are in ～ agreement. **5** real: Was what you saw something ～ or only a ghost?

sub·stan·tial·ly /-ʃəlɪ/ adv: Your efforts contributed ～ly (= considerably) to our success.

sub·stan·ti·ate /səb`stænʃɪeɪt/ vt give facts to support (a claim, statement, charge, etc).

sub·stan·ti·ation /səb`stænʃɪ`eɪʃən/ n

sub·sti·tute /`sʌbstɪtjut US: -tut/ n [C] person or thing taking the place of, acting for or serving for another: S～s for rubber can be made from petroleum. □ vt,vi use, serve, as a substitute: ～ margarine for butter.

sub·sti·tu·tion /ˌsʌbstɪ`tjuʃən US: -`tuʃən/ n [U]

sub·stra·tum /`sʌb`strɑːtəm US: -`streɪt-/ n [C] (pl -ta /-tə/) **1** level lying below another: a ～ of rock. **2** (formal) foundation: The story has a ～ of truth.

sub·struc·ture /`sʌbstrʌktʃə(r)/ n [C] foundation (the usual word).

sub·sume /səb`sjum US: -`sum/ vt (formal) include (an example, etc) under a rule or in a particular class.

sub·ter·fuge /`sʌbtəfjudʒ/ n [C,U] (formal) trick; [U] trickery.

sub·ter·ranean /ˌsʌbtə`reɪnɪən/ adj (formal) = underground.

sub·title /`sʌbtaɪtl/ n [C] **1** secondary title (of a book). **2** translation of a foreign language film, printed on the film.

subtle /`sʌtəl/ adj **1** difficult to perceive or describe because fine or delicate: a ～ distinction. **2** clever; complex: a ～ argument. **3** quick and clever at seeing or describing small differences: a ～ observer.

subtlety n [C,U] (pl -ies)

sub·tly /`sʌtəlɪ/ adv

sub·tract /səb`trækt/ vt take (a number, quantity) away from (another number, etc): ～ 6 from 9.

sub·trac·tion /səb`trækʃən/ n [C,U]

sub·tropi·cal /`sʌb`trɒpɪkəl/ adj nearly tropical.

sub·urb /`sʌbɜːb/ n [C] residential district round the outside of a town or city.

sub·ur·ban /sə`bɜːbən/ adj of or in a suburb.

sub·ur·bia /sə`bɜːbɪə/ n [U] (usually derogatory) (kind of life lived by, characteristic outlook of, people in) suburbs.

sub·ver·sion /səb`vɜːʃən US: -`vɜːʒən/ n [U] act of subverting.

sub·vers·ive /səb`vɜːsɪv/ adj tending to subvert: ～ literature/speeches/policies.

sub·vert /`sʌb`vɜːt/ vt destroy, overthrow (religion, a government) by weakening people's trust, confidence, belief.

sub·way /`sʌbweɪ/ n [C] **1** underground passage or tunnel, e g used to get from one side of a street to another. **2** (US) = underground(1).

suc·ceed /sək`sid/ vi,vt **1** do what one is trying to do: ～ in passing an examination. The attack ～ed. **2** come next after and take the place of: Who ～ed Kennedy as President? **3** inherit (a title, position, etc): On George VI's death, Elizabeth II ～ed (to the throne).

suc·cess /sək`ses/ n **1** [U] succeeding; the gaining of what is aimed at: meet with ～. **2** [U] prosperity: have great ～ in life. **3** [C] person or thing that succeeds: The plan/play/lecturer was a great ～.

suc·cess·ful /-fəl/ adj having success: ～ful candidates.

suc·cess·fully /-fəlɪ/ adv

suc·ces·sion /sək`seʃən/ n **1** [U] the coming

of one thing after another in time or order: *the ~ of the seasons.* **in succession,** one after the other. **2** [C] number of things in succession: *a ~ of defeats.* **3** [U] (right of) succeeding to a title, the throne, property, etc; person having this right: *Who is first in ~ to the throne?*

suc·cess·ive /sək'sesɪv/ *adj* coming one after the other in an uninterrupted sequence: *Liverpool won eleven ~ games.*

suc·cess·ive·ly *adv*

suc·ces·sor /sək'sesə(r)/ *n* [C] person or thing that succeeds another: *appoint a ~ to a headmaster.*

suc·cinct /sək'sɪŋkt/ *adj* expressed briefly and clearly.

suc·cinct·ly *adv*

suc·cinct·ness *n* [U]

suc·cour (*US* = **-cor**) /'sʌkə(r)/ *n* [U] (*literary*) help given in time of need. □ *vt* give such help to.

suc·cu·lent /'sʌkjʊlənt/ *adj* **1** (of fruit and meat) juicy; tasting good: *a ~ steak.* **2** (of stems, leaves) thick and fleshy; (of plants) having fleshy stems and leaves. □ *n* [C] succulent plant, e g a cactus.

suc·cumb /sə'kʌm/ *vi* yield (to death, temptation, flattery, etc).

such /sʌtʃ/ *adj* (*Note:* there is no comparative or superlative; not placed between the *a* and a noun.) **1** of the same kind or degree (as): *All ~ people are respected; poets ~ as Keats and Shelley; ~ poets as Keats and Shelley; ~ an occasion/on an occasion ~ as this. I've never heard of ~ a thing!* **2** *such as it is,* (used to suggest that something is of poor quality, of little value, etc): *You can use my bicycle, ~ as it is.* **3** *such (...) that: His behaviour was ~ that everyone disliked him. S~ was the force of the explosion that all the windows were broken.* **4** (Compare the positions of *such and so* in these examples): *Don't be in ~ a hurry,* in so much of a hurry, in so great a hurry. *I haven't had ~ an enjoyable evening* (= so enjoyable an evening) *for months.* **5** (used in exclamatory sentences): *It was ~ a long time ago! We've had ~ a good time!* **6** this, that, these, those (as already stated, etc): *S~ were his words. S~ is life!* Life is like that. □ *pron* person(s) or thing(s) of the same kind, etc: *I may have hurt feelings but ~* (= that) *was certainly not my intention.*

'such·like *adj* (*informal*) people, things, of the same kind: *I have no time for pop concerts and ~like.*

suck /sʌk/ *vt,vi* **1** draw (liquid) into the mouth by the use of the lip muscles: *~ the juice from an orange.* **2** hold (something) in the mouth and lick, move, squeeze, etc with the tongue: *The child still ~s its thumb.* **3** *suck sth up,* absorb: *plants ~ up moisture from the soil.* **4** (of a whirlpool, etc) pull in: *The canoe was ~ed (down) into the whirlpool.* □ *n* [C] act or process of sucking:

have/take a ~ at a lollipop.

sucker /'sʌkə(r)/ *n* [C] **1** person who, that which, sucks. **2** organ of some animals so that they can rest on a surface by suction **3** rubber device, e g a rubber disc, that can be used to fix an object to a surface by suction **4** unwanted shoot from the roots of a tree shrub, etc. **5** (*informal*) person foolish enough to be deceived by salesmen, advertisements, etc.

suckle /'sʌkəl/ *vt* feed with milk from the breast or udder.

suc·tion /'sʌkʃən/ *n* [U] **1** action of sucking **2** removal of air, liquid, etc from a cavity so as to produce a partial vacuum and enable air-pressure from outside to force in liquid or dust: *Vacuum-cleaners work by ~.* **3** similar process, e g in a rubber disc, a fly's foot, producing a vacuum that causes two surfaces to be held together.

sud·den /'sʌdən/ *adj* happening, coming done, unexpectedly, quickly, without warning: *a ~ shower.* □ *n* (only in) *all of a sudden,* unexpectedly.

sud·den·ly *adv*

sud·den·ness *n* [C]

suds /sʌdz/ *n pl* mass of tiny bubbles on soapy water.

sue /su/ *vt,vi* **sue for,** **1** make a legal claim against: *~ a person for damages.* **2** beg (the usual word): *suing for mercy.*

suede, suède /sweɪd/ *n* [U] kind of soft leather without a shining surface.

suet /'suɪt/ *n* [U] hard fat round the kidneys of sheep and oxen, used in cooking.

suf·fer /'sʌfə(r)/ *vi,vt* **1** *suffer (from),* feel or have pain, loss, etc. *~ from* (= often have) *headaches. His business ~ed while he was ill,* His business did not do well. **2** experience (something unpleasant): *~ pain/ defeat.* **3** put up with: *How can you ~ such insolence?*

suf·ferer, person who suffers.

suf·fer·ing, (a) [U] pain of body or mind. (b) (*pl*) feelings of pain, unhappiness, etc: *a prisoner's ~ings.*

suf·fer·ance /'sʌfrəns/ *n* [U] with permission implied by the absence of objection: *He's here on ~.*

suf·fice /sə'faɪs/ *vi,vt* **1** be enough (the more usual words): *Will £10 ~ for your needs?* **2** meet the needs of: *One meal a day won't ~ a growing boy.*

suf·fi·ciency /sə'fɪʃənsɪ/ *n* (usually with *a, an*) sufficient quantity: *a ~ of fuel*

suf·fi·cient /sə'fɪʃənt/ *adj* enough: *Have we ~ food for ten people?*

suf·fi·cient·ly *adv*

suf·fix /'sʌfɪks/ *n* [C] letter(s), sounds or syllable(s) added at the end of a word to make another word.

suf·fo·cate /'sʌfəkeɪt/ *vt,vi* **1** cause or have difficulty in breathing: *The fumes were suffocating me.* **2** kill, choke, by making breathing impossible.

suf·fo·ca·tion /ˌsʌfəˈkeɪʃən/ n [U]

sugar /ˈʃʊgə(r)/ n [U] sweet substance obtained from the juices of various plants, used in cooking and for sweetening drinks. □ vt sweeten or mix with sugar.

`sugar daddy, (informal) rich, elderly man who is generous to a young woman.

sugary adj (a) tasting of sugar. (b) (fig) (of music, etc) too sweet.

sug·gest /səˈdʒest US: səɡˈdʒ-/ vt 1 put forward for consideration, as a possibility: I ∼ed a visit/∼ed going/that we should go to the theatre. 2 bring (an idea, possibility, etc) into the mind: That cloud ∼s an old man.

sug·ges·tion /səˈdʒestʃən US: səɡˈdʒ-/ n (a) [U] suggesting: at the ∼ion of my brother; on your ∼ion. (b) [C] idea, plan, etc that is suggested: What a silly ∼ion! (c) [C] slight indication: a ∼ion of a French accent.

sug·ges·tive /səˈdʒestɪv US: səɡ-/ adj (a) tending to bring ideas, etc into the mind: ∼ive remarks. (b) tending to suggest(2) something indecent: ∼ive jokes.

sug·ges·tive·ly adv

sui·cidal /ˌsuːɪˈsaɪdəl/ adj 1 of suicide. 2 very harmful to one's own interests: ∼ policies.

sui·cide /ˈsuːɪsaɪd/ n 1 [U] murder of oneself: commit ∼; [C] instance of this: three ∼s last week; [C] person who does this. 2 [U] action destructive to one's interests or welfare: economic ∼, e g adoption of policies that will ruin the country's economy.

suit¹ /suːt/ n [C] 1 set of articles of outer clothing of the same material: a man's ∼, jacket (waistcoat) and trousers. 2 (formal) request made to a superior, esp to a ruler: press one's ∼. 3 = lawsuit. 4 any of the four sets of cards (spades, hearts, diamonds, clubs) used in many card games. **follow suit,** (fig) do what somebody else has done.

`suit·case, portable case with flat sides for clothes, used when travelling.

suit² /suːt/ vt, vi 1 satisfy; meet the needs of; be convenient to or right for: Does the climate ∼ you/your health? Will Thursday ∼ (you), be convenient? **suit oneself,** act according to one's own wishes. 2 (esp of articles of dress, hair styles, etc) look well; be appropriate for: Does this hat ∼ me? 3 **be suited (to/for),** be fitted, have the right qualities: That man is not ∼ed for teaching/to be a teacher.

suit·able /ˈsuːtəbəl/ adj right for the purpose or occasion: ∼ clothes for cold weather.

suit·ably /-əblɪ/ adv: suitably dressed.

suit·abil·ity /ˈsuːtəˈbɪlətɪ/ n [U]

suite /swiːt/ n [C] 1 group of personal attendants of an important person (e g a ruler). 2 complete set of matching articles of furniture: a `bedroom ∼. 3 set of rooms (e g in a hotel): the `bridal ∼. 4 (music) orchestral composition made up of three or more related parts

suitor /ˈsuːtə(r)/ n [C] 1 person bringing a lawsuit. 2 (dated) man courting a woman.

sulk /sʌlk/ vi be in a bad temper amd show this by refusing to talk.

sulky adj (-ier, -iest) unsociable.

sul·len /ˈsʌlən/ adj 1 silent and angry: ∼ looks. 2 dark and gloomy: a ∼ sky

sul·len·ly adv

sul·len·ness n [U]

sul·phur (US = **sul·fur**) /ˈsʌlfə(r)/ n [U] light-yellow non-metallic element (symbol S) that burns with a bright flame and a strong smell, used in medicine and industry.

sul·phu·ric (US = **sul·fu·**) /sʌlˈfjʊərɪk/ adj: ∼ic acid.

sul·tan /ˈsʌltən/ n [C] Muslim ruler.

sul·tan·ate /ˈsʌltəneɪt/, position, period of rule of, territory ruled by, a sultan.

sul·tana /sʌlˈtɑːnə US: -ˈtænə/ n [C] (pl ∼s) kind of small seedless raisin used in puddings and cakes.

sul·try /ˈsʌltrɪ/ adj (-ier, -iest) 1 (of the atmosphere, the weather) hot and oppressive. 2 (of a person's temper) passionate.

sul·trily /-trəlɪ/ adv

sum /sʌm/ n [C] 1 (also **sum total**) total obtained by adding together items, numbers or amounts. 2 problem in arithmetic: good at ∼s. 3 amount of money: save a nice little ∼ each week. □ vt, vi (-mm-) 1 give the total of. 2 express briefly (the chief points of what has been said): The judge ∼med up (the evidence). 3 form a judgement or opinion of: He ∼med up the situation at a glance, realized it at once.

sum·mar·ize /ˈsʌməraɪz/ vt be or make a summary of.

sum·mary /ˈsʌmərɪ/ adj (formal) 1 brief; giving the chief points only: a ∼ account. 2 done or given without delay or attention to small matters: ∼ justice. □ n [C] (pl -ies) brief account giving the chief points.

sum·mer /ˈsʌmə(r)/ n [C,U] (in countries outside the tropics) the warmest season of the year: in (the) ∼; this/next/last ∼; (as an adjective) ∼ weather; the ∼ holidays.

`sum·mer·time, the season of summer.

`summer time, time as recognized in some countries where clocks are put forward one hour so that darkness falls an hour later.

sum·mery adj like, suitable for, summer: a ∼y dress.

sum·mit /ˈsʌmɪt/ n [C] 1 highest point; top: reach the ∼, of a mountain. 2 (fig): the ∼ of his power.

`summit talk/meeting, (modern use) at the highest level (i e between heads of States).

sum·mon /ˈsʌmən/ vt 1 call or send for: ∼ a person to appear as a witness, e g in a law court. 2 gather together: ∼ up all one's courage.

sum·mons /ˈsʌmənz/ n [C] (pl ∼es) 1 order to appear before a judge or magistrate; document with such an order: issue a ∼ 2 command to do something or appear somewhere. □ vt serve a summons(1) on.

sun /sʌn/ n **1 the ~,** the heavenly body from which the earth gets warmth and light. **2 the ~,** light and warmth from the sun: *sit in the ~. under the sun,* (anywhere) in the world: *the best wine under the ~.* **3** [C] any fixed star with satellites: *There are many ~s larger than ours.* □ vt (-nn-) put in, expose (*oneself*) to, the rays of the sun: *The cat was ~ning itself on the path.*

`sun-baked adj made hard by the heat of the sun: ~baked fields.

`sun-bathe vi expose one's body to sunlight.

`sun-beam, ray of sunshine.

`sun-burn, (place where there is a) reddening and blistering caused by too much exposure to the sun. Hence, `sun-burnt adj.

`sun-dial, device that shows the time by the sun producing a shadow on a marked surface.

`sun-drenched adj exposed to great light and heat from the sun: ~-drenched beaches.

`sun-dried adj (of fruit, etc) dried naturally, by the sun, not by artificial heat.

`sun-fish, large fish almost spherical in shape.

`sun-glasses, with dark-coloured glass to protect the eyes from bright sunshine.

`sun-god, sun worshipped as a god.

`sun-lamp, lamp that gives out ultra-violet rays used for artificial sunbathing.

`sun-light, the light of the sun.

`sun-lit adj lit by the sun: a ~lit room.

`sun-rise, (time of) the sun's rising.

`sun-set, (time of) the sun's setting.

`sun-shade, parasol (like an umbrella) to keep off the sun.

`sun-shine, light of the sun.

`sun-spot, (a) (astronomy) dark patch on the sun. (b) (informal) place that has a sunny climate (e g for holidays).

`sun-stroke, illness caused by too much exposure to the sun, esp on the head.

`sun-tan, browning of the skin from exposure to sunlight: `~tan lotion/oil.

`sun-worship, (informal) fondness for sunbathing.

sun-less adj receiving little or no sunlight.

sunny adj (-ier, -iest) (a) bright with sunlight: a ~ny room. (b) cheerful: a ~ny smile.

Sun-day /ˈsʌndɪ/ n the first day of the week. *a month of sundays,* a long period of time.

sun-dries /ˈsʌndrɪz/ n pl various small items.

sung /sʌŋ/ pp of sing.

sunk /sʌŋk/ pt,pp of sink².

sunk-en /ˈsʌŋkən/ pp of sink².

sunny /ˈsʌnɪ/ adj ⇨ sun.

sup /sʌp/ vi,vt (-pp-) (esp Scot and N Eng) drink in small amounts. □ n [C] small quantity (of liquid).

super /ˈsuːpə(r)/ adj (informal) excellent;

splendid.

super– /ˈsuːpə(r)–/ prefix **1** above, over: *superimpose.* **2** superior to: *superhuman.*

super-an-nu-ate /ˈsuːpərˈænjʊeɪt/ vt give a pension to (an employee) when he is old or unable to work.

super-an-nu-ation /ˈsuːpərˈænjʊˈeɪʃən/ n [U] pension (the usual word).

su-perb /suːˈpɜːb/ adj magnificent; first class.

su-perb-ly adv

super-cili-ous /ˈsuːpəˈsɪlɪəs/ adj (formal) snobbish and indifferent: *nose high in the air, looking ~.*

super-cili-ous-ly adv

super-cili-ous-ness n [U]

super-fi-cial /ˈsuːpəˈfɪʃəl/ adj **1** of or on the surface only: *a ~ wound.* **2** not thorough or deep: *have only a ~ knowledge of a subject.*

super-fici-ally /-ʃəlɪ/ adv

su-per-flu-ous /suːˈpɜːflʊəs/ adj more than is needed or wanted.

su-per-flu-ous-ly adv

super-hu-man /ˈsuːpəˈhjuːmən/ adj exceeding ordinary human power, size, knowledge, etc: *by a ~ effort.*

super-im-pose /ˈsuːpərɪmˈpəʊz/ vt put (one thing) on top of something else.

super-in-tend /ˈsuːpərɪnˈtend/ vt,vi watch and direct (work, etc).

super-in-ten-dence /-əns/ n [U]

super-in-ten-dent /-ənt/ n [C] (a) person who superintends. (b) police officer above a chief inspector in rank.

su-per-ior /səˈpɪərɪə(r)/ adj **1** better than the average: *~ intelligence; ~ grades of coffee.* **2** greater in number: *The enemy attacked with ~ forces.* **3** *superior to,* (a) better than. (b) higher in rank or position than. **4** snobbish: *a ~ look.* □ n [C] **1** person of higher rank, authority, etc than another, or who is better, etc than another (in doing something): *Napoleon had no ~ as a general.* **2** (in titles) *the Father S~,* abbot; *the Mother S~,* abbess

su-per-ior-ity /səˈpɪərɪˈɒrətɪ US: -ˈɔːr-/ n [U] state of being superior: *the ~ity of one thing to another.*

su-per-la-tive /suːˈpɜːlətɪv/ adj **1** of the highest degree or quality: *a man of ~ wisdom.* **2** (gram) *the ~ degree,* the form of an adjective or adverb expressing the highest degree, e g *best, worst, highest, most foolish*(ly). □ n [C] superlative form of an adjective or adverb.

super-mar-ket /ˈsuːpəmɑːkɪt/ n [C] large self-service store selling food, household goods, etc.

super-natu-ral /ˈsuːpəˈnætʃrəl/ adj spiritual; of that which is not controlled or explained by physical laws: *~ beings,* e g angels.

super-sede /ˈsuːpəˈsiːd/ vt take the place of; put or use a person or thing in the place of: *Motorways have ~d ordinary roads for* *long-distance travel.*

super·son·ic /ˈsupəˈsɒnɪk/ *adj* **1** (of speeds) greater than that of sound. **2** (of aircraft) able to fly at supersonic speed.

super·sti·tion /ˈsupəˈstɪʃən/ *n* [C,U] (idea, practice, etc based on) belief in magic, witchcraft, etc.

super·sti·tious /ˈsupəˈstɪʃəs/ *adj* of, showing, resulting from, believing in, superstitions: *superstitious beliefs/ideas/people.*
super·sti·tious·ly *adv*

super·struc·ture /ˈsupəstrʌktʃə(r)/ *n* [C] structure built on the top of something else.

super·vise /ˈsupəvaɪz/ *vt,vi* watch and direct (work, workers, an organization).
super·vi·sor /-zə(r)/, person who supervises.
super·vi·sion /ˈsupəˈvɪʒən/, supervising: *under the supervision of,* supervised by.

sup·per /ˈsʌpə(r)/ *n* [C,U] last meal of the day.

sup·plant /səˈplɑnt US: -ˈplænt/ *vt* **1** supersede (the usual word). **2** take the place of (a person): *The Prime Minister was ~ed by his rival.*

supple /ˈsʌpəl/ *adj* (-r. -st) easily bent; not stiff: *the ~ limbs of a child.*

supple·ment /ˈsʌpləmənt/ *n* [C] **1** something added later to improve or complete, e g a dictionary. **2** extra and separate addition to a newspaper or other periodical: *The Times Literary S~.* □ *vt* /ˈsʌpləmənt/ make an addition or additions to: *~ one's ordinary income by writing books.*

supple·men·tary /ˈsʌpləˈmentrɪ/ *adj* additional; extra: *~ estimates,* e g for additional expenditure.

supply /səˈplaɪ/ *vt* (*pt,pp* -ied) **1** give or provide (something needed or asked for): *~ children with money for books.* **2** meet (a need): *Should the government ~ the need for more houses,* help to provide them (e g by making loans)? □ *n* **1** [U] supplying; [C] (*pl* -ies) that which is supplied; stock or amount of something which is obtainable: *Have you a good ~ of clothes for the holiday?* *in short supply,* scarce (the more usual word). **2** (*pl*) (esp) stores necessary for some public need: ˈmedical supplies.
sup·plier, person or firm supplying goods, materials, etc.

sup·port /səˈpɔt/ *vt* **1** bear the weight of; hold up or keep in place: *Is this bridge strong enough to ~ heavy lorries?* **2** provide a person or thing with what is necessary: *~ a political party,* agree with its policies; *a hospital ~ed by voluntary contributions; an accusation not ~ed by proofs.* **3** provide for: *He has a large family to ~.* □ *n* **1** [U] supporting or being supported: *I hope to have your ~ in the election. Mr X spoke in ~ of the motion. The divorced wife claimed ~* (i e a regular financial contribution) *for her children from her ex-husband.* **2** [C] person who, that which, supports: *Dick is the chief*

~ of the family, earns the money for the family.
sup·porter, person who, device which, supports.

sup·pose /səˈpəʊz/ *vt* **1** let it be thought that; take it as a fact that: *Let us ~ (that) the news is true. Everyone is ~d to know the rules,* It is assumed that we all know the rules. **2** guess; think: *What do you ~ he wanted? 'Will he come?'—'Yes, I ~ so'/ 'No, I ~ not'/'No, I don't ~ so'.* **3** *be supposed to,* (a) be expected or required to (by customs, duty, etc): *Is he ~d to clean the outside of the windows or only the inside?* (b) (*informal*) (in the negative) not be allowed to: *We're not ~d to play football on Sundays.*
sup·pos·ing *conj* if: *Supposing it rains, what shall you do?*
sup·pos·ed·ly /-ɪdlɪ/ *adv* according to what is/was supposed(2).

sup·po·si·tion /ˈsʌpəˈzɪʃən/ *n* **1** [U] supposing: *This newspaper article is based on ~,* on what the writer supposes to be the case, not on fact. **2** [C] guess: *Our ~s were fully confirmed.*

sup·pos·i·tory /səˈpɒzɪtrɪ US: -tɔrɪ/ *n* [C] (*pl* -ies) medical preparation (in a soluble capsule) inserted into the rectum or vagina and left to dissolve.

sup·press /səˈpres/ *vt* **1** put an end to the activity or existence of: *~ a rebellion.* **2** prevent from being known or seen: *~ the truth/a yawn/one's feelings.*
sup·pres·sion /səˈpreʃən/ *n* [U]
sup·pres·sive *adj* tending to, designed to, suppress.
sup·pres·sor /-sə(r)/, something that suppresses; (esp) a device fitted to electric apparatus to prevent interference with radio and television reception.

su·prem·acy /səˈpreməsɪ/ *n* [U] being supreme over; highest authority: *His ~ was unchallenged.*

su·preme /səˈprim/ *adj* **1** highest in rank or authority: *the S~ Commander; the S~ Court,* highest in one of the States of the US or in the whole of the US; *the S~ Being,* God. **2** most important; greatest: *make the ~ sacrifice,* die (e g in war).
su·preme·ly *adv* extremely: *~ly happy.*

sur·charge /ˈsɜtʃɑdʒ/ *n* [C] **1** payment demanded in addition to the usual charge, e g for a letter with insufficient postage paid on it. **2** excessive or additional load. □ *vt* **1** overload. **2** demand a surcharge(1) on or in.

sure /ʃʊə(r)/ *adj* **1** free from doubt; having confidence; knowing and believing; having, seeming to have, good reason for belief: *I think he's coming, but I'm not quite ~. You're ~ of* (= certain to receive) *a welcome. I'm not ~ why he wants it.* *be/feel sure (about sth),* have no doubts (about): *I think the answer's right, but I'm not ~ (about it).* *be sure to,* don't fail to: *Be ~ to* *write and give me all the news.* **make sure that/of sth,** (a) feel sure: *I made ~ he would be here.* (b) satisfy oneself; do what is necessary in order to feel sure, to get something, etc: *I think there's a train at 5 o'clock, but you'd better make ~,* e g by looking up trains in a timetable. **2** proved or tested; reliable: *a ~ cure for colds.* □ *adv* **1** **sure enough,** certainly: *I said it would happen, and ~ enough it did.* **2** **as sure as,** as certain as: *as ~ as my name's Bob.*

sure·ly /ˈʃʊəlɪ/ *adv* **1** with certainty: *He was working slowly but ~.* **2** if experience or probability can be trusted: *S~ this wet weather won't last much longer! You didn't want to hurt his feelings, ~!*

surety /ˈʃʊərtɪ US: ˈʃʊərtɪ/ *n* [C,U] (*pl* -ies) (something given as a) guarantee; person who makes himself responsible for the conduct or debt(s) of another person: *stand ~ for a debtor.*

surf /sɜːf/ *n* [U] waves breaking in white foam on the seashore, on sand-banks or reefs.

ˈsurf-board board used for surfing.

surfing, ˈsurf-riding, sport in which one balances oneself on a long narrow board while being carried along by heavy surf.

sur·face /ˈsɜːfɪs/ *n* [C] **1** the outside of any object, etc; any of the sides of an object: *Glass has a smooth ~. A cube has six ~s.* **2** top of a liquid: *The submarine rose to the ~.* **3** outward appearance; what is seen or learnt from a quick view or consideration: *His faults are all on the ~. When you get below the ~, you find that he is generous.* **4** (as an *adjective*) of the surface only: *~ impressions,* received quickly or casually, with no depth of thought, observation, etc. □ *vt,vi* **1** give a surface to: *~ a road with tarmac.* **2** (of a submarine, skin-diver, etc) (cause to) come to the surface.

ˈsurface mail, sent by land or sea, not airmail.

sur·feit /ˈsɜːfɪt/ *n* [C] (usually with *a, an*) too much of anything, esp food and drink: *have a ~ of curry while in Madras.* □ *vt* (cause to) take too much of anything: *be ~ed with pleasure.*

surge /sɜːdʒ/ *vi* move forward, roll on, in or like waves: *The floods ~d over the valley. The crowds ~d out of the sports stadium.* □ *n* [C] forward or upward movement: *the ~ of the sea; a ~ of anger/pity.*

sur·geon /ˈsɜːdʒən/ *n* [C] doctor who performs medical operations.

sur·gery /ˈsɜːdʒərɪ/ *n* (*pl* -ies) **1** [U] the science and practice of treating injuries and disease by operations: *qualified in both ~ and medicine.* **2** [C] (*GB*) doctor's or dentist's room where patients come to consult him: *~ hours, 4pm to 6pm.* **3** **political surgery,** (*informal*) where constituents can consult a member of Parliament.

sur·gi·cal /ˈsɜːdʒɪkəl/ *adj* of, by, for, sur-

gery: *~ instruments.*

sur·gi·cal·ly /-klɪ/ *adv*

sur·ly /ˈsɜːlɪ/ *adj* (-ier, -iest) bad-tempered and unfriendly.

sur·mise /səˈmaɪz/ *vt,vi* guess (the usual word). □ *n* /ˈsɜːmaɪz/ [C] guess.

sur·mount /səˈmaʊnt/ *vt* **1** overcome (difficulties); get over (obstacles). **2** **be surmounted by/with,** have on or over the top: *a spire ~ed by a cross.*

sur·mount·able /-əbəl/ *adj* that can be overcome or conquered.

sur·name /ˈsɜːneɪm/ *n* [C] person's hereditary family name: *Smith is a very common English ~.* ⇨ **given name, Christian name** and **forename.**

sur·pass /səˈpɑːs US: -ˈpæs/ *vt* (*formal*) do or be better than: *~ him in strength/speed/skill.*

sur·pass·ing *adj* (*formal*) excellent: *of ~ing beauty.*

sur·plice /ˈsɜːplɪs/ *n* [C] loose-fitting (usually white) gown with wide sleeves worn by (some) priests (over a cassock) during church services.

sur·plus /ˈsɜːpləs/ *n* **1** [C] amount (of money) that remains after needs have been supplied. **2** amount (of anything) in excess of requirements: *Brazil had a ~ of coffee last year.* **3** (as an *adjective*) more than what is needed or used: *~ population,* for which there is not enough food, employment, etc.

sur·prise /səˈpraɪz/ *n* **1** [C,U] (feeling caused by) something sudden or unexpected: *What a horrible/wonderful ~! He looked up in ~.* **2** (as an *adjective*) unexpected; made, done, etc without warning: *a ~ visit/attack.* □ *vt* **1** give a feeling of surprise to: *She was more ~d than frightened.* **2** experience surprise: *We were ~d at the news/~d to hear the news.* **3** come upon suddenly, without previous warning: *~ a burglar in a house.*

sur·pris·ing *adj* causing surprise.

sur·pris·ing·ly *adv*

sur·ren·der /səˈrendə(r)/ *vt,vi* **1** give up (oneself, a ship, a town, etc) to the enemy, the police, etc): *We shall never ~.* **2** give up under pressure or from necessity; abandon possession of: *We shall never ~ our liberty.* **3** give way to (a habit, emotion, influence, etc): *He ~ed to despair and committed suicide.* □ *n* [U] surrendering or being surrendered: *demand the ~ of all weapons.*

sur·rep·ti·tious /ˌsʌrəpˈtɪʃəs US: ˈsɜːrəp-/ *adj* (*formal*) (of actions) done secretly.

sur·round /səˈraʊnd/ *vt* be, go, all round, shut in on all sides: *a house ~ed with/by trees.* □ *n* [C] edge, e g of a floor.

sur·round·ing *adj* which is around about: *York and the ~ing countryside.*

sur·round·ings *n* (*pl*) everything around and about a place; conditions that may affect a person: *living in pleasant ~ings. You don't see animals in their natural ~ings at a zoo*

sur·veil·lance /sə`veɪləns/ n [U] close watch kept on persons suspected of doing wrong, etc: *under police* ~.

sur·vey /sə`veɪ/ vt 1 take a general view of: ~ *the countryside from the top of a hill.* 2 examine the general condition of: *The Prime Minister* ~*ed the international situation.* 3 measure and map out the position, size, boundaries, etc of (an area of land, a country, coast, etc): ~ *a parish/a railway.* 4 examine the condition of (a building, etc): *Have the house* ~*ed before you offer to buy it.* □ n /`sɜveɪ/ [C] 1 general view: *make a general* ~ *of the situation/subject.* 2 (map, record of) land-surveying; *an aerial* ~ *of Africa,* made by photography from aircraft. **sur·vey·ing,** the work of surveying(3,4). **sur·vey·or** /sə`veɪə(r)/, person who surveys(3,4).

sur·vival /sə`vaɪvəl/ n [U] state of continuing to live or exist; surviving: *the* ~ *of the fittest,* the continuing existence of those animals and plants which are best adapted to their surroundings, etc; (as an *adjective*) *a* ~ *kit,* package of necessities for a person after a disaster, etc (e g at sea).

sur·vive /sə`vaɪv/ vt,vi continue to live or exist; live or exist longer than: ~ *an earthquake/shipwreck. The old lady has* ~*d all her children.*

sur·vivor /-və(r)/, person who has survived: *send help to the survivors of an air crash.*

sus·cep·ti·ble /sə`septəbəl/ adj 1 easily influenced by feelings: *a* ~ *nature.* 2 easily affected, influenced, by: ~ *to pain.*

sus·cep·ti·bil·ity /sə`septə`bɪlətɪ/ n (pl -ies) (a) [U] sensitiveness: ~ *to colds.* (b) (pl) sensitive points of a person's nature: *We must avoid wounding their susceptibilities.*

sus·pect /sə`spekt/ vt 1 have an idea or feeling (concerning the possibility or likelihood of something): *She has more intelligence than we* ~*ed.* 2 feel doubt about: ~ *the truth of an account.* 3 have a feeling that a person may be guilty (of): *He is* ~*ed of telling lies.* □ n /`sʌspekt/ [C] person suspected of doing wrong, etc: *Are political* ~*s kept under police observation in your country?* □ adj /`sʌspekt/ of doubtful character: *His statements are* ~.

sus·pend /sə`spend/ vt 1 hang up (from): *lamps* ~*ed from the ceiling.* 2 (of solid particles, in the air or other fluid medium) be or remain in place: *dust/smoke* ~*ed in the air.* 3 stop for a time; delay: ~ *judgement,* postpone giving one. 4 announce that (a person) cannot be allowed to perform his duties, enjoy privileges, etc for a time: ~ *a (professional) football player,* e g because of breaking the rules.

sus·pend·ers /sə`spendəz/ n pl (also *a pair of* ~) 1 (GB) elastic band for keeping up a sock or stocking. 2 (US) = braces(4).

sus·pense /sə`spens/ n [U] uncertainty anxiety (about news, events, decisions, etc): *We waited in* ~ *for the doctor's opinion.*

sus·pen·sion /sə`spenʃən/ n [U] suspending or being suspended(4): *the* ~ *of a member of Parliament.*

sus`pension bridge, bridge hanging on steel cables supported from towers.

sus·pi·cion /sə`spɪʃən/ n 1 [C,U] feeling that a person has when he suspects; suspecting or being suspected; feeling that something is wrong: *I have a* ~ *that he is dishonest. He was arrested on (the)* ~ *of having stolen the money. above suspicion,* of such good reputation that suspicion is out of the question. 2 (*sing* with *a* or *an*) slight taste or suggestion: *There was a* ~ *of sadness in her voice.*

sus·pi·cious /sə`spɪʃəs/ adj having, showing or causing suspicion: *The excuse is* ~ *to me. He's a* ~ *character,* There is reason to suspect that he is dishonest, etc. **sus·pi·cious·ly** adv. *behave* ~*ly.*

sus·tain /sə`steɪn/ vt 1 keep from falling or sinking: *Will this light shelf* ~ *(the weight of) all these books?* 2 (enable to) keep up, maintain: ~*ing food,* that gives strength; ~ *an argument/attempt;* ~ *a note,* continue to sing or play the note without faltering; *make a* ~*ed effort.* 3 suffer; undergo: ~ *a defeat/an injury.* 4 (*legal*) give a decision in favour of: *The court* ~*ed his claim/*~*ed him in his claim.*

sus·ten·ance /`sʌstɪnəns/ n [U] (*formal*) (nourishing quality of) food or drink: *There's more* ~ *in cocoa than in tea.*

swab /swob/ n [C] 1 mop or pad for cleaning, e g floors, decks. 2 piece of absorbent material, etc for medical use; specimen taken with a swab: *take throat* ~*s.* □ vt (-bb-) clean with a swab: ~ *an injury.*

swag·ger /`swægə(r)/ vi walk or behave in a self-important or self-satisfied manner. □ n [C] swaggering walk or way of behaving: *with a* ~.

swal·low[1] /`swoləʊ/ n [C] kinds of small, swift-flying bird with a forked tail. **`swallow-tailed** adj (of butterflies, birds) with a deeply forked tail.

swal·low[2] /`swoləʊ/ vt,vi 1 cause or allow to go down the throat: ~ *one's food.* 2 take in; exhaust; cause to disappear; use up: *earnings that were* ~*ed up by lawyers' bills.* 3 (*fig*): ~ *an insult,* accept it meekly. *swallow sth whole,* believe it without argument, doubt. *swallow one's words,* express regret for them. □ n [C] act of swallowing; amount swallowed at one time.

swam /swæm/ pt of **swim.**

swamp /swomp/ n [C,U] (area of) soft wet land; marsh. □ vt 1 flood, soak, with water: *A big wave* ~*ed the boat.* 2 (*fig*) overwhelm: *We are* ~*ed with work.* **swampy** adj (-ier, -iest) having swamps.

swan /swon/ n [C] large, graceful, long-necked (and usually white) water-bird. □ vi

(-nn-) (*informal*) move, go in a slow, often aimless manner: *I suppose you're ~ning off to Paris for the weekend.*

`swan-song, last performance, appearance, work before death of a poet, musician, etc.

swap /swɒp/ *vt,vi* (-pp-) = swop.

swarm /swɔːm/ *n* [C] large number, of insects, birds, etc moving about together: *a ~ of ants/locusts/bees.* □ *vi* 1 (of bees) move or go in large numbers round a queen bee for emigration to a new colony. 2 (of places) be crowded: *The beaches were ~ing with people.* 3 be present in large numbers: *When the rain started the crowds ~ed into the cinemas.*

swarthy /ˈswɔːðɪ/ *adj* having a dark skin.

swat /swɒt/ *vt* (-tt-) slap with a flat object: *~ a fly.* □ *n* [C] 1 slap of this kind: *Give that fly a ~.* 2 implement with a handle for swatting (flies, etc): *a* `fly-~ (also `fly-~ter).

sway /sweɪ/ *vi,vt* 1 (cause to) move, first to one side and then to the other: *The branches of the trees were ~ing in the wind.* 2 control or influence; govern the direction of: *a speech that ~ed the voters.* □ *n* [U] 1 swaying movement. 2 rule or control: *under the ~ of Rome*, ruled by Rome (in ancient times).

swear /sweə(r)/ *vt,vi* (*pt* swore /swɔː(r)/, *pp* sworn /swɔːn/) 1 say solemnly or emphatically: *He swore to tell the truth/ swore that he would tell the truth.* 2 (cause (a person) to) take an oath. **swear sb in,** cause him to take the oath of office. **swear sb to secrecy,** make him swear to keep a secret. 3 **swear by sth, (a)** appeal to as a witness or witnesses: *~ by all the gods that...* **(b)** (*informal*) use and have great confidence in: *He ~s by strictness for discipline.* 4 make an affirmation after having taken an oath: *sworn evidence/statements.* 5 use curses and bad language: *The captain swore at his crew.*

`swear-word, word used in swearing(5).

swearer, person who swears(5).

sweat /swet/ *n* 1 [U] moisture that is given off by the body through the skin: *wipe the ~ off one's brow.* 2 (with *a, an*) condition of a person or animal (esp a horse) when covered with sweat: *be in a ~.* □ *vt,vi* give out sweat: *The long hot climb made him ~.*

`sweat shirt *n* = T-shirt.

sweaty *adj* (-ier, -iest) (making) damp with sweat.

sweater /ˈswetə(r)/ *n* [C] knitted jacket or jersey, usually of thick wool.

swede /swiːd/ *n* [C,U] kind of turnip.

sweep[1] /swiːp/ *n* [C] 1 act of sweeping with, or as with, a broom, etc: *Give the room a good ~.* **make a clean sweep of sth,** get rid of what is unwanted completely: *They made a clean ~ of their old furniture and bought new things.* 2 sweeping movement: *with one ~ of his arm.* 3 space, range, covered by a sweeping movement: *The*

radar has a ~ (= range) *of 100 miles.* 4 long unbroken stretch, esp curved, on a road, river, coast, etc or of sloping land: *a fine ~ of country.* 5 steady uninterrupted flow: *the ~ of the tide.* 6 = chimney-sweep.

`sweep-stake, form of gambling on horse-races, the money staked by all those who take part being divided among those who have drawn tickets for the winners.

sweep[2] /swiːp/ *vt,vi* (*pt,pp* swept /swept/) 1 clear (dust, dirt, etc) away with, or as with, a brush or broom; clean by doing this: *~ the carpets/the floor; ~ up the crumbs.* 2 clean or move as with a broom: *The current swept the logs along.* **be swept off one's feet,** (*fig*) be overcome by feeling, filled with enthusiasm. 3 pass over or along, esp so as to overcome obstacles: *A huge wave swept over the deck.* 4 move in a dignified or stately manner: *She swept out of the room.* 5 extend in an unbroken line, curve or expanse: *The coast ~s northwards in a wide curve.* 6 pass over (as if) to examine or survey: *The searchlights swept the sky.* 7 move over lightly and quickly: *Her dress swept the ground.* 8 make (a bow, curtsey) with a sweeping movement: *He swept her a bow.*

sweeper, (a) person or thing that sweeps: `street ~ers. **(b)** (*football*) defender who covers the backs, tackling any opponent who passes them.

sweep-ing *adj* far-reaching; taking in very much: *~ing changes/reforms; a ~ing statement.*

sweet /swiːt/ *adj* (-er, -est) 1 (opposite of *sour*) tasting like sugar or honey: *It tastes ~*, has a sweet taste. **have a sweet tooth,** like things that taste sweet. 2 fresh and pure: *keep a room clean and ~; ~ breath.* 3 having a fragrant smell: *Don't the roses smell ~!* 4 pleasant or attractive: *a ~ face; a ~ voice. Isn't the baby ~!* □ *n* [C] 1 small piece of something sweet (boiled sugar, etc chocolate, etc). 2 dish of sweet food (puddings, tarts, jellies, trifles, etc) as one of the courses of a meal. 3 (*dated*) (as a form of address) darling: *Yes, my ~.*

`sweet-bread, pancreas of a calf or lamb used as food.

`sweet-heart, (*dated*) either of a pair of lovers: *David and his ~heart.*

`sweet-meat, (*dated*) piece of food tasting sweet (usually made of sugar or chocolate).

'sweet po`tato, tropical climbing plant with thick edible roots, cooked as a vegetable.

sweet-ly *adv*

sweet-ness *n* [U]

sweeten /ˈswiːtən/ *vt,vi* make or become sweet.

sweet-en-ing /ˈswiːtənɪŋ/ *n* [C,U] that which sweetens e g food.

swell /swel/ *vi,vt* (*pt* ~ed /sweld/ *pp* swollen /ˈswəʊlən/) 1 (cause to) become greater in volume, thickness or force: *Wood* often ~s when wet. *His face began to* ~, e g *from toothache.* **have/suffer from a swollen head,** be conceited. Hence, `**swollen-headed** adj. **2** have, cause to have, a curved surface: *The sails* ~*ed out in the wind. The wind* ~*ed the sails.* □ *n* [C] **1** gradual increase in the volume of sound: *the* ~ *of an organ.* **2** (*sing* only) slow rise and fall of the sea's surface after a storm: *There was a heavy* ~ *after the storm.* □ *adj* (*informal*) excellent; fashionable.

swell·ing, (esp) swollen place on the body, e g the result of a toothache.

swel·ter /ˈsweltə(r)/ *vi* be uncomfortably warm: *a* ~*ing hot day.*

swept /swept/ *pt,pp* of sweep².

swerve /swɜːv/ *vi,vt* (cause to) change direction suddenly: *The car* ~*d to avoid knocking the boy down.* □ *n* [C] swerving movement.

swift¹ /swɪft/ *adj* (-er, -est) quick; fast; prompt: *a* ~ *revenge.*

swift·ly *adv*

swift·ness *n* [U]

swift² /swɪft/ *n* [C] kinds of small bird with long wings, similar to a swallow.

swill /swɪl/ *vt,vi* **1** rinse by pouring liquid into, over or through: ~ *out a dirty tub.* **2** (*informal*) drink greedily: *The workmen were* ~*ing tea when they ought to have been working.* □ *n* **1** [C] rinsing: *Give the bucket a good* ~ *out.* **2** [U] waste food, mostly liquid, e g as given to pigs.

swim /swɪm/ *vi,vt* (*pt* swam /swæm/, *pp* swum /swʌm/) (-mm-) **1** move the body through water by using arms, legs, fins, the tail, etc: *Fishes* ~. *Let's go* ~*ming. He swam across the river.* **2** cross by swimming: ~ *the English Channel;* take part in (a race) in this way; compete in this way: ~ *a race;* ~ *two lengths of the pool.* **3** be covered (with), overflowing (with), or (as if) floating (in or on): *eyes* ~*ming with tears; meat* ~*ming in gravy.* **4** seem to be moving round and round; have a dizzy feeling: *The room swam before his eyes. His head swam.* □ *n* [C] **1** act or period of swimming: *have/go for a* ~. **2** (*sing* with *the*) main current of affairs. **be in/out of the swim,** be/not be taking part in, aware of, what is going on.

swim·mer, person who swims.

`**swim·ming bath/pool,**` pool for swimming in.

`**swim·ming costume,**` `**swim-suit,**` one-piece garment worn by women and girls for swimming.

`**swim·ming-trunks**` *n pl* shorts worn by boys and men for swimming.

swindle /ˈswɪndəl/ *vt,vi* cheat; get (money, etc) by cheating: ~ *money out of a brother;* ~ *a child out of his money.* □ *n* [C] piece, act of swindling, e g something sold, etc that is less valuable than it is described to be: *This new radio is a* ~; *the quality of the sound is bad.*

swin·dler /ˈswɪndlə(r)/ person who swindles.

swing /swɪŋ/ *vi,vt* (*pt,pp* swung /swʌŋ/) **1** (of something having one end or one side fixed and the other free) move, cause to move, forwards and backwards or in a curve: *His arms swung as he walked. The door swung shut/swung to.* **2** turn, cause to turn, in a curve: *He swung* (= turned quickly) *round and faced his accusers.* □ [C] **1** swinging movement: *the* ~ *of the pendulum.* **2** strong rhythm. **in full swing,** active; in full operation. **3** seat held by ropes or chains for swinging on; act, period, of swinging on such a seat.

swipe /swaɪp/ *vt* (*informal*) **1** hit hard: *The batsman* ~*d the ball into the grandstand.* **2** steal. □ *n* [C] swinging blow: *have/take a* ~ *at the ball.*

swirl /swɜːl/ *vi,vt* (of water, air, etc) (cause to) move or flow at varying speeds, with twists and turns: *dust* ~*ing about the streets.* □ *n* [C] swirling movement: *the* ~ *of the tide.*

swish /swɪʃ/ *vt,vi* **1** move (something) through the air with a hissing or brushing sound; cut (something off) in this way: *The horse* ~*ed its tail. He* ~*ed off the tops of the thistles with his whip.* **2** make, move with, a sound like that of something moving through the air: *Her long silk dress* ~*ed as she came in.* □ *n* [C] sound of, like, swishing: *We heard the* ~ *of a cane.*

switch /swɪtʃ/ *n* [C] **1** device for making and breaking a connection at railway points (to allow trains to go from one track to another). **2** device for making and breaking an electric circuit: *a* `light-~`. **3** thin twig, etc, e g as used for urging a horse on. **4** bunch of false hair. **5** transfer; change-over: *a* ~ *from Liberal to Labour.* □ *vt,vi* **1** use a switch(2) to turn (electric current) on/off: ~ *the light/radio, etc on.* **2** **switch sb on,** (*sl*) cause a person to feel happy, excited: *That music really* ~*es me on!* **3** move (a train, tram, etc) on to another track: ~ *a train into a siding.* **4** shift; change: ~ *over to a Socialist Government.* **5** use a switch(3).

swivel /ˈswɪvəl/ *n* [C] device used to join two parts (e g a chain and hook) so that one part can turn without turning the other. □ *vt,vi* (-ll-, US also -l-) turn on or as on a swivel: *He* ~*led round in his chair.*

swiz /swɪz/ *n* [C] (*informal*) fraud.

swob /swɒb/ *n, vt* (-bb-) = swab.

swol·len /ˈswəʊlən/ *pp* of swell, esp as an *adjective*: *a* ~ *ankle.*

swoon /swuːn/ *vi* (*dated*) faint. □ *n* [C] fainting fit.

swoop /swuːp/ *vi* come down on with a rush: *The eagle* ~*ed down on the rabbit.* □ *n* [C] swooping movement; sudden attempt to snatch and carry off something.

swop (also **swap**) /swɒp/ *vt,vi* (-pp-) (*informal*) exchange by bargaining: ~

foreign stamps. **swop places with sb,** exchange seats, jobs, etc. □ *n* [C] exchange by bargaining.

sword /sɔd/ *n* [C] long steel blade fixed in a hilt, used as a weapon, or worn by army officers, etc as part of a uniform or as court dress.

`**sword-dance,** dance over swords put on the ground, or one in which they are waved or clashed.

`**sword-fish,** large sea-fish with a long upper jaw.

swore, sworn ⇨ swear.

swum /swʌm/ *pp* of swim.

swung /swʌŋ/ *pt,pp* of swing.

syca·more /ˈsɪkəmɔ(r)/ *n* 1 [C] large tree valued for its wood. 2 [U] its hard wood.

syl·labic /sɪˈlæbɪk/ *adj* of or in syllables.

syl·lable /ˈsɪləbəl/ *n* [C] minimum rhythmic unit of spoken or written language. '*Arithmetic*' *is a word of four* ∼s.

syl·la·bus /ˈsɪləbəs/ *n* [C] (*pl* ∼es) outline or summary of a course of studies; programme of lessons.

syl·lo·gism /ˈsɪlədʒɪzm/ *n* [C] form of reasoning in which a conclusion is reached from two statements, e g: *All men must die; I am a man; therefore I must die.*

sym·bol /ˈsɪmbəl/ *n* [C] sign, mark, object, etc looked on as representing something: *mathematical* ∼s, e g ×, ÷, +, −; *phonetic* ∼s.

sym·bolic /sɪmˈbɒlɪk/ *adj* of, using, used as, a symbol.

sym·boli·cally /-klɪ/ *adv*

sym·bol·ize /ˈsɪmbəlaɪz/ *vt* be a symbol of; make use of a symbol for.

sym·me·try /ˈsɪmətrɪ/ *n* [U] (beauty resulting from the) correct correspondence of parts; quality of harmony or balance (in size, design, etc) between parts: *mathematical* ∼.

sym·met·ric /sɪˈmetrɪk/, **sym·met·ri·cal** /-kəl/ *adj* having symmetry; (of a design) having (usually two) exactly similar parts on either side of a dividing line.

sym·met·ri·cally /-klɪ/ *adv*

sym·path·etic /ˌsɪmpəˈθetɪk/ *adj* having or showing sympathy; caused by sympathy: ∼ *looks/words/smiles; be/feel* ∼ *to/towards someone.*

sym·path·eti·cally /-klɪ/ *adv*

sym·path·ize /ˈsɪmpəθaɪz/ *vi* feel or express sympathy (with): *Tom's parents do not* ∼ *with his ambition to be an actor.*

sym·path·izer, person who sympathizes, e g one who supports a political party.

sym·pathy /ˈsɪmpəθɪ/ *n* (*pl* -ies) 1 [U] (capacity for) sharing the feelings of others, feeling pity and tenderness: *send her a letter of* ∼; *feel* ∼ *for her.* 2 (*pl*): *My sympathies are with the miners in this dispute,* I agree with them.

sym·phonic /sɪmˈfɒnɪk/ *adj* of, like a symphony.

sym·phony /ˈsɪmfənɪ/ *n* [C] (*pl* -ies)

(long) musical composition in (usually) three or four parts (called *movements*) for (usually a large) orchestra.

symp·tom /ˈsɪmptəm/ *n* [C] 1 change in the body's condition that is a sign of illness: ∼*s of measles.* 2 sign of the existence of something: ∼*s of political discontent.*

symp·to·matic /ˌsɪmptəˈmætɪk/ *adj* serving as a symptom: *Headaches may be* ∼*atic of many kinds of trouble.*

symp·to·mati·cally /-klɪ/ *adv*

syna·gogue /ˈsɪnəgɒg/ *n* [C] (building used for an) assembly of Jews for religious teaching and worship

syn·chron·ize /ˈsɪŋkrənaɪz/ *vt,vi* (cause to) happen at the same time, agree in time speeds, etc: ∼ *the clocks in a building.*

syn·chron·iz·ation /ˌsɪŋkrənaɪˈzeɪʃən *US.* -nɪˈz-/ *n* [U]

syn·di·cate /ˈsɪndɪkət/ *n* [C] 1 business association that supplies articles, cartoons, etc to periodicals. 2 combination of commercial firms associated to forward a common interest. □ *vt* /ˈsɪndɪkeɪt/ publish (articles, strip-cartoons, etc) in numerous periodicals through a syndicate(1).

syn·drome /ˈsɪndrəʊm/ *n* [C] (*medical*) number of symptoms which indicate an illness, etc.

synod /ˈsɪnɒd/ *n* [C] meeting of church officers to discuss and decide questions of policy, government, teaching, etc.

syn·onym /ˈsɪnənɪm/ *n* [C] word with the same meaning as another in the same language but often with different implications and associations.

syn·ony·mous /sɪˈnɒnɪməs/ *adj*

syn·op·sis /sɪˈnɒpsɪs/ *n* [C] (*pl* -opses /-siz/) summary or outline (of a book, play etc).

syn·op·tic /sɪˈnɒptɪk/ *adj*

syn·tac·tic /sɪnˈtæktɪk/ *adj* of syntax.

syn·tac·ti·cally /-klɪ/ *adv*

syn·tax /ˈsɪntæks/ *n* [U] (*linguistics*) (rules for) sentence-building.

syn·thesis /ˈsɪnθəsɪs/ *n* [C,U] (*pl* -theses /-siz/) combination of separate parts, elements, substances, etc into a whole or into a system; that which results from this process: *produce rubber from petroleum by* ∼.

syn·thetic /sɪnˈθetɪk/ *adj*

syph·ilis /ˈsɪfəlɪs/ *n* [U] infectious venereal disease.

syphon *n* = siphon.

syr·inge /sɪˈrɪndʒ/ *n* [C] kinds of device for drawing in liquid by suction and forcing it out again in a fine stream, used for injecting liquids into the body, etc: *a hypodermic* ∼ □ *vt* clean, inject liquid into, apply liquid, with a syringe.

syrup /ˈsɪrəp *US:* ˈsɜrəp/ *n* [U] thick sweet liquid made from sugar-cane juice or by boiling sugar with water.

sys·tem /ˈsɪstəm/ *n* [C] 1 group of things or parts working together in a regular relation:

the ˋnervous ∼; *the diˋgestive* ∼; *a* ˋ*railway* ∼. **2** ordered set of ideas, theories, principles, etc: *a* ∼ *of government; a comˋputer* ∼. **3** [U] organization: *You mustn't expect good results if you work without* ∼.

sys·tem·atic /ˌsɪstəˋmætɪk/ *adj* methodical; based on a system: *a* ∼*atic analysis*.

sys·tem·ati·cally /-klɪ/ *adv*

Tt

T, t /ti/ (*pl* **T's, t's** /tiz/) the twentieth letter of the alphabet

ˋ**T-junction,** place where two roads, pipes, wires, etc meet to form a T

ˋ**T-shirt,** short-sleeved, collarless cotton shirt like a vest, worn informally.

ˋ**T-square,** T-shaped instrument for drawing right angles.

ta /tɑ/ *int* (*informal*) thank you.

tab /tæb/ *n* [C] **1** small piece or strip of cloth, etc fixed to a garment, etc as a badge or distinguishing mark or (as a loop) for hanging up a coat, etc. **2** (*informal*) account. **keep tabs on sth/sb,** keep under observation.

tab·er·nacle /ˋtæbənækəl/ *n* [C] **1 the T**∼, the portable structure used by the Jews as a sanctuary during their wanderings before they settled in Palestine. **2** place of worship, e g a Baptist Church or Mormon temple.

table /ˋteɪbəl/ *n* [C] **1** piece of furniture consisting of a flat top with (usually four) supports (called legs): *a* ˋ*dining-*∼; *a* ˋ*kitchen-*∼. **2** (*sing* only) people seated at a table: *jokes that amused the whole* ∼. **3** list, orderly arrangement, of facts, information, etc: *a* ∼ *of contents,* summary of what a book contains; *a* ˋ*time-*∼. **4 turn the tables on sb,** gain a position of superiority after having been defeated or in a position of inferiority. □ *vt* **1** put (a proposal, etc) forward for discussion: ∼ *a motion/a Bill.* **2** put in the form of a table(3).

ˋ**table-cloth,** one (to be) spread on a table.

ˋ**table-knife,** knife for eating with.

ˋ**table-mat,** one to be placed under a hot dish on a table.

ˋ**table-spoon,** large spoon for serving food from a dish, etc.

ˋ**table-spoon·ful,** as much as a tablespoon holds.

ˋ**table-talk,** conversation during a meal.

ˋ**table tennis,** game with bats and a ball, similar to tennis but played on a table.

ˋ**table-ware,** dishes, silver, cutlery, etc used for meals.

tab·let /ˋtæblət/ *n* [C] **1** flat surface with words cut or written on it, e g one fixed to a wall in memory of a person or thing. **2** num-

ber of sheets of writing-paper fastened together along one edge. **3** lump of hard soap. **4** small, shaped piece of compressed medicine: *two* ∼*s of aspirin.*

tab·loid /ˋtæblɔɪd/ *n* [C] newspaper with many pictures, strip cartoons, etc and with its news presented in a form easily understood

ta·boo /təˋbu *US:* tæˋbu/ *n* **1** [C,U] (among some primitive races) something which religion or custom regards as forbidden, not to be touched, spoken of, etc: *That tree is under (a)* ∼. **2** [C] general agreement not to discuss or do something. □ *adj* under a taboo: *Unkind gossip ought to be* ∼.

taˋboo word, one which convention prohibits (e g marked △ in this dictionary). □ *vt* forbid, esp on moral or religious grounds.

tabu·lar /ˋtæbjʊlə(r)/ *adj* arranged in tables(3).

tabu·late /ˋtæbjʊleɪt/ *vt* arrange (facts, figures, etc) in tables(3).

tabu·la·tion /ˌtæbjʊˋleɪʃən/ *n* [U]

tacit /ˋtæsɪt/ *adj* understood without being put into words: ∼ *consent/agreement.*

tacit·ly *adv*

taci·turn /ˋtæsɪtɜn/ *adj* (*formal*) (in the habit of) saying very little.

tack /tæk/ *n* [C] **1** small, flat-headed nail (e g used for securing carpet to a floor). ⇨ thumb-tack. **2** long, loose stitch used in fastening pieces of cloth together loosely or temporarily. **3** sailing-ship's direction as fixed by the direction of the wind and the position of the sails. **on the right/wrong tack,** (*fig*) following a wise/unwise course of action. □ *vt, vi* **1** fasten with tacks(1): ∼ *down the carpet.* **2** fasten with tacks(2): ∼ *a hem.* **3** make a tack(3).

tackle /ˋtækəl/ *n* **1** [C,U] set of ropes and pulleys for lifting weights, etc. **2** [U] equipment, apparatus, for doing something: ˋ*fishing* ∼, a rod, line, hooks, etc. **3** [C] act of seizing and bringing down an opponent with the ball (in Rugby and American-style football); act of taking the ball from an opponent (in Association football). □ *vt, vi* **1** deal with, attack (a problem, a piece of work): *I don't know how to* ∼ *this problem,* how to start on it. **tackle sb about/over sth,** speak to him frankly (about a problem, etc). **2** seize, e g a thief or a player who, in Rugby, has the ball: *He* ∼*s fearlessly.* **3** take the ball from (an opponent, in Association football).

tact /tækt/ *n* [U] (use of) skill and understanding shown by a person who handles people and situations successfully and without causing offence: *show/have great* ∼.

tact·ful /-fəl/ *adj* having or showing tact

tact·fully /-fəlɪ/ *adv*

tact·less *adj* lacking tact.

tact·less·ly *adv*

tac·tic /ˋtæktɪk/ *n* [C] **1** means of achieving an aim. **2** (*pl*) (often used with a *sing verb*) art of placing or moving fighting forces for

or during battle. **2** (*pl*) (*fig*) plan(s) or method(s) for carrying out a policy: *These ～s are unlikely to help you.*
tac·ti·cal /-kəl/ *adj* of tactics: *a ～al error.*
tact·i·cally /-klɪ/ *adv*
tac·ti·cian /tækˈtɪʃən/ *n* [C] expert in tactics.
tac·tile /ˈtæktaɪl US: -təl/ *adj* of, experienced by, the sense of touch: *～ greetings,* e g kissing.
tad·pole /ˈtædpəʊl/ *n* [C] form of a frog or toad from the time it leaves the egg to the time when it takes its adult form.
tag /tæg/ *n* [C] **1** metal or plastic point at the end of a shoelace, string, etc. **2** label (e g for showing prices, addresses) fastened to or stuck into something. **3** any loose or ragged end. **4** [U] game in which one child chases and tries to touch another. □ *vt,vi* (-gg-) **1** fasten a tag(2) to. **2** **tag along/behind/ after,** follow closely: *T～ along with us* (= Come with us) *if you like.* **3** join: *～ old articles together to make a book.*
tail /teɪl/ *n* [C] **1** long movable part at the end of the body of a bird, some animals, fish or reptiles. *Dogs wag their ～s when they are pleased.* **turn tail,** run away. **2** something like a tail in position: *the ～ of a kite/ aircraft.* **3** (*pl*) side of a coin opposite to that in which there is the head of a monarch. **4** (*informal*) person employed to follow and watch another person, e g a suspected criminal: *put a ～ on him.* □ *vt,vi* **1** **tail after sb,** follow close behind. **2** **tail sb,** follow him closely, e g because he is suspected to be a criminal. **3** **tail off/away,** **(a)** become smaller in number, size, etc. **(b)** (of remarks, etc) end in a hesitating or inconclusive way. **(c)** fall behind or away in a scattered line.
ˈtail-ˈend, (usually with *the*) final part: *at the ～-end of the procession.*
ˈtail-gate, door or flap at the rear of a motor-vehicle which can be opened for loading and unloading.
ˈtail-light, light at the end of a train, bus or other vehicle.
ˈtail-spin, spiral dive of an aircraft in which the ～ makes wider circles than the front.
tail·less *adj* having no tail: *a ～less cat.*
-tailed /-teɪld/ *suffix:* ˈlong-ˈ～ed, having a long ～.
tailor /ˈteɪlə(r)/ *n* [C] maker of coats, suits, etc. □ *vt* **1** cut out and sew: *a well-～ed suit.* **2** adapt: *～ed for a particular age-group.*
ˈtailor-ˈmade *adj* **(a)** (esp of a woman's coat and skirt) made by a tailor, with special attention to exact fit. **(b)** (*fig*) appropriate, suitable: *He seems ～-made for the job.*
taint /teɪnt/ *n* [C,U] trace of some bad smell, decay or infection: *There was a ～ of insanity in the family.* □ *vt,vi* make or become infected: *～ed meat.*
take /teɪk/ *vt,vi* (*pt* took /tʊk/, *pt* taken /ˈteɪkən/) (For use with a large number of

nouns, ⇨ **15** below. For special uses with *adverbial particles* and *prepositions* ⇨ **16** below.) **1** get or hold with the hand(s) or any other part of the body, e g the arms, teeth or with an instrument: *～ her hand; ～ a man by the throat; He took her in his arms,* embraced her. **2** capture; catch; win (in a contest, etc): *～ a town,* in war; *～ 500 prisoners; be ～n prisoner,* be caught and be made a prisoner. *Her horse took* (= was awarded) *the first prize.* **take sb's fancy,** please, delight: *The new play really took the public's fancy.* **be taken ill,** become ill. **take sb unawares/by surprise,** approach or discover him doing something when he does not know that one sees him, etc. **3** use; use or borrow without permission; steal: *Who has ～n my bicycle?* **4** carry something, go (away) with somebody from a place: *～ letters to the post; ～ a friend home in one's car. T～ her some flowers.* **5** get, have; eat or drink; allow oneself: *～ a holiday/a walk/a bath/a quick look round/a deep breath. Do you ～ sugar in your coffee?* **take a chair/a seat,** sit down. **6** accept; receive: *Will you ～ £450 for the car,* sell it for this sum? ⇨ **takings.** *I'm not taking any more of your insults,* I refuse to listen to them. **take a chance (on sth),** accept the possibility of not getting it: *I'll ～ a chance on finding him at home,* will call hoping to find him there. **take it from me; take my word for it,** believe me when I say: *T～ it from me, there'll be some big changes made in the coming year.* **be able to take it; can take it,** be able to endure suffering, punishment, attack, etc without showing weakness, without admitting defeat, easily etc. **7** receive and pay for regularly: *Which newspapers do you ～?* **8** make a record of: *～ notes of a lecture; ～ a letter,* from dictation; *～ a photograph.* **9** need, require: *The work took four hours. These things ～ time.* **take one's time (over sth),** use as much time as one needs. **10** suppose; consider to be: *I took you to be an honest man. Do you ～ me for a fool?* **take sth for granted,** ⇨ **grant,** *v*(2). **11** find out (by inquiry, measurement, etc): *The doctor took my temperature.* **12** treat or regard in a specified way: *～ it/things easy,* not work too hard or too fast. **13** be in charge and act: *～ a class,* give the class its lesson, etc. **14** be successful: *That smallpox injection did not ～.* **15** (uses with *nouns*) (For examples of these uses ⇨ the *noun* entries, e g **account** (7), **advantage**, **aim** (2), **care** (2), **charge** (5), **confidence**(1), **courage**, **degree**(5), **delight**(1), **dislike**, **effect**(1), **exception**(3), **fancy** (3), **hand** (13), **head** (19), **heart**(2), **heed**, **heel** (1), **hint**, **interest**(1), **leave** (3), **liberty**(2), **liking**, **mind** (2), **notice**(3), **oath**(1), **offence**(2), **opportunity**, **pains**, **part** (4), **place** (1), **risk**(1), **stock** (1), **task**, **trouble**(3).)

16 (special uses with *adverbial particles* and *prepositions*):

be taken aback, ⇨ aback.

take after sb, resemble (esp a parent or relation) in features or character: *Your daughter does not ~ after you in any way.*

take sth apart, separate it (machinery, etc) into its (component) parts.

take away, (of a meal) take out of a restaurant to eat at home. Hence, **take-away** *adj:* *~away meals.* **take sth/sb away (from sb/sth),** remove: *Not to be ~n away, e g books from a library. The child was ~n away from school,* not allowed to attend.

take sth back, (a) retreat or withdraw (what one has said) as an admission of error, as an apology, etc: *I ~ back what I said.* (b) agree to receive back: *Shops will not usually ~ back goods after they have been paid for.*

take sb back (to), carry or conduct to an earlier period: *These stories took him back to his childhood days,* brought them back to his mind.

take sth down, (a) write down: *The reporters took down the speech.* (b) lower; get by lifting down from (a shelf, etc): *~ down a book from the top shelf; ~ down a mast.* (c) pull down; get into separate parts: *~ down the scaffolding round a building.*

take from, ⇨ take (away) *from* above.

take sth in, (a) receive (work) to be done in one's own house for payment: *She earns money by taking in sewing.* (b) reduce the size, length or width of (a garment, sail, etc): *This dress needs to be ~n in (= made smaller) at the waist.* (c) include, e g in one's journey or route: *a tour that ~s in six European capitals.* (d) understand: *They listened to my lecture, but how much did they ~ in, I wonder?* (e) see at once: *She took in every detail of the other woman's clothes.* (f) listen to, watch, with excitement: *The children took in the whole spectacle openmouthed.* **take sb in,** (a) receive, admit: *make a living by taking in guests.* (b) deceive: *Don't let yourself be ~n in by these politicians.*

take off, (a) make a start in jumping. (b) (of an aircraft) leave the ground and rise. Hence, **take-off** *n* [C] (a) (also *jump-off,* esp in show-jumping) place at which the feet leave the ground in jumping. (b) (of aircraft) leaving the ground and rising: *a smooth ~-off.* **take sth off,** (a) remove: *~ off one's hat.* (b) withdraw (from service): *The 7 a m express to Bristol will be ~n off next month,* will not run. **take sth off (sth),** (a) lift and move to another position: *T~ your hand off my shoulder.* (b) deduct: *~ 50p off the price.* **take sb off,** (a) lead away somewhere: *He was ~n off to prison.* (b) imitate: *Alice is clever at taking off the headmistress.* Hence, **take-off** *n* [C] caricature: *a good ~-off of the Prime Minister.* **not/never take one's eyes off sth/sb,** look at constantly: *He never took his eyes off her,* looked at her all the time.

take sth on, (a) undertake: *~ on extra work/heavy responsibilities.* (b) put on (a quality, appearance): *The chameleon can ~ on the colours of its background.* **take sb on,** (a) accept as an opponent: *~ him on at golf.* (b) employ: *~ on twenty more workers.* (c) (of a train, etc) allow to enter: *The bus stopped to ~ on some children.*

take sth out, (a) extract; remove: *have a tooth ~n out.* (b) obtain: *~ out an insurance policy/a driving licence.* **take sb out,** conduct; accompany: *~ the children out for a walk.* **take it out of sb,** leave him weak and exhausted: *His recent illness/All that hard work has ~n it out of him.* **take it out on sb,** show one's anger, disappointment, etc by being angry, etc with somebody else: *He came home angry at losing his job and took it out on his wife.*

take sb over, carry from one place to another: *Mr White took me over to the island in his launch.* **take sth over,** assume control of; succeed to the management or ownership of (a business, etc): *When Mr Green retired his son took over the business.* Hence, **take-over** *n* [C] change of control of a firm or company, e g after another has made a successful bid to buy its stock: *a `~over bid.* **take over (from sb),** accept duties, responsibilities, etc: *The new Chancellor took over (i e from his predecessor) yesterday.*

take to sth, (a) adopt as a practice or hobby, etc; get into a habit: *~ to gardening when one retires.* (b) take refuge in; use as a means of escape: *~ to the woods/the jungle,* go to the woods, etc, to avoid capture. **take to sth/sb,** have a liking for: *That boy will never ~ to cricket.*

take sth up, (a) pick up; raise: *~ up one's pen/book/gun.* (b) interest oneself in: *~ up photography.* (c) continue (something unfinished): *Harry took up the tale at the point where John had left off.* (d) occupy (time, space): *This table ~s up too much space.* **take sth up with sb,** speak or write to: *I will ~ the matter up with the Ministry,* e g by asking for information, or by making a protest.

take sth upon oneself, assume responsibility; undertake: *You mustn't ~ upon yourself the right to make decisions.*

take² /teɪk/ *n* **1** [C] amount (of money) taken. **2** (film industry) scene that has been or is to be photographed. **3** act of taking.

taker /ˈteɪkə(r)/ *n* [C] person who, that which, takes, esp one who takes a bet: *There were no ~s,* no one willing to take bets.

tak·ing /ˈteɪkɪŋ/ *adj* attractive; captivating. □ *n* (*pl*) money taken in business; receipts.

tal·cum powder /ˈtælkəm paʊdə(r)/ *n* [C] perfumed powder for the skin.

tale /teɪl/ *n* [C] **1** story: *~s of adventure.* **2**

report; account. *tell tales,* tell something about another person that he wishes to be kept secret, e g something he has done wrong.

tal·ent /'tælənt/ *n* **1** [C,U] (particular kind of) natural power to do something well: *a man of great ~; have a ~ for music/not much ~ for painting.* **2** [C] measure of weight, unit of money, used in ancient times among the Greeks, Romans, Assyrians, etc.

tal·ented *adj* having talent; skilled: *a ~ed musician.*

talk¹ /tɔk/ *n* **1** [C,U] conversation; discussion: *I've had several ~s with the headmaster about my boy.* ⇨ small talk. **talk of the town,** something or somebody that everyone is talking about. **2** [C] informal speech: *give a ~ on a holiday in Asia.*

talk² /tɔk/ *vi,vt* **1** say things; speak to give information; discuss something, etc: *He was ~ing to* (less often *with*) *a friend. What are they ~ing about? Were they ~ing in Spanish or in Portuguese?* **be/get oneself talked about,** be made the subject of gossip. **talk down to sb,** talk in a way that suggests that the speaker is superior. **Talking of...,** While on the subject of: *T~ing of travel, have you been to Munich yet?* **talk sth over,** discuss it. **talk round sth,** discuss a subject without reaching the point or a conclusion. **2** have the power of speech: *Can the baby ~ yet?* **3** be able to use (a language): *~ English/Spanish.* **4** discuss: *We ~ed music all evening.* **5** express in words: *~ sense/nonsense/treason.* **6** bring into a certain condition by talking: *~ oneself hoarse,* talk until one's throat hurts. **talk sb into/out of doing sth,** persuade him to do/not to do it: *She ~ed her husband into having a holiday in France.* **7** (various uses): *Don't do anything indiscreet—you know how people ~,* gossip. *Has the accused man ~ed yet,* given information, e g under torture or threats?

talking point, topic likely to cause discussion.

talka·tive /'tɔkətɪv/ *adj* fond of talking.

talker, (esp with an *adjective*) person who talks: *a good/poor ~er.*

tall /tɔl/ *adj* (-er, -est) **1** (of persons) of more than average height; (of objects such as a tree whose height is greater than its width) higher than the average or than surrounding objects: *She is ~er than her sister.* **2** of a specified height: *Tom is six foot ~.* **3** *a tall order,* an unreasonable request; a task difficult to perform. *a tall story,* one that is difficult to believe.

tall·ish /-ɪʃ/ *adj* rather tall.

tal·low /'tæləʊ/ *n* [U] hard (esp animal) fat used for making candles, etc.

tally /'tælɪ/ □ *vi* (*pt,pp* -ied) (of stories, amounts, etc) correspond; agree: *The two lists do not ~. Does your total ~ with mine?*

talon /'tælən/ *n* [C] claw of a bird, e g an

eagle.

tam·bour·ine /ˌtæmbə'rin/ *n* [C] small shallow drum with metal discs in the rim, played by striking with the knuckles and shaking it at the same time.

tame /teɪm/ *adj* (-er, -est) **1** (of animals) brought under control and/or accustomed to living with human beings; not wild or fierce: *a ~ monkey.* **2** (of a person) easily controlled or persuaded: *Her husband is a ~ little man.* **3** dull: *The story/film has a ~ ending.* □ *vt* make tame: *~ a lion.*

tamer, (usually in compounds) person who tames animals: *a 'lion-~r.*

tame·ly *adv* (of a person) acting, speaking, without spirit.

tame·ness *n* [U]

tam·per /'tæmpə(r)/ *vi* **tamper with,** interfere with: *Someone has been ~ing with the lock.*

tan /tæn/ *n* [C], *adj* yellowish brown; brown colour of sunburnt skin: *~ leather shoes/gloves; get a good ~* (on one's skin). □ *vt,vi* (-nn-) **1** (of an animal's skin) make, be made, into leather. *tan sb's hide,* (*sl*) give him a good beating. **2** make or become brown with sunburn: *Some people ~ quickly.*

tan·ner, workman who tans skins.

tan·nery /'tænrɪ/, place where skins are tanned.

tan·dem /'tændəm/ *n* [C] bicycle made for two persons to ride one behind the other, with pedals for both. □ *adv* (of horses in harness or two persons on a tandem) one behind the other: *drive/ride ~.*

tang /tæŋ/ *n* [C] sharp taste or flavour, esp one that is characteristic of something: *the salty ~ of the sea air.*

tan·gent /'tændʒənt/ *n* [C] straight line touching a curve. **go/fly off at a tangent,** (*fig*) change suddenly from one line of thought, action, etc to another.

tan·ger·ine /'tændʒə'rin *US:* 'tændʒərin/ *n* [C] small, sweet-scented, loose-skinned orange.

tan·gible /'tændʒəbəl/ *adj* **1** that can be known by touch. **2** clear and definite: *~ proof.*

tan·gibly /-əblɪ/ *adv*

tangle /'tæŋɡəl/ *n* [C] **1** confused mass (of string, hair, etc): *brush the ~s out of a dog's hair.* **2** confused state: *The traffic was in a frightful ~.* □ *vt,vi* **1** make or become confused; disordered: *~d hair.* **2** (*informal*) be/become involved in a fight or quarrel: *Don't ~ with Peter—he's bigger than you.*

tango /'tæŋɡəʊ/ *n* [C] (*pl* ~s) (music for a) S American dance with strongly marked rhythm and a variety of steps.

tank /tæŋk/ *n* [C] **1** (usually large) container for liquid or gas: *the 'petrol-~ of a car; an 'oil-~.* **2** armoured fighting vehicle with guns, moving on endless belts. □ *vi* **get tanked up,** (*sl*) get drunk (on beer).

tan·ker, (a) ship or aircraft for carrying petroleum. **(b)** heavy road vehicle with a large cylindrical tank for carrying oil, milk or other liquid.

tank·ard /ˈtæŋkəd/ n [C] large drinking mug, esp one for beer.

tan·ner, tan·nery, ⇨ tan.

tan·ta·lize /ˈtæntəlaɪz/ vt raise hopes that cannot (yet) be realized; keep just out of reach something that a person desires: *a tantalizing smell of food.*

tan·ta·mount /ˈtæntəmaʊnt/ adj **tantamount,** equal in effect to: *The Queen's request was ~ to a command.*

tan·trum /ˈtæntrəm/ n [C] (pl ~s) fit of temper or anger: *He's in one of his ~s again.*

tap¹ /tæp/ n **1** device for controlling the flow of liquid or gas from a pipe, barrel, etc: *Turn the ~ on/off. Don't leave the ~s running,* i e turn them off. **on tap,** (fig) available when needed. **2** plug used to close the opening of a cask. □ vt (-pp-) **1** draw out liquid through the tap of a (barrel): ~ (off) *cider from a cask.* **2** cut (the bark of a tree) and get (the sap, etc): ~ *rubber-trees.* **3** extract or obtain: ~ *a man for information;* ~ *a telephone/wire/line,* make a connection so as to intercept messages.

tap² /tæp/ n [C] **1** quick, light touch or blow: *a ~ on the window/at the door.* **2** (pl) (US armed forces) last signal of the day (by drum or bugle) for lights to be put out. □ vt,vi (-pp-) give a tap or taps (to): ~ *a man on the shoulder.*

tap-dancing, with rhythmical tapping of the foot.

tape /teɪp/ n [C,U] **1** (piece, length of) narrow strip of material used for tying up parcels, etc or in dressmaking: *three metres of linen ~.* ⇨ also *insulating tape, magnetic tape, red tape.* **2** length of tape stretched between the winning-posts on a race-track. □ vt **1** fasten, tie together, with tape. **2** record (sound) on magnetic tape. **3** **have sth/sb taped,** (informal) understand it/him thoroughly.

tape deck, tape recorder (without speakers or amplifiers) as a component in a hi-fi system.

tape-measure, length of thin, flexible metal or of strengthened cloth marked for measuring things with.

tape recorder, apparatus for recording sound on, and playing sound back from, magnetic tape.

tape-worm, kinds of many-jointed, long, flat worm that lives during its adult stage as a parasite in the intestines of man and other animals.

taper¹ /ˈteɪpə(r)/ n [C] length of string with a covering of wax, burnt to give a light.

taper² /ˈteɪpə(r)/ vt,vi make or become gradually narrower towards one end: *One end ~s/is ~ed off to a point.*

tap·es·try /ˈtæpɪstrɪ/ n [C,U] (pl -ies) (piece of) cloth into which threads of coloured wool are woven by hand to make designs and pictures, used for covering walls and furniture.

tapi·oca /ˈtæpɪˈəʊkə/ n [U] food (hard, white grains) used to make a milk pudding.

ta·pir /ˈteɪpə(r)/ n [C] animal like a pig of Central and S America with a long, flexible nose.

tar /tɑ(r)/ n [U] black substance, hard when cold, thick and sticky when warm, obtained from coal, etc used to preserve timber (e g in fences and posts), in making roads, etc. □ vt (-rr-) cover with tar. **tar and feather sb,** put tar on him and then cover them with feathers as a punishment. **tarred with the same brush,** having the same faults.

tar·mac, mixture of tar and gravel, as used for road surfaces.

ta·ran·tula /təˈræntjʊlə US: -tʃʊlə/ n [C] large, hairy, poisonous spider of S Europe.

tar·get /ˈtɑgɪt/ n **1** something to be aimed at in shooting-practice; any object aimed at. **2** thing, plan, etc against which criticism is directed: *This book will be the ~ of bitter criticism.* **3** objective (set for savings, production, etc); total which it is desired to reach.

tar·iff /ˈtærɪf/ n [C] **1** list of fixed charges, esp for meals, rooms, etc at a hotel. **2** list of taxes on goods imported or (less often) exported.

tar·mac /ˈtɑmæk/ n ⇨ tar.

tarn /tɑn/ n [C] small mountain lake.

tar·nish /ˈtɑnɪʃ/ vi,vt **1** (esp of metal surfaces) lose, cause the loss of, brightness: *Brass ~es easily.* **2** (fig) lessen the quality of: *His reputation is ~ed.* □ n [U] dullness.

tar·pau·lin /tɑˈpɔlɪn/ n [C,U] (sheet or cover of) canvas made waterproof, esp by being tarred.

tar·ra·gon /ˈtærəgən US: -gɒn/ n [U] herb with sharp-tasting leaves.

tarry¹ /ˈtɑrɪ/ adj covered, sticky, with tar.

tarry² /ˈtærɪ/ vt (literary) **1** stay, remain: ~ *a few days.* **2** be slow in coming, going, appearing.

tart¹ /tɑt/ adj **1** acid; sharp in taste: *a ~ flavour.* **2** (fig) bitter: ~ *humour.*

tart·ly adv

tart·ness n [U]

tart² /tɑt/ n [C] circle of pastry cooked with fruit or jam on it.

tart³ /tɑt/ n [C] (sl) girl or woman of immoral character. □ vt **tart sth/sb up,** (informal) dress like a tart; dress, decorate, (too) brightly.

tar·tan /ˈtɑtən/ n [U] Scottish woollen fabric woven with coloured crossing stripes; [C] this pattern, e g of a Scottish clan.

tar·tar¹ /ˈtɑtə(r)/ n [U] **1** chalk-like substance deposited on the teeth. **2** substance deposited on the sides of casks from fermented wine.

task /tɑsk US: tæsk/ n [C] piece of (esp hard) work (to be) done: *set a boy a ~*. **take sb to task (about/for sth)**, scold him: *It's wrong of you to take the child to ~ for such a silly offence.*

'task-force, specially organized unit (of police, etc) for a special purpose.

'task-master/-mistress, one who imposes tasks, esp a strict overseer.

tas·sel /ˈtæsəl/ n [C] bunch of threads, etc tied together at one end and hanging (from a flag, hat, etc) as an ornament.

tas·sel·led (*US* = **tas·seled**) *adj* having tassels.

taste[1] /teɪst/ n 1 [U] (with *the*) sense by which flavour is known: *sweet/sour to the ~*. 2 [C,U] quality of a substance made known by this sense, e g by putting some on the tongue: *Sugar has a sweet ~*. 3 (usually *sing* with *a, an*) small quantity (of something to eat or drink): *Won't you have a ~ of this cake/wine? Give him a ~ of the whip*, (*fig*) enough to be a sample of what it feels like to be whipped. 4 [C,U] liking or preference: *She has expensive ~s in clothes.* **There's no accounting for tastes,** We cannot explain why different people like different things. 5 [U] ability to enjoy beauty, esp in art and literature; ability to form judgements about these; ability to choose and use the best kind of behaviour: *She has excellent ~ in dress/dresses in perfect ~*.

taste·ful /-fəl/ *adj* showing good taste(5).

taste·fully /-fəlɪ/ *adv* in a tasteful manner: *~fully decorated with flowers.*

taste·less *adj* (a) (of food) having no flavour. (b) without taste(5).

taste·less·ly *adv*

tasty *adj* (-ier, -iest) having a pleasant flavour.

taste[2] /teɪst/ *vt,vi* 1 be aware of the taste of something: *Can you ~ anything strange in this soup?* 2 have a particular taste or flavour: *~ sour/bitter/sweet.* 3 test the taste of: *She ~d the soup to see if she had put enough salt in it.* 4 experience: *~ happiness/the joys of freedom.*

tat /tæt/ n ⇨ tit[2].

ta ta /ˈtɑ ˈtɑ/ *int* (baby language) goodbye.

tat·ters /ˈtætəz/ n pl pieces of cloth, paper, etc torn off or hanging loosely from something: *in ~, torn badly.*

tattle /ˈtætəl/ *vi,vt* chatter, gossip. □ n [U] idle talk.

tat·too[1] /təˈtu US: tæˈtu/ n [C] (*pl ~s*) 1 (*sing* only) beating of drum(s) to call soldiers back to quarters; hour at which this is sounded: *beat/sound the ~.* 2 [C] continuous tapping: *He was beating a ~ on the table with his fingers.* 3 [C] public entertainment, with music, marching, etc by soldiers.

tat·too[2] /təˈtu US: tæˈtu/ *vt* mark (a person's skin) with permanent designs or patterns by pricking it and putting in dyes or stains: *The sailor had a ship ~ed on his arm.* □ n [C] (*pl ~s*) mark or design of this kind.

tatty /ˈtætɪ/ *adj* (-ier, -iest) (*sl*) untidy and worn.

taught /tɔt/ *pt,pp* of teach.

taunt /tɔnt/ n [C] remark intended to hurt a person's feelings: *listen to the ~s of a successful rival.* □ *vt* attack (a person) with taunts: *They ~ed the boy with being a coward.*

taunt·ing·ly *adv*

Taurus /ˈtɔrəs/ n the Bull, second sign of the zodiac.

taut /tɔt/ *adj* (of ropes, nerves, etc) tightly stretched: *pull a rope ~*.

taut·ly *adv*

taut·ness n [U]

tauto·logi·cal /ˌtɔtəˈlɒdʒɪkəl/ *adj* of, containing, tautology.

taut·ol·ogy /tɔˈtɒlədʒɪ/ n [U] the saying of the same thing again in different ways without making one's meaning clearer or more forceful; [C] (*pl -ies*) instance of this.

tav·ern /ˈtævən/ n [C] (*old use*) public house for the supply of food and drink (to be consumed on the premises).

taw·dry /ˈtɔdrɪ/ *adj* (-ier, -iest) brightly coloured or decorated, but cheap or in bad taste: *~ jewellery/dresses*

taw·drily /-əlɪ/ *adv*

tawny /ˈtɔnɪ/ *adj* brownish yellow.

tax /tæks/ n 1 [C,U] (sum of) money (to be) paid by citizens (according to income, value of purchases, etc) to the government for public purposes: *state/local ~es; direct ~es*, i e on income; *indirect ~es*, e g paid when one buys goods. 2 *a tax on* (*sing* only) something that is a burden or strain: *a ~ on one's strength/health/patience.* □ *vt* 1 put a tax on; require (a person) to pay a tax: *~ luxuries/incomes/rich and poor alike.* 2 be a tax on: *~ a person's patience*, e g by asking him many silly questions. 3 *tax sb with sth*, accuse: *~ her with neglect of/ with having neglected her work.*

'tax-'free *adj* (a) not subject to taxation. (b) (of dividends or interest) on which tax has been deducted before distribution.

'tax-collector, official who collects taxes.

'tax-payer, person who pays taxes.

tax·able /-əbəl/ *adj* to be taxed· *~able income.*

tax·ation /tækˈseɪʃən/ n [U] (system of) raising money by taxes; taxes (to be) paid.

taxi /ˈtæksɪ/ n [C] (*pl ~s*) motor-car, esp one with a meter, which may be hired for journeys. □ *vi,vt* (of an aircraft) (cause to) move on wheels along the ground (or on floats, etc on the surface of water): *The plane ~ed/was ~ing across the tarmac.*

'taxi-cab, (common abbr *cab*) = taxi.

'taxi rank, place where taxis wait to be hired.

tea /ti/ n 1 [U] (dried leaves of an) evergreen shrub of eastern Asia, India, etc; drink made by pouring boiling water on these leaves: *a cup of* ~; *make* (*the*) ~, prepare it. *not my cup of tea,* not the sort of thing I like. **2** [C,U] occasion (in the late afternoon) at which tea is drunk: *We have* ~ *at half-past four.* ⇨ high tea.

`tea bag,` small bag with enough tea-leaves for use in a teacup.

`tea-break,` (in an office, factory, etc) short period when work is stopped for tea drinking.

`tea-caddy,` air-tight box in which to keep a supply of tea for daily use.

`tea-cake,` flat, sweetened cake, usually eaten hot with butter at tea.

`tea-chest,` large wooden box in which tea is packed for export.

`tea-cloth,` cloth used for drying cups, etc when they are washed.

`tea-cosy,` cover for keeping the contents of a teapot warm.

`tea-cup,` cup in which tea is served. *a storm in a teacup,* a lot of fuss about something unimportant.

`tea-pot,` vessel in which tea is made.

`tea-room,` restaurant which serves tea and light refreshments.

`tea-service/-set,` set of cups, saucers, plates, with a teapot, milk-jug, etc.

`tea-spoon,` small spoon for stirring tea.

`tea-spoon·ful /-fʊl/,` as much as a teaspoon can hold.

`tea-strainer,` device for sieving tea.

`tea-things,` (*informal*) things needed for having tea round a table.

`tea-time,` time at which tea is usually taken in the afternoon.

`tea-tray,` one on which a tea-set is used or carried.

teach /titʃ/ *vt,vi* (*pt,pp* taught /tɔt/) give instruction to (a person); cause (a person) to know or be able to do something; give a person (knowledge, skill, etc); give lessons (at school, etc); do this for a living: ~ *children;* ~ *French/history, etc;* ~ *a child* (*how*) *to swim. She is* ~*ing the piano to children. He* ~*es for a living. I will* ~ *you* (*not*) *to…,* (*informal*) (used as a threat) I will punish you, show you, the risk or penalty of…

`teach-in,` (*informal*) discussion of a subject of topical interest (as held in a college, with students, staff and other speakers).

teach·able /-əbəl/ *adj* that can be taught.

teacher, person who teaches.

teach·ing, (**a**) [U] work, profession of a teacher: *earn a living by* ~*ing.* (**b**) (usually *pl*) that which is taught; *the* ~*ings of Jesus.*

teak /tik/ *n* [C] tall, evergreen tree of India, Malaysia, etc; [U] its hard wood, used for making furniture, etc.

team /tim/ *n* [C] **1** two or more oxen, horses, etc pulling a cart, plough, etc together. **2** number of persons playing together and forming one side in some games, e g football, cricket, hockey and

sports, e g relay races. **3** group of people working together: *a* ~ *of surgeons in the operating theatre.* □ *vi* **team up (with),** (*informal*) make an effort in co-operation (with); work together (with).

`team-work,` combined effort; organized co-operation: *succeed by means of good* ~*-work.*

`team-mate,` fellow member of a team(2).

'team 'spirit, spirit in which each member of a team thinks of the success, etc of the team and not of personal advantage, glory, etc.

tear[1] /tɪə(r)/ *n* [C] drop of salty water coming from the eye: *Her eyes filled with* ~*s. The sad story moved us to* ~*s,* made us cry. *The girl burst into* ~*s,* began to cry.

`tear-drop,` single tear.

`tear-gas,` gas that causes severe watering of the eyes (used by the police to disperse a mob of demonstrators, etc).

tear·ful /-fəl/ *adj* crying; wet with tears: *a* ~*ful face.*

tear·fully /-fəlɪ/ *adv*

tear[2] /teə(r)/ *vt,vi* (*pt* tore /tɔ(r)/, *pp* torn /tɔn/) **1** pull apart or to pieces; make (a slit in something), damage, by pulling sharply: ~ *a sheet of paper in two/*~ *it to pieces/to bits. He tore the parcel open.* **tear sth up,** tear it into small pieces. **2** cause (something) to be out of place (*down, off, away, etc*) by pulling sharply: ~ *a page out of a book. She could scarcely* ~ *herself away from the scene,* to leave. **3** destroy the peace of: *a country torn by civil war; a heart torn by grief.* **torn between,** unable to choose between (conflicting demands, wishes, etc). **4** become torn: *This material* ~*s easily.* **5** go in excitement or at great speed: *The children tore out of the school gates.* □ *n* [C] torn place.

`tear-away,` aggressive youth.

tease /tiz/ *vt* **1** make fun of (a person) playfully or unkindly: *She* ~*d her father about his bald head. Molly was teasing the cat,* e g by pulling its tail. **2** separate, loosen, into separate fibres; fluff up the surface of (cloth, etc) by doing this: ~ *flax.* □ *n* [C] person who is fond of teasing others: *What a* ~ *she is!*

teaser, person who often teases.

teat /tit/ *n* [C] nipple(2) (esp an artificial one).

tech·ni·cal /'teknɪkəl/ *adj* **1** of, from, technique. **2** of, connected with, special to, one of the mechanical or industrial arts (e g printing, weaving) or with methods used by experts and artists: *a* `~ *college,* for engineering, etc.

tech·ni·cally /-klɪ/ *adv*

tech·ni·cal·ity /'teknɪ'kælətɪ/ *n* [C] (*pl* -ies) technical word, phrase, point, etc: *The judge explained the legal technicalities of the case to the jury.*

tech·ni·cian /tek'nɪʃən/ *n* [C] expert in the

technique(s) of a particular art, etc; highly skilled craftsman or mechanic.

tech·nique /tek'nik/ n **1** [U] technical or mechanical skill in art, music, etc. **2** [C] method of doing something expertly; method of artistic expression in music, painting, etc.

tech·noc·racy /tek'nokrəsɪ/ n [C,U] (pl -ies) (state where there is) organization and management of a country's industrial resources by technical experts.

tech·no·crat /'teknəkræt/ n [C] supporter, member, of a technocracy.

tech·no·logi·cal /ˌteknə'lodʒɪkəl/ adj of technology: ~ problems.

tech·nol·ogist /tek'nolədʒɪst/ n [C] expert in, student of, technology.

tech·nol·ogy /tek'nolədʒɪ/ n [U] **1** study, mastery and using of manufacturing methods and industrial arts. **2** systematic application of knowledge to practical tasks in industry: study engineering at a college of ~.

tedi·ous /'tidɪəs/ adj wearying; uninteresting: a ~ lecture/lecturer; ~ work.
tedi·ous·ly adv
tedi·ous·ness n [U]

te·dium /'tidɪəm/ n [U] (informal) boredom.

tee /ti/ n **1** (golf) place from which a player starts at each hole; specially shaped piece of wood or rubber used for this. **2** mark aimed at in certain games, such as quoits. **to a tee,** perfectly; exactly: She suits him to a ~. □ vt,vi **1** tee (up), put the ball on a tee(1). **2** **tee off,** drive(9) from a tee.

teem¹ /tim/ vi **1** be present in large numbers: Fish ~ in this river. **2** **teem with,** have in great numbers: His head is ~ing with bright ideas.

teem² /tim/ vi (of rain) fall heavily; pour: It was ~ing with rain.

teen·age /'tinerdʒ/ adj: ~ fashions, for persons in their teens.

teen·ager /'tinerdʒə(r)/ n [C] boy or girl in his or her teens or up to 21 or 22 years of age: a club for ~s.

teens /tinz/ n pl the ages 13 to 19: girls in their ~.

tee–shirt /'ti ʃət/ n [C] = T-shirt.

tee·ter /'titə(r)/ vi stand or walk unsteadily: ~ing on the edge of disaster.

teeth /tiθ/ pl of tooth.

teethe /tið/ vi (of a baby) be getting its first teeth.
teething troubles, (fig) problems which may occur during the early stages of a task.

tee·to·tal /ˌti'təʊtəl/ adj not drinking, opposed to the drinking of, alcoholic liquor.
tee·to·tal·ler (US also **tee·to·taler**) n [C] person who does not drink alcoholic liquor.

tele·com·muni·ca·tions /'telɪkə'mjuːnɪ'keɪʃənz/ n pl communications by cable, telegraph, telephone, radio or TV.

tele·gram /'telɪgræm/ n [C] message sent by telegraphy.

tele·graph /'telɪgrɑf US: -græf/ n [C] means of, apparatus for, sending messages by the use of electric current along wires or by radio. □ vi,vt send (news, etc) by telegraph.

tel·egra·pher /tə'legrəfə(r)/, operator who sends and receives messages by telegraph.

tele·graphic /ˌtelɪ'græfɪk/ adj sent by, suitable for, of, the telegraph.

tel·egra·phy /tə'legrəfɪ/ n [U] art, science, process, of sending and receiving messages by telegraph.

tel·epa·thy /tə'lepəθɪ/ n [U] transference of thoughts or ideas from one mind to another without using speech, signs, etc.
tele·pathic /ˌtelɪ'pæθɪk/ adj

tele·phone /'telɪfəʊn/ n (usual abbr phone in speech) **1** [U] means, system, of transmitting the human voice by electric current, usually through wires. **2** [C] apparatus (with receiver and mouthpiece) for this purpose: You're wanted on the ~. □ vt,vi send (a message to a person) by telephone.
telephone booth, (also 'phone booth or 'call-box), small enclosure with a coin-operated public telephone.
telephone directory, (informal = 'phone book) list of names with telephone numbers and addresses.
telephone exchange, place where telephone connections are made.

tel·ephon·ist /tə'lefənɪst/ n [C] operator in a telephone exchange.

tel·eph·ony /tə'lefənɪ/ n [U] method, process, of sending and receiving messages by telephone.

tele·scope /'telɪskəʊp/ n [C] long instrument with lenses for making distant objects appear nearer and larger. □ vt,vi make or become shorter by means of or in the manner of sections that slide one within the other: When the trains collided, the first two cars of one of the trains ~d/were ~d.

tele·scopic /ˌtelɪ'skopɪk/ adj (a) of, containing, able to be seen with, a telescope: a telescopic view of the moon, seen through a telescope. (b) having sections which slide one within the other: a telescopic aerial, e g as part of a portable radio.

tele·vi·sion /'telɪvɪʒən/ n (abbr **TV**) **1** [U] process of transmitting pictures by radio waves with sound at the same time: Did you see the news on (the) ~? **2** [C] (also '~ set) apparatus for receiving and showing these pictures and sound.

tele·vise /'telɪvaɪz/ vt send by television: The Olympic Games were televised.

tell /tel/ vt,vi (pt,pp told /təʊld/) **1** make known (in spoken or written words); give information concerning or a description of: I told him my name. T~ me where you live. I can't ~ you how happy I am, can't find words that are adequate. **I told you so,** I warned you that this would happen, etc and now you see that I'm right: Things have *gone wrong but please don't say 'I told you so!'* **2** express with words: ~ *a lie;* ~ *the children a story.* **tell tales,** ⇨ tale(2). **3** order; direct: *You must do as you're told. T~ him to wait.* **4** (esp with *can/could/be able to*) identify: *Can you* ~ *Tom from his twin brother? They look exactly the same; how can you* ~ *which is which?* **5** learn by observation; become aware (of something): *How do you* ~ *which of these keys to use?* **tell the time,** (be able to) read (or say) the time from a clock, etc: *Can Mary* ~ *the time yet? Can you* ~ *me what time it is?* **there is/was, etc no telling,** it is impossible or difficult to know: *There's no* ~ing *what may happen/where she's gone/what he's doing.* **6 tell sb off (for sth/for doing sth),** (*informal*) scold him: *He told me off for making so many careless mistakes.* **7** have a marked effect on; influence the result of: *All this hard work is* ~ing *on him,* is affecting his health. **8** (*informal*) inform against: *John told on his sister.* **9** tell a secret: *You promised not to* ~ *and now you've done so!*

tel·ler, (a) person who receives and pays out money over a bank counter. (b) man who counts votes, e g in the House of Commons.

tell·ing *adj* impressive: *a* ~ing *argument/ blow.*

'telling-`off, instance of being scolded. ⇨ **6** above.

tell·tale /'telteɪl/ *n* [C] **1** person who tells about another's private affairs, makes known a secret, etc. **2** (often as an *adjective*) circumstances, etc that reveal a person's thoughts, activities, etc: *a* ~tale *blush.*

telly /'telɪ/ *n* (*informal*) (abbr for) television: *I saw it on* (*the*) ~.

te·mer·ity /tɪ'merətɪ/ *n* [U] (*formal*) rashness.

tem·per [1] /'tempə(r)/ *n* [C] **1** state or condition of the mind: *in a good* ~, calm and pleasant; *in a bad* ~, angry, impatient, etc. **get/fly into a temper,** become very angry. **keep/lose one's temper,** keep/fail to keep one's temper under control. **2** [C] (of steel, etc) degree of strength, hardness, etc.

-tem·pered /'tempəd/ *suffix* having or showing a certain kind of temper: *a* `bad-/ `good-/ `hot-~ed man.*

tem·per [2] /'tempə(r)/ *vt,vi* **1** give, come to, the required temper(2) by heating and cooling. **2** soften or modify: ~ *justice with mercy,* be merciful when giving a just punishment.

tem·pera·ment /'temprəmənt/ *n* **1** [C,U] person's personality or nature, esp as this affects his way of thinking, feeling and behaving: *a girl with a nervous/an artistic* ~. **2** [U] (without an *adjective*) kind of personality that is easily excited, not easily controlled, e g as in some actresses and opera singers.

tem·pera·men·tal /'temprə'mentəl/ *adj* (a) caused by temperament: *a* ~al dislike for

study. (**b**) quickly changing moods: *a* ~al tennis player.

tem·pera·men·tally /-təlɪ/ *adv*

tem·per·ance /'tempərəns/ *n* [U] **1** self-control in speech, behaviour and (esp) in the use of alcoholic drinks. **2** total abstinence from alcoholic drinks.

tem·per·ate /'tempərət/ *adj* **1** showing, behaving with, self-control: *Be more* ~ *in your language, please.* **2** (of climate, parts of the world) free from extremes of heat and cold: *the north* ~ *zone,* between the Tropic of Cancer and the Arctic zone.

tem·per·ate·ly *adv*

tem·pera·ture /'temprətʃə(r)/ *US:* 'tem-pərtʃʊər/ *n* [C,U] degree of heat and cold: *The nurse took the* ~s *of all the patients,* measured their body temperatures with a thermometer. **have/run a temperature,** have a fever.

tem·pest /'tempɪst/ *n* **1** [C] violent storm. **2** (*fig*) violent agitation: *A* ~ *of anger swept through the crowd.*

tem·pes·tu·ous /tem'pestʃʊəs/ *adj* (of the weather and *fig*) violent; stormy.

temple [1] /'tempəl/ *n* [C] **1** building used for the worship of a god. **2** (applied occasionally to a) place of Christian worship (*church* and *chapel* are the usual words). **3** any of the three successive religious centres of the Jews in ancient Jerusalem.

temple [2] /'tempəl/ *n* [C] flat part of either side of the forehead.

tempo /'tempəʊ/ *n* [C] (*pl* ~s or, in music, tempi /-pɪ/) (*It*) **1** rate of movement or activity: *the tiring* ~ *of city life.* **2** speed at which music is (to be) played.

tem·poral /'tempərəl/ *adj* (*formal*) **1** of, existing in, time. **2** of earthly human life; of this physical life only, not spiritual.

tem·por·ary /'tempərɪ/ *US:* -pəreɪ/ *adj* lasting for, designed to be used for, a short time only: ~ *employment; a* ~ *bridge.*

tem·por·ar·ily /'tempərəlɪ/ *US:* 'tempə'rerəlɪ/ *adv*

tempt /tempt/ *vt* **1** (try to) persuade (a person) to do something wrong or foolish: *Nothing could* ~ *him to agree that torture is a necessary evil.* **2** attract (a person) to have or do something: *The warm weather* ~ed *us to go for a swim.*

temp·ter, person who tempts.

temp·tress /-trəs/, woman who tempts.

tempt·ing *adj* attractive: *a* ~ing *offer.*

temp·ta·tion /temp'teɪʃən/ *n* **1** [U] tempting or being tempted: *yield/give way to* ~. *Don't put* ~ *in my way.* **2** [C] that which tempts or attracts: *Clever advertisements are* ~s *to spend money.*

ten /ten/ *n* [C], *adj* (of) the number 10. **ten to one,** very probably: *T~ to one he will arrive late.*

tenth /tenθ/ *n* [C], *adj* (abbr *10th*) (of) the next after the 9th or one of 10 equal parts

tenth·ly *adv*

`ten·fold` *adv* ten times as many or much.

`ten·pence` *n* [C,U] (*GB* coin with the) value of ten pennies.

ten·able /ˈtenəbl/ *adj* **1** that can be defended successfully: *His theory is hardly* ~. **2** (of an office or position) that can be held (*by* a person): *The lectureship is* ~ *for a period of three years.*

ten·acious /təˈneɪʃəs/ *adj* (*formal*) holding tightly, refusing to let go: *a* ~ *memory;* ~ *of our rights.*

`ten·acious·ly` *adv*

`ten·acious·ness, ten·ac·ity` /təˈnæsətɪ/ *n* [U]

ten·ancy /ˈtenənsɪ/ *n* [U] **1** use of land, etc as a tenant: *during his* ~ *of the farm.* **2** (with *a, an*) length of time during which a tenant uses land, etc: *hold a* `life ~ *of a house.*

ten·ant /ˈtenənt/ *n* [C] person who pays rent for the use of land, a building, a room, etc.

tend[1] /tend/ *vt* watch over; attend: *shepherds* ~*ing their flocks.*

tend[2] /tend/ *vi* be inclined to move; have as a characteristic or direction: *Prices are* ~*ing upwards. He* ~*s to make too many mistakes.*

ten·dency /ˈtendənsɪ/ *n* [C] (*pl* -ies) turning or inclination: *Business is showing a* ~ *to improve.*

ten·den·tious /tenˈdenʃəs/ *adj* (*formal*) (of a speech, a piece of writing, etc) having an underlying purpose, aimed at helping a cause; not impartial: *Countries at war often send out* ~ *reports,* reports designed to show their cause in a favourable light, win sympathy, etc.

`ten·den·tious·ly` *adv*

ten·der[1] /ˈtendə(r)/ *adj* (-er, -est) **1** delicate; easily hurt or damaged; quickly feeling pain: ~ *blossoms,* e g easily hurt by frosts; *a* ~ *heart,* easily moved to pity. Hence, `tender-ˈhearted` *adj.* **2** (of meat) easily chewed; not tough: *a* ~ *steak.* **3** kind, loving: ~ *looks;* ~ *parents.*

`ten·der·loin,` tender part of the loin of beef or pork.

`ten·der·ly` *adv*

`ten·der·ness` *n* [U]

ten·der[2] /ˈtendə(r)/ *n* [C] **1** person who looks after, watches over, something. ⇨ bartender. **2** small ship attending a larger one. **3** wagon for fuel and water behind a steam locomotive.

ten·der[3] /ˈtendə(r)/ *vt,vi* **1** offer; present: *He* ~*ed his resignation to the Prime Minister.* **2** make an offer (to carry out work, supply goods, etc) at a stated price: ~ *for the construction of a new motorway.* □ *n* [C] **1** statement of the price at which one offers to supply goods or services, or to do something: *invite* ~*s for a new bridge.* ⇨ legal tender.

ten·don /ˈtendən/ *n* [C] tough, thick cord that joins muscle to bone.

ten·dril /ˈtendrɪl/ *US:* -drəl/ *n* [C] part like a thread of a plant, e g a vine, that twists round any nearby support.

ten·ement /ˈtenəmənt/ *n* [C] **1** large house for the use of many families at low rents. **2** (*legal*) any dwelling-house; any kind of permanent property.

tenet /ˈtenet *US:* ˈtenɪt/ *n* [C] (*formal*) principle; belief; doctrine.

ten·nis /ˈtenɪs/ *n* [U] game for two or four players who hit a ball backwards and forwards across a net.

`tennis-court,` marked area on which tennis is played.

`tennis-ˈelbow,` inflammation of the elbow caused by playing tennis.

tenor /ˈtenə(r)/ *n* [C] **1** (music for, singer with, the) highest normal adult male voice: (as an *adjective*) ~ *voice; the* ~ *part.* **2** (of instruments) with a range about that of the tenor voice: *a* ~ *saxophone.*

tense[1] /tens/ *adj* (-r, -st) tightly stretched or strained: ~ *nerves; a moment of* ~ *excitement.* □ *vt,vi* make or become tense: *He* ~*d his muscles for the effort.*

`tense·ly` *adv*

`tense·ness` *n* [U]

tense[2] /tens/ *n* [C,U] (*gram*) verb form that shows time: *the present/past/future* ~.

ten·sion /ˈtenʃən/ *n* [U] **1** state of, degree of, being tense: *If you increase the* ~ *of the rope it will break.* **2** stretching or being stretched. **3** mental, emotional or nervous strain; condition when feelings are tense, when relations between persons, groups, states are strained: *political* ~. **4** voltage: *Keep away from those high* ~ *wires or you'll be electrocuted.*

tent /tent/ *n* [C] shelter made of canvas supported by poles and ropes, esp as used by campers, scouts, soldiers, etc. ⇨ oxygen tent.

ten·tacle /ˈtentəkəl/ *n* [C] long, slender, boneless growth on certain animals used for touching, feeling, holding, moving, etc.

ten·ta·tive /ˈtentətɪv/ *adj* made or done as a trial, to test the effect: *make a* ~ *offer.*

`ten·ta·tive·ly` *adv*

tenth /tenθ/ *n, adj* ⇨ ten.

tenu·ous /ˈtenjʊəs/ *adj* (*formal*) **1** thin; slender: *the* ~ *web of a spider.* **2** (of distinctions) subtle.

ten·ure /ˈtenjʊə(r) *US:* -jə(r)/ *n* [C,U] (period, time, condition of) holding (e g political office) or using (land): *The farmers want security of* ~, to be secure in their tenancies.

tepid /ˈtepɪd/ *adj* lukewarm.

term /tɜːm/ *n* [C] **1** fixed or limited period of time: *a long* ~ *of imprisonment; during his* ~ *of office as President.* **2** (of schools, universities, etc) one of the periods (usually three) into which the academic year is divided: *end-of-*~ *examinations; during* `~-time.* **3** (*legal*) period during which a Court holds session. **4** (*pl*) conditions offered or agreed to: ~*s of surrender.* e g offered to a defeated enemy. ⇨ reference(1). **come to terms (with sb),** reach an agreement. **come to terms with sth,** accept finally: *come to ∼s with a difficult situation.* **5** (*pl*) **be on good/friendly/bad terms (with sb),** be friendly, etc with him. ⇨ speak(2). **6** words used to express an idea, esp a specialized concept: *technical/ scientific/legal ∼s.* **7** (*pl*) mode of expression: *How dare you speak of her in such abusive ∼s?* **8** (*maths*) part of an expression joined to the rest by + or −: *The expression* $a^2 + 2ab + b^2$ *has three ∼s.* □ *vt* name; apply a term to: *He has no right to ∼ himself a professor.*

ter·min·able /ˈtɜːmɪnəbəl/ *adj* that may be terminated.

ter·minal /ˈtɜːmɪnəl/ *adj* **1** of, taking place, each term(1,3): *∼ examinations/accounts.* **2** of, forming, the point or place at the end: *∼ cancer,* incurable; *the ∼ ward,* (in a hospital) for persons who cannot be cured and must soon die. □ *n* [C] **1** end of a railway line, bus route, etc; centre (in a town) used by passengers departing for, or arriving from, an airport: *the 'West 'London `Air T∼.* **2** point of connection in an electric circuit: *the ∼s of a battery.*

ter·min·ally *adv*

ter·min·ate /ˈtɜːmɪneɪt/ *vt,vi* bring to an end; come to an end: *∼ his contract.*

ter·mi·na·tion /ˌtɜːmɪˈneɪʃən/ *n* **1** [C,U] ending: *the ∼ of a contract.* **2** [C] final syllable or letter of a word.

ter·mi·nol·ogy /ˌtɜːmɪˈnɒlədʒɪ/ *n* [C,U] (*pl -ies*) (science of the) proper use of terms(6); terms used in a science or art: *medical/ grammatical ∼.*

ter·mi·no·logi·cal /ˌtɜːmɪnəˈlɒdʒɪkəl/ *adj*

ter·mi·nus /ˈtɜːmɪnəs/ *n* [C] (*pl -ni* /-naɪ/ or *∼es*) station at the end of a railway line, bus route, etc.

ter·mite /ˈtɜːmaɪt/ *n* [C] insect (popularly called *white ant*), which makes large hills of hard earth.

ter·race /ˈterəs/ *n* [C] **1** level(led) area of ground with a vertical or sloping front or side; a series of these, separated by sloping banks, rising one above the other, eg as a method of irrigation on a hillside. **2** flight of wide, shallow steps (eg for spectators in a football stadium). **3** continuous row of houses in one block. □ *vt* (usually as a *pp*) form into terraces: *a ∼d lawn; ∼d houses,* (long line of) houses joined together.

terra-cotta /ˌterə ˈkɒtə/ *n* [U] hard, reddish-brown pottery; the colour reddish-brown.

ter·rain /teˈreɪn US: tə-/ *n* [C] stretch of land, esp regarding its natural features: *difficult ∼ for walking.*

ter·res·trial /təˈrestrɪəl/ *adj* **1** of, on, living on, the earth or land: *the ∼ parts of the world.* **2** (opposite of *celestial*) of the earth.

ter·rible /ˈterəbəl/ *adj* **1** causing great fear

or horror: *a ∼ war/accident.* **2** causing great discomfort; extreme: *The heat is ∼ in Baghdad during the summer.* **3** (*informal*) extremely bad: *What ∼ food they gave us!*

ter·ribly /-əblɪ/ *adv* (*informal*) extremely: *How terribly boring he is!*

ter·rier /ˈterɪə(r)/ *n* [C] kinds of small and lively dog.

ter·rific /təˈrɪfɪk/ *adj* **1** causing fear. **2** (*informal*) very great; extreme: *driving at a ∼ pace.*

ter·rifi·cally /-klɪ/ *adv* extremely.

ter·rify /ˈterɪfaɪ/ *vt* (*pt,pp -ied*) fill with fear: *The child was terrified of being left alone in the house. What a ∼ing experience!*

ter·ri·torial /ˌterɪˈtɔːrɪəl/ *adj* **1** of land, esp land forming a division of a country: *∼ possessions.* **2** **T∼,** of any of the US Territories: *T∼ laws.* **3** (*GB*) of the force of mostly non-professional soldiers organized for the defence of Great Britain and trained in their spare time: *the T∼ Army.* □ *n* [C] member of the Territorial Army.

terri'torial `waters, the sea near a country's coast, over which special rights are claimed e g for fishing.

ter·ri·tory /ˈterɪtrɪ US: -tɔːrɪ/ *n* (*pl -ies*) **1** [C,U] (area of) land, esp land under one ruler or Government: *Is this American ∼?* **2** [C] land or district; [U] extent of such land, etc: *How much ∼ can he cover* (= travel across) *in a day?*

ter·ror /ˈterə(r)/ *n* **1** [U] great fear: *run away in ∼.* **2** [C] instance of great fear; (person or thing that causes) great fear: *have a ∼ of fire.*

`ter·ror·ism /-ɪzm/ *n* [U] use of violence and intimidation, esp for political purposes.

`ter·ror·ist /-ɪst/ *n* [C] supporter of, participant in, terrorism.

`ter·ror·ize /-aɪz/ *vt* fill with terror by threats or acts of violence.

terse /tɜːs/ *adj* (of speech, style, speakers) brief and to the point.

terse·ly *adv*

terse·ness *n* [U]

ter·ti·ary /ˈtɜːʃərɪ US: -ʃɪerɪ/ *adj* third in rank, order, occurrence, importance.

test /test/ *n* [C] (often as an *adjective*) examination or trial (of something) to find its quality, value, composition, etc; trial or examination (of a person, his powers, knowledge, skill, etc): *methods that have stood the ∼ of time; a `blood ∼,* e g at a hospital, for infection, etc; *a `driving ∼; an in`telligence ∼.* □ *vt* examine; make a trial of: *have one's eyesight ∼ed. The long climb ∼ed* (= was a test of) *our strength.*

`test case, (in law) one that shows the principle involved (even though it may not be important in itself).

`test drive** *n* [C] drive in a car one thinks of buying, to judge its qualities, worth, etc. Hence, **`test-drive *vt*

'test flight, (to judge the performance of a new aircraft).

'test match, one of the matches in any of the cricket or Rugby tours arranged between certain countries.

'test-tube, slender glass tube, closed at one end, used in chemical experiments.

tes·ta·ment /'testəmənt/ *n* **1** [C] (often *last Will and T~*) statement in writing saying how a person wishes his property to be distributed after his death. **2** Old T~, New T~, the two main divisions of the Bible.

tes·ti·cle /'testɪkəl/ *n* [C] each of the two glands of the male sex organ that secrete spermatozoa.

tes·ti·fy /'testɪfaɪ/ *vt,vi* (*pt,pp* -ied) **1** give evidence: *He testified under oath that he had not stolen the bike. The teacher testified to the boy's ability.* **2** serve as evidence of: *Her tears testified her grief.*

tes·ti·mo·nial /ˌtestɪ'məʊnɪəl/ *n* [C] **1** written statement testifying to a person's merits, abilities, qualifications, etc. **2** something given to a person to show appreciation of services: *a ~ match,* for a football player.

tes·ti·mony /'testɪmənɪ *US:* -məʊnɪ/ *n* [U] **1** declaration, esp in a law court, testifying that something is true: *The witness's ~ is false.* **2** declarations; statements: *According to the ~ of the medical profession, the health of the nation is improving.*

tes·tis /'testɪs/ *n* [C] (*pl* -tes /-tiz/) = tes·ticle.

tether /'teðə(r)/ *n* [C] rope or chain by which an animal is fastened while grazing. **at the end of one's tether,** (*fig*) at the end of one's patience, etc. □ *vt* fasten with a tether: *He ~ed his horse to the fence.*

text /tekst/ *n* **1** [U] printed words in a book (contrasted with notes, diagrams, illustrations, etc). **2** [C] original words of an author, apart from anything else in a book. **3** [C] short passage, sentence, esp of the Bible, etc, as the subject of a sermon or discussion. **'text·book,** book used to learn a subject: *an algebra ~book; a ~book on grammar.*

tex·tual /'tekstʃʊəl/ *adj* of, in, a text: *~ual errors.*

tex·tile /'tekstaɪl/ *adj* of the making of cloth: *the ~ industry.* □ *n* [C] cloth.

tex·ture /'tekstʃə(r)/ *n* [C,U] **1** the arrangement of the threads in a cloth: *cloth with a loose/close ~.* **2** arrangement of the parts that make up something: *the ~ of a mineral.*

than /ðən *rarely heard strong form:* ðæn/ *conj* introducing the second part of a comparison: *John is taller ~ his brother. I know you better ~ he (does),* ie than he knows you. *I know you better ~ him,* ie than I know him. *He is several years older ~ me.* **rather than,** ⇨ rather(1). **sooner than,** ⇨ soon(3,4).

thank /θæŋk/ *vt* express gratitude: *~ a person for his help. There's no need to ~ me. Thank you,* formula for accepting something or expressing thanks. *No, thank you,* formula used to decline an offer. □ *n* (*pl*) (expression of) gratitude: *T~s for the meal; kneel and give ~s to God. No, thanks,* (*informal*) No, thank you. **thanks to,** as the result of: *T~s to your help we were successful.*

'thanks-'giving, (a) expression of gratitude, esp to God; form of prayer for this. **(b)** (*US*) (also '*T~s-'giving Day*) day set apart each year to thank God for His goodness (usually the fourth Thursday in November).

thank·ful /-fəl/ *adj* grateful: *You should be ~ful that you have escaped with minor injuries.*

thank·fully /-fəlɪ/ *adv*

thank·less *adj* not feeling or expressing gratitude or winning appreciation: *a ~less task,* one which brings no thanks, appreciation or reward.

that /ðæt/ *adj, pron* (*pl* those /ðəʊz/) (contrasted with *this, these*) **1** the person or thing pointed to or drawn attention to, named or understood to be known: *Look at ~ man/those men. What is ~? What are those? What was ~ noise? What noise was ~? This book is much better than ~ (one). These are much better than those. Those who do not wish to go need not go. Throw away all those (which are) too old. I don't like ~ new secretary of his.* **2** (used as a collective *sing*): *What about ~ five pounds you borrowed from me last month?* □ *adv* (*informal*) to such a degree; so: *I can't walk ~ far,* = as far as that. *It's about ~ high,* ie as high as that.

that /ðət *rarely heard strong form:* ðæt/ *conj* **1** (introducing *noun* clauses): *She said (~) she would come. The trouble is ~ we are short of money.* **2** **so that; in order that,** (introducing clauses of purpose): *Bring it nearer so ~ I can see it better.* **3** (introducing clauses of manner): *His behaviour was so bad ~ we all refused to talk to him.* **4** (introducing clauses of condition): *on condition ~...*

that /ðət *rarely heard strong form:* ðæt/ *relative pron* (*pl* unchanged) (*Note:* when *that* is in parentheses in examples, it is often omitted.) **1** (used as the subject of the *verb* in a clause): *The letter ~ came this morning is from my father.* **2** (*who* is usually preferred to *that* for a person, but *that* is preferred to *who* after superlatives, *only, all, any,* and *it is* or *it was*): *Newton was one of the greatest men ~ ever lived. You're the only person ~ can help me.* **3** (used as the object of the *verb* in the clause): *The pen (~) you gave me is very nice. Is this the best (~) you can do?* **4** (used after an expression of time.): *the year (~) my father died.* **5** (used as the object of a preposition): *All the people (~) I wrote to agreed to come. Is this the book (~) you were looking for?*

thatch /θætʃ/ *n* [U] roof covering of dried

straw, reeds, etc. □ *vt* cover (a roof, etc) with thatch.

thaw /θɔ/ *vi,vt* **1** (of snow and ice) begin to melt. **2** (cause anything frozen to) become liquid or soft again: *leave frozen food to* ~ *before cooking it.* **3** (of persons, their behaviour) (cause to) become less formal, more friendly: *After a good dinner he began to* ~. □ *n* (usually *sing*) (state of the weather causing) thawing: *Let's go skating before a* ~ *sets in.*

the /ðə *strong form:* ði/ *definite article* **1** (used as a less specific form of *this, these, that, those,* applied to person(s), thing(s), event(s), etc already referred to or being discussed. Note the changes from *a, an* to *the* in these sentences): *An old man lived in a small hut near a forest. One day* ~ *old man left* ~ *hut and went into* ~ *forest to gather wood.* **2** (used when the situation is sufficient to make clear who or what is referred to): *Please close* ~ *window,* i e the window that is open. **3** (used with a *noun* when it stands for something unique): ~ *sun;* ~ *moon;* ~ *year 1989;* ~ *universe.* **4** (used with *nouns* such as *sea, sky,* when there is no *adjective*): *T*~ *sea was calm. Isn't* ~ *wind strong!* **5** (used with a *noun* if it is shown by the context to be unique): ~ *back of* ~ *house.* (*Note:* in many phrases *the* is or may be omitted: *from beginning to end; from* (~) *top to* (~) *bottom; in* (~) *future.*) **6** (used with a superlative): ~ *best way to get there.* (*Note: the* is not needed after the *verb 'be'* when the superlative is used without a *noun: It is wisest* (= The wisest plan is) *to avoid the centre of the town.* When *most* means 'very', *the* is not used: *T*~ *story was most exciting. This is a most useful dictionary.*) **7** (used before (a) names of seas and oceans: ~ *Mediterranean,* ~ *Red Sea;* ~ *Atlantic* (*Ocean*). **(b)** names of rivers and canals: ~ *Nile;* ~ *Suez Canal.* **(c)** *pl* geographical names: ~ *Alps;* ~ *West Indies.* **(d)** in a few geographical names: ~ *Sudan;* ~ *Sahara.*) **8** (used to indicate all members of a class): ~ *rich;* ~ *dead.* **9** (used with musical instruments): *to play* ~ *piano/*~ *violin/*~ *guitar,* but not with names of games: *to play tennis, football.* **10** (used with *nouns* expressing a unit): *This car does thirty miles to* ~ *gallon,* i e to each gallon of petrol. □ *adv* by so much; by that amount: *T*~ *more he has* ~ *more he wants. T*~ *more he reads* ~ *less he understands.*

the-atre (*US* = **the-ater**) /ˈθɪətə(r)/ *n* [C] **1** building, etc for the performance of plays, for dramatic events, etc: *go to the* ~ *to see a Shakespeare play.* **2** hall or room with seats in rows rising one behind another for lectures, scientific demonstrations, etc. **3** = operating theatre. **4** scene of important events: *a* ~ *of war.* **5** (usually *sing* with *the*) the writing and acting of plays, esp when

connected with one author, country, period, etc: *a book about the Greek* ~.

`**theatre-goer,** person who (often) visits theatres.

the-atri-cal /θɪˈætrɪkəl/ *adj* **(a)** of, for, the theatre: *theatrical costumes.* **(b)** (of behaviour, manner, way of speaking, persons, etc) designed for effect; exaggerated, not natural.

the-atri-cally /-klɪ/ *adv*

theft /θeft/ *n* [C,U] (the act of, an instance of) stealing.

their /ðeə(r)/ *adj* belonging to them: *They have lost* ~ *dog. They have a house of* ~ *own.*

theirs /ðeəz/ *possessive pron: That dog is* ~*s, not ours. It's a habit of* ~*s,* one of their habits.

them /ðəm *strong form:* ðem/ *personal pron* (object form of *they*): *Give* ~ *to me. It was kind of* ~.

theme /θiːm/ *n* [C] **1** topic; subject of a talk or a piece of writing. **2** (*music*) short melody which is repeated, expanded, etc e g in a sonata or symphony.

`**theme song,** one that is often repeated in a musical play, film, etc.

them·selves /ðəmˈselvz/ *pron* **1** (*reflex*): *They hurt* ~. *They kept some for* ~. **(all) by themselves, (a)** without help: *They did the work by* ~. **(b)** alone: *They were by* ~ *when I called.* **2** (used for emphasis): *They* ~ *have often made that mistake.*

then /ðen/ *adv* **1** at the time (past or future): *I was still unmarried* ~. **(every) now and then,** ⇨ now(3). **2** (used after a *preposition*): *from* ~ (= from that time) *onwards; until* ~; *since* ~. **3** next; after that; afterwards: *We spent a week in Rome and* ~ *we went to Naples.* **4** in that case; that being so: *A: 'It isn't here.'—B: 'T*~ *it must be in the next room.' You say you don't want to be a doctor.—T*~ *what do you want to be?* **5** and also: *T*~ *there's Mrs Green—she must be invited to the wedding.*

theo·lo·gian /ˈθɪəˈləʊdʒən/ *n* [C] advanced student of theology.

theo·logi·cal /ˈθɪəˈlɒdʒɪkəl/ *adj* of theology.

theo·logi·cally /-klɪ/ *adv*

the·ol·ogy /θɪˈɒlədʒɪ/ *n* [U] formation of a series of theories about the nature of God and of the foundations of religious belief.

the·orem /ˈθɪərəm/ *n* [C] (*pl* ~s) **1** statement which logical reasoning shows to be true. **2** (*maths*) statement for which a reasoned proof is required.

the·or·etic, -i·cal /θɪəˈretɪk, -kəl/ *adj* based on theory, not on practice or experience.

theor·eti·cally /-klɪ/ *adv*

the·ory /ˈθɪərɪ/ *n* (*pl* -ies) **1** [C,U] (explanation of the) general principles of an art or science (contrasted with practice): *Your plan is excellent in* ~, *but would it succeed*

in practice? **2** [C] reasoned account offered to explain facts or events: *Darwin's ~ of evolution.* **3** [C] something offered as an opinion, not necessarily based on reasoning: *He has a ~ that wearing hats makes men bald.*
the·or·ist /-ɪst/, person who forms theories.
the·or·ize /ˈθɪərɪz/ *vi* form theories.

thera·peutic /ˌθerəˈpjuːtɪk/ *adj* connected with the art of healing, the cure of disease.

thera·pist /ˈθerəpɪst/ *n* [C] specialist in therapy, esp psychotherapy.

ther·apy /ˈθerəpɪ/ *n* [U] curative treatment (esp of a kind shown by a preceding word): *occupational ~,* the curing of an illness by means of exercise. ⇨ **psychotherapy.**

there¹ /ðeə(r)/ *adv* of place and direction (contrasted with *here*) **1** in, at or to, that place: *We shall soon be ~. We're nearly ~,* have nearly arrived. *I've never been to Rome but I hope to go ~ next year.* **2** (used in exclamations; always stressed): *T~ goes the last bus! T~ they go!* **3** (used to call attention; always stressed): *T~'s the bell for lunch. T~'s gratitude for you!* Note how grateful/ungrateful he, she, etc is! **4** at, in connection with, that point (in an action, story, argument, etc): *Don't stop ~! T~ you are mistaken.* **5** (in phrases): **here and there,** ⇨ here(3). **there and back,** to a place and back again: *Can I go ~ and back in one day?* **over there,** (of a place farther than is shown by using *there* alone): *I live here, Mr Green lives ~,* and Mr Brown *lives over ~,* on the other side of the river.

there² /ðeə(r)/ *adv* (always unstressed) (used as an introduction in a sentence of which the *verb,* esp '*be*' precedes the subject) **1** (used with '*be*'): *T~'s a man at the door.* **2** (used with other verbs, esp *seem* and *appear*): *T~ seems (to be) no doubt about it. T~ comes a time when...*

there³ /ðeə(r)/ *int* (always stressed) **1** (used to comfort): *T~! T~! Never mind, you'll soon feel better.* **2** (used to suggest that the speaker was right, or to show triumph, dismay, etc according to the context): *T~, now! What did I tell you,* You now see that I was right! *T~! You've upset the ink!*

there·about(s) /ˈðeərəbaʊt(s)/ *adv* (usually preceded by *or*) near that place, number, quantity, degree, etc: *in 1978 or ~; £5/15 metres/3 o'clock or ~.*

there·after /ðeərˈɑːftə(r) *US:* -ˈæf-/ *adv* (*formal*) = afterwards.

there·by /ðeəˈbaɪ/ *adv* (*formal*) by that means; in that connection.

there·fore /ˈðeəfɔː(r)/ *adv* for that reason.

there·of /ðeərˈɒv/ *adv* (*formal*) from that source.

there·upon /ˌðeərəˈpɒn/ *adv* (*formal*) as the result of that.

therm /θɜːm/ *n* [C] (100 000 GB thermal units as a) unit of heat as used for measuring the consumption of gas (coal-gas or natural gas).

ther·mal /ˈθɜːml/ *adj* of heat: *~ springs,* of warm or hot water. □ *n* [C] rising current of warm air (as needed by a glider to gain height).

thermo- /ˈθɜːməʊ/ *prefix* of heat, temperature.

'thermo·dy·'nam·ics *n pl* (usually used with a *sing verb*) science of the relations between heat and mechanical work.

'thermo·'nu·clear *adj* (e g of weapons) of, using, the high temperatures released in nuclear fission: *the ~-nuclear bomb.*

'thermo·stat /ˈθɜːməstæt/ *n* [C] device for automatically regulating temperature by cutting off and restoring the supply of heat (e g in central heating).

ther·mom·eter /θəˈmɒmɪtə(r)/ *n* [C] instrument for measuring temperature.

ther·mos /ˈθɜːmɒs/ *n* (also `~ *flask*) (P) vacuum flask.

the·sau·rus /θɪˈsɔːrəs/ *n* [C] (*pl* ~es or -ri /-raɪ/) (esp) a book or collection of words, phrases grouped together according to similarities in their meanings.

these /ðiːz/ *pl* of this.

the·sis /ˈθiːsɪs/ *n* [C] (*pl* theses /-siːz/) statement or theory (to be) put forward and supported by arguments, submitted (as part of the requirements) for a university degree.

they /ðeɪ/ *personal pron* (subject form, *pl,* of *he, she, it*): *T~* (= People in general) *say that the government will have to resign. What a lot of questions ~* (= those in authority) *ask in this form!* ⇨ them.

thick /θɪk/ *adj* (-er, -est) **1** (opposite of *thin*) of relatively great or a specified measurement in diameter, from one side to the other, or from the front to the back: *a ~ line; ice three metres ~.* **2** having a large number of units close together: *~ hair; a ~ forest.* **3** (of a hedge) with bushes, etc closely planted. **4** **thick with,** full of or packed with: *The air was ~ with dust.* **5** (of liquids) semi-solid: *~ soup;* (of the air, etc) not clear; dense: *a ~ fog.* **6** (*informal*) stupid. **7** (*informal*) **as thick as thieves,** very friendly. **8** (*informal*) **a bit thick,** beyond what is reasonable or endurable: *Three weeks of heavy rain is a bit ~.* **lay it on thick,** be extravagant (with compliments, etc). □ *n* [U] **1** most crowded part; part where there is greatest activity: *We were in the ~ of it.* **through thick and thin,** under any kind of conditions, good or bad. **2** thick part of anything: *the ~ of the thumb.* □ *adv* thickly: *You spread the butter too ~.*

'thick-'headed *adj* stupid.

'thick-'set *adj* (a) (of a person) short and solid. (b) (of hedges, etc) closely planted.

'thick-'skinned *adj* (*fig*) not sensitive to criticism, insults, etc.

thick·ly *adv*

thick·ness, (a) [U] quality or degree of being thick: *four centimetres in ~ness.* (b) [C] layer: *two ~nesses of wollen cloth.*

thicken /ˈθɪkən/ vt,vi make or become thick: ∼ the gravy.

thicket /ˈθɪkɪt/ n [C] group of trees, shrubs, growing thickly together.

thief /θiːf/ n [C] (pl thieves /θiːvz/) person who steals, esp secretly and without violence.

thieve /θiːv/ vi,vt steal (the usual word).

thigh /θaɪ/ n [C] 1 part of the human leg between the knee and the hip. 2 corresponding part of the back legs of other animals.

thimble /ˈθɪmbəl/ n [C] cap (of metal, etc) used to protect the end of the finger when pushing a needle through cloth, etc.

thin /θɪn/ adj (-ner, -nest) 1 (opposite of thick) having opposite surfaces close together; of small diameter: a ∼ sheet of paper; a ∼ piece of string. 2 not full or closely packed: ∼ hair; a ∼ audience, with more seats empty than occupied. 3 (opposite of fat) having not much flesh: rather ∼ in the face. 4 (of liquids) having not much substance; watery: ∼ soup; ∼ blood, as when weakened by illness, etc; (of the air, etc) not dense: a ∼ mist. 5 not having some important ingredient; poor in quality: a ∼ excuse, not very convincing; a ∼ disguise, easily seen through. □ adv so as to be thin: You've spread the butter very ∼. □ vt,vi (-nn-) make or become thin: We had better wait until the fog ∼s, becomes less dense. At last the crowd ∼ned.

thin·ly adv in a thin manner: Sow the seed ∼ly.

'thin-'skinned adj (fig) sensitive to criticism, insults, etc.

thin·ness /ˈθɪnnəs/ n [U]

thing /θɪŋ/ n [C] 1 any material object: What are those ∼s on the table? 2 (pl) belongings; articles of which the nature is clear (or thought to be clear) from the context: Bring your swimming ∼s (= your swimming-suit, towel, etc) with you. Have you packed your ∼s (= clothes, etc) for the holiday? 3 subject: There's another ∼ (= something else) I want to ask you about. 4 **be 'seeing things,** have hallucinations. 5 situation; event; course of action: That only makes ∼s worse. I must think ∼s over, consider what has happened, what has to be done, etc. What's the next ∼ to do? What must be done next? **for 'one thing,** (used to introduce a reason): For one ∼, I haven't any money; for another… 6 (used of a person or an animal, expressing an emotion of some kind): She's a sweet little ∼/a dear old ∼. Poor ∼, he's been ill all winter. 7 (sing with the) just what will be best in the circumstances: A holiday will be the very ∼ for you. He always says the right/wrong ∼, makes the most suitable/unsuitable remark or comment. 8 (phrases) **the 'thing 'is,** the question to be considered is: The ∼ is, can we get there in time? **first thing,** before anything else; early: We must do that first ∼

in the morning. **a near thing,** a narrow escape (from an accident, missing a train, etc). **have a thing about,** (informal) be obsessed by.

think[1] /θɪŋk/ vi,vt (pt,pp thought /θɔːt/) (For special uses with adverbial particles and prepositions, ⇨ 7 below.) 1 use, exercise, the mind in order to form opinions, come to conclusions: You should ∼ (= not be hasty) before doing that. Do you ∼ in English when you speak English? **think aloud,** say one's thoughts as they occur. 2 consider; be of the opinion: Do you ∼ it will rain? Yes, I ∼ so. The child thought there was no harm in picking flowers in your garden. It will be better, don't you ∼, to start early. I thought it better to stay away. **think fit.** ⇨ fit[1] (2). 3 (negative with can/could) imagine: I can't ∼ what you mean. 4 have a vague intention: I ∼ I'll go for a swim. 5 reflect: She was ∼ing (to herself) how strange the children were. 6 expect; intend: I thought as much, That is what I expected or suspected.

7 (special uses with adverbial particles and prepositions):
think about sth, (a) examine, consider (esp a plan, idea, to see whether it is desirable, practicable, etc): She's ∼ing about emigrating to Canada. (b) reflect on: She was ∼ing about her childhood days.

think of sth, (a) consider; take into account: We have a hundred and one things to ∼ of before we can decide. (b) consider (without reaching a decision or taking action): We're ∼ing of going to Venice for Easter. (c) imagine: Just ∼ of the cost/danger! (d) have, entertain, the idea of (often with could, would, should, and not or never, with dream as a possible substitute for think): He would never ∼ of marrying a girl like you! (e) remember: I can't ∼ of his name at the moment. (f) suggest: Can you ∼ of a good place for a weekend holiday? **think highly/well/little, etc of sb/sth,** have a high/good/poor, etc opinion of: His work is highly thought of by the critics. He ∼s the world of her, loves her dearly. **think nothing of,** consider insignificant or unremarkable: Barbara ∼s nothing of walking 10 or 20 miles a day.

think sth out, consider carefully and make a plan for: It seems to be a well-thought out scheme.

think sth over, consider further (before reaching a decision, etc): Please ∼ over what I've said.

think sth up, invent, devise (a scheme, etc): There's no knowing what he'll ∼ up next.

think[2] /θɪŋk/ n (informal) occasion of, need for, thinking: He's got another ∼ coming. will need to think again.

thinker /ˈθɪŋkə(r)/ n [C] (with an adjective): person who thinks: a great ∼.

think·ing /ˈθɪŋkɪŋ/ *adj* who think: *all ~ men,* those people who think (about public affairs, etc). □ *n* [U] thought; way of reasoning: *do some hard ~,* think deeply.

third /θɜːd/ *adj, n* [C] (abbr *3rd*) (of) the next after the two or one of three equal parts: *the ~ month of the year,* i e March; *on the ~ of April; every ~ day; a ~ of the cake; two~s of a litre.*

'**third de'gree,** prolonged or hard questioning, use of torture (as used by the police in some countries to get confessions or information).

'**third 'party,** another person besides the two principals: (as an *adjective*) *~-party insurance,* of/to a person other than the person insured, which the insurance company undertakes to meet.

'**third-'rate** *adj* of poor quality.

the 'Third 'World, the developing countries not aligned with Communist or Western countries.

third·ly *adv*

thirst /θɜːst/ *n* [U, and with *a, an* as in examples] **1** feeling caused by a desire or need to drink; suffering caused by this: *They lost their way in the desert and died of ~.* **2** (*fig*) strong desire (*for*): *a ~ for knowledge.* □ *vt* **1** have thirst. **2** be eager (for); *~ for revenge.*

thirsty *adj* (-ier, -iest) having or causing thirst: *be/feel ~y.*

thir·teen /ˈθɜːˈtiːn/ *adj, n* [C] (of) 13.

thir·teenth /ˈθɜːˈtiːnθ/ *adj, n* [C] (abbr *13th*) (of) the next after twelve or one of twelve equal parts.

thirty /ˈθɜːtɪ/ *adj, n* [C] (of) 30.

thir·ti·eth /ˈθɜːtɪəθ/ *adj, n* [C] (abbr *30th*) (of) the next after twenty-nine or one of thirty equal parts.

this /ðɪs/ *adj, pron* (*pl* these /ðiːz/) (contrasted with *that, those*) **1** the person or thing nearby, touched, etc or drawn attention to, named or understood to be known: *Look at ~ box/these boxes. What's ~? What are these? T~ (one) is larger than that. These are better than those. He will be here ~ day week,* in a week's time. *T~ boy of yours seems very intelligent.* **2** (in narrative) a certain: *Then ~ funny little man came up to me.* □ *adv* (*informal*) so: *It's about ~ high. Now that we have come ~ far (= as far as this) ..*

thistle /ˈθɪsəl/ *n* [C] (sorts of) wild plant with prickly leaves and yellow, white or purple flowers.

tho' /ðəʊ/ *adv, conj* = though.

thong /θɒŋ/ *n* [C] narrow strip of leather, e g as a fastening, the lash of a whip.

tho·rax /ˈθɔːræks/ *n* [C] **1** part of an animal's body between the neck and the belly, e g in a man, the chest. **2** middle of the three main sections of an insect (with the legs and wings).

thorn /θɔːn/ *n* **1** [C] pointed growth on the stem of a plant. *a thorn in one's flesh/*

side, (*fig*) constant source of irritation **2** [C,U] kinds of shrub or tree with thorns.

thorny *adj* (-ier, -iest) (**a**) having thorns (**b**) (*fig*) full of trouble and difficulty; *a ~y problem.*

thor·ough /ˈθʌrə US: ˈθɜːrəʊ/ *adj* complete in every way; not forgetting or overlooking anything; detailed: *a ~ worker; be ~ in one's work.*

'**thorough-going** *adj* complete. *a ~-going revision.*

thor·ough·ly *adv*

thor·ough·ness *n* [U]

thor·ough·bred /ˈθʌrəbred US: ˈθɜːrə-/ *n* [C], *adj* (animal, esp a horse) of pure breed.

thor·ough·fare /ˈθʌrəfeə(r) US: ˈθɜːrə-/ *n* [C] road or street, esp one much used by the traffic and open at both ends: *Broadway is New York's most famous ~.*

those /ðəʊz/ *pl* of that.

though /ðəʊ/ *conj* **1** (also **al·though** /ɔːlˈðəʊ/) in spite of the fact that: *T~ they are poor, they are always neatly dressed. He passed the examination al~ he had been prevented by illness from studying.* **2** (introducing an independent statement) and yet; all the same: *I'll try to come, ~ I don't think I shall manage it.* **as though,** ⇨ as ²(11). □ *adv* however: *He said he would come; he didn't, ~.*

thought ¹ /θɔːt/ *pt,pp* of think ¹.

thought ² /θɔːt/ *n* **1** [U] (power, process of) thinking: *He was lost/deep in ~,* thinking so deeply as to be unaware of his surroundings, etc. **2** [U] way of thinking characteristic of a particular period, class, nation, etc: *Scientific/Greek ~.* **3** [U] care, consideration: *He often acts without ~.* **4** [C,U] idea, opinion, intention, etc formed by thinking: *That boy hasn't a ~ in his head. He keeps his ~s to himself,* does not tell anyone what he thinks. *She says she can read my ~s. He had no ~ (= intention) of hurting your feelings.* **on second thoughts,** after further consideration. **give sb/sth a thought,** think about before deciding, be sympathetic, etc according to context. **spare a thought for,** ⇨ spare(2).

thought·ful /-fəl/ *adj* (**a**) full of, showing, thought: *~ful looks.* (**b**) considerate; thinking of the needs of others: *It was ~ful of you to warn me of your arrival.*

thought·fully /-fəlɪ/ *adv*

thought·less *adj* (**a**) careless; unthinking: *Young people are often ~less for the future* (**b**) selfish; inconsiderate (*of* others): *a ~less action.*

thought·less·ly *adv*

thou·sand /ˈθaʊzənd/ *adj, n* [C] **1** (of) 1 000. **2** great number: *A ~ thanks for your kindness. He made a ~ and one excuses.* **a thousand to one (chance),** a remote possibility. **one in a thousand,** a rare exception.

thousand·fold /-fəʊld/ *adj, adv* a thousand times (as much or many).

thou·sandth /ˈθaʊzənθ/ *adj, n* [C] (abbr *1000th*) (of) the next after 999 or one of 1000 parts.

thrash /θræʃ/ *vt,vi* **1** beat with a stick, whip, etc: *He threatened to ~ the life out of me*, beat me thoroughly **2** (*informal*) defeat (a team, etc) in a contest. **3 thrash sth out,** (a) clear up (a problem, etc) by discussion. (b) arrive at (the truth, a solution, etc) by discussion. **4** (cause to) toss, move violently: *The swimmer ~ed about in the water.*

thrash·ing, (a) beating; *give/get a good ~ing.* (b) defeat, e g in games.

thread /θred/ *n* **1** [C,U] (length of) spun cotton, silk, flax, wool, etc esp for use in sewing and weaving: *a needle and ~.* **2** something like a thread: *A ~ of light came through the keyhole.* **3** [C] chain or line (connecting parts of a story, etc): *lose the ~ of one's argument.* **4** spiral ridge round a screw or bolt. □ *vt* **1** pass a thread through the eye of (a needle); put (beads, pearls, etc) on a thread. **2 thread one's way through,** make one's way (through a crowd, etc). **3** (of hair) streak: *black hair ~ed with silver,* with streaks of silver hair in it.

`thread·bare` /-beə(r)/ *adj* (of cloth) worn.

threat /θret/ *n* [C] **1** statement of an intention to punish or hurt a person, esp if he does not do as one wishes: *carry out a ~; be under the ~ of expulsion,* e g from a university. **2** sign or warning of coming trouble, danger, etc: *There was a ~ of rain in the dark sky.*

threaten /ˈθretn/ *vt,vi* **1** use threats: *~ an employee with dismissal.* **2** give warning of: *The clouds ~ed rain.* **3** seem likely to occur or come: *Knowing that danger ~ed, I kept an extra careful watch.*

threat·en·ing *adj: a ~ sky.*

threat·en·ing·ly *adv*

three /θri/ *adj, n* [C] (of) 3.

`three-ˈcornered` *adj* triangular: *a ~-cornered contest/fight,* with three contestants or competitors, e g in a Parliamentary election.

`three-ˈD,` (abbr for) three-dimensional.

`three-diˈmensional` *adj* having, or appearing to have, three dimensions (length, breadth and depth).

`three-ˈfigure` *adj* (of numbers, amounts) between 100 and 999 (inclusive).

`three-ˈpiece` *n* [C], *adj* set of three garments (e g a suit); set of furniture (usually a sofa and two armchairs).

`three-ˈply` *adj* (of wool, thread) having three strands.

`three-ˈscore,` sixty.

`three·some` /-səm/ *n* [C] (game played by) three persons.

thresh /θreʃ/ *vt,vi* beat (the grain out of) wheat, etc: *~ corn by hand.*

`thresh·ing-machine,` one for threshing grain.

thresher, person who, machine that, threshes.

thresh·old /ˈθreʃhəʊld/ *n* [C] **1** stone or plank under a doorway in a dwellinghouse, church, etc: *cross the ~.* **2** (*fig*) start, beginning: *He was on the ~ of his career.*

threw /θru/ *pt* of throw¹.

thrice /θraɪs/ *adv* (*rare*) three times.

thrift /θrɪft/ *n* [U] care, economy, in the use of money or goods.

thrifty *adj* (-ier, -iest) economical (the usual word).

thrill /θrɪl/ *n* [C] (experience causing an) excited feeling passing like a wave along the nerves: *a ~ of joy/pleasure/horror.* **the thrill of a lifetime,** excitement that has never been experienced before. □ *vt,vi* cause a thrill in: *The film ~ed the audience. We were ~ed with horror/joy.* **2** feel a thrill: *We ~ed at the good news.*

thril·ler, novel, play or film in which excitement and emotional appeal are the essential elements.

thrive /θraɪv/ *vi* (*pt* throve /θrəʊv/ *pp* thriven /ˈθrɪvən/) prosper; succeed; grow strong and healthy: *Children ~ on good food. He has a thriving business.*

thro', thro /θru/ = through.

throat /θrəʊt/ *n* [C] **1** front part of the neck: *I gripped him by the ~.* **2** passage in the neck through which food passes to the stomach and air to the lungs: *A bone has stuck in my ~.* **force/thrust sth down sb's throat,** try to make him accept one's views, beliefs, etc. **stick in one's throat,** (*fig*) not be readily acceptable.

throb /θrob/ *vi* (-bb-) (of the heart, pulse, etc) beat, esp beat more quickly than usual: *His head ~bed, He had a bad headache.* □ *n* [C] throbbing or vibration: *~s of joy.* ⇨ heart-throb.

throb·bing *adj* that throbs: *a ~bing pain/ sound.*

throne /θrəʊn/ *n* [C] **1** ceremonial chair or seat of a king, queen, bishop, etc. **2 the ~,** royal authority: *come to the ~,* become king/queen.

throng /θrɒŋ *US*: θrɔŋ/ *n* [C] crowd. □ *vt,vi* make, be, a crowd: *People ~ed to see the new play.*

throttle /ˈθrɒtl/ *vt,vi* **1** seize (a person) by the throat and stop his breathing; strangle: *~ the guard and then rob the bank.* **2** control the flow of steam, etc in an engine; lessen the speed of (an engine) by doing this. □ *n* [C] valve controlling the flow of steam, etc in an engine.

through¹ (*US* also **thru**) /θru/ *adv* (For special combinations with *verbs,* e g *get ~,* ⇨ the *verb* entries.) **1** from end to end, beginning to end, side to side: *They wouldn't let us ~,* e g pass the gate. *Did your brother get ~,* e g pass the examination? *He slept the whole night ~,* all night. **all through,** all the time (something was happening, etc): *I knew that all ~.* **2** to the very end. **be through (with), (a)** finish (with): *When will you be ~ with your work?* **(b)** (*informal*) have had enough of; be tired of: *I'm ~ with this job; I must find something more interesting.* **(c)** (*informal*) no longer be in love: *I'm ~ with her.* **see sth through,** continue (to help) with a series of events, etc until the end. **'through and `through,** in all parts; completely: *He's a reliable man ~ and ~.* **3** all the way to: *This train goes ~ to Paris.* **4** (as an *adjective*) (used in the sense of 3): *a ~ train to Paris; ~ traffic,* road traffic which is going through a place (contrasted with local traffic). **5** (telephoning) **(a)** (*GB*) connected: *I will put you ~ to the manager,* connect you. **(b)** (*US*) finished; not wishing to continue the call.

'through-put /-pʊt/, amount of material put through a process.

through² (*US* also **thru**) /θruː/ *prep* (for combinations with *verbs*, e g *go through,*⇨ the *verb* entries.) **1** (of places) from end to end or side to side of; entering at one side, on one surface, etc and coming out at the other: *The River Thames flows ~ London. There is a path ~* (= across) *the fields. He was looking ~ a telescope.* **2** (*fig*): *He went ~/has come ~* (= experienced) *many hardships. We must go ~* (= examine) *the accounts.* **3** (of time) from beginning to end of: *He won't live ~ the night,* He will die before morning. **4** (showing the agency, means or cause) because of: *The accident happened ~ no fault of yours.* **5** without stopping for: *Don't drive ~ a red light.* **6** (*US*) up to and including: *Monday ~ Friday.*

through-out /θruːˈaʊt/ *adv* right through; in every part; in all ways or respects: *The house needs painting ~.* □ *prep* all or right through; from end to end of: *~ the country; ~ the war.*

throve /θrəʊv/ *pt* of thrive.

throw¹ /θrəʊ/ *vt,vi* (*pt* threw /θruː/, *pp* thrown /θrəʊn/.) (For special uses with *adverbial particles* and *prepositions,* ⇨ **11** below) **1** cause (something) to go through the air, usually with force, by a movement of the arm or by mechanical means: *Don't ~ stones at my dog! He threw the ball to his sister.* **2** put (articles of clothing) (*on, off, over,* etc) quickly or carelessly: *~ a coat over one's shoulders.* **3** move (one's arms, legs, etc) (*out, up, down, about*) energetically: *~ one's chest out; ~ one's head back.* **4** **(a)** (of a horse) cause the rider to fall to the ground: *Two of the jockeys were ~n in the second race.* **(b)** (of a wrestler) force (an opponent) to the floor. **5** (of dice) drop on to the table (after shaking them in something); get by doing this: *~ three sixes.* **6** (*fig*) cause to be noticed as if by throwing: *He threw me an angry look.* **7** shape (pottery) on

a potter's wheel. **8** (*informal*) **throw a party,** give a (dinner, cocktail, etc) party. **throw a fit,** ⇨ fit²(2). **9** **throw sth open (to),** make (e g a competition) open to all persons. **10** (used with *nouns*) ⇨ cold¹(1), doubt(1), light³(5), dust¹(1), gauntlet, weight(2).

11 (special uses with *adverbial particles* and *prepositions*):
throw sth about, scatter: *Don't ~ waste paper about in the park.* **throw money about,** (*fig*) spend it carelessly.
throw sth away, (a) lose by foolishness or neglect: *~ away an opportunity.* **(b)** (of words spoken by actors, broadcasters, etc) say in a casual way, with conscious underemphasis.
throw back, show characteristics of, revert to, a remote ancestor. Hence, **'throw-back** *n* [C].
throw oneself down, lie down at full length.
throw sth in, (a) give something extra, without an addition to the price: *You can have the guitar for £20, with the case ~n in.* **(b)** put in (a remark, etc) casually. **(c)** (football) throw the ball in after it has gone out of play. Hence, **'throw-in** *n* [C]. **throw in the towel,** (*informal*) admit defeat.
throw oneself into sth, begin to work hard at.
throw sb/sth off, manage to get rid of; become free from: *~ off a cold/a pursuer.*
throw oneself on sb/sth, put one's trust in: *~ oneself on the mercy of the court.*
throw sth out, (a) say (esp casually): *~ out a hint/suggestion.* **(b)** reject (a Bill in Parliament, etc).
throw sb over, desert, abandon: *~ over one's girlfriend.*
throw sth together, assemble (too) quickly: *That dress seems to have been ~n together.*
throw sth up, (a) vomit (food). **(b)** resign from: *~ up one's job.* **throw up one's hands (in horror),** express horror by doing this.
throw oneself upon sb/sth, = throw on.

throw² /θrəʊ/ *n* [C] throwing; distance to which something is or may be thrown: *a well-aimed ~,* e g cricket, to get a batsman out. **within a `stone's throw (of),** near (to).

thru /θruː/ (*US*) = through.

thrush /θrʌʃ/ *n* [C] sorts of songbird, esp the `song-~.

thrust /θrʌst/ *vt,vi* (*pt,pp ~*) push suddenly or violently; make a forward stroke with a sword, etc: *He ~ his hands into his pockets/a coin into my hand.* □ *n* **1** [C] act of thrusting; (in war) strong attempt to push forward into the enemy's positions; (in debate, etc) attack in words. **2** [U] stress or pressure on a neighbouring part of a structure (e g an arch); force directed forward in a jet-engine.

thud /θʌd/ n [C] dull sound as of a blow on something soft: *He fell with a ~ to the carpet.* □ *vi* (-dd-) strike, fall, with a thud.

thug /θʌg/ n [C] violent and dangerous person.

thumb /θʌm/ n [C] short, thick finger set apart from the other four. **under sb's thumb**, under his influence and control. **rule of thumb**, method or procedure based on experience and practice. □ *vt* 1 turn over (pages, etc); make dirty by doing this: *~ the pages of a dictionary; a well-~ed book.* 2 **thumb a lift,** = hitch-hike.

`**thumb-tack,** (*US*) = drawing-pin.

thump /θʌmp/ *vt,vi* 1 strike heavily; hit with the fists: *He ~ed (on) the door. The two boys began to ~ one another. He was ~ing out a tune on the piano,* playing noisily. 2 beat(7) heavily: *His heart ~ed with excitement.* □ *n* [C] (noise of, or as of, a) heavy blow (esp one given with the fist): *Give him a friendly ~ on the back.*

thun·der /θʌndə(r)/ n [U] 1 noise which usually follows a flash of lightning: *a loud crash/a long roll of ~.* 2 (also *pl*) loud noise like thunder: *the ~ of the guns.* **steal sb's thunder,** spoil his attempt to be impressive by anticipating him. □ *vi,vt* 1 (impersonal): *It was ~ing and lightening.* 2 make a noise like thunder: *Someone was ~ing at the door,* beating at it. 3 speak in a loud voice. attack violently in words.

`**thunder·bolt,** (a) flash of lightning with a crash of thunder. (b) (*fig*) unexpected and terrible event.

`**thunder·clap,** sudden noise of thunder.

`**thunder·storm,** storm of thunder and lightning, usually with heavy rain.

`**thunder·struck** *adj* (*fig*) amazed.

thun·der·ous /-əs/ *adj* making a noise like thunder: *~ous applause.*

Thurs·day /θɜzdɪ/ n fifth day of the week.

thus /ðʌs/ *adv* in this way; so: *~ far,* to this point.

thwack /θwæk/ *vt, n* = whack.

thwart /θwɔt/ *vt* obstruct, frustrate: *be ~ed in one's ambitions/aims.*

thyme /taɪm/ n [U] kind of herb.

thy·roid /θaɪrɔɪd/ n [C] (also `~ gland**) gland in the front part of the neck, producing a substance which affects the body's growth and activity.

ti·ara /tɪˈɑrə/ n [C] (*pl* ~s) 1 coronet for a woman. 2 triple crown worn by the Pope.

tibia /tɪbɪə/ n [C] (*pl* ~e /-bɪɪ/) (*anat*) inner and thicker of the two bones between the knee and the foot.

tic /tɪk/ n [C] involuntary twitching of the muscles (esp of the face).

tick[1] /tɪk/ n [C] 1 light, regularly repeated sound, esp of a clock or watch. 2 (*informal*) moment: *I'll be with you in a couple of ~s.* 3 small mark (often √) to show that something is correct. □ *vi,vt* 1 (of a clock, etc)

make ticks(1): *The child put the watch to its ear and listened to it ~ing.* **What makes him/it tick,** (*informal*) What makes him/it act, behave, etc like that? 2 (of a clock): *~ away the hours.* 3 **tick over, (a)** (of an internal-combustion engine) be operating with gears disconnected. **(b)** (*fig*) be active but slow: *Business is ~ing over.* 4 put a tick(3) against: *~ off a name/the items on a list.* **tick sb off,** (*informal*) tell him off: *give her a good* `*~ing-*`*off.*

tick[2] /tɪk/ n [C] small parasite that fastens itself on the skin and sucks blood.

ticker /tɪkə(r)/ n [C] 1 telegraphic machine which automatically prints news on paper tape (called `**ticker-tape**). 2 (*sl*) heart.

ticket /tɪkɪt/ n [C] 1 written or printed piece of card or paper giving the holder the right to travel in a train, bus, ship, etc or to a seat in a cinema, concert hall, etc: *Do you want a single or a return ~?* 2 piece of card or paper, label, attached to something and giving information, e g about the price, size of clothing, etc. 3 printed notice of an offence against traffic regulations (e g a parking offence): *get a (`parking) ~.* 4 **(just) the ticket,** (*informal*) the proper thing to do. □ *vt* put a ticket(2) on; mark with a ticket.

`**ticket-collecter,** person who collects (railway) tickets.

tickle /tɪkəl/ *vt,vi* 1 excite the nerves of the skin by touching lightly, esp at sensitive parts, often so as to cause laughter: *~ him in the ribs.* 2 please (one's sense of humour, etc): *I was ~d to death/~d pink,* (= very amused and delighted) *at the news.* 3 have, feel, cause, an itching or tingling sensation: *My nose ~s.*

tick·ler /tɪklə(r)/, (esp) puzzling question.

tick·lish /tɪklɪʃ/ *adj* **(a)** (of a person) easily made to laugh when tickled. **(b)** (of a problem, piece of work, etc) needing delicate care or attention: *be in a ticklish situation.*

ti·dal /taɪdəl/ *adj* of a tide or tides: *a ~ river,* in which the tide rises and falls.

`**tidal wave,** great ocean wave, e g one that is (thought to be) caused by an earthquake.

tid·dler /tɪdlə(r)/ n [C] (*informal*) 1 very small fish. 2 small young child.

tide /taɪd/ n 1 [C,U] regular rise and fall in the level of the sea, caused by the attraction of the moon: *at high/low ~.* 2 [C] flow or tendency (of public opinion, feeling, etc): *The Socialists hoped for a turn of the ~,* that public opinion might turn in their favour. □ *vt* **tide sb over (sth),** help him to get through or survive (a period of difficulty, etc): *Will £5 ~ you over until you're paid?*

`**tide-mark,** highest point reached by a tide on a beach.

tid·ings /taɪdɪŋz/ n pl (*literary*) (used with a *sing* or *pl verb*) news: *glad ~.*

tidy /taɪdɪ/ *adj* (-ier, -iest) 1 arranged neatly and in order; having the habit of placing and keeping everything in its right place:

a ∼ *room/boy*. **2** (*informal*) fairly large (esp of money): *a* ∼ *sum of money*. □ *n* [C] (*pl* -ies) receptacle for odds and ends: *a* `sink- ∼, for bits of kitchen waste. □ *vt,vi* make tidy: *You'd better* ∼ (*up*) *the room before the guests arrive.*

ti·di·ly /ˈtaɪdɪlɪ/ *adv*

ti·di·ness *n* [U]

tie[1] /taɪ/ *n* [C] **1** something used for fastening. **2** (*fig*) something that holds people together: *the* ∼*s of friendship; family* ∼*s*. **3** something that takes up one's attention and limits one's freedom of action: *Mothers often find their small children a* ∼. **4** equal score in a game, etc: *The game ended in a* ∼, *2—2*. **5** band of material worn round the neck of a shirt and knotted in front.

tie[2] /taɪ/ *vt,vi* (*present participle* tying, *pt,pp* tied) **1** fasten or bind (with string, rope, wire, etc): ∼ *a man's feet together;* ∼ *up a parcel.* **2** fasten by means of the strings, etc of: ∼ *on a label.* **3** arrange (a ribbon, etc) in the form of a bow or knot: ∼ *one's shoelaces.* ∼ *a ribbon/scarf;* ∼ *the ribbon in(to) a bow.* **4** make by tying: ∼ *a knot in a piece of string.* **5** be fastened: *Does this sash* ∼ *in front or at the back?* **6** (of players, teams, candidates in a competitive examination) make the same score (as): *The two teams* ∼*d. They* ∼*d for first place* (*in the examination*).

7 (used with *adverbial particles* and *prepositions*):

tie sb down, restrict his freedom: *He's not in a hurry to get married; he doesn't want to get* ∼*d down.* **tie sb down to sth,** restrict him to (the terms of a contract, etc).

tie (sth) in with sth, link, agree, with: *Doesn't this* ∼ *in with what we were told last week?*

tie sth up, (**a**) invest (capital) so that it is not easily available. (**b**) ensure that (property, e g land, buildings) can be used, sold, etc only under certain conditions. **be/get tied up (with sth/sb),** (**a**) be, get, involved (with it/him) so that one has no time for other things: *I'm afraid I can't help you now—I'm too* ∼*d up with other things.* (**b**) be, become, linked with: *Isn't this company* ∼*d up with Vickers-Armstrong?* Hence, `tie-up *n* [C] link; merger; partnership.

tier /tɪə(r)/ *n* [C] row (esp of seats) parallel to and rising one above another, e g in a theatre or stadium.

tiff /tɪf/ *n* [C] slight quarrel.

ti·ger /ˈtaɪgə(r)/ *n* [C] large, fierce animal of the cat family, yellow-skinned with black stripes, found in Asia (and also called the jaguar and puma).

ti·ger·ish /-ɪʃ/ *adj* like, cruel as, a tiger.

ti·gress /ˈtaɪgrəs/ *n* [C] female tiger.

tight /taɪt/ *adj* (-er, -est) **1** fastened, fixed, fitting, held, closely: *a* ∼ *knot. The drawer is so* ∼ *that I can't open it.* **2** (esp in compounds) made so that something cannot get

out or in: `water-/`air-`∼ **3** packed so as to occupy the smallest possible space or to get in as much as possible: *Make sure that the bags are filled/packed* ∼. **4** (*informal*) having had too much alcoholic drink: *He gets* ∼ *every pay-day.* **5** fully stretched: *a* ∼ *rope.* **6** produced by pressure; causing difficulty.

in a tight corner/spot, (*fig*) in a difficult or dangerous situation. **a tight schedule,** one that it is difficult to keep to. **a tight squeeze,** condition of being uncomfortably crowded: *We got everyone into the bus, but it was a* ∼ *squeeze.* **7** (of money) not easily obtainable, e g on loan from banks: *Money is* ∼. □ *adv* = tightly: *squeeze/hold it* ∼ **sit tight,** ⇨ sit(1).

`tight-`fisted, miserly.

`tight-`laced *adj* = strait-laced.

`tight-`lipped *adj* (*fig*) saying little or nothing.

`tight-rope, one on which acrobats perform.

tight·ly *adv*

tight·ness *n* [U]

tighten /ˈtaɪtən/ *vt,vi* make or become tight(er): ∼ (*up*) *the screws;* ∼ *the ropes of the tent.*

tights /taɪts/ *n pl* **1** close-fitting (usually nylon) garment covering the hips, legs and feet, as worn by girls and women. **2** skintight garment covering the legs and body, worn by acrobats, ballet-dancers, etc.

tilde /tɪld/ *n* [C] the mark (∼) as used in this dictionary to replace the headword in the example sentences.

tile /taɪl/ *n* [C] (usually square or oblong) plate of baked clay for covering roofs, walls, etc, often painted with designs or pictures.

be (out) on the tiles, (*sl*) out drinking, etc. □ *vt* cover (a roof, etc) with tiles.

till[1] /tɪl/ (also **until** /ʌnˈtɪl/) (*Note:* the choice between *till* and *until* is chiefly a matter of personal preference, though *until* is often considered more formal.) *conj* up to the time when: *Go straight on* ∼ *you come to the post-office and then turn left. She won't go away* ∼ *you promise to help her.* □ *prep* up to the time when; up to; down to: *I shall wait* ∼ *ten o'clock. He works from morning till night, day after day.*

till[2] /tɪl/ *n* [C] money-drawer in a cash-register.

till[3] /tɪl/ *vt* cultivate (land).

till·age /ˈtɪlɪdʒ/ *n* [U] act or process of tilling; tilled land.

tiller /ˈtɪlə(r)/ *n* [C] lever (like a long handle) used to turn the rudder of a small boat.

tilt /tɪlt/ *vt,vi* (cause to) come into a sloping position (as by lifting one end); tip: *Don't* ∼ *the table.* □ *n* [C] tilting; sloping position.

tim·ber /ˈtɪmbə(r)/ *n* **1** [U] wood prepared for use in building, etc: *a* `∼-yard, place where timber is stored, bought and sold, etc. **2** [U] growing trees thought of as containing wood suitable for building, carpentry, etc:

time / tin

The fire destroyed thousands of acres of ~
3 [C] large piece of shaped wood, beam, forming a support (e g in a roof or a ship).

tim·bered *adj* (of buildings) made of timber.

time[1] /taɪm/ *n* **1** [U] all the days of the past, present and future: *past, present and future* ~. *The world exists in space and* ~. **2** [U] the passing of all the days, months and years, taken as a whole: *T*~ *will show who is right.* **3** [U] (also with *a, an* and an *adjective*) portion or measure of time: *Six o'clock is a point of* ~; *six hours is a period of* ~. *What a (long)* ~ *you have been! Take your* ~ *over it, Don't hurry.* **all the time, (a)** during the whole period in question: *I looked all over the house for that letter, and it was in my pocket all the* ~, *while I was searching.* **(b)** at all times; first and last: *He's a business man all the* ~, *has no other interests in life.* **half the time, (a)** as in: *He did the work in four hours; I could have done it in half the* ~, *in two hours.* **(b)** very often; nearly always: *He says he works hard, but he's asleep half the* ~. **behind time,** late: *The train is ten minutes behind* ~. **for the time being,** ⇨ be[3](4). **on time,** not late, punctual(ly): *The train is/came in on* ~. **in no time,** very soon; very quickly. **play for time,** delay doing something in the hope that the situation will improve. **4** [U] point of time stated in hours and minutes of the day: *What* ~ *is it? What's the* ~? **5** [U] time measured in units (years, months, hours, etc): *The winner's* ~ *was 11 seconds.* **pass the time of day (with...),** exchange a greeting, say 'Good morning!', etc. **6** [C,U] point or period of time associated with, or available or suitable for, a certain event, purpose, etc: *by the* ~ *we arrived home; every* ~ *I looked at her. It's* `*lunch-*~. *It's* ~ *I was going/*~ *for me to go, I ought to leave now.* **at the same time, (a)** together: *to laugh and cry at the same* ~. **(b)** notwithstanding; nevertheless. **from time to time; at times,** occasionally; now and then. **at all times,** always. **in time, (a)** not late; early enough: *We were in* ~ *to catch the train.* **(b)** sooner or later: *You will learn how to do it in* ~. **do time,** (*informal*) go to prison for a period. **7** [C] occasion: *this/that/next/another* ~; *the* ~ *before last; for the first/last* ~. **time and again; times without number,** again and again; repeatedly. **8** (*pl*) (used to show multiplication): *Three* ~s *five is/are fifteen,* $3 \times 5 = 15$. **9** [C] (often *pl*) period of time, more or less definite, associated with certain events, circumstances, persons, etc: *in ancient/prehistoric* ~s. **10** [C] (often *pl*) the conditions of life, the circumstances, etc of a period characterized by certain qualities, etc: *We lived through terrible* ~s *during the war years. T*~s *are good/bad,* (often meaning that it is easy/difficult to make a living). **behind the**

times, old-fashioned. **have a good time,** enjoy oneself. **have the time of one's life,** (*informal*) experience a period of exceptional happiness or enjoyment. **11** [U] **Greenwich / local / summer / standard time,** ⇨ these entries. **12** (*music*) measurement depending on the number of rhythmic beats in successive bars of a piece of music. **beat time,** show the rhythm by movements made with the hand or a stick (*baton*).

`**time-bomb,** designed to explode at some time after being dropped, placed in position.

`**time-card/-sheet,** one for a record of workmen's hours of work.

`**time-honoured** (*US* = **-honored**) *adj* respected because of its age.

`**time-keeper, (a)** one who, or that which, records the time spent by workers at their work. **(b)** (of a watch, etc) one that keeps time well, etc; *a good/bad* ~*keeper.*

`**time-lag,** interval of time between two connected events (e g between a flash of lightning and the thunder).

`**time-limit,** limited period of time; last moment of this: *set a* ~*-limit for the completion of a job.*

`**time-piece,** (*dated*) clock.

`**time-saving** *adj* serving to save time: *a* ~*-saving idea.*

`**time-signal,** signal (e g a series of pips) for telling the time (in a radio programme).

`**time-switch,** switch set to operate at a desired time (e g to turn a heating system on or off).

`**time-table,** list showing the days or hours at which events will take place, work will be done, etc esp a list showing the times at which trains, buses, etc will arrive and depart.

time[2] /taɪm/ *vt* **1** choose the time or moment for; arrange the time of: *He* ~*d his journey so that he arrived before dark.* **2** measure the time taken by or for (a race, runner, an action or event). **3** regulate: ~ *the speed of a machine.*

tim·ing *n* [U] act of determining or regulating the (order of) occurrence of an action, event, etc to achieve the desired results: *The timing of last night's performance was excellent.*

time·ly /taɪmlɪ/ *adj* (-ier, -iest) occurring at just the right time.

timid /tɪmɪd/ *adj* easily frightened: *He's as* ~ *as a rabbit.*

tim·id·ity /tɪˈmɪdətɪ/ *n* [U]

timid·ly *adv*

tim·or·ous /tɪmərəs/ *adj* timid.

tim·or·ous·ly *adv*

tim·pani /tɪmpənɪ/ *n pl* set of kettledrums (e g of an orchestra).

tim·pan·ist /tɪmpənɪst/, player of a kettledrum.

tin /tɪn/ *n* **1** [U] soft, white metal (symbol **Sn**) used in alloys and for coating iron sheets. **2** [C] (*US* = **can**) tin-plated airtight

694

container for food: *a* ~ *of sardines/beans*. □ *vt* (-nn-) **1** put a coating of tin on. **2** (= *can*) pack (food, tobacco, etc) in tins(2): ~*ned peaches.*

`tin-foil,` tin in thin, flexible sheets, used for wrapping and packing cigarettes, confectionery, etc.

`tin-opener,` device for opening tins.

tinny *adj* (-ier, -iest) of or like tin (e g in sound): *a* ~ *piano.*

tine /taɪn/ *n* [C] **1** point, prong (e g of a fork, etc). **2** branch of a deer's antler.

tinge /tɪndʒ/ *vt* **1** colour slightly (with red etc). **2** (*fig*) (esp in *pp*) affect slightly: *admiration* ~*d with envy.* □ *n* [C] slight colouring or mixture (*of*): *There was a* ~ *of sadness in her voice.*

tingle /ˈtɪŋgəl/ *vi* have a pricking or stinging feeling in the skin: *His fingers* ~*d with the cold. The children were tingling with excitement.* □ *n* [C] tingling feeling.

tin·ker /ˈtɪŋkə(r)/ *n* [C] **1** worker who repairs kettles, pans, etc. **2** attempt to repair; work: *have an hour's* ~ *at the radio,* try to mend it. □ *vi* work in an inexpert way (at): *Please don't* ~ *with my car engine.*

tinkle /ˈtɪŋkəl/ *vi,vt* (cause to) make a succession of light, ringing sounds, e g of a small bell. □ *n* (*sing*) such sounds: *the* ~ *of a bell.*

tin·sel /ˈtɪnsəl/ *n* [U] **1** glittering metallic substance made in sheets, strips and threads, used for ornament: *trim a Christmas tree with* ~. **2** cheap, showy brilliance. □ *vt* (-ll-, US also -l-) trim with tinsel.

tint /tɪnt/ *n* [C] (esp pale or delicate) shade or variety of colour: ~*s of green in the sky at dawn.* □ *vt* give a tint to; put a tint on.

tiny /ˈtaɪni/ *adj* (-ier, -iest) very small.

-tion /-ʃən/ (also **-sion** /-ʃən/, **-ation** /-eɪʃən/, **-ition** /-ɪʃən/) *suffix* (*verb* + ~ = *noun*): *relation; confession; hesitation; competition.*

-tional /-nəl/ *adj*

-tion·ally /-nəli/ *adv*

tip /tɪp/ *n* [C] **1** pointed or thin end of something: *the* ~*s of one's fingers/the* `finger-` ~*s.* **(have sth) on the tip of one's tongue,** (be) just going to say (it), just about to remember (it). **2** small piece put at the end of something: *cigarettes with filter-* ~*s.* □ *vt* (-pp-) supply with a tip(2): ~*ped cigarettes.*

`tip-toe` *adv* **on tiptoe,** on the tips of one's toes: *be on* ~*toe with excitement.* □ *vi* walk on tiptoe: *She* ~*toed out of the bedroom.*

`tip-top` *adj, adv* (*informal*) (colloq) first-rate: *in* ~*-top condition.*

tip /tɪp/ *vt,vi* (-pp-) **1** **tip (sth) up,** (cause to) rise, lean or tilt on one side or at one end: *The table* ~*ped up.* **tip sth (over),** (cause to) overbalance or overturn: *Careful! You'll* ~ *the canoe over.* **tip the scale (at),** (a) be just enough to cause one scale or pan (of a balance) to go lower than the other. **(b)** (*fig*)

be the deciding factor (for or against). **(c)** weigh: *He* ~*ped the scale at 70 kilos.* **2** empty (the contents of something) out of/ into: *No rubbish to be* ~*ped here,* a warning put up in open spaces. *She* ~*ped the water out of the bowl into the sink.* □ *n* [C] **1** (not US) place where rubbish may be tipped(2): *a* `refuse` ~. **2** hill of waste material from a coalmine, etc. **3** (*informal*) untidy place: *This room is a* ~*!*

tip /tɪp/ *vt* (-pp-) **1** touch or strike lightly: *His bat just* ~*ped the ball.* **2** give a tip to (1,2 below): ~ *the waiter.* **tip sb off,** (*informal*) give him a warning, information or a hint. Hence, `tip-off` *n* [C] hint or warning: *give the police a* ~*-off.* **tip the winner,** name the winner (of a horse-race) before the event takes place. □ *n* [C] **1** gift of money to a porter, waiter, etc for services: *leave a* ~ *on the table,* e g at a restaurant. **2** piece of advice on something, esp information about the probable winner of a horse-race, about a person wanted by the police, etc: *If you take my* ~ (= advice) *you'll say your sorry.* **3** tap(1).

tipple /ˈtɪpəl/ *n* [U] (usually alcoholic) drink: *My favourite* ~ *is sherry.*

tip·ster /ˈtɪpstə(r)/ *n* [C] person who gives tips about races. ⇨ tip(2).

tipsy /ˈtɪpsi/ *adj* (*informal*) slightly drunk.

ti·rade /taɪˈreɪd/ *n* [C] long, angry or scolding speech.

tire /ˈtaɪə(r)/ *n* [C] (*US*) = tyre.

tire /ˈtaɪə(r)/ *vt,vi* make or become weary, in need of rest, etc: *The long walk* ~*d the child/* ~*d him out/made him* ~*d.* **be tired of,** have had enough of: *be* ~*d of boiled eggs,* have had them too often.

tired /ˈtaɪəd/ *adj* weary in body or mind: *feel* ~*d after a long climb.* **tired out,** completely exhausted.

`tired·ness` *n* [U]

tire·less *adj* **(a)** not easily tired: *a* ~*less worker.* **(b)** continuing a long time: ~*less energy.*

`tire·some` /-səm/ *adj* troublesome; tedious.

tis·sue /ˈtɪʃu/ *n* [C,U] mass of cells and cell-products in an animal body: `muscular` ~. **2** [C,U] (also `~ paper`) thin, soft paper for wrapping things, protecting delicate articles, etc. **3** [C,U] (*dated*) woven fabric. **4** [C] (*fig*) series: *a* ~ *of lies.*

tit /tɪt/ *n* [C] kinds of small bird.

tit /tɪt/ *n* (only in) **tit for tat,** blow for blow.

tit /tɪt/ *n* △ (*vulgar sl*) nipple; woman's breast.

tit·bit /ˈtɪtbɪt/ *n* [C] attractive bit (*of* food, news, gossip, etc).

tit·il·late /ˈtɪtɪleɪt *US:* ˈtɪtəleɪt/ *vt* stimulate or excite pleasantly.

tit·il·la·tion /ˌtɪtɪˈleɪʃən/ *n* [U]

titi·vate (also **titti-**) /ˈtɪtɪveɪt/ *vt,vi* (*informal*) make smart: *She was titivating herself in front of the mirror.*

title /ˈtaɪtəl/ *n* **1** [C] name of a book, poem,

picture. etc. **2** [C] word used to show a person's rank, occupation, status, etc, e g Lord, Prince, Professor, Dr, Miss. **3** [C,U] (*legal*) right or claim, esp right to the possession of a position, property: *Has he any ~ to the land?* **4** = credit titles.

`title-role, part in a play that gives the play its name: *a performance of 'Othello' with Olivier in the ~-role*, with Olivier as Othello.

`title-deed, document proving a title(3) to property.

titled /ˈtaɪtəld/ *adj* having a title of nobility: *a ~d lady*, e g a duchess.

tit-ter /ˈtɪtə(r)/ *vt, n* [C] (give a) silly little laugh.

titu-lar /ˈtɪtjʊlə(r) *US*: -tʃʊ-/ *adj* **1** held by virtue of a title: *~ possessions*. **2** existing in name but not having authority or duties: *the ~ ruler*.

tizzy /ˈtɪzɪ/ *n* **be in a tizzy**, (*informal*) in a nervous state.

T-junction /ˈtiː dʒʌŋkʃən/ *n* [C] ⇨ T,t.

TNT /ˌtiː en ˈtiː/ *n* (= trinitrotoluene) powerful explosive.

to¹ /tuː/ *adverbial particle* **1** to or in the usual or required position, esp to a closed or almost closed position: *Push the door ~.* **2** *to and fro*, ⇨ fro. **3** ⇨ come(15), bring(6), and fall ²(14).

to² /tə *before vowels and strong-form:* tuː/ *participle* (marking the *infinitive*) **1** (used after many *verbs* but not after *can, do, may, must, shall, will*): *He wants ~ go.* **2** (used with *adverbs* of functions, purpose, result, outcome): *They came (in order) ~ help me. He lived ~ be ninety.* **3** (limiting the meanings of *adjectives* and *adverbs*): *The book is easy ~ understand. He's old enough ~ go to school.* **4** (a subsequent fact): *The good old days have gone never ~ return,* and will never return. *He awoke ~ find himself* (= and found himself) *in a strange room.* **5** (used with an *infinitive* as a *noun*): *It is wrong ~ steal.* **6** (used as a substitute for the *infinitive*): *We didn't want to go home but we had ~,* i e had to go home.

to³ /tə *before vowels and strong-form:* tuː/ *prep* **1** in the direction of; towards: *walk ~ work; point ~ it; hold sth (up) ~ the light; turn ~ the right.* **2** (*fig*) towards (a condition, quality, etc): *a tendency ~ laziness; slow ~ anger.* **3** (introducing the *indirect object*): *Who did you give it ~? The man I gave it ~ has left.* **4** as far as: *from beginning ~ end; count (up) ~ ten.* **5** before: *a quarter ~ six.* **6** until: *from morning ~ night. I didn't stay ~ the end of the meeting.* **7** (of comparison, ratio, reference): *I prefer walking ~ climbing. We won by six goals ~ three.*

toad /təʊd/ *n* [C] animal like a frog that lives on land except when breeding.

`toad-stool, kinds of fungus, some of them poisonous.

toast¹ /təʊst/ *n* [U] (slice of) bread made brown and crisp by heating: *two slices of ~.* □ *vt,vi* **1** (of bread) make or become brown and crisp by heating. **2** warm (oneself, one's toes, etc) before a fire.

`toaster, electric device for toasting bread.

toast² /təʊst/ *vt* wish happiness, success, etc to (a person or thing) while raising a glass of wine: *~ the bride and bridegroom.* □ *n* [C] act of toasting; person, etc toasted: *propose/drink a ~.*

to-bacco /təˈbækəʊ/ *n* [U] (plant having) leaves which are dried, cured and used for smoking (in pipes, cigars, cigarettes) or as snuff; (*pl*, for kinds of tobacco leaf): *This is a mixture of the best ~s.*

to-bac-co-nist /təˈbækənɪst/, shop, person, selling tobacco, cigarettes, etc.

to-bog-gan /təˈbɒgən/ *n* [C] long, narrow sledge without runners for sliding on ice. □ *vi* go down a snow- or ice-covered slope on a toboggan.

to-day /təˈdeɪ/ *adv, n* [U] **1** (on) this day: *T~ is Sunday. Have you seen ~'s newspaper? We're leaving ~ week/a week ~,* in one week's time. **2** (at) this present age or period: *the writers/the young people of ~.*

toddle /ˈtɒdl/ *vi* walk with short, uncertain steps as a baby does.

tod-dler /ˈtɒdlə(r)/, baby who can toddle.

toe /təʊ/ *n* [C] **1** each of the five divisions of the front part of the foot; similar part of an animal's foot. *tread/step on sb's toes*, (*fig*) offend him. *from top to toe,* from head to foot, completely. *on one's toes,* (*fig*) alert, ready for action. *on tiptoes,* ⇨ tip(1). **2** part of a sock, shoe, etc covering the toes. □ *vt* touch, reach, with the toes. *toe the line,* (*fig*) behave properly; obey orders given to one as a member of a group or party.

`toe-nail, nail of the toe of a human being.

toffee /ˈtɒfɪ *US*: ˈtɔːfɪ/ *n* [C,U] (piece of) hard, brown sticky sweet made by boiling sugar, butter, etc.

tog /tɒg/ *vt* (-gg-) (*informal*) put on smart clothes.

togs *n pl* (*informal*) clothes: *swimming ~s.*

toga /ˈtəʊgə/ *n* [C] (*pl ~s*) loose flowing outer garment worn by men in ancient Rome.

to-gether /təˈgeðə(r)/ *adv* **1** in company: *They went for a walk ~. together with,* as well as; in addition to; and also: *These new facts, ~ with the evidence you have already heard, prove the prisoner's innocence.* **2** so as to be in the same place, to be in contact, to be united: *Tie the ends ~. The leader called his men ~. put your/our, etc heads together,* consult with each other (to find a solution, make plans, etc). **3** at the same time: *All his troubles seemed to come ~.*

to-gether-ness *n* [C] friendship; feeling of unity.

togs /tɒgz/ *n pl* ⇨ tog.

toil /tɔɪl/ *vi* work long or hard (at a task); move with difficulty and trouble: ~ *up a steep hill.* □ *n* [U] hard work: *after long* ~
toiler, hard worker.

toilet /ˈtɔɪlət/ *n* [C] **1** process of dressing, arranging the hair, etc: *She spent only a few minutes on her* ~. **2** (as an *adjective*): *a* ~ *set,* ~ *articles,* such things as a hairbrush comb, etc. **3** lavatory; water-closet.
ˈtoilet-paper, for use in a lavatory.
ˈtoilet-roll, roll of toilet-paper.

to·ken /ˈtəʊkən/ *n* [C] **1** sign, evidence, guarantee or mark: *I am giving you this watch as a* ~ *of my affection.* ⇨ book token. **2** (as an *adjective*) acting as a preliminary or small-scale substitute: *The enemy offered only a* ~ *resistance,* did not resist seriously.
ˈtoken ˈpayment, payment of a small part of what is owed, made to show that the debt is recognized.
ˈtoken ˈstrike, for a few hours only (as a warning that a long strike may follow).

told /təʊld/ *pt,pp* of tell.

tol·er·ance /ˈtɒlərəns/ *n* [U] quality of tolerating opinions, beliefs, customs, behaviour, etc different from one's own: *religious/racial* ~.

tol·er·ant /ˈtɒlərənt/ *adj* having or showing tolerance: *Mr X is not very* ~ (*of criticism*).
tol·er·ant·ly *adv*

tol·er·ate /ˈtɒləreɪt/ *vt* **1** allow or endure without protest: *I won't* ~ *your impudence/ your doing that.* **2** endure the company of: *How can you* ~ *that rude girl?*
tol·er·able /ˈtɒlərəbəl/ *adj* (*formal*) that can be tolerated; fairly good: *tolerable food.*
tol·er·ably /-əblɪ/ *adv*

tol·er·ation /ˌtɒləˈreɪʃən/, tolerance, esp the practice of allowing religious freedom.

toll¹ /təʊl/ *n* [C] **1** payment required for the use of a road, bridge, harbour, etc. **2** (*fig*) something paid, lost or suffered: *The war took a heavy* ~ *of the nation's men.*
ˈtoll-bar/-gate, bar/gate across a road at which a toll is payable.
ˈtoll-house, house for the man in charge of a toll-bar.

toll² /təʊl/ *vt,vi* (of a bell) (cause to) ring with slow, regular strokes: *The funeral bell* ~*ed solemnly.* □ *n* (*sing* only) tolling stroke of a bell.

tom·ato /təˈmɑːtəʊ *US:* təˈmeɪtəʊ/ *n* [C] (*pl* ~es) (plant with) soft, juicy, (usually) red fruit: (as an *adjective*) ~ *juice.*

tomb /tuːm/ *n* [C] place dug in the ground, cut out of rock, etc for a dead body, esp one with a monument over it.
ˈtomb-stone, inscribed stone over a tomb.

tom·boy /ˈtɒmbɔɪ/ *n* [C] girl who likes rough, noisy games and play.

tom·cat /ˈtɒmkæt/ *n* [C] male cat.

tome /təʊm/ *n* [C] (*formal*) large, heavy book.

to·mor·row /təˈmɒrəʊ/ *adv, n* [C,U] (on)
the day after today: *If today is Monday,* ~ *will be Tuesday and the day after* ~ *will be Wednesday. The announcement will appear in* ~*'s newspapers.*

ton /tʌn/ *n* [C] **1** measure of weight (2 240 lb in GB, 2 000 lb in the US); *metric ton,* 2 204·6 lb or 1 000 kg. **2** (*informal*) large weight, quantity or number: *He has* ~*s of money.*

to·nal /ˈtəʊnəl/ *adj* (*music*) of tone or tones.

to·nal·ity /təʊˈnælətɪ/ *n* [C] (*pl* -ies) (*music*) character of a melody, depending upon the scale in which it is written, etc.

tone¹ /təʊn/ *n* **1** [C] sound, esp with reference to its quality, pitch, duration, feeling, etc: *the sweet* ~(*s*) *of a violin; a serious* ~ *of voice.* **2** [C] the pitch aspect of a (usually stressed) syllable; rise, fall, etc of the pitch of the voice in speaking: *In 'Are you ill?' there is a rising* ~ *on 'ill'.* **3** (*sing* only) general spirit, character, morale, of a community, etc: *The* ~ *of the school is excellent.* **4** [C] shade (of colour); degree (of light): *a carpet in* ~*s of brown.* **5** [C] (*music*) any one of the five larger intervals between one note and the next. **6** [U] proper and normal condition of (parts of) the body: *good muscular* ~.
tone·less *adj* not having colour, spirit, etc; dull: *answer in a* ~*less voice.*
tone·less·ly *adv*

tone² /təʊn/ *vt,vi* **1** give a particular tone of sound or colour to. **2** make or become less intense: *The artist* ~*d down the brighter colours. You'd better* ~ *down some of the offensive statements in your article.* **3** tone (sth) up, make or become more healthy, intenser, brighter, etc: *Exercise* ~*s up the muscles.* **4** tone in (with), (esp of colours) be in harmony: *These curtains* ~ *in well with your rugs.*

tongs /tɒŋz/ *n pl* (often *a pair of* ~) one of various kinds of U-shaped tool for taking up and holding something: `ˈsugar` ~. *be/go at it hammer and tongs,* ⇨ hammer(1).

tongue /tʌŋ/ *n* **1** [C] movable organ in the mouth, used in talking, tasting, licking, etc: *Don't put your* ~ *out at me!* **have sth on the tip of one's tong,** ⇨ tip¹(1). **have one's tongue in one's cheek,** say something that one does not intend to be taken seriously. **have lost one's tongue,** be too shy to speak. **hold one's tongue,** be silent, stop talking. **2** [C] language: *one's mother* ~, one's native language. **3** [C,U] animal's tongue as an article of food: *ham and* ~ *sandwiches.* **4** something like a tongue in shape or use, e g the strip of leather under the laces of a shoe, a flame.
ˈtongue-tied *adj* silent; unable or unwilling to speak through shyness, fear, etc.
ˈtongue-twister, word or succession or words difficult to say quickly and correctly

tonic /ˈtɒnɪk/ *n* [C], *adj* **1** (something, e g, medicine) giving strength or energy: *get a* bottle of ~ from the doctor. Praise can be a mental ~. **2** (music) keynote. **3** = tonic water: a gin and ~.

`tonic water, (bottled) water with quinine: a gin and ~.

to·night /tə`naɪt/ adv, n [U] (on) the night of today: last night, ~, and tomorrow night; ~'s radio news.

ton·nage /`tʌnɪdʒ/ n [U] **1** internal cubic capacity of a ship (1 ton = 100 cu ft). **2** total tonnage(1) of a country's merchant shipping. **3** charge per ton on cargo, etc for transport.

ton·sil /`tɒnsəl/ n [C] either of two small oval masses of tissue at the sides of the throat, near the root of the tongue.

ton·sil·itis /ˌtɒnsəl`aɪtɪs/ n [U] inflammation of the tonsils.

too /tu/ adv **1** also; as well; in addition: I, ~, have been to Paris, e g I, as well as he, you, etc. I've been to Paris ~, e g to Paris as well as to Rome, Milan, etc. **2** moreover: There was frost last night, and in May ~! **3** to, in, a higher degree than is allowable, required, etc: We've had ~ much rain lately. You're driving ~ fast for safety. These shoes are much ~ small for me. **4** (phrases) **go/carry sth too far,** ⇨ far ²(2). **all too soon/quickly, etc,** sooner, more quickly, etc than is desired: The holidays ended all ~ soon. **none too soon, etc,** not at all too soon, etc: We were none ~ early for the train, We caught the train with very little time to spare. **one too many,** ⇨ many(1). **be too much (for),** ⇨ much ¹ **only too** (+ adj), ⇨ only ².

took /tʊk/ pt of take ¹(1).

tool /tul/ n [C] **1** instrument held in the hand(s) and used by workmen, e g gardeners and carpenters. **2** person used by another for dishonest purposes: He was a mere ~ in the hands of the dictator.

toot /tut/ n [C] short, sharp warning sound from a horn, whistle, trumpet, etc. □ vi, vt (cause) to give out a toot.

tooth /tuθ/ n [C] (pl teeth /tiθ/) **1** each of the hard, white structures rooted in the gums, used for biting and chewing: have a ~ out (US: have a ~ pulled), i e by a dentist. **in the teeth of,** against the full force of; in opposition to. **armed to the teeth,** completely and elaborately armed. **long in the tooth,** old; experienced. **escape by the skin of one's teeth,** have a narrow escape. **fight tooth and nail,** fiercely, with a great effort. **get one's teeth into sth,** attack (a job) vigorously. **have a sweet tooth,** ⇨ sweet(1). **show one's teeth,** take up a threatening attitude. **2** part of a comb, saw or rake like a tooth. **go over/through sth with a fine-tooth comb,** examine it closely and thoroughly. **3** (pl) (informal) effective force: When will the new legislation be given some teeth, be made effective?

`tooth·ache, (sing only, with or without a/

the) ache in a tooth or teeth.

`tooth-brush, one for cleaning the teeth

`tooth-paste/-powder, for cleaning the teeth.

`tooth-pick, short, pointed piece of wood, etc, for removing bits of food from between the teeth.

tooth·less adj without teeth: a ~less grin

tootle /`tutəl/ vi, n [C] toot softly or continuously, as on a flute.

top ¹ /tɒp/ n **1** (usually sing with the) highest part or point: at the ~ of the hill; the hill~. **on top,** above: The green book is at the bottom of the pile and the red one is on ~. **on (the) top of, (a)** over, resting on: Put the red book on (the) ~ of the others. **(b)** in addition to: He borrowed £50 from me for the journey and then, on ~ of that, asked me if he could borrow my car, too. **from top to bottom,** completely. **from top to toe,** from head to foot. **blow one's top,** (informal) explode in rage. **2** upper surface, e g of a table: polish the ~ of a table. **on top of the world,** (informal) extremely happy, satisfied with everything: I'm feeling on ~ of the world today! **on top of things/one's work,** (informal) able to cope. **3** highest rank, foremost (or most important) place: He came out at the ~ of the list, e g of examination results. **come to the top,** (fig) win fame, success, etc. **reach/be at the top of the ladder/tree,** the highest position in a profession, career, etc. **4** utmost height or degree: **shout at the ~ of one's voice,** ⇨ voice, n(3). **5** highest in position or degree: on the ~ shelf; at ~ speed; charge ~ prices. **6** (motoring) in top, in top (the highest) gear. **7** the big top, very large circus tent.

`top `brass, senior management.

`top-coat, overcoat.

`top `dog, (sl) master, winner, etc.

`top drawer, the highest social class.

`top-`flight/-`notch adj (informal) firstrate; best possible: ~-flight French authors.

`top `hat, tall silk hat.

`top-`heavy adj over-weighted at the top so as to be in danger of falling.

`top-`hole adj (dated sl) excellent; firstrate.

`top-knot, knot of hair, bunch of feathers, etc on the top of the head.

`top·most /-məʊst/ adj highest

`top `people, those at the top of their profession, holding the highest positions, etc.

`top-`ranking adj of the highest rank.

`top secret, completely secret.

`top soil, soil on the surface.

top·less adj (of a woman's garment) leaving the breasts bare: a ~less swimsuit.

top ² /tɒp/ vt (-pp-) **1** provide a top for; be a top for; be a top to: a cake ~ped by/with icing. **2** top (sth) up, fill up (a partly empty container): ~ up with oil, add oil; ~ up a *drink*, refill a partly filled glass. **3** surpass, be taller or higher than: *Our exports have just ～ped the £80 000 mark.* **to top it all,** add the last (and surprising, etc) touch. **4** cut the tops off: *lift and ～ carrots,* take them from the ground and cut off the leaves.

top³ /tɒp/ *n* [C] toy that spins and balances on a point. **sleep like a top,** sleep deeply.

to·paz /ˈtəʊpæz/ *n* [U] transparent yellow mineral; [C] gem cut from this.

topic /ˈtɒpɪk/ *n* [C] subject for discussion.

topi·cal /-kəl/ *adj* of present interest: *～al news.*

topi·cally /-klɪ/ *adv*

top·og·ra·phy /təˈpɒɡrəfɪ/ *n* [U] (description of the) features, e g rivers, valleys, roads, of a place or district.

topo·graphi·cal /ˈtɒpəˈɡræfɪkəl/ *adj*

topo·graphi·cally /-klɪ/ *adv*

topple /ˈtɒpəl/ *vi,vt* (cause to) be unsteady and fall (over): *The pile of books ～d over/ down. The dictator was ～d from power.*

tor /tɔː(r)/ *n* [C] small hill; rocky peak.

torch /tɔːtʃ/ *n* [C] **1** (*GB*) electric light held in the hand. **2** piece of wood, etc soaked in oil, etc for carrying or using as a flaming light. **3** (*fig*) something that gives enlightenment: *the ～ of learning.*

`torch·light, light of a torch: *a ～light procession.*

tore /tɔː(r)/ *pt* of tear².

tor·ea·dor /ˈtɒrɪədɔː(r)/ *US:* `tɔr-/ *n* [C] bullfighter (usually on a horse).

tor·ment /ˈtɔːment/ *n* [C,U] (something that causes) severe bodily or mental pain or suffering: *be in ～; suffer ～(s) from an aching tooth.* □ *vt* /tɔːˈment/ cause severe suffering to; annoy: *～ed with pain/hunger.*

tor·men·tor /-tə(r)/, person who, that which, torments.

torn /tɔːn/ *pp* of tear².

tor·nado /tɔːˈneɪdəʊ/ *n* [C] (*pl* ～es) violent and destructive whirlwind.

tor·pedo /tɔːˈpiːdəʊ/ *n* [C] (*pl* ～es) cigar-shaped self-propelling shell filled with explosives and travelling below the surface of the sea, used to attack ships. □ *vt* **1** attack or destroy with a torpedo. **2** (*fig*) attack (a policy, institution, etc) and make it ineffective: *Who ～ed the Disarmament Conference?*

tor·rent /ˈtɒrənt/ *US:* `tɔr-/ *n* [C] **1** violent, rushing stream of liquid (esp water): *mountain ～s; ～s of rain.* **2** (*fig*) violent outpouring: *a ～ of abuse/insults.*

tor·ren·tial /təˈrenʃəl/ *adj* of, like, caused by, a torrent: *～ial rain.*

torso /ˈtɔːsəʊ/ *n* [C] (*pl* ～s) (statue of a) human body without head, arms and legs.

tor·toise /ˈtɔːtəs/ *n* [C] slow-moving, four-legged land (and fresh-water) varieties of turtle with a hard shell.

tor·tu·ous /ˈtɔːtʃʊəs/ *adj* **1** full of twists and bends: *a ～ path.* **2** (*fig*) not straightforward: *a ～ argument/politician*

tor·tu·ous·ly *adv*

tor·ture /ˈtɔːtʃə(r)/ *vt* cause severe suffering to: *～ a man to make him confess; ～d with anxiety.* □ *n* **1** [U] infliction of severe bodily or mental suffering: *instruments of ～.* **2** [C,U] pain caused or suffered; method of torturing: *suffer ～ from the secret police.*

tor·turer, person who tortures.

Tory /ˈtɔːrɪ/ *n* [C] (*pl* -ies) = Conservative

toss /tɒs/ *US:* tɔs/ *vt,vi* **1** throw up into or through the air: *He ～ed the beggar a coin/ ～ed a coin to the beggar. The horse ～ed its head.* **toss a coin,** send a coin spinning up in the air and guess which side will be on top when it falls. **toss sb for sth,** use the method of tossing a coin to decide something: *Who's to pay for the drinks? Let's ～ for it.* **2** (cause to) move restlessly from side to side or up and down: *The ship (was) ～ed about on the stormy sea.* **3** **toss sth off,** produce it quickly and without much thought or effort: *～ off a letter.* □ *n* [C] **1** tossing movement: *a ～ of the head; take a ～,* (esp) be thrown from the back of a horse. **2** **win/ lose the toss,** guess correctly/incorrectly when a coin is tossed.

`toss-up, tossing of a coin; (hence) something about which there is doubt: *It's a ～-up whether he will get here in time.*

tot¹ /tɒt/ *n* [C] **1** (often **tiny tot**) very small child. **2** (*informal*) small glass of liquor.

tot² /tɒt/ *vt,vi* (-tt-) **tot (sth) up,** (*informal*) add up: *～ up a column of figures.*

to·tal /ˈtəʊtəl/ *adj* complete; entire: *～ silence.* □ *n* [C] total amount: *Our expenses reached a ～ of £20.* □ *vt,vi* (-ll-, *US* also -l-) find, reach, the total of: *The visitors to the exhibition ～led 15 000.*

to·tally /ˈtəʊtəlɪ/ *adv* completely: *～ly blind.*

to·tal·ity /təʊˈtælətɪ/ *n* [U] entirety.

to·tali·tar·ian /ˈtəʊtælɪˈteərɪən/ *adj* of a system in which only one political party and no rival loyalties are permitted.

tot·ter /ˈtɒtə(r)/ *vi* **1** walk with weak, unsteady steps; get up unsteadily: *The wounded man ～ed to his feet.* **2** be almost falling; seem to be about to collapse: *The tree ～ed and then fell.*

tou·can /ˈtuːkæn/ *n* [C] kinds of tropical American bird with brightly coloured feathers and a large beak.

touch¹ /tʌtʃ/ *n* [C] **1** act or fact of touching: *I felt a ～ on my arm.* **2** [U] (sense giving) feeling by touching: *soft/rough to the ～,* when touched. **3** [C] stroke made with a brush, pen, etc: *add a few finishing ～es* (to a drawing or any piece of work). **4** [C] slight quantity, trace: *a ～ of frost in the air; a ～ of sadness in his voice.* **5** [C] style or manner of playing a musical instrument, of workmanship (in art), etc: *have a light ～,* e g on a piano, a typewriter. **6** [U] communication. **in/out of touch (with),** in/not in regular communication (with); having/not having information about: *keep in* ∼ *with old friends*; *be out of* ∼ *with the political situation*. **lose touch (with),** be out of touch (with): *If we correspond regularly we shan't lose* ∼. **7** (*football*) part of the pitch outside the side-lines: *The ball is in/out of* ∼.

'**touch-and-'go** *adj* risky; of uncertain result: *It was* ∼*-and-go whether the doctor would arrive in time.*

touch² /tʌtʃ/ *vt,vi* (For special uses with *adverbial particles* and *prepositions*, ⇨ 11 below.) **1** (cause to) be in contact with; bring a part of the body (esp the hand) into contact with: *One of the branches is* ∼*ing the water. Can you* ∼ (= reach with your hand) *the top of the door?* (eg in a museum) *are requested not to* ∼ *the exhibits.* **touch bottom,** (a) reach the bottom: *The water isn't deep here; I can just* ∼ *bottom,* i e with my feet. (b) (*fig*) reach the lowest level of value, misfortune, etc. **touch wood,** touch something made of wood to avoid bad luck: *I've never been in a road accident—*∼ *wood.* **2** apply a slight or gentle force to: *He* ∼*ed the bell,* rang it by pressing the button. **3** (in the negative) compare with; be equal to: *No one can* ∼ *him as an actor of tragic roles.* **4** (in the negative) take (food, drink): *He hasn't* ∼*ed food for two days.* **5** affect (a person or his feelings); concern: *The sad story* ∼*ed us/our hearts.* **6** have to do with: *As a pacifist I refuse to* ∼ (= invest money in) *shares of armament firms.* **7** injure slightly: *Luckily the paintings were not* ∼*ed by the fire.* **8** (*pp* ∼**ed**) slightly mad or deranged: *He seems to be a bit* ∼*ed.* **9** cause a painful or angry feeling in; wound: *The remark* ∼*ed him deeply;* cause a feeling of gratitude: *I was so* ∼*ed by your letter of sympathy.* ⇨ **touching.** **10** deal with; cope with; get a result from: *Nothing I have used will* ∼ (= get rid of) *these grease spots. She couldn't* ∼ (= even begin to answer) *the first two questions in the biology paper,* i e in an examination.

11 (special uses with *adverbial particles* and *prepositions*):

touch down, (of aircraft) come down to land. Hence, '**touch-down** *n* [C]

touch sb for sth, (*sl*) get money from (by begging): *He* ∼*ed me for a fiver* (i e £5).

touch sth off, (*fig*) cause to start: *The arrest of the men's leaders* ∼*ed off a riot.*

touch on sth, mention (a subject) briefly.

touch sth up, make small changes in (a picture, a piece of writing) to improve it.

touch-able /ˈtʌtʃəbəl/ *adj* that may be touched.

touch-ing /ˈtʌtʃɪŋ/ *adj* pathetic; causing gratitude, sympathy, etc: *a* ∼ *request for help.* □ *prep* concerning.

touch-ing-ly *adv*

touchy /ˈtʌtʃɪ/ *adj* (-ier, -iest) easily or quickly offended.

tough /tʌf/ *adj* (-er, -est) **1** (of meat) hard

to cut or get one's teeth into. **2** not easily cut, broken or worn out: *as* ∼ *as leather.* **3** strong; able to endure hardships: ∼ *soldiers.* **4** (of persons) rough and violent: *a* ∼ *criminal.* **a tough customer,** (*informal*) a difficult person to deal with. **5** stubborn; unyielding. **be/get tough (with sb)**: *The employers got* ∼ *with/adopted a get-*'∼ *policy towards their workers.* **6** hard to carry out; difficult: *a* ∼ *job/problem.*

'**tough 'luck,** (*informal*) bad luck.

'**tough-ly** *adv*

'**tough-ness** *n* [U]

toughen /ˈtʌfən/ *vt,vi* make or become tough.

tou-pee /ˈtuːpeɪ *US:* tuːˈpeɪ/ *n* [C] false hair worn to cover a bald patch.

tour /tʊə(r)/ *n* [C] **1** journey out and home again during which several or many places are visited: *a round-the-world* ∼; *conducted* ∼*s,* made by a group conducted by a guide. **2** brief visit to or through: *a* ∼ *of the palace.* **3** period of duty or employment (overseas): *a* ∼ *of three years as a lecturer in the University of Ibadan.* **4** round of (official) visits to institutions, units, etc: *The Director leaves tomorrow on a* ∼ *of overseas branches.* **5** number of visits to places made by a theatrical company, etc: *take a company on* ∼ . □ *vt,vi* make a tour (of): ∼ *western Europe. The play will* ∼ *the provinces in the autumn.*

tour-ing *n, adj*: *a* '∼*ing party.*

tour-ism /ˈtʊərɪzm/ *n* [U] organized touring: *foreign exchange from* ∼*ism,* from the money brought in by tourists.

tour-ist /ˈtʊərɪst/ *n* **1** [C] person making a tour for pleasure: *London is full of* ∼*s in summer.* **2** (as an *adjective*) of or for tours: *a* '∼ *agency;* '∼ *class,* (on liners, airliners) second class.

tour-na-ment /ˈtʊənəmənt *US:* ˈtɜːn-/ *n* [C] series of contests of skill between a number of players: *a* '*tennis*/'*chess* ∼.

tour-ni-quet /ˈtʊənɪkeɪ *US:* ˈtɜːnɪkɪt/ *n* [C] device for stopping a flow of blood through an artery by twisting something tightly around a limb.

tousle /ˈtaʊzəl/ *vt* (*formal*) make (esp the hair) untidy: *a girl with* ∼*d hair.*

tout /taʊt/ *n* [C] person who encourages others to buy something, use his services, etc, esp one who sells information about racehorses: *a* '*ticket* ∼, eg selling tickets for a major football match at a greatly inflated price. □ *vi* act as a tout: *There were men outside the railway station* ∼*ing for the hotels.*

tow /təʊ/ *vt* pull along by a rope or chain: ∼ *a damaged car to the nearest garage.* □ *n* [C,U] towing or being towed: *Can we give you a* ∼? **in tow,** (*informal*) also with (a person). **on tow,** being towed.

to-ward(s) /təˈwɔːd(z) *US:* tɔːd(z)/ *prep* **1** approaching; in the direction of: *walking* ∼ *the sea; first steps* ∼ *the abolition of arma-*

ments. **2** as regards; in relation to: *What will the Government's attitude be* ~ *the plan?* **3** for the purpose of (helping): *We must save money* ~ *the children's education.* **4** (of time) near: ~ *the end of the century.*

towel /'taʊəl/ n [C] piece of cloth, etc for drying or wiping something wet (e g one's hands or body): *a* `bath-~; a paper ~.* **throw in the towel,** ⟹ throw ⟹(11). □ vt (-ll-, *US* -l-) dry or rub (oneself) with a towel.

towel-ling (*US* = **toweling**) n [U] material for towels.

tower /'taʊə(r)/ n [C] **1** tall building, either standing alone (e g as a fort, *the T~ of London*) or forming part of a church, castle or other large building (e g a college). **2** *a* **tower of strength,** (*fig*) a person who can be relied upon for protection, strength or comfort in time of trouble. **3** = water tower. ⟹ cooling-tower. □ vi rise to a great height, be very tall, esp in relation to the height of the surroundings: *the skyscrapers that* ~ *over New York.* **tower above sb,** (*fig*) (of persons) greatly exceed in ability, in intellectual or moral qualities: *a man who* ~*s above his contemporaries.*

`**tower-block,** high block of flats or offices.

town /taʊn/ n **1** [C] centre of population larger than a village, esp one that has not been created a city (and often used in contrast to *country*): *Would you rather live in a* ~ *or in the country?* **paint the town red,** ⟹ red(1). **2** [U] the business, shopping, etc part of a town (contrasted with the suburbs, etc): *go to* ~ *to do some shopping. He's in* ~ *today.* ⟹ downtown. **go out on the town,** go out and enjoy the entertainment facilities of a town. **go to town,** (*sl*) act, behave, without inhibitions, e g by spending money, having a spree. **3** [U] the chief city or town in the neighbourhood (esp, in England, London): *He's gone up to* ~ *for the weekend.* **4** [U] (*sing* with *the*) the people of a town: *The whole* ~ *was talking about it.* **the talk of the town,** ⟹ talk (1). **5** (*sing* with *the*) towns in general: *Farm workers are leaving the country in order to get better paid work in the* ~.

`**town `centre,** area around which public buildings, e g the town hall, the public library, main shops, are grouped.

`**town `clerk,** official who keeps town or city records and advises on certain legal matters.

`**town `council,** governing body of a town.

`**town `councillor,** member of a town council.

`**town `hall,** building with offices of local government.

`**town house,** house in town, of a particular style or belonging to a person who also has a house in the country.

`**towns-folk,** people who live in town or the town referred to.

toxic /'toksɪk/ *adj* poisonous (the usual word).

toy /tɔɪ/ n **1** something, e g a doll, for a child to play with. **2** (as an *adjective*): ~ *soldier,* one made as a toy(1); ~ *dog/spaniel, etc,* small kinds kept as pets. □ vi **1** think not very seriously about: *He* ~*ed with the idea of buying a new car.* **2** = fiddle(2): ~*ing with a pencil.*

`**toy-shop,** shop where toys are sold.

trace[1] /treɪs/ n [C] **1** mark, sign, etc showing that a person or thing has been present, that something has existed or happened: ~*s of an ancient civilization. We've lost all* ~ *of them,* don't know where they are. **2** very small amount: *There were* ~*s of poison in his blood.*

trace[2] /treɪs/ *vt,vi* **1** draw, sketch, the course, outline, etc of: ~ (*out*) *one's route on a map.* **2** copy (something), e g by drawing on transparent paper the lines, etc on (a map, design, etc) placed underneath. **3** follow or discover (a person or thing) by looking at marks, tracks, evidence, etc: *I cannot* ~ (= cannot find) *any letter from you dated 1st June.* **trace (sth/sb) back (to sth),** (a) find the origin of by going back in time: *He* ~*s his ancestors back to an old Scottish family.* (b) find the origin of by going back through evidence: *The rumour was* ~*d back to a journalist,* It was discovered that he had started it.

trace-able /-əbəl/ *adj* capable of being traced (*to*).

trac-ing, reproduction (of a map, design, etc) made by tracing(1).

tracery /'treɪsərɪ/ n [C,U] (*pl* -ies) ornamental arrangement of designs (e g as made by frost on glass, or of stonework in a church window).

tra·chea /trə'kɪə *US:* 'treɪkɪə/ n [C] (*pl* ~e /-kiː/) (*anat*) = windpipe.

track /træk/ n [C] **1** line or series of marks left by a vehicle, person, animal, etc in passing along; path made by persons/animals: ~*s in the snow,* e g footprints; `*sheep-~s across the moor.* **be on sb's track/on the track of sb,** be tracking: *The police are on the* ~ *of the thief.* **cover up one's tracks,** hide one's movements or activities. **have a** `*one-track `mind,** give all one's attention to one topic or thought. **keep/lose track of sb/sth,** keep in/lose touch with; follow/fail to follow the course or development of: *read the newspapers to keep* ~ *of current events.* **off the track,** (*fig*) following a wrong line of action. ⟹ beaten. **2** course; line taken by something (whether marked or not): *the* ~ *of a storm/spacecraft.* **3** set of rails for trains, etc: *The train left the* ~, was derailed. **4** path prepared for racing (e g made of cinders, etc): *a* `*motor-racing/*`cycling/ `*running* ~. **5** = caterpillar(2). **6** band for recording sound (on magnetized tape); section of something recorded (on a record or tape). □ *vt* follow the track of: ～ *an animal to its den.* **track sb/sth down,** find by searching: ～ *down a bear/a reference.*

`**track event,** athletic contest, e g running, on a track(4).

`**track suit,** loose-fitting warm suit worn by an athlete.

`**track·ing station,** one which, by radar or radio, maintains contact with space-vehicles, etc.

`**tracker,** person, esp a hunter, who tracks wild animals.

tract¹ /trækt/ *n* [C] **1** stretch or area (*of* forest, farmland, etc): *the wide* ～*s of desert in N Africa.* **2** system of related parts in an animal body: *the di`gestive/re`spiratory* ～.

tract² /trækt/ *n* [C] short printed essay, esp on a moral or religious subject.

tract·able /'træktəbəl/ *adj* (*formal*) easily controlled or guided.

trac·tion /'trækʃən/ *n* [U] (power used in) pulling or drawing something over a surface: *electric/steam* ～.

trac·tor /'træktə(r)/ *n* [C] motor-vehicle used for pulling agricultural machinery (ploughs, etc), or other heavy equipment, over rough ground.

trade¹ /treɪd/ *n* **1** [U] buying and selling of goods; exchange of goods for money or other goods: *T*～ *was good last year.* **2** [C] particular branch of buying and selling: *He's in the* `*furniture/*`*book* ～. **3** [C,U] occupation; way of making a living, esp a handicraft: *He's a carpenter/tailor by* ～. *Shoe-making is a useful* ～. ⇨ jack.

the Trades, trade-winds.

`**trade-mark, (a)** design, special name, etc used to distinguish a manufacturer's goods from others. **(b)** (*fig*) distinguishing characteristics: *He leaves his* ～*mark on all his activities.*

`**trade name,** name given to a manufactured article.

`**trade price,** price charged by a manufacturer or wholesaler to a retailer.

`**trades·man,** shopkeeper (the usual word).

'**trade-'union,** (also less often **trades-union**) organized association of workers in a trade formed to protect their interests, improve their conditions, etc.

'**Trade 'Union 'Congress,** (abbr **TUC**) association of British trade unions.

'**trade-'unionist,** member of a trade-union.

`**trade-wind,** strong wind blowing always towards the equator from the S E and N E.

trade² /treɪd/ *vi,vt* **1** engage in trade(1); buy and sell: *Britain* ～*s with many European countries.* **2** exchange: *The boy* ～*d his skates for a cricket bat.* **3 trade sth in,** give (a used article) in part payment for a new purchase: *He* ～*d in his car for a new one.* Hence, `**trade-in** *n*. **4** take a wrong advantage of, use, in order to get something for oneself: ～ *on her sympathy.*

trader, person who trades(1).

tra·di·tion /trə'dɪʃən/ *n* **1** [U] (handing down from generation to generation of) opinions, beliefs, customs, etc. **2** [C] opinion, belief, custom, etc handed down.

tra·di·tional /-nəl/ *adj*

tra·di·tion·ally /-nəlɪ/ *adv*

traf·fic /'træfɪk/ *n* [U] **1** (movement of) people and vehicles along roads and streets, of aircraft in the sky: *There was a lot of/not much* ～ *on the roads yesterday.* **2** transport business done by a railway, steamship line, airline, etc. **3** illegal trading: *the drug* ～. □ *vi* (-ck-) trade: ～ *in hides (with...).*

`**traffic indicator** = **trafficator.**

`**traffic island,** platform in the centre of a busy road, for pedestrians when crossing.

`**traffic warden,** official controlling the parking of cars and use of parking-meters.

traf·fi·ca·tor /'træfɪkeɪtə(r)/ *n* [C] flickering yellow light used on a motor-vehicle to show the direction in which the vehicle is about to turn.

tra·gedy /'trædʒədɪ/ *n* (*pl* -ies) **1** [C] play for the theatre, cinema, TV, of a serious kind, with a sad ending. **2** [U] branch of the drama with this kind of play. **3** [C,U] very sad event, action, experience, etc in real life.

tra·gedian /trə'dʒiːdɪən/ *n* [C] writer of, actor in, tragedy.

tra·gedi·enne /trə'dʒiːdɪ'en/ *n* [C] actress in tragedy.

tra·gic /'trædʒɪk/ *adj* of tragedy: *a* ～ *actor/event.*

tragi·cally /-klɪ/ *adv*

trail /treɪl/ *n* [C] **1** line, mark or series of marks, drawn or left by a person or thing that has passed by: *a* ～ *of smoke,* (from a railway steam-engine); *a* ～ *of destruction,* e g left by a violent storm. **2** track or scent followed in hunting. **hot on the trail (of),** close behind. **3** path through rough country. □ *vt,vi* **1** pull, be pulled, along: *Her long skirt was* ～*ing along the floor.* **2** = track. **3** (of plants) grow over or along the ground, etc: *roses* ～*ing over the walls.*

trailer, (a) transport-vehicle hauled by a tractor or truck. **(b)** caravan drawn by a motor-vehicle. **(c)** trailing plant. **(d)** series of short extracts from a film to advertise it in advance.

train¹ /treɪn/ *n* **1** [C] (locomotive and) number of railway coaches, wagons, etc joined together: `*passenger/*`*goods/*`*freight* ～*s; travel by* ～*; get on/off a* ～. **2** number of persons, animals, carriages, etc moving in a line: *a* ～ *of camels.* **3** series or chain: *A knock at the door interrupted my* ～ *of thought.* **4** part of a long formal dress or robe that trails on the ground.

train² /treɪn/ *vt,vi* **1** give teaching and practice to (e g a child, a soldier, an animal) in order to bring to a desired standard of behaviour, efficiency or physical condition: ～ *a horse for a race/circus. There is a shortage of* ～*ed nurses.* **2** cause to grow in a required direction: ∼ *roses against/over a wall*. **3** point, aim: ∼ *a gun on the enemy's positions*.

trainee /treɪˈniː/, person undergoing some form of (usually industrial) training.

trainer, person who trains (esp athletes, race-horses, etc).

train·ing, in/out of training, in/not in good physical condition (e g for athletic contests).

trait /treɪt/ *n* [C] distinguishing quality or characteristic: *Two good* ∼s *in the American character are generosity and energy*.

trai·tor /ˈtreɪtə(r)/ *n* [C] person who betrays a friend, is disloyal to a cause, his country, etc.

trai·tor·ous /-əs/ *adj* treacherous (the usual word).

tram /træm/ *n* [C] (*US* = ∼`street-car`) (also `∼car`) public transport powered by electricity on rails in the road surface.

tramp /træmp/ *vi,vt* **1** walk with heavy steps: *He* ∼ed *up and down the platform waiting for the train*. **2** walk through or over (esp for a long distance): ∼ *through the mountains;* ∼ *over the hills. They* ∼ed (*for*) *miles and miles*. □ *n* **1** (*sing* with *the*) sound of heavy footsteps: *I heard the* ∼ *of marching soldiers*. **2** [C] long walk: *go for a* ∼ *in the country*. **3** [C] homeless person who goes from place to place and does no regular work: *There's a* ∼ *at the door begging for food*.

`tramp-steamer`, cargo boat which goes to any port(s) where cargo can be picked up.

trample /ˈtræmpəl/ *vt,vi* **1** tread heavily on with the feet: *The children have* ∼d (*down*) *the flowers/* ∼d *the grass down*. **2** (*fig*) affect badly and thoughtlessly: ∼ *on his feelings*. □ *n* [C] sound, act, of trampling.

tram·po·line /ˈtræmpəlin/ *n* [C] strong canvas on a spring frame, used by gymnasts for acrobatic leaps.

trance /trɑns *US*: træns/ *n* [C] **1** condition like sleep: *be/fall/go into a* ∼. **2** abnormal, hypnotic, state: *send her into a* ∼.

tran·quil /ˈtræŋkwɪl/ *adj* (*formal*) calm; quiet: *a* ∼ *life in the country*.

tran·quilly /-wɪlɪ/ *adv*

tran·quil·lity (*US* also **tran·quil·ity**) /træŋˈkwɪlətɪ/ *n* [U] calm, quiet state.

tran·quil·lize (*US* also **tran·quil·ize**) /ˈtræŋkwɪlaɪz/ *vt* make calm, quiet.

tran·quil·liz·er (*US* also **tran·quil·izer**) *n* [C] drug that produces a calm mental state.

trans- /trænz-/ *prefix* **1** across: *transatlantic*. **2** to a changed state: *transform*.

trans·act /trænˈzækt/ *vt* (*formal*) conduct, (business, etc).

trans·ac·tion /trænˈzækʃən/ *n* **1** [U] (*sing* with *the*) transacting: *the* ∼ *of business*. **2** [C] piece of business: *cash* ∼s. **3** [pl] (records of the) proceedings of (esp a learned society, e g its meetings, lectures): *the* ∼s *of the Royal Archaeological Society*.

trans·at·lan·tic /ˌtrænzətˈlæntɪk/ *adj* **1**

beyond, crossing, the Atlantic: *a* ∼ *voyage/flight*. **2** concerning (countries on) both sides of the Atlantic: *a* ∼ *treaty/trade agreement*.

tran·scend /trænˈsend/ *vt* go or be beyond or outside the range of (human experience, reason, belief, powers of description, etc).

tran·scen·den·tal /ˌtrænsenˈdentəl/ *adj* not based on experience or reason; going beyond human knowledge; that cannot be discovered or understood by practical experience: ∼ *meditation*.

tran·scen·den·tally /-təlɪ/ *adv*

trans·con·ti·nen·tal /ˌtrænzˈkɒntɪˈnentəl/ *adj* crossing a continent: *a* ∼ *railway*.

tran·scribe /trænˈskraɪb/ *vt* **1** copy in ordinary writing, esp from shorthand notes or from speech recorded on magnetic tape. **2** write in a special form: ∼d *into phonetics*.

tran·script /ˈtrænskrɪpt/ *n* [C] something transcibed.

tran·scrip·tion /trænˈskrɪpʃən/ *n* [C,U]

tran·sept /ˈtrænsept/ *n* [C] (either end of the) transverse part of a cross-shaped church.

trans·fer[1] /ˈtrænsfə(r)/ *n* **1** [C,U] (instance of) transferring. **2** [C] document that transfers a person or thing; drawing, plan, etc transferred from one surface to another.

trans·fer[2] /trænsˈfɜː(r)/ *vt,vi* (-rr-) **1** change position, move: *The head office has been* ∼red *from York to London*. **2** hand over the possession of (property, etc to): ∼ *rights to a son*. **3** convey (a drawing, design, pattern, etc) from one surface to another (e g from a wooden surface to canvas). **4** change from one train, bus, etc to another. **5** move from one occupation (usually within the same profession), position, company, etc to another: *He has been* ∼red *to the Sales Department*.

trans·fer·able /-əbəl/ *adj* that can be transferred: *These tickets are not* ∼able, cannot be given to anyone else.

trans·fer·ence /ˈtrænsfərəns *US*: trænsˈfɜːrəns/ *n* [U]

trans·fix /trænsˈfɪks/ *vt* (*formal*) **1** pierce through: ∼ *a leopard with a spear*. **2** cause (a person) to be unable to move, speak, think, etc: *He stood* ∼ed *with horror*.

trans·form /trænsˈfɔːm/ *vt* change the shape, appearance, quality or nature of: *Success and wealth* ∼ed *his character. A steam-engine* ∼s *heat into energy*.

trans·form·able /-əbəl/ *adj* that can be transformed.

trans·form·ation /ˌtrænsfəˈmeɪʃən/ *n* (a) [U] transforming or being transformed. (b) [C] instance of this: *He has undergone a great* ∼*ation since he was married*.

trans·for·mer, person or thing that transforms, e g apparatus that increases or decreases the voltage of an electric power supply.

trans·fuse /trænsˈfjuːz/ *vt* (esp) transfer the

blood of one person to another.

trans·fu·sion /træns'fjuːʒən/ n [U] act or process of transfusing; [C] instance of this: *The injured man was given a blood transfusion.*

trans·gress /træns'gres/ vt,vi (*formal*) 1 go beyond (a limit or bound): ~ *the bounds of decency.* 2 break (a law, treaty, agreement). 3 sin.

trans·gres·sion /trænz'greʃən/ n [C,U] (instance of) transgressing.

trans·gres·sor /-sə(r)/, person who transgresses; sinner.

tran·si·ent /'trænzɪənt US: 'trænʃənt/ adj (*formal*) lasting for a short time only: ~ *happiness.*

tran·sis·tor /træn'zɪstə(r)/ n [C] 1 small electronic device, used in radios, hearing aids and other kinds of electronic apparatus. 2 transistorized radio.

tran·sis·tor·ized /-aɪzd/ adj having transistors, not valves: *a ~ized computer.*

tran·sit /'trænsɪt/ n [U] sending, carrying or being sent, across, over or through. *In transit,* while being carried or sent from one place to another.

'transit camp, one for the use of persons (esp soldiers) who are in transit from one place to another.

'transit visa, visa allowing passage through (but not a stay in) a country.

tran·si·tion /træn'zɪʃən/ n [C,U] changing, change, from one condition or set of circumstances to another: *Adolescence is the period of ~ between childhood and manhood.*

tran·si·tional /-nəl/ adj

tran·si·tive /'trænsətɪv/ adj (*gram*) (of a verb) taking a direct object.

tran·si·tory /'trænsɪtrɪ US: -tɔrɪ/ adj = transient.

trans·late /trænz'leɪt/ vt 1 give the meaning of (something said or written) in another language: ~ *a book from English into French.* 2 interpret, explain (a person's behaviour, etc): *How would you ~ his silence,* What do you think it means?

trans·la·tor /-tə(r)/, person who translates.

trans·la·tion /'trænz'leɪʃən/ n [U] translating: *errors in ~;* [C] something translated: *make/do a ~ into French.*

trans·lu·cent /trænz'luːsnt/ adj allowing light to pass through but not transparent: *Frosted glass is ~.*

trans·mis·sion /trænz'mɪʃən/ n 1 [U] transmitting or being transmitted: *the ~ of news/a TV programme.* 2 [C] clutch, gears and drive which help to send power from the engine to the wheels (of a motor-vehicle).

trans·mit /trænz'mɪt/ vt (-tt-) 1 pass or hand on; send on: ~ *a message by radio;* ~ *a disease.* 2 allow through or along: *Iron ~s heat.*

trans·mit·ter, person, that which, transmits, esp (part of a) radio apparatus for sending out signals, messages, music, etc.

trans·mute /trænz'mjuːt/ vt change the

---

shape, nature or substance of: *We cannot ~ base metals into gold.*

trans·par·ency /træn'spærənsɪ/ n (*pl* -ies) 1 [U] state of being transparent. 2 [C] framed diagram, picture, etc on photographic film (to be projected on to a screen).

trans·par·ent /træn'spærənt/ adj 1 allowing light to pass through so that objects (or at least their outlines) behind can be distinctly seen: *Ordinary glass is ~.* 2 about which there can be no mistake or doubt: *a man of ~ honesty.* 3 clear; easily understood: *a ~ style of writing.* 4 (*informal*) (of a person, his behaviour) obviously lying, insincere, etc.

trans·par·ent·ly adv

tran·spire /træn'spaɪə(r)/ vi,vt (*formal*) 1 (of an event, a secret) come to be known: *It ~d that the President had spent the weekend golfing.* 2 (*dated*) happen.

trans·plant /træns'plɑːnt US: -'plænt/ vt,vi 1 take up (plants, etc) with their roots and plant in another place. 2 transfer (tissue, or an organ, eg a heart or kidney) from one person to another. 3 (*fig*) (of people) move from one place to another. □ n /'trænsplɑːnt US: -plænt/ [C] instance of transplanting(2): *a 'kidney ~.*

trans·port¹ /'trænspɔːt US: 'træn-/ n 1 [U] carrying (to another place) or being carried; means of carrying: *the ~ of troops by air; road ~.* 2 (as an *adjective*) of or for carrying (to another place): *London's ~ system; ~ charges.*

trans·port² /træn'spɔːt US: træn-/ vt 1 carry (goods, persons) from one place to another: ~ *goods by lorry.* 2 (in former times) send (a criminal) to a distant colony as a punishment: ~*ed to Australia.*

trans·port·able /-əbl/ adj that can be transported.

trans·por·ta·tion /'trænspɔː'teɪʃən US: 'træn-/ n [U]

trans·porter /træn'spɔːtə(r) US: træn-/ n [C] person or thing that transports, eg a long vehicle for carrying several motor-vehicles from a factory.

trans·pose /træn'spəʊz/ vt 1 cause (two or more things) to change places. 2 (*music*) put into another key.

trans·po·si·tion /'trænspə'zɪʃən/ n [C,U]

tran·sub·stan·ti·ation /'trænsəb'stæn-ʃɪ'eɪʃən/ n doctrine that the bread and wine in the Eucharist are changed into the body and blood of Christ.

trans·verse /trænz'vɜːs/ adj lying or placed across.

trans·verse·ly adv

trap /træp/ n [C] 1 device for catching animals, etc: *a 'mouse-~.* 2 (*fig*) plan for deceiving a person; trick or device to make a person say or do something he does not wish to do or say: *The employer set a ~ for the man by putting marked money in the till.* 3 U-shaped or other section of a drain-pipe which prevents a return flow of water (e g under a lavatory). **4** light, two-wheeled vehicle pulled by a horse or pony. **5** device (e g a box) from which an animal or object can be released, e g greyhounds at the start of a race. **6** (*sl*) mouth. □ *vt* (-pp-) **1** catch in a trap. **2** capture by a trick.

trap·per, person who catches animals, esp for their fur.

tra·peze /trə`piz *US*: træ-/ *n* [C] horizontal bar or rod supported by two ropes, used by acrobats and for gymnastic exercises.

tra·pezium /trə`pɪzɪəm/ *n* [C] (*pl* ~s) (*geom*) (*GB*) four-sided figure having two sides parallel.

trap·ezoid /`træpəzɔɪd/ *n* [C] (*geom*) (*GB*) four-sided figure having no sides parallel.

trap·pings /`træpɪŋz/ *n pl* (*fig*) ornaments or decorations, esp as a sign of public office: *He had all the ~ of high office but very little power.*

trapse (*US* = **traipse**) /treɪps/ *vi* (*informal*) walk wearily: ~ *round the shops.*

trash /træʃ/ *n* [U] **1** worthless material or writing. **2** (*US*) rubbish; refuse. **3** worthless people.

trashy *adj* (*informal*) worthless: ~*y novels.*

trauma /`trɔmə *US*: `traʊmə/ *n* (*pl* ~s or -mata /-mətə/) **1** diseased condition of the body produced by a wound or injury. **2** emotional shock.

trau·matic /trɔ`mætɪk *US*: traʊ-/ *adj* (a) of or for (the treatment of) a wound or injury. (b) (of an experience) distressing and unforgettable.

travel /`trævəl/ *vi,vt* (-ll-; *US* -l-) **1** make (esp long) journeys: ~ *round the world;* ~ (*for*) *thousands of miles;* ~ (*over*) *the whole world.* **2** go from place to place as a salesman: *He ~s in cotton goods.* **3** move; go: *Light ~s faster than sound.* **4** pass from point to point: *Her mind ~led over recent events.* □ *n* **1** [U] travelling: *He is fond of ~.* **2** (*pl*) journeys, esp abroad: *write a book about one's ~s.*

`travel agent, person who makes arrangements for travel, by selling tickets, reserving accommodation, etc. Hence, `travel-agency/-bureau *n* [C]

trav·el·led, (*US* = **trav·eled**) *adj* **1** having made many long journeys: *a ~led man.* **2** used by people who travel: *a much ~led part of the country.*

trav·el·ler, (*US* = **trav·eler**) /`trævlə(r)/, (a) person on a journey. (b) = commercial traveller.

`traveller's cheque (*US* = `traveler's check), one issued by a bank or tourist agency for the convenience of travellers.

trav·elogue (also **-log**) /`trævəlɒg *US*: -lɔg/ *n* [C] film or lecture describing travels.

tra·verse /`trævɜs/ *vt* (*formal*) travel across; pass over: *Searchlights ~d the sky.* □ *n* [C] **1** (mountaineering) sideways movement across the face of a steep slope of ice,

etc. **2** change of direction in a trench to prevent the enemy from firing along it.

trav·esty /`trævəstɪ/ *n* [C] (*pl* -ies) imitation or description of something that is, often on purpose, unlike and inferior to the real thing: *His trial was a ~ of justice.* □ *vt* (*pt,pp* -ied) make or be a travesty of.

trawl /trɔl/ *vi,vt* fish (with a large net).

trawl·er, boat, fisherman, that trawls.

tray /treɪ/ *n* [C] flat piece of wood, metal, etc with raised edges, for carrying light articles.

treach·er·ous /`tretʃərəs/ *adj* **1** false or disloyal (to a friend, cause, etc). **2** not to be relied upon: ~ *weather.*

treach·er·ous·ly *adv*

treach·ery /`tretʃərɪ/ *n* (*pl* -ies) [U] being treacherous; (*pl*) treacherous acts.

treacle /`trikəl/ *n* [U] thick, sticky, dark liquid produced while sugar is being refined.

treacly /`trikəlɪ/ *adj*

tread /tred/ *vi,vt* (*pt* trod /trod/, *pp* trodden /`trodən/) **1** walk, put the foot or feet down (on): *Don't ~ on the flowers.* **tread on sb's toes,** (*fig*) offend him. **2** stamp or crush; push (down, etc) with the feet: ~ *out a fire in the grass;* ~ *grapes,* when making wine. **3** make by walking: *The cattle had trodden a path to the pond.* **4** walk along: ~ *a dangerous path,* (*fig*) follow a risky course of action. **tread water,** keep oneself afloat in deep water by moving the feet up and down (as if working the pedals of a bicycle). □ *n* [C] **1** way or sound of walking: *with a heavy/loud ~.* **2** part of a step or stair on which the foot is placed. **3** grooved part of a tyre which touches the ground.

treadle /`tredəl/ *n* [C] pedal or lever that drives a machine, e g a lathe or sewing-machine, worked by pressure of the foot or feet. □ *vi* work a treadle.

trea·son /`trizən/ *n* [U] betrayal of one's country or ruler; disloyalty.

trea·son·able /-əbəl/ *adj*

trea·son·ably /-əblɪ/ *adv*

treas·ure /`treʒə(r)/ *n* **1** [C,U] (store of) gold and silver, jewels, etc; wealth: *The pirates buried their ~.* **2** highly valued object or person: *The National Gallery has many priceless `art ~s. She says her new secretary is a perfect ~.* □ *vt* **1** store for future use: ~ *memories of one's youth.* **2** value highly: *He ~s the watch she gave him.*

`treasure-house, building where treasure is stored.

`treasure-trove, treasure found hidden in the earth and of unknown ownership.

treas·urer /`treʒərə(r)/ *n* [C] person in charge of money, etc belonging to a club or society.

treas·ury /`treʒərɪ/ *n* (*pl* -ies) **1 the T~,** (in *GB*) department of State controlling public revenue. **2** [C] (place for the) funds of a society, organization, etc: *The ~ of our tennis club is almost empty.* **3** [C] person, book,

705

etc looked on as containing valuable information or as a valued source: *The book is a ~ of information.*

treat /triːt/ *vt, vi* **1** act or behave towards: *He ~s his wife badly.* **2** consider: *We had better ~ it as a joke,* instead of taking it seriously. **3** discuss; deal with: *The lecturer ~ed his subject thoroughly.* **4** give medical or surgical care to: *Which doctors are ~ing her for her illness?* **5** put (a substance) through a process (in manufacture, etc): *~ wood with creosote.* **6** supply (food, drink, entertainment, etc) at one's own expense (to): *I shall ~ myself/you to a good weekend holiday.* □ *n* **1** [C] something that gives pleasure, esp not often enjoyed or unexpected: *It's a great ~ for her to go to the cinema.* **2** act of treating(6): *This is to be my ~,* I'm going to pay.

treat·ise /ˈtriːtɪz US: -tɪs/ *n* [C] book, etc that deals systematically with one subject.

treat·ment /ˈtriːtmənt/ *n* [C,U] (particular way of) treating a person or thing; what is done to obtain a desired result: *Is the ~ of political prisoners worse than it used to be? They are trying a new ~ for cancer.*

treaty /ˈtriːtɪ/ *n* (*pl* -ies) **1** [C] (*formal*) agreement made and signed between nations: *a `peace ~.* **2** [U] agreement or negotiation between persons: *sell a house by private ~.*

treble[1] /ˈtrebəl/ *adj, n* [C] three times as much or as many (as): *He earns ~ my salary.* □ *vt, vi* make or become treble: *He has ~d his earnings/His earnings have ~d during the last few years.*

'**treble `chance,** method of gambling on football chance, by predicting all the drawn games (these having higher points value), and then wins for away and home matches (these having less value).

treble[2] /ˈtrebəl/ *n* [C] (boy's voice with, instrument that takes, the) highest part in a piece of music.

tree /triː/ *n* [C] **1** plant with a single self-supporting trunk of wood with (usually) no branches for some distance above the ground: *cut down ~s for timber.* **2** = family tree. **3** piece of wood for a special purpose: *a `shoe-~,* for keeping a shoe in shape while not being worn.
tree·less *adj* without trees.

tre·foil /ˈtriːfɔɪl/ *n* [C] **1** kinds of three-leaved plant, e g clover. **2** similar ornament or design.

trek /trek/ *vi* (-kk-) make a long journey, by ox-wagon, pony or on foot. □ *n* [C] journey of this kind; any long, hard journey. ⇨ safari.

trel·lis /ˈtrelɪs/ *n* [C] light upright structure of strips of wood, etc esp as used for supporting climbing plants. □ *vt* furnish with, support on, a trellis.

tremble /ˈtrembəl/ *vi* **1** shake involuntarily (as from fear, anger, cold, physical weakness, etc): *His voice ~d with anger. We*

were *trembling with cold/excitement.* **2** shake: *The bridge ~d as the heavy lorry crossed it.* **3** be in a state of anxiety: *I ~ to think what has happened to him,* am deeply worried. □ *n* [C] uncontrollable shaking: *There was a ~ in his voice.*

tre·men·dous /trəˈmendəs/ *adj* **1** very great; enormous; powerful: *a ~ explosion; travelling at a ~ speed.* **2** (*informal*) extraordinary: *He's a ~ eater/talker.* **3** (*informal*) first rate: *a ~ concert/performance/meal.*
tre·men·dously *adv* (esp *informal*) extremely: *~ly grateful.*

tremor /ˈtremə(r)/ *n* [C] shaking or trembling: *`earth ~s,* as during an earthquake; *a ~ of fear.*

trench /trentʃ/ *n* [C] ditch dug in the ground, e g for the draining of water, for a latrine, as a protection for soldiers against enemy fire. □ *vt, vi* surround, strengthen, with a trench.

trend /trend/ *n* [C] general direction; tendency: *The ~ of the coastline is to the south. The ~ of prices is still upwards.* **set the trend,** start a style, etc which others follow. Hence, `**trend-setter** *n* [C], `**trend-setting** *n* [C,U]. □ *vi* have a certain trend: *The road ~s towards the west.*

trendy *adj* (-ier, -iest) showing, following, the latest fashion, etc.

trepi·da·tion /ˌtrepɪˈdeɪʃən/ *n* [U] (*formal*) alarm: *in fear and ~.*

tres·pass /ˈtrespəs/ *vt* **1** go on to privately owned land without right or permission: *~ on someone's (private) property.* **2** make too much use of: *~ on my time/hospitality/privacy.* □ *n* [U] trespassing(1); [C] instance of this.
tres·pas·ser, person who trespasses(1): *T~ers will be prosecuted.*

tress /tres/ *n* [C] (*poetic* or *literary*) **1** (*pl*) hair (esp of a woman's or girl's head). **2** plait or braid of hair.

trestle /ˈtresəl/ *n* [C] horizontal beam of wood with two legs at each end, used in pairs to support planks, a table top, a workman's bench, etc.
'**trestle-`table,** one made by laying planks on trestles.

tri- /traɪ-/ *prefix* three: *triangle.*

trial /ˈtraɪəl/ *n* **1** [U] testing, trying, proving; [C] instance of this: *give a new typist a ~,* give her a chance to show her skill. **on trial,** (a) for the purpose of testing: *Take the machine on ~ and then, if you like it, buy it.* (b) when tested: *The new clerk was found on ~ to be incompetent.* **trial and error,** method of solving a problem by making tests until there are no more errors. **2** (as an *adjective*) for the purpose of testing: *a ~ flight,* e g of a new aircraft. **3** [C,U] examination in a law court before a judge (or judge and jury): *The ~ lasted a week.* **be/ go on trial (for sth),** be tried in a court of law (for an offence). **bring sb to trial; put sb on trial,** cause him to be tried in a court of law. **stand (one's) trial,** be tried. **4** [C] troublesome or annoying person or thing, esp thought of as a test of one's patience: *Life is full of little ~s.*

tri-angle /ˈtraɪæŋgəl/ n [C] **1** plane figure with three straight sides. **2** group of three. **the eternal triangle,** the situation existing when two persons are in love with the same person of the opposite sex.

tri-angu-lar /traɪˈæŋgjʊlə(r)/ adj **(a)** in the shape of a triangle. **(b)** in which there are three persons, etc: *a triangular contest in an election,* with three candidates.

tri-bal /ˈtraɪbəl/ adj of a tribe or tribes: *~ dances.*
tri-bal-ism /-ɪzm/ n [U]

tribe /traɪb/ n [C] racial group, esp one united by language and customs, living as a community under one or more chiefs: *the Indian ~s of America.*
'tribes-man, member of a tribe.

tribu-la-tion /ˌtrɪbjʊˈleɪʃən/ n [C,U] (formal) (cause of) trouble, grief: *trials and ~s.*

tri-bu-nal /traɪˈbjuːnəl/ n [C] place of judgement; board of officials or judges appointed for special duty, e g to hear appeals against high rents.

tri-bune /ˈtrɪbjuːn/ n [C] **1** official chosen by the common people of ancient Rome to protect their interests. **2** (later use) popular leader.

tribu-tary /ˈtrɪbjʊtəri US: -teri/ adj (of a river) flowing into another. □ n [C] (pl -ies) (esp) tributary river.

trib-ute /ˈtrɪbjuːt/ n [C,U] **1** (regular) payment which one government or ruler exacts from another: *Many conquered nations had to pay ~ to the rulers of ancient Rome.* **2** something done, said or given to show respect or admiration: *The actress received numerous floral ~s,* bunches of flowers.

trice /traɪs/ n **in a trice,** instantly.

trick /trɪk/ n [C] **1** something done in order to deceive or done to make a person appear ridiculous: *He got the money from me by a ~.* **the tricks of the trade,** ways of attracting customers, gaining advantages over rivals, etc. **2** practical joke: *The children are always up to amusing ~s.* **play a trick on sb,** ⇨ play²(3). **3** feat of skill with the hands, etc: *conjuring ~s. Are you clever at card ~s? do the trick, (sl)* make it possible to get something done, finished: *One more turn of the screwdriver should do the ~,* fasten the screw securely. **4** strange or characteristic habit, mannerism, etc: *He has a ~ of pulling his left ear when he is thinking out a problem.* **5** (cards played in) one round of bridge, etc): *take/win/lose a ~.* □ vt deceive: *He ~ed the poor girl out of her money/~ed her into marrying him by pretending that he was rich.*
trick-ery /-əri/, deception; cheating.

tricky adj (-ier, -iest) **(a)** (of persons and their actions) deceptive: *a ~y politician.* **(b)** (of work, etc) having hidden or unexpected difficulties: *a ~y problem/job.*

trickle /ˈtrɪkəl/ vi,vt (cause to) flow in drops or in a thin stream: *The tears ~d down her cheeks.* □ n [C] weak or thin flow: *~ of blood.*

tri-cycle /ˈtraɪsɪkəl/ n [C] three-wheeled cycle.

tried /traɪd/ ⇨ try¹.

tri-en-nial /traɪˈenɪəl/ n [C], adj (something) lasting for, happening or done every, three years.

trier /ˈtraɪə(r)/ n ⇨ try¹.

trifle /ˈtraɪfəl/ n **1** [C] thing, event, etc of little value or importance: *It's silly to quarrel over ~s.* **2** [C] small amount of money: *It cost me only a trifle.* **3 a trifle,** adv a little: *This dress is a ~ too short.* **4** [C,U] sweet dish made of cream, white of eggs, cake, jam, etc: *make a ~; eat too much ~.* □ vi,vt behave lightly or insincerely towards: *It's wrong to ~ with the girl's affections,* make her think that you love her when you don't.
trif-ling /ˈtraɪflɪŋ/ adj unimportant: *a trifling error.*

trig-ger /ˈtrɪgə(r)/ n [C] lever for releasing a spring, esp of a gun, rifle. □ vt **trigger sth off,** be the immediate cause of (something serious or violent): *Who/What ~ed off the rebellion?*

trig-on-om-etry /ˌtrɪgəˈnɒmətri/ n [U] branch of mathematics that deals with the relations between the sides and angles of triangles.

tri-lat-eral /ˌtraɪˈlætərəl/ adj having three sides or parts: *a ~ treaty.*

trilby /ˈtrɪlbi/ n [C] (pl -ies) soft felt hat with a narrow brim and a dent in the top.

trill /trɪl/ n [C] **1** shaky or vibrating sound made by the voice or as in bird song. **2** (music) quick alternation of two notes a tone or a semitone apart. **3** vibrating speech sound (e g Spanish 'r'). □ vi,vt sing or play (a musical note) with a trill.

tril-lion /ˈtrɪlɪən/ n [C], adj **1** (GB) million million million. **2** (US, Fr) million million.

tril-ogy /ˈtrɪlədʒi/ n [C] (pl -ies) group of three plays, novels, operas, etc having a common subject.

trim /trɪm/ adj (-mer, -mest) in good order; neat and tidy: *a ~ little garden.* □ n [U] trim state; readiness; fitness: *Everything was in good/proper ~.* □ vt,vi (-mm-) **1** make trim, esp by taking or cutting away uneven, irregular or unwanted parts: *~ one's beard.* **2** decorate or ornament (a dress, etc): *a hat ~med with fur.* **3** make (a boat, ship, aircraft) evenly balanced by arranging the position of the cargo, passengers, etc; set (the sails) to suit the wind.
trim-ming n [C] (usually pl) something used for trimming(2): *lace ~mings.*

tri-nitro-tolu-ene /ˌtraɪˈnaɪtrəʊˈtɒljuːiːn/ n

[U] (usually **T N T**) powerful explosive.

trin·ity /'trɪnətɪ/ n [C] (pl -ies) group of three. **the T~,** (in Christian teaching) union of three persons, Father, Son and Holy Ghost, one God.

trin·ket /'trɪŋkɪt/ n [C] ornament or jewel of small value.

trio /'triːəʊ/ n [C] (pl ~s) **1** group of three. **2** (musical composition for a) group of three singers or players.

trip /trɪp/ vi,vt (-pp-) **1** *trip over sth,* catch one's foot, etc in an obstacle and fall: *He ~ped over the root of a tree. trip (sb) up,* (a) (cause to) fall or make a false step: *He ~ped up and nearly fell.* (b) (fig) cause to make an error. **2** (poetic) walk, run or dance with quick, light steps: *She came ~ping down the garden path.* □ n [C] **1** journey, esp for pleasure: *a day ~ to the seaside.* **2** fall. **3** experience resulting from taking a hallucinatory drug.

trip·per, person making a (short) journey for pleasure: *weekend ~pers.*

tri·par·tite /'traɪ'paːtaɪt/ adj **1** (of an agreement) in which three parties have a share. **2** having three parts.

tripe /traɪp/ n [U] **1** part of the wall of the stomach of an ox or cow used as food: *a dish of stewed ~ and onions.* **2** (sl) useless talk, writing, ideas, etc: *Stop talking ~!*

triple /'trɪpəl/ adj made up of three (parts or parties): *the ~ crown,* the Pope's tiara. □ vt,vi make, become, be, three times as much or many.

trip·let /'trɪplət/ n **1** (pl) three children born at one birth: *One of the ~s is ill.* **2** [C] set of three.

trip·li·cate /'trɪplɪkət/ adj of which three copies are made. □ n [C] one of three like things, esp documents: *drawn up in ~,* one original and two copies. □ vt /'trɪplɪkeɪt/ make in triplicate.

tri·pod /'traɪpɒd/ n [C] three-legged support, e g for a camera.

trip·per /'trɪpə(r)/ n ▷ trip.

trite /traɪt/ adj (of remarks, ideas, opinions) ordinary (and so dull).

trite·ly adv

trite·ness n [U]

tri·umph /'traɪʌmf/ n [C,U] (joy or satisfaction at a) success or victory: *return home in ~; shouts of ~.* □ vi win a victory (over); show joy because of success: *~ over a defeated enemy.*

tri·um·phal /traɪ'ʌmfəl/ adj of, for, expressing, triumph: *a ~al arch,* one built in memory of a victory.

tri·um·phant /traɪ'ʌmfənt/ adj (celebrating at) having triumphed.

tri·um·phant·ly adv

triv·ial /'trɪvɪəl/ adj **1** of small value or importance: *a ~ offence.* **2** ordinary (and so dull): *a ~ speech.* **3** (of a person) superficial: *Don't marry a ~ young man.*

triv·ially /-ɪəlɪ/ adv

triv·ial·ity /'trɪvɪ'ælətɪ/ n [U] state of being trivial; [C] (pl -ies) trivial idea, event, etc: *talk/write ~ities.*

trod, trod·den /trɒd, 'trɒdən/ ▷ tread.

troll /trəʊl/ n [C] (in Scandinavian mythology) supernatural giant, or, in later tales, a mischievous but friendly dwarf.

trol·ley /'trɒlɪ/ n [C] (pl ~s) **1** two- or four-wheeled handcart. **2** small, low truck running on rails, e g one used by workers on a railway. **3** small table on wheels, used for serving food.

trol·lop /'trɒləp/ n [C] prostitute.

trom·bone /trɒm'bəʊn/ n [C] large brass musical instrument with a sliding tube.

trom·bon·ist /trɒm'bəʊnɪst/, trombone player.

troop /truːp/ n [C] **1** company of persons or animals, esp when moving: *a ~ of Boy Scouts.* **2** (pl) soldiers. **3** unit of cavalry, armoured vehicles or artillery (under the command of a lieutenant). □ vi,vt (used with a pl subject) come or go together in a group: *children ~ing out of school.*

'troop-carrier, ship or large aircraft for transporting troops.

'troop-ship, ship for transporting troops.

trooper, soldier in a cavalry or armoured regiment. *swear like a trooper,* swear a great deal.

trophy /'trəʊfɪ/ n [C] (pl -ies) **1** something kept in memory of a victory or success (e g in hunting, sport, etc). **2** prize, e g for winning a tournament: *'tennis trophies.*

tropic /'trɒpɪk/ n **1** [C] line of latitude 23°27' north (T~ *of Cancer*) or south (T~ *of Capricorn*) of the equator. **2 the ~s,** the parts of the world between these two latitudes.

tropi·cal /-kəl/ adj of, or as of, the tropics: *a ~al climate.*

tropi·cally /-klɪ/ adv

trot /trɒt/ vi,vt (-tt-) **1** (of horses, etc) go at a pace faster than a walk but not so fast as a gallop. **2** move with short steps. **3** *trot sth out,* recite without feeling or sincerity: *~ out an excuse.* **4** cause to: *~ a person off his legs,* take him walking, e g sight-seeing, until he is exhausted. □ n (sing only) **1** trotting pace: *go at a steady ~.* **on the trot,** (sl) one after the other: *five whiskies on the ~.* **2** period of trotting: *go for a ~.*

trot·ter, (a) horse bred and trained to trot. (b) (usually pl) pig's or sheep's foot eaten as food.

trouble /'trʌbəl/ vt,vi **1** cause worry, discomfort, anxiety or inconvenience to: *be ~d by bad news; ~d with a nasty cough.* **2** ask a person to do something inconvenient: *May I ~ you for a match?* **3** (esp in the negative or in a question) inconvenience oneself: *Don't ~ to meet me at the station.* **4** (esp pp) disturb: *~d looks.* □ n **1** [C,U] worry; unhappiness; difficulty: *She's always making ~ for her friends. He has been through much ~/*

has had many ~s. *The ~ is that...*, The difficulty is that... *in trouble*, suffering, or likely to suffer, anxiety, punishment etc, e g because one has done wrong. *ask/look for* **trouble**, (*informal*) behave in such a way that trouble is likely: *It's asking for ~ to associate with criminals*. *get into trouble*, do something deserving punishment, etc. *get sb into trouble*, cause a person to be in trouble. *get a girl into trouble*, (*informal*) make her pregnant. **2** [C] nuisance: *I don't want to be any ~ to you.* **3** [U] (extra) work; inconvenience: *Did the work give you much ~? Thank you for all the ~ you've taken to help my son.* **4** [C,U] political or social unrest: *'Labour ~(s)* (e g strikes) *cost the country enormous sums last year.* **5** [C,U] illness: `liver ~.

`trouble-maker, person who causes trouble (e g in industry).

`trouble-some /-səm/ *adj* causing trouble: *a ~some child/headache/problem.*

trough /trɒf *US:* trɔːf/ *n* [C] **1** long open box for animals to feed or drink from. **2** long open box in which a baker kneads dough for bread. **3** region of lower atmospheric pressure between two regions of higher pressure.

trounce /traʊns/ *vt* (*dated*) defeat: *Our team was ~d on Saturday.*

troupe /truːp/ *n* [C] company, esp of actors or of members of a circus.

trouper, member of a theatrical troupe: *He's a good ~r*, a loyal and uncomplaining colleague.

trousers /traʊzəz/ *n pl* **1** (often *a pair of ~s*) two-legged outer garment reaching from the waist to the ankles. **2** (*sing*) (as an *adjective*) of or for trousers: `trouser pockets.

trous-seau /truːsəʊ/ *n* [C] (*pl* ~s) outfit of clothing, etc, for a bride.

trout /traʊt/ *n* [C] (*pl* unchanged) freshwater fish valued as food and for the sport of catching it.

trowel /traʊəl/ *n* [C] **1** flat-bladed tool for spreading cement, etc. **2** tool with a curved blade for lifting plants, etc.

troy /trɔɪ/ *n* [U] British system of weights, used for gold and silver, in which one pound = 12 ounces.

tru·ant /truːənt/ *n* [C] child who stays away from school without permission. *play truant*, be a truant.

tru·ancy /truːənsɪ/ *n* [C,U] (*pl* -ies) (instance of) playing truant.

truce /truːs/ *n* [C] (agreement for the) stopping of fighting for a time.

truck[1] /trʌk/ *n* **1** (*GB*) open railway wagon for heavy goods. **2** (esp *US*) lorry.

trudge /trʌdʒ/ *vi* walk wearily or heavily: *trudging through the deep snow.* □ *n* [C] long, tiring walk.

true /truː/ *adj* (-r, -st) **1** according to, in agreement with, fact: *Is the news ~? come true*, (of a hope, dream) really happen,

become fact. **2** loyal, faithful: *be ~ to one's word/promise*, do what one has promised to do. **3** in accordance with reason; genuine: *T~ friendship should last for ever.* **4** *true to type*, being, behaving, etc as expected. **5** accurately fitted or placed: *Is the wheel ~?* **6** exact; accurate: *a ~ copy of a document.* □ *n* (only in) *out of true*, not in its exact or accurate position: *The door is out of ~.* □ *adv* (used with certain *verbs*) truly: *aim ~; tell me ~.*

`true-`blue *n* [C], *adj* (person who is) firmly loyal.

`true-`born *adj* legitimate.

`true-`love, (expression of love to a) boyfriend, girlfriend.

tru·ism /truːɪzm/ *n* [C] statement that is obviously true and need not have been made: *It's a ~ to say that you are alive.*

truly /truːlɪ/ *adv* **1** truthfully: *speak ~.* **2** sincerely: *feel ~ grateful. yours truly*, (used at the close of a letter, before the signature). **3** genuinely; certainly: *a ~ brave action.*

trump /trʌmp/ *n* [C] (in card-games such as whist, bridge) each card of a suit that has been declared as having higher value than the other three suits: *Hearts are ~s. turn up trumps*, (*informal*) **(a)** have a better result than was expected. **(b)** have a stroke of good luck. □ *vt,vi* **1** play a trump(1) on: *~ the ace of clubs.* **2** invent (an excuse, a lie, etc) in order to deceive: *He was arrested on a ~ed-up charge.*

trum·peter, trumpet player.

trum·pet /trʌmpɪt/ *n* **1** brass musical instrument played by blowing into it. **2** sound (as) of a trumpet: *the ~ of a elephant.* **3** something like a trumpet in shape (e g a flower). □ *vt,vi* (esp of an elephant) make loud sounds.

trun·cheon /trʌntʃən/ *n* [C] short thick stick (as used by the police).

trunk /trʌŋk/ *n* [C] **1** main stem of a tree (contrasted with the branches). **2** body (not the head, arms or legs). **3** main part of any structure. **4** large box with a hinged lid, for clothes, etc while travelling. **5** long nose of an elephant. **6** (*pl*) man's garment covering the lower part of the trunk(2), worn for swimming. **7** (*US*) = boot(2).

`trunk call, telephone call to a distant place, with charges according to distance.

`trunk line, **(a)** main line of a railway. **(b)** long-distance telephone line.

`trunk road, main road.

truss /trʌs/ *n* [C] **1** (*GB*) bundle (of hay, straw). **2** framework supporting a roof, bridge, etc. **3** padded belt worn by a person suffering from hernia. □ *vt* **1** tie or fasten up: *~ up a chicken*, pin the wings to the body before boiling or roasting it. **2** support (a roof, bridge, etc) with a truss(2).

trust[1] /trʌst/ *n* **1** [U] confidence, strong belief, in the goodness, strength, reliability of a person or thing: *A child usually has perfect ~ in its mother.* **on trust, (a)** without proof: *You'll have to take my statement on ~.* **(b)** on credit. **2** [U] responsibility: *a position of great ~.* **3** [C] (*legal*) property held and managed by one or more persons (*trustees*) for the benefit of another or others; [U] the legal relation between the trustee(s) and the property: *By his will he created ~s for his children.* **4** [C] association of business firms for e g reducing competition, maintenance of prices.

trust·ful /-fəl/, **trust·ing** *adj* ready to have trust in others; not suspicious.

trust·fully /-fəlɪ/, **trust·ing·ly** *adv*

trust·worthy /ˈtrʌstwɜːðɪ/ *adj* dependable.

trust² /trʌst/ *vt,vi* **1** believe in the honesty and reliability of: *He's not the sort of man to be ~ed/not a man I would ~.* **2** have confidence in: *~ in God.* **3** allow (a person) to do or have something, go somewhere, etc knowing that he will act sensibly, etc: *Do you ~ your young daughters to go to pop concerts with any sort of men?* **4** allow credit to a customer: *I wonder whether the newsagent will ~ me.*

trustee /trʌˈstiː/ *n* [C] person who has charge of property in trust(3) or of the business affairs of an institution.

trus·tee·ship /-ʃɪp/, position of a trustee.

truth /truːθ/ *n* (*pl* ~s /truːðz/) **1** [U] quality or state of being true: *There's no ~/not a word of ~ in what he says.* **2** [U] that which is true: *tell the ~.* **to tell the truth...**, (formula used when making a confession): *To tell the ~, I forgot all about it.* **3** [C] fact, belief, etc accepted as true: *scientific ~s.*

truth·ful /-fəl/ *adj* **(a)** (of persons) in the habit of telling the truth. **(b)** (of statements) true.

truth·fully /-fəlɪ/ *adv*

truth·ful·ness *n* [U]

try¹ /traɪ/ *vi,vt* (*pt,pp* tried) **1** make an attempt: *I don't think I can do it, but I'll ~. I've tried and tried* (= tried a great deal) *but its no use. He's ~ing his hardest,* making great efforts. *T~ to/T~ and behave better.* **2** make an attempt to get or win (esp a position): *~ for a job overseas.* **3** use or do something, as an experiment or test, to see whether it is satisfactory: *Have you tried sleeping on your back as a cure for snoring? ~ the garden if nobody hears you.* **try sth on, (a)** put on (clothes, etc) to see whether it fits, looks well, etc. **(b)** (*informal*) make a bold or impudent attempt to discover whether something will be tolerated: *It's no use your ~ing it on with me, I shall stand no nonsense from you.* **try sth out,** use it, experiment with it, in order to test it: *The idea seems good but it needs to be tried out.* Hence, **try-out** *n* [C] test of ability, qualification, etc, e g of an athlete. **try one's hand at sth,** ⇨ hand¹ (5). **4** inquire into (a case) in a court of law: *He was tried and found*

guilty of murder. **5** cause to be tired, exhausted, out of patience, etc: *His courage was severely tried.*

try·ing *adj* (⇨ **5** above) causing tiredness, exhaustion, impatience, etc: *have a ~ing day.*

try² /traɪ/ *n* [C] (*pl* tries) **1** attempt: *He had three tries and failed each time.* **2** (*Rugby*) touching down the ball behind the opponents' goal-line.

tsetse /ˈsetsɪ/ *n* [C] (also `~-fly) blood-sucking fly (in tropical Africa) carrying and transmitting (often fatal) disease in cattle, horses, etc.

T-shirt /ˈtiː ʃɜːt/ *n* ⇨ T, t.

T-square /ˈtiː skweə(r)/ *n* ⇨ T, t.

tub /tʌb/ *n* [C] **1** large open vessel, used for washing clothes, holding liquids, growing plants in, etc. **2** = tubful. **3** (*informal*) bath-tub.

`tub·ful /-fʊl/, as much as a tub holds.

tuba /ˈtjuːbə *US:* ˈtuː-/ *n* [C] (*pl* ~s) large musical instrument of brass playing deep notes.

tubby /ˈtʌbɪ/ *adj* (-ier, -iest) fat and round: *a ~ little man.*

tube /tjuːb *US:* tuːb/ *n* [C] **1** long hollow cylinder of metal, glass or rubber, esp for holding or carrying liquids, etc: *the `inner ~ of a bicycle/car tyre,* of rubber, filled with air at pressure. **2** soft metal container with a screw-cap, used for pastes, paints, etc: *a ~ of toothpaste.* **3** (in London) underground railway: *travel to the office by ~ every morning.* **4** hollow cylindrical organ in the body: *the bronchial ~s.*

tub·ing *n* [U] material in the form of a tube: *copper tubing.*

tube·less *adj* having no inner tube: *~less tyres.*

tu·ber /ˈtjuːbə(r) *US:* ˈtuː-/ *n* [C] enlarged part of an underground stem, e g a potato.

tu·ber·cu·lar /tjuːˈbɜːkjʊlə(r) *US:* tuː-/ *adj* of, affected by, tuberculosis.

tu·ber·cu·lo·sis /tjuːˌbɜːkjəˈləʊsɪs *US:* tuː-/ *n* [U] (common abbr **TB**) disease affecting various parts of the body's tissues, esp the lungs.

tu·bu·lar /ˈtjuːbjʊlə(r) *US:* ˈtuː-/ *adj* having, consisting of, tubes or tubing: *~ furniture,* with parts made of metal tubing.

tuck /tʌk/ *n* **1** [C] flat, stitched fold of material in cloth, for shortening or for ornament. **2** [U] (*GB sl*) food, esp the cakes, pastry, etc that children enjoy. □ *vt,vi* **1** draw together into a small space; put or push into a desired or convenient position: *Your shirt's hanging out; ~ it in to your trousers. He sat with his legs ~ed up under him. The map is ~ed away in a pocket at the end of the book. She ~ed him up in bed,* pulled the bed-clothes up round him. **2 tuck in,** (*dated*) eat a lot quickly.

`tuck-shop, shop (esp at a school) where tuck is sold.

-tude /tjuːd/ *US:* -tud/ *suffix* (used to form a *noun*) condition: *magnitude.*

Tues·day /ˈtjuːzdɪ *US:* ˈtuː-/ *n* third day of the week, next after Monday.

tuft /tʌft/ *n* [C] bunch of feathers, hair, grass, etc growing or held together at the base.

tufted *adj* having, growing in, tufts.

tug /tʌg/ *vt,vi* (-gg-) pull hard (*at*): *We ~ged so hard that the rope broke.* □ *n* [C] **1** sudden hard pull: *I felt a ~ at my sleeve.* **2** (also `~-boat`), small powerful boat for towing ships, etc.

'tug of 'war, contest in which two teams pull against each other on a rope.

tu·ition /tjuˈɪʃən *US:* tuː-/ *n* [U] (fee for) teaching: *have private ~ in mathematics.*

tu·lip /ˈtjuːlɪp *US:* ˈtuː-/ *n* [C] bulb plant with a large bell-shaped flower on a tall stem.

tumble /ˈtʌmbəl/ *vi,vt* **1** fall, esp quickly: *tumbling down the stairs/off a bicycle.* **2** move up and down, to and fro, in a restless or disorderly way: *The puppies were tumbling about on the floor.* **3** be in a weak state (as if ready to fall): *The old barn is tumbling down.* **4** cause to fall: *The accident ~d us all out of the bus.* **5 tumble to sth,** (*informal*) realize (an idea, etc): *At last he ~d to what I was hinting at.* □ *n* [C] **1** fall: *have a nasty ~.* **2** confused state: *Things were all in a ~.*

tum·bler /ˈtʌmblə(r)/ *n* [C] **1** drinking-glass without a handle or stem. **2** part of the mechanism of a lock which must be turned by a key before the lock will open.

tu·mes·cent /tjuˈmesənt *US:* tuː-/ *adj* (*formal*) swelling; swollen.

tummy /ˈtʌmɪ/ *n* [C] (*pl* -ies) (*informal*) (used by and to children) stomach; belly.

tu·mour (*US* = **tu·mor**) /ˈtjuːmə(r) *US:* ˈtuː-/ *n* [C] diseased growth in some part of the body.

tu·mult /ˈtjuːmʌlt *US:* ˈtuː-/ *n* [C,U] **1** great disturbance: *the ~ of battle.* **2** confused and excited state of mind: *be in a ~.*

tu·mul·tu·ous /tjuˈmʌltʃʊəs *US:* tuː-/ *adj* (*formal*) noisy and energetic: *a ~ welcome.*

tu·mul·tu·ous·ly *adv*

tuna /ˈtjuːnə *US:* ˈtuːnə/ *n* [C] (*pl* with or without *s*) large seafish used as food.

tun·dra /ˈtʌndrə/ *n* [C] (*pl ~s*) wide, treeless plain of the arctic regions (of Russia, Siberia).

tune /tjuːn *US:* tuːn/ *n* **1** [C] succession of notes forming a melody (of a song, etc). **2** [U] quality of having a strong melody: *music with very little ~ in it.* **3** [U] in/out of tune, at/not at the correct pitch: *sing/play in ~.* **4** [U] (*fig*) harmony: *be in/out of ~ with one's surroundings/companions.* **change one's tune,** change one's way of speaking, behaviour, etc (e g from insolence or respect). **to the tune of,** to the amount of: *He was fined* (e g for a motoring offence) *to the ~ of £30.* □ *vt,vi* **1** adjust the strings, etc (of a musical

instrument) to the right pitch: *~ a guitar.* **2** **tune in (to),** (a) adjust the controls of a radio to a particular frequency/station: *~ in to the BBC.* (b) (*fig*) be aware of what other people are saying, feeling, etc: *He's not very well ~d in to his surroundings.* **3** adjust or adapt the engine of a motor-vehicle so that it gives its best, or a special, performance.

tune·ful /-fəl/ *adj* having a pleasing tune.

tune·fully /-fəlɪ/ *adv*

'tuning-fork, small steel instrument like a fork which produces a musical note when struck.

tuner /ˈtjuːnə(r) *US:* ˈtuː-/ *n* **1** person who tunes musical instruments: *a piˈano-~.* **2** (part of) a radio, etc which receives the signals.

tu·nic /ˈtjuːnɪk *US:* ˈtuː-/ *n* [C] **1** close-fitting jacket as worn by policemen, soldiers, etc. **2** loose, pleated dress gathered at the waist with a belt.

tun·nel /ˈtʌnəl/ *n* [C] underground passage (esp through a hill or mountain, for a road, railway, etc). □ *vi,vt* (-ll-, *US* also -l-) dig a tunnel (through/into something).

tunny /ˈtʌnɪ/ *n* [C] (*pl* -ies or unchanged) = tuna.

tur·ban /ˈtɜːbən/ *n* **1** man's headdress made by winding a length of cloth round the head (as worn in some Asian countries). **2** similar woman's close-fitting hat.

tur·bine /ˈtɜːbaɪn/ *n* [C] engine or motor whose driving-wheel is turned by a current of water, steam or air.

tur·bu·lence /ˈtɜːbjʊləns/ *n* [C] state of being turbulent.

tur·bu·lent /ˈtɜːbjʊlənt/ *adj* violent; disorderly; uncontrolled: *~ waves/passions.*

tur·bu·lent·ly *adv*

turf /tɜːf/ *n* (*pl* turves) **1** [U] soil with grass growing in it. **2** [C] piece of turf. □ *vt* **1** cover or lay (a piece of land) with turf. **2** **turf sb or sth out,** (*GB sl*) throw out.

tur·key /ˈtɜːkɪ/ *n* [C] (*pl ~s*) large bird valued as food; [U] its flesh.

Tur·kish bath /ˈtɜːkɪʃ ˈbɑːθ/ *n* [C] bath of hot air or steam, followed by a shower and massage.

tur·moil /ˈtɜːmɔɪl/ *n* [C,U] (instance of) trouble, disturbance: *The town was in a ~ during the elections.*

turn[1] /tɜːn/ *n* [C] **1** act of turning; turning movement: *a few ~s of the handle.* **done to a turn,** cooked just enough, neither underdone nor overdone. **2** change of direction: *sudden ~s in the road.* **at every turn,** (*fig*) very frequently: *I've been coming across old friends at every ~ at the dance.* **3** change in condition: *The sick man/My affairs took a ~ for the better/worse.* **4** occasion or opportunity for doing something, esp in one's proper order among others: *It's your ~ to read now, John.* **in turn,** (of two persons) one after the other; (of more than two persons) in succession: *The boys were asked in*

A a

~ *to see the examiner*. **out of turn**, before or after the permitted time: *You mustn't speak out of (your)* ~. **take turns at sth**, do it in succession: *Mary and Helen took* ~s *at babysitting*. **5** action regarded as affecting a person: *do her a good* ~, *be helpful, etc*. **6** natural tendency: *a boy with a me`chanical* ~, *interested in, clever at, mechanical things*. **7** short period of activity: *I'll take a* ~ *at the wheel if you want a rest (from driving)*. **8** short performance on the stage.

turn² /tɜːn/ *vt, vi* (For special uses with *adverbial particles* and *prepositions*, ⇨ **5** below.) **1** (cause to) move round a point; (cause to) move so as to face in a different direction: *The earth* ~s *round the sun. He* ~ed *away from me. He* ~ed *to look at me. He* ~ed *(to the) left. When does the tide* ~, *begin to flow in/out?* **turn the corner**, ⇨ corner(1). **turn a deaf ear (to)**, ⇨ ear¹(1). **turn one's hand to sth,** (be able to) do (a task, etc): *He can* ~ *his hand to most jobs about the house*. **turn one's mind/ thoughts/attention to sth**, direct one's mind, etc to: *Please* ~ *your attention to something more important*. **2** (cause to) change in nature, quality, condition, etc: *Frost* ~s *water into ice. Caterpillars* ~ *into* (= become) *butterflies. His hair has* ~ed *grey*. **turn sb's head**, make him vain: *The excessive praise the young actor received* ~ed *his head*. **3** reach and pass: *He has* ~ed (= reach the age of) *fifty. It has just* ~ed *two, is just after two o'clock*. **4** shape (something) on a lathe, etc: ~ *a bowl on a potter's wheel*.

5 (special uses with *adverbial particles* and *prepositions*):

turn (sb) against sb, (cause to) become hostile to: *He tried to* ~ *the children against their mother*.

turn (sb) away, (cause to) turn in a different direction so as not to be facing; refuse to look at, welcome, help, admit (to a place): *She* ~ed *away in disgust. We had to* ~ *away hundreds of fans, eg from a stadium, because all seats were sold*.

turn (sb/sth) back, (cause to) return the way one has come: *It's getting dark—we'd better* ~ *back*.

turn (sth) down, (a) (cause to) fold down: ~ *down one's coat collar*. (b) reduce (the brilliance of a light) by turning a wheel or tap. **turn sb/sth down**, refuse to consider (an offer, a proposal, or the person who makes it): *He asked Jane to marry him but she* ~ed *him down*.

turn in, (*informal*) go to bed. **turn sb in,** (*informal*) surrender him to the police. **turn (sth) in,** (cause to) fold or slant inwards: *His toes* ~ *in*.

turn (sth) inside out, (cause to) become inside out: *The wind* ~ed *my old umbrella inside out*.

turn off, change direction; leave (one road)

for another: *Is this where we* ~ *off?* **turn sth off,** stop the flow of (liquid, gas, current) by turning a tap or other control: ~ *off the water/lights/radio/T V*. **turn (sb) off,** (*sl*) (cause sb to) lose interest, desire, etc: *He/ This music really* ~s *me off!*

turn sth on, start the flow of (liquid, gas, current) by turning a tap, etc: *T*~ *the lights/ radio on*. **turn (sb) on,** have, give to him, great pleasure or excitement: *What kind of music* ~s *you on? Some psychedelic drugs* ~ *you on very quickly, change your mental or emotional state*. **turn on sth,** depend on: *The success of the debate* ~s *on the Liberal vote*. **turn on sb,** attack: *The dog* ~ed *on me and bit me in the leg*.

turn out (well, etc), prove to be; be in the end: *Everything* ~ed *out well/satisfactory. As it* ~ed *out...,* As it happened in the end... **turn (sth) out,** (cause to) point outwards: *His toes* ~ *out*. **turn sth out,** (a) extinguish by turning a tap, etc: *Please* ~ *out the lights*. (b) empty (a drawer, one's pockets, a room, etc) when looking for something, etc: ~ *out all the drawers in one's desk*. **turn sb out (of/from sth),** expel by force, threats, etc: ~ *a tenant out* (= from his house) *for not paying the rent*. **turn sb/sth out,** produce: *Our new factory is* ~ing *out large quantities of goods. The school has* ~ed *out some first-rate athletes*. **turn (sb) out,** (cause people to) assemble for some event, or for duty: *Not many men* ~ed *out to watch the match*. Hence, `turn- out, (a)** persons who have turned out (assembled): *There was a good* ~*-out at the meeting*. (b) occasion when one turns out a drawer, etc. (c) equipment; clothes and accessories: *in a smart* ~*-out*.

turn (sb/sth) over, (cause to) fall over, upset; change the position of: *He* ~ed *over in bed*. **turn sth over in one's mind,** think about it (before making a decision). **turn sth/sb over (to sb),** give the control or conduct of it or him to: *I've* ~ed *over the management of my affairs to my brother. The thief was* ~ed *over to the police*. **turn sth over,** do business to the amount of: *Mr Smith/His business* ~s *over £500 a week*. Hence, `turn-over, (a)** amount of money made in business within a period of time or for a particular transaction: *a profit of £1 000 on a* ~*over of £10 000*. (b) rate of renewal: *There is a higher* ~*over of teachers in big cities*.

turn (sth/sb) round, (cause to) face another way, be in another direction: *T*~ *round and let me see your new hairstyle*.

turn `to, get busy: *The design staff* ~ed *to and produced a set of drawings in twenty-four hours*. **turn to sb,** go to: *The child* ~ed *to its mother for comfort*.

turn up, (a) make one's appearance; arrive: *He promised to come, but hasn't* ~ed *up yet*. (b) be found, esp by chance: *The book*

you've lost may ~ up one of these days. (c) (of an opportunity, etc) happen: *He's still waiting for something* (e g a job, a piece of good luck) *to ~ up.* **turn (sth) up.** (a) (cause to) slope upwards: *~* (= roll) *up one's shirt sleeves.* (b) expose; make visible: *He ~ed up some buried treasure on the beach.* **turn up one's nose at sth,** (fig) express a superior and critical attitude towards: *She ~ed up her nose at the suggestion.* **'turn-up,** (a) turned fold at the bottom of a trouser-leg. (b) surprising and unexpected event: *Fancy seeing you after all these years. What a ~-up for the book!* What a great surprise!
turn upon sb/sth, = turn on.

turn·coat /ˈtɜːnkəʊt/ n [C] person who deserts one group for another.

turn·stile /ˈtɜːnstaɪl/ n [C] revolving gate that allows one person through at a time.

turner /ˈtɜːnə(r)/ n [C] person who works a lathe.

turn·ing /ˈtɜːnɪŋ/ n [C] place where a road turns, esp where one road branches off from another: *Take the first ~ on/to the right.* **'turning-point,** (fig) point in place, time, development, etc which is critical: *reach a ~-point in history/in one's life.*

tur·nip /ˈtɜːnɪp/ n [C] (plant with a) large round root used as a vegetable and as food for cattle.

tur·quoise /ˈtɜːkwɔɪz/ n [C,U] (colour of a) greenish-blue precious stone.

tur·ret /ˈtʌrət/ n [C] 1 small tower, esp at a corner of a building or defensive wall. 2 [C] steel structure protecting gunners.

turtle /ˈtɜːtəl/ n [C] sea-animal with a soft body protected by a hard shell like a tortoise.

turves /ˈtɜːvz/ n pl ⇨ turf.

tusk /tʌsk/ n [C] long-pointed tooth, esp one coming out from the closed mouth, as in the elephant, walrus or wild boar.

tussle /ˈtʌsəl/ n [C], vi (have a) difficult struggle or fight (*with*).

tut /tʌt/, **tut-tut** /ˈtʌt ˈtʌt/ int used to express impatience.

tu·te·lage /ˈtjuːtəlɪdʒ *US:* ˈtuː-/ n [U] (*formal*) guardianship.

tu·tor /ˈtjuːtə(r) *US:* ˈtuː-/ n [C] 1 private teacher of a single pupil or a very small class. 2 (*GB*) university teacher who guides the general performance of a student. □ vt teach as a tutor.

tu·tor·ial /tjuːˈtɔːrɪəl *US:* tuː-/ adj of a tutor of his duties: *~ial classes.* □ n [C] teaching period for a small group of university students.

tux·edo /tʌkˈsiːdəʊ/ n [C] (pl ~s) (*US*) = dinner-jacket.

twaddle /ˈtwɒdəl/ n [U] foolish talk.

twang /twæŋ/ n [C] 1 sound of a tight string or wire being pulled and released: *the ~ of a guitar.* 2 harsh, nasal tone of voice: *speak with a ~.* □ vt,vi (cause to) make this kind of sound: *He was ~ing a banjo.*

'twas /twɒz *weak form:* twəz/ (*old use*) = it was.

tweak /twiːk/ vt pinch and twist: *~ a child's nose.* □ n [C] act of tweaking.

tweed /twiːd/ n 1 [U] (often as an *adjective*) thick, soft, woollen cloth of mixed colours: *a ~ coat.* 2 (pl) (suit of) clothes made of tweed: *dressed in Scottish ~s.*

tweet /twiːt/ n [C], vi (of a bird) = chirp.

tweez·ers /ˈtwiːzəz/ n pl (also *a pair of ~*) tiny pair of tongs for picking up or pulling out very small things, e g hairs from the eyebrows.

twelfth /twelfθ/ n [C], adj (abbr 12th) (of) the next after the 11 or one of 12 equal parts. **'twelfth-night,** eve of the festival of Epiphany, celebrated with festivities.

twelve /twelv/ n [C], adj (of) 12.

twen·ti·eth /ˈtwentɪəθ/ n [C], adj (abbr 20th) (of) the next after the 19 or one of 20 equal parts.

twenty /ˈtwentɪ/ n [C], adj (of) 20.

twice /twaɪs/ adv two times: *~ as much/as many. He's ~ the man he was,* healthier, stronger, more confident, more capable, etc. *think twice about doing sth,* hesitate, think carefully, before deciding to do it.

twiddle /ˈtwɪdəl/ vt,vi twist or turn idly: *~ one's thumbs; ~ a ring on one's finger.*

twig[1] /twɪg/ n [C] small shoot on or at the end of a branch (bush, plant).

twig[2] /twɪg/ vt,vi (-gg-) (*GB informal*) notice; understand: *I soon ~ged what he was up to,* saw the trick he was trying to play.

twi·light /ˈtwaɪlaɪt/ n [U] 1 faint light before sunrise or after sunset: *go for a walk in the ~.* 2 (fig) period about which little is known: *in the ~ of history.*

twill /twɪl/ n [U] strong cotton cloth.

twin /twɪn/ n 1 [C] either of two children or animals born together of the same mother: (as an *adjective*) *~ brothers.* 2 (as an *adjective*) completely like, closely associated with, another: *~ beds,* two identical single beds.
'twin-set, woman's jumper and long sleeved cardigan of the same colour and style.

twine /twaɪn/ n [U] thin string made by twisting two or more yarns together. □ vt,vi twist; wind: *vines that ~ round a tree.*

twinge /twɪndʒ/ n [C] sudden, sharp pain: *a ~ of toothache.*

twinkle /ˈtwɪŋkəl/ vi 1 shine with a light that gleams unsteadily: *stars that ~ in the sky.* 2 (of eyes) sparkle: *Her eyes ~d with amusement/mischief.* □ n 1 [U] twinkling light: *the ~ of the stars.* 2 sparkle: *There was a mischievous ~ in her eyes.*
twink·ling /ˈtwɪŋklɪŋ/, (*sing* only) *in a twinkling of an eye,* in an instant.

twin·ned /twɪnd/ adj paired (with): *a town in England ~ with a town in France,* for cultural, educational, etc exchanges.

713

twirl /twɜːl/ vt,vi **1** (cause to) turn round and round quickly: *He sat ∼ing his thumbs.* **2** curl: *He ∼ed his moustache (up).* □ n [C] quick circular motion.

twist /twɪst/ vt,vi **1** wind or turn (a number of threads, strands, etc) one around the other: *∼ pieces of straw into a rope.* **2** make (a rope, a garland, etc) by doing this. **3** turn, esp by the use of force; turn the two ends of (something) in opposite directions: *∼ the cap off a tube of toothpaste. He fell and ∼ed his ankle.* **twist sb's arm,** (fig) put (friendly or unfriendly) pressure on him to do something. **twist sb round one's little finger,** (informal) get him to do what one wants him to do. **4** force (a person's words) out of their true meaning: *The police tried to ∼ his words into a confession of guilt.* **5** give a spiral form to (a rod, column, etc); receive, have, move or grow in, a spiral form: *∼ed columns,* as in architecture. **6** turn and curve in different directions; change position or direction: *The road ∼s and turns up the side of the mountain.* **7** dance the twist, ⇨ **5** below. □ n **1** [C] turning or being turned: *Give the rope a few more ∼s. There are many ∼s in the road.* **2** [C] something made by twisting: *a rope full of ∼s.* **3** [C,U] thread, string, rope, etc made by twisting together two or more strands. **4** peculiar tendency of mind or character: *He has a criminal ∼ in him.* **5** dance (popular in the 1960's) in which there is twisting of the arms and hips.

twister, difficult task, problem, etc.

ˋtongue-twister, word or phrase difficult to pronounce.

twit /twɪt/ n [C] (sl) foolish person.

twitch /twɪtʃ/ n [C] **1** sudden, quick, usually uncontrollable movement of a muscle. **2** sudden quick pull: *I felt a ∼ at my sleeve.* □ vi,vt (cause to) move in a twitch(1): *The horse ∼ed its ears.*

twit·ter /ˈtwɪtə(r)/ vi **1** (of birds) make a succession of soft short sounds. **2** (of persons) talk rapidly through excitement, nervousness, etc. □ n [C] chirping: *the ∼ of sparrows.*

two /tuː/ adj, n [C] (of) 2. **break/cut sth in two,** into two parts. **put two and two together,** infer something from what one sees, hears, learns, etc.

ˈtwo-ˈfaced adj (fig) insincere.

ˈtwo-fold adj, adv double, doubly.

ˈtwo-pence /ˈtʌpəns US: ˈtupens/ n [U] sum of two pence (esp pre-decimal currency).

ˈtwo-penny /ˈtʌpnɪ US: ˈtupeni/ adj costing twopence.

ˈtwo-ˈpiece, set of clothes of similar or matching material, e g skirt and jacket, trousers and jacket: *(as an adjective) a ∼-piece bathing-suit.*

ˈtwo-ˈply adj of two strands or thicknesses: *∼-ply wool/wood.*

ˈtwo-ˈseater, car, aircraft, etc with seats for two persons.

ˈtwo-ˈtime, vt,vi (sl) deceive.

ˈtwo-timing adj (sl) deceitful.

ˈtwo-ˈway (a) (of a switch) allowing current to be switched on or off from either of two points. **(b)** (of a road or street) in which traffic may move in both directions. **(c)** (of radio equipment, etc) for both sending and receiving.

ty·coon /taɪˈkuːn/ n [C] (modern informal) wealthy and powerful business man or industrialist: *ˈoil ∼s.*

ty·ing /ˈtaɪɪŋ/ present participle of tie².

type¹ /taɪp/ n **1** [C] person, thing, event, etc considered as an example of a class or group: *Pele was a fine ∼ of football player.* **2** [C] class or group considered to have common characteristics: *men of this ∼.* **true to type,** ⇨ true(4). **3** [U] letters, etc cast in blocks of metal for use in printing; [C] one of these blocks.

ˈtype-script, typewritten copy (prepared for printing, etc).

ˈtype-write vt,vi (pt -wrote /-rəʊt/, pp -written /-rɪtn/) = type (the usual word).

ˈtype-writer, machine with which one prints letters on paper, using the fingers on a keyboard.

type² /taɪp/ vt,vi **1** use, write with, a typewriter: *∼ a letter. She ∼s well.* **2** determine the type(2) of something: *∼ a virus.*

ty·pist /ˈtaɪpɪst/, person who types(1).

type-cast /ˈtaɪpkɑːst US: -kæst/ vt (pt,pp typecast) cast (a person) for a part in a play, etc which seems to fit his/her own personality. □ adj (of a person) very suited to what he is doing.

ty·phoid /ˈtaɪfɔɪd/ n [U] (also ∼ fever) infectious disease which attacks the intestines.

ty·phoon /taɪˈfuːn/ n [C] violent hurricane.

ty·phus /ˈtaɪfəs/ n [U] infectious disease marked by fever and purple spots on the body.

typi·cal /ˈtɪpɪkəl/ adj serving as a type; representative or characteristic.

typi·cally /-klɪ/ adv

typ·ify /ˈtɪpɪfaɪ/ vt (pt,pp -ied) **1** be a symbol of; be representative of.

ty·pist /ˈtaɪpɪst/ n [C] ⇨ type².

ty·ran·ni·cal /tɪˈrænɪkəl/ adj of, like, a tyrant; acting like a tyrant.

tyr·an·nize /ˈtɪrənaɪz/ vi,vt rule cruelly and unjustly: *∼ (over) the weak.*

tyr·an·nous /ˈtɪrənəs/ adj = tyrannical.

tyr·anny /ˈtɪrənɪ/ n (pl -ies) **1** [U] cruel or unjust use of power; [C] instance of this. **2** [C,U] (instance of, country with, the) kind of government existing when a ruler has complete power, esp when this power has been obtained by force and is used unjustly: *live under a ∼.*

ty·rant /ˈtaɪrənt/ n [C] cruel or unjust ruler, esp one who has obtained complete power by force.

tyre (*US* = **tire**) /taɪə(r)/ n [C] band of rubber on the rim of a wheel, esp (*pneumatic* ~) the kind on bicycle and motor-car wheels.

tzetze /ˈsetsɪ/ n [C] = tsetse.

Uu

U, u /juː/ (*pl* U's, u's/juːz/) the 21st letter of the English alphabet.

'**U-ˈturn,** one of 180°: *No U-turns!* (as a traffic notice on motorways).

ubi·qui·tous /juːˈbɪkwɪtəs/ adj (*formal*) present everywhere or in several places at the same time.

ud·der /ˈʌdə(r)/ n [C] part of a cow, goat or other animal, from which milk comes.

ugh /ɜ *made with the lips either spread or rounded very strongly and one's facial expression showing disgust*/ int (used to show disgust).

ugly /ˈʌglɪ/ adj (-ier, -iest) **1** unpleasant to look at: ~ *men/furniture*. **2** threatening; unpleasant: *The situation looks* ~.

ug·li·ness n [U]

uku·lele /ˈjuːkəˈleɪlɪ/ n [C] Hawaiian four-stringed guitar.

ul·cer /ˈʌlsə(r)/ n [C] **1** open sore forming poisonous matter (on the outside or inside surface of the body). **2** (*fig*) corrupting influence or condition.

ul·cer·ate /-eɪt/ vt,vi form, convert into, an ulcer.

ul·cer·ous /-əs/ adj

ulna /ˈʌlnə/ n [C] (*pl* -nae /-niː/) (*anat*) inner of the two bones of the forearm.

ul·ter·ior /ʌlˈtɪərɪə(r)/ adj beyond what is first seen or said.

ulˈterior ˈmotive, motive other than what is expressed or admitted.

ul·ti·mate /ˈʌltɪmət/ adj last, furthest, basic: ~ *principles/truths; the* ~ *deterrent* (used of nuclear weapons).

ul·ti·mate·ly adv finally; in the end.

ul·ti·ma·tum /ˌʌltɪˈmeɪtəm/ n [C] (*pl* ~s or -ta /-tə/) final statement of conditions to be agreed without discussion, e g one sent to a student threatening expulsion.

ultra- /ˈʌltrə-/ prefix beyond, to excess: ~*violent*.

ultra·sonic /ˈʌltrəˈsɒnɪk/ adj of sound waves above normal human hearing.

ultra·vio·let /ˈʌltrəˈvaɪələt/ adj of the invisible part of the spectrum beyond the violet.

um·bili·cal /ʌmˈbɪlɪkəl/ adj (also ~ *cord*) cord connecting a foetus at the navel with the placenta.

um·brella /ʌmˈbrelə/ n [C] (*pl* ~s) **1** folding frame covered with cotton, etc used to shelter the person holding it from rain. **2** (*fig*) protection: *under the* ~ *of the U N O*.

um·laut /ˈʊmlaʊt/ n [C] (in Germanic languages) vowel change shown by two dots over the vowel (as in the German plural *Männer* of *Mann*).

um·pire /ˈʌmpaɪə(r)/ n [C] person chosen to act as a judge in a dispute, to see that the rules are obeyed in cricket, baseball, tennis and other games. (*Note: referee* for football and boxing.) □ vt,vi act as an umpire: ~ *a cricket match*.

ump·teen /ˈʌmpˈtiːn/ adj (*sl*) many: *I've warned you* ~ *times.*

ump·teenth /ˈʌmpˈtiːnθ/ adj: *for the* ~*th time*, for I don't know how many times.

un- /ʌn-/ prefix **1** (used with an *adjective* or *noun*) not: *unable; untruth.* **2** (used with a *verb*) negative, reverse, opposite of: *uncover; unpack; undress.*

un·abated /ˈʌnəˈbeɪtɪd/ adj (of a storm, etc) (continuing) as strong, violent, etc as before.

un·able /ʌnˈeɪbəl/ adj *unable to do sth,* not able to.

un·accom·pan·ied /ˈʌnəˈkʌmpənɪd/ adj **1** without a companion: ~ *luggage*, sent separately. **2** (*music*) performed without an accompaniment.

un·ac·count·able /ˈʌnəˈkaʊntəbəl/ adj in a way that cannot be accounted for or explained.

un·ac·count·ably /-əblɪ/ adv

un·ac·cus·tomed /ˈʌnəˈkʌstəmd/ adj **1** not accustomed to: ~ *as I am to speaking in public.* **2** not usual: *his* ~ *silence.*

un·ad·vised /ˈʌnədˈvaɪzd/ adj (esp) not discreet or wise.

un·ad·vised·ly /ˈʌnədˈvaɪzɪdlɪ/ adv rashly.

un·af·fec·ted /ˈʌnəˈfektɪd/ adj **1** sincere. **2** not affected.

un·alien·able /ʌnˈeɪlɪənəbəl/ adj that cannot be taken away or separated: ~ *rights.*

un·al·ter·ably /ʌnˈɔːltərəblɪ/ adv in a way that cannot be changed.

una·nim·ity /ˈjuːnəˈnɪmətɪ/ n [U] complete agreement or unity.

unani·mous /juːˈnænɪməs/ adj in, showing, complete agreement: *He was elected by a* ~ *vote/with* ~ *approval.*

unani·mous·ly adv

un·an·nounced /ˈʌnəˈnaʊnst/ adj without having been announced.

un·an·swer·able /ʌnˈɑːnsərəbəl *US:* -ˈæn-/ adj (esp) against which no good argument can possibly be brought: *His case is* ~.

un·an·swered /ʌnˈɑːnsəd *US:* -ˈæn-/ adj not replied to: ~ *letters.*

un·ap·proach·able /ˈʌnəˈprəʊtʃəbəl/ adj (esp, of a person) difficult to approach (because too stiff or formal).

un·armed /ʌnˈɑːmd/ adj without weapons or means of defence.

un·asked /ʌnˈɑːskt *US:* -ˈæs-/ adj (esp) without being requested: *helping* ~.

un·as·sum·ing /ˌʌnəˈsjuːmɪŋ US: -ˈsuː-/ adj not drawing attention to oneself; modest.
un·as·sum·ing·ly adv

un·at·tached /ˌʌnəˈtætʃt/ adj 1 not connected or associated with a particular person, group, organization, etc; independent. 2 not married or engaged to be married.

un·at·tended /ˌʌnəˈtendɪd/ adj not attended to; with no one to give care or attention to: *Would you leave small children at home ~ while you went to the cinema?*

un·auth·or·ized /ʌnˈɔːθəraɪzd/ adj not authorized; illegal.

un·avail·ing /ˌʌnəˈveɪlɪŋ/ adj without effect or success.

un·avoid·able /ˌʌnəˈvɔɪdəbəl/ adj that cannot be avoided.
un·a·void·ably /-əblɪ/ adv: *He was unavoidably absent.*

un·aware /ˌʌnəˈweə(r)/ adj not knowing; not aware.
un·awares /-ˈweəz/ adv (a) by surprise: *take him ~s.* (b) unconsciously: *She probably dropped the parcel ~s.*

un·bal·anced /ʌnˈbælənst/ adj (esp of a person, the mind) not sane or normal.

un·bear·able /ʌnˈbeərəbəl/ adj that cannot be borne or tolerated: *I find his rudeness ~.*
un·bear·ably /-əblɪ/ adv in a way that cannot be endured: *unbearably hot/rude.*

un·beaten /ʌnˈbiːtən/ adj (esp) not having been defeated or surpassed: *an ~ record for the 1 000 metres race.*

un·be·com·ing /ˌʌnbɪˈkʌmɪŋ/ adj not appropriate.

un·be·liev·er /ˌʌnbɪˈliːvə(r)/ n [C] (esp) person who does not believe in God.

un·bend /ʌnˈbend/ vi,vt (pt,pp unbent /-ˈbent/) 1 behave in a way free from strain, formality: *After teaching I ~.* 2 relax: *~ one's mind.*
un·bend·ing adj (esp) determined.

un·bi·as·sed (also **-biased**) /ʌnˈbaɪəst/ adj impartial.

un·block /ʌnˈblɒk/ vt remove obstruction from.

un·born /ʌnˈbɔːn/ adj not yet born; future: *~ generations.*

un·bro·ken /ʌnˈbrəʊkən/ adj (esp) 1 (e g of a horse) not tamed. 2 not interrupted: *six hours of ~ sleep.* 3 (of records, etc) not beaten.

un·buckle /ʌnˈbʌkəl/ vt undo the buckle(s) of.

un·built /ʌnˈbɪlt/ adj not (yet) built.

un·bur·den /ʌnˈbɜːdən/ vt relieve of a burden: *~ one's conscience*, e g by making a confession.

un·called-for /ʌnˈkɔːld fɔː(r)/ adj not justified, desirable or necessary: *Such rude comments are ~.*

un·canny /ʌnˈkænɪ/ adj not natural, mysterious: *an ~ ability to predict disaster.*
un·canni·ly adv

un·cared-for /ʌnˈkeəd fɔː(r)/ adj neglected: *~ children.*

un·ceas·ing /ʌnˈsiːsɪŋ/ adj going on all the time.
un·ceas·ing·ly adv

un·cer·emo·ni·ous /ˌʌnˈserəˈməʊnɪəs/ adj 1 informal. 2 lacking in courtesy.
un·cer·emo·ni·ous·ly adv
un·cer·emo·ni·ous·ness n

un·cer·tain /ʌnˈsɜːtən/ adj 1 not reliable: *~ weather; a man with an ~ temper.* 2 not certainly knowing or known: *be/feel ~ (about) what to do next; ~ of/about/as to one's plans for the future.*
un·cer·tain·ly adv

un·cer·tainty /ʌnˈsɜːtəntɪ/ n (pl -ies) 1 [U] state of being uncertain. 2 [C] something which is uncertain: *the uncertainties of employment in many countries.*

un·chari·table /ʌnˈtʃærɪtəbəl/ adj (esp) severe or harsh (in making judgements of the conduct of others).

un·checked /ʌnˈtʃekt/ adj not restrained. *~ anger.*

un·christian /ʌnˈkrɪstʃən/ adj not Christian; contrary to Christian principles.

un·civil /ʌnˈsɪvəl/ adj impolite (the usual word).

un·claimed /ʌnˈkleɪmd/ adj that has not been claimed: *~ letters/parcels* (at the post office).

uncle /ˈʌŋkəl/ n 1 brother of one's father or mother. 2 husband of one's aunt.

un·clouded /ʌnˈklaʊdɪd/ adj (fig) free from care: *a life of ~ happiness.* ⇨ cloudless.

un·coloured (US = **-colored**) /ʌnˈkʌləd/ adj (fig) not exaggerated: *an ~ description of events.*

un·com·mit·ted /ˌʌnkəˈmɪtɪd/ adj not committed; free, independent.

un·com·mon /ʌnˈkɒmən/ adj unusual (and so remarkable).
un·com·mon·ly adv (esp) remarkably: *a ~ly intelligent boy.*

un·com·pro·mis·ing /ʌnˈkɒmprəmaɪzɪŋ/ adj not prepared to make any compromise; firm: *an ~ member of the committee.*

un·con·cerned /ˌʌnkənˈsɜːnd/ adj 1 not involved (in); not (emotionally) concerned (with). 2 free from anxiety.
un·con·cern·ed·ly /-ˈsɜːnɪdlɪ/ adv

un·con·di·tional /ˌʌnkənˈdɪʃənəl/ adj absolute; not subject to conditions: *We demanded ~ surrender.*
un·con·di·tion·ally /-nəlɪ/ adv

un·con·di·tioned /ˌʌnkənˈdɪʃənd/ adj (esp): *~ reflex*, instinctive response.

un·con·scious /ʌnˈkɒnʃəs/ adj not conscious (all senses). □ n the ~, (psychology) that part of one's mental activity of which one is unaware, but which can be detected and understood through the skilled analysis of dreams, behaviour, etc.
un·con·scious·ly adv

un·con·sid·ered /ˌʌnkənˈsɪdəd/ adj 1 (of

words, remarks) spoken, made, thoughtlessly. **2** disregarded (as if of little value or worth).

un·cork /ʌnˈkɔk/ vt draw the cork from (a bottle).

un·couple /ʌnˈkʌpəl/ vt unfasten: ~ a *locomotive from a train.*

un·couth /ʌnˈkuːθ/ adj (of persons, their behaviour) rough, awkward, uncultured.
un·couth·ly adv
un·couth·ness n

un·cover /ʌnˈkʌvə(r)/ vt **1** remove a cover or covering from. **2** (fig) make known: *The police ~ed a plot against the President.*

un·cros·sed /ʌnˈkrɒst US: -ˈkrɔːst/ adj (esp, of a cheque) not crossed.

un·dated /ʌnˈdeɪtɪd/ adj not having a date: *an ~ cheque.*

un·daunted /ʌnˈdɔːntɪd/ adj fearless.

un·de·cided /ˈʌndɪˈsaɪdɪd/ adj not yet having made up one's mind.

un·de·fended /ˈʌndɪˈfendɪd/ adj (esp of a lawsuit) in which no defence is offered.

un·de·mon·stra·tive /ˈʌndɪˈmɒnstrətɪv/ adj not showing feelings of affection, interest, etc.

un·de·ni·able /ˈʌndɪˈnaɪəbəl/ adj undoubtedly true: *of ~ value.*
un·de·ni·ably /-əblɪ/ adv: *undeniably true.*

un·der[1] /ˈʌndə(r)/ adv in or to a lower place, position, etc: *The ship went ~, sank.*
down under, (*GB informal*) in Australia and New Zealand.

un·der[2] /ˈʌndə(r)/ prep **1** in or to a position lower than: *The cat was ~ the table. There's nothing new under the sun,* (*proverb*), nothing new anywhere. **2** in and covered by: *He hid ~ the bedclothes.* **3** less than; lower (in rank) than: *children ~ fourteen years of age; incomes ~ £1000; run a hundred metres in ~ ten seconds; no one ~ (the rank of) a captain.* (*Note:* opposites are *above* or *over.*) *under age,* ⇨ age. **4** (showing various conditions): *road ~ repair,* being repaired; *~ discussion,* being discussed; *be ~ the impression that,* have the idea or belief that.

under- /ˈʌndə(r)/ prefix **1** located beneath: *undergrowth.* **2** not enough: *undersized.* **3** lower in rank or importance: *understudy.*

under·act /ˈʌndərˈækt/ vt,vi act with too little energy, enthusiasm.

under·arm /ˈʌndərɑːm/ adj, adv (hitting or throwing a ball) with the hand kept below the level of the elbow.

under·bid /ˈʌndəˈbɪd/ vt (*pt,pp* unchanged) **1** make a lower bid than (another person). **2** (in card-games) bid less on (a hand of cards) than its strength demands.

under·car·riage /ˈʌndəkærɪdʒ/ n [C] (usually with *the*) landing gear of an aircraft.

under·charge /ˈʌndəˈtʃɑːdʒ/ vt charge too little for or to. □ n [C] /ˈʌndətʃɑːdʒ/ charge that is too small.

under·clothes /ˈʌndəkləʊðz US: -kləʊz/ n

pl clothing worn next to the skin.
under·cloth·ing /ˈʌndəkləʊðɪŋ/ n [U] = underclothes.

under·cover /ˈʌndəˈkʌvə(r)/ adj secret: *an ~ agent,* person who associates with suspected criminals, etc to get evidence against them.

under·cur·rent /ˈʌndəkʌrənt US: -kɜːrənt/ n [U] **1** current of water flowing beneath the surface. **2** (*fig*) tendency (of thought or feeling) lying below what is apparent: *an ~ of hatred.*

under·cut /ˈʌndəˈkʌt/ vt (*pt,pp* undercut) (-tt-) offer (goods, services) at a lower price than competitors.

under·de·vel·oped /ˈʌndədɪˈveləpt/ adj not yet fully developed: *~ muscles/ countries.*

under·dog /ˈʌndədɒg US: -dɔːg/ n [C] usually with *the*) (*fig*) person who is considered the poorest, weakest, the probable loser in a struggle, etc.

under·done /ˈʌndəˈdʌn/ adj (esp of meat) not completely cooked throughout.

under·esti·mate /ˈʌndərˈestɪmeɪt/ vt form too low an estimate or opinion of: *~ the enemy's strength.* □ n /-mət/ [C] estimate which is too low.

under·fed /ˈʌndəˈfed/ adj having had too little food.

under·foot /ˈʌndəˈfʊt/ adv under one's feet: *It is very hard ~,* eg when the ground is frozen hard.

under·go /ˈʌndəˈgəʊ/ vt (*pt* -went /-ˈwent/, *pp* -gone /-ˈgɒn US: -ˈgɔːn/) experience: *The explorers had to ~ much suffering.*

under·grad·uate /ˈʌndəˈgrædʒʊət/ n [C] university student working for a bachelor's degree.

under·ground /ˈʌndəgraʊnd/ adj **1** under the surface of the ground: *~ passages/ caves.* **2** secret (esp of political movement or one for resisting enemy forces in occupation of another country): *~ workers.* □ adv (also) /ˈʌndəˈgraʊnd/ (in the senses of the adj): *He went ~* (= into hiding) *when he heard the police were after him.* □ n **1** the U~, London's underground railway system. **2** resistance movement: *men of the French ~.*

under·growth /ˈʌndəgrəʊθ/ n [U] shrubs, bushes, low trees, growing among taller trees.

under·hand /ˈʌndəˈhænd/ adj, adv deceitful(ly).

under·lay /ˈʌndəleɪ/ n [U] material (felt, rubber, etc) laid under a carpet.

under·lie /ˈʌndəˈlaɪ/ vt form the basis of (a theory, of conduct, behaviour, doctrine).

under·line /ˈʌndəˈlaɪn/ vt **1** draw a line under (a word, etc). **2** (*fig*) emphasize. □ n /ˈʌndəlaɪn/ [C] line drawn under a word or words.

under·ling /ˈʌndəlɪŋ/ n [C] person in an unimportant position compared to others.

717

under·man·ned /ˈʌndəˈmænd/ adj (of a ship, factory, etc) having not enough men to do all the work that needs to be done.

under·men·tioned /ˈʌndəˈmenʃənd/ adj mentioned below or later (in an article, etc).

under·mine /ˈʌndəˈmaɪn/ vt 1 make a hollow or tunnel under: cliffs ∼d by the sea. 2 weaken gradually: His health was ∼d by drink.

under·neath /ˈʌndəˈniθ/ adv, prep beneath; below; at or to a lower place.

under·nour·ished /ˈʌndəˈnʌrɪʃt US: -ˈnɜːrɪʃt/ adj not provided with sufficient food for good health and normal growth.

under·pants /ˈʌndəpænts/ n pl male underwear covering the lower part of the body.

under·pass /ˈʌndəpɑːs US: -pæs/ n [C] section of a road that goes under another road or railway.

under·pay /ˈʌndəˈpeɪ/ vt (pt,pp -paid /-ˈpeɪd/) pay (workmen, etc) inadequately. **under·pay·ment** n [C,U].

under·pin /ˈʌndəˈpɪn/ vt (-nn-) 1 place a support of stone, etc under (a wall, etc). 2 (fig) support, form the basis for (an argument, etc).

under·privi·leged /ˈʌndəˈprɪvəlɪdʒd/ adj not having had the educational and social advantages enjoyed by more fortunate people, social classes, nations, etc.

under·rate /ˈʌndəˈreɪt/ vt place too low a value or estimate on: ∼ an opponent, fail to realize his abilities, strength, etc.

under·sec·retary /ˈʌndəˈsekrətrɪ US: -terɪ/ n [C] (pl -ies) (esp) (Parliamentary U∼) member of the Civil Service and head of a Government Department.

under·sell /ˈʌndəˈsel/ vt (pt,pp -sold /-ˈsəʊld/) sell (goods) at a lower price than (competitors).

under·signed /ˈʌndəˈsaɪnd/ pp: We, the ∼ed..., We whose signatures appear below...

under·sized /ˈʌndəˈsaɪzd/ adj of less than the usual size.

under·skirt /ˈʌndəskɜːt/ n [C] petticoat.

under·staffed /ˈʌndəˈstɑːft US: -stæft/ adj having too small a staff.

under·stand /ˈʌndəˈstænd/ vt,vi (pt,pp -stood /-ˈstʊd/) 1 know the meaning, nature, explanation, of (something): ∼ him/ French/a problem. He didn't ∼ me/what I said. 2 learn (from information received): I ∼ that you are now married. **under·stand·able** /-əbəl/ adj that can be understood: His refusal to agree is ∼able.

under·stand·ing adj (good at) realizing other persons' feelings or points of view: with an ∼ing smile. □ n (a) [U] power of clear thought, for seeing something from another's point of view, etc. (b) (often with a, an, but rarely pl) agreement; realization of another's views or feelings towards oneself: reach/come to an ∼ing with the

bank-manager. **on the understanding that...**, on condition that...

under·state /ˈʌndəˈsteɪt/ vt fail to state fully or adequately: They exaggerated the enemy's losses and ∼d their own. **under·state·ment** /ˈʌndəsteɪtmənt/ n [C,U].

under·stock /ˈʌndəˈstɒk/ vt equip with less stock than is necessary.

under·study /ˈʌndəstʌdɪ/ n [C] (pl -ies) person learning to, able to, take the place of another (esp an actor). □ vt (pt,pp -ied) study (a part in a play) for this purpose; act as an understudy to (an actor): He is ∼ing Macbeth.

under·take /ˈʌndəˈteɪk/ vt (pt -took /-ˈtʊk/, pp -taken /-ˈteɪkən/) 1 make oneself responsible for; agree, promise, (to do something): He undertook to finish the job by Friday. 2 start (a piece of work).

under·tak·ing /ˈʌndəˈteɪkɪŋ/ n [C] (a) work that one has agreed to do. (b) promise; guarantee.

under·taker /ˈʌndəteɪkə(r)/ n [C] one whose business is to prepare the dead for burial or cremation and manage funerals.

under·tone /ˈʌndətəʊn/ n [C] (formal) 1 low, quiet tone: talk in ∼s, talk quietly. 2 underlying quality: an ∼ of sadness.

under·took /ˈʌndəˈtʊk/ pt of undertake.

under·value /ˈʌndəˈvælju/ vt value at less than the true worth. **under·valu·ation** /ˈʌndəˈvæljuˈeɪʃən/ n [U]

under·vest /ˈʌndəvest/ n [C] = vest.

under·water /ˈʌndəwɔːtə(r)/ adj below the surface of the water: ∼ swimming.

under·wear /ˈʌndəweə(r)/ n [U] underclothes.

under·went /ˈʌndəˈwent/ pt of undergo.

under·world /ˈʌndəwɜːld/ n [C] 1 (Greek myth, etc) place of the departed spirits of the dead. 2 part of society that lives by vice and crime.

under·write /ˈʌndəˈraɪt/ vt (pt -wrote /-ˈrəʊt/, pp -written /-ˈrɪtən/) undertake to take responsibility for all or part of possible loss (by signing an agreement about insurance, esp of ships). **under·writer**, person who underwrites policies of (esp marine) insurance.

un·de·sir·able /ˈʌndɪˈzaɪərəbəl/ adj (esp of persons) of a kind not to be welcomed in society. □ n [C] undesirable person.

un·de·ter·red /ˈʌndɪˈtɜːd/ adj not discouraged: ∼ by the weather/by failure.

un·de·vel·oped /ˈʌndɪˈveləpt/ adj not developed: ∼ land, not yet used (for farming, etc).

un·did /ʌnˈdɪd/ pt of undo.

un·dies /ˈʌndɪz/ n pl (informal) women's underclothes.

un·dis·charged /ˈʌndɪsˈtʃɑːdʒd/ adj 1 (of a cargo) not unloaded. 2 (of a debt) not paid.

undo /ʌnˈduː/ vt (pt undid /ʌnˈdɪd/, pp undone /ʌnˈdʌn/) 1 untie, unfasten, loosen (knots, buttons, etc): My shoelace has come *undone.* **2** bring back the state of affairs that existed before: *He has undone the good work of his predecessor.*

un·do·ing, (cause of) ruin: *Drink was his ～.*

un·done *adj* not finished: *leave one's work undone.*

un·dom·es·ti·cated /ˌʌndəˈmestɪkeɪtɪd/ *adj* not trained or interested in household affairs: *His wife/Her husband is ～.*

un·doubted /ʌnˈdaʊtɪd/ *adj* certain; accepted as true: *show an ～ improvement in health.*

un·doubt·ed·ly *adv*

un·dreamed-of /ʌnˈdriːmd əv/ *adj* not thought of or imagined: *～ wealth.*

un·dreamt-of /ʌnˈdremt əv/ = undreamed-of.

un·dress /ʌnˈdres/ *vt,vi* **1** remove the clothes of: *Jane ～ed her doll.* **2** take off one's clothes: *～ and get into bed/get ～ed and go to bed.* □ *n* [U] *in a state of undress,* naked.

un·due /ʌnˈdjuː US: -ˈduː/ *adj* improper: *with ～ haste.*

un·duly /ʌnˈdjuːlɪ US: -ˈduːlɪ/ *adv* too: *unduly pessimistic.*

un·du·late /ˌʌndjʊleɪt US: -dʒʊ-/ *vi* (of surfaces) have a wave-like motion or look: *undulating land,* that rises and falls in gentle slopes.

un·du·la·tion /ˌʌndjʊˈleɪʃən US: -dʒʊ-/ *n* [C,U]

un·dy·ing /ʌnˈdaɪɪŋ/ *adj* everlasting: *～ love.*

un·earned /ʌnˈɜːnd/ *adj* **1** not gained by work or service: *～ income,* e g inherited. **2** not deserved: *～ praise.*

un·earth /ʌnˈɜːθ/ *vt* discover and bring to light: *～ new evidence.*

un·earth·ly /ʌnˈɜːθlɪ/ *adj* **1** supernatural. **2** mysterious; ghostly: *～ screams.* **3** (*informal*) unreasonable: *Why do you wake me up at this ～ hour?*

un·easy /ʌnˈiːzɪ/ *adj* (-ier, -iest) uncomfortable in body or mind: *have an ～ conscience; an ～ sleep.*

un·eas·ily /ʌnˈiːzɪlɪ/ *adv*

un·easi·ness *n* [U]

un·eaten /ʌnˈiːtən/ *adj* not eaten.

un·edu·cated /ʌnˈedʒʊkeɪtɪd/ *adj* (suggesting a person is) not educated: *an ～ mind/voice.*

un·em·ploy·able /ˌʌnɪmˈplɔɪəbəl/ *adj* that cannot be employed.

un·em·ployed /ˌʌnɪmˈplɔɪd/ *adj* **1** not working, not able to get work: *～ men.* **2** not being used: *～ capital.* □ *n the ～,* those who are (temporarily) without work.

un·em·ploy·ment /ˌʌnɪmˈplɔɪmənt/ *n* [U] state of being unemployed: *U～ is a serious social evil.* **2** amount of unused labour: *There is more ～ now than there was six months ago.* **3** (as an *adjective*): *～ pay/benefit,* money paid to a worker who cannot

get employment.

un·end·ing /ʌnˈendɪŋ/ *adj* everlasting; continuous.

un·en·light·ened /ˌʌnɪnˈlaɪtənd/ *adj* uneducated; not well-informed.

un·equal /ʌnˈiːkwəl/ *adj* **1** not equal. **2** (esp of work such as writing) variable in quality. **3** not capable, strong, etc enough: *I feel ～ to the task.*

un·equal·ly /-kwəlɪ/ *adv*

un·equal·led /ʌnˈiːkwəld/ *adj* unrivalled.

un·equivo·cal /ˌʌnɪˈkwɪvəkəl/ *adj* (*formal*) having one only possible meaning.

un·err·ing /ʌnˈɜːrɪŋ/ *adj* (*formal*) accurate: *fire with ～ aim.*

un·ex·cep·tion·able /ˌʌnɪkˈsepʃənəbəl/ *adj* (*formal*) beyond criticism.

un·fail·ing /ʌnˈfeɪlɪŋ/ *adj* never coming to an end.

un·fail·ing·ly *adv* at all times: *～ly honest.*

un·fair /ʌnˈfeə(r)/ *adj* unjust: *～ competition.*

un·fair·ly *adv*

un·fair·ness *n* [U]

un·faith·ful /ʌnˈfeɪθfəl/ *adj* **1** not true to one's duty, a promise, etc. **2** not faithful to marriage vows: *Her husband is ～ to her.*

un·faith·fully /-fəlɪ/ *adv*

un·faith·ful·ness *n* [U]

un·fal·ter·ing /ʌnˈfɔːltərɪŋ/ *adj* not hesitating: *with ～ courage.*

un·fam·il·iar /ˌʌnfəˈmɪlɪə(r)/ *adj* **1** not well known: *That face is not ～ to me,* I feel that I know it. **2** not acquainted with: *He is still ～ with this district.*

un·fath·om·able /ʌnˈfæðəməbəl/ *adj* **1** so deep that the bottom cannot be reached. **2** (*fig*) too strange or difficult to be understood.

un·fit /ʌnˈfɪt/ *adj* not fit or suitable: *He is ～ for driving/～ to be a doctor/medically ～.*

un·fold /ʌnˈfəʊld/ *vt,vi* **1** (of something folded) open out: *～ a newspaper.* **2** reveal, make known; become known or visible: *as the story ～s (itself).*

un·for·get·table /ˌʌnfəˈgetəbəl/ *adj* that cannot be forgotten: *an ～ experience.*

un·for·tu·nate /ʌnˈfɔːtʃʊnət/ *adj* **1** unlucky: *an ～ expedition.* **2** regrettable: *an ～ remark.*

un·founded /ʌnˈfaʊndɪd/ *adj* without proof: *～ rumours.*

un·fre·quented /ˌʌnfrɪˈkwentɪd/ *adj* visited rarely.

un·friend·ly /ʌnˈfrendlɪ/ *adj* not friendly.

un·frock /ʌnˈfrɒk/ *vt* (of a priest guilty of bad conduct) dismiss from the priesthood.

un·fruit·ful /ʌnˈfruːtfəl/ *adj* **1** not bearing fruit. **2** (*fig*) without results or success.

un·furl /ʌnˈfɜːl/ *vt,vi* unroll, spread out: *～ the sails.*

un·fur·nished /ʌnˈfɜːnɪʃt/ *adj* (esp) without furniture: *a house to let ～.*

un·gain·ly /ʌnˈgeɪnlɪ/ *adj* clumsy; awkward.

719

un·gen·er·ous /ʌn`dʒenrəs/ adj not generous.

un·god·ly /ʌn`gɒdlɪ/ adj 1 not religious. 2 (informal) unreasonable: Why did you phone me at this ~ hour?

un·gov·ern·able /ʌn`gʌvənəbəl/ adj that cannot be controlled: an ~ temper.

un·grate·ful /ʌn`greɪtfəl/ adj not showing gratitude.

un·guarded /ʌn`gɑdɪd/ adj (esp of a person and what he says) careless; indiscreet.

un·happy /ʌn`hæpɪ/ adj (-ier, -iest) not happy.

un·healthy /ʌn`helθɪ/ adj harmful to bodily or mental health.

un·heard /ʌn`hɜd/ adj 1 not heard. 2 not allowed a hearing. **go unheard,** (esp) have no-one willing to listen to it: Her request for help went ~.

un·heard-of /ʌn`hɜd əv/ adj without an equal: ~-of wealth.

un·hinged /ʌn`hɪndʒd/ adj (informal) mentally ill.

un·hook /ʌn`hʊk/ vt undo the hooks of (a dress, etc): Please ~ my dress.

un·hoped-for /ʌn`həʊpt fɔ(r)/ adj unexpected: ~ luck.

uni- /juːnɪ-/ prefix one, the same: uniform.

uni·corn /`juːnɪkɔn/ n [C] (in old stories) animal like a horse with one long horn.

un·iden·ti·fied /ʌnaɪ`dentɪfaɪd/ adj which cannot be identified: The dead man is still ~.

uni'dentified 'flying `object, (abbr UFO) object (thought to have been) seen in the sky and (claimed to have been) sent from another planet.

uni·form /`juːnɪfɔm/ adj not varying in form, quality, etc: ~ temperature. □ n [C,U] (style of) dress worn by all members of an organization, e g the police, the armed forces. **in uniform,** wearing such dress: He looks handsome in (his) ~.

uni·form·ly adv without varying in quality, timing, etc.

uni·form·ity /`juːnɪ`fɔmətɪ/ n [U] condition of being the same throughout.

unify /`juːnɪfaɪ/ vt (pt,pp -ied) 1 form into one; unite. 2 make uniform.

uni·fi·ca·tion /`juːnɪfɪ`keɪʃən/ n [U]

uni·lat·eral /`juːnɪ`lætrəl/ adj of, on, affecting, done by, one side or party only: a ~ declaration of independence, (abbr UDI); ~ repudiation of a treaty, by one of the parties that signed it, without the consent of the other party or parties.

uni·lat·er·al·ly /-rəlɪ/ adv

un·im·agin·ative /`ʌnɪ`mædʒənətɪv/ adj (formal) not having, using, imagination.

un·im·peach·able /`ʌnɪm`piːtʃəbəl/ adj that cannot be questioned or doubted: news from an ~ source.

un·in·formed /`ʌnɪn`fɔmd/ adj (esp) not having, made without, adequate information: ~ criticism.

un·in·hib·ited /`ʌnɪn`hɪbɪtɪd/ adj without inhibitions; unconventional.

un·in·spired /`ʌnɪn`spaɪəd/ adj dull: ~ singing.

un·in·ter·ested /ʌn`ɪntrɪstɪd/ adj 1 having, showing no interest. 2 having no personal concern in something.

union /`juːnɪən/ n 1 [U] uniting or being united; joining or being joined; [C] instance of this: the ~ of the three towns into one. 2 [U] state of being in agreement or harmony; [C] instance of this: a happy ~, e g a happy marriage. 3 [C] association formed by the uniting of persons, groups, etc. ⇨ trade-union.

the 'Union `Jack, the British national flag.

Union·ist /-ɪst/, (esp) supporter of the Federal Government of the US during the Civil War.

unique /juː`niːk/ adj having no like or equal; being the only one of its sort.

unique·ly adv

unique·ness n [U]

uni·sex /`juːnɪseks/ adj (of clothes) of a style designed for, or to be worn by, both sexes.

uni·son /`juːnɪsən/ n [U] **in unison,** together; in the same pitch: sing in ~

unit /`juːnɪt/ n [C] 1 single person, thing or group regarded as complete in itself. 2 quantity or amount used as a standard of measurement: The metre is a ~ of length. 3 the number 1.

Uni·tar·ian /`juːnɪ`teərɪən/ n [C] member of a Christian church which rejects the doctrine of the Trinity and believes that God is one person. □ adj of the Unitarians: the U~ Church.

unite /juː`naɪt/ vt,vi 1 make or become one; join: the common interests that ~ our two countries, that bring them together. 2 act or work together: Let us ~ to fight for human rights.

united adj (a) joined e g by love and sympathy: a ~d family. (b) resulting from association for a common purpose: make a ~d effort. (c) joined politically: the U~d Kingdom.

United Kingdom, Britain and Northern Ireland.

United Nations, (since 1942) international organization for peace and mutual aid.

United States (of America), nation in North America.

united·ly adv

unity /`juːnɪtɪ/ n (pl -ies) 1 [C,U] the state of being united; (an) arrangement of parts to form a complete or balanced whole: The figure on the left spoils the ~ of the painting. 2 [U] agreement (of aims, feelings, etc): political ~.

uni·ver·sal /`juːnɪ`vɜsəl/ adj of, belonging to, done by, affecting, all: War causes ~ misery.

uni·ver·sally /-səlɪ/ adv

uni·verse /`juːnɪvɜs/ n **the U~,** (a), everything that exists everywhere; all the stars, planets, their satellites, etc. (b) the whole creation and the Creator; mankind.

uni·ver·sity /ˌjuːnɪˈvɜːsətɪ/ n [C] (pl -ies) **1** (colleges, buildings, etc of an) institution for advanced teaching, conferring degrees and engaging in academic research. **2** members of such an institution collectively. **3** (as an adjective): a ~ student.

un·kempt /ˌʌnˈkempt/ adj = untidy (the usual word).

un·kind /ˌʌnˈkaɪnd/ adj lacking in, not showing, kindness: an ~ remark.
un·kind·ly adv in an unkind manner.

un·know·ing /ˌʌnˈnəʊɪŋ/ adj unaware.
un·know·ing·ly adv unawares.

un·known /ˌʌnˈnəʊn/ adj not known or identified: the tomb of the ~ warrior, of an unknown soldier buried in memory of those killed in World Wars I and II.

un·leash /ˌʌnˈliːʃ/ vt (fig) set free (to attack): ~ one's temper.

un·leav·ened /ˌʌnˈlevənd/ adj (of bread) made without yeast.

un·less /ənˈles/ conj if not: You will fail ~ you work harder.

un·like /ˌʌnˈlaɪk/ adj, prep not like; different from.

un·like·ly /ˌʌnˈlaɪklɪ/ adj not likely to happen or be true: an ~ event/story.

un·load /ˌʌnˈləʊd/ vt,vi **1** remove a load, cargo from: ~ a ship. The ship is ~ing. **2** get rid of (somebody, something not wanted): Don't try to ~ all your boring girl-friends on me!

un·looked-for /ˌʌnˈlʊkt fɔː(r)/ adj unexpected.

un·loose /ˌʌnˈluːs/ vt let loose; make free.

un·man·ly /ˌʌnˈmænlɪ/ adj **1** weak; cowardly. **2** effeminate.

un·man·ned /ˌʌnˈmænd/ adj having no crew: send an ~ spacecraft to Mars.

un·mask /ˌʌnˈmɑːsk US: -ˈmæsk/ vt,vi **1** remove a mask (from). **2** (fig) show the true character or intentions of: ~ a traitor.

un·match·able /ˌʌnˈmætʃəbəl/ adj that cannot be equalled.

un·matched /ˌʌnˈmætʃt/ adj without an equal.

un·men·tion·able /ˌʌnˈmenʃənəbəl/ adj so bad, shocking, etc that it may not be spoken of.

un·mind·ful /ˌʌnˈmaɪndfəl/ adj forgetful; oblivious: ~ of the time.

un·mis·tak·able /ˌʌnmɪˈsteɪkəbəl/ adj clear; about which no mistake or doubt is possible: Are black clouds an ~ sign of rain?
un·mis·tak·ably /-əblɪ/ adv

un·miti·gated /ˌʌnˈmɪtɪgeɪtɪd/ adj (formal) complete; absolute: an ~ rascal.

un·moved /ˌʌnˈmuːvd/ adj (esp) indifferent.

un·natu·ral /ˌʌnˈnætʃrəl/ adj not natural or normal.

un·nec·es·sary /ˌʌnˈnesəsrɪ US: -serɪ/ adj

not necessary.

un·nec·es·sar·ily /ʌnˈnesəˈserəlɪ/ adv

un·nerve /ˌʌnˈnɜːv/ vt cause to lose self-control, power of decision, courage.

un·not·iced /ˌʌnˈnəʊtɪst/ adj not observed or noticed: Her sadness went ~.

un·num·bered /ˌʌnˈnʌmbəd/ adj **1** more than can be counted. **2** having no number(s): ~ tickets.

un·ob·tru·sive /ˌʌnəbˈtruːsɪv/ adj not too obvious or easily noticeable.

un·of·fi·cial /ˌʌnəˈfɪʃəl/ adj not official: an ~ strike, not authorized by the union.

un·or·tho·dox /ˌʌnˈɔːθədɒks/ adj not in accordance with what is orthodox, conventional, traditional: ~ teaching methods.

un·pack /ˌʌnˈpæk/ vt,vi take out (things packed): ~ one's clothes/a suitcase.

un·par·al·leled /ˌʌnˈpærəleld/ adj having no equal: an ~ disaster.

un·pick /ˌʌnˈpɪk/ vt take out (stitches).

un·pleas·ant /ˌʌnˈplezənt/ adj not pleasant.
un·pleas·ant·ness n [U] unpleasant feeling (between persons); [C] quarrel.

un·prece·dented /ˌʌnˈpresɪdentɪd/ adj never done or known before.

un·preju·diced /ˌʌnˈpredʒədɪst/ adj free from prejudice.

un·pre·ten·tious /ˌʌnprɪˈtenʃəs/ adj modest; not trying to seem important.

un·prin·cipled /ˌʌnˈprɪnsəpəld/ adj without moral principles; dishonest.

un·pro·fes·sional /ˌʌnprəˈfeʃnəl/ adj (esp of conduct) contrary to the rules or customs of a profession.

un·prompted /ˌʌnˈprɒmptɪd/ adj (of an answer, action) not said, done, etc as the result of a hint, suggestion, etc.

un·pro·voked /ˌʌnprəˈvəʊkt/ adj without provocation: ~ aggression/attacks.

un·quali·fied /ˌʌnˈkwɒlɪfaɪd/ adj **1** not limited or restricted; absolute: ~ praise. **2** not qualified: ~ to speak on the subject.

un·ques·tion·able /ˌʌnˈkwestʃənəbəl/ adj beyond doubt; certain.
un·ques·tion·ably /-əblɪ/ adv

un·quote /ˌʌnˈkwəʊt/ (v, imperative only) (in a telegram, a telephoned message, etc) end the quotation: The rebel leader said (quote) 'We shall never surrender' (~).

un·ravel /ˌʌnˈrævəl/ vt,vi (-ll-; US -l-) **1** separate the threads of; pull or become separate: The cat has ~led the knitting. **2** solve: ~ a mystery.

un·real /ˌʌnˈrɪəl/ adj imaginary; not real.

un·reas·on·able /ˌʌnˈriːzənəbəl/ adj not reasonable.

un·re·lent·ing /ˌʌnrɪˈlentɪŋ/ adj not becoming less in intensity, etc: ~ pressure/attacks.

un·re·li·able /ˌʌnrɪˈlaɪəbəl/ adj that cannot be relied on; not to be trusted.

un·re·mit·ting /ˌʌnrɪˈmɪtɪŋ/ adj (formal) unceasing: ~ efforts.

un·re·quit·ed /ˌʌnrɪˈkwaɪtɪd/ adj not

returned or rewarded: ~ *love*.

un·re·serv·ed·ly /ˌʌnrɪˈzɜːvɪdlɪ/ *adv* without reservation or restriction; openly: *speak* ~.

un·rest /ʌnˈrest/ *n* [U] (esp) disturbed condition(s): *political* ~.

un·re·strained /ˌʌnrɪˈstreɪnd/ *adj* not kept under control: ~ *hatred/laughter*.

un·re·stricted /ˌʌnrɪˈstrɪktɪd/ *adj* without restriction(s); (esp of a road) not having a speed limit for traffic.

un·ri·valled (*US* = **-ri·valed**) /ʌnˈraɪvəld/ *adj* having no rival: ~ *in courage*.

un·ruffled /ʌnˈrʌfəld/ *adj* calm; not upset or agitated: *He was* ~ *by all the criticisms*.

un·ruly /ʌnˈruːlɪ/ *adj* (-ier, -iest) not easily controlled; naughty: *an* ~ *child*.

un·said /ʌnˈsed/ *adj* not expressed: *Some things are better left* ~.

un·sa·voury (*US* = **-sa·vory**) /ʌnˈseɪvərɪ/ *adj* (esp) nasty; disgusting: ~ *stories/scandals*.

un·scathed /ʌnˈskeɪðd/ *adj* unharmed; unhurt.

un·scru·pu·lous /ʌnˈskruːpjʊləs/ *adj* not guided by conscience (not to do wrong).
un·scru·pu·lous·ly *adv*

un·seas·oned /ʌnˈsiːzənd/ *adj* 1 (of wood) not matured. 2 (of food) not flavoured with seasoning.

un·seat /ʌnˈsiːt/ *vt* 1 remove from office: *Mr X was* ~*ed at the General Election*, lost his seat in the House of Commons. 2 throw from a horse: *Several riders were* ~*ed at the last fence*.

un·seem·ly /ʌnˈsiːmlɪ/ *adj* (of behaviour, etc) not proper.

un·seen /ʌnˈsiːn/ *adj* not seen; invisible.

un·settle /ʌnˈsetəl/ *vt* make troubled, anxious or uncertain: ~*d weather*, changeable weather.

un·sight·ly /ʌnˈsaɪtlɪ/ *adj* unpleasant to look at: ~ *litter*.

un·skilled /ʌnˈskɪld/ *adj* 1 (of work) not needing special skill. 2 (of workers) not having special skill or special training.

un·soph·is·ti·cated /ˌʌnsəˈfɪstɪkeɪtɪd/ *adj* not sophisticated; inexperienced.

un·sound /ʌnˈsaʊnd/ *adj* 1 unsatisfactory: *an* ~ *argument/building*. 2 *of unsound mind*, mentally disordered.

un·spar·ing /ʌnˈspeərɪŋ/ *adj* liberal; holding nothing back: *be* ~ *in one's efforts*; ~ *of praise*.

un·speak·able /ʌnˈspiːkəbəl/ *adj* that cannot be expressed or described in words: ~ *joy/sadness*.

un·stuck /ʌnˈstʌk/ *adj* 1 not stuck or fastened: *The flap of the envelope has come* ~. 2 fail to work according to plan: *Our plan has come* ~.

un·sung /ʌnˈsʌŋ/ *adj* not celebrated (in poetry or song). *go unsung*, (*informal*) (of a person, his actions) be unknown, not thanked, praised.

un·swerv·ing /ʌnˈswɜːvɪŋ/ *adj* (esp of

aims, purposes) not changing: ~ *loyalty*.

un·think·able /ʌnˈθɪŋkəbl/ *adj* not to be considered: *Such a possibility is* ~!

un·thought-of /ʌnˈθɒt əv/ *adj* unexpected; not imagined.

un·tidy /ʌnˈtaɪdɪ/ *adj* (-ier, -iest) (of a room, desk, person etc) not tidy.

un·til /ənˈtɪl/ *prep*, *conj* ⇨ till.

un·tir·ing /ʌnˈtaɪərɪŋ/ *adj* continuing to work without getting tired or causing tiredness: *his* ~ *efforts*.

un·told /ʌnˈtəʊld/ *adj* (esp) too many or too much to be counted, measured, etc: ~ *wealth*.

un·truth /ʌnˈtruːθ/ *n* [U] lack of truth; [C] (*pl* ~s /-ˈtruːðz/) lie.
un·truth·ful /-fəl/ *adv*
un·truth·ful·ly /-fəlɪ/ *adv*

un·used[1] /ʌnˈjuːzd/ *adj* never having been used.

un·used[2] /ʌnˈjuːst/ *adj* *unused to*, not accustomed to: *The children are* ~ *to city life*.

un·veil /ʌnˈveɪl/ *vt*,*vi* 1 remove a veil (from). 2 reveal.

un·wieldy /ʌnˈwiːldɪ/ *adj* awkward to move or control because of shape, size or weight.

un·wind /ʌnˈwaɪnd/ *vt*,*vi* (*pt*,*pp* -wound /-ˈwaʊnd/) 1 untwist (a ball of wool, etc); slacken (a spring, etc). 2 (*informal*) relax after a period of tension, exhausting work, etc. ⇨ wind[2] (6).

un·zip /ʌnˈzɪp/ *vt* (-pp-) unfasten or open by pulling a zip-fastener.

up /ʌp/ *adverbial particle* (contrasted with *down*) (for special uses with *verbs*, e g *throw up*, ⇨ the *verb* entries.) 1 to or in an erect or vertical position (esp as suggesting readiness for activity): *He's already* ~, out of bed. *It's time to get* ~, out of bed. *Stand* ~! *up and about*, out of bed and active (esp of a person recently ill). 2 to or in a high(er) place, position, degree, etc: *Lift your head* ~. *Prices are still going* ~, rising. *pull one's socks up*, ⇨ sock[1] (1). 3 to a place, town, of importance; to a place in or to the north: *He has gone* ~ *to London for the day*. *We're going* ~ *to Edinburgh*. 4 (used vaguely, in a way similar to the use of *down*, *round*, *over*, *across*) to the place in question, or in which the speaker is, was, will be: *He came* ~ (*to me*) *and asked the time*. 5 (used to show completeness, finality): *The stream has dried* ~, has become completely dry. *We've eaten everything* ~. *Lock/Tie/Fasten/Chain/Nail it* ~, *Make it fast*, secure, safe, etc by locking, tying, etc. 6 (used to show an increase in intensity, etc): *Speak/Sing* ~! ie with more force. 7 *up against* (*it*), faced with (difficulties, obstacles, etc). *be up before*, appear in court (before a magistrate, etc). *up and down*, (a) forward and back: *walking* ~ *and down the station platform*. (b) so as to rise and fall: *The boat bobbed* ~ *and down on* *the water.* **up for, (a)** being tried (for an offence, etc): ~ *for exceeding the speed limit.* **(b)** being considered for; on offer: *The house is ~ for sale.* **up to, (a)** occupied or busy with: *What's he ~ to? He's ~ to no good.* **(b)** capable of: *I don't feel ~ to going to work today.* **(c)** as far as: ~ *to now/then.* **(d)** required, looked on as necessary: *It's ~ to us* (= It is our duty) *to give them all the help we can.* □ *prep* (in the senses of the *adverb*): *climb ~ a mountain; walk ~ the stairs.*

'up-and-'coming, (of a person) making good progress, likely to succeed, in his profession, career, etc: *an ~-and-coming young doctor.*

'ups and 'downs, (*fig*) good and bad fortune.

up- /ʌp-/ *prefix* to a higher or better state: *uphill; upgrade.*

up-bring-ing /ˈʌpbrɪŋɪŋ/ *n* [U] training and education during childhood: *a good ~.*

up-coun-try /ʌpˈkʌntrɪ/ *adj, adv* (esp in a large thinly populated country) towards the interior; inland.

up-date /ʌpˈdeɪt/ *vt* bring up to date: ~ *a dictionary.*

up-grade /ʌpˈgreɪd/ *vt* raise to a higher grade. □ *n* /ˈʌpgreɪd/ (esp) **on the upgrade,** making progress.

up-heaval /ʌpˈhiːvəl/ *n* [C] great and sudden change: *political/social ~s.*

up-held /ʌpˈheld/ *pt,pp* of uphold.

up-hill /ʌpˈhɪl/ *adj* **1** sloping upward; ascending: *an ~ road.* **2** (*fig*) difficult; needing effort: *an ~ task.* □ *adv* up a slope: *walk ~.*

up-hold /ʌpˈhəʊld/ *vt* (*pt,pp* upheld /-ˈheld/) **1** support or approve (a person, his conduct, a practice, etc): *I cannot ~ such conduct.* **2** confirm (a decision, a verdict).

up-hol-ster /ʌpˈhəʊlstə(r)/ *vt* provide (seats, etc) with padding, springs, covering material, etc.

up-hol-sterer, person who upholsters.

up-hol-stery /-stərɪ/ *n* [U] (materials used in, business of) upholstering.

up-keep /ˈʌpkiːp/ *n* [U] (cost of) keeping something in good order and repair: *The ~ of this large garden is more than I can afford.*

up-land /ˈʌplənd/ *n* (often *pl*) higher part(s) of a region or country.

up-lift /ʌpˈlɪft/ *vt* raise (spiritually or emotionally): *His soul was ~ed by the Bach cantatas.* □ *n* /ˈʌplɪft/ [U] moral or mental inspiration.

up-most /ˈʌpməʊst/ *adj* = uppermost.

upon /əˈpɒn/ *prep* = on (which is more usual).

up-per /ˈʌpə(r)/ *adj* (contrasted with *lower*) higher in place; situated above: *the ~ lip; the ~ arm.* **have/get the upper hand (of sb),** have/get an advantage or control of. □ *n* [C] part of a shoe or boot over the sole.

'upper case, capital letter(s).

the 'upper class, top levels of society.

the 'Upper House, (in Parliament) the House of Lords.

up-per-most /-məʊst/ *adj* highest: *Thoughts of the holidays were ~most in their minds.* □ *adv* on, to, at, the top or surface: *say whatever comes ~most,* whatever one thinks first.

up-right /ˈʌpraɪt/ *adj* **1** erect; placed vertically (at an angle of 90° to the ground): *an ~ post.* **2** honourable; straightforward in behaviour: *an ~ man/judge.* □ *n* [C] upright support in a structure.

up-ris-ing /ʌpˈraɪzɪŋ/ *n* [C] revolt; rebellion.

up-roar /ˈʌprɔː(r)/ *n* [U] (with *a, an*) (outburst of) noise and excitement: *The meeting ended in (an) ~.*

up-roari-ous /ʌpˈrɔːrɪəs/ *adj* very noisy, esp with loud laughter and great good humour: ~*ious laughter.*

up-roari-ous-ly *adv*

up-root /ʌpˈruːt/ *vt* pull up with the roots: *The gale ~ed numerous trees.*

up-set /ʌpˈset/ *vt,vi* (*pt,pp* ~) (-tt-) **1** tip over; overturn: *Don't ~ the boat.* **2** trouble; cause (a person or thing) to be disturbed: ~ *the enemy's plan;* ~ *one's stomach by eating too much rich food. She is easily ~ emotionally.* □ *n* /ˈʌpset/ [C] **1** upsetting or being upset: *have a 'stomach ~.* **2** (*sport*) unexpected result.

up-shot /ˈʌpʃɒt/ *n* (*sing* with *the*) outcome; result: *What will be the ~ of it all?*

up-side-down /ˈʌpsaɪd ˈdaʊn/ *adv* **1** with the upper side underneath or at the bottom. **2** (*fig*) in disorder: *The house was turned ~ by the burglars.*

up-stairs /ʌpˈsteəz/ *adv* **1** to or on a higher floor: *go/walk ~.* **2** (as an *adjective*) belonging to, situated on, an upper floor: *an ~ room.*

up-stand-ing /ʌpˈstændɪŋ/ *adj* standing erect; strong and healthy: *fine ~ children.*

up-start /ˈʌpstɑːt/ *n* [C] person who has suddenly risen to wealth, power or higher social position, esp one who is arrogant.

up-stream /ʌpˈstriːm/ *adv* up a river; in the opposite direction to the stream or current.

up-surge /ˈʌpsɜːdʒ/ *n* [C] growth (of emotion): *an ~ of anger/indignation.*

up-tight /ʌpˈtaɪt/ *adj* (*sl*) extremely tense or nervous: ~ *about an interview.*

up-to-date /ˈʌp tə ˈdeɪt/ *adj* of the present time; of the newest sort.

'up-to-the-'minute *adj* very modern; latest.

up-turn /ˈʌptɜːn/ *n* [C] **1** upward turn. **2** change for the better: *an ~ in profits.*

up-ward /ˈʌpwəd/ *adj* moving or directed up: *an ~ glance.* □ *adv* (often **up-wards**) towards a higher place, level, etc.

ura-nium /jʊˈreɪnɪəm/ *n* [U] heavy white metal (symbol **U**) with radioactive properties, a source of atomic energy.

Ura·nus /jʊˈreməs/ n (astron) planet seventh in order from the sun.

ur·ban /ˈɜbən/ adj of or in a town: ~ areas.

'urban gueˈrilla, member of a small armed group fighting (political) opposition in towns.

ur·ban·ize /-aɪz/ vt change from a rural to an urban character.

ur·ban·iz·ation /ˌɜbənaɪˈzeɪʃən US: -nɪˈz-/ n [U]

ur·bane /ɜˈbeɪn/ adj (formal) polite; refined in manners.

ur·bane·ly adv

ur·chin /ˈɜtʃɪn/ n [C] 1 mischievous small boy. 2 poor destitute child.

urge /ɜdʒ/ vt 1 push or drive on: The crowd ~d the tennis star on to win. 2 request earnestly; try to persuade: 'Buy it now,' he ~d. 'Prices will soon rise.' 3 stress (the importance of) requests and arguments: He ~d on his pupils the importance of hard work. □ n [C] (rarely pl) strong desire: He has/feels an ~ to travel.

ur·gency /ˈɜdʒənsɪ/ n [U] importance of, need for, haste or prompt action: a matter of great ~.

ur·gent /ˈɜdʒənt/ adj 1 needing prompt decision or action: It is most ~ that the patient should get to hospital. 2 (of a person, his voice, etc) showing that something is urgent.

ur·gent·ly adv

uri·nary /ˈjʊərɪnrɪ US: -nerɪ/ adj of urine: ~ infection.

uri·nate /ˈjʊərɪneɪt/ vi discharge urine.

urine /ˈjʊərɪn/ n [U] waste liquid which collects in the bladder and is discharged from the body.

urn /ɜn/ n [C] 1 vase with a stem as used for holding the ashes of a person whose body has been cremated. 2 large metal container in which a drink such as tea or coffee is made or kept hot, e g in canteens.

us /əs strong form: ʌs/ pron object form of we: We hope you will visit ~ soon.

usage /ˈjuːzɪdʒ US: ˈjus-/ n 1 [U] way of using something; treatment: Machines soon wear out under rough ~. 2 [C,U] conventions governing the use of a language (esp those not governed by grammatical rules): Such ~s are not characteristic of educated speakers.

use¹ /juːs/ n 1 [U] using or being used; condition of being used: the ~ of electricity for cooking. **in use**, being used. **come into use**, begin to be used: When did the word 'transistor' come into common ~? **out of use**, not being, no longer, used. 2 [C,U] purpose for which a person or thing is or may be employed; work that a person or thing is able to do: a tool with many ~s; find a ~ for it; have no further ~ for it. 3 [U] value; advantage: Is this paper of any ~ to you? 4 [U] power of using: lose the ~ of

one's legs, become unable to walk. 5 [U] right to use: give a friend the ~ of one's bike.

use·ful /ˈjuːsfəl/ adj helpful; producing good results: Are you a ~ful member of society?

use·fully /-fəlɪ/ adv

use·ful·ness n [U]

use·less adj (a) of no use; worthless: A car is ~less without petrol. (b) without result; unrewarding: It's ~less to argue with them.

use·less·ly adv

use·less·ness n [U]

use² /juːz/ vt (pt,pp ~d /juːzd/) 1 cause to act or serve for a purpose: You ~ your legs when you walk. May I ~ (= quote) your name as a reference, e g in an application for a job. 2 have the use of (until nothing is left): How much coal did we ~ last winter? He has ~d up all his strength. 3 behave towards: U~ others as you would like them to ~ you.

used /juːzd/ adj no longer new: ~d cars.

user, person or thing that uses: There are more 'telephone ~rs in the USA than in any other country.

used /juːst/ anomalous finite (irregular pt and pp of use) (indicating a constant or frequent practice in the past, or, in the construction there used to be, the existence of something in the past): That's where I ~ to live when I was a child. Life isn't so easy here as it ~ to be.

used to /ˈjuːst tə before vowel sounds: tu/ adj having become familiar to by habit or custom: You will soon be/get ~ it.

usher /ˈʌʃə(r)/ n [C] person who shows people to their seats in theatres, cinemas, etc. □ vt 1 lead, conduct: The girl ~ed me to my seat (in a cinema). 2 announce: The change of government ~ed in a period of prosperity.

usher·ette /ˌʌʃəˈret/, girl or woman usher(1).

usual /ˈjuːʒʊəl/ adj such as commonly happens: He arrived later than ~.

usu·ally /ˈjuːʒʊlɪ/ adv in the ordinary way: What do you ~ly do on Sundays?

usurer /ˈjuːʒərə(r)/ n [C] person whose business is lending money for profit.

usurp /juːˈzɜp/ vt wrongfully take (a person's power, authority, position): ~ the chairman's authority.

usurper, person who does this.

usury /ˈjuːʒərɪ/ n [U] (practice of) lending money, esp at a high rate of interest.

uten·sil /juːˈtensəl/ n [C] instrument, tool, etc, esp for use in the house: 'household ~s, e g pots, pans, brushes.

uterus /ˈjuːtərəs/ n [C] (pl ~es) (anat) = womb.

utili·tar·ian /ˌjuːtɪlɪˈteərɪən/ adj characterized by usefulness rather than by beauty, truth, goodness.

util·ity /juːˈtɪlətɪ/ n (pl -ies) 1 [U] quality of being useful: (as an adjective) '~ van, one that can be used for various purposes. **2** [C] public service such as the supply of water or a bus service.

util·ize /ˈjuːtɪlaɪz US: -təl-/ vt make use of; find a use for.

util·iz·ation /ˌjuːtɪlaɪˈzeɪʃən US: -təlɪˈz-/ n [U]

ut·most /ˈʌtməʊst/ adj most extreme; greatest: with the ~ care. □ n (sing only) the most that is possible: I shall do my ~ to see justice is done.

ut·ter[1] /ˈʌtə(r)/ adj complete; total: ~ darkness.

ut·ter·ly adv completely: She's ~ly bored with him.

ut·ter[2] /ˈʌtə(r)/ vt **1** make (a sound or sounds) with the mouth: ~ a sigh/a cry of pain. **2** say: the last words he ~ed. **3** put (counterfeit money, etc) into circulation.

ut·ter·ance /ˈʌtərəns/ n **(a)** (sing only) (formal) way of speaking: a clear ~ance. **(b)** [C] spoken word or words. **(c)** [U] give ~ance to (one's feelings, etc), express in words.

ut·ter·most /ˈʌtəməʊst/ adj, n = utmost.

Vv

V, v /viː/ n (pl V's, v's) **1** the 22nd letter of the English alphabet. **2** the Roman numeral 5.

vac /væk/ n [C] (informal) = vacation.

va·cancy /ˈveɪkənsɪ/ n (pl -ies) **1** [U] condition of being empty or unoccupied. **2** [C] unoccupied space. **3** [U] lack of ideas, intelligence or concentration. **4** [C] position in business, etc for which a person is needed: good vacancies for typists.

va·cant /ˈveɪkənt/ adj **1** empty: gaze into ~ space. **2** not occupied by anyone: a ~ room, e g in a hotel; apply for a ~ position, e g in an office. **3** (of time) not filled with any activity. **4** (of the mind) without thought; (of the eyes) showing no signs of thought or interest: a ~ expression.

va·cant·ly adv

va·cate /vəˈkeɪt US: ˈveɪkeɪt/ vt **1** give up living in: ~ a house. **2** leave unoccupied: ~ one's seat.

va·ca·tion /vəˈkeɪʃən US: veɪ-/ n **1** [C] weeks during which universities and law courts stop work: the summer ~. **2** [C] (esp US) = holiday.

vac·ci·nate /ˈvæksɪneɪt US: -səneɪt/ vt protect (a person) (against smallpox, etc) by injecting vaccine.

vac·ci·na·tion /ˌvæksɪˈneɪʃən/ n [C,U] (instance of) vaccinating.

vac·cine /ˈvæksiːn US: vækˈsiːn/ n [C,U] substance from the blood of a cow, used to

protect persons from smallpox by causing them to have a slight, but not dangerous, form of the disease.

vac·il·late /ˈvæsɪleɪt/ vi hesitate; be uncertain (in opinion, etc): ~ between hope and fear.

vac·il·la·tion /ˌvæsɪˈleɪʃən/ n [C,U]

vac·uum /ˈvækjʊəm/ n [C] (pl ~s or, in science, vacua /-jʊə/) **1** space completely empty of substance or gas(es). **2** space in a container from which the air has been pumped out.

vacuum cleaner, apparatus which takes up dust, dirt, etc by suction.

vacuum-flask, one having a vacuum between its inner and outer walls, keeping the contents at an unchanging temperature.

vaga·bond /ˈvægəbɒnd/ adj having no fixed living-place: live a ~ life. □ n [C] vagabond person.

va·gary /ˈveɪgərɪ/ n [C] (pl -ies) (formal) strange, unusual act or idea, esp one for which there seems to be no good reason: the vagaries of fashion.

va·gina /vəˈdʒaɪnə/ n [C] (pl ~s) (anat) passage (in a female mammal) from the external genital organs to the womb.

vag·inal /vəˈdʒaɪnəl/ adj

va·grant /ˈveɪgrənt/ adj leading a wandering life: ~ tribes. □ n [C] vagrant person.

vague /veɪg/ adj (-r, -st) **1** not clear or distinct: I haven't the ~st idea what they want. **2** (of persons, their looks, behaviour) uncertain, suggesting uncertainty (about needs, intentions, etc).

vague·ly adv

vague·ness n [U]

vain /veɪn/ adj (-er, -est) **1** without use, value, meaning or result: a ~ attempt; ~ hopes/promises. **2** in vain, **(a)** without the desired result: All our work was in ~. **(b)** without due reverence, honour or respect: take a person's name in ~, use it disrespectfully. **3** having too high an opinion of one's looks, abilities, etc: He's as ~ as a peacock, very vain.

vain·ly adv

vale /veɪl/ n [C] (literary) = valley.

val·en·tine /ˈvæləntaɪn/ n [C] (letter, card, etc, sent on St Valentine's Day, 14 Feb, to a) sweetheart.

valet /ˈvælɪt/ n [C] member of (hotel) staff employed to dry-clean or press clothes. □ vt act as valet to.

val·iant /ˈvælɪənt/ adj brave (the usual word).

val·iant·ly adv

valid /ˈvælɪd/ adj **1** (legal) effective because made or done with the correct formalities: a ~ claim/marriage. **2** (of contracts, etc) having force in law: a ticket ~ for three months. **3** (of arguments, reasons, etc) well based; sound: raise ~ objections to a suggestion.

va·lid·ly adv

va·lid·ity /vəˈlɪdətɪ/ n [U] state of being valid.

vali·date /ˈvælɪdeɪt/ vt make valid: ~ a claim.

va·lise /vəˈliz US: vəˈlis/ n [C] small leather bag for clothes, etc during a journey.

val·ley /ˈvælɪ/ n [C] (pl ~s) stretch of land between hills or mountains, often with a river flowing through it.

val·our (US = **valor**) /ˈvælə(r)/ n [U] (formal) bravery, esp in war.

valu·able /ˈvæljuəbəl/ adj of great value, worth or use: a ~ discovery. □ n (usually pl) something of much value, e g jewels.

valu·ation /ˌvæljuˈeɪʃən/ n 1 [U] process of deciding the value of a person or thing. 2 [C] the value that is decided on: The surveyors arrived at widely different ~s.

value /ˈvælju/ n 1 [U] quality of being useful or desirable: the ~ of walking as an exercise. 2 [U] worth of something when compared with something else: This book will be of great/little/some/no ~ to him in his studies. 3 [C,U] worth of something in terms of money or other goods for which it can be exchanged: Is the ~ of the American dollar likely to decline? 4 [U] what something is considered to be worth (contrasted with the price obtainable): I've been offered £350 for my old car but its ~ is much higher. 5 (in music) full time indicated by a note: Give the note its full ~. 6 (pl) standards: moral/ethical ~s. □ vt 1 estimate the money value of: He ~d the house for me at £17500. 2 have a high opinion of: Do you ~ her as a secretary?
value·less adj worthless.
valuer, person whose profession is to estimate the money value of property, land, etc.

valve /vælv/ n [C] 1 (sorts of) mechanical device for controlling the flow of air, liquid, gas, etc in one direction only: the ~ of a bicycle tyre. 2 structure in the heart or in a blood-vessel allowing the blood to flow in one direction only. 3 vacuum tube used in a radio, allowing the flow of electrons in one direction. 4 device in musical wind instruments, e g a cornet, for changing the pitch by changing the length of the column of air.
val·vu·lar /ˈvælvjʊlə(r)/ adj of valves(2).

vam·pire /ˈvæmpaɪə(r)/ n [C] corpse that comes to life and leaves its grave at night and sucks the blood of sleeping persons.
vampire bat, sort of blood-sucking bat.

van[1] /væn/ n [C] 1 roofed motor-vehicle for carrying and delivering goods: a `furniture ~. 2 (GB) roofed railway carriage for goods: the `luggage ~.

van[2] /væn/ n [C] 1 front or leading part of an army or fleet in battle. 2 those persons who lead a procession or (fig) a movement: in the ~ of scientific progress.
van-guard, advance party of an army, etc as a guard against surprise attack.

van·dal /ˈvændəl/ n [C] person who delib-

erately destroys works of art or public and private property.
van·dal·ism /-ɪzm/ n [U] behaviour characteristic of vandals.

vane /veɪn/ n [C] 1 arrow or pointer on the top of a building, turned by the wind so as to show its direction. 2 blade of a propeller, or other flat surface acted on by wind or water.

van·guard /ˈvængɑd/ n ⇨ van[2].

va·nilla /vəˈnɪlə/ n 1 [C] (pods or beans of) plant with sweet-smelling flowers. 2 [U] flavouring substance from vanilla beans or synthetic product used for it: two ~ ices.

van·ish /ˈvænɪʃ/ vi suddenly disappear; fade away gradually; go out of existence: The thief ran into the crowd and ~ed.

van·ity /ˈvænətɪ/ n (pl -ies) 1 [U] having too high an opinion of one's looks, abilities, etc: do something out of ~. 2 [U] quality of being unsatisfying, without true value: the ~ of pleasure; [C] vain, worthless thing or act: the vanities of life.

van·quish /ˈvæŋkwɪʃ/ vt defeat (the usual word).

va·pour (US = **va·por**) /ˈveɪpə(r)/ n 1 [U] steam; mist; gaseous form to which certain substances may be reduced by heat: `water ~. 2 [C] something imagined: the ~s of a disordered mind.

vari·able /ˈveərɪəbəl/ adj varying; changeable: ~ winds; ~ standards. □ n [C] variable thing or quantity; factor which may vary, e g in an experiment.
vari·abil·ity /ˌveərɪəˈbɪlətɪ/ n [U]
vari·ably /-əblɪ/ adv

vari·ant /ˈveərɪənt/ adj different or alternative: ~ spellings of a word (e g 'programme' and 'program'). □ n [C] variant form (e g of spelling).

vari·ation /ˌveərɪˈeɪʃən/ n 1 [C,U] (degree of) varying or being variant: ~(s) of temperature. 2 [C] (music) simple melody repeated in a different form: ~s on a theme by Mozart. 3 [U] (biology) change in bodily structure or form caused by new conditions, environment, etc; [C] instance of such change.

vari·col·oured (US = **-col·ored**) /ˈveərɪˌkʌləd/ adj of various colours.

vari·cose vein /ˈværɪkəʊs ˈveɪn/ adj vein that has become permanently swollen or enlarged.

var·ied /ˈveərɪd/ adj 1 of different sorts: the ~ scenes of life. 2 full of changes or variety: a ~ career.

varie·gated /ˈveərɪgeɪtɪd/ adj marked irregularly with differently coloured patches: The flowers of pansies are often ~.
varie·ga·tion /ˌveərɪˈgeɪʃən/ n [U]

var·iety /vəˈraɪətɪ/ n (pl -ies) 1 [U] quality of not being the same, or not being the same at all times: a life full of ~. 2 (sing only) number or range of different things: for a ~ of reasons. 3 [C] (biology) subdivision of a species. 4 [C] kind or sort which differs from

others of the larger group of which it is a part: *rare varieties of early postage stamps.*
5 [U] kind of entertainment consisting of singing, dancing, comedy, etc: *a ` ~ act.*

var·i·ous /ˈveərɪəs/ *adj* different; of a number of different sorts: *for ~ reasons; at ~ times.*

vari·ous·ly *adv*

var·nish /ˈvɑːnɪʃ/ *n* [C,U] (particular kind of) (liquid used to give a) hard, shiny, transparent coating on a surface. □ *vt* put a coating of varnish on: *Some women ~ their toenails.*

vars·ity /ˈvɑːsətɪ/ *n* [C] (*pl* -ies) (*GB informal*) = university.

vary /ˈveərɪ/ *vi,vt* (*pt,pp* -ied) be, become, cause to become, different: *They ~ in weight from 3 to 5 kilos.*

vas·cu·lar /ˈvæskjʊlə(r)/ *adj* (*anat*) of, made up of, containing, vessels or ducts through which blood, lymph or sap flows: *~ tissue.*

vase /vɑːz *US:* veɪs/ *n* [C] vessel of glass, pottery, etc for holding cut flowers, or as an ornament.

va·sec·tomy /vəˈsektəmɪ/ *n* [C,U] (*pl* -ies) surgical operation to make a man sterile.

vast /vɑːst *US:* væst/ *adj* immense; extensive: *~ sums of money; a ~ expanse of desert.*

vast·ly *adv*

vast·ness *n* [U]

vat /væt/ *n* [C] large vessel for holding liquids, esp in brewing, dyeing.

vault[1] /vɔːlt/ *n* [C] **1** arched roof; series of arches forming a roof. **2** underground room or cellar (with or without an arched roof) as a place of storage (`*wine–~s*), or for burials (eg under a church), or for keeping valuables safe: *keep one's jewels in the ~ at the bank.*

vault[2] /vɔːlt/ *vi,vt* jump in a single movement, with the hand(s) resting on something, or with the help of a pole: *~ (over) a fence.* □ *n* [C] jump made in this way.

`**vault·ing-horse,** apparatus for practice in vaulting.

vaulter, person who vaults: *a `pole–~er.*

veal /viːl/ *n* [U] flesh of a calf eaten as food.

veer /vɪə(r)/ *vi* change direction: *The wind ~ed round to the north. Opinion ~ed in our favour.*

veg·etable /ˈvedʒtəbəl/ *adj* of, from, relating to, plants or plant life: *~ oils.* □ *n* [C] plant, esp one used for food, eg potatoes, cabbages, carrots.

veg·etar·ian /ˌvedʒɪˈteərɪən/ *n* [C] person who eats no meat: (as an *adjective*) *a ~ diet.*

veg·etate /ˈvedʒɪteɪt/ *vi* lead a dull life with little activity or interest.

veg·eta·tion /ˌvedʒɪˈteɪʃən/ *n* [U] plants generally and collectively: *a desert with no sign of ~ anywhere.*

ve·he·ment /ˈviːəmənt/ *adj* (*formal*) **1** (of feelings) strong, eager. **2** (of persons, their

speech, behaviour, etc) filled with, showing, strong or eager feeling: *~ passions.*

ve·he·ment·ly *adv*

ve·hicle /ˈviːɪkəl/ *n* [C] **1** carriage (car, lorry, van, bus, etc) (usually wheeled) for moving goods or passengers on land (and in space). **2** means by which thought, feeling, etc can be carried: *Art may be used as a ~ for/of propaganda.*

ve·hicu·lar /vɪˈhɪkjʊlə(r)/ *adj* **1** related to, consisting of, carried by, vehicles: *The road is closed to vehicular traffic.* **2** *vehicular language,* one used as a means of communication between people with different languages, eg English in Nigeria.

veil /veɪl/ *n* [C] **1** covering of fine net or other material to protect or hide a woman's face: *She lowered her ~.* **2** (*fig*) something that hides or disguises: *a ~ of mist.* □ *vt* **1** put a veil over: *Not all Muslim women are ~ed.* **2** (*fig*) hide: *He could not ~ his distrust.*

veil·ing, light material used for making veils.

vein /veɪn/ *n* [C] **1** blood–vessel along which blood flows from all parts of the body to the heart. **2** one of the lines in some leaves or in the wings of some insects. **3** coloured line or streak in some kinds of stone, eg marble. **4** (*fig*) characteristic: *There is a ~ of madness in him.* **5** crack in rock, filled with mineral or ore: *a ~ of gold.* **6** mood; train of thought: *in an i`maginative ~.*

vel·oc·ity /vəˈlosətɪ/ *n* (*formal*) = speed.

ve·lours, ve·lour /vəˈlʊə(r)/ *n* [U] fabric like velvet.

vel·vet /ˈvelvɪt/ *n* [U] cloth wholly or partly made of silk with a thick soft pile on one side.

vel·vety *adj* smooth and soft like velvet.

ve·nal /ˈviːnəl/ *adj* **1** (of persons) ready to do something dishonest (eg using influence or position) for money: *~ politicians.* **2** (of conduct) influenced by, done for, (possible) payment: *~ practices.*

ve·nally /-nəlɪ/ *adv*

ve·neer /vɪˈnɪə(r)/ *n* **1** [C,U] (thin layer of) fine quality wood glued to the surface of cheaper wood (for furniture, etc). **2** (*fig*) surface appearance (of politeness, etc) covering the true nature: *a ~ of kindness.* □ *vt* put a veneer on: *~ a desk.*

ven·er·able /ˈvenərəbəl/ *adj* **1** deserving respect because of age, character, associations, etc: *a ~ abbot.* **2** (Church of England) title of an archdeacon. **3** (Church of Rome) title of a person who is in the process of being canonized.

ven·er·ate /ˈvenəreɪt/ *vt* regard with deep respect: *They ~ the old man's memory.*

ven·er·ation /ˌvenəˈreɪʃən/ *n* [U]

ve·nereal /vɪˈnɪərɪəl/ *adj* of, communicated by, sexual intercourse: *~ diseases.*

ven·geance /ˈvendʒəns/ *n* **1** revenge; the return of injury for injury: *take ~ on an enemy.* **2** (*informal*) to a greater degree than is normal, expected or desired: *The rain came down with a ∼*.

venge·ful /ˈvendʒfəl/ *adj* showing a desire for revenge.

ve·nial /ˈviːnɪəl/ *adj* (of a sin, error, fault) excusable.

ven·ison /ˈvenɪsən/ *n* [U] deer meat.

venom /ˈvenəm/ *n* [U] **1** poisonous fluid of certain snakes. **2** (*fig*) hate; spite.
ven·om·ous /ˈvenəməs/ *adj* deadly; spiteful: *∼ous snakes/criticism.*
ven·om·ous·ly *adv*

ve·nous /ˈviːnəs/ *adj* **1** (*anat*) of the veins: *∼ blood.* **2** (*botany*) having veins: *a ∼ leaf.*

vent /vent/ *n* [C] **1** hole serving as an inlet or outlet for air, gas, liquid, etc, e g a hole in the top of a barrel, for air to enter as liquid is drawn out. **2** means of escape: *The floods found a ∼ through the dykes.* **3** (*sing* only) outlet for one's feelings. **give vent to,** give free expression to: *He gave ∼ to his feelings in an impassioned speech.* □ *vt* find or provide an outlet for: *He ∼ed his anger on his long-suffering wife.*

ven·ti·late /ˈventɪleɪt US: -təl-/ *vt* cause (air) to move in and out freely: *∼ a room.*
ven·ti·la·tor /ˈventɪleɪtə(r) US: -təl-/, device for ventilating.
ven·ti·la·tion /ˌventɪˈleɪʃən US: -təl-/ *n* [U]

ven·ture /ˈventʃə(r)/ *n* [C,U] undertaking in which there is risk: *a ˈbusiness ∼.* □ *vt,vi* **1** take the risk of, expose to, danger or loss: *∼ too near the edge of a cliff.* **2** go so far as, dare: *∼ (to put forward) an opinion; ∼ a guess.*

Venus /ˈviːnəs/ *n* (*astron*) planet second in order from the sun.

ve·ran·dah, ve·randa /vəˈrændə/ *n* [C] roofed and floored open space along the side(s) of a house, sports pavilion, etc.

verb /vɜːb/ *n* [C] (abbr *v* used in this dictionary) word showing what a person or thing does, what state he or it is in, what is becoming of him or it. ⇨ **phrasal verb; intransitive, transitive.**

ver·bal /ˈvɜːbəl/ *adj* **1** of or in words: *have a good ∼ memory,* be able to remember well the exact words of a statement, etc. **2** spoken, not written: *a ∼ statement.* **3** word for word, literal: *a ∼ translation.* **4** of verbs: *a ∼ noun* (e g *swimming* in the sentence 'Swimming is a good exercise').
ver·bally /ˈvɜːbəlɪ/ *adv* in spoken words, not in writing.

ver·bal·ize /ˈvɜːbəlaɪz/ *vt* put into words.

ver·ba·tim /vɜːˈbeɪtɪm/ *adv* exactly as spoken or written: *report a speech ∼.*

ver·bi·age /ˈvɜːbɪdʒ/ *n* [U] (use of) unnecessary words for the expression of an idea, etc.

ver·bose /vɜːˈbəʊs/ *adj* using, containing, more words than are needed: *a ∼ speech/speaker.*
ver·bose·ly *adv*
ver·bos·ity /vɜːˈbɒsətɪ/ *n* [U]

ver·dict /ˈvɜːdɪkt/ *n* [C] **1** decision reached by a jury on a question of fact in a law case: *The jury brought in a ∼ of guilty/not guilty.* ⇨ **open verdict. 2** decision or opinion given after testing, examining, or experiencing something: *The popular ∼* (= The opinion of people in general) *was that it served him right.*

verge /vɜːdʒ/ *n* **1** [C] edge; border (e g strip of grass at the side of a road). **2** (*sing* with **the**) **be on the verge of,** very close to, on the border of: *The country is on the ∼ of disaster.* □ *vi* approach closely, border (on): *Such ideas ∼ on stupidity.*

verger /ˈvɜːdʒə(r)/ *n* [C] **1** (C of E) official with various duties (e g opening pews for worshippers). **2** officer who carries a staff before a bishop in a cathedral, a vice-chancellor in a university, etc.

ver·ify /ˈverɪfaɪ/ *vt* (*pt,pp* -ied) **1** test the truth or accuracy of: *∼ a report/statement.* **2** (of an event, etc) show the truth of: *Subsequent events verified my suspicions.*
veri·fi·able /ˈverɪfaɪəbəl/ *adj* that can be verified.
veri·fi·ca·tion /ˌverɪfɪˈkeɪʃən/ *n* [U]

veri·table /ˈverɪtəbəl/ *adj* rightly named: *a ∼ liar.*

ver·mil·ion /vəˈmɪlɪən/ *adj, n* [U] bright red (colour).

ver·min /ˈvɜːmɪn/ *n* [U] (used with a *pl* verb, but not with numerals) **1** wild animals (e g rats, weasels, foxes) harmful to plants, birds and other animals. **2** parasitic insects (e g lice) sometimes found on the bodies of human beings and other animals. **3** (*fig*) human beings who are harmful to society or who prey on others.
ver·min·ous /-əs/ *adj*

ver·nacu·lar /vəˈnækjʊlə(r)/ *adj* (of a word, a language) of the country in question: *a ∼ language,* native language; *a ∼ poet,* one who uses a vernacular language. □ *n* [C] language or dialect of a country or district.

ver·sa·tile /ˈvɜːsətaɪl US: -təl/ *adj* interested in and clever at many different things; having various uses: *a ∼ mind/invention.*
ver·sa·til·ity /ˌvɜːsəˈtɪlətɪ/ *n* [U]

verse /vɜːs/ *n* **1** [U] (form of) writing arranged in lines, each conforming to a pattern of accented and unaccented syllables: *prose and ∼.* ⇨ **blank verse. 2** [C] group of lines of this kind forming a unit in a rhyme scheme: *a poem/hymn of five ∼s.* **3** [C] one line of verse with a definite number of accented syllables: *a few ∼s from Tennyson.* **4** one of the short numbered divisions of a chapter in the Bible.

versed /vɜːst/ *adj* **versed in,** skilled or experienced in: *well ∼ in mathematics/the arts.*

ver·sion /ˈvɜːʃən US: ˈvɜːrʒən/ *n* [C] **1** account of an event, etc from the point of view of one person: *There were three ∼s of what happened/of what the Prime Minister* *said*. **2** translation into another language: *a new ~ of the Bible*

ver·sus /ˈvɜːsəs/ *prep* (*Latin*) (in law and sport; often shortened to *v* in print) against: *Robinson v Brown; England v Brazil*.

ver·te·bra /ˈvɜːtibrə/ *n* [C] (*pl* ~e /-briː/) any one of the segments of the backbone.

ver·te·brate /ˈvɜːtibrət/ *n* [C], *adj* (animal, bird, etc) having a backbone.

ver·ti·cal /ˈvɜːtikəl/ *adj* (of a line or plane) at a right angle to the earth's surface or to another line or plane: *a ~ take–off aircraft*, one that can rise vertically. □ *n* [C] vertical line.

ver·ti·cal·ly /-klɪ/ *adv*

verve /vɜːv/ *n* [U] enthusiasm, spirit, vigour (esp in artistic or literary work).

very¹ /ˈverɪ/ *adj* **1** itself and no other; truly such: *At that ~ moment the phone rang. You're the ~ man I want to see.* **2** extreme: *at the ~ end/beginning.*

very² /ˈverɪ/ *adv* **1** (used to show intensity with *adverbs, adjectives*): *~ quickly/little.* **very well,** (often used to show agreement after persuasion or argument, or obedience to a command, request, etc): *V~ well, doctor, I'll give up smoking.* **2** (with a superlative) in the highest possible degree: *at the ~ latest.*

vessel /ˈvesəl/ *n* [C] **1** hollow receptacle, esp for a liquid, e g a bucket, bowl, bottle, cup. **2** ship or large boat. ⇨ blood-vessel.

vest¹ /vest/ *n* [C] **1** (*GB*) undergarment worn on the upper part of the body next to the skin. **2** (*US*) = waistcoat.

vest² /vest/ *vt, vi* furnish or give as a fixed right: *~ a man with authority/rights in an estate.*

ves·tige /ˈvestɪdʒ/ *n* [C] **1** trace or sign; small remaining bit of evidence of what once existed: *There is not a ~ of truth in the report.* **2** (*anat*) organ, or part of one, which is a survival of something that once existed: *A human being has the ~ of a tail.*

vest·ment /ˈvestmənt/ *n* [C] ceremonial robe as worn by a priest in church.

ves·try /ˈvestrɪ/ *n* [C] (*pl* -ies) **1** part of a church where vestments are kept. **2** room in a non-conformist church used for Sunday School, prayer meetings, etc.

vet¹ /vet/ *n* [C] (*informal*) (abbr for) veterinary surgeon.

vet² /vet/ *vt* (-tt-) (*informal*) **1** give (a person) a medical examination. **2** (*GB*) examine closely and critically, e g qualifications, etc: *He must be thoroughly ~ted before he's given the job.*

vet·eran /ˈvetərən/ *n* [C] **1** person who has had much or long experience, esp as a soldier: *a ~ teacher.* **2** (of cars) of the years before 1916: *a ~ Rolls Royce.* **3** (*US*) any ex-service man.

vet·erin·ary /ˈvetrɪnərɪ *US:* -nerɪ/ *adj* of or concerned with the diseases and injuries of (esp farm and domestic) animals: *a ~ surgeon/college.*

veto /ˈviːtəʊ/ *n* [C] (*pl* ~es) constitutional right of a sovereign, president, legislative assembly or other body, or a member of the United Nations Security Council, to reject or forbid something; statement that rejects or prohibits something: *exercise a power of ~.* □ *vt* put a veto on: *The police ~ed the demonstration that the workers wanted.*

vex /veks/ *vt* (*formal*) annoy; distress; *He was ~ed at his failure.*

vex·ation /vekˈseɪʃən/ *n* [U] state of being vexed; [C] something that vexes.

via /ˈvaɪə/ *prep* (*Latin*) by way of: *travel from London to Paris ~ Dover.*

vi·able /ˈvaɪəbəl/ *adj* capable of existing, developing and surviving: *Is the newly-created State ~?*

vi·abil·ity /ˈvaɪəˈbɪlətɪ/ *n* [U]

vi·aduct /ˈvaɪədʌkt/ *n* [C] long bridge (usually with many arches) carrying a road, railway, or canal across a valley.

vial /ˈvaɪəl/ *n* [C] small bottle, esp for liquid medicine.

vi·brant /ˈvaɪbrənt/ *adj* vibrating: *the ~ notes of a 'cello.*

vi·brate /vaɪˈbreɪt *US:* ˈvaɪbreɪt/ *vi, vt* **1** (cause to) move quickly and continuously backwards and forwards: *The house ~s whenever a heavy lorry passes.* **2** (of stretched strings, the voice) throb; quiver: *The strings of a piano ~ when the keys are struck.*

vi·bra·tion /vaɪˈbreɪʃən/ *n* [C,U] vibrating movement: *We felt ~s as the train passed.*

vicar /ˈvɪkə(r)/ *n* [C] **1** (C of E) clergyman in charge of a parish. **2** (R C Church) deputy; representative: *the ~ of Christ,* the Pope.

vicar·age /ˈvɪkərɪdʒ/ *n* [C] vicar's residence.

vi·cari·ous /vɪˈkeərɪəs *US:* vaɪˈk-/ *adj* (*formal*) done, experienced, by one person for another or others: *the ~ sufferings of Jesus.*

vi·cari·ous·ly *adv*

vice¹ /vaɪs/ *n* [C,U] (any particular kind of) evil conduct or practice: *Torture is a ~.*

vice² (*US* = **vise**) /vaɪs/ *n* [C] apparatus with strong clamps in which things can be held tightly while being worked on.

vice– /vaɪs-/ *prefix* person who is next in rank to and may act for another: *vice-president.*

vice versa /ˈvaɪsə ˈvɜːsə/ *adj* (*Latin*) the other way round; with the terms or conditions reversed: *We gossip about them and ~,* and they gossip about us.

vi·cin·ity /vɪˈsɪnətɪ/ *n* (*pl* -ies) **1** [U] nearness; closeness of relationship: *in close ~ to the church.* **2** [C] neighbourhood: *There isn't a good school in the ~.*

vi·cious /ˈvɪʃəs/ *adj* **1** evil (the usual word): *a ~ life.* **2** given or done with evil intent: *a ~ kick/look.*

'vicious 'circle, state of affairs in which a cause produces an effect which itself produces the original cause, e g *War breeds hate, and hate leads to war again.*

vi·cious·ly *adv*

vi·cious·ness *n* [U]

vic·tim /ˈvɪktɪm/ *n* [C] **1** living creature killed and offered as a religious sacrifice. **2** person, animal, etc suffering injury, pain, loss, etc because of circumstances, an event, war, an accident, etc: *the ∼s of the earthquake.*

vic·tim·ize /-aɪz/ *vt* select for ill treatment because of real or alleged misconduct, etc: *Trade union leaders claimed that some of their members had been ∼ized,* e g by being dismissed.

vic·tim·iz·ation /ˌvɪktəmaɪˈzeɪʃən US: -mɪˈz-/ *n* [U]

vic·tor /ˈvɪktə(r)/ *n* [C] person who conquers or wins.

vic·tori·ous /vɪkˈtɔːrɪəs/ *adj* having gained the victory.

vic·tori·ous·ly *adv*

vic·tory /ˈvɪktəri/ *n* [C,U] (*pl* -ies) (instance, occasion, of) success (in war, a contest, game, etc): *gain/win a ∼ over the enemy; lead the troops to ∼.*

video /ˈvɪdɪəʊ/ [C,U] *prefix* recording and reproducing vision: *∼ cassettes.*

video recorder, for using video tape.

video tape, magnetic tape for recording sound and vision, e g of television programmes.

vie /vaɪ/ *vi* **vie with sb/for sth,** rival or compete (the usual word): *The two boys ∼d with one another for the first place.*

view[1] /vjuː/ *n* **1** [U] state of seeing or being seen; field of vision: *The speaker stood in full ∼ of the crowd, could see them and could be seen by them.* **in view of,** considering, taking into account: *In ∼ of the facts, it seems useless to continue.* **on view,** being shown or exhibited: *The latest summer fashions are now on ∼ in the big shops.* **come into view,** become visible: *As we came round the corner the lake came into ∼.* **2** [C] (picture, photograph, etc of) natural scenery, landscape, etc: *a house with a fine ∼ of the mountains.* **3** [C] opportunity to see or inspect something: *a private ∼,* e g of paintings, before public exhibition. **4** [C] personal opinion; mental attitude; thought or observation (on a topic, subject): *She had/ expressed strong ∼s on the subject of equal pay for men and women.* **5** aim; intention; purpose **with a/the view to/of,** with the intention or hope: *with a ∼ to saving trouble.*

view·point, 'point of view, ⇨ point[1].

view-finder, device in a camera showing the area, etc that will be photographed.

view[2] /vjuː/ *vt* look at; examine; consider: *The subject may be ∼ed in various ways. How do you ∼ the situation? What do you think about it?*

viewer /ˈvjuːə(r)/, (esp) television *∼ers,*

persons watching a television programme.

vigil /ˈvɪdʒɪl/ *n* **1** [U] staying awake to keep watch or to pray: *keep ∼ over a sick child.* **2** (*pl*) instances of this: *tired out by her long ∼s.* **3** [C] eve of a religious festival, esp when observed with prayer and fasting.

vigi·lance /ˈvɪdʒɪləns/ *n* [U] watchfulness: keeping watch: *exercise ∼.*

vigi·lant /ˈvɪdʒɪlənt/ *adj* watchful.

vigi·lant·ly *adv*

vig·our (*US* = **vigor**) /ˈvɪɡə(r)/ *n* [U] mental or physical strength; energy; forcefulness (of language).

vig·or·ous /ˈvɪɡərəs/ *adj* strong; energetic

vig·or·ous·ly *adv*

vile /vaɪl/ *adj* (-r, -st) **1** shameful and disgusting: *∼ habits/language.* **2** (*informal*) very bad: *∼ weather.*

vile·ly /ˈvaɪlli/ *adv*

vile·ness *n* [U]

vil·ify /ˈvɪlɪfaɪ/ *vt* (*pt,pp* -ied) say evil things about (a person).

vil·ifi·ca·tion /ˌvɪlɪfɪˈkeɪʃən/ *n* [U]

villa /ˈvɪlə/ *n* [C] (*pl* ∼s) **1** (in *GB*) detached or semi-detached house, esp one on the outskirts of a town: *No 13 Laburnum Villas.* **2** country house with a large garden, esp in Italy or S France.

vil·lage /ˈvɪlɪdʒ/ *n* [C] place smaller than a town, where there are houses and shops, and usually a church and school: (as an *adjective*) *the ∼ post office.*

vil·lager /ˈvɪlɪdʒə(r)/, person who lives in a village.

vil·lain /ˈvɪlən/ *n* [C] **1** (esp in drama) wicked person. **2** rascal.

vil·lain·ous /ˈvɪlənəs/ *adj* evil: *∼ous acts.*

vil·lainy *n* (*pl* -ies) [U] evil conduct; (*pl*) evil acts.

vin·di·cate /ˈvɪndɪkeɪt/ *vt* show or prove the truth, justice, validity, etc (of something that has been attacked or disputed): *∼ a claim Events have ∼d his judgement/actions.*

vin·di·ca·tion /ˌvɪndɪˈkeɪʃən/ *n* [C,U]

vin·dic·tive /vɪnˈdɪktɪv/ *adj* having or showing a desire for revenge.

vin·dic·tive·ly *adv*

vin·dic·tive·ness *n* [U]

vine /vaɪn/ *n* [C] **1** climbing plant whose fruit is the grape. **2** any plant with slender stems that trails or climbs (e g melons, peas)

vin·ery /ˈvaɪnəri/, greenhouse for vines.

vine·yard /ˈvɪnjəd/, area of land planted with grape-vines.

vin·egar /ˈvɪnɪɡə(r)/ *n* [C] acid liquor (made from malt, wine, cider, etc) used in flavouring food and for pickling.

vin·egary /ˈvɪnɪɡəri/ *adj* like vinegar.

vin·tage /ˈvɪntɪdʒ/ *n* **1** [C] (rarely *pl*) (period or season of) grape harvesting: *The ∼ was later than usual last year.* **2** [C,U] (wine from) grapes of a particular year: *of the ∼ of 1973; a ∼ year,* one in which good wine was made. **3** (as an *adjective*) of a period in the past and having a reputation for high quality: $a \sim car$, one built between 1916 and 1930.

vint·ner /ˈvɪntnə(r)/ n [C] wine-merchant.

vi·nyl /ˈvaɪnɪl/ n [C,U] (kinds of) tough, flexible plastic, used for coverings, clothing, etc

vi·ola /vɪˈəʊlə/ n [C] tenor violin, of larger size than the ordinary violin.

vi·ol·ate /ˈvaɪəleɪt/ vt **1** break (an oath, a treaty, etc); act contrary to (what one's conscience tells one to do, etc). **2** act towards without respect: $\sim a$ person's privacy. **3** commit rape.
 vi·ol·ation /ˌvaɪəˈleɪʃən/ n [C,U].

vi·ol·ence /ˈvaɪələns/ n [U] state of being violent; violent conduct: robbery with $\sim$.

vi·ol·ent /ˈvaɪələnt/ adj **1** using, showing, accompanied by, great force: $a \sim wind/$ attack/temper. **2** caused by a brutal attack: meet $a \sim death$. **3** severe: $\sim toothache$.
 vi·olent·ly adv

vi·olet /ˈvaɪələt/ n **1** [C] small wild or garden plant with sweet-smelling flowers. **2** [U] bluish-purple colour (of wild violets).

vi·olin /ˌvaɪəˈlɪn/ n [C] four-stringed musical instrument played with a bow.
 vi·olin·ist /-ɪst/, player of a violin.

vi·olon·cello /ˌvaɪələnˈtʃeləʊ/ n [C] (pl $\sim$s) (usual abbr **cello** /ˈtʃeləʊ/) large bass violin held between the player's knees.

vi·per /ˈvaɪpə(r)/ n [C] kinds of poisonous snake, esp the common $\sim$, the adder.

vir·gin /ˈvɜːdʒɪn/ n [C] girl or woman who has not experienced sexual union. □ adj **1** pure and chaste. **2** pure and untouched: $\sim snow$. **3** in the original condition; unused: $\sim soil$, soil never before used for crops.
 vir·gin·ity /vəˈdʒɪnətɪ/ n [U] state of being a virgin.

vir·ginal /ˈvɜːdʒɪnəl/ adj of, suitable for, a virgin.

Virgo /ˈvɜːgəʊ/ n the Virgin, sixth sign of the zodiac.

vir·ile /ˈvɪraɪl US: ˈvɪrɪl/ adj **1** having or showing strength, energy, manly qualities: $a \sim style$ (of writing). **2** (of men) sexually potent.
 vir·il·ity /vɪˈrɪlətɪ/ n [U] masculine strength and vigour; sexual power.

vir·tual /ˈvɜːtʃʊəl/ adj being in fact, acting as, what is described, but not accepted openly or in name as such: $a \sim defeat/$ confession.
 vir·tu·ally /-tʃʊlɪ/ adv

vir·tue /ˈvɜːtʃuː/ n **1** [C,U] (any particular kind of) goodness or excellence: Patience is $a \sim$. **2** [U] chastity, esp of women: a woman of easy $\sim$, one who is promiscuous. **3** [U] ability to produce a definite result: Have you any faith in the $\sim$ of herbs to heal sickness? **4** advantage: The great $\sim$ of the scheme is that it costs very little. **5 by/in virtue of,** by reason of; because of: He claimed a pension in $\sim$ of his long military service.

vir·tu·ous /ˈvɜːtʃuəs/ adj having, showing,

virtue(1).
 vir·tu·ous·ly adv

vir·tu·os·ity /ˌvɜːtʃʊˈosətɪ/ n [U] special artistic skill.

viru·lent /ˈvɪrʊlənt/ adj **1** (of poison) strong; deadly. **2** (of ill feeling, hatred) extremely bitter. **3** (of words, etc) full of hatred. **4** (of diseases, etc) poisonous.
 viru·lent·ly adv

vi·rus /ˈvaɪərəs/ n [C] (pl $\sim$es) any of various poisonous elements, smaller than bacteria, causing the spread of infectious disease.

visa /ˈviːzə/ n [C] (pl $\sim$s) stamp or signature put on a passport to show that it has been examined and approved by the officials of a foreign country which the owner intends to visit (ˈentrance or ˈentry $\sim$) or leave (ˈexit $\sim$). □ vt put a visa in: get one's passport $\sim$ed /ˈviːzəd/ before going to Poland.

vis·count /ˈvaɪkaʊnt/ n [C] nobleman higher in rank than a baron, lower than an earl.

vis·count·ess /-es/ n [C] wife of a viscount; female viscount.

vise /vaɪs/ n (US) vice[2].

vis·ible /ˈvɪzəbəl/ adj that can be seen; that is in sight: The eclipse will be $\sim$ to observers in western Europe.
 vis·ibly /-əblɪ/ adv in a visible manner: She was visibly annoyed.

vis·ibil·ity /ˌvɪzəˈbɪlətɪ/ n [U] (esp) condition of the atmosphere for seeing things at a distance: The aircraft returned because of poor visibility.

vi·sion /ˈvɪʒən/ n **1** [U] power of seeing or imagining, looking ahead, grasping the truth: the field of $\sim$, all that can be seen from a certain point; a man of $\sim$. **2** [C] something seen or imagined, dreamt, etc: Have you ever had $\sim$s of great wealth and success?

vi·sion·ary /ˈvɪʒənrɪ US: -nerɪ/ adj **1** existing only in a vision or the imagination; unpractical: $\sim schemes$. **2** (of persons) having grand ideas; dreamy. □ n [C] (pl -ies) visionary person.

visit /ˈvɪzɪt/ vt,vi **1** go to see (a person); go to (a place) for a time: $\sim a$ friend; $\sim Rome$. **2** go to in order to inspect or examine officially: Restaurant and hotel kitchens are $\sim$ed regularly by officers of public health. □ n [C] act, time, of visiting: pay $a \sim$ on a friend/a patient; $a \sim$ of several hours.

vis·it·ing n [U] paying visits: ˈ$\sim$ing hours at a hospital.

visi·tor /ˈvɪzɪtə(r)/ n [C] person who visits; person who stays at a place: summer $\sim$s, e g at a holiday resort.

visi·ta·tion /ˌvɪzɪˈteɪʃən/ n **1** [C] official visit, e g one made by a bishop or priest. **2** [C] trouble, disaster, looked on as punishment from God: The famine was a $\sim$ of God for their sins.

vi·sor /ˈvaɪzə(r)/ n [C] **1** (in former times)

movable part of a helmet, covering the face.
2 peak of a cap or similar part of a crash-helmet.

vis·ta /ˈvɪstə/ n [C] (pl ∼s) **1** long, narrow view: a ∼ of the church at the end of an avenue of trees. **2** (fig) series of scenes, events, etc which one can look back on or forward to: a discovery that opens up new ∼s.

vis·ual /ˈvɪʒʊəl/ adj concerned with, used in, seeing: She has a ∼ memory, is able to remember well things she sees.
'**visual** '**aids,** (e g in teaching) e g pictures, film-strips, films.
vis·ually /ˈvɪʒʊəlɪ/ adv
vis·ual·ize /-aɪz/ vt imagine (as a picture): I remember meeting the man two years ago but can't ∼ize him, remember what he looked like.

vi·tal /ˈvaɪtəl/ adj **1** of, connected with, necessary for, living: Air is ∼ for all animals. **2** supreme; indispensable: of ∼ importance.
'**vital** '**sta'tistics,** (a) figures relating to the duration of life, and to births, marriages and deaths. (b) (modern informal) woman's measurements at bust, waist and hips.
vi·tally /ˈvaɪtəlɪ/ adv

vi·tal·ity /vaɪˈtælətɪ/ n [U] **1** capacity to endure, survive, perform functions: Can an artificial language have any ∼? **2** energy, liveliness: the ∼ of young children.
vi·tal·ize /ˈvaɪtəlaɪz/ vt put vigour into.

vit·amin /ˈvɪtəmɪn US: ˈvaɪt-/ n [C] any of a number of organic substances which are present in certain foods and are essential to the health of man and other animals.

vit·reous /ˈvɪtrɪəs/ adj of or like glass: ∼ rocks.

vit·riolic /ˌvɪtrɪˈɒlɪk/ adj (of words, feelings) full of abuse.

vi·va·cious /vɪˈveɪʃəs/ adj lively; high-spirited: a ∼ girl.
vi·va·cious·ly adv
vi·vac·ity /vɪˈvæsətɪ/ n [U]

viva voce /ˌvaɪvə ˈvəʊsɪ/ adj, adv oral(ly): a ∼ examination □ n [C] oral examination.

vivid /ˈvɪvɪd/ adj **1** (of colours, etc) intense; bright: a ∼ flash of lightning. **2** lively; active: a ∼ imagination. **3** clear and distinct: have ∼ recollections of a holiday in Italy.
vivid·ly adv

vivi·sect /ˈvɪvɪsekt/ vt operate or experiment on (living animals) for scientific research.
vivi·sec·tion /ˌvɪvɪˈsekʃən/ n [C,U]
vivi·sec·tion·ist /-ɪst/, person who vivisects or considers vivisection justifiable.

vixen /ˈvɪksən/ n [C] **1** female fox. **2** bad-tempered woman.

vo·cabu·lary /vəˈkæbjʊlərɪ US: -lerɪ/ n [C] (pl -ies) **1** total number of words which (with rules for combining them) make up a language: No dictionary could list the total

∼ of a language. **2** [C,U] (range of) words known to, or used by, a person, in a profession, etc: a writer with a large ∼. **3** [C] book containing a list of words; list of words used in a book, etc. usually with definitions or translations.

vo·cal /ˈvəʊkəl/ adj of, for, with or using, the voice: the ∼ organs, lips, tongue, etc.
vo·cally /-əlɪ/ adv
vo·cal·ist /ˈvəʊkəlɪst/ n [C] singer.
vo·cal·ize /-aɪz/ vt say or sing.

vo·ca·tion /vəʊˈkeɪʃən/ n **1** (sing only) feeling that one is called to (and qualified for) a certain kind of work (esp social or religious): Nursing, said Florence Nightingale, is a ∼ as well as a profession. **2** [U] special ability (for): He has little or no ∼ for teaching. **3** [C] person's trade or profession.
vo·ca·tional /-nəl/ adj of or for a vocation(3): ∼al courses, e g at a polytechnic.

vodka /ˈvɒdkə/ n [C,U] (portion of) strong Russian alcoholic drink distilled from rye, etc.

vogue /vəʊg/ n **1** current fashion; something currently being done or used: Are maxi-skirts still the ∼? **2** popularity; popular use or acceptance: The Beatles had a great ∼ many years ago. **be in/come into vogue; be/go out of vogue,** be/become (un)fashionable, (un)popular: When did the mini-skirt come into/go out of ∼?

voice /vɔɪs/ n **1** [U] sounds made when speaking or singing: He is not in good ∼, not speaking or singing as well as usual. **2** [C] power of making such sounds: He has lost his ∼, cannot speak or sing properly, e g because of a bad cold. **3** [C,U] sounds uttered by a person, esp considered in relation to their quality: in a loud/soft ∼. They gave ∼ to their indignation. **shout at the top of one's voice,** shout as loudly as one can. **4** [U] **have/demand a voice in sth,** a right to express an opinion on: I have no ∼ in the matter. **5** [C] anything which may be compared or likened to the human voice as expressing ideas, feelings, etc: the ∼ of God, conscience. **6** [U] (gram) the contrast between active and passive as shown in the sentences: The dog ate the meat and The meat was eaten by the dog. □ vt put into words: The spokesman ∼d the feelings of the crowd.

void /vɔɪd/ adj **1** empty; vacant. **2** **void of,** without: a subject ∼ of interest. **3** **null and void,** (legal) without force; invalid: The agreement, not having been signed, was null and ∼. □ n [C] space: There was an aching ∼ in his heart, (fig) a feeling of sadness. □ vt (legal) make void(3).

vol·atile /ˈvɒlətaɪl US: -təl/ adj **1** (of a liquid) that easily changes into gas or vapour. **2** (of a person, his mood) changing quickly or easily from one mood or interest to another.
vol·atil·ity /ˌvɒləˈtɪlətɪ/ n [U]

vol·ca·no /vɒl`keɪnəʊ/ n [C] (pl ~es or ~s) hill or mountain with openings (⇨ crater) through which gases, lava, ashes, etc come up from below the earth's crust (in *an active* ~), or may come up after an interval (in *a dormant* ~), or have long stopped coming up (in *an extinct* ~).
vol·can·ic /vɒl`kænɪk/ adj of, from, like, a volcano.

vole /vəʊl/ n [C] animal like a mouse or rat, esp *a `water-*~, large water-rat.

vo·li·tion /və`lɪʃən US: vəʊ-/ n [U] act, power, of using one's own will, of choosing, making a decision, etc: *do something of one's own* ~.

vol·ley /`vɒlɪ/ n [C] **1** throwing or shooting of a number of stones, arrows, bullets, etc together. **2** succession of oaths, curses, questions. **3** (*tennis*) stroke which returns the ball to the sender before it touches the ground. □ vt, vi **1** (of guns) sound together. **2** return a tennis-ball across the net before it touches the ground.
`**volley·ball**, game in which players on each side of a high net try to keep a ball in motion by hitting it with their hands back and forth over the net without letting it touch the ground.

volt /vəʊlt/ n [C] (abbr **v**) unit of electrical force.
volt·age /`vəʊltɪdʒ/ n [C,U] electrical force measured in volts.

vol·uble /`vɒljʊbəl/ adj talking, able to talk, very quickly and easily; (of speech) fluent.
vol·ubly /-jʊblɪ/ adv
vol·ubil·ity /`vɒljʊ`bɪlətɪ/ n [U]

vol·ume /`vɒljum US: -jəm/ n [C] **1** book, esp one of a set of books; number of sheets, papers, periodicals, etc bound together: *an encyclopedia in* 20 ~*s*. **2** [U] amount of space (expressed in cubic metres, etc) occupied by a substance, liquid or gas: *the* ~ *of wine in a magnum bottle*. **3** [C] large mass, amount or quantity: *the* ~ *of business/work, etc*. **4** [C] (esp pl) masses of steam or smoke: ~*s of black smoke*. **5** [U] (of sound) power; strength: *Your radio has a* ~ *control*.
vol·umi·nous /və`luminəs/ adj (*formal*) **1** (of writing) great in quantity: *a* ~ *work/history*. **2** (of an author) producing many books. **3** occupying much space: ~ *skirts*.

vol·un·tary /`vɒləntrɪ US: -terɪ/ adj **1** doing or ready to do things, willingly, without being forced; (something) done in this manner: ~ *work/helpers; a* ~ *confession*. **2** carried on, supported by, voluntary work and gifts. **3** (opposite = *involuntary*) (of bodily, muscular, movements) controlled by the will.
vol·un·tar·ily /`vɒləntrəlɪ US: `vɒlən`terəlɪ/ adv

vol·un·teer /`vɒlən`tɪə(r)/ n [C] **1** person who offers to do something, esp unpleasant or dangerous. **2** soldier who is not conscripted: (as an *adjective*) *a* ~ *corps*. □ vt, vi

come forward as a volunteer: *He* ~*ed some information/~ed to get some information*.

vo·lup·tu·ous /və`lʌptʃʊəs/ adj of, for, arousing, given up to, sensuous or sensual pleasures: ~ *beauty*.
vo·lup·tu·ous·ly adv

vomit /`vɒmɪt/ vt, vi **1** bring back from the stomach through the mouth: *He* ~*ed everything he had eaten. He was* ~*ing blood*. **2** send out in large quantities: *factory chimneys* ~*ing smoke*. □ n [U] food that has been vomited.

voo·doo /`vudu/ n [U] form of religion, with sorcery and witchcraft, practised by some Negroes in the West Indies, esp Haiti.
voo·doo·ism /-ɪzm/ n [U] this practice.

vo·ra·cious /və`reɪʃəs/ adj (*formal*) very hungry or greedy: *a* ~ *appetite; a* ~ *reader*, one who reads many books.
vo·ra·cious·ly adv in a voracious manner.
vo·racity /və`ræsətɪ/ n [U]

vor·tex /`vɒteks/ n [C] (pl ~es or vortices /-tɪsiz/) **1** mass of whirling fluid or wind, esp a whirlpool. **2** (*fig*) whirl of activity; system, pursuit, viewed as something that tends to absorb people or things: *the* ~ *of politics/war*.

vote /vəʊt/ n [C] **1** (right to give an) expression of opinion or will by persons for or against a person or thing, esp by ballot or by putting up of hands: *I'm going to the polling-booth to record/cast my* ~. *Mr Smith proposed a* ~ *of thanks to the principal speaker*, asked the audience to show, by clapping their hands, that they thanked him. **2** total numbers of votes (to be) given (e g at a political election): *Will the Labour* ~ *increase or decrease at the next election?* **3** money granted, by votes, for a certain purpose: *the Army* ~. □ vi, vt **1** vote for/against sb/sth, support/oppose by voting.
vote on sth, express an opinion by voting. **2** grant money (to): ~ *a sum of money for Education*. **3** (*informal*) declare, by general opinion: *He was* ~*d a fine teacher*, The children gave this as their opinion. **4** suggest, propose: *I* ~ (that) *we avoid him in future*.
voter, person who (by right) votes.

vouch /vaʊtʃ/ vi **vouch for sb/sth**, be responsible for, express confidence in (a person, his honesty, etc): ~ *for him/his ability*.

voucher /`vaʊtʃə(r)/ n [C] receipt or document showing payment of money, correctness of accounts, etc. ⇨ gift voucher.

vouch·safe /vaʊtʃ`seɪf/ vt (formal) be kind enough to give, to do (something): *He* ~*d to help*.

vow /vaʊ/ n [C] solemn promise or undertaking: `*marriage* ~*s; a* ~ *of chastity; break a* ~, not do what one promised. □ vt make a vow; promise or declare solemnly: *He* ~*ed to avenge/that he would avenge the insult*.

vowel /ˈvaʊəl/ n [C] **1** vocal sound made without audible stopping of the breath. **2** letter or symbol used to represent such a sound (e g the letters *a, e, i, o, u*; the phonetic symbols /i, ɪ, e, æ, ɑ, ɒ, ɔ, ʊ, u, ʌ, ɜ, ə/).

voy·age /ˈvɔɪdʒ/ n [C] journey by water, esp a long one in a ship: *a ∼ from London to Australia; during the ∼ out/home; on the outward/homeward ∼.* □ vi go on a voyage: *∼ through the South Seas.*

voy·ager /ˈvɔɪədʒə(r)/ n [C] person who makes a voyage (esp of those who, in former times, explored unknown seas).

vul·gar /ˈvʌlɡə(r)/ adj **1** in bad taste: *∼ language/behaviour/ideas; a ∼ person.* **2** (*formal, rare*) in common use: *∼ errors/ superstitions.*

ˈvulgar ˈfraction, one written in the usual way (e g ⅔), contrasted with a decimal fraction.

vul·gar·ity /vʌlˈɡærətɪ/ n (pl -ies) (**a**) [U] vulgar behaviour. (**b**) (pl) vulgar acts, words, etc.

vul·gar·ly adv

vul·ner·able /ˈvʌlnrəbəl/ adj that is capable of being damaged; not protected against attack: *a position ∼ to attack; people who are ∼ to criticism.*

vul·ner·abil·ity /ˌvʌlnrəˈbɪlətɪ/ n [U]

vul·ture /ˈvʌltʃə(r)/ n [C] **1** kinds of large bird that live on the flesh of dead animals. **2** (*fig*) greedy person who profits from the misfortunes of others.

vy·ing /ˈvaɪɪŋ/ ⇨ vie.

Ww

W, w /ˈdʌbəlju/ (pl W's, w's) the 23rd letter of the English alphabet.

wad /wɒd/ n [C] **1** lump of soft material for keeping things apart or in place, or to stop up a hole: *∼s of cotton-wool.* **2** collection of banknotes, documents, etc folded or rolled together. □ vt (-dd-) stop up, hold in place, with a wad.

waddle /ˈwɒdəl/ vi walk with slow steps as a duck does: *The baby ∼d across the room.* □ n (sing only) this kind of walk.

wade /weɪd/ vi,vt **1** walk with an effort (through water, mud or anything that makes progress difficult); walk across (something) in this way: *He ∼d across the stream.* **2** *wade in,* make a strong attack. *wade into sth,* attack it with force.

ˈwading bird, long-legged water-bird that wades (opposite to web-footed birds that swim).

wader, = wading bird.

wa·fer /ˈweɪfə(r)/ n [C] **1** thin flat biscuit (as eaten with ice-cream). **2** small round piece

of bread used in Holy Communion.

waffle¹ /ˈwɒfl/ n [C] small cake made of batter baked in a special apparatus with two parts hinged together.

waffle² /ˈwɒfl/ vi (GB informal) talk vaguely, unnecessarily, and without much result: *What's she waffling about now?* □ n [U] talk or writing which (even when it sounds impressive) means little or nothing.

waft /wɒft US: wæft/ vt carry lightly and smoothly through the air or over water: *The scent of the flowers was ∼ed to us by the breeze.* □ n [C] light breeze, smell: *∼s of fresh air through the window.*

wag /wæɡ/ vt,vi (-gg-) (cause to) move from side to side or up and down: *The dog ∼ged its tail.* □ n [C] wagging movement: *with a ∼ of the tail.*

wage¹ /weɪdʒ/ n [C] (now usually pl except in certain phrases and when used as an *adjective*) payment made or received for work or services: *His ∼s are £50 a week. The postal workers have asked for a ∼ increase/rise of £25 a week.* ⇨ fee(1), pay¹, salary.

ˈwage-earner, person who works for wages (contrasted with the salaried classes).

ˈwage-freeze, official control of wage increases.

wage² /weɪdʒ/ vt engage in (*war, etc*).

wa·ger /ˈweɪdʒə(r)/ n [C], vt,vi bet (the usual word).

waggle /ˈwæɡəl/ vt,vi = wag¹.

wag·gon (US usually **wagon**) /ˈwæɡən/ n [C] **1** four-wheeled vehicle for carrying goods, pulled by horses or oxen. ⇨ cart. **2** (US = freight car) open railway truck (e g for coal). ⇨ station-wagon.

wa·gon-lit /ˈvægɒŋ ˈli US: ˈvægɑŋ/ n [C] (pl wagons-lit) sleeping-car (as on European railways).

waif /weɪf/ n [C] homeless child: *∼s and strays,* homeless and abandoned children.

wail /weɪl/ vi,vt **1** cry or complain in a loud voice: *a ∼ing child.* **2** make a similar sound (e g of a siren): *an ambulance racing through the streets with sirens ∼ing.* **3** (of the wind) make similar sounds. □ n [C] wailing cry: *the ∼s of a newborn child.*

wain·scot /ˈweɪnskət/ n [C] wooden panelling (on the lower half of the walls of a room).

waist /weɪst/ n [C] **1** part of the body between the ribs and the hips: *measure 60 centimetres round the ∼.* **2** that part of a garment that goes round the waist. **3** middle and narrow part: *the ∼ of a violin.*

waist·coat /ˈweɪskəʊt US: ˈweskət/, close-fitting sleeveless garment worn under a coat or jacket, buttoned down the front (US = vest).

ˈwaist-band, part of a skirt, etc that fits round the waist.

ˈwaist-ˈdeep adj, adv up to the waist: *∼-deep in the mud.*

'waist-'high adj, adv high enough to reach the waist: The wheat was ~-high.

'waist-line, part of the body, a dress, etc at the smallest part of the waist: a dress with a narrow ~line.

wait¹ /weɪt/ n [C] 1 act or time of waiting: We had a long ~ for the bus. 2 [U] lie in wait for, be in hiding in order to attack, etc: The cat lay in ~ for the bird to fly down.

wait² /weɪt/ vi,vt 1 stay where one is, delay acting, until a person or thing comes or until something happens: Please ~ a minute. How long have you been ~ing? We are ~ing for better weather. We ~ed (in order) to see what would happen. keep sb waiting, fail to meet him or be ready at the appointed time: His wife never keeps him ~ing. 2 (= await the usual word): He is ~ing his opportunity. 3 wait on sb, fetch and carry things for. wait on sb hand and foot, ⇨ hand (1). 4 wait at, act as a waiter etc: ~ at table.

'wait-ing list, list of persons who will be served, treated, etc later, if possible: Put me on a ~ing list for two concert tickets.

'wait-ing room, (a) room in a railway-station, etc used by people who are waiting for trains. (b) room (eg in a doctor's or dentist's house or office) where people wait until they can be attended to.

waiter, man who serves food, etc in a restaurant, hotel dining-room, etc.

wait-ress /'weɪtrəs/, female waiter.

waive /weɪv/ vt (say that one will) not insist on (a right or claim): ~ a right.

waiver /'weɪvə(r)/, (legal) (written statement) waiving (a right, etc): sign a ~ of claims against a person.

wake¹ /weɪk/ vi,vi (pt woke /wəʊk/, pp woken /'wəʊkən/) 1 stop sleeping: What time do you usually ~ (up)? He woke up with a start, suddenly. 2 cause to stop sleeping: Don't ~ the baby. The noise woke me (up). 3 stir up from inactivity, inattention, etc: He needs someone to ~ him up, make him active, energetic.

wak-ing adj being awake: waking or sleeping, while awake or asleep.

waken /'weɪkən/ vt,vi (cause to) wake.

wake² /weɪk/ n [C] 1 (usually pl; often `W~s Week) annual holiday in N England, esp in the manufacturing towns of Lancashire. 2 (in Ireland) all-night watch with a corpse before burial, with grieving and drinking of alcoholic liquor.

wake³ /weɪk/ n [C] track left by a ship on smooth water, eg as made by propellers. in the wake of, after; following: Traders arrived in the ~ of the explorers.

walk¹ /wɔːk/ n [C] 1 journey on foot, esp for pleasure or exercise: go for a ~. The station is ten minutes' ~ from my house. 2 manner or style of walking: I recognized him at once by his ~. 3 path or route for walking: my favourite ~s in the neighbourhood. 4 walk of life, profession, occupation: They interviewed people from all ~s of life.

walk² /wɔːk/ vi,vt (for uses with adverbial particles and prepositions, ⇨ 5 below.) 1 (of persons) move by putting forward each foot in turn, not having both feet off the ground at once; (of animals) move at the slowest pace: He ~ed five miles. He was ~ing up and down the station platform. 2 cause to walk: He ~ed his horse up the hill. walk sb off his feet/legs, tire him out by making him walk far. 3 go over on foot: I have ~ed this district for miles round. 4 (used with various nouns): ~ the plank, ⇨ plank. ~ the streets, be a prostitute (a `street-~er).

5 (special uses with adverbial particles and prepositions):

walk about, walk in various directions, eg as a tourist.

walk away with sth, win (a competition) easily: The Russian team ~ed away with the gymnastics competition.

walk off with sth, take (either on purpose or unintentionally): Someone has ~ed off with my umbrella.

walk in, enter.

walk into, meet with accidentally: ~ into an ambush.

walk out, go on strike: The workers ~ed out yesterday. `walk-out n [C].

walk out on sb, (informal) desert him (at a time when he is expecting help, etc).

walk over sb, (informal) defeat him easily: She ~ed all over the other competitors. Hence, `walk-over n [C] easy victory.

walk up, (a) (imperative) (used as on invitation to enter (a circus, show, etc). (b) walk along: ~ up the High Street. (c) walk upstairs. (d) approach: A stranger ~ed up (to me) and asked me the time.

wall /wɔːl/ n 1 continuous, usually vertical, solid structure of stone, brick, concrete, wood, etc forming one of the sides of a building or room, or used to enclose, divide or protect something (including land): Hang the picture on that ~. Some old towns have ~s right round them. with one's back to the wall, ⇨ back (1). be/go up the wall, (sl) be/become very angry. go to the wall, be defeated, especially financially. 2 (fig) something like a wall: a ~ of fire; the abdominal ~. □ vt 1 (usually pp) surround with walls: a ~ed garden. 2 wall sth up/off, fill or close up with bricks, etc: ~ up a window.

`wall-flower, (a) common garden plant with sweet-smelling flowers. (b) woman who does not dance because not asked.

`wall-paper, paper with a coloured design, for covering the walls of rooms.

wal-laby /'wɒləbɪ/ n [C] (pl -ies) sorts of small kangaroo.

wal-let /'wɒlɪt/ n [C] folding case of leather, etc for banknotes, credit-cards, etc.

wal-lop /'wɒləp/ vt (sl) beat severely; hit

735

hard. □ *n* [C] heavy blow; crash: *Down he went with a* ~!

wal·low /ˈwɒləʊ/ *vi* **1** roll about (in mud, dirty water, etc): *pigs ~ing in the mud.* **2** (*fig*) take great delight in: *~ing in success.* □ *n* [C] place to which animals (e g buffaloes) go regularly to wallow.

wal·nut /ˈwɔːlnʌt/ *n* **1** [C] (tree producing a) nut with an kernel that can be eaten. **2** [U] the wood, used for making furniture.

wal·rus /ˈwɔːlrəs/ *n* [C] (*pl* ~es) large sea-animal of the arctic regions with two long tusks.

waltz /wɔːls *US:* wɒlts/ *n* [C] (music for a) slow ballroom dance. □ *vi, vt* (cause to) dance a waltz: *She ~es divinely.*

wan /wɒn/ *adj* (-nn-) **1** (of a person, his looks, etc) looking ill, sad, tired, anxious: *a ~ smile.* **2** (of light, the sky) pale; not bright.
wan·ly *adv*

wand /wɒnd/ *n* [C] slender stick or rod as used by a conjurer, fairy or magician.

wan·der /ˈwɒndə(r)/ *vi, vt* **1** go from place to place without any special purpose or destination: *~ up and down the road; ~ (through/over) the world.* **2** leave the right path or direction: *Some of the sheep have ~ed away,* are lost. *We ~ed (for) miles and miles in the mist.* **3** allow the thoughts to go from subject to subject: *Don't ~ from the subject/point. His mind is ~ing.*
wan·derer, person or animal that wanders.
wan·der·ings *n pl* (a) long travels; journeys: *tell the story of one's ~ings.* (b) confused speech during illness (esp high fever).

wan·der·lust /ˈwɒndəlʌst/ [U] strong desire to travel.

wane /weɪn/ *vi* **1** (of the moon) show a decreasing bright area after full moon. ⇨ wax²(1). **2** become less or weaker: *His strength/reputation is waning.* □ *n* esp **on the wane,** waning.

wangle /ˈwæŋɡl/ *vt* (*sl*) get, arrange something, by using improper influence, by trickery, persuasion, etc: *~ an extra week's holiday.* □ *n* [C] act of wangling.

want¹ /wɒnt/ *n* **1** [U] scarcity; state of being absent: *The plants died from ~ of water. Your work shows ~ of thought/care.* **2** [U] need; absence of some necessary thing: *The house is in ~ of repair.* **3** [C] (usually *pl*) desire for something as necessary to life, happiness, etc; thing to be desired: *We can supply all your ~s.*

want² /wɒnt/ *vt, vi* **1** be in need of: *That man ~s a wife to look after him,* needs to marry a woman who will look after him. *I don't ~ (= I object to having) women meddling in my affairs.* **2** wish for; have a desire for: *She ~s to go to Italy. She ~s me to go with her. He is ~ed by the police,* i e because he is suspected of having done wrong. (*Note: want* is used for something possible to get, *wish* is used for something

impossible or unlikely.) **3** need, ought (as in the notes to the examples): *Your hair ~s cutting,* needs to be cut. *You ~ (= ought) to talk to your teacher about that problem.* **4** (progressive tenses only) **be wanting (in sth),** (with human subject) be lacking: *He's ~ing in politeness,* is impolite. **be found wanting:** *He was put to the test and found ~ing,* inadequate. **5 want for nothing,** have all one needs.

wan·ton /ˈwɒntən/ *adj* **1** playful; irresponsible: *in a ~ mood.* **2** wild: *a ~ growth* (of weeds, etc). **3** deliberate: *~ destruction/ damage.* **4** immoral: *a ~ woman.*
wan·ton·ly *adv* in a wanton manner.

war /wɔː(r)/ *n* **1** [C,U] (state created by the use of armed forces between countries or ('civil war') rival groups in a nation: *We have had two world ~s in this century.* **at war,** in a state of war. **declare war (on),** announce that a state of war exists (with another state). **go to war (against),** start fighting. **have been in the wars,** (*informal*) have suffered injury, misfortune, etc. **2** [U] science or art of fighting, using weapons, etc: *the art of ~,* strategy and tactics. **3** (*fig*) any kind of struggle or conflict: *the ~ against poverty; a ~ of nerves/words.* □ *vi* (-rr-) fight; make war.
war-cry, word or cry shouted as a signal in battle.
war-dance, one by tribal warriors before going into battle, to celebrate a victory, or (in peace) to represent fighting.
war·fare /ˈwɔːfeə(r)/, making war; condition of being at war; fighting: *the horrors of modern ~fare.*
war-god, god (e g Mars) worshipped as giving victory in war.
war·head, (of a torpedo, shell, etc) explosive head.
war·like /ˈwɔːlaɪk/ *adj* (a) ready for, suggesting, war: *~like preparations.* (b) fond of war: *a cruel, ~like people.*
war·monger, person who encourages war.
war·path, (only in) **on the warpath,** ready for, engaged in, a fight or quarrel.
war·ship, ship for use in war.
war·time /ˈwɔːtaɪm/, time when there is war: *in ~time;* (as an *adjective*) *~time regulations.*
war-torn *adj* exhausted by, worn out in, war.
war-widow, woman whose husband has been killed in war.

warble /ˈwɔːbl/ *vi, vt* (esp of birds) sing with a gentle trilling note: *a blackbird warbling in a tree.* □ *n* [C] warbling.
war·bler /ˈwɔːblə(r)/, (kinds of) bird that warbles.

ward /wɔːd/ *n* **1** [C] division of, separate room in, a building, esp a hospital: *the children's ~.* **2** [C] division of a local government area, each division being represented by one Councillor. **3** [U] state of being in custody or under the control of a guardian: *a child in* ~. **4** [C] person under the guardianship of an older person or of law authorities. □ *vt* **ward sth off,** keep away, avoid: ~ *off a blow/danger.*

-ward(s) /-wədʒ/ *suffix* in the direction of: *backward(s).*

war·den /ˈwɔdən/ *n* [C] **1** person having control or authority: *the* ~ *of a youth hostel.* ⇨ **traffic warden. 2** (*US*) warder.

war·der /ˈwɔdə(r)/ *n* [C] (*GB*) person acting as guard in a prison.

ward·ress /ˈwɔdrəs/, woman warder.

ward·robe /ˈwɔdrəub/ *n* **1** cupboard with pegs, shelves, etc for clothes. **2** stock of clothes: *My* ~ *needs to be renewed,* I must buy some new clothes. **3** stock of costumes of a theatrical company.

ware /weə(r)/ *n* **1** (as a *suffix*) manufactured goods: `silver~, `iron~, `hard~. **2** (*pl*) articles offered for sale: *advertise one's* ~s.

ware·house /ˈweəhaus/ *n* [C] building for storing goods before distribution to retailers. □ *vt* store in a warehouse.

war·fare /ˈwɔfeə(r)/ ⇨ **war.**

warm[1] /wɔm/ *adj* (-er, -est) **1** having a medium degree of heat (between *cool* and *hot*): *Come and get* ~ *by the fire.* **2** (of clothing) serving to keep the body warm: *Put your* ~*est coat on.* **3** (of colours) bright; suggesting heat: *Red and yellow are* ~ *colours.* **4** enthusiastic, hearty: *give a speaker a* ~ *welcome.* **5** sympathetic; affectionate: *He has a* ~ *heart.*

'warm-'blooded, (a) (of animals) having warm blood. (b) (of a person) showing feelings, passion.

'warm-'hearted, kind and affectionate.

warm·ly *adv* in a warm manner: ~*ly dressed;* thank them ~*ly.*

warm[2] /wɔm/ *vt,vi* make or become warm or warmer: ~ *oneself/one's hands by the fire.* Please ~ (*up*) *this milk.* **warm to one's work/task, etc,** become more interested and involved. □ *n* (usually *sing* with *a*) act of warming: *Come near the fire and have a* ~.

warmth /wɔmθ/ *n* [U] state of being warm: *He was pleased with the* ~ *of his welcome.*

warn /wɔn/ *vt* give (a person) notice of possible danger or unpleasant consequences; inform in advance of what may happen: *He was* ~*ed of the danger. He* ~*ed me that there were pickpockets in the crowd/*~*ed me against pickpockets.*

warn·ing /ˈwɔnɪŋ/ *adj* that warns: *They fired some* ~ *shots.* □ *n* **1** [C] that which warns or serves to warn: *Let this be a* ~ *to you,* let this p nishment, accident, misfortune, etc teach you to be careful in future. **2** [U] action of warning; state of being warned: *The speaker sounded a note of* ~, spoke of possible danger.

warp /wɔp/ *vt,vi* **1** (cause to) become bent or twisted from the usual or natural shape:

Some metals ~ *in very hot weather.* **2** (*fig*) make evil; twist: *His judgement is* ~*ed,* biassed because of possible advantage for himself. *He has a* ~*ed sense of humour,* e g that is cruel, evil, abnormal, etc. □ *n* [C] **1** twisted or bent condition in timber, etc caused by shrinking or expansion. **2** threads over and under which other threads (the *weft*) are passed when cloth is woven on a loom.

war·rant /ˈwɔrənt *US:* ˈwɔr-/ *n* **1** [U] justification or authority: *He had no* ~ *for saying so/for what he did.* **2** [C] written order giving official authority: *a* ~ *to arrest a suspected criminal/for his arrest.* □ *vt* **1** be a warrant(1) for: *His interference was certainly not* ~*ed.* **2** guarantee (the more usual word). **3** (usually *pp*) justified: *His anger is not* ~*ed.*

war·ran·tee /ˈwɔrənˈti: *US:* ˈwɔr-/, person to whom a warranty is made.

war·ran·tor /ˈwɔrəntɔ(r) *US:* ˈwɔr-/, person who makes a warranty.

war·ranty /ˈwɔrəntɪ *US:* ˈwɔr-/, (written or printed) guarantee (e g to repair or replace defective goods): *The car is still under* ~*y.*

war·ren /ˈwɔrən *US:* ˈwɔr-/ *n* [C] **1** area of land in which there are many burrows in which rabbits live and breed. **2** (*fig*) building or district in which it is difficult to find one's way about: *lose oneself in a* ~ *of narrow streets.*

war·rior /ˈwɔrɪə(r) *US:* ˈwɔr-/ *n* [C] (*literary*) soldier; fighter: (as an *adjective*) *a* ~ *tribe.*

wart /wɔt/ *n* [C] small, hard, dry growth on the skin.

wart·hog /ˈwɔthɒg/ *n* [C] kinds of African pig with two large tusks and growths like warts on the face.

wary /ˈweərɪ/ *adj* (-ier, -iest) in the habit of being careful about possible danger or trouble: *be* ~ *of giving offence/of strangers.*

war·ily /-əlɪ/

was /wəz *strong form:* wɒz *US:* wʌz/ ⇨ **be.**

wash[1] /wɒʃ *US:* wɔʃ/ *n* **1** (*sing* only, usually with *a, an*) act of washing; being washed: *Will you give the car a* ~, please. **2** (*sing* only) clothing, sheets, etc (to be) washed or being washed: *When does the* ~ *come back from the laundry?* **3** (*sing* with *the*) movement or flow of water; sound made by moving water: *the* ~ *of the waves.* ⇨ also **eyewash, whitewash.**

wash[2] /wɒʃ *US:* wɔʃ/ *vt,vi* (for use with *adverbial particles* and *prepositions,* ⇨ **7** below.) **1** make clean with or in water or other liquid: ~ *one's hands/clothes. He never* ~*es* (i e washes himself) *in cold water,* **wash one's hands of sth/sb,** ⇨ hand[1](1). **2** (of materials) be capable of being washed without damage or loss of colour: *Does this material* ~ *well?* **3** (*fig*) be acceptable, bear examination: *That* *argument/excuse will not* ~. **4** (of the sea or a river) flow past or against: *The sea ~es the base of the cliffs.* **5** (of moving liquid) carry away, or in a specified direction: *He was ~ed overboard by a huge wave.* **6** go flowing, sweeping or splashing (*along, out, in, into, over,* etc): *We heard the waves ~ing against the sides of our boat. Huge waves ~ed over the deck.*

7 (special uses with *adverbial particles* and *prepositions*):

wash sth away, remove by washing: ~ *away stains.* **be washed away,** be removed by the movement of the sea, a river, etc: *The cliffs are gradually being ~ed away.*

wash sth down, clean by washing, e g with a hosepipe: ~ *down a car/the deck of a ship.*

wash sth down (with), swallow (liquid) with: *bread and cheese ~ed down with beer.*

wash sth out, clean by washing: ~ *out a dress.* **washed out,** (a) (*fig*) exhausted; pale: *feel ~ed out.* (b) (of games, sport) cancelled because of heavy rain. (c) (of roads, etc) ruined by rain: flooded. ⇨ wash-out below.

wash sth up, wash plates, knives, forks, pans, etc: ~ *up the breakfast things.* Hence, **'washing-'up** *n* (with *the*). **be washed up,** carried on to the beach (by waves, etc): *The empty boat was ~ed up on the beach.* (**sl**) **washed up,** (*informal*) ruined.

wash-³ /wɒʃ *US:* wɔʃ/ *prefix* (often used as a substitute for *washing*):

'wash-basin, basin for holding water in which to wash one's face and hands.

'wash-hand-basin, = wash-basin.

'wash-hand-stand, = wash-stand.

'wash-out *n* (a) place in a road, etc where a flood or heavy rain has carried away earth, etc and interrupted communications. (b) (*informal*) useless or unsuccessful person; complete failure.

'wash-room, (*US*) lavatory (esp in a public building, etc).

'wash-stand, piece of furniture with a basin, jug, etc formerly used for washing in a bedroom.

'wash-tub, large wooden bowl in which to wash clothes.

wash-able /ˈwɒʃəbəl/ *adj* that can be washed without being spoiled.

washer /ˈwɒʃə(r) *US:* ˈwɔ-/ *n* [C] **1** machine for washing clothes, or (`dish-~) dishes. **2** small flat ring of metal, plastic, rubber or leather for making a joint or screw tight.

wash-ing /ˈwɒʃɪŋ *US:* ˈwɔ-/ *n* [U] **1** washing or being washed. **2** clothes being washed or to be washed: *hang out the ~ on the line to dry.*

'washing-machine, power driven machine for washing clothes.

'washing-'up, ⇨ wash sth up at wash²(7).

washy /ˈwɒʃɪ *US:* ˈwɔ-/ *adj* **1** (of liquids) thin, watery. **2** (of colours) looking faded; pale. **3** (of feeling, attitude) lacking in strength.

wasp /wɒsp *US:* wɔsp/ *n* [C] kinds of flying insect with a powerful sting in the tail.

wast-age /ˈweɪstɪdʒ/ *n* [U] amount wasted; loss by waste.

waste¹ /weɪst/ *adj* **1** (of land) that is not or cannot be used; no longer of use: ~ *land,* not occupied or used for any purpose. **lay waste** ⇨ lay¹(4). **2** useless; thrown away because not wanted: `~ `paper.

'waste-land, (a) barren, desolate or unused land. (b) land destroyed by war, etc. (c) (*fig*) life, society, looked on as culturally and spiritually barren.

waste² /weɪst/ *n* **1** [U] wasting or being wasted: *It's a* ~ *of time to wait any longer.* **go/run to waste,** be wasted: *What a pity to see so many ideas going to* ~*!* **2** [U] waste material; refuse. **3** area of waste land, etc: *the ~s of the Sahara.*

'waste-'paper-basket, basket or other container for scraps of paper, etc.

'waste-pipe, pipe for carrying off (used) water.

waste-ful /-fəl/ *adj* causing waste; using more than is needed: ~*ful habits/processes.*

waste-fully /-fəlɪ/ *adv*

waste³ /weɪst/ *vt, vi* **1** make no use of; use without a good purpose; use more of (something) than is necessary: ~ *one's time and money. All his efforts were ~d,* had no result. **2** make (land) waste. **3** (cause to) lose strength by degrees: *He's wasting away.*

watch¹ /wɒtʃ/ *n* **1** [U] act of watching, esp to see that all is well. **be on the watch (for),** be watching for (a person or thing, esp possible danger). **2** (in former times) (usually *sing* with *the*) body of men employed to go through the streets and protect people and their property, esp at night. **3** (in ships) period of duty (4 or 2 hours) for part of the crew. **keep watch,** be on watch or watching.

'watch-dog, dog kept to protect property.

'watch-man, (*modern use*) man employed to guard a building (e g a bank, block of offices, factory) against thieves, esp at night.

watch-ful /-fəl/ *adj* (esp) wide-awake.

watch-word /-wɜd/, (a) password. (b) slogan.

watch² /wɒtʃ/ *vt, vi* look at; keep the eyes on: *W~ me carefully. W~ what I do and how I do it. We sat there ~ing the cricket. I'll ~ over* (= look after) *her while you go shopping.* **watch one's step,** (*fig*) be careful not to make an error, let a person win an advantage, etc, e g in negotiations.

watcher, person who watches.

watch³ /wɒtʃ/ *n* [C] small instrument for telling the time that can be carried in the pocket or worn on the wrist.

watch-maker, person who makes or repairs watches.

water[1] /ˈwɔtə(r)/ n (pl only as shown in examples below) **1** [U] liquid (H_2O) as in rivers, lakes, seas and oceans: *Fish live in (the)* ~. *by water,* by boat, ship, etc. *in deep water(s),* experiencing difficulty or misfortune. *under water,* flooded: *The fields were under* ~ *after the heavy rain. like a fish out of water,* feeling uncomfortable, behaving awkwardly, because of unfamiliar surroundings, an unfamiliar situation, etc. *be in/get into hot water,* have/get into trouble (esp because of foolish behaviour, etc). *hold water,* (of a theory) be sound when tested. *keep one's head above water,* avoid (esp financial) troubles or misfortunes. *spend money, etc like water,* extravagantly. *throw cold water on (a plan, etc),* discourage (it). *tread water,* ⇨ tread v(4). **2** [U] the state of the tide: *at high/low* ~. **3** (pl) seas as shown by a preceding word: *Home* ~s, the seas near the country to which a ship belongs. **4** (usually pl) mass of water: *the (ˈhead-)* ~s of *the Nile,* the lake from which it flows. **5** [U] solution of a substance in water: `rose-~.`

water-bird, kinds of bird that swim or wade in water.

water-biscuit, thin, hard biscuit eaten with butter and cheese.

water-borne adj (a) (of goods) carried by water. (b) (of diseases) passed on by the use of contaminated water.

water-buffalo, the common domestic buffalo of India, Indonesia, etc.

water-closet, (common abbr **WC**) small room with a lavatory.

water-colour (*US* = **-color**), (a) (pl) paints (to be) mixed with water, not oil. (b) picture painted with water-colours. (c) (pl or sing) the art of painting such pictures.

water-cress, creeping plant that grows in running water, with hot-tasting leaves used in salads.

water-fall, fall of water, esp where a river falls over rocks or a cliff.

water-front, land at the water's edge, esp the part of a town facing the sea, the harbour, a lake, etc.

water-hole, shallow depression in which water collects (esp in the bed of a river otherwise dry, and to which animals go to drink).

water-ice, frozen, flavoured water.

water-level, surface of water in a reservoir, etc esp as a measurement of depth.

water-lily, kinds of plant with broad, flat leaves floating on the surface of the water.

water-logged, adj (a) (of wood) so saturated with water that it will not float. (b) (of a ship) so full of water that it will not float. (c) (of land) thoroughly soaked with water.

water-main, main pipe in a system of water-supply.

water-mark, (a) manufacturer's design in some kinds of paper, seen when the paper is held against light. (b) mark which shows how high water (e g the tide, a river) has risen or how low it has fallen.

water-melon, (plant with) large, smooth-skinned melon with juicy pink or red flesh.

water-mill, mill whose machinery is turned by water-power.

water-polo, game played by two teams of swimmers who try to throw a ball into a goal.

water-power, power obtained from flowing or falling water, used to drive machinery or generate electric current.

water-proof adj which does not let water through: ~*proof material.* □ n [C] waterproof coat. □ vi make waterproof.

water-rat/-vole, animal like a rat living in, near, water.

water-rate, (*GB*) charge made (usually quarterly) for the use of water from a public water-supply.

water-shed, (a) line of high land separating river systems. (b) (fig) division between events which take different courses.

water-side, edge of the coast, a river-bank, etc: *go for a stroll along the* ~*side.*

water-ski vi ski on water while being towed at speed by a fast motor-boat. Hence, **water-skiing** n.

water-spout, (a) pipe or spout from which water is discharged, e g rainwater from a roof. (b) whirlwind over the sea which draws up a spinning column of water.

water-supply, system of providing and storing water, amount stored, for a district, town, building, etc.

water-table, level below which the ground is saturated with water: *The* ~*table has been lowered by drought.*

water-tight adj (a) so that water cannot get in or out: ~*tight boots.* (b) (fig) (of an agreement, etc) so that there can be no escape from any of the provisions; leaving no possibility of misunderstanding.

water tower, one supporting a large tank which maintains the pressure for a water-supply.

water-way, navigable channel (e g a canal).

water-wheel, one turned by a flow of water, used to work machinery.

water-works, (used with a *sing* or pl *verb*) (a) system of reservoirs, pumping stations, for supplying water. (b) ornamental fountains. (c) (*informal*) (working of the) bladder: *Are your* ~*works all right?* Can you pass urine normally? (d) (*informal*) tears: *Let's not have the* ~*works again!* Let's have no more crying!

water-worn adj (of rocks, etc) made smooth by the action of water.

water[2] /ˈwɔtə(r)/ vt,vi **1** put water on; sprinkle with water: ~ *the lawn/the plants.*

2 give water to: ~ *the horses.* 3 (of the eyes or mouth) fill with water; have much liquid: *The smoke made my eyes* ~. *The smell from the kitchen made my mouth* ~, made me feel hungry. 4 **water sth down, (a)** add water to: *This whisky has been* ~ed (*down*). **(b)** (*fig*) weaken: *The story has been* ~ed *down*.

`water·ing-can,` container with a long spout, used for watering plants.

`water·ing-place, (a)` water-hole. **(b)** spa. **(c)** seaside resort.

wat·ery /ˈwɔːtərɪ/ *adj* (-ier, -iest) 1 of or like water; (esp of cooked vegetables) containing, cooked in, too much water: ~ *soup.* 2 (of colour) pale. 3 (of the eyes or lips) running with, covered with, water.

watt /wɒt/ *n* [C] unit of electrical power: *a 60* ~ *light-bulb.*

wattle¹ /ˈwɒtəl/ *n* [U] structure of woven sticks or twigs used for fences, walls, etc.

wattle² /ˈwɒtəl/ *n* [C] red flesh hanging down from the head or throat of a bird, esp a turkey.

wave /weɪv/ *vi,vt* 1 move to and fro, up and down: *flags/branches waving in the wind.* 2 cause (something) to move in this way (e g to make a signal or request, to give a greeting, etc): ~ *one's hand/a flag. She* ~d *goodbye to us.* 3 cause (a person) to move in a certain direction by waving: *He* ~d *us away.* **wave sth aside,** (*fig*) dismiss: *My objections were* ~d *aside.* 4 (of a line or surface, of hair) be in a series of curves (〜〜〜): *Her hair* ~s *beautifully.* 5 cause to be in a series of curves: *She's had her hair permanently* ~d. □ *n* [C] 1 long ridge of water, esp on the sea, between two hollows; such a ridge curling over and breaking on the shore. **in waves,** in successive lines like waves: *The infantry attacked in* ~s. 2 act of waving(2 above); waving movement: *with a* ~ *of his hand.* 3 curve like a wave of the sea: *the* ~s *in her hair.* 4 steady increase and spread: *a* ~ *of enthusiasm/hatred.* ⇨ crime-wave, heat-wave. 5 motion like a wave by which heat, light, sound or electricity is spread or carried.

`wave-length,` distance between the highest point (the crest) of one wave(5) and that of the next. *(not) on the same wavelength,* (*fig*) (not) in agreement.

wavy *adj* (-ier, -iest) having curves: *a wavy line; wavy hair.*

wa·ver /ˈweɪvə(r)/ *vi* 1 move uncertainly or unsteadily: ~*ing shadows/flames.* 2 be or become unsteady; begin to give way: *His courage* ~ed. 3 hesitate: ~ *between two opinions.*

wa·verer, person who wavers.

wax¹ /wæks/ *n* [U] soft yellow substance produced by bees (`bees`~) and used for making honeycomb cells; kinds of substance similar to beeswax (e g as obtained from petroleum), used for making candles, etc: (as

an *adjective*) *a* ~ *candle.* ⇨ sealing-wax. □ *vt* cover, polish or treat with wax: ~ *furniture/a wooden floor.*

wax² /wæks/ *vi* (esp of the moon, contrasted with *wane*) show a larger bright area.

way /weɪ/ *n* 1 [C] road, street, path, etc: *a* ~ *across the fields. There's no* ~ *through.* ⇨ highway, railway, etc. **pave the way for,** (*fig*) prepare for, prepare people to accept (reforms, etc). 2 [C] route, road (to be) used (*from* one place *to* another): *Which is the best/right/quickest/shortest* ~ *there? Can you find your* ~ *home? Which is the* ~ *in/out?* **go one's way(s),** depart. **go out of one's way (to do sth),** make a special effort: *He went out of his way to be rude to me/to help me.* **lead the way, (a)** go in front as leader. **(b)** show by example how something may be done. **make one's way in life,** succeed. **pay one's way, (a)** keep out of debt. **(b)** pay one's share of expenses instead of letting others pay. **by the way of,** using a route through: *He came by* ~ *of Dover.* **out of the way,** exceptional, uncommon: *He has done nothing out of the* ~ *yet.* 3 **on the/one's way,** being engaged in going or coming: *They're still on the/their* ~. **by the way, (a)** during a journey. **(b)** (*fig*) incidentally (often used to introduce a remark not connected with the subject of conversation). **on the way out,** (*fig*) (*informal*) going out of fashion. 4 [C] method or plan; course of action: *the right/wrong/best* ~ *to do/of doing something. The work must be finished (in) one* ~ *or another.* **Where there's a will there's a way,** (*proverb*) If we want to do something, we will find a method of doing it. **ways and means,** methods, esp of providing money. **have/get one's own way,** get/do what one wants. **go/take one's own way,** act independently, esp against advice. 5 (*sing* only) distance between two points; distance (to be) traversed: *It's a long* ~ *off/a long* ~ *from here. This will go a long* ~ (= will be very helpful) *in overcoming the difficulty.* 6 [C] direction: *He went this/that/the other* ~. *Look this* ~, *please. Such opportunities never come/fall my* ~, come to me. 7 [U] advance in some direction; progress (esp of a ship or boat). **be under way,** (of a ship) be moving through the water. **get under way,** start to move forward. 8 [U] space for forward movement, for passing ahead; freedom to go forward: *Don't stand in the/my* ~. **be/put sth out of harm's way,** in a safe place. **get sth out of the way,** settle it, dispose of it. **give way (to sth/sb),** ⇨ give¹(10). **make way (for),** allow space or a free passage: *All traffic has to make* ~ *for an ambulance.* **see one's way (clear) to doing sth,** (esp) feel justified in doing something: *I don't see my way clear to helping you.* 9 [C] custom; manner of behaving; personal peculiarity: *English/Chinese* ~ *of living; the* ~ *of the* *world*, what appears to be justified by custom. *I don't like the ～* (= manner in which) *he looks at me.* **mend one's ways**, improve one's manners, behaviour, etc. **to `my way of thinking**, in my opinion. **10** [C] respect; point or detail: *He's a clever man in some ～. He's a nice man in his (own) ～.* **11** [C] condition, state, degree: *Things are/She's in a bad ～.* **in a small way**, on a small scale: *help in a small ～.* **have it both ways**, choose first one and then the other of alternatives in order to suit one's convenience, argument, etc. **12** [C] ordinary course: *do something in the ～ of business.* **13 by way of**, (a) as a substitute for or as a kind of: *say something by ～ of an apology/introduction.* (b) for the purpose of, with the intention of: *make inquiries by ～ of learning the facts of the case.* (c) in the course of: *by ～ of business.* ⇨ also **2** above.

'way-a`head *adj* (*informal*) ahead of current fashion: *clothes ～-ahead of the fashion.*

'way-`out *adj* (*informal*) = way-ahead: *～-out clothes.*

way-far-er /ˈweɪfeərə(r)/ *n* [C] (*literary*) traveller, esp on foot.

`way-far-ing /-feərɪŋ/ *adj* travelling: *a wayfaring man.*

way-side *n* [C] side of a road: *by the ～;* (as an *adjective*) *～ flowers.*

way-lay /weɪˈleɪ/ *vt* (*pt,pp* -laid /-ˈleɪd/) (wait somewhere to) attack, rob (a person), approach (a person) unexpectedly (with a request): *He waylaid me with a request for a loan.*

way-ward /ˈweɪwəd/ *adj* not easily controlled or guided: *a ～ child.*

we /wi/ *pron* (⇨ **us**) **1** (used by a speaker or writer referring to himself and another or others): *Can ～ all come to visit you?* **2** (used by a royal person in proclamations instead of *I*).

weak /wik/ *adj* (-er, -est) **1** (opposite of *strong*) lacking in strength; easily broken; unable to resist strong use, opposition, etc: *too ～ to walk; ～ in the legs; a ～ team; the ～ points of an argument/plan.* **2** (of health, etc) below the usual standard: *a ～ heart.* Hence, **'～-`sighted**, **'～-`minded**, **'～-`headed**. **3** (of mixed liquids or solutions) having little of some substance in relation to the water, etc: *～ tea/beer.* **4** not good; not efficient: *～ in spelling/grammar.*

'weak-`kneed *adj* (*fig*) weak in character.

'weak form (of the pronunciation of some words), form occurring in an unstressed position, usually by the use of a different vowel sound or by the absence of a vowel sound or consonant (e g /ənd/ for *and*).

'weak `verb, (*gram*) one inflected by additions to the stem, not by vowel change (e g *walk, walked*).

weak-ling, weak person or animal.

weak-ly *adv* in a weak manner. □ *adj* deli-

cate in health: *a ～ly child.*

weak-ness *n* (a) [U] state of being weak: *the ～ness of old age.* (b) [C] fault or defect of character: *We all have our little ～nesses.* (c) **have a weakness for**, a special or foolish liking for: *He has a ～ness for icecream.*

weaken /ˈwikən/ *vt,vi* make, become, weak(er).

weal /wil/ *n* [C] mark on the skin made by a blow from a whip, stick.

wealth /welθ/ *n* [U] **1** (possession of a) great amount of property, money, etc: *a man of ～.* **2** (*sing* only with *a, an* or *the*) great amount or number of: *a book with a ～ of illustrations; the ～ of phrases and sentences to illustrate meanings in this dictionary.*

wealthy *adj* (-ier, -iest) rich.

wean /win/ *vt* **1** accustom (a baby, a young animal) to food other than its mother's milk. **2** (*fig*) cause (a person) to turn away (from a habit, bad companions, etc): *～ a person off/away from drugs.*

weapon /ˈwepən/ *n* [C] something designed for, or used in, fighting or struggling (e g swords, guns, fists, a strike by workmen).

weapon-less *adj* unarmed (the usual word).

weap-onry *n* [U] weapons collectively.

wear¹ /weə(r)/ *n* [U] **1** wearing or being worn; use as clothing: *This coat is beginning to look the worse for ～*, shows signs of having been worn for a long time, so that it is no longer in a good or useful condition. **2** damage or loss of quality from use: *The carpet is showing signs of ～.* **wear and tear**, damage, loss in value, because used. **3** capacity to endure: *There's not much ～ left in these shoes*, they cannot be worn much longer. **4** (used chiefly in compounds or in terms used by tradesmen) things to wear: *`under～; `ladies'/`men's/`children's ～.*

wear² /weə(r)/ *vt,vi* (*pt* wore /wɔ(r)/, *pp* worn /wɔn/) **1** have on the body, carry on one's person or on some part of it: *He was ～ing spectacles/heavy shoes/a ring on his finger. She never ～s green*, ie green clothes. *She used to ～ her hair long*, used to have long hair. **2** (of expressions) have on the face: *～ a smile.* **3** (cause to) become less useful or to be in a certain condition, by being used: *I have worn my socks into holes. This material has worn thin. The stones were worn by the constant flow of water.* **4** make (a hole, groove, etc) in by rubbing or attrition: *～ holes in a rug/one's socks. In time a path was worn across the field.* **5** remain in a certain condition (after use): *Good leather will ～ for years. This cloth has worn well/badly. Old Mr Smith is ～ing well*, still looks well in spite of his advanced age.

6 (uses with *adverbial particles* and *prepositions*):

wear away, (a) become broken, thin, weak, as the result of constant use: *The inscription* on the stone had worn away, the words were difficult to read. (b) (of time) pass slowly: *as the evening wore away.* **wear sth away**, use up or damage something by constant use, etc: *The footsteps of thousands of visitors had worn away the stones.*

wear down, become gradually smaller, thinner, weaker, etc: *The heels of these shoes are ∼ing down.* **wear sth down**, cause to wear down. **wear sb/sth down**, weaken by constant attack, nervous strain, etc: *These noisy children do ∼ me down!*

wear off, pass away: *The novelty will soon ∼ off.*

wear on, (of time) pass.

wear (sth) out, (cause to) become useless, worn thin, exhausted: *Cheap shoes soon ∼ out. His patience had/was at last worn out.* **wear sb out**, exhaust, tire out: *I'm worn out by all this hard work.* Hence, **'worn-'out** *adj*: *a worn-out coat.*

wear·able /'weərəbəl/ *adj* that can be, or is fit to be worn.

weary /'wɪərɪ/ *adj* (-ier, -iest) **1** tired: *feel ∼; be ∼ of his constant grumbling.* **2** causing tiredness: *a ∼ journey.* **3** showing tiredness: *a ∼ sigh.* □ *vt,vi* make or become weary: *∼ of living alone.*

wear·ily /-əlɪ/ *adv*

weari·ness *n* [U]

weari·some /'wɪərɪsəm/ *adj* tiring; long and dull.

wea·sel /'wizəl/ *n* [C] small, fierce animal with red-brown fur.

weather[1] /'weðə(r)/ *n* [C] conditions over a particular area and at a particular time with reference to sunshine, temperature, wind, rain, etc: *He stays indoors in wet ∼. She goes out in all ∼s* (pl here = all kinds of ∼). (*Note*: *climate* is used when referring to a long period of time, e g a season.) **be/feel under the weather**, (*informal*) unwell. **make heavy weather of sth**, find it difficult.

weather-beaten *adj* showing marks or signs which come from exposure to the sun, wind, rain, etc: *a ∼-beaten face.*

weather-bound *adj* unable to make or continue a journey because of bad weather.

weather-chart/-map, diagram showing details of the weather over an area.

weather forecast, ⇨ forecast.

weather-man, (*informal*) man who reports and forecasts the weather.

weather-proof *adj* able to stand exposure to all types of weather.

weather-ship, one at sea to make observations of the weather.

weather-station, building where the weather is observed.

weather-vane, = vane(1).

weather[2] /'weðə(r)/ *vt,vi* **1** (*literally and fig*) come through successfully: *∼ a storm/ crisis.* **2** sail to the windward of: *∼ a cape.* **3** expose to the weather: *∼ wood*, leave it in the open air until it is properly shrunk and ready for use. **4** (cause to) discolour, become worn, by the weather: *rocks ∼ed by wind and rain.*

weave /wiv/ *vt,vi* (*pt* wove /wəʊv/, *pp* woven /'wəʊvən/) **1** make (by hand or by machine) (threads) into cloth, etc; make (cloth, etc) from threads: *∼ cotton yarn into cloth.* **2** make (garlands, baskets, etc) by a similar process: *∼ flowers into a wreath; ∼ a garland of flowers.* **3** (*fig*) put together, compose (a story, romance, etc): *∼ a plot.* **get weaving (on sth)**, (*sl*) make an energetic start (on a task, etc). **4** twist and turn: *The driver was weaving (his way) through the traffic.* □ *n* [C] style of weaving: *a loose/tight ∼.*

weaver, person who weaves cloth.

web /web/ *n* [C] **1** something made of threads by a spider or other spinning creature: *a spider's ∼.* ⇨ cobweb. **2** (usually *fig*): *a ∼ of lies.* **3** skin joining the toes of some waterbirds, e g ducks, and some water-animals, e g frogs. Hence, **'web-footed** *adj.*

web-bed *adj* having the toes joined by webs.

wed /wed/ *vt,vi* (*pt* ∼ded, *pp* ∼, ∼ed) **1** marry. **2** unite: *simplicity ∼ to beauty.* **wedded to**, devoted to; unable to give up: *He is ∼ded to his own opinions and nothing can change him.*

we'd /wid/ = we had/would.

wed·ding /'wedɪŋ/ *n* [C] marriage ceremony (and festivities connected with it): *attend/invite one's friends to a ∼; the ∼ dress.*

wedding breakfast, meal for the bride and bridegroom, their relatives, friends, etc between the wedding ceremony and departure for the honeymoon.

wedding-ring, ring placed on the bride's or groom's finger at a wedding.

wedge /wedʒ/ *n* [C] **1** V-shaped piece of wood or metal, used to split wood or rock (by being hammered), to widen an opening, or to keep two things separate. **the thin end of the wedge**, (*fig*) a small change or demand likely to lead to big changes or demands. **2** something shaped like or used like a wedge: *∼ heels (on shoes).* □ *vt* fix tightly (as) with a wedge: *∼ a door open*, by placing a wedge under it. *be tightly ∼d between two fat women on the bus.*

wed·lock /'wedlɒk/ *n* [U] condition of being married: *born out of ∼*, illegitimate.

Wed·nes·day /'wenzdɪ/ *n* fourth day of the week.

wee[1] /wi/ *adj* very small: *just a ∼ drop of brandy in my coffee.*

wee[2], **wee-wee** /'wi) wi/ *n* [U] (used by and to small children) urine. □ *vi* urinate.

weed /wid/ *n* [C] **1** wild plant growing where it is not wanted (e g in a garden). **2** (*fig*) thin, tall, weak-looking person. □ *vt,vi*